D1627615

COPINGER AND SKONE JAMES

on

COPYRIGHT

VOLUME ONE

AUSTRALIA
LAW BOOK CO.—SYDNEY

CANADA and **USA**
CARSWELL—TORONTO

HONG KONG
SWEET & MAXWELL ASIA

NEW ZEALAND
BROOKERS—WELLINGTON

SINGAPORE and **MALAYSIA**
SWEET & MAXWELL ASIA
SINGAPORE AND KUALA LUMPUR

ISBN 0-421-87650-6

9 780421 876507

COPINGER AND SKONE JAMES

on

COPYRIGHT

FIFTEENTH EDITION

BY

KEVIN GARNETT, M.A.
One of Her Majesty's Counsel

GILLIAN DAVIES, D.L., Ph.D.
Barrister

GWILYM HARBOTTLE, B.A. (Oxon)
Barrister

LONDON
SWEET & MAXWELL
2005

Published in 2005 by Sweet & Maxwell Limited
of 100 Avenue Road, London, NW3 3PF
(www.sweetandmaxwell.co.uk)
Typeset by Sweet & Maxwell's electronic publishing system
Printed and bound in Great Britain by Bath Press, UK

No natural forests were destroyed to make this product,
only farmed timber was used and replanted

A CIP catalogue record for this book is available from the British Library

ISBN 0421 876 506

FOREWORD

While the revisions contained in this edition have not been as great as in the fourteenth edition, the work involved has nevertheless been substantial. Quite apart from absorbing the Supplement published in 2002, which ran to nearly 600 pages, the biggest single item we have had to deal with has of course been the 2003 Regulations which implemented the 2001 Directive on the Harmonisation of Certain Aspects of Copyright and Related Rights in the Information Society (which we have referred to simply as the Information Society Directive). Its tendrils extend throughout the 1988 Act and thus through many chapters of the work. Other changes are described in more detail, below. There have also been a number of relevant decisions of the House of Lords since the last edition and over a dozen important cases in the Court of Appeal. At the same time, there have been numerous first instance and Commonwealth decisions, not forgetting decisions of the European Court of Justice. We have also had to cope with the explosion since the last edition of online reporting, which has meant that almost no utterance of any Judge in this field, however unguarded, passes unnoticed.

Turning to the detail of what is new, while Chapter 3 (Requirements for Copyright Protection) deals with the changes to the regime of wireless, cable and internet broadcasting, the opportunity has been taken to rewrite the early sections, dealing with protected subject matter and the originality requirements. Chapter 7 (The Rights of a Copyright Owner: Primary Infringements) includes a treatment of the new communication to the public right as well as digesting the substantial body of new case law. Chapter 9 (Permitted Acts) has been extensively revised to take into account the changes on implementation of the Information Society Directive and numerous reported decisions in the area. In Chapter 10 (Crown, Parliamentary and Other Rights) the section on enforcement of Crown copyright has been rewritten to cover the wholesale revisions of HMSO's licensing structure which have taken place over the last few years. This Chapter also has a new section dealing with the Directive on the Re-use of Public Sector Information. Chapter 13 (Design Right, Unregistered Community Design and the Protection of Works of Industrial Application), as well as dealing with the new case law since the last edition, covers the Community Unregistered Design Right and the difficult decision of the Court of Appeal in *Lambretta Clothing*. Chapter 15 (Circumvention of Protection Measures and Rights Management Information) has been substantially rewritten following implementation of the Information Society Directive and the cases of *Sony v Owen* and *Sony v Ball* are discussed at length. The scope of the Chapter has also been extended to include a separate section on rights management information. In Chapter 18 (Database Right), we have been able to take account of the decisions of the European Court of Justice in *The British Horseracing Board v William Hill Organisation Ltd* and *Fixtures Marketing Ltd v Oy Veikkaus Ab*. Chapter 22 (Civil Remedies) has been generally updated to take into account the Civil Procedure Rules and includes a new section on pre-action behaviour. It contains rewritten sections on interim injunctions (covering important cases such as *Ashdown v Telegraph Group, A v B,* the *Ashworth Hospital* litigation and *Cream Holdings v Banerjee*) and damages (discussing the cases of *Blayney v Clogau* and *Nottinghamshire Healthcare* amongst others). It also contains new sections on the conduit, caching and hosting defences, injunctions against service providers and non-exclusive licensees' rights of action. In Chapter 23 (Criminal Remedies and Customs Seizure) there is a revised treatment of the burden of proof in the light of *R v Johnstone, Attorney General's Reference No. 4 of 2002* and the Human Rights Act, together with a discussion of sentencing, now that the penalties for offences have been dramatically increased. The section on customs seizure has been substantially rewritten to take account of two new Community Regulations and one new UK Regulation. Chapter 24 (International Treaties) contains new sections on the Three-Step Test of the Berne Convention, which applies to exceptions to reproduction rights and has been extended to the WCT, WPPT and the TRIPs Agreement, in the context of which it has been the subject of a WTO Panel decision on section 110(5) of the United States Act. The section on the TRIPs Agreement now deals with the question of the direct effect of TRIPs and the section on Council of Europe Conventions covers a number of new instruments, including the Convention on Cybercrime. Chapter 25 (Community Law) takes into account the entry into force of the Treaty of Amsterdam and covers the considerable body of new relevant case law from the European Court of Justice. It naturally deals in depth with the Directives which are new since the last edition, including the Directives on the Information Society, Artists' Resale Right and Enforcement. More generally, with 14 Directives in 12 years, the chapter describes the ambitious programme of harmonisation of copyright undertaken by the EC Commission to date as well as prospects for further harmonisation and possible codification in the future. Chapter 26 (The Protection of Copyright Works Abroad) takes into account no fewer than 38 entirely new national copyright laws and amendments to a further 44. Chapter 27 (Exploitation of Rights in Particular Industries) has been substantially revised to take into account recent developments, such as ever increasing internet use and controversial issues such as file sharing. Chapter 28 covers the latest proposals for EC action to regulate collecting societies. In Chapter 29 (Control of the Exercise of Copyrights and Related Rights), the competition section has been rewritten to take account of the comprehensive institutional changes, both European and domestic, introduced since the last edition. The revised discussion of Article 81 covers the rash of recent Commission decisions on sports broadcasting, together with the *IFPI Simulcasting* case and developments in respect of the Santiago agreement. The important case of *IMS Health* is considered in depth.

Volume 2, as before, contains a comprehensive collection of materials. The 1988 Act is in danger of sinking under the encrustation of amendments and is in need of statutory restatement. The notes to the various sections set out the earlier versions of the Act where this will be helpful in understanding how it has evolved.

We have had considerable help from others in preparing this new edition and our thanks are due to them. Apart from our Specialist Editors, who are all listed on the Editors' page, we have had great assistance from colleagues in Hogarth Chambers, in particular, Ashley Roughton with Chapter 23 (Criminal Remedies) and Chapter 29 (Control of Rights), George Hayman with Chapter 21 (Rights of Confidence), Alexander Learmonth with Chapter 21 (Goodwill), Nicholas Saunders with Chapter 18 (Database Right) and Victoria Jones with research on a myriad of points and at the proof-reading stage. We also received considerable help with Chapter 15 (Copy Protection Circumvention) and Chapter 16 (Fraudulent Reception) from John Cahir (Herchel Smith Research Fellow, Queen Mary Intellectual Property Research Institute, University of London). The Patent Office was extremely open and helpful in discussing the thinking behind some of the amendments to the 1988 Act made on implementation of the Information Society Directive and was also very efficient in allowing us to look at the consultation submissions on the implementing Regulations. We would also like to thank Guy Holborn and the staff of Lincoln's Inn Library for their help and unfailing enthusiasm in running down some of the more obscure material.

We are indebted to our publishers at Sweet & Maxwell who have done an extraordinary job in turning our manuscript into the finished product in a very short space of time. It is a tribute to them that we have been able to include a discussion of the European Court of Justice's decisions in the *British Horseracing Board* and *Fixtues Marketing* cases, which were only published on November 9, 2004. As with the last edition, the present edition is also available online via Westlaw UK, as part of the practice area specific Westlaw UK Intellectual Property service.

We occasionally receive comments from readers and these are always very welcome and almost always helpful. With regular Supplements planned we are able to take these comments into account reasonably promptly. We encourage readers to contact us at Hogarth Chambers, 5 New Square, Lincoln's Inn, London WC2A 3RJ or by email to *barristers@hogarthchambers.com*, marked "Copinger".

We have attempted to state the law as at September 1, 2004, although where possible we have included subsequent developments.

Kevin Garnett QC
Gillian Davies
Gwilym Harbottle

CONTENTS

CHAPTER FOUR
AUTHORSHIP OF COPYRIGHT WORKS

CHAPTER FIVE
THE CHAIN OF TITLE

CHAPTER SIX
DURATION OF COPYRIGHT

PART V—MISCELLANEOUS RIGHTS

CHAPTER FOURTEEN
SEMICONDUCTOR TOPOGRAPHIES

CHAPTER FIFTEEN
CIRCUMVENTION OF PROTECTION MEASURES AND
RIGHTS MANAGEMENT INFORMATION

CHAPTER SIXTEEN
FRAUDULENT RECEPTION OF TRANSMISSIONS

PART VI—REMEDIES

CHAPTER TWENTY TWO
CIVIL REMEDIES

CHAPTER TWENTY THREE
CRIMINAL REMEDIES AND CUSTOMS SEIZURE

PART VII—INTERNATIONAL ASPECTS

CHAPTER TWENTY FOUR
INTERNATIONAL TREATIES

CHAPTER TWENTY FIVE
COMMUNITY LAW

CHAPTER TWENTY SIX
THE PROTECTION OF COPYRIGHT WORKS ABROAD

PART VIII—EXPLOITATION AND CONTROL OF RIGHTS

CHAPTER TWENTY SEVEN
EXPLOITATION OF RIGHTS IN PARTICULAR INDUSTRIES

CHAPTER TWENTY EIGHT
COLLECTING SOCIETIES

Chapter Twenty Nine
Control of the Exercise of Copyrights and Related Rights

Chapter Thirty
Taxation

CONTENTS FOR VOLUME TWO

PART A

PART B

RELATED LEGISLATION AND MATERIALS

PART C

ORDER IN COUNCIL

PART D

TABLE OF PARLIAMENTARY DEBATES

PART E

REPEALED STATUTES

PART F

COPYRIGHT CONVENTIONS AND AGREEMENTS

PART G

TREATY OF ROME

PART H

EC DIRECTIVES

PART I

EC COUNCIL DECISION

PART J

PRECEDENTS AND COURT FORMS

TABLE OF CASES

References are to paragraph numbers. This table includes European, Commonwealth and American cases.

TABLE OF STATUTES

References are to paragraph numbers

TABLE OF STATUTORY INSTRUMENTS

References are to paragraph numbers

TABLE OF TREATIES

References are to paragraph numbers

TABLE OF CONVENTIONS

References are to paragraph numbers

TABLE OF AGREEMENTS

References are to paragraph numbers

TABLE OF EUROPEAN LEGISLATION

References are to paragraph numbers

DECISIONS

TABLE OF INTERNATIONAL LEGISLATION

References are to paragraph numbers

CHAPTER ONE

INTRODUCTION—CLASSIFICATION AND SCOPE OF THE PROTECTION OF COPYRIGHT, RELATED RIGHTS AND DESIGN RIGHTS

Contents

Copyright is the Cinderella of the law. Her rich older sisters, Franchises and Patents, long crowded her into the chimney-corner. Suddenly the fairy godmother, Invention, endowed her with mechanical and electrical devices as magical as the pumpkin coach and the mice footmen. Now she whirls through the mad mazes of a glamorous ball.[1]

1–01 Copyright is one of the three main branches of the law of intellectual property, along with patent law and trade mark law. Overshadowed for much of its history by the greater economic worth of patents and trade marks, at the beginning of the twenty-first century copyright has overtaken both in economic importance. The law of copyright, originally conceived to provide protection against unauthorised reproduction of books, faces unprecedented challenges from the accelerating pace of technological innovation. Since copyright gives the owner the exclusive right to authorise or prohibit certain uses of his work by others, it is central to providing right owners with some element of control over the exploitation of their works in the new global networks of the information age.

1–02 Works protected by copyright and the rights related thereto discussed in this work represent a constantly increasing sector of the national economy[2] and of

---

[1] Z. Chafee, "Reflections on the Law of Copyright", XLV *Columbia Law Rev.* 503 and 719 (1945), 1.

[2] In 2001, the copyright industries that are substantially dependent on copyright accounted for up to 6 per cent of GDP (gross domestic product) in the UK and employed more than 1.3 million people. Exports contribute around £10.3 billion to the balance of trade and these industries are

world trade.[3] In the modern world, the law of copyright provides the legal framework not only for the protection of the traditional beneficiaries of copyright, the individual author, composer or artist, but also for the investment required for the creation of works by the major cultural industries, the publishing, film, broadcasting and recording industries, and the computer software industry. Copyright is important not only to the individuals and industries which depend upon it for their livelihood but it also impinges one way or another on the daily life of members of the public and business. Copyright protects a vast array of everyday items, including, for example on the private level, letters, photographs and home videos, and in business, all manner of advertisements, brochures, designs, documents, graphics, manuals and reports published or used by every firm in the country. No business can afford to be ignorant of the implications of copyright in its daily work. These implications are twofold: on the one hand, there is the copyright material created every day which is the subject of protection and of potential value and, on the other hand, there is the copyright protected material which is made use of in some way and in which rights must be cleared. For example, a newspaper proprietor publishes a daily paper in which copyright subsists; that paper, however, contains many articles, cartoons and photographs in which individual authors own the copyrights, all of which must be cleared and paid for before the newspaper can publish them. When an entrepreneur organises a concert, it is not enough to hire the performers and to ensure that their rights in the performance are respected; a licence to perform the musical works publicly must also be obtained.

1. CLASSIFICATION OF THE RIGHTS DEALT WITH IN THIS WORK

A. COPYRIGHT GENERALLY

1–03   **The 1988 Act.** This work is about the law of copyright in the United Kingdom under the present copyright statute, the Copyright, Designs and Patents Act 1988 (the 1988 Act, as amended), and under the various international conventions and treaties on the subject to which the United Kingdom is party. Certain rights related to copyright also provided for under the 1988 Act, such as moral rights, rights in performances, design rights, rights in databases and rights in published editions are also covered. A number of other specific rights provided for by special legislation outside the 1988 Act and having a connection with copyright, such as the Public Lending Right (PLR) are also dealt with. The various topics discussed in this book are listed below in paras 1–07, *et seq.*

Copyright is the term used in English-speaking countries to describe the bundle of rights that are granted by statute, for limited periods of time and subject to certain permitted exceptions, in respect of original literary, dramatic, musical or artistic works, such as novels, plays, poems, musical compositions, paintings, sculptures, as well as of sound recordings, films, broadcasts and typographical arrangements of published editions. These are proprietary rights, giving the owner the right to do and to authorise other persons to do the acts restricted by the copyright law. Under the 1988 Act, these restricted acts include copying the work, issuing copies thereof to the public, renting or lending the work to the public, performing, showing or playing the work in public, communicating the work to

---

growing at a rate of 5 per cent per annum, twice the national average (*cf. Creative Industries Mapping Document 2001* (Department for Culture, Media and Sport (DCMS), March 2001).

[3] The annual volume of international trade in goods protected by intellectual property was estimated by WIPO to be US$600 billion in July 1998 (World Sources Online, July 22, 1998).

the public and making an adaptation of the work or doing any of the acts restricted by copyright in relation to an adaptation. Communication to the public includes the broadcasting of the work and the making available to the public of the work by electronic transmission in such a way that members of the public may access it from a place and at a time individually chosen by them.

The 1988 Act deals separately with original literary, dramatic and musical works, databases, artistic works, sound recordings, films, broadcasts, published editions, and rights in performances and designs. A literary work has been given a definition in the Act that is broader than the normal concept of "a literary work". It is defined as meaning any work, other than a dramatic or musical work, which is written, spoken or sung, and including a table or compilation, a computer program, preparatory design material for a computer program, and a database. A dramatic work includes a work of dance or mime and a musical work means a work consisting of music, exclusive of any words or action intended to be sung, spoken or performed with the music. The term artistic work means a graphic work, photograph, sculpture or collage, irrespective of artistic quality, a work of architecture and a work of artistic craftsmanship.

For each category of work, the Act establishes the conditions under which copyright is to subsist, the duration of the protection and the acts restricted by the copyright.

(i) Distinction between authors' rights and related rights

Extent of protection. There are differences in the extent of protection afforded to these various categories of works, due partly to the international classification of the rights into so-called *authors' rights* in literary, dramatic, musical or artistic works, on the one hand, and so-called *related rights*, on the other hand. Authors' rights are protected in accordance with the Berne Convention for the Protection of Literary and Artistic Works 1886 (the Berne Convention) and the Universal Copyright Convention 1952 (the UCC) as well as the more recent WIPO Copyright Treaty 1996 (the WCT). The expression related rights in the narrow sense applies to the rights prescribed by the Rome Convention for the Protection of Performers, Producers of Phonograms and Broadcasting Organisations 1961 (the Rome Convention). Related rights in this narrow sense are sometimes also called "neighbouring rights", derived from the French expression *droits voisins du droit d'auteur*. Both expressions are used at the international level in a broader sense to describe not only the rights of beneficiaries of the Rome Convention but other newly introduced rights, such as, for example, certain rights afforded to publishers with respect to published editions and databases. In the United Kingdom, and other common law countries, the rights afforded to producers of sound recordings and broadcasters have always been described as "copyright", whereas in civil law countries these rights are generally described as related or neighbouring rights as opposed to authors' rights. The property rights that performers now enjoy in the United Kingdom are equivalent to copyright; in civil law countries, performers' rights are also considered to be related rights. The rights of two of the beneficiaries of the Rome Convention, performers and producers of phonograms, are also now protected under the WIPO Performances and Phonograms Treaty 1996 (the WPPT). **1–04**

International classification of rights. The international classification of the above rights is founded on the distinctions between the principles governing copyright protection in common law countries and those governing authors' rights (*droit d'auteur, derecho de autor, Urheberrecht*) in countries with a civil law tradition. Common law copyright has historically emphasised the protection of the "work" and has embraced new kinds of work, such as films, sound record- **1–05**

ings, photographs and computer programs, as they have developed from advances in technology, admitting as the authors of such works both individuals and legal entities. Civil law authors' rights systems, by contrast, put emphasis on the individual author who is the creator of the work and, as a general rule, do not consider legal entities as eligible to be authors, since the author is considered to be the creator of the work in a personal sense, the work being deemed to emanate from the authors' personality.[4]

In the past, these distinctions had little impact on the domestic law of the United Kingdom. However, the wide-ranging harmonisation programme of the European Commission in the area of copyright and related rights law, which has now been in full swing for some years and is continuing, has had the effect of bridging the gaps between the common law and civil law systems in the Member States, and certain elements of the authors' rights approach to copyright have already found their way into United Kingdom law. An example of the introduction of such an element into United Kingdom law is the new right of the principal director of a film to be one of the authors of a film, along with the producer.[5]

(ii) Copyright as intellectual property

1–06   **Copyright and industrial property distinguished.** Copyright as currently in force in the United Kingdom is defined in Chapter 2, below. It belongs to the category of rights known as "Intellectual Property Rights", which concerns property rights granted for the results of creative activity, *i.e.* creations of the human intellect. Intellectual property rights comprise two main branches, copyright and industrial property. This work is concerned with copyright and rights related thereto; industrial property is concerned with the protection of inventions (patent law), industrial designs, trade marks, service marks and commercial names and designations as well as the law against unfair competition. International protection for industrial property is provided under the Paris Convention for the Protection of Industrial Property 1883, which affords protection to patents, utility models (petty patents), industrial designs, trademarks, service marks, trade names, indications of source or appellations of origin and the repression of unfair competition.[6]

B. SUBJECT-MATTER OF THIS WORK

1–07   This work is concerned with copyright in the broad sense of authors' and related rights as well as certain other rights connected thereto and covers the topics discussed below.

(i) Copyright

(a) *Authors' rights under the Berne Convention*

1–08   As seen in para.1–04, above, this covers original literary, dramatic, musical and artistic works protected in accordance with both the Berne and Universal Copy-

---

[4] This and other differences between the two approaches are discussed in paras 25–42 *et seq.*, below.
[5] 1988 Act, s.9(2)(ab); originally introduced by the Copyright and Related Rights Regulations 1996 (SI 1996/2967) December 1, 1996.
[6] Stockholm Act 1967.

right Conventions and includes cinematographic works (films). The expression literary and artistic works is defined as follows by the Berne Convention[7]:

> "The expression 'literary and artistic works' shall include every production in the literary, scientific and artistic domain, whatever may be the mode or form of its expression, such as books, pamphlets and other writings; lectures, addresses, sermons and other works of the same nature; dramatic or dramatico-musical works; choreographic works and entertainments in dumb show; musical compositions with or without words; cinematographic works to which are assimilated works expressed by a process analogous to cinematography; works of drawing, painting, architecture, sculpture, engraving and lithography; photographic works to which are assimilated works expressed by a process analogous to photography; works of applied art; illustrations, maps, plans, sketches and three-dimensional works relative to geography, topography, architecture or science".

The expression "literary and artistic works" thus must be understood as including all such works capable of being protected. The definition lists a number of different kinds of works but the list is not exhaustive. The words "such as" shows that the list is purely illustrative and not limitative.[8] The United Kingdom as a member of the Berne Convention is obliged to afford protection to the works listed but is not prevented from providing copyright protection to other works. These works are protected in the United Kingdom for 70 years from the end of the calendar year in which the author dies, the period of protection having been increased from 50 years as a result of EC legislation adopted in 1993.[9] Rights in these works as provided by the 1988 Act are described in Chapters 3, 7 and 8, below.

(b) *Rome Convention rights*

Copyright in the United Kingdom also provides protection to broadcasts and sound recordings; these rights include the protection guaranteed to producers of phonograms and broadcasters under the Rome Convention but are much more extensive than the minimum rights provided for therein. The period of protection of these works in the United Kingdom is 50 years from the end of the calendar year in which the work is made or first released[10] to the public. The rights in these works are also described in Chapters 3, 7 and 8, below.

1–09

The other beneficiary of the Rome Convention, performers, do not benefit from copyright protection, as such, in the United Kingdom but enjoy non-property and property rights which also provide a higher level of protection than the Rome Convention. Rights in performances are discussed in Chapter 12, below.[11]

As mentioned in para.1–04, above, performers and producers of phonograms also enjoy protection under the WPPT.

(c) *Other copyrights*

The 1988 Act also protects typographical arrangements of published editions as copyright works. Published editions are protected for a period of 25 years from

1–10

---

[7] Berne Convention, Art.2(1).

[8] *Guide to the Berne Convention* (World Intellectual Property Organisation, Geneva, 1978), para.2.6.

[9] Council Directive 93/98 [1993] O.J. L290/9. The term of protection provided for by the Berne Convention is 50 years *post mortem auctoris* (pma).

[10] A recording is released when it is first published, played or shown in public, broadcast or included in a cable programme service.

[11] See also paras 1–13, below.

the end of the calendar year in which they were first published. The rights in these works are described in Chapters 4, 6 and 7, below.

(ii) Authors' unwaivable right to rental remuneration

1–11 A right to equitable remuneration is guaranteed to any author who transfers his rental right concerning a sound recording or a film to the producer of the sound recording or film. Thus, even when the author has assigned or otherwise transferred his rental right to such a producer, he retains the right to equitable remuneration for the rental. This right to equitable remuneration may not be assigned at all except to a collecting society. This applies in the case of an author of a literary, dramatic, musical or artistic work, and the principal director of a film. The idea behind this provision is to protect authors who are perceived as being in a weak negotiating position *vis á vis* producers and therefore in need of a safeguard to prevent them giving up their rights. This right is described in para.7–89, below.

(iii) Moral rights of authors

1–12 Moral rights constitute certain specific rights that the author of an original literary, dramatic, musical or artistic work, and the director of a film, enjoys in his creation. Only the author personally can exercise these rights during his lifetime, since they are not assignable. Moreover, certain of these rights subsist in favour of the author, whether or not he is the owner of the copyright. These rights are distinct from the economic rights of authors and guarantee the personal connection between the author and his work. As a general rule, they continue to subsist until the copyright in the work has expired.

They include the following rights:

(a) Right to be identified as author or director of a work.
(b) Right to object to derogatory treatment of a work.
(c) Right to object to false attribution of authorship or directorship.
(d) Right to privacy of certain photographs and films.

These rights are described in Chapter 11, below.

(iv) Rights in performances

1–13 Part II of the 1988 Act confers rights on performers and persons having recording rights.

(a) *Performers' rights in their performances*

1–14 These rights are designed to protect performers against unauthorised recording or live transmission of their live performances and to guarantee them adequate control over and remuneration for the exploitation of recordings of their performances. Thus, performers enjoy non-property rights with respect to certain uses of their live performances and recordings made without consent and certain property rights similar to copyright in their fixed performances. Hence, their consent is required for copying a recording, issuing copies thereof to the public and for the rental or lending of such copies to the public. Consent is also required for making a recording of a performance available to the public by electronic transmission in such a way that members of the public may access the recording from a place and at a time individually chosen by them. This is a new right known as "the making available right". They are also entitled to equitable remuneration from the owner of the copyright in the sound recording for the exploitation of a commercially published sound recording of their performance by means of public performance or communication to the public otherwise than by being made available as described in connection with the making available right, such as by inclusion in a broadcast or cable programme service and rental. This right to equitable remuneration may not be assigned, except to a collecting society for the purpose of enabling it to enforce the right on the performer's behalf. The rights expire 50 years from the end of the calendar year in which the performance takes place or is released to the public. These rights are described in Chapter 12, below.

(b) *Exclusive recording rights*

These rights, introduced for the first time in the 1988 Act, benefit persons entitled **1–15** to the exclusion of all other persons (including the performer) to make recordings of one or more of the performances of a performer with a view to their commercial exploitation, *i.e.* by sale, letting for hire, or showing or playing in public. In practice, this means a producer of sound recordings, who is party to and has the benefit of an exclusive recording contract to which the performance is subject, or to whom the benefit of such a contract has been assigned. The rights are infringed by anyone who, without the consent of the person having the recording rights or the performer, makes a recording of the whole or any substantial part of the performance or exploits a performance. The duration of these rights is the same as with respect to performers' rights in performances. These rights are also described in Chapter 12, below.

(v) Design right in original designs

Design right is a property right subsisting in an original design of any aspect of **1–16** the shape or configuration (whether internal or external) of the whole or part of an article. The designer is the person who creates it. In the case of a computer-generated design, the person by whom the arrangements necessary for the creation of the design are undertaken is taken to be the designer. A design must be original in the sense that it must not be "commonplace". To qualify for protection the design does not have to be registered, but it either must have been recorded in a design document or an article must have been made to the design. Design right is infringed by anybody copying or making an article from the design without consent. The right lasts for a period of only 15 years from the end of the calendar year in which the design was first recorded or an article made therefrom. This right is described in Chapter 13, below.

(vi) Miscellaneous other specific rights

(a) *Semiconductor design right*

A design right in original semiconductor topographies (the etched patterns which **1–17** make the electrical circuitry of integrated circuits) is provided by the Design Right (Semiconductor) Regulations 1989. A semiconductor product is a device performing an electronic function, utilising semiconducting properties of its constituent semiconductor layer(s). A semiconductor topography is a pattern which is either fixed or is intended to be fixed in a semiconductor layer or a layer of material provided over the semiconductor layer for the manufacture of a semiconductor device, and also includes an arrangement of such patterns in relation to each other. The requirement that a semiconductor topography must be original means that it must not be commonplace in the design field in question at the time of its creation. This right is dealt with in Chapter 14, below.

(b) *Devices designed to circumvent copy protection*

1–18 Copies of copyright works of all kinds are now commonly made available to the public in an electronic form which is copy protected, in order to prevent and discourage unauthorised reproduction or piracy of works. Copy protection systems include technological protection devices or means intended to prevent or restrict copying of a work or to impair the quality of copies made. The 1988 Act provides legal protection for technical measures used by right holders to protect their works against unauthorised reproduction and other copyright infringements and in this respect the relevant provisions of the EU Information Society Directive[12] have been transposed into UK law. The 1988 Act gives owners of copyright in computer programs the same rights against a person who makes or otherwise deals in devices or means specifically designed or adapted to circumvent copy-protection systems as they have in respect of an infringement of copyright, including the right to delivery up and seizure of such articles. In relation to works other than computer programs, a new civil remedy has been introduced against any person who deliberately circumvents without authority effective technological measures used by right holders to protect their works. A new offence has also been created in relation to the dealing in devices and services which circumvent effective technological measures as well as a civil remedy in relation to that dealing. These civil and criminal remedies are available in respect of measures intended to protect rights in performances, publication rights and database rights, as well as copyright, and are available to the owner of the right as well as to the person issuing copies to the public. These rights are described in Chapter 15, below.

(c) *Fraudulent reception of transmissions*

1–19 The 1988 Act has made it a criminal offence to fraudulently receive a programme included in a broadcasting service provided from a place in the United Kingdom with intent to avoid payment of any charge applicable to the reception of the programme. Similarly, it is an offence to make or otherwise deal in unauthorised decoders designed or adapted to enable an encrypted transmission, or any service of which it forms part, to be accessed in an intelligible form without payment of the fee charged by the person making the transmission (whether by the circumvention of any conditional access technology related to the transmission or service or by any other means). There are no civil remedies against the dishonest receiver of programmes or services. These provisions are described in Chapter 16, below.

(d) *25-year publication right*

1–20 This right, introduced by the Copyright and Related Rights Regulations 1996,[13] gives a person who, after the expiry of copyright protection, publishes[14] a previously unpublished work for the first time in the European Economic Area a property right equivalent to copyright for a limited period of 25 years. The right is granted without formality and supplements the rights publishers have in the typographical arrangement of their published editions. "Work" for the purpose of the right means a literary, dramatic, musical or artistic work, or a film. The right is described in Chapter 17, below.

---

[12] Directive 2001/29 of the European Parliament and of the Council of May 22, 2001 on the Harmonisation of Certain Aspects of Copyright and Related Rights in the Information Society (O.J. L167, June 22, 2001), transposed into UK law by the Copyright and Related Rights Regulations 2003 (SI 2003/2498).

[13] SI 1996/2967.

[14] The publisher of the work must be, at the time of first publication, a national of an EEA state.

(e) *The new sui generis Database right*

A database under the 1988 Act is a collection of independent works, data or other **1–21** materials which are arranged in a systematic or methodical way, and which are individually accessible by electronic or other means. Such a database is now to be considered to be a literary work only if it is original in the sense that, by reason of the selection or arrangement of its contents, the database constitutes the author's own intellectual creation. There are, however, many databases which do not qualify as original literary works, because they are mere compilations of data. The creation of such databases may require considerable investment and labour and, therefore, deserve some degree of protection against unauthorised reproduction. For this reason, in response to EC legislation (the EC Council Directive on the legal protection of databases),[15] the Copyright and Rights in Databases Regulations 1997[16] incorporated into UK law the criterion of originality defined in the Directive for databases protected as literary works and introduced in addition a new *sui generis* property right in databases, which do not meet that criterion (non-original databases) but in respect of which there has been a substantial investment in obtaining, verifying or presenting the contents of the database. It is an infringement of this right to extract or reutilise without consent all or a substantial part of the contents of the database. The right subsists for 15 years from the end of the calendar year in which the making of the database was completed. These rights are described in Chapter 18, below.

(f) *Public lending right*

The Public Lending Right Act 1979 set up a scheme to provide remuneration to **1–22** be paid out of public funds to authors of books lent out to the public by local library authorities in the United Kingdom. This is not a copyright but an assignable property right for the benefit of authors of books only; no other category of author may benefit from it. Authors must be nationals or residents of a country within the European Economic Area. The right subsists from the date of the book's first publication until 50 years from the end of the year of the author's death.[17] The scheme is described in Chapter 19, below.

(g) *Rights of confidence*

The law of breach of confidence is based on equity and has been developed by **1–23** case law; the 1988 Act provides that any rule of equity relating to breaches of trust or confidence is not affected thereby.[18] According to this judge-made doctrine, he who has received information in confidence must not use it or publish it in breach of the obligation of confidence. The right to restrain the publication of a work on the ground of breach of confidence is in some ways broader than copyright, because it may protect ideas and information which copyright does not protect, thus raising questions relating to the public interest and freedom of expression. The law of breach of confidence and its relationship with copyright are discussed in Chapter 20, below.

(h) *Authors' and copyright owners' goodwill*

The tort of passing off may be committed in relation to copyright works without **1–24**

---

[15] Directive 96/9 of March 11, 1996.
[16] SI 1997/3032.
[17] Public Lending Right Act 1979, ss.1(7), 4(2) and 6.
[18] CDPA 1988, s.171(1)(e).

infringing copyright but by causing damage to the interests of the author or owner of the copyright. For example, questions commonly arise in relation to copyright works as to the protection of titles of works, the names of the authors and fictional characters, and the general goodwill and reputation attaching both to the copyright work and its author. The law relating to passing off is discussed in Chapter 21, below.

C. INTELLECTUAL PROPERTY RIGHTS NOT DEALT WITH IN THIS WORK

(i) Registered designs

1–25   Design right in original designs, referred to in para.1–16 above, is to be distinguished from the protection conferred on registered designs under the Registered Designs Act 1949, which is not discussed in this work. In that Act, design means features of shape, configuration, pattern or ornament applied to an article *by any industrial process*, being features which in the finished article appeal to and are judged by the eye (eye appeal). Features of an article which are dictated by its function, or which are dependent on the appearance of another article of which the article is intended by the author of the design to form an integral part, are excluded from protection. The topic is discussed in a little more detail in Chapter 13, below, in connection with rights in designs generally.

(ii) Patents for inventions

1–26   Under the Patents Act 1977,[19] the patent system provides monopoly protection for a period of 20 years from the date of filing an application for a patent for an invention which is susceptible of industrial application, new and involves an inventive step. Patents are granted only after search and examination procedures designed to ensure that inventions meet those requirements of patentability. The patent law of the United Kingdom is in line with the European Patent Convention 1973 (EPC), which established a common system of law for the grant of patents in the Contracting States.[20] The United Kingdom became party to the EPC on October 7, 1977. Thus, applicants for patents in the United Kingdom may apply for a national patent at the United Kingdom Patent Office and/or for a European patent at the European Patent Office, designating whichever of the currently 28 Member States of the EPC in which protection is sought, including the United Kingdom, if desired. If a European patent is granted, it confers on its proprietor (with effect from the date of the mention of its grant in the European Patent Bulletin) in each Contracting State in respect of which it is granted the same rights as would be conferred by a national patent. At the international level, patents are protected under the Paris Convention for the Protection of Industrial Property 1883, to which the United Kingdom is also party.

There are a number of exclusions from patentability under the law of the United Kingdom and the EPC. The following may not be regarded as inventions: discoveries, scientific theories and mathematical methods; aesthetic creations;

---

[19] On patent law in the UK, see Thorley, *et al., Terrell on the Law of Patents* (15th ed., Sweet and Maxwell, 2000.

[20] On the law and practice relating to the EPC, see G. Paterson, *The European Patent System* (2nd ed., Sweet and Maxwell, 2001); R. Lunzer, *Singer: The European Patent Convention* (revised English ed., Sweet and Maxwell, 1995); Singer and Stauder, *The European Patent Convention: A Commentary* (3rd ed., Sweet and Maxwell/Carl Heymanns Verlag KG, 2003). As of August 20, 2004, the EPO had the following Contracting States: Austria, Belgium, Bulgaria, Cyprus, Czech Republic, Denmark, Estonia, Finland, France, Germany, Greece, Hungary, Ireland, Italy, Liechtenstein, Luxembourg, Monaco, Netherlands, Poland, Portugal, Romania, Slovakia, Slovenia, Spain, Sweden, Switzerland, Turkey and the United Kingdom.

schemes, rules and methods for performing mental acts, playing games or doing business and programs for computers, as such; as well as, finally, presentations of information.[21] Computer programs are, as seen above, considered to be literary works in terms of copyright protection; this means that the expression of the computer program is protected but not its underlying idea. This situation has come under increasing criticism because since 1981 patent protection for computer programs, as such, has been available in the United States of America[22] and there has been a perception that European industry is put at a disadvantage by the lack of patent protection for such programs in Europe.[23] The European Union, seeking to clarify the issue, has recently reached political agreement on a common position on a proposal for a Directive on the patentability of computer-implemented inventions stipulating that for a computer-implemented invention to be patentable it must meet the other requirements of patentability, namely, industrial applicability, novelty and inventive step.[24] This will confirm the present position under the EPC. The EPC is a Convention which was adopted in 1973 outside the framework of European Community law. Its 29 Contracting States are not the same as those of the European Union, the EPC having several Contracting States which are not to date members of the European Union.[25] EC legislation on this subject will therefore have a mandatory effect on EU Member States and their national legislation but a Diplomatic Conference would have to be held to amend the EPC in this respect.

(iii) Registered trade marks

The third main branch of intellectual property law concerns trade marks.[26] A   **1–27**
registered trade mark is an item of personal property and acts as a distinctive sign to protect the value of reputation and goodwill in trade and to distinguish the goods and services of one trading enterprise from those of another. A trade mark can be a very valuable item of intellectual property because it can come to be associated in the minds of the public with the reputation of a company and the quality of the goods and services it provides. Trade marks also protect the consumer. Trade mark law has been harmonised within the European Community[27] and this EC legislation was implemented by the Trade Marks Act 1994. The Act defines a trade mark as being "any sign capable of being represented graphically which is capable of distinguishing goods or services of one undertaking from those of another" and gives examples, such as, words (including personal names), designs, letters, numerals, or the shape of goods or their packaging. There is a registration system for trade and service marks, following examination of the distinctiveness of the mark and search and examination of prior registrations for the same goods and services and those of the same description. The Act also provides for the registration of collective marks, which are marks distinguishing the goods or services of members of the association which is the proprietor of the mark from

---

[21] EPC, Art.52(2).

[22] Following the US Supreme Court decision in *Diamond v Diehr*, 450 U.S.175, 67 L. Ed. 2d 155, 101 SCt. 1048, 209 USPQ I (1981).

[23] The perception is not altogether accurate. The European Patent Office does grant patents for computer programs but only where the program is used in a technical process and has a technical effect, *cf.* T 208/84 (*"VICOM"*) (O.J. EPO 1987, 14) and T 1173/97 (*IBM/Computer program product*) (O.J. EPO 1999, 609).

[24] Council of the European Union, Press Release, 2583rd Council Meeting, Brussels May, 17 and 18 2004.

[25] Bulgaria, Iceland, Monaco, Liechtenstein, Romania, Switzerland and Turkey.

[26] See R. Jacob ed., *Kerly's Law of Trade Marks and Trade Names* (13th ed., Sweet and Maxwell, 2000).

[27] Council Directive of December 21, 1988 to approximate the laws of Member States relating to trade marks [1989] O.J. L40/1.

those of other undertakings. The duration of registration is 10 years from the date of filing.

A European Community Trade Mark Office has been established at Alicante in Spain and began to accept applications for registration on January 1, 1996, following the entry into force of the Council regulation on the Community Trade Mark in 1994.[28] Only marks which can have effect throughout the Community as a whole will be accepted, since the Community trade mark has a unitary character having equal effect throughout the Community.

(iv) Malicious falsehood

1–28   Malicious falsehood, also referred to as injurious falsehood, is a tort which is available to provide protection against forms of unfair trading, such as false statements which are damaging to a trader's reputation or business.[29] The basis of the action is an untrue statement maliciously published about a plaintiff's business which is calculated to cause pecuniary damage. Under the Defamation Act 1952, proof of special damage is not necessary if the statement was calculated to cause pecuniary damage to the plaintiff and was published in writing or some other permanent form, or was made in respect of any office, profession, calling, trade or business held or carried on by him at the time of publication.

(v) Plant Varieties Act 1997

1–29   The protection of plant varieties is now governed by the Plant Varieties Act 1997, which replaced the Plant Varieties and Seeds Act 1964. The 1964 Act had created a special scheme outside the patent system and provided a monopoly right to breeders or discoverers of plant varieties The new Act brings the law of the United Kingdom on this subject into line with the revised 1991 version of the Convention for the Protection of New Varieties of Plants 1961(UPOV), and with the EC Regulation on Plant Variety Protection 1997.[30] Plant breeders' rights may be granted for varieties of all plant genera and species. "Variety" means a plant grouping within a single botanical taxon of the lowest known rank having certain defined characteristics, *i.e.* that it can be: (i) defined by the expression of the characteristics resulting from a given genotype or combination of genotypes, (ii) distinguished from any other plant grouping by the expression of at least one of those characteristics, and (iii) considered as a unit with regard to its suitability for being propagated unchanged. To qualify for protection, a variety must be distinct, uniform, stable and new. Plant breeders' rights are granted to applicants after official testing by the Controller of the Plant Variety Rights Office. The United Kingdom is party to the Convention for the Protection of New Varieties of Plants 1961 (UPOV), as revised in 1991.

(vi) Protection of the Olympic Symbol

1–30   The Olympic Symbol, etc. (Protection) Act 1995[31] establishes a right, the Olympics association right, which confers exclusive rights in relation to the use of the Olympic symbol, the Olympic motto and certain words associated with the

---

[28] [1994] O.J. L11.

[29] See *Copinger* (13th ed.), paras 21–50 *et seq.*

[30] Regulation 2100/94, which came into operation on April 27, 1995. See also the UK Patents and Plant Variety Rights (Compulsory Licensing) Regulations 2002.

[31] Olympic Symbol, etc. (Protection) Act 1995 (c.32), brought into force by SI 1995/2472, September 20, 1995.

Olympic games, such as Olympic, Olympiad and Olympian. The right is infringed by any person who, in the course of trade, uses a representation of the Olympic symbol, the Olympic motto or a protected word, or uses a representation of something so similar as to be likely to create in the public mind an association with it. The Act provides for certain permitted acts in relation to the right as well as for civil remedies and criminal sanctions in relation to infringement of the right. The Olympic symbol is also protected under the terms of an international agreement, the Treaty on the Protection of the Olympic Symbol, adopted at Nairobi on September 26, 1981. The Treaty prescribes that States party thereto are obliged to refuse or to invalidate the registration as a mark and to prohibit by appropriate measures the use, as a mark or other sign, for commercial purposes, of any sign consisting of or containing the Olympic symbol, except with the authorisation of the International Olympic Committee. The United Kingdom is not a party to the Treaty; nor did it sign the Treaty at the time it was open for signature.[32]

2. SCOPE OF SUCH RIGHTS GENERALLY

A. INTER-RELATIONSHIP OF RIGHTS

Copyright as bundle of rights. Copyright gives the copyright owner a bundle of property rights. Thus, the owner has the right to do or to authorise other persons to do the various acts restricted by the copyright law, including, for example, *inter alia* to reproduce, rent out and broadcast the work and to communicate it to the public. The right to control each of these acts is generally exercisable separately. However, these rights may overlap with other rights such as moral rights, so that in a given situation there may be infringement of the right of reproduction as well as of the moral right to be identified as the author. Rarely, the exercise of rights is mutually exclusive, as in the case of the protection given to those original designs which are not protected by copyright but which are protected by means of the separate registered design right described above.

1–31

Similarly, where more than one right owner has rights in a work, these rights subsist and may be exercised independently. For example, in relation to a sound recording, separate rights subsist with respect to: (a) the music and lyrics embodied in it; (b) the fixation of the performances recorded on it; and (c) the sound recording itself. Someone who wishes to exploit the sound recording must, therefore, acquire or clear all these separate rights. Any unauthorised exploitation will be actionable by any individual right owner.

Copyright is essentially not a positive but a negative right. Thus, for example, no provision of the Copyright Act confers on the owner of copyright in a literary work the right to publish it. The Act gives the owner of the copyright the right to *prevent* others from doing that which the Act recognises the owner alone has the right to do.[33]

B. EXCLUSIVITY AND EXCEPTIONS

Checks and balances on exclusive rights. Copyright is not a monopoly, since it does not prevent competition from similar works which have been created independently. However, the rights afforded by copyright and related rights are

1–32

---

[32] The Treaty was open for signature at Nairobi until December 31, 1982, and at Geneva until June 30, 1983. As of January 15, 2004, the Treaty had 41 Member States (for up-to-date status see the WIPO website at *www.wipo.int*).

[33] *Ashdown v Telegraph Group Ltd* [2001] EWCA Civ 1142; [2002] Ch. 149.

exclusive property rights, which, if exercised oppressively to prevent access to works, or to make such access too expensive, could be contrary to the public interest. The need for a balance between the rights owners, on the one hand, and the interest of the public in access to protected works, on the other hand, has given rise to various statutory limitations on and exceptions to copyright and related rights. The most important limitation is the restriction of the term of protection of copyright and other rights. Other limitations, often referred to as exceptions, restrict the exclusive rights of the owner of the rights with regard to certain uses of his work. The main such exceptions in the United Kingdom are certain permitted acts, for example, for research and private study and for the purposes of criticism and review. There are also statutory exemptions in favour of education and libraries. Finally, the licensing of works by rights owners and their respective collecting societies is subject to the control of the Copyright Tribunal to prevent potential abuse of exclusive rights.

C. MODERN PERCEPTION OF RATIONALE FOR PROTECTION

1–33   **Purpose of copyright and related rights.** Works protected by copyright are generally the expression of creative authorship. Copyright provides the framework required to induce authors and other right owners to create and to reward them for their work, *i.e.* one purpose of copyright is to encourage and reward human endeavour. It acts as an incentive also to publishers and others to invest in the dissemination and exploitation of works for the ultimate benefit of the public. A second rationale for copyright is that stimulating creativity benefits the public. The rationale for copyright is equally valid for related rights. Thus, these rights are regarded as worthy of protection in the public interest. It follows, that, where there is a conflict between the interests of right owners in receiving adequate reward and those of the public in access to works, there is a need to balance the conflicting interests.[34]

1–34   **Balancing private and public interests.** The question of balance is an increasingly delicate matter. Copyright law has been adapted continually to technological advances, as new works and new uses of works have resulted from technical progress. Technical advances accelerated throughout the twentieth century and are continuing to do so. The most recent developments, combining digital and telecommunications technologies, make it possible to distribute copyright works instantaneously throughout the world and to reproduce them at will. This makes the role of Government in balancing the need to define and guarantee the core rights of copyright owners, on the one hand, with the interest of the general public in obtaining access to works, on the other hand, correspondingly difficult. The plethora of legislation adopted by the European Community and the United Kingdom on the subject in the past 15 years bears witness to the constant need to adapt copyright to new circumstances resulting from technical advances and to the difficulty of this process. One controversial area where it is particularly difficult to establish a proper balance is that of private use, since works are now disseminated in digital form so widely and recording techniques make high-quality copying of copyright works so easy.

D. TERRITORIALITY AND ENFORCEMENT OF RIGHTS

1–35   **Territorial nature of rights.** As a rule, copyright and related rights are granted with respect to a particular territory only and give protection to nationals of that

---

[34] The rationale for copyright is discussed in more detail in para. 2–05, below.

territory alone; protection and the possibility of enforcing rights stops at the national borders except in so far as protection is extended outside the territory by bilateral or multinational treaties with other countries. The protection of works of foreign origin within the territory will also depend on such treaties.[35]

Enforcement. The law of the United Kingdom as regards enforcement of rights is described in Chapters 22 and 23, below. The extent to which the rights of United Kingdom nationals may be enforced abroad depends on a network of international treaties and regional and bilateral agreements, mentioned at paras 1–38 *et seq.*, below and described in more detail in Chapter 24, below. However, in recent years, the trade implications associated with the marketing of copyright goods have multiplied, mainly because the problems associated with the enforcement of intellectual property rights generally have escalated. In 1998, the Organisation for Economic Co-operation and Development (OECD) estimated that more than 5 per cent of world trade is in articles infringing intellectual property. Meanwhile, violations of intellectual property as a whole are estimated to have grown to as much as 9 per cent of world trade.[36]   **1–36**

International measures. This state of affairs led to intellectual property rights becoming an important issue in the trade negotiations of the GATT Uruguay Round, which resulted in the adoption of the Agreement on Trade- Related Aspects of Intellectual Property (TRIPs) in 1994.[37] The TRIPs Agreement set minimum standards of protection for intellectual property rights generally, including copyright and related rights, and provided for improved international enforcement measures to fight against international piracy of copyright protected material. The past 15 years has also seen a great deal of activity on the international copyright front which resulted in the adoption in December 1996 of the WIPO Copyright Treaty (WCT) and the WIPO Performances and Phonograms Treaty (WPPT),[38] the aim of which is to give right owners a better level of international protection in the digital age against piracy of all kinds. The Treaties are frequently referred to as the WIPO Internet Treaties. The resulting international obligations imposed on the United Kingdom and the vastly increased trade in copyright goods mean that these rights are no longer a matter for the domestic law of the United Kingdom alone. Moreover, as mentioned at paras 1–39 *et seq.*, below, the United Kingdom's membership of the European Union and the creation of the single market have made it necessary for the copyright law to be adapted to the laws of its European partners.   **1–37**

E. INTERNATIONAL STANDARDS FOR THE PROTECTION OF COPYRIGHT AND RELATED RIGHTS

(i) International treaties

Principal influential treaties. Towards the end of the nineteenth century, the expansion of international trade resulting from the industrial revolution fostered a recognition of the need for reciprocal protection of works between countries,   **1–38**

---

[35] Regarding the protection of UK works abroad, see Ch.26, below; as regards the protection of foreign works in the UK, see Chs 3 and 24, below.
[36] H. Vithlani, *The Economic Impact of Counterfeiting* (OECD, Paris, 1998), p.4: see also *Financial Times*, March 11, 2002, p.18.
[37] The Agreement on Trade-Related Aspects of Intellectual Property Rights (the TRIPs Agreement) is Annex 1C to the Agreement establishing the World Trade Organisation adopted at Marrakesh on April 15, 1994. See D. Gervais, *The TRIPs Agreement* (2nd ed., Sweet and Maxwell, 2003).
[38] The WCT and the WPPT came into force respectively on March 6, 2002 and May 20, 2002.

and this led in the first place to the adoption of the Berne Convention in 1886.[39] The Berne Convention is based on the principle of national treatment, according to which each Member State affords the protection of its national law to nationals of the other Member States. This principle did not basically interfere with the territorial nature of copyright law. The other major international conventions in this field, including the Universal Copyright Convention 1952 (UCC) (which provides a lower level of protection than the Berne Convention for authors and therefore a refuge for countries unwilling to accept the obligations of Berne), and the Rome Convention for the Protection of Performers, Producers of Phonograms and Broadcasting Organisations 1961 (the Rome Convention) are also based on national treatment. The history and scope of these Conventions, as well as the Convention for the Protection of Producers of Phonograms against the Unauthorised Duplication of their Phonograms 1971 (the Phonograms Convention), the Convention relating to the Distribution of Programme-carrying Signals Transmitted by Satellite 1974 (the Satellite Convention) and the TRIPs Agreement (mentioned above) are described in Chapter 24, below. All these treaties set minimum standards of protection for the categories of rights owner which they aim to protect, and these standards must be implemented by any state which adheres to the treaty in question. Should a Contracting State fail to meet its obligations under these treaties, generally there is no remedy; only the TRIPs Agreement carries sanctions with it.

The more recently adopted WCT and WPPT are also analysed at paras 24–66 *et seq.* and paras 24–119 *et seq.*, below.

(ii) European Union

1–39   **Impact of EC law.** The accession of the United Kingdom to the present European Union in 1973 and the establishment of the single market within the European Community has also had a considerable impact on trade in copyright goods and on the law of copyright. The application of the principle of the free flow of goods within the single market, according to which once such goods have been put on the market in one country with the consent of the rights owner they may be freely exported to another, meant that problems arose in connection with the differences in copyright protection in the various Member States. In the mid-1980s the Commission of the European Communities recognised the need for some measure of harmonisation of the laws of copyright and related rights, and embarked on a programme of approximation of laws which is continuing. This programme, including the legislation already adopted in the form of Directives and future legislation currently under consideration, as well as its likely impact on United Kingdom copyright law, is described in Chapter 25, below. The impact of EC law generally, and in particular competition law, on the exercise of rights under the 1988 Act is also explained in Chapter 25, below.

(iii) Regional and bilateral treaties

1–40   **Regional treaties.** Until the UCC was adopted in 1952, the United States of America and many Latin American countries remained outside the international copyright community. Instead, a series of Pan-American conventions were adopted between 1889 and 1946 to provide a degree of reciprocal protection for copyright as between the Contracting Parties. These are described at paras 24–163 *et seq.*, below.

---

[39] As regards The Berne Convention, see paras 24–04 *et seq.*, below.

There are also a number of Conventions concerned with the protection of copyright and related rights adopted under the auspices of the Council of Europe between 1958 and 2001, which are dealt with at paras 24–166 *et seq.*, below.

Bilateral treaties. In the nineteenth century, as a rule, national copyright laws 1–41 denied any protection to works of foreign authors, and what protection did exist resulted from bilateral treaties. The importance of these treaties has been superseded by the international conventions mentioned above. However, the European Union and the United States of America both make a point of including requirements for the respect of copyright and related rights in bilateral trade agreements which they enter into with third countries.

3. GENERAL SCHEME OF PROTECTION

Scheme of Protection

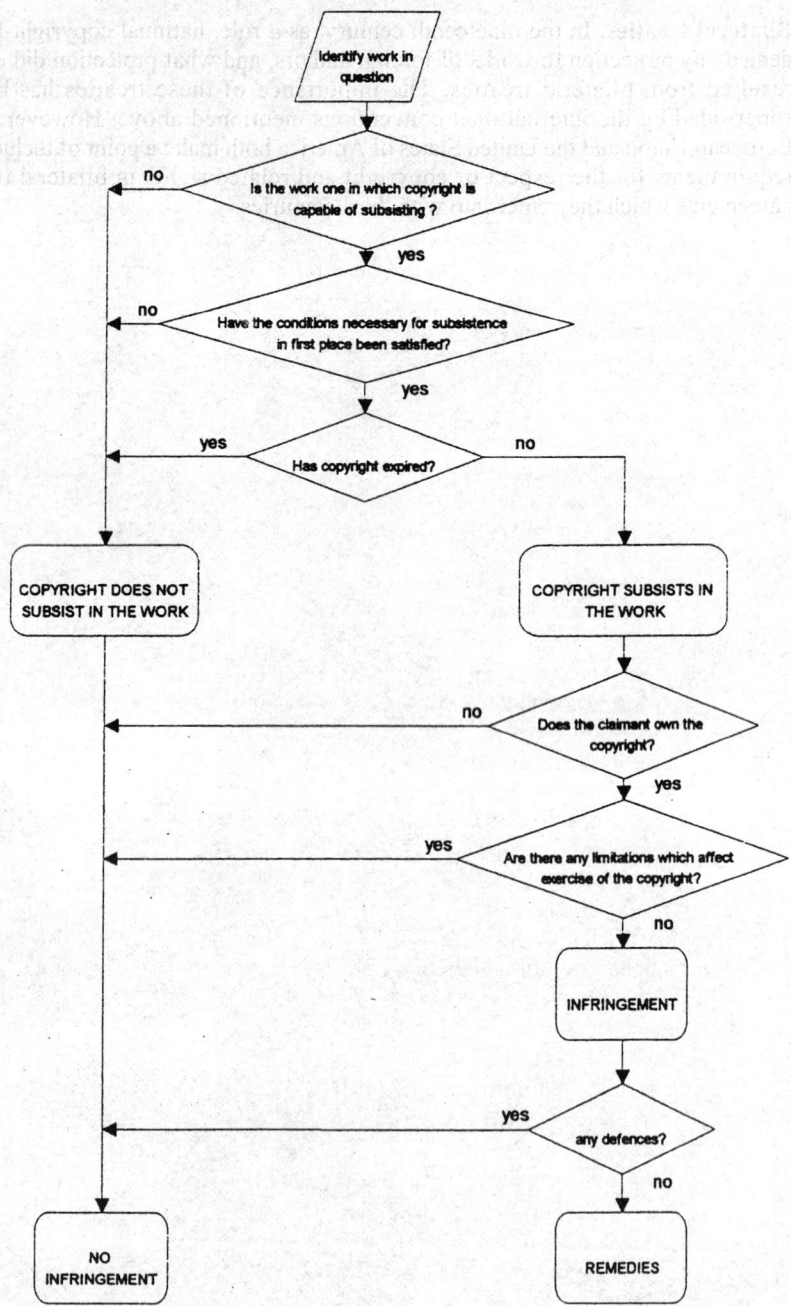

1–42 **Approaching a copyright problem.** The reader who is faced with a copyright problem, or a problem concerning any of the related and other rights described above, will no doubt hope to find the answers to any queries regarding the law in this work. The following guide aims to assist the reader to analyse his problem in such a way that he can identify the relevant chapter and find the information he needs. The steps are described in terms of copyright but they are equally applicable to problems arising out of the other rights discussed in this work.

First, the reader should identify the work in question. Might it be a literary, dramatic, musical or artistic work, or a film, a sound recording, a broadcast or musical work or other subject matter of protection? The subject-matter of copyright protection is discussed at paras 3–02 *et seq.*, below.

Then the following questions should be asked:

1. Is the work in fact one in which copyright is capable of subsisting, *i.e.* does it fit within the definitions of the works protected by the 1988 Act? (*cf.* paras 3–02 *et seq.*, below).

2. Does copyright subsist in the work now (*i.e.* at the time the question is posed)? The answer to this depends on the answers to the next two questions:

    (a) Were the conditions necessary for its subsistence in the first place satisfied? Was the work reduced to writing or fixed in some other material form? (*cf.* paras 3–105 *et seq.*, below). Were the originality requirements satisfied? (*cf.* paras 3–123 *et seq.*, below). Did the work qualify for protection either by reason of the nationality of its author or, if published, the place of publication? (*cf.* paras 3–152 *et seq.*, below). As regards the nationality of the author, is the author a British national, a national of the European Economic Area (EEA) or of a country to which protection has been extended under one or other of the international conventions to which the United Kingdom is party? (*cf.* paras 3–190 *et seq.* and Chapter 24, below). Are there any other qualifying conditions for subsistence of copyright? (*cf.* paras 3–152 *et seq*, below).

    (b) Has the copyright expired? In the case of a work in which the duration is connected with the life of the author, the question is whether the author is still alive and, if not, whether he has been dead for more than 70 years or not. In the case of a broadcast, performance or sound recording, the question is when was the work first made or released to the public? For other works, *e.g.* typographical arrangements of published editions, the crucial question is when was the work first published? (*cf.* Chapter 6, below).

3. Who is the author of the work (*cf.* Chapter 4, below)? Who owns the copyright (*cf.* Chapter 5, below)? These questions may be straightforward to answer but are not necessarily so. These rights are transferable and each constituent part of the bundle of rights which make up copyright may be assigned separately.

    To find out who owns the relevant right at any particular time, it is necessary to pose the following questions:

    (a) Who was the first owner of the copyright in question? (*cf.* Chapter 1). To determine this it is usually necessary to know who the author of the work was (*cf.* Chapter 4, below).

    (b) Has ownership of the particular right in which the reader is interested since been transmitted to another person? Assignments of copyright only take effect if they are in writing, signed by or on behalf of the assignor. Questions relating to the chain of ownership are discussed in Chapter 5, below.

4. What rights does the copyright *prima facie* include, *i.e.* what are the acts restricted by the copyright? The 1988 Act establishes a specific list of restricted acts for each category of work (*cf.* Chapters 7 and 8, below). What are the moral rights of the copyright owner? (*cf.* Chapter 11, below). How long do all these rights last? (*cf.* Chapters 6 and 11, below).

5. In the particular circumstances, are there any reasons why such exclusive rights are not available for dealing with in a non-litigious context or are there any defences to an infringement claim in a litigious context? This question concerns the limitations imposed by statute on the exercise of copyright. Apart from limitations on the duration of protection, the 1988 Act also limits the scope of copyright protection by providing for exceptions by means of certain permitted acts (*cf.* Chapter 9, below). In relation to infringement of copyright, a number of statutory defences are available. These questions are discussed in Chapter 22, below.

6. Are the rights, although exercisable, subject to any form of control? Collective licensing of rights through collecting societies representing one or more categories of right owner is common practice. Such societies provide a convenient mechanism for licensing and administering those rights which it would be difficult for right owners to exercise individually, such as, broadcasting and public performance rights. These societies normally represent the vast majority of a particular category of right owner and the danger exists that they could abuse what amounts to a monopolistic position. The Copyright Tribunal exists to control the licensing practices of these societies; any party to a negotiation may in certain circumstances refer a dispute to the Tribunal for resolution. The law relating to collecting societies is discussed in Chapter 28, below, and that concerning control of the exercise of copyrights and related rights in Chapter 29, below.

7. In the case of infringement, what remedies are available? The enforcement of rights by action in civil and criminal proceedings and other enforcement measures are dealt with in Chapters 22 and 23, below.

PART I

COPYRIGHT

CHAPTER TWO

NATURE AND HISTORY OF COPYRIGHT

Contents   *Para.*
1.   Nature of copyright   2–01
2.   History of copyright   2–08

1. NATURE OF COPYRIGHT

Copyright defined. Copyright under the Copyright, Designs and Patents Act   **2–01**
1988 ("the 1988 Act") is a property right which subsists in a number of different
kinds of works, such as original literary, dramatic, musical or artistic works,
sound recordings, films or broadcasts and the typographical arrangement of
published editions.[1] A "copyright work" means any such work in which copyright subsists.[2] Literary, dramatic, musical and artistic works must comply with
the criterion of originality in order to be protected. In United Kingdom law,
"original" means that the work must originate from its author and must not be
copied from another work.[3] It does not mean that the work must be the expression of original or inventive thought; the originality required relates to the expression of the thought.[4] The standard of originality is low and depends on the author
having expended sufficient independent skill, labour and judgement to justify
copyright protection for the result.[5]

Copyright springs into life immediately on creation of the work. Thus, the
work is protected as soon as it is recorded, in writing or otherwise, on paper,
canvas, tape, disc, film or other recording medium from which it is capable of being reproduced.[6] Unlike the case of other intellectual property rights, such as
patents and trade marks, there are no formalities required for copyright to subsist
and no system of registration of rights.[7] Thus, it is not necessary to apply to any
authority in order to enjoy copyright protection: "The law of copyright rests on a
very clear principle: that anyone who by his or her own skill and labour creates
an original work of whatever character shall, for a limited period, enjoy an

---

[1] CDPA 1988, s.1(1). A new publication right was introduced by the Copyright and Related Rights
Regulations 1996 (SI 1996/2967) s.16; this gives a person who, after the expiry of copyright
protection, publishes for the first time a previously unpublished work a property right equivalent
to copyright for a period of 25 years (see Ch.17, below).

[2] CDPA 1988, s.1(2).

[3] *University of London Press Ltd v University Tutorial Press Ltd* [1916] 2 Ch. 601 at 608. As
regards the criterion of originality in other jurisdictions, see paras 25–42 *et seq.*, below.

[4] See para. 2–06, below.

[5] *Kelly v Morris* (1866) L.R. 1 Eq. 697; *Karo Step* [1977] R.P.C. 255 at 273. As to originality generally, see paras 3–123, *et seq.*, below. Note that a higher criterion of originality is required in the
case of databases: "A literary work consisting of a database is original if, and only if, by reason
of the selection or arrangement of the contents of the database the database constitutes the
authors' own intellectual creation", (CDPA 1988, s.3A(2)).

[6] CDPA 1988, s.3(2) in relation to literary, dramatic and musical works.

[7] This was not always the case. Registration (originally with the Stationers' Company) was required
to acquire copyright under the first copyright law, the Statute of Anne 1709 (*cf.* para. 2–16,
below). After the copyright law was revised in 1842 (*cf.* para. 2–19, below), the requirement of
registration was maintained not as a pre-condition for statutory copyright but as a condition precedent to taking an enforcement action. The copyright arose automatically on publication (Copyright Act 1842, ss.13, 24).The requirement of registration was abolished by the 1911 Act to
comply with the UK's international obligations under the Berlin Act of the Berne Convention.

exclusive right to copy that work. No one else may for a season reap what the copyright owner has sown".[8]

Copyright gives the owner of the copyright in a work of any description the exclusive right to do certain acts in relation to the copyright work. This includes the right to copy the work itself and also to use the work in other ways protected under the law. These protected uses are issuing copies of the work to the public, renting or lending copies of the work to the public, performing, showing or playing the work in public, communicating the work to the public and making an adaptation of the work, or doing any of the above in relation to an adaptation. Communication to the public includes the broadcasting of the work and the making available to the public of the work by electronic transmission in such a way that members of the public may access it from a place and at a time individually chosen by them. These acts are known as the acts restricted by copyright[9] and are also often referred to as the copyright owner's economic rights. A person who does any of the acts restricted by copyright without the licence (*i.e.* agreement) of the copyright owner infringes the copyright in the work, unless the acts are otherwise excused,[10] and is liable to have legal action taken against him. Both civil remedies and criminal penalties are available for the enforcement of copyright.[11] In addition to these economic rights, so-called "moral rights" subsist in favour of the author, director or commissioner of certain descriptions of copyright work, irrespective of whether he is the owner of the copyright. These rights include the right to be identified as the author of a literary, dramatic, musical or artistic work or as director of a film, the right to object to derogatory treatment of certain copyright works and the right to object to having a work falsely attributed to oneself as author, as well as the right to privacy of certain photographs and films.[12]

2–02   The meaning of the expression "copyright" has changed over the years with the development of copyright law to extend protection to new subject-matter and to extend the classes of acts which constitute infringement. Before the 1911 Act, the expression "copyright" was confined to the right of multiplying copies and did not include the performing right in dramatic or musical works.[13] At that time, copyright subsisted at common law in respect of unpublished works (except for drawings, paintings and photographs) and by statute for published works (including unpublished drawings, paintings and photographs)[14] and it is uncertain whether the expression "copyright" was used before that date only in relation to the right to restrain publication of published works, or so as to include also the right of an author to restrain publication of his unpublished works.[15]

After the 1911 Act, the expression "copyright" in the United Kingdom came to be used to mean all the rights conferred by the 1911 Act upon authors, composers and artists in respect of their literary, dramatic, musical and artistic works.[16] Copyright, however, although now expressed as the exclusive right to do certain acts,[17] essentially gives the right owner the right to restrict others from doing those acts or to authorise them to do them, and, when copyright is referred to as

---

[8] See *Designers Guild Ltd v Russell Williams (Textiles) Ltd* [2001] F.S.R. 11, HL at para.2, *per* Lord Bingham of Cornhill.

[9] CDPA 1988, s.16.

[10] Because the acts constitute "permitted acts", see Ch.9, below.

[11] CDPA 1988, Ch.VI, ss.96, *et seq.*

[12] CDPA 1988, s.2 and Ch.IV, ss.77, *et seq.* (and see Ch.11, below).

[13] See *Pollock CB, Chappell v Purday* [1845] 14 M. & W. 303.

[14] Fine Arts Copyright Act, 1862 (25 & 26 Vict. c.68).

[15] *Re Dickens* [1935] Ch. 267.

[16] See Copyright Act 1911, s.1(2).

[17] CDPA 1988, s.16(1).

"an exclusive right", the emphasis is on the word "exclusive". Thus, the 1988 Act, whilst not defining "copyright" otherwise than as a property right,[18] which is transmissible as personal or moveable property,[19] provides that the owner of the copyright in a work has the exclusive right to do the acts restricted by the copyright in a work of that description specified in the 1988 Act.[20] Copyright is infringed by a person who, without the licence of the copyright owner, does, or authorises another to do, any of the restricted acts[21] set out in various sections of the 1988 Act.[22]

Thus, the essence of copyright is the owner's right to take action to prevent others from engaging in specified kinds of activity without the owner's permission. Under the 1988 Act, that right is limited to activities taking place in the United Kingdom.[23] Although usually classified as a moveable,[24] copyright shares some of the characteristics of immoveables in the sense that the rights are territorially limited, and from this it follows that copyright is situate in the country whose law governs its existence. Given that the relevant provisions of the 1988 Act extend to England and Wales, Scotland and Northern Ireland[25] this means that what is often referred to as "United Kingdom copyright" is situate or located in the United Kingdom.[26] Copyright is thus territorial in extent and, as a matter of United Kingdom law, there is no such thing as global or world-wide copyright.[27]

Ownership of copyright. According to the 1988 Act, the author, in relation to a work, means the person who creates it.[28] In relation to a literary, dramatic, musical or artistic work, the author will be the individual who wrote the book or play, composed the music or painted or created the artistic work. In the case of literary, dramatic, musical or artistic work which is computer-generated,[29] the author is taken to be the person by whom the arrangements necessary for making the work are undertaken. In relation to other copyright works, the author and person who creates the work is taken to be the producer in the case of sound recordings; the producer and the principal director in the case of films; the person making the broadcast in the case of broadcasts, or, in the case of a broadcast which relays another broadcast by reception and immediate re-transmission, the person making that other broadcast,[30] and, in the case of typographical arrangements of published editions, the publisher.[31] The author of a work is the first owner of copyright in it, except where a literary, dramatic, musical, artistic work or film is made by an employee in the course of his employment, in which case, subject to any agreement to the contrary, his employer is the first owner of any copyright in the work.[32] Copyright is generally alienable and may be transferred or assigned, in whole or

2–03

---

[18] s.1(1).

[19] s.90(1). See also Ch.5, below.

[20] ss.2(1) and 16(1). See also Chs 7 and 8, below.

[21] s.16(2).

[22] ss.17–21.

[23] s.16(1).

[24] s.90(1).

[25] s.207.

[26] See *Peer International Corp. v Termidor Music Publishers Ltd* [2002] EWHC 2675, ChD, paras 22, 23, citing Dicey and Morris, *The Conflict of Laws* (13th ed.), para.22–051 and *Novello & Co. Ltd v Hinrichsen Addition Ltd* [1951] Ch. 595.

[27] *Peer International Corp. v Termidor Music Publishers Ltd* [2002] EWHC 2675, Ch. The decision on these aspects was not affected by the decision on appeal in *Peer* [2003] EWCA Civ. 1156.

[28] CDPA 1988, s.9(1). See also Ch.4, below.

[29] s.9((3).

[30] s.9(2)(b).

[31] s.9(2)(d).

[32] s.11.

in part, and the owner of copyright may license one or more specific uses of his work.[33]

2–04   Limitations on copyright. Copyright protection is limited in duration as well as in other respects, certain exceptions being permitted to the exclusive rights it affords. The term of protection for an original literary, dramatic, musical or artistic work and for films generally expires at the end of the period of 70 years from the end of the calendar year of the death of the author or authors, and in the case of works of unknown authorship, from making or making the work available to the public.[34] As regards computer-generated works, sound recordings and broadcasts (*i.e.* works where the author is generally a corporate body rather than an individual), copyright subsists for a period of 50 years from making or making available to the public.[35] The duration of copyright in typographical arrangements of published editions subsist for 25 years from the end of the calendar year in which the work was first published.[36] Other limitations on copyright protection include numerous exceptions in favour of the general public, such as, for example, fair dealing for the purpose of research and private study, criticism, review and reporting current events and certain acts done for the purpose of instruction in educational establishments and done in libraries,[37] and many others.

Since copyright law does not create a monopoly, it has been argued that the basic protection which the law of copyright affords, namely that of preventing unlawful reproduction, should extend without limit of time. Prior to the 1911 Act, unpublished literary (and other) works had a perpetual right at common law. But such right ended on publication, after which an author had to base his claim for protection upon his statutory right, if any.[38] However, common law copyright was abolished by the 1911 Act, which provided that no person should be entitled to copyright or any similar right otherwise than under and in accordance with the provisions of that Act, or of any other statutory enactment for the time being in force.[39] The 1956 Act[40] and the 1988 Act[41] contain similar provisions. Nevertheless, an unlimited statutory term for unpublished literary (and other) works was created by the 1911 Act,[42] and continued by the 1956 Act,[43] but not by the 1988 Act, except in the case of works of unknown authorship.[44] However, a new property right equivalent to copyright has recently been introduced for persons who, after the expiry of copyright protection, publish for the first time a previously unpublished work.[45] The 1988 Act[46] also ended the perpetual copyrights granted to universities and colleges by the Copyright Act 1775,[47] which had been preserved by the 1911 Act,[48] as well as by the 1956 Act.[49]

---

[33] See paras 5–63 *et seq.* and 5–194 *et seq.*, below. Note, however, that certain moral rights and rights to equitable remuneration are not alienable.
[34] CDPA 1988, ss.12(1) and 13B. See also Ch.6, below.
[35] ss.12(7), 13A and 14.
[36] SI 1996/2967, s.16(6) and CDPA 1988, s.15.
[37] CDPA 1988, Ch.III, ss.28, *et seq.* See also Ch.9, below.
[38] *Donaldson v Beckett* [1774] 4 Burr. 2408; as to other works, see *Albert (Prince) v Strange* (1849) 1 M. & G. 25. See also para. 2–17, below.
[39] Copyright Act 1911, s.31.
[40] Copyright Act 1956, s.46(5).
[41] CDPA 1988, s.171(2).
[42] Copyright Act 1911, s.17(1).
[43] Copyright Act 1956, ss.2(3), 3(4).
[44] CDPA 1988, ss.9(4), (5), 12 and Sch.1, para.12. See paras 6–46 *et seq.*, below.
[45] The Copyright and Related Rights Regulations 1996, s.16.
[46] CDPA 1988, Sch.1, para.13.
[47] 15 Geo. 3, c.53 and see paras 6–81 *et seq.*, below.
[48] Copyright Act 1911, s.33.

Justifications for copyright. The underlying principles on which the modern **2–05** international system of copyright and authors' rights is founded are generally considered to be fourfold: natural law, just reward for labour, stimulus to creativity and social requirements.[50] According to natural law, the author has an exclusive natural right of property in the results of his labour and should have control over the publication of his work as well as the right to object to any unauthorised modification or other attack on the integrity of his work. The principle of just reward for labour supposes that authors deserve to be remunerated when their work is exploited. Moreover, copyright provides the economic basis for the investment required to create some works, such as films, sound recordings and works of architecture and to publish others. These investments will not be made unless there is a reasonable expectation of obtaining a return on them. Just reward for labour in turn provides a stimulus to creativity; copyright presupposes that the guarantee of protection and the possibility of controlling and being paid for the exploitation of works encourages authors to create. As Anthony Trollope said: "Take away from English authors their copyrights, and you would very soon take away from England her authors".[51]

Finally, it is considered a social requirement in the public interest that authors and other rights owners should be encouraged to publish their works so as to permit the widest possible dissemination of works to the public at large. These four fundamental principles are cumulative and interdependent and are applied in the justification of copyright in all countries, although different countries give varying emphasis to each of them. To generalise, it is true to say that in the development of modern copyright laws, the economic and social arguments are given more weight in the Anglo-American laws of common-law tradition, whereas, in Continental law countries with civil law systems, the natural law argument and the protection of the author are given first place.

In the United Kingdom, the justifications for copyright legislation have centred historically on the economic and social arguments. While the need to protect the natural rights of the author and to encourage creativity by protecting the products of his mind has always been recognised, as well as the need to ensure an adequate reward for authors and creators for their efforts, the copyright system aims to encourage the dissemination of ideas and knowledge to the general public. There is also a concern to balance the interest of the author in protection of his works, on the one hand, with the interest of the public in access to works on the other. Thus, the copyright law in the United Kingdom has created rights and regularly adapted the law to provide authors and other owners of rights with protection with respect to new developments in technology, but at the same time conditions and limitations have been imposed on these rights. The protection of copyright, along with other intellectual property rights,[52] is considered as a form of property worthy of special protection because it is seen as benefiting society as a whole and stimulating further creative activity and competition in the public interest.[53]

---

[49] Copyright Act 1956, s.46(1). In this regard, it is, perhaps, surprising that the CDPA 1988 created a new perpetual non-copyright right. Such right is a right for the Hospital for Sick Children, Great Ormond Street, to receive royalties in respect of certain acts of exploitation of the play Peter Pan by Sir James Matthew Barrie, notwithstanding that the copyright in such work expired on December 31, 1987. CDPA 1988, ss.149 and 301 and Sch.6 and see para. 6–50, below.

[50] S.M. Stewart, *International Copyright and Neighbouring Rights* (2nd ed., Butterworths, London, 1989), paras 1.01 *et seq.*; G. Davies, *Copyright and the Public Interest* (2nd ed., Sweet & Maxwell, 2002), p.9 *et seq.*

[51] A. Trollope, *Autobiography*, Ch.6.

[52] See Introduction, para. 1–06, above.

[53] "The exclusive rights which are granted by national copyright, patent, trademark and design laws are granted because it is in the public interest to grant them": *Copyright and Designs Law*, Report of the Committee to consider the Law on Copyright and Designs, Chairman: The Honourable Mr Justice Whitford (the Whitford Report), March 1977, HMSO, Cmnd.6732, para.84. "The

2–06 **No copyright in ideas.** Copyright is a property right,[54] but copyright law is concerned, in essence, with the negative right of preventing the copying of material.[55] It is not concerned with the reproduction of ideas, but with the reproduction of the form in which ideas are expressed.[56] "Ideas, it has always been admitted, … are free as air."[57] Copyright is not a monopoly, unlike patents and registered designs, which are.[58] Thus, if it can be shown that two precisely similar works were in fact produced wholly independently of one another, there can be no infringement of copyright by one of the other.[59] The position is that, if the idea embodied in the plaintiff's work is sufficiently general, the mere taking of that idea will not infringe. If, however, the idea is worked out in some detail in the plaintiff's work and the defendant reproduces the expression of that idea, then there may be an infringement.[60] In such a case, it is not the idea which has been copied but its detailed expression.[61] In the recent decision in the House of Lords, *Designers Guild*, Lord Hoffmann in his judgment discussed the question of what is really meant by the notion that there is no copyright in ideas, and what is the basis of the so-called ideas/expression dichotomy.[62] He first pointed out that all copyright works have as their *basis* an idea, in that all works are the expression of the author's ideas, represented by his decision to use certain modes of expression rather than others. The point usually made is a different one, or rather two different ones, since the distinction which the cases make between ideas and the expression of ideas in fact has two quite separate elements:

(1) A work may express certain "ideas" but those ideas are not protected by the copyright which subsists in the work because they have no connection with the particular subject-matter of the work, whether it be literary, dramatic, musical or artistic, etc. Thus, a literary work which describes a system or invention does not entitle the copyright owner to protection for

Government's broad aims in this revision of copyright law are to ensure continued protection for those who create copyright works while at the same time recognising that the public has a substantial interest in the availability of their works": *Intellectual Property and Innovation*, DTI White Paper, April 1986, HMSO, Cmnd.9712, para.4.

[54] CDPA 1988, ss.1(1), 90(1) and 96(2); *cf.* Copyright Act 1956, s.36(1) and Copyright Act 1842, s.25.

[55] *George Hensher Ltd v Restawhile Upholstery (Lancs.) Ltd* [1976] A.C. 64 at 98; *Fraser v Thames Television Ltd* [1984] Q.B. 44 at 60; *Performing Right Society Ltd v Rangers FC Supporters Club* [1975] R.P.C. 626 at 633; *British Leyland Motor Corporation v Armstrong Patents Co. Ltd* [1986] R.P.C. 279 at 302.

[56] See *Jefferys (C) v Boosey (T)* (1855) 4 H.L.C. 815; *Donoghue v Allied Newspapers Ltd* [1938] Ch. 106 at 109 and 110; *Gleeson v H. R. Denne Ltd* [1975] R.P.C. 471; *Gomme (E.) Ltd v Relaxateze Upholstery Ltd* [1976] R.P.C. 377; *Catnic Components Ltd v Hill & Smith Ltd* [1978] F.S.R. 405; *LB (Plastics) Ltd v Swish Products Ltd* [1979] R.P.C. 551, HL; *LA Randall Pty Ltd v Millman Services Pty Ltd* (1977–78) 17 A.L.R. 140; *Kleeneze Ltd v DRG (UK) Ltd* [1984] F.S.R. 399; *George Ward (Moxley) Ltd v Richard Sankey Ltd* [1988] F.S.R. 66; *Green v Broadcasting Corp. of New Zealand* [1989] R.P.C. 700; *Designers Guild Ltd v Russell Williams (Textiles) Ltd* [2001] F.S.R. 11, HL, para.24. And see CDPA 1988, s.3(2).

[57] A. Birrell, *The Law and History of Copyright in Books* (Cassell and Co., London, etc., 1899), p.167.

[58] See *British Leyland Motor Corporation v Armstrong Patents Co. Ltd* [1986] R.P.C. 279, at 361; *LB (Plastics) Ltd v Swish Products Ltd* [1979] R.P.C. 551, HL, at 570. Although, *cf. Tate v Fulbrook* [1908] 1 K.B. 821 at 832, 833 and *Green v Broadcasting Corp. of New Zealand* [1989] 2 All E.R. 1056 at 1058.

[59] *Corelli v Gray* (1913) 29 T.L.R. 570; *Rees v Melville* [1911–16] Mac. C.C. 96 at 168; *Hollinrake v Truswell* [1894] 3 Ch. 420; *Libraco Ltd v Shaw Walker Ltd* (1913) 30 T.L.R. 22; *Wesman v McNamara* [1923–28] Mac. C.C. 121; *Francis Day & Hunter Ltd v Bron* [1963] Ch. 587; and see paras 7–13 *et seq.*, below.

[60] See *Ibcos Computers Ltd v Barclays Mercantile Highland Finance Ltd* [1994] F.S.R. 275.

[61] See also para. 7–13, below.

[62] *Designers Guild Ltd v Russell Williams (Textiles) Ltd* [2001] F.S.R. 11, HL, *per* Lord Hoffmann, at para.24.

the invention.[63] In such cases, the expression of the idea in the literary work may well attract copyright protection but the operation of the system itself, or the working of the inventive process, will not reproduce the literary expression which is the subject- matter of copyright.

(2) A work may contain the expression of an "idea" but that expression, as contained in the work, may not be protected because it is not original or so commonplace as not to form a substantial part of the work. The example given was the case of *Kenrick & Co. v Lawrence & Co.*,[64] where the subject-matter was an artistic work representing a human hand in the act of voting. This category should, it is suggested, in fact be understood as applying to a number of separate types of cases, namely those, (a) where because the idea was so well known to the author from the work of others that its expression required no sufficient skill and labour (an unusual type of case in practice), or (b) where the idea has been expressed in such a trivial manner as not to satisfy the originality test and thus to merit protection, or (c) where, and this is the most usual type of case, the expression of the idea merits copyright protection but the defendant has not appropriated the skill and labour of the author in giving form to that expression. This was the situation in *Kenrick v Lawrence*. If the defendant there had made greater borrowing of the plaintiff's skill in representing a voter's hand, there would have been an infringement. Applied to the facts of *Designers Guild*, one of the features of the claimant's work consisting of a design for fabric was the combination of evenly spaced stripes over which flowers were scattered. If that was all that had been copied, the mere idea of combining stripes and flowers in a design would not have represented sufficient skill and labour as to merit protection from copying. "Particularly in relation to cases of artistic copyright, the more abstract and simple the copied idea, the less likely it is to constitute a substantial part. Originality tends to lie in detail with which the basic idea is presented."

So also, in *Designers Guild Ltd*, Lord Hoffmann emphasised that while an artistic technique, such as a type of brushstroke, could not be protected by copyright, the results of a particular technique, in terms of the visual effects produced using them, could be.[65]

Development of law of copyright. Copyright law was first introduced in the United Kingdom in response to the need to protect the new printing trade against the unauthorised copying of books (piracy). Ever since, it has developed to keep pace with the introduction of new technologies. As copyright law developed in the eighteenth and nineteenth centuries it was mainly concerned with the field of literature and the arts but, following the advances in technology of the twentieth century, the protection given by copyright law has been considerably expanded over the years, both with respect to the subject-matter of protection and also to the classes of acts which constitute infringement. Thus, today, not only is protection given to literary, dramatic, musical and artistic works (with, for instance, computer programs and databases being protected as literary works[66]), but also to sound recordings, films, broadcasts, and the typographical arrangements of

2–07

---

[63] See, *e.g. Kleeneze Ltd v DRG (U.K.) Ltd* [1984] F.S.R. 399
[64] (1890) 25 Q.B.D. 99.
[65] *Designers Guild Ltd v Russell Williams (Textiles) Ltd* [2001] F.S.R. 11, HL, at para.20.
[66] CDPA 1988, s.3. A literary work now, expressly, includes preparatory design material for a computer program. See paras 3–11 *et seq.*, below.

published editions.[67] Infringement of copyright was originally limited to copying but the acts restricted by copyright now cover the issue of copies to the public, the rental or lending of works to the public, the performance, showing or playing the work in public, communicating the work to the public and making an adaptation of the work or doing any of the above in relation to an adaptation.

2. HISTORY OF COPYRIGHT

2–08   **Antiquity.** It is helpful to an understanding of the modern law of copyright to study its history—to see how it has developed from its origins to the present day.

Copyright is a comparatively modern concept, born in the late fifteenth century, following the invention of printing, which for the first time made it possible to produce multiple copies of books quickly and comparatively cheaply. The classical world did not recognise copyright as such; there is no mention of any such concept in Justinian although there is plenty of evidence that Greek and Roman authors were greatly concerned to be identified as the author of their works and that their authorship should be recognised.[68] The word plagiarism, the practice of copying the work of another and passing it off as the copier's own, derives from the Latin *plagiarius*, an abductor or kidnapper, and has been condemned as an immoral and contemptible practice from the earliest historical times, but in those days there was no law against it. In today's terms, classical authors were concerned that their moral rights be respected, but they enjoyed no economic rights. The earliest copyright case of which there is any record is an Irish sixth-century case involving St Columba, who, while on a visit to the monastery of his former teacher, Abbot Finnian, copied the latter's psalter; Finnian demanded the return of the copy and getting no satisfaction referred the dispute to the King, who ruled in his favour: "to every cow her calf and consequently to every book its copy".[69]

Before the invention of printing, there was little practical need for legal protection of authors against the copying of their works. To start with, the bulk of the population was illiterate and had no use for books. Moreover, the copying of manuscripts was a painstaking and time-consuming occupation mainly done by monks and limited to the copying of religious works for religious orders and the royal courts of Europe. The possibility of printing multiple copies of books cheaply resulted in a new market for books for a public which had not previously had access to the manuscripts which, in the past, had been available only to the most privileged members of society.

2–09   **Early control of printing.** Throughout its history, as already noted, copyright law has been closely linked to developments in technology. It was only after the introduction of printing that any serious question as to the copyright in literary works could be expected to arise. An early statute of Richard III in 1483[70] encouraged the printing of books, and permitted their importation, but this statute was repealed 50 years later on protectionist grounds, it being alleged, in the preamble

---

[67] See paras 3–02 *et seq.*, below.

[68] A. Birrell, *The Law and History of Copyright in Books* (Cassell and Co., London, etc., 1899), pp.41 *et seq.* S.M. Stewart, *International Copyright and Neighbouring Rights* (2nd ed., Butterworths, London, 1989), p.13. G.H. Putnam, *The Question of Copyright* (2nd. ed., The Knickerbocker Press, New York, 1896).

[69] R.R. Bowker, *Copyright, its history and its law* (Houghton Mifflin, 1912), p.3; and see G. Putnam, *Books and their makers during the Middle Ages, 1476–1600* (New York, 1962).

[70] 1 Ric. 3, c.9.

of the repealing statute in 1533,[71] that such a "marvellous number of printed books" were imported into the realm to the prejudice of the "King's natural subjects", who "have given themselves so diligently to learn and exercise the said craft of printing, that at this day there be within this realm a great number cunning and expert in the said science or craft of printing as able to exercise the said craft in all points as any stranger in any other realm or country". A similar plea was urged on behalf of the bookbinders, who, "having no other faculty wherewith to get their living, be destitute of work and likely to be undone, except some reformation herein be had".[72]

As the number of printers increased in England, the King assumed a prerogative of granting printing privileges, and the earliest copyright protection took the form of printers' licences granted by the Sovereign to regulate the book trade and to protect printers against piracy.[73] These privileges became a source of considerable profit to the Crown[74] and in time were used as an instrument of censorship by the authorities.

Original charter of the Stationers' Company. In 1556, the original charter of the Stationers' Company was granted by the Catholic Queen Mary and her consort, Philip II of Spain.[75] It was the declared object of the Crown at that time to prevent the propagation of the reformed religion, and it seems to have been thought that this could be brought about most effectively by imposing the severest restrictions on the publishing trade and the press to prevent the publishing of seditious and heretical books and pamphlets. Until 1640, the Crown, using the Star Chamber as its instrument, rigorously enforced several decrees and ordinances of that Chamber regulating the manner of printing, the number of presses permitted to operate throughout the Kingdom, and prohibiting all printing against the force and meaning of any of the statutes or laws of the realm. This restrictive jurisdiction was enforced by the use of summary powers of search, confiscation and imprisonment, free of any obstruction from Parliament.

2–10

Decrees of the Star Chamber. In the same year 1556, by a decree of the Star Chamber, it was forbidden, amongst other things, to print contrary to any ordinance, prohibition, or commandment in any of the statutes or laws of the realm, or any injunction, letters patent, or ordinances set forth, or to be set forth, by the Queen's grant, commission or authority. By a later decree, this time in the reign of Mary's Protestant sister, Elizabeth I, dated June 23, 1585, every book was required to be licensed, and all persons were prohibited from printing: "any book, work, or copy against the form or meaning of any restraint contained in any statute or laws of this realm, or in any injunction made by Her Majesty, or her Privy Council; or against the true intent and meaning of any letters patent, commissions, or prohibitions under the great seal, or contrary to any allowed ordinance set down for the good government of the Stationers' Company".

2–11

In 1623, a proclamation was issued to enforce this decree; reciting that it had been evaded, amongst other ways "by printing beyond the sea such allowed books, works, or writings, as have been imprinted within the realm, by such to whom the sole printing thereof by letters patent or lawful ordinance or authority doth appertain".

---

[71] 25 Hen. 8, c.15.

[72] This statute is the prototype of the American "manufacturing clause", which provided that foreign works were protected only if printed in the USA. This clause was repealed only by the US Copyright Act 1976.

[73] An Act of Henry VIII (*Cum privilegio regali as imprimendum solum*) set up the system of privileges for the printing of books in England in 1529.

[74] For a discussion of the prerogative and its residual status in the UK, see *Monotti* in [1992] 9 E.I.P.R. 305.

[75] Confirmed by Elizabeth I in 1559.

In 1637, the Star Chamber codified its law on book licensing and printing and again decreed that "no person is to print or import (if printed abroad) any book or copy which the Company of Stationers, or any person, hath or shall, by any letters patent, order or entrance in their register book, or otherwise, have the right, privilege, authority, or allowance, solely to print".[76]

2–12   **First Licensing Act.** In 1640, however, the Star Chamber was abolished; with the Cromwellian revolution, the King's authority was set at naught; all the regulations of the press, and restraints previously imposed upon unlicensed printers by proclamations, decrees of the Star Chamber and charter powers given to the Stationers' Company were deemed, and certainly were, illegal. The scandalous nature of some libellous publications induced Parliament to pass an ordinance in 1643 which prohibited printing, unless the book was first lawfully licensed and entered in the register of the Stationers' Company. The ordinance prohibited printing of any such licensed book without the consent of the owner, or importing it (if printed abroad), upon pain of forfeiting the same to the owner or owners of the copies of the said books, and "such further punishment as shall be thought fit". The provision necessarily presupposed the property to exist; it would have been of no effect if there had been no admitted owner. An owner could not at that time have existed otherwise than by common law. In 1647, 1649 and 1652 further ordinances were passed in similar terms.[77] Finally, in 1662 the Licensing Act was passed[78] which likewise prohibited the printing of any book unless first licensed and entered in the register of the Stationers' Company. It ordered that no person should presume to print "any heretical, seditious, schismatical, or offensive books or pamphlets, wherein any doctrine or opinion shall be asserted or maintained which is contrary to the Christian faith, or the doctrine or discipline of the Church of England, or which shall, or may, tend to be to the scandal of religion or the church, or the government or governors of the church, state, or commonwealth, or of any corporation or particular person or persons whatever". It further prohibited the publication of unlicensed books, prescribed regulations as to printing and empowered the King's messengers, and the master and wardens of the Stationers' Company, to seize books suspected of containing matters hostile to the Church or Government. It was necessary to print at the beginning of every licensed book the certificate of the licenser to the effect that the books contained nothing "contrary to the Christian faith, or the doctrine or discipline of the Church of England, or against the state and government of this realm, or contrary to good life or good manners, or otherwise, as the nature and subject of the work shall require". To prevent fraudulent changes in a book after it had been licensed, a copy was required to be deposited with the licenser when application was made for a licence.

The Act further prohibited any person from printing or importing, without the consent of the owner, any book which any person had the sole right to print by virtue of letters patent, or "by force or virtue of any entry or entries thereof duly made or to be made, in the register book of the said Company of Stationers, or in the register book of either of the universities". The penalty for piracy was forfeiture of the books and six shillings and eight pence for each copy, half to go to the King, and half to the owner. The sole property of the owner is here acknowledged in express terms as a common law right; and so the legislature which passed that

---

[76] 4 Burr. 2312.

[77] It has been questioned whether these clauses were applicable to anybody other than members of the Stationers' Company— *i.e.* whether they were more than by-laws for the regulation of the members *inter se*, but it is doubtful whether any such restricted interpretation can be put upon their scope.

[78] 13 & 14 Car. 2, c.33.

Act must have recognised the concept that the productions of the brain could be the subject-matter of property. To support an action on this statute, ownership of the book had to be proved or the plaintiff could not have recovered, because the action was to be brought by the owner who was to have a half share of the penalty. The various provisions of this Act in effect prevented piracy, without actions at law or Bills in equity. Cases of disputed property did, however, arise. Some of them were between different patentees of the Crown; in some the point was whether the property belonged "to the author, from his invention and labour, or the King, from the subject-matter".

End of the Licensing Acts. The Licensing Act 1662 was continued by several Acts of Parliament, but expired in May 1679. The system had fallen into disrepute because the power of members of the Stationers' Company to claim copyright in perpetuity had led to high prices and a lack of availability of books. Powerful arguments were also being heard in favour of freedom of the press. The control of the book trade exercised by the Stationers' Company was broken with the result that piracy flourished. Soon thereafter, a case is reported in Lilly's Entries of Hilary Term,[79] in which action was brought for printing 4,000 copies of the Pilgrim's Progress, of which the plaintiff was the true proprietor, as a result of which he had lost the profit and benefit of his copy. **2–13**

Ordinances of the Stationers' Company. In 1681, all legislative protection having ceased, the Stationers' Company adopted an ordinance, or byelaw of its own, which recited that several members of the company had "great part of their estates in copies", that by ancient usage of the company, when any book or copy was duly entered in their register to any member, such person had always been reputed and taken to be the proprietor of such book or copy, and ought to have the sole printing thereof. The ordinance further recited that this privilege and interest had of late been often violated and abused; and it then provided a penalty against such violation by any member or members of the company, where the copy had been duly entered in their register. This ordinance was an attempt by the members of the Stationers' Company, who on finding their property in copies of books ("their estates in copies, which belonged to them by the common law") no longer under the protection of the Licensing Act, to provide for the failure of legislation and to regulate the printing trade themselves, although the ordinance was, of course, only applicable to their own members. The ordinance, however, shows what the common law right was then deemed to be. The situation was much the same as if an association of persons were to agree that any one of their number should pay a penalty for violating the acknowledged rights of property of any other person in the association, provided such rights were duly entered in their common records. It would not be an attempt to create the right, but it would justly be regarded as acknowledgment of the existence of such a right.[80] **2–14**

In another byelaw, passed in 1694, it was stated that copies were constantly bargained and sold amongst the members of the company as their property, and bequeathed to their children and others for legacies and to their widows for maintenance; and it was provided that, if any member should, without the consent of the member by whom the entry was made, print or sell the same, he should pay a fine of 12 pence for every copy.

New legislation sought. Parliament was regularly petitioned, therefore, for a new Licensing Act. The booksellers argued that failure to continue exclusive **2–15**

---

[79] 31 Car. 2, B.R. *Ponder v Brady, Lilly's Entries*, 67; see Carter, 89; 4 Burr. 2317; Skinner 234; 1 Mod. 257.
[80] *Curtis on Copyright*, p.38.

rights of printing had resulted in disincentives to writers. Without some form of protection to encourage authors, the public interest would be harmed by the decreased flow of works.[81]

To the submissions of the members of the Stationers' Company were added in 1690 the plea of the philosopher, John Locke, who, although opposed to licensing as leading to unreasonable monopolies injurious to learning, demanded a copyright for authors which he justified by the time and effort expended in the writing of the work which should be rewarded like any other work.[82]

In one of the petitions presented to the House of Commons in support of applications to Parliament in 1709 for a Bill to protect copyright, the last clause or paragraph was as follows:

"The liberty now set on foot of breaking through this ancient and reasonable usage is no way to be effectually restrained but by an Act of Parliament. For by common law, a bookseller, can recover no more costs than he can prove damage, but it is impossible for him to prove the tenth, nay, perhaps, the hundredth part of the damage he suffers; because a thousand counterfeit copies may be dispersed into as many hands over the kingdom, and he not be able to prove the sale of them. Besides, the defendant is always a pauper, and so the plaintiff must lose his costs of suit. (No man of substance has been known to offend in this particular, nor will any ever appear in it.) Therefore, the only remedy by the common law is to confine a beggar to the rules of the King's Bench or Fleet, and there he will continue the evil practice with impunity. We therefore pray that confiscation of counterfeit copies be one of the penalties to be inflicted on offenders".[83]

2–16   **The Statute of Anne 1709.** In response to these applications, in 1709, the first Copyright Act was passed and came into force on April 10, 1710.[84] The Statute of Anne was the first copyright law, as such, in the world and it is the foundation on which the modern concept of copyright was built.[85] Two of the principles established by the Statute of Anne were revolutionary at the time: recognition of the author as the fountainhead of protection and adoption of the principle of a limited term of protection for published works.[86] It was not the first English statute to deal with copyright but the first to be adopted by Parliament as opposed to royal decree and the first to be unconnected with censorship. According to its Preamble, the Act responded to several objectives: the encouragement of learning, the prevention of the practice of piracy for the future, and for the "encouragement of learned men to compose and write useful books". The Act gave authors of books already printed the sole right and liberty of printing them for a term of 21 years from the date of entry into force of the Act, and of books not then printed the sole right of printing for 14 years, with a proviso that, after the expiration of

[81] L. Patterson, *Copyright in Historical Perspective* (Vanderbilt University Press, Nashville, 1968), p.142.

[82] J. Locke, *Two Treatises of Government* (1690), P. Laslett, ed. (Cambridge University Press, 1988), para.27. And see J. Locke, "Memorandum to Edward Clark", cited in M. Rose, *Authors and Owners, the Invention of Copyright* (Harvard University Press, 1994), pp.32, 33. Ahead of his time, Locke also advocated limiting the term of protection to a period of from 50 to 70 years after the death of the author.

[83] 4 Burr. 2318.

[84] 8 Anne, c.19.

[85] "The unfortunately conceived and unhappily expressed statute of Queen Anne, which, however, has the honour of being the first copyright statute at law to be found in the *Corpus Juris* of any State, either of ancient or modern times", *per* A. Birrell, *The Law and History of Copyright in Books* (Cassell and Co., London, etc., 1899), p.68; *cf.* also G. Davies, *Copyright and the Public Interest* (2nd ed., Sweet & Maxwell, 2002), p.11 *et seq.*

[86] Lord Hailsham of St. Marylebone in *Halsbury's Laws of England* (4th ed., Butterworths, London, 1974), Vol.9.

the said term of 14 years, the sole right of printing or disposing of copies should return to the authors thereof, if they were then living, for another term of 14 years. Thus the statutory copyright was not to be limited to the members of the Guild and it was not to exist in perpetuity.

The title to the copy of a book had to be registered before publication with the Stationers' Company, and nine copies had to be delivered to certain libraries. Penalties for infringement were severe: infringing books were subject to forfeiture and a fine of a penny for every sheet copied. This resulted in a steep fine when many copies of a substantial book were pirated. The fine was divided equally between the Crown and the complainant. It is of interest to note that the Act also expressly provided that the importation and sale of books in Greek and other foreign languages printed "beyond the seas" should remain unaffected by its provisions. The idea that foreign authors also merited protection was not yet ripe.

The question of literary property. In 1731, 21 years after the Statute of Anne came into force, the stationers' monopoly on printing books already in print when the Statute had come into force expired. Printers in Scotland and in the provinces issued new editions of old books and the London booksellers sought means to prevent this in a series of cases brought before both the English and Scottish courts.[87] The booksellers argued that, at common law, and regardless of the expiry of the statutory period of protection, authors had a perpetual right to authorise printing, rights which had been assigned to them.[88] It was not disputed that the manuscript of a work was the property of the author and that prior to publication his right to it could continue indefinitely. The question was posed only with regard to published works and the argument raged over whether copyright was an inalienable form of property arising from the act of creation or a limited right of control or monopoly bestowed by Statute. The issue was first decided in favour of the perpetual right by a majority of the Court of King's Bench in the case of *Millar v Taylor* in 1769.[89] The Court held that there was a common law right of an author to his copy stemming from the act of creation and that that right was not taken away by the Statute of Anne. The decision was finally overturned, however, by the House of Lords in *Donaldson v Beckett*[90] in 1774, a case which decided that copyright was the deliberate creation of the Statute of Anne and thereafter treated as statutory property. Thus, the effect of the Statute of Anne was to extinguish the common law copyright in published works, while leaving the common law copyright in unpublished works unaffected. Such rights were abolished by the 1911 Act.[91]

The universities and colleges, alarmed at the consequence of this decision, ap-

2–17

---

[87] *Millar v Taylor*, 4 Burr. 2301; *Donaldson v Beckett*, 4 Burr. 2407; *Hinton v Donaldson* (1773) Mor 8307. For accounts of English cases in the mid-eighteenth century see A. Birrell, *The Law and History of Copyright in Books* (Cassell and Co., London, etc., 1899), pp.99 *et seq.;* D. Saunders, "Purposes or Principle? Early Copyright and the Court of Chancery", [1993] 12 E.I.P.R. 452. The Scottish cases are described in H.L. MacQueen, "Copyright, Competition and Industrial Design", (2nd ed.) *Hume Papers on Public Policy: Vol.3, No.2* (Edinburgh University Press, 1995). See also R.S. Tompson, "Scottish Judges and the Birth of British Copyright", *The Juridical Review*, Pt 1 (1992) 1.

[88] B. Kaplan, *An Unhurried View of Copyright* (Columbia University Press, 1967), p.12. See also M. Rose, "Author as Proprietor: Donaldson v Beckett and the Genealogy of Modern Authorship", in *Of Authors and Origins, Essays on Copyright Law*, B. Sherman and A. Strowel (eds) (Clarendon Press, Oxford, 1994).

[89] *Millar v Taylor*, 4 Burr. 2301.

[90] (1774) 4 Burr. 2407.

[91] See para. 2–28, below.

plied for and, in 1775, obtained an Act of Parliament[92] establishing in perpetuity their right to all the copies given or bequeathed to them or which might thereafter be given to or acquired by them. Such rights were abolished by the 1988 Act.

2–18   **Copyright Acts 1709/1833.** The Statute of Anne remained in force, virtually unchanged, until superseded by the Copyright Act of 1842, although it was amended from time to time to add to the list of protected works. The 1709 Act protected only "books and other writings" but gradually engravings, prints, lithographs and works of sculpture were added.[93] In 1777, musical and dramatic compositions were held to be books within the meaning of the Statute of Anne.[94] However, the duration of copyright was somewhat varied by section 4 of the Copyright Act 1814,[95] which replaced the two contingent 14-year periods of protection by a single term of 28 years, calculated from the day of first publication, or the natural life of the author, if he was still living at the expiration of that period. In 1833, the Dramatic Copyright Act[96] provided for a public performance right in dramatic works.

2–19   **Copyright Act 1842.**[97] The 1709 and 1814 Acts were repealed by the Copyright Act 1842. From 1837 to 1842, in spite of the opposition of Lord Macaulay, the celebrated historian and politician, Mr Serjeant Talfourd had used his best endeavours and expended all his eloquence to accomplish its passing. In contending for an extension of the period during which protection was afforded to literary works to 60 years after the death of the author, he argued:

> "There is something peculiarly unjust in bounding the term of an author's property by his natural life, if he should survive so short a period as 28 years. It denies to age and experience the probable reward it permits to youth—to youth, sufficiently full of hope and joys to slight its promises. It gives a bounty to haste, and informs the laborious student, who would wear away his strength to complete some work which the world will not willingly let die, that the more of his life he devotes to its perfection, the more limited shall be his interests in its fruits. It stops the progress of remuneration at the moment it is most needed; and when the benignity of nature would extract from her last calamity a means of support and comfort to the survivors—at the moment when his name is invested with the solemn interest of the grave—when his eccentricities or frailties excite a smile or a shrug no longer—when the last seal is set upon his earthly course, and his works assume their place among the classics of his country—your law declares that his works shall become your property, and you requite him by seizing the patrimony of his children".[98]

Macaulay opposed extending the period of protection beyond the life of the author at all, being convinced that to do so would "inflict grievous injury on the public, without conferring any compensating advantage on men of letters". He emphasised that "no natural right of property" could survive the original proprietor. "The system of copyright has great advantages, and great disadvantages ... The advantages ... are obvious. It is desirable that we should have a supply of good books; we cannot have such a supply unless men of letters are liberally remunerated: and the least objectionable way of remunerating them is by a

---

[92] 15 Geo. 3, c.53: and see Copyright Act 1801 (41 Geo. 3, c.107).
[93] See paras 2–19 to 2–24, below.
[94] *Bach v Longman* (1777), 2 Cowp. 623 and see paras 2–21 and 2–22, below.
[95] 54 Geo. 3, c.156.
[96] Dramatic Literary Property Act 1833 (3 & 4 Will. c.15).
[97] 5 & 6 Vict. c.45.
[98] *Hansard*, Vol.56, cols 1841, 342/3.

monopoly. Yet monopoly is an evil. For the sake of the good we must submit to the evil; but the evil should not last a day longer than is necessary for the purpose of securing the good."[99]

The 1842 Act as adopted represented a compromise, extending the period of literary copyright to the life of the author and seven years after his death, or a term of 42 years from publication, whichever should be the longer, or, if published after the author's death, 42 years from publication. Literary copyright covered material such as books and pamphlets, sheet music, maps, charts and plans. The performing right extended for the same period. The 1842 Act contained provisions for registration at Stationers' Hall. This was not compulsory, but had to be done before any action could be brought against infringers. In spite of its defects, both in substance and in draftsmanship, the 1842 Act remained the governing statute as to literary copyright until it was repealed by the 1911 Act.[1]

Engraving copyright. In the realm of artistic copyright, engravings were the first to receive legislative protection. In 1734, the Engraving Copyright Act[2] was passed, conferring copyright upon these for a term of 14 years.   **2–20**

No provision was made in this Act for the protection of any work of which the engraver was not also the designer; and this has been accounted for by the fact that Hogarth, by whose influence the Act was introduced,[3] was invariably the designer as well as the engraver of his celebrated works.

The Engraving Copyright Act of 1766[4] was passed to remedy this oversight, and extended protection to any person making an engraving from the original work of another, provided that they bore the copyright owner's name and the publication date. It also prolonged the period of protection to 28 years from the date of first publication. A further Act, the Prints Copyright Act of 1777,[5] improved the remedies for piracy; the Prints Copyright Act of 1836[6] extended the provisions of the Engravings Acts to Ireland, and the International Copyright Act of 1852[7] to prints taken by lithography or other mechanical process.

Sculpture copyright. Works of sculpture were the next to be protected, by the Sculpture Copyright Act 1814,[8] the term of protection being 14 years from first publication, with a further reversionary term of 14 years to the author, if then living and provided he had not meanwhile divested himself of the copyright.   **2–21**

Musical and dramatic copyright. Musical and dramatic compositions were held to be "books" within the meaning of the Copyright Acts relating to literary works[9]; but the performing right was not statutorily protected until the year 1833, when the Dramatic Copyright Act, commonly known as Bulwer Lytton's Act,[10] conferred an exclusive right of public performance for 28 years, with a reversionary period to the author for the residue of his life, provided the work was printed and published; if the work was not printed or published, the term of protection was uncertain.   **2–22**

---

[99] *Hansard*, Vol.56, cols 1841, 344.
[1] 1 & 2 Geo. 5, c.46.
[2] 8 Geo. 2, c.13.
[3] Hogarth's series of engravings "Marriage à la mode", had been very popular and widely pirated.
[4] 6 Geo. 3, c.38.
[5] 17 Geo. 3, c.57.
[6] 6 & 7 Will. 4, c.59.
[7] 15 & 16 Vict. c.12, s.14.
[8] 54 Geo. 3, c.56.
[9] *Bach v Longman* (1777) 2 Cowp. 623, *Storace v Longman* (1809) 2 Camp. 26, note; and see para. 2–18, above.
[10] 3 & 4 Will. 4, c.15.

Bulwer Lytton's Act only referred to dramatic pieces, but section 20 of the Literary Copyright Act 1842[11] dealt with the performing rights in both musical and dramatic pieces, and extended protection to the performing rights in both classes of works for a similar period to that provided for the duration of copyright in books, namely, a period of 42 years from first public representation or performance, or the life of the author and seven years after, whichever should be the longer: and 42 years from first public representation or performance for posthumous pieces.

Certain abuses arose with respect to the performing rights in musical works. In particular, a man named Wall gained considerable notoriety by purchasing performing rights and enforcing payment of "penalties" (royalties)—which were fixed at 40s. a performance by Bulwer Lytton's Act—from innocent infringers. This led to the passing of the Copyright (Musical Compositions) Acts of 1882 and 1888,[12] which required that notice of reservation of rights of public performance of any musical composition should be printed on every published copy thereof and left the question of payment of costs and amount of penalties to the discretion of the court.

2–23   Owing to the injury caused to proprietors of the copyright in musical compositions by the practice of selling pirated copies of songs and music through street hawkers, and the difficulty of finding any substantial person to proceed against for infringement, the Musical (Summary Proceedings) Act 1902, and the Musical Copyright Act 1906,[13] were passed providing summary methods of procedure against infringers of musical copyright. Both these last-mentioned Acts remained unrepealed by the 1911 Act, but were repealed by the 1956 Act.

2–24   **Painting, drawing and photographic copyright.** Paintings, drawings and photographs were protected, for the first time, by the Fine Arts Copyright Act, 1862.[14] This Act sought to protect paintings, drawings and photographs for the term of the life of the author and seven years after his death, but to obtain the full benefit of the Act, registration at Stationers' Hall was necessary. However, the wording of the Act was such as to produce the somewhat remarkable result that, unless the work was commissioned, so as to vest the copyright initially in the person commissioning the work, the copyright was lost altogether upon the first sale of the work unless, on that occasion, there was some written instrument signed by the artist dealing with the copyright, either by way of express assignment to the purchaser, or by way of express retention by the artist.[15] This requirement probably also applied to works of foreign origin, the copyright in which was secured in the United Kingdom by Convention or Order in Council, though it seems unlikely that foreign artists would have been aware of this peculiar provision of English law on a first sale to a dealer in their own country.

2–25   **Royal Commission of 1875.** Having regard to the number of Acts in force dealing with different branches of the law of copyright, a consolidating statute was urgently required. In 1875, a Royal Commission was appointed to inquire into the working of the Copyright Acts, and the Commissioners presented their Report in 1878.[16] In this Report they stated[17]:

"The first observation which a study of the existing law suggests is that its

---

[11] 5 & 6 Vict. c.45. Lectures were protected by the Lectures Copyright Act 1835 (5 & 6 Will. 4, c.65).
[12] 45 & 46 Vict. c.40; 51 and 52 Vict. c.17.
[13] 2 Edw. 7, c.15; 6 Edw. 7, c.36.
[14] 25 & 26 Vict. c.68.
[15] *Copinger* (4th ed.), pp.366, 367.
[16] Report of the Commissioners, C.2036, HMSO (1878).

form, as distinguished from its substance, seems to us bad. The law is wholly destitute of any sort of arrangement, incomplete, often obscure, and, even when it is intelligible upon long study, it is in many parts so ill-expressed that no one who does not give such study to it can expect to understand it. The common law principles, which lie at the root of the law, have never been settled. The well-known cases of *Millar v Taylor*, *Donaldson v Beckett*, and *Jefferys v Boosey* ended in a difference of opinion amongst many of the most eminent judges who have ever sat upon the Bench. The 14 Acts of Parliament which deal with the subject were passed at different times between 1735 and 1875.[18] They are drawn in different styles, and some are drawn so as to be hardly intelligible. Obscurity of style, however, is only one of the defects of these Acts. Their arrangement is often worse than their style. Of this the Copyright Act of 1842 is a conspicuous instance".

The Commission recommended that the law should be codified and clarified and entertained "no doubt that the interest of authors and the public alike requires that some specific protection should be afforded by legislation to owners of copyright". It is also of interest to note that the Commission made a strong recommendation to the Government of the day to enter into a bilateral copyright agreement with the United States of America in order to provide for reciprocal protection for British and US authors.[19]

The Berne Convention. Despite the recommendations of the Commission, no **2–26**
consolidating statute was passed and it was the involvement of this country in the preparatory work on the Berne Convention which finally gave the necessary impetus for reform. In 1886, the United Kingdom was represented at the Conference of Powers held at Berne, which resulted in the framing of the Berne Convention for the Protection of Literary and Artistic Works (the Berne Convention),[20] which the United Kingdom ratified with effect from December 5, 1887. Prior to the Conference, the International Copyright Act, 1886,[21] was passed, making the necessary alterations and additions to the International Copyright Act 1844[22] to enable the United Kingdom to give the required protection to foreign authors. The main changes to the existing copyright law were, first, that registration and deposit in the United Kingdom of foreign works were no longer required; second, an exclusive right to produce or import translations was granted in respect of foreign works, extending for the full term of the copyright in the original work. A further effect of the 1886 Act was to apply British copyright law to works originating in British possessions. This meant that a work produced in one of the possessions received protection not only in the United Kingdom but in all of the rest of them.[23]

However, the Berne Convention did not give rise to a comprehensive reform of the United Kingdom law at that stage. It was not until after the revision conference in Berlin held in 1908, where a number of modifications were introduced to the Berne Convention, including the principle that protection under the Conven-

---

[17] Report of the Commissioners, C.2036, HMSO (1878), paras 7, 8, 9.

[18] Several more were added between 1875 and 1910.

[19] There was at the time no protection for British authors in the USA and British works were being widely pirated; see Report of the Commissioners, C.2036, HMSO (1878), paras 233–252.

[20] *cf.* paras 24–04 *et seq.*, below. See also I. Davis, "A Century of Copyright: the United Kingdom and the Berne Convention", (1986), *Copyright*, p.177.

[21] 49 & 50 Vict. c.33.

[22] 7 & 8 Vict. c.12. This empowered the Crown to issue orders in Council extending copyright protection in the UK to cover works first published in foreign countries. Orders could specify shorter terms of copyright for foreign works than for British ones, and registration and deposit were required to secure protection for foreign works.

[23] On November 28, 1886, an Order in Council was issued under the 1886 Act extending the protection of the Berne Convention to all British dominions.

tion should be free from compliance with any formalities and a period of protection of the life of the author and 50 years thereafter, that it was recognised that the law had to be revised if the United Kingdom was to join with the other Powers and be in a position to give foreigners the protection required by the revised Act of the Convention.

2–27   **1909 Copyright Committee.** In 1909, therefore, a Committee was appointed to consider and make recommendations for changes to the copyright law required by the Berlin Act. The Committee examined the Berlin Act article by article to see which, if any, amendments were required to the law of this country. After hearing evidence, it reported to Parliament,[24] generally approving the provisions of the Berlin Act, and recommending the passing of a consolidating and amending Act, saying: "It would be a great advantage if the British law were placed on a plain and uniform basis, and that basis were one which is common so far as practicable to the nations which join in the Convention".[25]

2–28   **Copyright Act 1911.** The Copyright Act 1911, which was aimed at giving effect to these recommendations, received the Royal Assent on December 16, 1911.[26] This Act repealed all previous statutes on the subject of literary and artistic copyright, with the exception of the Musical (Summary Proceedings) Copyright Act of 1902 and the Musical Copyright Act of 1906,[27] and one section of the Fine Arts Copyright Act of 1862.[28] The 1911 Act came into force on July 1, 1912.[29]

The 1911 Act brought about several major reforms in order to comply with the Berlin Act of the Berne Convention on all points where it conflicted with the previous law of the United Kingdom. The requirement for registration, a leftover from the days of the Stationers' Company, was abolished altogether in conformity with one of the main principles of the Berne Convention, namely that protection under the Convention should not be subject to any formalities; the Act extended the term of protection to the international standard of life plus 50 years and gave authors of literary, dramatic, or musical works, the sole right to make any record, perforated roll, cinematograph film, or other contrivance by means of which the work could be mechanically performed or delivered.[30] Works of architecture were protected as artistic works and choreographic works as dramatic works. For the first time, the Act also provided that copyright should subsist in records, perforated rolls, and other contrivances by means of which sounds may be mechanically reproduced (sound recordings), in like manner as if such contrivances were musical works. The term of copyright for such contrivances was 50 years from making.[31]

The adoption of the term of protection of 50 years *post mortem auctoris* (pma) to conform with the Berlin Act and international practice was subject to an important proviso. At any time after the expiration of 25 years from the death of the author of a published work, a compulsory licence permitted reproduction subject to payment by the publisher to the author's heirs of a 10 per cent royalty.[32] There was a similar provision under which, at any time after the death of the author of a literary, dramatic or musical work which had been published or

---

[24] Report of the Committee on the Law of Copyright, Cmd.4976 (1909).

[25] Report of the Committee on the Law of Copyright, Cmd.4976 (1909), p.7.

[26] 1 & 2 Geo. 5, c.46. For a survey of the law of copyright immediately prior to the Copyright Act 1911, see *Copinger* (12th ed.), pp.1105–1333.

[27] See paras 2–22 and 2–23, above.

[28] See para. 2–24, above.

[29] Copyright Act 1911, s.37(2)(a).

[30] s.1(2)(d).

[31] s.19.

[32] s.3.

performed in public, application could be made to the Judicial Committee of the Privy Council to require the owner of the copyright to grant a licence allowing reproduction or performance of the work in public, if he had refused consent.[33]

Films were not specifically protected but that gap was remedied by the courts in 1912, when it was held that each frame of a film was a photograph, *i.e.* an artistic work.[34] In addition to the new rights given to authors to make cinematographic films and sound recordings of their works, certain doubtful areas of the law were clarified, the author being given a dramatisation right, a translation right and a public performance right in musical works. In 1934, the courts held that the copyright in sound recordings, of which the maker or producer was the author, also included a performance right separate from that in the works recorded.[35]

2–29

Abolition of common law copyright. The 1911 Act also abolished common law copyright in unpublished works.[36] Except in the cases of paintings, drawings and photographs,[37] unpublished works received no statutory protection prior to the commencement of the 1911 Act,[38] but were protected, if at all, under the common law.[39] This was a perpetual right for unpublished works which ceased on publication, after which an author had to base his claim for protection upon his statutory right, if any. The nature of this common law protection was fully discussed in *Re Dickens*,[40] in which one of the questions at issue was whether the common law right in an unpublished manuscript passed under a bequest, taking effect before the passing of the 1911 Act, of "all my private papers". The Court of Appeal held that the right was an incorporeal right existing independently of the property in the manuscript and one which did not pass to a legatee or donee on a bequest or gift of the manuscript itself.

2–30

Committee of 1951. The influence of the Berne Convention continued to make itself felt. The Convention was further revised at Rome in 1928 and at Brussels in 1948.[41] Following the Brussels Conference, in 1951, a further Committee was appointed "to consider and report whether any, and, if so, what changes are desirable in the law relating to copyright in literary, dramatic, musical and artistic works with particular regard to technical developments and to the revised international convention for the protection of literary and artistic works signed at Brussels in June 1948 and to consider and report on related matters". The Committee also took into consideration the preparatory work on the Universal Copyright Convention (UCC) which was subsequently signed at Geneva in 1952 under the auspices of UNESCO.[42] This Committee, after hearing evidence, reported to Parliament[43] recommending that Her Majesty's Government should accede to the Convention as revised at Brussels in 1948, and proposing a number of changes in the law.

2–31

[33] s.4.
[34] *Barker v Hutton* (1912) 28 T.L.R. 496.
[35] *Gramophone Co. Ltd v Stephen Cawardine & Co.* [1934] Ch. 450.
[36] See para. 2–17, above.
[37] *Tuck & Sons v Priester* [1887] 19 Q.B.D. 48; Fine Arts Copyright Act 1862 (25 & 26 Vict. c.68), s.1.
[38] Copyright Act 1911, s.37(2)(a).
[39] *Donaldson v Beckett* (1774) 4 Burr. 2408; *Millar v Taylor* (1769) 4 Burr. 2303; *Jefferys v Boosey* [1855] 4 H.L.C. 815; *Beckford v Hood* (1798) 7 T.R. 620; *Mayall v Higbey* (1862) 1 H. & C. 148; *Macmillan & Co. v Dent* [1907] 1 Ch. 107; *Mansell v Valley Printing Co.* [1908] 2 Ch. 441; *Bowden Bros. v Amalgamated Pictorials Ltd* [1911] 1 Ch. 386; *Albert (Prince) v Strange* (1849) 1 M. & G. 25.
[40] [1935] Ch. 267.
[41] *cf.* in general paras 24–04 *et seq.* and specifically para. 24–08, below.
[42] As a result this Convention is variously referred to as the Universal, Geneva or UNESCO Convention.
[43] Report of the Committee on the Law of Copyright, Cmd.8662 (1952).

2–32 **Copyright Act 1956.** A Bill to give effect to these recommendations received the Royal Assent on November 5, 1956.[44] This Act repealed the 1911 Act (except ss.15, 34 and 37[45]), the Musical (Summary Proceedings) Copyright Act of 1902 and the Musical Copyright Act of 1906 as well as the outstanding section of the Fine Arts Copyright Act of 1862. It came into force on June 1, 1957,[46] and was amended by the Design Copyright Act 1968.

The 1956 Act duly repealed the compulsory licence provisions of sections 3 and 4 of the 1911 Act, which were no longer permitted under the Brussels Act of the Berne Convention and made other limited changes to the law to enable the United Kingdom to ratify it. For example, it introduced a specific right to object to false attribution of authorship.[47] In addition, it introduced reforms to deal with technical advances affecting copyright since the passage of the 1911 Act. For the first time, specific protection for 50 years from publication for films (cinematographic works), for sound and television broadcasts and for published editions of works was introduced. The performance right in sound recordings recognised by the *Cawardine* case in 1934 was confirmed. The Act also established the Performing Right Tribunal to which disputes over the terms of broadcasting and public performance licences for the use of musical works and sound recordings by broadcasters and others could be referred.

2–33 **No protection for performers.** Performers were not protected under the 1956 Act.

Protection under the criminal law against misappropriation of their performances was first introduced in 1925. A series of statutes—the Performers' Protection Acts 1958–72—subsequently extended the protection available to them, establishing summary offences against making recordings or films of performances, performing them in public and broadcasting performances without the written consent of the performer.

2–34 **Committee of 1973.** The pace of technical development, allied to the continuing evolution of the Berne Convention, which was revised in Stockholm in 1967 and again in Paris in 1971, prompted the setting up of a new departmental Committee in 1973 to consider and report whether any, and if so what, changes were desirable in the law relating to copyright as provided in particular by the 1956 Act and the Design Copyright Act 1968, including the desirability of retaining the system of protection of industrial designs by the Registered Designs Act 1949. There was specific exclusion from the terms of reference of "any consideration of the merits of lending to the public as one of the acts restricted by copyright in a work". The Public Lending Right Act 1979 in fact established a non-copyright scheme to provide authors with remuneration paid out of public funds in respect of the lending of books in an entirely separate legislative process.[48]

The Committee, after receiving written and oral evidence, reported to Parliament.[49] The report proposed simplification of the general structure of the Copyright Act 1956 and a whole series of reforms aimed at rationalising and updating the law. Apart from recommending the repeal of registered design monopoly protection as then provided by the Registered Designs Act 1949, other major recommendations were made to take account of the problems raised by

---

[44] 4 & 5 Eliz. 2 c.74.

[45] ss.34 and 37(2) were repealed by the Statute Law (Repeals) Act 1986 (c. 12); s.15 concerned the delivery of copies to the British Museum and other libraries.

[46] SI 1957/863, see *Copinger* (12th ed.), para.1735.

[47] 1956 Act, s.43 (*cf.* CDPA 1988, s.84).

[48] See Ch.19, below and Vol.2 at B3.i.

[49] Report of the Committee to consider the Law on Copyright and Designs, Cmnd.6732 (1977).

new technical developments since the 1951 Committee had reported. Attention was drawn to the impact of this new technology on the methods by which works could be reproduced, on the techniques for recording sounds and sequences of visual images and on computer technology. The report also contained recommendations in relation to the United Kingdom's obligations under various international conventions having regard, in particular, to the revision of the Berne Convention at Stockholm in 1967 and at Paris in 1971, and of the Universal Copyright Convention at Paris in 1971 as well to the Rome Convention for the Protection of Performers, Producers of Phonograms and Broadcasting Organisations (the Rome Convention), which had been adopted in 1961.[50]

The report was acclaimed as a highly valuable contribution to the copyright debate but legislation did not follow for over a decade. During this period, the Government legislated on an ad hoc basis to amend the Copyright Act 1956 to deal with such urgent matters as improved remedies against piracy, which had become a real scourge as a result of new technology facilitating reproduction techniques, and the protection of computer software and cable programmes; these measures were contained in particular in the Copyright Act 1956 (Amendment) Act 1982, the Copyright (Amendment) Act 1983, the Cable and Broadcasting Act 1984 and the Copyright (Computer Software) Amendment Act 1985. The Government also produced a series of consultative documents on copyright law reform.[51] These culminated only in 1986 with a White Paper outlining the Government's legislative intentions.[52]

Semiconductor products. By the Semiconductor Products (Protection of Topography) Regulations 1987[53] a topography right, similar to copyright, was given to the designs of semiconductor products. These regulations were made on August 20, 1987, and came into force on November 7, 1987.

2–35

Copyright, Designs and Patents Act 1988. In October 1987, a Bill was introduced into the House of Lords which, as its title suggests, was not limited to copyright. In fact, it contained seven parts, only one of which was concerned with copyright and new statutory moral rights, the others being concerned with such matters as new statutory performers' rights, a new design right and amendments to the Registered Designs Act 1949. Other provisions were concerned with patents and Patent Agents and Trade Mark Agents. The Bill received the Royal Assent on November 15, 1988.[54]

2–36

The 1988 Act, *inter alia*, repealed the whole of the 1956 Act, the Copyright (Computer Software) Amendment Act 1985, and the Performers' Protection Acts 1958, 1963 and 1972, but did not repeal section 15 of the 1911 Act (concerning the delivery of copies of newly published books to the British Museum and other libraries) which was left unrepealed by the 1956 Act and the Statute Law (Repeals) Act 1986.[55]

The 1988 Act incorporated the previous ad hoc amendments to the 1956 Act which had dealt with remedies against piracy and protection with respect to computer software and cable programmes. It also introduced specific protection with respect to satellite broadcasting and cable programmes for their operators and for

---

[50] See Ch.24, below.
[51] Reform of the Law relating to Copyright, Designs and Performers' Protection, Cmnd.8302, HMSO, July 1981. Intellectual Property Rights and Innovation, Cmnd.9117, December 1993. The Recording and Rental of Audio and Video Copyright Material, Cmnd.9445, February 1985.
[52] Intellectual Property and Innovation, Cmnd.9712, HMSO, 1986.
[53] SI 1987/1497: see *Copinger* (13th ed.), para.A–565 and Ch.14, below.
[54] c. 48: see Vol.2 at A1.
[55] c. 12.

right owners, granted the right to control rental to the authors of films and phono-grams (under United Kingdom law at the time in both cases the producers) and computer programs, created moral rights for authors and film directors to enable the United Kingdom to ratify the Paris Act of the Berne Convention, replaced the Performing Right Tribunal with a Copyright Tribunal with extended powers over collecting societies and provided civil rights of action for performers and produc-ers of phonograms against unauthorised exploitation of performances. More controversially, it created a new perpetual non-copyright right in favour of the Hospital for Sick Children, Great Ormond Street.[56]

2–37   Another controversial issue, which the 1988 Act failed to legislate upon, was so-called private copying, *i.e.* the non-commercial copying of sound recordings and audiovisual works for personal and domestic use. By the 1980s, private copying had become a major unauthorised use of copyright works, a use which still escapes the control of the copyright owners. In 1977[57] the Whitford Committee had recommended that a "levy" on recording equipment, similar to that operated in the Federal Republic of Germany at the time, should be implemented. The Government in its Green Paper published in 1981,[58] then invited public debate on the issue, but said that it was not convinced of the need for a levy.

Following this consultation, the Government published a White Paper in 1986[59] in which it stated that it had decided to introduce a "levy" on blank audio tapes. This decision, which was announced in the Queen's speech[60] setting out the Government's programme in June 1987, was subsequently overturned and the subject was dropped from the Bill introduced later that year and, in spite of major discussions of the issue in both Houses of Parliament, remained excluded from the 1988 Act.[61] The issue has remained controversial and, to date, the Govern-ment has maintained its opposition to the introduction of any royalty or levy system to provide remuneration to right owners for private copying.

2–38   **Semiconductor products.** There have also been new regulations concerned with the design of semiconductor products[62] which revoked the earlier regulations.[63] Further amendments have been made by the Design Right (Semiconductor Topographies) (Amendment) Regulations 1991 (SI 1991/2237), the Design Right (Semiconductor Topographies) (Amendment) Regulations 1992 (SI 1992/400) and the Design Right (Semiconductor Topographies) (Amendment) Regulations 1993 (SI 1993/2497).[64]

2–39   **Developments.** In the 16 years since the 1988 Act entered into force, it has been amended continuously, mainly to implement EC Directives on the subject of copyright and related rights resulting from the European Commission's pro-gramme for the harmonisation of such laws within the European Union. This pro-gramme, the resulting Directives and their implementation in the United Kingdom, is described in detail in Chapter 25 of this work. Suffice it to say here

---

[56] CDPA 1988, s.301 and Sch.6.
[57] *Copyright and Designs Law*, Report of the Committee to consider the Law on Copyright and Designs; Chairman, the Hon. Mr Justice Whitford, Cmnd.6732 (1977).
[58] *Reform of the Law Relating to Copyright, Designs and Performer's Protection: A Consultative Document*, Cmnd.8302 (1981) Ch.3, para.23.
[59] *Intellectual Property and Innovation, presented to Parliament by the Secretary of State for Trade and Industry by Command of Her Majesty*, Cmnd.9712 (1986).
[60] Queen's Speech: June 25, 1987. The Copyright Bill, without provisions for royalties for private copying was introduced in October 1987.
[61] *cf.* para. 25–99, below.
[62] SI 1989/1100 as amended by SI 1989/2147 (see Vol.2 at B10.i) and SI 1990/1003.
[63] SI 1987/1497: see para. 2–32, above and Ch.14, below.
[64] See Ch.14, below.

that the amendments required to the 1988 Act have concerned the provisions regarding the legal protection of computer programs, the protection of performers, producers of sound recordings and films and broadcasting organisations, rental and lending rights, rights concerning satellite broadcasting and cable retransmission, rights in databases and, most importantly of all, the period of protection, which has been extended to 70 years pma with respect to literary, artistic and musical works, including films and computer programs.[65]

More recently, the United Kingdom has transposed into the 1988 Act the EC Directive on the harmonisation of certain aspects of copyright and related rights in the information society.[66] The Directive harmonises rights in certain key areas, primarily to meet the challenge of the internet and e-commerce, and digital technology in general. It also deals with exceptions to these rights and legal protection for the technological aspects of rights management systems. The Copyright and Related Rights Regulations 2003 therefore amended the 1988 Act in the following respects: the definition of broadcasting has been updated to take account of new electronic transmission techniques and the internet; a new restricted act of communication to the public of a work has been defined; performers have been accorded a making available right; the permitted acts in relation to copyright works and rights in performances, the so-called exceptions to copyright have been amended to conform with the Directive; protection for right owners against the circumvention of technical protection measures applied to copyright works and against the removal or alteration of electronic rights management information is introduced. Further substantial amendments to the 1988 Act were made by the Broadcasting Act 1990,[67] including the creation of two new forms of compulsory licence concerned with the inclusion of sound recordings (but not the music on the sound recordings) in broadcasts and cable programmes, and the provision of information about broadcast programmes.[68] The Broadcasting Act 1990 has itself been amended by the Broadcasting Act 1996, which in turn further amended the 1988 Act.

The future. The 1988 Act in the form in which it was first adopted may be seen as the last copyright legislation to be passed in the United Kingdom free of the influence of the harmonisation programme of the European Commission. Historically, since preparatory work began in the 1870s on the international standards later incorporated in the Berne Convention, the law of copyright in the United Kingdom has developed taking account of international norms and obligations under the various copyright and related rights conventions which have entered into force in the meantime. However, since the United Kingdom was traditionally influential in the intergovernmental negotiations leading to the adoption of

2–40

---

[65] See paras 25–76 *et seq.*, below. SI 1992/3233 on Copyright—The Copyright (Computer Programs) Regulations 1992 (came into force January 1, 1993) implementing Council Directive 91/250 of May 14, 1991 on the legal protection of computer programs; SI 1995/3297, the Duration of Copyright and Rights in Performances Regulations (came into force January 1, 1996) implementing Council Directive 93/98 of October 29, 1993 harmonising the term of protection of copyright and certain related rights. SI 1996/2967, Copyright and Related Rights Regulations (came into force December 1, 1996) implementing the Directive on rental right and lending right and on certain rights related to copyright in the field of intellectual property of November 19, 1992 (92/100 [1992] O.J. L346/61) and the Directive on the co-ordination of certain rules concerning copyright and rights related to copyright applicable to satellite broadcasting and cable retransmission of September 27, 1993 (93/83 [1993] O.J. L248/15); SI 1997/3032, the Copyright and Rights in Databases Regulations 1997 (came into force January 1, 1998) implementing Directive of the Parliament and Council 96/9 [1996] O.J. L77/20.

[66] Directive 2001/29 (O.J. L167/10, 22.6.2001), transposed into UK law by the Copyright and Related Rights Regulations 2003, SI 2003/2498, which came into force on October 31, 2003.

[67] c. 42. The provisions of this Act came into force on various dates: see the Broadcasting Act 1990 (Commencement No.1 and Transitional Provisions) Order 1990 (SI 1990/2347 (c.61)); see also Vol.2 at A2.ii.

[68] Broadcasting Act 1990, ss.175 and 176.

the multinational conventions, and many other countries throughout the English-speaking world and the Commonwealth had copyright laws based on that of the United Kingdom, the conventions as adopted took account of the British tradition of copyright and were broadly compatible with it. Moreover, the Berne and UCC Conventions, in particular, the Rome and Phonograms Conventions and the most recent TRIPs Agreement, did not impose doctrinal approaches to the protection of authors and other beneficiaries of copyright, but left it to national legislators to implement the standards required as they saw fit. Thus, for example, over 100 years' membership of the Berne Convention, while, as has been seen, having considerable influence on the development of the United Kingdom's copyright law, did not fundamentally alter the approach of the copyright law. The Convention evolved in such a way as to provide a bridge between the approaches of the common law and civil law systems in many respects. The influence of the harmonisation programme of the European Commission, however, on the United Kingdom's copyright law is altogether more far-reaching, introducing elements of the civil law authors' rights approach.[69] This process will continue, since the harmonisation programme of the Commission is not yet complete and areas of copyright law not so far affected will be dealt with. As mentioned above and described in detail in Chapter 25, below, the new EC Directive on copyright and related rights in the information society was adopted in April 2001[70] and has been implemented in the United Kingdom. The Directive deals with issues relevant to the use of copyright material in the information society, the internet and e-commerce, in particular, the rights of reproduction and communication to the public (electronic transmission, including digital broadcasting and "on demand" services). It also limits the type and scope of permitted exceptions to these rights and provides legal protection for technological measures used to safeguard rights and identify and manage copyright material (such as copy protection systems and digital watermarks and encryption systems). One of its main aims was to bring the laws of the EU Member States into conformity with the new international Treaties adopted in December 1996, the WIPO Copyright Treaty (WCT) and the WIPO Performances and Phonograms Treaty (WPPT). The Directive required Member States to transpose its provisions into their national laws before December 22, 2002; the United Kingdom failed to meet this deadline but the Directive was transposed into the law of the United Kingdom by the Copyright and Related Rights Regulations 2003.[71]

Another important area where recent EC harmonisation will require changes to the UK copyright law is the artist's resale right (not so far recognised under the law of the United Kingdom) following the adoption in July 2001 of the Directive on the resale right for the benefit of the author of an original work of art.[72] The European Commission has also announced plans for future legislation to harmonise the law relating to collecting societies.[73] Furthermore, in a recent review of the EC legal framework in the field of copyright and related rights the Commission announced that it is working towards the objective of codifying the *acquis communautaire*, *i.e.* the existing body of EC law in this field.[74]

The challenges to copyright presented by the digital and online environment of the information society, with the possibility of works protected by copyright being recorded, stored and made available on demand in digital form all over the

---

[69] *cf.* Introduction, para. 1–05 , above, and paras 25–64 *et seq.*, below.
[70] See para. 2–39 n.66, above.
[71] Copyright and Related Rights Regulations (SI 2003/2498), *cf.* para. 2–39 n.66, above.
[72] *cf.* Ch.25, below, paras 25–91 *et seq.*
[73] *cf.* Ch.25, below, paras 25–100 *et seq.*
[74] *cf.* Ch.25, below, paras 25–102 *et seq.*

world through electronic communications networks such as the internet, and with the threat of unlimited, perfect-quality copies being made of them, are not therefore a matter for the United Kingdom alone. Indeed, even a harmonised legislative response from the European Union will not suffice to protect rights owners adequately. Only a global approach will provide the protection required; the WCT and WPPT need to attract a membership at least as wide as that of the Berne Convention in a very short time-span if the present lack of protection is to be brought under control. Technology provides the capability for rights owners to use digital tools, such as encryption, copy protection devices and embedded rights management information, with which to control exploitation of their works, and effective measures to protect these systems against circumvention devices designed or marketed for infringement purposes are envisaged by the WCT and WPPT and the EC Information Society Directive.

Technical advance has long been the motor for the development of the law of **2–41** copyright. The legislator must ensure that the basic principles of copyright protection are applied to and enforced in the new digital environment, if rights owners are to be persuaded to provide content for online services. It is also in the interest of service providers and the general public that there should be certainty about the extent of the rights available, so as to facilitate contractual arrangements and rights management so that the potential of the information society can be realised.

CHAPTER THREE

REQUIREMENTS FOR COPYRIGHT PROTECTION

1. INTRODUCTION

Introduction. This chapter deals with the question of whether copyright subsists   **3–01**
in a particular subject matter. Today, this matter is governed by the Copyright,

Designs and Patents Act 1988.[1] The first stage of the inquiry is to identify whether the particular subject matter is capable of being a copyright work under the 1988 Act; the second stage is to consider whether the requirements laid down in the Act for subsistence of copyright in such subject matter are met. The first stage is dealt with in Section 2, "Subject Matter of Protection", and the second stage is dealt with in Sections 3, 4, and 5, "Fixation", "Originality" and "Qualifying Conditions". Section 6 deals with "Foreign Works", and Section 7 with the circumstances in which protection may be denied to works.

2. SUBJECT MATTER OF PROTECTION

A. INTRODUCTION: COPYRIGHT WORKS

3–02   **Introduction: copyright works.** The approach of the 1988 Act is to provide that copyright can subsist, subject to the conditions for subsistence being met,[2] only in specified categories of what in the Act are referred to as "works". In every case, therefore, the question whether copyright subsists in a particular subject matter first involves the question whether the subject matter falls within one of the specified categories of works. The works in which copyright can subsist under the 1988 Act are described in section 1(1) of the 1988 Act as follows:

(a) original literary, dramatic, musical or artistic works,

(b) sound recordings, films or broadcasts,[3] and

(c) the typographical arrangement of published editions.

Works of these descriptions in which copyright subsists are referred to in the 1988 Act as copyright works.[4] Each of these categories of works is discussed in turn in this Section.

3–03   **Categorisation of works.** The history of statutory copyright protection[5] is a history of steady enlargement of the extent of protection by the addition of new categories of protected subject matter, as technology advances or a need is perceived to protect the fruits of human endeavour. Statutory protection was first accorded to books (1709) (which included musical and dramatic compositions), then to engravings (1734), sculptures (1814), prints and lithographs (1852), paintings, drawings and photographs (1862), mechanical contrivances for the reproduction of sound (1911), films (in their own right), broadcasts and typographical arrangements of published works (1956), cable programmes (1985)[6] and computer programs (1985). The introduction of specific legislation to deal with a particular category of work has often been preceded by attempts to fit the work into an existing category, sometimes successfully and other times not. Although the origins of this categorisation lie in the piecemeal development of the extension of protection to new subject matter, the need to retain such categorisation has been driven, first, by the need to define, so as to be able to determine what falls within and what falls outside protection, and, secondly, by the need to make different provisions for different kinds of works.

It is a legacy of this piecemeal development that the description given to the

---

[1] See s.1. As to works made before the commencement of the 1988 Act, see para. 3–07, below.

[2] CDPA 1988, ss.1(1) and 153.

[3] Cable programmes are now subsumed under the general heading of broadcasts. See paras 3–82 *et seq.*, below.

[4] CDPA 1988, s.1(2). Note that in the civil law copyright systems, subject matters such as sound recordings, broadcasts and some films are not regarded as "works", this being an expression reserved for the creation of human authors.

[5] As to common law copyright in unpublished works, see Ch.2.

[6] Now protected under the heading of broadcasts: see para. 3–82.

categories into which a particular subject matter is subsumed may often be misleading. Thus, the terms literary and artistic works in the context of the Berne Convention must be given a much wider meaning than those terms have traditionally been given in the United Kingdom legislation, including, as they do, musical works, dramatic works and films. In the United Kingdom, the example can be given of the protection of computer programs and tables of figures as literary works. An earlier example was the protection of sound recordings as musical compositions under the 1911 Act.

Are the categories always mutually exclusive? In some cases, the 1988 Act **3–04** makes it clear that certain categories of copyright work are mutually exclusive or what the boundaries of certain works are. Thus it is expressly stated that a literary work cannot be a dramatic or musical work; a musical does not include any words or action intended to be sung, spoken or performed with the music; a photograph cannot also be part of a film;[7] and a soundtrack associated with a film is part of the film.[8] Occasionally, a subject matter may appear to fall into several categories at the same time but on closer examination it turns out to be a composite creation in which there is embodied more than one copyright work. So, for example, in relation to a song, there will be separate protection for the words and for the music.[9] Other works may embody a number of underlying works, for example a film, where in addition to the copyright in the film itself[10] there will be independent protection for the score, the screenplay and other works such as any novel on which the film is based.

Apart from cases where the Act specifically provides for mutual exclusion and apart from "composite" creations, it now seems clear that a single subject matter of creation can, depending on the circumstances, fall at the same time into two or more categories of copyright work. Unless the categories are expressly stated by the Act to be mutually exclusive, the only question is whether the subject matter in fact falls within the descriptions in question. Thus in *Norowzian v Arks Ltd (No.2)*,[11] the Court of Appeal held that the categories in subsections 1(1)(a) ("original literary, dramatic, musical or artistic works") and 1(1)(b) ("sound recordings, films or broadcasts") were not mutually exclusive. It followed that since the proper definition of a dramatic work is a work of action, with or without words or music, which is capable of being performed before an audience,[12] and a film could in appropriate circumstances fit this description, a film can be protected both as a "film" and as a dramatic work, assuming the work satisfies the definitions of each kind of work. The reasons why the court took the view that these categories were not mutually exclusive were simply that (a) there was no express requirement of mutual exclusivity in the 1988 Act[13] and (b) the absence of any requirement of originality in subsection 1(b) was sufficient ground for no exclusion to be implied.[14] This is consistent with the earlier view expressed by Jacob J.

---

[7] CDPA, ss.3(1), 3(2) and 4(2), respectively.

[8] CDPA, s.5B(2).

[9] *Redwood Music Ltd v B. Feldman & Co Ltd* [1979] R.P.C. 385; *Electronic Techniques (Anglia) Ltd v Critchley Components Ltd* [1997] F.S.R. 401, 413. Contrast the position in France, where words which accompany music are treated as part of a single musical work (with the consequence, in the past, of benefiting from the longer term of protection accorded to musical works).

[10] As to which, see para. 3–77, below.

[11] [2000] F.S.R. 363.

[12] See para. 3–35, below.

[13] The fact that the 1956 Act, s.48(1) expressly provided that a dramatic work did not include a cinematograph work whereas the 1988 Act was silent on the point was also said to support the conclusion, although Nourse L.J. thought that it would be unsafe to base any construction of the provisions of the 1988 Act on those of the 1956 Act.

[14] Buxton L.J. also considered that the United Kingdom's obligations under the Berne Convention

in *Anacon Corp Ltd v Environmental Research Technology Ltd*[15] that the visual part of a circuit diagram might be both a literary work and an artistic work (the literary work consisting of the table or compilation of information to be read from the diagram, namely the components, and how the components were interconnected).[16] It seems that this view was regarded as wrong in *Electronic Techniques (Anglia) Ltd v Critchley Components Ltd*,[17] where Laddie J., although accepting[18] that a circuit diagram could be a literary and an artistic work provided information could be read from it, and thus holding that the particular circuit diagram in that case was a literary work to the extent that it listed six components, said:[19] "... although different copyrights can protect simultaneously a particular product and an author can produce more than one copyright work during the course of a single episode of creative effort, ... it is quite another thing to say that a single piece of work by an author gives rise to two or more copyrights in respect of the same creative effort. The categories of copyright work are, to some extent, arbitrarily defined .... In the case of a borderline work, I think there are compelling arguments that the author must be confined to one or other of the possible categories. The proper category is that which most nearly suits the characteristics of the work in issue." Laddie J. took the view that the circuit diagram in *Anacon* was correctly regarded as a literary work to the extent that it consisted of a list or compilation of components whose identity could be read from the diagram but that the information as to how one component was connected to another, which could be deduced from the lines representing the connecting wiring, was not part of any literary work since it was purely visual information. As was pointed out in *Sandman v Panasonic U.K. Ltd*,[20] however, it is not clear that this is a correct reading of *Anacon* or why, if it is legitimate to look at written symbols for components to ascertain their nature, the lines which interconnect the symbols on a circuit diagram are not merely symbols for interconnections which can be "read" in order to understand their starting points and ending points and how they cross over each other or connect together. The conflict which exists between *Anacon* and *Electronic Techniques* was examined by Pumfrey J. in *Sandman*,[21] where he reached the conclusion that two such copyrights might subsist side by side. He gave as examples an e.e. cummings poem about a cat, written in the shape of a two-dimensional cat, and a Chinese calligraphic work.

Part of the confusion arises because of the way in which the question is often expressed, for example, by asking whether a work (in the singular) can be both a literary work and an artistic work. The better approach in such a case is to ask whether a single form of expression can, for example, be both a literary work and an artistic work. It is suggested that, to the extent that the subject matter comes within the definition of a literary work in that it conveys information or ideas in a form which can be written, spoken or sung,[22] it is a literary work and, to the extent that it comes within the meaning of an artistic work in that it conveys

---

required that any work of cinematography within the meaning of the Berne Convention was included within a "dramatic work", as that expression was to be understood in the 1988 Act. See para. 3–35, below.

[15] [1994] F.S.R. 659, although acknowledging that he had not heard proper argument on the point.

[16] See also *Comprop Ltd v Moran* [2002] J.L.R. 222 (Royal Ct of Jersey) where it was noted that a map might be both an artistic work and a literary work, the literary work consisting in the written information which could be read from the map.

[17] [1997] F.S.R. 401.

[18] [1997] F.S.R. 401 at 412.

[19] [1997] F.S.R. 401 at 413.

[20] [1998] F.S.R. 651.

[21] Although again without full argument.

[22] See para. 3–11, below.

purely visual information or ideas,[23] it is an artistic work. It is suggested that there is no objection in principle to a single form of expression being protected as both kinds of work: it is both a literary work and an artistic work.

At first sight, difficulties might be thought to arise as a result of the same subject matter being classified as two different kinds of work.[24] Thus, for example, the rights associated with a copyright work vary according to the description of the work,[25] as do the acts in relation to a copyright work which are permitted (and thus which do not amount to an infringement of copyright).[26] Again, the categorisation of works also has importance beyond copyright protection, as the same descriptions of works are used in relation to moral rights protection[27] and rights in performances.[28] However, the question in each case is whether the subject matter is a literary work, or an artistic work, etc. and to the extent that it is one or more of these, then the statutory consequences will follow.

What categories are not exclusive? It follows from the above that the categories of literary and artistic works are not mutually exclusive and also that a single form of expression can be both a dramatic work and a film. Since, like a film, some broadcasts can be described as works of action, with or without words or music, which are capable of being performed before an audience, it seems that the same subject matter can be both a dramatic work and a broadcast. Apart from cases in which the 1988 Act expressly delimits categories of works, most, if not all other categories are mutually exclusive simply because of the way in which they are defined.

3–05

What amounts to a "work"? For many purposes, it is important to identify precisely the "work" in question, for example because infringement is defined to take place when an unlicensed act takes place in relation to the "work as a whole or any substantial part of it".[29] This question is partly tied up with such questions as what amounts to a *literary*, etc. work,[30] and partly with what amounts to an *original* work.[31] A "work" is a thing which satisfies the statutory description of a literary, dramatic, etc. work. At the end of the particular process of creation, one must look at what has been created and assess whether it is a literary, etc. work and then whether it is an original work. The creation of a work may of course extend over a period of time, and be the subject to revisions. At each interval in the process of creation there is likely to have been created a new copyright work, even though as yet incomplete in the mind of the author.[32] Assuming this is so, it is not, however, appropriate to say of the final product of creation that it is composed of a number of separate works, each corresponding to a stage in the creative process. It is a single work,[33] albeit that there are also a number of ante-

3–06

---

[23] See paras 3–51 *et seq.*, below.
[24] As recognised in *Electronic Techniques (Anglia) Ltd v Critchley Components Ltd* [1997] F.S.R. 401.
[25] see Ch.7, below.
[26] See Ch.9, below.
[27] See CDPA 1988, s.77(1).
[28] CDPA 1988, s.180(2).
[29] See s.16(3)(a) of the 1988 Act and paras 7–23 *et seq.*, below.
[30] As to which see, *e.g.* paras 3–11 *et seq.*, below.
[31] As to which see paras 3–123 *et seq.*, especially 3–133, below.
[32] *Brighton v Jones* [2004] EWHC 1157 (Ch) (first scenes of a dramatic work); *Taylor v Rive Droite Music Ltd* [2004] EWHC 1605 (Ch), para.247.
[33] In *Ladbroke (Football) Ltd v William Hill (Football) Ltd* [1964] 1 W.L.R. 273, the House of Lords refused to regard a work of compilation as made up of its constituent elements for the purposes of an infringement claim.

cedent works.[34] A claimant cannot choose to divide up the subject matter into small parts, claiming that each part is "a work".[35]

3–07 **Old works: transitional provisions**. What is the position of a work made before the commencement of the 1988 Act (August 1, 1989)? To be a protected work, it must fall within the description of protected subject matter under the 1988 Act itself. Since, however, the Act provides that copyright in a pre-1988 Act work only subsists after commencement if copyright subsisted in it immediately before commencement,[36] it follows that in theory one must ask whether the work also fell within one of the descriptions of protected subject matter under the previous Copyright Act, namely the Copyright Act 1956.[37] Save in relation to works for which there are special transition provisions,[38] there is, however, no need to go through this step because the 1988 Act has been framed in such a way as to include all previous descriptions of protected subject matter. If a work falls within one of the descriptions of protected work under the 1988 Act, one can therefore safely assume that it fell within one of the descriptions of protected work under the pre-existing law.[39]

B. LITERARY WORKS

(i) History of protection

3–08 **Oldest category of protected works.** As already pointed out,[40] the category of literary works is the oldest category of protected works. Historically, it was not a category which was capable of exhaustive definition. Even in the early days of statutory protection for this category, when the protected subject matter was described as "books", it was necessary to add a definition which extended the category beyond what would ordinarily have been understood by that expression.[41]

3–09 **Literary works under the 1911 and 1956 Acts.** Neither statute attempted a complete definition of the term "literary work". The 1911 Act merely stated that

---

[34] In *CCH Canadian Ltd v Law Society of Upper Canada* [2002] 4 F.C. 213 (Canada Fed CA) (reversed on appeal, but not on this point, at [2004] S.C.C. 13), the question as to what is a "work" was answered by the Federal Court of Appeal of Canada as follows: "... one must decide whether the material in question is capable of existing outside of the context in which it is published, communicated, displayed, performed or otherwise disseminated. If a production is distinctive and reasonably able to stand alone, then it may be deemed a work in itself rather than a part of another work. However, if a production is dependent upon surrounding materials such that it is rendered meaningless or its utility largely disappears when taken apart from the context in which it is disseminated, then that component will instead be merely a part of a work" (Linden J.A., Sharlow J.A. agreeing). Rothstein J.A. suggested that a work was something which was complete or perhaps substantially complete. It is suggested that neither of these tests is correct. A work is something which conforms to the statutory description of the particular kind of work.

[35] *Coogi Australia Pty Ltd v Hysport International Pty Ltd* (1998) 157 A.L.R. 247 (Fed Ct of Aus).

[36] CDPA 1988, Sch.1, para.5(1).

[37] The approach under the 1956 Act was different to that under the 1988 Act. The 1956 Act provided a self-contained code as to protected works, making certain adjustments to that code in relation to works made before the 1956 Act came into force. See Sch.7 of that Act.

[38] As, for example, in the case of films, which became protected for the first time as such by the 1956 Act. See para. 3–79, below.

[39] Note that although CDPA 1988, Sch.1, para.35 provides that every work in which copyright subsisted under the 1956 Act immediately before commencement is to be deemed to satisfy the requirements of Pt I of the Act "as to qualification for copyright protection", this only refers to the qualification provisions referred to in s.9(3), not the question of whether the work falls within one of the descriptions of protected works.

[40] See para. 3–03, above.

[41] The Literary Copyright Act 1842 (5 & 6 Vict. c.45), s.2 defined books as every volume, part, or division of a volume, pamphlet, letterpress sheets, music sheets, maps, charts and plans.

a literary work included maps, charts and plans as well as table and compilations.[42] The inclusion of maps, charts and plans followed the previous categorisation of these works as literary works[43] and compilations were expressly included to ensure that such works, which had previously been protected as "books", remained protected.[44] The 1956 Act repeated this, as to tables and compilations, consigning maps, charts and plans to the more logical category of artistic works, as part of the definition of a drawing.[45]

The Berne Convention. By the time the composite definition of literary and artistic works came to be formulated in the Berne Convention, a lengthy list of examples had to be included, in order to demonstrate the width of these two expressions. The definition of "literary and artistic works" in Article 2(1) thus includes "every production in the literary, scientific and artistic domain, whatever may be the mode or form of its expression, such as books, pamphlets and other writings; lectures, addresses, sermons and other works of the same nature".

3–10

(ii) Literary works in general

Statutory definition: literary work. By section 3(1) of the 1988 Act, a literary work is defined to mean any work, other than a dramatic or musical work, which is written, spoken or sung. The definition continues by stating that a literary work includes a table or compilation (other than a database), a computer program, preparatory design material for a computer program, and, separately, a database. These specific examples of literary works are discussed below. Writing is further defined[46] as including any form of notation or code,[47] whether by hand or otherwise and regardless of the method by which, or the medium in or on which it is recorded.[48] The reference to a work which is written, spoken or sung clearly limits the nature of the protected subject matter to expressions by means of words.[49]

3–11

Exclusion of musical and dramatic works. The express exclusion of dramatic and musical works from the definition of literary work was new in the 1988 Act.[50] The way the exclusion is formulated means that if the work is properly a dramatic

3–12

---

[42] Copyright Act 1911, s.35(1).

[43] See para. 3–08, above.

[44] Parliamentary Debates, Fifth Series, House of Lords (1911) Vol.X, HMSO, at 211, Lord Gorell.

[45] Copyright Act 1956, s.48(1): "'literary work' includes any written table or compilation". But see *Comprop Ltd v Moran* [2002] J.L.R. 222 (Royal Ct of Jersey), as to logic of the 1911 Act in classifying a map as a literary work.

[46] CDPA 1988, s.178, and the term "written" is to be construed accordingly.

[47] Notation was included in the definition under the 1956 Act, s.48(1). The reference to code was new in the 1988 Act. The principal dictionary definition (OED) of notation is any set of symbols or characters used to represent numbers, quantities, etc. Presumably, also, a set of symbols or characters, such as the alphabet, used to represent words is equally a form of notation. If so, it is not clear what the addition of the word "code" in the 1988 Act adds.

[48] This part of the definition also enlarged the processes by which the notation can be written. The definition in the 1956 Act referred to "whether by hand or by printing, typewriting or any similar process". This made the distinction clear between something which was in handwriting, and something which was typed or printed, both of which processes may involve the use of the hand. The current definition is less elegant, in that the reference to "by hand" must presumably be read as "in handwriting"; the last part, however, clearly is intended to cover writing by means of a word processor or other electronic process, where the writing may be stored in computer memory or other electronic carrier.

[49] Sounds which are sung, but which do not consist of words in any human language, would, it is suggested, be a musical work, and therefore would be excluded from being a literary work.

[50] Whilst it had been recognised that in the case of songs under the 1956 Act the words and music were the subject of separate copyrights as literary and musical works, respectively, and to that extent the categories were mutually exclusive (see *Redwood Music Ltd v B. Feldman & Co Ltd* [1979] R.P.C. 385), this was not necessarily so between dramatic and literary works.

or musical work then it cannot be a literary work. This is unlikely to give rise to much difficulty in practice, nor, today, does much turn on whether a work is a literary work or a dramatic or musical work.[51]

3–13   **Protected subject matter.** As has been seen, under both the 1911 and 1956 Acts the protected subject matter was a "literary work", and what was protected was an "original literary work". This expression "original literary work" could be broken down into its constituent words, each of which added a shade of meaning to the composite whole. In particular, the word "original" has a particular significance in a copyright context,[52] so that in the past the analysis sometimes proceeded by asking whether the subject matter was a "literary work" and then whether it was an "original literary work". Even the expression "literary work" could be broken down by asking whether the subject matter came within the adjectival description of being "literary" and then whether it constituted a work,[53] although this was more unusual. In fact, in some of the cases it is not easy to deduce whether the issue being addressed was whether the work was a literary work or an original literary work.[54] Although a warning was given against treating the expression "original literary work" other than as a composite expression,[55] the need to do so was sometimes unavoidable.[56] The 1988 Act now legitimises a compartmentalised analysis, since a literary work is now defined "as *meaning* any *work*, other than a dramatic or musical work, which is written, spoken or sung …", thereby emphasising the need for there to be "a work" in the first place, the words "written, spoken or sung" going to the issue of whether or not the work is a literary or some other kind of work. Originality is a separate requirement of section 1(1)(a). Despite this change in the way in which literary work is defined, it seems likely, however, that the pre-1988 Act cases will remain

---

[51] The distinction, which had been of some importance under the 1911 Act, was already less important under the 1956 Act. Under the 1988 Act, the distinction has little importance, save possibly in the realm of infringement and as regards the restricted act of making an adaptation of a work, the definition of which is different in the case of each category of work (see CDPA 1988, s.21(3)(a) and (b)).

[52] See paras 3–123 *et seq.*, below.

[53] As in *Exxon Corporation v Exxon Insurance Consultants International Ltd* [1982] Ch. 119, at 143, *per* Stephenson L.J.: "I am not sure whether this can be said to be a 'work' at all; I am clearly of the opinion that it cannot be said to be a literary work"; and at 132, where Graham J. observed that the word "Jabberwock" could not be a "literary *work*" (his emphasis). See also *Apple Computer v Computer Edge* [1984] F.S.R. 481 at 495 (Fed Ct of Aus).

[54] Of course, if it was held that the work was entitled to copyright protection as an *original* literary work, it must have been a necessary part of the decision, or a matter of concession, that the work was a literary work.

[55] *Exxon Corporation v Exxon Insurance Consultants International Ltd* [1982] Ch. 119, *per* Stephenson L.J. at 139 ("… it is the expression as a whole in the context of the Act which has to be construed.") and *per* Oliver L.J. at 144 ("… for my part I do not think that the right way to apply a composite expression is, or at any rate is necessarily, to ascertain whether a particular subject matter falls within the meaning of each of the constituent parts, and then to say that the whole expression is merely the sum total of the constituent parts. In my judgment it is not necessary, in construing a statutory expression, to take leave of one's commonsense ….").

[56] For example, under s.84 the right to complain of false attribution arises in relation to a literary work, not an original literary work. See *Noah v Shuba* [1991] F.S.R. 14, where the same kind of issue arose under s.43 of the 1956 Act.

relevant,[57] although today increased emphasis will have to be placed on whether or not the subject matter is a "work".[58]

Written, spoken or sung. These words are not concerned with the question of fixation of the work.[59] Their purpose is to define what is a *literary* work. The common theme underlying the words "written, spoken or sung" is that of the expression of ideas or information by means of words. The reference to the possibility of the work being sung does not mean that the music of a song can be a literary work,[60] merely that singing is one possible means of expression using words. In the case of a spoken or sung work, the form of communication will necessarily involve the use of an ordinary human language. Whilst the voice need not be a human voice,[61] a communication by sign language would not appear to be capable of being a literary work (even if the requirement of fixation were satisfied by the communication being recorded on film), unless and until the work is written, spoken or sung. In the case of a written communication, the extended definition of writing so as to include any form of notation or code makes it clear that the writing need not be in the form of a human language, provided it conveys something and is capable of being understood, and indeed, the communication need not be in a form which is directly readable or intelligible to a human being.[62] The "writing" may even take the form of a diagram, provided information can be read from it.[63] In every case, the question is what is the work which lies behind, and is the subject of the communication. What matters is the message, not the medium. A message, expressed in writing, speech or song, will be capable of being a literary work. That is not, however, to confuse the expression of the message with its contents. It is with the expression and the form of that expression that copyright is concerned, not the content. This has particular consequences in relation to the issue of originality,[64] but in the present context it is this which distinguishes ideas and works, the latter being the subject matter of protection, not the former.[65]

3–14

Two points arise from this. First, a work conceived in the mind of a person, even though he uses words in his mind to formulate his thoughts, is not a literary work. It remains, at this stage, in the realm of ideas which have not been given any expression. The definition requires the work to be written, spoken or sung; it

---

[57] Not least because of s.172(2) of the 1988 Act, which provides that a provision of Pt I of the Act which corresponds to a provision of the previous law is not to be construed as departing from the previous law merely because of a change of expression. Nevertheless, care should be taken when considering cases decided before the 1911 Act because what was at issue there was not whether the work was a literary work but whether it was a "book" within the meaning given to that expression (see para. 3–08, above and *Exxon Corporation v Exxon Insurance Consultants International Ltd* [1982] Ch. 119, *per* Graham J., at 130).

[58] See, *e.g. R. Griggs Group Ltd v Evans* [2003] EWHC 2914 (Ch), para.17, where it was said that copyright could not exist in the expression "Dr Martens" because it was not a "work".

[59] This is the concern of CDPA 1988, s.3(2); see paras 3–105 *et seq.*, below.

[60] This is made clear by s.3(1), which defines a musical work as a work consisting of music, exclusive, *inter alia*, of any words intended to be sung with it.

[61] A person who speaks with the assistance of a computer-generated voice is expressing his thoughts in speech.

[62] Examples of other forms of notation or code are Braille, Morse code, shorthand, and computer-readable code; a work "written" in any of these will be a literary work.

[63] *Anacon Corp Ltd v Environmental Research Technology Ltd* [1994] F.S.R. 659. See, further, para. 3–17, below.

[64] See paras 3–105 *et seq.*, below.

[65] See, for a helpful discussion as to the distinction between the concept of a work and its expression in a detailed and concrete form, *Plix Products Ltd v Frank M. Winstone (Merchants)* [1984] 3 I.P.R. 390 at 418, *per* Pritchard J.: [1986] F.S.R. 63; affirmed [1985] 1 N.Z.L.R. 376, CA; [1986] F.S.R. 608. See also para. 3–18, below.

does not refer to a work which is *intended* to be written, spoken or sung.[66] Secondly, once a work is written, spoken or sung, it does not matter, for the purposes of its being a literary work, whether it was thought out as to its form and content before it was written, spoken or sung.[67] Thus, a person who gives an oral description from memory of an event is using speech to communicate information, and what is spoken by him will be a literary work, as this term is defined for the purposes of the 1988 Act, just as much as it would be if the person, being mute, communicated his recollection in writing.[68] Whether the spoken recollection is a copyright work will depend on whether it remains merely a spoken recollection, or becomes fixed, by being recorded in some way.[69] Similarly, a person who delivers a carefully thought out (but not previously written down) speech is delivering a literary work, as is a judge who delivers an *ex tempore* judgment.[70]

3–15   **"Literary" work.** The term "literary" work has never implied any requirement that the work must have any literary style or merit.[71] Rather, the word "literary" refers to the nature of the work, that is, one in which the expression is conveyed by means of words.[72] This point is now given statutory force by the fact that the word "literary" does not appear in the statutory definition of literary work in the 1988 Act at all: the only requirement is that it be a "work" which is "written, spoken or sung".

As already noted, in decisions under previous Acts little emphasis was placed on the individual words "literary" and "work" as opposed to the composite expression "literary work". Nevertheless, these cases provide a clear idea of what amounts to a literary work, namely something which is intended to afford another pleasure in the form of literary enjoyment or which is intended to convey information or instruction through the medium of writing, speech or song.[73] Although this definition will serve most purposes, and helps in borderline cases, it is clearly not exhaustive in that a work written for purely personal reasons, and without any intention of it being communicated to anyone, and thus not intended to afford another person literary pleasure, instruction or information, is nevertheless clearly

---

[66] This is irrespective of the lack of fixation of such work; but contrast the position of a musical work, discussed as para. 3–47, below.

[67] The issue of originality is a separate matter, and is discussed below.

[68] In *Gould Estate v Stoddart Publishing* [1996] Can. Abr. 3000, it was held that copyright did not subsist in an oral statement, because it was not a literary creation. The decision appears to have been based on the lack of permanence of such expression, but this is to confuse the requirement of fixation with the nature of the work itself.

[69] See further paras 3–113 *et seq.*, below.

[70] It had been suggested that a literary work under the 1956 Act was required to be expressed in some form of notation (see *Copinger* (12th ed.), pp.53, 85); the introduction of the words spoken or sung into the definition of a literary work in the 1988 Act makes it clear that there is no such requirement (following the recommendation of the 1977 Copyright Committee, Cmnd.6732, para.609 (viii)). See *Hansard*, HL Vol.490, cols 828–829 and Vol.493, cols 1058–1059. For a discussion of the problems in connection with copyright in spoken words, see Phillips in [1989] E.I.P.R. 231.

[71] See, *e.g. University of London Tutorial Press Ltd v University Tutorial Press Ltd* [1916] 2 Ch. 601 at 608, approved in *Ladbroke (Football) Ltd v William Hill (Football) Ltd* [1964] 1 W.L.R. 273, *per* Lord Pearce at 291; *Winterbottom v Wintle* (1947) 50 W.A.L.R. 58 (no literary merit required for a list).

[72] See *University of London Tutorial Press Ltd* [1916] 2 Ch. 601, *per* Peterson J., at 608: "The word 'literary' seems to be used in a sense somewhat similar to the use of the word 'literature' in political or electioneering literature and refers to written or printed matter" and *Ladbroke (Football) Ltd v William Hill (Football) Ltd* [1964] 1 W.L.R. 273, *per* Lord Pearce at 291: "[The words] are used to describe work which is expressed in print or writing ...". Today, of course, these statements should be understood as extending to spoken or sung matter, the emphasis being on the fact that the communication is by means of words.

[73] *Exxon Corporation v Exxon Insurance Consultants International Ltd* [1982] Ch. 119, in which the Court of Appeal approved the definition of a literary work given by Davey L.J. in *Hollinrake v Truswell* [1894] 3 Ch. 420 at 427–428 as being something which "is intended to afford either information and instruction or pleasure in the form of literary enjoyment".

capable of being a literary work.[74] A computer program is also not intended to convey instruction or information to another *person* but probably always was,[75] and is now expressly, a literary work. In most cases, however, whether or not a work satisfies this requirement will not present any particular problem and, as will be seen, there is a vast array of different types of works which without argument have been afforded protection as literary works. What are more instructive are those cases, few in number, in which protection has been denied on this ground. So, for example, protection was denied to the single invented word "Exxon" on the grounds that by itself it conveys no information, provides no instruction, gives no pleasure and is simply an "artificial combination of four letters of the alphabet which serves a purpose only when used in conjunction with other English words ...".[76] To similar effect is the observation that the word "Jabberwock" is not a literary work, only becoming part of a literary work and having meaning when it is embodied in Lewis Carroll's poem.[77] In South Africa, protection has been similarly denied to the invented single word "LePacer" on the grounds that it is meaningless.[78] Protection as a literary work was also denied to the layout of the body of the diary, *i.e.* the way in which the days and dates were set out with spaces for notes, etc.[79] Before the 1911 Act, protection was denied to a cardboard device in the shape of a sleeve for the human arm intended for use in dressmaking[80] since by itself it conveyed no information or instruction;[81] simple

---

[74] As noted in *International Business Machines Corporation v Spirales Computers Inc* (1984) 12 D.L.R. (4th) 351 (Fed Ct of Can). As to the definition in *Exxon* not being exhaustive, see also *Apple Computer v Computer Edge* [1984] F.S.R. 481 at 495 (Fed Ct of Aus).

[75] See para. 3–27, below.

[76] *Exxon Corporation v Exxon Insurance Consultants International Ltd* [1982] Ch. 119, *per* Oliver L.J. at 144. And see Graham J., at first instance, at 130: "... though invented and therefore original, [it] has no meaning and suggests nothing in itself. To give it substance and meaning, it must be accompanied by other words or used in a particular context or juxtaposition." Since the word could be written, spoken or sung, presumably today the case would be decided on the grounds that it was not a "work", as to which, see Stephenson L.J. at 143G.

[77] *Exxon Corporation v Exxon Insurance Consultants International Ltd* [1982] Ch. 119, *per* Graham J. at 132.

[78] *Kinnor (Pty) Ltd v Finkel T/A Harfin Agencies* (June 1, 1990, WLD 9059/90, Sup Ct of S.A.), leaving open the question whether the expression "Le Pacer" (two words) should be regarded differently as meaning, in the context of watches, a watch that paces other watches. *Sed quaere*, since by itself the expression means virtually nothing, and conveys no literary pleasure, instruction or information. See also *Proctor & Gamble Pharmaceuticals v Novopharm* [1996] Can. Abr. 299, in which it was held that it was arguable that copyright could subsist in the invented name "ASACOL".

[79] *G. A. Cramp & Sons Ltd v Frank Smythson Ltd* [1944] A.C. 329. This decision appears to have been reached independently of any question of originality.

[80] The device was curved so as to represent a human arm above and below the elbow and had printed on it the words "top curve line; under curve line; under arm curves; measure round the thick part of the arm; measure round the thick part of the elbow; measure round the knuckles of the hand;" together with curved lines relating to the words "under arm curves" and scales of inches and half-inches relating to the words "measure round the thick part of the arm," and "measure round the thick part of the elbow". The device also had certain holes in it and was intended for actual use in cutting out sleeves, and was not merely a set of instructions as to how to do so.

[81] *Hollinrake v Truswell* [1894] 3 Ch. 420. Lord Herschell and Lindley L.J. decided the case on the basis that the words and figures were not merely directions for the use of the device but were a part of the device itself, without which it could not be used, and except in connection with which they had no use. It was not therefore a "volume, part or division of a volume, pamphlet, sheet of letterpress, sheet of music, map, chart, or plan separately published" within the meaning of the 1842 Act, not being separately published nor being a publication complete in itself, but only a direction on a device, to be understood and used with it. And see also *Davis v Comitti* 52 L.T. (N.S.) 539 (printed portions for use on face of barometer, such as "high winds", etc.— meaningless unless used with barometer). There is no objection in principle, however, to instructions for use of a device being the subject of copyright: see *Meccano Ltd v Anthony Horden & Sons Ltd* [1918] S.R. (N.S.W.) 606. Davey L.J. decided *Hollinrake v Truswell* on what would now be regarded as the conventional ground that the sleeve chart gave no information or instruction and was not calculated to afford literary enjoyment or pleasure. As noted in *Meccano Ltd v*

instructions pasted on the outside of moneyboxes as to what to do with it;[82] an article described as a child's trick, consisting of an envelope with some simple words printed on the outside and, inside, a cardboard device and a verse by Longfellow.[83]

From this it might be thought that provided the words in question convey at least some information or instruction, even if they are unlikely to give any pleasure, then they will amount to a literary work. This is not the correct position, however, in that protection has been denied to expressions which, although they clearly have some meaning by themselves, have been considered too trivial.[84] Thus it was held that instructions on the use of a product, namely: "Follow clinic procedure for aftercare. If proper procedures are followed, no risk of viral infections can occur" did not, on their own, afford *sufficient* information, instruction or literary enjoyment to qualify for protection.[85] There must be doubt, however, whether the decision was correct since the instructions did convey information or instruction, and the issue of sufficiency should, it is suggested, go to the question of originality, not literary work. It is suggested that the decision can only have been justified on the grounds that the instructions were of such a banal nature that no one would pay any attention to them or thus receive information or instruction from them. The same comment can be made about the observation that the expression "Avoid the predicament of being without your glasses" was too trivial to merit protection.[86]

In accordance with these principles, virtually every product of writing, speech or song is likely to be a literary work and a vast array of works have been protected as such, whether the product of substantial creative endeavour such as a novels, newspaper articles or examination papers or more mundane things such as ordinary letters, written advertisements, rules for games and formulae. In this area of protected subject matter, the issue is usually whether the work is original or not, so that cases in which the point has been argued have been relatively rare.[87] Leaving aside cases about compilations and tables,[88] the following types of works have been protected: ordinary business letters;[89] examination papers;[90] a

Anthony Horden & Sons Ltd, the claimant was in effect seeking to copyright a tool. The instructions, apart from the tool, were meaningless.

[82] *Warren v Foster Bros. Clothing Co* (1906) 51 Sol. Jo. 145, on the basis, following *Hollinrake v Truswell* [1894] 3 Ch. 420, that the words only had use in relation to the box and therefore formed part of the box, and were thus not to be separately published. It was expressly left undecided whether the words had any literary merit on the grounds that the result would be the same either way.

[83] *Cable v Marks* (1882) 52 L.J. 107. The device cast a shadow resembling da Vinci's "Ecce Homo". The words were: "Entered at Stationers' Hall. Key enclosed. The Christograph: The Christian's Puzzle. Suitable for all sects and denominations—Every family should have it. Price, with Key, sixpence."

[84] These decisions therefore appear to give emphasis to the word "work" rather than the word "literary", although arguably this is something that might be better left to the issue of originality.

[85] *Noah v Shuba* [1991] F.S.R. 14 at 32, 33. This part of the decision was, however, *obiter*.

[86] *Kirk v J & R. Fleming Ltd* [1928– 35] Mac.C.C. 44. This comment was made as part of a wider decision on whether a number of commonplace sentences (of which the one quoted in the text formed part) strung together for the purposes of an advertisement constituted an original literary work. The basis of the decision as a whole appears to have been lack of originality, rather than the inherent inability of such phrases to amount to a literary work. See para. 3–129, below.

[87] The full variety of cases in which the subject matter has accepted without argument as a literary work can be seen from the cases on originality: see paras 3–129 *et seq.*, below.

[88] As to which, see para. 3–21, below.

[89] *British Oxygen Co Ltd v Liquid Air Ltd* [1925] Ch. 383, applied in *Tett Bros. Ltd v Drake & Gorham Ltd* [1928–35] Mac.C.C. 492. See also "Copyright in Letters" printed as an addendum in [1905–10] Mac.C.C.

[90] *University of London Press Ltd v University Tutorial Press Ltd* [1916] 2 Ch. 601.

manual of instructions for a toy, being complete in itself;[91] a form for use in correspondence courses;[92] material included in a diary consisting of the months, dates and days, with a three-month calendar;[93] a formula using symbols and numbers;[94] and a programme and a race card for greyhound racing.[95] A host of other mundane works have been protected without any argument on the point, for example, trade circulars,[96] consignment notes[97] the rules of a game,[98] and rules of a trade association.[99]

Names and titles as literary works. In the same vein is the reluctance of English courts to confer copyright protection on titles of newspapers, magazines, books and the like. In relation to books in particular, the title normally forms part of a copyright work consisting of the book as a whole and the issue here may be whether the copying of the title amounts to the taking of a substantial part of the whole work.[1] General statements can nevertheless be found in non-copyright cases to the effect that there is no property in a name or title standing alone unless it is the subject of goodwill or a registered trade mark.[2] In *Chilton v Progress Printing and Publishing Co*,[3] what amounted to a claim to copyright in individual names for horses was refused.[4] Much the same approach has been applied in relation to titles for books, newspapers, etc.[5] sometimes coupled with the expression

3–16

---

[91] *Meccano Ltd v Anthony Horden & Sons Ltd* [1918] S.R. (N.S.W.) 606, distinguishing *Hollinrake v Truswell* [1894] 3 Ch. 420.

[92] *Southern v Bailes* [1894] 38 S.J. 681, although it is not clear precisely what the copyright work was.

[93] *Waylite Diaries CC v First National Bank Ltd* [1993] (2) S.A. 128, (High Ct of S.A.).

[94] *Bookmakers' Afternoon Greyhound Services Ltd v Wilf Gilbert (Staffordshire) Ltd* [1994] F.S.R. 723 (formula describing how to do a calculation, and which could be set out at length using ordinary language). Copyright did not subsist, however, in the dividend forecasts which were produced by using the formula.

[95] *Bookmakers' Afternoon Greyhound Services Ltd v Wilf Gilbert (Staffordshire) Ltd* [1994] F.S.R. 723. Such a programme is probably more accurately classified as a compilation.

[96] *Coral Index Ltd v Regent Index Ltd* [1970] R.P.C. 147

[97] *Van Oppen & Co Ltd v Leonard Van Oppen* (1903) R.P.C. 617.

[98] *Caley (A. J.) & Son Ltd v Garnett (G.) & Sons Ltd* [1936–45] Mac.C.C. 99.

[99] *Co-operative Union Ltd v Kilmore, etc. Ltd* (1912) 47 I.L.T. 7.

[1] Which will almost invariably not be the case. See, *e.g. Francis Day and Hunter Ltd v Twentieth Century Fox Corp Ltd* [1940] A.C. 112; *Ladbroke (Football) Ltd v William Hill (Football) Ltd* [1964] 1 W.L.R. 273.

[2] See, *e.g. Taverner Rutledge Ltd v Trexapalm Ltd* [1975] F.S.R. 479, at 483 (no copyright or other property in the invented name "Kojak" by itself); *Miss World (Jersey) Ltd v James Street Productions Ltd* [1981] F.S.R. (C.A.) 309 at 311 (no property or copyright in a title such as "Miss World"); *Kean v McGivan* [1982] F.S.R. 119 (no property in the name "Social Democratic Party"); *Mirage Studios v Counter-Feat Clothing Co Ltd* [1991] F.S.R. 145, at 154 ("... there is a rule in copyright that you can have no copyright in a name ...").

[3] [1895] 2 Ch. 29.

[4] The claimant published in its newspapers the names of horses which were tipped to win races in the forthcoming week; each day the defendant published the names of horses which were tipped to win that day by various tipsters, including the claimant's tip. The basis of the decision was that the announcement of the name of a horse was not a protectable subject matter, being only an expression of the tipster's opinion. There is, however, nothing in principle to prevent the expression of someone's opinion being a literary work and today the case would probably be decided on the basis that while the claimant's newspaper as a whole was entitled to copyright, the taking of a single word from it could not amount to an infringement. For further comment on the case, see *Independent Television Publications Ltd v Time Out Ltd* [1994] F.S.R. 64.

[5] *Dick v Yates* (1881) 18 Ch. D. 76 (James L.J.: "... there cannot in general be any copyright in the title or name of a book."); *Licensed Victuallers' Newspaper Co v Bingham* (1888) 38 Ch. D. 139 (Bowen L.J.: "... there is no copyright in the title of a newspaper"); *Francis Day and Hunter Ltd v Twentieth Century Fox Corp Ltd* [1940] A.C. 112 at 123 ("... a title is not by itself a proper subject matter of copyright. As a rule a title does not involve literary composition, and is not sufficiently substantial to justify a claim to protection"). These cases overruled the earlier cases of *Weldon v Dicks* (1878) 10 Ch. D. 247 and *Mack v Petter* (1872) L.R. 14 Eq. 431, where such protection was conferred but which can be explained as passing off cases, as the law is now

of a fear of conferring a monopoly on part of the English language.[6] On this
basis, copyright protection has been denied to titles such as *Splendid Misery* for a
book,[7] *The Lawyer's Diary 1986* for a diary,[8] *The Licensed Victuallers' Mirror*
for a newspaper,[9] "The Man Who Broke the Bank at Monte Carlo" as the title for
a song,[10] *Opportunity Knocks* for a television game-show,[11] and "Dr Martens" for
the name of boots.[12] The courts have, however, been careful not to rule out the
possibility of such protection in appropriate circumstances,[13] although in practice
no case has ever gone this far. The only concrete example which has been given
judicially is the now archaic practice of the title-page of a book consisting of an
extended passage of text.[14] In *Lamb v Evans*,[15] protection was granted to an elaborate series of headings arranged alphabetically in a trade directory and provided
in four languages but this may have been a compilation case rather than a pure
"title" case.[16] It has been held arguable that a headline on a website consisting of
the words "Bid to Save Centre after Council Funding Cock-up", which had been
put together for the purpose of imparting information, was protected by copyright,[17] but this was based on a concession that a headline could be a literary
work.

3–17   **Literary work: code and other forms of notation**. It is not necessary that the
work should convey any information to the ordinary reader. A work which is

---

understood. See *Dick v Yates* and *Francis Day and Hunter Ltd v Twentieth Century Fox Corp Ltd.*
[6] See, *e.g. Rose v Information Services Ltd* [1978] F.S.R. 254 at 255.
[7] *Dick v Yates* (1881) L.R. 18 Ch.D. 76. It may well have been, however, that protection was denied on the grounds of lack of originality rather than because the title was not capable of protection: see the judgments of Jessel M.R. and Lush L.J.
[8] *Rose v Information Services Ltd* [1978] F.S.R. 254. Again, however, the ground of the decision may have been lack of originality.
[9] *Licensed Victuallers' Newspaper Co v Bingham* (1888) L.R. 38 Ch.D. 139.
[10] *Francis Day and Hunter Ltd v Twentieth Century Fox Corp Ltd* [1940] A.C. 112, where the House of Lords, at 123, apparently considered that although there might have been a certain amount of originality in choosing the title it was not a literary work.
[11] *Green v Broadcasting Corp of New Zealand* [1989] R.P.C. 469, at 475.
[12] *R. Griggs Group Ltd v Evans* [2003] EWHC 2914 (Ch), para.17 (*obiter*).
[13] See, *e.g. Francis Day and Hunter Ltd v Twentieth Century Fox Corp Ltd* [1940] A.C. 112, above, at 123, noting that the general rule "does not mean that in particular cases a title may not be on so extensive a scale, and so important in character, as to be the proper subject of protection against being copied", citing *Dick v Yates* (1881) L.R. 18 Ch.D. 76; *Ladbroke (Football) Ld v William Hill (Football) Ltd* [1964] 1 W.L.R. 273 (*per* Lord Hodson at 286, saying that *Dick v Yates* and *Francis Day and Hunter* "do not support the proposition that, as a matter of law, copyright can- not subsist in titles. No doubt they will not as a rule be protected, since alone they would not be regarded as a sufficiently substantial part of the book or other copyright document to justify the preventing of copying by others." See also Graham J. at first instance in *Exxon Corp v Exxon In- surance Ltd* [1982] Ch. 119 at 131: "Nothing I have said above is intended to suggest that I consider that a word which is used as a title can, as a matter of law, never in any circumstances be the subject of copyright, and I would disagree with dicta in previous cases to the contrary effect. Such a word would, however, I think, have to have qualities or characteristics in itself, if such a thing is possible, which would justify its recognition as an original literary work rather than merely as an invented word. It may well turn out not to be possible in practice, but, as at present advised, I consider that the mere fact that a single word is invented and that research or labour was involved in its invention does not in itself, in my judgment, necessarily enable it to qualify as an original literary work …".
[14] See *Dick v Yates* (1881) L.R. 18 Ch.D. 76 approved on this point in *Francis Day and Hunter Ltd v Twentieth Century Fox Corp Ltd* [1940] A.C. 112 at 123.
[15] [1893] 1 Ch. 218.
[16] Bowen L.J., however said that the headings were "the result of literary labour, both as regards *the composition of the headings themselves* and their collocation or concatenation in the book" (emphasis added) and in *Ladbroke (Football) Ltd v William Hill (Football) Ltd* [1964] 1 W.L.R. 273 Lord Hodson cited *Lamb v Evans* [1893] 1 Ch. 218 as good authority for the protection of headings in a proper case. For a more modern case in which *Lamb v Evans* was applied, see *Desktop Marketing Systems Ltd v Telstra Corp Ltd* 55 I.P.R. (2002) 1.
[17] *The Shetland Times v Wills* [1997] F.S.R. 604; [1997] E.M.L.R. 277.

written in code is "in writing"[18] and is thus protectable even though it may mean nothing to the person who does not have the key. In the "code cases"[19] protection was conferred on lists of short words which had been carefully selected in order that, when transmitted in Morse code, mistakes were less likely to occur with them than with other words. Users of the codes attributed their own meanings to the words, and thus used the lists simply as a source of appropriate code words. By itself, each word had no particular meaning[20] and the cases are therefore properly regarded as compilation cases rather than authorities for the proposition that a work written in code is protectable.[21] Nevertheless, they are relevant because the argument that nothing could qualify as a literary work which did not involve an appreciation of the meaning of words was rejected.[22] In the same way, a work written in a foreign language that few people would understand is nonetheless a literary work, as is a work of which the only embodiment or record is a digital one stored in computer memory, such that it cannot be appreciated without the aid of suitable equipment. It has also been suggested that lists of electrical components identified on a wiring diagram using only their technical symbols are literary works,[23] and on this basis it seems that even a line on such a diagram may be protected as part of a literary work if it would be understood as an instruction to connect component A to component B.[24]

Copyright in ideas. It is often stated that there is no copyright in ideas (the "ideas/expression dichotomy") but without further explanation it is a dangerous proposition: no work will be denied copyright protection simply because it can be categorised as one which "only" expresses ideas. In a general sense, of course, all copyright works have as their basis an idea, in that all works are the expression of the author's ideas, represented by his decision to use certain modes of expression rather than others.[25] As discussed above, however, it is not the concern of copyright to protect ideas unless and until the ideas have found expression in the form of a work of a category recognised as deserving of protection.[26] The expression of ideas in writing, speech or song will almost always produce a literary work save in the rare cases discussed in the preceding paragraphs. The protection given by copyright to the expression of those ideas then becomes a matter of

3–18

---

[18] CDPA 1988, s.178.

[19] *Anderson (D. P.) & Co Ltd v The Lieber Code Co* [1917] 2 K.B. 469; *Ager v P. & O. Steam Navigation Co* (1884) 26 Ch. D. 637; *Ager v Collingridge* (1886) 2 T.L.R. 291.

[20] In *Anderson (D.P.) & Co Ltd v The Lieber Code Co* [1917] 2 K.B. 469, the words were made up and had no inherent meaning; in the *Ager* cases (*Ager v P. & O. Steam Navigation Co* (1884) 26 Ch. D. 637 and *Ager v Collingridge* (1886) 2 T.L.R. 291), the words had been selected from various languages.

[21] See, *e.g.* Graham J. in *Exxon Corporation v Exxon Insurance Consultants International Ltd* [1982] Ch. 119, at 129, noting that it was the whole collection of many thousand words that was protected. Similarly, in *Pitman v Hine* (1884) 1 T.L.R. 39, a large collection of examples of shorthand words was protected, although the issue there was not subsistence but copying.

[22] This formed part of the *ratio* in *Anderson (D.P.) & Co Ltd v The Lieber Code Co* [1917] 2 K.B. 469. In *Ager v P. & O. Steam Navigation Co* (1884) 26 Ch. D. 637 copyright in the lists was not in issue and, in *Ager v Collingridge, Anderson* (1886) 2 T.L.R. 291 was merely applied.

[23] *Anacon Corp Ltd v Environmental Research Technology Ltd* [1994] F.S.R. 659; *Electronic Techniques (Anglia) Ltd v Critchley Components Ltd* [1997] F.S.R. 401.

[24] See the analysis of *Anacon Corp Ltd v Environmental Research Technology Ltd* [1994] F.S.R. 659, and *Electronic Techniques (Anglia) Ltd v Critchley Components Ltd* [1997] F.S.R. 401, in *Sandman v Panasonic U.K. Ltd* [1998] F.S.R. 651.

[25] *Designers Guild Ltd v Russell Williams (Textiles) Ltd* [2000] 1 W.L.R. 2416, *per* Lord Hoffmann at 2422.

[26] See, *e.g. Donoghue v Allied Newspapers Ltd* [1938] Ch. 106, *per* Farwell J., at 109: "This at any rate is clear beyond all question, that there is no copyright in an idea, or in ideas. A person may have a brilliant idea for a story, ... and which appears to him to be original; but if he communicates that idea to an author ..., the production which is the result of the communication of the idea to the author ... is the copyright of the person who has clothed the idea in form ..., and the owner of the idea has no rights in that product."

the scope of the exclusive rights which are conferred on the copyright owner in the work, in particular, what amounts to infringement by way of the taking of a substantial part of the work. It follows that once the ideas have been expressed in the form of a literary work, it is the form of expression which is the subject of protection, not the ideas, which themselves may be freely extracted from the work and absorbed and used by others to produce their own works so long as the form of expression of the copyright work is not also taken.[27] There are a number of further aspects to this. First, although a work may express certain ideas, it may be that those ideas are not protected by the copyright which subsists in the work because they have no connection with the particular subject matter. Thus a literary work which describes a system or invention does not entitle the copyright owner to protect the invention since the operation of the system or the working of the invention does not reproduce the literary expression which is the subject of copyright.[28] Again, the particular expression of ideas may not be protected because the expression is not original or the ideas are so commonplace that the expression which has been copied does not form a substantial part of the work.[29] As to this, the idea may have been so well known to the author from the work of others that its expression required no sufficient skill and labour (an unusual type of case in practice), or the idea may have been expressed in such a trivial fashion that the expression does not form a substantial part of the work as a whole. The most usual type of case is where the expression of the idea may merit protection but the defendant has not appropriated the author's skill and labour in giving form to that expression.[30] As already stated, these issues in the end all relate to questions of infringement, not subsistence of copyright, and are considered in Chapter 7.

3–19 **Copyright in news.** The same kind of considerations apply to literary works whose principal purpose is to communicate news, and indeed it is often stated that there is no copyright in news.[31] Again, however, taken by itself this is not a correct statement of UK law: the fact that the content of a literary work is news does not prevent that work from being capable of protection by copyright. What is protected is the form of expression of that content.[32] In general terms, the information itself, once stripped of its particular form of expression and robbed of any

---

[27] See, again, for example, *Donoghue v Allied Newspapers Ltd* [1938] Ch. 106, *per* Farwell J. at 110: "... that in which copyright exists is the particular form of language by which information which is to be conveyed is conveyed .... It is not until [the idea] is ... reduced into writing or into some tangible form that there is any copyright, and the copyright exists in the particular form of language in which ... the information or the idea is conveyed to those who are intended to read it ...". In this respect, however, it is to be noted that the form of expression of a literary work does not mean only the actual language in which that work is written; it may include the selection, and arrangement in a particular order, of incidents, whether factual or fictional. See, for an example of the extent of protection given to a traditional literary work, *Ravenscroft v Herbert and New English Library* [1980] R.P.C. 193.

[28] *Designers Guild Ltd v Russell Williams (Textiles) Ltd* [2000] 1 W.L.R. 2416, citing the example of *Kleeneze Ltd v D.R.G. (U.K.) Ltd* [1984] F.S.R. 399. For a further discussion on this point, see para. 7–12, below.

[29] *Designers Guild Ltd v Russell Williams (Textiles) Ltd* [2000] 1 W.L.R. 2416, citing as an example *Kenrick v Lawrence & Co* (1890) 25 Q.B.D. 99.

[30] This was the situation in *Kenrick v Lawrence & Co* (1890) 25 Q.B.D. 99. If the defendant there had made greater borrowing of the artist's skill in representing the voter's hand, there would presumably have been an infringement. See paras 7–55 *et seq.*, below, for further discussion of this point generally.

[31] For example, Art.2(8) of the Berne Convention provides that the protection of the Convention is not to apply to "news of the day or to miscellaneous facts having the character of mere items of press information."

[32] *Walter v Steinkopff* [1892] 3 Ch. 489, *per* North J.; *Wilson v Lukepy* [1875] 1 V.L.R. 127; and see *Football League Ltd v Littlewoods Pools Ltd* [1959] Ch. 637, *per* Upjohn J., at 651 ("... there can be no copyright in information or in an opinion *per se*. Copyright can only be claimed in the composition or language which is chosen to express the information or opinion").

work of compilation with other material, may be freely used, as with any other literary work. Again, however, this issue relates to the question of infringement, not subsistence of copyright.[33] Newspapers themselves are more properly regarded as compilations of literary and (usually) artistic works. News can also sometimes be protected as confidential information before publication.[34]

Copyright in information. Much the same can be said about statements that there can be no copyright in "mere" information. Merely because the work consists in essence of pure information, even if the work is the only source of that information, does not mean that copyright does not subsist in it.[35] See the following paragraphs, however, as to information in the form of tables, compilations or databases.   **3–20**

(iii) Tables, compilations and databases

Tables, compilations and databases. Whether called a table, compilation or database, such works have long been protected as copyright works, but copyright protection has never been conferred on systems as such, or on methods of indexing or retrieval of such material.[36] Until January 1, 1998, section 3(1) of the Act defined a literary work as including a table or compilation[37] and made no express reference to databases, which would normally have come within the description of either a table or a compilation. With effect from this date, the Act was amended to exclude a database from the description "table or compilation", and a database is now a separate category of literary work.[38] Thus, as the Act now stands, a literary work is defined to include (a) a database and (b) a table or compilation other than a database.[39] Since tables or compilations may often be databases, and vice versa, it may be wondered why it is necessary to make a distinction between tables and compilations which are databases and those which are not. The reason is to be found in the Database Directive[40] which as well as creating a new *sui generis* right in databases[41] also provided that copyright should subsist in databases if, but only if, by reason of the selection or arrangement of its contents, the database constituted the author's own intellectual creation.[42] This test is almost certainly higher than the normal originality requirement for such works under   **3–21**

---

[33] See para. 7–40, below.

[34] Such news was protected before the 1911 Act either on this basis or under common law copyright in the wire service cases, *e.g. Exchange Telegraph Co Ltd v Central News Ltd* [1897] 2 Ch. 48; *Exchange Telegraph Co Ltd v Gregory & Co* [1896] 1 Q.B. 147; *Press Association Ltd v Northern and Midland Reporting Agency* [1905–10] Mac. C.C. 306.

[35] *Football League Ltd v Littlewoods Pools Ltd* [1959] Ch. 637. The plaintiff had created the fixture lists for all the professional football leagues, and so a person who wished to reproduce a substantial part of the fixture lists would inevitably infringe, absent any defence such as fair dealing or, today, public interest or anti-competitive practices. See also *Fraser v Evans* [1969] 1 Q.B. 349 at 362, *per* Lord Denning, M.R.: Information is not the subject of copyright, but only "the literary form in which the information is dressed".

[36] See *Libraco Ltd v Shaw Walker Ltd* (1913) 30 T.L.R. 22 (a card index system with cards of different colours and headings for filing particulars of employees, and carrying only simple words such as "name" and "address": "useless and conveyed no meaning"). See also *Cartwright v Wharton* [1912] O.L.R. 357 (system of indexing).

[37] s.48(1) of the 1956 Act referred to "any" rather than "a" table or compilation, but it was not considered that this altered the previous law: *Football League Ltd v Littlewoods Pools Ltd* [1959] Ch. 637 at 650, *per* Upjohn J. Tables and compilations had been included in the category of literary works under the 1911 Act: s.35(1); see para. 3–09, above.

[38] By the Copyright and Rights in Databases Regulations 1997 (SI 1997/3032).

[39] CDPA 1988, ss.3(1)(d) and (a) respectively.

[40] Council Directive 96/9 of March 14, 1996 on the legal protection of databases.

[41] See generally as to database rights, Ch.18, below.

[42] Database Directive 96/9, Art.3(1).

United Kingdom copyright law[43] and so it became necessary to introduce a two-tier system of copyright protection: protection for databases (which, as defined, will include many tables and compilations) which satisfy the new and higher test of originality, and protection for tables and compilations which are not also databases as defined. Tables and compilations which are also databases but which, although satisfying the traditional, low United Kingdom test of originality, do not satisfy the new higher test of originality therefore no longer qualify for copyright protection.[44] They may of course qualify for database right protection.

3–22 **Databases: statutory definition**. Since it is now of fundamental importance to know whether a table or compilation is also a database, it is logical to consider what amounts to a database within the meaning of the Act before considering what amounts to a table or compilation.[45] A database is defined as a collection of independent works, data or other materials, arranged in a systematic or methodical way and individually accessible by electronic or other means.[46] The reference to a collection of independent works, data or other materials embraces the items which may be the subject of a compilation, and the reference to collection and arrangement in a systematic or methodical way covers the acts of selection, compilation and arrangement of those things. The definition has to be considered alongside the Database Directive and its Recitals, which provide[47] that a database should be understood to include (a) literary, artistic, musical or other collections of works, (b) collections of other material such as texts, sounds, images, numbers, facts and data, and (c) collections of independent works, data or other materials, the common requirement being that such collections should be systematically or methodically arranged and individually accessible. The Directive and Recitals also make it clear that certain types of works are specifically excluded from protection as a database; for example, computer programs used in the making or cinematographic, literary or musical works as such, do not fall within the scope of the Directive.[48] It is also stated that "as a rule, the compilation of several recordings of musical performances on a CD[49] does not come within the scope of the Directive, both because, as a compilation, it does not meet the conditions for copyright protection and because it does not represent a substantial enough investment to be eligible under the *sui generis* right".[50] The definition has been considered by the European Court of Justice[51] and is clearly of wide ambit. Since a database is defined in the same terms for the purposes of copyright protection and for database right protection, the reader is referred to the discussion in Ch.18.

3–23 **Table or compilation**. The dictionary definition of a table is an arrangement of numbers, words or items of any kind, in a definite and compact form, so as to ex-

---

[43] As to which, see paras 3–128 and 3–145, below.

[44] As to the transitional position, see para. 3–144, below.

[45] In theory, there may be databases which are not tables or compilations, but it is hard to imagine an example.

[46] CDPA 1988, s.3A(1); introduced by the Copyright and Rights in Databases Regulations 1997 (SI 1997/3032) with effect from January 1, 1998, and derived from the wording of the Database Directive, Art.1(2).

[47] Recital (17).

[48] Directive, Art.1(3) and Recitals (17) and (23).

[49] Nevertheless, it seems that electronic databases may include devices such as CD-ROMs, CD-Is, and presumably DVDs, pursuant to Recital (22) of the Directive.

[50] Directive, Recital (19). It follows that such compilations may be databases, as defined, but will not generally receive protection.

[51] Case C-444/02 *Fixtures Marketing Ltd v Organismos prognostikon agonon podosfairou AE(O-PAP)*, decision of the ECJ, November 9, 2004, unreported. See also the joined case of Case C-203/02 *The British Horseracing Board Ltd v William Hill Organisation Ltd*, decision of the ECJ, November 9, 2004, unreported.

hibit some set of facts, or relations, in a distinct and comprehensive way.[52] The dictionary definition of the verb "to compile" is to construct a written or printed work out of materials collected from various sources.[53] Whilst the two terms clearly overlap, and the term compilation is often used in this work to cover both, the essential characteristic of the former lies in what determines the arrangement between the items contained in the table, that of the latter lies in the gathering together of the items. Thus a collection of literary works in an anthology is a clear example of a compilation but any collection of separate items which can be written, spoken or sung will qualify too. As a matter of terminology, the phrase "table or compilation" is clearly apt to cover a database, which will consist of a compilation of items, usually arranged in a particular order by reference to a particular characteristic, and databases were previously protected as compilations.

The items which are arranged together in a table or assembled in a compilation may, individually, be entitled to copyright; such individual copyright remains independent of the separate copyright in the table or compilation.[54]

Compilations of literary and artistic works. Although a compilation is included in the category of a literary work, it is suggested that the items which are compiled together need not either exclusively, or at all, themselves be literary material, and that a compilation may consist of a mixture of literary and artistic material, or even exclusively of artistic material.[55] Newspapers and magazines are obvious examples of such works, as are atlases, books of street maps, catalogues, art gallery and exhibition guides,[56] and a story told in a series of pictures.[57] Indeed, if it were otherwise, where skill and labour has been expended in choosing and arranging artistic works as part of a larger composite work, the result would not be protected. Such works were protected as books under the pre-1911 Copyright Acts,[58] so that protection was given to works consisting entirely of illustrations with no, or virtually no, text, such as trade catalogues,[59] as well as trade catalogues consisting of text and illustrations,[60] and also map books[61] and other

3–24

---

[52] *Oxford English Dictionary.* So a table of measurements for machine parts was a "table": *Purefoy Engineering Co v Sykes Boxall & Co* (1955) 72 R.P.C. 89, at 102.

[53] *Oxford English Dictionary.*

[54] See, *e.g. Purefoy Engineering Co Ltd v Sykes Boxall & Co Ltd* [1955] 72 R.P.C. 89; *Longman Group Ltd v Carrington Technical Institute Board of Governors* [1991] 2 N.Z.L.R. 574; (1990) 20 I.P.R. 264 (High Ct of NZ). In the same way, the making of the table or compilation will require the licence of the owner of the copyright in the individual items, unless less than a substantial part of that work is taken.

[55] *The Football Association Premier League Ltd v Panini UK Ltd* [2003] EWCA Civ. 995, *per* the "provisional view" of Mummery L.J. (*obiter*, and acknowledging that the point had not been argued). It is suggested that Mummery L.J.'s provisional view is correct and it accords with Art.2(5) of the Berne Convention, which requires protection to be given to collections of literary or artistic works, which, by reason of the selection and arrangement of their contents, constitute intellectual creations.

[56] All cited as examples by Mummery L.J. in *The Football Association Premier League Ltd v Panini UK Ltd* [2003] EWCA Civ. 995.

[57] Each picture will constitute a separate artistic work. However, the structure and plot of the story, the creation of which may itself be presumed to have involved time, skill and labour, are found only in the arrangement of the pictures, one with another, and there seems no reason why this effort should not give rise to a separate copyright as a compilation.

[58] Although "books" had an extended definition: see para. 3–08, above.

[59] *Grace v Newman* (1875) L.R. 19 Eq. 623; *Maple & Co v Junior Army and Navy Stores* (1882) 21 Ch.D. 369, overruling *Cobbett v Woodward* (1872) L.R. 14 Eq. 407; *Davis v Benjamin* [1906] 2 Ch. 491).

[60] *Bogue v Houlston* 5 De G. & Sm. 267; *Hotten v Arthur* (1863) 1 H. & M. 603; *W. Marshall & Co Ltd v A.H. Bull Ltd* (1901) 85 L.T. 77.

[61] *Cary v Longman & Rees* [1801] 1 East. 358; 102 E.R. 139; *Cary v Kearsley* [1802] 4 Esp. 168; 170 E.R. 679; *Cary v Faden* (1799) 5 Ves. Jun. 23; 31 E.R. 453, although it is not clear to what extent these contained artistic works in the form of maps as opposed to itineraries, information about distances, etc.

works containing both text and illustrations.[62] In relation to these works, even where the work contained text, copyright was held to be infringed where artistic material only had been taken,[63] showing that protection must have extended to the selection of the artistic material as part of the book. Protection for such works, now as compilations, continued after the passing of the 1911 Act.[64]

The only doubt about the point arises under the present wording of the 1988 Act, which defines a literary work as meaning a work which is *written*,[65] spoken or sung, and "accordingly" as including compilations (other than databases). Arguably, a work which partly or wholly consists of artistic material is not, or to the extent that it consists of artistic material is not, "written". If, however, such works were no longer compilations under the 1988 Act, this would represent a change in the law and it seems unlikely that Parliament intended to remove protection for this category of work. It is suggested that the express inclusion of "compilation" in the definition, a word which has a well-established meaning in a copyright context, carries much greater force than the argument that the word "accordingly" restricts compilations to works which are wholly written.[66]

3–25 **Tables and compilations other than databases**. Any database will inevitably be a table or compilation but it may be wondered whether there can be a table or compilation which is not also a database. The reference to a database being a collection of independent works, data or other materials[67] would seem to cover all forms of tables or compilations[68] and so the only points of departure can be tables or compilations in which the materials are either (a) not arranged in a systematic or methodical way or (b) not individually accessible by electronic or other means. Most tables or compilations are arranged according to some system or method, if only an alphabetical or chronological one. Although it is not clear, it would seem that it is (b) which is critical. Although a collection of poems or a newspaper in ordinary hard copy form is a compilation, presumably they are not databases within the meaning of the Directive or the Act. Although technically each item is individually accessible by looking in an index or opening the pages, presumably it is not the intention of the Directive to bring within its scope such works.[69]

3–26 **Protected tables, compilations and databases.** Historically, the issue in cases involving compilations, etc. has seldom been whether the essential characteristic of a compilation is satisfied, but rather whether the work is original[70] or has been

[62] *e.g. Comyns v Hyde* (1895) 72 L.T. 250.
[63] *Bogue v Houlston*, 5 De G. & Sm. 267; *W. Marshall & Co Ltd v A.H. Bull Ltd* (1901) 85 L.T. 77; *Comyns v Hyde* (1895) 72 L.T. 250.
[64] See *Masson, Seeley & Co Ltd v Embosotype Manufacturing Co* (1924) 41 R.P.C. 160 (catalogue of type consisting of drawings plus text; the argument that a catalogue was not protected as a literary work because the law had been changed by the omission of "book" as a protected subject matter was rejected, applying the meaning given to "literary work" in *University of London Press v University Tutorial Press* [1916] 2 Ch. 601). *Purefoy Engineering Co Ltd v Sykes Boxall & Co Ltd* [1955] 72 R.P.C. 89 (trade catalogue comprising literary and artistic elements). The same result was achieved under the equivalent provisions of the Australian statute: *Kalamazoo (Aust.) Pty Ltd v Compact Business Systems Pty Ltd*, [1990] 1 Qd. R. 231; (1985) 5 I.P.R. 213 (Sup Ct of Queensland): accounting forms consisting of words, lines and boxes held to be a compilation.
[65] For this purpose, something which is written includes something in notation or code, by hand or otherwise: CDPA 1988, ss.178, 3(1).
[66] And see CDPA 1988, s.172(2). But see *Monotti* [1993] E.I.P.R. 156, arguing that a collection made up wholly of artistic material cannot now be a compilation while collections of literary and artistic material may be, the position being unclear.
[67] CDPA 1988, s.3A(1).
[68] See para. 3–23, above. The word "independent" appears to refer merely to the materials having a significance or existence apart from each other, a feature of any table or compilation.
[69] See the discussion at para. 18–05, below.
[70] As to which, in the case of compilations, see paras 3–144 *et seq.*, below.

infringed.[71] Provided the subject matter can reasonably be called a table, compilation or database, it will almost always fall within the statutory description.[72] Ultimately, however, the test remains the same as the general test for a literary work, namely whether the subject matter provides information, instruction or pleasure in the form of literary enjoyment.[73] Thus on the one hand copyright has been denied to a list of names which conveys no useful information,[74] and a card index system with cards of different colours and headings for filing particulars of employees, and carrying only simple words such as "name" and "address";[75] but on the other hand copyright was conferred on tables comprising grids of five-letter sequences for a monthly newspaper competition since they provided information to a competitor, telling him whether he had won or lost.[76] Arguments that there can be no copyright in "mere" information or lists have been rejected.[77] Examples of the variety of cases where compilations have been protected, often without argument, are: schedules of broadcasting programmes,[78] school text-books consisting of compilations of different materials,[79] a book of scientific questions and answers,[80] directories of all kinds,[81] trade brochures,[82] a report on various collieries, with plans and an appendix,[83] lists of registered bills of sale and deeds of arrangement extracted from publicly available sources,[84] a list of foxhunts and associated information,[85] a list of Stock Exchange prices,[86]

---

[71] As to which see Ch.7, below.

[72] In *Ladbroke (Football) Ltd v William Hill (Football) Ltd* [1964] 1 W.L.R. 273, at 278, Lord Reid pointed out that cases in which copyright has been denied to a compilation are comparatively few.

[73] *Express Newspapers v Liverpool Daily Post and Echo* [1985] 1 W.L.R. 1089; *Real Estate Institute of N.S.W. v Wood* (1923) 23 S.R. (N.S.W.) 349 (copyright in a compilation if it supplies "intelligible information"). In *Kalamazoo (Aust.) Pty Ltd v Compact Business Systems Pty Ltd*, [1990] 1 Qd. R. 231; (1985) 5 I.P.R. 213 (Sup Ct of Queensland), however, this test was rejected when conferring copyright on accounting forms consisting of words, lines and boxes which conveyed no information or instruction by themselves, it being said that the relevant test was whether there was intellectual input in the forms, it being the case on the facts that they were designed and presented in a way which would produce meaningful results for the user. This, however, would seem to go to the issue of originality.

[74] *Weatherby & Sons v International Horse Agency and Exchange Ltd* [1910] 2 Ch. 297 at 304.

[75] See *Libraco Ltd v Shaw Walker Ltd* (1913) 30 T.L.R. 22 (index was "useless and conveyed no meaning"). See also *Cartwright v Wharton* [1912] O.L.R. 357 (system of indexing).

[76] *Express Newspapers v Liverpool Daily Post and Echo* [1985] 1 W.L.R. 1089, distinguishing *Exxon Corporation v Exxon Insurance Consultants International Ltd* [1982] Ch. 119.

[77] *British Broadcasting Co v Wireless League Gazette Publishing Co* [1926] Ch. 433 (applying *University of London Press v University Tutorial Press* [1916] 2 Ch. 601), followed in *Independent Television Publications Ltd v Time Out Ltd* [1984] F.S.R. 64.

[78] *British Broadcasting Co v Wireless League Gazette Publishing Co* [1926] Ch. 433; *Independent Television Publications Ltd v Time Out Ltd* [1984] F.S.R. 64; *RTÉ v Magill TV Guide* [1990] F.S.R. 561 (High Ct of Ireland). There may be copyright in a written schedule of programmes, but not in a compilation of the programmes as they are broadcast during the day in accordance with the schedule: *FWS Joint Sports Claimants v Copyright Board* (1992) 22 I.P.R. 429; (1991) 81 D.L.R. 412 (Fed CA of Canada). For a full discussion of some of the television listings cases in the United Kingdom, Australia, New Zealand and Europe, see Watts and Durie in [1992] 4 Ent. L. R. 133.

[79] *Educational Co of Ireland Ltd v Fallon Bros Ltd* [1919] 1 I.R. 62; *Ghafur v Jwala* [1921] A.I.R. All. 95; *Leanie v Pillans* [1843] 5 Dunl. (Ct of Sess.) 416.

[80] *Jarrold v Houlston* (1857) 3 K. & J. 708.

[81] *Kelly v Morris* (1866) L.R. 1 Eq. 697; *Morris v Ashbee* (1868) L.R. 7 Eq. 34; *Morris v Wright* (1870) 5 Ch. 279; *Matthewson v Stockdale* (1806) 12 Ves. 270; *Fax Directories (Pty) Ltd v S.A. Fax Listings C.C.* (1990) 2 S.A.L.R. 164 (Sup Ct of S.A.).

[82] *Maple & Co v Junior Army and Navy Stores* (1882) 21 Ch.D. 369.

[83] *Kenrick v Danube Collieries, etc. Co Ltd* (1891) 39 W.R. 473.

[84] *Trade Auxiliary Co v Middlesbrough, etc. Association* (1889) 40 Ch. D. 425; *Cate v Devon, etc. Newspaper Co* (1889) 40 Ch.D. 500; *T.M. Hall & Co v Whittington & Co* [1892] 18 V.L.R. 525.

[85] *Cox v Land and Water Journal Co* (1869) L.R. 9 Eq. 324.

[86] *Exchange Telegraph Co Ltd v Gregory & Co* [1896] 1 Q.B. 147.

biographical notes of prominent golfers published in a golf annual,[87] a list of brood mares with their sires and a list of stallions with daughters at stud,[88] a list of weights and acceptances for horse racing,[89] a list of recently published books,[90] a list of characteristics of racehorses,[91] a list of customers,[92] a price list,[93] a manual of classified information for the use of motor car insurers,[94] a business manual,[95] an alphabetical list of railway stations,[96] chronological fixture lists of football clubs,[97] football pool coupons,[98] columns of birth and death announcements in a newspaper,[99] contract forms,[1] forms of writs,[2] a series of book-keeping forms,[3] sheets of election results,[4] tables comprising grids of five-letter sequences for a monthly newspaper competition,[5] a list of three letter mnemonics,[6] and an electronic circuit diagram.[7]

(iv) Computer programs and preparatory design material for a computer program

3–27   **History of protection of computer programs.** Computer programs were not expressly referred to in the United Kingdom copyright legislation until 1985,[8] nor in any major copyright convention until 1996.[9] However, by the time of the 1977 Copyright Committee,[10] there was already a widely-held view, not only in the United Kingdom, but also internationally, that computer programs should be considered as falling within the category of literary works. The Committee recommended that computer programs should be treated as literary works under United Kingdom copyright law.[11] This approach was followed in several inter-

---

[87] *Nisbet (J.) & Co Ltd v The Golf Agency* (1907) 23 T.L.R. 370.
[88] *Weatherby & Sons v International Horse Agency and Exchange Ltd* [1910] 2 Ch. 297.
[89] *Winterbottom v Wintle* (1947) 50 W.A.L.R. 58.
[90] *J. Whitaker & Sons Ltd v Publishers' Circular Ltd* [1946–47] Mac. C.C. 10.
[91] *Portway Press Ltd v Hague* [1957] R.P.C. 426, and see *Caboverbury Park Race Course Co Ltd v Hopkins* (1932) 49 W.N. (N.S.W.) 27; *Demerara Turf Club v Phang* (1963) 6 W.I.R. 177 and *Ascot Jockey Club Ltd v Simons* (1968) 64 W.W.R. 411.
[92] *Flocast Australia Pty Ltd v Purcell* 39 I.P.R. 177.
[93] *Payen Components South Africa Ltd v Bovis Gaskets C.C.* (1996) 33 I.P.R. 406 (South Africa).
[94] *Underwriters Survey Bureau Ltd v Amer. Home Fire Ass. Co* (1939) 4 D.L.R. 89
[95] *Flocast Australia Pty Ltd v Purcell* 39 I.P.R. 177.
[96] *Blacklock (H.) & Co Ltd v Arthur Pearson (C.) Ltd* [1915] 2 Ch. 376; *Leslie v Young (J.) & Sons Ltd* [1894] A.C. 335.
[97] *Football League Ltd v Littlewoods Pools Ltd* [1959] Ch. 637.
[98] *Ladbroke (Football) Ltd v William Hill (Football) Ltd* [1964] 1 W.L.R. 273.
[99] *John Fairfax & Sons Pty Ltd v Australian Consolidated Press Ltd* [1960] S.R. (N.S.W.) 413.
[1] *Capital Finance Co v Bowmaker (Commercial) Ltd* [1964] R.P.C. 463; *Capital Finance Co v Lombank Ltd* [1964] R.P.C. 467; *Real Estate Institute of N.S.W. v Wood* (1923) 23 S.R. (N.S.W.) 349
[2] *Alexander (W.) v Mackenzie (R.)* (1846) 9 Sess. Cas.D. 748.
[3] *Kalamazoo (Aus.) Pty Ltd v Compact Business Systems Pty Ltd* [1990] 1 Qd. R. 231 (Sup Ct of Queensland).
[4] *Press Association Ltd v Northern and Midland Reporting Agency* [1905–10] Mac. C.C. 306.
[5] *Express Newspapers v Liverpool Daily Post and Echo* [1985] F.S.R. 306; [1985] 1 W.L.R. 1089. Each of the 750 tables was a separate work.
[6] *Microsense Systems Ltd v Control Systems Technology Ltd* noted at [1992] I.P.D. 15006 (the three-letter mnemonics comprised the language code for communication with a pelican crossing controller).
[7] *Anacon Corporation Ltd v Environmental Research Technology Ltd* [1994] F.S.R. 659 (the diagram showed a large amount of writing and symbols and was a list of components together with information as to how they were connected).
[8] Copyright (Computer Software) Amendment Act 1985 (c.41).
[9] WIPO Copyright Treaty, adopted December 1996.
[10] Cmnd.6732, Ch.9.
[11] 1977 Copyright Committee, para.520(i).

locutory decisions in the first half of the 1980s.[12] The Copyright (Computer Software) Amendment Act 1985 removed any residual doubt about the protection of software under United Kingdom copyright law by confirming that the 1956 Act applied to computer programs, including programs made before the 1985 Act,[13] as it applied in relation to a literary work, regardless of any other copyright protection which also subsisted. The 1985 Act did not attempt to define a computer program. The 1988 Act dealt with computer programs slightly differently, but to the same effect, by introducing a computer program as a specific type of literary work in the definition of literary work in section 3(1).

The need to harmonise the treatment of computer programs under the national laws of the Member States led to the adoption of the Directive on the legal protection of computer programs,[14] which required Member States to protect computer programs as literary works within the meaning of the Berne Convention. The Directive was implemented in the United Kingdom with effect from January 1, 1993 by the Copyright (Computer Programs) Regulations 1992.[15] Specific aspects of the implementation of the Directive in the United Kingdom are discussed elsewhere,[16] but it should be noted that although some provisions of the Directive have been implemented more or less *verbatim*, some provisions of the Directive were apparently considered not to differ from current United Kingdom law, with the result that no change was made to the language of the Act. In considering copyright protection for computer programs in United Kingdom law, therefore, it may be necessary to refer back to the Directive; this is particularly so in relation to the scope of protection and the requirement of originality.

What is a computer program? In an area of rapidly changing technology, there are obvious difficulties in providing definitions of any specificity. Neither the 1988 Act, nor the Copyright (Computer Software) Amendment Act 1985, attempted any definition of a computer program.[17] The Directive provides only a partial definition, by including preparatory design material within the term.[18] However, the Directive does give some further guidance as to what is a computer program by providing that protection under the Directive shall apply to a computer program in any form[19] and expressed in any form,[20] and it thus includes a version of a computer program in source code[21] as well as in other forms. In general terms, however, the protectable subject matter of a computer program is the language or code written by programmer and the design and the structure of the

3–28

---

[12] Reported decisions in which the issue arose include *Gates v Swift* [1982] R.P.C. 339, *Sega Enterprises v Richards* [1983] F.S.R. 73 and *Thrustcode Ltd v W.W. Computing Ltd* [1983] F.S.R. 502.

[13] *Milltronics Ltd v Hycontrol Ltd* [1990] F.S.R. 273.

[14] Council Directive 91/250, adopted on May 14, 1991, [1991] O.J. L122/42. For a discussion of the background to the Directive, see paras 25–44 *et seq.*, below.

[15] SI 1992/333.

[16] See, as to originality and permitted acts, paras 3–130 and 9–132 *et seq.* respectively.

[17] *cf.* the definition introduced into the Australian Copyright Act 1968 by amendment in 1984: a set of statements or instructions to be used directly or indirectly in a computer in order to bring about a certain result. As to this, see *Australian Video Retailers Association Ltd v Warner Home Video Pty Ltd* (2002) 53 I.P.R. 242 (Fed Ct of Aus); *Autodesk Inc v Dyason (No.1)* (1992) 104 A.L.R. 563; [1992] R.P.C. 575 (High Ct of Aus).

[18] Computer Programs Directive 91/250 Art.1(1); and see para. 3–29, below.

[19] Recital (7), including a program which is incorporated into hardware.

[20] Art.1(2).

[21] *Ibcos Computers Ltd v Barclays Mercantile Highland Finance Ltd* [1994] F.S.R. 275 at 296, disapproving the statement in *Total Information Processing Systems Ltd v Daman Ltd* [1992] F.S.R. 171 at 181 to the contrary. In *Saphena Computing Ltd v Allied Collection Agencies* [1995] F.S.R. 616, it was assumed that separate copyrights attach to the source code and object code of a computer program. Whether this is so will depend on whether each is original.

program.[22] The Directive provides that protection does not extend to ideas and principles which describe any elements of a computer program, including those which underlie its interfaces.[23] The background to this exclusion of ideas and principles is elaborated in the recitals to the Directive. Recital (9) outlines the desirability of standardisation and interoperability; recital (14) confirms that to the extent that logic, algorithms and programming languages comprise ideas and principles, those ideas and principles are not protected. However, the nature and scope of protection for programming language is a particularly complex issue.[24] This aspect of the Directive was not expressly incorporated into United Kingdom copyright law on the implementation of the Directive, presumably on the basis that the distinction between idea and expression was already an established part of United Kingdom copyright law. This is, therefore, an area in which it is particularly important to refer back to the Directive when applying the 1988 Act to computer programs, to ensure that the proposed application is consistent with the terms of the Directive.[25]

The lack of a comprehensive definition of a computer program gives rise to questions about boundaries.[26] In particular, it is often unclear where the boundary lies between programs and data. In Australia, a computer program which formed part of a DVD has been held to consist of those parts which caused or enabled visual and caption content to be heard and shown, but not the content itself.[27] This problem is accentuated by certain modern programming techniques,[28] which associate program properties with data. The potential for tension between protection of programs and closely associated data and data structures is acknowledged in the Database Directive,[29] which specifically provides that copyright protection should not apply to computer programs used in the making or operation of databases accessible by electronic means.[30]

There are also considerable uncertainties about the scope of protection for computer programs, as such, in terms of user interface and inputs[31] and outputs. A question which frequently arises is whether screen displays are protected as part of the program which generates them, or only to the extent that they are, or are part of, a separate copyright work? There are several bases on which screen displays may be protected as non-program copyright works. A display in the

---

[22] *Cyprotex Discovery Ltd v The University of Sheffield* [2003] EWHC 760 (TCC), [2004] RPC 4, para.78 (upheld on appeal, although this point was not in issue: [2004] EWCA Civ 380, [2004] R.P.C. 43).

[23] Computer Programs Directive 91/250, Art.1(2). It has been suggested that where the expression of an idea is inseparable from its function, it forms part of the idea and is not entitled to copyright protection. See *Total Information Processing Systems Ltd v Daman Ltd* [1992] F.S.R. 171 at 181, citing *Kenrick & Co v Lawrence & Co* (1890) 25 Q.B.D. 99. This notion, however, is derived from a line of United States authorities such as *Lotus Development Corp v Paperback Software International* (1990) 740 F. Supp. 37 (Massachusetts Dist Ct); (1990) 18 I.P.R. 1 at 25 and *Computer Associates International Inc v Altai Inc* (1992) 23 I.P.R. 385 (US CA) (and see also *Autodesk Inc v Dyason* [1992] R.P.C. 575 at 583 (High Ct of Aus)). It has subsequently been disapproved, correctly so, it is suggested, by Jacob J. in *Ibcos Computers Ltd v Barclays Mercantile Highland Finance Ltd* [1994] F.S.R. 275 at 290–292.

[24] See, for example, *Data Access Corporation v Powerflex Services Pty Ltd* (1996) 33 I.P.R. 233 (Fed Ct of Western Australia).

[25] Notably, no reference was made to the Directive in *Ibcos v Barclays Finance Ltd* [1994] F.S.R. 275 (a decision on non-literal infringement) although judgment was given after implementation of the Computer Programs Directive 91/250.

[26] For example, between hierarchies in a computer program and the computer program itself.

[27] *Australian Video Retailers Association Ltd v Warner Home Video Pty Ltd* (2002) 53 I.P.R. 242 (Fed Ct of Aus).

[28] For example, so-called object-oriented programming.

[29] Directive 96/6 of the European parliament and Council, adopted on March 11, 1996; [1996] O.J. L77/20; see para. 3–21, above.

[30] Database Directive 96/9, Art.1(3).

[31] It is unclear in what circumstances, if any, the use of, for example, particular key strokes on a keyboard to trigger certain functions, could be part of the protected program.

form of a series of words and numbers, for example, may be a compilation, and protected as such as a literary work.[32] A display with moving images, as in a video game or multimedia product, may well be protected as a film.[33] A single graphic image on screen may be an artistic work.[34] However, inquiry as to the nature of the protection is far from academic, given that the rules under the 1988 Act as to authorship, ownership, duration, infringement, permitted acts and moral rights may all vary to different degrees, depending on the category of work which is protected.

Finally, the exclusion from the definition of literary work of a dramatic or musical work may cause particular problems in the context of computer programs. If a computer program can be said to be, in whole or in part, a dramatic or musical work, is it excluded from protection as a computer program? Music software for computers, digital synthesisers and music data files for use with both of these are commonplace. The definition of musical work under the Act may leave some room for distinguishing program elements as being in the nature of action, while treating pure music data on which the program is to operate as non-program musical works, but such a theoretical exercise may be difficult to perform in certain programming environments.

Preparatory design material for a computer program. The Directive specifically provides that the term computer program should include preparatory design material for computer programs.[35] This is slightly amplified in the recitals to the Directive, which explain that preparatory design work is included provided that the nature of the preparatory work is such that a computer program can result from it at a later stage.[36] This requirement was implemented in the United Kingdom by the addition of a new category of literary work, referred to as preparatory design material for a computer program.[37]

3–29

At a practical level, given the relatively low originality threshold applied in United Kingdom copyright law, it is unclear what additional protection is given by the express inclusion of preparatory design materials as a separate category of protectable literary works. Written notations produced in preparation for writing a computer program would have been entitled to protection in any event as a literary work. There are no transitional provisions in relation to preparatory design materials, giving rise to the question of what protection is available for such materials produced before 1993 and not otherwise entitled to protection.[38]

---

[32] CDPA 1988, s.3(1)(a); see paras 3–21 et seq., above.

[33] CDPA 1988, s.5B(1); see paras 3–77 et seq., below. Visual displays of computer games programs have been protected as films under the South African Copyright Act: *Nintendo Co Ltd v Golden China TV Game Centre* (1993) 28 I.P.R. 313 (Sup Ct of S.A.) (the computer instructions for the video game were stored as firmware on a ROM chip; different sequences of images were produced depending on the action of the games player); see also *Sega Enterprises Ltd v Galaxy Electronics Pty Ltd* 139 A.L.R. 518. See as to the protection of multimedia CD-ROM as a film: *Turner* [1995] E.I.P.R. 107.

[34] CDPA 1988, s.4(1); see paras 3–49 et seq., below. It has been held that copyright does not subsist in the screen display as a literary work, the screen display being a product of the program, not the program itself: *John Richardson Computers Ltd v Flanders* [1993] F.S.R. 497 at 527.

[35] Computer Programs Directive 91/250, Art.1(1).

[36] Recital (7).

[37] CDPA 1988, s.3(1)(c). Viewed strictly, the implementation may be defective in this respect, in that such materials should be treated as a computer program, rather than as a separate type of literary work; see, for example, the definition of adaptation, which applies to a computer program, but makes no reference to preparatory materials for a computer program: s.21(3)(ab).

[38] The Computer Programs Directive expressly provides that its provisions shall apply to programs (which term in the Directive includes preparatory design material) created before January 1, 1993: Art.9(1).

C. DRAMATIC WORKS

(i) History of protection

3–30   **History of protection.** In order to understand the nature of the protection currently given to dramatic works, it is particularly important to understand the history of their protection. Dramatic works were protected under the early copyright statutes as literary works, but the performing right in such works was not given statutory protection until the Dramatic Copyright Act 1833.[39] The protection was extended to musical works by the Literary Copyright Act 1842.[40] To constitute a dramatic work, it had to be more than just "dramatic", in particular it had to be a work of action. A work which was intended to be sung by a singer in character costume but without action could not therefore be a dramatic work.[41] Under these Acts, a dramatic work also had to be capable of being printed and published to obtain copyright protection,[42] so that no dramatic copyright subsisted in scenic effects, the make-up of the actors or any unscripted "stage-business"[43] or other unscripted pantomime or dumb show[44] or dance.[45] As will be seen, the need for the existence of some work capable of being printed and published disappeared under the 1911 Act, and therefore such old cases are of limited help in establishing what constitutes a dramatic work under the modern law.

3–31   **The 1911 Act.** By the time of the 1911 Act, protection under the Berne Convention extended to dramatic and dramatico-musical works, choreographic works and entertainments in dumb show, the acting form (or "*mise en scène*") of which was fixed in writing or otherwise.[46] These terms were reflected in the definition of a dramatic work in the 1911 Act, which was defined to include any piece for recitation, choreographic work or entertainment in dumb show, the scenic arrangement or acting form of which was fixed in writing or otherwise.[47] The definition was clearly not exclusive, since it did not refer to the most common type of dramatic work, namely a play consisting of words and action intended to be performed in front of an audience. The Act clearly now for the first time extended protected to works without words, such as works of dance and mime; it is unclear to what extent scenic arrangements or effects were protected.[48]

---

[39] 3 & 4 Will. 4, c.15, under which the performing right was given to authors of any tragedy, comedy, play, opera, farce or other dramatic piece of entertainment.

[40] 5 & 6 Vict., c.45, which also now defined the protected subject matter, namely "dramatic piece", to mean and include every tragedy, comedy, play, opera, farce or other scenic, musical, or dramatic entertainment (s.2).

[41] *Fuller v Blackpool Winter Gardens* [1895] 2 Q.B. 429 (CA); *Tate v Fullbrook* [1908] 1 K.B. 821 at 832, *per* Farwell L.J. The work would be a literary work, as to any words, and a musical work as to the music.

[42] *Tate v Fullbrook* [1908] 1 K.B. 821;

[43] *Tate v Fullbrook* [1908] 1 K.B. 821, although contrary to the dictum of Brett J. in *Chatterton v Cave* (1876) as reported in 33 L.T. 255: situations and scenic effects "are more peculiarly the subject of copyright than words themselves."

[44] *Karno v Pathé Frères Ltd* (1908) 99 L.T. 114, applying *Tate v Fullbrook* [1908] 1 K.B. 821. An appeal was dismissed on other grounds: (1909) 100 L.T. 260. In *Lee v Simpson* (1847) 3 C.B. 871, the written introduction to an otherwise unscripted pantomime was protected, but it is not clear that the protection extended to the pantomime itself.

[45] *Bishop v Viviana & Co* [1905–10] Mac. C.C. 211, again applying *Tate v Fullbrook* [1908] 1 K.B. 821.

[46] Berne Convention, Art.2.

[47] Copyright Act 1911, s.35(1).

[48] In *Tate v Thomas* [1921] 1 Ch. 503, it seems to have been held that no copyright could subsist in mere scenic effects since they could not be printed or published, relying on *Tate v Fullbrook* [1908] 1 K.B. 821. But this represented the pre-1911 position, which did not apply under the wording of the 1911 Act. It may be that the real ground of the decision in *Tate v Thomas* was that

Films as dramatic works. A further change under the 1911 Act was that a   **3–32**
dramatic work was also defined to include any cinematograph production where
the arrangement or acting form or the combination of incidents represented gave
the work an original character.[49] While the individual frames of a film could
therefore be protected as photographs,[50] a film which satisfied these additional
requirements of originality could therefore also be protected as a dramatic work[51]
and be "performed" by being shown to an audience.[52] A film of a sporting event
was held not to be a dramatic work because it did not involve any acting form or
arrangement, and was therefore not a "cinematograph *production*", and even if it
was a "production" it had no original character.[53] Even an edited film of a sporting event was held not to be a dramatic work, since the editing did not give rise to
the drama, which was inherent in the event itself,[54] although a suitably edited version of a naturally occurring event might be.[55]

The 1956 Act. To an extent, the 1956 Act maintained this approach, defining   **3–33**
dramatic work as including a choreographic work or entertainment in dumb show
if reduced to writing in the form in which the work or entertainment was to be
presented.[56] The Act no longer contained any reference to scenic arrangements
and was assumed to have limited the scope of the definition and to confine protection to something which had dramatic action without regard to any elements of
background or production.[57] In addition, a dramatic work was now expressly
defined to exclude a cinematograph film (as distinct from a scenario or script for
a cinematograph film),[58] and a new form of copyright protection was conferred
on cinematograph films of all kinds, whether having a degree of original character
or not.[59] A film could not therefore also be a dramatic work.

The Berne Convention. Dramatic and dramatic-musical works, and choreo-   **3–34**
graphic works and entertainments in dumb show are all protectable under the
general rubric of "literary and artistic works", as are cinematograph works and

---

the relevant elements in the drama were not sufficiently certain or fixed. See the judgment at 511.
The *mise en scène* was held to be the subject of copyright in *Perkin v Ray* [1911–16] Mac.C.C.
288, where there was clearly a reasonably well-defined script, consisting of a number of sketches
loosely hung together, with scripted jokes.

[49] Copyright Act 1911, s.35(1). This "new" category of dramatic work and the wording followed
from the 1908 Berlin Revision to the Berne Convention, by which it was provided that cinematograph productions should be protected as literary or artistic works, if, by the arrangement of the
acting form or the combination of the incidents represented, the author had given the work a
personal and original character (Art.14(2)). As has been pointed out (Ricketson, *The Berne
Convention for the Protection of Literary and Artistic Works, 1886–1989* (Kluwer, 1987), p.551),
the necessity for such a provision was questionable since such works should already have been
protected as dramatic or dramatico-musical works, albeit expressed in what was then a novel
form, and the requirement of personal and original character was implicit for such works.

[50] As an artistic work: Copyright Act 1911, s.35(1). See *Pathé Frères v Bancroft* [1928–35]
Mac.C.C. 403.

[51] *Nordisk Films Co Ltd v Onda* [1917–23] Mac.C.C. 337.

[52] *Copinger* (5th ed.), p.80.

[53] *Canadian Admiral Corp Ltd v Rediffusion Inc* (1954) 20 C.P.R. 75 (Excheq Ct of Can), citing
Copinger (8th ed.), p.221.

[54] *Australian Olympic Committee v Big Fights Inc* (1999) 46 I.P.R. 53 (Fed Ct of Aus).

[55] *Australian Olympic Committee v Big Fights Inc* (1999) 46 I.P.R. 53 (Fed Ct of Aus).

[56] Copyright Act 1956, s.48(1).

[57] *Copinger* (9th ed.), p.61.

[58] *Copinger* (9th ed.), p.61.

[59] Copyright Act 1956, s.13. The 1952 Gregory Committee Report (Cmnd.8662) had noted that the
requirement of original character in s.35(1) of the 1911 Act was probably to deprive films such as
newsreels of any protection, and took the view that the Berne Convention did not require that
films should have an original character. See para.100. Pre- 1956 Act films which had qualified
under the 1911 Act as dramatic works continued to be treated as dramatic works under the 1956
Act (1956 Act, Sch.7, para.15) and did not qualify as cinematograph films (*ibid.*, Sch.7, para.14).

works expressed by an analogous process.[60] Article 14 *bis* of the Convention also provides that cinematograph works are to be protected as original works, and that the owner of the copyright in them is to enjoy the same rights as the owners of other original works.

(ii) Under the 1988 Act

3–35   **Meaning of "dramatic work".** The 1988 Act continues the general approach of the earlier Acts in that, unlike the cases of literary and musical works, it does not attempt a comprehensive definition of a dramatic work, merely stating that it includes a work of dance or mime.[61] Although it is expressly provided that a literary work cannot be a dramatic work,[62] there is no express exclusion, unlike in the case of the 1956 Act, of the possibility of a film being a dramatic work. Whether or not this was deliberate,[63] the effect has been to reintroduce the possibility of a film being a dramatic work.[64] As to what comes within the general description of "dramatic work", the expression is at large and should therefore be given its natural and ordinary meaning, which is that it is a work of action, with or without words or music, which is capable of being performed before an audience.[65] This definition brings out the point that a distinguishing characteristic of a dramatic work is that it must be capable of being performed, but also that not all works which are capable of being performed are dramatic works. It is possible, in one sense, to perform a literary work (for example, by reciting a poem), or a musical work (for example, by singing a song), or even an artistic work (for example, by the once popular entertainment of recreating well-known paintings or statues with living actors, in suitable attitudes but silent and motionless (*tableaux vivants*), but these possibilities do not make such works dramatic works: they are not works of action. A work consisting of words intended to be spoken or sung, whether in costume or not, would not therefore be a dramatic work unless the performance of the words is to be accompanied by action.[66] Similarly, the assembly of a scene to be viewed or to be the subject of a photograph, even if incorporating human actors, does not constitute a dramatic work, as it lacks the necessary element of action.[67] For the same reason, backdrops and scenic arrangements produced as the setting in which a play is to be performed do not themselves constitute, nor are part of, a dramatic work.[68] No matter how "dramatic" the work, however, it must be one which is capable of performance if it is to be protected as a dramatic work. So where a film had been made of a man dancing but had then been edited (or "jump-cut") in such a way that the dancer's movements as portrayed in the film could not have been performed by a human

---

[60] Berne Convention, Art.2(1).

[61] CDPA 1988, s.3(1).

[62] s.3(1).

[63] There was no recommendation in the 1977 Whitford Committee Report (Cmnd.6732) that this be done, and no reference to the point in the subsequent White Paper or Parliamentary debates.

[64] See para. 3–37, below.

[65] *Norowzian v Arks Ltd (No.2)* [2000] F.S.R. 363, CA *per* Nourse L.J., said by him to be substantially a distillation of existing dictionary and textbook definitions. See also the cases decided under the earlier Acts, referred to above.

[66] Contrast works of dance and mime, which clearly predicate action in their performance.

[67] *Creation Records v News Group Newspapers* [1997] E.M.L.R. 444 (the arrangement of a scene including members of a group and other props to be photographed for the cover of their album). The same applies to *tableaux vivants*.

[68] Although they may, of course, be protected as artistic works, either in themselves (*e.g.* the painted backdrop) or as based on prior drawings (*e.g.* the stage layout). As noted above, the position has altered with successive Copyright Acts.

actor, the actions which had been recorded in the edited film were not themselves a dramatic work because they were not capable of performance.[69]

Dramatic and musical works. Whilst a dramatic work cannot, by definition,[70] also be a literary work, the same is not the case as between a dramatic and a musical work. If a dramatic work includes music, the musical elements are capable of copyright protection as a musical work,[71] but it would seem that the work as a whole is still capable of protection as a dramatic work.[72] The importance of the distinction between a dramatic work or musical work, and a literary work, already much less important under the 1956 Act than it had been under the law prior to 1911, ceases to be of any importance under the 1988 Act. **3–36**

A film as a dramatic work. As has been seen, the status of a film as a possible dramatic work has altered with successive Copyright Acts. The removal of the exclusion which existed under the 1956 Act which prevented a dramatic work also being a film[73] means that a film can once more be a dramatic work, provided that it is a work of action.[74] The requirement that a dramatic work be capable of performance can be satisfied in the case of a film, since its visual and acoustic presentation to an audience will amount to performance.[75] As to what distinguishes films which are works of action from other films, it does not seem that there is any requirement that in order to be a dramatic work the film should record the actions of a human being.[76] If this is right, films in which the action is portrayed by animals or by cartoon characters may therefore be dramatic works, provided there is action, as also, it would seem, may a film which consists entirely of a record of naturally occurring events, such as a volcano erupting, particularly where the film has been edited to increase the dramatic impact.[77] Again, there seems no reason why a film of a sporting event should not be a dramatic work, particularly where it has been edited to increase its impact. In contrast, a documentary film or a filmed interview will generally not be a work of action. If the film records action which is taking place in front of the lens, it will be a dramatic work; whether or not it will be an *original* dramatic work will depend, it seems, on whether the filmmaker adds anything of dramatic significance to the action which is taking place, for example, by choice of camera angle, lighting or **3–37**

[69] *Norowzian v Arks Ltd (No.2)* [2000] F.S.R. 363 at 367. Although the Court of Appeal held that the film was not a recording of a dramatic work, it ruled that the film itself was a dramatic work. See para. 3–37, below. The observation in *Aristocrat Leisure Industries Pty Ltd v Pacific Gaming Pty Ltd* 50 I.P.R. (2001) 29 (Fed Ct of Aus), that a *script* for an animated cartoon could be a dramatic work does not represent the position under UK law although, as noted in para. 3–37, the cartoon film itself might be.
[70] CDPA 1988, s.3(1); see paras 3–04 and 3–12, above.
[71] Which will exclude any words or action intended to be sung, spoken or performed with it: s.3(2).
[72] In the terminology of the Berne Convention, the work is a dramatico-musical work (Art.2(1)).
[73] CDPA 1988, s.48(1); see above.
[74] *Norowzian v Arks Ltd (No.2)* [2000] F.S.R. 363. Buxton L.J. also considered that the United Kingdom's obligations under the Berne Convention required that any work of cinematography within the meaning of the Berne Convention was included within a "dramatic work", as that expression was to be understood in the 1988 Act. As noted elsewhere (para. 3–04), the Court of Appeal held that there was no objection to a film being protected both as a film under CDPA 1988, s.5B and as dramatic work under s.3. To be protected as a dramatic work, it must of course be an *original* dramatic work. Further, *per* Buxton L.J., the United Kingdom's obligations under the Berne Convention required that any work of cinematography within the meaning of the Berne Convention was included within a "dramatic work", as that expression was to be understood in the 1988 Act.
[75] *Norowzian v Arks Ltd (No.2)* [2000] F.S.R. 363 This was also the position under the 1911 Act: see above.
[76] In *Norowzian v Arks Ltd (No.2)* [2000] F.S.R. 363, the sequence of actions recorded on the edited film could not have been performed in the same way by a human being.
[77] See, further, para. 3–32, above.

editing.[78] The possibility of a film being a dramatic work is of general significance because the film copyright will only be infringed by the copying of the actual record of sounds and visual images, that is, tape-to-tape copying and the like.[79] If copyright also subsists in the film as a dramatic work, this copyright may be infringed by the re-creation of a substantial part of the dramatic work without any copying of the actual record of the images and sounds.

Many films of action are also recordings of a dramatic work. This dramatic work may already have been recorded, for example in a screenplay, or may have been recorded for the first time when the film was shot. Nevertheless, the fact that almost all films in their final version are the product of editing means that the film itself will often be a dramatic work distinct from the earlier or underlying dramatic works. This will be so particularly in the case of films containing sequences made using special effects or editing which could not be performed by live actors.[80]

3–38   **Pre-1988 Act films as dramatic works.** The protection which previously existed for films which had qualified as dramatic works under the 1911 Act[81] continues: they are still protected as dramatic works under the 1988 Act.[82] This is clearly significant for the protection of old (pre-1956 Act) films. The position of films made under the 1956 Act, *i.e.* between June 1, 1957 and August 1, 1989, is more difficult. Even though a film made in this period could not have enjoyed any protection as a dramatic work, is the effect of the 1988 Act to confer copyright for the first time on such films if they qualify as dramatic works? The Act contains no transitional provisions which expressly deal with the point, only the general provision that copyright does not subsist in a work which was made before August 1, 1989 unless copyright subsisted in it immediately before that date.[83] In one sense, copyright may have subsisted in such a film before commencement *qua* cinematograph film under section 13 of the 1956 Act, even if not as a dramatic work under section 2. It is suggested, however, that the transitional provision should be read as meaning that copyright does not subsist in a dramatic work which was made before August 1, 1989 unless copyright subsisted in it as a dramatic work immediately before that date, so that films made in this period cannot also be dramatic works. Otherwise, the effect of the Act, apparently unintended, will have been to create a whole new raft of copyright works when arrangements and agreements may have been entered into on the basis that no such copyright existed.

3–39   **A broadcast as a dramatic work.** On the same basis that a film can be a dramatic work, a broadcast which is a work of action can also, it seems, be a dramatic work.[84]

3–40   **No requirement as to form.** There is no particular requirement as to the form which a work has to take in order to be a dramatic work. In many cases it is obvious whether a work is a dramatic work, in the sense discussed above. A play is a

---

[78] As to originality in dramatic works, see paras 3–123 *et seq.*, below.

[79] *Norowzian v Arks Ltd (No.1)* [1998] F.S.R. 394.

[80] For further discussion on the issues raised, see Stamatoudi, "'Joy' for the Claimant: Can a film be protected as a dramatic work?" [2000] I.P.Q. 117; Arnold, "Joy: A Reply" [2001] I.P.Q. 10.

[81] See para. 3–32, above. After repeal of the 1911 Act, protection for such films continued under the 1956 Act: Sch.7, para.15.

[82] Sch.1, para.7(2). The protection extends to films made before June 1, 1957: *ibid.*

[83] Sch.1, para.5(1).

[84] See the observation of Somers J. in *Green v Broadcasting Corp of New Zealand* [1989] R.P.C. 469 (High Ct of NZ), at 477, that the actual broadcast programme of each game show might have been a dramatic work, even though the court held that there was no dramatic copyright in any scripts.

prime example of a dramatic work and a screenplay is another.[85] Further, as with a literary work, what has to be considered for present purposes is the message, not the medium. Leaving aside the separate requirement of fixation of the work before copyright can subsist in it,[86] there is nothing in the modern law which requires a play to be written down before it can constitute a dramatic work. An author may, therefore, conceive the entirety of a play in his head, and get the actors to perform it by oral instruction and direction. Such a work is nonetheless a dramatic work for the purposes of the 1988 Act. Similarly, a piece of mime which the originator has developed in his mind and perfected by practice is a dramatic work, notwithstanding that he has never written down any part of it.

Elements or features of a dramatic work. The elements or features which make a work a dramatic work are many and varied, and in the case of an obvious example of a dramatic work, such as a play or a screenplay, will be readily identifiable as the dialogue and the acting directions, usually found in the stage directions. However, in order for a work to constitute a dramatic work there must be sufficient certainty of its subject matter.[87] In the case of a play or a screenplay, this presents little problem, since what knits the separate incidents together so that they can be performed as an entity is the structure of the work, or the plot, which comprises the setting, the characters, and their inter-relationship and development. In the case of subject matter which does not fall into any of the obvious types of dramatic work, however, this requires not only that there should be identifiable with sufficient certainty elements or features in such subject matter which are of a dramatic nature in the sense discussed above, but also that those features or elements should be sufficiently linked or connected so as to be capable of performance.[88] This ultimately turns on the facts of the particular case, but in applying this test it has been held that a sports game did not constitute a choreographic work (and therefore was not a dramatic work), even though parts of the game were intended to follow a pre-determined plan.[89] There seems no reason in principle, however, why other features commonly found in dramatic presentations, such as sound and light effects, should not be capable of being part of a dramatic work, provided they are sufficiently certain and capable of being linked together with other elements of the action.

3–41

Television show formats. It is sometimes said that there can be no copyright in television show formats, particularly game show formats. This conclusion is often said to follow from the decision in *Green v Broadcasting Corporation of New Zealand*,[90] where effectively a claim to the copyright in the format for the game show *Opportunity Knocks* failed. However, the claim there suffered from a

3–42

---

[85] See the discussion in *Hansard*, HL Vol.490, col.830.

[86] See further paras 3–115 *et seq.*, below.

[87] *Green v Broadcasting Corporation of New Zealand* [1989] R.P.C. 700 (where this was a further reason why the format in that case failed to qualify as a dramatic work); *Tate v Thomas* [1921] 1 Ch. 503. See also *Tate v Fullbrook* [1908] 1 K.B. 821 (a case under the pre-1911 law in which it was held that "gags" inserted into the piece by the performer and which were changed from time to time by the performer, could not be the subject of protection as a dramatic work).

[88] This latter requirement was identified by the Privy Council in *Green v Broadcasting Corporation of New Zealand* [1989] R.P.C. 700; in that case the features claimed as constituting the format of a television show, being unrelated to each other except as accessories to be used in the presentation of some other dramatic or musical performance, lacked the essential characteristic of sufficient unity to be capable of performance.

[89] *FWS Joint Sports Claimants v Copyright Board* (1991) 22 I.P.R. 429 (Fed CA of Canada), citing *Tate v Fulbrook* [1908] 1 K.B. 821 and *Green v Broadcasting Corporation of New Zealand* [1989] R.P.C. 700.

[90] [1989] R.P.C. 700.

number of fundamental defects. No scripts were available at trial,[91] and all that could be inferred was that such scripts as there had been did no more than express a general idea or concept for a talent quest. The characteristic features of the show which were repeated in each performance and in respect of which a claim was made for the dramatic format consisted merely of the title, the use of the catch phrases "For_____[name of the competitor] opportunity knocks", "This is your show folks, and I do mean you" and "Make up your mind time", the use of a "clapometer" to measure audience reaction to competitors' performances and the use of sponsors to introduce competitors. The other material (the acts of the performers in the talent show, the questions and answers in the quiz show, etc.) changed with each broadcast and there was therefore no sufficient certainty as to their subject matter. As to the fixed elements, they were unrelated to each other except as accessories to be used in the presentation of some other dramatic or musical performance and therefore lacked sufficient unity to be capable of performance.[92] There is no reason in principle, however, why a format should not be protectable as a dramatic work if it contains a sufficient record of how the show is to be presented.[93] Today, such formats, in addition to recording the central idea of the show or game, will often contain scripted spoken elements, directions for what the participants should do at particular stages, and details for the staging, lighting and sound effects. A useful test to determine whether there is a protectable dramatic work is to ask whether, using the written script or other record as a basis, it is possibly to present a coherent and meaningful show which is capable of being performed.[94] Whether another game show infringes will depend on whether or not a substantial part has been taken.[95]

3–43 **Nature of copyright in a dramatic work.** As with a literary work,[96] the idea for a dramatic work is not itself protected by copyright. What is protected is the form in which that idea is expressed. Whilst, as discussed above, a work will only be a dramatic work if it is a work of action capable of being performed before an audience, the *performance* of any actors must be distinguished from the *work*. The work may enjoy protection as a dramatic work; the performance of any actors may give rise to quite separate rights under Part II of the Act.[97] A copyright dramatic work confers on the owner the exclusive rights to do various acts in relation to the work as a whole or a substantial part of it; a qualifying performance confers on the owner of the performers' right various rights in relation to the performance. The unauthorised copying of a performance of a dramatic work may thus separately infringe the rights of the owners of the copyright and the performers' right. Again, a person may give a performance which is an ad-lib performance. This may either be as part of a work, as where the author has left

[91] Although there was evidence that there had once been some scripts, no reconstructions were produced.
[92] Similarly, it has been held that news and current affairs programmes comprising video clips, interviews and discussion, lacked the choreography required to constitute them dramatic works: *Television N.Z. v Newsmonitor Services* [1994] 2 N.Z.L.R. 91 (High Ct of NZ). Under the New Zealand Act, s.2, a dramatic work is defined to include a chorographic work if reduced to writing in the form in which it is to be presented; a film cannot be a dramatic work. Of course, the script for a television broadcast for a news or current affairs programme could itself constitute a literary work: *ibid.*
[93] Despite lobbying, the Government has resisted efforts to make specific provision for the protection of game show formats. Although consultation has taken place (see, *e.g.* the 1994 and 1996 DTI Consultation Papers), nothing has come of this.
[94] *Hutton v Canadian Broadcasting Corporation* (1989) 29 C.P.R. (3rd) 398 (High Ct of Canada) in which it was held that there was sufficient dramatic incident and seminal storyline in the concept of a television series to qualify it as a dramatic work.
[95] As to which, see para. 7–52, below.
[96] See para. 3–19, above.
[97] See Ch.2.

the performer to improvise without direction from the author, or it may constitute the entire performance. In the former case, the improvisation may be part of the dramatic structure of the work, but what the actor actually does while improvising cannot, it is suggested, be part of the original dramatic work.[98]

D. MUSICAL WORKS

(i) History of protection

Early protection. Musical scores were protected under the early Copyright Acts only as literary works, and thus only from unauthorised reproduction in printed or sheet music form. When a performing right was first introduced under the Dramatic Copyright Act 1833,[99] it applied only to dramatic, not musical works. This was remedied by the Literary Copyright Act 1842.[1] Such statutes contained no definition of a musical work.[2] Musical works were protected as a separate category of works under the 1911 Act and under the 1956 Act, but again neither Act contained a definition of a musical work.

3–44

Berne Convention. Musical works are protected under the Berne Convention as musical compositions, with or without words.[3]

3–45

(ii) Under the 1988 Act

Statutory definition: musical work. The 1988 Act defines a musical work as a work consisting of music, exclusive of any words or action intended to be sung, spoken or performed with the music.[4] The dictionary definition of music is sounds in melodic or harmonic combination, whether produced by voice or instruments,[5] but this definition is too restrictive for present purposes, as sounds which are neither in melodic nor harmonic combination may equally be recognised to be music. While an essential ingredient of a musical work is obviously that it be capable of being sensed by the human ear, mere sounds are not necessarily music. It is suggested that music is that which is regarded by a reasonable body of persons as music, as to which evidence would be admissible, or that which is reasonably regarded by the composer as being music.[6] As with a literary work, aesthetic appreciation is irrelevant to whether a work qualifies as a musical work. For these purposes, music is more than mere melody and more than that which is represented by notes written on a score; it includes all material which has an effect on the human ear, for example, harmonies, orchestration, ornamentation,

3–46

---

[98] Although it may become part of a new dramatic work if recorded. In the case of a truly improvised and unrecorded performance, whilst this will not be a performance of a dramatic work, it is suggested that this will still be a dramatic performance for the purposes of Pt II of the 1988 Act, given the subtle difference between the wording of s.180(2)(a) and(c), which seems designed to cover this very possibility. Note that a performance of a variety act or similar presentation (which would often contain much unscripted material) is specifically such a performance: s.180(2)(d).

[99] 3 & 4 Will. 4, c.15.

[1] 5 & 6 Vict., c.45.

[2] In a number of cases, the question arose whether a particular work was a dramatic piece as well as a musical work: *Russell v Smith* (1848) 12 Q.B. 217; *Clark v Bishop* (1872) 25 L.T. 908; *Roberts v Bignell* (1887) 3 T.L.R. 552; *Fuller v The Blackpool Winter Gardens, etc. Co Ltd* [1895] 2 Q.B. 429.

[3] Berne Convention, Art.2(1).

[4] CDPA 1988, s.3(1); as already noted there was no definition of musical work in the Copyright Act 1911 or in the Copyright Act 1956.

[5] *Oxford English Dictionary*. The now repealed Musical (Summary Proceedings) Copyright Act 1902 (2 Edw. 7, c.15,) s.3, defined a musical work as any combination of melody and harmony.

[6] *cf.* what amounts to a work of artistic craftsmanship: para. 3–63, below.

figuring and performance directions.[7] It is also suggested that such things as tempi and phrasing can form part of a musical work, provided they are sufficiently certain and can be appreciated by the human ear.[8] To the extent that notation or words are written down and are intended to represent sounds which qualify as music in the above sense, it seems that they are excluded from the definition of literary work, even though they can in one sense be read.[9] While words which are sung with music do not form part of the musical work, the sound that a human voice makes when singing the words does do so.[10] A passage of silence set within musical sounds and intended to be appreciated as part of those sounds is clearly part of the musical work as a whole. It is doubtful that a passage of silence by itself is capable of being a musical work, even if claimed by the author or critics to be such.

3–47 **No requirement as to form.** There is no requirement in the statutory definition of a musical work that the music must be expressed in writing or other notation. However, as with a literary and a dramatic work, for music to be the subject matter of copyright it must satisfy the requirement as to fixation.[11] A composer who composes a piece of music entirely in his head, therefore, will be creating a musical work for the purposes of the 1988 Act.[12] Equally, where a musician plays music which has not previously been composed, what is produced is a musical work. In any such case, however, no copyright will be capable of subsisting in such work until it is fixed, and for the purposes of the 1988 Act the date the musical work is made will be the date it is first fixed, not when it was first conceived or performed.[13]

3–48 **Musical work also a dramatic work.** The definition of a musical work makes it clear that it does not include words intended to be sung or spoken with the music or action intended to be performed with the music.[14] It is presumed, first, that the intention being referred to is the intention of the author of the music and, secondly, that the material time for establishing the intention is the time the author creates the music. Any such words, if they constitute a literary work,[15] are treated as a separate work, entitled to a separate copyright, and the mutually exclusive nature of the two types of works is strictly maintained. However, as already pointed out,[16] a dramatic work may include music: the music will be entitled to a separate copyright, notwithstanding that the music also forms an integral part of the dramatic work, as in the case of a work of dance written to music, or an opera. This question is of little importance, since the owner of copyright in a dramatic work has the same rights as those enjoyed by the owner of copyright in a musical work.

---

[7] *Sawkins v Hyperion Records Ltd* [2004] EWHC 1530 (Ch). Although see *Hansard*, Vol.490, col.837, suggesting that words instructing a musician how to play do not form part of the music.

[8] Although *cf.* the concession apparently made in *Sawkins v Hyperion Records Ltd* [2004] EWHC 1530 (Ch), para.66, that matters of speed directions were not part of the musical work.

[9] See CDPA 1988, s.3(1). And see the statement by Jacob J. in *Anacon Corp v Environmental Research Technology* [1994] F.S.R. 659 at 663, where, having suggested that a diagram could be a literary work provided it was all written down and contained information which could be read by somebody, as opposed to being appreciated simply with the eye, he said: "Similarly musical notation is written down but needs expressly to be taken out of the definition of 'literary work'".

[10] *Hayes v Phonogram Ltd* [2002] EWHC 2062 (Ch).

[11] By being recorded in writing or otherwise: CDPA 1988, s.3(2); see para. 3–117, below.

[12] Contrast the position with a literary work, discussed at para. 3–14, above.

[13] s.3(2).

[14] CDPA 1988, s.3(1). This provision was introduced to avoid any doubt about the distinction between the music itself, on the one hand, and words to be sung or performed with music on the other: *Hansard*, Vol.490, col.837.

[15] See para. 3–15, above.

[16] See para. 3–36, above.

E. ARTISTIC WORKS

(i) History of protection

Early protection. Artistic works have successively become the subject of protec-   **3–49**
tion under the Copyright Acts as new processes have developed. Engravings,
prints and lithographs were the earliest group of such works to be given protection, under the Engraving Copyright Acts of 1734 and 1766[17] and the Prints Copyright Act 1777.[18] Sculptures followed, under the Sculpture Copyright Act 1814,[19]
and paintings, drawings and photographs were first protected under the Fine Arts
Copyright Act 1862.[20] Works of artistic craftsmanship and works of architecture
first became separately entitled to copyright protection under the 1911 Act.

Berne Convention. With the exception of works of architecture, all such works   **3–50**
were included in the original definition of literary and artistic works in the Berne
Convention.[21]

(ii) Artistic works in general

Statutory definition: artistic work. By section 4(1) of the 1988 Act, an artistic   **3–51**
work means:

   (a) a graphic work, photograph, sculpture or collage, irrespective of artistic
       quality;
   (b) a work of architecture being a building or a model for a building; or
   (c) a work of artistic craftsmanship.

Artistic quality. Works described under sub-paragraph (a) are artistic works,   **3–52**
regardless of whether they have any artistic quality.[22] The definition of an artistic
work under the 1911 Act did not contain such words,[23] but it was generally
considered that the word "artistic" was merely used as a generic term to include
the different processes of creating works set out in the definition section and that,
provided that a work was produced by one of such processes, and that its creation
involved some skill or labour on the part of the artist, it was protected.[24] The use
of the word "artistic" was thought to equate to the use of the word literary in connection with literary works, which, as already pointed out,[25] was held to refer
only to the nature of the material being written or printed and not to its literary

---

[17] 8 Geo. 2, c.13; 7 Geo. 3, c.38.
[18] 17 Geo. 3, c.57.
[19] 54 Geo. 3, c.56.
[20] 25 & 26 Vict., c.12.
[21] Berne Convention, Art.2(1). Works of architecture were first included in the Berlin Act (1908).
   Art.2(1) of the Convention now includes within the description of "artistic works" every production in the artistic domain, whatever may be the mode or form of its expression, such as works of
   drawing, painting, architecture, sculpture, engraving and lithography, photographic works and
   works "expressed" by a process analogous to photography, works of applied art, illustrations,
   maps, plans, sketches and three-dimensional works "relative" to geography, topography,
   architecture or science.
[22] This was also the position under the Copyright Act 1956, s.3(1)(a). These words were deliberately
   retained in the 1988 Act, so as to avoid any doubt that artistry was not a requirement for protection as an artistic work: *Hansard*, HL Vol.490, cols 839, 840.
[23] Copyright Act 1911, s.35(1).
[24] Thus, merely commercial designs were protected under the Copyright Act 1911: *Waters v Huy-
   gen (M.A.) & Co* [1923–28] Mac. C.C. 17; *Purefoy Engineering Co Ltd v Sykes, Boxall & Co Ltd*
   (1955) 72 R.P.C. 89.
[25] See para. 3–15, above.

quality. This contrasts with the position in the case of artistic works falling within sub-paragraphs (b) and (c), where such words do not occur.[26]

3–53 Nature of copyright in artistic works. The essential nature of an artistic work is that it is a thing to be *looked* at in some manner or other. What matters is that which is *visually* significant.[27] It follows from this and ordinary copyright principles that the ideas conveyed by an artistic work, however original, are not protected by copyright, only the expression of those ideas in the form of an artistic work,[28] although of course every element in the expression of an artistic work will usually be the expression of an idea on the part of the artist, representing his choice to paint one thing rather than another, or to use one colour or brush technique rather than another, and so on, and it is the expression of these ideas which is protected.[29] In the case of simple artistic works, the protection given by copyright is therefore relatively weak, as shown by *Kenrick & Co v Lawrence & Co*[30] There, the claimant had the idea of producing cards on which were printed a hand holding a pencil in the act of making a cross within a square, to be used at elections by illiterate voters. The defendants then published similar cards with a hand holding a pencil, but the hand in the defendants' cards was in a slightly different position, though the idea was clearly taken from the claimant's cards. It was held that the defendants had not infringed the claimant's copyright. There was no copyright in the idea; the defendants' work did not substantially reproduce the form of the claimant's, and the claimant was not entitled to prevent anyone from producing such a simple design as a hand in a square in any form.[31]

3–54 Simple artistic works. Provided that the subject matter can be fairly said to fall within one of categories of protected subject matter (drawing, diagram, etc.), it will in principle be protectable, even though it is elementary or commonplace,[32] the issue in the case of simple works being one rather of originality.[33] All that it is necessary is that there be some visual significance in the product of the artist's

---

[26] As to these works, see paras 3–60 and 3–63, below.

[27] *Anacon Corp v Environmental Research Technology* [1994] F.S.R. 659, applying *Interlego AG v Tyco Industries Ltd* [1988] R.P.C. 343 at 373, *per* Lord Oliver, himself drawing on the phrase "visually significant" used by Whitford J. in *Rose Plastics GmbH v William Beckett & Co (Plastics) Ltd* [1989] F.S.R. 113.

[28] See, e.g. *Entec (Pollution Control) v Abacus Mouldings* [1992] F.S.R. 332, *per* Nicholls L.J. at 348; *Donoghue v Allied Newspapers Ltd* [1938] Ch. 106, *per* Farwell J., at p.109: "This at any rate is clear beyond all question, that there is no copyright in an idea, or in ideas. A person may have a brilliant idea ... for a picture ..., and which appears to him to be original; but if he communicates that idea to ... an artist ..., the production which is the result of the communication of the idea to the ... artist ... is the copyright of the person who has clothed the idea in form, ... and the owner of the idea has not rights in that product." And again, at 110: "... that in which copyright exists is the particular form of language by which information which is to be conveyed is conveyed. If the idea, however original, is nothing more than an idea, and is not put into ... any form of expression such as a picture, then there is no such thing as copyright at all. It is not until it is ... reduced into ... some tangible form that there is any copyright, and the copyright exists in ... the particular form of the picture by which ... the information or the idea is conveyed to those who are intended to look at it."

[29] *Designers Guild Ltd v Russell Williams (Textiles) Ltd* [2000] 1 W.L.R. 2416, at 2423.

[30] (1890) 25 Q.B.D. 99.

[31] But there was copyright in the claimant's drawing and if the drawing had been more closely reproduced, copyright would no doubt have been infringed. See also *George Ward (Moxley) Ltd v Richard Sankey Ltd* [1988] F.S.R. 66, where Whitford J. adopted a similar approach to the copying of an idea for the design of flower pots; *Entec (Pollution Control) Ltd v Abacus Mouldings* [1992] F.S.R. 332 at 348 (Nicholls L.J.) (drawings for a septic tank comprising simple pencil sketches of commonplace shapes with dimensions on them: what were crucial were the dimensions written on the drawings and it was these that had been copied) and *Mirage Studios v Counter-Feat Clothing Co Ltd* [1991] F.S.R. 145 at 154 (where Browne-Wilkinson V.-C. observed that the concept of a humanoid turtle of an aggressive nature receiving protection was a "difficult concept").

[32] *British Northrop Ltd v TexteamBlackburn Ltd* [1974] R.P.C. 344.

[33] As to which, see para. 3–129, below.

work. It may be that certain very simple creations are not protectable at all[34] but the boundary here is not very clear.[35] It has been suggested that the notion of an "artistic *work*" carries with it the notion of the exercise of some degree of skill and labour[36] but it is suggested this is an issue best left to the question of originality.

(iii) Graphic works

Statutory definition: graphic work. The term graphic work was new in the **3–55** 1988 Act, and is defined to include any painting, drawing, diagram, map, chart or plan, engraving, etching, lithograph, woodcut or similar work.[37]

A painting is not further defined, but is a word in ordinary usage in the English language, and should be given its ordinary meaning.[38] One meaning given in the dictionary[39] is a representation of objects or figures by means of colours laid on a surface. This is clearly too restrictive, in referring to a representation of objects or figures, to act as a comprehensive definition for the purposes of the 1988 Act, since it would exclude much abstract art, where the use of colour alone may be the essential element of the painting. Nevertheless, applying this definition, it has been held that the term did not embrace facial make-up.[40]

A drawing does not cease to exist because the original lines have been cut around to produce a paper pattern without lines,[41] and it appears that it does not even require production by means of a pen or pencil or similar means, but that it denotes that the work is a product of an artist who represents his ideas by use of line or delineation. Thus it has been held that labels made by cutting out various parts and sticking them on the appropriate background were capable of constituting a drawing.[42] A diagram can include such things as a circuit diagram[43] and a flow chart.[44] The meaning of drawings or diagrams has been stretched to include works which, although containing some visually significant elements, are in reality little more than written instructions for creating an article that has visual ap-

---

[34] *British Northrop Ltd v Texteam Blackburn Ltd* [1974] R.P.C. 344, at 68 (a line drawn with a ruler stated to be not "a very promising subject for copyright"; *Karo Step Trade Mark* [1977] R.P.C. 255 (straight line or circle not protectable); *Rose v Information Services Ltd* [1987] F.S.R. 254 (single vertical line doubted to be a work of originality).

[35] See, *e.g. Waylite Diaries CC v First National Bank Ltd* [1993] (2) S.A. 128, (High Ct of S.A.), where the straight lines dividing up the pages of an ordinary diary were held to be artistic works.

[36] *Karo Step Trade Mark* [1977] R.P.C. 255.

[37] CDPA 1988, s.4(2); encompassing the works defined in s.3(1)(a) of the 1956 Act as artistic works, together with the further definitions of drawing and engraving in s.48(1) of the Act (as to the omission of a print, see further in the text).

[38] *Merchandising Corporation of America Inc v Harpbond Ltd* [1983] F.S.R. 32.

[39] *Oxford English Dictionary*.

[40] *Merchandising Corporation of America Inc v Harpbond Ltd* [1983] F.S.R. 32 (facial make-up of pop singer Adam Ant), decided in part on the basis that facial make-up was not painting on a surface. However, there is no requirement as to fixation in relation to artistic works (see para. 3–119, below) and even then there would seem to be no good reason in principle why the face or any part of the body should not be considered a surface, so that facial or body make-up should constitute an artistic work (consider the example of a clown's particular facial make-up, which is his personal "trade mark").

[41] *Radley Gowns Ltd v Spyrou* [1975] F.S.R. 455 at p.466.

[42] *Ornstin Ltd v Quality Plastics* (Aldous J.) noted only at [1990] I.P.D. 13027. Such a work would also appear to be a collage (see para. 3–59, below).

[43] But, where the diagram showed a large amount of writing and symbols and was a list of components together with information as to how they were connected, it was held also capable of protection as a compilation (which gave wider protection against unlicensed copying): *Anacon Corporation Ltd v Environmental Research Technology Ltd* [1994] F.S.R. 659; see para. 3–17, above. As to whether the same work can be both a literary work and artistic work, see para. 3–04, above.

[44] A flow chart produced as preparatory design material for a computer program will now be capable of protection as a literary work; see para. 3–29, above.

peal,[45] but it is suggested that to the extent that a work includes material that can be read rather than appreciated visually, it can only be a literary work.[46] If it were otherwise, purely written instructions describing how to make an artistic work could be protected as an artistic work, and infringed by the making of the artistic work, which is clearly not the correct position.[47]

A map, chart or plan may be of real or imaginary things.[48] A map may be protected as both an artistic work and as a literary work, and, as to the latter it seems, either as a compilation of written and artistic material[49] or, to the extent that it contains information that can be read, purely as a literary work.[50]

Engravings, etchings, lithographs, and woodcuts are all works intended to produce a representation by a similar or analogous process. In the case of an engraving, the representation is made by incisions on a surface, traditionally being wood, metal or stone, but this could include rubber or plastic.[51] Dies and moulds for making products have been held to be protectable as engravings,[52] although it is difficult to see what aspect of the process of engraving is employed in making such moulds or dies. The better view would seem to be that engraving requires some process of cutting, incision, marking or otherwise working a surface, and that a mould or die made in the ordinary way would not be an engraving.[53] An engraving is typically made on a flat surface but need not be.[54] What constitutes an engraving is not limited to the appearance of that which is left by cutting away the surface but includes the internal shape and texture of cuts below the surface and any other part that affects the final appearance of the print made from it.[55] Nevertheless, not all cutting away of material from a plate constitutes engraving,

[45] *Lerose Ltd v Hawick Jersey International Ltd* [1973] F.S.R. 15 (point patterns for knitting machines containing, in addition to a visual representation of the pattern, instructions in the form of hieroglyphics, figures in the margins and words appearing underneath to enable a machine operator to set a knitting machine so that what emerges from it has the pattern reproduced upon it); *Vermaat v Boncrest Ltd* [2001] F.S.R. 43 (drawings for patchwork bedspread covers and cushions consisting of drawings in the form of grids of numbered squares and a border, on each of which was placed a code-number corresponding to the numbers of differently coloured swatches of material, which were also fixed to the drawing).
[46] See *Interlego AG v Tyco Industries Inc* [1989] A.C. 217 at 265C.
[47] See paras 7–12 and 7–34, below.
[48] As to protection of maps and plans of imaginary things, see *Braithwaite Burn & Co v Trustees of the Port of Madras* (1956) 2 Mad. L.J. 486.
[49] See para. 3–24.
[50] *Comprop Ltd v Moran* [2002] J.L.R. 222 (Royal Ct of Jersey).
[51] *James Arnold and Co Ltd v Miafern Ltd* [1980] R.P.C. 397 (rubber stereos used for printing onto transfer paper).
[52] *Wham-O Manufacturing Co v Lincoln Industries Ltd* [1985] R.P.C. 127 (High Ct of NZ) (moulds for making frisbees); *Mayceys Confectionery Ltd v Beckmann* (High Ct of NZ), noted at [1995] E.I.P.R. D- 101 (rubber moulds taken from plaster of Paris model for confectionery "crocodiles"—the report at 30 I.P.R. 331 is concerned with *quantum* only; subsistence was not in issue on the appeal, reported at 33 I.P.R. 543
[53] See *Gabrin v Universal Music Operations Ltd* [2003] EWHC 1335 (Ch), para.30; *Greenfield Products Pty Ltd v Rover-Scott Bonnar Ltd* (1990) 95 A.L.R. 275 (Fed Ct of Aus) (discussed by Ricketson in [1990] E.I.P.R. 421); *Talk of the Town Pty Ltd v Hagstrom* (1990) 19 I.P.R. 649 at 655 (Fed Ct of Aus)), not following *Wham-O Manufacturing Co v Lincoln Industries Ltd* [1985] R.P.C. 127 (High Ct of NZ).
[54] *Talk of the Town Pty Ltd v Hagstrom* (1990) 19 I.P.R. 649 (Fed Ct of Aus), correcting the statement on this point in *Greenfield Products Pty Ltd v Rover-Scott Bonnar Ltd* (1990) 95 A.L.R. 275 (Fed Ct of Aus).
[55] *Hi-Tech Autoparts Ltd v Towergate Two Ltd (No.1)* [2002] F.S.R. 15, para.39 (steel plate which had been worked with a boring tool to produce grooved circles with circular and conical edges, to be used as a stamp to produce rubber, anti-slip mats, held to be an engraving). The court also rejected the argument that what is protected in the category of "any engraving, etching, lithograph, woodcut or similar work" are works which are concerned with the final appearance of the two-dimensional print taken from the work as a plate, such that the protectable skill and labour is only that which has any impact on the appearance of the print.

so that, for example, cutting a rod into sections would not qualify.[56] There is no requirement that an engraving must be something that could be regarded as the work of an artist.[57] Not only is the plate whose surface has been cut into with an engraving tool an "engraving", but so also is the object produced by using this plate, since "engraving" can and usually does mean an image produced from an engraved plate.[58] The position was clearer on this point under the 1956 Act, which defined an engraving to include not only any etching, lithograph or woodcut, but also any "print or similar work". Under the 1988 Act, the relevant protected works are "any engraving, etching, lithograph, woodcut or similar work", without any further definition of "engraving" and without any reference to a "print". It would be surprising, however, if the 1988 Act had the effect of abolishing copyright in works in which copyright subsisted immediately before commencement,[59] and presumably the position in relation to prints under the 1988 Act remains as it was before.[60] In the case of an etching, the process involves the eating away of the surface, usually by the use of an acid. It is not clear what is added by reference to a lithograph and a woodcut, since these are usually understood to be no more than examples of these processes carried out on particular surfaces, namely stone and wood, respectively.

Examples of graphic works. As with other composite categories of work, examples of works which have been held to fall within the category merely go to illustrate the wide variety of types of work which have gained protection. Further, many of the cases are now mainly of historical significance only, given the effect of the restriction placed on the copyright in designs for the shape or configuration of articles by section 51 of the Act, and protection of such designs now falls mainly within the scope of design right.[61]

3–56

In the case of graphic works, examples demonstrate that simplicity is not enough to prevent copyright subsisting in a graphic work as an artistic work, and drawings for screws, studs, bolts, metal bars, rivets and washers (all carefully drawn to scale) have been held protectable.[62] Drawings for standard parts for vehicles such as engines and gearboxes[63] and exhausts,[64] and engineering drawings generally,[65] have been held capable of protection as artistic works. Protection has been conferred on the artistic part of a simple trade mark,[66] designs for

---

[56] *Hi-Tech Autoparts Ltd v Towergate Two Ltd (No.1)* [2002] F.S.R. 15.

[57] *Hi-Tech Autoparts Ltd v Towergate Two Ltd (No.1)* [2002] F.S.R. 15; *cf. Metix (U.K.) Ltd v G.H. Maughan (Plastics) Ltd* [1997] F.S.R. 718, as to which see para. 3–58, below.

[58] *Hi-Tech Autoparts Ltd v Towergate Two Ltd (No.1)* [2002] F.S.R. 15, paras 36 and 39; *Hi-Tech Autoparts Ltd v Towergate Two Ltd (No.2)* [2002] F.S.R. 16, para.16, following James *Arnold & Co Ltd v Miafern Ltd* [1980] R.P.C. 397 at 403, and *Wham-O Manufacturing Co v Lincoln Industries Ltd* [1985] R.P.C. 127.

[59] Copyright does not automatically subsist under the 1988 Act in works in which copyright subsisted under the 1956 Act; para.35 of Sch.1 to the 1988 Act relates only to the requirements as to qualification for protection, not categories of protected works.

[60] The point appears to have been glossed over in *Hi-Tech Autoparts Ltd v Towergate Two Ltd* [2002] F.S.R. 15; [2002] F.S.R. 16. Nevertheless, the requirement that in order for copyright to subsist the engraving should be original obviously presents problems in the case of such derivative prints. See para. 3–135, below.

[61] See para. 9–142 and Ch.13, below.

[62] *British Northrop Ltd v Texteam Blackburn Ltd* [1974] R.P.C. 344, and see para. 3–54, above, as to simplicity in general. But even if simple, such drawings must be original, see further paras 3–129 *et seq.*, below.

[63] *Nichols Advanced Vehicle Systems Inc v Rees* [1979] R.P.C. 127.

[64] *L.B. (Plastics) Ltd v Swish Products Ltd* [1979] R.P.C. 551; *Kwik Lok Corporation v W.B.W. Engineers Ltd* [1975] F.S.R. 237; *British Leyland Motor Corp v T.I. Silencers Ltd* [1981] F.S.R. 213; *British Leyland Motor Corp v Armstrong Patents Co Ltd* [1972] F.S.R. 481.

[65] See cases cited in the previous footnote.

[66] *Karo Step Trade Mark* [1977] R.P.C. 255 (a circle contained with four quarter-arcs of circles);

packaging,[67] mastheads and newspaper logos,[68] and to a signature and Union emblem.[69]

Point patterns for knitted fabrics,[70] and drawings for clerical shirts[71] have been protected as artistic works. In cases concerned with dress designs, infringement used often to be alleged in the design sketch, cutting patterns and prototype garment.[72] Such a sketch is undoubtedly a work in which copyright is capable of subsisting.[73] Where cutting patterns have been made by first drawing an outline of the pattern, copyright is capable of subsisting in them as graphic works,[74] and in theory copyright is capable of subsisting in a prototype garment as a work of artistic craftsmanship.[75]

Typeface designs are clearly protectable under the 1988 Act.[76] They were also considered capable of protection under the 1956 Act as artistic works, at least as to designs of individual letters, although doubt was expressed as to whether designs for fonts (*i.e.* complete sets of lettering) qualified as artistic works.[77] Designs for individual letters were protected under the 1911 Act as artistic works,[78] as also were fonts.[79]

(iv) Photographs

3–57   **Statutory definition: photograph.** A photograph is defined to mean a recording of light or other radiation on any medium on which an image is produced or from

---

[66] *AUVI Pte Ltd v Seah Siew Tee* (1991) 24 I.P.R. 41; [1995] F.S.R. 288 (High Ct of Singapore) (logo consisting of four letters in a stylised form); *R. Griggs Group Ltd v Evans* [2003] EWHC 2914 (Ch), para.18 (logo for boots, being word or phrase drawn in stylised way). Compare *Kinnor (Pty) Ltd v Finkel T/A Harfin Agencies*, W.L.D. 9059/90, Stranex Judgments on Copyright 352, and noted at [1990] 5 Ent. L.R. E-84, (Sup. Ct of S.A.), where it was held that a representation of a logo for "LePacer", with the loop of the "P" being elongated for the full length of the word, was not an original artistic work, being simply a different way of writing what was still the letter "P".

[67] *Charles Walker & Co Ltd v The British Picker Co Ltd* [1961] R.P.C. 57; *Taverner Rutledge Ltd v Specters, Ltd* [1959] R.P.C. 83; *Frank & Hirsch (Pty) Ltd v A. Roopanand Brothers (Pty) Ltd* (1994) 29 I.P.R. 465 (CA of S.A.) (artwork for audio cassette wrappers).

[68] *IPC Magazines Ltd v MGN Ltd* [1998] F.S.R. 431 (the logo "Woman" used as the masthead of a magazine). In *News Group Newspapers Ltd v Mirror Group Newspapers (1986) Ltd* [1989] F.S.R. 126, it was assumed that the masthead of *The Sun* was capable of being protected as an artistic work, subject to its originality. In *Emap National Publications Ltd v Security Publications Ltd* [1997] F.S.R. 891 it was conceded that copyright subsisted in the claimant's oval lozenge logo for its publication *Popular Classics*.

[69] *Daily Telegraph*, March 1, 1977 (use of facsimile of Mr Clive Jenkins' signature and his Union's emblem).

[70] As to diagrams: *Lerose Ltd v Hawick Jersey International Ltd* [1973] F.S.R. 15. But see para. 3–55, above.

[71] *Gleeson v H.R. Denne Ltd* [1975] R.P.C. 471.

[72] *Radley Gowns Ltd v Costas Spyrou* [1975] F.S.R. 455 is just one example.

[73] See. *e.g. J. Bernstein Ltd v Sidney Murray Ltd* [1981] R.P.C. 303, 328.

[74] See *Radley Gowns Ltd v Costas Spyrou* [1975] F.S.R. 455; *Merlet v Mothercare Plc* [1984] F.S.R. 358. The point was conceded in *House of Spring Gardens Ltd v Point Blank Ltd* [1983] F.S.R. 213 (High Ct of Ireland).

[75] See paras 3–63 *et seq.*, below.

[76] The 1988 Act proceeds on the assumption that designs for typefaces qualify for protection as artistic works: see *e.g.* ss.54 and 55 and *Hansard*, HL Vol.490, col.844; HL Vol.493, col.1068. S.78 defines "typeface" as including an ornamental motif used in printing, and see paras 9–145 *et seq.*, below. Designs for typefaces are excluded from the effect of s.51 (see s.51(1) and para. 9–142, below). See generally on the protection of software fonts, *Watts & and Blakemore* [1995] E.I.P.R. 133. The 1977 Whitford Committee Report recommended (Cmnd.6732, para.538) that the UK should ratify the Vienna Agreement on the Protection of Typefaces, signed by the UK on June 12, 1973 (Cmnd.5754, set out in Vol.2 at F9), but to date the UK has not done so.

[77] See the Whitford Committee Report, paras 524 and 529.

[78] *Millar & Lang Ltd v Polak* [1908] 1 Ch. 433 (designs of distinctive individual letters for Christmas cards; *Roland Corporation v Lorenzo & Sons (Pty) Ltd* (1991) 22 I.P.R. 245 (Fed Ct of Aus) (logo devices consisting of depictions of single letters).

[79] *Stephenson, Blake & Co v Grant, Legros & Co Ltd* (1916) 33 R.P.C. 406, following *Maple & Co v Junior Army and Navy Stores* (1882) 21 Ch. D. 369 and *Davis v Benjamin* [1906] 2 Ch. 491.

which an image may by any means be produced, and which is not part of a film.[80] Save for the last clause, this definition is new and is so worded to ensure that such things as holograms are capable of protection as artistic works by being photographs.[81] The definition also covers a photograph recorded digitally, since what is recorded is still light or other radiation, and the reference to the medium is unrestricted. The reference to light or other radiation ensures that a photograph taken by x-ray or infra-red or other process is nonetheless a photograph for the purposes of the Act. The last clause of the definition, which in this respect follows the definition in the 1956 Act, excludes a single frame of a film from being capable of protection as a photograph. A single frame of a film is, however, protectable as part of a film.[82]

(v) Sculptures

Statutory definition: sculpture. Sculpture is defined in the 1988 Act to include a cast or model made for purposes of sculpture,[83] but the 1988 Act does not otherwise define what is a sculpture. The expression therefore bears its ordinary dictionary meaning:[84] the art of sculpture is the art of forming representations of objects or abstract designs in the round or in relief by chiselling stone, carving wood, modelling clay, casting metal or similar processes.[85] Thus, plaster shapes made for the production of the die-casting moulds for the manufacture of the heating plates for sandwich toasters have been held to be sculptures.[86] In contrast, an arrangement of a scene for the purpose of a photograph being taken for the cover of a record album did not constitute a sculpture, as no element in the composition had been carved, modelled or made in any of the other ways in which a sculpture was made.[87] Whilst a carved wooden model produced to enable moulds to be made for moulding plastic, as a step in the process of manufacturing Frisbees, has been held to qualify as a sculpture,[88] it has been held that models or casts fashioned in plasticine or some other suitable modelling material which were no more than steps in the production, first of prototypes, and later in the manufacturing of tooling, and which were not intended to have any permanent existence, did not fall within the definition of sculpture.[89] The precise purpose for which such a work was made would, however, seem to be irrelevant when deciding whether the work satisfies the statutory description,[90] as is the issue of whether a work is intended to have a short or long existence, and it has subsequently been confirmed that something which has a transient existence may be a work of

3–58

---

[80] CDPA 1988, s.4(2). Compare the definition in the Copyright Act 1956, s.48(1): any product of photography or any process akin to photography, other than a part of a cinematograph film.
[81] See *Hansard*, HL Vol.495, col.1065.
[82] CDPA s.17(4) and para. 7–70, below.
[83] CDPA 1988, s.4(2), repeating the definition in s.48(1) of the Copyright Act 1956.
[84] *Breville v Thorn EMI* [1995] F.S.R. 77.
[85] *Oxford English Dictionary*.
[86] *Breville v Thorn EMI* [1995] F.S.R. 77. In *Mayceys Confectionery Ltd v Beckmann* (High Ct of NZ), noted at [1995] E.I.P.R. D- 101 it was conceded that a plaster of Paris model for confectionery "crocodiles" was a sculpture.
[87] *Creation Records v News Group Newspapers* [1997] E.M.L.R. 444. See also *Jarman & Platt Ltd v I. Barget Ltd* [1977] F.S.R. 260, CA: the headnote only records that at trial it had been held that settings or arrangements of furniture were not capable of attracting copyright but it is not clear under what category of artistic work protection was claimed.
[88] *Wham-O Manufacturing Co v Lincoln Industries Ltd* [1985] R.P.C. 127 (CA of NZ). The moulded discs themselves did not qualify.
[89] *Davis (J & S) (Holdings) Ltd v Wright Health Group Ltd* [1988] R.P.C. 403 (dental impression trays).
[90] See, *e.g. Wham-O Manufacturing Co v Lincoln Industries Ltd* [1985] R.P.C. 127 (CA of NZ), above.

sculpture.[91] There is further authority that a work of sculpture is something made by an artist's hand, so that where there was nothing to suggest that the persons who created moulds used to make certain industrial items considered themselves to be artists when designing the moulds, or were in any way concerned with the shape or appearance of what they were making, save for the purpose of achieving a precise functional effect, copyright could not subsist in the moulds as sculptures.[92] Again, it is suggested that this is to apply too restrictive an approach to the question of what is an artistic work, and ignores the force of the statutory disregard of whether the work has any artistic quality, contained in the definition of these works in section 4(1)(a).[93]

(vi) Collages

3–59   **Collages.** A collage is now specifically included as an artistic work.[94] No definition of a collage is provided or was apparently considered to be necessary,[95] and the dictionary definition of collage is "an abstract form of art in which photographs, pieces of paper, newspaper cuttings, string, etc. are placed in juxtaposition and glued to the pictorial surface".[96] Consistent with this, it has been held that a collage involves the use of glue or adhesive in the process of making a work of visual art.[97] There is no necessary requirement that the result should be a work of art;[98] the result may be a purely functional product.[99]

(vii) Works of architecture

3–60   **History of protection of works of architecture.** Works of architecture, as distinct from the plans, drawings and sketches of such works, were first made the subject of copyright protection under the 1911 Act.[1] This followed the revision of the Berne Convention in 1908, as a result of which the definition of literary and artistic works was extended to require protection to be granted to illustrations, maps, plans, sketches and three-dimensional works "relative", *inter alia*, to architecture.[2] Under the 1911 Act, an artistic work was therefore defined to

---

[91] *Metix (UK) Ltd v G.H. Maughan* [1997] F.S.R. 718, making the point that a sculpture in ice is nonetheless a sculpture, although see *Merchandising Corporation of America Inc v Harpbond Ltd* [1983] F.S.R. 32 (no copyright in short-lived fixation of painting) and the comment on this case in para. 3–155, above.

[92] *Metix (UK) Ltd v G.H. Maughan* [1997] F.S.R. 718, above. The items were flow mixers, cartridges and "closure" caps.

[93] See para. 3–52, above. And see *Hi-Tech Autoparts Ltd v Towergate Two Ltd (No.1)* [2002] F.S.R. 15, para.47, echoing these doubts about *Metix (UK) Ltd v G.H. Maughan* [1997] F.S.R. 718. It should be noted, however, that *Metix* turned on a pleading point, there being no direct pleading of a work of sculpture, only a plea that certain moulds were sculptures. It was held that if this plea was sufficient, it meant that any mould would be a sculpture, which was clearly not the case.

[94] There was some doubt as to whether a collage fell within the definition of an artistic work under the 1956 Act. If not, then it seems there is no protection created before August 1, 1989. See CDPA 1988, Sch.1, para.5(1).

[95] *Hansard*, HL Vol.495, col.1067.

[96] *Oxford English Dictionary*.

[97] *Creation Records v News Group Newspapers* [1997] E.M.L.R. 444, holding that the arrangement of a scene for the purpose of a photograph being taken for the cover of an album could not constitute a collage. It was also suggested that the intrinsically ephemeral nature of the assemblage prevented it being a collage, *sed quaere*.

[98] See para. 3–52, above.

[99] For example, the labels made by cutting out various parts and sticking them on the appropriate background, which were the subject of *Ornstin Ltd v Quality Plastics* (Aldous J.), noted at [1990] I.P.D. 13027.

[1] Copyright Act 1911, s.35(1).

[2] Berlin Act, Art.2(1).

include "architectural works of art",[3] this expression being in turn defined to mean any building or structure having an artistic character or design, in respect of such design, or any model for such building or structure, but the protection given by the Act was confined to the artistic character and design, and did not extend to processes or methods of construction.[4] Copyright could therefore now subsist in a building, as distinct from a copyright in the plans on which the building was based.[5] Under the 1956 Act, an artistic work was defined to include works or architecture, being either buildings or models for buildings,[6] a building being defined to include any structure.[7] Express reference to artistic character or design, and to the nature of protection, was now omitted but it is thought that this did not produce any substantial alteration in the law. While drawings were protected "irrespective of artistic quality",[8] the omission of these words in respect of architectural works maintained, in effect, the requirement under the 1911 Act that such works, in order to be architectural works, must have some artistic character.

Statutory definition: work of architecture. A work of architecture is defined by the 1988 Act as being a building or a model for a building,[9] and a building is defined as including any fixed structure, or a part of a building or fixed structure.[10] The reference to a part of a building or structure was introduced to remove any doubt that an extension to a building is included.[11] Although the word "building" is found in a number of other Acts, probably little help as to what constitutes a building is to be obtained from them: the definition was deliberately wide, and was intended to include structures designed by engineers, rather than architects, such as a bridge.[12] It is suggested that a building or structure must be of such a character as is usually erected upon, or constructed under the ground and that in each case it involves something of substance, with an element of permanence. If a building or structure has these characteristics, then it will be entitled to protection, not only as a whole, but in individual architectural features, including internal features of design.[13] On this basis a chimney-piece might, it is thought, be entitled to copyright and it has been held that a garden, consisting of a layout including steps, walls, ponds and other structures in stone, was capable of protection as "a structure".[14]

In view of what has been said, it is questionable whether the introduction in the 1988 Act of the qualification "fixed" to the term "structure" is helpful.[15] Presumably fixed means fixed to the ground, and is intended to denote a degree of permanence,[16] but the term may itself introduce argument as to the degree and duration of fixation which is envisaged and could result in some arbitrary distinc-

3–61

---

[3] Copyright Act 1911, s.35(1)—although the remedies for the infringement of those works were considerably curtailed: s.9.

[4] Copyright Act 1911, s.35(1).

[5] *Meikle v Maufe* [[1941] 3 All E.R. 144.

[6] Copyright Act 1956, s.3(1)(b).

[7] s.48(1).

[8] s.3(1)(a).

[9] CDPA 1988, s.4(1)(b), in identical terms to the definition in s.3(1)(b) of the Copyright Act 1956.

[10] CDPA 1988, s.4(2).

[11] *Hansard*, HL Vol.493, col.1069.

[12] *Hansard*, HL Vol.493, col.1071.

[13] *Meikle v Maufe* [1941] 3 All E.R. 144.

[14] *Vincent v Universal Housing Co Ltd* [1928–35] Mac. C.C. 275.

[15] The word "fixed" was intended to distinguish protected structures from those which were not intended to be protected, such as moveable engineering structures (*e.g.* a ship): *Hansard*, HL Vol.493, col.1071.

[16] It is suggested that, for example, a building constructed as part of a garden display at the Chelsea Flower Show would satisfy this requirement, even though it was intended to be demolished at the end of the show (and consider the example of the Crystal Palace, erected in Hyde Park for the duration of the Great Exhibition).

tions between works capable of protection as architectural works and others which are not. For example, a construction such as a summer house, which rested by its own weight on the ground but was not otherwise fixed to the ground, would, unless it was a "building", seem by this requirement to be excluded from being a work of architecture, although it would be capable of being a work of architecture if fixed to the ground in any way (even if such fixing was intended to be only temporary).

A model will be protected as a work of architecture if it is a model "for" a building. It is suggested that this is deliberately different from a model "of" a building. The word "for" implies a purposive connection between the making of the model and the intended building. In this respect a model is, like architects' plans and drawings, a preparatory work in the process of producing the design for the building or structure. This would exclude from a work of architecture a model made as a model (whether of an existing or imaginary building) which was not made for the purpose of showing the architectural form of the intended building or structure. Such a model would be capable of protection, if at all, as a work of artistic craftsmanship.[17]

3–62   **Artistic character or design of architectural work.** The necessity under the 1911 and 1956 Acts that a work of architecture should have an artistic character or design has already been noted and it is suggested that the position is the same under the 1988 Act.[18] It is suggested that such artistic character need not involve any aesthetic judgment,[19] but may reside in the process of design of the building or structure. In the case of the vast majority of structures in respect of which the issue might arise as to whether they were works of architecture, this is, in practice, likely not to be a problem. It is, however, possible to conceive of a structure which would require to be designed but which might not be considered to qualify as a work of architecture.[20]

(viii) Works of artistic crafstmanship

3–63   **Early protection for works of artistic craftsmanship.** Protection was first given to such works by the 1911 Act.[21] Previously, protection in this area was given only to works of "the fine arts"[22] and the intention of the 1911 Act was to extend protection to works produced under the influence of the Arts and Crafts movement, with its emphasis on the applied or decorative arts.[23] Although the term was not defined in the 1911 Act, the intention was thus to give protection to works of genuine artistry such as pottery, embroidery, and other forms of craftsmanship which might not otherwise be protected as artistic works.[24] The

---

[17] See para. 3–63, below.

[18] As with the 1956 Act, the 1988 Act, although stating that an artistic work includes a graphic work, photograph, sculpture or collage, "irrespective of artistic quality" (s.4(1)(a)), makes no such qualification in the case of a work of architecture.

[19] In *Blake v Warren* [1928–35] Mac.C.C. 268 (an official referee's decision), it was held that the requirement of "artistic character or design" in the 1911 Act required something apart from the "common stock of ideas", rather something that "strikes the eye as uncommon". But it is suggested that this is to apply a test which is virtually one of novelty, which was not the correct position.

[20] For example, an underground concrete water sump, or the foundations for a building, comprising the concrete raft and the piles to be driven into the ground.

[21] Copyright Act 1911, ss.1 and 35(1).

[22] *i.e.* to paintings, drawings and photographs under the Fine Arts Copyright Act 1862; and see the preamble to the Act.

[23] *George Hensher Ltd v Restawile Upholstery (Lancs) Ltd* [1976] A.C. 64, *per* Lord Simon at 90.

[24] The latter point was confirmed, in the case of the 1956 Act at least, by the fact that an artistic

1956 Act continued this protection and, similarly, provided no definition of this category of artistic work.[25]

Berne Convention. Work of artistic craftsmanship is not a term which is derived from the Berne Convention.[26]   **3–64**

Works of artistic craftsmanship under the 1988 Act. As with the previous Acts, the 1988 Act does not attempt to define this description of artistic work. Indeed, it was considered that no satisfactory definition of what is a work of artistic craftsmanship could be given in the statute.[27] In addition to this, matters are not helped by the fact that the leading case, in the House of Lords,[28] was handicapped by what was probably a mistaken concession,[29] and that even then the House of Lords did not speak with one voice.[30] The starting point[31] for considering whether a work is a work of artistic craftsmanship is that the phrase imports two separate requirements combined in the same work: artistic quality and craftsmanship. Had the intention merely been to protect works of craftsmanship, irrespective of artistic quality, the word artistic would have been omitted from the phrase. This is emphasised by the absence, in relation to this description of artistic work, of the words "irrespective of artistic quality", which accompany the description of artistic works included in section 4(1)(a) of the 1988 Act.[32] Although shades of meaning can be extracted from both the words "artistic" and "craftsmanship",[33] the phrase "work of artistic craftsmanship" is in the end a composite phrase that should be construed as a whole.[34] For a work to be regarded as one of artistic craftsmanship, it should be possible to say that the creator was both a craftsman and an artist.[35]   **3–65**

Craftsmanship. Obviously, unless the work is one of craftsmanship it cannot qualify for protection at all.[36] Did the work's creation reflect an exercise of craftsmanship, a concept in part requiring "a manifestation of pride in sound workmanship" and a "rejection of the shoddy, meretricious, the facile"?[37] A craftsman can be regarded as someone who makes a thing in a skilful way, as   **3–66**

---

work was defined to include works of artistic craftsmanship "not falling within either of the preceding paragraphs", *i.e.* paras 3(1)(a) and (b), setting out the other categories of artistic works. The omission, in the 1988 Act, of these extra words is not considered to have effected any change in the law.

[25] Copyright Act 1956, s.3(1)(c).

[26] Berne Convention, Art.2(1) merely refers to works of "applied art" as being included in the definition of literary and artistic works.

[27] See *Hansard*, HL Vol.490, col.847.

[28] *George Hensher Ltd v Restawile Upholstery (Lancs) Ltd* [1976] A.C. 64.

[29] The defendants had conceded at trial, probably wrongly in the view of each of the members of the House of Lords, that a prototype for piece of "knock-up" furniture was a work of craftsmanship. The only issue was thus whether it was a work of " *artistic* craftsmanship".

[30] As was pointed out by Lord Kilbrandon in *George Hensher Ltd v Restawile Upholstery (Lancs) Ltd* [1976] A.C. 64 at 98, the House of Lords rejected definitions of "artistic" framed by the trial judge, the Court of Appeal, counsel for the claimants and two by counsel for the defendants; further, each member of the House of Lords hearing the appeal provided a definition of his own.

[31] For a helpful review of the cases, see *Coogi Australia Pty Ltd v Hysport International Pty Ltd* (1998) 157 A.L.R. 247 (Fed Ct of Aus).

[32] Although in *George Hensher Ltd v Restawile Upholstery (Lancs) Ltd* [1976] A.C. 64 at 95, Lord Simon observed that it was no doubt because the Act is concerned with works of artistic craftsmanship, and not with artistic works of craftsmanship, that it was unnecessary to repeat these words, which refer to artistic merit.

[33] See paras 3–66 and 3–67, below.

[34] *George Hensher Ltd v Restawile Upholstery (Lancs) Ltd* [1976] A.C. 64, *per* Lord Simon at 91.

[35] *Bonz Croup (Pty) Ltd v Cooke* [1994] 3 N.Z.L.R. 216, followed in *Vermaat v Boncrest Ltd* [2001] F.S.R. 43.

[36] *George Hensher Ltd v Restawile Upholstery (Lancs) Ltd* [1976] A.C. 64 at 80.

[37] *George Hensher Ltd v Restawile Upholstery (Lancs) Ltd* [1976] A.C. 64 at 91, *per* Lord Simon; *Merlet v Mothercare plc* [1986] R.P.C. 115; *Bonz Group (Pty) Ltd v Cooke* [1994] 3 N.Z.L.R.

well as taking a justified pride in his workmanship,[38] so that a work of craftsmanship will involve the exercise of skill on the part of the creator in using the materials of which the article is made and the devices by which those materials are turned into an article.[39] It has been said that such a work presupposes special training, skill and knowledge for its production.[40] Such skills are not confined to handicraft skills but may involve skills in the use of machines,[41] even a computer-controlled machine, provided the resulting work is a manifestation of the creator's skill with the machine, knowledge of materials and pride in workmanship.[42] The issue in each case will be one of fact, on which lay and expert evidence will be admissible.[43]

3–67   **Artistic.** Clearly, not all works of craftsmanship are works of artistic craftsmanship.[44] What is required is that the work should have some real artistic or aesthetic quality,[45] that it be a work of art,[46] but not that it is a "work of fine art".[47] It should therefore be possible to regard the creator as an artist as well as a craftsman[48] and an artist has been described as someone with creative ability who produces something which has aesthetic appeal.[49] The requirement of artistic quality clearly requires a judgment by the court as to whether the work is artistic or not, but this does not mean that it is for the court to make its own value judgment as to whether the work has this quality. The issue is one of fact to be determined in the light of the evidence[50] on an objective basis.[51] The evidence may be of various types. First, evidence of the intentions of the maker, in particular whether or not he had the conscious purpose of creating a work of art, is relevant and important, although not a paramount or determining consideration.[52] If

---

216; *Guild v Eskandar Ltd* [2001] F.S.R. 645. It has been said that a work of craftsmanship suggests a durable, useful, handmade object (*Hensher, per* Lord Reid, at 77), but clearly this is not a definition, and does not apply in all cases: see the further discussion in the text.

[38] *Bonz Group (Pty) Ltd v Cooke* [1994] 3 N.Z.L.R. 216; *Vermaat v Boncrest Ltd* [2001] F.S.R. 43.

[39] *Bonz Group (Pty) Ltd v Cooke* [1994] 3 N.Z.L.R. 216; *Vermaat v Boncrest Ltd* [2001] F.S.R. 43.

[40] *George Hensher Ltd v Restawile Upholstery (Lancs) Ltd* [1976] A.C. 64 at 91 per Lord Simon, following *Cuisenaire v Reed* [1963] V.L.R. 719 and *Cuisenaire v South West Imports Ltd* [1968] 1 Ex.C.R. 493 514. But it is suggested in particular that special training is not necessarily required.

[41] *George Hensher Ltd v Restawile Upholstery (Lancs) Ltd* [1976] A.C. 64 at 90, 91, *per* Lord Simon.

[42] *Coogi Australia Pty Ltd v Hysport International Pty Ltd* (1998) 157 A.L.R. 247 (Fed Ct of Aus).

[43] See the discussion as to evidence in relation to "artistic", para. 3–67, below.

[44] See the discussion of different kinds of craftsmanship by Lord Simon in *George Hensher Ltd v Restawile Upholstery (Lancs) Ltd* [1976] A.C. 64 at 91.

[45] *George Hensher Ltd v Restawile Upholstery (Lancs) Ltd* [1976] A.C. 64 at 85H, 8E, 96G; *Cuisenaire v Reed* [1963] V.L.R. 719 at 730; *Merlet v Mothercare plc* [1986] R.P.C. 115 at 124 (does the work have artistic appeal in itself?); *Bonz Group (Pty) Ltd v Cooke* [1994] 3 N.Z.L.R. 216 at 224.

[46] *Merlet v Mothercare plc* [1986] R.P.C. 115 at 125, analysing what was the majority view of the House of Lords in *George Hensher Ltd v Restawile Upholstery (Lancs) Ltd* [1976] A.C. 64, adopted in *Guild v Eskandar Ltd* [2001] F.S.R. 645.

[47] The purpose of the provision was originally to extend to works of applied art the protection formerly given to works of fine art: *Coogi Australia Pty Ltd v Hysport International Pty Ltd* (1998) 157 A.L.R. 247 (Fed Ct of Aus)

[48] *Bonz Group (Pty) Ltd v Cooke* [1994] 3 N.Z.L.R. 216; adopted in *Vermaat v Boncrest Ltd* [2001] F.S.R. 43.

[49] *Bonz Group (Pty) Ltd v Cooke* [1994] 3 N.Z.L.R. 216; adopted in *Vermaat v Boncrest Ltd* [2001] F.S.R. 43.

[50] *George Hensher Ltd v Restawile Upholstery (Lancs) Ltd* [1976] A.C. 64, at 78C, 87B, 94G, 96H; *Merlet v Mothercare plc* [1986] R.P.C. 115, Walton J. adopting the approach which he considered favoured by the majority of the House of Lords in *Hensher*.

[51] *George Hensher Ltd v Restawile Upholstery (Lancs) Ltd* [1976] A.C. 64 at 81F/G.

[52] *George Hensher Ltd v Restawile Upholstery (Lancs) Ltd* [1976] A.C. 64 at 78F, 81G, 95B; *Merlet v Mothercare plc* [1986] R.P.C. 115 at 126.

he did have this intention, then provided he has not manifestly failed, it will be.[53] Second, evidence from ordinary members of the public that they do or would value the work for its appearance or get pleasure or satisfaction from it, whether on an emotional or intellectual level, is relevant.[54] Third, expert evidence will be admissible from those who have special capabilities or qualifications for forming an opinion, and whose evidence will command respect,[55] in particular those who are acknowledged artist-craftsmen or who teach in the field.[56] If the maker already has other works to his name which are acknowledged to be artistic, this will be relevant.[57] The fact that it is also a utilitarian article does not mean that it cannot have artistic or aesthetic qualities[58] nor is the presence of non-functional features the test of aesthetic quality.[59] The level of aesthetic appeal to be applied is, however, higher than mere visual appeal.[60] The question is therefore not concluded by evidence that the appearance of the work is such that some members of the public are motivated to acquire the article "on especial account" thereof;[61] it must have some aesthetic quality, and the fact that a segment of the public can be found who have been motivated to buy the work simply because of its visual appeal is not enough.[62] Whether a work is one of artistic craftsmanship must be decided by looking at the work in isolation, not when placed in juxtaposition with something else, where the ensemble may be "artistic".[63]

Other points. A work intended to be reproduced in articles of mass-production can as a matter of principle be a work of artistic craftsmanship, although this fact may cast doubt on whether it is truly one of artistic craftsmanship.[64] In the case, for example, of a mass-produced run of fabric which repeats a design, if any part is to be a work of artistic craftsmanship, copyright first subsists when the first fixation of the work is made. Copyright does not subsist in every length of fabric bearing the design.[65] It is not essential for such a work to be the product of the efforts of a single artist-craftsman. It is enough that two or more people have combined to design and make the ultimate product if it satisfies the two criteria of

3–68

---

[53] *George Hensher Ltd v Restawile Upholstery (Lancs) Ltd* [1976] A.C. 64 at 81; *Merlet v Mothercare plc* [1986] R.P.C. 115 at 126; *Bonz Group (Pty) Ltd v Cooke* [1994] 3 N.Z.L.R. 216.

[54] *George Hensher Ltd v Restawile Upholstery (Lancs) Ltd* [1976] A.C. 64 at 78, 87. But note the warning against mere "eye-appeal" being sufficient, below.

[55] *George Hensher Ltd v Restawile Upholstery (Lancs) Ltd* [1976] A.C. 64 at 82, 87.

[56] *George Hensher Ltd v Restawile Upholstery (Lancs) Ltd* [1976] A.C. 64 at 94.

[57] *George Hensher Ltd v Restawile Upholstery (Lancs) Ltd* [1976] A.C. 64.

[58] *George Hensher Ltd v Restawile Upholstery (Lancs) Ltd* [1976] A.C. 64, at 79, 86; *Coogi Australia Pty Ltd v Hysport International Pty Ltd* (1998) 157 A.L.R. 247 (Fed Ct of Aus).

[59] *Coogi Australia Pty Ltd v Hysport International Pty Ltd* (1998) 157 A.L.R. 247 (Fed Ct of Aus), and see the observation of Lord Simon in *George Hensher Ltd v Restawile Upholstery (Lancs) Ltd* [1976] A.C. 64 at 93B that in the context of the arts and crafts movement, the antithesis between function and beauty is a false one.

[60] *George Hensher Ltd v Restawile Upholstery (Lancs) Ltd* [1976] A.C. 64, at 79C, 81E, 84F, 86, 93E, 95F.

[61] *Coogi Australia Pty Ltd v Hysport International Pty Ltd* (1998) 157 A.L.R. 247 (Fed Ct of Aus).

[62] *Coogi Australia Pty Ltd v Hysport International Pty Ltd* (1998) 157 A.L.R. 247 (Fed Ct of Aus).

[63] *Merlet v Mothercare plc* [1986] R.P.C. 115 at 124 (rain-cape for mother and baby not to be viewed as worn by mother and child). In *Guild v Eskandar Ltd* [2001] F.S.R. 645 at 700, Rimer J. questioned whether it was not at least permissible to view a garment as arranged on a mannequin.

[64] In *George Hensher Ltd v Restawile Upholstery (Lancs) Ltd* [1976] A.C. 64, Lord Reid at 77 said that he found it difficult to conceive a work of artistic craftsmanship as being an object which was only intended as a step in a commercial operation and which had no value in itself, although he made it clear that this was not intended to be an authoritative statement. In *Guild v Eskandar Ltd* [2001] F.S.R. 645, simple garments made as prototypes for mass production were held to be neither artistic nor works of craftsmanship.

[65] *Coogi Australia Pty Ltd v Hysport International Pty Ltd* (1998) 157 A.L.R. 247 (Fed Ct of Aus).

craftsmanship and aesthetic quality,[66] provided, it is suggested, that the authors are joint authors of the work.[67]

3–69   **Examples: copyright conferred**. There are relatively few cases in which copyright has been conferred on works under this heading.[68] Works in respect of which protection has been conferred include: hand-knitted woollen sweaters,[69] fabric with a highly textured surface comprising a complex multi-coloured design with 3-D elements, produced using a computer-controlled knitting machine to realise the creative idea,[70] a range of pottery,[71] items of dinnerware[72] and a sculpture consisting of a plug for a yacht.[73]

3–70   **Examples: copyright denied**. There have been many failed attempts made to bring works within this category. They include a prototype sofa for a range of "knock-up" furniture,[74] a set of rods, specifically designed for teaching mathematics,[75] a prototype of a cape for a mother and child,[76] a frock,[77] sample garments made as prototypes for mass production,[78] "moving sand pictures",[79] a lounge suite,[80] sample patchwork bedspreads and cushion covers,[81] and a corkscrew.[82]

---

[66] *Bonz Group (Pty) Ltd v Cooke* [1994] 3 N.Z.L.R. 216; *Vermaat v Boncrest Ltd* [2001] F.S.R. 43.

[67] A single copyright work cannot have more than one author unless the authors are joint authors: para. 4–06, below. For a work to qualify as a work of joint authorship, the contribution of each must not be distinct from that of the other: see paras 4–39 and 4–44, below. If, therefore, one author is responsible for the elements of artistry and the other for the elements of craftsmanship, and their contributions are distinct, then it seems that there cannot be a work of artistic craftsmanship. And see *Burke etc. Ltd v Spicers Dress Designs* [1936] Ch. 400: any copyright which might have subsisted in the prototype garment did not vest in the firm which executed the design because the firm's servants, who made the garment from a third party's design, did not originate any artistic element which might subsist.

[68] In several cases, the issue has been held arguable at the interim stage, *e.g. Radley Gowns Ltd v Costas Spyrou* [1975] F.S.R. 455 at 466 (prototype garments); *Shelley Films Ltd v Rex Features Ltd* [1994] E.M.L.R. 134 (a film set).

[69] *Bonz Group (Pty) Ltd v Cooke* [1994] 3 N.Z.L.R. 216; *cf.* the cases referred to below where protection has been denied to prototype garments.

[70] *Coogi Australia Pty Ltd v Hysport International Pty Ltd* (1998) 157 A.L.R. 247 (Fed Ct of Aus). The operator was skilled in textile computer-aided machine operation and had used his knowledge of the material properties of textiles.

[71] *L. & J.E. Walter Enterprises (Pty) Ltd v Kearns* (High Ct of Zimbabwe) noted at [1990] 4 Ent. L. R. E-61.

[72] *Commissioner of Taxation v Murray* (1990) 92 A.L.R. 671 (Fed Ct of Aus).

[73] *Swarbrick v Burge* (2004) 208 A.L.R. 19 (it was relevant that the creator had intended the work to have aesthetic value).

[74] *George Hensher Ltd v Restawile Upholstery (Lancs) Ltd* [1976] A.C. 64, where the evidence was wholly inadequate to establish that the furniture in question merited the epithet "artistic".

[75] *Cuisenaire v Reed* [1963] V.R. 719; *Cuisenaire v South West Imports Ltd* [1968] 1 Ex.C.R. 493; 37 Fox's C.P.C. 81 (no craftsmanship in the making of the rods as no skill was involved in cutting or colouring them; nor were they artistic).

[76] *Merlet v Mothercare plc*, [1984] F.S.R. 358, not a work of art, but a basic commodity.

[77] *Burke etc. Ltd v Spicers Dress Designs*, [1936] Ch. 400: although the claim in fact failed on the question of title.

[78] *Guild v Eskandar Ltd* [2001] F.S.R. 645 (simple machine-made garments for which there was no evidence of any special elements of craftsmanship going into their manufacture and no sufficient evidence that their designer intended to create works of art or regarded herself as an artist. Even if all that was necessary to qualify as a work of art simply was that the work satisfied the aesthetic emotions of a substantial section of the public, there was no adequate evidence of this either); *Muscat v Le* (2004) 204 A.L.R. 335.

[79] *Komesaroff v Mickle* [1988] R.P.C. 204 (Sup Ct of Victoria).

[80] *Dress Designs (Pty) Ltd v G. Y. Lounge Suite Mfgs (Pty) Ltd* (1991) 2 S.A.L.R. 455 (Sup Ct of S.A., Witwatersrand Local Division)—a utilitarian product only.

[81] *Vermaat v Boncrest Ltd* [2001] F.S.R. 43: although the making of the articles by the seamstress might have been a work of craftsmanship, it was not sufficiently artistic.

[82] *Sheldon and Hammond Pty Ltd v Metrokane Inc* (2004) 61 I.P.R. 1.

F. Sound recordings

(i) History of protection

Pre-1912. Reproduction of sounds first became a copyright issue in 1886, the year of the Berne Convention. However, the issue was not whether protection should be granted to such reproductions, which by their very nature fell outside the scope of the Convention,[83] but whether the rights of authors of musical compositions should extend to prevent the unauthorised mechanical reproduction of their compositions. The issue was resolved against the mechanical reproduction of musical airs being regarded as an infringement of copyright.[84] At that time, the only mechanical means generally known for reproducing music were musical boxes and "Barbary" organs, and musical composers did not feel that they were abandoning rights of any great value by agreeing to this derogation of their rights.[85] It was not long, however, before instruments were being invented which were capable of reproducing not one or two tunes, but any number of tunes and even the words of songs, by means of perforated rolls, discs and cylinders. The popularity of such devices was soon established, to the concern of composers, who sought to test whether the manufacture and sale of these contrivances was an infringement of their copyright. The result, in the United Kingdom, was that such actions failed.[86]

3–71

The 1911 Act. At the conference in Berlin in 1908, the Berne Convention was revised to require protection to be given to composers against reproductions of their works by mechanical means.[87] By this time, a considerable industry for the manufacture of such mechanical contrivances had developed in the United Kingdom. The manufacturers lobbied the Parliamentary Committee, formed in 1909 to report to Parliament on what changes to British law were required to implement the Berlin Act for the introduction of a form of compulsory licence, but the majority of the Committee recommended allowing musical composers full control over the reproduction of their works by mechanical means.[88] The Copyright Bill was originally drafted to this effect. However, further lobbying by the manufacturers achieved the introduction of what became section 19 of the 1911 Act, the short effect of which was to compel a musical composer, if he had granted a licence to one person to reproduce his work mechanically, to grant to any other person a licence to reproduce the same work in like manner upon payment of a certain royalty.

3–72

It was section 19 of the 1911 Act which also gave to the manufacturers of such mechanical contrivances the protection they had sought against unauthorised copying of their devices, by according protection to records, perforated rolls and other contrivances by means of which sounds might be mechanically reproduced. The 1911 Act did not, however, create a new category of copyright work for this purpose, but provided that such mechanical contrivances were to be protected in

---

[83] The aim of the Convention was to protect the rights of authors in their literary and artistic creations; devices for the reproduction of music involved technical or industrial rather than artistic creativity.

[84] By the declaration contained in Art.3 of the Final Protocol.

[85] This provision had been requested by the Swiss delegates, to protect what was a Swiss national industry.

[86] See *Boosey v Whight* [1899] 1 Ch. 836, affirmed on appeal: [1900] 1 Ch. 122; *Newmark v The National Phonograph Co Ltd* (1907) 23 T.L.R. 439; *Monckton v The Gramophone Co Ltd* (1912) 106 L.T. 84. The composers had better success in Italy and Belgium, and partial success in France (the provision was interpreted as not permitting reproduction of the words of a song).

[87] Berlin Act, Art.13.

[88] Cd.4976 (1909).

the same manner as if they were musical works.[89] This effectively gave the maker of the contrivance the same exclusive rights as were enjoyed by the author of a musical composition.[90] The protection was extended to such contrivances as already existed at July 1, 1912, when the 1911 Act took effect.[91]

3–73   **The 1956 Act.** The link between mechanical contrivances and musical compositions became increasingly anomalous, with the development of technology and the manufacture and sale of recordings of other than musical works. Following the recommendation of the 1952 Copyright Committee, the 1956 Act introduced a separate regime of protection for sound recordings in their own right.[92] A sound recording was defined as the aggregate of the sounds embodied in and capable of being reproduced by means of a record of any description.

Under the 1911 Act, the soundtrack of a film enjoyed its own protection as a mechanical contrivance under section 19. Under the 1956 Act, a film soundtrack was excluded from the definition of a sound recording[93] and was treated as part of the film.[94]

3–74   **The Rome Convention.** Protection for sound recordings first became the subject of international convention under the Rome Convention.[95] This defines a phonogram as any exclusively aural fixation of sounds of a performance or of other sounds.[96] The Convention requires signatories to grant national treatment to producers of sound recordings who are nationals of a contracting state or where the sound was recorded in a contracting state or published in a contracting state. The United Kingdom's adherence to the Convention did not require amendment to be made to the 1956 Act.

(ii) Under the 1988 Act

3–75   **Statutory definition: sound recording.** Sound recordings are protected as a separate description of works under section 1(1)(b) of the 1988 Act.[97] A sound recording is defined as a recording either of sounds from which the sounds may be reproduced, or of the whole or any part of a literary, dramatic or musical work, from which sounds reproducing the work or part of the work may be produced.[98] The first limb of the definition is intended to cover a recording where there is no underlying work, such as a recording of people talking, or of other sounds such as the sounds of wildlife, whereas the second limb is intended to cover the recording of the performance of works which may themselves be the subject of separate copyrights. There is clearly a large degree of overlap between these two

---

[89] Copyright Act 1911, s.19(1).

[90] Including the performing right, although this was not fully appreciated until the decision in *Gramophone Co Ltd v Stephen Cawardine & Co* [1934] Ch. 450.

[91] Copyright Act 1911, s.19(8).

[92] Copyright Act 1956, s.12(1) and (2).

[93] Copyright Act 1956, s.12(9).

[94] Copyright Act 1956, s.13(10).

[95] The International Convention for the Protection of Performers, Producers of Phonograms and Broadcasting Organisations signed at Rome on October 26, 1961. See, generally, Ch.24.

[96] Art.3(b); for the text of the Convention, see Vol.2 at F5.

[97] Following the position adopted under the 1956 Act, s.12(1) and (2). This had not been the position under the 1911 Act; see para. 3–72, above.

[98] CDPA 1988, s.5A; re-enacting the previous definition which was contained in s.5(1). The renumbering is a consequence of the introduction by the Duration of Copyright and Rights in Performances Regulations 1995 (SI 1995/3297) of the new provisions as to films, now contained in s.5B.

limbs of the definition.[99] In the case of a recording of a performance of a work, the protection granted to the sound recording is separate from any rights in the performance itself and to any recording rights which may exist in relation to the performance.[1]

The definition makes it clear that the nature of the carrier, that is the physical medium on which the sound recording is stored, is irrelevant, as is also the method by which the sounds are reproduced or produced.[2] As a matter of definition, therefore, a film soundtrack (that is the sound recording accompanying a film and synchronised onto the film) is a sound recording for the purposes of the 1988 Act.[3]

Soundtracks of films. The 1988 Act, as originally enacted, introduced a change   3–76
in the treatment of soundtracks of films by including them in the definition of sound recordings. Under the 1956 Act, soundtracks were expressly excluded from the definition of sound recordings,[4] and the definition of a cinematograph film under that Act included sounds embodied in any soundtrack associated with the film.[5] The position from August 1, 1989, therefore, was that the soundtrack of a film, including a soundtrack existing at that date,[6] was entitled to copyright protection as a sound recording.[7]

However, since January 1, 1996, the position has reverted to what it was under the 1956 Act, in that although the definition of a sound recording remains unaltered, a soundtrack accompanying a film, including a soundtrack in existence at that date,[8] is, since such date, to be treated as part of the film for the purposes of Part I of the 1988 Act.[9]

G. FILMS

(i) History of protection

The position pre-1912. At the time of their early development, at the end of the   3–77
nineteenth century, films were not protected in their own right, but only as a series of photographs.[10] Photographs were required to be protected under the Berne Convention,[11] although not then included in the principal category of liter-

---

[99] This was accepted during the debate of this provision: see *Hansard*, HL Vol.490, col.855. Since the definition in the 1956 Act was equally apt to cover both sorts of recordings, it is not clear why it was thought necessary to change the definition from the shorter and simpler one contained in the 1956 Act, s.12(9), which was: the aggregate of the sounds embodied in and capable of being reproduced by means of a record of any description.

[1] *i.e.* rights granted under Pt II of the 1988 Act; as to which see Ch.12.

[2] CDPA 1988, s.5A.

[3] This was not the position under the 1956 Act, s.12(9), which expressly excluded a soundtrack associated with a cinematograph film. But see, as to the position now, para. 3–76, below.

[4] Copyright Act 1956, s.12(9).

[5] Copyright Act 1956, s.13(9).

[6] CDPA 1988, Sch.1, para.8(1); subject to the provisions of para.8(2).

[7] This reverted to the position under the 1911 Act, under which the soundtrack of a film was separately protected as a contrivance by means of which sounds might be mechanically reproduced.

[8] reg.26(1) of the Duration of Copyright and Rights in Performances Regulations 1995 (SI 1995/3297).

[9] CDPA 1988, s.5B(2); introduced by the Duration of Copyright and Rights in Performances Regulations 1995 (SI 1995/3297).

[10] Under the Fine Arts Copyright Act 1862 (25 & 26 Vict., c.68). There was no protection for the acting performance as a dramatic work under the Dramatic Copyright Act 1833 (3 & 4 Will. 4, c.15), because of the requirement that such a work had to be capable of being printed and published: *Tate v Fullbrook* [1908] 1 K.B. 821.

[11] Berne Convention, Art.3.

ary and artistic works.[12] Cinematograph productions were first required to be protected under Berne as a result of revision of the Convention at the Berlin Conference in 1908.[13] Protection was to be granted to cinematograph productions as literary or artistic works if, by the arrangement of the acting form or the combination of the incidents represented, the author gave the work a personal and original character.

3–78   **The position under the 1911 Act.** Under the 1911 Act, there was still no copyright in a film as such. As had been the position before, a film was regarded as a series of photographs, each photograph being capable of protection as an artistic work.[14] Protection was maintained by the 1911 Act in respect of any films so protected immediately before July 1, 1912.[15] In addition, under the 1911 Act the production was protected as a dramatic work where the arrangement or acting form, or the combination of incidents represented, gave the work an original character.[16] The soundtrack was protected as a contrivance by means of which sounds might be mechanically reproduced.[17] There was also a separate literary or dramatic copyright in any scenario or script.[18]

3–79   **The position under the 1956 Act.** Following the recommendation of the 1952 Copyright Committee, the 1956 Act introduced a separate regime for the protection of cinematograph films in their own right.[19] A cinematograph film was defined as any sequence of visual images recorded on material of any description (whether translucent or not) so as to be capable, by the use of that material, either of being shown as a moving picture, or of being recorded on other material (whether translucent or not) by the use of which it can be so shown.[20] This definition made it clear that the work which was the subject of protection was the content of the film, that is, the sequence of visual images, regardless of the medium on which it was recorded. The definition expressly made a film soundtrack part of the film.[21]

(ii) Under the 1988 Act

3–80   **Statutory definition: film.** Under the 1988 Act, a film is defined as a recording on any medium from which a moving image may by any means be produced.[22] This definition retains the essential element of a moving image,[23] found in the definition of a cinematograph film contained in the 1956 Act,[24] but is otherwise in

---

[12] Berne Convention, Art.2.

[13] Berlin Act, Art.14(2).

[14] *Pathé Pictures Ltd v Bancroft* [1928–35] Mac. C.C. 403; *Barker, etc. Ltd v Hulton (E.) & Co Ltd* (1912) 28 T.L.R. 496; *Nordisk Films Co Ltd v Onda* [1917–23] Mac. C.C. 337.

[15] Copyright Act 1911, s.24(1).

[16] Copyright Act 1911, s.35(1), reflecting Art.14(2) of the Berlin Act.

[17] Copyright Act 1911, s.19(1).

[18] *Milligan v The Broadway Cinema Productions Ltd* (1923) S.L.T. 35.

[19] Copyright Act 1956, s.13.

[20] s.13(10).

[21] s.13(9).

[22] CDPA 1988, s.5B(1); re-enacting the previous definition which was contained in s.5(1). The renumbering is a consequence of the introduction by the Duration of Copyright and Rights in Performances Regulations 1995 (SI 1995/3297) of new provisions as to authorship of films and duration of the term of copyright in films.

[23] A single frame of a film cannot therefore itself constitute a film, nor is it protectable as a photograph (see para. 3–57, above), although it is protectable as part of a film: see CDPA 1988, s.17(4) and para. 7–70, below. As to the position under the 1956 Act, see *Spelling Goldberg Productions Inc v B.P.C. Publishing* [1981] R.P.C. 283.

[24] See para. 3–79, above.

a much simplified form which removes any doubt that may have existed as to whether the definition under the 1956 Act covered video recordings.[25]

Soundtracks of films. Film soundtracks, protected under the 1956 Act as part of the film,[26] became entitled to copyright separately as sound recordings under the 1988 Act as originally enacted,[27] but since January 1, 1996 are to be treated, once again, as part of the film.[28]   **3–81**

H. Broadcasts

(i) History of protection

(a) *Introduction.*

Today, there are gathered together under the one heading of "broadcasts" what had previously been two separate protected subject matters, namely broadcasts consisting of wireless transmissions (which were called simply broadcasts) and broadcasts by cable (which were called cable programmes). With effect from October 31, 2003, there is a single protected subject matter only, namely broadcasts. This history of protection deals with each in turn.   **3–82**

(b) *History of protection of wireless broadcasts*

No protection of broadcasts under 1911 Act. The 1911 Act gave no protection to broadcasts as such.[29]   **3–83**

Position under the 1956 Act. As a result of strong representations made to it, the 1952 Copyright Committee recommended that a broadcasting authority should have the right to prevent the copying of its programmes and should also have a performing right in television programmes, but not in sound programmes.[30] These recommendations were partly taken up in section 14 of the 1956 Act,[31] which conferred a variety of exclusive rights by way of copyright in respect of television and sound broadcasts made by the British Broadcasting Corporation or by   **3–84**

---

[25] Following the recommendation of the 1977 Copyright Committee, Cmnd.6732, paras 889 and 916, that this should be made clear, notwithstanding their view that video recordings were within the definition in the 1956 Act. As to video games and multimedia products, being films, see para. 3–28, above. Note that a film, if it is a work of action, may be protected both as a "film" within the meaning of the Act and as a dramatic work: *Norowzian v Arks Ltd (No.2)* [2000] F.S.R. 363. See para. 3–37, above, for a discussion of this case.

[26] See para. 3–73, above.

[27] CDPA 1988, s.5(1).

[28] Following the introduction of s.5B(2) by the Duration of Copyright and Rights in Performances Regulations 1995 (SI 1995/3297).

[29] In so far as a programme which was broadcast included a literary, dramatic or musical work in which copyright subsisted, the act of broadcasting did not infringe that copyright but the public performance of the material which has broadcast, or its reproduction on a record or other device, would have constituted an infringement of that copyright, if unlicensed. In so far as the material which was broadcast did not enjoy copyright protection itself, a performance by a person who received the broadcast in a public place did not involve an infringement of copyright, nor was it an infringement of copyright to record the performance on a record or other device. This applied, in particular, to broadcasts of outside events, such as sporting events, processions, and historic occasions.

[30] Cmnd.8662, paras 117, 186 and 192.

[31] The Act went further than the recommendations and conferred a performing right protecion on sound recordings.

the Independent Broadcasting Authority[32] from a place in the United Kingdom. This right was conferred, however, only in respect of television and sound broadcasts made after June 1, 1957.[33]

3–85   Broadcasts under the 1988 Act as originally enacted. This protection continued under the 1988 Act, although the distinction between television and sound broadcasts was abandoned in favour of a single composite definition. A broadcast was defined as a transmission by wireless telegraphy[34] of visual images, sounds or other information which was either capable of being lawfully received by members of the public, or was transmitted for presentation to members of the public.[35]

(c) Cable transmissions

3–86   No protection until January 1, 1985. Cable programme services, or diffusion services as they were originally known, were not the subject of copyright protection in the United Kingdom either under the 1911 Act, or under the 1956 Act as originally enacted. This led to the 1977 Copyright Committee recommending that cable companies should enjoy a copyright in originated transmissions, just as broadcasters did under the 1956 Act.[36] This recommendation was implemented by the introduction into the 1956 Act of section 14A by the Cable and Broadcasting Act 1984.[37] The new right did not apply to cable programmes included in a cable programme service before January 1, 1985.[38]

3–87   The 1988 Act, as enacted. This regime was altered by the 1988 Act. The protected subject matter was now called a cable programme and comprised what was transmitted by cable.[39] However, not all transmissions by cable were protectable as cable programmes, only those items included in a "cable programme service".[40] A cable programme service was defined as a service consisting wholly or mainly in sending visual images, sounds or other information by means of a telecommunications system[41] other than one which was a transmission by wireless telegraphy.[42] In order to give rise to a cable programme in which copyright could subsist, the cable service had to be aimed at an audience of more than one, in that it had to be a service for sending information for reception either at two or more places (whether for simultaneous reception or at different times in response

---

[32] Formerly the Independent Television Authority: Sound Broadcasting Act 1972 (c.31), s.1, repealed and replaced by Independent Broadcasting Authority Act 1973 (c.19), ss.1, 38 and 39.

[33] Copyright Act 1956, Sch.7, para.17.

[34] Defined as the sending of electro-magnetic energy over paths not provided by a material substance constructed or arranged for that purpose: CDPA 1988, s.178. This definition was amended with effect from December 1, 1996 to exclude transmissions of microwave technology between terrestrial fixed points (reg.8 of the Copyright and Related Rights Regulations 1996 (SI 1996/2967)). This amendment had little effect on what was a broadcast, given the further requirement that a broadcast had to be intended for reception by the public.

[35] CDPA 1988, s.6(1).

[36] Cmnd.6732, para.468(x).

[37] c.46.

[38] The commencement date of s.22 of the Cable and Broadcasting Act 1984; see Copyright Act 1956, s.14A(11).

[39] CDPA 1988, s.1(1)(b).

[40] CDPA 1988, s.7(1), as enacted; this had also been the position under s.14A of the 1956 Act.

[41] CDPA 1988, s.7(1). A telecommunications system was defined by s.178 to be a means for conveying visual images, sounds or other information by electronic means.

[42] CDPA 1988, s.7(1) and see s.178 for the definition of wireless telegraphy. This exclusion ensured that the subject matter of a transmission could not qualify for copyright protection both as a broadcast and as a cable programme.

to requests by different users) or for presentation to members of the public.[43] An internet website, which allowed information to be sent to members of the public who accessed the website, was considered arguably to satisfy this definition and to be a cable programme service.[44]

A number of services were excluded from the definition of cable programme service by section 7(2) of the 1988 Act.[45] The first exception was aimed at interactive services. Thus there was excepted a service or part of a service which had as an essential feature not only the transmission of visual images, sounds or other information to the recipient but also the reception from the recipient of information (other than signals sent for the operation or control of the service).[46] The words in brackets ensured that the service was not excepted merely because the recipient could exercise a choice as to what was transmitted to him, for example, by selecting, in the case of a video on-demand cable service, the particular film or programme which he wished to see. The effect of this exception, together with those words, was to ensure that those parts of an interactive service in which sound, images or other information were conveyed to the user were within the definition of a cable programme service, so that those elements transmitted were capable of being protected as cable programmes, whilst those elements that were genuinely interactive (the placing of an order or the inputting of data) were not part of a cable programme service, and therefore were not capable of being protected by copyright as a cable programme.[47] The remaining exceptions dealt with services which were not truly aimed at the public. They included: a service run for the purposes of a business, or by an individual for domestic purposes, and which was entirely within the control of such business or individual, and was not connected to any other telecommunications system[48]; a service operating in or connecting premises in single occupation (except where the services formed part of the amenities provided for residents or inmates of premises run as a business) and not connected to any other telecommunications system[49]; and a service run for persons providing broadcasting or cable programme services or programmes for such services.[50]

---

[43] CDPA 1988, s.7(1). This aspect of the definition would, it is suggested, have excluded an email service from qualifying as a cable programme service, notwithstanding that the electronic signals were conveyed by cable. It would in any event have been excluded by the provisions of s.7(2)(a), as to which see later in the text. See, in this respect, *Hansard*, HL Vol.495, col.616.

[44] See *The Shetland Times v Wills* [1997] E.M.L.R. 277, approved, *obiter*, in *Sony Music Entertainment (UK) Ltd v Easyinternetcafe Ltd* [2003] EWHC 62; [2003] F.S.R. 48 (Ch), at para.47. The website contained articles and photographs taken from a local newspaper.

[45] CDPA 1988, s.7(1) excluded any service which was excepted, or to the extent that it was excepted, by s.7(2) of the 1988 Act. The reference to the extent to which a service was excepted meant that merely because some elements of the service fell within an exception, the remainder of the service was not excluded from being a cable programme service. Thus, an item transmitted as part of the service which was not excepted was a cable programme, whilst an item transmitted as part of the service which was excepted has not.

[46] CDPA 1988, s.7(2)(a).

[47] See *Hansard*, HL Vol.138, cols 113, 114 and Vol.501, cols 204–206.

[48] CDPA 1988, s.7(2)(b) and (c). The latter was intended to ensure that a system which was entirely domestic, *i.e.* comprising equipment in the private home which was not linked to any outside cable system, was not a cable programme service: *Hansard*, HL Vol.490, col.867. The exception excluded therefore, an internal telephone system in domestic or business premises, but not if it was linked to British Telecom's network or to some other network.

[49] CDPA 1988, s.7(2)(d). This exception excluded a computer network in an office, provided it was not connected to an external network, but the words in brackets ensured that cable systems in hotels, hostels, residential homes, etc. were not excepted, so that items transmitted on such services (for example, announcements of interest to the residents concerning activities, weather, local news, etc.) were capable of being cable programmes in which copyright might subsist.

[50] CDPA 1988, s.7(2)(e). Programmes made for broadcast are often transmitted by cable to the place from which they are to be broadcast; similarly, broadcasts may be transmitted by cable to a cable operator, for inclusion in that cable operator's service; this exception ensured that when

(d) *International Conventions*

3–88   **The protection of broadcasts under international conventions.** The first international convention to deal with broadcasts was the European Agreement on the Protection of Television Broadcasts.[51] This Convention applied to the visual and sound elements of television broadcasts, but not to sound-only broadcasts. The Rome Convention[52] provided protection for all forms of broadcasting, defined as the transmission by wireless means for public reception of sounds, or of images and sounds.[53] These Conventions did not require any amendment to be made to the 1956 Act, but resulted in protection being applied to foreign broadcasts by Orders in Council made under the 1956 Act.

(e) *European Directives*

3–89   The Copyright and Related Rights Directive,[54] the Satellite and Cable Directive[55] and subsequently the Information Society Directive,[56] required Member States to grant broadcasting organisations various rights in relation to their broadcasts,[57] and thus recognised broadcasts as being entitled to protection (as a "related right"). Cable broadcasters were to some extent regarded as broadcasters for these purposes.[58] No amendment needed to be made to the definitions of the protected subject matter in order to implement these Directives but, as will be seen, substantial amendments to their definitions became necessary as part of the implementation of the Information Society Directive.

(f) *The 1988 Act, as amended*

3–90   **Introduction.** Under the 1988 Act as enacted, as under the 1956 Act, the definitions used in relation to the protected subject matters of a broadcast and a cable programme were also used to determine what amounted to an infringement of copyright (*i.e.* to define the acts restricted by copyright) by way of the unlicensed broadcasting or cable transmission of a work.[59] Thus, for example, a "broadcast" was defined for the purposes of the protected subject matter, and the same definition was used when it came to the restricted act of "broadcasting" a work. The same applied to the protected subject matter of "cable programme" and the restricted act of including a work in a "cable programme service". The Information Society Directive[60] required the United Kingdom to alter the nature of these restricted acts, particularly in relation to transmission of a work by means of an on-demand service, and this in turn caused the United Kingdom to alter the definitions of the protected subject matter. The result has been that the link which had previously existed between the protected subject matter and the acts restricted by

---

such transmissions were made by others as part of a service provided for the programme maker and broadcaster, respectively, such a service was not itself treated as a cable programme service.
[51] Concluded at Strasbourg on June 22, 1960 and which was ratified by the UK on October 30, 1963 and entered into force on May 18, 1964. For the text of this Convention see Vol.2 at F3.
[52] The International Conventions for the Protection of Performers, Producers of Phonograms and Broadcasting Organisations, signed at Rome on October 26, 1961, and which was also ratified by the UK on October 30, 1963 and entered into force on May 18, 1964. See Ch.24. For the text, see Vol.2 at F5.
[53] Rome Convention, Art.3(f).
[54] Directive 92/100.
[55] Directive 93/83.
[56] Directive 2001/29.
[57] See Arts 6–9 and Arts 2, 3 respectively.
[58] See Art.6(2) and (3) of the Rental and Related Rights Directive.
[59] *i.e.* in CDPA 1988, s.20.
[60] Directive 2001/29.

copyright has been broken. These amendments were made by the Copyright and Related Rights Regulations 2003.[61]

Broadcast: basic definition. With effect from October 31, 2003, a broadcast **3–91** means an electronic transmission of visual images, sounds or other information which (a) is transmitted for simultaneous reception by members of the public and is capable of being lawfully received by them, or (b) is transmitted at a time determined solely by the person making the transmission for presentation to members of the public, and which is not an excepted internet transmission.[62] The subject matter of protection under section 1(1)(b) of the 1988 Act is therefore the transmission, not the works which happen to be included in the transmission. The essential element of this definition, namely that copyright is capable of subsisting in visual images, sounds and information which are broadcast, remains as before. The definition is intended to be technologically neutral, that is, it should embrace both wireless transmissions and cable transmissions of a broadcast character.[63] The definition therefore no longer contains any reference to wireless telegraphy and requires simply that the transmission be an electronic one.[64] Thus it covers both wireless transmissions and transmissions by cable and the like, or those which are partly one and partly the other.

Broadcast to "the public". It is implicit in the concept of a broadcast as a means **3–92** of communication that the communication should be intended for wide simultaneous dissemination, that is, to more than one person at the same time. This is made clear by the fact that in order for a transmission to be a broadcast for these purposes, it must either be transmitted for simultaneous reception by members of the public or be transmitted for presentation to members of the public. While the expression "the public" has a wide meaning,[65] the relevant sector is cut down by other parts of the definition, considered in the following paragraphs.

Transmission of visual images, sounds or other information. These were the **3–93** expressions used in the 1988 Act in the case of both a broadcast and a cable programme. "Other information" was probably intended to cover data transmissions of the kind sent in the vertical blanking interval.[66]

Broadcast: the first limb. The expressions "transmitted for simultaneous recep- **3–94** tion by members of the public" and "capable of being lawfully received by them" are grounded in the original definition of broadcast in the 1988 Act.[67] It clearly covers the traditional form of broadcast, where there is no possibility of the recipient being able to influence the time or content of the transmission. Capability of reception implies merely that the electronic signals can be captured and reproduced by members of the public by means of appropriate equipment.[68]

---

[61] SI 2003/2498, coming into force on October 31, 2003.

[62] CDPA 1988, s.6(1), as amended. References to broadcasting are to be construed accordingly: *ibid.* As to excepted internet transmissions, see para. 3–99, below.

[63] See the Government Conclusions on the Patent Office's Consultation Paper of August 7, 2002, para.3.6.

[64] Electronic is defined as meaning actuated by electric, magnetic, electro-magnetic, electro-chemical or electro-mechanical energy: CDPA 1988, s.178.

[65] See, *e.g.* the expression "to the public", considered in Ch.7.

[66] A business sprang up in the 1980s whereby BBC Worldwide sold data carrying capacity in the BBC's broadcasts to companies and other organisations that needed to transmit data to recipients located across the country.

[67] CDPA 1988, s.6(1)(a): "a 'broadcast' means a transmission by wireless telegraphy ... which is capable of being received by members of the public".

[68] Reception, in this context, also includes reception of the broadcast relayed by means of a telecommunications system, such as a cable network (CDPA 1988, s.6(5)). Telecommunications system

3–95   **Capable of lawful reception.** The requirement that the broadcast should be capable of being lawfully received introduces an important qualification. In the present context, it has two aspects: first, it prevents those transmissions which are not intended for public consumption from falling within the definition of a broadcast, particularly those transmissions by wireless telegraphy which are not intended for public reception; and secondly, encrypted broadcasts. As to the first aspect, in the United Kingdom it remains illegal to use wireless telegraphy apparatus, which includes a radio receiver, without a licence under the Wireless Telegraphy Act 1949, unless the use of the apparatus is exempted by regulation.[69] Apparatus used only for the reception of messages sent by authorised broadcasting stations or by licensed amateur stations is exempt, and therefore the use by a member of the public of equipment which is lawfully available for purchase for the purpose of receiving such signals is lawful without a licence. However, the use of such equipment for the reception of other radio transmissions without a licence remains unlawful. This will include transmissions by the police and emergency authorities, irrespective of whether such transmissions are unencrypted or not. There are therefore many transmissions which are capable of being received by members of the public on equipment which can be lawfully purchased in this country, but which are nevertheless excluded from being broadcasts for the purposes of the 1988 Act, because reception of such broadcasts by a member of the public is illegal in the United Kingdom. It is also illegal intentionally to intercept a communication in the course of its transmission by means of a public telecommunication system.[70] Communications by and to mobile telephones cannot therefore fall within the definition of a broadcast, as they may not be lawfully received except by the member of the public for whom they are intended.[71] A licence is, however, required for the lawful use of a television receiver, but since such licence is available to any member of the public, on payment of the required fee, any broadcast which can be received on such a television set is capable of being lawfully received by members of the public, for the purposes of this definition.

3–96   **Lawful reception of encrypted broadcast.** Section 9(2) of the 1988 Act contains special provisions defining what amounts to lawful reception in the case of encrypted broadcasts. The Act does not define an encrypted broadcast but in general it is a broadcast transmitted in an encoded form such as not to be receivable in an intelligible form without the reception being passed through appropriate decoding equipment. Encryption enables the broadcaster to control access to its broadcast, by controlling the supply of the appropriate decoding equipment, and thus to obtain payment by subscription or on the basis of use. Without further provision, the mere reception of an encrypted broadcast would not amount to unlawful reception. In the case of such a transmission, therefore, the Act provides that test of capability of reception by the public is satisfied only if the decoding equipment necessary to unscramble the signals has been made available to members of the public by or with the authority of the person making the transmission or the person providing the contents of the transmission.[72] If, therefore, decoding equipment which enables the broadcast to be viewed or heard has been

---

means a system for conveying visual images, sounds or other information by electronic means (s.178).

[69] See the Wireless Telegraphy Act 1949, s.1(1); see also *ibid.* s.5(1)(b)(i) under which it is an offence to use any wireless telegraphy apparatus with intent to obtain information as to the content of any message (whether sent by means of wireless telegraphy or not) of which neither the person using the apparatus nor the person on whose behalf he is acting is an intended recipient.

[70] Regulation of Investigatory Powers Act 2000, s.1.

[71] A different conclusion was reached by the High Court of Australia on the wording of the Australian Copyright Act 1968, in the light of its legislative history. *Telstra Corporations Ltd v Australia Performing Rights Associations Ltd* [1997] I.P.R. 294. See also the discussion in *Hansard*, HL Vol.490, cols. 860–866.

[72] CDPA 1988, s.6(2).

available to the public, for example by the issue of smart cards to subscribers, the broadcast becomes one which is lawfully capable of reception and therefore a protectable subject matter, whether or not any particular individual who receives the signal has lawful possession of a smart card.[73] Making the necessary decoding equipment available only to specific individuals (or companies) would not, it is suggested, be making it available to members of the public, and therefore would not satisfy this limb of the definition of a broadcast.[74]

Broadcast, the second limb: transmitted for presentation to the public. This limb is also grounded in the original definition of broadcast in the 1988 Act.[75] It is designed to bring within the definition transmissions which are intended by the transmitter to be played or shown to the public rather than simply being received by them.[76] It is clearly meant to include transmissions of a different kind from those covered by the first limb and does not refer to the ordinary kind of broadcasts which are transmitted for simultaneous reception by members of the public and which may also happen to be shown or played to members of the public by the recipient, for example in a pub.[77] Rather it is intended to cover those transmissions which are not transmitted for general reception by the public but by particular individuals or companies for presentation to the public. The definition does not specify how the broadcast might be presented to the public. One obvious example is the broadcast by encrypted satellite transmission of a sporting event to specific locations where the public is invited to attend for the purpose of viewing the broadcast. In such a case, the necessary decoding equipment will have been supplied to the locations, but will not have been made available to the public generally. Such a transmission is clearly a broadcast, in that it satisfies the second limb of the definition (but not the first). Similarly, an encrypted transmission of music to specific locations such as shops, pubs, restaurants, arcades, etc. for presentation to the public as background music at such locations, where the necessary decoding equipment is made available only to those locations,[78] will qualify as a broadcast under the second limb of the definition (but not, it is suggested, under the first).

3–97

On-demand services. The requirements that the transmission either be for simultaneous reception by the public or for reception at a time determined solely by the person making the transmission means that an on-demand or on-request transmission is not a broadcast for this purpose, except in the unlikely event of a request triggering a general transmission.[79] This marks a major change from the protection previously given to on-request or on-demand cable transmissions,

3–98

---

[73] There are various offences relating to the unauthorised use and supply of decoding equipment (see CDPA 1988, ss.297, 297A, etc and Ch.15) but these do not affect the question of whether the broadcast itself is protected by copyright.

[74] But, if the transmission was intended for presentation to the public via these individuals or companies by means of the decoding equipment, then the second limb of the definition would be satisfied; see para. 3–97, below.

[75] CDPA 1988, s.6(1)(b): "a 'broadcast' means a transmission by wireless telegraphy ... which is ... transmitted for presentation to members of the public."

[76] See the Government's conclusions on the Patent Office's Consultation Paper of August 7, 2002, para.3.9.

[77] Such transmissions are not "transmitted... *for* presentation to members of the public." If it had been the intention simply to refer to this kind of broadcast, there would be no need for the second limb at all.

[78] A service known as narrowcasting, in contrast to broadcasting.

[79] Although the Government seems to have taken a different view (see the Government's conclusions on the Patent Office's Consultation Paper of August 7, 2002, para.3.9, explaining the reason for introducing the words "at a time determined solely by the person making the transmission"), the requirement under the second limb that the transmission be for presentation to members of the public would in any event rule out virtually all on-demand transmissions.

which were protected under section 7 as enacted[80] and which are thus no longer protected.[81] It also represents one of the key distinctions now made between broadcasting as a protected subject matter and the new restricted act of communication of a work to the public. As will be seen, internet transmissions are in general excluded from broadcasts, leaving only internet transmissions of a broadcast character. "Near on-demand" services, by which programmes are repeatedly transmitted at frequent intervals, clearly fall within the definition of a broadcast.[82]

3–99   Excepted internet transmissions. "Internet transmissions" are generally excepted from the definition of broadcast by section 9(1A). The only kind of "internet transmission" which qualifies as a broadcast is: (a) a transmission taking place simultaneously on the internet and by other means, or (b) a concurrent transmission of a live event, or (c) a transmission of recorded moving images or sounds forming part of a programme service offered by the person responsible for making the transmission, being a service in which programmes are transmitted at scheduled times determined by that person.[83] The Act contains no definition of "internet transmission" or "the internet". The general intention is said to have been to include within the protected subject matter internet transmissions or webcasts which are in the nature of a conventional broadcast and not, for example, the transmission of ordinary web pages.[84] The obvious type of internet transmission included under (a) is a webcast where a simultaneous conventional broadcast of the material is taking place by radio or television, but it is not confined to cases where the simultaneous transmission is a broadcast as defined, the only requirement being that it should be a transmission other than on the internet. A single simultaneous transmission to a private person, and not generally to or for reception by the public, would appear to be sufficient. It does not have to be a broadcast. As to the second case, (b), there is no definition of "live event", but it no doubt refers to any event happening in real time, such as a sports event, an unfolding news item or a simple piece spoken live to the camera, and thus excludes any transmission of an event which has been pre-recorded (except to the extent that the recording forms part of a "live event"). It will include webcasts of live events where there is no simultaneous conventional broadcast. The third category, (c), will include a webcast of any pre-recorded material provided it is transmitted as part of a service and in accordance with a pre-determined schedule. It does not appear that the schedule must be one that has been published (although usually it will be), only that such a schedule has been fixed by the person responsible for the transmission and that the transmission is in accordance with that schedule. The essential point is that the transmission must not be part of an on-demand service, that is, as to both as to its timing and content, it is not transmitted in direct response to a request from the recipient.

---

[80] Under which a cable programme service was defined, amongst other things, as a service for reception at two or more places at different times in response to requests by different users.

[81] The reason given for this is that such services, which will inevitably rely on the transmission of recordings, will usually already contain protectable subject matter such as films and sound recordings, if not also other underlying works. It was therefore considered that there was no need to protect a cable programme as a species of copyright work, as apposed to its contents, unless it was in the nature of a broadcast: See the Government Conclusions on the Patent Office's Consulation Paper of August 7, 2002, para.3.6. While this may true, it does not necessarily follow that the "broadcaster" will be the owner of such rights.

[82] See the Government Conclusions on the Patent Office's Consultation Paper of August 7, 2002, para.3.11.

[83] CDPA 1988, s.6(1A).

[84] See the Government's conclusions on the Patent Office's Consultation Paper of August 7, 2002, para.3.11. The transmission of emails is already effectively excluded by the lack of any transmission to the public: *ibid*, para.3.11.

Immediate re-transmissions. The Act, as now amended, also provides that the **3–100** relaying of a broadcast by its reception and immediate re-transmission is to be regarded as a separate act of broadcasting from the making of the broadcast which is so re-transmitted.[85] The effect of this is that the re-transmission is itself a protectable broadcast. This was previously the position in relation to wireless broadcasts[86] but was not the position in relation to cable programmes.[87]

Transitional provisions. The amended provisions of the Act apply to works **3–101** made before October 31, 2003[88] and so a broadcast which satisfies the above provisions of section 9 as amended but which did not fall within the unamended provisions will have been protectable as from October 31, 2003. The main category of newly protected works would appear to be immediate cable retransmission of broadcasts, in which copyright now subsists.[89] Nevertheless, no act done before this date is to be regarded as an infringement of any such new broadcasting right.[90] Further, nothing in the amending regulations is to affect any agreement made before December 22, 2002 and no act done after October 31, 2003 in pursuance of an agreement made before December 22, 2002, is to be regarded as an infringement of any new broadcasting right.[91] As to works which qualified as broadcasts or cable programmes but which no longer do so, there are no saving provisions and it appears that they are no longer entitled to copyright. This is not likely to affect any old-style (wireless) broadcasts, but only cable programmes which were not of a broadcast nature.

I. TYPOGRAPHICAL ARRANGEMENTS OF PUBLISHED EDITIONS

Background to protection for typographical arrangements. The origin of this **3–102** right can be traced to two developments in the publishing industry, one of them artistic and the other technological. The first was the great improvement in typographical design which was associated with the arts and crafts movement in the last two decades of the nineteenth century and the first two of the twentieth. A new font could be registered as a design but the typographic layout of a particular book, which may have taken considerable skill and effort, was not as such protected. The second was the development since the First World War of the technique of photo-lithography, which enabled printing plates to be made by photographic means. The skill and labour which had gone into the typographical design of fine editions of classical works (themselves out of copyright) could be appropriated by other publishers who used photo-lithography to make facsimile copies.[92] The 1952 Copyright Committee therefore recommended protection for typographical arrangements[93] and this was brought about by section 15(1) of the 1956 Act, which gave copyright protection to typographical arrangements of published editions of one or more literary, dramatic or musical works.

Although the United Kingdom has therefore given copyright protection to typographical arrangements of published editions since 1957, such protection is not required under the terms of the Berne Convention or any European Directive,

---

[85] CDPA 1988, s.6(5A).
[86] Copyright was only denied to broadcasts which *infringed* the copyright in another broadcast or cable programme: s.6(6).
[87] Copyright was denied to a cable programme if it was included in a cable programme service by reception and immediate re-transmission of a broadcast: s.7(6)(a).
[88] Copyright and Related Rights Regulations 2003, r.31(1).
[89] See para. 3–100, above.
[90] Copyright and Related Rights Regulations 2003, reg.31(2).
[91] Copyright and Related Rights Regulations 2003, regs 32(1), (2).
[92] *Newspaper Licensing Agency Ltd v Marks & Spencer plc* [2001] UKHL 38; [2003] 1 A.C. 551.
[93] Cmnd.8662, paras 308 and 310.

and has not generally existed in other countries,[94] including many other European Member States. Similar considerations to those which led to the introduction of this protection in the United Kingdom resulted, however, in the creation throughout the Community of a publication right,[95] to protect those who first publish a previously unpublished work at a time when copyright in the work has expired. Whilst the term of protection under this right and under the typographical arrangement right is the same,[96] the two provisions are, however, different in their application. In some ways the publication right is of wider application, in that it covers first publication of previously unpublished artistic works and films,[97] but in others it is of narrower application, in that it applies only to first publication of works in which copyright has expired.[98]

3–103   **Statutory definition: typographical arrangement of a published edition.** Typographical arrangements of published editions are protected under section 1(1)(c) of the 1988 Act. For the purposes of that provision, "published edition" means a published edition of the whole or any part of one or more literary, dramatic or musical works.[99] The reference to the edition having been published must be construed in accordance with the definition of publication in the Act.[1] It is to be noted that there is no requirement that the work itself should still be, or indeed should ever have been, the subject of copyright,[2] although it must qualify under the Act as a literary, dramatic or musical work.[3] The definition deliberately excludes typographical arrangements of artistic works from protection. Typographical arrangement implies the layout of words or symbols on the printed page, to which the publisher has made a contribution. Where artistic works are included in a book, the publisher merely reproduces the work. In such a case, the protection of the copy of the artistic work rests solely on the copyright in the original work.[4]

3–104   **Published edition.** In this context, the term "published edition" is the language of the publishing trade.[5] In the context of works comprising a number of literary works, such as newspapers, the "edition" referred to in the expression "published edition" is therefore the product, generally between covers, which the publisher offers to the public.[6] The words "one or more" in the definition of a published edi-

---

[94] A similar type of provision was tabled by WIPO for inclusion in its model Copyright Act, but was abandoned in 1987; see *Hecker* [1995] E.I.P.R. 75.

[95] Pursuant to Art.4 of Council Directive 93/98, harmonising the term of protection of copyright and certain related rights; see, generally, Ch.25. This aspect of the Directive was implemented by reg.16 of The Copyright and Related Rights Regulations (SI 1996/2967), with effect from December 1, 1996.

[96] *i.e.* 25 years from the end of the year of publication; see Chs 6 and 17, respectively.

[97] Typographical arrangements of published editions do not include artistic works (see para. 3–103, below), or films.

[98] Neither subsistence of copyright, nor its expiry, in the work is a requirement for protection for the typographical arrangement of a published edition; see para. 3–103, below. Also, each new typographical arrangement of a published edition is entitled to its own protection, whereas the publication right applies only on the first publication of the previously unpublished work.

[99] CDPA 1988, s.8(1), in the same terms as s.15(1) of the 1956 Act.

[1] CDPA 1988, s.175(1). See paras 3–172 *et seq.*, below.

[2] Compare the new publication right, granted in respect of the first publication of a previously unpublished work after copyright in the work has expired; see generally Ch.17.

[3] See *Machinery Market Ltd v Sheen Publishing Ltd* [1983] F.S.R. 431.

[4] See *Hansard*, HL Vol.490, cols 870, 871. In *X Ltd v Nowacki* [2003] EWHC (Ch) 1928 at para.52, the layout of wording designed to be stamped on the underside of tableware, the words being set in various different fonts, was held to be an artistic work, and thus a separate copyright work from any copyright that might subsist in typographical arrangement of the words under CDPA 1988, s.1(1)(c).

[5] *Newspaper Licensing Agency Ltd v Marks & Spencer plc* [2001] UKHL 38; [2003] 1 A.C. 551.

[6] *Newspaper Licensing Agency Ltd v Marks & Spencer plc* [2001] UKHL 38, approving *Nationwide*

tion[7] show that one may have a single published edition of more than one literary work and that there is therefore no necessary congruence between the concept of an edition and the underlying works.[8] "Published edition" does not therefore refer to the published edition of each literary work appearing in the newspaper[9] but to the published edition of the whole newspaper.[10] While there may be borderline cases in which two or more distinct products are offered simultaneously at a single price, such as a newspaper with typographically distinct supplements or "inserts", it is unlikely that the point will matter in practice, because it is unlikely to affect the question of infringement (see para.7–74, below). Similarly, in the case of a work such as an anthology of poems, the published edition copyright will subsist in the typographical arrangement of the entire collection contained between the two covers, and not of a number of copyrights consisting of the typographical arrangement of each poem.[11]

3. FIXATION

A. Fixation in General

Introduction. It is a long established principle of copyright law that copyright does not subsist in a work unless and until the work takes some material form. This principle is known as the requirement of fixation. The reasons for this principle are practical. Since copyright is a form of monopoly in relation to the subject matter which is protected, there must be certainty as to what that subject matter is.[12] This is necessary both so as to be able to prove the existence of the work and to establish what the work consists of, so that it can be judged whether the work has been copied or otherwise infringed. Fixation also provides a limit to the monopoly, ensuring that the protection accorded to the work does not extend beyond the expression of the work to the ideas or information contained or represented in it. This is necessary in holding a balance between the author's interests and society's interests. Further, fixation provides a defined moment when the work takes existence, essential for the purpose of applying the rules as to the status of its author.

3–105

Fixation under the Berne and Rome Conventions. The principle of fixation is of general application, and is referred to both in the Berne Convention[13] and in the Rome Convention.[14] Of the subject matter protected under the Rome Conven-

3–106

News Pty Ltd v Copyright Agency Ltd (1995) 128 A.L.R. 285 (Fed Ct of Aus) and disapproving *Machinery Market Ltd v Sheen Publishing Ltd* [1983] F.S.R. 431, which had proceeded on the unchallenged but incorrect assumption that copyright subsisted in the typographical arrangement of a single advertisement appearing in a newspaper, *i.e.* in the arrangement of a single literary work rather than the whole newspaper.

[7] "'published edition' ... means a published edition of the whole or any part of one or more literary, dramatic or musical works".

[8] *Newspaper Licensing Agency Ltd v Marks & Spencer plc* [2001] UKHL 38; [2003] 1 A.C. 551.

[9] With the consequence that the newspaper as a whole does not consist of many published editions.

[10] *Newspaper Licensing Agency Ltd v Marks & Spencer plc* [2001] UKHL 38; [2003] 1 A.C. 551.

[11] *Newspaper Licensing Agency Ltd v Marks & Spencer plc* [2001] UKHL 38; [2003] 1 A.C. 551.

[12] See *Tate v Fullbrook* [1908] 1 K.B. 821; *Tate v Thomas* [1921] 1 Ch. 503; and *Green v Broadcasting Corporation of New Zealand* [1989] R.P.C. 700, PC, discussed at para. 3–41, above, in relation to dramatic works.

[13] Berne Convention, Art.2(2), which provides that it is for Union Countries to prescribe any requirements of fixation.

[14] In various Articles relating to the protection of performances and phonograms. However, the principle has most application in relation to works protected under Berne, that is, in the United Kingdom, to literary, dramatic, musical, artistic and cinematograph works.

tion, fixation is a requirement in the definition of a phonogram.[15] It has no application to a broadcast, which is essentially of an ephemeral nature.

3–107   **Distinction between fixation and requirement as to form of a work.** Whilst the principle of fixation requires that the work be reduced to a material form (for example in the case of a literary work, that it be recorded, in writing or otherwise), this is a separate matter from any requirement as to the form a particular work should take (in the case of a literary work, that it be written, spoken or sung). The requirement as to a particular form is an integral part of the description of the work; unless it is in that form, it does not constitute a work of that description. The requirement as to reduction to a material form is part of the conditions which the designated work must satisfy in order to qualify for copyright protection. Where there is a requirement as to a particular form, and this is met, the requirement as to fixation may also be met, but this is not necessarily so,[16] and this coincidence, when it does occur, should not obscure the distinction between the two. The distinction has not always been clear under earlier Copyright Acts,[17] which tended to describe any requirement as to fixation as being a requirement as to the particular form of the work, but this distinction is clearly made in the 1988 Act.

3–108   **Material not in a permanent form.** The courts have often experienced a difficulty in according a work copyright protection where the first embodiment of the work is considered to have or to have had a transient or ephemeral existence.[18] This is to confuse the requirement that the work should take a material form before copyright subsists with a requirement that such form should be permanent, or have a degree of permanence. It also confuses the physical material on or in which the work is first reduced to a material form with the copyright work, which continues to exist whatever happens to the first embodiment of the work. There is no reason in principle why a work which was always intended to have a fleeting existence should not be protected by copyright, if it otherwise satisfies the conditions for copyright to subsist in it.

3–109   **Separate existence of work and material on which fixed.** It follows from what has been said that the work, once fixed, continues to have a separate, disembodied, existence from the material form in which it is fixed. The record of the work may, indeed, be entitled to its own copyright as a separate work.[19] This is so even in those cases where the statute has prescribed a particular form as part of the description of the work itself. Destruction of the material form in which the work was fixed does not destroy the work itself, nor the copyright which came into existence upon its being fixed.[20] This is equally so in the case where the expression of the work which qualifies it as a work takes the material form in which the work is fixed, as is the case in many artistic works, for example a painting or a sculpture.

3–110   **Immaterial by whom fixed.** Since fixation addresses the issue of the definition

---

[15] It is referred to in relation to a performance, but is not a requirement for protection of a performance.

[16] See, *e.g. Hadley v Kemp* [1999] E.M.L.R. 589 (words and music of songs in existence before being recorded for the first time).

[17] For a good example, see the discussion in para. 3–116, below in relation to dramatic works.

[18] This has particularly been the case where an intermediate work made in the course of an industrial process is sought to be protected as a work of sculpture; see the discussion at para. 3–58, above. See also *Merchandising Corporation of America Inc v Harpbond* [1983] F.S.R. 32, where the court apparently took the view that no copyright could subsist in a face painting because it was too ephemeral.

[19] *e.g.* a dramatic work first recorded on film.

[20] If this were not so, copyright in a painting could not be infringed if the painting had been destroyed, since infringement is defined by reference to the exclusive right of the copyright owner to "copy the work": see CDPA 1988, s.16(1)(a).

of the work, and proof as to its existence and content, there is no reason of principle why the person who creates the work and the person who fixes the work should be the same. The functions of creation and fixation are distinct, as in the case of a person who first records the spoken words of another. Copyright protects the of skill and labour of the author, and once he has created and expressed his work, it is immaterial how his work comes to be fixed.

Fixation under the 1988 Act. As will be seen, prior to the 1988 Act, the require- **3–111** ment of fixation tended to be expressed as an aspect of the definition of a particular work. The 1988 Act gives clear expression to the requirement of fixation as a separate requirement and in doing so reflects the principles as to fixation discussed above.

B. LITERARY, DRAMATIC AND MUSICAL WORKS

Fixation is now an express requirement for copyright to subsist in a literary, **3–112** dramatic or musical work, the Act providing that copyright does not subsist in a literary, dramatic or musical work until it is recorded, in writing or otherwise.[21] The form of fixation required by the Act for these works is thus expressed in wide terms. The width is in the "or otherwise", which makes it clear that the nature of the medium on which the record is made is irrelevant.[22] The Act also makes it clear that the work may be recorded for the purposes of fixation by someone other than the author, and that it is immaterial whether this takes place with the author's consent or not.[23]

Fixation of a literary work. In the case of a literary work, the definition of the **3–113** work as being a work which is written, spoken or sung[24] makes it clear that the definition of the work does not now contain its own requirement as to fixation, since writing is only one form which such a work can take, and speaking and singing, whilst forms of expression, are not a reduction of the work to a recorded form. This definition means that an original *ex tempore* speech, lecture or judgment is capable of being protected as a literary work once delivered, provided that some record of it, whether in shorthand or by mechanical means such as a tape recorder, was made when it was delivered. Similarly, the lyrics of a song, even though not previously written down, are capable of being protected as a literary work once they are sung, provided that the singing is recorded, as will often be the case when such performance is given as part of a recording session in a studio.

Since it is immaterial by whom the literary work is in fact recorded,[25] if an author dictates to a stenographer, he will acquire copyright in his material as a literary work at the moment it is recorded in the notation of shorthand. This is on the basis that the person dictating the material is in fact the author of it; it is immaterial that the shorthand writer is not an employee.[26] Similarly, in the case of an original *ex tempore* speech, lecture or judgment which is recorded by another either by shorthand or on a tape recorder, the person delivering the same is entitled to copyright in the speech, lecture or judgment, whilst the person recording the same will be entitled to a separate (but necessarily dependent) copyright in the record as a literary work if in shorthand, or as a sound recording if on tape.

---

[21] CDPA 1988, s.3(2).
[22] The definition of writing is discussed at para. 3–11, above.
[23] CDPA 1988, s.3(3), following the recommendation of the 1977 Copyright Committee, Cmnd.6732, para.609(viii).
[24] Discussed at para. 3–14, above.
[25] CDPA 1988, s.3(3).
[26] See *Donoghue v Allied Newspapers Ltd* [1938] Ch. 106, and para. 4–11, below.

Again, the pop musician who performs a song comprising lyrics composed in his head creates a literary work when he sings such lyrics in a recording studio and they are recorded, and it is immaterial that the sound recording is made by the recording studio or the record company. In such cases, there will be separate copyrights, often in separate ownership, in the literary work and the recording.

3–114   **Fixation of literary works under earlier Acts.** The 1956 Act did not contain any such clear requirement as to fixation but contained provisions relating to the time when a literary, dramatic or musical work was "made",[27] and it would seem that a work had to be "made" before copyright could subsist in it.[28] In this context, references to the time at which a work was made were to be taken as references to the time at which it was first reduced to writing or some other material form.[29] It was unclear whether, for example, the recording on tape of a literary work amounted to reduction of the work to some material form; the view expressed in earlier editions of *Copinger* was that some form of notation was required.[30] Under equivalent provisions of the Irish Act it has been decided that reduction of the work onto tape is not sufficient on the grounds that "the symbol which comprises the notation must be capable without more of being understood"[31] but this seems doubtful. There is no requirement that the literary content of the material form be directly accessible by a human being. The 1911 Act contained no equivalent provision and the position under that Act is uncertain. Under the earlier Acts, statutory copyright did not subsist in mere spoken words.[32]

3–115   **Fixation of a dramatic work.** Under the 1988 Act, any form of recording of a dramatic work is sufficient to satisfy the requirement of fixation.[33]

3–116   **Fixation of dramatic works under earlier Acts.** Under the 1911 Act, a dramatic work was expressly defined as something which was fixed in writing or otherwise.[34] Although expressed as a requirement of the form of a dramatic work, this requirement was really no more than a fixation requirement, since it acknowledged that a dramatic work could exist independently of the particular form in which it was fixed. Under the 1956 Act,[35] however, a dramatic work was required to be reduced to writing. This requirement therefore operated much more restrictively than a mere requirement as to fixation, and effectively restricted the description of the work to one particular form in which a dramatic work could take material form. The result was that a work which was considered to be a dramatic work in which copyright subsisted under the 1911 Act, such as a sketch which was not written down, but was recorded on film at the moment of performance, was not a dramatic work under the 1956 Act. The 1988 Act has restored the position, in this respect, to what it was under the 1911 Act.

---

[27] See Copyright Act 1956, ss.2(1) (qualification), 4(2), 4(4) (ownership).

[28] See, *e.g.* the 1977 Whitford Committee Report, Cmnd.6732, at para.590: "Speeches and lectures delivered extempore do not acquire copyright unless and until fixed."

[29] Copyright Act 1956, s.49(4). Writing was defined to include any form of notation, whether by hand or by printing, typewriting or any similar process: s.48(1).

[30] *Copinger* (12th ed.), pp.53, 85. But see Somers J. in *Green v Broadcasting and Corporation of New Zealand* [1989] R.P.C. 469 (High Ct of NZ.), at 477: "There is much force in the submission that writing is but one method of giving a work the degree of certainty necessary to justify the monopoly conferred by the Act and that the same security can be obtained by fixing it in other tangible forms."

[31] *Gormley v EMI Records Ltd* [2000] E.C.D.R. 31 (Sup Ct of Ireland).

[32] For a review of the position, see Brennan and Christie, "Spoken Words and Copyright Subsistence in Anglo-American Law" [2000] I.P.Q. 309.

[33] See s.3(2) and para. 3–112, above.

[34] Copyright Act 1911, s.35(1).

[35] Copyright Act 1956, s.48(1).

Fixation of a musical work. In contrast to a literary work, which must be **3–117** expressed in writing, speech or singing before it can exist as a literary work, a musical work may exist as such in the mind of its composer as well as when it has been merely played or sung.[36] However, such work cannot be the subject of copyright under the 1988 Act until it is fixed, in any of the same ways that literary and dramatic works may also be fixed, that is, by it being recorded, in writing or otherwise.[37] The approach in the 1988 Act to fixation is of particular importance in relation to much modern music, which is played straight onto a recording device without having first been written down. So, as with the lyrics,[38] the pop musician who performs a song comprising music composed in his head creates a copyright musical work when he plays such music in a recording studio and it is recorded, and it is immaterial that the sound recording is made by the recording studio or the record company. In such cases, there will be separate copyrights, often in separate ownership, in the musical work and in the recording.

It follows from the combination of section 3(1) and (2) of the 1988 Act that if A improvises a tune in B's presence, then A has created a musical work. However, at that point the tune is not protected by copyright, as it is neither written down nor otherwise recorded. If B carries the tune away in his head and subsequently records it, then by such act by B the tune may become protected by copyright. However, B is not the author of the tune, as he is not the person who created it.[39] Although it is B's act in recording the tune which caused the tune to be the subject of copyright, upon such recording taking place it would seem clear that A is the owner of any copyright thereby subsisting in the tune and could therefore sue B for infringing his copyright.[40]

Fixation of musical works under earlier Acts. The position is the same as in re- **3–118** lation to literary works, considered above.

Fixation of artistic works. Artistic works are not made subject to a specific **3–119** requirement of fixation under the 1988 Act, but the nature of each of the types of work which fall within the definition of artistic work is such that the work will have taken a material form.[41] The position was the same under the earlier Acts.[42]

C. Sound Recordings, Films, Broadcasts and Typographical Arrangements

Sound recordings and films. The 1988 Act contains no express requirement of **3–120** fixation in relation to these works; their nature is such that it is unnecessary to specify separately any fixation requirement, since such works can only exist in some material form.[43] Thus the Act defines each work by reference to a "record-

---

[36] *Hadley v Kemp* [1999] E.M.L.R. 589 (music of songs in existence before being recorded for the first time).

[37] CDPA 1988, s.3(2).

[38] See para. 3–113, above.

[39] See CDPA 1988, s.9(1), and Ch.4.

[40] Subject to the evidential difficulty that A would face in proving that he, and not B, was in fact the author of the tune.

[41] The conception of a work of art, such as a painting or a sculpture, does not itself constitute the making of an artistic work for the purposes of the 1988 Act. It is the execution of the concept by painting the scene or sculpting the form which produces the artistic work. Drawings or sketches produced in preparation for the execution of such a work may, of course, be entitled to copyright as artistic works in their own right.

[42] CDPA 1988, s.49(4) did not apply to artistic works.

[43] Cinematograph works are classed as literary and artistic works under the Berne Convention, and Art.2(2) therefore applies to them. Sound recordings are specifically described in terms of fixation in the Rome Convention: Art.3(b).

ing"[44] which must, of course, therefore exist in a material form. The definitions provide, following the principle of fixation discussed above, that the medium on which the recording exists in each case is irrelevant.[45] Again, therefore, this makes it clear that the work has an existence independent of the medium. The position was the same under the 1956 Act. No copyright subsists in a film as such made before the commencement of the 1956 Act; and under the 1911 Act, copyright subsisted in sound recordings as if they were musical works.[46]

3–121 **Fixation of broadcasts.** The 1988 Act requires no fixation for broadcasts. The position was the same under the 1956 Act.

3–122 **Fixation of typographical arrangements of published editions.**

Fixation is not specifically referred to as a requirement for subsistence of copyright in a typographical arrangement of a published edition, but the nature of a typographical arrangement satisfies the principle of fixation. The position was the same under the 1956 Act.

4. ORIGINALITY

A. LITERARY, DRAMATIC, MUSICAL AND ARTISTIC WORKS

(i) Introduction

3–123 **Statutory provision.** Under section 1(1)(a) of the 1988 Act it is a requirement for the subsistence of copyright in a literary, dramatic, musical and artistic work that the work should be original. This was the position under the equivalent provisions of the 1956[47] and 1911 Acts.[48] As with these earlier Acts, there was no definition of "original" in the 1988 Act as originally enacted, and this remains the position as regards a definition of general application; a definition of originality was introduced by amendment[49] specifically in relation to a database, when a database was itself introduced as a new sub-category of a literary work.[50] Decisions on the question of originality under the 1911 and 1956 Acts therefore remain valid under the 1988 Act.[51]

3–124 **History of requirement of originality.** Under the piecemeal legislation which existed before the 1911 Act, there was no general statutory requirement of originality for copyright works. On the one hand, neither the Literary Copyright Act 1842,[52] nor the Engravings Copyright Act 1766,[53] used the expression "original" while, on the otherhand, the Sculpture Copyright Act 1814,[54] and the Fine Arts Copyright Act 1862,[55] referred respectively to "original sculptures" and "every original painting, drawing and photograph". So far as the 1842 Act was

---

[44] CDPA 1988, ss.5A(1), 5B(2).
[45] CDPA 1988, ss.5A(1), 5B(2).
[46] Copyright Act 1911, s.19(1).
[47] Copyright Act 1956, ss.2(1) and (2), and 3(2) and (3).
[48] Copyright Act 1911, s.1(1).
[49] CDPA 1988, s.3A(2); introduced by the Copyright and Rights in Databases Regulations 1997 (SI 1997/3032) with effect from January 1, 1998.
[50] See para. 3–144, below.
[51] And see CDPA 1988, s.171(3).
[52] 5 & 6 Vict., c.45; this gave copyright protection to books, which were defined to include not only books in the ordinary sense, but other printed material such as pamphlets and letterpress sheets, and also music sheets, maps, charts and plans.
[53] 7 Geo. 3, c.38.
[54] 54 Geo. 3, c.56.
[55] 25 & 26 Vict., c.68.

concerned, only a low level of creativity on the part of the author was required. This was demonstrated by the House of Lords decision in *Walter v Lane*,[56] where it was held that a reporter was entitled to copyright in his *verbatim* report of a public speech. Since the statute did not contain any express requirement as to originality,[57] it might have been thought that the introduction of an express statutory requirement of originality by the 1911 Act brought about a change in the law. Decisions under the 1911 Act, however, established that the test of originality remained a low one, and the better view was therefore that there had been no change in the law.[58] The matter was resolved in *Express Newspapers plc v News (U.K.) Ltd*,[59] where the court held that *Walter v Lane* remained good law.

The Berne Convention. Originality is not expressed to be a requirement for protection under the Berne Convention. The concept behind the Convention is, however, to accord protection to authors in respect of their intellectual creations.[60] This implies that the product so created is the result of the individual's own intellectual efforts, and, therefore, in this sense is original to him. The degree of originality required for the protection of works the subject of Berne varies widely amongst the countries adhering to Berne, as also does the approach to different types of works.[61] The United Kingdom has, from before 1911, adopted a low threshold of originality as qualifying a work for protection.[62] **3–125**

---

[56] [1900] A.C. 539.

[57] Lord Halsbury L.C. specifically referred as a basis for his decision in *Walter v Lane* [1900] A.C. 539 to the absence of "original" in the statute (*ibid.* at 594) but Lord Davey considered that the fact no originality or literary skill was required for the report had less to do with this than the principle that a person should not avail himself of another's skill, labour and expense, by copying his work (*ibid.* at 552).

[58] See earlier editions of *Copinger*; *cf. Roberton v Lewis* [1976] R.P.C. 169 (decided in 1960), where Cross J. suggested that in view of the introduction of the word "original" into the 1911 and 1956 Acts, it was at least arguable that *Walter v Lane* [1900] A.C. 539 was no longer good law. The point was left open in *Sifam Electrical Instrument Co Ltd v Sangamo Weston Ltd* [1973] R.P.C. 899, at 910. In *L.B. (Plastics) Ltd v Swish Products Ltd* [1979] R.P.C. 551, Whitford J., noting the point, nevertheless observed that the cases since the 1911 Act had established that no originality of thought was required for subsistence of copyright.

[59] [1990] F.S.R 359 (Browne-Wilkinson V.-C.), following the decision of the High Court of Australia in *Sands McDougall Proprietary Ltd v Robinson* (1917) 23 C.L.R. 49.

[60] See, for example, Berne Convention, Art.2(5), in relation to compilations. See Ricketson, *The Berne Convention for the Protection of Literary and Artistic Works: 1886–1996* (Kluwer, 1987), para.6.15.

[61] In *CCH Canadian Ltd v Law Society of Upper Canada* [2004] S.C.C. 13, the differences were summarised by the Supreme Court of Canada, as follows: "There are competing views on the meaning of 'original' in copyright law. Some courts have found that a work that originates from an author and is more than a mere copy of a work is sufficient to ground copyright. See, for example, *University of London Press Ltd v University Tutorial Press Ltd*, [1916] 2 Ch. 601; *U & R Tax Services Ltd v H & R Block Canada Inc* (1995), 62 C.P.R. (3d) 257 (F.C.T.D.). This approach is consistent with the "sweat of the brow" or "industriousness" standard of originality, which is premised on a natural rights or Lockean theory of "just desserts", namely that an author deserves to have his or her efforts in producing a work rewarded. Other courts have required that a work must be creative to be "original" and thus protected by copyright. See, for example, *Feist Publications Inc v Rural Telephone Service Co*, 499 U.S. 340 (1991); *Tele-Direct (Publications) Inc v American Business Information Inc*, [1998] 2 F.C. 22, CA. This approach is also consistent with a natural rights theory of property law; however it is less absolute in that only those works that are the product of creativity will be rewarded with copyright protection. It has been suggested that the "creativity" approach to originality helps ensure that copyright protection only extends to the expression of ideas as opposed to the underlying ideas or facts. See *Feist, supra,* at p. 353."

[62] This is criticised by Ricketson, *The Berne Convention for the Protection of Literary and Artistic Works: 1886–1996* (Kluwer, 1987), para.6.15 as being contrary to the spirit, if not the letter, of the Convention. But note the comment by McGechan J. in *Glogau v Land Transport Safety Authority of New Zealand* [1999] 1 N.Z.L.R. 257 (CA of NZ) that where the degree of originality is low it is unlikely that anything other than almost exact copying will be an infringement.; conversely in the case of works involving a high degree of originality (as to the correlation between the degree or originality and the substantial part test for infringement, see paras 7–25 and 7–27, below.) In consequence, applying a low threshold test of originality causes no real harm.

3–126   **EC Directives.** As part of the harmonisation of national copyright laws, two of the Directives adopted by the EC contain what amounts to a definition in similar terms of originality for the purposes of their respective subject matter. The first was the Directive on the legal protection of computer programs[63] ("the Software Directive") and the second was the Directive on the legal protection of databases ("the Database Directive").[64] The Software Directive requires that a computer program shall be protected if it is original in the sense that it is the author's own intellectual creation, and specifies that no other criteria, in particular as to the qualitative or aesthetic merits of the program, shall be applied in determining whether or not a computer program is an original work.[65] No change was made to the 1988 Act when the Directive was implemented, presumably on the basis that the law under the 1988 Act was considered to be already in line with the requirements of the Directive. The Database Directive adopted a similar approach to the Software Directive, and provided that copyright protection should be accorded to databases which, by reason of the selection or arrangement of their contents, constitute the author's own intellectual creation, and that no other criteria should be applied to determine their eligibility for copyright protection.[66] When, however, the Database Directive was implemented,[67] a definition of originality was introduced into the 1988 Act in relation to a database to reflect the terms of the Directive.[68] Whether the United Kingdom was correct not to make any amendment in relation to computer programs is considered further below.[69] The reference in both Directives to the work being the author's own intellectual creation reflects the use of this phrase in the Berne Convention.[70] It should be noted that a third Directive[71] (the Term Directive) provided that photographs "which are original in the sense that they are the author's own intellectual creation" should be protected.[72] Since, however, Member States were permitted to provide for the protection of other photographs,[73] the United Kingdom was not required to make any change on implementation, even assuming that this test was different from that applied by the 1988 Act in relation to photographs.[74]

(ii) Principles of originality

3–127   **Expression, not content.** Copyright protection is given to literary, dramatic, musical and artistic works and not to ideas,[75] and therefore it is original skill or labour in execution of the work, and not originality of thought, which is required.[76] Original, in this connection, does not mean that the work must be the expression of original or inventive thought; the originality required relates to the expression

[63] Council Directive 91/250, adopted on May 14, 1991; [1991] O.J. L122/42.
[64] Directive 96/9 of the European Parliament and Council, of March 11, 1996; [1996] O.J. L77/20.
[65] Software Directive 91/250, Art.1(3).
[66] Directive 96/9; Recital (16) adds that no aesthetic or qualitative criteria shall be applied in determining eligibility for protection.
[67] By the Copyright and Rights in Databases Regulations 1997 (SI 1997/3032). As to the new database right introduced by these Regulations, see Ch.18.
[68] As part of the new s.3A. See para. 3–146, below.
[69] See para. 3–130, below.
[70] See, e.g. Art.2(5).
[71] Directive 93/98 Harmonising the Term of Protection of Copyright and Certain Related Rights.
[72] Term Directive 93/98, Art.6.
[73] Term Directive 93/98, Art.6.
[74] See para. 3–142, below.
[75] See para. 3–18, above, and the discussion in *Plix Products Ltd v Frank M. Winstone (Merchants)* [1986] F.S.R. 63 at 92.
[76] *L.B. (Plastics) Ltd v Swish Products Ltd* [1979] R.P.C. 551 at 567. The sentence in the text was cited with approval in *Martin v Polyplas Manufacturers Ltd* [1969] N.Z.L.R. 1046 at 1050.

of thought.[77] The position in this respect under the Copyright Acts may be contrasted with the standard required for registered designs under the Registered Designs Act 1949, which is generally one of novelty, so that, if a design in fact resembles an existing design, it may not be registered, even though the designer of the second design arrived at this design entirely independently of the first design.

Nature of skill or labour required.[78] There are two interconnecting strands **3–128** involved.[79] First, the work must originate from the author, in the sense that it must not be copied from another work, for, as discussed below, a mere copyist does not obtain copyright in his copy.[80] As will be seen, however, the work may nevertheless be original even though the author has drawn on knowledge common to himself and others,[81] or has used already existing material.[82] Second, whether or not the author has drawn on other material, what is required is the expenditure of more than negligible or trivial effort or relevant skill in the creation of the work.[83] As to this, while it is clear that the standard of originality required by the Copyright Acts is a low one,[84] it is otherwise almost impossible to state in any precise terms the amount of knowledge, labour, judgment, skill or taste which the author of a work must bestow on its creation in order for the work to acquire copyright.[85] There is no guiding principle as to the *quantum* of labour, skill or judgment required.[86] It is a question of fact and degree and thus has to be determined on the facts of the particular case.[87] United Kingdom law has traditionally regarded mere labour in the creation of a work as sufficient to make it original, whether or not there is also skill involved.[88] As to what is meant by skill or judgment in this context, the following is a helpful statement by the Supreme Court of Canada:

"By skill, I mean the use of one's knowledge, developed aptitude or practised ability in producing the work. By judgment, I mean the use of

---

[77] *University of London Press Ltd v University Tutorial Press Ltd* [1916] 2 Ch. 601 at 608, *per* Petersen J., cited with approval in: *Macmillan & Co Ltd v Cooper (K. & J.)* (1923) 40 T.L.R. 186 at 190; *British Broadcasting Co v Wireless League Gazette Publishing Co* [1926] Ch. 433 at 440; *Ladbroke (Football) Ltd v William Hill (Football) Ltd* [1964] 1 W.L.R. 273 at 277; and see *Ascot Jockey Club Ltd v Simons* (1968) 64 W.W.R. 411.

[78] Sometimes the cases refer to labour, skill or *judgment* being required. In this work, judgment will for the most part be treated as being an aspect of the skill required for creation of a work.

[79] See *Ultra Marketing (UK) Ltd v Universal Components Ltd* [2004] EWHC 468 (Ch) at para.51, where the question of originality was correctly broken down into these two stages.

[80] *British Northrop Ltd v Texteam Blackburn Ltd* [1974] R.P.C. 344 at 68, approved by the Privy Council in *Interlego A.G. v Tyco Industries Inc* [1989] A.C. 217 at 261. See also *per* Lord James in *Walter v Lane* [1900] A.C. 539 at 554; *Leslie v Young (J.) & Sons* [1894] A.C. 335; *Barfield v Nicholson* (1824) 2 Sim.St. 1; and para. 3–131, below.

[81] *University of London Press Ltd v University Tutorial Press Ltd* [1916] 2 Ch. 601 at 608, *per* Petersen J.; *Macmillan & Co Ltd v Cooper (K. & J.)* (1923) 40 T.L.R. 186 at 188, in which Lord Atkinson cited with approval *Emerson v Davies*, Storey's U.S. Rep. 768 (1845); *Ladbroke (Football) Ltd v William Hill (Football) Ltd* [1964] 1 W.L.R. 273, at, *e.g.* 291 (Lord Pearce). And see *Dutt (S.K.) v Law Book Co* [1954] A.L.J. 125; *Gouindan v Gopalakrishna Kone* (1955) Mad.W.N. 369.

[82] See further paras 3–132 *et seq.*, below.

[83] *Ladbroke (Football) Ltd v William Hill (Football) Ltd* [1964] 1 W.L.R. 273 at 287; *Autospin (Oil Seals) v Beehive Spinning* [1995] R.P.C. 683, at 694 (drawings of oil seals).

[84] See some of the examples cited later in the text.

[85] See, *per* Lord Atkinson in *Macmillan & Co Ltd v Cooper (K. & J.)* (1923) 40 T.L.R. 186, PC; the decision of the Privy Council was approved by the House of Lords in *G.A. Cramp & Sons Ltd v Frank Smythson Ltd* [1944] A.C. 329 at 335, and *Ladbroke (Football) Ltd v William Hill (Football) Ltd* [1964] 1 W.L.R. 273 at 179, 282.

[86] As was pointed out by Maugham J. in *Cambridge University Press v University Tutorial Press Ltd* (1928) 45 R.P.C. 335.

[87] *Macmillan & Co Ltd v Cooper (K. & J.)* (1923) 40 T.L.R. 186, *per* Lord Atkinson; *G.A. Cramp & Sons Ltd v Frank Smythson Ltd* [1944] A.C. 329, at p.335; *Biotrading & Financing v Biohit* [1996] F.S.R. 393 at 395; [1998] F.S.R. 109, CA at 116.

[88] See, *e.g.* the compilation cases at para. 3–144, below.

one's capacity for discernment or ability to form an opinion or evaluation by comparing different possible options in producing the work. This exercise of skill and judgment will necessarily involve intellectual effort. The exercise of skill and judgment required to produce the work must not be so trivial that it could be characterized as a purely mechanical exercise. For example, any skill and judgment that might be involved in simply changing the font of a work to produce 'another' work would be too trivial to merit copyright protection as an 'original' work."

And in conclusion:

"The exercise of skill and judgment required to produce the work must not be so trivial that it could be characterized as a purely mechanical exercise. While creative works will by definition be 'original' and covered by copyright, creativity is not required to make a work 'original'."[89]

Simplicity, as such, is not enough to prevent copyright subsisting unless extreme, such as in a straight line,[90] or a circle[91] and indeed there are relatively few cases in which copyright has been denied on the grounds of lack of originality.[92] Copyright has been denied to a work written when drunk,[93] but in principle there is no reason why a work created under the influence of alcohol or drugs should not be regarded as original if it has some meaning or significance and is not simply gibberish.[94] Also, as already noted,[95] it is sometimes difficult to know whether cases have been decided on the basis that the work is not a *literary*, etc. work or that it is not an *original* work, and the reader is referred to the earlier discussion on this point and the cases referred to there. It has sometimes been said that as a rough practical test "what is worth copying is worth protecting",[96] but this should be applied with caution since otherwise the most trivial of works will be protected if copying has taken place.[97]

(iii) Non-derivative works

3–129   Where an author creates a work without reference to any existing subject matter, it will be rare that it will lack originality merely by reason of its simplicity or

---

[89] *CCH Canadian Ltd v Law Society of Upper Canada* [2004] SCC 13 (Sup Ct of Can). Note, however, that the court decided that, under the Canadian statute, originality required more than mere labour, and thus a higher test of originality than that laid down in *University of London Press Ltd v University Tutorial Press Ltd* [1916] 2 Ch. 601, (and lower than the test laid down by the US court in *Feist Publications Inc v Rural Telephone Service Co* 199 U.S. 340 (1991)). In this, Canadian law is thus different from UK law.

[90] *British Northrop Ltd v Texteam Blackburn Ltd* [1974] R.P.C. 344.

[91] *Karo Step Trade Mark* [1977] R.P.C. 255; *Gleeson v H.R. Denne Ltd* [1975] R.P.C. 471, at 482 (suggesting that there could be no copyright in simple figures such as squares, circles or crosses); *Duriron Inc v Hugh Jennings Ltd* [1984] F.S.R. 1 (no originality in rough and inaccurate representation of pipe of varying size, not drawn to scale); but see *Solar Thomson Engineering Co Ltd v Barton* [1977] R.P.C. 537 (copyright probably subsisted in drawing of three concentric circles, drawn to precise measurements).

[92] See para. 3–129, below.

[93] *Fournet v Pearson Ltd* (1897) 14 T.L.R. 82.

[94] What of Coleridge's *Kubla Khan*?

[95] See para. 3–13, above.

[96] *University of London Press Ltd v University Tutorial Press Ltd* [1916] 2 Ch. 601 at 610, *per* Peterson J.; *Ladbroke (Football) Ltd v William Hill (Football) Ltd* [1964] 1 W.L.R. 273, (per Lord Reid at 279: "I think that there is much wisdom in the reference by Petersen J. to the "rough practical test that what is worth copying is prima facie worth protecting—in *University of London Press Ltd* ...").

[97] *Ibcos Computers Ltd v Barclays Mercantile Highland Finance Ltd* [1994] F.S.R. 275; *Network Ten Pty Ltd v TCN Channel None Pty. Ltd* [2004] HCA 14; (2004) 59 I.P.R. 1 . See also para. 7–28, below.

banality. Copyright has been denied to simple phrases,[98] titles for books and magazines,[99] and the general arrangement and layout of a diary (*i.e.* the ways in which the days and dates were set out, with spaces for notes).[1] In relation to artistic works, simple divisions of a diary page, although regarded as artistic works, have been denied copyright on this ground.[2] While it has been doubted that copyright could subsist in simple drawings such as squares, circles or crosses,[3] and copyright has been denied to a rough and inaccurate representation of a pipe,[4] and to sketches of designs for a flag,[5] copyright has been held to subsist in a series of circles drawn in a regular array,[6] logos,[7] and held "probably" to subsist in a precise drawing of three concentric circles.[8] Originality may lie in the mere selection of the elements to use in a work, as where the creator is presented with a choice between two different versions or even where a variant has been created by a mistake.[9] Originality can also subsist in the mere selection of colours to be used in an artistic work.[10] Where the author has created a work by following some method, design or formula, it is irrelevant that by the same process another person could produce, or has already produced, an identical work, provided the author has worked out the result for himself. Thus works such as mathematical tables have been protected, even though identical tables have previously been published.[11] Although the idea or information embodied in the tables may not be novel, the result of the author's labour of compilation is a set of tables upon which the author has done original work. Again, for example, a collection of precedents constructed by following the general directions of a statute will be entitled to copyright, although any two persons with a knowledge of the subject would be bound to arrive at a similar result.[12] The same point can be made in re-

---

[98] *Kirk v J. & R. Fleming Ltd* [1928–35] Mac.C.C. 44; *R. Griggs Group Ltd v Evans* [2003] EWHC 2914 (Ch), para.17 ("Dr Martens").

[99] See para. 3–16, above.

[1] *Frank Smythson Ltd v G.A.Cramp & Sons Ltd* [1943] Ch. 133, CA. These aspects of the diary were regarded as a literary work, and was probably a table or compilation. For the decision on the further compilation aspects of the case in the House of Lords, see para. 3–145, below.

[2] *Waylite Diaries CC v First National Bank Ltd* [1993] (2) S.A. 128 (High Ct of S.A.) following the Court of Appeal decision in *Frank Smythson Ltd v G.A.Cramp & Sons Ltd* [1943] Ch. 133 (the diary, devised for bank managers, consisted of (a) lines dividing up pages and (b) months, dates and days, and a three-month calendar); *cf. Artifakts Design Group Ltd v N.P. Rigg Ltd* [1993] 1 N.Z.L.R. 196 (copyright subsisted in original artwork for the covers and other parts of corporate diaries).

[3] *Gleeson v H.R. Denne Ltd* [1975] R.P.C. 471 at 482.

[4] *Duriron Inc v Hugh Jennings Ltd* [1984] F.S.R. 1.

[5] *Commercial Signs v General Motors Products of Canada Ltd* (1937) 2 D.L.R. 310. The design consisted of four stars and were merely enlargements of an original drawing with colouring and lettering added.

[6] *Hi-Tech Autoparts Ltd v Towergate Two Ltd* [2002] F.S.R. 15 at para.17.

[7] See para. 3–56, above, and also *R. Griggs Group Ltd v Evans* [2003] EWHC 2914 (Ch) at para.18 (skill and labour used to draw word or phrase in a stylised way).

[8] *Solar Thomson Engineering Co Ltd v Barton* [1977] R.P.C. 537.

[9] *Guild v Nabavi* [2002] EWCA Civ 316. In that case, the feature had been introduced by an error in the manufacture of a prototype. The decision proceeded on the basis that the "adoption of the mistake may not contribute much by way of labour but it can certainly be the product of skill" (see para.47). Where the feature is merely one of a number of features which go to make up the whole work, such that a judgment is made between different possible versions, the decision seems unobjectionable. Caution needs to taken not to extend the principle too far. See, *e.g. A. Fulton Co Ltd v Grant Barnett & Co Ltd* [2001] R.P.C. 257 at para.42. If a machine makes a substantial change to a work, there may in reality be no human author of what results. As to computer generated works, see para. 3–147.

[10] *Coogi Australia Pty Ltd v Hysport International Pty Ltd* (1998) 157 A.L.R. 247 (Fed Ct of Aus).

[11] *Bailey v Taylor* (1830) 1 Russ. & My. 73 (tables of values of leases and annuities; subsistence of copyright was not, however, in issue).

[12] *Alexander (W.) v Mackenzie (R.)* (1846) 9 Sc.Sess.Cass. (2nd Ser.) 748, at 755 (held, although the work was not one of genius, or novel, it required care and exertion of mind).

lation to works of reference, such as directories or maps, where it is irrelevant that two persons can in theory independenly arrive at the same result.[13]

3–130   **Computer programs.** Computer programs are protected as literary works and as such are subject to the ordinary requirement of originality of the 1988 Act. No amendment was made to the Act on the implementation of the Software Directive, despite the requirement in the Directive that a computer program "shall be protected if it is original in the sense that it is the author's own intellectual creation" and that "no other criteria shall be applied to determine its eligibility for protection."[14] From this it can only be concluded that it was thought that such a requirement was fully consistent with the meaning of "original" in the 1988 Act, as it has come to be interpreted by the courts in relation to works generally. Since aesthetic and merit judgments have never been part of the requirement for copyright protection of these works (excluding works of artistic craftsmanship and works of architecture),[15] and since the requirement of originality has been viewed as meaning no more than that the work must be the product of the author's own skill and labour,[16] it is certainly arguable that this conclusion is correct. The European Commission has noted the fact that the United Kingdom has not expressly implemented this part of the Directive and has observed that it remains to be seen whether this will lead to an over-extensive protection of computer programs in the United Kingdom.[17] To date, no point has been taken in any reported case that a computer program lacks originality.

(iii) Derivative works

3–131   **Mere copy.** Skill, labour and judgment merely in the process of copying cannot confer originality, and a mere copyist cannot have protection for his copy.[18] This is despite the fact that copying, for example of an artistic work, even in the same medium, often requires a higher degree of skill and judgment than the mere reproduction of a literary work. Particularly, therefore, where the copy is in the same medium as the original, there must be more than an exact reproduction or facsimile enlargement or reduction if the copy is to secure copyright[19]; there must be some element of material alteration or embellishment which suffices to make the totality of the work an original work.[20] In this, the quality of the alteration is likely to be more important than the quantity. In the case of a literary work, what is significant is the form of literary expression[21] and, in the case of an artistic work, the visual impact of the alteration or embellishment on the work as a whole is more important than its technical significance.[22] It is originality in relation to

---

[13] As to such works, see paras 3–144 et seq., below.

[14] Software Directive 91/250, Art.1(3).

[15] As to which, see paras 3–62 and 3–67, above. Note that the eighth recital of the Software Directive provides that in respect of the criteria to be applied in determining whether or not a computer program is an original work, no tests as to the qualitative or aesthetic merits of the program are to be applied.

[16] See para. 3–128, above.

[17] See the Commission's report of April 10, 2000 (COM/2000/0199 final) on the implementation and effects of the Software Directive.

[18] per Lord Oliver in Interlego A.G. v Tyco Industries Inc [1989] A.C. 217 at 262H–263A.

[19] The Reject Shop v Manners [1995] F.S.R. 870 (facsimile enlargement).

[20] Interlego A.G. v Tyco Industries Inc [1989] A.C. 217 at 262H–263A.

[21] Gormley v EMI Records Ltd [2000] E.C.D.R. 31 (Sup Ct of Ireland) (child's endeavours to repeat a Bible story resulted in some change of language but did not create an original literary work: the story was told in the same way).

[22] Ornstin Ltd v Quality Plastics noted at [1990] I.P.D. 13027 (Aldous J.)

visually significant matters that is important here.[23] Mere change of scale will therefore not normally be regarded as visually significant.[24] If the original, in the case of an artistic work, is used merely as a model to give the idea of the new work, then the new work may well be entitled to protection, but if the result is simply a slavish copy, it will not be protected. Thus, protection has been denied to precise copies of existing drawings for children's building bricks,[25] tracings made from sections cut from a three-dimensional casting,[26] and an engraving copied from an existing engraving.[27]

Photographs, which in one sense will always be a copy of a scene, and which may more specifically be a copy of an existing artistic work, create their own problems as regards originality, and the principles discussed above are not easily applied to them; they are discussed separately below.[28]

Other use of existing subject-matter. As has been seen, where the author has produced his result without reference to any pre-existing subject-matter, it is immaterial that the result is not novel, or that anyone else could have produced the same result, or that the idea or scheme from which the result has been produced is open to the public. But where the author has made use of existing subject-matter, more difficulty arises, and it has to be determined whether he has expended sufficient independent skill and labour to justify copyright protection for his result.[29] In determining whether the work is original and entitled to copyright, the work must be looked at as a whole and if, notwithstanding that the author has used existing subject-matter, he has expended a degree of independent skill, labour and judgment, he will be entitled to copyright protection for his work as a whole.[30] It is wrong to attempt to isolate parts which are not original and argue that copyright subsists only in the remainder.[31]

3–132

Works in the course of creation. Many works are not created in their final form at one sitting. The status of a work in the course of creation will depend on the degree of skill and labour applied at any particular stage.[32] As soon as sufficient skill and labour have been devoted to it to make it an original work, copyright will subsist in it even though the work may be incomplete and the author intends to do further work on it. Thus even the first section of the first chapter of a literary work may qualify as a copyright work. As sections are added to the work, new copyright works will come into existence provided, in each case, the additions

3–133

---

[23] *Ultra Marketing (UK) Ltd v Universal Components Ltd* [2004] EWHC 468 (Ch) at para.10.
[24] *Drayton Controls (Engineering) Ltd v Honeywell Control Systems Ltd* [1992] F.S.R. 245, *per* Knox J. at 260.
[25] *Interlego A.G. v Tyco Industries Inc* [1989] A.C. 217 at 263 D/E.
[26] *J. & S. Davis (Holding) Ltd v Wright Heath Group Ltd* [1988] R.P.C. 403 at 412.
[27] *Re Martin (T.J.)* (1884) 10 V.L.R. 196.
[28] See para. 3–142, below.
[29] *Cala Homes (South) v Alfred McAlpine Homes East Ltd* [1995] F.S.R. 818; *Martin v Polyplas Manufacturers Ltd* [1969] N.Z.L.R. 1046.
[30] *Ladbroke (Football) Ltd v William Hill (Football) Ltd* [1964] 1 W.L.R. 273; *Redwood Music Ltd v Chappell & Co Ltd* [1982] R.P.C. 109. Examples of cases where this test has been satisfied include: *Macmillan Publishers Ltd v Thomas Reed Publications Ltd* [1993] F.S.R. 455 (sufficient work and skill in producing nautical charts from admiralty charts); *Cala Homes (South) v Alfred McAlpine Homes East Ltd* [1995] F.S.R. 818 (architect expended sufficient effort and skill in producing a new design with a combination of features from preceding designs); *Kilvington Bros Ltd v Goldberg* (1957) 8 D.L.R. (2d) 768 (artistic designs for tombstones original even though containing many features of existing designs: the creator's designs came from his own mind).
[31] *Ladbroke (Football) Ltd v William Hill (Football) Ltd* [1964] 1 W.L.R. 273; *Nouveau Fabrics Ltd v Voyage Decoration Ltd* [2004] EWHC 895 (Ch). Nevertheless, an analysis of what parts of a work were truly original and what parts were derived from existing material may become relevant when it comes to deciding the issue of substantial part for infringement purposes. See para. 7–27 at (j), below.
[32] See also para. 3–06, above.

are the product of sufficient skill and labour. The final work should, however, be regarded as a single copyright work, although technically there will remain in the background a family of underlying works.[33]

3–134   **Successive versions.** A similar point arises where a work goes through successive revisions in the course of its creation and development. Successive revisions to a complete work, as in the case of revisions to an author's manuscript, may of course result in separate copyright works if the revisions are the product of new skill and labour.[34] The important issue is usually the originality of later versions, although copyright continues to subsist in the earlier versions, whatever use is made of the material contained in it.[35] The issue as to the originality of later versions, or whether the claimant has identified the correct work to rely on, used frequently to arise in relation to revisions of engineering drawings.[36] One question is whether it is only the revision, rather than the whole of the revised drawing, which is entitled to the newly created copyright. In *L.B. (Plastics) Ltd v Swish Products Ltd*,[37] it was held that where there has been a previous drawing or a model from which a new drawing is prepared, or some sketches have been made which are in part redrawn, the new drawing will be entitled to copyright as a whole where there has been sufficient relevant skill and labour in producing it. Whether it is so entitled to copyright depends on whether there has been the addition of some element of material alteration or embellishment which suffices to make the totality of the work an original work.[38] This is a matter of fact and degree; even an alteration or addition which is quantitatively small may, if material, suffice to create an original work.[39] However, there is no single test for deciding whether or not a drawing is original by reference to how much skill or labour has been expended on its creation; a distinction must be made between what is visually significant, where skill and labour expended are highly important, and work which is not visually significant, where skill and labour involved is not relevant.[40] Even if such a revised or updated drawing is entitled to copyright, there may be problems in establishing infringement of such a work in that the courts, in considering whether a substantial part has been taken, will disregard the parts which have been taken without alteration from the pre-existing works.[41] Generally, however, a defendant can expect to receive short shrift from the court where he attempts to take points about successive versions of work, for example arguing that the earliest works have not been produced and that the later ones must be unoriginal, being copies of the earlier drawings with only insignificant alterations.[42] The reality, as has been pointed out, is that either the later drawings will as a whole be original or, if not, they are evidence of what earlier, and origi-

---

[33] See *Sweeney v Macmillan Publishers Ltd* [2002] R.P.C. 35 at para.33. See also *A v B* [2001] E.M.L.R. 1006, where it was pointed out that the first entry, and each successive entry in a diary, will be entitled to copyright protection on its own, as well as the diary as a whole, provided each entry was the product of sufficient skill and labour.

[34] *Sweeney v Macmillan Publishers Ltd* [2002] R.P.C. 35, at para.34.

[35] *L.A. Gear Inc v Hi-Tec Sports plc* [1992] F.S.R. 121, CA, followed in *Biotrading & Financing v Biohit* [1998] F.S.R. 109, CA. See also *Ray v Classic FM* [1998] F.S.R. 622; *Macmillan Publishers Ltd v Thomas Reed Publications Ltd* [1992] F.S.R. 455; *Ultra Marketing (UK) Ltd v Universal Components Ltd* [2004] EWHC 468 (Ch) at para.19.

[36] The problem may still arise in relation to design right, which has supplanted copyright in such cases. See Ch.13, below.

[37] [1979] R.P.C. 551.

[38] *Interlego A.G. v Tyco Industries Inc* [1989] A.C. 217 at 263C, *per* Lord Oliver.

[39] See para. 3–131, above.

[40] *Drayton Controls (Engineering) Ltd v Honeywell Control Systems Ltd* [1992] F.S.R. 245, *per* Knox J. at 259, applying *Interlego A.G. v Tyco Industries Inc* [1989] A.C. 217. See also *Biotrading & Financing v Biohit* [1996] F.S.R. 393; [1998] F.S.R. 109, CA.

[41] See *Warwick Film Productions Ltd v Eisinger* [1969] Ch. 508; and see para. 7–27 at (j), below.

[42] *L.A. Gear Inc v Hi-Tec Sports plc* [1992] F.S.R. 121, CA at 136, (followed in *Biotrading &*

nal, drawings looked like. Occasionally, however, the point becomes important, for example because the earlier works are no longer entitled to copyright or because the claimant does not own the copyright in the whole chain of works.[43]

Change of medium or form. It is often said that changing the expression of a work from one medium or form to another will entitle the new work to copyright. As a generalisation, this is true but it is no more than another way of saying that skill and labour expended on the creation of a work confers originality. The work of a reporter in faithfully reporting a speech delivered orally is an example of the expenditure of skill and labour in connection with a change of medium which has been held to entitle a work to protection.[44] An example of a change of form is the work of a translator, which has long been entitled to protection.[45]

3–135

In relation to artistic works, a change of medium will often entitle a reproduction of an existing artistic work to independent protection. Thus it has been said that a drawing of a three-dimensional object would qualify as an original work.[46] A further example is an engraving, which is often a copy, but the engraver's work will usually be original in the sense that he has employed skill and judgment in its production,[47] even where the engraving is a close copy of an existing work such as a painting or drawing. An engraver of the classical kind uses means which are very different from those of the painter or draughtsman whose work he copies, producing his effect by the management of light and shade (the "chiaroscuro"), using different lines and dots,[48] which usually requires a high degree of skill and labour.[49] Even in the case of an engraving of a mundane kind,[50] there will usually be skill and labour involved,[51] but copyright has been denied to an engraving which was merely a copy of another engraving.[52] As noted earlier,[53] it seems that the meaning of "engraving" is wide enough to include prints and other forms of work made from an engraved plate or stamp, these forms of work therefore being capable of attracting copyright as engravings in their own right. In a number of cases in which this point has been made, consideration does not, however, appear to have been given to the question of originality in relation to

---

Financing v Biohit [1998] F.S.R. 109, CA), where the point that each successive drawing was entitled to copyright was described as "so obvious that it needs no authority to support it", even though each drawing might have contained only a minor variation or been just a copy. See *per* Nourse L.J. at 136.

[43] *Biotrading & Financing v Biohit* [1996] F.S.R. 393 at 395; *Ultra Marketing (UK) Ltd v Universal Components Ltd* [2004] EWHC 468 (Ch) (where the claimant did not own the copyright in the later drawings).

[44] See *Walter v Lane* [1900] A.C. 539.

[45] *Byrne v Statist Co* [1914] 1 K.B. 622; *Wyatt v Barnard* (1814) 3 V. & B. 77 (translation of patent specification). Translations are required to be protected under Art.2(3) of the Berne Convention. For a general discussion of the position of the translator, see *Vaver* in [1994] E.I.P.R. 159.

[46] *L.B. (Plastics) Ltd v Swish Products Ltd* [1979] R.P.C. 551 at 568–569, *per* Whitford J.; this seems to have been accepted as correct in *Interlego A.G. v Tyco Industries Inc* [1989] A.C. 217.

[47] Engravings were the first works in the field of artistic copyright to receive statutory protection, by the Engraving Copyright Act 1734. See para. 2–20, above. Despite the wording of the earlier Acts, which referred to something that was invented and designed, it was never necessary that an engraving be of a totally new subject to qualify for protection, so that engravings of things taken from nature, or of buildings, were always protected: *Blackwell v Harper* (1740) 2 Atk. 92.

[48] *Newton v Cowie* (1827) 4 Bing. 234 at 246.

[49] *Martin v Polyplas Manufacturers Ltd* [1969] N.Z.L.R. 1046 (copyright in three-dimensional engravings of two-dimensional designs for coins, requiring "great delicacy and intense application").

[50] As to what constitutes an engraving, see para. 3–55, above.

[51] As in *Hi-Tech Autoparts Ltd v Towergate Two Ltd* [2002] F.S.R. 15, where an engraver had copied a plan drawing of a series of circles in a regular array to produce a three-dimensional plate having grooved circles with conical and vertical sides. The skill and labour resided in designing the grooves and in combining the grooved circles with the final layout of the circles. See para.32.

[52] *Re Martin* (1884) 10 V.L.R. 196.

[53] See para. 3–55.

the print.[54] In most cases, particularly where the prints are made by some kind of industrial process, it seems doubtful that any print could be an original work. The question will turn on what skill and labour, rather than mechanical acumen, is involved in realising that which is visually different between the plate and the print.

3–136 **New version of existing work.** In the case of a new edition of an existing work, the issue will be whether any original work has been done by the editor.[55] Such work may consist of additions to, or alterations of, the text which, if they are not merely trivial, but are material so as to make the totality of the work original, will be protected in the same way as any original literary work, whether they form a substantial part of the complete work or not.[56] Alternatively, such work may consist of a new arrangement of the existing subject matter. It follows, therefore, that where a work not out of copyright is edited, there may be two copyrights, that in the original text and that in the new edition. Exploitation of the new edition will require the consent of the owners of the copyright in both works. In the same way, there will often be originality in a new or revised version of an existing dramatic work,[57] provided more than just a few words are added.[58] Where a claimant reconstructed an ancient text from a large number of incomplete fragments (the Dead Sea Scrolls) by using his knowledge of linguistics and religious law to interpolate missing sections, the result was an original work, even though the intention was to recreate, as nearly as possible, the ancient text.[59]

3–137 **New arrangement or adaptation of music.** Any substantially new arrangement or adaptation of an existing piece of music is entitled to copyright.[60] What matters in relation to a musical work is its sound as appreciated by the human ear[61] and thus, in the present context, what is important is the contribution made to the sound by the arranger or adapter. If A makes a piano score of the music of B's opera,[62] or if he writes an arrangement of an existing melody,[63] A has, in each case, produced an original musical work. The work does not have to be inventive,

---

[54] See, *e.g. Hi-Tech Autoparts Ltd v Towergate Two Ltd (No.1)* [2002] F.S.R. 15; *Hi-Tech Autoparts Ltd v Towergate Two Ltd (No.2)* [2002] F.S.R. 16; *James Arnold & Co Ltd v Miafern Ltd* [1980] R.P.C. 397; and *Wham-O Manufacturing Co v Lincoln Industries Ltd* [1985] R.P.C. 127.

[55] The distinction drawn in the cases on this topic before 1911 is not now relevant. Under the Literary Copyright Act 1842, no action could be brought in respect of infringement of copyright in a book unless the book was duly registered at Stationers' Hall. Consequently, if a new edition was registered, and the date of publication entered as the date of its publication of the new edition, the question was whether the new edition, regarded as a whole, was a new book or not. If it was, the registration was correct, and an action for infringement of the book could be brought; if it was not, and the new edition was merely the old book with slight variations, then the registration was invalid. See *Thomas v Turner* (1886) 33 Ch.D. 292; *Black (A. & C.) Ltd v Murray (A.) & Son* (1870) 9 Sc. Sess. Cas. (3rd Ser.) 341; *Hedderwick v Griffin* (1841) 3 Dunl. (Ct of Sess.) 383.

[56] *Interlego A.G. v Tyco Industries Inc* [1990] A.C. 217, PC, *per* Lord Oliver at 263C, and see *Black v Murray* (1870) 9 Ct. Sess. (3rd series) (new edition of works of Walter Scott, with notes); *Jogesh Chandra Chaudhuri v Mohim Chandra Rai* [1914] C.W.N. 1078. The position is much the same as in relation to an author's successive revisions to his manuscript. See para. 3–134, above.

[57] *Hatton v Keane* (1859) 7 C.B. 268 (new version of one of Shakespeare's plays, with certain alterations in the text, original music, scenic effects, and other accessories); *Tree v Bowkett* (1896) 74 L.T. 77 (play altered by addition of two scenes, and so altered as to make it the plaintiff's; *Christoffer v Poseidon Film Distributors Ltd* [2000] E.C.D.R. 487 (Homer's *Odyssey* subjected to considerable reworking).

[58] *Tree v Bowkett* (1896) 74 L.T. 77; *Ashmore v Douglas-Home* [1987] F.S.R. 553 (no sufficient additions).

[59] *Eisenman v Qimron* [2001] E.C.D.R. 73 (Sup Ct of Israel). It follows, perhaps curiously, that if the reconstruction ultimately produces a work which is identical to the original work, the reconstruction will be a new copyright work. See also para. 3–137, below as to musical works.

[60] *Redwood Music Ltd v Chappell & Co Ltd* [1982] R.P.C. 109.

[61] See para. 3–46, above.

[62] *Wood v Boosey* (1867) L.R. 3 Q.B. 223, affirming (1866) L.R. 2 Q.B. 340, where it was held, under the pre- 1911 Act law, that the test was whether the arrangement was a new and substantive work in itself. In *Redwood Music Ltd v Chappell & Co Ltd* [1982] R.P.C. 109, at 116, it was

in the sense of creating music which did not exist before.[64] Painstaking work in restoring a score to what the composer probably intended, and correcting errors and filling in omissions may therefore qualify as original work, provided the resulting sound is different from existing versions of the musical work which the restorer worked on.[65] There is therefore no reason why technical skill alone should not in appropriate circumstances be sufficient and, for example, in relation to an arrangement, no great skill or labour is required for the purpose of conferring copyright.[66] It is not clear whether the work of transcribing a piece of music into notation is original. Even though the transcriber may not have created new sounds, the work would seem to be original on the basis of *Walter v Lane*.[67]

Abridgments, précis and abstracts. These are all examples of the same process, by which a larger work is reduced to a shorter summary.[68] Copyright will subsist in such works if they required skill and labour in their creation. However, the reduction of the size of a work merely by copying some of its parts and omitting others without the application of any skill or labour in the selection of what to retain and what to reject generally confers no copyright.[69]   **3–138**

Headnotes and case summaries. The digest of a law report in the form of a headnote or a case summary is a species of abridgment. Whether viewed as a separate brief report or as an independent deduction from the report, in principle there is clearly sufficient exertion of skill and labour to render a headnote or case summary the subject of copyright. It is something for which much skill and thought is often required, so as to express in clear and concise language the principle of law to be deduced from the decision, or the facts and circumstances which bring the case within some principle or rule of law or of practice:[70] "The authors must select specific elements of the decision and can arrange them in numerous different ways. Making these decisions requires the exercise of skill and judgment. The authors must use their knowledge about the law and developed ability to determine legal *ratios* to produce the headnotes. They must also use their capacity for discernment to decide which parts of the judgment warrant inclusion in the headnotes. This process is more than just a mechanical exercise."[71]   **3–139**

---

held that this test was consistent with the originality requirement of the 1911 Act. It is suggested, however, that although an arrangement which is a new and substantive work in itself will clearly be original, this is not the determining test. See also *Boosey v Fairlie* (1877) 7 Ch.D. 301.

[63] *Austin v Columbia Gramophone Co Ltd* [1917–23] Mac. C.C. 398; *Lover v Davidson* (1856) 1 C.B. (N.S.) 182; *Leader v Purday* (1848) 7 C.B. 4.

[64] *Sawkins v Hyperion Records Ltd* [2004] EWHC 1530 (Ch) at para.65.

[65] *Sawkins v Hyperion Records Ltd* [2004] EWHC 1530 (Ch). See also para. 3–136, above and the case of *Eisenman v Gimron* [2001] E.C.D.R. 73 (Sup Ct of Israel) referred to there.

[66] *Redwood Music Ltd v Chappell & Co Ltd* [1982] R.P.C. 109; *Godfrey v Lees* [1995] E.M.L.R. 307.

[67] [1900] A.C. 539. This was doubted by Cross J. in *Roberton v Lewis* [1976] R.P.C. 169, but the observation seems to have been based partly on an arguably wrong view of *Walter v Lane*.

[68] Note that the 1988 Act, in the defence provided under s.60 in relation to the copying of abstracts of articles on scientific or technical subjects, recognises that an abstract of an article can be entitled to its own copyright. It used to be important to know what constituted a true abridgment since a true abridgment, being a new and useful work, was often not regarded as an infringement. See *Gyles v Wilcox* (1740) 2 Atk. 141; *Ganga'vishnu Shrikisanda's v Moreshuar Ba'Puj Hegishte* [1889] I.L.R. 13 Bom. 358; *Macmillan & Co Ltd v Cooper (K. & J.)* (1923) 40 T.L.R. 186, citing earlier editions of this work. The same is not true today. See para. 7–28 at (e), below.

[69] As in *Macmillan & Co Ltd v Cooper (K. & J.)* (1923) 40 T.L.R. 186. See also the discussion of this case in relation to compilations at para. 3–145, below.

[70] *Sweet v Benning* (1855) 16 C.B. 459 at 491; *Ragunthan v All India Reporter Ltd* [1971] 4 A.I.R. Bom. 48.

[71] *CCH Canadian Ltd v Law Society of Upper Canada* [2004] SCC 13 (Sup Ct of Can). For this purpose, the headnote was taken to include the summary of the case, catchlines, statement of the

3–140 **Indexes.** An index will often be a work of separate creation from the main work. As such, the decision as to what to include will usually require the exercise of skill and judgment. The creator must choose the headings and then both decide what to include under those headings and how to describe the items included by a short summary.[72]

3–141 **Works infringing other works.** Copyright can, as a matter of principle, subsist in an infringing work.[73] Whether it does so or not will depend on whether the pirated work has involved the expenditure by its author of time, skill and labour, and it is suggested that this is so whether the entire work consists of pirated material, or merely part of it, provided that its originator has expended time, skill and labour on the material pirated. A particular example of such a pirated work is an unauthorised translation of a copyright work, where the translator may have expended considerable time, skill and labour in producing the translation, entitling the translation to its own copyright.[74] Such works may give rise to particular problems when it is alleged that this copyright has itself been infringed; the result may depend on whether what has been copied was the subject of edited or unedited copying.[75]

(iv) Photographs and films as dramatic works

3–142 **Photographs present their own problems in relation to originality.**[76] The essence of a photograph is that it should capture something for the purpose of its being reproduced for subsequent viewing. In one sense a photocopy is always, therefore, a copy of something. Photography is a process which is a mixture between a mechanical process and a creative process. The balance between these two elements may vary enormously in any given case, yet the product is in each case a photograph. In the United Kingdom, copyright law has never distinguished between a photograph which is the result of a purely mechanical process, that is the operation of the shutter caused by the button being depressed, and that which is the result of the expenditure of much time and skill by the photographer in obtaining the right conditions for the photograph that he wishes to achieve.[77] Although Article 6 of the Term Directive[78] required Member States to protect photographs which are original "in the sense that they are the author's own intellectual creation", Member States were permitted to protect "other" photographs. The United Kingdom did not amend the 1988 Act in this respect when implementing the Directive, or introduce a lesser category of photographs, and so the law as to what amounts to an original photograph was not altered.

---

case, case title and case information. Case summaries were similarly regarded as original, since a "summary of judicial reasons is not simply a copy of the original reasons. Even if the summary often contains the same language as the judicial reasons, the act of choosing which portions to extract and how to arrange them in the summary requires an exercise of skill and judgment".

[72] *CCH Canadian Ltd v Law Society of Upper Canada* [2004] SCC 13 (Sup Ct of Can) (index of legal cases); *Blacklock (H.) & Co Ltd v Arthur Pearson (C.) Ltd* [1915] 2 Ch. 376 at 384 (index to a new edition of a railway timetable).

[73] See the discussion at para. 3–263, below.

[74] It will of course remain dependent on the copyright in the work infringed in the sense that the exploitation of the translation will require the licence of the owner of the copyright in the original; see para. 3–263, below.

[75] See, for example, *Warwick Film Productions Ltd v Eisinger* [1969] Ch. 508; *ZYX Music GmbH v King* [1995] 3 All E.R. 1 (on appeal, but not on this point: [1997] 2 All E.R. 129, CA).

[76] Particularly in the context of infringement, when it has to be determined what aspects of a photograph are protected by the copyright which subsists in it. As to what is protected by the copyright in a photograph, see *Bauman v Fussell* [1978] R.P.C. 485 (decided in 1953) and para. 7–60, below. For a full discussion of the topic, see Michalos, *The Law of Photography and Digital Images* (Sweet & Maxwell, London, 2004).

[77] For a discussion as to the differing approaches of other Union Countries, to the protection of photographs, see Ricketson, *The Berne Convention for the Protection of Literary and Artistic Works: 1886–1996* (Kluwer, 1987), para.6.33.

[78] Council Directive 93/98 harmonising the term of protection of copyright and related rights.

In terms of what is original for the purpose of determining whether copyright subsists in a photograph, the requirement of originality is again low. So, photographs of various antiques were held to be original where they were taken with a view to exhibit particular qualities of the objects, including their colours, features (for example, glaze in pottery) and other details.[79] It was assumed for these purposes that some degree of skill was involved in the lighting, angling and judgment of the positions and the selection of the objects.[80] In fact, it seems that the test of originality may be satisfied by little more than the opportunistic pointing of the camera and the pressing of the shutter button[81] and there seems no reason of principle why there should be any distinction between the photograph which is the result of such a process and a photograph which is intended to reproduce a work of art, such as a painting or another photograph.[82] Provided that the author can demonstrate that he expended some small degree of time, skill and labour in producing the photograph (which may be demonstrated by the exercise of judgment as to such matters as the angle from which to take the photograph, the lighting, the correct film speed, what filter to use, etc.), the photograph ought to be entitled to copyright protection, irrespective of its subject matter.[83] Nevertheless, it has been decided by a court in the United States that, as a matter of English law, such a photograph is not original.[84] Since there was no element of "material alteration or embellishment" from the original work (see the words of Lord Oliver in *Interlego AG v Tyco Industries Inc*[85]), it was held that the photographs were effectively no different from photocopies.[86] Admittedly, in *Interlego* Lord Oliver said: "Take the simplest case of artistic copyright, a painting or a photograph. It takes great skill, judgment and labour to produce a good copy by painting or to produce an enlarged photograph from a positive print, but no one would reasonably contend that the copy painting or enlargement was an 'original' artistic work in which the copier is entitled to claim copyright. Skill, labour or judgment merely in the process of copying cannot confer originality." Lord Oliver was not, however, concerned in *Interlego* with photographs or this particular issue, and no argument was addressed to the Privy Council on the point. In any event, his *obiter* remarks about photographs were directed at the making of an enlargement from a positive, not the taking of a photograph itself. It is also suggested that the analogy of a photocopier made in the *Bridgeman* decision is a poor one, given the disparity of the skill and labour involved.[87]

Film or broadcast as a dramatic work. It has already been seen that a film or   **3–143**

---

[79] *Antiquesportfolio.com v Rodney Fitch & Co Ltd* [2001] F.S.R. 23.

[80] *Antiquesportfolio.com v Rodney Fitch & Co Ltd* [2001] F.S.R. 345.

[81] *Antiquesportfolio.com v Rodney Fitch & Co Ltd* [2001] F.S.R. 345, approving a paragraph in the previous edition of this work containing this statement.

[82] See *Graves' Case* (1869) 4 L.R.Q.B. 715, in which copyright was held to subsist under the Fine Arts Copyright Act 1862 in photographs of engravings, themselves made from paintings. See also *Hansard*, HL Vol.493, col.1073. "The question whether one photograph is a copy of another of the same subject matter will have to be decided by the usual test—is it original? Has it involved skill and effort on the part of the photographer?".

[83] cf. *The Reject Shop v Manners* [1995] F.S.R. 870, where copyright was held not to subsist in an enlarged photocopy.

[84] *The Bridgeman Art Library Ltd v Corel Corp*, 25 F. Supp. 2d 421 (S.D.N.Y.) 1998 and 36 F. Supp. 2d 191.

[85] [1989] A.C. 217.

[86] i.e. applying *The Reject Shop plc v Manners* [1995] F.S.R. 870, on this point. *Graves' Case* (1869) L.R. 4 Q.B. 715, was distinguished on the grounds of its antiquity and the "subsequent development" of the law of originality, presumably a reference to *Interlego*.

[87] See further on the point: Garnett, "Copyright in Photographs" [2000] E.I.P.R. 229; Deazley, "Photographing Paintings in the Public Domain: A Response to Garnett" [2001] E.I.P.R. 179; Stokes, "Graves' case revisited in the USA—The Bridgeman Art Library v. The Corel Corporation" [2000] Ent. L.R. 104; Stokes, letter, [2001] E.I.P.R. 354; Michalos, *The Law of Photography and Digital Images* (Sweet & Maxwell, London, 2004).

broadcast, if it is a work of action, will also be a dramatic work.[88] From the point of originality, such works are similar in some respects to photographs. Taking a film as an example, where the action in the film has been produced or enhanced by the process of editing, no particular problem arises. Where, however, the action takes place in front of the lens, presumably the resulting film will only be original if the filmmaker has added something of dramatic significance, for example by way of camera angle, lighting or editing.

(vi) Compilations, tables and databases

3–144   **Compilations, tables and databases.** The labour and skill employed in gathering, selecting or arranging existing subject-matter has traditionally resulted in copyright protection being given to the resulting work. Such protection was originally conferred either by way of a table or a compilation[89] but with effect from January 1, 1998 there are now two categories of work to be considered, namely (a) databases and (b) tables and compilations which are not databases: for works made on or after March 27, 1996 the test of originality differs in relation to each category.[90] In particular, although the Database Regulations[91] apply to databases created before as well as after January 1, 1998,[92] where a database was created before March 27, 1996[93] and copyright subsisted in it immediately before January 1, 1998, copyright will continue to subsist in the database for the remainder of its copyright term.[94] It follows that the "old" originality test is to be applied in relation to all compilations and tables made before March 27, 1996 and to tables and compilations made after this date if they are not also databases. The "new" originality test must be applied to all compilations and tables made after this date which are also databases (as well as any other work which is a database). The "old" test will be discussed first.

3–145   **The "old" originality requirement.** The relevant skill and labour may be directed to the compiling of the contents, their selection from a larger number of items, or to their arrangement.[95] Originality in this context will depend upon the degree of skill, labour and judgment involved in preparing the compilation.[96] In particular, since the nature of a compilation or table is that it supplies intelligible information[97], it is skill and labour directed to this object which is relevant. As to selection, there are only a few cases in which the labour of selection was regarded as so negligible that copyright protection was refused. For example, copyright was denied to the selection of various common tables for insertion into a pocket

---

[88] See para. 3–37, above, and *Norowzian v Arks Ltd (No.2)* [2000] F.S.R. 363.

[89] CDPA 1988, s.3(1)(a); Copyright Act 1911, s.35; Copyright Act 1956, s.48(1).

[90] This is the effect of the amendments introduced by the Copyright and Rights in Databases Regulations 1997 (SI 1997/3032), implementing the Database Directive 96/9. See para. 3–21, above, for a discussion of these categories.

[91] See the previous footnote.

[92] reg.27. Member States were required to implement the Database Directive by this date: Art.16(1).

[93] The date of the Directive was March 11, 1996.

[94] reg.29(1).

[95] Although Art.2(5) of the Berne Convention stipulates that protection is to be conferred on collections of literary or artistic works such as encyclopedias and anthologies which, by reason of the selection and arrangement of their contents, constitute intellectual creations, it does not follow that only such compilations are to be protected, since the Convention imposes minimum standards only.

[96] *Interlego A.G. v Tyco Industries Inc* [1989] A.C. 217 at 262, referring to *Macmillan & Co Ltd v Cooper* 40 T.L.R. 186; *G.A. Cramp & Son Ltd v Frank Smythson Ltd* [1944] A.C. 329; and the speeches of Lord Reid and Lord Hodson in *Ladbroke (Football) Ltd v William Hill (Football) Ltd* [1964] 1 W.L.R. 273 at 277, 285, 287.

[97] *Real Estate Institute of N.S.W. v Wood* (1923) 23 S.R. (N.S.W.) 349. See para. 3–26, above.

diary,[98] a local railway timetable relating to a particular town compiled from a larger timetable,[99] a selection of passages from North's translation of Plutarch's life made simply by omitting certain passages,[1] a list of greyhounds written down in the order in which they were drawn from a hat[2] and to the linking together of three computer programs.[3] By contrast, protection has been given under this head to a wide variety of works and originality has seldom been in issue, the argument usually being about infringement. Thus, compilations of works of literature, such as selections of poems or prose compositions have been protected as original works,[4] as have selections of incidents from real life[5] and selections of quotations from an interview.[6] Equally, trade directories,[7] telephone directories,[8] maps,[9] trade catalogues,[10] lists of horses,[11] race cards,[12] soccer fixture lists,[13] listings of

---

[98] *G.A. Cramp & Sons Ltd v Frank Smythson Ltd* [1944] A.C. 329 (the claimants claimed original- ity in a choice of seven tables for the diary: (a) a calendar for the year, (b) a selection of "days and dates" for the year, (c) postal rates, (d) equivalents of metric and imperial weights and measures, (e) lighting-up times, (f) an empire and foreign timetable (*i.e.* the equivalent time to noon at Greenwich), and (g) a percentage table. The compiler was dead and no evidence was called as to the process of selection.)

[99] *Leslie v J. Young & Sons* [1894] A.C. 335, HL (although the timetable was "convenient and use- ful for the inhabitants of that town, ... it does not require either such labour or such ingenuity in its preparation as to render it fit subject-matter for copyright". See the comment of Lord Macmil- lan on the case in *G.A. Cramp & Sons Ltd v Frank Smythson Ltd* [1944] A.C. 329 at 337. A compilation of circular journeys from the town was, however, held to be original).

[1] *Macmillan & Co Ltd v K. & J. Cooper* (1924) 40 T.L.R. 186 (North's translation contained about 40,000 words, of which about 20,000 words were selected. On the other hand, various notes to the selected text were protected, though of a commonplace nature and at least in part themselves selected from older sources.)

[2] *Greyhound Racing Association Ltd v Shallis* [1923–28] Mac. C.C. 370.

[3] *Total Information Processing Systems Ltd v Daman Ltd* [1992] F.S.R. Note, however, that in *Ib- cos Computers Ltd v Barclays Mercantile Highland Finance Ltd* [1994] F.S.R. 275 at 290, Jacob J. considered that the general proposition that copyright cannot subsist in a compilation of com- puter programs was wrong.

[4] *Macmillan & Co v Suresh Chunder Deb* (1890) 17 Indian L.R. (Calcutta) 951 (PC) (Palgrave's *Golden Treasury*).

[5] See *Harman Pictures N.V. v Osborne* [1967] 1 W.L.R. 723 (choice of incidents from the Charge of the Light Brigade); *Poznanski v London Film Production Ltd* [1936–45] Mac. C.C. 107 (book about Catherine the Great); *MacGregor v Powell* [1936–45] Mac. C.C. 233 (compilation about the evacuation of St Kilda in 1930, although the headnote appears to go further than the report); and *Ravenscroft v Herbert & Anor* [1980] R.P.C. 193. In none of these cases, however, was originality of the work in issue.

[6] *Express Newspapers plc v News (UK) Ltd* [1990] F.S.R. 359 at 360 (sufficient skill and judgment in selection of quotations from an interview lasting over eight and a half hours).

[7] e.g. *Kelly v Morris* (1886) L.R. 1 Eq. 697; *Morris v Ashbee* (1868) L.R. 7 Eq 34. For further examples of directory cases, see other footnotes to this paragraph and para. 7–44, below.

[8] *Desktop Marketing Systems Ltd v Telstra Corp Ltd* 55 I.P.R. (2002) 1.

[9] *Macmillan Publishers Ltd v Thomas Reed Publications Ltd* [1992] F.S.R. 455 (sufficient work in selection of information such as depth soundings, geographical features, buoys etc. in producing nautical charts).

[10] *Hotten v Arthur* (1863) 1 H. & M. 603 (list of rare books, manuscripts, etc. relating to an estate, with anecdotes, comments and descriptions); *Grace v Newman* (1875) L.R. 19 Eq. 623 (compila- tion of sketches of tombstones); *Maple & Co v Junior Army and Navy Stores* (1882) 21 Ch.D. 369 (overruling *Cobbett v Woodward* (1872) L.R. 14 Eq. 407, to the contrary); *Harpers Ltd v Barry, Henry & Co Ltd* (1892) 20 Sess. Cas. (4th Ser.) 133; *Collis v Cater Ltd* (1898) 78 L.T. 613, *Lamb v Evans* [1893] 1 Ch. 218 (list of advertisements). Illustrations in trade catalogues may be individually protected as artistic works, although text and illustrations together may be protected as a compilation; see para. 3–24, above.

[11] *Weatherby & Sons v International Horse Agency and Exchange Ltd* [1910] 2 Ch. 297.

[12] *Bookmakers' Afternoon Greyhound Services Ltd v Wilfred Gilbert (Staffordshire) Ltd* [1994] F.S.R. 723, following *Demerara Turf Club v Phang* [1963] W.I.R. 177 (Sup Ct of British Guy- ana); *Ascot Jockey Club Ltd v Simons* [1968] 64 W.W.R. 411 (Sup Ct of Can); *British Columbia Jockey Club v Standen (Winibar Publications)* [1984] 4 W.W.R. 537 (Sup Ct of Brit. Columbia), distinguishing *Greyhound Racing Association Ltd v Shallis* [1923–28] Mac. C.C. 370, noted earlier in this paragraph, where the list was compiled merely by drawing the names from a hat.

[13] *Ladbroke (Football) Ltd v William Hill (Football) Ltd* [1964] 1 W.L.R. 273.

programmes to be broadcast,[14] bridge tallies[15] and other mundane material[16] can be the subject-matter of copyright as original compilations. It is, of course, always open to question whether the component parts of a catalogue are original or merely taken from a common source, but a catalogue is generally a compilation upon which the compiler will have exercised skill and judgment in its creation. As to the gathering of information into a table or compilation, it has never been the position under English law that compilations compiled merely using "sweat of the brow" and not involving skill and judgment in the selection of their constitutent parts were not protected as original works.[17] This can be seen, for example, from *Collis v Cater*[18] where it was held that copyright subsisted in a "dry" list of ordinary medicines sold by a chemist, arranged in alpabetical order, which had required labour, or expense and trouble, but no literary skill, in its compilation. The same is true of the directory cases,[19] where originality may lie in the humdrum though painstaking accumulation of information. Another example is *Football League Ltd v Littlewood Pools Ltd*,[20] where copyright was held to subsist in a chronological list of football matches taken from a larger list, painstaking hard work and attention to accuracy being all that was required in its creation.[21]

It is sometimes argued that a distinction should be made between the skill and labour required for the compiling of information and the skill and labour required for the presentation of it, only the latter being relevant for the purposes of the originality requirement and copyright protection. Thus, with regard to the creation of a Football League fixture list, which required skill to arrange the dates on which the teams should play each other, it was argued that the working out of the dates had been done for the purposes of the League's activities and not for the compilation of its fixture list.[22] Again, in the case of the creation of football pool coupons, it was argued that while skill and labour might have been involved in working out which bets to offer, there was no sufficient skill and labour in writing out the bets.[23] The argument is usually founded on a statement of Lord Evershed's in *Purefoy Engineering Company Ltd v Sykes, Boxall & Co Ltd*.[24] There, the claimants made standard parts to be used by customers in the manufacture of jigs, and the defendants copied these jigs, as they were entitled to do. The claimants also made a catalogue of their parts, and it was argued that the defendants had copied the catalogue indirectly, by copying the claimants' parts. In the course of rejecting the argument, Lord Evershed said: "… the contents of the catalogue described the parts made and offered by the plaintiffs. And the considerable skill

---

[14] *British Broadcasting Co v Wireless League Gazette Publishing Co* [1926] 1 Ch. 433; 42 T.L.R. 370; *Independent Television Productions Ltd v Time Out Ltd* [1984] F.S.R. 64.

[15] *Stevenson (A.) v Crook (H.F.)* [1938] Ex. (Can.) 299 (tables of combinations of the players worked out so as to avoid repetition of partners, much skill and labour being involved in their creation; originality *was* in issue).

[16] *e.g. Skybase Nominees Pty Ltd v Fortuity Ltd* (1996) 36 I.P.R. 529 (Fed Ct of Aus) (compilation of weight loss programmes, requiring great skill and judgment, and expense); *Olympic Amusements Pty Ltd v Milwell Pty Ltd* (1998) 162 A.L.R. 199 (scales of prizes to be awarded by gaming machines to standard poker hands, whose working out was a complex and highly skilled affair).

[17] In this the law of the UK differs from that of the US, as laid down in such decisions as *Feist Publications Inc v Rival Telephone Service Co* 499 U.S. Ct. 340 (1991).

[18] (1898) 78 L.T. 613, approved in *Purefoy Engineering Co Ltd v Sykes Boxall & Co Ltd* (1955) 72 R.P.C. 89, CA at 99 and *Ladbroke (Football) Ltd v William Hill (Football) Ltd* [1964] 1 W.L.R. 273.

[19] See the cases cited earlier in this paragraph. For a very full and modern discussion of the prinicples in such cases, see *Desktop Marketing Systems Ltd v Telstra Corp Ltd* 55 I.P.R. (2002) 1 (Fed Ct of Aus).

[20] [1959] Ch. 637.

[21] [1959] Ch. 637 at 656.

[22] *Football League Ltd v Littlewoods Pools Ltd* [1959] Ch. 637 at 653ff.

[23] *Ladbroke (Football) Ltd v William Hill (Football) Ltd* [1964] 1 W.L.R. 273 at 278.

[24] (1955) 72 R.P.C. 89. The issue in the case was not, however, subsistence of copyright but whether the defendants had copied. See paras 7–31 and 7–34, below.

and labour devoted by the plaintiffs in making their selection was devoted to the selection of the range of goods in which the plaintiffs were to trade and not for the purpose of bringing into existence the literary work, namely, the catalogue. No doubt skill and labour were employed for the latter purpose, but skill and labour of a different order. The selected range of goods existed or was capable of existing for trading purposes independently altogether of the plaintiffs' catalogue or of any catalogue." Although such a defence is theoretically possible,[25] arguments of this kind have invariably failed, the reasons given being that the purpose of accumulating the information has in fact been to reduce it to a written or otherwise protectable form[26] and that a line cannot be drawn between the effort involved in developing ideas and that minimal effort required in setting those ideas down on paper.[27]

The "new" originality requirement for databases. As already noted, as far as copyright protection is concerned, databases are now excluded from the category of a table or compilation, and are to be treated as a separate type of literary work.[28] For most practical purposes, this change will only be relevant for databases created after March 27, 1996.[29] A database is the only work to be singled out in the 1988 Act to have its own definition of originality. Echoing the wording of Article 3(1) of the Database Directive, section 3A(2) of the 1988 Act now provides that a database is original if, and only if, by reason of the selection or arrangement of the contents of the database, the database constitutes the author's own intellectual creation.[30] As has already been pointed out, when a similar definition of originality was required to be applied to computer programs by the Software Directive, no alteration of the 1988 Act in this respect was made, presumably on the basis this requirement of the Directive was already satisfied in relation to United Kingdom law. The fact that an amendment has been made in relation to databases suggests that United Kingdom law would not have complied with the terms of the Database Directive. In particular, it would appear that the law may not have been compliant to the extent that United Kingdom copyright was conferred on compilations or tables which were the product only of "sweat of the brow" and not the product of skill or labour in the selection or arrangment of the contents. Thus, the definition of originality here would seem to require that the author's time, skill and labour be directed to the selection and arrangement of the database, and not the mere gathering of information.[31] To this extent the law has been altered.[32] Apart from this, it is suggested that the law has not been changed, since the United Kingdom law of originality already required, except in mere "sweat of the brow" cases, that the creation of a compilation, table or database be the result

3–146

[25] *Ladbroke (Football) Ltd v William Hill (Football) Ltd* [1964] 1 W.L.R. 273, *per* Lord Hodson at 287: "It may well be that there are cases in which expenditure of time and money has been laid out which cannot properly be taken into account as skill and labour involved in bringing into existence the literary work, be it catalogue or other compilation."
[26] *Football League Ltd v Littlewoods Pools Ltd* [1959] Ch. 637 at 655, followed in *Ladbroke (Football) Ltd v William Hill (Football) Ltd* [1964] 1 W.L.R. 273.
[27] *Ladbroke (Football) Ltd v William Hill (Football) Ltd* [1964] 1 W.L.R. 273, *per* Lord Hodson at 287. A further example is *Autocaps (Aust.) Pty Ltd v Pro-Kit Pty Ltd* (1999) 46 I.P.R. 339 (Fed Ct of Aus), where the compilation consisted of a list of replacement radiator and fuel tank caps, with an indication of which vehicles they were suitable for. It was held that preparatory work in determining which cap suited a particular vehicle was relevant for the purposes of originality.
[28] See paras 3–21 *et seq.*, above.
[29] In theory it may also affect databases created on or before this date but which were not then in copyright. See reg.29(1) of the Database Regulations.
[30] The use of the words "if, and only if" reflect the additional requirement in Art.3(1) of the Database Directive 96/9 that "no other criterial shall be applied to determine their eligibility for that protection." The wording of the Directive is also found in Art.5 of the 1996 WIPO Copyright Treaty, dealing with compilations of data or other material.
[31] In contrast to being the subject of database right; see Ch.18.
[32] See also the discussion at para. 18–03, below.

of the author's own intellectual creation, even if the standard of intellectual creation was a low one. Whether a database qualifies for copyright protection therefore depends on how the database was made, that is to say, whether sufficient relevant effort was put into its creation. Although there is no requirement to demonstrate aesthetic or qualitative criteria, there must be a quantitative baseline of originality before protection is acquired.[33]

(vii) Computer generated works

3–147   The 1988 Act contemplates that there may be literary, dramatic, musical or artistic works that are generated by computer in circumstances that there is no human author of the work in the ordinary sense. Where this is the case, the author is to be taken as the person by whom the arrangements necessary for the creation of the work are undertaken,[34] and this can clearly be a company as well as a human being. It is not clear how the requirement of originality is to be applied in these circumstances, in particular the requirement that the work be the product of at least some skill and labour. The difficulty will often be overcome by a readiness to find a human author, even in a process which is highly computer assisted,[35] but in principle there will always remain a class of works in respect of which this is not possible. It is suggested that the relevant skill and labour is that of the person by whom the arrangements necessary for the creation of the work were undertaken.

B. SOUND RECORDINGS AND FILMS

3–148   **Sound recordings and films: copies of previous sound recordings or films.** Originality, as such, is not a requirement for the subsistence of copyright in sound recordings or films,[36] and the 1988 Act only provides that copyright does not subsist in a sound recording or film which is, or to the extent that it is, a copy taken from a previous sound recording or film.[37] This applies whether such copy was authorised or not. Under the 1956 Act there was no requirement of originality and no equivalent provision.

C. BROADCASTS

3–149   **Broadcasts.** There is no originality requirement as such in relation to broadcasts. The 1988 Act merely provides that copyright does not subsist in a broadcast which infringes, or to the extent that it infringes, the copyright in another broadcast.[38] The 1988 Act therefore adopts a different approach in relation to broadcasts than it does in relation to sound recordings and films.[39] Although a broadcast which is an authorised repeat of an earlier broadcast is thus entitled to its own copyright,[40] it is provided that such copyright expires at the same time as

---

[33] See *British Horseracing Board Ltd v William Hill Organisation Ltd* [2001] R.P.C. 31.

[34] CDPA 1988, s.9(3).

[35] See, *e.g. Express Newspapers plc v Liverpool Daily Post & Echo plc* [1985] F.S.R. 306.

[36] An amendment to the original Bill seeking to introduce the requirement of originality as regards sound recordings, films, broadcasts and cable programmes and typographical arrangements of published editions was opposed, on the basis that lack of originality in content for such works was irrelevant, and all that was required was to exclude copyright to the extent that the work was taken from an existing work: *Hansard*, HL Vol.493, cols 1057.

[37] CDPA 1988, ss.5A(2), 5B(4). See *Hansard*, HL Vol.493, cols 1073, 1074 as to how these provisions came to be worded as they are.

[38] CDPA 1988, s.6(6).

[39] The reason for the different wording is explained in *Hansard*, HL SCE, col.50.

[40] The rationale of this provision is that a repeat broadcast is not made from a recording of the first

that in the original broadcast.[41] It would seem that where the broadcast repeats an earlier broadcast but contains new material, the entirety of the subsequent broadcast will be protected as such for its own full term of copyright.[42]

Cable programmes. With effect from October 31, 2003, cable programmes are no longer protected as a separate subject matter,[43] and the rights in relation to such works have since that date been subsumed within the enlarged category of a "broadcast". The amendments to the 1988 Act which have brought this about apply to works, and thus cable programmes, which were made before October 31, 2003,[44] and so the above provisions relating to "broadcasts" must be applied to those works which were formerly regarded as cable programmes and which are now protected as broadcasts.

3–150

D. Typographical arrangements

Copies of previous typographical arrangements. Under section 8(2) of the 1988 Act, copyright does not subsist in the typographical arrangement of a published edition if, or to the extent that, it reproduces the typographical arrangement of a previous edition.[45] Reproduction is not now a defined term under the 1988 Act,[46] and, strictly, the reference should have been to copying, not reproducing, since copying is defined, in relation to typographical arrangements, as the making of a facsimile copy of the arrangement.[47] In the context, this is clearly what was intended, and no doubt "reproduces" in section 8(2) will be so construed.

3–151

5. QUALIFYING CONDITIONS

A. Introduction

Qualification for copyright protection. The 1988 Act, after enumerating the descriptions of works in which copyright may subsist,[48] provides, in relation to all such works, that copyright does not subsist in such works unless the requirements set out in Chapter IX of the Act with respect to qualification for copyright protection are met.[49] Chapter IX contains a common set of provisions for the subsistence of copyright in published and unpublished works of all descriptions,[50] with special provision being made in the case of broadcasts.[51] These provisions apply to works coming into existence on or after August 1, 1989. Works which already existed at that date, and which are referred to in this section of this work

3–152

---

broadcast. It will be made from a recording made at the same time as or even before the first broadcast. For copyright protection to be adequate, therefore, each repeat must be given its own copyright, albeit for an abbreviated time. See *Hansard*, HL Vol.490, col.1163.

[41] CDPA 1988, s.14(5) and (6).

[42] This would appear to follow from general principles, and s.14(5) of the 1988 Act does not use the phrase "or to the extent that it is a repeat".

[43] See paras 8–82 *et seq.*, above.

[44] The Copyright and Related Rights Regulations 2003 (SI 2003/2498), reg.31(1).

[45] CDPA 1988, s.8(2); re-enacting Copyright Act 1956, s.15(1), proviso.

[46] As it was under the 1956 Act (s.48(1)).

[47] CDPA 1988, s.17(5); facsimile is defined as including a copy which is reduced or enlarged in scale (s.178).

[48] CDPA 1988, s.1(1); see paras 3–02 *et seq.*, above.

[49] CDPA 1988, ss.1(3) and 153(1). The scheme of the 1956 Act was different, in that qualifying conditions were set out in the sections dealing with each category of works: Copyright Act 1956, ss.2(1) and (2), 3(2) and (3), 12(1) and (2), 13(1) and (2), 14(1) and 15(1).

[50] CDPA 1988, ss.154 and 155; see para. 3–153, below.

[51] CDPA 1988, s.156; see para.3–182, below.

as existing works,[52] are subject to a different regime and, as a general rule, copyright under the 1988 Act subsists in such a work only if copyright subsisted in it immediately before August 1, 1989, that is, under the 1956 Act.[53] It is therefore necessary to deal separately with works coming into existence on or after August 1, 1989[54] and those in existence at that date.[55]

B. WORKS COMING INTO EXISTENCE ON OR AFTER AUGUST 1, 1989

(i) Introduction

3–153   **Two bases of qualification.** For all descriptions of works coming into existence on or after August 1, 1989,[56] the 1988 Act provides two bases on which copyright protection may be obtained. The first basis is by reference to the status of the author, irrespective of whether the work has been published or not.[57] The requirements, broadly, relate to the nationality, citizenship or residence of the author. The second basis, which applies to works which have been published, is by reference to the country in which the work was first published being met.[58] The requirements, broadly, are that the country should be one to which the provisions of the 1988 Act extend,[59] or have been applied in recognition of that country's protection of works of United Kingdom origin. In the case of broadcasts, the 1988 Act maintains this dual basis of qualification, but replaces the concept of publication (which, as it involves the issue of copies of the work to the public, has no application to such works) with that of the making of a broadcast, and the second basis for qualification for such works is by reason of the requirements being met as to the country from which the broadcast is made (*i.e.* transmitted).[60]

3–154   **Origin of two bases.** The two bases reflect the fact that in the early days of the development of copyright protection there were two parallel systems of protection: that accorded under statute, and that accorded under the common law. So far as early statutory protection was concerned, this was aimed exclusively at works which were published,[61] and, before the advent of international conventions to protect copyright works of other countries, it was natural that only those works which were published in the United Kingdom should be protected. Unpublished works continued to be protected by common law copyright,[62] where what mattered was whether the individual was subject to the common law, which was so in the case of an individual who was a subject of the Crown or who lived in England under the protection of the common law. This distinction between published and unpublished works also found expression in the Berne Conven-

---

[52] CDPA 1988, Sch.1, para.1(3). This term, however, can have different meanings in different statutory contexts; see para. 6–12, below.

[53] Sch.1, para.5. This general rule is subject to the important exception that an existing work may first gain protection under the 1988 Act by virtue of first publication in a relevant country or by the inclusion, for the first time, of the country of its author's nationality in an Order made under s.159 of the Act: Sch.1, para.5(2)(a) and (b); see further para. 3–189, below.

[54] Section B, paras 3–153 *et seq.*, below.

[55] Section C, paras 3–183 *et seq.*, above.

[56] Except in respect of works the copyright in which belongs to the Crown to which special provisions apply: see Ch.10.

[57] CDPA 1988, s.154; and see paras 3–158 *et seq.*, below.

[58] s.155; and see paras 3–172 *et seq.*, below.

[59] See para. 3–157, below.

[60] s.153(1)(c) and 156; and see para. 3–182, below.

[61] This continued to be so until the 1911 Act, with the exception of the Fine Arts Copyright Act 1862 (25 & 26 Vict., c.68), which applied to paintings, drawings and photographs, whether published or unpublished, whose author was a British subject or resident in the British Dominions.

[62] Such protection was lost on publication: *Donaldson v Beckett* (1774) 4 Burr. 2408; *Beckford v Hood* (1798) 7 T.R. 620; *Jefferys (C.) v Boosey (T.)* (1855) 4 H.L.C. 815.

tion, which required protection to be extended to works of authors who were nationals of a country of the Union, if unpublished or if first published in a country of the Union.[63] This was the position adopted in the United Kingdom under the 1911 Act, which abolished common law copyright and provided that copyright should subsist under that Act in the case of published works only if first published in the United Kingdom or a country to which the Act extended, and in the case of unpublished works only if the author was at the date of the making of the work a British subject or resident within a country to which the Act extended.[64]

Time at which qualification requirements must be met. The qualification requirements themselves all relate to a situation at a specific time (generally when the work was made or first published, as the case may be), from which it would follow that, if those requirements are met at the required time, later events (for example, the author ceasing to be a qualifying person or the country of first publication ceasing to be one to which the 1988 Act extends) are irrelevant to the continued subsistence of copyright. That this is the case in relation to works made on or after August 1, 1989, is made clear, in that the 1988 Act specifically provides that it is sufficient for copyright to subsist in a work if the qualification requirements of Chapter IX[65] are once satisfied in respect of that work, and that copyright does not cease to subsist in that work by reason of any subsequent event.[66]

3–155

Alternative nature of the two bases: published works. Under the 1988 Act, the two bases are entirely independent of each other. In the case of unpublished works, the only possible basis for qualification remains by reference to the status of the author. In the case of published works, the two bases are now true alternatives, in that all that is necessary for copyright to subsist in a published work is that the requirements relating to one basis should be satisfied. Although, for the reasons discussed above, publication has been historically the more important basis, as regards most types of work coming into existence after August 1, 1989, the application of the provisions of the 1988 Act to an increasing number of countries[67] and the loosening of the link required between an individual and such a country means that it is much more probable that inquiry as to the status of the author will prove the easier basis on which to establish subsistence of copyright under the 1988 Act. This is therefore the basis which is discussed first below.

3–156

Extension and application of the provisions of the 1988 Act. Before setting out the different bases on which copyright protection may be obtained under the 1988 Act, it is necessary to explain briefly the difference between the extension and the application of the provisions of the Act to other countries.[68] Extension is used to describe the situation where the provisions of the Act apply in a country because they are the law of that country. Under the 1911 Act and, to a lesser extent, under the 1956 Act, the provisions of those Acts were extended to a

3–157

---

[63] Berne Convention, Art.4(1).
[64] Copyright Act 1911, s.1(1).
[65] The reference to the requirements of CDPA 1988, Ch.IX means that this principle does not apply in the case of works made before August 1, 1989, which are not governed by Ch.IX, but by the rules in force under the 1956 Act (see *ibid.*, Sch.1, para.5).
[66] CDPA 1988, s.153(3). This was not so under the 1956 Act, since a work entitled to copyright by reason of the nationality of its author would subsequently have lost protection by first publication in a country to which the 1956 Act was not extended or applied; see *Copex Establishment v Flegon, The Times*, August 18, 1967, and *Bodley Head v Flegon* [1972] R.P.C. 587.
[67] See para. 3–157, below.
[68] These matters are discussed more fully in Section 6, Foreign Works, paras 3–190 *et seq.*, below.

number of colonies and dependent territories,[69] but Part I of the 1988 Act extends only to England and Wales, Scotland and Northern Ireland.[70] Application is used to describe the situation where the provisions of the Act are made applicable to a country to which they do not extend, so that works which are first published in that country or are made by authors who, in the case of individuals, are citizens or subjects of, or are domiciled or resident in, such country, or, in the case of companies, are incorporated under the laws of that country, will be treated in the same way as works first published in the United Kingdom or made by a qualifying person.[71]

(ii) By reference to the status of the author

3–158   **Two bases on which status of author may qualify work for protection.** There are two different routes by which the status of the author may qualify the work for protection under the 1988 Act. Both depend on the nature of the link which the author has with a particular country. The first is by reason of the author being a qualifying person, where the link is with the United Kingdom;[72] the second is by reason of the link the author has with a country to which the provisions of the 1988 Act have been applied by Order in Council made under section 159 of the Act.[73] In each case the link required may be broadly summarised as nationality of, or domicile or residence in, that country, or, in the case of a legal person, incorporation under the laws of that country.

3–159   **Qualifying person.** A work[74] qualifies for copyright protection if its author was at the material time a qualifying person.[75] In the case of an individual, this means a person who enjoys what may be described for brevity as an extended form of British nationality, or who is domiciled or resident in the United Kingdom or in a country to which the relevant provisions of the Act extend.[76] In the case of a body corporate, this means a body incorporated under the laws of the United Kingdom or of another country to which the relevant provisions of the Act extend.[77]

3–160   **British nationality.** The extended form of British nationality comprises the terms British citizen, British overseas territories citizen, British national (Overseas), British overseas citizen, British subject and British protected person as these are defined in the British Nationality Act 1981.[78]

---

[69] See paras 3–230 et seq., below.

[70] CDPA 1988, s.157(1). Although there is power to extend Pt I to the Channel Islands, the Isle of Man or any colony (s.157(2)) by Order in Council, no such Order has been made; for the current position in the Channel Islands, the Isle of Man and Hong Kong, see further paras 3–255—3–258, below.

[71] By an Order in Council made under CDPA 1988, s.159. As to Orders made under this section, and the countries to which Pt I has been applied, see paras 3–219 et seq., below.

[72] CDPA 1988, s.154(1); the subsection refers to a country to which Pt I extends, but this effectively means England and Wales, Scotland and Northern Ireland.

[73] CDPA 1988, s.154(2); see para. 3–157, above.

[74] These provisions apply to all descriptions of works; broadcasts could not qualify for protection under the 1956 Act by reason of their author being a qualified person; see further para. 3–74, above.

[75] The term used in the 1956 Act was "qualified person" (see Copyright Act 1956, ss.2(1), 3(2), 12(1) and 13(1)), but the concept remains the same (see Copyright Act 1956, s.1(5)).

[76] CDPA 1988, s.154(1). This effectively means England and Wales, Scotland and Northern Ireland, see para. 3–182, below.

[77] CDPA 1988, s.154(1). This effectively means England and Wales, Scotland and Northern Ireland, see para. 3–158, above. The 1956 Act adopted the same test for corporate bodies being qualified persons, but the 1911 Act had referred to such bodies "having an established place of business". This remains the test in relation to certain existing works: see para. 3–157, above.

[78] 1981 (c.61) (as amended); the Act came into force on January 1, 1983 and repeals the definitions

British citizen. This status is principally acquired through birth in the United **3–161** Kingdom to a parent who is a British citizen or who is settled, that is ordinarily resident, in the United Kingdom; other methods of acquisition include by descent, that is birth outside the United Kingdom to a person who is a British citizen, by adoption, by naturalisation or, in appropriate circumstances, by registration.[79]

British overseas territories citizen. This status is conferred on citizens of a **3–162** number of specified countries.[80]

British National (Overseas). This means a person who is so defined under the **3–163** Hong Kong (British Nationality) Order 1986.[81]

British Overseas citizenship. This is a residual category for citizens of the **3–164** United Kingdom and Colonies who do not acquire, under the 1981 Act, British citizenship or British Dependent Territories citizenship.[82]

British subject. A British subject under the 1981 Act[83] is a person who im- **3–165** mediately before that Act came into force was a British subject without citizenship or was a British subject by virtue of being a former citizen of Eire, under the British Nationality Act 1948,[84] or was a British subject by registration under the British Nationality Act 1965.[85]

British protected person. This means a person declared to be such by an Order **3–166** in Council made in relation to any territory which was a former protectorate, protected state or United Kingdom trust territory within the meaning of those terms under the British Nationality Act 1948[86] and who is *not* a citizen of certain specified territories mentioned in Schedule 3 to the British Nationality Act 1981.[87]

---

of British subject and Commonwealth citizen formerly contained in the Interpretation Act 1978 (c.30), Sch.1.
[79] British Nationality Act 1981, ss.1–14 and see the British Nationality (Hong Kong) Act 1990 (c.34), the British Nationality (Hong Kong) Act 1997 and the Hong Kong (War Wives & Widows) Act 1996 (c.41).
[80] British Overseas Territories Act 2002, (c.8), s.1(1); British Nationality Act 1981, ss.16–25 (ss.19–21 repealed by the Nationality, Immigration and Asylums Act 2002, ss.15, 161, Sch.2, para.1(d) and Sch.9). The countries are those specified in Sch.6, namely: Anguilla, Bermuda, British Antarctic Territory, British Indian Ocean Territory, Cayman Islands, Falkland Islands and Dependencies, Gibraltar, Hong Kong (since removed with effect from July 1, 1997, by the Hong Kong (British Nationality) Order 1986 (SI 1986/948) as amended by the Hong Kong (British Nationality) (Amendment) Order 1993 (SI 1993/1795)), Montserrat, Pitcairn, Henderson, Ducie and Oeno Islands, St Christopher and Nevis (since removed by the Saint Christopher & Nevis Modification of Enactments Order 1983 (SI 1983/882)), St Helena and Dependencies, South Georgia and South Sanwich Islands (inserted by British Nationality Act 1981 (Amendment of Schedule 6) Order 2001 (SI 2001/3497), art.2(b)), Sovereign Base Areas of Akrotiri and Dhekelia, Turks and Caicos Islands and Virgin Islands.
[81] SI 1986/948 as amended by the Hong Kong (British Nationality) (Amendment) Order 1993 (SI 1993/1795) and the British Overseas Territories Act 2002.
[82] British Nationality Act 1981, ss.26–29; as to the status of citizenship of the United Kingdom and Colonies, see the British Nationality Act 1948 (11 & 12 Geo. 6, c.56) now almost entirely repealed by the British Nationality Act 1981.
[83] British Nationality Act 1981, ss.30–35.
[84] British Nationality Act 1948, ss.2, 13 and 16, now repealed by the British Nationality Act 1981.
[85] 1965 (c.34), repealed by the British Nationality Act 1981.
[86] British Nationality Act 1948, ss.30 and 32, now repealed (save as to s.32(3)) by the British Nationality Act 1981.
[87] British Nationality Act 1981, s.38; the territories mentioned are: Antigua and Barbuda, Australia, The Bahamas, Bangladesh, Barbados, Belize, Botswana, Brunei (inserted by the British Nationality (Brunei) Order 1983 (SI 1983/1699), Cameroon (inserted by the British Nationality (Cameroon and Mozambique) Order 1998 (SI 1998/3161), art.2), Canada, Republic of Cyprus, Dominica, Fiji, The Gambia, Ghana, Grenada, Guyana, India, Jamaica, Kenya, Kiribati, Lesotho, Malawi, Malaysia, Maldives (inserted by the Brunei & Maldives Act 1985, s.1, Sch., para.8),

3–167   **Domicile.** No attempt is made, in the 1988 Act, to define domicile, the meaning of which is therefore left to the general law to determine.[88] Domicile may be obtained either by birth, operation of law,[89] or by choice. Domicile of origin prevails in the absence of a domicile of choice, that is, if a domicile of choice has never been acquired or, if once acquired, has been abandoned. Further, a domicile of choice is acquired when a person fixes voluntarily his sole or chief residence in a particular place with an intention of continuing to reside there for an unlimited time.[90] A domicile of choice may be abandoned when, after departure from a country, a person no longer has an intention to return there.[91]

3–168   **Residence.** As with the concept of domicile, the 1988 Act does not attempt to define residence, and the meaning of residence in the 1988 Act is therefore left to the general law.[92] Where there is nothing to show that the term residence is used in a more extensive sense, it denotes the place where an individual eats, drinks and sleeps, or where his family or his servants eat, drink and sleep.[93] It seems clear that it implies something more permanent than a visit, but the degree of permanence is hard to define.[94] It is suggested that it will be sufficient to show that the author, at the time the work was made, was living at a place within the country in question as his home.[95]

3–169   **Foreign works.** An author who is a citizen or subject of, or domiciled or resident in, or, in the case of a corporate body, is incorporated under the law of a foreign country to which Part I of the 1988 Act has been applied by an Order under section 159, is not by such fact brought within the definition of a qualifying person (although he may be a qualifying person if he otherwise satisfies the requirements of that definition). The works of such authors qualify independently for copyright protection by virtue of the author being, at the material time, a citizen or subject of, or domiciled or resident in or, in the case of a corporate body, incorporated under the law of such country.[96]

Malta, Mauritius, Mozambique (inserted by the British Nationality (Cameroon and Mozambique) Order 1998 (SI 1998/3161), art.2), Namibia (inserted by the Namibia (British Nationality) Order 1990 (SI 1990/1502), Nauru, New Zealand, Nigeria, Pakistan (inserted by the Pakistan (British Nationality) Order 1989 (SI 1989/1331), Papua New Guinea, Saint Lucia, Saint Vincent and the Grenadines, Saint Christopher & Nevis (inserted by the Saint Christopher & Nevis Modification of Enactments Order 1983 (SI 1983/882), Seychelles, Sierra Leone, Singapore, Solomon Islands, South Africa (inserted by the British Nationality (South Africa) Order 1994 (SI 1994/1634), Sri Lanka, Swaziland, Tanzania, Tonga, Trinidad and Tobago, Tuvalu, Uganda, Vanuatu, Western Samoa, Zambia, Zimbabwe. Under the British Nationality Act 1981, s.37, citizens of these territories are Commonwealth citizens and will not, as from the commencement of that Act, by the fact of their citizenship of that country be British subjects (as they were under s.1(3) of the British Nationality Act 1948).

[88] Other statutory definitions for particular purposes (see for example, Civil Jurisdiction and Judgments Act 1982 (c.27), ss.41–46, defining domicile for the purposes of that Act) may not therefore be of much assistance. For a fuller discussion of domicile, see Dicey & Morris, *Conflict of Laws* (13th ed., Sweet & Maxwell, London, 2000), Ch.6, sections 1 and 3.

[89] See Domicile and Matrimonial Proceedings Act 1973 (c.45).

[90] *In the Estate of Fuld, decd. (No.3)* [1968] P. 675; *Plummer v I.R.C.* [1988] 1 W.L.R. 292.

[91] See *Buswell v I.R.C.* [1974] 1 W.L.R. 1631; *Re Flynn* [1968] 1 W.L.R. 103; and *I.R.C. v Bullock* [1976] 1 W.L.R. 1178.

[92] For a fuller discussion of residence, see Dicey & Morris, *Conflict of Laws* (13th ed., Sweet & Maxwell, London, 2000), Ch.6, section 3.

[93] *R. v The Overseers of Norwood* (1866) L.R. 2 Q.B. 457; *Sinclair v Sinclair* [1968] P. 189; *R. v Barnet L.B.C. Ex p. Shah* [1983] 2 A.C. 309, HL.

[94] See *MacRae v MacRae* [1949] P. 397 and *Stransky v Stransky* [1954] P. 428.

[95] For cases on residence decided under the Income Taxes Acts, see: *Lloyd (T.) v S.I.R.* (1883) 11 Sess. Cas. (4th Ser.) 687; *Levene v C.I.R.* [1928] A.C. 217; *C.I.R. v Lysaght* [1928] A.C. 234; and *Reed v Clark* [1986] Ch. 1; and see *Cicutti v Suffolk* [1981] 1 W.L.R. 558 (a case under the Education Act) and *R. v Sec. State Ex p. Margueritte* [1983] 1 Q.B. 180 (a case under the British Nationality Act).

[96] Under CDPA 1988, s.154(2); whether a person is a citizen or subject of, or domiciled in, a

Material time. The material time for the purposes of satisfying the test as to the **3–170** author of a literary, dramatic, musical or artistic work being a qualifying person is, in the case of an unpublished work, when the work was made, or if the making of the work extended over a period, a substantial part of that period,[97] and, in the case of a published work, when the work was first published, or, if the author had died before first publication, immediately before his death.[98] A literary, dramatic or musical work is made when it is recorded in writing or otherwise;[99] there is no equivalent definition as to when an artistic work is made.[1] In the case of an artistic work which is completed, there would seem to be no difficulty in treating it as being made, for these purposes, when the making of the work is completed.[2] However, there seems no reason why a work which the artist leaves unfinished (for whatever reason) should be denied copyright protection,[3] and such a work should be treated as made for these purposes when the artist abandons finishing the work or when he dies. The material time for the purposes of satisfying the test as to the author of sound recordings, films and broadcasts being a qualifying person is also when they were made.[4] In the case of films and sound recordings, as with artistic works, there is no definition of when such works are made,[5] nor is there any specific provision, such as in the case of literary, dramatic, musical and artistic works,[6] to deal with the situation (which is likely to be the case for most films) where the making extends over a period of time. It is suggested, again, that such works should be treated as made for these purposes when their making is complete.[7] In the case of a wireless broadcast, the definition as to the place where it is made, contained in section 6(4) of the 1988 Act, also effectively defines the moment when it is made, which is when the programme-carrying signals are introduced into an uninterrupted chain of communication.[8] In relation to cable broadcasts, the broadcast is no doubt made when the signals are introduced into the cable network leading to the recipient. In relation to typographical arrangements of a published edition, the work is made when the edition was first published.[9]

---

foreign country will depend on the application of that country's law, these being matters of a person's status under that law; it is suggested that residence is a factual concept, and will be judged by what the term means in English law, as to which see para. 3–168, above.

[97] CDPA 1988, s.154(4)(a). As to who is the author of such works, see *ibid.*, s.9(1) and paras 4–10 *et seq.*, below.

[98] s.154(4)(b).

[99] s.3(2), re-enacting s.49(4) of the 1956 Act; writing includes any form of notation or code, whether by hand or otherwise: CDPA 1988, s.178. Making is not therefore the same as the first creation of the work, *e.g.* music may be composed, and even performed, before it is "made" for the purposes of the 1988 Act; see paras 3–152 and 3–182, above.

[1] Nor was there under the 1956 Act. In *Mak Hau-Shing v Oriental Press Group Ltd* [1996] 1 H.K.L.R. 245 it was held that copyright subsisted in a photograph as soon as the shutter had opened and closed.

[2] Compare the general provision in relation to works in existence at August 1, 1989 that when the making extended over a period the work shall be taken to have been made when its making was completed: CDPA 1988, Sch.1 para.1(3).

[3] See paras 3–06 and 3–133, above.

[4] CDPA 1988, s.154(5)(a) and (b). As to who is the author of such works, see *ibid.*, s.9(2) and paras 4–48 *et seq.* and 4–56 *et seq.*, below.

[5] *cf.* Copyright Act 1956, s.12(8), which provided that a sound recording was made when the first record embodying the recording was produced.

[6] See earlier in this paragraph.

[7] Compare the general provision in relation to works in existence at August 1, 1989 that when the making extended over a period the work shall be taken to have been made when its making was completed: CDPA 1988, Sch.1 para.1(3).

[8] Which, in the case of a satellite broadcast, includes the uplink. As to who is the author of such works, see CDPA 1988, s.9(2) and paras 4–73 *et seq.*, below.

[9] CDPA 1988, s.154(5)(d). As to who is the author of such works, see *ibid.*, s.9(2) and paras 4–77 *et seq.*, below.

3–171   **Works of joint authorship.** Where the work is a work of joint authorship,[10] the work qualifies for copyright protection if at the material time any of the authors satisfies the above requirements, but only those authors who satisfy such requirements are taken into account when determining ownership and duration of the copyright so subsisting.[11]

(iii) By reference to the place of first publication

(a) *Publication in general*

3–172   **Publication: generally.** As stated above, a literary, dramatic, musical or artistic work, typographical arrangement of a published edition, a sound recording or a film qualifies for copyright protection if it is first published in the United Kingdom, or in another country to which the relevant provisions of the 1988 Act have been applied.[12] Publication, in relation to all works in which copyright may subsist under the 1988 Act, means the issue of copies of the work to the public.[13] It follows that a work cannot be orally published.[14] The reference to copies in the plural is deliberate, and there can be no publication of a work of which there exists only a single example.[15] Indeed, the issue of copies must be such that it is intended to satisfy the reasonable requirements of the public and not be merely colourable, or else it does not constitute publication.[16] It is suggested that this remains the position, notwithstanding the amendment[17] of the expression "issue of copies", in the context of the restricted act of issue of copies to the public, but expressed to apply to references to the expression in Part I, to include reference to the issue of the original.[18] The term "copy"' must be construed in accordance with the provisions contained in section 17 of the 1988 Act defining copying and copies.[19] For the issue of copies to constitute publication, it must have been done by or with the licence of the copyright owner.[20]

3–173   **First publication: simultaneous publication.** Publication for these purposes means first publication of the work. The 1988 Act provides that publication in one country shall not be regarded as other than the first publication by reason of simultaneous publication elsewhere, and for this purpose publication elsewhere within the previous 30 days shall be treated as simultaneous.[21] What is frequently in copyright law described as simultaneous publication therefore means any two or more publications which take place within a period of 30 days. Under the 1911

---

[10] As to which see Ch.4, below.
[11] CDPA 1988, s.154(3); and also for the purpose of determining whether the work is anonymous or pseudonymous under s.57.
[12] CDPA 1988, s.155(1) and (2). See para. 3–157, above and para. 3–219, below.
[13] CDPA 1988, s.175(1).
[14] Thus delivery of a lecture from notes does not constitute publication of the notes: see para. 3–178, below. Public performance of a dramatic work had been held to be publication of the work, prior to the 1911 Act changing the law in this respect: see para. 3–178, below.
[15] Save, now, in the case of a work of architecture: CDPA 1988, s.175(3); see para. 3–178, below. A writer of a private letter does not publish the letter by sending it to his correspondent, although by sending it to a newspaper for publication he would be licensing its publication by the newspaper. Compare the amendment of the restricted act of issuing copies of the work to the public (CDPA 1988, s.18(1)).
[16] CDPA 1988, s.175(5), re-enacting s.49(2)(b) of the 1956 Act; see further, para. 3–176, below.
[17] By the Copyright and Related Rights Regulations 1996 (SI 1996/2967) with effect from December 1, 1996.
[18] CDPA 1988, s.18(4).
[19] s.17(1); see further para. 3–179, below.
[20] ss.175(6) and 178.
[21] CDPA 1988, s.155(3). As did the Copyright Act 1956: s.49(2)(d).

Act, the relevant provision provided a period of 14 days only.[22] This period continued to apply under the 1956 Act,[23] in the case of a publication taking place before June 1, 1957, and, by virtue of the transitional provisions in the 1988 Act,[24] this period still remains applicable in relation to existing works published before such date.[25]

Copies of the work. Publication involves the issue of copies of the work to the public. "Copies" must be construed in accordance with section 17 of the 1988 Act.[26] Section 17 provides specific rules as to what are to be treated as copies in the case of various different categories of works. Whilst these rules are expressed in the context of the acts restricted by copyright, they are clearly equally applicable to the question of what are copies for the purposes of publication under section 175 of the Act. The question remains, however, as to how exact the copies of the work issued to the public must be in order to constitute publication of that work. In this respect, the general provision that the doing of a restricted act in relation to a work is to be taken to include the doing of that act in relation to a substantial part of the work,[27] has no application. If the "substantial part" test does not apply, do the copies have to be copies of the entirety of the work in order for their issue to constitute publication of the work? It is suggested that minor variations between the copies and the original will not prevent issue of the copies being publication of the original and that the test should be whether the whole work has in substance been made available to the public. If what has been made available is something different in material respects from the original work, then the latter work has not been made available to the public and so has not been published. At most, what has been published is the work in the form of the copies.[28]

3–174

When copies of a work are issued to the public. In order for a work to be published, not only must the copies of the work be made, but they must be issued to the public.[29] Issue for the purposes of sale is not essential,[30] although, if copies are issued for such a purpose, that would amount to publication.[31] A presentation of copies on the part of the author to individuals, or to a limited class,[32] or even the sending of advance copies to the press for review, would not, it is thought, be publication, but gratuitous circulation generally would seem to be so.[33] Thus, in *Prince Albert v Strange*,[34] Queen Victoria and Prince Albert had given to their close friends lithographic copies of drawings and etchings which they had made for their own amusement, but this was held not to amount to publication of the

3–175

---

[22] Copyright Act 1911, s.35(3).

[23] Copyright Act 1956, Sch.7, para.33(1).

[24] CDPA 1988, Sch.1, para.5(1) and para.35.

[25] See further as to existing works, paras 3–183 *et seq.*, below.

[26] CDPA 1988, s.17(1).

[27] CDPA 1988, s.16(3).

[28] See, *e.g. Sweeney v Macmillan Publishers Ltd* [2002] RPC. 35 at para.42, confirming that for this purpose publication means publication of the whole work, not just a substantial part of it. If what is published is the latest in a series of revisions to a work, then what is published is the text set out in that latest, published version and not the text of the previous versions, which will remain unpublished.

[29] See, as to sufficiency of evidence of publication, *Warner Bros Inc v The Roadrunner Ltd* [1988] F.S.R. 292.

[30] See *British Northrop Ltd v Texteam Blackburn Ltd* [1974] R.P.C. 344.

[31] *White v Geroch* (1819) 2 B. & Ald. 298; *Blanchett v Ingram* (1887) 3 T.L.R. 687.

[32] For example, the issue of copies of the Oscar statuette to Acadamy Award winners was held not to be publication: *Oscar Trade Mark* [1980] F.S.R. 429.

[33] *Novello v Sudlow* (1852) 12 C.B. 177; subject to the requirement that the issue of copies must be intended to satisfy the reasonable requirements of the public and not be merely colourable, as to which see para. 3–176, below.

[34] (1849) 1 M. & G. 25.

works. In *Infabrics Ltd v Jaytex Shirt Co Ltd*,[35] the Court of Appeal thought that an offer or exposure for sale would not be publication but that any consequent sale which resulted in the issue of reproductions of the work to the public would constitute publication. However, it is suggested that if such offer or exposure for sale is sufficient to show that there was an intention to satisfy the demands of the public, should such demand arise, then that will be treated as publication.[36]

3–176 **Colourable publication.** For the issue of copies of the work to the public to constitute publication it must be intended to satisfy the reasonable requirements of the public and not be merely colourable.[37] The question as to what is a merely colourable publication arose in *Francis, Day & Hunter v Feldman & Co*,[38] in which the claimants claimed to be the owners of the copyright in a song. On May 5, 1913 they sent one copy to the British Museum and filed one copy at their London office. They also sent four copies to the agent for receiving copies for the university libraries. They exposed six copies for sale on the counter in the retail department of their business premises in London. They did not advertise the song, and there was no immediate demand for it, but subsequently it became a great success and was the subject of large sales. It was held that the publication in England, on May 5, 1913, was not "colourable only", and that it was sufficient to show that there was an intention to satisfy the demands of the public if such demand should arise.[39]

On the other hand, where the nature of the publication deliberately disregards the requirements of the public, it will not amount to publication.[40]

3–177 **Place of publication.** In cases where the place of first publication is material, it would appear that it is the place where copies are first put on offer to the public.[41] In the Canadian case of *Grossman v Canada Cycle Co*[42] the posting in Canada of copies of a newspaper to subscribers in the United Kingdom was held not to amount to publication in the United Kingdom. However, since the persons receiving the newspapers in the United Kingdom were subscribers, and had therefore requested to be supplied with the newspapers, it is difficult to see why this would not constitute publication in the United Kingdom, subject to the quantity of copies being sufficient in accordance with the cases discussed above, particularly if the subscriptions had been obtained by reason of advertisement in the United Kingdom of the availability of the newspaper by subscription.

---

[35] [1980] Ch. 282, *per* Buckley L.J. at 292 (expressing the same view as to a sale by private treaty); reversed on appeal as to the meaning of publication for the purposes of infringement: [1982] A.C. 1, HL.

[36] See *British Northrop Ltd v Texteam Blackburn Ltd* [1974] R.P.C. 344 and see *Francis Day & Hunter v Feldman & Co* [1914] 2 Ch. 728 discussed at para. 3–176, below.

[37] CDPA 1988, s.175(5), re-enacting Copyright Act 1956, s.49(2)(b) and Copyright Act 1911, s.35(3).

[38] [1914] 2 Ch. 728.

[39] In *Copex Establishment v Flegon, The Times*, August 18, 1967, 169 copies of the claimant's book in the Russian language had been placed on sale at more than 50 booksellers in the United Kingdom. On the first occasion of sale the demand did not exceed the supply, but, since the publicity given to the case, there had been extra demand which had exceeded the supply and it was intended to satisfy that demand. It is suggested that this satisfied the test of publication (the issue was not determined as undertakings were given).

[40] See the example of the samizdat publication in *Bodley Head v Flegon* [1972] R.P.C. 587, which, being clandestine, was considered deliberately to disregard the requirements of the Russian public, because such requirements could neither be lawfully voiced by potential readers nor satisfied by the author.

[41] *British Northrop Ltd v Texteam Blackburn Ltd* [1974] R.P.C. 344. As to publication in parts, see *Low v Ward* (1868) L.R. 6 Eq. 415. The Court of Appeal in *Infabrics Ltd v Jaytex Shirt Co Ltd* [1980] Ch. 282, *per* Buckley L.J. at 292, expressed the view that offer for sale would not be publication.

[42] [1901–04] Mac. C.C. 36.

(b) *Literary, dramatic, musical and artistic works and typographical arrangements of published editions*

**Publication: literary, dramatic, musical and artistic works and typographi-   3–178
cal arrangements of published editions.** In addition to the general definition of publication,[43] the 1988 Act provides that in the case of a literary, dramatic, musical or artistic work, publication includes making such a work available to the public by means of an electronic retrieval system.[44] In relation to literary, dramatic, musical and artistic works, a copy means a reproduction of the work in any material form, including one stored electronically.[45] The issue of records embodying such a work is therefore also publication under the 1988 Act.[46]

The performance or communication to the public[47] of a literary, dramatic or musical work does not constitute publication.[48] Where lectures, addresses, speeches and sermons have been recorded in writing or some other form, and are thus capable of being protected as literary works,[49] they do not become published by being delivered in public, since such delivery falls within the definition of performance of such works,[50] and is therefore excluded from constituting publication.[51] However, such works may be published by the issue of reports, or even of copies of notes, with the licence of the author. A lecturer would probably be held to license publication if he delivered his lectures knowing reporters were present, subject to any express or implied obligation on the part of those hearing the lecture to the contrary.[52]

An artistic work is not published by being exhibited.[53] Although, in relation to three-dimensional artistic works, a copy includes a copy in two dimensions,[54] a work of architecture in the form of a building or a model for a building, a sculpture or a work of artistic craftsmanship is not published by the issue to the

---

[43] CDPA 1988, s.175(1); see para. 3–172, above.

[44] s.175(1)(b).

[45] s.17(1), (2).

[46] This was excluded from being publication under the 1956 Act: s.49(2)(a).

[47] "Communication to the public" has a special meaning, namely communication to the public by electronic transmission, and it includes (a) the broadcasting of the work and (b) the making available to the public of the work by electronic transmission in such a way that members of the public may access it from a place and at a time individually chosen by them (*i.e.* by way of an on-demand service). See CDPA 1988, s.20(2) and para. 7–98, below, for a full discussion. In order to achieve consistency with s.175(1)(b), however (see the earlier text of this paragraph), there is excepted from this exclusion any such communication for the purposes of an electronic retrieval system (s.175(4)(a)(ii)).

[48] CDPA 1988, s.175(4)(a); this follows the position under the 1956, and 1911, Acts. The 1911 Act effected a change in this respect, in that public performance of a dramatic work had previously been held to constitute publication: *Boucicault v Delafield* (1863) 1 H. & M. 597; *Boucicault v Chatterton* (1877) 5 Ch.D. 267; *Caird v Sime* (1887) 12 App.Cas. 326; *Walter v Lane* [1900] A.C. 539; *Falcon v The Famous Players Film Co Ltd* [1926] 2 K.B. 474, CA.

[49] *University of London Press Ltd v University Tutorial Press Ltd* [1916] 2 Ch. 601; and see para. 3–151, above.

[50] CDPA 1988, s.19(2); re-enacting the previous position in relation to such works, under the Copyright Act 1956, ss.49(2)(a) and 48(1), and, before that, the Copyright Act 1911, s.1(3).

[51] CDPA 1988, s.175(4)(a)(i).

[52] See *Nicols v Pitman* (1884) 26 Ch.D. 374; *Caird v Sime* (1887) 12 App. Cas. 326 and, now, CDPA 1988, s.58. In an American case, *Keene (L.) v Kimball (M.)* (1860) 16 Gray (82 Mass.) 545, Hoar J. said: "The student who attends a medical lecture may have a perfect right to remember as much as he can, and afterwards to use the information thus acquired in his own medical practice, or to communicate it to students or classes of his own, without involving the right to commit the lecture to writing, for the purpose of subsequent publication in print or by oral delivery."

[53] CDPA 1988, s.175(4)(b)(i). This was also the case under the 1956 Act: see s.49(2)(a). It was held, prior to 1911, that exhibition of a painting in a public gallery, the rules of which forbade the public to copy, was not a publication of the work: *Turner v Robinson* (1860) 10 Ir.Ch. 121 at 510.

[54] CDPA 1988, s.17(3); as under the 1956 Act, s.48(1).

public of copies of a graphic work representing, or photographs of, such work.[55] Having regard to these provisions, therefore, a three-dimensional artistic work, or a work of artistic craftsmanship, can only be published by the issue of three-dimensional copies of such a work; for example, in the case of a work of sculpture, by copies cast from the original work. A work of architecture in the form of a building, or an artistic work incorporated into a building, is treated as published when constructed.[56] The issue to the public of copies of a film including an artistic work,[57] and the communication to the public of the work,[58] do not constitute publication of the artistic work.[59]

In relation to typographical arrangements of published editions, copy is defined as meaning a facsimile copy of the arrangement.[60] Facsimile is not itself defined, other than as including a copy which is reduced or enlarged in scale,[61] but its ordinary meaning is an exact reproduction. From this it necessarily follows that the copies must be identical (save for any enlargement or reduction) to the original typographical arrangement, but, again, if the copies only relate to part of the typographical arrangement and not the whole, their issue will not constitute publication of the typographical arrangement as a whole.[62]

3–179   **What is a reproduction?** Although, therefore, the 1988 Act refers, for the purposes of publication of a literary, dramatic, musical or artistic work, to the issue of copies,[63] because of the terms of section 17 of that Act which define copying and copies in relation to such works by reference to reproduction,[64] it remains necessary to consider, for the purposes of publication of such works, what is a reproduction. Since it was considered necessary to provide specifically that the issue of copies of graphic works representing, and of photographs of, works of architecture, sculptures and works of artistic craftsmanship should not constitute publication,[65] it appears to have been considered by the legislature that such graphic works and photographs would have been copies, and therefore reproductions, for the purposes of publication. Thus, the issue to the public of authorised graphic works or photographs of a painting, which, it would follow, are reproductions for these purposes, would constitute publication of such painting. Similarly, by excluding publication by the issue to the public of copies of a film in which the artistic work is included,[66] it appears to have been considered that such inclusion would have constituted reproduction for the purposes of publication.[67] This approach to "reproduction" for the purposes of publication is in accordance with

---

[55] CDPA 1988, s.175(4)(b)(ii). As to the meaning of graphic work, see s.4(2) and para. 3–55, above.

[56] CDPA 1988, s.175(3). This was not so under the 1956 Act: s.49(2)(a). It was doubted whether such a work could ever be published under the 1956 Act, save possibly by the issue to the public of paintings or drawings of the work: see *Copinger* (12th ed.), pp.265, 266.

[57] CDPA 1988, s.175(4)(b)(iii); "inclusion" is not defined, but this is not intended to cover the situation where the film is properly a reproduction of the work, for example a cartoon film which reproduces each of the artistic works comprising the drawings for the film; such drawings are published by the issue of copies of the film in which they are reproduced: *Warner Bros Inc v The Roadrunner Ltd* [1988] F.S.R. 292.

[58] Otherwise than for the purpose of an electronic retrieval system: CDPA 1988, s.175(4)(b)(iv). As to the meaning of "communication to the public" in this context, see paras 7–105 *et seq.*, below.

[59] CDPA 1988, s.175(4)(b)(iv).

[60] s.17(5).

[61] s.178.

[62] See s.16(3)(a) and para. 3–174, above; it is suggested that such issue would constitute publication of the copied part.

[63] CDPA 1988, s.175(1)(a); *cf.* Copyright Act 1956, s.49(2)(c). See para. 3–172, above.

[64] s.17(2).

[65] s.175(4)(b)(ii); re-enacting, as regards works of architecture and sculptures, the former provisions of the 1911 Act (s.1(3)) and of the 1956 Act (s.49(2)(a)).

[66] CDPA 1988, s.175(4)(b)(iii).

[67] This would remain so, however, in the case of a cartoon film, which in the true sense is a copy of

the decision under the 1956 Act in *Merchant Adventurers Ltd v M. Grew & Co Ltd*,[68] that drawings for light-fittings were published by the sale to the public of the three-dimensional fittings made from the drawings on the basis that "reproduction" in section 49(2)(c) of the 1956 Act should not be given a more restricted meaning than "reproduction" in section 48(1) of that Act where it was defined as including three-dimensional reproductions of two-dimensional artistic works. Nevertheless, questions may arise in relation to other works. For instance, if A were to translate his manuscript work and publish the translation before the original, would that be a publication of the original? It is suggested that it would not, and that the proper view of the matter is that where what is published so differs from the original that it is capable of existing as a separate copyright work, it is this separate copyright work which is published, not the original. This reasoning would apply to a dramatisation of an unpublished novel as well as to a translation. Thus, it is suggested that the publication of a pianoforte arrangement of an opera, or that of a few of the orchestral parts, would not be a publication of the opera itself.[69] These views are confirmed by the fact that the making of an adaptation of a work is treated as distinct from reproduction.[70]

(c) *Sound recordings and films*

Publication: sound recordings. Copy is not further defined in the 1988 Act in relation to sound recordings. Nor does the 1988 Act provide a specific definition of publication in relation to sound recordings.[71] Although the issue of records reproducing the whole sound recording clearly remains the issue of copies of the recording, and therefore publication of the sound recording under the 1988 Act, it is less clear whether, under the 1988 Act, the issue of records which reproduce part only of a sound recording is a publication of the whole sound recording, as it was under the 1956 Act.[72] Playing a sound recording in public does not constitute publication, nor does its communication it to the public.[73]   **3–180**

Publication: films. Similarly, the 1988 Act contains no definition of publication specifically in relation to films other than the general definition of issue of copies to the public. The definition given in the 1956 Act as the sale, letting on hire, or offer for sale or hire, of copies of the film to the public,[74] is not repeated in the 1988 Act. This definition was wider than the ordinary definition of publication (issue of copies to the public), but still gave rise to the question whether letting on hire of copies merely to exhibitors, rather than to the general public, constituted publication. The absence in the 1988 Act of any specific definition of publication in relation to films would appear to resurrect all the problems previously   **3–181**

---

the drawings produced for the film; such drawings would be published by the issue of copies of the film to the public: see *Warner Bros Inc v The Roadrunner Ltd* [1988] F.S.R. 292.

[68] [1972] Ch. 242; and see *Sifam Electrical Instruments Co Ltd v Sangamo Weston Ltd* [1971] F.S.R. 337 and *British Northrop Ltd v Texteam Blackburn Ltd* [1974] R.P.C. 344.

[69] *Boosey v Fairlie* (1877) 7 Ch.D. 301.

[70] CDPA 1988, ss.17(1) and 21(1).

[71] The definition given in the 1956 Act, s.12(9), as the issue to the public of records embodying the recording or any part of it, is not repeated in the 1988 Act.

[72] By virtue of the words "or any part thereof" included in the definition in s.12(9) of the 1956 Act; *cf.* CDPA 1988, s.172, is the omission of these words in the 1988 Act "merely a change of expresson"? Contrast the position in relation to literary, dramatic, musical and artistic works and typographical arrangements, discussed at para. 3–174, above. It is suggested that the better view is that this change of wording is deliberate, and intended to bring sound recordings into line with the position applying to other works in this respect.

[73] CDPA 1988, s.175(4)(c). For the meaning of communication to the public in this context, see para. 7–106.

[74] Copyright Act 1956, s.13(10).

thought to exist under the 1911 Act,[75] as to what constitutes publication of a film, since, in particular, the first issue of copies is usually the letting of copies on hire to exhibitors. In relation to a film, a copy includes a photograph of the whole or a substantial part of any image forming part of such work.[76] Showing a film in public does not constitute publication, nor does its communication to the public.[77]

(iv) By reference to the place of transmission

3–182   **Broadcasts.** As stated above, whilst the general qualifying conditions otherwise applicable to all works by reference to the author are applicable to broadcasts,[78] the nature of a broadcast means that the alternative basis of qualification by reference to the place of first publication requires modification, to refer to the place of transmission.[79] Thus, copyright subsists in a broadcast if it is made from a place which is either in the United Kingdom,[80] or in a country to which the relevant provisions of the 1988 Act have been applied.[81] The place where a wireless broadcast is made is defined as the place where the programme-carrying signals are introduced into an uninterrupted chain of communication, which in the case of a satellite broadcast includes the uplink.[82] The place where a cable broadcast is made is not defined, but is no doubt the place where the signals are introduced into the cable network that leads to the recipient.

C. EXISTING WORKS

3–183   **Qualification by reference to country of first publication.** Under the 1911 Act, the subsistence of copyright in a published work depended solely on the place of first publication, and consequently copyright could often be lost or gained by publication. This was so, in particular, in relation to works emanating from the United States of America, since, by Order in Council, copyright was extended to the unpublished works of subjects or residents of the United States, but not to works first published there.[83] The position was different under the 1956 Act, and subsistence of copyright in published works depended, not only upon the place of first publication but also, whatever that place, on whether the author was a qualified person when the work was first published or, if he died before publication, on whether he was a qualified person immediately before his death.[84]

3–184   **Importance of determining when a work is published: existing works.** The new provisions of the 1956 Act, referred to in paragraph 3–183 above, did not

---

[75] Prior to the 1956 Act enlarging the definition of publication in relation to films, films had been regarded as unpublished works, because of the definition of publication in the 1911 Act (s.1(3)) as issue of copies to the public.
[76] CDPA 1988, s.17(4); it was open to question under the 1956 Act whether a single frame could be a copy of a film for the purposes of publication (see *Spelling Goldberg Productions Inc v B.P.C. Publishing* [1981] R.P.C. 283); if the present definition applies equally for the purposes of subsistence as for infringement, then this question would seem to be answered, but such a result would be so anomalous that it is suggested that such a construction of copies for the purposes of subsistence by publication cannot be correct (*cf.* the position in relation to sound recordings discussed at para. 3–180, above).
[77] CDPA 1988, s.175(4)(c). For the meaning of communication to the public in this context, see para. 7–106.
[78] CDPA 1988, s.155; see para. 3–153, above.
[79] s.156.
[80] s.156(1).
[81] s.156(2); as to the countries to which the relevant provision have been applied, see paras 3–214 *et seq.*, below.
[82] s.6(4), replacing with effect from December 1, 1996 the provision as originally enacted, which was to similar effect but applied only to satellite broadcasts.
[83] S.R. & O. 1915 No.130.
[84] Copyright Act 1956, ss.2(2), 3(3).

apply to works which were first published before the commencement of the 1956 Act.[85] Consequently, it remained, under the 1956 Act, of substantial importance to determine whether or not a work was published. Even in the case of an existing work published after the commencement of the 1956 Act,, the date for determining whether or not the author was a qualified person was different, so that if the work was not first published in the United Kingdom or in another country to which the relevant provisions of the 1988 Act extended, it was necessary to ascertain different information about the author to that which was relevant while the work remained unpublished. Moreover, the term of copyright in certain cases ran from first publication.[86] While the term of copyright in relation to photographs taken after the commencement of the 1988 Act now does not run from first publication,[87] and the position is now different in relation to works first published in the United States of America, following that country becoming a signatory to the Berne Convention,[88] whether a work was published, and if so when and where, are questions which remain important under the 1988 Act in many cases in respect of works in existence before the commencement of that Act, particularly in relation to the term of copyright in such works.[89]

Existing works. An existing work, for the purposes of the 1988 Act, is a work the making of which was both begun and completed before August 1, 1989.[90] Unlike the definition of material time for the purposes of satisfying the test as to the requirements for subsistence of copyright by reference to a work's author,[91] in the case of a work the making of which extended over a period of time, it is the time of completion of the making of the work alone which governs whether the new provisions of the 1988 Act as to subsistence apply to the work. Nevertheless, where the making of the work was begun before, but completed after, August 1, 1988, it may still be necessary to consider the position during the making of the work prior to such date in order to determine whether copyright subsists in the work by reference to the requirements as to authorship being satisfied.[92]   **3–185**

Subsistence of copyright in existing works. The 1988 Act provides that copyright subsists in an existing work after August 1, 1989 only if it subsisted immediately before such date, or if it is published after such date in accordance with the requirements as to first publication contained in section 154 of that Act.[93] The new provisions as to subsistence of copyright introduced by the 1988 Act are, therefore, not to apply to events which occurred before August 1, 1989.[94] For example, if copyright did not subsist under the 1956 Act in a musical work, but records reproducing that work had been released in the United Kingdom prior to August 1, 1989,[95] such release does not operate to confer copyright on the work after commencement. Similarly, copyright will not subsist by virtue of publication under the 1988 Act in a work of architecture in the form of a building which   **3–186**

---

[85] *i.e.* June 1, 1957: Copyright Act 1956, Sch.7, para.1.
[86] *e.g.* published photographs and sound recordings.
[87] See para. 6–07, below.
[88] See para. 3–227, below.
[89] CDPA 1988, Sch.1, para.5(1) and para.12, and see Ch.6, below.
[90] CDPA 1988, Sch.1, para.2.
[91] See para. 3–152, above.
[92] See para. 3–152, above.
[93] CDPA 1988, Sch.1, para.5(1) and (2)(a); but see, as to foreign works, para. 3–188, below.
[94] Save in respect of works which are not existing works, because although their making began before commencement it was completed after such date: see para. 3–185, above.
[95] An act which did not constitute publication of the musical work under the Copyright Act 1956, (s.49(2)(a)), but which does under the 1988 Act; see para. 3–178, above.

was constructed prior to commencement.[96] On the other hand, if copyright did subsist in an existing work under the 1956 Act, then copyright continues to subsist under the 1988 Act, irrespective of whether the requirements for subsistence set out in the 1988 Act are in fact satisfied in relation to such work.[97] This approach to existing works in effect preserves the importance of the previous law under the 1956 Act in relation to such works. Thus, in relation to photographs taken, and sound recordings made, before June 1, 1957, the requirement as to qualification by reference to the author where it is a corporate body being incorporated under the laws of a country, continues to mean, under the 1988 Act, in relation to such works, a reference to such body having its established place of business in such country.[98]

3–187   Existing works: special provisions. The general approach of the 1988 Act to existing works, discussed above,[99] is supplemented by specific transitional provisions to ensure that copyright is not conferred on certain existing works which did not enjoy copyright protection under the Copyright Act 1956.

Thus, copyright does not subsist under the 1988 Act in an artistic work made before June 1, 1957, which at the time it was made constituted a design capable of registration under the Registered Designs Act 1949 and was used, or intended to be used, as a model or pattern to be multiplied by industrial process.[1]

The same approach of maintaining the existing law is taken in relation to certain existing films, film soundtracks and broadcasts. Thus no copyright subsists under the 1988 Act in films as such made before June 1, 1957, but provision is made for preserving the dramatic and artistic copyright in such films corresponding to the rights so subsisting by virtue of the 1911 Act.[2] Film soundtracks made before August 1, 1989 are now treated as sound recordings, not, as previously, as part of the film. However, for certain purposes, including subsistence of copyright, they continue to be treated as if they were part of the film.[3] Wireless broadcasts made before June 1, 1957 and broadcasts by cable before January 1, 1985 are not entitled to copyright protection.[4]

3–188   Foreign existing works. The only exception to the principle that events occurring before August 1, 1989 cannot entitle existing works to copyright protection if they did not enjoy such protection under the 1956 Act,[5] is in relation to existing foreign works, which may qualify for copyright protection after commencement by virtue of an Order made under section 159 of the 1988 Act applying Part I of that Act to a country to which those provisions do not extend.[6]

The point is of most significance in relation to existing American works made before June 1, 1957, in particular old American films, and which did not qualify for copyright protection under the 1956 Act until the adherence of the United States of America to the Berne Convention led to the inclusion of that country in

---

[96] CDPA 1988, s.175(3); and see para. 3–178, above.

[97] CDPA 1988, Sch.1, para.35.

[98] This being the definition of qualified persons which were corporate bodies under the 1911 Act, as preserved under the Copyright Act 1956, Sch.7, para.39(4).

[99] See para. 3–186, above.

[1] CDPA 1988, Sch.1, para.6; this maintains the position as it was under the Copyright Act 1956, Sch.7, para.8 and Sch.8, para.2.

[2] CDPA 1988, Sch.1, para.7; this maintains the position as it was under the Copyright Act 1956, Sch.7, paras 14, 15 and 16.

[3] CDPA 1988, Sch.1, para.8.

[4] CDPA 1988, Sch.1, para.9, as amended; this maintains the position as it was under the Copyright Act 1956, Sch.7, para.17 and s.14A (added, with effect from January 1, 1985, by the Cable and Broadcasting Act 1984, ss.22–24 (now repealed)).

[5] *i.e.* the principle underlying CDPA 1988, Sch.1, para.5(1) discussed at para. 3–186, above.

[6] CDPA 1988, Sch.1, para.5(2); and see paras 3–190 *et seq.*, below.

Schedule 1 of the Order applying the 1956 Act to such works.[7] The wording of that Order made it clear that such previously unprotected works could qualify for copyright protection under the 1956 Act either by virtue of a publication which took place in the United States of America before June 1, 1957, or by reason of the author being a citizen, resident or subject of such country.[8] This alteration in protection afforded to foreign existing works has greatly diminished the importance previously attributed to the question of whether it was possible to publish old American films, a question upon which the copyright protection in the United Kingdom of such films in turn depended.[9]

The position under the 1988 Act is the same, originally by virtue of the provisions of an Order made under section 159 of the Act.[10] Such Order contained its own "transitional" provisions intended to deal with the situation where, prior to such work becoming protected in the United Kingdom, a person committed himself to investment with a view to exploitation of the work in a way which was, after the work became protected, an infringement of copyright.[11]

Unprotected work qualifying for protection. Although the Orders in Council   **3–189** made under the Copyright Acts to comply with the Berne Convention and Universal Copyright Convention must make the event more unusual than in the past,[12] circumstances may still occur in which an unpublished work was unprotected in the United Kingdom, but subsequently became protected by reason of its publication here.[13] For instance, apart from international arrangements, a foreign artist does not, by exhibiting his painting in the United Kingdom, become entitled to copyright here. Until he has issued copies to the public, any person is at liberty (unless acting in breach of confidence or contract) to photograph, engrave, or otherwise copy the original work and to sell those copies in the United Kingdom. This, being done without the licence of the artist, does not constitute publication of the work,[14] and therefore, if the artist himself subsequently issues reproductions to the public in the United Kingdom (or another country to which the 1988 Act is applied or to which its provisions are extended), he thereby gains copyright in the United Kingdom in his original. What then is the position of the first copyist? Clearly, he cannot be sued for piracy merely because he has in his possession copies of the work, for those copies were lawfully made and the subsequent acquisition of copyright by the author cannot, *prima facie*, have a retrospective effect so as to render an act unlawful which was perfectly lawful at the time it was committed.[15] It is equally clear that the copyist cannot make or print any further copies (even from the copies he has already made). However, it is not so clear whether he can dispose of copies which he has on hand at the date when the artist acquired his copyright. Under the 1956 Act, it was suggested that the

---

[7] The Copyright (International Conventions) Order 1979 (SI 1979/1715) as amended with effect from March 8, 1989 by the Copyright (International Conventions) (Amendment) Order 1989 (SI 1989/1570).

[8] Copyright (International Conventions) Order 1979 (SI 1979/1715), Sch., para.6.

[9] See *Copinger* (12th ed.), p.797.

[10] The Copyright (Application to Other Countries) (No.2) Order 1989 (SI 1989/1293), paras 2(1) and (2). See now the Copyright (Application to Other Countries) Order 1999 (SI 1999/1751) and para. 3–226, below.

[11] See para.7(1) and (2) of the 1979 Order and now para.7(1) and (2) of the 1999 Order.

[12] But, as to the particular problem caused in relation to existing works by the retrospective effect given under the Order in Council to the United States of America becoming a signatory to the Berne Convention, see para. 3–227, below.

[13] See *Copex Establishment v Flegon*, *The Times*, August 18, 1967, where the authoress was Mrs Svetlana Alliluyeva, Stalin's daughter; and see *Bodley Head v Flegon* [1972] R.P.C. 587.

[14] CDPA 1988, ss.175(6) and 178.

[15] This is the approach taken under the various Orders in Council in relation to acts which were lawful when done, where previously unprotected works become protected in the United Kingdom; see para. 3–188, above.

test remained whether copies were lawfully made when made, and, if so, their subsequent sale could not give rise to an infringement.[16] The case was considered to be analogous to that of a person who has assigned his copyright, or granted a licence to publish for a term which has expired. It was held, under the old law, that an assignor could dispose of copies manufactured before the date of his assignment, and that a licensee could do the same with regard to copies manufactured before his licence ran out.[17] The position would appear to be different under the 1988 Act, in that the putting into circulation of copies not previously put into circulation now constitutes an infringement, if done without the copyright owner's licence, irrespective of whether the copies were infringing copies when made.[18]

6. FOREIGN WORKS

A. PROTECTION OF WORKS OF FOREIGN ORIGIN: APPLICATION OF ACT

(i) General

(a) Position before the 1911 Act

3–190   **Implementation of treaties, conventions and agreements.** It is clear that the parties to treaties, conventions and agreements can give effect to them, either by making the treaty part of the municipal law of the country, or by making separate legislation to carry its provisions into effect. This country, prior to the 1911 Act, had adopted the first alternative in respect of copyright since, by Orders in Council made under the International Copyright Acts of 1844 and 1866, the original Berne Convention and the Act of Paris were given full effect in this country and were interpreted by the courts.[19] These Acts, however, were repealed by the 1911 Act in the dominions to which that Act applied, and the scheme of the 1911 Act, the 1956 Act and the 1988 Act is to give to British works rights as large as those required by the Convention and, by Orders in Council, to give these rights to foreign works.[20]

The method of giving such rights to foreign works by Order in Council is to apply the provisions of the relevant Act to such works, thereby giving such works equivalent protection in this country to British works. This is to be distinguished from extending the provisions of the relevant Act to a country by Order in Council, thereby making that Act the law of that country. Extension is dealt with in Section 3 of this Chapter. Foreign works can, however, obtain protection in this country by other routes than the Orders in Council, for instance by simultaneous publication in the United Kingdom and elsewhere.

---

[16] See Copyright Act 1956, s.5(3).

[17] *Taylor v Pillow* (1869) L.R. 7 Eq. 418 (a case of assignment); *Howitt v Hall* (1862) 6 L.T. 348 (a case of licence); *cf.* the dicta to the contrary with regard to gramophone records under the Copyright Act 1911, s.2(2): *Monckton v Pathé Frères Ltd* [1914] 1 K.B. 395.

[18] CDPA 1988, s.18.

[19] *e.g.* in *Hanfstaengl v Empire Palace* [1894] 3 Ch. 109.

[20] In case of ambiguity see *Hogg v Toye and Co Ltd* [1935] Ch. 497 at 520 and *Warwick Film Productions Ltd v Eisinger* [1969] 1 Ch. 508 at 521; see also *Cheney v Conn* [1968] 1 W.L.R. 242 and *Monte Ulia (Owners) v Banco (Owners)* [1971] P. 137. See, however, as to the Treaty of Rome, Ch.25, below.

(b) *Position under the 1911 Act*

Orders in Council under the 1911 Act. A general Order in Council was made **3–191** on June 24, 1912[21] for the purpose of applying the 1911 Act, in accordance with section 29, to works originating in countries of the Copyright Union, and subsequent Orders were made, as necessity arose, by reason of countries joining the Union or altering their reservations to the Convention. By an Order in Council[22] dated March 16, 1933, all previous Orders were revoked, but without prejudice to existing rights, and the provisions of section 29 of the Act were applied to all countries of the Copyright Union. Under this Order, as under previous Orders, the term of protection was limited to that conferred by the law of the country of origin of the work, and limitations were imposed in respect of those countries which had made reservations to the Convention. In respect of existing works, it was provided that rights extinguished by virtue of section 5 of the International Copyright Act 1886, that is by virtue of non-publication in the English language within 10 years, should not be revived by the Order, and that the copyright in musical works should include mechanical rights where no contrivances had been made or sold in His Majesty's dominions before the dates mentioned in the Schedule.

Preservation of Orders in Council made under the 1911 Act. In order to **3–192** prevent Orders in Council made under the 1911 Act lapsing immediately upon the commencement of the 1956 Act and its repeal of the 1911 Act, it was provided, in paragraph 40 of Schedule 7 to the 1956 Act,[23] that such Orders, and all the provisions of the 1911 Act required for the purposes of any proceedings arising out of the operation of such continuance, were to continue in force until the occurrence of whichever of the following events first occurred, that was to say:

(a) the revocation of the Order under the 1911 Act;

(b) the coming into operation of an Order under the 1956 Act in the case of the foreign country in question; and

(c) the expiration of the period of two years from the repeal of the 1911 Act.

(c) *Position under the 1956 Act*

Power to apply the 1956 Act to other countries. By section 32 of the 1956 Act, **3–193** Her Majesty[24] was authorised, by Order in Council, to make provision for applying any of the provisions of that Act, in the case of a country to which those provisions did not extend, so as to secure that those provisions:

(a) applied in relation to literary, dramatic, musical or artistic works, sound recordings, cinematograph films or editions first published in that country as they applied to such works first published in the United Kingdom;

(b) applied in relation to persons who, at a material time, were citizens or subjects of that country as they applied in relation to British subjects;

(c) applied in relation to persons who, at a material time, were domiciled or resident in that country as they applied in relation to persons domiciled or resident in the United Kingdom;

(d) applied in relation to bodies incorporated under the laws of that country as they applied in relation to bodies incorporated under the laws of any part of the United Kingdom;

---

[21] S.R. & O. 1912 No.913.

[22] S.R. & O. 1933 No.253; *Copinger* (8th ed.), p.459.

[23] Copyright Act 1956, Sch.7, para.40, was repealed by Statute Law (Repeals) Act 1986 (c.12).

[24] See, as to the extension of s.32, Copyright Act 1956 to Hong Kong, para. 3–258, below.

(e) applied in relation to television broadcasts and sound broadcasts made from places in that country by one or more organisations constituted in or under the laws of that country as they applied in relation to television broadcasts and sound broadcasts made by the British Broadcasting Corporation or the Independent Broadcasting Authority;[25] and

(f) applied in relation to cable programmes sent from places in that country as they applied in relation to cable programmes sent from places in the United Kingdom.[26]

Any such Order in Council could have been made subject to exceptions and modifications, and could have applied either generally or in relation to specified classes of works or classes of cases.

3–194   **Limitation on power to apply the 1956 Act.** The power to make such Orders was, however, limited, in that an Order was not to be made applying any of the provisions of the 1956 Act in the case of a country, other than a country which was a party to a Convention relating to copyright to which the United Kingdom was also a party; "unless Her Majesty is satisfied that, in respect of the class of works or other subject-matter to which those provisions relate, provision has been or will be made under the laws of that country whereby adequate protection will be given to owners of copyright under this Act". This limitation was in slightly different language from that contained in the similar provisions in section 29 of the 1911 Act, which stated that, before making an Order: "His Majesty shall be satisfied that that foreign country has made, or has undertaken to make, such provisions, if any, as it appears to His Majesty expedient to require for the protection of works entitled to copyright under this Act".

3–195   **Self-governing dominions.** Whilst section 29 of the 1911 Act enabled Orders in Council to be made in respect of works originating in "a foreign country", section 32 of the 1956 Act applied to works originating in any country. This is because the 1911 Act extended, or was capable of being extended, throughout the British Empire, including the self-governing dominions, whereas the 1956 Act was only capable of being extended to the Isle of Man, the Channel Islands and any colony.[27]

Consequently, protection of works originating in a self-governing dominion or member of the Commonwealth had to be provided by Order in Council in the same way as in the case of a foreign country.

3–196   **Power to curtail protection.** The 1956 Act gave[28] power to deprive citizens or subjects of countries not giving adequate protection to British works, of copyright under that Act. That power arose if the laws of a country failed to give adequate protection to British works, or to one or more classes of such works. A "British work", for this purpose, meant a work of which the author, at the time when the work was made, was a qualified person.[29] Where the circumstances contemplated arose, an Order in Council could have been made providing that copyright under the 1956 Act should not subsist in works, or classes of works, first published after a date specified in the Order, if at the time of their first publication the authors were citizens or subjects of the country designated by the Order, and not at that time persons domiciled or resident in the United Kingdom, or in another country to which that Act extended, or were bodies incorporated under the laws of the country designated by the Order. Such an Order could have been

---

[25] See Independent Broadcasting Authority Act 1973 (c.19), ss.1, 38 and 39; repealed by Broadcasting Act 1981 (c.68), s.65(4) and Sch.9, but 1973 Act amendment preserved by 1981 Act, para.7, Sch.8.

[26] Sub-para.(f) was added by the Cable and Broadcasting Act 1984 (c.46).

[27] Copyright Act 1956, s.31, and see para. 3–241, below.

[28] Copyright Act 1956, s.35.

[29] s.35(5).

made in respect of literary, dramatic, musical and artistic works, sound recordings and cinematograph films. However, no such Order was ever made. The section only applied to published works because the unpublished works of foreign
authors could, in any case, only have obtained protection by an Order in Council
under section 32 of the 1956 Act, and could have been penalised merely by revoking or varying such an Order. What this section contemplated was the exclusion
from copyright protection of works first published in the United Kingdom which
would otherwise have obtained automatic protection under the main provisions
of the 1956 Act.

International organisations. Section 33 of the 1956 Act also provided for the   **3–197**
conferring of copyright by Order in Council upon original literary, dramatic,
musical or artistic works made by or under the direction or control of an
international organisation, and whether or not such organisation had the legal
capacity of a body corporate.[30] The section also applied where such a work was
first published by or under the direction or control of such an organisation. Such
section also dealt with duration and ownership of such copyright.

Orders in Council under section 32 of the 1956 Act   **3–198**
   (i) Countries other than Taiwan, Singapore and Indonesia. By an Order in
Council made under section 32 of the 1956 Act, and coming into operation on
September 27, 1957,[31] the 1956 Act was applied to works originating in the
countries specified in Schedule 1 to that Order, being countries which had adhered
to the Berne or Universal Copyright Conventions, in relation to all classes of
works then covered by that Act other than television broadcasts and sound
broadcasts. Replacement Orders and amendments were made from time to time.[32]
. Dealing first with works, including for this purpose sound recordings, cinematograph films and published editions, the 1956 Act was applied in relation to such
works first published in such countries, and in relation to the citizens or subjects
of such countries, and to persons domiciled or resident in such countries, and in
relation to bodies incorporated under the laws of such countries.[33] The general effect of the Order, therefore, was that all such works were to be treated as if they
had been first published in the United Kingdom, or had been made by British
subjects, persons domiciled or resident in the United Kingdom, or United
Kingdom companies, as the case may have been. It will be recalled that, under
sections 2(2) and 3(3) of the 1956 Act, a published work could have enjoyed
copyright protection, not only by reason of the place of publication, but also
because the author was a qualified person when the work was first published, and
similar provision was made in regard to sound recordings, cinematograph films
and published editions.[34] Consequently, under the Order, copyright could have
been enjoyed in the United Kingdom in respect of published works, not only
because they had been first published in a country to which the Order applied, but
also, if not so published, because the author, maker or publisher fell within the
provisions of the Order.

---

[30] This did not apply to works made or published before the commencement of the 1956 Act (
   Sch.7, para.27). See Copyright (International Organisations) Order 1957 (SI 1957/1524),
   Copinger (12th ed.), p.2116.
[31] SI 1957/1523. *Copinger* (12th ed.), p.2105. The date is the date on which the Universal Copyright Convention took effect so far as Great Britain is concerned.
[32] See the Copyright (International Conventions) Order 1964 (SI 1964/690), *Copinger* (12th ed.),
   para.2117; the Copyright (International Conventions) Order 1972 (SI 1972/673), *Copinger* (12th
   ed.), p.2128; and the Copyright (International Conventions) Order 1979 (SI 1979/1715), and see
   Milltronics Ltd v Hycontrol Ltd [1990] F.S.R. 273.
[33] Certain countries adhered to Conventions subsequent to the 1957 Order and accordingly the
   1964, 1972 and the 1979 Orders applied to them as from later dates.
[34] Copyright Act 1956, ss.12(1), 13(1) and 15(1).

3–199   **Works made after Order.** So far as concerns works or subject-matters made after the commencement of the 1957 Order, there were only two respects in which the copyright in such works differed from that in a work of United Kingdom origin. The first concerned the term of such copyright and was general, and the second was of a limited character in respect of the copyright in sound recordings.

3–200   **(a) Term of copyright.** It was provided in the 1957 Order that the term of copyright in a work protected under the provisions of that Order was not to exceed that granted by the country of origin of the work without formality, other than that specified in the Universal Copyright Convention, to a British work of the same class. "British work" meant a work made by a British subject resident in the United Kingdom, or by a company incorporated under the laws of the United Kingdom, and which, if published, was first published in the United Kingdom.

However, this provision was cancelled by an Order[35] coming into operation on August 11, 1958, so that the normal term under the 1956 Act was applicable to all such works. But this amending Order was not to revive copyrights, so that it may still be necessary to consider the provisions of the original Order if, under such provisions, the term would have expired between September 27, 1957, and August 11, 1958. This will involve knowledge of the relevant foreign law, and of the meaning of "country of origin" in the Order. It is assumed that the revocation of the 1957 and 1958 Orders by the 1964 Order, and of the 1964 Order by the 1972 Order, and of the 1972 Order by the 1979 Order, did not revive copyrights.[36]

3–201   **Meaning of "country of origin".** Owing to the requirements of the various Conventions and the complications ensuing as a result of the simultaneous publication of works in a number of countries, the expression "country of origin" received a complicated definition in the 1957 Order which may be shortly summarised as follows:

In the case of a work which was published in a country belonging to either of the Conventions it meant, if first published in such a country and not simultaneously published elsewhere, that country.

In the case of simultaneous publication, which meant, in the case of publications occurring before the commencement of that Order, publications within 14 days of one another, and, in any other case, within a period of 30 days of one another, there were four classes of case. If a work was simultaneously published in a Berne country and a non-Berne country, the country of origin was the Berne country. If the work was simultaneously published in a Universal Copyright Convention country and a country which was not a member of either Convention, the country of origin was the Universal Copyright Convention country. If a work was simultaneously published in several Berne countries, the country of origin was the country giving the shortest term of protection. If a work was simultaneously published in a number of Universal Copyright Convention countries and not in a Berne country, the country of origin was the country giving the shortest term of protection.

In the case of a work which was unpublished or first published in a country which did not belong to either Convention, the country of origin was the country whose laws gave the longest term of protection to such a work of the following, namely, the country of which the author was a subject or citizen, the country in which the author was domiciled, the country in which the author was resident or, where the author or maker was a body corporate, the country in which such body was incorporated.

---

[35] The Copyright (International Conventions) (Amendment) Order 1958 (SI 1958/1254).
[36] See art.11, 1964 Order and art.2(2) 1972 Order and Interpretation Act 1889, s.38 (52 & 53 Vict., c.63) and Interpretation Act 1978 (c.30), ss.16, 21, 23.

(b) Sound recordings. The provision about sound recordings was that, in rela- **3–202**
tion to any country other than Australia, Austria, Barbados, Brazil, Burkina Faso,
Chile, Colombia, Congo (People's Republic), Costa Rica, Cyprus, Czechoslovakia, Denmark, Dominican Republic, Ecuador, El Salvador, Federal Republic of
Germany (and Berlin (West)), Fiji, Finland, France, Guatemala, India, Republic
of Ireland, Israel, Italy, Luxembourg, Mexico, Monaco, New Zealand, Niger,
Nigeria, Norway, Pakistan, Panama, Paraguay, Peru, Philippines, Spain, Sri
Lanka (Ceylon), Sweden, Switzerland and Uruguay, the acts restricted by the
copyright in a sound recording were not to include causing the recording to be
heard in public or broadcasting the recording.[37]

Existing works. The provisions of the 1979 Order applied to works existing at **3–203**
the commencement of the 1957 Order, subject to the exceptions already noted
and to certain further qualifications:

(a) In the first place, copyright was not to subsist by virtue of the 1979 Order
in any work by reason only of its publication before a specified date in a
country which was a party to the Universal Copyright Convention, but
which was not a country of the Berne Copyright Union.[38] This, combined
with the operation of paragraph 1 of Schedule 7 to the 1956 Act, article 4
and Schedule 2 to the 1972 Order, article 2 and Schedule 2 to the 1964
Order and paragraph 5 of Schedule 4 to the 1957 Order, had the effect that
works first published in a Universal Copyright Convention country, not
being a Berne Convention country, before the specified date, would not
have enjoyed United Kingdom copyright, notwithstanding that their
authors may have been subjects of a country to which the 1957, 1964,
1972 and 1979 Orders applied at the date of publication.

(b) There was an exception to this in the case of works first published in the
United States during the periods of the two world wars which already
enjoyed copyright in the United Kingdom by virtue of the Wartime Orders
mentioned below.[39] Such works would also have enjoyed the full term of
United Kingdom copyright, notwithstanding the provisions about the term
of copyright mentioned above.[40]

(c) There was also an exception in respect of Bahamas, Barbados, Belize,
Cyprus, Fiji, Ghana, Kenya, Malawi, Malta, Mauritius, Nigeria, Trinidad
and Tobago, St Vincent and the Grenadines, Zambia and Zimbabwe.[41]

Provisions relating to translations and broadcasts **3–204**
(a) Translations. It was provided by the 1979 Order[42] that nothing in the 1956
Act, as applied by that Order, was to be construed as reviving any right to make,
or restrain the making of, or any right in respect of, translations, if such right had
ceased before the commencement of that Order. This referred, in particular, to
certain provisions of the Order in Council (Copyright (Rome Convention) Order

[37] Copyright (International Conventions) Order 1979 (SI 1979/1715), art.5 and Sch.3 as amended; and see Copyright (International Conventions) Order 1972 (SI 1972/673) art.5 and Sch.3 as amended, Copyright (International Conventions) Order 1964 (SI 1964/690), art.3 and Sch.3 as amended, and Copyright (International Conventions) Order 1957 (SI 1957/1523) art.1 proviso (iii) as amended.
[38] Copyright (International Conventions) Order 1979 (SI 1979/1715), art.4(1) and (2) and Sch.2.
[39] SI 1979/1715, art.4(3)(b). See para. 3–229, below.
[40] See para. 3–200, above.
[41] SI 1979/1715, art.4(3)(a) as amended.
[42] SI 1979/1715, art.7; see also art.1 proviso (v), Copyright (International Conventions) Order 1957 (SI 1957/1523), art.6, Copyright (International Conventions) Order 1964 (SI 1964/690) and art.7, Copyright (International Conventions) Order 1972 (SI 1972/673).

1933) made under the 1911 Act restricting the translation rights in works originating in certain countries because these countries also restricted translation rights.[43]

3–205 **(b) Broadcasts.** The 1979 Order provided[44] that the provisions of section 14 of the 1956 Act, so far as they related to sound broadcasts, were to apply in relation to sound broadcasts made from places in a number of named countries by any organisation constituted under the laws of such countries. It also provided[45] that the provisions of section 14 of the 1956 Act, so far as they related to television broadcasts, were to apply in relation to television broadcasts made from places in another series of countries by any organisation constituted under the laws of suchcountries.

3–206 **1956 Act was to apply as if references to commencement of Act were references to specified date.** There was a general provision in the 1979 Order,[46] as in the 1972 Order[47] and the 1964 Order[48] that, in Schedule 7 to the 1956 Act, references to the commencement of that Act, or to the repeal of any provision of the 1911 Act were to be treated, in relation to any work or other subject-matter in which copyright subsisted by virtue of the 1979 Order, as references to the dates specified.

3–207 **Preservation of existing rights.** Finally, the 1957, 1964, 1972 and 1979 Orders contained general provisions preserving existing rights of persons who, before the commencement of each Order, had incurred expenditure or liability in connection with the reproduction or performance of any work or other subject-matter.[49]

3–208 **Unrepeated provisions of 1957 Order**
    (a) As to royalty terms for recorded music. The 1957 Order contained provisions[50] affecting the right to record music on royalty terms, which had the effect that, in the case of works published before certain dates set out in a Table to the Order, such works might be recorded on royalty terms, notwithstanding that they had not been previously recorded in the United Kingdom. Furthermore, in the case of such works which had been recorded and records sold in the United Kingdom before the relevant date, such works should be freely recorded. Where copyright was conferred by the Order for the first time on a musical work, then, for the purposes of the last-mentioned provision, the date of the Order was to be the relevant date. This provision was not repeated in the 1964, 1972 and 1979 Orders.

3–209 **(b) As to copyright in sound recordings.** There was also in the 1957 Order a provision[51] about the copyright in sound recordings. This referred back, through paragraph 13 of Schedule 7 to the 1956 Act, to section 19(8) of the 1911 Act which gave copyright under the 1911 Act, in respect of existing sound recordings, provided that the making thereof would not have infringed copyright in

---

[43] S.R. & O. 1933 No.253, art.2, proviso (ii); see also proviso (vi).

[44] Copyright (International Conventions) Order 1979 (SI 1979/1715), art.8 and Sch.4, and see Copyright (International Conventions) Order 1972 (SI 1972/673), art.8 and Sch.4 and Copyright (International Conventions) Order 1964 (SI 1964/690), art.8 and Sch.5.

[45] SI 1979/1715, art.9 and Sch.5; and see 1972 Order, art.9 and Sch.5 and 1964 Order, Art.9 and Sch.6.

[46] Copyright (International Conventions) Order 1979 (SI 1979/1715), art.4 and Sch.2.

[47] Copyright (International Conventions) Order 1972 (SI 1972/673), art.4 and Sch.2.

[48] Copyright (International Conventions) Order 1964 (SI 1964/690), art.2 and Sch.2.

[49] 1979 Order, art.6; 1972 Order, art.6; 1964 Order, arts 4 and 10; and 1957 Order, art.2.

[50] Copyright (International Conventions) Order 1957 (SI 1957/1523), art.1, proviso (iv) and Sch.4.

[51] Copyright (International Conventions) Order 1957 (SI 1957/1523), art.1, proviso (iv) and Sch.4.

some other sound recording if that Act had been in force at the time of the making thereof. This provision of the 1957 Order seemed intended to apply the dates mentioned in Schedule 4 of that Act, or the date of the commencement of that Order, as the case might be, for the date of the commencement of the 1911 Act in paragraph 13 of Schedule 7 to the 1956 Act. This provision also was not repeated in the 1964, 1972 and 1979 Orders.

(c) As to revocation of previous Orders. The 1957 Order[52] revoked all the **3–210** previous Orders in Council relating to works of foreign origin, but it was provided that where, by virtue of any of such Orders, copyright subsisted in a work immediately before the commencement of the 1957 Order and copyright did not subsist therein by the 1957 Order, it should continue to subsist as if such Order had not been revoked. The effect of this provision was not altogether clear. The intention clearly was to keep alive copyright in works of foreign origin in which copyright subsisted at the commencement of the 1957 Order, but which would not acquire copyright under the 1956 Act by virtue of the prior provisions of that Order. It seems that the only effect of this provision was to preserve the copyright in such works during the two years mentioned in paragraph 40(2)(c) of Schedule 7 to the 1956 Act.[53] It, also, was not repeated in the 1964, 1972 and 1979 Orders.

(ii) Taiwan. By an Order in Council made under section 32 of the 1956 Act, and **3–211** coming into operation on December 17, 1985,[54] the 1956 Act was applied to works originating in Taiwan in relation to all classes of works covered by that Act, other than television broadcasts, sound broadcasts and cable programmes. As to works, including for this purpose sound recordings, cinematograph films and published editions, the 1956 Act was applied in relation to such works first published in Taiwan, and in relation to citizens or subjects of China, being citizens or subjects who were resident or domiciled in Taiwan, and in relation to bodies incorporated under the laws of Taiwan. The general effect of this Order was that all such works were to be treated as if they had been first published in the United Kingdom, or had been made by British subjects or companies. This Order contained no restriction on the copyright in sound recordings,[55] but it did contain a provision excluding from section 2(5)(f) of the 1956 Act the right to make a translation of the work. The Order contained a provision that, in Schedule 7 to the 1956 Act, for references to the commencement of that Act there were substituted references to July 10, 1985, and that copyright was not to subsist by virtue of such Order in any work or other subject matter by reason only of its publication in Taiwan before that date. Finally such Order contained a general provision preserving existing rights of persons who, before the commencement of such Order, had incurred expenditure or liability in connection with the reproduction or performance of any work or other subject matter. The provisions of the 1988 Act have now been applied to Taiwan.[56]

(iii) Singapore. By another Order in Council made under section 32 of the 1956 **3–212** Act, and coming into force on June 18, 1987,[57] the 1956 Act was apparently applied in relation to all classes of works and subject-matters covered by that Act originating in Singapore. It would appear that television broadcasts, sound

---

[52] Copyright (International Conventions) Order 1957 (SI 1957/1523), art.3.
[53] para.40, Sch.7, Copyright Act 1956 was repealed by the Statute Law (Repeals) Act 1986 (c.12).
[54] SI 1985/1777.
[55] See para. 3–202, above.
[56] Currrently, by as the Copyright (Application to Other Countries) Order 1999 (SI 1999/1751), as amended by the Copyright (Application to Other Countries) (Amendment) Order 2003 (SI 2003/774).
[57] SI 1987/940.

broadcasts and cable programmes were to be included since these were not expressly excluded although, if included, the Order did not make clear how the provisions as to broadcasts, for instance, were to be applied, and from when.[58] As to works, including for this purpose sound recordings, cinematograph films and published editions, the 1956 Act was applied in relation to such works first published in Singapore, and in relation to residents in Singapore, and in relation to bodies incorporated under the laws of Singapore. The general effect of this Order was that all such works were to be treated as if they had been first published in the United Kingdom, or had been made by British residents or companies. Citizens of Singapore were not referred to as they were qualified persons.[59] This Order contained a restriction on the copyright in sound recordings, namely that the acts restricted by the copyright in a sound recording were not to include causing the recording to be heard in public, broadcasting the recording or including it in a cable programme.[60] Finally such Order contained a general provision preserving existing rights of persons who, before the commencement of such Order, had incurred expenditure or liability in connection with the reproduction or performance of any work or other subject matter. The provisions of the 1988 Act have now been applied to Singapore.[61]

3–213   *(iv) Indonesia.* By another Order in Council made under section 32 of the 1956 Act, and coming into force on May 26, 1988,[62] the provisions of section 12 of the 1956 Act (copyright in sound recordings) and all the other provisions of that Act relevant to that section were applied to give protection to sound recordings originating in Indonesia. Thus these provisions were applied in relation to sound recordings first published in Indonesia, and in relation to makers of sound recordings who were citizens or subjects of or resident in Indonesia, or bodies incorporated under the laws of Indonesia. The general effect of this Order was that all such sound recordings were to be treated as if they had been first published in the United Kingdom, or had been made by British subjects, or United Kingdom residents or companies. Sound recordings protected under this Order were entitled to full sound recordings copyright. Finally, such Order contained a general provision preserving existing rights of persons who, before the commencement of the Order, had incurred expenditure or liability in connection with the making of a record embodying a sound recording, or causing a sound recording to be heard in public, or the broadcasting of a sound recording or its inclusion in a cable programme. The provisions of the 1988 Act have now been applied to Indonesia.[63]

(d) Position under the 1988 Act

3–214   **Power to apply the 1988 Act to other countries.** By section 159 of the 1988 Act, Her Majesty is authorised, by Order in Council, to make provision for applying any of the provisions of Part I of the Act dealing with copyright, in the case of

---

[58] See para. 3–205, above.
[59] Copyright Act 1956, s.1(5).
[60] See para. 3–202, below.
[61] Currrently, by as the Copyright (Application to Other Countries) Order 1999 (SI 1999/1751), as amended by the Copyright (Application to Other Countries) (Amendment) Order 2003 (SI 2003/774).
[62] SI 1988/797.
[63] Currrently, by as the Copyright (Application to Other Countries) Order 1999 (SI 1999/1751), as amended by the Copyright (Application to Other Countries) (Amendment) Order 2003 (SI 2003/774).

a country[64] to which such Part does not extend, so as to secure that those provisions:

(a) apply in relation to persons who are citizens or subjects of that country or are domiciled or resident there, as they apply to persons who are British citizens or are domiciled or resident in the United Kingdom, or

(b) apply in relation to bodies incorporated under the law of that country as they apply in relation to bodies incorporated under the law of a part of the United Kingdom, or

(c) apply in relation to works first published in that country as they apply in relation to works first published in the United Kingdom, or

(d) apply in relation to broadcasts made from that country as they apply in relation to broadcasts made from the United Kingdom.

Any such Order can be made subject to exceptions and modifications, and may apply either generally or in relation to specified classes of works or classes of cases. A statutory instrument containing an Order in Council under section 159 is subject to annulment in pursuance of a resolution of either House of Parliament.

These provisions correspond to those of section 32 of the 1956 Act as amended.[65] Further, the provisions of the 1988 Act dealing with qualification for copyright protection expressly provide for cases where an Order has been made under section 159.[66]

Limitation on power to apply the 1988 Act. The power to make such Orders is, as it was under section 32 of the 1956 Act,[67] limited in that an Order is not to be made in relation to a country,[68] other than a Convention country or another Member State of the European Economic Community, unless Her Majesty is satisfied that provision has been or will be made under the law of that country in respect of the class of works to which the Order relates, giving adequate protection to the owners of copyright under Part I of the 1988 Act. A Convention country is a country which is a party to a Convention relating to copyright to which the United Kingdom is also a party.[69]   **3–215**

Power to curtail protection. Section 160 of the 1988 Act, like section 35 of the 1956 Act,[70] gives power to deprive citizens or subjects of countries not giving adequate protection to British works, of copyright under the 1988 Act. This power arises if the laws of a country[71] fail to give adequate protection to British works, or to one or more classes of such works. A British work is a work of which the author was a qualifying person at the material time within the meaning of section 154 of the 1988 Act.[72] In the given circumstances, an Order in Council can be made providing, either generally or in respect of specified classes of cases, that works first published after a date specified in the Order do not qualify for copyright protection by virtue of such publication if at the time of their first publication the authors are citizens or subjects of the country designated by the Order and not domiciled or resident in the United Kingdom or another country to which   **3–216**

---

[64] "Country" includes any territory: CDPA 1988, s.178.

[65] See para. 3–193, above.

[66] CDPA 1988, ss.154(2) and (3), 155(2) and 156(2). As to existing works, see Sch.1, para.5, in particular para.5(2)(b), and para.35.

[67] See para. 3–194, below.

[68] See para. 3–193, above.

[69] CDPA 1988, s.159(3) and (4).

[70] See para. 3–196, above.

[71] See para. 3–193, above.

[72] See paras 3–158 et seq., above.

the relevant provisions of Part I of the 1988 Act extend,[73] or are bodies incorporated under the laws of the designated country. Such an Order may be made in respect of literary, dramatic, musical and artistic works, sound recordings and films. No such Order has yet been made. A statutory instrument containing an Order in Council under section 160 of the 1988 Act is subject to annulment in pursuance of a resolution of either House of Parliament.

3–217   **International organisations.** Section 168 of the 1988 Act[74] contains provisions for conferring copyright on original literary, dramatic, musical and artistic works made by officers or employees of, or published by an international organisation and which do not qualify for copyright protection under sections 154 or 155 of the 1988 Act.[75] In such circumstances the organisation is to be the first owner of such copyright.[76] Such copyright subsists until the end of the period of 50 years from the end of the calendar year in which the work was made or such longer period as may be specified by Order in Council for the purpose of complying with the international obligations of the United Kingdom.[77] Any work in which copyright subsisted by virtue of section 33 of the 1956 Act immediately before commencement of the copyright provisions of the 1988 Act is to be deemed to satisfy the requirements of section 168(1) of the 1988 Act, but otherwise section 168 does not apply to works made or, as the case may be, published before such commencement. Copyright in any such work which is unpublished continues to subsist until the date on which it would have expired in accordance with the 1956 Act, or the end of the period of 50 years from the end of the calendar year in which the copyright provisions of the 1988 Act come into force, whichever is the earlier.[78]

An international organisation means an organisation the members of which include one or more states,[79] and the international organisations to which section 168 of the 1988 Act applies are those to which Her Majesty has by Order in Council declared that it is expedient that such section should apply.[80] Such an organisation is to be deemed to have, and to have had at all material times, the legal capacities of a body corporate for the purpose of holding, dealing with and enforcing copyright and in connection with all legal proceedings relating to copyright.[81] A statutory instrument containing an Order in Council under section 168 of the 1988 Act is subject to annulment in pursuance of a resolution of either House of Parliament.[82]

The 1988 Act also contains provisions relating to moral rights in works in which copyright originally vested in an international organisation.[83]

3–218   **Anonymous unpublished works: folklore.** Section 169 of the 1988 Act contains new provisions conferring copyright, in certain circumstances, on unpublished

---

[73] See, as to countries ceasing to be colonies, CDPA 1988, s.158(2)(a).
[74] For the corresponding provision of the Copyright Act 1956, s.33.
[75] See CDPA 1988, s.153(2) and (3).
[76] s.168(1), and see s.11(3).
[77] s.168(3), and see s.12(5).
[78] Sch.1, para.44.
[79] s.178.
[80] s.168(2). By the Copyright (International Organisations) Order 1989 (SI 1989/989), s.168 was applied to the United Nations, the Specialised Agencies of the United Nations and the Organisation of American States; see Vol.2, C1.i and CDPA 1988, s.302 as to the giving of financial assistance to international organisations.
[81] s.168(4). See, as to presumptions, CDPA 1988, ss.104(2)(b) and (3) and 107(6). See, as to exceptions from infringement, s.57(2)(b).
[82] s.168(5).
[83] ss.79(7)(b) and 82(1)(c) and (2): "sufficient disclaimer" s.178.

literary, dramatic, musical or artistic works of unknown authorship[84] where there is evidence that the author (or, in the case of a joint work, any of the authors) was a qualifying individual by connection with a country outside the United Kingdom. A qualifying individual is a person who at the material time (within the meaning of section 154 of the 1988 Act)[85] was a person whose works qualified under that section for copyright protection.[86] Section 169(2) of the 1988 Act further provides that if under the law of that country a body is appointed to protect and enforce copyright in such works, Her Majesty may by Order in Council designate that body for the purposes of that section. No such Order has yet been made. Such a designated body is to be recognised in the United Kingdom as having authority to do in place of the copyright owner anything, other than assign copyright, which it is empowered to do under the law of that country, in particular bringing proceedings in its own name.[87] Section 169 of the 1988 Act does not apply if there has been an assignment of copyright in the work by the author of which notice has been given to the designated body, and nothing in that section is to affect the validity of an assignment of copyright made, or licence granted, by the author or a person lawfully claiming under him.[88] A statutory instrument containing an Order in Council under section 169 of the 1988 Act is subject to annulment in pursuance of a resolution of either House of Parliament.[89]

Order in Council under section 159 of the 1988 Act 3–219

(a) **Generally.** By successive Orders in Council made under section 159 of the 1988 Act,[90] various provisions of the 1988 Act are applied in various ways, to various works originating in various foreign countries, including Taiwan, Singapore and Indonesia. This Order, though similar to, is more complicated than the Orders made under section 32 of the 1956 Act,[91] and it is important, at the outset, to bear in mind two matters. The first is that article 6 of the current Order provides that nothing in the Order is to be taken as derogating from the effect of paragraph 35, Schedule 1 to the 1988 Act, which provides that every work in which copyright subsisted under the 1956 Act immediately before August 1, 1989 is to be deemed to satisfy the requirements of Part I of the 1988 Act as to qualification for copyright protection. Part I includes sections 153–156, dealing with qualification for copyright protection. The second is that the Articles of the Order granting protection (articles 2, 3 and 4) are made subject to article 7. This article applies to (a) a work made before the commencement of the Act (August 1, 1989), but in which copyright did not subsist under the 1956 Act when it was made and (b) to a work made after commencement, but in which copyright did not subsist under the 1988 Act when the work was made, but where, in either case, copyright now subsists in the work by virtue of the Order. In these cases, where a person incurs or has incurred any expenditure or liability in connection with, for the purpose of or with a view to the doing of an act which at the time is not or was not an act restricted by any copyright in the work, the doing, or continued doing, of that act after copyright subsequently subsists in the work by virtue of articles 2(1), 3, 4(1)

---

[84] As to "unknown authorship", see CDPA 1988, s.9(4) and (5). "Folklore" is not referred to in s.169, only in the side note thereto.
[85] See paras 3–158 *et seq.*, above.
[86] CDPA 1988, s.169(5).
[87] s.169(3).
[88] s.169(6).
[89] s.169(4).
[90] Currently, the Copyright (Application to Other Countries) Order 1999 (SI 1999/1751), as amended. See Vol.2, C1.iv. For previous Orders, see the Copyright (Applications to Other Countries) Order 1993 (SI 1993/942), the Copyright (Application to Other Countries) (No.2) Order 1989 (SI 1989/1293), as amended. See, as to the unification of Germany, para. 24–65, below.
[91] See paras 3–198 *et seq.*, above.

or 4(5) is not be an act restricted by the copyright unless the owner of the copyright or his exclusive licensee (if any) pays such compensation as, failing agreement, may be determined by arbitration.[92]

3–220 **(b) Works.** The 1988 Act protects, as works, literary, dramatic, musical and artistic works, sound recordings, films, broadcasts, and the typographical arrangement of published editions.

3–221 **(c) Literary, dramatic, musical and artistic works, films and the typographical arrangements of published editions.** The Order, article 2(1), provides that sections 153, 154 and 155 of the 1988 Act are to apply in relation to:

  (i) persons who are citizens or subjects of a country specified in Schedule 1 to the Order[93] or are domiciled or resident there as they apply to persons who are British citizens or are domiciled or resident in the United Kingdom;

  (ii) bodies incorporated under the law of such a country as they apply in relation to bodies incorporated under the law of a part of the United Kingdom; and

  (iii) works first published in such a country as they apply in relation to works first published in the United Kingdom.

"First published" includes simultaneous publication under section 155(3) of the 1988 Act. This *prima facie* entitlement to copyright is then withdrawn, by article 2(2), in respect of certain works because of circumstances relating to their first publication. Where copyright does subsist in a work by virtue of article 2(1), then article 2(3) provides that the whole of Part I of the 1988 Act, including Schedule 1, applies in relation to the work, save in the case of designs of typefaces, as to which there are limitations.

3–222 **(d) Sound recordings.** By article 3 of the Order, foreign sound recordings are to be protected in the same way as foreign films are protected under article 2, subject to certain modifications. These have the effect of excluding from infringement of the copyright in a sound recording, playing in public, communicating to the public,[94] secondary infringement under section 26 of the 1988 Act and the summary offences under section 107(3) of that Act, unless either at least one of the countries relevant to the work for the purposes of article 2(1) is specified in Schedule 2 to the Order,[95] or the sound recording in question is a film soundtrack accompanying a film. No doubt the latter was occasioned by reason of the fact that film soundtracks were protected under the 1988 Act (as originally enacted) as sound recordings.

3–223 **(e) "Broadcasts".** Article 4(1) of the Order provides that, in relation to "broadcasts",[96] sections 153, 154 and 156 of the 1988 Act apply in relation to:

  (i) persons who are citizens or subjects of a country specified in Schedule 3

---

[92] Art.7(2).

[93] These are all countries which are parties to the Berne Copyright Convention and/or the Universal Copyright Convention and/or the Agreement establishing the World Trade Organisation (TRIPS) and/or are Member States of the European Community or otherwise give adequate protection under their law.

[94] The order (SI 1999/1751) indicates that s.20 of CDPA 1988 relates to the broadcasting and the inclusion in a cable programme of a work, but these are no longer restricted acts; the restricted act under s.20 is the communication of the work to the public. See paras 7–98 *et seq.*

[95] These countries are either parties to the Rome Convention for the Protection of Performers, Producers of Phonograms and Broadcasting Organisations and/or are Member States of the European Community or otherwise give adequate protection under their law.

[96] The Copyright (Application to Other Countries) Order 1999 (SI 1999/1715) has not yet been amended to reflect the fact that under the 1988 Act there are no longer separate protected subject matters of "broadcasts" and "cable programmes", but only one protected subject matter, namely

to the Order[97] or are domiciled or resident there as they apply to persons who are British citizens or are domiciled or resident in the United Kingdom;

(ii) bodies incorporated under the law of such a country as they apply in relation to bodies incorporated under the law of a part of the United Kingdom; and

(iii) broadcasts made from such a country as they apply to broadcasts made from the United Kingdom.

If a broadcast was made before the "relevant date", as defined by article 4(4),[98] copyright will not subsist in it by virtue of these provisions: article 4(2). Where copyright does subsist in a broadcast by virtue of article 4(1), then article 4(3) provides that the whole of Part I of the 1988 Act including Schedule 1 thereto apply in relation to the broadcast, subject to provisions dealing with the duration of copyright in repeats under section 14(5) of the 1988 Act. In addition, in relation to certain countries (indicated by an asterisk in Schedule 3) (a) the issuing of copies of the broadcast to the public, (b) the communication of the broadcast to the public insofar as it relates to inclusion of the broadcast in a "cable programme service" and (c) the performing, showing or playing of a non-television broadcast in public are not restricted acts.[99]

(f) "Cable programmes". In relation to the countries listed in Schedule 4 of the Order,[1] the above provisions relating to broadcasts apply to "cable programmes"[2] as they apply to broadcasts.[3]

3–224

(ii) United States

Position under old law. There was no treaty between Great Britain and the United States dealing with copyright, and it was not until 1891, after the passage of the "Chace Act", that British authors could obtain any effective protection for their works in that country. The Chace Act was repealed by the Copyright Act 1909, under which British authors could obtain some protection for their works, by virtue of a proclamation by the President of the United States to the effect that the British law granted to citizens of the United States the benefit of copyright on substantially the same basis as its own citizens.[4] American citizens were in fact able to obtain copyright in their works by first publishing them in England, or

3–225

"broadcasts", which encompasses both wireless broadcasts and cable broadcasts. See paras 3–82 *et seq.* Presumably art.4(1) should be read as applying to wireless broadcasts.

[97] These countries are either parties to the Rome Convention for the Protection of Performers, Producers of Phonograms and Broadcasting Organisations and/or the European Agreement on the Protection of Television Broadcasts and/or the Agreement establishing the World Trade Organisation (including TRIPs) and/or are Member States of the European Community or otherwise give adequate protection under their law.

[98] The "relevant date" is the date or (as the case may be) the earliest of the dates specified in Sch.3 to the Order (SI 1999/1751) in respect of the relevant country. For some countries, different dates are specified for television and non-television broadcasts.

[99] See Sch.5, para.3of SI 1999/1751. These derogations also apply to Cyrpus, but only in respect of non-television broadcasts: Sch.5, para.4.

[1] See para. 3–223, above. Presumably, art.4(5) of the Copyright (Application to Other Countries) Order 1999 (SI 1999/1715) should be read as relating to cable broadcasts.

[2] These countries are all either Member States of the European Community or otherwise give adequate protection under their law.

[3] Except that in relation to the application of art.4(2) (copyright not to subsist if made before the relevant date), the relevant date is January 1, 1985: arts 4(5), 5 and Sch.5.

[4] See *Copinger* (13th ed.), para.18–23.

simultaneously[5] in England or a Convention country and America; and they could, no doubt, sue in England in respect of any publication in breach of trust or confidence.[6] Further, by an Order in Council dated February 3, 1915,[7] made under section 29 of the 1911 Act, the protection of that Act was extended to works of classes (b) and (c) of that section, that is, unpublished works.[8] But works first published in America had no protection in this country.

3–226   **Wartime legislation.** By an Order in Council dated February 9, 1920,[9] the 1911 Act was applied to works first published in the United States between August 1, 1914 and the termination of the war, which had not been republished in the British Empire (except the self-governing dominions[10]) prior to February 2, 1920, provided the work was published in such area not later than six months after the termination of the war. It would appear that, if an authorised publication was made in the area in question after the 14 days allowed by the 1911 Act, but before February 2, 1920, advantage could not be taken of this Order. By an Order in Council dated August 6, 1942, as amended by an Order in Council[11] dated October 9, 1950, the 1911 Act was applied to works first published in the United States between September 3, 1939, and December 29, 1950, which had not been published in the same area[12] within 14 days of the publication in the United States. In order to take advantage of this Order publication must have been made not later than December 28, 1950.[13] The 1942 Order came into operation on the date of its publication in the *London Gazette*, March 10, 1944. While persons taking action before the commencement of the 1942 Order, on the assumption that no copyright existed, are given certain protection for accrued rights and interests, it remained obscure whether, if an authorised publication was in fact made, the owner thereof had a title by relation back.

3–227   **Present position of United States' works.** Copyright under the 1956 Act was originally conferred in respect of works of United States' origin by reason of that country's adherence to the Universal Copyright Convention, but the provisions of the Orders conferring this right were not retrospective in relation to published works except in so far as such works had already acquired copyright under these wartime Orders. However, this position changed after the United States acceded to the Paris Act of the Berne Convention with effect from March 1, 1989. This was because the most recent Order concerned with conferring copyright under the 1956 Act on works of United States origin was amended, as from March 8, 1989, in such a way as to remove United States' works from the qualification on protection in such Order of works first published in America before September 27, 1957,[14] other than in accordance with the wartime Orders. As this amendment granted copyright to works not previously entitled thereto, the amending Order

---

[5] As to the meaning of this expression, see para. 3–173, above. The time for publication was extended during the war by an Order of February 9, 1920.

[6] Ch.20, below.

[7] S.R. & O. 1915/130. See *Copinger* (8th ed.), p.468.

[8] *Oscar Trade Mark* [1979] R.P.C. 173, on appeal to the Court from the Registrar [1980] F.S.R. 429.

[9] S.R. & O. 1920/257.

[10] In *Warner Brothers Inc v The Roadrunner Ltd* [1988] F.S.R. 292, it was held that, under the 1942 Order, this area did include the self-governing dominions: but see Copyright Act 1911, ss.25 and 29, and para. 3–228, below.

[11] S.R. & O. 1942 No.1579; SI 1950/1641. The four Orders were repealed by the 1957 Order, but see para. 3–203, above and para. 3–227, below.

[12] See para. 3–219, above.

[13] See *Plantation Wood (Lancing) Ltd's Applications for a Trade Mark* [1958] R.P.C. 400.

[14] The Copyright (International Conventions) Order 1979 (SI 1979/1715), as amended by The Copyright (International Conventions) (Amendment) Order 1989 (SI 1989/157) and see para. 3–226, above.

contained a general provision preserving existing rights of persons who, before the commencement of such Order, had incurred expenditure or liability in connection with the reproduction or performance of any work or other subject-matter. Further, this amendment would appear to make reliance on the wartime Orders of less importance. Of course many existing works would have obtained United Kingdom protection, under the 1956 Act, by having been simultaneously published in the United Kingdom or a Berne Convention country, without the necessity of reliance upon such Orders in Council. Works originating in the United States or of which United States citizens, etc. are the authors, are now protected by Order in Council made under section 159 of the 1988 Act .[15]

(iii) Works of enemy origin

1914–1918 War legislation. Prior to the commencement of the 1914–1918 War,   **3–228** Germany, as a member of the Berne Convention, and Austria-Hungary by a special copyright treaty,[16] had been given, by Orders in Council, rights in this country in respect of works published in those countries, or whose authors were subjects of, or residents in those countries. Where works were made or published before the outbreak of the war, the copyright in this country, if the property of an enemy, became liable, under the Trading with the Enemy Acts 1914 to 1918, to be vested in the Public Trustee as the Custodian of Enemy Property.[17] With regard to works made or published in an enemy country after the outbreak of the war, it was doubted whether any copyright in this country was acquired, though the Orders in Council creating such copyright do not appear to have been revoked. To remove these doubts it was provided, by the Trading with the Enemy (Copyright) Act 1916,[18] that the copyright created by these Orders in Council in enemy works should subsist and should be vested in the Custodian of Enemy Property. A large number of enemy copyrights were vested in the Custodian in the course of the war, and licences were granted in respect of the publication of such works in this country. The Treaties of Peace provided for the revesting of such copyrights, but subject to severe disabilities. The terms upon which the revesting took place are set out, as regards Germany and Austria, in an Order in Council of November 9, 1920,[19] made under the powers conferred by the Trading with the Enemy Act 1914, and the Treaty of Peace Orders 1919 and 1920, and, as regards Hungary, in an Order in similar terms dated August 16, 1921. These Orders reserved power to the Board of Trade to grant licences, but the provisions of these Orders were revoked in 1930,[20] so that, subject to any licences which may have been granted, it appears that the owner of the work is now again beneficially entitled to it. In order, however, to follow the title to such works, it may still be necessary to consider the effect of this legislation upon German, Austrian and Hungarian works made or published before the termination of the war, that is, in the case of Germany, before January 10, 1920,[21] in the case of Austria, July 16, 1920, and in the case of Hungary, August 31, 1921,[22] since such works, if vested in the Custodian at any time, became revested, subject to the disabilities and

---

[15] See para. 3–219, above.
[16] This treaty, and the Order in Council made in conformity with it, will be found set out in full in *Copinger* (5th ed.).
[17] 4 & 5 Geo. 5, c.87, s.4(1); 8 & 9 Geo. 5, c.31, s.8.
[18] 6 & 7 Geo. 5, c.32; and see paras 3–000, *et seq.*, above.
[19] S.R. & O. 1920/2119.
[20] Order in Council May 17, 1930 (S.R. & O. 1930/341).
[21] By Order in Council of February 9, 1920, made under the Termination of the Present War (Definition) Act 1918 (8 & 9 Geo. 5, c.59).
[22] By Order in Council August 10, 1921, made under that Act.

restrictions created by the Peace Treaties and set out in the Orders in Council above referred to.

3–229   1939–1945 War legislation. By section 5 of the Patents, Designs, Copyright and Trade Marks (Emergency) Act 1939,[23] provision is made for the preservation of enemy copyrights and the continuing in force of Orders in Council made under the Copyright Act in relation to enemy countries. The result is that the war did not affect the creation or continuance of British copyrights in works originating in enemy countries. The 1939 Act[24] also continued in force licences granted by enemies to persons resident in the United Kingdom, subject to control. The 1939 Act[25] also gave power to the comptroller to grant licences in respect of enemy copyrights, and to vary existing licences.[26] In consequence of these provisions, few copyrights were vested in the Custodian under the ordinary trading with the enemy legislation, matters being dealt with by leaving the copyrights vested in enemies and granting licences as required. Certain German copyrights might, however, have been affected by virtue of the Enemy Property Act 1953,[27] in consequence of the exercise by, or on behalf of, the Crown of the rights thereby conferred.

B. Protection of Works Originating in the British Commonwealth: extension of Act

(i) Position before the 1911 Act

3–230   Colonial Conference 1910. At the Colonial Conference of 1910, resolutions were passed generally recognising the desirability of obtaining a uniform code of copyright laws which should apply throughout the King's dominions but insisting at the same time, that, at any rate, self-governing colonies ought not to be bound by any Imperial Copyright Act, or be made party to any convention or treaty entered into by the home government, without the assent of those colonies, and that all colonies ought to have the right to make local modifications in the law.[28] Accordingly, the 1911 Act was extended in general terms throughout HM dominions, but the self-governing dominions were given rights to decide whether or not it should operate within their territories. In fact, as will be seen, they all adopted the 1911 Act and, in consequence, the 1911 Act operated throughout the British Commonwealth. The 1956 Act, however, was framed so that it could only extend to the United Kingdom, the Isle of Man, the Channel Islands, colonies and protected territories. The 1988 Act can only extend to the United Kingdom (including United Kingdom territorial waters and British ships, aircraft and hovercraft), the Channel Islands, the Isle of Man and colonies.

3–231   Law prior to 1911 Act. Having regard to questions of title affecting older works, it is still necessary to understand the law as it existed prior to the 1911 Act. The Literary Copyright Act 1842 expressly extended copyright to every part of the

---

[23] (2 & 3 Geo. 6, c.107). The 1939 Act was amended by the CDPA 1988 (s.303(1) and (2) and Schs 7 and 8) to take account of design right: and see Copyright Act 1956, Sch.7, para.44(b), CDPA 1988, Sch.1, para.4(2). See also paras 3–191 *et seq.*, above.

[24] Patents, Designs, Copyright and Trade Marks (Emergency) Act 1939, s.1.

[25] ss.1 and 2.

[26] The nature and effect of these powers was discussed in *Novello & Co Ltd v Eulenburg (E.) Ltd* [1950] 1 All E.R. 44 and *Novello & Co Ltd v Hinrichsen Edition Ltd* [1951] Ch. 595, 1026.

[27] (1 & 2 Eliz. 2, c.52), most of which was repealed by the Statute Law (Repeals) Act 1976 (c.16).

[28] Report of Colonial Conference 1910 (Cd.5272).

British dominions,[29] but none of the Acts relating to artistic or dramatic copyright contained any similar provision. The Fine Arts Copyright Act 1862 did refer to the British dominions, giving copyright in all works made in the British dominions or elsewhere,[30] but it was held that there was nothing in that Act to extend the copyright throughout the British dominions, the provisions of sections 8 and 10 providing for the recovery of the penalties in England, Scotland and Ireland, and forbidding the importation into the United Kingdom of copies made in any part of the British dominions indicating a contrary intention.[31]

Whilst, therefore, a British author publishing a literary work in the United Kingdom obtained, under the Literary Copyright Act 1842, an imperial copyright extending throughout the British dominions, and was thus enabled to prevent piracies in any colony, a British artist, first publishing in the United Kingdom, obtained no imperial copyright, but, if he desired to prevent infringements in a colony, needed to acquire local copyright according to the laws of the particular colony.

Rights of colonial authors in United Kingdom. Conversely, it was held that the Literary Copyright Act 1842 did not confer copyright in the United Kingdom on works first published in the colonies.[32] This grievance was, however, removed by the International Copyright Act 1886, which, by section 8, provided that the Copyright Acts should, subject to the provisions of the Act of 1886, apply to a literary or artistic work first produced in a *British possession* in like manner as they applied to a work first produced in the United Kingdom: provided (a) that the enactments respecting the registry of the copyright in such work should not apply if the law of such possession provided for the registration of such copyright; and (b) that where such work was a book, the delivery to any persons or body of persons of a copy of any such work should not be required. If, therefore, in the particular colony there was no provision for registration, then the registration needed to be effected in this country.   3–232

The result, therefore, was that any work produced in the colonies became entitled to the same copyright as it would have obtained if it had been first produced in the United Kingdom, but that, although literary works published in the United Kingdom obtained copyright throughout the dominions, this was not the case with regard to artistic works.

Foreign reprints. By section 17 of the Literary Copyright Act 1842, all persons, other than the proprietor of the copyright or persons authorised by him, were forbidden to import into any part of the British dominions, for sale or hire, any printed book first composed or written or printed and published within the United Kingdom, in which there should be copyright, and reprinted in any country or place out of the British dominions, under penalty of £10, and double the value of the books.[33] Complaints arose, especially from Canada, with regard to this prohibition. It was contended that, in the sparsely populated colonies, where the circulating library system did not prevail, the price of English books was practically prohibitive, whilst English publishers were afraid to issue special cheap colonial editions, because they would not be able to prevent their re-importation into Great Britain. With a view to remedying these grievances, the Act com-   3–233

---

[29] (5 & 6 Vict., c.45) s.29.
[30] (25 & 26 Vict., c.68) s.1.
[31] *Graves (Henry) & Co Ltd v Gorrie* [1903] A.C. 496.
[32] *Routledge v Low* (1868) L.R. 3 H.L. 100.
[33] And see the Customs Consolidation Act 1876 (39 & 40 Vict., c.36), ss.151 and 152; and *Black v Imperial Book Co Ltd* (1903) 5 Ontario L.R. 184; (1905) 21 T.L.R. 540.

monly known as the Foreign Reprints Act was passed in 1847,[34] enabling the Crown, by Order in Council, to suspend the prohibition against importation into the colonies of English copyright works, subject to their making suitable provisions for the protection of British authors. Under this Act, numerous Orders in Council were issued by virtue of which cheap foreign reprints of copyright works were permitted to be imported into various colonies.

(ii) Position under the 1911 Act

3–234   **Provisions of the 1911 Act.** The provisions of the 1911 Act relating to the British possessions were contained in sections 25 to 28. The countries subject to the Crown were divided into three classes: (a) dominions of the Crown, other than self-governing colonies; (b) self-governing colonies, meaning thereby the Dominion of Canada, the Commonwealth of Australia, the Dominion of New Zealand, the Union of South Africa, and Newfoundland[35]; and (c) protectorates and Cyprus.

3–235   **Non self-governing colonies and protectorates.** The provisions of the 1911 Act relating to the colonies, other than the self-governing dominions, and to the protectorates and Cyprus, were comparatively simple. Section 25(1) enacted that that Act, "except such of the provisions thereof as are expressly restricted to the United Kingdom,[36] shall extend throughout His Majesty's dominions", subject to a saving in respect of a self-governing dominion. Section 28 enabled His Majesty by Order in Council to extend the 1911 Act to any territories under his protection, and to Cyprus, "and, on the making of any such Order, this Act shall, subject to the provisions of the Order, have effect as if the territories to which it applies or Cyprus were part of His Majesty's dominions to which this Act extends." The legislature of any British possession to which the 1911 Act extended had, however, power to modify, or add to, any of the provisions of that Act in its application to the possession.[37]

Thus, for the purposes of copyright, the colonies, other than the self-governing colonies, were treated as parts of the United Kingdom, and British copyright extended to all such colonies, and, vice versa, colonial copyright extended to the United Kingdom, except those modifications and additions to the British Act which the legislature of any colony should make, those only applying locally. Similarly, the following protectorates, to which by an Order in Council[38] dated June 24, 1912, the British Act was extended, were equally considered for copyright purposes to be part of the United Kingdom, namely, Cyprus, the Bechuanaland Protectorate, East Africa Protectorate, Gambia Protectorate, Gilbert and Ellice Islands Protectorate, Northern Nigeria Protectorate, Northern Territories of the Gold Coast, Nyasaland Protectorate, Northern Rhodesia, Southern Rhodesia, Sierra Leone Protectorate, Somaliland Protectorate, Southern Nigeria Protectorate, Solomon Islands Protectorate, Swaziland and Uganda Protectorate. Further, the British Act was extended to Palestine by an Order in Council of March 21, 1924, to Tanganyika by an Order in Council of April 16, 1924, to the Federated Malay States by Order in Council[39] of February 12, 1931, and to British Cameroons by Order in Council of March 16, 1933. Most of such colonies and

---

[34] Its official title is the Colonial Copyright Act 1847 (10 & 11 Vict., c.95).
[35] Copyright Act 1911, s.35(1).
[36] *i.e.* Copyright Act 1911, ss.11 and 12, relating to summary remedies.
[37] Copyright Act 1911, s.27: and see *Rediffusion (Hong Kong) Ltd v Att-Gen of Hong Kong* [1970] A.C. 1136, and *Butterworth and Co (Publishers) Ltd v Ng Sui Nam* [1987] R.P.C. 485.
[38] S.R. & O. 1912 No. 912.
[39] S.R. & O. 1931 No.105.

protectorates passed local laws regarding the seizure by the customs of infringing copies and introducing penal provisions similar to those contained in section 11 of the 1911 Act, such laws being authorised by section 27 of that Act.

The 1911 Act came into force in the above-mentioned possessions (including the Channel Islands other than Jersey) on July 1, 1912, except that it came into force in the Isle of Man on July 5, 1912, in India on October 30, 1912, in Papua on February 1, 1913, and in Jersey on March 8, 1913. The 1911 Act came into force in the above-mentioned protectorates at the dates referred to in the respective Orders.

Self-governing dominions. The self-governing dominions all became dominions to which the 1911 Act extended.[40] Section 25(1) of the 1911 Act provided that that Act should not extend to the self-governing dominions unless declared by the legislature of any dominion so to apply, either without modifications, or with modifications relating exclusively to procedure and remedies, or necessary for its application to the dominion. Newfoundland adopted the 1911 Act without modifications. The Commonwealth of Australia and the Union of South Africa made certain modifications.

3–236

Canada and New Zealand did not adopt this procedure, but passed independent Acts on similar lines to the 1911 Act. By section 25(2) of the 1911 Act it was provided that, if the Secretary of State certified, by notice published in the *London Gazette*, that any self-governing dominion had passed legislation under which works, the authors whereof were, at the date of the making of the works, British subjects resident elsewhere than in the dominion or (not being British subjects) were resident in the parts of His Majesty's dominions to which that Act extended, enjoyed within the dominion rights substantially identical with those conferred by that Act, then, whilst such legislation continued in force, the dominion should, for the purposes of the rights conferred by that Act, be treated as if it were a dominion to which that Act extended.

The Canadian Act of 1921 complied with the provisions of this section in its terms, and the New Zealand Act of 1913 also complied with them when coupled with an Order of the Executive Council made thereunder of March 27, 1914. The Secretary of State in fact certified, in respect of both dominions, under section 25(2), in 1923 as to Canada and in 1914 as to New Zealand.[41]

The Republic of Ireland. By an Order in Council dated October 27, 1930, made in pursuance of the Irish Free State (Consequential Provisions) Act 1922,[42] the Irish Free State was deemed to be a self-governing dominion for the purposes of the 1911 Act, and, by a further Order in Council dated October 27, 1930, made in pursuance of section 26(3) of the 1911 Act, the 1911 Act was declared to apply to works first published in the Irish Free State and to works of which the authors were, at the time of making the work, resident in the Irish Free State, provided that there was to be no right to prevent the translation into English of literary or dramatic works in Irish if an authorised translation was not made within 10 years from publication. This Order in Council was preserved by the provisions of paragraph 40(4) of Schedule 7 to the 1956 Act,[43] but was repealed by the Copy-

3–237

[40] As regards the Republic of Ireland, see para. 3–237, below.
[41] See *Mansell v Star Printing, etc. Ltd* [1937] A.C. 872 and *Walt Disney Productions v (H.) John Edwards Publishing Co Pty Ltd* (1954) 71 W.N.(N.S.W.) 150.
[42] 13 Geo. 5, c.2.
[43] Repealed by Statute Law (Repeals) Act 1986 (c.12), but see s.2 thereof.

right (International Conventions) Order 1957[44] which applied the 1956 Act to the Republic of Ireland as a Berne Convention country.

The 1911 Act was repealed in the Irish Free State by an Irish Free State Act[45] passed in 1927 but, since this was thought to create doubts as to subsisting copyrights,[46] a further Act was passed in 1929[47] declaring that, so far as was necessary for the subsistence in the Irish Free State of copyrights, the 1911 Act and every Order made thereunder should be deemed to continue to have full force and effect in the Irish Free State. A new Copyright Act was passed on April 8, 1963, to replace the existing law.[48]

3–238   **International arrangements with dominions.** With regard to any international arrangements which were made by the United Kingdom, it was provided that any Order in Council made under section 29 of the 1911 Act[49] was to apply to all His Majesty's dominions, except the self-governing dominions and any other possession specified in the Order.[50] Accordingly, the various Orders in Council which were made under that section applied the Order to all the dominions, colonies and possessions of the Crown, with the exception of the self-governing dominions, and also to Cyprus and the protectorates to which the Copyright Act was by Order in Council extended.[51] With regard to the self-governing dominions the 1911 Act authorised the Governor in Council of any such dominion to which that Act extended to make, as respects that dominion, the like Orders as the Crown in Council was, under sections 29 and 30 of that Act, authorised to make with regard to dominions other than self-governing dominions, and the provisions of those sections were, with the necessary modifications, to apply accordingly.[52] Orders in Council were, under this power, or a similar power in their own Acts, made by Australia, New Zealand, Newfoundland and the Union of South Africa, while the same effect was produced by the terms of the Canadian Act itself.

3–239   **Repeal by dominions of pre-1911 legislation.** It is to be noted that section 26(1) of the 1911 Act gave to the legislature of any self-governing dominion power to repeal any enactment relating to copyright, including the 1911 Act. All the dominions repealed the legislation prior to the 1911 Act which applied to them.

(iii) Position under the 1956 Act

3–240   **Repeal of the 1911 Act in the United Kingdom.** Paragraph 41 of Schedule 7 to the 1956 Act provided that, in so far as the 1911 Act, or any Order in Council made thereunder, formed part of the law of any country other than the United Kingdom at a time after that Act had been wholly or partly repealed in the law of the United Kingdom, it should, so long as it formed part of the law of that country, be construed and have effect as if that Act had not been so repealed.[53] The repeal of the 1911 Act in the United Kingdom, therefore, did not affect its operation, either in colonial territories, or in the self-governing dominions.

---

[44] *Copinger* (12th ed.), p.2105: see Copyright (International Conventions) Order 1979 (SI 1979/1715), as amended.

[45] Industrial and Commercial Property (Protection) Act 1927, No.16 of 1927. See *Copinger* (9th ed.), App.E.

[46] *Performing Right Society Ltd v Bray U.D.C.* [1930] A.C. 377.

[47] Copyright (Preservation) Act 1929, S.R. & O. No.25 of 1929. See *Copinger* (9th ed.), App.E.

[48] Copyright Act (S.R. & O. No.10 of 1963).

[49] See para. 3–191, above.

[50] Copyright Act 1911, s.30(1) and (3).

[51] See para. 3–235, above.

[52] Copyright Act 1911, s.30(2).

[53] See, as to repeal of the 1911 Act as part of the law of any country in the Commonwealth, the Copyright Act 1956 (Transitional Extension) Order 1959 (SI 1959/103).

Extension of the 1956 Act to other countries. Power was given, by section 31 **3–241** of the 1956 Act, to extend that Act and Orders in Council made under that Act, by Order in Council, to the Isle of Man, any of the Channel Islands, any colony,[54] any country outside HM dominions in which for the time being Her Majesty had jurisdiction, and any country consisting partly of one or more colonies and partly of one or more such countries as are last mentioned. Such Orders in Council could have extended the 1956 Act subject to exceptions and modifications. By extending provisions of the Act they become the law of the country to which they have been extended. This is to be contrasted with applying provisions of the Act to foreign works whereby they are given equivalent protection in this country to British works, which is dealt with in Part 2 of this Chapter. No Order in Council was made extending the main provisions of the 1956 Act to the Channel Islands, and so the 1911 Act remained in force there.[55]

Extension Orders under the 1956 Act **3–242**

  (i) Orders in Council under the 1956 Act were extended to various countries, either by the Orders in Council themselves,[56] or by other Orders in Council.[57] The 1956 Act and various Orders in Council thereunder were extended, by Orders in Council, to the following countries: the Isle of Man as from May 31, 1959,[58] Sarawak as from January 1, 1960,[59] Gibraltar as from June 1, 1960,[60] Fiji as from February 1, 1961,[61] Uganda as from January 1, 1962,[62] Zanzibar as from January 1, 1962,[63] Bermuda as from August 6, 1962,[64] North Borneo as from August 6, 1962,[65] the Bahamas as from October 11, 1962,[66] the Virgin Islands as from October 11, 1962,[67] the Falkland Islands as from June 10, 1963,[68] St Helena and dependencies as from June 10, 1963,[69] Seychelles as from June 10, 1963,[70]

---

[54] See *Rediffusion (Hong Kong) Ltd v Att-Gen of Hong Kong* [1970] A.C. 1136.

[55] Copyright Act 1911, ss.25(1) and 37(2)(c). The date the Act of 1911 came into operation in the Channel Islands was July 1, 1912, except for Jersey when the date was March 8, 1913. S.37(2) was repealed by Statute Law (Repeals) Act 1986 (c.12).

[56] See, for instance, the Copyright (International Conventions) Order 1979 (SI 1979/1715) as amended and the Copyright (Singapore) Order 1987 (SI 1987/940).

[57] See, for instance, the Copyright (Singapore) (Amendment) Order 1987 (SI 1987/1030), the Copyright (Taiwan) (Extension to Territories) Order 1987 (SI 1987/1826), the Copyright (Taiwan Order) (Isle of Man Extension) Order 1987 (SI 1987/1833) and the Copyright (Singapore) (Amendment) Order 1988 (SI 1988/1297).

[58] The Copyright (Isle of Man) Order 1959 (SI 1959/861), the Copyright (Isle of Man) Order 1970 (SI 1970/1437) and the Copyright (Isle of Man) Order 1971 (SI 1971/1848): these three Orders were revoked and repealed by the Copyright (Isle of Man) Order 1986 (SI 1986/1299). See also the Copyright Act 1956 (Transitional Extension) Order 1959 (SI 1959/103).

[59] The Copyright (Sarawak) Order 1959 (SI 1959/2215).

[60] The Copyright (Gibraltar) Order 1960 (SI 1960/847), as amended by the Copyright (Gibraltar) (Amendment) Order 1985 (SI 1985/1986).

[61] The Copyright (Fiji) Order 1961 (SI 1961/60).

[62] The Copyright (Uganda) Order 1961 (SI 1961/2462).

[63] The Copyright (Zanzibar) Order 1961 (SI 1961/2463), as amended by the Copyright (Zanzibar) (Amendment) Order 1962 (SI 1962/629).

[64] The Copyright (Bermuda) Order 1962 (SI 1962/1642), as amended by the Copyright (Bermuda) (Amendment) Order 1985 (SI 1985/1985). The Copyright (Bermuda) Order 1962 has been revoked by the Copyright (Bermuda) Order 2003 (SI 2003/1517). The 2003 Order extends various provisions of Pt 1 of the 1988 Act, subject to modifications, to Bermuda.

[65] The Copyright (North Borneo) Order 1962 (SI 1962/1643).

[66] The Copyright (Bahamas) Order 1962 (SI 1962/2184).

[67] The Copyright (Virgin Islands) Order 1962 (SI 1962/2185), as amended by the Copyright (Virgin Islands) (Amendment) Order 1985 (SI 1985/1988).

[68] The Copyright (Falkland Islands) Order 1963 (SI 1963/1037).

[69] The Copyright (St Helena) Order 1963 (SI 1963/1038).

[70] The Copyright (Seychelles) Order 1963 (SI 1963/1039).

Kenya as from July 4, 1963,[71] Mauritius as from May 21, 1964,[72] Montserrat as from November 5, 1965,[73] St Lucia as from November 5, 1965,[74] Bechuanaland as from December 4, 1965,[75] Cayman Islands as from December 4, 1965,[76] Grenada as from January 1, 1966,[77] British Guiana as from February 5, 1966,[78] British Honduras as from June 16, 1966,[79] Saint Vincent as from July 5, 1967,[80] Hong Kong as from December 12, 1972[81]. and the British Indian Ocean Territory as from May 14, 1984.[82] Each Order contains exceptions and modifications which vary according to local circumstances.

(ii) The Copyright (Computer Software) Amendment Act 1985[83] was to be construed as one with the 1956 Act[84] so that the provisions thereof could be extended to other countries like the provisions of the 1956 Act. The provisions of the 1985 Act were accordingly extended to the Isle of Man[85] and to a number of other countries.[86]

3–243 **Effect where the 1956 Act was so extended.** Copyright was defined, in section 1(1) of the 1956 Act, as the exclusive right to do and authorise others to do certain acts in the United Kingdom or in any other country to which the provisions of that Act extended, and, to the extent that the 1956 Act and Orders in Council thereunder had been so extended, common conditions for obtaining copyright protection existed throughout the area to which that Act and Orders in Council were so extended. Thus, the definition of "qualified person", in section 1(5) of the 1956 Act, included a person domiciled or resident in the United Kingdom or in another country to which any provision of that Act extended, and a body incorporated under the laws of any such country. Further, "first publication", in sections 2(2) and 3(3) of that Act, included first publication in the United Kingdom or in another country to which the section extended. Similar provisions occurred in sections 12(2), 13(2) and 15(1) of the 1956 Act and also as to infringement, in sections 1(2), 5 and 16. Further, by section 36(2)(b) of the 1956 Act, an assignment of copyright could be limited so as to apply to any one or more, but not all, of the countries in relation to which the owner of the copyright had by virtue of that Act the exclusive right to do certain acts.

The advantages of having such common conditions for obtaining and enforcing copyright throughout that area were, however, diminished by reason of some countries in that area becoming independent and in some cases enacting their

---

[71] The Copyright (Kenya) Order 1963 (SI 1963/1147).
[72] The Copyright (Mauritius) Order 1964 (SI 1964/689).
[73] The Copyright (Montserrat) Order 1965 (SI 1965/1858), as amended by the Copyright (Montserrat) (Amendment) Order 1985 (SI 1985/1987).
[74] The Copyright (St Lucia) Order 1965 (SI 1965/1859).
[75] The Copyright (Bechuanaland) Order 1965 (SI 1965/2009).
[76] The Copyright (Cayman Islands) Order 1965 (SI 1965/2010).
[77] The Copyright (Grenada) Order 1965 (SI 1965/2158).
[78] The Copyright (British Guiana) Order 1966 (SI 1966/79).
[79] The Copyright (British Honduras) Order 1966 (SI 1966/685).
[80] The Copyright (St Vincent) Order 1967 (SI 1967/974).
[81] The Copyright (Hong Kong) Order 1972 (SI 1972/1724), as amended by the Copyright (Hong Kong) (Amendment) Order 1979 (SI 1979/910) and the Copyright (Hong Kong) (Amendment) Order 1990 (SI 1990/588).
[82] The Copyright (British Indian Ocean Territory) Order 1984 (SI 1984/541).
[83] c.41.
[84] Copyright (Computer Software) Amendment Act 1985, s.4(2).
[85] The Copyright (Isle of Man) Order 1986 (SI 1986/1299).
[86] The Copyright (Computer Software) (Extension to Territories) Order 1987 (SI 1987/2200).

own copyright legislation.[87] A further consequence of independence was that many such countries became countries to which the provisions of the 1956 Act were applied,[88] rather than extended.

Power of such other countries to modify the 1956 Act. While the legislature of any country to which any provisions of the 1956 Act had been extended, as aforesaid, could have modified or added to those provisions in their operation as part of the law of that country, no such modifications or additions, except in so far as they related to procedure and remedies, were to be made so as to apply to any work or other subject-matter unless the qualification of authorship or publication arose with reference to that other country.[89] In fact numerous modifications of a minor character were embodied in the Orders in Council.

3–244

Proceedings in the United Kingdom. It was further provided[90] that, for the purposes of any proceedings under the 1956 Act in the United Kingdom, where the proceedings related to an act done in a country to which any provisions of that Act extended subject to exceptions, modifications or additions, the procedure and remedies were to be in accordance with that Act in its operation as part of the law of the United Kingdom; but, if the act did not constitute an infringement of copyright in its operation as part of the law of the country where the act was done, it was not to be treated as constituting an infringement of copyright under that Act in its operation as part of the law of the United Kingdom. Presumably the usual conditions would have applied in respect of service out of the jurisdiction but, subject to this, it appears that a defendant could have been sued in the United Kingdom in respect of an infringement in a colony, provided that the act of infringement would have been an infringement by the law of the colony if the proceedings had been brought there, but the procedure and remedies would have been those of the United Kingdom.

3–245

Position as to colonial territories and self-governing dominions distinguished. So far as the colonial territories are concerned, the making of the necessary Orders in Council created a similar situation to that existing under the 1911 Act. But, so far as concerns the self-governing dominions, these were outside the operation of the 1956 Act, and works originating in their territory were only protected in the United Kingdom in the same manner as works originating in foreign countries were protected, that is to say, by Order in Council under section 32 of the 1956 Act, applying the provisions of the 1956 Act to works originating in such countries.[91]

3–246

Position in period before Orders in Council made. To provide for the interim period after the commencement of the 1956 Act, and before Orders were made extending or applying that Act to colonial and self-governing territories, provision was made in paragraph 39 of Schedule 7 to that Act. The effect of this paragraph appeared to be that, until any such Order was made, for the purposes of construing any reference in any provision of that Act to countries to which that provision extended, such provision was treated as extending to the territory in question whether it was a self-governing territory or not. The Copyright (International Conventions) Order 1957, which came into operation on September

3–247

---

[87] See para. 3–249, below.
[88] See the Copyright (International Conventions) Order 1979 (SI 1979/1715), as amended.
[89] Copyright Act 1956, s.31(3): and see *Rediffusion (Hong Kong) Ltd v Att-Gen of Hong Kong* [1970] A.C. 1136.
[90] Copyright Act 1956, s.31(4).
[91] See para. 3–198, above.

27, 1957,[92] applied the 1956 Act in respect of works originating in the self-governing dominions, that position being continued by the Copyright (International Conventions) Order 1964,[93] then by the Copyright (International Conventions) Order 1972,[94] and then by the Copyright (International Conventions) Order 1979.[95] Works originating in other Commonwealth territories would have remained protected by virtue of paragraph 39 until the making of Orders in Council extending the 1956 Act to them.

3–248   **The Republic of Ireland.** As stated above,[96] the Republic of Ireland was treated as a self-governing dominion to which the 1911 Act did not extend, and copyright protection was afforded to works originating in that country by an Order in Council made under section 26(3) of the 1911 Act. After the commencement of the 1956 Act, therefore, paragraph 40(4) of Schedule 7 to that Act[97] applied in relation to the Irish Republic, and it was accordingly treated as a foreign country in respect of which an Order in Council under section 29 of the 1911 Act had been made. But the Republic of Ireland was one of the countries in respect of which protection was given by virtue of the Copyright (International Conventions) Order 1957,[98] then by the Copyright (International Conventions) Order 1964,[99] then by the Copyright (International Conventions) Order 1972,[1] and then by the Copyright (International Conventions) Order 1979.[2] The 1956 Act itself, in defining "qualified person", included an individual who was a citizen of the Republic of Ireland, but not a body corporate incorporated under the laws of the Republic, and the Republic of Ireland was not a country to which that Act extended for the purpose of the provisions regarding first publication.

3–249   **International arrangements with dominions.** As the 1956 Act could not have been extended to the self-governing dominions, international protection there depended upon the 1911 Act, and Orders in Council made under that Act, so long as that Act was in force there. In so far as the self-governing dominions passed new Copyright Acts of their own, the nature of international protection there will fall to be determined according to the provisions of those Acts.[3]

(iv) Position under 1988 Act

3–250   **Extension of the 1988 Act to other countries.** Power is given, by section 157 of the 1988 Act,[4] to extend the copyright provisions of the 1988 Act and Orders in Council made thereunder, by Order in Council to any of the Channel Islands, the

---

[92] SI 1957/1523.
[93] SI 1964/690.
[94] SI 1972/673.
[95] SI 1979/1715.
[96] See para. 3–237, above.
[97] Repealed by Statute Law (Repeals) Act 1986 (c.12), but see s.2 thereof.
[98] SI 1957/1523.
[99] SI 1964/690.
[1] SI 1972/673.
[2] SI 1979/1715.
[3] See also the Copyright (Status of Former Dependent Territories) Order 1990 (SI 1990/1512).
[4] This power is more limited than that under Copyright Act 1956, s.31; see para. 3–241, above. See also CDPA 1988, s.304(3), (4) and (5).

Isle of Man or any colony.[5] The extending Orders in Council can extend such provisions and Orders in Council subject to exceptions and modifications.[6]

Power of such other countries to modify the 1988 Act. The legislature of any **3–251** country to which the copyright provisions of the 1988 Act have been extended may, under section 157 of the 1988 Act, as under section 31 of the 1956 Act,[7] modify or add to such provisions in their operation as part of the law of that country. But such modifications or additions are limited to adapting such provisions to the circumstances of the country concerned as regards procedure and remedies or as regards works qualifying for copyright protection by virtue of a connection with that country.[8]

Effect where the 1988 Act is so extended. As has been seen,[9] where the 1956 **3–252** Act and Orders in Council thereunder had been extended, common conditions for obtaining copyright protection existed throughout the area to which that Act and Orders in Council were so extended, with the advantages resulting therefrom.

However, the situation does not appear to have been continued in its entirety by the 1988 Act. Thus, by section 157(1) of the 1988 Act, that Act is to extend to England and Wales, Scotland and Northern Ireland,[10] and the countries to which the 1988 Act can be extended are more limited than under the 1956 Act.[11] Further, copyright under the 1988 Act does not, as under the 1956 Act, appear to cover the right to do and restrain the doing of certain acts in countries to which the Act has been extended, as well as in the United Kingdom. Thus, by section 2 of the 1988 Act, the copyright owner is given the exclusive right to do the restricted acts specified in Chapter II of that Act, and the various sections in Chapter II, which also cover infringement, appear to be limited to the doing of acts in the United Kingdom.[12] Again, section 90(2) of the 1988 Act does not, like section 36(2)(b) of the 1956 Act, contain a provision for partial assignments as to one or more countries. Finally, the 1988 Act contains no provision similar to section 31(4) of the 1956 Act[13] under which proceedings could be brought in the United Kingdom in respect of an act done in a country to which the 1988 Act has been extended.

On the other hand, certain of the conditions for qualifying for copyright protection under the 1988 Act are similar to those under the 1956 Act[14] in that, for instance, by section 154(1) of the 1988 Act, individuals domiciled or resident in a country to which the copyright provisions of the 1988 Act have been extended and bodies incorporated under the law of such a country are included. Also included, by section 155(1) of the 1988 Act, are works first published in such a country as are, by section 156(1) of that Act, broadcasts made from a place in such a country.

---

[5] CDPA 1988, s.157(2) and (3): and see s.304(6). Various provisions of Pt 1 of the 1988 Act, subject to modifications, have been extended to Bermuda. See the Copyright (Bermuda) Order 2003 (SI 2003/1517).

[6] CDPA 1988, s.157(2) and (3).

[7] See para. 3–244, above.

[8] CDPA 1988, s.157(4).

[9] See para. 3–243, above.

[10] See CDPA 1988, s.161 and para.38, Sch.1 as to the territorial waters of the UK and the UK sector of the continental shelf. See also s.162 and para.39, Sch.1 as to British ships, aircraft and hovercraft.

[11] See paras 3–242 and 3–249, above.

[12] See CDPA 1988, ss.16–27, in particular ss.16, 18, 22, 24 and 27, and compare Copyright Act 1956, ss.1(1) and (2), 5 and 16.

[13] See para. 3–245, above.

[14] See, for instance, Copyright Act 1956, ss.1(5), 2(1) and (2), 3(2) and (3), 12(1) and (2), 13(1) and (2) and 15(1).

The result of this would appear to be that, although the relevant provisions of the 1988 Act can be extended to another country, as could the provisions of the 1956 Act, and although, as under the 1956 Act, a person resident in a country to which the 1988 Act has been extended, for instance, may get copyright under the 1988 Act, nonetheless whereas under the 1956 Act, an act done in a country to which the 1956 Act had been extended could be an infringement of copyright under the 1956 Act as well as of copyright under the 1956 Act as extended to that country, it will not now be an infringement of copyright under the 1988 Act to do an act in a country to which the 1988 Act has been extended. This will, if at all, only be an infringement of that country's law, that is the 1988 Act as extended to that country.

3–253   **Countries ceasing to be colonies.** Section 158 of the 1988 Act contains certain provisions applicable where the country to which the copyright provisions of that Act have been extended ceases to be a colony of the United Kingdom.[15] If that happens, such a country is, as from the date on which it ceases to be a colony, not to be treated as a country to which such copyright provisions extend for the purposes of section 160(2)(a)[16] and of sections 163 and 165.[17] Nonetheless it is to continue to be treated as a country to which such copyright provisions extend for the purposes of qualification for copyright protection[18] until an Order in Council is made in respect of that country under section 159 of the 1988 Act,[19] or an Order in Council is made declaring that it shall cease to be so treated by reason of the fact that such copyright provisions as part of the law of that country have been repealed or amended.[20] A statutory instrument containing such a declaratory Order in Council is subject to annulment in pursuance of a resolution of either House of Parliament.[21]

3–254   **Self-governing dominions and the Republic of Ireland.** Self-governing dominions do not fall within the extending provisions of the 1988 Act. The position was the same under the 1956 Act.[22] Protection of works originating in the self-governing dominions will, therefore, depend on an Order in Council being made under section 159 of the 1988 Act applying the copyright provisions of that Act to such works.

The 1988 Act, s.154(1), does not, as did the 1956 Act, in the definition of "qualified person",[23] include citizens of the Republic of Ireland in the definition of "qualifying person", nor does the 1988 Act, s.157(2), include the Republic of Ireland as a country to which the 1988 Act can be extended for the purposes of qualification by place of first publication, for instance.[24] Works originating in the Republic of Ireland are protected by the Order in Council made under section 159.[25]

3–255   **Dependent Territories**
    (i) General. As has been seen, the 1956 Act was extended to the Isle of Man

---

[15] CDPA 1988, s.158(1) and (2).
[16] See para. 3–216, above.
[17] See Ch.10.
[18] CDPA 1988, ss.154–156.
[19] See para. 3–214, above.
[20] CDPA 1988, s.158(3). As to countries in which the 1911 Act or the 1956 Act is in force ceasing to be a colony, see , CDPA 1988, Sch.1, para.36(5).
[21] CDPA 1988, s.158(4).
[22] See paras 3–246 and 3–249, above.
[23] Copyright Act 1956, s.1(5) and see paras 3–159 and 3–248, above.
[24] CDPA 1988, ss.155 and 156.
[25] *i.e.* currently the Copyright (Application to Other Countries) Order 1999, as amended. See para. 3–219, above.

and a number of other countries,[26] but not, except to a limited extent, to the Channel Islands, where the 1911 Act remained in force.[27] The 1988 Act, para.36, Sch.1, contains provisions dealing with what are defined as dependent territories, that is any of the Channel Islands, the Isle of Man or any colony.[28]

(ii) Channel Islands. Paragraph 36(1), Schedule 1 to the 1988 Act, provides that the 1911 Act is to remain in force as part of the law of any dependent territory in which it was in force immediately before the commencement of the copyright provisions of the 1988 Act, such as the Channel Islands, until such provisions come into force in that territory by virtue of an Order under section 157 of the 1988 Act (extension),[29] or in the case of the Channel Islands, the 1911 Act is repealed by Order under paragraph 36(3). Certain provisions of the 1956 Act were, in fact, extended to the Channel Islands, (as well as to the Isle of Man and certain other countries), by Order in Council,[30] and paragraph 36(2), of Schedule 1 to the 1988 Act provides that an Order in Council in force immediately before such commencement which extends to any dependent territory any provisions of the 1956 Act shall remain in force as part of the law of that territory until the copyright provisions of the 1988 Act come into force in that territory by virtue of an Order under section 157 of the 1988 Act (extension), and while it remains in force such an Order may be varied under the provisions of the 1956 Act under which it was made. It would appear, therefore, that, until an Order is made under the 1988 Act, the position in the Channel Islands remains the same. At the moment no such Orders have been made.

3–256

As to the future, presumably the Order in Council extending certain provisions of the 1956 Act to the Channel Islands[31] will go if, and when, an Order is made in respect of the Channel Islands under section 157 of the 1988 Act. So far as the 1911 Act is concerned, this will remain in force in the Channel Islands until an Order is made under section 157 or the Act is repealed by an Order under paragraph 36(3). Paragraph 36(3) provides that, if it appears to Her Majesty that provision with respect to copyright has been made in the law of any of the Channel Islands otherwise than by extending the copyright provisions of the 1988 Act, Her Majesty may by Order in Council repeal the 1911 Act as it has effect as part of the law of that territory. However, if such an Order is made, it will be made, apparently, in a situation where the copyright provisions of the 1988 Act have not been extended to the Channel Islands. If that be so, it is unclear what is to happen to the Order extending certain provisions of the 1956 Act to the Channel Islands,[32] since, although paragraph 36(3) also refers to revoking an Order extending the 1956 Act, this appears, when taken with paragraph 36(2)(b), only to relate to the Isle of Man.[33]

Finally, paragraph 36(4) provides that a dependent territory in which the 1911 or 1956 Act remains in force is to be treated, in the law of the countries to which the copyright provisions of the 1988 Act extend, as a country to which such provisions extend. Further, that those countries are to be treated in the law of such a territory as countries to which the 1911 Act or, as the case may be, the 1956 Act extends. The Channel Islands are dependent territories but, again, this is not

---

[26] See para. 3–242, above.

[27] See para. 3–241, above.

[28] CDPA 1988, Sch.1, para.36(6).

[29] See para. 3–250, above, and see CDPA 1988, s.157(5). Certain non-copyright provisions of the 1988 Act have been extended to Guernsey under s.304(5) by The Copyright, Designs and Patents Act 1988 (Guernsey) Order 1989 (SI 1989/1997).

[30] The Copyright Act 1956 (Transitional Extension) Order 1959 (SI 1959/103).

[31] The Copyright Act 1956 (Transitional Extension) Order 1959 (SI 1959/103).

[32] The Copyright Act 1956 (Transitional Extension) Order 1959 (SI 1959/103).

[33] See paras 3–241 and 3–243, above.

entirely clear since certain provisions of the 1956 Act have been extended to the Channel Islands.[34]

3–257 **(iii) Isle of Man.** Paragraph 36(2), Schedule 1, to the 1988 Act, provides that an Order in Council in force immediately before the commencement of the copyright provisions of the 1988 Act which extends to any dependent territory, such as the Isle of Man, any of the provisions of the 1956 Act is to remain in force as part of the law of that territory until such provisions come into force in that territory by virtue of an Order under section 157 of the 1988 Act (extension), or in the case of the Isle of Man, the Order is revoked by Order under paragraph 36(3), and while it remains in force such an Order may be varied under the provisions of the 1956 Act under which it was made.

Although certain non-copyright provisions of the 1988 Act were extended to the Isle of Man, the principal provisions of the Act were not applied until July 1, 1992, when an Order was made under section 159 of the Act applying sections 153 to 156 of the Act to the Isle of Man.[35]

3–258 **(iv) Hong Kong; dependent territories.** By reason of paragraph 36(1)(a) and (2)(a) of Schedule 1 to the 1988 Act, the position will remain the same until an Order is made under section 157 of the 1988 Act extending the copyright provisions of the 1988 Act and Orders in Council made thereunder to such territories. No such Orders have yet been made, and as to Hong Kong, no such Order will be made. Thus, certain provisions of the 1956 Act, not including section 32 of that Act, were extended to Hong Kong by Orders in Council.[36] Further, paragraph 36(2) of Schedule 1 to the 1988 Act, which provides that such Orders in Council are to remain in force until an Order is made under section 157 of the 1988 Act, also provides that, while they remain in force, they may be varied under the provisions of the 1956 Act under which they were made. Such a variation was made by a further Order in Council with effect from April 12, 1990.[37] The effect of this further Order in Council was to extend to Hong Kong section 32 of the 1956 Act suitably amended. Section 32 of the 1956 Act enabled Her Majesty, by Order in Council, to apply the provisions of the 1956 Act to countries to which they did not extend,[38] and the amended section 32 extended to Hong Kong enabled the Governor of Hong Kong by Order to apply provisions of the 1956 Act to such countries. Further, whereas certain Orders in Council applying provisions of the 1956 Act were extended to Hong Kong,[39] the only Order in Council made applying provisions of the 1988 Act[40] was not extended to Hong Kong.[41] Paragraph 36(4) deals with the relationship between a dependent territory and other countries whilst the 1911 or 1956 Act remains in force in such territory.

3–259 **Non-dependent territories.** Under section 31(1) of the 1956 Act, that Act could

---

[34] The Copyright Act 1956 (Transitional Extension) Order 1959 (SI 1959/103).
[35] The Copyright (Application to the Isle of Man) Order 1992 (SI 1992/1313). At the same time the Copyright (Isle of Man) (Revocation) Order 1992 (SI 1992/1306) revoked the Copyright (Isle of Man) Order 1986, pursuant to para.36(3) of Sch.1 to the 1988 Act. The extension of non-copyright provisions of the 1988 Act is effected under CDPA 1988, s.304(4) and (6) by the Copyright, Designs and Patents Act 1988 (Isle of Man) (No.2) Order 1989 (SI 1989/1292); by the CDPA 1988 (Isle of Man) Order 1990 (SI 1990/1505); and by CDPA 1988 (Isle of Man) (No.2) Order 1990 (SI 1990/2293).
[36] The Copyright (Hong Kong) Order 1972 (SI 1972/1724) and the Copyright (Hong Kong) (Amendment) Order 1979 (SI 1979/910).
[37] The Copyright (Hong Kong) (Amendment) Order 1990 (SI 1990/588).
[38] See paras 3–193 et seq., above.
[39] See, for instance, the Copyright (International Conventions) Order 1979 (SI 1979/1715) as amended, and the Copyright (Singapore) Order 1987 (SI 1987/940).
[40] The Copyright (Application to Other Countries) (No.2) Order 1989 (SI 1989/1293) as amended.
[41] See para. 3–219, above.

be, and was, extended to certain countries.[42] Also, by virtue of paragraph 39(2) of Schedule 7 to the 1956 Act, certain countries were to be treated as countries to which the 1956 Act extended.[43] Paragraph 37 of Schedule 1 to the 1988 Act contains provisions dealing with such of those countries which were not immediately before the commencement of the copyright provisions of the 1988 Act dependent territories. Dependent territory means any of the Channel Islands, the Isle of Man or any colony,[44] and paragraph 37(1) provides that Her Majesty may by Order in Council conclusively declare for the purposes of paragraph 37 whether a country[45] was a country to which the 1956 Act extended or was treated as such a country.[46]

Paragraph 37(2) provides that a country to which paragraph 37 applies is to be treated as a country to which the copyright provisions of the 1988 Act extend for the purposes of sections 154 to 156 of the 1988 Act (qualification for copyright protection) until an Order in Council is made in respect of that country under section 159 of the 1988 Act (application),[47] or an Order in Council is made declaring that it shall cease to be so treated by reason of the fact that the provisions of the 1956 Act or, as the case may be, the 1911 Act, which extended there as part of the law of that country have been repealed or amended. A statutory instrument containing an Order in Council under paragraph 37 is subject to annulment in pursuance of a resolution of either House of Parliament.[48]

7. WORKS DENIED PROTECTION

Copyright is a creature of statute. The 1988 Act accords copyright to the works described in section 1(1) which meet the requirements for subsistence of copyright set out in section 153 and Chapter IX of the Act, discussed above. Nowhere in the 1988 Act[49] is the existence of that right qualified by considerations such as public policy, which do not, therefore, affect the question of the subsistence of copyright in a work. Thus, copyright will subsist in a work which otherwise satisfies the requirements of the Act, even though the work may be considered by some to be libellous, immoral, obscene, scandalous, irreligious, to involve deception of the public or where its exploitation would otherwise be contrary to public policy.[50]

3–260

Although copyright will subsist in such works, the court retains a jurisdiction to refuse to enforce some or all of the rights of a copyright owner, on the grounds of public interest or otherwise.[51] It had previously been held that the courts had only a limited, residual jurisdiction to decline to allow its process to be used in cases relating to the nature of the work, and that otherwise the permitted act pro-

---

[42] See para. 3–241, above.

[43] See para. 3–247, above.

[44] CDPA 1988, Sch.1, para.36(6), and see para. 3–255, above.

[45] "Country" includes any territory: CDPA 1988, s.178.

[46] See the Copyright (Status of Former Dependent Territories) Order 1990 (SI 1990/1512).

[47] See para. 3–214, above.

[48] CDPA 1988, Sch.1, para.37(3).

[49] The position has been the same in successive copyright enactments.

[50] Note, however, that in *Glyn v Weston Feature Film Co Ltd* [1916] 1 Ch. 261, at 269, Younger J. stated said that copyright could not subsist in a work of a grossly immoral tendency, but it is suggested that the better view is that copyright subsists but will not necessarily be enforced.

[51] *Ashdown v Telegraph Group Ltd* [2001] EWCA (Civ) 1142, which establishes that a defence of public interest is generally available to copyright claims. See further in the text. The jurisdiction to deny relief is preserved by CDPA 1988, s.171(3): "Nothing in this Part affects any rule of law preventing or restricting the enforcement of copyright, on grounds of public interest or otherwise". The equivalent provision under the 1956 Act (s.46(4)) was rather more limited, referring only to any rule of equity relating to breaches of trust or confidence.

visions of the Act[52] provided a complete code striking the balance between the interests of the public and the copyright owner.[53]This residual jurisdiction was said to apply in cases where the work was: (i) immoral, scandalous or contrary to family life; (ii) injurious to public life, public health and safety or the administration of justice; or (iii) liable to incite or encourage others to act in a way referred to in (ii).[54] While the court has refused to enforce copyright claims in a variety of such cases, it is now established that the limits of the defence of public interest in particular are not circumscribed or confined to these categories and the circumstances in which public interest can override rights of copyright are not capable of precise categorisation or definition.[55] Indeed, a further category of public interest has now been identified, namely, cases where the rights of the copyright owner must give way to the right to freedom of expression under Article 10 of the European Convention on Human Rights.[56] While these are all matters which in principle go to a defence to a copyright claim rather than issues of subsistence of copyright, they are for convenience dealt with here.

Historically, this jurisdiction has been founded on the rule that is against public policy to enforce the exclusive rights of copyright where the exploitation of such rights would itself be against the public interest.[57] Before the fusion of the courts of equity and law, the decisions took the form of a refusal by a court of equity to grant an injunction, leaving the copyright owner to pursue such remedy as he might have at law,[58] although sometimes all forms of relief were denied.[59] Today, no doubt, the nature of the exercise of the jurisdiction will vary according to the circumstances. Sometimes it will be sufficient to deny a claimant an injunction, leaving him to such remedy as he may have in damages; sometimes public policy will require that any pecuniary remedy be denied as well. Further, there is no reason in principle why, in relation to the same work, relief should not be refused in some circumstances but granted in others. So, for example, if a claimant is seeking to restrain dissemination of a grossly immoral or pornographic work in order to preserve the market for himself, an injunction might no doubt be refused, but if the work was always intended to be kept private or the claimant has come to regret having made it in the first place, there seems no good reason in principle why an injunction should not be granted,[60] and indeed it would be in the public interest to do so. Again, while an injunction to restrain dissemination of a confidential document may be refused where there is an overriding right to freedom of expression, which requires that the contents of the document be made public, once the contents have received sufficient publicity and the public interest requirement has been satisfied, there is no reason in principle to deny relief in respect of others who seek to make a profit out of further exploitaion of the work.

---

[52] See Ch.9.

[53] *Hyde Park Residence Ltd v Yelland* [2001] Ch. 143, Mance L.J. dissenting. The jurisdiction was said to relate to the nature of the work itself and not the particular use intended to be made of it, since copyright is assignable: see *per* Aldous L.J., at para.66.

[54] See *Hyde Park Residence Ltd v Yelland* [2001] Ch. 143, *per* Aldous L.J. at para.66. It had already been established that the defence was not confined to cases in which the claimant had been guilty of some inquity or wrongdoing. See *Lion Laboratories Laboratories v Evans* [1985] Q.B. 526 at 537, 538, 550. In previous editions of this work, the jurisdiction was described as consisting of cases where the court had considered the work to be libellous, immoral, obscene, scandalous or irreligious, or to involve deception of the public.

[55] *Ashdown v Telegraph Group Ltd* [2001] EWCA (Civ) 1142.

[56] *Ashdown v Telegraph Group Ltd* [2001] EWCA (Civ) 1142.

[57] See, *e.g. Stockdale v Onwhyn* (1826) 5 B. & C. 173.

[58] See, *e.g. Walcot v Walker* (1802) 7 Ves. 1; *Lawrence v Smith* (1822) Jac. 471.

[59] See, *e.g. Stockdale v Onwhyn* (1826) 5 B. & C. 173; *Glyn v Weston Feature Film Co Ltd* [1916] 1 Ch. 261.

[60] *Southey v Sherwood* (1817) 2 Mer. 435, 438.

Works immoral, scandalous or contrary to family life. There have been vari-   **3–261**
ous cases where the courts have refused to grant relief on these grounds. For
example, works have been denied protected on the grounds of gross immorality
or indecency,[61] or their libellous[62] or irreligious[63] content. In one curious case,
relief was granted in respect of leaflet purporting to be the imaginary will of
Adolf Hitler.[64] Such readiness on the part of the judges in the past to apply their
own views in deciding what works should be refused protection gave rise to
criticism.[65] In the present day, in which the public perception of such matters is
different, the courts can be expected to reflect this difference and to take an attitude which is far less protective of the public. Attitudes to what amounts to unacceptable irreligious material have changed,[66] and at least in relation to sexual
conduct protection is only likely to be refused to a work considered as having a
grossly immoral tendency by present-day standards.[67]

Works injurious to public life, public heath and safety, or the administration   **3–262**
of justice. Examples of cases in this category are those where the work involves
a deception of the public. Thus, a claim failed where the copyright work was
falsely held out to be a translation from the German of an author who had a high
reputation for works of that kind, and the object had been to deceive purchasers
and to give the work a value which it would not otherwise have had.[68] The same
principle was applied where the claimant published an illustrated catalogue of
trucks, trolleys and barrows made by him which contained pages headed "Inven-
tor, patentee, and sole maker" and "Slingsby's Patents", despite the claimant having no English patent for the various articles represented.[69] The catalogue also
contained pictures of buildings on which the claimant's name was written in
large letters, although the claimant did not occupy the whole of them. The defendant had copied the claimant's catalogue, but the claimant was refused an injunction on the grounds that the catalogue was calculated to deceive the public (as to

---

[61] *Stockdale v Onwhyn* (1826) 5 B. & C. 173 (a book of memoirs of Harriette Wilson, a courtesan); *Glyn v Weston Feature Film Co Ltd* [1916] 1 Ch. 261 (work of "grossly immoral tendency"); *Goeie Hoop Vitgewers (Ecendoms) B.P.K. v Central News Agency* (1953) (2) S.A. 843 (morbid presentation of sordid details of practice and acts of prostitution, likely to corrupt the young and inexperienced). But *cf. Pastickniak v Dojacek* [1923–28] Mac.C.C. 423 (book's contents merely "coarse and nasty", rather than suggesting lust, sexual passion or gross indecency).
[62] *Walcot v Walker* (1802) 7 Ves. 1 (criminally libellous publication); *Southey v Sherwood* (1817) 2 Mer. 435; *Stocksdale v Onwhyn* (1826) 5 B. & C. 173 (where the book also contained passages that were slanderous); *Hime v Dale* (1809) 2 Camp. 27n (no protection if work contained so gross a libel as to affect public morals).
[63] *Lawrence v Smith* (1822) Jac. 471; *Murray v Benbow* (1822) Jac. 474n. (injunction refused in respect of Lord Byron's poem "Cain").
[64] *A. Bloom & Sons Ltd v Black* [1936–45] Mac.C.C. 274 (the leaflet was described as coarse and nasty, and deprived of merit of any sort).
[65] Story J., in referring to Lord Eldon's decisions in cases cited on this point, said (2 Story's Eq. Jur. at 938): "If a court of equity, under colour of its general authority, is to enter upon all the moral, theological, metaphysical, and political inquiries, and if it is to decide dogmatically upon the character and bearing of such discussions, and the rights of authors growing out of them, it is obvious that absolute power is conferred over the subject of literary property, which may sap the very foundations on which it rests, and retard, if not entirely suppress, the means of arriving at physical as well as at metaphysical truth".
[66] See *R. v Lemon* [1979] A.C. 617, involving an alleged blasphemous libel concerning the Christian religion published in the magazine *Gay News*.
[67] This was the view adopted by Browne-Wilkinson V.-C. in *Stephens v Avery* [1988] Ch. 449 (a confidential information case), noting the difficulty caused by the fact that there no longer exists an accepted code of sexual morals. In *Mak Hau-Shing v Oriental Press Group Ltd* [1996] 1 H.K.L.R. 245, the court said that it would refuse to enforce copyright in photographs if they were indecent, obscene or otherwise of a grossly immoral tendency, or perhaps where, if they were merely mildly pornographic, the subject of the photographs had been subjected to coercion.
[68] *Wright v Tallis* (1845) 1 C.B. 893.
[69] *Slingsby v Bradford Patent Truck, etc. Co* [1905] W.N. 122; [1906] W.N. 51, approved in *Att.-Gen. v Guardian Newspapers Ltd (No.2)* [1990] 1 A.C. 109, *per* Lord Jauncey at 294. In *Hayward Bros v Lely & Co* (1887) 56 L.T. 418, the claimant's catalogue included one item which was described as patented, which indeed it had been, but the patent expired a short time after publication. An injunction was refused as to those parts where a mistatement was made.

the claimant having patents and as to its building), and that the claimant was attempting to obtain trade regardless of the manner in which it was obtained. No doubt relief would be refused in respect of a work intended to be used to further some illegal purpose, such as unlawful betting[70] or an unlawful restraint of trade,[71] or for a work written in breach of confidence.[72]

3–263   **Works infringing other works.** Today it is clear that copyright can subsist in a work which itself infringes copyright in an earlier work,[73] and the issue is whether the court will enforce such copyright. As to this, a work which itself is an infringement of an earlier work, but which otherwise satisfies the requirements for copyright to subsist in the work,[74] will normally be entitled to protection, subject to the right of the owner of the earlier copyright work to receive a share of any sum recovered.[75] The position might possibly be different if some moral obloquy was involved in the creation of the later work.[76]

3–264   **Copyright and freedom of expression.** Where the right to freedom of expression under Article 10 of the European Convention on Human Rights comes into potential conflict with the rights of a copyright owner, the permitted act provisions of the 1988 Act, in particular the fair dealing provisions, will usually provide a defence. There may, however, be exceptional and rare cases where this is not the case, even construing the 1988 Act as generously as possible to accommodate the right. In such circumstances, and where the Article 10 right is paramount in the public interest, a court would be bound to deny the copyright owner any relief the effect of which would be to prevent that freedom of expression.[77] Usually, this will involve the denial of an injunction, although not a claim to damages or an account of profits.[78] The topic is considered in more detail elsewhere.[79]

---

[70] This seems to have been accepted in *Barnard v White & Co* [1923–28] Mac.C.C. 218, although there the particular activity involved, namely credit betting on football matches, was not unlawful and so relief was granted.

[71] Again, this seems to have been accepted in *British Oxygen Co Ltd v Liquid Air Ltd* [1925] Ch. 383, although there it was held that the copyright work being relied on, a business letter, had been written as a legitimate act in furtherance of trade.

[72] See *Att-Gen v Guardian Newspapers Ltd (No.2)* [1990] 1 A.C. 109, HL at 262, 275–276, 294, although Lord Griffiths, at 276, considered that the copyright would in those circumstances have belonged to the person to whom the confidence was owed (in that case, the Crown), so that presumably there would have been no objection to the Crown relying on copyright to prevent dissemination of the work. Lord Jauncey, at 294, considered that no one could have been prevented from copying the work.

[73] *Redwood Music Ltd v Chappell & Co Ltd* [1982] R.P.C. 109 at 120 (Goff J.), applying *Wood v Boosey* (1866) L.R. 2 Q.B. 340; (1867) L.R. 3 Q.B. 223 at 229 (arrangement of a score of an opera held to be subject of copyright, notwithstanding that its publication without the authority of the composer of the original opera would be an infringement).

[74] As to whether such a work qualifies as original, see para. 3–141, above. In some of the older cases, relief was refused on the ground that the work was infringing: see *e.g. Cary v Faden* (1799) 5 Ves. 23. *Sailendra Nath De v Chayanika Chire Mandir* (1950) 55 Cal.W.N. 713; *Gouindan. v Gopalakrishna Kone* [1955] Mad.W.N. 369.

[75] *ZYX Music GmbH v King* [1995] F.S.R. 566; [1995] 3 All E.R. 1 at 9h to 11b, *per* Lightman J.

[76] *ZYX Music GmbH v King* [1995] 3 All E.R. 1, at 10g. See also *Cary v Faden* (1799) 5 Ves. 23.

[77] *Ashdown v Telegraph Group Ltd* [2001] EWCA (Civ) 1142.

[78] *Ashdown v Telegraph Group Ltd* [2001] EWCA (Civ) 1142. An earlier case where this occurred was *Lion Laboratories v Evans* [1985] Q.B. 526, where an injunction restraining publication of confidential memoranda which cast doubt on the accuracy of the breathalysers, and thus the safety of convictions, was refused on the grounds of public interest. A fair dealing defence was not, however, argued and today it seems likely that such a defence would succeed, obviating the need for reliance on a separate public interest defence.

[79] See para. 22–82, below.

AUTHORSHIP OF COPYRIGHT WORKS

1. INTRODUCTION

This chapter is concerned with who is to be regarded as the "author" of the vari-   **4–01**
ous categories of copyright works. Establishing the identity of the author of a
copyright work is important for a number of reasons:

(a) Whether a work qualifies for protection at all may depend on the status of
    the author.[1]

(b) It is usually necessary to know who the author of the work was in order to
    determine who was the first owner of the copyright.[2]

(c) For many works, the term of copyright is calculated by reference to the
    date of death of the author.[3]

(d) In the case of many copyright works, the author has important moral rights
    and a right to remuneration from rental of certain copies of his works.[4]

It is particularly important to keep in mind the distinction between the author
of a work and the owner of the copyright in it. Thus, for example, the author of a
work created by an employee is the employee but the first owner of the copyright
in the work will generally be the employer.[5] Again, confusion can arise unless it
is remembered that the term of copyright is not dependent on the identity of the
owner of the copyright but in general only on the identity of the author. So too,

---

[1] See Ch.3, above.
[2] See Ch.5, below. But note that the author will not necessarily be the first owner of the copyright.
[3] See Ch.6, below.
[4] As to moral rights, see Ch.11, below. As to the unwaivable right to remuneration, see paras 5–11
and 7–89, below.
[5] As to works of employees, see paras 5–11 *et seq.*, below.

although copyright may be transferred by assignment or operation of law, the moral rights of the author and his right to remuneration from rental of copies cannot be transferred in this way. They remain with the author until his death.[6]

4–02   **Authorship a matter of status.** Authorship is a question of status and fact, not agreement. An agreement between parties as to who the author is, or should be, cannot therefore confer the status of authorship on someone who was not in law the author.[7]

4–03   **Conflict with civil law systems of copyright.** For many years there has existed a conflict between common law and civil law systems of copyright law in the approach to the status of an author and indeed what works qualify for copyright protection.[8] Although this conflict has not in the past been of great practical significance to practitioners in the United Kingdom, it is becoming increasingly important, particularly with the steps being taken to harmonise the copyright laws of the Member States of the European Union.[9] The conflict has its origins in the different approach to the rationale of copyright protection. In the civil law, or *droit d'auteur*, systems, a work must be a work of personal, intellectual creation to be worthy of "author's right" protection. The works protected by author's right are therefore original literary, dramatic, musical and artistic works.[10] As such, they are regarded as part of the personality of the author. An author has both economic rights, enabling him to benefit from the exploitation of his work, but also, and no less significant, moral rights, enabling him to decide whether his work should be published at all and, if it is published, to control the form of publication, to prevent his work from being distorted or mutilated ("the right of integrity"), and the right to be identified as its creator ("the paternity right"). In relation to his economic rights, the civil law systems recognise that authors may have a weak bargaining position and so tend to place obstacles in the way of out-and-out alienation of the author's right. These may take the form of restrictions or presumptions against alienation[11] or the conferring on an author of the right to receive remuneration from the exploitation of his work, a right which cannot be alienated. A further economic right of authors which to date has been alien to the common law system[12] is the so-called *droit de suite*, which gives authors of certain works a right to a continuing interest on successive sales of their work. One consequence of the attitude that author's right is a personal right which springs from an individual's creativity is that copyright works cannot be created

---

[6] CDPA 1988, ss.93B, 94. As to the transfer of moral rights on death, see CDPA 1988, s.95. As to moral rights generally, see Ch.11, below. As to the transfer of the unwaivable right to remuneration on death, see s.93B(2) and, generally, para. 7–89, below.

[7] An agreement between two people as to who is to be regarded as the author may nevertheless create an estoppel as between them, as was argued in *Beggars Banquet Records Ltd v Carlton Television Ltd* [1993] E.M.L.R. 349.

[8] Inevitably, the distinction between common law and civil law systems is not cut and dried. At the extremes are, on the one hand, the laws of France (the ideological source), Italy, Spain, Portugal and the countries of Latin America and, on the other, those of the United Kingdom, together with countries which have been part of the British Commonwealth, and the United States. Countries such as Germany, Austria, Switzerland, the Nordic countries and Japan, while owing their ideology to other civil law systems, have developed certain aspects of it in different ways. See Stewart, *International Copyright and Neighbouring Rights* (2nd ed.), paras 1.13 *et seq*, and also Burkitt,. "Copyright Culture—The History and Cultural Specificity of the Western Model of Copyright" [2001] I.P.Q. 146.

[9] For a survey of the position, see para. 25–66 *et seq.*, below.

[10] Films form a hybrid category. See at para. 4–57, below.

[11] The German and Austrian laws do not allow assignment of the author's right. French law provides that the author's right in the work of an employee belongs to him unless expressly assigned to the employer. As to the contrasting position under United Kingdom law, see paras 5–11 *et seq.*, below.

[12] But see para. 24–44, below, for the EC Resale Right Directive, the implementation of which will introduce such a right into UK law, and Article 14 *ter* of the Berne Convention.

by a corporation, so that record producers, film producers and broadcasters are not entitled to any author's right in the sound recordings, films or broadcasts that they produce. To the extent that such things are protected, they are generally protected by way of related (or neighbouring[13]) rights.[14]

The common law system, on the other hand, has taken a more commercial and pragmatic view towards copyright, the rationale being to reward those who spend time, skill and effort in creating intangible property of the kind which can be exploited by being reproduced, performed, broadcast, etc. This is done by conferring copyright on their works and thus the exclusive right to control their exploitation. Further, in the purest form of the system, market forces are given a free hand in relation to matters of ownership and transferability of the copyright. Although, therefore, the actual intellectual creator of literary, dramatic, musical and artistic works is accorded the status of author, he may well have no "economic" rights. An example would be where the work was created by him in the course of his employment. Until the 1988 Act, he had few moral rights either[15] and it was only with the passing of that Act that the United Kingdom belatedly introduced a code of such rights, albeit subject to many limitations.[16] Again, "works" such as sound recordings, films and broadcasts are protected as copyright works, the right generally being conferred in the first instance on those who have assumed the financial risk of their creation. The framers of the 1988 Act had no ideological difficulty in describing such persons as "authors".[17]

4–04

The conflicts between the two systems have clearly emerged in the framing of the EC Directives dealing with the term of copyright[18] and the rental right.[19] Thus, the United Kingdom has been obliged to accede to directors of films the status of author[20] and to authors an unwaivable right to remuneration in respect of the rental of certain copies of their works.[21] Other tensions are emerging, for example in relation to the question of the originality required as a condition for subsistence of copyright in a work. Whereas common law systems tend to confer copyright protection on any work on which substantial skill or labour has been expended,[22] civil law systems often impose a higher test.[23] This divergence has, for example, seen the creation of a two-tier Community scheme of protection for databases.[24]

4–05

More than one author. Where more than one person has been involved in the process of creation, a number of different regimes may apply:

4–06

    (a) What they produce may consist of a number of distinct parts or works, as

---

[13] "Related" is the EC terminology.

[14] Together with the rights of performers. A film is a hybrid category, sometimes being protected by author's right, being regarded as the product of the intellectual creation of the director, screenplay writer, film crew, leading actors, composer of the music, etc. sometimes by way of a related or neighbouring right, and sometimes both. See Stewart, *International Copyright and Neighbouring Rights* (2nd ed.).

[15] As to the limited range of these which existed before the 1988 Act, see Ch.11, below.

[16] See generally, Ch.11, below.

[17] CDPA 1988, s.9(1). In reality, however, the expression is used as a shorthand and not in the ordinary meaning of that word. The 1956 Act used the expression "maker" in relation to such works. See paras 4–51 *et seq.*, below.

[18] Directive 93/98.

[19] Directive 92/100.

[20] See para. 4–58, below.

[21] See paras 5–111 and 7–89, below.

[22] Although note the rejection in the United States of a "sweat-of-the-brow" test for copyright in compilations: *Feist Publications Inc. v Rival Telephone Service Co.* 499 U.S. Ct 340.

[23] The case of photographs is a particular example. See Stewart, *International Copyright and Neighbouring Rights* (2nd ed.).

[24] See Ch.18, below.

for example with an encyclopedia, of which each part has a separate author.[25]

(b) Successive persons may have worked separately to produce successive versions of a work, each building on the efforts of his predecessor: each version is a separate work and each version has a separate author.[26]

(c) The efforts of the various persons in producing a work may have been collaborative and not distinct, in which case authorship of the work will be joint.[27]

(d) The contributions of some of the individuals may be of such a slight nature that they are not in law "authors" at all.[28]

4–07 **Transitional provisions.** The law relating to authorship of copyright works has changed from time to time. Save in relation to moral rights, the 1988 Act is framed so as to avoid any retrospective change in the identity of the author of a work caused by an alteration of the law. This is achieved by a transitional provision in the 1988 Act[29] to the effect that the law which was in force when a work was made must be applied to determine who was the author of the work. The effect is shown by the following table.

Date when work made	Act to be applied
On or after August 1, 1989	The 1988 Act
On or after June 1, 1957 but before August 1, 1989	The 1956 Act
On or after July 1, 1912, but before June 1, 1957	The 1911 Act
Before July 1, 1912	The Acts then in force.[30]

For this purpose, where the making of a work extended over a period, the work is to be taken as having been made when its making was completed.[31] The position is different in relation to moral rights, where the identity of the author of a work made before August 1, 1989 must be determined in accordance with the provisions of the 1988 Act alone.[32]

4–08 **Works of unknown authorship.** Problems can arise, for example in relation to the calculation of the term of copyright, if it is not possible to establish who the author was. Special provision is made for such cases.[33]

4–09 **Presumptions.** Various statutory presumptions can be relied on, in legal proceedings, to discharge the burden of proving who was the author of a work. These are considered elsewhere.[34]

---

[25] But note that there will usually also be a separate copyright work consisting of the encyclopedia as a whole, considered as a compilation, with its own author or authors. See para. 4–44, below.

[26] See para. 4–40 et seq., below, and, for example, *Robin Ray v Classic FM Plc* [1998] F.S.R. 622 at 638; *Brighton v Jones* [2004] EWHC 1157 (Ch).

[27] As to works of joint authorship, see paras 4–37 et seq., below.

[28] See para. 4–40, below.

[29] CDPA 1988, Sch.1, para.10.

[30] See para. 4–36, below.

[31] CDPA 1988, Sch.1, para.1(3).

[32] Sched.1, para.10.

[33] See, for example, CDPA 1988, ss.12(3) (duration of copyright) and 57 (acts permitted on assumption as to expiry of copyright or death of author). See below at paras 6–46 and 9–152, respectively.

[34] See para. 22–210, below.

2. LITERARY, DRAMATIC, MUSICAL AND ARTISTIC WORKS

The 1988 Act defines "author" generally as meaning the person who creates the work.[35] In the case of literary, dramatic, musical and artistic works, no further definition of this expression is given.[36] With limited exceptions,[37] the 1956, 1911 and earlier Acts contained no definition of "author" at all but in the light of the interpretation given to the expression "author" under these earlier Acts, there has not been any change in the law in terms of who is to be regarded as the author of a work of these types.[38] The question of authorship of these categories of work can therefore be considered without reference to the date when the work was created.   **4–10**

Meaning of "author". In the present context, it will not normally be hard to determine who is the person who created the work and therefore who was the author of it. As is discussed elsewhere,[39] copyright is concerned with the protection of the original expression in some material form of ideas, information, etc. and not the ideas, information, etc. themselves.[40] In general terms, therefore, the author of a work is the person who originates the protectable elements of the work, whether the language used, dramatic incident, musical content or design, as the case may be. Although this will usually be the person who puts down the work on the page, etc. it need not necessarily be so, as can be appreciated from the example of a shorthand secretary or an amanuensis, who clearly is not the author of the work in question.[41] The author is therefore not necessarily the person responsible for the actual fixation of the work (although he usually will be) but rather the person who is responsible for creating, selecting or gathering together the detailed concepts, data or emotions which are found in the work.[42]   **4–11**

With very limited exceptions,[43] the "author" of these categories of work must be a natural person.[44] The fact that one person is acting as employee of another cannot affect the question of authorship.[45] Nor can the fact that one person is an agent for another unless, perhaps, he acts in accordance with his principal's precise instructions, so as to be, in effect, an extension of his principal's hand in recording his principal's work. In the same way, a designer who is head of a design team is not the author of drawings made by other members of the team.[46]   **4–12**

---

[35] CDPA 1988, s.9(1).

[36] Save in relation to computer generated works. As to these, see para. 4–17, below.

[37] Relating to photographs and mechanical contrivances. See paras 4–34 and 4–53, below, respectively.

[38] "The word 'author' has never been defined, although it has always been taken to be the person who created the work." See, *e.g.* the Whitford Committee Report (Cmnd. 6732), para.539. Note also CDPA 1988, s.172, which provides for the general continuity of the law.

[39] See para. 7–13, below.

[40] As to the meaning of "original" in this context, see paras 3–127 *et seq.*, above.

[41] See para. 4–20, below.

[42] *Cala Homes (South) Ltd v Alfred McAlpine Homes East Ltd* [1995] F.S.R. 818; *Ray v Classic FM* [1998] F.S.R. 622 (emphasising the need for direct responsibility for what is recorded). See the further discussion on this point later in this Chapter.

[43] Relating to computer-generated works and old photographs. See paras 4–17 and 4–34, below.

[44] See, *e.g.* CDPA 1988, s.12(1) and *Fax Directories (Pty) Ltd v SA Fax Listings CC* [1990] 2 S.A.L.R. 164 (Local Division of Sup. Ct of SA).

[45] *Shepherd v Conquest* (1856) 17 C.B. 427, where the employer merely suggested the subject matter and had no share in the design or execution of the work, which, so far as any originality belonged to it, flowed from the mind of the person employed. Employment, may however, affect the separate question of ownership: see paras 5–11 *et seq.*, below.

[46] *Nichols Advanced Vehicle Systems Inc. v Rees* [1979] R.P.C. 127 at 139.

4–13 **Author of non-language content.** Although true for most cases, statements that whoever originates the language of a literary or dramatic work is the author need to be regarded with caution where the real essence, or protectable element, of the copyright work consists of or includes elements such as plot or structure. A typical example of such a case is where one person suggests details of a plot for a dramatic work and another clothes the plot with words and stage directions. This is considered in more detail below,[47] but in principle a person who suggests the plot of a dramatic work may be one of its authors provided his suggestions are sufficiently substantial, well defined and original. This will be a matter of degree. In the same way, the person responsible for originating the structure of a computer program may be one of the authors of the computer program.[48] A case where someone contributes detailed incidents of plot, characterisation, etc. but not the actual language, to a "pure" literary work, such as a novel, is less likely to arise in practice. Nevertheless, there is no reason in principle why a person who makes such a contribution should not be an author of the work, provided again that what he contributes is sufficiently defined, detailed and original.[49] In all such cases, it is necessary to identify the products of the skill and labour which made the work "original", and thus protected, and then ask who was responsible for them.

4–14 **Derivative works.** In many cases a work is derived from an existing work. Common examples are a translation of a work, the dramatisation of a novel, a photograph of a painting and an arrangement of a musical work, but a derivative version can take many forms, even a simple revision of the earlier work. Whether in such cases a new copyright work is created will depend on whether sufficient skill and labour was expended upon it[50] but, assuming that it was, the person who was responsible for that skill and labour will be the author of the new work. So where A's work is independently translated by B, B is the author of the translation.[51] A of course remains the author of his original work but he is not the co-author or joint author with B of the translation.[52] The same is true where B simply revises A's work, for example, by correcting and improving it. The final position will depend on the amount and value of the corrections and improvements. If the independent skill and labour expended by B is such as to create a new copyright work, then he will be author of it.[53] If not, there will be no new copyright work and A will remain the author of the original work. B will have been the author of the alterations but their nature will not have been such as to attract any protection under the law of copyright. If B's contribution was substantial in the above sense and it was the result of collaboration with A and the contributions of each were not distinct, then they will have been joint authors.[54]

4–15 Where a new copyright work is created by B from A's work, the rights of the owner of the copyright in A's work will depend upon how much of A's work remains in B's work. If B's work contains a substantial reproduction of A's work, then A's licence will be required to exploit it, as well as B's, for otherwise such

---

[47] See para. 4–27, below.

[48] See para. 4–25, below.

[49] See, *e.g. Ibcos Computers Ltd v Barclays Mercantile Highland Finance Ltd* [1994] F.S.R. 275 at 302.

[50] See para. 3–132, above.

[51] *Byrne v Statist Co.* [1914] 1 K.B. 622.

[52] As to joint authorship, see paras 4–37 *et seq.*, below.

[53] As in *Tree v Bowkett* (1896) 74 L.T. 77, where the claimant had made additions and alterations to an existing dramatic work, principally one entirely new scene and one altered scene. Clearly the work which he had done was substantial.

[54] As to joint authorship, see paras 4–37 *et seq.*, below.

exploitation will amount to an infringement of A's copyright. If B's work does not contain a substantial reproduction of A's work, then A's licence is not required.[55]

Some of the earlier cases on the point are confusing:

4–16

In *Springfield v Thame*[56] the claimant journalist (A) had sent an account of an incident he had witnessed to a newspaper. For the purposes of publication, a sub-editor (B) of the newspaper compiled an account of the facts in abbreviated form, reducing A's piece from 83 lines to 18 lines in length and such that it became in substance a different statement of the facts. The piece was copied and published by the defendant (C) in another newspaper with only slight further alterations. A's action against C failed on the ground that B was the "author" of the published version, not A. While this was clearly correct on the facts, it is suggested that this approach confuses the issue of authorship and infringement. A could not in any event have been the author of the published piece since he was not responsible for the alterations, although he was of course the author of the original account. An alternative and, it is suggested, better way of looking at the point would have been to say that the piece published by C did not infringe the copyright in A's original account.[57]

In *Samuelson v Producers Distributing Co. Ltd*,[58] an actor (B) made alterations to the script for a dramatic sketch which had been written by A, the altered version then being performed on the stage with considerable success. B's work amounted to a reconstruction of the original with alterations and omissions. Although the script was different, various phrases or passages from the old script remained the same, together with the characters and staging. It was held that A was the "author" of the altered sketch. It is, however, important to see what the issue in the case was. The defendant had produced a film which had been misrepresented in advertisements to be a film of the sketch as performed. Although the question of authorship was in issue on the pleadings, it being alleged that A was the owner of the copyright in the final version (B's), the cause of action by the date of trial was passing off, it being conceded that the film did not infringe the copyright in the sketch. At issue was whether A was entitled to be recognised as the author of the sketch and thus whether he had a cause of action in passing off.[59] It is suggested that the decision is not helpful on the issue of authorship of a copyright work. In fact, A had been credited as the "author" of the sketch as performed on the stage and B made no claim to own the copyright in his version. It is suggested that had infringement of copyright been in issue, the true analysis is that A was the author of the work consisting of the original script and B was the author of the work consisting of the resulting sketch.

Computer-generated works. Few people would have any difficulty with the concept that someone who uses word processing software to write a document is the author of that document. The software is a tool for writing, it does not supply the necessary ingredient of "originality", *i.e.* the skill and labour required for the composition of the document. Software can, however, assist in the creative process to a much greater degree. Computer-aided design ("CAD") software, for example, enables complex images and structures to be designed with the assistance of graphical libraries and rules. Software can perform increasingly complex

4–17

---

[55] The examples assume that A and B are the owners of the copyright in their respective works.
[56] (1903) 89 L.T. 242
[57] (1903) 89 L.T. 242, at 243: what C had published was news, not the claimant's expression of it (see para. 7–40, below).
[58] (1932) 48 R.P.C. 580.
[59] As to this claim, see Ch.21, below.

calculations to generate data for scientific and other uses, and from this generate increasingly complex outputs, including music, still or moving images and other computer programs. The question then arises as to whether a work written with the aid of such software has a human author, and if so, who it is. In many cases, of course, the software will merely be a tool used by an individual to create a work.[60] When framing the 1988 Act, however, it was recognised that there may be circumstances, when it may be impossible to identify a human author of such a work, the only immediate human involvement perhaps being the activation of a machine. Against this eventuality, the 1988 Act provides for a special category or works, namely those which are "computer-generated", being those works generated by a computer in circumstances such that there is no human author.[61] In relation to such works, the author is to be taken to be the person by whom the arrangements necessary for the creation of the work are undertaken.[62] This definition uses the same terminology as is used in relation to the definition of "producer" in the context of determining the author of a sound recording and a film.[63] The differences between such works and works of which there is a human author are significant. Not only is the question of authorship and thus ownership affected but also there is a problem in understanding how a computer-generated work could satisfy the requirement of originality under the Act.[64] In addition, the term of protection for such works is only 50 years from the end of the calendar year in which the work was made.[65]

4–18 Pre-1988 Act computer-generated works. It is not clear whether there were in fact any such works, but since the 1956 Act contained no such provision it would appear that in cases where there was no human author, there was no copyright in the work under that Act. There can thus be no copyright in the work under the 1988 Act.[66]

A. LITERARY WORKS

4–19 Cases of difficulty sometimes arise where one person is responsible for the fixing of the work in some material form for the first time[67] but another may have contributed some or all of the content. At one extreme is the case of a secretary who records another's spoken words. At the other is the case of a writer who uses the idea for a story which has been given to him.[68] Inevitably there are intermediate cases. The various situations are considered in turn.[69]

4–20 The secretary or amanuensis. It is clear that a secretary who merely takes down, word for word, the text of a work originated and dictated by another is not the

---

[60] As in *Express Newspapers plc v Liverpool Daily Post & Echo plc* [1985] F.S.R. 306, a case decided under the 1956 Act, where it was held that the computer and computer programs used to produce a work were simply tools of the person controlling them, just as with a conventional pen.
[61] CDPA 1988, s.178.
[62] s.9(3).
[63] See paras 4–49 and 4–59, below.
[64] See paras 3–127 et seq., above.
[65] CDPA 1988, s.12(3). See para.6–47.
[66] See CDPA 1988, Sch.1, para.5(1).
[67] No copyright will subsist in a literary, dramatic or musical work until it is recorded, in writing or otherwise. CDPA 1988, s.3(2). As to fixation, see para. 3–111, above. As to artistic works, see para. 3–119, above.
[68] The person who had the idea may be able to prevent its use by the person to whom he communicated it on the grounds of breach of confidence; see Ch.20, below.
[69] The question can also be approached from the perspective of joint authorship. See paras 4–40 et seq., below.

author of the work which is thus recorded.[70] The secretary, sometimes referred to as a mere amanuensis,[71] has not played any part in originating the expression of the ideas or information contained in the work. In the same way, where A extemporises and B reduces the results to some permanent form, either simultaneously or, relying on his memory, later, A is the author of the work which is thus created.[72]

Reporters and others as authors. Another category of cases is where a person (B), although in one sense merely reproducing the words of another (A), exercises substantial skill and labour in reducing it into some material form. As has been pointed out[73] in such cases, there may be two copyright works in existence. First, that of which A is the author, he being the originator of the words spoken by him. If he is speaking from a prepared text, copyright may already subsist; if he is speaking extempore, copyright will only come into existence when the first record of the words is made by B. The second copyright work is B's record, of which B is the author, having exercised substantial skill and labour in reducing it into that form. So, a reporter who exercises sufficient skill and labour in reporting the words spoken by another is to be regarded as the author of his work.[74] So too, where a medium wrote down what she claimed had been told her by a spirit, doing so at great speed and reproducing in archaic English what she said was communicated to her in an unknown tongue, she was clearly the author of the resulting work.[75] The difference between this type of case and the work of a mere amanuensis is that the amanuensis has exercised no relevant skill and labour in rendering the spoken word into a more permanent form. The secretary's work is not original.

4–21

Biographies, reminiscences and "ghosted" works. Accounts of the lives of famous personalities are often written on the basis of information supplied by them to a writer. In many cases ghost writers are employed to write such stories in the name of, or "with", the personality in question, who may not have the literary ability or time to do so himself. The normal principle applies in relation to such accounts, whether "ghosted" or not, namely that the author is the person who originated the literary expression. If, as often happens, the subject of the account provides details of incidents from his own life as the basis of articles or stories in which these incidents are written up by another, but does not take any part in producing the particular form of language in which the information is conveyed and which is the subject-matter of copyright, he is not the author of the written work.[76] But the position may be different if the writer uses the words actually spoken by the personality to a significant extent.[77]

4–22

---

[70] *Donoghue v Allied Newspapers Ltd* [1938] Ch. 106 at 109.
[71] See, *e.g. Donoghue v Allied Newspapers Ltd* [1938] Ch. 106 at 109.
[72] It may well be that the record of the work created by B will be a separate copyright work, of which B is the author. See the next paragraph.
[73] See paras 3–113 and 3–124 *et seq.*, above.
[74] *Walter v Lane* [1900] A.C. 539; *Express Newspapers plc v News (U.K.) plc* [1991] F.S.R. 36; *Cala Homes (South) Ltd v Alfred McAlpine Homes East Ltd* [1995] F.S.R. 818.
[75] *Cummins v Bond* [1927] 1 Ch. 167. The result would have been the same if the source of the communication had been a real person. Eve J. rejected the suggestion that the spirit, who had been "domiciled on the other side of the inevitable river" for some 1,900 years was the true author, this being a matter for solution by others "more competent" to decide than he.
[76] *Evans v E. Hulton & Co. Ltd* [1923–28] Mac.C.C. 51 (a freelance detective); *Donoghue v Allied Newspapers Ltd* [1938] Ch. 106 (a famous jockey); *Housden v Marshall* [1959] 1 W.L.R. 1 (another jockey); *Chaplin v Leslie Frewin (Publishers) Ltd* [1966] Ch. 71 (Charlie Chaplin's son).
[77] This possibility was left open in *Thrustcode Ltd v WW Computing Ltd* [1983] F.S.R. 502 at 507. If both are responsible for the final form of the language, then they may be joint authors. See paras 4–37 *et seq.*, below. Where what is recounted are the actual words spoken in conversation

4–23   Originator of plot of a novel. The copyright in a novel can be infringed if its plot is taken and turned into a dramatised version without any language copying.[78] It is only where the plot is worked out in some detail that this is likely to be so[79] but it follows that the person who originated these details, and who may not have been the same person as the person who clothed it in words, is one of its authors. Where the two have collaborated they are likely to joint authors[80] but if one person has recorded details of the plot and another has independently worked them up into a novel there will be two copyright works, each with its own author.[81] A dramatisation of the novel which takes sufficient incidents of plot will require the consent of the owner of the copyright in the first work.

4–24   "Author" of collective or composite work. In the case of collective or composite works, such as encyclopedias, there will be distinct copyrights, namely, the copyright in the entire work and the copyright in the various separate contributions. The person who gathers together and arranges the entire work will be the author of the whole work, considered as a compilation.[82] The fact that he is assisted in this by others will not make him any the less the author if it is he who compiled and arranged the information.[83] As to the separate contributions, the authors of these will be the persons who wrote them. Thus where a person has written the entries in a work such as a directory using information supplied by others he will be the author of those entries, unless he has done nothing more than simply copy such information verbatim.[84][85]

4–25   Author of computer program. No changes to the basic rules of authorship were required to implement the authorship requirements of the Computer Software Directive.[86] Computer programs are often written by more than one person and it is common for questions to arise as to whether they are works of joint authorship

---

by others, no doubt these will not be original to the writer, but in practice it is unlikely that such account would be verbatim.

[78] *i.e.* by making an "adaptation" of it. See CDPA 1988, s.21, *Kelly v Cinema Houses Ltd* [1928–35] Mac.C.C. 362 at 367 and para. 7–124, below..

[79] The point is more clearly illustrated in the cases relating to dramatic works since plot detail is a well established element of a dramatic work. See para. 7–52, below.

[80] As to joint authors, see paras 4–37 *et seq.*, below.

[81] See also paras 4–40 and 4–42, below.

[82] In *Waterlow Publishers Ltd v Rose* [1995] F.S.R. 207, the Court of Appeal considered that the provisions of s.20 of the 1956 Act, which provided for certain presumptions as to authorship in civil proceedings (see now CDPA 1988, s.104), contemplated that there might be cases in which there was no identifiable author of a compilation, in which case the presumptions would apply. However, it is hard to understand why this should be so. It may be difficult as a matter of fact to identify the author of a compilation (although no more so than with many other works) and the presumptions may help to prove authorship, but these are different matters.

[83] *Scott v Stanford* (1867) L.R. 3 Eq. 718, cited with approval in *Elanco Products Ltd v Mandops (Agricultural Specialists) Ltd* [1980] R.P.C. 213.

[84] *James Nisbet & Co. Ltd v The Golf Agency* (1907) 23 T.L.R. 370. In *Black (A and C) Ltd v Claude Stacey Ltd* [1929] 1 Ch. 177 it was held that even if the written information provided by third parties for such entries was used verbatim, the author of each contribution was the compiler of the directory who had asked for the information and not the third party. It is doubted whether this can be correct. The subject matter was *Who's Who* and the ruling was based on the proposition that where material is given to a compiler for publication by him, the provider cannot be the author. With respect this confuses the issues of authorship and the right to use material. The decision purportedly followed that in *James Nisbet & Co. Ltd v The Golf Agency*, above, which concerned a similar publication. There, however, the compilers of the entries had sent out written questionnaires from which the entries were compiled. They did not simply copy what was sent to them. It is clear, therefore, that the compilers were responsible for the language used. Had they simply copied the material, the position might have been different (see 371).

[85] In relation to a copyright database, as defined in the 1988 Act, it will be necessary to identify the person who has created the original, and then protectable, subject matter, in respect of which such works now receive protection. See para. 3–146, above.

[86] Directive 91/250 of December 16, 1986. Art.2.1 provides that: "The author of a computer program shall be the natural person or group of natural persons who has created the program …".

or whether the program, or package of programs, are distinct works.[87] Often, contributions are at different levels, one person being mainly responsible for the overall structure of the program, another for the detailed coding.

Computer programs are written in programming languages, some of which contain a high level of inbuilt intelligence which is carried through into the final program by use of terms from the language. The use of such complex programming languages may in an extreme position raise the issue as to whether the resulting program has a human author or is a computer-generated work.[88]

4–26

B. DRAMATIC WORKS

The author of a dramatic work will be the person who has originated the protectable elements of the work. It is sometimes said that a person who suggests the plot of a dramatic work is not an author, but the statement needs to treated with care.[89] Thus, it is established that the copyright in a dramatic work may be infringed by the copying of its plot, even where the language itself is not taken.[90] It follows that the person who originates the protectable elements of plot is an author. Clearly, however, someone who has a mere idea for a play, however good, is not an author if it is not he who has clothed it with the form in which the idea is realised.[91] So, for example, it was not enough to make a person an author where he had suggested an idea and some dramatic incidents for a dramatic sketch,[92] or even a few catch lines, together with some scenic effects and "stage business".[93] Again, where one person (A) suggested to another that he, B, write a dramatic version of an existing book and A then made critical suggestions which led to whole scenes being rewritten, helped with the stage craft but contributed nothing to the eventual dialogue apart from an occasional line and idea, A was not an author.[94] Even more clearly, where a theatre proprietor sent a writer to see and adapt an existing play, the proprietor was not the author of the result, having had no part in the design or execution of that which gave it its originality.[95] Where the dramatic work takes the form of a film,[96] the author will be the person or persons who were directly responsible for originating the action which is portrayed by the film: this will usually include the director and the editor of the film. The author of the screenplay, and of any other underlying works such as a novel, will not, it is suggested, be "authors" of the dramatic work which is the film. They are authors of their separate dramatic or literary works. The film itself,

4–27

---

[87] As to joint authorship, see paras 4–37 *et seq.*, below.

[88] As to which, see para. 4–17, above.

[89] It is suggested that the reasoning in *Hatton v Kean* (1859) 7 C.B. (N.S.) 268, where the claimant provided the defendant with the elements of music for a dramatic work, that it was the defendant who was the author of the whole work and that the claimant was not an author, would not be followed today, the distinction not being drawn there between the issues of authorship and ownership.

[90] See para. 7–52, below.

[91] *Donoghue v Allied Newspapers Ltd* [1938] Ch. 106

[92] *Tate v Fullbrook* [1908] 1 K.B. 821. To the same effect is *Bagge v Miller* [1917–23] Mac.C.C. 178, where only the idea for a one-act dramatic sketch was provided, all the work of its execution being another's.

[93] *Tate v Thomas* [1921] 1 Ch. 503.

[94] *Wiseman v Weidenfeld & Nicolson Ltd* [1985] F.S.R. 525.

[95] *Shepherd v Conquest* (1856) 17 C.B. 427.

[96] As to a film being a dramatic work, see para. 3–37, above. Note that the author of the dramatic work which takes the form of a film may be different from the author of the separate copyright work which is the film. As to the author of the copyright work which is a film, see para. 4–56 *et. seq.*, below.

if it is a work of action,[97] will be a new dramatic work, although based on the underlying works, and the authors of this new dramatic work will be those who realised the transformation of the underlying works onto film, often adding further dramatic material of their own in the process.[98]

C. MUSICAL WORKS

4–28 Disputes as to authorship of musical works are relatively common, particularly in the field of popular music where a good deal of informality often accompanies their creation. Disputes where one person claims to have been involved in making a contribution to the final form of a piece of music usually arise in the context of a work of joint authorship, which is dealt with separately,[99] but problems can arise where one person claims to have arranged an existing musical work. If the arrangement is sufficiently original to qualify as a new copyright work,[1] then the "arranger" will be the author of it.

D. ARTISTIC WORKS

4–29 **"Author" of artistic works.** In the case of artistic works the author will be the person who is most nearly the effective cause of the final representation.[2] Others may have had the idea for the work but what is relevant is what is done in creating the material form in which the idea is expressed.[3] To be an author, a person must have played a substantial role in putting the artistic work on the material in question.[4] In the ordinary case it will be the person whose hand fixes the picture upon the paper, canvas, etc. who is the author. So for example, where a person conceived of the idea of a card to help illiterate voters, consisting of a picture of a hand holding a pencil in the act of completing a cross but, being unable to draw, employed another, under his direction, to execute the idea, the latter was the author of the work.[5] In contrast, in theory, no doubt a person might have such close control over the application of pencil or paint to paper by another that he might be the sole author but it seems unlikely to arise often in practice. An example might be the case where an artist directs his apprentice precisely where and how to apply paint to a partially completed work. A more likely outcome in most cases will be joint authorship, as where a person who, although he did not actually put pen to paper, made such an input into the work, by way, for example,

---

[97] See para. 3–37, above.
[98] Although the film may be based on underlying works, it will almost inevtiably be original, not least because of the skill and labour involved in the change of medium and in realising a screenplay.
[99] See paras 4–37 et seq., below.
[1] As to which, see para. 3–123 et seq., above.
[2] *Nottage v Jackson* (1883) 11 Q.B.D. 627, where Brett M.R. also observed at 631: "Persons who draw Acts of Parliament will sometimes use phrases that nobody else uses .... Whoever, in ordinary life, talks of 'the *author*' of a painting?". The expression, however, now has a clear meaning in copyright law, and Brett M.R. went on: "Yet one can easily make out what is meant by the author of a painting or a drawing. The author of a painting is the man who paints it; and the author of a drawing is the man who draws it".
[3] *Plix Products Ltd v Frank M Winstone (Merchants)* [1986] F.S.R. 63, 81 (High Ct of NZ).
[4] *Kenrick & Co. v Lawrence & Co.* (1890) 25 Q.B.D. 99. Note, however, that unlike literary, dramatic and musical works, there is no express requirement that as a condition of subsistence an artistic work must be reduced to some material form, but presumably until it is fixed in some form it cannot be said to exist. See CDPA 1988, s.3(2) and para. 3–111, above.
[5] *Kenrick & Co. v Lawrence & Co.* (1890) 25 Q.B.D. 99. The possibility of the two being joint authors was left open, although this seems unlikely to have been the correct position on the facts. See para. 4–42, below. In *Nottage v Jackson* (1883) 11 Q.B.D. 627, to the same effect, the illustration was given of one person saying to another: "Go and draw that lady with a dog at her feet, and in one hand holding a flower". The former would not be one of the authors of the resulting drawing.

of providing preliminary sketches, stipulating the form of the final design and shepherding the design as it evolved, that he could be said to have provided part of the skill and effort involved in creating the detailed design which was found on the paper.[6] The fact that a person may have used computer-aided design (CAD) software as a tool to assist him in creating the drawing will not make him any the less the author of it.[7]

Derivative artistic works. Artistic works are often based on pre-existing works. Historically important examples are engravings and lithographs made for the purpose of the mass reproduction of illustrations in books and periodicals. With modern printing techniques, the process of reproducing illustrations for publication tends to be largely mechanical but problems can still arise today, for example in relation to an existing artistic work which is photographically reproduced. In such cases, the main question is usually whether a new copyright work has been created, that is, whether the new work is original.[8] Hand produced engravings and lithographs will usually be so.[9] If a new copyright work is in fact created, the author will be the person who made it, notwithstanding that the work may be derived from an earlier work.   **4–30**

Works of architecture. It will be recalled that for the purpose of the Copyright Acts, a work of architecture consists of either a building or structure, or a model for a building or structure.[10] It does not include any architectural drawing.[11] As also explained elsewhere,[12] copyright will only subsist in a work of architecture if it has some artistic character.[13] The author will be the person who was the effective cause[14] of the shape and design of the building.[15] In most cases this will be the same person as the author of any plans, certainly where the building is constructed following such plans. In cases where a builder constructs the building without reference to any plans, the builder will be the author of any work of architecture which results.   **4–31**

Photographs. Photographs form a special category of work in that not only is the general concept of authorship sometimes difficult to apply but also under the 1911 and 1956 Actsthe meaning of author was modified by express provision . As already noted,[16] the law which was in force when a work was made must be applied to determine who was the author of the work. The position under the 1988 Act is examined first.   **4–32**

Photographs: the 1988 Act. The provisions of the 1988 Act determine who is the author of a photograph made on or after August 1, 1989. In contrast to the   **4–33**

---

[6] *Cala Homes (South) Ltd v Alfred McAlpine Homes East Ltd* [1995] F.S.R. 818. As to joint authorship, see paras 4–37 *et seq.*, below.

[7] *Husqvarna Forest & Garden Ltd v Bridon New Zealand Ltd* (1997) 38 I.P.R. 513 (High Ct of NZ). As to the general problem of computer-assisted works, see para. 4–17, above.

[8] As to this question, see paras 3–123 *et seq.*, above.

[9] See para. 3–135, above.

[10] CDPA 1988, s.4(1)(b); Copyright Act 1956, s.3(1)(b); Copyright Act 1911, s.35(1). See para. 3–61, above.

[11] An architectural drawing is of course capable of protection, but as a drawing or plan and not as a work of architecture. See para. 3–60, above.

[12] See para. 3–62, above.

[13] Further, under the 1911 Act, copyright only subsisted *to the extent* of any artistic character or design. See s.35(1) and para. 7–65, below.

[14] See para. 4–29, above.

[15] *Meikle v Maufe* [1941] 3 All E.R. 144, where the argument that the builder was the author was rejected. Earlier editions of *Copinger* note the unreported case of *Jackson v Jones* (1934), where Farwell J. is reported to have held that the author was the builder and not the architect, but the factual basis of the decision is unknown.

[16] See para. 4–07, above.

1911 and 1956 Acts, the 1988 Act contains no special provisions as to authorship of photographs. The general principle therefore applies, namely, that the author of a photograph is the person who creates it.[17] This represents a return to the position which existed before the passing of the 1911 Act, which simply used the expression "author" in this context.[18] In most cases there will be no difficulty in identifying the author of a photograph: it will be the "photographer". In some cases, however, the subject matter of the photograph may have been carefully arranged or composed by one person and the shutter operated by another. In such a case it will be the former who is the author, he being the effective cause of the final result,[19] and in general terms the author of a photograph will be the person who expended relevant skill and labour in its production.[20] What amounts to sufficient skill and labour to make a person an author of a photograph will be a question of degree in each case. Merely showing the photographer where photographs should be taken from is unlikely to be enough.[21] No doubt if the person who operated the shutter also made a contribution to the final result by, for example, choosing particular camera settings, he too would be an author.[22] The important, and sometimes difficult, step is to determine what it is that makes the photograph original,[23] but once this is done, the author can then be identified as the person responsible for those elements in the work.[24]

4–34   **Photographs: the 1911 and 1956 Acts.** Specific definitions of "author" were contained in the 1911 and 1956 Acts in the case of photographs such that any problem in identifying the "author" of a photograph was largely avoided,[25] although certainty was achieved at the price of potential capriciousness. The position is as follows:

(a) In relation to photographs taken on or after July 1, 1912, but before June

---

[17] CDPA 1988, s.9(1).

[18] Fine Arts Copyright Act 1862, s.1. The change effected by the 1988 Act followed the recommendation of the Whitford Committee that the author of a photograph should be defined as the person responsible for its composition (see Cmnd. 6732, para.587). For a detailed discussion of this topic, see Garnett and Abbott, "Who is the 'Author' of a Photograph?", [1998] 6 E.I.P.R. 204.

[19] *Nottage v Jackson* (1883) 11 Q.B.D. 627 at 632, 637, applied in *Wooderson v Raphael Tuck & Sons* (1887) 4 T.L.R. 57. In *Melville v Mirror of Life Co.* [1895] 2 Ch. 531, the claimant's son undertook most of the arrangement and execution of a portrait photograph. The claimant, who ran a photographic business, for the most part stood by and looked on. It was held that the claimant was the author since everything had been done under his direction and by his agent. If the basis of the decision was that the son was merely carrying out his father's directions as to the posing of the subject, etc. then the decision is unexceptional (see, for example, *Nottage v Jackson*, at 632). If, however, as seems to have been the case on the facts, the steps taken by the son were not so directed then it is suggested that the true position was that the son was an author. (Since the father had held up his hand at the critical moment to indicate the direction in which the subject was to look they may in fact have been joint authors, assuming this to have added significantly to the final effect.) The fact that one person may have been acting on behalf of another in such circumstances may affect the question of ownership, but this is a different issue.

[20] *Ellis v Marshall (H) & Son* (1895) 64 L.J.Q.B. 757; *Creation Records Ltd v News Group Newspapers Ltd* [1997] E.M.L.R. 444 at 450.

[21] *Stackemann v Paton* [1906] 1 Ch. 774 at 779. In this case, however, authorship of one of the photographs was denied to the person who had arranged members of a school cricket team into poses as if they were playing a match. It is suggested that this must have been a borderline case and might be decided differently today.

[22] In the course of the passage of the Copyright Bill through Parliament, an amendment which would have had the effect of making the "photographer" the author in all circumstances was resisted, it being pointed out on behalf of the Government that: "In certain cases someone other than the person who operates the camera will make a substantial creative contribution to the final image—perhaps in the darkroom, perhaps in composing the picture through the viewfinder without actually pressing the button—and it would not be right to deny him a copyright in it on the grounds that he was not the actual photographer". (*Hansard*, HL Vol.490, col.883).

[23] See para. 3–142, above.

[24] See *Baumann v Fussell* [1978] R.P.C. 485 at 487.

[25] See *Nottage v Jackson* (1883) 11 Q.B.D. 627, where Brett M.R. observed: "I should like to know whether the person who drew this Act of Parliament [the Fine Arts Copyright Act 1862, 25 & 26 Vict. c.68] was clear in his mind as to who can be the *author* of a photograph."

1, 1957, the 1911 Act applies. This Act defined the author as the person who owned the original negative from which the photograph was directly or indirectly derived at the time when such negative was made.[26]

(b) In relation to photographs taken on or after June 1, 1957 but before August 1, 1989, the 1956 Act applies. This Act defined the author as being the person who, at the time when the photograph was taken, was the owner of the material on which it was taken.[27]

There is in practice no difference in the two definitions. It will be noted that the author of a photograph as defined for these purposes may have been someone quite different from the person who would have been the author had the 1988 Act applied.[28] Indeed the "author" may have had little relation to the actual photographer and may have been a company.[29]

Pre-1988 Act photographs and the Term Directive. Under the Regulations[30] which extended the term of United Kingdom copyright, photographs were in general granted an extended term of copyright for the life of the author and 70 years thereafter. The Regulations contain transitional provisions whose effect is to extend and in certain cases revive the copyright in some works in existence at the commencement date of the Regulations, in particular for present purposes, some photographs made while the 1911 and 1956 Acts were in force.[31] As has been seen, under the 1911 and 1956 Acts, the author, as defined by those Acts, may not have been a natural person yet the Regulations defined the new term of copyright in such works by reference to the date of the author's death. By a subsequent clarifying regulation,[32] the author of such works is to be taken to be, for the purpose of the Regulations relating to the extended or revived term only, the author as determined in accordance with the 1988 Act, namely, the person who created it.[33] This will in all cases be a natural person, identified in accordance with the principles stated above. The identity of the author for all other purposes is not affected.

4–35

E. PRE-1911 ACT WORKS

There will still be many copyright works in existence which were made before the coming into force of the Copyright Act 1911 on July 1, 1912. This is not simply because of the longevity of some authors. Even before the extension of the term of copyright to life and 70 years,[34] a copyright work written by a 20-year-old in 1910, who died in 1960, would have remained in copyright until 2010.[35] Furthermore, at the passing of the 1988 Act there were many unpub-

4–36

---

[26] s.21.

[27] s.48(1).

[28] For example the case of a press photographer using film stock belonging to a newspaper proprietor. And see *Australian Olympic Committee v Big Fights Inc.* (1999) 46 I.P.R. 53 (Fed. Ct of Aus.), for a case where the question of ownership of original film stock had to be investigated many years after the event (the 1956 Olympic Games in Melbourne).

[29] The use of the word "person" clearly included such a possibility. See, for example, the wording of s.21 of the 1911 Act. This possibility did not raise any difficulty when determining the term of copyright in photographs since this was to be reckoned without reference to the date of death of any author. It has, however, caused a problem with the implementation of the Term Directive. See the next paragraph.

[30] The Duration of Copyright and Rights in Performances Regulations 1995 (SI 1995/3297), Vol.2 at A3.ii. These implemented the Directive 93/98 harmonising the term of copyright.

[31] For a full discussion of the effect of these Regulations, see Ch.6, below.

[32] Copyright and Related Rights Regulations 1996 (SI 1996/2967), reg.19.

[33] See para. 4–33, above.

[34] See Ch.6, below.

[35] And will now remain in copyright until 2030.

lished, pre-1911 Act copyright works which still had a potentially indefinite term of copyright, or whose period had only started to run in recent years.[36]

There is no difficulty in principle in stating who was the author of an unpublished work protected at common law: it will have been the creator of it. As to works protected by statute, the various statutes generally either simply referred to the "author" of the various works, or, as noted below, dealt only with who was the first owner of the copyright. The relevant Acts and works dealt with are as follows[37]:

(a) "Books" (defined to mean every volume, part or division of a volume, pamphlet, sheet of letter-press, sheet of music, map, chart, or plan separately published) and dramatic works (*i.e.* every tragedy, comedy, play, opera, farce, or other scenic, musical or dramatic entertainment): Literary Copyright Act 1842.[38]

(b) Lectures: Lectures Copyright Act 1835.[39]

(c) Tragedies, comedies, plays, operas, farces or any other dramatic piece of entertainment: Dramatic Copyright Act 1833.[40]

(d) Engravings, etchings and workings in mezzotinto or chiaroscuro, prints taken by lithograph, or any other mechanical process for multiplying prints: Engravings Copyright Acts 1734, 1766; International Copyright Act 1852.[41]

(e) Sculptures: Sculpture Copyright Act 1814.[42]

(f) Paintings, drawings and photographs: Fine Arts Copyright Act 1862.[43]

3. JOINT AUTHORSHIP: LITERARY, DRAMATIC, MUSICAL AND ARTISTIC WORKS

4–37   **Introduction.** As has been noted,[44] circumstances may arise where there are joint authors of a work. Since the passing of the 1911 Act, the concept of joint authorship has been defined by statute. Before that date it was not defined. Despite slight differences in wording between the 1911, 1956 and 1988 Acts,[45] there has

---

[36] See paras 6–50 *et seq.*, below. The works which had an indefinite term of copyright were, broadly, literary, dramatic and musical works and engravings which had not been published in the author's lifetime. Although the term of copyright in all such works has now started to run, it will be many years before such terms expire.

[37] See Vol.2 at E5 , for these Acts and paras 6–21 *et seq.*, below, for a discussion of the term of copyright in these works.

[38] 5 & 6 Vict. c.45. See Vol.2 at E5.vii . Musical scores and books of words were protected under this Act.

[39] 5 & 6 Will. 4 c.65. See Vol.2 at E5.vi.

[40] 3 & 4 Will. 4 c.15. See Vol.2 at E5.v. As noted in the text of point (a), above, musical scores and books of words were protected under the Literary Copyright Act 1842. The performing rights in dramatic works only were protected by the 1833 Act, but ss.20 and 21 of the 1842 Act extended the protection to both musical and dramatic compositions.

[41] 8 Geo. 2 c.13 ("… every person who shall invent and design, engrave, etch, or work … or from his own works shall cause to be designed and engraved, etched, or worked … [any print] shall have the sole right and liberty of printing and reprinting the same …"), 7 Geo. 3 c.38 and 15 & 16 Vict. c.12, respectively. See Vol.2 at E5.i and E5.ii. The 1734 Act did not make provision for protection of any work of which the engraver was not also the designer. This was remedied by the 1766 Act, which extended protection, subject to conditions, to the work of any person making an engraving from the original work of another. s.14 of the 1852 Act brought prints taken by lithograph, etc. within the scope of the earlier Acts relating to engravings.

[42] 54 Geo. 3 c.56 ("… every person who shall make or cause to be made any new and original sculpture … shall have the sole right and property …"). See Vol.2 at E5.iv.

[43] 25 & 26 Vict. c.68. See Vol.2 at E5.ix.

[44] See para. 4–06, above.

[45] See 149 to 156, below.

not been any change in the law in relation to this issue[46] and indeed the Acts reflect the position as it existed before the passing of the 1911 Act.[47] Nevertheless, it is technically still necessary to bear in mind that the question of joint authorship must be approached in accordance with the law in force when the work was made.[48]

Importance of distinction between joint authors and co-authors.[49] Whether a work is one of joint authorship or whether there are co-authors is not a merely academic question but has important consequences. For example, the term of copyright in work will depend on the question, as will issues of ownership and infringement. **4–38**

Definition. A work of joint authorship is defined by the 1988 Act to mean "a work produced by the collaboration of two or more authors in which the contribution of each author is not distinct from that of the other author or authors."[50] It is not necessary that all should contribute to the same extent.[51] As to these requirements[52]: **4–39**

(a) To be a work of joint authorship, all the collaborators must answer the description of an "author", as that concept is properly to be understood.[53]

(b) Since collaboration is required, a work is not a work of joint authorship unless it is made in furtherance of some common design.[54]

(c) If the contributions are distinct or separate, it is not a work of joint authorship.[55]

There is no additional requirement that there must be a joint intention to create a joint work, in the sense that each author must intend the other to be a joint author.[56] The above three issues are considered in turn below. Whether a work is a work of joint authorship is a question of fact not agreement.[57]

---

[46] The point was conceded, with apparent judicial approval, in *Cala Homes (South) Ltd v Alfred McAlpine Homes East Ltd* [1995] F.S.R. 818.

[47] See *Copinger's Law of Copyright* (4th ed.), p.109.

[48] See para. 4–07, above.

[49] The expression "co-authors" is used here to describe, *e.g.* the case where two or more authors make distinct contributions to a work. See para. 4–06, above, and, *e.g.* the second limb of the definition of "collective work" in CDPA 1988, s.178.

[50] CDPA 1988, s.10(1). The definition in the 1956 Act, s.11(3), was the same except that the word "separate" was used, rather than "distinct". (Note that one of the O.E.D. definitions of "distinct" is "separate" and also CDPA 1988, s.172, which provides that a provision corresponding to a provision of the previous law should not be construed as departing from previous law merely because of a change of expression.) The 1911 Act also used the word "distinct", defining a work of joint authorship as "a work produced by the collaboration of two or more authors in which the contribution of one author is not distinct from the contribution of the other author or authors" (s.16(3)). The expression "collective work" as used in the Copyright Act 1911, s.35(1), and CDPA 1988, ss.79(6), 81(4), 116(4)(a) and 178 has a different meaning. See para. 5–114, below.

[51] *Levy v Rutley* (1871) L.R. 6 C.P.

[52] See *Ray v Classic FM* [1998] F.S.R. 622l at 636 for an equivalent formulation of these three principles.

[53] See para. 4–40, below.

[54] *Levy v Rutley* (1871) L.R. 6 C.P. 523; *Heptulla v Orient Longman Ltd* [1989] F.S.R. 598 (Delhi High Ct); *Glogau v Land Transport Safety Authority of New Zealand* [1997] 3 N.Z.L.R. 353 (High Ct of NZ). See, further, para. 4–43, below.

[55] See para. 4–44, below.

[56] *Beckingham v Hodgens* [2003] EWCA Civ 143, not following *Neudorf v Nettwerk Productions* [1999] R.P.C. 935 (Sup. Ct of British Columbia). As to the statement in *Levy v Rutley* (1871) L.R. 6 C.P., that for a work to be one of joint authorship there should be a "joint labouring in furtherance of a common design", the "common design" referred to there is not an intention that the work should be one of joint authorship but is a reference to the need for a joint process in the creation of the work.

[57] See para. 4–45, below and, for example, *Samuelson v Producers Distributing Co. Ltd* (1932) 48 R.P.C. 580 at 586 and *Wiseman v George Weidenfeld & Nicolson Ltd* [1985] F.S.R. 525.

4–40   All collaborators must be "authors". All must therefore make some contribution to the literary, dramatic, musical or artistic form in which copyright subsists.[58]
The question is whether the collaborator takes a part in producing the matter
which is the subject of copyright,[59] *i.e.* whether he has contributed the right kind
of skill and labour and in sufficient amount.[60] It may helpful to break this requirement down into four elements: (1) the collaborator must make a contribution of
some sort[61]; (2) it must have been significant[62]; (3) it must have been original; and
(4) it must have been a contribution to the creation of the work.[63] The last element may often be crucial, in the sense that a contribution which does not find
itself expressed in the final work will not be relevant.[64] In general as to this
requirement, the skill and labour need not be contributed in an amount equal to
that of the other co-author or co-authors,[65] and need not be of the same kind, so
that, for example, someone whose principal role is to arrange the songs written
by his collaborators can be a joint author.[66] It will be a matter of fact and degree
whether his contribution was large enough to make him a joint author.[67] It follows that if one person is merely the medium for transmitting to paper, canvas,
etc. the original work of another, the former is not an author and the work is not a
work of joint authorship. Looking at the other side of the coin, a person who
merely suggests the idea, without contributing anything to the literary, dramatic
or other form in which copyright subsists, is not a joint author. A situation can
clearly arise, however, where two people make a contribution to the work's final
expression, one being the person actually responsible for committing the work to
paper, the other providing an input to what is recorded.[68] But the fact that two
persons may have divided up the labour of creating a work will not make them
joint authors if only one person is responsible for the skill and labour involved in
final expression of their efforts.[69] For the same reason, a person who revises and
makes minor additions to an existing work cannot be a joint author.[70]

4–41   Examples of cases where this principle has been established include those where
one person (A) had recounted the events of his life to another (B), who had agreed
to write A's biography, B making notes from which drafts were prepared which
A and B then went over together, making amendments, A correcting the final

---

[58] *Wiseman v George Weidenfeld & Nicolson Ltd* [1985] F.S.R. 525.

[59] *Evans v E Hulton & Co. Ltd* [1923–28] Mac.C.C. 51 at 56; *Ray v Classic FM* [1998] F.S.R. 622
at 636.

[60] *Fylde Microsystems Ltd v Key Radio Systems Ltd* [1998] F.S.R. 449; *Godfrey v Lees* [1995]
E.M.L.R. 307 (a joint author must make a significant and original contribution to the creation of
the work).

[61] So the fact that an author needed to obtain the approval of a government department for the
contents and form of a work, and that the department laid down certain requirements, did not
make the department a joint author of the work: *Glogau v Land Transport Safety Authority of
New Zealand* [1999] 1 N.Z.L.R. 257 (Ct of App. of NZ).

[62] Emphasised in *Brighton v Jones* [2004] EWHC 1157 (Ch), para.34(1).

[63] *Hadley v Kemp* [1999] E.M.L.R. 589.

[64] As to this fourth element, and for emphasis on the fact that the author must contribute to the
expression which the law protects, as opposed simply to "ideas", see also *Brighton v Jones*
[2004] EWHC 1157 (Ch); *Neudorf v Nettwerk Productions Ltd* [2000] R.P.C. 935 (Sup. Ct of
British Columbia).

[65] *Levy v Rutley* (1871) L.R. 6 C.P. 523; *Godfrey v Lees* [1995] E.M.L.R. 307.

[66] *Godfrey v Lees* [1995] E.M.L.R. 307 .

[67] *Stuart v Barrett* [1994] E.M.L.R. 448; *Fylde Microsystems Ltd v Key Radio Systems Ltd* [1988]
F.S.R. 449.

[68] *Cala Homes (South) Ltd v Alfred McAlpine Homes East Ltd* [1995] F.S.R. 818; *Brighton v Jones*
[2004] EWHC 1157 (Ch).

[69] *Fylde Microsystems Ltd v Key Radio Systems Ltd* [1998] F.S.R. 449; *Ray v Classic FM* [1998]
F.S.R. 622. The principle needs to be applied with caution in the case of works of compilation,
where the relevant skill and labour will often include the gathering or selection of material. See
para. 4–24, above.

[70] He would also of course not be a joint author if there were no collaboration and their contributions were distinct.

draft line by line[71]; where three people all took part in the design of new models of chairs and settees, one being primarily responsible for the conception but all three taking part in the realisation of that conception in consultation with each other[72]; where two people who were intimately associated and contemplating marriage had collaborated on a book on poliomyelitis, having both worked in a hospital treating an epidemic, one supplying much information to the other and it being impossible to tell who had written which lines[73]; where members of a pop group sat down and composed pieces of music together[74]; where one person contributed the orchestral arrangements to songs otherwise written by members of a pop group[75]; where one architect engaged another to help him produce house designs and gave precise instructions as to the features to be incorporated into each house, often with the aid of sketches, checked each drawing produced and marked on it or otherwise made clear the alterations which he required.[76]

Examples of cases in which the claim of joint authorship has not been made out **4–42** include those where one person had suggested the title of a dramatic sketch, together with various incidents and a few catch lines and odd words but others had actually written the material[77]; where one person recounted his life's adventures to another, the latter being solely responsible for the form of words[78]; where one person (A) suggested to another (B) that he B write a dramatic version of an existing book and A made critical suggestions which led to whole scenes being rewritten, helped with the stage craft but contributed nothing to the eventual dialogue apart from an occasional line and idea[79]; where the claimant had written software for the defendant's mobile telephones and the defendant claimed joint authorship on the basis that he had made an extensive and technically sophisticated contribution in that he had provided (a) the specification for the software (but without saying how the specification was to be achieved), (b) the technical information to enable the software to communicate with the hardware, (c) various parameters for the software, (d) help in developing the software by testing and reporting faults and bugs, and (e) suggestions as to what was the cause of some of the faults (but without providing the software solution to them)[80]; where the defendant had made a number of suggestions as to what a cataloguing system for classical music broadcasts should contain but where the claimant had been responsible for all the final content[81]; where the claimants were members of a pop group to whom the defendant, another member, brought virtually finished

---

[71] *Heptulla v Orient Longman Ltd* [1989] F.S.R. 598 (Delhi High Ct).

[72] *George Hensher Ltd v Restawhile Upholstery (Lancs.) Ltd* [1975] R.P.C. 31 at 39, 40.

[73] *Taylor v Prior*, (1956) *The Author*, LXVII, No.3 at 60.

[74] *Stuart v Barrett* [1994] E.M.L.R. 448. In contrast, mere "tinkering" by a member with a song written before he joined did not make him a joint author.

[75] *Godfrey v Lees* [1995] E.M.L.R. 307.

[76] *Cala Homes (South) Ltd v Alfred McAlpine Homes East Ltd* [1995] F.S.R. 818, described as an exceptional case in *Ray v Classic FM* [1998] F.S.R. 622, and one in which the actual draftsmen were essentially only "scribes" of the architect.

[77] *Tate v Thomas* [1921] 1 Ch. 503. The former's contributions to the subject matter of the copyright work were described as "insignificant and negligible". To similar effect are *Tate v Fullbrook* [1908] 1 K.B. 821, where the contributions consisted of the general ideas on which the sketch was based, and *Bagge v Miller* [1917–23] Mac.C.C. 178, where only the bare idea for a one-act dramatic sketch was provided, all the work of execution of the idea being another's. But see, as to plot, para. 4–27, above.

[78] *Evans v E Hulton & Co. Ltd* [1923–28] Mac.C.C. 51. *cf. Heptulla v Orient Longman Ltd* [1989] F.S.R. 598 (Delhi High Ct).

[79] *Wiseman v Weidenfeld & Nicolson Ltd* [1985] F.S.R. 525.

[80] *Fylde Microsystems Ltd v Key Radio Systems Ltd* [1998] F.S.R. 449. For a similar case where a claim to joint authorship of computer programs failed, see *Cyprotex Discovery Ltd v The University of Sheffield* [2003] EWHC 760 (TCC), [2004] R.P.C. 4, para.84 (upheld on appeal, although this point was not in issue: [2004] EWCA Civ 380, [2004] R.P.C. 43).

[81] *Ray v Classic FM* [1998] F.S.R. 622.

songs, and the claimants then applied their skills as performers to the playing of the songs (as a result of which they were recorded for the first time) but did not make any significant contribution to the words or music of them[82]; where a director of a play suggested changes to a play but the playwright was responsible for turning the suggestions into the words and action which appeared in the script.[83] In *Kenrick v Laurence*,[84] where one person had conceived the idea for a drawing but it had been executed by another, it was suggested[85] that they might be joint authors. Unless, however, the former had made an actual contribution to final artistic form, which clearly was not the case on the facts, it is suggested that this would have been wrong.

4–43   **Collaboration required.** There must be collaboration for authorship to be joint. The work of the authors must be in prosecution of a joint design or joint labouring in furtherance of a common design.[86] So where an author was commissioned to write a play by a theatre proprietor who subsequently made alterations to the author's work, without reference to him, the resulting work was not one of joint authorship.[87] Again, if an existing musical work composed by A is independently arranged by B, the resulting work is not a work of joint authorship. The proper analysis is that is that A is the author of the original work and B is the author of the arrangement.[88]

4–44   **Contributions distinct.** The fact that the contribution can be identified in the final work does not mean it is distinct; the issue is whether it forms an integral part of the work, without which the work would be different in character.[89]If the contributions of each author are distinct, then what is produced will not be a work of joint authorship but works of separate authorship, even if they were acting pursuant to a common design. Each person will be the author of the part which he has contributed, each being a separate work.[90] An example would be an encyclopedia where there will usually be a large number of copyright works consisting of the individual entries, each having its separate author. In the case of such works it will be unusual if there is not also a further copyright work, being the encyclopedia considered as a whole, with its own author or authors who have brought the works together.

4–45   **Agreement as to joint authorship.** There is some authority for the proposition that where there has been some collaboration, a person can be a joint author if

---

[82] *Hadley v Kemp* [1999] E.M.L.R. 589.

[83] *Brighton v Jones* [2004] EWHC 1157, Ch.D.

[84] (1890) 25 Q.B.D. 99 (see para. 4–29, above).

[85] (1890) 25 Q.B.D. 99, at 106.

[86] *Levy v Rutley* (1871) L.R. 6 C.P. 523; *Heptulla v Longman Orient Ltd* [1989] F.S.R. 598 (Delhi High Ct); *Glogau v Land Transport Safety Authority of New Zealand* [1997] 3 N.Z.L.R. 353C (High Ct of NZ); *Neudorf v Nettwerk Productions Ltd* [2000] R.P.C. 935 (Sup. Ct of British Columbia).

[87] *Levy v Rutley* (1871) L.R. 6 C.P. 523. To the same effect is *Samuelson v Producers Distributing Co. Ltd* (1932) 48 R.P.C. 580, where an actor made alterations to a dramatic sketch he had been sent. As to the actual decision in this case, see para. 4–16, above.

[88] See *Brighton v Jones* [2004] EWHC 1157, Ch D and para. 4–14, above, for a general discussion of derivative works, where it is pointed out that the consent of the owner of the copyright in the original work will of course be required for the exploitation of the arranged version.

[89] So, a violin part which had been written specially by the claimant for a song was not distinct from the other contributions to the music. Although it was possible to identify the violin part separately in terms of musical notation, the part was dependent on what was already there. It would have sounded odd and have lost meaning played on its own. The final musical expression, which is what audiences would hear, was a joint one. See *Beckingham v Hodgens* [2003] E.C.D.R. 6, para.46.

[90] In *Levy v Rutley* (1871) L.R. 6 C.P. 523, it was said, *obiter*, that if two persons, in prosecution of a preconcerted joint design, had written different portions of a play such that each portion was the sole production of one or the other, they might be "co-authors".

this is something which has been agreed, even though he was not one of the authors of the work in the legal sense.[91] It is suggested that this cannot be right. Authorship is a question of status and fact, not agreement[92] and each person must answer the description of author. In the same way, if one person is solely responsible for the creation of a work, the fact that he made the work pursuant to a common design with another for its creation cannot make that other person one of the authors of the work.

Rights of joint authors *inter se* and against third parties. So far as concerns copyright, the question of the rights of co-authors as between themselves or as against third parties arises in the context of ownership of copyright rather than authorship, and is therefore considered in Chapter 5. The regulation of moral rights as between co-authors is considered in Chapter 11.   **4–46**

4. SOUND RECORDINGS, FILMS, BROADCASTS AND TYPOGRAPHICAL ARRANGEMENTS

Introduction. It has already been noted that the use in the 1988 Act of the term "author" in relation to these classes of works is not generally a happy one, and has been the subject of criticism. Save now in relation to films, however, the expression is not in fact used otherwise than as shorthand in the process of identifying the first owner of the copyright. As to this, the first owner is broadly identified with whoever was responsible for the financial risk behind the creation of the work, although the position in relation to films has now changed. Consistently with this approach, no person is granted any moral rights in respect of these works save, since the passing of the 1988 Act, the director of a copyright film.[93]   **4–47**

A. SOUND RECORDINGS

Sound recordings have been protected as such since the passing of the 1956 Act. Under the 1911 Act they were in effect protected as musical works, although with the passing of the 1956 Act these existing works became protectable as sound recordings rather than as musical works.[94] The copyright in all pre-1911 Act sound recordings will by now have expired.[95]   **4–48**

The 1988 Act. The question of authorship of sound recordings made after August 1, 1989 is governed by the authorship provisions of the 1988 Act.[96] As to this, the general principle under the 1988 Act, namely that the author of a work means the   **4–49**

---

[91] See, *e.g. Prior v Lansdowne Press Pty Ltd* [1977] R.P.C., discussed at 191, below.
[92] See *Levy v Rutley* (1871) L.R. 6 C.P. 523 at 531. The point was accepted on all sides in *Wiseman v George Weidenfeld & Nicolson Ltd* [1985] F.S.R. 525 at 529. The confusion often arises because of the close connection in many cases between the concepts of authorship and ownership. Thus where two or more persons each provide some input to the final form of a work, it will often be agreed between them, expressly or impliedly, that they will own the copyright jointly. As to whether such agreement will in fact make them joint owners, either at law or in equity. In *Prior v Lansdowne Press Pty Ltd* [1977] R.P.C. 511 (Sup. Ct of Victoria) one person had made no contribution to the text of a book but had helped to compile the material, and was a party with the two actual contributors to the publishing agreement in which they were all collectively described as "the Author" and was named in the book as published as one of its authors. He was held to be a joint author. At issue was the share of the damages which one of the other writers was entitled to. It is suggested that the decision that he was joint author was wrong, although it may well have been correct to treat him as a joint owner.
[93] See Ch.11, below.
[94] Copyright Act 1956, Sch.7, para.11.
[95] Sch.7, para.11
[96] See para. 4–07, above. The one exception relates to sound recordings made after August 1, 1989

person who created it, is modified such that this person is to be taken to be the producer, defined as the person by whom the arrangements necessary for the making of the recording are undertaken.[97] This latter expression is also to be found in the provisions of the 1988 and 1956 Acts dealing with films, so that the authorities in that context[98] are relevant here. In the normal commercial context of producing a sound recording, this person will usually be the person who has, for example, engaged or hired the equipment, studio, record producer, engineer, session musicians and any other personnel. In many cases this will be a record company but clearly many permutations are possible. The word "undertaken" implies that it is the person directly responsible for such arrangements, particularly in the financial sense, who is the author.[99] One who merely commissions or finances the making of the recording, not being directly responsible for making the various payments, is unlikely to be the author.[1] The wording of the 1988 Act is clearly directed at the usual situation of the making of a commercial sound recording. The wording is less apt to cover the case where, for example, a recording is informally made by a person who simply turns on a tape recorder when others are performing. In such a case presumably it will the person who is responsible for bringing the tape recorder and making any necessary adjustments to it who will be the "author".

4–50   In each case the issue will be one of fact. For example, in one case a person (A), requiring some recordings to be made for a particular purpose, engaged a musician (B) to make them. B was to set up a studio and musicians at his own expense in return for a fee that would enable him to make a profit. B (1) commissioned and paid for the musical arrangements that were made, (2) booked, arranged for and paid all the musicians and engineers and (3) discharged all the incidental expenses. A was nevertheless held to be the author.[2] The person who "made" the recording clearly will not necessarily be the person by whom the arrangements necessary for the making of the recording were undertaken.[3]

---

but whose making was commissioned before that date. The provisions of the 1956 Act apply to such recordings. As to these, see para. 4–51, below.

[97] CDPA 1988, ss.9(2)(aa), 178. The expression "producer" was introduced into the 1988 Act with effect from December 1, 1996 by the Copyright and Related Rights Regulations 1996 (SI 1996/2967) and derives from Art.2.1 of the Rental and Related Rights Directive (92/100). Previously s.9(2)(a) of the 1988 Act simply defined the author of a sound recording as being the person by whom the arrangements necessary for the making of the recording were undertaken. The effect of the amendment is to introduce an extra layer of definition but not to change the substantive law.

[98] See para. 4–59, below.

[99] Re FG (Films) Ltd [1953] 1 W.L.R. 483.

[1] *Beggars Banquet Records Ltd v Carlton Television Ltd* [1993] E.M.L.R. 349.

[2] *A&M Records Ltd v Video Collection International Ltd* [1995] E.M.L.R. 25. The facts of the case must have been very close to the borderline. The real issue was the ownership of the copyright in the sound recording and it was held in the alternative that A was entitled in equity to the copyright on the basis of an implied term of B's engagement by A (as to which see para. 5–173, below). Had the case been decided under the 1956 Act it would have been possible to achieve the same result by applying the commissioning provisions of the Act (s.12(4)). See para. 5–43, below.

[3] *A&M Records Ltd v Video Collection International Ltd* [1995] E.M.L.R. 25. In *Beggars Banquet Records Ltd v Carlton Television Ltd* [1993] E.M.L.R. 349 (a case concerning films rather than sound recordings) it was said that the words of the section must be construed in the light of the words of CDPA 1988, , s.9(1), which provides that the expression author "means the person who creates" the work. If by this it was intended to mean that it is relevant to consider who was responsible for the intellectual creation of the results of the recording it is suggested that this is wrong. CDPA 1988, s.9(2) redefines "author" without reference to any direct responsibility for the creative process and the suggestion is contrary to the authorities cited here and in relation to films on the wording of s.9(2).

The 1956 Act. There is no one who can properly be described as the "author" of   **4–51**
a sound recording made before August 1, 1989.[4] The 1956 Act used the expression "maker" rather than "author". It is, however, convenient to consider the provisions here.

The 1956 Act provided that the maker of a sound recording was the person who   **4–52**
owned the first record embodying the sound recording at the time when the recording was made.[5] This person is clearly not necessarily the same as the person who made the arrangements necessary for the making of the recording,[6] so that the positions under the 1956 and 1988 Acts are different. Thus, in many cases where a recording studio was hired and recording tape supplied by the studio as part of its hire services, the studio will have been the maker although not responsible for any other costs or creative input.[7] Nice questions as to the title to the tape may thus affect the question of who was the maker.[8]

1911 Act sound recordings. As noted above, these became protectable under the   **4–53**
1956 Act as sound recordings rather than musical works and this treatment is continued by the 1988 Act. Nevertheless, the 1911 Act must now be referred to in order to determine who the authors of such works were.[9] Unlike the 1956 Act, the 1911 Act actually spoke in terms of an "author" of such works, since they were equated with musical works.[10] The author was, however, deemed to be the person who was the owner of the original "plate"[11] from which the recording was derived, at the time when it was made.[12] The definition was therefore to the same effect as the equivalent provision in the 1956 Act.

Pre-1911 Act sound recordings. As noted above, the copyright in such works   **4–54**
will by now have expired.

Film sound tracks. The question of the authorship of film sound tracks is   **4–55**
considered under its own heading, below.

B. FILMS

Introduction. The treatment of films, and their "authorship", has been the subject   **4–56**
of much change over the years.[13] In effect, three different regimes have existed:

   Regime 1. That which has applied since July 1, 1994, the effective date of

---

[4] Or whose making was commissioned before that date. See CDPA 1988, Sch.1, para.11(2).

[5] Copyright Act 1956, s.12(8).

[6] In *Springsteen v Flute International Ltd* [1999] E.M.L.R. 180, tape recordings of an artist's performance were made by a partnership as part of its preparations for the promotion of the artist. On the assumption that one of the partners had bought the tapes, it was held that he had done so on behalf of the partnership and that they had become the property of the partnership. It was irrelevant whether or not he had been reimbursed.

[7] Note, however, that the potentially capricious effect of the Act was lessened by s.12(4), thereby a person who commissioned the making of a sound recording became the owner of the copyright (see para. 5–43, below).

[8] Precisely this kind of problem arose in *Springsteen v Flute International Ltd* [1999] E.M.L.R. 180. The dispute concerned the ownership of sound recordings made over 25 years previously. One party had made the arrangements for the recordings to be made at a recording studio and had duly paid the studio (although not in circumstances amounting to a commissioning). Although it was probable that the recording studio had provided the blank tapes which were used, it was held, in the absence of any evidence to the contrary, that the arrangement was that the blank tapes would become the property of the other party immediately before they were used for recording purposes.

[9] See para. 4–07, above.

[10] See the Copyright Act 1911, s.19(1).

[11] "Plate" was defined *inter alia* to mean any appliance by which records, perforated rolls or other contrivances for the acoustic representation of any work were intended to be made. See Copyright Act 1911, s.35(1).

[12] Copyright Act 1911, s.19(1).

[13] Note that in relation to a work made after the commencement of the 1988 Act, a film which is a

the amendments made to the 1988 Act to implement the Rental and Related Rights Directive.[14]

Regime 2. That which applied between June 1, 1957, the date of the coming into force of the 1956 Act, and July 1, 1994. In this period, the 1956 Act and 1988 Act, as unamended, were successively in force, but their effect was the same.

Regime 3. That which applied before June 1, 1957, relating to films made before the coming into force of the 1956 Act, when films were not protected as such and only the constituent elements, namely the dramatic work embodied in the film, the photographs forming the frames and the sound track were capable of individual protection.

4–57   Under the 1956 Act and the 1988 Act as originally enacted, the United Kingdom did not treat films as works having a true author, in the sense of having an individual who was responsible for the intellectual creation of the subject matter of the film, and in general terms conferred copyright on the person most closely responsible for the financial risk involved in making of the film.[15] Other systems, particularly civil law systems, have regarded films differently and have treated them as true authors' works, having "authors" properly so-called, for example, the screenplay writer, director, lighting cameraman, leading actors and composers of musical works for the film.[16] This difference in approach first came to a head with the Rental and Related Rights Directive,[17] which required, for the purpose of conferring the rental right,[18] that the principal director of a cinematographic or audiovisual work be considered as its author or one of its authors.[19] In fact before implementing the Rental Directive, the United Kingdom implemented the Directive harmonising the term of copyright,[20] which contained a similar requirement,[21] although when implementing the Term Directive, the United Kingdom merely enacted a provision whereby the term of copyright in a film was to be calculated by reference to the date of death of various specified individuals, including the principal director, and did not alter the law as to authorship.[22] However, the Term Directive required the United Kingdom to make the principal

---

work of action may also be protected as a dramatic work. See para. 3–37, above. The author of the dramatic work which takes the form of a film may be different from the author of the separate copyright work which is the film. As to the author of a dramatic work, see para. 4–27, above.

[14] Directive 92/100.

[15] See para. 4–59, below.

[16] See Stewart, *International Copyright and Neighbouring Rights* (2nd ed.), p.129. The Berne Convention had applied to cinematograph works since 1908, but from the outset adherence to the Convention left Member States free to determine authorship of films. See Art.14 *bis*(2)(a) and Ricketson, *The Berne Convention for the Protection of Literary and Artistic Works: 1886–1986*, paras 10–3 to 10–10.

[17] Directive 92/100.

[18] As to this right, see para. 7–81, below.

[19] Art.2.2. Fears had been expressed by the United Kingdom, amongst other Member States, that the requirement in the Directive that the principal director of a film be recognised as one of its authors would cause difficulties with regard to a film's exploitation. As part of a compromise when reaching a common position on the Directive, the Commission therefore agreed to produce a report on the question, this being finally produced on December 9, 2002 (IP/02/1824). The report concluded that the fears had been unfounded and that any potential difficulties had been or could be overcome by contractual arrangements between films producers and directors. See the report at *www.europa.eu.int/comm/internal_market/en/intprop/news/index.htm*.

[20] Directive 93/98.

[21] Directive 93/98, Art.2.1. The Community was faced with conflicting systems of law in relation to the treatment of films and particularly how the term of copyright was calculated. The fact that the principal director had already been accorded a rental right was one of the factors which influenced the decision to calculate the term of copyright in films by reference, *inter alia*, to the date of death of the principal director. See, *e.g.* Dworkin, "Authorship of Films and the European Commission Proposals for Harmonising the Term of Copyright", [1993] E.I.P.R. 151.

[22] CDPA 1988, s.13B, as amended by the Duration of Copyright and Rights in Performances Regulations 1995 (SI 1995/3297).

an author for all purposes by July 1, 1997 and although the Rental and Related
Rights Directive only required the principal director be made an author for the
limited purpose of the rental right, the law relating to authorship was duly
changed when implementing the Rental Directive.

Regime 1

Films made on or after July 1, 1994.[23] In relation to such films, but only as from   **4–58**
December 1, 1996,[24] the definition of author in the 1988 Act as being the person
who created the work[25] is further defined such that the author or authors are to be
taken to be the producer and the principal director of the film.[26] Unless the producer and the principal director were the same person, a film is to be treated as a
work of the joint authorship of these two persons.[27]

Producer. The producer is defined to be the person by whom the arrangements   **4–59**
necessary for the making of the film were undertaken.[28] This expression has already been considered in the context of sound recordings.[29] This definition was
also used in the 1956 Act in the context of films, the expression "maker" in that
Act being the equivalent of "producer",[30] so that decisions under that Act are still
relevant in this context. The producer, as so defined, will normally be the producer as that expression is also understood in the film industry, rather than, for
example, the camera operator.[31] He will be the person responsible for the arrangements, particularly in the financial sense.[32] For example, where a shell
company acted purely as nominee and agent for another company, which was in
reality providing the finance and control, the shell company was not the maker.[33]
In contrast, where a company (A), whose promoters had had the idea for a film
and were the joint directors, paid for the purchase of the film stock and the fares
for the crew and participants, A was the maker of the film, notwithstanding that
the finance was in fact provided by a television company for whom the film was
being made. Everything which was done in the making of the film was done on
A's behalf. An individual who had been engaged as cameraman and who may
have played some part in the direction of the film, and another company associated with him which was to have been responsible for the cutting and editing,
were not co-makers and had no interest in the copyright.[34] So, again, where a
company had initiated a project for a film, organised the activity necessary for it
to be made and paid for it, that person was the maker and not the local company

---

[23] Where the making of the film extended over a period, it is to be taken to have been made when its
making was completed. See reg.25(2).
[24] The Copyright and Related Rights Regulations 1996 (SI 1996/2967), reg.36(1). The starting date
of July 1, 1994 derives from Art.13.4 of the Rental and Related Rights Directive. See para. 4–61,
below, as to transitional provisions.
[25] s.9(1).
[26] s.9(2)(ab).
[27] s.10(1A). As to joint authorship of films generally, see para. 4–70, below.
[28] CDPA 1988, s.178, as amended.
[29] See para. 4–49, above. As with sound recordings, the expression "producer", although new to
United Kingdom law (cf. in the context of the Rome and Berne Conventions), simply forms an
extra layer of definition.
[30] See para. 4–62, below.
[31] *Adventure Film Productions Ltd v Tulley* [1993] E.M.L.R. 376.
[32] *Re FG (Films) Ltd* [1953] 1 W.L.R. 383.
[33] *Re FG (Films) Ltd* [1953] 1 W.L.R. 483, a case decided under the Cinematograph Films Act
1938, where the relevant expression, as in the 1956 Act, was in fact "maker" rather than
"producer". See para. 4–62, below.
[34] *Adventure Film Productions SA v Tulley* [1993] E.M.L.R. 376, decided under the 1956 Act. See
para. 4–70, below, as joint authorship in such circumstances.

whose help had necessarily been invoked to help shoot the film in mainland China.[35]

4–60   **The principal director.** This expression, which is derived from Article 2.1 of the Rental Directive, is not further defined.[36]

4–61   **Transitional.** Although the new provisions only took effect as from December 1, 1996, they apply to films made after July 1, 1994,[37] a provision which has some difficult consequences. These, however, relate mainly to the question of ownership of the copyright and so are considered in the next chapter.

Regime 2

4–62   In this period, two different statutes apply, although they are to the same effect:

(a) **Films made before July 1, 1994: the** 1988 Act. In relation to films made after August 1, 1989 but before July 1, 1994, the original provisions of the 1988 Act apply. These provided that the person who created a film, and who was thus the author of it, was to be taken to be the person by whom the arrangements necessary for the making of the film were undertaken.[38] The meaning of this expression has already been considered.

(b) **The 1956 Act.** The provisions of the 1956 Act, which apply to all films made between June 1, 1957 and August 1, 1989,[39] were to the same effect, namely, that the maker of a cinematograph film was the person by whom the arrangements necessary for the making of the film were undertaken.[40]

Regime 3

4–63   **Pre-1956 Act films.** There is no copyright in cinematograph films as such made before June 1, 1957.[41]

C. FILM SOUNDTRACKS

4–64   **Introduction.** The position of film soundtracks has been complicated by the changes which have been made from time to time in the way they are treated. The dilemma is as follows. Should a soundtrack be treated as part of the film copyright, or should it be treated as a separate copyright work, that is, a sound recording, even when part of the film? It is the varying answers to this question that have produced the complications.[42]

4–65   **Film soundtracks made on or after August 1, 1989: the 1988 Act as amended.** With effect from January 1, 1996, but in relation to all soundtracks,[43] the 1988 Act now provides that the soundtrack accompanying a film is to be treated as part

---

[35] *Century Communications Ltd v Mayfair Entertainment U.K. Ltd* [1993] E.M.L.R. 335.
[36] A new presumption is available in proceedings to help prove who was the principal director. See CDPA 1988, ss.105(5) and (6) and para. 22–217, below.
[37] See the Copyright and Related Rights Regulations 1996, reg.36(1).
[38] CDPA 1988, s.9(2)(a).
[39] See para. 4–07, above.
[40] s.13(10). It will be recalled that the expression "maker" rather than "author" was used in the 1956 Act.
[41] CDPA 1988, Sch.1, para.7(1).
[42] See para. 3–76, above, for a fuller discussion of the position of soundtracks.
[43] Note that in relation to questions of authorship and ownership, the 1988 Act is only of relevance to works made on or after August 1, 1989. See para. 4–07, above. See below as to the treatment of film soundtracks made before this date.

of the film.[44] This is not, however, to affect any copyright subsisting in a film soundtrack as a sound recording.[45] Copyright therefore subsists independently in a sound recording which forms the soundtrack of a film and, in the usual way, its author will be the producer, that is, the person by whom the arrangements necessary for its making were undertaken.[46] The film copyright will, however, also include the soundtrack. The film, taken as a whole and therefore including the soundtrack, will have its own author or authors. These will be the producer and, in relation to films made on or after July 1, 1994, the principal director.[47]

The position can be illustrated as follows. If the recording of sounds was made **4–66** separately, and not as part of the record of moving images, the recording will be a sound recording in the normal way and have its own author. It will remain as a separate copyright work with its own author even when the sound recording is united with the record of moving images, although the separate copyright work consisting of the film will now include the recording which forms the soundtrack. As to this, the author of the film must be determined, amongst other matters,[48] by asking who undertook the arrangements necessary for the making of the film as a whole, which will include the uniting of the sound recording with the film. Depending on whether the sound recording was made specially for the film or whether it was a pre-existing recording or recordings, this will involve asking who undertook the necessary arrangements for the making of a new sound recording or the selection of the existing sound recording, respectively, and then in each case who then undertook the arrangements necessary to have the recording united with the record of moving images. Where, alternatively, the soundtrack was made in the course of a live shoot, there will still be two copyright works created, the film, with its soundtrack, and the sound recording which is embodied in the soundtrack of the film. Each will have its own author or authors, determined according to the above rules, although in this case they will often be one and the same person or persons.

Film soundtracks made on or after August 1, 1989 but before January 1, **4–67** **1996: the transitional position under the 1988 Act as amended.** As has been seen, the amended provisions of the 1988 Act apply as from January 1, 1996 to those earlier soundtracks. What is the position of these works?[49] Under the original provisions of the 1988 Act, copyright subsisted in a film soundtrack as a sound recording in its own right and the film copyright did not include the soundtrack.[50] In the usual way, the author of the soundtrack was the person by whom the arrangements necessary for the making of the soundtrack were undertaken.[51] The film, which was not to be regarded as including the soundtrack for these purposes, would have had its own author or authors, determined in accordance with the normal rules. The effect of the amendments to the 1988 Act as they apply to these existing works was therefore to enlarge retrospectively the

---

[44] CDPA 1988, s.5B(2), inserted by Duration of Copyright and Rights in Performances Regulations 1995 (SI 1995/3297). The effective date is provided for by reg.26(1). This treatment of soundtracks only applies for the purposes of Pt I of the Act, *i.e.* the provisions dealing with copyright and moral rights.

[45] s.5B(5).

[46] See para. 4–49, above.

[47] See paras 4–56 *et seq.*, above.

[48] The role of the principal director must not be overlooked in relation to films made on or after July 1, 1994.

[49] It should be remembered that this discussion is not concerned with soundtracks made before August 1, 1989, since the authorship provisions of the 1988 Act only apply to works made on or after that date. See para. 4–07, above.

[50] CDPA 1988, s.5.

[51] See para. 4–49, above.

scope of the film copyright and thus possibly to alter or enlarge retrospectively the class of persons who were the authors of such films. The possible effect of this on the ownership of the film copyright and its consequences are considered when dealing with the question of first ownership of the copyright.[52]

4–68   **Film soundtracks made on or after June 1, 1957 but before August 1, 1989: the 1956 Act.** Under the 1956 Act the sounds embodied in any sound track associated with a cinematograph film were to be taken to be included in the film.[53] Copyright therefore subsisted in such a soundtrack as part of the copyright in the cinematograph film and not as a separate sound recording. The maker of the film was therefore the person who undertook the necessary arrangements for the making not only of the record of visual images but also the soundtrack. Again, however, a sound recording made separately from the film would have had its own, separate copyright, with its own "maker". The 1988 Act now provides that film soundtracks to which the 1956 Act applied are to be treated as sound recordings and not as part of the film.[54] This might have created difficulties with regard to the ownership of the copyright in such sound recordings but the 1988 Act provides that the "author" of such a film is to be treated as having been the "author" of the sound recording.[55] Thus, it seems, whoever was the maker of the cinematograph film[56] will be treated as having been the "author" of the soundtrack which is now to be regarded as a sound recording.

4–69   **Film soundtracks: the 1911 Act.** Copyright does not subsist in a film as such made before June 1, 1957[57] so that film soundtracks made before this date are protected as sound recordings and their author will be determined accordingly.[58]

D. JOINT AUTHORSHIP OF SOUND RECORDINGS AND FILMS

4–70   **The 1988 Act.** In general, sound recordings and films to which the 1988 Act applies may be works of joint authorship.[59] If the overall agreement between two persons is that one of them is to be the producer of a film, the fact that the other makes the arrangements for a particular location will not make the two of them joint authors in this sense.[60] As already seen,[61] a film made on or after July 1, 1994, will always be a work of joint authorship unless the producer and principal director are one and the same person.

4–71   **The 1956 Act: films.** It was implicit that the express provisions of the 1956 Act relating to joint authorship related only to literary, dramatic, musical and artistic works since it was only in relation to such works that the expression "author"

---

[52] See para. 5–563, below.

[53] Copyright Act 1956, ss.12(9), 13(9).

[54] CDPA 1988, Sch.1, para.8(1). This provision has not been altered by the changes introduced to the treatment of film soundtracks by Duration of Copyright and Rights in Performances Regulations 1995.

[55] CDPA 1988, Sch.1, para.8(2). The use of the expression "author" in relation to such 1956 Act works appears to be inappropriate.

[56] *i.e.* the person who undertook the arrangements necessary for its making.

[57] CDPA 1988, Sch.1, para.7(1).

[58] See para. 4–53, above.

[59] A difficulty may be thought to arise because a work of joint authorship is defined as meaning "a work produced by the collaboration of two or more authors in which the contribution of each author is not distinct from that of the other author or authors" (s.10(1)), and the author of a sound recording or film may not actually "produce" the work at all. It is suggested there is nothing in this. See, *e.g.* s.10(1A) of the 1988 Act. The possibility of joint authorship was accepted without argument in *Beggars Banquet Records Ltd v Carlton Television Ltd* [1993] E.M.L.R. 349.

[60] *Adventure Film Productions Ltd v Tulley* [1993] E.M.L.R. 376.

[61] See para. 4–58, above.

could be applied.[62] Since a 1956 Act film did not have any "authors", it could not have been a work of joint authorship but there seems no reason why there should not have been joint "makers" of a film.[63]

1956 Act and 1911 Act sound recordings. Again, there seems no reason why there should not have been joint makers or authors, respectively, of sound recordings made under these Acts, where the original recording or plate, respectively, was jointly owned.[64]   **4–72**

E. BROADCASTS

The 1988 Act. It has already been seen[65] that with effect from October 31, 2003,   **4–73**
the definition of "broadcast" has been altered in the course of implementation of the Information Society Directive, and the expression now also includes within its scope what used to be cable programmes.

As with sound recording and films, the concept of an "author" of a broadcast is an uneasy one but the expression is used only as a means to identify the first owner of the copyright. Thus, in relation to broadcasts made on or after August 1, 1989, the 1988 Act provides that the person who creates the work, and who is thus the author of it, is to be taken to be the person making the broadcast or, in the case of a broadcast which relays another broadcast by reception and immediate retransmission, the person making that other broadcast.[66] The 1988 Act further provides that references to the person making the broadcast are to the person transmitting the programme if he has responsibility to any extent for its contents, and to any person providing the programme who makes with the person transmitting it the arrangements necessary for its transmission.[67] In this context, the reference to a "programme" is to any item included in a broadcast. This definition applies to broadcasts, as now defined, whether made before or after October 31, 2003, the effective date of the Regulations which amended the defintion of the "broadcast".[68] Since the new definition includes within in it everything that was a broadcast under the 1988 Act as enacted, this does not give rise to any difficulties.

Cable programmes. In relation to cable programmes which are "broadcasts"   **4–73A**
within the new definition of this expression, the author is the person set out above. As to those cable programmes which came into existence between August 1, 1989 and October 31, 2003 which are still entitled to copyright,[69] the author was previously defined to be the person providing the cable programme service in which the programme was included.[70] This definition has, however, been repealed along with section 7 of the Act, and in relation to these cable programmes, which are now to be regarded as broadcasts, the new, general definition of author of a broadcast apparently applies. It is not clear whether there will have been any cable programmes in respect of which the person providing the cable programme service in which the programme was included will have been someone different from the person "making" the transmission, as that expression is defined. If so, it

---

[62] See the wording of s.11(3) of the 1956 Act.
[63] As suggested in *Adventure Film Productions Ltd v Tulley*, [1993] E.M.L.R. 376. The Whitford Committee noted that there were no provisions in the 1956 Act dealing with "joint makers" of films and sound recordings, in contrast to the provisions relating to joint authors, and recommended the making of equivalent provision (see Cmnd. 6732, para.584).
[64] See the previous last footnote to para. 4–71, above.
[65] See para. 3–91, above.
[66] CDPA 1988, s.9(2)(b).
[67] s.6(3).
[68] The Copyright and Related Rights Regulations 2003 (SI 2003/2498), para.31(1).
[69] See para. 3–91, above.
[70] CDPA 1988, s.9(2)(c).

seems that as at October 31, 2003 there will have been a retrospective change of authorship of the work and potentially, therefore, of ownership.

4–74   Joint authors. Where more than one person is to be taken as making the broadcast in accordance with the above definition, then the broadcast is to be treated as a work of joint authorship.[71]

4–75   The 1956 Act. The 1956 Act did not use the expression "author" in relation to what were broadcasts as defined under that Act, identifying only the person who was entitled to first ownership, namely the BBC or the IBA, as the case may have been.[72] In relation to what were described as cable programmes, there was no copyright in cable programmes included in a cable programme service before January 1, 1985.[73] As to cable programmes which came into existence after this date, the 1956 Act, as amended, did not make provision for any person to be the author of a cable programme, simply stating that the person providing the cable programme service in which a cable programme was included should be entitled to the copyright in such a work.[74]

4–76   Pre-1956 Act broadcasts. There is no copyright in broadcasts made before June 1, 1957.[75]

G. TYPOGRAPHICAL ARRANGEMENTS

4–77   The 1988 Act. In relation to a typographical arrangement of a published edition made after August 1, 1989, the person who created the work, and who is thus the author of it, is to be taken to be the publisher of it.[76]

4–78   The 1956 Act. The 1956 Act, which applies to typographical arrangements made before August 1, 1989,[77] did not provide for an author of such works. The Act simply stated that the publisher was to be entitled to the copyright subsisting in a published edition under that Act.[78]

4–79   Pre-1956 published editions. It appears that the 1956 Act applied to pre-1956 Act published editions, since that Act contained no relevant transitional provisions. However, the 25-year term in respect of such works[79] will have expired.

[71] CDPA 1988, s.10(2).
[72] Copyright Act 1956, s.14(2).
[73] s.14A(11), as inserted by the Cable and Broadcasting Act 1984; CDPA 1988, Sch.1, para.9(b).
[74] Copyright Act 1956, s.14A(3), as inserted by the Cable and Broadcasting Act 1984.
[75] CDPA 1988, Sch.1, para.9(a).
[76] CDPA 1988, s.9(2)(d). As to the meaning of "publisher", see s.175(1).
[77] See para. 4–07, above.
[78] Copyright Act 1956, s.15(2).
[79] Copyright Act 1956, s.15(2).

THE CHAIN OF TITLE

1. THE FIRST OWNER OF COPYRIGHT

A. INTRODUCTION

Introduction. In many circumstances it will be important to know who is the   **5–01**
owner of the copyright in a work. This involves asking, first, who was the first
owner of the legal title to the copyright and, secondly, whether that title has since

devolved on some other person. The question of first ownership is considered in this section, the issue of devolution of title in the next. It must also be borne in mind that although the legal title may be vested in one person, some other person may be entitled to the copyright in equity. This will often have significant consequences and is considered in the later section on equitable title.

5–02 **Distinction between ownership of copyright and physical material.** It is important to bear in mind that, subject to limited exceptions,[1] the identity of the first owner of the copyright in a work may be quite different from the person who is owner of the physical material or other medium on or in which the copyright work is first recorded or fixed. The question arises more usually in the context of transfer of title, where the principle is the same, namely that the transfer of the medium on which the work was first fixed does by itself operate to transfer the copyright.[2] Usually, of course, the author will own the paper, ink, canvas, paint, etc, by means of which the work is fixed but even where he does not, this does not affect the question of first ownership.

5–03 **Transitional provisions.** The rules relating to first ownership of copyright have altered from time to time. As with authorship, the provisions of the 1988 Act have been framed so as to avoid any retrospective alteration in the identity of the first owner of the copyright. This is achieved by a transitional provision to the effect that the law which was in force when the work was made must be applied to determine who was the first owner of the copyright.[3] The effect is shown by the following table:

Date when work made	Act to be applied
On or after August 1, 1989	The 1988 Act
On or after June 1, 1957 but before August 1, 1989	The 1956 Act
On or after July 1, 1912, but before June 1, 1957	The 1911 Act
Before July 1, 1912	The Acts then in force[4]

For this purpose, where the making of a work extended over a period, the work is to be taken as having been made when its making was completed.[5]

5–04 **Presumptions.** Various presumptions can be applied, in civil proceedings, to determine who the owner of the copyright was at certain times.[6] These are considered elsewhere.[7]

5–05 **Crown and Parliamentary copyright, copyright of certain international organisations.** A quite separate regime applies to these works, which is considered elsewhere.[8]

B. LITERARY, DRAMATIC, MUSICAL AND ARTISTIC WORKS

(i) Author as first owner

5–06 **The general rule.** The general rule under all the Copyright Acts in relation to

---

[1] *i.e.* first ownership of pre- 1988 Act photographs and sound recordings. See paras 4–34, above (with 5–06) and 5–42, below, respectively.
[2] See para. 5–65, below.
[3] CDPA 1988, Sch.1, para.10.
[4] See para. 5–40 , below.
[5] CDPA 1988, Sch.1, para.1(3).
[6] CDPA 1988, ss.104–106.
[7] See paras 22–210 *et seq.*, below.
[8] See Ch.10, below.

these works has always been that the author is the first owner of the copyright.[9]
The question of who the author of these works is has already been considered.[10]
The remainder of this chapter is concerned with exceptions to this general rule.

Joint authors. As an extension of this principle, where the authors are joint   **5–07**
authors,[11] then the general rule is that these authors will be the first owners of the
copyright, holding as joint owners.[12]

(ii) Works of employees

Introduction. In contrast to the position under many civil law or *droit d'auteur*   **5–08**
systems,[13] it has for many years been the position under United Kingdom law, as
an exception to the general rule stated above, that an employer is *prima facie*
entitled to the copyright in the work made by his employee.[14]

The 1988, 1956 and 1911 Acts. The full statement of the rule under all these   **5–09**
Acts is that where a literary, dramatic, musical or artistic work is or was made by
an employee in the course of his employment under a contract of service or apprenticeship, his employer is the first owner of any copyright in the work, subject
to any agreement to the contrary.[15] The rule is subject to qualification in relation
to pre-1988 Act works of employees of proprietors of newspapers and the like,
and certain other contributions to newspapers.[16] Save in relation to such works,
however, the rule is the same in relation to all works made on or after July 1,
1912. The position in relation to works before that date is considered separately.[17]

Equitable ownership and licence. It must always be borne in mind that, even if   **5–10**
the legal title to the copyright does not vest in the employer as first owner under
these rules, it will often be a term of the contract of the author's engagement that
the "employer" should own the copyright or at least have some rights to use the
work. A number of possibilities then arise:

   (a) If the contract amounts to a valid assignment of future copyright,[18] the
      copyright will vest in the "employer" as soon as it comes into existence.

   (b) If the contract does not amount to such an assignment but it is neverthe-
      less a term of the contract, express or implied, that the "employer" should
      own the copyright, then although the legal title will remain with the

---

[9] CDPA 1988, s.11(1); Copyright Act 1956, s.4(1); Copyright Act 1911, s.5(1); as to the earlier
Acts, see para. 5–40, below.

[10] See Ch.4, above.

[11] As to joint authorship, see para. 4–37, above.

[12] CDPA 1988, ss.11(1), 10(3); Copyright Act 1956 s.4(1), Sch.3, para.6. The 1911 Act contained
no such express provisions but it is suggested the position is clear. As to the incidents of co-
ownership, see para. 5–69, below.

[13] See para. 4–03, above.

[14] This position reflects the views of the Whitford Committee in its report (Cmnd. 6732) that "... as
a matter of principle, if a person is employed to do a job of work and paid for his services according to the nature of those services, the product of his labour should, subject to any agreement to
the contrary, belong to his employer ...". See para.571 of the report and also para. 5–26, below.
The Committee rejected submissions that the general rule should always be that the author/
employee should be the first owner of the copyright in his work. The Committee's recommendation (para.574) that, if a work was exploited by the employer in a way not in the contemplation of
the parties at the time of its making, the employee should have a statutory right to an award, was
not accepted. *cf.* the position under the Patents Act 1977, s.40, as amended.

[15] CDPA 1988, ss.11(2), 178; Copyright Act 1956, ss.4(4), (5); Copyright Act 1911, s.5(1)(b).

[16] See paras 5–29 and 5–30, below.

[17] See paras 5–31 *et seq.*, below.

[18] As to which, see paras 5–105 *et seq.*, below.

author, the "employer" will own the copyright in equity provided he is entitled to enforce the contract.[19]

(c) Alternatively, it may appear from the terms of the author's engagement that even though the "employer" was not to be the owner of the copyright, the "employer" was to be entitled to use the results of the author's work to some extent. The result of this will be that the "employer" will have a licence to use the work, the terms of which, including whether it is sole and exclusive, will depend on the terms of the engagement.[20]

5–11   **Employees' works: The issues.** The rule stated above raises the following questions:

(a) Was the author employed under a contract of service?

(b) Was the work made in the course of the author's employment?

(c) Was there a relevant agreement to the contrary?

In practice, it can sometimes be difficult to be sure of the answers to these questions andthis can cause a dilemma where, for example, a prospective employer-claimant is contemplating seeking urgent interim relief. There are four possible courses of action: first, to take the risk that the contract is one of service, etc, and sue in the employer's name alone; secondly, to obtain an assignment from the author (together with accrued causes of action) before issuing proceedings in the name of the employer; thirdly, to join the author as co-claimant; fourthly, where there is a dispute between them or the author is not willing to co-operate, to join the author as a defendant.[21] The first course of action clearly contains the greatest risk.

5–12   **Was the author employed under a "contract of service"?**[22] There are many cases outside the copyright field on this issue,[23] and the concepts of an employee and a contract of service are well understood and have the same meanings in the 1988 Act as they do elsewhere.[24] The distinction is between a "contract of service" and a "contract for services".[25] The two expressions indicate, for example, the distinction between a person engaged to do some specific work under a considerable measure of control, extending not only to the work which he does but also to the way in which he does it, on the one hand, and that of a person engaged more in the capacity of an independent contractor, for example professionally, on the other.[26] A contract of service will exist if three conditions are satisfed: (a) the servant agrees that, in consideration of a wage or other remuneration, he will provide his own work and skill in the performance of some work for his master; (b) he agrees, expressly or impliedly, that in the performance of that

---

[19] See para. 5–170 et seq., below.

[20] As to licences, see paras 5–194 et seq., below

[21] This option assumes that if he is not the legal owner of the copyright then, at worst, the "employer" is either the equitable owner or an exclusive licensee within the meaning of the 1988 Act (as to which, see para. 5–203, below). If he is none of these things, the action for infringement of copyright will fail. The need to join the author as defendant arises from the requirement that the legal owner or the exclusive licensor, as the case may be, must be joined as a party, although note that an interim injunction may nevertheless be obtained in these cases without having joined the author. See the separate treatment of these two situations at paras 5–186 and 5–206, below.

[22] The recommendation of the Whitford Committee (Cmnd. 6732, para.575), that the only question should be whether the work was made in the course of employment, was not accepted. The Committee's comment (para.568) was that the expression "contract of service", if intelligible at all, is only intelligible to lawyers.

[23] Often in the field of income tax and previously in the field of the Workman's Compensation Acts.

[24] Ultraframe (UK) Ltd v Fielding [2003] EWCA Civ 1805, para.19 (a design right case).

[25] Beloff v Pressdram Ltd [1973] R.P.C. 765 at 769.

[26] Stevenson Jordan & Harrison Ltd v Macdonald & Evans [1952] 1 T.L.R. 101, per Evershed M.R.

work he will be subject to the other's control in a sufficient degree to make that other master; and (c) the other provisions of the contract are consistent with its being a contract of service.[27] As to these, the degree of control is important, but is no longer regarded as the determining factor.[28] There must, however, be some degree of control, not necessarily in the sense of direction and control exercised by actual supervision, or the possibility of such supervision, but in the sense of ultimate authority over the worker in the performance of his work so that he is subject to the employer's orders and directions.[29] One feature of the difference is that under a contract of service, a person is usually employed as part of the business, and the work is done as an integral part of the business, whereas under a contract for services, the work, although done for the business, is not integrated into it, but is only an accessory to it.[30] But these represent the extreme positions and a more useful test is whether the person who performed the work did so as a person in business on his own account. In answering this question, no strict rules can be laid down as to the relative weight which should be attached to the various considerations which apply. As already stated, the degree of control is important but is no longer regarded as the determining factor. Other factors which may be important are whether the person provides his own equipment, hires his own helpers, what degree of financial risk he takes, what degree of responsibility for investment and management he has, and whether and how far he has an opportunity of profiting from sound management in the performance of his task.[31] A contract of employment may be casual rather than regular.[32] Evaluation of the position is not a mechanical exercise of checking off the various factors but of evaluating the whole picture painted from the accumulation of detail.[33] The terms of the contract as a whole need to be looked at, giving attention particularly to the substantive obligations and rights of each party, so as to determine whether they are more strongly indicative of one form of relationship rather than the other.[34] The test of whether the person is in business on his own account may not be so helpful in the case of a person carrying on a profession or vocation, when it may be more important to bear in mind the traditional contrast between a servant and an independent contractor, the extent to which he is dependent upon or independent of a particular paymaster for the financial exploitation of his talents being of significance.[35] Whether a person is engaged under a contract of service or not is a question of law depending upon the facts,[36] and although parties cannot alter the nature of their relationship by putting a new label on it, where the situation is in doubt or ambiguous, so that it can be brought under one relationship or the other,

---

[27] *Ready Mixed Concrete (South East) Ltd v Minister of Pensions and National Insurance* [1968] 2 Q.B. 497, taken to be "the safest starting point" in *Montgomery v Johnson Underwood Ltd* [2001] I.C.R. 819 and applied in *Ultraframe (UK) Ltd v Fielding* [2003] EWCA Civ 1805, para.21.

[28] Particularly in the case of professional persons, who are often employed under contracts of service. See *Morren v Swinton and Pendlebury Borough Council* [1965] 1 W.L.R. 576; *Whittaker v Minister of Pensions and National Insurance* [1967] 1 Q.B. 156.

[29] *Humberstone v Northern Timber Mills* (1949) 79 C.L.R. 389, 404, applied in *Montgomery v Johnson Underwood Ltd* [2001] I.C.R. 819.

[30] *Humberstone v Northern Timber Mills* (1949) 79 C.L.R. 389, *per* Denning L.J.

[31] *Market Investigations Ltd v Minister of Social Security* [1969] 2 Q.B. 173 at 184, 185. Approved in *Lee Ting Sang v Chung Chi-Keung* [1990] 2 A.C. 374 at 382, PC.

[32] *Hall v Lorimer* [1994] 1 W.L.R. 209, CA.

[33] *Hall v Lorimer* [1994] 1 W.L.R. 209 at 216, CA.

[34] *Barnett v Brabyn* [1996] S.T.C. 716.

[35] *Hall v Lorimer* [1994] 1 W.L.R. 209 at 218, CA, where it was pointed out that a self-employed author working at home may have none of the usual trappings of a business.

[36] *O'Kelly v Trusthouse Forte plc* [1984] Q.B. 90. Where the entire contract is contained in a written agreement, the matter is purely one of law. See, *e.g. McMeechan v Secretary of State for Employment* [1995] I.C.R. 444, EAT. Otherwise it will be necessary to determine, as a question of fact, what the contract was. An appellate court should only interfere with the trial court's finding of fact if there was no evidence to support the finding. See *Lee Ting Sang v Chung Chi-Keung* [1990] 2 A.C. 374, PC.

it is open to the parties, by agreement, to stipulate what the legal situation between them should be.[37]

A number of examples in the copyright and related fields show that each case
turns on its own facts:[38]

Cases where a contract of service established

5–13
(a) A "dress editress" of a periodical, engaged to recommend artists, visit
shops, supervise fashion artists, to write dress articles and correspondence, her duties being of a general nature.[39]

(b) A chief dancer of a ballet company, engaged as choreographer as well as a
dancer, who was required to give his exclusive services to the company,
attend all performances as required and superintend all necessary rehearsals, in return for a monthly salary.[40]

(c) A part-time interviewer for a market research company, required to follow the company's detailed instructions on interviewing and as to who to
interview (although beyond the company's actual control when in the
field), but free as to when to do the work within a given period and to
work for other organisations.[41]

(d) The full-time political and lobby correspondent of a national newspaper,
paid an annual salary, who was an active member of the editorial staff
with an office in the newspaper building, who would discuss the content
of her articles with, but was not dictated to by, the editor.[42]

(e) A designer of cars employed as chief engineer and designer for a fixed
term and at an annual salary.[43]

(f) A professional, salaried dancer engaged full-time during specified hours
by Sadlers Wells, the company having first call on his services but, subject
to that, he being permitted to obtain outside work.[44]

No contract of service

5–14
(a) A person engaged by a fashion magazine at a monthly salary to supply
fashion drawings and not to do any other work until such work was
completed, working at her home or her studio and doing odd jobs for others; not a "servant" within the meaning of the Companies (Consolidation)
Act 1908, s.209. Nor was a writer engaged to provide weekly articles for
the magazine, but not on an exclusive basis and not being required to attend its offices.[45]

(b) University examiners employed to prepare examination papers and mark
the answers, for which they received a lump sum, they being free to do so
at their own convenience, subject to a deadline, it being left to their own
skill and judgment to decide what questions to be asked having regard to
the syllabus and standard of examination, and not being part of the staff of

---

[37] *Massey v Crown Life Insurance Co* [1978] 1 W.L.R. 676.
[38] Quite apart from the fact that each case turns on its own facts, care must be taken in relying on
the earlier cases, decided when the degree of control exercised was considered a decisive factor.
[39] *Re Beeton & Co* [1913] 2 Ch. 279. She was therefore a "servant" within the meaning of the
Companies (Consolidation) Act 1908, s.209.
[40] *Massine v De Basil* [1936–45] Mac.C.C. 223.
[41] *Market Investigations Ltd v Minister of Social Security* [1969] 2 Q.B. 173.
[42] *Beloff v Pressdram Ltd* [1973] R.P.C. 765.
[43] *Nichols Advanced Vehicle Systems Inc v Rees* [1979] R.P.C. 127.
[44] *Fall v Hitchen* [1973] 1 W.L.R. 286.
[45] *Re Beeton & Co* [1913] 2 Ch. 279. *Cf.* example (a) ("dress editress"), above.

the university and having regular employment in other educational establishments.[46]

(c) Two newspaper reporters, one employed to attend certain sporting meetings and provide reports for which he was paid a rate *per diem*, the other employed to write a number of weekly sporting articles for which he was paid an annual salary. Neither worked at the newspaper's offices, nor were they bound to render their exclusive services to the newspaper, nor were they under the newspaper's general control.[47]

(d) A music hall artiste engaged to appear with another artiste as a comedy duo at a specified theatre for one week, subject to a large number of regulations designed for the proper working of the theatre, but his performance depending entirely on his skill, personality and artistry, with which the management had no right to interfere, the amount and degree of control being the significant factor.[48]

(e) A person engaged as a screenplay writer for a sequel to a successful film, with various milestones for its preparation being specified, the production company having the right to require revisions but not to tell him how to go about his work or what he was to do, the writer being paid a fee payable by instalments and a share of the net profit.[49]

(f) A member of what was in effect a co-operative of musicians forming an orchestra. Although technically engaged by a company, each member was a shareholder and if asked: "Who is your employer," would have replied: "We don't have a boss, we run ourselves through a company, and we hire 11 administrators to do it."[50]

(g) Freelance musicians engaged by an orchestra company on a session-by-session basis, being free to accept or refuse engagements as they wished.[51]

(h) A well-known expert in classical music, engaged at an hourly rate to advise on the composition and compilation of a radio station's repertoire, the contract making provision for him to pursue other business interests and to work when and where he wanted, without supervision or control.[52]

Company directors. The position of a company director sometimes causes difficulty because a director will not necessarily be employed under a contract of service, even where he is an executive director.[53] The fact that a managing director, as part of his management activities, from time to time acts as if he were a servant or employee does not make him an employee for this purpose.[54] If he is so employed, the ordinary rule applies. If he is not, the legal title to the copyright will not vest in the company but the fiduciary duties which he owes as a director and officer will usually mean that he holds on trust for the company any copyright in work he does *qua* director.[55]   **5–15**

Owner-directors of companies. Where a person owns the entire share capital of   **5–16**

---

[46] *University of London Press Ltd v University Tutorial Press Ltd* [1916] 2 Ch. 601.
[47] In *Re Ashley & Smith Ltd* [1917–23] Mac.C.C. 54.
[48] *Gould v Minister of National Insurance* [1951] 1 K.B. 731.
[49] *Hexagon Pty Ltd v Australian Broadcasting Commission* [1976] R.P.C. 628.
[50] *Winfield v London Philharmonic Orchestra Ltd* [1979] I.C.R. 726.
[51] *Addison v London Philharmonic Orchestra Ltd* [1981] I.C.R. 261.
[52] *Ray v Classic FM plc* [1998] F.S.R. 622. The contract also expressly stated that the relationship was one of an independent contractor providing services and not that of employer and employee.
[53] *Parson v Albert J. Parson & Sons Ltd* [1979] F.S.R. 254. In *Gardex Ltd Sorata Ltd* [1986] R.P.C. 623, it was held that the work was done in the course of a managing director's employment, but it is not clear that there was any evidence of a contract of employment.
[54] *Antocks Lairn Ltd v I. Bloohn Ltd* [1972] R.P.C. 219 at 221; *Wilden Pump & Engineering Co v Fusfield* (1985) 8 I.P.R. 250.
[55] *Antocks Lairn Ltd v I. Bloohn Ltd* [1972] R.P.C. 219. See para. 5–176, below.

a company or a controlling interest and is also a director or shadow-director, it can be even more difficult to know whether he has a contract of employment with the company.[56] The first question may be whether there is a genuine contract between the director and the company at all, as to which, facts such as how and for what reasons the alleged contract came into existence and what each party did in relation to the contract are likely to be important. The next question will usually be whether any such contract, assuming it is not a sham, was a contract of employment, as to which the above types of considerations will be relevant. This issue is not determined by the fact that he owns a controlling shareholding, and it will be relevant to ask whether there are directors other than, or additional to the shareholder and whether the constitution of the company gives him rights such that in reality he is answerable only to himself and incapable of being dismissed. If he is a director, it may be relevant to ask whether he is entitled under the articles to vote on matters on which he is personally interested, such as his contract of employment. Again the conduct of the parties under the contract may well be relevant.[57] As a practical matter, it may be useful to ask questions such as: Was the individual, as shareholder and director, under an obligation to be at work a certain number of hours a week, or to do things such as create copyright works in return for wages?[58]

5–17   **Partners.** A partner of a firm is not "employed" by his partners or the partnership and so the partner will be the first owner of the legal title to a work created by him.[59] On the other hand, the copyright in a work created by an employee of the firm in the course of his employment under a contract of service will vest in the partners.[60]

5–18   **Course of employment.** In order for the copyright to vest in an employer, it is not sufficient merely that the work is made by an author who is employed under a contract of service. It must also be made in the course of that employment. This involves asking, first, whether the work which was done was the kind of work which the employee was engaged to do and, if it was, whether the work was in fact done in the course of that employment at all. The questions often merge into one another.

5–19   **Scope of employment.** This involves a consideration of the terms of the contract of service. Where there is no express contract of employment or no definitive statement of the employee's duties, it will be relevant to consider whether the work was done during normal office hours and using materials provided at the employer's expense and for his benefit and at his request, but these are not conclusive factors[61] since an employee will often do things for his employer which he is not expressly contracted to do.[62] Each case must, of course, depend on its own facts. The question to ask is, was the author employed to do the kind of work in question? Under the contract, could he have been ordered to do the work and would it have been a breach of contract for the employee then not to do it?[63]

5–20   **Work done outside course of employment.** The fact that work is done outside

[56] On this question generally, see *Ultraframe (UK) Ltd v Fielding* [2003] EWCA Civ 1805.
[57] *Ibid.*, para.20.
[58] *Ibid.*, para.25.
[59] As to the equitable title, see para. 5–177, below.
[60] As to the rights of the partners amongst themselves, see, again, para. 5–177, below.
[61] *Intercase UK Ltd v Time Computers Ltd* [2003] EWHC (Ch) 2988.
[62] *Stevenson Jordan and Harrison Ltd v MacDonald & Evans* [1952] 1 T.L.R. 101 at 111.
[63] *Stevenson Jordan and Harrison Ltd v McDonald & Evans* [1952] 1 T.L.R. 101, at 113. In *Sun Newspapers Ltd v Whippie* (1928) 28 S.R. (N.S.W.) 473, an illustration made by an employee

normal working hours does not necessarily mean that the work is not done in the course of employment. Indeed for many employees today there is no clear demarcation of the hours of work. The problem is often acute where an employee does work outside normal working hours which clearly has some connection with his employment. It is suggested that if the work is within the scope of employment[64] and was done for the benefit of the employer, it will have been done in the course of employment.

Work done outside course of employment: "Moonlighting". Where the work falls within the scope of employment but is not done in the course of employment, for example, being done outside office hours and not for the employer's benefit, and the results of which might later be used in competition, the employee may be in breach of his fiduciary duty by not disclosing the work to his employer. Although an employee may make use of his leisure for his profit, he may not secretly set himself up to do in his spare time something which would inflict harm on his employer's business.[65] The consequence of this may either be that the copyright is held on constructive trust for the employer, or the employee will not be allowed to set up a claim that the work was not done in the course of his employment.[66] **5–21**

Work done in breach of contract of employment. It does not follow from the fact that an employee has acted in breach of his contract of employment that he is also in breach of a fiduciary duty. Contractual duties of good faith and loyalty, or trust and confidence, are not automatically to be equated with fiduciary obligations. In all cases it is necessary to examine the particular duties of the employee and see whether in the circumstances he must act solely in the interests of his employer. In the case of the creation of copyright works, the question may be whether the employee had a duty to use his skill and expertise for his employer's benefit alone and thus create such works for his employer.[67] So, where an employee, working undercover for a film maker, had secretly filmed events inside his employer's film parlour, there had been no breach which brought this principle into operation. There was no breach of confidence involved and he was therefore free to describe what he had seen, whether in writing or otherwise. He could thus not be a trustee of such a description and for the same reason he could not be a trustee of a photograph or film he had made, whether covert or not.[68] **5–22**

Course of employment: Examples. Examples help to illustrate the point: **5–23**
    (a) A person permanently employed on the editorial staff of a newspaper and

---

was beyond the scope of his employment and he could have refused to do it. Nevertheless the employer was held to have acquired the legal title. This was on the basis that the "respective rights of the parties in the original drawing were intended to be the same as their rights in the drawings made under the contract", so that the drawing was "considered to have been made in the course of his employment". It is suggested that this conclusion was wrong, although no doubt the employer was entitled to the copyright in equity.

[64] See the previous paragraph.

[65] *Hivac Ltd v Park Royal Scientific Instruments Ltd* [1946] 1 Ch.169 at 178, cited in *Ultra Marketing (UK) Ltd v Universal Components Ltd* [2002] EWHC (Ch) 2285, where an employee was not held to be in breach of any duty by creating a copyright work outside his employment. The employee was known to have personal interests and the work he created would never have been part of an actual or intended business of the company.

[66] See *Missing Link Software v Magee* [1989] F.S.R. 361; *Service Corp plc v Channel Four Television Corp*, The Independent, May 14, 1998. As to an equitable title, see paras 5–175 *et seq.*, below.

[67] *Nottingham University v Fishel* [2001] R.P.C. 367. It was accepted that an employer might be entitled in equity to the copyright in a work created by an employee otherwise than in the course of his employment if it had been created in breach of his fiduciary duty to his employer, for example in breach of his contractual duty to use his expertise for his employer alone or where the work contained confidential information belonging to his employer.

[68] *Service Corp International PLC v Channel Four Television Corp* [1999] E.M.L.R. 83.

who was specially requested by the proprietors to translate and summarise a speech, which he did in his own time, independently of his ordinary duties and for a separately negotiated fee, was not acting in the course of his employment. What he had done was not in pursuance of any duty owed to his employer.[69]

(b) A management consultant, who prepared and wrote lectures for delivery to universities and societies dealing with the business in which he was employed, did not do so in the course of his employment.[70] This was so notwithstanding that (1) the giving of lectures was helpful to the company in that it served as an advertisement and, on that account, he was paid the expenses he incurred and (2) that it was, in a sense, part of the services rendered by him for the benefit of the company. It was not part of his regular duties and he could not have been ordered to give the lectures. On the other hand, a report which he had written for a client about its business when on assignment to the client was written in the course of his employment even though it was written largely after hours. The difference was that this was written as part of his work as a servant of the company but the lectures were written as an accessory to the contract and not as part of it. The decision was made having regard to the general consideration that someone engaged to deliver a series of lectures would, in the absence of clear terms to the contrary, be entitled to the copyright in them.[71]

(c) A consultant epidemiologist who wrote, at home, in the evenings and at weekends but not at the instigation of his employers, a guide on hygiene in relation to skin-piercing activities, did not do so in the course of his employment.[72] This was so notwithstanding that he had not undertaken the writing of the book in any private capacity and its preparation was part of his official duties which fell within the terms of his conditions of service and was his employer's publication.

5–24 **Unincorporated association.** The legal title in the copyright in a work created by a member of an unincorporated association will usually belong to that member but its ownership will be subject to the rules of the association.[73]

5–25 **Apprenticeship.** An apprentice is someone who is engaged to another for the purpose of learning his trade or calling, the nature of the contract being that the master teaches and the other serves the master with the intention of learning.[74] The purpose of apprenticeship is to learn a craft, trade or a profession such that

---

[69] *Byrne v Statist Co* [1914] 1 K.B. 622. Having paid for the work, the newspaper proprietor was no doubt entitled to the copyright in equity. See para. 5–173, below.

[70] *Stevenson, Jordan & Harrison Ltd v Macdonald & Evans* [1952] 1 T.L.R. 101.

[71] *Stevenson, Jordan & Harrison Ltd v Macdonald & Evans* [1952] 1 T.L.R. 101 at 107, citing the example of Professor Maitland's law lectures to students at Cambridge. Further examples given were lectures or lessons given orally to students by a doctor on the staff of a hospital or a teacher on the staff at a school who, for his own convenience, puts the lectures into writing, this being useful as an accessory to his contracted work but not part of it. See p.111 of the report.

[72] *Noah v Shuba* [1991] F.S.R. 14, following *Stevenson, Jordan & Harrison Ltd v Macdonald & Evans* [1952] 1 T.L.R. 101. Note that because the presumption of ownership contained in s.20(2) of the 1956 Act applied, the burden of proof to show that the claimant had made the work in the course of employment was on the defendant.

[73] In *Massie & Renwick Ltd v Underwriters' Survey Bureau Ltd* [1940] S.C.R. 218 (Can.), it was held that in the particular circumstances, the copyrights belonged to the members as tenants in common.

[74] *Clapham v St Pancras* (1860) 6 Jur.(N.S.) 700; *Horan v Hayhoe* [1904] 1 K.B. 288 (in which the element of instruction is again emphasised).

when the apprenticeship is completed the apprentice becomes qualified in that trade or profession.[75]

Agreement to the contrary. The 1988 Act provides, as did the 1956 and 1911 Acts, that these employment provisions are subject to any agreement to the contrary.[76] The agreement must have been made before the work came into existence.[77] Such a term may be express, whether in writing[78] or oral, or implied, for example, as a result of a long-standing practice adopted by an employer whereby the employee retains the copyright.[79] The agreement must be one such that (a) notwithstanding the existence of a contract of employment, the title to works created during its course should not vest in the employer, and (b) it is legally effective.[80] Generally, it will no doubt be hard for an employee to establish such an implied term. The normal inference from employment and payment will be that copyright should belong to the employer.[81]

5–26

Employees as joint authors. The position as to first ownership where one of the authors is acting in the course of his employment under a contract of service and the other is not, or is employed by a different employer, is unclear. Arguably the provisions of the Copyright Acts making the employer the first owner of the copyright[82] do not apply since the references in the 1988 and 1956 Acts to the author of a work are to be taken to be references to all authors in the case of a work of joint authorship.[83] Whatever the position as to the legal title in such circumstances, however, the employer will almost inevitably be entitled in equity to his employee's interest in the work.

5–27

(iii) Works made for publication in a newspaper, magazine or similar periodical

For many years, special provision was made regarding the ownership of copyright in works made by employees for publication in newspapers, etc. The 1988 Act makes no such provision for this category of work, so that the general rule under the Act relating to works of employees[84] applies. In relation to such works made before August 1, 1989, however, the rules under the earlier Acts are still relevant. The regime under these Acts was a half-way house between that applying to employees in general and that relating to non-employees. Under the provisions, newspaper and other proprietors acquired a limited or restricted copyright, extending only to press publication. The absence of such a provision in the 1988 Act effected a substantial change in the law in this area. As will be seen, the 1988

5–28

---

[75] *Wiltshire Police Authority v Wynn* [1981] Q.B. 95.

[76] CDPA 1988, s.11(2); Copyright Act 1956, s.4(5); Copyright Act 1911, s.5(1).

[77] *Noah v Shuba* [1991] F.S.R. 14. A contract made afterwards may, of course, amount to an assignment or an agreement to assign.

[78] As in *Christopher Bede Studios Ltd v United Portraits Ltd* [1958] N.Z.L.R. 250.

[79] *Noah v Shuba* [1991] F.S.R. 14.

[80] *Ray v Classic FM plc* [1998] F.S.R. 622. Presumably for this purpose a "legally effective" agreement means an agreement which has the force of a contract.

[81] *Lawrence & Bullen Ltd v Aflalo* [1904] A.C. 17, applying *Sweet v Benning* (1855) 16 C.B. 459, followed in *Lamb v Evans* [1893] 1 Ch.D. 218, all cases decided under s.18 of the Copyright Act 1842, as to which, see para. 5–31, below. See also the remarks of the Whitford Committee in its report, quoted in the footnote to para. 5–08, above.

[82] See para. 5–08, above.

[83] CDPA 1988, s.10(3); Copyright Act 1956, Sch.3, para.6. The 1911 Act did not contain any such express provision.

[84] See para. 5–08, above.

Act also brought about a major change in the existing rights to these works made under the 1911 Act.[85]

5–29   **The 1956 Act.** The provisions of this Act must be applied in relation to all such works made between June 1, 1957, and August 1, 1989.[86] The Act provided that where a literary, dramatic or artistic work was made by the author in the course of the author's employment by the proprietor of a newspaper, magazine or similar periodical under a contract of service or apprenticeship, and was so made for the purpose of publication in a newspaper, magazine or similar periodical, then the proprietor should be entitled to the copyright in the work in so far as the copyright related to publication of the work in any newspaper, magazine or similar periodical, or to reproduction of the work for the purpose of its being so published; but in all *other* respects the author should be entitled to any copyright subsisting in the work by virtue of that Act.[87]

What is meant by "in the course of employment" under a "contract of service or apprenticeship" has already been discussed.[88] It should be noted that this provision did not apply to musical works. In the equivalent provision of the Australian Copyright Act, it was held that a "newspaper" was a publication containing a narrative of recent events and occurrences, published regularly at short intervals from time to time.[89] Supplementary advertising material and "fliers" inserted in newspapers can also be part of a newspaper, if they are of the kind of material apt to be found as an integral part of it.[90] The newspaper proprietor's copyright does not include the right to make photocopies of the journalist's work for use in a press clippings service, since this does not constitute publication or reproduction for the purposes of publication in a newspaper.[91] It is suggested that for the same reason the right of storage and exploitation of a journalist's work in an online data retrieval service is not within the proprietor's copyright.

While the operation of the subsection might have been excluded by agreement, it could not have been extended by an agreement. Thus the proprietor could not, merely by agreement, acquire the legal title to more than the newspaper right in the work under this section unless the agreement amounted to a valid assignment of the balance of the copyright[92] or, where, for example, the agreement was only oral, an equitable title to it.[93] If the work was not made by an employee under a contract of service, but by a paid independent contributor, there is an argument that the equitable right to the entire copyright ought not to have vested in the proprietor unless there was something more than mere engagement and payment from which a contract to that effect could be inferred. Otherwise such a contributor would have been in a worse position than one who was employed under a contract of service, for the latter was deemed to have the general rights of publi-

---

[85] See para. 5–30, below. It was submitted to the Whitford Committee that this type of provision in fact reflects a fair balance between the interests of employer and employee in all cases. The Committee's conclusion in relation to all works of employees, however, was that certainty and practicability were important and that it was generally undesirable to separate ownership of the various rights comprised in the copyright, this being best left to agreement between the parties in individual cases (Cmnd. 6732, para.574).

[86] See para. 5–03, above.

[87] s.4(2). The subsection had effect subject to any agreement excluding its operation and to Part VI of the Act, which includes provisions relating to devolution of title: s.4(5), (6).

[88] See paras 5–11 *et seq.*, above.

[89] *De Garis v Nevill Jeffress Pidler Pty Ltd* (1990) 18 I.P.R. 292 (Fed. Ct of Aus.), applying *D.C.T. v Rotary Offset Press Pty Ltd* (1971) 45 A.L.J.R. 518 (High Ct of Aus.).

[90] *John Fairfax & Sons Ltd v D.C.T.* (1988) 15 N.S.W.L.R 620C (Sup. Ct of N.S.W.) followed in *De Garis v Nevill Jeffress Pidler Pty Ltd*, above.

[91] *De Garis v Nevill Jeffress Pidler Pty Ltd*, above.

[92] As to which, see paras 5–80 *et seq.*,below.

[93] As to the acquisition of an equitable title, see paras 5–173 *et seq.*,below.

cation reserved to him. In the end, however, the question will depend on what were the terms of the contract, express or implied.

The 1911 Act. The provisions of this Act must be applied in relation to all such works made on or after July 1, 1912, but before June 1, 1957.[94] This Act contained a similar provision to that found in the 1956 Act, namely, that where a work made in the course of employment by an employee under a contract of service or apprenticeship was an article or other contribution to a newspaper, magazine or similar periodical, there was to be deemed to be reserved to the author a right to restrain the publication of the work otherwise than as part of a newspaper, magazine or similar periodical.[95] The effect of this provision was to give the copyright to the employer while apparently giving the employee a bare statutory right to restrain publication by his employer[96] and others.[97] The employer was entitled to restrain infringements by others, relying on his copyright.[98] The effect of this provision has not been continued by the 1988 Act.[99] It therefore appears that today the author has no rights and the employer is to be regarded as having been the first owner of the entire copyright in such works. If correct, this represents a substantial change brought about by the 1988 Act.

5–30

Pre-1911 Act works. The Literary Copyright Act 1842 contained an ill-drafted section[1] under which the copyright in an "encyclopaedia, review, magazine, periodical work, or work published in a series of books or parts, or any book whatsoever" vested in the proprietor in certain circumstances. The proprietor had to prove that (a) he employed the writer to compose the articles; (b) the articles were composed on terms that the copyright should belong to the proprietor; and (c) the articles were paid for by him.[2] It is thought that this section applied only to works of the character of encyclopaedias, magazines and periodicals.[3] It was held that such a term could be implied and need not be express. Whether a term could be implied depended in the usual way upon the inferences of fact to be drawn from the nature of the contract and all the circumstances.[4] The general rule was that it was unreasonable to suppose that a person paid for the right to publish another's contributions in an encyclopaedia leaving it open to the other to publish his contributions the next day in a separate form.[5] The section also provided that the author was to be at liberty, after the lapse of 28 years from the date of publication, to publish his articles in a separate form. The 1988 Act continues this right, by providing that where a work made before July 1, 1912, consists of an essay, article or portion forming part of and first published in a review, magazine or

5–31

[94] See para. 5–03, above.
[95] s.5(1)(b).
[96] *Nicol v Barranger* [1917–23] Mac.C.C. 219; *Sun Newspapers Ltd v Whippie* (1928) 28 S.R. (N.S.W.) 473.
[97] *Nicol v Barranger* [1917–23] Mac.C.C. 219. This point was left open in *Sun Newspapers Ltd v Whippie* (1928) 28 S.R. (N.S.W.) 473, but seems clear.
[98] *Nicol v Barranger* [1917–23] Mac.C.C. 219 at 228.
[99] The 1911 Act was repealed by the 1956 Act and although the effect of this provision was continued by the 1956 Act (see, Sch.7, para.3 and Sch.8, para.1), the 1956 Act was itself repealed by the 1988 Act without equivalent provision being made.
[1] s.18.
[2] Actual payment was necessary: *Richardson v Gilbert* (1851) 1 Sim. (N.S.) 336; *Brown v Cooke* [1874] 16 L.J. Ch. 140; *Collingridge v Emmott* [1887] 57 L.T. 864.
[3] See, *e.g. Copinger* (4th ed.), p.110 and wording of the complementary right conferred on the author, as now preserved by the 1988 Act (see below, in the body of the text). *Cf. Ward, Lock & Co Ltd v Long* [1906] 2 Ch. 550, deciding that the section extended to books generally.
[4] *Lawrence, etc., Ltd v Aflalo* [1904] A.C. 17, following *Sweet v Benning* (1855) 16 C.B. 459. To the same effect is *Lamb v Evans* [1893] 1 Ch. 218; *Chantrey, etc., Co v Dey (T.H.)* (1912) 28 T.L.R. 499. No such term was made out or sufficiently pleaded in *Bishop of Hereford v Griffin* (1848) 16 Sim. 190 or *Walter v Howe* (1881) 17 Ch.D. 708.
[5] *Lawrence, etc., Ltd v Aflalo* [1904] A.C. 17.

other periodical or work of a like nature, the copyright is subject to any right of publishing the essay, article or portion in a separate form to which the author was entitled at the commencement of the 1911 Act, or would, if that Act had not been passed, have become entitled under s.18 of the 1842 Act.[6]

(iv) Commissioned artistic works

Commissioned works generally

5–32   None of the Copyright Acts has ever contained a general provision relating to the commissioning of all categories of works. Subject therefore to the special provisions made in the pre-1988 Acts which are discussed below, the general rule is that the first legal owner of the copyright in a work whose making was commissioned will be the author, *i.e.* the person who creates it.[7] Even where this general rule applies, it should nevertheless be borne in mind that in many cases where a work is made pursuant to a contract of commission, it will be a term of the contract, express or implied, that the commissioner will be entitled to the copyright. Provided that the commissioner is entitled to enforce the contract, he will thus be the equitable owner of the copyright.[8] Alternatively, if the agreement on its true construction amounts to an assignment of future copyright and complies with the relevant formalities, then the copyright will vest in the commissioner on the coming into existence of the copyright.[9] At its lowest, the commissioner is likely to have some sort of licence to use the work.[10]

Although containing no general rule, the earlier Copyright Acts contained important provisions relating to the commissioning of particular categories of works, and these still continue to apply in relation to works made before August 1, 1989.[11] Those relating to artistic works are considered here. Commissioned sound recordings are considered when dealing with sound recordings.[12] While the 1988 Act did not continue the regime relating to the first ownership of copyright in certain commissioned works,[13] the Act does contain other sections which relate to commissioning. Thus, the Act creates a moral right entitling a person to a right of privacy in respect of photographs which were commissioned for private and domestic purposes.[14] The ownership of design right may also be affected where the design was commissioned.[15] Decisions under the earlier Acts as to what amounts to commissioning may therefore also be applicable in construing these provisions.

5–33   **Commissioned artistic works under the1956 Act.** The provisions of the 1956 Act apply to determine questions of first ownership of copyright in works made

---

[6] CDPA 1988, Sch.1, para.18. Similar transitional provisions were contained in the Copyright Act 1911, Sch.1 and the Copyright Act 1956, Sch.7, para.37.

[7] See para. 5–06, above.

[8] As to equitable title, see para. 5–174, below.

[9] See CDPA 1988, s.91 and the Copyright Act 1956, s.37 and para. 5–105, below.

[10] See the similar discussion in relation to works made for an "employer", para. 5–10, above.

[11] CDPA 1988, Sch.1, para.11(2).

[12] See para. 5–43, below.

[13] The majority recommendation of the Whitford Committee, which was not accepted, was that, subject to any agreement to the contrary, the author should retain the copyright in all cases, subject to the commissioner having an exclusive licence to use the work for the purposes contemplated by the parties, and also the right to restrain other exploitation to which he could reasonably have objected (Cmnd. 6732, para.577).

[14] CDPA 1988, s.85(1).

[15] See paras 13–87 and 13–108, below.

between June 1, 1957 and August 1, 1989.[16] The 1956 Act provided that, where a person commissioned the taking of a photograph, or the painting or drawing of a portrait, or the making of an engraving, and paid or agreed to pay for it in money or money's worth, and the work was made in pursuance of that commission, the person who so commissioned the work should be entitled to any copyright subsisting under that Act.[17] This provision was expressed to be subject to provisions of the Act relating to the works of employees of newspaper proprietors and the like.[18] It was also subject to any agreement excluding the operation of the section[19] and to Pt VI of the Act, which included provisions relating to devolution of title.[20]

The 1956 Act. Various points arise under these provisions: 5–34

(a) *"Engraving", "photograph" and "portrait".*[21] "Engraving" was defined as including any etching, lithograph, woodcut, print, or similar work, not being a photograph, and "photograph" was defined as any product of photography or any process akin to photography, other than part of a cinematograph film.[22] There was no definition of a "portrait" in the Act.[23] Whether a picture is a portrait or not will no doubt depend upon what is the main purpose of the picture.[24] If it is to represent the likeness of a person, it is nonetheless a portrait because of the presence of subordinate accessories in the picture. It is fairly clear that a portrait may include the likeness of more than one individual, but that, on the other hand, the mere fact that real persons happen to be delineated in a picture does not necessarily make that picture a portrait.[25] So, a picture of the Duke of Schomberg sitting, clad in armour, upon horseback, a battle scene forming the background of the picture, was a portrait.[26] Again, a picture painted by a spiritualist medium of a dead person whom he had not seen, was a "portrait". This was because it was intended to represent the deceased

---

[16] See para. 5–03, above. The commissioning provisions of the 1956 Act also apply to works made after August 1, 1989 but which were commissioned before that date (CDPA 1988, Sch.1, para.11(2)). Where a work was made after June 1, 1957, but pursuant to a contract made before that date, the provisions of the 1911 Act apply (Copyright Act 1956, Sch.7, para.3), as to which, see para. 5–35, below.

[17] s.4(3).

[18] See para. 5–29, above. The application of this saving is unclear but presumably the intention was to make it clear that where, for example, a newspaper proprietor requested an employee to take a particular photograph, the split ownership provisions of s.4(2), considered above, should apply.

[19] See s.4(5). The parties might therefore agree, expressly or impliedly, that the copyright should remain with the author, as was found to be the case in *Gabrin v Universal Music Operations Ltd* [2003] EWHC 133 5 (Ch), para.25.

[20] s.4(6). The effect of this saving was presumably to make it clear that the parties to the commissioning might effectively transfer the title to some third party or that the commissioner himself might do so.

[21] Vaisey J. pointed out in *Leah v Two Worlds Publishing Co Ltd* [1951] Ch. 393, without drawing any conclusions, that whereas engravings and photographs involve particular methods of production, the word "portrait" can cover all methods of pictorial representation. In its report (Cmnd. 6732), the Whitford Committee noted that, portraits aside, no one had been able to suggest any valid ground for treating photographs and engravings differently from other commissioned works. See para.561 of the report.

[22] 1956 Act, s.48(1). Cinematograph film was itself defined as any sequence of visual images recorded on material of any description (whether translucent or not) so as to be capable, by the use of that material (a) of being shown as a moving picture or (b) being recorded on other material (whether translucent or not) by the use of which it can be shown): s.13(10).

[23] The dictionary definition of the word is "a figure drawn, painted or carved upon a surface to represent some object, now, almost always, a likeness of a person, especially of the face, made from life ..." (Shorter O.E.D.) Clearly, however, a portrait does not necessarily have to made from "life". See *Leah v Two Worlds Publishing Co Ltd* [1951] Ch. 393, discussed below.

[24] See *Apple Corps Ltd v Cooper* [1993] F.S.R. 286 at 293.

[25] *Duke of Leeds v Earl Amherst* (1845) 14 L.J. Ch. 73. The issue arose on the construction of a will.

[26] *Duke of Leeds v Earl Amherst* (1845) 14 L.J. Ch. 73.

person as that person was when living, and that it was nonetheless a portrait because the "model" that the artist used was entirely subjective.[27] On the other hand, a picture, although said to be "of" a real person but not based on any life study or representation of him and therefore not bearing any likeness, would not be a portrait.[28]

(b) *When did the copyright vest?* The copyright will have vested as soon as the work came into existence.[29] It follows that the commissioner became the owner of the copyright whether or not the work was accepted[30] or even completed.[31]

(c) *What amounts to a commissioning?* In general, the word "commission" means "order".[32] This means more than "request" or "encourage".[33] There must therefore come into existence a contract with mutual obligations, namely an obligation to create the work and an obligation to pay.[34] While well-known personalities will often agree to their photograph being taken, even in a studio, without any commission by them being made, this is less likely to happen in the case of people in the ordinary walk of life, since in the latter case the photographer is unlikely to take the risk of no prints being ordered.[35] Of course, if there was either payment or an agreement to pay, it will normally be easy to conclude that a work was commissioned but it does not necessarily follow that this was so. The commissioning must obviously have taken place before the work is made.[36]

(d) *Work subcontracted.* If a person ordered a work to be made by another, who then subcontracted the necessary labour, the person ordering the work would in the normal case have been entitled to the copyright in the work. This is on the basis that the person ordering the work commissioned all necessary articles to be made even though unaware of the need for them.[37] This principle assumes, however, that the subcontracted work was itself subject to the commissioning provisions of the Act.[38] The position would be different if, for example, the subcontractor had reserved the copyright.[39]

(e) *Was there an agreement to pay?*[40] While a commissioning does not necessarily imply an obligation to pay, it will often do so. Indeed, the usual meaning of "commission" involves both the ordering of work to be done and the coming under an obligation to pay for that work, irrespective of

---

[27] *Leah v Two Worlds Publishing Co Ltd* [1951] Ch. 393 (decided under the 1911 Act, as to which, see below).
[28] *Duke of Leeds v Earl Amherst*, above, at 81.
[29] *Apple Corps Ltd v Cooper* [1993] F.S.R. 286.
[30] *Apple Corps Ltd v Cooper* [1993] F.S.R. 286.
[31] *Art Direction Ltd v U.S.P. Needham (N.Z.) Ltd* [1977] 2 N.Z.L.R. 12, decided under the similar provision of the New Zealand Act.
[32] *Plix Products Ltd v Frank M. Winstone (Merchants)* [1986] F.S.R. 63.
[33] *Plix Products Ltd v Frank M. Winstone (Merchants)* [1986] F.S.R. 63.
[34] *Ultraframe (UK) Ltd v Fielding* [2003] EWCA Civ)1805, para.30. As to the obligation to pay, see further in the text.
[35] *Sasha Ltd v Stoenesco* (1929) 45 T.L.R. 350.
[36] *Plix Products Ltd v Frank M. Winstone (Merchants)* [1986] F.S.R. 63; *Apple Corps Ltd v Cooper* [1993] F.S.R. 286.
[37] *James Arnold and Co Ltd v Miafern Ltd* [1980] R.P.C. 397.
[38] See the reservation in *Apple Corps Ltd v Cooper* [1993] F.S.R. 286 at 297.
[39] See 1956 Act, s.4(5).
[40] Note that the 1988 Act, when dealing with commissions in relation to the moral right of privacy in relation to photographs and films, refers only to commissioning, without the further requirement of an agreement to pay (s.85(1)). The provision dealing with the design right, however, refers to a "commission for money or money's worth" (s.263(1)).

whether any product of that work is purchased.[41] Everything, however, will depend on the circumstances as to whether any agreement was made at all and, if so, whether it included a provision for payment. In the case of a portrait photograph, for example, the question will be whether, if the sitter declines to buy any copies of the photograph, the photographer is entitled to a fee or the cost of the work and labour done in the making of the copyright work.[42] In the ordinary case where a professional photographer, painter or engraver is commissioned, the court will readily imply that the commissioner is to pay for the work.[43] But a professional photographer will often be willing to attend occasions such as a wedding or the taking of a school photograph without any agreement for payment but simply in the expectation that people will order prints from him. In such a case, he will have retained the copyright. As already noted, in the case of well-known personalities, a photographer may also be willing to take photographs without any commission or assurance of payment.[44] An agreement to pay, of course, requires a consensus so that where the commissioner had an intention to pay, perhaps only if requested, but this was not known to the maker of the work, this will not suffice. Neither will expectation of payment by the maker if the commissioner had not agreed to pay.[45]

(f) *What the payment must have been for.* The payment or agreement to pay must have been for the making of the copyright work, not the physical embodiment of the work itself. The payment is the *quid pro quo* for the copyright.[46] In the context of a photograph, for example, the fact that prints or even the negative was paid for will not therefore be sufficient, although clearly the cost of the work of taking the photograph may in fact be built into the price of making copies.[47] So, too, the fact that the creator of the work is commissioned and paid for his time and expenses, and payment is also made for a licence to use the works, will not be sufficient if the payment was not also for the making of the works.[48] Again, in the context of an engraving, payment for a run of the finished product with a built-in or separate charge for the costs of tooling will not necessarily be payment for the making of the work.[49] Such cases will turn on the nice question of precisely what the payment was to be for.

(g) *Money or money's worth.* Under the earlier Acts, the issue was whether "valuable" or "good" consideration had been given. These cases are considered below but it is suggested that they are not of great assistance when considering the provisions of the 1956 Act. "Money's worth" refers to the case where the price or consideration for the making of the work was something other than money, for example services to be rendered or property other than money.[50] Whether the giving of access to private premises or a famous personality will amount to payment in money's worth will depend on the precise circumstances, although usually it will

[41] *Plix Products Ltd v Frank M. Winstone (Merchants)* [1986] F.S.R. 63.
[42] *Sasha Ltd v Stoenesco* (1929) 45 T.L.R. 350; *Hartnett v Pinkett* (1953) 103 L.J. 204 (Cty Ct).
[43] *Boucas v Cooke* [1903] 2 K.B. 227, analysed in *Apple Corps Ltd v Cooper* [1993] F.S.R. 286 citing the example of a sitter approaching the photographer without any prior invitation.
[44] *Sasha Ltd v Stoenesco* (1929) 45 T.L.R. 350.
[45] *Apple Corps Ltd v Cooper* [1993] F.S.R. 286.
[46] *Apple Corps Ltd v Cooper* [1993] F.S.R. 286.
[47] *Sasha Ltd v Stoenesco* (1929) 45 T.L.R. 350.
[48] *Gabrin v Universal Music Operations Ltd* [2003] EWHC 1335 (Ch), para.24.
[49] *Plix Products Ltd v Frank M. Winstone (Merchants)* [1986] F.S.R. 63.
[50] See *Secretan v Hart* [1969] 1 W.L.R. 1599.

not. In any event it is likely to be rare that such access will have been provided by way of payment for the making of the photographs.[51]

(h) *When must the agreement to make the work and to pay, or payment, have been made?* Since the vesting of the copyright in the commissioner takes place, if at all, when the work is first made, all the elements referred to in the section must be present at this moment. It follows that the commissioning and thus also either the payment or the agreement to pay must have been made before this time.[52] Payment made after the event without obligation will not, therefore, of itself have operated to vest the copyright in the commissioner.[53] In such circumstances, the copyright will only have been transferred to the commissioner if it was part of a separate transaction by which the legal title was validly assigned.[54] Alternatively in such a case, the commissioner may thereby have acquired an equitable title if the payment was part of an agreement which included, expressly or impliedly, the acquisition of the copyright.[55]

5–35   **Commissioned artistic works under the 1911 Act.** The provisions of the 1911 Act apply to determine questions of first ownership of copyright in works made between July 1, 1912, and June 1, 1957.[56] The 1911 Act provided[57] that where, in the case of an engraving,[58] photograph[59] or portrait,[60] the plate[61] or other original was ordered by some other person than the author, and was made for valuable consideration in pursuance of that order, then, in the absence of any agreement to the contrary, the person by whom such plate or other original was ordered was the first owner of the copyright. The 1911 and 1956 Acts, although expressed in different words seem generally to have been to the same effect, although it is possible that "money or money's worth" in the 1956 Act had a narrower meaning than "valuable consideration", which is considered below. The above discussion as to what amounted to a "commissioning" under the 1956 Act is relevant in considering what amounted to an "ordering" under the 1911 Act.[62]

5–36   **Valuable consideration.** This expression was also used in the 1862 Act, considered below, which in addition used the expression "good" consideration. Valuable consideration usually consists of some right, interest, profit or benefit accruing to one party, or some forbearance, detriment, loss or responsibility

---

[51] The cases under the earlier Acts in which such questions arose are considered below.

[52] *Apple Corps Ltd v Cooper* [1993] F.S.R. 286; *Ultraframe (UK) Ltd v Fielding* [2003] EWCA Civ 1805, para.30. See also *Gabrin v Universal Music Operations Ltd* [2003] EWHC 1335 (Ch), para.24, where no agreement to acquire and pay for any of the photographs was made before they were taken. The agreement to acquire the copyright in particular photographs was made after the event, and for a further consideration.

[53] *Leah v Two Worlds Publishing Co Ltd* [1951] Ch. 393, where the agreement to pay for a portrait was only made after it had been seen.

[54] As to assignments of copyright, see paras 5–80 *et seq.*, below.

[55] As to equitable titles, see para. 5–174, below.

[56] See para. 5–03, above. The 1911 Act also applied to works made after June 1, 1957 but which were commissioned by a contract made before that date (see the footnotes to para. 5–33, above).

[57] s.5(1)(a).

[58] Defined to include etchings, lithographs, wood-cuts, prints and other similar works, not being photographs: s.35(1). This is identical to the 1956 Act definition.

[59] Defined to include a photo-lithograph and any work produced by any process analogous to photography: s.35(1). This is similar to the 1956 definition, except that the 1956 Act excluded any photograph forming part of a cinematograph film. Under the 1911 Act, films were not protected as such but the individual frames were protected as photographs.

[60] As to the meaning of this, see the earlier discussion of the 1956 Act provisions.

[61] Defined to include any stereotype or other plate, stone, block, mould, matrix, transfer, or negative used or intended to be used for printing or reproducing copies of any work: s.35(1).

[62] See, for example, *Boucas v Cooke* [1903] 2 K.B. 227 and *Sasha Ltd v Stoenesco* (1929) 45 T.L.R. 350, referred to above in the discussion of the 1956 Act provisions.

given, suffered or undertaken by the other.[63] It clearly includes money or money's worth, but excludes a consideration which is illusory or merely nominal. Some of the cases on this point are not easy to reconcile:

(a) Where a claimant was in the business of taking and selling photographs of well-known sporting celebrities and requested and was allowed to take a photograph of one such person, on terms that the photographer be allowed to print and sell copies, the celebrity was held thereby to have given good and valuable consideration.[64]

(b) Where a celebrity agreed to a request by a photographer to sit for her photograph, without any charge being made by the photographer, this did not amount to good or valuable consideration.[65]

(c) Where a firm of photographers took photographs of school premises and pupils with the permission of the proprietors, it being clearly understood that no one was compelled to buy any prints, the photographers reasonably speculating that they would in fact make sales to pupils and others, it was held that the proprietors had given "good", although apparently not "valuable", consideration by permitting the photographers to have access to private premises and showing them around.[66]

The 1911 Act: "Other original". The meaning of this expression is unclear. It seems that it was not just the copyright in the engraving, photograph or portrait which the commissioner acquired. Thus, a sketch produced with the intention of its being reproduced in a newspaper was held to be within the section on the basis that it was the "original" of the newspaper illustration.[67] A sketch which, had it been accepted, was intended by its maker for use as the original of an engraving would not be an "original" if it was never in fact accepted or so used.[68]

5–37

Pre-1911 Act commissioned artistic works. There was a similar provision in the Fine Arts Copyright Act 1862[69] to the effect that, where a painting, drawing or the negative of any photograph was "made or executed for or on behalf of any person for a good or a valuable consideration", the copyright belonged to "the

5–38

---

[63] *Fleming v New Zealand Bank* [1900] A.C. 577.

[64] *Melville v Mirror of Life Co* [1895] 2 Ch. 531. The claim that the copyright had vested in the celebrity failed, however, on the wording of the 1862 Act in that the photograph had not been made or executed "for or on his behalf". See below.

[65] *Ellis v Marshall (H.) & Son* (1895) 64 L.J.Q.B. 757. Again, the claim also failed because the photographs were not taken "for or on her behalf". *Melville v Mirror of Life Co* [1895] 2 Ch. 531, was decided 15 days earlier and not cited.

[66] *Stackemann v Paton* [1906] 1 Ch. 774. *Melville v Mirror of Life Co* [1895] 2 Ch. 531 was apparently not cited. *Ellis v Marshall (H.) & Son* (1895) 64 L.J.Q.B. 757 was distinguished on the basis that the Judge there had found that the only consideration given by the celebrity was that he had taken the trouble to walk up to the photographer's room and sit in his chair, and this was neither good nor valuable. It is suggested that even if the decision that the proprietors of the school had given good consideration was correct, the case was wrongly decided since the photographs had not been made "for or on behalf of" the proprietors (see, again, the wording of the 1862 Act, below). Farwell J. seems to have been influenced by the conclusion that the proprietors would not conceivably have allowed a photographer to publish photographs of the inside of a girls' school (including that of the French governess in her bedroom), a factor which, it is suggested, was irrelevant on this point.

[67] *Nicol v Barranger* [1917–23] Mac.C.C. 219. Although it is not clear from the report, it seems that an engraving was made from the sketch so that it could be reproduced in the newspaper, and thus that the sketch was the "original" of the engraving (see the specific reference to "engravings" in the quotation of s.5(1)(a) at p.226). In *Con Planck Ltd v Kolynos Inc* [1925] 2 K.B. 804, a sketch which was intended to be reproduced by lithographic process for advertisement purposes was held itself to be a "lithograph". *Sed quaere.*

[68] *Toronto Carton Co v Manchester McGregor Ltd* [1935] 2 D.L.R. 94, decided under the similar provisions of the Canadian Act. It seems, although this was not decided, that the sketches were also not made for valuable consideration in pursuance of any order, having been made in the hope only that they would be accepted and paid for.

[69] 25 & 26 Vict. c.68.

person for or on whose behalf the same shall be so made or executed."[70] Under this Act it was necessary, if the commissioned author wished to retain the copyright, for him to do so in writing. The differences between the 1911 Act and the 1862 Act were that: (1) under the 1911 Act writing was not required if the artist desired to retain his copyright—the proviso only said "in the absence of any agreement to the contrary"; (2) the 1862 Act referred to a work "made" for another, whereas the 1911 Act spoke of a plate or original "ordered" by some other person; (3) as already noted, the 1862 Act used the expression "a good or a valuable consideration," whereas the 1911 Act only had the words "valuable consideration"; (4) the 1862 Act referred to any painting or drawing, not just a portrait.

5–39 **Limits as to commissioning.** It has already been pointed out that the provisions of the Copyright Acts relating to commissioned works are limited in scope. Generally, it was only commissioned engravings and photographs that vested in the commissioner, together with commissioned portraits, by whatever means produced. This was capable of producing unexpected severances of copyright in the case of commercial art. Consider, for example, the case of an advertiser who placed an order for an advertisement. He would have been the owner of the final engraving or photograph comprising the advertisement, having commissioned it. But the advertisement probably started life as a sketch or drawing, unaffected by this subsection,[71] so that there will have been an outstanding copyright in the sketch or drawing which will not have vested in the advertiser as a result of the commission and which might have caused trouble if the advertiser wished to repeat the main design in a new advertisement.[72]

(v) Pre-1911 Act works

5–40 **Pre-1911 Act works.** The position of pre-1911 Act works has already been discussed in the context of authorship.[73] As to unpublished works which were protected at common law, the author will have been the first owner. As to works protected by statute, the general position was that the author was the first owner, the exceptions being:

(a) *Books, etc,*[74] protected under the Literary Copyright Act 1842.[75] Where the work was published posthumously, the copyright belonged to the owner of the manuscript.[76]

(b) *Encyclopaedias, reviews, magazines, periodical works, works published in a series of books or parts, or any book* protected under the Literary Copyright Act 1842.[77] This exception is considered in the section dealing with works made for publication in a newspaper etc.[78]

---

[70] As to this provision, see above and *Petty v Taylor* [1897] 1 Ch. 465; *Boucas v Cooke* [1903] 2 K.B. 227.
[71] Although see the discussion of the expression "other original" in the 1911 Act, above.
[72] See, for example, the comments in *Plix Products Ltd v Frank M. Winstone (Merchants)* [1986] F.S.R. 63. It is doubtful whether many such problems remain today. In any event, it should be remembered that the equitable title to the copyright in the sketch or drawing may nevertheless have vested in the advertiser, or at least he is likely to have acquired some form of licence. See para. 5–174, below.
[73] See para. 4–36, above.
[74] See para. 4–36, above, for what was included within this description.
[75] 5 & 6 Vict., c.45.
[76] Copyright Act 1842, s.3. See para. 5–130, below, as to the effect of a bequest of a manuscript.
[77] 5 & 6 Vict., c.45.
[78] See para. 5–31, above.

(c) *Lectures*, protected under the Lectures Copyright Act 1835.[79] The first owner was the author or the person to whom he had sold or otherwise conveyed "the copy thereof".[80]

(d) *Engravings, etchings, lithographs, etc*, protected under the Engravings Copyright Acts 1734, 1766 and the International Copyright Act 1852.[81] The first owner was the person who either engraved etc., any work or who caused it to be engraved, etc.[82] Thus a person who had arranged for lithographs to be made to help follow the course of the Franco-Prussian war and who provided the engraver with rough sketches and other materials was the first owner of the copyright in the engraving, even though he could not draw himself.[83]

(e) *Paintings, drawings and photographs* protected under the Fine Arts Copyright Act 1862.[84] The exception made for commissioned works has already been considered in the context of commissioned works generally.[85]

(f) *Sculptures*, protected under the Sculpture Copyright Act 1814.[86] The first owner was the person who made or caused the work to be made.[87]

C. SOUND RECORDINGS AND FILMS

(i) Sound recordings

The 1988 Act. With one exception,[88] the question of first ownership of copyright in sound recordings made after August 1, 1989 is governed by the provisions of the 1988 Act. As with other works, these provide that the first owner is the author.[89] As has already been discussed, this person is to be taken to be the producer, that is, the person by whom the arrangements necessary for the making of the recording are undertaken.[90] The meaning of this expression has already been considered.[91] There are no provisions dealing with the case where the arrangements are made by an employee in the course of his employment since where this happens clearly it will be the employer who is the "producer".   **5–41**

The 1956 Act. This Act applies in the case of sound recordings made on or after June 1, 1957 but before August 1, 1989, or whose making was commissioned before the latter date.[92] The 1956 Act provided that, save in relation to commissioned sound recordings, the first owner of the copyright was the "maker". As already seen, the maker of a sound recording was defined to be the person who   **5–42**

---

[79] 5 & 6 Will. 4, c.65.

[80] See Lectures Copyright Act 1835, s.1.

[81] 8 Geo. 2, c.13, 7 Geo. 3, c.38 and 15 & 16 Vict., c.12, respectively.

[82] See ss.1 of the 1734 and 1766 Acts.

[83] *Stannard v Harrison* (1871) 19 W.R. 811.

[84] 25 & 26 Vic., c.68.

[85] See para. 5–38, above.

[86] 54 Geo. 3, c.56.

[87] See Sculpture Copyright Act 1814, s.1.

[88] See the next paragraph.

[89] CDPA 1988, s.11(1).

[90] CDPA 1988, s.9(2)(aa). The expression "producer" was introduced into the 1988 Act by the Copyright and Related Rights Regulations 1996 and derives from the Rental and Related Rights Directive (92/100/EEC). The effect of the amendment was to introduce an extra layer of definition but not to change the law. See the footnote to para. 4–49, above.

[91] See para. 4–49, above.

[92] See CDPA 1988, Sch.1, para.11(2).

owned the first record embodying the sound recording at the time when the recording was made.[93]

5–43 **1956 Act commissioned sound recordings.** In a case where a person commissioned the making of a sound recording and paid or agreed to pay for it in money or money's worth, and the record was made in pursuance of that commission, that person and not the maker was the first owner of the copyright, in the absence of any agreement to the contrary.[94] The question of commissioning has already been discussed in relation to artistic works.[95] The same principles apply. As already noted, this provision tempered the potentially capricious effect of the "maker" provisions, above.

5–44 **The 1911 Act.** As already noted,[96] these works became protectable under the 1956 Act as sound recordings rather than musical works and this treatment is continued by the 1988 Act. Nevertheless, the 1911 Act must now be referred to in order to determine who the first owner of the copyright in these works was.[97] As has been seen, the author and thus the first owner was deemed to be the person who was the owner of the original "plate"[98] from which the recording was derived, at the time when it was made.[99] There were no provisions in the 1911 Act relating to commissioned sound recordings.

5–45 **Pre-1911 Act sound recordings.** The copyright in such works will by now have expired.[1]

5–46 **Film soundtracks.** The topic of film soundtracks is considered under its own heading, below.

(ii) Films

5–47 **Introduction.** As already seen,[2] three different regimes in effect operate in relation to films: first, those made on or after July 1, 1994; secondly those made before July 1, 1994 but on or after June 1, 1957; thirdly, those made before this date.

(a) Regime 1

5–48 **Films made on or after July 1, 1994.** The consequence of the authorship provisions of the 1988 Act, as amended,[3] is that as from December 1, 1996,[4] the first owners of the copyright in such films will be the producer and the principal direc-

---

[93] Copyright Act 1956, s.12(8). See para. 4–52, above. The Whitford Committee did not recommend any change in this area, noting that the industry seemed content with the position as it was, no doubt in the light of the commissioning provisions, considered below (Cmnd. 6732, para.581).

[94] Copyright Act 1956, s.12(4). For an example of a decision as to who, on the facts, owned the record, see *Silly Wizard Ltd v Shaughnessy* [1984] F.S.R. 163 (Ct of Sess.).

[95] See paras 5–32 *et seq.*, above.

[96] See paras 4–48 and 4–53, above.

[97] See para. 5–03, above.

[98] Plate was defined, *inter alia*, to mean any appliance by which records, perforated rolls or other contrivances for the acoustic representation of any work were intended to be made. See the Copyright Act 1911, s.35(1).

[99] Copyright Act 1911, s.19(1).

[1] See the Copyright Act 1956, Sch.7, para.11.

[2] See para. 4–56, above.

[3] See para. 4–58, above.

[4] The Copyright and Related Rights Regulations 1996 (SI 1996/2967), reg.36(1). The starting date of July 1, 1994 derives from Art.13(4) of the Rental Directive (92/100). See the next paragraph in the text as to transitional provisions.

tor, or where employed, etc, his or their employers.[5] The expressions "producer" and "principal director" have already been considered.[6] Unless the producer and the principal director are the same person, these first owners will be joint owners.[7]

Transitional. Although these provisions only apply as from December 1, 1996, they apply in relation to films made on or after July 1, 1994.[8] This creates a potential difficulty in that between July 1, 1994 and December 1, 1996 there will have been films brought into existence whose copyright first belonged to whoever undertook the arrangements necessary for their making. Such a person may well have entered into arrangements relating to the copyright, whether the granting of licences or the assignment of the copyright. What is the effect of the fact that, as from December 1, 1996, the principal director is also to be regarded as one of the authors of these films and that therefore he, or his employer and also the employer of the producer, if any, are to be regarded as first owners of the copyright? The Regulations contain a limited saving provision, providing that it is not an infringement of the principal director's interest to do anything after December 1, 1996 in pursuance of arrangements for the exploitation of the film made before November 19, 1992.[9] The effect seems to be that as from November 19, 1992, parties are to be taken to have known that the law would be changed and thus that arrangements made after this date without the principal director's consent will not bind him so far as anything done after December 1, 1996 is concerned.

5–49

(b) *Regime 2*

Two statutes applied successively during this period but their effect is the same:

5–50

  (a) **Films made before July 1, 1994: the 1988 Act.** In relation to films made on or after August 1, 1989 but before July 1, 1994, the effect of the 1988 Act is that the first owner of the copyright is the person by whom the arrangements necessary for the making of the film were undertaken.[10]

  (b) **The 1956 Act.** The provisions of the 1956 Act, which apply to all films made between June 1, 1957 and August 1, 1989,[11] were to the same effect. Thus the Act provided that the first owner of the copyright was the maker, namely the person by whom the arrangements necessary for the making of the film were undertaken.[12]

---

[5] CDPA 1988, ss.9(2)(ab), 11(2) (IP/02/1824—see para. 4–58, above) on the question of authorship of cinematograph or adudiovisual works, the Commission has stated its view that the effect of s.11(2) "seem[s] to exclude the principal director from having rights in the work". The Commission therefore stated its intention to examine how far this was consistent with the provisions of the Rental Directive (92/100) which stipulate that the principal director is to be regarded as one of the authors of a film. Section 11(2) is of course expressly made subject to any agreement to the contrary, and there is also nothing in the Directive which prohibits an employer or film producer acquiring the principal director's interest in the film copyright. Indeed, the main thrust of the Report is that the existence of contractual arrangements between film producers and directors has avoided any potential obstacles to the normal exploitation of films.

[6] See para. 4–58, above.

[7] CDPA 1988, s.10(1A). As to joint authorship of films generally, see para. 4–70, above.

[8] The Copyright and Related Rights Regulations (SI 1996/2967), reg.36(1).

[9] The date of the Rental and Related Rights Directive 9/100 which lead to the introduction of these provisions.

[10] CDPA 1988, ss.11(1) and 9(2)(a), as enacted. See para. 4–62, above.

[11] See paras 4–07 and 5–03, above.

[12] Copyright Act 1956, s.13(10). It will be recalled that the expression "maker" rather than "author" was used in the 1956 Act.

(c) *Regime 3*

5–51 **Pre-1956 Act films.** There is no copyright in cinematograph films as such made before June 1, 1957.[13]

(iii) Film soundtracks

5–52 **Film soundtracks made on or after August 1, 1989: the1988 Act as amended.** The complicated provisions relating to "authorship" of film soundtracks have already been considered.[14] It will be recalled that a soundtrack accompanying a film is now to be treated as part of the film but this is not to affect any copyright subsisting in the film soundtrack as a sound recording.[15] The present position is therefore that the first owner of the copyright in a sound recording which forms the soundtrack of a film will be the author of the sound recording, namely, the person by whom the arrangements necessary for its making were undertaken (the "producer").[16] In relation to films made on or after July 1, 1994, the first owner or owners of the copyright in the film, of which the soundtrack is now to be treated as forming part, will be, as from December 1, 1996, the producer and principal director or their employers. In relation to films made after August 1, 1989 but before July 1, 1994, the first owner will have been the producer alone. The meaning of these expressions in the context of film soundtracks has already been discussed.[17]

5–53 **Film soundtracks made on or after August 1, 1989 but before January 1, 1996: the transitional position under the 1988 Act as amended.** The new provisions in the 1988 Act whereby a soundtrack which accompanies a film is to be taken to be part of the film were introduced with effect from January 1, 1996 but are to apply to soundtracks made before that date.[18] As has been seen, under the original provisions of the 1988 Act, copyright subsisted in a film soundtrack as a sound recording in its own right and the film copyright did not include the soundtrack.[19] Who owns that part of the film copyright which includes the soundtrack? What is the position about acts done in relation to the sound recording before January 1, 1996? Transitional provisions provide that whoever was the owner of the copyright in the film immediately before January 1, 1996 is to have from that date what are termed "corresponding rights" as copyright owner in the existing soundtrack which is now to be treated as part of the film.[20] The "corresponding rights" are presumably the rights which correspond to those which the owner of the copyright has in a film, with accompanying soundtrack, made after January 1, 1996. These rights are without prejudice to the rights of the owner of the sound recording copyright which exists in the soundtrack.[21] Generally acts done and arrangements made in relation to the sound recording before this date are saved. Thus the Regulations provide that anything done under or in relation to the copyright in the sound recording continues to have effect, so far as concerns

---

[13] CDPA 1988, Sch.1, para.7(1).

[14] See paras 4–64 *et seq.*, above.

[15] CDPA 1988, s.5B(2), (5). It will be recalled that in relation to questions of authorship and first ownership, it is only in relation to works made after August 1, 1989 that the 1988 Act applies.

[16] CDPA 1988, s.9(2)(aa). See para. 4–49, above.

[17] See paras 4–65 *et seq.*, above.

[18] Duration of Copyright and Rights in Performances Regulations 1995, reg.26(1).

[19] CDPA 1988, s.5. This discussion of the ownership provisions of the 1988 Act of course only relates to works made after August 1, 1989.

[20] Duration of Copyright and Rights in Performances Regulations 1995, reg.26(2). This provision obviously includes the particular case under consideration, that is, first ownership.

[21] reg.26(2) and see also CDPA 1988, s.5B(5).

the soundtrack, in relation to the film as in relation to the sound recording.[22] A licence to exploit the sound recording as a film soundtrack would therefore remain good. Again, anything done after January 1, 1996 in pursuance of arrangements for the exploitation of the sound recording made before that date will not infringe the copyright in the film.[23]

Film soundtracks: the 1956 Act. The position of these works has already been considered.[24] The 1988 Act provides that film soundtracks to which the 1956 Act applied[25] are now to be treated as sound recordings and not as part of the film and further provides that the first owner of the copyright in such a film is to be treated as having been the first owner of the copyright in the sound recording.[26] Thus, it seems, whoever was the maker of the cinematograph film[27] will be treated as having been the first owner of the soundtrack which is now to be regarded as a sound recording rather than a film.   **5–54**

Film soundtracks: the 1911 Act. Copyright does not subsist in a film as such made before June 1, 1957[28] so that film soundtracks made before this date are protected as sound recordings and the first owner of copyright will be determined accordingly.[29]   **5–55**

(iv) Joint first ownership of copyright in sound recordings and films

The 1988 Act. Sound recordings and films to which the 1988 Act applies may be the works of joint authorship and thus joint first ownership.[30] As already seen,[31] a film made after July 1, 1994, will always be a work of joint first ownership unless the producer and principal director are one and the same person.   **5–56**

   The 1956 Act: films. As already noted,[32] there seems no reason why there should not have been joint makers and thus joint first owners of the copyright in these works.

   The 1956 and 1911 Acts: sound recordings. Since an original "plate" or recording could in principle have been jointly owned, there seems no reason why such works could not have had joint first owners.[33]

D. BROADCASTS

The 1988 Act. It has already been seen[34] that with effect from October 31, 2003, the definition of "broadcast" has been altered as part of the amendments to implement the Information Society Directive, and the expression now also includes within its scope cable broadcasts and internet transmissions transmissions which are in the nature of broadcasts. In relation to broadcasts made after August 1, 1989, the 1988 Act provides that the first owner of the copyright is the author and thus the person making the broadcast or, in the case of a broadcast which relays   **5–57**

---

[22] reg.26(3).
[23] reg.26(4).
[24] See para. 4–68, above.
[25] *i.e.* those made between June 1, 1957 and August 1, 1989.
[26] CDPA 1988, Sch.1, para.8(2).
[27] As to which, see para. 4–62, above.
[28] CDPA 1988, Sch.1, para.7(1).
[29] See para. 4–63, above.
[30] See para. 4–70, above.
[31] See para. 4–48 , above.
[32] See para. 4–71, above.
[33] As to the ordinary rule relating to first ownership of such works, see paras 4–42 and 4–44, above.
[34] para. 3–91, above.

another broadcast by reception and immediate re-transmission, the person making that other broadcast.[35] The question of who is the person making the broadcast has already been considered.[36]

5–57A   **Cable programmes**. In relation to cable programmes which constitute "broadcasts" within the new definition of this expression, the first owner of the copyright is the person determined in accordance with the above rule. This now applies to all cable broadcasts coming into existence after August 1, 1989. As to those cable programmes which came into existence between August 1, 1989 and October 31, 2003 which are now entitled to copyright as broadcast,[37] the author and thus first owner of the copyright was previously defined as the person who created the cable programme, being the person providing the cable programme service in which the programme was included.[38] This definition has, however, now been repealed along with s.7 of the Act, and in relation to these cable programmes, which are now to be regarded as broadcasts, the new, general definition of author and thus first owner apparently applies. As pointed out when dealing with the authorship provisions,[39] it is not clear whether there will have been any cable programmes in respect of which the person providing the cable programme service in which the programme was included will have been someone different from the person "making" the transmission, as that expression is defined. If so, it seems that as at October 31, 2003 there will have been a retrospective change of authorship of the work and potentially, therefore, of ownership.

5–58   **Joint authors.** Where more than one person is to be taken as making the broadcast in accordance with the above definition, then the broadcast is to be treated as a work of joint authorship and thus joint first ownership.[40]

5–59   **The 1956 Act.** Under the 1956 Act the BBC or the IBA, as the case may have been, were the persons entitled to the copyright in broadcasts made by them.[41] In relation to what were described as cable programmes, there is no copyright in cable programmes included in a cable programme service before January 1, 1985.[42] As to cable programmes made after this date, the 1956 Act, as amended, stated that the person providing the cable programme service in which a cable programme was included should be entitled to the copyright in such a work.[43]

5–60   **Pre-1956 Act broadcasts.** There is no copyright in broadcasts made before June 1, 1957.[44]

F. TYPOGRAPHICAL ARRANGEMENTS

5–61   **The 1988 Act.** In relation to a typographical arrangement of a published edition made after August 1, 1989, the first owner of copyright is the author, that is, the publisher of it.[45]

---

[35] CDPA 1988, s.9(2)(b).
[36] See para. 4–73, above.
[37] See para. 3–91, above.
[38] CDPA 1988, s.9(2)(c).
[39] See para. 4–73A, above.
[40] CDPA 1988, s.10(2).
[41] Copyright Act 1956, s.14(2). See para. 4–75, above.
[42] s.14A(11), as inserted by the Cable and Broadcasting Act 1984; CDPA 1988, Sch.1, para.9(b).
[43] Copyright Act 1956, s.14A(3), as inserted by the Cable and Broadcasting Act 1984.
[44] CDPA 1988, Sch.1, para.9(a).
[45] CDPA 1988, s.9(2)(d). As to the meaning of "publisher", see s.175(1).

The 1956 Act. Under the 1956 Act, the publisher was to be entitled to the copy-   **5–62**
right subsisting in a published edition.[46]

2. TRANSMISSION OF TITLE

A. INTRODUCTION

Today, copyright is a statutory property right,[47] being a thing in action,[48] which is   **5–63**
transmissible by assignment or by operation of law as personal or moveable
property.[49] This section is concerned with transfers of the legal title. Transfers of
the equitable title are dealt with later.

The root of title. Copyright has two features which combine to create difficulties   **5–64**
when it comes to establishing title. The first is the potential longevity of many
works, the period of copyright for literary, dramatic, musical and artistic works
and films now being the lifetime of the author plus 70 years. Many works made
in the nineteenth century are therefore still in copyright. The second is the absence
of any system of registration of title,[50] or the existence of any rule whereby a
good title can be deduced from a transfer made at least a certain number of years
ago,[51] or a concept equivalent to a possessory title to land.[52] The result is that, if
required, the title to a work has to be proved by establishing a chain of title from
the first owner through to the present claimant.[53] If the work is an old one, or is
one which has passed through the hands of several owners this may present difficulties in obtaining the necessary evidence and is also likely to be expensive.
Apart from insurance, however, there is no short cut if a purchaser requires title
to be fully deduced. In the context of litigation, suggestions that the burden of
proof be altered such that the defendant should be required to prove that the
claimant does *not* own the copyright have been rejected.[54] A claimant has two
means of mitigating the problem as the law stands today, neither of them usually
being very effective in practice. The first is to serve a notice to admit the various
facts which establish the claimant's title,[55] thereby throwing the risk of having to
pay the costs of proving title on the defendant, whatever the result of the action.
The second, where the appropriate material is available, is to seek to rely on one
or more of the various statutory presumptions.[56] Occasionally, too, a claimant
may be able to invoke the maxim *omnia paesumunter rite esse acta.* So, for
example, where a party has "acquired" the copyright by purchase and there has
been a long course of dealing by him on the basis that he owns the copyright,
without objection from anyone who might have a rival claim, a court may be able

---

[46] Copyright Act 1956, s.15(2).
[47] CDPA 1988, s.1(1).
[48] *Orwin v Attorney-General* [1998] F.S.R. 415 at 421.
[49] CDPA 1988, s.90.
[50] Compare patents, registered trade marks and registered designs.
[51] Compare, in the case of unregistered land, the Law of Property Act 1925, s.23.
[52] There can be no "possession" of copyright: *Chaplin v Leslie Frewin (Publishers) Ltd* [1966] Ch.
71.
[53] It may of course be the case that an old agreement can no longer be found or is known to have
been lost. In such circumstances, it is permissible to adduce secondary evidence of it and its
contents, and the court will attach such weight to that evidence as is appropriate in all the
circumstances. The old "best evidence" rule no longer applies: *Springsteen v Masquerade Music
Ltd* [2001] E.M.L.R. 654, CA.
[54] See, *e.g.* the Gregory Committee Report in 1952 (Cmnd. 8662, para.286) and the Whitford Committee Report in 1977 (Cmnd. 6732, para.729). In general, the Gregory Committee concluded
that the burden which a copyright owner may have to labour under is something he has to expect
in return for the great benefits conferred by a copyright system that requires no registration or fee.
[55] *i.e.* under CPR Rule 32.18.
[56] As to these, see paras 22–210 *et seq.*, below.

to infer that everything was done to carry out the intention of the parties, and that therefore title was transferred by a valid assignment.[57]

5–65   **Distinction between transfer of title to copyright and to physical material.** It is important to recognise that ownership of copyright in a work is distinct from the ownership of the physical material in which the copyright work may happen to be embodied. Just as the owner of the physical material on or in which a copyright work is first recorded is not necessarily the first owner of the copyright,[58] so the transfer of title to the original physical material does not by itself to operate to transfer the title to the copyright[59] any more than an assignment of copyright operates by itself transfer title to the physical material on which the work may be embodied. Copyright is not a chattel and so cannot be passed by delivery.[60] Thus, to take an obvious example, the purchaser of a book or DVD becomes the owner of the physical article but he does not thereby become the owner of any part of the copyright in the works reproduced in it. The copyright in the literary work remains with the copyright owner, who enjoys and is entitled to enforce all the exclusive rights of copying, publication, adaptation, sale, rental and so on conferred on him by copyright law. The purchaser does not acquire by his purchase any right, either by way of assignment or licence, to exercise any of those exclusive rights. In the case of the purchase of the physical material on which the copyright work was first fixed, for example an author's manuscript or an original painting, it may not be so obvious that the mere fact of purchase includes neither the right to make copies of it nor the right to prevent the author or artist or anyone else from making copies.[61] It is, nevertheless, the fact that such a purchaser can only obtain the right to make copies of the work he has purchased by taking an assignment of copyright or entering into some form of licence. It has been said that there are occasions when the retention of the copyright by the vendor of an article, such as a picture, involves an "unnatural dissociation of two kinds of property" and, consequently, the court will lean towards construing a document given at the time of the sale as an assignment of copyright.[62] It is, however, suggested that today, with perhaps a greater appreciation of the commercial value of copyright and the ease of duplication, there are few if any works of which it can be said that the separation of the copyright and its physical embodiment involves any unnatural dissociation. In the end, and in the absence of any express terms, the issue will be what terms, if any, are to be implied from the circumstances of the sale.[63]

In the same way, the sale of an article by means of which a work can be easily reproduced (for example, a copy of it in digital form or of artwork in the form of negatives) does not by itself convey the copyright in the work.[64] The contract of sale may of course expressly or impliedly include a term whereby the copyright

---

[57] *Dennison v Ashdown* (1897) 13 T.L.R. 226, following *Dennison v Boosey* (unreported) to the same effect. The copyright work had been purchased at an auction of a music publishers' plates and copyrights.

[58] See para. 5–02, above.

[59] *Nicol v Barranger* [1917–23] Mac.C.C. 219.

[60] *Performing Right Society Ltd v London Theatre of Varieties Ltd* [1924] A.C. 1 at 26.

[61] Unless the purchaser can frame an action in, for example, contract, confidence or trust.

[62] *London Printing, etc., Alliance Ltd v Cox* [1891] 3 Ch. 291 at 304. In fact, there was no dispute that the contract included the sale of the copyright as one of its terms, the only issue being whether the copyright was intended to pass at once or later.

[63] See *Wilson v Weiss Art Pty Ltd* (1995) 31 I.P.R. 423 at 432 (Fed. Ct of Aus.).

[64] *Cooper v Stephens* [1895] 1 Ch. 567 (where the sale of printing blocks included a licence for the purchaser, but no one else, to use them), followed in *Marshall (W.) & Co Ltd v Bull (A.H.) Ltd* (1901) 85 L.T. 77, CA.

is also agreed to be sold.[65] More frequently, a contract of sale of such an article will, by necessary implication, include a licence to use the article for some limited purposes and thus to do what would otherwise be an infringement. This subject is dealt with elsewhere.[66] There are also circumstances in which the courts will hold that the vendor of an article may not derogate from his grant by asserting his copyright against a purchaser in order to prevent him from repairing the article. This is also considered elsewhere.[67]

Letters, manuscripts, etc. For the same reasons, while the property in a letter will usually pass to the recipient,[68] the copyright will remain with the writer. Ownership of copyright apart, and depending on the circumstances, the recipient may at one extreme have a licence to publish it[69] or, at the other, be liable in an action for breach of confidence for disclosing its contents.[70] The position in relation to manuscripts submitted to a publisher is considered elsewhere.[71]   **5–66**

Bequest of original materials. The one exception to this general rule applies in the case of a bequest of the original material on which a work is recorded or embodied. This exception is considered in detail below.[72]   **5–67**

Transfer of title by one joint owner. Where the legal title of one joint owner is assigned to a third party, the third party will become the joint legal owner of the copyright together with the other joint owners.   **5–68**

Transfer of copyright by "foreign" transaction. Whether, and to what extent, United Kingdom copyright is assignable is a matter of the law of the United Kingdom.[73] Where the proper law of the instrument is foreign law, the instrument must therefore comply with the formal requirements of the 1988 Act[74] if it is to transfer United Kingdom copyright but at the same time if, as an agreement, it is invalid under that law (for example because some formality has not been observed) it will not be effective to transfer the United Kingdom copyright.[75] An act purporting to expropriate United Kingdom copyright which is not recognised by English law will be of no effect.[76]   **5–69**

Transfer of foreign copyrights. An assignment may, on its true construction, show an intention to pass foreign copyrights, or rights equivalent to United Kingdom copyright, as well as the copyright conferred by the Copyright, Designs and Patents Act 1988. It should be borne in mind that the rules relating to the transfer of such foreign rights will be governed by the law of the particular foreign system and not that of the United Kingdom.   **5–70**

Summary of law affecting transfers of title. Before considering what amounts   **5–71**

---

[65] Even so, the copyright will only be transferred if the formalities for an assignment of the legal title are satisfied, and this will depend on the form and substance of the contract. As to formalities, see para. 5–82, below.

[66] See para. 5–213, below.

[67] See para. 5–231, below.

[68] *Pope v Curl* (1741) 2 Atk. 341; *Oliver v Oliver* (1861) 11 C.B. (N.S.) 139.

[69] As with a letter written to a newspaper for publication. See para. 5–220, below.

[70] See Ch.20, below.

[71] See paras 27–55 *et seq.*, below.

[72] See para. 5–127, below.

[73] *Peer International Corp v Termidor Music Publishers Ltd* [2002] EWHC 2675 (Ch); [2004] RPC 22, para.24, citing Dicey & Morris, *The Conflict of Laws*, (13th ed.,) Rule 118(1)(b) and *Campbell Connolly & Co Ltd v Noble* [1963] 1 W.L.R. 252 at 255.

[74] CDPA 1988, s.90(3). See para. 5–82, below.

[75] *Peer International Corp v Termidor Music Publishers Ltd* [2002] EWHC 2675 (Ch); [2004] RPC 22, para.25 and [2003] EWCA Civ 1156; [2004] Ch. 212, CA, para.7.

[76] *Peer International Corp v Termidor Music Publishers Ltd* [2003] EWCA Civ 1156; [2004] Ch. 212, CA.

to an effective transfer of the legal title, it is convenient to summarise the legal effect of the various kinds of possible transaction.

5–72   *Transmission of legal title.* In the case of an effective and immediate transmission of the legal title, whether of the whole or part of the copyright:[77]

    (a) If the transferee was a bona fide purchaser for value without notice he will take free of any prior equitable interests, including those of any equitable assignee. He will also take free of any earlier licences granted by the copyright owner.[78] In all other cases, he will take subject to such equities or licences. His title will be secure against anyone to whom his assignor subsequently purports to assign the copyright or to grant any licence, whether or not the latter had notice of the previous transfer.

    (b) The transferee can sue for infringement in his own name without adding any other party.[79]

5–73   *Creation of equitable title.* An event which does not pass the legal title immediately may nevertheless result in the creation of an equitable title in the transferee. This commonly arises in the following situations:[80]

    (a) A purported but defective assignment of the legal title will usually be construed as an agreement to assign and thus operates as an equitable assignment of the copyright, provided it is specifically enforceable, in particular, provided that it is supported by consideration.

    (b) Whether or not it satisfies the technical requirements for an assignment of the legal title, the transaction may on its true construction amount to an agreement to assign rather than a purported immediate assignment. If the agreement is specifically enforceable, the assignee will again be entitled to the copyright in equity. Where such an agreement amounts to an agreement to assign the copyright in an existing work at some future time,[81] the assignee's equitable title will arise when that time comes.

The position of someone who acquires an equitable title only can be summarised as follows:[82]

    (a) He can rely on his equitable title to bring proceedings for infringement but usually he can only succeed at trial if he has by then perfected his legal title by taking an assignment from the legal owner or, in the absence of such an assignment, if he has joined the legal owner of the copyright, either as claimant or defendant.

    (b) His title is not binding on a bona fide purchaser of the legal title without notice of the equitable title. He is therefore liable to be sued and otherwise have his rights defeated by such legal owner.

    (c) Except as against such a purchaser of the legal title, however, he will have a defence of consent to any action for infringement brought by the legal owner.

These various situations are discussed in more detail in the following sections of this work.

5–74   *Licence only.* Alternatively, the effect of the transaction, while not amounting to an assignment either in law or equity, may amount to a licence. This may be:

---

[77] See, as to partial assignments, paras 5–93 *et seq.*, below.

[78] See CDPA 1988, s.90(4) and para. 5–75, below.

[79] But see para. 5–91, below, as to accrued causes of action, and paras 5–203 *et seq.*, below, as to exclusive licensees.

[80] See paras 5–171 *et seq.*, below, for a full discussion of this topic.

[81] As to the special case of an assignment of the copyright in a "future work", see para. 5–105, below.

[82] Again, see paras 5–186 *et seq.*, below, for a full discussion of this topic.

(a) An exclusive licence, which, depending on its form, may give the licensee a right to bring an action for infringement against third parties;[83] or

(b) A non-exclusive licence which complies with the requirements of s.101A of the 1988 Act,[84] which will confer on the licensee a right to bring an action for infringement against third parties but which will otherwise merely provide a defence to an action for infringement brought by the copyright owner; or

(c) Some lesser licence, which will merely provide a defence to an action for infringement brought by the copyright owner.[85]

The effect of a valid transfer of the legal title. The position in outline has already been discussed, but an owner generally has an unfettered right to transfer his copyright and the transferee will take free of any obligations or burdens to which he was subject. This general rule is subject to three limitations. **5–75**

(a) First, where there are outstanding equitable interests[86] then, except in the case of a bona fide purchaser for value without actual or constructive notice, the transferee will take subject to such equities. Thus if the owner held the legal title on trust for another or, for example, had granted an option to another to acquire the copyright, the transferee is liable to be divested of the copyright at the suit of the owner of the equitable right.

(b) Secondly, and again except in the case of a bona fide purchaser for value without actual or constructive notice, a transferee will be bound by any licence granted by the copyright owner.[87]

(c) Thirdly, a transferee may possibly be bound by contractual obligations of his predecessor under the doctrine of "benefit and burden". This is considered in more detail in the next paragraph.

Equities and licences created by a predecessor of the transferor will similarly bind the transferee unless, at some stage in the chain, the legal title has been acquired by a purchaser for value without notice.[88] These rules are obviously a trap for an assignee, who takes the risk of not investigating his assignor's title.

Agreement not to assign. If the copyright owner has contracted not to assign the copyright, it is suggested that an assignment in breach of that agreement will not be effective to transfer the legal title. The same is true where he has agreed not to assign the copyright without first obtaining consent. The opposite conclusion has, however, been reached in New Zealand, on the grounds that an agreement, express or implied, not to assign rights *in personam*, or not to assign them without consent, should generally be specifically enforced as between the immediate parties, unless there is some strong reason why that course should not be adopted.[89] However, the reasoning does not appear to give full weight to the fact that copyright is a property right. The fact that a copyright owner has agreed to pay royalties or share profits with another will not by itself be sufficient to give rise to an implied term not to transfer the copyright.[90] **5–76**

Assignor's rights to royalties, etc. In general, where an owner assigns copyright **5–77**

---

[83] See paras 5–203 *et seq.*, below.
[84] As to which, see paras 5–209, below.
[85] See para. 5–194, below.
[86] As to such interests, see paras 5–170 *et seq.*, below
[87] CDPA 1988, s.90(4).
[88] As to this rule in relation to licences, see CDPA 1988, s.90(4).
[89] *New Zealand Payroll Software Systems Ltd v Advanced Management Systems Ltd* [2003] 3 N.Z.L.R. 1, applying *Linden Gardens Trust Ltd v Lenesta Sludge Disposals Ltd* [1994] 1 A.C. 85.
[90] *Sims v Marryat* (1851) 17 Q.B. 281.

in return for a promise to pay royalties, he cannot sue a third party to whom the copyright has been assigned for those royalties unless a novation of the original contract has taken place: no privity of contract exists between them.[91] The assignor retains his contractual rights against his assignee but obviously these may be worthless in the event of the assignee's insolvency.[92] In *Barker v Stickney*,[93] various grounds were advanced for making the subsequent purchaser liable for royalties but were all rejected:

(a) An unpaid vendor's lien. *Held*: the assignor/vendor had accepted the assignee/purchaser's covenant to pay royalties in satisfaction of his claim for the price and was therefore not an unpaid vendor.

(b) A charge on the copyright. *Held*: a charge could only arise if it had been clearly and expressly created, and this was not the case.[94]

(c) A burden which ran with the copyright, on the general principle stated in *De Mattos v Gibson*.[95] *Held*: since it was settled law[96] that a purchaser of a chattel is not bound by mere notice of stipulations entered into by his vendor, and there was nothing to distinguish a chose in action such as copyright from chattels or land, a person acquiring copyright was not bound by notice of his predecessor's promise.

As to the burden of the obligation to pay royalties running with the copyright, it has since been confirmed that the *De Mattos v Gibson* principle would not, even at its fullest extent, assist because it only enables negative restrictions to be enforced, not positive obligations.[97] An alternative argument which possibly still remains open is the principle of "benefit and burden".[98] In order to succeed here, however, it seems that it will be necessary to show that on the transfer from the original assignee the copyright had been transferred subject to the transferee discharging the obligation to pay royalties.[99] A simple transfer of the copyright, or of the benefit of the contract, which did not make it clear that the original assignee did not intend to remain liable for payment of royalties, would, it seems not be enough.[1] This rule is mitigated somewhat for assignments made after May 11, 2000 by the Contracts (Rights of Third Parties) Act 1999. This permits some types of third party to enforce a term of a contract either if the contract expressly provides that he may[2] or if the term purports to confer a benefit on him.[3] However, the original assignor is not normally able to ensure that subsequent assignments will be in terms that confer rights on him under the Act. For this and other reasons,

---

[91] *Bagot Pneumatic Tyre Co v Clipper Pneumatic Tyre Co* [1902] 1 Ch. 146 and see *Beswick v Beswick* [1968] A.C. 58.

[92] As in *Re Grant-Richards Ex p. Deeping* [1907] 2 K.B. 33. The limited protection given by the Bankruptcy Act 1914 given to an author in the case of a publisher's insolvency is discussed at para. 5–79, below.

[93] [1919] 1 K.B. 121. But see Adams, "*Barker v Stickney* revisited" [1998] I.P.Q. 113, arguing that *Barker v Stickney* was wrongly decided.

[94] But see Adams, *Barker v Stickney* revisited" [1998] I.P.Q. 113, suggesting that today a court may be more ready to imply a charge.

[95] (1859) 4 De G. & J. 276.

[96] Applying *Taddy & Co v Sterious & Co* [1904] 1 Ch. 354; *McCruther v Pitcher* [1904] 2 Ch. 306; and *Dunlop Tyre Co Ltd v Selfridge & Co Ltd* [1915] A.C. 847.

[97] See *Swiss Bank Corp v Lloyds Bank Ltd* [1979] Ch. 548.

[98] See *Tito v Waddell (No. 2)* [1977] Ch. 106.

[99] See *Tito v Waddell (No. 2)* [1977] Ch. 106 at 302 and *Law Debenture Corp. v Ural Caspian Oil CorpLtd* [1993] 1 W.L.R. 138 at 147.

[1] But see *John v James* [1991] F.S.R. 397 where it seems to have been taken for granted that an assignee who acquires the benefit of an original publisher's rights will take subject to any burden of exploitation, including the ordinary burden of accounting to the writer for his contractual entitlement to royalties.

[2] Contracts (Rights of Third Parties) Act 1999, s.1(1)(a).

[3] s. 1(1)(b). This subsection does not apply if "on a proper construction of the contract it appears that the parties did not intend the term to be enforceable by the third party" — s.1(2).

therefore, it is always in the interests of an author who depends upon the continued payment of royalties or performance of other contractual obligations, to enter into a licence for the exploitation of his work rather than an assignment.

The fiduciary duties of a publisher-assignee. A publisher who takes an assign-   **5–78**
ment of copyright in return for an agreement to pay royalties may be subject to fiduciary duties in addition to his contractual duties. The existence and scope of any such duty will be subject to the express terms of the agreement,[4] but, where the agreement is silent, the nature of the duty will have to be worked out from the other terms and surrounding circumstances. Generally, it seems that a publisher will have a fiduciary duty to account for monies received and to exploit the copyright only in a way which the publisher honestly considers to be for the joint benefit of the parties.[5] Other duties may be implicit from the relationship, for example, one not to make any profit for himself which is not brought into account when computing the writer's royalties, such that the publisher will be in breach by setting up overseas subsidiaries to deduct greater sums than are justified by the work involved. Factors which may be relevant here include:[6]

(a) whether the agreement is to endure for the full term of copyright;

(b) whether the works in question comprise all works written by the author during the term of the agreement;

(c) whether the entire copyright is assigned to the publisher;

(d) whether the publisher has complete control over the method of exploitation;

(e) whether the exploitation is for the benefit of the publisher alone or for their joint benefit, such that the agreement is in the nature of a joint venture, the author having to place trust and confidence in the publisher over the manner in which the publisher discharges its exploitation functions;

(f) whether it is implicit that the publisher is to account for a fixed share of royalties from only one pool, including sales from home and overseas markets, such that it is implicit that there would not be some other pool, for example sums earned by wholly owned overseas subsidiaries, in which the author is not to share.

Bankruptcy Act 1914. This Act gave some protection to authors by preventing a   **5–79**
publisher's trustee in bankruptcy from selling or authorising the sale of copies of his work or dealing with his interests in the copyright except on terms which ensured that the author would receive such royalties as would have been payable by the publisher.[7] The provision has been repealed,[8] but continues to have effect in relation to any transaction entered into before the commencement of the Insolvency Act 1986.[9]

---

[4] *Kelly v Cooper* [1993] A.C. 205 at 215, PC.

[5] *John v James* [1991] F.S.R. 397.

[6] These were the factors considered relevant in *John v James* [1991] F.S.R. 397 in imposing such a duty on the publisher.

[7] Bankruptcy Act 1914, s.60. The section did not apply where the publisher was a company (*Re Health Promotion Ltd* [1932] 1 Ch. 65). As to whether the provision was applicable where the publisher had a mere licence, see *Henham v Alston Rivers Ltd* [1911–16] Mac.C.C. 330 and *Copinger* (12th ed.), para.1162.

[8] Insolvency Act 1985, as replaced by the Insolvency Act 1986.

[9] Insolvency Act 1986, Sch.11, para.15.

B. TRANSFER OF LEGAL TITLE BY ASSIGNMENT

(i) General

5–80 **Introduction.** As already noted, copyright is today transmissible by assignment as personal or moveable property.[10]

5–81 **Transitional.** It may be necessary in the case of old works to consider the effect of transactions entered into before the passing of the 1988 Act. With the exceptions which will be noted, the law on assignments under the 1988 Act is to the same effect as that under the previous Acts. The 1988 Act provides that any document made before August 1, 1989, which affected the ownership of the copyright in a work made before that date (an "existing work"), or which transferred an interest or right in respect of the copyright in such a work, is to have the corresponding operation in relation to copyright in the work under the 1988 Act.[11] The effect of this is that if an assignment was effective to transfer the copyright or an interest in the copyright conferred under the earlier Acts, then it is effective to transfer the copyright or the corresponding interest conferred by the 1988 Act. The Act also provides that expressions used in pre-August 1, 1989 documents are to be construed in accordance with their effect immediately before this date.[12]

There should also be borne in mind the general provisions contained in the 1988 Act for securing the continuity of the law so far as the new copyright provisions (*i.e.* the provisions of the 1988 Act relating to copyright[13]) re-enact, with or without modification, earlier provisions. The following general principles are laid down:[14]

(a) A reference in an instrument or other document to copyright, or to a work or other subject matter in which copyright subsists, which apart from the 1988 Act would be construed as referring to copyright under the 1956 Act, is to be construed, so far as may be required for continuing its effect, as being, or as the case may require, including, a reference to copyright under the 1988 Act or to works in which copyright subsists under that Act.[15]

(b) A reference (express or implied) in an instrument or other document to a provision repealed by the 1988 Act is to be construed, so far as may be required for continuing its effect, as a reference to the corresponding provision of that Act.[16]

(ii) Requirements for a valid assignment

5–82 **Requirements for valid assignment of the legal title: the 1988 Act.** An assignment of the legal title to copyright is not effective unless it is in writing signed by

---

[10] CDPA 1988, s.90.

[11] CDPA 1988, Sch.1, para.25(1). The effect of this provision, no more but no less, is to preserve the legal effect of a pre-commencement assignment or agreement to assign. It does not attempt to legislate as to the effect of such a document and only preserves such effect as the document originally had. See *Novello & Co Ltd v Keith Prowse Music Publishing Co Ltd* [2004] EWHC 766 (Ch), para.9. The 1956 Act (Sch.7, para.28(1)) contained a provision to similar effect. As to the 1911 Act, see s.24(1) and paras 5–148 *et seq.*, below.

[12] CDPA 1988, Sch.1, para.25(2). See the previous footnote as to this provision's effect, which is the same as para.25(1). Sch.7, para.28(2) of the 1956 Act was to similar effect, adding that this was so "notwithstanding that a different meaning is assigned to them for the purpose of this Act."

[13] CDPA 1988, Sch.1. para.1(1).

[14] These general principles have effect subject to any specific transitional provision or saving and to any express amendment made by the 1988 Act. See Sch.1, para.4(6).

[15] CDPA 1988, Sch.1, para.4(2).

[16] Sch.1, para.4(5).

or on behalf of the assignor.[17] "Writing" includes any form of notation or code, whether by hand or otherwise and regardless of the method by which, or medium in, or on which, it is recorded.[18] No notice to anyone is required to perfect the transfer.[19] Minors[20] can own and dispose of copyrights in the same way as adults, but subject to the usual rules as to infants' contracts.[21] In the case of a body corporate, the requirement that the assignment should be signed by or on behalf of any person is satisfied by the affixing of its seal.[22] An assignment may also of course be executed by a company by it being signed by someone on the company's behalf. If the assignment is signed on behalf of the assignor, the person so signing must obviously have the authority of the assignor in order to transfer the copyright.[23] A receiver appointed by the court over partnership assets, which include copyrights, will usually have authority to sign an assignment of any copyright "on behalf of" the partners.[24] A receiver appointed out of court under a debenture will invariably have sufficient authority by virtue of the terms of the debenture to enable him to dispose of the company's property and execute documents on its behalf.

Assignments under the 1956 and 1911 Acts. The provisions under these Acts relating to the formal requirements for an assignment of existing copyright were to the same effect as those of the 1988 Act.[25]   **5–83**

What words will effect an assignment? An assignment of copyright does not have to be in any special form, other than in writing, signed by or on behalf of the assignor.[26] Thus any written, signed instrument may constitute an assignment of copyright even though the word "copyright" is not used in the document if, on its true construction, it was intended that the copyright should thereby pass.[27] Thus, for example, the copyright would be carried by general expressions such as "all right and title in the business" or "the assets" of the business if the copyright formed part of the assets of that business and it is apparent from the surrounding circumstances that this is what was intended.[28] In the same way, it is not necessary that the words "grant" or "assign" be used if an intention to assign the copy-   **5–84**

---

[17] CDPA 1988, s.90(3). See Vol.2 at J1.i, for a precedent of an assignment of copyright.

[18] s.178.

[19] *Performing Right Society Ltd v London Theatre of Varieties Ltd* [1924] A.C. 1. As to assignment of accrued causes of action, see para. 5–91, below.

[20] See Family Law Reform Act 1969 (c.46).

[21] *Chaplin v Leslie Frewin (Publishers) Ltd* [1966] Ch. 71.

[22] CDPA 1988, s.176(1). This provision was new in the 1988 Act. Where the company does not have a common seal, a document signed by a director and the secretary, or by two directors, and expressed to be executed by the company, has the same effect as if executed under the company's common seal. See the Companies Act 1985, s.36A(4).

[23] *Beloff v Pressdram Ltd* [1973] 1 All E.R. 241; *Heptulla v Orient Longman Ltd* [1989] F.S.R. 598 at 610.

[24] *Murray v King* [1986] F.S.R. 116 (Fed. Ct of Aus.). The reasoning (pp.129, 137) was that although the receiver was not the agent of the partners and was not in "possession" (*sic*—see the footnote to para. 5–64, above) of the copyright, the partners must nevertheless have been taken to have anticipated the possibility of a receiver being empowered by the court to sell the assets in a receivership (p.129), since otherwise they might not obtain that to which they were entitled (p.137). The sale could therefore be said to be on the partners' behalf.

[25] Copyright Act 1956, s.36; Copyright Act 1911, s.5(2). As to pre- 1911 Act assignments, see paras 5–92 *et seq.*, below.

[26] See para. 5–82, above.

[27] *Cray Valley Ltd v Deltech Europe Ltd* [2003] EWHC (Ch) 728, para.69; *Murray v King* [1986] F.S.R. 116 (Fed. Ct of Aus.); *Greenfield Products Ltd v Rover-Scott Bonnar Ltd* [1990] A.I.P.C. 90–667. As already noted (see para. 5–69, above), whether, and to what extent, United Kingdom copyright is assignable is a matter of United Kingdom law. Where the agreement is governed by foreign law, it must be construed in accordance with that law.

[28] *Cray Valley Ltd v Deltech Europe Ltd* [2003] EWHC (Ch) 728, para.69; *Murray v King* [1986] F.S.R. 116 (Fed. Ct of Aus.) *Greenfield Products Ltd v Rover-Scott Bonnar Ltd* [1990] A.I.P.C. 90–667.

right can be gathered from the context.[29] Many transactions are informal in nature and it is often difficult to determine whether the intention of the party in signing a document was to transfer the copyright or simply grant or confirm the grant of a licence. This topic is dealt with elsewhere,[30] but in general the whole background may need to be looked at to discover the parties' true intention. Where the signed document forms part of a transaction in which a copyright work was made for a purchaser, and where it is clear that it was contemplated by both that the purchaser was to have exclusive use of the work, it may be easy to conclude that copyright was intended to pass with the physical subject matter. On this basis, the wording on mere invoices[31] or receipts[32] has been held to amount to an assignment

5–85 **Assignment of "copyright": extent of assignment.** Copyright is made up of a bundle of various rights. The extent to which a partial assignment of these rights is permissible is considered below but in general an assignment of "copyright" will operate, in the absence of contrary intention, to convey to the assignee all the rights which go to make up the copyright.[33] An assignor should therefore always take care that the assignment is drawn in such a way as not to carry rights in excess of those intended to be assigned.

5–86 **Future rights.** In general, an assignment expressed to include future rights cannot operate to transfer the legal title to such rights and will at best operate as an agreement to assign, *i.e.* an equitable assignment.[34] A statutory exception exists in relation to "future copyright." The topic is considered in more detail later in this chapter.[35]

Subject matter of grant. If there is ambiguity in the subject matter of the grant, extrinsic evidence may be adduced to identify it.[36]

5–87 **Extent of assignment: new technologies.** It is not always clear whether an assignment includes rights which are exercisable by means of technologies which were not known at the date of the assignment. This is a question which more frequently arises in the context of commercial licences, and is considered there.[37]

5–88 **Assignor may not reproduce the work.** An author who has assigned the copyright in his work may, like any other person, be restrained by the assignee from

---

[29] See *Lacy v Toole* (1867) 15 L.T. 512 (an agreement to "let A have" a certain work in discharge of a debt owing to A, sufficient to pass the copyright in the work to A); *British Actors Film Co Ltd v Glover* [1918] 1 K.B. 299 (agreement by the copyright owner to let, and by the defendant to hire, the "right of performing" a comic opera for a term construed as an assignment (or at least an equitable assignment)).

[30] See para. 5–202, below.

[31] As in *London Printing, etc., Alliance Ltd v Cox* [1891] 3 Ch. 291 (the words on an invoice, "For pastel picture and entire copyright, 'On the Threshold', £52 10s." sufficient to pass the copyright, the circumstances of the case showing that the title to the copyright was intended to pass at the same time as the picture itself); *Ornamin (UK) Ltd v Bacsa Ltd* [1964] R.P.C. 293 (invoice expressed to be for "two designs for children's plates").

[32] As in: *Savory (E.W.) Ltd v The World of Golf Ltd* [1914] 2 Ch. 566, where the words on a receipt, "Received of Messrs. E.W.S., Ltd, the sum of £2 6s. 6d. for five original card designs, inclusive of all copyrights. Subjects: Four Golfing subjects; one Teddy Bear painting" were held to be a sufficient assignment of the copyright; *Glogau v Land Transport Safety Authority of New Zealand* [1997] 3 N.Z.L.R. 353 (High Ct of N.Z.): "This receipt is to be regarded as full and final payment for unencumbered ownership of the intellectual property and copyright ..."; *Comprop Ltd v Moran* [2002] J.L.R. 222 (Royal Ct. of Jersey), where the vendor wrote: "I hereby acknowledge receipt of the sum of £25,614.00 ... for the purchase of all copyrights ...".

[33] See, for example, CDPA 1988, ss.1(1), 2(1).

[34] See paras 5–105 and 5–173 *et seq.*, below.

[35] See paras 5–105 *et seq.*, below.

[36] *Savory (E.W.) Ltd v The World of Golf Ltd* [1914] 2 Ch 566; *The Photocrom Co Ltd v H. & W. Nelson Ltd* [1923–28] Mac.C.C. 293; *Comcorp (Pty) Ltd v Quipmor CC* (1997) 2 S.A. 599.

[37] See paras 5–202 *et seq.*, below.

reproducing or authorising others to reproduce the work.[38] There is no reservation of such a right in the assignment unless it can be shown that, in the circumstances of the case, it is necessary to imply it to give business efficacy to the transaction.[39]

Separate assignments of derivative works. Where an author has created a second work by using material derived from an earlier work, what is the effect of separate assignments of each work? The point may arise where an author has created several drafts or sketches before the final version of the work. Where the first assignment in time is of the earlier work, the second assignment cannot operate to vest in the assignee any rights which the assignor no longer owns and thus cannot vest in the assignee rights of copyright in the earlier work. He will only have exclusive rights in relation to material which is found only in the later work. Thus, if in exploiting the later work he reproduces a substantial part of the earlier work, he will infringe. His rights as against the first assignee and third parties extend only to the right to complain of exploitation of a substantial part of the new material contained in his work. He cannot of course complain about exploitation of the earlier work itself. If the later work is so far removed from the earlier that although references from the one can be found in the other, the later work does not in fact reproduce any substantial part of it, then they are two independent copyright works and can be exploited independently.

5–89

Where the first assignment in time is of the later work, then its effect will depend on its construction but *prima facie* an assignee of the copyright in the later work can maintain an action for infringement against a person using the first work to the extent it can be said to "reproduce" the later work.[40] This is on the basis that the assignment of the second work must generally be taken to include an assignment of the copyright in the preceding works to the extent that they are found in the final work. Otherwise the assignment would be valueless if confined only to what was new in the final work. The assignment could of course be expressly framed to have this effect.

A similar problem can arise if there is a single assignment of copyright which does not expressly state what is the subject matter of the assignment. Does the assignment extend to all works or only the latest in time? The answer depends on the intention of the parties as gathered from the words used in the assignment when construed against the factual background.[41] Relevant factors may include whether the parties are likely to have contemplated that the assignor should be free to exploit the earlier work and the consequences of the titles to the distinct copyright works becoming separated.

Assignment not bona fide: a sham. The court will always look behind the legal form to the reality of the transaction. The court will regard an assignment as bogus if, though in proper legal form, it was intended to take effect otherwise than as an assignment in substance and reality.[42] The court will, however, give effect to an assignment which is intended to be in all respects an out and out assign-

5–90

---

[38] CDPA 1988, s.64 provides a limited exception in the case of artistic works. See para. 9–174, below.

[39] *Performing Right Society Ltd v Harlequin Record Shops Ltd* [1979] F.S.R. 233 at 241.

[40] *Metzler & Co (1920) Ltd v Curwen (J.) & Sons Ltd* [1928–35] Mac.C.C. 127. Technically, of course, material taken from the earlier work will not reproduce the later work, there being no causal connection.

[41] *Comprop Ltd v Moran* [2002] J.L.R. 222 (Royal Ct. of Jersey), para.104.

[42] *Landeker & Brown v Woolff (L.)* (1907) 52 S.J. 45 (assignment of copyright executed subject to an undertaking that assignee would not reproduce the work without the assignor's consent, the purpose being to enable the assignee to bring an action without joining the assignor, who was a foreigner); *Dennison v Ashdown* (1897) 13 T.L.R. 226; *Beloff v Pressdram Ltd* [1973] R.P.C. 765 at 779.

ment, even though it was contemplated at the time of the assignment that the assignee would thereby be assisted or enabled to bring proceedings for infringement of the copyright against a third party.[43]

5-91 **Assignment of accrued causes of action.** Where litigation is contemplated and an assignment of copyright is taken to enable an action to be brought or the claimant's legal title perfected, care should also be taken to assign accrued causes of action in respect of past infringements. Otherwise a claimant may be met by a defence that he is not entitled to relief in respect of these acts. The legal title to such accrued causes of action may be passed by an absolute assignment in writing under the assignor's hand coupled with the giving of express notice in writing of the assignment to the infringer.[44] If suitably drafted,[45] therefore, and once notice has been given, the same instrument can be effective in law to transfer not only the copyright but also the rights of action accrued to and vested in the assignor in respect of past infringements of that copyright. Where there is no express mention in the assignment of accrued causes of action, it will be a matter of construction to determine whether the parties in fact intended to transfer such rights. Until notice is given to the infringer,[46] the assignment of the accrued causes of action will only operate in equity[47] so that, as a matter of caution, notice of such assignment should be given to the prospective defendant before the issue of proceedings.[48]

5-92 **Pre-1911 Act assignments.** The copyright in unpublished works protected at common law could seemingly be transferred orally.[49] An assignment of the copyright in a published literary work either had to be in writing[50] or, if the title had been registered at Stationers' Hall, could be effected by making an entry of the assignment in the register.[51] As regards published musical and dramatic works, the musical scores and books of words were protected as literary works,[52] but an assignment of the copyright did not convey the performing right unless an entry to that effect was made in the register at Stationers' Hall.[53] The assignment of the copyright in an engraving probably had to be in writing, attested by two witnesses,[54] and in a work of sculpture, by deed, attested by two witnesses.[55] In the

---

[43] *Beloff v Pressdram Ltd* [1973] R.P.C. 765; *Husqvarna Forest & Garden Ltd v Bridon New Zealand Ltd* (1997) 38 I.P.R. 513 (High Ct of N.Z.) (assignment to local distributor with (apparently)a right to call for a reassignment).

[44] *i.e.* under the Law Property Act 1925, s.136. Such an assignment will rarely savour of maintenance or champerty since an assignment of a cause of action simultaneously with a property right to which it is ancillary, or of a cause of action in respect of which the assignee has a genuine commercial interest in taking and enforcing for his own benefit, is valid. See *Trendtex Trading Corp v Crédit Suisse* [1982] A.C. 679 at 703 (*per* Lord Roskill). What is objectionable is trafficking in litigation: *Camdex International Ltd v Bank of Zambia* [1998] Q.B. 22.

[45] As, *e.g.* in *Beloff v Pressdram* [1973] R.P.C. 765; *Infabrics Ltd v Jaytex Shirt Co Ltd* [1978] F.S.R. 451 at 461. For a precedent, see Vol.2 at J1.i.

[46] An assignment of copyright does not of course require the giving of notice.

[47] No consideration is required: *Holt v Heatherfield Trust Ltd* [1942] 2 K.B. 1 at 4.

[48] The assignee may nevertheless commence an action relying on his equitable title: *Weddell v J.A. Pearce & Major* [1988] Ch. 26 at 41. If by no other means, it seems that the legal title will usually be perfected in the course of the action by the assignment being referred to or disclosed: *Weddell v J.A. Pearce & Major*, above. See also *The Aiolos* [1983] 2 Lloyd's Rep.25 at 34, but *cf. Compania Colombiana de Seguros v Pacific Steam Navigation Co* [1965] 1 Q.B. 101.

[49] See *Copinger* (4th ed.), p.142.

[50] *Leyland v Stewart* (1876) 4 Ch.D. 419. It was generally considered that such an assignment did not have to be attested. See *Cumberland v Copeland* (1862) 1 Hurl. & C. 194; but see 8 Jur.(N.S.), Part II, p.148.

[51] Literary Copyright Act 1842, s.13.

[52] *i.e.* under the Literary Copyright Act 1842, ss.20, 21.

[53] Literary Copyright Act 1842, s.22.

[54] See the reasoning in *Jefferys v Boosey* (1854) 4 H.L.C. 815 at 994, 995.

case of a painting, drawing or photograph, it had to be in writing, signed by the proprietor of the copyright or his agent.[56]

(iii) Partial assignments

(a) *Extent of permissible assignments*

Partial assignments. A copyright owner will often wish to divide up the copyright, parcelling out different rights to different persons and, in general, it is permissible to do this. Thus, the 1988 Act makes it clear that there can be separate and independent owners of the copyright in respect of the doing of different acts, or different classes of acts, and at different times. Where different persons are in consequence of partial assignments entitled to different aspects of copyright in a work, the "copyright owner" for the purposes of, for example, infringement, is the person who is entitled to the aspect of the copyright relevant for the purpose of the Act.[57] The Act thus creates separate rights which can be dealt with separately.[58] The divisions which a copyright owner may desire to make will be into different modes of exploitation, different periods of time and different territories. These are considered in turn, below.

5–93

Extent of permissible assignments: the 1988 Act. The 1988 Act provides that an assignment may be partial, that is, limited so as to apply:

(a) to one or more, but not all, of the things the copyright owner has the exclusive right to do;

(b) to part, but not the whole, of the period for which the copyright is to subsist.[59]

As already noted, such a partial assignment will vest in the assignee a proprietary interest in the copyright and enable him to sue in his own name for infringement of that right by third parties.

5–94

Particular means of exploitation. As already stated, the 1988 Act provides that an assignment of copyright may be "limited so as to apply to one or more, but not all, of the things the copyright owner has the exclusive right to do." S.16 of the Act sets out the various "acts" which he has the exclusive right to do, for example, the right to copy the work, perform it in public, broadcast it, etc. The word "things", rather than "acts", was used in s.90(2)(a) with the intention of making it clear that an assignment of copyright may be limited to narrower classes of exploitation than these principal categories of "acts".[60] So, as well as divisions into such rights as the reproduction, public performing or broadcasting right,[61] further subdivisions are possible, for example the right to reproduce a work on records (often referred to as the "mechanical right"), broadcast it by satellite, and so on. By way of further example, there seems no reason why an assignment cannot be made of the right to perform a work "professionally".[62]

It seems clear that it was the intention to be able to sub-divide copyright not

5–95

---

[55] Sculpture Copyright Act 1814 (54 Geo. 3, c.56), s.4.

[56] Fine Arts Copyright Act 1862 (25 & 26 Vict. c.68), s.3.

[57] CDPA 1988, s.173(1).

[58] *J. Albert & Sons Pty Ltd & Others v Fletcher Construction Co Ltd* [1976] R.P.C. 615 (Sup.Ct of N.Z.).

[59] CDPA 1988, s.90(2).

[60] See *Hansard*, H.L. Vol.493, col.1342; H.L. Vol.495, cols 667 and 668.

[61] As to the primary rights of a copyright owner, see Ch.7, below.

[62] *British Actors Film Co Ltd v Glover* [1918] 1 K.B. 299, decided under the 1911 Act but which seems to have been to the same effect. See para. 5–97, below.

just into different modes of exploitation, as above, but also into exploitation for different purposes in relation to particular modes, for example, the right to reproduce and publish the work in book form,[63] or in hardback or paperback form. In previous editions of this work,[64] doubt was expressed as to whether this was possible, taking the case of the example of a grant of "serial rights", and arguing that since the infringing act of reproduction took place, if at all, when printing took place, it could not be determined at that stage whether the pages would be bound up for a single publication or for publication in parts over a period, so that it would be impossible to know at that stage whether an infringement had occurred or who was the proper claimant. It is suggested, however, that establishing the purpose for which the work was printed would be a matter for evidence. Such an approach is adopted elsewhere in the 1988 Act.[65] Certainly under the earlier Acts, which appear to have been to the same effect, the validity of such a division was accepted without argument.[66]

5–96   **Particular means of exploitation: the 1956 Act.** The 1956 Act was to the same effect. Thus, the structure of the 1956 Act was that various acts, such as the reproduction of a work, its performance in public, broadcasting, etc, were "restricted" by the copyright, the copyright owner having the exclusive right to do these acts.[67] The Act then provided that an assignment might be limited to one or more, but not all, of the classes of acts which the owner of the copyright had the exclusive right to do, including any one or more classes of acts not separately designated as being restricted by the copyright, but falling within any of the classes of acts so designated.[68]

5–97   **Particular means of exploitation: the 1911 Act.** The effect of the 1911 Act was the same. The Act provided that the right of copyright, being the sole right to do various acts, for example, to reproduce a work or perform it in public,[69] might be assigned either wholly or partially.[70] The right so given to part with the copyright limited as to the means of exploitation was clearly recognised.[71]

5–98   **Time.** It is clear that copyright may be assigned for a period less than the whole term of copyright.[72] This may be for a fixed term starting immediately or in the future. The position was the same under the earlier Acts.[73] A common problem which arises under such a grant is the right of the assignee, after the end of the

---

[63] See *Hansard*, H.L., Vol.493, col.1342; H.L. Vol.495, cols 667 and 668.

[64] See, *e.g. Copinger* (13th ed.), para.5–19.

[65] So that, for example, whether the decompilation of a computer program amounts to an infringement apparently depends on the purpose for which the decompilation is carried out. See CDPA 1988, s.50B, especially subs.(3)(d).

[66] See para. 5–97, below.

[67] See Copyright Act 1956, s.1(1).

[68] Copyright Act 1956, s.36(2)(a). Note, for example, that s.4(2) of the Act expressly provided for such a split of the copyright. Again, the assignee of such a limited right was then to be taken to be the owner of the copyright in respect of its application to the particular limited class of act: s.49(5).

[69] Copyright Act 1911, s.1(2).

[70] s.5(2); and where an assignee became entitled to any right comprised in the copyright, he was to be treated, as respects the right so assigned, as the owner of the copyright: s.5(3).

[71] *British Actors Film Co Ltd v Glover* [1918] 1 K.B. 299 (right to perform a work "professionally"); *Jonathan Cape Ltd v Consolidated Press Ltd* [1954] 1 W.L.R. 1313 (right to publish in "volume form"); *Canadian Performing Right Society v Famous Players Canadian Corp Ltd* (1927) 60 O.L.R. 280 and 614 (assignment of performing right).

[72] CDPA 1988, s.90(2).

[73] See the Copyright Act 1956, s.36(2)(c), the Copyright Act 1911, s.5(2) and, as to the earlier acts, *Copinger* (4th ed.), p.147 and, for example, *Horrit v Hall* (1862) 6 L.T. 348.

term, to continue to deal with articles made by him during the term. This is dealt with elsewhere.[74]

Different territories: the 1988 Act. It is a common feature of international copyright for a copyright owner to want to divide up the right between different territorial areas, whether by assignment or grant of exclusive licences. This may be because the copyright owner does not have the means to exploit the work abroad himself, and so must find another to take this burden on, or for other commercial reasons.[75] Two points need to be borne in mind in this connection. First, the assignment of the rights conferred under foreign systems of law will be governed by those systems. As to this, the present treatment is concerned only with the question of whether it is possible to effect a subdivision of the limited territorial copyright conferred by the 1988 Act. Secondly, the partition of an intellectual property right between different territories in an attempt to create separate markets may fall foul of rules relating to the free movement of goods and anti-competitive practices. The latter topic is dealt with elsewhere.[76]

5–99

The 1988 Act confers on the copyright owner the exclusive right to do various acts "in the United Kingdom".[77] It is suggested that the copyright conferred by the 1988 Act cannot be sub-divided into rights for the different countries which make up the United Kingdom or even smaller areas. This is because, firstly, the Act, while making express provision for partial assignments in terms of different acts and different times, makes no provision as to different areas. Secondly, although the copyright can be divided up into one or more of the "things" which the copyright owner has the exclusive right to do, the things which the copyright owner has the exclusive right to do are set out in s.16, and these confer the exclusive right to do various acts "in the United Kingdom", and not "or in part thereof". Thirdly, if United Kingdom copyright could be so divided it would apparently mean, for example, that the owner of the copyright "in Scotland" would have the right to prevent the making of copies of a work in England, relying on the provision in s.16 that the owner of the copyright has the exclusive right to copy the work "in the United Kingdom". This result could only be prevented by adding words to the statute so as to limit the rights of the copyright owner to the territory of his grant.[78] Again, it is difficult to see how the owner of the copyright "in Scotland" could prevent the "importation" into Scotland of copies unlawfully made in England, since the Act only makes it an infringement to import infringing copies "into the United Kingdom". *A fortiori*, it is suggested that the division of the copyright into smaller areas, for example counties, is not possible. The effect of a purported assignment of the copyright in "England" would, it is suggested, not be to vest any proprietary interest in the "assignee". At best he would only obtain contractual rights against the "assignor".

Different territories: the 1956 Act. At a first reading, the effect of the provisions of the 1956 Act might appear to have been to produce a different result. It is suggested, however, that this was not the case. Thus the Act expressly provided that an assignment of copyright might be limited to one or more of the countries in re-

5–100

---

[74] See para. 27–66, below.

[75] For example, it is common for music publishers and recording companies to operate through a system of assignments or exclusive licences of the copyright in favour of different companies in different territories.

[76] See Ch.29, below.

[77] See CDPA 1988, s.16(1). The United Kingdom consists of England, Wales, Scotland and Northern Ireland: Interpretation Act 1978, Sch.1.

[78] It is suggested that s.173(1) is insufficient to do this.

lation to which the owner had the exclusive right.[79] The different wording arises because under the 1956 Act (and the 1911 Act), unlike the 1988 Act, the Act as a whole, including the infringement provisions, might be extended to other countries.[80] An assignment might therefore be limited to one of these other countries but could not, it is suggested, and for the same reasons as apply to the 1988 Act, have been limited to a territory smaller than the United Kingdom.

5–101   **Different territories: the 1911 Act.** It is suggested that the position was the same under the 1911 Act, which permitted an assignment "either wholly or partially, and either generally or subject to limitations to the United Kingdom or any self-governing Dominion or other part of His Majesty's Dominions to which this Act extends".[81] There is, however, some authority to suggest that local divisions of the copyright were possible. For example, it was said that since the Act recognised the right to part with the copyright subject to restrictions as to time, place or otherwise, so as to make the grantee of the limited right which he acquired the actual owner of that limited part of the copyright, an assignee of the right to perform a work "in the provinces" was therefore the owner of the copyright to that extent.[82] But the point was not argued,[83] and it is suggested that the better view is that an assignment could not have been made in respect of an area smaller than the United Kingdom (or one of the Dominions).[84]

5–102   **Pre-1911 Act assignments.** It is not clear whether, under the law prior to 1911, copyright was divisible as to territory. It is thought that statutory copyright was not.[85]

(b) *Presumption of transfer of rental right*

5–103   **Presumption of transfer of rental in case of film production agreement.** The EC Directive on Rental, Lending and Related Rights[86] required Member States to confer on authors and performers an unwaivable right to remuneration from the rental of fixations of their works and performances on sound recordings and films where they had parted with such rental right. Although Member States were at the same time required to provide for a presumed transfer of a performer's rental right on the conclusion of a film production agreement, it was left to the discretion of Member States whether to make a similar provision in the case of authors. After consultation, the United Kingdom chose to exercise this option by introducing provisions which mirror those which apply to performers.[87]

Section 93A thus provides that where an agreement concerning film produc-

---

[79] Copyright Act 1956, s.36(2)(b).

[80] See the Copyright Act 1956, ss.31 and 1(2). As to the extension of the Copyright Acts to other countries generally, see paras 3–230 *et seq.*, above.

[81] Copyright Act 1911, s.5(2).

[82] *British Actors Film Co Ltd v Glover* [1918] 1 K.B. 299.

[83] The argument was whether, because of its other provisions, the grant took effect as a licence only. It was not argued that an assignment limited to a particular area was not possible at all. See p.305.

[84] See, for example, *Copinger* (8th ed.), p.109.

[85] See *Copinger* (4th ed.), p.146 and *Jefferys (C.) v Boosey (T.)* (1855) 4 H.L.C. 815 at 993 (copyright conferred on every part of British Dominions not divisible; assignment limited to United Kingdom or smaller regions therefore void); *Taylor v Neville* (1878) L.J. Q.B. 254 (no legal right to present a work "in London" can be assigned); *cf. Holt v Woods* (1896) 17 N.S.W.R. 36 (distinction drawn between right to reproduce a work—not divisible—and right to present performance of a work—divisible; right to perform a work in Australia therefore assignable).

[86] Directive 92/100.

[87] See CDPA 1988, s.191F and para. 12–48, below.

tion is concluded between an author and a film producer,[88] the author is to be presumed, unless the agreement provides to the contrary, to have transferred to the film producer any rental right[89] in relation to the film arising by virtue of the inclusion of a copy of the author's work in the film.[90] For this purpose, "author" means an author, or prospective author, of a literary, dramatic, musical or artistic work.[91] The section therefore does not apply to an agreement between a film producer and the principal director of the film, even though the principal director is now to be taken as one of the authors of a film.[92] Nor does it apply, for example, to an agreement between the film producer and the "author" of any sound recording used in the film.

The presumption does not apply to any rental right in relation to the film arising by virtue of the inclusion in the film of a screenplay, dialogue or music specifically created for and used in the film.[93] This will exclude the operation of the section in the case of many of the works in relation to which a film production agreement is usually concluded. Often of course, such an agreement will be concluded in relation to a work, such as a novel or a piece of music, which already exists and was not written specifically for the film. In the case of such works, and works created specifically for and used in the film other than the screenplay, dialogue or music, the question is then whether the agreement "concerns" film production. This expression is vague[94] but clearly is intended to refer to an agreement between an author and film producer relating to the use of the author's work in a particular film.

The section therefore appears to provide an exception to the general rule relating to assignments, namely that an assignment of copyright must be in writing and signed by or on behalf of the copyright owner. Thus, it seems that any agreement, whether written or oral, and if written, whether or not signed, will be sufficient to bring the section into play and effect a transfer of the rental right by virtue of the presumption of an effective transfer. Some doubt is thrown on this conclusion, however, by the wording of subs.(4), which provides that where s.93A applies, the absence of signature by or on behalf of the author does not exclude the operation of the s.91(1). This latter section provides that an agreement by which "future copyright" is purported to be assigned will be effective to vest the legal title in the assignee if the agreement is signed by or on behalf of the prospective owner.[95] In relation to a work which is not yet in existence, s.93A(4) therefore makes it clear that the presumption of a transfer will apply even in the absence of a signed agreement. It might be thought to follow from this specific provision and the omission of any corresponding provision in relation to existing works that the absence of signature from an agreement relating to existing works was fatal to the operation of s.93A. There seems no logical justification for such a conclusion: indeed it seems likely that these provisions of the Directive were intended to apply to oral agreements as well as written ones in all cases.[96] If an *effective* transfer is to be presumed then, the presumption must be that the transfer

---

[88] A film "producer" means the person by whom the arrangements necessary for the making of the film are undertaken. CDPA 1988, s.178.

[89] "Rental right" means the exclusive right of a copyright owner to authorise or prohibit the rental of copies of the work. See CDPA 1988, s.178, and para. 7–81 *et seq.*, below.

[90] CDPA 1988, s.93A(1).

[91] s.93A(2).

[92] See s.9(2)(ab) and para. 4–58, above. As an author, however, he will potentially be able to bargain for a share in any profits made from rental of the film.

[93] s.93A(3).

[94] The wording is taken from Art.2.5 of the Rental Directive.

[95] For a full discussion of the section, see para. 5–105 *et seq.*, below.

[96] See, *e.g.* Reinbothe & von Lewinski, *The EC Directive on Rental and Lending Rights and on Piracy* (Sweet & Maxwell, London, 1993), p.57.

was made by means sufficient to vest the legal title in the film producer, *i.e.* by an assignment in writing signed by or behalf of the copyright owner. Probably the wording of s.93A(4) was inserted out of unnecessary caution.

Although the section refers to a "presumption" (the word used in the Directive), the presumption is rebuttable if the agreement provides to the contrary. The use of the concept of a presumption was imported from the Directive, but the section appears to be similar in effect, if not in wording, to the employment provision in s.11(2) of the 1988 Act, which provides that where a work is made by an employee in the course of his employment, his employer is the first owner of the copyright subject to any agreement to the contrary. The new section does not say whether the agreement to the contrary must be express or can be implied but it is suggested that an implied agreement to the contrary will be enough.[97] In practice of course, such agreements will usually contain express provision dealing with the rights granted to the film producer.

5–104   The Act further provides that the reference in the section to an agreement concluded between an author and a producer includes any agreement having effect between those persons, whether made by them directly or through intermediaries.[98] It is not clear what the purpose or result of these words is, since if the agreement has "effect" between the parties, whether concluded directly or through "intermediaries" (*i.e.* presumably, agents), it will amount in law to an agreement "concluded" between them. The Directive requires, in the similar provision relating to performers,[99] that the presumption is to apply where the agreement is concluded "individually or collectively" between the parties, the latter presumably referring to the possibility of some kind of collective bargaining,[1] and this may be the reason for the wording in the Act.[2]

Section 93A applies to an agreement whenever made[3] although in relation to an agreement concluded before December 1, 1996 there is no exclusion of the presumption in relation to screenplay, dialogue or music specifically created for the film under s.93A(3).[4]

(iv) Assignments of "future" copyright and future rights

(a) *"Future" copyright works*

5–105   Where parties enter into arrangements concerning a work to be made in the future, it is often highly convenient if the vesting of the legal title can be dealt with at the

---

[97] Compare, for example, the operation of s.11(2), where an implied agreement to the contrary is sufficient to oust the employer/employee provisions of the section (see *Noah v Shuba* [1991] F.S.R. 14) and of the Copyright Act 1842, where an implied agreement was held sufficient for the purposes of s.18: see *Lawrence, etc., Ltd v Aflalo* [1904] A.C. 17, following *Sweet v Benning* (1855) 16 C.B. 459. To the same effect is *Lamb v Evans* [1893] 1 Ch. 218 and *Chantrey, etc., Co v Dey (T.H.)* (1912) 28 T.L.R. 499. See generally, para. 5–31, above. Note that Art.2.5 of the Rental Directive speaks in terms of "contractual *clauses* to the contrary", but it is not thought this terminology was intended to exclude the operation of any implied term. See, *e.g.* Reinbothe & von Lewinski, *The EC Directive on Rental and Lending Rights and on Piracy* (Sweet & Maxwell, 1993), p.58.

[98] CDPA 1988, s.93(A)(5).

[99] Directive (92/100), Art.2.5. And see also CDPA 1988, s.191F.

[1] See, *e.g.* Reinbothe & von Lewinski, *The EC Directive on Rental and Lending Rights and on Piracy* (Sweet & Maxwell, 1993), p.58.

[2] *cf.*The more usual form in, *e.g.* s.90, that an assignment be signed "by or on behalf of" the assignor.

[3] See the Copyright and Related Rights Regulations 1996 (SI 1996/2967), reg.32(1). It appears that reg.27(1), which provides that, except as otherwise expressly provided, nothing in the Regulations is to affect an agreement made before November 19, 1992, is overridden by reg.32(1).

[4] Copyright and Related Rights Regulations 1996 (SI 1996/2967), reg.32(1).

time, rather than having to deal with this by a separate assignment once the work has been created. This may, for example, happen where a work is being commissioned or where an author is regularly creating copyright works and he has entered into an agreement for their exploitation or control by a publisher or a collecting society. Statute apart, however, the general law is that a work must be in existence before its ownership can be assigned at law.[5] An assignment of an expectancy, if made for consideration, will only be treated as a contract to assign. If, on creation of the subject matter, the legal ownership duly vests in the assignor, the beneficial interest and thus equitable ownership will be all that vests in the assignee.[6] Under the general law, therefore, an assignment of the copyright in all works then or thereafter belonging to the assignor would amount to a valid assignment of the legal title in respect of all copyrights vested in the assignor at the date of the assignment and an agreement to assign future and after-acquired copyrights. As seen below, however, this general rule was expressly altered by the 1956 Act, enabling parties to enter into an agreement which will effect the vesting of the legal title in the assignee as soon as a future work is created.

Transitional. The 1988 Act applies to all relevant agreements made after June 1, 1957 but not to any assignment or agreement made before that date.[7] The normal rule therefore applies to these earlier assignments: the legal title cannot have been passed in this way.   **5–106**

Transfer of future copyright: the 1988 Act. Subsection 91(1) of the 1988 Act provides that: **5–107**

> "Where by an agreement made in relation to future copyright, and signed by or on behalf of the prospective owner of the copyright, the prospective owner purports to assign the future copyright (wholly or partially) to another person, then if, on the copyright coming into existence, the assignee or another person claiming under him would be entitled as against all other persons to require the copyright to be vested in him, the copyright shall vest in the assignee or his successor in title by virtue of this subsection."[8]

A number of points arise under this provision: **5–107A**

(a) "Future copyright" is defined as copyright which will or may come into existence in respect of any future work or class of works or on the occurrence of a future event.[9] "Prospective owner" is to be construed accordingly and includes a person who is prospectively entitled to copyright by virtue of such an agreement as is mentioned in the provision.[10]

(b) Assignments of future copyright can only be made by written agreement. Purported assignments which fall outside this description will at best operate as equitable assignments.[11]

(c) Unlike an assignment of existing copyright, which does not require consideration or an "agreement", it seems that a specifically enforceable agreement is necessary under the section. This follows not only from the

---

[5] *Sweet v Shaw* (1839) 8 L.J. Ch. 216; *Colburn v Duncombe* (1838) 9 Sim. 151.

[6] *Performing Right Society Ltd v London Theatre of Varieties Ltd* [1924] A.C. 1; *Wah Sang Industrial Co v Tackmay Industrial Co Ltd* [1980] F.S.R. 303 at 309.

[7] CDPA 1988, Sch.1, para.26(1). The provisions of s.37 of the 1956 Act were substantially to the same effect, and altered the existing law, hence the transitional date.

[8] See Vol.2 at J1.ii for a precedent of an assignment of future copyright.

[9] CDPA 1988, s.91(2). As to the reference to the occurrence of a future event, a work may be in existence but not yet entitled to copyright because none of the qualifying conditions for subsistence has yet been satisfied.

[10] s.91(2).

[11] See para. 5–171, below.

use of the word "agreement", in contrast to "writing" in the case of an assignment of existing copyright,[12] but also from the fact that the title will only vest if the assignee is entitled, as against all other persons, and thus including the assignor, to require the title to be vested in him by the assignor.[13] An assignment of future copyright must therefore not only be in writing but also be supported by sufficient consideration. An assignment by way of deed only will not suffice.

(d) It might be thought to follow that if, when the work comes into existence, the assignee has lost the right to specific performance of the agreement, for example, because he has failed to honour relevant obligations of the agreement on his side, no automatic vesting under s.91(1) will take place. However, in *Peer International Corp v Editora Musical de Cuba*,[14] it was held that an assignment of future copyright was good to transfer the equitable title despite the fact that the contract had by virtue of a foreign decree been abrogated before the copyright came into existence.[15]

(e) The expression "entitled as against all other persons" apparently refers to the rules of priority which would have applied apart from the Act if the assignee had been claiming specific performance of the agreement to assign the copyright to him. So, for example, where the prospective owner purports to assign the future copyright to two persons by separate assignments, the first in time will become the owner unless he has so acted to cause his equity to be postponed.

(f) The section is not limited to cases where the prospective owner is the author of the work. Thus, an employer may make an effective assignment of the copyright in a work to be made by his employee.[16]

(g) It also follows from the definition of "prospective owner" that an effective assignment may be made not only by the prospective first owner, but also by the prospective assignee of the future copyright from him, and so on.

(h) Since the legal title vests in the assignee the moment the work is created, the subsequent avoidance of the agreement, for example on the grounds that the assignor was an infant, will not operate to revest the title in the assignor.[17]

5–108 **Assignments made under the 1956 Act.** As already noted, assignments of future copyright made under the 1956 Act are now governed by the 1988 Act. In fact, the 1956 Act, although worded slightly differently, was, apart from one provision, to the same effect.[18] The only difference is that the 1956 Act expressly dealt with the case where the person who would have been entitled to the copyright died before the copyright came into existence, the Act providing that the copy-

[12] See CDPA 1988, s.90(3).
[13] The drafting of the section seems clearly to have started from the position which existed before the passing of the 1956 Act, under which an assignee of future copyright could at most acquire an equitable title. The section also appears to be somewhat tautologous in that if the section operates at all, the title will automatically vest and so there will be no one against whom the assignee can assert the right to require vesting of the copyright. Presumably the words "apart from the operation of this section" should be read into subs. (1) after the words "would be entitled".
[14] [2002] EWHC 2675 (Ch), [2004] R.P.C. 22 (not affected on this point by the decision on appeal [2003] EWCA Civ 1156. [2004] Ch. 212, CA.
[15] This decision was reached relying on *Re Lind, Industrials Finance Syndicate Ltd v Lind* [1915] 2 Ch. 345 (not following *Collyer v Isaacs* (1881) 19 Ch.D. 342), for the general principle that such an assignment creates an equitable charge arising immediately upon the property coming into existence, and thus is an independent and higher right than the contractual right to an assignment.
[16] As to works of employees, see paras 5–08 et seq., above.
[17] *Chaplin v Leslie Frewin (Publishers) Ltd* [1966] Ch. 71. The assignor may of course be able to establish grounds, for example, undue influence, for an order that the copyright be revested in him.
[18] Copyright Act 1956, s.37.

right was then to devolve as if it had subsisted immediately before his death and he had then been the owner of the copyright.[19] The effect of this provision has been preserved.[20]

Pre-1956 Act assignments. As already noted, the provisions of the 1988 Act re-   **5–109**
lating to assignments of future copyright do not apply to agreements made before June 1, 1957. As to these, the provisions of the earlier Acts relating to assign-ments[21] had no application to a document purporting to assign the copyright in a future copyright work, since there was no owner in existence who could execute an assignment.[22] The legal title therefore vested in the author or other first owner when the work came into existence, although a purported assignment might be enforced as an equitable assignment.[23]

(b) *Assignments of future rights*

Although a copyright work may exist at the date of the assignment, new or   **5–110**
extended rights may subsequently be brought into existence by statute in relation to that work. Recent examples are the rental right,[24] the extended rights in respect of the extended and revived term of copyright,[25] the extended rights in sound recordings,[26] and the newly formulated communication to the public right.[27] The effect of a pre-existing grant on these rights will depend in the first instance on any transitional provisions. For example, in the case of rights to the extended and revived terms of copyright which came into being as a result of the increase in the term of copyright from life and 50 years to life and 70 years, and to the extended rights in sound recordings, express provision is made.[28] As to the example of the rental right as a new right, it is clear that the right subsists in rela-tion to works made before the coming into force of the amending Regulations.[29] The same is true in relation to the communication to the public right.[30] Since there are no other relevant transitional provisions, it therefore appears to follow that a pre-amendment assignment of the "copyright" will carry with it the rental right and the communication to the public right in the absence of any contrary intention in the assignment: it is part of the "copyright" in the work. This can be more clearly seen in relation, for example, to the exclusive right to issue copies

---

[19] s.37(2).

[20] Thus, although this provision has been repealed, its repeal does not affect its operation in relation to an agreement made before commencement of the 1988 Act on August 1, 1989. See CDPA 1988, Sch.1, para.26(2).

[21] For example, the Copyright Act 1911, s.5(2), (3).

[22] *Performing Right Society Ltd v London Theatre of Varieties Ltd* [1924] A.C. 1. The position was the same before the 1911 Act. See *Colburn v Duncombe* (1838) 9 Sim. 151; *Sweet v Shaw* (1839) 3 Jur. 217. The decision in *Ward, Lock & Co Ltd v Long* [1906] 2 Ch. 550, might suggest the con-trary, Kekewich J. holding that, in the context of a publishing agreement, "an agreement to assign in matters of this kind is quite as good as a direct assignment in words, is enforceable in equity, and as between businessmen is complete", with the consequence that an equitable title prevailed over that of a later assignee of the legal title. It is suggested that as a matter of principle the deci-sion was wrong.

[23] As to equitable ownership generally, see para. 5–170, below.

[24] *i.e.* the right of a copyright owner to authorise or prohibit the rental of copies of the work. See para. 7–81, below.

[25] See para. 6–11 *et seq.*, below.

[26] See para. 6–55 *et seq.*, below.

[27] See para. 7–98 *et seq.*, below.

[28] See paras 5–133 *et seq.* and 5–142 *et seq.*, below, respectively, where it is explained that the po-sition is the same in relation to the increased term of copyright introduced by the Copyright Act 1911.

[29] See the Copyright and Related Rights Regulations 1996 (SI 1996/2967), reg.26(1), and para. 7–88, below.

[30] The Copyright and Related Rights Regulations 2003 (SI 2003/2498), reg.31(1).

of the work to the public,[31] a right which was first introduced in its present form by the 1988 Act.[32] Again, this right clearly exists in relation to works which were made before the commencement of the 1988 Act.[33] The effect of the transitional provisions in the Act is that any assignment of the "copyright" made before commencement will, subject to any term in the assignment to the contrary effect, carry the copyright as conferred by the 1988 Act,[34] and thus the complete bundle of rights included within the copyright, including the exclusive right to issue copies of a work to the public. The general effect of the 1956 Act seems to have been the same, for example in relation to the exclusive right to broadcast a work which the Act introduced.[35] An example to the opposite effect was the new mechanical right introduced by s.19 of the 1911 Act. Under the previous law, the owner of the copyright in a musical work did not enjoy the exclusive right to make copies of it in the form of sound recordings, or "mechanical contrivances".[36] This position was changed by the 1911 Act[37] but at the same time it was provided that an assignment of the copyright in a musical work made before commencement should not carry the new mechanical right, which was instead to belong to the author or his personal representatives.[38]

Although, therefore, as a matter of general law a present assignment of future rights cannot operate to transfer the legal title to such rights and will only operate as an agreement to assign,[39] this rule may be altered by transitional provisions. Certainly, the use of such expressions in an assignment as "the whole of the property, copyright and interest, present or future, vested or contingent" will often be wide enough to show an intention to assign such future rights.[40]

(v) Limitations on the right to assign

(a) *Right to equitable remuneration where rental right transferred*

5–111 Substantial amendments were made to the 1988 Act to implement the EC Directive on rental and lending rights,[41] one effect of which was to confer on an owner of copyright a comprehensive right to control the rental and lending of copies of the copyright work. At the same time, there was created in favour of an author of a literary, dramatic, musical or artistic work, and the principal director of a film, a right to receive equitable remuneration for such rental where the rental right concerning a sound recording or film had been transferred to the producer of the sound recording or film.[42] This right ("the equitable remuneration right") is not strictly a right of copyright and is considered further elsewhere,[43] but it should be noted here that the Act places restrictions on the ability of the author to assign

---

[31] See CDPA 1988, s.18, paras 7–76 *et seq.*, below.
[32] Under the 1956 Act, an exclusive right of first publication existed, which was rather different in its effect. See the footnotes to para. 7–76, below.
[33] CDPA 1988, Sch.1, para.3.
[34] Sch.1, para.25(1).
[35] See the Copyright Act 1956, s.2(5)(d) and Sch.7, para.28(1).
[36] *Boosey v Whight* [1900] 1 Ch. 122.
[37] Copyright Act 1911, s.1(2)(d).
[38] s.19(7)(c).
[39] See, *e.g.* para. 5–105, above.
[40] See *Redwood Music Ltd v B. Feldman & Co Ltd* [1978] R.P.C. 429 at 444; [1979] R.P.C. 385, CA at 394.
[41] Council Directive 92/100 as implemented by the Copyright and Related Rights Regulations 1996 (SI 1996/2967).
[42] A similar right was created in favour of performers. See CDPA 1988, s.191G and para. 12–48, below.
[43] See para. 7–89, below.

such right, hence the use of the expression "the unwaivable right to remuneration."[44]

Thus, s.93B of the Act now provides that the equitable remuneration right may not be assigned by the author except to a collecting society for the purpose of enabling the society to enforce the right on his behalf.[45] Although the right cannot be assigned by the author, it is however transmissible by testamentary disposition or by operation of law as personal or moveable property.[46] Any person into whose hands the right passes on such a transmission may himself assign or transmit it.[47] No formalities are prescribed,[48] but presumably such an assignment can be effected in law by a transfer complying with s.146 of the Law of Property Act 1925, and in equity by a more informal assignment.[49]

(b) Reversionary rights under the 1911 Act

The 1911 Act contained a limitation on the power of an author to part with his interest in his copyright for longer than 25 years after his death, making any attempt to do so by him ineffective. The object of this limitation was to protect authors and their heirs from the consequences of the imprudent disposition of the fruits of their special talent and, originality,[50] but for the reasons which are discussed below, the benefits conferred by this limitation were largely illusory. Following a recommendation of the Gregory Committee in 1952,[51] the provision was repealed by the 1956 Act but its effect was continued in respect of assignments entered into before the Act's commencement. This state of affairs has been continued by the 1988 Act, with some further amendments and clarification. This limitation, therefore, still has important implications for agreements entered into before June 1, 1957 and can be something of a trap.

5–112

As the limitation now stands,[52] its effect is that where the author of literary, dramatic, musical or artistic work was the first owner of the copyright in it, no assignment of the copyright or grant of any interest in it by him (otherwise than by will) made after the passing of the 1911 Act[53] and before June 1, 1957 is to be operative to vest in the assignee or grantee any rights with respect to the copyright in the work beyond the expiration of 25 years from the death of the author.[54] This means that, unless some further assignment has been made since June 1, 1957 (see below), any such assignment or grant will only have operated until the end of this 25-year period.

---

[44] See Art.4 of Directive 92/100.

[45] CDPA 1988, s.93B(2). For this purpose, a collecting society means a society or other organisation which has as its main object, or one of its main objects, the exercise of the equitable remuneration right on behalf of more than one author. See s.93B(7).

[46] s.93B(2).

[47] s.93B(2).

[48] cf. the formalities prescribed for an assignment of copyright by s.90(3).

[49] See Snell, *Principles of Equity* (30th ed., Sweet & Maxwell), para.5–12 *et seq.*

[50] *Redwood Music Ltd v B. Feldman & Co Ltd & Others* [1979] R.P.C. 385 at 402; *Chappell & Co Ltd v Redwood Music Ltd* [1981] R.P.C. 337.

[51] Cmnd. 8662. In fact the reasons for the repeal were other than the illusory nature of the benefit. See further, below, para. 5–120, below.

[52] As now set out in CDPA 1988, Sch.1, para.27, which governs the position today: *Novello & Co Ltd v Keith Prowse Music Publishing Co Ltd* [2004] EWHC (Ch) 766, para.7. The provision was originally contained in the proviso to s.5(2) of the 1911 Act and its effect was continued by the 1956 Act, Sch.8, para.6 and Sch.7, para.28.

[53] *i.e.* on December 16, 1911.

[54] CDPA 1988, Sch.1, para.27(1). Given the fact that para.25 of Sch.1 preserves the effect of pre-1988 Act assignments (see para. 5–81, above), para.27 may have been unnecessary, but it follows the pattern of the 1956 Act and may in any event have been necessary to preserve the statutory vesting of the reversionary interest in the author's personal representatives (see para. 5–113A, below): *Novello & Co Ltd v Keith Prowse Music Publishing Co Ltd*, above, para.11.

5–113   **"Grant of any interest".** It is unclear what these words mean in this context. Their use derives from the original provisions of the 1911 Act which provided, first, that the owner of the copyright in a work might assign the right, either wholly or partially, and might grant "any interest in the right by licence", but that no such assignment or grant should be valid unless it was in writing and signed by the owner or his agent.[55] The words of the reverter proviso then went on to apply in the case of any "assignment" or "grant of any interest" in the copyright by the author/first owner. It was clear that a mere consent, even oral or implied from conduct, although always a defence to a claim for infringement,[56] did not amount to the grant of an interest in the copyright such that, for example, the person with the benefit of the consent could sue a third-party infringer.[57] It seems, therefore, that a distinction was being drawn between such consents and some other, more formal licences in writing by which a proprietary interest in the copyright was granted coupled with a licence to exercise it.[58] What might have amounted to such a grant has always been unclear,[59] but it is suggested the section was intended to apply to a grant which, although it could have been the subject of an assignment, was in fact by way of exclusive licence.[60]

5–113A   **Further Points.** The following further points should be noted:

(a) A first assignment of copyright or grant of an interest in respect of pre-1956 Act works made by the author on or after June 1, 1957 are unaffected by the limitation. The assignee or grantee takes freely under the terms of the instrument. The position of an author who on or after June 1, 1957 deals with the reversionary interest in a work which was the subject of pre-June 1, 1957 assignment or grant by him is considered below.[61]

(aa) As the law stood under the 1911 Act, an author could not assign the legal title to the copyright in a "future" work of his, such an assignment at best operating as an agreement to assign, creating an equitable interest in the assignee.[62] To the extent that an author purportedly assigned or granted an interest in the last 25 years of the term of copyright in a future work of his, including a work made on or after June 1, 1957, it will have been inoperative to do so.[63]

(b) As a general rule, the reversionary interest in the copyright expectant on the determination of the 25-year period will, on the death of the author, devolve on his legal personal representatives as part of his estate.[64] If, however, the author executes a further assignment on or after June 1,

---

[55] Copyright Act 1911, s.5(2).

[56] See the 1911 Act, s.2(1) and para. 5–194, below.

[57] See para. 5–194, below.

[58] See *British Actors Film Co Ltd v Glover* [1918] 1 K.B. 299 at 307, 308.

[59] In cases where the question might have arisen, the agreement was construed as an assignment and not a licence, and so did not have to be answered. See *British Actors Film Co Ltd v Glover* [1918] 1 K.B. 299; *Jonathan Cape Ltd v Consolidated Press Ltd* [1954] 1 W.L.R. 1313. But see *Kinekor Film (Pty) Ltd v Movie Time* [1976] (1) S.A. 649.

[60] See *Copinger* (8th ed.), p.115. Note that today, an exclusive licence in writing from the copyright owner confers procedural but not proprietary rights on the licensee. See paras 5–203 *et seq.*, below. See further, as to the 1911 Act and exclusive licences, para. 5–208, below.

[61] As to assignments made before the passing of the 1911 Act, see further, para. 5–116, below.

[62] Such an agreement, or any purported assignment, could not in any event have been effective at that time to transfer the legal title to the promisee. See para. 5–105, above.

[63] This was made clear by the wording of the proviso to s.5(2) of the 1911 Act, which provided that any agreement entered into by the author as to the disposition of the reversionary interest was to be null and void. See *Novello & Co Ltd v Keith Prowse Music Publishing Co Ltd* [2004] EWHC 766 (Ch), para.21.

[64] CDPA 1988, Sch.1, para.27(2), thus effecting a statutory revesting of the reversionary period without the need for any re-assignment. See *Novello & Co Ltd v Keith Prowse Music Publishing Co Ltd* [2004] EWHC 766 (Ch), para.10.

1957 which includes the reversionary interest, this will now take full effect. This is made clear by express statutory provision in the case of assignments made on or after August 1, 1989,[65] and has been established also to be the position in the case of an assignment made between June 1, 1957 and August 1, 1989.[66] An author who had purported to assign away the copyright in his work for the full term before June 1, 1957 may therefore at any time since then freely dispose of his reversionary interest.

(c) Nothing in these provisions affects three kinds of assignment relating to reversionary interests, namely[67]:

   (i) An assignment of the reversionary interest by a person to whom it has been assigned. A person to whom the reversion had been assigned by the personal representatives (see next paragraph) might therefore have himself assigned it at any time, as may a person to whom the author, after June 1, 1957 has assigned the reversion (see previous paragraph).

   (ii) An assignment of the reversionary interest after the death of the author by his personal representatives or any person becoming entitled to it. Any such assignment by the personal representatives is therefore valid, even made while the 1911 Act was in force.[68] There is therefore no requirement that the personal representatives must wait until the reversion falls in. The purpose of the Act was only to prevent a disposal by the author.[69]

   (iii) Any assignment of the copyright after the reversionary interest has fallen in.

(d) Nothing in the provision is to be construed as applying to the assignment of the copyright in a collective work, or to a licence to publish a work or part of a work as part of a collective work.[70]

(e) The limitation applied to partial assignments of copyright just as it did to assignments of the whole copyright in a work.[71]

(f) The reverter provision applies not only to an assignment of the copyright, but also to the "grant of any interest in [the copyright]", such as, for example, the grant of an exclusive licence extending into the period starting 25 years after the death of the author.[72]

(g) The reverter only applies in cases where the author was the first owner of the copyright. The author may not have been the first owner where the work was made by him in the course of his employment or where the

---

[65] CDPA 1988, Sch.1, para.27(2).

[66] *Novello & Co Ltd v Keith Prowse Music Publishing Co Ltd* [2004] EWHC 766 (Ch). The Whitford Committee thought that whether an author could assign the reversion after the commencement of the 1956 Act was not free from doubt and recommended that, to the extent it was not already clear, it ought to be provided that an author might be able to do so at any time. See Cmnd. 6732, paras 620, 622. The draftsman of the 1988 Act presumably also thought that the position was unsettled but took the view that any doubt should be resolved by the courts rather than risk altering established rights by statute. This is probably why the 1988 Act only makes express provision for the position after the commencement of that Act. See *Novello & Co Ltd v Keith Prowse Music Publishing Co Ltd* [2004] EWHC 766 (Ch), para.13.

[67] CDPA 1988, Sch.1, para.27(3). These provisions were not contained in the 1911 or 1956 Acts but their inclusion in the 1988 Act did not, it is thought, change the existing position. They were inserted for clarification. See the Whitford Committee Report, Cmnd. 6732, paras 620, 622.

[68] *Chappell & Co Ltd v Redwood Music Ltd* [1981] R.P.C. 337 at 347.

[69] As to the consequence of this in practice, see para. 5–119, below.

[70] CDPA 1988, Sch.1, para.27(4). See, further, para. 5–114, below.

[71] *Redwood Music Ltd v Francis Day & Hunter Ltd* [1978] R.P.C. 429 at 449.

[72] See, for example, the reference in subpara.(4) to a licence to publish a work as part of a collective work. See para. 5–113 , above, as to the meaning of "grant of any interest".

work was a commissioned engraving, photograph or portrait.[73] The first owner of the copyright in such cases was at liberty to assign it for the full term.

5–114   **Reverter does not apply to collective works.** The reverter does not apply "to the assignment of the copyright in a collective work or a licence to publish a work or part of a work as part of a collective work."[74] A collective work means: (a) an encyclopaedia, dictionary, year book, or similar work; (b) a newspaper, review, magazine, or similar periodical; and (c) any work written in distinct parts by different authors, or in which works or parts of works of different authors are incorporated.[75] In a collective work, there may be several distinct copyrights, namely, the copyright in the complete work, considered as a whole, in addition to the various copyrights in the distinct contributions to the work. Thus, an anthology enjoys a copyright of its own, as a compilation arising out of the original literary effort and judgment involved in the selection and arrangement of the subject-matter of the compilation. The copyright in the compilation is additional to, and independent of, and different from whatever copyright or copyrights may subsist in the component parts of the compilation. On the other hand, in the case, for example, of a song, there is no copyright in it as an entity: the words and the music each attract separate copyrights. A disposition of the copyright in a compilation, as distinct from the disposition of the copyright in the separate parts, is excepted from the application of the reverter provision.[76] An "assignment" of the copyright in a compilation, if a collective work, could therefore have been made for the full period of copyright, as could a licence to publish a contribution as part of the collective work. But assignments of the copyright in the contributions themselves could not have been made for the full period. The expression "the copyright in a collective work" refers only to that "compilation copyright" which exists, if at all, in addition to and apart from any separate copyright which may exist in the constituent parts of the collective work: it does not refer to the copyright in the separate constituent parts. Thus, in the case of a song, assignments of the distinct copyrights in the words and music written by different persons will not have been effective beyond the expiration of 25 years after the death of the respective authors. There is no independent copyright attributable to a song as a compilation and, therefore, nothing to fall within the exception to the proviso. What purports, however, to be an assignment of copyright in a work for use only as part of a collective work may amount to no more than a licence for that purpose and fall within the second half of the exception.[77]

5–115   **Works of joint authorship.** Although the reverter provision does not apply to collective works it does apply to works of joint authorship.[78] The 1911 Act provided that "references in this Act to the period after the expiration of any specified number of years from the death of the author shall be construed as references to the period after the expiration of the like number of years from the death of the author who dies first or after the death of the author who dies last, which-

---

[73] Copyright Act 1911, s.5(1)(a) and (b). See paras 5–09 and 5–35, above, respectively.
[74] CDPA 1988, Sch.1, para.27(4).
[75] *ibid.* Sch.1, para.27(5). The wording repeats that of the 1911 Act, s.5(2), proviso, hence the particular language.
[76] *Chappell & Co Ltd v Redwood Music Ltd* [1981] R.P.C. 337; *Redwood Music Ltd v B. Feldman & Co Ltd* [1979] R.P.C. 385; *Redwood Music Ltd v Chappell & Co Ltd* [1982] R.P.C. 109.
[77] *Chappell & Co Ltd v Redwood Music Ltd* [1981] R.P.C. 337; *Redwood Music Ltd v B. Feldman & Co Ltd* [1979] R.P.C. 385; *Redwood Music Ltd v Chappell & Co Ltd* [1982] R.P.C. 109.
[78] *Redwood Music Ltd v B. Feldman & Co Ltd* [1979] R.P.C. 1, and [1979] R.P.C. 385 at 406.

ever period may be the shorter."[79] The effect of this would appear to be that, where the reversion takes place, it takes place in respect of the shares of both joint authors at the same time. The date of reversion is ascertained by substituting, for the period after the expiration of 25 years from the death of the author referred to in the reverter provision, either the period after the expiration of 25 years from the death of the author who dies first, or the period after the death of the author who dies last, whichever period is the shorter. The operation of the provision in the case of published joint works is illustrated in the following two examples in which A and B are joint authors of the relevant work:

(a) A dies first. B dies five years later. The period of copyright remaining after B's death was 45 years (now 65 years), whereas the period remaining after the expiration of 25 years from the death of A will be only 25 (now 45) years and will therefore be the shorter period. Reversion will therefore take place 25 years after the death of A.

(b) A dies first. B does not die until 30 years later. In this case, the shorter remaining period of copyright is the period of 20 years (now 40) after the death of B. Reversion will therefore take place on the death of B.

It follows from these examples that it is impossible to know at the time of A's death when the reversion will occur, or, indeed, if it will occur at all. This can only be known on the death of B, the author who dies last.

The 1988 Act provides that any document made before August 1, 1989 which had any operation affecting the ownership of the copyright in an existing work or creating, transferring or terminating any interest, right or licence in respect of the copyright in an existing work, has the corresponding operation in relation to copyright in the work under the 1988 Act.[80] The position was the same under the 1956 Act.[81] Thus an assignment of a share in the copyright in a work of joint authorship to which the reverter provision applied, operates, in relation to the copyright subsisting under the 1988 Act, as it would have done in relation to the copyright subsisting under the 1911 Act.[82] The position under the 1956 Act was the same. It would also appear that, where an assignment was made in respect of a work of joint authorship before 1956, and the copyright was still subsisting at the commencement of the 1956 Act, then the work enjoyed the extended term, ascertained by reference to the author who died last.

Reverter applies to pre-1911 Act works, but not to pre-1911 Act assignments. **5–116**
The references in the reverter provision contained in the 1911 Act to "the copyright" referred to the copyright as conferred by the 1911 Act and not the rights which existed previously.[83] An assignment or grant made before the commencement of the 1911 Act which dealt with the copyright in an existing work was therefore unaffected by the reverter provision.[84] This is clearly so in the case of assignments made before the passing of the Act but even in the case of assignments made between the passing and commencement of the Act, the express reference in the reverter provision to an assignment made "after the passing" of the Act did not affect assignments made in this period of the pre-1911 Act rights. It concerned only assignments of the future copyright in works which might come

---

[79] Copyright Act 1911, s.16(1).
[80] CDPA 1988, Sch.1, para.25(1).See also *Novello & Co Ltd v Keith Prowse Music Publishing Co Ltd* [2004] EWHC 766 (Ch).
[81] Copyright Act 1956, Sch.7, para.25(1).
[82] *Redwood Music Ltd v B. Feldman & Co Ltd* [1979] R.P.C. 1, and [1979] R.P.C. 385 at 406.
[83] *Coleridge-Taylor v Novello & Co Ltd* [1938] Ch. 850.
[84] Such assignments were, however, governed by the provisions of s.24 of the 1911 Act. See paras 5–148 *et seq.*, below.

into existence after the commencement of the Act.[85] On the other hand, the provision applies to assignments made by an author after commencement in respect of pre-commencement works, since the subject matter of the assignment will necessarily have been the new copyright which was conferred by the 1911 Act on such works.[86]

5–117   **Doubt as to photographs.** It is uncertain whether the reverter provision applies to photographs, the copyright in which was for a period of 50 years from the date of the making of the negative, and which first vested in the owner of the negative, who was "deemed" to be the author of the work.[87] It would seem that the draftsman of the reverter provision overlooked the fact that in the case of these works, the period of copyright protection bore no relation to the life of the author, and that the author might have been a company. Although, therefore, the words of the reverter provision are *prima facie* wide enough to cover photographs, it is suggested that it does not in fact apply to such works.[88] One reason for excluding photographs from the provision is that, as noted, a corporation could have been the "author" of such works and, in such a case, the reverter provision could have no possible application. Again, one reason for fixing the period of 25 years from the death of an author as the limit of the assignability of copyright was because, at that date, a work ceased to have exclusive copyright, and any person—including, of course, the assignee of the copyright, who then ceased to have the benefit of his assignment—could have reproduced the work for sale upon a royalty basis.[89] It is, however, doubtful whether a photograph could have been exploited upon this basis.[90] The assignee of the copyright in a photograph whose author died shortly after the making of the negative or plate would therefore be in a worse position as compared to an assignee of, say, literary copyright. Again, the provision refers to the interest of the author after the termination of the period of his assignment as "the reversionary interest in the copyright expectant on the termination of that period". If works for which the existence of any reversionary period was problematical (for the author of a photograph might live for 25 years after the making of the photograph) were intended to be included, it might have been expected that there would have been added, after the words "reversionary interest", the words "if any".

5–118   **Arrangements and adaptations.** After the copyright in the work had been assigned by the author-first owner, original arrangements or adaptations of the work may have been made by or with the licence of the assignee and given rise to fresh and independent copyrights in the arrangements or adaptations. These copyrights will vest in the person who made the arrangements or adaptations, or his employer, assignee, etc. At the end of the 25-year period they do not revert to the author of the original work from which the arrangements or adaptations were made because he was not the first owner of the copyright in them. All that reverts to him is the copyright in the underlying work of which he was the author and first owner. This is the case even with arrangements and adaptations which were

---

[85] *Coleridge-Taylor v Novello & Co Ltd* [1938] Ch. 850. Such an assignment could pass the equitable title but not the legal one.

[86] *Chappell & Co Ltd v Redwood Music Ltd* [1982] R.P.C. 109.

[87] Copyright Act 1911, ss.19 and 21.

[88] A similar doubt previously existed in relation to "mechanical contrivances", which were protected under the 1911 Act as musical works (see s.19 of the 1911 Act). Such 1911 Act works are now protected as sound recordings and are thus clearly outside the scope of the reverter provision, which applies only to literary, dramatic, musical and artistic works.

[89] 1911 Act, s.3, proviso. See *Copinger* (12th ed.), paras 296 *et seq.*

[90] See *Copinger* (12th ed.), para.303.

made without the licence of the author-first owner after the reversion has taken place.[91]

Illusory nature of the benefits conferred by the reverter. The reverter provi- **5–119** sion was inserted in the 1911 Act in the interest of an author's family, to prevent, if possible, a successful author from making improvident contracts for the fruits of his talent and originality to the detriment of his dependants.[92] The reversionary interest became an asset of the author's estate and assignable immediately upon his death by his personal representatives or by a beneficiary after assent.[93] It might therefore have been sold by his personal representatives for the payment of his debts and, even if not required for that purpose, it was frequently the duty of the executors to realise the interest for the purpose of winding up the author's estate.[94] Even where the author made a specific bequest of his reversionary interest in his copyright, the specific legatee would probably be ready to sell that interest at once, rather than wait for a chance of income 25 years later. The amount which a purchaser would be prepared to give for a reversionary interest in a copyright falling into possession 25 years later was not likely to have been very large, particularly bearing in mind that he would in any event be entitled to publish the work upon payment of a royalty and also that, if he did purchase, he could for the same reason not acquire an exclusive right.[95] It was also the fact that in the case of works originating in the United States of America, the descendants of a deceased author often executed assignments in favour of publishers with the primary purpose of transferring to the publishers the renewal rights in the works arising under American law at the expiration of 28 years from the date of first publication. Such agreements may, on their true construction according to the proper law of the agreements, have been effective to transfer to the publishers the reversionary copyright arising under English law.[96]

Recommendation of 1952 Copyright Committee. The Gregory Committee **5–120** recommended that this provision should not be continued on the ground that since it was recommending the omission of the right to publish works on compulsory royalty terms at the end of the 25-year period,[97] the reverter provision should also go, taking the view that it had been inserted so as to give the compulsory royalty to the personal representatives of the author.[98] These recommendations were carried into effect by the 1956 Act, together with transitional provisions which, together with clarifications and further amendment, are contained in the 1988 Act, as discussed above.

C. TRANSMISSION BY TESTAMENTARY DISPOSITION AND OPERATION OF LAW

As has been seen, the 1988 Act provides that copyright is transmissible by **5–121** testamentary disposition or by operation of law, as personal or moveable

---

[91] *Redwood Music Ltd v Chappell & Co Ltd* [1982] R.P.C. 109.

[92] *Redwood Music Ltd v B. Feldman & Co Ltd* [1979] R.P.C. 385 at 402; *Chappell & Co Ltd v Redwood Music Ltd* [1981] R.P.C. 337 at 344.

[93] *Chappell & Co Ltd v Redwood Music Ltd* [1981] R.P.C. 337 at 344.

[94] For instance, the rule well known to equity lawyers as the rule in *Howe v Lord Dartmouth* (1802) 7 Ves. 137 would apply. *cf. Pickering v Evans* [1921] 2 Ch. 309.

[95] Copyright Act 1911, s.3.

[96] Although there is no necessary implication that they do so when they are executed in the context of American renewal rights. See *Redwood Music Ltd v B. Feldman & Co Ltd* [1979] R.P.C. 385 at 403; *Chappell & Co Ltd v Redwood Music Ltd* [1981] R.P.C. 337 at 350.

[97] 1911 Act, s.3. see para. 5–156, below.

[98] Cmnd.8662, para.23.It is unclear from the Parliamentary debates at the time that this was in fact the case. See also para. 5–112, above, as to the objective of the reverter provision.

property.[99] On such a transmission, copyright may be divided up in the same way as it can be by a partial assignment.[1] Note that title to United Kingdom copyright, being property situate in the United Kingdom, cannot be taken away by foreign governmental decree or act. This is simply an application of the wider rule that English law will not enforce foreign laws which purport to have extra-territorial effect.[2]

(i) Death

5–122   On the death of an owner, his copyrights will devolve on his personal representative.[3] Subject to payment of debts and administration expenses, the copyrights will be held by the personal representative for the benefit of the person to whom the owner has bequeathed them or, if he died intestate, his next-of-kin.

5–123   **In whom vested on death.** Where a person dies testate and domiciled in England or Wales, having appointed an executor who survives him, his copyrights will vest on his death in his executor.[4] A subsequent grant of probate does not operate to vest the copyrights in him: they are already vested. The grant is merely the proof which an English court requires to establish his appointment.[5] On the other hand, where a person domiciled in England or Wales dies intestate, or dies testate but without having appointed an executor entitled to probate, or an executor who survives him,[6] his copyrights will vest by operation of law in the Public Trustee on death.[7] It is only on the grant of letters of administration that the copyrights will vest in the administrator,[8] whose title does not in general relate back to the date of death.[9]

The distinction between the two situations is crucial. Since an executor's title dates from the moment of death, he may start an infringement action without obtaining a grant. If his title is put in issue, he will merely have to obtain a grant by the date of the trial to prove it.[10] For the same reason, an executor has sufficient title to assign the copyright before obtaining a grant. On the other hand, if an infringement action is started by a prospective administrator before obtaining a grant, he will have had no title at the date of the issue of the writ and the action is likely to be irremediably bad.[11] The subsequent obtaining of the grant will not

[99] CDPA 1988, s.90(1). s.36(1) of the 1956 Act made the same provision. There was no express provision to this effect in the 1911 Act but it is thought it was to the same effect.
[1] CDPA 1988, s.90(2). As to such assignments, see paras 5–93 et seq., above.
[2] See Peer International Corp v Termidor Music Publishers Ltd [2003] EWCA Civ 1156, applying Bank voor Handel en Scheepvaart NV v Slatford [1953] 1 Q.B. 248 and holding Lorentzen v Lydden & Co Ltd [1942] 2 K.B. 202 to have been wrongly decided. In Peer, a decree of the communist government of Cuba made in 1960 had the purported effect of divesting owners of their copyright, but was held to be of no effect in relation to United Kingdom copyright.
[3] Williams, Mortimer and Sunnucks on Executors, Administrators and Probate (18th ed.), p.467 et seq.
[4] Williams, Mortimer and Sunnucks on Executors, Administrators and Probate (18th ed.), p.467.
[5] Williams, Mortimer and Sunnucks on Executors, Administrators and Probate (18th ed.), p.458.
[6] No grant of probate will be issued in these circumstances, only a grant of letters of administration with the will annexed. See In the Goods of Pryse (Deceased) [1904] P. 301.
[7] Administration of Estates Act 1925, s.9, as amended by s.14 of the Law of Property (Miscellaneous Provisions) Act 1994.
[8] Administration of Estates Act 1925, s.9.
[9] Williams, Mortimer and Sunnucks on Executors, Administrators and Probate (18th ed.), p.468.
[10] In some circumstances a party may be able to obtain a stay of the action pending a grant.
[11] Redwood Music Ltd v B. Feldman & Co Ltd [1979] R.P.C. 1. As to the sufficiency of title at the date of the writ generally, see para. 22–31, below. For the exceptional cases in which title of an administrator is regarded as "relating back" to a time before the grant, see Williams, Mortimer and Sunnucks on Executors, Administrators and Probate (18th ed.), p.469.

save it. In the same way he has no title to assign.[12] Where urgent action needs to be taken and there is no executor, the appropriate course is to obtain a limited or special grant (*ad colligenda bona*) or obtain the appointment of a receiver by the court. Whether title is claimed by an executor or administrator, the primary way of proving the grant is the production of the grant itself. In its absence, secondary evidence is admissible, but may be of little weight.[13]

Death of person with foreign domicile. The position as to the immediate vesting of the copyrights of a person dying domiciled abroad is not very clear and is complicated by the fact that, unlike the position under English and other common law systems, civil law systems generally provide for the immediate and automatic transmission of property to the heirs or universal legatee.[14] The position seems to depend on whether the question is one of administration or succession. On the one hand, questions regarding the succession of moveables (which for this purpose would include copyright[15]) are governed by the law of the deceased's domicile. On the other, under English law, questions regarding the administration of an estate are treated as governed by the law of the country from which the personal representative derives his authority. A grant issued by a foreign court has no operation in England or Wales, so to establish title here a personal representative will need to obtain an English grant and thus the administration will be governed by English law. It is suggested that under English law, the immediate vesting of a deceased person's property is a matter of administration not succession.

5–124

As to the authorities, where a foreigner dies testate, appointing an executor who survives him, and the law of his domicile on this issue is the same as the law of England, it seems that his copyrights vest in the executor.[16] An action may therefore be started by him, or by persons claiming through him, before obtaining a grant. Where a foreigner dies intestate or without appointing an executor who survives him, it appears that his English copyrights vest in the Public Trustee until a grant is obtained.[17] No action may therefore be brought before such a grant is obtained.

Literary executors. It is common practice for an author to appoint separate executors of his literary estate, often having particular experience in the field.[18] Where no relevant trusts are declared by the will, the executors' primary obliga-

5–125

---

[12] Although if he subsequently obtains a grant, the title may be perfected by virtue of the doctrine of "feeding the estoppel".

[13] *Gabrin v Universal Music Operations Ltd* [2003] EWHC (Ch) 1335 (although wrongly holding that the old "best evidence" rule applies—see para. 5–64, above, and *Springsteen v Masquerade Music Ltd* [2001] E.M.L.R. 654, CA).

[14] See Cheshire and North, *Private International Law* (13th ed. 1999, Butterworths), p.975.

[15] Although the 1988 Act states that copyright is transmissable as personal or moveable property (s.90(1)), copyright shares some of the characteristics of immoveables in the sense that the rights of copyright are territorially limited, so that copyright is regarded as situate in the country whose law governs its existence. United Kingdom copyright is therefore situate in the United Kingdom. See *Peer International Corp v Termidor Music Publishers Ltd* [2002] EWHC (Ch) 2675 and para. 2–02, above.

[16] *Redwood Music Ltd v B. Feldman & Co Ltd* [1979] R.P.C. 1. But note that the decision appears to have proceeded on the basis that the issue of the vesting was governed by the law of domicile (the State of Michigan). *cf. Mackay v Mackay* [1912] 2 S.L.T. 445.

[17] *Novello & Co Ltd v Hinrichson Edition Ltd* [1951] Ch. 595 (executor dying before testator); *Redwood Music v Feldman*, above; *Novello & Co Ltd v Eulenburg (E.) Ltd* [1950] 1 All E.R. 44 at 46, CA. The decisions were, however, *obiter*.

[18] The literary estate will of course be available, with the testator's other property, for the payment of debts and expenses in the course of administration: Administration of Estates Act 1925, s.32(1).

tion will be to sell the property in order to wind up the estate,[19] but there is never-theless a discretion to postpone sale for its better administration.[20] This power may be particularly valuable where the immediate sale of the literary estate would not realise its full potential.[21] A properly drawn will appointing literary executors will vest in the literary executors not only the author's copyrights but also his manuscripts and the benefit of his publishing contracts and provide for express powers to postpone sale and manage the exploitation of the copyrights.

5–126   **Title from personal representative.** Title may be derived from a personal repre-sentative by assignment or assent. Where the personal representative sells the copyright, title should be passed by way of assignment. Where copyright has been bequeathed, title should be made by assent. An assent, although usually in writing, may be oral or even implied from conduct,[22] and operates to vest the property in the beneficiary by operation of law. Where a personal representative has died with copyright still vested in him, the title will devolve on his personal representative. If he has no executor, a special grant will be needed.[23]

(ii) Bequest of an unpublished work

5–127   The 1988 Act supplies a rule of construction affecting the title to copyright works where the physical object originally embodying the work passes under a specific or general bequest in a will. It therefore operates as a limited exception to the general principle that a transfer of the ownership of a physical object embodying a copyright work does not operate to transfer the copyright. Earlier Acts contained rules of more limited application and in order to preserve the effect of these rules the provisions of the 1988 Act therefore vary, depending on the date of death.

5–128   **Death on or after August 1, 1989.** This rule applies where a person is entitled under a specific or general bequest to an original document or other thing record-ing or embodying a literary, dramatic, musical or artistic work which was unpub-lished before the testator's death. In such a case, unless a contrary indication ap-pears from the will or codicil, the bequest is to be construed as including the copyright in the work in so far as the testator was the owner of the copyright im-mediately before his death.[24] A similar rule applies in the case of an unpublished sound recording or film where a person is entitled under a bequest to the original thing containing the recording or film.[25] The rule applies whether or not the testa-tor is the author and thus it applies, for example, where an assignee of the copy-right owns original manuscripts. The rule applies whether the bequest is specific or general and whether the person is entitled under the bequest beneficially or otherwise, for example, as trustee on trust.

5–129   **Death before August 1, 1989 but after June 1, 1957.** The rule is more limited, applying only to a bequest of an original document embodying a work, and thus

---

[19] And where life interests are involved, the rule in *Howe v Lord Dartmouth* (1802) 7 Ves. 137 will need to be considered.

[20] Administration of Estates Act 1925, s.39(1)(iii) and, in the case of an intestate, s.33(1). As to the effect of this power on the power to trade or carry on a business, see Williams, Mortimer and Sunnucks on *Executors, Administrators and Probate* (18th ed.), p.753.

[21] It will often be the case that the market for the literary estate will in practice be limited to the author's publisher.

[22] Williams, Mortimer and Sunnucks on *Executors, Administrators and Probate* (18th ed. Sweet & Maxwell), p.1072; *Redwood Music Ltd v B. Feldman & Co Ltd* [1979] R.P.C. 1.

[23] See generally, Williams, Mortimer and Sunnucks on *Executors, Administrators and Probate* (18th ed.), pp.346 *et seq.*

[24] CDPA 1988, s.93.

[25] s.93.

only to literary, dramatic, musical and artistic works.[26] This reflects the more limited provision which was contained in the 1956 Act.[27]

Death before June 1, 1957. The above provisions do not apply where a testator died before the commencement of the 1956 Act.[28] In such an event, the rule is even more limited, applying only to the author of an unpublished or unperformed literary, dramatic or musical work. Here, the ownership after his death of a manuscript of his is *prima facie* proof of the copyright being with the owner of the manuscript where such ownership was acquired under a testamentary disposition made by the author.[29] This provision reflects the position under the 1911 Act[30] and perhaps that which existed before then.[31] It had no application to bequests by anyone other than the author, in particular, assigns from him, or to artistic works.

5–130

(iii) Bankruptcy

On an owner's bankruptcy, the copyright in a work is held initially by the Official Receiver as receiver and manager,[32] and, on the appointment of the trustee in bankruptcy of the copyright owner passes, to him by operation of law without any assignment in writing.[33] The copyright in any work acquired by or, devolving on the bankrupt after the commencement of his bankruptcy and before his discharge does not automatically vest in the trustee, but may be the subject of a claim by him.[34] Although the benefit of an unexecuted contract for personal services by the bankrupt will not vest in a trustee,[35] the trustee is entitled to sums of money such as publishing royalties or distributions from collecting societies due in respect of works completed before the bankruptcy and not depending on performance of further obligations on the author's part.[36] In the absence of any claim to post-bankruptcy works themselves, the trustee is not entitled to sums arising from such works.[37]

5–131

(iv) Execution

There is no process whereby copyright can be directly taken in execution by a judgment creditor of the copyright owner[38] even, it seems, by the appointment of a receiver by way of equitable execution.[39] Of course, royalties due to the judgment debtor may be subject to process of execution, such as attachment in garnishee proceedings.

5–132

---

[26] CDPA 1988, Sch.1, para.30(1)(b).
[27] Copyright Act 1956, s.38 and Sch.7, para.29(1).
[28] CDPA 1988, Sch.1, para.30(1)(a).
[29] Sch.1, para.30(2).
[30] Copyright Act 1911, s.17(2).
[31] See *Wilis v Curtois* (1838) 1 Beav. 189. Note, also, the provisions of s.3 of the Copyright Act 1842, under which the copyright in every "book" published after the author's death was to belong to the proprietor of the manuscript.
[32] Insolvency Act 1986, s.287.
[33] CDPA 1988, s.90(1) and the Insolvency Act 1986, ss.283, 306.
[34] Insolvency Act 1986, s.307.
[35] *Bailey v Thurston & Co Ltd* [1903] 1 K.B. 137 at 145–146.
[36] *Performing Right Society Ltd v Rowland* [1997] 3 All E.R. 336.
[37] *Performing Right Society Ltd v Rowland* [1997] 3 All E.R. 336.
[38] See *Re Baldwin* (1858) 2 De G. & J. 230. Cf. *Planet Earth Productions Inc v Rowlands* (1990) 69 D.L.R. (4th) 715 (Ontario S.C.), although there the wording of the relevant statute included choses in action.
[39] *Edwards & Co v Picard* (1909) 78 L.J. K.B. 1108 (a patent case).

3. RIGHTS IN EXTENDED AND REVIVED TERMS OF COPYRIGHT

A. THE EXTENDED AND REVIVED TERMS UNDER THE TERM DIRECTIVE

(i) Introduction

5–133   As discussed elsewhere,[40] compliance with the Council Directive 93/98 harmonising the term of copyright required the United Kingdom to extend the term of copyright for many works[41] to the life of the author and 70 years after his death.[42] This was achieved by the Duration of Copyright and Rights in Performances Regulations 1995, which came into force on January 1, 1996. In the case of works which were the subject of existing United Kingdom copyright protection on this date, this meant extending the term for a further 20 years. In addition, where the United Kingdom term of copyright had already expired by December 31, 1995 but the work was, on July 1, 1995, still protected in another EEA state under legislation relating to copyright or related rights, the United Kingdom copyright in such works was revived for the remainder of the 70-year post mortem term.[43] It followed that the Regulations needed to deal with two separate issues, namely, ownership of the copyright during the extended term and ownership of the revived term of copyright.

The Directive did not stipulate who such owners should be. In each case, there were two obvious alternative candidates: first, the original author or first owner of the copyright, who otherwise stood to be deprived of the windfall of the extended or revived term; secondly, the owner of the copyright immediately before the expiry of the old term. As will be seen, in respect of the extended term, the Regulations confer the extended copyright on the person who is the owner of the copyright at the end of the old term. In respect of the revived term, the general effect of the Regulations is to confer the right either on the person who was the owner of the copyright immediately before it expired or, if that person had died or ceased to exist before January 1, 1996, the original author or his personal representatives. In this respect, the Regulations appear to operate in a rather arbitrary manner.

(ii) Ownership of the extended and revived terms

5–134   **Ownership of the extended term generally.** In the case of works which were the subject of United Kingdom copyright on December 31, 1995, the person who was the owner of the copyright at that date is to be, as from January 1, 1996, the owner of the full, extended term.[44] Thus whoever was the owner of the copyright on December 31, 1995, whether he was the original, first owner or someone deriving title from him, became the owner of the new, longer term. The exception to this rule is where the copyright owner on December 31, 1995 was owner for a term less than the full, old term of life and 50 years, for example under an assignment for a more limited period. In this case, whoever was entitled to the rever-

---

[40] See Ch.6, below.

[41] *i.e.* literary, dramatic, musical and artistic works, and films.

[42] More precisely, to a term being the author's life and a period ending 70 years from the end of the calendar year in which the author died. See CDPA 1988, s.12(1) as amended by the Duration of Copyright and Rights in Performances Regulations 1995 (SI 1995/3297). Previously, the term of copyright for such works was a period ending 50 years from the end of the calendar year in which the author died.

[43] For a full discussion of the effect of the Regulations, see Ch.6, below.

[44] Duration of Copyright and Rights in Performances Regulations 1995 (SI 1995/3297), reg.18(1).

sionary interest expectant on the termination of the lesser term became entitled to the extended term.[45]

Ownership of the revived term. In the first instance, the Regulations provide that the person who was the owner of the copyright in the work immediately before the copyright expired is, as from January 1, 1996, the owner of any revived copyright.[46] Effectively, therefore, the last owner of the expired copyright will be the owner of copyright for the rump of the *post mortem* period, even if he only acquired the copyright a short time before the expiry of the old term. Where, however, this person had died before January 1, 1996, or being a legal person, such as a company, had ceased to exist before this date, the revived term is to belong to the author of the work or his personal representatives,[47] except in the case of a film, when the right is to belong to the principal director of the film or his personal representatives.[48] Where the right vested in personal representatives in this way, it is to be held by them for the benefit of the person who would have been entitled to the right had it been vested in the deceased person immediately before his death and devolved as part of his estate.[49] This provision has two notable effects. First, whether or not the revived copyright vests in the author depends entirely on whether the former copyright owner died or ceased to exist before January 1, 1996, an event which has no bearing on who has the greater moral claim to the benefit of the revived term. The second is that where the former owner has died, then, except in the case of films, it is the author or his estate, which benefits.[50] This is so even where the author never owned the copyright, for example where the work was made by him in the course of his employment under a contract of service. The position is similar in relation to films where the former copyright owner has died or ceased to exist: the revived right belongs to the principal director, a person who previously would have had no interest in the copyright.

5–135

(iii) Transitional provisions

(a) *Pre-commencement assignments and licences*

Pre-commencement assignments. Since the owner of the extended term is the owner "as from" January 1, 1996 ("commencement"), he may assign or deal with the extended term of copyright, together with his interest in what was the remainder of the old term, from that date. What, however, is the effect of attempted dealings in the extended term before that date? In general, the legal title to property which is not yet in existence cannot be passed, and a purported assignment will at best take effect as an agreement to assign,[51] so that all that can be achieved by such an assignment, if it was given for consideration, is the passing of the equitable title to the extended or revived term. The position is to some extent dealt with by the Regulations, which provide that:

"Where, by an agreement made before commencement in relation to

5–136

---

[45] reg.18(2).

[46] Duration of Copyright and Rights in Performances Regulations 1995 (SI 1995/3297), reg.19(1)(b).

[47] As to the vesting in an author's personal representatives, see the similar wording of the proviso to the 1911 Act, s.5(2) proviso, now re-embodied in CDPA 1988, Sch.1, para.27(2). As to the effect of this proviso, see paras 5–113A *et seq.*, above.

[48] Duration of Copyright and Rights in Performances Regulations 1995 (SI 1995/3297), reg.19(2)(a).

[49] reg.19(3).

[50] It is only in the case of films that the author might still be alive.

[51] See para. 5–105, above.

extended or revived copyright,[52] and signed by or on behalf of the prospective owner of the copyright, the prospective owner purports to assign the extended or revived copyright (wholly or partially) to another person, then if, on commencement the assignee or another person claiming under him would be entitled as against all other persons to require the copyright to be vested in him, the copyright shall vest in the assignee or his successor in title by virtue of this paragraph".[53]

It follows that where this paragraph applies, the legal title to the extended or revived term will have vested in the assignee on January 1, 1996. It should be noted that an agreement for which there was no consideration will not carry such rights since the assignee would not be entitled to a decree of specific performance vesting the copyright in him.[54] The wording of the Regulation is similar to that used elsewhere in the Act in relation to the assignment of future rights and, perhaps partly as a result, is not as clear as it might be.[55] First, it is not clear what is added by the qualifying condition that the agreement should be one "in relation to" extended or revived copyright. If the prospective owner purports to assign such copyright, then presumably the agreement will have been one "in relation to" such copyright; if not, the provision is of no operation anyway. In any event, the main issue is likely to be whether the prospective owner purported to deal with the revived or extended copyright. This will be a matter of construing the agreement in the light of the surrounding circumstances. Many assignments include as a matter of standard form words such as "all extensions and renewals of copyright" in defining the subject matter of the grant and such words may help in reaching the conclusion that the extended or revived term was intended to be included. Even in such a case, however, there may still be an issue as to whether there was an intention to assign "the" extended or revived term of United Kingdom copyright when neither party had it in contemplation as opposed, for example, to any extensions under existing foreign systems of law. Many assignments, of course, simply define the subject matter of the grant as "the copyright". It is suggested that the normal meaning to be placed on such words is that all possible rights were intended to be assigned so that such an assignment will carry the extended or revived term.

The second issue arises on the further requirement that the assignee or his successor should have been entitled on January 1, 1996 to have "the copyright" vested in him. It is here that the repetition of the wording used in s.91(1) and elsewhere in the 1988 Act gives rise to difficulties. The common case which will arise in practice is no doubt the one of a pre-commencement assignment of copyright, the issue being whether it will carry the extended or revived right. In such a case, "the copyright", as it existed before commencement, will already be vested in the assignee. It therefore seems inappropriate to speak in terms of the assignee still being entitled on commencement to require "the copyright" to be vested in him. This comment applies even in the case of a pre-commencement assignment expressly limited to the extended or revived term. Clearly, a purposive construction must be given to the provision and it therefore seems that the words "the copyright" should be understood as referring to the extended or revived copyright.

---

[52] "Extended copyright" is defined to mean any copyright which subsists by virtue of the provisions of the 1988 Act as amended by the Regulations ("the new provisions") after the date on which it would have expired under the 1988 Act as unamended ("the 1988 provisions"). Similarly, "revived copyright" is defined to mean any copyright which subsists by virtue of the new provisions after having expired under the 1988 provisions or any earlier enactment relating to copyright. See Duration of Copyright and Rights in Performances Regulations 1995 (SI 1995/3297), reg.17.

[53] reg.20(1).

[54] cf. the similar situation in respect of assignments of future copyright. See para. 5–107A, above.

[55] cf. CDPA 1988, ss.91 (future copyright–see para. 5–107, above), 191C (future performer's property rights—see para. 12–43, below) and s.223 (future design right—see para. 13–117, below).

Licences by prospective owners. Provision is made as to who is bound by   **5–137**
licences granted by prospective owners of the extended or revived terms. Thus it
is provided that a licence granted by a prospective owner of extended or revived
copyright is binding on every successor in title to his interest, or prospective
interest, in the right, except a purchaser in good faith for valuable consideration
and without actual or constructive notice of the licence or a person deriving title
from such a purchaser.[56] For this purpose, a prospective owner also includes a
person who is prospectively entitled to any extended or revived copyright by
virtue of such an agreement.[57] Thus, licences granted in respect of the extended
or revived term by a person to whom the extended or revived term was
prospectively assigned will bind his successors. Again, the wording of the relevant regulation has been imported from s.91(3) of the 1988 Act without, perhaps,
sufficient thought being given to its new context. Clearly, the reference to the
prospective owner includes all pre-commencement owners of the copyright since
they were, unknowingly, prospective owners of the new rights. Again, presumably the reference to the licence granted by such an owner must be a reference to
a licence granted by him in respect of the extended or revived term. Usually, no
doubt, a licence agreement will have made no express reference to the extended
or revived term. Separate provision is made as to the effect of existing licences in
relation to the extended term, considered below, and the interrelationship of the
two provisions is not clear. No provision is made in relation to the revived term.[58]

The effect of existing licences and agreements: the extended term. Before   **5–138**
January 1, 1996 many copyright owners will have granted a licence or entered
into an agreement affecting the right to exploit a work. What is the effect of this
in relation to the extended term? Two different but interrelated regulations have
to be considered in such cases.

(a) First, it is provided that where any copyright licence or any term or condi-
    tion of an agreement relating to the exploitation of a copyright work
    subsisted immediately before January 1, 1996 in relation to a work in
    which copyright then subsisted, and was not to expire before the old pe-
    riod of copyright, then it is to have effect during the period of any extended
    period of copyright, subject to any agreement to the contrary.[59] So where,
    for example, a licence was granted for the whole of the old term of copy-
    right, it will continue for the extended term unless the agreement provided
    otherwise. In the same way, any terms or conditions of the licence, for
    example as to payment, will continue for the extended term. The position
    is the same where the licence, or the terms or conditions of the agreement,
    were imposed by the Copyright Tribunal.[60] One odd effect of these provi-
    sions is that if a pre-commencement licence was granted for some future
    term expiring at the end of the old term of copyright, but which had not
    yet started to run at commencement, the licence will not continue to have
    effect into the extended period.

(b) Secondly, as has already been seen, a licence granted by a prospective
    owner of the extended term in respect of the interest will generally bind
    his successors in title. If, therefore, the licence granted continues to have
    effect during the extended period, successors to the original licensor will
    be bound.

---

[56] Duration of Copyright and Rights in Performances Regulations 1995 (SI 1995/3297), reg.20(2).
[57] reg.20(3).
[58] But note that a licence of right is available in respect of the revived term. See para. 5–141 ,
below.
[59] Duration of Copyright and Rights in Performances Regulations 1995 (SI 1995/3297), reg.21(1).
No doubt the agreement may be express or implied. *cf.* para. 5–152, above.
[60] reg.21(2).

(b) *Effect of things done in relation to revived copyright before commencement*

5–139   Where the copyright in a work had expired, acts may well have been done in relation to the work on the basis that it was, and would remain, in the public domain
and therefore no licence to do the acts was required from anybody. Article 10(3)
of the Term Directive provides that any revival of the term is to be without prejudice to any acts of exploitation performed before implementation of the Directive
and that Member States are required to adopt measures to protect acquired rights
of third parties. The detail of such measures, however, is a matter left to the
discretion of Member States, provided that they do not have the overall effect of
preventing the application of the new terms of protection laid down by the
Directive.[61] To achieve this, the Regulations therefore had to deal with a number
of situations.

    (a) First, it is provided that no act done before commencement[62] is to be
regarded as an infringement of any revived copyright in a work.[63] It follows that no copying of the work before this date will have been an infringement and such copies will not be infringing copies for the purposes
of any act of sale, etc, whether pre- or post-commencement.[64] *Prima facie*,
however, the issue of such copies to the public after commencement would
be an infringement, but the extent to which this will be so is limited, as
discussed below.

    (b) Secondly, it is not an infringement to do anything after commencement in
pursuance of arrangements made before January 1, 1995 at a time when
copyright did not subsist in the work.[65] Provided therefore that relevant
"arrangements" were made before this date, it will not be an infringement
to do anything "in pursuance" of those arrangements. For this purpose,
"arrangements" means arrangements for the exploitation of the work.[66]
So, for example, if steps were taken to stage a performance of a public
domain work, such as the hiring of a venue, the engagement of the
performers and the building of sets, it will not be an infringement of copyright to perform the work pursuant to those arrangements after
commencement. It is not clear whether this would still be the case if the
public demand for the work led to an extended run of several years and in
different venues, although if the arrangements which were made contemplated such a possibility, it is suggested it would. As to what will suffice
as "arrangements", they are not limited to arrangements by way of contract
but do not extend to all kinds of acts done, or steps of any kind taken: the
acts must be of some degree of solidity or certainty, such that it can be
said that acts done later are done "in pursuance of" the arrangements.[67]
So, where a defendant had done a great deal of work on a new edition of a
book which was then out of copyright, and had had various encouraging
discussions with publishers but had not yet concluded a contract with
them, neither the discussions nor the work on the new edition amounted to
"arrangements" within the meaning of the regulations.[68] Where, however,
all or a great deal of the preparatory work had been done before January 1,

---

[61] *Butterfly Music Srl v Carosello Edizioni Musicali E Discografichi Srl* [1999] E.M.L.R. 847;
[2000] E.C.D.R. 1 (E.C.J.).
[62] *i.e.* January 1, 1996.
[63] Duration of Copyright and Rights in Performances Regulations 1995 (SI 1995/3297), reg.23(1).
[64] As to infringement by dealing in infringing copies, see Ch.8.
[65] reg.23(2)(a).
[66] reg.23(5).
[67] *Sweeney v Macmillan Publishers Ltd* [2002] R.P.C. 35, at para.57.
[68] *ibid.*

1995 on the basis of an understanding or negotiations between the author and publisher relating to its publication, this would probably suffice.

(c) Thirdly, it will not be an infringement to issue to the public copies of the work made before July 1, 1995[69] at a time when copyright did not subsist in the work.[70] So, in the case of the example given above in relation to the printing of copies of the work, provided those copies were made before July 1, 1995, the issue of those copies to the public will not be an infringement. As already pointed out, such copies will not be infringing copies.

It may well have happened that while a work was in the public domain, other **5–139A** works were made which incorporated the public domain work. The exploitation of the new work could thus be prevented by the revival of copyright if no provision were made dealing with this. The Regulations therefore provide that in two circumstances it is not an infringement of the revived copyright in a work (the "old work") to do anything after commencement in relation to a literary, dramatic, musical or artistic work or a film made before commencement, or made in pursuance of arrangements made[71] before commencement (a "new work"), which contains a copy of the old work or is an adaptation of the old work:

(a) The first circumstance is where the new work was made before July 1, 1995[72] at a time when copyright did not subsist in the old work.[73] So, where a book was written before July 1, 1995 incorporating material from an old work in which copyright has since revived, it will not be an infringement to print and distribute copies of that book or do anything else "in relation to" it, for example, make a film based upon it. The Regulation will apply where, for example, the work is incorporated into a play or film although not where it is incorporated into a sound recording. The Regulation contemplates that there must be a new "work" brought into existence in which there will be found a copy or adaptation of the public domain work.

(b) The second circumstance is where the new work was made in pursuance of arrangements made before July 1, 1995 at a time when copyright did not subsist in the old work.[74] Thus even if the new work was not itself made before July 1, 1995, provided it was made in pursuance of arrangements made before this date, nothing done in relation to the new work will be an infringement.

(c) *The revived term: further provisions*

Revived copyright: owner not known. It can often be difficult to establish the **5–140** identity of a copyright owner, particularly in relation to an old work. This problem is accentuated in cases of revived copyright since (a) the work may have been out of copyright for some time so that there will have been no authorised publisher or other person exploiting the work in the market in recent years who can be found and (b) where the revived copyright belongs to the author or his personal

---

[69] This is the date by which Member States were required to implement the Directive. See Art.13(1)
[70] reg.23(1)(b).
[71] See the text earlier in the paragraph as to the meaning of "arrangements made".
[72] As already noted, this is the date by which Member States were required to implement the Directive.
[73] reg.23(3)(a).
[74] reg.23(3)(b).

representatives rather than the last owner of the copyright,[75] it may be very difficult to establish who the new copyright owner actually is. To alleviate this problem, the Regulations provide that it is not an infringement of the revived copyright in a work to do, after 1995, anything which is a restricted act in relation to the work if the act is done at a time when, or is done in pursuance of arrangements made[76] at a time when, the name and address of the person entitled to authorise the act cannot by reasonable inquiry be ascertained.[77]

5–141   **Use of revived copyright work as of right.** The rights of the revived copyright owner are substantially cut down by the availability of a compulsory licence to anyone who gives notice of his intention to exploit the work. In order to avail himself of such a licence, a person merely has to give reasonable notice of his intention to the copyright owner, stating when he intends to begin such acts. The licence will be subject to the payment of such reasonable royalty or other remuneration as may be agreed or determined in default of agreement by the Copyright Tribunal but the licence will come into effect whether or not the parties have come to any agreement as to royalties or other remuneration and whether or not this has been determined by the Tribunal. It appears that the requirement of "reasonable" notice is of little significance, not least because the copyright owner can do nothing to stop the intended acts once notice in proper form is given, and that thus very short notice is sufficient.[78] These provisions are considered in more detail elsewhere.[79]

B. RIGHTS IN THE EXTENDED TERM OF COPYRIGHT IN SOUND RECORDINGS UNDER THE INFORMATION SOCIETY DIRECTIVE

(i) Introduction

5–142   As discussed elsewhere,[80] one of the possible effects of the implementation of the Information Society Directive,[81] with its amendment of Article 3(2) the Term Directive,[82] was to extend the term of copyright in sound recordings. Because of this, the implementing regulations[83] contained transitional and other provisions which are similar to those in the regulations relating to the more general extension of the term of copyright dealt with in the previous section ("the Term Regulations").[84] For this purpose, the Regulations define the expression "extended copyright" to mean any copyright in a sound recording which subsists by virtue of the amended Act after the date on which it would have expired before amendment.[85]

(ii) Ownership of the extended copyright

5–143   The Regulations provide that the person who was the owner of the copyright in a

---

[75] See Duration of Copyright and Rights in Performances Regulations 1995 (SI 1995/3297), reg.19(2) and para. 5–135, above.

[76] See para. 5–139, above, as to the meaning of "arrangements made".

[77] reg.23(4).

[78] *Sweeney v Macmillan Publishers Ltd* [2002] R.P.C. 35, at para.63.

[79] See paras 29–41 *et seq.*, below.

[80] See para. 6–55, below.

[81] 2001/29.

[82] 93/100, amended by Art.11(2) of the Information Society Directive 2001/29.

[83] The Copyright and Related Rights Regulations 2003 (SI 2003/2498).

[84] There is no question of any revival of copyright under the regulations being considered in the present section.

[85] reg.30(1C).

sound recording immediately before October 31, 2003 shall be, as from that date, the owner of any extended copyright in that sound recording.[86] This provision therefore differs from that in the Term Regulations relating to the general extension of copyright, so far as concerns a person who was, on October 31, 2003, the owner of the copyright for *less* than the old term.[87] In this, the Regulations seem rather arbitrary.

(iii) Transitional provisions

(a) *Pre-commencement assignments, licences and agreements*

Pre-commencement assignments. The Regulations contain a provision dealing with the effect of an agreement made before October 31, 2003 whereby the prospective owner of the extended copyright in a sound recording purports to assign the extended copyright. If, on commencement, the assignee or person claiming under him would be entitled to require the copyright to be vested in him, the copyright shall vest automatically.[88] The provision is similar to that contained in the Term Regulations, and the same comments apply.[89]   **5–144**

Licences by prospective owners. As with the Term Regulations, a licence granted by a prospective owner of the extended copyright in a sound recording is binding on successors in title, except a purchaser for value without actual or constructive notice of the licence.[90]   **5–145**

The effect of existing licences and agreements. Any copyright licence or any term or condition of an agreement relating to the exploitation of a sound recording which subsisted immediately before October 31, 2003 and would not have expired before the end of the term of copyright under the unamended provisions of the Act, is to continue to have effect during the period of any extended copyright, subject to any agreement to the contrary.[91] . The same applies to any licence, term or condition imposed by order of the Copyright Tribunal.[92] The Term Regulations contain identical provisions.[93]   **5–146**

(b) *Effect of things done in relation to extended copyright before commencement*

The Regulations make a number of savings similar to those found in the Term Regulations: (1) no act done before October 31, 2003 is to be regarded as an infringement of any extended copyright;[94] (2) nothing in the Regulations is to affect any agreement made before December 22, 2002;[95] (3) no act done after October 31, 2003, in pursuance of an agreement made before December 22, 2002, is to be   **5–147**

---

[86] Copyright and Related Rights Regulations 2003 (SI 2003/2498), reg.36.
[87] See para. 5–134, above.
[88] Copyright and Related Rights Regulations 2003 (SI 2003/2498), reg.37(1)
[89] See para. 5–136, above.
[90] Copyright and Related Rights Regulations 2003 (SI 2003/2498), reg.37(2). "Prospective owner" is defined in reg.30(1). See the comment on the similar provisions of the Term Regulations in para. 5–137, above.
[91] Copyright and Related Rights Regulations 2003 (SI 2003/2498), reg.38(1).
[92] reg.38(2).
[93] See para. 5–138, above.
[94] Copyright and Related Rights Regulations 2003 (SI 2003/2498), reg.31(2).
[95] reg.32(1).

regarded as an infringement of any extended copyright.[96] . The comments made in relation to the equivalent provisions of the Term Regulations apply equally to these provisions, except that it should be noted that the expression used now is "in pursuance of any agreement" rather than "in pursuance of any arrangements",[97] clearly a more strict test.[98]

C. Rights in the extended term under the 1911 Act

5–148 **Introduction.** The term of copyright conferred by the 1911 Act in respect of published works was longer than that subsisting under the pre-existing law,[99] and this longer term was conferred on existing works which were still in copyright at the commencement date of the 1911 Act.[1] Subject to the important transitional provisions considered below, whoever was the owner of the relevant right immediately before commencement became entitled to the corresponding copyright conferred by the 1911 Act, including, therefore, the copyright during the period of any extended term. This meant that where the author had assigned or granted an interest in the old right for the whole of the old term, a windfall might have been produced for the assignee or grantee. In such a case, it was therefore provided that the assignment or grant continued until the old period of copyright would have run out, at which date the unexpired term of copyright revested in the author or his personal representatives, subject to two alternative rights of the original assignee or grantee to continue to exploit the work. The 1956 Act sought to maintain the rights of the various interested parties and the 1988 Act continues this regime. To understand the position today it is necessary, first, to examine the nature of the provisions in the 1911 Act and then to see how these have been carried through by the 1956 and 1988 Acts.

5–149 **The substituted rights under the 1911 Act.** As to the provisions of the 1911 Act, first, it is important to examine how the Act operated generally in the case of pre-1911 Act rights. Before the passing of the 1911 Act, a right of copyright existed at common law to restrain the publication of and other dealings with certain categories of unpublished works. Copyright also subsisted by force of statute in published works of various descriptions (and certain unpublished works), giving the owner the right to restrain reproduction etc., of such works. Further, in relation to works which could be performed, namely musical and dramatic works, there similarly existed two distinct public performance rights, namely a right at common law to restrain the public performance of works which had not previously been performed in public, and a statutory right to restrain performance of works which had been publicly performed. Under the 1911 Act, these rights were coalesced into one, "substituted", right of copyright. Thus the owner of the pre-1911 Act copyright, whether statutory or common law, became entitled to the substituted right of copyright conferred by the 1911 Act, and common law copyright was abolished.[2] As to the performing right, a person who before the 1911 Act was the owner, whether at common law or under statute, of the performing right, but not the copyright, in a musical or dramatic work became

---

[96] reg.32(2).
[97] reg.23(2)(a) of the Term Regulations, dealing with revived copyright.
[98] See the discussion at para. 5–139, above.
[99] So, for example, whereas the term for published works under the Literary Copyright Act 1842 was the life of the author and seven years, or 42 years from publication, whichever was the longer, the term of copyright for such works under the 1911 Act was the lifetime of the author and 50 years after his death. The period of copyright in many unpublished works under the pre- 1911 Act law was perpetual.
[1] Copyright Act 1911, s.24(1).
[2] Copyright Act 1911, s.24(3).

the owner of a substituted right of copyright, being the sole right to perform the work in public, to the exclusion of all other rights comprised in the copyright. Similarly, a person who owned the copyright, but not the performing right, in a musical or dramatic work, became the owner of a substituted right of copyright, being the copyright to the exclusion of the sole right to perform the work or any substantial part of it in public.[3] Again, the common law performing right was abolished.

Ownership of the 1911 Act term. In general terms, the 1911 Act provided that whoever was entitled to a pre-1911 Act right which was still subsisting at commencement[4] became the owner of the substituted right, or to the same interest in such substituted right, for the term for which it would have subsisted had the 1911 Act been in force when the work was made. In general terms, this meant that the owner of the old right as at commencement became the owner of the new, substituted right of copyright for the whole of the new term of copyright.

5–150

The revesting proviso. As already indicated, the one qualification to this applied where an author, being the first owner of the old right, had assigned or granted an interest for the whole of the old term. In such a case, the 1911 Act provided[5] that where the author of a pre-1911 Act right which was subsisting at commencement[6] had assigned the right or granted any interest in it for the whole term of the right, then at the date when, but for the passing of the Act, the right would have expired, the substituted right conferred by the Act should, in the absence of express agreement, pass to the author of the work.[7] Any interest in the work created before commencement, and still then subsisting, determined.[8] The general intention was therefore to preserve the extended term for the benefit of authors or their estates.

5–151

Express agreement. The words "in the absence of express agreement" meant "in the absence of an agreement expressly referring to the substituted right identified as such".[9] The agreement must therefore have been one made in clear contemplation of these provisions of the Act. It follows that an agreement made before the passing of the 1911 Act referring in general terms to copyright, however wide, for example, "present or future, vested or contingent", would not fall within this description.[10] However, a further assignment, after commencement, of the "copyright" would *prima facie* have carried the full, extended term.

5–152

Relation to 1911 Act reverter provision. As has been seen,[11] the 1911 Act contained a provision whereby authors were unable to dispose of their interest in their works for the last 25 years of the term of copyright. Any attempt to do so resulted in the copyright reverting to their personal representatives at the beginning of this period. However, the references in this reverter provision to "the copyright" referred to the copyright as conferred by the 1911 Act and not the rights which existed previously.[12] An assignment or grant made before the commencement of the 1911 Act which dealt with the copyright in an existing work was therefore unaffected by the reverter provision.

5–153

---

[3] s.24, Sch.1.
[4] July 1, 1912.
[5] Copyright Act 1911, s.24(1), proviso.
[6] July 1, 1912.
[7] For this purpose, the expression "author" included the legal personal representatives of a deceased author. See s.24(2).
[8] s.24(1), proviso.
[9] *Chappell & Co Ltd v Redwood Music Ltd* [1981] R.P.C. 337.
[10] *Chappell & Co Ltd v Redwood Music Ltd* [1981] R.P.C. 337.
[11] See para. 5–112, above.
[12] *Coleridge-Taylor v Novello & Co Ltd* [1938] Ch. 850.

5–154 **Partial assignment or grant for less than old term.** The above provision only applied to the case of an assignment or grant of an interest covering the whole term of copyright. If, therefore, the author had parted with his copyright for a period less than the whole of the original term, he had a reversionary interest which would automatically confer upon him the substituted right, which would become exercisable by him upon the falling in of his reversion. It is unclear whether the proviso applied in the situation where the author had assigned or granted a right to one person for a portion of the old term, and then to another for the residue of that term. It is suggested that, in accordance with the policy underlying the section, it did apply.[13] The proviso must also have applied where the assignment or grant was made at some time after the work was created, so that it will not strictly have been for the "whole term of the right", but for the whole of the remaining term of the right. Otherwise the proviso would have been of almost no application.

5–155 **Assignment by a person other than the author.** It is important to note that the proviso only applied to a case where the assignment or grant was made by "the author" of the work. Where the copyright vested in the first instance in any person other than the author,[14] then a suitably worded pre-1911 Act assignment or grant by such person would have been effective to pass to the assignee or grantee the benefit of the extended term conferred by the 1911 Act.

5–156 **Rights of assignee or grantee notwithstanding revesting.** Although the benefit of any extended term of copyright conferred by the 1911 Act *prima facie* vested in the original author of the work, and not in his assignee or grantee, it was considered unfair to deprive the assignee or grantee of the right to reap any advantage from the market which he might have created. The 1911 Act therefore provided that the person who, immediately before the date when the copyright would have expired under the repealed statutes, was the owner of any right or interest in the copyright was entitled to two, alternative options, as follows:

> *First option.* He was entitled to call for an assignment of the right or the grant of a similar interest in it for the remainder of the extended term of the right. This right had to be exercised by notice and was to be for such consideration as, failing agreement, was determined by arbitration.[15] The notice referred to had to be given not more than one year, and not less than six months, before the date on which the right would have so expired, and to be sent by registered post to the "author"[16] or, if the author could not with reasonable diligence be found, advertised in the London Gazette and in two London newspapers.[17] It is suggested that the true construction of this option was that a person who had obtained an assignment of the old term of copyright was entitled to an assignment of the right, but not to the grant of an interest, and, similarly, that a person who had obtained a grant of an interest for the whole of the old term was entitled to a "similar" grant for the residue of the new term, but not to an assignment of the right.

> *Second option.* Alternatively, he was entitled, without taking any such as-

---

[13] But note that the transitional provisions of the 1956 Act, which summarise the application of the revesting proviso, refer to the grant of "an" interest in the right, rather than "any" interest. See the Copyright Act 1956, Sch.7, para.38(a).

[14] As, for example, in the case of articles written for collective works, where in certain circumstances the copyright first vested in the proprietor. See the Literary Copyright Act 1842, s.18 and para. 5–31 and 5–40, above.

[15] The giving of this notice presumably bound the person giving it to purchase the right or interest.

[16] As noted, this expression included his personal representatives: see Copyright Act 1911, s.24(2).

[17] It is not clear how the assignment or grant, as the case may have been, was to be obtained if the author or his personal representatives could not be found. The person giving the notice, however, would presumably obtain at least an equitable title.

signment or grant, to continue to reproduce or perform the work on a non-exclusive basis,[18] subject to the payment of royalties to the author, if demanded, but otherwise in the same manner as before.[19] No notice had to be given by the assignee or grantee and the demand for such royalties had to be made by the author within three years after the date on which the right would have expired, otherwise any right was forfeited. The royalties were to be of such amount as, failing agreement, was determined by arbitration.

The second option and collective works. Where the assignee or grantee took the second option, the rights of the author were further qualified in the case of collective works.[20] As to pre-1911 Act collective works, it often happened that the copyright in an article contributed to a collective work vested, *ab initio*, in the proprietor of the work.[21] In that case there would have been no assignment by "the author", and the proviso had no application.[22] The extended term of copyright would belong to the proprietor of the collective work.[23] If, however, the copyright did not originally vest in the proprietor of the collective work, but was the property of the author, then, in accordance with the revesting proviso, the benefit of the extended term would belong to the author or his personal representatives, notwithstanding any subsequent assignment or grant for the whole term. In this situation, the Act provided that where the assignee or grantee for the whole term was also the proprietor of the collective work, he was to be entitled, during the extended term of copyright, to continue to reproduce the work without any payment to the author.[24] He could, however, only reproduce "in like manner as theretofore", so that under this option he could not reproduce an article contributed to the collective work, except as part of that collective work. **5–157**

Provisions of the 1956 Act. When the 1956 Act was passed, two classes of cases had to be considered, namely (a) cases in which the pre-1911 Act copyright term would by then have expired but the extended term under the 1911 Act had not yet done so and, (b) cases in which the pre-1911 Act term would not yet have expired (and where the term conferred by the 1911 Act had not done so either). **5–158**

The 1956 Act: where the pre-1911 Act term would have already expired. In this situation, the substituted right would already have revested in the author in accordance with the proviso, either unencumbered or subject to the rights of the former assignee or grantee under one or other of the two options. These rights will usually have either been exercised or been forfeited, although there may have been a number of cases where the old term would have expired only shortly before commencement of the 1956 Act[25] so that they remained exercisable. The transitional provisions of the 1956 Act provided that, if before commencement any event had occurred or notice had been given which, in accordance with the terms of the revesting proviso, had any operation affecting the ownership of the right conferred by the 1911 Act in relation to the work, or creating, transferring or terminating an interest, right or licence in respect of that right, that event or **5–159**

---

18 *Loew's Inc v Littler* [1958] Ch. 650.
19 *Loew's Inc v Littler* [1958] Ch. 650.
20 For the definition of "collective work", see s.35 of the 1911 Act and para. 5–114, above.
21 *i.e.* under s.18 of the Literary Copyright Act 1842. See paras 5–31 and 5–40, above, and *Lawrence, etc., Ltd v Aflalo* [1904] A.C. 17.
22 See para. 5–151, above.
23 Subject to the concurrent right of the author, if the collective work was of a periodical nature, and not otherwise, to publish his article in "separate form" when 28 years had elapsed since the original publication. See the note to Sch.1 to the 1911 Act and para. 5–31, above.
24 Copyright Act 1911, s.24, proviso (a)(ii).
25 On June 1, 1957.

notice was to have the corresponding operation in relation to the copyright in the work under the 1956 Act. It followed, therefore, that where the copyright under the 1911 Act had revested in the author or his personal representative under the proviso, the copyright conferred by the 1956 Act vested in him also, and the operation of any notice given under the first option was also preserved. It was further provided that any right which, at a time after the commencement of the 1956 Act, would, by virtue of the revesting proviso, have been exercisable in relation to the work or to the right conferred by the 1911 Act, if the 1956 Act had not been passed, should be exercisable in relation to the work, or to the copyright therein under the 1956 Act, as the case might be.[26] This preserved the right conferred upon the assignee under the second option, and the right to exercise the first option, if still available.

5–160   **The 1956 Act: where the pre-1911 Act term would not yet have expired.** In this situation, the assignee or grantee would, immediately before commencement, still have been entitled to his interest for the remainder of the old term. As to this, the 1956 Act provided that if the substituted right conferred by the 1911 Act would have reverted to the author or his personal representatives at the end of the pre-1911 Act term in accordance with the revesting proviso, and this date fell after the commencement of the 1956 Act, then on that date:

(a) the copyright in the work conferred by the 1956 Act was to revert to the author or his personal representatives as the case might be; and

(b) any interest of any other person in that copyright which subsisted on that date, by virtue of any document made before the commencement of the 1911 Act, was thereupon to determine.[27]

Nevertheless, as already seen, any right which after the commencement of the 1956 Act would have been exercisable if the 1956 Act had not been passed, was to be exercisable in relation to the copyright conferred by the 1956 Act. This preserved the right of the assignee or grantee under the two options. The effect of the 1956 Act was therefore to continue the regime of the 1911 Act.

5–161   **Provisions of the 1988 Act.** The 1988 Act continues the effect of these provisions. Thus:

(a) If, before the commencement of the 1988 Act (August 1, 1989), any event occurred or notice was given which, by virtue of the above transitional provisions of the 1956 Act, had any operation in relation to copyright in the work under that Act, the event or notice has the corresponding operation in relation to copyright conferred by the 1988 Act.[28] This preserved the revesting of copyright which had already taken place and the corresponding rights of assignees and grantees under the two options.

(b) Any right which, immediately before commencement of the 1988 Act, would by virtue of these provisions of the 1956 Act have been exercisable in relation to the work or copyright in it, is exercisable in relation to the work or copyright in it under the 1988 Act.[29] This preserves the rights of assignees and grantees in the future to exercise the two options.

(c) Finally, if in accordance with the above provisions of the 1956 Act, copyright would, on a date after the commencement of the 1956 Act, have reverted to the author or his personal representatives and that date falls after August 1, 1989, the copyright in the work is to revert to the author or

---

[26] Copyright Act 1956, Sch.7, para.38(3).
[27] *ibid.* Sch7. para.38(4),.
[28] CDPA 1988, Sch.1, para.28(2).
[29] Sch.1, para.28(3).

his personal representatives, as the case may be, and any interest of any other person in the copyright which subsists on that date, by virtue of any document made before the commencement of the 1911 Act, is to thereupon determine.[30] This provides for the revesting of copyright in accordance with the proviso where the old term would have come to an end after the commencement of the 1988 Act.

4. JOINT AUTHORS AND JOINT OWNERS

The topic of joint authorship and ownership is dealt with in detail as it arises in connection with various issues such as authorship, ownership, etc. A summary of the important points only is given here.   **5–162**

Joint authorship.[31] A work of joint authorship is one produced by the collaboration of two or more authors in which the contribution of each author is not distinct from that of the other or others.[32] This requires that (a) each contributor must answer the description of an "author", (b) there must have been collaboration between them and (c) their contributions must not have been distinct. A film will now always be a work of joint authorship of the producer and principal director, unless they are one and the same person.[33]   **5–163**

Subsistence of copyright in works of joint authorship. Where the subsistence of copyright depends on the author satisfying one of the qualifying conditions of the 1988 Act, then if any one of the authors satisfies those requirements the work will qualify for copyright protection.[34] Where a work qualifies for protection by this route, however, only those authors who satisfy the requirements are to be taken into account in deciding who is the first owner of copyright, determining the duration of copyright and whether the defence under s.57 of the Act (anonymous or pseudonymous works) applies.[35]   **5–164**

Joint authors as first owners of copyright. Where a work is one of joint authorship, the general rule is that the authors will be joint first owners of the copyright.[36] As such, they will usually hold the copyright as tenants in common rather than as joint tenants, this being the natural inference in the context of the creation of a copyright work. The matter, however, is one of agreement and the circumstances may show a contrary intention.[37] For example, there may be a strong inference that the property of husband and wife was intended to be held as joint tenants.[38] Where the first owners hold the copyright as tenants in common, the shares will   **5–165**

---

[30] Sch.1, para.28(4).

[31] See paras 4–37 *et seq.*, above, for a detailed treatment of joint authorship.

[32] CDPA 1988, s.10(1).

[33] s.10(1A).

[34] CDPA 1988, s.154(3). See Ch.3, above, for a detailed treatment of this topic.

[35] s.154(3).

[36] See para. 5–07, above. The exception is where the authors were employed under contracts of service. As to this situation, see para. 5–08, above.

[37] The statement in *Lauri v Renad* [1892] 3 Ch. 402 at 413, *per* Kekewich J., to the effect that this is always so is, it is suggested, wrong and is based on an incorrect reading of *Powell v Head* (1879) L.R. 9 Ch. 518. In this latter case, the owners in question were each assignees of a share of the copyright from the first owner and so were clearly tenants in common. It is also suggested that a similar statement in previous editions of this work, upon which the dicta in *Prior v Lansdowne Press Pty Ltd* [1977] R.P.C. 511, *Dixon Projects Pty Ltd v Masterton Homes Pty Ltd* (1996) 36 I.P.R. 136 and *Acorn Computers Ltd v MCS Microcomputer Systems Pty Ltd* (1984) 4 I.P.R. 214 were built, and the statement in *Ray v Classic FM plc* [1998] F.S.R. 622 that joint authors hold copyright as tenants in common, were also wrong.

[38] *Mail Newspapers plc v Express Newspapers plc* [1987] F.S.R. 90 (copyright in wedding photographs).

usually be equal,[39] but there is no rule as to this[40] and the circumstances may indicate otherwise, for example where the authors are parties to a publishing agreement which provides for an unequal split in royalties.[41]

5–166   **Transmission of title.** One joint owner may assign his interest in the copyright.[42] On the death of one joint tenant, his interest in the copyright will pass to his co-owners by survivorship.[43] On the death of one tenant in common, his interest passes to his personal representatives as part of his estate.[44]

5–167   **Term of copyright.** The present position under the 1988 Act is that the copyright in a literary, dramatic, musical or artistic work of joint authorship expires 70 years after the death of the last of the authors to die.[45]

5–168   **Licence by one joint owner only.** One of several joint owners cannot grant a licence which is binding on his co-owners.[46] Nor can he grant a statutory exclusive licence to a third party, since he is not "the" copyright owner.[47]

5–169   **Rights of co-owners *inter se*.** One co-owner can sue his co-owners for infringement of copyright for doing any of the acts restricted by the copyright which have been committed without his licence. This is because the reference in s.16(2) to acts done without the "licence" of the copyright owner is to be taken as a reference to all the copyright owners.[48] One co-owner therefore has no right to exercise the rights of a copyright owner alone, not even if he accounts to his co-owners for a share of any profits: the rights of his co-owners are not limited to an account.[49] One co-owner can also sue third parties for infringement and obtain an injunction and damages without joining his co-owners.[50] Probably, one tenant in common can only recover damages for the injury done to his share.[51]

5. EQUITABLE OWNERSHIP

5–170   It happens frequently that the legal and beneficial titles to a copyright work become separated. This Chapter is concerned with the circumstances in which this occurs, how the equitable title can be transferred and what the incidents of equitable ownership are.

---

[39] As in *Redwood Music Ltd v B. Feldman & Co Ltd* [1979] R.P.C. 1 at 4.

[40] *Bamgboye v Reed* [2002] EWHC (QB) 2922, para.40.

[41] As in *Prior v Lansdowne Press Pty Ltd* [1977] R.P.C. 511 (Sup. Ct of Victoria). Again, it is suggested that the statement in *Ray v Classic FM plc* [1998] F.S.R. 622 that joint authors hold the copyright as tenants in common in equal shares is wrong.

[42] See para. 5–68, above. The effect of an assignment by one joint tenant will be to sever the joint tenancy.

[43] See *Mail Newspapers plc v Express Newspapers plc* [1987] F.S.R. 90.

[44] As to transmission on death generally, see para. 5–121, above.

[45] CDPA 1988, s.12(8). This only summarises the present position. The reader is referred to Ch.6, below, for the detailed discussion on the term of copyright.

[46] CDPA 1988, s.173(2). The earlier Copyright Acts did not make express provision for this but the position was the same. See *Copinger* (12th ed.), para.372 and *Powell v Head* (1879) 12 Ch. D. 686.

[47] See CDPA 1988, s.173(2). As to statutory exclusive licences, see paras 5–204 *et seq.*, below. It is suggested that the statement in *Mail Newspapers plc v Express Newspapers plc* [1987] F.S.R. 90 that this follows from the fact that one co-owner cannot prevent his co-owners from doing of any of the acts restricted by the copyright is incorrect. He *can* do so (see the following paragraph).

[48] CDPA 1988, ss.16(2), 173(2); *Ray v Classic FM plc* [1998] F.S.R. 622. The position was the same under the earlier Acts, although not so explicit. See *Cescinsky v George Routledge & Sons Ltd* [1916] 2 K.B. 325.

[49] *Ray v Classic FM plc* [1998] F.S.R. 622, above.

[50] *Lauri v Renad* [1892] 3 Ch. 402; *Prior v Lansdowne Press Pty Ltd* [1977] R.P.C. 511; *Acorn Computers Ltd v MCS Microcomputer Systems Ltd* (1985) A.L.R. 389; *Waterlow Publishers Ltd v Rose* [1995] F.S.R. 207; *Cala Homes (South) Ltd v Alfred McAlpine Homes East Ltd* [1995] F.S.R. 818 at 836; *Dixon Projects Pty Ltd v Masterton Homes Pty Ltd* (1996) 36 I.P.R. 136.

[51] *Prior v Lansdowne Press Pty Ltd* [1977] R.P.C. 511.

A. CREATION OF AN EQUITABLE TITLE

There are no set rules which determine the circumstances in which an equitable **5–171** title arises. By definition, it occurs on an event which results in the legal and beneficial titles becoming separated. Although an express declaration of trust is the clearest example of the creation of an equitable interest,[52] the usual commercial cases arise either on the creation of the work or on a later, ineffective, attempt to transfer the legal title. Writing is not necessary to create an equitable interest, whether created by trust or otherwise, although it is necessary for the purpose of assigning such interest.[53]

(i) Equitable title arising on creation of a work

The identity of the first legal owner of the copyright in a work is determined by **5–172** the application of the relevant statutory provisions, which have already been considered. In many cases, however, the circumstances in which the work is made mean that the beneficial owner is in fact some person other than the legal owner, either because this is what the parties agreed[54] or as a consequence of some fiduciary or trust relationship that exists between them.

Equitable title by virtue of contract. There is no limit to the variety of **5–173** contractual situations in which parties may agree that the copyright in a work yet to be created will belong to someone other than the first legal owner. Contracts pursuant to which the making of a work is commissioned are a common example, and are considered separately, below. If the contract contains a valid assignment of the future legal title in the work to be created, then the legal title will vest in the assignee when the work is made.[55] Often, however, the agreement is silent or ineffectual to transfer the future legal title, but if the intention of the parties, express or implied, is that a party other than the first legal owner should be entitled to the copyright, then that party will acquire an equitable title in the copyright when the work is made, provided that he is entitled to enforce his claim in equity to have the title vested in him by the legal owner.[56] This will often be the case where the author was paid to create the work.[57] The consequence of such an arrangement will be that the copyright is held on trust by the legal owner,[58] and the legal owner must transfer the legal title if called upon to do so.[59] Thus the agreement may contain an express provision that the copyright in the work should

---

[52] For an example of such a declaration in a commercial context, see *The Photocrom Co Ltd v H. & W. Nelson Ltd* [1923–28] Mac.C.C. 293.

[53] See para. 5–185, below.

[54] The identity of first legal owner is determined by statute. It cannot be altered by agreement, save in relation to employees' works and "future" works (as to which see paras 5–26 and 5–105, above, respectively).

[55] As to such an assignment of the future copyright, see para. 5–105, above.

[56] Note that it seems that the equitable title may remain good even if the assignee has lost the right to enforce the contract before the legal title is perfected. See *Peer International Corp v Editora Musical de Cuba* [2002] (Ch) EWHC 2675, where the contract in question had been abrogated by virtue of a foreign decree. Presumably, however, the equitable title would be lost if the assignee had lost the right to specific performance of the agreement because of his own conduct. The decision on these aspects was not affected by the decision on appeal, [2003] EWCA Civ 1156.

[57] *Massine v de Basil* [1936–45] Mac.C.C. 223; *John Richardson Computers Ltd v Flanders* [1993] F.S.R 497.

[58] *Nichols Advanced Vehicle Systems Inc v Rees* [1979] R.P.C. 127 at 139; *John Richardson Computers Ltd v Flanders* [1993] F.S.R 497 at 516.

[59] *R. Griggs Group Ltd v Evans* [2003] EWHC 2914 (Ch), para.33. Note the suggestion in that case (para.56) that if the commissioned author had been mistaken as to scope of the project and had undercharged as a result, he might be able to resist a demand that he assign the copyright without being paid an increased fee.

belong to the other party[60] amounting to an agreement to sell it,[61] or merely an implied term to this effect.[62] In this context, a purported assignment of future copyright which is for some reason ineffectual to transfer the legal title when the work is made[63] will be construed as an agreement to assign the copyright[64] and, if supported by consideration, will therefore be sufficient to vest an equitable title in the assignee as soon as the work comes into existence. Alternatively, the agreement may be to assign the copyright when called upon to do so, in which case the equitable title will arise when a request to assign is made.[65] It follows that an agreement for which there is no sufficient consideration will be ineffective to create an equitable title, as will a contract in respect of which the right to specific performance has been lost.[66] On the other hand, an oral agreement supported by sufficient consideration can clearly be effective to do so, whether or not the consideration has been executed.[67]

5–174   **Commissioned works.** It has already been seen that, except in certain pre-1988 Act cases,[68] a person who commissions a work to be made by another does not thereby become the first legal owner of the copyright. His interest in the copyright, if any, will depend on the terms of the contract. Where the terms expressly deal with the copyright, little difficulty usually arises.[69] Where, on the other hand, the matter is one of implication it can be very hard to determine what the true position is. There are many circumstances where a work is prepared by A for B which do not result in B acquiring any interest in the copyright: the result of the transaction may simply be that B becomes entitled to the property in the physical material created and to a licence to use it for the particular purpose envisaged by the parties, but does not become equitable owner of the copyright.[70] In accordance with general principles, a term to the effect that the commissioner is to be entitled to the copyright will only be implied where it is necessary to give business efficacy to the contract and the implied term satisfies the officious bystander test. Almost inevitably, however, some term will have to be implied, even if only that the commissioner is licensed to use the work, for the general principle is that "the engagement for reward of a person to produce material of a nature which is capable of being the subject of copyright implies a permission, or consent, or licence in the person giving the engagement to use the material in the manner and for the purpose in which and for which it was contemplated between the parties that it would be used at the time of the engagement".[71] The question will be whether the term to be implied is one for a non-exclusive licence, an exclusive licence or an assignment of the copyright, in whole or part: on the facts, was the

---

[60] As in *University of London Press Ltd v University Tutorial Press Ltd* [1916] 2 Ch. 601. But such an agreement may of course, on its true construction, and if the formalities are complied with, amount to a valid assignment.

[61] *Simms v Marryat* (1851) 17 Q.B. 281.

[62] Most commonly, this arises in the context of commissioned works, which are considered below, together with the topic of when such a term can be implied.

[63] As to which see para. 5–107, above.

[64] *Performing Right Society v London Theatre of Varieties Ltd* [1924] A.C. 1; *Wah Sang Industrial Co v Takmay Industrial Co Ltd* [1980] F.S.R. 303.

[65] *Hexagon Pty Ltd v Australian Broadcasting Commission* [1976] R.P.C. 628.

[66] *Levy v Rutley* (1871) L.R. 6 C.p.523.

[67] *Western Front Ltd v Vestron Inc* [1987] F.S.R. 66; *Wah Sang Industrial Co v Takmay Industrial Co Ltd* [1980] F.S.R. 303.

[68] See paras 5–33 *et seq.* and 5–43, above.

[69] As in *Ward, Lock & Co Ltd v Long* [1906] 2 Ch. 550; *Hazlitt v Templeman* (1866) 13 L.T. 593 (agreements to assign the copyright in a book yet to be written, a very common example).

[70] See, *e.g. Nicol v Barranger* [1917–23] Mac.C.C. 219; *Cooper v Stephens* [1895] 1 Ch. 567. See para. 5–217, below, as to the further examples of such licences.

[71] *Beck v Montana Constructions Pty Ltd* [1964–65] N.S.W.R. 229 approved in *Blair v Osborne & Tomkins* [1971] 2 Q.B. 78, CA.

agreement one whereby the author sold his copyright[72] or merely one whereby he granted some form of licence? In accordance with modern, general principles, the term implied should go no further than is necessary to fill the lacuna in the express terms of the contract, so that if the implication of a licence of some kind will meet this need, no agreement to assign should be implied.[73] It might be thought that the difficulty with the rigid application of this principle is that in almost every case in which it would be otherwise appropriate to imply an agreement to assign (as to which, see the next paragraph), business efficacy could be given to the agreement by implying the grant of an exclusive licence, since in such a case the grantee would be entitled to exploit the work to the exclusion of all others, including the grantor.[74] This is not so, however, since it is only in the case of a statutory exclusive licence that the licensee obtains rights which, for present purposes, are sufficiently close to those of an assignee of the copyright, in particular, a right to sue in his own name for infringements by third parties. In many cases, the agreement in question will not satisfy the requirements for the grant of a statutory exclusive licence, which must be in writing and signed by or on behalf of the owner of an existing copyright work.[75] In any event, the remedies of an exclusive licensee are not necessarily as good as those of a copyright owner.[76] If, therefore, the commissioner may need to enforce the copyright against third parties and have exclusive control over the work, this will point to it being implicit that he should own the copyright.[77]

Circumstances in which an agreement to assign the copyright are likely to be implied include those where the work is made specifically for the commissioner's business and at his expense and neither party can have contemplated that the maker of the work would have any genuine use for it himself.[78] It will be necessary to consider in particular the price paid, the impact of an assignment on the maker and whether it could sensibly have been intended that he should retain the copyright.[79] The fact that the maker may have made use of underlying works supplied and owned by the commissioner, such as preliminary drafts or sketches, so that the commissioned work could not be used by the maker without infringing the copyright in these underlying works, will also support such an implication.[80] Again, where the maker works as part of a team with employees of the commissioner, this may justify the implication.[81] On the other hand, where it is

---

[72] See, e.g. *Ironside v H.M. Attorney-General* [1988] R.P.C. 197 and *Ray v Classic FM plc* [1998] F.S.R. 622 at 640, which contains a review of the relevant principles.
[73] *Ray v Classic FM plc* [1998] F.S.R. 622, at 642, applying *Liverpool City Council v Irwin* [1977] A.C. 239.
[74] And see *Ray v Classic FM plc* [1998] F.S.R. 622 at 644, suggesting that today an assignment is rarely likely to be implied, an exclusive licence usually being sufficient.
[75] CDPA 1988, s.92(1). See para. 5–204, below, for a detailed discussion of the formalities required for the grant of an exclusive licence.
[76] *R. Griggs Group Ltd v Evans* [2003] EWHC (Ch) 2914, para.58.
[77] *R. Griggs Group Ltd v Evans* [2003] EWHC 2914 (Ch), *Durland v Molino* [2000] E.C.D.R. 320.
[78] As in *A&M Records Ltd v Video Collection International Ltd* [1995] E.M.L.R. 25; *Harold Drabble Ltd v The Hycolite Manufacturing Co* (1928) 44 T.L.R. 264 (although note the suggestion in *Ray v Classic FM plc* [1998] F.S.R. 622, that the decision may only have been that a licence was implied); *Warner v Gestetner Ltd* (unreported but cited in *Saphena Computing Ltd v Allied Collection Agencies Ltd* [1995] F.S.R. 616 at 634), and also cited as an example in *Ray v Classic FM plc* [1998] F.S.R. 622, at 642; *Pasterfield v Denham* [1999] F.S.R. 168 (advertising leaflets commissioned by a local authority to promote a local tourist attraction); *Durland v Molino* [2000] E.C.D.R. 320 (commissioned painting of restaurateur and others participating in restaurant business, reproductions of it and the original to be used in the business).
[79] *Ray v Classic FM plc* [1998] F.S.R. 622, at 642.
[80] Again, cited as an example in *Ray v Classic FM plc*, above, at 642.
[81] *Ray v Classic FM plc* [1998] F.S.R. 622, citing as examples *Nichols Advanced Vehicle Systems Inc v Rees* [1979] R.P.C. 127 at 139, and *Sofia Bogrich v Shape Machines*, unreported, November 4, 1994.

contemplated that the work may be sold by the maker to others[82] or where it incorporates elements that the maker is likely to use again in his business, such as standard routines employed by a software writer, together with additions that are specific to the commissioner's business, an intention that the commissioner should own the entire copyright is unlikely to be implied. Obviously the fact that the maker disowns any claim to any beneficial interest will make it easier in practice for the commissioner to establish his equitable title.[83] Care may need to be taken with some of the older cases, decided when the modern principles relating to the implication of terms into a contract had not yet been worked out or in which they were not rigorously applied, for example with such statements as:

> "... where a man employs another to write an article, or to do anything else for him, unless there is something in the surrounding circumstances, or in the course of dealing between the parties, to require a different construction, it is to be understood that the writing or other thing is produced on terms that the copyright shall belong to the employer".[84]

5–175 **Employee not under a contract of service.** The legal title to most works made by an author in the course of his employment under a contract of service will belong to his employer.[85] Where this is not the case, the work may nevertheless have been made in circumstances that a term is to be implied that the copyright should belong to whoever has engaged or employed the author.[86]

5–176 **Company directors and other fiduciaries.** Where the work is created by someone who stands in a fiduciary relationship with another, such that he cannot be heard to say that he created the work for his own benefit, he will usually hold the copyright in trust for that other person. So, for example, a director or *de facto* director of a company who is not employed under a contract of service[87] may nevertheless hold the copyright in works he makes for the company on trust and will have to assign the copyright to the company when called upon to do so.[88] This will usually be so because the director will have created the work for the company's business, using the company's property and in the company's time.[89] There is, however, no rule that works created by a director for his company are always held on trust: it will depend on what, if anything, has been agreed.[90] In particular, it is always open to the shareholders of a company to agree that a

---

[82] *Saphena Computing Ltd v Allied Collection Agencies Ltd* [1995] F.S.R. 616.

[83] As in *Merchant Adventurers Ltd v M. Grew & Co Ltd* [1973] R.P.C. 1.

[84] *Sweet v Benning* (1855) 16 C.B. 459, *per* Maule J. Note also that the suggestion in *Ray v Classic FM plc* [1998] F.S.R. 622, at 643, that cases decided before the passing of the 1956 Act are generally likely to be of little guidance since before then an exclusive licensee had no right to sue in his own name (see para. 5–207 to 5–208, below). As seen above, however, it will often not be possible to create a statutory exclusive licence by implication.

[85] CDPA 1988, s.11(2). See paras 5–209 *et seq.*, below.

[86] As in *Massine v De Basil* [1936–45] Mac.C.C. 223; *Sweet v Shaw* (1839) 8 L.J. Ch. 216 (law reports prepared for future publication). See also the reasoning in *Sweet v Benning* (1855) 16 C.B. 459, quoted in para. 5–174, above.

[87] As, *e.g.*, in *Parsons v Albert J. Parsons & Sons Ltd* [1979] F.S.R. 254; *Wilden Pump & Engineering Co v Fusfield* (1985) 8 I.P.R. 250 and *Ultraframe (UK) Ltd v Fielding* [2003] EWCA Civ 1805. Where a work is made by a director in the course of his employment under a contract of service, the copyright will, of course, subject to any agreement to the contrary, belong to the company. See paras 5–15 *et seq.*, above, and *Gardex Ltd v Sorata Ltd* [1986] R.P.C. 623; *Erica Vale Australia Pty Ltd v Thompson & Morgan (Ipswich) Ltd* (1994) 29 I.P.R. 589 at 632.

[88] *Antocks Lairn Ltd v I. Bloohn Ltd* [1971] F.S.R. 490; *Kambrook Distributing Pty Ltd v Delaney* (1984) 4 I.P.R. 79 at 89; *A-One Accessory Imports Ltd v Off Road Imports Pty Ltd* (1994) 34 I.P.R. 306 (Fed. Ct of Aus.), suggesting that work done by two persons intended to be for the benefit of a company which they later acquired and became directors of was held in trust for the company.

[89] See the analysis in *Ultraframe (UK) Ltd v Fielding* [2003] EWCA Civ 1805.

[90] *Wilden Pump & Engineering Co v Fusfield* (1985) 8 I.P.R. 250 (director of one-man company receiving royalties for designs from company: inconsistent with holding copyright in trust).

director should retain property he has created or to relieve him of any liability for any breach of duty, provided that to do so is not *ultra vires* the company or a fraud on its creditors.[91] In the case of a sole shareholder-director, however, it will often be difficult to show that the company has agreed to this.[92] Again, where a work is made by an employee outside office hours, but in breach of his fiduciary duty to his employer, the employer may be entitled to the copyright in equity.[93] It is an open question whether an employer is entitled in equity to the copyright in a former servant's work containing information which he remained under a duty of confidence to keep secret.[94]

Partners. Where a work is made by one partner in the ordinary course of the partnership business and for the purposes of the partnership, the copyright in the work will become partnership property, in the sense that as between the partners it is to be regarded as an asset of the partnership.[95] In the absence of a written assignment, however, the legal title will remain with the partner who was the author and will not devolve upon the partners. The other partners' right is to have the copyright applied for the benefit of the partnership.[96] The same will apply to copyright brought into the partnership as capital.[97]

5–177

(ii) Equitable title arising subsequent to creation of work

There are many circumstances in which the legal and equitable titles become separated on an event subsequent to the creation of a copyright work. Most frequently this happens in a transaction which amounts to an agreement to assign the copyright.

5–178

Agreement to assign. Where an agreement made for consideration contains an obligation to assign the copyright in an existing work, an equitable title will be created.[98] The agreement may be oral or implied. A vesting order may be made to transfer the legal title.[99] Where the obligation arises at some future time, the assignee will acquire an equitable title when that time comes,[1] assuming the agree-

5–179

---

[91] *Ultraframe (UK) Ltd v Fielding* [2003] EWCA Civ 1805, at para.39. It will, however, be *ultra vires* the company to distribute assets to a shareholder otherwise than by distribution of a profit lawfully made or by lawful reduction or return of capital, and allowing a shareholder-director to retain rights of copyright will normally involve either one or other of these steps: *Ultraframe*, at para.39.

[92] *Ultraframe (UK) Ltd v Fielding* [2003] EWCA Civ 1805.

[93] *Missing Link Software v Magee* [1989] F.S.R. 361; *Service Corp International plc v Channel Four Television Corp*, The Independent, May 14, 1998.

[94] See *Attorney-General v Guardian Newspapers Ltd (No. 2)* [1990] 1 A.C. 109 at 263A, HL; *Att-Gen v Blake* [1998] Ch. 439; [1997] Ch. 84. In *A-G v Blake*, at first instance, Sir Richard Scott V.C. indicated that although he would have felt constrained by *Lister & Co v Stubbs* (1890) 45 Ch. D. 1 and *Halifax Building Society v Thomas* [1996] Ch. 217 to hold that the employer (in that case the Crown) was not so entitled, his view was that in the light of Privy Council decision in *Att-Gen for Hong Kong v Reid* [1994] 1 A.C. 324, disapproving *Lister*, the law should be otherwise. For the decision in the House of Lords, see [2001] 1 A.C. 268.

[95] *Meikle v Mauffe* [1941] 3 All E.R. 144; *Roban Jig & Tool Co Ltd v Taylor* [1979] F.S.R. 130; *Murray v King* [1986] F.S.R. 116 (Fed. Ct of Aus.); *Ibcos Computers Ltd v Barclays Mercantile Highland Finance Ltd* [1994] F.S.R. 275; cf. *Coffey's Registered Designs* [1982] F.S.R. 227, where the partnership business was not concerned with producing designs.

[96] *O'Brien v Komersaroff* (1982) 56 A.L.J.R. 681.

[97] *Ibcos Computers Ltd v Barclays Mercantile Highland Finance Ltd* [1994] F.S.R. 275.

[98] See *The Photocrom Co Ltd v H. & W. Nelson Ltd* [1923–28] Mac.C.C. 293. s.90(3) is only concerned with transfers of the legal title: *Lakeview Computers plc v Steadman* (unreported, November 26, 1999, CA).

[99] *Lakeview Computers plc v Steadman* (November 26, 1999, CA, unreported).

[1] *Hexagon Pty Ltd v Australian Broadcasting Commission* [1976] R.P.C. 628.

ment then to be specifically enforceable.[2] The obligation to assign may arise at some fixed, future time or be a matter of the assignee's choice.[3] Until that time arrives, the assignee has a sufficient equitable interest in the copyright to entitle him to protection, for example, to prevent disposal of the copyright by the assignor.[4] Except as against a purchaser of the legal title for value without notice, the assignee will be entitled to the copyright against anyone to whom the legal owner has assigned the copyright in breach of his contract with the assignee.

5–180 **Imperfect legal assignment.** The requirements for a valid, immediate assignment of the legal title to a copyright work have already been considered,[5] as has the special case of an assignment of a future copyright work.[6] An invalid assignment of the legal title to an existing work will be treated as an agreement to assign, and thus an equitable assignment, if supported by sufficient consideration.[7]

5–181 **Assignment of after-acquired works.** It is a common feature of music publishing and other similar agreements that a party agrees to assign not only works which he owns at the date of the assignment but also works which he subsequently acquires from other parties. Such an agreement will rarely operate as a legal assignment of the title to the works when they are acquired[8] and at best the assignee will therefore usually only acquire an equitable title.[9] Such agreements should therefore always contain a covenant for further assurances.

(iii) Other equitable interests: options, pre-emptions and equitable mortgages

5–182 **Option to acquire.** Although an agreement whereby a party is granted an option to acquire the copyright in a work will not create any equitable title to the copyright before exercise of the option, it will create a sufficient equitable interest to entitle the grantee to an injunction to restrain exploitation of the work by a third-party assignee from the grantor, unless the third party is a purchaser for value without notice.[10] Such options are a common feature of publishing agreements in the literary and music fields, and in the film industry.

5–183 **Right of pre-emption or first refusal.** It is common in many fields for the copyright owner to grant another the right of pre-emption or first refusal to a work. Such a grant, if given for consideration, will give the grantee an equitable interest which can be enforced against not only the grantor but also all others except a purchaser for value without notice.

---

[2] But see *Peer International Corp v Editora Musical de Cuba* [2002] EWHC (Ch) 2675 and the comment in the footnotes to para. 5–173, above, on this case.

[3] As in *Hexagon Pty Ltd v Australian Broadcasting Commission* [1976] R.P.C. 628; *Colburn v Duncombe*, 9 Sim. 151 (agreement to deliver a "regular assignment" when called upon to do so). As to an assignment of the copyright in a "future work", see para. 5–105, above.

[4] *Macdonald (E.) Ltd v Eyles* [1921] 1 Ch. 631.

[5] See para. 5–82, above.

[6] See para. 5–105, above.

[7] *Wah Sang Industrial Co v Takmay Industrial Co Ltd* [1980] F.S.R. 303 (Ct of Appeal of Hong Kong).

[8] The provisions of CDPA 1988, s.91, relating to assignments of future copyright, will only catch such works if they are works of "future copyright" and the assignor is a "prospective owner" within the meaning of the section (see para. 5–107, above).

[9] *Performing Right Society Ltd v London Theatre of Varieties Ltd* [1924] A.C. 1 at 13.

[10] *Macdonald (E.) Ltd v Eyles* [1921] 1 Ch. 631.

Equitable mortgage. The creation of, and rights incidental to, an equitable **5–184** mortgage are considered elsewhere.[11]

B. TRANSFER OF EQUITABLE INTEREST

Although no formalities are required for the creation of an equitable interest, the **5–185** assignment of an equitable title to copyright is governed by the Law of Property Act 1925, which provides that a disposition of an equitable interest subsisting at the time of the disposition must be in writing, signed by the person disposing of the same, or by his agent lawfully authorised in writing or by will.[12] The combined effect of the 1988 Act and the Law of Property Act 1925 is therefore that any assignment of copyright, whether it be of the legal or equitable interest, must be in writing.[13] As with the legal title, the disposal of the physical property in which the copyright work may happen to be embodied, such as a manuscript or painting, does not carry with it the equitable title.[14]

C. INCIDENTS OF EQUITABLE OWNERSHIP

Right to bring proceedings. An equitable owner is entitled to institute proceed- **5–186** ings for infringement of copyright and to obtain an interim injunction, thereby protecting his interest.[15] Normally, however, an equitable owner by himself cannot obtain judgment at trial,[16] even a final injunction, because of the risk to the defendant that he will be exposed to a second claim by a legal owner, in particular a bona fide purchaser for value without notice claiming under the legal owner.[17] Before judgment, therefore, the equitable owner must either perfect his title by taking an assignment from the legal owner or, alternatively, join the legal owner, either as claimant or defendant.[18] Until he does so, the proceedings are liable to be stayed.[19] This is, however, a rule of practice not law, although it will be departed from only very sparingly. Thus, there may be special cases where the equitable owner can sue alone, for example because of the impossibility of getting an assignment from the legal owner and the great inconvenience of joining

---

[11] See para. 5–192, below.

[12] Law of Property Act 1925, s.53(1)(c); *Lakeview Computers plc v Steadman* (unreported, November 26, 1999, CA); *Comprop Ltd v Moran* [2002] J.L.R. 222 (Royal Ct of Jersey) at para.97.

[13] *Roban Jig & Tool Co Ltd v Taylor* [1979] F.S.R. 130 at 143; see *Performing Right Society Ltd v London Theatre of Varieties Ltd* [1924] A.C. 1 at 18; *Wah Sang Industrial Co v Takmay Industrial Co Ltd* [1980] F.S.R. 303 at 309 (Ct of Appeal of Hong Kong).

[14] *Nicol v Barranger* [1917–23] Mac.C.C. 219. See also para. 5–65, above.

[15] *Mawman v Tegg* (1826) 2 Russ. 385; *Sweet v Shaw* (1839) 8 L.J. Ch. 216; *Sweet v Cater* 11 Sim. 572; *Hodges v Welsh* (1840) 2 Ir. Eq. R. 266; *Performing Right Society Ltd v London Theatre of Varieties Ltd* [1924] A.C. 1 at 14, 35; *Merchant Adventurers Ltd v Grew & Co* [1972] Ch. 242 at 252; *Roban Jig & Tool Co Ltd v Taylor* [1979] F.S.R. 130 at 135; *Wah Sang Industrial Co v Takmay Industrial Co Ltd* [1980] F.S.R. 303; *Orwin v Attorney-General* [1998] F.S.R. 415.

[16] See *University of London Press v University Tutorial Press* [1916] 2 Ch. 601; *Orwin v Attorney-General*, above.

[17] *Performing Right Society Ltd v London Theatre of Varieties Ltd* [1924] A.C. 1 at 14; *Weddell v J.A. Pearce & Major* [1988] Ch. 26; *Batjac Productions Inc v Simitar Entertainment (UK) Ltd* [1996] F.S.R. 139, at 150.

[18] *Orwin v Attorney-General* [1998] F.S.R. 415 at 423; *Batjac Productions Inc v Simitar Entertainment (UK) Ltd* [1996] F.S.R. 139, at 152; *Three Rivers District Council v Bank of England* [1996] Q.B. 292, at 309. Note that an equitable assignor can only bring proceedings by himself if, with the agreement of the assignee, he sues as trustee for the assignee, and in that event his representative capacity should be revealed in accordance with CPR, r.16.2(3). If he sues, attempting to recover for himself, the assignee must be joined. See *Three Rivers District Council v Bank of England* at 308B.

[19] *Weddell v J.A. Pearce & Major* [1988] Ch. 26.

him, his conduct,[20] or other exceptional circumstances.[21] An important factor will be the evaluation of the risk to the defendant of a further claim by the legal owner. A helpful parallel may be drawn with the power of the court to grant leave to an exclusive licensee to proceed without joining the copyright owner.[22]

5–187   **Rights as against legal owner.** By definition, except as against a purchaser of the legal title for value without notice, the equitable owner has a right to an assignment of the legal title, which may be enforced by a decree for specific performance or an order vesting the copyright in him.[23] Even before such assignment, it seems that he is entitled to the remedies available under the 1988 Act as against the bare legal owner.[24]

5–188   **Rights as between equitable owners.** The normal equitable rule applies, namely that the title of the first equitable owner in time will prevail, except that the first owner may lose his prior claim through his own misconduct.[25] Except in such circumstances, therefore, the first owner in time will be entitled to an assignment of the legal title from the legal owner in priority to the second owner, and to an injunction against the second owner.[26]

5–189   **Defence to an action for infringement.** An equitable owner will have a defence to a claim for infringement, except one brought by a *bona fide* purchaser of the legal title for value without notice.

6. MORTGAGES AND CHARGES

5–190   The express giving of security over a specific copyright work or works has historically not been a common feature of copyright law but is becoming more so. An exception has been the film and related industries where the sums required to fund the making of a film are such that the financiers will usually require some form of security (usually a mortgage) over the film and underlying works (such as the screenplay) to protect their investment. Apart from this, it is of course an everyday feature of commercial life for companies to provide fixed and floating charges over their assets by way of a debenture to secure bank or other loans. Caught up in such charges will be any copyright works belonging to the company.

5–191   **Mortgages.** As with any mortgage, the characteristic of a mortgage of copyright is the transfer of the copyright to another as a security for the payment of a debt or the discharge of some other obligation for which it is given.[27] A legal mortgage of copyright is formally effected by an assignment of the copyright by the mortgagor coupled with a covenant by the mortgagee to reassign on repayment of the debt or discharge of the obligation.[28] A legal mortgage must therefore be in

---

[20] *Performing Right Society Ltd v London Theatre of Varieties Ltd* [1924] A.C. 1 at 18.
[21] As in *William Brandt's Sons & Co v Dunlop Rubber Co* [1905] A.C. 454 at 462, where the defendant disclaimed a wish to have the legal owner joined.
[22] See CDPA 1988, s.102(1) and para. 5–206, below.
[23] See, *e.g.* the Trustee Act 1925, s.51; *R. Griggs Group Ltd v Evans No.1* [2003] EWHC (Ch) 2914, para.34; *R. Griggs Group Ltd v Evans No.2* [2004] EWHC (Ch) 1088, para.51.
[24] See *Cableship Ltd v Williams*, noted at [1991] I.P.D. 14205; *John Richardson Computers Ltd v Flanders* [1993] F.S.R. 497. It is not clear whether the remedies were granted there as a matter of equity. In *Ibcos Computers Ltd v Barclays Mercantile Highland Finance Ltd* [1994] F.S.R. 275, no point was taken.
[25] See Snell, *Principles of Equity* (29th ed., Sweet & Maxwell), pp.57 *et seq.*
[26] *Sims v Marryat* (1851) 17 Q.B. 281 at 292.
[27] *Santley v Wilde* [1899] 2 Ch. 474.
[28] See Snell, *Principles of Equity* (30th ed., Sweet & Maxwell), para.22–15.

writing, signed by or on behalf of the mortgagor-copyright owner.[29] Where it is contemplated that the mortgagor will need to exploit the work during the term of the mortgage, the mortgage will need to include a grant back of a licence, usually an exclusive licence, to allow for this. Where finance is being provided for the making of a work, a legal mortgage can be created relying on the provisions of s.91 of the 1988 Act.[30] An attempt to create a mortgage otherwise than by these means will at best create an equitable mortgage, the rights of the equitable mortgagee then being at risk as against a person who bona fide acquires the legal title by way of purchase for value (whether on a sale or, for example, another mortgage) without notice of the equitable mortgagee's interests. It should be noted that a purported assignment by way of mortgage may not, on its proper construction, be effective to pass the legal title to the copyright, so that the mortgage created thereby will be merely equitable.[31]

A legal mortgagee, having the legal title vested in him, can sue in his own name for infringements of copyright, although in his conduct of the action he must bear in mind that he holds the copyright as a mere security for his debt. The mortgagor, who retains an interest in the copyright by way of the equity of redemption, also has a sufficient title to start proceedings to restrain infringements of copyright and thus protect his interest,[32] but must join the mortgagee or redeem the mortgage before trial.[33] Where the mortgage includes the grant back of an exclusive licence to the mortgagor, the mortgagor will have additional title to sue.[34]

Equitable mortgages. An equitable mortgage may arise on an ineffectual attempt to create a legal mortgage, for example, where the mortgage has not been signed by, or on behalf of the mortgagor, or is merely oral. An equitable owner of copyright may mortgage his interest; such a mortgage must also be in writing signed by, or on his behalf.[35] **5–192**

Charges. An equitable charge over copyright is created when the owner agrees to give another rights over the copyright as security for a loan or other obligation.[36] This is formally effected by the owner agreeing that the copyright should stand charged with the repayment of the loan or discharge of the obligation, but the same result is achieved where the owner agrees to pay a debt out of the copyright or its proceeds of sale.[37] In the case of many company debentures, the charge will be a floating one,[38] enabling the company to deal freely with copyright works created or acquired in the course of the business until the charge crystallises. Neither **5–193**

---

[29] See CDPA 1988, s.90(3) and para. 5–82, above. For a precedent of a legal mortgage, see Vol.2 at J1.vii.

[30] This section enables the legal assignment of "future copyright". See para. 5–107, above.

[31] See *Chitty on Contracts* (29th ed.), para.19–004 , for a discussion of the circumstances in which a purported assignment of a chose in action may not be an effective legal assignment. Section 90(1) of the 1988 Act does not expressly provide that an assignment must be "absolute" or "not by way of charge only" (*cf.* s.136 of the Law of Property Act 1925), but it would seem that a purported assignment of copyright which is conditional (for example, expressed to be only until the debt is repaid, or only to take effect on default) will not be an "assignment" within s.90(1). See, *e.g. Hearst Corp v Stark*, 639 F. Supp.970 (N.D. Cal. 1986) and *Pantone, Inc v A.I. Friedman Inc* 294 F. Supp.545 (1968). However, a mortgage in ordinary form with a proviso for reassignment upon repayment of the mortgage is an absolute assignment for the purposes of Law of Property Act 1925, s.136. See *Tancred v Delagoa Bay and East Africa Rly Co* (1889) 23 Q.B.D. 239; *Hughes v Pump House Hotel Co* [1902] 2 K.B. 190.

[32] *Hardacre v Armstrong* [1905–10] Mac.C.C. 1.

[33] See para. 5–186, above.

[34] As to an exclusive licensee's right to bring proceedings, see para. 5–205, below.

[35] *i.e.* so as to satisfy the Law of Property Act 1925, s.53(1)(c). See para. 5–185, above.

[36] *London County and Westminster Bank Ltd v Tompkins* [1918] 1 K.B. 515.

[37] See *Swiss Bank Corp v Lloyds Bank Ltd* [1979] Ch. 548 at 569.

[38] The usual form of debenture often does not include copyrights in the property secured by way of

the legal nor equitable title is transferred to the chargee and in principle the chargee merely has the right to have the copyright realised by judicial process to obtain repayment of the loan.[39] A well-drafted charge will, however, provide remedies such as the power to appoint a receiver to enable the chargee to realise his security without recourse to proceedings.

7. LICENCES AND RELATED ISSUES

A. INTRODUCTION

5–194   The 1988 Act confers on the copyright owner the exclusive right to do the various acts restricted by the copyright.[40] An infringement of copyright occurs if one of those acts is done without his licence.[41] A licence therefore passes no interest but merely makes lawful that which would otherwise be unlawful;[42] it is a permission which carries with it immunity from proceedings.[43] A mere licence from the copyright owner confers no proprietary interest on the licensee enabling him, for example, to bring proceedings in his own name,[44] unless coupled with the grant of some other interest, for example, the right to take property away.[45] Statute apart, even an exclusive licence, which is merely the leave to do a thing coupled with a promise not to do, or give anyone else permission to do, that thing, gives the licensee no right to sue in his own name for infringement nor any other proprietary interest.[46] In copyright law, this general rule is altered by statute in the case of exclusive licences which comply with prescribed formalities.[47] The 1998 Act confers on such a licensee a procedural status which enables him to bring proceedings but otherwise the rule is unchanged: an exclusive licensee has no proprietary interest in the copyright.[48]

5–195   **Formalities.** Except in relation to the particular procedural status conferred by statute on certain licensees,[49] there is no requirement that a licence be in writing or comply with other formalities. A licence can therefore be oral, or be implied into a contract, whether on the grounds of business efficacy or trade practice and custom. It may be gratuitous and inferred from conduct only.

---

fixed charge or mortgage; more normally this is included in a floating charge of the undertaking and all other assets of the company, both present and future.

[39] See Snell (30th ed.), para.21–03.

[40] CDPA 1988, s.16(1).

[41] s.16(2).

[42] *Canon Kabushiki Kaisha v Green Cartridge Co (Hong Kong) Ltd* [1997] A.C. 728 at 735 (P.C.), citing *Thomas v Sorrell* (1674) Vaughan 330, 351. See also *Muskett v Hill* (1840) 5 Bing. N.C. 694; *Nicol v Barranger* [1917–23] Mac.C.C. 219 at 243; *Frisby v B.B.C. Ch. 932* at 948.

[43] *British Actors Film Co Ltd v Glover* [1918] 1 K.B. 299.

[44] *Neilson v Horniman* (1909) 26 T.L.R. 188 (sole licence), following *London Printing and Publishing Alliance (Ltd) v Cox* [1891] 3 Ch. 291 and *Heap v Hartley* (1889) 42 Ch. D. 461. The suggestions in *Young v Odeon Music House Pty Ltd* (1976) 10 A.L.R. 153 at 161, and *Sega Enterprises Ltd v Galaxy Electronics Pty Ltd* (1997) 39 I.P.R. 577, based on a passage in *Halsbury's Laws of England* (4th ed), Vol.9, para.880, that a non-exclusive licensee may sue for infringement if the copyright owner is joined as co-claimant, are submitted to be wrong, and based on a mistaken reading of *Neilson v Horniman*.

[45] *Heap v Hartley* (1889) 42 Ch.D. 461 at 470 (a patent case).

[46] *Heap v Hartley* (1889) 42 Ch.D. 461; *C.B.S. United Kingdom Ltd v Charmdale Record Distributors Ltd* [1980] F.S.R. 289 at 295. It is suggested that the statement in *Wilson v Weiss Art Pty Ltd* (1995) 31 I.P.R. 423 (Fed. Ct of Aus.) at 433 that: "The grant of an irrevocable and exclusive licence for consideration must create, in equity, in favour of the licensee, an interest in the copyright, no different from that created in favour of an assignee by an equitable assignment, except for the right, in an appropriate case, to call for a legal assignment" is incorrect.

[47] See CDPA 1988, s.101, and paras 5–204 and 22–20, below. CDPA 1988, s.101A also confers precedural remedies on certain non-exclusive licensees. See paras 5–209 and 22–23, below.

[48] *C.B.S. United Kingdom Ltd v Charmdale Record Distributors Ltd* [1980] F.S.R. 289.

[49] See paras. 5–205 and 5–211, below.

Licence granted by one joint owner. A licence granted by one of several joint **5–196**
owners will not bind the others, and a person acting on the strength of it will be
liable to the others in an infringement action.[50]

Position of licensee. A licence granted by a copyright owner is binding on every **5–197**
successor in title to his interest in the copyright, except a purchaser in good faith
for valuable consideration and without notice (actual or constructive) of the
licence, or a person deriving title from such a purchaser.[51] References to doing
anything with or without the licence of the copyright owner are to be construed
accordingly.[52] The licensee of copyright, to the extent of the licence, can therefore
do acts restricted by the copyright as against the owner and anyone claiming
under the owner, except a purchaser for value without notice. Where the licence
permits the licensee to authorise others to do acts restricted by the copyright or to
grant sub-licences to others, then those other persons will be in a similar position
in relation to acts done within the scope of their authorisation or sub-licence.[53]

Transitional. The 1988 Act provides that any document made, or event occur- **5–198**
ring, before August 1, 1989 which had any operation creating, transferring or
terminating any licence in respect of the copyright in any work made before that
date will have the corresponding operation in relation to the work under the 1988
Act.[54] Generally, licences granted before this date have the same effect in relation
to copyright conferred under the 1988 Act as do licences granted after this date.
A number of exceptions are considered separately, below.

Compulsory licences. There are a number of cases in which a licence, or a right **5–199**
to call for one, is conferred by statute, rather than arising by agreement. These are
considered elsewhere.[55]

B. ASSIGNMENT OR LICENCE?

A frequent problem in this area is to determine whether a particular agreement **5–200**
amounts to an assignment of copyright, in whole or part, or merely a licence, in
particular, an exclusive licence.

Importance of the distinction. Given that an exclusive licensee may, if the **5–201**
agreement complies with the statutory formalities,[56] have sufficient title to sue
infringers, it might be thought that it is of little importance today whether the

---

[50] CDPA 1988, s.173(2).
[51] CDPA 1988, s.90(4). This statutory rule was first introduced by the 1956 Act (s.36(4)). Before
then it had been established that an assignee for value without notice took free of any licence (see
London Printing, etc, Alliance Ltd v Cox [1891] 3 Ch. 291 at first instance—the decision was reversed on other grounds on appeal) and although it was, assumed that a purchaser *with* notice
took subject to the licence (see, *e.g. Copinger* (8th ed), p.114), it is not clear what the basis for
this was since a mere licence did not create an equitable interest. The point was left open at first
instance in the *London Printing* case. It is suggested that the need for the statutory rule indicates
that a mere licence would not otherwise bind a subsequent assignee.
[52] CDPA 1988, s.90(4). A licence granted by the prospective owner of copyright, including the prospective owner of any extended or revived copyright, is similarly binding upon every successor
in title to his interest (or prospective interest) in the right: CDPA 1988, s.91(3), the Duration of
Copyright and Rights in Performances Regulations 1995 (SI 1995/3297), reg.20(2), and the
Copyright and Related Rights Regulations 2003 (SI 2003/2498), reg.37(2).
[53] The 1956 Act contained express provision to this effect (s.49(7)) which is not repeated in the
1988 Act, but presumably the law has not changed.
[54] CDPA 1988, Sch.1, para.25(1). The effect of this provision is to preserve the legal effect of a pre-
commencement licence. It does not attempt to legislate as to the effect of such a document and
only preserves such effect as the document originally had. See *Novello & Co Ltd v Keith Prowse
Music Publishing Co Ltd* [2004] EWHC 766 (Ch), para.9.
[55] See Ch.29, below.
[56] See para. 5–205, below.

instrument amounts to an assignment or exclusive licence.[57] In many respects, however, the distinction is vital and has important consequences. The differences arise from the proprietary nature of an assignee's title as opposed to that of a licensee. They can be summarised as follows:

(a) The rights of a licensee, whether exclusive or non-exclusive, are not proprietary: they derive only from his contract, if any, together with such extra protection as the 1988 Act gives him. Thus his licence will not bind a purchaser from the copyright owner acting in good faith for valuable consideration and without notice of the licence. In contrast, an assignee's title, being a proprietary one, is good against all subsequent dealings, including of course a purported, subsequent purchaser from his assignor.

(b) An exclusive licensee's right to assign the benefit of his licence or grant sub-licences will be subject to the terms of his licence. Even if he is entitled to assign the benefit of the licence, the right to exercise the licence will remain subject to whatever terms were originally imposed. In contrast, an assignee has a proprietary title which he can assign,[58] and his assignee will take the copyright free of any contractual restrictions or other encumbrances which may exist, save only any subsisting licences or other equities, these binding all except a bona fide purchaser without notice. Thus, for example, a failure to pay royalties due under the original agreement may, in the case of a licence, enable a licence to be revoked but, in the case of an assignment, cannot lead to recovery of the copyright which has been assigned. This distinction is highly significant, for example in relation to the different consequences on the death or insolvency of an assignee and a licensee.[59]

(c) As a matter of the general law, a licensee has no title to sue. The right to sue given to certain licensees is a statutory right only and in the case of exclusive licensees is subject to the procedural limitation that without leave he cannot proceed with the action unless he joins his licensor. An assignee, whether of whole or part of the copyright, can sue in his own name.[60]

(d) In his dealings with the copyright work, an exclusive licensee must act within the scope of the licence. Otherwise he will infringe. So, for example, he may not alter the work if the licence does not permit this. On the other hand, an assignee of the copyright and his successors may deal with the work as they please, for example by altering or adapting it, subject only to any moral rights which the author has[61] and, in the assignee's case, to any contractual restrictions which bind him.

(e) A statutory exclusive licensee cannot himself grant an exclusive sub-licence which will enable the sub-licensee to sue in his own name.[62]

For these reasons, therefore, it is always in the interests of an author who depends upon the continued payment of royalties or performance of other contractual obligations to enter into an exclusive licence for the exploitation of his work rather than an assignment.

---

[57] See, e.g. *Chaplin v Leslie Frewin (Publishers) Ltd* [1966] Ch. 71 at 93. Sometimes, of course, it does not matter, as in *Ironside v HM Att-Gen* [1988] R.P.C. 197, where the defence of either (equitable) assignment or licence was sufficient to defeat the claim.

[58] He may, of course, be in breach of contract, for example of a term granting option or pre-emption rights, by doing so.

[59] See para. 5–77, above, as to the obligations which may bind a successor in title.

[60] Except where he has granted an exclusive licence of concurrent rights, when without leave he may not proceed with the action unless he joins the exclusive licensee. See CDPA 1988, s.102(1).

[61] As to such rights, see Ch.11, below.

[62] The position is the same in relation to non-exclusive licensees who have a right to sue by virtue of CDPA 1988, s.101A. See para. 5–210, below.

Principles of construction. In each case it is of course a matter of construction   **5–202** of the instrument in question whether the parties intended that there should be transferred a proprietary interest in the copyright or merely that the grantee should be given a permission to exploit the work, coupled perhaps with contractual restraints on the grantor as to his own exploitation. The distinction is often a fine one.[63] The position is made complicated by the fact that rights of the copyright owner are defined in terms of the "exclusive right" to do the various acts restricted by the copyright.[64] A grant of "exclusive" or "sole and exclusive rights" is therefore ambiguous,[65] being equally consistent with an assignment or a licence. Where such an expression is used, as it often is, the other terms of the agreement must be considered to determine whether the grant was intended to operate by way of assignment[66] or licence.[67]

The following limited principles can be extracted from the cases:

(a) An assignment need not use the word "assign" or "grant", provided the intention to assign otherwise appears from the context.[68] Obviously, however, the use of words such as "assign" or "licence" helps to indicate the parties' intentions one way or the other,[69] but even then they are not conclusive.[70] Generally, parties may not disguise the reality of the transaction by applying inappropriate labels to it.[71]

(b) The commercial significance to either party of the grant operating either as a licence or an assignment will be a relevant factor.[72]

(c) If the word "copyright" is used elsewhere in the agreement but not in the words of grant, this may point to a licence on the principle that since the

---

[63] See the comments in *Western Front Ltd v Vestron Inc* [1987] F.S.R. 66 at 75–76.

[64] CDPA 1988, s.16(1). The wording of the 1956 Act was the same (s.1(1)). The 1911 Act defined copyright as the "sole" right to do various acts.

[65] *Re "Clinical Obstetrics"* [1905–10] Mac.C.C. 176; *Booth v Richards* [1905–10] Mac.C.C. 284.

[66] Cases where such a grant has been construed as an assignment include: *Messager v British Broadcasting Corp* [1929] A.C. 151 (the grant of the sole and exclusive right of representing and performing a play—other provisions insufficient to cut down this "plain grant"); *Jonathan Cape Ltd v Consolidated Press Ltd* [1954] 1 W.L.R. 1313 (a grant of the exclusive right to print and publish a work in volume form); *Loew's Incorporated v Littler* [1958] Ch. 650 (sale and purchase of sole rights of production of a work in the English language); *Chaplin v Leslie Frewin (Publishers) Ltd* [1966] Ch. 71 (agreement that publishers should have the exclusive right of producing, publishing and selling a work in volume form).

[67] Cases where such a grant has been construed as an exclusive licence include: *Stevens v Benning* (1855) 1 K. & J. 168, affirmed at 6 D.M. & G. 223 (grant construed as sole licence to print and publish); In *re Jude's Musical Compositions* [1907] 1 Ch. 651 (grant of sole and exclusive right to print and publish in volume form); *"Clinical Obstetrics"* [1905–10] Mac.C.C. 176 (an agreement giving another the whole (*sic*) and exclusive right to print and publish a work); *Sampson Low, Marston & Co, Ltd v Duckworth & Co* [1923–28] Mac.C.C. 205 (an agreement ceding and assigning to another the exclusive right to publish a work, including the right to arrange any translation or reprint in whatever manner thought fit); *C.I.R. v Longmans Green & Co Ltd* [1928–35] Mac.C.C. 345 (the grant of the exclusive right of translation and publication); *Frisby v British Broadcasting Corp* [1967] Ch. 932 (exclusive right to televise a play).

[68] *Stevens v Benning* (1855) 1 K. & J. 168, affirmed at 6 D.M. & G. 223; *Chaplin v Leslie Frewin (Publishers) Ltd* [1966] Ch. 71 at 94. And see also *British Actors Film Co Ltd v Glover* [1918] 1 K.B. 299 (agreement by A to let, and by B to hire, the right of performing a work: partial assignment); *Bairstow v Terry* [1924] 2 Ch. 316 (agreement for A to have entire rights in play inalienably: assignment of performing right).

[69] *Neilson v Horniman* (1909) 25 T.L.R. 684 (grant of "sole licence" not an assignment). In both *"Clinical Obstetrics"* [1905–10] Mac.C.C. 176 and *Sampson Low, Marston & Co, Ltd v Duckworth & Co* [1923–28] Mac.C.C. 205, the absence of any reference to "assigns" of the grantee was held to point to a licence.

[70] *Messager v British Broadcasting Corp* [1929] A.C. 151 (parties to assignment described as "licensors and "licensees").

[71] *Street v Mountford* [1985] A.C. 809; *A.G. Securities v Vaughan* [1900] 1 A.C. 417. *cf. Massey v Crown Life Insurance Co* [1978] 1 W.L.R. 676, CA.

[72] *Wilson v Weiss Art Pty Ltd* (1995) 31 I.P.R. 423 (Fed. Ct of Aus.)

parties had the concept of copyright in mind they would have used the word in the grant if copyright was intended to pass.[73]

(d) Sometimes, the fact that the agreement has continuing obligations, for example to pay royalties as opposed to a one-off lump sum, has influenced a decision that the agreement was a licence[74] but again this is not conclusive.[75] Probably little weight would be given to this fact today since many agreements which are clearly assignments do provide for payments of royalties rather than a lump sum.

(e) Agreements for profit sharing generally indicate a licence.[76]

(f) The fact that the circumstances show that the grantor relied on the personal skill and discretion of the grantee points to a licence.[77] Nevertheless, agreements of this kind often contain an unambiguous assignment.

(g) The fact that the agreement provides for the "reversion" of the right in certain events indicates an assignment,[78] but the absence of such a clause is not fatal to an assignment, since, if necessary, it can be implied.[79]

(h) Assistance can sometimes be obtained if the agreement provides for who is to sue in case of an infringement. Since, however, the parties often do not understand the principles involved, this can be of limited help.

C. EXCLUSIVE LICENCES

(i) Introduction

5–203   A sole licence is often understood to be one where the licence is coupled with a contractual promise that the licensor will not grant a licence to any other party, the licensor himself remaining free to exercise the licensed rights. In contrast, a sole and exclusive licence, or, more shortly, an exclusive licence, is one where there is included a promise that the licensor will not himself exercise any of the rights the subject of the licence. As has been seen,[80] as a matter of general law an exclusive licence, whether oral or written, confers no proprietary interest in the copyright, merely the usual incidents of a licence but coupled with contractual remedies against the licensor in the event of any breach of exclusivity provisions. So for example, statute apart, an exclusive licensee has no right to bring an action in his own name and no remedy against a third party to whom the licensor may have subsequently granted a licence or assigned the copyright. Exclusive licences are, however, of great commercial convenience and since the passing of the 1956

---

[73] As in *"Clinical Obstetrics"* [1905–10] Mac.C.C. 176; *Sampson Low, Marston & Co, Ltd v Duckworth & Co* [1923–28] Mac.C.C. 205.

[74] *Re Jude's Musical Compositions* [1906] 2 Ch. 595, affirmed on slightly different grounds at [1907] 1 Ch. 651; *Sampson Low, Marston & Co, Ltd v Duckworth & Co* [1923–28] Mac.C.C. 205. See also *R. Griggs Group Ltd v Evans* [2003] EWHC (Ch) 2914, para.58, noting that an exclusive licence is more appropriate where the consideration is payment of royalties rather than a lump sum.

[75] As in, *e.g. Messager v British Broadcasting Corp Ltd* [1929] A.C. 151 (although not one of the grounds relied on by the court).

[76] *Stevens v Benning* (1855) 1 K. & J. 168, affirmed at 6 D.M. & G. 223; *Reade v Bentley* (1858) 3 K. & J. 271; *Hole v Bradbury* (1879) 12 Ch.D. 886; *Sampson Low, Marston & Co Ltd v Duckworth*, above.

[77] *Re "Clinical Obstetrics"* [1905–10] Mac.C.C. 176; *Sampson Low, Marston & Co, Ltd v Duckworth & Co* [1923–28] Mac.C.C. 205.

[78] *Messager v British Broadcasting Corp. Ltd* [1929] A.C. 151, at 155; *Loew's Incorporated v Littler* [1958] Ch. 650 at 663.

[79] *Chaplin v Leslie Frewin (Publishers) Ltd* [1966] Ch. 71. Note also that a provision for a reverter may not be necessary at all, since copyright can be assigned for part only of the term of copyright. See CDPA 1988, s.90(2)(b) and para. 5–98, above.

[80] See para. 5–194, above.

Act such licensees have enjoyed a statutory procedural status entitling them to bring actions against infringers in their own name.[81]

(ii) Statutory exclusive licences

Statutory exclusive licence: the 1988 Act. For the purposes of the 1988 Act, an **5–204** "exclusive licence" is a licence in writing, signed by or on behalf of the copyright owner, authorising the licensee to the exclusion of all other persons, including the person granting the licence, to exercise a right which would otherwise be exercisable exclusively by the copyright owner.[82] Since an exclusive licensee has the same rights and remedies as if the licence had been an assignment,[83] it follows that the rights granted by such a licence must be such as to be capable of forming the subject matter of a valid assignment of copyright and, likewise, that whatever is capable of forming the subject matter of a valid assignment of copyright is capable of being the subject of an exclusive licence.[84] The extent to which copyright is divisible by way of assignment is dealt with elsewhere[85] but it should be noted that an assignment of copyright cannot be made in respect of, for example, "England" or some smaller area, such as London. It follows that a statutory exclusive licence cannot be granted covering such a limited area either and that will take effect in contract only. Two matters also follow from the requirement that the licence be signed "by or on behalf of the copyright owner"—first, that a statutory exclusive licensee cannot himself grant a statutory exclusive licence by way of sub-licence. If such a grant is permitted by the terms of the head licence, it will of course create a valid contractual sub-licence, giving the sub-licensee protection in an infringement action brought by the copyright owner and contractual rights against his own licensor. Secondly, it seems that a statutory exclusive licence cannot be granted in respect of a future copyright work:[86] at the date of the grant there is no "copyright owner" by whom or on whose behalf the licence can be granted.[87] A statutory exclusive licence may be granted in respect of any act which the copyright owner has the exclusive right to do and is not limited to those acts which fall within s.16 of the Act. A statutory exclusive licence may therefore be granted in respect of the importation of infringing copies,[88] but not the right to sell licensed copies of a work since the right to sell such copies is not an exclusive right of the copyright owner.[89] No doubt, however, such an agreement could often be construed as a grant of the exclusive right to issue copies of the work to the public,[90] which would amount to a statutory exclusive licence. Where the licensor reserves to himself rights which are also the subject of the grant to the licensee, the licence obviously is not exclusive.

[81] The position of an exclusive licensee before the passing of the 1956 Act was uncertain. See para. 5–208, below.
[82] CDPA 1988, s.92(1).
[83] s.101(1).
[84] *Sega Enterprises Pty Ltd v Galaxy Electronics Pty Ltd* (1998) 39 I.P.R. 577.
[85] See para. 5–93, above.
[86] See CDPA 1988, s.92 and *cf.* the wording of s.91.
[87] *cf.* the similar problem which arose before the 1956 Act in respect of assignments of future copyright. See *Performing Right Society Ltd v London Theatre of Varieties Ltd* [1924] A.C. 1 and para. 5–109, above.
[88] *Biotrading & Financing OY v Biohit Ltd* [1998] F.S.R. 109.
[89] See the wording of CDPA 1988, s.92(1) and also *Avel Pty Ltd v Multicoin Amusements Pty Ltd* (1990) 18 I.P.R. 443 (High Ct of Aus.). *cf. Broderbund Software Inc v Computermate (Australia) Pty Ltd* (1991) 22 I.P.R. 215. In *PM Sulcs & Associates Pty Ltd v Detroit Diesel-Allison Australia Pty Ltd* (1997) 39 I.P.R. 328 (Fed. Ct of Aus.), the point whether an exclusive licence to use and license the use of a computer program was capable of amounting to an exclusive licence to reproduce the work was held not sufficiently clear for summary determination.
[90] See CDPA 1988, s.18.

Where some rights are reserved, it will depend on the construction of the licence whether there is any overlap with the rights granted.[91]

5–205　**Rights of statutory exclusive licensee.** A statutory exclusive licensee has, except against the copyright owner, the same rights and remedies in respect of matters occurring after the grant of the licence as if the licence had been an assignment.[92] Such rights and remedies are concurrent with the rights and remedies of the copyright owner, and references to the copyright owner are to be construed accordingly.[93] These provisions are purely procedural, entitling the exclusive licensee to enforce the proprietary rights of the copyright owner. The exclusive licensee is not himself the owner of the copyright, is not treated as such owner (otherwise than for procedural purposes) and is not entitled to the copyright.[94]

Generally, the right of a statutory exclusive licensee to sue for infringement of copyright is exercisable only against third-party infringers but not assignees or licensees claiming under the copyright owner. As to licensees from the copyright owner, this follows from s.101(3) of the 1988 Act, which provides that, in any action brought by the exclusive licensee, a defendant may avail himself of any defence which would have been available to him if the action had been brought by the copyright owner. It also follows that if the owner of the copyright has granted or subsequently grants a licence conflicting with the exclusive licence, the other licensee will be protected in proceedings for infringement of copyright brought by the exclusive licensee, since he could have relied upon his licence in an action brought by the owner of the copyright. In such a case, the only remedy of the exclusive licensee is in damages against the owner of the copyright,[95] and possibly an injunction to restrain him from granting further licences.

As against a licensor who acts in conflict with the exclusive licence, the licensee's remedies are restricted to claims for breach of contract. As against the licensor's assigns, the licensee would, statute apart, have no remedy. This is because even though the assignee might take subject to the licence,[96] he would not assume the burden of the contractual obligations of the licensor nor, since he is the copyright owner, would he be liable in an action for infringement of copyright.[97] To deal with this situation, it is provided that a licensee under an exclusive licence has the same rights as against a successor in title who is bound by the licence[98] as he has against the person granting the licence.[99] The effect of this seems to be that the contractual obligations of the licensor are imposed by statute on his successors, except a bona fide purchaser for value without notice and his successors. This provision was new in the 1988 Act and does not apply in relation to an exclusive licence granted before August 1, 1989.[1]

---

[91] See, *e.g. Sega Enterprises Pty Ltd v Galaxy Electronics Pty Ltd* (1998) 39 I.P.R. 577, where the grant of the exclusive right to exhibit films in games arcades, coupled with a reservation to enable the licensor to supply its own arcades, was held capable of being a grant of a valid exclusive licence to exhibit in arcades other than those of the licensor. See also *Young v Odeon Music House Pty Ltd* (1976) 10 A.L.R. 153.

[92] CDPA 1988, s.101(1).

[93] s.101(2).

[94] *C.B.S. United Kingdom Ltd v Charmdale Record Distributors Ltd* [1980] F.S.R. 289. Nevertheless, an exclusive licensee is often spoken of as having an "interest" in the copyright. See *e.g. Chaplin v Leslie Frewin (Publishers) Ltd* [1966] Ch. 71 at 94.

[95] *See Simms v Marryat* (1851) 17 Q.B. 281 (grant of exclusive right impliedly including a warranty of sufficient title).

[96] See CDPA 1988, s.90(4) and para. 5–197, above.

[97] See s.101(1) and also s.16(2).

[98] *i.e.* anyone other than a bona fide purchaser for value without notice and his successors. See CDPA 1988, s.90(4) and para. 5–197, above.

[99] s.92(2).

[1] Sch.1, para.29.

Necessity to join owner of copyright as party. Where an action for infringe- **5–206** ment of copyright brought by the copyright owner or an exclusive licensee relates to an infringement in respect of which they have concurrent rights of action, the copyright owner or, as the case may be, the exclusive licensee, may not, without the leave of the court, proceed with the action unless the other is either joined as a claimant or added as a defendant.[2] In many cases the copyright owner will be unwilling to join in the action as co-claimant or take any active part in the action. In such a case, if he is joined as a defendant, he will not be liable for any costs in the action unless he takes part in the proceedings.[3] These provisions requiring joinder of the copyright owner do not affect the granting of interim relief on an application by a copyright owner or exclusive licensee alone.[4] An exclusive licensee may therefore start an action and obtain interim relief without joining the copyright owner (and vice versa). Thereafter, he may proceed in the absence of the owner of the copyright only with the leave of the court and will usually be required to join the owner, for otherwise the defendant will be at risk from a subsequent claim by the owner.[5] Leave to proceed without the copyright owner may be particularly appropriate where he is dead and no grant has been taken to his estate or he cannot be found or is otherwise unavailable.[6]

Special provisions as to damages and account of profits. The fact that both the **5–207** copyright owner and the exclusive licensee have a concurrent right of action means that special provision has to be made for the assessment of damages or an account of profits in such cases. These provisions apply whether or not the copyright owner and the exclusive licensee are both parties to the action. They are as follows:[7]

(a) *Damages.* In such cases, the court, in assessing damages, must take into account the terms of the licence and any pecuniary remedy already awarded or available to either the copyright owner or the exclusive licensee in respect of the infringement.

(b) *Account of profits.* No account of profits shall be directed if an award of damages has been made, or an account of profits has been directed, in favour of the other of them in respect of the infringement. If an account of profits is directed, the court must apportion the profits between the copyright owner and the exclusive licensee as the court considers just, subject to any agreement between them.

(c) *Delivery up and right of seizure.* Special provision is also made for applying for delivery up orders and for the exercise of the right of seizure of infringing copies. The copyright owner is under an obligation to notify any exclusive licensee having concurrent rights before applying for a delivery up order or exercising the right of seizure of infringing copies. The court may on the application of the licensee make such order for delivery up or, as the case may be, prohibiting or permitting the exercise by the copyright owner of the right of seizure, as it thinks fit having regard to the terms of the licence.[8]

Transitional. The 1988 Act provides that in relation to any document or event **5–208** occurring before August 1, 1989 which had any operation in creating any inter-

---

[2] CDPA 1988, s.102(1).
[3] s.101(2).
[4] s.102(3).
[5] *cf.* the requirement that an equitable owner must join the legal owner before judgment. See para. 5–186, above.
[6] See *Bodley Head Ltd v Flegon* [1972] R.P.C. 587, where, by consent, leave was given to proceed without joining the copyright owner, the dissident author Solzhenitsyn.
[7] CDPA 1988, s.102(4).
[8] s.102(5).

est, right or licence in respect of a work which was then in existence, it is to have the corresponding operation in relation to copyright in the work under the 1988 Act.[9] The effect of licences entered into before this date therefore needs to be considered.

(a) *The 1956 Act.* The provisions of the 1956 Act were to substantially the same effect as those now contained in the 1988 Act.[10] The procedural status conferred on exclusive licensees by the 1988 Act is therefore also conferred on licensees under a statutory exclusive licence granted between June 1, 1957 and August 1, 1989.

(b) *The 1911 Act.* There were no provisions relating to exclusive licences contained in the 1911 Act which correspond to those contained in the 1988 Act. *Prima facie*, therefore, an exclusive licensee under a grant made between July 1, 1912 and June 1, 1957 enjoys no special status today. The 1911 Act, however, provided that a copyright owner might "grant any interest in the right by licence".[11] It was never resolved what this provision meant and in particular whether it was sufficient to confer on a licensee, particularly an exclusive licensee, a legal interest in the copyright such as would, for example, enable him to sue in his own name.[12] An argument against such a construction is that whereas the Act expressly provided that the assignee under a partial assignment was to be treated as the owner of such part, no such provision was made in relation to a grantee by way of licence.[13] In *British Actors Film Co Ltd v Glover*,[14] the view was expressed, *obiter*, that the expression referred to the case of grant of an interest coupled with a licence to exercise it, as distinct from an assignment or partial assignment on the one hand or a simple consent on the other. It is not clear, however, what the former might have been, other than an assignment. If the true effect of the 1911 Act was indeed to confer a proprietary interest on an exclusive licensee, then the licence is to have a "corresponding operation" under the 1988 Act. It seems doubtful, however, that this can be the procedural status which is now conferred by the 1988 Act on exclusive licensees, since this status does not correspond to the operation of a pre-1956 Act exclusive licence, whatever this might have been.

(c) *Pre-1911 Act.* Before the passing of the 1911 Act, an exclusive licensee

---

[9] CDPA 1988, Sch.1, para.25(1). The effect of this provision is to preserve the legal effect of a pre-commencement licence. It does not attempt to legislate as the effect of such a document and only preserves such effect as the document originally had. See *Novello & Co Ltd v Keith Prowse Music Publishing Co Ltd* [2004] EWHC (Ch) 766, para.9.

[10] Copyright Act 1956, s.19. The exception is that the 1956 Act did not contain a provision which corresponds to s.92(2) of the 1988 Act, which gives an exclusive licensee rights against a successor in title to his licensor who is bound by the licence. See para. 5–205 , above. Sch.1, para.9, of the 1988 Act expressly provides that s.92(2) does not apply to a licence granted before August 1, 1989.

[11] Copyright Act 1911, s.5(2). No such grant was valid unless it was in writing signed by the owner of the relevant right: *ibid.*

[12] It was because of this uncertainty that the Gregory Committee recommended in 1952 that the status of an exclusive licensee be made clear, as was done by the 1956 Act. See Cmnd.8662, para.276. See also para. 5–113, above.

[13] See Copyright Act 1911 s.5(3). It was suggested in previous editions of this work that the legislature inserted the provision to cover the case of a grant which was, in substance, a partial assignment but, in form, was expressed as a licence, and that the real effect of this provision was to make it easier to construe such a document as a partial assignment. This would not affect the law relating to documents which were licences only in the narrower sense, either because they were not exclusive or because they purported to deal with rights which were not susceptible of separate assignment.

[14] [1918] 1 K.B. 299. The point was left open in *Jonathan Cape Ltd v Consolidated Press Ltd* [1954] 1 W.L.R. 1313.

had no proprietary interest in the copyright enabling him to sue in his own name.[15]

D. LICENCES GRANTED UNDER SECTION 101A

Introduction. When the Information Society Directive[16] was implemented by the Copyright and Related Rights Regulations 2003,[17] a new s.101A was inserted giving certain non-exclusive licensees the right to bring proceedings for infringement of copyright. The original thinking behind this provision was to enable service providers and others to act against those using their networks to transmit infringing material in circumstances where they are neither the owners nor exclusive licensees of rights in the content they transmit, but the owner of copyright in the content wishes them to be able to act.[18] In fact, the provision is of general scope and not restricted to service providers or licences to transmit works in networks.

5–209

Applicable licences. A non-exclusive licensee may now bring proceedings, provided the licence (i) is in writing and is signed by or on behalf of the copyright owner; and (ii) expressly grants the non-exclusive licensee a right of action under the section.[19] The first limb uses the same wording as is found in s.92(1), defining exclusive licensee, and means that to be effective the licence must be signed by or on behalf of the copyright owner, and not for example by an exclusive licensee. The second limb is likely to reduce greatly the application of the section, since it appears that there must be an express reference to the section in the licence for it to be effective. It is unlikely to become a matter of standard drafting to include such a reference, because in most commercial cases, the copyright owner will not wish to give the licensee a right to sue independently of him.

5–210

The right to bring proceedings. The section limits the circumstances in which such a licensee can bring proceedings. He may only bring an action if the infringing act "was directly connected to a prior licensed act of the licensee".[20] This rather curiously worded provision presumably means that the infringing act must be one which would fall within the scope of the licence, and must have been committed at a time when the licence was in force. It is not clear, however, whether it means something more. In particular, is it necessary that the licensee has previously done an act which falls within the scope of his licence? In other words, in order to trigger the right to sue, must the licensee be already acting pursuant to the licence? It is also not clear what is the intended effect of the words "*directly connected* to the prior licensed act" and, in particular, whether anything more is intended than that the infringing act must fall within the scope of the licence, or, if anything more is intended, precisely what. In the case of a defendant using a service provider's network to transmit infringing material, it is unlikely that the defendant's act of infringement will have any kind of connection with the licensed actions of the service provider other than use of its network.

5–211

---

[15] *Heape v Hartley* (1889) 42 Ch.D. 461; *The London Printing and Publishing Alliance Ltd v Cox* [1891] 3 Ch. 291; *Neilson v Horniman* (1909) 26 T.L.R. 188.

[16] Directive 2001/29.

[17] SI 2003/2498.

[18] See Government's Conclusions on the Patent Office's Consulation Paper of August 7, 2002 and the Transposition Notice accompanying the Regulations.

[19] CDPA 1988, s.101A(1)(b). For these purposes, a non-exclusive licensee is defined to mean the holder of a licence authorising him to exercise a right which remains exercisable by the copyright owner: s.101A(6). A s.101A licence may therefore be granted by a partial owner of copyright in respect of his partial interest, or some lesser interest; the s.101A right will come to an end when the copyright owner's interest terminates (which would be the usual position in any event).

[20] CDPA 1988, s.101A(1)(a).

Generally, this seems a confusingly worded provision if the intention was to simply to enable "service providers [and others] to be able to act against infringements connected to their activities in circumstances where they are neither the owner nor exclusive licensee of rights in content they transmit, but the owner of copyright in the content wishes them to be able to act".[21]

5–212　**Procedural provisions.** The other provisions are more straightforward and follow the example of s.92 and the rights of exclusive licensees. Thus, the non-exclusive licensee is to have the same rights and remedies available to him as the copyright owner would have had if he had brought the action,[22] and the licensee's rights are to be concurrent with those of the copyright owner.[23] Further, in any action brought by the licensee, a defendant may avail himself of any defence which would have been available to him if the action had been brought by the copyright owner.[24] Finally, the procedural provisions of ss.102(1) to (4) are to apply to the non-exclusive licensee as they apply to an exclusive licensee.[25]

E.　IMPLIED AND INFORMAL LICENCES

5–213　**Implied licences.** Implied licences frequently cause difficulties. Since it will be the defendant who will have raised the issue of licence as a defence, no doubt the onus will be upon him to establish its existence and extent.[26] Where the licence is alleged to arise in a contractual context, a term will only be implied if it is necessary to give business efficacy to the contract and it satisfies the "officious bystander" test, and not simply because it is reasonable.[27] The test is an objective one.[28] Where a work is made by an independent contractor to be used by another for certain purposes, in circumstances such that the copyright is retained by the contractor,[29] some licence to use the work must be implied in favour of the latter if the contract is otherwise silent on the point. In such cases the principle to be applied is that "the engagement for reward of a person to produce material of a nature which is capable of being the subject of copyright implies a permission, or consent, or licence in the person giving the engagement to use the material in the manner and for the purpose in which and for which it was contemplated between the parties that it would be used at the time of the engagement".[30] The implied licence extends no further than the minimum which is necessary to give business

---

[21] See the Government's Conclusions on the Patent Office's Consultation Paper of August 7, 2002, para.8.6.

[22] CDPA 1988, s.101A(2).

[23] s.101A(3). References in the relevant provisions of Part I of the Act to the copyright owner are to be construed accordingly: *ibid.*

[24] s.101A(4).

[25] s.101A(5).

[26] *Noah v Shuba* [191] F.S.R. 14; *De Garis v Neville Jeffries Pidler Pty Ltd* (1990) I.P.R. 292 at 302 (Fed. Ct of Aus.). Technically, however, it will be for the claimant to establish his cause of action by proving that the acts in question were done without licence. See *Computermate Products (Aust) Pty Ltd v Ozi-Soft Pty Ltd* (1988) 83 A.L.R. 492; *Avel Pty Ltd v Multicoin Amusements Pty Ltd* (1990) 97 A.L.R. 19 (High Ct of Aus.); *Devefi Pty Ltd v Mateffy Pearl Nagy Pty Ltd* [1993] R.P.C. 493 (Fed. Ct of Aus). Usually, however, this evidential burden is discharged by the claimant's formal evidence that consent was not given.

[27] *Liverpool City Council v Irwin* [1977] A.C. 239; *Shell UK Ltd v Lostock Garage Ltd* [1976] 1 W.L.R. 1187 at 1200; *Sport International Bossum B.V. v Hi-Tec Sports Ltd* [1988] R.P.C. 329. *Ray v Classic FM plc* [1998] F.S.R. 622.

[28] *Redwood Music Ltd v Chappell & Co Ltd* [1982] R.P.C. 109 at 128.

[29] For example, because the contract expressly so provides or where it is not a term of the contract (express or implied) that the copyright should belong to the other.

[30] *Beck v Montana Constructions Pty Ltd* [1964–65] N.S.W.R. 229, approved by the Court of Appeal in *Blair v Osborne & Tomkins* [1971] 2 Q.B. 78. See also, *e.g. Ironside v HM Att-Gen* [1988] R.P.C. 197.

efficacy to the contract.[31] In a case where the licence is gratuitous and informal, however, the position is different. Thus, where the work is supplied knowing that it will be used for a particular purpose, the licence may be limited to that purpose,[32] but where the purpose is left vague, the extent of the licence is unlikely to be confined to the immediate purposes which the parties had in mind.[33] No doubt the test is objective: for what purposes would a reasonable person in the shoes of the licensee consider he could use the work?

Licences implied from trade practice or custom. It is clearly possible that a trade custom or practice may exist whereby works are accepted on all sides as being liable to be copied, etc. The usual difficulty will be to show that the usage or custom is invariable, certain and general,[34] as opposed to mere common practice.[35]   **5–214**

Licences implied from conduct. A licence can also arise as a result of conduct, without the existence of any contractual relation. So, for example, the payment and acceptance of royalties or other sums in respect of the exploitation of the copyright can evidence the recipient's consent to the acts of the payer.[36] In such a case, the test is an objective one, namely whether, viewing the facts objectively, the words and conduct of the alleged licensor, as made known to the alleged licensee, indicated that the licensor consented to what the licensee was doing.[37]   **5–215**

Effect of estoppel and acquiescence. Where a copyright owner stands back and allows another to assume that no objection will be taken to the exploitation of the work, the effect may be that the copyright owner will become estopped from asserting that there was no consent or that any consent has been revoked. The ordinary principles of estoppel or acquiescence will operate.[38] Mere delay, after knowledge of an infringement, falling short of acquiescence, will not deprive a claimant of the right to a final injunction.[39]   **5–216**

Examples of implied licences. As already noted, where a copyright work is made by A at the request of B but in circumstances that the copyright does not belong either in law or in equity to B, some licence must usually be implied if use is to be made of the work for the purposes contemplated by both parties. There are many examples of such implied licences and each case turns on its own facts and is subject to whatever other contractual terms may have been agreed. For   **5–217**

---

[31] *Stovin-Bradford v Volpoint Ltd* [1971] Ch. 1007; *R. & A. Bailey & Co Ltd v Boccaccio Pty Ltd* (1988) 77 A.L.R. 177; *De Garis v Neville Jeffries Pidler Pty Ltd* (1990) I.P.R. 292 (Fed. Ct of Aus.); *Ray v Classic FM plc* [1998] F.S.R. 622.

[32] See *Trumpet Software Pty Ltd v Ozemail Pty Ltd* (1996) 34 I.P.R. 481 at 500.

[33] *Brighton v Jones* [2004] EWHC (Ch) 1157, para.76.

[34] See *Chitty on Contracts* (29th ed.), para.13–018. In *Express Newspapers Plc v News (U.K.) Ltd* [1990] F.S.R. 359, the suggestion that there was a trade custom between newspaper publishers that one newspaper was free to reproduce news stories appearing in another, particularly the quoted words of an interviewee, was held sufficiently arguable to go to trial.

[35] *De Garis v Neville Jeffries Pidler Pty Ltd* (1990) I.P.R. 292 (Fed. Ct of Aus.). Such a licence will not be implied from the fact that copying habitually takes place: *Walter v Steinkopff* [1892] 3 Ch. 489; *USP Strategies v London General Holdings Ltd* [2002] EWHC (Ch) 2557. See also *Banier v News Group Newspapers Ltd* [1997] F.S.R. 812 (where it was said to be common practice, after one newspaper has published a photograph, for other newspapers to publish without waiting to obtain a formal licence; *held*: the practice, if it existed, amounted to the taking of a commercial risk and was unlawful). As to any custom in the Press, see para. 5–220, below.

[36] *Redwood Music Ltd v Francis Day & Hunter Ltd* [1978] R.P.C. 429; *Redwood Music Ltd v Chappell & Co Ltd* [1982] R.P.C. 109.

[37] *Redwood Music Ltd v Chappell & Co Ltd* [1982] R.P.C. 109.

[38] See, *e.g. Godfrey v Lees* [1995] E.M.L.R. 307; *Ibcos Computers Ltd v Mercantile Highlands Finance Ltd* [1994] F.S.R. 275; *Baillieu v Australian Electoral Commission* (1996) 33 I.P.R. 494 (Fed. Ct of Aus.). The argument failed on the facts in *Banier v News Group Newspapers Ltd* [1997] F.S.R. 812; *KMA Corp Pty Ltd v G & F Productions Pty Ltd* (1997) 38 I.P.R. 243; *Beckingham v Hodgens* [2003] E.C.D.R. 6 and *Brighton v Jones* [2004] EWHC (Ch) 1157.

[39] *Hogg v Scott* (1874) L.R. 18 Eq. 444.

example, the production of an advertisement by an advertising agency for a client was held to include a licence to use the advertisement for as long as the client wished,[40] and the commission of designs of coins to include a licence from the designer to use the designs for the coinage and proof sets.[41] Depending on the circumstances, the supply of source code by a software house to a customer may imply a licence to use it to fix errors in the object code.[42] A common situation which gives rise to the implication of a licence is the sale of an article by means of which a work can be easily reproduced.[43] Again, the extent of any implied term will turn on the minimum terms that are required to give the contract business efficacy and to satisfy the "officious bystander" test, and not on some lesser test of what is reasonable.[44] Neither will the court imply a licence to reproduce a work for commercial purposes from the sale of an article simply because there is no express restriction on the use of a copyright work which is embodied in it.[45] The following examples in this field can be noted: the retail sale of a pattern book containing knitting patterns generally includes a licence to make garments for personal use but not in commercial quantities;[46] of a directory, to obtain information from it but not the right to copy it for the purpose of producing a rival directory;[47] of a book of legal precedents, the right to reproduce the precedents in the ordinary course of practice but not in a competing work; of a book of code words, the right to reproduce the code in sending messages but not the right to publish a competing work;[48] of printing blocks, the right of the purchaser, but not others, to use them.[49] A further situation which has given rise to a body of case law is the case of architects' drawings and is considered separately, below.[50]

Betts v Willmott. As already indicated, the courts, when implying a term, have generally drawn the line at what is necessary to give a contract business efficacy. Commonwealth courts, in particular, have refused to import the so-called "*Betts v Willmott*" principle from patent law, which is to the following effect:

> "When a man has purchased an article he expects to have control of it, and there must be some clear and explicit agreement to the contrary to justify the vendor in saying that he has not given the purchaser his licence to sell the article, or to use it wherever he pleases as against himself".[51]

In rejecting this approach, the courts have pointed to the traditional form of a grant of letters patent, which gives the patentee the exclusive right to "make, use exercise and vend" the invention, which requires the implication of some such term into the contract of sale of a patented article if the sale is not to be futile. In contrast, the law of copyright does not prevent the ordinary use of a copy of a

---

[40] *Drabble (Harold) Ltd v The Hycolite Manufacturing Co* (1928) 44 T.L.R. 264.

[41] *Ironside v HM Att-Gen* [1988] R.P.C. 197.

[42] *Saphena Computing Ltd v Allied Collection Agencies Ltd* [1995] F.S.R. 616 at 637 (the statutory right of a lawful user of a computer program under CDPA 1988, s.50C to copy it for the purpose of correcting errors only applies to errors in *that* program).

[43] Whether in these circumstances the seller in fact has the right to grant any licence is of course a separate issue.

[44] *Creative Technology Ltd v Aztech Systems Pte Ltd* [1997] F.S.R. 491 (CA of Singapore); *Ray v Classic FM plc* [1998] F.S.R. 622.

[45] *Roberts v Candiware Ltd* [1980] F.S.R. 352.

[46] *Roberts v Candiware Ltd* [1980] F.S.R. 352

[47] *Waterlow Directories Ltd v Reed Information Services Ltd* [1992] F.S.R. 409.

[48] *Ager v Peninsular & Oriental Steam Navigation Co* (1884) 26 Ch.D. 637.

[49] *Cooper v Stephens* [1895] 1 Ch. 567; *Marshall (W.) & Co Ltd v Bull (A.H.) Ltd* (1901) 85 L.T. 77.

[50] See paras 5–228 *et seq.*, below.

[51] See *Betts v Willmott* (1871) L.C. 6 Ch. App. 239 at 245 and also *National Phonograph Co of Australia Ltd v Menck* [1911] A.C. 336.

copyright work and therefore no similar implication is required.[52] So, the sale of an article in one jurisdiction without any territorial restriction on resale does not imply or carry the right to import it into another jurisdiction and to do so may therefore infringe the importation right.[53] Again, the ordinary retail sale of test or diagnostic software as part of a larger software package does not include a licence to run the software for the purpose of understanding its functionality so as to make a competing product.[54]

Computer programs. Computer programs are unlike most other copyright works in that in the course of their ordinary use they are almost inevitably copied. Clearly some licence to use the program for ordinary purposes is implied into the normal contract of sale and purchase if no express provision is otherwise made.[55] In fact, amendments made to the 1988 Act to implement the Software Directive[56] provide that certain acts in relation to computer programs are permitted and therefore not infringing, so that the question of licence does not arise. These provisions are considered in detail elsewhere[57] but in summary the following acts are not infringements:

    (a) The making of back-up copies by a lawful user, any contractual term to the contrary being void;[58]

    (b) The decompilation of a program by a lawful user to obtain necessary information for the creation of an independent program, any contractual term to the contrary being void;[59]

    (c) The observation, study or testing of the functioning of the program by a lawful user in order to determine the ideas and principles which underlie any element of the program, if the user does so while performing any of the acts of loading, displaying, running, transmitting or storing the program which he is entitled to do, any contractual term to the contrary being void;[60]

    (c) To copy the program in the course of lawful use or to correct errors, subject to any contractual term to the contrary.[61]

5–218

Databases. In the same way, amendments to the 1988 Act to implement the Database Directive[62] have introduced a class of permitted act in relation to the use of databases that might otherwise have been covered by licence. Thus, the Act provides that it is not an infringement of copyright in a database for anyone who has a right to use it to do anything which is necessary for the purposes of access to and use of its contents, any contractual term to the contrary being void.[63]

5–219

Letters and the Press. The nature of the agreement to be implied when an author

5–220

---

[52] *Time-Life International (Nederlands) B.V. v Interstate Parcel Express Co Pty Ltd* [1978] F.S.R. 251 at 270 (High Ct of Aus.); *Creative Technology Ltd v Aztech Systems Pte Ltd* [1997] F.S.R. 491 (Ct of App. of Singapore).

[53] *Time-Life International (Nederlands) B.V. v Interstate Parcel Express Co Pty Ltd* [1978] F.S.R. 251; *R. & A. Bailey & Co Ltd v Boccaccio Pty Ltd* (1988) 77 A.L.R. 177.

[54] *Creative Technology Ltd v Aztech Systems Pte Ltd* [1997] F.S.R. 491.

[55] As to the effect of "shrink-wrap" and "click-wrap" licences, see *Beta Computers (Europe) Ltd v Adobe Systems (Europe) Ltd* [1996] F.S.R. 367 (Ct of Sess.), and para. 27–331, below.

[56] Council Directive 91/250.

[57] See paras 9–132 *et seq.*, below.

[58] CDPA 1988, ss.50A, 296A.

[59] ss.50B, 296A.

[60] ss.50BA, 296A.

[61] ss.50C.

[62] Council Directive 96/9.

[63] CDPA 1988, ss.50D, 296B.

submits an article or other manuscript for publication is considered elsewhere.[64] Since, when a letter is written to a newspaper with a view to publication, the copyright remains with the writer, a licence to publish is clearly implied.[65] As to other letters, whether the recipient of a letter has a licence to reproduce and publish it will obviously depend upon the circumstances, but *prima facie* such publication will be an infringement.[66] Before the 1911 Act, letters might be published to vindicate the character of the receiver[67] but it is thought that no such defence could now be relied upon in an action for infringement of copyright:[68] a defendant would have to establish that his conduct amounted to fair dealing or was within one of the other classes of permitted acts,[69] or was in the public interest.[70] Commonly photographic agencies will submit prints or transparencies to newspapers on the understanding that the paper is at liberty to use them, when a recognised fee will be paid. The legal effect of this arrangement will usually be that the agency makes an offer to permit the newspaper to use the photograph in return for a fee, which offer is accepted by publication.[71] Like all offers made without consideration, however, it may be revoked by notice, and thereafter the newspaper has no right to publish photographs which have already been submitted.[72] There may be a custom in the Press that one newspaper may copy from another the quoted words of a third party,[73] but otherwise a licence will not be implied from the fact that copying, for example by one newspaper of another, is habitually carried on.[74]

F. CONSTRUCTION AND TERMS OF LICENCES

5–221   Difficulties usually arise where the licence is either wholly implied, in which case all the terms have to be worked out, or only partly express, leaving other terms to be implied. The important questions to decide are usually: what persons are entitled to the benefit of the licence; the extent of the permitted use; and the licence's duration.

5–222   **Persons entitled to benefit.** The original licensee may be the only person entitled to the benefit of the licence[75] or it may extend beyond him, for example, to his workmen or professional advisers.[76] A licence may even be so expressed as to extend to the world at large.[77] In all cases, the licence will need to be construed carefully.[78]

---

[64] See paras 27–55 *et seq.*, below.
[65] The extent to which alterations may be made is considered, see para. 5–224, below.
[66] See, *e.g. British Oxygen Co Ltd v Liquid Air Ltd* [1925] Ch. 383; *Tett Bros Ltd v Drake & Gore-ham Ltd* [1928–35] Mac.C.C. 492 (commercial correspondence).
[67] *Perceval (Lord and Lady) v Phipps* (1813) 2 V. & B. 19; *Lytton (Earl of) v Devy* (1884) 52 L.T. 121; *Labouchere v Hess* (1898) 77 L.T. 559; *Folsom v Marsh* (1841) 2 Story (Amer.) 100; *How-ard v Gunn* (1863) 32 Beav. 462. *cf. Palin v Gathercole* (1844) 1 Col.C.C. 565.
[68] See *British Oxygen Co Ltd v Liquid Air Ltd* [1925] Ch. 383.
[69] See Ch.9, below.
[70] See para. 22–82, below.
[71] *Bowden Bros v Amalgamated Pictorials Ltd* [1911] 1 Ch. 386.
[72] *Bowden Bros v Amalgamated Pictorials Ltd* [1911] 1 Ch. 396.
[73] *Express Newspapers plc v News (U.K.) Ltd* [1990] F.S.R. 359, where, on an application for summary judgment, the point was treated as being arguable.
[74] *Walter v Steinkopff* [1892] 3 Ch. 489; *Banier v News Group Newspapers Ltd* [1997] F.S.R. 812.
[75] As in *Cooper v Stephens* [1895] 1 Ch. 567.
[76] *Blair v Osborne & Tomkins* [1971] 2 Q.B. 78
[77] *Mellor v Australian Broadcasting Commission* [1940] A.C. 491; *Computermate Products (Aust) Pty Ltd v Ozi-Soft Pty Ltd* (1988) 83 A.L.R. 492; *cf. Plix Products Ltd v Frank M. Winstone (Merchants)* [1986] F.S.R. 63. Note that a general licence has been granted in respect of the reproduction of the designs for the Euro coins. See [2002] O.J. C318, November 13, 2002, p.3.
[78] As in *Booth v Edward Lloyd Ltd* (1909) 26 T.L.R. 549, where a licence to A to print and publish

Licence personal or otherwise not assignable. The benefit of a licence may be   **5–223**
assignable or the circumstances of the grant of the licence and its terms may
justify the conclusion that it was intended to be personal to the licensee and not
capable of vicarious performance. Thus a licence will not be assignable where it
was granted to the licensee because of his personal skill or reputation,[79] as is
often the case with publishing contracts and other agreements where the licensee
is entrusted with the exploitation of a work made by the licensor.[80] The fact that
the licensee is a partnership[81] or even a limited company[82] or that the agreement
is made with a publisher "and his assigns"[83] does not mean that the identity of the
licensee was irrelevant and that the licence may therefore be assigned. Where a
licence is on its terms not assignable, or is assignable only on certain conditions,
for example only with the licensor's consent, a purported assignment which does
not comply with the licence terms will not, as against third parties, vest any rights
in the assignee.[84]

Alterations. Whether a party who is not the copyright owner and who has only a   **5–224**
licence to reproduce a work is entitled to make alterations to it will in part depend
upon the terms of the licence and will now also turn on an author's right not to
have his work subjected to derogatory treatment, a topic which is considered
elsewhere.[85] As to the terms of the licence, the licence may expressly or impliedly
require that use of the work be in an unaltered form or that no substantial
alteration be made, and a court will readily imply a term into any contract limiting the right to make alterations[86] particularly, it is thought, in cases where matters of judgment or opinion are involved.[87] In cases of a more commercial
character, it is suggested that a limitation on the right to make at least insubstantial
alterations and additions will be less easily implied. In the absence of any prohibition or limitation, however, the licensee may make alterations, even substantial
ones.[88] The position of a licensee should be contrasted with that of an assignee,
who is generally free to alter a work as he sees fit, subject only to any moral
rights of the author and the law of passing off and defamation.

  Thus the alteration of even one line in a play may be beyond the scope of a

---

was held to permit A to print and supply books to B, with B's name as printer and publisher, for
sale to the public by B, the reason given being that if a licensor wished to restrict his licensee to
printing and publishing *in his own name*, he should expressly do so. *Sed quaere*: and surely B
was the "publisher".

[79] *Stevens v Benning* (1855) 1 K. & J. 168; *Reade v Bentley* 3 K.& J. 271 (licences to publishers);
Messager v British Broadcasting Corp. Ltd [1927] 2 K.B. 543, reversed on other grounds [1929]
A.C. 151 (licence by composer to theatrical agent); *Dorling v Honnor Marine Ltd* [1964] Ch. 560
at 568 (licence to build sailing dinghies).

[80] In *Hales v T. Fisher Unwin Ltd* [1923–28] Mac.C.C. 31, the licence was held to be personal even
though the author admitted that he was so poor he would agreed to anyone publishing his work if
promised a royalty.

[81] *Hole v Bradbury* (1879) 12 Ch.D. 886; *Sampson Low, Marston & Co, Ltd v Duckworth* [1923–
28] Mac.C.C. 205, where the licence was construed to extend to the partnership as it might be
constituted from time to time but not to a limited company formed to take over the business.

[82] *Griffith v Tower Publishing Co Ltd* [1897] 1 Ch. 21; *Hales v T. Fisher Unwin Ltd* [1923–28]
Mac.C.C. 31.

[83] See *Booth v Richards* [1905–10] Mac.C.C. 284.

[84] *Hospital for Sick Children v Walt Disney Productions Inc* [1966] 1 W.L.R. 1055 at 1074; *Devefi
Pty Ltd v Mateffy Pearl Nagi Pty Ltd* [1993] R.P.C. 493 (Fed. Ct of Aus.); *Beck v Montana
Constructions Pty Ltd* [1964–65] N.S.W.R. 229; and, generally, *Linden Gardens Trust Ltd v Lenesta Sludge Disposals Ltd* [1994] 1 A.C. 85; *Hendry v Chartsearch Ltd*, The Times, September
16, 1998.

[85] See Ch.11, below.

[86] *Frisby v British Broadcasting Corp* [1967] Ch. 932; *Messager v British Broadcasting Corp Ltd*
[1927] 2 K.B. 543.

[87] See *Joseph v National Magazine Co Ltd* [1959] Ch. 14; *Gilbert v Workman* [1905–10] Mac.C.C.
235 (where the point was conceded).

[88] *Frisby v British Broadcasting Corp* [1967] Ch. 932; *Cox v Cox* (1853) 11 Hare 118.

production company's licence,[89] but insubstantial changes to an architect's plans may be permitted.[90] A limited consent to alter an article submitted for publication may be implied, for example to reduce it in length to fit the available space,[91] particularly perhaps where it has been prepared hurriedly to meet a deadline. A court will readily imply a term that no substantial alteration may be made to a signed article without the author's consent.[92] In the case of a letter to a newspaper written for publication, the newspaper not only has the implied right to publish it but also, by customary implication, the right to alter it, so long as the alterations are not of a nature to affect the credit or literary reputation of the writer. Today, the letters page of a newspaper usually sets out terms on which letters are accepted for publication.

5–225 **New technologies.** Questions frequently arise both in the context of licences and assignments as to whether a grant made before the advent of a particular technology extends to exploitation by use of that technology. Thus, should the grant be limited to what was known to the parties at the time or should it extend to the new technology if the words of the grant are in fact wide enough to cover it? The answer to this question is a matter of construction. Modern agreements often grant the right to exploit works using such expressions as "by all means whether known or unknown" and here the intention is clearly to cover future technologies. The difficult cases are where no such expression is used.

If the grant is wide enough in its terms to include the new technology, then it is capable of including the new rights even if such rights were unknown or the parties did not have such a possibility in mind.[93] So, a grant of the "exclusive right of production" of a play in 1880 included the right to make a film of it, even though films were then unknown.[94] Again, a grant (or reservation) of "moving picture rights" made in 1919 was capable of carrying the right to make a sound film[95] since talkies were a species of moving pictures with essentially the same form and area of exploitation.[96] But this conclusion will yield to the parties' intention as drawn from the actual agreement, as where the new rights were unknown and the parties contemplated a single exercise of the principal right,[97] the agreement containing a warranty that the author owned all "cinematograph rights", but the grant being only of "moving picture" rights, the former clearly meaning something more than the latter, and it being impossible to make a "moving picture" of the voice.[98] Where the right granted is exclusive or amounts to an assignment and the new right cannot be exploited separately from the old (as with the right to make a talking picture, which cannot be exploited without the moving

---

[89] *Frisby v British Broadcasting Corp* [1967] Ch. 932. But the line was considered by the author to be the key line of the play.

[90] See the cases discussed below in relation to architects' plans.

[91] As was conceded in *Joseph v National Magazine Co Ltd* [1959] Ch. 14.

[92] *Joseph v National Magazine Co Ltd* [1959] Ch. 14, approved in *Frisby v British Broadcasting Corp* [1967] Ch. 932.

[93] *Hospital for Sick Children v Walt Disney Productions Inc* [1968] Ch. 52. It is suggested that the views to this effect expressed by the Court of Appeal at 65, 73 and 78, although *obiter*, and differing from those of the trial judge ([1966] 1 W.L.R. 1055), were correct.

[94] *Serra v Famous-Lasky Film Service Ltd* (1922) 127 L.T. 109.

[95] *Serra v Famous-Lasky Film Service Ltd* (1922) 127 L.T. 109.

[96] *L.C. Page & Co v Fox Film Corp* (1936) 83 Fed. Rep.(2d.) 196. See also *J.C. Williamson Ltd v Metro-Goldwyn-Mayer Theatres Ltd* (1937) 56 C.L.R. 567 (High Ct. of Aus.)—grant in 1924 excluding all motion picture film rights, although future use of talkies by this time contemplated. Both decisions were followed in *Hospital for Sick Children v Walt Disney Productions Inc* [1968] Ch. 52. "Talkies" first became a technological possibility in about 1923 and a commercial reality in about 1927.

[97] *e.g.* the making of a single film, as in *Hospital for Sick Children v Walt Disney Productions Inc* [1968] Ch. 52.

[98] *Pathé Pictures Ltd v Bancroft* [1928–35] Mac.C.C. 403.

picture rights), it may be helpful to ask whether it is likely that the parties really intended to divide the right to exploit the new right between them.[99] Obviously all other terms of the agreement need to be considered.[1] If the agreement provides for the payment of royalties on sales, and the royalty provisions are not workable in the case of sales in the new medium, this may indicate that the parties did agree to exploitation by this means. Where a licence to exploit a work has to be implied, it will extend no further than to acts which were in the contemplation of the parties at the time and what was necessary to give business efficacy to the agreement.[2] An implied licence will therefore seldom, if ever, extend to technologies which were unknown at the date of the agreement.

Effect of non-compliance with licence terms. A licence will usually contain terms, express or implied, relating to its exercise, for example that agreed fees be paid or that no alterations be made. The question then often arises as to the position of a licensee who does not observe such terms. If he simply does something for which he does not have permission, he will be acting beyond the terms of the licence and thus infringing. Thus a person may have a licence to print and sell copies of a work but not to authorise its public performance,[3] to use another's work but not to claim it as his own,[4] nor to make alterations,[5] with the result that if he does these latter things he infringes. Alternatively, a term may amount to a condition precedent to the exercise of the licence so that failure to comply with the term will again mean that what is done is an infringement. Thus it may be a condition precedent for the right to use a song in a film that the composer be credited, or at least that someone else should not be credited.[6] On the other hand, if the licence is given in return for a promise by the licensee, the licensor's only remedy may be in damages. This will often be the position where the promise in question is to make a one-off payment by the licensee.[7] Whether or not such a term is a condition precedent, or a term whose breach will allow the licensor to revoke the licence, will depend upon the proper construction of the licence agreement.[8] Where the licence contains continuing obligations on the part of the licensee, for example to pay royalties, it is suggested that non-payment or other default amounting to a repudiation of the contract will usually entitle the licensor to accept the repudiation and thus bring the licence to an end on the basis that, as a matter of construction, the licence was granted only so long as the licensee adhered to the terms of the agreement.[9]

5-226

Revocation and termination. A licence, if coupled with a contract not to revoke it (for example, a contractual licence for a fixed term) is irrevocable[10] except in accordance with its express terms or on the occasion of a relevant breach by the licensee (see below). If a contractual licence does not provide for its duration, it

5-227

---

[99] *J.C. Williamson Ltd v Metro-Goldwyn-Mayer Theatres Ltd* (1937) 56 C.L.R. 567.

[1] For a discussion of some of the cases on the point in the United States, as they apply to the acquisition of internet rights, see Radcliffe, "New Media Convergence: Acquiring Rights to Existing Works for the Internet under U.S. Law" [2001] E.I.P.R. 172.

[2] *Ray v Classic FM plc* [1998] F.S.R. 622 at 643.

[3] *Williams v Feldman* [1911–16] Mac.C.C. 98.

[4] *Blair v Osborne & Tomkins* [1971] 2 Q.B. 78.

[5] *Frisby v British Broadcasting Corp* [1967] Ch. 932.

[6] *Miller v Cecil Film Ltd* [1937] 2 All E.R. 464.

[7] *Ng v Clyde Securities Ltd* [1976] N.S.W.L.R. 443.

[8] *Ng v Clyde Securities Ltd* [1976] N.S.W.L.R. 443.

[9] See, *e.g. Jay v Benning* (1855) 1 K. & J. 168 at 174; *"Clinical Obstetrics"* [1905–10] Mac.C.C. 176.

[10] *Hurst v Picture Theatres Ltd* [1915] 1 K.B. 1; *British Actors Film Co Ltd v Glover* [1918] 1 K.B. 299; *Williams v Feldman* [1911–16] Mac.C.C. 98; *Winter Garden Theatre (London) Ltd v Millennium Productions Ltd* [1948] A.C. 173; *Hounslow London Borough Council v Twickenham Garden Developments Ltd* [1971] Ch. 233.

is revocable on reasonable notice, as is a gratuitous licence.[11] A licence which is personal and thus unassignable by the licensee[12] will terminate on the licensee's insolvency[13] or death.[14] To be effective, a notice must purport to revoke the licence or otherwise make it clear that the licensor considers the licence to be at an end and not, for example, simply propose terms for its continuance.[15] A letter from a licensor which is in fact a repudiation of a licence agreement does not constitute a notice to terminate the licence pursuant to an express or implied term unless it is otherwise clear that the licence is being revoked.[16] Thus, if the licensor purports to revoke a revocable licence, but gives no notice or insufficient notice of revocation, the licensee cannot ignore the revocation and treat the licence as subsisting.[17] On the other hand, the licensee cannot be treated as a wrongdoer for continuing to do what the licence permitted him to do until the expiry of the period which would have constituted reasonable notice.[18] Although a gratuitous licence may in general be revoked at any time, where the licensor has led the licensee to believe that it would not be revoked and the licensee has acted on that basis, the licensor may find himself estopped from revoking it, or from asserting his equitable and legal rights after any revocation.[19] Where there is a dispute as to title, the person revoking the licence should be in a position to produce proof of his title to the copyright before he can effectively revoke the licence.[20]

G. ARCHITECTS' PLANS AND WORKS OF ARCHITECTURE

5–228   Many of the problems connected with licences are illustrated by cases concerning architects' plans.[21] Although the property in the physical plans prepared by an architect for a client usually belongs to the client,[22] the architect will usually remain the owner of the copyright in them.[23] The architect may also of course own the copyright in models for the building, or the building itself, as works of architecture. Unless the client has acquired the copyright in such works, he may not copy any of them unless he has some licence to do so. If nothing is said, it is usually clear that some licence to use the plans must be implied but, first, what is the extent of the use covered by the licence? For example, is it limited to an application for planning permission alone, or does it extend to obtaining planning permission and thereafter for use in constructing and repairing the building in ac-

---

[11] *Edwards v Cotton* (1903) 19 T.L.R. 34; *Hart v Hayman, etc, Ltd* [1911–16] Mac.C.C. 301. See further, below.

[12] See para. 5–223, above.

[13] *Lucas v Moncrieff* (1905) 21 T.L.R. 683.

[14] *Messager v British Broadcasting Corp Ltd* [1927] 2 K.B. 543, reversed on other grounds: [1929] A.C. 151.

[15] *Redwood Music Ltd v Chappell & Co Ltd* [1982] R.P.C. 109.

[16] *Decro-Wall S.A. v Marketing Ltd* [1971] 1 W.L.R. 361 at 382 (letter purporting to accept repudiation, itself amounting to a repudiation, not sufficient notice under agreement terminable on 12 months' notice).

[17] *Dorling v Honnor Marine Ltd* [1964] Ch. 560; *Godfrey v Lees* [1995] E.M.L.R. 307. The distinction between this situation and a *Decro-Wall* type of case can be a fine one.

[18] *Dorling v Honnor Marine Ltd* [1964] Ch. 560 at 567; *Martin-Baker Aircraft Co Ltd v Canadian Flight Equipment Ltd* [1955] 2 Q.B. 556.

[19] As in *Godfrey v Lees* [1995] E.M.L.R. 307. But the incurring of expenditure by the licensee will not automatically make the licence irrevocable: *Hart v Hayman, Christy and Lilly Ltd* [1911–16] Mac.C.C. 301.

[20] *Redwood Music Ltd v Chappell & Co Ltd* [1982] R.P.C. 109.

[21] Today, use of an architect's plans will usually be governed by standard terms of the architect's engagement, such as the RIBA conditions. See para. 5–230, below.

[22] *Gibbon v Pease* [1905] 1 K.B. 810; *Inala Industries Pty Ltd v Associated Enterprises Pty Ltd* [1960] Q.S.R. 562. The property in all notes, sketches and other material used by the architect in preparation of the plans will usually remain with the architect: *Leicestershire County Council v Faraday & Partners Ltd* [1941] 2 K.B. 205; *Chantrey Martin v Martin* [1953] 2 Q.B. 286.

[23] The standard term of the RIBA conditions so provides.

cordance with the plans, perhaps as modified?[24] Secondly, who is entitled to the benefit of the licence? Is it the original client, or the original client and for instance anyone to whom he sells the site with the benefit of the planning permission, and in either case is the licence dependent upon the architect having been paid his fee?

Examples. A claimant had prepared plans for a client for the purpose of obtaining full planning permission to build two houses on a site and had been paid the full-scale fee under the RIBA conditions for that work. The site was sold after planning permission had been obtained and the plans were then used by another firm in erecting houses on the site. It was held that in the circumstances the claimant had impliedly licensed the use of the plans for all purposes connected with the erection of that building on that site in substantial accordance with them, whether by the client or by the purchasers of the plot, and by their surveyors or workmen, and such that they might make copies of the plans for that purpose.[25] This conclusion was reached on a consideration of the then RIBA conditions under which the architect was paid for his work in stages and which envisaged that the architect's engagement might not run its full course, so that it would be wrong in principle for the architect to be able to hold the client to ransom such that the client would almost inevitably have to retain him, particularly where the scale fees fully compensated the architect for the work actually done.[26] The principle applied was that "the payment for sketch plans includes a permission or consent to use those sketch plans for the purpose for which they were brought into existence, namely, for the purpose of building a building in substantial accordance with them and for the purpose of preparing any necessary drawings as part of the task of building the building".[27] But where an architect charged a nominal amount purely for the purposes of preparing plans for a planning application, the amount being much less than the appropriate scale fee, no licence was implied further than one enabling the plans to be used for that purpose.[28] The reason why a nominal fee will be charged in many such cases is that if the planning application is refused the money spent by the client will be thrown away, whereas if it is granted the architect may expect to be engaged under the building contract and earn substantial fees,[29] or at least to be further compensated.[30] Every case will, however, depend upon its own facts,[31] and it may be that a licence would be implied even if the architect had not been paid full-scale fees for the work done up to a particular stage, but had been asked to remain as architect for the project and had refused or demanded unreasonable terms for doing so.[32]

Where the architect has retained the copyright, there will often be sound reasons for this. For example, he may thereby be able to prevent the plans being used for purposes other than the specific building contemplated.[33] But where a licence can be implied for all purposes connected with the erection of buildings in accordance with plans, the licence will usually extend to making changes to

5–229

---

[24] It should be remembered that the reconstruction of a building will not infringe the copyright in any plans at all. See CDPA 1988, s.65 and para. 9–176, below.

[25] *Blair v Osborne & Tomkins* [1971] 2 Q.B. 78.

[26] See the analysis in *Stovin-Bradford v Volpoint Ltd* [1971] Ch. 1007.

[27] *Blair v Osborne & Tomkins* [1971] 2 Q.B. 78, the Court of Appeal citing with approval this passage from *Beck v Montana Constructions Pty Ltd* [1964–65] N.S.W.R. 229.

[28] *Stovin-Bradford v Volpoint* [1971] Ch. 1007.

[29] *Stovin-Bradford v Volpoint* [1971] Ch. 1007, *per* Salmon L.J. at 1019.

[30] *Stovin-Bradford v Volpoint* [1971] Ch. 1007, *per* Megaw L.J. at 1022.

[31] *Stovin-Bradford v Volpoint* [1971] Ch. 1007.

[32] *Stovin-Bradford v Volpoint* [1971] Ch. 1007, *per* Megaw L.J. at 1022, and *per* Salmon L.J. at 1019, citing the example of an architect of wide renown; and see also *Beck v Montana Constructions Pty Ltd,* [1964–65] N.S.W.R. 229.

[33] *Blair v Osborne & Tomkins,* [1971] 2 Q.B. 78, *per* Widgery L.J. at 86.

them which are not substantial or to adding detail to them, for example for the purpose of obtaining building regulation approval.[34] The licence will usually extend to successors in title to the property,[35] or the assignees from the original client,[36] and will extend to reproducing the plans in a leaflet intended to be shown to prospective purchasers of the building.[37] It will usually enable the owner and his successors in title and contractors to repair or renovate the building, particularly where this has become necessary because of the architect's own fault.[38] It will not, however, extend to permit someone to remove the architect's name from the plans and put them forward as his own, although in such cases the damage resulting may be small.[39]

Whether the architect can stop the use of his plans where he is unpaid will depend upon whether payment was a condition precedent, or whether non-payment can be treated as a repudiatory act allowing the architect to terminate any licence. It has been said that one of the purposes of the architect retaining copyright is to enable him to prevent the use of his work by others who have paid him no fee,[40] but in the usual type of case, particularly where payment is not expected to be made at the outset, it is thought that the correct analysis will be that the licence is given in return for a promise to pay, recoverable by action.[41] Where the original client has become insolvent, and the site has passed into another's hands, this remedy may of course be worthless.[42] Where, however, the architect's consent has been given gratuitously, he may later withdraw it.[43]

5–230 **Current RIBA conditions.** The terms on which a client may use an architect's plans may of course be regulated by the express terms of his appointment. The current (1992) edition of the RIBA standard conditions of appointment makes more detailed provision than the conditions considered in the earlier cases. Thus they provide that the client may reproduce the plans in executing the particular building project[44] provided that:

   (a) this is restricted to the site to which the plans relate;
   (b) the architect has completed a "scheme design"[45] or provided detailed design and production information;
   (c) any fees, expenses and disbursements have been paid.

Until these conditions are satisfied, it appears that any reproduction of the plans will be an infringement.[46] Where the architect's services have been limited to making and negotiating planning applications, the client is not to reproduce the

---

[34] *Blair v Osborne & Tomkins* [1971] 2 Q.B. 78; see also *Barnett v Cape Town Foreshaw Board* [1978] F.S.R. 176 (Cape Div. Ct) but *cf. Netupsky v Dominion Bridge Co Ltd* (1969) 68 W.W.R. 529. The point was left open in *Hunter v Fitzroy Robinson and Partners* [1978] F.S.R. 167. Regard should also be had to an architect's right to object to derogatory treatment of his work. See Ch.11, below.

[35] *Blair v Osborne & Tomkins,* [1971] 2 Q.B. 78.

[36] *Hunter v Fitzroy Robinson and Partners* [1978] F.S.R. 167.

[37] *Robert Allan & Partners v Scottish Ideal Homes* (1972) S.L.T. (Shire Court Reports) 32. The use of drawings or photographs of buildings in such circumstances may now also be permissible by virtue of s.63 of the 1988 Act. See para. 9–172, below.

[38] *ADI Ltd v Destein* (1983) 141 D.L.R. (3d) 370.

[39] *Blair v Osborne & Tomkins* [1971] 2 Q.B. 78, where the claimant was awarded £2. Note that there is also an architect's moral right to be identified as the author of his work. See Ch.11, below.

[40] *Blair v Osborne & Tomkins,* [1971] 2 Q.B. 78, *per* Widgery L.J. at 86.

[41] *Ng v Clyde Securities Ltd* [1976] N.S.W.L.R. 443.

[42] As in *Ng v Clyde Securities Ltd,* [1976] N.S.W.L.R. 443.

[43] *Katz v Cytrynbaum* (1984) 2 D.L.R. (4th) 52, following *Hart v Hayman, Christy & Lilly Ltd* [1911–16] Mac.C.C. 301.

[44] Including for the purpose of any maintenance, repair or renewal of the building.

[45] Broadly, the stage of developing the outline proposal up to the detailed design stage.

[46] The RIBA conditions, having laid down these conditions for the reproduction of the plans, rather

plans without consent (such consent not to be unreasonably withheld) and the payment of "any additional fees".[47] Generally, the benefit of the agreement, and therefore any licence, is stated not to be assignable without the consent in writing of the architect. This is obviously a powerful weapon in the hands of the architect and a trap for any successor to the client.

H. THE RIGHT TO REPAIR

Implied licence: the right to repair. Before the decision of the House of Lords in *British Leyland Motor Corp Ltd v Armstrong Patents Co Ltd*,[48] there were a number of decisions to the effect that a purchaser of an article was entitled, by virtue of an implied licence from the vendor, to reproduce a copyright work if this was done in the course of repair of the article. Such decisions were reached by analogy with patent cases where the form of the letters patent[49] forced the court to imply some licence to enable the purchaser of a patented article to use it and thus repair it. The licence in such cases extended no further than enabling the purchaser to prolong the life of the article by repair but not to entitle him to make a new article under the cover of repair.[50] The cases decided in relation to copyright established that such a licence extended to enable the purchaser to make spare parts himself and to have such parts made for him,[51] and probably to have two or more made at the same time against the future breakdown of the article.[52] The licence did not, however, extend to the world at large so as to enable a manufacturer to make spare parts in anticipation of future orders,[53] nor to enable the manufacturer to copy any plans to which he might have had access, as opposed to working backwards from the part which he was going to replace.[54]

5–231

Non-derogation from grant: the right to repair. The use by the courts of an implied licence theory was artificial and gave rise to obvious difficulties, for example, where there was no privity of contract between the manufacturer of the original article and its owner or the spare part manufacturer. The principle was largely abandoned by the House of Lords in the *British Leyland* case, where the question arose whether an independent manufacturer of replacement car exhaust systems could be stopped by the owner of the copyright in the manufacturing drawings for such systems. Two alternative bases were propounded for denying such a remedy. First, that the purchaser of an article such as a car has an inherent right to repair it, so that the common law will not allow a copyright owner to assert a monopoly right to detract from the rights of ownership, thus affecting the

5–232

---

confusingly go on to state that: "Where the architect has not completed a scheme design, the Client shall not reproduce the design by proceeding to execute the Project without the consent of the Architect".

[47] It would appear that any such fees must have been specifically agreed.

[48] [1986] A.C. 577.

[49] "To make, use, exercise and vend" the invention.

[50] *Dunlop Pneumatic Tyre Co v Neal* [1899] 1 Ch. 807; *Sirdar Rubber Co Ltd v Wallington Weston & Co* (1907) 24 R.P.C. 539. The concept of an implied licence to repair in the case of patented articles has now been abandoned. The question in all cases is whether the defendant has "made" the patented article. See *United Wire Ltd v Screen Repair Services (Scotland) Ltd* [2001] R.P.C. 439, HL.

[51] *Solar Thomson Engineering Co Ltd v Barton* [1977] R.P.C. 537; *Gardner & Sons Ltd v Paul Sykes Organisation Ltd* [1981] F.S.R. 281, and *Weir Pumps Ltd v C.M.L. Pumps Ltd* [1984] F.S.R. 33.

[52] *British Leyland Motor Corp Ltd v Armstrong Patents Co Ltd* [1984] F.S.R. 591; *Hoover plc v George Hulme Ltd* [1982] F.S.R. 565.

[53] *British Leyland Motor Corp Ltd v Armstrong Patents Co Ltd* [1984] F.S.R. 591; *Hoover plc v George Hulme Ltd* [1982] F.S.R. 565.

[54] *i.e.* by reverse engineering. See *Weir Pumps Ltd v C.M.L. Pumps Ltd,* [1984] F.S.R. 33.

value and use of the article sold.[55] Secondly, by an extension of the principle of non-derogation from grant, it was held that a grantor would not be allowed to derogate from his grant by using intellectual property retained so as to render property granted by him unfit or materially unfit for the purpose for which the grant was made.[56]

The full extent of this doctrine as applied to the field of copyright was never fully worked out[57] and now that the transitional provisions relating to the introduction of design right[58] and the corresponding restriction on the ability to rely on copyright in relation to designs for spare parts[59] have worked themselves out,[60] the principle is likely to be of little importance. This is because s.51 essentially abolished industrial copyright as it had previously been recognised under the 1956 Act, so that there is no further need for a spare part exception in relation to industrial designs since there is no right from which the exception is needed.[61] In addition, there is no room for a spare part exception in relation to design right,[62] because the question of spare parts was specifically considered by Parliament when introducing design right and no such right was provided for. Nor is there any room for it in relation to computer programs or database right, since these have both been the subject of complete statutory codes following implementation of the respective Community Directives.[63][64] In relation to other forms of copyright work, the Information Society Directive[65] permits Member States to make an exception to the reproduction and distribution rights in connection with the repair of equipment,[66] and while the United Kingdom did not introduce any provision taking advantage of this on implementation, it is arguable that any residual right to repair under United Kingdom law would come within this.[67] What follows is therefore a summary of the law on this topic as it stood before its development was arrested.

It was recognised by the House of Lords in *British Leyland Motor Corp Ltd*[68] that it was a novel application of the principle of non-derogation from grant to prevent a party exercising a statutory right and indeed subsequently the Privy Council has suggested that the true basis of the decision was one of public policy, namely to prevent a manufacturer from controlling the after-market in spare parts.[69] Thus any suggestion that it should be extended will be treated with caution.[70] Certainly, the principle does not go so far as to enable the owner of the

---

[55] *per* Lord Bridge at 625.

[56] *per* Lord Templeman at 641, relying on *Browne v Flower* [1911] 1 Ch. 219.

[57] There is nothing in the 1988 Act which apparently affects the general application of the *British Leyland* principle (see, *e.g.* CDPA 1988, s.172(3)), but see the further discussion in the text.

[58] See Ch.13, below. The defence was not taken away with the passing of the 1988 Act: *Flogates Ltd v Refco Ltd* [1996] F.S.R. 935.

[59] *i.e.* CDPA 1988, s.51. See paras 13–278 *et seq.*, below.

[60] CDPA 1988, Sch.1, para.19. See para. 13–317 *et seq.*, below.

[61] *Mars U.K. Ltd v Teknowledge Ltd* [2000] F.S.R. 138.

[62] See Ch.13, below.

[63] Namely, the Software Directive (91/250) and the Database Directive (96/9).

[65] Directive 2001/29

[66] Art.5(3)(l). Generally, however, the Directive is without prejudice to provisions concerning design rights (see Art.9). See Ch.9, below, for a discussion on the effect of the Directive on the exceptions to rights permitted to Member States.

[67] Any such exception would, however, have to comply with the three-step test in Art.5, *i.e*, it should only apply in certain special cases which do not conflict with a normal exploitation of the work or other subject-matter and do not unreasonably prejudice the legitimate interests of the right-holder. As to this, see para. 24–33, below.

[68] [1986] A.C. 577 at 627.

[69] *Canon Kabushiki Kaisha v Green Cartridge Co (Hong Kong) Ltd* [1997] A.C. 728.

[70] *Canon Kabushiki Kaisha v Green Cartridge Co (Hong Kong) Ltd* [1997] A.C. 728; *Mars UK Ltd v Teknowledge Ltd* [2000] F.S.R. 138.

article to do whatever is necessary to keep it in running order,[71] and neither is it sufficient to ask mechanistically whether the "spare part" can properly be regarded as a separate entity or as an accessory of a larger entity.[72] The true basis of the principle combines two features. First, does the manufacture of the part constitute repair of a kind which the ordinary man who bought the article would assume he could do without infringing any rights of the manufacturer? Secondly, would the exercise of the property right unquestionably operate against the interests of consumers? Evaluation of the second feature may require asking whether the purchaser of the original article would normally evaluate the cost of purchasing the replacement parts during the lifetime of the article when making his decision to purchase.[73] Various other principles can be stated:

(a) In a case where a question of patent protection simultaneously arose,[74] the principles applicable in such cases still applied and the principle of non-derogation from grant did not and perhaps should not have been invoked.[75]

(b) None of the "repair" cases decided under the implied licence principle were disapproved on their facts and the result in each case was presumably not wrong.

(c) The principle enabled the owner of an article to have a replacement part made either by himself or by another, as before, but also enabled a supplier to manufacture such stock in advance of anticipated orders.[76]

(d) The principle appears to go further than that applied in relation to patent cases in that the copyright owner was not entitled to complain of the manufacture of an entirely new part as opposed to simply the repair of an existing one.[77]

(e) The distinction between the two principles is further emphasised by the fact that the right to repair and thus reproduce copyright works could not apparently be withheld even by express terms of the contract of purchase.[78]

(f) A subcontractor who designed a part for a manufacturer, knowing the purpose for which it was to be used, could not assert his copyright against the purchaser.[79]

(g) The right did not permit a defendant to take copies of the claimant's drawings directly[80] or, presumably, to make articles from such copies.

---

[71] *Canon Kabushiki Kaisha v Green Cartridge Co (Hong Kong) Ltd* [1997] A.C. 728.

[72] *Canon Kabushiki Kaisha v Green Cartridge Co (Hong Kong) Ltd* [1997] A.C. 728 citing *Dennion Manufacturing Co v Alfred Holt and Co Ltd* (1987) 10 I.P.R. 612 (plastic tags for attaching price labels to garments by means of a gun not "spare parts" for gun).

[73] Compare the position in *British Leyland* where the decision as to what make of car to buy was probably not influenced by the cost of occasional replacement of the exhaust, with that in the *Canon Kabushiki* case, where the cost of replacement printer cartridges was substantial in relation to the cost of the whole printer and was likely to have been an important part of the choice between rival makes. The principle suggests that the argument of the claimant in *Flogates Ltd v Refco Ltd* [1996] F.S.R. 935 that the defence did not apply to parts which were regularly worn out and whose replacement cost was a major factor for a prospective buyer was probably correct.

[74] As it did in the *Solar Thomson Engineering Co Ltd v Barton* [1977] R.P.C. 537.

[75] *British Leyland Motor Corp Ltd v Armstrong Patents Co Ltd* [1986] A.C. 577, *per* Lord Bridge at 625. Lord Templeman, who gave the other leading speech, did not expressly deal with the point. See also *Dellareed Ltd v Delkim Developments* [1988] F.S.R. 329. Note, however, that principle in patent cases no longer rests on the concept of an implied licence: *United Wire Ltd v Screen Repair Services (Scotland) Ltd* [2001] R.P.C. 24, HL.

[76] *British Leyland Motor Corp Ltd v Armstrong Patents Co Ltd* [1986] A.C. 577 at 625.

[77] As in the *British Leyland* case itself. This also appears to have been the position established under the implied licence cases. See *Gardner & Sons Ltd v Paul Sykes Organisation Ltd* [1981] F.S.R. 281 and *Weir Pumps Ltd v C.M.L. Pumps Ltd* [1984] F.S.R. 33.

[78] *British Leyland Motor Corp Ltd v Armstrong Patents Co Ltd,* [1986] A.C. 577 at 643.

[79] *British Leyland Motor Corp Ltd v Armstrong Patents Co Ltd* [1986] A.C. 577 at 643.

[80] *Warman International Ltd v Envirotech Australia Pty Ltd* (1986) 67 A.L.R. 253 (Fed. Ct of Aus.).

(h) Where the purchaser would not normally have been able or have expected to repair the article, the principle did not apply.[81]

(i) The right did not permit a purchaser to repair goods which were not of merchantable quality. His remedy was to return the goods or claim damages.[82]

(j) The copying of a work to help produce a compatible and competing product did not fall within the principle.[83]

I. TRANSITIONAL PROVISIONS

5–233 **General principles.** As has already been noted, any document made or event occurring before the commencement of the 1988 Act (*i.e.* August 1, 1989) which had any operation affecting the ownership of the copyright in an existing work or creating, transferring or terminating an interest, right or licence in respect of the copyright in an existing work, has the corresponding operation in relation to copyright in the work under the 1988 Act.[84] In addition, expressions used in such documents are to be construed in accordance with their effect immediately before commencement.[85] The general effect of these provisions is therefore that one should first consider the operation of a pre-commencement licence when it was created. It is then to have the corresponding operation under the 1988 Act. Although these provisions of the 1988 Act apply in general to all existing works (*i.e.* works made before commencement of the 1988 Act), including works in existence at the commencement of the 1911 Act or the 1956 Act, there are modifications in special cases in the application of certain provisions of the 1988 Act to existing works. These are now summarised.

5–234 **Exclusive licences.** The effect of an exclusive licence granted before the 1956 Act came into force has already been considered,[86] as has the fact that s.92(2) of the 1988 Act, dealing with the rights of an exclusive licensee against successors in title to the licensor, does not apply in relation to a licence granted before August 1, 1989.[87]

5–235 **1911 Act reversionary rights.** It has already been seen that assignments under the 1911 Act were in certain cases subject to a proviso limiting the ability of an author to assign the last 25 years of the term of copyright. This limitation also applied to those licences which amounted to a grant of an interest in the copyright.[88] The effect of this limitation has already been considered when dealing with assignments.[89]

5–236 **1911 Act, s.24.** It has been seen that since the term of copyright under the 1911 Act was, in general, longer than that subsisting under the pre-existing statute law, the 1911 Act contained provisions under which assignments or licences subsisting at the commencement of that Act should determine when the old period of copyright ran out, and the 1911 Act copyright thereafter revested in the author or his personal representatives. The continuing effect of these provisions has been dealt with in the section dealing with assignments.

---

[81] *Saphena Computing Ltd v Allied Collection Agencies Ltd* [1995] F.S.R. 616.
[82] *Fylde Microsystems Ltd v Key Radio Systems Ltd* [1998] F.S.R. 449.
[83] *Creative Technology Ltd v Aztech Systems Pte Ltd* [1997] F.S.R. 491 (Ct of App.of Singapore).
[84] CDPA 1988, Sch.1, para.25(1).
[85] Sch.1, para.25(2).
[86] See para. 5–233, above.
[87] See paras 5–205 and 5–233, above.
[88] See the proviso to s.5(2) of the Copyright Act 1911, as now re-enacted in CDPA 1988, Sch.1, para.27. As to the meaning of the "grant of any interest", see paras 5–113 and 5–233, above.
[89] See para. 5–113, above.

CHAPTER SIX

DURATION OF COPYRIGHT

Contents

1. INTRODUCTION

Introduction. The need to establish the duration of copyright in a particular   **6–01**
work may arise in a variety of contexts. Thus, itmay be important to establish that
copyright in a particular work has already expired before undertaking an act of
exploitation of that work which would otherwise need to be licensed. In an infringement action, it will be necessary to establish not only that the requirements
for copyright to subsist in the work have been met, but that copyright continued
or continues to subsist throughout the period of alleged infringement. It may also
be important to establish for how long in the future the work may be expected to
enjoy protection, a matter as much of concern to those on both sides of transactions involving the copyright in the work as to those who are waiting for the
copyright to expire, so that they may freely exploit the work once it falls into the
public domain.

In the case of a recently created work in which copyright is established to
subsist, the question of the duration of copyright in such work is a relatively
straightforward matter. It involves identifying the appropriate description of the
work for the purposes of the 1988 Act,[1] ascertaining (in the case of some works)

---

[1] See CDPA 1988, s.1(1), and Ch.3, above.

the identity of its author[2] and, if dead, the year of his death, or, in the case of other works, the date of the creation or first exploitation of the work, and identifying the rule applying to the particular work amongst the rules as to duration contained in sections 12 to 15A of the 1988 Act.

However, in relation to all but the most recently created works, the question of the duration of copyright subsisting in the work is a much more complex matter, since the identification of the applicable period of protection will involve considering the rules as to duration not only under the current statutory regime, but under each preceding statutory regime, back to that which was in force when the work was created. This is not because successive Copyright Acts have maintained in force the earlier statutory regime as to duration for existing works,[3] since each Act has proceeded on the general principle that its own rules as to duration apply as much to new works as to existing works. However, the history of the term of copyright protection in the United Kingdom is one of progressive extensions to the term, and as each successive statutory regime as to duration has replaced its predecessor, it has usually retained, through transitional provisions, certain aspects of the previous regime, which continue to apply to works created under that previous regime. Since, until the amendments made to the 1988 Act in 1996,[4] each regime has replaced its predecessor, it was, before this latest amendment of the 1988 Act, necessary only to consider the transitional provisions in the 1988 Act in order to determine whether the current rules are modified in their application to a particular existing work, whatever the date of creation of that work.

However, the very question of the subsistence of copyright under the current regime, in a work created before that regime was introduced, requires consideration as to whether that work remained protected immediately prior to the commencement of the subsequent regime, and this in turn requires consideration of the duration of protection applied to that work under the preceding regime. If the work was created before that preceding regime came into force, then the same consideration has to be given to the duration of protection applied to the work under the earlier preceding regime. For this purpose, it has always been necessary to consider not only the principal rules of that earlier regime, but also its transitional provisions.

It is this retrospective aspect which makes the question of the duration of the copyright in a work under the current provisions of the 1988 Act a matter of considerable complexity, which is increased as the date of the creation of the work falls within each earlier period in the following table:

[2] As to who is the author of a work, see Ch.4, above.

[3] As is the case, for example, regarding the question of who is the author of a work; see para. 4–07, above.

[4] As explained in para. 6–14, below, the transitional provisions of the Regulations, which amended the CDPA 1988, did not follow this practice, and require the position to be considered also under the CDPA 1988 as it was before amendment by the Regulations.

Date when work made	Provisions to be considered
On or after January 1, 1996	(i) the 1988 Act as amended[5]
On or after August 1, 1989 but before January 1, 1996	(i) as above; and (ii) the 1988 Act as originally enacted and the transitional provisions contained in regulations 12 to 16 of the Duration Regulations[6]
On or after June 1, 1956 but before August 1, 1989	(i) and (ii) as above; and (iii) the transitional provisions contained in paragraph 12 of Schedule 1 to the Act; (iv) the 1956 Act and the transitional provisions contained in paragraphs 2, 11 and 14 of Schedule 7 to the Act
On or after July 1, 1912 but before June 1, 1956	(i), (ii), (iii) and (iv) as above; and (v) the 1911 Act
Before July 1, 1912	(i), (ii), (iii), (iv) and (v) as above; and (vi) the Acts then in force

The scheme of this chapter is to describe the history of the term of protection that has applied in the United Kingdom, first, against the background of international developments, and then making certain points of general application to existing works under each of the regimes that has applied since before 1911, before setting out the specific rules as to the duration of copyright in the different descriptions of works protected by copyright under the 1988 Act, dealing in each case with the current rules and then any particular rules applicable to existing works of that description under the transitional provisions of the 1988 Act.

2. THE HISTORY OF THE DEVELOPMENT OF THE TERM OF COPYRIGHT PROTECTION

What is a fair term for copyright? The history of the development of the term   **6–02**
of copyright protection in the United Kingdom is one of progressive extension of the term of protection,[7] and might be thought to reflect a development towards a consensus as to what is considered to be the fair term for such protection. The debate as to what should be the proper period of protection, which was first raised in the United Kingdom when literary works were first accorded copyright under statute, by the Statute of Anne 1709,[8] has continued over the succeeding years without any general consensus emerging. In the early days of the debate, the argument was between those who contended, in the interest of literature, for a very short period; and others who contended, in the same interest, for perpetuity.

---

[5] By the Duration of Copyright and Rights in Performance Regulations 1995 (SI 1995/3297), see para. 6–11, below.

[6] The transitional provisions of the Duration Regulations amending the CDPA 1988 do not follow this practice, and require the position to be considered also under the CDPA 1988 as it was before amendment by the Duration Regulations, see also para. 6–12, below.

[7] As has been the case with most other countries adhering to Berne; a notable exception was the reduction in the term accorded to Berne works by Spain in November 1987; see the footnotes to para. 6–08, below.

[8] 8 Anne, c.19; see para. 2–16, above, and see generally as to the history of the development of copyright, Ch.2 above, and A. Robinson "The Life and Terms of UK Copyright in Original Works" [1997] 2 Ent. L.R. 60.

The Gregory Committee was faced with these conflicting views.[9] The debate has been rekindled on each occasion that copyright protection has been extended to a new description of work, or when attempts are made to revise the term of protection at international level through the revision of the various international conventions. The 1977 Copyright Committee considered submissions that the term should be extended to a period of life of the author plus 70 years thereafter, but concluded that the case for extension had not been made out, and that the then current period should remain.[10] The debate has recently been revived in the context of the extension of the term of protection required in the United Kingdom, and throughout the territory of the European Union by Council Directive 93/98,[11] in relation to works of EEA origin.[12]

Those who argue in favour of a restricted period for copyright speak of it as a monopoly;[13] whilst upholders of copyright in perpetuity speak of the author's right to prevent others multiplying copies of his work as a right of property. The issue of what is a fair term of copyright cannot be decided by such attempts to categorise copyright, but by a consideration of opposing public interests which are to be balanced. On the one hand, there is the public interest in ensuring access to creative works,[14] which argues for limiting the term of protection. On the other hand, there is the public interest in encouraging creative effort and its dissemination, which argues for extending the term of protection so as both to provide adequate rewards for the author and his publisher for their creative and business endeavour, and to protect the author's right to maintain the integrity of his work.[15]

Thus, whilst it is generally accepted, today, that the liberal arts cannot be expected to flourish in a country possessing inadequate copyright laws, at the same time clearly some limit must be set on copyright protection. The longer the period of protection, the greater the practical difficulty of tracing title to a kind of property of which there can be no physical possession.[16] Also, at least as regards published works, it is unreasonable to give to the remote successors of the author, long after his death, a monopoly in what has in fact been made public by exploitation. That is particularly so in relation to works which by their nature involve an element of industrial enterprise, as distinct from individual literary, musical or artistic creativity, and the tendency has been to accord such works a shorter, usually fixed, period of protection.

---

[9] Perpetuity at one extreme, a fixed period of 15 years from publication at the other. The Gregory Committee itself was of the view that all periods of copyright are arbitrary, there being no ideal period: Report of the Committee on the Law of Copyright, 1952, Cmnd.8662, para.16.

[10] Report of the Committee to consider the Law on Copyright and Designs, Cmnd.6732, para.637; and see, generally, paras 625–636.

[11] [1993] O.J. L290/9, and see paras 6–09 to 6–08, below. As to the interrelationship between the European Union and the European Economic Area, see para. 25–01, below.

[12] See, for example, S. Ricketson "The Copyright Term" (1992) 6 I.I.C. 755; S. von Lewinski in (1992) 6 I.I.C. 785; G. Dworkin "Authorship of Films and the European Commission Proposals for Harmonising the Term of Copyright" [1993] 5 E.I.P.R. 151; P. Parrinder "The Dead Hand of European Copyright" [1993] 11 E.I.P.R. 391; L. Kurlantzick "Harmonisation of Copyright Protection" [1994] 11 E.I.P.R. 463; G. Davies "Copyright and the Public Interest" (2nd ed., Sweet & Maxwell, 2002); Mr Justice Laddie "Copyright: Over-strength, Over-regulated, Over-rated?" [1996] 5 E.I.P.R. 253; J. Antill and P. Coles "Copyright Duration: The European Community Adopts 'Three Score Years and Ten'" [1996] 7 E.I.P.R. 379.

[13] As to how far this is correct, see para. 1–31, above.

[14] Embodied in Art.27(1) of the Declaration Human of Rights, which provides: "Everyone has the right freely to participate in the cultural life of the community, to enjoy the arts and to share in scientific advancement and its benefits". See also para. 1–33, above.

[15] Protection of the author's economic and moral rights is also embodied in the Declaration of Human Rights, Art.27(2) of which provides: "Everyone has the right to the protection of the moral and material interests resulting from any scientific, literary or artistic production of which he is the author". See also para. 1–33, above.

[16] See para. 5–64, above.

The adoption of a term of 50 years pma. At the Conference of the Powers held   **6–03**
at Berlin in 1908 for the purpose of considering what modifications ought to be
made to the Berne Convention,[17] it was decided that the minimum period of
protection accorded to an author of a literary or artistic work[18] should be 50 years
post mortem auctoris,[19] that is, during his life and for a period of 50 years after
his death.[20] This was accordingly the term adopted by the United Kingdom in the
Copyright Act 1911 for all literary, dramatic, musical and artistic works, with
certain minor exceptions.[21] This position had the very considerable advantage
over the position under the law in the United Kingdom before 1911, in that the
date of publication no longer had any bearing on the period of copyright protection, save in certain excepted cases. Under the law prior to 1911, which gave an
alternative period of copyright for literary works, either for the life of the author
and seven years after his death or a gross period of 42 years from the date of publication, whichever should be the longer,[22] the works of the same author were liable to fall into the public domain at different times. The change introduced by
the 1911 Act has been followed in subsequent Copyright Acts, so that since 1911
all the literary, dramatic, musical and artistic works of the same author will, save
in certain excepted cases,[23] fall into the public domain at the same time.
Furthermore, since such date the term has depended on proof of the date of death,[24]
which is generally much easier to secure than proof of date of first publication.

Brussels Act. The Brussels Act, resulting from a further conference to revise the   **6–04**
Berne Convention held at Brussels in 1948, maintained the standard period of 50
years from the death of the author.[25] However, the definition of literary and artistic
works was revised expressly to include cinematographic and photographic
works,[26] and in respect of these works the term of protection was to be that given
by the law of the country in which protection was claimed, but was not to exceed
the term fixed in the country of origin of the work.[27] The Brussels Act provided
(with the object of removing any uncertainty which might otherwise arise through
difficulty in determining the precise date of death or other event) that the term of
protection should always be deemed to begin on January 1 of the year following
the event.[28] The necessary changes to give effect to this rule of calculation were
introduced in the 1956 Act. This rule has been maintained in subsequent revision

---

[17] The Convention of the International Union for the Protection of Literary and Artistic Works
signed at Berne on September 9, 1886; see Ch.24.

[18] Such expression in the Convention encompasses every production in the literary, scientific and
artistic domain, including dramatic and musical works: Art.2.

[19] Often abbreviated to "pma".

[20] This was therefore the period provided for in the Berlin Act (1908).

[21] Copyright Act 1911, s.3; photographs and sound contrivances were entitled to a straight term of
50 years from their making (ss.21 and 19 respectively) and literary, dramatic and musical works
first published after the death of the author were entitled to a term of 50 years from publication (
s.17).

[22] Under the Copyright Act 1842 (5 & 6 Vict. c.45); see para. 2–18, above.

[23] *i.e.* certain photographs and those literary, dramatic and musical works first published
posthumously, see n.19, above.

[24] Save in the case of works of unknown authorship, as to which see para. 6–46, below.

[25] Brussels Act, Art.7(1); and see Ch.24, below.

[26] Brussels Act, Art.2(1). Certain types of cinematographic works had been protected since the
Berlin Act 1908 (Art.14.(2)). Certain types of photographic works had been protected under the
Berne Convention since its inception, but photographic works in general were only included in
Art.2(1) in the Brussels Act 1948.

[27] Brussels Act, Art.7(3).

[28] Brussels Act, Art.7(6).

of the Berne Convention,[29] and has remained the rule in the United Kingdom under the 1988 Act.[30]

6–05 **Universal Copyright Convention.** The Universal Copyright Convention of 1952, provided, as does the Paris revision of 1971 of this Convention, that the Convention States should give to works of Convention nationals, or works first published in Convention States, protection for the period given to their own nationals, but in any event a minimum of 25 years.[31] As this minimum was less than that required by the Brussels Act (1948) (and by subsequent revisions of the Berne Convention), the United Kingdom, in formulating the term of protection under the 1956 and 1988 Acts in relation to such works, had regard to the Berne Convention as so revised.

6–05A **Revision to Berne Convention: Stockholm and Paris Acts.** The Berne Convention was further revised at conferences held at Stockholm in 1967 and Paris in 1971. The resulting Acts made no revision to the standard period of 50 years from the death of the author.[32] However, the Stockholm Act introduced a minimum term of protection in relation to films, which has been retained in the Paris Act, as an alternative to the standard period, of 50 years after the work was made available to the public.[33] As regards photographic works, the Stockholm Convention introduced a minimum term of 25 years from the making of such work, which has been retained in the Paris Act.[34]

6–06 **The Rome Convention.** Whilst films and photographs have been assimilated to literary and artistic works, so far as the provisions of the Berne Convention are concerned, sound recordings and other works which have become protected as new technology has developed in the course of the century following the ratification of the Berne Convention, such as broadcasts, have been the subject of other international conventions, principally the Rome Convention.[35] This Convention is based on the principle of according national treatment to the works originating in other Contracting States, and does not stipulate for a minimum term in respect of the protection of such works. Certain other international conventions relating to such works do stipulate for a minimum period, but that minimum has tended to be low, reflecting the lowest period adopted amongst the contracting states.[36]

6–07 **The 1988 Act as originally enacted.** The 1988 Act, as originally enacted, provided two basic periods for protection for works in which copyright subsists under the Act, reflecting the distinction, referred to above,[37] as to whether the creation of the work involved an element of industrial or technical enterprise, as

---

[29] See now Art.7(5) (Paris Act, 1971).

[30] This rule of calculation was adopted as mandatory under the Term Directive, Art.8; see para. 6–08, below.

[31] See Ch.24, below.

[32] Art.7(1) in each Act.

[33] Art.7(2) in each Act.

[34] Art.7(4) in each Act.

[35] The International Convention for the Protection of Performers, Producers of Phonograms and Broadcasting Organisations agreed at Rome, October 26, 1961; for the text see Vol.2 at F5.

[36] For example, the European Agreement on the Protection of Television Broadcasts agreed at Strasbourg, June 22, 1960, stipulated a minimum period of protection of 10 years in respect of television broadcasts: Art.2(1); for the text of the Agreement see Vol.2 at F3. This minimum was increased to 20 years by a Protocol agreed at Strasbourg on January 22, 1965; for the text, see Vol.2 at F3.i. The Convention for the Protection of Producers of Phonograms against Unauthorised Duplication of their Phonograms, agreed at Geneva October 29, 1971, stipulates for a minimum period of protection in respect of sound recordings of 20 years: Art.4; for the text see Vol.2 at F8.

[37] See para. 6–02, above; also reflecting the United Kingdom's international obligations under the different conventions discussed at paras 6–03 to 6–06, above.

distinct from individual literary, musical or artistic creativity. Thus, the 1988 Act originally provided for all[38] literary, dramatic, musical and artistic works a period of protection lasting until the end of the period of 50 years from the end of the calendar year in which the author died,[39] and for sound recordings, films, broadcasts and cable programmes a period of protection lasting until the end of the period of 50 years from the making of such work.[40] Solely in relation to typographical arrangements of published editions, the 1988 Act provided a period of 25 years from the end of the year in which the edition was first published.[41]

European harmonisation of the term of protection. Decisions of the European   **6–08** Court of Justice had highlighted the need for harmonisation in the national copyright laws of the Member States, if differences between such laws were not to continue to impede the establishment of an internal market.[42] This was particularly so as regards the differences which existed in the term of protection accorded under such laws.[43] This led to the adoption by the Council of the European Communities, on October 29, 1993, of Directive 93/98 harmonising the term of protection of copyright and certain related rights (the Term Directive).[44]

The objective of the Term Directive was to harmonise in the laws of the Member States:

(1) the period of copyright protection for authors to a period of 70 years after the death of the author;

(2) the period of related rights protection to a period of 50 years;

(3) the manner of calculation of the period of protection; and

(4) the protection afforded to the works of non-Community nationals.

The works required to be given the benefit of the extended term under (1) are those which are treated as literary or artistic works under the Berne Convention,[45] which are those works defined under the 1988 Act as literary, dramatic, musical and artistic works and films. The benefit of the extension is to be given to existing works which were protected in any Member State on January 1, 1995.[46]

The choice of a period of protection of 70 years after the author's death has been criticised as extending a term which many already considered to be too long.[47] The rationale expressed in the Duration Directive for this choice is that the minimum term of protection under Berne of life of the author and 50 years after his death was intended to provide protection for the author and the first two generations of his descendants, and that the average lifespan in the Community had grown longer to the point where this term was no longer sufficient to cover

---

[38] Following the recommendation of the 1977 Copyright Committee, Cmnd.6732, para.656, that such period should be the maximum period of protection for all such works.

[39] Subject to exceptions in the case of computer-generated works (see para. 6–47, below) and works of unknown authorship (see para. 6–46, below).

[40] This remains the position in relation to sound recordings (see para. 6–56, below) and broadcasts (see para. 6–76, below) but is no longer so in respect of films (see paras 6–67 et seq., below).

[41] This remains unchanged; see para. 6–80, below.

[42] See generally paras 25–37, et seq., below.

[43] See Case 341/87, *EMI Electrola GmbH v Patricia Im- und Export Verwaltungsgesellshaft GmbH* [1989] E.C.R. 79; [1989] 2 C.M.L.R. 413 and paras 25–38 et seq., below. And as to harmonisation generally in the European Union, see paras 25–41 et seq., below.

[44] [1993] O.J. L290/9. The text of the Directive is set out at Vol.2 at H5. See also the discussion of the Directive at para. 25–17, below.

[45] Term Directive, Art.1(1) and see Berne, Art.2, set out at paras 1–08 et seq., above.

[46] Term Directive, Arts 10(2) and 13(1); as also is the term provided for in (2).

[47] See, in particular, P. Parrinder "The Dead Hand of European Copyright" [1993] 11 E.I.P.R. 391; Mr Justice Laddie "Copyright: Over-strength, Over-regulated, Over-rated?" [1996] 5 E.I.P.R. 253.

two generations.[48] However, the reality of the matter is that the Commission, in formulating the proposal, had to take account of the fact that certain Member States had exercised their right under Berne to accord a longer period of protection.[49] Thus, the period of protection of such works after the death of the author varied from 70 years in Germany,[50] to 60 years in Spain,[51] in respect of all such works, to 70 years in France in respect of musical works, with or without words.[52] Faced with this disparity, there was little choice but to harmonise the term of protection upwards, otherwise transitional provisions which would have been required to protect vested rights would have effectively postponed, to a large extent and for far too long,[53] the progress to the smooth operation of the internal market which was the principal objective of the harmonisation.[54]

The term of related rights protection to be accorded under the Duration Directive is also to apply to works protected in any Member State on January 1, 1995.[55] Not surprisingly, given the low minimum terms required under international conventions in relation to works not falling within Berne, there was a much wider variation in the laws of the Member States in the term of protection accorded to such works. Thus, in relation to sound recordings, the period of protection varied from 20 years to 50 years,[56] calculated variously from creation (fixation) or release (publication).[57] There was an equally large disparity in the term of protection accorded to broadcasts.[58] Applying the same imperative, the Directive required harmonisation of the term upwards, to 50 years, in respect of sound recordings, broadcasts and films[59] (as distinct from the protection to be accorded to films as cinematographic or audiovisual works[60]).

For the same reason of ensuring that the harmonising effect of the Directive's provisions would not be unduly delayed, it was necessary to ensure that the extended term would apply equally throughout the Community to existing works, even if such works had fallen into the public domain in one or more Member States.[61] The Directive, therefore, expressly envisaged that its effect would, in certain cases, be to bring back into protection works which had fallen into the public domain in those Member States.[62]

---

[48] Even assuming the validity of the premise, the logic of the extension is open to challenge: see the articles by P. Parrinder and Mr Justice Laddie, cited in the previous footnote.

[49] Art.7(6) (Paris Act, 1971).

[50] A period which had been adopted in 1965.

[51] The term of protection in Spain had been reduced in November 1987 from 80 years pma (the period which had operated since 1879) to 60 years pma, but with transitional provisions continuing to protect vested rights.

[52] The Directive seeks to explain such longer terms as introduced to offset the effect of the world wars on the exploitation of authors' works (Duration Directive 93/98, recital (6)). This had certainly been given as the reason for Germany extending the term of protection from 50 years pma to 70 years pma in 1965. Other countries had introduced specific extensions for wartime works: Belgium, 10 years; Italy, 12 years (repealed by the law of February 6, 1996, implementing the Duration Directive); France, six and eight years respectively in relation to each World War and 30 years in respect of works whose author was killed in action.

[53] Term Directive, recital (9).

[54] Term Directive, recitals (2) and (11).

[55] Duration Directive, Arts 10(2) and 13(1).

[56] In 1993: 20 years (Luxembourg); 25 years (Germany); 30 years (Italy); 40 years (Spain); 50 years (Austria, Denmark, France, Greece, Ireland, the Netherlands, Portugal, United Kingdom).

[57] Fixation: Denmark, France, Greece, the Netherlands, Luxembourg, Portugal; publication: Ireland, Spain, United Kingdom. Germany applied both criteria, and Italy applied a criterion of deposit.

[58] Through 25 years (Germany, Norway, Finland, Iceland); 40 years (Spain); 50 years (Denmark, France, United Kingdom); to unlimited (Italy).

[59] Term Directive, Art.3(2), (3) and (4) respectively.

[60] Art.2(1); see further paras 6–66 and 6–67, below.

[61] Recital (25).

[62] Recital (27).

The Information Society Directive. Although not principally concerned with   **6–09**
further harmonisation of the term of copyright, this Directive[63] made a small
adjustment to the period of protection of sound recordings, in order to comply
with the 1996 WIPO Performances and Phonograms Treaty (see para.6–10,
below). This is considered in more detail later in this chapter.

Further international harmonisation of the term of protection. The harmoni-   **6–10**
sation brought about as between the laws of the Member States of the European
Union by the Term Directive in relation to the term of protection of copyright
and related rights has to some extent been mirrored by further progress at harmonisation at the international wider evel. Thus, as regards sound recordings and
broadcasts, the TRIPS agreement[64] provided for a minimum term of 50 years and
20 years for such works respectively.[65] The WIPO Performances and Phonograms Treaty[66] has completed this harmonisation by providing for a term of
protection of 50 years in respect of sound recordings.[67] As regards such works,
therefore, the position within the European Union is likely to be reflected on the
international level, as countries adopt legislation to give effect to this WIPO
Treaty.

That is not the position, however, as regards the term of protection in respect
of those authors' works which are the subject of the Berne Convention. Whilst
recent Community legislation has brought about harmonisation of the term of
protection as between the laws of the Member States of the European Union
upwards to the level of life plus 70 years, the standard period of protection for
those works outside the European Union remains the life of the author and the
period of 50 years after his death.[68] This is the standard adopted in the TRIPS
agreement[69] and subsequently in the WIPO Copyright Treaty.[70] It is unlikely at
present that the international community will progress to extending the period of
protection for works falling within Berne to life plus 70 years.

That there would be this disparity between the term of protection accorded
such works within the European Union and outside was recognised by the Duration Directive, which is deliberately framed to require Member States to accord
the extended term of protection only to works of Community origin.[71] In the case
of such works not of Community origin, Member States are required to apply
comparison of terms, rather than national treatment.[72] This requirement is subject
to any international obligation the Member States may otherwise have to accord
a longer period of protection to such works.[73]

---

[63] Directive 2001/29 of the European Parliament and of the Council on the harmonisation of certain
aspects of copyright and related rights in the information society (May 22, 2001). See Vol.2 at
H11.
[64] The Agreement on Trade-related Aspects of Intellectual Property Rights concluded at Geneva on
December 15, 1993: Art.9.
[65] Arts 14(2), (3) and (5).
[66] Concluded at the WIPO Diplomatic Conference in Geneva, December 20, 1996.
[67] Art.17(2).
[68] See para. 6–05, above. The United States is a notable exception, where, following the increase in
the term applied by Member States in Europe and the application of "comparison of terms" (see
further in the text and para. 6–17, below), the standard term was also increased to life and 70
years pma.
[69] The Agreement on Trade-related Aspects of Intellectual Property Rights concluded at Geneva on
December 15, 1993: Art.9.
[70] Concluded at the WIPO Diplomatic Conference in Geneva, December 20, 1996: Art.1(4). An
earlier suggestion that the term should be similarly increased under the Berne Convention was
not carried through; see paras 25–62, below.
[71] Term Directive, recital (22) and Art.7.
[72] Term Directive, Art.7(1); see further paras 6–16 to 6–18, below.
[73] Term Directive, Art.7(2) and (3).

3. THE PRESENT POSITION UNDER THE 1988 ACT AS AMENDED

6–11   **Implementation of the Duration Term Directive in the United Kingdom.** Member States were given until July 1, 1995 to introduce the provisions necessary to implement the Term Directive.[74] The United Kingdom did so by the Duration of Copyright and Rights in Performances Regulations 1995 (the Duration Regulations),[75] with effect from January 1, 1996.[76] The 1988 Act did not require amendment to provide for a term of 50 years for related rights, or as to the manner of calculation of the period of protection, as its original provisions were already in accordance with the requirements of the Directive in these respects.[77] Some amendment was required to deal with the protection afforded to the works of non-Community nationals,[78] and extensive amendment and new provisions were required to deal with the extension of the period of protection to 70 years and its application to existing works.[79] Before dealing with the present position in the United Kingdom with respect to the different descriptions of works protected by copyright under the 1988 Act as so amended, some comments of general applicability to all such works, except typographical arrangements, are necessary in order to understand the full implications of the amended provisions, particularly for works made before January 1, 1996.

6–12   **The transitional provisions of the Duration Regulations.** In addition to the amendments required to sections 12 to 15 of the 1988 Act in order to give effect to the Term Directive in respect of works coming into existence after January 1, 1996, transitional provisions were also required, to ensure, in accordance with the policy mentioned above which lies behind the Directive,[80] that the benefit of the extended term is applied in the United Kingdom to any work of EEA origin protected under the law of any one EEA state on July 1, 1995. The Duration Regulations achieve this by providing that the 1988 Act as amended[81] is to apply not only to works coming into existence after commencement[82] but also to three categories of existing works. An existing work, for the purposes of the Regulations, is one made before January 1, 1996,[83] irrespective of when, before that date, it was made. The three categories of existing works to which the new provisions are to be applied are:

---

[74] Art.13(1).

[75] SI 1995/3297. The relevant sections of the 1988 Act, both before amendment and as amended, are set out at Vol.2 at A1. The text of those provisions of the Regulations not incorporated into the Act is set out at Vol.2 at A3.ii. For the discussion in Parliament of the Regulations, see *Hansard*, H.C. Vol.268, cols 1254–1272, December 18, 1995.

[76] The United Kingdom was therefore late in implementing the Directive, in theory exposing the United Kingdom to an action by private parties for damages: see, as to the effect of Directives, Cases C-6 and C-9/90, *Frankovich v Italy* and *Boniface v Italy* [1991] E.C.R. 5357. The delay was explained by the Government as due to the complexity of the drafting and consultative exercise which was required: *Hansard*, H.C. Vol.268, col. 1254, December 18, 1995. Implementation throughout the Union has been piecemeal (see the table of implementation at para. 25–90, below), with other countries being late (out of the 15 countries, only Belgium, Denmark, Germany and Ireland implemented the Directive before July 1, 1995).

[77] That is in respect of the matters set out in (2) and (3) in paras 6–08, above; see paras 6–04 and 6–07, above.

[78] See paras 6–15 to 6–18, below.

[79] See, as to literary, dramatic, musical and artistic works, paras 6–51 and *et seq.*, below, as to sound recordings, para. 6–55 *et seq.*, below and as to films paras 6–66 *et seq.*, below. The particular problems as to ownership of the extended (and revived) term of copyright created by the Regulations and the protection of acquired rights are dealt with at paras 5–133 *et seq.*, above.

[80] See paras 6–09 to 6–08, above.

[81] The provisions of the Act as so amended are referred to as "the new provisions": reg.12(2).

[82] reg.16(a); the Regulations came into force on January 1, 1996: reg.1(2).

[83] reg.14(1)(a). The term "existing work" is therefore used to describe both works existing before January 1, 1996 and also works existing before August 1, 1989 (see CDPA 1988, Sch.1, para.1(3)), depending on the context. In this part of the work, it is used with the former meaning.

(i) existing works first qualifying for protection after January 1, 1996;[84]

(ii) existing works in which copyright subsisted immediately before that date;[85] and

(iii) existing works in which copyright expired before December 31, 1995 but which were protected on July 1, 1995 in another EEA state.[86]

Existing works first brought into protection by the Regulations. Given the   **6–13**
extent of copyright protection accorded by the 1988 Act (and its predecessors) prior to January 1, 1966, there is no obvious example which can be given of an existing work which had not enjoyed copyright protection at any time before that date, but which is brought within protection by the new provisions. No doubt this class of existing work was included out of caution, and emphasises the objective that, whatever the position which governed before January 1, 1996, the new provisions are to govern the position thereafter.

Existing copyright works. Existing copyright works are defined as those exist-   **6–14**
ing works in which copyright subsisted immediately before January 1, 1996.[87] In the case of the principal category of authors' works, previously benefiting from a term of 50 years pma, this would include all the works of authors who died on or after January 1, 1945. The application of the new provisions to this class of existing works is, however, subject to the important qualification that if copyright would have subsisted in the work under the provisions of the 1988 Act before amendment for a longer period, then that is the period which continues to apply to the work.[88] Whilst this qualification will not apply to the majority of existing copyright works, it has particular application to existing copyright works which had not, prior to January 1, 1996, been published or otherwise commercially exploited, and were enjoying a period of protection under the 1988 Act, as unamended, which was not limited in time.[89] This qualification nevertheless has the unfortunate consequence, already described, that it is in all cases necessary to consider the position of an existing copyright work under the two distinct regimes, before the current period of its term of protection can be determined with certainty.[90]

The further period of protection which, subject to this qualification, will apply to existing works (20 years in the case of existing literary, dramatic, musical and artistic works and a potentially longer period in the case of films) is referred to in the Regulations as "extended copyright",[91] and is subject to special rules as to its ownership[92] and savings in respect of existing licences, agreements, etc.[93]

**Existing works in the public domain in the United Kingdom but protected in   6–15
another EEA state on July 1, 1995.** Before the amendment of the 1988 Act by the Duration Regulations, the determination of the term of protection of a work in the United Kingdom was entirely a matter of applying the relevant rules of the law of the United Kingdom, and this was so whether the country of origin of that

---

[84] reg.16(b); see para. 6–13, below.
[85] reg.16(c); see para. 6–14, below.
[86] reg.16(d); see paras 6–15 *et seq.*, below.
[87] reg.14(1)(b). Time is a continuum, and this therefore includes works in which copyright would otherwise have expired at midnight on December 31, 1995; see *Hansard*, H.C. Vol.268, col.1265, December 18, 1995.
[88] reg.16(c) and reg.15(1).
[89] See further, paras 6–51 to 6–54, below.
[90] See the beginning of the Chapter: para. 6–01, above.
[91] reg.17.
[92] regs 18 and 20; discussed at para. 5–133, above.
[93] reg.21; discussed at para. 5–138, above.

work was the United Kingdom or a foreign country. This was because the United Kingdom had not, as a general rule, exercised the right under Berne to apply comparison of terms to the works of other Berne Convention countries, but simply applied, through the inclusion of such countries in the relevant Order in Council under section 159, national treatment to such works.

Under the 1988 Act as amended, and in relation to works made before January 1, 1996, it is now necessary to consider the position as to the term under the regime applicable in the United Kingdom, and then, if that leads to the conclusion that copyright in the United Kingdom had expired before December 31, 1995 (that is had expired on December 31, 1994 or before), it remains necessary to consider the position of that work under the laws of the other EEA states.[94] If the work continues to benefit from copyright protection in any one of those countries, then it must be given a revived term of protection in the United Kingdom, so that copyright expires in that work throughout the whole of the EEA at the same time.

As indicated above, a degree of harmonisation as to the manner of calculation of the term in respect of authors' works had been achieved amongst Berne Convention countries.[95] For those EEA states that had, like the United Kingdom, adopted that method of calculation,[96] the reference to copyright subsisting in another EEA state on July 1, 1995 effectively refers to works which remained in protection on January 1, 1995.

Since, however, as indicated above,[97] a number of EEA states have accorded a term of protection for certain categories of authors' works of 70 years pma, the effect of this provision was to bring back into copyright in the United Kingdom a large number of such works of authors who died on or after January 1, 1925 and before January 1, 1945. The period of copyright which such works enjoy is that part of the period of 20 years which remains, depending on how recently before January 1, 1945 the author died. The further period of protection which applies to such works is referred to in the Regulations as "revived copyright".[98]

In the case of an author who died on January 1, 1925, and benefited from a period of protection for his works of 70 years pma in Germany, for example, that work would have fallen into the public domain in the United Kingdom as from January 1, 1976. Such a work should, under the Term Directive,[99] have enjoyed a revived period of copyright in the United Kingdom until December 31, 1995. However, because of the late implementation of the Directive in the United Kingdom, the effect of the provisions is effectively to deny such work any period of revived copyright.[1] So far as the United Kingdom is concerned, therefore, the shortest period of revived copyright will have been from January 1, 1996 to December 31, 1996, applicable in the case of an author who died on or after January 1, 1926 and before January 1, 1927, and whose work benefited from a period of 70 years pma in, for example, Germany. At the other end of the scale is the case of the author who died on or after January 1, 1944 and before January 1,

---

[94] An EEA state is a state which is a contracting party to the Agreement on the European Economic Area signed at Oporto on May 2, 1992, as adjusted by the Protocol signed at Brussels on March 17, 1993: CDPA 1988, s.172A..

[95] See para. 6–04, above.

[96] A few had not, calculating the term from the date of death or other event, for example Belgium (and also Iceland and Liechtenstein).

[97] See paras 6–08, above. Austria, also, amongst EEA states, had applied a period of 70 years pma since 1936.

[98] reg.17.

[99] Arts 10(2) and 13(1).

[1] reg.16(d) applies to such a work, but such revived copyright is effectively nullified by reg.23(1), which provides that nothing done before January 1, 1996 shall infringe revived copyright in a work.

1945 and whose work benefited from a period of protection of 70 years pma in Germany. In his case, the work will benefit from revived copyright under reg.16(d) for a period of 19 years lasting from January 1, 1996 until December 31, 2014.

Revived copyright is subject to special rules as to its ownership,[2] savings in respect of moral rights,[3] and for acts done when the work was in the public domain,[4] and is subject to a form of statutory licence.[5]

The *Phil Collins* Case. The discussion above of Regulation 16(d) has concentrated on the application of the new provisions in the United Kingdom to a work which was still in copyright in another EEA state in 1995, but which had fallen into the public domain in the United Kingdom before that date. The examples given to demonstrate the application of this provision were of works which benefited from the longer period of protection granted in another EEA state, for example Germany, which that state granted under its own laws. Unlike the United Kingdom, such countries have traditionally applied comparison of terms to the works of other nationals or of which the country of origin was another Berne Convention country, as they were entitled to do. Thus, whilst the work of a German author who died in 1944 was entitled to a term of copyright in Germany expiring on December 31, 2014, a comparable work of an English author was entitled, under the comparison of terms approach, to a term of protection in Germany expiring on December 31, 1974.

6–16

However, for an EEA state to apply comparison of terms to such effect is a breach of its obligations under European law, in that it amounts to discrimination on the basis of nationality. The Court of Justice, in its decision in the joined cases of *Phil Collins v Imtrat HandelsGmbH* and *Verwaltung-gesellschaft mbH v EMI Electrola GmbH*[6] held that such discrimination was not permissible as being contrary to what is now Art. 6 of the Treaty.[7] It is, therefore, not only the works of the nationals of such countries, or even the works of which such a country is the country of origin, which benefit from the revival in the United Kingdom of copyright, pursuant to Art.10(2) of the Term Directive, but all works of which the authors are nationals of an EEA state or of which such a state is the country of origin.[8]

Country of origin: authors' works. The concept of the country of origin of a work has existed under Berne as a means of determining which foreign works a Convention country is obliged to treat under its own laws as enjoying protection.[9] However, this concept has not previously required definition in United Kingdom Copyright Acts, as the policy of the 1988 Act and its predecessors has been to apply the same term of protection to a work which qualifies by reason of its being first published in, or its author being domiciled or resident in, a country to which the relevant provisions of the 1988 Act have been applied,[10] as to a work of that type which qualifies by reason of its being first published in, or its author being a

6–17

---

[2] regs 19 and 20; discussed at para. 11–81, below.

[3] reg.22; discussed at para. 5–139, above.

[4] reg.23; discussed at para. 5–141, above.

[5] regs 24 and 25; discussed at para.5–144, above.

[6] Cases 92 & 326/92, [1993] 3 C.M.L.R. 773.

[7] For the text of Art.6, see Vol.2 at G, below. The prohibition against discrimination by a Member State applies equally in cases where the author has died before the EEC Treaty comes into force in the Member State concerned: *Land Hessen v G Ricordi & Co Bühnen- und Musikverlag GmbH* (C360/00) [2003] E.C.D.R. 1.

[8] For a discussion of the effect of this decision in the context of the Term Directive, see the article by Dworkin and Sterling in [1994] E.I.P.R. 187.

[9] See Brussels Act, Art.4(3), and now Paris Act (1971), Art.5(4).

[10] *i.e.* by an Order in Council under CDPA 1988, s.159. A definition of country of origin was contained in the Copyright (International Conventions) Order 1957 (SI 1957/1523), para.4(2). See *Copinger* (12th ed.), para.1392.

British subject or being domiciled or resident in the United Kingdom.[11] This is no longer the position, and the 1988 Act has now introduced comparison of terms, in that in respect of works of non-EEA origin, the normal rule of life plus 70 years is not to apply unless that is the term which applies in the country of origin. The term of protection for such a work in the United Kingdom is limited to the term which that work enjoys in the country of origin. This change has been required in order to implement the Term Directive.[12]

The country of origin of a work for the purposes of the application of the provisions relating to duration of copyright[13] is determined by new provisions, contained in section 15A of the 1988 Act,[14] which follow closely the provisions in Berne. Thus, the country of origin of a work first published in a Berne Convention country[15] is that country;[16] if the work is first published simultaneously[17] in two or more countries only one of which is a Berne Convention country, then that country is the country of origin of the work.[18]

6–18   **Country of origin: EEA states.** Since the only purpose in introducing the concept of the country of origin into the 1988 Act is to be able to distinguish between works whose country of origin is an EEA state[19] and those whose country of origin is not, further rules are contained in section 15A defining the country of origin in the case of EEA states. If the work is published simultaneously in two or more countries, of which two or more are Berne Convention countries, then if any one of those countries is an EEA state, that country is the country of origin,[20] but if not, then that Berne Convention country which grants the shorter or shortest period of copyright protection is the country of origin.[21] Where the work is unpublished, or is first published in a country which is not a Berne Convention country, then the general rule is that the country of origin of the work is that country of which the author is a national.[22] The general rule is subject to exceptions in the case of films, where the country of origin is that country in which the maker of the film has his headquarters, is domiciled or resident,[23] and works of architecture or artistic works incorporated into a work of architecture, where the country of origin is that country in which the work of architecture is situated.[24] In both cases the exception applies only if that country is a Berne Convention country.

6–19   **Country of origin: other works.** The 1988 Act does not refer to the country of origin other than in respect of works defined in the Berne Convention (which

---

[11] Whilst the United Kingdom could consistent with its international obligations have applied comparison of terms to such works, it has traditionally favoured applying national treatment. As to application of the provisions of the 1988 Act to foreign works generally, see paras 3–190 *et seq.*, above.

[12] See para. 6–08, above.

[13] Stated to be generally for the purposes of Pt I of the CDPA 1988, but the concept has no relevance other than in relation to term.

[14] Introduced by the Duration Regulations.

[15] That is a country which is a party to any Act of the International Convention for the Protection of Literary and Artistic Works signed at Berne on September 9, 1886: CDPA 1988, s.15A(6)(a).

[16] CDPA 1988, s.15(2); Berne, Art.5(4)(a).

[17] That is, published within 30 days of first publication: CDPA 1988, s.15A(6)(b).

[18] CDPA 1988, s.15A(3); Berne (Paris Act, 1971), Art.5(4)(b).

[19] An EEA state is a state which is a contracting party to the Agreement on the European Economic Area signed at Oporto on May 2, 1992, as adjusted by the Protocol signed at Brussels on March 17, 1993: CDPA 1988, s.172A.

[20] CDPA 1988, s.15A(4)(a). Presumably, in the case where two or more are EEA states, then "those countries" are the "country of origin".

[21] CDPA 1988, s.15A(4)(b), following, by analogy, Berne Convention, Art.5(4)(a).

[22] CDPA 1988, s.15A(5)(c).

[23] CDPA 1988, s.15A(5)(a).

[24] CDPA 1988, s.15A(5)(b).

include films).[25] In respect of sound recordings and broadcasts, the Act refers to the author of such works being a national of an EEA state.[26] The construction of references in the 1988 Act to an EEA state is subject to special transitional provisions, which are designed to ensure that the benefit of the new provisions is applied to works whenever any EEA state regards that work as published in an EEA state,[27] or as originating in an EEA state,[28] or regards its author as a national of an EEA state.[29]

4. THE EFFECT OF TRANSITIONAL PROVISIONS ON THE TERM OF EXISTING WORKS

Introduction. Before dealing with the current rules as to the duration of copyright in the different descriptions of work in which copyright subsists under the 1988 Act, it is necessary, for the reasons described above,[30] to provide an outline of the development of the term of protection in the United Kingdom through the various Acts leading up to the 1988 Act, and to describe how each Act has dealt, through transitional provisions, with works existing at the date of its commencement. Since, in the case of works made under earlier regimes, it is necessary to consider each successive regime, it is convenient to start with the position before 1912 and end with the position under the transitional provisions of the 1988 Act.

6–20

A. THE LAW BEFORE THE 1911 ACT

Unpublished works. The 1911 Act abolished common law copyright[31] with effect from July 1, 1912. Unpublished works were previously protected at common law, and, therefore, any work[32] unpublished on July 1, 1912 was protected under the 1911 Act.

6–21

Literary copyright. The governing statute was the Literary Copyright Act 1842,[33] which provided in relation to "books" (that is every volume, part, or division of a volume, pamphlet, letterpress sheet, music sheet, map, chart and plan[34]) a period of protection of the longer of seven years after the death of the author or 42 years from publication.[35] The protection accorded to such works included the literary rights in musical and dramatic works. Any such work published on or after July 1, 1870, or any work the author of which died on or after July 1, 1905, was, therefore protected under the 1911 Act,[36] notwithstanding that there had been no registration of the copyright.[37]

6–22

---

[25] See CDPA 1988, s.12(6) and 13B(7).
[26] See CDPA 1988, s.13(4) and 14(3).
[27] In the case of a work first published before July 1, 1995: reg.36(1)(a).
[28] In the case of a film made before July 1, 1995 and whose maker was regarded by such state as domiciled or resident in that state: reg.36(1)(b).
[29] In the case of the author of a work made before July 1, 1995: reg.36(1)(c).
[30] See paras 6–01, above.
[31] Copyright Act 1911, s.31.
[32] But see para. 6–27, below as to paintings, drawings and photographs.
[33] 5 & 6 Vict. c.45.
[34] Literary Copyright Act 1842, s.2.
[35] Literary Copyright Act 1842, s.3; as to the terms and conditions applying to such copyright, see *Copinger* (12th ed.) paras 1107 and 1108.
[36] See para. 6–29, below.
[37] *Savory (E.W.) Ltd v The World of Golf Ltd* [1914] 2 Ch.566.

6–23   Lectures. Limited protection was granted to published lectures under the Lecturers Copyright Act 1835.[38] The period of protection was 28 years from publication.[39] Speeches and lectures delivered in public and without restrictions lost all right to protection, unless certain onerous formalities were complied with.[40] But a report of a speech might be entitled to copyright.[41]

6–24   Musical and dramatic works. Musical scores and books of words were protected as literary works under the Literary Copyright Act 1842.[42] The statutes relating to the performing rights were the Dramatic Copyright Act 1833,[43] which originally only applied to dramatic works, and sections 20 and 21 of the Literary Copyright Act 1842, which applied to both musical and dramatic compositions.The effect of these provisions was to protect the performing rights in a musical or dramatic work which had been published as a book for the longer of seven years after the death of the author or 42 years from the date of the first public representation or performance of the work. If the work had not been published as a book, but was in manuscript form only, the term of the performing rights was doubtful.[44] In the case of musical, but not dramatic works, it was essential to the preservation of performing rights that a notice of reservation of those rights should be printed on the title page of every publication of work published after 1882.[45] No musical work, therefore, published after 1882, but before July 1, 1912, which omitted to print such notice of reservation obtained any performing rights under the 1911 Act.

6–25   Engravings, prints and lithographs. As regards engravings and prints, the main statutes in force before the 1911 Act were the Engraving Copyright Acts of 1734 and 1766[46] and the Prints Copyright Act 1777.[47] Prints taken by lithograph, or any other mechanical process for multiplying prints, were brought under the earlier Acts relating to engravings by the International Copyright Act 1852.[48] The term of protection was 28 years from the date of publication, provided the name of the author and the date of first publication was engraved on the plate and printed on each copy.[49] In order, therefore, to be entitled to protection under the 1911 Act, engravings must have been published since June 30, 1884, and have had the name of the author and date of first publication printed on every copy.

6–26   Sculptures. Works of sculpture were protected under the Sculpture Copyright Act 1814.[50] The term of protection was 14 years from first publication, and a further 14 years if the first proprietor was then living and had not divested himself of the copyright. The name of the sculptor and date of first publication had to be put on the work.[51] The following works of sculpture made before July 1, 1912, therefore, received no protection under the 1911 Act: (a) all works published before July 1, 1884; (b) all works published between June 30, 1884 and July 1

[38] 5 & 6 Will. 4, c.65.
[39] Lecturers Copyright Act 1835, s.4.
[40] See *Copinger* (12th ed.) para.1112.
[41] *Walter v Lane* [1900] A.C. 539; and see para. 3–135, above.
[42] See para. 6–22, above.
[43] 3 & 4 Will. 4, c.15.
[44] The Dramatic Copyright Act 1833 did not prescribe any term in such a case, and it is not clear that this was altered by the Literary Copyright Act 1842.
[45] For the terms and conditions applying to such copyright, see *Copinger* (12th ed.), paras 1114 and 1115.
[46] 8 Geo. 2, c.13; 7 Geo. 3, c.38.
[47] 17 Geo. 3, c.57.
[48] 15 & 16 Vict. c.12; s.14.
[49] As to terms and conditions applying to such copyright, see *Copinger* (12th ed.), para.1120.
[50] 54 Geo. 3, c.56.
[51] As to terms and conditions applying to such copyright, see *Copinger* (12th ed.), para.1121.

1898, unless the author was then living; and (c) all works published before July 1, 1912, which did not bear the name of the sculptor and the date of first publication.

Paintings, drawings and photographs. By the Fine Arts Copyright Act 1862,[52] a painting, drawing or photograph made in the British Dominions or elsewhere was entitled to a term of protection (if its author was a British subject or resident in the British Dominions) for the period of the life of the author and seven years after his death. The statutory term of protection commenced from the date of the making of the work, whether the same was published or not; although, if the work was unpublished, a common law copyright existed in parallel to the statutory copyright, which probably expired at the same time as the statutory protection. Further, except in the case of works executed on commission, copyright was liable to be destroyed if the author did not, upon the first sale of his work, reserve the copyright to himself in writing.[53] It consequently follows that no painting, drawing or photograph made before July 1, 1912 was entitled to protection under the 1911 Act if the author had died before July 1, 1905, or if he had failed to reserve the copyright in the work on its first sale (in the case of a work not executed on commission). Non-registration under the 1862 Act did not disentitle the work to copyright (although it prevented an infringement action being brought in respect of the period prior to registration).[54]

6–27

Non-protected works. Works of architecture (except architects' plans, which were protected as artistic works), choreographic works, pantomimes and musical and other records were not entitled to any copyright under the law before July 1, 1912, and with the exception of mechanical contrivances for reproducing sounds,[55] none of these works, if made or published before July 1, 1912, was entitled to protection under the 1911 Act.

6–28

B. THE 1911 ACT

General position under the 1911 Act: existing works. The approach of the 1911 Act to works in existence at its commencement[56] was to provide that any person entitled to copyright under the previous law at that date thereupon obtained copyright, as defined by the Act of 1911, subject to certain modifications in respect of rights forming part of the copyright under the 1911 Act which had not previously existed. In relation to works in existence before July 1, 1912, it therefore remains necessary to consider the law as it stood before that date in order to determine whether there was a subsisting copyright at that date. This differs from the approach in both the 1956 and 1988 Acts, under which all questions of subsistence and term in relation to existing works depend upon the provisions, respectively, of those Acts.

6–29

General rule as to term. The term adopted under the 1911 Act for all literary, musical, dramatic and artistic works, with certain exceptions, was the period of the life of the author and 50 years after his death.[57] The period was calculated from the date of death. The exceptions were photographs and certain works first published posthumously, and contrivances for the reproduction of sounds.

6–30

Photographs. Photographs, which included films (which were treated as a series

6–31

---

[52] 25 & 26 Vict. c.68.
[53] As to the terms and conditions applying to such copyright, see *Copinger* (12th ed.), para.1123.
[54] See *Copinger* (12th ed.), para.1122.
[55] Such works were protected under the 1911 Act by virtue of s.19(8).
[56] July 1, 1912.
[57] Copyright Act 1911, s.3.

of photographs), were granted a fixed period of protection of 50 years from the date of the making of the original negative.[58]

6–32   Posthumous works. Literary, dramatic and musical works and engravings, in which copyright subsisted at the date of the death of the author, and which remained unpublished at that date, were entitled under the 1911 Act to an unlimited period of copyright until first publication of the work, when they became entitled to a further period of 50 years from that date. Publication, in this context, included, in the case of a dramatic or musical work, being performed in public, and, in the case of a lecture, being delivered in public.[59]

6–33   Mechanical instruments. Records, perforated rolls and other contrivances by means of which sounds might be mechanically reproduced, were protected in the same manner as if they were musical works, but were granted a period of protection of 50 years from the making of the original plate from which the contrivance was derived.[60]

6–34   Films. As stated above, films were protected under the 1911 Act as a series of photographs.[61] Films were also capable of protection as dramatic works,[62] and a film in which copyright subsisted as a dramatic work was entitled to the standard period of protection for such works, namely the life of its author and the period of 50 years after his death.

C. THE 1956 ACT

6–35   General position under the 1956 Act: existing works. The approach adopted by the 1956 Act to works in existence at its commencement[63] was to treat its provisions as having always applied to such works, subject to any modifications contained in Schedule 7 to the Act.[64]

6–36   General rule as to term. The 1956 Act made no change in the standard period of protection for literary, musical, dramatic and artistic works, which remained the period of the life of the author and 50 years after his death. However, under the 1956 Act, this period was calculated from the end of the year in which the death or other relevant event occurred.[65] The general rule was subject to exceptions in the case of certain works first published posthumously, and photographs.

Literary, dramatic and musical works,[66] and engravings[67] which remained unpublished at the author's death were entitled to protection for an unlimited period until first published, when they became entitled to a further fixed period of 50 years from the end of the year in which publication took place.

Photographs were entitled to protection for a fixed period of 50 years from the end of the year in which they were first published.[68]

Sound recordings were granted protection of unlimited duration while they

---

[58] Copyright Act 1911, s.21.
[59] Copyright Act 1911, s.17(1).
[60] Copyright Act 1911, s.19(1).
[61] See para. 6–31, above.
[62] The definition of dramatic work under the 1911 Act included any cinematograph production where the arrangement or acting form or the combination of incidents represented gave the work an original character: s.35(1). See para. 3–32, above.
[63] June 1, 1957.
[64] Copyright Act 1956, Sch.7, para.45(1).
[65] Copyright Act 1956, ss.2(3) and 3(4).
[66] Copyright Act 1956 proviso to s.2(3).
[67] Copyright Act 1956 proviso (a) to s.3(4).
[68] Copyright Act 1956, s.3(4), proviso (b).

remained unpublished, and on publication became entitled to protection for a further period of 50 years from the end of the year in which publication occurred.

Films became subject to their own regime, and, in general,[69] were granted protection of unlimited duration while they remained unpublished, and on publication became entitled to protection for a further period of 50 years calculated from the end of the year in which publication occurred.

Broadcasts, which were first given protection under the 1956 Act, were granted a fixed period of 50 years after the end of the year in which they were first broadcast.

Transitional provisions. In the case of works existing at June 1, 1957 the general rules as to term therefore applied to such works, with modification in the case of existing photographs and in the case of joint works. Exceptions were also made in the case of existing sound recordings and films.   **6–37**

Existing photographs. The term of copyright in a photograph taken before June 1, 1957 was the period of 50 years from the end of the year in which it was taken, and not from the end of the year in which the photograph was published.[70]   **6–38**

Existing works of joint authorship. There was no copyright under the 1956 Act[71] in a work of joint authorship in which the copyright expired before June 1, 1957 under the provisions of the 1911 Act as to joint works,[72] which provided for such works a term which was the longer of (a) the period of 50 years from the death of the author who died first or (b) the life of the author who died last.   **6–39**

Existing sound recordings. In respect of sound recordings existing before June 1, 1957, the term of protection was fixed at 50 years from the end of the year in which they were made.[73]   **6–40**

Existing films. Films made before June 1, 1957 were excluded from copyright as films, but retained their protection as a series of photographs and as dramatic works, as under the 1911 Act.[74]   **6–41**

D. THE 1988 ACT

General position under the 1988 Act: existing works. The general approach of the 1988 Act to works existing at August 1, 1989[75] was to apply its provisions to such works as they apply in relation to works coming into existence after that date, subject to any express provision to the contrary contained in the transitional provisions of Schedule 1 to the Act.[76] The general principles underlying the schedule were stated to be that existing copyright should not be lost; that existing works not in copyright should not suddenly acquire it; that existing copyright owners should not suddenly find themselves with a right substantially less valuable than already enjoyed; and that others exploiting or dealing with existing works should not find themselves unable to continue.[77] Although this statement of principles would not have prevented the extension of the rights of owners of copyright in existing works in which copyright subsisted immediately before   **6–42**

---

[69] Depending on whether they were registrable or not.
[70] Copyright Act 1956, Sch.7, para.2.
[71] Copyright Act 1956, Sch.7, para.10.
[72] Copyright Act 1911, s.16(1).
[73] Copyright Act 1965, Sch.7, para.11.
[74] Copyright Act 1965, Sch.7, paras 15 and 16.
[75] The date of commencement of the 1988 Act.
[76] CDPA 1988, Sch.1, para.3.
[77] *Hansard*, H.L. Vol.492, col. 582.

August 1, 1989, the approach taken in the 1988 Act as regards duration is to preserve the position which existed under the previous applicable legislation by specific provisions contained in paragraph 12 of Schedule 1 to the Act.

6–43   **General rule as to term.** The 1988 Act retained as the standard period of protection for Berne works, other than films, the period of the life of the author and a further period of 50 years after the end of the year of his death.[78] This term of protection was for the first time applied to photographs, which had hitherto enjoyed a fixed period of protection, not dependent on the life of their author.

The period of protection accorded to sound recordings, films, broadcasts and cable programmes[79] remained the same as it had been under the 1956 Act,[80] save that the possibility for sound recordings and films to enjoy protection for an unlimited time while they remained unpublished, was removed.

6–44   **Transitional provisions.** The application of the general rules as to duration contained in sections 12 to 15 of the Act is therefore modified in relation to existing works by the specific provisions contained in paragraph 12 of Schedule 1 to the Act, affecting posthumous works, photographs, works of unknown authorship, sound recordings and films. These exceptions are dealt with more fully in the following sections of this chapter, in respect of each of the works concerned.

5. LITERARY, DRAMATIC, MUSICAL AND ARTISTIC WORKS

A. WORKS MADE ON OR AFTER JANUARY 1, 1996

6–45   **General position.** By section 12(2) of the 1988 Act,[81] the normal period of protection for literary, dramatic, musical and artistic works coming into existence after commencement of the Duration Regulations[82] lasts until the end of the period of 70 years from the end of the calendar year in which the author died. In the case of a work of joint authorship, this means the death of the last of the authors to die.[83] This remains the period whether or not at the author's death such works have been published or otherwise publicly exploited.[84] This general rule is subject to special provisions applying to works of unknown authorship;[85] computer-generated works;[86] and works the copyright in which belongs to the Crown,[87] to the Houses of Parliament,[88] or to certain international organisations.[89] The new

---

[78] CDPA 1988, s.12.

[79] CDPA 1988, ss.13 and 14. As to cable programmes, see below.

[80] As amended, in the case of cable programmes, which became protected by the amendments introduced by the Cable and Broadcasting Act 1984.

[81] As amended by the Duration Regulations (SI 1995/3297) which came into force January 1, 1996: reg.1(2).

[82] For the purposes of the Regulations, "commencement" means January 1, 1996: reg.12(1). The new provisions as to term apply to such works by virtue of reg.16(a).

[83] CDPA 1988, s.12(8), and see generally paras 4–37 *et seq.*, above.

[84] This was the position under the CDPA 1988 before amendment. Under the 1956 Act, the period was different depending on whether on not publication or other public exploitation had taken place before the author's death; see paras 6–36, above, and para. 6–51, below.

[85] CDPA 1988, s.12(3); and see para. 6–46, below.

[86] CDPA 1988, s.12(7) and see para. 6–47, below.

[87] CDPA 1988, s.12(9) and see para. 10–01, below.

[88] CDPA 1988, s.12(9) and see para. 10–36, below.

[89] CDPA 1988, s.12(9) and see para. 3–231, above.

provisions apply to all photographs, irrespective of whether they involve the author's own intellectual creation.[90]

Works of unknown authorship. The right of an author to preserve his anonymity in relation to his work, without thereby forfeiting copyright protection for the work, is recognised under the Berne Convention.[91] This creates a practical difficulty in applying the normal rule as to term, being fixed as it is by reference to the date of death of the author. The 1988 Act provides a distinct regime for determining the term of protection of anonymous and pseudonymous works, at the same time providing that acts which would otherwise infringe the copyright in such works are in certain circumstances permitted.[92] Such works coming into existence after commencement of the Duration Regulations[93] enjoy a period of copyright protection lasting for 70 years from the end of the year in which the work was made,[94] unless within that period the work has been made available to the public, in which case the period lasts for 70 years from the end of the year in which it was first made available to the public.[95]

6–46

A work is of unknown authorship if it is not possible for a person to ascertain the identity of the author by reasonable inquiry.[96] Once the identity of an author is known, it shall not subsequently be treated as unknown.[97] If the identity of the author becomes known before the end of the 70-year period from the end of the year in which the work was made, or in which it was first made available to the public, as the case may be, then the term of protection for such work becomes subject to the normal rule, that is 70 years from the end of the year in which the author died.[98] In the case of a work of joint authorship, it is only to be treated as a work of unknown authorship if all the authors are unknown; if the identity of any one or more authors is known, then the term is determined by applying the normal rule under section 12(2) of the 1988 Act to that author or authors.[99]

The phrase "first made available to the public" clearly covers publication, that is the issue of copies to the public,[1] but is wider in that it also includes public performance of a literary, dramatic or musical work, public exhibition of an artistic

---

[90] As was the case under the 1988 Act before amendment. The United Kingdom has never made a distinction as regards the term of protection between photographs involving the author's intellectual creation and others, such as news photographs. Such a distinction was permissible under the Berne Convention (Paris Act, 1971, Art.7(4)) and remained permissible under the Term Directive, Art.6. See, for a discussion of the history of protection of photographs under the Berne Convention, S. Ricketson, *The Berne Convention for the Protection of Literary and Artistic Works: 1886–1986* (Kluwer, 1987) paras 6.33–6.43.

[91] See now Art.7(3) and also Art.15 (Paris Act, 1971).

[92] See CDPA 1988, s.57, and para. 9–152, below.

[93] January 1, 1996; see regs 12(1), 1(2)..

[94] CDPA 1988, s.12(3)(a); prior to the amendment of s.12, the equivalent provision in s.12(2) referred not to the making of the work, but to when it was first made available to the public, thus effectively giving such a work which was never made available to the public a perpetual copyright. This provision, together with s.57(1), before it was amended by the Duration Regulations (which permitted acts in respect of anonymous and pseudonymous works on the assumption as to the expiry of copyright), was in accordance with Art.7(4) of Berne (Paris Act, 1971). The change was required in order to bring the position into line with Art.1(4) of the Term Directive. See further as to existing anonymous and pseudonymous works, para. 6–51, below.

[95] CDPA 1988, s.12(3)(b).

[96] , CDPA 1988, s.9(5).

[97] CDPA 1988, s.9(5)

[98] CDPA 1988, s.12(4). This provision does not repeat the express provision in s.12(2) as originally enacted that this shall not apply if the identity of the author becomes known after the end of that period, but this is clearly implicit from the wording of s.12(2); it was not expressed in the equivalent provision in the 1956 Act (see Copyright Act 1956, Sch.2, para.2) but was considered implicit., and see *Hansard*, H.L. Vol.493, cols 1083, 1084.

[99] CDPA 1988, s.9(4) and s.12(8)(a)(ii) and (b).

[1] As to what is publication of such works, see paras 3–121 *et seq.*, above. That availability to the public was intended to include, but be wider than, publication was confirmed in the debate on this provision: *Hansard*, H.L. Vol.490, col.1158; H.C. SCE, cols 116–120.

work or of a film in which it is included, and the communication to the public of any such work, provided in each case that no account is taken of any unauthorised act.[2] The definition of the term "first made available to the public" is specific to section 12.[3] The provision is silent as to whether it is sufficient that a substantial part of the work should have been made available to the public through such means, rather than the work in its entirety, in order for the extended term to apply. In the context of infringement, that is the doing without the necessary licence of an act which is restricted by the copyright,[4] it is sufficient for the act to be done in relation to a substantial part of the work, rather than as to its entirety.[5] The acts referred to as constituting making the work available to the public are all acts which are in themselves restricted by the copyright in such works, and it might be argued therefore that the opening words of section 16(3)[6] apply to such acts in the context of section 12. However, it is thought that the better view is that the provision contained in section 16(3) is specific to the context of infringement, where it is understandable that it should be enough to do the restricted act in relation to a substantial part of the work. The context of section 12 is more similar to the context of publication for the purposes of subsistence of copyright, rather than for the purposes of infringement. As was the position under the 1956 Act in relation to publication,[7] there is no reason of policy why the statutory "substantial part" test should apply in the context of determining whether the work is entitled to the extended period of protection. Nevertheless, if, as it is suggested is correct, the substantial part test does not apply, there clearly must be some degree to which the work as performed, or broadcast, etc., is not in every respect required to be identical to the whole work, or else a performance would rarely constitute making the work available. It is suggested that the test is whether in substance the whole work has been made available to the public. If the work performed or broadcast, etc. is different in material respects from the whole work, then the latter work has not been made available by this means to the public. At most, a different, lesser work, has been made available to the public.[8]

6–47   Computer-generated works. Computer-generated literary, dramatic, musical and artistic works, that is works generated by a computer in circumstances such that there is no human author of the work,[9] are subject to a special rule, reflecting

[2] CDPA 1988, s.12(5). "Communication to the public" has a defined meaning for these purposes, namely the communication to the public of the work by electronic transmission, which includes (a) the broadcasting of the work and (b) the making available to the public of the work by electronic transmission in such a way that members of the public may access it from a place and at a time individually chosen by them (*i.e.* by way of an on-demand service). See s.20(2). For a full discussion of the term, see para. 7–106 *et seq.*, below. For the meaning of unauthorised, see CDPA 1988, s.178.

[3] CDPA 1988, s.12(5).

[4] *i.e.* under CDPA 1988, s.16; and see paras 7–23 *et seq.*, below.

[5] CDPA 1988, s.16(3)(a).

[6] "References in this Part to the doing of an act restricted by the copyright in a work ...".

[7] See the Copyright Act 1956, s.49(1) proviso and s.49(2), the effect of which was to exclude the application of the substantial part test in the context of publication.

[8] Since in such a case the alteration to the work has been authorised (or else the question does not arise), it may therefore be that this other work is the work which enjoys the extended period of protection, while the work as a whole does not, although this presents difficult conceptual problems.

[9] CDPA 1988, s.178.

the fact that they do not have a human author,[10] and are entitled only to a fixed period of 50 years from the end of the year in which the work was made.[11]

Works of non-EEA origin. Where the country of origin of the work is not an **6–48** EEA state[12] and the author of the work is not a national of an EEA state,[13] the new provisions require the application of the principle of comparison of terms, in that the term of protection for such work is that to which it is entitled in the country of origin of the work, provided that such term does not exceed the standard period for such works or the period applicable to works of unknown authorship under section 12, as may be appropriate.[14]

B. WORKS MADE BEFORE JANUARY 1, 1996

General position. The new provisions of the 1988 Act apply to literary, musical, **6–49** dramatic and artistic works made before January 1, 1996[15] and which first qualify for copyright protection after that date[16] or in which copyright subsisted immediately before that date,[17] irrespective of whether the work was made before August 1, 1989. These existing works (other than computer-generated works[18]) therefore benefit from the extended term of protection lasting until the end of the period of 70 years from the end of the calendar year in which the author died. In the case of existing copyright works, the application of the new provisions is subject to the important qualification that if the period of protection for a work under the 1988 Act before its amendment by the Duration Regulations would have been longer, then that period continues to apply to the work.[19] Thus, in respect of such works, it remains necessary to consider the rules for the duration of the term of protection both under the Act as amended and as originally enacted, in order to determine which provides the longer term.

General position under the 1988 Act (before amendment). The general approach of the 1988 Act to works existing at August 1, 1989[20] was to apply its provisions to such works as they apply in relation to works coming into existence after that date, subject to any express provision to the contrary.[21] **6–50**

It was the general policy of the 1988 Act to abolish the possibility for perpetual copyright, previously enjoyed by certain works. Where the 1988 Act achieved this, it substituted a fixed term of 50 years commencing on January 1, 1990.

In accordance with this policy,[22] the 1988 Act abolished the perpetual copyrights which were enjoyed by universities and colleges, originally under the

---

[10] That is, as the work's creator in the sense meant by s.9(1) of the 1988 Act. Such a work may nevertheless be treated as having a human author by reason of s.9(3) of the 1988 Act, where such person undertakes the arrangements necessary for the creation of the work; see generally as to authorship of computer-generated works, para. 4–17, above.

[11] CDPA 1988, s.12(7), to the same effect as s.12(3) as originally enacted.

[12] As to which see para. 6–17, above.

[13] As to which see para. 6–18, above.

[14] CDPA 1988, s.12(6);

[15] The commencement date for the Duration Regulations (SI 1995/3297); see para. 6–12, above.

[16] Duration Regulations, reg.16 (b); see generally para. 6–13. above.

[17] Defined as existing copyright works: reg.16(c); this means works in which copyright subsisted from January 1, 1995 to December 31, 1995, and includes those works in which, apart from the effect of the Duration Regulations, copyright would have expired at midnight on December 31, 1995; see para. 6–14, above.

[18] Which remain entitled to a fixed term of 50 years from the end of the year in which they were made; see para. 6–22, above.

[19] reg.16(c) and reg.15(1); see para. 6–14, above.

[20] The date of commencement of the 1988 Act.

[21] CDPA 1988, Sch.1, para.3. See, generally, paras 6–42 to 6–44, above.

[22] And following the recommendation of the 1977 Copyright Committee, Cmnd.6732, para.656(iii).

346   DURATION OF COPYRIGHT

Copyright Act 1775,[23] in respect of certain works, providing that such rights shall continue to subsist until December 31, 2039 and will then expire.[24] Given the nature of these works, this remains the position under the 1988 Act as amended.

The 1988 Act also abolished,[25] with exceptions, the perpetual copyright previously possible for unpublished literary, dramatic, musical works and engravings and photographs,[26] and transitional provisions, found in pararaph 12 of Schedule 1 to the 1988 Act, apply this rule to works existing at August 1, 1989. However, the new provisions now apply to such works, and in relation to existing works of unknown authorship,[27] posthumously published existing works[28] and photographs,[29] it is necessary to consider the effect of these transitional provisions in the light of the amendment of the 1988 Act.

On the other hand, the 1988 Act introduced a new exception[30] in relation to the play "Peter Pan" by Sir James Barrie, the copyright in which expired on December 31, 1987, by giving to the trustees of The Hospital for Sick Children, Great Ormond Street, London a perpetual right to receive a royalty in respect of the public performance and certain other forms of exploitation[31] of such work, so long as the Hospital continues to have a separate identity and have purposes which include the care of sick children.[32] Whilst these provisions remain unaffected by the amendments made to the 1988 Act by the Duration Regulations, the play itself is a work which benefits from a revived copyright under the new provisions, which will expire on December 31, 2007. During the period of revived copyright, therefore, the trustees will benefit from the more extensive rights available to the copyright owner under section 16 of the 1988 Act,[33] rather than the limited right granted under Schedule 6.

6–51   **Existing literary, dramatic, musical and artistic works (except photographs) of unknown authorship.** The amended provisions relating to literary, dramatic, musical and artistic works of unknown authorship apply to existing anonymous and pseudonymous works.[34] However, the new provisions are different, in setting the initial period of copyright protection by reference to a period calculated from the end of the year in which the work was made.[35] The previous provisions referred to a period calculated from the end of the year in which the work was first made available to the public by being published or otherwise publicly exploited,[36] thus providing an unlimited period of protection for such works until they became publicly exploited.

However, under the transitional provisions of the 1988 Act,[37] such literary, dramatic, musical and artistic works (except photographs) of unknown author-

---

[23] 15 Geo. 3, c.53; and see further paras 6–81 *et seq.*, below.
[24] CDPA 1988, Sch.1, para.13.
[25] Following the recommendation of the 1977 Copyright Committee, Cmnd.6732, para.656.
[26] Copyright Act 1956, ss.2(3) and 3(4) (works posthumously published) and Sch.2, para.2 (works of unknown authorship).
[27] See para. 6–51, below.
[28] See paras 6–52 and 6–53, below.
[29] See para. 6–54, below.
[30] CDPA 1988, s.301 and Sch.6.
[31] *i.e.* commercial publication or communication to the public: CDPA 1988, Sch.6, para.2(1).
[32] CDPA 1988, Sch.6, para.7(2).
[33] But subject to the general limitations applicable to all revived copyrights; see para. 6–15, above.
[34] See para. 6–46, above, but see para. 6–54, below, as to photographs.
[35] CDPA 1988, s.12(3)(a) (as amended); this change was required in order to implement Art.1(3) of the Term Directive 93/98.
[36] CDPA 1988, s.12(2) (as originally enacted); as to what constitutes being made available to the public, see para. 6–46, above.
[37] CDPA 1988, Sch.1, para.12(3); as to existing photographs of unknown authorship, see para. 6–54, below.

ship made before August 1, 1989, and which had been published[38] before August 1, 1989 continued to enjoy the period of protection that they would have enjoyed under the 1956 Act, that is for a period of 50 years from the end of the year in which the work was first published.[39] In the case of such works, therefore, the term will be calculated under the new provisions, as the longer period of 70 years from the end of the year in which they were first published.

The potentially unlimited period of protection for such works made before August 1, 1989 and not published before that date was taken away by the transitional provisions of the 1988 Act.[40] In its place, such works were given a fixed period of 50 years from January 1, 1990, unless made available to the public within that period, when the term would continue for a period of 50 years from the end of the year in which that occurred. In the case of such works made before January 1, 1970, therefore, the initial term will be 50 years from January 1, 1990, this being longer than 70 years from the end of the year in which they were made. In the case of such works made on or after January 1, 1970, the new provisions will provide the longer initial term of 70 years from the end of the year in which they were made. In each case, the initial term will be extended if the work is made available to the public within the initial term, but in the case of a work governed by the old provisions, for a further period of 50 years, and in the case of a work governed by the new provisions, for a further period of 70 years.

In the case of works of unknown authorship made on or after August 1, 1989 and before January 1, 1996, the possibility of an unlimited initial term of copyright remains.[41] In respect of such works, therefore, it will be necessary to wait and see whether the new or the old provisions will provide the longer term. This will depend on whether the work is made available to the public within the period of 70 years from the end of the year in which it was made; if it is, then the new provisions will provide the longer term, (because the second period will be a further 70, not 50 years), but if it is not, then the old provisions will inevitably provide the longer term.

Posthumously published existing literary, dramatic and musical works. In   **6–52**
the case of works of a known author made after August 1, 1989, the date of publication of such works is not relevant to the term of their protection and neither, therefore, is any distinction made between such works published during the life of their author and those published posthumously. However, a distinction was made under the 1956 Act, and literary, dramatic and musical works which at the author's death had not been published, performed in public, offered for sale to the public on records, broadcast or included in a cable programme, continued to enjoy copyright protection until the end of the period of 50 years from the end of the calendar year in which they were first published or otherwise publicly exploited in any of those ways.[42] This distinction is maintained by the transitional provisions of the 1988 Act in relation to works made before August 1, 1989. Where such works had been publicly exploited in this manner before August 1, 1989, and the 50-year period had begun to run, the 1988 Act maintained that pe-

---

[38] That is the previous narrower criterion, not the new wider criterion of being made available to the public.

[39] Copyright Act 1956, Sch.2, para.2.

[40] CDPA 1988, Sch.2, para.12(3)(b), as amended by the Copyright and Related Rights Regulations 2003 (SI 2003/2498) to correct the errors made on the original implementation of the Term Directive.

[41] This is difficult to understand, in the light of the removal of the possibility of unlimited protection for such works made before August 1, 1989.

[42] Copyright Act 1956, proviso to s.2(3); this included doing such acts in relation to an adaptation of the work: *ibid.*, s.2(4).

riod as the term of protection for such works.[43] The new provisions accord such works the standard period of 70 years pma. The term for such works will therefore now depend on whether they were first publicly exploited within 20 years of the author's death, in which case the new provisions will provide the longer term, but if not, then the old provisions will provide the longer term.

Where such works had not been publicly exploited before August 1, 1989, the 1988 Act substituted a fixed term of protection for such works, of 50 years from January 1, 1990.[44] In respect of such works, therefore, the term will depend on whether the author died on or after January 1, 1969. If he did, then the new provisions will provide the longer term of 70 years pma, but if he died before that date, then the old provisions will apply, as providing the longer term.

The discussion above would appear to apply equally to such works made before June 1, 1957 as made after that date, as the 1956 Act contained no relevant transitional provisions.[45]

6–53   **Posthumously published existing engravings.** The provisions relating to posthumously published works in the 1956 Act did not apply in general to artistic works, but similar provisions applied to engravings.[46] Engravings which at the author's death had not been published continued to enjoy copyright protection until the end of the period of 50 years from the end of the calendar year in which they were first published.[47] These provisions were maintained in relation to engravings made before August 1, 1989 by the transitional provisions of the 1988 Act. In the case of such engravings which had been published before August 1, 1989, and in respect of which the 50-year period had begun to run, the 1988 Act maintained that period as the term of protection for such works.[48] The new provisions accord such works the standard period of 70 years pma. The term for such works will therefore now depend on whether they were first publicly exploited within 20 years of the author's death, in which case the new provisions will provide the longer term, but if not, then the old provisions will provide the longer term.

Where such engravings had not been published before August 1, 1989, the 1988 Act substituted a fixed term of protection for such works, of 50 years from January 1, 1990.[49] In respect of such engravings, therefore, the term will depend on whether the author died on or after January 1, 1970. If he did, then the new provisions will provide the longer term of 70 years pma, but if he died before that date, then the old provisions will apply, as providing the longer term.

The discussion above would appear to apply equally to such engravings made before June 1, 1957 as made after that date, as the 1956 Act again contained no relevant transitional provisions.[50]

6–54   **Existing photographs.** As indicated above,[51] photographs taken on or after August 1, 1989 became assimilated to other artistic works, enjoying a term of

---

[43] CDPA 1988, Sch.1, para.12(2)(a).
[44] CDPA 1988, Sch.1, para.12(4)(a).
[45] These provisions were substantially to the same effect as s.17(1) of the Copyright Act 1911, save that the issue of records of a work may not have constituted publication of the work under that Act.
[46] See para. 6–36, above.
[47] Copyright Act 1956, s.3(4), proviso, sub-para.(a).
[48] CDPA 1988, Sch.1, para.12(2)(b).
[49] CDPA 1988, Sch.1, para.12(4)(b).
[50] See also paras 6–37 et seq., above.
[51] See para. 6–43, above.

protection calculated from the death of the author.[52] Under the 1988 Act as originally enacted, this was a period of 50 years from the end of the calendar year in which the author dies.[53] Under the new provisions, that term is increased to a period of 70 years from the end of the calendar year in which the author dies.[54]

Under the 1956 Act, photographs had enjoyed indefinite protection while they remained unpublished, and once published enjoyed a period of protection of 50 years from the end of the year in which publication occurred,[55] and, accordingly, the question of whether the identity of the author was known or not did not arise. The transitional provisions of the 1988 Act maintain this distinction in relation to photographs made before August 1, 1989, and whether the identity of their author is known or not does not affect their term.[56]

In the case of photographs taken on or after June 1, 1957 (whether or not of unknown authorship) and which had been published before August 1, 1989, and in respect of which the 50-year period had therefore begun to run, the 1988 Act retained that period as the term of protection for such works.[57] The new provisions accord such photographs the standard period of 70 years pma, and apply the general provisions as to works of unknown authorship. Which provision will provide for the longer term will depend on the respective dates of publication and of the author's death. For example, in the case of a photograph taken in 1960, and whose author dies in 1961, and which is published in 1980, the old provisions provide a term which expires on December 31, 2030 (end of 50 years after the end of the calendar year in which publication took place), and the new provisions provide a term which expires on December 31, 2031 (end of 70 years from the end of the year in which the author died, assuming his identity is known). The new provisions will therefore apply to such photographs.

In the case of photographs taken on or after June 1, 1957 but which remained unpublished at August 1, 1989, the 1988 Act removed the indefinite protection and substituted a fixed period of 50 years from January 1, 1990.[58] The new provisions accord such photographs the standard term of 70 years after the end of the year in which the author dies. As regards such photographs, therefore, unless the author died before January 1, 1969, the new provisions will provide the longer term.

As regards photographs taken before June 1, 1957, these were accorded a fixed term of protection of 50 years from the end of the year in which they were taken.[59] This term was retained in respect of such photographs under the 1988 Act and applied whether the photograph had been published or not.[60] The new provisions of the 1988 Act accord such photographs the standard period of 70 years pma. As regards such photographs, therefore, whether the new provisions or the old provisions as to term will apply to them, will depend on the respective dates of when the photograph was taken and of the author's death. For example, a photograph

[52] Following the recommendation of the 1977 Copyright Committee, Cmnd.6732, para.656. The general provisions as to works of unknown authorship contained in s.12(2) (as unamended) therefore became applicable to photographs.
[53] CDPA 1988, s.12(1) (before amendment).
[54] See para. 6–45, above. The new provisions as to works of unknown authorship contained in s.12(3) apply to photographs.
[55] Copyright Act 1956, s.3(4), proviso, sub-para (b).
[56] CDPA 1988, Sch.1, para.12(3).
[57] CDPA 1988, para.12(2)(c); the purpose of the transitional provisions being to maintain the shorter period of protection in force when the photograph was taken.
[58] CDPA 1988, Sch.1, para.12(4)(c).
[59] Copyright Act 1956, Sch.7, para.2. This in substance maintained the period of protection accorded to such photographs under the Copyright Act 1911, s.21 (50 years from the making of the original negative from which the photograph was directly or indirectly derived); see para. 6–38, above.
[60] CDPA 1988, Sch.1, para.12(2)(c).

taken in 1955 and whose author died in 1995 would have a term of protection expiring on December 31, 2005 under the old provisions, and on December 31, 2065 under the new provisions, which would therefore apply to such a photograph to accord it a considerable period of extended copyright.[61]

As has been explained above, when the 1988 Act introduced the change, in respect of photographs, from a fixed term of protection to a term of 50 years pma, the new term did not apply to photographs which had been taken before August 1, 1989. The amendment of the 1988 Act, as indicated above, is not so restricted, with the effect that the new term of 70 years pma will become applicable to many photographs which had already fallen into the public domain in the United Kingdom. For example, in the case of a photograph taken in 1918 by an author who died in 1990, such photograph would have had a term of protection under the 1956 Act expiring on December 31, 1968. The photograph would have remained in the public domain in the United Kingdom after August 1, 1989, notwithstanding that its author was still alive. However, on January 1, 1996, such a photograph became entitled to revived copyright in the United Kingdom, (assuming that it remained in copyright in at least one EEA state[62] on July 1, 1995)[63] expiring on December 31, 2060.[64]

6. SOUND RECORDINGS

6–55   **Introduction.** The position of sound recordings has been complicated by a number of factors. First, as enacted, the 1988 Act dealt with films and sound recordings together, but separate treatment was then required in order to implement the Term Directive. Second, the Information Society Directive[65] made minor changes to the treatment of phonograms in the Term Directive in order to give effect to the 1996 WIPO Phonograms and Performances Treaty. This is turn required minor changes to be made to the 1988 Act, and at the same time provisions had to be made to deal with the possibile extension of copyright in sound recordings which resulted.[66]

A. SOUND RECORDINGS MADE ON OR AFTER JANUARY 1, 1996

6–56   **General position.** In relation to a sound recording made after commencement of the Duration Regulations,[67] copyright expires at the end of the period of 50 years from the end of the calendar year in which it was made,[68] or, if published before the end of that period, 50 years from the end of the calendar year in which it was published,[69] or that if during that period the recording is not published but is made available to the public by being played in public or communicated to the public,[70] 50 years from the end of the calendar year in which it was first so made available.[71] In determining whether a sound recording has been published, played

---

[61] As to which see para. 6–14, above.
[62] See para. 6–18, above.
[63] By reg.16(d) of the Duration Regulations (SI 1995/3297).
[64] As to the limitations of revived copyright, see para. 6–15, above.
[65] Directive 2001/29 of the European Parliament and of the Council of May 22, 2001 on the harmonisation of certain aspects of copyright and related rights in the information society. See Vol.2, H11.
[66] See para. 6–57, et seq., below.
[67] January 1, 1996; reg.12(1).
[68] CDPA 1988, s.13A(2)(a).
[69] CDPA 1988, s.13A(2)(b). As to the meaning of published, see CDPA 1988, s.175.
[70] As to the meaning of this expression, see para. 7–106, below.
[71] CDPA 1988, s.13A(2)(c).

in public or communicated to the public, no account is to be taken of any unauthorised act.[72]

History of amendments. Before amendment of the 1988 Act to implement the   **6–57**
Information Society Directive,[73] copyright in a sound recording was to expire at
the end of the period of 50 years from the end of the calendar year in which it was
made,[74] or, if released before the end of that period, 50 years from the end of the
calendar year in which it was released. These provisions reproduced the previous
provisions in the 1988 Act as originally enacted,[75] save that they only applied to
sound recordings (films being treated similarly to other works covered by the
Berne Convention and being given their own separate rules as to duration[76]) and
were made subject to the new provisions relating to works which are not of EEA
origin.[77] The concept of a "release" of a sound recording had been introduced by
the 1988 Act in relation to sound recordings (and films), to define the acts of public exploitation upon which the sound recording (and film) became entitled to the
further term of copyright. Following the amendment of the 1988 Act by the Duration Regulations, this concept remained, with some modification, applicable to
sound recordings but not to films, which were given their own rules as to
duration.[78] The amendment made on implementation of the Information Society
Directive replaces the concept of release with the acts of publication, playing in
public and communication to the public. Because this gives rise to the possibility
of the term being extended, provision is made as to ownership of the extended
term[79] and as to existing licences and agreements.[80] Similarly, because these
amendments also give rise to the possibility of the term being otherwise shortened, it is expressly provided that copyright in an existing sound recording is to
continue to subsist until the date it would have expired under the Duration
Regulations 1995[81] if that date is later than the date on which copyright would
expire under the Act as now amended.[82]

The possibility of the further term of protection being accorded to sound
recordings from the date of their public exploitation had existed under the 1956
Act, but was triggered by publication, reflecting the similar position in relation to
literary, dramatic, musical and artistic works. However, publication of a sound
recording occurred only when records embodying the sound recording were issued to the public, and did not occur when the sound recording was played or
shown in public, or was broadcast or included in a cable programme service.[83]
Before amendment to implement the Information Society Directive, that was still
the position as regards publication.[84] The concept of release introduced by the
1988 Act included, but was wider than, publication and under the provision before
its amendment, a sound recording or film was released not only when it was first
published, but also when it was broadcast or included in a cable programme service or, in the case of a film or film soundtrack, when the film was first shown in

---

[72] CDPA 1988, s.13A(3).
[73] By the Copyright and Related Rights Regulations 2003 (SI 2003/2498), reg.29, with effect from
October 31, 2003.
[74] CDPA 1988, s.13A(2)(a).
[75] CDPA 1988, s.13(1) (as originally enacted).
[76] s.13B and see para. 6–67, below.
[77] CDPA 1988, s.13A(4) and (5) and see para. 6–59, below.
[78] See para. 6–67 *et seq.*, above.
[79] By the Copyright and Related Rights Regulations 2003, (SI 2003/2498), regs.36, 37, . See para.
5–143, above.
[80] reg.38. See para. 5–144 *et seq.*, above.
[81] *i.e.* under reg.15.
[82] Copyright and Related Rights Regulations 2003, (SI 2003/2498), reg.39.
[83] Copyright Act 1956, s.12(9); the same position applied in relation to films: s.13(10).
[84] CDPA 1988, s.175(4)(c).

public,[85] provided that in each case no account was to be taken of any unautho-rised act.[86] The substituted provision which defined, with effect from January 1, 1996, what constituted release of a sound recording repeated the previous provi-sion, but in addition included the act of playing the sound recording in public, an act which had not previously caused the sound recording to be released. As al-ready seen, the Act as it now stands contemplates the further period of protection arising once a sound recording is either published, played in public or com-municated to the public.[87]

6–58   **Limit imposed on term.** The second difference introduced by the 1988 Act was that, whilst under the 1956 Act copyright in unpublished sound recordings (and films) continued without limit in time until they were first published, and then expired at the end of 50 years from first publication,[88] the 1988 Act set a limit on the term for unreleased sound recordings of 50 years from the end of the calendar year in which they were made.[89] This remains the position. It is only if a sound recording is published, played in public or communicated to the public within such period that it will then enjoy copyright protection for a further period of 50 years from the end of the calendar year in which such act occurs.[90] The maximum possible period of copyright protection for a new sound recording or film is therefore 101 years.[91]

6–59   **Works of non-EEA origin.** Where the author of a sound recording[92] is not a national of an EEA state,[93] the Act as amended requires the application of the principle of comparison of terms, in that the term of protection for such a work is that to which it is entitled in the country of which the author is a national, provided that such term does not exceed the standard period for such works under section 13A.[94] This rule is subject to exception, to the extent that it would place the United Kingdom in breach of an international obligation assumed before October 29, 1993,[95] in which case the standard rule applies.[96] In the present context, this is effectively a reference to the United Kingdom's obligations under the Rome Convention,[97] under which the United Kingdom is obliged to accord national treatment to the sound recordings produced by nationals of, or first published in, other Contracting States.[98] In relation to such sound recordings, therefore, the United Kingdom will continue to accord them the standard term under section

[85] CDPA 1988, s.13(2).

[86] CDPA 1988, s.13(2); for the full meaning of unauthorised, see s.178.

[87] The concept of a sound recording being included in a cable programme service has now been as-similated into the single act of communication to the public. See para. 7–106, below, as to the meaning of this.

[88] Copyright Act 1956, ss.12(1) and (3), and 13(1) and (3) (although a limit of 50 years after registra-tion was set in respect of films required to be registered under certain enactments: s.13(3)(a), as amended by the Films Act 1985 (c.21), s.7(2)).

[89] See now, CDPA 1988, s.13A(2)(a). This changed followed the recommendation of the 1977 Copyright Committee, Cmnd.6732 para.656(ii).

[90] CDPA 1988, ss.13A(2)(b), (c).

[91] CDPA 1988, ss.13A(2)(b), (c). Taking the extreme example of a sound recording made on Janu-ary 1 in one year and not, for example, published until some time in the 51st year after that; for example: made January 1, 1996, published December 31, 2046, copyright expires December 31, 2096.

[92] As to who is the author of a sound recording, see para. 4–48, above.

[93] As to which see paras 6–18 and 6–19, above.

[94] CDPA 1988, s.13A(4);

[95] That is the date the Term Directive was adopted.

[96] CDPA 1988, s.13A(5).

[97] International Convention for the Protection of Performers, Producers of Phonograms and Broadcasting Organisations, signed at Rome, October 26, 1961, ratified by the United Kingdom on October 30, 1963.

[98] Art.5.

13A(2), through the inclusion of such Contracting States in Orders in Council made under section 159 of the Act.[99]

Film soundtracks. Under the 1956 Act, a film soundtrack was treated as part of
6–60
the film and not as a sound recording.[1] This was reversed by the 1988 Act as originally enacted.[2] The effect of the Duration Regulations was to restore the position to that which existed under the 1956 Act, and a soundtrack accompanying a film is to be treated as part of the film for the purposes of Part I of the Act.[3] The amended provisions applying to films therefore apply to film soundtracks.[4]

B. SOUND RECORDINGS MADE BEFORE JANUARY 1, 1996

General position. The provisions of the 1988 Act following amendment by the
6–61
Duration Regulations applied to sound recordings made before January 1, 1996[5] and which first qualified for copyright protection after that date[6] or in which copyright subsisted immediately before that date,[7] irrespective of whether the sound recording was made before August 1, 1989. The amended provisions introduced no change in the duration of the standard term of protection for sound recordings, but amended the concept of release to include playing the record in public.[8] This amendment in the Act to the concept of release was not stated to be applicable only prospectively, and the deliberate general retrospective application of the new provisions[9] would suggest that the amended concept applied to events taking place before January 1, 1966. This was subject to the overriding principle that such application was not to result in a shorter term of protection being applicable to an existing sound recording in which copyright subsisted immediately before January 1, 1996.[10] The same applies following the further amendment to replace the concept of release with the acts of publication, playing in public and communication to the public.[11] Thus, in respect of such works, it remains necessary to consider the rules for the duration of the term of protection both under the Act as amended and as originally enacted, in order to determine which provides the longer term.

Sound recordings made on or after August 1, 1989 and before January 1,
6–62
1996. A sound recording made between such dates and which has been played in public or communicated to the public before January 1, 1996, but has not otherwise published, broadcast or included in a cable programme service, will therefore now be treated as released on the date on which such act took place, with the consequence that the 50-year term will run from the end of the calendar

---

[99] See further para. 3–213, above.

[1] See para. 3–76, above. The 1956 Act reversed the previous position, under which film soundtracks were treated as recordings: 1911 Act, s.19(1).

[2] CDPA 1988, s.5(1); and see para. 3–76, above.

[3] CDPA 1988, s.5B(2); as to the problems to which this gives rise, see P. Kamina, "The Protection of Film Soundtracks under British Copyright after the Copyright Regulations 1995 and 1996" [1998] Ent. L.R. 153.

[4] See further para. 6–69, below.

[5] The commencement date for the Duration Regulations, reg.1(2).

[6] Duration Regulations, reg.16(b); see generally para. 6–13, above.

[7] Duration Regulations, reg.16(c); this means works in which copyright subsisted from January 1, 1995 to December 31, 1995, and includes those works in which, apart from the effect of the Duration Regulations, copyright would have expired at midnight on December 31, 1995; see para. 6–14, above.

[8] CDPA 1988, s.13A(3), now repealed (see below); and see para. 6–57, above.

[9] reg.16(c).

[10] reg.16(c) and reg.15(1).

[11] Copyright and Related Rights Regulations 2003, reg.39. The possibility of the term being extended has also been noted, in para. 6–57, above.

year in which the act took place.[12] However, the retrospective effect of the amended provisions cannot result in a shorter term of protection than would otherwise have applied under the 1988 Act before its amendment.[13]

6–63 **Sound recordings made on or after June 1, 1957 and before August 1, 1989.** These sound recordings are existing works for the purposes of the 1988 Act.[14] The general approach of the 1988 Act in treating existing works in the same way as new works[15] is modified by the transitional provisions of the Act,[16] which preserve in relation to such works the former distinction based on publication,[17] so that under the 1988 Act as originally enacted the wider concept of release did not therefore apply to such works.

6–64 **Existing published sound recordings.** Thus, the term of copyright for a sound recording made on or after June 1, 1957 and before August 1, 1989 and which was published[18] before August 1, 1989 continues until the date on which it would have expired under the 1956 Act;[19] that is until the end of 50 years from the end of the calendar year in which it was so published.[20] Whether the term of protection for such a sound recording is shorter under the new provisions, therefore, will depend on whether any acts are done in relation to the sound recording which amount to its playing in public or communication to the public before the sound recording was published. If so, then the old provisions may provide the longer term, depending on the respective dates of making of the sound recording and its eventual publication. If, as will often be the case, broadcasting and playing of the sound recording in public take place at the same time as records of the sound recording are issued to the public, then there will be no distinction between the term under the new and old provisions. Nevertheless, there will be cases where the distinction is material. For example, in the case of a recording made in 1940 of a public performance which was then broadcast in 1940, but which was not published by the issue of records of the recording until 1988, the new provisions provide a term expiring on December 31, 1990, whilst the old provisions provide a term expiring on December 31, 2038, which is therefore the applicable term.

6–65 **Existing unpublished sound recordings.** Sound recordings made on or after June 1, 1957 and before August 1, 1989, and which remained unpublished at that date,[21] were given a further period of protection of 50 years from January 1, 1990, regardless, therefore, of how long ago they were made.[22] At the end of that period the term of copyright expires, unless publication takes place during that period, when protection continues for a further period of 50 years after the calendar year in which publication took place.[23] Whether the term of protection for such a sound recording will be that under the new provisions or the old provisions will depend on whether the recording has been published, and, if so, the respective dates of the making of the recording and its being first published. Thus, in the case of a recording made in 1960 of a public performance but which has not to date been published or released, the copyright in that recording will expire

[12] CDPA 1988, s.13A(2)(b), (c).
[13] See para. 6–61, above.
[14] CDPA 1988, Sch.1, para.1(3).
[15] CDPA 1988, Sch.1, para.3.
[16] Sch.1, para.12(2)(d) and para.12(5)(a).
[17] Copyright Act 1956, s.12(9).
[18] That is, in accordance with the definition in Copyright Act 1956, s.12(9).
[19] CDPA 1988, Sch.1, para.12(2)(d).
[20] See Copyright Act 1956, s.12(3).
[21] The criterion remains that of publication, not release; see para. 6–69, above.
[22] CDPA 1988, Sch.1, para.12(5)(a).
[23] CDPA 1988, Sch.1, para.12(5)(a).

under the old provisions on December 31, 2039, unless by then it has been published, in which case the copyright will expire 50 years after the end of the year in which it is published, and will expire under the new provisions on December 31, 2010, unless by then it has been played in public or communicated to the public, in which case copyright will expire 50 years after the end of the year it which such an act takes place. Unless such recording is published,[24] therefore, before December 31, 2010, the old provisions will be applicable providing the longer term. In the case of a recording which was made in 1960 of a public performance and which was broadcast later in 1960, but was not published by the issue of records of the recording until 1995, the new provisions provide a term expiring on December 31, 2010, whilst the old provisions provide a term expiring December 31, 2045, which is therefore the applicable term.

Sound recordings made before June 1, 1957. The 1988 Act as originally enacted maintained, by its transitional provisions,[25] the term of protection accorded to such sound recordings under the 1956 Act,[26] which was the fixed period of 50 years from the end of the year in which the recording was made.[27] Thus, under the old provisions of the 1988 Act copyright in all sound recordings made before January 1, 1945 will have expired on December 31, 1994, at the latest, the period of protection not being affected or extended by any subsequent publication of the sound recording. The amended provisions will not apply to such a sound recording, since copyright did not subsist in it immediately before January 1, 1996.[28] This assumes that the sound recording was not still in copyright on July 1, 1995 in another EEA state.[29] On the other hand, the amended provisions will apply to a sound recording made on or after January 1, 1945 and before June 1, 1957.[30] The term of protection for such a recording will inevitably be either the same or longer under the amended provisions, and this is so whether the recording has been published or not. In the case of such recordings which have been published, the difference between the term under the amended provisions and the old will be the greater the longer the interval between the making of the recording and its first being published. Thus, in the case of a sound recording made in 1945 and first published in 1995, copyright expires under the old provisions on December 31, 1995, but on December 31, 2045 under the amended provisions, which is therefore the applicable term. In the case of a sound recording made in 1957 (before June 1, 1957), and first published in 1995, copyright expires on December 31, 2007 under the old provisions and on December 31, 2045 under the amended provisions, which is therefore the applicable term. In the case of a sound recording made in 1957 (before June 1, 1957) and published in 1958, copyright expires on December 31, 2007 under the old provisions, and on December 31, 2008 under the amended provisions, which is still therefore the applicable term.

6–66

---

[24] By the issue of copies to the public, not by any other act which constitutes release.

[25] CDPA 1988, Sch.1, para.12(2)(d).

[26] Copyright Act 1956, Sch.7, para.11. By *ibid.*, para.13 the term of protection was maintained for works made before July 1, 1912, provided they had enjoyed copyright under the 1911 Act, by virtue of s.19(8) of that Act. However, copyright in all such recordings expired under the 1956 Act by July 1, 1962, at the latest.

[27] This was the period that had been accorded such works under the Copyright Act 1911, s.19(1), save that it ran from the date of making of the recording.

[28] SI 1995/3297, reg.14(1)(b) and reg.16(c).

[29] Whilst no other EEA state has accorded sound recordings a greater term than 50 years, it is possible that differences in the criterion as to when such period commences might result in such a sound recording being still protected on July 1, 1995 in an EEA state, in which case the new provisions would apply to it by virtue of reg.16(d).

[30] And possibly in the case of one made on or after January 1, 1944 and before January 1, 1945; see the previous footnote.

7. FILMS

A. FILMS MADE ON OR AFTER JANUARY 1, 1996

6–67   **General position.** The amended provisions introduced by the Duration Regulations brought about a major change in the period of protection accorded to films. Previously, films were treated in the United Kingdom not as authors' works, covered by the Berne Convention, enjoying a term of protection calculated by reference to the life of the author, but rather as works protected by related rights under the Rome Convention, entitled to a fixed term of protection in accordance with the distinction between works involving industrial or technical creativity and those involving literary, musical and artistic creativity.[31] Under the amended provisions, films are now treated similarly to other authors' works.

In relation to a film made after January 1, 1996, therefore, the term of protection is to last until the end of 70 years from the end of the calendar year in which the last of a number of designated persons dies. The persons designated for this purpose are: the principal director, the author of the screenplay, the author of the dialogue and the composer of music specially created for and used in the film.[32] If there is no-one falling within this list of designated persons, then the film is to be entitled to a fixed period of protection of 50 years from the end of the year in which it was made.[33]

This list of designated persons follows the list set out in the Term Directive,[34] which also provides that the designation of such persons is irrespective of whether they are co-authors of the film. The earlier Rental Directive[35] had already provided that Member States should harmonise their laws as to authorship of films to provide that the principal director should be designated as the author or one of the authors of a film,[36] and this requirement was repeated in the Term Directive.[37] Section 9 of the 1988 Act was amended by the Regulations implementing the Rental Directive to provide that the authors of a film are to be taken to be the producer and the principal director.[38]

The scheme of the Term Directive would appear to provide for two distinct sets of rights in films, one in films as cinematographic or audiovisual works, to be treated as authors' works, the other in films as the recording of the work, to be treated as a work protected by related rights. Thus, the Directive provided a term of 70 years after the end of the year in which the last of the designated list of persons dies[39] and, separately, a fixed term of 50 years after fixation in respect of the first fixation of the film,[40] which was to belong to the producer of the film.[41] Before the amendment of the 1988 Act, the United Kingdom granted the rights in

---

[31] See para. 6–02, above.

[32] CDPA 1988, s.12(2) (as amended).

[33] CDPA 1988, s.13B(9). An example of such a film might be a home movie; this will depend on the meaning given to "the principal director".

[34] Art.2(2).

[35] Council Directive 92/100 on rental right and lending right and on certain rights related to copyright, November 19, 1992, [1992] O.J. L346/61; see para. 25–52, below.

[36] Rental Directive, Art.2(2).

[37] Term Directive, Art.2(1).

[38] CDPA 1988, s.9(2)(ab), as amended with effect from December 1, 1996, by the Copyright and Related Rights Regulations 1996 (SI 1996/2967).

[39] Art.2(2), referred to above.

[40] Defined as a cinematographic or audiovisual work or moving images, whether or not accompanied by sound: Art.3(3).

[41] Art.3(3).

the film, protected as a recording, to the producer of the film, as its sole author.[42] In amending the authorship provisions to include the principal director as a co-author, and changing the term of protection to the period of 70 years pma, the United Kingdom has implemented the provisions of the Term Directive, but in doing so it has amalgamated what would appear to be considered by the Term Directive as two different sets of rights in two different works into one set of rights in a single work.[43]

Films of unknown "authorship". Before the amendment of the 1988 Act, films **6–68** were granted a fixed period of protection not dependent on the life of an author, and the provisions as to works of unknown authorship were not applied to films. As a consequence of the change in the period of protection of films now being dependent on the lives of various individuals, new provisions had to be introduced by the Duration Regulations dealing with films where the identity of the designated individuals is unknown. As noted above,[44] of these persons, only the principal director is treated as an author of the film, so the provisions contained in section 13B (3) to (6) of the 1988 Act are different from, but closely reflect, the similar provisions applying to literary, dramatic, musical and artistic works of unknown authorship.[45] The identity of any of the individuals is only to be treated as unknown if it is not possible to ascertain the identity of that person by reasonable enquiry.[46] If the identity of any such person is once known, it shall not subsequently be treated as unknown.[47]

These provisions only apply where the identity of none of the designated persons is known.[48] If the identity of any one of the designated persons is known, then the period of 70 years is to run from the death of that person.[49] If the identity of none of the designated persons is known, then the period of protection is a fixed period of 70 years from the end of the year in which the film was made,[50] unless within that period the film has been made available to the public, in which case the period lasts for 70 years from the end of the year in which it was first made available to the public.[51] As with literary, dramatic, musical and artistic works of unknown authorship, if the identity of any of the designated persons becomes known during the period of protection (but not afterwards), then the period of protection will be the period of 70 years from the end of the year in which that person, or the last of those persons, died.[52]

For the purposes of these provisions, a film is made available to the public not only when it is published by the issue of copies of the film to the public, but also when it is shown in public or communicated to the public.[53]

---

[42] CDPA 1988, s.9(2)(a) (as unamended).

[43] Whether this properly implements the Duration Directive is questionable; see P. Kamina "Authorship of Films and Implementation of the Term Directive: The Dramatic Tale of Two Copyrights" [1994] 8 E.I.P.R. 319, and "British Film Copyright and the Incorrect Implementation of the EC Copyright Directives" [1998] Ent. L.R. 109; see also G. Dworkin, "Authorship of Films and the European Commission Proposals for Harmonising the Term of Copyright" [1993] 5 E.I.P.R. 151.

[44] See para. 6–67, above.

[45] See para. 6–46, above.

[46] CDPA 1988, s.13B(10); to the same effect as s.9(5), which does not apply since the provisions do not refer to the identity of the author being unknown.

[47] CDPA 1988, s.13B(10).

[48] CDPA 1988, s.13B(3). This is not, of course, the same as there being no such persons, as to which see para. 6–67, above.

[49] CDPA 1988, s.13B(3)

[50] CDPA 1988, s.13B(4)(a).

[51] CDPA 1988, s.13B(4)(b).

[52] CDPA 1988, s.13B(5).

[53] CDPA 1988, s.13B(6). For the meaning of communicated to the public, see para. 7–106, below, for the meaning of unauthorised see s.178. This parallels the definition of "making available to

6–69 **Film soundtracks.** As indicated above,[54] a film soundtrack is treated under the amended provisions of the 1988 Act as part of the film, thus reversing the position under the 1988 Act as originally enacted, and restoring the position to that which existed under the 1956 Act, which itself had reversed the position existing under the 1911 Act. The primary purpose of treating a soundtrack as part of the film is to harmonise the regimes applicable to the audio and visual elements of a film.[55]

6–70 **Films of non-EEA origin.** Where the country of origin of a film[56] is not an EEA state,[57] the amended provisions require the application of the principle of comparison of terms, in that the term of protection for such a film is that to which it is entitled in its country of origin, provided that such term does not exceed the period which would apply under the rules discussed in paragraphs 6–67, above.

B. FILMS MADE BEFORE JANUARY 1, 1996

6–71 **General position.** The amended provisions of the 1988 Act apply to films made before January 1, 1996[58] and which first qualify for copyright protection after that date,[59] or in which copyright subsisted immediately before that date.[60] This remains subject to the overriding principle that such application is not to result in a shorter term of protection being applicable to an existing sound recording in which copyright subsisted immediately before January 1, 1996.[61] Thus, in respect of such works, it remains necessary to consider the rules for the duration of the term of protection both under the Act as amended and as originally enacted, in order to determine which provides the longer term.

6–72 **Films made on or after August 1, 1989 and before January 1, 1996.** A film made on or after August 1, 1989 and before January 1, 1996 was entitled to a period of protection of 50 years from the end of the year in which it was made,[62] or if released during that period, to a further period of 50 years from the end of the year in which it was released.[63] The amended provisions apply to such a film, and, assuming that there is at least one person falling within the list of designated persons for that film, the amended provisions will usually provide the longer term. However, in the case of a film made in 1995, in respect of which there is no designated person,[64] and which is not released until 2045, the period of protection under the amended provisions will expire on December 31, 2045, and under the original provisions on December 31, 2095, which is therefore the applicable term. Similarly, in the case of a film made in 1995, in respect of which the last of

the public" in relation to literary, dramatic, musical and artistic works in s.12(5); see para. 6–46, above.
[54] See para. 6–58, above.
[55] As to the problems which the assimilation of the soundtrack to the film creates, see P. Kamina, "The Protection of Film Soundtracks under British Copyright after the Copyright Regulations 1995 and 1996" [1998] Ent. L.R. 153.
[56] As to which see paras 6–17 and 6–18, above.
[57] As to which see para. 6–18, above.
[58] The commencement date for the Duration Regulations; reg.1(2).
[59] Duration Regulations, reg.16(b); see generally para. 6–13, above.
[60] Duration Regulations, reg.16(c); this means works in which copyright subsisted from January 1, 1995 to December 31, 1995, and includes those films in which, apart from the effect of the Duration Regulations, copyright would have expired at midnight on December 31, 1995; see para. 6–14, above.
[61] reg.16(c) and reg.15(1).
[62] CDPA 1988, s.13(1)(a) (as unamended).
[63] CDPA 1988, s.13(1)(b) (as unamended). As to what constitutes release of a film for these purposes, see para. 6–55, above.
[64] See para. 6–67, above.

the designated persons died in 2010, and which is not released until 2045, the period of protection under the amended provisions will expire on December 31, 2080, and under the original provisions on December 31, 2095, which is therefore the applicable term.

Films made on or after June 1, 1957 and before August 1, 1989. A film made   **6–73** on or after June 1, 1957 and before August 1, 1989, if registrable,[65] was entitled to a period of protection of 50 years from the end of the year in which it was registered.[66] If the film was not registrable, it was entitled to a period of protection of unlimited duration while it remained unpublished, and thereafter for a further 50 years from the end of the year in which it was published.[67] Under the transitional provisions of the 1988 Act, such a film, if registrable, or if not registrable but which had been published before August 1, 1989, remains entitled to the period of protection which it enjoyed under the 1956 Act.[68] Publication in the case of a film means by the issue of copies of the film to the public.[69] In the case of a film which was not registrable, and which had not been published before August 1, 1989, such a film remains entitled to a further fixed period of protection expiring on December 31, 2039, unless before that date it is published, in which case it will enjoy a further period of protection of 50 years from the end of the year in which it is published.[70]

Films made before June 1, 1957. Films made before June 1, 1957 were not   **6–74** entitled to protection as films, but as a series of photographs and as dramatic works.[71] The period of protection to which such a film is entitled under the old provisions of the 1988 Act is therefore that applicable to photographs[72] and to dramatic works[73] made before that date. The amended provisions are expressly made to apply to films made before June 1, 1957, in so far as they are protected as photographs or dramatic works.[74] Each set of provisions will therefore have to be applied to the facts relating to such a film, which will include ascertaining who is to be treated as the author of such works,[75] before its term can be ascertained.

Film soundtracks. The amended provisions relating to the treatment of film   **6–75** soundtracks apply to film soundtracks existing at January 1, 1996 as to film soundtracks made on or after that date, but with transitional rules relating to ownership and to acts done before January 1, 1996.[76]

8. BROADCASTS

General position. Under the 1988 Act as amended, copyright in a broadcast   **6–76** expires at the end of the period of 50 years from the end of the calendar year in

---

[65] Under Pt III of the Cinematograph Films Act 1938 (1 & 2 Geo. 6, c.17) or Pt II of the Films Act 1960 (8 & 9 Eliz. 2, c.57): Copyright Act 1956, s.31(1).

[66] Copyright Act 1956, s.13(3)(a); as amended by the Films Act 1960 and the Films Act 1985 (c.21), s.7(2) (which repealed the Films Act 1960).

[67] Copyright Act 1956, s.13(3)(b).

[68] CDPA 1988, Sch.1, para.12(2)(e).

[69] As to what constitutes publication of a film, see para. 3–130, above.

[70] CDPA 1988, Sch.1, para.12(5)(b).

[71] See para. 6–41, above.

[72] See para. 6–54, above.

[73] See para. 6–50, above.

[74] Duration Regulations, reg.13.

[75] As to which see above at paras 4–34 *et seq.*, (photographs) and paras 4–27 *et seq.*, (dramatic works).

[76] Duration Regulations, reg.26(1) and see para. 5–53, above.

which the broadcast was made.[77] As has been seen,[78] the definition of broadcast has been altered as part of the implementation of the Information Society Directive, with the result that cable programmes are no longer protected as such: cable broadcasts are now protected simply as broadcasts, whenever they were made. The ordinary term of copyright in broadcast therefore applies to those cable broadcasts which are now protected simply as broadcasts.

6–77   **Broadcasts existing before January 1, 1996.** The current provision of the 1988 Act as to the standard term of protection of broadcasts in effect re-enacts without alteration the provision as it was before the 1988 Act was amended by the Duration Regulations.[79] No distinction therefore requires to be made in considering the term of protection of broadcasts between those existing before January 1, 1996 and those coming into existence after that date. The same provision applies to broadcasts made before commencement of the 1998 Act.[80] Wireless broadcasts were first accorded protection in the United Kingdom under the 1956 Act,[81] which did not apply to wireless broadcasts made before June 1, 1957. The transitional provisions of the 1988 Act applied only to existing wireless broadcasts in which copyright subsisted before August 1, 1989,[82] and expressly maintain this position as to wireless broadcasts made before June 1, 1957.[83] No distinction therefore requires to be made in considering the term of protection of wireless broadcasts between those existing before August 1, 1989 and those coming into existence after that date. The position in relation to those cable programmes which are now protected as broadcasts appears to the same, in that they are simply to be regarded as "broadcasts." It should be noted, however, that cable programmes were first accorded protection in the United Kingdom only under the 1956 Act[84] as amended by the Cable and Broadcasting Act 1984,[85] which did not apply to cable programmes included in a cable programme service before January 1, 1985.[86] The transitional provisions of the 1988 Act applied only to existing cable programmes in which copyright subsisted before August 1, 1989,[87] and expressly maintain this position as to broadcasts made by cable before January 1, 1985.[88]

6–78   **Repeat broadcasts.** Copyright in a repeat broadcast expires at the same time as the copyright in the original broadcast.[89] A repeat broadcast is one which is a repeat of a broadcast previously made,[90] but disregarding any wireless broadcast, whether sound or television, made before June 1, 1957, and broadcasts by cable

---

[77] CDPA 1988, s.14(2).

[78] See para. 3–90, above.

[79] CDPA 1988, s.14(1).

[80] CDPA 1988, Sch.1, para.12(6).

[81] Copyright Act 1956, s.14.

[82] CDPA 1988, Sch.1, para.12(6).

[83] CDPA 1988, Sch.1, para.9, as amended by the Copyright and Related Rights Regulations 2003 (SI 2003/2498), Sch.1, para.16; preserving, in respect of broadcasts, the effect of Sch.7, para.18 of the 1956 Act.

[84] Copyright Act 1956, s.14A.

[85] c.46

[86] The commencement date of s.22 of the Cable and Broadcasting Act 1984; see Copyright Act 1956, s.14A(11).

[87] CDPA 1988, Sch.1, para.12(6).

[88] CDPA 1988, Sch.1, para.9, as amended by the Copyright and Related Rights Regulations, (SI 2003/2498), Sch.1, para.16 .

[89] CDPA 1988, s.14(5) (as amended), re-enacting in similar terms *ibid.*, s.14(2) (as originally enacted), to the same effect as the Copyright Act 1956, ss.14(3) and 14A(4).

[90] CDPA 1988, s.14(6) (as amended), re-enacting in similar terms *ibid.*, s.14(3) (as originally enacted), to the same effect as Copyright Act 1956, ss.14(3) and 14A (4).

made before January 1, 1985.[91] This means, in effect, that no addition to the term of copyright can be acquired by virtue of a repetition of a broadcast. However, if a repetition involves any substantial alteration of the material, then presumably the broadcast will be a new broadcast, and, at least as regards the additional material, will be entitled to a new copyright having its own term of 50 years from broadcast.[92] The rationale of this provision is that a repeat broadcast is not made from a recording of the first broadcast. It will be made from a recording made at the same time as, or even before the first broadcast. For copyright protection to be adequate, therefore, each repeat must be given its own copyright, albeit for an abbreviated time.[93]

Works of non-EEA origin. Where the author of a broadcast[94] is not a national of an EEA state,[95] the new provisions require the application of the principle of comparison of terms, in that the term of protection for such a work is that to which it is entitled in the country of which the author is a national, provided that such term does not exceed the standard period for such works under section 14.[96] This rule is subject to exception, to the extent that it would place the United Kingdom in breach of an international obligation assumed before October 29, 1993,[97] in which case the standard rule applies.[98] In the present context, this is effectively a reference to the United Kingdom's obligations under the Rome Convention,[99] under which the United Kingdom is obliged to accord national treatment to the broadcasts either made by a broadcasting organisation whose headquarters is situated in another Contracting State, or transmitted from another Contracting State.[1] In relation to such broadcasts, therefore, the United Kingdom will continue to accord them the standard term under section 14(2), through the inclusion of such Contracting States in Orders in Council made under section 159 of the Act.[2]

6–79

9. TYPOGRAPHICAL ARRANGEMENTS OF PUBLISHED EDITIONS

Typographical arrangements. Copyright in the typographical arrangement of a published edition expires at the end of the period of 25 years from the end of the calendar year in which the edition was first published.[3] The same provision applies to typographical arrangements of an edition published before commencement.[4] Protection for typographical arrangements of published editions was first provided by the 1956 Act[5] and although it appeared that the protection was accorded to such works whether they first came into existence before or

6–80

---

[91] CDPA 1988, Sch.1, para.9.

[92] See further paras 3–149 and 3–150, above.

[93] See *Hansard*, H.L. Vol.490, col.1163.

[94] As to who is the author of such a work, see para. 5–57, above.

[95] As to which see para. 6–18, above.

[96] CDPA 1988, s.14(3).

[97] That is the date the Duration Directive 93/98 was adopted.

[98] CDPA 1988, s.14(4).

[99] International Convention for the Protection of Performers, Producers of Phonograms and Broadcasting Organisations, signed at Rome, October 26, 1961, ratified by the United Kingdom on October 30, 1963.

[1] Rome Convention, Art.6.

[2] See further para. 3–219, above.

[3] CDPA 1988, s.15. Such works are not literary or artistic works within the meaning of Art.2 of the Berne Convention, and this provision remained unamended by the Duration Regulations (SI 1995/3297); it is in the same terms as s.15(2) of the 1956 Act.

[4] CDPA 1988, Sch.1, para.12(6); and see para. 4–78, above.

[5] See para. 3–102, above.

after June 1, 1957,[6] given the limited period of protection granted to such works, protection for any such works first published before June 1, 1957 had already expired before August 1, 1989.[7]

The protection accorded to typographical arrangements of published editions now exists alongside the new publication right, introduced by the Rental Regulations.[8]

10. RIGHTS OF CERTAIN UNIVERSITIES AND COLLEGES

6–81   **Perpetual copyrights.** The Copyright Act 1775[9] had conferred on certain universities and colleges perpetual copyrights in books which were given or bequeathed to them for the advancement of learning and other purposes of education. The 1775 Act and the rights which it had created survived a succession of subsequent Copyright Acts,[10] until the Act was repealed by the Copyright Act 1911, which provided that no person was to be entitled to copyright or any similar right otherwise than in accordance with the provisions of the 1911 Act or another statutory enactment for the time being in force.[11] Nevertheless, the 1911 Act preserved those copyrights which the universities and colleges had already acquired under the 1775 Act.[12] With the repeal of the 1775 Act, no further copyrights could be acquired by those institutions after July 1, 1912. Section 33 of the 1911 Act, along with virtually the whole of the Act, was repealed by the 1956 Act, which similarly provided that no copyright or right in the nature of copyright should subsist otherwise than by virtue of the 1956 Act or some other enactment in that behalf.[13] Nevertheless, again, the existing rights of these universities and colleges were preserved by the 1956 Act.[14]

6–82   **Abolition of the perpetual copyrights.** The 1977 Copyright Committee considered that these surviving perpetual copyrights enjoyed by the universities and colleges were anomalous, served little purpose and, although probably harmless, should be abolished.[15] This recommendation was implemented by the 1988 Act. The 1988 Act repealed the 1956 Act and, like its two predecessors, provided in section 171(2) that, subject to certain saved rights listed in section 171(1), no copyright right or right in the nature of copyright shall subsist otherwise than by virtue of Part I of the 1988 Act or some other enactment in that behalf. Section 171(1) did not include those existing rights of the universities and colleges amongst the list of saved rights. Nonetheless, these rights were preserved by the transitional provisions in the 1988 Act for a further limited period of 50 years

---

[6] See *Copinger* (12th ed.), para.181.

[7] No doubt this is why the transitional provisions of the 1988 Act do not make any reference to such works, although Sch.1, para.12(6) would ensure that s.15 applied to such works in any event.

[8] The Copyright and Related Rights Regulations 1996 (SI 1996/2967), reg.16, implementing the Duration Directive 93/98, Art.4; see generally as to the publication right, Ch.17.

[9] 15 Geo. 3, c.53.

[10] See, as to the intervening history, para. 6–84, below.

[11] Copyright Act 1911, s.31.

[12] Copyright Act 1911, s.33. The remedies and penalties for infringement of those rights were those granted under the 1911 Act.

[13] Copyright Act 1956, s.46 (5).

[14] Copyright Act 1956, s.46(1); proceedings for infringement now had to be brought under the 1956 Act.

[15] Report of the Committee to consider the Law on Copyright and Designs; Cmnd.6732, paras 648, 649.

from the end of the year in which the 1988 Act came into force.[16] Thus the rights conferred on universities and colleges by the Copyright Act 1775 continue to subsist until December 31, 2039. During this final period, the rights are subject to other provisions in Pt I of the Act, namely: c.III (acts permitted in relation to copyright works;[17]) c.VI (remedies for infringement), c.VII (provisions with respect to copyright licensing) and c.VIII (the Copyright Tribunal).[18]

Origin of the rights. In 1534, Henry VIII granted letters patent to the University of Cambridge empowering the Chancellor, Masters and Scholars of that University to appoint University printers although, apparently, no printing actually took place until 50 years later. Similar letters patent were granted to the University of Oxford by Charles I in 1632, although Oxford University had, it seems, begun printing in 1585. The granting by the Crown to the Universities of Oxford and Cambridge of patents to print Bibles and Prayer Books is dealt with elsewhere.[19] Immediately after, and in consequence of, the decision in *Donaldson v Beckett*,[20] the universities secured the passing of the Copyright Act 1775[21] enabling the two universities in England (Oxford and Cambridge), the four universities in Scotland (St Andrews, Glasgow, Edinburgh and Aberdeen), and the several colleges of Eton, Westminster, and Winchester, to hold in perpetuity the copyright in books given or bequeathed to them for the advancement of useful learning and other purposes of education.   **6–83**

The right was to exist in all such books as had been before 1775, or should thereafter be, given or bequeathed by the authors of the same, or their representatives, to or in trust for those universities, or any colleges, or any of them, for the beneficial purpose of education within them or any of them.

The privilege in favour of the universities and colleges was to extend only to their own books, so long as they were printed at the college press and for their sole benefit. A power was given to the universities and colleges by the Act, to sell or dispose of the copyright given or bequeathed to them, but if they should delegate, grant, lease, or sell the copyright of any book, or allow any person to print it, their privilege was to cease to exist. The copyright of any work presented to the universities was required to be registered at Stationers' Hall within two months after any such gift came to the knowledge of the officers of the university or college. Special penalties were imposed for any infringement of copyright.

Subsequent history of the rights. By the Copyright Act 1801,[22] a similar right to copyright was given to Trinity College, Dublin. The Literary Copyright Act 1842 Act[23] repealed the 1801 Act, but not the 1775 Act. Nevertheless, by section 27 of the 1842 Act, the rights of the universities (including Trinity College, Dublin) and of the colleges were saved from the operation of that Act. As indicated above,[24] the 1775 Act was repealed by the 1911 Act, which also repealed the 1842 Act. The effect of this repeal was therefore that in so far as any rights of Trinity College, Dublin, were saved by the 1842 Act, they appear to have been lost altogether upon the 1911 Act coming into force.   **6–84**

---

[16] CDPA 1988, Sch.1, para.13(1).
[17] But in relation to the acts permitted by CDPA 1988, s.57, it is provided that the assumption in s.57(1)(b)(i) as to expiry of copyright is not to apply in relation to such rights: *ibid.*, Sch.1, para.15(2)(b).
[18] CDPA 1988, Sch.1, para.13(2).
[19] See para. 10–03, below.
[20] (1774) 4 Burr. 2408; and see para. 2–16, above.
[21] 15 Geo. 3, c.53.
[22] 41 Geo. 3, c.107.
[23] 5 & 6 Vict. c.45.
[24] See para. 6–79, above.

11. ABANDONMENT OF COPYRIGHT

6–85   It has been said that an author may by his conduct, or by his express desire, abandon his copyright, and give to the public a right to publish his work before the time when his copyright would expire.[25] There is no direct authority on the point,[26] and it is difficult to say what amount of evidence the courts would require as to the fact of a dedication of a copyright to the public. Clearly mere non-exploitation by the copyright proprietor of his rights will not give grounds for such a plea of abandonment.[27] The argument that British Leyland had abandoned its copyright in its drawings of exhaust pipes was advanced in *British Leyland Motor Corp v Armstrong Patents Co Ltd*, but was rejected by Foster J. who considered that it was extremely difficult to divest oneself of a legal right.[28] A similar argument that the claimant's predecessor in title had released its copyright to the public domain, or had licensed the world to make copies, was rejected by the High Court of New Zealand in *Plix Products Ltd v Frank M. Winstone (Merchants)*.[29]

In *Catnic Components Ltd v Hill & Smith Ltd*,[30] Whitford J. expressed the view that a patentee, by applying for a patent must be deemed, upon publication, to have abandoned his copyright in drawings the equivalent of the patent drawings. The basis for this view was that a patentee in applying for a patent necessarily makes an election accepting that, in return for a potential monopoly, the material disclosed by him in the specification must, upon publication, be deemed to be open to be used by the public, subject only to such monopoly rights as he may acquire on his application for the patent and during the period for which his monopoly remains in force, whatever be the reason for the determination of the monopoly rights. This view was, however, *obiter* to the actual decision in the case, and the Court of Appeal, whilst upholding the learned judge's finding of non-infringement, declined to comment on the question of abandonment.[31] The view expressed by Whitford J. has not subsequently been the subject of a decision in the English courts,[32] although in cases in various other jurisdictions, where it has been referred to in support of the argument of abandonment, the courts

---

[25] In *Millar v Taylor* (1769) 4 Burr. 2303 at 2346; *Platt v Button* (1813) 19 Ves.447; *Rundell v Murray* (1821) Jac. 311 at 316. As to the separate issue of whether an author can ever abandon his manuscript, see *Moorhouse v Angus & Robertson (No.1) Pty* [1981] 1 N.S.W.L.R. 700 and para. 27–56, below.

[26] See *Mellor v Australian Broadcasting Commission* [1940] A.C. 491; *Romesh Chowdhry v Kh. Ali Mohamad Nowsheri* [1965] A.I.R. Jammu and Kashmir 101.

[27] See *Weldon v Dicks* (1878) 10 Ch.D. 247, in which the argument that the proprietor of the copyright in a book had lost his copyright by non-publication for a period of 12 years, during which the book had been allowed to remain out of print, was rejected.

[28] *British Leyland Motor Corp v Armstrong Patents Co Ltd* [1982] F.S.R. 481 at 492; although it would appear that *Millar v Taylor* (1769) 4 Burr. 2303 at 2346; *Platt v Button* (1813) 19 Ves.447; *Rundell v Murray* (1821) Jac. 311 were not cited to the judge. See also CDPA 1988, s.153(3) which, in the context of qualification for copyright protection, provides that, once the qualification requirements are satisfied, copyright does not cease to subsist by reason of any subsequent event.

[29] [1986] F.S.R. 63 at 87–88; affirmed on appeal (but this point not being the subject of the appeal): [1986] F.S.R. 608. See also para. 5–222, above, and the cases cited there.

[30] [1978] F.S.R. 405. The 1977 Copyright Committee, Cmnd.6732, para.915, recommended that any copyright in drawings reproduced in a patent specification should cease when the patent ceases to be in force.

[31] [1979] F.S.R. 619, CA.

[32] The point was treated as arguable by Slade J. in *General Electric Co v Turbine Blading Ltd* [1980] F.S.R. 510, on an application in a copyright action for discovery of patent drawings, and Falconer J. distinguished Catnic (*Catnic Components Ltd v Hill & Smith Ltd* [1978] F.S.R. 405) on its facts, without deciding its correctness on this point in *Gardex Ltd v Serata Ltd* [1986] R.P.C. 623. See also Whitford J. in *Rose Plastics GmbH v William Beckett & Co (Plastics) Ltd* [1989] F.S.R. 113 at 123–4.

have rejected the argument,[33] pointing out that in *Werner Motors Ltd v A.W. Gamage Ltd*[34] (which was not referred to in *Catnic*), the Court of Appeal had held that there was no basis for putting an applicant to an election between a patent for an article and registration of a design for shape of a similar article.

---

[33] *House of Spring Gardens Ltd v Point Blank Ltd* [1983] F.S.R. 213 at 269 (High Court of Ireland, affirmed on appeal: [1985] F.S.R. 327); *Ogden Industries Pty Ltd v Kis (Australia) Ltd* [1983] F.S.R. 619 (Supreme Court of New South Wales); *Wham-O Manufacturing Co v Lincoln Industries Ltd* [1982] R.P.C. 281 at 297 (High Court of New Zealand); and in particular *Interlego AG v Tyco Industries Inc* [1987] F.S.R. 409 where the point was fully discussed at 455 (Court of Appeal of Hong Kong).

[34] (1904) 21 R.P.C. 621.

CHAPTER SEVEN

THE RIGHTS OF A COPYRIGHT OWNER: PRIMARY INFRINGEMENT

Contents Para.

1. INTRODUCTION

Copyright is a statutory property right, the rights of property granted being the **7–01** exclusive right to do various "restricted acts" in relation to the copyright work. Being a property right, the rights of a copyright owner can be sold or licensed. In a commercial context, therefore, it is common to ask what are the *rights* of a copyright owner which are available or need to be obtained. As to enforcement of those rights, the remedy for invasion of a copyright owner's exclusive rights by a third party is, by statutory definition, an action for infringement. In the context of litigation, therefore, it is common to ask what are the acts that amount to an *infringement*. These two viewpoints merely represent a different side of the same coin. Infringement only occurs if one of the exclusive rights of the copyright owner has been invaded.

Primary and secondary infringement. This chapter is concerned with the **7–02** exclusive rights which are conferred on a copyright owner and what amounts to an infringement of those rights. In addition, however, the 1988 Act provides additional remedies to copyright owners in respect of various dealings in relation to copyright works and infringing copies. The common and necessary ingredients of these remedies are that (a) they only arise when some other infringing act has occurred or is assumed to have occurred ("the primary infringement") and (b) the liability of a defendant is dependent on establishing some degree of "guilty" knowledge on his part. The acts in respect of which these remedies are available are also classified as infringements and although they are not strictly invasions of any of the exclusive property rights which are expressly conferred on the copyright owner, yet in some sense these remedies do constitute additional rights of the copyright owner.[1] It is common to classify these infringements as "secondary" infringements,[2] being secondary to the primary act of infringement which takes place. Secondary infringements are discussed in the next chapter.

7–03   European Directives. A number of Directives have prescribed a patchwork of rights in the copyright and related rights fields. Most recently, the Information Society Directive[3] has prescribed a coherent scheme for a number of basic rights for various rights owners, namely (1) an exclusive right of reproduction, (2) an exclusive right of communication to the public and (3) an exclusive right of distribution of copies. There were already in existence a number of Directives prescribing a piecemeal scheme of protection for rights owners, namely, and in historical order, the Software Directive,[4] the Rental and Related Rights Directive,[5] the Satellite and Cable Directive[6] and the Database Directive.[7] The effect of these Directives will be considered in relation to the various rights of copyright owners under United Kingdom law as they arise.

7–04   The rights: basic definitions. The rights of the copyright owner are defined to be the exclusive right to do the following acts in the United Kingdom[8]:

(a) copy the work ("the reproduction right"[9]);

(b) issue copies of the work to the public ("the distribution right");

(c) rent or lend the work to the public ("the rental and lending rights");

(d) perform, show or play the work in public ("the public performance right"[10]);

(e) communicate the work the work to the public ("the communication to the public right");

(f) make an adaptation of the work, or to do any of the above acts in relation to an adaptation of the work ("the adaptation right").

These various rights are described as the acts "restricted by the copyright" in a work.[11] They are the subject of more detailed statutory definition as discussed later in this chapter.

7–05   Infringement: the basic definitions. Copyright is infringed by a person who, without the licence of the copyright owner, does, or authorises another to do, any of the acts restricted by the copyright.[12] Not only is copyright therefore infringed by anyone who does one of the restricted acts without licence, but also by anyone who without licence *authorises* the doing of any such act.[13] An infringing act of

---

[1] They can, for example, be the subject of a licence: *Biotrading & Financing OY v Biohit Ltd* [1998] F.S.R. 109.

[2] See, *e.g.* the heading to CDPA 1988, ss.22 *et seq.*

[3] Directive 2001/29.

[4] Or Computer Program Directive, 91/250.

[5] Directive 92/100.

[6] Directive 93/83.

[7] Directive 96/9.

[8] CDPA 1988, ss.2(1), 16(1).

[9] This and the following descriptions of the various rights are used as a convenient shorthand but are not, apart from the rental right, part of any statutory definition.

[10] Caution should taken when speaking of the public performance right since in some circumstances, for example in relation to the administration of rights by the Performing Rights Society Ltd, the expression performing right includes other rights, *e.g.* the right to broadcast.

[11] CDPA 1988, s.16(1).

[12] CDPA 1988, s.16(2).

[13] In addition, of course, the ordinary rules as to liability for inciting or procuring the commission of a tort apply. See paras 22–35 *et seq.*, below.

authorisation is a separate tort from the infringing act so authorised.[14] In addition, copyright is infringed:

  (a) by the doing of any of these acts not only in relation to the whole of a work but also in relation to any substantial part of it[15];

  (b) by the doing of any of these acts indirectly as well as directly, it being immaterial whether any intervening acts themselves infringe copyright.[16]

The doing of any of these acts by any person other than the copyright owner or one who has his permission is therefore an infringement unless the act falls within one of the statutory permitted acts[17] or is otherwise excusable.[18] Each wrongful exercise of an exclusive right constitutes a separate tort. Apart from these acts, however, other dealings with a work do not constitute a primary infringement. It is thus not an infringement of copyright to read a hard copy of a book[19] or to resell a copy which was purchased in a bookshop.[20]

Licence; permitted acts. It is a necessary ingredient of the tort that the act in question was done without the licence of the copyright owner. This topic is considered in detail elsewhere.[21] There is also a large class of so-called permitted acts which, although falling within the description of one or more of the restricted acts, may be done without infringing copyright. These acts are considered in Chapter 9.   **7–06**

Innocence or ignorance not a defence. It is a characteristic of all these rights of the copyright owner that the right is infringed whether or not the defendant appreciated that what he was doing infringed copyright. Copyright is a proprietary right and is infringed by invasion of the right, except to the extent that the statute provides otherwise. Innocence is therefore not a defence to a claim for primary infringement of copyright.[22] A limited defence to a claim in damages (but not to any other relief) is available where the defendant proves that at the time of the infringement he did not know, and had no reason to believe, that copyright subsisted in the work in question.[23] The defence is of very limited application.[24]   **7–07**

Infringement actionable without damage. Copyright is a right of property and is actionable without having to show damage, this not being one of the ingredients of the tort.[25]   **7–08**

2. THE REPRODUCTION RIGHT

A. Introduction

The exclusive right to prevent copying or reproduction of a work is the most fundamental, and historically the oldest, right of a copyright owner.   **7–09**

---

[14] *Ash v Hutchinson & Co (Publishers) Ltd* [1936] Ch. 489.
[15] CDPA 1988, s.16(3)(a). As to the meaning of substantial part, see paras 7–23 *et seq.*, below.
[16] CDPA 1988, s.16(3)(b). See para. 7–15, below.
[17] See para. 7–06, below.
[18] *e.g.* because it is in the public interest. See para. 22–82, below.
[19] Reading a copy of a book stored in digital form raises other issues, because reproduction of the work inevitably takes place in the process. See para. 7–20, below.
[20] But note that to put into circulation a licensed copy of a work which had not previously been put into circulation is an infringement. See CDPA 1988, s.18 and paras 7–76 *et seq.*, below.
[21] See paras 5–00, *et seq.*
[22] See, *e.g. Mansell v Valley Printing Company* [1908] 2 Ch. 441; *Lee Simpson* (1847) 3 C.B. 871. See, further, para. 7–22, below.
[23] CDPA 1988, s.97(1).
[24] See paras 22–64 *et seq*, below.
[25] See the definition of infringement in CDPA 1988, s.16(2) and *Weatherby & Sons v International Horse Agency & Exchange Ltd* [1910] 2 Ch. 297, at 305, applied in *Hawkes & Son (London) Ltd v Paramount Film Service Ltd* [1934] Ch. 593.

7–10   **European Directives.** A number of Directives have dealt with various aspects of the reproduction right. Most recently, and most importantly, the Information Society Directive[26] has defined the scope of the acts covered by the reproduction right which Member States are obliged to confer in relation to authors' works[27] and related rights subject matter,[28] the intention being to ensure legal certainty within the internal market.[29] Thus the Directive provides for an exclusive right to authorise or prohibit the direct or indirect, temporary or permanent reproduction of such subject matter by any means and in any form, in whole or in part.[30] Before that, a number of other Directives had made piecemeal provision relating to the reproduction of various types of subject matter. Thus, the Software Directive[31] provides for an exclusive right of the permanent or temporary reproduction of computer programs, by any means and in any form, in part or in whole, including situations where the loading, displaying, running, transmission or storage of the program necessitated such reproduction.[32] Next, the Rental and Related Rights Directive[33] provided, in relation to phonogram producers for their phonograms, film producers for their films and broadcasting organisations for their broadcasts, for an exclusive right to authorise or prohibit direct or indirect reproduction.[34] Finally, the Database Directive[35] provides, in relation to copyright databases, for an exclusive right to carry out or authorise the temporary or permanent reproduction of the database by any means and in any form, in whole or in part.[36] In relation to all of these requirements, United Kingdom law as contained in the 1988 Act was already compliant with them, such that no amendment to the reproduction right was required when other provisions of these Directives were implemented.

7–11   **Common considerations.** In one form or another, the reproduction right exists today in relation to every category of copyright work.[37] Each such category is considered in turn in this chapter[38] but some points are common to all categories, namely:

(1) The right is the exclusive right of *copying*.[39] For the right to be infringed, two elements have to be established, (a) a sufficient degree of objective similarity between the copyright work and the alleged infringement and (b) that this was the result of the copyright work having been copied, *i.e.* that there is a causal connection between the two.

(2) As with all rights of a copyright owner, the exclusive right relates not only to the entire work but also any substantial part of it.

---

[26] Directive 2001/29.

[27] *i.e.* the rights in Berne copyright works, namely, literary, dramatic, musical, artistic works, and works of cinematography considered as authors' works.

[28] *i.e.* rights conferred on producers of sound recordings and films, and broadcasters. The rights of performers are considered separately, in Ch.12, below.

[29] See Recital 21 of Directive 2001/29.

[30] Art.2.

[31] Directive 91/250.

[32] Art.4.

[33] Directive 92/100.

[34] Art.7. This Article has now been deleted and replaced by Arts 2(b), (c), (d) and (e) of the Information Society Directive (2001/29), above, to equivalent effect.

[35] Directive 96/9.

[36] Art.5.

[37] CDPA 1988, s.17(1).

[38] The basic right is the subject of different statutory rules of interpretation in relation to each category, these rules being part definition and part elucidation.

[39] The right is necessarily limited to the exclusive right to do an act whereby a copy comes into existence which did not exist before. The right does not include an exclusive right to alter a version of a work without producing a new copy. See *Théberge v Gallerie d'Art du Petit Champlain Inc* 210 DLR (4th) 385 (Sup Ct of Can) and para. 7–55, below.

(3) Again, as with all other such rights, the exclusive right is the right to copy the work either directly or indirectly.

(4) In relation to all categories of work, the exclusive right extends to the making of copies which are transient or incidental to some other use of the work.[40]

These issues are considered separately in this introductory section.

Sufficient similarity. As already stated, there must be a sufficient objective similarity between the copyright work and alleged copy. This has two aspects: **7–12**

(a) First, the allegedly infringing work must in some real sense represent the claimant's.[41] Thus a literary work consisting of instructions will not be infringed by the making of an article in accordance with those instructions[42] and an artistic work such as a circuit diagram will not be infringed by describing it or its contents in words, no matter how detailed.[43] Another example, from the law as it stood before 1911, is that piano rolls and cylinders for music boxes did not amount to "copies" of sheet music.[44] The question in these cases is not whether the defendant has used the claimant's work, but whether he has reproduced it, a question that should be answered from a common sense point of view.[45]

(b) Secondly, even if the defendant's work does represent the claimant's in this sense, there will be no infringement if there is no *sufficient* objective similarity between it and the copyright work.[46] Even if a copyright work has been used as a reference or is the inspiration for what the defendant has done, this by itself is not enough if there is no such similarity. For example, a defendant may have derived his work from the claimant's, but may have done so in such a way, either deliberately or through incompetence, that what he produces does not amount to a copy in law.[47] The issue here is whether a substantial part of the copyright work has been copied,[48] an issue which is perhaps the most common and often the most difficult question arising in everyday copyright law. This is considered further, below.

Ideas versus expression. In dealing with the question of copying, there should be borne in mind the well established principle that there is no copyright in mere ideas, concepts, schemes, systems or methods.[49] Rather, the object of copyright is to prevent the copying of the particular form of expression in which these things **7–13**

---

[40] CDPA 1988, s.17(6). But note the permitted act in relation to the making of transient and incidental copies provided for by s.28A. See para. 9–56, below and see, further in para. 7–19, below.

[41] *Purefoy Engineering Co Ltd v Sykes Boxall & Co. Ltd* (1955) 72 R.P.C. 89 at 99.

[42] *Interlego A.G. v Tyco Industries Inc* [1989] A.C. 217 at 265. See the discussion in relation to literary works at para 7–34, below, for further examples.

[43] *Anacon Corp Ltd v Environmental Research Technology Ltd* [1994] F.S.R. 659. This is not to say that something made by following a written or verbal description of an artistic work may not infringe the copyright in the artistic work. See below.

[44] *Boosey v Whight* [1900] 1 Ch. 122. Sheet music was protected as a "book" under the Literary Copyright Act 1842. The law is now different.

[45] *Designers Guild Ltd v Russell Williams (Textiles) Ltd* [2001] 1 W.L.R. 2416. Originality, and thus protection, tends to lie in the detail with which a basic idea is presented, *per* L.J. Hoffmann at para.26. See also paras 2–06 and 7–13, above, for a discussion of the ideas/expression dichotomy and *Autospin (Oil Seals) Ltd v Beehive Spinning* [1995] R.P.C. 683, which contains a provocative discussion of the problem.

[46] *Francis Day & Hunter Ltd v Bron* [1963] Ch. 587 at 614.

[47] *Billhöffer Maschinenfabrik GmbH v Dixon & Co Ltd* [1990] F.S.R. 105.

[48] This applies both to the case where a part of the work has been taken and to the case where the whole work has been copied, but in an altered form.

[49] There are many statements in the cases to this effect. For modern examples, see *L.B. (Plastics) Ltd v Swish Products Ltd* [1979] R.P.C. 551 at 619, 633, HL; *Johnstone Safety Ltd v Peter Cook*

are conveyed. If the expression is not copied, copyright is not infringed.[50] Thus, to be liable, the defendant must have made a substantial use of the form of expression; he is not liable if he has taken from the work the essential idea, however original, and expressed the idea in his own form, or used the idea for his own purposes. Protection of this kind can only be obtained, if at all, under patent law or the law relating to confidential information. This principle finds expression in many of the cases, to the effect, for example, that it is no infringement of the copyright in a literary or dramatic work to take its basic idea or plot[51] or of an artistic work to take the general idea.[52] As with all such general statements of principle, however, it must be treated with caution and not taken too far. It is not a correct statement of English law that because a copyright work contains the expression of an idea it may be copied; nor that if there is only one way of expressing an idea, then that way cannot be the subject of copyright[53]; nor that where the expression of an idea is inseparable from its function, it forms part of the idea and is not entitled to copyright protection.[54] The correct position is that although copyright cannot prevent the copying of a general idea, where the idea has been worked out in detail in the form of writing, drawings, etc. it will be an infringement if the labour which went into the expression of the idea is appropriated. In such a case, it is not the idea which has been copied but its detailed expression.[55] Thus the law of copyright is concerned not with originality of ideas but with the original expression of thought (in the case of a literary work, for example, the expression in writing).[56] The originality which is required, and thus the protection conferred, relates to the expression of thought.[57] In each case, it will be a matter of degree whether the line which divides the copying of an idea from copying of its expression has been overstepped.[58] For the same reason, care should be taken when it is said that there is no copyright in news. The original

---

[Int.) *Plc* [1990] F.S.R. 161, CA (functional concepts); *Harman Pictures N.V. v Osborne* [1967] 1 W.L.R. 723 at 728. For older examples, see *Hollinrake v Truswell* [1894] 3 Ch. 420; *McCrum v Eisner* (1917) 87 L.J. Ch. 99.

[50] *Hollinrake v Truswell* [1894] 3 Ch. 420 at 424, 427.

[51] *Wilmer v Hutchinson & Co Ltd* [1936–45] Mac. C.C. 13. There are many similar examples in the field of dramatic works. See paras 7–52 *et seq.*, below.

[52] *Kenrick & Co v Lawrence & Co* (1890) 25 Q.B.D. 99 (drawing of hand filling in voting slip, made to help illiterate voters, not infringed by use of the same concept); *Gleeson v H.R. Denne Ltd* [1975] R.P.C. 471 (idea for design of ecclesiastical collar). See further, para. 7–58, below.

[53] See the criticisms of *Total Information Processing Systems Ltd v Daman Ltd* [1992] F.S.R. 171 and *John Richardson Computers Ltd v Flanders* [1993] F.S.R. 497 in *Ibcos Computers Ltd v Barclays Finance Ltd* [1994] F.S.R. 275.

[54] Such statements are often made in relation to computer programs, drawing on United States authorities. See, *e.g. Autodesk Inc v Dyason* [1992] R.P.C. 575 at 583 (High Ct of Aus) citing *Lotus Development Corp v Paperback Software International* (1990) 18 I.P.R. 1 at 25 (U. Dis Ct).

[55] *L.B. (Plastics) Ltd v Swish Products Ltd* [1979] R.P.C. 551 at 619, 633, HL; *William Hill (Football) Ltd v Ladbroke (Football) Ltd* [1980] R.P.C. 539 at 546; *Leco Instruments (U.K.) Ltd v Land Pyrometers Ltd* [1982] R.P.C. 140 (an idea put into permanent form may be the subject of copyright).

[56] *Ibcos Computers Ltd v Barclays Finance Ltd* [1994] F.S.R. 275.

[57] *University of London Press Ltd v University Tutorial Press Ltd* [1916] 2 Ch. 601 at 608, cited with approval in *Ladbroke (Football) Ltd v William Hill (Football) Ltd* [1964] 1 W.L.R. 273 at 277.

[58] *Ibcos Computers Ltd v Barclays Finance Ltd* [1994] F.S.R. 275. So, in *Bowater Windows Ltd v Aspen Windows Ltd* [1999] F.S.R. 780, a particular technique for selling double glazing had been given expression in the form of documents used by salesmen used in the course of their "pitch". Only the form in which the technique had been expressed in the documents could be protected, not the technique itself. In that case the sales technique was common in the industry and the defendant had not copied the detailed expression of the technique from the claimant's documents. There was therefore no infringement even though the claimant's documents had been the inspiration for the defendant's. (Although there had been some copying of expression from the claimant's documents, there had been no sufficient skill and labour expended on these parts to make the amount copied a substantial part.)

expression of a news story is certainly capable of being the subject matter of copyright and of being infringed by the appropriation of that expression.[59]

Causal connection. As has been pointed out,[60] where the claimant's and the defendant's works are similar, there are four possible explanations: the defendant's work was copied from the claimant's; the claimant's from the defendant's; both from a common source; or mere chance or coincidence.[61] It is only in the first case that an infringement of the claimant's work can have occurred. Although the concept of copying is expressed differently in relation to the different categories of work, the underlying principle is that there can be no infringement unless use has been made, directly or indirectly, of the copyright work.[62] Copyright is not a monopoly right and no infringement occurs by an act of independent creation.[63] This is often expressed as saying there must be a causal connection between the copyright work and an infringing work.[64] This is one of the ways in which copyright differs from true monopoly rights such as patents and registered designs. In the case of the latter rights, a person can infringe even though he has arrived at his result by independent creation.

7–14

Indirect copying. Although there must be a causal connection between the claimant's and the defendant's work for there to be any infringement, this connection need not be direct. The 1988 Act makes clear what has always been the position, namely, that copyright may be infringed indirectly by copying something which is itself a copy of the claimant's work.[65] Indeed, in most cases of alleged infringement the copying is done indirectly, the plagiarist never having seen the original manuscript, drawing, etc. only the published work or other thing derived from the original work. The position is the same whether or not the intervening work is of a nature capable of enjoying copyright or is itself an infringement of copyright[66] and even if there is no intervening work as such at all. Thus an artistic work is capable of being infringed where the link between it and the copy is a written[67] or verbal[68] description, if the description is nevertheless sufficient to enable a copy of the artistic work to be made. The latter point underlines the risk that, even if an independent designer is employed in an attempt to avoid infringement, it may be necessary to give him so much informa-

7–15

---

[59] The matter is considered further at para. 7–40, below.

[60] *Corelli v Gray* (1913) 29 T.L.R. 570.

[61] The possibility of coincidence should never be ruled out, for: "We constantly in life meet with coincidences which suggest a common origin, but which, when investigated and examined, are found to be nothing but coincidences. Experience shews that it is not merely probable, but certain, that improbable events will happen." See *Lucas v Cooke* (1879) 13 Ch.D. 872 at 879. Of course, the more commonplace the subject matter, the less improbable is the explanation of coincidence.

[62] *L.B. (Plastics) Ltd v Swish Products Ltd* [1979] R.P.C. 551, HL.

[63] *L.B. (Plastics) Ltd v Swish Products Ltd* [1979] R.P.C. 551, HL, at 619; *Francis Day & Hunter Ltd v Bron* [1963] Ch. 587 at 617; *Corelli v Gray* (1913) 29 T.L.R. 570; *Wesman v McMara* [1923–28] Mac.C.C. 121.

[64] *Francis Day & Hunter Ltd v Bron* [1963] Ch. 587, at 614.

[65] CDPA 1988, s.16(3)(b). It has always been the law that it is irrelevant by what intermediate sources the defendant copied. See, *e.g. British Leyland Motor Corp. Ltd v Armstrong Patents Co Ltd* [1986] A.C. 577, HL; *King Features Syndicate Inc v O. & M. Kleeman Ltd* [1940] Ch. 523 at 806, CA (the point was no longer in issue by the time the case reached the House of Lords). As to examples of pre- 1911 Act cases, see *Ex p. Beal* [1868] L.R. 3 Q.B. 387; *Cate v Devon, etc. Newspaper Co* [1889] 40 Ch.D. 500; *Hanfstaengl v H.R. Baines & Co. Ltd* [1895] A.C. 20, HL.

[66] *Hanfstaengl v H.R. Baines & Co. Ltd* [1895] A.C. 20, HL (copies of claimant's paintings made via *tableaux vivants*, not themselves capable of amounting to an infringement).

[67] *Plix Products Ltd v Frank M. Winstone (Merchants) Ltd* [1986] F.S.R. 63 at 608 (CA of NZ).

[68] *Ultra Marketing (UK) Ltd v Universal Components Ltd* [2004] EWHC 468 (Ch), para.15, applying *Plix Products Ltd v Frank M. Winstone (Merchants) Ltd* [1986] F.S.R. 63, and *Solar Thomson Engineering Co Ltd v Barton* [1977] R.P.C. 537. See also *Gleeson v H. R. Denne Ltd* [1975] R.P.C. 471 (no infringement, on the facts).

tion that the work he produces is still a copy.[69] A defendant may even infringe by giving a designer very loose instructions and then prompting him to produce, for example by trial and error, a result which eventually resembles the copyright work.[70] Where it is alleged that the original copyright work has been copied via some intervening work, care must be taken in comparing the alleged infringing work with the intervening work, since the vital comparison is between the alleged infringement and the original work.[71]

Even though copying may take place indirectly, it is still necessary to prove an unbroken chain between the claimant's and the defendant's work. It must therefore be shown that the intermediate copy is itself either a direct or indirect copy of the copyright work.[72] Often this turns out not to be the case, particularly where the claimant's work is derived from another work or article and the defendant has copied that other work or article.[73] This situation frequently arises where the claimant's work, for example a drawing, turns out not to be at the head of the chain but to have been made to record an existing article, the latter being what the defendant has actually copied.[74] The "intermediate" stage must in some real and intelligible sense be a copy or description of the work in which copyright subsists. Thus where a defendant compiled a catalogue from the range of machinery parts sold by the claimant, thereby bringing into being a catalogue substantially similar to the claimant's, the copyright in the claimant's catalogue was not infringed. This was because the machinery parts offered by the claimant did not in any proper sense amount to a reproduction of the descriptions of those parts in the catalogue.[75]

7–16   **Access.** The need for a causal connection obviously implies the need to show that the alleged infringer had access, either directly or indirectly, to the copyright work.[76] The issue of proof of copying is considered below, but if there is sufficient similarity between the works, this will raise a *prima facie* case of access and thus causation.[77]

7–17   **Proof of copying.**[78] It is for the claimant to prove copying, this being a question of fact,[79] the standard being the ordinary civil standard.[80] In most cases copying can only be deduced by inference from all the surrounding circumstances because normally there will be no evidence from anyone "being present and looking over the [defendant's] shoulder" at the time he designed or made his work.[81] The case will therefore normally start with establishing substantial similarity combined

---

[69] *Solar Thomson Engineering Co Ltd v Barton* [1977] R.P.C. 537.

[70] *House of Spring Gardens Ltd v Point Blank Ltd* [1983] F.S.R. 213 (High Ct of Ireland); *LED Builders Pty. Ltd v Eagle Homes Ltd* (1996) 35 I.P.R. 215 (Fed Ct of Aus).

[71] As in *Johnstone Safety Ltd v Peter Cook (International) plc* [1990] F.S.R. 161.

[72] *Johnstone Safety Ltd v Peter Cook (International) plc* [1990] F.S.R. 161; *Billhöffer Maschinenfabrik GmbH v Dixon & Co Ltd* [1990] F.S.R. 105 at 108.

[73] Examples are *Toole v Young* [1873] 9 Q.B. 523; *Schlesinger v Bedford* (1890) 63 L.T. 762 (in both cases, the defendant's independent dramatisation of a novel had not been copied from claimant's dramatisation); *Lucas v Cooke* (1879) 13 Ch.D. 872 (copyright in engraving of painting not infringed by subsequent copy taken from painting); *The Duriron Co Incorp v H. Jennings & Co. Ltd* [1984] F.S.R. 1 (claimant's articles not made from drawings relied on).

[74] *Autospin (Oil Seals) Ltd v Beehive Spinning* [1995] R.P.C. 683.

[75] *Purefoy Engineering Co Ltd v Sykes Boxall & Co Ltd* (1955) 72 R.P.C. 89. The skill and labour of the claimant which had been copied was that which had gone into selecting the parts and not into compiling the catalogue.

[76] *L.B. (Plastics) Ltd v Swish Products Ltd* [1979] R.P.C. 551, HL.

[77] *Francis Day & Hunter Ltd v Bron* [1963] Ch. 587 at 612.

[78] See also para. 7–56, below, for a discussion of this issue in relation to artistic works.

[79] *Ibcos Computers Ltd v Barclays Finance Ltd* [1994] F.S.R. 275 at 296.

[80] *Biotrading & Financing OY v Biohit Ltd* [1998] F.S.R. 109 at 121.

[81] *Sifam Electrical Instrument Co. Ltd v Sangamo Weston Ltd* [1973] R.P.C. 899.

with the possibility of access.[82] Where there is substantial similarity, this is *prima facie* evidence of copying[83] and also of access.[84] Once a *prima facie* case is established in this way, a shift in the evidential burden takes place which the party charged may refute by evidence of independent creation[85] or by giving some alternative explanation for the similarities.[86] The task of the judge is then to decide, on the evidence as a whole, whether or not there has been copying.[87] This can be summarised by saying that proof of sufficient similarity, coupled with proof of the possibility of access, raises a *prima facie* case or inference of copying for the defendant to answer.[88] This shifting of the burden of proof is merely one of plain, rational thought.[89]

Naturally, even if an inference of copying can be drawn, it may be rebutted by the defendant's evidence that he did not copy.[90] The fact that the defendant denies copying is some evidence to rebut the inference but is obviously not conclusive[91]: it has to be weighed against all the other evidence. A bare denial of copying without any explanation of the similarities is, however, unlikely to be convincing.[92] On the other hand, where there is a respectable defence of, for example, common source, functional necessity or hackneyed theme, the absence of other tell-tale similarities may mean that the defendant's evidence can easily be accepted.[93] Thus where two works are claimed to have been based on earlier materials, similarities in incident and situations, although affording *prima facie* evidence of copying, may not be sufficient to override a denial of copying coupled with an explanation of similarities by reference to the sources.[94] While for the purposes of the "substantial part" test it is the similarities between the works which matter, not the differences,[95] in the context of copying, the unimportant parts of two works may contain unexplained similarities which are probative of copying.[96] Again, although an alleged infringing article and a copyright drawing may appear similar when viewed from one angle, when viewed from another they may appear so dissimilar that any inference of copying is dispelled.[97] Evidence of unlikely similarities will usually have to be of the most cogent kind before it can be preferred to the sworn evidence of a respectable and responsible

---

[82] In *L.B. (Plastics) Ltd v Swish Products Ltd* [1979] R.P.C. 551 at 619, Lord Wilberforce speaks of "proof" of access but it is suggested that this goes too far. Proof of the possibility of access is surely enough.

[83] *King Features Syndicate v O. & M. Kleeman Ltd* [1941] A.C. 417 at 436.

[84] *Francis Day & Hunter Ltd v Bron* [1963] Ch. 587 at 612. Of course, if it is very unlikely that a defendant could have had access to the claimant's work, this will weaken the inferential case.

[85] *L.B. (Plastics) Ltd v Swish Products Ltd* [1979] R.P.C. 551; *King Features Syndicate Inc v O. & M. Kleeman* [1941] A.C. 417. If the defendant calls no evidence, a court is therefore entitled to find copying proved: *Mathieson v Universal Stock Exchange* [1901–04] Mac.C.C. 80; *Cadieux v Beauchimin* [1901–04] Mac.C.C. 4 (Sup Ct of Can).

[86] *Billhöffer Maschinenfabrik GmbH v Dixon & Co Ltd* [1990] F.S.R. 105 at 107.

[87] *L.B. (Plastics) Ltd v Swish Products Ltd* [1979] R.P.C. 551, at 619, 621, HL.

[88] *Francis Day & Hunter Ltd v Bron* [1963] Ch. 587, at 612, 614; *Designers Guild Ltd v Russell Williams (Textiles) Ltd* [2001] 1 W.L.R. 2416, *per* Lord Millett at para.39.

[89] *Ibcos Computers Ltd v Barclays Finance Ltd* [1994] F.S.R. 275 at 297; cited with approval in *Creative Technology Ltd v Aztech Systems Pte. Ltd* [1997] F.S.R. 491 at 501 (CA of Singapore).

[90] *De Manduit v Gaumont, etc. Corp. Ltd* [1936–45] Mac.C.C. 292.

[91] *Francis Day & Hunter Ltd v Bron* [1963] Ch. 587, at 614.

[92] *Harman Pictures N.V. v Osborne* [1967] 1 W.L.R. 723.

[93] As in *Deeks v Wells* [1928–35] Mac.C.C. 353; *Thomas Forman & Sons Ltd v Balding & Mansell* [1928–35] Mac.C.C. 501.

[94] See, *e.g. Poznanski v London Film Production Ltd* [1937–45] Mac.C.C. 107.

[95] *Entec (Pollution Control) Ltd v Abacus Mouldings* [1992] F.S.R. 332. See para. 7–27, below at (g).

[96] *Billhöfer Maschinenfabrik GmbH v Dixon & Co Ltd* [1990] F.S.R. 105; *Ibcos Computers Ltd v Barclays Mercantile Highland Finance Ltd* [1994] F.S.R. 275.

[97] *Gomme Ltd v Relaxateze Upholstery Ltd* [1976] R.P.C. 377.

person which the court would otherwise accept.[98] On the other hand, the similarities may be so great that his evidence could never be believed.[99] The fact that a witness who denies copying is disbelieved will not necessarily prove copying[1] since it constitutes no positive evidence,[2] but it can clearly be brought into the balance.[3] The fact that the defendant has copied other works before may be probative.[4] The type of evidence which will help prove copying obviously varies with each case, but unexplained similarities in style, content and so on usually play a part.[5] Indeed it is often in the repetition of mistakes, redundancies, idiosyncrasies and the like that a plagiarist is caught out, for "… it is the resemblances in *inessentials*, the small, redundant, even mistaken elements of the copyright work, which carry the greatest weight. This is because they are least likely to have been the result of independent design"[6] and may "shed a flood of light on the real source of the more substantial similarities."[7] Obviously, where a number of passages in a work are proved to have been copied (*e.g.* because of mistakes), other passages which are the same in both works may be assumed also to have been copied.[8] In limited circumstances, similar fact evidence may be relied upon to rebut the suggestion of coincidence.[9]

7–18   **The role of expert witnesses.** Expert witnesses are often called in infringement actions.[10] Their usual function will be to examine the similarities which are said to exist between the two works, where necessary explaining the technicalities involved, and help the court reach a conclusion on whether and to what extent the similarities are or are not probative of copying. This may involve setting the similarities against what is usual or commonly done in the field and an examination of other sources which were available to the defendant.[11] In cases of technical complexity, such as computer software infringement, they may be essential in order to explain the presence and significance of what seem to be similarities between the two works.[12] In music copyright cases, expert evidence is invariably called to educate the court in the nuances of melody, rhythm, orchestration and so on, and to identify and explain common or unusual musical figures. This is so even though similarities between two musical works are often apparent to the most uneducated in music. Such witnesses can also play a role in identifying what is important or essential about a work and therefore help the court decide whether a substantial part of the claimant's work has been reproduced, where this

---

[98] *Deeks v Wells* [1928–35] Mac.C.C. 353, CA.

[99] *Robl v Palace Theatre (Ltd)* (1911) 28 T.L.R. 69.

[1] *L.B. (Plastics) Ltd v Swish Products Ltd* [1979] R.P.C. 611 at 620, HL.

[2] *Johnstone Safety Ltd v Peter Cook (International) Plc* [1990] F.S.R. 161 at 175; *Billhöffer Maschinenfabrik GmbH v Dixon & Co Ltd* [1990] F.S.R. 105.

[3] *Designers Guild Ltd v Russell Williams (Textiles) Ltd*, [2000] 1 W.L.R. 2416, at p.2419, recording the approach of the trial judge.

[4] See para. 22–222, below.

[5] There are many examples of such cases and it is not helpful to cite individual examples.

[6] *Billhöfer Maschinenfabrik GmbH v T.H. Dixon & Co Ltd* [1990] F.S.R. 105 at 123; cited in *Ibcos Computers Ltd v Barclays Finance Ltd* [1994] F.S.R. 275 at 297 and *Creative Technology Ltd v Aztech Systems Pte. Ltd* [1997] F.S.R. 491 at 501 (CA of Singapore).

[7] *L.B. (Plastics) Ltd v Swish Products Ltd* [1979] R.P.C. 551, *per* Lord Hailsham.

[8] *Mawman v Tegg* (1826) 2 Russ. 385; *Ibcos Computers Ltd v Barclays Finance Ltd* [1994] F.S.R. 275 at 303. Proof of copying of an insubstantial part may therefore support the proof of copying a substantial part.

[9] See para. 22–222, below.

[10] As to the ordinary duties of an expert witness, see *"The Ikarian Reefer"* [1993] F.S.R. 562; *Cala Homes (South) Ltd v Alfred McAlpine Homes East Ltd* [1995] F.S.R. 818; *Autospin (Oil Seals) Ltd v Beehive Spinning* [1995] R.P.C. 683.

[11] *Baumann v Fussell* [1978] R.P.C. 485. An example is *Nicol v Barranger* [1917–23] Mac.C.C. 219.

[12] As in *Ibcos Computers Ltd v Barclays Finance Ltd* [1994] F.S.R. 275.

issue arises.[13] Although an expert's opinion as to whether or not copying has taken place is admissible,[14] it is important to appreciate the limitations of the expert's role, which is not to decide the issues of copying or substantial part, these being for the court and the court alone.[15]

Transient and incidental copying; copying by electronic means. The making   **7–19** of transient copies can constitute infringement just as much as the making of copies of a more permanent form.[16] Unless it constitutes a permitted act,[17] any fleeting but unlicensed copying of a work will therefore infringe, whether, for example, taking the form of writing on a blackboard or the presentation of text or an image on a computer screen or television monitor.[18] As will be seen, in relation to literary, dramatic, musical and artistic works, copying also expressly includes the storing of the work in any medium by electronic means.[19] The combination of the two provisions makes it clear that the fleeting copying of such works in computer memory is one of the exclusive rights of the copyright owner. In each case, however, it will be necessary to examine precisely what has been copied. A difficult issue arises where very small fragments of a work have been successively copied in RAM or other temporary memory as part of the incidental processing of the whole of the work for some other use. An example might be a DVD player which in the course of displaying a film on a screen reads data from the DVD and copies small fragments to RAM which are held there only fleetingly before being replaced by further fragments. Another example is the buffering which takes place in RAM when a broadcast is streamed over the internet. On one view, each fragment is so small that at any one time there cannot be said to be a "copy" of the film or any substantial part of the film in RAM, and so no copying of the film will have taken place for the purposes of the Act.[20] It is suggested that this view is correct. The process is not really analogous to copying out

---

[13] See *Ibcos Computers Ltd v Barclays Finance Ltd* [1994] F.S.R. 275, at 301, where the importance was emphasised of an expert separating the two issues: (1) are there any indicia of copying? (2) if so, has a substantial part been taken?

[14] Civil Evidence Act 1972, s.3 allows the giving of expert evidence on *any* issue in the proceedings; *Designers Guild Ltd v Russell Williams (Textiles) Ltd* [1998] F.S.R. 803, at 811; *IPC Media Ltd v Highbury Leisure Publishing Ltd* [2004] EWHC 1967 (Ch), para.15.

[15] *Deeks v Wells* [1928–35] Mac.C.C. 353, CA; *Baumann v Fussell* [1978] R.P.C. 485.

[16] CDPA 1988, s.17(6).

[17] Particularly, in this context, an act permitted by s.28A. See para. 9–56, below.

[18] This was the case even under the 1956 Act, which did not contain such an express provision. See *Bookmakers' Afternoon Greyhound Services Ltd v Wilf Gilbert (Staffordshire) Ltd* [1994] F.S.R. 723 at 738. An older example was the representation of a painting or sculpture by human figures, *i.e.* as a *tableau vivant*. See para. 7–55, below.

[19] CDPA 1988, s.17(2). It has been clear that under UK copyright law, storage in computer memory has been a restricted act since at least 1985, and probably before. The Copyright (Computer Software) Amendment Act 1985, s.2, provided that "[r]eferences in the Copyright Act 1956 ... to the reproduction of any work in a material form, shall include reference to storage of that work in computer." Art.2 of the Information Society Directive (2001/29) also provides that the reproduction right provided for there is to include the exclusive right of direct, indirect, temporary or permanent reproduction by any means and in any form, in whole or in part. It was not necessary to alter UK law to give effect to this. An attempt to include in the 1996 WIPO Copyright Treaty and WIPO Performances and Phonograms Treaty provisions to the effect that temporary and transient copying were restricted acts was abandoned in the face of opposition, although in an "Agreed Statement on the Reproduction Right" it was confirmed that: "The reproduction right ... and the exceptions permitted thereunder, fully apply in the digital environment, in particular to use of works in digital form. It is understood that the storage of a protected work in digital form in an electronic medium constitutes a reproduction ...". In other words, notwithstanding a clear statement that digitisation is an infringing act, the position with respect to temporary and transient storage is left open so far as the international treaty position is concerned. For a detailed discussion of these Treaties, see paras 24–66 and 24–119, below.

[20] *Australian Video Retailers Association Ltd v Warner Home Video Pty Ltd* (2002) 53 I.P.R. 242 (Fed Ct.of Aus). Under the Australian legislation, however, the restricted act of copying a work in any material form is modfied to the extent that "material form" is defined to include any form of storage from which the work *can be reproduced*.

small fragments of a work onto separate pieces of paper since at the end of this process a new copy of the work will exist, albeit scattered amongst separate pieces of paper. In the case of the fragmentary copying into RAM, at no point does there exist anything which can be realistically be said to be a copy. Admittedly, the restricted act is the "copying" of the work, not the making of a "copy", but if a copy is not produced at some stage of the process it seems unrealistic to say that copying has taken place. Arguably, this could be a situation in which the principle of "little and often" could be adopted,[21] with the result that copying should be regarded as having taken place, but this is an unsatisfactory basis for the reaching this conclusion.

7–20   Works recorded in digital form. The growth of digital storage and transfer of works via the internet and other information carriers has a number of copyright implications. Whereas, traditionally, most works can be enjoyed simply and freely by, for example, reading the book in which the work has been printed, or watching or listening to the work being performed,[22] works which are recorded in digital form usually cannot be sensibly enjoyed without being copied again for the particular purpose, for example into transient computer memory (and often again onto a screen). The restricted act of copying is therefore usually implicated in uses of works recorded in digital form. Thus, although the traditional enjoyment of works has not required any form of licence, enjoyment of works in digital form will often do so. Usually, of course, such use is impliedly licensed on the sale of a physical carrier of the digital copy, but where the material is supplied online, it raises the possibility of a charge being made for each use, and the spectre of a "licence to read". Even in the case where use is licensed on the sale of a physical carrier, such licence may be limited in extent.[23]

7–21   Who commits the act of copying? In the era of electronic communications and the use of other new technologies, it may often be crucial to know who commits the actual act of copying which is the exclusive right of the copyright owner. The question may arise in the comparatively simple case of a fax transmission: who is the "person who … *does*" the restricted act of copying the work.[24] A more complex case is where digital information is sent via an electronic network such as the internet, when it will usually be stored transiently in computers provided by intermediate service providers, before being stored more permanently, although still in electronic form, by the eventual recipient. Although such intermediaries will often now be able to rely on the protection conferred on them following the implementation into United Kingdom law of both the E-Commerce Directive[25] and the Information Society Directive[26], the threshold question may still arise in such cases as to who does the act of copying. The problem may be acute, not only because in the course of such a transfer copying may take place in several jurisdictions, but also because the service providers will generally have no means of knowing whether the copies which are being made in their computers are licensed or not, and will often be unable to control what is passed through or received by their computers. The primary act of infringement by copying is a tort of strict liability, so that the consequences are clearly of fundamental

---

[21] See para. 7–29, below.

[22] Public performance, etc. of most works is of course a restricted act, for which the performer is responsible.

[23] For example, an article may be sold in one territory on terms that it is for use in that territory only, in which case any use in another territory which involves reproduction of a copyright work will be unlicensed. See *Sony Computer Entertainment v Owen* [2002] E.W.H.C. 45 (Ch).

[24] See CDPA 1988, ss.16(2), (1).

[25] See para. 22–88, below.

[26] See para. 9–15, below.

importance.[27] These questions require the application of copyright law in a new context but this does not mean that the ordinary principles should not be applied. The question always remains the same: who "does" the act of copying? Who is the human person who is the most proximate cause of the act being done? Thus, in the simple example of a photocopier provided by a library, a member of the public who uses the photocopier to make a copy is clearly the person who copies the work, not the librarian nor the owner of the library nor the supplier of the photocopying equipment. In the technically more complex case of the sending of a fax, where the sender causes a copy to be made automatically by the recipient's remote fax machine, it is suggested that the sender is the person who is responsible for copying the work which is sent, not the person in control of the receiving fax machine.[28] In the case of network transmissions, the problem is in essential respects no different.[29] Although the service provider makes available the facilities for making the copy, it is suggested its employees, servants or agents do not themselves copy the work if this is done as a result of an automatic process which is activated by the receipt of a transmission. Other potential grounds of liability need to be considered in all these cases, of course, in particular whether the defendant has authorised the copying of the work,[30] or is liable as a joint infringer, or for having procured or incited the copying.[31] In the case of a service provider which has enabled the onward transmission of the work through its networks, consideration will also need to be given as to whether it has communicated the work to the public.[32] In relation to these potential grounds of liability, it will be necessary to examine the facts of each case, particularly the relationship between the service provider and the third parties involved, whether the service provider assumes responsibility to any extent for policing what is stored, for example by way of monitoring the content or reserving the right to intervene. It is suggested, however, that a purely passive service provider would not be liable for the act of copying.

Ignorance no excuse; subconscious copying. As already pointed out, since copyright is a proprietary right, ignorance is no defence to a infringement claim.[33] If, therefore, the defendant's work has been copied from the claimant's, either directly or indirectly, the fact that the defendant was unaware that the work he was copying in this way existed, or was the claimant's or was the subject of copyright, or whether he thought he had a licence, provides no defence to a claim

7–22

---

[27] It was for this reason, of course, that the liability of service providers was modified by the E-Commerce (2000/31) and Information Society (2001/29) Directives.

[28] See the observations of Peter Smith J. in *Sony Music Entertainment (UK) Ltd v Easyinternetcafe Ltd* [2003] EWHC 62 (Ch); [2003] F.S.R. 48, at para.33, although he appears to have taken the view that the owner of the machine would not be liable because he would be "an involuntary copier". It is suggested, however, that he is not a copier at all. Note, however, the provisions of CDPA 1988, s.24(2), which create a liability in the case of a person who transmits a work by means of a telecommunication system, knowing or having reason to believe that infringing copies will be made by means of the reception of the transmission. It is arguable that this provision is for the most part unnecessary.

[29] *Sony Music Entertainment (UK) Ltd v Easyinternetcafe Ltd* [2003] EWHC 62 (Ch); [2003] F.S.R. 48.

[30] See generally *C.B.S. Songs Ltd v Amstrad plc* [1988] A.C. 1013, HL and *Amstrad Consumer Electronics plc v British Phonographic Industry Ltd* [1986] F.S.R. 159, CA, and see paras 7–130, *et seq.*, below, for a detailed discussion of authorisation.

[31] See para. 22–35, below. Note also the possibility of the sender being liable for the secondary act of infringement under CDPA 1988, s.24(2), (see para. 8–15, below) and see CDPA 1988, s.97A and para. 22–108, below, for the possibility of obtaining an injunction against the service provider.

[32] *i.e.* within the meaning of CDPA 1988, s.20. The issue used to be whether the provider was operating a cable programme service (see para. 7–73, below), as held arguably to be the case in *Shetland Times Ltd v Wills* [1997] F.S.R. 604 (approved, *obiter*, in *Sony Music Entertainment (UK) Ltd v Easyinternetcafe Ltd* [2003] EWHC 62 (Ch); [2003] F.S.R. 48, at para.47.

[33] See para. 7–07, above.

for primary infringement although, in very limited circumstances, it may affect the remedy.[34] Nor would a blind person, or someone who was illiterate or who simply chose not to look at the thing he is copying, have a defence.[35] It also follows that a defendant's intentions, whether it was to copy or infringe copyright or not, are irrelevant. It is sometimes alleged that there has been "subconscious copying" that is, subconscious use of the claimant's work rather than conscious use by deliberate copying. Such a possibility often arises in musical copyright cases, where a songwriter may have been exposed to many melodies and other musical devices over the years which he may subconsciously call on when writing a work. Since the issue of copying does not depend on any question of "knowledge" but, in this respect, only causation, it is suggested that if the reason for the substantial similarity between two works is that the maker of the defendant's work unconsciously or subconsciously drew on the claimant's work as his source, then copying will have occurred. The possibility has in fact been accepted in a number of cases without argument.[36] In the one case where the matter has been argued, the result was inconclusive,[37] although it was emphasised that the fact that the maker of the defendant's work did not believe there was any causal connection between the two works is irrelevant.[38] The problem will in most cases be one of proof. With a work of any complexity, it is unlikely that a person who remembered enough of it to be able to recreate it would be unaware of what he was doing. With a more simple work such as a popular song, if the evidence that no conscious copying took place is accepted then it may be difficult to prove that the reason for the similarity is a causal link between the two works rather than an independent creation, particularly in a field where almost every musical device can be found to have been used somewhere else before. A particularly difficult situation may arise where the defendant is accused of copying an earlier work of his own which he no longer has the right to reproduce, since it may be very hard for him to put out of his mind completely the earlier work.[39]

B. SUBSTANTIAL PART

7-23   Introduction. The law has never allowed a defendant to escape liability on the

---

[34] See CDPA 1988, s.97(1) and para. 22–76, below.

[35] *Sony Music Entertainment (UK) Ltd v Easyinternetcafe Ltd* [2003] EWHC 62 (Ch); [2003] F.S.R. 48, at para.36 (*obiter*).

[36] *Sinanide v La Maison Kosmeo* (1927) 44 T.L.R. 371 (reversed on other grounds on appeal); *Gleeson v Denne (H.R.) Ltd* [1975] R.P.C. 471; *Johnstone Safety Ltd v Peter Cook (International) Ltd* [1990] F.S.R. 161; *John Richardson Computers Ltd v Flanders* [1993] F.S.R. 497; *EMI Music Publishing Ltd v Papathanassiou* [1993] E.M.L.R 306. In *G. Ricordi & Co v Clayton & Waller Ltd* [1928–35] Mac.C.C. 154, the possibility of subconscious copying was accepted but not established on the facts. In *Rees v Melville* [1911–16] Mac.C.C. 168, it was established that the defendant might unconsciously (or indeed consciously) have retained some recollection of the claimant's play but as no substantial part was reproduced, there was no infringement. Subconscious misuse of information has been held sufficient to found a breach of confidence claim: *Seager v Copydex Ltd* [1967] 1 W.L.R. 923 at 921.

[37] *Francis Day & Hunter Ltd v Bron* [1963] Ch. 587. Willmer L.J. expressed the opinion (at 614) that whether or not the defendant was consciously aware of a causal connection was irrelevant. Diplock L.J. felt unable to deal with the matter without evidence of the mental processes involved. Upjohn L.J. declined to express a view. *G. Ricordi & Co (London) Ltd v Clayton & Waller Ltd ibid.* was apparently cited as the only English authority on the point (see at 612), although a number of United States authorities were relied on. In *Andritz Sprout-Bauer Australia Pty Ltd v Rowland Engineering Sales Pty Ltd* (1993) 28 I.P.R. 29 (Fed Ct of Aus), the concept was clearly accepted.

[38] *Francis Day & Hunter Ltd v Bron* [1963] Ch. 587, *per* Diplock L.J. at 625.

[39] *Industrial Furnaces Ltd v Reeves* [1970] R.P.C. 605 at 623 (conscious copying found in the facts); *Galago Publishers (Pty) Ltd v Erasmus* [1989] 1 S.A. 276 at 293. Note that in the case of artistic works there is a limited defence under CDPA 1988, s.64 for an artist who does not repeat or imitate the main design of his earlier work. See para. 9–174, below.

grounds that he has not copied the claimant's work exactly; less than complete copying has always been an infringement. In this, the underlying rationale of the law of copyright is to protect and adequately reward the interests of authors and copyright owners and to prevent others from unfairly appropriating the benefit of the effort, skill and labour which went into a work's creation.[40] On the other hand, it has never been the law that copying of any part of a work, no matter how small, is unlawful; copyright should not be allowed to become an instrument of oppression and extortion.[41] Some use of a copyright work is clearly permissible, for the Act does not prohibit use of "any" part, even if that part was the product of skill and labour,[42] only a "substantial part".[43] It is in arriving at the dividing line that the difficulty arises. Although the difficulty arises in relation to all the exclusive rights of the copyright owner, not merely the reproduction right, it most often arises and is mostly easily discussed in the present context.

The use which has been made of the claimant's work can usually be characterised as (a) the exact use of part of the work only (as where extracts from a literary work have been taken *verbatim*) or (b) some reworking of the whole of it (as where the whole of a literary work has been paraphrased, dramatised or translated into another language; an entire artistic work imitated in some way; or a complete musical work altered) or (c) a combination of these. As to these:

(a) The issue in the first category is simply whether the part which has been taken is a substantial part, applying the tests set out below.

(b) Where the whole work has been imitated, modified or otherwise altered without exact copying of any part, the issue has historically sometimes been treated as being whether the use amounts to the copying of the whole of the claimant's work[44] and sometimes whether the copying is of a substantial part,[45] These cases were sometimes characterised as ones of "colourable imitation" or "colourable alteration" of the claimant's work.[46] The use of the expression was continued in the 1911 Act, which defined

---

[40] *Designers Guild Ltd v Russell Williams (Textiles) Ltd* [2001] 1 W.L.R. 2416, at 2432 (Lord Scott) and *per* Lord Bingham at 2418: "The law of copyright rests on a very clear principle: that anyone who by his or her own skill and labour creates an original work of whatever character shall, for a limited period, enjoy an exclusive right to copy that work. No one else may for a season reap what the copyright owner has sown". See also, *e.g. Hanfstaengl v Empire Palace* [1894] 3 Ch. 109 at 128, CA; *Hawkes & Son (London) Ltd v Paramount Film Service Ltd* [1934] Ch. 593 at 602.

[41] *Hanfstaengl v Empire Palace* [1894] 3 Ch. 109 at 128, CA; *Hawkes & Son (London) Ltd v Paramount Film Service Ltd* [1934] Ch. 593 at 602, and also *Chappell & Co v D.C. Thompson & Co* [1928–35] Mac.C.C. 467. Admittedly, in *Hanfstaengl* one of the examples of oppression and extortion of which Lindley L.J. was thinking was the possibility of preventing fair reviews of plays, etc. a matter which then fell to be decided under the heading of copying, but which would now be dealt with under the heading of fair dealing (see paras 9–19 *et seq.*, below). This does not apply to the other examples he cites, or the decisions in *Hawkes* and *Chappell*, decided under the 1911 Act.

[42] *Electronic Techniques (Anglia) Ltd v Critchley Components Ltd* [1997] F.S.R. 401 at 409. In *Designers Guild Ltd v Russell Williams (Textiles) Ltd* [2001] 1 W.L.R. 2416, at 2418, Lord Bingham described the substantial part test as amounting to the realistic recognition that no real injury is done to the copyright owner if no more than an insignificant part of the copyright work is copied.

[43] CDPA 1988, s.16(3)(a). Note that the Information Society Directive 2001/29, Art.2, refers to reproduction "in whole or in part". It was nevertheless assumed that this did not require Member States to provide an exclusive right of reproduction literally in relation to any part, but only to any "creative" part, which it was considered essentially corresponded with the United Kingdom substantial part test. See the Government Conclusions on the Patent Office's Consulation Paper of August 7, 2002.

[44] As in *Sillitoe v McGraw-Hill Book Co (U.K.) Ltd* [1983] 545 at 550. And see the analysis in *Spectravest Inc v Aperknit Ltd* [1988] F.S.R. 161 at 170.

[45] As in *King Features Syndicate Inc v O. & M. Kleeman* [1941] A.C. 417, HL, at 424; *Bauman v Fussell* [1978] R.P.C. 485, CA.

[46] Thus in early editions of this work, for example, infringements were classified as: (1) reprinting the whole verbatim; (2) reprinting a part verbatim; (3) imitating the whole or part or by reproduc-

an infringing copy as including any copy or colourable imitation of a work[47] (in addition to defining "copyright" as the sole right to produce or reproduce the work or any substantial part of it[48]) but was no longer included as part of the definition of infringement in the 1956 or 1988 Acts.[49] Although the expression is sometimes still used,[50] it is suggested that since the ordinary meaning of colourable is that the change is designed to disguise the fact that use has been made of the claimant's work,[51] it does not add to the discussion of what amounts to impermissible copying. The defendant's state of mind, in particular whether the changes were made deliberately in an attempt to throw off the suspicion of copying, is irrelevant. The only relevant question is whether there has been a copying of a substantial part of the claimant's work. In order to answer this question, it is necessary to identify, first, what elements or features of the copyright work have been taken and then, secondly, to ask whether those elements amount to a substantial part of the copyright work, applying the tests set out below.[52] The approach is therefore no different in principle to that applied in relation to the first category of cases, although more difficult to apply because of the requirement to identify, as a first step, the elements or features which have been taken. It may be tempting, particularly in cases of artistic or musical works where it is often difficult to describe in words what has been taken, to ask whether the offending work looks or sounds like the copyright work or, conversely, to reach a conclusion that since it does *not* look or sound like the copyright work, no substantial part has been taken. This approach is incorrect, however, and may lead to the wrong conclusion.[53]

(c) In the third class of case, it is again necessary to identify what part or parts of the copyright work have been copied and then ask whether they amount to a substantial part of the whole work.

Although, therefore, types of copying can be differently categorised, the test remains the same.

7–24   **Substantial part and permitted uses.** The question of what amounts to a substantial part is not answered simply by balancing the interests of the author or copyright owner against the general public interest in being able to reproduce parts of a work for certain purposes, since this latter interest can to a large extent be assumed to be safeguarded by the various permitted acts to which today the

---

ing the whole or part with colourable alterations; (4) reproduction under an abridged form and; (5) translation. See *Copinger* (4th ed., 1904), pp.155(a) and 170(b).

[47] s.35(1).

[48] s.1(2).

[49] Although the expression is still used in the separate context of what constitutes publication of a work for the purposes of satisfying the qualification provisions of the Act. Thus CDPA 1988, s.175 states that references to publication "do not include publication which is merely colourable and not intended to satisfy the reasonable requirements of the public".

[50] See, *e.g. Designers Guild Ltd v Russell Williams (Textiles) Ltd* [2001] 1 W.L.R. 2416, *per* Lord Millett, at 2425 ("The reproduction may be exact or it may introduce deliberate variations involving altered copying or colourable imitation as it is sometimes called."); *Sillitoe v McGraw-Hill Book Co (U.K.) Ltd* [1983] 545 at 550, where passages of the claimant's work had been rendered into *oratio obliqua*: "... 'reproduction' for copyright purposes, embraces a colourable imitation", and also *Norowzian v Arks Ltd* [1998] F.S.R. 394 (a colourable imitation to "all intents and purposes is a copy of the original work, albeit that there might be certain relatively minor changes to it").

[51] See, *e.g. Catnic Components Ltd v Hill & Smith Ltd* [1982] R.P.C. 183 and *Rodi and Weinenberger A.G. v Henry Showell Ltd* [1969] R.P.C. 367 at 467, both patent cases, and also *Emerson v Davies* (1845) 3 Story (Amer.) 768 at 793.

[52] *Designers Guild Ltd v Russell Williams (Textiles) Ltd* [2001] 1 W.L.R. 2416.

[53] As happened in the Court of Appeal in *Designers Guild Ltd v Russell Williams (Textiles) Ltd*, reported at [2000] F.S.R. 121.

rights of the copyright owner are subject. Indeed, these two issues have been kept separate since the passing of the 1911 Act. Thus copyright is only infringed if a substantial part of the claimant's work has been taken. If this issue is decided against a defendant, the question may then arise as to whether his actions fall with any of the permitted acts. The extent of such acts is today the subject of a defined code.[54]

Substantial part: the test. The essential test is whether the defendant's work has been produced by the substantial use of those features of the claimant's work which, by reason of the knowledge, skill and labour employed in their production, constitute it an original copyright work. The test has been put in a number of similar ways. Has the infringer incorporated a substantial part of the independent skill, labour, etc. contributed by the original author in creating the copyright work?[55] Has the defendant made a substantial use of those features of the claimant's work in which copyright subsists?[56] Has there been a substantial appropriation of the independent labours of the author?[57] Has there been an appropriation of a part of the work on which a substantial part of the author's skill and labour was expended?[58] Has there been an over-borrowing of the skill, labour and judgment which went into the making of the claimant's work?[59] It is therefore often important to ask what are the features of the claimant's work which made it an original work and thus which gave rise to its protection under the law of copyright. For example, with a literary work it may be the skill or effort in expressing thoughts or information in words, or the collecting together and presentation of other material; with a dramatic work, the working out of details of character and plot; with a musical work, the composition of a melody or its orchestration; with an artistic work, the arrangement and representation of subject matter; and so on. If substantial use has been made of these features, then infringement will have occurred. **7–25**

Old law. As already noted, although it has always been the law that a defendant could not escape infringement by using less than the whole of the claimant's work, it was only with the passing of the 1911 Act that the "substantial part" test was expressly included as part of the statutory definition of infringement.[60] Although this was intended to give effect to previous decisions, which are therefore sometimes still good authority,[61] caution must be used in referring to pre-1911 Act cases since the issue of what might properly be taken of a claimant's work was often bound up with questions which would now fall within the description of "fair dealing" or permitted acts, again a topic which was not then part of any statutory code. Thus the question often asked, before the 1911 Act, was whether any "unfair use" had been made of the claimant's work.[62] **7–26**

---

[54] See CDPA 1988, ss.28–00 and Ch.9.

[55] *Designers Guild Ltd v Russell Williams (Textiles) Ltd* [2001] 1 W.L.R. 2416, *per* Lord Scott at 2431.

[56] *Krisarts S.A. v Briarfine Ltd* [1977] F.S.R. 557, at 562.

[57] *Ladbroke (Football) Ltd v William Hill (Football) Ltd* [1964] 1 W.L.R. 273 at 288.

[58] *Cantor Fitzgerald v Tradition (U.K.) Ltd* [2000] R.P.C. 95.

[59] *Ibcos Computers Ltd v Barclays Finance Ltd* [1994] F.S.R. 275. Although in *Cantor Fitzgerald v Tradition (U.K.) Ltd*, *ibid.*, it was thought not helpful to rephrase the test by asking whether there has been an "overborrowing", since this does not add any further useful criteria.

[60] Copyright Act 1911, s.1(2). Under the Literary Copyright Act of 1842, which granted the exclusive right to print or otherwise multiply copies of "books", a book was defined to include every "volume, part or division of a volume". See s.2.

[61] *Chappell & Co v D.C. Thompson & Co* [1928–35] Mac.C.C. 467.

[62] See, *e.g. Weatherby & Sons v International Horse Agency and exchange Ltd* [1910] 2 Ch. 297.

7–27   **Substantial part: a question of mixed fact and law.** The issue of substantial part is a mixture of law and fact in the sense that it requires the court to apply a legal standard to the facts as found.[63] It is a matter of degree in each case[64] and has to be considered having regard to all the circumstances. In the end it is often a matter of impression,[65] in the sense that it generally involves taking into account a number of factors of varying degrees of importance and deciding whether they are sufficient to bring the whole within the legal description of "substantial part", as to which it may be difficult to give precise reasons for arriving at a conclusion one way or the other.[66] There are always borderline cases over which reasonable minds may differ.[67] For these reasons, and since the question involves the application of a not altogether precise legal standard to a combination of features of varying importance, an appeal will not lie against the decision unless the judge misdirected himself[68] or there was no evidence to support it.[69] It can be a matter which is suitable for determination on an application for summary judgment if this is the only live issue and no further relevant evidence will be available at trial.[70]

Although it is perhaps the most common and difficult of all questions which arise in copyright cases, limited assistance is obtained from the authorities. This is because after the application of the general principles discussed below, the matter, as already noted, often becomes one of impression. A court will therefore frequently move from a citation of one or more of the general principles and an enunciation of the relevant factors to a conclusion on the particular facts of the case without further analysis. Generally, therefore, it is not useful to refer to particular decisions as to the quantity taken.[71] As to the general principles, the application of the substantial part test varies with the type of work, whether literary, dramatic, musical, artistic and so on. These categories will be considered separately, but some general propositions can be stated:

   (a) As already stated, the overriding question is whether, in creating the defendant's work, substantial use has been made of the skill and labour

---

[63] *Designers Guild Ltd v Russell Williams (Textiles) Ltd* [2001] 1 W.L.R. 2416, *per* Lord Hoffmann at 2423, although in *King Features Syndicate Inc v O. & M. Kleeman* [1941] A.C. 417, HL, *per* Viscount Maugham at 424, it was described as a question of fact. In the past, it has been described as a jury question (*Beere v Ellis* (1889) 5 T.L.R. 330, applying *Planche v Braham* 4 Bing. N.C. 19), although no doubt the jury has to be directed as to the law.

[64] *Ladbroke (Football) Ltd v William Hill (Football) Ltd* [1964] 1 W.L.R. 273 at 283; *Leco Instruments (U.K.) Ltd v Land Pyrometers Ltd* [1982] R.P.C. 140.

[65] *Merchandising Corporation of America v Harpbond* [1983] F.S.R. 32.

[66] *Designers Guild Ltd v Russell Williams (Textiles) Ltd* [2001] 1 W.L.R. 2416, at 2420, 2426.

[67] *Designers Guild Ltd v Russell Williams (Textiles) Ltd* [2001] 1 W.L.R. 2416.

[68] *ibid.*, at 2418, 2423, applying *Pro Steben Media A.G. v Carlton U.K. Television Ltd* [1999] 1 W.L.R. 605, 612–613, and *Norowzian v Arks Ltd (No. 2)* [2000] F.S.R. 363, 370. See also *Bauman v Fussell* [1978] R.P.C. 485 at 487, 490, where the actual decision may have been surprising on its facts but the Court of Appeal, having come to the conclusion that the trial judge had correctly approached the issue as one of fact, was not prepared to interfere with his finding. Note also that where the decision on substantial part is based partly on assistance given by expert witnesses, the trial judge may be in a better position than the Court of Appeal to assess the importance of various elements of the claimant's work, even if the credibility of witnesses is not in issue. This may be an additional reason for the Court of Appeal not to interfere with the trial judge's decision. See *Designers Guild Ltd v Russell Williams (Textiles) Ltd, ibid.*, at para.28, *per* Lord Hoffmann.

[69] *Bauman v Fussell* [1978] R.P.C. 485, at 489.

[70] Sometimes the application is by the alleged infringer who seeks a declaration of non-infringement, arguing that even if all other matters, such as copying, were established, the material which is alleged to have been taken still does not amount to a substantial part. Usually the judge hearing such an application will be in as good a position as the trial judge to reach a decision on the point, assuming that the copyright owner is not able to persuade the court that, for example, disclosure may throw light on the extent of copying, as in *Leco Instruments (U.K.) Ltd v Land Pyrometers Ltd* [1982] R.P.C. 140 (*sed quaere*). Generally, see para. 22–209, below.

[71] See, *e.g. Bramwell v Halcomb* (1836) 3 My. & Cr. 737 at 738: "It is useless to refer to any particular cases as to quantity."

which went into the creation of the claimant's work and thus those features which made it an original work.

(b) The quality or importance[72] of what has been taken is much more important than the quantity.[73] The issue thus depends therefore not just on the physical amount taken but on its substantial significance[74] or importance to the copyright work,[75] so that the quality, or importance, of the part is frequently more significant than the proportion which the borrowed part bears to the whole. In this context, expressions such as "quality" or "importance" need to be properly understood. A literary work may convey a very important idea but, as already discussed, the law of copyright is concerned with the protection of the expression of such ideas, not the idea itself. In the same way, a drawing may contain important information, but it is the draftsman's work which the law protects, not the information as such.[76] Quality and importance must therefore be understood in terms of the features of the work which made it an original work in the first place. It follows that the quality relevant for the purposes of substantiality in the case of a literary work refers to the literary originality of that which has been copied. In the case of an artistic work, it is the artistic originality of that which has been copied.[77]

(c) Depending on the circumstances, the question may depend on whether what has been taken is novel or striking, or is merely a commonplace arrangement of words or well known material.[78] In this respect it may be a helpful shortcut to ask whether the part taken could itself be the subject of copyright,[79] although this should not be used as a substitute for the proper and full test of substantial part.[80] In any event it is in reality merely a restatement of the basic question, which is whether use has been made of those features of the claimant's work which, by reason of the skill and labour employed in their production, constitute it an original copyright work.

(d) As a corollary of the last point, the more simple or lacking in substantial originality the copyright work, the greater the degree of taking will be needed before the substantial part test is satisfied. In the case of works of little originality, almost exact copying will normally be required to amount to infringement.[81]

(e) The more abstract and simple a copied idea, the less likely it is to constitute a substantial part. Originality, in the sense of the contribution of the

---

[72] *Catnic Components Ltd v Hill & Smith Ltd* [1982] R.P.C. 183 at 223.

[73] There are statements in many authorities to this effect. See, *e.g. Ladbroke (Football) Ltd v William Hill (Football) Ltd* [1964] 1 W.L.R. 273 at 276; *Designers Guild Ltd v Russell Williams (Textiles) Ltd* [2001] 1 W.L.R. 2416, at 2422, 2425, 2431. See also *Bramwell v Halcomb* (1836) 3 My. & Cr. 737 (all the "vital part of another's book, though it might be but a small proportion of the book in quantity").

[74] *Ladbroke (Football) Ltd v William Hill (Football) Ltd* [1964] 1 W.L.R. 273, at 283.

[75] *Designers Guild Ltd v Russell Williams (Textiles) Ltd* [2001] 1 W.L.R. 2416, *per* Lord Millett, at 2426.

[76] The difficult subject of what is protected by an artistic work is considered more fully later in this chapter.

[77] *Designers Guild Ltd v Russell Williams (Textiles) Ltd* [2001] 1 W.L.R. 2416, and see the comment on this aspect of the case in *Newspaper Licensing Agency Ltd v Marks & Spencer plc* [2001] 3 W.L.R. 290.

[78] *Ladbroke (Football) Ltd v William Hill (Football) Ltd* [1964] 1 W.L.R. 273, at 276.

[79] So, in *A v B* [2001] E.M.L.R. 1006, copies of two pages from a personal daily diary were held to amount to a substantial part of the whole diary since the first entry in the diary, and each successive entry, would have been entitled to copyright protection on their own.

[80] *Ladbroke (Football) Ltd v William Hill (Football) Ltd* [1964] 1 W.L.R. 273 at 277.

[81] *Glogau v Land Transport Safety Authority of New Zealand* [1999] 1 N.Z.L.R. 257 (CA of NZ).

author's skill and labour, tends to lie in the detail with which the basic idea is presented.[82]

(f) In general it is wrong to dissect the claimant's work, taking each part which has been copied and asking whether each part could be the subject of copyright if it had stood alone. It is the work as a whole which must be considered,[83] particularly where the originality of the work lies in the creation of the work as a whole. If there is no originality in the creation of the work as a whole, for example where the work is simply a collection of subsidiary works assembled without any sufficient skill or labour, the proper analysis is that there is not one work but rather a number of works. In such a case it would be proper to take each subsidiary work by itself.[84] But this is not a question of substantial part but of identifying the real copyright work or works in issue. A claimant cannot divide up "the work" into small sections, so as to improve his case by arguing that a substantial part of a small section has been taken.[85]

(g) It is wrong to concentrate on the dissimilarities between the works: what is important is a comparison between the copyright work considered as a whole and those elements which have been taken from it.[86] The extent to which the defendant's work is different from the claimant's is irrelevant and, in the context of artistic works for example, it is wrong to ask whether the defendant's work looks like the claimant's.[87]

(h) At this stage it is also wrong merely to compare the similarities between the works where not all the similarities are due to copying. What matters is the significance of what has been copied.

(i) If copying is established or admitted, it is wrong to jump to the conclusion that a substantial part was taken,[88] for copying can clearly occur which falls short of the taking of a substantial part. Nevertheless, where a finding of copying has been made as a result of the inference drawn from the similarities between the two works, it is likely to follow that a substantial part has been taken, although the question still needs to be considered independently.[89] While a finding of copying based in inference may not conclude the issue of copying, in many cases it is almost bound to do so.[90] An exception to this general approach will be where copying has been established because of the presence of a small and non-substantial number of unexplained similarities, the only explanation for which is copying.[91] The court may of course go on to make a finding, based on this small

---

[82] *Designers Guild Ltd v Russell Williams (Textiles) Ltd* [2001] 1 W.L.R. 2416, at 2423, *per* Lord Hoffmann: "Copyright law protects foxes better than hedgehogs".

[83] *ibid.*, at 2421.

[84] As in *Leslie v Young & Sons* [1894] A.C. 335.

[85] *Coogi Australia Pty Ltd v Hysport International Pty Ltd* (1998) 157 A.L.R. 247 (Fed Ct of Aus).

[86] *Designers Guild Ltd v Russell Williams (Textiles) Ltd* [2001] 1 W.L.R. 2416, at 2418, 2422. See also *Entec (Pollution Control) Ltd v Abacus Mouldings* [1992] F.S.R. 332; *Biotrading & Financing OY v Biohit Ltd* [1998] F.S.R. 109 at 121.

[87] *Designers Guild Ltd v Russell Williams (Textiles) Ltd* [2001] 1 W.L.R. 2416; *Baumann v Fussell* [1978] R.P.C. 485; *Spectravest Inc v Aperknit Ltd* [1988] F.S.R. 161 at 170; *Monsoon Ltd v India Imports of Rhode Island Ltd* [1993] F.S.R. 486. An examination of the differences may of course highlight the similarities: *Biotrading & Financing OY v Biohit Ltd* [1998] F.S.R. 109.

[88] *Ibcos Computers Ltd v Barclays Finance Ltd* [1994] F.S.R. 275 at 301.

[89] *Designers Guild Ltd v Russell Williams (Textiles) Ltd* [2001] 1 W.L.R. 2416, at 2418, Lord Bingham, 2426, *per* Lord Millett.

[90] *Designers Guild Ltd v Russell Williams (Textiles) Ltd* [2001] 1 W.L.R. 2416: *cf.* the view of Lord Scott, that such a finding would be determinative of the issue of substantialilty as well as copying. The other Law Lords do not appear to have agreed, and it is suggested that it is wrong as a matter of principle.

[91] As often happens in the case of directories, where deliberate mistakes, or "sleepers", are placed in the copyright work in order to detect infringers.

number of points in common, that copying on a larger scale has taken place,[92] but unless it does so, the court will not be justified in a holding that there has been copying of a substantial part.

(j) If what has been taken from the claimant's work is material which was not original to the maker of the work, because for example it was copied from another work, then it should be disregarded in deciding this issue.[93] If, however, part of the originality of the claimant's work consisted of the choosing and collecting together of unoriginal material, and the defendant has made unfair use of *this* labour and skill, then the test will be satisfied. This can often be seen in compilation cases,[94] but other types of works will also often contain elements taken from earlier works but combined in a new way. In such cases, "old" material which has been copied should not be disregarded: all of what was copied should be taken into account, keeping in mind what it was that made the claimant's work original.[95] On the other hand, "that which would not attract copyright except by reason of its collocation will, when robbed of that collocation, not be a substantial part of the copyright".[96] It is, therefore, often important to isolate what it is the real worth of a work from the copyright point of view, in particular what parts of the work constitute the original contribution of the author and thus represent the skill or labour of his creation.

(k) Although statements to precisely the opposite effect can be found,[97] the relevant question is not whether the part which has been taken forms a substantial part of the defendant's work but whether a substantial part of the claimant's work has been taken. Indeed, whether the part taken forms a small or a substantial part of the defendant's work is irrelevant.[98] Of course, if the defendant's work is of any substance and a large proportion of it has been copied from the claimant's, it may easily follow that an unlawful appropriation of the claimant's labours had been made.

(l) In the case of some works, such as works of reference, it may be that a greater amount of copying is permissible than with other works, such as novels. This is on the basis that one of the purposes of the author was to add to the stock of human knowledge, so that there may be attributed to him an intention that the material in his work, if it is not to become sterile, may be used by the reader with the consequence that the law will allow wider use of such a work.[99] It is suggested, however, that the principle, if it exists, is of limited application, perhaps to historical works only,[1] and is certainly not applicable to all reference works.[2] There seems no good reason why the normal rule should not be that the copyright owner is presumed to have intended that such use should be made of his work as the law generally allows in the case of copyright works and no more. Any wider right to use could only be the subject of one of the permitted acts or some implied licence, a limited concept.

---

[92] As in *Comprop Ltd v Moran* [2002] J.L.R. 222 (Royal Ct of Jersey).

[93] *Warwick Film Productions Ltd v Eisinger* [1969] Ch. 508.

[94] See para. 7–44, below.

[95] *Biotrading & Financing OY v Biohit Ltd* [1998] F.S.R. 109 at 122 (designs for parts of pipettes including shapes taken from earlier drawings but combined with new shapes).

[96] *Ladbroke (Football) Ltd v William Hill (Football) Ltd* [1964] 1 W.L.R. 273 at 293.

[97] e.g. *Neale v Harmer* (1897) 13 T.L.R. 209.

[98] *Designers Guild Ltd v Russell Williams (Textiles) Ltd* [2001] 1 W.L.R. 2416, *per* Lord Millett, at 2425. The same point is made in *Cantor Fitzgerald v Tradition (U.K.) Ltd* [2000] R.P.C. 95, at 133.

[99] *Ravenscroft v Herbert* [1980] R.P.C. 193 at 205.

[1] This was the subject matter in *Ravenscroft*.

[2] *Comprop Ltd v Moran* [2002] J.L.R. 222 (Royal Ct of Jersey).

7–28   **Other considerations.** A number of other considerations are sometimes put forward as helping to decide whether a substantial part has been taken but today need to be treated with caution:

(a) Are the two works in competition? Has the value of the claimant's work been diminished? Is the market for the claimant's work likely or unlikely to be affected? Tests of these kind are sometimes applied[3] but it is suggested that today they need to be used with caution. Obviously, if it can be seen that the market for lawful reproductions of the claimant's work has been adversely affected, this may be because a substantial part has been taken, particularly if the reason for this is that the public regards the defendant's work as an adequate substitute for the claimant's.[4] Care needs to be taken, however, since this decline may simply be the result of lawful (*i.e.* non-infringing) competition. Conversely, it is possible to imagine many cases where the businesses of the claimant and the defendant do not compete, but unfair advantage of the claimant's skill and labour may yet have been taken.[5] In such a case it is difficult to see why the absence of competition should help answer the question in favour of the defendant. Where, however, the two works are clearly in the same market and compete, and the claimant's work would be expected to suffer if a substantial part had been taken, the absence of any injury may be a helpful indication.

(b) A rough practical test which is sometimes applied is: "what is worth copying is worth protecting".[6] An indication of the value of what was taken may, of course, be the fact that the defendant has chosen to take it rather than rely on his own efforts.[7] Clearly, however, the test needs to be applied with caution since otherwise the copying of any part of a work would amount to an infringement: it should serve as a guide only.[8] The practice of "sampling" musical works and sound recordings, discussed later, and the use of 'Ringtones', may be appropriate cases for the application of this

---

[3] See the statement Story J. quoted above in *Folsom v Marsh* (1841) 2 Story 100 at 116, cited with approval in *Scott v Stanford* (1867) L.R. 3 Eq. 718, that: "… we must, in deciding questions of this sort, look to … [*inter alia*] … the degree in which the use may prejudice the sale, or diminish the profits, or supersede the objects, of the original work". In *Weatherby & Sons v International Horse Agency and Exchange Ltd* [1910] 2 Ch. 297, Parker J. stated that the nature of the two works and the likelihood or unlikelihood of competition was not only relevant but might be the determining factor in a case. But see the next but one footnote as to this case. Another example is *Cambridge University Press v University Tutorial Press Ltd* (1928) 75 R.P.C. 335, where this factor was described as useful, although not determinative. Older cases on the point include *Dodsley v Kinnersely* (1737) 1 Amb. 402; *Gyles v Wilcox* (1740) 2 Atk. 141; *Hawkesworth v Newbery* (1776) Lofft. 755; *Bell v Whitehead* (1839) 8 L.J. Ch. 141; *cf. e.g. Dickens v Lee* (1844) 8 Jur. 183, suggesting that the claimant is the best person to judge whether his work is harmed.

[4] As, *e.g.* with an abridgment or other edited version.

[5] Thus in *Weatherby & Sons v International Horse Agency and Exchange Ltd* [1910] 2 Ch. 297, Parker J. went on to say (see the previous but one footnote) that unfair use of the claimant's work might be made even where there is no likelihood of competition, since copyright is a right of property. For an example, see *Kipling v Genatosan Ltd* [1917–23] Mac.C.C. 203, where four lines from Kipling's "If" were used in an advertisement for the defendant's medicinal preparation. Held: an infringement.

[6] *University of London Press Ltd v University Tutorial Press Ltd* [1916] 2 Ch. 601 at 610, cited with approval in *Ladbroke (Football) Ltd v William Hill (Football) Ltd* [1964] 1 W.L.R. 273 at 288.

[7] *Campbell v Scott* (1842) 11 Sim. 31, *per* Shadwell V.-C. at 39: "I do not think that it is necessary for me to consider whether the selections in this case are the very cream and essence of all that [the claimant] ever wrote; but it is pretty plain that they would not have been inserted in the Defendant's work, unless the party who selected them thought that they were very attractive in themselves".

[8] *Ibcos Computers Ltd v Barclays Mercantile Highland Finance Ltd* [1994] F.S.R. 275; *Cantor Fitzgerald v Tradition (U.K.) Ltd* [2000] R.P.C. 95, at 133; *Network Ten Pty Ltd v TCN Channel None Pty Ltd* [2004] HCA 14, 59 I.P.R. 1 (2004).

principle. The test can also have no real application where the whole point
of the defendant's work was to refer to works such as the claimant's, for
example, in a work of criticism or reference.

(c) On the same principle, it has been said that the basis of copyright law is
the Seventh Commandment: "Thou shalt not steal",[9] but this is not
particularly helpful since it does not identify what it is permissible to take.
As a statement it can neither enhance the rights of an owner nor extend
the ambit of infringement.[10] It also does not emphasise the real basis of
copyright law, which is that one man must not be permitted to appropriate
the result of another's labour.[11]

(d) Has there been an *animus furandi*[12] on the part of the defendant, in the
sense of an intention on his part to take for the purpose of saving himself
labour?[13] Historically, this test was sometimes applied,[14] but it is suggested that today the defendant's intentions are irrelevant,[15] as is whether
use of the claimant's work is openly acknowledged or not.[16]

(e) Has the defendant expended a sufficient amount of skill and labour on his
work such that it qualifies as an original work itself? Is the defendant's
work itself a useful work, not being just a copy of the claimant's? This
test was often applied in the older cases[17] but today is no longer good
law.[18]

"Little and often". A problem arises where a defendant regularly takes a small   **7–29**
amount of material from the claimant's works, for example, a few statistics each
week from figures published by the claimant. Assuming that the taking of the material from just one issue is not enough of itself to amount to an infringement,
does the defendant infringe by his cumulative actions? There are two types of situation to be considered, first, where the takings are made from different copyright
works, secondly, where the takings are all made from the same copyright work:

(1) In *Trade Auxiliary Co v Middlesborough, etc. Association*,[19] the claimant
published a nationwide weekly list of all bills of sale and deeds of arrangement which had been registered, running to about 400 items. The
defendant took details which were of local interest to readers of its publi-

---

[9] *e.g. MacMillan & Co. Ltd v Cooper* (1923) 40 T.L.T. 186, PC, at p.187.
[10] *C.B.S. Songs Ltd v Amstrad plc* [1988] A.C. 1013, *per* Lord Templeman at 1057.
[11] *L.B. (Plastics) Ltd v Swish Products Ltd* [1979] R.P.C. 611, HL. And see *Autospin (Oil Seals) Ltd v Beehive Spinning* [1995] R.P.C. 683, *per* Laddie J. at 700 suggesting that it is because the claimant has so often blatantly stolen the results of the claimant's labours in many cases that the courts have applied this principle with "almost evangelical fervour".
[12] *i.e.* an intention of stealing.
[13] *Jarrold v Houlston* (1857) 3 K. & J. 708. The distinction made is usually between those cases where a defendant has taken the claimant's work and promulgated it as his own, and works of criticism, abridgement, etc. where there is no disguise of the source.
[14] See, *e.g. Carey v Kearsley* (1802) 4 Esp. 168; *Mawman v Tegg* (1826) 2 Russ. 385; *Lewis v Fullarton* (1839) 2 Beav. 6; *Reade v Lacy* (1861) 1 J. & H. 524. However, the principle was also applied in the relatively modern case of *Ravenscroft v Herbert* [1980] R.P.C. 193, at 203, 207.
[15] See para. 7–07, above.
[16] This only becomes relevant in the context of fair dealing. See paras 9–19 *et seq*, below.
[17] A sample of such cases includes: *Gyles v Wilcox* (1740) 2 Atk. 141; *Carey v Kearsley* (1802) 4 Esp. 168; *Wilkins v Aikin* (1810) 17 Ves. 422; *Mawman v Tegg* (1826) 2 Russ. 385; *Bramwell v Halcomb* (1836) 3 My. & Cr. 737; *Dickens v Lee* (1844) 8 Jur. 183; *Spiers v Brown* (1858) 6 W.R. 352; *Hotten v Arthur* (1863) 1 H. & M. 603. *Glyn v Weston Feature Film Co* [1916] 1 Ch. 261 is a later example.
[18] *Schweppes Ltd v Wellingtons Ltd* [1984] F.S.R. 210, followed in *Williamson Music Ltd v Pearson Partnership* [1987] F.S.R. 97. The headnote in *Joy Music Ltd v Sunday Pictorial Newspapers (1920) Ltd* [1960] 2 Q.B. 60 is incorrect: *Williamson Music.*
[19] (1889) 40 Ch.D. 425.

cation, amounting to about four per week, and was held to have infringed.[20] In *Cate v Devon and Exeter Constitutional Newspaper Co*,[21] brought by the same claimants, the defendant similarly took a small number of entries for its local readership[22] and was held to have infringed on the ground that all that was material for the purpose of the defendant's newspaper had been taken and copied exactly and systematically, week by week, as of right. It is suggested, however, that in so far as each work is a separate copyright work, each must be looked at separately to see whether a substantial part of *that* work has been taken. It is not legitimate to combine separate works and ask whether a substantial part of the combination has been appropriated. If, of course, the claimant's work can be regarded as one serial work published in instalments, the position may be different,[23] but it is suggested that this is likely to be an artificial solution.[24] It is also not easy to see why, as a matter of principle, if a defendant acts lawfully by taking an extract from one publication, his actions should become unlawful if repeated in relation to successive publications, however aggravating his conduct might be to the claimant.[25] These two cases have since been explained as having been decided at a time when the relevant statute contained no reference to substantial part, and the only issue was whether the infringement was sufficiently minimal as not to warrant the grant of an injunction: they did not decide that a "substantial part", as that expression is now understood, had been taken.[26] Whether or not this is correct, it is suggested that the cases would not be decided in the same way today. So, where there had been regular copying of small extracts (each not a substantial part in itself) from successive editions of newspapers, and thus separate copyright works, it was held that this did not cumulatively amount to the taking of a substantial part.[27]

(2) In *Football League Ltd v Littlewoods Pools Ltd*,[28] the claimant had produced a chronological list of the 2,000 or so weekly Football League championship fixtures to be played in the season. Each fortnight, the defendant copied the list of the fixtures being played by the 90 or so clubs for that fortnight for the purpose of preparing its pools coupons. There was, therefore, only one copyright work which was alleged to have been infringed, the case being that small amounts had been repeatedly taken. The defendant was held to have infringed, relying on *Cate v Devon and Exeter Constitutional Newspaper Co*, and the decision has since been regarded as correctly decided on the basis that the statutory requirement of substantial part was satisfied by the repeated, systematic copying from the same work, such that the entire list was in the end copied.[29] On the facts, however, it is suggested that each fortnightly list was clearly an infringement of the whole chronological list and it was unnecessary to call

---

[20] The then relevant Act, the 1842 Act, contained no express "substantial part" test. The defendant argued that the use was *de minimis*.

[21] (1889) 40 Ch.D. 500.

[22] In one case, a single entry only. See p.507 of the report.

[23] See the suggestion to this effect made in *Electronic Techniques (Anglia) Ltd v Critchley Components Ltd* [1997] F.S.R. 401.

[24] For example, if the various lists made for the claimant in the two cases had been made by different authors, although each employed by the claimant, they would clearly be different works.

[25] See *Electronic Techniques (Anglia) Ltd v Critchley Components Ltd* [1997] F.S.R. 401 for a discussion of some of the illogical results which follow from the decision in *Cate*.

[26] *Newspaper Licensing Agency Ltd v Marks & Spencer plc* [2001] R.P.C. 76, CA.

[27] *Newspaper Licensing Agency Ltd v Marks & Spencer plc* [2001] R.P.C. 76, CA..

[28] [1959] Ch. 637.

[29] *Newspaper Licensing Agency Ltd v Marks & Spencer plc* [2001] R.P.C. 76, CA.

in aid the cumulative effect of the defendant's actions. In contrast, if, for example, a local newspaper had each week published the details of the one match being played by its local club, the publication of that one fixture in the first week would surely not infringe, and the newspaper's actions could surely not become infringing in the future by some process of accumulation.[30] Otherwise, presumably it would follow that an infringement would occur once the cumulative amount taken went past the threshold of a substantial part. Presumably, it would then also follow that at this point all previous copying would retrospectively become an infringement, and that what was previously not an infringing copy would now become an infringing copy. This type of conclusion shows the difficulty with the point. The position might well be different if, at the beginning of the season, the newspaper had published a complete list of all matches to be played by the club that season. It has been pointed out elsewhere[31] that it is possible to apply this principle in the difficult case of the transient copying of small fragments of a work in RAM or other temporary computer memory.

Parodies and burlesques. The fact that a defendant's work may be a parody or burlesque of the claimant's is not a relevant consideration when considering the issue of substantial part.[32] The test remains the same, whether in the context of literary,[33] dramatic,[34] musical[35] or artistic works.[36] The point is discussed further in relation to these classes of works.   **7–30**

C. LITERARY, DRAMATIC, MUSICAL AND ARTISTIC WORKS

In relation to literary, dramatic, musical and artistic works, the exclusive right of copying is defined to mean the right of reproducing the work in any material form.[37] For this purpose, reproducing a work in material form includes storing it in any medium by electronic means[38] and making transient copies or ones which are incidental to some other use.[39] Although in other contexts the word "reproduce" is sometimes used in the neutral sense of producing something similar, whether by copying or not,[40] it is clear that in the present context that the word   **7–31**

---

[30] See, again, *Electronic Techniques (Anglia) Ltd v Critchley Components Ltd* [1997] F.S.R. 401, for a discussion of the illogicalities involved. Laddie J. there suggested that a defendant's conduct might be viewed as one continuous act, a proposition which is again suggested to be artificial. As Laddie J. himself points out at 409, a small amount of copying is permissible, even though the labour of the claimant is thereby appropriated.

[31] See para. 7–19, above.

[32] *Schweppes Ltd v Wellingtons Ltd* [1984] F.S.R. 210; *Williamson Music Ltd v Pearson Partnership* [1987] F.S.R. 97. Whether there can be a "fair dealing" defence in the case of parodies is considered elsewhere. See para. 9–41, below.

[33] *Williamson Music Ltd v Pearson Partnership* [1987] F.S.R. 97.

[34] *Glyn v Weston Feature Film Co* [1916] 1 Ch. 261; *Carlton v Mortimer* [1917–23] Mac.C.C. 194.

[35] *Francis Day & Hunter Ltd v Feldman & Co* [1914] 2 Ch. 728; *Williamson Music Ltd v Pearson Partnership* [1987] F.S.R. 97.

[36] *Twentieth Century Fox Film Corp. Ltd v Anglo Amalgamated Film Distributors Ltd, The Times,* January 22, 1965; *Schweppes Ltd v Wellingtons Ltd* [1984] F.S.R. 210; *A.G.L. Sydney Ltd v Shortland County Council* [1990] A.I.P.C. 90–661 (Fed Ct of Aus) (parody of advertisement by advertisement).

[37] CDPA 1988, s.17(2).

[38] CDPA 1988, s.17(2)

[39] CDPA 1988, s.17(6).

[40] In *Purefoy Engineering Co. Ltd v Sykes, Boxall & Co. Ltd* (1954) 72 R.P.C. 89, Evershed M.R. at 99, gave the example of the effects a naturally occurring event, such as a storm, being "reproduced" by a later storm.

"reproduce" essentially means "copy".[41] However, even though the two words are now often used interchangeably in this context, historically the expression "reproduce in any material form" encompassed a wider class of act than simply "copy". For example, under the law before the 1911 Act, a musical work was not copied by the making of a mechanical device which could reproduce the musical work in terms of sound.[42] The later Acts made clear that in the case of literary, dramatic or musical works, references to reproducing a work were to include their reproduction in the form of a record or film.[43] Although the 1988 Act does not contain such express provision, there can be no doubt that the law has not changed on this point.[44]

7–32 **Reproduction versus adaptation.** In relation to literary, dramatic and musical works, there exists a separate category of restricted act, namely the making of an adaptation, this being expressly defined, but including for example in relation to a literary work, a translation or a dramatisation of it.[45] The whole topic is discussed in more detail under the heading of "Adaptation"[46] but it is suggested, although the point is not clear, that in some cases at least, a version of a work may amount to both a reproduction of it and an adaptation of it.

(i) Literary works

(a) *Introduction*

7–33 The general principles have already been considered. As has been pointed out, copying of a literary work may take place not only when the work is reproduced in the same medium, for example in writing or in print, but also when reproduction occurs in some other material form. So, for example, a song lyric is copied when it is reproduced on a sound carrier such as a compact disc and a written work is copied when it is stored in digital form on the hard disk of a computer. As with all categories of works, the making of transient or incidental copies amounts to copying just as much as the making of permanent copies.[47]

7–34 **Defendant's work must represent claimant's.** It has already been pointed out that in general terms a work is not reproduced unless what has been produced represents the work in some real sense. A description in a novel of a scene from nature is thus not infringed by a drawing made to depict that scene. So, in the context of a literary work, the copyright in a book which described a method of teaching mathematics was not infringed by making a series of coloured rods

---

[41] *British Leyland Motor Corp. Ltd v Armstrong Patents Co. Ltd* [1986] A.C. 577, *per* Lord Griffiths at 646; *Ladbroke (Football) Ltd v William Hill (Football) Ltd* [1964] 1 W.L.R. 273 at 276; *Purefoy Engineering Co. Ltd v Sykes, Boxall & Co. Ltd* (1954) 72 R.P.C. 89; *Norowzian v Arks Ltd* [1998] F.S.R. 394 (the words "reproducing the work in any material form" is a "commonsense explanation of what copying in relation to a literary work must mean. What is protected is the work itself").

[42] See *Boosey v Whight* [1900] 1 Ch. 122, decided under the 1842 Copyright Act, where it was held that perforated rolls for mechanical organs were not "copies" of the claimant's sheet music. However, under the 1842 Act, the claimants were the owners not of a musical work as that expression would now be understood but of the copyright in sheet music, and thus the exclusive right of multiplying copies of those sheets, *i.e.* essentially as a book. The law was changed by the 1911 Act. See s.1(2)(b) of that Act.

[43] Copyright Act 1956, s.48(1). The Copyright Act 1911, s.1(2)(d) was to the same effect.

[44] *Norowzian v Arks Ltd* [1998] F.S.R. 394. And see also CDPA 1988, s.172(2) (no departure from previous law merely as a result of a change of expression).

[45] CDPA 1988, s.21.

[46] See para. 7–121, below.

[47] CDPA 1988, s.17(6). See, however, s.28A and para. 9–15, below, as to the permitted act of making transient or incidental copies.

which demonstrated that method,[48] the copyright in written instructions for the making of a garment was not infringed by making the garment,[49] and the copyright in the words and numerals in knitting guides was not infringed by making garments to those instructions.[50] Again the copyright in a book of recipes is not infringed by making a dish according to one of the recipes.[51]

The problem can also arise in relation to literary works that consist of tables or compilations. Such works are obviously infringed by their unlicensed and substantial reproduction in the form of another written table or compilation, but do other forms of copying amount to a reproduction in a material form? In particular, is a list of components or articles reproduced for these purposes by assembling those components, either loosely or in the form of composite article amount to a reproduction? The question was discussed, although not answered, in *Anacon Corp. Ltd v Environmental Research Technology Ltd*,[52] where Jacob J. held that copyright subsisted in a circuit diagram both as an artistic work[53] and a literary work, the literary work consisting of the written information which the diagram contained, even though it was largely in the form of code (*i.e.* symbols for electrical components and how they interconnected). It was held that the literary copyright was infringed by the making of a "net list", that is, a list of all the components, and what other components they were connected to and where, since the net list reproduced the information found in the literary work. Whether the literary copyright was also infringed by the making of a circuit from the circuit diagram was left undecided, but with the indication that while the mere presence of the components on a circuit board would not make it an infringement, if the components were marked then it might do so, on the grounds that one could then read the information from the circuit board. In *Sandman v Panasonic U.K. Ltd*,[54] Pumfrey J. expressed the view that a circuit would be a reproduction of a circuit diagram as a literary work because it would contain all the literary content of the copyright work, even though it would require analysis for it to be extracted. It is not clear whether Pumfrey J. was referring to a case in which the components were marked, and indeed he adds that the question might turn on the facts. If the question turns on whether the components are marked or not, it is suggested that this is an artificial distinction, for there seems no good reason to distinguish between cases where the components carry a written description, or one where the components are, for example, colour-coded in accordance with industry conventions or the manufacturer's system, or one where they are unmarked and require destructive analysis to determine what they are. It also is artificial, because if interconnects are part of the literary information which makes up the literary work[55] such interconnects will not be "marked" but could be "read" by a visual inspection of their layout.

(b) *Substantial part: general considerations*

Wholly new versus derivative works. The general question of what amounts to a substantial part has already been considered. Two separate types of cases can

7–35

---

[48] *Cuisenaire v Reed* [1963] V.R. 719; *Cuisenaire v South West Imports Ltd* [1968] 1 Ex.C.R. 493.
[49] *Lambretta Clothing Co Ltd v Teddy Smith (UK) Ltd* [2003] EWHC 1204 (Ch), at para.78 (first instance only).
[50] *Brigid Foley Ltd v Ellott* [1982] R.P.C. 433.
[51] *J & S Davis (Holdings) Ltd v Wright Health Group Ltd* [1988] R.P.C. 403 at 414; *Edge Pty Ltd v Apple Computer Inc* (1986) 65 A.L.R. 33 at 61.
[52] [1994] F.S.R. 659.
[53] Which had not been infringed: see para. 7–55, below.
[54] [1998] F.S.R. 651.
[55] See para. 3–17, above.

be identified in relation to literary works, first, where the claimant's work is essentially a new work, such as a novel, poem, etc. where no part of it was derived from other sources, and, secondly, where the claimant's work is to some extent derivative, having been created by drawing on earlier works or other source material. Where the claimant's work is wholly original in the first sense, the question of substantial part is uncomplicated by the presence in the claimant's work of unoriginal material. In the case of a derivative work on the other hand, a number of complicating factors may arise. The first is that an explanation of independent creation rather than copying as the reason for similarities in the works may be more credible. The second is that a work of this kind may be protected on two levels, (a) the actual language used to convey the information, etc. and (b) the work of compilation in assembling and presenting the materials. Copyright in such a work may be infringed if there has been substantial copying of the work of compilation although little language copying.[56] Thirdly, and related to this, where the claimant's work contains extracts from other works, it may be necessary to examine closely what it is that the defendant has taken and what it was that made the claimant's work original, *i.e.* what was the nature of the labour or skill which the claimant contributed. If what has been taken was not original to the claimant's work, because for example it was itself taken from another work, there will be no infringement unless the originality of the claimant's work consisted of the choosing and bringing together of such material and it is this labour and skill which has been appropriated.

7–36   **Non-literal or non-textual copying.** It is not essential for the purposes of infringement that the very words used in the claimant's work have been taken. As the cases about précis, etc. discussed below, clearly show, so-called non-textual copying may amount to an infringement just as much as literal copying. The principle is not confined to précis and the like, however, but extends to any case in which there has been a substantial taking of the original skill and labour of the author in expressing his ideas, thoughts, etc. Thus the copyright in a historical work was infringed where there was a substantial taking of the information which the author had assembled,[57] a novel may be infringed where a substantial amount of the incident, plot and characterisation has been copied in another novel.[58] Most of the cases on the point relate to dramatic works, or the dramatisation of literary works,[59] but the general point of principle is the same.

7–37   **Wholly "new" literary work: verbatim extracts.** Quantity is not the appropriate test. Thus the taking of four lines out of 32 from a serious poem may be an infringement,[60] yet four lines consisting of some 20 quite simple words having no sort of literary merit taken from the refrain of a popular song may not be.[61]

---

[56] The copyright protection afforded to compilations is considered in the next section.

[57] *Ravenscroft v Herbert* [1980] R.P.C. 193.

[58] *Designers Guild Ltd v Russell Williams (Textiles) Ltd* [2001] 1 W.L.R. 2416, *per* Lord Hoffmann at 2422; *Cantor Fitzgerald v Tradition (U.K.) Ltd* [2000] R.P.C. 95; *Brighton v Jones* [2004] EWHC 1157 (Ch); *Christoffer v Poseidon Film Distributors Ltd* [2000] E.C.D.R. 487, citing *Ravenscroft v Herbert* [1980] R.P.C. 193, and *Harman Pictures NV v Osborne* [1967] 1 W.L.R. 723, although on the facts *Christoffer* appears to have been a case of the copying of a dramatic work by the making of a film and other preparatory acts; *Autospin (Oil Seals) Ltd v Beehive Spinning* [1995] R.P.C. 683 at 697, although citing the example of a novel being turned into a play, a clear case of infringement by making an adaptation. See para. 7–124, below.

[59] See paras 7–52 and 7–124, below.

[60] *Kipling v Genatosan Ltd* [1917–23] Mac.C.C. 203: the four lines forming the "essential part of the crescendo" of Kipling's "If".

[61] *Chappell & Co v D.C. Thompson & Co* [1928–35] Mac.C.C. 467. The decision was clearly influenced by the fact that the words were being used by the defendant as part of a serial story and therefore caused no damage to the claimant's work as part of a popular song.

Abstracts, préçis and other abridgments. A version of another work, whether   7–38
it involves the verbatim reproduction of the actual language of part of another
work or is merely a paraphrase of it will, if it in any real sense acts as a substitute
for the original, almost inevitably involve the reproduction of a substantial part of
it. So, in a modern case,[62] the copyrights in two novels and a play were infringed
by study notes produced for schools which reproduced either verbatim or in *oratio obliqua* between five and 10 per cent of the works. It was under this heading
that the question in many of the early cases arose as to whether copying a part of
the claimant's work was an infringement[63] but few of the cases are good law
today, turning as they often did on whether the claimant's work had been
prejudiced or whether the defendant's work itself had involved independent judgment or was useful.[64]

More difficult are the cases where a work has been summarised, not with the
purpose of being a substitute, but to provide an outline of the contents. No rule
can be laid down but it is suggested that if the author of the préçis has not simply
taken the shortcut of repeating various passages from the claimant's work, and
thus used another's labours, but instead by his own efforts and in his own words
distilled the essence of the ideas being expressed into a short piece, infringement
is unlikely.[65] In contrast, where a work is summarised in detail so as give a
complete picture of the claimant's work, infringement is likely.[66] A helpful
example is *Valcarenghi v The Gramophone Co. Ltd*,[67] where the plots of various
operas had been summarised in the defendant's publication, along with other
historical details about the works. The defendant was held not to have infringed
where the plots had been summarised, some in very bare outline only, others in
more detail, but in neither case having the effect of transposing them into short
stories.

Parodies, etc. The general principle here has already been discussed. The fact   7–39
that the defendant's intention may have been to parody the claimant's work is no
defence if what has been taken is a substantial part of it, the test being unaffected
the defendant's motives. Of course, with most parodies of literary works it will
be the style rather than the actual words which has been copied. Unless there has
been substantial copying of language, there will be no infringement.[68]

---

[62] *Sillitoe v McGraw-Hill Book Co. (U.K.) Ltd* [1983] F.S.R. 545.

[63] Some of the old cases include: *Gyles v Wilcox* (1740) 2 Atk. 141 (work colourably shortened
only); *Bell v Walker* (1784) 1 Brick 450 and *Story v Holcombe* (1847) 4 McLean 306 (facts, and
terms in which they were related, the same); *Butterworth v Robinson* (1801) 5 Ves. 709 (law
reports repeated verbatim, leaving out only the headnotes); *D'Almaine v Boosey* (1835) 1 Y. & C.
Ex. 288 (whole chapters taken); *Sweet v Benning* (1855) 15 C.B. 459 (headnotes from law reports
repeated verbatim); *Saunders v Smith* (1883) 3 My. & Cr. 711 (law reports).

[64] See para. 7–28, above for a discussion of some of the factors which are suggested not to be relevant today.

[65] Rightly or wrongly, much is likely to depend on the perceived purpose of the defendant's work,
in particular whether it was to take advantage of the claimant's work for his own benefit. Note
also the permitted act contained in CDPA 1988, s.60 which allows the copying of the claimant's
own abstract of a scientific or technical article, where there is one. See para. 9–163, below.

[66] See, *e.g. Sillitoe v McGraw-Hill Book Co (U.K.) Ltd* [1983] F.S.R. 545, where the copyright in a
play was held to be infringed by detailed, scene-by-scene summaries, described by the judge as
"more than a synopsis of the play". Admittedly the infringement amounted to an adaptation of
the play (*i.e.* conversion into a non-dramatic work) rather than a reproduction, but it is suggested
the same result would have followed if the claimant's work been a literary rather than a dramatic
work.

[67] [1928–35] Mac.C.C. 301. Again, strictly, the case was concerned with infringement by the making of an adaptation (*i.e.* turning a dramatic work into a non-dramatic one) rather than by
reproduction.

[68] Which was the position in *Williamson Music Ltd v Pearson Partnership* [1987] F.S.R. 97 where
the words of Oscar Hammerstein II's lyrics for "There is Nothin' Like a Dame" were parodied,

7–40   **Newspaper reports.** Although it is often said that there is no copyright in news, just as there is no copyright in ideas or information, copyright can clearly subsist in the form in which news is expressed[69] and will be infringed if the expression of that story has been reproduced.[70] The difficult balance here is between protecting a journalist's literary effort as against the wider public interest in dissemination to the public at large.[71] It has been pointed out that if the law is too restrictive in this area, a newspaper which obtained a scoop from an exclusive and confidential source would have a monopoly in the story.[72] So where a news story about a drowning man was reduced from a piece of some 83 lines to one of 18, becoming in effect a restatement of the facts, there was no infringement.[73] On the other side of the line, where one newspaper had taken from another verbatim quotations attributed to an interviewee running to some 154 words, infringement was established.[74] As always, it is important to analyse the true nature of the claimant's work. Thus, if the originality lies in the collecting together and presentation of information, so that the work has elements of a "compilation copyright"[75] then an infringement is likely if the defendant, in covering the same story, has simply saved the effort of doing this work himself. So, a wire news service was held to have infringed the copyright in three cocoa crop reports on the basis that the most important and interesting parts of the reports had been taken, including a number of direct quotations and statistical information.[76]

(c) *Compilations, databases and other works of reference*

7–41   **Compilations generally.** Disputes frequently arise over whether a work containing information or material obtained from elsewhere has been copied or, if this is admitted or proved, as to what use can properly be made of such a work. Copying is often suspected because compilations relating to the same subject matter will of necessity often have similarities. It should be borne in mind in this area that although a claimant's work may contain much material that is not original, the value of the work may lie in the searching out and selection of such material. The general principle, discussed in more detail below, is that even where two works will inevitably contain similarities, the maker of the second must do for himself

---

but not copied, in an advertisement for a bus service. (The music for the advertisement was, however, sufficiently like Richard Rogers' to attract an interim injunction.)

[69] *Walter v Steinkopff* [1892] 3 Ch. 489. See para. 3–19, above.

[70] The cases in this area are mostly concerned with the question of whether copyright subsists in a news story, rather than whether substantial reproduction has occurred.

[71] CPDA 1988, s.30(2) provides that fair dealing with a work for the purpose of reporting current events is not an infringement if accompanied by a sufficient acknowledgment. See generally para. 9–44, below. But as between trade rivals, the dealing may not be fair and it may be inappropriate to provide any acknowledgment.

[72] *Express Newspapers plc v News (U.K.) Ltd* [1990] 1 W.L.R. 1320 at 1325. Sir Nicolas Browne-Wilkinson V.-C. suggested that the escape from a finding of infringement might lie in the fair dealing provisions (see above) or the implication of an implied licence. Both these solutions have difficulties in practice and it is suggested the first question must always be whether a substantial part of the journalist's work has been reproduced.

[73] *Springfield v Thame* (1903) 89 L.T. 242. In fact, the case was decided on the rather confusing ground that the author of the original piece was not the author of the rewritten version (as to which, see para. 4–16, above), but the point was also made that what the defendant had published was news, not the claimant's expression of it.

[74] *Express Newspapers plc v News (U.K.) Ltd* [1990] 1 W.L.R. 1320. Although there is no discussion of the point, it is implicit in the judgment that a substantial part had been taken. And see also *Walter v Steinkopff* [1892] 3 Ch. 489, where substantial passages were taken from the claimant's newspaper.

[75] See para. 7–44, below.

[76] *PCR Ltd v Dow Jones Telerate Ltd* [1998] F.S.R. 170.

what was done in the making of the first.[77] A defendant is not entitled to make unfair use of the labour or skill which was expended on the production of the claimant's work. It is in this area that copying can often be detected by the repetition of mistakes, redundant features and even innocuous material deliberately included to trap pirates ("seeds" or "sleepers").

Databases. Many literary works include, to a greater or lesser extent, material   **7–42**
which has been gathered from other sources. Such works may range from "pure" literary works, for example, works, through anthologies, of a historical nature, to a bare list of data, amounting to a table, compilation or database.[78] In considering this topic today, it must be borne in mind that following the implementation of the Database Directive[79] databases are treated differently from other literary works of this kind. The topic is considered in detail elsewhere[80] but in outline:

(a) Although tables and compilations are not defined by the 1988 Act, they generally comprise works in which information or ideas have been gathered from other sources and presented in a single work. From a copyright point of view, their value lies in the labour of compiling or making the selection of the material. Historically, such works were treated as original and thus protected even though their creation might have involved no intellectual effort but only mere labour.[81] As will be seen in the next paragraph, databases are now excluded from the class of literary works consisting of a "table or compilation".

(b) Historically, a "database" would have fallen within the description of a table or compilation, but databases, as defined by the Act, are now excluded from this category and treated as a separately defined category of literary work.[82] A database for this purpose is defined to be a collection of independent works, data or other materials which (a) are arranged in a systematic or methodical way and (b) are individually accessible by electronic or other means.[83] As to this:

   (i) A "database", so defined, will be protected as a literary work provided that it satisfies a modified originality test, namely, that by reason of the selection and arrangement of its contents it constituted the author's own intellectual creation.[84] "Sweat-of-the-brow" works which fall within the definition of database but which are not original in this sense are therefore now excluded from copyright protection.

   (ii) A database within this definition but now excluded from copyright protection because it fails the modified originality test may yet be protected under the separate, *sui generis* database extraction right if there was substantial investment in obtaining, verifying or presenting the contents of the database.[85]

---

[77] *Kelly v Morris* (1866) L.R. 1 Eq. 697. See para. 7–44, below.
[78] See CDPA 1988, s.3(1). A historical work which includes information which has been collected from other sources can of course be regarded, *pro tanto*, as a compilation.
[79] Council Directive 96/9, implemented by the Copyright and Rights in Databases Regulations 1997 (SI 1997/3032).
[80] See Ch.18, below.
[81] So called "sweat-of-the-brow" works. See para. 3–145, above.
[82] CDPA 1988, s.3(1).
[83] Precisely what is included within this definition is discussed elsewhere. See paras 3–22, above and 18–05, below.
[84] CDPA 1988, s.3A(2). As to the requirement of originality, see paras 3–144 *et seq.*, above.
[85] See the Copyright and Rights in Databases Regulations 1997, reg.13(1) and Ch.18, below.

7–43 **Databases: transitional.** A database which was made on or before March 27, 1996[86] and was in copyright on January 1, 1998[87] (*i.e.* which satisfied the old originality test) will continue to enjoy copyright protection for its full term under section 12 of the 1988 Act.[88]

The present discussion is therefore concerned with literary works of all kinds, including tables, compilations and databases, except those databases made after March 27, 1996 which do not satisfy the modified originality requirements. Even within these confines, it may still be important to ask whether the work alleged to be infringed is a database properly so-called under the Act or is a table or compilation. This is because, although the definition of infringement by reproduction is the same for all these classes of works, in other respects they are treated differently. Thus the exclusive right of making an adaptation of a work has a different meaning in relation to a database than for other literary works.[89] In addition, databases are treated differently in relation to some of the permitted acts.[90]

7–44 **Compilations: substantial part.** The test is the same in all cases. The test will vary, depending on whether or not the work is a post-March 27, 1996 database. This is because the threshold originality requirement is different for such works.[91] In the case of such works, whether a substantal part has been taken must be assessed by reference to the author's work of intellectual creation in selecting or arranging the contents of the database.[92] In general terms, however, a defendant may not unfairly take advantage of the labour which has been expended by another in making the compilation: "No man is entitled to avail himself of the previous labour of another for the purpose of conveying to the public the same information."[93] The defendant must himself therefore carry out the work which is necessary to produce the compilation,[94] or at least do so by some other means than taking the shortcut of using the claimant's work.[95] Even to copy the claimant's work but then to go to the source to check that the information is correct will be an infringement.[96] It is irrelevant that the plan, arrangement or layout of the claimant's work may not have been copied if the labour of compilation has been appropriated.[97] The fact that the information in the claimant's work is not available from any other source, as for example in case of television programme schedules or football fixture lists, does not excuse copying.[98]

This is not to say that no part of the claimant's labour may be used: a single piece of information may be taken since this will not represent a substantial part of the claimant's work.[99] Again, many other legitimate uses may of course be made of such works, particularly if they were intended to be used as reference

---

[86] Copyright and Rights in Databases Regulations 1997, reg.29(1)(a).

[87] *i.e.* the commencement date of the Database Regulations.

[88] Copyright and Rights in Databases Regulations 1997, regs 29(1), (2).

[89] See CDPA 1988, s.21(3)(ac).

[90] See CDPA 1988, ss.29(1A) and 50D and Ch.9, below.

[91] See para. 3–146, above.

[92] See para. 3–287b, above.

[93] *Scott v Sandford* (1867) L.R. 3 Eq. 723.

[94] *Kelly v Morris* (1866) L.R. 1 Eq. 697 ("he must count the milestones for himself"); *Cox v Land and Water Journal Co* (1869) L.R. 9 Eq. 324 ("... it is information they must get at their own expense, as a result of their own labour, and they are not to be entitled to the results of the labours undergone by others").

[95] *Independent Television Publications Ltd v Time Out Ltd* [1984] F.S.R. 64 at 69.

[96] *Kelly v Morris* (1866) L.R. 1 Eq. 697; *Morris v Ashbee* (1868) L.R. 7 Eq. 34; *Moffat and Paige Ltd v Gill* (1902) 86 L.T. 465, CA; *Waterlow Publishers Ltd v Rose* [1995] F.S.R. 207.

[97] *Kelly v Morris* (1866) L.R. 1 Eq. 697; *Morris v Ashbee* (1868) L.R. 7 Eq. 34; *Moffat and Paige Ltd v Gill* (1902) 86 L.T. 465, CA; *Waterlow Publishers Ltd v Rose* [1995] F.S.R. 207.

[98] *Independent Television Publications Ltd v Time Out Ltd* [1984] F.S.R. 64 at 69; *Football League Ltd v Littlewoods Pools Ltd* [1959] 1 Ch. 637.

[99] The statement in *Kelly v Morris* (1866) L.R. 1 Eq. 697 at 702 that a defendant may not take a

works. Thus, a person may use a claimant's work to find sources which he might not otherwise have thought of,[1] and he is then entitled to quote from those sources provided that the end result is not simply to reproduce the claimant's work of compilation.[2] Again, the claimant's work may be consulted and used to check the accuracy of what the defendant has himself done,[3] or to check whether there is anything which he has forgotten.[4] There will of course be no infringement if no copying or other restricted act takes place. A person may therefore use a work such as directory to contact the listed names as many times as he wishes. If, however, in the course of doing so or afterwards he writes down or makes some other record of a substantial amount of the information obtained from the claimant's work, then he is likely to have infringed. On the other hand, if having contacted the names and obtained information from them, he publishes that information without reproducing the compilation of names and contact details, he will not infringe. Although no case directly decides the point,[5] it is suggested that infringement may occur even where the copying occurs by the recording of the names and addresses on separate pieces of paper, for example on envelopes to be sent out as part of a mail-shot. It is suggested that the real issue here will often not be whether a substantial part of the claimant's work has been reproduced but whether such use was licensed. In particular, the important point may be whether the use was for a competing purpose, for example to compile a rival directory, or whether it was for a legitimate purpose such as to canvass non-competing business from those identified in the directory. In the former case, whether the names and addresses were copied out onto one or separate pieces of paper cannot alter the fact that the defendant has appropriated the labour and skill of the claimant's work of compilation. In the latter case, it may be strongly arguable that the defendant is using the directory for the very purpose for which it was made available by the claimant, so that such use is licensed. An important distinction can also be made between different kinds of compilations. A work such as a trade directory is intended to be used in a different manner from a work such as an anthology of poetry. The limits of any such implied licence are, however, reasonably clear: in no case will use of the claimant's work be authorised for the production of a second work of a competing nature.[6]

A difficult point is whether any distinction is to be drawn between the labour involved in gathering or compiling the information and that involved in presenting it. Compilation cases have been said to be based essentially upon a claimant being able to establish the requisite degree of skill and labour in making the compilation, as distinct from that of ascertaining that information,[7] and, again, that "... it is the product of the labour, skill, and capital of one man which must not be appropriated by another, not the elements, the raw material ... upon which the labour and skill and capital of the first have been expended".[8] Clearly no copyright protection could be claimed for a work consisting simply of a figure for

---

single word from a map or single line from a directory without infringing goes too far. It is suggested that the doubt about this statement expressed in *Waterlow Directories Ltd v Reed Information Services Ltd* [1992] F.S.R. 409 is clearly correct.

[1] *Jarrold v Houlston* (1857) 3 K. & J. 708.

[2] *Morris v Wright* (1870) L.R. 5 Ch. App. 279; *Pike v Nicholas* (1870) L.R. 5 Ch. App. 251.

[3] *Kelly v Morris* (1866) L.R. 1 Eq. 697; *Scott v Stanford* (1867) L.R. 3 Eq. 718.

[4] *Jarrold v Houlston* (1857) 3 K. & J. 708.

[5] The point was left open in *Waterlow Directories Ltd v Reed Information Services Ltd* [1992] F.S.R. 409.

[6] *Waterlow Directories Ltd v Reed Information Services Ltd* [1992] F.S.R. 409.

[7] *Elanco Products Ltd v Mandops (Agricultural Specialists) Ltd* [1980] R.P.C. 213; *PCR Ltd v Dow Jones Telerate Ltd* [1998] F.S.R 170. But see the reservations expressed by Whitford J. in *Independent Television Publications Ltd v Time Out Ltd* [1984] F.S.R. 64, at 69.

[8] *Macmillan & Co Ltd v Cooper* (1924) 40 T.L.R. 186 at 188, cited with approval in *Interlego A.G. v Tyco Industries Inc* [1989] A.C. 217 at 260, although the words were spoken in the context of

the height of a mountain, no matter how much skill, effort and labour had gone into the survey and calculations required.[9] With compilations, however, it is clearly not simply the skill and labour of the author of the work in presenting the information in a digestible or useful way which is protected. The whole merit of many works of this kind is that someone has spent substantial time and effort in collecting together or choosing the raw material which is the basis of the compilation, and it is this skill and effort which the law protects.[10] The skill and effort is not literary in any conventional sense, but as a matter of convenience it is protected as a literary work.[11]

7–45   **Examples.** These principles may be illustrated by reference to some of the cases:

(a) *Directories: the older cases.* Three leading nineteenth-century cases illustrate many of the points. In *Kelly v Morris*[12] the claimant published a street directory for London, including the names and addresses of residents. The defendant infringed where a large number of entries had been copied from the claimant's directory and canvassers were then sent to the addresses to see if the information was correct. This information was then copied into the defendant's rival directory, even where it had not been possible to verify the information. The same result followed in *Morris v Ashbee*,[13] where the claimant's work consisted of a London trade directory giving the names and occupations of merchants, traders and businessmen, arranged in a classified list in alphabetical order. The defendant cut out entries from this directory and then sent representatives to call on each person to verify the information and obtain permission to use it. This information was then printed in his own directory. In contrast, in *Morris v Wright*,[14] although the defendant had similarly cut out the entries from the claimant's directory and sent out representatives, he had not yet published his directory and at the date of the interim hearing there was no evidence that he had actually copied any entry, this issue being left to trial. There was therefore no infringement established.[15]

(b) *Directories: modern cases.* The claimant compiled a directory of names and addresses of lawyers. The defendant copied 1,600 out of 12,620 entries onto a word processor and, using these, sent out canvassing letters for the purpose of preparing its own directory. Held: an infringement.[16] The same result followed where a defendant used the claimant's directory to send out 50,000 forms to solicitors containing proposed entries for the recipients to approve and correct.[17] Thus in directory cases it is the effort

---

the requirement of originality generally, and particularly, in *Interlego*, in the context of whether a mere copy is capable of being an original work.

[9] See, *e.g. Bookmakers' Afternoon Greyhound Services Ltd v Wilf Gilbert (Staffordshire) Ltd* [1994] F.S.R. 723, at 735 (no copyright in individual dividend forecast).

[10] *Autospin (Oil Seals) Ltd v Beehive Spinning* [1995] R.P.C. 683 at 698.

[11] *Autospin (Oil Seals) Ltd v Beehive Spinning* [1995] R.P.C. 683.

[12] (1866) L.R. 1 Eq. 697.

[13] (1868) L.R. 7 Eq. 34.

[14] (1870) L.R. 5 Ch. 279.

[15] The defendant had altered his *modus operandi* in the light of the decision in *Morris v Ashbee* (1868) L.R. 7 Eq. 34. See the analysis of these three cases in *Waterlow Directories Ltd v Reed Information Services Ltd* [1992] F.S.R. 409. Other older cases include *Mathewson v Stockdale* (1806) 2 Russ. 385; *Kelly v Hooper* (1840) 4 Jur. 21; *Cornish v Upton* (1861) 4 L.T. 862.

[16] *Waterlow Directories Ltd v Reed Information Services Ltd* [1992] F.S.R. 409. It was the copying of the claimant's list onto a word processor which was held to amount to an infringement. As noted above, the question as to whether the printing of the names and addresses onto separate envelopes was also an infringement was left open.

[17] *Waterlow Publishers Ltd v Rose* [1995] F.S.R. 207. See also *Fax Directories (Pty) Ltd v S.A. Fax Listings* [1990] 2 S.A.L.R. 164; (1992) S.A. 64 (D) (Sup. Ct of S.A.).

and skill expended in finding out who lives where, etc. which merits protection.[18]

(c) *Catalogues.* The claimant published a number of works on fruiting plants. The defendant compiled his own catalogue of plants, in the course of which he put specimens of fruit trees in front of him and compared their appearance with the descriptions in various publications, including the claimants'. Where the description tallied exactly, he copied the claimant's description, otherwise making the necessary alterations. Where he could not obtain a specimen, he copied the description from the claimant's work. Held: an infringement.[19]

(d) *Statistical information.* The claimant compiled statistical information as part of a crop forecasting service, the information consisting of details of the growing crop, weather and soil information, and so on. The information was presented as part of a report to subscribers. The defendant infringed by passing on to commodity traders the "essential" part of the information extracted from the reports.[20]

(e) *Technical data.* The claimant published information about a chemical on labels on the outside of containers, the information having been compiled from a number of public domain sources. The defendant infringed by producing a label which contained much of the same information and which had been obtained from the claimant's label. The result would have been different if the defendant had itself looked at all the available information, including that on the claimant's label, and then made its own choice about what to include and how to express it, even though the result might have been very similar to the claimant's. What it was not entitled to do was to take advantage of the skill and judgment of the claimant and save itself the trouble and cost of assembling the information.[21]

(f) *Dictionaries, encyclopaedias, etc.* The claimant produced an educational scientific book in the form of questions and answers. The concept was not new and the material itself not original. The defendant infringed where he had used portions of the book mixed in with his own labour.[22]

(g) *Anthologies, etc.*

(1) The defendant infringed where he copied the selection of poems in Palgrave's *Golden Treasury*, the selection requiring "extensive reading, careful study and comparison, and the exercise of taste and judgment."[23] Again, where the claimant had prepared an annotated, potted version of *As You Like It* for use in schools, the defendant infringed by copying the substance of the work. It was said that, in relation to a series of quotations, to take the reference given by the claimant and to go and see if it is correctly copied and, if so, to use it with other added material:

"... is to leave out the whole merit; the felicity of the quotation; its adaptability to a particular end; its illustration of a particular characteristic. All these things enter into the choice of one quotation as apart from another. This is a pro-

---

[18] *Autospin (Oil Seals) Ltd v Beehive Spinning* [1995] R.P.C. 683, at 698.

[19] *Hogg v Scott* (1873) L.R. 18 Eq. 444.

[20] *PCR Ltd v Dow Jones Telerate Ltd* [1998] F.S.R. 170. See also *Scott v Stanford* (1867) L.R. 3 Eq. 718 (statistics of coal imports).

[21] *Elanco Products Ltd v Mandops (Agrochemical Specialists) Ltd* [1980] R.P.C. 213.

[22] *Jarrold v Houlston* (1857) 3 K. & J. 708. See also *Mawman v Tegg* (1826) 2 Russ. 385; *cf. Jarrold v Heywood* (1870) 18 W.R. 279 (on the facts, no copying).

[23] *MacMillan & Co v Suresh Chunder Deb* (1890) 17 I.L.R. 951 (Calcutta), approved in *MacMillan & Co Ltd v Cooper* (1923) 40 T.L.R. 186, PC.

cess which may involve gifts both of knowledge and intelligence. The aptness of quotation does not depend on the particular page or number of lines in which it is found … it does not entitle you to annexe the skill and judgement and taste which has dictated the selection."[24]

(2) But where the claimant's work consisted of the life of Alexander, compiled by taking selected passages amounting to about one-half of the standard translation of Plutarch's work and knitting them together with a word or two of connecting material to make a connected narrative, the defendant did not infringe by reproducing those passages, there being no sufficient skill or taste in what had been done by the author of the claimant's work in this respect.[25]

(3) A more difficult case arose where a study of Hazlitt's essays had been published consisting of 13 of the 127 published essays, chosen to represent his work, together with a lengthy introduction and notes, the whole work being prescribed for an examination course. Of the 127 essays, 30 to 40 were well known and likely to be the starting point for any edition, and of which four or five were so well known as to be inevitably included in such a collection. Other collections had also been published, for example one of 23 essays containing 12 of the claimant's 13. The defendant published a selection of 20 essays, including the 13 chosen by the claimant (albeit in a different order), and which were marked with an asterisk to indicate that they were prescribed. In a decision which was described as being close to the line,[26] it was held that there was no infringement, relevant factors being that the claimant's introduction and notes (which were part of the prescribed materials) had not been taken; part of the merit of the claimant's work lay in its arrangement, which had not been copied; the inclusion of the 13 essays was not motivated to gain an advantage from the choice made in the claimant's work but to cater for the needs of students; the claimant's work was much more elaborate and knowledgeable and its sales unlikely to be affected by the defendant's.

(h) *Historical works.* Although there is no monopoly in historical facts, protection will be given to a work which is the result of skill and effort in researching and presenting the material.[27] Thus where the claimant's work consisted of a historical account of the charge of the Light Brigade, compiled from the various sources, it appeared that the defendant's film script had made extensive use of that work, thus saving the labour of the research and presentation, even though much other material was added:

---

[24] *Moffat and Paige Ltd v Gill* (1902) 86 L.T. 465, CA. See also *Blackie & Sons Ltd v The Lothian Book Publishing Co, etc. Ltd* (1921) 29 C.L.R. 396 (annotated version of *King Henry V*).

[25] *MacMillan & Co Ltd v Cooper* (1923) 40 T.L.T. 186, PC. However, the defendant infringed by copying the notes which accompanied the text. See also *Longman v Winchester* (1809) 16 Ves. 269 at 271.

[26] *Cambridge University Press v University Tutorial Press Ltd* (1928) 75 R.P.C. 335. The case was clouded by the fact that the defendant had published an earlier edition which clearly infringed, and was obviously partly motivated by the wish to publish a work which contained the prescribed essays.

[27] Although note that slightly greater leeway may be given to the borrowing of material from historical works than from other kinds. See para. 7–27, above, at (l) and *Ravenscroft v Herbert* [1980] R.P.C. 193.

injunction granted.[28] Again, where a claimant had written a semi-historical, semi-mystical account of the spear which pierced the side of Christ, the defendant's novel infringed where about four per cent of the claimant's work had been copied in order to give the defendant's book historical authenticity, there being both language and non-language copying.[29] In contrast, where the defendant had used the claimant's work to find sources for his book on the origin of the English nation, and had then gone to those sources and quoted from them and not the claimant's work, he did not infringe, even though in the result the works were quite similar.[30]

(i) *Maps, etc.* As well as being artistic works, maps may also be regarded as compilations.[31] The general topic of maps is, however, considered in relation to artistic works.

(j) *Fixture lists.* The claimant produced a list of League football matches for the entire season. The defendant produced a fortnightly pools coupon having taken the matches for that fortnight from the claimant's list. Held: an infringement.[32]

(k) *Programme schedules.* Where the claimant produced a schedule of forthcoming television programmes, the defendant's listings magazine compiled using information from the claimant's schedules infringed.[33]

(l) *Betting coupons, etc.* A defendant infringed where it had copied the layout and betting system worked out by the claimant for its pools coupons.[34]

(m) *Computer programs.* While each computer program may be entitled to protection in its own right,[35] a suite of computer programs may be protected quite independently as a compilation if sufficient labour and skill has been expended in assembling them.[36]

"Little and often." Compilations are particularly susceptible to having small amounts regularly taken from them for a defendant's specialist needs. This general problem had already been discussed.[37] **7–46**

Rearrangement or scrambling of compilations. Sometimes a defendant takes a list of data prepared by another and presents it in a different order. It is suggested that whether or not this amounts to an infringement will depend upon where the originality of the claimant's work lay. If at least part of the originality lay in compiling or assembling the information, then the defendant will infringe by us- **7–47**

---

[28] *Harman Pictures N.V. v Osborne* [1967] 1 W.L.R. 723. The decision was an interim one only but a strong case of copying was made out in the absence of any explanation from the defendant.

[29] *Ravenscroft v Herbert* [1980] R.P.C. 193.

[30] *Pike v Nicholas* (1869) L.R. 5 Ch. App. 251. It seems that a feature which led to both works being similar was that both were written as entries to a competition and it was likely that the prize committee would favour an entry written with a particular slant.

[31] *Anacon Corp. Ltd v Environmental Research Technology Ltd* [1994] F.S.R. 659; *Comprop Ltd v Moran* [2002] J.L.R. 222 (Royal Ct of Jersey).

[32] *Football League Ltd v Littlewood Pools Ltd* [1959] Ch. 637. The case was decided having relied on the "little and often" principle (see para. 7–29, above), but it is suggested that the material taken each fortnight was a substantial part of the season's list. For examples of race card cases, see *Bookmakers' Afternoon Greyhound Services Ltd v Wilf Gilbert (Staffordshire) Ltd* [1994] F.S.R. 723; *Demerara Turf Club v Phang* [1963] W.I.R. 177 (Sup Ct of Brit Guyana); *Ascot Club Ltd v Simoms* [1968] 64 W.W.R. 411 (Sup Ct of Canada); *British Columbia Jockey Club v Standen* [1984] 4 W.W.R. 537 (Sup Ct of Brit Columbia).

[33] *Independent Television Publications Ltd v Time Out Ltd* [1984] F.S.R. 64. But as to programme listings now, see the Broadcasting Act 1990, s.176 and Sch.17 and paras 29–09, below *et seq.*

[34] *Ladbroke (Football) Ltd v William Hill (Football) Ltd* [1964] 1 W.L.R. 273.

[35] See para. 7–48, below.

[36] *Ibcos Computers Ltd v Barclays Mercantile Highland Finance Ltd* [1994] F.S.R. 275, disapproving *Total Information Processing Systems Ltd v Daman Ltd* [1992] F.S.R. 171.

[37] See para. 7–29, above.

ing the results of that labour even in a rearranged form.[38] If, on the other hand, this was not the case, for example because the information was readily available or was gathered without any labour or skill in selection, but the originality lay in the manner of its presentation, which the defendant has not copied, there will be no infringement.

(d) *Computer programs*

7–48   One of the features of a computer program that sets it apart from other literary works is that for most practical purposes it cannot be perceived, accessed or used without being copied into computer memory, albeit invisibly to the user. Since it is made clear that reproduction of a computer program includes transient or incidental copying,[39] as well as the storing of the program in any medium by electronic means, the restricted act of copying is likely to be committed in every form of use. Not only will the storage of a program inevitably involve its reproduction in computer memory,[40] but even the ordinary acts of transient copying between different parts of a computer system incidental to the running of the programme will do so. This approach is consistent with the Computer Software Directive,[41] Article 4(a) of which provides that, subject to exceptions, the exclusive rights of the owner of copyright in a computer program "shall include the right to do or to authorize ... the permanent or temporary reproduction of a computer program by any means and in any form, in part or in whole. In so far as loading, displaying, running, transmission or storage of the computer program necessitate such reproduction, such acts shall be subject to authorization by the rightholder."[42] The result is that for all practical purposes any unlicensed use of a computer program is liable to be an infringement if not subject to one of the permitted acts.[43] This protection for computer programs is a very valuable weapon in the hands of copyright owners, given the ease of copying of such works and, to a lesser extent, the uncertainty about the efficacy of the mass-market software practice of "shrinkwrap" and "clickwrap" licensing.[44] The need for users to have a licence to use the program provides a strong foundation for controlling use, to be compared, for example, with the rights of owners of copyright in other works, who, presented with a defendant who is using a suspected pirate copy of a work, may need to be sure that the knowledge requirements applicable to acts of secondary infringement are satisfied before effective action can be taken.[45]

The general principles in relation to infringement of computer programs are no

---

[38] See, *e.g. Independent Television Publications Ltd v Time Out Ltd* [1984] F.S.R. 64; *British Columbia Jockey Club v Standen* (1986) 22 D.L.R. (4th) 467. In *Demerara Turf Club v Phang* (1963) W.I.R. 177, it was held that the publication in the defendant's coupon of a list of names of horses in a race, taken from the claimant's programme and coupon, but in a scrambled form, was an infringement. The point was left open in *Football League Ltd v Littlewoods Pools Ltd* [1959] Ch. 637.

[39] CDPA 1988, s.17(6).

[40] *Ocular Sciences Ltd v Aspect Vision Care Ltd* [1997] R.P.C. 289 at 418.

[41] Directive 91/250 of May 14, 1991.

[42] No change to the infringement sections of the 1988 Act was required to comply with this provision of the Computer Software Directive.

[43] As to such acts, it should be borne in mind that there are a number of permitted acts which are specific to computer programs, namely the making of back-up copies; decompilation to make a compatible program; observing, studying and testing the functioning of a program; and acts necessary for the lawful use of a program, including error correction: see CDPA 1988, ss.50A–50C and paras 9–132, below *et seq*. Note, however, that the permitted act provisions of s.28A, which relate to the making of transient or incidental copies, do not apply to computer programs (or databases).

[44] As to this, see para. 27–331, below.

[45] In particular, possession in the course of business, knowing or having reason to believe the article is an infringing copy. See Ch.8, below.

different from those relating to other types of literary works.[46] Neither the 1988 Act nor the Software Directive defines a "computer program", and it should be borne in mind that such things as data files and suites of programs may other kinds of copyright works as well as, or rather than, a computer program.[47] What must of course be compared is the claimant's program with the alleged infringing work, usually another program.[48] It is not necessary to examine every part of the defendant's program to establish reproduction of a substantial part. A comparison of samples will be sufficient if they are representative.[49] The fact that two devices produce the same output in response to a command or produce the same result does not necessarily mean that there is any similarity between the two computer programs: each may be structured and written entirely differently.[50]

Copying may take the form of: (a) the exact or literal reproduction of all or part of the program, (b) reproduction of the program in a re-written form, perhaps in a different language,[51] (c) reproduction on a higher level, for example the reproduction of the structure of the program.

Proof of copying. With computer programs in particular, it is the presence of similar redundancies, mistakes and idiosyncrasies in coding, as opposed to standard routines, which reveal the hand of the copyist.[52] Computer code typically evolves, both during initial development and subsequently through testing and upgrading. As a result, it is common to find that there is residual and redundant code left within the program. Just as some directory and list publishers introduce "sleepers" or "seed" entries into their works,[53] some programmers also deliberately include "smoking guns" into their code, with no function other than to assist in proving copying. In addition, true and permanent deletion of computer code is difficult. "Deleted" files are often merely re-indexed rather than being deleted, and can be readily retrieved. More sophisticated tools exist for endeavouring to retrieve files which have been deliberately overwritten. Copies of programs and data are also routinely made and stored as part of computer or network backups, and may provide useful snapshot proof of the development process, despite deliberate attempts to destroy the evidence. Careful analysis of code can also reveal evidence of copying at the level of comments and notes in the human-generated program code.[54] It follows that, although copying may be easier in the digital world, proof of copying may also be easier.

7–49

In the common case of flagrant piracy of a computer program, there will usually be exact reproduction of the whole program by simple duplication, and proving identity is a purely mechanical task. Where there has been literal copying of

---

[46] It should be noted that where an arrangement or altered version of the program is made, or a version of the program is made in which it is converted into or out of a computer language or code, or into a different computer language or code, this will amount to an adaptation of the program as well, perhaps, as a reproduction of it. See CDPA 1988, ss.21(3)(ab), (4).

[47] See, *e.g. Ibcos Computers Ltd v Barclays Mercantile Finance Ltd* [1994] F.S.R. 275.

[48] *Thrustcode Ltd v W.W. Computing Ltd* [1983] F.S.R. 502; *Apple Computers Inc. v Mackintosh Computers Ltd* (1990) 71 D.L.R. 95.

[49] *Ibcos Computers Ltd v Barclays Mercantile Highland Finance Ltd* [1994] F.S.R. 275; *Accounting Systems 2000 (Developments) Pty Ltd v C.C.H. Australia Ltd* (1993) 114 A.L.R. 355 (Fed Ct of Aus)

[50] *John Richardson Computers Ltd v Flanders* [1993] F.S.R. 497; *Autodesk Inc v Dyason* [1992] R.P.C. 575 (High Ct of Aus); *News Datacom Ltd v Satellite Decoding Systems* [1995] F.S.R. 201; *Admar Computers Pty Ltd v Ezt Systems Pty Ltd* (1997) 38 I.P.R. 659.

[51] Although again this would normally constitute an adaptation of the program as well. See para. 7–127, below.

[52] As in *Ibcos Computers Ltd v Barclays Mercantile Highland Finance Ltd* [1994] F.S.R. 275; *Creative Technology Ltd v Aztech Systems Pte. Ltd* [1997] F.S.R. 491 (Ct of App of Singapore); *Cantor Fitzgerald v Tradition (U.K.) Ltd* [2000] R.P.C. 95.

[53] See paras 7–41 and 7–17, above.

[54] As happened in *Ibcos Computers Ltd v Barclays Mercantile Highland Finance Ltd* [1994] F.S.R. 275.

part only of the program, however, the issue is whether that part constitutes a substantial part, the question here being no different than in other cases. The function of the law of copyright is to protect the relevant skill and labour of the author, so that infringement occurs if there has been an appropriation of a part of the work on which a substantial part of the author's skill and labour was expended.[55] The copying of a small amount of code is unlikely to amount to an infringement[56] particularly if, for example, the writing of that part involved no great skill or labour, as in the case of commonplace routines. In the context of computer software, it is also dangerous to import tests sometimes used in relation to other types of works, such as, how important or essential is the part taken when compared to the whole of the claimant's work?[57] This is because in relation to a computer program, the slightest semantic error may cause the program not to run or cause it to produce the wrong result. In this sense, the smallest part of a program, and one containing no relevant originality, may be vitally important.[58] Controversially, in *Autodesk Inc v Dyason*,[59] the High Court of Australia held that the copying of a 127-bit "look-up table", a series of numbers stored within a program and being part of a "lock-and-key" security device, amounted to an infringement, even though the numbers had been randomly generated and thus had required no programming skill to create them and were unlikely to have qualified for copyright protection had they stood alone. The decision does not form part of English law.[60]

Where it represents a substantial part of the skill and labour of the programmer of the copyright work, infringement may occur by the reproduction of the structure of the program, including its overall structure at a high level of abstraction,[61] although it may be more difficult in practice to decide whether such copying has occurred. Here, a useful analogy can be drawn between computer programs and dramatic works, where infringement can clearly occur even where language copying has not taken place,[62] although the analogy can be difficult to apply because of the relatively unfamiliar medium and the functional nature of a computer program. In each case, it will be a matter of degree, applying the usual tests, whether a substantial part has been taken. In the end, this will be a matter for the court's value judgment, helped, especially in this field, by expert evidence. In practice, the analysis is not usually as theoretical as the problem suggests. As already noted, the evidence will often show numerous examples of unexplained similarities, such as similar spelling mistakes, identical column headings and file record names, and the presence of redundant coding.

---

[55] *Cantor Fitzgerald v Tradition (U.K.) Ltd* [2000] R.P.C. 95; *Ibcos Computers Ltd v Barclays Mercantile Highland Finance Ltd* [1994] F.S.R. 275, although there Jacob J. propounded the test as being whether there has been an "overborrowing" of the author's skill and labour, a test which was doubted by Pumfrey J. in *Cantor Fitzgerald v Tradition (U.K.) Ltd*, since it did not add any further useful criteria.

[56] See *Creative Technology Ltd v Aztech Systems Pte. Ltd* [1997] F.S.R. 491 (two sections of code consisting of seven and 12 lines respectively and forming about four per cent of the total program were not enough to amount to a substantial part).

[57] See para. 7–27, above at (b).

[58] *Cantor Fitzgerald v Tradition (U.K.) Ltd* [2000] R.P.C. 95.

[59] [1992] R.P.C. 575.

[60] *Cantor Fitzgerald v Tradition (U.K.) Ltd* [2000] R.P.C. 95. For further criticism of the decision, see *Lahore* [1992] E.I.P.R. 428, *Prescott* [1992] E.I.P.R. 191 and the doubts expressed in *Autodesk Inc v Dyason (No.2)* [1993] R.P.C. 259.

[61] *Ibcos Computers Ltd v Barclays Mercantile Highland Finance Ltd* [1994] F.S.R. 275; *John Richardson Computers Ltd v Flanders* [1993] F.S.R. 497; *Cantor Fitzgerald v Tradition (U.K.) Ltd* [2000] R.P.C. 95 (no substantial copying of these elements on the facts).

[62] See para. 7–52, below. The same is, however, true for literary works generally. See para. 7–36, above.

Ideas only? It is sometimes argued that what has been taken from the claimant's program amount to ideas or concepts only,[63] but as has been seen,[64] this is often an oversimplified approach. Only where the idea embodied in the claimant's work is very general can it safely be said that the taking of the idea will not infringe. Where the idea is worked out in any detail in the claimant's program and the defendant has reproduced the expression of that idea, then it is likely he will have infringed.

7–50

"Abstraction and filtration." The extent to which protection should be given to elements such as ideas, functionally driven material and work gathered from the public domain has been raised frequently in the United States in this field, but only on a limited number of occasions in the United Kingdom. Generally, however, it is wrong in this context to incorporate jurisprudence from the United States,[65] particularly insofar as this involves carrying out an "abstraction and filtration" process whereby there is first systematically excluded from consideration various elements of the claimant's program, as follows: (1) elements which result from the expression of an idea where there is only one way to express that idea, (2) elements which result from the description of the same facts which can only be described in a particular way, and lastly (3) elements taken from the public domain, and then, when this process is complete, what is left of the claimant's program is compared with the defendant's work. The law of the United States differs from the United Kingdom in this area,[66] not least in denying protection to "any idea, procedure, process, system, method of operation, concept, principle, or discovery, regardless of the form in which it is described, explained, illustrated or embodied".[67] Under United Kingdom law:

7–51

(a) Where an idea, function or concept is sufficiently worked out and expressed in computer code, being the result of independent skill and labour, that expression is protected and the copying of a substantial part of that expression is a restricted act.[68] Although mere general ideas or general principles may not be protected, their detailed expression is.

(b) Where the circumstances are such that there will inevitably be similarities in two independently written pieces of coding, this does not mean that there is no copyright in that coding: copyright will subsist if it was the product of substantial skill and labour. The circumstances may explain the similarities but do not excuse copying.

(c) Where particular coding is in the "public domain", or more probably, is a standard piece of coding in which no one claims copyright, while a claimant may not be able to claim any originality for it, if he has combined it with other coding using skill and labour, the copying of that piece of "public domain" coding in combination with the other coding is likely to be an infringement.[69]

(ii) Dramatic works

In the case of dramatic works which are written or otherwise recorded in words,

7–52

---

[63] And note that Art.1.1 of the Software Directive (91/250) specifies that "ideas and principles which underlie any element of a computer program, including those which underlie its interfaces, are not protected by copyright under this Directive."

[64] See para. 7–13, above.

[65] As was done in *John Richardson Computers Ltd v Flanders* [1993] F.S.R. 497, applying the principles adopted in *Computer Associates Ltd v Altai Inc* 23 U.S.P.Q. 2d. 1241 (2nd. Cir. 1992).

[66] *Ibcos Computers Ltd v Barclays Mercantile Highland Finance Ltd* [1994] F.S.R. 275.

[67] s.102 of the US Code.

[68] See *Ibcos Computers Ltd v Barclays Mercantile Highland Finance Ltd* [1994] F.S.R. 275 and para. 7–13, above.

[69] See para. 7–27, at (j), below.

if the language itself has been copied, no special considerations apply. However, a basic distinction between literary works and dramatic works is that the choice of dramatic incident and the arrangement of situation and plot may constitute, to a much greater extent, the real value of a dramatic work. This section of the chapter is primarily concerned with whether infringement of a dramatic work can occur where only situations and plot, but not language, have been reproduced. This commonly happens, for example, where a play is based on another play, or a film upon a play. Infringement by turning a dramatic work into a non-dramatic work, and vice versa, is considered under the heading of infringement by making an adaptation, but here too the question can arise as to whether copying of incident and plot, without language copying, can amount to an infringement. It should be remembered that dramatic works include not only plays and screenplays but also works of dance and mime.[70]

A dramatic work may be infringed by a second dramatisation which reproduces dramatic incidents without using or imitating language.[71] It is thus not necessary that the words in the dialogue should be the same, for the situations and incidents, and the way in which the ideas are worked out and presented, may form a part of the real value of the whole work. Regard should be had to the dramatic value and importance of what has been taken, even though the part may in fact be small and the actual language not copied. On the other hand, the fundamental idea that two plays may be the same, but if worked out separately and on independent lines they may be so different as to bear no real resemblance to one another.[72]

Care should be taken in reaching the conclusion that copying has taken place simply because of the presence in both works of stock incidents, whether found in other dramatic works or drawn from historical or fictional sources.[73] If there are incidents in common between the two works which can be found in other sources or which are well-used dramatic ideas, it may be that no copying took place or, even if there was copying, there may be no infringement if there was no originality in the part copied or the defendant's piece has been worked out in a different way.[74] More of the reported cases fail on these grounds[75] than have succeeded. In this area, help as to what amounts to protectable elements of plot

---

[70] CDPA 1988, s.3(1).

[71] *Designers Guild Ltd v Russell Williams (Textiles) Ltd* [2000] 1 W.L.R. 2416; *Cantor Fitzgerald v Tradition (U.K.) Ltd* [2000] R.P.C. 95, at 133; *Christoffer v Poseidon Film Distributors Ltd* [2000] E.C.D.R. 487 (copying of a dramatic work by the making of a film and other preparatory acts); *Brighton v Jones* [2004] EWHC 1157 (Ch) (incorporation of scenes from prepatory script into final script). Cases decided before the passing of the 1911 Act must be read with caution because there was some doubt whether the copyright in a dramatic work could be infringed unless actual words and phrases were used or colourably imitated. If scenes or points of drama were taken (*Chatterton v Cave* (1878) 3 App. Cas. 483) or, in the case of a musical drama, words of some of the songs (*Planché v Braham* (1838) 4 Bing. N.C. 17), but not the embodiment of the plot in words to any substantial extent, there was no infringement (*Schlotz v Amasis Ltd & Fenn* [1905–10] Mac.C.C. 216; but see *Nethersole v Bell* [1901–04] Mac.C.C. 64). See *Sutton Vane v Famous Players Film Co Ltd* [1928–35] Mac.C.C. 6 and *Kelly v Cinema Houses Ltd* [1928–35] Mac.C.C. 362 for a review of the position.

[72] *Rees v Melville* [1911–16] Mac.C.C. 96 and 168. See also *Sutton Vane v Famous Players Film Co. Ltd* [1928–35] Mac.C.C. 6; *Bolton v British International Pictures Ltd* [1936–45] Mac.C.C. 20; *Poznanski v London Film Production Ltd* [1936–45] Mac.C.C. 107; *Ashmore v Douglas-Home* [1987] F.S.R. 553; *Harman Pictures N.V. v Osborne* [1967] 1 W.L.R. 723; *Telstra Corp Ltd v Royal & Sun Alliance Insurance Ltd* I.P.R. 57 (2003) 453.

[73] *Harman Pictures N.V. v Osborne* [1967] 1 W.L.R. 723 at 728.

[74] In the unusual case of *Norowzian v Arks Ltd (No.2)* [2000] F.S.R. 363, the technique used in the claimant's work had been copied, but the actual dramatic story told by the defendant's work was quite different.

[75] Examples of such cases are: *Rees v Melville* [1911–16] Mac.C.C. 96 and 168; *Robl v Palace Theatre* (1911) 28 T.L.R. 69; *Bagge v Millar* [1917–23] Mac.C.C. 179; *Dagnall v British and Dominion Film Corporation Ltd* [1928–35] Mac.C.C. 391; *Wilmer v Hutchinson & Co Ltd* [1936–45] Mac.C.C. 13; *Bolton v British International Pictures Ltd* [1936–45] Mac.C.C. 20; *Poznanski v London Film Production Ltd* [1936–45] Mac.C.C. 107; *De Manduit v Gaumont, etc. Corp. Ltd* [1936–45] Mac.C.C. 292; *Ashmore v Douglas-Home* [1987] F.S.R. 553.

and situation can be also obtained from cases concerned with infringement by adaptation, whether the dramatisation of a non-dramatic work or vice versa.[76] Of course in every case copying must be proved. Thus even if there are sufficient similarities between the two works to establish an inference of copying, this inference can be rebutted by the defendant's evidence that no copying took place.[77]

(iii) Musical works

As with literary and dramatic works, the copying of a musical work can take place not only by its reproduction in the form of sheet music but also by its reproduction in the form of recordings of the music, whether on conventional sound carriers such as records, tapes, CDs and films, but also in data files stored in computer memory. If a musical work has been arranged or transcribed, this may also constitute infringement by making an adaptation of it,[78] a topic which is considered separately. In dealing with questions of infringement of musical works by copying, it should be remembered that words or action intended to be sung, spoken or performed with the music are not included within the definition of a musical work: they are protected as literary or dramatic works.[79]

7-53

As to whether a substantial part of a musical work has been copied, the question remains whether the alleged infringement has made use of a substantial part of the skill, labour and taste of the original composer.[80] It is common practice in music copyright cases to call expert evidence to identify and explain the significance of similarities and differences between the works.[81] Although the court is often helped by such evidence, the issue of substantial part does not depend solely on a note for note comparison but must be determined by the ear as well as by the eye,[82] for the most uneducated in music can recognise that an altered work of music is, in effect, the same as or is derived from the original work.[83] In undertaking the comparison, the works as a whole should be considered, and it is wrong to isolate certain features and concentrate on those.[84] It is clear that a relatively short part of a work can amount to a substantial part,[85] particularly if what has been taken is the vital or essential part of the work,[86] as opposed to being musical commonplace.[87] A relevant question may be whether the amount

---

[76] See, e.g. Corelli v Gray (1913) 29 T.L.R. 570; Harman Pictures N.V. v Osborne [1967] 1 W.L.R. 723, and paras 7–124 and 7–125, below.

[77] As in Sutton Vane v Famous Players Film Co Ltd [1928–35] Mac.C.C. 6; De Manduit v Gaumont, etc. Corp Ltd [1936–45] Mac.C.C. 292.

[78] i.e. under CDPA 1988, s.21(3)(b).

[79] CDPA 1988, s.3(1).

[80] Francis Day & Hunter Ltd v Bron [1963] Ch. 587.

[81] As to the role of expert evidence generally, see paras 7–18, above and 22–223, below.

[82] D'Almaine v Boosey (1835) 1 Y. & C. Ex. 288; Austin v Columbia Gramophone Co Ltd [1917–23] Mac.C.C. 398; Francis Day & Hunter Ltd v Bron [1963] Ch. 587. Other cases on the point include Boosey v Fairlie (1877) 7 Ch.D. 301; on appeal (1879) 4 App. Cas. 711; see also Leader v Purday (1848) 7 C.B.4; Wood v Boosey (1867) L.R. 2 Q.B. 340; L.R. 3 Q.B. 223.

[83] D'Almaine v Boosey (1835) 1 Y. & C. Ex. 288; Francis Day & Hunter Ltd v Bron [1963] Ch. 587.

[84] Betsen v CBS United Kingdom Ltd [1994] E.M.L.R. 467 (drum and bass line only of popular song alleged to be similar).

[85] Austin v Columbia Gramophone Co Ltd [1917–23] Mac.C.C. 398; G. Ricordi & Co., etc. Ltd v Clayton and Waller Ltd [1928–35] Mac.C.C. 154 (eight bars sufficient, although not in fact copied); Hawkes & Son (London) Ltd v Paramount Film Service Ltd [1934] Ch. 593 (28 bars of "Colonel Bogey" copied, amounting to just under a minute's worth of composition lasting about four minutes); Francis Day & Hunter Ltd v Bron [1963] Ch. 587.

[86] Francis Day & Hunter Ltd v Bron [1963] Ch. 587.

[87] EMI Music Publishing Ltd v Papathanasiou [1993] E.M.L.R. 306.

taken is so small that it is impossible to recognise the original work,[88] or whether it can still be recognised, but where the part taken has been added to other material it is important not to fall into the trap of asking whether the defendant's work sounds like the claimant's. The correct comparison is between the part taken by the defendant and the claimant's work, not between the defendant's work and the claimant's work.[89] Where the claimant's work contains material that was not original to him, then in the usual way these parts should be left out of the comparison exercise and attention centred on those parts which were original.[90]

Particularly in the field of popular music, the vital or essential part of the work may be a short refrain or hook line. The problem here becomes even more acute with the modern practice of "sampling", whereby a short piece of music is taken and often repeated many times in the making of a new recording. The same point arises in relation to 'ringtones'. The piece taken is often a distinctive part of the original work and thus immediately recognisable, which is of course the reason why it was taken. In cases of this kind, although it will be relevant to ask whether the piece which was copied was the result of any particular inventiveness on the part of the original author or was, for example, merely a hackneyed phrase,[91] it is suggested that it will often be appropriate in these cases to apply the rule of thumb that "what is worth copying is worth protecting".[92]

Even where the material in common is sufficient to amount to a substantial part, it of course still has to be established that the reason for this is copying.[93] It is in the field of music copyright cases in particular that the difficult issue of subconscious copying can often arise.[94]

(iv) Artistic works

7-54   **Designs for articles.** The whole topic of the copying of artistic works cannot today be discussed without an appreciation of the fundamental changes to the law in this area made by the 1988 Act. Before the 1988 Act, the gradual appreciation that copyright was capable of subsisting in artistic works such as engineering drawings and other designs for utilitarian objects, and might be infringed by indirectly copying the three-dimensional objects which had been made from those drawings, resulted in a good deal of controversy, culminating judicially in the House of Lords' decision in *British Leyland*.[95] In response, section 51 of the 1988 Act effected a fundamental change in the approach to works of this kind by cutting down the ambit of the copyright in relation to such works while at the same time providing a more limited form of protection by way of design right. The matter is considered in detail elsewhere[96] but can be summarised as follows:

(a) Certain works are now classified as design documents, namely those which contain any record of a "design", whether in the form of a drawing,

---

[88] *Hawkes & Son (London) Ltd v Paramount Film Service Ltd* [1934] Ch. 593.

[89] *Designers Guild Ltd v Russell Williams (Textiles) Ltd* [2001] 1 W.L.R. 2416.

[90] *Sawkins v Hyperion Records Ltd* [2004] EWHC 1530 (Ch).

[91] See, *e.g. EMI Music Publishing Ltd v Papathanasiou* [1993] E.M.L.R. 306, not a sampling case but where the only thing in common was a four-note sequence, described as "musical commonplace".

[92] As to this rule of thumb, see para. 7–28, above at (b). The problem also arises in relation to the copying of sound recordings (see para. 7–68, below).

[93] See, *e.g. G. Ricordi & Co, etc. Ltd v Clayton and Waller Ltd* [1928–35] Mac.C.C. 154 (substantial similarity but defendant's evidence of no copying accepted).

[94] As to subconscious copying, see para. 7–22, above.

[95] *British Leyland Motor Corp v Armstrong Patents Co Ltd* [1986] A.C. 850. Note that the Court of Appeal, [1986] A.C. 577, rejected the argument that the prevention of three-dimensional reproduction of functional designs by way of copyright protection was unlawful under Art.30 of the Treaty of Rome: see *Entec (Pollution Control) Ltd v Abacus Mouldings* [1992] F.S.R. 332.

[96] See Ch.13, below.

a written description, a photograph, data stored in a computer or otherwise. For this purpose a "design" means the design of any aspect of the shape or configuration (whether internal or external) of the whole or part of an article, other than surface decoration. A drawing for a machine part is therefore a design document, since it contains a record of the shape and configuration of the whole of an article.

(b) With certain exceptions, the Act then provides that in relation to a design document as so defined, it is not an infringement of any copyright in it to make an article to the design or to copy an article made to the design.[97] It is therefore not an infringement of the copyright in a drawing for a machine part to make a machine part from it. Nor is it an infringement of the copyright in the drawing to make a machine part by copying another machine part which was itself made from the drawing.

(c) The exceptions referred to above concern design documents or models recording or embodying a design for an artistic work or a typeface. These are still infringed by making an article to that design or by copying an article made to that design. Thus the copyright in a design document consisting of preliminary sketches for a sculpture is infringed by the unlicensed making of a sculpture to that design, since the design document records a design for an artistic work. A design for a machine part does not fall within this exception because a machine part is not an artistic work.

(d) It is also not an infringement of the copyright to issue to the public, or include in a film or broadcast, anything the making of which was, by virtue of the above provisions, not an infringement of that copyright.

These provisions must therefore be borne in mind when approaching any question of infringement concerning an artistic work which consists of a representation of an article, or which is itself a three-dimensional work. The provisions apply not merely to functional or utilitarian objects such as machine parts but also, for example, to designs for items of clothing in so far as the design relates to aspects of shape or configuration. It also follows that many of the earlier cases relating to infringement of artistic works, and which are referred to below, will be of no direct application today and are useful only in so far as they exemplify general principles. The 1988 Act contained transitional provisions such that works made before the commencement of the Act (August 1, 1989) were unaffected by these provisions for a period of 10 years from that date, although in the last five years of this period, licences of right were available.

Reproduction: general principles. The copying of an artistic work can take place by its reproduction in any material form,[98] even for example in a form by which it cannot be directly seen, such as data stored in computer memory.[99] The 1988 Act also specifically provides that a two-dimensional artistic work may be infringed by the making of a copy in three dimensions and a three-dimensional work infringed by making a copy in two dimensions.[1] An artistic work consisting of a two-dimensional representation of a three dimensional object is therefore

7–55

---

[97] CDPA 1988, s.51.

[98] CDPA 1988, s.17(2).

[99] CDPA 1988, s.17(2). And see *Autospin (Oil Seals) Ltd v Beehive Spinning* [1995] R.P.C. 683 at 698.

[1] CDPA 1988, s.17(3). There was some doubt about this prior to the 1911 Act (see *Hanfstaengl v Empire Palace* [1894] 2 Ch. 1, where it was held on the facts of that case that *tableaux vivants* were not infringements of copyright in pictures, although the House of Lords considered that as a matter of law this was possible: see [1895] A.C. 20), but any doubt about this was laid to rest by the 1911 Act: see *Bradbury, Agnew & Co v Day* (1916) 32 T.L.R. 349 and *King Features Syndicate v O. & M. Kleeman Ltd* [1940] 1 Ch. 531 (at first instance) and [1941] A.C. 417, fol-

infringed by copying it in the form of the three-dimensional object, whether directly (*i.e.* from the artistic work itself) or indirectly (*e.g.* by copying an object itself made from the artistic work).[2] The copyright in a drawing of a human figure may thus be infringed by copying it in the form of a sculpture, and the copyright in a sculpture infringed by taking a photograph of it.[3] The change of medium or dimension may make it more difficult to see that the three-dimensional work is a copy, but this is only a question of degree.[4] It makes no difference, it is suggested, that after it was made the copy became bound up with other items such that it no longer resembles the copyright work or a substantial part of it. Before alteration it was a copy and if it can be disassembled it can be seen to be a copy again.[5] It has already been pointed out[6] that copying can take place where the link between the artistic work and the copy is only a written or verbal description, and that a work may also be infringed by the designer being given very loose instructions and then corraled into producing something which eventually resembles the copyright work. There is no copying, however, where no new copy of the work is brought into existence. So where a defendant transferred an image from a poster onto canvas, by physically lifting the ink from the poster, leaving a blank piece of paper behind, there was no copying.[7]

The 1956 Act contained a special defence such that the copyright in a two-dimensional artistic work was not infringed by a three-dimensional copy if the copy did not appear to a non-expert to be a reproduction of the two-dimensional work.[8] This provision was not repeated in the 1988 Act but its abolition has not widened the scope of what constitutes a reproduction of an artistic work.[9]

In order to see whether an artistic work has been reproduced, it is permissible to examine a greatly magnified form of the alleged infringing article.[10] However, the copy must in some real sense represent the artistic work, so that the copyright in an artistic work such as a map or diagram which contains information in a vi-

---

lowed in *Walt Disney Productions v H. John Edwards Publishing Co Pty Ltd* (1954) 71 W.N. (N.S.W.) 150. Although see *Autospin (Oil Seals) Ltd v Beehive Spinning* [1995] R.P.C. 683, suggesting that there was never any doubt.

[2] *British Leyland Motor Corp v Armstrong Patents Co Ltd* [1986] A.C. 577, HL; *Canon Kabushiki Kaisha v Green Cartridge Co. (Hong Kong) Ltd* [1997] A.C. 401.

[3] Although note the defence provided by CDPA 1988, s.62.

[4] *King Features Syndicate v O. & M. Kleeman Ltd* [1940] Ch. 523 (at first instance). But note *Burke, etc. Ltd v Spicers Dress Designs* [1936] Ch. 400 (dress held not to amount to a reproduction of perspective drawing), a case decided very much on its own facts, and not followed in *Gleeson v H.R. Denne Ltd* [1975] R.P.C. 471; *Radley Gowns Ltd v Coftas Spyrou* [1975] F.S.R. 455; *J. Bernstein Ltd v Sidney Murray Ltd* [1981] R.P.C. 303.

[5] See *Muscat v Le* (2004) 204 A.L.R. 335, disapproving *Merlet v Mothercare Plc* [1984] F.S.R. 358, where Walton J. had held that a cape was not a reproduction of a cutting pattern because in its sewn-up form it did not resemble the pattern.

[6] See para. 7–15, above.

[7] *Thèberge v Gallerie d'Art du Petit Champlain Inc* 210 D.L.R. (4th)385 (Sup Ct of Can). See also *Benchmark Building Supplies Ltd v Mitre 10 (New Zealand) Ltd* (2004) 58 I.P.R. (stickers superimposed on claimant's posters) and *Frost v Olive Series Publishing Co* (1908) 22 TLR 649 (mounted pictures from pamphlets sold as cards).

[8] Copyright Act 1956, s.9(8), which provided that: "The making of an object of any description which is in three dimensions shall not be taken to infringe the copyright in an artistic work in two dimensions, if the object would not appear, to persons who are not experts in relation to objects of that description, to be a reproduction of the artistic work." There were few cases in practice where the defence succeeded, although see, *e.g.* the remarks in *S.W.Hart Ltd v Edwards Hot Water Systems* [1986] F.S.R. 575 (High Ct of Aus). The section came under repeated criticism for the difficulties in its interpretation.

[9] *Anacon Corp. Ltd v Environmental Research Technology Ltd* [1994] F.S.R. 659, rejecting the argument that s.9(8) of the Copyright Act 1956 recognised that there might be certain kinds of artistic works which only an expert could recognise as infringements, so that certain things are now infringements which were not before. However, it must also be arguable that any case which would have come within the old s.9(8) defence should still not be an infringement, since if the alleged infringing article cannot be seen by anyone other than an expert to "reproduce" the copyright work, why should a court find it to be so?

[10] *Guildford Kapwood Ltd v Embassy Fabrics Ltd* [1983] F.S.R. 567, where the court compared a

sual as opposed to a literary form is not infringed by reproducing the data in a literary form, such as a table.[11] Nor is the copyright in such an artistic work infringed by producing something which has a wholly different visual appearance, even though the information conveyed may be the same.[12] Again, there is no artistic copyright in such matters as dimensions or other written material recorded on an artistic work, so that if these are all that the defendant has copied, the artistic copyright will not be infringed: a reproduction must in some way be a copy or representation of the original.[13] Written instructions and other material may of course be referred to, to see whether there is any causal link between the three-dimensional work and the drawing.[14] Associated drawings may be looked at together to see if there has been an infringement,[15] but where it is alleged that the copyright in two separate drawings has been infringed by one composite work, each drawing must be considered separately.[16] Where a claimant's works consist of a large number of similar drawings, as in the case of characters created for a cartoon series, a defendant may well not have copied any one particular drawing but rather an amalgam of the distinguishing features of a character. In such cases, a defendant will not escape by arguing that the claimant cannot identify the particular work copied.[17] There is a problem where the "artistic work" is recorded in the form of a data file: is the record of dimensions, etc., an artistic or a literary work (being a table, etc.), and if the latter, is copyright infringed by reproducing the data in a form recognisable to the human eye as an artistic work? The approach to such problems should be a common sense one, namely has the work been reproduced?[18]

If an artistic work consists of the representation of some internal part of an object which is not directly visible, it is permissible to dissect the object, for example to make a cross section. If from the sectioned article, the artistic work can be seen to have been copied, this is sufficient for the purposes of

greatly magnified version of the defendant's garment with the claimant's lapping diagram, used in a particular knitting process.

[11] *Anacon Corp. Ltd v Environmental Research Technology Ltd* [1994] F.S.R. 659. But in such a case it is important to bear in mind that copyright may subsist in the data as a separate literary work (namely a table or compilation) and, if so, the copyright in this work may be infringed by reproduction of the data. See paras 3–17 *et seq.* and 7–34 above at (i). See also *Sandman v Panasonic U.K. Ltd* [1998] F.S.R. 651.

[12] Copyright in an artistic work consisting of a circuit diagram will thus not be infringed by copying it in the form of another circuit diagram with a wholly different visual appearance, or by copying it in the form of a circuit board which has a wholly different visual appearance. See the cases cited in the previous footnote. Note, however, that in *Mackie Designs Incorporated v Behringer Specialised Studio Equipment (U.K.) Ltd* [1999] R.P.C. 717, a circuit diagram was held to be design document within the meaning of s.51 and therefore the copyright in such a diagram would in any event not be infringed by making an article to that design. See Ch.13 and para. 13–294, below. As to the possibility of infringement of the literary work which may be recorded in a circuit diagram, see para. 7–34, above.

[13] *Catnic Components Ltd v Hill & Smith Ltd* [1982] R.P.C. 183 at 223, approved in *Interlego Industries A.G. v Tyco Industries Inc* [1989] A.C. 217. See also *The Duriron Company Inc v Hugh Jennings & Co Ltd* [1984] F.S.R. 1; *Brigid Foley Ltd v Ellott* [1982] R.P.C. 433 (written knitting guides not infringed by manufacture of garments); *Davis (J & S) (Holdings) Ltd v Wright Health Group Ltd* [1988] R.P.C. 403 at 414. See, generally, on this point, para. 7–34, above.

[14] *British Leyland Motor Corporation v Armstrong Patents* [1984] F.S.R. 591, CA; *Interlego A.G. v Tyco Industries Inc* [1987] F.S.R. 409 (CA, Hong Kong) and [1989] A.C. 217, 265, PC. This point often arose in connection with s.9(8) of the 1956 Act, referred to above.

[15] *Rose Plastics GmbH v William Beckett & Co. (Plastics) Ltd* [1989] F.S.R. 113, relying on *Solar Thomson Engineering Co v Barton* [1977] R.P.C. 537 at 559. See also *Merchant Adventurers Ltd v M. Grew & Co Ltd* [1972] R.P.C. 242.

[16] *Biotrading & Financing OY v Biohit Ltd* [1998] F.S.R. 109; *UPL Group Ltd v Dux Engineers Ltd* [1989] 3 N.Z.L.R. 135 at 143.

[17] *King Features Syndicate Inc v O. & M. Kleeman Ltd* [1941] A.C. 417, applied in *BBC Worldwide Ltd v Pally Screen Printing Ltd* [1998] F.S.R. 665.

[18] See *Autospin (Oil Seals) Ltd v Beehive Spinning* [1995] R.P.C. 683. Arguably, the data file can be regarded as an artistic work because it is simply the record of the shape, etc of the work, just as are the lines drawn on a page.

infringement.[19] The same applies where the drawing is itself a sectional drawing of a three dimensional object,[20] although the application of both these principles has been greatly reduced by section 51 of the 1988 Act, considered above.

7–56   **Proof of copying.** Whether or not copying has taken place is established using the usual forensic means already discussed.[21] In a case where the court is asked to infer copying by reason of the similarities between the works, the first step should be to identify those features of the defendant's work which it is alleged have been copied from the copyright work. The court should then undertake a visual comparison of the two works, noting the similarities and the differences. The purpose of this examination is to judge whether the particular similarities relied on are sufficiently close, numerous or extensive to be more likely to be the result of copying than coincidence, not to see whether the overall appearance of the two designs is similar. Similarities which are commonplace, unoriginal, the result of common subject matter or external constraints, such as dimensions to which both works are subject,[22] or consist of general ideas can usually be disregarded at this stage because they are not probative of copying. This is not a hard and fast rule, however, because an overall impression of sufficient similarity, leading to an inference of copying, can arise from a combination of elements which by themselves are not original.[23] If the claimant demonstrates sufficient similarity, not in the works as a whole but in the features which he alleges have been copied, and establishes that the defendant had prior access to the copyright work, the burden passes to the defendant to satisfy the judge that, despite the similarities, they did not result from copying. Although this inquiry is directed to the similarities rather than the differences, the differences may nevertheless be important because they may indicate an independent source and so rebut any inference of copying. But differences in the overall appearance of the two works due to the presence of features of the defendant's work about which no complaint is made are not material.[24]

7–57   **Inexact reproduction: imitation and substantial part.** Once it has been established that the defendant's work represents the claimant's in the sense discussed above and that the similarities between the works are the result of copying, then, except in the case of exact copying, the question will be whether the defendant's work is a copy of a substantial part of the claimant's. The general principles relating to inexact reproduction have already been discussed. Since it is the object of copyright in cases of this kind to ensure that the skill and effort of the creator are rewarded,[25] it has to be determined whether the maker of the defendant's work used a substantial part of those features of the claimant's work upon the creation of which skill and labour was employed. Have the essential features and substance of the copyright work been adopted?[26] As to this, in accordance with general principles, the elements or features which have been copied

---

[19] *Solar Thompson Engineering Co Ltd v Barton* [1977] R.P.C. 537.

[20] There are many examples in the cases. See, *e.g. Johnstone Safety Ltd v Peter Cook (International) plc* [1990] F.S.R. 161.

[21] See para. 7–17, above.

[22] *Nicol v Barranger* [1917–23] Mac.C.C. 219, CA.

[23] *Nouveau Fabrics Ltd v Voyage Decoration Ltd* [2004] EWHC 895 (Ch), pointing out that otherwise an inference of copying could never be made where the originality of the copyright work lay in its combination of existing elements or features.

[24] This paragraph is based on the speech of Lord Millett in *Designers Guild Ltd v Russell Williams (Textiles) Ltd,* [2000] 1 W.L.R. 2416 at 2425.

[25] *British Leyland Motor Corp Ltd v Armstrong Patents Co Ltd* [1983] F.S.R. 50 (at first instance).

[26] *Hanfstaengl v Baines & Co* [1895] A.C. 20 at 31; *Merchant Adventurers Ltd v M. Grew & Co Ltd* [1973] R.P.C. 1; *Drayton Controls (Engineering) Ltd v Honeywell Control Systems Ltd* [1992] F.S.R. 245.

must first be identified and then compared with the copyright work as whole.[27] A claimant is not entitled to select only parts of his work, claiming copyright in those, so as to establish infringement by reproduction of just those parts.[28] By the same token, a defendant is not entitled to dissect the copyright work, taking each part which has been copied and asking whether each part could be the subject of copyright if it had stood alone. The inquiry should be directed to what has been reproduced rather than what has not.[29] Because of this, it is wrong to decide the question by asking whether the defendant's work looks like the claimant's.[30] An action for infringement of copyright is not concerned with the appearance of the defendant's work but with its derivation. The basis of the complaint is not that the defendant's work resembles the copyright work but that the defendant has copied all or a substantial part of it. Thus the overall appearance of the defendant's work may be very different from the copyright work, but it does not follow that the defendant's work does not infringe the plaintiff's copyright.[31] A visual comparison of the two designs is therefore not only unnecessary, but likely to mislead.[32] It used to be said[33] that the question of substantial part could generally be answered merely by a comparison of the two works, and that a useful test of a copy was something which came so near to the original as to give every person seeing it the idea created by the original[34] or, alternatively, was that which comes so near to the original as to suggest that original to the mind of every person seeing it.[35] This must now be regarded as wrong,[36] certainly to the extent that it suggests that if the defendant's work does *not* give the idea of or suggest the copyright work, the substantial part test is not satisfied. Obviously, if the defendant's work does give the idea of or suggest the copyright work, this may be because there has been substantial copying, but even this may not be the case for the reasons given below. This kind of approach is more appropriate in relation to the threshold question of whether there has been copying.[37]

In deciding the question of substantial part, it may be helpful to bear in mind that the essential nature of an artistic work is that it is a thing to be looked at, and

[27] *Designers Guild Ltd v Russell Williams (Textiles) Ltd* [2001] 1 W.L.R. 2416. In *Spectravest Inc v Aperknit Ltd* [1988] F.S.R. 161, Millett J., as he then was, suggested, citing *Baumann v Fussell* [1978] R.P.C. 485, that it may be a useful approach to start by identifying that part of the copyright work which is *alleged* to have been reproduced and deciding first whether that part constitutes a substantial part of the copyright work, applying the usual qualitative test, and then deciding whether that part *is* a copy. In the light of what was said in *Designers Guild Ltd v Russell Williams (Textiles) Ltd*, however, to which Lord Millett was a party, this is not the right approach.
[28] *Merchandising Corporation of America Inc v Harpbond Ltd* [1983] F.S.R. 32.
[29] *Designers Guild Ltd v Russell Williams (Textiles) Ltd* [2001] 1 W.L.R. 2416; *Baumann v Fussell* [1978] R.P.C. 485.
[30] *Designers Guild Ltd v Russell Williams (Textiles) Ltd* [2001] 1 W.L.R. 2416; *Baumann v Fussell* [1978] R.P.C. 485.
[31] *Designers Guild Ltd v Russell Williams (Textiles) Ltd* [2001] 1 W.L.R. 2416, *per* Lord Millett, at 2425.
[32] *Designers Guild Ltd v Russell Williams (Textiles) Ltd* [2001] 1 W.L.R. 2416, at p.2426.
[33] See, *e.g. Copinger*, 14th ed., para.7–82.
[34] *West v Francis* (1822) 5 B. & Ald. 737 at 743; cited with approval in the House of Lords in *King Features Syndicate v O. & M. Kleeman Ltd* [1941] A.C. 417, although note that this form of definition is not complete, as it does not take into account the necessity of proving actual copying: see *Merchant Adventurers Ltd v M. Grew & Co Ltd* [1971] F.S.R. 233 at 237.
[35] *Hanfstaengl v W.H. Smith & Sons* [1905] 1 Ch. 519 at 524; see *Catnic Components Ltd v Hill & Smith Ltd* [1975] F.S.R. 529; [1979] F.S.R. 619, CA; *Lerose Ltd v Hawick Jersey International Ltd* [1973] F.S.R. 15; *Antocks Lairn Ltd v I. Bloohn Ltd* [1971] F.S.R. 490; and see *Twentieth Century Fox Film Corp v Anglo Amalgamated Film Distributors Ltd*, *The Times*, January 22, 1965.
[36] See *Designers Guild Ltd v Russell Williams (Textiles) Ltd* [2000] 1 W.L.R. 2416 and the general discussion of the "substantial part" issue, para. 7–27, above.
[37] See para. 7–56, above.

what is important is what is visually significant.[38] In this context "visually significant" means visually significant to the person to whom the work would normally
be addressed.[39] In the case of an artistic work, whether the part reproduced is
substantial may therefore depend upon how important that part is to the recognition and appreciation of the work.[40] Where the purpose of the artistic work is to
convey information, the importance of the part reproduced may thus fall to be
judged by how far it contributes to the conveying of that information.[41] Nevertheless, it must be born in mind that what is protected is the skill and labour devoted
to making the artistic work, not the skill and labour devoted to developing the
idea or invention communicated.[42] The limit of protection in the case of an artistic
work is its visual characteristics, not the technical ideas that it embodies.[43]

7–58   Since the question of substantiality has to be judged by asking whether there has
been a substantial taking of those features of the copyright work upon the creation of which skill and labour was employed, it follows that if the defendant has
merely reproduced a part of the copyright work on which no skill and labour was
expended, so that it had no originality, there will be no infringement.[44] Thus if the
copyright work is based partly upon an earlier work, and all that has been appropriated is the work of the earlier artist, there will have been no substantial
copying of the copyright work.[45] Again, there is no copyright in an idea or
functional concept as such, so that if this is all the defendant has copied, and he
has not appropriated the claimant's labour in expressing that idea in the form of
an artistic work, there will be no infringement.[46] Generally speaking, the more
abstract and simple the copied idea, the less likely it is to constitute a substantial
part of the copyright work. Originality, in the sense of the contribution of the
author's skill and labour, tends to lie in the detail with which the basic idea is
presented.[47] Copyright protection is no broader where the work embodies a novel
or inventive idea than where it represents a commonplace object.[48] But where an
idea or concept has been expressed in some artistic work using sufficient skill and
labour to make it a copyright work, then the copyright will be infringed by copying that expression.[49] Artistic techniques and skills, for example types of
brushwork, cannot generally be the subject of copyright, so if this is all that has

---

[38] *Rose Plastics GmbH v William Beckett & Co (Plastics) Ltd* [1989] F.S.R. 114, adopted in *Interlego Industries A.G. v Tyco Industries Inc* [1989] A.C. 217 and applied in *Johnstone Safety Ltd v
Peter Cook (International) plc* [1990] F.S.R. 161.
[39] *Billhöfer Machinenfabrik GmbH v T. H. Dixon & Co. Ltd* [1990] F.S.R.105: in the case of an
engineering drawing, "visually significant" means visually significant to an engineer and not an
ordinary member of the public.
[40] *Catnic Components Ltd v Hill & Smith Ltd* [1982] R.P.C. 183 at 223, approved in *Interlego
Industries A.G. v Tyco Industries Inc* [1989] A.C. 217 and applied in *Johnstone Safety Ltd v Peter Cook (International) plc* [1990] F.S.R. 161.
[41] *Entec (Pollution Control) Ltd v Abacus Mouldings* [1992] F.S.R. 332 (at first instance: in the case
of a manufacturing drawing, reproduction of a substantial part means reproduction of the dimensions and spatial arrangements which are important for the purpose of manufacturing the article).
[42] *Catnic Components Ltd v Hill & Smith Ltd* [1982] R.P.C. 183 at 223, approved in *Interlego
Industries A.G. v Tyco Industries Inc* [1989] A.C. 217.
[43] *Ultra Marketing (UK) Ltd v Universal Components Ltd* [2004] EWHC 468 (Ch), para.51.
[44] *Merchandising Corporation of America Inc v Harpbond Ltd* [1983] F.S.R. 32.
[45] See, *e.g.* para. 7–27, above at (j).
[46] *L.B. (Plastics) Ltd v Swish Products Ltd* [1979] R.P.C. 611; *Johnstone Safety Ltd v Co v Peter
Cook (International) plc* [1990] F.S.R. 161; *Mono Pumps (N.Z.) v Amalgamated Pumps* [1992] 1
N.Z.L.R. 728.
[47] *Designers Guild Ltd v Russell Williams (Textiles) Ltd* [2001] 1 W.L.R. 2416, at 2423: "Copyright
law protects foxes better than hedgehogs." See the footnote to para. 7–27, above at (e).
[48] *Catnic Components Ltd v Hill & Smith Ltd* [1979] F.S.R. 619, CA.
[49] *Catnic Components Ltd v Hill & Smith Ltd* [1979] F.S.R. 619, CA; *Leco Instruments (U.K.) Ltd v
Land Pyrometers Ltd* [1982] R.P.C. 140, CA. For examples of cases where the idea has been copied but not the expression, see *Kenrick & Co v Lawrence & Co* (1890) 25 Q.B.D. 99 (idea of illustration of human hand in the act of voting, as an aid to illiterate voters); *Gleeson v H.R. Denne*

been copied, this will not amount to the taking of a substantial part. The principle cannot be taken too far, however, because the use of techniques will result in visual effects forming part of the artistic work and if these effects have been reproduced, this will be relevant to the overall issue of substantial part.[50] Again, in the case of a drawing of a utilitarian article, it is not correct to attempt to separate the skills of the creator of the copyright work into those which were purely "artistic" and those which were directed to giving the article its operational efficiency, perhaps at the direction of an engineer, and thus argue that if no use has been made of the former skills there will have been no infringement.[51] The fact that the claimant's work may have been the inspiration for the defendant's will not of itself make the defendant's work an infringement,[52] although if the "feeling and character" of the claimant's work has been taken this will be a relevant, but not conclusive, consideration.[53] Again as has been seen, the test of infringement is not affected by the fact that the defendant's work may be a parody of the claimant's.[54]

Once it is established that there has been a substantial use of the claimant's work, it does not matter that the defendant has used a different medium, or that the infringing work has been derived indirectly from the claimant's. It is equally an infringement of copyright whether the size of the copy has been increased or reduced,[55] or the dimensions altered.[56] A copy of another's work will not escape infringement merely by the omission or substitution by the defendant of features in the claimant's work,[57] or by combining part of the claimant's work with his own or another's in producing the final result.[58] Minor or trivial differences will not prevent one work from being a reproduction of another.[59]

Simple artistic works. Where the work is simple, or one representing ordinary objects, the first issue is usually whether the work is sufficiently original to make it a copyright work.[60] Once this had been established, the fact that the work may be described as simple does not help a defendant if he has in fact copied, that is,

7–59

Ltd [1975] R.P.C. 471 (concept for design of clerical collars); *Kleeneze Ltd v D.R.G. (U.K.) Ltd* [1984] F.S.R. 399 (concept for draught excluder); *George Ward (Moxley) Ltd v Richard Sankey Ltd* [1988] F.S.R. 66 (idea of sleeve for "nested" flower pots). For a general discussion of the problem of idea *versus* expression, see para. 7–13, above.

[50] *Designers Guild Ltd v Russell Williams (Textiles) Ltd* [2001] 1 W.L.R. 2416. There, the creator of the claimant's work had used a technique that had produced a distinctive impression of looseness and boldness combined with lightness and fragility, and this effect had been copied: see p.2421.

[51] *British Leyland Motor Corp Ltd v Armstrong Patents Co Ltd* [1986] A.C. 577 at 621, HL, although cases of this kind will now usually only be relevant in the case of design right. It has been said that where the claimant's design has been indirectly copied but only to the extent of features that are purely functional, there is no infringement: see *George Ward (Moxley) Ltd v Richard Sankey Ltd* [1988] F.S.R. 66, *per* Whitford J., citing the dissenting judgment of Lord Griffiths in *British Leyland*. It is suggested that this is clearly wrong.

[52] *Baumann v Fussell* [1978] R.P.C. 485.

[53] *Baumann v Fussell* [1978] R.P.C. 485; *Brooks v Religious Tract Society* (1897) 45 W.R. 476; *Antiquesportfolio.com v Rodney Fitch & Co Ltd* [2001] F.S.R. 345 at 355 (photographs).

[54] *Twentieth Century Fox Film Corporation v Anglo Amalgamated Film Distributors Ltd, The Times*, January 22, 1965.

[55] *Johnstone Safety Ltd v Peter Cook (Int.) plc* [1990] F.S.R. 161 at 174; *Auvi Trade Mark* [1995] F.S.R. 288 at 296; *Antiquesportfolio.com v Rodney Fitch & Co Ltd* [2001] F.S.R. 345.

[56] *Wham-O Manufacturing Co v Lincoln Industries Ltd* [1985] R.P.C. 127 (CA of NZ); *Johnstone Safety Ltd v Peter Cook (Int.) plc* [1990] F.S.R. 161; *Alan Nuttall v Equipashop Ltd*, noted at [1992] I.P.D. 15097 (what is substantial cannot be defined by inches or measurement).

[57] *Brooks v Religious Tract Society* (1897) 45 W.R. 476.

[58] *London Stereoscopic, etc. Co Ltd (The) v Kelly* (1888) 5 T.L.R. 169; *Weldons Ltd v United Press Ltd* [1905–10] Mac.C.C. 293.

[59] *British Northrop Ltd v Texteam Blackburn Ltd* [1974] R.P.C. 57; *S.W. Hart & Co Pty Ltd v Edwards Hot Water Systems* [1986] F.S.R. 575; *Interlego A.G. v Tyco Industries Inc* [1987] F.S.R. 409.

[60] As to which, see para. 3–129, above.

taken advantage of the skill and labour of the claimant in making the work.[61] On the other hand, where the work is indeed simple, a defendant may more easily be able to show that while he may have copied the concept, he did not take advantage of the claimant's labour in expressing it, *i.e.* did not copy what was visually significant, but rather did this by his own efforts.[62] Thus the more simple and commonplace the drawing, the more clearly must the alleged infringement adhere to it if liability is to be established,[63] and in the case of works of little originality, almost exact copying will normally be required to establish infringement.[64] It follows that in the case of simple drawings, the labour of creation may have been so slight that there will be no infringement unless there is an almost exact reproduction of the drawing.[65]

7–60   **Reproduction of photographs.** Photographs are commonly reproduced photographically or by some other facsimile process, but they may also be reproduced by a drawing, painting or even by another photograph for which the subject matter was specially posed or selected.[66] These cases sometimes cause difficulties, and it is important to understand what it is that the copyright in a photograph protects, namely the author's work of origination.[67] Thus where a photographer takes a photograph of some public event or naturally occurring scene, a defendant who uses the photograph to obtain an accurate impression of the relative positions of the individuals or objects in the scene, but otherwise recreates the scene in his own style, will usually not infringe. This is because the relative positions of the individuals or objects are not the work of the photographer.[68] This may even be the case where the scene is not commonplace and the photograph may have been the inspiration for the defendant's work.[69] But where the defendant has in addition recreated the feeling and artistic character of the claimant's work this may be sufficient to amount to an infringement if a substantial portion of the claimant's skill and labour has thereby been taken.[70] So also where the photographer has arranged the subject-matter of the photograph to create a particular design[71] or has composed his photograph to include a particular selection of features which the defendant has copied.[72] In each case it is a matter of degree.[73] The copying, however, must be of the photograph. Thus where a defendant took a photograph of a scene which had been arranged by the claimant, he did not

---

[61] *Cala Homes (South) Ltd v Alfred McAlpine Homes East Ltd* [1995] F.S.R. 818.

[62] *Entec (Pollution Control) Ltd v Abacus Mouldings* [1992] F.S.R. 332.

[63] *Constructions Pty Ltd v Foskett Pty Ltd* (1991) 20 I.P.R. 666 (Fed Ct of Aus.); *Dixon Investments Pty Ltd v Hall* (1990) 18 I.P.R. 481 (Fed Ct of Aus).

[64] *Glogau v Land Transport Safety Authority of New Zealand* [1999] 1 N.Z.L.R. 257 (CA of NZ).

[65] *Politechnika Ipari Szovetkezet v Dallas Print Transfers Ltd* [1982] F.S.R. 529.

[66] *Antiquesportfolio.com v Rodney Fitch & Co Ltd* [2001] F.S.R. 345, at 355, approving this passage, although only *obiter.*

[67] As to the author of a photograph, see paras 4–32 *et seq.*, above. For a full discussion of the various issues, see Michalos, *The Law of Photography and Digital Images* (London, Sweet & Maxwell, 2004).

[68] *Baumann v Fussell* [1978] R.P.C. 485.

[69] *Baumann v Fussell* [1978] R.P.C. 485

[70] *Brooks v Religious Tract Society* (1897) 45 W.R. 476; *Baumann v Fussell* [1978] R.P.C. 485.

[71] *Baumann v Fussell* [1978] R.P.C. 485.

[72] *Krisarts S.A. v Briarfine Ltd* [1977] F.S.R. 557.

[73] The equivalent passage in the 14th ed., down to this point, was approved in *Antiquesportfolio.com v Rodney Fitch & Co Ltd* [2001] F.S.R. 345, at 355, with a particular emphasis on the points that it is the "author's work of origination which is protected", and that there may be infringement where the defendant has "recreated the feeling and artistic character of the [claimant's] work". The case contains a number of examples of copying of photographic works.

infringe the copyright in the claimant's photograph of the same scene because there was no causal link between the two photographs.[74]

Reproduction of scenes from painting, etc. The same kind of problem may arise where the claimant's work is a painting or drawing of a scene. Even if the scene is a well-known one, the artist may well have made an original contribution to his picture by his choice of viewpoint, the balance of features in the foreground, middle ground and background, and the other details. A defendant who makes a substantial use of these features will infringe.[75]   **7–61**

Maps and diagrams. The normal rules apply to what might be called the purely artistic features of a map.[76] In the case of maps, however, copyright will subsist not only in the outlines of the various features but also in the selection, arrangement and presentation of the various parts, such as towns, lakes, rivers, etc. If the defendant has copied the claimant's selection, amounting to a substantial part, he will have infringed.[77] It should also be borne in mind that such works are usually not only artistic works, but in some respects are also compilations of information, and in this respect are to be treated as literary works.[78] The artistic copyright may therefore be infringed by reproduction in the form of a substantially similar map and the literary work may be infringed by the reproduction in some other form, for example a table of the information which the map contains. In either case, to escape infringement a defendant must himself carry out the survey, gather the information and do whatever else is necessary to compile the work, and not simply appropriate the claimant's labour.[79]   **7–62**

Architects plans and works of architecture. Copyright may subsist in both architects' plans and in works of architecture themselves (*i.e.* buildings or models for buildings[80]). Although architects may therefore be concerned with infringements of a number of different rights, disputes in this area most usually concern infringements of plans by the making of other plans and the construction of buildings from such plans.   **7–63**

Infringement of plans. Copyright in an architect's plan is infringed if a substantial part of the skill and labour used in creating the work has been taken.[81] The copying of the same methods of construction, if they do not find expression in the claimant's artistic work and the defendant's plan or building, will not constitute an infringement. Naturally it will be more difficult to establish copying of a design for an ordinary building since the similarities may be explained by the fact that each architect has drawn on common experience or sources.[82] However, this only goes to the matter of proof: if a claimant's design for an ordinary build-   **7–64**

---

[74] *Creation Records Ltd v News Group Newspapers Ltd* [1997] E.M.L.R. 444. There was also no copyright in the scene itself.

[75] *Krisarts S.A. v Briarfine Ltd* [1977] F.S.R. 557.

[76] Some of the older cases include *Carnon v Bowles* 2 Bro.C.C. 80; *Cary v Longman* (1801) 1 East. 357; *Cary v Faden* 5 Ves. 24.

[77] *Geographia Ltd v Penguin Books Ltd* [1985] F.S.R. 208; see also *General Drafting Co Inc v Andrews* 37 F. 2d 54.

[78] *Anacon Corp Ltd v Environmental Research Technology Ltd* [1994] F.S.R. 659.

[79] *Longman v Winchester* (1809) 16 Ves. 269 (two maps, if both accurate, may be much the same, but the labour and expense of a survey must be undertaken by each); *Kelly v Morris* (1866) L.R. 1 Eq. 697, is to the same effect.

[80] CDPA 1988, s.4(1)(a).

[81] *Cala Homes (South) Ltd v Alfred McAlpine East Ltd* [1995] F.S.R. 818.

[82] See, *e.g. Beck v Montana Constructions Pty Ltd* [1964–5] N.S.W.R. 229 at 232.

ing has been copied, the fact that the design is simple does not afford a defence.[83] In the usual way, the alleged infringement, even if derived from the claimant's work, must bear a sufficient resemblance to the part copied.[84]

An architect's plans may be copied in the form of a building which reproduces the plans. Thus a drawing of an elevation for a building can be infringed by a building which reproduces the elevation, this being a reproduction of the claimant's work in a "material form".[85] The more difficult case is where floor plans are copied. Here it may be thought more difficult to say that the plans have been infringed if the only way to see the resemblance would be either to demolish the building to floor level or to recreate the floor plan by measurement of the building. Nevertheless it seems reasonably clear that if it can be proved by such means, or by reference to the plans which it is proved the defendant used to construct the building, that the layout is substantially similar, then the copyright in the claimant's plans will have been infringed by the construction of the building, since the plans will have been reproduced in a "material form".[86]

7–65   Infringement of building or model for building. It should be born in mind that, unlike other artistic works, copyright does not subsist in a building or model for a building "irrespective of artistic quality".[87] It is suggested that infringement is therefore confined to copying that in which copyright subsists, namely the features of the building having artistic quality.[88] It should also be borne in mind that the copyright in a building is not infringed by making a graphic work,[89] photograph or film of it, or broadcasting a visual image of it.[90] Infringement is therefore largely confined to making a three-dimensional copy, whether in the form of another building or a model. The same applies to a model for a building if it is situated in a public place or in premises open to the public.[91]

7–66   Other permitted acts. It should also be noted that the copyright in a building, or in any drawings or plans in accordance with which the building was lawfully constructed, is not infringed by anything done for the purposes of reconstructing that building.[92]

D.   SOUND RECORDINGS

7–67   There is no extended definition in the 1988 Act of "to copy" in relation to sound recordings. It is therefore an infringement of the copyright in a sound recording

---

[83] *Cala Homes (South) Ltd v Alfred McAlpine East Ltd* [1995] F.S.R. 818 (see the Annexes to the report for an analysis and illustrations of the designs held to infringe).

[84] *Collier Constructions Pty Ltd v Foskett Pty Ltd* (1991) 20 I.P.R. 666 (Fed Ct of Aus)—copyright in floor plans for a house, which included the room divisions, windows, entrances and various fittings, not infringed by the reproduction of the outline only in an advertisement comparing overall sizes). See also *Dixon Investments Pty Ltd v Hall* (1990) 18 I.P.R. 481 (Fed Ct of Aus) and the cases cited there; *Eagle Homes Pty Ltd v Austec Homes Pty Ltd* (1997) 39 I.P.R. 565.

[85] *Chabot v Davies* (1936) 155 L.T. 525; [1936] 3 All E.R. 221.

[86] This was accepted without argument in *Cala Homes (South) Ltd v Alfred McAlpine East Ltd* [1995] F.S.R. 818. Note also that it is permissible to examine a cross section of what the defendant has made to establish infringement. See para. 7–55, above. See also *Lend Lease Homes Pty Ltd v Warrigal Homes Pty Ltd* [1970] 3 N.S.W.R. 265, where the difficult case of *Burke, etc. Ltd v Spicers Dress Designs* [1936] Ch. 400 was distinguished.

[87] See CDPA 1988, s.4(1)(a).

[88] See *Meikle v Maufe* [1941] 3 All E.R. 144, although note that under the 1911 Act copyright was conferred on a building or structure having an artistic character or design *in respect of such character or design*. See s.35(1).

[89] This expression includes a painting, drawing or plan. For the full definition, see CDPA 1988, s.4(2).

[90] See CDPA 1988, s.62, and para. 9–169, below for a fuller discussion of these permitted acts.

[91] CDPA 1988, s.62, and para. 9–169, below for a fuller discussion of these permitted acts.

[92] CDPA 1988, s.65. See para.9–00.

to copy it[93] or a substantial part of it,[94] either directly or indirectly[95] and whether transiently or incidentally to some other use.[96] Although the Act does not expressly state that copying may take place by storing the sound recording in a medium by electronic means,[97] it is suggested that such an act nevertheless does amount to copying.[98]

What is protected by the copyright in a sound recording is the particular recording of sounds on the sound carrier.[99] The copyright in a sound recording is therefore infringed by making a copy of those sounds, directly or indirectly, from that recording but not by making a new recording of identical or similar sounds independently, for example by recording a new performance by musicians of the same music.[1] Nor is it an infringement of the copyright in a sound recording to make a transcription in some form of notation of the sounds which have been recorded, for example in the form of sheet music. In any of these cases, of course, the copyright in a work which is recorded on the recording may be infringed by such means.

Substantial part. The issue of what amounts to a substantial part of a sound recording now frequently arises because of the practice of "sampling", that is, the process of taking a small part of a recording and repeating it, together with other material, to form a new recording. The problem is a difficult one because a very small and musically unexceptional part of a recording of a popular piece of music may yet be instantly recognisable. Indeed, this is usually the very reason why the part has been taken and, by the repeated use of the extract, the defendant draws on the popularity of the claimant's work to attract the public for his own benefit. It is suggested that this is an appropriate occasion for the application of the rule of thumb that "what is worth copying is worth protecting".[2]   **7–68**

Film soundtracks. The treatment of film soundtracks has changed over the years.   **7–69**
The topic is discussed in detail elsewhere, but for present purposes the soundtrack accompanying a film is today to be treated as part of the film.[3] This does not, however, affect any copyright which subsists in a film soundtrack as a sound recording.[4] Where, therefore, a film soundtrack has been copied, this is to be regarded as the copying of a film rather than of a sound recording.

---

[93] CDPA 1988, ss.16(1)(a), 17(1).
[94] s.16(3)(a).
[95] s.16(3)(b).
[96] s.17(6), although note the permitted act provisions of s.28A in relation to transient or incidental use.
[97] cf. s.17(2), which only applies in the case of copying of literary, dramatic, musical and artistic works.
[98] Copying of sound recordings by such means is a common feature of present-day recording techniques.
[99] "Sound recording" means: (a) a recording of sounds, from which the sounds may be reproduced, or (b) a recording of the whole or any part of a literary, dramatic or musical work, from which sounds reproducing the work or part may be produced. See CDPA 1988, s.5A(1).
[1] *Norowzian v Arks Ltd* [1998] F.S.R. 394; *CBS Records Australia Ltd v Telmak Teleproducts (Aust.) Pty Ltd* (1988) 79 A.L.R. 604; *Polygram Records Inc v Raben Footwear Pty Ltd* (1996) 35 I.P.R. 426 (Fed Ct of Aus).
[2] See para. 7–28, at (b), and compare the position in relation to musical works, para. 7–53, above. For a US case, see *Grand Upright Music Ltd v Warner Bros. Records Inc* 91 Civ. 7648(US Dist Ct). See also *Tackaberry* in [1990] Ent. L.R. 87 (for a review of the Canadian authorities) and *Bently and Sherman* in [1992] Ent. L.R. 158.
[3] CDPA 1988, s.5B(2).
[4] CDPA 1988, s.5B(5).

E. FILMS

7–70 It is an infringement of the copyright in a film to make a copy of it,[5] or a substantial part of it,[6] whether directly or indirectly[7] and whether transiently or incidental to some other use.[8] This includes making a photograph of the whole or any substantial part of any image forming part of the film.[9] As with a sound recording, it is not expressly stated that copying of a film includes storing it by electronic means, but again it is suggested that it does. Again, the copyright in a film is infringed if the recorded moving images are directly or indirectly copied but not if the same or similar images are created independently, for example by reshooting the subject matter of the film.[10] Again, however, underlying works such as the screenplay may be infringed by such means.

It has been seen that in relation to films made after July 1, 1994 the author of a film is to be taken, as from December 1, 1996 to be the principal director of the film, as well as the producer.[11] This is clearly likely to have an effect on the ownership of the copyright in such films and thus on the question of infringement. Transitional provisions therefore provide that where arrangements were made before November 19, 1992[12] for the exploitation of any such film, the rights which the principal director now has are not infringed by anything done after December 1, 1996 in pursuance of such arrangements.[13]

7–71 **Film soundtracks**. As already noted, for present purposes the soundtrack accompanying a film is today to be treated as part of the film.[14] Where, therefore, a film soundtrack has been copied, this is to be regarded as the copying of a film rather than of a sound recording.

F. BROADCASTS

7–72 No further definition of "copying" in relation to a broadcast is given in the 1988 Act other than that it includes making a photograph of the whole or any substantial part of any image forming part of the broadcast.[15] It should be noted, however, that the making in domestic premises for private and domestic use of a photograph of the whole or any part of an image forming part of a broadcast, or a copy of such a photograph, does not infringe any copyright in the broadcast.[16] In the usual way, it will also be an infringement to copy the whole or any substantial

[5] CDPA 1988, ss.16(1)(a), 17(1).
[6] CDPA 1988, s.16(3)(a).
[7] CDPA 1988, s.16(3)(b).
[8] CDPA 1988, s.17(6), although note the permitted act provisions of s.28A in relation to transient or incidental use.
[9] CDPA 1988, s.17(4). This gives statutory effect to the judicial interpretation of the 1956 Act. See *Spelling Goldberg Productions Inc v B.P.C. Publishing Ltd* [1981] R.P.C. 283.
[10] *Norowzian v Arks Ltd* [1998] F.S.R. 394; *Zeccola v Universal City Studios Inc.* (1982) 46 A.L.R. 189 and *Telmak Teleproducts Australia Pty Ltd v Bond International Pty Ltd* (1985) 5 I.P.R. 203 (although see the subsequent decision in the case reported at (1987) 9 I.P.R. 440, where the question was left open). A film is defined as a recording on any medium from which a moving image may by any means be produced. See CDPA 1988, s.5B(1).
[11] See CDPA 1988, s.9(2)(ab) and para. 4–58, above.
[12] The effective date of the Rental and Related Rights Directive.
[13] The Copyright and Related Rights Regulations 1996 (SI 1996/2967), reg.36(2).
[14] CDPA 1988, s.5B(2).
[15] CDPA 1988, s.17(4).
[16] s.71. See para. 9–196, below.

part of the broadcast,[17] whether directly or indirectly[18] or transiently or incidentally to some other use.[19]

Cable programmes. It has already been noted that, with effect from October 31, 2003, there is no longer a separate category of copyright work consisting of a cable programme, only a "broadcast".[20] Since that date, any work in which copyright may have subsisted as a cable programme can now only be protected as a broadcast, provided of course that it satisfies the qualifying conditions for a broadcast under the amended provisions of the 1988 Act.[21] In relation to any acts taking place before that date which amounted to an infringment of the copyright in a cable programme, the right to bring proceedings in respect of such infringement will still exist.[22] As to this, no further definition of "to copy" in relation to a cable programme was given in the Act other than it included the making of a photograph of the whole or any substantial part of any image forming part of the cable programme.[23] As with broadcasts, the making for private and domestic use of a photograph of the whole or any part of an image forming part of a cable programme, or a copy of such a photograph, did not infringe any copyright in the cable programme.[24]

7-73

G. TYPOGRAPHICAL ARRANGEMENTS

The Act provides that in relation to the typographical arrangement of a published edition, copying means making a facsimile copy of the arrangement.[25] "Facsimile copy" is defined as including a copy which is reduced or enlarged in scale.[26] The ubiquitous photocopying and faxing of published works are everyday examples of such infringements. Where the text of a published work is electronically scanned and the image then converted into a text file by character recognition software, the act of scanning will amount to copying of the typographical arrangement but the subsequent conversion or storage of the text will not do so. This is because the software will generate the typographical arrangement afresh.

7-74

Substantial part. As seen elsewhere,[27] the protected work in the case of typographical arrangement copyright is the whole of the product which a publisher offers to the public whether, in the case of a book, that which is between the covers or, in the case of a newspaper, the whole newspaper. The issue of substantial part must be judged by applying the normal rule that substantiality is about quality rather than quantity. As to the relevant quality, this again must be considered by reference to the reason why copyright protection is conferred on the work, which is to protect and reward the investment of skill and labour in the presentation and layout of the edition.[28]

The question is therefore whether there has there been a copying of sufficient

7-75

---

[17] s.16(3)(a).
[18] s.16(3)(b).
[19] s.17(6).
[20] See paras 3–82 et seq., above.
[21] See paras 3–90 et seq., above.
[22] Interpretation Act 1978, s.16.
[23] CDPA 1988, s.17(4).
[24] CDPA 1988, s.71.
[25] CDPA 1988, s.17(5). In *Machinery Market Ltd v Sheen Publishing Ltd* [1983] F.S.R. 431, decided under the 1956 Act, the defendants were held liable although it was their printers who had made the reproductions. It is not clear whether the printers were treated simply as the defendants' agents, although no doubt the defendants were liable for having authorised the infringement.
[26] CDPA 1988, s.178.
[27] See para. 3–104, above.
[28] *Newspaper Licensing Agency Ltd v Marks & Spencer* [2001] UKHL 38; [2003] 1 A.C. 551, ap-

of the relevant skill and labour expended on the creation of the edition's typographical arrangement. This depends not upon the proportion which the part taken bears to the whole but on whether the copy can be said to have appropriated the presentation and layout of the edition. In the case of traditional book publishing,[29] the skill and labour involved is the skill in designing the pages and the labour and capital in setting up the type and keeping it standing. In the case of a newspaper, the skill and labour devoted to the typographical arrangement is principally expressed in the overall design. It is not the choice of a particular typeface, the precise number or widths of the columns, the breadth of margins or the relationship of headlines and strap lines to the other text, the number of articles on a page or the distribution of photographs and advertisements, but the combination of all of these into pages which give the newspaper as a whole its distinctive appearance. In some cases, that appearance will depend upon the relationship between the pages; for example, having headlines rather than small advertisements on the front page. Usually, however, it will depend upon the appearance of any given page. It is therefore unlikely that the skill and labour which has gone into the typographical arrangement of a newspaper will be sufficiently expressed in anything less than a full page since the particular fonts, columns, margins and so forth are "the typographical vocabulary in which the arrangement is expressed".[30] So, where a defendant had made reprographic copies of individual articles from newspapers, this did not amount to the copying of a substantial part of the typographical arrangement of the whole newspaper. The defendant had not "reproduced anything that could be regarded as either resembling the newspaper concerned or having newspaper-like qualities".[31]

3. THE ISSUE OF COPIES TO THE PUBLIC: THE DISTRIBUTION RIGHT

7–76   The distribution right. One of the acts restricted by the copyright in all works is the issue of copies of the work to the public, often called the "distribution right". Broadly, this means the act of first release onto the market of any particular copy of the work, including "the original". Infringement by issue of copies to the public was a new concept introduced by section 18 of the 1988 Act and represented a substantial departure from the previous law, under which "publication" of a literary, dramatic, musical or artistic work was an infringement.[32] Decisions under the earlier law are of little assistance in interpreting section 18.

7–77   The Berne and Rome Conventions. There has been little consistency amongst the countries which are parties to these Conventions in their approach to a right

---

proving *Nationwide News Pty Ltd v Copyright Agency Ltd* (1994) 30 I.P.R. 159, (1995) 34 I.P.R. 53 (Fed Ct of Aus).

[29] This was the field of activity in mind when this form of protection was originally created by the 1956 Act and the purpose of the copyright was originally to protect the publisher against competition from pirate photo-lithographic copies of his edition.

[30] *Newspaper Licensing Agency Ltd v Marks & Spencer* [2001] UKHL 38, *per* Lord Hoffmann at para.23; [2003] 1 A.C. 551.

[31] *Newspaper Licensing Agency Ltd v Marks & Spencer* [2001] Ch. 257, CA *per* Mance L.J. and approved by the House of Lords [2001] UKHL 38; [2003] 1 A.C. 551.

[32] The expression "publishing" in this context did not simply mean the issuing of works to the public, but rather making public what had previously not been made public in the United Kingdom: *Infabrics Ltd v Jaytex Ltd* [1982] A.C. 1. A defendant could therefore only be liable under this head if copies of the work had never before been made public in the United Kingdom. For confirmation of the change in the law, see *The British Phonographic Industry Ltd v Mechanical-Copyright Protection Society Ltd (No. 2)* [1993] E.M.L.R. 86 at 98, n.9.

to control the distribution of works and related rights subject matter, and thus the Conventions do not lay down any general exclusive right in this area.[33]

EC Directives. The distribution right has been the subject of a number of EC Directives, two of which have necessitated amendments to section 18,[34] namely the Computer Software Directive, which dealt with computer programs,[35] and the Rental and Related Rights Directive, which dealt with related rights subject matter.[36] Most recently, Art.4 of the Information Society Directive[37] has required Member States to provide for a general distribution right[38]but no change to the 1988 Act was required to implement this aspect of the Directive.   **7–78**

Issue to the public: meaning.[39]As section 18 now stands, the expression "the issue to the public of copies of a work" means: **7–79**

(a) The act of putting into circulation in the EEA[40] copies not previously put into circulation in the EEA by or with the consent of the copyright owner; or

(b) The act of putting into circulation outside the EEA copies not previously put into circulation in the EEA or elsewhere.[41]

For this purpose, "issue to the public of copies of a work" does not include:

(c) any subsequent distribution, sale, hiring or loan of copies previously put into circulation[42] or

(d) any subsequent importation of such copies into the United Kingdom or another EEA state,

except insofar as paragraph (a) above applies to putting into circulation in the EEA copies previously put into circulation outside the EEA.[43]

Further, the expression "the issue of copies" is to be understood as including the issue of the "original" work.[44] Thus the putting into circulation of an original painting for the first time is a restricted act. The section originally made further provision for the case of rental of copies of certain works, but rental is now exclusively the subject of the separate rental right under section 18A, considered later in this chapter.

---

[33] For a full discussion, see Ricketson, *The Berne Convention for the Protection of Literary and Artistic Works: 1989–1996* (Kluwer, 1987), p.400, *et seq.*

[34] As to the transitional provisions relating to these amendments, see *Copinger* (14th ed.), para.7–110.

[35] Art.4 of the Directive required Member States to provided the rightholder with an exclusive right in relation to any form of distribution to the public of the original program or copies. It was implemented by the Copyright (Computer Programs) Regulations 1992 (SI 1992/3233).

[36] Art.9 of the Directive required Member States to provide an exclusive distribution right in respect of sound recordings, films (the producer's right) and broadcasts. It was implemented by the Copyright and Related Rights Regulations 1996 (SI 1996/2967).

[37] Directive 2001/29.

[38] The right is directed to the control of distribution of a work incorporated in a tangible article. See Recital 28, which provides: "Copyright protection under this Directive includes the exclusive right to control distribution of the work incorporated in a tangible article. The first sale in the Community of the original of a work or copies thereof by the rightholder or with his consent exhausts the right to control resale of that object in the Community. This right should not be exhausted in respect of the original or of copies thereof sold by the rightholder or with his consent outside the Community. Rental and lending rights for authors have been established in Directive 92/100/EEC. The distribution right provided for in this Directive is without prejudice to the provisions relating to the rental and lending rights contained in Ch.I of that Directive."

[39] See generally on the distribution right, Philips and Bently, "Copyright Issues: The Mysteries of Section 18" [1999] E.I.P.R. 133.

[40] The "EEA" means the European Economic Area: CDPA 1988, s.172A(1).

[41] CDPA 1988, s.18(2).

[42] But see CDPA 1988, s.18A: infringement by rental or lending.

[43] CDPA 1988, s.18(3).

[44] CDPA 1988, s.18(4). See also Art.4 of the Information Society Directive.

The section therefore makes the act of putting particular copies of a work into circulation in the United Kingdom for the first time a restricted act, even where the work has already been published in the sense that other copies of the work have previously been put into circulation in the United Kingdom. So, for example, the putting into circulation of a further 10 copies of a work which has already been published is a restricted act. It is also clear that it does not matter for this purpose whether the further copies are licensed or unlicensed.[45] A trader who therefore acquires a number of copies of a work which were made with the licence of the copyright owner but who does not have the owner's express or implied licence to put them into circulation will infringe if he does so.[46]

7–80   On the wording of the section, it might appear that copyright could be infringed by the act of putting copies into circulation outside the United Kingdom, not only anywhere in the EEA but even anywhere in the world outside the EEA. It is suggested that this cannot be correct. Not only is the whole basis of copyright, both as generally understood under United Kingdom law and internationally, territorial[47] but the words of section 18 are subject to the general words of section 16, namely that "[the] owner of the copyright in a work has, in accordance with the following provisions of this Chapter, the exclusive right to do the following acts *in the United Kingdom* … (b) to issue copies of the work to the public."[48] As originally enacted, section 18(2) provided that "References in this Part to the issue to the public of copies of a work are to the act of putting into circulation copies not previously put into circulation, in the United Kingdom or elsewhere, and not to (a) any subsequent distribution, sale, hiring or loan of those copies, or (b) any subsequent importation of those copies into the United Kingdom …". The change introduced to give effect to the Computer Software Directive[49] did not materially affect the sense of the section.[50] It was only the changes made as part of the implementation of the Rental and Related Rights Directive[51] which introduced the present wording. There is nothing in the Directive itself or the purposes which underlie it which suggests that a revolutionary broadening of the territoriality of the scope of infringement was intended. It is suggested that the present wording has come about because the draughtsman concentrated on giving effect to the Community principle of exhaustion of rights, while seeking to deny any question of international exhaustion, that is, to make it clear that while the act of putting a copy of a work into circulation in the EEA should exhaust that right within the EEA, the act of putting that copy into circulation anywhere outside the EEA should not do so. In doing so, the draughtsman focused on dealing with the past history of the copy (*i.e.* whether it had been put into circulation

[45] *Nelson v Rye* [1996] F.S.R. 313 at 339.
[46] Assuming that those copies had not previously been put into circulation. Normally, of course, he will have an implied if not express licence to do so. See *Nelson v Rye* [1996] F.S.R. 313, at 339.
[47] *i.e.* the right which each state confers by way of copyright is essentially domestic, and is concerned with the rights of the owner within that state.
[48] As to the territorial scope of United Kingdom copyright see *Peer International Corp v Termidor Music Publishers* [2002] EWHC 2675 (Ch), [2004] R.P.C. 22. And see *ABKCO Music v Music Collection International Ltd* [1995] R.P.C. 657 on the difference in the territorial scope of CDPA 1988, s.16 (limited to the United Kingdom) and the tort of authorisation (not so limited).
[49] By the Copyright (Computer Programs) Regulations 1992 (SI 1992/3233).
[50] The 1992 Regulations introduced, after the words "References in this Part to the issue to the public of copies of a work are", in CDPA 1988, s.18(2), the words "except where the work is a computer program" and a further subsection relating to computer programs: "(3) References in this Part to the issue to the public of copies of a work where the work is a computer program are to the act of putting into circulation copies of that program not previously put into circulation in the United Kingdom or any other member State, by or with the consent of the copyright owner, and not to (a) any subsequent distribution, sale, hiring or loan of those copies, or (b) any subsequent importation of those copies into the United Kingdom; except that the restricted act of issuing copies to the public includes any rental of copies to the public."
[51] By the Copyright and Related Rights Regulations 1996 (SI 1996/2967).

and, if so, where) and overlooked that, in doing so, the clarity of the geographic limitation of the basic exclusive right had been lost. It is therefore suggested that the effect of the section is as follows:[52]

(a) If the copy of the work has never before been put into circulation anywhere in the world, the act of putting it into circulation in the United Kingdom for the first time is a restricted act.

(b) If the copy has previously been put into circulation within the EEA by or with the consent of the copyright owner, then the act of putting it into circulation in the United Kingdom is not a restricted act. In Community terms, the distribution right is exhausted by the consensual first act of distribution.

(c) If the copy has previously been put into circulation in a country outside the EEA, but not within the EEA, then the act of putting it into circulation in the United Kingdom is a restricted act.

(d) Whether the act of putting the copy into circulation in a country other than the United Kingdom is an infringement of copyright is a matter for the law of that state, not that of the United Kingdom.

As to what acts amount to issuing to the public, or putting a copy into circulation, the latter expression is not further defined but suggests a release of a copy onto the market such that it may be passed on to other members of the public. It is not clear whether for this purpose the plural includes the singular, so that the release of a single copy is a restricted act,[53] but as a matter of principle there seems no good reason why it should not do so. Some help as to what acts might be included within the expression is provided by the references in subsections (3)(a) and (b) to acts of importation, distribution, sale, hire and loan, the inference being that any such act can amount to putting a copy into circulation (provided that it is not "subsequent" to an earlier issue to the public). In the case of acts of sale and distribution, it is easy to see that such acts might well have the effect of releasing copies onto the market. In the case of the acts of loan or hire, although such acts might not have the effect of releasing copies into *free* circulation, it would seem that they must be taken as amounting to putting copies into circulation. For this purpose, presumably the loan or hire of the copy must be to a member of the public and not by way of private transaction. Since the rental and lending of copies of a work to the public is also a restricted act under section 18A,[54] it would seem that the first rental or lending to a member of the public is capable of being an infringement under both section 18 and section 18A.[55] Finally, as to importation, it is difficult to see how the mere act of importation could amount to putting copies into circulation, particularly if, for example, the

---

[52] Section 18 should no doubt be construed consistently with the provisions of the Information Society Directive (2001/29), under which Member States are required to provide for authors, in respect of the original of their works or of copies of them, with the exclusive right to authorise or prohibit any form of distribution to the public by sale or otherwise: Art.4 (the distribution right in relation to related rights subject matter is dealt with in similar terms by Art.9 of the Rental and Related Rights Directive, 92/100). The right is directed to the control of distribution of a work incorporated in a tangible article (Recital 28) and is not to be exhauted within the European Community in respect of the original or copies of the work, except where the first sale or other transfer of ownership in the Community of that object is made by the rightholder or with his consent (Art.4.2 and Recital 28). On the other hand, first sale outside the Community is not to exhaust this right (Recital 28).

[53] This is clearly so in the case of the rental and lending right, and some support is given by the fact that the issue of the "original" is now a restricted act. The point was left open in *Microsoft Corp v Electro-wide Ltd* [1997] F.S.R. 580.

[54] As to this, see further below.

[55] The words in parenthesis in CDPA 1988, s.18(3)(a) appear to confirm this.

copies were not then released to the public.[56] It would appear that the act of offering or exposing copies for sale is not capable of amounting to putting copies into
circulation, this following from the ordinary meaning of the words and from the
absence of any reference to such acts in subsection (3).[57]

It is less clear what constitutes the restricted act of putting copies into circulation where there is a chain of distribution. Thus in the common type of case, the
chain of distribution will start with the producer or importer of the goods, which
are then sent to a wholesaler, who in turn distributes them to retailers, who then
make them available to the public. Who, in this chain, puts the goods into circulation? The producer or importer at the head of the chain no doubt is the principal
cause of the goods being put into eventual circulation, and it is suggested that it is
this person who is liable for the primary act of infringement of issuing copies of
the work to the public, even though it is not he who deals directly with the public.
This is given some support by the express provision that any *subsequent* distribution, sale, hiring or loan of copies previously put into circulation does not amount
to an infringement, indicating perhaps that it is only the person at the head of the
distribution chain who is liable under this section. The only other person who
might sensibly be described as putting the copies into circulation is the retailer at
the end of the distribution chain, being the person who has direct contact with the
public. As will be seen,[58] however, in relation to the acts of importation, sale and
distribution of infringing copies, the persons responsible for such acts are generally liable only if they have knowledge, actual or constructive, that they are dealing with infringing copies. A construction which made the person at the end of
the distribution chain liable for the primary act of infringement of issuing copies
to the public would thus render the requirement of guilty knowledge nugatory in
the case of dealings with infringing copies.[59]

4. THE RENTAL AND LENDING RIGHTS

7–81   **Background.** Historically, the right to control the rental or lending of legitimate
copies was not one of the rights conferred on copyright owners.[60] The 1988 Act
as enacted contained a limited exclusive right to control the rental of copies of
certain works. Thus in relation to sound recordings, films and computer programs,
the exclusive right of issuing copies to the public under section 18 included the
exclusive right of rental of copies of such works to the public.[61] No such right
was given in relation to the literary, dramatic, musical or artistic works which

---

[56] While the inclusion of this act in CDPA 1988, s.18(3)(b) suggests that there are circumstances
where importation could amount to an issue to the public, the better view is that this is also the
result of muddled drafting. The intention as expressed in Parliament seems clearly to have been
that mere importation could not amount to infringement. See *Hansard*, cols 214, 215 (November
2, 1988) (Lord Young).

[57] *cf.* CDPA 1988, s.24(1)(d), under which such acts in relation to infringing copies can amount to a
secondary infringement.

[58] See Ch.8, below.

[59] Note that in *The Football Association Premier League Ltd v Panini UK Ltd* [2003] EWCA Civ.
995, Munnery L.J. assumed that where a defendant had imported copies and then distributed
them to distributors, it was the distributors who issued the copies to the public, not the defendant
(presumably the distributors sold direct to the public, and there were no further distributors in the
chain). Thus the defendant might have been liable for importing, selling, distributing, etc., infringing copies, with knowledge, or for authorising the issue of copies to the public by the distributors,
but not for the act of issue to the public itself. The point, however, had not been argued. The *obiter* view of Paterson J., in *Video Ezy International (NZ) Ltd v Roadshow Entertainment (NZ) Ltd*
[2002] N.Z.L.R. 855, at 862, was to the same effect. See, again also, Philips and Bently, "Copyright Issues: The Mysteries of Section 18" [1999] E.I.P.R. 133.

[60] Although they had the right to control such dealings in infringing copies. See the Copyright Act
1956, s.5(3)(a).

[61] CDPA 1988, s.18(2). For this purpose "rental" included any arrangement under which a copy of
a work was made available (a) for payment (in money or money's worth), or (b) in the course of a

might be included in such media or which were otherwise the subject of rental, for example in the form of books. However, under the Public Lending Right Act 1979 as implemented by the Public Lending Right Scheme 1982, a separate right had been conferred on a limited class of authors under which they were entitled to payment out of a central fund in respect of books lent to the public by local library authorities. The public library lending of computer programs, sound recordings and films did not fall within the Public Lending Right Scheme but was treated as rental under section 18, even though no payment might be made.[62] Implementation of the Rental and Related Rights Directive required the United Kingdom to grant an exclusive right of rental and lending in relation to a much wider class of works than those referred to above.[63] Although Member States were *prima facie* required to provide an exclusive right of lending in respect of such works, they were permitted to derogate from this right in respect of "public lending", provided that authors obtained remuneration for this. The United Kingdom chose to exercise this right of derogation, and such remuneration is now provided under an amended Public Lending Right Scheme.[64] The necessary amendments to the 1988 Act were made with effect from December 1, 1996.[65] The scheme of the 1988 Act, as amended, is that both rental and lending of copies of a work to the public are now restricted acts, that is, they are two of the exclusive rights of the copyright owner, but if the lending of a book by a public library is within the Public Lending Right Scheme, or is by a prescribed library or archive, it amounts to a permitted act and is therefore not an infringement.[66] Provision is also made for the Secretary of State to provide for the lending to the public of defined categories of works to be treated as licensed, subject only to payment of a reasonable royalty.[67] As already pointed out, it appears that the first rental or lending of a work may be an act restricted not only by the rental and lending right but also by the distribution right.

The Berne and Rome Conventions. There has been little consistency amongst countries which are parties to these Conventions in their approach to a right to control the rental or lending of works and related rights subject matter, and thus the Conventions do not lay down any general exclusive right in this area.[68]   **7–82**

Applicable works. The rental and lending right only applies to certain categories of works, namely (a) literary, dramatic and musical works (b) artistic works other than works of architecture in the form of a building or a model for a building, or works of applied art and (c) films and sound recordings. As to the works excluded from these categories, the Rental and Related Rights Directive provides that the rights should not extend to "buildings",[69] the intention being to exclude the possibility of an architect or copyright owner being able to control the leasing of   **7–83**

---

business, as part of services or amenities for which payment was made, in either case on terms that it would or might be returned. See s.178 as enacted. Whether the first act of rental of copies of these and other types of work might constitute issue to the public was unclear; s.18 was amended, with effect from January 1, 1993, to introduce a new subs.(3) dealing solely with computer programs, but under which the rental of copies to the public remained a restricted act. See the Copyright (Computer Programs) Regulations 1992 (SI 1992/3233).

[62] See CDPA 1988, Sch.7, para.8, as enacted.

[63] For a detailed discussion of the background to the Rental Directive, see Reinbothe & von Lewinski, *The EC Directive on Rental and Lending Rights and on Piracy* (1993).

[64] See Ch.19, below.

[65] By the Copyright and Related Rights Regulations 1996 (SI 1996/2967).

[66] CDPA 1988, s.40A. See para. 9–108, below.

[67] CDPA 1988, s.66. See paras 9–178 and 29–45, below.

[68] For a discussion, see Ricketson, *The Berne Convention for the Protection of Literary and Artistic Works: 1989–1996* (Kluwer, 1987), p.401.

[69] Directive 92/100, Art.2.3.

property.[70] In fact, the 1988 Act goes further than the Directive in that models for buildings are also excluded. The exception in the case of works of "applied art" is also provided for by the Directive,[71] the expression not being defined further either by the Directive or the 1988 Act. It is an expression that is also found in the Berne Convention,[72] and refers broadly to articles to which an artistic work has been applied, usually by an industrial process. The distinction is between works of applied art and works of pure art. The intention is again to prevent the owner of the copyright in designs for such articles as cars or items of crockery from controlling their rental.[73]

7–84   **Rental right.** The rental of copies of any of the above categories of works, or the original,[74] to the public is a restricted act. For this purpose, rental means making a copy of the work available for use, on terms that it will or may be returned, for direct or indirect economic or commercial advantage.[75] The section is therefore aimed at the ordinary commercial rental of a work. The reference to a term that the work "may" be returned will include an arrangement whereby a copy of a work is sold to a purchaser but on terms that it can be brought back and some part of the money refunded or another work taken in exchange. The more limited provisions of the 1988 Act as enacted made it clear that rental included the making available of a work in the course of a business, as part of services or amenities for which payment was made.[76] This was clearly aimed at including the making available of copies of videos to hotel guests. The existing provisions are not so explicit but it is suggested that the words "indirect economic or commercial advantage", would catch such rental.[77] The 1988 Act appears to go further than the Directive in that whereas under the Directive "rental" means the making available for a limited period of time, under the 1988 Act the period of rental is potentially unlimited. The European Court of Justice has made it clear that rental right is not exhausted by the sale or other acts of release into circulation of a copy of the work,[78] nor by other acts of rental.[79]

7–85   **The lending right.** The lending of copies of any of the above categories of works, or the original,[80] to the public is also a restricted act. For this purpose, "lending" means making a copy of the work available for use, on terms that it will or may be returned, otherwise than for direct or indirect economic or commercial advantage, through an establishment which is accessible to the public. The word "establishment" is not defined but again is taken directly from the Directive.[81] The expression clearly includes, but is not limited to, public libraries. Although the restricted act is confined to lending to the public, the Act nevertheless expressly provides that lending between establishments accessible to the public,

---

[70] See Reinbothe & von Lewinski, *The EC Directive on Rental and Lending Rights and on Piracy* (1993), p.53.

[71] Directive 92/100, Art.2.3.

[72] See Art.2(1) of Directive 92/100, and especially Art.2(7). See Ricketson, *The Berne Convention for the Protection of Literary and Artistic Works: 1886–1986* (Kluwer, 1987), paras 6.44, *et seq.*

[73] Reinbothe & von Lewinski, *The EC Directive on Rental and Lending Rights and on Piracy* (1993), p.53.

[74] CDPA 1988, s.18A(6).

[75] CDPA 1988, s.(2)(a).

[76] CDPA 1988, s.178, as enacted.

[77] The expression "for direct or indirect commercial advantage" is taken directly from Directive 92/100. See Art.1.2.

[78] *Metronome Musik GmbH v Music Point Hokamp GmbH* [1999] F.S.R. 576, [2000] E.C.D.R. 11, ECJ.

[79] *Foreningen AF Danske Videogramdistributorer v Laserdisken* [1999] E.M.L.R. 681, ECJ.

[80] CDPA 1988, s.18A(6).

[81] Directive 92/100, Art.1.3.

for example from one library to another, is not a restricted act.[82] As to what constitutes direct or indirect economic or commercial advantage, the Act makes it clear that the mere making of a payment which does not go beyond what is necessary to cover the operating costs of the establishment is not to amount to such an advantage.[83]

Common considerations. In the case of both the rental and the lending right, the rights only apply where copies are made available "to the public". This expression clearly requires that the public at large has access to the work, whether by means of a high-street rental outlet, library or mail order scheme. It apparently excludes the rental or loan of the work or a copy by one private individual or concern to another. Both rights only concern the making available "for use". In most cases, of course, the copy will have been made available in order to be read, listened to or otherwise enjoyed. It would seem that in relation to an artistic work, "use" would include the lending of it to members of the public so that it can be viewed or enjoyed in private.[84]   **7–86**

Excluded acts. Three classes of acts are excluded from both the rental and lending rights: **7–87**

(a) The making available of the original work or copies for the purpose of public performance, playing or showing in public, or communication to the public[85] Thus, for example, the rental of a film to a cinema for public showing is not a restricted act.[86]

(b) The making available of the work or copies for the purpose of exhibition in public.[87]

(c) The making available of the work or copies for on-the-spot reference use.[88] Thus an organisation which allows users to have access to a work but not to take it away does not rent or lend the work for this purpose.

Transitional. Section 18A, by which the rental and lending right was conferred, came into force on December 1, 1996[89] and is subject to transitional provisions, most of which will now have worked themselves out.[90] Two provisions only need to be mentioned here. First, the amended provisions apply to works made both before and after this date.[91] The second depends on an understanding of the distinction made in the transitional provisions between "new" and other rights. A new right is a right which arose by virtue of the implementing Regulations to authorise or prohibit an act in relation to a copyright work, but excluding a right which corresponded to a right which existed immediately before commencement of the Regulations. Thus the exclusive rights of rental in relation to literary works (other than computer programs), dramatic and musical works and the limited class of artistic works were all new rights, unlike the exclusive right of rental in   **7–88**

---

[82] CDPA 1988, s.18A(4). This provision is derived from Recital (13) of Directive 92/100.

[83] CDPA 1988, s.18A(5). The wording of this subsection is taken directly from Recital (14) of Directive 92/100.

[84] The making available of the work or copy for the purpose of exhibition in public is expressly excluded. See para. 7–87, below.

[85] CDPA 1988, s.18A(3)(a). Again, this provision is derived from Recital (13) of Directive 92/100.

[86] Of course, the showing in public of the film would itself require the consent of the owners of the copyright in the film and of the underlying rights. See CDPA 1988, s.19 and paras 7–121 *et seq.*, below.

[87] CDPA 1988, s.18A(3)(b) and Recital (13) of Directive 92/100.

[88] CDPA 1988, s.18A(3)(c) and Recital (13) of Directive 92/100.

[89] Copyright and Related Rights Regulations 1996 (SI 1996/2967), regs 1(2), 4.

[90] For these provsions, see *Copinger*, 14th ed., para.7–117.

[91] Copyright and Related Rights Regulations 1996 (SI 1996/2967), reg.26(1).

relation to computer programs, films and sound recordings.[92] In relation to the lending right, all such rights were new rights.[93] In a case where before December 1, 1996 the owner or prospective owner of the copyright in a literary, dramatic, musical or artistic work authorised another to make a copy of that work, the new rental and lending rights in relation to that copy are to belong not to the copyright owner but to the person so authorised, subject to any agreement to the contrary.[94]

7–89   Unwaivable right to remuneration. It is a feature of the rental right,[95] but not the lending right, that with effect from December 1, 1996[96] authors of certain works are entitled to limited "unwaivable" rights to remuneration in respect of rental of their work. The authors in question are the authors of literary, dramatic, musical and artistic works, and the principal directors of films. Where such an author transfers the rental right, so far as it concerns use of the work in a sound recording or film, to the producer of the sound recording or film, he retains the right to "equitable remuneration" for any rental of his work.[97] Thus, for example, an author who assigns the right to use his screenplay in a film to the film producer, where such assignment includes the right to rent copies of the film to the public, retains a right to remuneration from such rental. This right cannot be excluded or restricted by contract.[98] The limitations on the ability to assign this right are considered elsewhere[99] as are the provisions of the Act for determining the amount of such remuneration.[1] The right of the author to remuneration appears to be a *sui generis* right and is not strictly a right of copyright, since his rights are limited to his claim for remuneration and he cannot, for example, prevent the further rental of copies if he is not paid. His only right is a claim for remuneration against the owner of the rental right for the time being, that is, the person to whom the rental right was transferred or his successor in title.[2]

7–90   Transitional. The right to equitable remuneration arose with effect from December 1, 1996.[3] No act done before this date, however, is to give rise to any right to such remuneration.[4] In addition, where a right to equitable remuneration would otherwise have arisen on the transfer by an author of his rental right under section 93B, no such right shall in fact arise in respect of any rental of a sound recording or film before April 1, 1997 or in respect of any rental after that date of a sound recording or film made in pursuance of an agreement entered into before July 1, 1994.[5] The only exception is where, before January 1, 1997, the author or

---

[92] Although the definition of "rental" under the 1988 Act as enacted (see the footnotes to para. 7–81, above) was slightly different from the current definition, it is suggested that the rights in relation to these works now conferred by s.18A do "correspond" to the rights conferred under CDPA 1988, s.18, as enacted.

[93] The new lending right does not correspond to the rights of certain authors under the Public Lending Right Scheme, since those rights do not include any right to authorise or prohibit the lending of their works. Again, it is suggested that the rights of copyright owners in respect of the public library lending of computer programs, sound recordings and films, which was treated as rental under CDPA 1988, s.18 and which did not fall within the Public Lending Right Scheme (see para. 7–81, above), do not correspond to the new lending right.

[94] Copyright and Related Rights Regulations 1996 (SI 1996/2967), reg.31.

[95] *i.e.* the exclusive right to rent or authorise the rental of the work. CDPA 1988, s.178.

[96] For transitional provisions, see the Regulations and *Copinger*, 14th ed., para.7–119.

[97] CDPA 1988, s.93B(1).

[98] CDPA 1988, s.93B(5).

[99] See para. 5–111, above.

[1] See para. 29–130, below. In the absence of agreement, it will be determined by the Copyright Tribunal. See CDPA 1988, s.93C.

[2] CDPA 1988, s.93B(3).

[3] Copyright and Related Rights Regulations 1996 (SI 1996/2967), regs.1(1) and (4).

[4] Reg.26(2).

[5] Reg.33.

any successor in title of his notified the person by whom the remuneration would be payable that he intended to exercise such right.[6]

5. PERFORMANCE, SHOWING OR PLAYING OF A WORK IN PUBLIC: THE PUBLIC PERFORMANCE RIGHT

Literary, dramatic and musical works. It is an act restricted by the copyright in a literary, dramatic or musical work to perform the work in public.[7] For this purpose, "performance" is defined to include delivery in the case of lectures, addresses, speeches and sermons[8] and, in general, includes any mode of visual or acoustic presentation, including presentation by means of a sound recording, film or broadcast of the work.[9] These latter expressions are all further defined.[10] Thus, in addition to the obvious ways in which such works may be performed, a literary or musical work embodied in a sound recording may be performed by its being played by means of the sound recording. In relation to a dramatic work, if the incidents of the plot are visually presented to a substantial degree, this will amount to an infringement, even though the same language is not used.[11] In the usual way, it is not only an infringement to do such acts in relation to the work as a whole but also in relation to any substantial part of it.[12] Again, it is a separate infringement to authorise such acts.[13]

7–91

Sound recordings, films and broadcasts. In relation to a sound recording, film or broadcast, the playing or showing of the work in public is a restricted act.[14] Thus, for example, the playing of a sound recording in public by means of a record player or juke box would amount to a public performance not only of the literary or musical works embodied in it, but also of the sound recording itself. Again, these rights are infringed by doing such acts in relation to a substantial part of the work and by authorising such acts.

7–92

Communication to the public versus performance. It is clear that the expressions "performance", "playing" and "showing" used in the above senses include the doing of such acts by means of a radio or television set.[15] Thus, for example, the playing of a radio or television in public will amount to a public performance of works of the above descriptions embodied in the broadcast, and of the broadcast itself.[16] However, the act of broadcasting is not itself a public performance of the works included in the broadcast but amounts to the separate restricted act of communication of the works to the public.[17]

7–93

The person liable for the infringement. In the case of a public performance through the human agency of actors, singers, etc. there will usually be no dif-

7–94

---

[6] Reg.33.

[7] CDPA 1988, s.19(1).

[8] CDPA 1988, s.19(2)(a).

[9] CDPA 1988, s.19(2)(b).

[10] "Sound recording": CDPA 1988, s.5A(1); "film": s.5B(1); "broadcast": s.6(1).

[11] See para. 7–52, above.

[12] CDPA 1988, s.16(3)(a).

[13] CDPA 1988, s.16(2).

[14] CDPA 1988, s.19(3).

[15] *i.e.* apparatus for receiving visual images or sounds conveyed by electronic means. See, *e.g.* CDPA 1988, s.19(2)(b) and the wording of s.19(4). See s.178 for the definition of "electronic."

[16] See the various cases referred below in relation to the expression "in public", and *Australasian Performing Right Association Ltd v Tolbush Pty Ltd* (1986) 62 A.L.R. 521 (Sup Ct of Queensland).

[17] See paras 7–98 *et seq.*, below and CDPA 1988, s.20.

ficulty in determining who is the performer. Again, where recorded music is played in a dance club it will be the operator of the equipment who is primarily liable for the performance of the lyrics and music, and the playing of the sound recording. Where the works are played by the use of such means as radios, televisions or juke boxes, the person liable for the primary act of infringement will be the person who actually operates the apparatus by means of which the sounds or images are produced.[18] Other persons may of course be liable for having authorised such acts of primary infringement,[19] and persons who provide the premises or apparatus for such performances may be liable for acts of secondary infringements.[20] The Act makes it clear that in the case of a performance, playing or showing of a work in public by means of an apparatus for receiving visual images or sounds conveyed by electronic means, neither the person by whom the visual images or sounds are sent (e.g. a broadcaster) nor, in the case where the work is performed by individuals, the performers themselves, are to be regarded as responsible for the infringement.[21]

7–95   **"In public."** The expression "in public", was also used in this context in the 1956 and 1911 Acts,[22] and has been the subject of numerous decisions. Whether a particular performance takes place in public or not is in one sense a question of law, in that the true meaning of the words "in public" is a matter of law, but in every case it is obviously a question of fact whether the facts of the case do or do not fall within that meaning.[23] The chief guide in answering the question should be common sense.[24]

The distinction to be made is between performances which are public and those which are domestic or quasi-domestic in character, that is, those in which the members of the audience are present in their capacity as members of the particular home circle.[25] A useful test is whether the persons coming together to form the audience are bound together by a domestic or private tie, or by an aspect of their public life.[26] In drawing this distinction, it is also the character of the audience which is crucial[27] and in particular it is the relationship of the audience to the owner of copyright which is important rather than its relationship to the

---

[18] See, e.g. Performing Right Society Ltd v Hammond's Bradford Brewery Co Ltd [1934] Ch. 121, followed in Canadian Performing Right Society Ltd v Ford Hotel [1935] 2 D.L.R. 391 and Performing Right Society Ltd v Gillette [1943] 1 All E.R. 413. See also Messager v British Broadcasting Co Ltd [1929] A.C. 151.

[19] See paras 7–130 et seq., below.

[20] i.e. under CDPA 1988, ss.25 and 26. These secondary acts of infringement are considered in Chapter 8.

[21] CDPA 1988, s.19(4). There was some doubt whether under the 1911 Act broadcasting itself constituted a public performance of the works embodied in it. See Messager v British Broadcasting Co Ltd [1927] 2 K.B. 543; Performing Right Society Ltd v Hammond's Bradford Brewery Co Ltd [1934] Ch. 121. cf. Mellor v Australian Broadcasting Commission [1940] A.C. 491. See also Canadian Admiral Corporation Ltd v Rediffusion Inc (1954) Ex. C.R. 382; Chappell & Co. Ltd v Associated Radio Co of Australia Ltd [1925] V.L.R. 350; Remick (J.H.) & Co v American Auto-Accessories Co [1923–1928] Mac.C.C. 173. Under the 1956 Act, broadcasting or including a work in a cable programme was expressly excluded from the definition of performance (s.48(5)) and was a separate act of infringement.

[22] Copyright Act 1956, ss.2(5)(c), 12(5)(b), 13(5)(b), 14(4)(c); Copyright Act 1911, s.1(2). Under the law before 1911, the performance, to be an infringement of copyright, had to be presented at a place of dramatic entertainment. But it was held that this condition was fulfilled if the performance was at any place in public (Russell v Smith (1848) 12 Q.B. 217). The 1911 Act gave effect to the decisions under the earlier law. See, for example Glenville v Selig Polyscope Co (1911) 27 T.L.R 554.

[23] Jennings v Stephens [1936] Ch. 469; Harms (Inc) Ltd v Martins Club Ltd [1927] 1 Ch. 526.

[24] Ernest Turner, etc. Ltd v Performing Right Society Ltd [1943] Ch. 167.

[25] Duck v Bates (1884) 13 Q.B.D. 843; Jennings v Stephens [1936] Ch. 469.

[26] Australian Performing Right Association Ltd v Commonwealth Bank of Australia (1992) 25 I.P.R. 157 at 171.

[27] Jennings v Stephens [1936] Ch. 469.

performer.[28] If it can be said that the audience is one which the owner of the copyright might fairly consider as part of his public then this indicates that the performance was "in public",[29] particularly where the members of the audience are enjoying the work under conditions where they would normally pay for the privilege in one form or another.[30] It has been said that the key to the construction of these words is that what is intended to be protected is the value of the author's invention.[31] Consistent with this, it has also been said that it is the duty of the court to protect the rights of persons such as authors and composers, according to a fair construction of the Act, such that it is important to ask whether the public's demand for their works may be affected by such performances.[32]

Always bearing in mind that it is the character of the audience and its relationship to the copyright owner which is crucially important, various other tests have been discussed in the cases. Thus, clearly, if the public at large is freely admitted, the performance will almost certainly be in public, but the performance may also be in public if only a limited portion of the public is allowed to attend, for example the members of a club and their guests.[33] On the other hand, the mere fact that guests are present at what would otherwise be a private performance will not make it public.[34] The number of persons present is a relevant consideration, but nevertheless a performance may be in public even though the audience is very small.[35] Whether the performance is given with a view to monetary profit may be relevant,[36] but it is of very limited importance whether the actual performers are paid. Thus performers often give their services to the public free, whereas they are often paid when the occasion is undoubtedly private.[37] The fact that no charge is made for admission is of itself also of little importance.[38] The kind of place at which the performance occurs may be an indication of the type of performance, but clearly a private performance may be given in what is normally a public room, and a public performance may be given in a private house.[39] As already noted, it is important to consider whether the performance is likely to injure the owner of the copyright in the sense that some of the audience might be willing to pay to see or hear such a performance,[40] and whether the demand for the author's work might otherwise be diminished.[41] Thus if the person responsible for the performance would be likely to pay for a licence rather than have such performance stopped, then clearly the copyright owner will suffer by an unlicensed performance,[42] although obviously it is not in every such case that the performance will be in public.

While bearing in mind that each case must be considered separately on its own facts, the following are examples of cases in which performances have been regarded as having taken place in public: the putting on of a drama by an amateur   **7–96**

---

[28] *Jennings v Stephens* [1936] Ch. 469; *Ernest Turner, etc. Ltd v Performing Right Society Ltd* [1943] Ch. 167; *Performing Right Society Ltd v Rangers F.C. Supporters Club* [1975] R.P.C. 626.

[29] *Jennings v Stephens* [1936] Ch. 469.

[30] *Performing Right Society Ltd v Rangers F.C. Supporters Club* [1975] R.P.C. 626.

[31] *Duck v Bates* (1884) 13 Q.B.D. 843.

[32] *Jennings v Stephens* [1936] Ch. 469.

[33] *Harms (Inc.) Ltd v Martans Club Ltd* [1927] 1 Ch. 526.

[34] *Jennings v Stephens* [1936] Ch. 469.

[35] *Jennings v Stephens* [1936] Ch. 469

[36] *Harms (Inc.) Ltd v Martans Club Ltd* [1927] 1 Ch. 526.

[37] *Jennings v Stephens* [1936] Ch. 469.

[38] *Harms (Inc.) Ltd v Martans Club Ltd* [1927] 1 Ch. 526.

[39] *Jennings v Stephens* [1936] Ch. 469.

[40] *Harms (Inc.) Ltd v Martans Club Ltd* [1927] 1 Ch. 526.

[41] *Jennings v Stephens* [1936] Ch. 469.

[42] *Performing Right Society Ltd v Harlequin Record Shops Ltd* [1979] 1 W.L.R. 851.

company for a charitable object, the public being admitted upon payment of money or by the issue of tickets generally[43]; the performance of music by a dance band at a proprietary dinner and dance club at which members and their guests were present, the membership being selective and by election but being drawn by invitation to the public[44]; a dramatic performance given at a village Women's Institute, even though the performers were all members of a neighbouring Institute, no one was present except members and no charge was made (all the adult female members of the village were, however, in practice eligible to join the Institute)[45]; the playing of gramophone records and the radio over loudspeakers to workers at a factory during working hours[46]; the playing of video cassettes in the presence of 11 employees, the general public being unable to see or hear, the purpose being to instruct the employees[47]; the performance of orchestral music in the lounge of a hotel, the audience consisting of residents of the hotel and members of the public who had dined there[48]; the playing of a radio in a public house's private room, but which the public was freely able to use as a saloon bar[49]; the playing of a radio in a private room of a public house, but which could be heard in the adjoining public bar[50]; the playing of a radio in a private room adjoining a restaurant, but which could be heard in the restaurant, the principle being that the performance took place wherever it could be heard[51]; the performance of music to an audience consisting of members of a social club and their guests[52]; the playing of records in record shops to which the public was encouraged to enter without payment or invitation, the purpose and effect being to increase the sale of records, the evidence being that most record shop proprietors would pay for the necessary licence rather than be prevented from playing such records.[53]

On the other hand, the putting on of a play by children or adults at home would obviously not be in public, being domestic and private.[54] The same would apply to a play put on for friends in a house hired for the occasion.[55] A performance given by an amateur dramatic club to nurses, attendants and others connected with a hospital, to which admission was free, the expenses being born by the governors of the hospital, was held not to be in public.[56]

7–96A   Hotel bedrooms etc. An unresolved question is whether, for example, where

---

[43] Given as an example in *Duck v Bates* (1884) 13 Q.B.D. 843.

[44] *Performing Right Society Ltd v Hammond's Bradford Brewery Co Ltd* [1934] Ch. 121.

[45] *Jennings v Stephens* [1936] Ch. 469.

[46] *Ernest Turner, etc. Ltd v Performing Right Society Ltd* [1943] Ch. 167. This case is reported jointly with *Performing Right Society Ltd v Gillette Industries Ltd*, where the facts were very similar.

[47] *Australian Performing Right Association Ltd v Commonwealth Bank of Australia* (1992) 25 I.P.R. 157.

[48] *Performing Right Society Ltd v Hawthornes Hotel (Bournemouth) Ltd* [1933] Ch. 855.

[49] *Performing Right Society Ltd v George* (unreported, but referred to in *Performing Right Society Ltd v Camelo* [1936] 3 All E.R. 557).

[50] *Performing Right Society Ltd v George*, obiter, but relied on in *Performing Right Society Ltd v Camelo* [1936] 3 All E.R. 557; and see *Australian Performing Right Association Ltd v Canterbury-Bankstown League Club Ltd* [1964–65] N.S.W.R. 138.

[51] *Performing Right Society Ltd v Camelo* [1936] 3 All E.R. 557.

[52] *Performing Right Society Ltd v Rangers F.C. Supporters Club* [1975] R.P.C. 626.

[53] *Performing Right Society Ltd v Harlequin Record Shops Ltd* [1979] 1 W.L.R. 851. See also *Canadian Admiral Corporation Ltd v Rediffusion Inc* [1954] Ex. C.R. 382; *Australasian Performing Right Association Ltd v Tolbush Pty Ltd* (1986) 62 A.L.R. 521; and see *South African, etc. Ltd v Trust Butchers (Pty) Ltd* [1978] 1 S.A.L.R. 1052.

[54] Given as an example in *Duck v Bates* (1884) 13 Q.B.D. 843.

[55] *Duck v Bates* (1884) 13 Q.B.D. 843.

[56] *Duck v Bates* (1884) 13 Q.B.D. 843, described there by Brett M.R. as a borderline and extreme case; see also the comments on this decision in *Jennings v Stephens* [1936] Ch. 469 and *Harms (Inc.) Ltd v Martans Club Ltd* [1927] 1 Ch. 526.

music or a television programme is relayed to hotel bedrooms, in which the music or programme is then listened to or watched by the occupants, this amounts to a public performance.[57] It has been decided in the Exchequer Court of Canada[58] that the performance of material by way of television in private homes, the material having been received by subscribers to a cable service, did not amount to public performance on the grounds that the character of the audience was purely domestic, and even a large number of "private" performances could not be in public. It might therefore be argued that the character of the audience in separate hotel bedrooms is similar, each hotel bedroom being the occupant's "home" for the night, and each performance being "private".[59] In a decision of the Supreme Court of New South Wales,[60] however, the issue arose whether the watching of television sets by the occupants of motel rooms, to which films were relayed by means of a video cassette recorder and cables, amounted to public performance. The plaintiff's case was argued primarily on the basis that the presentation of a film in a single room, even to only one person, amounted to public performance. It was held that such presentation was in fact in public since the character of the audience was as guests of the motel and not as individuals in a private or domestic situation. In that capacity the guests were paying for the accommodation and the benefits which went with it. It is thought that for the same reasons the performance of works to inmates of prisons is "in public".

Permitted acts. There are important exceptions relating to the public performance of sound recordings and broadcasts, which are considered elsewhere.[61]   **7–97**

6. THE COMMUNICATION TO THE PUBLIC RIGHT

The new communication to the public right. With effect from October 31,   **7–98**
2003, and as part of the implementation of the Information Society Directive, section 20 of the 1988 Act has been amended to introduce a new exclusive right, the communication to the public right, in place of the two separate exclusive rights which previously existed, namely, the broadcasting right and the cable programme right. As will be seen, the new right has broadly assimilated these two separate rights, but it is now clear that the new right also extends to what may loosely be called the on-demand availability right, particularly as it relates to communications via the internet.[62]

(a) Historical background

The broadcasting right and the cable programme right. The exclusive right   **7–99**
of broadcasting a work to the public via a wireless service was first provided for by the Copyright Act 1956, and the exclusive right of transmitting a work to the public via a cable service was first provided for following amendment to the 1956

---

[57] Whether the operation of such a system amounts to the communication of works to the public is a separate matter. See CDPA 1988, s. 20, and paras 7–98 *et seq*, above.

[58] *Canadian Admiral Corporation Ltd v Rediffusion Inc* [1954] Ex.C.R. 382.

[59] See, *e.g. Mellor v Australian Broadcasting Commission* [1940] A.C. 491 at 500; but *cf. Messager v British Broadcasting Co. Ltd* [1927] 2 K.B. 543.

[60] *Rank Film Production Ltd v Dodds* [1983] 2 N.S.W.L.R. 553; see also *Hotel Mornington AB v Föreningen Svenska Tonsättares Internationella Musikbyrö (STIM)* [1982] E.C.C. 171 (Sup Ct of Sweden); *Teosto v A Taxi Driver* [2004] E.C.D.R. 3 (Sup. Ct. of Finland) (provision of music by taxi driver to his customers); *Garware Plastics and Polyester Ltd v M/s Telelink* [1989] A.I.R. (Bombay) 331 (as to the meaning of "communication to the public" in the Indian Copyright Act).

[61] *i.e.* under CDPA 1988, ss.67, 72. See Ch.9, below.

[62] The extent to which such transmissions fell with the cable programme right was never entirely clear. See para. 7–105, below.

Act by the Cable and Broadcasting Act 1984.[63] These rights were separate and distinct from the exclusive right of performing a work in public. At the same time, broadcasts and cable programmes were themselves protected as "works". This scheme was broadly continued under the 1988 Act as originally enacted, which provided that broadcasting a work and including a work in a cable programme service were both restricted acts. "Cable programme service" was given a convoluted definition but broadly meant a service consisting of sending visual images, sounds or other information by means of a telecommunications system.

(b) International Obligations

7–100   **The Berne Convention and the 1996 WIPO Copyright Treaty.** The 1971 Paris Act of the Berne Convention provides an incomplete regime in this field. Thus, Article 11 *bis* of the Convention provides that in relation to Berne literary and dramatic works there is to be an exclusive right of authorising the broadcasting of these authors' works, or their communication to the public by any other means of wireless duffusion, and of authorising the communication of these works to the public by wire. Art.11 of the Convention provides that in relation to Berne dramatic, dramatico-musical and musical works, there is to be an exclusive right of authorising the communication to the public of the *performance* of these author's works, by any means of any process. Art.8 of the 1996 WIPO Copyright Treaty[64] was intended to provide a more comprehensive regime, with the result that in relation to literary and artistic works there is to be an exclusive right of authorising any communication to the public, by wire or wireless means, including the right of making the works available to the public in such a way that members of the public may access them from a place and at a time individually chosen by them (the "on-demand availability right"), this being intended to cover internet and similar transmissions.

7–101   **The Rome Convention and 1996 WIPO Performances and Phonograms Treaty.** Under the Rome Convention, phonogram producers are provided only with the *possibility* of a limited right to equitable remuneration in the case of the broadcasting or communication to the public of their commercially published phonograms,[65] but not with a general broadcasting or communication to the public right. The 1996 WIPO Performances and Phonograms Treaty goes further than this by providing that phonogram producers *shall* have a right to equitable remuneration in respect of the broadcasting or communication to the public of their commercially published recordings,[66] and an exclusive right in relation to the making available of their recordings via an on-demand service.[67] No general exclusive right of communication to the public is provided for. Under the Rome Convention, broadcasters are to be provided with an exclusive right in relation to the rebroadcasting of their works and a limited communication to the public right in the case of television broadcasts.[68]

(c) European Directives

7–102   **The Rental and Related Rights Directive.** In this area, the scope of the Rental

---

[63] See ss.2(5)(d), (e), 3(5)(c), (d), 12(5)(c), 13(5)(c), (d), 14(4)(d) of the 1956 Act as amended. The cable right was originally described as the right to include a work in a diffusion service and latterly as the right to include a work in a cable programme service.

[64] As to the WIPO Copyright Treaty, see para. 24–66, below.

[65] Rome Convention, Art.12.

[66] WIPO Copyright Treaty, Art.15.

[67] WIPO Copyright Treaty, Art.14.

[68] WIPO Copyright Treaty, Art.13.

and Related Rights Directive was limited. It merely prescribed a right for phonogram producers to share in equitable remuneration for the broadcasting of their commercially published sound recordings.[69]

The Directive on Satellite Broadcasting and Cable Retransmission. This Directive was also of limited scope. Authors were to have an exclusive right in relation to the broadcasts of their works by satellite.[70] **7–103**

The Information Society Directive. One of the objectives of the Information Society Directive was to give effect to the 1996 WIPO Treaties. Article 3(1) of the Directive therefore provides that in relation to authors' rights works, Member States are to provide an exclusive right to authorise or prohibit any communication to the public of the work, by wire or wireless means (*i.e.* broadcasting generally),[71] as well as an "on-demand right", that is, the right to make a work available to the public by wire or wireless means in such a way that members of the public may access it from a place and at a time individually chosen by them.[72] In relation to related rights subject matter, as has been seen, an equitable right of remuneration for producers of phonograms in respect of the broadcasting or communication to the public of their commercially published phonograms had already been provided for by the Rental and Related Rights Directive. The Information Society Directive did not make any further provision concerning a broadcasting right related to this and other related rights subject matter, but required that an exclusive on-demand right be provided for in respect of such subject matter.[73] **7–104**

(d) *The new communication to the public right: introduction*

Implementation of the Information Society Directive. Although the restricted act of inclusion of a work in a cable programme service in the 1988 Act probably extended to "on request" services,[74] the definition of a cable programme service was extremely convoluted and was not considered by the Government to be a particularly "clear or transparent" way of ensuring that the requirements of the Information Society Directive were fulfilled.[75] A new right has therefore been introduced which includes within in it both the exclusive right to broadcast a work, whether by wireless means or by cable, and the on-demand right prescribed by the Directive. In doing so, the link which previously existed between, on the one hand, the protected subject matters of a "broadcast" and a "cable programme" and, on the other, the restricted acts of broadcasting a work or including a work in a cable programme service, has been abandoned. On the one hand, there now exists the single protected subject matter of a "broadcast", which includes within it wireless broadcasts and cable transmissions in the nature of broadcasts, but not internet transmissions of a non-broadcast kind, in particular, not on-demand transmissions. On the other, there is now an exclusive right of communicating a work to the public by electronic means, which includes wireless and cable broadcasts and, in addition, on-demand transmissions by electronic means, whether wireless or by wire, or partly one and partly the other. **7–105**

The right defined. With effect from October 31, 2003, it is an act restricted by **7–106**

---

[69] Directive 92/100, Art.8(2).
[70] Directive on Satellite Broadcasting and Cable Retransmission, Art.2.
[71] Information Society Directive, Art.3(1)
[72] Information Society Directive, Art.3(1)
[73] Information Society Directive, Art.3(2).
[74] *Shetland Times Ltd v Wills* [1997] F.S.R. 604 (Ct of Sess).
[75] See the Government Conclusions on the Patent Office's Consultation Paper of August 7, 2002, para.3.1.

the copyright in all categories of work, apart from a published edition of a typographical arrangement, to communicate the work to the public.[76] Communication to the public is for this purpose defined to mean the communication to the public by electronic transmission, and to include:

(a) The broadcasting of the work;

(b) The making available to the public of the work by electronic transmission in such a way that members of the public may access it from a place and at a time individually chosen by them.[77]

It is important to appreciate that although two particular instances of communication to the public by electronic means are specified, *any* act which falls within the description of a communication to the public by electronic means is an act restricted by the copyright in a work. The discussion which follows will deal first with the two particular instances and then the more general definition of the restricted act.

Acts which fall within the description of communication to the public under section 20 are different in nature from the restricted acts of performing, or showing or playing, a work in public under section 19. The restricted act of communication to the public is concerned with cases where a work is communicated to a public which is not present at the place where the communication originates,[78] whereas the restricted act of public performance, etc. is concerned with performances which take place in the presence of a public audience. In a case where a work is peformed in public by means of a broadcast,[79] the communication is to be regarded as orginating in the loudspeaker of the television or radio set where the public is present, and not at the place of transmission of the broadcast.

7–107   **Works subject to the right.** The communication to the public right is a right which subsists in relation to literary, dramatic, musical and artistic works, and sound recordings, films and broadcasts.[80] It therefore does not subsist in relation to typographical arrangements of published editions, which was also the position in relation to the pre-amendment rights.[81]

7–108   **Transitional provisions.** The Regulations implementing the Information Society Directive contain a number of transitional provisions. Those relating to acts committed before October 31, 2003 are considered below. In general, however, the amendments apply to works made before this date as well as after it,[82] so that in relation to any act committed on or after October 31, 2003, the relevant question for present purposes is whether that act constituted an infringement of the communication to the public right as defined in section 20.

(e) *Broadcasting*

7–109   **Broadcasting the work.** The definition of "broadcast" has already been considered in relation to the protected subject matter of a broadcast.[83] The earlier discussion is not repeated here, except to say that a broadcast means an electronic

---

[76] CDPA 1988, s.20(1), as amended by the Copyright and Related Rights Regulations 2003 (SI 2003/2498).

[77] CDPA 1988, s.20(2).

[78] See Recitals 22 and 23 of the Information Society Directive 2001/29 and Art.3, which refers to communication by wire or wireless means. The point is made clear by CDPA 1988, s.20, which refers to communication by electronic transmission.

[79] See paras 7–91 and 7–94, above.

[80] CDPA 1988, s.20(1).

[81] Such a right was not within the scope of Directive 2001/29.

[82] The Copyright and Related Rights Regulations 2003, reg.31(1).

[83] See paras 3–91 *et seq.*, above.

transmission of visual images, sounds or other information which is transmitted for simultaneous reception by members of the public and is capable of being lawfully received by them, or is transmitted at a time determined solely by the person making the transmission for presentation to members of the public.[84] It therefore includes both wireless transmissions and transmissions by wire, *i.e.* cable transmissions, and to some extent has assimilated the previous restricted acts of: (a) broadcasting (which was limited to a transmission by wireless telegraphy) and (b) inclusion in a cable programme service. Excepted from this definition of broadcasting, however, is any internet transmission unless it is: (a) a transmission taking place simultaneously on the internet and by other means, or (b) a concurrent transmission of a live event, or (c) a transmission of recorded images or sounds forming part of a programme service offered by the person responsible for making the transmission, being a service in which programmes are broadcast at scheduled times by that person.[85] Such internet transmissions are similar in nature to "ordinary" broadcasts and for this reason are included within the scope of a broadcast. To the extent that internet transmissions are excluded from the definition of broadcast, they may still fall within the making available right, considered further below.[86]

Who is the person who broadcasts? The person who is liable for the restricted **7–110** act of communicating a work to the public, in the case where the communication takes place by way of a broadcast, is obviously the person who broadcasts the work. It is not so obvious, however, who this person actually is. Is it, for example, the person who operates the transmission equipment, or the person who has responsibility for feeding the programme-carrying signals into the transmission process, or the person who is responsible for the programme content, or some other person? The Information Society Directive says nothing about who is to be regarded as communicating a work to the public. Before amendment, the position was reasonably clear. Thus, section 6(3) of the Act provided that references to the person: (a) making the broadcast (which then meant a wireless broadcast but not a cable broadcast), (b) broadcasting a work, or (c) including a work in a broadcast, were to the person transmitting the "programme" (which meant any item included in the broadcast) if that person had responsibility to any extent for its contents.[87] In addition to that person, where any other person provided the programme (which meant any item included in the broadcast) and made the arrangements necessary for its transmission with the person transmitting it, that other person was also be taken to have broadcast the work.[88] It seemed clear that this definition of "broadcasting a work" applied to the restricted act of broadcasting the work under section 20.[89] Section 6(3) therefore provided an extended definition of who was the broadcaster in the case of wireless broadcasts. The position following amendment is no longer as clear as it was, both in relation to wireless broadcasts and cable broadcasts. Thus, although section 6(3) still provides that references to a person "making a broadcast or a transmission which is a broadcast" (which now includes both wireless and cable transmissions of the defined kind) are to the persons referred to above,[90] it does not now say anything about who is to be regarded as "broadcasting" the work. The principal purpose of

---

[84] CDPA 1988, s.6(1).

[85] CDPA 1988, s.6(1A).

[86] The distinction may be important for performers, although not for owners of copyright in commercially published sound recordings, because if the transmission is a broadcast but not an ondemand transmission, there will only be a right to equitable remuneration.

[87] CDPA 1988 s.6(3).

[88] CDPA 1988 s.6(3).

[89] See the words "in this Part" in CDPA 1988, s.6(3).

[90] *i.e.* to the person transmitting the "programme" if that person had responsibility to any extent for

the definition in section 6(3) of the person who "makes" a broadcast appears to be identify the author of, and thus first owner of, the copyright in a broadcast.[91] In contrast, and on a litereral reading, the restricted act of broadcasting is not concerned with who "makes" the broadcast but who broadcasts the work. It is nevertheless the case that for the purposes of broadcasting by satellite, which is a sub-class of the restricted act of broadcasting, the broadcaster is clearly to be regarded as the person who "makes" the broadcast.[92] Under the 1956 Act, where there were no precisely equivalent definitions, the broadcaster was held to include anyone participating in the broadcast, for example, the programme contractors and even, it seems, the performers.[93] While it is suggested that performers are not properly to be regarded as broadcasters, it is less clear who is.

7–111   **Where does the act of broadcasting take place?** There has been a prolonged debate over whether a broadcast should be regarded as occurring at the place where the signals are transmitted (the "emission theory") or at the place where they are received, or both. As far as the European Community and satellite broadcasts are concerned, this debate was resolved in favour of the emission theory by EC Directive 93/83 on Satellite Broadcasting and Cable Retransmission[94]. Effect was given to the Directive by amendments made to the 1988 Act by the Copyright and Related Rights Regulations 1996, as now refined following implementation of the Information Society Directive. In fact, the 1988 Act goes further than the Directive and expressly applies the emission theory to wireless broadcasts of all kinds, not just satellite broadcasts. The position in relation to broadcasts by cable is not expressly provided for and is less clear.

First, in the case of a wireless broadcast, the 1988 Act now provides that the place from where the broadcast is made is the place where, under the control and responsibility of the person making the broadcast, the programme signals are introduced into an uninterrupted chain of communication ending with the receiver.[95] In the case of a satellite transmission, this chain is to include the chain leading to the satellite and down towards the earth.[96] These provisions make it clear that in the case of wireless transmissions, what matters for the purposes of infringement is the place from which the signals are first introduced into the chain of communication and not the place where a signal is receivable or its footprint falls. The fact that the signal may not be receivable in the United Kingdom therefore does not affect a broadcaster's potential liability under the 1988 Act if the chain of communication of the signals starts in the United Kingdom. By the same token, the fact that a broadcast can be received in the United Kingdom does not mean that the restricted act of broadcasting is taking place in the United Kingdom: it will not do so if the broadcast was made from another country in accordance with the above rules.

---

its contents and also to any other person who provides the programme and who makes the arrangements necessary for its transmission with the person transmitting it.

[91] See, *e.g.* the wording of CDPA 1988, s.9(2)(b).

[92] See CDPA 1988, s.6A.

[93] *Independent Television Companies Association Ltd v Performing Right Society Ltd, The Times,* February 23, 1982; *The Association of Independent Radio Contractors Ltd v Phonographic Performance Ltd* (1980) (unreported). Again, broadcasting was limited to tranmissions by wireless telegraphy.

[94] See Directive 93/83, Art.1.2(a), (b).

[95] CDPA 1988, s.6(4), as amended with effect from December 1, 1996 by the Copyright and Related Rights Regulations 1996 (SI 1996/2967). The Directive only required this definition in the case of broadcasts by satellite, but the amendment applied to all types of wireless broadcast, presumably on the basis that the emission theory correctly represented the law in the case of terrestrial wireless broadcasts as well. S.6(4), as enacted, provided that the place from which a broadcast was made was, in the case of a satellite transmission, the place from which the signals carrying the broadcast were transmitted to the satellite.

[96] CDPA 1988, s.6(4), as amended with effect from December 1, 1996 by the Copyright and Related Rights Regulations 1996 (SI 1996/2967).

There are two situations in which a satellite broadcast which is made from outside the EEA in accordance with the above definition is in fact treated as being made from within the EEA.[97] In the context of United Kingdom copyright law, this becomes important when the place from which the broadcast is made is treated as being within the United Kingdom when otherwise it would not be so. Both situations arise where the law of the country from which the broadcast is actually made fails to provide a minimum level of protection for authors and performers, and in particular fails to provide:

(a) Exclusive rights in relation to broadcasting equivalent to the exclusive rights of broadcasting conferred on authors of literary, dramatic, musical and artistic works, films and broadcasts by section 20 of the 1988 Act[98];

(b) A right in relation to live broadcasting equivalent to that conferred on a performer in relation to the live broadcasts of his performances under section 182(1)(b) of the 1988 Act[99]; and

(c) A right for authors of sound recordings and performers to share in a single equitable remuneration in respect of the broadcasting of such sound recordings.[1]

The first situation is where the broadcast is made from such a country but the place from which the programme-carrying signals are transmitted to the satellite ("the uplink station") is located in an EEA State. In this situation, the latter place is treated as being the place from which the broadcast is made and the person operating the uplink station is treated as being the person making the broadcast. Where this place is within the United Kingdom, therefore, the unlicensed broadcast is liable to be an infringement under the 1988 Act for which the person operating the uplink is liable. The second situation is where the uplink station is not located in an EEA State but a person who is established within an EEA State has commissioned the making of the broadcast. In this situation, he will be treated as making the broadcast and the place in which he has his principal establishment in the EEA shall be treated as the place from which the broadcast was made. Again, therefore, an infringement under the 1988 Act may occur where this place is within the United Kingdom.

7–112

As to broadcasts by cable (*i.e.* by wire), neither the Act nor any Directive makes any provision as to where the broadcast takes place.[2] Where the broadcast is initiated in one country and received in another (for example between the Republic of Ireland and Northern Ireland), where does the broadcast take place? Since the United Kingdom has applied the emission theory to wireless broadcasts of all kinds, it is suggested that the theory is also to be applied to broadcasting by cable, so that broadcasting by this means occurs at the place where the signals originate. All such transmissions are now "broadcasts" and it is suggested that no distinction should be drawn between different types of transmission.

Re-broadcasts. Where a broadcast is relayed by its reception and immediate re-transmission, this is to be regarded as a separate act of broadcasting from the

7–113

---

[97] These two cases are prescribed by the Satellite and Cable Directive. See Recital (20) and Art.1(2)(d).

[98] *i.e.* the section presently under consideration.

[99] See Ch.12, below.

[1] Again, in fact the United Kingdom confers no such right on authors of sound recordings, although the owner of the copyright in a sound recording has the exclusive right to control its exploitation. Performers have such a right by virtue of CDPA 1988, s.182D.

[2] CDPA 1988, s.6(4), which states where a broadcast takes place from, applies only to wireless broadcasts.

making of the original broadcast.[3] It was always the case that rebroadcasting a work fell within the restricted act of broadcasting. An important exception exists, however, in the case of cable re-transmission of wireless broadcasts by cable.[4]

(f) Making the work available on demand

7–114   **The on-demand right.** The second category of communication to the public right (the so-called on-demand right) is the act of making available a work to the public by electronic transmission in such a way that members of the public may access it from a place and at a time individually chosen by them.[5] The wording of this provision follows closely that of Articles 3.2 and 3.3 of the Information Society Directive, which are themselves based on Article 8 of the 1996 WIPO Copyright Treaty and Articles 10 and 14 of the 1996 WIPO Performances and Phonograms Treaty. The Directive states expressly that the transmission may be by wire or wireless means, so that the right encompasses both wireless transmissions and transmissions by cable, but this is implicit in section 20 from the fact that the communication must be by electronic transmission. The essential difference between this right and the "broadcasting" right is of course that in the case of the broadcasting right the work is transmitted at a time determined by the broadcaster with a view to its simultaneous reception by the public at large, whereas in relation to the on-demand right the transmission is to a single recipient, who initiates the transmission and chooses when and where to receive it.

7–115   **What constitutes the act of making a work available and who is liable?** Neither the Act nor the Directive says anything further about this. The important point to emphasise is that it is the act of making a work available to the public *by electronic transmission*, and *in such a way that the public can access it*, which matters. Thus, where A makes a work available to B, an internet service provider, so that B can make it available to the public in this way, it is suggested that it is the act of B in making it available by electronic transmission such that the public can access it which is the restricted act. Although A has made the work available, he has not made the work available to the public by electronic transmission, etc. although of course he may be liable for having authorised that act or as a joint tortfeasor. In each case, it will be necessary to examine the facts to see who has committed the restricted act.[6]

7–116   **When does the act of making available occur?** Unlike the restricted act of broadcasting, there appears to be no requirement that any transmission actually takes place before the restricted act takes place: the restricted act is the making available of the work so that members of the public "may" access it. For example, therefore, it is suggested that as soon as a work becomes available on an internet service provider's servers, the restricted act is committed, and will continue to be committed until the work is no longer available.[7]

7–117   **Where does the act of making available take place?** This will often be a vital point where the transmission in question has occurred across national boundaries.

---

[3] CDPA 1988, s.6(5A). This provision was introduced to establish that such a broadcast also qualifies for copyright protection.

[4] *i.e.* under CDPA 1988, s.73. See para. 9–205, below.

[5] CDPA 1988, s.20(2)(b).

[6] It is important to note, however, that a person who makes a work available within the meaning of section 20 may have a defence available to him, particularly of "hosting", "caching" or "mere conduit" under the E-Commerce Regulations (see paras 22–88 *et seq.*, below).

[7] In the same way, an infringement can continuously take place by the exposure of an infringing copy for sale under CDPA 1988, s.24(1).

In principle it resurrects the arguments which existed as to the place where a broadcast should be regarded as occurring. Again, however, since the restricted act is defined by reference to the "making available" of the work, and not its actual transmission or reception, it is suggested that the place where the apparatus is situated and from where access to the work can be obtained is the place where the restricted act occurs.[8]

Members of the public. Although the Act refers to the work being made available to "the public", in the usual way this does not mean that the restricted act is only committed when the public at large can obtain access to it. Where the work is only available to subscribers to an internet service, the subscribers will qualify as "the public" for this purpose. **7–118**

(g) *Other forms of communication to the public by electronic means*

The acts of broadcasting a work and making it available on-demand are merely two specified kinds of the more general restricted act of communication of a work to the public by electronic means. As to what acts might fall outside two specified kinds but within the more general restricted act, it is easier to say what acts do not fall within the general restricted act at all. For example, the reference to a communication to the public means that point-to-point electronic communications initiated by the sender, such as emails, will not fall within the scope of the restricted act. **7–119**

(h) *The old law: transitional provisions*

As already explained, in relation to acts taking place on or after October 31, 2003, the new law, as set out above, must be applied.[9] In relation to acts taking place before this date, whether or not they amounted to an infringement of copyright will depend on whether they infringed the Act as it stood before amendment.[10] Readers are referred to the previous edition of this work in relation to such acts.[11] **7–120**

7. THE ADAPTATION RIGHT

One of the acts restricted by the copyright in any literary, dramatic or musical work is the right to make an adaptation of the work.[12] Further consideration is given below as to the meaning of "adaptation" in this context, but there is an unclear dividing line between what amounts to a reproduction of a work and what amounts to an adaptation of a work. Thus, for example, although the making of a translation of a literary or dramatic work is expressly included within the definition of making an adaptation, it can clearly be argued that a translation is also a reproduction of the original work, assuming that a substantial use was **7–121**

---

[8] The Government declined to make express provision in relation to this question, taking the view that it was neither necessary or appropriate given that Directive 93/98 was silent on the point. See the Government Conclusions on the Patent Office's Consulation Paper of August 7, 2002, para.3.5.

[9] This is confirmed by the transitional provisions in reg.31(2) of the Copyright and Related Rights Regulations (SI 2003/2498), which provide that no act done before October 31, 2003 shall be regarded as an infringement of any new or extended right arising by virtue of the Regulations.

[10] Interpretation Act 1978, s.16(1).

[11] See *Copinger* (14th ed.), paras 7–132 to 7–137.

[12] CDPA 1988, ss.16(1)(e), 21(1).

thereby made of the skill and labour of its author.[13] Other acts expressly brought within the definition of making an adaptation, considered below, provide even clearer examples. The concept of an exclusive right to make an adaptation of a work was first introduced by the 1956 Act, partly to bring under one head a number of separate exclusive rights provided for under the 1911 Act,[14] and partly to make it clear that certain other acts were also within the exclusive rights of the copyright owner.[15] The concept has been continued by the 1988 Act and in subsequent amendments made to it. The Act provides that no inference is to be drawn from the provisions relating to the making of an adaptation as to what does or does not amount to copying of a work,[16] and since there is no reason in principle why the same act cannot fall within two separate classes of restricted act, it is suggested that in some cases the same act may infringe both the reproduction right and the adaptation right.

In general, an adaptation is made when it is recorded, in writing or otherwise.[17] If the restricted act extended no further than the *making* of an adaptation, the right would be of limited value but the Act provides that not only is the making of an adaptation a restricted act but it is also a restricted act to reproduce an adaptation in any material form, issue copies of it to the public, perform it in public or communicate it to the public.[18] For this purpose it is immaterial whether the adaptation itself was recorded in the above sense when any such further act was done.[19] This provision makes it clear, for example, that copyright in a musical work may be infringed by performing an adaptation of it on stage, even though the adaptation itself is never recorded.

In the usual way, it is a restricted act not only to do any of the above acts in relation to the work as a whole but also in relation to any substantial part of it. Further, copyright is infringed not only by anyone who does one of these restricted acts without the licence of the copyright owner, but also by anyone who authorises the doing of such an act without licence.

Literary and dramatic works

7–122   The expression "adaptation" is defined by reference to particular categories of work. Thus, in relation to a literary or dramatic work, other than a computer program or a database, the 1988 Act defines "adaptation" to mean:

   (a) a translation of the work;

   (b) a version of a dramatic work in which it is converted into a non-dramatic work or, as the case may be, a version of a non-dramatic work in which it is converted into a dramatic work;

   (c) a version of the work in which the story or action is conveyed wholly or mainly by means of pictures in a form suitable for reproduction in a book, or in a newspaper, magazine or similar periodical.[20]

---

[13] But note that there is some authority, referred to below, that a translation of a literary work is not a "copy" of it.

[14] *i.e.* the "translation" and "dramatisation" rights (see ss.1(2)(a), (b) and (c) of the Copyright Act 1911).

[15] *i.e.* the "strip-cartoon" right and the right to make an arrangement or transcription of a musical work (see ss.2(6)(a)(iv) and (b) of the Copyright Act 1956).

[16] CDPA 1988, s.21(5).

[17] CDPA 1988, s.21(1). For this purpose, writing includes any form of notation or code, whether by hand or otherwise and regardless of the method by which, or medium in or on which, it is recorded. CDPA 1988, s.178.

[18] CDPA 1988, s.21(2).

[19] CDPA 1988, s.21(2).

[20] CDPA 1988, s.21(3)(a).

Translation.[21] Although "translation" commonly means the turning of a work   **7–123**
from one human language into another, it is suggested that the word is wide
enough to include the conversion of a work into code or Braille.[22] It should be
noted that two separate rights may exist where there has been a translation,
namely the right of the owner of the copyright in the original work to restrain
reproduction, etc. of the original or any translated form, and the right of the
owner of the copyright in the translation to restrain reproduction of his translation.
Anyone wishing to reproduce a particular translation should therefore obtain a
licence from the owner of the copyright in both the original and the translation.[23]
The position will be the same even where the translation was unauthorised since,
although an infringement, it will be entitled to copyright.[24]

Dramatisation of non-dramatic works. Infringements of this kind may occur   **7–124**
when a novel is turned into a play or a screenplay for a film.[25] In such cases there
may of course be sufficient copying of language for the defendant's dramatic
work to be a reproduction of the plaintiff's work. However, even where there is
no language copying but, for example, the defendant has to a substantial extent
taken the incidents and plot from the plaintiff's novel and turned them into a
dramatic work, this will amount to an infringement by the making of an
adaptation.[26] The issues which arise here are similar to those which arise in relation to the reproduction of one dramatic work by another.[27] Thus the question is
whether the situations or plot have been copied from the novel and then
represented in dramatic form.[28] This is not to say that mere ideas or a character
can be protected in this way, certainly if the character or ideas are not novel,[29] but
if the combination of events which has been taken is not merely trivial, but
amounts to a substantial part, there will be an infringement.[30] Examples from the
cases include infringements by dramatising a novel in the form of a play, a

---

[21] Pre- Copyright Act 1911 cases on this point need to be approached with caution since there was
some doubt, prior to the 1911 Act, whether copyright in a work could be infringed by making a
translation of it: *Burnett v Chetwood* (1817) 2 Mer. 441; *cf. Cate v Devon, etc. Newspaper Co*
(1889) 40 Ch. D. But see *Copinger* (4th ed.), pp.187, *et seq.*, arguing strongly for the opposite
view. The 1911 Act made it clear that the exclusive rights to produce, reproduce, perform and
publish a work included the exclusive right to do these acts in relation to any translation of the
work (see s.1(2)(a)). As noted above, the Copyright Act 1956 introduced the concept of the
restricted act of making an adaptation of a work, which was defined to include the making of a
translation (see ss.2(5), (6)(a)(iii)).
[22] If not, then such acts must presumably be regarded as amounting to a reproduction of a work,
since otherwise they would not be restricted acts at all, a curious result. But see *Apple Computer,
Inc v Mackintosh Computers Ltd* (1988) 44 D.L.R. (4th) 74.
[23] *Murray v Bogue* (1853) 1 Drew. 353 at 368.
[24] *Redwood Music Ltd v Chappell & Co Ltd* [1982] R.P.C. 109; *ZYX Music v King* [1995] 3 All
E.R. 1 (at first instance); and see para. 3–263, above.
[25] Again, care must be taken with the earlier cases on this point. Before the passing of the Copyright
Act 1911, it did not constitute an infringement to convert a novel or other non-dramatic work into
a dramatic work, provided there was no substantial language copying (see *Read v Conquest*
(1861) 9 C.B. (N.S.) 755; *Tinsley v Lacey* (1863) 32 L.J. Ch. 535; *Warne & Co v Seebohm* (1888)
39 Ch.D. 73. Under the Copyright Act 1911 it was expressly provided that the exclusive rights to
produce, reproduce, perform and publish a work included the right to convert a non-dramatic
work into a dramatic work, and vice versa (see ss.1(2)(b), (c)). The law was thus changed: see
Corelli v Gray (1913) 30 T.L.R. 116. The Copyright Act 1956 introduced the concept of the
restricted act of making an adaptation of a work, which was defined to include similar rights (
ss.2(6)(i), (ii)). However, to turn a novel into a film would have been to reproduce the novel, not
to have made an adaptation of it (see s.48(1)—definitions of "dramatic work" and "reproduction").
[26] *Corelli v Gray* (1913) 30 T.L.R. 116. Again, arguably it will also amount to copying of the work,
where part of the merit of the literary work was its plot, characterisation, etc.
[27] See para. 7–52, above.
[28] *Kelly v Cinema Houses Ltd* [1928–35] Mac.C.C. 362.
[29] *Kelly v Cinema Houses Ltd* [1928–35] Mac.C.C. 362; *Dagnall v British and Dominion Film
Corporation Ltd* [1928–35] Mac.C.C. 391 (a case of infringement of a dramatic work by
reproduction); *Harman Pictures N.V. v Osborne* [1967] 1 W.L.R. 723
[30] *Kelly v Cinema Houses Ltd* [1928–35] Mac.C.C. 362; *Fernald v Jay Lewis Productions Ltd*

sketch,[31] a script for a film or a film itself,[32] or a short story in the form of a ballet.[33] In the case of a historical work, which the claimant has compiled from various sources, it will in the usual way be necessary to examine whether the incidents in common between the two works which the defendant has dramatised have been taken by him from the claimant's work or from those other sources.[34]

7–125   **Conversion of dramatic into non-dramatic work.**[35] As in the case of non-dramatic works, a dramatic work may be infringed simply by its language being reproduced to a substantial extent. Even where there has not been such copying, however, the copyright in a dramatic work may be infringed if it is converted into a non-dramatic form. Thus where the events and conversations in a play were described in detail, scene by scene, constituting more than just a synopsis, this was held to be an adaptation.[36] It made no difference that the descriptions formed part of a larger work and were interspersed with commentaries and other writings. On the other hand, short synopses of operas are unlikely to be infringements of the operatic works if the operas are described shortly and in very bare outline.[37] The position would presumably be different if numerous incidents were reproduced.

7–126   **Strip cartoon.** As has been seen, in relation to a literary or dramatic work, "adaptation" includes a version of the work in which the story or action is conveyed wholly or mainly by means of pictures in a form suitable for reproduction in a book, or in a newspaper, magazine or similar periodical.[38] A pictorial representation of the plot of a book or a play will therefore constitute infringement even though no words are used in the representation.

7–127   **Computer programs.** In the early days of the debate about software protection, there was concern whether infringement could be avoided by arguments about the distinctions between the levels of code involved in the translation from what was written by the human author (source code) to the lowest level of code, on which the computer operated (machine code), or by arguing that there was no infringement if a program was re-written in a different computer language. The Copyright (Computer Software) Amendment Act 1985 addressed these issues by specifically providing that a version of a program in which it was converted into or out of a computer language or code, or into a different computer language or code, was an adaptation of the program.[39] This approach was substantially repeated in the 1988 Act, by means of a special definition of "translation", and thus adaptation, so far as computer programs were concerned.[40] As part of the

---

[1975] F.S.R. 499; *cf. MacGregor v Powell* [1936–45] Mac.C.C. 233; *De Mandnit v Gaumont British Picture Corporation Ltd* [1936–45] Mac.C.C. 292.

[31] *Corelli v Gray* (1913) 30 T.L.R. 116.

[32] *Fernald v Jay Lewis Productions Ltd* [1975] F.S.R. 499 (infringement by taking a single episode from a semi-fictional story, itself consisting of 12 episodes, and dealt with in only four out of 126 pages of the book); *Zeccola v Universal City Studios Inc* (1982) 46 A.L.R. 189.

[33] *Holland v Vivian Van Damm Productions Ltd* [1936–45] Mac.C.C. 69.

[34] *Harman Pictures N.V. v Osborne* [1967] 1 W.L.R. 723.

[35] See the footnotes to para. 7–124, above, dealing with the earlier law.

[36] *Sillitoe v McGraw-Hill Book Co (U.K.) Ltd* [1983] F.S.R. 545.

[37] *Valcarenghi v The Gramophone Co Ltd* [1928–35] Mac.C.C. 301, where it was found that the defendants had not infringed, not having transposed the work into a novel or short story.

[38] This right was expressly included for the first time in the Copyright Act 1956. Before then there was doubt whether such an act amounted to an infringement.

[39] Copyright (Computer Software) Amendment Act 1985, s.1(2).

[40] S.21(4), as enacted, provided that: "In relation to a computer program a 'translation' includes a version of the program in which it is converted into or out of a computer language or code or into a different computer language or code, otherwise than incidentally in the course of running the program".

implementation of the Computer Software Directive,[41] the wording was modified to mirror more closely the wording of Article 4(b) of the Directive. Thus the 1988 Act now provides that in relation to a computer program, "adaptation" means an arrangement or altered version of it, or a translation of it, a translation for these purposes including a version of the program in which it is converted into or out of a computer language or code or into a different computer language or code.[42] Perhaps because of the pervasiveness of copying in the digital environment, relatively little attention has been given to this restricted act.[43] The section clearly covers cases where, as with the translation of a traditional literary work from one human language to another, a program written in one programming language is rewritten in another, with similarities of structure and nomenclature, where these are consistent with the programming environment.

Database. In relation to a copyright database, adaptation means an arrangement or altered version of the database, or a translation of it.[44] The expression "translation" is not further defined in relation to database and so has the ordinary meaning used in relation to literary and dramatic works other than computer programs.   **7–128**

Musical works. In relation to musical works, the 1988 Act defines adaptation to mean an arrangement or transcription of the work.[45]   **7–129**

8. AUTHORISATION

As already noted, copyright is infringed not only where an act restricted by the copyright in a work is done without consent, but also where a person authorises the doing of such an act.[46] The meaning of "authorised" in this context is discussed below, but where a person is liable for having authorised an infringement he will also often be liable as a joint tortfeasor or for having procured the infringing act.[47] Also, of course, he may be vicariously liable for the acts of his servants or agents done with his authority.[48] "Authorisation" is a separate act of infringement from the act which is itself authorised.[49] It does not apply to indirect acts of infringement.[50]   **7–130**

---

[41] 91/250, as implemented by the Copyright (Computer Programs) Regulations 1992 (SI 1992/3233).

[42] CDPA 1988, ss. 21(3)(ab), (4). Provision is now made by CDPA 1988, s.50C for the incidental running of a program.

[43] The cases are usually treated as ones of mere reproduction.

[44] CDPA 1988, s.21(3)(ac). The subsection was introduced by the Copyright and Rights in Databases Regulations 1997 (SI 1997/3032). See paras 7–41 et seq., above as to infringement of copyright databases.

[45] CDPA 1988, s.21(3)(b).

[46] CDPA 1988, s.16(2). The position was the same under the 1956 and 1911 Acts: Copyright Act 1956, s.1(1); Copyright Act 1911, s.1(2).

[47] As to which, see CBS Songs Ltd v Amstrad plc [1988] A.C. 1013 at 1057, HL; Amstrad Consumer Electronics plc v British Phonographic Industry Ltd [1986] F.S.R. 159, CA and paras 22–35 et seq., below.

[48] Performing Right Society Ltd v Mitchell and Booker, etc. Ltd [1924] 1 K.B. 762; Canadian Performing Right Society v Canadian National Exhibition Association [1934] 4 D.L.R. 154. It was questioned whether the word "authorise" added anything to the law when first introduced in the 1911 Act (see, e.g. Performing Right Society v Ciryl Theatrical Syndicate Ltd [1924] 1 K.B. 1), but it had been held before then that a person was only liable for infringements committed by his servants or agents (see, e.g. Karno v Paté Frères Ltd (1909) 100 L.T. 260) and the effect of the Copyright Act 1911 was clearly to overrule this (Falcon v Famous Players Film Co [1926] 2 K.B. 474). See also Fiel v Lemaire (1939) 4 D.L.R. (Can.) 561

[49] Ash v Hutchinson and Co. (Publishers) Ltd [1936] Ch. 489; ABKCO Music v Music Collection International Ltd [1995] R.P.C. 657.

[50] Although the Report of Whitford Committee, Cmnd. 6732, recommended at para.749(iii) that it should.

7–131   Jurisdiction. Although no infringement is committed by the doing of any of the restricted acts unless the act takes place in the United Kingdom,[51] infringement by authorisation of any of those acts occurs even if the act of authorisation takes place outside the jurisdiction.[52]

7–132   Meaning of "authorise". Authorisation means the grant or purported grant, which may be express or implied, of the right to do the act complained of, whether the intention is that the grantee should do the act on his own account, or only on account of the grantor.[53] An expression which has often been used as equivalent to the word "authorise" is "sanction, approve and countenance",[54] but this must be treated with caution, particularly in so far as the word "countenance" is equivalent to the word "condone".[55] Thus, in general, an authorisation "can only come from someone having or purporting to have authority, and an act is not authorised by someone who merely enables or possibly assists or even encourages another to do that act, but does not purport to have any authority which he can grant to justify the doing of the act".[56] Some of the older cases need to be read with caution in the light of this modern statement of the law.

Clearly a person will have authorised an act if he formally grants the right to do the act in contemplation that it will in fact be done,[57] or simply gives permission for it to be done.[58] Likewise, a person who asks another to do an act, the former having the power to give or refuse permission to do that act, will usually be taken to have authorised it,[59] and a person who commissions another to produce an article will usually impliedly grant him the right to make it and thus authorise him to do so.[60] Cases where a person simply puts the means of doing the infringing act into another's hands are more difficult.[61] A person does not necessarily authorise an act to be done merely because he intentionally puts into another's hands the means by which the infringing act can be done if those means can also be used for a perfectly legitimate purpose,[62] even where it is known that they will in fact inevitably be used for an infringing purpose.[63] This will be so particularly if the supplier has no control over how the means will be used,[64] since it is the essence of a grant or purported grant that the grantor has some degree of actual or

---

[51] CDPA 1988, s.16(1).

[52] *ABKCO Music v Music Collection International Ltd* [1995] R.P.C. 657.

[53] *CBS Songs Ltd v Amstrad plc* [1988] A.C. 1013, HL citing, with apparent approval, Atkin L.J.'s statement in *Falcon v Famous Players Film Co.* [1926] 2 K.B. 474 at 499.

[54] *Falcon v Famous Players Film Co.* [1926] 2 K.B. 474, *per* Bankes L.J., following *Monckton v Pathé Frères Pathephone Ltd* [1914] 1 K.B. 395 and *Evans v E. Hulton & Co. Ltd* (1924) 131 L.T. 534. The phrase is meant to be read conjunctively: *Pensher Security Door Co Ltd v Sunderland City Council* [2000] R.P.C. 249, CA.

[55] *Amstrad Consumer Electronics plc v British Phonographic Industry Ltd* [1986] F.S.R. 159, CA, *per* Lawton L.J. at 207, approved in *CBS Songs Ltd v Amstrad plc* [1988] A.C. 1013 at 1055. It has been said that in this context "countenance" must be understood in its strongest dictionary meaning, namely, "give approval to, sanction, permit, favour, encourage": *CCH Canadian Ltd v Law Society of Upper Canada* [2004] S.C.C. 13 (Sup. Ct. of Canada), citing *The New Shorter Oxford English Dictionary* (1993), vol.1, p.526.

[56] *per* Whitford J. in *CBS Inc v Ames Records & Tapes Ltd* [1982] Ch. 91 at 106, approved in *Amstrad Consumer Electronics plc v British Phonographic Industry Ltd* [1986] F.S.R. 159 at 211, CA and in *CBS Songs Ltd v Amstrad plc* [1988] A.C. 1013 at 1055, HL.

[57] *Evans v E. Hulton & Co Ltd* (1924) 131 L.T. 534.

[58] As in *ABKCO Music v Music Collection International Ltd* [1995] R.P.C. 657.

[59] *Standen Engineering Ltd v A. Spalding & Sons Ltd* [1984] F.S.R. 554, held in *Pensher Security Door Co Ltd v Sunderland City Council* [2000] R.P.C. 249, CA, not to have been impliedly overruled by *CBS Songs Ltd v Amstrad plc* [1988] A.C. 1013.

[60] *Pensher Security Door Co Ltd v Sunderland City Council* [2000] R.P.C. 249.

[61] Whether or not the supply of equipment amounts to authorisation, such acts may well amount to secondary infringement. This is considered elsewhere; see paras 8–19 *et seq.*, below.

[62] See the cases cited in the examples given below at para. 7–133, below.

[63] *Amstrad Consumer Electronics plc v British Phonographic Industry Ltd* [1986] F.S.R. 159 at 211, CA, and *CBS Songs Ltd v Amstrad plc* [1988] A.C. 1013, HL, disapproving *RCA Corporation v John Fairfax & Sons Ltd* [1982] R.P.C. 91 (Sup Ct of New South Wales) on this point.

[64] *Vigneux v Canadian Performing Right Society Ltd* [1945] A.C. 108, cited with approval by Law-

apparent right to control the relevant actions of the grantee.[65] But where he retains control over the means in question, the facts may warrant a finding of implicit authorisation.[66] The older cases state that: (a) authorisation may be inferred from acts which fall short of being positive and direct; (b) even indifference may be sufficient[67]; and (c) whether what the defendant has done amounts to an authorisation will often be a matter of impression,[68] particularly in the case of advertisements which appear to encourage a particular activity.[69] In each case, it is no doubt a question of fact as to the true inference to be drawn from the conduct of the defendant,[70] but today it is likely to be a rare case that a sufficient inference can be drawn from such actions (or inaction). The mere failure to prevent infringement taking place when it could have been stopped will not amount to authorisation.[71] Ignorance of the fact that what will be done will be an infringement does not affect the question of liability.[72]

Examples of "authorisation". Many of the older reported cases are concerned with authorisation of the public performance of works. Where this question arises in the context of a performance in a place of public entertainment, the question of liability under section 25 of the Act will usually also arise.[73] As to authorisation, where a person engages performers for a public occasion, but in his absence and without his knowledge and without him suspecting, they perform works in infringement of copyright, he is clearly not liable for authorising, even though he has the power to direct them what to perform and to dismiss them if they refuse.[74] The older cases suggest that the position may be different if that person does not care whether the performance is an infringement or not and is present when it is given,[75] and also that where a person engages performers, and then approves a list of proposed titles which they submit, this will amount to authorisation.[76] These examples, must however, be regarded with caution in the light of the modern approach in *CBS Songs v Amstrad*, above. The facts of each case need to be looked at to see whether, for example, the performers looked to the person engag-

7–133

---

ton and Glidewell LL.J. in the Court of Appeal in *Amstrad Consumer Electronics plc v British Phonographic Industry Ltd* [1986] F.S.R. 159, whose judgments were themselves approved by the House of Lords in *CBS Songs Ltd v Amstrad plc* [1988] A.C. 1013, HL.

[65] *per* Slade L.J. in *Amstrad Consumer Electronics plc v British Phonographic Industry Ltd* [1986] F.S.R. 159, whose judgment was approved by the House of Lords, in *CBS Songs Ltd v Amstrad plc* [1988] A.C. 1013, HL. See also *RCA Corporation v John Fairfax & Sons Ltd* [1982] R.P.C. 91.

[66] *Moorhouse v University of New South Wales* [1976] R.P.C. 15, and *Amstrad Consumer Electronics plc v British Phonographic Industry Ltd* [1986] F.S.R. 159 at 211.

[67] *Performing Right Society v Ciryl Theatrical Syndicate Ltd* [1924] 1 K.B. 1.

[68] *RCA Corporation v John Fairfax & Sons Ltd* [1982] R.P.C. 91.

[69] *WEA International Inc v Hanimex Corporation Ltd* (1987) 77 A.L.R. 456.

[70] *WEA International Inc v Hanimex Corporation Ltd* (1987) 77 A.L.R. 456

[71] *Durand v Molino* [2000] E.C.D.R. 320 (occupier of premises who at the public unveiling of a painting did not act to prevent a photographer taking a photograph of it did not thereby authorise its reproduction).

[72] *Performing Right Society Ltd v Bray U.D.C.* [1930] A.C. 377, PC. Although note *Brintons Ltd v Feltex Furnishings of New Zealand Ltd* [1991] 2 N.Z.L.R. 677 (High Ct of NZ) where it was held that a person who merely authorised another to make an article could not be liable for infringement unless he knew that the article was a copy of another work. The decision was apparently being based on the proposition that "there can only be copying if the infringer knows he is copying." This is not a correct statement of the law under CDPA 1988.

[73] See para. 8–17, below.

[74] *Performing Right Society v Ciryl Theatrical Syndicate Ltd* [1924] 1 K.B. 1.

[75] *Monaghan v Taylor* (1885) 2 T.L.R. 685, a case decided before the Copyright Act 1911, where the issue was whether the defendant had caused or permitted a place to be used for public entertainment. See also *Bolton v London Exhibitions Ltd* (1898) 14 T.L.R. 550; *Green v Irish Independent Co Ltd* [1899] 1 I.R. 386; *Colburn v Simms* (1843) 2 Ha. 543 at 547.

[76] *Performing Right Society Ltd v Bray U.D.C.* [1930] A.C. 377, PC. See also *Australasian Performing Right Association Ltd v Canterbury-Bankstown Leagues Club Ltd* [1964–65] N.S.W.R. 138; and *Australasian Performing Right Association Ltd v Koolman* [1969] N.Z.L.R. 273.

ing them to give them the necessary permission to perform the material; or whether this was regarded as the performers' responsibility; or whether, for example, this was a matter to which no thought was given by either party. It is suggested that it is only in the first of these cases that there can have been authorisation. Simply approving a list of works to be performed can hardly amount to authorisation, since it does not reveal enough about what the assumptions were. It has been said that a broadcaster who knows that his broadcast will be performed in public at hotels and other public places authorises such public performance, but this cannot be correct.[77]

As already indicated, cases in which the defendant provides the means by which the infringement is committed sometimes cause difficulties. Again, in this context the question will sometimes also arise as to whether an act of secondary infringement under sections 24 or 26 has been committed.[78] Where a person places an order for the manufacture of an article upon another, the former having the power to prevent such manufacture, and supplies an example of the article to be copied, this will usually amount to authorisation.[79] Again, where a person sold the rights in a manuscript with a view to its publication, such publication being bound to infringe, this amounted to authorisation.[80] Where defendants hired out to a cinema proprietor a film whose exhibition was bound to be an infringement, they were held to have authorised that act.[81] It has been held that the seller of a record authorises its use,[82] which may on the particular facts be true, but whether he authorises its infringing use is a different question, since it may be used for non-infringing purposes, for example, performance in private.[83] The mere sale of a record would not today be held to be an authorisation of the public performance of the musical work embodied in it. Thus where a record library lent out records and simultaneously offered blank tapes for sale at a discount, it was held that no authorisation of home taping had occurred.[84] Usually a seller of a computer program will authorise its use,[85] and since any use of a program will inevitably involve its reproduction,[86] it is likely that where such use is unlicensed, or is not subject to one of the permitted acts,[87] and is thus an infringement, the seller will also infringe by authorising such use.

In *Amstrad*,[88] where the defendant sold hi-fi systems which included the facility for the high-speed duplication of cassette tapes, this was held not to amount to authorisation even though the almost inevitable consequence would be that purchasers would use such equipment to make infringing copies. Again, in *Vi-*

[77] *per* Viscount Maugham in *Mellor v Australian Broadcasting Commission* [1940] A.C. 491. The point was not argued. A broadcaster has no control over whether or not an appropriate public performance licence is obtained.
[78] See paras 8–15 and 8–19, below.
[79] *Standen Engineering Ltd v A. Spalding & Sons Ltd* [1984] F.S.R. 554.
[80] *Evans v E. Hulton & Co. Ltd* (1924) 131 L.T. 534.
[81] *Falcon v Famous Players Film Co.* [1926] 2 K.B. 474; *Fenning Film Service Ltd v Wolverhampton, etc. Cinemas Ltd* [1914] 3 K.B. 1171; compare, prior to the Copyright Act 1911, *Glenville v Selig Polyscope Co* (1911) 27 T.L.R. 554; see also *Karno v Pathé Frères Ltd* (1909) 100 L.T. 260.
[82] *Monckton v Pathé Frères Pathephone Ltd* [1914] 1 K.B. 395.
[83] The proposition from *Monckton* cited in the text was apparently approved by the House of Lords in *CBS Songs Ltd v Amstrad plc* [1988] A.C. 1013, on the basis that in the *Monckton* case "a performance of the musical work by the use of the record was bound to be an infringing use and the record was sold for that purpose." But only a *public* performance of a musical work is bound to be an infringement. Playing the record in private will not be.
[84] *CBS Inc v Ames Records & Tapes Ltd* [1982] Ch. 91. See also *A. & M. Records Inc v Audio Magnetics Incorporated (U.K.) Ltd* [1979] F.S.R. 1; *Paterson Zochonis Ltd v Merfarken Packaging Ltd* [1983] F.S.R. 273.
[85] *Ibcos Computers Ltd v Barclays Mercantile Highland Finance Ltd* [1994] F.S.R. 275.
[86] See para. 7–20, above.
[87] See Ch.9, below.
[88] *CBS Songs Ltd v Amstrad plc* [1988] A.C. 1013.

gneux,[89] the supply of a coin-operated juke box on hire for a fixed rent to a restaurant, and of the records for use in it, did not, on the facts, amount to authorisation of public performance, the supplier having no control over the use of the machine or as to whether it was available to customers. But a case on similar facts was distinguished in the later Australian decision of *Winstone*, where it was held that the fact that the defendant supplied the records for use in the juke box gave the defendant sufficient control over its use to amount to authorisation.[90] Again, in *Moorhouse*,[91] another Australian case, where a university provided copying machines close to its library, retaining control over them and over the books which were copied using the machines, and having reasonable grounds to suspect that infringements might occur if no adequate precautions to prevent this happening were taken, this was held to amount to authorisation. *Moorhouse* has not been followed by the Supreme Court of Canada in *CCH Canadian*[92] in a similar factual situation, the important points being that not all works in the library were copyright works, some users would have had a defence of fair dealing, and the library had posted a notice above the photocopiers disclaiming responsibility for infringing copies. How an English court would decide cases on these facts today is uncertain[93] but each case has to be looked at on its own facts. If a defendant supplies music equipment to another on the basis the user must obtain whatever licences are necessary to play the music in public,[94] this could hardly justify a finding of authorisation.[95] If, however, the basis on which the equipment was supplied by the defendant was that music could be played without fear of any infringement, since all necessary permissions had been obtained, the position would be different. As already noted, the 1988 Act widened the categories of secondary infringements to include the provision of apparatus, with knowledge, for the purpose of an infringing performance.[96] In the case of a photocopier made available by a library or photocopy shop, it is suggested that the decision in *CCH Canadian* is a better guide than that in *Moorhouse*.

---

[89] *Vigneux v Canadian Performing Right Society Ltd* [1945] A.C. 108. The case was decided under the special provisions of the Canadian Act and the decision on "authorisation" was strictly *obiter*, but affirmed by the Supreme Court of Canada in *Muzak Corp v Composers, Authors and Publishers Association of Canada* [1953] S S.C.R. 182. See also *Georges de Tervagne v Town of Beloeil*, (1993) 50 C.P.R. (3d) 419, and the next footnote.

[90] *Winstone v Wurlitzer, etc.* [1946] V.L.R. 338. However, in *Vigneux*, the defendant also supplied the records for use in the juke box and to this extent the case seems hard to distinguish on the facts, although this was not a matter which was commented on by the court. See also the comments of Whitford J. in *CBS Inc v Ames Records & Tapes Ltd* [1982] Ch.91. *Vigneux* was also distinguished in *Winstone* on the ground that in *Winstone* the juke box was provided on a profit-sharing arrangement rather than a fixed fee, so that the arrangement was a joint venture for which the defendant was liable.

[91] *Moorhouse v University of New South Wales* [1976] R.P.C. 151 (High Ct of Aus). There are extensive provisions in the CDPA 1988 regulating the extent of copying permitted by libraries. See paras 9–100 *et seq.*, below.

[92] *CCH Canadian Ltd v Law Society of Upper Canada* [2004] SCC 13 (Sup Ct), stating that *Moorhouse* was not consistent with the previous British and Canadian approaches to the question. The court also applied the principle, extracted from Canadian authorities, that courts should presume that a person who authorises an activity does so only so far as it is in accordance with the law, although this presumption may be rebutted if it is shown that a certain relationship or degree of control existed between the alleged authoriser and the persons who committed the copyright infringement. It is suggested that this is not a principle of English law.

[93] Dicta from *Vigneux* were cited in the Court of Appeal and the House of Lords in the *Amstrad* decisions, but the decision on the facts was not commented upon. *Winstone* was cited to the House of Lords in *CBS Songs Ltd v Amstrad* [1988] A.C. 1013 but not commented upon. *Moorhouse* appears to have been regarded in *Amstrad Consumer Electronics plc v British Phonographic Industry Ltd* [1986] F.S.R. 159 as correct on its own facts, which justified a finding of implicit authorisation: at 211.

[94] For example from Performing Right Society Ltd or Phonographic Performance Ltd (as to which see paras 28–59 and 28–60, below, respectively).

[95] See, *e.g. Keays v Dempster* [1994] F.S.R. 554 (author merely choosing photographs for his book, leaving it to the publisher to clear any rights).

[96] See paras 8–19 *et seq.*, below.

7–134   **Other matters**. Obviously, unless the act authorised is itself an infringement, no act of authorisation can amount to an infringement either.[97] It is unclear whether, in order for the tort of authorisation to be complete, the act authorised must itself have been committed. There is authority that this is the correct position,[98] and if it were otherwise an instruction to do an act which was revoked before the act was carried out would be an infringement, although in suitable circumstances a case for a *quia timet* injunction could no doubt be made out.[99] So, where a defendant had the copyright owner's consent to distribute a film, and had consequently authorised its showing in public by third-party exhibitors, he was not liable for authorisation where the copyright owner later revoked his consent before the showings had taken place.[1] Nevertheless, the point must be in doubt following the decision in *MCA Records Inc v Charly Records Ltd*[2] There, a licence had been granted by a defendant more than six years before the writ had been issued, but some infringing acts committed under the licence had taken place within the six-year period. The issue was whether the acts of authorisation had also taken place within this period. By analogy with cases concerning the grant of an unlawful subtenancy, it was held that the authorisation was a one-off event which had taken place on the grant of the licence and was not renewed from time to time as each act of infringement was committed. Further, and probably *obiter*, it was held that authorisation "is complete when the authorisation is effected; it is not a tort which is completed only once an infringing act is carried out in pursuance of the authorisation". However, none of the above cases to the contrary effect are referred to in the judgment, and it is not clear whether they were cited to the court.[3] Of course, such a ruling has attractions as a matter of practice, not least because otherwise a licensor might be liable over the full term of the licence, which might last as long as the term of copyright in the work or works in question. Against this, the copyright owner will usually have no means of knowing of the act of authorisation until, at the earliest, an act of infringement under the licence is committed. Again, from the copyright owner's point of view, a licensor is often of greater financial worth than a licensee when it comes to pursuing any claim for damages or profits.

It has been said that it is necessary to plead some specific authorisation of an actual breach of copyright affecting a particular claimant, and that it is not sufficient to plead authorisation at large.[4] However, it is submitted that there is no reason in principle why a sufficiently clear act of authorisation should not amount to an infringement even though not addressed to a specific person.

---

[97] *ABKCO Music & Records Inc v Music Collection International Ltd* [1995] R.P.C. 657 at 660; *Nelson v Rye* [1996] F.S.R. 313; *Composers, Authors and Publishers Association of Canada Ltd v CTV Television Network Ltd*, [1968] S.C.R. 676, at 680.

[98] *Performing Right Society Ltd v Mitchell and Booker, etc. Ltd* [1924] 1 K.B. 762 at 773; *Moorhouse v University of New South Wales* [1975] R.P.C. 454 at 467; *RCA Corporation v John Fairfax & Son Ltd* [1982] R.P.C. 91; *Copyright Agency Ltd v Haines* [1982] F.S.R. 331; *WEA International Inc v Hanimex Corp. Ltd* (1987) 77 A.L.R. 456.

[99] *RCA Corporation v John Fairfax & Sons Ltd* [1982] R.P.C. 91 (*quia timet* injunction refused); *WEA International Inc v Hanimex Corp. Ltd* (1987) 77 A.L.R. 456.

[1] *Century Communications Ltd v Mayfair Entertainment U.K. Ltd* [1993] E.M.L.R. 335.

[2] [2000] E.M.L.R. 743. *Fenning Film Service Ltd v Wolverhampton, etc. Cinemas Ltd* [1914] 3 K.B. 1171 may be authority to the same effect (see, *e.g. Performing Right Society Ltd v Mitchell and Booker, etc. Ltd* [1924] 1 K.B. 762).

[3] See further, Dickens, "When Is an Authorisation an Authorisation?" [2000] E.I.P.R. 339.

[4] *A. & M. Records Inc v Audio Magnetics Incorporated (U.K.) Ltd* [1979] F.S.R. 1.

SECONDARY INFRINGEMENT OF COPYRIGHT

Contents   *Para.*

1. INTRODUCTION

The 1988 Act provides for a class of secondary infringements, the principal **8–01** characteristic of which is that it is a necessary ingredient of the tort that the defendant must have a degree of "guilty knowledge" before he can be liable. The acts are termed secondary because they generally depend upon a primary act of infringement having first taken place, for example the making of an infringing copy.[1] The 1988 Act does not provide that a person who authorises a secondary act of infringement is liable, although a person may nevertheless be liable for such an act under the common law, for example as a joint tortfeasor.[2]

The 1988 Act provides for three broad classes of secondary infringement. The first consists of various dealings with infringing copies, the second of providing the means for making infringing copies and the third of permitting or enabling infringing performances to take place. The three classes will be considered in turn.

2. DEALINGS IN INFRINGING COPIES

A. INTRODUCTION

The main acts of secondary infringement concern dealings with infringing copies. **8–02** Thus the copyright in a work is infringed by any person who, without the licence of the copyright owner:

  (a) possesses in the course of a business,
  (b) sells or lets for hire, or offers or exposes for sale or hire,
  (c) in the course of a business exhibits in public or distributes, or
  (d) distributes otherwise than in the course of a business to such an extent as to affect prejudicially the owner of the copyright,

an article which is, and which he knows or has reason to believe is, an infringing

---

[1] This is an oversimplification in the case, *e.g.* of importation. See para. 8–05, below.

[2] As to authorisation, see para. 7–130, above, and as to joint tortfeasors see para. 22–35, below. Note that the 1977 Copyright ("Whitford") Committee, Cmmd.6732, para.749(iii), recommended that persons authorising indirect infringements should be liable.

copy of the work.[3] The copyright in a work is also infringed by any person who, without the licence of the copyright owner, imports into the United Kingdom, otherwise than for his private and domestic use, an article which is, and which he knows or has reason to believe is, an infringing copy of the work.[4] These provisions are principally directed, not to manufacturers, but to third parties who deal in infringing articles supplied to them,[5] and enable a copyright owner to limit the further dissemination of such copies. The need for a plaintiff to prove the element of "guilty knowledge" reflects the fact that traders and others may handle infringing copies without necessarily suspecting or having the means of knowing that they are infringing. As already noted, there may be circumstances in which someone who sells or distributes infringing copies is also liable for the primary act of infringement of issuing copies to the public,[6] in respect of which "guilty knowledge" is not an element. The point is discussed in relation to the treatment of issue to the public.[7] To an extent, these secondary rights granted to copyright owners can be regarded as an aspect of the distribution right although, of course, they only relate to infringing copies and not legitimate copies.

B. INFRINGING COPY

8–03   An article is an infringing copy if its making constituted an infringement of the copyright in the work in question.[8] An article is also an infringing copy if:

(a) it has been or is proposed to be imported into the United Kingdom, and

(b) its making in the United Kingdom would have constituted an infringement of the copyright in the work in question, or a breach of an exclusive licence agreement relating to that work.[9]

There are also a number of provisions in the 1988 Act whereby copies of works whose making did not constitute an infringement of copyright, because statutory exemptions applied, are nevertheless to be treated as infringing copies in certain subsequent events.[10] These provisions are dealt with elsewhere.[11] Where in any proceedings it is proved that an article is a copy of a work, and that copyright subsists or has at any time subsisted in the work, then for the purposes of deciding whether the article is an infringing copy it is to be presumed until the contrary is proved that the article was made at a time when copyright subsisted in the work.[12] An article such as a door does not cease to be an "article" simply because it becomes integrated into a building.[13]

---

[3] CDPA 1988, s.23.

[4] s.22.

[5] *Paterson Zochonis Ltd v Merfarken Packaging Ltd* [1983] F.S.R. 273.

[6] *i.e.* under CDPA 1988, s.18.

[7] See para. 7–80, above.

[8] CDPA 1988, s.27(2). Although for the purposes of infringement the 1988 Act only applies in relation to acts done after August 1, 1989, the article dealt in may of course have been made before this date. For the purposes of determining whether an article is an infringing copy, the 1956 Act is to be applied in relation to an article made after June 1, 1957 and before August 1, 1989, and the 1911 Act is to be applied to an article made before June 1, 1957 (see CDPA 1988, Sch.1, para.14(3)). In relation to articles made on or after August 1, 1989, the 1988 Act is to be applied.

[9] s.27(3). As to the definition of an exclusive licence, see s.92(1) and para. 5–204, above.

[10] s.27(6).

[11] See Ch.9, below.

[12] CDPA 1988, s.27(4).

[13] *Pensher Security Door Co. Ltd v Sunderland City Council* [2000] R.P.C. 249, CA.

The making was an infringement. Little more needs to be said about this ingredient. The making of the copy will have been an infringement if the reproduction right was thereby infringed.[14]

8–04

Imported copies. An article will also be an infringing copy if its making in the United Kingdom would have constituted an infringement of copyright or a breach of an exclusive licence agreement relating to that work. This definition therefore proceeds on a hypothetical basis as to the place and circumstances in which the article was made. The assumption which has to be made is that the copy was made in the United Kingdom by the person who actually made it.[15] The section therefore covers the cases where:

8–05

(a) The article was made abroad by a third party who has no interest in the copyright and no licence of any kind.

(b) The article was made abroad by a person who owned the copyright in that territory (but not in the United Kingdom) or who had a licence in that territory (but not for the United Kingdom).

(c) The article was made abroad by a person who owned the copyright in the United Kingdom but who had granted an exclusive licence for the United Kingdom.[16] In this case, the making of the copy by the copyright owner in the United Kingdom would not have constituted an infringement of copyright but would have constituted a breach of the exclusive licence. It is therefore an infringing copy.[17]

Thus the owner of the United Kingdom copyright, or the United Kingdom exclusive licensee, can object to the importation of and subsequent dealings in copies made abroad without his licence, subject to European Community law principles.[18] This is so even though the articles made abroad were legitimately purchased there on the open market (so-called "grey copies"), since the sale of articles in the ordinary course of business in one territory without restriction on resale does not carry with it any implied licence to import and sell those articles in another territory. The purchaser obtains the same rights as the purchaser of any other chattel, and the rights which flow from acquisition and ownership do not involve any such implied licence.[19] United Kingdom copyright law has never recognised the principle of "international exhaustion", and is now bound by European Directives not to do so in relation to sales outside the European Community.[20]

The European Communities Act 1972. The 1988 Act expressly provides that nothing in the provisions of the 1988 Act shall be construed as applying to an article which may be lawfully imported into the United Kingdom by virtue of any enforceable Community right within the meaning of section 2(1) of the European

8–06

---

[14] As to the reproduction right, see CDPA 1988, s.17 and paras 7–09 et seq., above.

[15] See *C.B.S. Ltd v Charmdale Record Distributors Ltd* [1981] Ch. 91; *Polydor Ltd v Harlequin Record Shops Ltd* [1980] F.S.R. 194 and 362, CA. These cases were decided under the slightly different provisions of ss.5(2) and (3) of the 1956 Act.

[16] As to the meaning of exclusive licence, see CDPA 1988, s.92 and paras 5–204 et seq., above.

[17] The position under the 1956 Act was different. See *C.B.S. Ltd v Charmdale Record Distributors Ltd* [1981] Ch. 91 and *Polydor Ltd v Harlequin Record Shops Ltd* [1980] F.S.R. 194 and 362, CA.

[18] See para. 8–06, below.

[19] *Time-Life International (Nederlands) N.V. v Interstate Parcel Express Co. Pty Ltd* [1978] F.S.R. 251; *Polydor Ltd v Harlequin Record Shops* [1980] F.S.R. 362; *Penguin Books Ltd v India Book Distributors* [1985] F.S.R. 120; *R. & A. Bailey & Co. Ltd v Boccaccio Pty Ltd* (1988) 77 A.L.R. 177; *Computermate Products (Aus) Pty Ltd v Ozi-Soft Pty Ltd* (1988) 83 A.L.R. 492. As to implied licences generally, see para. 5–213 et seq., above.

[20] See para. 8–06, below.

Communities Act 1972.[21] Thus if an article is in free circulation within the European Economic Area it will not be an infringing copy for any purpose.[22] This point is reinforced by a number of provisions in European Directives in this field, dealing with the question of exhaustion of rights. Thus, most recently, Article 4(2) of the Information Society Directive[23] stipulates that the distribution right is not exhausted within the Community in respect of the original or copies of the work, except where the first sale or other transfer of ownership in the Community of that object is made by the rightholder or with his consent.This does not apply in relation to first sale outside the Community.[24] Similar provision had been made in earlier Directives dealing with computer programs,[25] related rights subject matter[26] and copyright databases.[27] The bare fact that an article has been sold in a Community territory, and the owner did not prevent it, will not be enough to raise a defence in the absence of any evidence that the copyright owner knew that the sale was taking place and could have prevented it, and by inference must be taken to have authorised it.[28]

C. Territorial Extent

8–07   Unlike the case of primary acts of infringement,[29] and the equivalent provisions of the 1956 Act,[30] the acts of secondary infringement, apart from importation, are not restricted in express terms in the 1988 Act to acts done in the United Kingdom. It is suggested, however, that it is clear that they are. This Part of the Act is extended in the first place only to England and Wales, Scotland and Northern Ireland,[31] and the general principle of statutory construction is that unless the contrary is expressly enacted, English legislation does not extend to acts of foreigners committed outside the jurisdiction.[32] Thus if an article whose making in the United Kingdom constituted an infringement of copyright, and which was thus an infringing copy, subsequently came into the hands of someone in a foreign jurisdiction, it would be surprising if the legislature intended that person should become liable under the 1988 Act for selling the article in the foreign jurisdiction even where he had the necessary knowledge.

In these circumstances, the provision that an "infringing copy" may include one which is "proposed" to be imported into the United Kingdom requires explanation, since it apparently expressly contemplates a situation in which a dealing with an article which has not yet been imported into the United Kingdom may be an infringement. First, although to "import" is not defined in the Act, it probably means to bring an article from abroad into port, such that the carriage is ended or its continuity is in some way broken.[33] Secondly, an act done on a British ship, aircraft or hovercraft will be treated as being done in the United King-

---

[21] CDPA 1988, s.27(5).

[22] As to the effects of Community law generally, see Ch.25, below.

[23] Directive 2001/29/EC.

[24] Recital 28.

[25] Computer Programs Directive 91/250, Art.5(c).

[26] Rental and Related Rights Directive 92/100, Art.9(2).

[27] Database Directive 96/9, Art.5(c).

[28] *EMI Records Ltd v The CD Specialists Ltd* [1992] F.S.R. 70.

[29] See CDPA 1988, s.16(1).

[30] Copyright Act 1956, ss.5(2), (3), 16(2), (3). See also *Def Lepp Music v Stuart-Brown* [1986] R.P.C. 273, confirming that the provisions of the 1956 Act were expressly confined to acts done in the UK or other countries to which the Act was extended. The same principle underlies the decision in *Pearce v Ove Arup Partnership Ltd* [2000] Ch. 403.

[31] CDPA 1988, s.157(1).

[32] See *Ex parte Blain* (1879) 12 Ch. D. 522; *Clark v Oceanic Contractors Inc.* [1983] 2 A.C. 130; *ABKCO Music v Music Collection International Ltd* [1995] R.P.C. 657.

[33] See para. 8–14, below, in relation to infringement by importation.

dom[34] and, in addition, the territorial waters of the United Kingdom are to be treated as part of the United Kingdom.[35] It follows that acts can be done in what is the United Kingdom for the purposes of the Act, for example on board a British ship, in relation to articles which are "proposed to be imported into the United Kingdom". If this is correct, then it would be an infringement of copyright to possess, with knowledge, a piratical article on board a British ship if it was proposed to import it into the United Kingdom, but it would not be an infringement to possess such an article on board a British ship if the article was neither made in the United Kingdom nor had ever been imported into the United Kingdom and it was not proposed to import it.

D. KNOWLEDGE

Necessity to prove knowledge. As has been seen, in relation to secondary infringements, it is necessary to prove that the defendant knew or had reason to believe he was dealing with an article which was an infringing copy of the work. Two states of mind are therefore sufficient for this purpose: actual knowledge or constructive knowledge. The 1988 Act effected a change of the law in this area: under the 1911 and 1956 Acts a defendant was liable only if he knew the making of the copy was an infringement,[36] although some of the cases decided under these provisions came close to making a defendant liable who had only constructive knowledge.[37] The clear intention behind these provisions of the 1988 Act was to relax the requirement of guilty knowledge in favour of a claimant.[38] Cases decided under the 1956 and 1911 Acts[39] are therefore generally not useful authorities for the purpose of construing the constructive knowledge limb of the 1988 Act.[40]

8–08

Actual knowledge.[41] The question is one of fact and will usually turn on the evidence of the defendant's actions and what he knew and did. The burden of proof is on the claimant and has been described as a heavy one.[42] Strictly, turning a blind eye, or "Nelsonian" knowledge, is a case of actual knowledge since the defendant merely averts his gaze from what he knows to be there. A person who deliberately refrains from inquiry and shuts his eyes to that which is obvious to him (and which he therefore knows) cannot therefore be heard to say that he lacks the requisite knowledge.[43] The provisions, however, contemplate specific knowledge about the circumstances in which a specific article was made and it may be that a defendant's general knowledge that an article may be an infringing copy will not be sufficient to fix him with knowledge, for example, where he is in

8–09

---

[34] CDPA 1988, s.162.

[35] s.161.

[36] Copyright Act 1956, ss.5(2), (3), 16(2), (3). For the cases decided on this point, see the next footnote and *Van Dusen v Kritz* [1936] 2 K.B. 176; *R.C.A. Corporation v Custom Cleared Sales Pty Ltd* [1978] F.S.R. 576; applied in *Politechnika v Dallas Print Transfers Ltd* [1982] F.S.R. 529; *Hoover Plc v George Hulme Ltd* [1982] F.S.R. 565 and *Hooi v Brophy* (1984) 52 A.L.R. 710. See also *International Business Machines Corp. v Computer Imports Ltd* [1989] 2 N.Z.L.R. 395.

[37] See, *e.g. Albert v Hoffnung & Co. Ltd* [1921] 22 S.R.(N.S.W.) 75, followed in *Infabrics Ltd v Jaytex Shirt Co. Ltd* [1978] F.S.R. 451 (at first instance). See also *Gramophone Co. Ltd v Music Machine (Pty) Ltd* [1973] 3 S.A.L.R. 188.

[38] See, *e.g.* the White Paper: Intellectual Property and Innovation, Cmnd.9712, para.12.12.

[39] Such as *Van Dusen v Kritz* [1936] 2 K.B. 176; *Hoover plc v George Hulme (Stockport) Ltd* [1982] F.S.R. 565.

[40] *LA Gear Inc. v Hi-Tec Sports plc* [1992] F.S.R. 121.

[41] Cases decided under the 1956 and 1911 Acts are potentially relevant, but borderline cases will no doubt usually be decided now under the constructive knowledge limb.

[42] *Infabrics Ltd v Jaytex Shirt Co. Ltd* [1978] F.S.R. 451 (at first instance); *Sillitoe v McGraw-Hill Book Co.* [1983] F.S.R. 545.

[43] *Columbia Picture Industries v Robinson* [1987] Ch. 38.

possession of a large number of articles, some of which he knows may infringe and some of which may not.[44] Under the 1956 Act, a defendant was taken to have had actual knowledge if he knew all the relevant facts but was under a mistake of law or ignorant as their effect.[45] This is still good law[46] although the point is now likely to be academic in the light of the alternative constructive knowledge limb.

It is reason to believe, not belief. Nuoveau: reason to suspect may evolve into reason to believe if no explanation

8–10   **Constructive knowledge.** The words "has reason to believe" should be construed in accordance with their ordinary meaning. In particular:

  (a) "Reason to believe" involves a concept of knowledge of facts from which a reasonable man would arrive at the relevant belief. The test is thus an objective one;

  (b) Facts from which a reasonable man might *suspect* the relevant conclusion are not enough;

  (c) The section connotes the allowance of a period of time to enable the reasonable man to evaluate the facts to convert them into a reasonable belief.[47]

The reasonable man will be taken to be a reasonable man in the position of the defendant and with his knowledge and experience.[48] If a defendant has knowledge of relevant facts giving grounds for belief that is all that is necessary: it is no defence that the defendant did not in fact believe the copies to be infringing[49] or for a defendant to say that although he knew the facts he nevertheless believed that as a matter of law no infringement would be committed, even if this was on the basis of legal advice.[50] Mere suspicion, however, is not enough.[51] Where a person is not aware that he is dealing in infringing goods, he must therefore be given notice of the facts, commonly by letter, before a *prima facie* case can be made that further dealings by him will amount to infringement. Sufficient information must be given to suggest to the recipient that an infringement will be committed if he continues to deal in the articles in question. The information must not be of such a general nature that the recipient can form no proper view as to what is being alleged.[52] Thus usually it will be necessary to identify the copyright work in question, and if a copy is not supplied then at least facilities should be offered for its inspection. It is not, however, necessary for a person to have seen a copy of the relevant copyright work before he can be said to have reason to believe that an article is an infringing copy. Each case will turn on its own facts. For example, where a claim of infringement is made against a person who knows that his article is similar to and has probably been copied from the claimant's corresponding article, and a reasonable man would know that the claimant's article was made from drawings in which copyright subsisted, he will

---

[44] *Columbia Picture Industries v Robinson* [1987] Ch. 38. The point is of limited importance now, given the alternative constructive knowledge test.

[45] *Sillitoe v McGraw-Hill Book Co.* [1983] F.S.R. 545 (decided under the 1956 Act). See also *International Business Machines Corp. v Computer Imports Ltd* [1989] 2 N.Z.L.R. 395 at 418.

[46] *ZYX Music GmbH v King* [1997] 2 All E.R. 129, CA, applying *Sillitoe v McGraw-Hill Book Co.* [1983] F.S.R. 545.

[47] *LA Gear Inc. v Hi-Tec Sports plc* [1992] F.S.R. 121, CA; *Linpac Mouldings Ltd v Eagleton Direct Export Ltd* [1994] F.S.R. 545, CA.

[48] *ZYX Music GmbH v King* [1995] F.S.R. 566 at 578 (knowledge of reasonable record distributor in defendant's position); *Raben Footwear Pty Ltd v Polygram Records Inc.* (1997) 37 I.P.R. 417 (regard to be had "to the knowledge, capacity and circumstances of the particular defendant").

[49] *Nouveau Fabrics Ltd v Voyage Decoration Ltd* [2004] EWHC 895, ChD.

[50] *ZYX Music GmbH v King* [1997] 2 All E.R. 129, CA, applying *Sillitoe v McGraw-Hill Book Co.* [1983] F.S.R. 545 (decided under the 1956 Act). See also *International Business Machines Corp. v Computer Imports Ltd* [1989] 2 N.Z.L.R. 395 at 418.

[51] *ZYX Music GmbH v King* [1995] 3 All E.R. 1.

[52] *Hoover Plc v George Hulme Stockport Ltd* [1982] F.S.R. 565.

have "reason to believe" for this purpose.[53] As to the period of notice, as already noted, a period of time must be allowed to enable the reasonable man to evaluate the facts to convert them into a reasonable belief[54] or, for what may be grounds for suspicion to harden into grounds for belief,[55] whether or not the defendant actually believes it. A person is not fixed with knowledge at the instant he receives notice of a claim. A period of 14 days is often taken as sufficient[56] but in each case it will be a question of fact.[57] A defendant is not bound to accept the claimant's assertions, although he cannot simply ignore them.[58] A defendant who does so, and who therefore is a person who has reason to *suspect*, is capable of becoming a person with reason to *believe* if he carries out no sensible inquiries, and does absolutely nothing in the face of continued assertions of the copyright by the owner.[59] What he must do is evaluate the assertions, a process which will, in many cases, require him to make reasonable inquiries, and the result of those inquiries will be taken into account in assessing whether he has reason to believe.[60] Sometimes a relatively long time may be needed for the defendant to make proper inquiries and obtain what information he can.[61]Where a defendant's knowledge consists only of assertions of infringement, or of disputed facts, whether made in correspondence or pleadings, this is not enough.[62] Thus where there is a dispute between A and B about whether certain articles infringe, and C deals in those articles knowing of the dispute but does not know and does not have the means of knowing what is the correct position, he does not have sufficient knowledge for this purpose should A's version of events subsequently turn out to be correct[63]: he does not have knowledge of the relevant facts. Probably the knowledge of an agent would be imputed to his principal.[64] It has been said, in a different context, that where a trader goes into the market and finds what appears to be a novel product, it is not incumbent upon him, in the absence of some special circumstance, to enquire of the person offering the product whether there are any copyright complications involved in dealing with the product. He is entitled to assume that the vendor is in a position to sell what he offers to sell.[65] The burden of satisfying the court that a defendant has sufficient knowledge lies on the claimant.[66]

[53] *Pensher Security Door Co. Ltd v Sunderland City Council* [2000] R.P.C. 249, CA.
[54] *L.A. Gear Inc. v Hi-Tec Sports plc* [1992] F.S.R. 121, CA. For the earlier cases, which were to the same effect, see, *e.g. Van Dusen v Kritz* [1936] 2 K.B. 176; *R.C.A. Corporation v Custom Cleared Sales Pty Ltd* [1978] F.S.R. 576.
[55] *Nouveau Fabrics Ltd v Voyage Decoration Ltd* [2004] EWHC 895, ChD.
[56] See, *e.g. Infabrics Ltd v Jaytex Ltd* (at first instance) [1978] F.S.R. 451.
[57] See, *e.g. Sillitoe v McGraw-Hill Book Co.* [1983] F.S.R. 545. Where the defendant had to make inquiries of manufacturers abroad, nine days was held insufficient in *Rexnold Inc. v Ancon Ltd* [1983] F.S.R. 662, but 21 days sufficient in *Monsoon Ltd v India Imports of Rhode Island Ltd* [1993] F.S.R. 21.
[58] *Nouveau Fabrics Ltd v Voyage Decoration Ltd* [2004] EWHC 895, ChD.
[59] *Nouveau Fabrics Ltd v Voyage Decoration Ltd* [2004] EWHC 895, ChD, although it is not clear, on this basis, when reason to suspect will become reason to believe.
[60] *Nouveau Fabrics Ltd v Voyage Decoration Ltd* [2004] EWHC 895, ChD.
[61] In *Nouveau Fabrics Ltd v Voyage Decoration Ltd* [2004] EWHC 895 , ChD, six months elapsed between the letter before action and the defendant having reason to believe.
[62] The paragraph down to this point in the 14th edition was approved as an accurate statement of the law in *Vermaat v Boncrest Ltd (No.2)* [2002] F.S.R. 21.
[63] *Hutchinson Personal Communications Ltd v Hook Advertising Ltd* [1995] F.S.R. 365; *Metix (UK) Ltd v G.H. Maughan (Plastics) Ltd* [1997] F.S.R. 718.
[64] *R.C.A. Corporation v Custom Cleared Sales Pty Ltd* [1978] F.S.R. 576.
[65] *Quaker Oats Co. Ltd v Alltrades Distributors Ltd* [1981] F.S.R. 9. The context was a consideration of factors relevant to the grant of interlocutory relief. As to the effect of a copyright notice on imported goods, see *Clarke, Irwin & Co. v C. Cole & Co.* (1960) 22 D.L.R. (2d) 183; and also *Godfrey, etc., Ltd v Coles Book Stores Ltd* [1974] 40 D.L.R. (3d) 346 and *Simon & Schuster Inc. v Coles Book StoresLtd* [1976] 61 D.L.R. (3d) 590.
[66] *Springsteen v Flute International Ltd* [1999] F.S.R. 180.

E. Particular Acts

8–11 **Possession.** Copyright in a work is infringed by any person who, without the licence of the copyright owner, and with the necessary knowledge, possesses an infringing copy in the course of a business.[67] "Business" is defined as including a trade or profession.[68] The business in question must be that of the possessor, and not that of some other person who sold it to him[69] for otherwise every member of the public who knowingly bought an infringing copy from a business would be liable for possession, which is clearly not the Act's intention. Although the business in question is not limited to that of doing business in articles of that kind,[70] possession of such articles must be part of the ordinary course of the business, so that possession which is only incidental to a business will not amount to possession in the course of that business.[71] Otherwise a party's solicitor might become liable if he came into possession of an infringing article while acting for him, which would be absurd.[72] In the case of a local authority, some of its activities can be properly described as business activities and some not. In each case it will depend on the nature of the activity. For example, a local authority carrying out its duty to provide street lighting is not engaged in a business activity but the ownership, management, regulation, control and letting of flats pursuant to a local authority's powers under the Housing Acts is a business activity.[73] "Possession" in this context is not confined to cases where a party is in possession of an article with a view to its dissemination to some other party. Possession with a view to retention is also an infringement.[74]

8–12 **Sale, etc.** It is an infringement to offer or expose for sale or hire an infringing copy, whether in the course of a business or not. The exhibition of an infringing article in public is also an infringement but only if done in the course of a business. It is not an infringement under these provisions to invite offers for sale, for example by sending out a price list.[75] Nor does a person infringe copyright who merely attempts to effect a sale but who does not in the course of doing so commit one of the specific acts of infringement, such as the offer or exposure of the copy for sale.[76] Where articles were concealed from view at a trade exhibition and were produced only to those who asked to see them, but were not for sale even though a brochure and price list referring to them were openly available, they were held to be neither offered for sale nor exposed for sale and, arguably, not even exhibited in public.[77] Whether a sale has taken place will be judged on the normal objective basis, and the fact that one party had no subjective intention to enter into a contract or legal relationship, for example on a trap purchase, is

[67] This provision was new in the 1988 Act. The Whitford Committee had recommended only that possession in the course of trade of imported copies should be an infringement: Cmnd.6732, para.749(ii).
[68] CDPA 1988, s.178.
[69] See *Reid v Kennett* (1986) Crim.L.R. 456, decided under the Copyright Act 1956, s.21(4A).
[70] *LA Gear Inc. v Hi-Tec Sports plc* [1992] F.S.R. 121, CA.
[71] *Pensher Security Door Co. Ltd v Sunderland City Council* [2000] R.P.C. 249, CA.
[72] *Pensher Security Door Co. Ltd v Sunderland City Council* [2000] R.P.C. 249, CA. This view is supported by a statement made by the Government when resisting an amendment to s.24. It was said that a person who was merely looking after an article for a friend would have "custody or control" of it, but that the friend would have "possession" of it. *Hansard*, HL, Vol.490, col.1216. (Note, however, that the words "in the course of a business" were subsequently added to the definition of the infringing act of possession.)
[73] *Pensher Security Door Co. Ltd v Sunderland City Council* [2000] R.P.C. 249, CA (possession of infringing doors an integral part of the council's business activity of managing and letting flats).
[74] *Pensher Security Door Co. Ltd v Sunderland City Council* [2000] R.P.C. 249, CA.
[75] *Norgren Co. v Technomarking, The Times*, March 3, 1983.
[76] *Wolff v Wood, The Times*, October 31, 1903; *Britain v Kennedy* (1903) 19 T.L.R. 122.
[77] *LA Gear Inc. v Hi-Tec Sports plc* [1992] F.S.R. 121, CA.

irrelevant.[78] Where a defendant has delivered copies of a work on a "sale or return basis" he is not liable for any subsequent sale because he cannot demand the return of the copies.[79]

Distribution. To be an infringement, the distribution must either be in the course 8–13 of a business or to such an extent as to affect prejudicially the owner of the copyright. It is not, however, easy to imagine a case in which distribution is neither in the course of a trade or business nor prejudicial to the owner of the copyright, except perhaps where only a few copies are distributed to persons who would never have bought the work anyway.

Importation. No definition of what amounts to importation is contained in the 8–14 Act. Generally, an article is imported when it is brought from abroad into port or, in the case of carriage by aircraft, landed.[80] It is thought that the carriage must be ended or its continuity in some way broken,[81] so that an article is not imported if the vessel in which it is carried merely enters a port of call on its way to its final destination.[82] Nor is an article imported if the vessel carrying it merely enters the territorial waters of the United Kingdom[83]; the goods must be physically received and become subject to the English Court's jurisdiction.[84] But an article will be imported even though it is landed only with the purpose of transporting it across the territory to another state.[85] The position may be different if the goods are landed involuntarily, for example, as a result of a hijack or bad weather.[86] The onus is on the importer to show, if he can, that the article was only imported for private or domestic use. Note that provision is also made for the owner of the copyright to restrict unlawful importation by giving notice to the Commissioners of Customs and Excise. The matter is dealt with elsewhere.[87]

3. PROVIDING THE MEANS OF MAKING INFRINGING COPIES

The Act contains provisions making persons liable who knowingly possess or 8–15 provide the means for making infringing copies. Whether or not such acts may also amount to the separate tort of authorising an infringement is dealt with elsewhere.[88] Thus the copyright in a work is infringed by a person who, without the licence of the copyright owner:

    (a) makes,

    (b) imports into the United Kingdom,

    (c) possesses in the course of a business, or

    (d) sells or lets for hire, or offers or exposes for sale or hire,

an article specifically designed or adapted for making copies of that work, know-

---

[78] *Phillips v Holmes* [1988] R.P.C. 613.

[79] *Schofield & Sims Ltd v Gibson (R.) & Sons Ltd* [1928–35] Mac.C.C. 64; but *cf. E.W. Savory Ltd v The World of Golf Ltd* [1910–16] Mac.C.C. 149.

[80] See, *e.g. Wilson v Chambers & Co. Pty Ltd* (1926) 38 C.L.R. 138. For a definition of when an article is imported for Customs and Excise purposes, see the Customs and Excise Management Act 1979, s.5.

[81] *Wilson v Chambers & Co. Pty Ltd* (1926) 38 C.L.R. 138.

[82] *Canada Sugar Refining Co. v R.* [1898] A.C. 735.

[83] *R. v Bull* (1974) 48 A.L.J.R. 232.

[84] *LA Gear Inc. v Hi-Tec Sports plc* [1992] F.S.R. 121, CA.

[85] *Mattel Inc. v Tonka Corp.* [1992] F.S.R. 28 (High Ct of Hong Kong); *Gramophone Company of India Ltd v Pandey* [1985] F.S.R. 136.

[86] *Mattel Inc. v Tonka Corp.* [1992] F.S.R. 28 (High Ct of Hong Kong).

[87] See para. 23–65 *et seq.*, below.

[88] See para. 7–130, above.

ing or having reason to believe that it is to be used to make infringing copies.[89] Again, a "business" is defined as including a trade or profession.[90] The reference to an article "specifically designed or adapted for making copies of that work" makes it clear that dealing in an article which is generally designed for making copies, such as a photocopier or tape-recorder, will not fall within this provision. Rather, the provision is directed to dealings in articles such as photographic negatives, moulds, master recordings and the like which may be used to make copies of specific works.[91] The article does not itself have to be an infringing copy.

The copyright in a work is also infringed by a person who, without the licence of the copyright owner, transmits the work by means of a telecommunications system (otherwise than by communication to the public), knowing or having reason to believe that infringing copies of the work will be made by means of the reception of the transmission in the United Kingdom or elsewhere.[92] "Telecommunications system" is defined as meaning a system for conveying visual images, sounds or other information by electronic means.[93] This provision will make it an infringement, for example, to fax a work knowing that infringing copies will then be made at the receiving end. In such a case, the person transmitting the work will often also have infringed by copying the work before, or in the course of, transmission. Where the transmission is by way of communication to the public, an act of primary infringement will of course also occur.[94] The provision that an infringement will occur under the present section if the sender knows or has reason to believe that infringing copies will then be made "elsewhere" than in the United Kingdom appears to be designed to prevent works being electronically exported for copying overseas. The provision appears to be of limited application, however, since the definition of "infringing copy" is generally limited to copies either made in the United Kingdom or which have been or are intended to be imported into the United Kingdom.

4. PERMITTING OR ENABLING PUBLIC PERFORMANCE

8–16   **Introduction.** As has been seen, the exclusive rights of performance, playing and showing of various works in public are primary rights, restricted by the copyright in such works. In addition to the general liability of persons who authorise such infringements, the 1988 Act also makes provision for secondary acts of infringement in cases where the defendant gave permission for premises to be used for performances or supplied the means by which such works were seen or heard in public. The wording of the 1988 Act makes it clear that a person can only be liable under these provisions where there is already some other person liable for the primary infringement.

8–17   **Permitting use of premises.** The Act provides that where the copyright in a literary, dramatic or musical work is infringed by a performance at a place of public entertainment, any person who gave permission for that place to be used for the

---

[89] CDPA 1988, s.24(1).

[90] s.178.

[91] An amendment during the passage of the Bill to alter the wording of the section to "an article designed for making copies of that class of works" was successfully resisted. See also *Hansard,* HL, Vol.490, col.1217, and the report of the debates of the House of Commons Standing Committee E in 1988, col.166.

[92] CDPA 1988, s.24(2). But see para. 7–21, above, suggesting that the sender may also be liable for the primary act of infringement by reproduction.

[93] s.178, where "electronic" is also defined.

[94] See para. 7–98, above.

performance is also liable for the infringement, unless when he gave permission he believed on reasonable grounds that the performance would not infringe copyright.[95] For this purpose, "place of public entertainment" includes premises which are occupied mainly for other purposes but are from time to time made available for hire for the purposes of public entertainment.[96] The effect of the Act appears to be to make the defendant liable for the actual act of infringement by performance, presumably jointly with whoever is liable for that infringement.

Permission. One of the crucial questions will often be whether permission was given for the use of the premises for the performance. The question whether the defendant committed the separate tort of authorising the performance will often arise at the same time.[97] As to permission, the giving of permission for use of the premises generally is not sufficient since the permission must be for the premises to be used for the performance complained of. Under the equivalent provisions of the 1911 Act it was said that a person does not permit what he cannot control, and does not permit the use of a place for the performance of a work if he does not know that the work is going to be performed.[98] Thus where a person permits premises to be used knowing which works will be performed, this will be sufficient to establish "permission", but not if the music to be performed is left to the performers and the defendant has no knowledge of what in fact will be performed.[99] Permission may be inferred from acts which fall short of being direct and positive, and may be inferred from indifference, but permission will not be inferred from a mere general authority to use a theatre for the performance of musical or dramatic works.[1] In an Australian case, it was held that the owners of a hall who, under the terms of their contract of letting, could not prevent the performance of which complaint is made, did not "permit" the performance.[2]   **8–18**

Provision of apparatus, etc. The 1988 Act makes further provision for secondary infringement where the copyright in a work is infringed by the public performance of a work or by the playing or showing of it in public. Thus various categories of person may also be liable where such infringement has occurred by means of apparatus for playing sound recordings, showing films or receiving visual images or sounds conveyed by electronic means.[3] Again, the wording of the 1988 Act makes it clear that a person can only be liable under these provisions where there is already some other person liable for the primary infringement.   **8–19**

First, a person who supplies the apparatus, or any substantial part of it, is liable for the infringement if, when he supplied the apparatus or part:

(a) he knew or had reason to believe that the apparatus was likely to be so used as to infringe copyright, or

(b) in the case of apparatus whose normal use involves a public performance,

---

[95] CDPA 1988, s.25(1).

[96] *ibid.*, s.25(2).

[97] As to which, see para. 7–130, above.

[98] *Performing Right Society Ltd v Ciryl Theatrical Syndicate Ltd* [1924] 1 K.B. 1.

[99] *Monaghan v Taylor* (1885) 2 T.L.R. 685, cited in *Performing Right Society Ltd v Ciryl Theatrical Syndicate Ltd* [1924] 1 K.B. 1.

[1] *Performing Right Society Ltd v Ciryl Theatrical Syndicate Ltd* [1924] 1 K.B. 1.

[2] *Australian Performing Right Association Ltd v Adelaide Corporation* (1928) 40 C.L.R. 481; see also *Canadian Performing Right Society v Canadian National Exhibition Association* (1934) 4 D.L.R. 154; but *cf. Australian Performing Right Association v Turner (J) & Son* (1927) 27 S.R. (N.S.W.) 344.

[3] CDPA 1988, s.26(1).

playing or showing, he did not believe on reasonable grounds that it would not be so used as to infringe copyright.[4]

Presumably, an infringement in the first case would occur where, for example, a person supplied a television for use in public, such as in a public house, knowing that no sufficient licence had been obtained. The second kind of case might arise where, for example, a juke box was supplied for use in public, or specialised equipment for use in a discotheque. Although the burden of proof as to the requisite degree of knowledge appears still to rest with the claimant, the intention in this latter kind of case appears to make that burden easier to discharge. In the ordinary type of case it will no doubt be sufficient to prove that the supply of apparatus has continued after a warning letter has been received.

8–20   Secondly, an occupier of premises who gives permission for the apparatus to be brought onto the premises is also liable for the infringement if, when he gave permission, he knew or had reason to believe that the apparatus was likely to be so used as to infringe copyright.[5] Again, this kind of case might arise where the occupier of a public house or discotheque allows equipment to be brought onto the premises knowing that no sufficient licence has been obtained.

Thirdly, a person who supplies a copy of the sound recording or film used to infringe copyright is also liable for the infringement if when, he supplied it, he knew or had reason to believe that what he supplied, or a copy made directly or indirectly from it, was likely to be so used as to infringe copyright.[6] Persons who knowingly supply records for use in jukeboxes are therefore likely to be caught by this provision.

---

[4] s.26(2).
[5] CDPA 1988, s.26(3).
[6] CDPA 1988, s.26(4).

CHAPTER NINE

PERMITTED ACTS

Contents   *Para.*

1. GENERAL INTRODUCTION

Chapter III, Part I, of the 1988 Act, containing some 65 sections, permits certain **9–01** acts which would otherwise amount to copyright infringement. Since the 1988 Act was originally enacted, various sections have been added and a large number of amendments made in order to comply with European legislation. These "permitted acts"[1] are in general designed to balance the interests of copyright owners with the public interest, and some of the provisions show up important conflicts between the two.[2] More generally, the permitted acts should be viewed alongside the requirement of substantial taking[3] and the restrictive way in which some of the exclusive rights of the copyright owner are drawn, in particular the exclusive right to perform a work, which only applies to performances in public. The possible existence of an implied licence needs also to be borne in mind.[4]

The Berne Convention, and the "3-step test". The Berne Convention[5] allows **9–02** for exceptions to be made to the rights in works protected under the Convention in certain specified cases.[6] The permitted act provisions take advantage of these provisions, which are dealt with as they arise in the course of this chapter. As well as allowing for such specific exceptions, however, the Berne Convention also contains in Article 9(2) a general dispensation in the following terms: "It shall be a matter for legislation in the countries of the Union to permit the reproduction of [literary[7] and artistic] works in certain special cases, provided such reproduction does not conflict with the normal exploitation of the work and does not unreasonably prejudice the legitimate interests of the author". The three requirements, namely that such permission may be granted (a) in certain special cases, where the reproduction (b) does not conflict with the normal exploitation of the work and (c) does not unreasonably prejudice the legitimate interests of the author, are known as the Berne "3-step" test. The meaning and significance of the 3-step test is considered elsewhere.[8] Although the 3-step test has never been incorporated into United Kingdom copyright legislation it has in principle been taken into account when framing a number of the permitted act provisions.[9]

---

[1] The various permitted acts are sometimes referred to as defences, but strictly speaking this is not the case, *cf.* CDPA 1988, s.97.

[2] Moreover, it is important to recognise that the permitted acts serve a number of disparate functions and take effect in a variety of ways. For example, a number of the provisions only take effect in the absence of a licensing agreement (see, *e.g.* CDPA 1988, ss.35, 36, 60, 74 and corresponding text, below).

[3] CDPA 1988 s.16(3)(a). See further, para. 7–23, *et seq.,* , above.

[4] See further, para. 5–213 *et seq*, above.

[5] See Ch.24, below.

[6] See Berne Convention, Arts 2 *bis* (1), (2), 10 and 10 *bis*.

[7] The concept of a literary or artistic work is wider under Berne than under United Kingdom legislation. See Ch.24, below.

[8] See paras 24–33 and 24–142, below.

[9] For examples of cases which are generally considered to fall within this permitted exception, see Ricketson: *The Berne Convention for the Protection of Literary and Artistic Works: 1989–1996,* (Kluwer, 1987), p.485.

9–03   **The Rome Convention.** The Rome Convention,[10] which for present purposes is concerned with the rights in relation to phonograms and broadcasts,[11] permits contracting states to provide for exceptions to such rights in cases of (a) private use, (b) use of short excerpts in connexion with the reporting of current events, (c) the ephemeral fixation by a broadcasting organisation by means of its own facilitites and for its own broadcasts and (d) use solely for the purposes of teaching or scientific research.[12] In addition to this, however, contracting states are also permitted to provide for the same kinds of limitations to these rights as they provide in connection with the protection of literary and artistic works.[13] As with the Berne Convention, the 1988 Act contains provisions taking advantage of these permitted exceptions, which are considered in this chapter as they arise.

9–04   **The TRIPS agreement.** The TRIPS agreement requires Members to confine limitations or exceptions to the protection granted to Berne Convention works to cases compying with the 3-step test[14] and, in the case of subject matter protected under the Rome Convention, to those provided for by the Rome Convention.[15]

9–05   **European Directives.** Various European Directives have made piecemeal provision affecting exceptions which Member States either must or may make to the various rights which are the subject matter of such Directives. First, Articles 5 and 6 of the Software Directive[16] required certain limited exceptions to be made to the rights relating to computer programs; no others were permitted. These exceptions either fell within existing permitted act provisions of the 1988 Act or were implemented by amendment.[17] Second, Article 5 of the Rental and Related Rights Directive[18] permits certain derogations from the public lending right, which the United Kingdom took advantage of by the introduction of sections 36A and 40A into the 1988 Act.[19] Article 10 of the same Directive permits specified exceptions to be made to the rights prescribed in relation to phonograms, films and broadcasts, but also permits Member States to make limitations of the same kind as are provided in the case of literary and artistic works. No amendments were made to the 1988 Act arising out these matters. Thirdly, the Database Directive[20] required Member States to make what was in effect an exception to rights of copyright in databases[21] and allowed Member States to provide for certain other limitations or exceptions to these rights, including exceptions of a kind that were traditionally allowed under national copyright laws.[22] Section 50D was introduced into the 1988 Act to give effect to the former requirement[23] but no other amendments were made. Fourth and finally, but most significantly, the Information Society Directive[24] attempted a degree of harmonisation across the whole field of permitted exceptions. This Directive is considered in more detail

---

[10] See Ch.24, below.
[11] As to the Rome Convention and performers, see Ch.12, below.
[12] Rome Convention, Art.15(1).
[13] Art.15(2).
[14] TRIPS, Art.13.
[15] TRIPS, Art.14(6).
[16] Directive 91/250.
[17] See paras 9–132 et seq., below.
[18] Directive 92/100.
[19] See paras 9–99 and 9–108, below, respectively.
[20] Directive 96/9.
[21] Art.6(1).
[22] Arts 6(2), (3)
[23] See para. 9–139, below.
[24] 2001/29/EC

below. It should also be borne in mind that the E-Commerce Directive[25] provides for horizontal, or across the board, defences whose aim is to limit the liability of intermediary internet service providers to actions of all kinds (and not just for copyright infringement) arising out of the transmission and storage of information in their electronic networks. Subject to various safeguards, liability in respect of any damages and for any other pecuniary remedy or for any criminal sanction is therefore to be excluded for the activities of "mere conduit", "caching" and "hosting" of information. These exclusions, which are in the nature of defences rather than permitted acts, have been implemented into United Kingdom law[26] and are discussed in more detail in Chapter 22.

The Information Society Directive. This Directive[27] merits discussion in greater   **9–06**
detail here. It had two objectives in the area of permitted acts. The first, which overlaps with that of the E-Commerce Directive, relates to the harmonisation provision in Article 2 of the Information Society Directive which requires Member States to provide rightholders with the exclusive right to prevent or authorise the temporary reproduction of the subject matter of their rights.[28] This exclusive right extends to temporary or transient reproductions in computer memory. It was considered that some provision had to be made, however, such that this right would not unduly interfere with the proper functioning of electronic networks or lawful use of works in electronic form. This has been achieved by a mandatory requirement in the Directive that liability for transient acts of reproduction in the course of the transmission of material through networks or lawful use is to be exempted from the reproduction right.[29] This objective, which was controversial,[30] is limited in scope in its implementation. It is considered in more detail later in this chapter.[31] The second objective was more general, and more ambitious. It was to achieve harmonisation amongst Member States across the entire range of permitted exceptions or limitations. A justification for the Directive in its final form can be found in Recital 31, where it is stated that the existing exceptions and limitations provided by Member States needed to be "reassessed in the light of the new electronic environment." Such differences, it was said, had "direct negative effects on the functioning of the internal market" which might well have "become more pronounced in view of the further development of trans-border exploitation of works and cross-border activities". In order to ensure the proper functioning of the internal market, such exceptions and limitations therefore needed to "be defined more harmoniously", although the degree of the harmonisation needed to be "based on the impact on the smooth functioning of the internal market".[32] In its first incarnations, the draft Directive provided

---

[25] Directive 2000/31.

[26] By the Electronic Commerce (EC Directive) Regulations 2002 (SI 2002/2013).

[27] Directive 2001/29.

[28] As to this right, see para. 7–19, above.

[29] Although there is an overlap here with the E-Commerce Directive, the provisions are complementary and operatate in parallel. See Recital 16 of the Information Society Directive 2001/29.

[30] There were those who argued that the exclusive right in respect of such transient reproduction in networks should not have been made part of the reproduction right in the first place. See, *e.g.* Dietz, "The Protection of Intellectual Property in the Information Age—The Draft EU Copyright Directive of November 1997" [1998] I.P.Q. 335.

[31] See para. 9–15 *et seq.*, below.

[32] Harmonisation to this degree has never been attempted by the signatories to the Berne Convention (see generally, Ricketson, *The Berne Convention for the Protection of Literary and Artistic Works: 1886–1996*, (Kluwer, 1987), or the Rome Convention, and it must also be doubted whether the workings of the Internal Market were in the past affected in any substantial way by the patchwork of exceptions which existed within the Community. Of course, the effects in the future in a digital environment are more uncertain.

for a small and closed class of exceptions.[33] As perhaps could have been predicted, the objective ran into opposition, with Member States arguing for retention of their own particular exceptions. In its final form, Recital 32 proclaims that the final list of exceptions takes due account of the different legal traditions in Member States, while at the same time aiming to ensure a functioning internal market. In reality, what has been achieved is a poor form of harmonisation, with no less than 19 separate permitted exceptions or limitations, many of which are of a general nature or have further subdivisions, coupled with a save-all provision which allows Member States to retain their existing exceptions in the case of analogue uses of minor importance, but not digital, uses. The Directive fails to achieve harmonisation because, save only the case of the exception mandated by Article 5(1) for the making of transient and incidental copies, referred to above, all the permitted exceptions are optional, that is, Member States are free to choose whether or not to take advantage of them. This part of the Directive is a harmonisation measure only in the sense that the class of permitted acts is closed, so that Member States are not able to provide exceptions outside these cases.[34] Particular, although perhaps predictable, areas of failure were in relation to private copying and reprographic copying, it being one of the principal original aims of the Directive to harmonise the laws of Member States in this area. In the end, no effective consensus could be achieved on these issues, and the matter has been left such that Member States may, but are not required to, permit private copying and reprographic copying. If they do so, however, it is only to be on terms that rightholders receive fair compensation.[35]

The various exceptions or limitations allowed by the Directive are dealt with in this chapter as they arise in the context of the various permitted acts. Some general comments can be made about them here, however. The first is that the permitted exceptions are concerned only with the exclusive rights which are the subject matter of the Directive, namely the reproduction right, the distribution right and the communication to the public right,[36] these being the rights prescribed by Articles 2, 3 and 4. The Directive is thus not directly concerned with exceptions which Member States may make to rights of public performance.[37] As already noted, earlier Directives have dealt with permissible or mandatory exceptions to the particular rights the subject of those Directives and for the most part the Information Society Directive leaves those Directives untouched.[38] Further, the Directive does not permit exceptions to all three rights indiscriminately. Thus, the first category of exceptions, in Article 5(2), are permitted only in relation to the reproduction and distribution rights,[39] while the second category, in

[33] See, e.g. the 1997 Proposal, COM (97) 628 final.

[34] See also Recital 32, which states that the Directive provides for an exhaustive enumeration of exceptions and limitations to the reproduction right and the right of communication to the public.

[35] For some of the extensive literature on the Information Society Directive and these exceptions, see Heide, "The Approach to Innovation under the Proposed Copyright Directive: Time for Mandatory Exceptions?" [2000] I.P.Q. 215; Wing & Kirk, "European/US Copyright Law Reform: Is a Balance Being Achieved?" [2000] I.P.Q. 138; Vinje, "Should We Begin Digging Copyright's Grave?" [2000] E.I.P.R. 551; Hugenholtz, "Why the Copyright Directive is Unimportant, and Possibly Invalid" [2000] E.I.P.R. 499.

[36] The exclusive right to communicate authors' works to the public (Art.3(1)) and the exclusive right to make related rights subject matter available to the public (Art. 3(2)) are in this chapter referred to together as the "communication to the public right", the compendious title given to these rights by the 1988 Act.

[37] See recitals 23, 24 of the Information Society Directive 2001/29.

[38] As will be seen, however, the Information Society Directive also amends provisions of the Rental and Related Rights Directive dealing with permitted exceptions or limitations, and this has affected the exceptions permitted in respect of the public performance of sound recordings. See paras 9–181 and 9–198, below.

[39] An exception to the distribution right is only permissible where a corresponding exception has

Article 5(3), are permitted in relation to all three rights.[40] An exception permitted only under Article 5(2) cannot therefore be applied in relation to the communication to the public right. Finally, Article 5(5) of the Directive restates the requirement of the 3-step test in Article 9(2) of the Berne Convention, by stating that the exceptions and limitations permitted by the Directive shall only be applied in certain special cases which do not conflict with a normal exploitation of the work or other subject-matter and do not unreasonably prejudice the legitimate interests of the rightholder.[41] When taking advantage of particular permitted exceptions Member States must therefore frame their legislation to comply with the 3-step test.

Amendments to the 1988 Act. While many of the existing permitted act provisions of the 1988 Act fell within these permitted exceptions many did not. In the latter case, the Act has been amended as discussed in detail later in this Chapter by reference to individual permitted acts. In cases where the Directive permits, but does not require, Member States to make exceptions and where there was no exisiting equivalent permitted act in the 1988 Act, the United Kingdom has taken a minimalist approach and not made any new provision not required by the Directive.[42] As with previous legislation in this field, the 1988 Act does not contain any express reference to the 3-step test, which the Directive requires to be applied. Rather, the legislation has been framed with this requirement in mind.[43] However, the fact that the 3-step is now part of European law means that it will be possible to challenge the implementation of the Directive by way of infraction proceedings in the European Court of Justice. A number of tidying up amendments have also been made to reflect the change to section 20, whereby the restricted acts of broadcasting a work and including a work in a cable programme service have been replaced by the composite restricted act of communicating a work to the public.   **9–07**

Transitional provisions. Regulations to amend the 1988 Act and implement the Information Society Directive came into force on October 31, 2003.[44] As a matter of the general law, whether or not an act committed before this date constituted an infringement or fell within the permitted act provisions must be determined in accordance with the law then in force.[45] In addition, however, the Regulations provide that the provisions of the 1988 Act as they stood *before* amendment shall continue to apply to anything done *after* commencement in completion of an act begun before commencement which was permitted by those unamended provisions.[46] A more general saving provides that nothing in the Regulations is to affect any agreement made before December 22, 2002[47] and no act done after October 31, 2003, in pursuance of an agreement made before December 22, 2002,   **9–08**

---

been made to the reproduction right, and then only to the extent justified by the purpose of the permitted act of reproduction. See Art.5(4).

[40] Although see the preceding note for the limitation on the distribution right.

[41] See para. 9–02, above.

[42] See *e.g.* the Patent Office's Consulation Paper of August 7, 2002 and the Analysis of Responses and Government Conclusions, and the Transposition Note to the Implementing Regulations (SI 2003/2498). No doubt this attitude was also influenced by the lack of Parliamentary time and Government's ability to make amendments to the 1988 Act by Statutory Instrument using its powers under the European Communities Act 1972, s.2.

[43] See the Analysis of Responses and Government Conclusions to the Patent Office's Consulation Paper of August 7, 2002, para.5.2 and the Transposition Note.

[44] The Copyright and Related Rights Regulations 2003 (SI 2003/2498).

[45] Interpretation Act 1978, s.16.

[46] SI 2003/2498, reg.33.

[47] As to this date, see Information Society Directive, Art.10.

shall be regarded as an infringement of any new or extended right arising by virtue of the Regulations.[48]

9–09   **Permitted exceptions and copy-protection devices.** A further problem which the Information Society Directive had to deal with was the conflict between the provisions of the Directive requiring or allowing exceptions to rights of copyright owners and related rightholders and the provisions of the Directive which aim to prevent the circumvention of copy-protection devices. For details of these latter provisions, which implement the 1996 WIPO Copyright and Performances and Phonograms Treaties, see Chapter 15. In brief, Member States are required to provide legal protection against the circumvention of copy-protection devices, and against the manufacture of and commercial dealings in products or services which achieve this. Where a work is available in electronic form, so that any access to it will inevitably involve copying, it follows that there may be a conflict between the general public policy of permitting uses of the work which do not unreasonably prejudice the rightholder and the rightholder's ability to control any use of the work via copy-protection devices. The Directive in the end offered no clear solution to this highly contentious issue and passed the problem on to Member States. Thus, the Directive requires that in relation to certain of the permitted exceptions, and in the absence of voluntary measures taken by rightholders, Member States are to take "appropriate measures" to ensure that rightholders make available to the beneficiary of the exception the means of benefiting from it.[49] These provisions are not, however, to apply to works or other subject-matter made available to the public on agreed contractual terms by way of an on-demand service.[50] The reasoning is that where material is available under licence by way of an on-demand service, the contractual provisions of the licence should prevail over any general right, although it is questionable whether this does not run against the whole spirit and purpose of permitted use in cases where this is founded on public interest.

9–10   **Implementation by the 1988 Act.** The United Kingdom's answer to the problems posed by Article 6 of the Directive is contained in section 296ZE of the Act, which is considered in more detail in Chapter 15. In short, where the presence of a copy-protection device prevents a person from carrying out one of a limited list of permitted acts[51] then a complaint can be made to the Secretary of State. If the Secretary of State establishes that there is no subsisting voluntary measure or agreement enabling such use, he may give directions so as to ensure that the means of carrying out the permitted act, to the extent necessary so as to benefit from the permitted act, are made available to the complainant.[52] These provisions do not apply to computer programs, which are subject to the different

---

[48] SI 2003/2498, reg.32.

[49] Information Society Directive, Art.6(4) and Recital 51. Such measures are to be made available only to the extent necessary to enable a benefit to be obtained from that exception and only where that beneficiary has legal access to the protected work or subject-matter concerned. Art.6(4) also provides that when Art.6 "is applied in the context of" the Rental and Lending Directive (92/100/EEC) and the Database Directive (96/9/EC), "this paragraph" is to apply *mutatis mutandis*. The apparent purpose of this is that in the case of the exceptions which those Directives provide for, a similar regime as to voluntary or appropriate measures is to apply, although presumably only where there is an equivalent exception.

[50] *i.e.* where the subject-matter is made available in such a way that members of the public may access it from a place and at a time individually chosen by them. See the penultimate paragraph of Art.6(4) and also Recital 53 of the Information Society Directive.

[51] Sch.5A to the 1988 Act sets out the list of the permitted acts to which these provisions apply, the intention being to conform with the list set out in Art.4 of the Information Society Directive.

[52] CDPA 1988, ss.296ZE(2), (3).

regime of permitted exceptions imposed by the Software Directive.[53] It is worth noting here that, amongst others, these provisions do not apply to the permitted acts of making temporary copies, under section 28A, or fair dealing for the purposes of criticism, review or news reporting. The Act leaves unanswered the question which the Directive itself failed to address, namely how are any means enabling the relevant permitted act to be limited to that purpose, as opposed to enabling access to or use of the work for all purposes?[54]

The Impact of the Human Rights Act on the Permitted Acts. The Human Rights Act 1998 came into force on October 1, 2000 and with it the European Convention on Human Rights, including the right under Article 10 to freedom of expression, became part of the domestic law of the United Kingdom. The right to freedom of expression may impinge on the 1988 Act in a number of ways: (1) it may affect the circumstances in which copyright will be enforced;[55] (2) it may affect the application of the permitted act sections of the Act; and (3) in circumstances where the permitted act sections of the Act do not apply, it may provide an additional defence, essentially on the grounds of public interest.[56] In the area of the permitted act sections of the 1988 Act, the impact of the Article 10 right of freedom of expression is most likely to be felt in relation to the fair dealing provisions of the Act. It is therefore considered under that heading, below.[57]   **9–11**

2. INTRODUCTORY PROVISIONS

The permitted acts are grouped together into 14 categories: general, (which includes the temporary copying and fair dealing exceptions)[58] visual impairment,[59] education,[60] libraries and archives,[61] public administration,[62] computer programs,[63] databases,[64] designs,[65] typefaces,[66] works in electronic form,[67] miscellaneous provisions relating to literary, dramatic, musical and artistic works,[68] miscellaneous provisions relating to the lending of works,[69] miscellaneous provisions relating to films, sound recordings and computer programs[70] and miscellaneous provisions relating to broadcasts.[71] This chapter considers each category in turn, with the exception of the provisions relating to designs and the provisions   **9–12**

---

[53] Directive 91/250, Arts 5 and 6.
[54] The rightholder is to make available means "to the extent necessary to benefit from that exception or limitation". See Art.6(4) of the Directive.
[55] See para. 3–260, above.
[56] See para. 22–82 *et seq*, below. The decision in *Hyde Park Residence Ltd v Yelland* [1999] R.P.C. 655, that the provisions of the 1988 Act spell out a complete code of exceptions to copyright, and that there is therefore no room for any more general defence that the acts of the defendant were in the public interest, must now be regarded as wrong: *Ashdown v Telegraph Group Ltd* [2001] EWCA Civ 1142 [2002].
[57] See para. 9–22, below.
[58] CDPA 1988, ss. 28A–31, paras 9–15 *et seq.*, below.
[59] ss.31A–31F, paras 9–63, *et seq.*, below.
[60] ss.32–36A, paras 9–88 *et seq.*, below.
[61] ss.37–44A, paras 9–100 *et seq.*, below.
[62] ss.45–50, paras 9–123 *et seq.*, below.
[63] ss.50A–50C, paras 9–132 *et seq.*, below.
[64] s.50D, paras 9–139 *et seq.*, below.
[65] ss.51–53, paras 9–141 *et seq.*, below.
[66] ss.54–55, paras 9–145 *et seq.*, below.
[67] s.56, para. 9–150, below.
[68] ss.57–65, paras 9–152 *et seq.*, below.
[69] s.66, paras 9–178 *et seq.*, below.
[70] ss.66A–67, paras 9–179 *et seq.*, below.
[71] ss.68–75, paras 9–186 *et seq.*, below.

establishing compulsory licences, which are only dealt with in outline.[72] Defences under European law and the E-Commerce Directive, and the public interest defence are dealt with elsewhere.[73] Finally, the Broadcasting Act 1990 imposes a statutory duty on broadcasters to supply information about their programmes and confers a statutory licence on publishers enabling such information to be reproduced and published.[74] Although the 1988 Act was not amended to give effect to this, the 1990 Act provides that the 1988 Act is to have effect as if the relevant provisions of the 1990 Act were included in Chapter III of the 1988 Act. These provisions are nevertheless considered under the topic of compulsory licences.[75]

The Act provides that the permitted acts are to be construed independently of each other, so that just because an act does not fall within one provision does not mean that it is not covered by another.[76] In addition, the Act expressly provides that the provisions are to apply to works of every description, except where a more limited class of works is specified.[77] Again, if, by virtue of the permitted acts, an act may be done in relation to a literary, dramatic or musical work and the work is itself an adaptation of another work there will be no indirect infringement of that other work.[78]

The fact that an act may be done without infringing copyright does not, however, mean that such an act will not be a breach of some other right or obligation, such as an express contractual term.[79] Thus if a work is supplied to a library under an agreement whereby no part of it is to be copied, but such a copy is made regardless, the library will be in breach of contract, even though there may be no infringement of copyright.[80]

Since the provisions only apply once infringement has been established, procedurally the onus will be on the defendant to prove that one of the exceptions applies.[81] As derogations from the owner's property rights, the courts have occasionally adopted the approach of construing these provisions strictly against the defendant.[82] The matter is one of ordinary statutory constuction, however,[83] and the permitted act provisions are to be regarded as an integral part of the Copyright Act, rather than a mere defence.[84] Indeed it is clear that the provisions

---

[72] They are considered in detail in Chs 13 and 29, respectively.

[73] See Chs 25 and 22, respectively.

[74] Broadcasting Act 1990, s.176 and Sch.17.

[75] See Ch.29, below.

[76] CDPA 1988, s.28(4).

[77] s.28(2).

[78] s.76.

[79] s.28(1).

[80] This seems entirely obvious, but research conducted during the passage of the Bill showed that there was considerable confusion over this issue: *Hansard* HL, Vol.501, cols 227–228. This provision has a more limited effect in relation to computer programs, databases and broadcasts.

[81] *Sillitoe v Mcgraw Hill Book Co.* [1983] F.S.R. 545 at 558.

[82] See *Beloff v Pressdram Ltd* [1973] 1 All E.R. 241; *Distillers Co. (Biochemicals) Ltd v Times Newspapers Ltd* [1975] Q.B. 613. Also see *The Longman Group Ltd v Carrington Technical Institute Board of Governors* [1991] 2 N.Z.L.R. 574 (High Court of NZ).

[83] *CCH Canadian Ltd. v Law Society of Upper Canada* [2002] 4 F.C. 213, Can. Fed. CA (for the next note for decision of the Supreme Court).

[84] See, *e.g. CCH Canadian Ltd. v Law Society of Upper Canada* [2004] SCC 13 (Can. Sup. Ct): "The fair dealing exception … is a user's right. In order to maintain the proper balance between the rights of a copyright owner and users' interests, it must not be interpreted restrictively... 'User rights are not just loopholes. Both owner rights and user rights should therefore be given the fair and balanced reading that befits remedial legislation.'," citing Vaver, *Copyright Law*, (Toronto, Irwin Law, 2000) p.171.

are to be construed liberally in favour of the defendant, particularly where there are freedom of expression considerations...[85]

Private use. Although not formally recognised in the structure of the Act, there are now a small number of permitted acts which relate to the use of a copyright work for private and domestic purposes. For example, there are provisions which permit the copying of a broadcast for the purpose of "time-shifting" and which allow photographs to be taken of part of a television broadcast.[86] Other permitted acts, whilst not specifically confined to the private sphere, are clearly relevant to the copying or use of a work in this context. Under this heading also fall exceptions relating to private study and to the playing of sound recordings for the purposes of a club or society. It should also be remembered that certain acts are not an infringement at all if either done in private (performance of a work, section 19) or done for private and domestic purposes (importation of an infringing copy, section 22). Taken together, these provisions are undoubtedly important, but it would be a mistake to view them as marking a clearly defined boundary between acceptable private use and activities which pose a substantial threat to the copyright owner's interests.[87] While it has been the ambition for some time to bring in European legislation to harmonise provisions relating to private copying, little progress has been made.[88] In particular, the Information Society Directive failed to achieve harmonisation in this respect, merely permitting, but not requiring, Member States to provide for a private copying exception on condition that the rightholder receive fair compensation.[89] The United Kingdom did not taken advantage of this permitted exception when implementing the Directive.

9–13

Criminal offences. The structure of the Act might suggest that the permitted acts can only be relied upon in civil actions, but they apply equally in the context of criminal offences,[90] since if the act was permitted it cannot have been an infringement or an offence.[91]

9–14

3. GENERAL PROVISIONS

A. THE MAKING OF TEMPORARY COPIES

Introduction: The Information Society Directive. The Directive requires that an exemption be made from the reproduction right in the case of certain transient or incidental reproductions. The requirement applies to all froms of subject-matter with which the Directive is concerned, but not to computer programs or databases.[92] As has already been seen,[93] the exemption was legislated for since it was felt that otherwise the temporary reproduction right required by Article 2

9–15

---

[85] See para. 9–22, below.

[86] CDPA 1988, ss.70 and 71, respectively. Similarly, in relation to rights in performances, there is an exception allowing a recording of a performance to be made where this is for the private and domestic use of the person making the recording: s.182(2). See further, Ch.12, below.

[87] In this context it should be noted that Government declined to introduce a levy on blank tapes as a solution to the ubiquitous problem of "home taping" of copyright works, either in the 1988 Act as enacted or when implementing the Information Society Directive (see 2001/29, Art.5(2)(b)). Subject to a fairly narrow set of exceptions, private copying therefore remains an infringing act.. For a comparative analysis of the problems in this area see Davies and Hung, *Music and Video Private Copying*, (Sweet and Maxwell, London, 1993).

[88] See the *Follow-Up to the Green Paper on Copyright and Related Rights in the Information Society* Com (96) 586 final, pp.9–12.

[89] See Information Society Directive, 2001/29, Art.5(2)(b).

[90] CDPA 1988, s.107 and see Ch.23, below.

[91] s.107(1)(e), (2)(b), (3)(b). Also see *Thames & Hudson Limited v Design and Artists Copyright Society Limited* [1995] F.S.R. 153.

[92] See Information Society Directive (2001/29), Art.1(2). Works of these types are subject to the

would unduly interfere with the proper functioning of electronic networks and lawful use.[94] Article 5(1) accordingly provides that temporary acts of reproduction, which are transient or incidental and an integral and essential part of a technological process and whose sole purpose is to enable (a) a transmission in a network between third parties by an intermediary, or (b) a lawful use of a work or other subject-matter to be made, and which have no independent economic significance, shall be exempted from the reproduction right provided for in Article 2.[95] It is the only mandatory "exception"[96] in the Directive and required the United Kingdom to amend the 1988 Act by the introduction of an entirely new section 28A, since under section 17(6) of the Act copying is defined to include the making of copies which are transient or incidental to some other use of the work. As will be seen, the wording of Article 5(1) was implemented virtually verbatim. The Government declined to refine the wording further to take into account the 3-step test which Article 5(5) imposes as a further requirement on this and all other exceptions,[97] it being the Government's understanding that the European Commission took the view that the test had already been taken into account when framing Article 5(1), such that it would be inappropriate to add the test.[98] Recital 33 of the Directive amplifies Article 5 by stating that to the extent that any use meets the above conditions, the exception "should include acts which enable browsing as well as acts of caching to take place, including those which enable transmission systems to function efficiently, provided that the intermediary does not modify the information and does not interfere with the lawful use of technology, widely recognised and used by industry, to obtain data on the use of the information". The Government also declined to implement any part of this wording on the grounds that, in line with what was understood to be the Commission's view, it was "inappropriate".[99]

9–16   **The 1988 Act as amended.** Section 28A of the 1988 Act implements Article 5(1) virtually verbatim. Thus, the section provides that copyright in a literary work (other than a computer program or a database), or in a dramatic, musical or artistic work, the typographical arrangement of a published edition,[1] a sound recording or a film, is not infringed by the making of a temporary copy which is

---

provisions of Arts 5 and 6 of the Software Directive and Art.5 of the Database Directive respectively, which provide their own code of exceptions. Art.5(1) of the Software Directive in particular provides that temporary acts of reproduction of a computer program shall not require authorization by the rightholder where they are necessary for the use of the computer program by the lawful acquirer in accordance with its intended purpose. The exceptions permitted in the case of computer programs are dealt with by ss.50A–50C and s.50D of the 1988 Act respectively.

[93] See para. 7–92, above.

[94] There were those who argued that the exclusive right in respect of such transient reproduction in networks should not have been made part of the reproduction right in the first place. See, e.g. Dietz, "The Protection of Intellectual Property in the Information Age—The Draft EU Copyright Directive of November 1997" [1998] I.P.Q. 335.

[95] Member States are, obviously perhaps, not permitted to make an exception to the distribution right in relation to copies so made, contrast to the position in relation to copies made by acts of reproduction permitted under in Arts 5(2) and (3): See Art.5(4).

[96] The terminology of the Art.5(1) is ambivalent, in that it speaks of tempory acts of reproduction as being being "exempted" from the right, whereas Arts 5(2) and (3) speak of the acts referred to there as being allowable "exceptions or limitations" to the relevant rights. Nevertheless, Art.5 is generally headed "Exceptions and Limitations" and Recital 33 speaks of the Art.5(1) as being an "exception". Presumably Member States are free to implement Art.5(1) either by defining the reproduction right in terms that exclude the exclusive right to do or authorise these temporary acts or by providing a separate exception, which is what the United Kingdom has done.

[97] As to this test, see paras 9–02, above and 9–24 to 9–33, below.

[98] See the Government Conclusions to the Patent Office's Consultation Paper of August 7, 2002, para.4.2. This is despite that fact that the Art.5(1) exception for temporary copies is made expressly subject to the 3-step test in Art.5(5).

[99] See the previous note.

[1] The copyright conferred on typographical arrangements of published editions by the United Kingdom (see para. 7–74 et seq., above) was not within the ambit of the Directive. Unless CDPA

transient or incidental, which is an integral and essential part of a technological process and the sole purpose of which is to enable:

(a) a transmission of the work in a network between third parties by an intermediary; or

(b) a lawful use of the work;

and which has no independent economic significance.

It will be noted, first, that in line with the Directive, the permitted act of making temporary copies does not extend to computer programs or copyright databases. More generally, the permitted act is directed to two quite different situations, namely copying which enables the transmission of a work in a network and copying which enables some lawful use of a work. In each case, however, there are common requirements:

(1) The permitted act only extends to the restricted act of copying. If, for example, as part of the same process, the work is communicated to the public via the internet, there is no defence under this provision to the act of communication.

(2) The permitted act only extends to the making of a temporary copy of the work. "Temporary" is not defined in the Act or in the Directive but necessarily implies that the copy will be deleted, destroyed or will otherwise disappear within some limited, although not necessarily short, time. An essential nature of a temporary copy is that it lacks permanance, usually, in the present context, by virtue of the nature of the physical copy in question. A copy made in RAM, which ceases to exist when a computer is turned off or when that part of memory is required for some other purpose, or a copy displayed on a computer screen, are both no doubt temporary copies in this sense. Recital 33 of the Directive, set out above, indicates that temporary copies made to enable browsing or caching are capable of falling within the exception. Copies made in RAM or on a computer screen to enable browsing will no doubt therefore normally fall within the exception. Presumably a cached copy may itself amount to a temporary copy and thus be permitted, although such copies may often be stored for substantial periods of time.[2]

(3) The copy must not only be temporary but also be transient or incidental. Transience reinforces the requirement that the copy be temporary, but also adds the notion that the lifetime of the copy is short or fleeting. "Incidental" connotes that the making of the copy is incidental to some other purpose, or is the means to some other end. A copy of a work displayed on a computer screen will normally be transient (although not if it remains displayed for a substantial length of time) but not incidental: the display of the copy is likely to be the very reason why the process has been initiated. A copy made in RAM in order that some process can be carried on it, in particular, in order that it may be transmitted in a network, may or may not be transient but will usually only be incidental to that larger purpose. Again, a cached copy will often be more than transient but perhaps can be regarded as being incidental in that it merely enables easier access to the work in the near future. In all of this, it must of course be remembered that the exception does not apply to computer programs or databases.

(4) The copying must take place as an integral and essential part of a

---

1988, s.28A extended to such works, however, the operation of the exception in the case of literary works in facsimile form (e.g. pdf format) would be seriously affected.

[2] The maker of cached copies will in any event normally have a defence under r.18 of the Electronic Commerce (EC Directive) Regulations 2002 (SI 2002/2013). See para. 22–96, below.

technological process. "Technological process" is not defined but is a very general term. A temporary copy made in writing on a piece of paper which is then thrown away might be temporary and transient, but it would not usually be part of a technological process. The requirement that it be integral implies that the copying is part of a process whereby the copying is integrated with other steps in the process. The requirement that the copying is an essential part of the process implies that without the copying the process will fail to achieve its designed objective.

(5) The making of the copy must have no independent economic significance. The important word to emphasise here is "independent", which presumably means independent of the network transmission or the lawful user. Some acts of temporary copying may well have economic significance. For example, some users may be willing to pay to be able to see the temporary display of a work on a screen. If, however, the display is to enable the lawful use of the work, it would seem that the display does not have an economic significance independent of the lawful use. As has been seen, recital 33 of the Directive contemplates that the exception should include acts which enable browsing to take place.

9–17 **Transmissions in networks.** Where the above conditions are satisfied, copying will be permitted when it is to enable the transmission of the work in a network between third parties by an intermediary. None of these expressions is defined.[3] This limb of the exception is obviously aimed primarily at copying which takes place by intermediaries such as service providers. Copying of a work other than the one to be transmitted is not permitted, nor is any alteration of the work by the intermediary.[4] It would also appear that the copying must be to enable transmission of the work *by* the intermediary. Copying of a work to enable transmission of the work *to* an intermediary for onward transmission to a further recipient is therefore not permitted. Nor does the section permit unlicensed copying by the further recipient. The fact that an infringement of copyright has been committed by the sender, or will be committed by the recipient of the transmission, does affect the intermediary's exemption from liability, even if he knows or has reason to believe that an infringement is taking place. In such circumstances, however, it may be possible to obtain an injunction against the service provider under section 191JA of the Act.[5] The E-Commerce Regulations,[6] which implement the E-Commerce Directive,[7] provide an overlapping defence in this area.

9–18 **Lawful use.** Again, where the conditions set out in section 28A are satisfied, temporary copying to enable "lawful use" will be permitted. Although the Act does not define lawful use, recital 33 of the Directive states that a use "should be considered lawful where it is authorised by the rightholder or not restricted by law". No doubt the latter type of use includes any case where another of the permitted act provisions applies or where some other defence can be relied on. As to "lawful use" generally, if the making of a temporary copy is to enable a use which is licensed, the making of that copy will often itself fall within the scope of the licence, so that the permitted act provisions of section 28A will not need to be relied on. Again, if the enabled use is lawful by virtue of a permitted act, for example the making of a copy of a work for the purpose of private study under

---

[3] Recital 33 of the Information Society Directive 2001/29 qualifies "transmission" with the word "efficient".

[4] Recital 33.

[5] See para. 22–108, below.

[6] The Electronic Commerce (EC Directive) Regulations 2002 (SI 2002/2013).

[7] Directive 2000/31.

section 29(1C), then the making of such a temporary copy would in any event usually be permitted under section 29(1C), since it would be likely to fall within the ambit of dealing with the work for the permitted purpose of private study.[8] The same appears to be true in relation to other permitted acts.Nevertheless, the effect of section.23A is to make the position clearer.

In relation to acts which are not expressly licensed there is often doubt about the full extent of the licence. In these cases, the effect of this permitted act provision is to make it clear that acts which "enable" lawful use will not be infringements of copyright, and so to avoid technical arguments about the scope of the licence. The key question will be whether the use is lawful.

4. THE FAIR DEALING PROVISIONS

A. OVERVIEW

Introduced in 1911, the fair dealing provisions provide three important limitations to owners' rights, namely, fair dealing for the purposes of non-commercial research or private study, fair dealing for the purposes of criticism or review and fair dealing for the purpose of news reporting. Before the 1911 Act there were no statutory exceptions to copyright infringement in the United Kingdom, unlike in many civil law countries, which have long provided such provisions.[9] Nevertheless, the question of what amounted to "fair dealing" frequently arose under the law prior to 1911 in determining whether the use which had been made of the plaintiff's work was sufficient to constitute infringement.[10] As such, this question was often not distinguished from the issue of whether a substantial part of the plaintiff's work had been taken.[11] Since the 1911 Act, the two issues have been quite distinct. It is only when the court has determined that a substantial part has been taken that any question of fair dealing arises.

9–19

As noted above, under the 1988 Act fair dealing is permitted for the purposes of private study or non-commercial research, criticism or review or the reporting of current events. Other types of dealing are not permitted no matter how "fair" they may be.[12] This restricted approach can be contrasted with the fair use provisions under United States law,[13] which only provides guidelines as to what amounts to fair use[14] and which are available in relation to all types of work. The Whitford Committee had recommended that a similar approach be adopted in the

---

[8] See para. 9–125 *et seq.*, below.

[9] English and French versions of some of these early provisions can be found in Birrell, *Seven Lectures on the Law and History of Copyright in Books* (Cassell & Co., London, 1899) pp.182–185.

[10] *e.g. Wilkins v Aikin* (1810) 17 Vesey 422; *Scott v Stanford* (1867) L. R. 3 Eq. 718; *Bradbury v Hotten* (1872) L.R. 8 Ex. 1; *Smith v Chato* (1874) 31 L.T. 77. Prior to the 1911 Act, however, no cases had arisen on the question of whether there was a right to copy a work for the purposes of private study.

[11] In particular see *Bradbury v Hotten* (1872) L.R. 8 Ex. 1, but *cf. Bell v Whitehead* (1839) 8 L.J., N.S. (Equity) 141. For a review of the whole history of the "fair use" exception, see Burrell: "Reining in Copyright Law. Is Fair Use the Answer?" [2001] I.P.Q. 361.

[12] "It is fair dealing directed to and consequently limited to and to be judged in relation to the approved purposes. It is dealing which is fair for the approved purposes and not dealing which might be fair for some other purpose or fair in general", *per* Ungoed-Thomas J. in *Beloff v Pressdram* [1973] 1 All E.R 241 at 262; "The provisions are not to be regarded as mere examples of a general wide discretion vested in the courts to refuse to enforce copyright where they believe such refusal to be fair and reasonable", *per* Laddie J. in *Pro Sieban Media AG v Carlton UK Television Ltd* [1998] F.S.R. 43 at 49 (reversed by the Court of Appeal, [1999] 1 W.L.R. 605; [1999] F.S.R. 610, but not with any disapproval of this statement) . For further discussion, see Griffiths "Preserving Judicial Freedom of Movement—Interpreting Fair Dealing in Copyright Law" [2000] I.P.Q. 164.

[13] Copyright Act 1976, 17 U.S.C., s.107.

[14] *Sony Corporation of America v Universal City Studios* (1984) 464 U.S. 417. This approach has

United Kingdom,[15] but this was rejected by the Government, together with a proposal to rename the defence "fair use" or "fair practice".[16] The argument against a codified system such as that in the United Kingdom is that a more flexible approach allows the courts to develop the law on a case-by-case basis as new problems emerge.[17]

9–20   **The Berne Convention.**[18] Article 10(1) of the Connvention provides that it is permissible to make "quotations" from a work which has already been lawfully made available to the public, provided that the making is compatible with fair practice, and their extent does not exceed that justified by the purpose, including quotations from newspaper articles and periodicals in the form of press summaries. Where such use is made, however, "mention" must be made of the source, and of the name of the author if it appears on the work.[19] "Lawfully made available to the public" is a broader concept than that of a "published work" and would include, for example, a public performance or electronic dissemination. Furthermore, there is no requirement under the Article that the work be made available to the public with the author's consent, only that this has been lawfully done. Thus "lawfully made available to the public" might include a situation where a work is made available by virtue of a compulsory licence. Presumably, however, it would not include a situation where a work has only been distributed to a narrow category of persons.[20] As to use for the purposes of reporting current events, a number of provisions of the Convention are in theory relevant. First, Article 2(8) excludes protection for "news of the day or to miscellaneous facts having the character of mere items of press information".[21] Secondly, Article 10 *bis*(1) provides for a limited class of exception, permitting "the reproduction by the press, the broadcasting or the communication to the public by wire of articles published in newspapers or periodicals on current economic, political or religious topics, and of broadcast works of the same character", provided a due acknowledgment is made. However, this is of little application in the present context since it does not apply if the right has been expressly reserved. Thirdly, Article 10 *bis*(2) states that it is for individual countries "to determine the conditions under which, for the purpose of reporting current events by means of photography, cinematography, broadcasting or communications to the public by wire, literary or artistic works seen or heard in the course of the event may, to the extent justified by the informatory purpose, be reproduced and made and available to the public". This Article is in effect dealing with incidental inclusion of works, and is not of general application in relation to reporting of current events.

9–21   **The Information Society Directive.** A number of provisions of the Directive apply in the area of fair dealing, and required several changes to be made to the

---

been criticised for ignoring the principle of statutory construction *noscitur a sociis* (*i.e.* that the meaning of a doubtful word may be ascertained by reference to the meaning of words associated with it). See Goldstein, *Copyright*, (Boston: Little, Brown & Co., 1989) para.10.2.1.

[15] Report of the Committee to Consider the Law on Copyright and Designs, Cmnd. 6732, paras 672–677.

[16] *Hansard*, HL Vol.491, cols 85–89. Although it was accepted that "dealing" is somewhat deceptive, in that it implies some form of transaction, it was retained on the grounds that the phrase is understood by lawyers and others in the field.

[17] See Weinreb, "Fair's Fair: A Comment on the Fair Use Doctrine," (1990) 103 Harv. L. Rev. 1137.

[18] For a full discussion of exceptions permitted under the Berne Convention, see para. 24–28 *et seq.*, below.

[19] Berne Convention, Art.10(3).

[20] As in *Hubbard v Vosper* [1972] 2 Q.B. 84, CA. See Ricketson, *The Berne Convention for the Protection of Literary and Artistic Works 1886–1986* (Kluwer, London, 1987) pp.491–493.

[21] As to the doubtful nature of the exception, see Ricketson, *The Berne Convention for the Protection of Literary and Artistic Works 1886–1986* (Kluwer, London, 1987), p.303.

1988 Act. First, whereas the 1988 Act originally provided that fair dealing with a work for the purposes of "research" was permitted, Article 5(3)(a) of the Directive in effect stipulates that such acts must be of a non-commercial nature. The Act has therefore been amended to restrict this permitted act to research for a "non-commercial" purpose. Secondly, Article 5(2)(b) effectively requires the private study provision to be restricted to private study of a non-commercial nature, and the Act has been amended to make this clear. Thirdly, whereas the Act originally provided that fair dealing with a work for the purposes of criticism or review was permitted where the work was either published or unpublished, Artcle 5(3)(d) of the Directive stipulates that such use shall be permitted only where the use relates to a work or other subject-matter which has already been lawfully made available to the public.[22] The Act has been amended accordingly. Fourth, although in some cases of fair dealing the Act required a "sufficient acknowledgment" of the work and its author to be made, no such acknowledgment was required in the case of fair dealing for the purposes of research or private study. The Directive has changed this. These amendments all take effect from October 31, 2003.[23]

The Human Rights Act.[24] Consideration is given to the Human Rights Act 1998 **9–22** elsewhere[25]but it has a potentially significant impact in the context of the fair dealing provisions, where the Article 10 right to freedom of expression will often overlap with the permitted acts of criticism, review and reporting of current events. In cases where it is necessary to reproduce a substantial part of a work for these purposes, the fair dealing provisions will usually permit this and thus the freedom of expression requirements of the Act will be satisfied. The requirement of fairness, particularly in the context of a dealing for the purposes of reporting current events, will normally be flexible enough to enable a court to reflect properly the public interest in freedom of expression and, in particular, the freedom of the press.[26] There may, nevertheless, be rare cases where the right of freedom of expression will come into irreconcilable conflict with the protection afforded by the 1988 Act, notwithstanding the express exceptions to be found in the Act, even when these expressions are construed liberally in favour of the user[27] and a flexible approach is adopted in relation to what is "fair" use. Examples might be where the reporting in question cannot realistically be said to be of "current events",[28] where the reporting of current events in the public interest can only effectively be done by the use of a photograph[29] or where there is a sufficient public interest in the criticism or review of a work which has not previously been made available to the public.[30] In these circumstances, a court would be bound, in so far as it is able, to apply the Act in a manner that accommodates the right of freedom of expression. The possible methods of doing so would be to

---

[22] This provision has clearly been taken from Art. 10(1) of the Berne Convention. See para. 9–20, below.

[23] The Copyright and Related Rights Regulations 2003 (SI 2003/2498), para.1.

[24] What follows in this paragraph is based on *Ashdown v Telegraph Group Ltd* [2001] EWCA Civ 1142 [2002].

[25] See paras 3–260, above and 22–82 *et seq.*, below.

[26] This approach requires that decisions made before the Human Rights Act came into force as to what amounts to "fair" dealing should not be regarded as inflexible, although they are still important. The question which needs to be asked is: are the facts of the case such that the importance of freedom of expression outweighs the conventional considerations established by the earlier authorities as to what is "fair"? See *Ashdown*.

[27] See para. 9–23, below.

[28] A case suggested in *Ashdown.*

[29] Such use falls outside the permitted act provisions. See para. 9–47, below.

[30] Again, such use falls outside the permitted act provisions. See para. 9–37, below. The facts of *Hubbard v Vosper* [1972] 2 Q.B. 84, CA might be such a case.

refuse the discretionary relief of an injunction, leaving the claimant to his remedy in damages (which will usually be the appropriate course), or by invoking the public interest defence.[31]

9–23 **Approach to construction.** Some consideration has already been given as to how the permitted act provisions should be construed.[32] In general, the fair dealing provisions involve issues on which a trial judge comes to a judgmental conclusion after taking into account a number of factors. As such, his decision should not be disturbed by the Court of Appeal unless it proceeded from some error of principle or is clearly unsustainable.[33] As to the various expressions, "criticism or review" and "reporting current events", these are expressions which should be interpreted liberally and their precise boundaries cannot be plotted: the nearer any use comes to the boundaries, unplotted as they are, the less likely is the use to be "fair".[34] All the fair dealing provisions use the words "for the purpose of". As to whether this expression imports an objective or subjective test, it is important to construe the composite phrases "for the purpose of non-commercial research" and "for the purpose of private study", etc. rather than each single word. When this is done, the precise mental element on the part of the user ceases to be of great importance. The words "in the context of" or "as part of an exercise in" could be substituted for "for the purpose of" without any significant change of meaning. The task of the court is to consider the use made of the work and then ascertain what was the perceived purpose of that use. The user's subjective intention might well be relevant on the issue of whether the dealing was "fair", but it is wrong for a court to put itself in the user's shoes to decide what the purpose was.[35]

9–24 **Preparatory dealings.** In cases where there has been dissemination of a work for the purposes of criticism, review or reporting of current events, there will usually be other, preparatory acts of copying, especially where dissemination takes place via one of the established forms of media. In such a case, the preparatory acts will also have been carried out "for the purpose" of the relevant act.[36] In those cases where a sufficient acknolwedgement is required, this raises a difficult issue

---

[33] *Pro Sieben Media AG v Carlton UK Television Ltd* [1999] 1 W.L.R. 605; [1999] F.S.R. 610, approved by the House of Lords in *Designers Guild Ltd v Russell Williams (Textiles) Ltd* [2001] F.S.R. 113.

[34] *Pro Sieben Media AG v Carlton UK Television Ltd* [1999] 1 W.L.R. 605; [1999] F.S.R. 610. The same is no doubt true of the expressions "non-commercial research" and "private study".

[35] *Pro Sieben Media AG v Carlton UK Television Ltd* [1999] 1 W.L.R. 605; [1999] F.S.R. 610. It was said there that to do so would, for example, encourage journalists to give implausible evidence as to their intentions if encouraged to think that a sincerely held belief as to the actual purpose would be sufficient. See *Pro Sieben*, above, at 620 and *Hyde Park Residence Ltd v Yelland* [2001] Ch. 143. If, however, the purpose is to discover whether the use fell within the ambit of the statute, there seems no good reason why both the user's actual intentions and also the impact of the use on the intended recipient should not be of help. If implausible evidence is given on behalf of the defendant, then it is unlikely to be believed.

[36] *Pro Sieben Media AG v Carlton UK Television Ltd* [1999] 1 W.L.R. 605; [1999] F.S.R. 610. There, the defendant had made a copy of the whole of the claimant's television programme before deciding to use a short extract. Although there was little evidence about the circumstances in which this was done, the Court of Appeal accepted that it was copied simply in order for it to be available to the editor to consider whether to use an extract from it. Since the ultimate use of the extract was for the purpose of criticism or review, the making of the complete copy was for the same ultimate purpose. See also *Time Warner Entertainment Ltd v Channel 4 Television Corporation Plc*, [1994] E.M.L.R. 1; *Television New Zealand v Newsmonitor Services Ltd* (1993) 27 I.P.R. 441 (High Ct of New Zealand) at 467.

as to whether the acknowledgment must be made in respect of these preparatory acts as well as the acts of dissemination.[37]

B. NON-COMMERCIAL RESEARCH AND PRIVATE STUDY

(i) Introduction

The general aim of these provisions is to give students and non-commercial researchers greater access to copyright works. By granting a limited right to copy articles and small sections of other works, these groups are repeatedly able to consult sources to which they may not have ready access, provided that the copying remains within the bounds of what is fair (see paragraph 9–00, below). As was the case under the 1956 Act, the exceptions apply only to literary, dramatic, musical and artistic works, thus "it is possible to make copies of parts of plays for the purposes of studying drama, but no equivalent loophole exists in relation to film footage".[38] This fails to reflect the increasing importance of non-textual media for both study and research and means, for example, that a researcher is not permitted to copy part of a sound recording under this section, even though there would be no infringement of the underlying musical work in his doing so.[39]

9–25

(ii) Non-commercial research

Introduction: the Information Society Directive. The Directive permits Member States to make an exception to the reproduction right, to the communication to the public right, and to the distribution right, in the case of use "for the sole purpose of scientific research, as long as the source, including the author's name, is indicated, unless this turns out to be impossible, and to the extent justified by the non-commercial purpose to be achieved".[40] Recital 42 also provides that when applying the exception or limitation for non-commercial scientific research purposes, the non-commercial nature of the activity in question should be determined "by that activity as such" and the organisational structure and the means of funding of the establishment concerned are not to be the decisive factors in this respect. A number of preliminary points can be made about this. First, although the Directive refers to "scientific" research, it is reasonably clear that this includes the humanities.[41] Secondly, the source of the work will usually have to be indicated. Thirdly, in the rather convoluted language of the Directive, it is clear that the purpose of the research must be non-commercial and the extent of any exception is to be limited to the extent justified by that non-commercial purpose.

9–26

The 1988 Act, as amended. The Act required amendment to comply with the non-commercial nature of the permitted exception and the requirement of recog-

9–27

---

[37] See, further, para. 9–29, below.

[38] *Pro Sieben Media AG v Carlton UK Television Ltd* [1998] F.S.R. 43 at 48, but note the limited educational exception that exists in relation to films: CDPA 1988, s.32(2) and see para. 9–92, below.

[39] Note that the combined effect of ss.19(1) and 2(1) of the 1911 Act was to permit such acts.

[40] Information Society Directive, 2001/29, Arts 5(3)(a), (4). An exception is permitted to the distribution right only to the extent justified by the purpose of the authorised act of reproduction: Art.5(4).

[41] Note that although Art.6 of Database Directive 96/9 also refers to scientific research, recital 36 of that Directive makes it clear that this term covers "both the natural sciences and the human sciences."

nition of the source. Thus, the Act now provides that fair dealing with a literary,[42] dramatic, musical or artistic work for the purposes of research for a non-commercial purpose does not infringe any copyright in the work, provided it is accompanied by a sufficient acknowledgement,[43] unless this is impossible, for reasons of practicability or otherwise.[44] Previously, fair dealing was permitted in the case of any form of research, other than in the case of a database.[45] As it happens, the Whitford Committee had recommmended that commercial research should be excluded from the scope of fair dealing[46] but this did survive lobbying from British industry.[47] In the case of the typographical arrangement of a published edition, fair dealing for the purposes of any form of research does not infringe copyright in the work, and no acknowledgment is required at all.[48]

9–28   **"Research for a non-commercial purpose."** The expressions "research" and "non-commercial purpose" no doubt have to be construed consistently with the Directive,[49] but in the end they are ordinary English words. In the equivalent Australian provision, "research" has been held to have its ordinary dictionary meaning, namely, the "diligent and systematic inquiry or investigation into a subject in order to discover facts or principles".[50] Quite what the limits are of *non-commercial* research is not clear. Although, as already noted, rectial 42 provides that the non-commercial nature of the activity in question should be determined "by that activity as such" and that the organisational structure and the means of funding of the establishment concerned (where there is one, presumably) are not the *decisive* factors in this respect, this does not provide a great deal of extra clarity. Presumably any research which, at the time it is conducted, is contemplated or intended should be ultimately used for a purpose which has some commercial value will not be within the permitted act. "Commercial" in general means engaged in commerce, which suggests an activity by way of trade, but the expression no doubt encompasses any activity conducted with a view to making a profit. What is relevant is the purpose of the research, not the larger purpose of the researcher. Thus, in the case of research carried out by an em-

---

[42] Note, however, that special rules apply to computer programs with the result that they are effectively taken out of this provision.See para. 9–34 , below.

[43] CDPA 1988, s.29(1), as amended.

[44] CDPA 1988, s.29(1B).

[45] As enacted, no distinction was made by the 1988 Act as to databases either. However, implementation of the Database Directive (96/9) required the permitted act of fair dealing with a database for the purpose to research to be restricted to non-commercial research, and also that such fair dealing be accompanied by a sufficient acknowledgment. See s.29(5), as introduced by the Copyright and Rights in Databases Regulations (SI 1997/3032). With the changes made to implement the Information Society Directive 2001/29, however, it was no longer necessary to distinguish between databases and other literary works, and s.29(5) has therefore been deleted.

[46] That this was the committee's view is evident from paras 676–677. Also see *Hansard*, HL Vol.491, col.93.

[47] See *Hansard*, HL Vol.493, cols 1153–1157. Reliance was placed on the transaction cost argument, that is to say, that any revenue raised from licensing agreements would be swallowed up by the costs of administrating such agreements (*Hansard*, HL Vol.491, cols 92–94). It is instructive to contrast the position in the United States, where the ready availability of licences has meant that the reproduction of single copies of articles for commercial research purposes does not amount to fair use (*American Geophysical Union v Texaco Inc.* 60 F.3d 913 (2d Cir. 1994)).

[48] CDPA 1988, s.29(2). Typographical arrangements are treated differently from other works under s.29 because they are not subject to the Information Society Directive. Although there has been an amendment to s.29(2), the effect is to preserve the position in relation to such works as it was before an amendment was made to s.29(1).

[49] The Government did not amend the section to restrict any dealing, in the words of the Directive, to "scientific" research, taking the view that the breadth of the term was such that it did not appear to add anything. See the Government Conclusions on the Patent Office's Consulation Paper of August 7, 2002, para.5.4.

[50] *De Garis v Neville Jeffress Pidler Pty Ltd* (1990) 18 I.P.R. 292 (Fed. Ct of Australia) at 298–299. Also see *Television New Zealand v Newsmonitor Services Ltd* (1993) 27 I.P.R. 441 (High Ct of New Zealand) at 463.

ployee of a not-for-profit organisation but with a view to raising funds for the organisation, it seems that the research would be for a commercial purpose. The purpose may no doubt be internal, that is, research to be used to produce something which has a commercial value (a product, or the supply of professional services, for example), or external, where the research is published as part of a larger commercial enterprise (the publication of a book with a view to profit, for example).

Sufficient aknowledgement. If it is not to be an infringment, the dealing must be   **9–29** accompanied by a sufficient acknowledgment, except "where this would be impossible for reasons of practicality or otherwise". This requirement was introduced as a result of Article 5(3)(a) of the Directive, which permits such use, "as long as the source, including the author's name, is indicated" unless "this turns out to be impossible". As will be seen, the basic requirement of sufficient acknowledgment was already part of United Kingdom law as applied to other cases of fair dealing, and is defined to mean an acknowledgment identifying the work in question by its title or other description and identifying the author unless (a) in the case of a published work, it is published anonymously[51]; or (b) in the case of an unpublished work, it is not possible to ascertain the identity of the author by reasonable inquiry.[52] In the case of section 29(1), the requirement therefore has two layers of dispensation. First, the general requirement of sufficient acknowledgment is dispensed with where the work is published anonymously or, in the case of an unpublished work, where the author cannot reasonably be ascertained. Secondly, even where, for example, the work was published under the author's name, acknowledgment is also dispensed with where it would be impossible for reasons of practicility or otherwise to name him. Such cases are likely to be rare, but may arise where the version of the work used for the dealing no longer bears the author's name. No doubt the words "for reasons of practicality or otherwise" were added in the Act because the wording of the Directive ("unless this turns out to be impossible"), taken literally, impose a test that could hardly ever be satisfied, and this was not the intention of the Directive. Dispensation in cases where acknowledgment would be "impossible for reasons of practicality" suggests a situation where it is not practical, using all reasonable endeavours, to establish the name of the author or title of the work in the time available before the dealing in question. Cases where it is "otherwise" impossible suggest a situation where no amount of inquiry would have revealed this information. It should be noted that although the Act does not require the work or author to be named where the work has been published anonymously, even where these details are in fact known, this is not consistent with the Directive, which requires identification in such circumstances. It might have been better simply to adopt the words of the Directive in the form "…as long as the source, including the author's name, is indicated, unless this turns out to be impossible for reasons of practicality or otherwise".

In other cases where acknowledgment is required by the Act, namely criticism, review and the reporting of current events, the "dealing" in question usually involves some form of public dissemination of the work, in which event the acknowledgment has some purpose and value for the author. In the case of research, however, the dealing may be wholly private.[53] Is the researcher required to place the name of the author of the work and the title on every copy he makes?

---

[51] For example, see *PCR Ltd v Dow Jones Telerate Ltd* [1998] F.S.R. 170, in particular, at 184.

[52] CDPA 1988, s.178.

[53] See para. 9–19, below, on the choice of the word "dealing." The making of a single copy in the course of research is clearly a dealing. If it were otherwise the act of copying could not be brought within the section at all.

It may be that the Directive, which refers to the source being "indicated", does not require this and only contemplates the source being named when some communication of the work to a another person actually takes place, but a literal reading of the Act requires an acknowledgment in the case of every dealing. In some cases of research of a private nature the dealing can no doubt be brought within the private study exception, which does not require acknowledgement[54] but this will not always be the position. It seems that in this latter type of case an acknowledgment is required to avoid infringement.

9–30   **Form of acknowledgment.** The acknowledgment of the work may take the form of identification of its title or some other description of it.[55] Identification of the author need not by reference to his proper name, particular if this would be unlikely to have any particular significance or would be meaningless to the bulk of the intended audience.[56] Use of a psuedonym by which an author is known to the public will therefore be sufficient. There is authority that the acknowledgment must recognise the position or claims of the author and that it is not sufficient that the title of the work and the identity of the author are immediately revealed in the text[57] but this seems doubtful. The Directive, for its part, merely requires that the source, including the author's name, be "indicated". It is important to emphasise that the acknowledgment must identify the author of the work, not the copyright owner.[58] If the part of the work which is used itself reproduces a substantial part of an underlying work then the underlying work must also be acknowledged. This may prove to be a trap for the unwary.[59]

(iii) Private study.

9–31   **The Directive.** Articles 5(2)(b) and (4) of the Information Society Directive permit Member States to provide an exception to the reproduction right and to the distribution right in the case of reproductions on any medium made by a natural person for private use and for ends that are neither directly nor indirectly commercial, on condition that the rightholder receive fair compensation. Although the existing provisions of the 1988 Act permitted fair dealing with a literary, dramatic, musical or artistic work for the purposes of private study,[60] it was clearly felt that this might not exclude private study for a commercial end. Logistically, the Directive also required that dealings for the purposes of commercial research be deal with differently from dealings for the purposes of private study. The Act has therefore been amended to place the private study exception in a new subsection[61] and to define private study so as to exclude any study which

---

[54] See para. 9–31 et seq., below.

[55] CDPA 1988, s.178.

[56] *Pro Sieben Media AG v Carlton UK Television Ltd* [1999] 1 W.L.R. 605; [1999] F.S.R. 610; *Newspaper Licensing Agency Ltd v Marks and Spencer plc* [1999] R.P.C. 536 (CA). See further as to the form of acknowledgment, para. 9–52, below.

[57] *Sillitoe v McGraw-Hill Book Co.* [1983] F.S.R. 545 at 565. In that case the defendant published study notes of various works to help students prepare for examination. It was quite clear what the title of work was and who was its author, but it was said that there was nothing by way of "acknowledgment"; the work was treated, so far as appearances went, as if it were a non-copyright work.

[58] *Express Newspapers Plc v News (UK) Ltd* [1990] F.S.R. 359 at 367.

[59] This does not apply where the work in question is an adaptation. In this instance only the adaptation itself need be acknowledged; the underlying work from which the adaptation is made need not be: CDPA 1988, s.76 and see para. 9–12, above.

[60] CDPA 1988, s.29(1). As with fair dealing for the purposes of research, an amendment was made to exclude databases but this is no longer relevant. See the notes to para. 9–27, below.

[61] s.29(1C).

is directly or indirectly for a commercial purpose.[62] No acknowledgment is required in the case of this permitted act. Again, in the case of the typographical arrangement of a published edition, fair dealing for the purposes of private study does not infringe copyright in such a work.[63] It will be noted that no amendment has been made to restrict this permitted act to dealings by way of copying and distribution of copies so made, no doubt on the premise that private study will not involve other classes of acts restricted by the copyright. More significantly, no amendment has been made to provide rightholders with any compensation for this form of copying. The Government's view was apparently that private copying of this kind does not prejudice rightsholders in any substantial way, so that "fair" compensation would either be zero or of such little amount that it would be swallowed up by the transaction costs involved in establishing and running any scheme.[64]

Private study and non-commercial purpose. In Australia, "study" has been held to have its ordinary meaning, namely: (1) The application of the mind to the acquisition of knowledge, as by reading, investigation or reflection; (2) The cultivation of a particular branch of learning, science or art (as in the study of law); (3) A particular course of effort to acquire knowledge (as in the pursuance of medical studies); (4) A thorough examination and analysis of a particular subject.[65] There is clearly some overlap with the expression "research", considered above. The meaning of commercial in this context has also already been considered in the context of research. The mere fact that a work is reproduced for the purposes of private study will not, in itself, mean that the use amounts to a fair dealing. Thus, for example, it was no defence under the previous provisions of the Act to reproduce a work in the form of study notes to be used by examination students[66] and the position would be the same today.   **9–32**

(iv) Common considerations

Copying by a person other than the student or researcher. The Act makes extensive provision as to the circumstances in which copies may be made for the purposes of private study or non-commercial research by others. In the case of libraries the Act provides that copying by a librarian or his agent is not permitted if it goes beyond what is permissible under the provisions which specifically relate to copying by such persons.[67] In addition, the Act provides that in any other case, copying by a person other than the researcher or student himself is not fair dealing if the person doing the copying knows or has reason to believe that it will   **9–33**

---

[62] s.178. This amendment was said to be "for the avoidance of doubt". See the Transposition Note on implementation.

[63] s.29(2). See the notes to para. 9–16, below.

[64] See the Government Conclusions on the Patent Office's Consulation Paper of August 7, 2002, para.5.6 and Transposition Note. The Government also relied on recital 35 of the Directive, which provides that "When determining the form, detailed arrangements and possible level of such fair compensation, account should be taken of the particular circumstances of each case. When evaluating these circumstances, a valuable criterion would be the possible harm to the rightholders resulting from the act in question. In cases where rightholders have already received payment in some other form, for instance as part of a licence fee, no specific or separate payment may be due. ... In certain situations where the prejudice to the rightholder would be minimal, no obligation for payment may arise." See, again, the Government Conclusions on the Consultation Paper and the Transposition Note.

[65] *De Garis v Neville Jeffress Pidler Pty Ltd* (1990) 18 I.P.R. 292 (Fed. Ct of Australia) at 298–299. Also see *Television New Zealand v Newsmonitor Services Ltd* (1993) 27 I.P.R. 441 (High Ct of New Zealand) at 463.

[66] *Sillitoe v McGraw Hill Book Co.* [1983] F.S.R. 545.

[67] CDPA 1988, s.29(3)(a). This relates to s.38 (copying by librarians: articles in periodicals) and s.39 (copying by librarians: parts of published works). See paras 9–106 and 9–107, below.

result in copies of substantially the same material being provided to more than one person at substantially the same time and for substantially the same purpose.[68] The Act, therefore, provides only a limited exception in the case of any copying done by a person other than the person actually engaged in the non-commercial research or private study. Thus it appears clear that there is no defence under this section if a teacher makes multiple copies of a work for use by classroom students. On the other hand, it seems that a student or researcher may ask another to make a copy of a work provided that the section is otherwise satisfied.

9–34   **Computer programs.** Two special provisions apply in the case of computer programs. The Software Directive[69] allows only a limited category of exceptions to the rights prescribed in relation to such works. Two exceptions are relevant in the present context of fair dealing. First, Article 5(3) stipulates that there is to be an exception to allow a person having a right to use a copy of a program to observe, study or test the functioning of the program in order to determine the ideas and principles which underlie any element of the program, if this is done while performing any of the acts of loading, displaying, running, transmitting or storing the program which he is entitled to do. At the time of implementation of the Software Directive, this requirement was clearly considered to be catered for by the provisions of section 29 as they then stood, which permitted fair dealing for the purposes of commercial as well as non-commercial research or private study. With the amendment of the Act to restrict this permitted act to non-commercial research or private study, this was no longer the case. New sections 29(4A) and 50BA have therefore been added to deal with this. Thus, section 50BA provides, in the words of the Directive, that it is not an infringement of copyright for a lawful user of a copy of a computer program to observe, study or test the functioning of the program in order to determine the ideas and principles which underlie any element of the program if he does so while performing any of the acts of loading, displaying, running, transmitting or storing the program which he is entitled to do. A line between acts permitted under section 50BA and those permitted under the fair dealing provisions is drawn by section 29(4A), which provides that it is not fair dealing to observe, study or test the functioning of a computer program in order to determine the ideas and principles which underlie any element of the program, these being acts which are permitted if they fall within section 50BA.

The second relevant exception prescribed by the Software Directive is to permit decompilation of a computer program so as to obtain information necessary to achieve interoperability between that program and another program. This topic is discussed elsewhere[70] but effect was given to this provision of the Directive by section 50B—introduced by the Copyright (Computer Programs) Regulations 1992.[71] A line was again drawn between the two categories of permitted acts, by a section 29(4), which provides that it is not fair dealing to convert a program expressed in a low-level language into a version expressed in a higher-level language or in the course of so doing to copy it, these being acts permitted if done in accordance with section 50B.

---

[68] s.29(3)(b).
[69] Council Directive 91/250/EEC.
[70] See para. 9–134, below.
[71] SI 1992/3233.

C. CRITICISM OR REVIEW

Introduction. Criticism or review of a work has always been permitted and since the 1911 Act has been the subject of statutory provision.[72]

9–35

The Information Society Directive. Articles 5(3)(d) and (4) of the Directive permit Member States to provide an exception to the reproduction, distribution and communication to the public rights in the case of quotations for purposes such as criticism or review, provided (a) that they relate to a work or other subject-matter which has already been lawfully made available to the public, and (b) that, unless this turns out to be impossible, the source, including the author's name, is indicated, and (c) that their use is in accordance with fair practice, and to the extent required by the specific purpose.[73] Except in one respect, the existing provision in section 30(1) of the 1988 Act allowing fair dealing for the purposes of criticism or review was consistent with the Directive. The expression "quotations" is clearly borrowed from the Article 10 of the Berne Convention[74] and no doubt includes use of a substantial part of a work in some form other than an unaltered textual quotation, and also use of an artistic work. The one respect in which the 1988 Act clearly did not comply with the Directive was that the Act permitted fair dealing with an unpublished work as well as a published work.[75] The Act has therefore had to be amended in this respect.

9–36

The 1988 Act. As the Act now stands, fair dealing with a work for the purpose of criticism or review, of that or another work or a performance of a work, does not infringe any copyright in the work provided that it is accompanied by a sufficient acknowledgment and provided that the work has previously been made available to the public.[76]

9–37

For the purposes of criticism or review. The proper approach to the construction of these expressions has already been considered.[77] In Australia, the words "criticism" and "review" have both been given their dictionary definitions. Thus "criticism" has been defined as: (1) The act or art of analysing and judging the quality of a literary or artistic work, etc. (as in literary criticism). (2) The act of passing judgment as to the merits of something. (3) A critical comment, article or essay.[78] "Review" has been defined as: "a critical article or report, as in a periodical, on some literary work, commonly some work of recent appearance; a critique".[79] "Criticism" can thus be seen as describing the "critical application of the mental faculties", whilst "review" describes the results of such a process.[80] Criticism may be strongly expressed and unbalanced, the issue then usually being whether the use is fair dealing.[81]

9–38

---

[72] Sometimes, it could no doubt be argued that review or criticism of a work is impliedly authorised by the copyright owner putting the work before the public. Without s.30, however, there is a danger that only favourable or insipid reviews would be permitted. *cf. Chatterton v Cave* (1878) 3 App.Cas. 483 at 492.

[73] An exception to the distribution right is permitted only to the extent justified by the purpose of the authorised act of reproduction: Art.5(4).

[74] See para. 9–12, below.

[75] The fact that the work was unpublished might, however, have affected the question of whether the dealing was fair. See para. 9–53 *et seq.*, below.

[76] CDPA 1988, s.30(1). Note that this provision applies to all categories of work (see s.28(2)).

[77] See para. 9–23, below.

[78] *De Garis v Neville Jeffress Pidler Pty Ltd* (1990) 18 I.P.R. 292 at 299.

[79] *De Garis v Neville Jeffress Pidler Pty Ltd* (1990) 18 I.P.R. 292.

[80] *De Garis v Neville Jeffress Pidler Pty Ltd* (1990) 18 I.P.R. 292.

[81] *Pro Sieben Media AG v Carlton UK Television Ltd* [1999] 1 W.L.R. 605, [1999] F.S.R. 610, CA.

9–39 **Criticism or review "of a work".** It is not necessary for the parts of the work selected for the criticism or review to be representative of the work as a whole. Criticism of a single aspect of a work is therefore capable of constituting fair dealing.[82] The requirement that the criticism or review be of "a work" or a performance of "a work" is construed liberally. The criticism or review need not be confined to the literary style or merit of the work but may extend to the thoughts underlying it, for example the doctrine or philosophy[83] or ideas and events[84] expounded in the work or, for example, to criticism of works constituting the fruits, and thus the practice, of "cheque-book" jounalism,[85] and even to criticism of a decision to withdraw a work from circulation.[86] Nevertheless, what is required is that the copying should take place as part of and for the purposes of criticising or reviewing the work in question. If it is done for some other purpose it will not suffice.[87] The fact that there is another purpose, such as education, as well as the purpose of criticism or review, will not, in itself, prevent the defence of fair dealing applying, although this may affect the question of fairness.[88]

9–40 **Work reproduced need not be the work criticised.** The exception is available whether the work reproduced is the work criticised or not.[89] Thus in criticising one work it is permissible to quote from other comparable works for the purpose of exemplifying the criticism. Again, in criticising a work in a foreign language, it is permissible to quote from an English translation even though there is no criticism of the translation as such. Nevertheless, under the 1956 Act the criticism or review had to be of a "work" and since a performance is not a "work" it followed that the defence probably could not have been relied upon when, for example, quoting passages of a play in reviewing a performance of it. Under the 1988 Act the defence is available in such circumstances.[90] There is no requirement that the work performed be a copyright work so that, for example, it would seem that the section would apply in the case of a review of an extempore performance of which no record is made.

9–41 **Caricature, parody or pastiche.**[91] Unlike some other countries, there has never been a specific statutory exception for these kinds of treatment in the United Kingdom. Although Article 5(3)(k) of the Information Society Directive permits Member States to provide an exception in the case of caricature, parody or pastiche, the United Kingdom has not taken advantage of this, except in so far as

---

An author's remedy for unbalanced criticism which still amounts to fair dealing will lie, if anywhere, in the law of defamation: *Pro Sieben*.

[82] *Time Warner Entertainment Ltd v Channel 4 Television Corporation Plc* [1994] E.M.L.R. 1.

[83] *Hubbard v Vosper* [1972] 2 Q.B. 84.

[84] *Distillers Co. (Biochemicals) Ltd v Times Newspapers Ltd* [1975] Q.B. 613.

[85] *Pro Sieben Media AG v Carlton UK Television Ltd* [1999] 1 W.L.R. 605, [1999] F.S.R. 610. The works criticised were the claimant's television programme and newspapers in general.

[86] *Time Warner Entertainment Ltd v Channel 4 Television Corporation Plc* [1994] E.M.L.R. 1. Although the film was arguably only reviewed in order to facilitate criticism of the plaintiff's decision to withdraw the work from circulation, there was still a review of the film, and the review of the film and the criticism of the decision not to allow the film to be shown in the United Kingdom were inseparable.

[87] *Ashdown v Telegraph Group Ltd*, [2001] EWCA Civ 1142; [2002] Ch.149 (no criticism or review of the copyright work, only of the actions of certain individuals); *Banier v News Group Newspapers Ltd* [1997] F.S.R. 812 (no defence of fair dealing for the purposes of criticism or review when a newspaper copied a rival's photograph since the defendant's purpose had been to report a news story).

[88] *Sillitoe v Mcgraw Hill Book Co.* [1983] F.S.R. 545, and see para. 9–53 *et seq.*, below.

[89] CDPA 1988, s.30(1); the position under the 1956 Act was the same: Copyright Act 1956, s.6(2).

[90] s.30(1). Fair dealing with a performance for the purpose of criticism or review, of that or another performance, will also not infringe any separate rights in the performance, s.189 and Sch.2, para.2.

[91] For an exploration of the different meanings attached to these and other terms see Gredley and Maniatis, "Parody: A Fatal Attraction? Part 1: The Nature of Parody and its Treatment in Copyright" [1997] 7 E.I.P.R. 339.

the existing United Kingdom law of criticism or review already permits such acts. As parody depends upon recognition of the work being parodied, the substantial part requirement will sometimes be satisfied.[92] Where this is the case the parody will infringe unless the dealing falls within one of the statutory exceptions, the most likely being fair dealing for the purpose of criticism or review. This issue has yet to be addressed directly by the courts in the United Kingdom,[93] but in the United States it is clear that a parody may fall within the fair use doctrine as a form of criticism.[94] However, even if parody were to be accepted as a form of criticism two difficulties would remain. First, there is the requirement of sufficient acknowledgment (see paragraph 9–43, below). Whilst such acknowledgment is by no means impossible,[95] it runs counter to ordinary publishing practice and imposes a rather artificial obligation on the parodist, as one of the benchmarks against which a parody can be judged is its success in making a connection with the work being parodied without any form of express reference. Moreover, the author of the work being parodied may well prefer not to be identified. The second obstacle is the possibility that the parody may amount to a derogatory treatment of the work,[96] as to which there is no fair dealing defence. The possibility of a derogatory treatment claim exists despite the fact that although a parody may be prejudicial to an author's reputation in a broad sense, it will not usually be presented as the creation of the author and is, therefore, much closer to an adverse review than to a case where a work is altered in order to meet some commercial objective.

Work must have been made available to the public. It has been seen that the   **9–42** Article 5(3)(d) of the Information Society Directive limits the permitted exception to criticism or review relating to subject-matter which has already been lawfully made available to the public, and the 1988 has had to be amended to comply with this requirement. The Government seems to have taken the view, correctly it is suggested, that the Directive prohibits substantial use of a work which has not been made available to the public for criticism or review of *that* work or another work (whether publicly available or not), but not use of a work which is publicly

---

[92] See paras 7–30 and 7–39, above, as the substantial part test in relation to infringement by parody. There is unlikely to be taking of a substantial part where there is a mere "conjuring up" of the work. See Gredley and Maniatis, "Parody: A Fatal Attraction? Part 1: The Nature of Parody and its Treatment in Copyright" [1997] 7 E.I.P.R. 339. In general, a substantial part of the work is much more likely to be taken when parodying an artistic work or a musical work than when parodying a literary work.

[93] In *Williamson Music v The Pearson Partnership Ltd* [1987] F.S.R. 97, the point seems to have been accepted as a possibility.

[94] In particular, see the judgment of the Supreme Court in *Campbell v Acuff-Rose Music, Inc.* (1994) 127 L. Ed 2d 500. Also see Nimmer, *Nimmer on Copyright* (Matthew Bender, New York, 1981) pp.13–212 to 13–230. More generally, see *The Parody Defence to Copyright Infringement: Productive Fair Use After Betamax*, (1984) 97 Harv. L. Rev. 1395. For a more critical view of parodies see Dube J. in *MCA Canada Ltd-MCA Canada Ltee et al. v Gillberry & Hawke Advertising Agency Ltd* (1976) 28 C.P.R. (2d) 52. If parody were to be accepted as a form of criticism then in one respect U.K. law would prove to be more flexible than its American counterpart. In some US cases a distinction has been drawn between cases where a work itself is parodied and cases of satire, where part of a work is used to provide a critique of individuals or institutions or society in general: *Metro-Goldwyn-Mayer, Inc. v Showcase Atlanta Coop. Productions Inc.* (1979) 479 F. Supp. 351; *MCA Inc. v Wilson* (1981) 677 F.2d 180; *Campbell v Acuff-Rose Music, Inc.* (1994) 127 L. Ed 2d 500 (*per* Justice Kennedy, concurring). The broad definition of criticism which has been adopted in the United Kingdom which allows the reviewer to look "behind" a work (see para. 9–38, above), would seem to make it more likely that some cases of satire would also fall within the fair dealing defence.

[95] Both the author and the publisher were acknowledged in *Campbell v Acuff-Rose Music, Inc.* (1994) 127 L. Ed 2d 500.

[96] See CDPA 1988, ss.80, 89 and see paras 11–41 *et seq.*, below, and Gredley and Maniatis, "Parody: A Fatal Attraction? Part 1: The Nature of Parody and its Treatment in Copyright" [1997] 7 E.I.P.R. 339. The author would have to establish that there was an addition to, deletion from or alteration to or adaptation of the work or some part of the work and that the parody distorted or mutilated the work or was otherwise prejudicial to his reputation.

available for the purposes of criticism or review of another work which is not publicly available.

The Act therefore now states that fair dealing with a work for the purposes of criticism or review is only permissible where the work has been made available to the public. For this purpose, a work is to be regarded as having been made available to the public if it has been made available by any means, including (a) the issue of copies to the public; (b) making the work available by means of an electronic retrieval system; (c) the rental or lending of copies of the work to the public; (d) the performance, exhibition, playing or showing of the work in public; (e) the communication to the public of the work.[97] The possibility of the right to freedom of expression under the Human Rights Act 1998 overriding the 1988 Act in the case of works not made available to the public has already been noted.[98]

9–43   **Sufficient acknowledgment.** As enacted, the 1988 Act required that any dealing with a work for the purpose of criticism or review had to be accompanied by a "sufficient acknowledgment".[99] No amendment was made to this provision on implementation of the Information Society Directive, which requires that in the case of criticism or review of a work the source, including the author's name, be indicated, unless this turns out to be impossible.[1] The meaning of "sufficient acknowledgment" and the extent to which this differs from the terms of the Directive have already been considered.[2]

D. REPORTING CURRENT EVENTS

9–44   **Introduction.** It has always been accepted that fair use of a work should be allowed for the purposes of news reporting and since the 1911 Act this has had statutory recognition.[3] The defence is intended to protect the role of the media in informing the public about matters of current concern to the public.[4] In many cases, of course, a news reporting exception is unnecessary since current events can be reported without infringing copyright, as the law of copyright does not confer a monopoly over a particular set of facts.[5] This would be to ignore, however, the authority which can be given to a news story by a quotation from an original document and thus the public interest in learning of the very words used.[6]

---

[97] CDPA 1988, s.30(1A), which also provides that in determining whether a work has been made available to the public no account is to be taken of any unauthorised act .

[98] See para. 9–22, below.

[99] CDPA 1988, s.30(1). This requirement was first introduced in the 1956 Act in order to bring the position in the United Kingdom in line with Art.10 of the Berne Convention: Report of the Copyright Committee, 1952 (Cm. 8662), para.42. Art.10 of the Berne Convention is itself intended to ensure protection for the author's paternity right: Ricketson, *The Berne Convention for the Protection of Literary and Artistic Works 1886–1986* (Kluwer, London, 1987) p.500. No acknowledgment or attribution of authorship was required under s.2(1)(i) of the 1911 Act: *Johnstone v Bernard Jones Publications Ltd* [1938] Ch. 599 at 606.

[1] Information Society Directive, 2001/29, Art.5(3)(d).

[2] See para. 9–29, below.

[3] Copyright Act 1911, s.2(1)(i), where the permitted act was "newspaper summary".

[4] *Ashdown v Telegraph Group Ltd* [2001] EWCA Civ 1142 [2--2] Ch.149. It was also observed there that a system of law whereby the media should have to pay compensation for the right to use a work might discourage the participation by the press in matters of public concern, applying the reasoning of *Bladet Tromso v Norway* [1999] 29 E.H.R.R. 125 and *Tolstoy Miloslavsky v United Kingdom* [1995] 20 E.H.R.R. 442. However, there has never been any question of applying a compulsory licence in this area. The important issue is the ability of the media to use material without the threat of an injunction.

[5] See paras 3--19 and 7--40, above.

[6] *Ashdown v Telegraph Group Ltd* [2001] EWCA Civ 1142 [2002] Ch.149.

Moreover, such quotations place readers in a better position to make their own judgment, rather than relying upon that of the journalist.[7]

The Berne Convention. The various provisions of the Berne Convention have already been noted.[8]   9–45

The Information Society Directive. Articles 5(3)(c) and (4) of the Information   9–46
Society Directive permit Member States to provide an exception to the reproduction, distribution and communication to the public rights in the case of use of works or other subject-matter in connection with the reporting of current events, to the extent justified by the informatory purpose and as long as the source, including the author's name, is indicated, unless this turns out to be impossible.[9] The Act needed only a slight amendment to the sufficient aknowledgement requirement in order for it to comply with the Directive.

The 1988 Act. The Act provides that fair dealing with a work (other than a   9–47
photograph) for the purpose of reporting current events does not infringe any copyright in the work provided that it is accompanied by a sufficient acknowledgment,[10] except where the reporting of current events is by means of a sound recording, film or broadcast, when no such acknowledgment is required where this would be impossible for reasons of practicality or otherwise.[11]

For the purpose of reporting current events. The general approach to the   9–48
construction of this provision has already been considered:[12] it is clear that the expression will be construed liberally. Substituting other expressions for "current events", such as "current affairs" or "news" does not provide much assistance.[13] Current events are not confined to specific and very recent happenings,[14] particularly where the ramifications of the event continue to be a matter of public debate and concern.[15] The exception is not confined to the reporting of current events in a general news programme and includes, for example, the reporting of sports events in a sports news bulletin.[16] The work itself need not be "current", provided that it is used properly to report current events.[17] The events reported must, however, be current and not just a newsworthy matter of history, so that a newspaper was not able to rely on this section in using the death of the Duchess

---

[7] For a general discussion of the problems in this area see Johnston, "Copyright and Freedom of the Media: A Modest Proposal" [1996] 1 E.I.P.R. 6.

[8] See para. 9–20, above.

[9] An exception to the distribution right is permitted only to the extent justified by the purpose of the authorised act of reproduction: Art.5(4). Art.5(3)(c) also provides for a more restricted exception in the case of reproduction by the press, communication to the public or making available of published articles on current economic, political or religious topics or of broadcast works or other subject-matter of the same character, in cases where such use is not expressly reserved, and as long as the source, including the author's name, is indicated.

[10] CDPA 1988, s.30(2).

[11] s.30(3).

[12] See para. 9–23, above.

[13] *Pro Sieben Media AG v Carlton UK Television Ltd* [1999] 1 W.L.R. 605; [1999] F.S.R. 610, CA.

[14] *Pro Sieben Media AG v Carlton UK Television Ltd* [1999] 1 W.L.R. 605; [1999] F.S.R. 610.

[15] *Ashdown v Telegraph Group Ltd* [2001] EWCA Civ 1142; [2002] Ch.149 (where the "event" consisted of a meeting which had taken place two years previously; while the issues identified by the defendant in its articles might not themselves have been "events", the existence of those issues could help to demonstrate the continuing public interest in the meeting). In *Hyde Park Residence Ltd v Yelland* [2001] Ch.143; [1999] R.P.C. 655; [2000] E.M.L.R. 363, the Court of Appeal considered that it was arguable that the events surrounding the death of Diana Princess of Wales were still current a year later, at a time when the investigation into the death was still continuing.

[16] *British Broadcasting Corp. v British Satellite Broadcasting* [1992] Ch. 141 and see the Broadcasting Act 1996, s.137 (see para. 9–51, below).

[17] *Associated Newspapers Group plc v News Group Newspapers Ltd* [1986] R.P.C. 515.

of Windsor as an excuse to reprint correspondence.[18] The fact that a work has recently been published will not, of itself, mean that it is fair to reproduce it for the purposes of commenting on that fact[19] but sometimes the media coverage of an event may itself be a current event which it is fair to report[20] although this will often be a "bootstraps" argument of little merit.[21] In deciding whether the work is being used for this purpose, a useful test may be whether it is reasonably necessary to refer to the work in order to deal adequately with the events in question.[22] The work must be used for "reporting current events" and not for editorial or other purposes.[23] It would seem that the "reporting" must consist of reporting to the public at large in some general sense and not the reporting to a closed circle for some commercial purpose.[24]

9–49   **Photographs.** As has been seen, photographs are excluded from the ambit of the permitted act. The reason for this is that it was said that use of photographs in the context of news reporting could never be fair, such that the matter needed to be put beyond doubt.[25] It is suggested, however, that while many of the situations which would cause concern, such as the use by newspapers of a rival's photograph, would in any event probably not be fair (see paragraph 9–53, below), it would have been preferable to leave the matter open to allow for the exceptional case.[26]

9–50   **The Human Rights Act.** It has already been noted[27] that the limitation in the fair dealing provision to the reporting of *current events,* and the exclusion of photographs from the ambit of section 30(2), may be the occasion, in a rare case, for the Article 10 right to freedom of expression overriding the provisions of the 1988 Act.

9–51   **Avoidance of certain terms relating to news reporting.** As has been seen,[28] in general the permitted acts only relate to the question of copyright infringement and do not affect any other right or obligation. It is therefore possible to exclude

---

[18] *Associated Newspapers Group plc v News Group Newspapers Ltd* [1986] R.P.C. 515

[19] *Associated Newspapers Group plc v News Group Newspapers Ltd* [1986] R.P.C. 515

[20] *Newspaper Licensing Agency Ltd v Marks and Spencer plc* [2001] Ch. 257; [2001] R.P.C. 76, CA, Peter Gibson L.J. disagreeing); *Pro Sieben Media AG v Carlton UK Television Ltd* [1999] 1 W.L.R. 605, [1999] F.S.R. 610 (volume and intensity of media interest sufficient to bring the media coverage itself within the ambit of the current events which were being reported); *Hyde Park Residence Ltd v Yelland* [2001] Ch.143, [1999] R.P.C. 655 (media coverage generated by statements made by Mr Al Fayed concerning the relationship between his son and Diana Princess of Wales); *PCR Ltd v Dow Jones Telerate Ltd* [1998] F.S.R. 170 (defendant's articles reported the fact that the plaintiff's commodity report had been published and that it had affected the market; held, the defendant's articles were written for the purpose of reporting current events).

[21] *Ashdown v Telegraph Group Ltd* [2001] EWCA Civ 1142 [2002] Ch.149.

[22] *Associated Newspapers Group plc v News Group Newspapers Ltd* [1986] R.P.C. 515 at 519.

[23] *Hyde Park Residence Ltd v Yelland* [2001] Ch. 143; [1999] R.P.C. 655.

[24] *Newspaper Licensing Agency Ltd v Marks and Spencer plc* [2001] Ch. 257; [2001] R.P.C. 76, CA, *per* Peter Gibson L.J.: Chadwick L.J. disagreed. Mance L.J. declined to express a concluded view, but indicated that it was difficult to extend the exception to the reporting of current events for private commercial purposes, and that although in some instances private reporting might be in the public interest (for example reporting to the Cabinet or other official bodies), an extension of the exception to all reporting for any purpose was "debatable".

[25] See next note.

[26] This was in fact the Government's original intention. In the event, resistance from the photographic community and the National Union of Journalists proved such that the Government thought better of it: *Hansard*, HL Vol.501, cols 236–237. Note that a photograph which is part of a film is not to be regarded as a photograph under the 1988 Act: CDPA 1988, s.4(2). *cf. Barker Motion Photography Ltd v Hulton and Co. Ltd* (1912) 28 T.L.R. 496. Also see *Banier v News Group Newspapers Ltd* [1997] F.S.R. 812: no defence of fair dealing for the purposes of criticism or review when a newspaper copied a rival's photograph since the defendant's purpose had been to report a news story.

[27] See para. 9–22, above.

[28] See para. 9–12, above.

the operation of the permitted acts contractually. However, in order to ensure that extracts of sports programmes remain available for news reporting purposes, a more restricted rule applies to broadcasts. The Broadcasting Act 1996 thus provides that a provision in an agreement is void in so far as it purports to prohibit or restrict the communication to the publicof any visual images taken from a broadcast, where the communication is covered by fair dealing for the purpose of reporting current events.[29]

Sufficient acknowledgment. As originally enacted, the 1988 Act required sufficient acknowledgment except where the news reporting was by means of a sound recording, film or broadcast. This exception reflected the practical difficulties which it was thought broadcasters and others might experience in identifying the work in question in the time available to them.[30] The Information Society Directive, however, requires acknowledgment in all circumstances in the context of reporting current events, unless this "turns out to be impossible",[31] and so the Act needed amendment. The result is something of a mess. The basic requirement of sufficient acknowledgment has been left unchanged but in the case of the reporting of current events by means of a sound recording, film or broadcast the Act now states that no acknowledgment is required where this would be impossible for reasons of practicaly or otherwise. The meaning of "sufficient acknowledgment" and the other implications of these requirements have already been considered.[32] In the case of the reporting of current events, the "author" of the work used may well be a company,[33] and in such a case the acknowledgment can properly take the form of the name by which the company is known to the intended readership or audience, rather than the full company name,[34] or even a simple logo.[35]

9–52

E. THE CONCEPT OF FAIRNESS

Introduction. The expression "fair dealing" was also used in the1956 and 1911 Acts. In addition to the above categories of dealing, the issue of fair dealing now has also to be considered in the context of educational use.[36] Although rather different policy considerations are involved with the various different fair dealing provisions, namely non-commercial research, private study, criticism, review, the reporting of current events and educational use, similar criteria of "fairness" are employed in considering whether the use in question amounts to "fair" dealing.[37] Unlike the position in the United States, there are no statutory criteria

9–53

---

[29] Broadcasting Act 1996, s.137 as amended by SI 2003/2498. This provision should be read alongside the provisions of that Act relating to listed events: ss.97–105.

[30] *Hansard*, HL Vol.491, cols 115–116.

[31] Information Society Directive, 2001/29, Art.5(3)(c).

[32] See para. 9–29, above.

[33] As in the case of sound recordings, films, broadcasts and typrographical arrangements of published editions.

[34] *Newspaper Licensing Agency Ltd v Marks and Spencer plc* [2001] Ch.257 (CA); [1999] R.P.C. 536 CA (newspaper publisher was sufficiently identified by the name of the newspaper which it published and with which it was identified in the public mind, rather than its actual name).

[35] *Pro Sieben Media AG v Carlton UK Television Ltd* [1999] 1 W.L.R. 605; [1999] F.S.R. 610 (the claimant sufficiently identified by its logo, consisting of a stylised figure 7, particularly in the light of the facts that it was the means by which it was accustomed to identify itself and the use of the full, correct name (Pro Sieben Media AG) would have been unlikely to have any particular significance to the bulk of the audience).

[36] Under CDPA 1988, s.32(2A) copyright in specified works is not infringed by copying in the course of instruction or of preparation for instruction, provided, amongst other things, the copying is fair dealing with the work. See para. 9–92, below.

[37] See *British Broadcasting Corp. v British Satellite Broadcasting* [1992] Ch.141, in particular, at 148.

of "fairness" under United Kingdom copyright law,[38] although the test that has been judicially developed incorporates a number of similar considerations. As already noted,[39] in cases where the dealing brings into play the Article 10 right to freedom of expression, pre-Human Rights Act cases as to what amounts to fair dealing should not be applied inflexibly. Considerations of public interest are paramount and it should be asked whether the facts of the case are such that the importance of freedom of expression outweighs the conventional considerations established by the earlier authorities.[40]

9–54   **An objective test.** Fairness should be judged by the objective standard of whether a fair-minded and honest person would have dealt with the copyright work in the manner in which the defendant did, for the relevant purposes.[41] Ultimately the decision must be a matter of impression.[42]

9–55   **Relevant considerations.** Relevant factors to be taken into account in judging whether the dealing was fair have been identified in various cases. None is determinative and the weight to be attached to them will vary from case to case. In particular, the various factors will carry different weight according to the type of dealing. Cases of fair dealing for purposes of criticism, review and the reporting of current events usually raise more difficult problems than cases of non-commerical research and private study. The three most important factors have been identified to be:[43]

     (1) The degree to which the alleged infringing use competes with exploitation of the copyright work by the owner. This is likely to be a most important factorl. Clearly, if a criticism or review of a work competes with it in the sense that the criticism or review will act as an acceptable substitute to the public, this will highly relevant. The test should be understood as referring not just to competition with the actual form of media in which the claimant exploits his work but any form of activity which potentially affects the value of the copyright work.[44] There mere existence of commercial rivalry is not conclusive, however. So, even where the claimant and defendant were both involved in the broadcasting of sports programmes their trade rivalry did not prevent the defendant's use of short

---

[38] *cf.* United States Copyright Act 1976, 17 U.S.C., s.107.

[39] See para. 9–22, above.

[40] *Ashdown v Telegraph Group Ltd* [2001] EWCA Civ 1142; [2002] Ch.149: .

[41] *Hyde Park Residence Ltd v Yelland* [2001] Ch.143 [1999] R.P.C. 655, applied in *Newspaper Licensing Agency Ltd v Marks and Spencer plc* [2001] Ch. 257 [2001] R.P.C. 76, CA.

[42] *Hubbard v Vosper* [1972] 2 Q.B. 84 at 92–95. Also see *Johnstone v Bernard Jones Publication* [1938] Ch.599.

[43] *Ashdown v Telegraph Group Ltd* [2001] EXCA Civ 1142; [2002] Ch.149. These correspond to the three factors identified by Lord Denning MR in *Hubbard v Vosper* [1972] 2 Q.B. 84, in the more limited context of fair dealing for the purposes of criticism or review, namely, (1) the number and the extent of the quotations and the extracts; (2) the use made of the quotations and the extracts: if they have been used for a rival purpose then that may well be unfair; (3) the proportion of the work consisting of quotations and extracts as compared with the proportion of the work consisting of comment and analysis. *cf.* United States Copyright Act 1976, U.S.C. 17, s.107 which lists four factors to be taken into consideration when deciding whether a use is fair: (1) The purpose and character of the use, including whether such use is of a commercial nature or is for non-profit educational purposes; (2) The nature of the copyrighted work; (3) The amount and substantiality of the portion used in relation to the copyrighted work as a whole; and (4) The effect of the use upon the potential market for or value of the copyrighted work.

[44] Thus contrast *Pro Sieben Media AG v Carlton UK Television Ltd* [1999] 1 W.L.R. 605; [1999] F.S.R. 610 (defendant's television programme criticising chequebook journalism did not in any real sense represent unfair competition with the claimant's exploitation of its rights) with *Ashdown v Telegraph Group Ltd* [2001] EWCA Civ 1142;; [2002] Ch.149 (the defendant's publication destroyed a part of the value of the claimant's memoirs which it had been his intention to sell).

THE FAIR DEALING PROVISIONS

extracts from some of the claimant's programmes being fair.[45] The mere fact that, in the case of critism, review or reporting of current events, the use is for a commercial purpose[46] clearly does not prevent the dealing from being fair.[47]

(2) Whether the work has been published or not. If the work is unpublished, any dealing is unlikely to be fair.[48] Since the amendment made to the 1988 Act to remove "unpublished" works altogether from ambit of fair dealing for the purposes of criticism or review,[49] this factor is only of relevance in cases of non-commercial research, private study, the reporting of current events and educational use. It seems that this principle may not be as relevant in the case of government documents.[50] Furthermore, even if a work has not been published to the world at large, it may have been circulated to a sufficiently wide circle so that it is fair to publish sections of it by way of reporting current events.[51]

(3) The extent of the use and the importance of what has been taken. In many cases this will be a highly important factor,[52] particularly if the defendant has taken the most interesting and valuable part from the claimant's work.[53] In most cases there will a grey area between the threshold of substantial part (below which no infringement occurs in any event) and a use which is so substantial as to be unfair. Here, a useful test may be whether it was necessary to use as much as the defendant did for the relevant purpose.[54] This reasoning should not be used, however, to attempt pare off "unnecessary" parts from defendant's work to make a case of unfair use: there will be no precise boundary line between what is fair and unfair. Occasionally, it may be fair to reproduce the whole of a work, particularly if it is very short[55] and it may well be fair to copy the whole of

---

[45] *British Broadcasting Corp. v British Satellite Broadcasting* [1992] Ch.141.

[46] In the case of research or private study of course, the fact that the dealing is for a commericial purpose will take it outside the permitted act provisions altogether.

[47] Although note that in *Newspaper Licensing Agency Ltd v Marks and Spencer plc* [2001] Ch. 257; [2001] R.P.C. 76 Chadwick L.J. considered that a dealing by a person for his own commercial advantage, and to the actual or potential commercial disadvantage of the copyright owner, would not be fair dealing unless there was some overriding element of public advantage which justified the subordination of the rights of the copyright owner. Peter Gibson L.J. considered that the dealing in that case (an internal news clippings service) would have been fair, since the commercial motives and intentions of the defendant could not be impugned and it was not in competition with the claimant, for example, by selling the material to others.

[48] *Ashdown v Telegraph Group Ltd* [2001] EWCA Civ 1142; [2002] Ch.149. In *British Oxygen Company Ltd v Liquid Air Ltd* [1925] Ch. 383 at 393, it was said that any dealing which resulted in publication of a previously unpublished document could not be fair, but this clearly goes too far. It is highly relevant factor only: *Beloff v Pressdram* [1973] 1 All E.R. 241 at 263.

[49] See para. 9–36, above. Strictly, it is where a work has not been "made available to the public" that the permitted act no longer applies.

[50] *Commonwealth of Australia v John Fairfax and Sons Ltd* [1981] 55 A.L.J.R. 45 at 50.

[51] *Hubbard v Vosper* [1972] 2 Q.B. 84 (although that case was concerned with criticism or review).

[52] See also as to this factor, *Pro Sieben Media AG v Carlton UK Television Ltd* [1999] 1 W.L.R. 605; [1999] F.S.R. 610, CA. It was said in *Independent Television Publications v Time Out* [1984] F.S.R. 64 at 75, that once it is established that a substantial part of a work has been taken then no defence of fair dealing will be likely to succeed, but this is clearly wrong as a matter of principle.

[53] See also the emphasis given by Mance L.J. to the intrinsic worth or merit of the work in question in *Hyde Park Residence Ltd v Yelland* [2001] Ch.143; [1999] R.P.C. 655 at 392.

[54] *PCR Ltd v Dow Jones Telerate Ltd* [1998] F.S.R. 170; *Associated Newspapers Group plc v News Group Newspapers Ltd* [1986] R.P.C. 515.

[55] See Megaw L.J. in *Hubbard v Vosper* [1972] 2 Q.B. 84 at 98 who gives the melancholy example of a parishioner who, wishing to complain about an epitaph on a tombstone, sets it out in full in a letter to the parish magazine.

a longer work if this is preparatory to making a decision as to which parts to use for a relevant dealing.[56]

Other relevant factors may be:

(4) The motives of the alleged infringer: for example, was the use merely dressed up in the guise of criticism or review?[57]

(5) The purpose of the use: was the use necessary at all to make the point in question?[58]

(6) The fact that the copy of a previously unpublished work was obtained by the defendant by theft or other misappropriation.[59] Where the work has previously been published, the method used to obtain the copy appears to be of little relevance.[60]

F. GENERAL PROVISIONS: INCIDENTAL INCLUSION OF COPYRIGHT MATERIAL

9–56   **Introduction.** Section 31 of the Act provides that the copyright in a work is not infringed by its incidental inclusion in an artistic work, sound recording, film or broadcast.[61] Where, by virtue of these provisions, the making of a copy was not an infringement of copyright in a work, then the issue to the public of such copies, or the playing, showing or broadcasting of anything whose making was not an infringement of copyright, will not infringe the copyright in the work either.[62]

There would seem to be three justifications for such a provision. First, in relation to photographers, film makers and broadcasters, it is justifiable on the grounds that it will often be very difficult to obtain permission from the owners of all the works reproduced in the photograph, film or broadcast. Consider the live broadcast of a sporting event. Without such a provision a broadcaster might infringe copyright by broadcasting a sound recording which is being played over the public address system or by including shots of an advertising hoarding.[63] A second justification is that the incidental use of a work will in any event not detract from the market for the original and in certain circumstances may even enhance it. This point has been accepted in a number of United States American cases, with the result that incidental inclusion has been held to fall within the fair use defence, there being no specific provisions in the UNited States Act dealing with this matter.[64] The third justification for such a provision is that it allows film makers and broadcasters a degree of artistic freedom by allowing them to set the

---

[56] *Pro Sieben Media AG v Carlton UK Television Ltd* [1999] 1 W.L.R. 605; [1999] F.S.R. 610; *Time Warner Entertainment Ltd v Channel 4 Television Corporation Plc*, [1994] E.M.L.R. 1. Also see *Television New Zealand v Newsmonitor Services Ltd* (1993) 27 I.P.R. 441 (High Ct of New Zealand) at 467: "In my view it is a fair dealing with a television broadcast to tape the whole program for the purpose of extracting material from it if that extraction does not go beyond the bounds of fair dealing and if the tape is not used for any other purpose and is then destroyed".

[57] *Pro Sieben Media AG v Carlton UK Television Ltd* [1999] 1 W.L.R. 605; [1999] F.S.R. 610.

[58] *Hyde Park Residence Ltd v Yelland* [2001] Ch.143; [1999] R.P.C. 655 (use of stills from video footage of Princess Diana not necessary to make the point).

[59] *Hyde Park Residence Ltd v Yelland* [2001] Ch.143; [1999] R.P.C. 655, *per* Mance L.J. at 393; *Ashdown v Telegraph Group Ltd* [2001] EWCA Civ 1142; [2002] Ch.149; *Beloff v Pressdram* [1973] 1 All E.R. 241.

[60] *Time Warner Entertainment Ltd v Channel 4 Television Corporation Plc* [1994] E.M.L.R. 1.

[61] The 1956 Act (which only applied to artistic works) was more restrictive in that it provided that there was no infringement of copyright if the work's inclusion "is only by way of background or is otherwise only incidental to the principal matters represented". Copyright Act 1956, s.9(5).

[62] CDPA 1988, s.31(2).

[63] See *Hansard*, HL Vol.491, col.123. Normally, of course, the intention of the advertiser will have been to have the hoarding included in the broadcast.

[64] See further, *Mura v Columbia Broadcasting Systems Inc.* (1965) 245 F. Supp. 587; *Italian Book Corp. v American Broadcasting Cos* (1978) 458 F. Supp. 65.

activities of their characters in a wide variety of settings. Thus no special permission is needed to film against the background of a play being performed in a theatre.[65] Indeed without some form of exception an artist, photographer, film maker or broadcaster could not even include images of a building in his work without infringing the architect's copyright.[66] Overall, these provisions have a great deal of importance for photographers, advertisers, film makers and broadcasters.

Berne Convention. The permitted act of incidental inclusion partly corresponds to Article 10 *bis*(2) of the Berne Convention. This Article states that it is for individual countries "to determine the conditions under which, for the purpose of reporting current events by means of photography, cinematography, broadcasting or communications to the public by wire, literary or artistic works seen or heard in the course of the event may, to the extent justified by the informatory purpose, be reproduced and made and available to the public". Section 31 is clearly wider than this, and presumably is justified under the general exception for special cases permitted by Article 9(2).[67] **9–57**

The Information Society Directive. The Directive permits Member States to provide an exception to the reproduction, distribution and communication to the public rights in the case of the incidental inclusion of a work or other subject-matter in other material.[68] This was consistent with the existing provisions of the 1988 Act and no amendment was therefore required, other than that brought about by the changed definition of broadcasting and the new right of communication to the public. **9–58**

Incidental. Special provision is made for what constitutes incidental inclusion in the case of a musical work but, apart from this, the word "incidental" is an ordinary descriptive English word and was deliberately left undefined in the Act.[69] It has been said that it is impossible to provide a definition that will be satisfactory for all purposes: what is incidental will depend on all the circumstances of the case.[70] Resort should not therefore be had to dictionaries, *Hansard*, the 1956 Act or substitute words or expressions.[71] "Incidental" in this context does not mean unintentional,[72] and indeed is not confined to unintentional or non-deliberate inclusion. Nor is a valid distinction to be made between use of a copyright work which is "incidental" and that which is "integral" to the work in which it is included, and there is no necessary dichotomy between the two in this context. Where, for example, an artistic work appears in a photograph because it is part of the setting in which the photographer finds his subject, it will necessarily appear in the photograph unless edited out, and in that sense may be said to be integral. But that does mean that its inclusion either is, or is not, incidental. The only question is whether the inclusion of the copyright work in the relevant **9–59**

---

[65] See also Sch.2, para.3(1): no infringement of rights in the performance.
[66] But also see s.62.
[67] See para. 9–02, above.
[68] Information Society Directive, 2001/29, Arts 5(3)(i), (4). The exception to the distribution right is permitted only to the extent justified by the purpose of the authorised act of reproduction: Art.5(4).
[69] *The Football Association Premier League Ltd v Panini UK Ltd* [2003] EWCA Civ. 995.
[70] *The Football Association Premier League Ltd v Panini UK Ltd* [2003] EWCA Civ. 995.
[71] *The Football Association Premier League Ltd v Panini UK Ltd* [2003] EWCA Civ. 995. The decision in *IPC Magazines Ltd v MGN Ltd* [1998] F.S.R. 431, that the word "incidental" bears its ordinary dictionary meaning of casual, inessential, subordinate, or merely background, *per* the Oxford Dictionary, must presumably be regarded as over-elaborate, although not wrong as such.
[72] *The Football Association Premier League Ltd v Panini UK Ltd* [2003] EWCA Civ. 995.This is clear from CDPA 1988, s.31(3), as to which, see para. 9–62, below.

artistic work, sound recording, film or broadcast was or was not incidental, and that turns on the question: why, having regard to the circumstances in which the relevant work was made, was the copyright work included?[73] Depending on the circumstances, consideration can be given not only to the aesthetic reasons for including it but also to the commercial ones. This is particularly so where the work was made primarily for commercial reasons.[74] For this purpose it will be irrelevant to consider the subjective intentions of the person creating the work in which the copyright work is included.[75]

9–60   **The relevant acts.** In relation to incidental inclusion it may be particularly important to focus on the relevant acts which are alleged to be an infringement. In a case in which articles or things have been made and then issued to the public or disseminated in some other way, such acts being the alleged infringing acts, it is important (a) to examine the circumstances when these things or articles were made, and (b) whether or not the articles or things are artistic works, sound recordings, films or broadcasts. As to (a), it is only the circumstances which existed at the time when the things were made which are relevant to the question of incidental inclusion, and not those which existed at the time of some antecedent act, for example when a preparatory copy of the copyright work was first made. As to (b), it is only where the copyright work is incidentally included in one of these categories of work that the exception in section 31 applies. Thus it should be noted, for example, that where artistic works are published as part of a newspaper, magazine, etc. the whole publication may be a compilation and thus a literary work.[76] The individual images as they appear in the compilation are artistic works in their own right but this does not prevent the entirety being a compilation. To the extent that the publication is a compilation it would seem that the section cannot apply so as to permit acts done in relation to the compilation.[77]

---

[73] *The Football Association Premier League Ltd v Panini UK Ltd* [2003] EWCA Civ. 995.

[74] *The Football Association Premier League Ltd v Panini UK Ltd* [2003] EWCA Civ. 995. Note also the suggestion in *IPC Magazines Ltd v MGN Ltd* [1998] F.S.R. 431, that it may be helpful to assess the impact of the defendant's work without the presence of the claimant's. There, the defendant had reproduced the front cover of the claimant's magazine (a copyright work) for the purposes of a comparative advertisement for its own magazine in a television programme. It was held that the inclusion was not incidental: the impact of the advertisement would have been lost entirely if the front cover of the claimant's magazine had not been used. Its inclusion was an essential and important feature of the advertisement.

[75] *The Football Association Premier League Ltd v Panini UK Ltd* [2003] EWCA Civ. 995, *per* Chadwick L.J. at para.27 and Mummery L.J. at para.39, where it was considered irrelevant to consider what might have been in the mind of the employee making the work or of those to whom it was distributed. In *IPC Magazines Ltd v MGN Ltd* [1998] F.S.R. 431 it was also held that whether or not the inclusion was "incidental" was an objective question, in the sense that it was not relevant to call evidence of the intentions of the defendant or of the perceptions of those who may have seen the use made. A different view was taken at first instance in *Panini* [2002] EWHC 2779 (Ch), namely that the question might be partly subjective and partly objective, on the grounds that for the purposes of CPDA 1988, s.31(3) (see para. 9–60, below) it is a relevant consideration that the work was deliberately included, a subjective matter, and that it would be odd if the test differed between the two subsections. This approach must presumably be regarded as having been overruled by the Court of Appeal although it is difficult to see why, if the intentions of the person making the subsidiary work are known, this should not be a relevant consideration.

[76] See para. 3–24, above.

[77] *The Football Association Premier League Ltd v Panini UK Ltd* [2003] EWCA Civ. 995, although the point was expressly left open by the Court of Appeal, not having been argued. The reason given for not advancing the argument was that it would be startling if a defence which was available in relation to the making and distribution of individual artistic works ceased when the artistic work was combined with other works. This reasoning was doubted by Mummery L.J. (who alone in the Court of Appeal dealt with the point), with good reason it is suggested. Any oddity in the result is due to the fact that the Act has prescribed a limited class of works to which the exception applies. Assuming that a collection of artistic works and written material can cor-

The decision in *Panini.* In *The Football Association Premier League Ltd v Pa-*   **9–61**
nini UK Ltd,[78] photographs of soccer players wearing their club strip were
reproduced in the form of stickers to be inserted into a collector's album, and in
the form of further images printed in the album itself. The photographs
reproduced the club or Premier League emblems or logos, which were copyright
artistic works. The stickers and albums had been made abroad and the acts of infringement alleged were (it seems) the importation of copies of copyright works,
and the offer for sale, sale and distribution of those copies to distributors, all with
the knowledge that they were infringing copies, and the authorisation of the issue
to the public by the distributors of the stickers and albums. The question identified by the Court of Appeal was whether the emblems and badges printed on the
players' strip had been incidentally included in the stickers and in the album
when those stickers and albums were made. This question was therefore to be
answered by examining the circumstances which existed at that time and not at
the time when the original photographs were made, or by asking what were the
subjective intentions, motives, views or states of mind of the photographer or the
employee producing the stickers or album, or the distributors or collectors. On
the facts, the answer to the question, namely, why were the logos and emblems
included in the stickers and the album, was self evident. The objective, when
creating the image of the player as it appeared on the sticker and the album was
to produce something that was attractive to the collector. As part of that objective
it was important that the players appeared in what was recognisably their
authentic club strip and for this purpose the club logos and emblems needed to be
apparent. The inclusion of these copyright works was essential to the object for
which the image of the players was produced on the stickers and albums.[79]

In *Panini* there was no claim brought against the original photographer alleging that the taking of his photographs had been an infringement.[80] If there had
been such a claim, then for the purposes of any defence under s.31(1) it would
clearly have been relevant to examine the circumstances as they existed at the
time when the photographs were made. It is possible (although highly unlikely in
a case such as *Panini*) that the making of the photographs would not have been
an infringement (because their inclusion then was incidental) but their reproduction on stickers would have been (because they were not incidentally included at
that stage), or vice versa. For example, the photographer might have chosen his
subject-matter for reasons having nothing to do with the included copyright material, and may even have been oblivious to it, but the eventual user might have
chosen the image precisely because the included material suited his commercial
purposes.

Musical works, etc. A musical work, words spoken or sung with music, and so   **9–62**
much of a sound recording or broadcast as includes a musical work or such words,
is not to be regarded as incidentally included if it is deliberately included.[81] Here,
it becomes relevant to know the subjective intentions of the maker of the artistic

rectly be described as a compilation (which, again, it is suggested is the case), there seems no
room for argument on the point.
[78] [2003] EWCA Civ. 995.
[79] As already noted, the collection of artistic works with other written material in the album was
arguably a compilation and thus a literary work. If this was correct, then whatever the position
may have been in relation to the stickers, acts relating to the making and distribution of the
albums as a whole could not have been within CDPA 1988, s.31. Since, however, the images
were clearly not incidentally included in the albums in any event, and the point had not been
argued, the question was left open by the Court of Appeal.
[80] See para.31 of the judgment.
[81] CDPA 1988, s.31(3). It seems that the phrase "words spoken or sung with music" must have been
intended to refer to words which are being spoken or sung to music at the time of their inclusion,
rather than referring to "a literary work consisting of words intended to be spoken or sung with
music", which is used in a later section of the Act (s.77(3)). However, this seems unnecessarily

work, sound recording, film or broadcast in which the work is included.[82] It would seem that the burden of proof lies on the person alleging infringement. This provision would prevent it from being argued that, for example, the intentional inclusion of background music (of whatever kind) in a film or television programme to add colour is not an infringement of copyright, but would generally allow the filming of an event at which music happens to be played if it was not the film-maker's intention that it should include music.[83] It may be relevant to ask: was the decision to start filming dictated to any extent by whether or not music was playing? This special provision was the result of lobbying by the music industry: other groups did not appear to see any grounds for concern, perhaps because they did not consider that non-musical works were likely to be used in the same way or to the same extent.[84] The extension of this exclusion to prevent the reproduction of a sound recording or broadcast in so far as either includes part of a musical work means that even if permission is obtained from the owner of the musical work for this use it would still not be possible to make a film with music deliberately playing in the background from a record player without obtaining the permission of the owner of the copyright in the sound recording.[85]

5. VISUAL IMPAIRMENT

(i) The core provisions

9–63   **Introduction.** Before the general implementation of the Information Society Directive, the 1988 Act had been prospectively amended by the Copyright (Visually Impaired Persons) Act 2002 to introduce a new series of permitted acts to enable versions of works to be made which are more accessible by visually impaired persons. Research had indicated that, with the exception of a few commercial publishers of large-print and audio books, most publishers do not find it economic to publish works adapted to suit the needs of visually impaired people. While rightholders do not on the whole insist on a royalty for the making of such versions, the process of obtaining consents on a case-by-case basis was often a long-drawn-out and thus expensive process. The fact that the making of these versions was not an activity which was of any real commercial significance for the majority of rightholders, and thus did not damage their economic interests, contributed to the shaping of the 2002 Act, which restricts the permitted acts to those of a non-commercial nature. Indeed, where publishers do make such versions available, the permitted act provisions do not apply. These permitted acts are thus designed to be compliant with the Berne 3-step test.[86] The Act came into force on October 31, 2003,[87] immediately after the Regulations implementing the

---

restrictive and would catch, for example, Tony Hancock's rendition of the words of a Government health campaign to the tune of *Lied Der Deutschen* (*The Blood Donor*, BBC Video, 1994).

[82] *The Football Association Premier League Ltd v Panini UK Ltd*, at first instance, [2002] EWHC 2779, Ch D.

[83] cf. *Hawkes and Son (London) Ltd v Paramount Film Service Ltd* [1934] Ch. 593 (newsreel of opening of the Royal Hospital School which included a snatch from "Colonel Bogey" played by a boys' band). Also see *Hansard*, HL Vol.491, cols 123, 124 and the Report of the Debates of the House of Commons Standing Committee E in 1988, cols 218–220.

[84] See *Hansard*, HL Vol.491, col.124.

[85] It is not clear why the nature of any underlying works should have a bearing on the way in which the sound recording or broadcast can be treated. It may be that this extension was intended to prevent a defendant from relying on the argument that it was the sound recording or broadcast that was deliberately included and not the underlying musical work.

[86] See paras 9–02, above and 24–33, below.

[87] The Copyright (Visually Impaired Persons) Act 2002 (Commencement) Order 2003 (SI 2003/

Directive.[88] The Act must be read in a way that is compatible with the requirements of the E-Commerce Regulations.[89]

The Information Society Directive. The Directive permits Member States to provide an exception to the reproduction right, to the communication to the public rights, and the distribution right, in the case of uses for the benefit of people with a disability, which are directly related to the disability and of a non-commercial nature, to the extent required by the specific disability.[90]   **9–64**

The core provisions. Sections 31A to 31F have three core provisions: (1) a provision enabling a "visually impaired person" to make an "accessible copy" of a work; (2) a provision enabling certain approved bodies to make accessible copies of a work for visually impaired persons; and (3) a provision enabling such approved bodies to hold "intermediate" copies of works, being copies necessarily created during the making of accessible copies. It can therefore be seen that there are two fundamental concepts: that of (a) a "visually impaired person" and (b) an "accessible" copy.   **9–65**

Visually impaired person. A visually impaired person is defined in section 31F(9) as a person: (1) who is blind; (2) who has an impairment of visual function which cannot be improved, by the use of corrective lenses, to a level that would normally be acceptable for reading without a special level or kind of light; (3) who is unable, through physical disability, to hold or manipulate a book; or (4) who is unable, through physical disability, to focus or move his eyes to the extent that would normally be acceptable for reading. The definition of a visually impaired person is therefore not restricted to persons whose visual functions are impaired. It extends, for example, to persons who cannot hold a book because of severe rheumatoid arthritis.   **9–66**

Accessible. The provisions are concerned with copies of works which are "accessible" to a visually impaired person. A copy of a copyright work is to be taken to be accessible to a visually impaired person only if it is as accessible to him as it would be if he were not visually impaired.[91]   **9–67**

Accessible copy. An accessible copy, in relation to a copyright work, is defined as meaning a version which provides improved access to the work for a visually impaired person.[92] From the use of the word "version" it follows that an accessible copy includes not only a version made by "copying" the work within the meaning of section 17(2) of the Act but also one by making an adaptation of the work within the meaning of section 21. Copying of a work could include the making of an enlarged photocopy or the making of a copy of a literary, dramatic or musical work in the form of a sound recording or film, such as a talking book, video cassette or DVD. The making of an adaptation of a work would include the   **9–68**

2499). For the background, see the Patent Office Consultation Paper (Copyright and Visually Impaired People, available at www.patent.gov.uk/about/consultations/index.htm).

[88] The Copyright (Visually Impaired Persons) Act 2002 (Commencement) Order 2003 (SI 2003/2499), para.2.

[89] The Electronic Commerce (EC Directive) (Extension) Regulations 2003 (SI 2003/115).

[90] See Information Society Directive, 2001/29, Arts 5(3)(b) and (4). The exception to the distribution right is permitted only to the extent justified by the purpose of the authorised act of reproduction: *ibid.* Note also recital 43 of the Information Society Directive, which provides that it is "important for the Member States to adopt all necessary measures to facilitate access to works by persons suffering from a disability which constitutes an obstacle to the use of the works themselves, and to pay particular attention to accessible formats".

[91] CDPA 1988, s.31F(2).

[92] CDPA 1988, s.31F(3).

making of a version of a work in braille.[93] For this purpose, an accessible copy also includes one which has facilities for navigating around the work, such as an index or search facilities, but does not include one which has: (a) changes that are not necessary to overcome problems caused by visual impairment; or (b) changes which infringe the right not to have the work subjected to derogatory treatment.[94]

9–69 **Lawful possession and lawful use.** Many of the new provisions are dependent on there being "lawful possession" or "lawful use" of a copy of a copyright work from which the accessible copy is made. Situations where this may occur include not only those where a retail copy has been bought by the user but also where a lawful copy has been lent to him, whether by another member of the public or a library.

9–70 **Other permitted acts.** It should be remembered, of course, that there are other provisions of the 1988 Act which permit dealings with copyright works (for example fair dealing for the purposes of private study) which may be applicable in the case of visually impaired persons. These are not affected.

(ii) Making for personal use of visually impaired person

9–71 **The main provisions.** Section 31A permits the making of an accessible copy of a copyright work for the personal use of a visually impaired person. The section recognises that in some cases the visually impaired person may easily be able to make the copy himself (as in the case of an enlarged photocopy) while in other cases he may not (the making of a copy in braille, for example). The section only applies where a visually impaired person already has lawful possession or lawful use of a copy (referred to as a "master copy") of the whole or part of a literary, dramatic, musical or artistic work, or a published edition, but which is not accessible to him because of his visual impairment.[95] In these circumstances, it is not an infringement of copyright in the work, or in the typographical arrangement of the published edition, for an accessible copy of the master copy to be made for the visually impaired person's personal use.[96] It follows that the copy does not have to be made by the visually impaired person, provided he had lawful possession or use of the master copy in the first place, and the copy is then made for him, and for his personal use, and from the master copy. A making of a copy in such circumstances by a friend or a copy shop would therefore not be an infringement. Where in such a case the person making the copy charges for it, the sum charged must not exceed the cost of making and supplying the copy.[97] Presumably the effect of this is to make the charging of an excessive sum unlawful and, if an excessive sum is paid, the excess will be recoverable. The exception is not restricted to published works. The requirements also make it clear that this section will not enable multiple copies to be made, either by a visually impaired person or for visually impaired persons generally.[98] As to the phrase "for his personal use", this can be distinguished from the phrase "for his private and do-

---

[93] *i.e.* a translation. See s.21(3)(a)(i).

[94] s.31F(4). As to changes which might infringe the right not to have the work subjected to derogatory treatment, see Ch.11, below.

[95] CDPA 1988, s.31A(1).

[96] s.31A(1).

[97] s.31A(5).

[98] This is emphasised both by the section heading ("Making a single accessible copy for personal use"), although this wording is not found in the section itself, and the exchanges in the Parliamentary debates, in which, as elsewhere, this exception has been referred to as the "one-for-one" exception.

mestic use" which is an expression used elsewhere in the Act.[99] Use for the visually impaired person's business or profession is therefore permitted provided the use is personal to him, and it seems that the section will also enable an employer to make an accessible copy for an employee who is a visually impaired person, assuming that the visually impaired person has possession of the master copy in the course of his employment and the accessible copy is for his personal use in the course of his employment.

Restrictions on the permitted act. There are certain restrictions to this exception. First, the exception does not apply where the master copy is of a musical work, or part of a musical work, and the making of an accessible copy would involve recording a performance of the work or part of it.[1] Thus accessible copies of musical works may not be made from sound recordings, and the rights in the sound recordings themselves and those of performers are thus preserved.[2] Second, the exception does not apply where the master copy is of a database, or part of a database, and the making of an accessible copy would infringe copyright in the database.[3] The reason for this is that the Database Directive[4] permits only limited derogations from any copyright which may subsist in a database[5] and none of these derogations are directly applicable to the case of visually impaired persons. In any event, any database will be usually be one in which the separate and parallel *sui generis* database right subsists, whether or not copyright also subsists in it,[6] so that the making of an accessible copy will *prima facie* infringe database right. Given the potentially wide meaning of a database, these are important limitations on the operation of these provisions. Thirdly, the exception does not apply in relation to the making of an accessible copy for a particular visually impaired person if, or to the extent that, copies of the copyright work are commercially available, by or with the authority of the copyright owner, in a form that is accessible to that person.[7] This is an important restriction on the permitted act. The reasoning for it is that if accessible copies of the work are commercially available then the ability to make further accessible copies by way of a permitted act would interfere with the normal exploitation of the work and thus contravene the Berne 3-step test. There is no requirement, however, that the commercially available copies should be available at a price which is either reasonable or one which the visually impaired person can afford.

9–72

Sufficient acknowledgment. The Act contains an ill-drafted provision dealing with information that must accompany an accessible copy. Thus, where an accessible copy is made under section 31A, the copy must be accompanied by (a) a statement that the copy has been made under the section and (b) a sufficient acknowledgment.[8] "Sufficient acknowledgment" has its usual meaning under the Act, namely an acknowledgment identifying the work in question by its title or other description, and identifying the author.[9] Presumably one of the intentions of this provision is to ensure, so far as reasonably possible, that such copies will not

9–73

---

[99] See, for example, s.22.

[1] CDPA 1988, s.31A(2)(a).

[2] Since an accessible copy is defined as a version which provides improved access to the work for a *visually* impaired person, this restriction seems hardly necessary.

[3] s.31A(2)(b). As to what constitutes a database, see s.3A(1), and para. 3–22, above.

[4] Database Directive 96/9.

[5] See Art.6.

[6] See para. 3–22, above.

[7] s.31A(3).

[8] CDPA 1988, s.31A(4).

[9] CDPA 1988, s.178. See also para. 9–29, above. The requirement is dispensed with in the case of anonymously published works and unpublished works where it is not possible to ascertain the identity of the author by reasonable inquiry: s.178.

be misused in the hands of third parties (as to which, see below). The requirement is not required by the Information Society Directive and seems onerous and a rather unrealistic in the case of one-off copies made by or for individual visually impaired persons. The effect of non-compliance is also obscure, since the section merely states that the accessible copy "must" be accompanied by the relevant statements. It would seem that at best all that is created is a statutory duty, a breach of which will be actionable at the suit of the copyright owner. By way of contrast, the effect of the fair dealing provisions of sections 29(1), 30(1) and (2) of the Act, which also require there to be a sufficient acknowledgment, is that unless there is such an acknowledgment the exceptions do not apply, so that the dealing will be an infringement, no matter how "fair".

(iii) Use of accessible copy

9–74 **Introduction.** A complicated and poorly drafted regime applies following the making of an accessible copy, the general effect of which is to restrict the use which may be made of such copies.[10] The basic position is of course that where an accessible copy is made by or for a visually impaired person under section 31A(1) it will not be an infringing copy, so that the holding of the copy, or the passing of the copy from the visually impaired person to another person, whether or not also a visually impaired person, would not be an infringement.[11] The Act alters this *prima facie* position in a number of ways.

9–75 **Holding of an accessible copy.** The Act deals first with the position of a person who "holds" an accessible copy made under section 31A(1). Section 31A(6) provides that if a person holds an accessible copy made under section 31A(1) when he is not entitled to have it made under that subsection, the copy is to be treated as an infringing copy. The use of the expression "when he is not entitled to have it made" is not very apt. Presumably what is meant is "when he would not be entitled to have such a copy made for him".[12] Obviously, if the provisions of section 31A(1) were not complied with when the copy was made it will always have been an infringing copy and the section is not directed to this. Rather, the section is directed to two situations: first, where the person in question is the visually impaired person who made or for whom the accessible copy was originally made; secondly, where the accessible copy comes into the hands of some other person. The general effect in either case is that if and so long as such a person is a visually impaired person who would have been able to make or have made another such copy for him for his personal use under section 31A(1), a non-infringing accessible copy will remain a non-infringing copy. Otherwise it will become an infringing copy. The wording makes it reasonably clear that this person must at all times also have lawful possession or lawful use of a "master copy".[13] This seems harsh. For example, where a visually impaired person borrows a book at his local library to make an enlarged copy to read at home, the

---

[10] As will be seen, the intended effect of the provisions is reasonably clear and was also partly explained by the Parliamentary Under Secretary of State for Trade and Industry in Parliament: "A visually impaired person may keep an accessible copy that they were entitled to have made, or are entitled to have transferred to them, only if they still have what is referred to in the Bill as a 'master copy' of the copyright material. It is not legal under the exception for a visually impaired person to make an accessible copy and pass it on to another visually impaired person who does not have a master copy. Nor is it possible for a visually impaired person to keep an accessible copy when they have handed on the master copy to someone else". (Standing Committee D, May 1, 2002, Col.16)

[11] Assuming that such acts did not amount to an issue of copies to the public within the meaning of CDPA 1988, s.18.

[12] Compare the rather happier wording of the CDPA 1988, s.31B(9), dealt with below.

[13] As to the meaning of "master copy", see para. 9–71, above.

copy will become an infringing copy once he gives the book back. Admittedly, his possession will not amount to an infringement nor will the copy be liable to be delivered up unless the possession happens to be in the course of a business.[14] It would appear that a copy can pass in and out of the status of being an infringing copy, depending on the position of the holder. It also follows that where an accessible copy is transferred from one visually impaired person to another, it will become an infringing copy in the transferee's hands unless (a) the copy also provides that person with improved access to the work, *i.e.* he suffers from a similar kind of impairment; (b) he also has lawful possession or use of a master copy of the work; and (c) the copy is for his personal use. In addition, it should be noted that under the provisions considered below, the copy may in fact already have become an infringing copy by virtue of the particular type of transfer.

Unless further provision were made, it would also follow from this that where a master copy had been supplied to a person for the purpose of making an accessible copy for a visually impaired person under section 31A(1), the accessible copy, when made, would be an infringing copy in the maker's hands. It is therefore provided that subsection (6) does not apply where the person holding the accessible copy is a person who has lawful possession of the master copy and intends to transfer the accessible copy to a visually impaired person who "is entitled to have the accessible copy made under subsection (1)".[15] The same comment as above can be made about the inapt wording of this provision.

Commercial dealings. The Act contains relatively straightforward provisions aimed at making commercial dealings with an accessible copy an infringement. Thus, if an accessible copy which, apart from section 31A(1), would be an infringing copy is subsequently dealt with: (a) it is to be treated as an infringing copy for the purposes of that dealing; and (b) if that dealing infringes copyright, it is to be treated as an infringing copy for all subsequent purposes.[16] For this purpose, "dealt with" means sold or let for hire or offered or exposed for sale or hire or communicated to the public.[17] This provision follows the form of similar provisions relating to other permitted acts.[18] A person who sells an accessible copy, knowing or believing it to be an infringing copy (which it will be by virtue of section 31A(9)—and ignorance of the law will not be a defence) will thus infringe, even if the sale is to a visually impaired person who would be entitled under section 31A(1) to have such a copy made for him. As will be seen, there is an uneasy overlap between this provision and the next set of provisions, dealing with other transfers of accessible copies.

9–76

Other transfers of accessible copies. Section 31A(7) deals with cases where a person who holds an accessible copy made under section 31A(1) "may" transfer it to some other person. Thus, it is provided that a person who holds an accessible copy made under subsection (1) "may" transfer it to two categories of transferee. First, under subsection (7)(a), to a visually impaired person "entitled to have the accessible copy made under subsection (1)", that is, presumably, to a person who would be entitled to have such a copy made for him. Secondly, under subsection (7)(b), to a person who has lawful possession of "the" master copy and intends to transfer the accessible copy to the first category of person. Taken by themselves, these provisions would appear to be of limited scope. Presumably the expression "may transfer" simply means that a person who carries out such an act does so

9–77

---

[14] See ss.24(1)(c) and 99(1)(a).
[15] See s.31A(6) and (7).
[16] CDPA 1988, s.31A(9).
[17] s.31A(10).
[18] See ss.32(5), 35(3), 36(5), 37(3)(b), 56(2), 63(2) and 68(4)).

without infringing copyright. The cases in which a person may hold an accessible copy without it becoming an infringing copy have already been considered. If the copy is not an infringing copy in the hands of the transferor then of course the transfer will not be an infringing act except in the perhaps rare case of the transfer amounting to the issue, rental or lending of "copies" to the public under sections 18 or 18A. The fact that the copy may become an infringing copy in the hands of the transferee under section 31A(6) will not affect this either way. If, on the other hand, the copy is an infringing copy in the hands of the transferor, the act of transfer would only be an infringement if the transfer amounted to a sale, letting for hire or distribution, with the requisite degree of knowledge, under section 23(d). Subsection (7) cannot, however, be read without reference to subsection (8), which provides for circumstances in which a transfer of an accessible copy "is" an infringement of copyright. It provides that the transfer by a person of an accessible copy made under subsection (1) to another person is an infringement of copyright by the transferor unless he has reasonable grounds for believing that the transferee is a person falling within subsection (7)(a) or (b) (as to which, see above). The subsection therefore appears to provide for a new category of infringement, namely the transfer of an accessible copy in the defined circumstances, whether or not the act of "transfer" also happens to be one of the existing acts of primary or secondary infringement. The reference to "another person" is clearly to a person who does not fall within subsections (7)(a) or (b). On such an infringing transfer, the accessible copy will necessarily become an infringing copy by virtue of the "holding" provisions of section 31A(6).

(iv) The making of multiple copies

9–78   **Introduction.** Section 31B enables the making of multiples copies for visually impaired persons. The general safeguard is that such copies can only be made by an approved body. For this purpose an approved body means an educational establishment or a body that is not conducted for profit.[19] As will be seen, there are circumstances in which the Secretary of State may deny the application of the section to certain approved bodies. Section 31B applies where an approved body has lawful possession of a copy (referred to, again, as a "master copy") of the whole or part of (a) a commercially published literary, dramatic, musical or artistic work; or (b) a commercially published edition. Section 31B therefore differs from section 31A in that it only applies where the work in question has been "commercially published".[20] In these circumstances, it is not an infringement of copyright in the work, or in the typographical arrangement of the published edition, for the body to make, or supply, accessible copies for the personal use of visually impaired persons to whom the master copy is not accessible because of their impairment. For this purpose, "supply" includes lending[21] and "lending" means making it available for use, otherwise than for direct or indirect economic or commercial advantage, on terms that it will or may be returned.[22] A loan is not to be treated as being for direct or indirect economic or commercial advantage if a charge is made for the loan which does not exceed the cost of making and supplying the copy.[23]If the approved body charges for supplying a copy made under

---

[19] CDPA 1988, s.31B(12). "Educational establishment" has its usual definition under s.174.
[20] As to this expression, see s.175 and para. 11–12, below.
[21] s.31B(13).
[22] s.31F(6).
[23] s.31F(6), (7). The definition of lending in s.18A does not apply: s.31F(8).

this section, the sum charged must not exceed the cost of making and supplying the copy.[24]

Restrictions. There are a number of restrictions which apply. First, there are   **9–79**
restrictions which are similar to those applying under section 31A. Thus section 31B(1) does not apply if the master copy is of a musical work, or part of a musical work, and the making of an accessible copy would involve recording a performance of the work or part of it.[25] Again, it does not apply if the master copy is of a database, or part of a database, and the making of an accessible copy would infringe copyright in the database.[26] Further, it does not apply in relation to the making of an accessible copy if, or to the extent that, copies of the copyright work are commercially available, by or with the authority of the copyright owner, in a form that is accessible to the same or substantially the same degree.[27] Finally, it does not apply in relation to the supply of an accessible copy to a particular visually impaired person if, or to the extent that, copies of the copyright work are commercially available, by or with the authority of the copyright owner, in a form that is accessible to that person.[28] Secondly, there are similar requirements as to information and acknowledgment. An accessible copy made under section 31B must be accompanied by (a) a statement that it is made under the section and (b) a sufficient acknowledgment.[29] Thirdly, where the approved body is an educational establishment, it "must" ensure that the copies will be used only for its educational purposes. Presumably the only remedy for non-compliance is for breach of statutory duty. Fourthly, if the master copy is in copy-protected electronic form, any accessible copy made of it under the section must, so far as it is reasonably practicable to do so, incorporate the same, or equally effective, copy protection, unless the copyright owner agrees otherwise.[30] Again, presumably the remedy for non-compliance is for a breach of statutory duty.

Subsequent dealings. As with section 31A, there are a number of provisions   **9–80**
which affect subsequent dealings. If an accessible copy which would be, but for the subsection, an infringing copy is subsequently dealt with, (a) it is to be treated as an infringing copy for the purposes of that dealing; and (b) if that dealing infringes copyright, is to be treated as an infringing copy for all subsequent purposes.[31] For this purpose, "dealt with" again means sold or let for hire or offered or exposed for sale or hire or communicated to the public.[32] Further, if an approved body continues to hold an accessible copy made under the subsection when it would no longer be entitled to make or supply such a copy under that subsection, the copy is to be treated as an infringing copy. Unlike section 31A, there are no other comparable provisions whereby accessible copies made under section 31B become infringing copies in the hands of other persons, or whereby certain transfers become infringements.

Approved bodies and the Secretary of State's powers. Although the Act speaks   **9–81**
in terms of "approved bodies", such bodies are not approved in any real sense of the word and the Act therefore contains provisions enabling the Secretary of State to take steps if there is evidence of abuse. Thus, the Secretary of State may

---

[24] s.31B(6).
[25] CDPA 1988, s.31B(2)(a).
[26] s.31B(2)(b).
[27] s.31B(3).
[28] s.31B(4).
[29] s.31B(5).
[30] s.31B(8). As to copy-protection devices, see Ch.15, below.
[31] CDPA 1988, s.31B(10).
[32] s.31B(11).

make an order under section 31E if it appears to him that the making of multiple copies by an approved body under section 31B has led to infringement of copyright on a scale which, in the Secretary of State's opinion, would not have occurred if section 31B had not been in force.[33] Such an order may prohibit one or more named approved bodies, or one or more specified categories of approved body, from acting under section 31B[34] and may disapply the provisions of section 31B in respect of the making of copies of a description so specified.[35] Such an order is exercisable by statutory instrument subject to annulment in pursuance of a resolution of either House of Parliament.[36] Where the Secretary of State is proposing to make an order he must first consult (a) such bodies representing copyright owners as he thinks fit; and (b) such bodies representing visually impaired persons as he thinks fit.[37] If the Secretary of State proposes to make an order which includes a prohibition he must, before making it, consult (a) if the proposed order is to apply to one or more named approved bodies, that body or those bodies; (b) if it is to apply to one or more specified categories of approved body, such bodies representing approved bodies of that category or those categories as he thinks fit.[38]

9–82   **Record keeping and notices.** An approved body must keep records of accessible copies made under section 31B and of the persons to whom they are supplied and allow the copyright owner or a person acting for him, on giving reasonable notice, to inspect the records at any reasonable time.[39] Further, within a reasonable time of making the accessible copy the approved body must (a) notify each relevant representative body; or (b) if there is no such body, notify the copyright owner.[40] For this purpose a relevant representative body is a body which (a) represents particular copyright owners, or owners of copyright in the type of copyright work concerned; and (b) has given notice to the Secretary of State of the copyright owners, or the classes of copyright owner, represented by it.[41] The Secretary of State has power by regulations to prescribe (a) the form in which or (b) the procedure in accordance with which any such notices must be given.[42] Such power is exercisable by statutory instrument subject to annulment in pursuance of a resolution of either House of Parliament.[43] The requirement to notify the copyright owner under the above provision does not apply if it is not reasonably possible for the approved body to ascertain the name and address of the copyright owner.[44] There are no prescribed sanctions for breaches of any of these provisions and presumably they are actionable as breaches of statutory duty.

(v) Intermediate copies

9–83   **Introduction.** Where multiple copies are made by an approved body under section 31B it may often be necessary to make relatively expensive intermediate copies as part of the manufacturing process. The policy of the Act is not to waste that expenditure if possible. Section 31C(1) therefore provides that an approved

---

[33] CDPA 1988, s.31E.
[34] s.31E(2).
[35] s.31E(3).
[36] s.31F(11).
[37] s.31E(4).
[38] s.31E(5).
[39] CDPA 1988, s.31C(6).
[40] s.31C(7).
[41] s.31C(8).
[42] s.31F(10).
[43] s.31F(11).
[44] s.31C(9).

body which is entitled to make accessible copies under section 31B "may hold" an intermediate copy of the master copy which is necessarily created during the production of the accessible copies. It seems clear from subsection (2) that the effect of the words "may hold" is that the intermediate copy is not to be treated as an infringing copy in the hands of the body while the conditions of the subsection continue to be satisfied. An intermediate copy is not itself defined but is clearly a copy which was made, directly or indirectly, from the master copy and from which, directly or indirectly, multiple copies are subsequently made, and which was a necessary and integral part of the manufacturing process. There is no reason why there may not be more than one intermediate copy in the manufacturing chain.

The subsection goes on to provide that the approved body "may hold" an intermediate only (a) if and so long as the approved body continues to be entitled to make accessible copies of that master copy; and (b) for the purposes of the production of further accessible copies. If the intermediate copy is held in breach of these provisions it is to be treated as an infringing copy.[45] It follows that if the approved body no longer has lawful possession of the master copy, or if the copies of the work in a form that is accessible to the same or substantially the same degree become commercially available, the intermediate copy will immediately become an infringing copy. A body holding such a copy in the course of a business and with the requisite degree of knowledge will thus become liable for infringement by possession. Although the Act states that the approved body may only hold the intermediate copy for the purposes of the production of further accessible copies, it is reasonably clear that once a manufacturing run has been completed the body may continue to hold the intermediate copy pending any decision to make further copies provided, of course, that meanwhile it does not use it for some other purpose.

Making intermediate copies available. The Act goes on to make provision enabling an approved body to make an intermediate copy available to other approved bodies for the same purpose. Thus section 31C(3) provides that an approved body "may lend or transfer" the intermediate copy to another approved body which is entitled to make accessible copies of the work or published edition under section 31B. Lending for this purpose has the same extended definition as it does for the purposes of section 31B.[46] The mere lending or transfer of such a copy would not ordinarily be an infringement unless it fell within the provisions of either section 18 or 18A but, as with sections 31B(7) and (8), it seems that section 31C(3), taken with section 31(4), creates a new act of infringement. Thus, section 31C(4) provides that the loan or transfer by an approved body of an intermediate copy to another person is an infringement of copyright by the lender or transferor unless he has reasonable grounds for believing that the borrower or transferee: (a) is another approved body which is entitled to make accessible copies of the work or published edition under section 31B; and (b) will use the intermediate copy only for the purposes of the production of further accessible copies. As with section 31B, the effect of these provisions is presumably that the loan or transfer to a person who does not fall within this description is an infringement unless the lender or transfor reasonably believes that he does so. The borrower or transferee will of course only be entitled to make further accessible copes if he has lawful possession of a master copy (whether from the lender or transferor, or another copy). As to whether he "will use the intermediate copy" only for this purpose, presumably it will be a question of fact whether this is his intention. If

9–84

---

[45] CDPA 1988, s.31C(2).
[46] As to which, see above and CDPA 1988, ss.31F(6), (7) and (8).

the approved body charges for lending or transferring the intermediate copy, the sum charged must not exceed the cost of the loan or transfer.[47]

Although the wording is not entirely happy, an approved body which holds an intermediate copy following such a loan or transfer presumably "may" continue to hold it under subsection (1) provided it remains entitled to make accessible copies and holds it for the purposes of doing so. It too may lend or transfer it to another approved body.[48]

9–85   **Record keeping and notices.** As with section 31B, there are requirements on approved bodies to keep records and give certain notices in relation to imtermediate copies. Thus an approved body must (a) keep records of any intermediate copy lent or transferred under this section and of the persons to whom it is lent or transferred; and (b) allow the copyright owner or a person acting for him, on giving reasonable notice, to inspect the records at any reasonable time.[49] Again, within a reasonable time of lending or transferring an intermediate copy under this section, the approved body must (a) notify each relevant representative body; or (b) if there is no such body, notify the copyright owner.[50]

(vi) Licensing schemes

9–86   **Introduction.** Just as the policy of the Act is not to permit the making of accessible copies where copies of the work in question are commercially available, it is also the policy of the Act not to permit such activities where a relevant licensing scheme is in force. Section 31D therefore provides that the ability of an approved body to make multiple copies under section 31B does not apply to the making of an accessible copy in a particular form if three conditions are satisfied: (a) a licensing scheme operated by a licensing body is in force under which licences may be granted by the licensing body permitting the making and supply of copies of the copyright work in that form; (b) the scheme is not unreasonably restrictive; and (c) the scheme and any modification made to it have been notified to the Secretary of State by the licensing body. For this purpose, a scheme is unreasonably restrictive if it includes a term or condition which: (a) purports to prevent or limit the steps that may be taken under section 31B or 31C; or (b) has that effect.[51] Nevertheless, subsection (2) does not apply if (a) the copyright work is no longer published by or with the authority of the copyright owner; and (b) there are reasonable grounds for preventing or restricting the making of accessible copies of the work.[52] Finally, if section 31B or 31C is displaced by a licensing scheme, the scheme can be referred to the Copyright Tribunal.[53] As with notices under section 31C, the Secretary of State has power by regulations to prescribe (a) the form in which or (b) the procedure in accordance with which any notice required under section 31D(1) must be given.[54]

9–87   **The Secretary of State's powers.** As with the provisions relating to the making of multiple copies by approved bodies, the Secretary of State has powers to make orders in the case of licensing schemes. Thus he may make an order if it appears to him that the making of copies under a licence granted under a licensing scheme

---

[47] s.31C(5).
[48] s.31C(3).
[49] CDPA 1988, s.31C(6)
[50] s.31C(7).
[51] CDPA 1988, s.31D(2).
[52] s.31D(3).
[53] s.31D(4). As to the reference of a scheme to the Copyright Tribunal, see para. 29–105 , et seq., below.
[54] s.31F(10).

that has been notified under section 31D has led to infringement of copyright on a scale which, in the Secretary of State's opinion, would not have occurred if the licence had not been granted.[55] Such an order may prohibit one or more named approved bodies, or one or more specified categories of approved body, from acting under a licence of a description specified in the order and the order may disapply the provisions of a licence, or a licensing scheme, of a description specified in the order in respect of the making of copies of a description so specified.[56] As with the powers in relation to section 31B, the power is exercisable by statutory instrument subject to annulment in pursuance of a resolution of either House of Parliament[57] and the Secretary of State must consult specified bodies before any such order is made.[58] Where an approved body is prohibited by an order from acting under a licence, it may not apply to the Copyright Tribunal under section 121(1) in respect of a refusal or failure by a licensing body to grant such a licence.[59]

6. EDUCATION

Introduction. One of the clearest examples of a strong public interest in limiting copyright protection is in the field of education. However, just because education is a worthy cause does not mean that some form of blanket exception to copyright should be allowed. It must be remembered that it is works made for educational purposes that will often be copied in educational establishments. A wide exemption would therefore undermine the market for such works, so that a publisher would be unlikely to invest in their production. In the event, the exceptions relating to education are in many respects quite limited, even when viewed alongside the available licensing agreements and other sections of the 1988 Act, such as the exceptions relating to libraries and fair dealing for the purposes of non-commercial research or private study. The exceptions are an expansion of the even more modest provision made in the 1956 Act and before that the 1911 Act.[60]   **9–88**

The Berne Convention. Article 10(2) of the Convention states that it is a matter for individual countries to permit the use of works for illustration in publications, broadcasts, sound recordings or films for teaching, provided this is compatible with fair practice. The acts permitted by the 1988 Act in this area appear to fall within this.   **9–89**

The Information Society Directive. Rectial 14 of the Directive states that the Directive should seek to promote learning and culture by protecting works and other subject-matter while permitting exceptions or limitations in the public interest for the purpose of education and teaching. Articles 5(2)(c) and (4) go on to permit Member States to make an exception to the reproduction and distribution rights in respect of specific acts of reproduction made by educational establishments, which are not for direct or indirect economic or commercial advantage.[61] Articles 5(3)(a) and (4) also permit an exception to be made to the reproduction right, to the communication to the public right, and the distribution   **9–90**

---

[55] CDPA 1988, s.31E(1).
[56] s.31E(2) and (3).
[57] s.31F(11).
[58] ss.31E(4) and (5).
[59] s.31E(6).
[60] See s.6(6) of the 1956 Act and s.2(1)(iv) of the 1911 Act.
[61] The exception to the disribution right is permitted only to the extent justified by the purpose of the authorised act of reproduction: Information Society Directive, 2001/29, Art.5(4).

right, for the sole purpose, amongst other things, of illustration for teaching, as long as the source, including the author's name, is indicated, unless this turns out to be impossible, to the extent justified by the non-commercial purpose to be achieved.[62] Recital 42 to the Directive indicates that when applying the exception or limitation for non-commercial educational purposes the non-commercial nature of the activity in question is to be determined by that activity as such. The organisational structure and the means of funding of the establishment concerned are not the decisive factors in this respect. Overall, these requirements have necessitated a number of changes to the permitted acts under the 1988 Act dealing with education, in particular to provide for sufficient acknowledgment and to restrict the permitted acts to non-commercial purposes.

9–91   **Educational establishment.** With the exception of section 32, which deals with instruction and examination in a broad sense (see paragraph 9–92, below), the education exceptions in sections 33 to 36A are confined to educational establishments. "Educational establishment" is defined by the Act as including any school, which is itself defined by reference to the various Education Acts.[63] Apart from any school, the term includes any other educational establishment specified by the Secretary of State under his powers under section 174(1)(b) of the 1988 Act.[64] In addition, these provisions have been extended to apply to teachers employed by a local authority to give instruction to pupils unable to attend an educational establishment.[65] While it was the Government's view that copying for educational purposes or instruction in educational establishments under these exceptions would very largely be for a non-commercial activity, it could not be confident that this would invariably be so, for example in relation to some educational activity in some further education establishments.[66] Amendments have therefore been made to various provisions to limit the permitted acts to a non-commerical activity. These are considered in turn, below.

A. DOING THINGS FOR THE PURPOSES OF INSTRUCTION OR EXAMINATION

9–92   **Instruction.** As the Act now stands, the copyright in a literary, dramatic, musical or artistic work is not infringed by its being copied in the course of instruction or of preparation for instruction, provided the copying (a) is done by a person giving or receiving instruction, (b) is not done by means of a reprographic process, (c) is accompanied by a sufficient acknowledgment, and provided that the instruction is for a non-commercial purpose.[67] No acknowledgment is required where this would be impossible for reasons of practicality or otherwise.[68] The requirements of sufficient acknowledgment and non-commercial purpose are new. "Repro-

---

[62] Again, the exception to the disribution right is permitted only to the extent justified by the purpose of the authorised act of reproduction.

[63] CDPA 1988, s.174(3). The Acts in question are the Education Act 1996 (c. 56), the Education (Scotland Act) 1962 (c.47) (see also the Education (Scotland Act) 1980 (c.44)) and the Education and Libraries (Northern Ireland) Order 1986 (SI 1986/594 (NI 3)).

[64] See the Copyright (Educational Establishments) (No.2) Order 1989 (SI 1989/1068), at Vol.2 at A4.v, which defines "educational establishment" very broadly to include universities, theological colleges and institutions providing further education within the meaning of s.41 of the Education Act 1944 (c.31); s.1(5) (b) of the Education (Scotland) Act 1980 (c.44) or Art.5c of the Education and Libraries (Northern Ireland) Order 1986.

[65] See the Copyright (Application of Provisions relating to Educational Establishments to Teachers) (No.2) Order 1989 (SI 1989/1067) at Vol.2 at A4.iv made under s.174(2) of the CDPA 1988.

[66] See the Government Conclusions on the Patent Office's Consulation Paper of August 7, 2002, para.5.8.

[67] CDPA 1988, s.32(1). As to the limited exception provided for reprographic copying, see CDPA 1988, s.36, para. 9–98, below.

[68] s.32(3A).

graphic process" is defined by the Act as meaning a process (a) for making fac-simile copies, or (b) involving the use of an appliance for making multiple cop-ies, and includes, in relation to a work held in electronic form, any copying by electronic means, but does not include the making of a film or sound recording.[69] Thus, for example, it seems that a teacher may copy onto a blackboard a substantial part of a literary work, and pupils may copy it down. The teacher may not, however, photocopy the same material for use by students in the absence of a licensing agreement. Similarly, a teacher would not be entitled to photocopy ma-terial onto an acetate for use on an overhead projector, even though the same ma-terial could be copied onto an acetate by hand. The meaning of sufficient acknowledgment has already been considered.[70] It should be noted that the acknowledgment does not have to be in writing, which may be important in the context of classroom teaching. As to the copying being "for a non-commercial purpose", this expression has also been considered in the context of fair dealing.[71] Strictly, what is relevant here is the purpose of the instruction, not the purpose of the copying or the purpose of the educational establishment, although no doubt these matters will be of some relevance in assessing the purpose of the instruction. The relevant purpose appears to be that of either the giver or the receiver of the instruction. In the case of the latter, instruction received by way of general school or university education is presumably not received for a commercial purpose but instruction received in the course of professional or other vocational training with a view to a qualification would appear to be received for a commercial purpose. As to the giver of the instruction, the requirement of non-commercial purpose would no doubt be satisfied in the case of most educational establish-ments but not in the case of commercial organisations offering courses to fee-paying students.

In relation to a sound recording, film or broadcast, copyright is not infringed by its being copied by making a film or film sound-track in the course of instruc-tion, or of preparation for instruction, in the making of films or sound-tracks, provided the copying (a) is done by a person giving or receiving instruction and (b) is accompanied by a sufficient acknowledgment, and provided that the instruc-tion is for a non-commercial purpose.[72]

In relation to a literary, dramatic, musical or artistic work which has been made available to the public, copyright is not infringed by its being copied in the course of instruction or of preparation for instruction, provided the copying (a) is fair dealing with the work, (b) is done by a person giving or receiving instruction, (c) is not done by means of a reprographic process, and (d) is accompanied by a sufficient acknowledgment.[73] There is clearly a large overlap between this provi-sion and section 32(1), and the section was introduced to take advantage of Article 5(3)(d) of the Information Society Directive, apparently on the basis that the Article is not limited to criticism or review, these being only examples of the permitted use.[74] The important difference with section 32(2A) is that copying in the course of instruction for a commercial purpose is permitting provided, of

---

[69] s.178, where "facsimile copy" and "electronic" are also defined.

[70] See para. 9–29, above.

[71] See para. 9–28, above.

[72] CDPA 1988, s.32(2). Again, no acknowledgment is required where this would be impossible for reasons of practicality or otherwise: s.32(3A).

[73] s.32(2A). No acknowledgment is required where this would be impossible for reasons of practicality or otherwise: s.32(3A). The meaning of "made available to the public" has the same meaning here as under the fair dealing provisions of s.30(1A): s.32(2B). As to permitted acts of reprographic copying in the case of educational uses, see s.36 and para. 9–98, below.

[74] This provision was introduced "to maintain existing flexibility in this area". See the Patent Office Consultation Paper of August 7, 2002 and the Transposition Note on implementation of the Directive by SI 2003/2498.

course, that the work has been made available to the public and it amounts to fair dealing. What amounts to fair dealing has already been considered.[75] In this, the fact that the instruction is for a commercial purpose will be a factor to be considered, but will not be conclusive. Also relevant will be the amount of copying and the reason for the copying.

9–93   **Examinations.** The Act also provides that copyright is not infringed by anything done for the purposes of an examination by way of setting the questions, communicating the questions to the candidates or answering the questions, provided that the questions are accompanied by a sufficient acknowledgment.[76] The requirement of sufficient acknowledgment is new and clearly raises an obstacle where the point of the question is to test the candidate's knowledge of the name of the work or its author. The provision does not extend to the making of a reprographic copy of a musical work for use by an examination candidate in performing the work.[77] "Reprographic copy" refers to copying by a reprographic process.[78] Thus it will not be permissible to photocopy sheet music for candidates taking a musical test instead of buying or hiring the sheet music.[79]

9–94   **Subsequent dealings with copies.** If by virtue of the above provisions the making of a copy of a work was not an infringement of copyright, but such a copy is subsequently dealt with, that is (a) sold, let for hire, offered or exposed for sale or hire, or (b) communicated to the public (unless that communication is itself, by virtue of section 32(3), not an infringement of copyright), then it is to be treated as an infringing copy for the purpose of that dealing.[80] Once such an infringement has occurred, the copy will be treated as an infringing copy for all subsequent purposes, and not just for the purpose of that dealing.[81] Thus, for example, possession in the course of business, with the requisite degree of knowledge, subsequent to such a dealing, will also amount to an infringement.[82] The purpose of these particular provisions is to prevent the commercial exploitation of copies made for educational purposes. As to the knowledge required to make such a dealing an infringement, in accordance with the usual principles it will be sufficient if the defendant has knowledge of the relevant facts. His ignorance of these particular provisions, being matters of law, will be irrelevant.[83] Thus, if the person dealing with a copy of a work knows or has reason to believe that it is a copy made for educational purposes, that dealing will almost inevitably amount to a secondary infringement under section 23 of the Act.

B. ANTHOLOGIES FOR EDUCATIONAL USE

9–95   The Act contains a very limited exception which allows for the inclusion of a "short passage" from a published literary or dramatic work in a collection which

---

[75] See para. 9–53, above.
[76] CDPA 1988, s.32(3). No acknowledgment is required where this would be impossible for reasons of practicality or otherwise: s.32(3A).
[77] s.32(4).
[78] s.178 and see para. 9–92, above.
[79] This provision reflects the vulnerability of this publishing sector. See further, Gurnsey, *Copyright Theft* (Aslib Gower, Aldershot, 1995).
[80] CDPA 1988, s.32(5), s.27(6). Communication to the public was introduced as a further form of dealing on implementation of the Information Society Directive because of the possible commercial nature of such acts. See the Government Conclusions on the Patent Office's Consulation Paper of August 7, 2002, para.5.11.
[81] s.32(5).
[82] s.23(a).
[83] See Ch.8, above.

is intended for use in educational establishments.[84] In order to fall within this exception four conditions must be satisfied. First, the collection must be described as being for use in educational establishments both in its title and in any advertisements issued by or on behalf of the publisher. Secondly, it must consist "mainly of material in which no copyright subsists". Thirdly, the work from which the passage is taken must itself not be intended for use in an educational establishment. Finally, the inclusion must be accompanied by a sufficient acknowledgment.[85] Moreover, even if the above conditions are satisfied, no more than two excerpts from copyright works by the same author may be published in collections by the same publisher over any period of five years.[86] In relation to any given passage this reference to excerpts from works by the same author (a) includes excerpts from works created by him in collaboration with another and (b) if the passage in question is from a collaborative work, "works by the same author" is to be taken to include excerpts from works by any of the authors.[87] Thus, within a five-year period, it seems that a publisher who had already taken an excerpt from a work by A and an excerpt from a work by B, could not take an excerpt from a work created by A and B, even though he could take another excerpt from a work created by A or B individually. The utility of this exception is further diminished by the lack of certainty involved in the concept of a "short passage". Logically this must refer to something greater than a "substantial part", but otherwise the concept is undefined. The courts may therefore be forced into a general consideration of the "fairness" of the use in question.[88] The requirement that the collection should "mainly consist of material in which no copyright subsists" (itself rather vague) is also extremely restrictive. It would not be possible, for example, for a publisher to rely on this section if he wished to include a short extract of a work in a collection consisting mainly of material in which he owns the copyright. A publisher might, however, be able to rely on fair dealing for the purposes of criticism or review in such circumstances.[89]

C. Performing, Playing or Showing a Work in the Course of Activities of Educational Establishments

The performance of a literary, dramatic or musical work before an audience consisting of teachers and pupils at an educational establishment and other persons directly connected with the activities of the establishment (a) by a teacher or pupil in the course of the activities of the establishment, or (b) at the establishment by any person for the purposes of instruction, is not to be regarded a public performance for the purposes of infringement of copyright.[90] Similarly, the playing or showing of a sound recording, film or broadcast before such an audience at an educational establishment for the purposes of instruction is not a playing or showing of the work in public for the purposes of infringement of copyright.[91] Reference has already been made to the definition of an "educational

9–96

---

[84] CDPA 1988, s.33(1). References in the section to the use of a work "in an educational establishment" are to any use for the purposes of such an establishment: s.33(4). The purpose of this subsection was to make sure that the exception applies to institutions such as the Open University, where use of the work would take place mostly in the home of the student rather than on the premises of the institution itself: *Hansard*, HL Vol.493, col.1166.

[85] See para. 9–29, above.

[86] s.33(2).

[87] s.33(3).

[88] See paras 9–53 *et seq.*, above.

[89] See paras 9–38 *et seq.*, above.

[90] CDPA 1988, s.34(1). The Information Society Directive is not concerned with the public performance right and so its provisions do not have to be taken into account in relation to s.34.

[91] s.34(2).

establishment."[92] "Teacher" and "pupil" are defined to mean any person who gives and any person who receives instruction respectively.[93] As to the persons who may be "directly connected with the activities" of such an establishment, the Act provides that a person is not for this purpose directly connected with the activities of the educational establishment simply because he or she is the parent of a pupil at the establishment.[94] This exclusion of parents was felt to be necessary in order to comply with the Berne Convention, which does not allow for the granting of exceptions in relation to a public performance.[95] Thus a school play to which all parents or the parents of participants are invited will constitute a public performance and may infringe copyright accordingly.[96] If, however, parents were present because they had some special role in relation to the particular performance, for example, by assisting backstage, they would seem to fall within the exception. In any event, the unforeseen presence of one or two parents would probably not, in itself, render the performance a public one.[97] Other persons "directly connected with the activities" of the establishment might include caretakers and similar employees.[98]

D. RECORDING OF BROADCASTS

9–97 Modern teaching methods make extensive use of visual media, particularly video, as this helps keep student attention by introducing an element of variety and on occasion allows information to be presented more efficiently. In recognition of this, the Act allows a recording of a broadcast, or a copy of such a recording, to be made by or on behalf of an educational establishment, provided that this is to be used for the educational purposes of that establishment, and provided that it is accompanied by a sufficient acknowledgment of the broadcast and that the educational purposes are non-commercial.[99] If these conditions are satisfied, such recording will not infringe copyright in the broadcast, or in any work included in it.[1] The requirements of sufficient acknowledgment and non-commercial purpose are new. Copyright is also not infringed where a recording of a broadcast or a copy of such a recording, whose making was by virtue of the above provisions not an infringement of copyright, is communicated to the public by a person situated within the premises of an educational establishment provided that the communication cannot be received by any person situated outside the premises of that establishment.[2] These provisions do not apply, however, if or to the extent that the Secretary of State has certified a licensing scheme for these purposes

---

[92] See para. 9–91, above.

[93] s.174(5).

[94] s.34(3).

[95] See *Hansard*, HL Vol.493, col.1167. This is presumably why, in the case of this "permitted" act, the 1988 Act does not speak in terms of it not being an infringement but redefines it so as not to amount to the restricted act of public performance.

[96] But see *Duck v Bates* (1884) 13 Q.B.D. 843. *cf. Jennings v Stephens* [1936] 1 Ch. 469. As to what constitutes a performance in public more generally, see para. 7–95 *et seq.*, above.

[97] See *Hansard*, HL Vol.493, col.1167.

[98] *Hansard*, HL Vol.493, col.1168. Although this example was given in Parliament it would be possible to argue that whilst caretakers and the like are connected with the running of the school they are not directly connected with its "activities".

[99] CDPA 1988, s.35(1). Such a recording can then be shown to students in accordance with s.34 (see para., above).

[1] s.35(1).

[2] s.35(1A). This provision was introduced because otherwise the deletion of s.7 would have meant that cable transmission within an educational establishment of recordings of broadcasts made under the s.35 exception would require authorisation, whereas it had previously been exempt by virtue of s.7(2)(d). See the Analysis of Responses and Government Conclusions on the Patent Office's Consultation Paper of August 7, 2002, para.5.9.

under section 143 of the Act.[3] Even if a scheme has been certified, however, the matter can still be referred to the Copyright Tribunal, should an educational establishment feel that the proposed terms are unreasonable. The Act thus provides an incentive to owners to offer licences on reasonable terms. In this instance the Act benefits educational establishments not by conferring a limited privilege upon them, but rather by strengthening their bargaining position as against copyright owners. The section also contains provisions of the kind already discussed making it an infringement to deal in copies made under the protection of this section.[4]

E. REPROGRAPHIC COPYING

Section 36 of the Act provides an exception to allow to a limited extent the mak- **9–98** ing of reprographic copies of passages from published literary, dramatic or musical works by or on behalf of an educational establishment for the purposes of instruction provided that they are accompanied by a sufficient acknowledgment and the instruction is for a non-commercial purpose.[5] The requirements of sufficient acknowledgment and non-commercial purpose are new. Reprographic copies of passages from published editions may also, to the same limited extent, be made without infringing any copyright in the typographical arrangement of the edition.[6] In this case, no acknowledgment is required and there is no restriction to non-commercial purposes.[7] Copies will be made "on behalf of" an educational establishment if they are made for the purposes of that establishment by any person.[8] The circumstances in which such copying will not amount to an infringement are that not more than 1 per cent of any work may be copied in any quarter, that is, in any period from January 1 to March 31, April 1 to June 30, July 1 to September 30 or October 1 to December 31.[9] However, copying is not permitted by this section if, or to the extent that, licences authorising the copying in question are available and the person making the copies knew or ought to have been aware of that fact.[10] But where the terms of such a licence purport to restrict the proportion of a work which may be copied to less than the above percentage, then such terms are to that extent of no effect.[11] This will be so whether or not the licence imposes terms for payment.[12] The section also contains provisions of the kind already discussed making it an infringement to deal in copies made with the protection of this section.[13] Overall, therefore, the real importance of this section,

---

[3] s.35(2) and see, as to licensing schemes so far certified, para. 29–78, below.

[4] s.35(3) and see para. 9–94, above. Under this section, however, "dealt with" means sold or let for hire, offered or exposed for sale or hire, or communicated from within the premises of an educational establishment to any person situated outside those premises.

[5] No acknowledgment is required where this would be impossible for reasons of practicality or otherwise: CDPA 1988, s.36(1A).

[6] s.36(1B).

[7] This is because the copyright in typographical arrangements is not subject to the provisions of the Information Society Directive, and the position of such works has therefore not been altered.

[8] s.174(6).

[9] s.36(2).

[10] s.36(3). Note that there is no equivalent requirement of knowledge in relation to s.35. Presumably this is because it will be easier to determine whether an appropriate scheme has been certified.

[11] s.36(4).

[12] s.36(4)

[13] s.36(5); para. 9–94, above. For the purposes of this section, "dealt with" means sold or let for hire, offered or exposed for sale or hire or communicated to the public. Communication to the public was introduced as a further form of dealing on implementation of the Information Society Directive because of the possible commercial nature of such acts. See the Government Conclusions on the Patent Office's Consulation Paper of August 7, 2002, para.5.11.

as with the provisions relating to the copying of broadcasts,[14] is in providing an incentive to owners to ensure that licences are available. In this case, however, there is no requirement that the Secretary of State must approve the scheme, although the specification of a minimum proportion of a work which is to be available for copying, together with the power to refer licences to the Copyright Tribunal, does afford educational establishments some security.[15]

F. LENDING OF COPIES BY EDUCATIONAL ESTABLISHMENTS

9–99 Section 36A provides that the copyright in a work is not infringed by the lending of copies of the work by an educational establishment.[16] This provision was introduced into the 1988 Act by the Copyright and Related Rights Regulations, 1996,[17] implementing the Rental and Related Rights Directive.[18] The provision corresponds to Article 5(3) of this Directive, which gives Member States the power to exempt entirely certain categories of establishment from the exclusive public lending right of authors and performers.[19] This provision was not affected by the Information Society Directive.[20]

7. LIBRARIES AND ARCHIVES

9–100 **Background and rationale.** Demands are frequently made upon public libraries for copies of articles or parts of periodicals and books in their possession. The fair dealing provisions relating to non-commercial research and private study will often not sufficiently cover this type of situation and, in particular, may not protect the librarian. The 1956 Act introduced provisions dealing with this problem, which in general terms are reproduced in the 1988 Act, together with a number of additional provisions dealing with other situations faced by librarians and archivists.[21] The increasing importance of on-line sources to the provision of library services was, however, not anticipated by the 1988 Act and the attraction of such sources has been further increased by cuts in library budgets. As a result, librarians are often frustrated by their inability to create databases of particular articles or fulfil library loans electronically.[22]

9–101 **The Berne Convention.** The Convention does not contain any specific provision dealing with libraries or archives but presumably the permitted acts under consideration here fall within Article 9(2), which allows countries of the Union to permit the reproduction of works in certain special cases, provided that such reproduction does not conflict with normal exploitation of the work and does not

---

[14] See *i.e.* under s.35.

[15] It is instructive to compare this provision with the position in the United States where the fair use doctrine will, in certain circumstances, cover the making of multiple copies for classroom use. Guidelines to this effect were agreed upon by authors, publishers and educational establishments. These set out the minimum amount which may be safely copied and were approved by Congress: H.R. Rep. No. 94–1476, 94th Congress, 2d Sess. 66–72 (1976).

[16] CDPA 1988, s.36A.

[17] SI 1996/2967.

[18] Council Directive 92/100 on rental and lending right and on certain rights related to copyright in the field of intellectual property [1992] O.J. L346/61.

[19] Art.5 of the Rental Rights Directive also gives Member States a more general discretion to derogate from the exclusive public lending right, "provided that at least authors obtain a remuneration for such lending": Art.5(1) and see CDPA 1988, s.40A (para. 9–108, below).

[20] See recital 40 and Art.1(2)(b) of the Information Society Directive, 2001/29.

[21] CDPA 1988, ss.37–44.

[22] As to some of the problems, see Norman, "The Electronic Environment: The Librarian's View". [1996] 2 E.I.P.R. 71.

unreasonably prejudice the legitimate interests of the owner (i.e. provided the 3-step test is satisfied[23]).

The Information Society Directive. Article 5(2)(c) permits Member States to make an exception to the reproduction and distribution rights in respect of specific acts of reproduction made by publicly accessible libraries, museums, or by archives, which are not for direct or indirect economic or commercial advantage.[24] This exception is directed at acts of reproduction by the relevant establishment itself, as opposed to users. The use of the word "specific" no doubt implies that to fall within the exception the copying must not be of a general kind, for example, every issue of a periodical.[25] It is not clear whether the expression "which are not for direct or indirect economic or commercial advantage" refers to the nature of the establishment or the nature of the acts of reproduction, etc. Some indication that it is the former is provided by recital 40, which states that "Member States may provide for an exception or limitation for the benefit of certain non-profit-making establishments, such as publicly accessible libraries and equivalent institutions, as well as archives". Recital 40 also states that the exception in favour of such establishments should not cover uses made in the context of online delivery of protected works or other subject-matter.

In addition, Article 5(3)(n) of the Directive permits Member States to make an exception to the reproduction right, to the communication to the public rights, and the distribution right, in cases where a work is communicated, for the purpose of research or private study, to individual members of the public by dedicated terminals on the premises of establishments of publicly accessible libraries, museums or archives, if the work is not subject to purchase or licensing terms which are contained in their collections. It would seem from the opening words of Recital 40 ("Member States may provide for an exception or limitation for the benefit of certain non-profit making establishments ...") that the exception is intended to be for the benefit of the establishment.

Amendments to the 1988 Act. Only a small number of amendments were made to the 1988 Act on implemetation of the Directive, with the aim of ensuring that copies supplied by librarians were only to be used for non-commercial research or private study.

Introductory provisions. The current provisions apply to libraries and archives of descriptions and in conditions prescribed by regulations made by the Secretary of State,[26] which, in the following sections, will be simply referred to as "the Regulations". In the remainder of this section "library" and "archive" will be used in this sense and 'librarian" and "archivist" will be used accordingly. In relation to different provisions of the 1988 Act different classes of library are prescribed by the Regulations. These are dealt with in turn, below, as they arise. A number of the provisions require the librarian or archivist to be "satisfied" of certain matters, and in such cases the Regulations provide for cases in which the librarian or archivist may rely on or must require a declaration signed by the person using the library's facilities (referred to here as the "reader") as to those

9–102

9–103

9–104

[23] See para. 9–02, above.
[24] The exception to the distribtion right is permitted only to the extent justified by the purpose of the authorised act of reproduction: Information Society Directive, Art.5(4).
[25] Recital 40 also states that the exception "should be limited to certain special cases covered by the reproduction right".
[26] See the Copyright (Librarians and Archivists) (Copying of Copyright Material) Regulations 1989 (SI 1989/1212) Vol.2 at A4.viii, made under ss.37 and 38–43 of the 1988 Act, as amended by the Scotland Act 1998 (Consequential Modifications) (No.1) Order 1999 and the The Copyright and Related Rights Regulations 2003 (SI 2003/2498), Sch.1, para.26.

matters.[27] If a reader makes such a declaration which is false in a material partic-ular and is then supplied with a copy which would have been an infringing copy if made by him, then that copy will be treated as an infringing copy and the reader will be liable for infringement as if he had made it himself.[28] In such circum-stances it seems clear that the librarian or archivist will not be liable for any infringement. In these provisions, references to a librarian or archivist include a person acting on his behalf.[29]

A. COPYING OF ARTICLES IN PERIODICALS AND PARTS OF PUBLISHED WORKS

9–105   **Overview.** The following two sections of this work should be read in conjunction with one another as they deal with provisions which perform essentially the same function and hence similar comments can be made in relation to both. "Prescribed library" here means those specified in Part A of Schedule 1 of the Regulations. These include the copyright libraries, libraries administered by a library author-ity, libraries administered by a local authority, school libraries and the libraries of other educational establishments,[30] libraries administered by Parliament or by a Government department and libraries conducted for the purposes of facilitating or encouraging the study of education, religion, philosophy, science (including the social sciences) and the arts. Libraries conducted for profit are, however, specifically excluded.[31] The primary importance of these provisions is in relation to the inter-library loans system and "distance lending", as most libraries now provide self-service photocopying facilities for their readers.[32] By permitting limited copying of articles in periodicals and small sections of other works the Act provides the foundations for the above system. These exceptions are, however, subject to a number of complex conditions,[33] compliance with which increases staff costs, whilst arguably doing little to prevent abuses of the system. In practice this may mean that the Regulations are often ignored, as happened with the Regulations which governed the similar provisions of the 1956 Act.[34]

B. ARTICLES IN PERIODICALS

9–106   **Copying by librarians.** Provided certain conditions are met, a librarian may make and supply a copy of an article in a periodical without infringing any copy-right in the text, in any illustrations accompanying the text or in the typographical arrangement.[35] For this purpose "article" includes an item of any description in a periodical.[36] The prescribed conditions are (a) that copies are supplied only to persons satisfying the librarian that they require them for the purposes of (i) research for a non-commercial purpose, or (ii) private study, and will not use

---

[27] CDPA 1988, s.37(2); regs 4(3), 7(3).

[28] s.37(3).

[29] s.37(6).

[30] As to "educational establishments", see para. 9–91, above.

[31] "Conducted for profit" in this context means a library which is established or conducted for profit or which forms part of, or is administered by, a body established or conducted for profit: SI 1989/1212, para.3(5).

[32] As shown by the decisions in *Moorhouse and Angus and Robertson (Publishers) Pty Ltd v University of New South Wales* [1976] R.P.C. 151 and *CCH Canadian Ltd v Law Society of Up-per Canada* [2004] SCC 13, librarians must still be careful as to what and how they allow their readers to copy if they are not to be liable for authorisation of copying. See further para. 7–132, *et seq.*, above.

[33] See para. 9–106 and para. 9–107, below.

[34] This was discussed by the Whitford Committee: The Report of the Committee to Consider the Law on Copyright and Designs, 1977 (Cmnd 6732), paras 242–250.

[35] CDPA 1988, s.38(1).

[36] s.178.

them for any other purpose; (b) that no person is furnished with more than one copy of the same article or with copies of more than one article contained in the same issue of a periodical; and (c) that persons to whom copies are supplied are required to pay for them a sum not less than the cost (including a contribution to the general expenses of the library) attributable to their production.[37] The production of multiple copies of the same material under this exemption is further restricted by a provision to the effect that a copy shall be supplied only to a person satisfying the librarian that his requirement is not related to any similar requirement of another person.[38] For this purpose the Regulations provide that a reader's requirements are to be regarded as similar to those of another reader if the requirements are for copies of substantially the same material at substantially the same time and for substantially the same purpose. The requirements of readers are to be regarded as related if they receive instructions to which the material is relevant at the same time and place.[39] This can cause problems where a class of students is referred by a lecturer to the same material, as copying by a librarian in these circumstances will clearly not fall within this exception, even though students may be able to copy the material for themselves.[40]

C. PARTS OF PUBLISHED WORKS

Copying by librarians. This section should be read together with the provisions relating to the copying of articles in periodicals (above). If prescribed conditions are complied with, a librarian may make and supply from a published edition a copy of part of a literary, dramatic or musical work (other than an article in a periodical) without infringing any copyright in the work, in any illustrations accompanying the work or in the typographical arrangement.[41] The prescribed conditions include restrictions similar in effect to those required for copying of articles in periodicals, save that no person is to be furnished with more than one copy of the same material or with a copy of more than a reasonable proportion of any work.[42] What amounts to a reasonable proportion is not further defined. Again, similar further restrictions are imposed on the production of multiple copies for similar or related uses by different persons as in the case of articles in periodicals.[43] When relying on this section librarians must be careful to avoid inadvertently copying the whole of a work, as might be the case where a photocopy is made of part of a collection of short stories or poems (each story or poem being a separate literary work).

9–107

D. LENDING OF COPIES BY LIBRARIES OR ARCHIVES

The Act provides that the copyright in a work of any description is not infringed by the lending of a book by a public library if the book is within the public lending right scheme.[44] For this purpose the "public lending right scheme" means the scheme in force under section 1 of the Public Lending Rights Act 1979.[45] A book is to be treated as being within the public lending right scheme if it falls within

9–108

---

[37] s.38(2), as amended following implementation of the Information Society Directive, and SI 1989/1212, reg.4(2).
[38] s.40(1) and SI 1989/1212, reg.4(2)(b).
[39] s.40(2) and SI 1989/1212, reg.4(2)(b).
[40] Relying on s.29 (fair dealing for the purposes of non-commercial research or private study). See paras 9–25 *et seq.*, above.
[41] CDPA 1988, s.39(1).
[42] s.39(2)(b).
[43] ss.40(1), (2) and SI 1989/1212, reg.4(2)(b).
[44] CDPA 1988, s.40A(1).
[45] s.40A(1)(a).

the eligibility criteria laid down by that scheme, irrespective of whether it actually qualifies for payment.[46] The Act further provides that copyright in a work is not infringed by the lending of copies of the work by a prescribed library or archive. For this purpose "prescribed library" means a non-public library which otherwise falls within paragraphs 2 to 6 of Part A of Schedule 1 of the Regulations.[47]

These provisions were introduced into the 1988 Act by the Copyright and Related Rights Regulations 1996,[48] implementing the Rental and Related Rights Directive,[49] no doubt with the intention of taking advantage of Article 5.[50]

E. SUPPLY OF COPIES TO OTHER LIBRARIES

9–109   In addition to the provisions relating to copying by librarians that have already been considered, the Act provides an exception to allow a librarian of a prescribed library to make and supply to another prescribed library a copy of an article in a periodical or the whole or part of a published edition of a literary, dramatic or musical work.[51] Provided that the "prescribed conditions" are complied with, the making and supply of the copy will not infringe copyright in the text of the article or, as the case may be, in the work, in any illustrations accompanying it or in the typographical arrangement.[52] Under the Regulations all libraries in the United Kingdom are "prescribed libraries" for the purpose of making and supplying copies under this section,[53] but the receiving library must either fall within the definition of prescribed library set out in Part A of Schedule 1 of the Regulations (see paragraph 9–105, above) or must be a library outside the United Kingdom which is not conducted for profit and which otherwise falls within Part B of Schedule 1.[54] The extent to which copying is permitted under this section depends on the material in question. Where the request is for a single article in an issue of a periodical this may be supplied on condition that only one copy is supplied and that the library receiving the copy pays a sum not less than the cost of producing the copy, including a contribution to the general expenses of the library.[55] This provision therefore appears to allow a library to make limited additions to its collection by acquiring for its readers articles from journals to which it does not subscribe. Where the request is for a copy of the whole or part of a published edition, or where the request is for more than one article in a single issue of a periodical then, again, only one copy may be supplied and the library receiving the copy must pay a sum not less than the cost of producing the copy.[56] In addition, however, a number of much more restrictive conditions must also be satisfied.

---

[46] See further, para. 19–09, below.

[47] Copyright and Related Rights Regulations 1996 (SI 1996/2967), reg.35. In effect "prescribed library" has a slightly narrower meaning in this context (*cf.* para. 9–105, above) in that libraries administered by a library authority and (other) public libraries are excluded from the definition.

[48] SI 1996/2967, reg.11.

[49] Council Directive 92/100 on rental and lending right and on certain rights related to copyright in the field of intellectual property ([1992] O.J. L346/61).

[50] Art.5(1) of the Rental Rights Directive gives Member States the power to derogate from the exclusive lending right in respect of public lending, provided that at least authors obtain a remuneration for such lending. However, it seems that CDPA 1988, s.40A may not comply in full with Art.5. See further, para. 19–02, below.

[51] CDPA 1988, s.41.

[52] s.41(1).

[53] SI 1996/2967, reg.3(2)

[54] reg.3(3). In order to fall within Pt B of Sch.1, a library outside the United Kingdom must be "conducted wholly or mainly for the purpose of facilitating or encouraging the study of bibliography, education, fine arts, history, languages, law, literature, medicine, music, philosophy, religion, science (including natural and social science) or technology".

[55] reg.5(2).

[56] reg.5(2).

Thus the section does not apply if at the time the copy is made the librarian making it knows, or could by reasonable inquiry ascertain, the name and address of a person entitled to authorise the making of the copy.[57] Moreover, the library requesting the copy must provide a written statement to the effect that it is a prescribed library and that it does not know and could not by reasonable inquiry ascertain, the name and address of a person entitled to authorise the making of the copy.[58] It seems that this provision is most likely to be useful in situations where a library wishes to acquire a copy of a book or journal and the publisher has gone out of business, as in these circumstances it can be very difficult to establish who is entitled to grant permission for such a copy to be made.

F. REPLACEMENT COPIES OF WORKS

Recognising that copies of works may become damaged or destroyed in circumstances where it would be difficult or impossible to purchase another original, the Act provides an exception to allow replacement copies to be made, thereby helping to preserve collections of important works.[59] Thus a librarian or archivist of a prescribed library or archive may make a copy from an item in the permanent collection of the library or archive (a) in order to preserve or replace that item by placing the copy in its permanent collection in addition to or in place of it, or (b) in order to replace in the permanent collection of another prescribed library or archive an item which has been lost, destroyed or damaged. In these circumstances the librarian or archivist will not thereby infringe the copyright in any literary, dramatic or musical work, in any illustrations accompanying such a work or, in the case of a published edition, in the typographical arrangement.[60] This exception only applies, however, to reference items; it does not apply to articles available for lending.[61] In addition, the prescribed conditions restrict the making of copies to cases where it is not reasonably practicable to purchase a copy of the item to fulfil the purpose in question.[62] It therefore seems that the operation of this section will be confined to out-of-print books where it would be difficult or disproportionately expensive to purchase a second-hand copy.[63]

9–110

G. COPYING OF UNPUBLISHED WORKS

Introduction. In many cases unpublished letters and manuscripts of historical or literary interest have been deposited with libraries or other institutions, and it may be in the general public interest that they should eventually be published.[64] Under the 1956 Act the copyright in such unpublished works might have been

9–111

---

[57] CDPA 1988, s.41(2) and SI 1996/2967, reg.5(2)(b).

[58] SI 1996/2967, reg.5(2)(b).

[59] CDPA 1988, s.42

[60] s.42(1). "Prescribed library" has, in relation to both the library that makes the copy and the receiving library, the same meaning as in s.41 of the 1988 Act (see para. 9–105, above). All archives in the United Kingdom are "prescribed archives" for the purpose of making and supplying copies under this section, but the receiving archive must not be conducted for profit.. "Conducted for profit" in this context means a library which is established or conducted for profit or which forms part of, or is administered by, a body established or conducted for profit: SI 1989/1212, para.3(5).

[61] SI 1996/2967, reg.6(2)(a).

[62] CDPA 1988, s.42(2) and SI 1996/2967, reg.6(2)(b). The library receiving the copy must also pay a sum not less than the cost of producing the copy, again including a contribution to the general expenses of the library: reg.6(2)(d).

[63] A similar exception exists in the United States where "the library or archive has, after a reasonable period, determined that an unused replacement cannot be obtained at a fair price": United States Copyright Act 1976, U.S.C. 17, s.108(c).

[64] Similar policy considerations lie behind the publication right, as to which, see Ch.17, below.

perpetual[65] and it was often impractical for anyone desiring to publish the material to find out with certainty in whom the copyright was vested. On the other hand, it might often have been difficult to find a publisher prepared to take the risk of publishing when a person might come forward, able to prove good title to the copyright. The 1956 Act therefore made provision to allow such works to be published, provided certain conditions were satisfied.[66]

The 1988 Act, as amended, altered the position relating to the period of copyright in unpublished works, so that perpetual copyright was abolished.[67] The provisions in the 1956 Act dealing with this problem were therefore not repeated. However, in the light of the transitional provisions dealing with the period of copyright in such works,[68] the 1988 Act contains transitional provisions such that the provisions of the 1956 Act continue to apply in modified form to works made before August 1, 1989.

At the same time, the 1988 Act included a new, more limited, exception to allow copies of unpublished works made on or after August 1, 1989 to be made by librarians and archivists and supplied for the purposes of research or private study. This has now been amended to restrict the purposes to non-commercial research and private study.

More generally, these provisions should be viewed alongside the "publication right" which is given to the first person to publish a previously unpublished literary, dramatic, musical or artistic work or a film which is no longer in copyright: the permitted acts now under consideration provide a degree of security for those who copy previously unpublished works (albeit for a limited purpose under the 1988 Act) and the publication right provides a financial incentive for the publication of such works.[69]

9–112　**Works made before August 1, 1989.** As already noted, the provisions of the 1956 Act continue to apply, in modified form,[70] in relation to works made before August 1, 1989.[71] For this purpose, where the making of a work extended over a period it is to be taken as having been made when its making was completed.[72]

The provisions of the 1956 Act (section 7(6)) apply where a manuscript or a copy of an unpublished literary, dramatic or musical work has been kept in a library, museum or other institution at which it is open to public inspection. Provided that more than 50 years have elapsed from the end of the calendar year in which the author died, and more than 100 years have elapsed after the making of the work, then the work may be reproduced for purposes of research or private study, or with a view to publication. Although these provisions primarily apply to literary, dramatic or musical works they also apply in respect of artistic works provided for explaining or illustrating the work in question.[73] Where a work is lawfully published under these provisions it may also lawfully be broadcast, performed in public or recorded.[74]

9–113　**Works made on or after August 1, 1989.** As has been seen, the relevant provi-

---

[65] Copyright Act 1956, s.2(3) proviso.

[66] ss.7(6)–(9).

[67] See further, paras 6–11 *et seq.*, above.

[68] CDPA 1988, Sch.1, para.12; and see para. 6–44, above.

[69] The publication right was introduced by the Copyright and Related Rights Regulations 1996 (SI 1996/2967). See further, Ch.17, below.

[70] The most important modification in that there is no longer a duty to give notice of intended publication: CDPA 1988, Sch.1, para.16. *cf.* Copyright Act 1956, s.7(7).

[71] CDPA 1988, Sch.1, para.16.

[72] Sch.1, para.1(3).

[73] Copyright Act 1956, s.7(9).

[74] s.7(8).

sions of the 1988 Act only apply to works made on or after August 1, 1989.[75] As to such works, the 1988 Act provides that, if prescribed conditions are complied with, the librarian or archivist of a prescribed library or archive may make and supply a copy of the whole or part of a literary, dramatic or musical work from a document in the library or archive without infringing any copyright in the work or any illustrations accompanying it.[76] The prescribed conditions are that this exception only applies if, (a) the copies are supplied only to persons satisfying the librarian or archivist that they require them for the purposes of (i) research for a non-commercial purpose, or (ii) private study, and will not use them for any other purpose; (b) that no person is furnished with more than one copy of the same material; and (c) the person receiving the copy is required to pay for it a sum not less than the cost attributable to its production, including a contribution to the general expenses of the library.[77] Moreover, this exception does not apply if at the time the copy is made the librarian or archivist making it is, or ought to be, aware of the fact that (a) the work had been published before the document was deposited in the library or archive, or (b) the copyright owner has prohibited copying of the work.[78]

H. LEGAL DEPOSIT LIBRARIES

Introduction. Section 15 of the Copyright Act 1911, which remained in force af- **9–114** ter that Act's general repeal, required publishers to deliver publications in print form to the Britsih Library for deposit and, on request, to any of five other specified legal deposit libraries.[79] The Legal Deposit Libraries Act 2003 (in this section 'the 2003 Act') has re-enacted section 15, making certain minor changes and, more significantly, has enabled equivalent measures to be made for the increasing volume of non-print material which is published.[80] The aim is to extend the provisions of the Act progressively to cover various non-print media as they develop, including off-line publications such as CD-ROMs and microforms, on-line publications such as e-journals, and other non-print materials. Section 15 of the 1911 Act was not in fact directly concerned with copyright issues but the 2003 Act has necessitated amendments to the 1988 Act to ensure that the various acts required or enabled by the 2003 Act do not infringe copyright.

The Information Society Directive. Article 9 of the Directive provides that the **9–115** Directive it is to be without prejudice to provisions concerning legal deposit requirements, so that the new provisions of the 1988 Act are permitted by the Directive.

Delivery of works published in print media. Where a copy of a work is **9–116** delivered to a legal deposit library, in whatever media, the 2003 Act provides that such delivery is to be taken not to infringe copyright, publication right or database right in relation to any part of the work (or any patent).[81] The 1988 Act has not itself been amended to provide for a defence or permitted act in this respect, but this provision of the 2003 Act presumably falls within the general scope of acts

---

[75] CDPA 1988, Sch.1, para.16.

[76] s.43(1). All libraries and archives in the United Kingdom are prescribed for the purposes of this section: SI 1996/2967, regs 3(2), 3(4).

[77] CDPA 1988, s.43(3), as amended; SI 1996/2967, reg.7.

[78] s.43(2).

[79] These were the National Libraries of Scotland and Wales, and the University libraries of Oxford, Cambridge and Trinity College Dublin.

[80] The Act came into force on February 1, 2004 (SI 2004/130). The Act is not to apply to works published before this date: s.16(4).

[81] Legal Deposit Libraries Act 2003, s.9(1)(b). Neither is it to constitute breach of any contract relating to any part of the work to which that person is a party: s.9(1)(a).

permitted under section 50 as being authorised by Act of Parliament.[82] In the case of works in the form of print media, it is hard to see how the mere act of delivery of a copy of a work to a legal deposit library could constitute an infringement of copyright, unless it were to constitute an issue to the public within the meaning of section 18 of the 1988 Act or unless, where it contains infringing material, it constituted a distribution within the meaning of section 23.

9–117 **Delivery of works published in non-print media.** Section 6 of the 2003 Act enables the Secretary of State to make regulations applying the provisions of that Act to works published in non-print media. Such regulations may make detailed provision regarding the manner of delivery and so on, including delivery by electronic means and as to the medium for delivery of a work published online.[83] The regulations may also require that, with the copy of the work, there is also delivered a copy of any computer program and any information necessary in order to access the work, and a copy of any manual and other material that accompanies the work and is made available to the public.[84] As with delivery of a copy of a work in print media, such delivery is to be taken not to infringe copyright, publication right or database right in relation to any part of the work.[85]

9–118 **Web harvesting.** It is clearly contemplated that deposit will not only take place by delivery by publishers but also by deposit libraries themselves taking material directly from the internet ("web harvesting"). The 1988 Act has therefore been amended to provide that copyright is not infringed by the copying of a work from the internet by a deposit library or person acting on its behalf if: (a) the work is of a prescribed description, (b) its publication on the internet, or a person publishing it there, is connected with the United Kingdom in a prescribed manner, and (c) the copying is done in accordance with any prescribed conditions.[86] No regulations prescribing such matters have yet been made.

9–119 **Acts done in relation to deposited non-print material.** The 2003 Act makes provision for particular acts that may and may not be done in relation to specified copies of a work delivered pursuant to these provisions. These copies are referred to as "relevant material" and are defined to mean: (i) a copy of a work published in a medium other than print; (ii) a copy of a computer program or a copy of any computer program and any information necessary in order to access the work, and a copy of any manual and other material that accompanies the work and is made available to the public; (iii) a copy of a work which has been published on the internet, where (a) the work is of a prescribed description, (b) the publication of the work on the internet, or a person publishing it there, is connected with the United Kingdom in a prescribed manner, and (c) the copy was made by a deposit library or person acting on its behalf copying the work from the internet in accordance with any prescribed conditions, and (iv) a copy (at any remove) of anything within any of these categories.[87] As to such material, the 2003 Act starts by stating what a deposit library or person acting on its behalf, or readers,[88] may not do, namely: (a) use the material (whether or not such use necessarily involves the

---

[82] See para. 9–131, below.

[83] See Legal Deposit Libraries Act 2003, s.6(2).

[84] s.6(2)(b).

[85] ss.9(1)(a), (2).

[86] CDPA 1988, s.44A(1), as inserted by the Legal Deposit Libraries Act 2003, s.8(1). Power to prescribe such matters is conferred by s.10 of the 2003 Act.

[87] Legal Deposit Libraries Act 2003, ss.7(5)(b), 10(6). Power to prescribe such matters is conferred by s.10 of the 2003 Act. No such regulations have yet been made.

[88] A reader is defined as a person who, for the purposes of research or study and with the permission of a deposit library, is on library premises controlled by it: s.7(5)(a).

making of a temporary copy of it), (b) copy the material (other than by making a temporary copy where this is necessary for the purpose of using the material), (c) in the case of relevant material comprising or containing a computer program or database, adapt it, (d) lend the material to a third party (other than lending by a deposit library to a reader for use by the reader on library premises controlled by the library), (e) transfer the material to a third party, or (f) dispose of the material.[89] Many such acts will constitute infringements of copyright but they are also now to constitute breaches of statutory duty.[90] The 2003 Act then continues by providing that the Secretary of State may nevertheless make provision by regulations permitting a deposit library or a person acting on its behalf, and readers, to do any of these activities in relation to relevant material, subject to such conditions as may be prescribed. Such conditions may deal with: (a) the purposes for which relevant material may be used or copied; (b) the time at which or the circumstances in which readers may first use relevant material; (c) the description of readers who may use relevant material; (d) the limitations on the number of readers who may use relevant material at any one time (whether by limiting the number of terminals in a deposit library from which readers may at any one time access an electronic publication or otherwise).[91] No regulations have yet been made prescribing for these matters. Finally, to give further effect to these provisions, the 1988 Act has been amended by insertion of a new section 44A(2) to provide that copyright is not infringed by the doing of anything which is so permitted.[92]

Excluded activities. A power has been inserted into the 1988 Act to make regulations to stop one or more of the permitted acts applying, or restrict the way they apply, to non-print material. The stated purpose of such regulations is so that a limit can be put on the application of any of the permitted acts under the 1988 Act to deposited material where, for example, such application gives rise to access that is more generous than that permitted for the same material that other libraries have had to purchase under a contract.[93] The power is nevertheless given in very broad terms. Thus, sections 44A(2) and (3) of the 1988 Act enable the Secretary of State to prescribe certain activitites, namely activities: (a) done for a prescribed purpose, (b) done by prescribed descriptions of reader, (c) done in relation to prescribed descriptions of relevant material, (d) done other than in accordance with prescribed conditions. In relation to such activities and in relation to relevant material (see above), the Secretary of State may by regulations exclude the application of such of the provisions of Chapter I of the 1988 Act as are prescribed. No such regulations have yet been made. **9–120**

Regulations. The 2003 Act contains a number of provisions dealing with regulations made under the Act. In general, such regulations may not be made unless the Secretary of State has consulted (a) the deposit libraries, and (b) the publishers appearing to the Secretary of State to be likely to be affected.[94] Regulations dealing with deposit of works in non-print media may not be made so as to apply to works published before the regulations are made[95] or unless the Secretary of State considers that the costs likely to be incurred as a result of the regulations by persons who publish works to which the regulations relate are not disproportion- **9–120A**

---

[89] s.7(1), (2).
[90] s.7(6).
[91] s.7(4).
[92] Inserted by s.8(2).
[93] *Hansard*, HL Vol.563 (2003).
[94] s11(2).
[95] s.11(3).

ate to the benefit to the public arising from the delivery of copies of such works.[96] Regulations dealing with the deposit of works in non-print media, the permitting of certain acts (*i.e.* so as to affect the scope of secion 44A(2) of the 1988 Act) or the exemption for deposit libraries for "web-harvesting" (i.e., under section 44A(1)), may not be made unless the Secretary of State considers that the regulations do not unreasonably prejudice the interests of persons who publish works to which the regulations relate.[97]

I. COPIES REQUIRED AS CONDITION OF EXPORT

9–121 **Export licensing for cultural goods: an overview.** Most countries seek to ensure that articles of cultural and artistic importance remain within their territory.[98] In the United Kingdom domestic legislation operates alongside European Union Regulations.[99] In brief, a licence must be obtained for practically all goods produced or manufactured more than 50 years ago. Either a United Kingdom or European licence may be required depending on the type of object, its value and its intended destination.[1] In either case the application has to be made to the United Kingdom authorities, who will apply the same criteria when deciding whether to grant an export licence.[2]

In many instances the burden of having to obtain a licence is substantially reduced by the existence of the system of Open General Export Licences. However, this system does not apply to goods which require a European licence,[3] nor does such a licence permit exports to an embargoed destination.[4] The Open General Export Licence (Antiques) allows goods to be exported without prior authorisation and no licence needs to be presented at the place of export.[5] It is only available for goods which fall below a certain value and it is not applicable to

---

[96] ss.11(3), (4).

[97] s.11(5).

[98] For further information, see the notice, *Export Licensing for Cultural Goods: Procedures and Guidance for Exporters of Works of Art and Other Cultural Goods* which is available from the Department for Culture, Media and Sport, Export Licensing Unit, 2-4 Cockspur Street, London SW1Y 5DH or on the Department's website: www.culture.gov.uk.

[99] The Export Control Act 2002 (c.28) empowers the Secretary of State to place restrictions on the export of any class of goods. Current restrictions on the export of antiques are to be found in the Export of Goods (Control) Order 1992 (SI 1992/3092), and current restrictions on the export of objects of cultural interest are to be found in the Export of Objects of Cultural Interest (Control) Order 2003 (SI 2003/2759). European controls are to be found in Council Regulation 92/3911 on the export of cultural goods ([1992] O.J. L395/1).

[1] Where the goods are being dispatched to another EU Member State, export restrictions do not apply to certain goods, including goods being exported by, and being the personal property of, their manufacturer or producer, or the spouse, widow or widower of that person; nor do they apply to letters written by or to the exporter or spouse of the exporter: Export of Goods (Control) Order 1992, Sch.1, Pt 1, reg.4 (antiques only), and Export of Objects of Cultural Interest (Control) Order 2003 (SI 2003/2759) Sch.1, Art.1, reg.1. Where the goods are being dispatched to a destination outside the EU, export restrictions do not apply to goods being exported by their "originator": Council Regulation 92/3911 on the export of cultural goods, annex 1, n.1. In the United Kingdom this is interpreted as meaning that restrictions do not apply to goods being exported by, and being the personal property of, their manufacturer or producer; nor do they apply to letters written by or to the exporter: *Export Licensing for Cultural Goods: Procedures and Guidance for Exporters of Works of Art and Other Cultural Goods*, p.15.

[2] Council Regulation 92/3911 on the export of cultural goods, Art.2(2). Application forms are available from the Export Licensing Unit at the above address. As to the criteria which are applied see *Export Licensing for Cultural Goods: Procedures and Guidance for Exporters of Works of Art and Other Cultural Goods*, pp.1–5.

[3] See s.11 of the Open General Export Licence (Antiques) (hereafter "OGEL (Antiques)"), 1 November 2002.

[4] See s.8 of OGEL (Antiques) 1/11/02: "embargoed destination means a destination to which an exportation ban applies by virtue of a prohibition contained in legislation implementing Eurpoean Union or United Nations sanctions".

[5] Save in respect of certain articles such as articles including a representation of the likeness of any British historical personage (made otherwise than by photography and excluding a coin) that has a value of £10,000 or above but less than £180,000, where a certificate must be produced to

certain goods including hand-produced manuscripts (including archives and documents) nor to hand-sanctionsproduced architectural, scientific and engineering drawings.[6] In all cases where an Open General Export Licence is not available, a specific licence must be applied for.

The permitted act. Where a specific licence is required this will usually be granted.[7] However, in the case of documentary or photographic material this licence may be made conditional upon a copy of the work being deposited in a library or archive, so that it will not be lost to British researchers. Access to the copy will then normally be denied for a period of seven years, unless the owner of the original consents to some lesser restriction.[8] In order to speed up applications for documentary material Government guidelines recommend that the applicant include a good-quality copy of the original with the licence application.[9] However, the guidelines also recognise that this will not always be possible because the work may still be in copyright and the applicant may well not be the copyright owner.[10] To cover the situation of a copy being required to be deposited as a condition of an export licence, the Act provides that where an article of cultural or historical importance or interest cannot lawfully be exported from the United Kingdom unless a copy of it is made and deposited in an appropriate library or archive,[11] it is not an infringement of copyright to make that copy.[12] The wording of this provision is broad enough to cover conditions contained in both United Kingdom and European licences, but it would not protect an applicant who voluntarily enclosed a copy of a work with his application. An applicant who wishes to speed up his application must therefore be diligent in ensuring that he does not infringe copyright.[13]

9–122

8. PUBLIC ADMINISTRATION

Introduction. The 1988 Act contains a number of provisions relating to public administration. These provisions rationalise and expand the similar provisions of the 1956 Act and can be divided into four categories. First, there are exceptions relating to Parliamentary and judicial proceedings and to the proceedings of Royal Commissions and statutory inquiries. The Act provides that copyright will

9–123

---

customs and excise at the place of export by either the Director of the National Portrait Gallery or the Keeper of the Scottish National Portrait Gallery stating that in his opinion the work is not of national importantance. See ss.3 and 4 of OGEL (Antiques) 1/11/02.

[6] Works in which copyright may subsist and for which an OGEL is available (irrespective of the intended destination) include photographs more than 50 years old valued at less than £10,000, paintings more than 50 years old in oil or tempera valued at less than £180,000, and portraits in any medium more than 50 years old of a British historical personage valued at less than £180,000. See further, *Export Licensing for Cultural Goods: Procedures and Guidance for Exporters of Works of Art and Other Cultural Goods.*

[7] Objections are made to applications relating to between 25 and 50 objects each year out of a total of 3,000–5,000 applications covering 8,000 to 10,000 objects: *Export Licensing for Cultural Goods: Procedures and Guidance for Exporters of Works of Art and Other Cultural Goods*, pp.4 and 5.

[8] *Export Licensing for Cultural Goods: Procedures and Guidance for Exporters of Works of Art and Other Cultural Goods.*

[9] *Export Licensing for Cultural Goods: Procedures and Guidance for Exporters of Works of Art and Other Cultural Goods.*

[10] *Export Licensing for Cultural Goods: Procedures and Guidance for Exporters of Works of Art and Other Cultural Goods*, and see the footnotes to para. 9–122, above, for the position where goods are exported by their manufacturer or producer.

[11] This is not limited to "prescribed libraries and archives" (*cf.* para. 9–104, above), but in practice the copy will have to be deposited with the British Library: *Export Licensing for Cultural Goods: Procedures and Guidance for Exporters of Works of Art and Other Cultural Goods.*

[12] CDPA 1988, s.44.

[13] This provision was new in 1988. As to the background to its introduction, see *Copinger*, (12th ed.), p.204, n.79.

not be infringed by anything done for the purpose of such proceedings or for the reporting thereof.[14] Secondly, there are exceptions allowing the copying of public records and material on a statutory register or on a register available for public inspection pursuant to a statutory requirement. Thirdly, there is an exception allowing the Crown to copy and issue to the public copies of previously unpublished works, where these have been communicated to the Crown in the course of public business. Finally, the Act makes it clear that an act done under specific statutory authority will not infringe copyright. The justification for these provisions is the general public interest in permitting the copying of works where this is necessary for effective public administration, in circumstances where the rights of the copyright owner are unlikely to be substantially prejudiced.

9–124   **The Berne Convention.** The Convention does not contain any specific provision dealing with acts of these kinds but presumably they all fall within Article 9(2), which allows countries of the Union to permit the reproduction of works in certain special cases, provided that such reproduction does not conflict with normal exploitation of the work and does not unreasonably prejudice the legitimate interests of the owner (*i.e.* provided the 3-step test is satisfied[15]).

9–125   **The Information Society Directive.** No amendments were made to these provisions of the Act on implementation of the Information Society Directive. Article 5(3)(e) of the Directive permits Member States to make an exception to the reproduction, distibution and communication to the public rights in the case of use for the purposes of public security or to ensure the proper performance or reporting of administrative, parliamentary or judicial proceedings. Article 9 also also provides that the Directive is to be without prejudice to provisions concerning access to public documents.

A. PARLIAMENTARY AND JUDICIAL PROCEEDINGS

9–126   The copyright in any work is not infringed by anything done for the purposes of parliamentary or judicial proceedings.[16] "Parliamentary proceedings" are defined as including proceedings of the Northern Ireland Assembly, or the Scottish Parliament, or of the European Parliament.[17] "Judicial proceedings" are defined as including proceedings before any court, tribunal or person having authority to decide any matter affecting a person's legal rights or liabilities.[18] This would cover the Copyright Tribunal and seemingly includes arbitration proceedings.[19] In addition, copyright is not infringed by anything done for the purposes of reporting such proceedings, but this is not to be construed as authorising the copying of a work which is itself a published report of the proceedings.[20] Thus it would not be permissible under this section for a journalist to copy a rival's Parliamentary sketch. The reports of *Hansard* and law reports are similarly protected. Whether a use falls within this permitted act is essentially an objective question and the expression "for the purposes of parliamentary or judicial proceedings" should be

---

[14] This provision does not, however, allow a work which is itself a published report of such proceedings to be copied (see para. 9–126 and para. 9–127, below).

[15] See para. 9–02, above.

[16] CDPA 1988, s.45(1).

[17] s.178.

[18] s.178.

[19] *London & Leeds Estates v Paribas Ltd (No.2)* [1995] 1 E.G.L.R. 102. In reaching this construction, Mance J. relied upon s.48(1) of the Copyright Act 1956, which defined judicial proceedings as "a proceeding before any court, tribunal or person having by law the power to hear, receive and examine evidence on oath".

[20] CDPA 1988, s.45(2). It must be assumed that "reporting" extends to include all the acts restricted by copyright including copying, issuing copies to the public and broadcasting.

construed as a whole, rather than focussing on individual words.[21] It was held that the equivalent provisions of the New Zealand Act applied only to specific proceedings existing at the time the reproduction was made and not to proceedings that were merely contemplated,[22] although this seems unduly restrictive and it has been held at least arguable that under the 1988 Act proceedings need not be in existence.[23] The court also left open the question, assuming that proceedings need not yet be in existence, of what the status of copies would be if the proceedings were never in fact brought. It is suggested, however, that the act of copying could not retrospectively become an infringement in this event, and so the copies made would not become infringing copies. Section 54 does not contain the type of provision to the latter effect found elsewhere in some of the permitted act provisions.[24]

B. ROYAL COMMISSIONS AND STATUTORY INQUIRIES

The copyright in any work is not infringed by anything done for the purposes of **9–127** the proceedings of a Royal Commission or statutory inquiry.[25] For this purpose, "Royal Commission" includes a Commission appointed for Northern Ireland by the Secretary of State in pursuance of the prerogative powers of Her Majesty delegated to him under section 7(2) of the Northern Ireland Constitution Act 1973.[26] "Statutory inquiry" means an inquiry held or investigation conducted in pursuance of a duty imposed or power conferred by or under an enactment.[27] Moreover, where a work, or material from it, is contained in a report of a Royal Commission or a statutory inquiry, the copyright in the work is not infringed by issuing copies of the report to the public.[28] Nor is the copyright in any work infringed by anything done for the purposes of reporting any such proceedings held in public, but this is not to be construed as authorising the copying of a work which is itself a published report of the proceedings.[29]

C. MATERIAL OPEN TO PUBLIC INSPECTION OR ON OFFICIAL REGISTER

The Act provides three related exceptions to allow for the copying of material **9–128** that is available for public inspection, thus facilitating the use of such material and promoting access to it. The first exception relates to material which is open to public inspection pursuant to a statutory requirement or which is on a statutory register. Any copyright in the material as a literary work is not infringed by the copying of so much of the material as contains factual information, provided this is done by or with the authority of the appropriate person and does not involve the issuing of copies to the public.[30] For these purposes "statutory requirement" means a requirement imposed by a provision made by or under an enactment and "statutory register" means a register maintained in pursuance of a statutory

---

[21] *A v B* [2000] E.M.L.R. 1006, applying *Pro Sieben Media AG v Carlton U.K. Television Ltd* [1999] 1 W.L.R. 605; [1999] F.S.R. 610.
[22] *Auckland Medical Aid Trust v Commissioner of Police* [1976] 1 N.Z.L.R. 485.
[23] *A v B* [2000] E.M.L.R. 1006.
[24] As to which, see s.27(6).
[25] CDPA 1988, s.46(1).
[26] s.46(4).
[27] s.46(4).
[28] s.46(3). Note that there is no exception to allow for the report to be performed in public or to be communicated to the public. It might not, therefore, be possible for the Commission to publish its report on the Internet. See further, Crown, "Copyright and the Internet," (1995) 11(6) Comp. L.&P. 169 at 170.
[29] s.46(2). As to the meaning of "reporting" see the note of s.45(2) in para. 9–126, above.
[30] CDPA 1988, s.47(1).

requirement.[31] The "appropriate person" is the person required to make the material open to public inspection or, as the case may be, the person maintaining the register.[32] This provision would presumably, for example, enable copies to be made of records kept for public inspection by the Registrar of Companies.[33] The second exception is confined to material open to public inspection pursuant to a statutory requirement. Provided that the appropriate person has given his authority, copyright in any work will not be infringed by the copying or issuing to the public of copies if this is for the purpose of enabling the material to be inspected at a more convenient time or place, or if this otherwise facilitates the exercise of any right for the purpose of which the statutory requirement of availability for inspection is imposed.[34] For example, planning documents could be copied for inspection at a more convenient time or place.[35] The third exception, like the first, relates both to material which is open to public inspection pursuant to a statutory requirement and material which is on a statutory register. Where such material contains information about matters of general scientific, technical, commercial or economic interest, copyright is not infringed by the copying or issuing to the public of copies if this is for the purpose of disseminating that information. Again this is dependent upon the authority of the appropriate person being given.[36] An example here would seem to be the copying and publication of a patent specification in so far as this contains material of "general interest". The Secretary of State may provide that these three provisions are only to apply to copies marked in a specified manner,[37] and may extend the provisions to material made open to public inspection by international organisations or under international agreements.[38]

D. Material Communicated to the Crown

9–129 In certain circumstances the Crown is permitted to make copies of a previously unpublished work and issue these to the public.[39] This exception applies whenever a literary, dramatic, musical or artistic work has been communicated to the Crown in the course of public business by or with the licence of the copyright owner and a document or other material thing recording or embodying the work is owned by or is in the custody or control of the Crown.[40] In such cases the Crown may, for the purpose for which the work was communicated to it, or any related purpose which could reasonably have been anticipated by the copyright owner, copy the work and issue copies of the work to the public without infring-

---

[31] s.47(6). An example of a statutory register is the Data Protection Register, as established by the Data Protection Act, 1984.

[32] CDPA 1988, s.47(6).

[33] See *Hansard*, HL Vol.501, col.242; Report of the Debates of the House of Commons Standing Committee E in 1988, col.234. The Registrar of Companies has in fact issued blanket licences giving authority to all persons to make copies under s.47(1), (2) and (3).

[34] CDPA 1988, s.47(2).

[35] *Hansard*, HL Vol.501, col.242.

[36] s.47(3).

[37] s.47(4). And see the Copyright (Material Open to Public Inspection) (Marking of Copies of Maps) Order 1989 (SI 1989/1099), at Vol.2 at A4.vii, which prescribes the marking to be applied to maps, and the Copyright (Material Open to Public Inspection) (Marking of Copies of Plans and Drawings) Order 1990 (SI 1990/1427), at Vol.2 at A4.xiii, which prescribes the marking to be applied to plans and or drawings copied under s.47(2).

[38] s.47(5). As to the definition of "international organisation," see s.178. And see the Copyright (Material Open to Public Inspection) (International Organisations) Order 1989 (SI 1989/1098), at Vol.2 at A4.vi, which extends the provisions to the European Patent Office and the World Intellectual Property Organisation.

[39] CDPA 1988, s.48. "Unpublished" in this context means unpublished otherwise than by virtue of this section: s.48(3). The Crown does not, however, have the right to perform a work in public or communicate the work to the public (see the footnotes to para. 9–127, above).

[40] s.48(1).

ing copyright,[41] subject to any agreement to the contrary.[42] For this purpose "public business" includes any activity carried on by the Crown,[43] and "the Crown" includes various health service bodies.[44] It was said during the passage of the Bill that "any related purpose which could reasonably have been anticipated by the copyright owner" might, for example, cover material submitted to a departmental committee which is subsequently included in the committee's report.[45] This can be contrasted with the position of an author who submits a manuscript to the authorities in order to prove that he is engaged in useful employment. The Crown would not be able to publish the work in these circumstances.[46]

These provisions provide the Crown with a remarkably wide exception. There is no restriction, for example, on the Crown using these provisions in order to make a profit at the copyright owner's expense. Making this exception subject to any agreement to the contrary is unlikely to afford much protection to copyright owners, as the communication of the material in question may otherwise be in the owner's interest, so that deciding not to communicate the material unless certain conditions are complied with may not be a viable option. It was suggested during the passage of the Bill that an owner might on occasion be able to rely on an obligation of confidence,[47] but ultimately it seems that the owner will often have to rely on the Crown's good will, a point that was in effect conceded by the Government.[48]

E. PUBLIC RECORDS

Public records within the meaning of the Public Records Acts 1958, the Public Records (Scotland) Act 1937 and Welsh public records (as defined in the Government of Wales Act 1998), the Public Records Act (Northern Ireland) 1923, which are open to public inspection, may be copied, and a copy may be supplied to any person, provided this is done by or with the authority of an officer appointed under one of those Acts.[49] Once again the justification for such a provision is to facilitate the use of certain material and to promote wider access to it. This exception can therefore be seen as supplementing the provisions relating to statutory registers and material open to public inspection pursuant to a statutory requirement.

9–130

F. ACTS DONE UNDER STATUTORY AUTHORITY

Where the doing of a particular act is specifically authorised by an Act of Parliament, whenever passed, then, unless the Act provides otherwise, the doing of that act does not infringe copyright.[50] This provision was new in the 1988 Act and seems unnecessary, as presumably the defence of statutory authority would always have been available and is in fact expressly preserved by the Act.[51] The reference to a "particular act specifically authorised by an Act of Parliament" is

9–131

---

[41] s.48(2).
[42] s.48(5).
[43] s.48(4).
[44] s.48(6).
[45] *Hansard*, HL Vol.495, col.641.
[46] *Hansard*, HL Vol.493, col.1178.
[47] *Hansard*, HL Vol.495, col.641. The permitted acts do not provide a defence to such an action: CDPA 1988, s.28(1) and see para. 9–12, above.
[48] *Hansard*, HL Vol.495, col.641.
[49] CDPA 1988, s.49. As amended by the Government of Wales Act 1998 (c.38), Sch.12, para.27.
[50] CDPA 1988, s.50(1) This provision also applies in relation to an enactment contained in Northern Ireland legislation as it applies in relation to an Act of Parliament CDPA 1988, s.50(2).
[51] s.50(3).

designed to exclude cases where a general activity is authorised by Parliament. Thus it could not be argued that because the Broadcasting Acts authorise broadcasting by independent television this amounts to Parliament having granted a blanket licence to use copyright material.[52] This can be contrasted with the duty placed on companies to provide a copy of its memorandum and articles of association to any member who requires it.[53] It was said during the passage of the Bill that, by virtue of this section, there would be no infringement of copyright in these circumstances, even though the copyright in such documents might not belong to the company concerned.[54]

9. COMPUTER PROGRAMS

9–132   **Introduction.** Amendments to the 1988 Act made by the Copyright (Computer Programs) Regulations 1992[55] included a series of permitted acts relating to computer programs. These amendments implemented Council Directive 91/250/EEC on the legal protection of computer programs[56] (in this section "the Directive"), which attempts to reconcile the copyright laws of the Member States of the European Union with some of the practical difficulties posed by copyright protection for computer programs. Prior to the implementation of the Directive, the Act only provided a limited exception relating to the transfer of works in electronic form.[57] Further amendment has been required on implementation of the Information Society Directive as a result of the change to the fair dealing provisions in section 29 of the Act but this has not resulted in any substantial change in the substantive law in this area.[58] In brief, the permitted acts contained in the Act relate to (a) the right of a "lawful user" of a computer program to make a back-up copy, (b) the right to decompile a program in order to create an independent compatible program, (c) the right of a lawful user to observe, study or test a computer program for certain purposes and (d) a limited right to copy or adapt a program where this is necessary for the lawful use of that program. In conjunction with these permitted acts, section 296A strikes down contractual terms which would frustrate these provisions.[59] It provides that where a person has the use of a computer program under an agreement, any term or condition in the agreement shall be void in so far as it purports to prohibit or restrict the right to make back-up copies, the right to decompile a program or the use of any device or method to analyse the ideas and principles which underlie any element of the program. It is worth emphasising that these provisions should be construed consistently with the Directive, as a number of key terms in both the Act and the Directive are left undefined.

A. BACK UP COPIES

9–133   In the absence of statutory provision, the making of a back up copy would be an infringement unless the owner had consented to such use. In practice an express

---

[52] *Hansard*, HL Vol.495, col.643.

[53] Companies Act 1985 (c.6), s.19.

[54] *Hansard*, HL Vol.495, col.643.

[55] SI 1992/3233. As to transitional provisions, see reg.12(2), which provides that the amendments are not to affect any agreement or any term or conditions of an agreement entered into before January 1, 1993. Otherwise, the Regulations apply equally in relation to computer programs created before this date. See also the Software Directive (91/250/EEC), Art.9(2).

[56] [1991] O.J. L122/42.

[57] CDPA 1988, s.56 (see para. 9–150, below).

[58] Indeed, it was expressly provided that the Information Society Directive was not to affect the Software Directive: 91/250, Art.1(2)(a).

[59] *cf.* CDPA 1988, s.28(1) and see para. 9–12, above.

right to make back up copies is often granted and in other cases it may be implied. The Directive whilst not expressly providing a right to make back up copies, does so implicitly by providing, under the heading "Exceptions to the restricted acts", that in the absence of contractual provisions the making of a copy of a program is not to require the authorisation of the rightholder where this is necessary for its use by the lawful acquirer in accordance with its intended purpose and, further, that the making of a back up copy by a person having a right to use the program may not be prevented by contract in so far as it is necessary for that use.[60] Section 50A provides more explicitly that: "It is not an infringement of copyright for a lawful user of a copy of a computer program to make any back up copy of it which is necessary for him to have for the purposes of his lawful use". A "lawful user" is defined as any person who has a right to use the program, whether under a licence to do any acts restricted by the copyright in the computer program or otherwise.[61] Clearly this would extend to a purchaser of a program who thereby acquires, expressly or impliedly, a licence to use the program and to any person claiming through the purchaser.[62] But where a term of the purchase contract expressly limits any licence to the purchaser alone, it seems that any other user would not be a lawful user, since the use of a program inevitably involves its reproduction.[63] Examples of cases where a person might have a "right" to use the program otherwise than under licence would presumably be where that person was exercising another of the permitted acts, or where that person had some other defence to an action for infringement. It is worth pointing out that this permitted act extends only to the making of back up copies of computer programs. It is not lawful to make a back up copy of something which includes works other than computer programs. This will often be the position in the case of computer games, which will contain other kinds of literary works, as well as artistic and musical works. The point underlines the importance which often arises of distinguishing a computer program from other works stored in digital form.

The Act does not attempt to define "back up copy," but presumably this refers to a copy made by the user as a reserve in case of loss of or damage to the original.[64] The European Commission has stated its opinion that the wording and objective of Article 5(2), under which "a" (*i.e.* only one) copy is permitted, means that the purpose may not be other than as a "back up" to ensure that normal use of the program can continue in the event of loss or defect of the original.[65] It is not entirely clear, however, when the making of a back up copy is to be regarded as "necessary": the Directive refers merely to acts which are necessary for the use of the program "in accordance with its intended purpose".[66] While the making of a back up copy is often no doubt highly desirable, it is arguable that it will often not be necessary. The provision would be of virtually no application, however,

---

[60] Information Society Directive, Arts 5(1), (2). The recitals do not deal specifically with back up copies. The 18th recital states only: "Whereas [recital 17] means that the acts of loading and running necessary for the use of a copy of a program which has been lawfully acquired, and the act of correction of its errors, may not be prohibited by contract; whereas, in the absence of specific contractual provisions, including when a copy of the program has been sold, any other act necessary for the use of the copy of a program may be performed in accordance with its intended purpose by a lawful acquirer of that copy".

[61] CDPA 1988, s.50A(2).

[62] As to the rights of such persons, see s.56 and para. 9–150, below.

[63] s.17(6), "Copying ... includes the making of copies which are transient or are incidental to some other use of the work". Also see para. 7–19, above.

[64] *The Shorter Oxford English Dictionary* defines a back up copy in this context as, "a duplicate copy of a disk, file, program, etc.".

[65] See the Commission's communication on the implementation and effect of the Software Directive (COM/2000/0199 final).

[66] Information Society Directive, Art.5(1). See also CDPA 1988, s.296A, which strikes down contractual terms probiting or restricting the making of a back-up copy "which it is necessary for [the user] to have *for the purposes of the agreed use*".

unless a reasonably liberal construction is given to it, such that the ordinary and prudent making of a back up copy is allowed. It has been said that the section is directed to the situation in which a person who has access to a computer program in the form, for example, of a physical copy such as a CD-ROM also has an express licence to use it, such that the licence will continue even if the original physical copy is lost or damaged. In this situation, the argument continues, the licence can be exercised if access can be had to some other lawful copy, such as a back up copy, assuming that the licence is not restricted to the original copy. The section is not directed, it is said, to the kind of case in which a person simply buys a computer program, for example a computer game in CD-ROM format, and with it acquires an obviously implied licence to use it. In this situation, if the physical carrier is lost or damaged there is no continuing licence and another copy must be purchased. It would not therefore have been "necessary" to make a back up copy.[67] While all this may be true, the suggestion does not throw any real light on why it should be "necessary", as opposed to desirable, to make a back up copy in the first kind of case[68] and the argument appears to depend on the precise nature of any express or implied licence. It would seem particularly difficult to argue that an additional copy was "necessary" if the program is supplied on a physical copy such as a CD-ROM with the intention that it should be copied onto and stored on a hard drive for its normal use. The original physical copy will remain available in case of loss or damage to the hard drive and serves the purpose of a back up copy. Where the program supplied in physical form is only loaded into RAM or other temporary memory in the course of ordinary use, the case is clearly stronger for arguing that it is "necessary" to make a back up copy within the spirit of the Directive. In the case of a program supplied via the internet without any accompanying physical copy, again the case is stronger for saying that it is necessary to make a back up copy.

B. DECOMPILATION

9–134   **Rationale.** Section 50B is designed to meet the "interoperability" requirements of the Software Directive. The final form of this part of the Directive was the result of intense negotiation and lobbying between the various interested parties, in particular major software houses, companies engaged in the production of compatible products and consumers.[69] The fundamental issue at stake was the extent to which designers of computer programs and computer-related products should be entitled to look at and study other programs to enable compatible products to be produced, particularly through knowledge of the program's interfaces. Without such knowledge, communication between two systems is generally impossible, and thus compatible non-infringing products such as application programs and peripheral devices cannot be developed. The nature of computer programs means that determining the nature of the interfaces will inevitably involve reproducing the program at some stage, since the program will normally only be available in machine code, from which these characteristics will not be apparent. The machine code must first be extracted and converted into a higher-level language[70], a process which would normally involve

---

[67] *Sony Computer Entertainment v Owen* [2002] EWHC 45 (Ch).

[68] It was not relevant for the purpose of the decision to explore this aspect further.

[69] See Dreier, "The Council Directive of 14 May 1991 on the Legal Protection of Computer Programs". [1991] 9 E.I.P.R. 319.

[70] *i.e.* it must be "decompiled": CDPA 1988, s.50B(1).

infringement.[71] Thus, without some form of exception to allow for the decompilation of a program, the copyright owner's monopoly would be extended beyond the boundaries of the "work" and would include the sole right to produce compatible products.[72]

The permitted act. To overcome the problem outlined above, section 50B **9–135** provides that: "It is not an infringement of copyright for a lawful user of a copy of a computer program expressed in a low level language to convert it into a version expressed in a higher level language, or incidentally in the course of so converting it to copy it".[73] However, this exception is subject to a number of conditions:

(1) It is only available to a lawful user. "Lawful user" has the same meaning here as in relation to the making of back up copies.[74]

(2) The decompilation must be necessary in order to obtain the information required to create an independent program which can be operated with the program decompiled or with another program (the "permitted objective").[75]

(3) The information acquired must not be used for any purpose other than that set out above.[76]

The Act goes on to give examples of cases where these conditions will not be satisfied. Thus the Act provides that these conditions will not be satisfied where the information required is "readily available" to the lawful user.[77] Such information will presumably be "readily available" if information regarding a program's interfaces is available from the program's manufacturers. The Act also provides that these conditions will not be satisfied if the user does not confine the decompiling to such acts as are necessary to achieve the permitted objective[78]; nor may the information be supplied to a person who does not require the information for that purpose.[79] Finally, the information must not be used to create a program which is "substantially similar in expression to the program decompiled or be used to do any act restricted by copyright".[80] At first it might appear as though this final restriction imposes two distinct limitations on the right to decompile a program, namely, (1) that the information must not be used to create a program which is substantially similar in expression to the program decompiled; and (2) that the information must not be used to do any act restricted by copyright. However, this last condition should be taken to implement Article 6(2)(c) of the

---

[71] s.21(4). It will also usually be necessary to copy the machine code onto some other medium at this stage.

[72] In the United States the problem of decompilation has been solved not by legislation but by the court's application of the "fair use" doctrine: *Atari Games Corp. v Nintendo of America, Inc.* (1992) 975 F.2d 832; *Sega Enterprises v Accolade, Inc.* (1992) 977 F.2d 1510. *cf. Creative Technology Ltd v Aztech Systems PTE Ltd* (CA, Singapore) [1997] F.S.R. 491. In the United Kingdom the defence of fair dealing for the purposes of non-commercial research or private study is specifically excluded in the case of decompilation: CDPA 1988, s.29(4).

[73] CDPA 1988, s.50B(1). "Low and "higher-level" languages are not defined, but machine code, assembly code and object or source code can be taken to represent ascending levels of language.

[74] s.50A(2). *cf.* Article 6(1)(a) of the Software Directive which provides that the right of decompilation may be exercised by "the licensee or by another person having a right to use a copy of the program, or on their behalf by a person authorised to do so".

[75] s.50B(2)(a). It is worth emphasising the latter point, *i.e.* that decompilation may be carried out with a view to creating a program to be operated with a program other than the one decompiled.

[76] s.50B(2)(b).

[77] s.50B(3)(a).

[78] s.50B(3)(b).

[79] s.50B(3)(c). It seems that this is to act as a condition subsequent, so that if decompilation takes place without infringement (because all the other conditions are met) but the decompiler subsequently supplies this information in contravention of this section, the original decompilation will become, retrospectively, an infringement.

[80] s.50B(3)(d).

Directive, which provides that the information obtained must not be used "for the development, production or marketing of a computer program substantially similar in its expression, or for any other act which infringes copyright". Whilst this seems relatively clear, a degree of uncertainty remains as to what "substantially similar in expression" means. In particular, it is not clear whether this test is the same as the ordinary test of infringement in the United Kingdom, namely, that the defendant's work must not reproduce "a substantial part" of the Claimant's work. The potential disparity arises because the Directive seems to have embraced the idea/expression dichotomy,[81] whilst courts in the United Kingdom have proved much more reluctant to do so.[82] It seems likely that courts in the United Kingdom will interpret the words "which is substantially similar in expression" as being equivalent to "which reproduces a substantial part." As with the "back up" exception, it should be noted that the decompilation exception applies only to computer programs and not to other works which may be embodied in electronic form along with the computer program. This will often restrict the utility of this exception.

9–136   **Lock and key routines**. Section 50B would on its face appear to enable a program to be decompiled in order to ascertain any "lock-and-key" routines contained within the program decompiled[83] provided this was done with the objective of creating an independent program which could be operated with the program decompiled or with another program. Whether the independent program could then have been written without infringing copyright would depend on whether the "key" written into it amounted to a substantial part of the target computer program, such that they were substantially similar in expression.[84] However, the lock-and-key routine will constitute a technical device within the meaning of section 296[85] and a person who manufactures for sale, sells, etc. means, the sole intended purpose of which is to facilitate the unauthorised circumvention of the lock-and-key routine will thus infringe the rights conferred by section 296. These issues are dealt with more fully in Chapter 15.

C. Observing, Studying and Testing of Computer Programs

9–137   Article 5(3) of the Software Directive provides that a person having a right to use a copy of a computer program shall be entitled, without the authorisation of the rightholder, to observe, study or test the functioning of the program in order to determine the ideas and principles which underlie any element of the program if he does so while performing any of the acts of loading, displaying, running, transmitting or storing the program which he is entitled to do. It was not considered necessary to amend the 1988 Act when implementing the Directive because section 29 of the Act already permitted fair dealing with a work, and thus a computer program, for the purposes of research or private study. The effect of the Information Society Directive was, however, to require this general permitted

---

[81] See further, recital 13 and Art.5(3) of the Software Directive.

[82] For example, see *Ibcos Computers Ltd v Barclays Bank Highland Finance Ltd* [1994] F.S.R. 275 at 292, 302. See further, para. 7–13, above. Moreover, it should be noted that even in jurisdictions where the idea/expression dichotomy is firmly entrenched, in particular the United States, attempting to distinguish between ideas and expression in the context of computer programs has proved exceptionally difficult. See, for example, *Whelan Associates Inc. v Jaslow Dental Laboratory Inc.* [1987] F.S.R. 1; *Computer Associates v Altai Inc.* (1992) 23 U.S.P.Q. 2d 1241.

[83] "Key" routines produce a data stream which, when detected and recognised by a device such as a games console, will "unlock" the device and allow it to be operated.

[84] See para. 7–148 , *et seq.*, above.

[85] In relation to a computer program, a technical device is defined to mean any device intended to prevent or restrict acts that are not authorised by the copyright owner of that computer program and are restricted by copyright: CDPA 1988, s.296(6).

act to be restricted to non-commercial research and also to exclude any private study which is directly or indirectly for a commercial purpose.[86] The result would in many cases have been to exclude the kind of acts covered by Article 5(3) of the Software Directive. The provisions of this Directive were expressly not to be affected by the Information Society Directive and so it was necessary for the United Kingdom to deal with the issue on implementation. This was done by the introduction of a new section 50BA, which enacts the provisions of the Software Directive verbatim. It provides that it is not an infringement of copyright for a lawful user[87] of a copy of a computer program to observe, study or test the functioning of the program in order to determine the ideas and principles which underlie any element of the program if he does so while performing any of the acts of loading, displaying, running, transmitting or storing the program which he is entitled to do.[88] At the same time, section 29 has been amended to provide a demarcation between these acts and those permitted under the fair dealing provisions. Thus, section 29(4A) provides that it is not fair dealing under that section to observe, study or test the functioning of a computer program in order to determine the ideas and principles which underlie any element of the program, these acts being acts which are permitted, if at all, if done in accordance with section 50BA. Once again, it should be noted that this exception does not permit the copying of works other than computer programs when observing, etc. computer programs.

D. OTHER ACTS PERMITTED TO LAWFUL USERS

Error correction and other lawful acts. Article 5(1) of the Software Directive   **9–138**
provides that, in the absence of specific contractual provisions, authorisation to do any of the acts restricted by copyright will not be necessary where the act in question is necessary for the use of a computer program by its lawful acquirer in accordance with its intended purpose. The Article goes on to provide expressly that this is to include the right to correct errors. Section 50C therefore provides that a lawful user[89] may copy or adapt a program where this is necessary for its lawful use and provided that this is not prohibited by a contractual term.[90] Like the Directive, the section then goes on to deal with error correction, by providing that, "It may, in particular, be necessary for the lawful use of a computer program to copy or adapt it for the purpose of correcting errors in it".[91] Although this section appears to implement Article 5 of the Directive fairly faithfully, there is a degree of ambiguity in the Directive as to whether it ought to be possible to exclude the right to correct errors by contract. This is because recital 18 of the Directive provides that "the act of correction of its errors may not be prohibited by contract", whereas Article 5 does appear to allow this right to be so restricted. As recitals are considered to be of considerable importance when interpreting

---

[86] See para. 9–21, above.

[87] "Lawful user" is again defined to mean any person who has a right to use the program, whether under a licence to do any acts resricted by the copyright in the computer program or otherwise: CDPA 1988, s.50A(2).

[88] s.50(BA)(2) goes on to provide that where an act is permitted under this section, it is irrelevant whether or not there exists any term or condition in an agreement which purports to prohibit or restrict the act. Such terms are void under s.296A, as now amended.

[89] "Lawful user" is again defined to mean any person who has a right to use the program, whether under a licence to do any acts resricted by the copyright in the computer program or otherwise: CDPA 1988, s.50A(2).

[90] s.50C(1).

[91] s.50C(2). Note that there is no room for any "right to repair" defence (see para. 5–23, et seq., above) in relation to computer programs, since this is now the subject of a complete statutory code following the implementation of the Software Directive 91/250: Mars UK Ltd v Teknowledge Ltd [2000] E.C.D.R. 99.

European legislation the effect of this inconsistency is uncertain.[92] The 1988 Act does not contain any provision striking down contractual terms prohibiting or restricting such acts.[93]

10. DATABASES

9–139   **Acts permitted in relation to databases.** The Database Regulations 1997[94] introduced a new section 50D into the Act, as required by Article 6(1) of the Database Directive.[95] The section provides that it is not an infringement of copyright in a database for a person who has a right to use the database to do, in the exercise of that right, anything which is necessary for the purposes of access to and use of the contents of the database.[96] In this context a "right to use a database" is to include a right to use any part of a database, and the permitted act applies to anything which is necessary to access and use that part.[97] The Act also makes it clear that the exception applies in all circumstances where a person has a right to use a database and not just where the use has been licensed.[98] This provision has to be understood in the context of the dual system of protection for databases introduced by the Database Directive and the Regulations. Except in the case of " existing" databases, copyright will only subsist in a database where the database satisfies the special originality test, that is, where "by reason of the selection or arrangement of the contents of the database the database constitutes the author's own intellectual creation".[99] In contrast, all databases whose production involved a "substantial investment in obtaining, verifying or presenting the contents" will qualify for *sui generis* database right,[1] which will subsist alongside any copyright.[2] It should be noted that the permitted act now under consideration only relates to the question of copyright infringement. However, the nature of database right is such that no equivalent provision is required.[3]

9–140   **Avoidance of certain terms relating to databases.** As has been seen, in general the permitted acts only relate to the question of infringement of copyright: they do not affect any other right or obligation. Hence it is ordinarily possible to exclude or restrict the operation of the permitted act provisions contractually. However, this was thought to be undesirable in the case of databases.[4] Thus, as with the provisions relating to computer programs (see para.9–132, above), section 296B strikes down contractual terms which would have the effect of nullify-

---

[92] As to the ECJ's approach to the interpretation of Directives and the emphasis placed on "contextual" interpretation, see Bengoetxea, *The Legal Reasoning of the European Court of Justice* (Clarendon, Oxford, 1993) pp.233, 240–270.

[93] *cf.* the provisions of CDPA 1988, s.296A.

[94] Copyright and Rights in Databases Regulations, 1997 (SI 1997/3032).

[95] Directive 96/9.

[96] CDPA 1988, s.50D(1). It was said that this permitted act was introduced to protect users of electronic databases who, in order to search a database, may find it necessary to download the whole or a substantial part of the database into the memory of a computer (see House of Commons Standing Committee on Delegated Legislation (Pt 1), December 3, 1997; *Hansard*, HL Vol.584, col.793). However, its general effect is wider than this; the permitted act was introduced to implement Art.6(1) of the Database Directive.

[97] s.50D(1).

[98] s.50D(1).

[99] See Ch.3, above. Existing databases (*i.e.* databases created on or before March 27, 1996) will, however, continue to enjoy copyright for the remainder of the copyright term: SI 1997/3032, reg.29.

[1] regs 13, 30.

[2] reg.13(2).

[3] As to the nature of the database right, see Ch.18, below.

[4] Art.8 of the Database Directive prohibits the database right owner from preventing a lawful user carrying out certain acts, but this appears to apply only to *sui generis* database right, not copyright. Recital 49 appears to be to the same effect. Art.6, which is concerned with copyright, merely

ing the permitted act. Section 296B thus provides "where under an agreement a person has a right to use a database or part of a database, any term or condition in the agreement shall be void in so far as it purports to prohibit or restrict the performance of any act which would but for section 50D infringe the copyright in the database".[5] This provision was designed to ensure that a contract for the use of an electronic database could not be used so as to stop it being downloaded if that were necessary in order to search it.[6] It should be read alongside regulation 19 of the Database Regulations, which provides that "Where under an agreement a person has a right to use a database, or part of a database, which has been made available to the public in any manner, any term or condition in the agreement shall be void in so far as it purports to prevent that person from extracting or re-utilising insubstantial parts of the contents of the database, or of that part of the database, for any purpose".[7]

11. DESIGNS

Introduction. Although the permitted acts relating to designs[8] are given extensive treatment elsewhere,[9] they are also briefly outlined below. The aim of these particular provisions is not so much to grant a set of exemptions to a special class of user but to mark out a boundary between copyright and designs law.   **9–141**

The Information Society Directive. Article 9 of the Directive, dealing with the continued application of other legal provisions, states that the Directive is to be without prejudice to provisions relating to designs. No amendment was therefore required to these permitted act sections.

A. DESIGN DOCUMENTS AND MODELS

The Act provides that it is not an infringement of any copyright in a design document or model recording or embodying a design for anything other than an artistic work or a typeface to make an article to the design or to copy an article made to the design.[10] Design in this context is defined in a very similar way as in relation to the unregistered design right. Thus, design "means the design of any aspect of the shape or configuration (whether internal or external) of the whole or part of an article, other than surface decoration".[11] A design document means any record of a design, whether in the form of a drawing, a written description, a photograph, data stored in a computer or otherwise.[12] This exception was introduced in order to prevent design owners from relying on artistic copyright to protect utilitarian three-dimensional objects. Essentially, the problem arises because copyright subsists in graphic works (which will include a large number of design documents) and sculptures (which may include hand-made design models[13]), irrespec-   **9–142**

---

states that acts necessary for access or normal use "shall not require the authorisation" of the rightholder.
[5] CDPA 1988, s.296B.
[6] *Hansard*, HL Vol.584, col.793.
[7] SI 1997/3032, reg.19(2). Also see para. 18–13, below.
[8] CDPA 1988, s.51–53.
[9] See further, Ch.13, below.
[10] CDPA 1988, s.51(1). Nor is it an infringement of copyright to issue to the public, or include in a film or communicate to the public anything whose making was, by virtue of s.51(1), not an infringement of copyright: s.51(2). Note that copyright in the document or model is not itself removed. See further para. 13–166, below.
[11] s.51(3).
[12] s.51(3).
[13] See *Wham-O Manufacturing v Lincoln* [1985] R.P.C. 127, CA of NZ.

tive of artistic quality.[14] As copyright may be infringed indirectly as well as directly,[15] and in relation to an artistic work includes the making of a copy in three dimensions of a two-dimensional work,[16] the copying of an end product might well infringe copyright in the design documents or models. This protection was seen as particularly problematic in that purely functional designs were able to enjoy the full copyright term, whereas the copyright in aesthetic (*i.e.* registrable) designs was restricted to a term of 15 years.[17] It was a desire to remove this anomaly that led Parliament to introduce the section now under consideration[18] which, together with the introduction of the new design right,[19] aims to ensure that functional designs receive a much more appropriate term of protection.

The exclusion from this section of documents or models embodying a design for an artistic work is intended to ensure that artists and sculptors can make preliminary sketches or models without losing copyright in their final work. However, designs for other, functional articles may also fall outside the scope of this section, providing they amount to designs for artistic works.[20] Many of these cases will, however, be caught by section 52 (considered below) with the result that copyright protection will be restricted to a term of 25 years. It should be noted that there is not necessarily a neat demarcation between elements of design which are protected by design right but not copyright (shape, configuration) and those that are protected by copyright but not design right (surface decoration) such that all elements receive some degree of protection.[21]

B. EXPLOITATION OF DESIGNS DERIVED FROM ARTISTIC WORKS

9–143 Section 52 was introduced to "truncate copyright where [an artistic] work has been exploited in the mass market".[22] This section applies where an artistic work has been exploited, by or with the copyright owner's consent, by making articles embodying a copy of the work by means of an industrial process,[23] provided such

---

[14] s.4(1)(a).
[15] s.16(3)(b).
[16] s.17(3).
[17] By virtue of the Design Copyright Act 1968 (c.68).
[18] Report of the Debates of the House of Commons Standing Committee E in 1988, cols 238–239.
[19] See Ch.13, below.
[20] For example, engravings for such things as rubber car-floor mats. See *Hi-Tech Autoparts Ltd v Towergate Two Ltd (No.1)* [2002] F.S.R. 15, paras 36 and 39; *Hi-Tech Autoparts Ltd v Towergate Two Ltd (No.2)* [2002] F.S.R. 16, para.16, following *James Arnold & Co. Ltd v. Miafern Ltd* [1980] R.P.C. 397, at p.403, and *Wham-O Manufacturing Co. v Lincoln Industries Ltd* [1985] R.P.C. 127 at 155, CA of NZ (engravings for plastic 'frisbees'). Precisely this example was raised during the passage of the Bill by Lord Lucas of Chilworth, who introduced an amendment which would have taken designs for all "functional articles" outside of this exception. Lord Beaverbrook, replying for the Government, stated that in most cases the distinction between an artistic work and a non-artistic work would be "self-evident". Where this is not the case the wording of the section "will allow the courts the freedom they need to reach sensible conclusions": *Hansard*, HL Vol.491, cols 185–186.
[21] See *Lambretta Clothing Co. Ltd v Teddy Smith (UK) Ltd* [2004] EWCA Civ 886, and para. 13–167, below.
[22] *Hansard*, HL Vol.491, col.189.
[23] An article is to be regarded as made by an industrial process if (a) it is one of more than 50 articles which all fall to be treated as copies of a particular artistic work and which do not together constitute a single set of articles (seof articles was defined in s.44(1) of the Registered Designs Act 1949 and although this section has now been repealed, it is assured the definition still applies); or (b) it consists of goods manufactured in lengths or pieces, not being handmade goods: The Copyright (Industrial Process and Excluded Articles) (No.2) Order 1989 (SI 1989/1070), r.2, (see Vol.2 at B8.ii).

articles have been marketed (in the United Kingdom or elsewhere).[24] In these circumstances, at the end of 25 years from the end of the year in which such articles were first marketed, copyright will not be infringed by making articles of any description, or by doing anything for the purposes of making articles of any description, or by doing anything in relation to copies so made.[25]

This section must, however, be read in conjunction with the Industrial Process Order.[26] This Order excludes from the operation of the section certain articles of "a primarily literary or artistic character".[27] As well as books and other printed material, the Order includes sculptures within this definition,[28] thus allowing sculptors to produce and sell their works in potentially large numbers.[29] The difficulty with this is that it is dependent upon being able to say with precision what is and what is not a sculpture and, in particular, being able to distinguish sculptures from other types of artistic works, such as engravings.[30] Under the terms of the Industrial Process Order, the former will gain the full copyright term, the latter will only get protection for 25 years from the end of the year in which articles embodying the work are first marketed.

C. THINGS DONE IN RELIANCE ON REGISTRATION OF DESIGN

The final permitted act relating to designs gives primacy to the registered design system, so that anyone who relies on the provisions of the Registered Designs Act, or on the accuracy of the register of designs, will not have to be concerned with any potential copyright infringement.[31] It should be noted that this provision is particularly important in relation to commissioned designs, as the owner of the registered design may well not be the owner of the copyright in such cases.[32] The Act thus provides that the copyright in an artistic work is not infringed by anything done (a) in pursuance of an assignment or licence made or granted by a person registered under the Registered Designs Act as the proprietor of a corresponding design, and (b) in good faith in reliance on the registration and without notice of any proceedings for the cancellation or invalidation of the registration or for rectifying the relevant entry into the register of designs.[33] This section applies notwithstanding the fact that the person registered as the proprietor was not entitled to be so registered.[34]

9–144

"Corresponding design" here means a design within the meaning of the Registered Designs Act, which, if applied to an article, would produce something which would be treated as a copy of the artistic work.[35]

12. TYPEFACES

Introduction. Designing a typeface is a skilled and time-consuming task, but once the design has been finished it can be copied at a fraction of the cost it

9–145

---

[24] CDPA 1988, s.52(1). "Marketed" here means selling an article or letting an article for hire or offering or exposing an article for sale or hire: s.52(6)(b).

[25] s.52(2).

[26] The Industrial Process Order 1989, (1989/1070).

[27] Note that the Act also expressly excludes films from the operation of this section: CDPA 1988, s.52(6)(a).

[28] The Industrial Process Order 1989, r.3(1)(a).

[29] Thus Claes Oldenberg might retain the full term of copyright protection for his "multiples".

[30] See para. 3–58, above.

[31] CDPA 1988, s.53.

[32] See further paras 13–000 et seq.

[33] s.53(1).

[34] s.53(1).

[35] s.53(2).

originally took to produce. Thus there is real justification for some form of intellectual property protection.[36] While copyright will *prima facie* subsist in the design for a single letter, copyright will not subsist in sets of lettering as such. The Johnson Committee[37] looked at this problem in 1962 and recommended that the 1956 Act be amended so that copyright protection be extended to cover original sets of lettering,[38] but this recommendation was never implemented. Protection is available under the Registered Designs Act 1949 and the Community Design Regulations for single letters and, it would seem, for a typeface as a whole.[39]

The Vienna Agreement[40] of 1973 was an attempt to set out a minimum international level of protection for typefaces and to provide for their reciprocal protection. Although the United Kingdom signed the Vienna Agreement it never ratified it and, as yet, the Agreement is still not in force. When the Whitford Committee came to look at typefaces it recommended, as had the Johnson Committee before it, that copyright protection be given to sets of lettering and that the United Kingdom should ratify the Vienna Agreement.[41] In the event, this part of the Whitford Committee's recommendations was never implemented, so that copyright still does not subsist in a set of lettering.[42] Nevertheless, it is clear that copyright can subsist in individual letters and characters as graphic works (or sculptures where the pieces are carved) and, as discussed below, the 1988 Act makes special provision in order to restrict the scope of copyright protection in such works.[43]

Whilst the rationale of these sections is relatively clear, it seems that the sections have been designed with mechanical methods of reproduction in mind.[44] Applying these provisions to electronic methods of reproducing a typeface poses a number of difficulties (see paragraph 9–149, below).[45]

9–146   **The Information Society Directive.** Article 9 of the Information Society Directive, dealing with the continued application of other legal provisions, states that the Directive is to be without prejudice to provisions relating to typefaces. No amendment was therefore required to these permitted act sections.

---

[36] The preamble to the Vienna Agreement for the Protection of Type Faces and their International Deposit (hereafter "the Vienna Agreement") of 1973 states that typefaces play a role in "the dissemination of culture". For a consideration of the ways in which typefaces (and typographical arrangements more generally) can help to convey meaning, see McGann, "Composition as Explanation (of Modern and Postmodern Poetries)" in Ezell, O'Brien and O'Keeffe (eds.) *Cultural Artifacts and the Production of Meaning* (University of Michigan Press, Ann Arbor, 1994).

[37] Report of the Departmental Committee on Industrial Designs, 1962 (Cmnd. 1808).

[38] Report of the Departmental Committee on Industrial Designs, 1962 (Cmnd. 1808), paras 160–163.

[39] See the Registered Designs Act 1949, s.1(3) as amended, and the Community Design Regulation EC 6/2002, in force on March 6, 2002, and Ch.13, below.

[40] See Vol.2 at F9.

[41] The Vienna Agreement is fairly flexible as regards the form protection should take and allows Member States to protect typefaces by means of a *sui generis* right, or by designs law, or by copyright: Vienna Agreement, Art.3.

[42] *cf. Plix Products Ltd v Frank M Winstone (Merchants) Ltd* [1986] F.S.R. 63, where Prichard J. seemed to indicate that copyright subsisted in the "Plix system" or range of products as a whole. Although the New Zealand Court of Appeal referred to this issue, it declined to consider the matter further.

[43] CDPA 1988, ss.54, 55. Note, however, that these sections refer to "copyright in an artistic work consisting of the design of a typeface". As "typeface" is usually taken to refer to "a set of printing type of a particular design" (*Oxford English Dictionary*, 2nd ed.) the wording of these sections seems better suited to describe copyright in a typeface as a whole, rather than protection for individual letters. The fact that copyright subsists in individual characters has to be inferred from general principles relating to artistic works.

[44] See further, *Hansard*, HL Vol.493, col.1181–1182.

[45] For a detailed consideration of these problems see Watts and Blakemore, "Protection of Software Fonts in UK Law", [1995] 3 E.I.P.R. 133.

A. TYPEFACES USED IN THE ORDINARY COURSE OF PRINTING

As has been seen, the design of a typeface will often be an artistic work in which **9–147** copyright subsists, and the use of such a typeface in, for example, a printer, will involve repeated reproduction of the artistic work. Where the owner of the typeface has licensed its reproduction in an article, such use would usually be the subject of an implied licence, and possibly the principle of non-derogation from grant.[46] However the Act goes further than this in an attempt to protect a purchaser who purchases an article which incorporates an infringing typeface.[47] Thus the Act provides that it is not an infringement of copyright in an artistic work consisting of the design of a typeface (a) to use the typeface in the ordinary course of typing, composing text, typesetting or printing, (b) to possess an article for the purpose of such use, or (c) to do anything in relation to material produced by such use; and this provision applies notwithstanding the fact that the article which is used, for example a typewriter key, is an infringing copy of the artistic work.[48]

The Act contains various provisions dealing with articles specifically designed or adapted for making copies of a work where they are to be used for making infringing copies. Thus section 24 makes it an infringement of copyright in a work to make, import, sell, etc., an article specifically designed or adapted for making copies of that work, knowing or having reason to believe that it is to be used for making infringing copies[49] sections 99 and 100; provide for delivery up and seizure of such articles in these circumstances; section 107(2) makes it a criminal offence to make or possess such an article with such knowledge; and section 108 provides for seizure of articles in such an event. These provisions apply whether or not the article is itself an infringing copy. If no further provision were made, these sections would be of no application in, for example, a case where a person dealt with an article incorporating a typeface knowing or having reason to believe that it was to be used without the copyright owner's consent to print material reproducing the typeface. This is because by virtue of section 54(1) infringing copies would not be produced as a result. Although the policy of the Act is to exempt the user of the typeface from liability for infringement in such circumstances, it was clearly thought that this exemption should not be extended to those who deal in typefaces. It is therefore provided by section 54(2) that the above provisions of the Act (sections 24, 99, 100, 107(2) and 108) apply in relation to persons making, importing or dealing with articles specifically designed or adapted for producing material in a particular typeface as if the production of material as is mentioned in subsection (1) did infringe copyright in the artistic work consisting of the design of the typeface. For this purpose "dealing with" an article means selling, letting for hire, or offering or exposing for sale or hire, exhibiting in public, or distributing the article.[50] A person who makes, imports or deals with such an article will therefore be liable under the above provisions of the Act if he knows or has reason to believe it will be used to make copies of the typeface without the copyright owner's consent. Although simple possession of an article for the purpose of using the typeface is not an infringement,[51] the provi-

---

[46] See, para. 5–639, above.
[47] See *Hansard*, HL Vol.495, col.646. Note that this provision applies even where the purchaser knows that the typeface infringes copyright. However, a person importing or dealing with articles that incorporate an infringing typeface may still be liable for secondary infringement (see below).
[48] CDPA 1988, s.54(1).
[49] See para. 8–15, above.
[50] s.54(3).
[51] s.54(1)(b).

sions are to apply in a similar way to the possession of such articles for the purpose of dealing with them.[52]

B. ARTICLES FOR PRODUCING MATERIAL IN PARTICULAR TYPEFACE

9–148   Where articles incorporating the typeface have been marketed by or with the licence of the copyright owner, the Act in effect limits the term of protection, thereby bringing typefaces into line with other artistic works that are industrially exploited.[53] Thus 25 years from the end of the calendar year in which the first such articles are marketed, the artistic work consisting of the design of the typeface may be copied by making further such articles or doing anything for this purpose.[54] Moreover, it will not be an infringement of copyright to do anything in relation to such articles.[55] In this context, "marketed" means sold, let for hire or offered or exposed for sale or hire whether in the United Kingdom or elsewhere.[56] It follows, for example, that after the 25-year period it would be permissible for anyone to make and sell replacement printer keys which reproduce the typeface used on the original printer.[57]

C. TYPEFACES IN ELECTRONIC FORM

9–149   In the interests of clarity, all the examples that have so far been considered relate to traditional, mechanical, methods of reproducing typefaces. In practice, however, typefaces are now more likely to be copied by means of an electronic process, in particular, as part of the use of a word processing program. It might be thought that there was a difficulty created by this transition to electronic methods of reproduction because of the use of the term "article" in both sections 54 and 55 of the Act, wording which might seem ill-suited to describe the use of software fonts. Where, however, software fonts are recorded or carried in the form of CD-ROMs, etc. or are copied to computer memory in whatever form, these items all constitute "articles".[58] Nevertheless, a difficulty remains in relation to section 55, as the restriction of the term of copyright only applies once articles designed or adapted for producing material in a particular typeface have been marketed. Thus were a font only to be sold over the internet it might be argued no "articles" would ever be marketed and the term of copyright would remain unaffected.[59] It seems likely, however, that the section would be given a liberal interpretation.

13. WORKS IN ELECTRONIC FORM

9–150   Where a work in electronic form is passed on by the first purchaser, the Act provides an exception to permit the transferee to use the work without infringing copyright.[60] Such a provision is required since, as has already been considered, the use of a work in electronic form will almost invariably involve its reproduc-

---

[52] s.54(2).

[53] CDPA 1988, s.55.

[54] s.55(2). Note that copyright in the typeface is not itself removed: *Hansard*, HL Vol.493, col.1182. Thus, for example, a sign writer who copies the typeface might still infringe.

[55] s.55(2).

[56] s.55(3).

[57] Note that where such articles have been marketed before August 1, 1989, the 25-year period only runs from December 31, 1989.

[58] *Sony Computer Entertainment Inc v Ball* [2004] EWHC 1738, Ch.

[59] See further, Watts and Blakemore, "Protection of Software Fonts in UK Law", [1995] 3 E.I.P.R. 133.

[60] CDPA 1988, s.56.

tion at some stage.[61] Thus the owner of the copyright could argue that in the absence of any legal relationship with the transferee any use of the work would infringe copyright. This provision therefore applies where a copy of a work in electronic form has been purchased on terms which expressly, impliedly or by virtue of any rule of law allow the purchaser to copy the work or to adapt it or to make copies of an adaptation of it, in connection with the purchaser's use of it.[62] Presumably "any rule of law" includes the principle of non-derogation from grant.[63] The provision applies to all works in "electronic form," which means a form usable only by electronic means,[64] and "electronic" itself is defined to mean actuated by electric, magnetic, electro-magnetic, electro-chemical or electro-mechanical energy.[65] In such cases, if there are no express terms (a) prohibiting the transfer of the copy by the purchaser, imposing obligations which continue after a transfer, prohibiting the assignment of any licence or terminating any licence on a transfer, or (b) providing for the terms on which a transferee may do the things which the purchaser was permitted to do, then anything which the purchaser was allowed to do may also be done without infringement of copyright by a transferee.[66] These provisions also apply where the original copy is no longer usable and a further copy used in its place is transferred.[67] Finally, they apply not only on the first transfer, but also on any subsequent transfer.[68]

The Act provides, however, that where the purchaser does not also transfer any copy, adaptation or copy of an adaptation made by him before the transfer, then such a copy is to be treated for all purposes as an infringing copy, as from the time of the transfer.[69] In practice, this means that the purchaser must ensure that he does not retain a back up copy or a copy on his hard disk.

The Information Society Directive. No amendments were made to this permit-ted act on implementation of the Directive. The Directive makes no express ref-erence to this kind of act and clearly the saving in Article 5(3)(o) for existing minor analogue exceptions does not apply. It would seem that the Government regarded this permitted act as an aspect of contract law within the meaning of Article 9 the Directive, although this seems doubtful.[70]   **9–151**

14. MISCELLANEOUS PROVISIONS: LITERARY, DRAMATIC, MUSICAL AND ARTISTIC WORKS

A. ANONYMOUS OR PSEUDONYMOUS WORKS: ACTS PERMITTED ON ASSUMPTIONS AS TO EXPIRY OF COPYRIGHT OR DEATH OF AUTHOR

The permitted acts. Where the identity of the author of a literary, dramatic, musical or artistic work is unknown it will normally be impossible to determine precisely when copyright expires. In recognition of this, the Act provides an   **9–152**

---

[61] See further, para. 7–20, above.
[62] s.56(1).
[63] See, para. 5–23, above.
[64] s.178.
[65] s.178.
[66] s.56(2). Also see *Beta Computers (Europe) Ltd v Adobe Systems (Europe) Ltd* [1996] F.S.R. 367 at 372. These provisions do not, however, apply in relation to a copy purchased before August 1, 1989: Sch.1, para.14(6).
[67] s.56(3).
[68] s.56(4).
[69] s.56(2).
[70] If the permitted act is to be viewed as an aspect of non-derogation from grant, such a principle is not applicable in a field where the position is covered by Community legislation: see para. 5–232, above.

exception to allow a work to be freely copied at a time when it is reasonable to assume that copyright has expired.[71] Thus the copyright in a literary, dramatic, musical or artistic work of unknown authorship[72] is not infringed by any act done, or in pursuance of any arrangements made at a time when, it is reasonable to assume either (a) that copyright has expired, or (b) that the author died 70 years or more before the beginning of the calendar year in which the act is done or the arrangements are made.[73] The latter provision does not, however, apply in relation to a work in which Crown copyright subsists, or a work in which copyright originally vested in an international organisation and in which a copyright period longer than 70 years has been specified.[74]

9–153   **Transitional provisions.** The Act also contains further, transitional, provisions which apply to works made before August 1, 1989. In relation to such works the assumption as to the expiry of copyright does not apply in relation to photographs or in relation to rights conferred on universities and colleges by virtue of the Copyright Act 1775.[75]

9–154   **The Information Society Directive.** The Directive does not contain any provision expressly covering this permitted act. No doubt, however, section 57 can be regarded as an administrative provision relating to the term of copyright in cases where this is uncertain, rather than as an exemption, exception or limitation to copyright within the ambit of the Directive.

B. USE OF NOTES OR RECORDINGS OF SPOKEN WORDS IN CERTAIN CASES

9–155   **Introduction.** The 1988 Act expressly recognises that copyright may subsist in a speaker's words when they are recorded by another person, irrespective of whether the speaker has consented to this "fixation".[76] To alleviate the difficulties this may cause, the Act provides an exception so as to allow the speaker's words to be used by journalists and broadcasters, such that where a person's spoken words are recorded, the subsequent use of that record cannot, in defined circumstances, be prevented by relying on any copyright "in the words as a literary work".[77] Thus, subject to certain conditions, the Act provides that where a record of spoken words is made, in writing[78] or otherwise, for the purpose (a) of reporting current events, or (b) of communicating to the public the whole or part of the

---

[71] CDPA 1988, s.57. Also see s.66A and para. 9–179, below.

[72] This phrase is not actually used, but this section virtually repeats the wording of an earlier section of the Act, which provides that, "a work is of unknown authorship if the identity of the author is unknown or, in the case of a work of joint authorship, if the identity of none of the authors is known": s.9(4). The identity of an author is to be regarded as unknown "if it is not possible to ascertain his identity by reasonable inquiry": s.9(5).

[73] s.57(1). In relation to a work of joint authorship the reference to "the author" having died is to be construed as a reference to all the authors having died: s.57(3)(b).

[74] s.57(2). Although these works will have a natural author, the term of copyright in such works is unrelated to the author's death. Whilst this is also true of certain other categories of work (such as works in which Parliamentary copyright subsists), it is only in cases where copyright subsists for longer than 70 years that an honest mistake as to the date of the author's death is likely to result in the reproduction of a work still in copyright. As to the duration of copyright more generally, see Ch.6, above.

[75] CDPA 1988, Sch.1, para.15(2). As to the rights conferred by the 1775 Act, see para. 6–81, above. Note that Sch.1, para.15(3) has been repealed by The Copyright and Related Rights Regulations 2003 (SI 2003/2498), following the amendment to Sch.1, para.12(3), by way of further implementation of the Term Directive.

[76] CDPA 1988, ss.3(2), (3) and see para. 3–135, above. See below as to the possible existence of a separate reporter's copyright.

[77] s.58.

[78] Writing is defined as including any form of notation or code, whether by hand or otherwise and regardless of the method by which, or the medium in or on which, it is recorded: s.178.

work, then it is not an infringement of any copyright in the words as a literary work to use the record or material taken from it (or to copy the record, or any such material, and use the copy) for that purpose.[79]

The conditions which must be complied with are that: (a) the record is a direct record of the spoken words and is not taken from a previous record or from a broadcast; (b) the making of the record was not prohibited by the speaker and, where copyright already subsisted in the work, did not infringe copyright; (c) the use made of the record or material taken from it is not of a kind prohibited by or on behalf of the speaker or copyright owner before the record was made; and (d) the use is by or with the authority of a person who is lawfully in possession of the record.[80]

The Information Society Directive. Although some aspects of this permitted act fall within the exception for the reporting of current events allowed by Article 5(3)(c), it clearly does not wholly do so, not least because the Act does not contain any requirement to acknowledge the source. No amendment to the section was made on implementation of the Directive. It seems that because the operation of the section depends largely on the absence of prohibition the Government regarded this permitted act as relating to a contractual matter within the spirit of Article 9 of the Directive, and thus allowed, but this seems doubtful.

9–156

Comment. This section of the Act should be compared with that providing for fair dealing for the purpose of reporting current events[81] and that for enabling published works to be read in public and then recorded or broadcast.[82] The section presents a number of difficulties of interpretation which are considered below.

9–157

The copyright work. The first problem is to identify the copyright work which is not infringed by virtue of the section. The section states that it is not an infringement "of any copyright in the words as a literary work" to use the record or material taken from it.[83] At first sight this provision may seem curiously worded, since no copyright can subsist in words as such, but only in the literary work which comes into existence once the words have been recorded, in writing or otherwise.[84] Presumably, however, the intention is that the provision should apply in the case where a person makes an extemporaneous speech which is recorded by another. In such circumstances two copyright works may come into existence at the same time. The first is the literary work consisting of the speaker's words which are recorded, the copyright in which will normally be owned by the speaker.[85] The permitted act no doubt applies to this work. The second work is the record itself which, if it is in writing, will be a literary work, or, if it is recorded on tape, will be a sound recording. The copyright in this will not normally be owned by the speaker.[86] It seems clear that the permitted order does not apply to this work, even where it is a literary work, since the Act expressly provides that the record must be a direct record of the spoken words and must not be taken

9–158

---

[79] s.58(1).
[80] s.58(2).
[81] CDPA 1988, s.30(2), paras 9–44 et seq., above.
[82] s.59, para. 9–161, below.
[83] CDPA 1988, s.58(1).
[84] s.3(2).
[85] See further, para. 5–06, above.
[86] See para. 5–41, above, and CDPA 1988, s.3(3).

from a previous record.[87] The licence of the copyright owner (*e.g.* the journalist) will therefore be required for the use of the record. There are, however, other works to which the provision applies. In particular, it seems that the provision also applies where copyright subsisted in "the words as a literary work" already, that is, before the words were spoken.[88] An example of this is the case where the speaker writes his speech beforehand, and then delivers it from memory or his prepared text. The speaker will usually be the owner of the copyright in his prepared text.

It is also important to consider the position where the speaker recites an extract from some other copyright literary work. Where the licence of the owner of the copyright was not obtained for the making of the record, then it seems the section will not apply, since such a work will not fall within the operation of this section and thus the making of the record will have infringed copyright.[89]

9–159   **The position of the speaker.** It is clear that the section applies whether the words were spoken in public or in private. It is also clear that the section will apply unless the making of the record was expressly prohibited by the speaker, so that it appears that the onus will be on the speaker to prohibit such acts and not upon the maker of the record to seek permission.[90] Nor does it appear that it is necessary that the speaker should even be aware that his words were being recorded. Moreover, even if the speaker was aware that his words were being recorded, it does not appear that it is necessary that he knew the use which would be made of the record. This raises the possibility of the speaker being deceived as to the purposes for which the record will be used, although in a case where, for example, a politician makes a statement "off the record" there would no doubt be a strong implication that publication of its contents was prohibited within the meaning of section 58(2)(c). If the making of the record or its use is to be prohibited by the speaker, this must be done before the record is made and any attempt to do so afterwards will apparently be of no effect.

9–160   **The permitted uses.** The purposes for which the record was made may either be for the reporting of current events or for broadcasting the whole or part of the work. The meaning of "reporting current events" has already been considered in the context of the fair dealing exceptions.[91] The advantage of the present exception in this context appears to be that it can be relied upon even if the dealing is not fair (for example because the extract used is too long),[92] or if there is a failure to provide sufficient acknowledgment.[93] As to broadcasting the work, presumably the words "the whole or part of the work" in subsection 58(1)(b) must refer to the work whose use is permitted by the section. It is not necessary that there be any element of reporting current events under this limb. The expression "for that purpose" in the concluding words of subsection (1) appears to indicate that if the

---

[87] s.58(2)(a) and see above, also note that in any event the use of the record must be by or with the authority of a person in lawful possession of the record.

[88] See the wording of s.58(2)(b).

[89] Unless reliance can be placed on another of the permitted acts, for example s.59, para. 9–161, below. Also note that the speaker may be the owner of the copyright in such a work.

[90] *cf. Nicols v Pitman* (1884) 26 Ch.374: implied understanding between lecturer and audience that notes taken during the course of a lecture delivered to an audience limited and admitted by tickets cannot be published for profit.

[91] See paras 9–44 *et seq.*, above.

[92] See paras 9–53 *et seq.*, above.

[93] See para. 9–52, above. Note that in any event no acknowledgment is required in connection with the reporting of current events by means of a sound recording, film or broadcast: CDPA 1988, s.30(3).

record is made for one of the defined purposes it may not be used for the other.[94] Yet it may not always be easy to tell for which purpose the record was made and in many cases it will be made for both purposes, for example the broadcasting of a current affairs programme. In this case it would appear permissible to reuse the record for either purpose, so that a record made for the purposes of such a programme could be reused in order to broadcast "the work", even though the record no longer related to "current events."

The use may be of the record itself or of material taken from it, or a copy of the record.[95] Thus where the record is in the form of a tape recording it appears permissible to transcribe it and print the transcript in a newspaper provided that this is for the purpose of reporting current events. Where the record is in writing it appears permissible to record that material on tape and broadcast the contents of the tape recording. The original "record" must, however, itself be a direct record of the spoken words and not taken, for example, from a broadcast of the spoken words. The express reference to it being permissible to copy the record, and to use the copy, raises the doubt, which might otherwise not have arisen, whether the making of third, fourth and later generation copies is permissible. Were it not for these words it would probably be implicit that the making of such further copies is permissible if for the defined purposes. In many cases a record of an interview will go through several generations of copies before it is printed or broadcast and it would clearly be highly inconvenient if such copying were restricted to the original record and only copies made directly from it. It is thought this cannot have been the intention of the legislature.[96]

C. PUBLIC READING OR RECITATION

The Act provides that the reading or recitation in public by one person of a reasonable extract from a published literary or dramatic work does not infringe any copyright in the work if it is accompanied by a sufficient acknowledgment.[97] The definition of "sufficient acknowledgment" has already been considered.[98] In addition, where a reading or recitation does not infringe copyright by virtue of this provision, the Act provides a limited exception to allow for the reading or recitation to be included in a sound recording or communication to the public. However, this latter provision only applies where the recording or communication consists mainly of material in relation to which it is not necessary to rely on this exception.[99] No further guidance is given as to the proportion of the recording or broadcast that may consist of copyright material, but during the passage of the Bill it was said that the purpose of this exception was to allow the televising of events such as eisteddfodau, where a speaker might unforeseeably recite an extract from a literary or dramatic work.[1]

9–161

The Information Society Directive. The Directive is not concerned with the public performing right in works,[2] and thus the acts of reading or recitation in public permitted by section 59(1) do not come within its ambit. The subsidiary permitted acts of inclusion of the work in a sound recording or broadcast do so,

9–162

---

[94] See further, *Hansard*, HL Vol.501, cols 198–200.

[95] CDPA 1988, s.58(1).

[96] In fact this provision was inserted to allow broadcasters to follow their usual practice of making copies of their original recordings for the purposes of their broadcasts: Report of the Debates of the House of Commons Standing Committee E in 1988 cols 484–5.

[97] CDPA 1988, s.59(1).

[98] See para. 9–29, above.

[99] s.59(2).

[1] *Hansard*, H.L. Vol. 501, col. 198.

[2] See Information Society Directive 2001/29, recitals 23 and 24.

however, and none of the exceptions permitted by the Directive corresponds precisely to this permitted act, although various permitted exceptions may apply on the facts of the particular case.[3] It some cases, the general exception in Article 5(3)(o) for existing analogue uses of minor importance may apply. Where this is not the case, it would seem that the Government relied on the Article 5(3)(d) to justify not making any amendment to this section. Article 5(3)(d) permits quotations for purposes such as criticism or review, and so it is arguable that the cases of criticism or review are illustrative only of the uses which may be made of quotations.

D. ABSTRACTS OF SCIENTIFIC OR TECHNICAL ARTICLES

9–163   Before the 1988 Act, it was common practice within the scientific and technical communities to copy abstracts accompanying an article and to circulate them, but in the absence of any express provision such copying almost invariably amounted to an infringement of copyright, as it seems that licences were very seldom obtained. Nevertheless, it was seen as desirable that such copying be allowed to continue and put on a proper basis, as databases of abstracts can greatly speed up research by allowing scientists and researchers to identify papers relevant to their work without having to look through individual journals.[4] The Act thus provides that where an article on a scientific or technical subject is published in a periodical accompanied by an abstract indicating the contents of the article, it is not an infringement of copyright in the abstract, or in the article, to copy the abstract or issue copies of it to the public.[5] For this purpose "article" includes an item of any description in a periodical.[6] "Copyright in the abstract or in the article" must be taken to include copyright in the typographical arrangement.[7] Less certain is the meaning of "technical" in this context. The legislative history suggests that a narrow definition be given to this term, so as only to include engineering subjects and applied sciences,[8] even if as a matter of principle there is no good reason not to extend this exception so as to include a broad range of disciplines.[9]

This provision does not, however, apply if or to the extent that there is a relevant licensing scheme certified under section 143 of the Act.[10] The Act thus provides an incentive to publishers to enter into a licensing agreement and an opportunity for them to receive income for an activity that was previously unregulated,[11] although as yet no such scheme has been certified.

9–164   **The Information Society Directive.** No amendment was made to section 60 on implementation of the Directive. Articles 5(3)(a) and (4) permit Member States to make an exception to the reproduction and distribution rights in the case of non-commercial scientific research, provided a proper acknowledgment is made. Section 60 clearly does not fall within this permitted exception. It would seem that the Government placed reliance on the general saving for existing analogue uses of minor importance permitted by Article 5(3)(o), making the assumption that all copying would be "analogue" and that the issue of copies of abstracts to

---

[3] For example the exceptions under Information Society Directive, Art.5(3)(c), (f) or (g).
[4] See further, *Hansard*, HL Vol.491, col.106.
[5] CDPA 1988, s.60(1).
[6] s.178.
[7] This is clear from the legislative history (see the next footnote) and see CDPA 1988, s.28(2) and see para. 9–12, above.
[8] See *Hansard*, HL Vol.491, cols 106, 110; Vol.495, col.628; HC Vol.138, cols 145–147.
[9] At the very least it is clear that Parliament intended "the humanities" to be excluded from the scope of this provision: HC Vol.138, col.147.
[10] CDPA, 1988, s.60(2).
[11] See further, *Hansard*, HL Vol.501, col.252; HC Vol.138, col.147.

the public could only take place by the issue of hard copies and so again must be analogue use.

E. RECORDINGS OF FOLKSONGS

Introduction. The Act contains provisions, which were new in the 1988 Act, relating to the recording for archival purposes of unpublished songs of unknown authorship,[12] and for the supply by the archivist of copies of such recordings for the purposes of non-commercial research or private study. These provisions should be considered alongside the exception allowing for fair dealing with literary and musical works for the purposes of non-commercial research and private study.[13]   **9–165**

The Information Society Directive. Articles 5(2)(c) and (4) permit Member States to make an exception to the reproduction and distribution rights in respect of specific acts of reproduction made by publicly accessible museums and archives, which are not for direct or indirect economic or commercial advantage. Presumably this extends to enabling copies to be made for such organisations as well as by them. The exception also falls partly within Articles 5(2)(b) and 5(3)(a) as regards copying and supplying to the public. An amendment was made to the Act to limit the permitted supply of copies for purposes of *non-commercial* research,[14] with the effect that section 61 now appears to comply with the Directive.   **9–166**

Making recordings. The Act provides that so long as certain conditions are met, a sound recording[15] of a performance of a song may be made for the purpose of including it in an archive maintained by a designated body without infringing any copyright in the lyrics or in the accompanying music.[16] For this purpose, a "designated body" is one designated by Order of the Secretary of State,[17] but the Secretary of State is not to designate such a body unless satisfied that it is not established or conducted for profit.[18] There are three conditions to be met: **9–167**

(1) First, as has been seen, the words of the song must be unpublished and of unknown authorship at the time when the recording is made.[19] For a literary or musical work to be unpublished in this context, copies[20] of the work must not have been issued to the public or made available by means of an electronic retrieval system,[21] but a work is not to be regarded as having been published by its being performed or communicated to the public

---

[12] The title "folksongs" is merely a signpost: *Hansard*, HC Vol.138, col.110.

[13] See paras 9–25 *et seq.*, above.

[14] At the same time, the definition of private study has been limited to exclude study for commercial purposes: CDPA 1988, s.178.

[15] For the definition of a sound recording see CDPA 1988, s.5A(1) and see para. 3–75, above.

[16] s.61(1).

[17] s.61(5)(a), (6). As to such designated bodies see The Copyright (Recordings of Folksongs for Archives) (Designated Bodies) Order 1989 (SI 1989/1012), see Vol.2 at A4.ii. Twelve bodies have so far been designated: The Archive of Traditional Welsh Music; The Centre for English Cultural Tradition and Language; The Charles Parker Archive Trust (1982); The European Centre for Traditional and Regional Cultures; The Folklore Society; The Institute of Folklore Studies in Britain and Canada; The National Museum of Wales, Welsh Folk Museum; The National Sound Archive, the British Library; The North West Sound Archive; The Sound Archives, British Broadcasting Corporation; Ulster Folk and Transport Museum; The Vaughan Williams Memorial Library; and The English Folk Dance and Song Society.

[18] s.61(5)(a).

[19] s.61(2)(a).

[20] For the definition of "copies", see ss.17, 178.

[21] s.175(1).

(other than for the purposes of an electronic retrieval system).[22] Neither will colourable publication, not intended to satisfy the reasonable requirements of the public, amount to publication,[23] nor will any unauthorised publication.[24] For the words to be of "unknown authorship" the identity of the author, or in the case of works of joint authorship,[25] all the authors, must be unknown,[26] and the identity of an author will be regarded as unknown if it is not possible for a person to ascertain his identity by reasonable inquiry, but if his identity is once known it is not to be regarded subsequently as unknown.[27]

(2) Secondly, the making of the recording must not infringe any other copyright.[28] It follows that it will not be possible to copy an existing copyright sound recording by virtue of this section.

(3) Finally, the making of the recording must not be prohibited by any of the performers.[29]

9–168   **Supply of copies.** Once such a recording has been included in a relevant archive, the Act provides that, subject to prescribed conditions, the archivist, or a person acting on his behalf,[30] may make and supply copies without infringing copyright in either the recording or the works included in it.[31] The conditions, prescribed by the Secretary of State, are (a) that copies are only supplied to persons satisfying the archivist that they require them for purposes of research for a non-commercial purpose or private study and will not use them for any other purpose,[32] and (b) that no person is furnished with more than one copy of the same recording.[33]

F. REPRESENTATION OF CERTAIN ARTISTIC WORKS ON PUBLIC DISPLAY

9–169   **The permitted acts.** The 1988 Act, as did the 1956 and 1911 Acts, makes provision enabling certain works on public display to be represented without infringing copyright.[34] The provisions of the 1988 Act apply to buildings (irrespective of location), and to models for buildings, sculptures and works of artistic craftsmanship, where these are permanently situated in a public place or in premises open to the public.[35] The Act provides that copyright in such a work is not infringed by making a graphic work representing it, or by making a photograph or film of it, or by making a broadcast of a visual image of it.[36] Furthermore, copyright is not infringed by the issue to the public of copies, or the communication to the public, of anything whose making was, by virtue of this

---

[22] s.175(4)(a).

[23] s.174(5). As to the meaning of "reasonable requirements of the public", see *Francis, Day and Hunter v Feldman* [1914] 2 Ch.728 and para. 3–176, above

[24] s.174(6). For the definition of "unauthorised", see s.178.

[25] For the definition of a work of "joint authorship", see s.10(1) and see para. 4–39 *et seq.*, above.

[26] s.9(4).

[27] s.9(5).

[28] s.61(2)(b).

[29] s.61(2)(c).

[30] CDPA 1988, s.65(1)(c).

[31] s.61(3).

[32] s.61(4)(a); The Copyright (Recordings of Folksongs for Archives) (Designated Bodies) Order 1989 (SI 1989/1012), reg.3(2)(a). See Vol.2 at A4.ii.

[33] s.61(4)(b); The Copyright (Recordings of Folksongs for Archives) (Designated Bodies) Order 1989 (SI 1989/1012), reg.3(2)(b).

[34] CDPA 1988, s.62. *cf.* Copyright Act 1956, ss.9(3), 9(4), 9(6); Copyright Act 1911, s.2(1)(iii).

[35] s.62(1). As to the definition and meaning of "buildings", "sculptures" and "works of artistic craftsmanship", see s.4 and see paras 3–61, 3–58 and 3–65, above, respectively.

[36] s.62(2).

provision, not an infringement of copyright.[37] In relation to anything made before August 1, 1989, it is to be assumed that these provisions were in force at all material times.[38] The expression "open to the public" presumably extends the section to premises to which the public are admitted only on licence or on payment and,[39] if so, there would seem to be nothing to prevent the owner of the premises imposing contractual conditions restricting the copying of the material exhibited.[40]

"In such a work." The words "in such a work" have the potential to limit the scope of this exception quite considerably. For example, someone who takes a photograph of a building might still infringe copyright in the architect's preliminary drawings or plans, since the words "in such a work" would seem to refer only to copyright in the building itself. However, whilst this conclusion may be inevitable given the wording of the Act, it should be noted that Parliament gave this section very little consideration during the passage of the Bill. The wording of this section therefore seems to be the result of the draftsman having paraphrased the wording of the 1956 Act which, it seems, was also not wide enough to cover copyright in preliminary drawings and plans. Yet it is clear that Parliament intended the provisions in the 1956 Act to have the same effect as those in the 1911 Act and these latter provisions were not so limited.[41]   **9–170**

The Information Society Directive. Articles 5(3)(h) and (4) permit Member States to make an exception to the reproduction, distribution and comuunication to the public rights, in the case of use of works, such as works of architecture or sculpture, made to be located permanently in public places. Section 62 appears to fall squarely within this.   **9–171**

G. ADVERTISEMENT OF SALE OF ARTISTIC WORK

The Act makes special provision to enable copies of artistic works to be made for the purpose of advertising their sale.[42] Thus the Act provides that it is not an infringement of copyright in an artistic work to copy it, or to issue copies of it to the public, for the purpose of advertising the sale of the work.[43] It is therefore permissible in the course of selling a painting to make and publish copies of it in a catalogue. In relation to such copies, however, if they are subsequently dealt with[44] for any other purpose, they are to be treated as infringing copies for the purposes of that dealing and, if that dealing infringes copyright, for all subsequent purposes.[45] Someone who so deals in such copies, and who has the requisite degree of knowledge, will therefore be liable for secondary infringement of   **9–172**

---

[37] s.62(3).

[38] Sch.1, para.14(4).

[39] In *Cawley v Frost* [1976] 1 W.L.R. 1207 it was held in relation to the Public Order Act 1936, that, where the public have access to premises, those premises should be considered in their entirety, so the fact that the public are denied access to certain areas will not, of itself, stop them being part of a public place.

[40] See CDPA 1988, s.28(1) and *Sports and General Press Agency Ltd v "Our Dogs" Publishing Co. Ltd* [1916] 2 K.B. 880; [1917] 2 K.B. 125.

[41] See *Hansard*, HL Vol.195, col.1048; Copyright Act 1956, ss.9(3), 9(4); Copyright Act 1911, s.2(1)(iii) and compare CDPA 1988, s.65(b) (see para. 9–176, below).

[42] CDPA 1988, s.63. This section was new in the 1988 Act.

[43] s.63(1).

[44] For this purpose, "dealt with" means sold or let for hire, offered or exposed for sale or hire, exhibited in public, distributed or communicated to the public. Communication to the public was introduced as a further form of dealing on implementation of the Information Society Directive 2001/29, because of the possible commercial nature of such acts. See the Government Conclusions on the Patent Office's Consulation Paper of August 7, 2002, para.5.11.

[45] s.63(2).

copyright.[46] This provision will therefore catch the practice of selling old auction catalogues.

9–173　The Information Society Directive. Articles 5(3)(j) and (4) permit Member States to make an exception to the reproduction, distribution and communication to the public rights in the case of use for the purpose of advertising the public exhibition or sale of artistic works, to the extent necessary to promote the event, excluding any other commercial use. Section 63 appears to fall squarely within this.

H. MAKING OF SUBSEQUENT WORKS BY SAME ARTIST

9–174　Artists often wish to copy aspects of their earlier works when creating a new work, but where the copyright in an earlier work has been assigned (or where the work was made in the course of employment) there is a danger that the artist will infringe copyright by doing so.[47] The Act provides a limited exception to allow artists to copy parts of their earlier works, such that where the author of an artistic work is not the copyright owner, he does not infringe the copyright by copying the work in making another artistic work, provided he does not repeat or imitate the main design of the earlier work.[48] This provision would not, however, affect a claim in contract against an artist who copied part of a work over which he had granted an exclusive licence, since (as has been seen) the exceptions only apply to the question of copyright infringement and the rights of the exclusive licensee against the owner of the copyright lie in contract only.[49] Whether the artist would in fact be liable to the exclusive licensee would depend on the terms of the contract. In the course of Parliamentary debates on this provision two examples of its intended effect were given. First, it was said that this provision would allow an architect to reproduce some part the original design, such as a staircase, in a subsequent building, provided he avoided repeating or imitating the main design. Secondly, it was said that it would allow the painter of a group portrait to reuse sketches to reproduce individual portraits.[50] In addition, it would seem that this section would protect a painter who reuses a "trade mark" object or motif.[51]

9–175　The Information Society Directive. Section 64 was not amended on implementation of the Directive, even though the Directive does not contain any permitted exception which corresponds to this permitted act. It would appear that the Government relied on the general saving for analogue uses of minor importance permitted by Article 5(3)(o) and assumed that any digital copying would be *de minimis*.

I. RECONSTRUCTION OF BUILDINGS

9–176　The Act provides that anything done for the purposes of reconstructing a building will not infringe two categories of copyright works. First, any copyright in the building; secondly, in any drawings or plans in accordance with which the build-

---

[46] See para. 8–02, above, and s.27(6).
[47] *cf. Gross v Seligman*, 212 F.930 (2d Cir. 1914) and see Hughes, "The Personality Interest of artists and inventors in Intellectual Property" (1998) 16 Cardozo Arts & Ent. L.J. 81.
[48] CDPA 1988, s.64. The Copyright Acts 1956, s.9(9), and 1911, s.2(1)(ii), contained broadly equivalent provisions.
[49] See para. 5–23, above.
[50] *Hansard*, HL Vol.491, col.191; Vol.493, col.1187.
[51] So, for example, Magritte's *bilboquets* might fall within this section.

ing was, by or with the licence of the copyright owner, constructed.[52] For this purpose, in relation to buildings constructed before August 1, 1989, the reference to the owner of the copyright in any drawings or plans is to the person who at the time of construction was the owner of the copyright in the drawings or plans under the 1956 or 1911 Acts, or earlier legislation, as the case may be.[53]

The Information Society Directive. Article 5(3)(m) permits Member States to make an exception to the reproduction, distribution and communicatin to the public rights, in the case of use of an artistic work in the form of a building or a drawing or plan of a building for the purposes of reconstructing the building. Section 65 appears to fall squarely within this permitted exception.

9–177

15. MISCELLANEOUS PROVISIONS: LENDING OF WORKS

LENDING TO PUBLIC OF COPIES OF CERTAIN WORKS

Lending: compulsory licences.[54] The public lending of copies of works is an act restricted by copyright in most types of work,[55] and thus an infringement of copyright unless the licence of the copyright owner has been obtained. By virtue of section 66, however, the Secretary of State has power to order that such lending is to be treated as licensed subject only to payment of a reasonable royalty or other payment.[56] This "permitted act" is thus in reality a compulsory licence and is dealt with in detail elsewhere.[57]

9–178

16. MISCELLANEOUS PROVISIONS: FILMS AND SOUND RECORDINGS

A. FILMS: ACTS PERMITTED ON ASSUMPTIONS AS TO EXPIRY OF COPYRIGHT

As has been seen, the term of copyright in films was extended by the Duration of Copyright and Rights in Performances Regulations 1995.[58] The term of copyright is now determined by reference to the date of death of the director, the author of the screen play, the author of the dialogue and the composer of any specially created music: copyright lasts for 70 years from the end of the year in which the last

9–179

---

[52] CDPA 1988, s.65. The Copyright Act 1956, s.9(10) contained a very similar provision. It is perhaps worth contrasting this provision with the "right to repair" established by case law. See paras 5–000 *et seq.*

[53] Sch.1, para.14(7).

[54] The heading, as amended by the Copyright and Related Rights Regulations 1996 (SI 1996/2967), actually reads, "Miscellaneous: lending of works and playing of sound recordings". However, this is misleading, as the Duration of Copyright and Rights in Performances Regulations (SI 1995/3297), grouped the miscellaneous provisions relating to the playing of sound recordings together with a new section dealing with assumptions as to the expiry of copyright in films (see para. 9–179, below).

[55] See further, CDPA 1988, s.18A: "the rental or lending of copies of the work to the public is an act restricted by copyright in (a) a literary, dramatic or musical work, (b) an artistic work, other than a work of architecture or a work of applied art, or (c) a film or sound recording." See further, para. 7–81, *et seq.*, above.

[56] s.66(1). s.66 in its present form was introduced by the Copyright and Related Rights Regulations 1996 (SI 1996/2967), which implemented the Rental and Lending Rights Directive (92/100). This new section replaces the original provision. s.66 as originally enacted was similar in operation, but it applied to the rental of works. It is considered elsewhere (see para. 29–45, below).

[57] See para. 29–45, below.

[58] SI 1995/3297. See Ch.6, above.

of these persons dies.[59] One effect of this amendment has been to make it more difficult to know precisely when copyright in a film has expired. The Duration of Copyright Regulations therefore introduced a new exception to allow a film to be copied at a time when it is reasonable to assume that copyright has expired.[60] The Act thus provides that copyright in a film is not infringed by an act done, or in pursuance of arrangements made, at a time when it is reasonable to assume either (a) that copyright has expired, or (b) that the last of the persons by reference to whom the copyright period is determined died 70 years or more before the beginning of the calendar year in which the act is done or the arrangements are made.[61] The latter provision does not, however, apply in relation to a film in which Crown copyright subsists, or a film in which copyright originally vested in an international organisation and in which a copyright period longer than 70 years has been specified.[62] These provisions are very similar to those governing the copying of works of unknown authorship,[63] except that there has been no need for complex transitional arrangements.

9–180   **The Information Society Directive.** The same comment can be made about this permitted act as was made in relation to the provisions governing the copying of works of unknown authorship.[64]

B. PLAYING OF SOUND RECORDINGS FOR PURPOSES OF CLUBS, ETC.

9–181   **The permitted act.** Section 67 of the 1988 Act provides that if certain conditions are met, it is not an infringement of the copyright in a sound recording to play it as part of the activities of, or for the benefit of, a club, society or other organisation.[65]

9–182   **The Information Society Directive.** The public performance right is not one of the rights with which the Directive is directly concerned.[66] However, Article 11(1) of the Directive amends the Rental and Related Rights Directive to introduce the Berne 3-step test requirement into the exceptions permitted by that Directive.[67] Before this amendment, Article 10 of the Rental and Related Rights Directive permitted a Member State to make exceptions or limitations to the rights of phonogram producers, including limitations which are of the same kind as the Member State makes in connection with the protection of copyright in literary and artistic works.[68] Section 67 was not amended on implementation of this Directive, the Government apparently taking the view that its terms were consistent with it.[69] With the amendment of Article 10 of the Rental and Related Rights Directive by the Information Society Directive, to require that these limitations

---

[59] CDPA 1988, s.13B(2), and see para. 6–67, above.

[60] s.66A.

[61] s.66A(1).

[62] s.66A(2).

[63] See para. 9–152, above.

[64] See para. 9–152, above.

[65] CDPA 1988, s.67(1). Note that the section only applies to sound recordings and not to any musical or literary works embodied in them. The section only comes into play of course if the playing of the recording amounts to the playing of it in public. See s.12(7) of the 1956 Act for the provision made under that Act in this area.

[66] See Information Society Directive 2001/29, Recitals 23 and 24.

[67] As to the Berne 3-step test, see paras 9–02, above, and 24–33 , below.

[68] The other permitted limitations are for (a) private use; (b) use of short excerpts in connection with the reporting of current events; (c) ephemeral fixation by a broadcasting organisation by means of its own facilities and for its own broadcasts; and (d) use solely for the purposes of teaching or scientific research. See Rental and Related Rights Directive, 92/100, Art.10. All these exceptions correspond to the exceptions permitted by Art.15 of the Rome Convention.

[69] This was a view which was apparently shared by the Commission. See the comment in *Phono-*

comply with the Berne 3-step test,[70] amendment was needed to section 67 to narrow the scope of its conditions relating to (a) the motives of the person playing the recording, (b) how the proceeds of any charges made for admission are applied and (c) how the proceeds from the sale of any goods or services made at the time are applied.[71]

Organisations to which the section applies. If section 67 is to apply, the organisation in question must be a club, society or other organisation which is not established or conducted for profit and whose main objects are charitable or otherwise concerned with the advancement of religion, education or social welfare.[72] Similar wording also appeared in section 8(1)(a) of the Rating and Valuation (Miscellaneous Provisions) Act 1955 and cases decided under that section are helpful in construing section 67.[73] The following principles apply:

9–183

(1) The word "organisation" does not have a wide, unrestricted meaning, since under the *ejusdem generis* rule the reference to clubs and societies colours and cuts down the sort of organisation that falls within the section.[74] The distinguishing characteristic of a club or society is that it consists of individuals who are bound together in some common activity or enterprise.[75]

(2) As to the requirement that the organisation should not be established or conducted for profit, an organisation will not be conducted for profit simply because it makes investments, provided such investments are only a means of achieving other, legitimate, objectives.[76]

(3) The organisation must be one whose main functions, or whose functions when viewed as a whole, are either charitable or otherwise concerned with the advancement of religion, education or social welfare. The fact that one of the main objects of an organisation is, for example, the

---

graphic Performance Ltd v Department of Trade and Industry [2004] EWHC 1795 (Ch), at para.7, a case where proceedings were brought against the Crown alleging failure to implement the Rental and Related Rights Directive. Although it is not particularly clear from the Directive itself, Art.8(2) effectively requires Member States to provide protection for owners of the copyright in sound recordings in respect of their public performance, this being a "communication to the public". See also Recitals 5 and 11, which respectively state that (a) the protection of the subject matter of related rights protection by communication to the public is to be considered as being of fundamental importance for the Community's economic and cultural development and (b) the Community's legal framework on certain rights related to copyright can be limited to establishing, amongst other things, the right to communication to the public for certain groups of rightholders in the field of related rights protection.

[70] See Information Society Directive, Art.11(1)(b), amending Rental and Related Rights Directive, Art.10(3) to provide: "The limitations shall only be applied in certain special cases which do not conflict with a normal exploitation of the subject-matter and do not unreasonably prejudice the legitimate interests of the rightholder".

[71] It was the Government's belief that these changes would prevent organisations seeking to benefit from the CDPA 1988, s.67 exception in relation to activities conducted on a quasi-commercial basis. See the Government Conclusions on the Patent Office's Consulation Paper of August 7, 2002, para.5.15.

[72] CDPA 1988, s.67(2)(a). This condition was not altered on amendment.

[73] *Phonographic Performance Ltd v. South Tyneside Metropolitan Borough Council* [2001] R.P.C. 594; [2001] E.M.L.R. 446. See also the Miners' Welfare Act 1952 (c.23), s.16, and the Recreational Charities Act 1958 (c.17), s.1.

[74] Unless the words "other organisation" were restricted in some such way, it would be of very wide ambit indeed, including all arms of national government, local government, local authorities, quangos, regional health trusts, etc: *Phonographic Performance Ltd v. South Tyneside Metropolitan Borough Council* [2001] R.P.C. 594; [2001] E.M.L.R. 446.

[75] *Phonographic Performance Ltd v South Tyneside Metropolitan Borough Council* [2001] R.P.C. 594; [2001] E.M.L.R. 446. The nature of the organisation is of course further qualified by CDPA 1988, s.67(2).

[76] *National Deposit Friendly Society (Trustees) v Skegness UDC* [1959] A.C. 293, HL *per* Lord Denning.

advancement of education is not enough.[77] In order to fall within the provision, all the main objects of the organisation must satisfy the requirements of section 67(2)(a), although provided each of the main objects satisfies at least one of the requirements (*i.e.* of charity, religion, education or social welfare), that is enough. If any of the organisation's main objects are held not to be charitable or akin to charitable objects then the organisation will fall outside the protection of this section.[78] However, provided the organisation's main objects satisfy the requirements of this section, the organisation may also have subsidiary objects, such as the benefit of its members.[79]

(4) Whether the objects of an organisation are charitable or not is a question of the general law of charity. Legal charities have to fall into one of four classes, namely, the relief of poverty,[80] the advancement of education,[81] the advancement of religion,[82] and other purposes beneficial to the community.[83] In addition to this there must be an element of public benefit so that, for example, a trust for the education of employees of a particular company is not a valid legal charity.[84]

(5) The words "or are otherwise concerned with the advancement of religion, education or social welfare" are intended to include activities which are quasi-charitable in nature.[85] The words "are otherwise concerned with the advancement of" impose a limitation on the words "religion, education or social welfare" which follow. They show that the section is concerned with objects which are of concern to charitable organisations but which for some reason or other fail to come under the definition of "charitable purposes" in the strictly legal sense.[86] The nature and effect of these words is therefore to extend the protection of this section to organisations which are charitable in the popular sense rather than in the strictly legal sense.[87] In general it has been said that it is impossible to provide a precise delimitation of organisations which might fall within this definition, so that each case must be considered on its merits.[88] "Social welfare" means the well-being (whether in the physical, mental or material sense) of individuals as members of society.[89] Thus the provision of benefits which tend directly to improve the health or conditions of life comes *prima facie* within the expression "social welfare";[90] there is no need for an eleemosy-

[77] *Phonographic Performance Ltd v South Tyneside Metropolitan Borough Council* [2001] R.P.C. 594; [2001] E.M.L.R. 446.
[78] In particular, see *Berry v St Marylebone BC* [1958] Ch.406.
[79] *National Deposit Friendly Society (Trustees) v Skegness UDC*, [1959] A.C. 293, HL *per* at 310 Lord Denning.
[80] See, *e.g. Re Coulthurst* [1951] Ch.661 at 665.
[81] See further, *Chartered Insurance Institute v London Corporation* [1957] 1 W.L.R. 867; *IRC v McMullen* [1981] A.C. 1.
[82] See further, *United Grand Lodge, etc. v Holborn BC* [1957] 1 W.L.R. 1080; *Berry v St Marylebone BC* [1958] Ch. 406; *Re South Place Ethical Society* [1980] 1 W.L.R. 1565.
[83] *Income Tax Special Purposes Commissioners v Pemsel* [1891] A.C. 531.
[84] *Oppenheim v Tobacco Securities Trust Co. Ltd* [1951] A.C. 297.
[85] *Phonographic Performance Ltd v South Tyneside Metropolitan Borough Council* [2001] R.P.C. 594; [2001] E.M.L.R. 446.
[86] *Phonographic Performance Ltd v South Tyneside Metropolitan Borough Council* [2001] R.P.C. 594; [2001] E.M.L.R. 446.
[87] *National Deposit Friendly Society (Trustees) v Skegness UDC* [1959] A.C. 293, HL *per* at 311 Lord Keith.
[88] *National Deposit Friendly Society (Trustees) v Skegness UDC* [1959] A.C. 293.
[89] *National Deposit Friendly Society (Trustees) v Skegness UDC* [1957] 2 Q.B. 573, CA *per* at 581 Parker L.J., CA; *Berry v St Marylebone BC* [1958] Ch. 406.
[90] *National Deposit Friendly Society (Trustees) v Skegness UDC* [1957] 2 Q.B. 573.

nary element.[91] The words "concerned with the advancement of" require that the organisation does more than enable individuals to advance their own welfare.[92] By analogy with the law of charities, there must be an intention to benefit the community.[93] It seems, however, that there is no need for public benefit in the narrow, technical, sense.[94]

(6) In determining the main objects of an organisation it seems that it may be permissible to look at the way the organisation's affairs have been conducted, as well as at its rules.[95] Where the organisation has a written constitution, however, it is to that and that alone to which the court should look to ascertain its objects for present purposes[96] and extrinsic evidence is not admissible to limit the proper meaning of the language used.[97]

Having regard to these principles, a local authority was held not to be an "organisation" within the meaning of s.67, since: (1) As a matter of impression, a normal user of the English language would not describe all of the main functions of a local authority, or the functions of a local authority viewed as a whole, as charitable or for the provision of social welfare. Although one of the main objects was undoubtedly the advancement of education, this was not enough. (2) A local authority is something quite different from a club or a society. (3) The objects of a local authority are neither charitable nor quasi-charitable in nature. (4) The function of a local authority is to carry out the administrative and governmental functions in respect of its area, to the extent that these have been devolved from national government. (5) As to the "main objects" of a local authority, these include education, housing, social and welfare services, control of planning, maintenance of the roads (including pavements and lighting), licensing activities and the raising of money by way of business rates and council tax payments under the provisions of the Local Government Finance Acts 1988 and 1992.[98]

Other conditions. There are three other conditions which have to be satisfied in order to come within the permitted act: **9–184**

(1) *The motives of the person playing the recording*. The sound recording must be played by a person who is acting primarily and directly for the benefit of the organisation and who is not acting with a view to gain.[99] This means that the hiring of a DJ or a Karaoke operator who is paid a fee will take the playing outside the section.

(2) *Application of charges made for admission*. The proceeds of any charge for admission to the place where the recording is to be heard must be applied solely for the purposes of the organisation.[1]

(3) *Application of proceeds from the sale of any goods or services*. The

---

[91] *Berry v St. Marylebone B.C.* [1958] Ch.406.

[92] *National Deposit Friendly Society (Trustees) v Skegness UDC* [1957] 2 Q.B. 573.

[93] *National Deposit Friendly Society (Trustees) v Skegness UDC* [1957] 2 Q.B. 573; *Independent Order of Oddfellows, etc. v Manchester Corporation* [1957] 1 W.L.R. 1059.

[94] *Skegness UDC v Derbyshire Miners' Welfare Committee* [1959] 2 All E.R. 258; *National Deposit Friendly Society (Trustees) v Skegness UDC* [1959] A.C. 293, *per* Lord Denning at 321.

[95] *National Deposit Friendly Society (Trustees) v Skegness UDC* [1959] A.C. 293, at 320.

[96] *Phonographic Performance Ltd v South Tyneside Metropolitan Borough Council* [2001] R.P.C. 594; [2001] E.M.L.R. 446.

[97] *Royal College of Nursing v St Marylebone BC* [1958] 1 W.L.R. 95 at 99–100. Also see *Berry v St Marylebone BC* [1958] Ch. 406.

[98] *Phonographic Performance Ltd v South Tyneside Metropolitan Borough Council* [2001] R.P.C. 594; [2001] E.M.L.R. 446. Sound recordings were played at aerobics and keep-fit lessons organised by the defendant authority which were open to the public.

[99] CDPA 1988, s.67(2)(b). These, and the succeeding conditions of CDPA 1988, s.67(2), were introduced on amendment, revoking and replacing the previous condition that the proceeds of any charge for admission to the place where the recording is to be heard were to be applied solely for the purposes of the organisation.

[1] s.67(2)(b).

proceeds from any goods or services sold by, or on behalf of, the organisation (i) in the place where the sound recording is heard, and (ii) on the occasion when the sound recording is played, must be applied solely for the purposes of the organisation.[2]

9–185 **Comment.** The exception applies whether the record is performed as part of the activities of the organisation, for example for the entertainment of those whose education, social welfare, etc. is being advanced, or it is performed for the benefit of the organisation, which would include a performance given to outsiders where the proceeds of the performance are applied solely for the purposes of the organisation. However, it is important to emphasise that these provisions only apply to the playing of sound recordings. They do not apply to any underlying musical or literary work. Thus the practical effect of this section is that organisations falling within this section will not have to seek a licence from Phonographic Performance Ltd but they will still need a licence from the Performing Rights Society Ltd, unless they are diligent in ensuring that they only play recordings of works which are out of copyright.

17. MISCELLANEOUS PROVISIONS: BROADCASTS

A. Incidental Recording for Purposes of Broadcast

9–186 **Introduction.** Section 68 of the Act enables a person who is entitled to broadcast a work to make temporary copies of the work for that purpose.[3] In practice the process of broadcasting a work will often involve the making of temporary copies and thus the aim of this section is to allow such copies to be made.[4] In distinction to the other permitted acts, section 68 operates by conferring a licence on the user rather than by stating that copyright is not infringed.

9–187 **The Berne Convention.** This provision directly corresponds to Article 11 *bis* (3) of the Berne Convention.[5]

9–188 **The Information Society Directive.** Article 5(2)(d) of the Directive permits the making of ephemeral recordings of works by broadcasting organisations by means of their own facilities and for their own broadcasts.[6] No amendment was required to the 1988 Act on implementation of the Directive.

9–189 **The permitted acts.** The exception applies in cases where by virtue of a licence or assignment of copyright a person is authorised to broadcast (a) a literary, dramatic or musical work, or an adaptation of such a work, (b) an artistic work, or (c) a sound recording or film.[7] In such cases that person is to be treated as licensed by the owner of the copyright in the work to do or authorise certain further acts for the purposes of the broadcast. In the case of a literary, dramatic or

---

[2] s.67(2)(c).

[3] CDPA 1988, s.68. The 1956 Act contained a similar, but more limited provision: Copyright Act 1956, s.6(7). It might be thought that the person having the right to broadcast a work would usually have an implied licence to make copies of the work for that purpose. However, in *Bishop v Stevens* (1990) 72 D.L.R. (4th) 97 the Supreme Court of Canada refused to imply such a term.

[4] These rights may have been assigned to different people. As such, this provision can also be seen as providing a degree of security for the purchaser of the broadcasting rights.

[5] Also see United States Copyright Act 1976, 17 U.S.C., s.112.

[6] Note that recital 41 of the Information Society Directive 2001/29, states that "when applying the exception or limitation in respect of ephemeral recordings made by broadcasting organisations it is understood that a broadcaster's own facilities include those of a person acting on behalf of and under the responsibility of the broadcasting organisation".

[7] CDPA 1988, s.68(1).

musical work, or an adaptation of such a work, the further acts are the making of a sound recording or film of the work or adaptation.[8] In the case of an artistic work the acts are the taking of a photograph or the making of a film of the work.[9] In the case of a sound recording or film, the acts are the making of a copy of it.[10] The licence is, however, subject to two conditions, namely, that the recording, film, photograph or copy in question (a) shall not be used for any other purpose, and (b) shall be destroyed within 28 days of being first used for broadcasting the work.[11] Where a recording, film, photograph or copy is made pursuant to the licence conferred by this section, but is then used for some purpose other than the broadcast in question, then when used for that other purpose, that article is to be treated as an infringing copy.[12] Similarly, any such article which is not destroyed within the specified 28-day period is also to be treated as an infringing copy for all purposes thereafter.[13] Any person who then deals with such an article with the requisite degree of knowledge will be liable for secondary infringement.[14]

In practice, broadcasters have found the requirement that they destroy copies within 28 days to be unduly onerous,[15] in particular, because it would be much cheaper for broadcasters if they were allowed to retain copies for repeated later use. This led the operator of a subscription music service transmitted by satellite to argue that it had a statutory right to make and retain copies for longer than 28 days by virtue of section 135C(1) of the 1988 Act.[16] This argument was rejected on the grounds that it is clear both as a matter of plain language and from the legislative history that section 135C(1) "is in nowise concerned with the making by the broadcaster of copies of sound recordings or the protection of the broadcaster from infringement proceedings in respect of the making of copies".[17]

B. RECORDING FOR PURPOSES OF SUPERVISION OF BROADCASTS, ETC.

The Act makes provision enabling broadcast programmes to be recorded for the purposes of supervision and control of such programmes. Thus copyright is not infringed by the making or use by the BBC, for the purpose of maintaining supervision and control over programmes broadcast by them, of recordings of those programmes.[18] Similarly, there are provisions relating to the supervision and control of Independent Television and Radio. However, with the changes introduced by the Broadcasting Acts 1990 and 1996, the original provisions of the 1988 Act relating to the control by the IBA and the Cable Authority had to be amended. The Act now provides that the copyright in a work is not infringed by anything done in pursuance of:

9–190

(a) The powers of the Independent Television Commission, the Radio

---

[8] s.68(2)(a).
[9] s.68(2)(b).
[10] s.68(2)(c).
[11] s.68(3).
[12] s.68(4)(a).
[13] s.68(4)(b). Also see *Phonographic Performance Ltd v AEI Rediffusion Music Ltd* [1998] Ch. 187.
[14] s.27(6) and see para. 8–02, above.
[15] It should be noted that the Whitford Committee saw "no absolute need to provide for destruction" (Whitford Committee: The Report of the Committee to Consider the Law on Copyright and Designs, 1977 (Cmnd. 6732) para.683), but any provision which allowed copies to be retained indefinitely would place the United Kingdom in breach of the Berne Convention.
[16] *Phonographic Performance Ltd v AEI Rediffusion Music Ltd* [1998] Ch. 187. Sections 135A–135G were inserted into the 1988 Act by the Broadcasting Act 1990. These sections give broadcasters a statutory licence to broadcast copyright sound recordings. See further, paras 29–25 *et seq.*, below.
[17] *Phonographic Performance Ltd v AEI Rediffusion Music Ltd* [1998] Ch. 187, at 194.
[18] CDPA 1988, s.69(1).

Authority, the Broadcasting Standards Commission and justices of the peace to make copies of recordings and to use these in pursuance of their duties.[19]

(b) A condition requiring that copies of broadcasts be made and kept which, by virtue of section 334(1) of the Communications Act 2003, is included in a licence granted under Part I or Part III of that Act or Part I or II of the Broadcasting Act 1996.[20]

(c) A direction given by OFCOM in accordance with its power to demand scripts and recordings prior to broadcast following a failure by a licence holder to comply with a condition of the licence or with a direction given by it.[21]

In addition, copyright is not infringed by the use by OFCOM, in connection with the performance of any of its functions under the Broadcasting Act 1990, the Broadcasting Act 1996 or the Communications Act 2003, of (a) any recording, script or transcript which is provided to it under or by virtue of any provision of those Acts or (b) any existing material which is transferred to it by a scheme made under section 30 of the Communications Act 2003.[22] For this purpose, "existing material" means any recording, script or transcript which was provided to the Independent Television Commission or the Radio Authority in connection with their functions under the 1990 or 1996 Broadcasting Acts, or any recording or transcript which was provided to the Broadcasting Standards Commission under the complaints procedure of the Broadcasting Act 1996.[23]

9–191   **The Information Society Directive.** Article 5(3)(d) of the Directive permits Member States to make an exception to the reproduction right for the purpose of "public security". Whether or not section 69 falls within this expression, it no doubt falls within the general spirit, if not the actual wording, of the general saving of Article 9.

C. RECORDING FOR PURPOSES OF TIME-SHIFTING

9–192   The use of domestic videocassette recorders to make recordings of broadcasts was widespread before the 1998 Act, although unlawful as the law then stood.[24] Section 70 of the 1988 Act legitimised this state of affairs by permitting a recording of a broadcast to be made with a view to enabling it to be listened to or viewed at a later date, such that the copyright in the broadcast and any work included in it will not be infringed.[25]

9–193   **The Information Society Directive.** The Directive does not contain any provision expressly permitting such an exception but Article 5(2)(b) allows Member States to make an exception to the reproduction and the distribution rights in respect of reproductions on any medium made by a natural person for private use and for ends that are neither directly nor indirectly commercial, on condition that the rightholders receive fair compensation. Apart from the requirement of compensation, section 70 as enacted fell broadly within the terms of this permit-

---

[19] s.69(2)(a).
[20] s.69(2)(b).
[21] s.69(2)(c); and see Broadcasting Act 1990, s.109(2).
[22] s.69(3).
[23] s.69(4).
[24] In much the same way as the unlawful act of "home taping" of audio recordings was prevalent.
[25] The same result has been achieved in the United States through an application of the fair-use doctrine. See further, *Sony Corporation of America v Universal City Studios* (1984) 464 U.S. 417.

ted exception,[26] although some tightening up was required on implementation to limit the permitted act more clearly to private and non-commercial use. No amendment was made, however, to introduce provisions for compensation to rightholders, the Government taking the view that any compensation was likely to be nil or at least of very small amount, and would in any event be swallowed up by the transaction costs of administering any compensation scheme,[27] such that reliance can be placed on recital 35 of the Directive. This states that in "certain situations where the prejudice to the rightholder would be minimal, no obligation for payment may arise".

The 1988 Act. The Act now provides that it is not an infringement of the copy-   **9–194**
right in a broadcast or in any work included in it to make in domestic premises a recording for private and domestic use if it is solely for the purpose of enabling it to be viewed or listened to at a more convenient time.[28] It has been said that the purpose of the section is to cover the case of an individual who makes a copy of a broadcast and uses it solely for his private and domestic use.[29] It has also been held that the relevant use is that of the copier, so that if the copy is made by one person for the private and domestic use of another, even for the sole purpose of enabling that other person to view it later, this would not fall within the section.[30] But in the same case the court also appears to have conceded that it would not be an infringement for a neighbour to make a copy of a broadcast for a person's private and domestic use. The case was decided on the wording of the Act as it stood before amendment, which was not particularly clear,[31] but now that the provisions have been tightened, it is suggested that there is no reason in principle or on policy grounds why the making of a recording by A, in domestic premises, for the private and domestic use of B, for the sole purpose of enabling B to view or listen to it at a more convenient time, should not fall squarely within the terms of the permitted act. In a case where an individual sets up a business in his own home of making and selling recordings to others, this activity will now be caught by the provisions considered in the next paragraph.

Subsequent dealings. As enacted, recordings made in this way did not become   **9–195**
infringing copies under the Act if subsequently dealt with. There was therefore nothing to stop private individuals selling such original copies, provided they had been made in accordance with section 70 and provided also that such acts did not constitute an issue to the public.[32]

This possibility is inconsistent with the Directive and so the Act has now been amended to provide that where such a copy is subsequently dealt with it is to be

---

[26] This is also the Government's view. See the Transposition Note on implementation of the Directive by the Copyright and Related Rights Regulations 2003 (SI 2003/2498).

[27] See the Analysis of Responses and Government Conclusions on the Patent Office's Consulation Paper of August 7, 2002, para.5.16.

[28] CDPA 1988, s.70(1). Or, apparently, a more convenient place: *Hansard*, HL Vol.501, col.267. The restriction to require the recording to be made in domestic premises was added by amendment on implementation of the Information Society Directive 2001/29. Had this amendment then been in force, it would have prevented any argument by the defendant in *Sony Music Entertainment (UK) Ltd v Easyinternetcafé Ltd* [2003] EWHC 62 (Ch); [2003] F.S.R. 48, that its activities fell within the section. In that case, members of the public were able to download music files from the internet onto the server at the defendant's internet café. The defence failed in any event. See below.

[29] *Sony Music Entertainment (UK) Ltd v Easyinternetcafé Ltd* [2003] EWHC 62; [2003] F.S.R. 48,.

[30] *Sony Music Entertainment (UK) Ltd v Easyinternetcafé Ltd* [2003] EWHC 62; [2003] F.S.R. 48,. The facts were rather extreme, but this seems to be the effect of the judgment.

[31] The section was added at a late stage of the Bill's passage through Parliament, and may not have received the attention it would otherwise have deserved.

[32] See CDPA 1988, s.18.

treated as an infringing copy for the purposes of that dealing and, if that dealing itself infringes copyright, as an infringing copy for all subsequent purposes.[33]

D. PHOTOGRAPHS OF BROADCASTS

9–196   While the 1988 Act provides that in relation to a broadcast, copying includes making a photograph of any image forming part of the broadcast,[34] section 71 of the Act permits the taking of a such photographs for private and domestic purposes. As with the time-shifting defence, this permitted act required tightening in order that it complied with the Information Society Directive.[35] Thus, the Act now provides that the making in domestic premises for private and domestic purposes of a photograph[36] of the whole or any part of an image forming part of a broadcast, or a copy of such a photograph, does not infringe any copyright in the broadcast or in any film included in it.[37] It should be noted that this exception does not cover the reproduction of an artistic work included in the broadcast. Thus the taking a photograph of a broadcast image which includes an artistic work will infringe copyright in the artistic work, unless the photographer can bring himself within one of the other exceptions, the most likely being incidental inclusion or one of the fair dealing provisions.[38]

9–197   **Subsequent dealings**. As with the permitted act of time-shifting, the Act has been amended to provide that, in the event of subsequent dealings with such copies, these become infringing copies.[39]

E. FREE PUBLIC SHOWING OR PLAYING OF BROADCAST

9–198   As enacted, section 72 of the 1988 Act contained a provision such that the showing or playing of a broadcast in public did not amount to an infringement of the broadcast or of any sound recording or film included in it, if it was not to a paying audience.[40] The permitted act was controversial[41] but in any event has been subject to substantial amendment on implementation of the Information Society Directive 2001/29.

9–199   **The Information Society Directive.** The application of the Information Society Directive and the Rental and Related Rights Directive in relation to the public performance of protected subject matter, and of sound recordings in particular, has already been considered in relation to section 67.[42] Much the same considerations apply to section 72, with the result that the section has been amended to cut down its provisions drastically as they apply to the free playing of broadcast sound recordings, with the aim of making the permitted act compliant with the 3-step test so far as concerns sound recordings.

---

[33] s.70(2). For this purpose, "dealt with" means sold or let for hire, offered or exposed for sale or hire or communicated to the public": s.70(3).

[34] CDPA 1988, s.17(4). See further, para. 7–72, above.

[35] *i.e.* so that it fell within the provisions of Information Society Directive, 2001/29, Art.5(2)(b).

[36] For the definition of "photograph," see. s.4(2) and see para. 3–57, above.

[37] s.71.

[38] s.31, and see paras 9–19 *et seq.* and 9–56, *et seq.*, above.

[39] CDPA 1988, ss.71(2), (3).

[40] The 1956 Act, ss.14(8), 14A(9) contained broadly equivalent provisions.

[41] In particular, because of the way the provision permitted the free public performance of broadcast sound recordings in shops, pubs and other places to which the public had access without paying. Separate proceedings have been brought against the United Kingdom by the Commission and Phonographic Performance Ltd alleging a failure to implement the Rental and Related Rights Directive 92/100. See *Phonographic Performance Ltd v Department of Trade and Industry* [2004] EWHC 1795 Ch D. The position is now different following implementation of the Information Society Directive.

[42] See para. 9–181, above.

The 1988 Act as amended: summary. As the Act now stands, sound recordings **9–200**
have been divided into two categories, namely "excepted" sound recordings and
all other sound recordings (which latter category will be referred to here as "non-
excepted" sound recordings). As will be seen, virtually all commercially released
sound recordings will fall into the category of excepted sound recordings. The
basic position then is that where a broadcast is without licence shown or played
in public to an audience who have not paid for admission to the place where the
broadcast is to be seen or heard, this will not infringe any copyright in (a) the
broadcast, or (b) any film included in it.[43] In addition, such an act will not infringe
any copyright in any *non-excepted* sound recording[44] but, in general, the copyright in any *excepted* sound recordings will be infringed.[45] All that is generally allowed by this form of permitted act (the "wider form") is therefore the showing
of the broadcast itself, the showing of any film included in it, and the playing of a
limited range of sound recordings.There are then two special or narrow cases in
which such an act will in addition not infringe the copyright in any excepted
sound recording (the "narrowes" permitted acts), namely (a) where the playing or
showing of the broadcast forms part of the activities of an organisation that is not
established or conducted for profit and (b) where the playing or showing of the
broadcast is necessary for the purposes of the repair or demonstration of television or radio equipment.[46] These provisions are discussed in further detail below.

It is irrelevant for the present purposes that the copyright in the sound recording or film was infringed by the orginal broadcast, although the fact that the
sound recording or film was heard or seen in pubic by the reception of the
broadcast is to be taken into account in assessing the damages for that
infringement.[47]

The overall effect of this section is that public houses, cafés, shops and the like
will need one or more licences to have a television or radio playing for the benefit
of customers unless the programme being broadcast does not include any copyright literary, dramatic or musical works or any commercially released sound
recordings (*i.e.* excepted recordings). Thus, for example, it may be possible to
show a broadcast sports event by virtue of this exception, although today such
programmes usually contain works of the above kinds.[48] It will not be possible
under this section to play a radio station which broadcasts popular music,[49] so
that a licence from the Performing Rights Society Ltd[50] will be required, nor,
save where one of the narrower permitted acts applies, will it be possible to do so
without a licence from Phonographic Performance Ltd.[51]

Excepted sound recordings and the wider permitted act. The underlying aim **9–201**
is therefore to provide that the public performance by means of broadcasts of
ordinary or commercially released sound recordings will require a licence except
in cases which fall within the narrower permitted acts. An "excepted sound recording" is defined as a sound recording (a) whose author is not the author of the
broadcast in which it is included, and (b) which is a recording of music with or

[43] CDPA 1988, s.72(1).
[44] s.72(1).
[45] s.72(1) and s.19(3).
[46] s.72(1B).
[47] s.72(4).
[48] Although see CDPA 1988, s.31(3) and see para. 9–62, above.
[49] *cf. Performing Rights Society Ltd v Camelo* [1936] 3 All E.R. 557.
[50] As to which, see para. 28–59, below.
[51] As to which, see para. 28–60, below. But see below, as to the notification of such licences.

without words spoken or sung.[52] As to (a), the author of a sound recording is the person who undertakes the arrangements necessary for the making of the work ("the producer")[53] and the author of a broadcast is the person who makes the broadcast.[54] Thus, the playing of sound recordings, of whatever kind, produced by the broadcaster itself will fall within the wider permitted act. Otherwise, only if the recording is of the spoken word alone, or of other sounds which do not include any music, can its playing fall within the wider permitted acts. Thus, virtually all commercially released sound recordings will fall outside the wider permitted act.

9–202   **The narrower permitted acts.** Having removed a large swathe of sound recordings from the ambit of the wider permitted act, the playing of such broadcast recordings is brought back within the ambit of the narrower permitted acts in two special situations. In relation to both situations, however, there remains the requirement that the audience should not have paid for admission to the place where the broadcast is to be seen or heard. The first situation is where the playing or showing of the broadcast forms part of the activities of an organisation that is not established or conducted for profit.[55] The nature of such an organisation has already been considered.[56] The second is where the playing or showing of the broadcast is necessary for the purposes of (i) repairing equipment for the reception of broadcasts; (ii) demonstrating that a repair to such equipment has been carried out; or (iii) demonstrating such equipment which is being sold or let for hire or offered or exposed for sale or hire.[57] So the playing of sound recordings in TV or radio repair, retail or hire shops will in general fall within the exception. The intention of both these exceptions is no doubt that, when coupled with the other requirements of the section, they will comply with the 3-step test. The second exception appears to be derived from Article 5(3)(l) of the Information Society Directive, which permits an exception to be made to the rights prescribed by that Directive in the case of use in connection with the demonstration or repair of equipment. What is relevant for the purposes of section 72, however, are the exceptions permitted by the Rental and Related Rights Directive, not those permitted by the Information Society Directive. Presumably the Government's thinking was that the exception permitted by Article 5(3)(l) must be an example of a case which satisfies the 3-step test.[58]

9–203   **Payment for admission.** The Act contains further provision as to the circumstances in which persons are to be treated as having paid for admission. Thus the Act rather cumbersomely provides that an audience is to be treated as having paid for admission to a place if they have paid for admission to a place of which that place forms part.[59] They are also to be treated as having paid for admission to a place if goods or services are supplied at that place (or a place of which it forms part) (a) at prices which are substantially attributable to the facilities afforded for seeing or hearing the broadcast, or (b) at prices exceeding those usually charged there and which are partly attributable to those facilities.[60] On the other hand, persons admitted as residents or inmates of a place are not, for this purpose, to be

[52] CDPA 1988, s.72(1A).
[53] ss.9(2)(aa), 178. See para. 4–49, above.
[54] s.9(2)(b). See para. 4–73, above.
[55] CDPA 1988, s.72(1B)(a).
[56] See para. 9–183, above.
[57] s.72(1B)(b).
[58] Even though the Article, as are all the permitted exceptions, is further qualified by the requirement of Article 5(5) that the exception conform to the 3-step test.
[59] CDPA 1988, s.72(2)(a).
[60] s.72(2)(b).

regarded as having paid for admission to that place,[61] nor are persons admitted as members of a club or society where the payment is only for membership of the club or society and the provision of facilities for seeing or hearing broadcasts is only incidental to the main purposes of the club or society.[62]

Notification of licences for excepted recordings. Given that the circumstances in which broadcasts are heard in commercial situations will vary considerably, and that the reasons for doing so may be different than in the case of a conscious or deliberate decision to play sound recordings in public by way of CDs, tapes and the like, the Government has introduced a new mechanism for regulating the licensing of the public performance of broadcast sound recordings. Thus, new sections 128A and 128B have been introduced which will require those collectively licensing the performance of sound recordings via broadcasts to notify the proposed licensing arrangements to the Secretary of State. He will then consider a number of matters, including the extent to which the licensing body has consulted affected parties and whether its proposals take account of factors such as the degree to which potential licensees will be using broadcasts containing recorded music. He then has the power to refer the proposals to the Copyright Tribunal for a determination of whether the arrangements are reasonable.[63]

9–204

F. RECEPTION AND RETRANSMISSION OF WIRELESS BROADCAST BY CABLE

Overview. Section 73 of the 1988 Act contains an exception to allow for the reception and immediate retransmission by cable of a wireless broadcast.[64] The original provisions of the 1988 Act dealing with this matter were amended to take into account the changes introduced by the Broadcasting Acts 1990 and 1996.[65] Further amendments have been necessary to take account of the changed treatment of broadcasts and cable programme services following implementation of the Information Society Directive. The provisions take effect partly by way of permitted act and partly by way of compulsory licence. The former aspect is dealt with below, the latter aspect is dealt with in detail elsewhere.[66]

9–205

Background. With the passing of the 1956 Act, it became an infringement of copyright in a literary, dramatic, musical or artistic work, or a sound recording or film, to broadcast a work by wireless means or by cable.[67] The 1956 Act also conferred copyright protection on wireless broadcasts themselves.[68] Thereafter difficult questions arose concerning the potential liability of a person who retransmitted a wireless broadcast by including it in a cable broadcast. Although

9–206

---

[61] s.72(3)(a).

[62] s.72(3)(b).

[63] See the Government Conclusions on the Patent Office's Consulation Paper of August 7, 2002, paras 5.20, 5.21. It is expected by the Government that the possibility for referral by this route will largely take the place of referral of proposed licensing arrangements by users to the Tribunal. The Government has also concluded that, for the time being at least, no action should be taken in relation to public performance of musical works via broadcasts (which is outside the scope of CDPA 1988, s.72 and was therefore already licensable), but will continue to monitor this aspect: see the Government's conclusion on the Consultation Paper, para.5.22. As to CDPA 1988, ss.128A and 128B, see further para. 29–80, below.

[64] As did the Copyright Act 1956, s.40.

[65] Broadcasting Act 1996 (c.55), s.138, Sch.9, para.1.

[66] See para. 29–48 *et seq.*, below.

[67] Copyright Act 1956, ss.2(5)(d), 3(5)(c), 2(5)(e) and 3(5)(d). That Act distinguished between broadcasts, which were defined to mean transmissions by wireless telegraphy (s.48(2)), and transmissions by means of a "cable programme service" or, previously, by means of a "diffusion service". See paras 3–82 and 7–98, above. Unless otherwise clear from the context, the present discussion uses the expression "broadcast" to include both forms of transmission.

[68] Copyright Act 1956, s.14.

authors and film makers were given a general right to control the cable broadcasting of their works, under section 40(3) of the 1956 Act they were deemed to have freely licensed the cable retransmission of BBC and IBA wireless broadcasts which included their material. Wireless broadcasters also had no right to control further cable transmission of their broadcasts. Consequently, cable operators were able to transmit domestic wireless broadcasts free of charge. Foreign broadcasts were subject to the jurisdiction of the Performing Rights Tribunal so that content owners' claims covered only the additional audience over and above that paid for by the foreign broadcaster.[69]

The Whitford Committee recommended that wireless broadcasting organisations be granted a cable transmission right, but also that section 40(3) should be extended to cover wireless broadcasts by the BBC or IBA, provided the cable retransmission was of the whole broadcast, was simultaneous and was confined to the area in which the broadcast was intended to be received.[70] Effectively, cable retransmission in the same area was to remain free. However, the Whitford Committee also recommended that the provisions relating to the cable retransmission of foreign broadcasts be abandoned.[71] The Cable and Broadcasting Act 1984 gave effect to many of these recommendations.

The 1988 Act originally provided two exceptions as regards cable retransmission, permitting retransmissions under the "must carry" provisions of the Cable and Broadcasting Act 1984 and retransmission within the original broadcast area (the "service area" exception). These exceptions were available both in relation to an action for infringement brought by the owner of the copyright in the wireless broadcast itself and the owners of copyright in works included in the wireless broadcast. However, as regards consent to cable retransmission of the broadcast itself (as opposed to consent to retransmit copyright works included in the broadcast) the service area defence did not apply to cable retransmission of either satellite or encrypted transmissions.

The "must carry" exception was repealed by the Broadcasting Act 1990.[72] This was because cable licences under that Act were no longer subject to "must carry" obligations. The service area exception was maintained. The Broadcasting Act 1996 reimposed "must carry" requirements and hence a "must carry" exception, albeit in a rather different form, was reintroduced. The opportunity was also taken to reform the service area exception.

9–207   **Justification.** A number of countries besides the United Kingdom have made provision to deal with the retransmission of broadcasts by cable.[73] However, the question of whether cable operators should have a right to retransmit broadcasts

---

[69] s.28.

[70] The Report of the Committee to Consider the Law on Copyright and Designs, 1977 (Cmnd. 6732) para.446. These recommendations were subsequently adopted by the Government: Green Paper 1981 (Cm. 8302), pp.27–32.

[71] The Report of the Committee to Consider the Law on Copyright and Designs, 1977 (Cmnd. 6732), paras 446, 448, 468(v).

[72] Broadcasting Act 1990, s.203(3), Sch.21.

[73] See further, Gendreau, *The Retransmission Right: Copyright and the Rediffusion of Works by Cable* (ESC, Oxford, 1990). A right to retransmit works is recognised under the Berne Convention (Art.11 *bis*(1)(ii)), but Art.11 *bis*(2) provides, "It shall be a matter for legislation in the countries of the Union to determine the conditions under which the rights mentioned in the previous paragraph [Broadcasting and Related Rights] may be exercised … but they shall not in any circumstances be prejudicial to the moral rights of the author, nor his right to obtain equitable remuneration". As regards the right to equitable remuneration in relation to retransmission within the original broadcast area (which takes effect by way of exception rather than by way of compulsory licence), it has been said that such remuneration will be obtained from the original broadcaster who will pay fees in respect of the whole audience within that area. See further, the Report of the Committee to Consider the Law on Copyright and Designs, 1977 (Cmnd. 6732) para.430–1.

and the question of whether this should take effect by way of outright exception or by way of compulsory licence has proved controversial.[74] Nevertheless, it is possible to identify at least three reasons why a retransmission right is justifiable in certain circumstances.

First, it can be argued that cable programmes offer better quality services, particularly in areas where reception is poor (so called "shadow zones") and in areas where there are restrictions on the use of individual outdoor aerials.[75] In such cases there would seem to be a general public interest in ensuring that cable services are readily available at an affordable rate. Requiring cable operators to negotiate with both broadcasters and the owners of works included in the broadcasts might impose extraordinarily high transaction costs upon the cable operator, with the result that such services would not be economically viable.

Secondly, it can be argued that such retransmissions do not harm the interests of traditional broadcasters. Indeed, in the case of broadcasters whose income depends upon advertising revenue, such retransmission may even increase profits by allowing the broadcaster to charge more for advertising time, as the advertisements will reach a larger audience. Moreover, in relation to the owners of works included in the broadcast, it is possible to view the act of simultaneous retransmission as part of the original broadcast and thus not an activity for which they are entitled to claim additional revenue. In particular, it is said that when negotiating a licence with a broadcaster the content owner will assume universal coverage within the broadcast area and will fix a price accordingly. From this perspective, it could even be said that granting content owners the right to claim additional revenue from cable operators would be unjust, in that the content owners would then be paid twice for what is essentially a single use of their work.[76]

Thirdly, it must be noted that in certain circumstances the operators of cable programme services are compelled by a "must carry" obligation to retransmit broadcasts as part of their services. Where cable operators are under such an obligation it might seem unfair to force them to pay for carrying material that they might well have preferred to omit. Moreover, allowing content owners to prevent their works from being retransmitted unless the cable operator agrees to pay royalties might prove to be self-defeating, in that the cable operator might then be able to avoid the "must carry" obligation simply by refusing to pay.

On the other hand, it is possible to identify a number of situations in which the above arguments either do not apply or in which there are other, overriding, policy considerations. For example, allowing cable retransmission of subscription or pay-per-view broadcasts would have very serious financial repercussions for the operators of such services. Similarly, the above justifications look much less convincing in a case where a cable operator records a transmission with a view to broadcasting it in a modified form at a later date (for example, after having substituted different advertisements). In such a case the cable operator may well be intending to compete directly with the broadcaster and thus to include such activities within the retransmission right might be to allow the cable operator to make a profit at the broadcaster's expense. Finally, there would seem to be little justification in allowing a cable operator to retransmit works outside of the broadcast's normal reception area. Such retransmissions would seem to be particularly unfair on the owners of works included in the broadcasts, as they are more directly deprived of an opportunity to charge for the use of their works.

9–208

---

[74] See the previous note.

[75] See further, Whitford Committee: The Report of the Committee to Consider the Law on Copyright and Designs, 1977 (Cmnd. 6732) para.422.

[76] It should be noted that the Tribunal has a duty to ensure that copyright owners are not rewarded twice over for the transmission of their works: CDPA 1988, s.134.

For these reasons the Act generally confines the retransmission right to the immediate retransmission of broadcasts within their normal area of reception. Such a restriction has not proved possible, however, in relation to cable operators operating under a "must carry" obligation who retransmit a broadcast outside of its normal area of reception. In these cases the Act provides that there is still no infringement of copyright in the broadcast, but in relation to works included in the broadcast, the Act provides that these are to be treated as licensed by the owner, subject to the payment of a reasonable royalty by the *broadcaster*. The latter provisions thus take effect by way of compulsory licence and are dealt with in detail elsewhere.[77]

9–209   **The permitted acts.** As the Act now stands, it makes provision for cases where a wireless broadcast[78] is made from a place in the United Kingdom and is received and immediately retransmitted by cable.[79] In such cases the Act provides that copyright is not infringed in two distinct circumstances.

(1) First, the Act provides that copyright in the broadcast, and copyright in any work included in the broadcast, is not infringed if and to the extent that the broadcast is made for reception in the area in which it is retransmitted by cable and forms part of a qualifying service.[80] "Qualifying service" here means a regional or national Channel 3 service, Channel 4, Channel 5, S4C, the public teletext service, S4C Digital, and the television broadcasting and teletext services of the BBC.[81] All other services fall outside the operation of this section.[82]

(2) Secondly, the Act makes provision to deal with the position of cable operators under a "must carry" obligation. To the extent that such an obligation results in works being retransmitted in the original broadcast area, the above provisions apply.[83] Where a cable operator retransmits a broadcast outside the original broadcast area the Act draws a distinction between the broadcast and any works included in the broadcast. The Act provides that copyright in the broadcast will not be infringed, just as if the retransmission had been confined to the original reception area.[84] However, any work included in the broadcast is to be treated as licensed by the owner of copyright in the work, subject to the payment of a reasonable royalty.[85] Thus, as noted above, this later provision takes effect by

---

[77] See paras 29–48 *et seq.*, below.

[78] A "wireless broadcast" is defined as a broadcast by means of wireless telegraphy: CDPA 1988, s.178, where "wireless telegraphy" is also defined.

[79] s.73(1). The expression "retransmission by cable" is not defined, save that it is to include the tranmssion of microwave energy between terrestrial fixed points: s.178. Such a transmission is excluded from the definition of wireless telegraphy and thus wireless broadcasts: s.178

[80] ss.73(2)(b), s.73(3), although where the making of the broadcast was an infringement of the copyright in the work, the fact that the broadcast was retransmitted by cable is to be taken into account in assessing the damages for that infringement: s.178 Note that the Secretary of State is given extensive powers to vary the operation of this subsection (s.73(9)), and may instead order that a compulsory licence is to be available in relation to works which currently fall within this subsection (s.73(10)). The Secretary of State also has power to make appropriate transitional provisions (s.73(11)).

[81] s.73(6).

[82] But note that the Secretary of State may by order add any service to, or remove any service from, the definition of "qualifying service": (s.73(8)), and is given further power to make appropriate transitional provisions: s.73(11).

[83] ss.73(2)(a), (7).

[84] s.73(2)(a).

[85] s.73(4).

way of compulsory licence and, accordingly, is dealt with in detail elsewhere.[86]

Retransmission of broadcasts made in other EEA States. It is important to emphasise that the provisions considered above only apply to cable retransmission of broadcasts made from a place in the United Kingdom.[87] They do not apply to the retransmission of foreign broadcasts. However, the Cable and Satellite Broadcasting Directive[88] makes provision so as to facilitate the retransmission of broadcasts made in another EEA Member State. In brief, content owners retain their copyright, but they can only exercise their rights through a collecting society. Moreover, where the content owner has not transferred the management of his rights to a collecting society, the collecting society which manages rights of the same category shall be deemed to be mandated to manage his rights.[89] This provision was implemented in the United Kingdom by section 144A of the 1988 Act.[90] These provisions do not, however, affect broadcasters, who retain full control over copyright in their broadcasts and in any work included in the broadcast which they happen to own.[91] Thus the operator of a retransmission service will normally have to enter into direct negotiations with the broadcaster in order to get permission to retransmit a foreign broadcast.

9–210

G. PROVISION OF MODIFIED COPIES OF BROADCAST

Section 74 of the Act makes provision for the supply of specially modified copies of broadcasts for people who are disabled in some way.[92] Thus a designated body may make, and issue or lend to the public, copies of television broadcasts which are sub-titled or otherwise modified to meet the special needs of people who are deaf or hard of hearing, or who are otherwise physically or mentally handicapped, without infringing any copyright in the broadcasts or in any work included in them.[93] For this purpose "designated body" means a body designated by Order of the Secretary of State, who is not to designate a body unless satisfied that it is not established or conducted for profit.[94] This provision does not apply, however, if, or to the extent that, there is a certified licensing scheme in operation providing for the grant of licences.[95]

9–211

The Information Society Directive. Articles 5(3)(b) and 4 of the Directive permit Member States to make an exception to the reproduction, distribution and communication to the public rights, in the case of uses, for the benefit of people with a disability, which are directly related to the disability and of a non-commercial nature, to the extent required by the specific disability. The permitted act of section 74 falls squarely within this.

9–212

---

[86] See Ch.29, below.

[87] CDPA 1988, s.73(1).

[88] Council Directive 93/83 on the co-ordination of certain rules concerning coyright and rights related to copyright applicable to satellite broadcasting and cable retransmission; [1993] O.J. L248/15.

[89] Council Directive 93/83, Art.9.

[90] This is considered in detail at para. 29–75, below.

[91] CDPA 1988, s.144A(6).

[92] As to the ability to make copies for visually impaired persons, see para. 9–63 et seq., above.

[93] CDPA 1988, s.74(1).

[94] s.74(2). The National Sub-titling Library for Deaf People has been designated for this purpose: Copyright (Sub-titling of Broadcasts and Cable Programmes) (Designated Body) Order 1989 (SI 1989/1013). See Vol.2 at A4.iii.

[95] s.74(4). As to such licensing schemes, see Ch.29, below, and, in particular, as to certification, para. 29–78, below.

H. RECORDING FOR ARCHIVAL PURPOSES

9–213   Section 75 of the Act makes provision enabling broadcasts to be recorded for archival purposes.[96] This section should be read alongside those provisions relating to libraries and archives which are aimed at preserving important works for the nation.[97] Thus a recording of a broadcast of a designated class,[98] or a copy of such a recording, may be made for the purpose of being placed in an archive maintained by a designated body without thereby infringing any copyright in the broadcast or in any work included in it.[99] "Designated" means designated by Order of the Secretary of State, and a body is not to be designated unless it is not established or conducted for profit.[1]

9–214   **The Information Society Directive.** Artcle 5(2)(b) of the Directive permits Member States to make an exception to the reproduction right in respect of specific acts of reproduction made by publicly accessible archives, which are not for direct or indirect economic or commercial advantage. Section 75 appears to fall squarely within this permitted exception.

---

[96] CDPA 1988, s.75.

[97] In particular, see ss.42 and 44. See further para. 9–110 and para. 9–122, above.

[98] All broadcasts other than encrypted transmissions have been designated for this purpose: The Copyright (Recording for Archives of Designated Class of Broadcasting and Cable Programmes) (Designated Bodies) Order 1993 (SI 1993/74), see Vol.2 at A4.xvi.

[99] s.75(1).

[1] Eight bodies have so far been designated: The British Film Institute, The British Library, The British Medical Association, The British Music Information Centre, The Imperial War Museum, The Music Performance Research Centre, The National Library of Wales and the Scottish Film Council: The Copyright (Recording for Archives of Designated Class of Broadcasting and Cable Programmes) (Designated Bodies) Order 1993 (SI 1993/74). See Vol.2 at A4.xvi.

CHAPTER TEN

CROWN, PARLIAMENTARY AND OTHER RIGHTS

Contents

1. CROWN RIGHTS

A. INTRODUCTION

Introduction. In the absence of special provision, the Crown, like any other legal   **10–01**
person, would no doubt have become entitled to the copyright in many works
under the general rules. Historically, however, the Crown has been entitled under
the royal prerogative to a special form of copyright in a limited number of types
of work. Where this prerogative copyright subsists, the normal rules as to subsistence, title and term do not apply. At the present date, prerogative copyright is
probably of practical importance only to the publishers of copies of the King
James translation of the Bible and the Book of Common Prayer. As well as
preserving prerogative copyright, the 1988 Act contains significant modifications
to the general rules so far as they apply to works created by Her Majesty, her officers and her servants. The effect of these modifications is that copyright subsists
in certain circumstances where it would not otherwise subsist and that copyright
vests in the Crown in certain circumstances where it would otherwise not do so.
Such copyright is called "Crown copyright". With these provisions go special
rules as to the term of Crown copyright in literary, dramatic, musical and artistic
works. The overall effect is to place the Crown in a uniquely privileged position
so far as copyright is concerned.

B. PREROGATIVE COPYRIGHT

History. Printing was originally considered to be a matter of State and accord-   **10–02**
ingly the Crown claimed the right by proclamations, prohibitions, charters of
privilege and finally by decrees of Star Chamber, to authorise publications of all

types.[1] This right was assumed by Parliament on the abolition of Star Chamber in 1640 but reverted to the Crown at the Restoration. Although the Crown finally lost this right in the 1690s, it nevertheless continued to claim the exclusive right to print and publish a limited number of categories of work. This right resembles copyright in that it is a right to print and publish and to license others to print and publish works of the kinds to which it extends.[2] On the other hand, no specific requirements need to be satisfied before the right subsists in respect of a particular work. Furthermore, the right lasts for an unlimited period and is probably not capable of being lost by non-use.[3] Prerogative copyright was preserved in its entirety by the 1911[4] and 1956 Acts[5] and (except in relation to Acts, Measures and Bills) the 1988 Act.[6] In the following paragraphs, the extent to which the right exists is considered separately in respect of each of the more important categories of work in which it has been claimed to exist.

10–03   **Bibles and prayer books.**[7] The Queen's Printers and the Universities of Oxford and Cambridge hold patents from the Crown under the royal prerogative for the printing of the Bible and other books containing the rites and ceremonies of the Church of England.[8] As long ago as 1828 Lord Lyndhurst L.C. was able to state in relation to a patent extending to Bibles, New Testaments, Psalm Books, the Book of Common Prayer, the Confessions of Faith and the greater and lesser Catechisms that the right of the Crown to grant such patents was a point not admitting of doubt or controversy.[9] A variety of reasons have been offered for the existence of this prerogative power. First, the fact that the Authorised Version of the Bible was commissioned by James I; secondly, the fact that the monarch is head of the Church of England; and thirdly the fact that the monarch, as chief executive officer of the Government, has a duty to superintend the publication of those works upon which the established doctrines of the Church of England are founded.[10]

10–04   **Bibles: the scope of the prerogative.** In the 300 years prior to 1963 no attempt was made to claim that the patents referred to in the previous paragraph extended to translations of the Bible other than the Authorised Version.[11] However, in 1961 a new translation known as the *New English Bible* was published by the Oxford and Cambridge University Presses. Shortly afterwards, the Queen's Print-

---

[1] See paras 2–09 *et seq.*, above.
[2] *Universities of Oxford and Cambridge v Eyre & Spottiswoode Ltd* [1964] 1 Ch. 736 at 748.
[3] There is no generally accepted principle that a prerogative power may be lost by non-use: Maitland, *Constitutional History of England* (1908) p. 418; De Smith and Brazier, *Constitutional and Administrative Law* (8th ed.), p. 136. See also the discussion in *Attorney-General for New South Wales v Butterworth & Co. (Australia) Ltd* (1938) 38 S.R. (N.S.W.) 195 at 226 and in Monotti, "Nature and Basis of Crown Copyright in Official Publications" [1992] 9 E.I.P.R. 305.
[4] Copyright Act 1911, s.18.
[5] Copyright Act 1956, s.46(2).
[6] CDPA 1988, s.171(1)(b). Note s.171(5).
[7] For a historical discussion and a review of some of the contemporary issues involved in the enforcement of copyright in religious works, see Syn, "Copyright God: Enforcement of copyright in the Bible and religious works" [2001] 10 E.I.P.R. 454.
[8] The patent relied on by the Queen's Printers in *Universities of Oxford and Cambridge v Eyre & Spottiswoode Ltd* [1964] 1 Ch. 736 covered, in addition to Bibles, "all Books of Common Prayer and Administration of the Sacraments and other Rites and Ceremonies of the Church of England … and also … all other Books whatsoever which we have commanded or hereafter shall command to be used in the service of God in the Churches of … England".
[9] *Manners v Hunter Blair* (1828) 3 Bligh (N.S.) 391 at 402. The case concerned a Scottish patent but this dictum was directed at the position in England.
[10] The last of these explanations was preferred by Lord Lyndhurst L.C. in *Manners v Hunter Blair* ((1828) 3 Bligh (N.S.) 391 at 402), citing Lord Camden in *Donaldson v. Beckett* (1774) 4 Burr. 2408, Chief Baron Skinner in *Eyre and Strahan v Carnan* (1781) 6 Bac. Abr. (7th Ed.) 509 at 511 and *Universities of Oxford and Cambridge v Richardson* (1802) 6 Ves. 689.
[11] *i.e.* the King James I Bible of 1611.

ers published an identical version. Proceedings were brought by the University Presses[12] and the Queen's Printers sought to rely on their patent by way of defence. It was common ground that the patents could not grant rights which were more extensive than the prerogative itself.[13] The court held that to permit the Queen's Printers to rely on their patent would amount to an expropriation without compensation of the copyright in the *New English Bible*. In the absence of express statutory authority, such an expropriation in the name of the royal prerogative was not permissible.[14] Accordingly, the royal prerogative did not include the right to print material which infringed copyright. It follows from this decision that in the case of the Bible, prerogative copyright is limited to the Authorised Version and that new translations in which copyright subsists cannot be claimed by the Crown or by persons claiming under it.

Statutes. Before the 1988 Act came into force, the royal prerogative extended to Acts of Parliament.[15] The rationale for this was usually stated to be the fact that as head of the executive the monarch had the right of promulgating to the people all acts of state and Government and therefore the exclusive privilege of printing legislation.[16] However, section 164 of the 1988 Act abolished the prerogative relating to statutes (whether passed before or after commencement) and made them subject to statutory Crown copyright.[17]   **10–05**

Judgments. Patents to print law reports were upheld in two seventeenth-century cases,[18] but there is no evidence of any later attempt to assert a royal prerogative in relation to judgments or law reports. It is true that law reporters initially had a practice of seeking judicial sanction before publication.[19] However, by the late eighteenth century this practice had come to be seen as having been without legal foundation and it was abandoned.[20] It is also true that until the late eighteenth century the House of Lords restrained publication of its decisions, but this was on the ground that such publication was a breach of privilege rather than on the basis of the royal prerogative.[21] Nevertheless, the two seventeenth-century cases have never been overruled and there is no general rule that the prerogative may be lost simply by non-use.[22] On the other hand, it would not be difficult for a court to reach a view that the seventeenth-century cases were decided at a time of "high   **10–06**

---

[12] *Universities of Oxford and Cambridge v Eyre & Spottiswoode Ltd* [1964] 1 Ch. 736.
[13] *Universities of Oxford and Cambridge v Eyre & Spottiswoode Ltd* [1964] 1 Ch. 736 at 749, citing *Basket v University of Cambridge* (1758) 1 Wm. Bl. 105, 121.
[14] Applying *Attorney-General v De Keyser's Royal Hotel Ltd* [1920] A.C. 508.
[15] *Company of Stationers* (1681) 2 Ch. Cas. 76; *Basket v University of Cambridge* (1758) 1 Bl. W. 105; *Baskett v Cunningham* (1762) 1 Bl. W. 370; *Attorney-General for New South Wales v Butterworth & Co. (Australia) Ltd* (1938) 38 S.R. (N.S.W.) 195. The latter case contains a thorough review of the authorities.
[16] See, *e.g. Company of Stationers* (1681) 2 Ch. Cas. 76; Chitty, *A Treatise on the Law of the Prerogatives of the Crown* (1820) p. 239.
[17] See para. 10–19, below. CDPA 1988, s.164(4) provides that no copyright or right in the nature of copyright other than Crown copyright subsists in an Act or Measure. This provision applies to existing, that is pre-commencement, Acts of Parliament: *ibid.*, Sch.1, para.42(1). Although CDPA 1988, s.171(1)(b) contains savings for the royal prerogative, those savings are to have effect subject to s.164(4): see s.171(5).
[18] *Atkins v Company of Stationers* (1666) Carter 89, cited in *Millar v Taylor* (1769) 4 Burr. 2303 at 2316; *Roper v Streater* (1685), cited in *Stationers' Company v Parker* (1685) Skinner 233 at 234 and in *Millar v Taylor* (1769) 4 Burr. 2303.
[19] Holdsworth, *A History of the English Law*, Vol. 12, p. 112.
[20] Holdsworth, *A History of the English Law*, Vol.12, p.113. Subsequently there were, however, occasional instances of judicial pressure being placed on reporters to omit cases from their reports: *ibid.*
[21] Holdsworth, *A History of the English Law*, Vol.12, p.573.
[22] Maitland, *Constitutional History of England* (1908), p.418; De Smith and Brazier, *Constitutional and Administrative Law* (8th ed.), p.136.

prerogative" and ought not to be followed.[23] It seems highly unlikely that any prerogative claim will now be asserted by the Crown in respect of judgments or law reports. Even if it was, it would no doubt be met with the contention that any prerogative copyright has been removed by section 45(2) of the 1988 Act, which provides that copyright is not infringed by anything done for the purposes of reporting judicial proceedings.

10–07   **The Latin grammar.** In the eighteenth century it was thought that the Crown had a prerogative copyright in the King Edward VI Latin grammar on the grounds that it had been compiled at the King's expense.[24] The reference in the authorities is to the specific publication which was extant at the time and accordingly this right (if any) is highly unlikely to be of any practical importance at the present day.

10–08   **Almanacs.** The control of almanacs was perceived to be of considerable importance to the Crown, since, in addition to astronomical and other information, they might contain copies of the ecclesiastical calendar of the Church of England.[25] In *The Company of Stationers v Seymour*,[26] the Court upheld a grant by the Crown to the Company of Stationers of the exclusive right to print almanacs. However, a century later, in *Stationers' Company v Carnan*[27] the same or a substantially identical grant was held invalid.[28] The report gives no reasons for the decision. However, the successful defendant had contended that *Seymour*'s case ought not to be followed both because it was decided "in the days of high prerogative, soon after the Licensing Act", and because "no solid ground of true prerogative" was stated in the decision. In the unlikely event that an issue as to almanacs were to be raised at the present day, it seems inevitable that *Carnan*'s case would be followed.

C. STATUTORY CROWN COPYRIGHT

(i) The position under the 1988 Act

(a) *Background*

10–09   **The Whitford Committee Report.** The 1956 Act contained detailed provisions in relation to Crown copyright.[29] The Whitford Committee was critical of a number of these provisions. First, it objected to the fact that the Crown obtained copyright not only in works made by its employees but also in works "made by or under the direction or control of Her Majesty or a Government department".[30] The Committee expressed the view that the breadth of this phrase was likely to

---

[23] See *Monotti* [1992] 9 E.I.P.R. 305 at 309 for a detailed discussion. *cf.* the judicial history of the prerogative claims over almanacs at para. 10–08, below.

[24] *Millar v Taylor* (1769) 4 Burr. 2303 at 2329, 2405. These dicta are *obiter* but of high authority. There seem to be no direct decisions on the point.

[25] The Court in *The Company of Stationers v Seymour* (1677) 1 Mod. 256 at 257 stated: "the almanack that is before the common-prayer proceeds from a public constitution; it was first settled by the *Nicene Council*; is established by the canons of the church; and is under the government of the *Archbishop of Canterbury*; so that almanacks may be accounted *prerogative copies*" (reporter's italics). The case is also reported sub nom. *The Corporation of Stationers v Seymour* in 3 Keble 79.

[26] (1677) 1 Mod. 256.

[27] (1775) 2 Wm. Bl. 1004.

[28] Despite the plaintiffs' contention that the regulation of time was a matter of state: report at 1006.

[29] See paras 10–21 *et seq.*, below.

[30] Copyright Act 1956, s.39(1). See para. 10–21, below.

lead to difficulty.[31] Secondly, the Committee objected to the fact that the Crown could obtain copyright in a work simply by virtue of being the first to publish it, thus extinguishing the author's copyright in it ("the first publication rule").[32] The Committee considered a number of arguments in favour of retaining Crown copyright, including the difficulty in keeping track of the large number of authors employed by the Crown, but ultimately concluded that there was no basis for giving the Crown a special status not accorded to other large organisations. Accordingly, the Committee recommended the abolition of statutory Crown copyright.[33]

The 1986 White Paper. The Government, in its 1988 White Paper, did not take up the Whitford Committee's recommendation that Crown copyright should be abolished. In fact, it proposed that Crown copyright should continue to subsist in works made by or under the direction or control of Her Majesty or a Government department and, on the assumption that the position as to commissioned works was unclear, should subsist in commissioned works in the absence of agreement to the contrary.[34] So far as the first publication rule was concerned, the Government stated in the White Paper that it recognised that the rule could work unfairly.[35] Accordingly, the White Paper contained a proposal for the rule to be abolished and replaced by a provision allowing the reproduction and publication by or under the authority of the Crown of unpublished material lawfully acquired in the course of Crown business.[36] Examples given in the White Paper of the kind of material the Government had in mind were evidence given to and findings of committees and statistical or industrial information given to Government Departments.[37] It was proposed that the new rule would operate subject to any agreement to the contrary.[38] In fact, as will be seen, only the second of the changes proposed in the White Paper (the replacement of the first publication rule) was destined to reach the statute book.[39]

10–10

The policy of the 1988 Act. The Parliamentary debates on the Bill indicate that in framing the Bill which became the 1988 Act, the Government accepted the Whitford Committee's objections to the first publication rule,[40] but not its recommendation that Crown copyright be abolished.[41] The Government's view was that statutory Crown copyright had worked well for over 75 years and had given rise to no practical problems.[42] Its abolition would have no discernible public benefit but would necessitate the employment of additional staff at considerable expense in order to keep track of all the authors concerned in the production of Government publications.[43] As had been foreshadowed in the 1986 White Paper,[44] the Bill originally contained express provision to extend Crown copyright to

10–11

---

[31] Cmnd. 6732, para.593. The Committee noted that the uncertainty of the law had enabled Government departments to claim the copyright in computer programs created at their request but without any direction or control (see para. 596).

[32] Cmnd. 6732, paras 595–6. The Committee recognised that this was a somewhat academic problem because the policy of HMSO was to obtain copyright clearance in all cases of doubt.

[33] Cmnd. 6732, para.600.

[34] *Intellectual Property and Innovation* Cmnd. 9712, para.16.6. See also *Hansard*, HL Vol. 491, col.553–4 and HL Vol. 493, col.1394 for the Government's view that the position as to commissioned works was unclear.

[35] para.16.7.

[36] para.16.8.

[37] para.16.7.

[38] para.16.7.

[39] As to the proposal in relation to commissioned works, see *Hansard*, HL Vol.501, col.193.

[40] *Hansard*, HL Vol. 493, col.1391.

[41] *ibid.*

[42] *ibid.*

[43] *ibid.*

[44] See para. 10–10, above.

commissioned works. This provision aroused considerable opposition in the House of Lords and was ultimately abandoned after consultations indicated that the Crown would not be seriously inconvenienced if it was not enacted.[45]

(b) *Works made on or after August 1, 1989*

10–12   **Subsistence and ownership.** The general provisions in the 1988 Act relating to subsistence and first ownership of copyright do not apply to works made by Her Majesty or by an officer or servant of the Crown[46] in the course of his duties.[47] Instead, section 163(1) of the 1988 Act provides that where a work[48] is made by Her Majesty or by an officer or servant of the Crown in the course of his duties, the work qualifies for copyright protection even if the ordinary qualification requirements are not satisfied,[49] and that Her Majesty is the owner of any copyright in the work.[50] Thus, for example, if a work is made by an employee of the Crown who is not a qualifying person because he is not domiciled or resident in the United Kingdom or another country to which the provisions of Part I of the 1988 Act extend, copyright will nevertheless subsist in the work. Of greater practical importance is the fact that Her Majesty becomes the owner of the copyright in all works created by her officers as well as by her employees provided of course that the works were made in the course of their duties.[51] It is provided that copyright in such a work[52] is referred to in Part I of the 1988 Act as "Crown copyright" even if it has been assigned by the Crown.[53]

10–13   **Term.** Section 163(3) of the 1988 Act provides for a special term in respect of Crown copyright in literary, dramatic, musical and artistic works.[54] That term depends on whether the work has been published commercially before the end of

---

[45] *Hansard*, HL Vol.495, col.678; *Hansard*, H.L Vol.501, cols 193–197. For current HMSO Guidance in relation to commissioned works, together with a draft commissioning agreement, see HMSO Guidance Note 5 (revised November 6, 2000), *www.hmso.gov.uk/copyright/guidance/gn_05.htm.*

[46] The expression "the Crown" includes the Crown in right of the Scottish Administration or of Her Majesty's Government in Northern Ireland or in any country outside the United Kingdom to which the copyright Part of the 1988 Act extends: CDPA 1988, s.178. For a list of the bodies considered by HMSO to have Crown status, see *www.hmso.gov.uk/copyright/policy/c_copyright/crown_bodies.htm.*

[47] CDPA 1988, ss.153(2) (subsistence) and 11(3) (first ownership). For these purposes, works made by Her Majesty include any sound recording, film or live broadcast of the proceedings of the National Assembly for Wales (including proceedings of a committee of the Assembly or of a sub-committee of such a committee) which is made under the direction and control of the Assembly; but a work shall not be regarded as made by or under the direction or control of the Assembly by reason only of its being commissioned by or on behalf of the Assembly: CDPA 1988, s.163(1A). This subsection is in similar (but not identical) terms to the provisions in relation to parliamentary copyright in works made under the direction or control of the House of Commons or the House of Lords, as to which see para. 10–72, below. CDPA 1988, s.163(1A) was inserted by para.28 of Sch.12 to the Government of Wales Act 1988 (c.38), with effect from April 1, 1999: see Government of Wales Act 1998 (Commencement No.4) Order 1999 (SI 1999/782). It was amended by reg.11(a) of the Copyright and Related Rights Regulations (SI 2003/2498) with effect from October 31, 2003 to delete the reference in the original text to live cable programme. Recordings of the other United Kingdom legislative bodies are subject to parliamentary copyright: see paras 10–72 and 10–73, below.

[48] For what may be a copyright work, see CDPA 1988, s.1.

[49] CDPA 1988, s.163(1)(a). For the ordinary qualification requirements, see CDPA 1988, s.153(1) and paras 3–152 *et seq.*, above.

[50] s.163(1)(b).

[51] The rule that an employer is the first owner of the copyright in a work made by his employees is subject to any agreement to the contrary, does not relate to all works, and does not apply to works made by officers: see CDPA 1988, s.11(3).

[52] *i.e.* a work made by Her Majesty or by an officer or servant of the Crown in the course of his duties.

[53] CDPA 1988, s.164(2): thus "once Crown copyright always Crown copyright".

[54] The term of Crown copyright was not altered by the Duration of Copyright and Rights in Performances Regulations 1995 (SI 1995/3297).

the period of 75 years from the end of the calendar year in which it was made. For a detailed discussion of the meaning of the term "commercial publication", see paragraph11–12, below. During the Parliamentary debates it was stated that the issue of photocopies to the public by the Public Record Office was excluded from the definition because copies were made on demand.[55] If the work has not been published commercially during this period of 75 years, the term of Crown copyright is 125 years from the end of the calendar year in which it was made.[56] In the Parliamentary debates on the Bill, the Government gave two reasons for arriving at this term of 125 years.[57] The first was that a term of life of the author plus 50 years was not practical since it would require a large bureaucracy to keep records of the date of death of all the authors of Crown copyright works.[58] The second was that official documents are not in the public domain for the first 30 years of their life (for Royal papers the period is 100 years) and such a term would provide a reasonable period of protection once the documents in question were in the public domain.[59] If, on the other hand, the work has been published commercially before the end of the period of 75 years from the end of the calendar year in which it was made, the term of copyright is 50 years from the end of the calendar year in which it was so published.[60] In relation to works other than literary, dramatic, musical or artistic works, the term is the normal term for the relevant category of work.[61] No publication right arises from the publication of a work in which Crown copyright subsisted.[62]

Works of joint authorship. In the case of works created jointly by Her Majesty   **10–14** or an officer or employee of Her Majesty on the one hand and a third party on the other, section 163 applies only in relation to Her Majesty, her officer or employee and the copyright subsisting by virtue of her or his contribution to the work.[63] Accordingly, in order to establish the subsistence of copyright in that part of the work to which the third party contributed, it is necessary to show that the ordinary qualifying requirements are satisfied.[64] Furthermore, the term of copyright in that part of the work to which the third party contributed will be the normal term.[65]

Application of Part I of the 1988 Act to Crown copyright. It is provided that   **10–15** with the exception of the special rules outlined above in relation to subsistence, title and term, and subject to any express exclusion elsewhere in Part I of the 1988 Act, the copyright part of the 1988 Act is to apply to Crown copyright as to other copyright.[66] Accordingly, for example, the ordinary rules will apply to any

[55] *Hansard*, H.L Vol.491, col.559.
[56] CDPA 1988, s.163(3)(a).
[57] Which, as was pointed out for the Government, was equivalent to that then proposed for the early works of a long-lived author: *Hansard*, HL Vol.491, col.559.
[58] See previous footnote.
[59] *ibid.*
[60] CDPA 1988, s.163(3)(b). The Parliamentary debates indicate that the Government considered that a term of 125 years from the date of publication would be excessive: *Hansard*, HL Vol.491, col.559.
[61] CDPA 1988, s.163(5) provides that except as provided in s.163 or expressly excluded elsewhere in Part I of the Act, the provisions of Part I apply in relation to Crown copyright as to other copyright. For the various terms, see the earlier chapters of this work.
[62] Copyright and Related Rights Regulations 1996 (SI 1996/2967), reg.16(5).
[63] CDPA 1988, s.163(4).
[64] As to which see paras 3–152 *et seq.*, above.
[65] A work of joint authorship is a work where the respective contributions of the joint authors are not distinct from each other: CDPA 1988, s.10(1). Difficulties may therefore arise in identifying the respective contributions of the joint authors for the purposes of establishing the term of the copyright in the various parts of the work.
[66] CDPA 1988, s.163(5).

dealings with Crown copyright[67] and the Crown or its assignee will be entitled to the ordinary remedies for infringement.[68] Moreover, in general, the permitted acts set out in sections 28A to 50 of the 1988 Act apply equally to works of Crown copyright.[69]

10–16   **Interrelationship with Parliamentary copyright.** It is provided that section 163 of the 1988 Act does not apply to a work if, or to the extent that, Parliamentary copyright subsists in it.[70]

(c) *Works made before August 1, 1989*

10–17   **Subsistence and ownership.**[71] The provisions of the 1988 Act apply to things existing at commencement as they apply to things coming into existence after commencement, subject to any express provision to the contrary.[72] In the case of Crown copyright, there are a number of express contrary provisions. First, the provisions of section 163 of the 1988 Act apply to works made before commencement only if section 39 of the 1956 Act[73] applied to the work immediately before commencement and the work is not one to which section 164, 165 or 166 of the 1988 Act applies.[74] Section 164 established a new statutory copyright in Acts and Measures.[75] Section 165 established Parliamentary copyright.[76] Section 166 provided for copyright in Parliamentary Bills.[77] Secondly, every work in which Crown copyright subsisted under the 1956 Act immediately before commencement is to be deemed to satisfy the requirements of the copyright part of the 1988 Act[78] as to qualification for copyright protection.[79] Thirdly, the first owner of copyright in such works is to be determined in accordance with the law in force at the time the work was made.[80] The two latter provisions are of particular importance in view of the narrower scope of Crown copyright under the 1988 Act.[81] The position under the 1956 Act is dealt with later.[82]

10–18   **Term.** The various terms of copyright in pre-commencement works to which section 163 of the 1988 Act applies are set out in paragraph 41 of Schedule 1 to the 1988 Act. In respect of many works different provisions apply depending on whether or not the work is a published work. The question which provision applies to a work is to be determined by reference to the facts immediately before commencement.[83] Accordingly, the question whether a work is a published work

---

[67] ss.90 to 93A.
[68] ss.96–115.
[69] HMSO Guidance Note No.3: Copyright in Public Records, para.11, *www.hmso.gov.uk/copyright/ guidance/gn__03.htm.*
[70] CDPA 1988, s.163(6). As to Parliamentary copyright, see paras 10–72 *et seq.*, below.
[71] What follows is confined to Crown copyright as defined in CDPA 1988, s.163. For pre-commencement Acts and Measures, Parliamentary copyright and copyright in Parliamentary Bills, see below at paras 10–20, 10–71 and 10–80 respectively.
[72] CDPA 1988, Sch.1, para.3.
[73] See paras 10–21 *et seq.*, below.
[74] CDPA 1988, Sch.1, para.40(1).
[75] See para. 10–19, below.
[76] See paras 10–72 *et seq.*, below.
[77] See paras 10–77 *et seq.*, below.
[78] *i.e.* Part I.
[79] CDPA 1988, Sch.1, para.35.
[80] Sch.1, para.11(1). Note also para. 11(2).
[81] As to which see para. 10–11, above.
[82] See paras 10–21 *et seq.*, below.
[83] *i.e.* August 1, 1989.

is to be determined as at the time immediately before commencement.[84] It is further provided that expressions used in paragraph 41 which were defined for the purposes of the 1956 Act have the same meaning as in that Act.[85] Copyright continues to subsist in a large number of categories of work until the date on which it would have expired in accordance with the 1956 Act. Those categories are as follows[86] : published literary, dramatic and musical works; artistic works other than engravings or photographs; published engravings; published photographs and photographs taken before June 1, 1957; published sound recordings and sound recordings made before June 1, 1957; published films and films falling within section 13(3)(a) of the 1956 Act.[87] Copyright in unpublished literary, dramatic and musical works continues to subsist until the date on which it expires in accordance with section 163(3)[88] or 50 years from the end of the calendar year in which the copyright provisions of the 1988 Act came into force,[89] whichever is the later.[90] Copyright in unpublished engravings and unpublished photographs taken on or after June 1, 1957 continues to subsist until the end of the period of 50 years from the end of the calendar year in which the 1988 Act came into force.[91] Copyright in films and sound recordings not falling into any of the above categories continues to subsist until the end of the period of 50 years from the end of the calendar year in which the 1988 Act came into force[92] unless the film or sound recording is published before the end of that period, in which case copyright expires 50 years from the end of the calendar year in which it was published.[93]

(d) Acts and Measures

Acts and Measures passed on or after August 1, 1989. Until the passing of the   **10–19**
1988 Act, the copyright in Acts of Parliament and Measures of the Synod of the Church of England was vested in the Crown by virtue of the royal prerogative.[94] The 1988 Act placed the Crown's rights on a statutory footing by providing that Her Majesty is entitled to copyright in every Act of Parliament and every Measure of the General Synod of the Church of England.[95] The reasons for this change are not clear, although it seems to have been connected with the introduction of the new Parliamentary copyright in respect of Bills.[96] Since May 6 and December 2, 1999 respectively, Her Majesty has been entitled to copyright in Acts of the Scottish Parliament[97] and of the Northern Ireland Assembly.[98] The copyright subsists from the date of Royal Assent until the end of the period of 50 years

---

[84] CDPA 1988, Sch.1, para.41(1).

[85] ibid.

[86] Sch.1, para.41(2).

[87] i.e. films registered under a former enactment requiring registration of films.

[88] i.e. at the end of the period of 125 years from the end of the calendar year in which the work was made or, if the work was published commercially before that date, at the end of the period of 50 years from the end of the calendar year in which it was so published.

[89] i.e. 50 years from December 31, 1989.

[90] CDPA 1988, Sch.1, para.41.

[91] Sch.1, para.41(4). The period is therefore 50 years from December 31, 1989.

[92] i.e. 50 years from December 31, 1989.

[93] CDPA 1988, Sch.1, para.40(5).

[94] See para. 10–05, above.

[95] CDPA 1988, s.164(1). The general provisions in the 1988 Act relating to subsistence and duration of copyright do not apply to copyright in Acts and Measures: ss.153(2) (subsistence) and 12(9) (duration).

[96] Hansard, HL Vol.501, cols 194–5.

[97] CDPA 1988, s.164(1), as amended by para.25(6) of Sch.8 to the Scotland Act 1998 (c.46). For commencement, see the Scotland Act 1998 (Commencement) Order 1998 (SI 1998/3178) para.2 and Sch.3.

[98] CDPA 1988, s.164(1), as amended by para.8(6) of Sch.13 to the Northern Ireland Act 1998. For

from the end of the calendar year in which Royal Assent was given.[99] No other copyright or right in the nature of copyright subsists in Acts or Measures, and accordingly the prerogative copyright in them is abolished.[1] With the above exceptions, the provisions of Part I of the 1988 Act apply in relation to copyright in Acts and Measures as they apply to other Crown copyright.[2]

10–20 **Acts and Measures passed before August 1, 1989.** The rules set out in the preceding paragraph apply to pre-commencement Acts and Measures including Church Assembly Measures.[3] This is subject to the general rule that copyright subsists in a pre-commencement work after commencement only if it subsisted in it immediately before commencement.[4] However, as has already been stated, copyright subsisted in Acts of Parliament before the commencement of the 1988 Act by virtue of the royal prerogative.[5]

(ii) The position under the 1956 Act

(a) *Literary, dramatic, musical and artistic works*

10–21 **Subsistence of copyright in works not otherwise protected.**[6] Section 39(1)(a) of the 1956 Act provided that copyright was to subsist in original literary, dramatic, musical and artistic works made by or under the direction or control of Her Majesty or a Government department even if copyright did not subsist in them under the general law.[7] Thus, for example, an unpublished work of which the author was not a qualified person[8] would nevertheless be protected if made under the direction of a Government department. The expression "made under the direction or control", which derives from the 1911 Act,[9] was not defined.[10] It was probably intended to be confer protection beyond works made under a contract of service to works commissioned by the Crown from independent contractors.[11] The term "Government department" was defined as any department of Her Majesty's Government in the United Kingdom or of the Government of

---

commencement, see the Northern Ireland Act 1998 (Commencement No.5) Order 1999 (SI 1999/3209), para.2 and Sch.

[99] CDPA 1988, s.164(2).
[1] s.164(4).
[2] s.163(3).
[3] CDPA 1988, Sch.1, para.42. The Church Assembly became the General Synod as from November 4, 1970: Synodical Government Measure 1969 (No.2), s.2.
[4] CDPA 1988, Sch.1, para.5.
[5] See para. 10–05, above.
[6] For the position under the 1911 Act and before, see the 13th edition of this work.
[7] For an example, see *Secretary of State for Defence v Guardian Newspapers* [1984] Ch. 156, CA.
[8] As defined in Copyright Act 1956, s.1(5).
[9] Copyright Act 1911, s.18.
[10] Its breadth was the subject of criticism by the Whitford Committee (Cmnd. 6731), paras 593 to 600. See para. 10–09, above.
[11] In *British Broadcasting Co. v Wireless League Gazette Publishing Co.* [1926] 1 Ch. 433 it was held on the facts that a list of programmes (the *Radio Times*) published by the BBC was not published under the direction or control of a Government department even though the programmes themselves were broadcast under a revocable licence from the Government and the publication of the list had been approved by the Postmaster-General. In *Land Transport Safety Authority of New Zealand v Glogau* [1999] 1 N.Z.L.R. 261, the New Zealand Court of Appeal held that the fact that log books for taxi drivers had to be in a form approved by the Crown did not mean that log books which were so approved had been made under the Crown's direction or control, even though the power to approve them gave the Crown a degree of direction and control over their content.

Northern Ireland, or any department or agency of any other country to which the section extended.[12]

Ownership of copyright. The 1956 Act contained separate provisions for works made by or under the direction or control[13] of the Crown on the one hand and works first published by or under the direction or control of the Crown on the other. Section 39(1)(b) of the 1956 Act provided that the Crown was entitled to the copyright in every original literary, dramatic, musical or artistic work made by or under the direction or control of Her Majesty or a Government department.[14] Section 39(2) of the 1956 Act provided that the Crown was entitled to the copyright in every original literary, dramatic, musical or artistic work first published in the United Kingdom or another country to which the provisions of the 1956 Act extended if first published by or under the direction of Her Majesty or a Government department.[15] Both these provisions were subject to any agreement made by or on behalf of Her Majesty or a Government department with the author of the work whereby it was agreed that the copyright should vest in the author or in another person designated in the agreement in that behalf.[16]

10–22

Term of Crown copyright. As regards literary, dramatic and musical works, section 39(3) of the 1956 Act provided that where the Crown was entitled to copyright by reason of the provisions set out in the preceding paragraph,[17] the term of copyright depended on whether or not the work had been published. Where the work was unpublished, copyright was to continue to subsist so long as it remained unpublished.[18] Where the work was published, copyright was to subsist (or, as the case might be, to continue to subsist) until the end of the period of 50 years from the end of the calendar year in which it was first published.[19] As regards artistic works other than engravings or photographs, section 39(4) of the 1956 Act provided that where the Crown was entitled to copyright by reason of the circumstances set out in the preceding paragraph,[20] copyright subsisted until the end of the period of 50 years from the end of the calendar year in which the work was made. For engravings and photographs, it was provided that copyright was to subsist until the end of the period of 50 years from the end of the calendar year in which the work was first published.[21] It would seem that if copyright in a work commissioned by the Crown was vested by agreement in the author rather than the Crown, then the normal term of copyright applied.[22]

10–23

(b) Sound recordings and films

Subsistence, ownership and term. Section 39(5) of the 1956 Act made similar provision as regards sound recordings and films. First, it provided that copyright was to subsist in sound recordings and films made by or under the direction or

10–24

[12] Copyright Act 1956, s.39(9).
[13] For the meaning of this term, see para. 10–21, above.
[14] For the definition of this expression, see para. 10–21, above.
[15] In *Catnic Components v Hill & Smith Ltd* [1978] F.S.R. 405 at 427 it was held, presumably on the basis of this provision, that drawings in a patent were Crown copyright. In *Ironside v H.M. Attorney-General* [1988] R.P.C. 197 it was held that the issue by the Chancellor of the Exchequer of a press release containing authorised photographs and descriptions of the new decimal coinage amounted to a publication under the direction or control of a government department.
[16] Copyright Act 1956, s.39(6).
[17] *i.e.* pursuant to Copyright Act 1956, s.39(1) or (2).
[18] s.39(3)(a).
[19] s.39(3)(b).
[20] *i.e.* pursuant to Copyright Act 1956, s.39(1) or (2).
[21] s.39(4).
[22] As to which, see Copyright Act 1956, ss.2 and 3.

control of Her Majesty or a Government department even if copyright did not subsist in them under the general law.[23] Secondly, it provided that in any case where a sound recording or film had been made by or under the direction or control of Her Majesty or a Government department, Her Majesty was to be entitled to the copyright in it.[24] Thirdly, it provided that the copyright should subsist for the same period as if it subsisted and was owned in accordance with the general provisions relating to copyright in sound recordings and films.[25]

(c) Pre-commencement works

10–25   **General.** The general transitional provisions applicable under the 1956 Act applied equally to Crown copyright. Accordingly, in general, the provisions discussed above applied in relation to works in existence at the commencement of the 1956 Act[26] as they applied in relation to works which came into existence after its commencement.[27] However, this general position was specifically modified in relation to photographs, sound recordings and films.

10–26   **Photographs, sound recordings and films.** In relation to photographs taken before the commencement of the 1956 Act, Crown copyright was to subsist until the end of the period of 50 years from the end of the calendar year in which they were made.[28] In relation to sound recordings made before commencement, Crown copyright was to subsist for the period of 50 years from the end of the calendar year in which they were made.[29] In relation to films made before commencement, it was provided that no Crown copyright subsisted in them as films. However, in so far as such a film was an original dramatic work as defined in the 1911 Act,[30] Crown copyright was to subsist in the film to the same extent that it would have subsisted if the film was an original dramatic work.[31] Moreover, in so far as such a film was made up of photographs, they were to be protected in the same way as other Crown copyright photographs made before commencement.[32]

(iii) Enforcement and management of Crown Copyright: the present position

10–27   **Administration.** Since October 1, 1996, the responsibility for control and administration of Crown copyright has rested with the Controller of Her Majesty's Stationery Office ("HMSO") who is appointed by the Queen by letters patent. The day to day administration of Crown copyright is now exercised by HMSO's Licensing Team[33] and, in relation to works made in the exercise of a function which is exercisable by any office-holder in or member of staff of the

---

[23] s.39(5)(a).

[24] s.39(5)(b).

[25] s.39(5)(b). The general provisions were Copyright Act 1956, ss.12 (sound recordings) and 13 (films).

[26] On June 1, 1957.

[27] Copyright Act 1956, Sch.7, para.45(1).

[28] Copyright Act 1956, Sch.7, para.30. Thus, pre-commencement photographs were equated with artistic works other than engravings.

[29] Sch.7, para.31(1). Thus, the normal period of 50 years from first publication (s.12(3) as applied by s.39(5)(b)) was disapplied.

[30] For a discussion of the position under the 1911 Act, see para. 3–32, above, and earlier editions of this work.

[31] Sch.7, para.31(2)(b).

[32] Sch.7, para.31(2)(c).

[33] See *About the Licensing Team*, www.hmso.gov.uk/about/licensing.htm, September 29, 2003 edition.

Scottish Administration, by the Queen's Printer for Scotland.[34] In general, Government departments may only deal with Crown copyright if they have the authority of the Licensing Division.[35] However, departments have the right to grant non-exclusive licences to private sector publishers to publish official material on their behalf.[36] Most government trading funds (government organisations which have been set up to run on a commercial basis[37]) have been granted delegations of authority to license the re-use of material which they originate.[38] Delegations will also be issued in the following specified circumstances:[39] first, where the department maintains an archive of photographs, films and other visual material; secondly, where the department wishes to license the re-use of its departmental logo provided it does not include the Royal Arms; thirdly, in some cases of reproduction of computer software and programs; and fourthly, where the copyright element of a work is subsidiary to that part of it which is subject to such other intellectual property rights as patents and design rights. HMSO administers delegations in accordance with the Information Fair Trader Scheme.[40]

Enforcement and management policy. Article 2(4) of the Berne Convention **10–28** provides in effect that the extent of the protection to be granted to official texts of a legislative, administrative and legal nature is a matter for the discretion of the country in question.[41] However, after the 1988 Act was passed, the European Commission expressed the view that the public sector should, to the highest extent possible, make use of this discretion to exempt from copyright texts of a legislative, administrative and legal nature.[42] In fact, Governments have long recognised that there is a public interest in proper access to certain types of official information and accordingly Crown copyright has never been fully enforced.[43]

The current framework derives from the 1999 White Paper *The Future*

---

[34] See *e.g.* Queen's Printer for Scotland Guidance Note 2: *Reproduction of Press Notices Issued by the Scottish Administration, www.oqps.gov.uk/copyright/guidance/gn_02.htm*, August 10, 2001 edition, para.4.

[35] See *Policy Arrangements on the Licensing of Government Information, www.hmso.gov.uk/ copyright/guidance/departments.htm*, November 28, 2001 edition, para.14.

[36] See *Policy Arrangements*, paras 8–10.

[37] Examples include: Ordnance Survey, NHS Estates and the Driving Standards Agency. For a list of government trading funds, see *www.hmso.gov.uk/copyright/guidance/ departments.htm#annexa.*

[38] See *Policy Arrangements*, para.21.

[39] See *Policy Arrangements*, para.24.

[40] See *www.hmso.gov.uk/copyright/regulation/ifts.htm.*

[41] See Volume 2 at F1.

[42] *Guidelines for improving the synergy between the public and private sectors in the information market* (European Commission Directorate-General for Telecommunications, Information Industries and Innovation, 1989, Cat. No.CD-54-88-126-EN-C), para. 18. The procedure for access to official documents of the European Union is governed by Regulation (EC) No 1049/2001 (O.J. L145/43, May 31, 2001) and implementation documents published by the Commission, Council and Parliament. There is a Commission report on the implementation of this Regulation: COM 2004/45 final. The Regulation is without prejudice to any existing rules on copyright which may limit a third party's right to reproduce or exploit released documents: Art.16. Official publications of the European Union are published by the Office for Official Publications of the European Communities, whose organisation and operation are governed by a decision dated July 20, 2000: O.J. L183/12, July 22, 2000. Most such publications carry a copyright notice which states that reproduction is authorised, provided the source is acknowledged, except where stated otherwise. Unpublished documents of the Commission may be reproduced, but only for non-commercial purposes: see *A Citizen's Guide: Access to Unpublished Documents*, europa.eu.int/comm/ secretariat_general/sgc/citguide, para.16.

[43] For a brief history of enforcement before the passing of the 1988 Act see the Green Paper *Crown Copyright in the Information Age: A consultation document on access to public sector information*, Cm. 3819, HMSO, paras 2.2–2.7. See also previous editions of this Work and *Attorney-General for New South Wales v Butterworth & Co. (Australia) Ltd* (1937–8) 38 S.R. N.S.W. 195 at 236.

Management of Crown Copyright.[44] The general policy is to improve and encourage access to the broad range of public sector information whilst at the same time maintaining the integrity and status of works produced within government.[45] In order to enable members of the public to locate such information, the Government has set up the Information Asset Register, which lists information resources held by the government and can be searched online.[46] At the same time, pursuant to the Freedom of Information Act 2000, public authorities are establishing publication schemes, which specify the classes of information they publish or intend to publish, how the information is or is intended to be published and whether there is any charge for it.[47] Finally, also pursuant to the Freedom of Information Act, as from January 1, 2005 each public authority will be obliged to comply with requests for the information that it holds unless an exemption from disclosure applies.

However, by no means all Crown copyright material may be reproduced, while in respect of the material which may be reproduced, there remains a complex patchwork of rights. Four degrees of access can be identified. First, in respect of certain specific categories of material, reproduction is generally permissible, subject to compliance with conditions (in some of these cases the copyright is said to have been "waived", albeit conditionally). The categories include: legislation,[48] some public records,[49] some court forms,[50] some national curriculum and similar material,[51] Government and Scottish Administration press notices[52] and the record of proceedings of the Welsh Assembly.[53] Second, in respect of "value-added" material, specific licences are required and may have to be paid for.[54] Third, in respect of much other material, there is a "Core licence"which is free of charge and subject to terms and conditions.[55] Finally, ad hoc provision exists in relation to certain specified works, such as articles written by Ministers or civil servants in journals and conference proceedings and the British passport.[56] These arrangements may need to be reviewed in the light of recent European legislation.[57] The procedures which HMSO will adopt in the event of a suspected infringement are set out on its website.[58]

10–29   Typographical arrangements. In October 1996, the publishing division of HMSO was privatised and began to be operated by The Stationery Office Limited. The copyright in the typographical arrangements of the vast majority of works published by HMSO before privatisation belongs to the Crown. However, the

---

[44] Cm. 4300.

[45] Cm. 4300, paras 1.3 and 2.2.

[46] See *www.inforoute.hmso.gov.uk/inforoute/about__iar.htm* and HMSO Guidance Note 18: Information Asset Register and Freedom of Information—a co-ordinated response to information access, *www.hmso.gov.uk/copyright/guidance/gn__18.htm*. There is also a bibliography of official publications: see HMSO Guidance Note 17: Maintaining the Bibliography of UK Official Publications, *www.hmso.gov.uk/copyright/guidance/gn__17.htm*.

[47] See *www.informationcommissioner.gov.uk/eventual.aspx?id=77*. The obligation is contained in s.19 of the Freedom of Information Act 2000. Of course, the supply of information does not give an automatic right to reuse: see HMSO Guidance Note 19: Freedom of Information Publication Schemes, *www.hmso.gov.uk/copyright/guidance/gn__19.htm*.

[48] Paras 10–30 to 10–31 below.

[49] Paras 10–32 to 10–34 below.

[50] Paras 10–35 to 10–36 below.

[51] Paras 10–39 to 10–41 below.

[52] Para. 10–42 below.

[53] Para. 10–43 below.

[54] Paras 10–44 to 10–45 below.

[55] Paras 10–46 to 10–48 below.

[56] Paras 10–49 and 10–50 below.

[57] See Directive 2003/98/EC of the European Parliament and of the Council of 17 November 2003 on the reuse of public sector information [2003] O.J. L345/90, below paras 10–51 to 10–57.

[58] See *www.hmso.gov.uk/copyright/licences/breach__flowchart.pdf*.

same is not necessarily true in relation to works published after privatisation. Accordingly, unless the relevant Government department has taken appropriate measures,[59] certain types of users will need to obtain a separate licence from the owner of that copyright. This problem does not arise in relation to legislation because the copyright in the typographical arrangement of legislation is owned by the Crown,[60] nor does it arise in relation to Government and Scottish Administration press notices.[61]

Legislation: background to and scope of the waiver. Prior to the White Paper, **10–30** Crown copyright legislative material could only be reproduced in limited circumstances and subject to stringent conditions.[62] In the White Paper, the Government announced its intention to waive Crown copyright in Acts of Parliament, Measures of the General Synod of the Church of England, Statutory Instruments from England and Wales and Statutory Rules of Northern Ireland.[63] In fact, the waiver now extends to all these categories as well as to Acts of the Northern Ireland Assembly and Scottish Parliament, Explanatory Notes to all these statutes and Scottish Statutory Instruments.[64] The waiver also extends to copyright in the typographical arrangements of the texts of all the categories of material to which it applies.[65]

Legislation: terms of the waiver. Provided certain conditions are complied **10–31** with, there are no restrictions whatsoever on how material which is subject to the waiver may be reproduced.[66] However, the waiver is conditional on compliance with those conditions, which are intended to protect the material against use in a misleading or derogatory manner.[67] The conditions are as follows.[68] First, all reproduction should be made from an official version. This means either the version published by the Queen's Printer, the Government Printer for Northern Ireland or the Queen's Printer for Scotland as the case may be, or the text featured on the relevant official legislation website (users wishing to reproduce the material from the Government's Statute Law Database or from any other value added legislation product or service provided by the Government, will need to enter into

---

[59] HMSO Guidance Note 1: Copyright in Typographical Arrangements, *www.hmso.gov.uk/copyright/guidance/gn__01.htm*, November 6, 2000 edition, recommends that the copyright position is clarified in each case where an external publisher or designer is engaged and points out that a failure to obtain an assignment of this copyright may limit access to the material.

[60] HMSO Guidance Note 6: Reproduction of United Kingdom, England, Wales and Northern Ireland Primary and Secondary Legislation, *www.hmso.gov.uk/copyright/guidance/gn__06.htm*, October 7, 2002 edition, para.8; Queen's Printer for Scotland Guidance Note 1, Reproduction of Acts of the Scottish Parliament, Explanatory Notes to Acts of the Scottish Parliament and Scottish Statutory Instruments, *www.oqps.gov.uk/copyright/guidance/gn__01.htm*, October 15, 2002 edition, para.6.

[61] HMSO Guidance Note 9: Reproduction of Government Press Notices for England, Northern Ireland and Wales, *www.hmso.gov.uk/copyright/guidance/gn__09.htm*, August 10, 2001 edition, para.6. Queen's Printer for Scotland Guidance Note 2: Reproduction of Press Notices Issued by the Scottish Administration, *www.oqps.gov.uk/copyright/guidance/gn__02.htm*, August 10, 2001 edition, para.5.

[62] See the previous edition of this work para. 10–29.

[63] Cm. 4300, para.5.2.

[64] HMSO Guidance Note 6, para. 8; Queen's Printer for Scotland Guidance Note 1, para.6.

[65] See para. 10–29, above.

[66] HMSO Guidance Note 6, para.10; Queen's Printer for Scotland Guidance Note 1, para.8.

[67] HMSO Guidance Note 6, para.9; Queen's Printer for Scotland Guidance Note 1, para.7.

[68] HMSO Guidance Note 6, para.12; Queen's Printer for Scotland Guidance Note 1, para.10. Some of the conditions are prefaced by "should", others by "must". However, the waiver is expressed to be conditional on their being complied with. Accordingly, it is thought that breach of a condition prefaced by "should" is just as likely to give rise to a withdrawal of the waiver as breach of one prefaced by "must".

separate and specific licensing arrangements).[69] Secondly, the material must be reproduced accurately. In the case of translations into other languages, a competent translator must be used where the translation is to be issued to the public. Thirdly, care should be taken that material reproduced is from the current or up-to-date version and that out-of-date material is not presented as current. Where out-of-date material is being reproduced for the purposes of drawing comparisons with current material or similar analysis, it should be made clear that the out-of-date material has been superseded, with appropriate cross-references to the current material. Fourthly, the material should not be used in a derogatory or misleading manner, nor should it be used for the purposes of advertising or promoting a particular product or service or for promoting particular personal interests or views.[70] Fifthly, the reproduced versions of the material should not be presented in a way which could imply that they have official status or that they are endorsed by any part of Government. Sixthly, all publisher imprints which are featured on the official versions of the material should be removed from any copies which are issued or made available to the public, whether in hard copy or in electronic form. The Royal Arms may only be reproduced where they form an integral part of the material being reproduced and are used in that context. For example, the cover of an Act of Parliament featuring the Royal Arms may be reproduced in a compendium or database product if the rest of the Act is being reproduced. Finally, the material must be appropriately acknowledged.[71]

10–32   **Unpublished public records: background.** Section 49 of the 1988 Act permits certain acts to be carried out in relation to material comprised in public records as defined by certain specified statutes.[72] Public records which are open to public inspection pursuant to any of those statutes may be copied by or with the authority of any officer appointed under the relevant statute and a copy may be supplied to any person by or with such authority, in each case without infringing copyright.[73] Under this provision, members of the public can obtain copies of public records from public record offices, but section 49 does not authorise any further use. In its White Paper, the Government indicated that this procedure would continue but announced its intention to waive copyright in Crown copyright public records which are available to public inspection provided they were unpublished on the date they were deposited with the record office in question.[74]

---

[69] HMSO Guidance Note 6, para.15; Queen's Printer for Scotland Guidance Note 1, para.13.

[70] Presumably a single-interest campaign which is supported by a significant number of other people would not be regarded as a "particular personal interest or view".

[71] There are two forms of acknowledgment, which apply where Crown copyright material is being published, circulated or issued to the others, including electronically. Where one specific item is being reproduced, the form is: "[Title of Publication] is reproduced under the terms of Crown Copyright Policy Guidance issued by HMSO": HMSO Guidance Note 6, para.14 (the Scottish form of acknowledgement is in the same terms except that the word "HMSO" is replaced by the words "the Queen's Printer for Scotland": Queen's Printer for Scotland Guidance Note 1, para.11). Where a range of material is being reproduced, the form is: "Crown Copyright material is reproduced with the permission of the Controller of HMSO and the Queen's Printer for Scotland": HMSO Guidance Note 6, para.15 (in the case of Scottish legislation, the acknowledgement simply refers to the permission of the Queen's Printer for Scotland: Queen's Printer for Scotland Guidance Note 1, para.11).

[72] The statutes are the Public Records Act 1958 (c.51), the Public Records (Scotland) Act 1937 (c.43), the Public Records Act (Northern Ireland) 1923 (c.20 (NI)) and the Government of Wales Act 1998 (c.38).

[73] See para. 9–130, above.

[74] Cm 4300, para.5.11.

Unpublished public records: scope of the waiver.[75] Obviously, the waiver only   **10–33**
covers Crown copyright. Users wishing to reproduce records which are not
Crown copyright will need to identify the copyright owner and obtain permission
to publish.[76] For the purposes of the waiver, public records are defined as "the records of central government in the United Kingdom and its constituent countries,
and of the central courts of law, including bodies under the government, such as
the national museums, the National Health Service, and national regulatory
authorities", which "have been selected for permanent preservation and are
preserved in record offices and other repositories in the United Kingdom" and
made available to the public under specified statutes.[77] The places where public
records are kept ("public record depositaries") are the National Archives, the
National Archives of Scotland, the Public Record Office of Northern Ireland and
some 240 places of deposit in England and Wales appointed by the Keeper of
Public Records.[78] The waiver of copyright only applies to material contained in
records which have been deposited in a public record depository, which were either unpublished at the time they were deposited or which contain material which
was unpublished at that time, and which are open to public inspection.[79] For these
purposes, "publication" is defined as the authorised issuing of copies of a work to
the public in any medium by the legal copyright holder or with his consent, except
in those cases where the term of copyright protection has expired.[80] The waiver
does not apply to "tradeable information", which in this context consists of two
categories.[81] First, unpublished records of the Ordnance Survey, the Ordnance
Survey of Northern Ireland and the United Kingdom Hydrographic Office, which
form the basis of maps, charts, mapping data and other related publications.
Secondly, copies of public records created by public record repositories in
microfilm, microfiche, digital and photographic form, but not the data they
contain, to which the waiver presumably therefore applies. The reproduction of
such "tradeable information" may be subject to formal licensing and payment of
fees.[82] Finally, public records that are available for inspection only after completion of a confidentiality undertaking will continue to have access and use
restricted on that basis.[83]

Unpublished public records: terms of the waiver. Users may "copy, quote,   **10–34**
index, transcribe, publish and broadcast" such material in all formats and media
throughout the world without needing to make any payment or to obtain a specific
licence.[84] However, the waiver of copyright is subject to certain conditions.[85]
First, the source of the Crown copyright material must be provided on any copies
of the material which are to be made available to the public and in any publication or broadcast reproducing or using the material. This is to be done by quoting
the archival document reference and the name of the public record repository
where the records are held. Secondly, the material must not be used in a mislead-

---

[75] See HMSO Guidance Note 3, Copyright in Public Records, *www.hmso.gov.uk/copyright/
guidance/gn__03.htm*, November 6, 2000 edition.
[76] HMSO Guidance Note 3, para.12.
[77] HMSO Guidance Note 3, para.4. The statutes are the Public Records Act 1958 (c.51), the Public
Records (Scotland) Act 1937 (c.43), the Public Records Act (Northern Ireland) 1923 (c.20 (NI))
and the Government of Wales Act 1998 (c.38).
[78] HMSO Guidance Note 3, para.4.
[79] HMSO Guidance Note 3, para.8.
[80] HMSO Guidance Note 3, para.4. The purpose of this exception is obscure: if copyright has
expired there is nothing to waive.
[81] HMSO Guidance Note 3, para.14.
[82] HMSO Guidance Note 3, para.15.
[83] HMSO Guidance Note 3, para.17.
[84] HMSO Guidance Note 3, para.5.
[85] HMSO Guidance Note 3, para.6.

ing context or in a derogatory manner. Finally, a complimentary copy of the product or publication in which the material is reproduced must be supplied to the Controller of HMSO and/or to the public record repository in which the material is held. In the case of electronic products and publications, the Controller and/or the public record repository should be provided with an appropriate end-user licence and password access. It should be noted that public record repositories retain the right to determine the means by which copies of public records are made available and the right to charge for the provision of such copies.[86]

10–35   **Court forms: background to and scope of the waiver.** Before the White Paper, court forms could be reproduced under the licensing scheme for quasi-legislative material. However, reproduction had to be in a value-added context and was subject to payment of a royalty.[87] In the White Paper, the Government stated that it was in its interest to make forms, both statutory and non-statutory, available as widely as possible.[88] In accordance with this approach, there is now a limited waiver in relation to court forms. At the time of writing, the waiver applies to practice and prescribed forms covered by a large number of pieces of subordinate legislation including the Civil Procedure Rules.[89] The list may be revised from time to time and HMSO advises regular confirmation of which forms are contained in it.[90] It may be a condition of use of new forms in the future that users submit their versions for approval by the Court Service.[91] The waiver only applies to official versions of the forms which appear in the Queen's Printer versions of legislation and to forms issued by the Department of Constitutional Affairs.[92]

10–36   **Court forms: terms of the waiver.** Users may carry out the following activities in relation to the forms: photocopying; publishing and selling alternative versions; including facsimile versions in text books; including the forms as part of a software-based forms package; distributing copies in all media; reproducing the forms on computers to enable completion of individual details on screen; featuring them on intranet sites; and establishing hypertext links to the Court Service's web site.[93] These activities are permitted provided the forms are reproduced in accordance with the relevant Rules and provided various conditions are complied with. The conditions are as follows.[94] First, all reasonable efforts must be made to ensure that the forms are reproduced accurately and in their entirety, except where the Court Service has stated that revisions may be made. Secondly, all reasonable efforts must be made to ensure that all forms used are current and have not been superseded or amended.[95] Thirdly, prescribed acknowledgments must

---

[86] HMSO Guidance Note 3, para.16.

[87] See para.10–31 of the previous edition.

[88] Cm 4300, para.5.5.

[89] HMSO Guidance Note 4: Reproduction of Court Forms *www.hmso.gov.uk/copyright/guidance/gn__04.htm*, November 6, 2000 edition. The full list is as follows: the Family Proceedings Rules 1991, the Family Proceedings Courts (Matrimonial Proceedings) Rules 1991, the Family Proceedings Courts (Children Act) Rules 1991, the Parental Responsibility Agreement Regulations 1991, the Enduring Powers of Attorney (Prescribed Forms) Regulations 1990, the Court of Protection (Enduring Powers of Attorney) Rules 1994, the County Court (Forms) Rules 1982, the Rules of the Supreme Court as amended up to 1998 and the Civil Procedure Rules and Protocols (1999): *ibid.*, para.4.

[90] HMSO Guidance Note 4, para.6.

[91] HMSO Guidance Note 4, para.9.

[92] HMSO Guidance Note 4, para.5.

[93] HMSO Guidance Note 4, para.7. The Court Service's website is at *www.courtservice.gov.uk*.

[94] HMSO Guidance Note 4, para.8.

[95] HMSO suggests that users check with the Lord Chancellor's Department at The Court Service,

be given.[96] Finally, all official publishing and printing imprints must be removed from the user's version.[97]

Birth, death and marriage certificates: background.[98] Anyone may purchase a birth, death or marriage certificate from the appropriate person on payment of the appropriate fee. Only a limited number of persons (including Registrars and the Registrar General) have the power to issue such certificates. It is an offence to make a copy and pass it off as genuine. Any number of certificates may be purchased provided they are not purchased for the purposes of issuing copies to the public. The prescribed forms of such certificates are subject to Crown copyright.

10–37

Birth, death and marriage certificates: what is permitted. The prescribed forms of such certificates may be reproduced provided that such reproduction is in accordance with HMSO guidance as to the reproduction of legislation[99] and no attempts are made to pass off such copies as official certificates or copies of official certificates.[1] However, government policy is not to authorise the copying of completed certificates except in certain limited circumstances as follows.[2] First, by government departments and local government for the purposes of public administration. Secondly, by individuals or organisations for their own record-keeping purposes, provided the copies are not passed to others as evidence of birth, death or marriage. Thirdly, within the context of legal proceedings (this provision appears to be largely otiose in view of the terms of section 45 of the 1988 Act, which provides that copyright is not infringed by anything done for the purposes of judicial proceedings). Fourthly, within works of genealogical research undertaken by or on behalf of the family concerned where the work in question will be given limited distribution only. A work will not be regarded as being given limited distribution if it is placed on the Internet. Fifthly, subject to prior formal written permission, for use within biographies or autobiographies or within academic, educational or historical works not covered by the previous exception. Finally, by the transcription and copying of the information contained in the certificate. The Guidance Note goes on to emphasise that the copying of certificates which contain personal details and the use of information taken from such certificates may be subject to other restrictions, such as the need for any public body to comply with its statutory powers and the provisions of the Human Rights Act 1998 and Data Protection Act 1998.[3]

10–38

National Curriculum and similar material: background. The responsibility for the policy and implementation of the National Curriculum in England rests with the Department for Education and Skills ("the DfES") and the Qualifications and Curriculum Authority ("the QCA"). The QCA is a body corporate established under the Education Act 1997. Both the DfES and the QCA create and publish material in the field. Material created by the DfES is Crown copyright. The QCA

10–39

Civil and Family Operations, Southside, 105 Victoria Street, London SW1E 6QT, Tel. 020 7210 2266.
[96] For reproduction as specimens, the acknowledgement is "© Crown copyright". Where the forms are being used or distributed for completion, it is "© Crown copyright. Published*/Reproduced*/ Issued* by [insert company name]" (* Delete as appropriate): HMSO Guidance Note 4, para.8.
[97] Note, however that the Royal Coat of Arms may be reproduced: HMSO Guidance Note 4, para.11. Artwork may be obtained from HMSO: *ibid.* para.12.
[98] See HMSO Guidance Note 7: Guidance on the Copying of Birth, Death and Marriage Certificates and Marriage Registers, *www.hmso.gov.uk/copyright/guidance/gn_07.htm*, September 23, 2003 edition.
[99] As to which, see para. 10–31, above.
[1] HMSO Guidance Note 7, para.7.
[2] HMSO Guidance Note 7, para.8.
[3] HMSO Guidance Note 7, para.9.

has assigned the copyright in certain material created by it to the Crown.[4] The Welsh equivalents of the DfES and the QCA are the National Assembly for Wales and the Qualifications, Curriculum and Assessment Authority for Wales ("ACCAC"). Like the QCA, the ACCAC has assigned the copyright in some material created by it to the Crown.[5] There is no statutory national curriculum in Scotland. National guidelines are produced by the Scottish Executive Education Department ("SEED") and Learning and Teaching Scotland ("LT Scotland"). Assessment materials are produced by the Scottish Qualifications Agency ("SQA"). Guidelines produced by SEED and LT Scotland are Crown copyright. The SQA has assigned the copyright in some of the material created by it to the Crown.[6]

10–40   **National Curriculum and similar material which may be reproduced freely subject to conditions.** The following material may be reproduced freely throughout the world on compliance with certain conditions. First, the National Curriculum Orders.[7] Second, the following English material: the National Literacy and Numeracy Documents;[8] the Programmes of Study and the explanatory material relating to them;[9] and the Attainment Targets.[10] Third, the following Welsh material: the programmes of study and explanatory material relating to them;[11] and the attainment targets. Fourth, the following Scottish material: the 5–14 Guidelines;[12] the 5–14 National Test Information for Teachers;[13] and the 5–14 National Test Exemplars.[14] The conditions under which such material may be reproduced are almost identical to the seven conditions applicable to the

---

[4] HMSO Guidance Note 8, *www.hmso.gov.uk/copyright/guidance/gn_08.htm*, November 6, 2000 edition, paras 1 to 7.

[5] HMSO Guidance Note 10, *www.hmso.gov.uk/copyright/guidance/gn_10.htm*, August 31, 2001 edition paras 1 to 6.

[6] Queen's Printer for Scotland Guidance Note 3, *www.oqps.gov.uk/copyright/guidance/gn_03.htm*, January 16, 2002 edition, paras 1 to 7.

[7] HMSO Guidance Note 8, para.8. These are the Statutory Instruments which give the National Curriculum statutory effect and are Crown copyright.

[8] HMSO Guidance Note 8, para.8. There are currently two, both of which are Crown copyright: *The National Literacy Strategy Framework for Teaching* (ISBN 0 85522 872 5) and *The National Numeracy Strategy Framework for Teaching Mathematics* (ISBN 0 85522 922 5).

[9] HMSO Guidance Note 8, para.8. The Programmes of Study are part of the official framework documents for the National Curriculum and set out for each subject what pupils should be taught. The QCA has assigned copyright in them to the Crown. Copyright in the explanatory material relating to them has been retained by the QCA but the QCA has agreed that this material may be reproduced under the same conditions as the Crown protected material provided an acknowledgment is given in the following form: " *Qualifications and Curriculum Authority copyright material is reproduced under the terms of HMSO Guidance Note 8*": HMSO Guidance Note 8, para.12.

[10] HMSO Guidance Note 8, para.8. Again, these are part of the official framework documents for the National Curriculum. They set out the expected standards of pupils' performance for each of the principal subjects studied in schools. Again, the QCA has assigned copyright in them to the Crown.

[11] The ACCAC has assigned copyright in the Programmes of Study to the Crown. Copyright in the explanatory material relating to them has been retained by the ACCAC but it has agreed that this material may be reproduced under the same conditions as the Crown protected material provided an acknowledgment is given in the following form: " *Qualifications, Curriculum and Assessment Authority for Wales. Reproduced under the terms of HMSO Guidance Note 10*": HMSO Guidance Note 10, para.11. A Welsh version of the acknowledgement may be used where appropriate.

[12] These guidelines are used by schools to describe the curriculum and assessment of pupils from primary 1 to secondary 2. They are Crown copyright: Queen's Printer for Scotland Guidance Note 3, paras 5, 6 and 8.

[13] The copyright in this has been assigned by the SQA to the Crown: Queen's Printer for Scotland Guidance Note 3 para.7.

[14] Again, the copyright has been assigned by the SQA to the Crown: see previous note.

reproduction of legislation.[15] Again, a prescribed acknowledgment must be given.[16]

National Curriculum Material and Literacy and Numeracy Strategy Mate-   **10–41**
rial which may be reproduced under licence. Two categories of material, namely the modules and teachers' notes for the Literacy and Numeracy Strategies and the Mathematical Vocabulary book, may only be reproduced with the formal permission of HMSO.[17] Material in certain other categories may only be reproduced with the formal permission of the QCA or ACCAC or SQA as appropriate. Those categories are, first, National Curriculum Tests and Tasks produced by the QCA or ACCAC which are set for pupils at Key Stages 1, 2 and 3, as described in the National Curriculum Documents;[18] secondly, the 5–14 test units;[19] thirdly, information, documentation and guidance originated by the QCA which supports the implementation of the National Literacy and Numeracy Strategies and the National Curriculum;[20] and finally, information, documentation and guidance originated by ACCAC which supports the implementation of the National Curriculum, the Personal and Social Education framework or the Work-Related Education framework.[21] In relation to material produced by the QCA, the Guidance Note states that specific permission is not required if the user has an appropriate licence from the Copyright Licensing Agency or the use is a permitted use under the 1988 Act; in either case an appropriate acknowledgment must be given.[22] In relation to material produced by ACCAC, the Guidance Note states that specific permission is not required if the use is a permitted use under the 1988 Act; again an appropriate acknowledgment must be given.[23]

Government Press Notices for England, Northern Ireland and Wales; Press   **10–42**
Notices issued by the Scottish Administration. In accordance with the change announced in the White Paper,[24] official press notices and releases issued by government departments and agencies and the Scottish Administration (including their typographical arrangements) may now be reproduced freely.[25] Where the notice contains a statement that copyright in specific material is not held by the Crown there is no right to reproduce that material.[26] The Guidance Notes do not cover press notices issued by public or private sector organisations which do not have Crown status.[27] The Crown asks[28] that users ensure that the material is reproduced accurately and not in a way that might confuse or mislead others, that

---

[15] See para. 10–31, above. For the precise terms, see the relevant Guidance Notes.

[16] The precise terms are set out in the relevant Guidance Notes.

[17] HMSO Guidance Note 8, para.5. Both these are Crown copyright.

[18] HMSO Guidance Note 8, para.13. HMSO Guidance Note 10, para.12.

[19] Queen's Printer for Scotland Guidance Note 3, para.12.

[20] HMSO Guidance Note 8, para.13.

[21] HMSO Guidance Note 10, para.12.

[22] HMSO Guidance Note 8 para.15 states that the "source" of the material must be "appropriately" acknowledged and that the acknowledgment must include a statement that the copyright in the material remains with the QCA.

[23] HMSO Guidance Note 10 para.14.

[24] Cm 4300, para.5.4.

[25] HMSO Guidance Note 9: Reproduction of Government Press Notices for England, Northern Ireland and Wales, *www.hmso.gov.uk/copyright/guidance/gn_09.htm*, August 10, 2001 edition, para 6. Queen's Printer for Scotland Guidance Note 2: Reproduction of Press Notices Issued by the Scottish Administration, *www.oqps.gov.uk/copyright/guidance/gn_02.htm*, August 10, 2001 edition, para.5.

[26] See previous note.

[27] *ibid.* For a list of bodies with Crown status, see *www.hmso.gov.uk/copyright/policy/c_copyright/crown_bodies.htm*.

[28] *Sic.* It is not clear whether failure to comply with this request will lead to infringement action.

it is correctly acknowledged in the form set out in the Guidance Notes and that the Royal Arms are removed when the material is published.[29]

10–43   **The Record of Proceedings of the National Assembly of Wales.** The National Assembly of Wales is a Crown body and the Official Record, having no doubt been made under its direction or control, is Crown copyright.[30] There is a general waiver, which is subject to conditions as follows: where the copy is being published, circulated or issued to others, prescribed copyright notices should be used; the source and version of the material should be indicated where practicable; there must be no use in connection with advertising, product endorsement or in any context which "could be viewed as undignified association"; there must be no use in any circumstances which are "knowingly or potentially" libellous or slanderous; the Royal Arms may only be used in context; the copy must not purport to be published by the authority of the Assembly or in such a way as to suggest that it has official status; and the proceedings must not be reproduced for "overtly political purposes".[31]

10–44   **Value added material.** In the White Paper, the Government announced its intention to retain a category of "tradeable information" for the reproduction of which users would be charged a licence fee.[32] Tradeable information has now become "value added information" and is defined as "information where value is added to raw data enhancing and facilitating its use and effectiveness for the user, for example through further manipulation, compilation and summarisation into a more convenient form for the end-user, editing and/or further analysis and interpretation, or commentary beyond that required for policy formulation by the relevant government department with policy responsibility. It also includes supplying retrieval software, or where the material is included as part of the compilation of related data, and where there is not necessarily a statutory or operational requirement for Government to produce the material."[33] "Value added material" will usually satisfy certain conditions. First, the material will bring together information from a variety of sources, including "core information". Secondly, value will often be added by means of commentary, analysis, indexing, search facilities and text retrieval software in ways which extend its usefulness as a reference tool. Thirdly, the fact that the material is issued by the Government will not be essential to its status but the material will be seen as authoritative. Fourthly, there may be similar competing services and products in the marketplace. Finally, the creation of the material is not vital to the workings of government. There will often be alternative suppliers of such information.[34] "Core information" is material which is likely to satisfy certain conditions as follows. First, it is essential to the business of government. Secondly, it explains government policy. Thirdly, it is the only source of the information. Fourthly, it sets out how the law must be complied with. Fifthly, citizens will consider the information to be key to their

---

[29] HMSO Guidance Note 9, para.8. Queen's Printer for Scotland Guidance Note 2, para.7.

[30] HMSO Guidance Note 15: Reproduction of the Record of Proceedings, the National Assembly for Wales, *www.hmso.gov.uk/copyright/guidance/gn_15.htm*, April 8, 2002 edition para.8 simply states that the Assembly has Crown status and therefore the Official Record qualifies for Crown copyright protection.

[31] HMSO Guidance Note 15, paras 10 to 16. Although some types of use would obviously break one or more of these conditions, the precise scope of phrases such as "could be viewed as undignified association", "potentially libellous" or "might suggest that the reproduced version has official status" is not particularly clear. Furthermore, the need for the final condition, which prevents use for "overtly political purposes" is difficult to understand.

[32] Cm. 4300, para.9.1–9.2.

[33] *Guidance for Departments: New Policy Arrangements on the Licensing of Government Information*, *www.hmso.gov.uk/copyright/guidance/departments.htm*, November 28, 2001 edition, para.18.

[34] *Guidance for Departments*, para.19.

relationship with the government. Finally, there may be a statutory requirement to produce or issue such information.[35] Examples of material which is considered by HMSO to be value added material include Official Histories published by the Cabinet Office, the Listed Buildings Database, the Manual to the Building Regulations, CD-ROM products published by the Health and Safety Executive, the Statute Law Database and the Census database.[36]

Value added material: licensing policy and prices. A specific licence is   **10–45**
required to reproduce value added material. However, such a licence will not necessarily be granted. In particular, the commercial reuse of the complete or substantial content of a value-added product or service will only be licensed where the user also adds value to it by using it as part of a compilation together with information drawn from a number of other sources or by adding commentary, analysis, indexing and search facilities.[37] The terms of any licence which is granted will depend on the use required to be made but are likely to include a payment.[38] A royalty is likely to be charged where the material is reused in a commercial product that is offered for sale, or where a substantial amount of material is being reused.[39] The normal royalty is 10 per cent of licensee income attributable to the Crown copyright element of the work.[40] By contrast, a fixed fee will be charged where the material is reused in a way that does not involve the offer for sale of a product or service to a customer; where the quantity of material being used is modest (in the case of text, up to 5,000 words); where the material will be made available free of charge; or where the material represents a small proportion of a large database product.[41]

Other material: the Core Licence. In the White Paper, the Government   **10–46**
undertook to introduce standard terms across government for the reproduction of Crown copyright protected material other than tradeable information and to feature the licensing terms on HMSO's website.[42] This has now been done and the licence is called "the Core Licence".[43] By the end of November 2003 over 4,000 such licences had been granted to a wide range of types of individual and organization.[44] The Core Licence does not apply to material in a large number of different categories. First, material in respect of which a waiver is in place.[45] Second, material published by certain departments which have trading fund status.[46] Third, material which is covered by security classification, legal or policy

---

[35] *Guidance for Departments*, para.15.
[36] See *Illustrative examples of value added material sorted by government department*, *www.hmso.gov.uk/copyright/licences/valueadded/va_examples.htm*.
[37] See *Charging for value-added material*, *www.hmso.gov.uk/copyright/licences/valueadded/charging.htm#royalties*, para.3.
[38] An electronic application form is at *www.hmso.gov.uk/copyright/licences/valueadded/appform.htm*; a standard form licence is at *www.hmso.gov.uk/copyright/licences/valueadded/va_terms.htm*; information about charges is at *www.hmso.gov.uk/copyright/licences/valueadded/charging.htm#royalties*.
[39] *Charging for value-added material*, para.8.
[40] *Charging for value-added material*, para.9. For translations into other languages, the rate is 7.5%.
[41] *Charging for value-added material*, para.10.
[42] Cm 4300, para.7.3.
[43] *www.hmso.gov.uk/copyright/licences/core/c_terms.htm*.
[44] See *www.hmso.gov.uk/about/website_info.htm#clickuseintro*.
[45] The list in cl.1.2 of the Core licence is as follows: legislation (see para. 10–31, above), unpublished public records (para. 10–33), Government press notices (para. 10–42, above), and National Curriculum Material for England and Wales (see para. 10–40, above).
[46] cl.5.1. They include: the Central Office of Information, Companies House, H.M. Land Registry, the Ordnance Survey, the Patent Office and the Vehicle Inspectorate: Core Licence, Annex A.

restrictions.[47] Fourth, material which includes personal information about named individuals.[48] Fifth, photographs and films held in photographic or film archives.[49] Sixth, material where there is a requirement for the reused version to be approved by a Department.[50] Seventh, value added material.[51] Eighth, computer programs and software.[52] Ninth, material in which the copyright is not wholly owned by the Crown.[53] Tenth, material including technical drawings and diagrams, which relates to wider Government intellectual property rights in patents, trade marks, design rights, registered designs and inventions.[54] Finally, material the licensing of which has been delegated by HMSO to departments.[55]

10–47   Core Licence: terms. The current edition of the Core Licence[56] constitutes an offer which may be accepted by completing an online application form.[57] Its "main purpose" is to provide users with a fast system that "lets you reuse" a wide range of material.[58] The rights granted include the following non-exclusive rights throughout the world:[59] publishing the material in any medium; authorising users and subscribers to access the material as part of electronic or digital products by means of an end-user licence; translating the material provided the translation is accurate and made by a competent translator; copying the material for the purposes of research and private study; conversion of the material to Braille and other formats for the visually impaired; and copying by libraries. Licensees incur certain obligations under the licence. They are as follows.[60] First, to provide accurate information on the application form and to notify HMSO of changes in those details. Secondly, to let HMSO know if they wish to cancel the licence (the licensee may cancel at any time).[61] Thirdly, to reproduce only material which falls within the scope of the licence. Fourthly, to reproduce the material accurately from the current official source except when the licensee makes clear that there is a more up-to-date version available. Fifthly, to identify the source of the material and to feature a prescribed copyright statement if the material is published.[62] Sixthly, not to use the material for the principal purpose of advertising or promoting a particular product or service or in a way which could imply endorsement by a Department or generally in a manner which is likely to mislead others. Seventhly, not to reproduce official imprints, departmental logos or badges, crests,

---

[47] cl.5.2. This includes personal identity documents such as driving licences and passports and information exempted from disclosure to the public under the Freedom of Information Act 2000: *ibid.*

[48] cl.5.3.

[49] cl.5.4. These items continue to be covered by existing licensing and supply arrangements: *ibid.*

[50] cl.5.5. This includes information appearing on Government websites which is subject to frequent change and where the re-use of out of date material could mislead the public: *ibid.* For a list of such items, see *www.hmso.gov.uk/copyright/licences/core/out__of__scope.htm.* This document also explains how licences may be applied for to reproduce departmental logos, military medals, badges and insignia and the Royal arms.

[51] cl.5.6. See para. 10–45, above.

[52] cl.5.7.

[53] cl.5.8. This is defined as follows: first, works that contain a statement that the copyright is held jointly by the Crown and another; secondly, works that contain a statement that the copyright is owned by someone other than the Crown; and thirdly, works in respect of which there is copyright in the typographical arrangement of published editions, except where it is shown that the copyright rests with the Crown.

[54] cl.5.9. The precise meaning and scope of this exception are unclear.

[55] cl.5.10. See para. 10–27, above.

[56] Version 2.0 dated July 27, 2001.

[57] Introduction and cl.3.

[58] cl.1.1.

[59] cl.6.

[60] cl.10.

[61] cl.12.2.

[62] The copyright statement is as follows: "Crown copyright material is reproduced with the permission of the Controller of HMSO and the Queen's printer for Scotland": cl.10.5.

medals and insignia of the Armed Forces.[63] Finally, to allow HMSO to inspect copies of any works which include the material to ensure that the terms of the licence have been complied with. HMSO reserves the right to change the terms of the licence although an existing licence will be honoured for the remainder of its term unless the licensee wishes to terminate it and take out a licence on the revised terms.[64] Both HMSO and the licensee have the right to terminate the licence if there is a material breach of its terms and the breach is not remedied within 60 days of notification of the nature of the breach.[65] The benefit of the licence may not be assigned.[66] The licensee agrees that use of the material under the licence is entirely at his or her risk and HMSO makes no warranty, representation or guarantee that the material will be error-free.[67]

Core Licence: procedure. A core licence may be applied for by registering with HMSO and then completing a simple form online.[68] The applicant will then receive a licence number and a start date.[69] Subject to the licensee's compliance with its conditions, the licence continues for five years unless terminated earlier by the licensee.[70] In most cases, the material may be reproduced from its official source by whatever means the licensee may choose.[71] Where this is not possible, or the licensee requires the material in a different format, and the department incurs costs in supplying the material, there may be a charge for its supply.[72] HMSO aims to confirm receipt of the application form promptly, to put right difficulties or answer queries quickly, to handle all licences in a manner that is fair and consistent and to provide licensees with details of any changes to the licence.[73] There is a complaints procedure.[74]

10–48

Articles written by Ministers and civil servants. There is a special scheme in relation to such articles.[75] It applies where a government department or agency wishes to submit such an article for publication in a journal or similar publication; or a publisher commissions an author to prepare such an article for publication; or a minister or civil servant gives a presentation at a conference or seminar and the organiser wishes to publish the text of the presentation in the conference proceedings. In such circumstances, the publisher must obtain the author's consent (in the case of a Minister this can be obtained from his or her Private Office) and obtain confirmation from the head of the department concerned or Agency Chief Executive that the article is consistent with departmental policy and may be published (again, in the case of a Minister, clearance from his or her Private Office will suffice). Once consent has been obtained, the article may be published in any format throughout the world for a period of up to 12 months from the grant of consent. The publisher may also sub-license his customers to access the article in the context of digital products and services; authorise the

10–49

---

[63] The Royal Arms may be reproduced only when they form an integral part of the material reproduced and they are reproduced in that context: cl.10.7.

[64] cl.11.

[65] cl.12.1. Given that licensees may terminate at any time under cl.12.2, it seems unlikely that they will wish to use this right.

[66] cl.13.

[67] cl.14.

[68] The registration form is at *www.click-use.hmso.gov.uk/online/p.Register.asp.*

[69] cl.3.2.

[70] cl.3.1.

[71] cl.7.

[72] cl.8.

[73] cl.9.

[74] *ibid.*

[75] HMSO Guidance Note 2: Publication of Articles written by Ministers and Civil Servants in Journals and Conference Proceedings, *www.hmso.gov.uk/copyright/guidance/articles.htm,* October 24, 2003 edition.

inclusion of the article in collective licensing schemes such as that operated by the Copyright Licensing Agency; and authorise the inclusion of the article as part of document delivery, abstracting and indexing services.[76] There are three further conditions. First, an appropriate acknowledgement must be given.[77] Second, the publication must not be for the purpose of advertising or promoting a particular product or source. Finally, the reproduction must be accurate and the article must not be amended without the author's approval.

10–50   **The British passport.** Again, there is a special scheme.[78] There are two circumstances in which the British passport may be reproduced. First, photocopies in black and white of the personal details page of a particular passport may be reproduced without a licence for the purposes of record-keeping only by: the holder or owner; notaries, solicitors, banks and government departments; or a person or institution subject to the requirements of the Money Laundering Regulations, a person certifying that identification checks required under these Regulations have taken place.[79] Secondly, the cover of the passport including the Royal Arms and the inside of the passport may also be reproduced as part of a work, including promotional and advertising works.[80] An application must be made and a fee paid and there are a number of specific conditions as to the precise manner in which the passport may be reproduced.[81]

10–51   **The future: the Directive on the reuse of public sector information.** The arrangements set out above may need to be revised once more in the light of European developments. On January 20, 1999, the European Commission published a Green Paper: Public Sector Information: a key resource for Europe.[82] On June 5, 2002, following a period of consultation, the Commission published a proposal for a Directive on the re-use and commercial exploitation of public sector documents.[83] The Directive was finally adopted on November 17, 2003.[84] It must be implemented by Member States by July 1, 2005.[85] The Department of Trade and Industry believes that the measures in the Directive include provisions which may require action by public sector organisations, but that the United Kingdom central government and the Scottish administration have already met most of the Directive's requirements.[86]

10–52   **The objects of the Directive.** The recitals to the Directive refer to the significance for individuals of the evolution towards an information and knowledge so-

---

[76] The Guidance Note does not expressly limit these uses to 12 months from the date consent is obtained, but presumably such a limitation is intended.
[77] The form is: "The article [Title] was written by [Name author(s)] of [Name department(s)]. It is published with the permission of the Controller of HMSO and the Queen's Printer for Scotland"
[78] HMSO Guidance Note 20: Reproduction of the British Passport, www.hmso.gov.uk/copyright/guidance/gn__20.htm, May 23, 2003 edition.
[79] HMSO Guidance Note 20, para.6.
[80] HMSO Guidance Note 20, para.7.
[81] HMSO Guidance Note 20, paras 7 and 8.
[82] COM (1998) 585.
[83] COM(2002) 207 final.
[84] Directive 2003/98/EC of the European Parliament and of the Council of November 17, 2003 on the reuse of public sector information: [2003] O.J. L 354/90.
[85] Art.12.
[86] See its Consultation Document at www.dti.gov.uk/industries/digital__content/consultation__doc__ria__sept__03.pdf, which was issued on September 12, 2003. The Consultation Document considers two alternatives for implementation (paras 14–19). The first is the establishment of a formal statutory regulatory framework. The second is a framework of legislation which would be implemented through codes of best practice like the European Information Fair Trader Scheme. The current preference is for the second option: ibid., para.20.

ciety and the fact that digital content plays an important role in this evolution.[87] They note that the public sector collects, produces, reproduces and disseminates a wide range of information in many areas of activity and that this information is an increasingly important primary material for the growing market in digital content products and services.[88] According to the recitals, there are considerable differences in the rules and practices relating to the exploitation of such information in the different Member States. These differences constitute barriers to the realisation of the full potential of this primary material, and especially to the development of Community-wide digital services. Accordingly, harmonisation in this field is expected to contribute to the achievement of the internal market and to preventing distortions of competition in the internal market.[89] In the absence of minimum harmonisation at Community level, there is thought to be a danger of further divergences between Member States.[90] Accordingly, the Directive establishes a minimum set of rules governing the reuse and the practical means of facilitating re-use of existing documents held by public sector bodies of the Member States.[91]

No effect on intellectual property rights. It should immediately be noted that the Directive is not intended to affect the intellectual property rights of public sector bodies or of third parties. Accordingly, it does not contain any obligation to allow the reuse of documents.[92] Rather, it lays down a general framework, based on minimum harmonisation, for the conditions governing reuse of those documents where such reuse is permitted by the public sector body in question.[93] Member States are permitted and indeed encouraged to go beyond the minimum standards of the Directive, thus allowing for more extensive reuse.[94] It is expressly provided that the Directive has no application to documents for which third parties hold intellectual property rights.[95]   **10–53**

"Public sector body" and "body governed by public law". The definitions of these terms are taken from various public procurement Directives.[96] "Public sector body" means the State, regional or local authorities, bodies governed by public law and associations of such authorities or bodies.[97] "Body governed by public law" means any body which satisfies three criteria (which are to be read conjunctively).[98] First, the body must have been established for the specific purpose of meeting needs in the general interest, not having an industrial or commercial character[99] (public undertakings are excluded from this definition[1]).   **10–54**

---

[87] Directive 2003/98, recitals 2 and 3.
[88] Recitals 4 and 5.
[89] Recitals 1 and 6.
[90] Recital 7.
[91] Art.1(1).
[92] Directive 2003/98, recitals 9, 22 and 24.
[93] Recital 9 and Arts 1(1), 1(3) and 3.
[94] Recitals 8, 9, 22.
[95] Art.1(2)(b).
[96] These are listed in Directive 2003/98, recital 10.
[97] Art.2(1).
[98] Art.2(2).
[99] Art.2(2)(a).
[1] Recital 10. The significance of this statement requires an understanding of certain well-established concepts of E.U. competition law. The term "undertaking" is a term of art. In very broad terms, it encompasses any entity engaged in an economic activity, regardless of its legal status and the way it is financed: Case C-41/90, *Höfner v Macroton* [1991] E.C.R. I-1979;, [1993] 4 C.M.L.R. 306, para.21. "Public undertakings" are "undertakings over which public authorities may exercise, directly or indirectly, a dominant influence by virtue of their ownership of it, their financial participation therein, or the rules which govern it. A dominant influence is to be

Secondly, the body must have legal personality.[2] Thirdly, the body must either be financed for the most part by the State, or by regional or local authorities, or by other bodies governed by public law; or be subject to management supervision by those bodies; or have an administrative, managerial or supervisory board, more than half of whose members are appointed by the State, regional or local authorities or other bodies governed by public law.[3]

10–55 **"Document".** The Directive applies to "documents". A document is defined as "any content whatever its medium (written on paper or stored in electronic form or as a sound, visual or audio-visual recording)" or any part of such content.[4] The apparent breadth of this definition is reduced by the recitals. First, the definition of "document" is not intended to cover computer programs.[5] Second, the definition covers "any representation of acts, facts or information—and any compilation of such acts, facts or information—whatever its medium".[6]

10–56 **Documents to which the Directive does not apply.** Documents in a number of different categories are excluded from the application of the Directive. The categories are as follows. First, documents the supply of which is an activity falling outside the scope of the public task of the public sector body concerned.[7] Secondly, documents covered by industrial property rights, such as patents, registered designs and trade marks.[8] Thirdly, documents for which third parties hold intellectual property rights.[9] Fourthly, documents which are excluded from access by virtue of access regimes in the Member States, including on grounds of the protection of national security, defence or public security or statistical or commercial confidentiality.[10] Fifthly, documents held by public service broadcast-

---

presumed when the public authority holds the major part of the undertaking's subscribed capital, controls the majority of votes attached to the shares issued or can appoint more than half the members of the undertaking's administrative, managerial or supervisory body": Cases 188–190/88, *France, Italy and the U.K. v Commission* [1982] E.C.R. 2545. However, a body will not be an "undertaking" to the extent that it is acting in the exercise of public or official authority, that is where the activity in question is a task in the public interest which forms part of the essential functions of the state: Case 30/87 *Corinne Bodson v Pompes Funèbres des Regions Libérées S.A.* [1988] E.C.R. 2479; [1989] 4 C.M.L.R. 984; Case C–343/95 *Calie Figli* [1997] E.C.R. I–1547; [1997] 5 C.M.L.R. 484. It follows that a "public undertaking", by definition, is likely to be excluded from the ambit of the Directive by Art.2(2)(a).

[2] Directive 2003/98, Art.2(2)(b).
[3] Art.2(2)(c).
[4] Directive 2003/98, Art. 2(3).
[5] Recital 9.
[6] Recital 7.
[7] Directive 2003/98, Art.1(2)(a). The scope of the public task is that defined by law or other binding rules in the Member State. In the absence of such rules, the scope of the public task is "as defined in line with common administrative practice in the Member State in question": *ibid.* These definitions are not particularly precise, but the broad aim appears to be to exclude from the scope of the Directive material which is produced by public sector bodies for commercial exploitation. Thus, recital 9 states that activities falling outside the scope of the public task will typically include the supply of documents which are produced and charged for exclusively on a commercial basis and in competition with others in the market. Without such an exclusion, the Directive would effectively make such activities impossible. Nevertheless, the Directive leaves considerable scope for argument as to whether the supply of a particular document is or is not within the public task.
[8] Curiously, this only emerges from recital 22 and is not stated in the body of Directive 2003/98.
[9] Art.1(2)(b). Since the Directive is totally inapplicable to documents covered by industrial property rights (see previous footnote), the term "intellectual property rights" means "copyright and related rights only (including *sui generis* forms of protection)": recital 22. Where a third party has rights in only part of a document, the effect of the definition of "document" in Art.2(3) (para. 10–55 above) appears to be that the Directive will apply to those parts of the document which are free of such rights.
[10] Art.1(2)(c). See also Art.4(5): such bodies are not required to respond to requests, whether positively or negatively.

ers, their subsidiaries and similar bodies.[11] Sixthly, documents held by educational and research establishments.[12] Seventhly, documents held by cultural establishments.[13] As has already been stated, computer programs are not "documents" at all.[14]

"Reuse". "Reuse" means the use by persons or legal entities of documents held by public sector bodies for commercial or non-commercial purposes other than the initial purpose within the public task for which the documents were produced.[15] The object of this definition is to ensure that public authorities that reuse documents in a manner which is outside the scope of their public task, for example to supply them on a purely commercial basis and in competition with others, can only do so on the same terms (in particular as to payment) as anyone else. This is intended to eliminate cross-subsidies.[16] The exchange of documents between public sector bodies purely in pursuit of their public task is not reuse.[17]   **10–57**

Other limitations. Three further limitations should be mentioned. First, the Directive does not apply in cases where applicants have to prove a particular interest under the access regime before they can obtain access to the documents.[18] Secondly, the Directive leaves intact and in no way affects existing rules about data protection.[19] Thirdly, the obligations imposed by the Directive apply only in so far as they are compatible with the provisions of international agreements on the protection of intellectual property rights and in particular the Berne Convention and the TRIPS Agreement.[20]   **10–58**

General principle. The general principle of the Directive is stated to be that Member States shall ensure that where the reuse of documents held by public sector bodies is allowed, those documents shall be re-usable for commercial or non-commercial purposes in accordance with the Directive.[21] Where possible, documents must be made available through electronic means.[22]   **10–59**

Processing of requests for reuse. The Directive obliges public sector bodies to process requests for reuse through electronic means where possible. The request will have to be processed and the document made available (or, where a licence is needed, a licence offer finalised) within a reasonable time that is consistent with any time-frames which have been laid down.[23] The recitals make clear that any time-frame which is laid down must be short enough to allow the full economic potential of the documents to be exploited. This is particularly important   **10–60**

---

[11] Art.1(2)(d). The Art.4(5) exclusion applies to these bodies as well.

[12] Art.1(2)(e). The Art.4(5) exclusion also applies to these bodies. The exclusion expressly applies to organisations established for the transfer of research results where relevant.

[13] Art.1(2)(f).

[14] See para. 10–55, above.

[15] Directive 2003/98, Art.2(4).

[16] Recital 9.

[17] Art.2(4).

[18] Directive 2003/98, Art.1(2)(3). This provision appears to give public authorities considerable scope for limiting access to their documents.

[19] Art.1(2) (4). In particular, it does not alter the obligations and rights set out in Directive 95/46/EC.

[20] Art.1(2) (5). As has already been stated, recital 22 and Art. 1(2)(b) preserve third-party intellectual property rights, while recital 24 makes clear that the intellectual property rights of public sector bodies are unaffected. Note also that recital 24 states that the Directive is without prejudice to the Information Society Directive (Directive 2001/29/EC) and the Database Directive (Directive 96/9/EC).

[21] Directive 2003/98, Art.3.

[22] Art.3. See also recital 15, under which Member States will be obliged to encourage the creation of online indices of available documents.

[23] Directive 2003/98, recital 12.

where content is dynamic and its economic value depends on its immediate availability.[24] In addition, specific time-limits are applicable if no time-frame has been laid down and these will presumably be regarded as a suitable benchmark for what is a reasonable time. Where no time-frame has been laid down, the document will have to be supplied or the licence offer finalised within 20 days of receipt of the request.[25] However, there will be an exception for "extensive or complex requests". In such cases, the time-frame will be capable of being extended by another 20 days but the applicant will have to be notified within three weeks after the initial request that more time is needed to process it.[26] It will clearly be in the interests of public sector bodies to lay down a longer period for processing requests than 20 days provided such a period will be capable of being justified as reasonable.

10–61   **Refusals and appeals.** In the event of a negative decision, the public sector body concerned will have to communicate the grounds for refusal on the basis of the relevant provisions of the access regime in the relevant member state or the national provisions adopted pursuant to the Directive.[27] Any negative decision will have to contain a reference to the means of redress in case the applicant wishes to appeal the decision.[28] No further explanation is offered as to the type of means of redress which might be considered satisfactory and it is not clear whether an internal right of appeal will suffice or whether there will need to be a right to apply to a court. However, public sector bodies will be obliged to ensure that applicants are informed of available means of redress relating to decisions and practices affecting them.[29] Public service broadcasters, their subsidiaries and similar bodies, educational and research establishments and cultural establishments will not be obliged to process any requests under the Directive or communicate any negative decision.[30]

10–62   **Conditions for reuse.** Public sector bodies will be obliged to make their documents available in any pre-existing format or language, through electronic means where possible and appropriate. However, there will be no obligation to create or adapt documents in order to comply with a request, nor to provide extracts where this would involve disproportionate effort, going beyond a simple operation.[31] Furthermore, the Directive will not oblige public sector bodies to continue to produce documents of a particular type.[32] Presumably the requirement that applicants are informed of the available means of redress relating to "practices" affecting them[33] implies a requirement that there be a means to challenge such practices; whether this is to be by reference to an internal procedure or by application to a court is unclear.

---

[24] Art.4(1). The example given is traffic data.

[25] Art.4(2).

[26] *ibid.*

[27] Directive 2003/98, Art.4(3).

[28] Art.4(4).

[29] Art.7.

[30] Art.4(5).

[31] Directive 2003/98, Art.5(1). To facilitate reuse, public sector bodies should make their documents available in a format which, as far as possible and appropriate, is not dependent on the use of specific software: recital 13. The possible use of documents by and for people with disabilities should also be taken into account: *ibid.*.

[32] Art.5(2). On the other hand, if a public sector body decides to cease making certain documents available for reuse, or to cease updating such documents, this decision must be made public at the earliest opportunity, via electronic means where possible: recital 18.

[33] Art.7.

Charges. Any applicable conditions and standard charges will have to be pre-established and published, through electronic means where appropriate.[34] The public body in question will be obliged to indicate on request which factors will be taken into account in the calculation of charges for atypical cases.[35] Where charges are made, the total income from supplying and allowing the reuse will not be permitted to exceed the cost of collection, production, reproduction and dissemination, together with a reasonable return on investment.[36] Charges "should be cost-oriented over the appropriate accounting period" and calculated in line with the accounting principles applicable to the public sector bodies involved.[37] Presumably the requirement that applicants are informed of the available means of redress relating to "practices" affecting them[38] implies a requirement that there be a means to challenge any charges which are imposed.

10–63

Licences. Public sector bodies will be permitted to allow for the reuse of documents without conditions, or to impose conditions, where appropriate through a licence.[39] Any conditions which are imposed will not be allowed to restrict unnecessarily the possibilities for reuse or to restrict competition.[40] Where licences are used, Member States will be obliged to ensure that standard licences, which can be adapted to meet particular licence applications, are available in digital format and capable of being processed electronically.[41] Member States will be obliged to encourage all public sector bodies to use the standard licences.[42]

10–64

Practical arrangements. Once the Directive is implemented, Member States will be obliged to ensure that practical arrangements are in place to facilitate the search for documents available for reuse.[43] These arrangments will have to include assets lists, preferably accessible online, of main documents and portal sites linked to decentralised assets lists.[44] For an outline of the steps which have already been in this direction in the United Kingdom, see paragraph 10–28, above.

10–65

Non-discrimination. Any applicable conditions for the reuse of documents will have to be non- discriminatory for comparable categories of reuse.[45] On the other hand, this is not intended to prevent two particular types of practice.[46] First, public authorities will be permitted to exhange information free of charge provided this is for the exercise of public tasks while at the same time charging other parties to re-use the same documents. Secondly, public authorities will be allowed to adopt a differentiated charging policy for commercial and non-commercial reuse.

10–66

---

[34] Directive 2003/98, Art.7.

[35] *ibid.*

[36] Art.6. Recital 14 contains relevant observations on this provision. First, it makes clear that in applying this formula, due regard shall be had to the self-financing requirements of the body concerned, where applicable. It goes on to state that "production" includes creation and collation while "dissemination" may include user support. Thirdly, it states that charges calculated in accordance with this formula are intended to represent the upper limit. Lower charges may be made or no charges at all. Finally, it states that Member States should encourage public sector bodies to make documents available at charges that do not exceed the marginal cost for reproducing and disseminating them. Recital 19 makes clear that public authorities will nevertheless be permitted to charge commercial reusers more than non-commercial reusers.

[37] Art.6

[38] Art.7.

[39] Directive 2003/98, Art. 8(1).

[40] *ibid.*

[41] *ibid.*

[42] *ibid.* Presumably the Core Licence, which is already available from HMSO (see para. 10–46, above), will have to be made available by other bodies.

[43] Directive 2003/98, Art.9.

[44] *ibid.*

[45] Directive 2003/98, Art.10(1).

[46] Recital 19.

If documents are reused by a public sector body as input for its commercial activities which fall outside the scope of its public tasks, the same charges and other conditions will apply to the supply of such documents for those activities as apply to other users.[47]

10–67   **Prohibition of exclusive arrangements**. The general principle is to be that the reuse of documents will be open to all potential actors in the market, even if one or more players already exploits value-added products based on these documents.[48] Accordingly, public sector bodies holding the documents will generally not be permitted to grant exclusive rights to third parties.[49] However, where the grant of an exclusive right is necessary for the provision of a service in the public interest, the grant will be permitted but the reason for the grant of the exclusive right will have to be reviewed regularly and in any event every three years.[50] An example of where such a grant would be necessary is where no commercial publisher would publish the information without such an exclusive right.[51] Any exclusive arrangements granted after the entry into force of the Directive will have to be transparent and made public.[52] Existing exclusive arrangements which do not qualify for the exception will have to be terminated at the end of the contract and in any case not later than December 31, 2008.[53] It is clear that the role of HMSO in the United Kingdom will have to be examined carefully in the light of these provisions.

D. MORAL RIGHTS

10–68   **Limited scope in relation to Crown works.** The rights created by the 1988 Act to be identified as author or director[54] and to object to derogatory treatment of a work[55] have only limited scope in relation to works in which Crown copyright subsists. The right to be identified as author or director does not apply in relation to a work in which Crown copyright subsists unless the author or director has been identified as such in or on published copies of the work.[56] It follows that the Crown[57] will effectively be able to determine whether this right can ever be asserted in relation to a work in which Crown copyright subsists. The right to object to derogatory treatment of a work in which Crown copyright subsists does not apply to anything done in relation to such a work by or with the authority of the copyright owner unless the author or director is identified at the time of the relevant act or has previously been identified in or on published copies of the work.[58] Even where the right applies, it is not infringed if there is a sufficient disclaimer.[59]

---

[47] Art.10(2).

[48] Directive 2003/98, Art.11(1).

[49] *ibid*.

[50] Art.11(2).

[51] Recital 20.

[52] Art.11(2).

[53] Art.11(3).

[54] CDPA 1988, s.77. See Ch.11.

[55] s.80. See Ch.11.

[56] s.79(7)(a). For the meaning of "publication" and related expressions, see s.175(1) and paras 3–172 *et seq.*, above.

[57] Or its assignee: Crown copyright continues to subsist in a work the copyright in which has been assigned by the Crown: CDPA 1988, s.163(2).

[58] s.82(2). For the meaning of "publication" and related expressions, see s.175(1) and paras 3–172 *et seq.*, above.

[59] s.82(2). For the meaning of "sufficient disclaimer", see CDPA 1988, s.178, and Ch.11, below.

E. DESIGN RIGHT

Special provisions in relation to the Crown. The Crown is a qualifying person   **10–69**
for the purposes of design right.[60] The provisions of the 1988 Act dealing with
Crown use of designs are dealt with elsewhere.[61]

2. PARLIAMENTARY RIGHTS

A. INTRODUCTION

The scheme of the 1988 Act. The 1988 Act created a new species of copyright   **10–70**
called parliamentary copyright, which subsists in works made by or under the
direction of the House of Commons or the House of Lords.[62] The Act also makes
special provision for the copyright in parliamentary bills to belong to one or both
Houses of Parliament.[63] For the purposes of holding, dealing with and enforcing
these types of copyright, each House of Parliament is to be treated as a body
corporate.[64] These provisions have now been extended to works made by or under
the direction of the Scottish Parliament or the Northern Ireland Assembly and to
bills introduced into those bodies.[65]

The policy of the 1988 Act. Under the 1956 Act, the Crown was entitled to the   **10–71**
copyright in every literary, dramatic, musical or artistic work which was first
published under the direction or control of Her Majesty or of a Government
department ("the first publication rule").[66] This rule enabled the Crown to obtain
the copyright in material produced by Parliament, including perhaps most
importantly, in *Hansard*, simply by being the first to publish it. The Whitford
Committee criticised the first publication rule on the grounds that it led to
potential injustice[67] and the Government proposed its abolition in its 1986 White
Paper.[68] However, at the same time it was considered that the abolition of the first
publication rule would give rise to uncertainty as to the ownership of the copyright in parliamentary material and in particular in *Hansard*.[69] The Government's
original intention was to make such material the subject of Crown copyright.[70]
However, following the introduction of the Bill which became the 1988 Act, it
concluded that to vest such copyright in the Crown would be undesirable, apparently because it would have the effect of vesting the control of parliamentary
papers with the controller of HMSO rather than with the House in question.[71]
Because the precise legal personalities of the Houses of Parliament were thought
to be unclear, it was considered to be necessary to endue them with a statutory
legal personality so that they could hold, deal with and enforce their copyright.[72]
For Scotland and Northern Ireland, the equivalent bodies are the Scottish
Parliamentary Corporate Body and the Northern Ireland Assembly Commission

---

[60] CDPA 1988, s.217(2). For the significance of this, see paras 13–91 *et seq.*, below.
[61] See paras 13–131 *et seq.*, below.
[62] CDPA 1988, s.165.
[63] s.166.
[64] s.167.
[65] See below at paras 10–73 and 10–82 respectively.
[66] Copyright Act 1956, s.39(2).
[67] See para. 10–09, above.
[68] *Intellectual Property and Innovation*, Cmnd. 9712, para.16.9.
[69] *ibid.*
[70] *ibid.*
[71] *Hansard*, HC, col.93 (S.C.E.); HL Vol.501, col.194.
[72] *Hansard*, H.L., Vol. 501, col. 194.

respectively.[73] The structure of the Parliamentary copyright provisions is similar to that of the provisions relating to statutory Crown copyright.[74]

B. PARLIAMENTARY COPYRIGHT

(i) Copyright in works other than Parliamentary Bills

10–72   **Subsistence, ownership and term.** The general provisions of the 1988 Act relating to subsistence, first ownership and duration of copyright do not apply to works made by or under the direction or control of either of the Houses of Parliament.[75] Instead, section 165(1) of the 1988 Act provides that where a work[76] is made by or under the direction or control of either House of Parliament, it qualifies for copyright protection even if the ordinary qualification requirements are not satisfied,[77] and that the House by which, or under the direction or control of which the work is made is the first owner of any copyright in the work.[78] If the work is made by or under the direction or control of both Houses, the two Houses are joint first owners of the copyright.[79] The term "direction and control", which was used in relation to Crown copyright in the 1956 Act,[80] was criticised by the Whitford Committee, which expressed the view that a provision in language of such width was likely to lead to difficulty.[81] Presumably with the object of reducing the likelihood of such difficulties, section 165 of the 1988 Act contains a limited definition of the term. Thus, it is provided that for the purposes of these provisions, works made by or under the direction or control of the House of Commons or House of Lords include any work made by an officer or employee of that House in the course of his duties[82] and any sound recording, film, live broadcast or live cable programme of the proceedings of that House.[83] On the other hand, a work is not to be regarded as made by or under the direction of either House by reason only of its being commissioned by or on behalf of that House.[84] It is provided that copyright in works made under the direction of the Houses of Parliament is referred to in Part I of the 1988 Act as "Parliamentary copyright" even if it has been assigned to another person.[85] Parliamentary copyright in a literary, dramatic, musical or artistic work continues to subsist until the end of the period of 50 years from the end of the calendar year in which the work was made.[86] In the absence of specific provision, the term of Parliamentary copy-

---

[73] See the Parliamentary Copyright (Scottish Parliament) Order 1999 (SI 1999/676) and the Parliamentary Copyright (Northern Ireland Assembly) Order 1999 (SI 1999/3146) respectively.

[74] *i.e.* CDPA 1988, s.163. See paras 10–12 *et seq.*, above.

[75] CDPA 1988, ss.153(2) (subsistence), 11(3) (first ownership) and 12(9) (duration).

[76] For what may be a copyright work, see CDPA 1988, s.1. Note that Parliamentary copyright may subsist in works of all classes.

[77] CDPA 1988, s.165(1)(a). For the ordinary qualification requirements, see *ibid.* s.153(1) and paras 3–152 *et seq.*, above.

[78] s.165(1)(b). The effect of this would seem to be that judicial decisions of the House of Lords are the subject of Parliamentary copyright.

[79] s.165(1).

[80] Copyright Act 1956, s.39(1).

[81] Cmnd. 6732, para.593.

[82] CDPA 1988, s.165(4)(a).

[83] s.165(4)(b). Note that these definitions are not exhaustive.

[84] s.165(4). Before the passing of the 1988 Act, the Government was of the view that it was unclear whether the words "work made ... under the direction or control of" extended to works which were commissioned: *Hansard*, HL Vol.491, cols 553–4.

[85] CDPA 1988, s.165(2).

[86] CDPA 1988, s.165(3).

right for all other works will be the normal term.[87] No publication right arises from the publication of a work in which Parliamentary copyright subsisted.[88]

Scottish and Northern Irish parliamentary copyright. The provisions of section 165 of the 1988 Act apply, subject to any exceptions or modifications specified by Order in Council,[89] to works made by or under the direction or control of any other legislative body of a country to which Part I of the 1988 Act extends and references to "parliamentary copyright" are to be construed accordingly.[90] By section 165(7) of the 1988 Act, the provisions of section 165 (which contains provisions as to the subsistence and term of parliamentary copyright) apply, subject to any exceptions or modifications specified by Order in Council, to works made by or under the direction or control of any other legislative body to which the copyright Part of the 1988 Act extends. By section 157(1), the 1988 Act extends to Scotland and Northern Ireland. Recent legislation creating devolved institutions in Scotland and Northern Ireland has made it necessary to provide for the application of section 165 to works made by or under the direction or control of those bodies. Accordingly, with effect from May 6, and December 2, 1999 respectively, section 165 of the 1988 Act applies to works made by or under the direction or control of the Scottish Parliament and the Northern Ireland Assembly with appropriate modifications to make the section applicable to these bodies.[91] The only significant modifications are that the first owner of Scottish parliamentary copyright is the Scottish Parliamentary Corporate Body,[92] while the first owner of Northern Irish parliamentary copyright is the Northern Ireland Assembly Commission.[93]

10–73

Works of joint authorship. In the case of works of joint authorship where one or more but not all of the authors are acting on behalf of, or under the direction or control of, one of the Houses of Parliament or of the Scottish Parliament or the Northern Ireland Assembly, section165 applies only in relation to those authors and the copyright subsisting by virtue of their contribution to the work.[94] Accordingly, in order to establish the subsistence of copyright in that part of the work contributed by a person who was not acting on behalf of or under the direction or control of one of the Houses, it will be necessary to show that the ordinary qualifying requirements are satisfied.[95] Furthermore, the term of copyright in that part of the work to which that person contributed will be the normal term.[96]

10–74

---

[87] As to which, see Ch.6.

[88] Copyright and Related Rights Regulations 1996 (SI 1996/2967), reg.16(5).

[89] A statutory instrument containing an Order in Council under this provision shall be subject to annulment in pursuance of a resolution of either House of Parliament: CDPA 1988, s.165(8).

[90] CDPA 1988, s.165(7).

[91] For the Scottish Assembly these modifications are effected by the Parliamentary Copyright (Scottish Parliament) Order 1999 (SI 1999/676), with effect from May 6, 1999: *ibid.*, para.1(1). For the Northern Irish Assembly the modifications are effected by the Parliamentary Copyright (Northern Ireland Assembly) Order 1999 (SI 1999/3146). The latter came into force on the day appointed for the commencement of Parts II and III of the Northern Ireland Act 1998, *i.e.* December 2, 1999: see the Northern Ireland Act 1998 (Appointed Day) Order 1999 (SI 1999/3208).

[92] SI 1999/676, para.2(b).

[93] SI 1999/3146, para.2(b).

[94] CDPA 1988, s.165(5). There is an apparent lacuna in this provision in that it refers only to authors acting on behalf of, or under the direction or control of the House of Commons or Lords. No provision is made in respect of works made jointly by the Houses themselves together with persons not acting on behalf of them or under their direction or control.

[95] As to which see CDPA 1988, s.153(1) and paras 3–152 *et seq.*, above.

[96] A work of joint authorship is a work where the respective contributions of the joint authors are not distinct from each other: CDPA 1988, s.10(1). Difficulties may therefore arise in identifying the respective contributions of the joint authors for the purposes of establishing the term of the copyright in the various parts of the work.

10–75   **Application of Part I of the 1988 Act to parliamentary copyright.** It is provided that with the exception of the special rules outlined above in relation to subsistence, title and term, and subject to any express exclusion elsewhere in Part I of the 1988 Act, the copyright Part of the 1988 Act is to apply to parliamentary copyright as to other copyright.[97] Accordingly, for example, the ordinary rules apply to any dealings with parliamentary copyright[98] and the Houses of Parliament, the Scottish Parliamentary Corporate Body, the Northern Ireland Assembly Commission or their assignees are entitled to the ordinary remedies for infringement.[99] It should, however, be noted that copyright is not infringed by anything done for the purposes of parliamentary proceedings or for the purposes of reporting such proceedings other than copying a published report of those proceedings.[1]

10–76   **Works made before August 1, 1989.** The only pre-commencement works to which the provisions of the 1988 Act creating parliamentary copyright apply are literary, dramatic, musical and artistic works which were created before August 1, 1989 and were unpublished on that date. Many of the published works created by or under the direction or control of the Houses of Parliament before August 1, 1989 were published by the Crown.[2] Accordingly, the copyright in these works remains vested in the Crown under the first publication rule contained in the 1956 Act.[3]

(ii) Copyright in Parliamentary Bills

10–77   **Subsistence.** Section 166 of the 1988 Act provides that copyright subsists in every Bill introduced into Parliament. In relation to public Bills, copyright subsists from the time when the text of the Bill is handed in to the House in which it is introduced.[4] In relation to private Bills, copyright subsists at the time when a copy of the Bill is first deposited in either House.[5] In relation to personal Bills, copyright subsists from the time when the Bill is given a First Reading in the House of Lords.[6] The copyright status of a Bill before it has been introduced into Parliament is not clear. The ordinary rules as to subsistence of copyright do not apply in relation to copyright under section 166.[7] However, copyright only subsists under section 166 when the Bill has been introduced into Parliament. It would seem to follow that the ordinary rules as to subsistence of copyright in literary works apply before the Bill has been introduced. Furthermore, it may be said that a Bill is not yet in any true sense a Bill until it has been introduced into Parliament. Finally, it is worth noting that although section 166(7) of the 1988 Act expressly provides that no copyright is to subsist in a Bill after it has once subsisted in accordance with section 166, there is no similar provision in relation to the position before such copyright comes into existence. If copyright subsists in Bills before they are introduced into Parliament, that copyright will almost invariably in the case of Government bills be owned by the Crown because they

---

[97] CDPA 1988, s.163(5).

[98] ss.90 to 92. See paras 5–63 *et seq.*, above.

[99] ss.96–115. See Chapters 22 and 23.

[1] s.45. See para. 9–126, above. "Parliamentary proceedings" includes proceedings of the Northern Ireland Assembly and of the Scottish Parliament: CDPA 1988, s.178.

[2] *Hansard*, HL Vol.501, col.194.

[3] Copyright Act 1956, s.39.

[4] CDPA 1988, s.166(2).

[5] s.166(3).

[6] s.166(4).

[7] s.153(2) provides that s.153(1) does not apply in relation to parliamentary copyright and contains a cross-reference to s.166. References to parliamentary copyright in Part I of the 1988 Act (except those in s.165) include references to copyright in Bills: s.166(6).

will have been drafted by officers or servants of the Crown in the course of their duties.[8] However, this will not necessarily be true of Bills drafted by or on behalf of private members or the promoters of private bills.

Ownership. The owner of the copyright in a Bill depends on the nature of the Bill itself. Thus, the copyright in a public Bill belongs in the first instance to the House in which it is introduced, but after the Bill has been carried to the second House, the copyright belongs to both Houses jointly.[9] The copyright in a private Bill belongs to both Houses jointly.[10] The copyright in a personal Bill belongs in the first instance to the House of Lords,[11] and after it has been carried to the House of Commons it belongs to both Houses jointly.[12]   **10–78**

Term. The time when copyright begins to subsist in a parliamentary Bill is discussed above.[13] So far as concerns the cessation of such copyright, the 1988 Act provides that the copyright automatically ceases on Royal Assent.[14] If the Bill does not receive Royal Assent, the copyright in it ceases on the withdrawal or rejection of the Bill at the end of the Session.[15] However, it is provided that copyright in a Bill which has been rejected in any Session by the House of Lords does not cease to subsist if, by virtue of the Parliament Acts 1911 and 1949, it remains possible for it to be presented for Royal Assent in that Session. It is further provided that no other copyright or right in the nature of copyright subsists in a Bill after parliamentary copyright has once subsisted in it.[16] However, this rule is without prejudice to the subsequent operation of section 166 in relation to a Bill which, having not passed in one session, is reintroduced in a subsequent session.[17] Accordingly, even though copyright will normally cease to subsist in a Bill which has been rejected by Parliament, such copyright will nevertheless come back into existence if the Bill is reintroduced at a later date.   **10–79**

Pre-commencement Bills. The provisions of the 1988 Act relating to parliamentary Bills have only a very limited application to Bills introduced into Parliament before the commencement of the Act on August 1, 1989. The precise extent of the application of these provisions depends on the nature of the Bill. The provisions do not apply to public Bills introduced into Parliament and published before commencement,[18] or to private Bills of which copies were deposited in either House before commencement,[19] or to personal Bills which had been given their First Reading in the House of Lords before commencement.[20] In relation to Bills to which the provisions of the 1988 Act do not apply, the normal provisions of   **10–80**

---

[8] CDPA 1988, s.163(1). Many draft Bills are created by the Law Commission, which is listed as a Crown body in HMSO's list of Crown bodies. The Law Commission claims that the material on its website is Crown copyright unless otherwise indicated. There is no contrary indication in the draft Bills annexed to its reports. It follows that the Law Commission believes that they are subject to Crown copyright.

[9] CDPA 1988, s.166(2).

[10] s.166(3).

[11] Such Bills are customarily presented in the House of Lords: 34 *Halsbury's Laws* (4th ed., reissue), "Parliament", para. 907.

[12] CDPA 1988, s.166(4).

[13] See para. 10–77, above.

[14] CDPA 1988, s.166(5)(a).

[15] s.166(5)(b).

[16] s.166(7).

[17] *ibid.*

[18] CDPA 1988, Sch.1, para.43(2)(a).

[19] Sch.1, para.43(2)(b).

[20] Sch.1, para.43(2)(c).

the 1988 Act (including its transitional provisions) will apply.[21] Accordingly, copyright may well subsist in them as literary works.

10–81 **Application of Part I of the 1988 Act to the copyright in arliamentary Bills.** It is provided that with the exception of the special rules outlined above in relation to subsistence, title and term, the copyright Part of the 1988 Act is to apply to copyright in parliamentary Bills as to other parliamentary copyright.[22] The extent to which this Part applies to Parliamentary copyright is dealt with above.[23]

10–82 **Bills of the Scottish Parliament and Northern Ireland Assembly.** Section 166A(1) of the 1988 Act[24] provides, with effect from May 6, 1999, that copyright in every bill introduced into the Scottish Parliament belongs to the Scottish Parliamentary Corporate Body. Copyright under this provision subsists from the time the text of the Bill is handed in to the Parliament for introduction until the Bill receives Royal Assent or, if it does not receive Royal Assent, until it is withdrawn or rejected or no further parliamentary proceedings may be taken in respect of it.[25] With the exception of the special rules outlined above in relation to subsistence, title and term, the copyright Part of the 1988 Act is to apply to copyright in Bills of the Scottish Parliament as to other parliamentary copyright.[26] No other copyright or right in the nature of copyright subsists in a Bill after copyright has once subsisted under section 166A. However, this is stated to be without prejudice to the subsequent operation of the section in relation to a Bill which, having not received Royal Assent, is later reintroduced into the Parliament.[27] With effect from December 2, 1999, section 166B of the 1988 Act makes almost identical provision in relation to Bills introduced into the Northern Ireland Assembly.[28] The copyright in such Bills belongs to the Northern Ireland Assembly Commission.[29]

(iii) Position of the Houses of Parliament and the Scottish and Northern Irish Assemblies

10–83 **Ownership and legal proceedings.** At the time the 1988 Act was being considered in Parliament, the precise legal personality of the Houses of Parliament was thought to be unclear. Accordingly it was considered necessary to provide each House with its own legal personality in order to permit it to hold, deal with and enforce its newly acquired copyright.[30] Thus, for the purposes of holding, dealing with and enforcing copyright, and in connection with all legal proceedings relating to copyright, each House of Parliament is to be treated as having the legal capacities of a body corporate.[31] This status is not to be affected either by a prorogation or by a dissolution.[32] By contrast, Scottish parliamentary copyright is owned by a separate entity, the Scottish Parliamentary Corporate

---

[21] Sch.1, paras 3 and 5.
[22] CDPA 1988, s.166(6).
[23] See para. 10–75, above.
[24] Introduced by para.25(6) of Sch.8 to the Scotland Act 1998 (c.46) with effect from May 6, 1999: see the Scotland Act 1998 (Commencement) Order 1998 (SI 1998/3178), para.2 and Sch.3.
[25] CDPA 1988, s.166A(2).
[26] s.166A(3).
[27] s.166A(4).
[28] Introduced by para.8(6) of Sch.13 to the Northern Ireland Act 1998 and para.2 of and Sch. to the Northern Ireland Act 1998 (Commencement No. 5) Order 1999 (SI 1999/3209).
[29] CDPA 1988, s.166B(1).
[30] *Hansard*, HL Vol.501, col.194.
[31] CDPA 1988, s.167(1).
[32] *ibid.*

Body, while Northern Irish parliamentary copyright is owned by the Northern Ireland Assembly Commission.[33]

House of Commons. The functions of the House of Commons as owner of copy- **10–84** right are to be exercised by the Speaker on behalf of the House.[34] If so authorised by the Speaker or if there is a vacancy in the office of Speaker, those functions may be discharged by the Chairman of Ways and Means or a Deputy Chairman.[35] On a dissolution of Parliament, a person who on the dissolution was Speaker of the House of Commons, Chairman of Ways and Means or a Deputy Chairman may continue to act until the corresponding appointment is made in the next session of Parliament.[36] Legal proceedings relating to copyright are to be brought by or against the House of Commons in the name of "The Speaker of the House of Commons".[37]

House of Lords. The functions of the House of Lords as owner of copyright are **10–85** to be exercised by the Clerk of the Parliaments on behalf of the House.[38] If so authorised by the Clerk of the Parliaments or, in the case of a vacancy in the office of Clerk of the Parliaments, those functions may be discharged by the Clerk Assistant or the Reading Clerk.[39] Legal proceedings relating to copyright are to be brought by or against the House of Lords in the name of "The Clerk of the Parliaments".[40]

(iv) Enforcement of parliamentary copyright

Administration. Under the terms of an agreement with the Speaker of the House **10–86** of Commons and the Clerk of the Parliaments,[41] Her Majesty's Stationery Office ("HMSO") administers a large proportion of Parliamentary material.[42] The day to day administration of this material is carried out by HMSO's Licensing Division, which reports to the Controller.[43] The material concerned includes: *Hansard*, including Official Reports of Commons Standing Committees; Bills of Parliament; the Journals of both Houses; the Lords Minute; the Commons Order Paper, Votes and Proceedings and other parts of the Vote bundle; Select Committee Reports; the Commons Public Bill List; lists relating to the progress of Statutory Instruments; lists relating to the progress of Deregulation Orders; the Weekly Information Bulletin of the House of Commons; the Sessional Information Digest; and House of Commons Library Documents.[44] Certain other material mainly intended for use within the two Houses is administered by the appropriate House

---

[33] CDPA 1988, s.166A(1) and 166B(1).
[34] CDPA 1988, s.167(3).
[35] *ibid.*
[36] *ibid.*
[37] s.167(5)(a).
[38] CDPA 1988, s.167(4).
[39] *ibid.*
[40] CDPA 1988, s.167(5)(b).
[41] On behalf of the House of Lords.
[42] *Dear Publisher letter: Reproduction of Parliamentary Copyright Material*, HMSO, ref. CO(P)48/1022 (March 9, 2001 revision), para.3.2 *www.hmso.gov.uk/copyrigth/guidance/publisher.htm*. The Government's expressed object in creating the new Parliamentary copyright was to ensure that the copyright in parliamentary papers, including *Hansard*, was controlled by the House concerned and not by HMSO. In practical terms, this object has clearly not been attained, although it is presumably open to the relevant officers to terminate their agreement with HMSO if they wish to do so.
[43] *Dear Publisher letter*, para.3.2.
[44] *Dear Publisher letter*, para.4.1.

official.[45] Finally, the rights to broadcast material which is subject to Parliamentary copyright are administered by the Supervisor of Parliamentary Broadcasting.[46]

10–87   **Policy of the Licensing Division.**[47] As is the case in relation to Crown copyright, not all Parliamentary copyright is strictly enforced.[48] Parliamentary copyright in United Kingdom Parliamentary Bills and Explanatory notes has been waived subject to conditions.[49] Some other Parliamentary copyright material may be reproduced free of charge and without prior permission while other material may be copied pursuant to standard licences which are readily available and in some cases gratuitous.[50] In other cases, the Licensing Division will normally seek a payment.[51]

10–88   **United Kingdom Parliamentary Bills and Explanatory Notes.** Following the waiver of Crown copyright in primary and secondary legislation,[52] HMSO has now waived parliamentary copyright in Bills presented to either House of Parliament and in Explanatory Notes relating to such Bills.[53] As is the case in relation to legislation, all forms of reproduction are permitted, subject, however, to conditions.[54] The conditions are slightly different from those applicable to legislation. They are as follows. First, reproduction must be from an official version, that is the text ordered to be printed by either House and bearing a House printing number or a Bill number or the text downloaded from any official source, including Parliament's website.[55] Secondly, the material must be reproduced accurately and in a manner and context which is not misleading as to its intended meaning and application.[56] Thirdly, the material must not be used in connection with advertising, endorsement or in any context which could be viewed as undignified association.[57] Fourthly, it must not be used in any circumstances which are knowingly or potentially libellous or slanderous of individuals, companies or organisations.[58] Fifthly, it must not purport to be published by authority of either House or in a form or style or using insignia or symbols which might suggest that the reproduced version has official status.[59] Sixthly, care should be taken to identify the relevant stage of a bill if an extract is reproduced.[60] Seventhly, all official publisher imprints which appear on the official version must be

---

[45] *Dear Publisher letter*, para.4.2.

[46] *Dear Publisher letter*, para.4.3.

[47] For the position under the Berne Convention and the European Commission's view, see para. 10–28, above.

[48] Nevertheless, HMSO has made clear that all parliamentary copyrights are reserved and will be exercised in appropriate cases: *Dear Publisher letter*, para.6.3.

[49] See para. 10–88, below.

[50] For the previous "General Notice" procedure, see earlier editions of this Work. Where a licence applies, it permits reproduction anywhere in the world in any language, but publishers are obliged to take reasonable steps to ensure that translations are correct: *Dear Publisher letter*, para.12.

[51] See paras 10–92 and 10–93, below.

[52] See para. 10–31, above.

[53] HMSO Guidance Note 14: Reproduction of Bills and Explanatory Notes to Bills of the United Kingdom Parliament, October 31, 2000, *www.hmso.gov.uk/copyright/guidance/gn__14.htm*.

[54] HMSO Guidance Note 14, para.9.

[55] HMSO Guidance Note 14, para.11.

[56] HMSO Guidance Note 14, para.12(a).

[57] HMSO Guidance Note 14, para.12(b).

[58] HMSO Guidance Note 14, para.12(c).

[59] HMSO Guidance Note 14, para.12(d).

[60] HMSO Guidance Note 14, para.13. Although the word used is "should", presumably this is intended to mean "shall".

removed.[61] Eighthly, in cases where reproduced versions are being made available to others, Parliamentary copyright must be acknowledged.[62] Finally, when translating text into another language, all reasonable steps should be taken to ensure that a competent translator undertakes the translation and the text is translated faithfully.[63]

Reproduction other than photocopying: general. The amount of reproduction by means other than photocopying which is permissible before a licence must be obtained depends partly on the nature of the proposed reproduction and partly on the nature of the work. However, the following general rules apply. First, any reproduction which is not intended to be in a "value-added context" requires specific prior permission from HMSO's Licensing Division.[64] Secondly, there are various rules to prevent what is considered to be improper exploitation of parliamentary copyright material. Accordingly, it is provided that such material must be reproduced accurately and in a fashion and context which is not misleading as to its intended meaning or application[65] ; that it may not be used in connection with advertising, endorsement or any form of "undignified" association[66] ; that it may not be used in circumstances which are knowingly or potentially libellous or slanderous of individuals, companies or organisations[67] ; that when reproduced it must not purport to be published by authority of Parliament or of either House or of HMSO or in a form or style which suggests it is the official version[68] ; and that it may not be reproduced for overtly political purposes.[69] Thirdly, in all cases where parliamentary copyright material is reproduced, an appropriate acknowledgement must be given.[70] What follows does not relate to broadcasting rights, which are administered separately.[71]

10–89

---

[61] HMSO Guidance Note 14, para.14. Again, the word "should" is presumably intended to mean "shall".

[62] HMSO Guidance Note 14, para.15. In most cases, the following words will be appropriate: " *The text of [this Bill] [these Explanatory Notes] and the typographical arrangement of the text are Parliamentary Copyright*": *ibid.*

[63] HMSO Guidance Note 14, para.16. Again, "should" is presumably intended to mean "shall". Para.16 goes on to state that the acknowledgment of Parliamentary Copyright "given at paragraph 14" (which is presumably a reference to para.15) should be given both in English and in the language into which the text has been translated.

[64] *Dear Publisher letter*, Annex A, General Condition (iii), Annex B, General Condition (ii). For these purposes, the term "value-added context" does not mean the same as the term "value-added material" in the context of Crown copyright (as to which, see para. 10–44, above). For these purposes it means "where the original text has had value added to it by compilation with other related text, analysis, commentary, annotation, indexing or cross-referencing (this may be taken as covering both commercially published and in-house databases)": *ibid.*, para.5.3.

[65] *Dear Publisher letter*, para.6.1(a). It is specifically provided that *Hansard* must be reproduced verbatim and must not be adapted or modified in any way whatsoever: *ibid.*, para.8. Moreover, publishers are obliged to take all reasonable steps to ensure that translations are undertaken by a competent translator and that the text is translated faithfully: *ibid.*, para.12.

[66] *Dear Publisher letter*, para.6.1(b).

[67] *Dear Publisher letter*, para.6.1(c).

[68] *Dear Publisher letter*, para.6.1(d). There is express prohibition on the reproduction of the Royal Arms and of official printing and publishing imprints, except where such use is incidental: *ibid.*, para.9. Para.9 gives as an example of use which is considered to be incidental, use as part of the front cover of a title reproduced in its entirety. There is also a prohibition on the use of parliamentary insignia and symbols, in particular the Parliamentary portcullis, on any publication, packaging or promotional material without specific prior approval: *ibid.*

[69] *Dear Publisher letter*, para.6.1(e).

[70] *Dear Publisher letter*, para.6.2. The acknowledgment will generally be as follows: "Parliamentary copyright material from [*insert categories of material if appropriate*] is reproduced with the permission of the Controller of Her Majesty's Stationery Office on behalf of Parliament": *ibid.*, para.10.

[71] Applications to broadcast Parliamentary copyright material must be made to the Supervisor of Parliamentary Broadcasting: *Dear Publisher letter*, Annex A, General Condition (vi); Annex B, General Condition (v).

10–90   **Reproduction other than photocopying: works which may be freely reproduced.** Subject to the general restrictions set out in the previous paragraph, two categories of Parliamentary copyright works may be freely reproduced without prior permission in any medium, including on the Internet, namely Standing Orders of the House of Commons[72] ; and House of Lords judgments.[73]

10–91   **Reproduction other than photocopying: Select Committee reports.** The position in relation to Select Committee Reports depends first on whether the reproduction is in a print or non-print medium, secondly on the extent of the reproduction, and thirdly on whether the report was made by a Select Committee of the House of Commons or the House of Lords. Up to 10 per cent of the text of any House of Commons or House of Lords Select Committee report may be freely reproduced in any one publication[74] in a print medium without prior permission.[75] Any other reproduction of such a report in a print medium requires a licence. In relation to House of Commons Select Committee reports, a fee or royalty will normally be payable for a licence for commercial reproduction.[76] In relation to House of Lords Select Committee reports a fee or royalty will not normally be payable.[77] Any reproduction of part or the whole of a Select Committee report of either House in a non-print medium requires a prior licence.[78] In relation to a report of a House of Commons Select Committee, a fee or royalty may be payable.[79] In relation to a report of a House of Lords Select Committee, a fee or royalty will not normally be payable.[80]

10–92   **Reproduction other than photocopying: other categories of material.** So far as concerns all other categories of parliamentary copyright material administered by HMSO, including *Hansard*,[81] the position again depends on the medium of the reproduction, the extent of the reproduction, and on whether the material emanates from the House of Commons or the House of Lords. Up to 30 per cent, or 2,500 words, whichever is the greater, of the text of any single publication, may be freely reproduced in any print medium in any one publication[82] without prior permission.[83] Any other reproduction in this manner of material in these categories in a print medium requires a licence.[84] In relation to House of Commons material, a fee or royalty will normally be payable for a licence for commercial reproduction.[85] In relation to House of Lords material a fee or royalty

---

[72] *Dear Publisher letter*, Annex A, item 4.

[73] *Dear Publisher letter*, Annex B, item 4.

[74] For these purposes, separate issues of a journal each constitute separate publications: *Dear Publisher letter*, Annex A, General Condition (v); Annex B, General Condition (iv).

[75] *Dear Publisher letter*, Annex A, item 3; Annex B, item 3.

[76] *Dear Publisher letter*, Annex A, item 3; Annex B, item 3. However, fees or royalties will normally be reduced or waived when reproduction takes place for non-commercial, technical or scientific purposes, including, *inter alia*, works of scholarship and articles in academic journals: *ibid.*, General Condition (ii).

[77] *Dear Publisher letter*, Annex B, item 3.

[78] *Dear Publisher letter*, Annex A, item 3; Annex B, item 3.

[79] *Dear Publisher letter*, Annex A, item 3. However, fees or royalties will normally be reduced or waived when reproduction is for non-commercial, technical or scientific purposes: *ibid.*, General Condition (ii).

[80] *Dear Publisher letter*, Annex B, item 3.

[81] This category also includes the following works: House of Commons Journals; Commons Order Papers, Votes and Proceedings and the Vote Bundle; Commons Public Bill Lists; Lists relating to the progress of Statutory Instruments; Lists relating to the progress of Deregulation Orders; the House of Lords Journal; and the Lords Minute: *Dear Publisher letter*, Annex A, item 1 and Annex B, item 1.

[82] For these purposes, separate issues of a journal each constitute separate publications: *Dear Publisher letter*, Annex A, General Condition (v), Annex B, General Condition (iv).

[83] *Dear Publisher letter*, Annex A, item 1; Annex B, item 1.

[84] *Dear Publisher letter*, Annex A, item 1; Annex B, item 1.

[85] *Dear Publisher letter*, Annex A, item 1. However, fees or royalties will normally be reduced or

will not normally be payable.[86] Extracts of House of Commons or House of Lords material which do not exceed 2,500 words may be reproduced in a non-print medium other than on an Open Network System (including the Internet) without a prior licence.[87] So far as reproduction of such extracts on Open Network Systems including the internet is concerned, a licence is required in respect of material from either House.[88] In respect of House of Commons material, a fee or royalty may be payable.[89] In respect of House of Lords material, a fee or royalty will not normally be payable.[90] All other reproduction of House of Commons or House of Lords material in a non-print medium requires a licence.[91] In relation to House of Commons material, a fee or royalty will normally be payable.[92] In relation to House of Lords material, a fee or royalty will not normally be payable.[93]

Photocopying of parliamentary copyright material. Photocopying of a large **10–93** number of categories of material is permitted free of charge provided it is within specified limits and that certain conditions are complied with.[94] The categories of material concerned are as follows: *Hansard*; House Business Papers including Journals of both Houses, Lords Minutes, the Vote Bundle, Commons Order-Books, the Commons Public Bills Lists and Statutory Instruments Lists, the Weekly Information Bulletin and the Sessional Information Digest; and other parliamentary Papers, including Command Papers and Reports of Select Committees of both Houses.[95] Photocopying of the text from any single title or document in its entirety is permitted provided that no more than one photocopy is made for any one individual and copies are not distributed to other individuals or organisations.[96] The making of unlimited multiple copies of extracts from any title or document is permitted provided that the extracts from any single work do not exceed 30 per cent or one chapter or equivalent, whichever is the greater.[97] There are various limitations on the purposes for which reproduction may occur. Reproduction is not allowed in connection with advertising or endorsement, nor in circumstances which in the view of HMSO's Licensing Division may be defamatory.[98] Parliamentary copyright material must not be reproduced in a way which gives rise to "unfair or misleading selection" or "undignified association".[99]

---

waived when reproduction is for non-commercial, technical or scientific purposes: *ibid.*, General Condition (ii).

[86] *Dear Publisher letter*, Annex B, item 1.

[87] *Dear Publisher letter*, Annex A, item 1; Annex B, item 1.

[88] *Dear Publisher letter*, Annex A, item 1; Annex B, item 1.

[89] *Dear Publisher letter*, Annex A, item 1. However, fees or royalties will normally be reduced or waived when reproduction is for non-commercial, technical or scientific purposes: *ibid.*, General Condition (ii).

[90] *Dear Publisher letter*, Annex B, item 1.

[91] *Dear Publisher letter*, Annex A, item 1; Annex B, item 1.

[92] *Dear Publisher letter*, Annex A, item 1. However, fees or royalties will normally be reduced or waived when reproduction takes place for non-commercial, technical and scientific purposes: *ibid.*, General Condition (ii).

[93] *Dear Publisher letter*, Annex B, item 1.

[94] See generally *Dear Librarian letter: Photocopying of Crown and Parliamentary Material*, March 9, 2001 revision, *www.hmso.gov.uk/copyright/guidance/librarian.htm*.

[95] *Dear Librarian letter*, para.4.1.

[96] *Dear Librarian letter*, para.4.2(a). Exceptionally, schools and places of higher education are permitted to provide a single copy to each student.

[97] *Dear Librarian letter*, para.4.2(b).

[98] *Dear Librarian letter*, para.4.3.

[99] *Dear Librarian letter*, para.4.3.

C. MORAL RIGHTS

10–94   **Limited scope in relation to parliamentary copyright works**. The rights created by the 1988 Act to be identified as author or director[1] and to object to derogatory treatment of a work[2] have only limited scope in relation to works in which
parliamentary copyright subsists. The right to be identified as author or director
does not apply in relation to a work in which parliamentary copyright subsists
unless the author or director has been identified as such in or on published copies
of the work.[3] It follows that the Houses of Parliament[4] will effectively be able to
determine whether this right can ever be asserted in relation to a work in which
parliamentary copyright subsists. The right to object to derogatory treatment of a
work in which parliamentary copyright subsists does not apply to anything done
in relation to such a work by or with the authority of the copyright owner unless
the author or director is identified at the time of the relevant act or has previously
been identified in or on published copies of the work.[5] Even where the right applies, it is not infringed if there is a sufficient disclaimer.[6]

3. THE RIGHTS OF INTERNATIONAL ORGANISATIONS

10–95   **Section 168 of the 1988 Act**. This section makes special provision in respect of
literary, dramatic, musical or artistic works which have been made by officers or
employees of certain international organisations or which have been published
by such organisations and which do not qualify for copyright protection under
sections 154 or 155 of the Act. The section is considered in paragraph
3–217, above.

---

[1] CDPA 1988, s.77. See paras 11–09 *et seq.*, below.

[2] s.80. See paras 11–34 *et seq.*, below.

[3] , s.79(7)(a). For the meaning of "publication" and related expressions, see s.175(1) and paras
3–172 *et seq.*, above.

[4] Or their assignees: parliamentary copyright continues to subsist in a work the copyright in which
has been assigned by the Houses of Parliament: CDPA 1988, s.165(2).

[5] CDPA 1988, s.82(2). For the meaning of "publication" and related expressions, see *ibid.*, s.175(1)
and paras 3–172 *et seq.*, above.

[6] CDPA 1988, s.82(2). For what may be a sufficient disclaimer, see *ibid.*, s.178, and para. 11–50,
below.

PART II

MORAL RIGHTS

MORAL RIGHTS

1. INTRODUCTION

Droit moral. The term "moral rights", introduced into English law by Chapter **11–01**
IV of the 1988 Act, has its origins in the *"droit moral"* enjoyed by authors in
various countries, notably France, Germany and Italy.[1] It refers collectively to a
number of rights which are concerned more with an author's relationship with his

---

[1] For a brief introduction to the development of the rights in these countries, see A. Dietz, *Copyright Law in the European Community* (Sijthoff & Noordhoff, 1978), p.66 *et seq.*; (for France) H. Desbois, "The Moral Right", XIX RIDA 121 (1958); (for Italy) A. Pojaghi, *Aperçu sur la protection du droit moral en Italie* (Congress of Antwerp, ALAI 1993), pp.160 *et seq.*; Ricketson, *The Berne Convention for the Protection of Literary and Artistic Works: 1886–1986* (Kluwer, 1987), pp.456 *et seq.*

work than the commercial value of them.[2] An author's moral rights in his work, which in general are regarded as inalienable, are therefore to be distinguished from his economic rights in his work, which in general are alienable.

11–02 **International background.** Historically, the protection given to the moral rights of authors in different countries, particularly those of continental Europe, varied widely. An attempt to bring some cohesion to this situation in the international field was first made in the revisions to the Berne Convention made by the Rome Act of 1928.[3] This required recognition of two rights of authors, first, the right, even after the transfer of copyright, to claim authorship of a work (the "paternity right") and, second, the right to object to any distortion, mutilation or other modification of his work which would be prejudicial to his honour or reputation (the "integrity right").[4] It was left to Contracting States to determine the way in which such protection was afforded. These provisions of the Berne Convention relating to moral rights were extended by the Brussels and Stockholm Acts of 1948 and 1967 respectively, and are now to be found in Article 6 *bis* of the Paris Act of 1971.[5] Other moral rights, conferred in various jurisdictions, such as the right of an author to choose whether his work should be published or not, the right to modify or withdraw a work (subject to compensation), the right to prevent excessive criticism, and a right to prevent false attribution of authorship, have never found an agreed place internationally.

11–03 **Moral rights in the United Kingdom.** The manner of implementation of the moral rights provisions of the Berne Convention has, as noted above, always been left to Contracting States. Before the introduction of an express code of moral rights by the 1988 Act, a patchwork of mostly common law rights, such as passing off, defamation and slander of goods,[6] as partly supplemented by statute,[7] was considered sufficient to give effect to Article 6*bis* in the United Kingdom. Thus when moral rights were first prescribed by the Rome Act, the United Kingdom made no changes to its law and, for example, the Gregory Committee of 1952 felt able to conclude that the Convention as then contained in the Brussels Act imposed no obligations on the United Kingdom to introduce any legislation to alter the law.[8] It became increasingly clear, however, that the law of the United Kingdom did not give effect to the Convention and the Whitford Committee of 1977[9] recommended that proper protection should be introduced. A statutory right of paternity and integrity was therefore introduced by the 1988 Act. At the same time, alterations were made to the existing right of a person to prevent a work being falsely attributed to him as author and a new right of privacy introduced in relation to photographs commissioned for private and domestic purposes, all under the rubric of "moral rights".

---

[2] Ricketson, *The Berne Convention for the Protection of Literary and Artistic Works: 1886–1986* (Kluwer, 1987), p.456, notes that the adjective "moral" has no precise English equivalent in this context, although the words "spiritual", "non-economic" and "personal" convey something of the same meaning.

[3] As to International Copyright and the Berne Convention, see Chs 24 and 25, below.

[4] Art.6 *bis* of the Rome Act.

[5] Although parties to the TRIPS agreement must comply with Arts 1–21 of the Berne Convention, there is an express exception in the case of the rights conferred by Art.6 *bis*. See TRIPS, Art.9.1.

[6] See, *e.g.* Dworkin, *The Moral Right of the Author, Moral Rights and the Common Law Countries* (Congress of Antwerp, ALAI 1993), p.81.

[7] Latterly, Copyright Act 1956, s.43, which dealt mainly with the separate right of false attribution of authorship, but which also granted an author rights where an altered version of an artistic work was dealt with as being his unaltered work. The section derived from the Fine Arts Copyright Act 1862, s.7.

[8] Report of the Copyright Committee, Cmnd.8662, paras 219–226. The same view can be found in the Preface to the 7th ed. (1936) of this work.

[9] Cmnd.6732, paras 50–57, 80(vi).

The rights. The moral rights conferred by the 1988 Act are as follows: **11–04**

- (1) the right of an author of a copyright literary, dramatic, musical or artistic work, or director of a film, to be identified as author or director respectively ("the paternity right");
- (2) the right of an author of such a work not to have it subjected to derogatory treatment ("the integrity right");
- (3) the right of any person not to have a work or film falsely attributed to him as author or director, respectively; and
- (4) the right of any person to privacy in respect of photographs which he commissioned for private and domestic purposes ("the privacy right").

All these rights are collectively referred to in the Act as "moral rights".[10]

Nature of rights. Some general remarks can be made about these rights: **11–05**

- (1) Although all are termed moral rights, only the first two, the paternity and integrity rights, are "authors' rights" as contemplated by the Berne Convention, whereas the other two rights are capable of being enjoyed by any person, author or not. In this context, the term "author" has the same meaning as in the context of copyright, namely the person who creates the work.[11] As will be seen, moral rights are capable of subsisting in works which were made before the commencement of the 1988 Act,[12] and although for the purposes of copyright the author of a work is to be determined in accordance with the law in force at the time when the work was made,[13] in the case of moral rights the author is to be determined in accordance with the current provisions of the 1988 Act, *i.e.* those in Part I. This means, for example, that the author of a pre-1988 Act photograph is to be taken for moral rights purposes to be the person who created it and not, as under the 1956 Act, the person who owned the material on which the photograph was taken and thus, possibly, a company.[14] Although as a matter of United Kingdom law, the author of a film is now to be taken to be "the principal director", as well as the producer,[15] it is only "the director" who is granted any moral rights in relation to a film. There is no statutory definition of the term "the director" of a film for this purpose; it appears that where there are directors of a film who do not fall within the description of principal director, each will have moral rights, provided the film was jointly directed.[16]
- (2) The paternity, integrity and privacy rights only exist in relation to a work which is a copyright work.[17] If, therefore, copyright does not subsist in the work, for example because the qualification conditions are not met[18] or the term of copyright has expired,[19] the author has no such moral rights in respect of it. In contrast, the right of a person not to have a work attributed to him as author applies, whatever the copyright status of the work,

---

[10] See, *e.g.* the heading of Ch.IV of the 1988 Act and s.94.

[11] CDPA 1988, ss.179, 9(1). As to authorship, see Ch.4. Note that the presumptions as to authorship contained in ss.104 and 105 can be applied.

[12] On August 1, 1989.

[13] CDPA 1988, Sch.1, para.10. See paras 4–07 *et seq.*, above.

[14] See, generally, as to such works, para. 4–34, above.

[15] CDPA 1988, s.9(2)(ab). See para. 4–58, above.

[16] See 11–78, below, as to a jointly directed film.

[17] See the wording of CDPA 1988, ss.77(1), 80(1) and 85(1) respectively. A copyright work is a work in which copyright subsists. See ss.178, 1(2).

[18] See Ch.3, above.

[19] See CDPA 1988, s.86(1). As to the term of copyright, see Ch.6, above.

provided that it at least qualifies as a "work".[20] So, where the work in question is alleged to be a literary work, it must satisfy the requirement that it affords sufficient information, instruction or literary enjoyment.[21]

(3) Although enjoyment of the paternity, integrity and privacy rights depends upon copyright subsisting in the work, it is important to appreciate that the person who is entitled to exercise these moral rights will often not be the same person as the owner of the copyright. Care must therefore always be taken that exploitation of the work by a copyright owner or his licensees does not infringe any of these moral rights. The rights are in some respects linked, but in others are quite distinct.

(4) The paternity and privacy rights apply in relation to any substantial part of the work as well as in relation to the whole of the work. The meaning of "substantial part" in this context is discussed below. In contrast, the integrity right and the right to prevent false attribution apply in relation to the whole or *any* part of a work.

(5) Moral rights are personal in nature and are not property rights. They are not, therefore, assignable, in contrast to copyright.[22] They can, however be, waived and are only infringed if there is no consent to the act in question.[23] Special provision is made as to exercise of the rights after the death of the person initially entitled to them.[24]

(6) Subject to exceptions, the paternity and integrity rights apply to works in existence before the commencement of the 1988 Act,[25] the most important exception being the case of works whose author had died before this date. The privacy right does not apply to photographs taken or films made before this date.

11–06 **The Information Society Directive.** This Directive[26] was not concerned with the moral rights of authors and so did not require any changes to be made to the treatment of moral rights by the 1988 Act. However, other changes to the Act which were made on implementation of the Directive, in particular those relating to broadcasts, cable programme services and on-demand transmissions, have meant that there has been some amendment to the moral rights provisions to bring them into line.

11–07 **EC Commission proposals.** The Commission's current view is that there is no need to harmonise moral rights protection in the Community. In its opinion, the international legal framework in practice provides an adequate level playing field for the markets to operate.[27]

11–08 **WIPO Performances and Phonograms Treaty.** By wording which bears similarities to Article 6 *bis* of the Berne Convention, the 1996 WIPO Performances and Phonograms Treaty[28] requires that independently of a performer's economic rights, and even after transfer of those rights, a performer should, as

---

[20] See the wording of CDPA 1988, s.84(1). As to the various types of "work", see Ch.3, above.
[21] *Noah v Shuba* [1991] F.S.R. 14 at 33, applying *Exxon Corporation v Exxon Insurance Consultants International Ltd* [1982] Ch. 119.
[22] CDPA 1988, s.94.
[23] See s.87(1).
[24] See para. 11–66, below.
[25] On August 1, 1989.
[26] Directive 2001/29.
[27] Document SEC(2004) 995 of July 17, 2004, Commission Staff Working Paper on the review of the EC legal framework in the field of copyright and related rights, para.3.5. See, further, para. 25–101, below.
[28] See Vol.2 at F14.

regards his live, "aural" performances or performances fixed in phonograms (a) have the right to be identified as the performer, except where omission is dictated by the manner of the use of the performance, and (b) to object to any distortion, mutilation or modification of this performance that would be prejudicial to his reputation.[29] The law of the United Kingdom will require change to implement these provisions.

2. THE RIGHT TO BE IDENTIFIED AS AUTHOR OR DIRECTOR

A. INTRODUCTION

The right. In general, the author of a copyright literary, dramatic, musical or artistic work has the right to be identified as the author of the work.[30] A similar right to be identified as the director of a copyright film work is conferred on the director.[31] As has been seen, the right is derived from Article 6 *bis* of the Berne Convention, which provides that independently of his "economic" rights,[32] and even after any transfer of those rights, an author "shall have the right to claim authorship" of his work.[33] The right belongs to the person who is the author or director of the work in the copyright sense, not the person who, not being such an author, nevertheless contributed ideas, etc. which find expression in the work.[34] The meaning of author in this context has already been discussed.[35] As already noted, the paternity right is only capable of subsisting if at the same time copyright subsists in the work. The right is infringed by the doing of any of the various acts specified in the relevant provisions[36] without the consent of the person entitled to the right.[37] This general statement is, however, subject to three important qualifications:

(1) the circumstances in which the right arises vary according to the type of copyright work;

(2) the right is not infringed unless it has been asserted in a specified manner; and

(3) the right is subject to numerous exceptions.

11–09

Transitional. The right applies to works made before commencement of the Act (August 1, 1989), except in two cases: first, the case of a film made before this date; secondly, in relation to the other kinds of copyright work, where the author had died before this date.[38] There are also further transitional provisions limiting the paternity right in respect of works made before commencement, which are considered later.

11–10

---

[29] See Directive 2001/29, Art.5(1).
[30] CDPA 1988, s.77(1).
[31] s.77(1).
[32] *i.e.* any copyright vested in him.
[33] Before the implementation of this right by the 1988 Act, the only effective means by which an author could acquire such a right was by contract (see, *e.g. Tolnay v Criterion Film Productions Ltd* [1936] 2 All E.R. 1625) or, where he was also the copyright owner, by making any exploitation of the work conditional upon him being identified (see, *e.g. Miller v Cecil Film Ltd* [1937] 2 All E.R. 464). Note also that since the passing of the 1956 Act, certain acts of fair dealing have only escaped being an infringement if there is a sufficient acknowledgement of the author. See paras 9–35 *et seq.*, above.
[34] *Anya v Wu* [2004] EWHC 386 (Ch).
[35] See para. 11–05, above.
[36] CDPA 1988, ss.77(2)–(8).
[37] CDPA 1988, s.87(1).
[38] CDPA 1988, Sch.1, para.23(2).

B. THE CIRCUMSTANCES IN WHICH THE RIGHT EXISTS

11–11   As with the other forms of moral rights, the paternity right is a passive right in the sense that it is only capable of being exercised where some form of exploitation of the work takes place, the particular form varying according to the type of copyright work. As will be seen, where the other conditions for infringement are satisfied, it is the person who carries out any of these acts of exploitation who infringes the right.

(i) Literary and dramatic works

11–12   The meaning of these expressions is considered elsewhere.[39] In the present context, however, words intended to be sung or spoken with music are treated in the same way as a musical work, not as a literary work.[40] The author of works of these types has the right to be identified whenever any of the following events occur[41]:

(1) *Commercial publication of the work.* "Commercial publication" is defined as the issue of copies of the work to the public "at a time when copies made in advance of the receipt of orders are generally available to the public."[42] The expression "issue to the public" of copies is itself further defined by a complex set of provisions[43] which are considered in detail elsewhere[44] but it broadly means putting into circulation copies which were not previously in circulation. It therefore refers to the first issue of any particular copy of a work. In the case of literary and dramatic works, "copy" refers to any reproduction of the work in material form,[45] which includes the issue of copies not only in the form of books, newspapers and so on but also in the form of sound recordings, films, etc.[46] Overall, therefore, the expression "commercial publication" contemplates that copies be generally available to the public, whether by way of sale or otherwise, for example in retail outlets, and not simply in response to orders.[47] Commercial publication in this context also includes the making of the work available to the public by means of an electronic retrieval system,[48] but it does not include the performance of the work, nor the communication to the public of the work (otherwise than for the purposes

---

[39] For the meaning of "literary work", see CDPA 1988, s.3(1) and paras 3–08 *et seq.*, above. For the meaning of "dramatic work", see paras 3–30 *et seq.*, above.
[40] CDPA 1988, s.77(2), (3). No doubt one of the reasons for this is because there is no right to be identified as the author of a musical work where it is, *e.g.* performed in public or broadcast (see below). Given this approach, it would not make sense to have to identify the author of any accompanying lyrics.
[41] s.77(2).
[42] s.175(2)(a).
[43] s.18(2), (3) & (4).
[44] See paras 7–76 *et seq.*, above. Although the definition of "the issue of copies to the public" is found in the provisions relating to infringement of copyright, it is defined for the purposes of "this Part", *i.e.* Pt I of the 1988 Act, which includes the moral rights provisions which are contained in Ch.IV of Pt I. See also s.178.
[45] CDPA 1988, s.17(2), which also applies in the case of musical and artistic works. This definition applies to the moral right provisions as well as those relating to copyright. See ss.179, 17(1).
[46] For a detailed discussion, see paras 7–31 *et seq.*, above.
[47] The reason for this distinction is probably that under Art.3(3) of the Berne Convention, "published works" means works published such that the availability of copies has been sufficient to satisfy the reasonable requirements of the public, having regard to the nature of the work. Availability in response to orders may not satisfy such requirements. See the *WIPO Guide to the Berne Convention (1978).*
[48] CDPA 1988, s.175(2)(b).

of an electronic retrieval system).[49] It should be noted that the paternity right is not exercisable in relation to the rental of copies of the work to the public.[50]

(2) *Performance of the work in public.* Performance in this context has the same meaning as in relation to copyright[51] and is considered in detail in that context.[52] In general it includes any mode of visual or acoustic presentation, including presentation by means of a sound recording, film or broadcast of the work.[53] It also includes delivery in the case of lectures, addresses, speeches and sermons.[54]

(3) *Broadcast of the work.* Again, this expression has the same meaning as in relation to copyright.[55] It means an electronic transmission of visual images, sounds or other information which (a) is transmitted for simultaneous reception by members of the public and is capable of being lawfully received by them, or (b) is transmitted at a time determined solely by the person making the transmission for presentation to members of the public.[56]Excepted from this definition, however, is any internet transmission unless it is (a) a transmission taking place simultaneously on the internet and by other means, (b) a concurrent transmission of a live event, or (c) a transmission of recorded moving images or sounds forming part of a programme service offered by the person responsible for making the transmission, being a service in which programmes are transmitted at scheduled times determined by that person.[57]

(4) *Inclusion of the work in films and sound recordings issued to public.* The meaning of the expression "issued to the public" has been briefly considered above and in more detail elsewhere.[58] There appears to be an overlap between this category of act and category (1) above, since, as noted there, the meaning of "copy" includes a reproduction of a work in the form of a film or sound recording. Often a work which is included in a film or sound recording and which has been issued to the public will have been commercially published in the sense considered above, but the present category of act is wider in that there is no limiting condition that "copies made in advance of orders be generally available to the public". Again, it should be noted that the paternity right is not exercisable in relation to the rental of copies of the work to the public.[59]

(5) *The doing of any of the above acts in relation to an adaptation of the work.* Adaptation in the context of a literary or dramatic work means (a) a translation of the work, (b) a version of a dramatic work in which it is converted into a non-dramatic work or, in the case of a non-dramatic work, in which it is converted into a dramatic work, or (c) a version of the work in which the story or action is conveyed wholly or mainly by means of pictures in a form suitable for reproduction in a book, or in a newspaper,

---

[49] s.175(4)(a). As to such acts, see however, the following paragraphs.
[50] *i.e.* by the doing of any of the acts falling within s.18A.
[51] Again, "performance" is defined in s.19 for the purposes of Pt I of the 1988 Act.
[52] See paras 7–92 *et seq.*, above.
[53] CDPA 1988, s.19(2)(b).
[54] s.19(2)(a).
[55] See ss.178, 6(1).
[56] s.6(1). For a full discussion of the meaning of the expression, see para. 3–91, above.
[57] s.6(1A).
[58] See paras 7–76 *et seq.*, above.
[59] *i.e.* by the doing of any of the acts falling within CDPA 1988, s.18A.

magazine or similar periodical.[60] In any of these cases, the author of the original work has the right to be identified as the author of that work.[61] If the adaptation is a new copyright work, as it often will be, the author of the adaptation may have a separate right to be identified as its author. The manner in which an author must be identified is considered generally below, but where the author of each work is entitled to be identified, care must be taken to distinguish between the two works and their two authors.

(ii) Musical works

11–13   The circumstances in which the author of a musical work, or of a literary work consisting of words intended to be sung or spoken with music, has a right of paternity are more restricted.[62] The right is limited to the following cases in which the work is exploited:

(1) *The commercial publication of the work.*[63] This type of exploitation will include the issue of copies not only in the form of sheet music or lyrics in book form but also in the form of sound recordings or film soundtracks.

(2) *The issue to the public of copies of the work in the form of sound recordings.* Again, there appears to be a potential overlap between this category and category (1) above. Although a film whose soundtrack contains a reproduction of the work is a "copy" of the work, the soundtrack is now to be treated as part of the film and not a sound recording,[64] and falls within category (4), below.

(3) *The showing in public of a film whose soundtrack includes the work.* The theatrical exhibition of a film whose soundtrack includes the author's music or lyrics is therefore an occasion for the exercise of the paternity right. Where such exhibition occurs by means, for example, of the public showing of a television broadcast of the film, it is not the broadcaster who "shows" the film but the person who is responsible for allowing the public to see the film.[65]

(4) *The issue to the public of copies of a film of which the soundtrack includes the work.* Again, there appears to be an overlap between this category and category (1) above. The common occasion when this category of act will take place is when video cassettes or DVDs are issued to the public.

(5) *The doing of any of the above acts in relation to an adaptation of the work.* The right in such an event is to be identified as the author of the work from which the adaptation was made. An adaptation in the context of a musical work means an arrangement or transcription of the work. The right is therefore to be identified as the author of the original work. Again, the author of the arrangement or transcription, where it is a separate copyright work, may have a separate right to be identified as the author of that work.

There is therefore no right to be identified as the author of a musical work where the work is performed in public (other than by the public showing of a film which includes it), broadcast, or on the rental or lending of copies of the work.

---

[60] CDPA 1988, s.21(3)(a).

[61] CDPA 1988, s.77(2) (assuming, of course, that the other conditions for the exercise of the right are satisfied).

[62] CDPA 1988, s.77(3).

[63] See para. 7–98, above for the meaning of this expression.

[64] See s.5B(2).

[65] In relation to infringement of copyright by showing a work in public, this is made clear by s.19(4). No equivalent provision applies in relation to moral rights but it is suggested that this is the correct position.

The reason for this is that it was thought unrealistic for broadcasters in particular to have to credit every songwriter when any piece of music was used.[66]

(iii) Artistic works

The author of an artistic work has the right to be identified whenever the work is published commercially, or exhibited in public, or a visual image of it is communicated to the public.[67] The right also arises whenever a film including a visual image of the artistic work is shown in public or copies of such a film are issued to the public.[68] The paternity right therefore differs from copyright in an important respect: the owner of the copyright in an artistic work has no control over the public exhibition of the original representation of the work or a non-infringing copy of it.[69]   **11–14**

Works of architecture, sculpture and artistic craftsmanship. There are further, special provisions relating to these particular classes of artistic work. In the case of a work of architecture in the form of a building[70] or a model for a building, or a sculpture[71] or a work of artistic craftsmanship,[72] the author has the right to be identified whenever copies of a graphic work[73] representing it, or a photograph of it, are issued to the public.[74] Once again, the issue of such copies will often also amount to commercial publication of the work. The author of a work of architecture in the form of a building also has the right to be identified on the building as constructed.[75] Where more than one building is constructed to the design (for example, on a housing estate), the right is to be identified on the first building to be constructed.[76]   **11–15**

(iv) Films

The director of a film[77] has the right to be identified whenever the film is shown in public, or is communicated to the public or copies of the film are issued to the public.[78]   **11–16**

C. THE MODE OF IDENTIFICATION

The mode of identification which is required also varies according to the character of the work and the manner of its exploitation: **11–17**

    (1) In the case of commercial exploitation of a work or the issue to the public of copies of a film or sound recording, the author or director, as the case

---

[66] See *Hansard*, HL Vol.493, col.1327.

[67] CDPA 1988, s.77(4)(a). For the meaning of communication to the public, see para. 7–98, above.

[68] s.77(4)(b). Again, the issue to the public of copies of a film which include the work will often also amount to the commercial publication of the work.

[69] It is an infringement of copyright to exhibit an infringing *copy* of an artistic work in public in the course of a business, knowing or having reason to believe it to be so. See s.23.

[70] A building includes any fixed structure, and a part of a building or fixed structure. See CDPA 1988, s.4(2).

[71] A "sculpture" includes a cast or model made for purposes of sculpture. See s.4(2).

[72] As to works of artistic craftsmanship, see paras 3–65 *et seq.*, above.

[73] A "graphic work" includes any painting, drawing, diagram, map, chart or plan, and any engraving, etching, lithograph, woodcut or similar work. See CDPA 1988, s.4(2).

[74] CDPA 1988, s.77(4)(c).

[75] See further at para. 11–17(2), below, as to the way in which the identification must be made.

[76] CDPA 1988, s.77(5).

[77] A "film" means a recording on any medium from which a moving image may by any means be produced. See CDPA 1988, s.5B and para. 3–80, above.

[78] CDPA 1988, s.77(6).

may be, must be identified in or on each copy.[79] The identification must be clear and reasonably prominent,[80] such that it is likely to come to the attention of a person acquiring the copy.[81] Identification in very small print or in a position which will not be apparent will thus not suffice. It would seem that the identification needs be outwardly apparent, for example to a prospective purchaser inspecting goods which are shrink-wrapped, since the identification must be such as to be likely to come to the attention of a person *acquiring* a copy. If identification "in or on" each copy is not appropriate, identification must be in some other manner which is likely to bring the identity of the author or director to the notice of a person acquiring a copy.[82] If, however, it is correct that the identification must be reasonably apparent before any purchase, it is hard to envisage a case where such identification could be otherwise in or on a copy.

(2) In the case of identification on a building, the author has the right to be identified by appropriate means visible to persons entering or approaching the building.[83] This is clearly satisfied by the common practice of displaying the architect's name in the stonework near the entrance to the building.

(3) In any other case that is public exhibition or performance, the communication to the public or showing of a film in public, the right is to be identified in a manner likely to bring the identity of the author or director to the attention of a person seeing or hearing the performance, exhibition, showing, or communication in question, as the case may be.[84] Thus, for example, in the case of a film which reproduces an author's literary work, the identification will usually take the form of a screen credit along with others involved in the making of the film.[85]

D. THE FORM OF IDENTIFICATION

11–18   Any reasonable form of identification may be used.[86] This will usually be done by stating the ordinary or professional name of the author or director, as the case may be, in words sufficient to indicate that he is the author or director of the work. If, however, the author or director in asserting his right to be identified[87] specifies a pseudonym, initials or some other particular form of identification, that form must be used.[88] It may also be reasonable to employ such a form of identification if it is in fact used by the author or director, even though it has not been specified on assertion of the right. The author must, however, be identified as the author of the work and not simply named.[89] He should also be named in such a manner that it is clear to all persons who are likely to see the form of

---

[79] CDPA 1988, s.77(7)(a).

[80] See the concluding words of s.77(7).

[81] See the concluding words of s.77(7)(a), considered further, below, "... some *other* manner likely to bring his identity to the notice of a person acquiring a copy".

[82] s.77(7)(a).

[83] s.77(7)(b). Again the identification must be clear and reasonably prominent.

[84] s.77(7)(c). Once again, the identification must be clear and reasonably prominent.

[85] See para. 27–230, below.

[86] CDPA 1988, s.77(8).

[87] As to this, see below.

[88] CDPA 1988, s.77(8); *Sawkins v Hyperion Records Ltd* [2004] EWHC 1530 (Ch), para.85 (the claimant had specified "© Copyright 2002 by Lionel Sawkins").

[89] *Sawkins v Hyperion Records Ltd* [2004] EWHC 1530 (Ch), above (an acknowledgement in the form "With thanks to Dr Lionel Sawkins for his preparation of performance materials for this recording" not sufficient since it was unclear and understated what the author had done.)

identification that he is the author, and it will not be sufficient if inside knowledge is required to work out that this is in fact the case.[90]

E. ASSERTION OF THE RIGHT

An important and controversial hurdle imposed by the 1988 Act as a precondition of the exercise of the right of paternity is the requirement that the right must first be formally asserted. Thus an author need not assert the right to be identified if he does not want to, but, if he wishes to enforce the right, he must first have asserted it both in the particular manner required and in such a way as to bind the person he wishes to hold liable for infringing the right. The reason for this requirement is that it was felt that users of copyright material should know where they stood in relation to the right.[91] Not only is assertion necessary, it is also important that the assertion should be made as soon as possible as, in an action for infringement of the right, the court, in considering remedies, must take into account any delay in doing so.[92]

11–19

Mode and effect of assertion of the right. The right may be asserted generally, or in relation to any specified act or description of act.[93] It may thus, for example, be asserted so as to require the author of a literary work to be named on the publication of his work in book form but not in relation to a film which reproduces the work. It may be asserted in one of two ways: either on an assignment of copyright or by some other instrument in writing which comes to the notice of the person sought to be made liable. Special further provision is made in relation to the public exhibition of an artistic work. These are all considered below. No particular form of words is required. An "assertion", in ordinary language, is simply an insistence or positive statement of a right or claim. The form of words commonly used is: "[the author] hereby asserts his right to be identified as the author of [the work]".[94]

11–20

(i) Assignment of copyright

The first method of asserting the right is on an assignment of copyright in the work by the author or director. It is done by including in the instrument effecting the assignment a statement that the author or director asserts, in relation to that work, his right to be identified. It is not necessary that the assignment be the first assignment of the copyright, nor that the author or director be the copyright owner-assignor, nor even, apparently, that he be a party to the assignment, merely that the assignment includes such a statement. It would even seem that such a statement will be effective if it is included without the author's or director's authority or without his knowledge but where he later wishes to rely on it. An assertion made in this manner is binding on the assignee[95]and on anyone claiming through the assignee, whether or not he has notice of the assertion.[96] It is therefore the most effective way of asserting the right, and an author or director who wishes to be as sure as possible of being identified should seek to have such an assertion

11–21

---

[90] *Sawkins v Hyperion Records Ltd* [2004] EWHC 1530 (Ch).

[91] It was considered that the requirement of assertion was not inconsistent with Art.6 *bis* of the Berne Convention, which only required that an author have the right to *claim* authorship. See *Hansard*, HL Vol.491, col.352.

[92] CDPA 1988, s.78(5).

[93] CDPA 1988, s.78(2).

[94] For a precedent, see Vol.2 at J1.v.

[95] CDPA 1988, s.78(4)(a).

[96] s.78(4)(a).

included in the first assignment of the copyright as a matter of course.[97] The possibility of this method of assertion also means that a purchaser of copyright who is concerned by the possible exercise of this right must investigate the entire chain of title if he wishes to be sure of his position.[98] As discussed elsewhere,[99] an assignment of copyright is not effective unless it is in writing signed by or on behalf of the assignor.[1] It may be limited so as to apply to particular acts or part of the copyright term.[2] Where the assertion is included in a partial assignment of copyright, the assertion will be effective in relation to the exercise of the rights assigned, but not other rights.[3]

(ii) Instrument in writing

11–22   An author or director may of course have had no opportunity for stipulating an assertion of his right in an assignment of copyright[4] or may not have taken the opportunity to do so.[5] In such a case, or for whatever other reason, the right may also be asserted by an instrument in writing[6] signed by the author or director.[7] An "instrument", in its ordinary meaning, includes any formal or informal document.[8] The assertion must be signed by the author or director himself, and not by someone on his behalf.[9] As with an assertion made on an assignment of copyright, the assertion made by this method may be made either generally or in relation to a specified act or description of acts. Whereas an assertion made on an assignment of copyright may only be made in relation to the work or works which are the subject of the assignment, it seems that an assertion made by this method may be made in relation to a number of the author's works, even future works. The main drawback with an assertion made by this method, however, is that it is binding only on persons to whose notice the assertion is brought.[10]

This method of making an assertion and the requirement that notice of it be brought home to any person before he can be made liable can create problems both for the author or director and for any person dealing with the work. For example, where copies of a work are made on the strength of the fact that no assertion has been made but the author then asserts his right before publication or other distribution of the copies, the publisher is in a difficult position. Commercial publication of the copies which does not include an assertion will amount to an infringement in such circumstances, and the publisher, if he chooses to take the risk of publishing without identifying the author, for example where to do so would cause significant expense or inconvenience, must hope that the author will

---

[97] In practice, where the author or director is the copyright owner-assignor, it will often depend on his relative bargaining position whether the assignment contains an assertion as opposed to a waiver of the right. As to waiver, see para. 11–76, below.

[98] Such an assignee or licensee who cannot find out what the position is should therefore seek a warranty from his assignor to the effect that no assertion has been made. The usual warranties relating to title to the copyright will not deal with this issue.

[99] See para. 5–82.

[1] CDPA 1988, s.90(3).

[2] s.90(2). See para. 5–93, above.

[3] See s.78(2).

[4] For example, because he was not the copyright owner and therefore was not a party to the assignment.

[5] Also of course, he may have assigned his copyright before the provisions of the 1988 Act came into force.

[6] "Writing" includes any form of notation or code, whether by hand or otherwise, and regardless of the method by which, or the medium in or on which, it is recorded:. CDPA 1988, s.178.

[7] CDPA 1988, s.78(2)(b). For a precedent, see Vol.2 at J1.v.

[8] *R v Registrar of Companies, ex p. Central Bank of India* [1986] Q.B. 1114 at 1174, 1179.

[9] *Beckingham v Hodgens* [2003] E.C.D.R. 6 (letters and pleadings signed on the author's behalf not sufficient).

[10] CDPA 1988, s.78(4)(b).

be denied his remedies on the special ground of the author's delay in making the assertion.[11] But this may not help the publisher where the author had in fact given notice earlier but to some other person, but only found out later about the assignment or licence under which the publisher is acting. In these circumstances, the special statutory ground for denying the author his remedies appears not to apply since the word "delay" usually implies a measure of fault on the part of the author. The unsatisfactory nature of an assertion which has to be made in this way is further shown by the fact that it may have to be repeatedly made. Thus there is no provision whereby an assertion once made, for example, to the copyright owner, will bind all those claiming under him and there is obviously no guarantee that the copyright owner will bring the assertion to the attention of such persons.

It is not clear whether an assertion once made by either of these methods can be formally withdrawn. In practice, however, the paternity right, once asserted, can be waived.[12]

(iii) Public exhibition of artistic works

Special additional provisions deal with the manner of assertion in relation to the public exhibition of an artistic work.[13] These provisions do not affect the validity of an assertion made by either of the two above methods in relation to this category of act but, as already noted, the public exhibition of the original fixation or a non-infringing copy of an artistic work is not a matter which falls within the scope of the copyright in an artistic work. A person who wishes to exhibit an artistic work therefore has no cause to investigate the title to the copyright and since he does not claim "through" the assignee,[14] he will not be bound by an assertion made in an assignment of the copyright. Of course, if he in fact has notice of an assertion made either by this method or in some other instrument he will be bound.   **11–23**

In relation to public exhibition of an artistic work, the right may be asserted by the following additional methods:

(A) First, when the author or other first owner of copyright parts with possession of the original, or of a copy made by him or under his direction or control, by securing that the author is identified on the original or copy, or on a frame, mount or other thing to which it is attached. A number of points can be made about this ill-drafted provision:

    (1) It appears to assume that whoever is the first owner of the copyright, whether the author or some other person, will be the first possessor of the original fixation. While this may often be the case (as with a painting made in the artist's studio), it will not necessarily be so.[15] It is only on the parting with possession of it by such first owner that the provision applies. Where the author is not the first owner, but is the first possessor of the work,[16] an identification on the work on parting with possession is apparently of no effect.

    (2) The author or first owner may of course part with possession of the work many times before irretrievably parting with possession of it, as where the work is frequently lent. It seems that an identification

---

[11] s.78(4)(b). See para. 11–72, below.
[12] See s.87 and para. 11–76, below.
[13] CDPA 1988, s.78(3)(a).
[14] See the wording of s.78(4)(a).
[15] See para. 5–02, above, as to the distinction between the first owner of the copyright in a work and the first owner of the physical embodiment of it.
[16] As for example, a work made by an employee and kept at his home.

which is on the work on any such occasion will allow the author to exercise his paternity right.

(3) Although this means is characterised as a way in which the right to be identified as author may be asserted, it does not, in fact, require any assertion of the right, only the identification of the author, for example, by his signature. In placing his signature on the work, the author may have had no knowledge that he was doing an act which amounted to an assertion of this aspect of his paternity right.[17] It follows that any person who exhibits an artistic work which bears the name of the artist in one of the relevant places should take the right to have been asserted and will infringe the author's paternity right unless the author's name is apparent to anyone seeing the exhibited work. The transitional provisions of the Act are dealt with separately below, but it should also be noted in this context that even where the relevant parting with possession took place before the commencement of the 1988 Act, an assertion made by this method is sufficient. The presence of the artist's name on any copyright artistic work should therefore be taken as a sufficient assertion unless, for example, it is known that the artist has waived his right.

(4) Again, the identification need not be made by the author himself nor, apparently, with his authority.

(5) In whatever manner such an identification is made, it will bind anyone into whose hands that original or copy comes and remains binding whether or not the identification is still present or visible.[18] This obviously presents a difficulty where the identification was made in the margin which has since been cropped or on a frame which has since been discarded.

(B) Secondly, the right may be asserted by including, in a licence by which the author or other first owner of copyright authorises the making of copies of the work, a statement signed by or on behalf of the person granting the licence that the author asserts his right to be identified in the event of the public exhibition of a copy made in pursuance of the licence.[19] In this case the assertion is binding on the licensee and on anyone into whose hands a copy made in pursuance of the licence comes. The assertion is binding whether or not that person has notice of it.[20] As to this:

(1) Again, it seems that it is only possible to make such an assertion on the granting of a licence by the first owner of the copyright, whether this be the author or another person. It cannot be made on the grant of a licence by a subsequent owner.

(2) For this type of assertion, the mere identification of the author is not sufficient: the assertion must be specific and relate to the public exhibition of the work.[21]

---

[17] An assertion in this form will only amount to an assertion of the right to be identified in relation to the public exhibition of the work.

[18] CDPA 1988, s.78(4)(c).

[19] s.78(3)(b).

[20] s.78(4)(d).

[21] If the licence contains a general assertion but is in fact signed by the author, it will of course satisfy CDPA 1988, s.78(2)(b).

(iv) Joint works

In the case of works of joint authorship,[22] the right must be asserted by each joint   **11–24**
author in relation to himself.[23] Where only one of two or more joint authors asserts his right, it therefore seems that only he must be identified as author. Where
a publisher takes this course, however, he may find himself in as bad a position as
if no author is identified at all, since the attribution of one person only as author
will clearly be false and he may find himself the subject of a claim in reverse
passing off.[24] The prudent course will be to name all authors.[25]

(v) Assertion and the revived and extended terms of copyright

The effect of the revival of copyright[26] on moral rights is considered later.[27]   **11–25**
However, any assertion of the paternity right which subsisted immediately before
the expiry of copyright is to continue to have effect during the period of revived
copyright.[28] Also, any assertion of the paternity right which (a) subsisted immediately before January 1, 1996[29] in relation to an existing copyright work,[30]
and (b) is not to expire before the end of the copyright period under the 1988 Act
as originally enacted, is to continue to have effect during the period of any
extended copyright, subject to any agreement to the contrary.[31]

F. EXCEPTIONS

The right to be identified is subject to exceptions of various kinds: (i) as to the de-   **11–26**
scription of work, (ii) as to the acts done in relation to a work and (iii) as to the
circumstances in which those acts are done.[32]

(i) Excepted descriptions of work

The right does not apply at all in relation to a computer program, the design of a   **11–27**
typeface,[33] or any computer-generated work. The paternity right was denied to
authors of computer programs and typefaces for reasons of practicality, since the
right was thought to lead to more problems than benefits for these works,[34] and of
course there is no human author of a computer-generated work.[35]

(ii) Qualified exception of works by reference to nature of copyright

The right to be identified does not apply in relation to a work in which Crown   **11–28**

---

[22] A work of joint authorship is one produced by the collaboration of two or more authors in which
the contribution of each author is not distinct from that of the other author or authors: CDPA
1988, s.10(1). See para. 4–37, above.
[23] CDPA 1988, s.88(1).
[24] See para. 21–11, below.
[25] The paternity right does not give an author any right *not* to be named as the author of a work of
his.
[26] *i.e.* effected by the Duration of Copyright and Rights in Performances Regulations 1995 (SI
1995/3297).
[27] See para. 11–80, below.
[28] See SI 1995/3297, reg.22(2).
[29] *i.e* the commencement date of SI 1995/3297.
[30] *i.e.* a work in which copyright subsisted immediately before that date. See SI 1995/3297,
reg.14(1).
[31] See SI 1995/3297, reg.21(1).
[32] CDPA 1988, s.79.
[33] The "design of a typeface" includes an ornamental motif used in printing: CDPA 1988, s.178.
[34] *Hansard*, HL 491, col.366.
[35] CDPA 1988, s.79(2). A computer-generated work is defined to be one that is generated by a computer in circumstances such that there is no human author of the work. See s.178.

copyright or Parliamentary copyright subsists, or a work in which copyright originally vested in an international organisation by virtue of section 168 of the 1988 Act, unless the author or director has previously been identified as such in or on published copies of the work.[36] It is not clear whether such previous identification must have been on all published copies: it is suggested that identification on any published copy will have been enough to preserve the right. Crown copyright subsists where a work is made by Her Majesty or by an officer or servant of the Crown in the course of his duties.[37]

Parliamentary copyright subsists when a work is made by or under the direction or control of the House of Commons or the House of Lords.[38] Parliamentary copyright extends to every Bill introduced into Parliament.[39] An international organisation is the first owner of copyright in every original literary, dramatic, musical or artistic work made by an officer or employee of, or published by, an international organisation as specified in an Order in Council.[40]

(iii) Authority of copyright-owning employer

11–29 The right does not apply to anything done by or with the authority of the copyright owner where the copyright in the work originally vested in the author's or director's employer by virtue of section 11(2) of the 1988 Act.[41] This exception is clearly of great significance. While an employee-author's right is retained in respect of anything done without the authority of the copyright owner, this is hardly likely to be of great practical importance since any such act will usually also be an infringement of copyright.[42] For example, employed journalists or photographers have no right to be identified as the author of their works published in a newspaper or magazine.[43] There will also clearly be a large number of more general employee works in respect of which the author has no right to be identified as author.

(iv) Pre-1988 Act works

11–30 There is a blanket exception to the paternity right in the case of works whose author died before commencement of the 1988 Act[44] and all pre-commencement films,[45] but there is a further exception in the case of pre-existing literary, dramatic, musical and artistic works whose author was alive at this date. Thus, the right does not apply where (a) copyright first vested in the author and (b) by virtue of an assignment or licence granted before commencement an act may be

---

[36] CDPA 1988, s.79(7).
[37] s.163(1). See para. 10–12, above.
[38] s.165(1). See para. 10–72, above.
[39] s.166(1).
[40] s.168(1). At present, these are the United Nations, the Specialised Agencies of the United Nations and the Organisation of American States. See the Copyright (International Organisations) Order 1989 (SI 1989/989), see Vol.2, C1.
[41] The position where the copyright vested in the author's employer by virtue of the earlier Acts is considered below. A mistake in the earlier drafting of this provision has now been corrected by the Copyright and Related Rights Regulations 2003 (SI 2003/2498), reg.18(1). See Copinger, 14th ed., para.11–31, n.40.
[42] Although not, for example, in the case of the public exhibition of an artistic work. In such a case it is not in any event clear why the authority of the copyright owner should be of any relevance.
[43] An even more significant exception which affects journalists, news photographers and other persons involved with reporting current events is contained in CDPA 1988, s.79(5), considered below.
[44] August 1, 1989.
[45] CDPA 1988, Sch.1, para.23(2).

done without infringing copyright.[46] Nor does the right apply in relation to such a work where (a) the copyright vested in someone other than the author and (b) an act is done by or with the licence of the copyright owner.[47] These restrictions are clearly likely to affect the exercise of the paternity right in relation to a large number of "old" works.

(v) Permitted acts

The right is not infringed by the doing of various acts which would amount to permitted acts in the context of infringement of copyright.[48] It should be noted that not every act which is permitted for copyright purposes will also escape infringement of the paternity right. On the contrary, the doing of many of the permitted acts will be capable of infringing the paternity right. The permitted acts which do not amount to an infringement of the paternity right are: fair dealing for the purpose of reporting current events by means of a sound recording, film or broadcast[49]; incidental inclusion of the work in an artistic work, sound recording, film or broadcast[50]; anything done for the purposes of an examination[51] by way of setting the questions, communicating the questions to the candidates or answering the questions[52]; anything done for the purposes of parliamentary or judicial proceedings[53] or reporting the same[54]; anything done for the purposes of the proceedings of a Royal Commission or statutory inquiry or for the purpose of reporting any such proceedings held in public[55]; making an article to the design, or copying an article made to the design, in a design document or model recording or embodying a design for anything other than an artistic work or a typeface[56]; copying an artistic work by making articles of any description after the end of the period of 25 years after the end of the calendar year in which the artistic work has been exploited by or with the copyright owner's licence by making articles by industrial process and marketing such articles in the United Kingdom and elsewhere[57]; and those cases where acts are permitted in relation to the copyright in an anonymous or pseudonymous work on the assumption that the copyright has expired or the author has died 70 years or more before the act is done.[58]

11–31

Reporting current events. In addition, the right does not apply in relation to any work made for the purpose of reporting current events.[59] The exception which applies to works of employees, and thus employed journalists, photographers and

11–32

---

[46] Sch.1, para.23(3)(a).

[47] Sch.1, para.23(3)(b).

[48] CDPA 1988, s.79(4).

[49] s.79(4)(a). But note that fair dealing for the purposes of reporting current events requires a sufficient acknowledgement, except where the reporting is by means of a sound recording, film or broadcast and acknowledgement would be impossible, for reasons of practicality or otherwise. The position here has changed following implementation of the Information Society Directive. See paras 9–35 et seq., above.

[50] CDPA 1988, ss.79(4)(b), and 31. See paras 9–56 et seq., above.

[51] s.32(3). See paras 9–93 et seq., above.

[52] s.79(4)(c).

[53] s.45. See para. 9–126, above.

[54] s.79(4)(d).

[55] ss.79(4)(e), 46(1), (2). See para. 9–127, above.

[56] ss.79(4)(f), 51. See para. 9–139, above.

[57] ss.79(4)(g), 52. See para. 9–143, above.

[58] ss.79(4)(h), 57 and 66A. Those are cases in which it is not possible by reasonable inquiry to ascertain the identity of the author. See para. 9–152, above.

[59] CDPA 1988, s.79(5). As to the meaning of "reporting current events", see the discussion of s.30(2) at para. 9–44, above.

others has already been noted.[60] A further exception which applies in relation to works published in newspapers, etc. is dealt with in the next paragraph. The present exception is wider in scope in that it applies not only to the work of employed and freelance journalists, photographers and film makers, but also to the use of their work in other news-reporting media, such as television and radio. These provisions were included particularly because of the perceived difficulties in attributing authorship in the case of news reporting and the like.[61]

(vi) Non-infringing publications

11–33 The right does not apply in relation to the publication in a newspaper, magazine or similar periodical or in an encyclopaedia, dictionary, yearbook or other collective work[62] of reference, of a literary, dramatic, musical or artistic work made for the purposes of such publication or made available with the consent of the author for the purposes of such publication.[63] Not only will this provision include the work of journalists, etc., but also of advertisers and correspondents.

3. THE RIGHT TO OBJECT TO DEROGATORY TREATMENT OF A WORK

11–34 In general, the author[64] of a copyright literary, dramatic, musical or artistic work, and the director of a copyright film, has the right not to have his work subjected to derogatory treatment ("the integrity right").[65] Again, this right is derived from Article 6 *bis* of the Berne Convention, which requires that independently of his economic rights, and even after the transfer of any such rights, an author of a work shall have the right to "object to any distortion, mutilation or other modification of, or other derogatory action in relation to, the said work, which would be prejudicial to his honour or reputation". The 1988 Act gives effect to this requirement by first defining a concept of "derogatory treatment" in relation to a work. The Act then provides that the right is infringed by the doing of a number of specified acts in relation to such derogatory treatment, where such acts do not have the consent of the person entitled to the right. As with the case of the paternity right, the right only applies in relation to a work in which copyright subsists, and the circumstances in which the integrity right is infringed vary according to the character of the copyright work. The right is also subject to various important exceptions and qualifications. There is, however, no requirement that this right should have been asserted as a prerequisite to liability for infringement. Before the integrity right was introduced by the 1988 Act, the only means by which an author might generally take action in respect of such treatment was under the law of libel.[66]

11–35 **Transitional.** The right applies to works made before commencement of the Act (on August 1, 1989), except in the case of a film made before this date or, in relation to the other kinds of copyright work, where the author had died before this

---

[60] *i.e.* that contained in s.79(3).

[61] See *Hansard*, HL Vol.493, cols 1312, 1313; Vol.495, cols 658, 659.

[62] A collective work is a work of joint authorship or a work in which there are distinct contributions by different authors or in which works or parts of works of different authors are incorporated. CDPA 1988, s.178. See para. 5–115, above.

[63] s.79(6).

[64] As to the meaning of "author", see para. 11–05, above.

[65] CDPA 1988, ss.80(1), 1(2). For a form of Statement of Claim, see Vol.2 at J2.v.

[66] See the cases cited below in relation to the discussion of "derogatory treatment".

date.[67] The Act contains further provisions limiting the right in relation to pre-commencement works, which are considered below.

In the case of a work of joint authorship, the right is a right of each joint author, his right is satisfied if he consents to the treatment in question.[68]

A. Derogatory treatment

In order to make good a claim of infringement of the integrity right, the author or director must first establish that his work has been subject to a "treatment" and then that such treatment is "derogatory".

11–36

Treatment. "Treatment" of a work means, in general, any addition to, deletion from or alteration to or adaptation of the work.[69] As already noted, the integrity right is not limited in its application to a substantial part of a work but applies to any part of it.[70] It follows that virtually any change to the work is covered by the expression, subject to the exceptions noted below. The alteration of a single word of a literary or dramatic work, a single note of a musical work, the slightest alteration to an artistic work or the cutting of a single frame from a film therefore amounts to a treatment.[71] Neither is a "treatment" confined to a physical embodiment of the altered work. As will be seen, public performance and broadcasting of a derogatory treatment are among the acts capable of infringing the integrity right.[72] By virtue of a specific exclusion, however, a translation of a literary or dramatic work does not qualify as a treatment.[73] Therefore, no matter how corrupt or damaging to an author's reputation such a translation may be, he has no remedy by way of infringement of a moral right. Neither does the expression "treatment" extend to an arrangement or transcription of a musical work involving no more than a change of key or register.[74] In both these cases, the justification was said to be that such changes would not affect the basic integrity of the work.[75] The definition does, however, include, by its use of the expression "adaptation",[76] the conversion of a dramatic work into a non-dramatic work and of a non-dramatic work into a dramatic work[77] and a version of a literary or dramatic work in which the story or action is conveyed wholly or mainly by means of pictures in a form suitable for reproduction in a book or in a newspaper, magazine or similar periodical.[78]

11–37

The right also extends to the treatment of parts of a work resulting from a previous treatment by a person other than the author or director, if those parts are

---

[67] CDPA 1988, Sch.1, para.23(2).

[68] s.88(2).

[69] CDPA 1988, s.80(2)(a).

[70] s.89(2).

[71] See, *e.g. Confetti Records Ltd v Warner Music UK Ltd* [2003] 1274 (Ch) ("rap" line added to a song); *Morrison Leahy Music Ltd v Lightbond Ltd* [1993] E.M.L.R. 144 (new recording made by taking short "snatches", lasting from between 10 to 65 seconds, from five songs which lasted from between three to seven minutes, and slight alterations made in the lyrics). Where the defendant had scaled down the size of the plaintiff's cartoons, this was conceded to amount to a treatment: *Tidy v Trustees of the Natural History Museum* (1995) 39 I.P.R. 501. The background colour had also been altered to pink and yellow from the original black and white.

[72] This gives effect to Art.6 *bis* of the Berne Convention, which provides that any "derogatory action" in relation to a work may be objected to by the author.

[73] CDPA 1988, s.80(2)(I).

[74] s.80(2)(a). It is not clear why this special exception was necessary since it is unlikely that a mere change of key or register would amount to a *derogatory* treatment. If it could do so, then there would seem to be good reason for bringing it within the integrity right.

[75] *Hansard*, HC, SCE, col.388.

[76] CDPA 1988, s.21(3). See paras 7–121 *et seq.*, above.

[77] s.21(3)(a)(ii). See paras 7–124 and 7–125, above.

[78] s.21(3)(a)(iii). See para. 7–126, above.

attributed to, or are likely to be regarded as the work of the author or director.[79] This means that if a work is subjected to a treatment by someone other than the author, for example in the course of the editing of a novel by a publisher, further alteration to it, for example by dramatising part of the edited version, will amount to treatment of the original work, but only if the result is seen to be the work of the original author.[80]

11–38 **"Derogatory" treatment.** This expression is at the core of the integrity right. A treatment of a work is "derogatory" if it amounts to distortion or mutilation of the work or is otherwise prejudicial to the honour or reputation of the author or director.[81] In the case of a treatment which is a distortion or mutilation of a work, a concept which is already pejorative, it must also be such as to be prejudicial to the honour or reputation of the author or director: a treatment which is a distortion or a mutilation but which is not prejudicial to the author's honour or reputation is not actionable as an infringement of the integrity right.[82] This follows from the use of the word "otherwise" in relation to the third category of derogatory treatment, indicating that this is a necessary qualification in relation to the first two, and from the wording of Article 6 *bis*, which section 80 was intended to implement.[83] Thus, in Article 6*bis*, the words "which would be prejudicial to his honour or reputation" qualify all the derogatory acts referred to. Indeed, unless some such objective qualification is imposed on the words "distortion" and "mutilation", the section would pose great difficulties in its application, since the words standing alone are highly subjective.[84] For example, an author's work may be edited in a way which he considers has seriously impaired its worth, and yet to others the alteration may not be significant or may even be thought to be an improvement.[85]

11–39 **Distortion, mutilation, or other prejudicial treatment.** As already noted, these words are pejorative and clearly further cut down the ambit of "treatment" from its defined meaning, namely any "addition to, deletion from or alteration to or adaptation of" a work. A distortion of a work, as a matter of ordinary language, involves some form of twisting or perversion of it.[86] Mutilation of a work involves some form of cutting or destruction so as to render it imperfect. As to the third category of derogatory treatment, the wording covers any addition to, deletion from or alteration to or adaptation of the work which, although not a distortion or mutilation, is nevertheless prejudicial to the honour or reputation of the author or

---

[79] s.80(7).

[80] Although note that in the example given, it could be argued that the dramatisation is itself a "treatment" of the original work. The apparent intention of the provision was to ensure that where A's work was subjected to a treatment by B, and B's work was then subjected to a treatment by C, C's actions could not be the subject of a claim by A, but only by B, if B's contribution was not taken to be the work of A. See *Hansard*, HL Vol.491, col.389.

[81] CDPA 1988, s.80(2)(b).

[82] *Confetti Records Ltd v Warner Music UK Ltd* [2003] 1274 (Ch), para.150; *Pasterfield v Denham* [1999] F.S.R. 168 (County Court).

[83] *Confetti Records Ltd v Warner Music UK Ltd* [2003] 1274 (Ch), para.150; *Pasterfield v Denham* [1999] F.S.R. 168 (County Court).

[84] Compare, for example, the difficulties experienced by the Australian court in answering, in a different context, the question whether an adaptation of a musical work "debases" the work. See *Schott Musik Int. GmbH & Co v Colossal Records of Australia Pty Ltd* (1997) 38 I.P.R. 1.

[85] So, in *Pasterfield v Denham* [1999] F.S.R. 168, the fact that the author might have been aggrieved by what had been done was irrelevant. However, in *Tidy v Trustees of the Natural History Museum* (1995) 39 I.P.R. 501, where the plaintiff's cartoons had been reduced in size, the question was treated as being whether this was either a distortion or was otherwise prejudicial to his honour or reputation.

[86] In *Tidy v Trustees of the Natural History Museum* (1995) 39 I.P.R. 501, the question of whether the treatment to which the plaintiff's works had been subjected (reduction in size) amounted to a distortion was held not suitable for summary judgment.

director. It is, however, not easy to conceive of examples of prejudicial treatment which could not also be said to amount to a distortion or mutilation in the general sense of these words.[87]

Prejudicial to honour or reputation. These words are taken from Article 6 *bis* itself and were intended to give effect to it.[88] In the original proposal for this Article, the right was defined as one to object to "any modification of the work which would be prejudicial to [the author's] moral interests".[89] This wording was altered as a result of representations from the British delegation to the effect that the concept of "moral interests" was too vague to have any clear meaning under English law, whereas those of "honour" and "reputation" had a close resemblance to existing personal rights under the laws of defamation and passing off.[90] It is therefore suggested that the words should be interpreted in this light. Thus "reputation" has an objective connotation, referring to what is generally said or believed about a person. "Honour", which is associated with both reputation and good name, is more a matter of respect for a person and his position. Quite clearly, not all additions to, deletions from, alterations to or adaptations of a work will be derogatory in the sense of the Act. Many such alterations can be made, even those with which the author may not agree, which will not amount to derogatory treatment. No doubt the alteration of an author's work so as to make him appear inept, untruthful, bigoted and so on are all examples of derogatory treatment. Much will depend on the evidence of the effect which the treatment had on the author's honour or reputation in the eyes of others.[91] It is not necessary that the treatment should have been carried out with the intention of subjecting the author's or director's work to derogatory treatment. An error which results in important passages of a work being omitted or the colours of an artistic work being poorly printed is capable of amounting to derogatory treatment even though the error was inadvertent. Earlier cases in the related fields of libel, passing off, etc. may serve as useful examples:

(1) Where a work was altered for serial publication by the making of cuts and additions, particularly to heighten interest at the end of each part, and the names of the characters were altered, this was found to be injurious to the author's reputation.[92]

(2) An expert in jade was entitled to refuse to allow publication of an article written by him which had been altered such that its style was no longer considered appropriate by him.[93]

(3) The publication of an author's work in a vulgar and offensive jacket was

11–40

[87] Limited help as to the ambit of this third category is obtained from Art.6 *bis* of the Berne Convention. The words "distortion" and "mutilation" are used in Art.6 *bis* itself, so that this category appears to be intended to cover the other acts referred to in Art.6 *bis*, namely any "other modification of, or other derogatory action in relation to" the work. The original provision of the Berne Convention relating to the integrity right, introduced by the Rome Act of 1928, provided that the author should have the right to object to any "distortion, mutilation or other modification [of his work] which would be prejudicial to his honour or reputation". The present form of the provision was introduced in 1948 by the Brussels Act.

[88] *Confetti Records Ltd v Warner Music UK Ltd* [2003] 1274 (Ch).

[89] See Ricketson, *The Berne Convention for the Protection of Literary and Artistic Works: 1886–1986* (Kluwer, 1987), p.460.

[90] See Ricketson, *The Berne Convention for the Protection of Literary and Artistic Works: 1886–1986* (Kluwer, 1987), p.460.

[91] *Tidy v Trustees of the Natural History Museum* (1995) 39 I.P.R. 501: *cf. Snow v Eaton Centre* (1982) 70 C.P.R. 105 (High Ct. of Ontario), suggesting that the expression "prejudicial to his honour or reputation" involves a subjective element or judgment on the part of the author, so long as it is reasonably arrived at.

[92] *Humphreys v Thomson & Co Ltd* [1905–10] Mac.C.C. 148.

[93] *Joseph v National Magazine Co Ltd* [1959] Ch. 14.

restrained on the basis that it made the untrue suggestion that the book was just as vulgar and offensive as the cover.[94]

(4) The omission of a few words from a play was arguably sufficient to weaken the whole structure.[95]

Since it is necessary to show that the treatment is prejudicial to the honour or reputation of the author or director, it is necessary to adduce evidence to this effect,[96] unless, perhaps, in an extreme case, it is obvious. Evidence should therefore normally be adduced that some members of the public do, or would be likely to, think less of the author or director because of the treatment. It need hardly be said that if the author does not give evidence complaining about the treatment, otherwise than for some good reason, the court is unlikely to find prejudice.[97] Since the issue is whether the treatment is prejudicial, and not whether the author's or director's reputation *has been prejudiced*, or whether the *acts* done in relation to treatment have cause his reputation to suffer, it seems that it does not matter that the witness in fact knows that the treatment was not done by the author, or that the treated work has been published anonymously or with a disclaimer.[98]

11–41 **Burlesques, parodies, etc.** A burlesque or parody may or may not involve a treatment of a claimant's work in the above sense.[99] Where it does not involve a treatment, no question of infringement of the moral right can arise. Where it does so, it will often be plain that the work is not actually that of the claimant and so, no matter how critical or contemptuous of the claimant the treatment is, it is suggested that an infringement is unlikely to arise. Perhaps one case in which it might do so is where those who read, hear or see the claimant's work will no longer be able to do so without calling to mind the parody, to the prejudice of his honour or reputation.[1] It is only where the treatment is made out to be the claimant's own work that there can be an infringement.[2]

11–42 **Destruction.** The deliberate and complete destruction of the original embodiment of a work, for example a work of art or an original manuscript, is often a controversial issue. While it almost certainly amounts to a treatment of the work, being a deletion from or alteration to it, it would not seem to be prejudicial to the author's honour or reputation. Unless, therefore, the above conclusion that the words "otherwise prejudicial" qualify the words "distortion" and "mutilation" is wrong, such an act would not amount to a derogatory treatment. In any event, as will be seen, the right is only infringed if one of a number of specified acts, such as publication, is done in relation to a derogatory treatment. The destruction of a work is not such an act. An exception might be where a work such as a painting is destroyed publicly as part of a statement about the artist which was prejudicial to him, and the act of destruction filmed and later broadcast such that the half

---

[94] *Mosely v Stanley Paul & Co* [1917–23] Mac.C.C. 341. But *quaere* whether this would amount to a "treatment".

[95] *Frisby v British Broadcasting Corp* [1967] Ch. 932.

[96] *Confetti Records Ltd v Warner Music UK Ltd* [2003] 1274 (Ch), para.157.

[97] *Confetti Records Ltd v Warner Music UK Ltd* [2003] 1274 (Ch), para.157.

[98] This conclusion also seems to follow from the provisions in the 1988 Act which provide for the making of a "sufficient disclaimer" (see ss.81(6), 82(2), 103(2)), which suggest that, but for the statutory provision, such a disclaimer would not prevent a treatment from being derogatory.

[99] A burlesque or parody usually involves imitation of the style of another, rather than a particular work.

[1] *cf.* the US case of *Campbell v Acuff-Rose Music Inc.* (1994) 127 L. Ed. 2d. 500 (U.S. Sup. Ct.), where the issue was whether a parody might amount to fair dealing. As to this see para. 9–41, above.

[2] This was the position in *Clark v Associated Newspapers Ltd* [1998] 1 All E.R. 959, but since it was the plaintiff's style which was being parodied rather that a particular work of his, no question of derogatory treatment arose.

destroyed work was shown. A private act of destruction could not, however, infringe the right.

Derogatory use must relate to treatment. What is the position where a work is   **11–43**
used in a context which may be highly injurious to the reputation of the author or director, for example, where a literary work is used in a pornographic film or an artistic work placed in a setting which is entirely inappropriate to it?[3] Is this capable of amounting to a derogatory treatment? On a first reading of the Act, the answer seems to be no, since the word derogatory relates to the treatment of the work, *i.e.* the addition, deletion, alteration, etc. and not to a use which is made of the unaltered work. In the above examples, although the use made of the work may be derogatory, the treatment of it itself is not. Thus consider the case of a work used in an unaltered form. Here, the work has clearly not been subjected to a treatment within its defined meaning and no matter what use is made of it such use will still not be a treatment, derogatory or otherwise. The same result would seem to follow if the same object were achieved by selecting extracts from the work in a non-derogatory way, since, although in this case the selection will amount to a treatment, the treatment itself is not derogatory, although the use made of it may be so. Although this appears to be the position on the wording of the Act, it does present difficulties in practice since whether or not a treatment is derogatory may often depend on how that treatment is used. It is also doubtful whether this interpretation is consistent with Article 6 *bis*, which stipulates that the author's right is to object, *inter alia*, to any derogatory "action" which would be prejudicial to his honour or reputation. In *Morrison Leahy Music Ltd v Lightbond Ltd*,[4] short extracts were taken from several recordings of the claimant's songs and compiled, with other material, into one recording. The argument appears to have turned on whether the compilation, rather than the way in which the songs had been cut, was derogatory. In any event, however, the juxtaposition of the short extracts with other material presumably amounted to an addition to or alteration of each work.

B. CIRCUMSTANCES IN WHICH THE RIGHT IS INFRINGED

Even when it has been established that a work has been subjected to a derogatory   **11–44**
treatment, it is only when the treatment is then subjected to some specified use that any question of infringement arises. The specified uses vary with the type of work. As already noted, the word "derogatory" apparently refers to the type of treatment which the work has been subjected to, and not the type of use to which the derogatory treatment is then subjected.

(i) Literary, dramatic and musical works

In the case of a literary, dramatic or musical work, the right is infringed by a   **11–45**
person who publishes commercially, performs in public or commincates to the public a derogatory treatment of the work.[5] It is also infringed by a person who issues to the public copies of a film or sound recording of, or including, a deroga-

---

[3] And consider, *e.g.* the facts of *Mosely v Stanley Paul & Co* [1917–23] Mac.C.C. 341 (plaintiff's book published in a vulgar and offensive dust jacket) and *Shostakovich v Twentieth Century Fox Film Corp* (1948) 80 N.Y.S.(2d) 575 (recordings of music used in settings of which the composers did not approve).
[4] [1993] E.M.L.R. 144.
[5] CDPA 1988, s.80(3)(a).

tory treatment of the work.[6] The expressions have already been considered in the context of the paternity right, as has the apparent overlap between them.

(ii) Artistic works

11–46   In the case of an artistic work, the right is infringed by a person who publishes commercially or exhibits in public a derogatory treatment of the work or communicates to the public a visual image of a derogatory treatment of the work.[7] The right is also infringed by a person who shows in public a film including a visual image of a derogatory treatment of a work or issues to the public copies of such a film.[8] Again, these expressions have already been considered when dealing with the paternity right. As noted there, public exhibition of an artistic work is an act which is not capable of amounting to infringement of copyright in an artistic work.

11–47   **Works of architecture, sculptures and works of artistic craftsmanship.** In the case of works of architecture in the form of a model for a building (but not in the form of a building itself), sculptures and works of artistic craftsmanship, a person infringes the right if he issues to the public copies of a graphic work[9] representing, or of a photograph of,[10] a derogatory treatment of the work.[11] As noted elsewhere in relation to other similar provisions, the issue to the public of such copies will often also amount to commercial publication. Where a work of architecture in the form of a building is the subject of derogatory treatment and its author is identified on the building, his only right is to require the identification to be removed.[12] The subjection of the building to the derogatory treatment is not itself an infringement,[13] so that where the architect is not identified he has no remedy. Neither, it seems, does he have any right to damages whilst his name remains on the building.

(iii) Films

11–48   In the case of a film, the right is infringed by a person who shows in public or communicates to the public a derogatory treatment of the film or issues to the public copies of a derogatory treatment of the film.[14]

C. OTHER PERSONS LIABLE FOR INFRINGEMENT

11–49   The integrity right is also infringed by persons possessing or dealing with infringing articles. For this purpose, an infringing article is a work or a copy of a work which has been subjected to derogatory treatment within the meaning of the Act and which has been, or is likely to be, the subject of any of the acts referred to

---

[6] ss.80(3)(a), (b).
[7] CDPA 1988, s.80(4)(a).
[8] s.80(4)(b).
[9] A graphic work includes a painting, drawing, diagram, map, chart or plan, or an engraving, etching, lithograph, woodcut or similar work. See CDPA 1988, s.4(2).
[10] A photograph means a recording of light or other radiation on any medium on which an image is produced or from which an image may by any means be produced, and which is not part of a film. See CDPA 1988, s.4(2).
[11] CDPA 1988, s.80(4)(c).
[12] s.80(5).
[13] Compare the wording of ss.80(4) and (5).
[14] CDPA 1988, s.80(6).

above which amount to an infringement of the integrity right.[15] This double requirement means that an article may change in character from a non-infringing to an infringing article, and even back again, depending on the use to which it is intended to be put. In relation to such an article, the right is infringed by a person who, knowing or having reason to believe that it is an infringing article[16]:

(1) possesses it in the course of a business;
(2) sells it or lets it for hire, or offers it or exposes it for sale or hire; or
(3) in the course of a business exhibits it in public or distributes it; or
(4) distributes it otherwise than in the course of a business so as to affect prejudicially the honour or reputation of the author or director.[17]

D. EXCEPTIONS

The right is subject to various exceptions depending upon: (a) the character of the work, (b) the acts done in relation to it, (c) the circumstances in which the various acts are done, and (d) whether the work was in existence before the commencement of the 1988 Act.   **11–50**

(A) *Excepted works.* The right does not apply to a computer program.[18] This is so notwithstanding that inept alterations to a computer program which are still likely to be regarded as the work of the original author because, for example, it still carries his name, may be highly damaging to his reputation. Neither does the right apply to any computer-generated work.[19]

(B) *Reporting current events.* The right does not apply to any work made for the purpose of reporting current events.[20] What is important here is the purpose for which the work was made, not the purpose for which the work is used. The work of a news journalist may therefore be edited, however ineptly, without infringing his integrity right.

(C) *Publications.* The right does not apply in relation to the publication in a newspaper, magazine or similar periodical, or in an encyclopedia, dictionary, yearbook or other collective work of reference, of a literary, dramatic, musical or artistic work made for the purposes of such publication or made available with the consent of the author for the purposes of such publication.[21] The right does not apply in relation to any subsequent exploitation elsewhere of such a work without any modification of the published version.[22]

(D) *Anonymous, pseudonymous works.* Sections 57 and 66A of the 1988 Act. The right is not infringed by an act which, by virtue of sections 57 or 66A, would not infringe copyright in the work.[23] That section refers to anonymous or pseudonymous works and to acts permitted on assumptions as to the expiration of copyright or death of the author.[24]

(E) *Certain purposes.* The right is not infringed by anything done for certain specified purposes, provided that, where the author or director is identified

---

[15] CDPA 1988, s.83(2).
[16] s.83(1). See paras 8–08 *et seq.*, above.
[17] See paras 8–11 *et seq.*, above, for a discussion of the meaning of these terms in relation to infringement of copyright.
[18] CDPA 1988, s.81(2)
[19] s.81(2). The exception is hardly surprising since a "computer-generated work" is one that is generated by computer in circumstances such that there is no human author of the work: s.178.
[20] s.81(3). See paras 9–35 and 9–44, above.
[21] s.81(4). As to a collective work, see s.178 and para. 5–115, above.
[22] s.81(4). As to a collective work, see s.178 and para. 5–115, above.
[23] s.81(5).
[24] s.57, 66A. See para. 9–152, above.

at the time of the relevant act or has previously been identified in or on published copies of the work, there is a "sufficient disclaimer".[25] Those purposes are:[26]

(1) avoiding the commission of an offence;

(2) complying with a duty imposed by or under an enactment; or

(3) in the case of the British Broadcasting Corporation, avoiding the inclusion in a programme broadcast by them of anything which offends against good taste or decency or which is likely to encourage or incite to crime or to lead to disorder or to be offensive to public feeling.

A "sufficient disclaimer" means a clear and reasonably prominent indication given at the time of the act, and if the author or director is then identified, appearing along with the identification, that the work has been subjected to treatment to which the author or director has not consented.[27]

(F) *Existing works.* As with the paternity right, there is a blanket exception to the integrity right in the case of works whose author died before commencement of the 1988 Act[28] and all pre-commencement films,[29] but there are further similar exceptions in the case of then-existing literary, dramatic, musical and artistic works whose author was alive at this date. Thus, the right does not apply where (a) copyright first vested in the author and (b) by virtue of an assignment or licence granted before commencement an act may be done without infringing copyright.[30] Nor does the right apply in relation to such a work where (a) the copyright vested in someone other than the author and (b) an act is done by or with the licence of the copyright owner.[31] These restrictions are clearly likely to affect the exercise of the integrity right in relation to a large number of "old" works.

E. QUALIFICATION OF THE RIGHT

11–51   In the case of certain works, the right is qualified.[32] Those works are:

(1) works in which copyright originally vested in the author's or director's employer by virtue of section 11(2)[33];

(2) works in which Crown copyright or Parliamentary copyright subsists; and

(3) works in which copyright originally vested in an international organisation by virtue of section 168.

In all these cases the right does not apply to anything done in relation to such work by or with the authority of the copyright owner, unless the author or director is identified at the time of the relevant act, or has previously been identified in or on published copies of the work. Where, in such cases, the right does apply, it is not infringed if there is a sufficient disclaimer.[34]

This qualification is clearly of substantial significance in so far as it relates to the works of employees where, as will usually be the case, the copyright first

---

[25] s.81(6).

[26] s.81(6).

[27] s.178.

[28] August 1, 1989.

[29] CDPA 1988, Sch.1, para.23(2).

[30] Sch.1, para.23(3)(a).

[31] Sch.1, para.23(3)(b).

[32] CDPA 1988, s.82.

[33] A mistake in the earlier drafting of this provision was corrected by the Copyright and Related Rights Regulations 2003 (SI 2003/2498), reg.18(2). See *Copinger* (14th ed.), para.11–56, n.27.

[34] CDPA 1988, s.82(2). For a definition of sufficient disclaimer, see CDPA 1988, s.178 and para. 11–50, above.

vests in the employer.[35] As in the case of the paternity right,[36] this limitation will apply in many cases since exploitation of the derogatory treatment will often have had the consent of the copyright owner: otherwise it will usually also be an infringement of his copyright.[37] The limitation is not, however, quite as wide in scope as that which relates to the paternity right, since the integrity right arises not only in cases where a substantial part of the work has been subjected to derogatory treatment but also where *any* part has been so treated.[38] Exploitation of a derogatory treatment which reproduces or is an adaptation of less than a substantial part of the original will not require the permission of the copyright owner. An author's or director's integrity right in such cases is therefore unaffected by the qualification in section 82. It is suggested that even if in such cases the thing done in relation to the derogatory treatment is done with the permission of the copyright owner, the qualification will still not bite since his *authority* was not required and therefore not given.[39]

Assuming, however, that the thing done in relation to the original work was done with the authority of the copyright owner, then if the employee is not identified as the author or director of the original work, whether at the time or on previously published copies, he has no right to complain even if he can establish derogatory treatment.[40] Even where the author or director has been so identified, he will still be unable to exercise the integrity right where a disclaimer is made.

4. FALSE ATTRIBUTION OF AUTHORSHIP OR DIRECTORSHIP

In general, a person has the right not to have a literary, dramatic, musical or artistic work falsely attributed to him as author, or a film falsely attributed to him as director.[41] The right is conferred on authors and non-authors alike,[42] although clearly such statements are most likely to be made in relation to persons who have established reputations, whether as authors, dramatists, composers or artists. The right applies in relation to the whole or any part of the work, not just a substantial part.[43] These provisions of the 1988 Act are largely based upon the equivalent provisions of the 1956 Act.[44] As already pointed out, this right is not prescribed by the Berne Convention. Alongside this statutory right, a person may have a claim in passing off or defamation in relation to such acts.[45]

The section therefore requires that there be an attribution of authorship or directorship and that the attribution be false. "Attribution" in relation to the relevant work means a statement, express or implied, as to who is the author or direc-

11–52

---

[35] It will only not do so where there was an agreement, express or implied, to the contrary. See CDPA 1988, s.11(2) and paras 5–11 *et seq.*, above.

[36] *i.e.* by virtue of the exception under CDPA 1988, s.79(3). See para. 11–29, above.

[37] *i.e.* the derogatory treatment will usually reproduce or be an adaptation of a substantial part of the original work.

[38] CDPA 1988, s.89(2).

[39] See, *e.g. C.B.S. Songs Ltd v Amstrad plc* [1988] A.C. 1013, HL, and paras 7–130 *et seq.*, above.

[40] On the other hand, there is no limitation on the nature of previously published copies which identified the author. Copies long out of print which identified the author will preserve the right.

[41] CDPA 1988, s.84(1).

[42] This follows from the wording of the Act but see also *Clark v Associated Newspapers Ltd* [1998] 1 All E.R. 959.

[43] CDPA 1988, s.89(2).

[44] See CDPA 1988, s.43. The ultimate source of the provisions is s.7 of the Fine Arts Copyright Act 1862 (25 & 26 Vict. c.68), which related only to artistic works.

[45] See, *e.g. Byron v Johnston* (1816) 2 Mer. 29; *Archbold v Sweet* (1832) 1 Moo. & R. 162; *Ridge v The English Illustrated Magazine Ltd* [1911–16] Mac.C.C. 91 (libel). The precise cause of action in some of the early cases is unclear. As to possibility of passing off in such cases, see Ch.21.

tor of the work.[46] For these purposes, the "work" is the whole work which is attributed to the claimant. So where words are added to the claimant's actual work and the whole attributed to him, the right is infringed.[47] Examples of false attribution include a newspaper article in the first person attributing to a person words which that person did not in fact use,[48] an article which in addition to quoting the actual words of the claimant added to the quote a further 17 words which were not his,[49] and a spoof diary column purporting to be by the claimant, a well known politician, and carrying his photograph, and held to contain a clear statement attributing the column to him.[50] In order to succeed, the representation relied on as conveying the message that the claimant was the author of the work must be construed to see what the single correct meaning of it is.[51] In this, the tort is like the tort of defamation[52] but is unlike passing off, where if the same representation may mean different things to different people it is sufficient to establish that one of those meanings at least deceives or causes confusion amongst a substantial number of people.

11–53   **False statement as to adaptation.** The right extends to cases where, contrary to the fact, a literary, dramatic or musical work is falsely represented as being an adaptation[53] of a work of a person.[54] Where, therefore, a play is falsely held out as being based on another's novel, such a statement will amount to a false attribution within the meaning of the Act, even when it is clear that the dramatisation itself is the work of another. Such a claim could conceivably arise where a play or film is misrepresented, by its title, to be based upon a well known book.[55]

11–54   **False statement as to copy of artistic work.** A false statement that a copy of an artistic work is a copy made by the author of the artistic work will also amount to a false attribution.[56] The application of this provision appears rather limited today, but clearly could apply where prints are represented as having been made by the artist himself.

11–55   **False statement as to alterations to artistic work.** Where an artistic work has been altered after the author has parted with possession of it, the right of the artist is infringed by a person who, in the course of a business, deals with the altered work as being the unaltered work of the author, or deals with a copy of such work as being a copy of the unaltered work of the author, knowing, or having reason to believe, that this is not the case.[57] Under the similarly worded provisions of the 1862 Act, it was held that the right only applied in the case of a material alteration,

---

[46] CDPA 1988, s.84(1).
[47] *Noah v Shuba* [1991] F.S.R. 14 at 32.
[48] *Moore v News of the World Ltd* [1972] 1 Q.B. 441.
[49] *Noah v Shuba* [1991] F.S.R. 14 at 32.
[50] *Clark v Associated Newspapers Ltd* [1998] 1 All E.R. 959. This was despite the statement carried in the column that the diary was how the writer imagined the claimant might have recorded certain events. This was held not to neutralise the main impression conveyed by the column as a whole.
[51] *Clark v Associated Newspapers Ltd* [1998] 1 All E.R. 959.
[52] See *Charleston v News Group Newspapers Ltd* [1995] 2 A.C. 65 at 71.
[53] For the meaning of adaptation in relation to these works, see CDPA 1988, s.21(3) and paras 7–121 *et seq.*, above.
[54] CDPA 1988, s.84(8).
[55] Although the section does not in terms refer to a false representation made in relation to a film, a film is capable of being a dramatic work. See para. 3–37, above.
[56] CDPA 1988, s.84(8).
[57] CDPA 1988, s.84(6).

not to something which was *de minimis*, and that an alteration was material if it might affect adversely the character or reputation of the artist.[58]

Joint authorship. The right is also infringed by any false statement as to the authorship of a work of joint authorship or by the false attribution of joint authorship in relation to a work of sole authorship.[59] Such a false attribution infringes the right of every person to whom authorship of any description is, whether rightly or wrongly, attributed.[60] If one person only is named as the author of a work of which two persons are the authors, the person who is named has the right to complain of false attribution, not the unnamed author. The right of the unnamed author is to assert his paternity right.[61] Where a work of sole authorship is attributed to two joint authors, the named person who was not the author clearly has the right to complain of false attribution. It seems that the person who was the actual author cannot claim false attribution but can assert a right of paternity, claiming the right to be identified as "the" author of the work, not as a joint author.   **11–56**

Infringing acts. Where a false attribution had been made, a person's rights are infringed by anyone who commits the following acts: **11–57**

(1) *Issue to the public.* This occurs if a person issues to the public copies of a literary, dramatic, musical or artistic work or a film, in or on which there is a false attribution.[62]

(2) *Public exhibition.* This occurs when a person exhibits in public an artistic work, or a copy of an artistic work, in or on which there is a false attribution.[63]

(3) *Public performance.* This occurs if, in the case of a literary, dramatic or musical work, a person performs the work in public or communicates it to the public as being the work of a person or, in the case of a film, shows it in public or communicates it to the public as being directed by a person. Infringement only occurs, however, if that person knows or has reason to believe that the attribution is false.[64]

(4) *Associated material.* The right is infringed by the issue to the public, or by the public display of material containing a false attribution in connection with any of the acts mentioned above.[65]

(5) *Indirect infringement.* The right is infringed by a person who, in the course of a business, possesses or deals with a copy of a literary, dramatic, musical or artistic work or a film in or on which there is a false attribution or, in the case of an artistic work, possesses or deals with the work itself when there is a false attribution in or on it. Liability is dependent on that person knowing or having reason to believe that there is such an attribution and that it is false.[66] The references to "dealing" are to selling or letting for hire, offering or exposing for sale or hire, exhibiting in public, or distributing.[67]

The meaning of these various expressions has already been considered.

---

[58] *Carlton Illustrators v Coleman & Co Ltd* [1911] 1 K.B. 771 at 780. Evidence was accepted that alterations in the size and colour of a work might so affect the author. An example of a *de minimis* alteration was said to be an alteration to the artist's signature. *Sed quaere.*
[59] CDPA 1988, s.88(4).
[60] s.88(4)
[61] See para. 11–24, above, as to the problem where one joint author only asserts his paternity right.
[62] CDPA 1988, s.84(2)(a).
[63] s.84(2)(b).
[64] s.84(3)(a),(b).
[65] s.84(4).
[66] s.84(3).
[67] s.84(7).

5. RIGHT TO PRIVACY OF CERTAIN PHOTOGRAPHS AND FILMS

11–58   There is no general right of privacy in English law.[68] Limited provisions relating to the use of photographs and films were introduced into the 1988 Act in response to the change in the law which meant that the commissioner of a photograph no longer automatically became entitled to the copyright.[69]

The Act provides that a person who, for private and domestic purposes, commissions the taking of a photograph[70] or the making of a film[71] has, where copyright subsists in the resulting work, a right to "privacy" in such work. The right does not apply in relation to photographs or films taken or made before the commencement of the 1988 Act.[72] In general, such a person has the right[73] not to have:

(1) copies of the work issued to the public;

(2) the work exhibited or shown in public; or

(3) the work communicated to the public.

These rights are infringed by a person who does, or authorises the doing of, any of these acts. The meaning of the various expressions has already been considered. What amounts to commissioning the taking of a photograph has also been considered in detail in relation to the ownership of copyright in pre-1988 Act photographs.[74] Whereas the right of the commissioner to the copyright in such a photograph depends on him not only having commissioned the taking of the photograph but also having paid or agreed to pay for it,[75] the privacy provisions of the 1988 Act do not in terms include a reference to payment. Normally, however, a commissioning connotes an obligation to pay.[76] In such circumstances it is clearly possible that the commissioner will not only have rights of privacy under the present provision but also be entitled to the copyright in the photograph or film, in equity at least.[77] The two rights are, however, independent.

11–59   **Private and domestic purposes.** The commissioning must have been for "private and domestic" purposes. This is an expression which is used elsewhere in the Act.[78] Although the limits of this expression may not be entirely clear, it is important to keep in mind that it qualifies the purposes of the commission and not the subject matter of the photographs. A wedding may to some extent be a public affair and not domestic, but it is suggested that the purposes for which wedding photographs are commissioned are normally both private and domestic, that is the recording of the event for family and friends. The words private and domestic are conjunctive: a photograph which is commissioned for private but not domestic purposes, for example for purposes relating to a person's private business affairs, will not fall within the section.

---

[68] As to the right of privacy and the law of confidential information, see Ch.20, below.

[69] As to the old law relating to commissioned photographs, see paras 5–33 *et seq.*, above.

[70] A photograph means a recording of light or other radiation on any medium on which an image is produced or from which an image may by any means be produced, and which is not part of a film. CDPA 1988, s.4(2).

[71] A film means a recording on any medium from which a moving image may by any means be produced. CDPA 1988, s.5(1).

[72] *i.e.* August 1, 1989. See CDPA 1988, Sch.1, para.24.

[73] CDPA 1988, s.85(1).

[74] See paras 5–33 *et seq.*, above.

[75] See the Copyright Act 1956, s.4(3).

[76] *Apple Corps Ltd v Cooper* [1993] F.S.R. 286.

[77] As to the rights in equity of a person who commissions the making of a copyright work, see paras 5–174 *et seq.*, above.

[78] See, *e.g.* CDPA 1988, s.22 (secondary infringement by importation).

Infringing acts. Although the photograph or film must have been commissioned   **11–60**
for private and domestic purposes, there is no requirement that the infringing act
be an invasion of a person's private or domestic affairs. In this sense the right
conferred, once the private and domestic purpose test is satisfied in relation to the
commissioning, is analogous to a right of copyright: the commissioner can withhold his consent to any of the specified uses for whatever reason. The exploitation for these purposes may therefore become deadlocked where the commissioner and copyright owner are different persons and each declines to consent to
its use.[79]

Substantial part. The right only applies in relation to the whole or any substantial   **11–61**
part of the work.[80] It is not clear whether these words will be construed in their
normal copyright sense[81] or whether they will be judged by the quality or
importance of the image in relation to a right of privacy. In theory, a small part of
a photograph, for example the image of one person taken from a large group,
may not amount to a substantial part of the photograph in the copyright sense, but
its use in a newspaper may amount to an invasion of privacy of the kind which
the section is designed to prevent. Although in practice a court may have little
difficulty in such a case in reaching the conclusion that, even if judged on the
copyright test, the section is satisfied, it is suggested that the words should be
construed bearing in mind the purpose of the section and therefore, if necessary,
in a sense favourable to the protection of a person's privacy in a domestic sphere.

Exceptions. The right is not infringed by an act which, by virtue of various pro-   **11–62**
visions, would not infringe copyright in the work. The provisions are those which
relate to the incidental inclusion of the work in an artistic work, film or broadcast[82]; parliamentary and judicial proceedings[83]; Royal Commissions and statutory inquiries[84]; acts done under statutory authority[85]; and anonymous or pseudonymous works and acts permitted on assumptions as to the expiry of copyright
or death of the author.[86] It is worth noting that no exception exists in relation to
any form of fair dealing and in particular any use of a photograph or film for the
purpose of reporting current events. As already noted, the right does not apply in
relation to photographs or films taken or made before the commencement of the
1988 Act.[87]

Joint commissions. In the case of a work made in pursuance of a joint commis-   **11–63**
sion, the right is that of each person who commissions the making of the work.[88]
Thus, the right of each is satisfied if he consents to the act in question,[89] and a
waiver by one of them under section 87 does not affect the rights of the others.[90]
Thus where one of two joint commissioners agrees to the publication of a
photograph, the rights of the other to object are not affected.

---

[79] Although this cannot happen in the case of the public exhibition or showing of the work, an act
which does not require the consent of the copyright owner (except in the case of an infringing
copy).
[80] CDPA 1988, s.89(1).
[81] As to which see paras 7–23 et seq., above.
[82] CDPA 1988, ss.5(2)(a), 31. See para. 9–56, above.
[83] CDPA 1988, ss.85(2)(b), 45. See para. 9–126, above.
[84] CDPA 1988, ss.85(2)(c), 46. See para. 9–127, above.
[85] CDPA 1988, ss.85(2)(d), 50. See para. 9–131, above.
[86] CDPA 1988, ss.85(2)(e), 57. See para. 9–144, above.
[87] i.e. August 1, 1989. See CDPA 1988, Sch.1, para.24.
[88] CDPA 1988, s.88(6).
[89] s.88(6)(a).
[90] s.88(6)(b). See paras 11–74 et seq., below.

6. DURATION OF MORAL RIGHTS

11-64 The question of how long moral rights should last has been a matter of controversy in the international treatment of these rights.[91] Article 6 *bis* of the Rome revision of the Berne Convention left the period of protection for the paternity and integrity rights unspecified.[92] The Brussels revision of 1948 made it clear that the rights should last for at least the author's lifetime and, to the extent that national legislation permitted,[93] at least until the copyright in the work expired. The Stockholm revision of 1967, now found in the Paris Act, made obligatory a *post mortem* term of 50 years, except for those countries whose legislation did not provide for such protection at the time of their ratification or accession to the Act.[94] Since the rights of paternity and integrity were put on a new, clear statutory basis by the 1988 Act, there was no impediment to the United Kingdom fully implementing Article 6 *bis*. The 1988 Act therefore provides that the right to be identified as author or director and the right to object to derogatory treatment of a work continues to subsist so long as copyright subsists in the work, as does the right to privacy in commissioned photographs and films.[95] The exercise of these rights after a person's death is considered below. The right of a person not to have works falsely attributed to him endures for a different period, namely until 20 years after a person's death.[96] Any infringement of the right occurring after the person's death is actionable by his personal representatives.[97]

11-65 **Extension and revival of copyright term.** With the amendments made to the 1988 Act to comply with the EC Directive harmonising the term of copyright to one of life and 70 years after the author's death,[98] provision also had to be made in relation to the period of protection for moral rights. The provisions relating to extension and revival of the term of copyright are considered in detail later.[99] Where the copyright has been extended or revived, the moral rights are exercisable so long as the copyright subsists.[1]

---

[91] The main controversy has been between the "monist" systems, which perceive moral rights and economic rights as being closely linked so that they should be of the same duration, and the "dualist" systems, which perceive them as being separate, so that while the economic rights should be limited in time, moral rights should be perpetual.

[92] The position of the United Kingdom was that since the paternity and integrity rights were adequately protected under the existing common law, and since causes of action such as defamation died with the author, the term of protection prescribed should be no longer than this.

[93] This escape clause was inserted at the insistence particularly of the United Kingdom delegation, which opposed any extension of the rights beyond the author's lifetime. See Ricketson, *The Berne Convention for the Protection of Literary and Artistic Works: 1886–1986* (Kluwer, 1987), p.465.

[94] The United Kingdom deposited its instrument of ratification of the Paris Act on September 29, 1989, with effect from January 2, 1990. The 1988 Act came into force on August 1, 1989.

[95] CDPA 1988, s.86(1).

[96] s.86(2).

[97] s.95(5).

[98] Directive 93/98 of October 29, 1993.

[99] See paras 11–80 *et seq.*, below. The distinction has to be made between cases where the term of UK copyright had not yet expired, in which case the term was in general simply extended from life and 50 years to life and 70 years, and cases in which the UK copyright had expired but had to be revived for the residue of the life and 70-year term.

[1] This follows from the words of CDPA 1988, s.86. Various transitional provisions are considered in the context in which they arise in this chapter.

7. TRANSMISSION OF MORAL RIGHTS

Moral rights are not assignable.[2] They are personal, not proprietary, rights. Since, however, they subsist beyond the lifetime of the author or director, provision has to be made for the exercise of these rights in the *post mortem* period. Article 6 *bis* leaves it to the legislation of each country to provide by whom the *post mortem* paternity and integrity rights should be exercised. The 1988 Act provides that on the death of a person who is entitled to be identified as author or director of a work, or to object to derogatory treatment of a work or to the right of privacy in respect of a photograph or film, the right passes to such persons as he may by testamentary disposition specifically direct.[3] Not only may an author or director appoint more than one person under this provision,[4] but it seems he may also appoint different persons in respect of the three different rights. If there is no specific testamentary disposition of the right in this way by the author or director, but the copyright in the work in question forms part of that person's estate, then the right passes to the person to whom the copyright passes,[5] whether under his will or on intestacy. If and to the extent that the right does not pass in either of these ways, it is exercisable by that person's personal representatives.[6] Presumably in any of these cases, the right can be similarly transmitted after the death of the person in whom the right becomes vested. Although special provision is made as to the exercise of these rights where there is more than one person entitled,[7] it is not clear whether on the death of one such person the entitlement passes to the survivor or survivors or whether it passes to the persons specified in section 95(1). Since this section is the only mechanism provided for the transmission of the rights, it is suggested that the latter is the correct answer in the case of the death of a person to whom the right has passed by virtue of either testamentary disposition or by following the copyright.[8] Where the right has been transmitted to personal representatives under subsection (c), it is suggested that the position is different and that the right becomes exercisable by the survivor or survivors of two or more personal representatives, and then, where the chain of representation continues, by the personal representative of the survivor.[9] Where the chain is broken, the right will be exercisable by whoever obtains a new grant to the original estate.

Unlike the various forms of property which, after the owner's death, vest in personal representatives and thereafter in beneficiaries or transferees,[10] these rights cannot be transferred or divested, even, for example, by personal

11–66

---

[2] CDPA 1988, s.94. *cf.* assignments of copyright. In relation to the paternity and integrity rights, Art.6 *bis* of the Berne Convention does not state this expressly but it is implicit.

[3] CDPA 1988, s.95(1)(a).

[4] See s.95(3) and para. 11–70, below.

[5] s.95(1)(b). See s.95(3) and para. 11–69, below, as to the position where the copyright is split on such a bequest. The provision does not appear very apt in the case of the privacy right (since the point of the section is that the benefit is conferred where the commissioner does *not* own the copyright).

[6] s.95(1)(c).

[7] See below.

[8] A problem with this might be thought to be that CDPA 1988, s.95 only provides for the transmission of the right "on the death of person entitled" to the rights conferred by ss.77, 80 and 85, and the persons entitled to the rights conferred by those sections are the original authors, directors or commissioners. However, it is suggested that any of the persons to whom the right passes under paras (a) or (b) are persons "entitled" to the right conferred.

[9] Note the difference in the wording between, on the one hand, paras (a) and (b) ("... the right passes ...") and, on the other, paras (c) ("if or to the extent that the right does not pass under paragraph (a) or (b) it is *exercisable* by his personal representatives".—emphasis added). As to the chain of representation, see Williams, Mortimer and Sunnucks, *Executors, Administrators and Probate* (18th ed., Sweet & Maxwell) p.46 .

[10] *cf.* the position in relation to copyright, para. 5–123, above.

representatives after administration of the estate is complete. Again, where the right passes to the person entitled to the copyright,[11] the right does not become attached to the copyright and pass with it on a subsequent assignment. It remains vested in that person until a subsequent transmission under section 95(1). It is unclear whether production of a grant is necessary to prove a person's title to these rights in an action, but it is suggested that it is.[12] Where the right passes to the person specifically appointed by testamentary disposition, the right apparently vests in such appointee immediately on death and not, for example, in his executors where he dies testate or in the Public Trustee where he dies intestate. Where the right passes with the copyright,[13] the position is more complicated. On the death of the copyright owner, the copyright will vest first in his executors, or in the Public Trustee and then in his administrators, depending on whether he died testate or intestate.[14] The copyright will then be subject to the usual trusts in the administration of the owner's estate and liable to be sold, along with his other assets, to pay his debts and testamentary expenses. Only if it is not sold in the course of administration will the copyright pass to the person beneficially entitled to it, whether under the will or under the intestacy rules, by assent or assignment, as the case may be.[15] Presumably the intention is that the right passes to whoever, incidents of administration apart, is or would have been beneficially entitled to the copyright.

11–67   **False attribution.** The above provisions affect only the transmission of the paternity, integrity and privacy rights. In the case of the right to prevent false attribution, which lasts for the shorter period of 20 years after a person's death,[16] the right becomes actionable by a person's personal representatives after his death.[17]

11–68   **Nature of transmitted right.** Although the statute does not say so expressly, the rights of paternity, integrity and the right to prevent false attribution which become vested in others by these means remains a right which is referable to the moral rights of the deceased author. Thus, in relation to the paternity right, the right is obviously to have the deceased author or director identified as the author or director of the work, and not the person by whom the right is now exercisable. In the same way, the integrity right which is exercisable after the author's or director's death is a right not to have a derogatory treatment of the deceased author's work exploited. The right of false attribution is a right not to have a work falsely attributed to the deceased person.[18] In contrast, a person who becomes entitled to exercise the privacy right after the commissioner's death simply has the right not to have the relevant photograph or film exploited in any of the specified ways. As already noted, in this respect the privacy right is more analogous to a right of copyright. Any damages recovered by personal representatives by virtue of these provisions in respect of an infringement occurring after a person's death devolve as part of his estate as if the right of action had subsisted and been vested in that person immediately before his death.[19]

---

[11] *i.e.* under para.95(1)(b).
[12] *cf.* the position following the death of an owner of copyright, discussed at para. 5–123, above.
[13] *i.e.* under CDPA 1988, s.95(1)(b).
[14] See para. 5–123, above.
[15] See para. 5–126, above.
[16] CDPA 1988, s.86(2). See para. 11–64, above.
[17] s.95(5).
[18] Of course the person entitled to exercise this right after the author's or director's death has a quite separate personal right not to have a work or film falsely attributed to *him*.
[19] CDPA 1988, s.95(6). See, further at para. 11–71, below.

Split copyright. During an author's or director's lifetime, any disposition of **11–69** copyright by him, whether partial or total,[20] will not affect the exercise of his moral rights relating to that work. The rights remain vested in him. Since, however, on death the author's moral rights may pass to the person entitled to the copyright,[21] a potential difficulty arises when different aspects of the copyright become vested in different persons. This may occur, for example, where a bequest is limited so as to apply to one or more, but not all of the things which the copyright owner has the exclusive right to do or authorise; or to part, but not the whole, of the period for which the copyright is to subsist.[22] By whom are the moral rights relating to these works to be exercised? The Act provides that where copyright forming part of a person's estate passes in part to one person and in part to another, any right which passes with the copyright by virtue of section 95(1) of the 1988 Act is correspondingly divided.[23] Taking the example of an author who has made a bequest of the right to reproduce his literary works in book form to one person (A) and to reproduce or dramatise them in the form of films to another (B), A but not B is entitled to assert the paternity right in relation to publication of the work in book form and to object to a derogatory treatment which is commercially published in book form, even though, in the latter case, the derogatory treatment may seriously damage the copyright vested in B. As already noted, these moral rights do not pass on any subsequent assignments of these partial rights of copyright. They remain vested in A and B until further transmitted in accordance with section 95(1).

Joint rights. The position of the exercise of the various moral rights in the case **11–70** of joint authors has already been considered in the context of each individual right. On transmission of the right following death, however, the right may be transmitted to more than one person jointly. The further transmission of such rights in such circumstances has already been considered, but how are the rights to be exercised in these circumstances? The Act provides that where by virtue of section 95(1)(a) or (b) of the 1988 Act a right becomes exercisable by more than one person:

(1) In the case of the right to be identified as author, it may be asserted by any of them[24];

(2) In the case of the integrity and privacy rights, the right is exercisable by each of them and is satisfied in relation to any of them if he consents to the treatment or act in question[25];

(3) In any case, any waiver of the right in accordance with section 87 of the 1988 Act by one of them does not affect the rights of the others.[26]

(4) A consent or waiver previously given or made binds any person to whom the right passes by virtue of section 95(1) of the 1988 Act.[27]

So, for example, where a right has been passed to A and B, A may assert the author's right to be identified independently of B, and B, it seems, may later bring an action for infringement relying on A's assertion. In the case of the integrity or privacy rights, either A or B may bring an action for infringement and any consent or waiver by B does not affect the exercise of the integrity or privacy right by A.

---

[20] As to partial assignments of copyright, see paras 5–93 et seq., above.
[21] i.e. under CDPA 1988, s.95(1)(b).
[22] ss.95(2)(a), (b).
[23] s.95(2).
[24] CDPA 1988, s.95(3)(a).
[25] s.95(3)(b).
[26] s.95(3)(c). See paras 11–74 et seq., below.
[27] s.95(4).

8. REMEDIES FOR INFRINGEMENT OF MORAL RIGHTS

11–71   An infringement of a moral right is actionable as a breach of statutory duty owed to the person entitled to the right without proof of damage.[28] An author will, in an appropriate case, be entitled to recover general and special damages and an injunction to restrain threatened future breaches of duty. Damages for infringement of the paternity right will no doubt usually be assessed on the basis of the loss of publicity and thus lost opportunity which the omission to name him has caused.[29] In the case of derogatory treatment, damages will, for example, be assessed by reference to the damage which the publicity has done to his career and loss of sales of his other works. False attribution is likely to lead to damages to an author's reputation and loss of future earnings by the association of his name with a work with which he is unconnected. As with similar cases in the field of passing off, the damage is often likely to be difficult to quantify and the important remedy will usually be an injunction, particularly an interim injunction. No provision is made for any award of additional damages in the case of flagrancy[30] although, presumably, an award of exemplary damages is now obtainable.

Cases where the claim is brought after the author's death raise peculiar difficulties. How, for example, is the measure of damages to be assessed? Infringement of the paternity or integrity rights may affect future sales of the author's or director's works, but this is a loss which will affect the copyright owner who will not necessarily be the person to whom the right has been transmitted. The point is underlined by the fact that it is only where the rights are exercisable by the personal representatives that any damages form part of the deceased's estate.[31] In all other cases, the damages belong beneficially to the person to whom the right has passed, and such person may have no other connection with the author, his estate or his copyright works.[32]

11–72   **Delay.** In relation to the paternity right, the court, in considering remedies, is to take into account any delay in asserting the right.[33] This provision was inserted because it was thought it might be unjust to grant an injunction or substantial damages if there was a late assertion of the right after the owner had spent money on exploitation.[34] The provision is clearly intended to go beyond the court's existing discretion to refuse relief on equitable grounds in cases, for example, of acquiescence.

11–73   **Disclaimer.** In proceedings for infringement of the right to object to derogatory treatment of a work, the court may, if it thinks it is an adequate remedy in the circumstances, grant an injunction on terms prohibiting the doing of any act unless a

---

[28] CDPA 1988, s.103(1) and *Clark v Associated Newspapers Ltd* [1998] 1 All E.R. 959. See Ch.22, below, as to remedies generally. For forms of Statement of Claim, see Vol.2 at J2.iv, v.

[29] For cases on claims in contract for failure to give credit: see *Marbé v George Edwardes (Daly's Theatre) Ltd* [1929] 1 KB 269; *Tolnay v Criterion Film Productions Ltd* [1936] 2 All E.R. 1625; *Herbert Clayton and Jack Waller Ltd v Oliver* [1930] AC 209; *Joseph v National Magazine Co Ltd* [1959] 1 Ch 14, CA; *Brighton v Jones* [2004] EWHC 1157 (Ch).

[30] *cf.* CDPA 1988, s.97(2) in the case of infringement of copyright.

[31] s.95(6). In such a case, the damages recovered devolve as part of his estate as if the right of action had subsisted and been vested in him immediately before his death. *ibid.*

[32] Often, no doubt an author or director will have appointed someone under CDPA 1988, s.95(1)(a) because trust was reposed in him to preserve his good name, not for any personal benefit.

[33] CDPA 1988, s.78(5).

[34] *Hansard*, HL Vol.491, col.365. See para. 11–22, above, for a discussion of some of the problems to which this can give rise.

disclaimer is made, in such terms and in such manner as may be approved by the court, dissociating the author or director from the treatment of the work.[35]

9. SUPPLEMENTARY PROVISIONS

A. CONSENT AND WAIVER OF RIGHTS

The Act distinguishes between two types of act which affect the exercise of moral rights, namely consent and waiver. The apparent intention was that a waiver would be appropriate in cases where a release from any claims was required on a long-term or formal basis, while a simple consent would be appropriate in one-off cases when the right might otherwise be infringed.[36]   **11–74**

Consent. It is not an infringement of any moral right to do any act to which the person entitled to the right has consented.[37] Consent may be given orally or in writing, formally or informally, and it may be express or implied from words or conduct. The mere fact that the work was commissioned from the author, setting up an equitable title to the copyright in the commissioner, does not mean that consent to do any of the acts within the scope of his moral rights can be inferred.[38]   **11–75**

Waiver. Any of the rights may also be waived by an instrument in writing signed by the person giving up the right.[39] A waiver by one joint author does not affect the rights of the other joint authors.[40] A waiver may relate to a specific work, to works of a specified description or to works generally, and may relate to existing or future works.[41] A waiver may also be conditional or unconditional and may be expressed to be subject to revocation.[42] If a waiver is made in favour of the owner or prospective owner of the copyright in the work or works to which it relates, the waiver is presumed to extend to his licensees and successors in title, unless a contrary intention is expressed.[43] The provisions as to formal waiver by instrument in writing do not exclude the operation of the general law of contract or estoppel in relation to an informal waiver or other transaction in relation to the right to be identified, the right to object to derogatory treatment and the privacy right.[44]   **11–76**

Waiver and the extended and revived terms. The effect of the extension and revival of the copyright term on moral rights is considered below. However, any waiver of a moral right which (a) subsisted immediately before January 1, 1996[45] in relation to an existing copyright work,[46] and (b) is not to expire before the end of the copyright period under the 1988 Act as originally enacted, is to continue to have effect during the period of any extended copyright, subject to any agreement to the contrary.[47] Also, any waiver of a moral right which subsisted immediately   **11–77**

---

[35] CDPA 1988, s.103(2). For the definition of "sufficient disclaimer", see CDPA 1988, s.178 and para. 11–50, above.

[36] *Hansard* HL Vol.491, col.395; HL Vol.493, col.1336.

[37] CDPA 1988, s.87(1).

[38] *Pasterfield v Denham* [1999] F.S.R. 168 (County Court).

[39] CDPA 1988, s.87(2). For a precedent of a waiver, see Vol.2 at J1.vi.

[40] s.88(3).

[41] s.87(3)(a).

[42] s.87(3)(b). It is not clear whether a waiver which is expressed to be irrevocable but which is not given for consideration is in fact revocable in the absence of any estoppel.

[43] s.87(3).

[44] s.87(4).

[45] *i.e.* the commencement date of SI 1995/3297.

[46] *i.e.* a work in which copyright subsisted immediately before that date. See SI 1995/3297.

[47] See See SI 1995/3297, reg.21(1).

before the expiry of copyright shall continue to have effect during the period of revived copyright.[48]

B. Joint directors

11–78   The various provisions applicable in relation to joint authorship of a work apply in relation to a film which was, or is alleged to have been, jointly directed.[49] A film is "jointly directed" if it is made by the collaboration of two or more directors, and the contribution of each director is not distinct from that of the other director or directors.[50] As already noted, although for copyright purposes one of the authors of a film is the "principal director",[51] for moral rights purposes the joint directors need not all be principal directors.

10. TRANSITIONAL PROVISIONS

A. Pre-1988 Act works

11–79   Some of the transitional provisions which apply in relation to works in existence before the commencement of the 1988 Act[52] have been considered as they arise in the context of the different moral rights but are summarised here. The paternity and integrity rights apply in relation to works in existence before commencement ("existing works"), but they do not apply in relation to a literary, dramatic, musical or artistic work the author of which died before the commencement, or in relation to a film made before the commencement, of the Act.[53]

In relation to an existing literary, dramatic, musical or artistic work:

(1) Where the copyright first vested in the author, the rights do not apply to anything which by virtue of an assignment of copyright made or licence granted before commencement may be done without infringing copyright.[54] So, for example, where the author was the first owner of the copyright but before commencement granted a licence to publish his work, the licensee may publish it without identifying the author if the licence is silent on the point, for to do so will not infringe the author's copyright. In the same way, if the licence permits the publisher to alter the work,[55] publication of the altered work will not infringe the author's integrity right.

(2) Where the copyright first vested in a person other than the author, the rights in relation to existing works do not apply to anything done by or with the licence of the copyright owner.[56] So where, for example, the copyright first vested in the author's employer, neither the employer nor any successor in title of his need identify the author or concern himself with the integrity right in relation to an act done by him. The same applies to acts done with his licence.

The rights do not apply to anything done in relation to a record made in pursu-

---

[48] See SI 1995/3297, reg.22(2).

[49] CDPA 1988, s.88(5). As to works of joint authorship, see s.10(1) and paras 4–37 *et seq.*, above.

[50] s.88(5). As to works of joint authorship, see s.10(1) and paras 4–37 *et seq.*, above.

[51] s.9(2)(ab). There is no reason in principle why there should not be joint "principal directors".

[52] August 1, 1989.

[53] CDPA 1988, Sch.1, paras 23(1), (2).

[54] Sch.1, para.23(3)(a).

[55] As to which, see para. 5–224, above.

[56] CDPA 1988, Sch.1, para.23(3)(b). In *Morrison Leahy Music Ltd v Lightbond Ltd* [1993] E.M.L.R. 144, the court assumed that where a composer had entered into a publishing agreement whereby the copyright in future compositions was to belong to the publisher, the copyright first vested in the publisher, not the composer. See *ibid.* s.91, and paras 5–105 *et seq.*, above.

ance of section 8 of the 1956 Act,[57] which provided for a statutory recording licence.

The right to privacy in relation to photographs and films does not apply to photographs taken or films made before the commencement of the 1988 Act.[58]

B. MORAL RIGHTS AND THE REVIVED AND EXTENDED TERMS OF COPYRIGHT

The implementation of the Term Directive[59] meant that the term of United Kingdom copyright was generally increased from the life of the author of the work and 50 years after his death to life and 70 years. In cases where the work was still in copyright in the United Kingdom, this meant simply extending the period for the new term. In certain other cases, where the United Kingdom term had expired but the work was still in copyright in another EEA State, copyright was revived for the remainder of the life and 70 year term.[60] Transitional provisions needed to be made to deal with the moral rights implications of these changes.

11–80

The extended term. In general, no special provisions apply. Moral rights are exercisable for the full, extended term in accordance with the provisions of the 1988 Act. However, any assertion of the paternity right or waiver of a moral right which (a) subsisted immediately before January 1, 1996[61] in relation to an existing copyright work,[62] and (b) is not to expire before the end of the copyright period under the 1988 Act as originally enacted, is to continue to have effect during the period of any extended copyright, subject to any agreement to the contrary.[63]

11–81

The revived term. In relation to all works which are the subject of revived copyright, the author will have died before the commencement of the 1988 Act. Nothing in the transitional provisions relating to the revived term is to affect the basic transitional provision of the 1988 Act that in such cases the paternity and integrity rights do not apply.[64] It would therefore appear that no paternity or integrity right can exist in relation to the revived term of copyright. Nevertheless, the Regulations make provision for such a case, and also in relation to the privacy right and right to prevent false attribution. Thus it is provided that where the copyright in a work has been revived, moral rights relating to it are also revived or come into being.[65] In such a case, the author or director of a revived copyright work is entitled to exercise the paternity and integrity rights as from its revival on January 1, 1996. Where the author or director had died before this date, the rights are exercisable by his personal representatives.[66] In the case of the privacy right, the draftsman of the Regulations also appears to have overlooked that it is not the author of the photograph or film who is entitled to the right, but the commissioner.[67] In all these cases, any damages recoverable by the personal representatives devolve as part of the author's, director's or commissioner's estate as if the right of action had subsisted and been vested in him immediately

11–82

---

[57] CDPA 1988, Sch.1, para.23(4).

[58] Sch.1, para.24.

[59] Council Directive 93/98 of October 29, 1993, implemented by SI 1995/3297.

[60] For a full discussion, see Ch.6, above.

[61] i.e. the commencement date of SI 1995/3297.

[62] i.e. a work in which copyright subsisted immediately before that date. See SI 1995/3297.

[63] See SI 1995/3297, reg.21(1).

[64] i.e. under CDPA 1988, Sch.1, para.23(2)(a). See SI 1995/3297, reg.22(6).

[65] As where the copyright had expired before August 1, 1989 so that no moral rights ever existed.

[66] This is so even where CDPA 1988, s.95(1)(a) or (b) applied.

[67] See the wording of SI 1995/3297, regs. 22(3) and (4): "(3) Moral rights are exercisable after commencement by the author of a work, or as the case may be, the director of a film in which revived copyright subsists ... (4) Where the author or director died before commencement—(a) the rights

before his death.[68] Again, the draftsman appears to have overlooked the fact that in the case of the right to complain of false attribution, the right is that of any person to whom a work has been falsely attributed as author or director, and does not depend on him being an author or director or there being any copyright work. The revival of copyright is therefore of no relevance to such a right.[69]

In addition to these provisions, the Act also provides that the revival of copyright is not to affect the other transitional provisions in the 1988 Act denying or limiting moral rights to works in existence at the commencement of the 1988 Act.[70] Again, this provision is of doubtful application.

Any assertion of the paternity right, and any waiver of any moral right, which subsisted immediately before the expiry of copyright is to continue to have effect during the period of revived copyright.[71]

11–83   The Regulations contain various savings for acts done on the basis that the copyright had expired and was thus in the public domain.[72] The provisions relating to savings for infringement of copyright are considered in detail elsewhere,[73] but where by virtue of these provisions an act does not constitute an infringement of copyright, neither does it infringe any moral right.[74]

C. SOUND RECORDINGS AND FILMS

11–84   One of the changes made by the Regulations implementing the Term Directive was to alter the treatment of film soundtracks, which are now to be treated as part of the film.[75] It is not an infringement of any moral right in a film to do anything after January 1, 1996 in pursuance of arrangements made before this date for the exploitation of the sound recording which is now to be treated as the soundtrack.[76]

---

conferred by ... CDPA 1988, section 85 ... are exercisable after commencement by his personal representatives."

[68] SI 1995/3297, reg.22(5).
[69] cf. the wording of SI 1995/3297, reg.22(4)(b).
[70] i.e. by virtue of CDPA 1988, Sch.1, paras 23 and 24. See para. 11–79, above.
[71] See SI 1995/3297, reg.22(2).
[72] See SI 1995/3297, reg.23.
[73] See paras 5–147 et seq., above.
[74] SI 1995/3297, reg.23(6).
[75] See paras 4–64 et seq., above, for a detailed discussion.
[76] SI 1995/3297, reg.26(4).

PART III

RIGHTS IN PERFORMANCES

RIGHTS IN PERFORMANCES

1. INTRODUCTION

A. HISTORICAL

Nature of performers' rights.[1] The performer is the direct intermediary between the author or composer and the public. A dramatic or musical work may be read but cannot be fully appreciated unless performed. Authors and other copyright owners are therefore dependent on the talent of performers to interpret their works and to bring them before the general public. There is no copyright as such in a performance[2] and until certain rights in performances were conferred on performers by the 1988 Act, as subsequently amended, there was no property right in the nature of copyright in a performance.

Neither the 1911 Act nor the 1956 Act created any copyright in respect of live performances although, as will be seen, some limited statutory protection existed. The extension of copyright or the grant of a similar right in respect of perfor-

12–01

---

[1] For a full treatment of performers' rights, see Arnold, *Performers Rights* (3rd ed., Sweet & Maxwell, 2004).

[2] *Apple Corps Ltd v Lingasong Ltd* [1977] F.S.R. 345 at 350.

mances had been considered by the Copyright Committee, which reported in 1951 on changes to the copyright law, following representations from performers' organisations. At that time, such protection was not thought to be justified on two grounds: first, it was considered that the essence of copyright was the protection against the copying of a work reduced to a material form (*i.e.* fixed in writing or otherwise) and performances, being ephemeral by their nature and never exactly repeated, were too elusive to give rise to a right of property and did not fit into the framework of copyright; second, that such a right would add to the number of licences needed for the exploitation of certain copyright works. The Committee to consider the law on copyright and designs, which reported in 1977 (the Whitford Committee), took the same view, emphasising that to give a performer a copyright in his performance could lead to considerable practical difficulties.[3] The Whitford Committee did, however, recommend making civil remedies such as an injunction and damages available to performers in respect of unauthorised reproduction of live and recorded performances.

In the long legislative process starting with the Whitford Committee report and completed by the adoption of the 1988 Act, the Government indicated first in a Green Paper issued in 1981[4] and finally in a White Paper issued in 1986,[5] its intention to make civil remedies available to performers. The 1988 Act duly conferred rights on performers, by requiring the performer's consent to the exploitation of his performance. Civil remedies for the enforcement of these rights was conferred by way of an action for breach of statutory duty, as well as criminal sanctions. Subsequently, the Act needed to be amended to confer additional property rights on performers in order to comply with the Rental and Related Rights Directive[6] and the result has been the creation of a two-tier system of protection. Although these new rights are not described as copyright, in effect a new copyright was conferred on performers.[7]

12–02   **Origins of performers' rights.** As the copyright system developed for the protection of authors, the question of the protection of performers did not arise for the simple reason that performances could not be reproduced and being ephemeral had no need of protection. Anyone wishing to see or hear a particular performer had to buy a ticket and attend a performance. The position changed early in the twentieth century in response to the increasing possibilities for the exploitation of performances made available as a result of new technical developments, such as sound recording, cinema and radio broadcasting, and the problem was raised in various international fora. Performers' organisations (in the United Kingdom, principally the Musicians' Union) were concerned by what they saw as the reduction in employment opportunities which the reproduction and dissemination of their live performances was likely to entail and they therefore sought protection against unauthorised uses of such performances. In due course, the impact of technological change on the performers' professions led to recognition of the need for some form of legal protection for performers and their cause was taken up by the International Labour Organisation (ILO)in the 1920s. Thereafter, the ILO continuously promoted an international solution to the problems of performers with a view to safeguarding their employment opportunities. These

---

[3] Report of the Committee on the Law of Copyright, Cmd.8662 (1952) paras 170, 172 and 177. See also 1977 Copyright Committee, Cmnd.6732 paras 406 *et seq*. And see *Groves* in [1990] 6 Ent. L.R. 202 & *Sherrard* in [1992] 6 Ent. L.R. 57.

[4] Cmnd.8302, Ch.6.

[5] Cmnd.9712, Ch.14.

[6] See below.

[7] On the evolution of performers' rights in the UK, see A. Plant, *Performers' Rights and Recording Rights*, (Sweet and Maxwell, 1998) Ch.1.

efforts led to the adoption of the Rome Convention for the Protection of Performers, Producers of Phonograms and Broadcasting Organisations (the Rome Convention) in 1961, which the United Kingdom ratified in 1963.[8]

Dramatic and Musical Performers' Act 1925. It was in the context of the intergovernmental discussions on the protection of performers that some measure of statutory protection came to be afforded to performers in the United Kingdom under the provisions of the Dramatic and Musical Performers' Protection Act 1925, which was modified by the 1956 Act and later repealed and re-enacted by the Dramatic and Musical Performers' Protection Act 1958. That Act was in turn amended by the Performers' Protection Act 1963, in order to give effect to the Rome Convention, and by that of 1972. The nature of the protection afforded by these Acts was to make certain unauthorised acts connected with performances criminal offences punishable by fines and/or imprisonment. Under these Acts, protection was afforded only to performers who performed literary, dramatic, musical or artistic works.[9]   **12–03**

The 1988 Act. All those Acts were repealed in their entirety by the 1988 Act,[10] Part II of which initially created two separate rights in performances: one for performers, which was personal and non-assignable ("performers' rights"); and one for persons having an exclusive recording contract with a performer, which was transferable by contractual assignment ("recording rights").[11] The performers' rights were not rights in the nature of copyrights. They were not assignable and imitation of a performance was not an infringement thereof. However, in 1992 the Rental and Related Rights Directive[12] required that performers should be afforded certain transferable property rights. As a result, in 1996 considerable additions and changes were made to the scheme of protection under the 1988 Act in order to implement such legislation in the United Kingdom and to meet other international obligations.[13] Yet further changes were required in 2003 on implementation of the Information Society Directive.[14] These are all discussed in further detail, below.   **12–04**

B. Summary of the Law Pre-1988 Act—Performers' Protection Acts 1958 to 1972

Pre-1988 Act law. Although these Acts have been repealed it is helpful to an understanding of the law as it now stands to summarise the position before the commencement of the 1988 Act.   **12–05**

(i) Criminal offences

The main method adopted for the protection of performances was the creation of criminal offences, punishable summarily or on indictment, for knowingly making and exploiting records, films and broadcasts of performances which had been   **12–06**

---

[8] Ratified by the UK on October 30, 1963, and entered into force on May 18, 1964. See para. 12–10, below; see also paras 24–88 *et seq.*, below, concerning the history and progress of the Rome Convention.

[9] See *Copinger*, (12th ed.), paras 688 *et seq.*

[10] CDPA 1988, s.303(2), Sch.8; See Vol.2 at E6.i, E6.ii and E6.iii. *et seq.* for the texts of the repealed Acts.

[11] See para. 12–20, below.

[12] Council Directive 92/100/EEC. See further, at para. 20–13, below.

[13] See para. 12–10, below.

[14] Directive 2001/29/EC of the European Parliament and of the Council. See further at para. 12–16, below.

made without the written consent of the performers. Although criminal sanctions remain for making, dealing with and using "illicit recordings" of performances,[15] they are not the main method for the protection of performers' rights today.

(ii) Private rights

12–07   Although the 1958 to 1972 Acts provided on their face only for penalties in criminal proceedings against a person found guilty of committing a statutory offence, it was held that those Acts, on their true construction, disclosed an intention to create private rights of action for the benefit of performers. This conclusion was reached because it was apparent from the provisions that the obligations and prohibitions were imposed for the benefit or protection of performers as a particular class of individuals. A performer was, therefore, entitled to bring a civil action for breach of statutory duty claiming an injunction and damages.[16]

(iii) Duration of the private right

12–08   It was also held that the private rights thereby conferred did not cease on the death of the performer. The right to consent to the recording and exploitation of a performance vested in the performer's personal representatives when the performer died. The Acts were not limited to the protection of the reputation and future employment prospects of a performer. They also enured for the protection of the performer's economic interests by ensuring that he was paid for the use of his performances.[17]

The consequence of this construction of the Act was that a performer enjoyed more extensive rights in respect of his performances than an author in respect of his works. The performer enjoyed a quasi-proprietary right akin to copyright, but without any of the safeguards and provisions in the 1956 Act which limited the duration of the right and provided other restrictions on enforcement.

(iv) Persons having exclusive recording rights

12–09   The protection of the Acts was, however, confined to performers. It did not extend to recording companies or other persons who had obtained exclusive recording contracts in respect of the artists' performances. They had no right of action under those Acts because they did not fall within the class for whose benefit the Acts were passed.[18] They had no cause of action at common law, even though the making and distribution of unauthorised "bootleg" records inflicted serious economic loss on recording companies. They could not claim effective relief for interference with contractual relations of the performers, because the "bootlegger" who made and sold the recording of a live performance of the artist did not interfere with the performance or induce the artist to act in breach of any of his contractual obligations to the recording companies.[19]

---

[15] CDPA 1988, s.198. See Ch.23, below.

[16] *Rickless v United Artists* [1988] Q.B. 40, applying *Lonrho Ltd v Shell Petroleum Ltd (No.2)* [1982] A.C. 173 at 185; *Grower v BBC* [1990] F.S.R. 595. *Cf. Musical Performers' Protection Association Ltd v Lingasong Ltd* [1977] F.S.R. 345.

[17] *Rickless v United Artists* [1988] Q.B. 40, applying *Lonrho Ltd v Shell Petroleum Ltd (No.2)* [1982] A.C. 173 at 185; *Grower v BBC* [1990] F.S.R. 595. *Cf. Musical Performers' Protection Association Ltd v Lingasong Ltd* [1977] F.S.R. 345.

[18] *R.C.A. Corporation v Pollard* [1983] Ch.135.

[19] *R.C.A. Corporation v Pollard* [1983] Ch.135

This position was remedied by the 1988 Act which creates recording rights in performances.[20]

C. The International Perspective

(i) The Rome Convention

On October 26, 1961, the International Convention for the Protection of Performers, Producers of Phonograms and Broadcasting Organisations was adopted at Rome.[21] By Article 7(1) of the Rome Convention, the United Kingdom, as one of the parties, undertook to protect certain rights of performers. The performer himself was to have rights which would make it possible for him to prevent unauthorised broadcasting, fixation and reproduction of fixations of his performances. The Rome Convention guarantees protection for a term of 20 years, from fixation, performance or broadcasting, as appropriate.[22] The 1963 Performers' Protection Act was passed to enable effect to be given to that Convention.

12–10

Principle of national treatment. Under the terms of the Convention, each Contracting State must apply national treatment in respect of the rights which it accords to performers, producers of sound recordings (phonograms) and broadcasting organisations. In addition, Contracting States are required to offer nationals of other States who are protected by the Convention certain minimum rights. In the case of sound recordings, these include an exclusive right to authorise all reproductions, direct or indirect, and also a right to equitable remuneration (which under national law could alternatively be paid to or shared with performers) for the use of recordings in broadcasts and public performance.[23] Performers acquired only "the possibility of preventing" various specified acts,[24] a distinction which was thought to allow the United Kingdom, in particular, to continue its approach of only protecting performers by criminal sanctions.[25] This article has no further application once the performer has consented to the incorporation of his performance in a visual or audiovisual fixation,[26] so the performer has no right to authorise or prevent secondary uses of a performance (for example, use in films).

12–11

(ii) European Community legislation

There has been considerable legislative activity as a result of the programme to create uniform and improved Community-wide protection for copyright and related rights. Four Council Directives have necessitated amendments to Part II of the 1988 Act, and a considerable strengthening of protection for performers has resulted.

12–12

The Rental and Related Rights Directive.[27] This provides that performers must have the exclusive right to authorise or prohibit the following acts:

12–13

---

[20] See paras 12–27 et seq., below.
[21] See paras 24–88 et seq. and for text see Vol.2 at F5. This Convention is not to be confused with the Rome Act of the Berne Convention.
[22] Rome Convention, Art.14.
[23] Rome Convention, Arts 5, 10–12. A complete reservation may, however, be made with regard to Art.12 (right to equitable remuneration).
[24] Broadcasting, fixation and the reproduction of fixations without consent: Art.7(1).
[25] Arts 4, 7–9.
[26] Art.19.
[27] Council Directive 92/100 on rental right and lending right and on certain rights related to copyright in the field of intellectual property, [1992] O.J. L346/61.

    (1) the fixation of their performances[28] ;

    (2) the direct or indirect reproduction of fixations of their performances[29] ;

    (3) the distribution of fixations of their performances[30] ;

    (4) the rental and lending of fixations of their performances[31] ;

    (5) the broadcasting by wireless and the communication to the public of their performances (except where the performance is itself already a broadcast performance or is made from a fixation).[32]

The limitations which Member States might allow to these rights were prescribed[33] and the reproduction, distribution and rental and lending rights were stated to be proprietary, in that they may be transferred, assigned or licensed.[34] As will be seen, the reproduction right has since been enlarged to make it clear that it covers temporary as well as permanent reproduction of fixations of perfomances.[35]

Performers are thereby ensured a reasonable degree of control over the exploitation of their performances and a share of royalties and other payments (such as "residuals"—fixed amounts payable for particular uses such as rebroadcasts) made for broadcasting or cable-casting sound recordings. There is an unwaivable right to equitable remuneration if the rental right is assigned,[36] and performers must share in a single equitable remuneration paid for the public performance or broadcasting of recordings of their performance.[37]

12–14   **The Satellite Broadcasting and Cable Retransmission Directive.** This requires that the rights given to performers under the Rental and Related Rights Directive apply also in relation to broadcasts of their performances by satellite.[38]

12–15   **The Term Directive.** This harmonises the term of protection of copyright and certain related rights, including performers' rights.[39] It also introduces a principle of reciprocal treatment for the protection of the performances of non-European Union nationals, in place of the principle of national treatment which previously applied in United Kingdom law.See paras 12–30 et seq., below.

12–16   **The Information Society Directive.** One of the main aims of this Directive, so far as performers were concerned, was to implement the 1996 WIPO Performances and Phonograms Treaty.[40] In this respect, the Directive did a number of things in the field of performers' rights with the aim of harmonising the reproduction, distribution and communication to the public rights. First, it replaced the existing reproduction right in the Rental and Related Rights Directive to make it clear that the reproduction right applied in relation to temporary as well as per-

---

[28] Art.6.

[29] Art.7, although this has since been repealed and replaced by Art.2(a) of the Information Society Directive. See further in the text of this paragraph.

[30] Art.9.

[31] Art.2.

[32] Art.8.

[33] Art.10

[34] Art.7(2), Art.9(4), Art.2(4).

[35] See para. 12–16, below.

[36] Art.4, which applies also to authors. See paras 12–19 et seq., below.

[37] Art.8(2), following Art.12 Rome Convention. See paras 12–45 et seq., below.

[38] Council Directive 93/83 on the co-ordination of certain rules concerning copyright and rights related to copyright applicable to satellite broadcasting and cable retransmission; [1993] O.J. L248/15, Art.4.

[39] Council Directive 93/98 harmonising the term of protection of copyright and certain related rights; [1993] O.J. L290/9.

[40] See para. 12–18, below.

manent reproductions of performances.[41] Second, it required that performers be granted an on-demand right in relation to fixations of their performances.[42] Finally, it made further provision for the limitations or exceptions which Member States may make to these rights.

(iii) TRIPs

The starting point of the TRIPs[43] provisions on copyright is that all Members **12–17** must comply with the substantive Articles (1–21) of the Berne Convention, other than the provision on moral rights.[44] By contrast, in the sphere of related rights, there is no equivalent incorporation of the Rome Convention. Instead the TRIPs agreement has its own code of obligations relating to performers.

Performers must be provided with exclusive rights covering fixation, reproduction, wireless broadcasting and public communication of live performances (as distinct from recordings thereof). Such rights must last for a minimum of 50 years from the end of the calendar year in which fixation was made or in which the performance took place.[45]

The TRIPs agreement is of great significance for performers' rights, since many more countries will offer reciprocal protection. The level of protection offered by the 1988 Act already exceeds the Article 14 requirement.

(iv) The WIPO Performances and Phonograms Treaty

The WIPO Performances and Phonograms Treaty was adopted at a Diplomatic **12–18** Conference in Geneva in December 1996.[46] It provides that performers must be accorded inalienable moral rights in respect of live aural performances and performances fixed in phonograms.[47] Audiovisual performances are excluded from protection under the Treaty.[48] Performers must be given the "exclusive right of authorising" broadcasting (except re-broadcasting), communication to the public (except where the performance is a broadcast performance) and fixation of live performances, direct or indirect reproduction of performances fixed in phonograms, distribution of performances fixed in phonograms, commercial rental of performances fixed in phonograms and making available on demand performances fixed in phonograms.[49] The term of protection for performers is 50 years from the end of the year in which the performance was fixed in a phonogram.[50] Moral rights must last at least until the expiry of performers' economic rights.[51] There are also provisions concerning copy protection measures, rights management information, and enforcement.[52] The Treaty entered into force on March 6, 2002.

---

[41] Information Society Directive, Arts 2, 11(1)(a).

[42] Information Society Directive, Art.3(2)(a).

[43] The Agreement on Trade-Related Aspects of Intellectual Property Rights (TRIPs) is annexed to and forms part of the Marrakesh Agreement Establishing the World Trade Organisation, signed by 124 nations on April 15, 1994.

[44] TRIPs, Arts 1–21 (omitting Art.6 *bis* of the Berne Convention).

[45] TRIPs, Arts 14(1), (5).

[46] See paras 24–119 *et seq.*, below.

[47] WIPO Performances and Phonograms Treaty, Art.5(1).

[48] For a discussion of this exclusion, see paras 24–119 *et seq.*, below.

[49] Arts 6–10.

[50] Art.17(1).

[51] Art.5(2).

[52] Arts 18, 19, 23.

2. THE SUBSTANTIVE RIGHTS

A. IMPLEMENTATION OF DIRECTIVES AND OVERVIEW

12–19   **Amendments to the 1988 Act.** The United Kingdom's obligations under the Rome Convention were fully addressed by the 1988 Act. However, the various Community measures referred to above necessitated significant additions and amendments to the Act. Changes were effected by means of three statutory instruments:[53] the Duration of Copyright and Rights in Performances Regulations 1995,[54] the Copyright and Related Rights Regulations 1996[55] and the Copyright and Related Rights Regulations 2003.[56] These successive alterations have resulted in something of a patchwork of rights, the reason for this being that implementation of these Directives has been effected by statutory instrument using the powers conferred by the European Communities Act 1972. This means that amendments have necessarily been restricted to changes that the Directives have required. Had the Act been amended by primary legislation a more coherent scheme could have been provided for.

12–20   **Present rights.** The new rights required by the Rental and Related Rights Directive were added to the existing scheme, leaving the original rights in place. Thus the present rights are as follows:

    (i) *Rights originally granted by the* 1988 Act

        (a) *Performers' non-property rights*:

            (i) fixation and live broadcasting of live performances (section 182);[57]

            (ii) public performance and communication to the public by means of a recording made without consent (section 183);[58]

            (iii) dealing in illicit recordings (section 184).

        (b) *Recording rights* of persons having exclusive recording contracts with performers (section 185).

        Under the terms of the 1988 Act as enacted, these rights were intended to be unlike copyright. There were various differences, notably that they could not be assigned, although performers' rights were transmissible on death.[59] These differences have been maintained in the Act as amended.[60] Infringements of these rights were actionable only as breaches of statu-

---

[53] All three of the Directives relevant to Part II of the 1988 Act were implemented after the dates required by their provisions. The Rental and Related Rights Directive (Dir.92/100) was due to be implemented by July 1, 1994, but was not implemented in the UK until December 1, 1996. The Duration Directive (Dir.93/98) was due to be implemented by July 1, 1995, but not implemented in the UK until January 1, 1996. The Information Society Directive was due to be implemented by December 2002, but was not implemented in the UK until October 31, 2003. Potential liability under *Francovich v Italy* ([1991] I E.C.R. 5357) and *Brasserie du Pêcheur SA v Germany* ([1996] 1 C.M.L.R. 889) has been limited by the drafting of the transitional provisions, which are generous to users.

[54] SI 1995/3297.

[55] SI 1996/2967.

[56] SI 2003/2498.

[57] As enacted, the rights were also infringed by the inclusion of the performance in a live cable programme service. The result of the implementation of the Information Society Directive has in effect been to bring cable transmissions within the ambit of broadcasts. See para. 7–73, above.

[58] Again, the result of implementation of the Information Society Directive has been to alter to original provisions of the 1988 Act to replace the broadcasting and cable programme rights by a new right (the communication to the public right) which includes broadcasting and on-demand transmissions. See para. 12–66, below.

[59] CDPA 1988, s.192 as enacted.

[60] ss.192A, 192B.

tory duty, and this too remains the same.[61] An important element of the original scheme of protection was its creation of criminal offences in relation to dealing with or using illicit recordings and certain other related acts, and this too has been retained.

(ii) *Further rights granted on amendment of the* 1988 Act

Performers' property rights. The Rental and Related Rights Directive requires that certain performers' rights be capable of transfer and assignment. The Act as amended therefore confers a category of 'performers' property rights'.[62] This is of particular significance when the rights are infringed, since these are now actionable in the same way as other property rights, including copyright. Performers' property rights are those conferred by sections 182A–C and consist of a reproduction right, distribution right, rental right and lending right.[63] The Rental and Lending Directive also requires that performers have an unwaivable right to equitable remuneration in certain circumstances. These rights are conferred by sections 182D and 191F–H.[64]

It should be noted that the rights conferred by Part II on performers are independent of any copyright in, or moral rights relating to, any work performed or any film or sound recording of, or broadcast including, the performance.[65] The rights are also independent of any other right or obligation arising otherwise than under Part II of the Act,[66] *e.g.* under another statutory provision or by reason of contractual provisions or as the result of a duty of confidence.

12–21

Transitional provisions. The rights conferred by Part II apply in relation to performances taking place before the commencement of Part II (August 1, 1989), but no act done before commencement, or in pursuance of arrangements made before commencement, is to be regarded as infringing those rights.[67] The various amendments made to the Act have necessitated a considerable number of further transitional provisions, found in the relevant statutory instruments. The transitional provisions of the Duration of Copyright and Rights in Performances Regulations 1995 are discussed with the substantive amendments to the provisions affecting the duration of Part II rights.[68] The Copyright and Related Rights Regulations 1996 apply to performances given before and after commencement, subject to any special transitional provisions and savings.[69] No act done before commencement is to be regarded as an infringement of any new right, or as giving rise to any right to remuneration arising by virtue of the 1996 Regulations.[70] There is a saving for existing agreements made before November 19, 1992, and (unless expressly provided) no act done in pursuance of such an agreement after commencement is to be regarded as an infringement of any new right.[71] Any new right is exercisable as from commencement by the performer or (if he has died) by the person who immediately before commencement was entitled by virtue of

12–22

---

[61] See para. 12–104, below.
[62] CDPA 1988, s.191.
[63] See para. 12–43, below.
[64] See para. 12–48, below.
[65] CDPA 1988, s.180(4)(a).
[66] s.180(4)(b).
[67] CDPA 1988, s.180(3).
[68] SI 1995/3297, Pt III. See paras 12–33 *et seq.*, below.
[69] SI 1996/2967, reg.26(1). Specific transitional provisions are discussed elsewhere, with the relevant material.
[70] reg.26(2).
[71] reg.27. This is the date of the adoption of Council Directive No.92/100/EEC.

section 192(2) to exercise the rights conferred on the performer by Part II in relation to that performance.[72]

As to amendments made by the 2003 Regulations,[73] implementing the Information Society Directive, the Regulations apply to performances given before as well as after the date the Regulations came into force (October 31, 2003).[74] No act done before commencement is to be regarded as an infringement of any new or extended right arising by virtue of the Regulations.[75] Nothing in the Regulations is to affect any agreement made before December 22, 2002[76] and no act done after commencement, in pursuance of an agreement made before December 22, 2002 is to be regarded as an infringement of any new or extended right arising by virtue of the Regulations.[77] Other transitional provisions are dealt with in this Chapter as they arise.

B. Protected Performances

(i) Definition of performance

12–23   There is no definition of a performer in the 1988 Act, but the meaning of that term can be gathered from the statutory definition of a performance. In Part II "performance" refers to live performances of various kinds given by one or more individuals.[78] The relevant kinds of performance are a dramatic performance, which includes dance and mime[79] ; a musical performance[80] ; a reading or recitation of a literary work[81] ; and a performance of a variety act or any similar presentation.[82] In general, sporting performances will not fall within these categories. There is no requirement that the performance be one in public; a performance in a private place such as recording studio will qualify.[83]

Part II applies to any such performance which is, or so far as it is, a live performance given by one or more individuals.[84] This definition thus excludes from protection under Part II the use of recorded material or material on film which might form part of, for example, a dramatic or musical presentation. If the performance is given by more than one individual, each performer is entitled to the rights conferred in relation to his or her performance:[85] there is no concept of a joint performance.[86] In most, if not all cases, the performance of each performer is distinct from the performance of the other or others.[87] Note that there is no requirement of originality, so that performers' rights can subsist in each separate performance of, say, the same dramatic work.

---

[72] reg.30(1).
[73] The Copyright and Related Rights Regulations 2003 (SI 2003/2498).
[74] reg.31(1).
[75] reg.31(2).
[76] reg.32(1). December 22, 2002 is the date when the Information Society Directive should have been implemented. See Art.13(1).
[77] Copyright and Related Rights Regulations (SI 2003/2498), reg.32(2).
[78] CDPA 1988, s.180(2); *Cf.* s.19(2) (definition of "performance" in relation to a work).
[79] s.180(2)(a); see s.3(1).
[80] s.180(2)(b); see s.3(1). The relatively simple performance was found to be a musical performance in *Bamgboye v Reed* [2002] EWHC 2922, QBD.
[81] s.180(2)(c); s.211(1).
[82] s.180(2)(d).
[83] *Bamgboye v Reed* [2002] EWHC 2922, QBD.
[84] CDPA 1988, s.180.
[85] *Bamgboye v Reed* [2002] EWHC 2922, QBD.
[86] *Bamgboye v Reed* [2002] EWHC 2922, QBD.
[87] CDPA 1988, s.180. *Cf.* s.10(1).

(ii) Qualifying performances of performers

No formalities (such as registration, deposit or notice) are required for the subsis- **12–24**
tence of performers' rights. However, performers' rights subsist only in relation
to a qualifying performance. A performance is a qualifying performance for the
purposes of Part II if it is either:

(1) given by a qualifying individual; or

(2) takes place in a qualifying country.[88]

A qualifying individual means a citizen or subject of, or an individual resident
in, a qualifying country.[89] A qualifying country means the United Kingdom[90] or
another member of the European Economic Community[91] or, to the extent that
any order under section 208 of the 1988 Act so provides, a country designated
under that section as enjoying reciprocal protection.[92]

The reference in the definition of a qualifying individual to a person being a
citizen or subject of a qualifying country is to be construed, in relation to the
United Kingdom, as a reference to his being a British citizen[93] and, in relation to
a colony of the United Kingdom, as a reference to his being a British Dependant
Territories' citizen by connection with that colony.[94]

(iii) Reciprocal protection

Her Majesty may, by Order in Council,[95] designate as enjoying reciprocal protec- **12–25**
tion under Part II a Convention Country[96] or a country as to which Her Majesty is
satisfied that protection has been made or will be made under the law giving adequate protection for British performances.[97] A Convention Country is a country
which is a party to a convention relating to performers' rights to which the United
Kingdom is also a party.[98] A British performance means a performance given by
an individual who is a British citizen or a resident in the United Kingdom, or taking place in the United Kingdom.[99] A large number of countries are currently
designated as Convention Countries.[1] As the TRIPs agreement continues to take
effect, more countries will offer reciprocal protection.

---

[88] CDPA 1988, s.181. See Ch.3, above.

[89] s.206(1).

[90] s.206(1)(a).

[91] s.206(1)(b).

[92] s.206(1)(c). See para. 12–25, below.

[93] s.206(2)(a).

[94] s.206(2)(b).

[95] A statutory instrument containing an Order in Council under s.208 of the 1988 Act is subject to
annulment in pursuance of a resolution of either House of Parliament: s.208(6).

[96] CDPA 1988, s.208(1)(a).

[97] s.208(1)(b). This power (i.e. in relation to "non-Convention countries") is exercisable in relation
to any of the Channel Islands, the Isle of Man or any colony of the United Kingdom as in relation
to a foreign country: CDPA 1988, s.208(5). If the law of a non-Convention country contains adequate protection only for certain descriptions of performance, an Order designating that country
must contain provision limiting to a corresponding extent the protection afforded by Pt II in relation to performances connected with that country: CDPA 1988, s.208(4). To date, the Isle of Man
has been designated. See Performances (Reciprocal Protection) (Convention Countries and Isle
of Man) Order 2003 (SI 2003), see Vol.2 at C1.v.

[98] CDPA 1988, s.208(2).

[99] s.208(3).

[1] See Performances (Reciprocal Protection)(Convention Countries and Isle of Man) Order 2003
(SI 2003), see Vol.2 at C1.v. Designated Convention countries are listed in the Schedule to the
Order. Pt II lists countries which are party to the Rome Convention (entitled to full protection
under Pt II of the 1988 Act). Pt III lists TRIPs signatories which are not party to the Rome
Convention (partial protection). See the Order, Art.3 and the Explanatory Note.

(iv) Territoriality

12–26   Part II of the Copyright, Designs and Patents Act 1988 extends to England and Wales, Scotland and Northern Ireland,[2] but not to the Channel Islands, the Isle of Man or any colony.[3]

For the purposes of Part II the territorial waters of the United Kingdom are treated as part of the United Kingdom.[4] Part II applies to things done in the United Kingdom sector of the continental shelf,[5] on a structure or vessel which is present there for purposes directly connected with the exploration of the sea bed or subsoil or the exploitation of their national resources as it applies to things done in the United Kingdom.[6]

Part II also applies to things done on a British ship, aircraft or hovercraft as it applies to things done in the United Kingdom.[7] A "British ship" means a ship which is a British ship for the purposes of the Merchant Shipping Acts (see section 2 of the Merchant Shipping Act 1988) otherwise than by virtue of registration in a country outside the United Kingdom.[8] "British aircraft" and "British hovercraft" mean an aircraft or hovercraft registered in the United Kingdom.

C. SUBSISTENCE OF RECORDING RIGHTS

(i) General

12–27   The 1988 Act also creates recording rights in relation to a performance. No right of this kind existed before the 1988 Act. The right is conferred on a person who is a party to and has the benefit of an exclusive recording contract to which the performance is subject[9] or to whom the benefit of the contract has been assigned[10] and who is a qualifying person. Such a person is referred to as a "person having recording rights". That person may be either an individual or a corporate entity.

If a person is subject to an exclusive recording contract, but the person who is a party to or has the benefit of it is not a qualifying person, then the person having the recording rights is any person who is licensed by such a person to make recordings of the performance with a view to their commercial exploitation[11] or any person to whom the benefit of such a licence has been assigned[12] and who is a qualifying person.

No formalities (such as a registration, deposit or notice) are required for the subsistence of recording rights.

(ii) Exclusive recording contract

12–28   An "exclusive recording contract" is defined as having certain characteristics[13] :
>   (1) it must be a contract;

---

[2] CDPA 1988, s.207.

[3] s.210(1).

[4] s.109(1).

[5] This is an area designated by order under the Continental Shelf Act 1964, s.1(7): CDPA 1988, s.209(3).

[6] CDPA 1988, s.209(2).

[7] s.210(1).

[8] s.210(2). Merchant Shipping Act 1988, s.2 has been repealed by the Merchant Shipping (Registration, etc.) Act 1993.

[9] CDPA 1988, s.185(2)(a).

[10] s.185(2)(b).

[11] s.185(3)(a).

[12] s.185(3)(b).

[13] CDPA 1988, s.185(1).

(2) it must be between a performer and another person;

(3) it must entitle that other person to make recordings of one of more of the performer's performances with a view to their commercial exploitation. The performances do not have to be qualifying performances within the meaning of the provisions.

(4) it must so entitle him to the exclusion of all other persons, including the performer. The expression "with a view to commercial exploitation" means with a view to the recordings being sold or let for hire, or shown or played in public.[14]

"Recording", in relation to a performance, means a film or sound recording:

(a) made directly from the live performance,

(b) made from a broadcast of the performance

(c) made directly or indirectly, from another recording of the performance.[15]

(iii) Qualifying person

A "qualifying person" means a qualifying individual or a body corporate or other body having legal personality which is formed under the law of part of the United Kingdom or another qualifying country,[16] and has in any qualifying country a place of business at which substantial business activity is carried on.[17] In determining whether substantial business activity is carried on at a place of business in any country, no account is to be taken of dealings in goods which are at all material times outside that country.[18]

12–29

D. DURATION OF RIGHTS

(i) General

As originally enacted, Part II of the 1988 Act provided simply that performers' rights and recording rights continued to subsist in a performance until the end of the period of 50 years from the end of the calendar year in which the performance took place.[19] However, the Duration Directive[20] required significant changes to this rule, and these were implemented by the Duration of Copyright and Rights in Performances Regulations.[21]

12–30

First, As the Act now stands, Part II rights expire at the end of a period of 50 years from the end of the calendar year in which the performance takes place, unless a recording of the performance is released during that period, in which case the rights expire 50 years from the end of the calendar year in which the recording is released.[22] A recording is "released" for these purposes when it is first published, played or shown in public or communicated to the public, and no account is to be taken of any unauthorised act.[23] Thus there is a potential extension of term where release does not take place within the same year as the performance.

---

[14] s.185(4).

[15] s.180(2); definitions as for Pt I: s.211(1), s.5A, s.5B.

[16] CDPA 1988, s.206(1)(a). See para. 12–24, above. See also Ch.3, above.

[17] s.206(1)(b).

[18] s.206(3).

[19] CDPA 1988, s.191.

[20] Directive 93/98 harmonising the term of protection of copyright and certain related rights; [1993] O.J. L290/9.

[21] SI 1995/3297. See Vol.2 at A3.ii.

[22] CDPA 1988, s.191(2).

[23] s.191(3), as amended on implemtation of the Information Society Directive to replace the reference to a record being broadcast or included in a cable programme service by its being "com-

12–31   Secondly, the Duration Directive adopts the principle of the "shorter term" to encourage other countries to adopt equivalent standards.[24] The effect of this is to introduce reciprocal treatment for non-EEA nationals. Thus, where a performer is a not a national of an EEA state,[25] the duration of the rights conferred by Part II is that to which the performer is entitled in the country of which he is a national, provided that this does not exceed the period which would apply if the performer were an EEA national.[26] In relation to performances given before July 1, 1995 the performer is to be treated as an EEA national if he was on July 1, 1995, regarded under the law of the United Kingdom or under the law of another EEA state relating to performers' rights as a national of that State.[27]

There is a derogation from this principle to allow Member States which (at the date of adoption of the Directive) granted a longer term of protection pursuant to their international obligations than would result from reciprocal treatment to continue to do so.[28] The implementing provision is section 191(5), which states that if or to the extent that the application of the reciprocal treatment provision (section 191(4)) would be at variance with an international obligation to which the United Kingdom became subject prior to October 29, 1993, the duration of Part II rights will be governed by the rules on national treatment.[29]

(ii) Application

12–32   The amended provisions relating to the duration of rights under Part II of the 1988 Act apply to performances before and after commencement, and may extend or revive performers' rights. Specifically, the new provisions apply:

    (a) to performances taking place after commencement (January 1, 1996)[30] ;

    (b) to "existing performances"[31] which first qualify for protection under Part II after commencement[32] ;

    (c) to "existing protected performances", subject to the general saving for any longer period applicable under the 1988 provision[33] ;

    (d) to "existing performances":

        (i) in which rights under Part II expired after commencement of that Part (August 1, 1989) and before December 31, 1995, or

        (ii) which were protected by earlier enactments relating to the protection of performers and in which rights under that Part did not arise by reason only that the performance was given at a date such that the rights would have ceased to subsist before the commencement of that part (*i.e.* more than 50 years before August 1, 1989),

    but which were on July 1, 1995 protected in another EEA state under legislation relating to copyright on related rights.[34]

An "existing performance" is one given before commencement (January 1,

---

municated to the public". As to the meaning of this expession, see CDPA 1988, ss.211 and 20(2), and para. 7–98, above.

[24] Duration Directive 93/98, Art.7(2).

[25] "EEA state" means a state which is a Contracting Party to the Agreement on the European Economic Area 1992 (see para. 25–01, below).

[26] CDPA 1988, s.191(4).

[27] Duration of Copyright and Rights in Performances Regulations (hereafter DCRP Regs), (SI 1995/3297), reg.36(2).

[28] Duration Directive, Art.7(3).

[29] CDPA 1988, ss.191(2), (3).

[30] DCRP Regs 1995, reg.29(a).

[31] reg.27(1)(a).

[32] reg.29(b).

[33] reg.29(c).

[34] reg.29(d).

1996).[35] An "existing protected performance" is a performance in relation to which rights under Part II of the 1988 Act subsisted immediately before commencement.[36] A general saving provides that any rights under Part II of the 1988 Act in an existing protected performance shall continue to subsist until the date on which they would have expired under the 1988 provisions, if that date is later than the date on which the rights would expire under the new provisions.[37]

(iii) Transitional provisions

Extensive transitional provisions are necessary to deal with rights in relation to performances which are extended or were revived as a result of the amended duration provisions. **12–33**

Extended performance rights. These are defined as rights under Part II which subsist by virtue of the amended provisions after the date on which they would have expired under the unamended 1988 provisions.[38] Any extended performance rights are exercisable from commencement by the person who was entitled to exercise those rights immediately before commencement, that is: **12–34**

  (a) in the case of performers' rights, the performer or (if he has died) the person entitled by virtue of section 192(2) of the 1988 Act to exercise those rights[39];

  (b) in the case of recording rights, the person who was within the meaning of section 185 of the 1988 Act the person having those rights.[40]

Revived performance rights. These are defined as rights under Part II which subsist by virtue of the amended provisions either: **12–35**

  (a) after having expired under the unamended 1988 provisions, or

  (b) in relation to a performance which was protected by earlier enactments relating to the protection of performers and in which rights under that Part did not arise because the performance was given at a date such that the rights would have ceased to subsist before the commencement of that Part. These latter are known as "revived pre-1988 rights".[41]

Any revived performance rights are exercisable as from commencement:

  (a) in the case of rights which expired after the commencement of the 1988 Act, by the person who was entitled to exercise those rights immediately before they expired[42];

  (b) in the case of revived pre-1988 performers' rights, by the performer or his personal representatives[43];

  (c) in the case of revived pre-1988 recording rights, by the person who would have been the person having those rights immediately before the death of the performer, applying the provisions of section 185 of the Act to the circumstances then obtaining.[44]

Any remuneration or damages received by a person's personal representatives by virtue of extended or revived performance rights devolves as part of that

---

[35] reg.27(1)(a).
[36] reg.27(1)(b).
[37] reg.28.
[38] DCRP Regs 1995, reg.30.
[39] reg.31(1)(a).
[40] reg.31(1)(b).
[41] DCRP Regs 1995, reg.30(b).
[42] reg.31(2)(a).
[43] reg.31(2)(b).
[44] reg.31(2)(c).

person's estate as if the right had subsisted and been vested in him immediately before his death.[45]

Existing licences relating to the exploitation of an existing protected performance which subsisted immediately before commencement, and which are not to expire before the end of the period for which rights under Part II subsist in relation to that performance are automatically extended for the period of any extended performance rights, subject to any agreement to the contrary.[46]

12–36   **Infringement.** There are a number of transitional provisions relating to infringement of revived performance rights, some of which remain potentially relevant. Thus, it is not an infringement of revived performance rights in a performance to do anything after commencement in pursuance of arrangements made before January 1, 1995 at a time when the performance was not protected, nor to issue to the public after commencement a recording of a performance made before July 1, 1995 at a time when the performance was not protected.[47] It is not an infringement of revived performance rights in a performance to do anything after commencement in relation to a sound recording or film made before commencement, or made in pursuance of arrangements made before commencement, which contains a recording of the performance if the recording of the performance was made before July 1, 1995 at a time when the performance was not protected, or the recording of the performance was made in pursuance of arrangements made before July 1, 1995 at a time when the performance was not protected.[48] It is not an infringement of revived performance rights in a performance to do after commencement anything at a time when, or in pursuance of arrangements made at a time when, the name and address of a person entitled to authorise the act cannot by reasonable inquiry be ascertained.[49]

12–37   **Licences of right.** Such licences are available in respect of revived performance rights. The potential licensee will be treated as having the right owner's consent to acts which require consent, subject only to the payment of such reasonable remuneration as may be agreed or determined in default of agreement by the Copyright Tribunal.[50] The potential licensee must give reasonable notice of his intention to the rights owner, stating when he intends to begin to do the acts.[51] If he does not give such notice, his acts will not be treated as having consent.[52] If he does give such notice, his acts will be treated as licensed, and reasonable remuneration will be payable in respect of them even if its amount is not agreed or determined until later.[53] Either the rights owner or the person claiming to be treated as having his consent may apply to the Copyright Tribunal to settle the remuneration payable.[54] Either party may subsequently apply to the Tribunal to vary the order, but only by special leave if the application is within 12 months of the original order.[55]

---

[45] reg.31(3).
[46] reg.32.
[47] DCRP Regs 1995, reg.33(2).
[48] reg.33(3).
[49] reg.33(4). "Arrangements" means arrangements for the exploitation of the performance in question (reg.33(5)). For a fuller discussion of this topic, see para. 9–152 et seq., above.
[50] DCRP Regs 1995, reg.34(1).
[51] reg.34(2).
[52] reg.34(3).
[53] reg.34(4).
[54] reg.35(1).
[55] reg.35(3)(4).

3. OWNERSHIP AND TRANSMISSION OF RIGHTS

A. OWNERSHIP

(i) Performers' rights

The first owner of performers' rights is the performer. There is a single exception to this rule, created by the Copyright and Related Rights Regulations.[56] Where, before commencement (December 1, 1996), the owner or prospective owner of performers' rights in a performance has authorised a person to make a copy of the recording of the performance, any new right (*i.e.* one created as a result of the 1996 Regulations) in relation to that copy vests in that person on commencement. **12–38**

(ii) Recording rights

[57] The right is conferred on a person who is party to and has the benefit of an exclusive recording contract to which the performance is subject[58] or to whom the benefit of the contract has been assigned[59] and who is a qualifying person. Such a person is referred to as a "person having recording rights". That person may be either an individual or a corporate entity. **12–39**

If a performance is subject to an exclusive recording contract, but the person who is a party to or has the benefit of it is not a qualifying person, then the person having the recording rights is any person who is licensed by such a person to make recordings of the performance with a view to their commercial exploitation[60] or any person to whom the benefit of such a licence has been assigned[61] and who is a qualifying person.

(iii) Equitable remuneration

A performer is entitled to equitable remuneration in two cases: firstly, where a sound recording is broadcast or otherwise communicated to the public; secondly, where the performer's rental right in a film or sound recording is transferred to its producer, the performer nevertheless retains a right to equitable remuneration for rental of the film or sound recording.[62] **12–40**

B. TRANSMISSION

(i) Performers' non-property rights

Performers' non-property rights are not assignable, although they are transmissible on death.[63] On the death of a person entitled to any such rights the right passes to such person as the performer may by testamentary disposition specifically direct, and if or to the extent that there is no such direction, the right is exercis- **12–41**

---

[56] SI 1996/2967, reg.31(b).
[57] See para. 12–27, above.
[58] CDPA 1988, s.185(2)(a).
[59] s.185(2)(b).
[60] s.185(3)(a).
[61] s.185(3)(b).
[62] CDPA 1988, s.191G(1); see paras 12–45 *et seq.*, below.
[63] CDPA 1988, s.192A(1).

able by his personal representatives.[64] Any damages recovered by personal representatives in respect of an infringement after a person's death devolve as part of his estate as if the right of action had subsisted and been vested in him immediately before his death.[65] Consent which is binding upon the deceased will bind the person or persons to whom the rights pass.[66]

(ii) Recording rights

12–42 As before, recording rights are not assignable or transmissible, even on the death of an indvidual who is entitled.[67] However, the contractual rights on which they depend are assignable and in such an event the assignee will become the person entitled to the recording rights.[68]

(iii) Performers' property rights

12–43 As has been seen, it was a requirement of the Rental and Related Rights Directive that certain rights be proprietary, and therefore a category of "performers'" property rights was created on implementation.[69]

A performer's property rights are those conferred by sections 182A–C: namely, the reproduction right, distribution right, rental right and lending right. These are transmissible by assignment, by testamentary disposition or by operation of law, as personal or moveable property.[70] There is a presumption of transfer of the rental right where there is a film production agreement,[71] but also a right to equitable remuneration where the rental right is transferred.[72] There is a similar right to equitable remuneration for exploitation of a sound recording.[73]

Assignments may be partial, that is, limited to certain acts or to a certain period.[74] An assignment must be in writing signed by or on behalf of the assignor.[75] Specific provision is made for cases where a performer or his agent assigns (or purports to assign) the performer's property rights in relation to a future recording of a performance to another person.[76] If on the rights coming into existence the assignee or another person claiming under him would be entitled as against all other persons to require the rights to be vested in him, they vest in the assignee or his successor in title.[77] This ensures that an assignee who would be entitled to specific performance of the agreement becomes the legal owner of the rights as soon as the recording is made. Equally, where the assignee is not entitled to specific performance, a purported assignment would be ineffective.

12–44 A licence granted by the owner of a performer's property right is binding on every successor in title to that interest (or prospective interest) in the rights,

---

[64] s.192A(2).
[65] s.192A(5).
[66] s.193(3).
[67] CDPA 1988, s.192B(1).
[68] ss.192B(2), s.185(2)(b), (3)(b).
[69] CDPA 1988, s.191A.
[70] s.191B(1).
[71] s.191F.
[72] s.191G, see para. 12–48, below.
[73] s.182D, see para. 12–46, below.
[74] s.191B(2). *cf.* CDPA 1988, s.90(2).
[75] s.191B(3).
[76] s.191C(1).
[77] s.191C(2). See para. 5–105, above, for a discussion of the equivalent provision in relation to assignments of future copyright.

except a purchaser in good faith for valuable consideration and without notice (actual or constructive) of the licence or a person deriving title from such a purchaser.[78] It is expressly provided that an exclusive licensee of a performer's property rights has the same rights and remedies as if the exclusive licence were a assignment.[79]

There is a presumption that a bequest of any material thing containing an original recording of a performance which was not published before the death of the testator shall include any performer's rights in relation to the recording to which the testator was entitled immediately before his death.[80]

(iv) Equitable remuneration

Two rights to equitable remuneration for performers were introduced as a result of the Rental and Related Rights Directive. The rights have been amended following implementation of the Information Society Directive. In outline, one gives the performer the right to claim equitable remuneration with respect of (a) the communication to the public of sound recordings (other than by way of an on-demand service) or (b) the public performance of sound recordings (but not films).[81] The other gives a right to equitable remuneration where the performer transfers (or is presumed to transfer) his rental right in a film or sound recording to the producer of the film or sound recording.[82]

12–45

Right to equitable remuneration for exploitation of a sound recording. The first right arises where a commercially published sound recording of the whole or any substantial part of a qualifying performance is played in public, or included in a communication to the public, other than by way of an on-demand service.[83] The meaning of "commercially published" is not entirely clear. As to the statutory definitions in the 1988 Act, for the purposes of Part II (Rights in Performances) "publication" is to have the same meaning as under Part I (Copyright), that is, the same meaning as in section 175, where it means, for present purposes, the issue of copies to the public.[84] Excluded from this meaning is any publication which is merely colourable and not intended to satisfy the reasonable requirements of the public, and any unauthorised act. Nothing, however, is said about the meaning of "commercial publication" where it appears in Part II, although it is defined in section 175 for the purposes of Part I, where it means either (a) the issuing of copies of the work to the public at a time when copies made in advance of the receipt of orders are generally available to the public; or (b) making the work available to the public by means of an electronic retrieval system.[85]

This definition is not, however, of any relevance for present purposes. In fact,

12–46

---

[78] CDPA 1988, ss.191B(4), 191C(3).

[79] ss.191L(1), 191D(1).

[80] s.191E.

[81] CDPA 1988, s.182D.

[82] s.191F–H.

[83] CDPA 1988, s.191F–H. In the present context, what this means in practice is thta the right will arise where the recording is broadcast. An on-demand service is used as shorthand in the text for a service whereby the recording is made available to the public by electronic transmission in such a way that members of the public may access it from a place and at a time individually chosen by them. See ss.211 and 20. Broadcast is defined in s.4. Where the recording is made available by way of an on-demand service, the peformer has a right to prevent this taking place altogether, not just to equitable remuneration: ss.182(C), 182D(1)(b). And see para. 12–66, below. As from October 31, 2003, performers have had no right to any equitable remuneration in respect of such a service. See the Copyright and Related Rights Regulations 2003 (SI 2003/2498), reg.34(1).

[84] As to the meaning of "issue to the public", see para. 7–76, above.

[85] See para. 11–12, above, for a discussion of the meaning of the expression "commercially published".

the expression "commercially published" in section 182D is derived from Article 8(2) of the Rental and Related Rights Directive, which states that Member States are to provide for equitable remuneration for performers in circumstances where use is made of a phonogram which has been "published for commercial purposes", or of a reproduction of such a phonogram. It is by reference to the wording and purpose of the Directive that the expression must be construed.

12–47 Where the rights arises, as described above, the performer is entitled to equitable remuneration from the owner of the copyright in the sound recording.[86] The right may not be assigned except to a collecting society for the purpose of enabling it to enforce the right on the performer's behalf.[87] However, the right is transmissible by testamentary disposition or by operation of law, and it may then be further assigned.[88] The amount payable is as agreed by or on behalf of the persons by and to whom it is payable.[89] In default of such agreement, application may be made to the Copyright Tribunal to determine the amount payable.[90] The Copyright Tribunal may also vary a previous agreement or determination.[91] The Tribunal may order any method of calculation and paying equitable remuneration as it may determine to be reasonable in the circumstances, taking into account the importance of the contribution of the performer to the sound recording.[92] An agreement purporting to exclude or restrict the right to equitable remuneration, or purporting to prevent a person questioning the amount of equitable remuneration or to restrict the powers of the Copyright Tribunal, is of no effect.[93] There is no provision to parallel section 191H(4), which states that in cases where the rental right is transferred, remuneration is not to be considered inequitable merely because it was paid as a single payment, or at the time of transfer of the right.

The right is not subject to any special transitional provisions. However, the general transitional provision under the Copyright and Related Rights Regulations 1996 applies, namely, that no act done before commencement (December 1, 1996) gives rise to any remuneration.[94] Note that the rights to equitable remuneration are not regarded as "new rights" for the purposes of the transitional provisions of the Copyright and Related Rights Regulations 1996, so the saving for agreements made before November 19, 1992, does not apply.[95]

12–48 **Right to equitable remuneration where rental right transferred.** Where a performer has transferred his rental right concerning a sound recording or a film to the producer of the sound recording or film, he retains the right to equitable remuneration for the rental.[96] An agreement purporting to exclude or restrict the right to equitable remuneration is of no effect.[97] This right may not be assigned by the performer, except to a collecting society for the purpose of enabling it to

---

[86] CDPA 1988, s.182D(1).

[87] s.182D(2). There is no restriction on the nature of the collecting society. cf. CDPA 1988, s.191G(6). As noted above, the right to equitable remuneration in respect of on-demand services was removed as from October 31, 2003. Any assignment made before this date which had effect under CDPA 1988, s.182D(2) is, as from that date, to cease to apply insofar as it relates to this on-demand right. See the Copyright and Related Rights Regulations 2003, reg.34(2).

[88] CDPA 1988, s.182D(2).

[89] s.182D(3).

[90] s.182D(4). As to the basis of assessing such remuneration, see para. 29–134, below, and *Stichting ter Exploitatie van Naburige Rechten v Nederlandse Omroep Stichting* E.C.J., Case C–245/00 [2003] R.P.C. 42.

[91] CDPA 1988, s.182D(5).

[92] s.182D(6).

[93] s.182D(7).

[94] Copyright and Related Rights Regulations 1996 (SI 1996/2967), reg.26(2).

[95] regs 25(3)(b), 27.

[96] CDPA 1988, s.191G(1).

[97] s.191G(5).

enforce the right on his behalf.[98] However, the right is transmissible by testamentary disposition or by operation of law, and it may then be further assigned.[99] The amount payable is as agreed by or on behalf of the persons by and to whom it is payable.[1] In default of such agreement, application may be made to the Copyright Tribunal to determine the amount payable.[2] The Copyright Tribunal may also vary a previous agreement or determination.[3] The Tribunal may order any method of calculation and paying equitable remuneration as it may determine to be reasonable in the circumstances, taking into account the importance of the contribution of the performer to the film or sound recording.[4] Remuneration shall not be considered inequitable merely because it was paid by way of a single payment or at the time of the transfer of the rental right.[5]

Where an agreement concerning film production is concluded between a performer and a film producer, the performer shall be presumed, unless the agreement provides to the contrary, to have transferred to the film producer any rental right in relation to the film arising from the inclusion of a recording of his performance in the film.[6] The right to equitable remuneration under section 191G applies where there is a presumed transfer as in the case of an actual transfer.[7]

The right is subject to both general and specific transitional provisions, some of which may still be relevant. Thus, the rights to equitable remuneration are not regarded as "new rights" for the purposes of the transitional provisions, so the saving for agreements made before November 19, 1992 does not apply.[8]   **12–49**

There is a specific transitional provision regarding the right to equitable remuneration applicable to rental after April 1, 1997. No right to equitable remuneration under section 191G (right to equitable remuneration where rental right transferred) arises:

(a) in respect of any rental of a sound recording or film before April 1, 1997, or

(b) in respect of any rental after that date of a sound recording or film made in pursuance of an agreement entered into before July 1, 1994, unless the performer (or a successor in title of his) before January 1, 1997 notified the person by whom the remuneration would be payable that he intended to exercise that right.[9]

4. CONSENT AND LICENSING

A. GENERAL

Consent. Consent for the purposes of Part II by a person having performers' non-property rights or by a person having recording rights may be given in relation to   **12–50**

---

[98] s.191G(2), (6). The collecting society must be an organisation "which has as its main object, or one of its main objects, the exercise of the right to equitable remuneration on behalf of more than one performer".

[99] s.191G(2).

[1] s.191G(3), (4).

[2] s.191H(1). As to the basis of assessing such remuneration, see para. 29–134, below, and *Stichting ter Exploitatie van Naburige Rechten v Nederlandse Omroep Stichting* E.C.J., Case C–245/00 [2003] R.P.C. 42.

[3] CDPA 1988, s.191H(2).

[4] s.191H(3).

[5] s.191H(4).

[6] s.191F(1).

[7] s.191F(4).

[8] Copyright and Related Rights Regulations 1996 (SI 1996/2967), regs 25(3)(b), 27.

[9] reg.33.

a specific performance, a specified description of performances or performances generally. Consent may relate to past or future performances.[10] It is suggested that the same principles apply to performers' property rights.

A person having recording rights in a performance is bound by any consent given by a person through whom he derives his rights under the exclusive recording contract or licence in question, in the same way as if the consent had been given by him.[11]

Where a performer's non-property right passes to another person, any consent binding on the person previously entitled binds the person to whom the right passes in the same way as if the consent had been given by him.[12]

B. POWERS OF THE COPYRIGHT TRIBUNAL

12–51   **The Copyright Tribunal.** The Tribunal has jurisdiction to hear and determine proceedings under various sections of the Act.[13] Its jurisdiction in relation to performers' rights has been expanded considerably since 1988, but it still has no jurisdiction at all in the case of recording rights. Significant changes were made as a result of the Rental and Related Rights Directive, notably the removal of the Tribunal's jurisdiction to consent on behalf of a performer where consent had unreasonably been withheld,[14] and by extending the Tribunal's jurisdiction in relation to the rights to equitable remuneration granted by the Rental and Lending Rights Directive.[15] Various statutory licences and licences of right are available.

(i) Compulsory licensing

12–52   **(1) Power to consent on behalf of a performer.** The 1988 Act as enacted gave the Copyright Tribunal power to give consent on behalf of a performer in two types of situation where a person wished to make a recording from a previous recording of a performance, either where the identity or whereabouts of the performer could not be ascertained, or where the performer unreasonably withheld consent. The Rental and Lending Rights Directive did not allow for compulsory licensing in a case where consent was withheld, and this provision was therefore deleted.[16]

Thus, the Tribunal may now give consent only in a case where the identity or whereabouts of the person entitled to the reproduction right cannot be ascertained by reasonable inquiry.[17] The reference to "person entitled to the reproduction right" replaces the original wording of "performer", to deal with cases where the identity and whereabouts of the performer is known, but not the identity or whereabouts of the present owner(s) of the reproduction right.[18] Application must be made by the person wishing to make a copy of a recording of the performance.[19] It is submitted that the explicit reference to the reproduction right is intended to exclude the distribution, rental and lending rights.

12–53   **(2) Reception and retransmission of a broadcast in a cable programme**

---

[10] CDPA 1988, s.193(1).
[11] s.193(2).
[12] s.193(3).
[13] CDPA 1988, s.205B.
[14] s.205B; paras 12–52 *et seq.*, below.
[15] s.205B; ss.182D, 191H; see para. 12–45, above.
[16] Copyright and Rights in Performances Regulations 1996 (SI 1996/2967) reg.23(2), deleting CDPA 1988, s.190(1)(b).
[17] CDPA 1988, s.190(1) as amended by SI 1996/2967, reg.23.
[18] A lacuna highlighted in *Ex p. Sianel Pedwar Cymru* [1993] E.M.L.R. 251.
[19] CDPA 1988, s.190(1).

service. Where a wireless broadcast made from the United Kingdom is received and immediately retransmitted by cable, Part II rights in a performance or recording included in the broadcast are not infringed if the broadcast is made for reception in the area in which it is retransmitted by cable.[20] Where the retransmission by cable is in pursuance of a relevant "must-carry" requirement,[21] but the area in which the retransmission by cable takes place falls outside the area for reception in which the broadcast is made, the above exception does not apply. In this case, the inclusion of any performance or recording is treated as licensed by the owner of the Part II rights, subject to the payment of a reasonable royalty or other payment. In default of agreement, this may be determined by the Copyright Tribunal, on the application of either the owner of the rights or the person making the broadcast.[22]

(3) Powers exercisable in consequence of competition report. Licences of   **12–54** right are available in respect of performers' property rights if the Secretary of State, the Competition Commission or the Office of Fair Trading reports that certain specified practices may be expected to operate or have operated against the public interest. The two specified practices are:

   (a) conditions in licences granted by the owner of a performer's property rights restricting the use to which a recording may be put by the licensee or the right of the owner to grant other licences;

   (b) a refusal of an owner of a performer's property rights to grant licences on reasonable terms.[23]

In such cases the above bodies have powers to cancel or modify such conditions or to provide that licences in respect of the performer's property rights shall be available as of right.[24] In default of agreement the terms of such a licence will be settled by the Copyright Tribunal.[25]

(4) Lending of certain recordings. The Secretary of State may by order provide   **12–55** that in the cases specified in the order the lending to the public of copies of films or sound recordings shall be treated as licensed by the performer subject only to the payment of a reasonable royalty or other payment.[26] In default of agreement the amount will be determined by the Copyright Tribunal.[27] The order may make different provision for different cases and may specify cases by reference to any factor relating to the work, the copies lent, the lender or the circumstances of the lending.[28] An application to settle the royalty or other sum payable in pursuance of paragraph 14A of Schedule 2 may be made to the Copyright Tribunal by either the owner of a performer's property rights or the person claiming to be treated as licensed by him.[29]

No order may be made under paragraph 14A of Schedule 2 if there is a licensing scheme certified for this purpose under paragraph 16 of Schedule 2A.[30] A person operating or proposing to operate a licensing scheme may apply to the

---

[20] CDPA 1988, Sch.2, para.19(2), as amended.
[21] Sch.2, para.19(3). See further as this provision, s.73.
[22] Sch.2, paras 19(3), 19A.
[23] CDPA 1988, Sch.2A, para.17(1).
[24] Sch.2A, para.17(1A).
[25] Sch.2A, para.17(4).
[26] CDPA 1988, Sch.2, para.14A(1). *Cf.* s.66.
[27] Sch.2, para.14A(1).
[28] Sch.2, para.14A(3).
[29] Sch.2A, para.15(1).
[30] Sch.2, para.14A(2).

Secretary of State to certify the scheme for the purposes of paragraph 14A.[31] The Secretary of State must certify the scheme by statutory instrument if satisfied that it enables the works to which it relates to be identified with sufficient certainty by persons likely to require licences, and sets out clearly any charges payable and the other terms on which licences will be granted.[32] The order shall be revoked if the scheme ceases to be operated, or may be if it is no longer being operated according to its terms.[33]

(ii) Collective licensing

12–56   Collective licensing bodies (or collecting societies) collect and distribute royalties, and issue licences. They also have an important role in monitoring and enforcement. The economies of scale which result benefit both owners and users, although the market power which can result poses a danger if abused. Part II of the 1988 Act as enacted did not contain any provision dealing with the collective licensing of performers' rights. Such provisions have now been added in relation to performers' property rights by the Copyright and Related Rights Regulations 1996. Schedule 2A now regulates the operation of "licensing schemes" and "licensing bodies" in relation to the licensing of performers' property rights, providing a framework similar to those schemes which already exist in relation to copyright. For a detailed treatment of these provisions and of the powers of the Copyright Tribunal, the reader is referred to Chapter 29, below. Details of collecting societies operating in the United Kingdom which represent performers and persons having recording rights may be found in Chapter 28, below.

5. INFRINGEMENT

12–57   **New rights.** Under the original scheme of the 1988 Act, infringements of performers' rights and recording rights were actionable only as breaches of statutory duty.[34] The Rental and Related Rights Directive requires that performers have certain transferable property rights, and the Act was amended accordingly by the 1996 Regulations which introduced the additional performers' property rights of distribution (issuing to the public), rental and lending.[35] Certain remedies are available for infringements of property rights which are not available for breach of statutory duty.[36]

A. INFRINGEMENT OF PERFORMERS' RIGHTS

12–58   Performers' rights in a qualifying performance are infringed by various acts done without the consent of the performer. As explained above, these rights are divided into either property or non-property rights, as identified in the treatment which follows, with the different consequences as to the juridical basis of any infringement and as to transmissibility of the right, etc.[37] What amounts to a qualifying recording has already been discussed.[38] Previously, various acts did not consti-

---

[31] Sch.2A, para.16(1).
[32] Sch.2A, para.16(2).
[33] Sch.2A, para.16(5).
[34] CDPA 1988, s.194 (as enacted).
[35] Copyright and Related Rights Regulations 1996 (SI 1996/2967).
[36] See paras 12–104 *et seq.* and Ch.22, below.
[37] See paras 12–41 and 12–43.
[38] See para. 12–27, above.

tute an infringement if they were done for a person's private and domestic use.[39] Such encroachments on the rights of performers was in effect an exception or limitation on the right and as such were not consistent with the Information Society Directive unless any such exception was expressly permitted by the Directive. In these cases, therefore, the "private and domestic use" provisions have been deleted and such use is now permitted, if at all, by virtue of the permitted act provisions which apply in relation to these rights.[40] These are considered later.

(i) Recording direct from live performance

It is an infringement for a person to make a recording of the whole or any substantial part of a performance directly from the live performance without consent.[41] As the section makes clear, this right refers to the direct recording from a live performance, and makes "bootleggers" infringers. It is a non-property right.[42]

12–59

(ii) Live broadcast of performance

It is an infringement to broadcast live the whole or any substantial part of a performance without consent.[43] For this purpose, the following persons are to be regarded as broadcasting a performance: the person transmitting the programme in question if he has responsibility to any extent for its contents; and/or any person providing the programme who makes the arrangements necessary for its transmission with the person transmitting it.[44] This is a non-property right.[45]

12–60

(iii) Recording from a broadcast of live performance

It is an infringement to make a recording of the whole or any substantial part of a performance directly from a broadcast of the live performance without consent.[46] This is a non-property right.[47]

12–61

(iv) Copying a recording of performance without consent (reproduction right)

It is an infringement to copy a recording of the whole or any substantial part of a performance without consent.[48] This right is referred to as the "reproduction right".[49] Although it was probably the case that this right, as originally introduced following implementation of the Rental and Related Rights Directive,[50] included transient or incidental copying,[51] the effect of the Information Society Directive

12–62

---

[39] See CDPA 1988, ss.182, 182A and 186.See also Art.10 of the Rental and Related Rights Directive.
[40] See para. 12–78 *et seq.*, below.
[41] CDPA 1988, s.182(1)(a).
[42] s.192A.
[43] CDPA 1988, s.182(1)(b).
[44] s.6(3), which applies to performers' rights expressly by virtue of s.211(2). Certain satellite broadcasts are subject to special rules under s.6A.
[45] s.192A.
[46] CDPA 1988, s.182(1)(c).
[47] s.192A.
[48] CDPA 1988, s.182A.
[49] s.182A(3). *Cf.* Rental and Lending Rights Directive, Art.7(1).
[50] See para. 12–13, above.
[51] Just as the reproduction right in the case of copyright almost certainly included transient copying

was to require this to be made clear.[52] The Act was therefore amended on implementation to provide that copying for this purpose includes the making of a copy which is transient or is incidental to some other use of the original recording.[53] At the same time, a permitted act has been introduced to enable temporary copies to be made to enable transmissions in networks and lawful use.[54] It is immaterial whether the copy is made directly or indirectly.[55] This is a property right.[56]

(v) Issuing copies of recording of a performance to the public

12–63   It is an infringement to issue to the public copies of a recording of the whole or any substantial part of a performance without consent.[57] This right to authorise or prohibit the issue of copies to the public is referred to as the "distribution right".[58] The word "copies" is expressly defined to include the issue of the original recording of the live performance.[59]

Issue to the public is defined as:

(a) the act of putting into circulation in the EEA copies not previously put into circulation in the EEA by or with the consent of the performer, or

(b) the act of putting into circulation outside the EEA copies not previously put into circulation in the EEA or elsewhere.[60]

Issue to the public does not include:

(a) any subsequent distribution, sale, hiring or loan of copies previously put into circulation (but see section 182C: consent required for rental or lending), or

(b) any subsequent importation of such copies into the United Kingdom or another EEA state,[61] except insofar as paragraph (a) of subsection (2) applies to putting into circulation in the EEA copies previously put into circulation outside the EEA.[62]

12–64   Thus, the distribution right is exhausted by distribution of copies in the EEA: once a specific copy has been put into circulation in the EEA, its subsequent importation, distribution or sale will not infringe, except where it is rented or lent

---

under the 1956 Act (see para. 7–19, above). There was, however, clearly an argument that the Act seemed to make a distinction between copying for the purposes of copyright infringement, which was expressly stated to include copying which was transient or incidental to some other use of the work (CDPA 1988, ss.17(2), (6)) and copying for the purposes of performers' rights, about which the Act was silent.

[52] Art.7 of the Rental and Related Rights Directive was silent on this point but the Information Society Directive repealed Art.7 (see Art.11(1)(a)). Art.2 of the Information Society Directive now takes its place.

[53] CDPA 1988, s.182A(1A).

[54] Sch.2, para.1A.

[55] s.182A(2). In *Mad Hat Music Ltd v Pulse 8 Records* [1993] E.M.L.R. 172 it was held to be arguable that, where a performer had consented to the making of the original recording, no further consent was needed to the making of records from that recording. Such an argument, it is submitted, is inconsistent with the definition of "recording" in s.180(2)(c) since in both the cases of the original and any subsequent recording the alleged offender "makes" a recording of the performance. This case was not followed in *Bassey v Icon Entertainment Plc* [1995] E.M.L.R. 596, and s.182A confirms that further consent is needed to the making of records from an original recording made with consent.

[56] CDPA 1988, s.192A.

[57] CDPA 1988, s.182B(1).

[58] s.182B(5). *cf.* Rental and Lending Rights Directive, Art.9(1).

[59] s.182B(4).

[60] s.182B(2).

[61] s.182B(3).

[62] s.182B(3). *Cf.* s.18, the equivalent provision in Part I. For a detailed treatment of these definitions, see the discussion on s.18 in paras 7–76 *et seq.*, above.

to the public in the United Kingdom. However, the distribution right is not exhausted by distribution of copies outside the EEA, so the distribution in the EEA of a copy imported from outside the EEA can be an infringement, even if it was put into circulation with the consent of the performer. This distinction follows from the Rental and Related Rights Directive, which envisages a principle of Community exhaustion, not one of international exhaustion.[63] "Issue to the public" is defined in the same way in relation to the issue of copies of works to the public in Part I of the 1988 Act (section 18) and the reader is referred to the discussion in Chapter 7. A discussion of the principles of Community and international exhaustion is contained in Chapter 25, below. This is a property right.[64].

(vi) Renting or lending copies of recording of a performance to the public

It is an infringement to rent or lend to the public copies of a recording of the whole or any substantial part of a performance without consent.[65] The rights to authorise or prohibit such rental and lending are referred to as the "rental right" and "lending right".[66] Again the word "copies" is expressly defined to include the issue of the original recording or the live performance.[67] "Rental" is defined as making a copy of a recording available for use, on terms that it will or may be returned, for direct or indirect economic or commercial advantage.[68] "Lending" is defined as making a copy of a recording available for use, on terms that it will or may be returned, otherwise than for direct or indirect economic or commercial advantage, through an establishment which is accessible to the public[69] but it does not include making available between establishments which are accessible to the public.[70] For this purpose, where lending by an establishment accessible to the public gives rise to a payment, if the amount of the payment does not go beyond what is necessary to cover the operating costs of the establishment, this is not to be regarded as being for direct or indirect economic or commercial advantage.[71] However, neither "rental" nor "lending" includes:

(a) making available for the purpose of public performance, playing or showing in public or communication to the public;

(b) making available for the purpose of exhibition in public;

(c) making available for on-the-spot-reference use.[72]

Note that where an agreement concerning film production is concluded between a performer and a film producer, the performer is to be presumed, unless the agreement provides to the contrary, to have transferred to the film producer any rental right in relation to the film arising from the inclusion of a recording of

12–65

---

[63] Rental Directive, Art.9.

[64] CDPA 1988, s.191A.

[65] CDPA 1988, s.182C. The rental and lending rights do not apply to a copy of a recording of a performance acquired before commencement of the Copyright and Related Rights Regulations 1996 (SI 1996/2967) for the purpose of renting or lending it to the public: reg.34(2).

[66] CDPA 1988, s.182C(7). *cf.* s.18A, the equivalent provision in Pt I. For a discussion of s.18A, see paras 7–81 *et seq.*, above.

[67] s.182C(6).

[68] s.182C(2)(a).

[69] s.182C(b).

[70] s.182C(4).

[71] s.182C(5).

[72] s.182C(3). These three exclusions are derived from recital 13 of Dir.92/100.

his performance in the film.[73] However, the performer retains the right to equitable remuneration for the rental.[74]

(vii) Making available recording of a performance by way of an on-demand service.

12–66 In a case where a performance has been recorded, the Rental and Related Rights Directive did not require that performers be given an exclusive right to authorise or prohibit the wireless broadcasting or communication to the public of the performance via that recording, only a right to remuneration. This is reflected in the equitable remuneration right in section 182D, which has already been considered.[75] The Information Society Directive does, however, require that performers be given an exclusive right to authorise or prohibit the making available of recordings of their performances by way of an on-demand service.[76] Effect has been given to this by section 182CA, it also being made clear that such acts do not fall within the equitable remuneration provisions.[77]

The Act therefore now provides that a performer's rights are infringed by a person who, without his consent, makes available to the public a recording of the whole or any substantial part of a qualifying performance by electronic transmission in such a way that members of the public may access the recording from a place and at a time individually chosen by them.[78] This is known as the "making available right",[79] and is a property right.[80]

12–67 Transitional. This new making available right became exercisable as from October 31, 2003.[81] The right is exercisable by the performer or, if he had died, by the person who immediately before this date was entitled under section 192A(2) to exercise the non-property rights in relation to that performance.[82] Any damages received by a person's personal representatives by virtue of this provision shall devolve as part of that person's estate as if the right had subsisted and been vested in him immediately before his death.[83] Generally, of course, the right is a property right and is transferable and will devolve as such.[84]

(viii) Use of recording made without consent

12–68 It is an infringement to show or play in public or communicate to the public the whole or any substantial part of a performance by means of a recording which was made without the consent of the performer and which the person doing that act knew or had reason to to believe was so made.[85] This is a non-property right.[86]

---

[73] s.191F(1) See para. 12–45, above.
[74] s.191G(1) See para. 12–48, above.
[75] See para. 12–45, above.
[76] Information Society Directive, Art.3(2)(a).
[77] See CDPA 1988, s.182D(1)(b), and para. 12–45.
[78] s.182CA(1). See para. 7–114, above, for the equivalent right in relation to copyright.
[79] s.182CA(2).
[80] s.191A.
[81] See the Copyright and Related Rights Regulations 2003 (SI 2003/2498), reg.35(1).
[82] See reg.35(1). The Regulations say "if he *has* died", but presumably, given that the right is a property right, the reference is intended to be to his death before commencement.
[83] reg.35(2).
[84] See para. 12–66, above.
[85] CDPA 1988, s.183 For the meaning of the expression "in public" see paras 7–95 *et seq.*, above. *cf.* ss.22, 23, 24, 26 where the same words are used to define secondary infringement of copyright. See Ch.8, above.
[86] s.192A.

(ix) Dealing with illicit recordings

It is an infringement to import into the United Kingdom, otherwise than for **12–69** private or domestic use, an "illicit recording".[87] It is also an infringement in the course of a business to possess, sell, let for hire, offer or expose for sale or hire, or distribute a recording which is an "illicit recording".[88] In each of these cases it must also be shown that the person knew or had reason to believe that it was an illicit recording.[89] This is a non-property right.[90]

An "illicit recording" is a recording of the whole or any substantial part of a performance if it is made, otherwise than for private purposes, without the performer's consent.[91] It is immaterial where the recording was made.[92] Certain recordings which were not originally illicit recordings by virtue of the permitted act provisions may become so if subsequently dealt with, by virtue of special provisions under Schedule 2.[93] These are: recordings made for purposes of instruction or examination[94]; recordings made by educational establishments for educational purposes[95]; recordings of performances in electronic form retained on transfer of the principal recording[96]; recordings made for the purposes of broadcast,[97] a recording made for the purposes of time shifting,[98] and photographs of broadcast.[99]

B. INFRINGEMENT OF RECORDING RIGHTS

The rights of the persons having recording rights in relation to a performance **12–70** may be infringed by various acts done without consent. The provisions as to the relevant consent vary according to the different acts.

(i) Recording

It is an infringement of the recording right to make a recording of the whole or **12–71** any substantial part of a performance without the consent of the person having such rights or that of the performer.[1] The performance does not have to be a qualifying performance.

(ii) Use of recording made without consent

It is an infringement, without the consent of the person having the recording **12–72** rights, or, in the case of a qualifying performance, that of the performer, to show or play in public the whole or any substantial part of a performance by means of a recording which was made without the appropriate consent.[2] It is also an infringement to communicate to the public the whole or any substantial part of the

---

[87] CDPA 1988, s.184(1)(a). The provisions are dealt with in more detail in section 6 of this Chapter ("Permitted Acts"). For Part I rights *cf.* s.22 and paras 8–05 *et seq.*, above.
[88] s.184(1)(b).
[89] s.184(1).
[90] s.192A.
[91] s.197(2).
[92] s.197(6).
[93] s.197(5).
[94] Sch.2, para.4(3).
[95] Sch.2, para.6(2).
[96] Sch.2, para.12(2).
[97] Sch.2, para.16(3).
[98] Sch.2, para.17A(2).
[99] Sch.2, para.17B(2)
[1] CDPA 1988, s.186(1).
[2] CDPA 1988, s.187(1)(a).

performance by means of a recording which was made without the appropriate consent.[3] In each of these cases it must also be shown that the person doing the act knew or had reason to believe that it was made without the appropriate consent.[4] The "appropriate consent" is that of the performer or the person who, at the time the consent was given, had recording rights in relation to the performance. If there was more than one such person the consent of all of them is necessary.[5]

(iii) Dealing with illicit recordings

12–73   It is an infringement, without the consent of the person having the recording rights or, in the case of a qualifying performance, that of the performer, to import into the United Kingdom, otherwise than for private and domestic use, a recording of a performance which is an illicit recording.[6] It is also an infringement in the course of business to possess, sell or let for hire, offer or expose for sale or hire, or distribute a recording of the performance which is an illicit recording.[7]

For the purposes of the rights of a person having recording rights, a recording of the whole or any substantial part of a performance subject to the exclusive recording contract is an "illicit recording" if it is made, otherwise than for private purposes, without his consent or that of the performer.[8] In each of these cases it must also be shown that the person knew or had reason to believe that it was an illicit recording.[9]

6. PERMITTED ACTS AND DEFENCES

A. General

12–74   Various acts may be done notwithstanding the rights conferred by Part II.[10] Those acts correspond broadly to those acts which are permitted notwithstanding copyright.[11] Permitted acts are dealt with in Schedule 2 to the 1988 Act. The provisions of the Schedule specify acts which may be done in relation to a performance or a recording. They relate only to the question of infringement of the rights conferred by Part II. They do not affect any right or obligation restricting the doing of any of the specified acts.[12] No inference is to be drawn as to the scope of the Part II rights from the description of any of the permitted acts.[13] The provisions of the Schedule are to be construed independently of each other. Thus, the fact that an act does not fall within one provision does not mean that it is not covered by another provision.[14]

12–75   **The Rental and Related Rights Directive and the Information Society Directive.** The Rental and Related Rights Directive permitted various exceptions

---

[3] s.187(1)(b).
[4] s.187(1). Cf. ss.22, 23, 24, 26 where the same words are used to define secondary infringement of copyright.
[5] s.187(2).
[6] CDPA 1988, s.188(1)(a).
[7] s.188(1)(b).
[8] s.197(3): cf., for performers' rights, s.197(2).
[9] s.188(1).
[10] CDPA 1988, s.189; Sch.2.
[11] See Ch.III of Pt I. See Ch.9, above.
[12] Sch.2, para.1(1).
[13] Sch.2, para.1(2).
[14] Sch.2, para.1(3).

or limitations to be made to the rights of performers.[15] There were four particular permitted exceptions, namely for private use, use of short excerpts in connection with the reporting of current events, ephemeral fixations by broadcasting organisations and use for teaching or scientific research, together with a further general exception which permitted a Member State to make the same kind of exceptions as it did in relation to Berne copyright works.[16] The permitted act provisions in relation to performers' rights were framed with these permitted exceptions in mind. As with the permitted acts in the copyright field, the provisions relating to performers' rights have been subject to substantial amendment on implementation of the Information Society Directive.[17] The reader is referred to Chapter 9 for a full discussion of the effects of the Directive on the various permitted acts,[18] since most of what is said there is equally applicable to performer's rights. In the context of performers' rights, as already noted,[19] the Act previously excluded from the scope of infringement certain acts done for a person's private and domestic use.[20] In order to make the Act compliant with the Information Society Directive, these provisions have been deleted and such acts are now only allowed, if at all, to the extent that they come within the permitted acts provisions. The Information Society Directive also amended the Rental and Related Rights Directive to limit the scope of any permitted exceptions or limitations to cases which complied with the "3-step test", *i.e.* to "certain special cases which do not conflict with a normal exploitation of the subject-matter and do not unreasonably prejudice the legitimate interests of the rightholder."[21] This test is discussed elsewhere.[22] Although the test has not been expressly incorporated into the 1988 Act, a number of the permitted acts have been framed or curtailed with the test in mind.[23]

Transitional. The unamended provisions of Schedule 2 of the Act (which set out the permitted acts in relation to performances, etc.) continue to apply to anything done after October 31, 2003 in completion of an act begun before this date which was permitted by those provisions.[24]   12–76

Circumvention of copy-protection devices. The provisions of Article 6(4) of the Information Society Directive, which deal with measures to resolve the conflict between the interests of beneficiaries of the various permitted exceptions and the rights of rightholders in respect of the circumvention of copy-protection devices, are considered elsewhere.[25] These provisions apply in relation to the permitted exceptions to the performers' reproduction and on-demand rights under the Information Society Directive. Article 6(4) of the Directive goes on to provide   12–77

---

[15] Rental and Related Rights Directive, Art.10.

[16] Art.10(2).

[17] By the Copyright and Related Rights Regulations 2003 (SI 2003/2498).

[18] See paras 9–05 and 9–06.

[19] See para. 12–58, above.

[20] As noted in the text, Art.10 of the Rental and Related Rights Directive permitted an exception or limitation from the Art.7 reproduction right in respect of private use, so that CDPA 1988, s.182A did not conflict with the Directive. Since Art.7 has now been deleted by the Information Society Directive and replaced with Art.2 of the latter Directive, this permitted limitation to the reproduction right no longer exists under the Rental and Related Rights Directive. The applicability of the various permitted exceptions under the Information Society Directive is discussed fully in Ch.9, above.

[21] Art.11(1)(b) of the Information Society Directive, amending Art.10(3) of the Rental and Related Rights Directive. Any exceptions permitted under the Information Society Directive must also comply with this test: Art.5(5).

[22] See para. 9–02, above.

[23] See, *e.g.* the Government Conclusions on the Patent Office's Consulation Paper of August 7, 2002, para.5.2.

[24] The Copyright and Related Rights Regulations 2003, reg.33.

[25] See paras 9–10, above, and para. 15–23, below.

that when Article 6 "is applied in the context of" the Rental and Related Rights Directive, "this paragraph" shall apply *mutatis mutandis*. The apparent purpose of this is that in the case of the exceptions which are governed by the Rental and Related Rights Directive, a similar regime as to voluntary or appropriate measures is to apply, although presumably only where there is an equivalent exception.

B. PARTICULAR ACTS

(i) Making of temporary copies

12–78   The Directive required the introduction of an entirely new permitted act dealing with the making of temporary copies. This was in reaction to the express right conferred on performers and owners of rights in recordings to prevent the making of transient or incidental copies.[26] Thus, it is now provided that the rights conferred by Part 2 are not infringed by the making of a temporary copy of a recording of a performance which is transient or incidental, which is an integral and essential part of a technological process and the sole purpose of which is to enable either (a) a transmission of the recording in a network between third parties by an intermediary, or (b) a lawful use of the recording, and which has no independent economic significance.[27]

(ii) Criticism, reviews and news reporting

12–79   Rights in performances and recordings are not infringed by fair dealing with a performance or recording

(a) for the purpose of criticism or review, of that or another performance or recording, or of a work, provided that the performance or recording has been made available to the public; or

(b) for the purpose of reporting current events.[28]

(iii) Incidental inclusion of performance or recording

12–80   By virtue of paragraph 3(1) of Schedule 2, the rights are not infringed by the incidental inclusion of a performance or recording in a sound recording, film or broadcast.[29] A performance or recording, so far as it consists of music or words spoken or sung with music, is not to be regarded as incidentally included in a sound recording or broadcast if it is deliberately included.[30] The rights are not infringed by anything done in relation to copies of, or the playing, showing or communication to the public of anything which was, by virtue of paragraph 3(1), not an infringement of those rights.[31]

(iv) Things done for purposes of instruction or examination

12–81   By virtue of paragraph 4(1) of Schedule 2 the rights are not infringed by the copying of a recording of a performance in the course of instruction, or of prepa-

---

[26] See para. 9–58, above.
[27] CDPA 1988, Sch.2, para.1A.See paras 9–15 *et seq.* for the equivalent provision in relation to copyright.
[28] CDPA 1988, Sch.2, para.2. Expressions have the same meaning as in s.30. See paras 9–35 *et seq.*, above.
[29] CDPA 1988, Sch.2, para.3(1). Expressions have the same meaning as in s.31; see paras 9–56 *et seq.*, above.
[30] Sch.2, para.3(3).
[31] Sch.2, para.3(2).

ration for instruction, in the making of films or film sound tracks, provided the copying is done by a person giving or receiving instruction and the instruction is for a non-commercial purpose.[32] The rights are not infringed by the copying of a recording of a performance for the purposes of setting or answering the questions in an examination or by anything done for the purposes of an examination by way of communicating the questions to the candidates.[33] Where a recording, which would otherwise be an illicit recording is made for the purposes of instruction or examination, but is subsequently dealt with, it is to be treated as an illicit recording for the purposes of that dealing. If that dealing infringes any right conferred by Part II it is to be treated as an illicit recording for all subsequent purposes. For this purpose, "dealt with" means (a) sold, let for hire, or offered or exposed for sale or hire, or (b) communicated to the public, unless that communication is itself by virtue of the above provisions,[34] not an infringement of the rights conferred by Part 2.[35]

(v) Playing or showing sound recording, film or broadcast at educational establishments

The playing or showing of a sound recording, film or broadcast at an educational establishment for the purposes of instruction before an audience consisting of teachers and pupils at the establishment and other persons directly connected with the activities of the establishment is not a playing or showing of a performance in public for the purposes of infringement of Part II rights.[36] A person is not for this purpose directly connected with the activities of the educational establishment simply because he is the parent of a pupil at the establishment.[37]

12–82

(vi) Recording of broadcasts by educational establishments

A recording of a broadcast, or a copy of such a recording, may be made by or on behalf of an educational establishment for the educational purposes of that establishment without thereby infringing any of the rights conferred by Part II in relation to any performance or recording included in it, provided the education purposes are non-commercial.[38] These rights are also not infringed where a recording of a broadcast or a copy of such a recording, whose making was by virtue of the above provisions not an infringement of such rights, is communicated to the public by a person situated within the premises of an educational establishment provided that the communication cannot be received by any person situated outside the premises of that establishment.[39] However, these provisions do not apply if or to the extent that there is a licensing scheme certified for those purposes under paragraph 16 of Schedule 2A providing for the grant of licences.[40] Where a recording of a broadcast which would otherwise be an illicit recording is made by an educational establishment in accordance with this provision, but is subse-

12–83

---

[32] CDPA 1988, Sch.2, para.4(1). Expressions have the same meaning as in s.32: see paras 9–88 et seq., above.

[33] Sch.2, para.4(2).

[34] i.e. anything done by way of communication of questions to candidates under CDPA 1988, Sch.2, para.4(2)(b)

[35] Sch.2, para.4(3).

[36] CDPA 1988, Sch.2, para.5(1). Expressions have the same meaning as in s.34: see paras 9–96 et seq., above.

[37] Sch.2, para.5(2).

[38] CDPA 1988, Sch.2, para.6(1). Expressions have the same meaning as in s.35: see paras 9–97 et seq., above.

[39] Sch.2, para.6(1A).

[40] Sch.2, para 6(1B).

quently dealt with, it is to be treated as an illicit recording for the purposes of that dealing. If that dealing infringes any right conferred by Part II it is to be treated as an illicit recording for all subsequent purposes. For this purpose, "dealt with" means sold, let for hire, offered or exposed for sale or hire, or communicated from within the premises of an educational establishment to any person situated outside those premises.[41]

(vii) Lending of copies by educational establishments, libraries and archives

12–84   The lending of copies of a recording of a performance by an educational establishment does not infringe Part II rights.[42] Similarly, the lending of copies of a recording of a performance by a prescribed library or archive (other than a public library) which is not conducted for profit, does not infringe Part II rights.[43]

(viii) Copy of work required to be made as condition of export

12–85   If an article of cultural or historical importance or interest cannot lawfully be exported from the United Kingdom unless a copy of it is made and deposited in an appropriate library or archive, it is not an infringement of any right conferred by Part II to make that copy.[44]

(ix) Parliamentary and judicial proceedings

12–86   The rights conferred by Part II are not infringed by anything done for the purposes of parliamentary or judicial proceedings or for the purposes of reporting such proceedings.[45]

(x) Royal Commissions and statutory inquiries

12–87   The rights conferred by Part II are not infringed by anything done for the purposes of the proceedings of a Royal Commission or statutory inquiry or for the purposes of reporting any such proceedings held in public.[46]

(xi) Public records

12–88   Material which is comprised in public records[47] which are open to public inspection in pursuance of the relevant legislation may be copied and a copy may be

---

[41] Sch.2, para.6(2).
[42] CDPA 1988, Sch.2, para.6A(1). Expressions have the same meaning as in s.36A; see paras 9–99 *et seq.*, above.
[43] Sch.2, para.6B(1). Expressions have the same meaning as in s.40A(2); and any provision under CDPA 1988, s.37 prescribing libraries or archives for the purposes of that section applies also for the purposes of this paragraph: see paras 9–108 *et seq.*, above.
[44] CDPA 1988, Sch.2, para.7(1). Expressions have the same meaning as in s.44: see paras 9–121 *et seq.*, above.
[45] CDPA 1988, Sch.2, para.8(1). Expressions have the same meaning as in s.45: see paras 9–126 *et seq.*, above.
[46] CDPA 1988, Sch.2, para.9(1). Expressions have the same meaning as in s.46: see paras 9–127 *et seq.*, above.
[47] As defined in the Public Records Act 1958, the Public Records (Scotland) Act 1937, the Public Records Act (Northern Ireland) 1923 or in Welsh public records, as defined by the Government of Wales Act 1998. See CDPA 1988, Sch.2, para.10(1).

supplied to any person, by or with the authority of any officer appointed under the relevant legislation, without infringing Part II rights.[48]

(xii) Acts done under statutory authority

Where the doing of a particular act is specifically authorised by an Act (including an enactment contained in Northern Ireland legislation),[49] whenever passed, then, unless the Act provides otherwise, the doing of the act does not infringe the rights conferred by Part II.[50] This provision is not to be construed as excluding any defence of statutory authority otherwise available under or by virtue of any enactment.[51]

12–89

(xiii) Transfer of copies of works in electronic form

Special provision is made for the case where a recording of a performance in electronic form has been purchased on terms which, expressly or impliedly or by virtue of any rule of law, allow the purchaser to make further recordings in connection with his use of the recording.[52]

12–90

If there are no express terms prohibiting the transfer of the recording by the purchaser, imposing obligations which continue after a transfer, prohibiting the assignment of any consent or terminating any consent on a transfer or providing for the terms on which a transferee may do the things which the purchaser was permitted to do, anything which the purchaser was allowed to do may also be done by a transferee without infringing Part II rights. But any recording made by the purchaser which is not also transferred is to be treated as an illicit recording for all purposes after the transfer.[53] The same applies where the original purchased recording is no longer usable for all purposes after the transfer and what is transferred is a further copy used in its place.[54]

These provisions also apply on a subsequent transfer, but do not apply in relation to a recording purchased before the commencement of Part II.[55]

(xiv) Use of recordings of spoken words in certain cases

Where a recording of the reading or the recitation of a literary work is made for the purpose of reporting current events, or of communicating to the public the whole or part of the reading or recitation, it is not an infringement of the Part II rights to use the recording or to copy the recording and use the copy for that purpose, provided that specified conditions are met.[56] Those conditions are that[57]:

12–91

   (a) the recording is a direct recording of the reading or recitation and is not taken from a previous recording or from a broadcast; and
   (b) the making of the recording was not prohibited by or on behalf of the person giving the reading or recitation; and

---

[48] CDPA 1988, Sch.2, para.10(1). Expressions have the same meaning as in s.49: see paras 9–130 *et seq.*, above.
[49] CDPA 1988, Sch.2, para.11(2).
[50] Sch.2, para.11(1). Expressions have the same meaning as in s.50: see paras 9–131 *et seq.*, above.
[51] Sch.2, para.11(3).
[52] CDPA 1988, Sch.2, para.12(1). Expressions have the same meaning as in s.56; see paras 9–150 *et seq.*, above.
[53] Sch.2, para.12(2).
[54] Sch.2, para.12(3).
[55] Sch.2, para.12(5).
[56] CDPA 1988, Sch.2, para.13(1). Expressions have the same meaning as in CDPA 1988, s.58: see paras 9–155 *et seq.*, above.
[57] Sch.2, para.13(2).

    (c) the use made of the recording is not of a kind prohibited by or on behalf of that person before the recording was made; and

    (d) the use is by or with the authority of a person who is lawfully in possession of the recording.

(xv) Recordings of folk songs

12–92   The recording of a performance of a song may be made for the purpose of including it in an archive maintained by a designated body without infringing any Part II rights. Certain conditions must, however, be met.[58] They are that,

    (a) the words are unpublished and of unknown authorship at the time the recording is made,

    (b) the making of the recording does not infringe any copyright,

    (c) its making is not prohibited by any performer.[59]

Copies of a recording made in reliance on these provisions and included in an archive maintained by a designated body may, if the prescribed conditions are met, be made and supplied by the archivist without infringing Part II rights.[60] The "prescribed conditions" means the conditions prescribed for the purposes of section 61(3). A designated body means a body designated for the purposes of section 61.[61]

(xvi) Lending of certain recordings

12–93   The Secretary of State may by order provide that in specified cases the lending to the public of copies of films or sound recordings shall be treated as licensed by the performer subject only to the payment of such reasonable royalty or other payment as may be agreed or determined in default of agreement by the Copyright Tribunal.[62] No such order shall apply if, or to the extent that there is a licensing scheme certified under paragraph 16 of Schedule 2A providing for the grant of licences.[63] This provision does not affect liability under section 184(1)(b) (secondary infringement: possessing or dealing with illicit recording) in respect of the lending of illicit recordings.[64]

(xvii) Playing of sound recordings for the purposes of clubs and societies

12–94   It is not an infringement of Part II rights to play a sound recording as part of the activities of or for the benefit of a club, society or other organisation provided that certain conditions are met.[65] Those conditions are that,

    (a) the organisation is not established or conducted for profit and its main objects are charitable or are otherwise concerned with the advancement of religion, education or social welfare,

    (b) that the sound recording is played by a person who is acting primarily and directly for the benefit of the organisation and who is not acting with a view to gain,

---

[58] CDPA 1988, Sch.2, para.14(1). Expressions have the same meaning as in s.61: see paras 9–165 *et seq.*, above.

[59] Sch.2, para.14(2).

[60] Sch.2, para.14(3).

[61] Sch.2, para.14(4). See SI 1989/1012; See Vol.2 at A4.ii.

[62] CDPA 1988, Sch.2, para.14A(1). Expressions have the same meaning as in s.66: see paras 9–178 *et seq.*, above.

[63] Sch.2, para.14A(2).

[64] Sch.2, para.14A(5).

[65] CDPA 1988, Sch.2, para.15(1). Expressions have the same meaning as in s.67: see paras 9–181 *et seq.*, above.

(c) that the proceeds of any charge for admission to the place where the recording is to be heard are applied solely for the purposes of the organisation, and

(d) that the proceeds from any goods or services sold by, or on behalf of, the organisation—

    (i) in the place where the sound recording is heard, and

    (ii) on the occasion when the sound recording is played,

are applied solely for the purposes of the organisation."[66]

(xviii) Incidental recording for purposes of broadcast

A person who proposes to broadcast a recording of a performance in circumstances not infringing Part II rights is to be treated as having consent for the purpose of Part II for the making of a further recording for the purposes of a broadcast.[67] That consent is subject to certain conditions. They are that the further recording shall not be used for any other purpose and shall be destroyed within 28 days of being first used for broadcasting the performance.[68]

    12–95

A recording made in accordance with these provisions is to be treated as an illicit recording for the purposes of any use in breach of the condition as to non-use for any other purpose and for all purposes after that condition or the condition as to destruction within 28 days is broken.[69]

(xix) Recordings for the purposes of supervision and control of broadcasts and other services

The rights conferred by Part II are not infringed by the making or use by the British Broadcasting Corporation, for the purpose of maintaining supervision and control over programmes broadcast by them, of recordings of those programmes.[70] The rights conferred by Part II are not infringed by anything done in pursuance of:

    12–96

(a) various provisions of the Broadcasting Acts 1990 and 1996 and Communications Act 2003 (maintenance of supervision and control over programmes and advertisements, etc.); or

(b) a condition which, by virtue of section 334(1) of the Communications Act 2003, section 11(2) or 95(2) of the Broadcasting Act 1990, is included in a licence granted under Part I or Part III of that Act or Part I or Part II of the Broadcasting Act 1996; or

(c) a direction given under section 109(2) of the Broadcasting Act 1990 (power of OFCOM to require production of recordings, etc.); or

(d) section 334(3) of the Communications Act 2003.[71]

The rights conferred by Part II are not infringed by :

(a) the use by OFCOM, in connection with the performance of any of their functions under the Broadcasting Act 1990, the Broadcasting Act 1996 or the Communications Act 2003, of any recording, script or transcript which is provided to them under or by virtue of any provision of those Acts; or

---

[66] Sch.2, para.15(2).
[67] CDPA 1988, Sch.2, para.16(1). Expressions have the same meaning as in CDPA 1988, s.68: see paras 9–186 et seq., above.
[68] Sch.2, para.16(2).
[69] Sch.2, para.16(3).
[70] CDPA 1988, Sch.2, para.17(1). See paras 9–190, above.
[71] Sch.2, para.17(2).

(b) any existing material which is transferred to them by a scheme made under section 30 of the Communications Act 2003.[72]

(xx) Recording for the purposes of time-shifting

12–97   The rights conferred by Part 2 in relation to a performance or recording included in the broadcast are not infringed by the making in domestic premises for private and domestic use of a recording of a broadcast solely for the purpose of enabling it to be viewed or listened to at a more convenient time.[73] Where a recording which would otherwise be an illicit recording is made in accordance with this provision but is subsequently dealt with, it is to be treated as an illicit recording for the purposes of that dealing; and if that dealing infringes any right conferred by Part 2, it is to be treated as an illicit recording for all subsequent purposes.[74] For this purpose, "dealt with" means sold or let for hire, offered or exposed for sale or hire or communicated to the public.[75]

(xxi) Photographs of broadcasts

12–98   The rights conferred by Part 2 in relation to a performance or recording included in the broadcast are not infringed by the making in domestic premises for private and domestic use of a photograph of the whole or any part of an image forming part of a broadcast, or a copy of such a photograph.[76] Where a recording which would otherwise be an illicit recording is made in accordance with this paragraph but is subsequently dealt with, it is to be treated as an illicit recording for the purposes of that dealing, and if that dealing infringes any right conferred by Part 2, it is to be treated as an illicit recording for all subsequent purposes.[77] For these purposes, "dealt with" means sold or let for hire, offered or exposed for sale or hire or communicated to the public.[78]

(xxii) Free public showing or playing of broadcast

12–99   The showing or playing in public of a broadcast to an audience who have not paid for admission to the place where the broadcast or programme is to be seen or heard does not infringe any Part II rights in relation to a performance or recording included in the broadcast, or any sound recording (except in so far as it is an "excepted sound recording") or film which is played or shown in public by reception of the broadcast.[79] In addition, in the case of the showing or playing in public of a broadcast to an audience who have not paid for admission to the place where the broadcast is to be seen or heard, the rights in relation to a performance or recording included in any excepted sound recording which is played in public by

---

[72] Sch.2, para.17(3). Expressions have the same meaning as in s.69: see paras 9–190 et seq., above. For these purposes, "existing material" means (a) any recording, script or transcript which was provided to the Independent Television Commission or the Radio Authority under or by virtue or provision of the Broadcasting Act 1990 or the Broadcasting Act 1996 and (b) any recording or transcript which was provided to the Broadcasting Standards Commission under section 115(4) or (6) or 116(5) of the Broadcasting Act 1996: CDPA 1988, Sch.2, para.17(4).

[73] CDPA 1988, Sch.2, para.17A. Expressions used have the same meaning as in CDPA 1988, s.70: see paras 9–192 et seq., above.

[74] Sch.2, para.17A(2).

[75] Sch.2, para.17A(3).

[76] CDPA 1988, Sch.2, para.17B. Expressions used have the same meaning as in s.71: see paras 9–196 et seq., above.

[77] Sch.2, para.17B(2)

[78] Sch.2, para.17B(3).

[79] CDPA 1988, Sch.2, para.18(1). Expressions have the same meaning as in s.72: see para. 9–198, above.

reception of the broadcast are not infringed if the playing or showing of that broadcast in public (a) forms part of the activities of an organisation that is not established or conducted for profit; or (b) is necessary for the purposes of (i) repairing equipment for the reception of broadcasts, (ii) demonstrating that a repair to such equipment has been carried out, or (iii) demonstrating such equipment which is being sold or let for hire or offered or exposed for sale or hire.[80]

The audience is to be treated as having paid for admission to a place in two sets of circumstances; first, if they have paid for admission to a place of which that place forms part and, secondly, if goods or services are supplied at that place (or a place of which it forms part) at prices which are substantially attributable to the facilities afforded for seeing or hearing the broadcast, or at prices exceeding those usually charged there and which are partly attributable to those facilities.[81]

In two cases persons are not regarded as having paid for admission to a place: first, persons admitted as residents or inmates of the place: secondly, persons admitted as members of a club or society where the payment is only for membership of the club or society and the provision of facilities for seeing or hearing broadcasts is only incidental to the main purposes of the club or society.[82]

(xxiii) Reception and retransmission of wireless broadcast by cable

Provision is made for the case where a wireless broadcast made from a place in the United Kingdom is received and immediately retransmitted by cable.[83] The rights conferred by Part II in relation to a performance or recording included in the broadcast are not infringed if and to the extent that the broadcast is made for reception in the area in which it is retransmitted by cable; but where the making of the broadcast was an infringement of those rights, the fact that the broadcast was retransmitted by cable shall be taken into account in assessing the damages for that infringement.[84]

12–100

Where:

(a) the retransmission by cable is in pursuance of a relevant requirement, but

(b) to any extent, the area in which the retransmission by cable ("the cable area") falls outside the area for reception in which the broadcast is made ("the broadcast area"),

the retransmission by cable (to the extent that it is provided for so much of the cable area as falls outside the broadcast area) of any performance or recording included in the broadcast shall be treated as licensed by the owner of the Part II rights in relation to the performance or recording, subject only to the payment by the person making the broadcast of a reasonable royalty or other payment in respect of the retransmission by cable of the broadcast as may be agreed or determined in default of agreement by the Copyright Tribunal.[85] This provision does not apply if, or to the extent that, the retransmission of the performance or recording by cable is (apart from sub-paragraph 19(3)) licensed by the owner of the Part II rights in relation to the performance or recording.[86]

The Secretary of State may by order provide that in specified cases paragraph 19(2) is to apply in relation to broadcasts of a specified description which are not

12–101

---

[80] Sch.2, para.18(1B).
[81] Sch.2, para.18(1).
[82] Sch.2, para.18(3).
[83] CDPA 1988, Sch.2, para.19(1). Expressions have the same meaning as in s.73: see paras 9–205 *et seq.*, above.
[84] Sch.2, para.19(2).
[85] Sch.2, para.19(3).
[86] Sch.2, para.19(4).

made as mentioned within it, or may exclude the application of section 19(2) in relation to broadcasts of a specified description made as mentioned within it.[87]

An application to settle the royalty or other sum payable in pursuance of section 19(3) may be made to the Copyright Tribunal by the owner of the Part II rights or by the person making the broadcast.[88]

(xxiv) Provision of sub-titled copies of broadcast

12–102   Certain bodies designated for the purposes of section 74 of the 1988 Act may, for the purpose of providing people who are deaf or hard of hearing, or physically or mentally handicapped in other ways, with copies which are sub-titled or otherwise modified for their special needs, make recordings of such broadcasts and copies of such recordings, and issue or lend copies to the public without infringing Part II rights in relation to a performance or recording included in the broadcast.[89] However, this provision does not apply if, or to the extent that, there is a licensing scheme certified for those purposes under paragraph 16 of Schedule 2A providing for the grant of licences.[90]

(xxv) Recording of broadcast for archival purposes

12–103   The recording of a broadcast of a designated class[91] or a copy of such a recording may be made for the purpose of being placed in an archive maintained by designated bodies without thereby infringing any right conferred by Part II in relation to a performance or recording included in the broadcast.[92]

7. REMEDIES AND PENALTIES FOR INFRINGEMENT OF RIGHTS

12–104   Performers' rights and recording rights may be enforced by means of an infringement action, including applications for delivery-up and forfeiture, and the right of seizure. The performers' property rights are enforceable by provisions which parallel the relevant copyright infringement provisions.

An infringement of a performer's property rights is actionable by the owner of the performer's property rights[93] or by an exclusive licensee.[94] An exclusive licensee has, except against the owner of the rights, the same rights and remedies in respect of matters occurring after the grant of the licence as if it were an assignment.[95] If the exclusive licensee sues, a defendant may avail himself of any defence which would have been available to him if the action had been brought by the rights owner.[96] Although the rights owner and the exclusive licensee have concurrent rights of action, neither may proceed beyond an application for interim relief without joining the other, except with leave of the court.[97] Where the other

[87] CDPA 1988, Sch.2, para.19(5).
[88] Sch.2, para.19A(1).
[89] CDPA 1988, Sch.2, para.20(1). Expressions have the same meaning as in s.74: see paras 9–211 *et seq.*, above.
[90] Sch.2, para.20(1A).
[91] See CDPA 1988, s.75, para. 9–213, above.
[92] Sch.2, para.21(1). Expressions have the same meaning as in s.75: see paras 9–213, above.
[93] CDPA 1988, s.191I(1).
[94] s.191L(1).
[95] s.191L(2).
[96] s.191L(3).
[97] s.191M(1), (3).

party is added as a defendant, he is not liable for any costs in the action unless he takes part in the proceedings.[98]

An infringement of a performer's non-property rights, or of any Part II right conferred on a person having recording rights, is actionable by the person entitled to the right as a breach of statutory duty.[99] An exclusive licensee of performers' non-property rights has no right of action in respect of any breach.

It is expressly provided that, in an action for infringement of performers' prop- **12–105** erty rights, all such relief by way of damages, injunctions, accounts or otherwise is available to the claimant as is available in respect of the infringement of any other property right.[1] Thus the remedies for infringement of these rights are assimilated to those available for infringement of copyright. Like all property rights, infringement is actionable without proof of damage. The court now has a power to grant an injunction against a service provider in the case of others using its service to infringe a performer's property right.[2]

For performers' non-property rights and recording rights the normal remedies for breach of statutory duty are available.[3] Express provision is made for the remedies of delivery up, seizure and forfeiture of illicit recordings.[4]

A detailed discussion of the remedies and penalties available for the infringement of performers' rights and recording rights is given in Chapters 22 and 23, below.

---

[98] s.191M(2).
[99] s.194.
[1] CDPA 1988, s.191I(2).
[2] para.191JA.
[3] s.194.
[4] ss.95–97.

PART IV

DESIGN RIGHT AND THE PROTECTION OF WORKS OF INDUSTRIAL APPLICATION

CHAPTER THIRTEEN

DESIGN RIGHT, UNREGISTERED COMMUNITY DESIGN AND THE PROTECTION OF WORKS OF INDUSTRIAL APPLICATION

1. THE SCHEME OF PROTECTION

A. INTRODUCTION

This Chapter will deal primarily with unregistered forms of protection for industrial designs—design right, unregistered Community design and copyright. Forms of registered protection—under the Registered Designs Act 1949 and registered Community design—are dealt with in outline only.   **13–01**

What is "industrial design"? A design is, in broad terms, the plan or scheme for the appearance of an article (or a part of an article). It is concerned with what an article looks like or is intended to look like. It is not concerned with how an article performs its function.[1] The design of an article may be recorded in a drawing, a photograph or a written description or it may be embodied in an actual article. "Industrial" in this context means that the design relates to the appearance of an article intended to fulfil a specific function and, usually, to be mass produced. An industrial design is, therefore, to be distinguished from a work of fine art (such as a painting) which performs no particular function other than to be enjoyed as an object in itself.   **13–02**

Scope of industrial design. Industrial design covers a wide field of activity. Some designs (such as the design of a machine cog) are dictated solely by the functions which the relevant articles are to perform and aesthetic considerations are of no significance. Others (such as the design for a chair), must mix functionality with aesthetic appeal.[2] In yet others (such as a design of soft toy, wallpaper and fabrics), functionality will play very little part but aesthetic appearance will be crucial. Finally, the design of some articles may be derived from a work (such as a painting) which started life as a purely artistic work in its own right and which was not intended to be a design for another article.   **13–03**

B. NATURE OF THE PROBLEM

Conflicting needs. The protection of industrial designs is and has always been controversial. At the heart of this controversy is how to balance two conflicting needs. On the one hand, the need to provide protection so as to reward human endeavour and creativity; on the other, the need to allow competition in the production of articles which fulfil a particular function or purpose.   **13–04**

The need to protect. As with any other form of industrial endeavour, there is a need to provide some protection for industrial designs. Protection encourages and rewards innovation and skill; without it, designers may not invest their skill, time or money in a design and, in particular, in a design which is expensive to develop but simple to copy.[3] Moreover, it may be thought that a person who has invested in a design should be entitled to enjoy the benefit of that investment. The design is, in this sense, a form of property.[4] If a work of pure art is to be protected, why   **13–05**

---

[1] This is the concern of patent law.

[2] A chair must perform the function of a chair so its design will include a leg or legs and a seat but other aspects of its design, such as its elegantly tapering and fluted legs, may be included simply to attract buyers to that particular product.

[3] See the Council Regulation 6/2002 on Community design (EC) No. 6/2002 at Recital (7).

[4] It was commented in Parliament that nothing could more properly be described as a man's property than the products of his mind, see *Hansard*, H.L. Vol.489, col.1476.

not a work of industrial art[5] or a purely functional design which may have involved the same degree of creative effort and probably more investment.[6]

13–06 **The need for competition.** On the other hand, because an industrial design (unlike a work of fine art) determines the shape or appearance of an article which is intended to perform a specific function, there is a need to allow some degree of competition. The greater the extent to which the appearance of an article is dictated by the article's function, the more likely it is that protection of the design will operate to prevent others making articles to fulfil that same function. In such cases, protection would allow the designer to create a monopoly in articles made to fulfil that function. It may also prevent a design idea from being fully developed and exploited, often by someone better suited to the task than its original creator. From this perspective, protection may stultify commercial progress and the development of ideas[7] and may deprive the public of a chance to choose an alternative, possibly cheaper, and possibly better product of the same or a similar design.

13–07 **Forms of protection.** If some protection is thought to be appropriate, then the form of that protection must take into account the need for competition. A monopoly in the use of a design[8] would provide the designer with strong protection and, as questions of copying would be irrelevant, would give competitors some certainty. It would, however, be very restrictive on competitors and public alike, for no one else could produce an article to that design even if they had acted independently. Moreover, monopolies are usually provided under a system of registration which is likely to be time-consuming, expensive and, for many types of design, impractical.[9] An alternative is to protect against copying. In its traditional copyright form, this appears to offer a good balance between protection and competition, in that it arises automatically whilst allowing a competitor to produce the same or a similar design provided he acted independently (without copying). However, such a form of protection requires proof of copying (often by inference) which often gives rise to uncertainty.

The period of protection is also likely to be important. Even if an industrial design is deserving of protection, the need for competition in producing articles to perform the function of the article in question suggests that the period of protection for the design should be both shorter and more easily ascertainable than the period of protection which applies to works of fine art. If protection is to be given to a functional design, then a relatively short period of protection (as in patent law) may be sufficient to allow the designer to make a return on his investment before competitors can enter the market. If, however, the protection relates to the more decorative aspects of the article's appearance, then a longer period of protection should not unduly restrict fair competition.

Given that designs vary from the purely technical to the almost purely artistic, a form and period of protection which is appropriate for one design may be

---

[5] *i.e.* a design which has features added by way of embellishment in order to make the article to which they are applied more attractive to consumers.

[6] To use the example given in the course of counsel's submissions on behalf of the plaintiff in *British Leyland Motor Corporation Ltd v Armstrong Patents Ltd* [1986] A.C. 577 at 597E, why should one assume that "there is more merit in creating the shape of Popeye, which attracts copyright protection, than in working out, with great skill and at great expense, the shape of an article of great commercial value and worth which does not 'appeal to the eye' and which is not patentable".

[7] See White Paper "Intellectual Property and Innovation" (Cmnd.9712). April 1986, para.3(b) of the Introduction and para.5 of the Preface to Part I. See also, the Council Regulation on Community design (EC) No. 6/2002 at Recital (10).

[8] *i.e.* a patent or a registered design type of protection.

[9] *e.g.* in those areas, such as the fashion industry, where designs change rapidly.

wholly inappropriate for another. As has already been noted, the need to allow competition is much more apparent in the case of functional designs (such as a machine cog) or in the case of the functional aspects of the mixed design (such as a chair) than it is for those designs (such as a child's toy) which are governed largely by aesthetic considerations.[10] Yet, if differing forms or degrees of protection are to be available for different types of design, the need to define clear boundaries between those different types of design becomes vital. The law has long decided that industrial designs should have some form of protection but it is the drawing of these boundaries which has caused difficulties.

C. BASES OF PROTECTION

Protection of unregistered designs. An unregistered industrial design may be protected against (broadly speaking) acts of copying under the following bases:　　**13–08**

　(1) **Design right.** A design which came into existence after August 1, 1989 may be protected by design right—a right introduced by the 1988 Act.

　(2) **(Unregistered) Community design.** A design may be protected as an unregistered Community design under the Community Design Regulation (Reg. 6/2002).

　(3) **Copyright.** Whilst copyright protection under the 1988 Act is of some very limited importance in relation to designs recorded or embodied in copyright works created after August 1, 1989,[11] it has some greater importance in relation to designs created before that date.[12]

Protection of registered designs. A stronger, monopoly form of protection is also available to industrial designs through registration on the following bases (which are only considered in outline in this work):　　**13–09**

　(4) **Registered Design.** A design may be protected if registered under the Registered Designs Act 1949.[13]

　(5) **(Registered) Community design.** A design may be protected if registered as a Community design under the Community Design Regulation (Reg.6/2002) under a system of registration introduced on April 1, 2003.

Other bases of protection. An industrial design may also be protected under the law relating to passing off or breach of confidence (which are dealt with elsewhere in this book[14]), or under patent and registered trade mark law (which are outside the scope of this book).　　**13–10**

D. HISTORY OF PROTECTION OF INDUSTRIALLY APPLIED WORKS

The history of protection for industrial designs prior to the 1988 Act shows the difficulties which arise in this area of law.[15] It is also useful to an understanding of the industrial design provisions of the Copyright Designs and Patents Act 1988.　　**13–11**

---

[10] There is usually little need for anyone else to reproduce aesthetic features, save in so-called "must match" situations, see paras 13–62 *et seq.*, below.

[11] The intention of the 1988 Act (as implemented by CDPA s.51) was, as much as possible, to remove industrial designs from the sphere of copyright protection, see para. 13–279, below.

[12] The application of the 1988 Act to works created before August 1, 1989 is subject to the transitional provisions contained in Sch.1 of that Act. See paras 13–315 *et seq.*, below.

[13] (c.88) as amended by the CDPA 1988, ss.265–273 and Sch.4, and by the Registered Designs Regulations 2001 (SI 2001/3949).

[14] See Ch 20 and 21, below.

[15] The history of protection was considered by the House of Lords in *British Leyland Motor Corporation v Armstrong Patents Co Ltd* [1986] A.C. 577 and by the Whitford Committee Report, Cmnd. 6732 (March 1977), at paras 89 to 104.

13–12   **Copyright protection before 1911.** Traditionally, copyright law was concerned with the protection of what may broadly be called works of fine art and not with industrial designs. Thus, prior to 1911, there was copyright protection partly under the common law and partly under statute for various categories of works (such as literary works, engravings, sculptures, paintings, drawings and photo-graphs[16]). The form of copyright protection, being automatic and potentially long lasting,[17] was well suited to works of fine art as there was no public interest in allowing "competing" artists to copy each others' works nor to provide them with certainty as to when it would be safe to do so. Whilst there was nothing expressly to exclude copyright from a work which embodied or recorded an industrial design, this was not considered to be a problem; many works of design were two dimensional (*e.g.* a drawing) and the concept of the infringement of a two dimensional artistic work by its reproduction in three dimensions had yet to be developed.[18]

13–13   **Registered design protection before 1911.** After some initial attempts to extend copyright protection to certain limited categories of design,[19] the first serious at-tempt to protect designs directly was by statutes passed in 1839 and 1842.[20] Instead of adopting a copyright form of protection, these statutes introduced a system of registration for a wide range of designs and gave the proprietor of a registered design a monopoly in that design lasting up to three years. This period was increased to five years in 1883.[21] Later, the Patents and Designs Act 1907[22] provided for the registration of new or original designs applicable to any article of manufacture by way of pattern, shape, configuration or ornament. It also increased the period of monopoly protection to a maximum of 15 years. Even at this relatively early stage, the needs of competitors in the field of industrial design were recognised by the form of the protection adopted. Thus, the registered design system provided some commercial certainty by giving the proprietor a monopoly in the use of a design, but only where that design had been registered; it also prevented a designer claiming too broad an area of protection for his efforts by requiring him to show that his design was new and by limiting the scope of protec-tion to the use of the design in relation to articles in respect of which it had been registered. It is worth noting, however, that, at this stage, purely functional designs were registrable.[23]

13–14   **Copyright Act 1911.** The Copyright Act 1911 brought all forms of copyright protection under a single statute for the first time and conferred protection for the life of the author plus 50 years[24] on most original literary, dramatic, musical and artistic works.[25] However, section 22 of the 1911 Act provided that no copyright would subsist in designs which were capable of being registered under the Patents

---

[16] The early history of copyright law has already been considered, see Ch.2, above.

[17] The period of statutory protection was, in general, fixed by reference to the life of the author.

[18] See *Interlego A.G. v Tyco International Inc* [1988] A.C. 217 at 251, HL and para. 13–16, below.

[19] Mostly types of fabric, *e.g.* the Designing and Printing of Linens Act 1787 (27 Geo.3, c.38) and the Linens Act 1794 (34 Geo. c.23).

[20] The Copyright and Designs Act 1839, repealed and replaced by the Designs Act 1842 (5 & 6 Vict. c.100).

[21] Patents, Trademarks and Designs Act 1883 (46 & 47 Vict. c.57), s.50(1).

[22] Patents and Designs Act 1907 (7 Edw. 7 c.29), s.93 (prior to its amendment by Patents and Designs Act 1919, s.19 as to which, see para. 13–15, below).

[23] It was only later that a requirement for "eye appeal" and an exclusion of designs dictated by func-tion became a part of the registered designs legislation, see paras 13–347 to 13–348, below. The requirement for eye appeal has now been dropped by reason of the amendments made by the Registered Designs Regulations 2001. See paras 13–254 *et seq.* below.

[24] Copyright Act 1911, s.3.

[25] Copyright Act 1911, s.1(1).

and Designs Act 1907[26] unless they were not used or intended to be used as models or patterns for industrial production.[27] The intention behind section 22 seems clear. Works of art were to be protected, if at all, by copyright; industrial designs, if at all, by registration. In the event, section 22 proved less than effective as a means of excluding copyright from the industrial sphere. This was due in part to the fact that it did not restrict or remove copyright protection from artistic works which had not been used and had not been intended to be used industrially at the time that they were made, but which had subsequently been used industrially.[28] It was also due in part to changes in the law of registered designs made after 1911.[29]

Developments in the law of registered designs. The changes made in the law of   **13–15**
registered designs after 1911 meant that fewer designs were capable of registration. As has been seen, when the Copyright Act 1911 was passed, a design was defined in broad terms for the purposes of registration and, it seems, a purely functional design was registrable.[30] However, this changed with the Patents and Designs Act 1919. For the purposes of registration, a design was defined by the 1919 Act as those features of shape, configuration, pattern or ornament which in the finished article appealed to and were judged solely by the eye but not any mode or principle of construction nor anything which was in substance a mere mechanical device.[31] Although the 1919 Act was replaced by the Registered Designs Act 1949,[32] the definition of a design in the 1949 Act (as it then was) remained substantially the same.[33] Designs which were not visually appealing or were functional were therefore excluded from registration.[34] At the other (more artistic) end of the industrial design spectrum, the Registered Design Rules 1949[35] excluded from registration designs for certain articles such as sculptures (other than casts or models to be applied industrially), wall plaques and medals, and printed matter primarily of a literary or artistic character (including, for example, book-jackets, dressmaking patterns, greetings cards, maps, plans, postcards, advertisements, cards, etc.).[36] Although these changes were understandable, the narrowing of the definition of a design for the purposes of registration served to reduce the effectiveness of section 22 of the Copyright Act 1911 in excluding copyright from industrial designs.[37]

Problems with section 22. As has been seen,[38] section 22 of the Copyright Act   **13–16**
1911 sought to exclude copyright from works embodying industrial designs by

---

[26] The meaning of "capable of being registered" was considered in *Interlego A.G. v Tyco Industries Inc* [1988] R.P.C. 343 at 359, 360, 362 and 364. For the position under the 1907 Act, see para. 13–347, below.

[27] Copyright Act 1911, s.22, see para. 13–16, below.

[28] See *King Features Syndicate Inc v O & M Kleeman Ltd* [1941] A.C. 417 and para. 13–16, below.

[29] See para. 13–15, below.

[30] See para. 13–13, above.

[31] (9 & 10 Geo. 5, c.80), s.19. It has been suggested that this new wording simply reflected the way in which the old law had been construed by the courts. It seems, however, that this was not the case, see paras 13–13, above and paras 13–347 to 13–348, below.

[32] The Registered Designs Act 1949, s.7 also provided monopoly protection lasting a maximum of 15 years against certain specified dealings in relation to articles in respect of which the design was registered and to which the design or a design not substantially different had been applied.

[33] The Registered Designs Act 1949, s.1(3). The wording of the definition followed the construction of the definition of a "design" under the 1919 Act adopted in *Kestos Ltd v Kempat Ltd* (1935) 53 R.P.C. 139 at 151. See para. 13–346, below.

[34] See *Amp Inc v Utilux Proprietary Ltd* [1972] R.P.C. 103 and *British Leyland Motor Corporation v Armstrong Patents Co Ltd* [1986] A.C. 577 at 617H–618E.

[35] Made under the Registered Designs Act 1949, s.1(4).

[36] Registered Design Rules 1949, r.26.

[37] See para. 13–16, below.

[38] See para. 13–13, above.

reference to whether the design was registrable. Thus, in so far as the changes in
the law of registered designs described above meant that certain designs were not
registrable, the works embodying those designs became capable of copyright
protection. In practice this was of little significance while the 1911 Act was in
force because the copyright works in which most unregistrable industrial designs
were recorded were categorised as "plans" which the 1911 Act treated as literary
works rather than artistic works.[39] As copyright in a literary work could not be
infringed by the making of the article described in that work,[40] designers could
not rely on copyright in most cases of industrial copying. It was, however, of significance where the relevant unregistrable industrial design was recorded in an
artistic rather than a literary work. This was the case in *King Features Syndicate
Inc v O & M Kleeman Ltd*[41] (the *Popeye* case) where the House of Lords was
concerned with copyright in cartoon sketches of Popeye the Sailor. The sketches
were drawn for publication in a newspaper but various Popeye dolls and brooches
had been made subsequently with the licence of the copyright owner. The defendant had copied these articles without licence and was held thereby to have
infringed the copyright in the sketches. The decision established several points of
importance; first, various members of the House of Lords commented that section 22 could never have applied to the sketches because the sketches were not
designs capable of registration.[42] Secondly, the Lords found that, even if the
sketches were designs capable of registration,[43] the question whether section 22
applied to exclude copyright from them was to be determined as at the time that
the work was created. If at that time the work was not used nor intended to be
used industrially, copyright would subsist and there was nothing in section 22 to
remove that copyright if the work was later applied industrially.[44] As there had
been no such use or intention at the time that the sketches were created, section
22 did not apply and the sketches retained full copyright protection despite the
extensive licensed use which had been made of them.[45] The Lords also accepted
that, under the 1911 Act, copyright in the sketches could be infringed by the
making of a copy in three dimensions[46] and also that it could be infringed
indirectly (*i.e.* by copying articles which had been made to the works).

13–17   **Copyright Act 1956.** The Copyright Act 1911 was replaced by the Copyright
Act 1956 under which copyright subsisted in every original literary, dramatic,
musical or artistic work.[47] The 1956 Act also restricted the protection given by
copyright to industrial designs but, unlike the 1911 Act, did not do so by exclud-

---

[39] Copyright Act 1911, s.35(1).

[40] See para. 7–34, above.

[41] [1941] A.C. 417.

[42] [1941] A.C. 417 at 429–430, 439–440 and 443. The basis for this was that, to be registrable, a
design had to be applicable to an article of manufacture. The sketches were not designs for
articles but were merely sketches for publication in a newspaper. The defendant did not seek to
argue the contrary.

[43] *i.e.* even if (contrary to the view of the House of Lords) the sketches could be seen as designs applicable to articles of manufacture.

[44] *King Features Syndicate Inc v O & M Kleeman Ltd* [1941] A.C. 417 at 429 and 431, 440–441,
434 and 451–452.

[45] This finding is not entirely easy to justify. Lord Bridge stated in *British Leyland Motor Corporation v Armstrong Patents Ltd* [1986] A.C. 577 at 620B that: "The phrase used in s.22 is not *used
or* intended to be used, etc .... It seems to me to be a little difficult to understand what significance the House's decision [in *King Features*] allowed to the words I have emphasised".

[46] Before the Copyright Act 1911, the making of an article was probably not an infringement of the
copyright in a two dimensional artistic work, see *Hanfstaengl v Empire Palace* [1894] 2 Ch. 1.
However, the introduction by s.1(2) of the 1911 Act of the words "sole right to produce or
reproduce the work ... in any material form whatsoever ..." made it clear that, thereafter, such an
act could constitute an infringement, see *Purefoy Engineering Co Ltd v Sykes Boxall & Co Ltd*
(1955) 72 R.P.C. 89 at 98, CA.

[47] See Copyright Act 1956, s.2(1) and 3(2).

ing copyright from the work in question. Instead, sections 9(8) and 10 of the 1956 Act sought to place limits on the type of act which could infringe copyright in the relevant work.[48] As to section 9(8) as has been seen, the 1911 Act had treated many of the works which recorded industrial designs as plans and thus as literary works, the copyright in which would not be infringed by the making of the article so described.[49] However, under the 1956 Act, diagrams, maps, charts and plans were treated as drawings and, therefore, as artistic works.[50] Given the decision in *King Features*,[51] this meant that the copyright in an industrial design drawing could be infringed by the making of articles to the design. It was to counter this that section 9(8) of the 1956 Act provided that the making of an object in three dimensions should not be taken as infringing the copyright in an artistic work in two dimensions if the object would not appear, to the non-expert eye, to be a reproduction of the artistic work. Section 10 was the principal means by which the 1956 Act sought to limit copyright protection for industrial designs. Section 10 applied to an artistic work where a corresponding design[52] had been registered under the Registered Designs Act 1949 or, if it had not been registered, where it had been applied industrially,[53] and articles to which the design had been applied had been marketed.[54] In very broad terms, the nature of the limitation imposed by section 10 was that the copyright in the relevant artistic work would not be infringed to the extent that the Registered Designs Act 1949 provided a remedy or would have provided a remedy had the design been registered.[55] The intention, clearly, was to encourage designers to use the system of registration rather than to rely on copyright.

Problems with the 1956 Act. In practice, sections 9(8) and 10 of the 1956 Act were only partly effective in excluding copyright from the industrial sphere. Both provisions were considered in *Dorling v Honnor Marine Ltd*,[56] a case concerning copyright in plans of a sailing dinghy. The defendant had made boats and kits of parts for boats to those plans. It was held that the plans were artistic works and that, unless one of the new defences applied, the copyright in them would have been infringed by the defendant's actions.[57] On the facts, the court found that section 9(8) did not provide a defence in relation to the making of the kits and it sug-

13–18

---

[48] These provisions largely adopted the recommendations of the 1952 Gregory Report (Cmnd. 8662).

[49] See para. 13–16, above.

[50] Copyright Act 1956, ss.48(1) and 3(1)(a).

[51] See para. 13–16, above.

[52] A "corresponding design" in relation to an artistic work was a design which, when applied to an article, resulted in a reproduction of that work, Copyright Act 1956, s.10(7).

[53] The industrial application had to be by or with the consent of the copyright owner, Copyright Act 1956, s.10(2). A design was applied industrially if it was applied to or reproduced on or in more than 50 articles, see the Copyright (Industrial Designs) Rules 1957 (SI 1957/867).

[54] Copyright Act 1956, s.10(2). Marketing in this context meaning that such articles had been sold or let for hire or offered for sale or hire, see Copyright Act 1956, s.10(2)(b).

[55] For the first 15 years, copyright protection was only excluded in relation to those acts covered by the actual registration (see s.10(1)(a)) or those acts which would have been covered had the design been registered for the articles marketed by or with the licence of the copyright owner (s.10(3)(a)). Thereafter, copyright was excluded in relation to all acts which would have been covered by the widest registration which would have been possible in relation to that design. See s.10(1)(b), s.10(3)(b) and s.10(6). See also, *British Leyland Motor Corporation v Armstrong Patents Co Ltd* [1986] A.C. 577 at 620G.

[56] [1965] Ch. 1.

[57] The decision in *Dorling v Honnor Marine Ltd* [1965] Ch. 1 has been criticised on the basis that a distinction should have been drawn between an act which actually reproduces an artistic work (whether in two or three dimensions), as had been the case in *King Features* [1941] A.C. 417 (see para. 13–16, above), and an act which merely amounts to the use of the information contained in an artistic work (such as a drawing) as instructions for making a three dimensional object. In the latter case, the object, although derived from the information, does not in any real sense reproduce it. The strength of this criticism was accepted in *Canon Kabushiki Kaisha v Green Cartridge Co*

gested, without deciding, that it would not have provided a defence in relation to the making of complete boats either.[58] The court also found that section 10 of the 1956 Act only applied to artistic works whose corresponding designs were either (a) registered,[59] or (b) unregistered but registrable and had been applied industrially.[60] The section, it was found, had no relevance to works whose corresponding designs were *unregistrable*. As the plans were unregistrable,[61] section 10 did not operate so as to limit copyright protection for them.[62] The decision had wide-ranging implications for it showed that artistic works embodying unregistrable designs (in particular, designs which were unregistrable because they were functional) had full copyright protection lasting for the life of the author plus 50 years.

13–19   **Design Copyright Act 1968.** The attempt to maintain a distinction between industrial design protection and artistic copyright protection was largely abandoned when the Design Copyright Act 1968 was enacted.[63] Notwithstanding the Report of the 1962 Designs Committee,[64] the 1968 Act amended section 10 of the 1956 Act such that an artistic work embodying a design was entitled to full copyright protection. The scope of this protection was only limited where a corresponding design was applied industrially.[65] In such a case, copyright protection for the work was reduced to 15 years.[66] As a result of the 1968 Act, a registrable design recorded in an artistic work became capable of dual protection under both the Registered Designs Act 1949 and the Copyright Act 1956 (albeit for a reduced period in the latter case in the event that it was applied industrially). However, the 1968 Act did not affect the position as regards unregistrable designs. An unregistrable design recorded in a qualifying work remained entitled to full copyright protection of life plus 50 years in accordance with the decision in *Dorling v Honnor Marine Ltd*[67]

13–20   **Further developments in the law of registered designs.** Further developments in the law of registered designs increased the significance of copyright protection for unregistrable industrial designs. As has been seen, designs dictated solely by function were excluded from registration under the Registered Designs Act

---

(Hong Kong) Ltd [1997] 3 W.L.R. 13 at 17B–E, PC but it was said to be "far too late" to depart from the construction of copyright law taken in *Dorling* and followed in *L.B. (Plastics) Ltd v Swish Products Ltd* [1979] R.P.C. 551 and *British Leyland Motor Corporation v Armstrong Patents Ltd* [1986] A.C. 577. Of course, under the 1911 Act, the plans would have been literary rather than artistic works, see para. 13–16, above, the law was (and remains) that copyright in a literary work would not, in general, be infringed by the making of an article to that design, see the cases cited at para. 7–34, above.

[58] [1965] Ch. 1 at 16–17, 21–22, CA. Defences based on s.9(8) of the Copyright Act 1956 also failed in *L. B. (Plastics) Ltd v Swish Products Ltd* [1979] R.P.C. 551 and *British Leyland Motor Corporation v Armstrong Patents Ltd* [1986] A.C. 577.

[59] Copyright Act 1956, s.10(1).

[60] ss.10(2) and (3). The fact that the limitation placed on copyright protection for unregistered designs by s.10(3) was defined by reference to the protection which would have been available under the registered designs legislation led the Court of Appeal in *Dorling* to the view that s.10(2) only applied to works whose corresponding designs were registrable see [1965] 1 Ch. 1 at 16 and 19E–F.

[61] [1965] 1 Ch. 1 at 14C–E and at 19F–G.

[62] [1965] 1 Ch. 1 at 13–15 and 19–20.

[63] See *British Leyland Motor Corporation Ltd v Armstrong Patents Ltd* [1986] A.C. 577 at 620H.

[64] Cmnd. 808. The Committee, by a majority, favoured a continuing limitation on the application of artistic copyright in cases where a design was used industrially.

[65] *i.e.* applied in the sense set out in Copyright Act 1956, s.10(2)(a) and (b) (as amended).

[66] After the 15-year period, copyright would not be infringed to the extent that the Registered Designs Act 1949 would have provided a remedy had the design been registered at the relevant time, see s.10(2) and (3) as amended.

[67] [1965] Ch. 1. See para. 13–18, above. For other cases where designs have been found to be unregistrable and, therefore, to enjoy full copyright protection, see para. 13–20, below.

1949.[68] In *Amp Inc v Utilux Pty Ltd*,[69] this exclusion was construed widely so as to apply to any design which was brought about by, or which was attributable only to, the function of the article. The exclusion would apply even if there could be articles to other designs which would perform that function.[70] On this construction,[71] the test for registration seemed even more stringent and the scope for copyright protection for industrial designs correspondingly greater. More recently, designs which were unregistrable under Registered Designs Rules[72] or because they did not comply with the registered design definition of "design"[73] or because the articles to which they were to be applied did not satisfy the Registered Design definition of an "article"[74] were all held to be entitled to full copyright protection.

Spare parts and *British Leyland v Armstrong Patents*. The law as it stood **13–21** caused particular problems in relation to spare parts. A spare part for a product will usually be in the same or substantially the same shape as the original part. If, however, the designer of the original part had produced design drawings,[75] copyright in those drawings (however basic and lacking in artistic merit they may be) could often be asserted so as to prevent the manufacture of spare parts by competitors. Further, as such designs were unlikely to be registrable, section 10 did not operate to reduce the period of copyright protection. Accordingly, copyright might allow its owner an effective monopoly in the supply of spare parts for the entire commercial life of the design as well as for the actual life of products with which the design was associated. The point arose directly in *British Leyland Motor Corporation Ltd v Armstrong Patents Ltd*[76] where the defendant was manufacturing spare exhaust pipes to fit the plaintiff's vehicles. The plaintiff claimed that these spares infringed the copyright in its drawings of exhaust pipes for the relevant vehicles. The House of Lords accepted that, as the design drawings were unregistrable, they were not caught by section 10 of the 1956 Act. It also accepted that, because most objects can be recognised from their drawings, section 9(8) of the 1956 Act was incapable of preventing copyright protection extending into areas far beyond its main or originally intended scope.[77] However, in an attempt to allow a measure of competition, the House of Lords accepted that the rights of the copyright owner were subject to an exception which became known as the "spare parts exception". This exception was formulated in various ways but, in essence, it operated to prevent the manufacturer of an article such as a car using his copyrights in a way which would interfere with the right of the owner of that article to have access to a free market for spares to repair it or to keep it in good working order.[78]

Semiconductor topographies. Shortly after the decision in *British Leyland*, **13–22**

---

[68] s.1(3) of the 1949 Act (prior to its amendment by the CDPA 1988). See para. 13–15, above.
[69] [1972] R.P.C. 103.
[70] [1972] R.P.C. 103 at 114–115, 118 and 122, HL. See also *Interlego A.G. v Tyco International Industries Inc* [1988] R.P.C. 343 at 355, HL.
[71] Which the House of Lords in *British Leyland Motor Corporation v Armstrong Patents Co Ltd* [1986] A.C. 577 declined to overrule, see at 614D and at 618H–619A.
[72] Rules made under s.1(4) of the Registered Designs Act 1949.
[73] See *Entec (Pollution Control) Ltd v Abacus Mouldings* [1992] F.S.R. 332 following *British Leyland Motor Corporation v Armstrong Patents Co Ltd* [1986] A.C. 577.
[74] See *Drayton Controls (Engineering) Ltd v Honeywell Control Systems Ltd* [1992] F.S.R. 245.
[75] As was increasingly the case.
[76] [1986] A.C. 577.
[77] [1986] A.C. 577 at 653C and 639C–D.
[78] The decision in *British Leyland Motor Corporation v Armstrong Patents Co Ltd* [1986] A.C. 577 and its formulation of the spare parts exception has been the subject of much criticism. See, for example, *Canon Kabushiki Kaisha v Green Cartridge Co (Hong Kong) Ltd* [1997] 3 W.L.R. 13.

there was a further development of significance in the field of industrial design. On December 16, 1986, the Council of the European Communities issued a Directive[79] concerning protection for the design or topography of semiconductor products. This Directive expressly recognised that semiconductor products were capable of being copied at a fraction of the cost which it took to develop them and that their topographies therefore required protection. The Directive was significant in that it included a requirement that the subject matter for protection (the topography) must be original, not only in the sense that it was the product of the creator's own intellectual effort, but also in the sense that it was not commonplace in the semiconductor industry. Further, the protection offered was more limited than that available to normal copyright works. The Directive was implemented in the United Kingdom by the Semiconductor Products (Protection of Topography) Regulations 1987[80] which by Regulation 9(1) provided that it was not an infringement of the copyright in an artistic work to reproduce a topography.

13–23   **Summary of the law as at 1988.** Thus, as at 1988, the law relating to the protection of industrial designs was in some disarray. Designs which were sufficiently novel were capable of registered design protection lasting 15 years. However, such protection was not proving popular[81] and the exclusion from registrability had, in any event, been construed widely.[82] Save where the uncertain spare parts exception applied,[83] automatic copyright protection, traditionally the preserve of the fine arts, was available to a very wide range of industrial designs provided only that they were recorded in a qualifying copyright work. This copyright protection lasted for the life of the author plus 50 years unless the corresponding design was both registrable under the Registered Designs Act 1949 and had been applied industrially, in which case the term of copyright protection was limited to 15 years.[84] As a result, the full term of copyright protection was available for the least "artistic" of designs[85] whilst the most artistic industrial designs (those which, being visually appealing and not being governed by functionality, were registrable under the Registered Designs Act 1949) had only 15 years' copyright protection. This often led to parties arguing that their designs were not registrable even, sometimes, where they had previously registered the design.[86] Finally, a completely separate system of protection was available for semiconductor topographies.

13–24   **Anomaly concerning three-dimensional works.** The use of copyright as a means of protecting industrial designs gave rise to other anomalies. In particular,[87] where an industrial design was recorded in a drawing, the drawing (and indirectly the design) had copyright protection regardless of its artistic merit and regardless of how functional or otherwise the design may be. If, however, the design was only recorded in a three dimensional article made to the design, then copyright protection was only available if the article itself fell within the defini-

[79] Council Directive 87/54 EEC.
[80] Now replaced by the Design Right (Semiconductor Topography) Regulations 1989. For the current position, see Ch.14, below.
[81] See paras 102 and 103 of the Whitford Report Cmnd.6732 (March 1977).
[82] See para. 13–20, above.
[83] See para. 13–21, above.
[84] Under Copyright Act 1956, s.10 (as amended by the 1968 Act), copyright was only limited to 15 years if the design had been industrially applied *and* was registered or registrable under the Registered Designs Act 1949. The mere fact that a design had been registered did not operate to limit copyright protection to 15 years.
[85] Such as, for example, rivets, screws, a bolt, a block of leather and a washer in *British Northrop Ltd v Texteam Blackburn Ltd* [1974] R.P.C. 57 at 68–69.
[86] See, for example, *Interlego A.G. v Tyco International Inc* [1988] R.P.C. 343.
[87] See para.197 of the Whitford Report Cmnd.6732 (March 1977).

tion of an artistic work and, in particular, only if it was a sculpture or a work of artistic craftsmanship—the meaning of the latter being very narrowly construed.[88] This meant that the availability of copyright protection for a design would often depend upon the chance of whether or not a preliminary sketch of the design had been made.

Proposals for reform. Many of the developments in the law which are discussed above were controversial and over the years various proposals for reform were put forward. The contrasting proposals reflected the difference between those who regarded the need for protection as paramount and who saw no need to distinguish between industrial designs and artistic works and those who believed that there was a need to allow more competition in relation to industrial designs than for works of art. Yet, even within the latter category, there was a wide variety of views as to how to meet that need.[89]   **13–25**

The Whitford Report 1977. The Whitford Committee report[90] dealt at length with the law relating to industrial designs[91] and with the differing submissions it had received from various interested parties on how best to balance protection against competition.[92] In its conclusions, the Committee unanimously recommended the repeal of the registered designs monopoly provided by the Registered Designs Act 1949. A majority was in favour of providing copyright protection without the need for registration for so-called "Category A" designs (designs which consisted only of a surface pattern and the shapes of three-dimensional articles of which the aesthetic appearance would influence a purchaser in making a purchase regardless of whether they started life in two or in three dimensions[93]). This protection would, however, be cut to 25 years once the design had been industrially applied. The committee was divided on how to treat designs which it called "Category B" designs (designs of three dimensional shapes with no such aesthetic appeal). Some felt that no protection was appropriate. Others thought that the protection should be the same as that for Category A designs. Others favoured a limited form of protection under a design deposit copyright system. All, however, were in favour of compulsory licences being available in respect of Category B designs, on the ground that the United Kingdom market was not being adequately supplied.[94]   **13–26**

The 1981 and 1983 Green Papers. After the Whitford Report, two green papers considered, *inter alia*, the protection of industrial designs. The 1981 Green Paper[95] favoured the removal of any protection (other than patent protection) from purely functional items, arguing that industrial progress was being hindered by the protection which the law afforded. By contrast, the 1983 Green Paper[96] accepted that novel designs of purely functional items should be given protection. Unlike the Whitford Report, it suggested that all designs could be protected through a   **13–27**

---

[88] See *George Hensher Ltd v Restawile Upholstery (Lancs.) Ltd* [1976] A.C. 64.
[89] This variety of views can be seen in the fact that some countries, such as France, have traditionally followed the so-called doctrine of the "unity of art" (that there should be no distinction between the protection of works or pure art and works of industrial art), whilst others, such as Italy, have traditionally adopted a more restrictive approach to protection, see para. 13–35, below.
[90] Cmnd. 6732 (March 1977).
[91] See paras 89–203 of the Report.
[92] See paras 129–164 of the Report .
[93] In order to remove the anomaly referred to in para. 13–24, above.
[94] See para.194 of the Report.
[95] Reform of the Law relating to Copyright, Designs and Performers' Protection (Cmnd. 8302). July 1981.
[96] Intellectual Property Rights and Innovation (Cmnd. 9117). December 1983.

system of registration rather than by a form of copyright (although it recommended that the costs of such a proposal be investigated).

13–28   **The 1986 White Paper.** The 1986 White Paper[97] rejected the suggestion in the 1983 Green Paper that all designs be registrable. It proposed, instead, that the Registered Designs Act 1949 be amended to protect only genuinely aesthetic designs but that the period of protection be increased to 25 years. For non-registrable designs, it considered, but rejected as uncertain, protection based on an "unfair copying" law and proposed, instead, a completely new "unregistered design right" based on copyright principles but without the more objectionable features associated with full copyright protection.[98] In particular, it suggested that the new design right provide protection for all original designs, including spare parts,[99] but not including artistic works,[1] and that the term of protection be only 10 years with provision for licences as of right in the last five years of the term.

13–29   **Copyright Designs and Patents Act 1988.** The Copyright Designs and Patents Act 1988 followed, with some important exceptions, the proposals contained in the 1986 White Paper. As with the 1911 and 1956 Acts, the intention behind the 1988 Act is to remove industrial designs from the sphere of copyright and to leave copyright as the preserve of what might properly be called artistic works.[2] The need to provide protection for industrial designs was, however, recognised. To achieve this, the 1988 Act created a wholly new right known as design right. Design right, like copyright, provides automatic protection against copying without any need for formalities such as registration. However, the scope of design right has been carefully limited so as to allow far more competition than the law of copyright allows. Thus, commonplace designs[3] are excluded from design right protection, as are designs which fall within the so-called "must fit" and "must match" exclusions.[4] Moreover, where design right subsists in a design, it only lasts for 15 years or, if articles made to the design are made available for sale or hire within five years from the end of the calendar year when the design was first recorded in a design document or when an article was first made to the design, for 10 years from the end of the calendar year in which that first occurred.[5] Finally, competitors are entitled to seek licences of right in relation to the design in the last five years of its term.[6] The 1988 Act also contained provisions amending the Registered Designs Act 1949[7] and, in particular, increasing the period of protection available to registered designs to 25 years.

The provisions and effect of the 1988 Act are analysed in detail below. However, its effect has been to reduce significantly the role of copyright in the protection of industrial designs. Moreover, although design right has many similarities to copyright, the limitations placed on it in the 1988 Act mean that it should not be regarded as being copyright by another name and that the scope of

---

[97] Intellectual Property and Innovation (Cmnd. 9712). April 1986.
[98] See para.3.26 of the White Paper.
[99] See paras 3.26 and 3.27 of the White Paper.
[1] The United Kingdom having obligations in respect of artistic works under the Berne Convention. See paras 13–35 et seq., below.
[2] See Hansard, H.L. Vol.491, cols 185, 186.
[3] CDPA 1988, s.213(4). See paras 13–70 et seq., below.
[4] CDPA 1988, s.213(3). See paras 13–56 et seq., below.
[5] CDPA 1988, s.216, see paras 13–100 et seq., below. In contrast, copyright now lasts for the lifetime of the author plus 70 years—see Ch.6, above.
[6] CDPA 1988, s.237. See paras 13–123 et seq., below.
[7] CDPA 1988, ss.265–273 and Sch.4.

its protection for industrial designs is much more limited than that previously offered by copyright.[8]

European Community design—the background. The protection of industrial   **13–30**
designs has also been the subject of considerable debate within the European
Community. The basis of this debate was that the Treaty establishing the
European Community provides for the establishment of an internal market,[9] the
abolition of obstacles to the free movement of goods in that market and the
institution of a system to ensure that competition in that market is not distorted.
The fact that the various Member States were providing widely differing levels of
protection for industrial designs was seen as being contrary to those aims.[10] As a
result, in June 1991, the European Commission produced a Green Paper on the
Legal Protection of Industrial Designs.[11] This Paper suggested the creation of a
completely new system to protect so-called Community designs and a measure of
harmonisation of the Member States' national design laws. The Green Paper was
followed by two proposals in December 1993—a proposed Directive on the Legal
Protection of Designs[12] and a proposed Regulation for Community designs[13] After a lengthy process and various amendments, the Directive was finally adopted
in 1998 and the Regulation in 2002.

The Directive on the Legal Protection of Designs—further changes to the   **13–31**
Registered Designs Act 1949. The Directive on the Legal Protection of Designs[14]
required Member States to harmonise their registered design law but did not affect the law of design right.[15] The Directive was implemented in the United
Kingdom by the Registered Design Regulations 2001[16] which came into force on
December 9, 2001. These Regulations made significant amendments to the
Registered Designs Act 1949. In brief,[17] a new wider definition of "design" was
adopted, but to be registrable, there were newly drafted requirements that a design
had to be new and have individual character. The amendments also brought in
newly drafted exclusions for designs dictated solely by technical function and
designs of interconnections. As a result of these amendments, many of the provisions of the 1949 Act are the same as those contained in the Regulation on Community designs which is considered below. However, these amendments have
removed many of the similarities in language that previously existed between the
law relating to United Kingdom registered design law and United Kingdom
design right.

---

[8] See Radcliffe and Caddick "Abbreviating the Scope of Design Right" [1997] E.I.P.R. 534.
[9] *i.e.* the "common" market.
[10] See Recitals (1) to (8) of the Regulation on Community designs (EC) No. 6/2002.
[11] III/F.5131/91.
[12] [1993] O.J. C345/14; COM. (93) 344 final—SYN 464.
[13] [1994] O.J. C29/20; COM. (93) 342 final—SYN 463.
[14] Directive 98/71.
[15] The position regarding the effect of the Directive on the copyright provisions of the CDPA 1988
is more complicated. Art.17 of the Directive provides that a design protected by way of registration must also be eligible for copyright protection under the relevant Member State's law—
although the extent of such protection and any conditions under which it is conferred remain a
matter for each Member State. No changes have been made to the 1988 Act as a result of the
Directive—presumably on the basis that the 1988 Act does not actually exclude the subsistence
of copyright in registrable designs albeit that ss.51 and 52 of the 1988 Act effectively remove
large swathes of the protection that copyright would otherwise provide for such designs. Given
that recital 8 to the Directive states that the principle of cumulation of registered design and
copyright protection is important, s.51 and possibly also s.52 may be the subject of future
harmonisation.
[16] SI 2001/3949.
[17] The law relating to registered designs is considered in outline at paras 13–251 *et seq.*, below.

13–32   The Community Design Regulation—protection for Community designs.
Under the Regulation on Community Designs,[18] a Community design can be
protected in two ways; first, automatic protection against copying lasting for
three years from the date of first marketing and, secondly, upon registration,
monopolistic protection lasting for up to 25 years. This two-tier system for the
protection of Community designs is intended to operate (for the time being at
least) alongside the national laws of the individual Member States. As mentioned
above, much of the language governing Community design is the same as that
which now applies to United Kingdom registered designs. The Regulation came
into effect on March 6, 2002 and it became possible to apply for registration of a
Community design on April 1, 2003.

E. PROTECTION REQUIRED BY INTERNATIONAL AGREEMENTS

13–33   In determining the level of protection for industrial designs, the international
treaty obligations to which the United Kingdom is subject must be borne in mind.

(i) Paris Convention for the Protection of Industrial Property

13–34   The Paris Convention for the Protection of Industrial Property,[19] to which the
United Kingdom is a signatory, provides for the establishment of a Union of
countries for the protection of industrial property, a phrase which the Convention
provides is to be understood in its broadest sense and which includes industrial
designs.[20] Article 2 provides that, in relation to industrial property, nationals of
any country of the Union shall enjoy in all other countries the advantages which
their respective laws then or thereafter may grant to their own nationals without
the imposition of any requirement as to domicile.[21] By Article 5 *quinquies* of this
Convention,[22] industrial designs are required to be protected in all countries of
the European Union.

   The 1988 Act. As has been seen, the protection of industrial designs under the
1988 Act is largely dealt with by way of design right. It would appear that the
intention of Parliament was that effect should be given to the United Kingdom's
obligations under the Paris Convention by way of Orders in Council made under
section 221 of the 1988 Act and providing for designs to qualify for design right
in order to fulfil an international obligation.[23] A similar arrangement applies in
relation to registered designs.[24]

---

[18] Regulation (EC) No. 6/2002.
[19] 1883. Revised at Brussels (1900), Washington (1911), the Hague (1925), London (1934), Lisbon
(1958) and Stockholm (1967).
[20] Paris Convention, Arts 1(1)–(3).
[21] *i.e.* the same protection and the same legal remedies against any infringement—assuming that the
conditions and formalities imposed on nationals are complied with, see Paris Convention,
Art.2(1).
[22] *i.e.* Art.5 of the Lisbon (1958) revision of the Paris Convention.
[23] See *Hansard*, H.L. Vol.491, cols 1128–1129. It would seem that Parliament took the view
(expressed in the earlier White Paper on Intellectual Property and Innovation (1986, Cmnd.
9712) at paras 2.27 and 3.34) that the Paris Convention applies only as regards aesthetic designs
of the kind which are registrable under the Registered Designs Act 1949 and not to the designs of
functional articles. This was a view based, presumably, on the terms of Arts 4 and 5 of the Paris
Convention.
[24] Registered Designs Act 1949, ss.13–15.

(ii) Berne Convention

Literary and artistic works—Article 2(1). The history and provisions of the **13–35** Berne Convention are considered elsewhere.[25] Under the Convention, the Convention states undertook to adopt measures necessary to protect literary and artistic works as defined by Article 2(1) of the Paris Act (1971) thereof. Article 2(1) starts with the general statement that such works include every production in the literary, scientific and artistic domain, whatever may be the mode or form of expression. It then sets out a list of specific types of work to be included. The list is prefaced by the words "such as" and is not, therefore, intended to be exhaustive. However, the type of works covered by the general statement to Article 2(1) must, it is suggested, be read in the light of the specific works listed. The listed works include (for present purposes) "... works of drawing, painting, architecture, sculpture, engraving and lithography; ... works of applied art; illustrations, maps, plans, sketches and three-dimensional works relative to geography, topography, architecture or science."

The category comprising "illustrations, maps, sketches and three-dimensional works relative to geography, topography, architecture or science" would not, it is suggested, include most industrial designs.[26] Moreover, the fact that those drafting the Convention saw fit to include this category in the Article 2(1) list of works suggests that the category of "works of drawing, painting (etc.)" referred to earlier in the list was not intended to encompass all types of drawing or painting but only such of those works which could properly be seen as artistic.[27] On this basis, purely technical "non-artistic" works would be outside the scope of both of these two categories[28] and also, presumably, outside the scope of the general statement referred to above. However, the position is rather different as regards the numerous types of industrial design where some "artistic" element is required to attract buyers and also as regards those works which started their lives as truly artistic works but which were subsequently applied industrially.[29] Initially, the Berne Convention contained no express provision as to such works and different states took differing views of their obligations to protect them as artistic works.[30] These differences in opinion were debated at various conferences called to revise the Convention[31] and led to a provision being added to the Convention at the Berlin Act (1908) to the effect that "works of art applied to industry are protected to the extent permitted by the internal legislation of each country". However, this still left Convention States free to determine whether such works should be treated as works of art on the one hand or as industrial designs or models on the other and to deny protection if they decided on the latter. It was not until the Brussels Act (1948) that the Convention was amended so as to include "works of applied art" within the definition of works for which

---

[25] See Ch.24, below.

[26] A design sketch for a chair or of a machine cog, for example, would not relate to geography, topography, architecture or science, see Ricketson *The Berne Convention for the Protection of Literary and Artistic Works: 1886–1986* at para.6.58.

[27] Ricketson, *The Berne Convention for the Protection of Literary and Artistic Works: 1886–1986*, at paras 6.28 and 6.29.

[28] Unless they related to geography, topography, architecture or science.

[29] Works, for example, such as a painting subsequently used as a pattern for wall paper or cartoon sketches subsequently used as a design for dolls and brooches (see *King Features Syndicate Inc v O. & M. Kleeman Ltd* [1941] A.C. 417—"the Popeye Case", see para. 13–16, above.

[30] The differences being between those countries (notably France) which saw no need to distinguish between works or pure art and works of industrial art and those (such as the United Kingdom) which either wished to exclude them from the copyright sphere or at least to limit the scope of their copyright protection.

[31] The history of the various debates concerning the protection of industrially applied works is discussed in full in Ricketson, *The Berne Convention for the Protection of Literary and Artistic Works: 1886–1986*, at paras 6.44–6.54.

the Convention (*prima facie*) requires protection. This is the position maintained by the Stockholm (1967) and also (as appears above) by the Paris (1971) Acts of the Convention.

13–36 **Qualifications on protection—Article 2(7).** Although the definition of literary and artistic works contained in Article 2(1) is potentially very wide and would, on its face, cover most industrial designs[32] or works applied industrially, the actual level of protection required by the Convention is significantly qualified by Article 2(7) of the Paris Act. This provides that it is for the Convention States to determine the extent of the application of their laws to works of applied art, industrial designs and models, as well as the conditions under which such works, designs and models shall be protected. Article 2(7) also provides that works protected in the country of origin solely as designs and models are entitled in another Convention State only to such special protection as is granted in that country to designs and models, but if no such protection is granted in that country, such works are to be protected as artistic works.[33] Article 2(7) is subject to Article 7(4) which provides that, whilst Convention States may determine the term of protection of works of applied art in so far as they are protected as artistic works, that term must be at least 25 years from the making of such a work.

13–37 **The 1988 Act.** It would seem that the 1988 Act complies with the United Kingdom's obligations under the Berne Convention. Under the 1988 Act, full copyright is retained in respect of articles which qualify as artistic works in their own right. Moreover, copyright continues to subsist in artistic works which constitute industrial designs; however, the limitation placed on the scope of protection for such works by section 51 of the 1988 Act is a limitation permitted by Article 2(7). Similarly, the 1988 Act allows copyright to subsist in artistic works which are industrially applied and the reduction in the period of copyright protection for such works brought about by section 52 of the 1988 Act—namely to 25 years—is permitted by Articles 2(7) and 7(4).[34]

(iii) Agreement on Trade-Related Aspects of Intellectual Property Rights ("TRIPS")

13–38 The history of and background to the Agreement on Trade-Related Aspects of Intellectual Property Rights ("TRIPS")[35] is considered elsewhere.[36] In outline, under its provisions, Member States agreed to give effect to the provisions of that Agreement (whilst being free to determine the appropriate method for so doing). They also agreed to accord the treatment provided for in the Agreement to the nationals of other Member States.[37] Under Article 25(1) of TRIPS, Member States must provide for the protection of independently created industrial designs that are new or original but they are entitled to provide that designs are not new or original if they do not significantly differ from known designs or combinations of known design features and also that protection need not extend to designs dictated by essentially technical or functional considerations. Article 26 of TRIPS deals

---

[32] Assuming they are not purely functional.

[33] Art.2(7) of the Stockholm (1967) and Paris (1971) Acts was derived from Art.2(5) of the Brussels (1900) but with the addition of the phrase commencing with the words "however, if no such protection ... (etc.)". See Ricketson, *The Berne Convention for the Protection of Literary and Artistic Works: 1886–1986*, at para.6.53.

[34] For detailed discussions of CDPA 1988, ss.51 and 52, see below at paras 13–278 *et seq.* and 13–297 *et seq.* respectively.

[35] Concluded at Geneva on December 15, 1993, GATT document MTN/FA II-AIC.

[36] See Ch.24, below.

[37] TRIPS, Art.1.

with the nature of the protection to be provided; the type of acts capable of being infringements,[38] limited exceptions from protection,[39] and a minimum period of protection lasting 10 years.[40] Part III of TRIPS sets out the way in which the relevant rights may be enforced and the type of remedies which may be provided.

The 1988 Act. It would seem that the United Kingdom's law of registered designs **13–39** complies with TRIPS.[41] If TRIPS applies in relation to the unregistered design right provisions of the 1988 Act, those too would seem to comply.[42]

2. DESIGN RIGHT: INTRODUCTION

Nature of design right. Design right is a property right which subsists in certain **13–40** original designs.[43] Like copyright, it is not a monopoly right but rather makes copying an infringement. Like copyright, it subsists automatically without the need for any formality such as registration or the deposit of documents. However, the scope of protection for industrial designs under design right is intended to be far narrower than that which copyright often provided before the 1988 Act. Thus, the 1988 Act places wide-ranging limitations on the type of designs which will attract design right protection.[44] Moreover, design right protection where it is available lasts for a maximum of 15 years and, in many cases, for nearer to 10 years.[45] In the last five years of its term, licences of right are available.[46]

Interrelationship of design right with copyright. Design right subsists in **13–41** certain designs; copyright in (*inter alia*) certain artistic and literary works. If, therefore, a design is recorded or embodied in such a work, there is a possibility that both design right and copyright will subsist. The 1988 Act does not prevent this but instead seeks to exclude dual protection by both design right and copyright. Thus, section 51 provides that most acts of industrial copying of industrial designs will not infringe any relevant copyright.[47] Such acts are actionable (if at all[48]) as infringements of design right. Where section 51 does not apply, section 236 provides that it is not an infringement of the design right to do anything which is an infringement of copyright. These provisions are considered in more detail later in this Chapter.

---

[38] To be an infringement, an act must be undertaken for commercial purposes , TRIPS, Art.26(1).

[39] Art.26(2) which also provides that such exceptions should not unreasonably conflict with the normal exploitation of protected industrial designs nor unreasonably prejudice the legitimate interests of the owner of the protected design, taking account of the legitimate interests of third parties.

[40] TRIPS, Art.26(3).

[41] For a brief discussion of registered designs see paras 13–251 *et seq.*, below.

[42] In *Re Azrak Hamway International Inc* [1997] R.P.C. 134, it was argued that the design right licence of right provisions were contrary to TRIPS because they could result in the reduction in the period of effective protection to less than the 10 years required by Art.26(3) and because they did not constitute limited exceptions within the meaning of Art.26(2). This argument was rejected on the grounds that TRIPS had no application in relation to unregistered design right provisions of the 1988 Act (as opposed to the registered design provisions of the Registered Designs Act 1949) and that, even if it did, the licence of right provisions (with their provision for licence fees) would not be contrary to Art.26. For a discussion of design right see paras 13–40 *et seq.*, below, and for licences of right see paras 13–123 *et seq.*, below.

[43] CDPA 1988, s.213(1).

[44] The design must be original and not commonplace. Further, any so-called "must fit" and "must match" features are excluded from protection.

[45] For the duration of design right see paras 13–100 *et seq.*, below. Copyright protection is now for the life of the artist plus 70 years.

[46] For the design right licence of right provisions see paras 13–123 *et seq.*, below.

[47] Under CDPA 1988, s.51, the copyright in a design document or model recording or embodying the design for anything other than an artistic work or typeface is not infringed by the making of articles to that design or by the copying of articles made to the design. For a full discussion of s.51 see paras 13–228 *et seq.*, below.

[48] The fact that CDPA 1988, s.51 operates does not mean that there must be a claim in design right; s.51 operates regardless of whether or not design right subsists in the relevant design.

13–42 **Interrelationship of design right and registered designs.** There are different definitions of a design for the purposes of design right on the one hand and for the purposes of registration under the Registered Designs Act 1949 on the other.[49] However, many designs will satisfy both definitions. The 1988 Act does nothing to prevent dual protection where this occurs. It should be noted that the proprietor of the registered design and the owner of the design right are not necessarily the same person[50] although, where they are, an assignment of the registered design would carry the design right with it unless the contrary appears.[51]

13–43 **Design right issues.** In approaching a design right case, the following questions may need to be addressed:

   (i) What is the actual design to be relied on—is it a "design" in which design right is capable of subsisting?

   (ii) Does design right actually subsist in the design—*i.e.* (1) were the necessary conditions for subsistence of design right satisfied when the design was created and, if so, (2) does design right still subsist or has the term expired?

   (iii) Who owns the design right—this involves asking (1) who was the first owner of the design right and (2) has ownership passed (in law or equity) to some other person?

   (iv) What rights does the design right owner have?

   (v) In the particular circumstances of the case, are there any reasons why the design right owner cannot assert his exclusive rights—*i.e.* do any of the usual defences to an action for infringement apply?

   (vi) Are his rights, although exercisable, subject to any form of control?—*i.e* are licences of right available?

   (vii) In the case of infringement, what remedies are available?

3. DESIGN RIGHT: SUBJECT MATTER OF PROTECTION

A. DEFINITION OF DESIGN

13–44 **Section 213(2)—definition of design.** For design right to subsist, there must be a design within the meaning of section 213(2) of the 1988 Act. This provides that "design" means the design of any aspect of the shape or configuration (whether internal or external) of the whole or part of an article.

13–45 **The "design".** This definition is extremely wide. For example, in the case of a teapot,[52] a plaintiff may choose to rely on the design of the whole pot but he may also rely on the design of one or more of its parts or aspects—such as the spout, the handle, the lid or even a part of the lid.[53] The width of this definition allows a claimant to define the design upon which he relies in a way that most closely

---

[49] For the design right definition of a design see paras 13–44 *et seq.*, below; for the Registered Design Act 1949 definition, see paras 13–255 *et seq.*, above.

[50] See paras 13–111 *et seq.*, below.

[51] CDPA 1988, s.224, see para. 13–118, below.

[52] The example used in *Ocular Sciences Ltd v Aspect Vision Care Ltd* [1997] R.P.C. 289 at 422.

[53] See *Farmers Build Ltd v Carier Bulk Materials Handling Ltd* [1999] R.P.C. 461, at 475 and 483–486, where the Court of Appeal upheld claims to design right in the design of the whole of a slurry-separating machine but also in the designs of certain component parts (both as articles in their own right and as parts of the machine). See also *Spraymiser Ltd v Wrightway Marketing Ltd* [2000] E.C.D.R. 349 (design for configurable wooden figure of a man) and *A. Fulton Co Ltd v Grant Barnett & Co Ltd* [2001] R.P.C. 257 at paras 36 and 38 (designs of handles and carrying cases for folding umbrellas).

matches what he believes the defendant to have taken.[54] It also allows the claimant to rely on a number of alternative designs. Thus, a claimant may assert design right in the design of an article as a whole and/or on the design of an article minus certain features and/or in the design of specified aspects of that article.[55] If the article is formed of component parts, the claimant can also rely on the designs of those components as articles in their own right, or as aspects of the design of the whole article.[56]

Given the width of this definition, it is important to identify clearly each separate design being relied upon. As will be seen, the precise identification of the design relied upon is important for a number of reasons. First, it is the design relied on which is tested for originality.[57] Thus a design which combines a number of features may be original even if some or even all of those component features would not be original if looked at individually.[58] Secondly, one must identify the design in question in order to identify its designer and, hence, the design right owner. In the case of an article on which a team of designers has worked, the design right in the overall design of the whole article may be jointly owned by all of the design team whereas the design rights in the designs of its various parts may be owned by different individuals.[59] Finally, the way in which the relevant design is identified may have serious implications when it comes to proving infringement.[60] A careful pleading of alternative designs is, therefore, advisable.

No requirement of artistic merit or eye appeal. As with copyright, the relevant design need not have any artistic merit nor need it appeal to the eye. Thus design right may subsist in a functional design as well as in one which is intended to be attractive.[61] It is suggested that the design may even be of something which is invisible to the naked eye in normal use.[62] Further, as a design may be described or defined by way of dimensions, very small changes in those dimensions may give rise to a separate design.[63]   **13–46**

Any aspect. It seems that the word "aspect" means something that is discernable or recognisable (although not necessarily visible to the naked eye) in the shape or   **13–47**

---

[54] See *Ocular Sciences Ltd v Aspect Vision Care Ltd* [1997] R.P.C. 289 at 422 and *A Fulton Co Ltd v Totes Isotoner (UK) Ltd* [2003] EWCA Civ 1514, at para.34 and also at para.23 where Jacob L.J. rejected the idea that this left the law ripe for abuse.

[55] Such as the umbrella case minus part of its cuff in *A Fulton Co Ltd v Totes Isotoner (UK) Ltd* [2003] EWCA Civ 1514 (a claim based on the design of the whole article failed so that the alternative plea was important) or the umbrella handle minus its protuberant rim in *A Fulton Co Ltd v Grant Barnett & Co Ltd* [2001] R.P.C. 257 at 270.

[56] See *Farmers Build Ltd v Carier Bulk Materials Handling Ltd* [1999] R.P.C. 461, at 475 and 483–486. *Novum (Overseas) Ltd v Iceland Foods plc* [2002] EWHC 53 shows the importance of pleading alternatives. There a claim based on the design of a freezer as a whole succeeded whereas claims based on the designs of the internal dividers of the freezer and of the gasket between its lid and main body failed (due, respectively, to the "must fit" and commonplace exclusions—see paras 13–57 and 13–58 *et.seq.*, below. For the problems which the choice of design may cause in relation to the "must fit" exclusion, see para. 13–58, below).

[57] CDPA 1988, s.213(1) and s.213(4).

[58] See *Farmers Build Ltd v Carier Bulk Materials Handling Ltd* [1999] R.P.C. 461 at 486 and *Ocular Sciences Ltd v Aspect Vision Care Ltd* [1997] R.P.C. 289 at 429–430. For a full discussion of originality, see paras 13–70 *et seq.*, below.

[59] See para. 13–85, below.

[60] See para. 13–149, below. The test for infringement in CDPA 1988, s.226(2) requires a court to ask whether the allegedly infringing *article* has been made wholly or substantially to the plaintiff's *design*. This is relatively straightforward where the plaintiff's design is of a whole article for there the comparison being made is usually of like with like. It is less straightforward where the design in question is of part of an article.

[61] Subject to the exclusion in relation to surface decoration. See paras 13–66 *et seq.*, below.

[62] Because, for example, it is too small or because it is internal and concealed. See *A Fulton Co Ltd v Totes Isotoner (UK) Ltd* [2003] EWCA Civ 1514 per Jacob L.J. at para.30.

[63] See *Ocular Sciences Ltd v Aspect Vision Care Ltd* [1997] R.P.C. 289 at 422.

configuration of an article.[64] As the teapot example shows, an article or even a part of an article may comprise many aspects of shape or configuration. Each of those aspects is capable of being a design for these purposes and, subject to the exclusions discussed below,[65] each is a design in which design right may subsist.

13–48 **Shape or configuration.** The relevant design must be of an aspect of the shape or configuration (whether internal or external) of an article or part of an article. The words "shape" and "configuration" are not defined by the 1988 Act. However, "shape" suggests the outward appearance or external form of an article whilst "configuration" suggests the arrangement of its various interrelating parts. For many years, the same words were included in the definition of a design for registered design purposes,[66] and in that context it was stated that they might for practical purposes be considered as synonymous.[67] However, this may not always be true. Thus, in *Cow & Co Ltd v Cannon Rubber Manufacturers Ltd*, it was stated that the ribbing on a hot water bottle might be configuration but not shape[68] although a better example of a distinction might be the polygonal patches that make up a patchwork quilt.[69] In the design right context, it has been decided that the word configuration may apply to the design of the components present in a circuit board and their interconnection even though a circuit board made to that design could have a wide range of shapes.[70]

As design right is concerned with "any aspect" of the shape or configuration of the whole or part of an article, there is no reason why the relevant design should not be of a two-dimensional aspect of shape (provided it does not fall within the surface decoration exclusion[71]). Thus, the design of a template used in dressmaking or of a stencil may be a design for these purposes.[72] However, the mere use of colour (even if it is not part of the surface decoration) would not be an aspect of configuration.[73]

---

[64] *A Fulton Co Ltd v Totes Isotoner (UK) Ltd* [2003] EWCA Civ 1514 per Jacob L.J. at paras 30 and 31.

[65] *i.e.* the exclusions set out in CDPA 1988, s.213(3), see paras 13–53 *et seq.*, below.

[66] Until it was amended by the Registered Designs Regulations 2001, the Registered Designs Act 1949, s.1 defined a design as "features of shape, configuration, pattern or ornament applied to an article ...".

[67] See *Kestos Ltd v Kempat Ltd* (1936) 53 R.P.C. 139 at 152.

[68] [1959] R.P.C. 240, per Lord Evershed M.R. at 244. It could be argued to the contrary that the ribbing did help define the shape of the bottle—see *Lambretta Clothing Co Ltd v Teddy Smith (UK) Ltd* [2004] EWCA Civ 886 at para.20 per Jacob L.J. (with whom Mance L.J. agreed on this point).

[69] The patchwork quilt example was criticised by Jacob L.J. in *Lambretta Clothing Co Ltd v Teddy Smith (UK) Ltd* [2004] EWCA (Civ) 886 at para.28. However, his reasoning is difficult to reconcile with his comments regarding two or three dimensional designs (at para.24). Moreover, a quilt is an article, and it is difficult to see why the patches that make up that quilt should not be seen an aspect of its configuration. It is submitted that, in this respect, the views of Sedley LJ in *Lambretta* (see para.89) are to be preferred.

[70] *Mackie Designs Inc v Behringer Specialised Studio Equipment (UK) Ltd* [1999] R.P.C. 717 where Pumfrey J. commented that the configuration of an article includes its relative arrangement of parts or elements (at p.721). In *Lambretta Clothing Co Ltd v Teddy Smith (UK) Ltd* [2004] EWCA (Civ) 886, Jacob L.J. commented that there may well be force in the criticism of *Mackie* on the basis that a mere schematic diagram is not the design of an article or part of an article. However, the reasoning in *Mackie* appears to be consistent with comments made by Laddie J. in *Occular Sciences Ltd v Aspect Vision Care Ltd* [1997] R.P.C. 289 at p.429 as regards semiconductor topographies.

[71] See paras 13–66 *et seq.*, below.

[72] It may be argued that a stencil made to the design is itself an artistic work within CDPA 1988, s.4(2)(b) ("engraving, etching, lithograph, woodcut or similar work"). If so, then s.51 would not apply and any design right protection would be excluded in favour of copyright protection, CDPA 1988, s.236. See paras 13–164 *et seq.*, below.

[73] *Lambretta Clothing Co Ltd v Teddy Smith (UK) Ltd* [2004] EWCA Civ 886 per Jacob L.J. at paras 14–29. On this point, Mance L.J. agreed with Jacob L.J. (see para.78) although Sedley L.J. did not (see para.88).

An article. The design must be of an aspect of the shape or configuration of the whole or part of an article. Although the word "article" is not defined by the 1988 Act,[74] the fact that the article has to have "shape or configuration" plainly suggests something which has its own separate physical form and which is, in that sense, three dimensional.[75] Thus a contact lens, a mobile phone case, a breast prosthesis are all articles.[76] Similarly, a car or an electrical transformer[77] are articles even though they are made up of various component parts each of which may also be an article in its own right. A chair leg may be an article if it is made separately from the rest of the chair, but not if it is made by shaping the same piece of metal used for the rest of the chair frame. A kitchen unit is an article but the complete fitted kitchen is not.[78] Although the word "article" suggests something in three dimensions, there seems to be no reason why it should exclude objects which are usually regarded as flat but which nevertheless have a physical form such as, for example, a paper template or a stencil.[79] It has been said that the word "article" is not intended to have a restricted meaning, that it could just as well be replaced by the word "thing" and could include a living or formerly living thing.[80]   **13–49**

Design right is concerned with the design not with the article. Although the design relied upon must be the design of the whole or part of an article, it is important to bear in mind that design right is concerned with the protection of the relevant design and not with the protection of the particular article on which that design happens to be recorded or to which that design happens to be first applied. The design may equally be applied to other articles.[81]   **13–50**

Design of the whole or part of an article. The design must also be of the whole or part *of* an article. In this regard, it is submitted that it is immaterial whether there is any intention that the design should actually be applied to such an article.[82] A sketch of an imaginary vase is a design *of* a vase even if the artist has no intention of making vases to his design. However, in such a case, the artist may well   **13–51**

---

[74] By contrast, before it was amended by the Registered Designs Regulations 2001, the Registered Designs Act 1949, s.44(1) defined an "article" (for registered design purposes) as "an article of manufacture and includes any part of an article if that part is made and sold separately." That definition was repealed by Sch.2 of the 2001 Regulations.

[75] The words "shape" and "configuration" by themselves have been said in the registered design context to signify something in three dimensions, see *Kestos Ltd v Kempat Ltd* (1936) 53 R.P.C. 139 at 152.

[76] Such articles being the subject matter of, respectively, *Ocular Sciences Ltd v Aspect Vision Care Ltd* [1997] R.P.C. 289; *Parker & Parker v Tidball* [1997] F.S.R. 680; and *Amoena (UK) Ltd v Trulife Ltd* (unreported) May 23, 1995.

[77] See, respectively, *Ford Motor Co Ltd and Iveco Fiat SpA's Applications* [1993] R.P.C. 399 (Registered Designs Appeal Tribunal) and [1994] R.P.C. 554 (Divisional Court) and *Electronic Techniques (Anglia) Ltd v Critchley Components Ltd* [1997] F.S.R. 401.

[78] See *Mark Wilkinson Furniture Ltd v Woodcraft Designs (Radcliffe) Ltd* [1998] F.S.R. 63 at 73 where the meaning of the word "article" was considered in the context of the "must match" exclusion (see CDPA 1988, s.213(3)(b)(ii) and para. 13–62, below).

[79] See para. 13–48, above. Further, the word "articles" is used in a copyright context to describe items such as greetings cards, maps, playing cards, etc. which, though flat, have a physical form, see the Copyright (Industrial Process and Excluded Articles) (No.2) Order 1989 (SI 1989/1070), Art.3(1)(c).

[80] *Ocular Sciences Ltd v Aspect Vision Care Ltd* [1997] R.P.C. 289 at 425 where the human eye (against which a contact lens must fit) was found to be an article for the purposes of the "must fit" exclusion (see CDPA 1988, s.213(3)(b)(i) and para. 13–58, below).

[81] See *Electronic Techniques (Anglia) Ltd v Critchley Components Ltd* [1997] F.S.R. 401 at 418 where the example given was of the design of a spoon with a non-commonplace handle. There was, it was said, no reason why the designer should only be entitled to protection for the application of his design to spoons when it was readily apparent that the same design could be applied to other articles, such as forks.

[82] It is suggested that it is for this reason that CDPA 1988, s.51, having defined "a design" in virtually identical terms to s.213(2) (*i.e.* the design ... *of* an article), then refers to such a design being "... *for* anything other than an artistic work or typeface", see para. 13–289, below.

be able to rely on copyright protection against the copying of his sketch as an artistic work rather than on design right.[83]

13–52   **Kits.** A person who designs or makes a kit of parts cannot necessarily be said to be designing or making the article which results from the assembly of the kit. Because of this, section 260 of the 1988 Act provides that the design right provisions apply in relation to a kit as they apply in relation to the assembled article; a "kit" being defined as a complete or substantially complete set of components intended to be assembled into an article.[84] However, this does not affect the question whether design right subsists in any of the components of the kit.[85] This provides some flexibility. It allows the designer of a kit of parts to choose whether to assert design right in the design of the completed article or to rely on the designs of the various component parts of the kit. The former may be preferable where it would otherwise be possible to avoid infringing by making complete articles. Conversely, the provision also allows the designer of a whole article to prevent others infringing his design right by the making and selling of kits.[86]

B. EXCLUDED DESIGNS

13–53   **Introduction.** Even if there is a design within the meaning of the definition discussed above, sections 213(3) and 213(5A) of the 1988 Act contain various exclusions from design right. The exclusions contained in section 213(3) play an important part in the scheme of the 1988 Act, namely to ensure that design right, whilst providing a limited amount of protection for original designs, did not unfairly restrict fair competition.[87]

13–54   **Section 213(3).** This provides that design right does not subsist in:

    (a) a method or principle of construction,
    (b) features of shape or configuration of an article which—
        (i) enable the article to be connected to, or placed in, around or against, another article so that either article may perform its function, or
        (ii) are dependent upon the appearance of another article of which the article is intended by the designer to form an integral part, or
    (c) surface decoration.

Before considering these exclusions in detail, it is important to note that these exclusions only operate to exclude design right from the sort of features set out above. Thus, where the design relied upon comprises a number of features only some of which fall within these exclusions, this does not mean that design right cannot subsist in the design as a whole. It simply means that design right cannot be claimed in those excluded features on their own.[88]

(i) A method or principle of construction

13–55   Under section 213(3)(a) of the 1988 Act, design right is excluded from "a method or principle of construction". It could be argued that this exclusion is unnecessary

---

[83] Although the sketch is a design *of* an article, it is not a design *for* an article other than an artistic work. Thus, CDPA 1988, s.51 would not exclude copyright protection and s.236 provides that an act will not infringe design right if it would infringe copyright, see paras 13–289 *et seq.*, below.
[84] See CDPA 1988, s.260(1).
[85] CDPA 1988, s.260(2).
[86] See *Hansard*, H.C. SCE, col.592.
[87] See para. 13–29, above, and *Hansard*, H.L. Vol.489, col.1479.
[88] See *Ultraframe UK Ltd v Fielding* [2003] R.P.C. 23 at paras 69–71 and 78 (a point not challenged on appeal, [2004] R.P.C. 24).

on the basis that a method or principle of construction is the process by which shape or configuration is imparted to an article, rather than being a design.[89] However, the exclusion (or one similar) was a part of registered design law for many years,[90] and it serves to emphasise that the law of design is only concerned with the appearance of an article (or part of an article) and not with the process by which the article is to be made. It is intended, therefore, to ensure that designers cannot create an effective monopoly over articles made in a particular way.[91]

This exclusion means that design right does not subsist in a "design" which requires an article to be made of a particular substance. Such a "design" is a method of construction. Thus, where the design of a pig-slurry-separating machine included as a component part a roller made of laminated rubber of varying degrees of hardness, the shape of the roller was protected, but the "design" of the type of materials used in constructing it was not because it was a method of construction.[92] In that case, the exclusion may have been unnecessary in that the "design" for the way in which the roller was made did not define its shape or configuration (thus, design right could never have subsisted in it). However, the exclusion will also apply where the way in which an article is made does have an impact on its shape or configuration. Thus, it has been held that the "design" for stitching together a mobile phone case with the seams turned in, whilst affecting the appearance of the case, would nevertheless be a method of construction from which design right is excluded.[93] By contrast, it has also been held that the design for outward pointing seams on a case for a folding umbrella was not a method of construction.[94] On the facts, it is easy to see why the courts reached these differing conclusions. However, if one starts from the assumption that both the inward and outward pointing seams were aspects of the design of their respective articles, it is not easy to define the legal basis on which the exclusion was found to operate in one case but not in the other.[95]

In the registered designs context, it has been held that the exclusion of a method or principle of construction did not apply to a design whereby the two diagonal hoops on a square baby's activity mat crossed at right angles to each other at the top. What the claimant was seeking to protect was not the method of construction by which the mat was put together, but rather its appearance when put together. It

---

[89] See *Kestos Ltd v Kempat Ltd* (1936) 53 R.P.C. 139 at 151, a registered design case.

[90] Although a process of manufacture was not expressly excluded by the Patents, Trademarks and Designs Act 1883 (46 & 47 Vict. c.57) or the Patents and Designs Act 1907 (7 Edw. 7, c.29), it was found to be implicit in the definitions of a design (being a design for the pattern, shape, configuration or ornament of an article) in s.60 of the 1883 Act and s.93 of the 1907 Act), see *Moody v Tree* (1892) R.P.C. 333 and *Bayer's Design* (1907) 24 R.P.C 65. The exclusion was made express when the 1907 Act was amended by the Patents and Designs Act 1919 (9 & 10 Geo. 5, c.80), s.19 and was carried over into the Registered Designs Act 1949, (see s.1(3) prior to its amendment by the CDPA 1988, and s.1(1)(a) thereafter). However, the exclusion has now been removed from registered design law by reason of the amendments to the 1949 Act made by the Registered Designs Regulations 2001. See paras 13–251 *et seq.*, below.

[91] See *Gardex Ltd v Sorata Ltd* [1986] R.P.C. 623 at 638.

[92] See *Farmers Build Ltd v Carier Bulk Materials Handling Ltd* (unreported) March 26, 1997, transcript at 19 and 29. The point was not raised in the Court of Appeal ([1999] R.P.C. 461).

[93] *Parker & Parker v Tidball* [1997] F.S.R. 680 at 696 where it was also doubted whether such a "design" was of an aspect of shape or configuration of an article.

[94] See *A. Fulton Co Ltd v Grant Barnett & Co Ltd* [2001] R.P.C. 257 at para.70.

[95] The distinction between the cases is probably due to the fact that the designer of the umbrella case in *Fulton* [2001] R.P.C. 257, had clearly intended to include the outward pointing seams as a part of his design whereas the designer of the phone case in *Parker & Parker v Tidball* [1997] F.S.R. 680, had probably not consciously "designed" the inward pointing seams or, if he had, that they were simply a "conception of some general characteristic of shape and configuration necessitated by the mode or principle of construction," and therefore excluded from protection (see *Pugh v Riley Cycle Co Ltd* (1912) 29 R.P.C. 196 at 202 and *Christopher Tasker's Design Right References* [2001] R.P.C. 3 at paras 28 and 33). However, this distinction does not appear clear from the judgments. It may be that the result in *Parker* illustrates the danger of assuming that the claimant's design must include all of the features that appear on an article made to that design.

would have been possible for the defendant to design a mat that worked in the same way but that looked different.[96] Under earlier registered designs legislation, an exclusion of designs amounting to a "mode of construction" was held to apply to a design for the "pattern of a basket consisting of osiers being working in singly with the butt ends being outside",[97] and to a design whereby a corset had "gores or gussets cut horizontally and from the front of the busk towards the back of the corset".[98] It did not apply, however, to a design whereby the two diagonal hoops on a square baby's activity mat crossed at right angles to each other at the top. What the claimant was seeking to protect was not the method of construction by which the mat was put together but rather its appearance when put together. It would have been possible for the defendant to design a mat that worked in the same way but which looked different.

(ii) The "must fit" and "must match" exclusions

13–56 The "must fit" and the "must match" exclusions reflect Parliament's wish to allow competition where there is no design freedom for either functional or aesthetic reasons.[99] Whilst they are clearly intended to permit competition in the supply of spare parts and assessories, they are of general application and are a significant limitation on the scope of design right. However, it is important to bear in mind that they only permit copying of those design features which satisfy the terms of the exclusions. The other features of the design may remain protected.[1]

(iii) The "must fit" exclusion

13–57 [2] Section 213(3)(b)(i) of the 1988 Act contains the so-called "must fit" or "interface" exclusion. It provides that design right will not subsist in "features of shape or configuration of an article which … enable the article to be connected to, or placed in, around or against, another so that either article may perform its function".

The wording of the exclusion falls into two parts; the first part requires that there be the requisite relationship between two articles. The second limits the scope of the exclusion by requiring that that relationship be made so that either article may perform its function.

---

[96] See *Isaac Oren v Red Box Factory* [1999] F.S.R. 785. This exclusion has been removed from the RDA 1949 by the Registered Designs Regulations 2001.

[97] See *Moody v Tree* (1892) 9 R.P.C. 33 at 335, a case decided under the Patents Trademarks and Designs Act 1883, where it was stated that such a "design" was not intended to represent a peculiar shape or pattern of a basket but, rather, the way in which it was to be made.

[98] See *Bayer's Design* (1907) 24 R.P.C 65 at 79, another registered design case decided under the Patents, Trademarks and Designs Act 1883 which cited *Moody v Tree* (1892) 9 R.P.C. 333 and where it was commented that one might as well seek to claim that the bonding together of bricks using iron bands was a design.

[99] See *Hansard*, H.L. Vol.489, col.1479; H.L. Vol.491, cols 1111–1113; H.L. Vol.494, col.109 and H.C. Vol.132, cols 597–598. In *Mars UK Ltd v Tecknowledge Ltd* [2000] F.S.R. 138, it was stated that, given the enactment of the "must fit" and "must match" exclusions, there is no place in design right cases for any common law spare parts defence. For further background, see paras 13–21 and 13–28, above.

[1] See *Ultraframe UK Ltd v Fielding* [2003] R.P.C. 23 at paras 69–71, 74 and 78. See also *Ultraframe (UK) Ltd v Eurocell Building PLastics Ltd* [2004] EWHC 1785 at para.113.

[2] In relation to registered designs, there is now an "interconnections" exclusion which appears to be somewhat more generous to designers than design right's "must fit" exclusion—see s.1C(2) of the 1949 Act (as amended) and paras 13–257 and 13–209, below.

The relationship between the two articles. The "must-fit" exclusion is **13–58** concerned with the relationship or "interface" between two articles.[3] The nature of this relationship is broadly defined and there is no reason why the word "article" should be construed narrowly. Indeed, it has been said that it could have been replaced by the word "thing"; and that it might include a living or a formerly living thing such as a human eye.[4]

The exclusion is of features of shape or configuration of an article. It is submitted that the "article" for these purposes (*i.e.* for the purposes of section 213(3)) need not be the same article by reference to which the design right claim is framed (*i.e.* for the purposes of section 213(2)). Thus, where a plaintiff relies on design right in a design of an article (the "composite article") made from various component articles, the "must fit" exclusion will apply to those features which allow the composite article to interface with another article. It is, however, unclear whether the exclusion will also apply to those features which allow its various component articles to interface with each other.[5] If it does, then where the plaintiff relies on the design of a car, the interface exclusion would not only apply to the external interface features of the car (if there are any), but would also apply to the numerous internal interface features of its many component parts.

So that either article may perform its function. The interface must be made so **13–59** that either article may perform its function. In this context, "function" has to be construed widely. Thus, the primary function of a contact lens is to correct the eye's focusing ability, but it is also a part of its function to fit properly and to remain in position in relation to the eyeball and eyelid and to allow oxygen to reach the conjunctiva. The primary function of the human eye is to see but it is also a part of its function to perform that function efficiently by being able to focus light, by being protected and kept clean (*e.g.* by the operation of the eyelid). Given this, various interface features of contact lenses (*i.e.* the back radius, diameters and bevelled edges) were found to be present so that both lens and eye could perform their functions. They were, therefore, excluded from protection.[6] By contrast, it was held that the exclusion did not apply to the design of a top cover for a valley assembly for a conservatory roof. Although the cover could be pushed down so that its outer edge touched the window frames, it was not clear

---

[3] *i.e.* the article embodying the design features in issue and the article with which it interfaces—see *Ocular Sciences Ltd v Aspect Vision Care Ltd* [1997] R.P.C. 289 at 425.

[4] See, *Ocular Sciences Ltd v Aspect Vision Care Ltd* [1997] R.P.C. 289 at 425.

[5] *Electronic Techniques (Anglia) Ltd v Critchley Components Ltd* [1997] F.S.R. 401 at 416–419 and *Ocular Sciences Ltd v Aspect Vision Care Ltd* [1997] R.P.C. 289 suggest that the exclusion will apply. Whilst this construction is hard to reconcile with the wording of s.213, it does give effect to the intention of the CDPA (to deny protection to spare parts) without doing violence to the infringement provisions in s.226. By contrast, in *Baby Dan AS v Brevi SRL* [1999] F.S.R. 377, at pp.381–383, it was held that, where a design right claim was framed by reference to a composite article, the "must fit" exclusion only applied to those features which allowed that article to interface with another article and not to those features which allowed its component parts to interface with each other. The difficulty with this is that it may well allow claimants to claim protection against the manufacturers of spare parts. To counter this difficulty, the court in *Baby Dan* suggested that if an alleged infringer was only making component parts, the only design on which the claimant could rely to show an infringement would be the design of the relevant component part. However, it is not clear on what basis the claimant could be prevented from framing his claim by reference to the relevant component part as an aspect of the design of the composite article. There is certainly nothing in s.226 to prevent him doing so. The reasoning in *Baby Dan* was adopted in *A. Fulton Co Ltd v Grant Barnett & Co Ltd* [2001] R.P.C. 257 at para.73. Also, faced with these conflicting decisions, the court in *Ultraframe (UK) Ltd v Eurocell Building Plastics Ltd* [2004] EWHC 1785 at para.21 felt obliged to follow *Baby Dan* (it being the more recent case). Nevertheless, it is submitted that *Electronic Techniques* is to be preferred.

[6] *Ocular Sciences Ltd v Aspect Vision Care Ltd* [1997] R.P.C. 289, (Laddie J.).

that that interface enabled either the cover or the window frames to perform any particular function.[7]

Several other points arise: first, a design feature that meets the interface criteria will be excluded from design right even if it also serves some other function (such as attracting customers).[8] Secondly, there is nothing in the wording to suggest that a design feature is only excluded from protection if it is the *only* way in which the necessary interface between the articles could be achieved. Instead, if a number of different design features could permit the interface, the exclusion will apply. It does not matter that a differently designed feature could have performed the same function.[9] Thirdly, there is some uncertainty as to whether the exclusion would apply only if the designer knew that the relevant features would enable the articles to interface or whether it was sufficient that the features do in fact enable the interface.[10] The latter construction avoids difficult questions of fact as to the designer's intentions. However, it would mean that a design feature may be excluded from protection simply because the defendant is able to show that it permits an interface never contemplated by the designer. The latter construction may also be difficult to reconcile with the words "enable" and "so that" (rather than, for example, the more passive words "allow" or "permit") which arguably suggest that section 213(3)(b)(i) was concerned with where a particular design feature was incorporated with a view to allowing the article to interface with another.

13–60   **Examples.** Construing the "must fit" exclusion may plainly give rise to difficulties and its operation may best be seen through examples.

(1) **Gasket**. A gasket was designed to fit between the lid and the body of a freezer. The only non-commonplace design feature was an upstanding "ear" which allowed the gasket to fit properly. The must fit exclusion operated. The design of the "ear" (like the design of the gasket as a whole) enabled it to interface with another article (the lid and the body of the freezer) and that interface enabled each of the articles to perform its function—namely to create a draught free and efficient freezer.[11]

(2) **Car exhaust.** The design of a car exhaust must have some design features which enable it to be connected to the engine exhaust manifold and other features which allow it to follow the contours of the car's chassis, to avoid the suspension and rear axle and to be attached at the appropriate points. These design features all satisfy the first part of the wording of the "must fit" exclusion and it seems clear that they also satisfy the second part.[12] For example, the features which allow the exhaust to connect to the engine exhaust manifold are there "so that" the exhaust and the engine may perform their functions, and the features which allow the exhaust to be attached to the chassis do, as a matter of fact, allow the articles to interface even though they may not all be essential or the only possible means of attaching the exhaust to the vehicle. The "must fit" exclusion would, therefore, apply to these design features. By contrast, the design of the internal layout of the exhaust's silencer box does not satisfy the first part

---

[7] *Ultraframe UK Ltd v Fielding* [2003] R.P.C. 23 at para.80 (also Laddie J.) (a point not raised on appeal, [2004] R.P.C. 24).

[8] *Ocular Sciences Ltd v Aspect Vision Care Ltd* [1997] R.P.C. 289 at 424.

[9] *Ocular Sciences Ltd v Aspect Vision Care Ltd* [1997] R.P.C. 289 at 424. See also *Parker & Parker v Tidball* [1997] F.S.R. 680 at 693 and *Ultraframe (UK) Ltd v Eurocell Building Plastics Ltd* [2004] EWHC 1785 at para.114.

[10] Contrast *A. Fulton Co Ltd v Grant Barnett & Co Ltd* [2001] R.P.C. 257 at para.75 with *Ocular Sciences Ltd v Aspect Vision Care Ltd* [1997] R.P.C. 289 at 426.

[11] *Novum Overseas Ltd v Iceland Foods plc* [2002] EWHC 53 at para.122.

[12] See para. 13–59, above.

of the exclusion, and the design for sporty looking twin exhaust outlets is unlikely to be within the first part of the exclusion and is almost certainly not within the second; these design aspects would not, therefore, fall within the "must fit" exclusion. Thus, if a supplier of spare parts was to copy the whole exhaust, he may be infringing design right in the design of the exhaust as a whole (as well as the designs of some parts of the exhaust) even though design right would have been excluded from the "must fit" aspects of that design.[13]

(3) **Car wheels.** The plaintiff has designed an attractive alloy spoke wheel for a car. The features which allow the wheel to be fitted to the car and to link with its braking and steering systems will be caught by the "must fit" exclusion. By contrast, the design of the spokes themselves is unlikely to be within the first part of the exclusion and is almost certainly not within the second.[14]

(4) **Table lamp.** A desk lamp must have a socket designed to be fitted with a bulb. The design of the socket would plainly be excluded from design right (as would the design of the bayonet or screw fitting of the bulb itself). If the lamp has an unusually shaped shade, those features of the design which allow that shade to fit around the bulb and to fit against the stand would be excluded. Other features of the shape of the shade and of the stand would not be.[15]

(5) **Traffic cones.** The design of traffic cones allows them to be placed on a road and to be visible to motorists. However, the design also includes features which allow the cones to be stacked. These features satisfy the first part of the wording of the exclusion. But is this an interface "so that [either of the cones] may perform its function"? The principal function of a traffic cone when in use is to provide a marker to guide or restrict the flow of traffic. However, as traffic cones are often in storage or in transit, an ability to be stacked is likely to be an important factor in their design and in a customer's decision to buy that design of cone in preference to a non-stacking design. In *C & H Engineering v F. Klucznik & Sons Ltd*,[16] the features of the plaintiff's pig fenders which enabled them to be stacked were referred to (in the context of testing for infringement) as "functionally significant".[17] This suggests (as does the approach *Ocular Sciences Ltd*[18]) that stackability should be treated as part of the cones' function, and that design features which allow stacking should be excluded from design right protection.

(6) **Plates.** The design of a dinner plate raises interesting questions as regards   **13–61** both parts of the exclusion. Most plates have a feature (their relative flatness) which means that one can be stacked on top of another. Is this, however, a feature which "enables" the plate to be stacked with other

---

[13] See, for example, *Novum Overseas Ltd v Iceland Foods plc* [2002] EWHC 53. There, the "must fit" exclusion operated in respect of the gasket (see Example (1)) and also in respect of certain design features of the internal dividers for the freezers (*i.e.* the hooks which allowed units to be hung inside the freezer—see para.123). Notwithstanding these exclusions, the design right claim succeeded in relation to the overall design of the freezer (see para.119).

[14] It may, however, be excluded by the "must match" provisions. See paras 13–64 *et seq.*, below.

[15] These may, however, be within the "must match" exclusion. See paras 13–64 *et seq.*, below. In *Ultraframe (UK) Ltd v Eurocell Building Plastics Ltd* [2004] EWHC 1785 at para.113, Lewison J. used the example of the light bulb.

[16] [1992] F.S.R. 421.

[17] [1992] F.S.R. 421 at 429.

[18] [1997] R.P.C. 289. See para. 13–59, above.

plates? The approach in *Ocular Sciences Ltd*[19] suggests that it is. On the other hand, it could be said that it is straining the meaning of the word "enable" to say that it is the design of a plate which "enables" it to be stacked, for the ability to be stacked is something inherent in the nature of a thing which fulfils the function of a plate (unlike traffic markers). Similarly, can it be said that the features which allow plates to be stacked are features which are present *so that* the plates can perform their function? Possibly; but as the ability to be stacked is something inherent in a plate, the position is much less clear than in the case of the traffic cones.

(7) **Lamp and bracket.** A person designs a lamp with a connecting bracket which allows it to be fitted to a bicycle. Those aspects of the design of the lamp and of the bracket which allow them to fit together are, therefore, excluded from protection. The exclusion of design right is absolute. It does not matter whether a rival uses the design features for the same or for different articles. Thus he is free (so far as design right is concerned) to make his own lamp of another overall design (or other device) to fit on to that bracket or his own bracket to fit that lamp.

(8) **A tow bar.** A "T"-shaped tow bar is designed to allow a recovery vehicle to tow a broken-down vehicle. At the ends of the head of the "T" are slots into which the wheels of the vehicle being recovered will fit whilst being towed. The design of those slots will be excluded.

(iv) The "must match" exclusion

13–62   The third exclusion is the so-called "must match" exclusion contained in section 213(3)(b)(ii) of the 1988 Act. This provides that design right will not subsist in "features of shape or configuration of an article which … are dependent upon the appearance of another article of which the article is intended by the designer to form an integral part". The wording shows that this exclusion is concerned with a dependency in the design of one article (in whose features the issue of design right arises) upon the appearance of another article of which it is intended to form an integral part. These articles may be referred to as, respectively, the component article and the composite article.[20] The background to this exclusion has already been considered but, in summary, its rationale is to allow a component article to be copied where the circumstances compelled copying for aesthetic reasons. In such a case, the intention of Parliament is that competition in the after-market should prevail.[21] However, the wording of the exclusion is ambiguous and obscure,[22] and various difficulties arise in relation to its construction.

13–63   **Intention to form an integral part.** For the exclusion to operate, the designer of an article must have intended that article to form an integral part of another article. The word "integral" suggests that the article in question must be intended to be incorporated into the other article so that together they form a complete or a whole article. The wording also seems to require that the designer has that other article in mind when creating his design. It is suggested that the exclusion would not apply where the intention was to design an article which could be incorporated into many different other articles for in such a case, the article was not intended to form an integral part of *another article*. Thus the exclusion would probably apply to the design of a car door for a particular model of car, but not to the design of a

---

[19] [1997] R.P.C. 289.

[20] The meaning of "article" has already been considered, see para. 13–49, above.

[21] See para. 13–56, above.

[22] As commented in *Ford Motor Co Ltd and Iveco Fiat SpA's Applications* [1993] R.P.C. 399 at 421.

removeable child's car seat. It is also submitted that the relevant time for determining whether there was the requisite intention is the time when the relevant design is created. Thus, if an article is designed to stand alone as an independent article, the fact that it is subsequently used to form a part of another article will not bring the exclusion into operation. If, for example, a designer designs an all-purpose strut which another person subsequently incorporates together with other matching struts in a design for a protective grill, the exclusion would not operate (assuming, of course, that at the time that the strut was designed, its designer did not intend it to form an integral part of the grill).[23]

Dependent upon the appearance of another article. For the exclusion to operate, the relevant features of shape or configuration of the component article must be dependent upon the appearance of the composite article. This issue of dependency (in contrast to the integral part issue) is not qualified by reference to the designer's intention and requires, it seems, an objective assessment as to whether the relevant design features of the component article had been governed or dictated by the appearance of the composite article. The mere fact that they are compatible with the appearance of the composite article will not be sufficient.

13–64

The approach to this issue adopted by the Registered Designs Appeal Tribunal[24] has been to ask whether the component part, objectively viewed, contributes to the overall shape of the composite article. If so, its design may be said to be dependent upon the design of the whole and to be subject to the exclusion. If, on the other hand, the component part (objectively viewed) could be replaced without substantially altering the appearance or identity of the composite article, then its design is unlikely to be dependent upon the appearance of the other article. The distinction was one which the Tribunal drew by asking whether, if the relevant part was to be replaced, it would have to be replaced, "as a matter of practical commonsense", by a part which is for all practical purposes the same as the original. To the extent that this was so, the Tribunal found that the shape and configuration of the component part was dependent upon the appearance of the composite article, and that the exclusion should apply because a competitor would have no design freedom to produce an alternative design. In applying the test for dependency, the Tribunal considered the appearance of the composite article with the relevant component part or parts in place[25] but where the relevant component article was one of a set of substantially identical parts all intended to form a part of the composite article, the Tribunal considered that the question was whether the design of the set was dependent upon the appearance of the composite article.[26]

Applying this approach in the case of spare parts and accessories for cars, the Registered Designs Appeal Tribunal decided that designs for body panels, doors, bonnet, grille, boot, bumper, instrument panel, spoiler and a windscreen were all designs dependent upon the appearance of the car as a composite article and were

---

[23] The all-purpose strut was the example used in Parliament, see *Hansard*, H.L. Vol.495, col.700.

[24] See *Ford Motor Co Ltd and Iveco Fiat SpA's Design Applications* [1993] R.P.C. 399 at 419–420, a case concerning the substantially identical "must match" exclusion in the Registered Designs Act 1949, s.1(1)(b)(ii) before it was amended by the Registered Designs Regulations 2001. The reasoning of the Tribunal was accepted by the Divisional Court upon judicial review (see [1994] R.P.C. 545 at 554). However, the House of Lords on appeal decided the case solely on the issue of whether the relevant component articles were "articles" within the meaning of s.44 of the 1949 Act and declined to consider the proper construction of the "must match" exclusion, see [1995] R.P.C. 167.

[25] The designer had, after all, intended that part to form an integral part of the composite article. See *Ford and Fiat's Applications* [1993] R.P.C. 399 at 420.

[26] *Ford and Fiat's Applications* [1993] R.P.C. 399 at 420.

all, therefore, excluded by the must match exclusion.[27] By contrast, it found that designs for articles such as a steering wheel, wing mirrors, wheels, wheel covers and seats[28] were not dependent on the appearance of the car as a whole and were not, therefore, covered by the exclusion.[29] The approach of the Tribunal appears to achieve broadly what Parliament seems to have intended by the must match exclusion and a similar approach was adopted in *A. Fulton Co Ltd v Grant Barnett & Co Ltd*[30] However, it is not entirely easy to reconcile this approach with the actual wording of the "must match" exclusion.

13–65   **Examples:**

(1) **A fountain pen cap.** A fountain pen cap is an article and is plainly intended to form an integral part of another article (the fountain pen as a whole). In some cases, certain features of the shape of the cap—for example, the contours—might be dependent upon the appearance of the pen as a whole. These would be excluded from protection. By contrast, other features such as the shape of a distinctive clip may have little to do with the appearance of the rest of the pen and everything to do with the identity of the manufacturer. Such features would not be excluded.

(2) **A chair leg.** A chair leg (assuming it is a separate article) will plainly be intended to form an integral part of another article (namely the chair) and, applying the test adopted in *Ford*,[31] falls more clearly into the category of being an essential part of the overall shape and appearance of the chair than into the category of accessories.[32] As the features of shape and configuration of the leg are in that sense dependent upon the appearance of the rest of the chair, those features will be excluded from design right. A competitor may, therefore, manufacture a replacement replica leg for that chair.

(3) **A set of chairs.** With a set of chairs, the design of one chair from a matching set of chairs is clearly likely to be dependent upon the appearance of the rest of the set. However, the rest of the set cannot be said to be "an article" of which the single chair can form an integral part. The exclusion would not, therefore, apply and a competitor is not free to make a whole new chair to replace one of the set. A similar point arose in *Mark Wilkinson Furniture Ltd v Woodcraft Designs (Radcliffe) Ltd*[33] where it was held that the exclusion did not apply to exclude design right from the design of one kitchen cupboard albeit that that cupboard had to match the rest of the kitchen. The judge accepted the submission that the complete kitchen was not an article for these purposes but was, instead, a series of matching articles none of which forms an integral part of another.

---

[27] *Ford and Fiat's Applications* [1993] R.P.C. 399 at 419–420.
[28] *i.e.* exactly the sort of articles which, the Tribunal found, were often substituted, often by the original manufacturer itself, in order (for example) to give the vehicle a more sporty appearance.
[29] Although on the facts of that case, the Tribunal found that the designs of wing mirrors and wheel covers were not dependent upon the appearance of the car as a whole, it is not difficult to envisage cases where the designs of such articles would play an important part in defining the overall appearance of the vehicle and where replacement with a matching part would, as a matter of commonsense, be of considerable importance.
[30] [2001] R.P.C. 257 (at para.77).
[31] [1993] R.P.C. 399. See para. 13–64, above.
[32] In other words, the chair legs are closer by analogy to the body panels of a car than to the wheels of a car.
[33] [1998] F.S.R. 62 at 73.

(v) Surface decoration

Section 213(3) also provides that design right does not subsist in "surface decoration".[34]   **13–66**

This exclusion serves to emphasise that what may be seen as a purely artistic aspect of design should be protected through copyright[35] or registered design[36] rather than through design right. Taken with the exclusion of methods or principles of construction,[37] it shows that design right is concerned with designs for the appearance of the basic form of an article and not with how it is made or embellished.

Plainly, therefore, the surface decoration exclusion means that design right will not subsist in a pattern or effect created by paint on the surface of an article. However, the exclusion can also apply where that same pattern or effect is created by, for example, a mosaic or by dyeing the material (even where the material is dyed right through).[38] The surface decoration exclusion might, therefore, apply to a three-dimensional design feature. However, as many articles are designed with a view to their aethestic appeal, it is not always easy to determine the point at which a three dimensional design feature ceases to be merely an aspect of the shape of that article and becomes part of its surface decoration.[39] Ultimately, determining whether a design feature is surface decoration involves a value judgment and will depend upon whether that feature is a significant part of the essential shape or configuration of an article.[40]

Examples: **13–67**

(1) **Desk top.** The design for a decorative pattern on a tooled leather desk top would constitute surface decoration.

(2) **Relief carving.** Despite the use of the word "surface", the surface decoration exclusion applies not only to two dimensional decoration but also to any aspect of design which may properly be seen as decorating the surface of an article. Thus relief carving on church choir stalls would be excluded as would a three dimensional pattern on the surface of a plate. If however, the carving or pattern ceases merely to decorate the surface of an article and, instead, becomes part of or defines the form or substance of the article then the exclusion will not operate.

(3) **Kitchen cupboards.** Certain aspects of the design of kitchen cupboard units have been held to constitute surface decoration. Thus, the painted

---

[34] CDPA 1988, s.213(3)(c).

[35] As an artistic work within CDPA 1988, s.4, assuming CDPA 1988, s.51 does not operate to exclude copyright protection. For a full discussion of s.51 and of the difficulties arising from *Lambretta Clothing Co Ltd v Teddy Smith (UK) Ltd* [2004] EWCA Civ 886, see paras 13–278 *et seq*, below.

[36] Being a feature of "...the lines, contours, colours, shape, texture or materials of the product or its ornamentation" within Registered Designs Act 1949, s.1(2) (as amended by the Registered Designs Regulations 2001.

[37] See paras 13–55 *et seq.*, above.

[38] *Lambretta Clothing Co Ltd v Teddy Smith (UK) Ltd* [2004] EWCA Civ 886 at para.30. In that case, the "design" consisted of a combination of coloured fabrics for a track top. Even if this was a design within the meaning of s.213 (contrary to the views of Jacob and Mance L.J.J. although not of Sedley L.J., see para. 13–48, above), the surface decoration exclusion would operate to exclude design right from the design. Jacob L.J. (using the example of a stick of Brighton Rock) commented that it made no difference that the dye went right through the fabric.

[39] See, for example, *Mark Wilkinson Furniture Ltd v Woodcraft Designs (Radcliffe) Ltd* [1998] F.S.R. 62 at 73, discussed in example (3), below.

[40] *A. Fulton Co Ltd v Grant Barnett & Co Ltd* [2001] R.P.C. 257 at para.79. See also *Hi-Tech Autoparts Ltd v Towergate Two Ltd* [2002] F.S.R. 270 where the small projections on the underside of rubber floor mats for a car were held not to be surface decoration but instead to be important parts of the configuration of the mats as a whole. They were functional features giving the mats a non-slip quality. They were not merely decorative features having an incidental functional quality.

finish, the cockbeading on the door frame and "V" grooves used to decorate the main frame were all excluded from protection. On the other hand, the cornice for the top of the cupboard, the rounded quadrant design for the corners of the cupboard and the recessed panels for its doors and sides were not treated as surface decoration. Rather than being surface decoration, they were features which were themselves liable to surface decoration.[41]

(4) **Pattern of holes, doilies and stencils.** In *Jo y Jo v Matalan Retail Ltd*[42] an issue arose as to whether the pattern of holes on the front of a garment was surface decoration. Although the judge did not decide this issue, he commented that it was arguable that it was not surface decoration because the holes were (by definition) devoid of surface. It is submitted that such argument was incorrect. The surface being decorated was the surface of the substance from which the holes were cut. If it were otherwise, a pattern on a desk created by tooled leather or by relief carving would be surface decoration whilst the same pattern created by holes would not be. There could be no logic in such a distinction. Thus, a pattern for a doily would be surface decoration. By contrast, the same pattern for a stencil would not be surface decoration for, in such a case, the pattern would not (and would not be intended to) decorate the stencil as such. It would, instead, be an inherent part of the shape of the stencil the application of which is intended to put decoration on something else (*i.e.* a wall).[43]

(5) **Fabrics.** Embroidery on the front of a garment was surface decoration (being the result of the application of stitches to the garment after it had otherwise been made). By contrast, the edging and welt of the garment were not surface decoration but were parts of the essential garment.[44]

(vi) Olympic symbols, etc.

13–68   **Section 213(5A)—Olympic symbols** Under this provision,[45] design right does not subsist in a design which consists of or contains a controlled representation within the meaning of the Olympic Symbol, etc. (Protection) Act 1995. This applies only to designs created on or after September 20, 1995.[46] A controlled representation for these purposes means (a) a representation of the Olympic symbol, the Olympic motto or a protected word or (b) a representation of something so similar to the Olympic symbol or motto as to be likely to create in the public mind an association with it.[47]

---

[41] *Mark Wilkinson Furniture Ltd v Woodcraft Designs (Radcliffe) Ltd* [1998] F.S.R. 62 at 73.

[42] [2000] E.C.D.R. 178.

[43] See also the perforated drum that was a part of the slurry machine in *Farmers Build Ltd v Carier Bulk Material Handling Ltd* [1999] R.P.C. 461 at 485 and in which design right subsisted.

[44] *Jo-y-Jo v Matalan Retail Ltd* [2000] E.C.D.R. 178, where the judge was influenced by the fact that the stitching was done after the garment was made, *i.e.* it was applied to a pre-existing surface. It is submitted that the time of application may sometimes be of assistance but it is by no means conclusive as to whether a design feature is surface decoration.

[45] Added to CDPA 1988 by the Olympic Symbol, etc. (Protection) Act 1995, s.14(1). The 1995 Act created a quasi-property right called "the Olympic Association Right" (see s.1). This right has been vested in the British Olympic Association.

[46] Olympic Symbol, etc. (Protection) Act 1995, s.14(2). For these purposes, a design is created on the first day on which (a) it is recorded in a design document or (b) an article is made to it; *ibid.*, s.14(3).

[47] Olympic Symbol, etc. (Protection) Act 1995, s.3(1). By s.18(1), the Olympic symbol is the symbol of five interlocking rings, the Olympic Motto is "Citius, altius, fortius". The following are protected words, namely Olympiad, Olympiads, Olympian, Olympians, Olympic, and Olympics, *ibid.*, s.18(2). References to the Olympic Motto or to a protected word include the motto or word in translation into any language, *ibid.*, s.18(3).

4. CONDITIONS FOR SUBSISTENCE

A. SUMMARY OF REQUIREMENTS

Assuming that design right is capable of subsisting in a design, the question then arises whether on the facts design right actually does subsist. For these purposes, the following conditions must be satisfied: **13–69**

- (i) The design must be original both in the copyright sense of the word and also in the sense that it is not commonplace in the relevant design field (see sections 213(1) and 213(4) of the 1988 Act).
- (ii) The design must have been recorded in a design document or an article must have been made to the design (see section 213(6) of the 1988 Act).
- (iii) The design must have been recorded in a design document or an article must have been made to the design after August 1, 1989 (see section 213(7) of the 1988 Act).
- (iv) The design must qualify for design right under the territorial qualification conditions (see section 213(5) of the 1988 Act).

B. ORIGINALITY

Section 213. By section 213(1) of the 1988 Act, design right subsists in "an original design". Further, section 213(4) provides that "[a] design is not 'original' for the purposes of this Part if it is commonplace in the design field in question at the time of its creation." **13–70**

The effect of these provisions is that originality must be considered in two stages. First, the design must be original in the copyright sense of the word. Secondly, the design must not be commonplace within section 213(4).[48] The use of the word "original" in relation to design right (a form of protection based on copyright) plainly suggests that it is intended to bear its copyright meaning.[49] Moreover, the negative form of wording used in section 213(4) suggests that that subsection was not intended to be an exhaustive definition as regards originality but, rather, to be an attempt to exclude some (commonplace) designs which would otherwise be treated as original.[50] As a result of the two-stage test, a work may qualify as original for copyright purposes yet a design embodied in that work may fail to qualify for design right for being commonplace. The commonplace exclusion is therefore a significant departure from the law of copyright and many designs recorded or embodied in copyright works will be excluded from design right protection as a result.

Originality and commonplace tests relate to *the design* relied on. It is important to note that it is *the design* relied on by the claimant (rather than the design document or article in which it is recorded or embodied) which must be original and which must not be commonplace.[51] Thus, if the design is of a single feature (*i.e.* a part of an article) then it must be ascertained whether that isolated design is original and if so, whether or not it is commonplace. If the design comprises a combination of features then the question is whether the overall **13–71**

---

[48] *Farmers Build Ltd v Carier Bulk Material Handling Ltd* [1999] R.P.C. 461 at 475 and 482.

[49] As to which, see para. 13–72, below.

[50] Given that the copyright test of originality is in no way concerned with whether or not a work is "commonplace", it seems strange that the 1988 Act decided to remove design right from commonplace designs by providing that such designs were not original rather than simply providing that design right should not subsist in them as it does with, for example, "must fit" and "must match" designs (as to which, see paras 13–56 *et seq.*, above).

[51] *Farmers Build Ltd v Carier Bulk Material Handling Ltd* [1999] R.P.C. 461 at 483.

design—*i.e.* the combination of features—is original and, if so, whether or not the combination is commonplace. In this latter case, the fact that some or even all of the constituent features taken individually would not be original or would be commonplace does not necessarily mean that the overall design must also be.[52] A new and exciting design can be produced from the most trite of ingredients although, plainly, in many cases, a run-of-the-mill combination of well known features will produce a commonplace combination of features.[53] Because it s the design that is tested, it seems that one must look at the whole design including "must fit" and "must match" features.[54]

13–72   **Originality in the copyright sense.** Originality for copyright purposes is considered in detail earlier in this work.[55] In summary, originality is "concerned not with any originality of ideas but with their form of expression, and it is in that expression that originality is requisite. That expression need not be original or novel in form but it must originate from the author and not be copied from another work ... A drawing which is simply traced from another drawing is not an original artistic work: a drawing which is made without any copying from anything originates from the artist."[56] Thus, the relevant design must not have been copied but must be the independent work of the designer.[57] Further, even if substantial parts of the design of an article have been copied from earlier articles, that design may still be original provided it is, taken as a whole, new and differs from the earlier designs in significant respects and provided it is the overall design that is the result of the independent work of its designer.[58] It has been held that where a design feature originated in a mistake, the decision to adopt that mistake may well involve a sufficient exercise of skill to constitute originality.[59]

13–73   **Commonplace in the design field at the time of its creation.** Even if a design is original in a copyright sense, section 213(4) provides that it will not be original for design right purposes if it is "commonplace in the design field in question at the time of its creation".

It was stated in Parliament that this provision was intended to prevent mundane, routine and well known designs from acquiring design right,[60] and it has been said that its effect is to exclude designs which are "trite, trivial, common-or-garden, hackneyed or of the type which would excite no peculiar attention in those in the relevant art".[61] As set out below, the commonplace exclusion requires the court to compare the design in issue with other designs in the relevant design field. Logically, therefore, the first issue is to identify the relevant design field.[62]

13–74   **Design field.** There is no statutory definition of "design field". However, the expression is clearly intended to set sensible limits to the scope of the inquiry

---

[52] See para. 13–45, above.
[53] *Farmers Build Ltd v Carier Bulk Material Handling Ltd* [1999] R.P.C. 461 at 486. See also *Ocular Sciences Ltd v Aspect Vision Care Ltd* [1997] R.P.C. 289 at 429–430.
[54] See *Ultraframe (UK) Ltd v Eurocell Building Plastics Ltd* [2004] EWHC 1785 at para.117, doubting a statement to the contrary in *Ultraframe (UK) Ltd v Fielding* [2003] R.P.C. 435 at 457.
[55] See Ch.3, above and *Interlego AG v Tyco Industries Inc* [1989] A.C. 217 at 262F–263E, (PC).
[56] *British Northrop Ltd v Texteam Blackburn Ltd* [1974] R.P.C. 57 at 68, a passage quoted with approval in *Interlego A.G. v Tyco Industries Inc* [1989] A.C. 217 at 261E.
[57] *C & H Engineering Ltd v F. Klucznick & Sons Ltd* [1992] F.S.R. 421 at 427.
[58] *Farmers Build Ltd v Carier Bulk Material Handling Ltd* [1999] R.P.C. 461 at 475 and 486 and para. 13–77, below.
[59] *Guild v Eskandar* [2002] EWCA Civ 316 at para.48.
[60] See *Hansard*, S.C.E. col.575.
[61] See *Ocular Sciences Ltd v Aspect Vision Care Ltd* [1997] R.P.C. 289 at 429. See also *Parker & Parker v Tidball* [1997] F.S.R. 680 at 693.
[62] *Lambretta Clothing Co Ltd v Teddy Smith (UK) Ltd* [2004] EWCA Civ 886 at para.43.

into whether a design is commonplace.[63] In some cases, the design field identified by the courts has been extremely narrow—such as the design field of long necked beer bottles[64] or of wooden configurable figures of the human form.[65] In *Mark Wilkinson Furniture Ltd v Woodcraft Designs (Radcliffe) Ltd*,[66] it was held that the design field was not "cabinetry generally" (even though the design features in question may have been better known in that wider field) but was instead fitted kitchen furniture as that was a discrete design field with its own particular problems and characteristics. However, as set out below, these cases may well have been somewhat too narrow in their approach.

In *Scholes Windows Ltd v Magnet Ltd*,[67] a case concerning a design feature for a U-PVC window, the Court of Appeal found that the relevant design field was that of window design generally—including the designs of traditional wooden "sash" windows. This was so even though the driving forces and design constraints that operate in relation to U-PVC windows were said to be quite different from those that operate for other types of window. More recently, in *Lambretta Clothing Co Ltd v Teddy Smith (UK) Ltd*,[68] the Court of Appeal stated that a "reasonably broad" approach is called for when identifying the relevant design field and that what matters are the sort of designs with which a notional designer of the article in question would be familiar. In that case, the design was of a "multi-purpose" garment—a tracktop intended for leisurewear but with a "sporty" image. Jacob L.J. commented that the designer would naturally look to and have as part of his background knowledge and experience, the design of sportswear. Accordingly, for the purposes of the commonplace provision, the relevant design field encompassed the design of well-known actual sportwear and the trial judge had been wrong to narrow the design field to that of "casual wear as distinct from sportswear". The position would have been different if the design had been for a "sportswear-only" garment (such as a wet suit).[69]

Although the 1988 Act does not make it clear, the fact that the 1988 Act is a territorial Act suggests that the relevant design field is limited to the United Kingdom.[70] However, this does not mean that the court must ignore the international position when determining what is or is not commonplace in the relevant design field. The issue is whether "the design" is commonplace and not whether an article made to that design is commonplace. Accordingly (and consistent with the approach in *Lambretta*), it may well be that a design for an article only marketed abroad has become sufficiently well known to designers and the informed public in the United Kingdom to become commonplace.

Commonplace. Having identified the relevant design field, the court must decide **13–75** whether the design in issue was commonplace in that design field. In deciding this, it is important to bear in mind that the issue is whether the design rather than

---

[63] *Scholes Windows Ltd v Magnet Ltd* [2002] F.S.R. 10 at para.31. In practice, a considerable amount of time and money is spent looking for and considering examples of similar designs in an effort to show that a particular design is or is not commonplace.

[64] *Round Imports v PLM Redfearn Ltd* (1999) 22(7) I.P.D. 22071.

[65] *Spraymiser Ltd v Wrightway Marketing Ltd* [2000] E.C.D.R. 349.

[66] [1998] F.S.R. 62 at 74.

[67] *Scholes Windows Ltd v Magnet Ltd* [2002] F.S.R. 10 at paras 31–38.

[68] *Scholes Windows Ltd v Magnet Ltd* [2002] F.S.R. 10 at paras 43–47.

[69] In such a case, the designer would not naturally look to designs from the leisurewear design field. Thus, the design field could properly be narrowed to that of wet suits or, at the very least, to water sportswear only.

[70] Or, perhaps, to the United Kingdom and any country to which the design right provisions have been extended under CDPA 1988, s.255.

the article is commonplace. For example, doors may be commonplace articles but a design for a door need not be a commonplace design.[71]

The meaning of "commonplace" was considered in detail in *Farmers Build Ltd v Carier Bulk Material Handling Ltd*[72] In that case, the Court of Appeal noted that the commonplace provision was not intended to be a means of limiting protection for spare parts (that was the function of s.213(3)(b)). The Court of Appeal also stated that the relatively short period, the narrow scope of design right protection and the fact that design right could extend to designs of functional articles suggested that the commonplace provision should be construed narrowly for, if it were construed broadly it would remove protection from many designs of functional articles. The rationale for the provision was to prevent claims arising where the functional nature of the design meant that there was bound to be a substantial similarity between designs. Accordingly, to have design right protection, a design must in some respects be different from other designs so that it could fairly and reasonably be described as not commonplace. However, the Court of Appeal emphasised that this was not to be equated with a requirement of novelty for to do so would remove the protection that design right had been intended to confer on functional designs.

With these comments in mind, the Court of Appeal laid down guidelines as to the approach which the court should adopt when faced with the argument that a design was not original because it was commonplace.[73] These guidelines were, in summary:

    (1) To compare the design of the article in which design right is claimed with other designs of other articles in the same design field as at the time of its creation (and also with the defendant's article).

    (2) To ensure that the claimant's design had not been copied from another design, *i.e.* to ensure that it was original in the copyright sense.

    (3) Assuming the claimant's design had not been copied, to compare it with other designs for similar articles in the same design field in order to assess how similar it is to them, *i.e.* the "commonplace" test.[74]

    (4) This comparison is to be conducted objectively and will depend on all of the circumstances. Assuming the claimant had not copied another design, then the closer the similarity, the more probable it is that there is only one way of designing the article and that the design can reasonably be called commonplace.

    (5) If the claimant's design has aspects not found in any other design in the field in question, the court is entitled to conclude that the design is not commonplace.

In carrying out the necessary comparisons, expert evidence is admissible to assist the court in appreciating the differences and similarities in the designs compared. However, it is not necessary to be an expert to make that appreciation or to form an opinion as to whether a design is commonplace. Ultimately, it is for the court and not not the experts to decide objectively on the available evidence

---

[71] See *Hansard*, S.C.E. col.575. See also, *Farmers Build Ltd v Carier Bulk Material Handling Ltd* [1999] R.P.C. 461 at 483 and *A. Fulton Co Ltd v Grant Barnett & Co Ltd* [2001] R.P.C. 257 at para.54.

[72] [1999] R.P.C. 461 at 483.

[73] [1999] R.P.C. 461 at 482–483. See also *Scholes Windows Ltd v Magnet Ltd* [2002] F.S.R. 10 (CA) at paras 27 *et seq.*

[74] In the report of *Farmers Build*, these other articles were said to be those made by persons other than the parties or persons unconnected with the parties. It appears that "unconnected" should read "connected", see *Ultraframe (UK) Ltd v Eurocell Building Plastics Ltd* [2004] EWHC 1785 at para.111.

whether a design is commonplace.[75] For this reason, the Court of Appeal will only interfere with the trial judge's conclusion on the issue if it is clear that he misdirected himself or erred in principle.[76]

At the time of its creation. To decide whether the design in issue is commonplace, that design must be compared with other designs in the relevant design field as at the time when it was created. For these purposes it does not matter whether those other designs were created many years before provided they can fairly and reasonably be said to be in the design field when the design in issue is created. Thus, in *Scholes Windows Ltd v Magnet Ltd*, the claimant's design (created in 1994) for an "S" shaped horn feature on its window frames was found to be commonplace when compared with pre-1915 designs for such features which, although no longer on the market, could still be seen by designers and interested members of the public on many houses and which were, therefore, still common in the built environment in 1994.[77]

13–76

Examples. Various decisions show how the courts have dealt with the commonplace exclusion.

13–77

(1) The addition of a metal roll bar to an otherwise commonplace pig fender distinguished that design for a pig fender design from other designs of pig fenders. It took that design outside the ordinary. The overall design was not, therefore commonplace.[78]

(2) The design for a new pig-slurry-separating machine had certain aspects which had been copied from earlier machines but also included features which differed in significant respects from any previous design. Thus the design of the new machine (as well as the designs of many of those additional features individually) was original in the copyright sense and was not commonplace.[79]

(3) The designs for various contact lenses included nothing "out of the ordinary" and all of the features were well known (save one which was more related to the lens' manufacture than to its design). Whether taken individually or in combination, the design features relied upon were commonplace.[80]

(4) Although it was commonplace for folding umbrellas to have rectangular handles, that did not mean that every design of a rectangular handle for such an umbrella would be commonplace. There was still considerable scope for detailed design work to create a handle with its own qualities, as the examples of so-called "prior part" showed.[81]

C. RECORDED IN A DESIGN DOCUMENT OR ARTICLE MADE

Section 213(6). Under section 213(6) of the 1988 Act, design right does not subsist "... unless and until the design has been recorded in a design document or an article has been made to the design". As will be seen, ascertaining when a design has been recorded in a design document or when an article has been made to the design is important not only as regards the subsistence of design right but

13–78

---

[75] *Scholes Windows Ltd v Magnet Ltd* [2002] F.S.R. 10, at para.49.

[76] *Lambretta Clothing Co Ltd v Teddy Smith (UK) Ltd* [2004] EWCA Civ 886 at para.49.

[77] See *Scholes Windows Ltd v Magnet Ltd* [2002] F.S.R. 10 at paras 39–44.

[78] *C & H Engineering Ltd v F. Klucznick & Sons Ltd* [1992] F.S.R.

[79] *Farmers Build Ltd v Carier Bulk Materials Handling Ltd* [1999] R.P.C. 461 at 485–486.

[80] *Ocular Sciences Ltd v Aspect Vision Care Ltd* [1997] R.P.C. 289 at 428–430.

[81] *A Fulton Co Ltd v Grant Barnett & Co Ltd* [2001] R.P.C. 257 at paras 49–60, where it was also commented (at paras 52) that the existence of one or two examples of reasonably obscure prior art does not necessarily mean that that design was commonplace.

also in order to determine when the design right will expire[82] and the date upon which licenses as of right will become available.[83]

13–79   **Design document.** Design right may subsist where the design has been recorded in a design document. For these purposes, a "design document" is defined as being "any record of a design, whether in the form of a drawing, a written description, a photograph, data stored on a computer or otherwise."[84] The words "any record of a design" and "otherwise" suggest that this definition should be construed widely and it has been held that the other words are not intended to be limiting but are rather examples of possible ways in which the record of an aspect of design can be made.[85] In particular, although no express reference is made to diagrams and plans (as opposed to drawings) there seems to be no reason why they should not constitute a sufficient record of a design. A list of the dimensions by which a design is defined or described can be a sufficient record,[86] so too could a digital record by way of data stored on a computer. As with copyright, there is no requirement that the design document should be of any particular artistic quality or aesthetic merit. As design right may subsist in the design of even a single aspect of the shape or configuration of a part of an article, it seems likely that the most simple or basic sketch will suffice.

13–80   **An article made to the design.** Design right may also subsist where an article has been made to the design. This wording is slightly awkward. As has already been discussed, the word "article" is not defined but is clearly a reference to something having its own physical form.[87] However, as the relevant design could be the design of any aspect of the shape or configuration of an article, it would have been preferable had the 1988 Act referred to the making of an article to the design or incorporating the design. Again, there is no requirement that the article made to the design be of any particular quality. In this respect, the 1988 Act has sensibly avoided one of the anomalies of the old law. Prior to the 1988 Act, where a design was recorded in a drawing it could have copyright protection regardless of the artistic merit of the drawing. Where however, the design was only recorded in the form of an article made to the design, there was only copyright protection if that article was itself an artistic work (*i.e.* either a sculpture or a work of artistic craftsmanship). As these terms had been restrictively construed, such designs were rarely protected.[88]

D. Recorded or made on or after August 1, 1989

13–81   By section 213(7) of the 1988 Act, design right will not subsist in a design unless the design was recorded in a design document or an article was made to the design after the commencement of the 1988 Act, which was on August 1, 1989.[89]

---

[82] For the duration of design right, see paras 13–100 *et seq.*, below.

[83] For licences of right see paras 13–123 *et seq.*, below.

[84] CDPA 1988, s.263(1).

[85] See *Mackie Designs Inc v Behringer Specialised Studio Equipment (UK) Ltd* [1999] R.P.C. 717 at 721.

[86] See *Ocular Sciences Ltd v Aspect Vision Care Ltd* [1997] R.P.C. 289 at 422–423.

[87] See para. 13–49, above.

[88] See *George Hensher Ltd v Restawile Upholstery (Lancs.) Ltd* [1975] R.P.C. 31 and para. 13–24, above.

[89] Although design right cannot subsist in a design document or article created before August 1, 1989 such document or article may be entitled to copyright protection as an artistic or literary work as to which, see paras 13–315 *et seq.* and 13–341 *et seq.*, below.

E. QUALIFYING CONDITIONS

Design right, like copyright, will only subsist if certain territorial conditions are satisfied. In order to determine whether a design satisfies these conditions, it may be necessary to establish the identity of the designer; whether the design was created in pursuance of a commission; and whether it was created in the course of employment. These matters will be considered before turning to the actual qualification provisions.

13–82

(i) The designer

The identity of the designer of a design is of importance in order to determine whether the design qualifies for design right[90] and also, if it does so qualify, in order to determine who is the first owner of that design right.[91]

13–83

Section 214(1). In the case of a design which is not a computer-generated design,[92] section 214(1) of the 1988 Act provides that "the 'designer', in relation to a design, means the person who created it". It is not wholly clear from this wording whether the person who created a design is the person who had the design idea or the person who first recorded it in a design document or made an article to it.[93] The word "created" may suggest the latter.[94] However, the design right provisions taken as a whole show that the creator for these purposes is the person who had the design idea and this is, it is submitted, the correct construction.[95] A design has a separate existence from the tangible form in which it is represented (*i.e.* the design document recording it or the article made to it)[96] and the definition of the designer clearly refers to the creator of the design rather than to the creator of the design document or of the article made to the design. As there is no requirement that the recording of the design need be done by or at the behest of the designer, it may happen that the designer and the person who records it are completely different persons. It will not, of course, always be easy to determine (as a matter of fact) whose idea a particular design was (particularly if a design has been through various stages of development and discussion), and a distinction must be drawn between persons whose contributions related to the design of the shape or configuration of the article (who are designers) and those whose contributions were, for example, in relation to matters of construction (who are not).[97]

13–84

Designers of joint designs. In the case of a joint design, any reference to the designer is a reference to all the designers of the design.[98] A joint design is defined by section 259(1) of the 1988 Act as "a design produced by the collaboration of two or more designers in which the contribution of each is not distinct from that of the other or others". This provision is substantially the same as that relating to

13–85

---

[90] Whether by reference to the designer himself under CDPA 1988, s.218 (see para. 13–91, below) or by reference to his commissioner or employer under CDPA 1988, s.219 (see paras 13–90, below).

[91] See CDPA 1988, s.215(1) and paras 13–106 *et seq.*, below.

[92] For the designer of computer generated designs, see para. 13–86, below.

[93] The same issue arises in relation to whether a design was commonplace in the field of design in question at the time of its creation—see para. 13–76, above.

[94] It suggests the production of something tangible (a creation) which records the design.

[95] This was the approach adopted in *C. & H Engineering Ltd v F. Klucznick & Sons Ltd* [1992] F.S.R. 421 at 428 where it was stated that "the creator is not necessarily the person who records the design but usually will be".

[96] See CDPA 1988, s.213(6) and paras 13–78 *et seq.*, above.

[97] See *Parker & Parker v Tidball* [1997] F.S.R. 680 at 701. See also *A. Fulton Co Ltd v Grant Barnett & Co Ltd* [2001] R.P.C. 257 at para.81.

[98] CDPA 1988, s.259(2).

copyright works of joint authorship and its meaning is considered in that context.[99] The collaboration must be in relation to the production of the relevant design rather than the production of an article to the design. Accordingly a court should ask who, as a matter of fact and degree, has made a significant contribution to the creation of the design and should disregard contributions which are more concerned with matters of construction than with design appearance.[1] Again, it is important to identify precisely the design with which one is concerned. Where an article is designed by a group, the design of the overall article may be a joint design. However, the design of individual parts or aspects of the article may be the work of a single designer and, therefore, not joint designs.

13–86   **Designer of a computer-generated design.** A computer-generated design is defined by section 263(1) of the 1988 Act as a design "generated by computer in circumstances that there is no human designer". If the design is a computer-generated design, section 214(2) provides that "the person by whom the arrangements necessary for the creation of the design are undertaken shall be taken to be the designer". Substantially the same words are used in the copyright provisions of the 1988 Act in relation to the authorship of a sound recording or film[2] and in relation to computer-generated literary, dramatic, musical and artistic works,[3] and are considered in those contexts.[4]

(ii) Design created in pursuance of a commission

13–87   In order to determine whether the design qualifies for design right[5] and, if so, who is its first owner,[6] it may also be necessary to ascertain whether a design was created "in pursuance of a commission".

The 1988 Act does not expressly state what the thing is which is being commissioned. Nor does the 1988 Act define the word "commission" save to say that it means a commission for money or money's worth.[7] The meaning of the word "commission" has already been considered in relation to the Copyright Act 1956 and the Copyright Act 1911.[8] However, some care is required when relying on copyright commissioning cases because the wording used in those earlier Acts was somewhat different to that used in the 1988 Act.[9] In the design right context, it has been decided that, for a design to have been created pursuant to a commission, there must have been a contract prior to the creation of the relevant design. This contract must involve mutual obligations; namely the obligation of the de-

---

[99] s.10(1)—see Ch.4, above.

[1] See *Parker & Parker v Tidball* [1997] F.S.R. 680 at 701.

[2] CDPA 1988, s.9(2)(a).

[3] s.9(3).

[4] See paras 4–58 *et seq.* and 4–17, respectively.

[5] See CDPA 1988, s.219 and paras 13–89 *et seq.*, below.

[6] s.215(2). See paras 13–106 *et seq.*, below.

[7] s.263(1). The Registered Designs Act 1949, s.2(1A) now contains the same definition. It seems that there is no requirement for the court to assess the adequacy of the consideration paid by way of commission. Thus, at first instance in *Farmers Build Ltd v Carier Bulk Materials Handling Ltd* (unreported) March 26, 1997, transcript at 29, it was held that it was irrelevant that the designer was not fully compensated for his design costs (the point was not raised on appeal, [1999] R.P.C. 461). Further, a designer who was not paid for his design work but who expected to recover his costs through being able to mass-produce articles to the design (and who would have charged for his design work if that production work had been given to someone) was held to have been commissioned to create the relevant design, see *Spraymiser Ltd v Wrightway Marketing Ltd* [2000] E.C.D.R. 349.

[8] See paras 5–32 *et seq.*, above.

[9] In particular, the 1988 Act may be more favourable to commissioners than the 1956 Act in that it covers *any* design made pursuant to the commission (clearly covering, for example, preparatory design sketches). The wording of the 1956 Act is somewhat more equivocal in that "the work" there may refer only to the actual commissioned work.

signer to create the design and the obligation of the commissioner to pay for it.[10] It seems clear, therefore, that the contract must be for the creation of a *design* and not merely for the supply of some product. Having said this, there are cases where the former can be inferred from the latter. For example, a contract for the supply of custom made office desks may well involve impliedly commissioning the design of those desks whereas a contract to be supplied with the manufacturer's standard range desks would not. Ultimately, the approach to any commissioning case under the 1988 Act is to identify the relevant commission and to ask whether the design in question was created "in pursuance" of it.[11]

(iii) Design created in the course of employment

The question whether a design was created in the course of employment is also relevant both as regards qualification for design right[12] and first ownership of such design right.[13] In this context, section 263(1) of the 1988 Act provides that "'employee', 'employment' and 'employer' refer to employment under a contract of service or of apprenticeship". Substantially the same wording appears in those provisions of the 1988 Act which deal with copyright works created by an employee in the course of his employment[14] and have been considered in detail in that context.[15] However, in summary, the first issue is whether the designer was employed under a contract of service or apprenticeship. In this regard, a contract of service will exist where (i) the servant has agreed that, in consideration of a wage or other remuneration, he will provide his own work and skill in the performance of some service for his master; and (ii) the servant has agreed, expressly or impliedly, that in performing that service he will be subject to the other's control in a sufficient degree to make that other the master; and (iii) the other terms of the agreement are not inconsistent with the contract being a contract of service.[16] If there is such a contract, then the second issue is whether the design was created in the course of the designer's employment under that contract.[17]

13–88

(iv) Qualification provisions

The provisions which govern whether a design qualifies for design right are contained in section 213(5) of the 1988 Act. In summary, a design may qualify for design right protection by reference to:

13–89

---

[10] *Ultraframe UK Ltd v Fielding* [2004] RPC 24 at paras 30–33.

[11] In *Farmers Build Ltd v Carier Bulk Materials Handling Ltd*, a commission to produce a machine was held to give the commissioner the design rights in the design. (Unreported, March 26, 1997, transcript p.29. Not challenged on appeal, [1999] R.P.C. 461). Similarly in *Apps v Weldtite Products Ltd* [2001] F.S.R. 39, the defendant had commissioned the claimant to produce a report on its bicycle stabilisers and to make recommendations as to any new stabiliser (if required). It was held that the claimant's designs for a new stabiliser were made pursuant to a commission in that it was inevitable that he would have to indicate at least the general configuration for a replacement stabiliser in order to fulfil the tasks he had been set. The defendant was, therefore, held to be the design right owner.

[12] CDPA 1988, s.219 (see para. 13–90, below).

[13] s.215(3), see paras 13–106 *et seq.*, below.

[14] ss.11(2) and 178.

[15] See paras 5–11 *et seq.*, above.

[16] This being the "well understood" meaning of "a contract of service"—see *Ultraframe UK Ltd v Fielding* [2004] R.P.C. 24 at para.21, where a director and 100 per cent shareholder was held not to be an employee. Contrast *A. Fulton Co Ltd v Grant Barnett & Co Ltd* [2001] R.P.C. 257 (at para.83) where the designer was the chairman, chief executive and a director, and where it was stated in the company's account that no director had a service contract but where, because he was taxed under PAYE and worked for no-one else, he was held to be an employee.

[17] For a case in which this issue was considered at length, see *Intercase UK Ltd v Time Computers Ltd* [2003] EWHC 2988 at paras 9–18.

(i) the person by whom the design was commissioned or with whom its designer was employed; or

(ii) its designer;

(iii) the person by whom and the country in which articles made to the design were first marketed; or

(iv) the provisions of any Order made under section 221 of the 1988 Act.

(v) Qualification by reference to commissioning or employment

13–90   Under section 219, a design qualifies for design right if it is created in pursuance of a commission from or in the course of employment with a qualifying person.[18] In the case of a joint commission or joint employment,[19] the design will qualify for design right protection if any of the commissioners or employers is a qualifying person.[20] The meaning of the term "a qualifying person" is considered below.[21] Whilst it is not entirely clear from the wording of section 219, it is submitted that for the design to qualify for design right by reference to employment, the employer must be a qualifying person at the time when the design is created otherwise the design could not be said to have been created "in the course of employment ... with a qualifying person". The position is less clear in relation to a commissioned design, but it is submitted that a commissioner too would have to be a qualifying person at the time that the design was created if the design is to qualify under this head. It should be noted that if a design was created in pursuance of a commission or in the course of employment, but the commissioner or employer is not a qualifying person, then that design cannot qualify by reference to its designer.[22] The two methods of qualification are mutually exclusive. However, such a design may still qualify by reference to first marketing or under section 221.[23]

(vi) Qualification by reference to the designer

13–91   If a design was not created in pursuance of a commission or in the course of employment, then it will qualify for design right protection under section 218 of the 1988 Act if the designer is a qualifying individual or, in the case of a computer-generated design, if the designer is a qualifying person.[24] If such a design was a joint design, it will qualify for design right protection provided one of the designers is a qualifying individual or (as the case may be) a qualifying person. The meaning of "a qualifying individual" and "a qualifying person" are considered below.[25]

(vii) Qualification by reference to first marketing

13–92   If a design does not qualify by reference to the designer, or the commissioner or employer, it may nevertheless qualify under section 220 if the first marketing of articles made to the design is by a qualifying person[26] who is exclusively authorised to put such articles on the market in the United Kingdom, and such first

---

[18] CDPA 1988, s.219(1).

[19] Unlike "joint design", the words "joint commission" and "joint employment" are not defined.

[20] CDPA 1988, s.219(2).

[21] See para. 13–98, below.

[22] For qualification of a design by reference to its designer, see para. 13–91, below.

[23] See, respectively, paras 13–92 et seq. and 13–95, below.

[24] CDPA 1988, s.218(1) and (2).

[25] See, respectively, paras 13–97 and 13–98, below.

[26] For the meaning of "qualifying person" see para. 13–98, below.

marketing takes place in the United Kingdom or in another country to which the design right provisions extend by virtue of an Order made under section 255,[27] or in another Member State of the European Economic Community.

Marketing. The reference to the marketing of articles is to their being sold or let for hire, or offered or exposed for sale or hire in the course of a business.[28] In order to prevent abuses, no account is taken of marketing "which is merely colourable and not intended to satisfy the reasonable requirements of the public".[29]   **13–93**

Exclusively authorised. Not only must the person who first markets the relevant articles be a qualifying person, he must also show that he was exclusively authorised to put the articles on the market in the United Kingdom. For these purposes, this means that he was authorised by the person who would have been the first owner of design right (whether as designer, commissioner or employer) if he had been a qualifying person or by a person lawfully claiming under such a person and that that authorisation was exclusive in the sense that its exclusivity is capable of being enforced by legal proceedings in the United Kingdom.[30] It will be noted that the requirement that the exclusivity be capable of enforcement in the United Kingdom may raise difficult issues on the choice and conflict of laws. It may also give rise to questions of enforceability under European competition law. Where the first marketing is done jointly by two or more persons, then the design will qualify for design right if any one of those persons is a qualifying person who is exclusively authorised to put the articles on the market in the United Kingdom.[31]   **13–94**

(viii) Qualification by Order made under section 221

Section 221 of the 1988 Act provides that Her Majesty may, with a view to fulfilling an international obligation, by Order in Council provide that a design qualifies for design right protection if such requirements as are specified in the Order are met. It was indicated in the course of Parliamentary debate[32] that this Order would be used to ensure that the United Kingdom complied with its obligations under, for example, the Paris Convention for the protection of industrial property.[33] To date, however, no such Order has been made.   **13–95**

(ix) Qualifying individuals, person and countries

As appears above, in order to ascertain whether a design qualifies for design right, it may be necessary to determine whether there is a qualifying individual, a qualifying person or a qualifying country.   **13–96**

Qualifying individual. A qualifying individual is defined by section 217(1) of the 1988 Act as "a citizen or subject of, or an individual habitually resident in, a qualifying country". The requirement that an individual be "a citizen or subject of a qualifying country" is construed, in relation to the United Kingdom, as a reference to the individual being a British citizen. In relation to a United Kingdom colony, it is construed as a reference to his being a British Dependent Territories   **13–97**

---

[27] See para. 13–99, below.
[28] CDPA 1988, s.263(2).
[29] s.263(2). The meaning of "colourable" is considered in detail in relation to the meaning of publication and commercial publication for copyright purposes; see para. 3–176, above, and CDPA 1988, s.175(5).
[30] CDPA 1988, s.220(4).
[31] s.220(2). For the meaning of "qualifying person" see para. 13–98, below.
[32] By Lord Beaverbrook—see *Hansard*, H.L. Vol.491, cols 1128–1129.
[33] (1883). See para. 13–34, above.

citizen by his connection with that colony.[34] The phrase "habitual residence" is not defined by the 1988 Act. However, it suggests a more stringent test than the simple residence test necessary to qualify for copyright protection.[35]

13–98 **Qualifying person.** A qualifying person is defined by section 217(1) of the 1988 Act as "a qualifying individual or a body corporate or other body having legal personality which (a) is formed under the law of a part of the United Kingdom or another qualifying country, and (b) has in any qualifying country a place of business at which substantial business activity is carried on." The word "business" includes a trade or profession,[36] and in determining whether substantial business activity is being carried on at a place of business in any country, no account is to be taken of dealings in goods which are at all times outside that country.[37] By requiring a body corporate to have a substantial business activity in a qualifying country, design right has again adopted a more stringent qualification test than that which applies in copyright.[38] However, it should be noted that there is no requirement that the relevant activity be in respect of any particular type of article. References to a qualifying person also include the Crown or the government of any other qualifying country.[39]

13–99 **Qualifying country.** A qualifying country is defined by section 217(3) of the 1988 Act as "(a) the United Kingdom,[40] (b) a country to which this Part extends by virtue of an Order made under section 255, (c) another Member State of the European Economic Community, or (d) to the extent that an Order under section 256 so provides, a country designated under that section as enjoying reciprocal protection". Under section 255 of the 1988 Act, an Order in Council may be made to extend the application of the design right provisions of the 1988 Act (subject to such exceptions and modifications as may be specified) to any of the Channel Islands, the Isle of Man or any colony. The legislature of any country to which the design right provisions are so extended may modify or add to those provisions so as to adapt the design right protection to the circumstances of that country, but not so as to deny design right protection in a case where it would otherwise exist.[41] If a country ceases to be a colony of the United Kingdom, it shall continue to be treated as such a country until an Order in Council is made designating it as a country enjoying reciprocal protection or an Order in Council is made declaring that it will cease to be so treated because the design right provisions as part of the law of that country have been amended or repealed.[42] As yet, no Order has been made under section 255 of the 1988 Act. By section 256, where the law of a country provides adequate protection for British designs, an Order in Council may be made designating that country as one enjoying reciprocal protection under the design right provisions of the 1988 Act. If that other country provides adequate protection for only certain classes of British design or only for designs applied to a certain class of article, then any Order made shall contain limiting provisions, limiting to a corresponding extent the protection afforded by the design right provisions of the 1988 Act to designs connected with that country. As yet, 16 countries (including the Channel Islands, the Isle of Man and various colonies) have been recognised as providing adequate protection for

---

[34] CDPA 1988, s.217(4).
[35] s.154(1)(b) and see Ch.3, above.
[36] CDPA 1988, s.263(1).
[37] s.217(5).
[38] s.154(1)(c).
[39] s.217(2).
[40] *i.e.* England and Wales, Scotland and Northern Ireland.
[41] CDPA 1988, s.255(4).
[42] s.255(5).

British designs and so have been designated as enjoying reciprocal protection under the design right provisions of the 1988 Act.[43]

5. DURATION

The position before the 1988 Act. One of the least satisfactory features of the law prior to the 1988 Act[44] was that a design which was unregistrable under the registered designs legislation (often because it was purely functional) was entitled to full copyright protection lasting for the lifetime of the author plus 50 years. This often allowed the designer an effective monopoly lasting for a considerable time and contrasted strangely with the protection for registrable designs which was then generally limited to a maximum of 15 years.[45]   **13–100**

The 1988 Act. Design right offers two alternative periods of protection.   **13–101**

   (i) **The 15-year rule.** By section 216(1)(a) of the 1988 Act, design right in a design will expire 15 years from the end of the calendar year in which that design document or that article came into existence (whichever first occurred).[46]

  (ii) **The 10-year rule.** However, by sections 216(1)(b) and 216(2) of the 1988 Act, if articles made to the design are made available for sale or hire anywhere in the world by or with the licence of the design right owner within five years from the end of the calendar year in which the design was recorded in a design document or in which an article is made to the design, then the design right will expire 10 years from the end of the calendar year in which the articles were first made available for sale or hire.

Thus, under these provisions, a design can never have protection for longer than 15 years from the end of the calendar year in which it was recorded in a design document or in which an article was made to the design, and will in most cases be reduced by the 10-year rule. If, of course, articles are made available for sale or hire almost immediately after design right starts to subsist, the period of design right may last only 10 years.

Example. On June 1, 2000, a designer created a design document recording his design for a revolutionary new aircraft wing. Design right subsisted in his design from that date. Whilst the 15-year rule applies, design right will expire at the end of 2015.[47] If, however, aircraft wings made to the design are made available for sale or hire at any time up to and including December 31, 2005, then the 10-year rule will operate. Thus, if wings were sold on (for example), October 1, 2002,   **13–102**

---

[43] Design Right (Reciprocal Protection) (No.2) Order (1989) (SI 1989/1294) see Vol.2, at C1.ii.

[44] See generally para. 13–23, above.

[45] Under the registered design legislation before its amendment by the CDPA 1988, a design which was registered had protection for up to 15 years, see Registered Designs Act 1949, s.8. Under the Copyright Act 1956, s.10 (as amended by the Design Copyright Act 1968), a registrable design which was applied industrially had copyright protection limited to 15 years. Since the CDPA 1988, the maximum period of protection available to registered designs has been increased to 25 years, see Registered Designs Act 1949, s.8 as amended.

[46] As has been seen, design right does not subsist in a design unless and until the design is recorded in a design document or until an article is made to the design, see CDPA 1988, s.213(6) and paras 13–78 et seq., above, and unless the design qualifies in accordance with s.213(5)—see paras 13–89 et seq., above. However, it is the former event that is important as regards the operation of the 15-year rule..

[47] i.e. 15 years from the end of the calendar year in which the design document was created.

then design right would expire at the end of 2012.[48] By contrast, if aircraft wings are first made available for sale or hire *after* December 31, 2005, then the 10-year rule will never operate and the 15-year period will continue.

13–103 **Articles made to the design made available for sale or hire.** In the context of the 10-year rule, the time when "articles made to the design are are [first] made available for sale or hire" is not further defined.[49] Nor is it clear whether more than one article must actually have been made to the design (and have been made available for sale or hire) before the 10 year rule will come into operation. The wording of section 216(1)(b) suggests that this might be so. However, it seems more likely that the intention of Parliament was that it was the offer to sell or hire articles (i.e. the placing of the design in the market) that was intended to trigger the operation of the 10-year rule and that this may apply even if, in fact, only a single articles had been made to the design.[50]

6. TITLE TO AND DEALINGS WITH DESIGN RIGHT

A. Introduction

13–104 **Property right.** Design right is a property right[51] and, subject to the provisions of 1988 Act, the usual principles of property law govern questions of title and how it may be transmitted. Design right (like copyright[52]) may have separate legal and equitable owners, and it may be co-owned either by joint tenants or by tenants in common. The title to design right may also be divided so that different people own different aspects of it.[53] As design right is a form of property in its own right, ownership of the design right must be distinguished from ownership of the design document which records the design or ownership of an article made to the design. A similar point has already been made in relation to copyright.[54] As with other forms of property, dealings which transfer title to design right must be distinguished from dealings which merely give another person the right (a licence) to do something in relation to the property which would otherwise be an actionable wrong. The latter form of dealing does not affect title to design right.[55]

13–105 **Scheme of this section.** This section will consider, first, who is the first owner of design right; secondly, ownership in other circumstances, in particular whether the first owner holds the design right on trust or subject to the rights of any other person; thirdly, the transmission of title to design right; fourthly, the grant of licences relating to design right; fifthly, the availability of licences of right and, finally, Crown use.

B. First owner of design right

13–106 **Definition of "first owner".** Section 215 determines who is the first owner of the design right in a design. It provides that:

---

[48] *i.e.* 10 years from the end of the calendar year in which articles made to the design were first made available for sale or hire.

[49] By contrast, in the case of copyright, some guidance as to when a work is "made available to the public" is given by CDPA 1988, s.12. See para. 6–46, above.

[50] For a similar point see CDPA 1988, s.226 and para. 13–146, below.

[51] CDPA 1988, s.213(1).

[52] See para. 5–01, above.

[53] Because, for example, of an assignment limited by way of time or of some only of the exclusive rights given by the CDPA 1988.

[54] See para. 5–02, above.

[55] Save that the CDPA 1988, s.222(4). provides that any licence granted by a design right owner will bind some of his successors in title (see para. 13–120, below) and CDPA 1988, s.225 also confers certain exceptional rights on exclusive licensees (see para. 13–121, below).

"(1) The designer is the first owner of any design right in a design which is not created in pursuance of a commission or in the course of employment.

(2) Where a design is created in pursuance of a commission, the person commissioning the design is the first owner of any design right in it.

(3) Where, in a case not falling within subsection (2) above, a design is created by an employee in the course of employment, his employer is the first owner of any design right in the design.

(4) If a design qualifies for design right protection by virtue of section 220 (qualification by reference to first marketing of articles made to the design), the above rules do not apply and the person by whom the articles in question are marketed is the first owner of the design right."

It is clear from this definition that the issue of the identity of the first owner of design right is closely linked to the question whether the design satisfies the qualification conditions and many of the relevant terms are considered in that context.[56] It should be noted, that the first owner of design right as defined by section 215 is the first legal owner of design right but is not necessarily the first owner in equity.[57]

Designer as first owner. Subject to section 215(4),[58] the designer is the first owner of design right in a design provided it was not created in pursuance of a commission or in the course of employment.[59] If the design was a joint design, then the first owners will be only those designers who are qualifying individuals or, as the case may be, qualifying persons.[60] The fact that a group of designers has together designed an article does not mean that they must all be joint first owners of any design rights which arise in relation to that article. As has been seen,[61] the design of component parts of the article may be attributable to different individuals. If so, those individuals are the designers of those parts and each will be the first owner of the design right in the design of each respective part. Each individual may (depending on the circumstances) hold the design right on trust for, or subject to the express or implied terms of a contract between himself and the other designers.[62]   **13–107**

Commissioner as first owner. Subject, again, to section 215(4),[63] the first owner of design right in a design created in pursuance of a commission will be the person who commissioned it.[64] The circumstances when a design may be said to have been created in pursuance of a commission have already been discussed.[65] Where a design was jointly commissioned, only those commissioners who are qualifying persons are first owners of the design right.[66] In providing that the commissioner is the first owner of design right, the 1988 Act has followed the ap-   **13–108**

---

[56] See paras 13–89 *et seq.*, above.

[57] For equitable ownership see para. 13–112, below.

[58] *i.e.* unless the design in question qualifies for design right under CDPA 1988, s.220, *i.e.* by reference to first marketing, as to which, see paras 13–92 *et seq.*, above.

[59] CDPA 1988, s.215(1). For the meaning of "designer", "commission" and "employment", see paras 13–83 *et seq.*, above.

[60] s.218(4). As to joint designs, see para. 13–85, above.

[61] See para. 13–85, above.

[62] See para. 13–112, below.

[63] *i.e.* unless the design qualifies under s.220—by reference to first marketing (see paras 13–92 *et seq.*, above).

[64] CDPA 1988, s.215(2). For a case where the commissioner was the first owner of design right in a design, see *Farmers Build Ltd v Carier Bulk Materials Handling Ltd* (unreported) March 26, 1997, transcript at 29.

[65] See para. 13–87, above.

[66] CDPA 1988, s.219(3). As to the meaning of "qualifying person" see para. 13–98, above.

proach which has long been adopted in the registered designs legislation rather than the approach adopted in relation to copyright.[67]

13–109   **Employer as first owner.** Subject again to section 215(4),[68] the first owner of design right in a design which was not created in pursuance of a commission,[69] but which was created by an employee in the course of his employment will be the employer.[70] The test for determining whether a person was acting in the course of his employment has already been considered.[71] In the case of joint employers, only those employers who are qualifying persons are first owners of that design right.[72]

13–110   **Person who first markets as first owner.** If a design qualifies for design right under section 220 of the 1988 Act (*i.e.* by reference to the first marketing of articles made to the design[73]) then, notwithstanding the other provisions as to first ownership, the first owner will be the person by whom those articles are marketed.[74] Where articles made to the design are first marketed by more than one person, only those who are qualifying persons and who are exclusively authorised to put the articles on the market in the United Kingdom will be first owners of the design right.[75] This first marketing provision contrasts with the other provisions as to first ownership. In linking first ownership to marketing rather than to the creation of the design, it means that the first owner may be someone wholly unconnected with the design idea. Accordingly, if foreign designers or, as the case may be, foreign commissioners or employers[76] wish their designs to have design right protection in the United Kingdom, they must not only take steps to ensure that the first marketing complies with all of the qualification requirements of section 220[77] but should also be aware that the first owner of the design right will be the person whom they exclusively authorise to market articles made to the design. They may, therefore, wish to provide by way of contract for an assignment of design right to themselves or for some form of trust so as to limit the first marketer's right to deal with and control the relevant design right.

13–111   **Differing first owners of design right, registered design and copyright.** As has already been seen,[78] there remains some overlap in the protection which may be afforded to a design by design right, by registration under the Registered Designs Act 1949 and by copyright. However, it should not be assumed that the first owner of the design right is the same person as the original proprietor for registered design purposes or the first owner of the copyright. The provisions for first ownership of design right are similar to those governing the original

---

[67] It was stated in Parliament that it was important that the ownership provisions for design right and for registered designs were the same because both rights can apply in respect of the same design—see *Hansard*, H.L. Vol.491, col.1116. The reason for this distinction was that design right (and, presumably registered designs) "... concerns the designs of articles, which are the very essence of industry. Consequently, it seems to us that he who pays the piper should call the tune", see *Hansard*, H.L. Vol.494, col.114.

[68] *i.e.* unless the design qualifies under s.220—by reference to first marketing (see paras 13–92 *et seq.*, above).

[69] See para. 13–87, above.

[70] CDPA 1988, s.215(3).

[71] See para. 13–88, above.

[72] CDPA 1988, s.219(3). As to the meaning of "qualifying person" see para. 13–98, above.

[73] See paras 13–92 *et seq.*, above.

[74] CDPA 1988, s.215(4).

[75] s.220(3). As to the meaning of "qualifying person", "market" and "exclusive authorisation" see paras 13–98 and 13–93 *et seq.*, above.

[76] *i.e.* a designer, a commissioner or an employer who is not himself a qualifying individual or (as the case may be) a qualifying person.

[77] See paras 13–92 *et seq.*, above.

[78] See para. 13–42, above.

proprietorship of a registered design under the Registered Designs Act 1949.[79] In particular, similar provisions govern ownership of designs made in pursuance of a commission or created in the course of employment,[80] and there will be no difference between the identity of the "author" of a design for registered design purposes and of its "designer" for design right purposes. Both are defined as the person who creates the design in question.[81]

However, the first ownership provisions for design right diverge from the original proprietor provisions for registered designs where a design qualifies for design right protection by virtue of the first marketing provisions in section 220 of the 1988 Act. In such a case, the first marketer will be the first owner of the design right[82] but, as there is no equivalent provision in respect of registered designs, a different person may be the original proprietor of the design for registered design purposes. As section 3(3) of the Registered Designs Act 1949 (as amended) states that an application for the registration of a design in which design right subsists must be made by the person claiming to be the owner of the design right, this would mean that there could be no registration of such a design until ownership of the two rights is in common hands (for example, after an assignment).

There are also circumstances in which copyright and design right co-exist but where there will be different first owners. In particular, the designer (the person who creates the design idea) may not be the person who records that idea in a design document or who makes an article to the design. In such a case, the first owner of the design right will not necessarily be the first owner of the copyright which subsists in the design document or (if the article is an artistic work) in the article. Further, the owner of design right in a design created pursuant to a commission is the commissioner; yet as there are now no commissioning provisions in relation to copyright,[83] the legal owner of copyright in a design drawing recording that design will be the author of the drawing. Accordingly, if the design right owner does not also own the copyright in the corresponding copyright work, then care must be taken not to use the design in a way which would infringe that copyright. In particular, care will be required when acting outside the scope of the exclusion in section 51.[84]

C. Ownership in other circumstances

Equitable ownership. The first ownership provisions of the 1988 Act determine who is the first legal owner of design right. However, that person may not be the first beneficial or equitable owner. Equitable title may vest in another person by virtue of a contract or by reason of a fiduciary relationship.[85] Such situations have already been considered in relation to equitable title to copyright at paragraphs 5–168 and 5–171 et seq., above.   **13–112**

D. Transmission of title

As design right is a property right, ownership of it (whether legal or equitable)   **13–113**

---

[79] Registered Designs Act 1949, s.2 as amended by the CDPA 1988.

[80] See CDPA 1988, s.215(2) and (3) and Registered Designs Act 1949, s.2(1A) and (1B) (as amended).

[81] See Registered Designs Act 1949, s.2(3) and CDPA 1988, s.214(1).

[82] See paras 13–92 et seq., above.

[83] See para. 5–32, above.

[84] CDPA 1988, s.51 provides that it is not an infringement of any copyright in a design document or model recording or embodying a design for anything other than an artistic work to make an article to the design, or copy an article made to a design, see paras 13–278 et seq., below.

[85] For a recent case on equitable ownership of designs created by the director of and 100 per cent shareholder in a company, see *Ultraframe UK Ltd v Fielding* [2004] R.P.C. 24.

may pass or be transmitted from one person to another. The law on the transmission of title to design right mirrors that which relates to copyright and has already been considered fully in that context.[86]

13–114   **Section 222(1).** Section 222(1) of the 1988 Act provides that design right is "transmissible by assignment, by testamentary disposition, or by operation of law, as personal or moveable property". This wording is identical to that used in relation to copyright, and the meaning of the phrases "transmission by operation of law" and "transmission by testamentary disposition" and the general nature of assignments have already been considered in that context.[87]

13–115   **Assignments in writing and equitable assignments.** Section 222(3) provides that an assignment of design right is not effective unless it is in writing and signed[88] by or on behalf of the assignor. The same wording is used in relation to copyright and its meaning has already been considered in that context.[89]

13–116   **Partial assignments of design right.** As with copyright, an assignment may be of the whole or of a part of the design right. By section 222(2), a partial assignment is an assignment limited so as to apply "(a) to one or more, but not all, of the things the design right owner has the exclusive right to do; (b) to part, but not the whole, of the period for which the right is to subsist".[90] A design right owner has the exclusive right to reproduce the design for commercial purposes by making articles to that design or by making a design document recording the design for the purpose of enabling such articles to be made.[91] Thus, an assignment of the right to reproduce the design by making one particular type of article would be a partial assignment. In the event of partial assignment, the different aspects of design right will have different design right owners.[92] Again, these provisions mirror those relating to copyright.[93]

13–117   **Assignment of future design right.** As a general rule, a person cannot legally assign future property,[94] and an attempt to do so amounts, at best, to an equitable assignment.[95] However, section 223 of the 1988 Act creates an exception to this rule in the case of future design right. It provides that where, under an agreement signed[96] by or on behalf of the prospective owner of a future design right, the prospective owner purports to assign the future design right (wholly or partially) then, upon the right coming into existence, title to it will vest in the purported assignee (or in a person claiming under him) provided he would be entitled as against all other persons to require the design right to be vested in him. It will be noted that under section 223 the assignee of a prospective owner may himself

[86] See, generally, Ch.5 and, in particular, paras 5–63 et seq. (legal title) and paras 5–185 et seq. (equitable title).
[87] CDPA 1988, ss.90(1). For the meaning of "transmission by testamentary disposition", see para. 5–121, above. For the meaning of "transmission by operation of law" see paras 5–131 et seq., above.
[88] In the case of a body corporate, the requirement for a signature is also satisfied by the affixing of its seal. CDPA 1988, s.261.
[89] CDPA 1988, s.90(3), see para. 5–82, above.
[90] The period for which the design right subsists is discussed at paras 13–100 et seq., above.
[91] CDPA 1988, s.226(1), see paras 13–145, below.
[92] s.258(1).
[93] ss.90(2) and 173(1). See paras 5–93 et seq., above.
[94] i.e. property which had not come into existence at the time of the purported assignment.
[95] On the basis that there was a promise to assign which if supported by consideration was enforceable by specific performance—see Snell's Principles of Equity (30th ed.) at paras 5–28–5–30.
[96] In the case of a body corporate, the requirement for a signature is also satisfied by the affixing of its seal. CDPA 1988, s.261.

further assign the future design right.[97] The equivalent provisions in relation to copyright have already been considered.[98]

Assignment of registered design carries with it the design right. The 1988 Act seeks to minimise instances of separate ownership of design right and a corresponding registered design. Thus, section 224 provides that "where a design consisting of a design in which design right subsists is registered under the Registered Designs Act 1949 and the proprietor of the registered design is also the design right owner, an assignment of the right in the registered design shall be taken to be also an assignment of the design right, unless a contrary intention appears". This provision only applies where the same person owns the registered design and the design right.[99] Further, it appears to apply only where the design which has been registered is the same as the design in which design right subsists. Because of the differences in the definitions of a design for registered design purposes and for design right purposes, the two designs may not be the same.[1] This, again, emphasises the need for care in determining precisely the design with which one is concerned. It also means that care must be taken with an assignment to ensure that it covers all such rights as are required in order to allow the exploitation of a design.

13–118

E. LICENCES

Nature of a licence. A licence must be distinguished from an assignment. In its widest sense, a licence is merely a permission to do something in relation to property which would otherwise be an actionable wrong. The 1988 Act does not require that a licence relating to design right be in writing.[2] The licence may be in writing or oral. It may be granted expressly or be implied from the circumstances, or arise by way of *estoppel*. Further, it may be gratuitous in which case it is prima facie revocable (subject to any issue of estoppel). It may be granted under a contract, in which case its extent is a matter of construction of that contract. Finally, it may arise as a result of the licence of right provisions of the 1988 Act. Save as regards licences of right, the law as regards licences of design right is substantially the same as that which relates to licences of copyright. This has already been considered in detail.[3]

13–119

Successors in title. The 1988 Act creates various design right exceptions to the general rule of law that a licence only binds the person who grants it. Thus section 222(4) provides that a licence granted by the owner of design right is binding on every successor in title of the title of the grantor except a purchaser in good faith for valuable consideration and without notice (actual or constructive) of the licences, or a person deriving title from such a purchaser. Under section 223(3), a licence granted by a prospective owner of design right will be similarly binding. Finally, section 225(2) provides that an exclusive licensee has the same rights

13–120

---

[97] s.223(2).

[98] s.91. See paras 5–110 *et seq.*, above. Where the section applies, the assignee will acquire (when the design right comes into existence) the full legal (and beneficial) title rather than the equitable title that he would have acquired under the general rule. He is, therefore, able to bring proceedings in his own name without the need to join the assignor.

[99] By reason of s.3(3) Registered Designs Act 1949 (as amended), the initial proprietor of a registered design should generally be the design right owner.

[1] See Registered Designs Act 1949, s.1(1) discussed at paras 13–251 *et seq.*, below and CDPA 1988, s.213(3), discussed at paras 13–44 *et seq.*, above. The changes in the definition of a design for registered design purposes have reduced the similarity in the wording of the definitions but have probably increased the similarity in their meaning.

[2] However, to qualify as an exclusive licence, the licence would have to be in writing and signed by or on behalf of the design right owner. See para. 13–121, below.

[3] See paras 5–194 *et seq.*, above.

against any successor in title who is bound by the licence as he has against the person granting the licence. The similar provision relating to licences granted under copyright are considered elsewhere.[4]

13–121   **Exclusive licences.** Design right, like copyright, may be the subject of an exclusive licence. Under section 225(1) of the 1988 Act, an exclusive licence is "a licence in writing signed[5] by or on behalf of the design right owner authorising the licensee to the exclusion of all other persons, including the person granting the licence, to exercise a right which would otherwise be exercisable exclusively by the design right owner".[6] The significance of an exclusive licence lies in the special rights which section 234 of the 1988 Act confers upon exclusive licensees and, in particular, the right to bring an action for infringement and to recover damages in his or her own name.[7] The definition of an exclusive licence and the nature of the special rights granted to an exclusive licensee are the same as those which apply in copyright and have already been considered in that context.[8]

13–122   **Other licences.** Save as is mentioned above, the 1988 Act contains no special provisions as regards gratuitous or contractual licences and the law regarding implied or inforaml licenses is as discussed in relation to licences of copyright.[9]

F. LICENCES OF RIGHT

13–123   **The 1986 White Paper.** When the 1986 White Paper on Intellectual Property[10] proposed the introduction of design right, it also made recommendations intended to ensure that design right did not create unfair monopolies. Thus it recommended that there should be a limited right for owners of equipment to repair that equipment. It also recommended that licences of right should be available in the last five years of the term of design right. This would, it was suggested, allow competition from other manufacturers reasonably early in the life of a design whilst allowing the original designer sufficient time to gain a market lead and to make a return on his design expenses. The White Paper also proposed that licences of right should be available at any time in the life of a design if the Monopolies and Mergers Commission found that design right was being exercised in a manner contrary to the public interest. In the event, the 1988 Act introduced the "must fit" and "must match" exclusions which were of much wider significance than the limited right to repair suggested by the White Paper[11] but nevertheless adopted in full the White Paper's proposals for licences of right.

13–124   **Section 237—licence of right in the last five years of design right.** The most important licence of right provision is section 237 of the 1988 Act. This provides that any person is entitled as of right to a licence in the last five years of the term of a design right.[12] This appears simple enough, but various difficulties are likely to arise. In particular, in order to determine when a licence of right becomes

---

[4] See para. 5–197, above.

[5] For a body corporate, the requirement for a signature is also satisfied by affixing the seal, CDPA 1988, s.261.

[6] *i.e.* any part of the right to reproduce the design for commercial purposes (a) by making articles to that design or (b) by making a design document recording the design for the purpose of enabling such articles to be made. See CDPA 1988, s.226.

[7] See para. 13–169, below.

[8] CDPA 1988, ss.92 and 101. See paras 5–203 *et seq.*, above.

[9] See para. 5–213 *et seq.*, above.

[10] Intellectual Property and Innovation (Cmnd. 9712). April 1986 at paras 3.26–3.39.

[11] See paras 13–28 and 13–29, above.

[12] CDPA 1988, s.237(1). It was stated in the course of debate in Committee that a period of five years exclusive rights is sufficient; "… it gives the original designer a lead in the market …

available, one must first ascertain whether the relevant design is subject to the 15-year term of protection or to the 10-year term. As has been seen,[13] the 10-year term applies when articles made to the design have been made available for sale or hire less than five years from the date when design right first subsisted in the design. Where it applies, the 10-year term runs from the end of the calendar year in which such articles were first made available.[14] A prospective licensee would, therefore, have to ascertain not only when design right came into subsistence[15] but also whether and, if so, when, articles made to the design were first made available for sale or hire. Without the co-operation of the design right owner, these matters may be difficult or impossible to establish. If the prospective licensee and the design right owner cannot agree as to subsistence of design right or as to its term or as to the identity of the person in whom it first vested, then such issues may be referred to the Comptroller for his decision.[16] The Secretary of State has power by Order to exclude the operation of section 237(1) if it appears to him to be necessary in order to comply with an international obligation or to secure or maintain reciprocal protection for British designs in other countries.[17]

Section 238—licence of right in the public interest. If, following a reference to the Competition Commission, whatever needs to be remedied, mitigated or prevented by the Secretary of State, or by the Competition Commission or by the Office of Fair Trading includes (a) conditions in licences granted by a design right owner restricting the use of the design by the licensee or the right of the design right owner to grant other licences or (b) a refusal by the design right owner to grant licences on reasonable terms, then section 238 of the 1988 Act (as modified by the Competition Act 2002) provides that the powers conferred by Schedule 8 of the Competition Act 2002 shall include the power to cancel or modify those conditions and instead, or in addition to, provide that a licence shall be available as of right. The terms of such licence would, in default of agreement, be fixed by the Comptroller[18] and it seems that such a licence may be made available at any time during the term of design right. However, the procedure is complicated and likely to be time consuming and costly. Further, it is submitted that it would require some very substantial abuse in order to justify the grant of such a licence earlier than in the last five years of the life of the design right. **13–125**

Terms of a licence of right. Where section 237 applies, a person is entitled to a licence of right to do anything which would otherwise infringe the design right.[19] Where section 238 applies, he is entitled to a licence to do the things in respect of which the relevant Order of the Secretary of State requires a licence to be made available.[20] Although such a licence cannot be denied,[21] it may, nevertheless, be granted on terms. The relevant terms should be agreed by the parties or, in default of agreement, settled by the Comptroller-General of Patents, Designs and Trade **13–126**

---

together with all the inherent advantages which the originator will have ...", see *Hansard*, H.C. SCE, col.596.

[13] For a discussion of the alternative periods of duration, see paras 13–100 *et seq.*, above.

[14] See para. 13–103, above.

[15] *i.e.* when the design was recorded in a design document or when an article was first made to the design, see paras 13–78 *et seq.*, above.

[16] CDPA 1988, s.246(1). See para. 13–188, below.

[17] s.237(3). As yet, no such Order has been made.

[18] CDPA 1988, s.238(3).

[19] CDPA 1988, ss.237(1) and 247(3)(a). This would not include, for example, the right to make articles to a design outside the United Kingdom. For the acts capable of infringing design right, see paras 13–149 *et seq.*, below.

[20] s.247(3)(b).

[21] By either the design right owner or by the Comptroller, s.247(3).

Marks.[22] The Secretary of State has power to prescribe by order factors to which the Comptroller must have regard in settling the terms of any licence.[23] However, no such order has yet been made and, in the absence of express guidance, the Comptroller has adopted the patent-licence-of-right test, namely that the terms should be those which protect the interests of the parties in a manner which is fair and reasonable and which would have been agreed in free negotiation by a willing licensor and a willing licensee.[24] It is submitted that this is the correct test. However, as the Patents Act 1977 contains various provisions governing the grounds upon which a patent licence of right may be granted and matters to which the Comptroller must have regard when exercising his powers,[25] which provisions were not adopted by the 1988 Act for design right licences of right, it is also submitted that some care must be exercised when relying on patent-licence-of-right cases and principles in design right cases.[26]

Because the licence of right to which a person is entitled under section 237 is a licence to do anything which would otherwise infringe the design right, neither the design right owner nor the Comptroller can refuse to grant a licence of right under that section, which permits sub-licensing (if that is what the prospective licensee seeks).[27] They may, however, impose such terms on the right to grant sub-licences as may be fair and reasonable to protect the interests of the parties. Such terms may include, for example, the obligation to provide the licensor with details of the persons to whom sub-licences are to be granted, of the articles which the sub-licensees are authorised to make and of any changes in the sub-licence arrangements.[28] Other terms imposed on licensees of right under section 237 have included a provision for the termination of the licence in the event of the licensee being in breach of the terms of the licence or being insolvent, and an obligation on the licensee to keep full and accurate records for inspection by the licensor (and to retain such records for three years after the licensor's right to inspect had expired). However, in another case, the Comptroller, taking account of the fact that the parties were competitors, ruled that certain sensitive information need not be disclosed to the licensor but to an independent accountant.[29]

13–127   **The licence fee.** The most important term in most licences of right is likely to be the fee payable by the licensee to the licensor. Again, this should be such sum as would be agreed between a willing licensor and licensee. This will plainly depend upon the nature of the proposed use. Where only limited use is intended, the payment may be by way of a lump sum but if the licensee proposes to manufacture articles to the design, the fee is more likely to be a royalty based on a percentage

---

[22] ss.237(2), 238(3) and 263(1). Where a decision of the Comptroller is reported in the Reports of Patent Cases (R.P.C.s), a copy of the licence granted is also set out in full. These provide useful guidance as to the sort of terms which have been accepted by parties or imposed by the Comptroller.

[23] s.247(4).

[24] See *Roger Bance and Anor's Licence of Right (Copyright) Application* [1996] R.P.C. 667 at 672; *Pioneer Oil Tools Ltd Licence of Right (Copyright) Application* [1997] R.P.C. 573 at 580; and *Sterling Fluid Systems Ltd's Licence of Right (Copyright) Application* [2000] R.P.C. 775 at 780. All these cases concerned copyright in a design document recording a design which was created before the commencement of the CDPA 1988. However, by reason of the transitional provisions (CDPA 1988, Sch.1 paras 19(2) and (3)), the design-right-licence-of-right provisions applied.

[25] Patents Act 1977, ss.48–50 (inclusive).

[26] See *Pioneer Oil Tools Ltd's Application* [1997] R.P.C. 573 at 580 and (in relation to the appropriate royalty rate) at 581.

[27] See *Roger Bance's Application* [1996] R.P.C. 667 at 672, 682–683 where the licensee wished for such a licence and *Pioneer Oil Tools Ltd's Application* [1997] R.P.C. 573 at 602 where it did not. It is, presumably, for the proposed licensee to ensure that the terms of the licence actually granted cover its anticipated activities.

[28] See *Roger Bance's Application* [1996] R.P.C. 667 at 672 and 682–683.

[29] *Sterling Fluid Systems Ltd's Application* [2000] R.P.C. 775 at 797.

of the sale price of each such article sold. The level of investment made by the original designer in the design is also likely to be important.[30] So too is the amount that it would cost the licensee to re-design his products so as to avoid the need to take a licence[31] and the fact that the designs were for articles competing with a number of similar products and that a large proportion proportion of their value lay in the materials used rather than in their design.[32] By contrast, the fact that a designer had had to use particular skill in creating the design or that the licensor might lose sales in his capacity as a manufacturer have been held to be irrelevant.[33] Ultimately, the question is one of market forces; of how much, when it comes down to commercial realities, a person would be prepared to pay for a licence to use the design.[34] In assessing this, the amount paid under comparable licences (if sufficiently similar licences exist[35]) or the amount agreed by the parties in other dealings may well be relevant.[36] There is no reason why the sum which would be payable under a patent licence[37] should be the starting point for a design right licence.[38] In particular, it appears that the "profits available" approach (*i.e.* to determine the licence fee by reference to the profits available to the licensee)[39] is reasonably firmly established in design right cases.[40] The profits available approach involves determining the net profit available to the licensee, and then deciding in what proportions a willing licensor and licensee would divide that profit. Thus, in one design right case where the licensee's anticipated available profit was 32 per cent of its anticipated sale price,[41] it was held that the licensor should get 25 per cent of that profit, *i.e.* eight per cent of the sale price.[42] This eight per cent was then uplifted to nine per cent to take account of the fact that the licensee had access to special markets not open to the licensor and could, therefore, sell goods made to the design at a premium.[43] The idea of dividing the available profit such that the licensee would receive its usual net profit margin on past trading—namely 3.3 per cent—was rejected on the ground that a willing li-

---

[30] See *Hansard*, H.C. SCE, col.596.

[31] *Sterling Fluid Systems Ltd's Application* [2000] R.P.C. 775 at 790–792.

[32] *Stafford Engineering Services Ltd's Licence of Right (Copyright) Application* [2000] R.P.C. 797 at 811–812 where this fact suggested that a low royalty of four per cent was justified.

[33] See *Stafford Engineering Services Ltd's Application* [2000] R.P.C. 797 at 810 and *E-UK Controls Ltd's Licence of Right (Copyright) Application* [1998] R.P.C. 833 at 840.

[34] See *Roger Bance's Application* [1996] R.P.C. 667 at pp.678–679 and *Pioneer Oil Tools Ltd's Application* [1997] R.P.C. 573 at 589.

[35] See *Pioneer Oil Tools Ltd's Application* [1997] R.P.C. 573 at 591 and *Sterling Fluid Systems Ltd's Application* [2000] R.P.C. 775 at 789.

[36] See *Roger Bance's Application* [1996] R.P.C. 667 at p. 674.

[37] Such royalty generally being five to seven per cent of the sale price of articles made using the relevant mechanical invention.

[38] See *Roger Bance's Application* [1996] R.P.C. 667 at 676 where the Comptroller commented that there was no clear justification (other than as "a certain gut reaction") for accepting the sum which would be payable under a patent licence of right as a starting point.

[39] In patent cases, there has been some reluctance to adopt the "available profits" approach—see, for example, *Smith Kline & French Laboratories Ltd's (Cimetidine) Patent* [1990] F.S.R. 203 and *Gerber Garment Technology Inc v Lectra Systems Ltd & Anor* [1995] R.P.C. 383 at 418 to 419, where the approach was nevertheless adopted because both parties suggested it and because there was no evidence of any sufficiently similar comparable licences, *ibid.* at 418–419.

[40] See *Sterling Fluid Systems Ltd's Application* [2000] R.P.C. 775 at 785 (where it was stated that this approach better reflected commercial reality), *E-UK Controls Ltd's Application* [1998] R.P.C. 833 and *Stafford Engineering Services Ltd's Application* [2000] R.P.C. 797 at 809. In *Pioneer Oil Tools Ltd's Application* [1997] R.P.C. 573 at 581, the Comptroller commented that one of the arguments against the use of the "profits available" approach in patent cases was the wording of Patents Act 1977 (c.37), s.50(1)(b) which requires that the royalty be fixed by reference to the licensor's remuneration rather than the licensee's. He pointed out that there is no comparable provison in the CDPA 1988 in relation to design right. In *Roger Bance's Application* [1996] R.P.C. 667, the "profits available" approach was used as a means to cross-check other figures.

[41] *Pioneer Oil Tool Ltd's Application* [1997] R.P.C. 573 at 588.

[42] *Pioneer Oil Tool Ltd's Application* [1997] R.P.C. 573 at 589.

[43] *Pioneer Oil Tool Ltd's Application* [1997] R.P.C. 573 at 590.

censee was unlikely to settle for so low a return.[44] In another case, the royalty rate fixed was 6.5 per cent of the invoiced price excluding VAT and transport costs.[45] In yet another, it was four per cent of that price less VAT, packaging and transport costs.[46]

13–128   **Application to Comptroller to settle terms.** In default of agreement by the parties,[47] the prospective licensee can apply to the Comptroller to settle the terms of the licence.[48] Such an application cannot be made earlier than one year before the licence of right first becomes available under that section.[49] The basis on which the Comptroller settles the terms of a licence has already been discussed above. Where the Comptroller settles the terms, the date on which the licence takes effect is either, in the case of an application made under section 237 and made before the earliest date on which a licence of right could take effect under that section, that date[50] or, in all other cases, the date of the application to the Comptroller.[51] An appeal against a decision of the Comptroller lies to the Registered Designs Appeal Tribunal.[52] No appeal lies against the decision of the Tribunal, the only remedy being judicial review by the Divisional Court.

13–129   **Terms of licence when design right owner is unknown.** If the identity of the design right owner cannot be discovered on reasonable inquiry, a person may still apply to the Comptroller to settle the terms of a licence and the Comptroller may order that the licence be free of any obligation to make any payment.[53] If such an order is made, the design right owner may apply to vary the terms of that licence but only with effect from the date when the application to vary is made.[54] Further, even if it emerges that a licence had not been available as of right,[55] the licensee is not liable for damages or an account of profits in respect of anything done at a time before the licensee was aware of any claim by the design right owner that a licence was not available. These limitations on the subsequent rights and remedies of the design right owner suggest that the Comptroller should examine with care the evidence adduced by the prospective licensee as to his attempts to identify the design right owner.

13–130   **Prohibition on the licensee claiming a connection with the owner.** The 1988 Act provides that a licensee under a licence of right shall not, without the consent of the design right owner, apply to goods marketed or to be marketed under the licence a trade description which indicates that he is a licensee of the design right

---

[44] *Pioneer Oil Tool Ltd's Application* [1997] R.P.C. 573 at 589.

[45] *Stafford's Engineering Service Ltd's Application* [2000] R.P.C. 797 at 809.

[46] *Sterling Fluid Systems Ltd's Application* [2000] R.P.C. 775.

[47] CDPA 1988, ss.237(2) and 238(3). Despite the wording of these sections, it is not thought that it is essential to be able to prove such default before making an application to the Comptroller—see *Roussel-Uclaf (Clemence & Le Martret's) Patent* [1987] R.P.C. 109 (a patent case) *per* Falconer J. at 117.

[48] CDPA 1988, s.247(1). An application may be made for a licence in respect of more than just one design, see *Split Roller Bearing Co Ltd's Licence of Right (Copyright) Application* [1996] R.P.C. 225 at 231. The prospective licensor has, it appears, no right to apply to the Comptroller under s.247.

[49] CDPA 1988, s.247(2).

[50] *i.e.* the date five years from the end of the term of design right, see para. 13–124, above.

[51] CDPA 1988, s.247(6).

[52] s.249.

[53] CDPA 1988, s.248(1) and (2).

[54] s.248(3).

[55] Because, for example, the design was not in the last five years of its term of protection.

owner nor use such a trade description in any advertisement in relation to such goods.[56] A breach of this prohibition is actionable by the design right owner.[57]

G. Crown use

Crown use not an infringement. Under section 240 of the 1988 Act, certain uses of a design by the Crown will not constitute an infringement of that design right even though such use was without the licence of the design right owner. Similar provisions exist under the Registered Designs Act 1949 and the Patents Act 1977.[58] Section 240 of the 1988 Act permits a government department[59] or a person authorised in writing by a government department to do anything for the purpose of supplying articles for the services of the Crown or to dispose of articles no longer required for the services of the Crown. Such use of a design is called "Crown use".[60] A person does not have to be authorised by a government department *before* he makes Crown use of a design on behalf of that department; the authorisation may be given before or after the use and whether or not the person is authorised (directly or indirectly) by the design right owner.[61] Furthermore, any person acquiring anything sold as a result of the exercise of the Crown use powers, is entitled to deal with it in the same manner as if the design right were held on behalf of the Crown.[62]

13–131

Services of the Crown. To be permitted, the relevant use must relate to "services of the Crown". This does not cover every area of Crown activity but only use for the defence of the realm, for foreign defence purposes and for health service purposes.[63] The supply of articles for foreign defence purposes means their supply for the defence of a country outside the realm in pursuance of an agreement or arrangement between the government of that country and the British Government; or their supply for use by armed forces in pursuance of a resolution of the United Nations.[64] "Health service purposes" include pharmaceutical services, general medical services or general dental services; that is services of those kinds under Part II of the National Health Service Act 1977 and equivalent provisions in Scotland[65] and Northern Ireland.

13–132

---

[56] CDPA 1988, s.254. "Trade description" and "advertisement" have the same meaning as in the Trade Descriptions Act 1968 (c.29).

[57] CDPA 1988, s.245(2): actionable as a breach of statutory duty.

[58] Registered Designs Act 1949 (c.88), s.12 and Patents Act 1977 (c.37), ss.55–59.

[59] "Government department" is defined as including a Northern Ireland department and any part of the Scottish Administration; see CDPA 1988, s.263(1) (as amended by the Scotland Act 1998 (Consequential Modifications) (No.2) Order 1999, SI 1999/1820). Since June 23, 1999, the power conferred by s.240(1) on a government department is also exercisable for the purposes of a visiting force or headquarters to the extent that it would have been exercisable if that visiting force or headquarters were a part of the home forces and references to "Crown use" in ss.240(5) to (7) shall be construed accordingly. This provision does not, however, authorise the doing of anything in relation to design right which is for foreign defence purposes or health service purposes within the meaning of ss.240(3) and (4). See The Visiting Forces and International Headquarters (Application of Law) Order 1999, SI1999/1736, art.3.

[60] CDPA 1988, s.240(5).

[61] s.240(6).

[62] *i.e.* where an article no longer required for the services of the crown is disposed of by sale, ss.240(1)(a) and 240(7).

[63] CDPA 1988, s.240(2). It appears that this definition is narrower than the equivalent Crown use provisions in the Registered Designs Act 1949 where "Crown use" is not defined save that is "deemed to include" certain defence and United Nations uses (see RDA 1949, Sch.1,para.1).

[64] CDPA 1988, s.240(3).

[65] National Health Service (Scotland) Act 1978 (c.29), Pt II.

13–133 **Crown use during emergency.** Section 244 of the 1988 Act contains special provisions which apply during a period of emergency[66] and which extend the scope of Crown use. They permit any act which would otherwise be an infringement of design right for any purpose which appears to the government department concerned necessary or expedient:

(a) for the efficient prosecution of any war in which the government is engaged;

(b) for the maintenance of supplies and services essential to the life of the community;

(c) for securing a sufficiency of supplies and services essential for the well-being of the community;

(d) for promoting the productivity of industry, commerce and agriculture;

(e) for fostering and directing export and reducing imports and generally redressing the balance of trade;

(f) generally for ensuring that the whole resources of the community are available for use; or

(g) for assisting the relief of suffering and the restoration and distribution of essential supplies and services in any country outside the United Kingdom which is in grave distress as a result of war.

13–134 **Notification of Crown use to design right owner.** Section 241(1) of the 1988 Act provides that, where Crown use is made, the government department concerned must (unless it is contrary to the public interest, or unless the identity of the design right owner cannot be ascertained) notify the design right owner of the Crown use and give the design right owner such information as to the extent of the Crown use as the design right owner may from time to time require.[67]

13–135 **Terms of Crown use.** Although Crown use will not constitute an infringement of the design right, section 241(2) of the 1988 Act provides that the use must be on terms to be agreed by the government department concerned and the design right owner with the approval of the Treasury. Such agreement may be made before or after the relevant use. In default of agreement, any party may refer the matter to the court for its determination of the terms for the Crown use.[68] In determining a dispute as to the terms for Crown use, a court must have regard to any remuneration which the design right owner is entitled to receive, directly or indirectly, from any government department in respect of the design and to whether the design right owner or the design right owner's predecessor in title has, in the court's opinion, without reasonable cause failed to comply with the department's request for the use of the design on reasonable terms.[69] This plainly suggests that the terms to be agreed by the parties or to be imposed by the court should be "reasonable" terms. It is submitted that the terms should be those which protect the interests of the parties in a manner which is fair and reasonable and which would be agreed by a willing licensor and a willing government department. Whilst this test resembles that for licences of right, it seems likely that the terms which a willing licensor might agree with a willing government department may well be rather different to those which would be agreed with a rival manufacturer. The

---

[66] The period of emergency being a period declared by Order in Council to be a period of emergency, see CDPA 1988, s.244(3).

[67] CDPA 1988, s.241(1). For the position where there is an exclusive licence in force in respect of the design, see para. 13–138, below.

[68] CDPA 1988, ss.241(2) and 252(1). The relevant court with jurisdiction to determine disputes as to the terms for Crown use are defined by s.252(6) as being (a) in England and Wales, the High Court or any patents county court having jurisdiction under s.287; (b) in Scotland the Court of Session and (c) in Northern Ireland, the High Court. For jurisdiction generally, see paras 13–195 *et seq.*, below.

[69] s.252(2).

terms may include provision for payment in addition to any sum which may be payable by way of compensation for loss of profit under section 243.[70] Where the identity of the design right owner cannot be ascertained on reasonable enquiry, the government department concerned may apply to the court which may order that no royalty or other sum should be payable in respect of the Crown use of the design until the owner agrees terms with the department or refers the matter to the court for determination.[71] It is, therefore, in the design right owner's interests to refer the matter to court as soon as possible once he becomes aware of the Crown use.

Compensation for loss of profit. In addition to any other terms which may be agreed or imposed by the court,[72] section 243 of the 1988 Act provides that, where Crown use is made of a design, the government department should pay compensation for any loss suffered by the design right owner or (if there is an exclusive licence in force in respect of the design) the exclusive licensee resulting from such person not being awarded a contract to supply the articles made to the design. Compensation is not payable for losses due to any failure to secure contracts for the supply of articles otherwise than for the services of the Crown.[73] However, although compensation is only payable to the extent that the design right owner or exclusive licensee could have met the contract from his existing manufacturing capacity, it is nevertheless payable even if there were circumstances which would have rendered the design right owner or the exclusive licensee ineligible to be awarded that contract.[74] In determining the level of compensation, regard must be had to the actual profit which would have been made on such a contract and to the extent to which any manufacturing capacity was under-used.[75] The actual level of compensation should be agreed between the design right owner or the exclusive licensee and the government department concerned, with the approval of the Treasury.[76] In the absence of agreement, any of the parties may refer the matter to the court for its determination.[77]

13–136

Rights of third parties in relation to Crown use. In many cases, third parties will have an interest in or in relation to the relevant design right. Accordingly, the 1988 Act provides that the provisions of any licence, assignment or agreement made between the design right owner (or his predecessors or successors in title) and any other person[78] are of no effect in relation to Crown use or any act incidental to Crown use insofar as they seek to restrict or regulate anything done in relation to the design or the use of any model, document or other information relating to the design or seek to provide for the making of payment in respect of, or calculated by reference to such use. Furthermore, the copying or issuing to the public of copies of any such model or document, or any such use, is deemed not to be an infringement of any copyright in the model or document.[79] However, this

13–137

---

[70] s.243(5), see para. 13–136, below.

[71] s.241(3).

[72] *i.e.* under CDPA 1988, s.241.

[73] s.243(4).

[74] s.243(2).

[75] ss.243(2) and 243(3).

[76] Unless the government department is any part of the Scottish Administration, see the Scotland Act 1998 (Consequential Modifications) (No.2) Order 1999 (SI 1999/1820), art.4, Sch.2, para.93(3).

[77] CDPA 1988, ss.243(5) and 252(1).

[78] Other than a government department, CDPA 1988, , s.242(1). See para. 13–131, above.

[79] s.242(1).

is not to be construed as authorising the disclosure of any model, document or information in contravention of the licence, assignment or agreement.[80]

13–138   **Exclusive licences.** Special provisions apply where an exclusive licence[81] has been granted in respect of the relevant design right. The provisions applicable depend upon whether or not the exclusive licence was granted for royalties.[82] Where the exclusive licence was granted for royalties, the licensee is plainly directly interested in the determination of the sum payable by the Crown in respect of Crown use. Accordingly, where such a licence is in force in respect of the relevant design, any agreement between the design right owner and a government department settling the terms for Crown use[83] will require the consent of the exclusive licensee.[84] Further, the exclusive licensee is entitled to recover from the design right owner such part of the payment for Crown use as may be agreed between the design right owner and the licensee. In default of such agreement, any party may refer the matter to the court for its determination.[85] The interest of a licensee under an exclusive licence granted for royalties is also apparent from the fact that a determination by the court of the amount of *any payment* to be made for Crown use is of no effect unless that licensee had been notified of the reference to the court and had been given an opportunity to be heard.[86] If the court is asked to determine the proportion payable to the exclusive licensee, the court is required to determine what would be just having regard to any expenditure incurred by the licensee in developing the design or in making payments to the design right owner in consideration of the licence (other than royalties or other payments determined by reference to the use of the design).[87] Where the licence was an exclusive licence not granted for royalties, the exclusive licensee takes the place of the design right owner for the purposes of being notified of the Crown use and in settling the terms for Crown use under section 241 of the 1988 Act.[88] However, section 241 will not apply in relation to the actions of the licensee by virtue of being authorised by a government department in respect of Crown use.[89]

13–139   **Assignments for royalties.** Special provisions also apply where the design right has been assigned to the design right owner in consideration of royalties. In these circumstances, the settlement of terms for Crown use under section 241 of the 1988 Act has to take into account both the design right owner and the assignor, and any payment for Crown use is to be divided between them in such proportion as may be agreed. In default of agreement, any party may refer the matter to the court for its determination.[90] In these circumstances, the provisions of section 241 do apply in relation to any act incidental to Crown use as they apply in relation to Crown use of the design.[91]

13–140   **Use of model, document or other information.** As mentioned above,[92] the provisions of any licence, assignment or agreement between the design right owner

---

[80] s.242(2).

[81] For the meaning of "exclusive licence", see para. 13–121, above.

[82] See CDPA 1988, s.242(3). "Royalties" include any benefit determined by reference to the use of the design, see s.242(6).

[83] *i.e.* an agreement under CDPA 1988, s.241(2).

[84] s.242(3)(a).

[85] ss.242(3)(a)(ii) and 252(1).

[86] s.252(4).

[87] s.252(5).

[88] s.242(3)(b)(i). For s.241, see para. 13–135, above.

[89] s.242(3)(b)(ii).

[90] CDPA 1988, ss.242(4) and 252(1).

[91] s.242(4)(b).

[92] CDPA 1988, s.242(1) and see para. 13–137, above.

and any person other than a government department are of no effect in relation to Crown use of a design so far as they restrict or regulate anything done in relation to the design, or the use of any model, document or other information relating to it. However, the person entitled to the benefit of such a provision which is thereby rendered inoperative is placed in the position of the design right owner as regards settlement of terms for Crown use.[93]

7. THE RIGHTS OF THE DESIGN RIGHT OWNER AND INFRINGEMENT

A. INTRODUCTION

This Chapter is concerned with the rights that the 1988 Act confers upon a design right owner (*i.e.* the rights to exploit or to deal with the design in a non-litigious context) and with the infringement of those rights. As with copyright, the rights and forms of infringement fall into two categories—primary and secondary. The former are concerned largely with the copying of a design for commercial purposes; the latter with commercial dealings in such copies.

13–141

B. EXCLUSIVE RIGHTS AND PRIMARY INFRINGEMENTS

Exclusive rights of design right owner. Primary infringements of design right are defined by reference to the exclusive rights of the design right owner. Those exclusive rights are set out in section 226(1) of the 1988 Act which provides that:

13–142

"The owner of the design right in a design has the exclusive right to reproduce the design for commercial purposes—
   (a) by making articles to that design, or
   (b) by making a design document recording the design for the purpose of enabling such articles to be made."

Primary infringement. Subject to certain statutory exceptions,[94] it is an infringement of design right for a person without the licence of the design right owner to do or to authorise another to do anything which is the exclusive right of the design right owner.[95] Whether a person has the necessary licence is, of course, a matter of fact to be determined in each case.[96] The meaning of the word "authorise" has already been considered in relation to infringements of copyright.[97]

13–143

Commercial purposes. The design right owner's exclusive rights are limited to the right to reproduce the design for commercial purposes. An act done in relation to an article is only done for commercial purposes if it is done with a view to that article being sold or hired in the course of business.[98] Although this definition does not fit entirely easily with the way in which section 226(1) is phrased, it seems clear enough that its inclusion means that a person who (for example) makes articles to a design intending to use them domestically does not thereby infringe design right. Even if such a person subsequently decides to sell or hire out the relevant articles in the course of business, that person would not be liable

13–144

---

[93] s.242(5).

[94] CDPA 1988, s.226(5) and ss.236–245, see paras 13–163 *et seq.*, below.

[95] s.226(3).

[96] For a discussion of design right licences, see paras 13–119 *et seq.*, above.

[97] See paras 7–130 *et seq.*, above. For a recent case on authorisation in the context of infringement of industrial copyright under the transitional provisions of the 1988 Act, see *Pensher Security Door Co Ltd v Sunderland City Council* [2000] R.P.C. 249 at 276–279 (CA).

[98] CDPA 1988, s.263(3).

for infringement.[99] This result seems, at first sight, strange. However, as a person is unlikely to make many articles with a view to non-commercial purposes, it should in practice create few problems.

(i) Making articles to the design

13–145 **Scope of exclusive right.** Under section 226(1)(a), the design right owner has the exclusive right to reproduce the design for commercial purposes by making articles to the design. The scope of this exclusive right and, therefore, the area of potential primary infringement is defined by section 226(2). This provides that "reproduction of a design by making articles to the design means copying the design so as to produce articles exactly or substantially to that design." It is clear from this that, like copyright, design right is concerned with an exclusive right to copy the design. However, the scope of this exclusive right is significantly different to that conferred by copyright. In copyright cases, the exclusive right is to copy the copyright work or a substantial part of that work.[1] By contrast, in design right cases, the exclusive right is to copy the design so as to produce articles exactly or substantially to that design. As the scope of the exclusive rights conferred by copyright and by design right are different, so too are the tests for infringement. In particular, for design right, it may not be enough that the defendant has copied a part (even a substantial part) of the claimant's design. Instead, one must look at the whole of that design and ask if the defendant's article is made to or substantially to that design.[2]

13–146 **Reproducing the design by "making articles".** The exclusive right relates to the making of articles. As design right is concerned with the protection of a design (*i.e.* with shape or configuration) and not with the particular substrate on which it is recorded nor with the article to which it is first applied, the exclusive right extends to the making of any article provided that article can be said to have been made exactly or substantially to the relevant design.[3] Thus, a person who designs a doll will (assuming design right subsists in the design) have the exclusive right to produce toothbrush holders exactly or substantially to that design.[4] Similarly, there is no reason why the designer of a spoon with a novel handle should not have the exclusive right to apply that design of handle to other articles.[5] On the wording of the 1988 Act, it appears that, provided design right subsists in a design (*i.e.* it was not commonplace in the design field in which it was created), then the design right owner can claim exclusive rights in other areas even if the design would be commonplace in those other areas. Thus, in the example given above, if design right subsisted in the design of the doll, the exclusive rights of the owner would extend to its use in relation to a toothbrush holder even if the design would have been commonplace had it originated in that

---

[99] The fact that the copying was not an infringement means that the copy cannot be an infringing article within CDPA 1988, s.228. Accordingly, dealings with the article will not constitute secondary infringements. As to secondary infringements, see paras 13–157 *et seq.*, below.

[1] CDPA 1988, s.16, see paras 7–23 *et seq.*, above.

[2] See *L. Woolley Jewellers Ltd v A & A Jewellery Ltd* [2003] F.S.R. 15 at paras 15 and 19 (CA). See also *Guild v Eskandar Ltd* [2003] F.S.R. 23 at paras 11 and 58 (CA). This is why careful pleading of the design relied on is essential and why claimants define that design or designs to reflect what the defendant has taken, see para. 13–45, above.

[3] See *Electronic Techniques (Anglia) Ltd v Critchley Components Ltd* [1997] F.S.R. 401 at 418. As to whether the relevant article has been made "exactly or substantially" to the relevant design, see paras 13–149 *et seq.*, below.

[4] This was the example used in the course of Parliamentary debate—see *Hansard*, H.L. Vol.491, cols 1131–1132 and H.L. Vol.495, col.703.

[5] See *Electronic Techniques (Anglia) Ltd v Critchley Components Ltd* [1997] F.S.R. 401 at 418. Whether the making of the other article is covered by the exclusive right will, of course, depend upon whether it has been made exactly or substantially to the relevant design.

design field. Although section 226 refers to the exclusive right to make "articles", it is submitted, both as a matter of statutory construction[6] and as a matter of common sense, that this exclusive right extends to and can be infringed by the making of just a single article to the design.[7] The meaning of the word "article" has already been considered; an article may be a simple article (such as a mug), it may be a composite article (such as a teapot or a car) which is made up of various component articles, or it may be one of those component articles (such as a teapot lid or an exhaust pipe).[8]

The test for infringement. Given the nature of the exclusive rights conferred on the design rights owner, the question of infringement of design right by the making of articles must be approached in two stages; the first is to determine whether there has in fact been copying; the second is to determine whether an article has been made by the alleged infringer either exactly or substantially to the claimant's design.[9]   **13–147**

Copying the design. Design right is not infringed by a person who makes an article or articles to a design which was created independently.[10] Copying must have occurred. Such copying may have been direct or indirect, and it is immaterial whether any intervening acts themselves infringe the design right.[11] Copying may also be established by direct evidence or, more often, by inference from the surrounding circumstances including the extent of the similarities between the claimant's design and the defendant's article.[12] However, the fact that a component article was "bought in" (off the shelf) by the defendant may defeat an inference of copying that might otherwise arise from such a similarity.[13]   **13–148**

Infringement by making articles exactly or substantially to the design. Proof of copying by itself is not enough. To establish an infringement, the claimant must also show that the alleged infringer has copied the design "so as to produce articles exactly or substantially to that design".[14] This plainly requires a comparison to be made. However, it is important to note that on the wording of section 226(2), the comparison to be made is between the allegedly infringing   **13–149**

---

[6] Under the Interpretation Act 1978, s.6(c).

[7] See *C & H Engineering Ltd v F. Klucznik & Sons Ltd* [1992] F.S.R. 421 at 428 ("allegedly infringing article or articles"). It might be argued to the contrary that the equivalent provision in the Registered Designs Act 1949, s.7(1) (as amended by the CDPA 1988) and also CDPA 1988, s.51 both refer to "an article" (*i.e.* in the singular) and that this suggests that the use of the plural in the design right provisions of the CDPA 1988 was deliberate. However, it seems unlikely that the exclusive rights of a design right owner were not intended to cover cases where a "one-off" article was made to a design. Significantly, the acts of secondary infringement are defined by reference to dealings with " *an* infringing article", see paras 13–157 *et seq*, below.

[8] See para. 13–49, above.

[9] See *C & H Engineering Ltd v F. Klucznik & Sons Ltd* [1992] F.S.R. 421 at 428.

[10] CDPA 1988, s.226(2) was added by amendment to the original Bill with the specific purpose of clarifying that the use of the term "reproduction" in design right meant (as it does in copyright) that proof of copying was essential to proving infringement, see *Hansard*, H.L. Vol.495, col.703. For other Parliamentary discussion on this point, see *Hansard*, H.L. Vol.491, cols 1132, 1133; and H.L. Vol.494, cols 125, 126.

[11] CDPA 1988, s.226(4). For a discussion of direct and indirect copying, see paras 7–14 *et seq*., above.

[12] See para. 13–150, below. The extent and nature of the similarities may raise the inference of copying and may shift the onus on to the defendant to prove that he did not copy (see *A. Fulton Co Ltd v Grant Barnett & Co Ltd* [2001] R.P.C. 257 at para.96). In *C & H Engineering Ltd v F. Klucznick & Sons Ltd* [1992] F.S.R. 421 at 429, the court was satisfied on the evidence that there had been copying whereas in *Ocular Sciences Ltd v Aspect Vision Care Ltd* [1997] R.P.C. 289 at 423–424, the alleged infringer was able to rebut the inference of copying by showing that it had gone through its own independent design process. The meaning of "copying" is also discussed in detail in relation to copyright at para. 7–17 *et seq*., above.

[13] *Baby Dan AS v Brevi SRL* [1999] F.S.R. 377 at 388.

[14] CDPA 1988, s.226(2).

article on the one hand and the claimant's design on the other, and the issue is whether the former has been made exactly or substantially to the latter. The allegedly infringing article does not have to be of the same type as that with which the relevant design was concerned.[15] However, it does have to be an article. The design, on the other hand, may be of the whole or of any part of an article.[16] Where the design is of a whole article, the required comparison should be relatively straightforward—particularly where the design is for the same type of article as the allegedly infringing article—for then the comparison is of like for like.[17] However, where the design relied on is the design of a part of an article, the comparison is likely to be more difficult. Taking the example of the teapot, it seems strange to argue that the defendant's allegedly infringing teapot can have been produced exactly or substantially to the claimant's design for the spout of a teapot. Nevertheless, the fact that the definition of "design" in section 213 allows a claimant to assert design right in a part of an article[18] suggests that section 226 should be construed as allowing such a design (the design of a part of an article) to be infringed by the making of an article, and this conclusion would appear to be supported by the authorities.[19] It also seems in keeping with the intention of Parliament.[20]

13-150 **Exactly or substantially.** Where the copying does not produce an article made exactly to the claimant's design, the question whether it has been made *substantially* to that design is to be determined objectively through the eyes of those persons to whom the claimant's design is directed.[21] On the one hand, any similarities, in particular similarities in respect of unusual or attractive design features, may lead to the conclusion that, despite any other differences, the allegedly infringing article has been made substantially to the claimant's design. It is submitted that an objective observer may form the view that an article has been made substantially to a design even though that design forms only a small part of the article in quantitative terms, provided it plays an important role in qualitative terms.[22] On the other hand, similarities in respect of features whose design is dictated solely or largely by the function which the article is to perform are likely

---

[15] See para. 13–146, above.

[16] See para. 13–44 *et seq.*, above.

[17] As in *C & H Engineering Ltd v F. Klucznik & Sons Ltd* [1992] F.S.R. 421 where the allegedly infringing pig fenders were compared with the claimant's design for a pig fender (see para. 13–161, below). These were the sort of cases referred to in the course of Parliamentary debate—see *Hansard*, H.L. Vol.495, col.703.

[18] See para. 13–45, above.

[19] See for example, *Scholes Windows Ltd v Magnet Ltd* [2002] F.S.R. 10, a case concerning a design for a small "S" shaped horn extension to the upper casement of a window which the defendant had copied in its windows. The trial judge stated that, if the design had not been commonplace, the defendant would have been liable for infringement of design right in the design. It would seem, therefore, that he accepted that the defendant's window had been produced exactly or substantially to that design (see [2000] F.S.R. 432 at 446–447). The Court of Appeal stated that it did not need to express any concluded view on the question of infringement but commented that it would have been reluctant to interfere with his conclusion (see [2002] F.S.R. 172 at para.51). See also the comments of Laddie J. in *Electronic Techniques (Anglia) Ltd v Critchley Components Ltd* [1997] F.S.R. 401 at p.418 and *Lambretta Clothing Co Ltd v Teddy Smith (UK) Ltd* [2004] EWCA Civ 886 at para.75.

[20] In the course of Parliamentary debate, the example used was of fins at the end of an aircraft wing which, whilst small, were plainly of great significance and should be capable of protection—see *Hansard* H.L. Vol.494, col.124. It is submitted that an alleged infringer whose aircraft wings incorporated the design of such fins would, therefore, be producing articles (*i.e.* the wings) *substantially* to the claimant's design (*i.e.* of the fins).

[21] *See C & H Engineering Ltd v F. Klucznik & Sons Ltd* [1992] F.S.R. 421 at 428 and *Baby Dan AS v Brevi SRL* [1999] F.S.R. 377 at 385.

[22] In Parliament, an example used was of fins at the end of an aircraft wing—see *Hansard* H.L. Vol.494, col.124. Such fins, whilst small, would plainly be of great significance and should be capable of protection. It is submitted that an alleged infringer whose aircraft wings incorporated

to be of little assistance to a claimant.[23] If the alleged infringer has used the design in making a different type of article, it may be that the impact of the design in that article is very different—particularly where the other features of shape and configuration of the article cause the whole article to seem very different to the design relied on.[24] In such a case, an objective observer may take the view that the article as a whole has not been made substantially to the design and the claim for infringement would, therefore, fail. Where the design is defined by reference to the most detailed and specific dimensions, then the mere fact that the allegedly infringing articles cannot be distinguished from the claimant's design by visual inspection is not enough; the claimant would have to show that the defendant had produced an extremely similar design in order to prove infringement.[25] By contrast, a circuit board made to a design recorded in a circuit diagram could take a number of forms. Thus visual similarities may not always be required in order to establish an infringement of design right.[26]

Treatment of commonplace and excluded features. Section 226 of the 1988 Act does not make clear how the court should approach the question of infringement of a design which includes features which taken individually would be commonplace or features from which design right is excluded.[27] Given that design right subsists in the whole of a design and not just in its non-commonplace features,[28] it is submitted that commonplace features should not be ignored for the purposes of making the comparison between the allegedly infringing article and the claimant's design, although a court would be unlikely to find that an allegedly infringing article has been made exactly or substantially to the claimant's design unless there are other more striking similarities than in respect of commonplace features.[29] The position is less clear where the design includes features from which design right is excluded but, again, there seems to be no reason why those features should be ignored when considering whether an allegedly infringing article has been made exactly or substantially to the claimant's design. Such features are a part of the overall design even though design right does not subsist in them themselves. If, of course, the only features of the design which have been copied are excluded features, then there can be no infringement of any design right.

    Given the nature of the test for infringement, a claimant should pay careful attention to the type of articles which the alleged infringer has made and would be well advised to frame his design right claim in the way which produces the most favourable comparison between his design and what he believes the alleged infringer has taken.[30]

13–151

---

the design of such fins would, therefore, be producing articles (*i.e.* the wings) *substantially* to the claimant's design (*i.e.* of the fins).

[23] As was the case in *C & H Engineering Ltd v F. Klucznik & Sons Ltd* [1992] F.S.R. 421 and para. 13–152, below. See also *Baby Dan SA v Brevi SRL* [1999] F.S.R. 377 at 390, where similarities in relation to features as simple as a hinge support and a hook were insufficient to show that the articles had been made substantially to the claimant's design.

[24] See *Electronic Techniques (Anglia) Ltd v Critchley Components Ltd* [1997] F.S.R. 401 at 418.

[25] See *Ocular Sciences Ltd v Aspect Vision Care Ltd* [1997] R.P.C. 289 at 424.

[26] See *Mackie Designs Inc v Behringer Specialised Studio Equipment (UK) Ltd* [1999] R.P.C. 717 at 719. See also *Ocular Sciences Ltd v Aspect Vision Care Ltd* [1997] R.P.C. 689 at p.429.

[27] *i.e.* by the exclusions contained in CDPA 1988, s.213(3).

[28] See para. 13–71, above.

[29] This appears to have been the approach adopted in *C & H Engineering Ltd v F. Klucznik & Sons Ltd* [1992] F.S.R. 421 where the court, when determining whether there had been an infringement, had regard to the whole of the claimant's fender despite having found that pig fenders without a roll bar were commonplace. For a detailed discussion of the decision in *C & H Engineering*, see para. 13–152, below.

[30] See *Ocular Sciences Ltd v Aspect Vision Care Ltd* [1997] R.P.C. 289 at 422.

13–152   *C & H Engineering v F. Klucznick & Sons.* The different ways in which the test for infringement may be applied can be seen from the decision in *C & H Engineering Ltd v Klucznik & Sons Ltd*.[31] There, the relevant design was of a whole article—namely a whole pig fender.[32] The design was not commonplace because it had incorporated a two-inch pipe acting as a roll bar on the top of an otherwise commonplace pig fender. The alleged infringer had also produced pig fenders with a roll bar and its incorporation of the roll bar had been the result of copying. Objectively viewed, however, the allegedly infringing fender was not made exactly or substantially to the design of the claimant's fender. Whilst there were similarities between the fenders, those similarities were in respect of features which pig fenders must have in order to perform their function as pig fenders. Further, an objective observer would be struck by the differences in the designs of the fenders and, in particular, by design features unique to the allegedly infringing fenders which allowed them to be stacked. Thus, despite the evidence of copying, the claimant's case failed.

It seems that *C & H Engineering Ltd* might (depending upon the precise facts) have been argued in several alternative ways. Although it seems unlikely that any of these would have led to a different result in that case, a discussion of these alternatives shows how the test in section 226 works and how claimants may be able to strengthen their position by framing their design right claims in the way which produces the closest comparison between their designs and the articles which the alleged infringer has made. Thus, instead of relying on the design of the whole fender, the claimant could have relied on the design of just the roll bar,[33] making it the claimant's design for the purposes of the comparison. This would have allowed the claimant to argue that other parts of its fender[34] were irrelevant for the purposes of making the comparison. Instead, the comparison would have been between the claimant's design of the roll bar on the one hand and the alleged infringer's article—being either the alleged infringer's fender or the alleged infringer's roll bar (assuming that it was itself a separate article)—on the other. However, on the facts of *C & H Engineering Ltd*, it is submitted that the claimant's case would still have failed. If the claimant's design of a roll bar was compared with the alleged infringer's fender, then that fender was plainly not an article made exactly to that design and was unlikely to have been an article made substantially to it.[35] Similarly, if the claimant's design of a roll bar was compared with the alleged infringer's roll bar, then it seems unlikely that the claimant could have persuaded the court that so functional a feature as a roll bar had been made exactly or substantially to that design.

13–153   *Parker & Parker v Tidball.* The difficulties which may arise in applying the test for infringement can be seen in *Parker & Parker v Tidball*[36] where the court was concerned with various design features of leather cases for mobile phones. Some of these were found to be commonplace and others were excluded by the must fit exclusion. However, each of the remainder (each being the design of a part of an article) was treated as a separate design in which design right subsisted. In approaching the question of infringement of each of these designs, the court first

---

[31] [1992] F.S.R. 421.

[32] *i.e.* the relevant design was of the entire pig fender and not of any individual part of it. As to the contrary view (*i.e.* that the relevant design was of the roll bar only), see *Parker & Parker v Tidball* [1997] F.S.R. 680 at 691 and see para. 13–153, below.

[33] On the basis that its design was the design of a part of an article (*i.e.* as part of the fender) or, if as appears to have been the case, the roll bar had its own separate form, as the design of an article in its own right. For the meaning of "an article", see para. 13–49, above.

[34] Including those, such as the stacking features, which the court found to be significant when looking at the whole article.

[35] Even on the basis that the word "substantial" has a qualitative meaning, see para. 13–150, above.

[36] [1997] F.S.R. 680.

asked whether the relevant design feature had been copied. It then compared the whole of the defendant's allegedly infringing mobile phone case with the whole of the plaintiff's mobile phone case in order to determine whether the defendant had made articles exactly or substantially to the plaintiff's design.[37] It is submitted that this approach was incorrect. First, the approach seems contrary to section 226 of the 1988 Act. The references in that section to *"a design"* and to *"that design"* are plainly references to the design relied upon by the claimant, and the issue is whether the alleged act of copying has produced an article exactly or substantially *"to that design"*. If the relevant design is the design of a part of an article then it is against that design—the design of the part of an article—that the allegedly infringing article must be compared. The wording of the section does not require and, indeed does not justify, any comparison being made with the article of which the claimant's design is a part. Moreover, whilst the judge in *Parker & Parker v Tidball* plainly considered himself to be following the approach in *C & H Engineering Ltd*, it is submitted that he misconstrued the decision in that case. The judge took the view that the relevant design in *C & H Engineering Ltd* had been the design of *a part of an article* rather than of a whole article—namely the design of just the roll bar rather than the design of a pig fender.[38] In fact, whilst the point is never expressly addressed, it would appear that the claimant in *C & H Engineering Ltd* was asserting design right in the whole of its drawing of a fender and not just in any part,[39] and that is why the court in that case compared the allegedly infringing fender with the whole of the claimant's fender.[40] On this basis, it is submitted that whilst a comparison with the whole of the plaintiff's mobile phone case would have been justified had the plaintiff been relying upon the design of the whole case, it was not justified when the plaintiff was relying on designs of *parts* of the case. It was suggested in *Parker & Parker v Tidball*[41] that the justification for testing for infringement of design right in the design of *a part* of an article by reference to the whole article is that there could otherwise be no infringement of the design of part of an article. However, it is submitted that this is not the case; whilst it may well be correct to say that a whole article cannot be made exactly to the design of a part of an article, an article may still be made *substantially* to the design of a part such that it would satisfy the test for infringement.[42] In any event, given the wide meaning of "article",[43] a claimant may, in those cases where an article is made up of various component parts which themselves qualify as articles, be able to tailor his design right claim so as to rely on the design right subsisting in one of those component parts.

A. Fulton v Totes Isotoner. The way in which a design right claim can be tailored can be seen in *A. Fulton Co Ltd v Totes Isotoner (UK) Ltd*[44] There the claimant had designed a umbrella case. The defendant's umbrella case was copied from that design but had a section cut out from its top cuff (where the umbrella was inserted). The claimant accordingly relied not only on the design of the whole

13–154

---

[37] [1997] F.S.R. 680 at 691 and 702–706.
[38] [1997] F.S.R. 680 at 691.
[39] [1992] F.S.R. 421, see the drawing reproduced at 422, the issue numbered (3) at 425 and the words of Aldous J. at 425.
[40] As the designs for the leather cases had some non-commonplace features, it is submitted that *Parker & Parker v Tidball* [1997] F.S.R. 680, above, could have been argued on the basis that the relevant design was the design of the whole case—albeit that design right was excluded from certain "must fit" features. However, it appears that this would have made no difference to the result.
[41] [1997] F.S.R. 680 at 691.
[42] See para. 13–150, above.
[43] See para. 13–49, above.
[44] [2003] EWCA 1514.

case but also on the design of the whole case minus a cut-out section—thereby matching what the defendant had taken. The claim based on the design of the whole case failed but the claim based on the design minus the cut-out succeeded.

(ii) Making a design document

13–155   Under section 226(1)(b), the design right owner has the exclusive right to reproduce the design for commercial purposes by making a design document recording the design for the purpose of enabling "such articles" to be made. In this context, the reference to "such articles" is a reference back to articles made to the design which are the subject of section 226(1)(a).[45] A person who does this or who authorises another to do this, without the licence of the design right owner, is liable for infringement of design right. The meaning of "commercial purposes", "authorises" and of "design document" have already been considered.[46] It is not clear whether the words "recording the design" mean that the design document in question must have recorded the whole of the claimant's design or whether the recording of some part of the design would be sufficient. On the one hand, the wording of section 226(1)(b) suggests that the record should be of the whole design because the making of the design document recording the design is not qualified by the words "exactly or substantially" in section 226(2). On the other hand, the court in *C & H Engineering Ltd*[47] seems to have accepted that there had been "copying [of] the design" for the purposes of section 226(1)(a) even though the evidence was only of the copying of a part of the design.[48] If the copying of a part was sufficient for these purposes, then why would the recording of a part of a design for the purposes of section 226(1)(b) not also be so? Given that the relevant design document must be created by the alleged infringer for the purpose of enabling articles to be made exactly or substantially to the claimant's design,[49] the latter interpretation would appear to be preferable.

13–156   **For the purpose of enabling articles to be made to the design.** Under section 226(1)(b), the making of the relevant design document must have been "for the purpose of enabling" articles to be made to the design right owner's design. This, it is submitted, would operate where a person makes or authorises another to make the relevant design document knowing or intending it to be used in the production process of the article in question. It would not, however, operate where at the time of creation, there was no intention so to use the document.[50] Whilst it is not clear, it would seem that the words "for the purpose" govern the word "making" so that a person who makes a design document at the request of another but without having any knowledge as to that other person's purpose would not be liable for infringement, although this would mean that the person making that request could not be liable for authorising.[51] Whether the relevant purpose is present must, it seems, be judged as at the time that the design document was

---

[45] For the meaning of "making articles to the design" under CDPA 1988, s.226(1)(a)—see para. 13–149, above.

[46] See paras 13–79, 13–143 and 13–144, above and CDPA 1988, s.263(1).

[47] [1992] F.S.R. 421.

[48] [1992] F.S.R. 421 at 429. It was only after making a finding of copying that the court in *C & H Engineering Ltd* then went on to consider whether the articles had been made exactly or substantially to the claimant's design. The finding of copying does not, therefore, appear to have been influenced by the reference later in s.226(2) to articles being made "substantially" to the design.

[49] See para. 13–156, below.

[50] Because, for example, it was created as an artistic work in its own right or even because it was created for a brochure.

[51] It is likely to be rare in industrial design cases that the maker of a design document would not realise that the document is to be used in the process of making articles to the design.

created. If at that time there was no intention to make articles to the design, then there could be no infringement under this head even if the document was subsequently used for that purpose.

C. SECONDARY INFRINGEMENTS

The acts of secondary infringement are defined by section 227(1) of the 1988 Act which provides that design right is infringed[52] by a person who, without the licence of the design right owner—   **13–157**

"(a) imports into the United Kingdom for commercial purposes,[53] or

(b) has in his possession for commercial purposes, or

(c) sells, lets for hire, or offers or exposes for sale or hire, in the course of a business,[54]

an article which is, and which he knows or has reason to believe is, an infringing article."

In summary, therefore, secondary infringements of design right involve some form of dealing with an infringing article by a person who has the requisite knowledge. This is very similar to the position in relation to copyright and many of the required elements have already been dealt with that context.[55] The words "commercial purposes" have already been considered in the context of primary infringement of design right.[56]

(i) An infringing article

A person is not liable for a secondary infringement of design right unless he knows or has reason to believe that the article with which he is dealing is an infringing article. An article is an infringing article in relation to a design either if its making to that design was an infringement of the design right in that design,[57] or if it has been or if it is proposed to be imported into the United Kingdom and its making to that design in the United Kingdom would have been an infringement of design right in the design or a breach of an exclusive licence agreement relating to the design.[58] On the other hand, a design document is not an infringing article even if the making of the design document was or would have constituted an infringement of design right.[59] Whilst this means that a person who imports or deals with[60] a design document will not be liable for a secondary infringement, that person's activities may justify the design right owner in seeking a *quia timet* injunction if there is evidence to suggest that the design document is to be used to make articles to the design.   **13–158**

Presumption as to time of making article. If it is shown that an article has been made to a design in which design right subsists or in which design right has   **13–159**

---

[52] Unless one of the exceptions applies, see paras 13–163 *et seq.*, below.

[53] In *Baby Dan AS v Brevi SRL* [1999] F.S.R. 377 at 391, it was stated that a foreign manufacturer which arranged and charged for transporting its goods to its UK distributor, would be jointly liable for importation of infringing articles.

[54] In *Baby Dan AS v Brevi SRL* [1999] F.S.R. 377, it was also held that a foreign manufacturer whose goods and catalogue were displayed at a UK trade fair and which supplied UK retailers through a UK corporate vehicle was liable for offering infringing articles for sale.

[55] CDPA 1988, ss.22 and 23, as to which see Ch.8, above.

[56] See para. 13–144, above. See also CDPA 1988 ss.23(a), (c) and (d).

[57] CDPA 1988, s.228(2). As to whether the making of the article was an infringement, see paras 13–146 *et seq.*, above.

[58] s.228(3).

[59] s.228(6).

[60] *i.e.* possesses the design document or sells, lets for hire or offers it for sale or hire.

subsisted at any time, then there is a presumption until the contrary is proved that the article was made at a time when design right subsisted.[61] The onus is, therefore, on the alleged infringer to show that the article was made at a time either before design right subsisted[62] or at a time after design right had expired.[63]

13–160   **Importation from European Community.** If an article may be lawfully imported into the United Kingdom under any enforceable European Community right within the meaning of section 2(1) of the European Communities Act 1972,[64] then that article is not an infringing article.[65]

(ii) Treatment of territorial waters and continental shelf

13–161   When considering whether there has been a secondary infringement and whether an article is an infringing article, the provisions of section 257 of the 1988 Act should be borne in mind and, in particular, the provision which treats the territorial waters of the United Kingdom as a part of the United Kingdom. The only act of infringement defined by reference to the United Kingdom is importation.[66] Whether bringing goods into the territorial waters can constitute importation has already been considered in relation to infringements of copyright.[67]

(iii) Knowledge or reason to believe

13–162   To establish a secondary infringement of design right, the claimant must prove that the person importing or dealing with the infringing article knew or had reason to believe that the article in question was an infringing article. The same requirement of knowledge or of reason to believe also forms a part of the definition of secondary infringements of copyright and has been discussed in detail in that context.[68]

8. EXCEPTIONS TO RIGHTS

A. Introduction

13–163   The rights of design right owners and the provisions as to infringement of design right are subject to the various exceptions set out in sections 236 to 245 of the 1988 Act.[69] These exceptions include the provisions relating to licences of right[70] and to Crown use of designs,[71] both of which have already been considered.[72] The other exceptions are (1) where there is parallel copyright protection (section 236) and (2) where the Secretary of State makes an appropriate Order under section 245.

---

[61] CDPA 1988, s.228(4).
[62] *i.e.* before the design was recorded in a design document, see para. 13–78, above, or at a time before the design qualified for design right, see para. 13–81, above.
[63] See paras 13–100 *et seq.*, above.
[64] c.68.
[65] CDPA 1988, s.228(5).
[66] CDPA 1988, s.227(1)(a).
[67] See para. 8–14, above.
[68] See Ch.8, above.
[69] CDPA 1988, ss.226(5) and 227(2).
[70] ss.237–239.
[71] ss.240–244.
[72] For licences of right see paras 13–123 *et seq.*, above. For Crown use, see paras 13–131 *et seq.*, above.

B. PARALLEL COPYRIGHT PROTECTION—SECTIONS 236 AND 51

Sections 236 and 51. As has been seen, the intention behind the 1988 Act was, as far as possible, to remove industrial design from the sphere of copyright.[73] Sections 236 and 51 are the means by which the 1988 Act attempts to draw the boundary between copyright protection for artistic works and design right protection for industrial designs and to make the two forms of protection mutually exclusive.[74] The need for these provisions arises from the fact that many designs are recorded in works in which copyright may subsist.   **13–164**

Statement of section 236 of the 1988 Act. Section 236 of the 1988 Act provides that "[w]here copyright subsists in a work which consists of or includes a design in which design right subsists, it is not an infringement of design right in the design to do anything which is an infringement of copyright in that work". In other words, the prospect of dual protection against any particular act is excluded. If that act infinges copyright, it will not also infringe design right. This would apply even in those cases where the copyright owner and the design right owner are different persons.[75]   **13–165**

Effect of section 51. The significance of the section 236 exception to design right protection is much more limited than may at first appear. This is because section 51 provides that "[i]t is not an infringement of any copyright in a design document or model recording or embodying a design for anything other than an artistic work or typeface to make an article to the design or to copy an article made to the design". Thus, where section 51 operates, the relevant acts cannot be infringements of copyright, accordingly section 236 would not prevent a person suing for infringement of such design right may subsist in the design.   **13–166**

Examples. The effect of section 51 is considered in detail later in this Chapter. For present purposes, the operation of sections 236 and 51 is best seen by way of examples.[76] In these examples, it is to be assumed that both copyright and design right subsist.   **13–167**

(1) A painting of an imaginary chair is an artistic work. It also records the painter's design *of* a chair. However, the painting is not a design document or model *for* anything. It is a thing in itself. Accordingly section 51 would not operate to exclude copyright protection and, by reason of section 236, there is no design right protection in respect of acts that would infringe copyright.

(2) A preliminary drawing of an imaginary chair produced by the artist prior to painting the picture referred to in (1) above would be an artistic work and would in one sense be recording the design *of* a chair.[77] However, the drawing is not a design *for* a chair. It is the design *for* an artistic work (the painting) so, again, section 51 would have no application. Again, by reason of section 236, there is no design right protection in respect of acts that would infringe copyright.

(3) A craftsman draws a design for a new style of chair which he intends to make by hand. The drawing would be an artistic work. It also records the design both *of* and also *for* a chair. However, it is likely that the chair

---

[73] See para. 13–29, above.

[74] See *Hansard*, H.L. Vol.491, col.1136.

[75] See para. 13–111, above.

[76] CDPA 1988, s.51 is considered in more detail at paras 13–278 *et seq.*, below.

[77] A similar example was used in the course of debate in Parliament, see *Hansard*, H.L. Vol.491, col.1136.

depicted would itself be an artistic work—being a work of artistic craftsmanship. If so, section 51 would not operate. Once again, by reason of section 236, there is no design right protection in respect of acts that would infringe copyright.

(4) An employee of a furniture warehouse draws a design for a chair which is to be mass-produced on a production line. The drawing is both the design *of* and *for* a chair but in this case that chair is unlikely to be a work of artistic craftsmanship.[78] Section 51 would apply and a person who makes a chair to that design or who copies a chair made to the design would not infringe the copyright in that drawing. Accordingly, section 236 would not exclude an action for infringement of design right by the design right owner in respect of those acts.

(5) The photocopying of the drawing referred to in (4) above would not be one of the acts to which section 51 applies. Thus, a person who makes such a photocopy would still infringe copyright and section 236 would defeat any action by the design right owner for infringement of design right.[79]

(6) By contrast, a person who photographs a chair made to the design drawing referred to in (4) above would probably be copying an article made to the design. Section 51 would, therefore, operate. However, if there was no infringement of copyright, section 236 would not operate to prevent the design right owner suing for infringement of design right.[80]

C. ORDER OF SECRETARY OF STATE—SECTION 245

13–168   Under section 245, the Secretary of State may, if it appears to him to be necessary in order to comply with an international obligation or to secure reciprocal protection for British designs in other countries, make an Order providing that acts of a description specified in the Order do not infringe design right.[81] The Order may make different provision for different descriptions of design or article.[82] To date, no such Order has been made.

9. PARTIES TO ACTION AND REMEDIES FOR INFRINGEMENT

A. THOSE ENTITLED TO SUE FOR INFRINGEMENT

13–169   The persons who may sue for infringement of design right have already been considered in Chapter 22 of this work. In summary, they include the following:

---

[78] See *George Hensher Ltd v Restawile Upholstery (Lancs.) Ltd* [1975] R.P.C. 454 and para. 13–24, above.

[79] This is the situation enviaged by Mance L.J. in *Lambretta Clothing Co Ltd v Teddy Smith (UK) Ltd* [2004] EWCA Civ 886 at para.84. Making the photocopy would usually, provided it is done for commercial purposes and with the purpose of enabling articles to be made to the design, amount to an infringement within CDPA 1988, ss.226(1)(b) and 263(1), *i.e.* the making of a design document recording the design.

[80] Again, assuming the photograph was taken for commercial purposes and with the purpose of enabling chairs to be made to the design, its taking would amount to an infringement within CDPA 1988, ss.226(1)(b) and 263(1).

[81] CDPA 1988, s.245(1).

[82] s.245(2).

namely, the legal owner of design right,[83] the equitable owner,[84] an exclusive licensee[85] and a joint owner.[86]

B. THOSE WHO MAY BE SUED

The position as regards those who may be sued is similar to that which applies in copyright.[87] They include the person who actually does the relevant act (including employees of companies) and, in the case of the primary infringements, a person who authorises that act (including, although depending upon their level of personal involvement, directors of companies). There may be one infringer or a number of joint tortfeasors.   **13–170**

C. REMEDIES

Section 229(2). Section 229(2) of the 1988 Act provides that, in an action for infringement: **13–171**

"... all such relief by way of damages, injunctions, accounts or otherwise is available to the plaintiff as is available in respect of the infringement of any other property right."

This provision is identically worded to section 96(2) which applies in respect of remedies for infringement of copyright. The nature of these remedies has already been fully considered in Chapter 22.[88] In this chapter, reference is made only to the particular sections of the 1988 Act relating to design right.

Damages. A design right owner or an exclusive licensee is entitled to claim damages for any infringement of design right, and section 229(3) provides that a court may, having regard to all the circumstances and in particular to the flagrancy of the infringement and any benefit accruing to the defendant by reason of the infringement, award such additional damages as the justice of the case may require.[89] The way in which the courts approach the question of damages has already been considered in detail in relation to copyright.[90] As with copyright, the damages recoverable for a primary infringement of design right may be limited where the defendant is an innocent infringer as defined in section 233(1).[91] Unlike copyright, there is also a provision limiting damages for secondary infringements where the defendant establishes that the infringing article in question was innocently acquired by him or his predecessor in title.[92] In such a case, section 233(2) provides that the only remedy available against that defendant for that infringement is damages not exceeding a reasonable royalty in respect of the act in   **13–172**

---

[83] See para. 22–15, below.

[84] See paras 22–17 *et seq.*, below. The legal owner must be joined (or an assignment of legal title obtained) before an equitable owner can obtain final relief.

[85] See paras 22–20 *et seq.*, below. The rights of an exclusive licensee are concurrent with those of the design right owner.

[86] See para. 22–29, below.

[87] As to which, see paras 22–32 *et seq.*, below.

[88] See paras 22–113 *et seq.*, below.

[89] For the identically worded provisions as to additional damages in copyright, see CDPA 1988, s.97(2).

[90] See paras 22–162 *et seq.*, below. In a recent design right case, it was stated that for the additional damages to be awarded, there must be some additional measure of turpitude in the actions of the defendant, see *Novum (Overseas) Ltd v Iceland Foods plc* [2002] EWHC 53 at paras 125–128.

[91] See para. 22–34, below.

[92] "Innocently acquired" means that the person acquiring the article did not know and had no reason to believe that the article in question was an infringing article, see CDPA 1988, s.233(3). The test for innocent acquisition is an objective one, see *Badge Sales v PSM International* (unreported, June 11, 2004).

respect of which complaint is made.[93] As with copyright, in a case where a design right owner has concurrent rights with an exclusive licensee, the court in assessing damages must take into account the terms of the licence and any pecuniary remedy already awarded or available to either in respect of the infringement.[94]

13–173 **Limitation on damages—where design right owner unknown.** As has been seen,[95] a person may seek a licence of right in respect of a design where the design right owner is unknown. Where such a licence is granted but it is subsequently discovered that the licence had not been available, the licensee will not be liable for damages (or an account of profits) for the period for which he was unaware that a licence was not available.

13–174 **Injunctions.** The principles upon which a court may grant final and interlocutory injunctions are dealt with elsewhere.[96] There are, however, various situations in which a court will not grant an injunction in a design right case. First, as has already been noted, an injunction may not be granted in an action for secondary infringement where the defendant can show that the infringing article in question had been acquired innocently.[97] Secondly, an injunction will not be granted in any action for infringement of design right in a design[98] where a licence of right is available under sections 237 or 238 of the 1988 Act[99] and where the defendant undertakes to take such a licence on terms to be agreed or, in default of agreement, settled by the Comptroller.[1] This limitation will not, however, preclude the grant of an injunction covering the period between the date of the Order and the time when the licence of right becomes available.

13–175 **Accounts.** As with cases of infringement of copyright, a plaintiff may opt for an account of profits instead of damages.[2] As has been seen,[3] an account is not available in a case of secondary infringement where the defendant establishes that the infringing article in question was innocently acquired by him or his predecessor in title. Further, where the defendant undertakes to take a licence of right or where the design right owner is unknown, the right to an account is limited in the same way that the right to damages was limited.[4] Where an action relates to an infringement where an exclusive licence has concurrent rights with the design right owner, no account of profits may be directed if an award of damages has been made or an account of profits directed in favour of the other person with concurrent rights. If an account of profits is ordered, then (subject to any other agreement) the court must apportion the profits as between the owners of the

---

[93] CDPA 1988, s.233(2). The burden of proof being on the defendant who seeks to rely on s.233(2), see *Badge Sales v PSM International* (unreported, June 11, 2004). There is no copyright equivalent to this provision.

[94] s.235(4)(a). This applies whether or not the design right owner and the exclusive licensee are both parties to the action. These provisions and their copyright equivalent, s.102(4), are discussed at para. 22–103, below.

[95] See para. 13–129, above.

[96] For the interlocutory relief available (including interlocutory injunctions, *Anton Piller* orders, orders to disclose the identity of infringers and *Mareva* injunctions), see paras 22–120 *et seq.*, below. For final injunctions, see paras 22–150 *et seq.*, below.

[97] See CDPA 1988, s.233(2) and see para. 13–172, above.

[98] *i.e.* whether primary or secondary infringement.

[99] For licences of right, see paras 13–123 *et seq.*, above.

[1] See CDPA 1988, s.239. See para. 13–176, below.

[2] For a full discussion of the principles upon which a court may order an account of profits, see para. 22–161 and para. 22–175 *et seq.*, below.

[3] See CDPA 1988, s.233(2)discussed in para. 13–172, above.

[4] See paras 13–176 and 13–180, below.

concurrent rights in such manner as it thinks just.[5] Again, this applies whether or not both the design right owner and the exclusive licensee were parties to the action.[6]

Effect of undertaking by defendant to take a licence of right. A defendant in   **13–176**
proceedings for infringement of design right may restrict the remedies available against him by giving an undertaking to take a licence of right (assuming one is available) on terms to be agreed or to be settled by the Comptroller. If the defendant gives such an undertaking, section 239(1) of the 1988 Act provides that no injunction shall be granted against him, no order for delivery up shall be made under section 230, and that the amount recoverable against him by way of damages or on an account of profits shall not exceed double the amount which would have been payable by him as licensee if such a licence on those terms had been granted before the earliest infringement.[7] It should be noted, however, that this limitation only applies to remedies otherwise available against the defendant in respect of an infringement committed after licences of right became available in respect of the relevant designs.[8]

The defendant may give such an undertaking at any time before a final order in the proceedings without any admission of liability.[9] Thus, despite giving an undertaking, the defendant may still contest matters at issue in the infringement proceedings[10] including, for example, whether design right subsists in the plaintiff's design and whether the defendant's activities constitute an infringement. This raises the question of the status of the licence if the proceedings are subsequently determined against the plaintiff. Clearly a term may be included in the licence making it clear that the licence will determine in the event that the defendant's actions were found not to infringe design right. The position is less clear as regards such money as may have already have been paid under such a licence. In *Roger Bance and Anor's Licence of Right (Copyright) Application*,[11] the Comptroller took the view that if a defendant chooses to take the potential benefits which section 239 gives those who undertake to take a licence,[12] then the defendant should not be entitled to recover sums paid under the licence if the plaintiff's action subsequently fails.[13] However, given the wording of section 239, it may be that this view is only partially correct. Section 239 refers to an undertaking given in "proceedings for infringement of design right in a design in respect of which a licence is available as of right ...". Whilst the Comptroller's view seems to be correct where the proceedings fail only because the plaintiff is unable to prove an act of infringement,[14] it seems harder to justify where the

---

[5] See CDPA 1988, s.235(4)(b) and (c).
[6] CDPA 1988, s.235(4).
[7] CDPA 1988, s.239(1)(c). As damages are usually calculated on the basis of the sum which would have been payable in return for a licence to do the wrongful act, this provision is unlikely to be of much significance to a defendant where the plaintiff is claiming damages. It might, however, be of some importance where the plaintiff seeks an account of profits.
[8] s.239(3).
[9] s.239(2).
[10] That this was the intention of Parliament was made clear in the course of debate, see *Hansard*, H.L. Vol.491, col.1156.
[11] [1996] R.P.C. 667.
[12] *i.e.* the limitation on the remedies available against him if the plaintiff succeeded.
[13] [1996] R.P.C. 667 at 686.
[14] In such a case, the proceedings would still have been "proceedings for the infringement of design right in a design in respect of which a licence is available as of right ..." notwithstanding the plaintiff's failure to show an actual act of infringement.

plaintiff's action fails because he was unable to prove any design right subsisted in his alleged design.[15]

13–177   **Delivery up.** Under section 230 of the 1988 Act, a design right owner[16] may apply to the court for an order for delivery up of certain articles. Very similar provisions apply as regards copyright.[17]

13–178   **Order for forfeiture, destruction, etc.** Under section 231(1) of the 1988 Act, an application may be made to the court[18] for an order that the infringing article or other thing delivered up under section 230 be forfeited to the design right owner, or destroyed, or otherwise dealt with as the court thinks fit, or for a decision that no such order should be made. This power and the corresponding powers relating to copyright and performers' rights (ss.104 and 204) have already been considered.[19]

10. THREATS

13–179   **Introduction.** In the commercial world, making a threat to bring infringement proceedings against another person may cause serious damage; the alleged infringer may feel obliged to stop making the article in question and, more importantly, if the threat is made known more widely, his customers may be reluctant to deal with him. The potential for such damage led to provisions being included in the Patents Act 1977[20] and in the Registered Designs Act 1949[21] allowing a person aggrieved by such a threat to bring an action seeking a declaration that the threat was unjustifiable, an injunction against further such threats, and an award of damages. However, one of the anomalies in the use of copyright to protect industrial designs prior to the 1988 Act was that there was no similar protection against groundless threats of copyright proceedings. The 1988 Act, therefore, includes provisions against the making of groundless threats of design right proceedings.[22]

13–180   **Section 253—threat of proceedings for infringement.** Section 253(1) of the 1988 Act provides that:

> "Where a person threatens another person with proceedings for infringement of design right, a person aggrieved by the threats may bring an action against him claiming—
>
> (a) a declaration to the effect that the threats are unjustifiable;
>
> (b) an injunction against the continuance of the threats;
>
> (c) damages in respect of any loss which he has sustained by the threats."

---

[15] In such a case, the proceedings were never "proceedings for infringement of design right in a design in respect of which a licence *is* available as of right ..." (emphasis added). If no design right subsisted, then no licence was ever available of right.

[16] Where there are concurrent rights, the term "design right owner" includes the exclusive licensee, see CDPA 1988, s.234(2).

[17] Delivery up is dealt with in Ch.22, below.

[18] As with CDPA 1988, s.230, the application under CDPA 1988, s.231 may be made in the County Court or, in Scotland, the sheriff court, see CDPA 1988, s.232(1) and (2).

[19] See paras 22–179 *et seq.*, below.

[20] (c.37), s.70.

[21] s.26.

[22] There are still no such provisions in relation to copyright. It was stated in Parliament that a change was unnecessary in the case of copyright because, it was considered, the position as regards ownership of copyright was usually clear—see *Hansard*, H.L. Vol.501, col.338. It is worth noting that the draft Civil Copyright and Unregistered Design Right Pre-Action Protocol contains a provision that states that a departure from the Pre-Action Protocol might be justified if the fact that the sending of a letter before action would expose the claimant to a threats action.

Form of threat. The 1988 Act does not require that the threat be in any particular **13–181**
form and there is no reason why it may not be oral as well as written; implied as
well as express.[23] A threat may be made in a private letter.[24] However, a threat
made in the course of without prejudice communications or without prejudice
meeetings cannot found a threats action.[25] To be actionable, the material relied on
as being a threat must be such that the recipient would reasonably see it[26] as being a threat of legal proceedings for infringement of design right (however innocently phrased that threat may have been made[27]). The threat must also, it
would seem, be for the bringing of proceedings in the United Kingdom.[28]

In determining whether something constitutes a threat, it must be seen in
context; thus a document which is not threatening when read in isolation may
well be when read in the context of the correspondence as a whole.[29] However,
mere notification that a design is protected by design right is not sufficient for
these purposes.[30] This would, it seems, allow a design right owner to say sufficient to put someone on notice of the design right owner's rights for the purposes
of subsequently proving secondary infringement if the recipient ignores those
rights. However, the borderline between a threat of proceedings and mere
notification of the existence of design right is often very fine, and design right
claimants and their professional advisers must clearly exercise care in the way in
which they assert claims if they wish to avoid the risk of a threats action being
brought against them.

Excluded threats. It is specifically provided[31] that an action cannot be brought **13–182**
under section 253 where the threat was to bring proceedings for the making of
something or for the importation of something. This provision recognises that the
real evil at which the "threats" provision is aimed is the making of threats to
customers and traders.[32] It is, however, important to bear in mind that the exclusion is defined not by reference to the identity of the person receiving the threat
but only by reference to the nature of the act in relation to which proceedings are

---

[23] The Patents Act 1977, s.70(1) and the Registered Designs Act 1949, s.26(1) both refer to the
threats being "by circulars, advertisements or otherwise ...". These words have been widely
construed, see *Speedcranes Ltd v Thomson* [1978] R.P.C. 221.

[24] *Skinner v Perry* (1893) 10 R.P.C. 1.

[25] See *Unilever plc v The Proctor & Gamble Co* [2000] 1 WLR 2436, [2000] F.S.R. 344 (CA). To
remain privileged, the threat must have been made in the context of a genuine attempt to resolve
or negotiate a settlement of a dispute. In *Kooltrade Ltd v XTS Ltd* [2001] F.S.R. 158, a letter
purporting to be without prejudice was sent at a time when there were no negotiations taking
place. Pumfrey J. found that the letter constituted a threat. He commented (at p.164) that the letter had not been "nothing whatever to do with negotiation and everything to do with making the
claimant's position with [its customer] as difficult as possible".

[26] See *C and P Development Co (London) Ltd v Sisabro Novelty Co Ltd* (1953) 70 R.P.C. 277 at
280 (a patent case). See also *Brain v Ingledew Brown Bennison & Garrett* [1997] F.S.R. 511 at
521 (another patent case) where it was stated that, in applying this test, the court must guard
against being led down a path of forensic analysis to a meaning which is narrower or broader
than would occur to an ordinary recipient.

[27] See *Hansard*, H.L. Vol.494, col.142.

[28] *Prince plc v Prince Sports Group Inc* [1998] F.S.R. 21 at 27, a trade mark case. However, the
same reasoning would apply given that design right arises under United Kingdom law.

[29] See *Brain v Ingledew Brown Bennison & Garrett* [1997] F.S.R. 511 at 521. See also *L'Oreal
(UK) Ltd v John & Johnson* [2000] F.S.R. 686—a case brought under s.21 Trade Marks Act
1994—where it was found to be at least arguable that a solicitor's letter (said to be the work of a
master of Delphic utterances) constituted a threat because, although it disclaimed making any
threat, its thrust could reasonably be taken to be a warning of possible future infringement
proceedings and this was how its recipient understood it. The threat might have been veiled and
muffled but it remained sufficient to unsettle the recipient.

[30] CDPA 1988, s.253(4).

[31] CDPA 1988, s.253(3).

[32] See *Hansard*, H.L. Vol.491, col.1162 and H.L. Vol.494, cols 142–143. The exclusion (which
also appears in the Patents Act 1977, s.70(4)) was added to the CDPA 1988 during the course of
debate. The CDPA 1988 also amended the Registered Designs Act 1949 so as to add the same
exclusion to s.26 of the 1949 Act, see s.26(2A).

threatened (*i.e.* manufacturing or importing). These excluded threats will usually (although not invariably) be made to the manufacturer or the importer, and their exclusion means that a design right owner may notify such persons of his claim[33] without running the risk of a threats action. It may be that he could even notify others of *that* threat but clearly very great care would be required in case this was construed as a threat of proceedings against persons in relation to acts other than the manufacture or importation of anything.[34]

13–183   **Person aggrieved.** The person entitled to bring an action under section 253 is "a person aggrieved by the threats". To be a person aggrieved, the claimant must personally have had a real as opposed to a fanciful, commercial interest which has been interfered with.[35] This does not, however, mean that he must have suffered actual damage; he may, for example, have been able to avert damage from the threat on that occasion but wish to prevent (by a declaration and injunction) any future recurrences of the threat which might cause actual damage.[36] Thus, a retailer of allegedly infringing articles who receives a threat of proceedings for infringement will clearly be a person aggrieved but so too would be the person who had supplied him with the relevant articles.[37] It may be that a director, an executive or a shareholder of a company may have sufficient personal interest in threats made to that company to make him a person aggrieved in respect of threats directed at that company. However, such a finding would require a close degree of identity between the fortunes of the company and of the individual concerned.[38]

13–184   **Person issuing threats.** The person against whom a threats action is brought is the person who makes the threat even if that person has no interest in the design right in question. Thus where a solicitor makes such a threat on his client's behalf, both the client and the solicitor himself could be sued for the threat.[39]

13–185   **Defences.** Once the plaintiff in a threats action proves that threats have been made and that he is a person aggrieved by them, then the onus is on the defendant to show that the threat had been justified, *i.e.* that the acts in respect of which the threat of proceedings was made did constitute (or if done would have constituted) an infringement of the design right concerned.

13–186   **Available relief.** If the threats action is successful, then section 253 makes clear that a court may make a declaration that the threat was unjustifiable, grant an injunction against the continuance of such threats and award damages in respect of any loss which has been caused by the threats. To recover damages, a claimant must show that it is more likely than not that the threat in fact resulted in the alleged damage. It must have been an effective or dominant cause of that damage.[40] Thus, if the matters said to constitute damage occurred because of the issue of

---

[33] According to Lord Beaverbrook, such notification may be in "strong and unambiguous terms", *Hansard*, H.L. Vol.494, col.143.

[34] See *Neild v Rockley* [1986] F.S.R. 3. See also *Cavity Trays Ltd v RMC Panel Products Ltd* [1996] R.P.C. 361 (a patent case) where Aldous L.J. stated that a person could safely threaten a person for manufacturing products but not for disposing of those products when manufactured.

[35] See *Brain v Ingledew Brown Bennison & Garrett* [1997] F.S.R. 511 at 519, a case decided under the Patents Act 1977, s.70 but where much of the reasoning was based on provisions (*e.g.* s.70(3) and (4)) which are in substantially similar terms to those relating to design right threats (see CDPA 1988, s.253(2) and (3)).

[36] *Brain v Ingledew Brown Bennison & Garrett* [1997] F.S.R. 511 at 516–521.

[37] As was the case in *Carflow Products (UK) Ltd v Linwood Securities (Birmingham) Ltd* [1996] F.S.R. 424, a case brought under Registered Designs Act 1949, s.26 and CDPA 1988, s.253(1).

[38] See *Brain v Ingledew Brown Bennison & Garrett* [1997] F.S.R. 511 at 524.

[39] However, in *Earles Utilities Ltd v Harrison* (1934) 52 R.P.C. 77, a statement by a solicitor that he would advise his client to commence proceedings was held not to be a threat.

[40] *Carflow Products (UK) Ltd v Linwood Securities (Birmingham) Ltd & others* [1996] F.S.R. 424.

proceedings against the recipient rather than as a result of the threat, then it was not the threat which caused that damage.[41]

11. JURISDICTION

Under the 1988 Act, the Comptroller-General of Patents, Designs and Trade Marks, the High Court, the Patents County Court and other county courts have varying degrees of jurisdiction in relation to certain design right issues.

13–187

A. COMPTROLLER-GENERAL OF PATENTS, DESIGNS AND TRADE MARKS

Section 246—disputes as to subsistence, term and first owner of design right. Section 246(1) of the 1988 Act provides that where there is a dispute as to (a) the subsistence of design right, (b) the term of design right or (c) the identity of the first owner of design right, a party to that dispute may refer the matter to the Comptroller-General of Patents, Designs and Trade Marks for his decision.[42] Moreover, under section 246(2), no other court shall decide such matters except (a) on a reference or appeal from the Comptroller, or (b) in infringement or other proceedings in which the issue arises incidentally,[43] or (c) in proceedings brought with the agreement of the parties or with the leave of the Comptroller. The Comptroller's decision on the matter referred to him is binding on the parties to the dispute,[44] but he also has jurisdiction to determine any incidental question of fact or law arising in the course of the reference.[45] The Comptroller may order (or, if both parties agree, must order) that the proceedings brought before him under section 246 or any question or issue (whether of fact or law) be referred to the High Court[46] on such terms as he may direct.[47] Where such a reference is made, the court may exercise the power otherwise conferred on the Comptroller and may, after its determination, refer any matter back to the Comptroller.[48] Under section 251(4), an appeal from any decision of the Comptroller in section 246 proceedings lies to the High Court.[49]

13–188

Section 247—terms of licence of right. Under section 247 of the 1988 Act, the Comptroller is also given jurisdiction to hear an application to settle the terms of a design right licence of right. The nature of such an application and the appeals process from the Comptroller's decision have already been considered.[50]

13–189

Although the judgment mentions the need to establish a "prima facie connection" between the threat and the alleged damage, the judgment as a whole shows that the burden is on the claimant to establish his claim according to the normal civil standard of proof (the balance of probabilities).

[41] *Carflow Products (UK) Ltd v Linwood Securities (Birmingham) Ltd & others* [1996] F.S.R. 424.

[42] The only reported case under s.246 is *Christopher Tasker's Design Right References* [2001] R.P.C. 3 where the Comptroller determined issues concerning the subsistence, duration and ownership of design right in various design features relating to a wardrobe system.

[43] *e.g.* a "threats" action brought under CDPA 1988, s.253.

[44] s.246(1).

[45] s.246(3).

[46] In Scotland, the Court of Session.

[47] CDPA 1988, s.251(1) and (2).

[48] s.251(3).

[49] In Scotland, the appeal is to the Court of Session. The extended jurisdiction of the Patents County Court does not include appeals from the Comptroller, see Patents County Court (Designation and Jurisdiction) Order 1994 (SI 1994/1609), Art.4 (see para. 13–195, below). As s.246 proceedings concern substantive matters in relation to design right, an appeal to the High Court was thought appropriate. By contrast, an appeal from the Comptroller in relation to the settlement of the terms of a licence of right (see s.247) is to the Appeal Tribunal constituted under Registered Designs Act 1949, s.28, a procedure thought to be less expensive and more appropriate for licensing matters, see *Hansard*, H.C. SCE, col.610.

[50] See paras 13–128 and 13–188, above.

13–190 **Rules of procedure before the Comptroller.** The procedure before the Comptroller is regulated by rules.[51] These allow the Comptroller to give such directions as to the conduct of the proceedings as he considers appropriate—including giving directions for a case management conference or a pre-hearing review, for witness statements and (in certain circumstances) witnesses and the variation of time limits. They also provide for the procedure and evidence at hearings before the Comptroller, for representation and rights of audience, and for costs. Finally, they allow for the Comptroller to appoint an adviser to assist in any proceedings before him.

B. THE COURT

13–191 **References and appeals from the Comptroller.** As has already been seen,[52] the High Court[53] has jurisdiction to hear references and appeals from the Comptroller in relation to the issues of subsistence, term and first ownership of design right.

13–192 **Crown use.** The High Court and a designated patents county court[54] have jurisdiction to determine any reference made to resolve disputes concerning Crown use of a design. These may include disputes as to the terms for Crown use, the rights of third parties in the case of Crown use, and compensation for Crown use.

13–193 **Delivery up, disposal, etc.** Any county court has jurisdiction[55] to hear proceedings seeking an order for delivery up in the circumstances provided for in section 230 of the 1988 Act, and also for an order under section 231 as to how an article delivered up should be dealt with.[56]

13–194 **Actions for infringement—High Court.** The High Court has unlimited jurisdiction to hear an action relating to infringement of design right.[57]

13–195 **Actions for infringement—patents county courts.** A designated patents county court[58] has special jurisdiction to hear and determine any action or matter relating to patents or designs over which the High Court would have jurisdiction, together with any claims or matters ancillary to, or arising from, such proceedings.[59] In these respects, therefore, its jurisdiction is not limited in any of the ways in which that of an ordinary county court is limited.[60] The reference to "designs" shows that the jurisdiction of a patent county court extends to actions relating to in-

---

[51] See the Design Right (Proceedings before Comptroller) Rules 1989 (SI 1989/1130), made under CDPA 1988, s.250 and subsequently amended (see SI 1990/1453; SI 1990/1699; SI 1992/615 and, most recently, SI 1999/3195). For the text of these Rules (as amended), see Vol.2, at B8.iii, below.

[52] CDPA 1988, s.251 and para. 13–188, above.

[53] In Scotland, the Court of Session.

[54] CDPA 1988, s.252(6). In Scotland, the relevant court is the Court of Session. The only county court presently designated as a patents county court under s.287 is the Central London County Court, see Patents County Court (Designation and Jurisdiction) Order 1994 (SI 1994/1609), revoking an earlier Order (SI 1990/1496) which had designated the Edmonton County Court. See para. 13–195, below.

[55] CDPA 1988, s.232, in Scotland, the sheriff's court. In Northern Ireland, a county court only has jurisdiction where the value of the relevant article does not exceed the county court's limit for actions in tort.

[56] For a discussion of ss.230 and 231, see Ch.22, below.

[57] Such actions are assigned to the Chancery Division, see Supreme Court Act 1981, Sch.1, para.1(i) (as amended by the CDPA 1988, Sch.7, para.28(3)).

[58] The only county court presently designated as a patents county court is the Central London County Court, see para. 13–192, above. For the practice and procedure of a patents county court, see County Court Rules, Ord.48A.

[59] Patents County Court (Designation and Jurisdiction) Order 1994, art.3.

[60] Since the High Court and County Courts Jurisdiction Order 1991 (SI 1991/724), art.2(1)(l), the jurisdiction of a county court in tort claims has not been limited by reference to the value of such claims. However, a limitation remains on a county court's jurisdiction in relation to the making of *Mareva* and *Anton Piller* orders, see County Court Remedies Regulations 1991 (SI 1991/

fringement of design right;[61] it has also been held to include actions for infringement of copyright in design documents created before the 1988 Act came into force and in respect of which copyright protection may still be available because of the postponement of the operation of section 51 effected by the transitional provisions of that Act.[62]

Actions for infringement—other county courts. The position as regards the jurisdiction of ordinary county courts to hear design right cases is less clear. Because section 287 expressly provides for a designated patent county court to have jurisdiction over proceedings relating to "patents and designs", and section 232 expressly provides that an ordinary county court may make orders for delivery up and disposal, etc. of certain infringing articles, it has sometimes been argued that the ordinary county courts have no jurisdiction to hear design right claims. It is submitted that this argument is wrong and that design right claims, like copyright claims, fall within the county court's tortious jurisdiction.[63] The need for section 287 arose from the fact that a county court would otherwise have no jurisdiction in relation to patents and registered designs.[64] The need for section 232 (and its copyright equivalent, section 115) arose from the fact that an order for delivery up or disposal of certain infringing articles would not have fallen within any of the powers conferred on the county court by the County Courts Act 1984. Accordingly, the inclusion of these provisions in the 1988 Act should not be taken as support for the proposition that the county court has no jurisdiction to hear design right claims.

13–196

12. UNREGISTERED COMMUNITY DESIGNS

A. INTRODUCTION

A design may qualify for protection as a Community design under the European Council Regulation on Community designs.[65] As has already been seen,[66] this Regulation created two forms of protection; a short three-year period of protection for unregistered Community designs (which is considered below) and a longer period of protection (up to 25 years) for registered Community designs (which will be considered in outline later in this Chapter). A Community design is enforceable in all Member States of the European Community.

13–197

1222) regs 2 and 3. This limitation does not apply to a patents county court, see *McDonald v Graham* [1994] R.P.C. 407 at 435.

[61] See *PSM International plc v Specialised Fastener Products (Southern) Ltd* [1993] F.S.R. 113 at 117. See also *McDonald v Graham* [1994] R.P.C. 407 at 435 where Ralph Gibson L.J. stated that, whilst it was unnecessary to make a finding on the point, he was inclined to the view that the word "designs" in relation to the jurisdiction of the patents county court was limited to rights arising under legislation dealing with designs; plainly this would include design right.

[62] See *PSM International plc v Specialised Fastener Products (Southern) Ltd* [1993] F.S.R. 113 at 116–117. It is submitted that this decision is correct and is not inconsistent with the comments of Ralph Gibson L.J. in *McDonald v Graham* [1994] R.P.C. 407 at 435. For example, the 1988 Act referred to the relevant transitional provisions relating to copyright in such works under the heading " *designs*". For the effect of the transitional provisions on CDPA 1988, s.51, see paras 13–315 *et seq.*, below.

[63] See *PSM International plc v Specialised Fastener Products (Southern) Ltd* [1993] F.S.R. 113 at 116. In *McDonald v Graham* [1994] R.P.C. 407 at 435–436, the Court of Appeal rejected the claim that an ordinary county court had jurisdiction to grant *Mareva* and *Anton Piller* orders in a copyright action but did not question that court's jurisdiction to hear the action itself. For the jurisdiction of a county court in relation to claims in tort, see County Courts Act 1984, s.15.

[64] The Patents Act 1977, s.130(1) and the Registered Designs Act 1949, s.27(1), unlike the CDPA 1988, expressly confer jurisdiction on the High Court only. Special provision was, therefore, required to confer jurisdiction on a patent county court in relation to such rights.

[65] Regulation (EC) No. 6/2002.

[66] See para. 13–30 *et seq.*, above.

The two types of protection created by the Regulation are intended to meet the differing needs of different sectors of industry in the Community. The unregistered form of protection is aimed at those sectors of industry where a requirement of registration would be burdensome and impractical and where the need for long-term protection may be less important, *e.g.* industries that produce large numbers of designs for products with (often) a short market life. By contrast, the registered form of protection is intended to meet the needs of those sectors of industry where the longer life of the products requires a longer period of protection and where registration provides greater certainty.[67] The Regulation came into force on March 6, 2002. However, the Regulation does not (unlike the 1988 Act[68]) provide that its provisions only apply to designs created after it came into force. It would seem, therefore, that Community design protection may well be available for a design which predates March 6, 2002—although this will be of far greater significance as regards the registration of a Community design (where the maximum period of protection is 25 years) than in the case of an unregistered Community design (where the period of protection is only three years).

13–198 **Nature of unregistered Community design.** As with copyright and design right, unregistered Community design is a property right which subsists automatically and which provides protection against the copying of the design.[69] As with national law, monopoly protection of a design is only available where the design is registered.

13–199 **Interrelation with design right.** As has also been seen, the protection for Community designs under the Regulation was not intended to replace United Kingdom design right. Thus, an unregistered design may be protected both as a Community design and also under design right.[70]

B. DEFINITION OF A COMMUNITY DESIGN

13–200 **Definition of design.** Under the Regulation, a design is very widely defined[71] as:

"... the appearance of the whole or a part of a product resulting from the features of, in particular, the lines, contours, colours, shape, texture and/or materials of the product itself and/or its ornamentation"

"product" for these purposes means:

"...any industrial or handicraft item, including *inter alia* parts intended to be assembled into a complex product, packaging, get-up, graphic symbols and typographic typefaces, but excluding computer programs"

and "complex product" means:

"...a product which is composed of multiple components which can be replaced permitting disassembly and re-assembly of the product."

The Community definition of a "design" is, therefore, concerned with the appearance of a product or of a part of a product.[72] The fact that the definition refers to a part of a product means that, like United Kingdom design right, a claimant

---

[67] See Recitals (15) to (17) of the Directive by which the national laws of Member States relating to registered designs were harmonised (91/71/EC).

[68] CDPA 1988, s.213(7).

[69] See, respectively, regs 27, 11 and 19(2) of Regulation (EC) No. 6/2002.

[70] See Art.96(2) of Regulation (EC) No. 6/2002 . The claimant would, of course, have to establish that he owns both rights.

[71] Art.3 of Regulation (EC) No. 6/2002. The limitation on the protection offered by Community design is achieved through the requirements of novelty and individual character, and through specific exclusions (as discussed below) rather than by narrowing the definition of a design.

[72] For an interesting argument that in context of the Design Directive (91/71/EC), the word "appearance" is not necessarily limited to appearance to the eye but may include appearance to the

need not rely on the design of the whole product but may rely on the design of one or more of its parts. In this way, the holder of a Community design right can improve his prospects of success in an infringement action by pleading alternative designs and by relying on designs that are as close as possible to the design of the defendant's product.[73] As with design right, there is no requirement that the design have any aethestic quality.[74] Thus, in principle, a functional design may be a Community design, although the significance of this is somewhat reduced by the fact that the Regulation also provides that, to be protected, a design must have "individual character"[75] and that Community design will not subsist in features dictated solely by the technical function of the product.[76]

In other respects, the definition of a design for these purposes is significantly wider than that for design right.[77] This is apparent not only from the list of relevant design features (lines, contours, colours, etc.) but also from the definition of a "product" and, in particular, the inclusion in that definition of get-up, graphic symbols and typographical typefaces. Clearly, therefore, the design can be two dimensional as well as three dimensional. Further, in contrast to the position under design right, the definition of a design for the purposes of Community design expressly includes appearance resulting from the ornamentation of the product. Accordingly, decorative features of design (whether surface or otherwise) may qualify for protection. Indeed, the definition also refers to colours.[78] In this regard, it is unclear whether a single colour would be treated as a design for these purposes—particularly where it is the only design feature relied upon.[79] Moreover, the fact that the definition refers to texture and materials shows that the appearance of a product as imparted by the substances from which that product is made can be a design.[80]

---

touch, see David Musker, *Community Design Law* (Sweet & Maxwell, London, 2002) at para.1–012. The argument may be slightly stronger in relation to unregistered Community design under the Regulation (EC) No. 6/2002 because the recitals to the Regulation do not include an equivalent to recital (11) to the Directive). The fact that the definition of design refers to appearance resulting from the features of texture and materials may lend some support to this argument for, if those words were to be construed as applying only where the texture or material had a visible effect, those words would otherwise appear to add little to the other words included in the definition (such as "lines", "contours" "shape", etc).

[73] See the discussion of this point in relation to design right at para. 13–45, above. The closer the designs are, the more likely it is that they would produce the same overall impression on an informed user (*i.e.* constitute an infringement—see para. 13–230, below). However, if too simple a design is chosen or if the design relied on has only a few features, a court may be inclined to find that such design is not novel or that it lacks individual character. It may also be difficult to establish copying.

[74] See recital (14) to the Directive (91/71/EC). There is no reason to think that the position would be different under the Regulation (EC) No. 6/2002 even though the Regulation does not have an equivalent recital.

[75] See Reg., Arts 4(1) and 6—discussed at paras 13–202 *et seq.*, below.

[76] See Reg., Art.8(1) discussed at paras 13–207 *et seq.*, below. In this respect, the position under Community design is similar to that under design right but differs from that which applied under the Registered Designs Act 1949 before it was amended in 2001.

[77] It is also much wider than the former definition of a design in the Registered Designs Act 1949. However, since the 1949 Act was amended by the Registered Designs Regulations 2001, its definition of "design" is almost identical to that in the Regulation.

[78] In *Lambretta Clothing Co Ltd v Teddy Smith (UK) Ltd* [2004] EWCA Civ 886, it was commented that the Community definition of design would "clearly" have covered the claimant's choice of colours for its track top (red of the body panels, blue with white stripes for the sleeves, and white for the zip). However, it appears that the claimant's design claim had to be based on UK design right—which claim failed as the design (*i.e.* a choice of colours) was not an aspect of "shape or configuration" of the top. See para. 13–48, above.

[79] It is likely to be difficult to establish that a defendant has copied a design when that design is simply a choice of colour without any other design features.

[80] This appears to differ from the position as it was under the Registered Designs Act 1949 before it was amended in 2001, see the old registered design cases discussed at para. 13–55, above, where such design features were excluded from protection for being modes of construction.

13–201   **Product.** This word is also broadly defined, and given the references to packaging, get-up, graphic symbols and typographical typefaces will clearly cover areas which, in English law, have generally been a matter for copyright[81] or trade mark law.[82] As is clear from the above definitions, the product may itself be a complex product, *i.e.* a product which is comprised of multiple components (each of which might also be a product) which can be replaced permitting assembly and re-assembly. An obvious example of a complex product would be a car.[83]

C. REQUIREMENTS OF NOVELTY AND INDIVIDUAL CHARACTER

13–202   **Requirement that a design be new and have individual character.** Whilst "design" is defined in wide terms, by reason of Article 4(1) of the Regulation, a design will only be protected by a Community design to the extent that it is new and has individual character. This provision and Article 4(2) (which lays down additional criteria by which the novelty and individual character of designs for component parts of complex products are assessed and which is considered below[84]) significantly limit the scope of Community design protection. There are two important points that arise in relation to this; first, that it is the *design* in issue that is tested for novelty and individual character rather than the product to which it has been applied or in which it is incorporated and, second, that the novelty and individual character of the design are tested as at the time that that design is made available to the public. It does not, therefore, matter when that design was created. The issue is whether it was new and had individual character compared with other designs at the time when it was made available to the public.

13–203   **Meaning of "new".** Under Article 5(1)(a) of the Regulation, an unregistered Community design will be considered new if no identical design has been made available to the public before the date on which the design for which protection is claimed was first made available to the public.[85] It seems clear that this provision means that the design in question must be compared with any other designs that have been made available to the public. For these purposes, Article 5(2) provides that the designs shall be deemed to be identical if their features differ only in immaterial details. Thus, to be "new", a design need only differ from any other design in some material respect and, as with design right, it seems clear that a design may be new even though some or even all of its component design features taken by themselves would not be.[86] The novelty test is not, therefore, a

---

[81] It may be that some "handicraft" items would also qualify for copyright protection in the UK as works of artistic craftsmanship, see paras 13–63 *et seq.*, above. Where copyright protection is available, the availability of unregistered Community design is of little benefit. However, the same definition of design applies to a registered Community design, and the protection offered to registered Community designs (being monopolistic) may well be of significant value to a designer.

[82] Community design protection may offer an useful alternative to a trade mark. Unlike trade mark, there is no need to prove that the design denotes the trade origin of goods, nor that it is distinctive (provided it is novel and has individual character). Nor does it matter whether or not the design results from the nature of the goods (provided it is not dictated solely by the technical function of the product). Further, the protection of an unregistered Community design is not by reference to a class of product for which it is registered.

[83] At first sight this appears to mirror the position under design right (see para. 13–49, above). However, in relation to design right, it was stated that whilst a kitchen unit was an article, the whole kitchen was not. There is a suggestion that the position may be different in relation to Community designs and that a complete kitchen may be treated as a complex product (see David Musker, *Community Design Law* (Sweet & Maxwell, London, 2002) at paras 1–019 and 1–1027).

[84] See para. 13–206, below.

[85] For a discussion of the date when a design is first made available to the public, see para. 13–205, below.

[86] See para. 13–71, above.

particularly onerous test for a designer.[87] However, Article 5 gives no guidance as to what material and immaterial details are. Nor does Article 5 state by whose eye the designs must be compared. One possibility is that it is by the eye of persons in the "circles specialising in the sector concerned, operating within the Community". Another possibility is that the eyes are those of the "informed user". However, as the issue appears to be essentially one of fact (*i.e.* are the designs identical or not), it is submitted that the issue is probably one for the judge to determine objectively, albeit that the judge might (as in design right cases) hear expert evidence to assist in determing whether any differences are or are not material.[88]

Meaning of individual character. To be protected as a Community design, a design must also have individual character. For these purposes, Article 6(1) of the Regulation provides that:

13–204

> "A design shall be considered to have individual character if the overall impression it produces on the informed user differs from the overall impression produced on such a user by any design which has been made available to the public ... before the date on which the design for which protection is claimed was first made available to the public."[89]

and Article 6(2) that:

> "In assessing individual character, the degree of design freedom of the designer in developing the design shall be taken into consideration."

Recital (14) to the Regulation provides the following guidance as to the test for individual character:

> "The assessment as to whether a design has individual character should be based on whether the overall impression produced on an informed user viewing the design clearly differs from the overall impression produced on him by the existing design corpus, taking into consideration the nature of the product to which the design is applied or in which it is incorporated, and in particular the industrial sector to which it belongs and the degree of freedom which the designer had in developing the design."

Clearly Article 6 requires a comparison to be made between the overall impressions produced by the relevant design and by any other design previously made available to the public. At first sight, this suggests that the comparison may be very broad ranging, in that such other design may be from a completely different sector of industry and may have been applied to a completely different type of product.[90] However, the scope of the enquiry is limited by the requirement that that other design against which the design in question is being compared must

---

[87] In this respect, the test resembles that which the courts undertake in assessing whether a design is commonplace for the purposes of design right—see *Farmers Build Ltd v Carier Bulk Material Handling Ltd* [1999] R.P.C. 461, discussed at paras 13–75 *et seq.*, above.

[88] See para. 13–75, above. Art.7 of Regulation (EC) No. 6/2002 requires one to look to the knowledge of people in the circles specialised in the sector concerned, operating within the Community (*i.e.* experts) when determining whether a design has been made available to the public (see para. 13–205, below). By contrast, Art.6 provides that the issue whether the design creates a different overall impression from any other design is determined by reference to the eye of the "informed user". It is not clear that either of these must apply to Art.5. Nor (if the Art.7 approach were to apply to Art.5) is it clear how Art.7 would work if the relevant designs are from different sectors. Whilst the "informed user" test in Art.6 would avoid this difficulty (because it seems clear that the user is the user of the product to which the design (*i.e.* the design in which Community right is applied), if that is the test applied for the purposes of Art.5, it is difficult to see what (if anything) the comparison under Art.5 would add to the comparison under Art.6. For more on the argument in favour of the Art.7 test applying to Art.5, see David Musker *Community Design Law* (Sweet & Maxwell, London, 2002) at para.1–045.

[89] For a discussion of the date when a design is first made available to the public, see para. 13–205, below.

[90] The test is, therefore, somewhat more onerous than the commonplace test under UK design right

itself have been made available to the public in the sense discussed below. Further, as Recital (14) makes clear, in making the comparison, the nature of the product to which the design has been applied and the industrial sector to which it belongs must be taken into consideration.[91]

The fact that the comparison is of the overall impressions produced by the relevant designs suggests that it would be wrong to try to deconstruct the various component elements of those designs and to analyse them separately. The issue, instead, is whether an informed user looking at those designs as a whole would see the overall designs as different or, taking the words of Recital (14) as clearly different. For these purposes, the "user" would appear to be the user of the type of product to which the design being tested for individual character has been applied. Further, the fact that the relevant impressions are those produced on a "user" (a user who is, according to Recital (14), "viewing the design") seems significant. The designs are being compared using the eyes of a customer rather than of a designer or of an expert in the relevant design field. This suggests that the test for individual character may involve considerations similar to those that arose under the test of eye appeal that used to be a part of United Kingdom registered design law.[92] Under that test, a design had eye appeal if there was something peculiar, distinctive, significant or striking about its appearance—something which would catch the eye of a customer and distinguish that design from any other.[93]

Although the comparison is in the eyes of a user, that user must be taken to be an "informed" user. This is, presumably, a reference to the fact that that person must be taken to be aware of other designs that have been made available to the public (in the sense considered below) and must be in a position to take into account the matters referred to in Recital (14), including the degree of design freedom enjoyed by designers in the relevant sector of industry. This reference to the degree of design freedom suggests that where there is little design freedom, more minor differences would satisfy the informed user that the design in question has individual character.[94]

13–205 **Made available to the public.** As appears from the above, in order to determine whether a design is new and whether it has individual character, it is necessary to look at other designs which have been "made available to the public" at the time that the design in question was made available to the public.[95] Article 7(1) of the Regulation provides that a design has been "made available to the public" if it has been published following registration or otherwise, or exhibited, used in trade or otherwise disclosed. Interestingly, Article 7(1) does not require that the design should have been made available "within the Community". Therefore, subject to the qualifications considered below, it would seem that an event taking place outside the Community might amount to publication.

There are two qualifications to Article 7. First, a design will not be treated as having been made available to the public if the event relied on could not reasonably have become known in the normal course of business to the circles spe-

---

where the design is compared with other designs from "the design field in question" (see paras 13–73 *et seq.*, above).

[91] If the relevant designs are from very different industrial sectors, an informed user may take the view that they produce different overall impressions.

[92] Before the 1949 Act was amended by the Registered Design Regulations 2001, see paras 13–267 and 13–330, below.

[93] See *Amp Inc v Utilux Proprietary Ltd* [1972] R.P.C. 103 at 108, 112–113 and 121.

[94] A somewhat similar concern to allow competition where the functional nature of the product permits no real design freedom is clearly apparent in UK design right decisions such as *Farmers Build Ltd v Carier Bulk Handling Ltd* [1999] R.P.C. 461, see paras 13–75 *et seq.*, above.

[95] For registered Community designs, the relevant date is the date of filing of the application for registration of the design for which protection is claimed or, if priority is claimed, the date of priority.

cialised in the sector concerned, operating within the Community. Given the language of Article 7, it seems probable that the relevant circles are the circles concerned with the type of product to which the design said to have been made available to the public has been applied and not the circles concerned with the type of product to which the design being tested for novelty and individual character has been applied (although this does beg the question why the informed user of the latter product should be taken to be aware of such other designs). Of course, the fact that the other design has been published outside the Community does not mean that it will not have become known within the relevant circles. The second qualification is that a design will not be deemed to have been made available to the public on the sole ground that it had been disclosed to a third person under explicit or implicit conditions of confidentiality.

Component parts of complex products. As mentioned above, Article 4(2) of the Regulation lays down additional criteria by which the novelty and individual character of designs for component parts of complex products[96] are assessed. It provides that:

> "A design applied to or incorporated in a product which constitutes a component part of a complex product shall only be considered to be new and to have individual character (a) if the component part, once it has been incorporated into the complex product, remains visible during normal use of the latter and (b) to the extent that those visible features fulfil in themselves the requirements as to novelty and individual character."

13–206

This provision (together with the technical function and interconnections exclusions considered below) was clearly intended to address concerns relating to "spare parts" and, in particular, automotive "spare parts". Thus, the exclusion of protection for the design of any component that is not visible in normal use will clearly mean that Community design protection is not available for the designs of "under the bonnet" car components. However, the provision is of general application. In this respect, Article 4(2) goes much further in limiting the scope of Community design than the 1988 Act goes in limiting United Kingdom design right. For design right, the definition of a design expressly refers to internal features, and the main limitations on protection are the "must fit" and "must match" exclusions.[97]

In determining whether a component part is visible during normal use, normal use is defined by Article 4(3) as meaning use by the end user, excluding maintenance, servicing or repair work. This test may not always be easy to apply. For example, it seems clear that the exclusion is intended to apply to "under the bonnet" parts that would be visible when the windscreen washer water reservoir or the engine oil for a car are topped up. But what about parts only visible when the petrol cap is opened to fill up with petrol? What about the parts of a fountain pen that are only visible when the pen is being refilled with ink? These would not appear to be acts of "maintenance". Yet it is not easy to see how those acts differ from the act of filling up with water or oil—each affects the ability of the product to perform its function.

D. OTHER EXCLUSIONS FROM PROTECTION

As well as excluding Community design from designs that are not novel or that do not have individual character, the Regulation has exclusions that apply in respect of features of appearance solely dictated by the technical function of the

13–207

---

[96] See Art.3 and para. 13–200, above.
[97] See paras 13–44 et seq., and paras 13–56 et seq., above.

product, and features allowing the interconnection of products and designs that are contrary to public policy or to accepted principles of morality. These exclusions are considered below.

(i) Designs dictated by their technical Function

13–208   Article 8(1) of the Regulation provides that:

> "A Community design shall not subsist in features of appearance of a product which are solely dictated by its technical function".

As appears from recital (10), where this exclusion applies, the relevant features should not be taken into consideration for the purpose of determining whether the other features of the design fulfil the requirements for protection as a Community design. However, the wording of Article 8(1) raises a number of issues. First, it is unclear whether the exclusion will only apply to a design if that is the only design by which the product in question could perform its function or whether it operates whenever a design was as a matter of fact dictated solely by the function of the product even though it was not the only design that was capable of allowing that function to be performed. Although English authority regarding the similarly worded exclusion in s.1(3) of the Registered Designs Act 1949 (prior to its amendment by the CDPA 1988) favoured the latter construction,[98] that construction had been the subject of much criticism and it is submitted that the former (narrower) construction of Article 8(1) is the correct one. In this regard, the wording of recital (10) is again significant; whilst it provides that "[t]echnological innovation should not be hampered by granting design protection to features dictated solely by a technical function", it also provides that "[i]t is understood that this does not entail that a design must have an aesthetic quality". This suggests that the technical function exclusion was intended to be construed narrowly and that it should be construed in a way that does not unduly restrict the availability of protection for non-aesthetic (*i.e.* functional) designs.[99] The second issue arising from the wording of Article 8(2) is the meaning of "technical function". This is clearly a reference to design features that are dictated by function rather than, say, the need to attract a customer. However, there seems to be no reason why the function of a product should be narrowly construed.[1]

(ii) The "interconnections" exclusion.

13–209   Under Article 8(2) of the Regulation:

> "A Community design will not subsist in features of appearance of a product which must necessarily be reproduced in their exact form and dimensions in order to permit the product in which the design is incorporated or to which it is applied to be mechanically connected to or placed in, around or against another product so that either product may perform its function".

Although this exclusion is called the "interconnections" exclusion, much of its wording mirrors that of the United Kingdom "must fit" exclusion for design right.[2] As with the "must fit" exclusion, Article 8(2) does not apply only to spare parts and, as the wording of recital (14) makes clear, it will also apply where

---

[98] See *Amp Inc v Utilux Pty Ltd* [1972] R.P.C. 103.

[99] This is supported by the comments of the Avocate General in *Philips v Remington* [2001] E.T.M.R. 509 and is also consistent with the comments of the European Economic & Social Committee, [1995] O.J. C110/12 (May 2, 1995).

[1] See, for example, the comments in *Ocular Sciences Ltd v Aspect Vision Care Limited* [1999] R.P.C. 289 at 425, regarding the function of contact lenses for the purposes of the must fit exclusion contained in s.213(3)(b)(i) of the 1988 Act. See para. 13–59, above.

[2] CDPA 1988, s.213(3)(b)(i) which is considered in detail at paras 13–56 *et seq*, above.

there is a need to allow the interoperability of products of different makes. However, the words "must necessarily be reproduced in their exact form and dimensions" suggests that this interconnections exclusion may be somewhat narrower in scope than the "must fit" exclusion.[3]

Modular products. The application of Article 8(2) is subject to Article 8(3)   **13–210**
which provides that notwithstanding Article 8(2) (and subject to satisfying the requirements of novelty and of having individual character):

> "... a Community design shall ... subsist in a design serving the purpose of allowing multiple assembly or connection of mutually interchangeable products within a modular system".

In this regard, Recital (11) states that:

> "The mechanical fittings of modular products may nevertheless constitute an important element of the innovative characteristics of modular products and present a major marketing asset, and therefore should be eligible for protection".

The interconnections exclusion will not, therefore, remove protection from "mutually interchangeable" products—such as children's building blocks.

(iii) Exclusions due to public policy or morality.

Article 9 of the Regulation provides that Community design shall not subsist in a   **13–211**
design which is contrary to public policy or to accepted principles of morality. This differs from the position under copyright and design right where the balance of authority suggests that a contravention of public policy or morality does not prevent copyright or design right subsisting, but only prevents its being enforced by the courts.[4]

The European Directive on the legal protection of designs[5] contains the same exclusion. However, the Directive also contains a recital (Recital (16)) which is not in the Regulation and which makes it clear that it was not the intention to harmonise national concepts of public policy or morality. This was, presumably, because the Directive was dealing with national laws whereas the Regulation was creating a Community-wide right. It is, therefore, unclear whose law resolves the issue of public policy or morality in the context of a Community design. It seems unlikely that it is the law of the country that is hearing the dispute, as that country may take a very different view to these issues than the country where the alleged infringement of the design occurred. The most likely meaning is that the design must not offend against any Member State's public policy or principles of morality.

E. GROUNDS FOR INVALIDITY

Introduction. A design will be invalid if it does not satisfy the definition of a   **13–212**
design in Article 3(a), or if it falls within one of the limitations and exclusions in Articles 4 to 9. There are, however, other grounds on which a Community design may be declared invalid. Articles 24 to 26 of the Regulation deal with invalidity, setting out the various grounds of invalidity, the manner in which these grounds can be raised and the consequences of invalidity.

---

[3] Contrast the position under design right, see para. 13–59, above.
[4] See paras 3–260 et seq., above.
[5] Directive 98/71/EC.

13–213   **Declaration of invalidity.** In the case of an unregistered Community design, Article 24(3) provides that a declaration of invalidity can be made by a Community design court on application or on the basis of a counterclaim in infringement proceedings.[6] Article 24(2) provides that such a declaration can be made even after the Community design has lapsed.

13–214   **Grounds of invalidity.** Article 25 lists the only grounds on which a Community design can be declared invalid. They are:

(a) That the design does not correspond with the definition (of design) in Article 3.

(b) That the design does not fulfil the requirements of Articles 4 to 9, *i.e.* the provisions relating to novelty, individual character, technical function, interconnections and public policy or morality.

(c) That the (alleged) right-holder is not entitled under Article 14 (see paragraphs 13–217 *et seq.*, below). Only the person who is entitled under Article 14 can rely on this ground.[7]

(d) —[8]

(e) That the design has used an already existing distinctive sign in circumstances where Community or national law (*e.g.* the law of passing off or trade mark law) would permit the right-holder of that sign to prohibit such use. Only the holder of that right can rely on this ground.[9]

(f) That the design constitutes an authorised use of a work protected under the copyright law of a Member State. Again, only the owner of that copyright can rely on this ground.[10]

(g) That the design constitutes an improper use of any of the items listed in Article 6*ter* of the Paris Convention for the Protection of Industrial Property or are badges, emblems and escutcheons other than those covered by Article 6 and which are of particular public interest in a Member State. Only the person or entity concerned by such use can rely on this ground.[11]

F. DURATION

13–215   **Duration—three years only.** Under Article 11(1), an unregistered community design is only entitled to a very short period of protection—namelyhree years from the date when the design is first made available to the public within the Community. This contrasts with the much longer periods of protection for a design under design right (15 years from when the design is first recorded or, where articles made to the design are marketed, 10 years from the date of first marketing) and for where a design is registered (up to 25 years). Another potentially important difference between Community design and design right is that, under Article 11(1), a design will not have Community design protection *before* it is first made available to the public. If, therefore, the defendant obtains details of and copies the design before that event, some other remedy would have to be found—such as copyright or design right.

13–216   **Date when design made available to the public.** The three-year protection for an unregistered Community design starts on the date when the design is first made available to the public within the Community. For these purposes, Article 11(2) provides that:

---

[6] For the meaning of Community design courts, see Regulation (EC) No. 6/2002, Art.80 and para. 13–245, below.

[7] See Regulation (EC) No. 6/2002. Art.25(2).

[8] This ground relates solely to registered Community designs.

[9] See Art.25(3).

[10] See Art.25(3).

[11] See Art.25(4).

"... a design shall be deemed to have been made available to the public within the Community if it has been published, exhibited, used in trade or otherwise disclosed in such a way that, in the normal course of business, these events could reasonably have become known to the circles specialising in the sector concerned, operating within the Community. The design shall not, however, be deemed to have been made available to the public for the sole reason that it has been disclosed to a third person under explicit or implicit conditions of confidentiality".

This is the same definition that applies under Article 7 and has been considered in that context.[12] Accordingly, it would seem that a design might be found to have been made available in the Community even though it had only been published (etc.) outside the Community. The only criteria is whether its publication (etc.) was such as to have become known in the relevant circles within the Community.

G. OWNERSHIP

Right to the Community design

Ownership of a Community design is governed by Article 14 of the Regulation. **13–217**

Employees. The starting point is to identify the designer. If the designer was an **13–218** employee and developed the design in the execution of his duties or following instructions given by his employer then, under Article 14(3), Community design will vest in the employer unless otherwise agreed or specified under national law. For these purposes, it would seem that any issue as to whether the designer was an employee, whether he had been acting in the execution of his duties or under instructions from his employer and whether there had been some contrary agreement or specification would be governed by the national law that governed the relationship between the relevant parties. The issue whether the designer had been acting in the execution of his duties would seem to correspond with the test under United Kingdom design right where the issue is whether the designer was an employee acting in the course of his employment.[13]

Ownership by agreement. Although Article 14 does not say, it seems clear that **13–219** where the relevant parties have reached an agreement as to ownership, then Community design would vest in accordance with that agreement.[14]

Commissioned designs. It is not clear what the position will be where a design is **13–220** developed by a self-employed person acting in the course of a commission. In English law, such a person would not be "an employee". However, it is possible that Article 14(3) was intended to cover this situation as well. In support of this, it could be argued that, if it were otherwise, it is difficult to see what the reference to an employee "following the instructions of his employer" would add to the reference to an employee acting "in the execution of his duties". The argument is not an easy one, and clearly where a design is commissioned, the parties would be best advised to agree between themselves who is to be entitled to any Community design in the design developed as a result.

---

[12] See para. 13–205, above.
[13] See para. 13–88, above.
[14] This corresponds with the position for design right under s.223 of the 1988 Act, see para. 13–117, above.

13–221   **Designer.** If Article 14(3) does not apply (because, for example, the designer was not an employee or because he was not acting in execution of his duties or under the instructions of his employer or because the parties or national law had specified otherwise), then the Community design would vest in the designer or his successor in title pursuant to Article 14(1).

13–222   **Joint developed designs.** Where two or more people jointly develop a design, Article 14(2) provides that the right to the Community design will vest in them jointly. These provisions appear similar to those that apply in UK design right.

13–223   **Who is the designer?** Although Article 14 talks in terms of the designer being the person who developed the design rather than the person who created it, there is no reason to think that the identity of the designer for these purposes will differ from the identity of the designer for the purposes of United Kingdom design right.[15]

13–224   **Disputes over entitlement to a Community design.** If a person who is not entitled to an unregistered Community design in the sense set out above discloses or claims an unregistered Community design, then Articles 15(1) and 15(2) of the Regulation provide that the person properly entitled to the Community design or jointly entitled to that design, may (without prejudice to any other remedy that may be open to him) claim to be recognised as the legitimate holder of the design or, as the case may be, the joint holder. There is, however, a significant difference to UK national law in that Article 15(3) of the Regulation also provides that legal proceedings to be recognised as the legitimate holder (but not, it seems any other rights) will be barred three years after the other person disclosed the unregistered design or after the publication of the registered design (unless the other person had acted in bad faith).[16] It seems clear that this limitation period is against the *commencement* of proceedings seeking recognition as the legitimate holder of the Community design after the relevant three-year period (rather than the continuation of existing proceedings).

H. DEALINGS WITH A COMMUNITY DESIGN

13–225   **Community design as a property right.** Articles 27 to 34 of the Regulation deal with the status of Community designs as objects of property.

13–226   **Dealing with a Community design—the governing law.** Article 27 of the Regulation lays down a code regarding dealings with a Community design and the law that will govern those dealings. Article 27(1) provides that:

"Unless Articles 28, 29, 30, 31 and 32 provide otherwise, a Community design as an object of property shall be dealt with in its entirety, and for the whole area of the Community, as a national design right of the Member State in which:

(a) the holder has his seat or his domicile on the relevant date; or

(b) where point (a) does not apply, the holder has an establishment on the relevant date".

Article 27(3) provides that:

"In the case of joint holders, if two or more of them fulfil the condition under paragraph 1, the Member State referred to in that paragraph shall be determined:

---

[15] See para. 13–84, above.

[16] For unregistered Community design, which only lasts three years from the date when the design was disclosed, this limitation is of little significance. However, the same restriction also applies to registered Community designs which can last for up to 25 years.

(a) in the case of an unregistered Community design, by reference to the relevant joint holder designated by them by common agreement...".[17]

Finally, Article 27(4) provides that where the previous paragraphs of Article 27 do not apply, "the Member State referred to in paragraph 1 shall be the Member State in which the seat of the Office is situated", *i.e.* Spain.

A number of points arise out of this. First, (unless one of Articles 28 to 32 applies) the Community design must be dealt with in its entirety and for the whole area of the Community.[18] This is an important restriction on the normal right of a property owner to deal with his property as he thinks fit, and it is clearly intended to help prevent Community designs becoming fragmented by having different owners in different countries. Second, although Community design is a Community-wide property right, a single national law will govern dealings with that right. The applicable national law is ascertained in accordance with Article 27 (unless Articles 28 to 32 provide otherwise[19]). Third, as is clear from Article 27, the applicable national law may change depending on the circumstances of the holder or holders.

Security, rights *in rem*, execution. Articles 29 and 30 of the Regulation provide that a registered Community design may be given as security or be the subject of rights *in rem* and may be levied in execution; on request, such dealings can be entered on the register. There are, however, no equivalent provisions in the case of unregistered Community designs. Given this, it seems probable that the general provision in Article 27(1) would operate so that any such dealing in relation to an unregistered Community design would only be permitted if it was a dealing for the design in its entirety and for the whole area of the Community. Again, the rationale for this would seem to be to prevent possible uncertainty arising from there being different property interests in a Community design in different Member States.

13–227

Insolvency proceedings. Under Article 31 of the Regulation, insolvency proceedings in which a Community design may be involved can only be opened in the Member State within the territory in which the centre of the debtor's main interests is situated. Where the debtor is a joint proprietor, this applies only to his share. By reason of Article 33(4), the effect of insolvency proceedings on any third parties shall be governed by the national law of the Member State in which those proceedings are first brought.

13–228

Licensing. As an exception to the general provision in Article 27 requiring Community designs to be dealt with in their entirety, Article 32(1) provides that a Community design may be licensed for the whole or part of the Community. Article 33(1) provides that the effects of a licence granted under Article 32 shall be governed by the law of the Member State determined in accordance with Article 27.[20] However, Article 32(1) provides that a licence may be exclusive or non-exclusive and, under Articles 32(3) and (4), exclusive and non-exclusive licensees have somewhat wider rights to sue for infringement than would be the

13–229

---

[17] It is not clear which law applies where only one of the joint holders has a seat or domicile or establishment in a Member State although commonsense suggests that the law of that Member State will apply.

[18] See also Regulation (EC) No. 6/2002, Art.1(3) which states that a Community design "shall have a unitary character. It shall have equal effect throughout the Community. It shall not be registered, transferred or surrendered or be the subject of a decision declaring it invalid, nor shall its use be prohibited, save in respect of the whole Community. This principle and its implications shall apply unless otherwise provided in this Regulation".

[19] Art.28 only applies to registered Community designs. For the position regarding Arts 29 and 30 see para. 13–227, below. For Arts 31 and 32 see below at paras 13–228 and 13–229, respectively.

[20] See para. 13–226, above.

case for licensees under United Kingdom design right. These wider rights are considered later in this chapter.[21]

Under English law, a licence is merely a permission to do that which would otherwise infringe some property right. Thus, a licensee who goes beyond the scope of his licence would be infringing the relevant property right. Article 32(2) adopts the same approach, providing that a licensee who contravenes any provision in his licence contract with regard to duration, or the form in which the design can be used, or the range of products for which the licence is granted, or the quality of products manufactured by the licensee is liable to be sued by the holder of the Community design.

I. RIGHTS CONFERRED BY A COMMUNITY DESIGN AND INFRINGEMENT

13–230   **Introduction.** An unregistered Community design, like copyright and design right, confers on its holder certain exclusive rights. These exclusive rights are to use the relevant design in any of the ways set out in Article 19(1) of the Regulation, provided such use results from copying of the protected design (see Article 19(2)). Significantly, by reason of Article 10, the scope of the protection offered by Community design is not limited to the protected design but extends to any other design that does not produce a different overall impression on the informed user. A person who, without the holder's consent, does one of the acts specified in Article 19 in respect of a design which falls within the scope of protection laid down in Article 10 will (unless he falls within one of the limitations set out in Articles 20 to 23) infringe Community design. In contrast to the position under copyright and design right, there are no categories of secondary infringement of Community design.

13–231   **Rights conferred by a Community design.** Article 19 of the Regulation sets out the rights conferred by a Community design on its holder and, therefore, defines the acts that are capable of infringing that Community design.

Article 19(1) deals with the position regarding registered Communty designs. It states that:

> "A registered Community design shall confer on its holder the exclusive right to use it and to prevent any third party not having his consent from using it. The aforementioned use shall cover, in particular, the making, offering, putting on the market, importing, exporting or using of a product in which the design is incorporated or to which it has been applied, or stocking such a product for those purposes."

In relation to unregistered Community designs, Article 19(2) provides that:

> "An unregistered Community design shall, however, confer on its holder the right to prevent the acts referred to in paragraph 1 only if the contested use results from copying the protected design.
>
> The contested use shall not be deemed to result from copying the protected design if it results from an independent work of creation by a designer who may be reasonably thought not to be familiar with the design made available to the public by the holder".

A number of points arise from Article 19. First, the types of use that fall within the exclusive rights and which are therefore capable of being infringements are very broadly defined—including even "using of" a product to which the design has been applied or in which the design is incorporated and "stocking" such product for any reason other than the stated purposes. Secondly, the exclusive rights to use a design are not limited to uses in respect of any particular product.

---

[21] See para. 13–241, below.

Thus, the holder of a Community design in the design for a handle of a spoon would have the exclusive right to apply that design to a fork or even to a vase. If someone else were to copy that design (without permission) by using it as the handle for a fork, they would making a product (the fork) to which the design (of a handle) had been applied and would be infringing unless they fell within one of the limitations contained in Articles 20 to 23.[22] Thirdly, to establish an infringement of an unregistered Community design, proof of copying is required. In this respect, the law reflects that for copyright and design right, and there is no reason to think that what has already been said in relation to those rights would not apply equally in an unregistered Community design case.[23] In fact, the second part of Article 19(2) clearly assumes that a presumption of copying can arise as a result of similarities between the designs. Further, the possibility of indirect copying of an unregistered Community design is recognised in Article 19(2) which provides that the presumption of copying can be rebutted by proof that the contested use was the result of an independent work of creation by a designer who may be reasonably thought not to be familiar with the protected design.

Scope of protection. The scope of protection offered to the holder of a Community design is not limited to uses of that particular design. Under Article 10(1) of the Regulation, it extends to any other design that does not produce on the informed user a different overall impression. Thus, for the purposes of Article 19, a person may infringe unregistered Community design if (by copying) he makes (or offers or to puts on the market, etc.) a product to which a design which does not produce a different overall impression to the relevant design has been incorporated or to which such a design has been applied.   **13–232**

The meaning of "informed user" and of "overall impression" and the significance of the designer's design freedom have already been considered in the context of whether a design has individual character.[24] However, in assessing the scope of protection for a design, Article 10(2) requires that the degree of freedom of the designer in developing his design must be taken into account. This is an important provision. If the designer had little design freedom (as is often the case with designs for more functional products), then two similar designs are less likely to produce the same overall impression on an informed user. Instead, that user would be likely to be influenced by small differences. Equally, where the designer has a greater degree of design freedom (as is the case with more aesthetic designs, *e.g.* of a toy) similarities are more likely to produce the same overall impression on the informed user.

Treatment of excluded features. In determining whether a design creates the same overall impression as the protected design, it is important to bear in mind that it is the *designs* that are being compared rather than the products to which they have been applied or in which they are incorporated. Further, although Article (10) provides that features solely dictated by function and interconnection features shall not be taken into account in determining whether other features fulfil the requirements for protection (*i.e.* whether the design is new and has individual character), because such features are nevertheless part of the design, there seems to be no reason why they should not be taken into account in deciding whether the protected design and any other design produce different overall impressions for the purposes of Article 10.   **13–233**

---

[22] In this respect, the approach to infringement for the purposes of Art.19 appears to be somewhat closer to the approach in copyright than to that in design right. As has been seen, for copyright the test is whether the defendant has copied the work or a substantial part of it. For design right, it is whether the defendant has made an article to or substantially to the design—see para. 13–149, above.

[23] See para. 13–148, above.

[24] See para. 13–204, above.

J. PERMITTED ACTS

13–234 **Permitted acts.** Articles 20, 21, 23 and, importantly, 110 of the Regulation lay down a number of limitations on the rights conferred on the holder of an unregistered Community design.

13–235 **Non-commercial acts.** Article 20(1) of the Regulation provides that:
"The rights conferred by a Community design shall not be exercised in respect of
   (a) acts done privately and for non-commercial purposes;
   (b) acts done for experimental purposes;
   (c) acts of reproduction for the purpose of making citations or of teaching, provided that such acts are compatible with fair trade practices and do not unduly prejudice the normal exploitation of the design, and that mention is made of the source".

These are plainly important limitations on the rights under a Community design. Many of the concepts are familiar from copyright and/or design right.

13–236 **Ships and aircraft temporarily entering the Community.** Article 20(2) of the Regulation provides that the rights conferred by a Community design shall not be exercised in respect of (a) the equipment on aircraft and ships registered in a third (*i.e.* non-Community) country when these temporarily enter Community territory; (b) the importation into the Community of spare parts and accessories for the purpose of repairing such craft; and (c) the execution of repairs to such craft.

13–237 **Exhaustion of rights.** Under Article 21 of the Regulation, the rights conferred by a Community design do not extend to acts relating to a product in which a design within the scope of protection is incorporated or to which it has been applied, when the product has been put on the market in the Community by the holder of the Community design or with his consent.

13–238 **Government use.** Under Article 23 of the Regulation, a provision in the law of a Member State allowing use of national designs by or for the Government, will apply to Community designs but only to the extent that the use is necessary for essential defence or security needs.

13–239 **Spare parts—transitional provision.** Another important limitation on Community design protection is the transitional provision contained in Article 110 of the Regulation. This deals with spare parts. It provides that protection as a Community design shall not exist for a design which constitutes a component part of a complex product used within the meaning of Article 19(1) for the purpose of the repair of that complex product so as to restore its original appearance.

This provision has similarities to the "must match" exclusion that applies in design right, and that formerly applied in United Kingdom registered designs—particularly in its concept of restoring the original design appearance of a product.[25] However, there are also important differences in wording. For example, the definition of a design to which the exclusion in Article 110 might apply is much wider than the definition of a design for the purposes of the "must match" exclusion. However, under the Regulation, the exclusion only applies to designs which may be used for the purpose of repair.

[25] See s.213(3)(b)(ii) of the 1988 Act and s.1(1)(b)(ii) of the Registered Designs Act 1949 (before its amendment by the Registered Designs Regulations 2001) and, in particular, *Ford Motor Co Ltd and Iveco Fiat SpA's Registered Design Applications* [1993] R.P.C. 339 (discussed at para. 13–64, above). The 1949 Act now has an exclusion in substantially the same terms as Article 110 of the Regulation—see s.7A(5) of the 1949 Act (as amended).

As mentioned above, Article 110 is a transitional provision, for it states that it shall only operate until the Regulation is amended following a proposal from the Commission. The background to this is that there is still considerable controversy as to whether the designs of spare parts should be afforded protection. Because of this controversy, the Directive on the legal protection of designs presently permits Member States to retain any existing protection for spare parts under national law (although not to increase such protection), but provides that, within three years of implementation, the Commission should submit an analysis of the consequences that this has had on consumers, on competition, and on the internal market, and is to consider harmonisation of the law in this area and the possibility of introducing a remuneration system and a more limited period of protection.[26] However, the Commission is clearly keen to remove such protection and, pending any proposal following such review, the Regulation excludes such spare parts from any protection under Community design (see recital (13) of the Regulation).

K. WHO CAN SUE

The Holder. By reason of Article 19 of the Regulation, the person primarily entitled to sue for infringement of unregistered Community design is the holder, *i.e.* the person in whom Community right is vested. This is the person identified under Article 14 of the Regulation or that person's successor in title.   **13–240**

Licensees. However, special provisions govern the position in respect of licensees. In this regard, Article 32(3) of the Regulation provides that: **13–241**

> "Without prejudice to the provisions of the licensing contract, the licensee may bring proceedings for infringement of a Community design only if the right holder consents thereto. However, the holder of an exclusive licence may bring such proceedings if the right holder in the Community design, having been given notice to do so, does not himself bring infringement proceedings within an appropriate period".

And Article 32(4) that:

> "A licensee shall, for the purpose of obtaining compensation for damage suffered by him, be entitled to intervene in an infringement action brought by the right holder in a Community design".

The position is, therefore, both similar and dissimilar to the position under copyright and design right.[27] It is similar in that the primary party entitled to sue remains the holder of the right, although an exclusive licensee may bring an action. It is dissimilar in that a non-exclusive licensee of a Community design may sue (provided he has the holder's permission to do so), and in that the holder need not, it seems be joined as a party when a licensee of a Community design sues. However, the underlying rationale is clearly the same as in English law—namely to prevent an infringer being exposed to a claim by both the holder and the licensee.

L. JURISDICTION AND REMEDIES

Introduction. Articles 79 to 94 of the Regulation contain extensive provisions dealing with issues of jurisdiction and enforcement in relation to Community designs.   **13–242**

---

[26] See Art.14 and recital (19) of the Design Directive (98/71/EC). This analysis should have been submitted in October 2004.

[27] See, respectively, paras 22–23 *et seq.*, below and para. 13–169, above.

13–243   Application of the Brussels Convention. First, Article 79 of the Regulation confirms that, as a general rule and subject to the provisions of the Regulation, the Brussels Convention on Jurisdiction and the Enforcement of Judgments in Civil and Commerial matters shall apply to proceedings relating to Community designs, as well as to proceedings relating to actions on the basis of Community designs and national designs enjoying simultaneous protection.[28] Thus, the general rule is that a person must be sued in his country of domicile—although there are other bases on which jurisdiction may be founded under the Convention.

13–244   Jurisdiction under Article 82. In essence, the approach of the Regulation is consistent with this general rule. Thus, under Articles 82(1), (2) and (3) of the Regulation, any action or claim for (a) infringement and threatened infringement of Community design, (b) a declaration of non-infringement of Community designs, (c) a declaration of invalidity of a Community design, and (d) counterclaims seeking a declaration of invalidity raised in connection with an action under (a) above, must be brought in:

(1) the courts of the Member State in which the defendant is domiciled or (if there is no such State) in which he has an establishment; or

(2) if the defendant has no such domicile or establishment, the courts of the Member State in which the plaintiff is domiciled or (if there is no such State), where the plaintiff has an establishment; or

(3) if plaintiff also has no such domicile or establishment, the courts of the State where the Office has its seat (*i.e.* Spain).

Article 82(4) provides that the parties may agree or accept the jurisdiction of the courts of another Member State. Finally, Article 82(5) provides that actions for infringement or threatened infringement and for a counterclaim for a declaration of invalidity brought within such actions may be brought in the courts of the Member State where an act of infringement has been committed or threatened, although, as set out below, where jurisdiction is based on this ground, it is limited to infringements occurring in that Member State.

13–245   Community design courts. For the purposes of Article 82 of the Regulation, the courts to which jurisdiction is given are the Community design courts of the Member State in question.[29] Community design courts are those national courts which the relevant Member State has designated under Article 80 of the Regulation.[30] Article 81 of the Regulation provides that these courts have exclusive jurisdiction in respect of the actions referred to in paragraph 13–244, above. In exercising their exclusive jurisdiction, the Community design court must apply the provisions of the Regulation, but in matters not covered by the Regulation shall apply its national law and rules of procedure.[31]

13–246   Jurisdiction—infringement. Article 83 of the Regulation deals with the extent of the jurisdiction conferred on a Community design court by Article 82 in respect of acts of infringement or threatened infringement. It provides that where jurisdiction is based on any of Articles 82(1), (2), (3) or (4), the relevant court has jurisdiction in respect of any acts or infringement committed or threatened within

---

[28] [1972] O.J. L299. The Brussels Convention has since been replaced by the Brussels Regulation 44/2001 (see [2001] O.J. L12/1–23).

[29] Non-Community design courts may hear actions relating to Community designs other than those referred to in Reg., Art.81 if the law of the relevant Member State permits. Otherwise, the courts of the State where the Office has its seat (Spain) have jurisdiction to hear such actions—see Reg., Art.93.

[30] In England for unregistered Community designs these are the Chancery Division of the High Court, the Patents County Court and a County Court where there is also a Chancery District Registry (see CPR r.63.13 and Practice Direction 63PD.18). In Scotland it is the Court of Session and in Northern Ireland, the High Court.

[31] Reg., Art.88.

the territory of any of the Member States. However, where jurisdiction is based on Article 82(5), the relevant court only has jurisdiction in respect of acts of infringement committed or threatened in the Member State where that court is situated.

In an action in respect of an infringement or threatened infringement of Community design, Article 85(2) provides that, if the right-holder proves that the conditions laid down in Article 11 have been met and indicates what constitutes the individual character of his Community design, the Community design court must treat the design as valid unless the defendant contests validity by way of a plea or with a counterclaim for a declaration of invalidity. It would seem that the reference to the "conditions laid down in Article 11" is a reference to proving that the design has been made available to the public in accordance with Artile 11(2).[32]

Where actions for infringement or threatened infringement involving the same cause of action and same parties are brought in the courts of different Member States, one seized on the basis of Community design, the other on the basis of a national design providing simultaneous protection, the court other than that first seized of the matter shall of its own motion decline jurisdiction in favour of that court. A Community design court should also reject an action if a final judgment on the merits has been given on the same cause of action and between the same parties on the basis of a design right providing simultaneous protection—and vice versa.[33]

Jurisdiction—claims or counterclaims for a declaration of invalidity. Article 84 of the Regulation deals with issues arising from a claim for invalidity. It provides that (1) an action or counterclaim for invalidity may only be based on the grounds set out in Article 25 of the Regulation;[34] (2) in the cases referred to in Articles 25(2), (3), (4) and (5), the action or counterclaim could only be brought by the person named in those provisions;[35] (3) if the counterclaim is brought in an action to which the holder of the Community design in question was not a party (because, for example, it was an action by the licensee), the holder must be informed and may be joined as a party; and (4) the validity of a Community design cannot be put in issue in an action for a declaration of non-infringement. Where a court declares that a Community design is invalid, that declaration is effective in all Member States.[36]   **13–247**

Remedies. Where a Community design court finds that a defendant has infringed or threatened to infringe a Community design, it must (unless there are special reasons for not doing so) order the following:[37]   **13–248**

(a) an order prohibiting the defendant proceeding with the acts that constituted or would constitute an infringement (*i.e.* an injunction).

(b) an order to seize the infringing products (delivery up).

(c) an order to seize materials and implements predominantly used in order to manufacture the infringing products (if their owner knew the effect for which such use was intended or if such effect would have been obvious).

(d) any other sanctions appropriate under the circumstances and permitted by

---

[32] If Reg., Art.85(2) also required the holder to prove that the conditions in Section 1 (*i.e.* Arts 3 to 9) were satisfied, then the requirement that he indicate what constitutes individual character would be otiose.

[33] Reg., Art.95.

[34] See paras 13–212 *et seq.*, above.

[35] See para. 13–214, above.

[36] Reg., Art.87.

[37] Reg., Art.89.

the national law of the Member State in which the acts of infringement or threatened infringement took place.

13–249 **Interim relief.** Article 90 of the Regulation provides that application may be made to a Community design court for such provisional measures (*i.e.* interim relief) as may be available under national law, even if a Community design court of another Member State has jurisdiction as to the substance of the case. Where such an application is made, the defendant is permitted to raise the issue of the validity of the Community design although not by way of a counterclaim seeking a declaration of invalidity. This is clearly because that is an issue for the court hearing the substance of the case.

13–250 **Appeals.** Appeals from a Community design court of first instance lies to a Community design court of second instance on such conditions as the national law of the Member State should provide. The national rules would also govern any further appeal from the court of second instance.[38]

13. REGISTERED DESIGNS AND REGISTERED COMMUNITY DESIGNS

A. INTRODUCTION

13–251 An industrial design may qualify for protection under the Registered Designs Act 1949 or as a registered Community design under the Council Regulation on Community designs.[39] A detailed discussion of the law of registered designs is outside the scope of this work and the following is merely an outline of some of the relevant law.[40] For a detailed discussion and, in particular a discussion as to process of registration and dealings involving the register, readers are referred to specialist works on the subject.[41]

13–252 **Background.** The history of registered protection for industrial designs and of the Registered Designs Act 1949 have already been described.[42] As has been seen, when the Copyright, Designs and Patents Act 1988 introduced design right, it also made amendments to the 1949 Act in an effort to rationalise the scheme of protection for industrial designs. However, further and more substantial amendments were made to the 1949 Act on December 9, 2001 when the Registered Design Regulations 2001[43] came into force. These amendments were made to implement the terms of the Directive on the Legal Protection of Designs[44] which required Member States of the European Union to harmonise their national laws on registered designs. Shortly thereafter, the Council Regulation on Community design was adopted[45] introducing a short (three-year) period of protection for unregistered Community designs[46] and a system of protection for registered Community designs. This protection for Community designs has not replaced national law. As a result, protection by registration is now available under both the 1949

---

[38] Reg., Art.92.
[39] Regulation (EC) No. 6/2002.
[40] *i.e.* under the RDA 1949, since its amendment by the Registered Design Regulations 2001, and under the Regulation.
[41] Such as *Russell-Clarke & Howe on Industrial Design* (7th ed., Sweet & Maxwell, 2005).
[42] See paras 13–11 *et seq*, above.
[43] SI 2001/3949.
[44] Directive 98/71/EC.
[45] Regulation (EC) No. 6/2002.
[46] The protection of unregistered Community designs has been considered in detail at paras 13–197 *et seq.*, above.

Act and the Regulation. Further, as set out below, much of the law governing registered designs is common to both the 1949 Act (as amended) and the Regulation.

Transitional provisions for the 1949 Act. The amendments to the Registered Designs Act 1949 came into effect on December 9, 2001 but are subject to transitional provisions.[47] In essence, the old law will continue to apply *only* in relation to (a) the determination of applications for registration that were pending on the date when the Regulations came into effect; (b) the cancellation or invalidation of registrations made in espect of any application made before that date; and (c) infringements occurring before that date. In all other respects, the new law applies.   **13–253**

B. THE NEW LAW

Summary of the new law. The Registered Designs Act 1949 in its amended (post-December 6, 2001) form and the Regulation on Community design (Reg. 6/2002) share many provisions in common. In particular, they share the same wide definition of a design, the same requirements for novelty and for individual character, and the same exclusions in respect of designs dictated solely by technical function, of designs of interconnections, and of designs which are contrary to public policy or morality. The scope of protection under the 1949 Act and under the Regulation is also the same—covering both the registered design itself and any other design that does not create a different overall impression on an informer user.   **13–254**

Definition of design. The Registered Designs Act 1949 (as amended) and the Regulation contain the same definition of a "design" for the purposes of registration.[48] That definition is also the same as that which applies for the purposes of unregistered Community design and has been considered in that context.[49]   **13–255**

Requirements of novelty and individual character; the period of grace. The Registered Designs Act 1949 (as amended) and the Regulation also share substantively the same requirements that the design be new and have individual character.[50] Much the same provisions apply to unregistered Community designs and have been considered in that context.[51] There are, however, the following important differences: **13–256**

(1) In the case of a registered design, in assessing whether a design is novel and also whether it has individual character, the required comparisons are between the design in question and other designs that have been made available to the public before the date of filing the application for registration of the design in question (or, if a priority is claimed, before the date of priority). Again, therefore, the issue is not when the design was created, but whether it was new and had individual character when compared with other designs that had been made available to the public as at that date.

---

[47] Registered Design Regulations 2001, SI 2001/3949, regs.11–14.
[48] RDA 1949, s.1(2) and (3) and Reg., Art.3.
[49] See paras 13–200 *et seq.*, above.
[50] RDA 1949, s.1B and Regulation (EC) No. 6/2002, Arts 4–6.
[51] See paras 13–202 *et seq.*, above.

(2) The 12-month so-called "period of grace".[52] By reason of this period of grace, certain disclosures of the design for which protection is claimed will not be treated as disclosures so as to deprive that design of novelty or individual character. This period of grace applies to any disclosure made during the 12 months immediately preceding the date of filing of the application for registration of that design provided that disclosure was made by (a) the designer, (b) his successor in title, or (c) a third person in consequence of information provided or action taken by the designer, or his successor in title.

13–257   **Exclusions.** The 1949 Act and the Regulation contain the same exclusions from protection. These exclusions have been considered above in relation to unregistered Community designs.[53] In brief, they apply in respect of designs solely dictated by the technical function of the product, the designs for interconnections and designs that are contrary to public policy or morality.[54]

13–258   **Duration.** The duration of registered design protection is the same as it was under the Registered Designs Act 1949 before it was amended, *i.e.* a maximum of 25 years. This is made up of an initial five years from registration and four further five-year periods for which the holder can apply (subject to the payment of the appropriate fee).[55]

13–259   **Ownership.** The provisions governing proprietorship of a design and of a registered design for the purposes of the Registered Designs Act 1949 remain unaltered. However, as set out below, those provisions differ from those of the Regulation.

Under the 1949 Act, the person who creates a design is its author. This person is the original proprietor of that design unless he was acting in pursuance of a commission or in the course of employment in which cases, his commissioner or employer is, respectively, the original proprietor. Where the design was generated by computer in circumstances where there is no human author, the author is taken to be the person who made the arrangements necessary for the creation of the design.[56] Title to the design may pass from the original proprietor by assignment, transmission or operation of law.[57] When a design is registered on the application of a person claiming to be the proprietor of the design, that person is registered as the proprietor of the registered design,[58] and title to the registered design may also pass by assignment, transmission or operation of law in which case the person who becomes entitled to it may apply to have notice of his interest entered on the register.[59]

Under the Regulation, the provisions governing ownership are somewhat different.[60] In brief, title will vest in the designer or (if the designer was an employee acting in execution of his duties or under instructions from his employer) in his employer. The positions relating to a commissioned work and to a work generated by computer are not dealt with expressly. The person in whose name the registered Community design is registered, or prior to registration, the person

---

[52] RDA 1949, s.1B(6)(c) and (d) and Reg., Art.7(2).
[53] See paras 13–207 *et seq.*, above.
[54] RDA 1949, ss.1B, 1C and 1D (as amended) and Reg., Arts 8 and 9.
[55] RDA 1949, s.8 (as amended) and Reg., Art.12. Renewals of Community design are governed by Reg., Art.13.
[56] RDA 1949, s.2(1), (1A), (3) and (4).
[57] As is clear from RDA 1949, s.2(2).
[58] RDA 1949, s.1(2) and s.17.
[59] RDA 1949, s.19.
[60] For the ownership of an unregistered Community designs, see paras 13–217 *et seq.*, above.

in whose name the application was filed is deemed to be the person entitled in any proceedings.[61] Title to a Community design can be transferred and the transferree's name entered on the register.[62] Further, the Regulation confers on the designer (even if he is not the owner of the design), the right to be cited as such before the Office and in the register.[63]

Monopoly rights conferred by registration, infringement and permitted acts.   **13–260**
The provisions of the Registered Designs Act 1949 (as amended) and of the Regulation defining the exclusive rights that registration confers on the proprietor (and, therefore, defining the acts capable of constituting an infringement) are in substance, the same. So too are the provisions relating to permitted acts.[64] Subject to two differences, these provisions are also the same as those which apply to unregistered Community designs and have been considered in that context.[65] One crucial difference is that for a registered design, the exclusive rights of the proprietor are monopolistic in nature. Thus, unlike copyright, design right and unregistered Community design, the issue of copying does not arise; if another person does an act covered by the proprietor's exclusive rights, that person may be infringing the registered design or registered Community design regardless of whether or not that person had copied that design. The other difference is that, under the Regulation, a right of prior use shall exist for any third person who can establish that, before the date of filing of the applciation, he had in good faith commenced use in the Community (or has made serious and effective preparations to that end) of a design included within the scope of protection of a registered Community design, which had not been copied from the latter.[66]

Interrelation with design right. A design capable of registration will often, but   **13–261**
will not invariably, also be a design for design right purposes. This is because of the different definitions of design, the different exclusions and the difference between the tests of novelty and individual character that apply to registered designs and the test of originality (including whether the design is commonplace) that applies in design right. Subject to this, a design may be entitled to both forms of protection. Indeed, section 224 of the 1988 Act recognises that the owner of the registered design may also be the owner of the design right and, in such a case, an assignment of the registered design will carry the design right with it unless the contrary appears.

Interrelation with copyright. The interrelation of registered designs with copy-   **13–262**
right has become much less complicated since the 1988 Act because the level of copyright protection for a work is no longer defined expressly by reference to the registration or registrability of any corresponding design.[67] However, sections 51 and 52 of the 1988 Act will in practice remove or limit the copyright protection for many registered or registrable designs. Moreover, under section 53, the copyright in an artistic work is not infringed by anything done in pursuance of an assignment or licence granted by the registered proprietor of a design corresponding to the copyright work and done in good faith in reliance upon the registration and without notice of any proceedings to cancel or rectify the registration. Thus where a person acts pursuant to rights granted by the registered design proprietor,

---

[61] Reg., Art.17.
[62] Reg., Art.28.
[63] Reg., Art.18.
[64] RDA 1949, ss.7 and 7A; Reg., Arts 10, 19–23 and 110.
[65] See paras 13–230 *et seq.*, above.
[66] Reg., Art.22.
[67] For the problems that arose before 1988, see paras 13–11 *et seq.*, above.

he has a defence to any action brought against him but a different person claiming to own the copyright in a corresponding artistic work.[68]

C. THE OLD LAW

13–263   **Summary of the old law under the** 1949 Act. As set out above, the old law (*i.e.* the Registered Designs Act 1949 in its pre-December 9, 2001 form) still governs (a) the determination of applications for registration that were pending on the date when the Regulations came into effect; (b) the cancellation or invalidation of registrations made in respect of any application made before that date; and (c) infringements occurring before that date. Under that old law, there had to be a design (which was more narrowly defined) applied to an article.[69] That design had to have eye appeal[70] and not be dictated solely by the function of the article nor dependent upon the appearance of another article of which it was intended to form an integral part.[71] The design had to be new.[72] Designs were registered in respect of articles or sets of articles. In contrast to design right and copyright, a designer need not satisfy any territorial qualification requirements in order to register his design.

13–264   **Meaning of "design".** Under the old law, a design was defined by section 1(1) of the Registered Designs Act 1949 (before its amendment) as:

"… features of shape, configuration, pattern or ornament applied to an article by any industrial process, being features which in the finished article appeal to and are judged by the eye, but does not include—

(a) a method or principle of construction, or

(b) features of shape or configuration of an article which—

(i) are dictated solely by the function which the article has to perform, or

(ii) are dependent upon the appearance of another article of which the article is intended by the author of the design to form an integral part".

The relevant design has, therefore, to be distinguished from the article to which it was applied. It did not even need to be the design of an entire article. The registrable design comprised only those features which appealed to and were judged by the eye and which were not within the specified exclusions.

13–265   **Shape, configuration, pattern or ornament.** The meaning of the words "shape" and "configuration" has already been considered,[73] and it has been said that the words "pattern" and "ornament" are practically synonymous, being substantially in two as opposed to three dimensions;[74] an article can exist without any pattern or ornament upon it, whereas it can have no existence at all apart from its shape and configuration.

13–266   **Applied to an article.** The relevant features of shape, configuration, pattern or ornament were to be applied to an article by any industrial process. For these purposes, an article meant an article of manufacture, and included any part of an

---

[68] Assuming that he acts in good faith and without knowledge of any proceedings for the cancellation or rectification of the registration.

[69] *i.e.* features of shape, configuration, pattern or ornament applied to an article by any industrial process—see RDA 1949, s.1(1).

[70] s.1(1).

[71] s.1(1)(b).

[72] s.1(2).

[73] See para. 13–48, above.

[74] See *Kestos Ltd v Kempat Ltd* (1936) 53 R.P.C. 139 at 152.

article, provided that part was made and sold separately.[75] The relevant design feature had to be applied to such an article, *i.e.* added to the article by making it to the shape or configuration, or with that feature of pattern or ornament.[76] The reference to the application of the design to an article being by any industrial process simply suggested the capability of the mass production of such articles whether by a machine or by a hand process.

Appeal to and be judged by the eye. Under the old law, the relevant design features had to be such that in the finished article they appealed to, and were judged by the eye. Before it was amended by the 1988 Act, the Registered Designs Act 1949 had referred to features which appeal to, and are judged *solely* by the eye,[77] but even after the 1988 Act, it seems that the test remained whether or not the feature in question was such as to cause a customer to prefer the appearance of the article to which it is applied over the appearance of another article.[78] There had to be something special, peculiar, distinctive, significant or striking about its appearance; something which caught and in that sense appealed to the eye.[79] This was determined according to the eye of the customer at whom the article was aimed. It did not appear to matter whether or not it was the object of the designer to achieve eye appeal nor that the design feature related to the article's function.[80] The relevant feature did not need to be immediately visible. Thus, a design for the interior of a chocolate egg had eye appeal; whilst it was not immediately visible, it would become apparent to a consumer, when the egg was being eaten and would, presumably, be attractive.[81]   **13–267**

Excluded designs. Various designs were specifically excluded from registration under the old law. Thus, a method or principle of construction was excluded as were design features that were dependent upon the appearance of another article of which the article was intended by the author of the design to form an integral part.[82] These exclusions mirrored those which apply in relation to design right and have been considered in that context.[83] The other exclusion under the old law for registered design was of features dictated solely by the function which the article had to perform. This not only excluded those features which allowed and which alone would allow the article to perform its function but also excluded any feature which the designer included solely to make the article work regardless of whether there were other ways in which the article could have been designed in order to perform that function.[84]   **13–268**

Exclusion of designs for articles of primarily literary or artistic character. Section 1(5) of the 1949 Act (in its pre-2001 form) provided for the making of rules to exclude from registration designs for articles of a primarily literary or artistic nature which, it was considered, more properly fell within the field of   **13–269**

---

[75] RDA 1949, s.44(1).

[76] See *Amp Inc v Utilux Proprietary Ltd* 1972 R.P.C. 103 at 108.

[77] See RDA 1949, s.1(3) (prior to amendment).

[78] See *Amp Inc v Utilux Proprietary Ltd* [1972] R.P.C. 103 at 108, 112–113 and 121.

[79] *Amp Inc v Utilux Proprietary Ltd* [1972] R.P.C. 103 at 121.

[80] As with the design features of "Lego" bricks in *Interlego A.G. v Tyco Industries Inc* [1989] A.C. 217. If, however, the only reason why the particular feature was attractive to the observer was that it made the article look best suited for its purpose, then despite having eye appeal, the design was excluded under the functionality exclusion discussed, below—see, for example, *Amp Inc v Utilux Proprietary Ltd* [1971] R.P.C. 103 at 118–119.

[81] See *Ferrero's Design* [1978] R.P.C. 473.

[82] See *Isaac Oren v Red Box Factory* [1998] F.S.R. 676.

[83] See paras 13–55 *et seq.*, above (method or principle of construction) and paras 13–62 *et seq.*, above (must match).

[84] *Amp Inc v Utilux Proprietary Ltd* [1972] R.P.C. 103 at 109–110, 113, 117–118 and 122.

copyright.[85] The application of the Rules made under this section was not always easy to justify. As has been seen,[86] plans for the assembly of a kit of parts for a sailing dinghy were treated as plans within the Rules and, therefore, fell outside the scope of registration.

13–270 **Materiality.** Under section 1(3) of the 1949 Act (in its pre-2001 form), a design could not be registered in respect of an article, if the appearance of the article was not material, *i.e.* if aesthetic considerations were not normally taken into account to a material extent by persons acquiring or using such an article and would not be taken into account if the design were applied to the article.[87]

13–271 **The design had to be "new".** In order to be registered under the old law, the design in question had to be new.[88] In this context, it is important to remember that it was the relevant design features relied upon that had to be new and not necessarily the design of the whole of the article to which they were to be applied.[89] Moreover, when testing for novelty, the question was not whether the particular design (*i.e.* the particular features of shape (etc.)) was novel in itself but whether its application to that particular kind of article was novel.[90]

Under section 1(4) of the 1949 Act (in its pre-2001 form), a design was not to be regarded as new if it was the same as a design registered in respect of the same or any other article in pursuance of a prior application,[91] or the same as a design published in the United Kingdom in respect of the same or any other article before the date of the application.[92] Nor would a design be regarded as new if it differed from such a design only in immaterial details or in features which were variants commonly used in the trade. Whether the differences were in more than just immaterial details was to be judged objectively and by eye by asking whether the design imparted a different appearance.

13–272 **Duration.** Under the 1949 Act (in its pre-2001 form), the initial period of protection provided by registration lasted for five years from registration. This could, however, be extended by four further periods each of five years by application to the registrar. The maximum period of protection was, therefore, 25 years from registration.[93]

---

[85] Under the Registered Design Rules 1995, r.26, designs for works of sculpture (other than casts or models used or intended to be used as models or patterns to be multiplied industrially), wall plaques, medals, medallions and printed matter primarily of a literary or artistic character, including (by way of example) book jackets, calendars, dress-making patterns, greeting cards, maps, plans, etc., are excluded from registration.
[86] *Dorling v Honor Marine Ltd* [1965] Ch. 1, see para. 13–18, above.
[87] RDA 1949, s.1(3).
[88] RDA 1949, s.1(2).
[89] Thus, if the design relied on was the pattern to be applied to the seat of a chair, it was that design and not the design of the chair which was tested for novelty.
[90] *i.e.* the kind of article having regard to its general character and use rather than to the strict categories of articles as set out in the schedule to the design rules—see *Saunder v Wiel* (1892) 10 R.P.C. 29 at 33 and *Re Clarke's Design* (1896) 13 R.P.C. 351.
[91] Under RDA 1949, s.4, an owner of a prior registered design could add to the articles in respect of which that design was registered. He could also apply to modify or vary the registered design provided he did not alter its character or substantially affect its identity.
[92] Under RDA 1949, s.6, certain forms of disclosure (disclosure in confidence or by a third party, etc.) did not, by themselves, prevent registration of the design. For example, where a copyright artistic work had a corresponding design, use of the artistic work (other than its industrial application through the marketing of articles made to the design) would not of itself mean that the design could not be"new" for the purposes of registration under the old law—see RDA 1949, ss.6(4) and (5).
[93] RDA 1949, s.8.

Ownership. The ownership of design under the old law was the same as under the new law and has already been considered.[94]   **13–273**

Infringements. Under the old law, a registered design was infringed by a person   **13–274** who, without licence of the registered proprietor of the design, (a) made or imported either for sale or hire or for use for the purposes of a trade or business or (b) sold, hired, or offered or exposed for sale or hire an article in respect of which the design was registered and to which that design or a design not substantially different from it had been applied.[95] It was also an infringement to make, without licence, anything for enabling such an article to be made in the United Kingdom or elsewhere.[96] Section 7(4) (in its pre-2001 form) dealt with the question of infringement in relation to a kit.[97]

14. COPYRIGHT AND WORKS OF INDUSTRIAL APPLICATION

A. INTRODUCTION

As has been seen,[98] the Copyright, Designs and Patents Act 1988 contains provi-   **13–275** sions intended to prevent copyright being used to protect works which fall more properly within the industrial than the artistic field. Despite this, copyright remains of some importance in relation to works of industrial application which were created after the 1988 Act came into force[99] and of considerable importance where such works were created before that date.

The nature of copyright protection for works of industrial application is best approached by reference to the date when the work in question was created. For these purposes, works fall into the following categories:

(1) Those created on or after August 1, 1989 (after the 1988 Act came into force);

(2) Those created on or after June 1, 1957 but before August 1, 1989 (*i.e.* whilst the Copyright Act 1956 was in force); or

(3) Those created before June 1, 1957 (*i.e.* at any time before the Copyright Act 1956 came into force).

The general law applicable to works created in each of these periods has already been considered in the main Copyright chapters of this work. This Chapter is concerned only with aspects of copyright law which particularly affect copyright works of industrial application.

15. COPYRIGHT WORKS OF INDUSTRIAL APPLICATION MADE ON OR AFTER AUGUST 1, 1989

A. INTRODUCTION

Copyright in works of industrial application. A copyright work of industrial   **13–276** application is likely to be an artistic work.[1] The subsistence of copyright in such a

---

[94] See para. 13–259, above.
[95] RDA 1949, s.7(1) and (2).
[96] RDA 1949, s.7(3).
[97] *i.e.* a complete or substantially complete set of components intended to be assembled into a kit.
[98] See paras 13–29 *et seq.*, above.
[99] August 1, 1989.
[1] *i.e.* (a) a graphic work, photograph, sculpture or collage irrespective of artistic quality; (b) a work

work is considered in the main Copyright section of this book.[2] In brief, the work would have to be original in the copyright sense of the word[3] and the relevant qualification requirements would have to have been satisfied.[4] The acts which (unless they fall within the categories of permitted acts discussed below[5]) constitute infringements of copyright under the 1988 Act have also already been considered in detail.[6]

13–277 **Permitted acts.** The 1988 Act provides for various permitted acts—acts which do not constitute infringements of copyright.[7] Many are of little or no relevance to works of industrial application. The following, however, are of particular importance and will be considered in detail below.

(1) Section 51—which provides that any copyright in a design document or a model recording or embodying a design for anything other than an artistic work will not be infringed by certain design-right-type acts of infringements. However, other acts may still infringe the copyright in such a work.

(2) Section 52—which provides that where an artistic work is exploited by or with the licence of the copyright owner through the making and marketing of articles which constitute copies of the work, then the period of copyright protection for the work is reduced in respect of a wide range of activities to a period of 25 years from the date of first marketing.

(3) Section 53—which provides that copyright in an artistic work is not infringed by anything done in pursuance of an assignment or licence by a person registered under the Registered Designs Act 1949 as the proprietor of a corresponding design and which is done in good faith in reliance upon that registration.

B. SECTION 51

(i) Statement of section 51(1)

13–278 **Section 51.** Section 51(1) of the 1988 Act provides that:
"It is not an infringement of any copyright in a design document or model recording or embodying a design for anything other than an artistic work or a typeface to make an article to the design or to copy an article made to the design".

(ii) Preliminary points

13–279 **Scheme of 1988 Act.** Section 51 is crucial to the 1988 Act scheme of protection for industrial designs under the 1988 Act. Broadly speaking, its aim is to remove industrial designs from the sphere of copyright protection.[8] To do this, section 51 distinguishes between works that record designs for artistic works or typefaces on the one hand, and works that record designs for anything else on the other.

---

of architecture being a building or a model for a building or (c) a work of artistic craftsmanship—CDPA 1988, s.4.
[2] See Ch.3, above.
[3] CDPA 1988, s.1(1)(a).
[4] s.1(3).
[5] See para. 13–277, below.
[6] See Chs 7 and 8, above.
[7] The permitted acts are set out in Ch.III of the CDPA 1988 and are discussed in the main copyright section of this book—see Ch.9, above.
[8] This was made clear in the course of Parliamentary debate—see *Hansard*, H.L. Vol.490, col.1175; H.L. Vol.491, col.185 and H.C., SCE, col.244. However, the difficulty in achieving this

Section 51 has no effect on the scope of copyright protection for the former but radically reduces the scope of copyright protection for the latter. The rationale for this is that where the work in question is the design for an end product which is itself an artistic work (or typeface) protected by copyright, then the work should also be protected by copyright. If, however, the end product is not an artistic work (or typeface) and thus has no copyright protection, then there is no reason why a document recording the design of that product should have such protection.

Partial exclusion. Although section 51 was intended to take industrial designs out of copyright,[9] it does not do this by providing that no copyright can subsist in a work which records or embodies an industrial design. Instead, it provides that certain acts[10] will not infringe copyright. Other acts may still infringe copyright.[11] It should be noted, however, that if the work is an artistic work which has been exploited industrially then even if copyright protection was not excluded by section 51, the term of copyright protection may be reduced to 25 years by section 52.[12]   **13–280**

No correlation between the operation of section 51 and the availability of design right protection. The wording of section 51 plainly shows that it is intended to exclude copyright protection from those areas in which design right is to operate. However, the fact that an act does not infringe copyright because of the operation of section 51 does not necessarily mean that that act must infringe design right instead. The limitation upon the copyright protection imposed by section 51 is not co-extensive with the existence of design right protection. There may well be cases where the copyright subsisting in a work recording an industrial design is unenforceable under section 51 but no design right subsists in the design. It may be, for example, that the design right does not subsist because the design is commonplace,[13] or because it is excluded by the must fit or must match provisions of section 213(3)(b),[14] or because the design right qualification requirements are not satisfied.[15] Similarly, the fact that the copying of a design document does not infringe design right does not necessarily mean that it must have infringed copyright in that document.[16]   **13–281**

Examples: **13–282**
(1) A drawing of a contact lens is original in the sense that the drawing is the designer's own work. Copyright will, therefore, subsist in the drawing. However, the design embodied in the drawing may not be original for design purposes because it is commonplace. If (as seems probable) the design drawing was created for the making of lenses, then section 51 will

---

aim is apparent from cases such as *Hi-Tech Autoparts Ltd v Towergate Two Ltd (No.2)* [2002] F.S.R. 270, see para. 13–290, example (11), below.

[9] See para. 13–279, above.

[10] *i.e.* the making of an article to the relevant design or the copying of an article made to that design. Broadly speaking, these are the design-right-type acts of infringement.

[11] In this respect, CDPA 1988, s.51 is similar to Copyright Act 1956, s.10—see para. 13–17, above.

[12] For a discussion of CDPA 1988, s.52, see paras 13–297 *et seq.*, below.

[13] See paras 13–73 *et seq.*, above.

[14] CDPA 1988, s.213(3) excludes design right from methods of construction, "must fit" and "must match" designs and surface decoration, see paras 13–56 *et seq.*, above. Copyright has no equivalent exclusions.

[15] See, for example, *Mackie Designs Inc v Behringer Specialised Studio Equipment (UK) Ltd* [1999] R.P.C. 717 where the claimant (a US company) sought (unsuccesfully) to rely on copyright in its drawings of circuit boards because it did not qualify for design right protection. For the differing qualification provisions for copyright and design right, see Ch.3 and paras 13–82 *et seq.*, above, respectively.

[16] It is not the case that if you do not have design right you must have copyright—see *Lambretta Clothing Co Ltd v Teddy Smith (UK) Ltd* [2004] EWCA Civ 886 at paras 35–38.

apply to limit copyright protection even though the design has no design right protection. The designer, therefore, can rely on neither copyright nor design right to prevent others making lenses to his design.[17]

(2) Copyright may subsist in design drawings of a car exhaust pipe. Section 51 will prevent the designer relying on that copyright to prevent others making exhausts to his design. However, the design right requirement of originality and its "must fit" exclusion may well mean that the design (or some of its features) has no design right protection.

(iii) Conditions for application of section 51

13–283 As indicated above, section 51 only operates to exclude copyright protection in respect of "a design document or model recording or embodying a design for anything other than an artistic work or a typeface."

13–284 **Design document.** For these purposes, a design document is defined by section 51(3) as "any record of a design, whether stored in the form of a drawing, a written description, a photograph, data stored on a computer or otherwise." The meaning of these words has already been considered in the context of design right.[18] In brief, the principal definition requires that it be any record of a design. There is no reason why this should be construed narrowly. For example, the definition refers expressly to a design being recorded in a drawing but there is no reason why it may not be recorded in a diagram or plan. The reference to "a written description" is curious,[19] but serves to emphasise the width of the definition of a "design document". The meaning of "a design" for these purposes is considered below.[20]

13–285 **Model.** The word "model" is not defined by the 1988 Act but in ordinary usage can mean a three dimensional representation of either a proposed or an existing structure or object.[21] Of course, section 51 is only concerned with models in which copyright is capable of subsisting—for example, a model which qualifies as a copyright work in its own right as a sculpture.[22]

13–286 **Illustrations**
(1) A model for an aircraft wing may be a sculpture or, possibly, a work of artistic craftsmanship. If so, it would be an artistic work in which copyright subsists. However, such a model would also be a design for a non-artistic work, namely an aircraft wing. Section 51 would, therefore, operate to limit its copyright protection.

(2) A plaster cast model for a marble carving of a head would probably be an artistic work[23] in which copyright subsists. As the marble carving would also be an artistic work, the plaster model embodies the design *for* an artistic work and section 51 would not operate to limit copyright in the model.

(3) Copyright subsists in the model for a building.[24] As the building itself is

[17] See *Ocular Sciences Ltd v Aspect Vision Care Ltd* [1997] R.P.C. 289.
[18] CDPA 1988, s.263(1) and para. 13–79, above.
[19] See para. 13–295, below.
[20] See paras 13–231 and 13–287 *et seq.*, below .
[21] See the *Shorter Oxford English Dictionary*.
[22] See para. 3–58, above.
[23] *i.e.* a sculpture or a work of artistic craftsmanship within CDPA 1988, s.4(1).
[24] s.4(1)(b).

also an artistic work in its own right,[25] the model would be a model for an artistic work. Again, section 51 would not operate in relation to the model.

Recording or embodying a design. For section 51(1) to operate, the relevant   **13–287** design document or model must be one "recording or embodying a design".[26] Reading into this the definition of "design" contained in section 51(3), this means that for section 51(1) to operate, the relevant design document or model must be one—

"recording or embodying a [design of any aspect of the shape or configuration (whether internal or external) of the whole or part of an article, other than surface decoration]"

The definition of "design" is very similar to that which applies in relation to design right.[27] Clearly, therefore, as a general rule, section 51 is intended to operate to limit copyright protection for designs of the shape and configuration of articles, *i.e.* for industrial designs.[28] There is, however, an important difference between section 51 and the design right provisions relating to a design. This is that section 51 has no equivalent to sections 213(3)(a) or (b) of the 1988 Act. This difference ensures that methods of construction and "must fit" and "must match" design features are not only excluded from design right protection (by reason of section 213(3)(a) and (b)), but that they are also excluded from the copyright protection that might otherwise be available to them when recorded in a design document.[29]

Another difference between section 51 and the design right provisions is that "surface decoration" is expressly excluded from the definition of a "design" for the purposes of section 51. By contrast, it is not excluded from the definition of a "design" for design right purposes. Instead, a separate subsection, section 213(3)(c), provides that design right does not subsist in surface decoration. This difference would not appear to be particularly significant and, subject to difficulties arising from *Lambretta Clothing Co Ltd v Teddy Smith (UK) Ltd,*[30] it seems clear that Parliament intended that where a design document records surface decoration, the designer should be able to claim copyright protection but not design right protection.[31]

Lambretta Clothing Co Ltd v Teddy Smith (UK) Ltd. As indicated above, certain   **13–288** difficulties have arisen in relation to section 51 as a result of the difference of views in the Court of Appeal in *Lambretta Clothing Co Ltd v Teddy Smith (UK) Ltd*[32] *Lambretta* concerned a design drawing showing a track top made up of red body panels, blue sleeves with white stripes and a white zip. The shape of the garment was not original (being based on an existing sample). However, the claimant claimed design right in the choice of colours, and copyright in the whole

---

[25] s.4(1)(b).

[26] CDPA 1988, s.51(1).

[27] s.213(2). See paras 13–44 *et seq.,* above.

[28] See *Jo-y-Jo v Matalan Retail Ltd* [2000] E.D.C.R. 178, where it was held that CDPA 1988, s.51 did not apply in relation to the design of the edging and welt of a garment because they were not aspects of the shape or configuration of the garment.

[29] See paras 13–281 and 13–282, example (2), above, and see *Lambretta Clothing Co Ltd v Teddy Smith (UK) Ltd* [2004] EWCA Civ 886 at para.80.

[30] [2004] EWCA Civ 886. See paras 13–288 *et seq.,* below.

[31] The reference to surface decoration was added to s.51(3) during Parliamentary debate. It was intended to ensure that surface decoration, such as relief carving, which might in one sense be said to be an aspect of shape or configuration, was not excluded from copyright protection. See *Hansard,* H.L. Vol.493, cols 1179–1180. In *Jo-y-Jo v Matalan Retail Ltd* [2000] E.D.C.R. 178, it was also held that s.51 did not exclude protection for the embroidery on the front of a garment because it was surface decoration.

[32] [2004] EWCA Civ 886.

of the design drawing as an artistic work. The design right claim was rejected (by a majority of the Court) on the basis that the choice of colours was not an aspect of shape or configuration and (unanimously) on the basis that, even if it was, it was commonplace as well as being surface decoration. There was, however, a difference of opinion regarding the application of section 51.

Jacob L.J. found that section 51 did operate. In his judgment, the drawing was a design document and the fact that "surface decoration" was excluded from the definition of a design made no difference. This was because the colours had no existence (either physically or conceptually) apart from the shape of the top. It was not as if that surface decoration could exist on other substrates in the way that a picture or logo could. Thus, if the claimant could assert artistic copyright in respect of the colours it would, in effect, be asserting copyright in the shape of the garment which was what section 51 was intended to prevent.[33]

Mance L.J. disagreed.[34] In his judgment, for section 51 to operate, it was necessary for the court to conclude "that the article was made, or was a copy of an article made, to the design meaning 'the design [as embodied in the drawing] of any aspect of the shape or configuration ... of the whole or part of an article, other than surface decoration.'" Even if this was satisfied, section 51 only operated to the extent that the article had been made or was copied from an article made to the design in the limited sense as defined by section 51(3). To the extent that the design in issue went beyond the design in that limited sense, copyright in the design document would remain enforceable. On this basis, because it was improbable that the defendant had copied the shape and configuration shown in the drawing but had at most copied the colours (which the Court of Appeal had found were not aspects of shape or configuration), section 51 could not operate. Mance L.J. went on to comment that he believed that his conclusions were consistent with the position regarding surface decoration which is excluded from design right by section 213(3)(c) but which is excluded by section 51(3) from the concept of a design for the purposes of section 51(1). Thus, copyright in a design document showing an article with surface decoration could still be infringed. In his judgment, the wording of section 51 did not provide any basis for limiting copyright protection for surface decoration to a situation where the surface decoration could be said itself to consitute a separate drawing.

Sedley L.J. said he agreed with Jacob L.J. However, he also stated that in his view, the colours were more than just surface decoration and were, in fact, part of the configuration of the top.[35] On that basis, section 51 would clearly apply and the issue of the colours having no existence apart from the shape of the top would be irrelevant.

It is difficult to determine what exactly (if any) is the *ratio* of *Lambretta* in relation to section 51 and, as Sedley L.J. commented, neither the approach of Jacob L.J. nor that of Mance L.J. is unproblematical. However, it is submitted that there is much to be said for the view of Mance L.J. The difficulty with the approach of Jacob L.J. is that the claimant was not asserting that the defendant had made an article to the design as defined by section 51(3). Instead, it was asserting that the defendant had copied the colours shown on its drawing—which colours were not part of the "design of any aspect of the shape or configuration ... of ... an article other than surface decoration".[36] To that extent, it is difficult to see why section 51(1) should operate to limit copyright protection for the drawing. Indeed, it

---

[33] [2004] EWCA Civ 886, para.39.

[34] [2004] EWCA Civ 886, at paras 79–85

[35] [2004] EWCA Civ 886, paras 88 and 89. If they were an aspect of the configuration, CDPA 1988, s.51 would clearly operate.

[36] As Jacob L.J. (and Mance L.J.) accepted for the purposes of the design right claim (see para.29).

seems strange that a claimant should be deprived of copyright protection for its design for the colouring of an article simply because its record of that design was recorded in a design document that depicted the whole article. Equally, it seems a strange result that colours found to be surface decoration for the purposes of design right were not treated as being surface decoration for the purposes of section 51. Whilst it might be correct to say that the colours in *Lambretta* were somehow limited by the shape of the top, there is nothing obvious in the wording of section 51 to suggest that they could not therefore still be treated as surface decoration for the purposes of section 51. Indeed, it could be argued that the colours were no more limited by the shape of the top than any other form of decoration would be when such decoration is designed to fit the shape of the surface to which it is to be applied (*e.g.* a face designed to cover the surface on a mug).

A design *for* anything other than an artistic work. For section 51 to operate, the relevant design document or model must not only record or embody a design, it must also be a design document or model "*for* anything other than an artistic work or typeface".   **13–289**

It is important to note that section 51 requires that the relevant design must be both the design *of* an article in the sense set out above, and also the design *for* an article (other than an artistic work or a typeface). The use of the word *for* suggests that the design document or model was produced as part of the process of producing something else; that it was a design[37] created as a precursor to an article rather than being created as an end in itself. The words "artistic work" will, presumably, bear their usual meaning as set out in section 4 of the 1988 Act.[38] Clearly, if the end product is an artistic work capable of protection by copyright, then it makes sense for any design documents for, and models of that product, to be similarly protected.[39] As appears from the examples set out below, it seems likely that one effect of section 51 will be an increase in the importance of the category of works of artistic craftsmanship as a type of artistic work.[40] However, as example (11) below shows, it is possible that the designs for some very functional and mass produced articles may still qualify for copyright protection on the ground that the articles are engravings and, hence, artistic works. This is plainly a serious limitation on the effectiveness of section 51 as a means of excluding copyright from the sphere of industrial designs.

The question whether the design was *for* anything other than an artistic work or typeface turns, it is submitted, on the intentions of the designer. If the work was intended to be used as the design document or model *for* a product which is neither artistic nor a typeface, then the section will operate; otherwise, it does not. Although the section does not expressly say so, it seems that this state of mind must be determined as at the time that the design document or model was created.[41] Thus, section 51 would not apply to a work which started life as a purely artistic work even if that work was subsequently used as the design basis for industrially exploited articles. In such a case, the only limitation on the copy-

---

[37] As recorded or embodied in the relevant design document or model.

[38] See Ch.3, above.

[39] See, generally, the explanation of CDPA 1988, s.51 given in the course of debate by Lord Beaverbrook, *Hansard*, H.L. Vol.491, cols 185–186. See also *Guild v Eskandar Ltd* [2001] F.S.R. 645 where certain items of designer ladies clothing were found not to be artistic works or works of artistic craftsmanship. Accordingly, s.51 operated to limit copyright protection for the designs for such items. This finding was not challenged on appeal ([2002] EWCA Civ 316).

[40] For a full discussion of the meaning of works of artistic craftsmanship see paras 3–63 *et seq.*, above.

[41] This would be consistent with the approach of the House of Lords in construing Copyright Act 1911, s.22 in *King Features Syndicate Ltd v O & M Kleeman Ltd* [1941] A.C. 417, see para. 13–16, above.

right protection would be that provided by section 52, which is considered below.[42]

13–290   **Examples.** The way in which section 51 operates is best understood by way of examples.

(1) A craftsman potter produces a one-off vase without producing any prior design documents or models. The vase is not a design document nor is it a model. It is the intended end product. Section 51 will not operate to limit any copyright which subsists in the vase as a work of artistic craftsmanship. Design right may also subsist in the design of the vase.[43] However, design right protection is excluded in favour of the copyright protection.[44]

(2) A craftsman potter produces a prototype vase with a view to mass producing vases to that design. Copyright may subsist in the prototype as a work of artistic craftsmanship. However, in contrast to illustration (1) above, this prototype *is* a model in that it records a design for future vases. Whether section 51 operates will depend upon whether or not those future vases are themselves artistic works (*i.e.* works of artistic craftsmanship). If they are not (because, for example, they are mass produced with no element of craftsmanship), section 51 will operate to limit copyright protection. It seems that this would also be so even if the design was rejected and never used. Another person may, therefore, make vases to this design without infringing copyright, although he may of course be infringing such design right as may subsist in the design.[45]

(3) A famous painter paints a picture featuring a rustic kitchen chair. Copyright will subsist in the painting as an artistic work. It might be argued that the painting is a design document in that it records the design of the shape and configuration *of* a chair.[46] However, the artist did not create the painting with a view to making chairs to that design. Accordingly the painting, whilst recording (arguably) the design *of* a chair, is not a design document *for* a chair. Section 51 will not operate and the painting will retain full copyright protection. If a manufacturer subsequently obtains the artist's permission to make chairs to the design shown in the painting, section 51 will still not apply (although section 52 would[47]). The painting was not a design document *for* a chair at the time that it was created.

(4) If the same artist had produced a sketch depicting a chair prior to producing his painting, then copyright would also subsist in that sketch as an artistic work. As in illustration (3) above, the sketch is the design document *of* a chair but it is plainly not the design document *for* a chair because it is not preparatory to the production of a chair. If the sketch can be said to be a design document *for* anything, it is *for* the painting which is an

---

[42] See paras 13–297 *et seq.*, below.

[43] The vase being an article made to the design, CDPA 1988, s.213(6), see para. 13–80, above. This assumes that the design right conditions for subsistence are satisfied.

[44] s.236.

[45] See the note to Example (1), above.

[46] On the other hand, it might be said that the whole essence of *a design* is that it is something which is preparatory to the creation of something else. Accordingly, as most artists create a painting intending it to be an end in itself, a painting cannot be said to be a *design* either *of* or *for* an object depicted in the painting. On this basis, as with illustration (1), above, CDPA 1988, s.51 would never be relevant. The difficulty with such a construction is that it begs the question why the word *"for"* (as opposed to the word "of") was then used in s.51. The fact is that the painting does depict the artist's idea of a chair, or it may record the shape or configuration of an actual chair (depending upon whether or not the artist is painting from real life). The painting records, in that sense, the design *of* a chair even though it is not the design *for* a chair.

[47] See paras 13–297 *et seq.*, below.

artistic work. Accordingly, section 51 would not operate to limit copyright.[48]

(5) Copyright may subsist in a painting or sketch created by a furniture designer of a chair intended for mass production. However, the work is not only a design document recording the design *of* a chair but is also a design document *for* a chair. As the chair is unlikely to be an artistic work in its own right,[49] section 51 would operate. Accordingly, another person who makes a chair to that design would not infringe copyright but may, of course, be infringing any design right which subsists in the design.[50]

(6) If the same furniture designer had sketched only a chair leg, the result would be the same as in (5) above. If the chair leg was an article in its own right, the sketch would be a design document recording the design *of* a chair leg and would also be a design document *for* a chair leg.[51] If the chair leg was not an "article" in its own right but is merely a part of a larger article,[52] then the sketch would be a design document recording the design of a chair leg but it would still be a design document *for* the chair to which the leg is to be fitted. In either event, as the chair *for* which the design was created is unlikely to be an artistic work,[53] section 51 would operate.

(7) An artist draws cartoon sketches of a futuristic car for a comic strip in a child's magazine. Copyright will subsist in these sketches as artistic works. Further, although the works are design documents in the sense that they record a design *of* a car, they are not design documents *for* anything other than an artistic work. There is no intention to apply them to a car. Section 51 does not, therefore, operate.[54]

(8) The same artist is asked to design a futuristic car which is to be built for and used in a new science fiction film. The artist's sketches will be design documents recording the design of a car and, as the futuristic car when made for the film may well be an artistic work,[55] they would also be design documents *for* a thing which is an artistic work. If so, section 51 would not operate.

(9) An artist draws cartoon sketches of an imaginary character to be used in a newspaper.[56] Copyright will subsist in the sketches as artistic works but, as with the vase in illustration (1) above, the sketches are not designs *for* anything other than an artistic work. Section 51 does not, therefore, operate.

(10) An interior designer makes a drawing of the proposed pattern to be ap-

---

[48] It could also be argued that the design is for the surface decoration of an article (*i.e.* the painting) and, therefore, that CDPA 1988, s.51 would not operate because surface decoration is excluded from the definition of a design by s.51(3) For the problems relating to surface decoration, see para. 13–288, above.

[49] Unless, which seems unlikely, the chair qualifies as a work of artistic craftsmanship—but see *George Hensher Ltd v Restawile Upholstery (Lancs) Ltd* [1976] A.C. 64 and para. 13–24, above.

[50] See the note to Example (1), above.

[51] Which is probably not an artistic work—see para. 13–24, above.

[52] *i.e.* a chair leg which is made separately from the rest of the chair rather than merely being a part of a larger article—see para. 13–49, above.

[53] See para. 13–24, above.

[54] See *BBC Worldwide Ltd v Pally Screen Printing Ltd* [1998] F.S.R. 665 at 672 where it was stated that if the relevant drawings had from the outset been intended to be used to decide the shape and appearance of three-dimensional children's television characters (the Teletubbies), section 51 would arguably operate whereas if they had been intended to be used as prototypes for a comic strip it would not.

[55] *i.e.* a work of artistic craftsmanship—see by way of analogy, *Shelley Film Ltd v Rex Features Ltd* [1994] E.M.L.R. 134.

[56] For example, sketches such as those of Popeye in *King Features Syndicate Ltd v O & M Kleeman Ltd* [1941] A.C. 417.

plied to a stencil. Copyright will subsist in the drawing as an artistic work. The drawing is not of surface decoration but is the design document recording the design of the actual shape or configuration *of* the stencil.[57] Further, it is also the design document *for* a stencil. However, as a stencil made to the design would probably be an artistic work,[58] section 51 would not operate.

(11) A designer creates drawings and an engraved metal plate to produce rubber floor mats for cars. The drawings and plate are, respectively, a design document and a model recording the design for the rubber mats. However, as the mats themselves were (strangely) artistic works (being engravings), section 51 did not operate to limit copyright protection for the designs.[59]

13–291   **Or a typeface**. Typefaces are also expressly excluded from the operation of section 51. The distinct copyright regime which applies to typefaces has already been considered.[60]

(iv) Permitted acts under section 51

13–292   Where section 51(1) applies, it is not an infringement of any copyright in the relevant design document or model to make an article to the design or to copy an article made to the design. However, these are only permitted acts in relation to the copyright in the work. A person who so acts may nevertheless infringe any design right which may subsist in the relevant design. Further, as has been pointed out,[61] other acts may still constitute infringements of copyright.

13–293   **To make an article to the design**. The phrase "to make an article to the design" is not defined for the purposes of section 51,[62] however, it clearly refers to the making of a three dimensional object to the design. Accordingly, using the examples set out in paragraph 13–282, above, the making of contact lenses in accordance with the drawings would amount to making articles to the design and would not infringe copyright by reason of section 51. Similarly, making exhausts to the drawings would not infringe copyright in the drawings. By contrast, the making of a photocopy of the drawings would remain an infringement of copyright. Whether or not the making of such a photocopy constituted the making of an article,[63] this would not be making an article *to the design* but would, instead, be copying the design document.

13–294   **To copy an article made to the design**. At first sight, this provision appears to add little to the previous provision which allows the making of an article to the

---

[57] See para. 13–67 (example 4), above.

[58] Being either an "engraving, etching, lithograph, woodcut or similar work" within CDPA 1988, s.4(2)(b) or, possibly, a work of artistic craftsmanship.

[59] See *Hi-Tech Autoparts Ltd v Towergate Two Ltd (No.2)* [2002] F.S.R. 270. Whilst this result seems strange, the finding that the mats were engravings was in accordance with the decisions in *Wham-O Manufacturing Co v Lincoln Industries Ltd* [1985] R.P. 127 and *Arnold (James) & Co Ltd v Miafern Ltd* [1980] R.P.C. 397. See para. 3–55, above.

[60] See para. 9–145, above.

[61] See para. 13–280, above.

[62] The same words are used in relation to primary infringements of design right—see CDPA 1988, s.226(1) and are, not entirely helpfully, defined in that context as "copying the design so as to produce articles exactly or substantially to that design"—see CDPA 1988, s.226(2) and paras 13–146 *et seq.*, above.

[63] There are good reasons for suggesting that a photocopy is not an article for these purposes. In this context, as in the design right context, an article should be seen as something with shape and configuration— *i.e.* a positive physical form—see para. 13–49, above. This conclusion is supported by *BBC Worldwide Ltd v Pally Screen Printing Ltd* [1998] F.S.R. 665 where the copying of a design by printing it on a T-shirt did not constitute the making of an article to the design.

design. However, the words "to copy" in section 51 are wider than the words "to make an article". They mean that, where section 51 operates, a competitor is not only permitted (for copyright purposes) to make an article by copying articles which the designer has made to his design[64] but also to produce his own design drawings[65] provided they have been copied from articles made to the design document rather than being copied direct from the designer's drawings.

In effect, this part of section 51(1) operates to exclude a copyright claim in respect of any act of copying of an article made to the design, whatever the result of that copying. It was on this basis that it was held to be arguable that section 51 excluded a copyright claim in *BBC Worldwide Ltd v PallyScreen Printing Ltd*[66] In that case, the defendants had made garments featuring pictures of the characters from the BBC television series "The Teletubbies". The picture on one group of garments had clearly been copied from a photograph of the Teletubby characters and it was arguable that the picture on the other group of garments had been copied from the Teletubby characters as they had appeared on television. In both cases, there had been indirect copying of the claimant's copyright drawings.[67] However, on the assumption that the drawings had been the design *for* the characters (and not, therefore, the designs *for* something that was an artistic work or typeface[68]), then what the defendants had done was to copy an article made to the design (*i.e.* the Teletubby shown in the photograph or on television). On this basis, it was arguable that section 51 operated.[69] Strangely, the result would have been different if the defendant had copied the drawings directly, for in such a case, the defendant would not have been copying an article made to the design nor would it have been making an article to the design within section 51.[70]

Making an article where the design document is a written description. As has been seen, the definition of a design document expressly includes a design recorded in the form of a "written description".[71] This inclusion is curious. As the making of a three dimensional article cannot infringe the copyright in a literary work,[72] it would seem that section 51 had no need to provide for such a design.[73]   **13–295**

Section 51(2). Finally, under section 51(2),[74] it is not an infringement of *the copyright* to issue to the public, or include in the film or communicate to the public, anything the making of which was, by virtue of section 51(1), not an infringement of that copyright. The reason for this provision is that, where section 51(1) applies, the article made to the design or a copy of an article made to the design is   **13–296**

---

[64] Such an action would also be covered by the right to make an article to the design.

[65] Which, as stated in para. 13–293, above, would not be covered by the permission to "make an article to the design".

[66] [1998] F.S.R. 665.

[67] In accordance with the decision in *King Features Syndicate Inc v O and M Kleeman Ltd* [1941] A.C. 417. See para. 13–16, above.

[68] See para. 13–293, above.

[69] In *Mackie Designs Inc v Behringer Specialised Studio Equipment (UK) Ltd* [1999] R.P.C. 717 at 723 it was said that the reasoning in *BBC Worldwide Ltd v Pally Screen Printing Ltd* [1998] F.S.R. 665 was said to be not just "arguable" but "compelling". In *Mackie* it was held that a defendant who had copied a circuit board made to the claimant's circuit diagram was indirectly copying the claimant's design but was doing so by copying an article made to that design. Hence, a copyright claim would be excluded by CDPA 1998, s.51.

[70] See *BBC Worldwide Ltd v Pally Screen Printing Ltd* [1998] F.S.R. 665, where it was commented that, with any attempt to draw a boundary between copyright and design right protection, there would inevitably be hard cases near the borderline.

[71] CDPA 1988, s.51(3).

[72] See para. 7–34, above.

[73] It may be that the words were intended to cover cases where the design comprises a drawing supplemented by a written description.

[74] Since October 31, 2003 when it was amended by the Copyright and Related Rights Regulations 2003 (SI 2003/2498).

not an infringing copy. Thus, most dealings with that article or copy could not amount to infringements of copyright.[75] However, as has been seen, the issue to the public of copies not previously in circulation would usually constitute a primary infringement of copyright even though the copies in question are not infringing copies. Accordingly, these and the other acts referred to in section 51(2) are expressly made permitted acts so far as copyright is concerned.

C. SECTION 52

(i) Introduction

13–297   Although section 51 of the 1988 Act will operate to limit the copyright protection available for many industrial designs, it does not deal with the problem of copyright protection for artistic works properly so-called (such as sculptures or paintings) or designs for such works which are subsequently exploited industrially. This is the purpose of section 52.

13–298   **Rationale.** What lies behind section 52 is the feeling that full copyright protection, whilst justified in the case of artistic works which remain in the artistic field, is not justified where the copyright owner chooses to exploit his work industrially. In such a case, there is no reason why the period of protection to which the copyright owner is entitled should be any longer than the period of protection available to the proprietor of a registered design. To achieve this, section 52 (where it applies) reduces the period of copyright protection in respect of most but not all acts of infringement to a period of 25 years from the end of the year in which the work in question was first exploited.[76]

13–299   **Interrelationship with** section 51. The operation of section 52 is not dependent upon, nor is it mutually exclusive with the operation of section 51. Where an artistic work is exploited industrially, section 52 may operate to reduce the period of whatever copyright protection is available for the work regardless of whether or not the types of acts capable of infringing that copyright have been limited by reason of section 51.

(ii) Statement of section 52

13–300   Section 52 provides:

"(1) This section applies where an artistic work has been exploited by or with the licence of the copyright owner, by—

(a) making by an industrial process articles falling to be treated for the purposes of this Part as copies of the work, and

(b) marketing such articles in the United Kingdom or elsewhere.

(2) After the end of the period of 25 years from the end of the calendar year in which such articles are first marketed, the work may be copied by making articles of any description, or doing anything for the purpose of making articles of any description, and anything may be done in relation to articles so made, without infringing copyright in the work".

---

[75] See Ch.8, above.

[76] In this sense, CDPA 1988, s.52 is similar in approach to Copyright Act 1956, s.10(2) and (3) (as amended by the Design Copyright Act 1968). However, in contrast to s.10, the operation of s.52 is not in any way dependent upon whether or not the design in question was registrable.

(iii) Conditions for application of section 52

Industrial process. For section 52 to operate, the relevant artistic work must   **13–301**
have been exploited by the making of articles by an industrial process.[77] Under
section 52(4), the Secretary of State may, by Order, provide for the circumstances
in which an article, or any description of an article, is to be regarded for the
purposes of section 52 as made by an industrial process. The relevant Order[78]
provides that:

> "An article is to be regarded for the purposes of section 52 ... as made by an
> industrial process if—
>> (a) it is one of more than fifty articles which—
>>> (i) all fall to be treated for the purposes of Part I of this Act as cop-
>>> ies of a particular artistic work, but
>>> (ii) do not all together constitute a single set of articles as defined in
>>> section 44 of the Registered Designs Act 1949; or
>> (b) it consists of goods manufactured in lengths or pieces, not being hand-
>> made goods".

Despite the reference to an industrial process, the wording of the Order makes
it clear that section 52 may apply whether the relevant articles have been made
by hand or by some mechanical process. The reference to industrial for these
purposes is a reference to the scale rather than the precise means of production.
There is, however, an exception in that section 52 will not apply to goods which
are manufactured in lengths or pieces and which are hand-made. This exception
may save full-term copyright in the case of, say, lengths of hand-shaped
architrave or pieces of a hand-made jigsaw.[79] It would seem that there is no reason why each of the 51 or more articles made need be identical provided they are
all copies of the relevant work.

Articles. For section 52 to operate, articles must have been made. The meaning   **13–302**
of "article" has been considered in relation to design right[80] and there is no reason
to believe that a different meaning should be adopted here. However, the making
of certain articles will not trigger the operation of section 52. First, section 52(6)
provides that references in section 52 to articles do not include films. Thus, the
making of multiple copies of a film of an artistic work will not amount to the
making of articles for the purposes of section 52. Accordingly, copyright protection for the artistic work will not be reduced as a result of the making of such
films.[81] Secondly, under section 52(4), the Secretary of State is empowered to
exclude from the operation of section 52 such articles of a primarily artistic or literary nature as he may think fit. The following articles are excluded by the relevant Order:[82]

> "(a) works of sculpture, other than casts or models used or intended to be
> used as models or patterns to be multiplied by any industrial process;
> (b) wall plaques, medals and medallions; and
> (c) printed matter primarily of a literary or artistic character, including

---

[77] CDPA 1988, s.52(1)(a).
[78] The Copyright (Industrial Process and Excluded Articles) (No.2) Order 1989 (SI 1989/1070),
para.2—Vol.2 at B8.ii, below.
[79] Both the architrave and the jigsaw may also qualify as "sculptures". If so, they would in any
event be excluded from the operation of s.52 by the Copyright (Industrial Process and Excluded
Articles) (No.2) Order 1989 (SI1989/1070), para.3(1)(a), see paras 13–302, below.
[80] CDPA 1988, s.213(2). See para. 13–49, above.
[81] See *Hansard*, H.L. Vol.501, cols 245–246.
[82] The Copyright (Industrial Process and Excluded Articles) (No.2) Order 1989 (SI 1989/1070),
para.3(1)—see Vol.2 at B8.ii.

book jackets, calendars, certificates, coupons, dress-making patterns, greetings cards, labels, leaflets, maps, plans, playing cards, postcards, stamps, trade advertisements, trade forms and cards, transfers and similar articles".

Thus, even if a work is industrially exploited by the making of any of these articles, section 52 will not operate. The same articles are also excluded from registration under the registered designs legislation[83] in which context it has been said that their protection was more naturally a matter for copyright than for registered design.[84] The meaning of the words "works of sculpture" and of "models" have already been considered.[85] In the last category—"printed matter of a literary or artistic character—the list of items is not intended to be exclusive[86] but the category does give rise to some difficulties. Thus, although wallpaper may be said to be an article of printed matter of an artistic nature, it has always been treated as otherwise in the context of the equivalent registered designs rule on the ground that it is not a similar article to the other articles listed in the rule.[87]

13–303   **Which are to be treated as copies of the work.** Section 52 only applies where the relevant articles fall to be treated as copies of the relevant artistic work for the purposes of Part I of the 1988 Act.[88] This is determined by reference to what constitutes copying for the purposes of section 17 of the 1988 Act.[89] Thus, where the artistic work is reproduced on only part of an article (for example, as a pattern on one side of a plate) the article would, nevertheless be treated as a copy for these purposes. Further, it would seem that an article will be treated as a copy of an artistic work when the copier has reproduced a substantial part of the work.[90] If this were otherwise, the value of section 52 in limiting the scope of copyright protection in the industrial field would be severely reduced.

13–304   **Marketing of such articles.** Before section 52 can operate, it must be shown that the relevant articles have been marketed in the United Kingdom or elsewhere.[91] References to the marketing of an article are defined[92] as being references to its being sold or let for hire or offered or exposed for sale or hire. The meaning of this has already been considered in the context of secondary infringements of copyright.[93] It should be noted, however, that section 52 operates whether or not the relevant act was done in the United Kingdom.

13–305   **Exploitation of part only.** It is clear from the terms of section 52(3) that a copyright owner may choose to exploit part only of his copyright work by making and marketing articles falling to be treated as copies of that part of the work. The significance of this is considered below.[94]

---

[83] Registered Designs Rules 1995 (SI 1995/2912), reg.26.
[84] See *Lamson Industries Ltd's Application* [1978] R.P.C. 1 at 7. See also *Hansard*, H.L. Vol.501, cols 245–246 and H.C., SCE, cols 249 and 250 where it was made clear that the intention was that s.52 should operate where the owner of the copyright in a painting chose to exploit that work by, say, reproducing it on tin trays but not where he reproduced it in the form of prints.
[85] See, respectively, paras 3–58 and 13–285, above.
[86] See *Lamson Industries Ltd's Application* [1978] R.P.C. 1 at 6.
[87] A wallpaper design may, therefore, be registered under the RDA 1949, see *Lamson Industries Ltd's Application* [1978] R.P.C. 1 at 6 and 8.
[88] *i.e.* the copyright provisions of the CDPA 1988.
[89] CDPA 1988, s.179 refers to CDPA 1988, s.17 for the definition of "copy and copying". For a detailed discussion of s.17 reference should be made to Ch.7, above.
[90] See paras 7–23 *et seq.*, above.
[91] CDPA 1988, s.52(1)(b).
[92] s.52(6)(b).
[93] s.23(b), considered in Ch.8, above.
[94] See para. 13–311, above.

(iv) Consequences of section 52 applying

Section 52(2). If an artistic work has been exploited within the meaning of section 52(1), then section 52(2) provides that "[a]fter the end of the period of 25 years from the end of the calendar year in which such articles are first marketed, the work may be copied by making articles of any description, or doing anything for the purpose of making articles of any description, and anything may be done in relation to articles so made, without infringing copyright in the work". Thus, section 52(2) only operates to reduce the period of copyright protection against certain specified acts. Copyright protection remains otherwise unaffected. If a rival steps outside the permitted areas, he may still infringe copyright over its full term. The period of 25 years is plainly intended to be analogous to the period of protection available to a registered design, the latter being 25 years from the date of application for registration. In effect, the act of marketing is treated as being the moment when the copyright owner takes his work out of the purely artistic sphere and into the industrial.

13–306

Work may be copied by making an article of any description. Where section 52 applies, section 52(2) allows a person, after the 25-year period, to copy the work by making an article[95] of any description without infringing copyright. Accordingly, subject to the specific exclusion discussed below, a person may copy the work in the form of whatever type of article he chooses. He is not limited to the type of articles by which the copyright owner had chosen to exploit his work. However, because section 52(6)(a) states that references to articles in section 52 do not include films, a person cannot copy the work in the form of a film after the 25-year period. What is less clear is whether, when section 52 applies, a person can make articles of the types which are specified by the Order of the Secretary of State made under section 52(4)(b).[96] On balance, it is submitted that a person can. Section 52(4)(b) provides that the relevant Order may be made "excluding [such articles] from the operation of this section". This wording suggests that the exclusion is intended to apply in relation to subsection (1), *i.e.* in determining the type of articles whose making and marketing would trigger the operation of section 52. It seems more difficult to argue that section 52 "operates" in relation to the articles the making of which is not to be an infringement by reason of subsection (2). Moreover, if articles of a primarily literary or artistic nature were intended to be excluded wherever a reference was made to "articles" in section 52, then the exclusion could and perhaps should have been contained in section 52(6) together with the exclusion of films.[97] Finally, as section 52(2) allows others to copy the work by making articles which are themselves artistic works, there seems to be no reason why others should be excluded from copying the work by making articles which are primarily of a literary or artistic character.

13–307

Illustrations.

(1) Where a painting has been exploited by the copyright owner within the meaning of section 52(1) in the form of making table mats, then 25 years after the end of the calendar year of first marketing of such mats, other

13–308

---

[95] The meaning of an "article" has already been considered—see para. 13–49, above.

[96] *i.e.* the articles of a primarily literary or artistic nature specified in the Copyright (Industrial Process and Excluded Articles) (No.2) Order 1989 (SI 1989/1070), see paras 13–302, above.

[97] Interestingly, the debate in Parliament shows that CDPA 1988, s.52(6)(a) was enacted because a film could not be called an article primarily of literary or artistic character within what is now s.52(4)(b). Thus, s.52(6)(a) was enacted to ensure that the making of multiple films did not trigger the operation of s.52. There was no reference to the significance of either provision as regards articles it was permitted to make under s.52(2). See *Hansard*, H.L. Vol.501, cols 245–246 and H.C., SCE, cols 249–250.

persons will be able to copy the work as a design on crockery, wallpaper or material fabric[98] as well as on table mats.

(2) An artist draws cartoon sketches of a futuristic car for a comic strip in a science fiction magazine. Copyright will subsist in these sketches as artistic works. As has been seen, section 51 does not operate in relation to such works. But if the artist subsequently allows toy cars of that design to be made and marketed in sufficient quantities, then section 52 will operate. After 25 years from first marketing, a rival manufacturer may make toy or real cars to the same design or make pencil erasers to the design.

13–309 **Doing anything for the purpose of making articles of any description.** Where section 52 applies, section 52(2) also permits the doing of anything for the purpose of making articles of any description.[99] This would, for example, allow a rival to prepare manufacturing drawings for an article, such drawings not themselves being "articles". However, it is important to note that the drawings would have to have been produced for the purpose of making the articles.

13–310 **Anything may be done with articles so made.** Section 52(2) also permits dealings with the articles of any description so made. The words "so made" are plainly a reference to articles which it is permissible to make after the 25 year period has expired.[1] Such articles may, therefore, be issued to the public without infringing copyright or included in a film or communicated to the public. The section does not permit dealings with articles made before the 25-year period has expired.

13–311 **Exploitation of part only.** As has been seen, a copyright owner may choose to exploit or to allow the exploitation of his work in part only. In such event, section 52(2) only applies in relation to that part. Any act in relation to the unexploited part will remain an infringement of copyright.

D. SECTION 53

13–312 Section 53 of the 1988 Act provides that:

"(1) The copyright in an artistic work is not infringed by anything done—

(a) in pursuance of an assignment or licence made or granted by a person registered under the Registered Designs Act 1949 as the proprietor of a corresponding design, and

(b) in good faith in reliance on the registration and without notice of any proceedings for the cancellation of the registration or for rectifying the relevant entry in the register of designs;

and this is so notwithstanding that the person registered as the proprietor was not the proprietor of the design for the purposes of the 1949 Act.

(2) In subsection (1) a 'corresponding design', in relation to an artistic work means a design within the meaning of the 1949 Act which, if applied to an article would produce something which would be treated for the purposes of this Part as a copy of the artistic work".

13–313 **Rationale.** This provision was intended to deal with those cases where a design is covered by both copyright and by registration under the Registered Designs Act 1949 and where a person acts under an assignment or licence from the pro-

---

[98] Assuming that CDPA 1988, s.52(4)(b) does not exclude articles of a primarily literary or artistic nature from the articles which can be made without infringing copyright under s.52(2), see para. 13–307, above.
[99] See para. 13–307, above.
[1] See para. 13–307, above.

prietor of the registered design. Normally, this will present no problem in that the owner of the copyright in a work will usually also be the proprietor of its corresponding registered design. In giving his permission as registered proprietor, he can hardly complain about the infringement of copyright. The difficulties arise where the owner and the proprietor are different. Previously this was dealt with by Schedule 1 to the Copyright Act 1956. Section 53 is intended to re-enact that provision.[2]

Conditions for application of section 53. The wording of section 53 is largely self-explanatory. To take advantage of the section, the relevant act must have been in pursuance of an assignment or licence. An act outside the scope of such assignment or licence may still infringe copyright in the relevant work. The assignment or licence must have been made by someone who was registered as the proprietor of the corresponding design even if he was not truly the proprietor for the purposes of the Registered Designs Act 1949.   13–314

16. COPYRIGHT WORKS OF INDUSTRIAL APPLICATION MADE ON OR AFTER JUNE 1, 1957 BUT BEFORE AUGUST 1989

A. INTRODUCTION

Copyright in existing works of industrial application. Any work created before August 1, 1989 is referred to by the 1988 Act as an existing work.[3] This Part of this Chapter is concerned only with the issues which arise where such works are of industrial application and were created during the period that the Copyright Act 1956 Act was in force, *i.e.* on or after June 1, 1957 but before August 1, 1989.   13–315

Permitted acts. Certain acts which would otherwise infringe the copyright in an existing work will, provided they occur after August 1, 1989, be permitted acts under the 1988 Act. For copyright works of industrial application, the most significant provisions are sections 51 to 53. Section 53 applies without any qualification in relation to works created before commencement of the 1988 Act.[4] However, the application of section 51 and of section 52 in the case of existing works is subject to the transitional provisions of the 1988 Act which are discussed below.   13–316

B. PERMITTED ACTS—POSTPONEMENT OF THE OPERATION OF SECTION 51

Limitation of protection for industrial designs—the transitional provisions. In the case of an existing work, the transitional provisions of the 1988 Act provided that section 51 would not apply for a period of 10 years after commencement, *i.e.* until August 1, 1999.[5] Thus, any existing copyright work which is a design document or model recording or embodying a design for anything other than an artistic work or typeface[6] retained its copyright protection against   13–317

---

[2] See *Hansard*, H.C. SCE, col.251.
[3] CDPA 1988, Sch.1, para.1(3).
[4] As to CDPA 1988, s.53, see paras 13–312 *et seq.*, above.
[5] CDPA 1988, Sch.1, para.19(1).
[6] For the meaning of "design document" and "model" see paras 13–283 *et seq.*, above.

the full range of possible acts of infringement until that date.[7] This protection was, however, subject to the operation of any rule of law preventing or restricting the enforcement of copyright in relation to a design.[8]

13–318   **Licences of right during the period of postponement.** The transitional provisions also provided that, during the 10-year period for which section 51 did not apply, the design right licence of right provisions would apply (subject to certain modifications) to any relevant copyright as they applied in relation to design right.[9] Under these provisions, any person was entitled to a licence of right in respect of any relevant copyright for the last five years of the ten-year period of postponement (*i.e.* after August 1, 1994[10]) until August 1, 1999,[11] the licence being to do those acts which would have been permitted by section 51 had the relevant work been a new work rather than an existing work.[12]

13–319   **After the period of postponement.** Since August 1, 1999, section 51 has applied to existing works just as it does to new works.[13]

13–320   **Rationale for transitional provisions.** The intention behind the transitional provisions relating to section 51 was plainly to ensure that, in general terms, the scope of protection for existing works[14] of industrial design was broadly the same as that for new works of that type. Before the 1988 Act, such works were entitled to copyright protection.[15] In the case of new works of the same type, copyright protection is effectively denied by section 51 and any protection is a matter for design right with its more limited duration, its licences of right and wide-ranging "must fit" and "must match" exclusions. However, design right cannot subsist in designs recorded or embodied in existing works.[16] Thus, if section 51 had applied to existing works of industrial design, many designs would have been left without protection. To avoid so drastic a change, the transitional provisions postponed the operation of section 51 for the 10 years to August 1, 1999[17] whilst providing for licences of right and the continuation of rules of law such as those in *British Leyland Motor Corporation v Armstrong Patents Co Ltd*[18] to ensure that this residual copyright did not result in the effective monopolies which copyright protection had previously created.

---

[7] Assuming, of course, that copyright in the relevant work does not expire before then.

[8] Sch.1, para.19(9). Such rules of law will include the "spare parts" exception, see *British Leyland Motor Corporation v Armstrong Patents Co Ltd* [1986] A.C. 577, see paras 5–231 and 13–21, above.

[9] See CDPA 1988, Sch.1, paras 19(2)–(7). The design right licence of right provisions are discussed at paras 13–123 *et seq.*, above.

[10] Sch.1, para.19(2), (3) and s.237.

[11] Since August 1, 1999, a licence to do the things permitted by s.51 has not been necessary.

[12] Sch.1 para.19(7). Thus, the terms of a s.238 licence of right arising in relation to an existing work may differ to those of a licence arising under the design right provisions. In the latter, the licence may be in respect of anything which the Order of the Secretary of State requires.

[13] For the application of CDPA 1988, s.51 to new works, see paras 13–228 *et seq.*, above.

[14] Again, "existing works" in this context means works which existed as at August 1, 1989 when the CDPA 1988 came into force.

[15] Assuming they were recorded in copyright works. Such copyright protection was subject to the largely ineffective s.9(8) of the 1956 Act, the "spare parts" exception put forward in *British Leyland Motor Corporation v Armstrong Patents Co Ltd* [1986] A.C. 577 and to a reduction in term to 15 years where s.10 of the 1956 Act (as amended by the Design Copyright Act 1968) applied.

[16] Design right only applies to designs created after August 1, 1989.

[17] *i.e.* a period roughly similar to the 10-year period of design right protection—see paras 13–100 *et seq.*, above.

[18] CDPA 1988, Sch.1, para.19(a) and [1986] A.C. 577.

C. PERMITTED ACTS—THE APPLICATION OF SECTION 52

(i) Industrial application of artistic works—the transitional provisions

Schedule 1, paragraph 20. In the case of existing works created whilst the 1956   **13–321**
Act was in force, the application of section 52 was subject to the transitional provisions contained in Schedule 1, paragraph 20 to the 1988 Act. These provided
that:

> "(1) Where section 10 of the 1956 Act[19] (effect of industrial application
> of design corresponding to artistic work) applied in relation to an artistic
> work at any time before commencement, section 52(2) of this Act applies
> with the substitution for the period of 25 years mentioned there of the rele-
> vant period of 15 years as defined in section 10(3) of the 1956 Act" and

> "(2) Except as provided in sub-paragraph (1), section 52 applies only
> where articles are marketed as mentioned in subsection (1)(b) after
> commencement".

The need for paragraph 20(1) arose from the repeal of the whole of the Copyright Act 1956. Where section 10 of the 1956 Act had applied to an artistic work,
it reduced the period of copyright protection to 15 years.[20] The transitional provisions of the 1988 Act effectively maintained that period of protection for those
works by providing that section 52(2) would apply to them but with a 15-year period of protection. Thus, no copyright can now subsist in such works—the very
latest date for such protection having expired being July 31, 2004. If, however,
section 10 did not apply to a work at any time (*i.e.* before August 1, 1989), then
paragraph 20(2) ensures that section 52 will not operate retrospectively and that
it will only apply if articles are marketed within the meaning of section 52(1)(b)
on or after August 1, 1989.[21] In such cases, section 52 will apply to the existing
work just as it does to new works.

The application of section 52 to existing works. Under the transitional provi-   **13–322**
sions, the following questions arise when considering the application of section
52 to a work of industrial application created whilst the 1956 Act was in force:

(1) Did section 10 of the 1956 Act apply to the work at any time prior to
   August 1, 1989?

(2) If so, what acts are now permitted by reason of section 52(2) as modified
   by paragraph 20(1)? and

(3) If section 10 did not apply to the work before August 1, 1989, have articles
   been marketed on or after August 1, 1989 within the meaning of paragraph
   20(2)?

These questions remain important, for if section 10 of the 1956 Act did not apply to the work and there has been no marketing of articles within the meaning of
section 52(1)(b) since July 31, 1989, the work would remain entitled to copyright
for its full term and copyright may still subsist.

---

[19] *i.e.* the Copyright Act 1956.

[20] See s.10(3) as amended by the Design Copyright Act 1968 (the 15-year period ran from the date
when articles made to the design were first marketed, see para. 13–323, below). For the reasons
discussed at para. 13–324, below, it is submitted that the question whether s.10 in its unamended
form ever applied to a work does not arise.

[21] See para. 13–304, above.

(ii) Did section 10 of the 1956 Act apply to the work at any time?

13–323 **History of section 10 of the Copyright Act 1956.** The first question is whether section 10 of the 1956 Act had applied to the work at any time. Before this question can be answered, it is necessary to consider the history of section 10 and its amendment by the Design Copyright Act 1968.[22] Prior to its amendment, section 10 applied to two types of work; (i) a work whose corresponding design had been registered under the Registered Designs Act 1949[23] and (ii) a work whose corresponding design was not registered but had been applied industrially through the making and marketing of articles to the designs.[24] It did not, however, apply to a work whose corresponding design was unregistrable.[25] Where section 10 applied, it excluded copyright protection in so far as protection was or would have been available through registration of the corresponding design.[26] The 1968 Act made substantial amendments to section 10 as a result of which section 10 only applied to one type of a work, *i.e.* one whose corresponding design had been applied industrially through the making and marketing of articles to the design.[27] Where the amended section 10 applied, the relevant artistic work retained its copyright protection for a period of 15 years from the date on which articles made to the design were first marketed.[28] After that period, copyright in the work would not be infringed to the extent that registration would have provided a remedy had the corresponding design been registered at the relevant time.[29] Despite these amendments, section 10 still only applied to an artistic work whose corresponding design was capable of registration.[30]

13–324 **The amended or unamended form of section 10.** As has been seen, paragraph 20(1) of the transitional provisions of the 1988 Act applies to an existing artistic work if section 10 of the 1956 Act had applied to that work "at any time" before

---

[22] See paras 13–17 *et seq.*, above. The 1968 Act came into force on October 25, 1968.

[23] Copyright Act 1956, s.10(1).

[24] Copyright Act 1956, s.10(2).

[25] See *Dorling v Honnor Marine Ltd* [1965] Ch. 1 at 16 and 19E-F. This was due to the nature of the limitations on the copyright protection (s.10(6)), see para. 13–18, above.

[26] The provisions limiting copyright protection were complicated. In essence, where s.10(1) applied, copyright protection was excluded in the 15 years after registration to the extent that the actual registration provided protection. Thereafter it was excluded to the extent that registration of the design in the widest possible terms would have provided protection. Where s.10(2) applied, copyright protection was excluded in the 15 years after articles made to the design were first marketed to the extent that registration in relation to that type of article would have provided protection. Thereafter, it was excluded to the extent that registration of the design in the widest possible terms would have provided protection. See Copyright Act 1956, s.10(1), (2), (3) and (6). One of the advantages of CDPA 1988, s.52 is the abandonment of this approach.

[27] Copyright Act 1956, s.10(2)(b) (as amended).

[28] Copyright Act 1956, s.10(3) (as amended).

[29] Copyright Act 1956, s.10(3) (as amended). Again, it was to be presumed that the widest possible registration was in place as at the time of the act of alleged infringement, see Copyright Act 1956, s.10(3) and (6).

[30] The definition of a "corresponding design" in Copyright Act 1956, s.10(7) was not amended by the 1988 Act and remained the same as that contained in the Registered Designs Act 1949, s.44(1) (which has now been repealed by the Registered Design Regulations 2001). Similarly, s.10(4) of the 1956 Act was not amended by the 1988 Act. Had the 1968 Act intended s.10 to apply to unregistrable designs as well as registrable designs, s.10(4) would have been deprived of any meaning or operation. For these reasons it has been held that s.10 as amended only applied to works whose corresponding designs were capable of registration, see *British Leyland Motor Corporation v Armstrong Patents Co Ltd* [1986] R.P.C. 279 at 308–309 and 314–316, CA and *Entec (Pollution Control) Ltd v Abacus Mouldings* [1992] F.S.R. 332 at 336. Further, as s.10(3) (as amended) still limited the scope of copyright (after the 15-year period) by reference to potential protection under the Registered Designs Act 1949, the reasoning in *Dorling v Honor Marine Ltd* [1965] Ch. 1 remained applicable, see *British Leyland Motor Corporation v Armstrong Patents Co Ltd* at 316.

August 1, 1989.[31] This presents no difficulty in the case of an artistic work which was created after section 10 was amended by the Design Copyright Act 1968. In such a case, the reference to section 10 in paragraph 20(1) must clearly be a reference to section 10 in its amended form. The question arises, however, how to treat a work created before the amendment of section 10.[32] It is submitted that, notwithstanding the words "at any time", the transitional provisions are only concerned with whether section 10 applied in its amended (post-1968 Act) form.[33] Paragraph 20(1) states that it applies "[w]here section 10 ... (effect of industrial application of design corresponding to artistic work) applied to an artistic work ...". The words in parentheses suggest that section 10 is being referred to in its amended form. As has been seen,[34] prior to its amendment, section 10 could apply to two types of work; a work whose corresponding design was registered, and a work whose corresponding design was not registered but had been applied industrially. The words in parentheses are not particularly appropriate as regards the first type of work. By contrast, after section 10 was amended, it only applied to a work whose corresponding design had been applied industrially. The words in parenthesis, therefore, describe accurately the only situation in which section 10 applied after its amendment. Further, paragraph 20(1) provides that if section 10 had applied, section 52(2) of the 1988 Act applies "with the substitution for the period of 25 years ... of the relevant period of 15-years as defined in section 10(3) of the 1956 Act". This again suggests that reference is being made to section 10 in its amended form. The 15-year period "as defined by section 10(3)" runs from the date on which relevant articles were first sold, let for hire or offered for sale or hire. There may have been no such date under section 10 in its unamended form because section 10 could then have applied simply because the corresponding design had been registered. Finally, such a construction is more consistent with the approach of the 1988 Act in relation to new works where copyright and registration may co-exist and where section 52 only applies if a design has been applied industrially.[35]

Section 10 (as amended). Accordingly, it is submitted that for the purposes of   **13–325**
the transitional provisions relating to section 52 of the 1988 Act, the question whether section 10 of the 1956 Act applied to an existing work at any time prior to August 1, 1989, must be answered by reference to section 10 as amended by the Design Copyright Act 1968. Section 10 (as so amended) applied:

"(2) Where copyright subsists in an artistic work, and—

(a) a corresponding design is applied industrially by or with the licence of the owner of the copyright in the work, and

(b) articles to which the design has been so applied are sold, let for hire, or offered for sale or hire whether in the United Kingdom or elsewhere".

There must, therefore, have been (1) an artistic work, (2) a corresponding design, (3) industrial application of the corresponding design and (4) relevant marketing of articles. In the absence of any of these factors, section 10 would not

---

[31] CDPA 1988, Sch.1, para.20(1),see para. 13–321, above.

[32] *i.e.* do the transitional provisions require one to ask whether s.10 of the 1956 Act applied in its unamended form to the work at any time before that date and in its amended form at any time after that date; or to ask simply whether s.10 applied in its amended form at any time.

[33] This was the approach in *Drayton Controls (Engineering) Ltd v Honeywell Control Systems Ltd* [1992] F.S.R. 245 at 256 where, in determining the application of the transitional provisions to drawings one of which preceeded the 1968 Act, the court only had regard to s.10 in its amended form.

[34] See para. 13–323, below.

[35] See, generally, paras 13–297 *et seq.*, above.

have applied and, therefore, the modified version of section 52 would not apply either.[36]

13–326   **A corresponding design.** For section 10 of the 1956 Act to have applied to an artistic work, that work had to have a "corresponding design". A corresponding design was defined by section 10(7) as a design which, when applied to an article, resulted in a reproduction of the relevant artistic work. For these purposes, a "reproduction" included a version produced by converting the work into a three-dimensional form or, if it were in three dimensions, by converting it into a two dimensional form.[37] Thus, the novel design of a chair depicted in a drawing could be a corresponding design[38] because a chair made to that design would reproduce the drawing.

13–327   **Limitations on the meaning of "corresponding design".** The scope of the definition of a corresponding design and, therefore, the application of section 10 was, however, subject to limitations. The most important of these, namely that the design in question be one capable of registration under the Registered Designs Act 1949, is considered in more detail below. Another was that the definition only applied to those designs embodied in an artistic work which, when applied to an article, would result in a reproduction of that work. Thus, in a case where the relevant artistic work was a drawing of a thermostatic radiator valve, a design consisting of the shape of one part of the valve (such as a bezel) was not a corresponding design because an article made to it would not be a reproduction of the drawing of the complete valve.[39] Finally, it would seem that the question whether a design was a corresponding design was subject to the effect of section 9(8) of the 1956 Act. Section 9(8) provided that the making of a three dimensional object should not be taken to infringe copyright in an artistic work in two dimensions if the object would not have appeared, to persons who were not experts in relation to objects of that description, to be a reproduction of that work. Although section 9(8) did not in terms qualify the meaning of a "reproduction", it effectively placed a limit on what would be regarded as a reproduction. Accordingly, it seems probable that if section 9(8) applied to a work, then the relevant design would not be a corresponding design because an article made to that design would not have been treated as a reproduction of that work.

13–328   **Corresponding design must be capable of registration.** The most important limitation on the application of section 10 was that a design, to be a corresponding design, must be a design capable of registration under the Registered Designs Act 1949. Although this was not a requirement expressly stated in section 10(7), it was clearly established by the authorities.[40] At the relevant time,[41] a "design" was defined by the 1949 Act as:

> "... features of shape, configuration, pattern or ornament applied to an article by any industrial process or means being features which in the finished article appeal to and are judged solely by the eye but does not include a

---

[36] *i.e.* CDPA 1988, s.52 as modified by Sch.1 para.20(1), see paras 13–321, above.

[37] Copyright Act 1956, s.48.

[38] Assuming that it was capable of registration, see para. 13–328, below.

[39] See *Drayton Controls (Engineering) Ltd v Honeywell Control Systems Ltd* [1992] F.S.R. 245, *per* Knox J. at 258 following the result in *Sifam Electrical Instrument v Sangamo Weston* [1973] R.P.C. 899 where the point was not argued.

[40] See, for example, *Drayton Controls Engineering Ltd v Honeywell Control Systems Ltd* [1992] F.S.R. 245, above, and *Entec (Pollution Control) Ltd v Abacus Mouldings* [1992] F.S.R. 332 at 336.

[41] For these purposes, the definition is that which applied before the 1949 Act was amended by the CDPA 1988 and by the Registered Design Regulations 2001 (SI 2001/3949).

method or principle of construction[42] or features of shape or configuration which are dictated solely by the function which the article to be made in that shape or configuration has to perform."[43]

Corresponding design—features of shape, configuration, pattern or orna-   **13–329**
ment applied to an article. It was said in one case,[44] that the words "shape" and "configuration" were, for practical purposes, synonymous as were the words "pattern" and "ornament". Shape and configuration both signified something in three dimensions; the form in which the article itself was fashioned. Pattern and ornament were substantially in two as opposed to three dimensions; an article could exist without any pattern or ornament upon it, whereas it could have no existence at all apart from its shape and configuration. Whilst there were also cases which suggested that "shape" and "configuration" should not always be regarded as synonymous,[45] this remains a convenient summary of the definition of a design for registered design purposes at the relevant time (*i.e.* before the 1988 Act). If the design did not satisfy this definition, section 10 of the 1956 Act would not have applied to the relevant work. Because an "article" was defined as any article of manufacture including any part of an article if that part was made and sold separately, the design of a part of an article would not have been registrable if that part was not intended to be sold separately from the rest of the article.[46]

Corresponding design—eye appeal. At the relevant time, to be capable of   **13–330**
registration, the design had to "appeal to and [be] judged solely by the eye".[47] This meant that, when judged by the eye of the customer, the design had to have an appeal created by a distinctiveness of shape, pattern or ornament calculated to influence a customer choice. The appeal need not have been aesthetic or artistic although, if it was, it would presumably have satisfied the requirement.[48] It did not necessarily matter that the designer did not consciously intend his design to have eye appeal[49] but plainly, his intention may be relevant. Thus, a design for a toy was likely by its very nature to have eye appeal[50] whereas the design for washer or a nut was unlikely to. It has been said that, in applying the test of eye appeal, the court should look at the design of the entire finished article and if *some* of its features had eye appeal, then the design of the whole article has eye

---

[42] The meaning of "methods or principles of construction" is considered in the context of design right, see paras 13–55 *et seq.*, above.

[43] Registered Designs Act 1949, s.1(3) (prior to its amendment by the 1988 Act).

[44] *Kestos Ltd v Kempat Ltd* (1936) 53 R.P.C. 139 at 152.

[45] See *Amp Inc v Utilux Proprietary Ltd* [1972] R.P.C. 103 at 108, *Gramophone Co Ltd v Magazine Holder Co* (1910) 27 R.P.C. 152 at 159, *P.B. Cow & Co Ltd v Cannon Rubber Manufacturers Ltd* [1959] R.P.C. 347 (where ribs on a hot-water bottle (designed to prevent a user being scalded) were held to be features of configuration but not shape) and *Somner Allibert (UK) Ltd v Flair Plastics Ltd* [1987] R.P.C. 599 (where grooves applied in the manufacturing process to the backs of plastic chairs were found to be features of configuration but not of shape). More recently, see the debate in *Lambretta Clothing Co Ltd v Teddy Smith (UK) Ltd* [2004] EWCA Civ 886 discussed in hte notes to para. 13–48, above.

[46] See *Drayton Controls (Engineering) Ltd v Honeywell Control Systems Ltd* [1992] F.S.R. 245 at 257–258 following *Sifam Electrical Instrument v Sangamo Weston* [1973] R.P.C. 899 at 913.

[47] The need for a design to appeal to the eye was introduced by the Patents and Designs Act 1919 (see para. 13–15, above and para. 13–347, below). The CDPA 1988 removed the word "solely" from the Registered Design Act 1949 definition of a design. For new designs (*i.e.* designs created after December 9, 2001), the requirement of eye appeal has been removed altogether by reason of amendments made by the Registered Designs Regulations 2001, see paras 13–251 *et seq.*, above.

[48] See *Interlego A.G. v Tyco International Inc* [1988] R.P.C. 343 at 355, PC. See also, *Amp Inc v Utilux Pty Ltd* [1972] R.P.C. 103, *British Leyland Motor Corporation v Armstrong Patents Co Ltd* [1986] R.P.C. 279; *Interlego A.G. v Alex Folley, etc. Ltd* [1987] F.S.R. 283 and *Gardex Ltd v Sorata Ltd* [1986] R.P.C. 623. See para. 13–267, above.

[49] See *Amp Inc v Utilux Pty Ltd* [1972] R.P.C. 103 at 110.

[50] See *Interlego A.G. v Tyco International Inc* [1988] R.P.C. 343 at 357–358, PC.

appeal.[51] However, it is not clear that this approach is consistent with the definition of a design for the purposes of registration at that time. Under that definition, the relevant registrable design may not be of the whole article. What was registrable was only those features of shape, configuration (etc.) to be applied to an article which had eye appeal (and which were not dictated solely by function).[52]

13–331   **Corresponding design—dictated solely by function.** At the relevant time, a design was not capable of registration if it was dictated solely by the function which the relevant article was to perform. This exclusion operated separately from the requirement of eye appeal, thus a design may have eye appeal yet nevertheless not be registrable because it was dictated solely by function.[53] It has been stated that, for the exclusion to have operated, each and every feature of the design must have been dictated solely by function so that, if some of its features were not dictated by function, the design as a whole would have been registrable even though the majority of features were so dictated.[54] It is submitted that this was wrong. As stated above, at the relevant time, the registrable design was of those features of shape or configuration (etc.) applied to an article which have eye appeal and which were not dictated solely by function. It was not the design of the whole article, even though the design is registered in respect of an article.[55] In determining whether a design was dictated solely by function, it was not necessary to show that the design in question was the only design by which the article could have performed its function. The exclusion could have applied in any case where the relevant features of shape were brought about by, or were attributable only to the function of the article even if that same function could be performed by an article of a different shape.[56]

13–332   **Corresponding design—excluded designs.** In addition to those designs which failed to meet the definition of "a design",[57] certain other categories of design were expressly excluded from registration at the relevant time. Section 10(4) of the 1956 Act provided that, for the purposes of section 10(2) and (3), no account should be taken of articles (primarily literary or artistic in character) in respect of which the design in question was excluded from registration by rules made under section 1(4) of the Registered Designs Act 1949. Under the relevant rules (since repealed), designs for the following articles were excluded from registration:[58]

"(1) works of sculpture other than casts or models used or intended to be used as models or patterns to be multiplied by any industrial process.

(2) wall plaques and medals.

(3) printed matter primarily of a literary or artistic character, including book jackets, calendars, certificates, coupons, dressmaking patterns, greet-

---

[51] See *Interlego A.G. v Tyco International Inc* [1988] R.P.C. 343 at 353.

[52] It appears that neither party in *Interlego* put forward this construction of the definition of a design in *Interlego A.G. v Tyco International Inc* [1988] R.P.C. 343 (see pp.353–354). However, it is submitted that this was not because this construction is wrong but because, on the facts of that case, it was not in the interests of either party to rely on it.

[53] *Interlego A.G. v Tyco International Inc* [1988] R.P.C. 343 at 355–356.

[54] *Interlego A.G. v Tyco International Inc* [1988] R.P.C. 343 at 353–356, especially at 354. This construction of RDA 1949, s.1(3) (in its unamended form) has been much criticised—see *Fellner on Industrial Design Law* at paras 2.040 to 2.045.

[55] See RDA 1949, s.1(1) (before its amendment by the 1988 Act) and s.1(2) after its amendment by that Act but before its amendment by the Registered Designs Regulations 2001.

[56] See *Interlego A.G. v Tyco International Industries Inc* [1988] R.P.C. 343 at 355 and *Amp Inc v Utilux Pty Ltd* [1972] R.P.C. 103 at 114–115, 118 and 122.

[57] See paras 13–328 *et seq.*, above.

[58] See r.26 of Designs Rules 1949 (SI 1949/2368), subsequently replaced by, in turn the Designs Rules 1984 (SI 1984/1989), the Registered Designs Rules 1989 (SI 1989/1105) and the Registered Designs Rules 1995 (SI 1995/2912) (as amended SI 1999/3196). Rule 26 has now been repealed by the Registered Designs (Amendment) Rules 2001 (SI 2001/3950).

ings cards, leaflets, maps, plans, postcards, stamps, trade advertisements, trade forms, and cards, transfers, and the like"

As the designs for such articles were excluded from registration, section 10 of the 1956 could not have applied to them, nor, therefore, can the modified version of section 52(2) of the 1988 Act.[59]

Corresponding design—no requirement of novelty. The question also arises whether section 10 could have applied to a work where the design in question, whilst being a design as defined above and not being within a category of excluded designs, was not registrable because it failed to satisfy the registered design requirement of novelty.[60] It is submitted that section 10 would have applied to such a work.[61]   **13–333**

Applied industrially. For section 10 of the 1956 to have applied to an artistic work, a corresponding design had to have been applied industrially prior to August 1, 1989[62] by or with the licence of the copyright owner. By rules made under section 10(5),[63] a design would have been applied industrially where it was applied by any process to or was reproduced on or in, more than 50 articles not together constituting a single set, or in goods manufactured in lengths or pieces other than hand-made goods. These rules were similar to those which now apply in relation to section 52 of the 1988 Act and have been considered in that context.[64] In brief, the word "industrially" merely suggested quantity rather than any particular method of production. It should be noted that when section 10(2) was amended by the Design Copyright Act 1968, the words "whether in the United Kingdom or elsewhere" were added to section 10(2)(b) but not to section 10(2)(a). This suggests that, whilst the marketing of articles may take place anywhere, the actual process of industrially applying the design to articles must have taken place within the United Kingdom.   **13–334**

Articles marketed in the UK or elsewhere. Finally, for section 10 of the 1956 Act to have applied, articles to which the corresponding design had been applied[65] had to have been sold, let for hire, or offered for sale or hire whether in the United Kingdom or elsewhere and prior to August 1, 1989. As mentioned above,[66] the relevant marketing of articles may take place anywhere.   **13–335**

(iii) Consequences of section 10 having applied

Application of modified section 52(2). If section 10 of the 1956 Act had applied at any time to an existing artistic work prior to August 1, 1989, then under the transitional provisions, section 52 of the 1988 Act applied to that work thereafter   **13–336**

---

[59] For the modified version of CDPA 1988, s.52(2) see paras 13–321, above.

[60] See Registered Designs Act 1949, s.1(2) (in pre-1988 unamended form).

[61] As has been seen, the authorities had established that the test for these purposes was whether there was a design "capable of registration" (see, for example, *Entec (Pollution Control) Ltd v Abacus Mouldings* [1992] F.S.R. 332 at 336). Although such words were not contained in s.10 itself, they had been used in Copyright Act 1911, s.22 in which context they were found to require only that the design in question possess the essential features of a "design" within the meaning of the Registered Designs Act 1949, s.1(3) and not to exclude designs which were denied protection for want of novelty or originality, see *Interlego A.G. v Tyco International Industries Inc* [1988] R.P.C. 343 at 361–364.

[62] *i.e.* before the Copyright Act 1956 was repealed.

[63] Copyright (Industrial Designs) Rules 1957 (SI 1957/867) (see *Copinger* (12th ed.) para.1742).

[64] See para. 13–301, above.

[65] *i.e.* applied industrially by or with the consent of the copyright owner—see above.

[66] See para. 13–334, above.

but with a period of 15 years (as defined in section 10(3) of the 1956 Act[67]) instead of the period of 25 years that applies to new works.

Section 52(2), with the substitution of the appropriate words from section 10(3) of the 1956 Act, provides that:

"After the end of the period of [15 years beginning with the date on which articles to which the design has been applied industrially were first sold, let for hire or offered for sale or hire in the United Kingdom or elsewhere[68]], the work may be copied by making articles of any description, or doing anything for the purpose of making articles of any description, and anything may be done in relation to articles so made, without infringing copyright in the work".

13–337   **15-year period of full copyright protection.** Thus, where the modified version of section 52(2) of the 1988 Act applied, it limited the period of full copyright protection for an existing work to the relevant 15-year period. As has already been noted, the substitution of the 15-year period was plainly intended to ensure that the works to which section 10 of the 1956 Act had previously applied continued to receive the same period of protection. It should also be noted that the 15-year period ran from the actual date of first marketing and not from the end of the calendar year in which the first marketing occurred[69] —something which it was not always be easy for competitors to ascertain. As mentioned above, the very latest date on which this 15-year period could have expired in relation to existing works was July 31, 2004.[70]

13–338   **Permitted acts after the 15-year period.** The 15-year period of protection has now expired for all works to which the modified version of section 52(2) applied. Accordingly, under section 52(2) any person may copy any such work by making articles of any description and do anything for the purpose of making articles of any description and do anything in relation to articles so made, without infringing copyright in such work. The nature of these permitted acts has already been considered in relation to the application of section 52(2) to new works.[71] In essence, most acts of industrial copying of the work are permitted. In other respects, the copyright remains unaffected and may be enforced for the rest of its usual term.[72]

13–339   **Interrelation with section 51.** The operation of the modified 52(2) of the 1988 Act is neither dependent upon nor mutually exclusive with the operation of section 51 of that Act after the end of the ten-year period of postponement which applies in relation to section 51 under the transitional provisions of the 1988 Act.[73]

(iv) Marketing of articles within paragraph 20(2)

13–340   If section 10 of the 1956 Act had not applied to an existing artistic work,[74] then section 52 of the 1988 Act will not apply to that work unless articles are marketed

---

[67] CDPA 1988, Sch.1, para.20(1). See para. 13–321, above.

[68] The words in brackets are derived from Copyright Act 1956, ss.10(3) and 10(2).

[69] This contrasts with the position under the unmodified version of CDPA 1988, s.52(2) but is consistent with the position as it had been under Copyright Act 1956, s.10.

[70] For Copyright Act 1956, s.10 to have applied to an existing work, the relevant act of first marketing must have occurred prior to August 1989. Thus, no existing work to which s.10 of the 1956 Act applied could retain full copyright protection after 15 years from that date.

[71] See paras 13–306 *et seq.*, above.

[72] *i.e.* for the life of the author plus 70 years—see Ch.6, above.

[73] See para. 13–299, above.

[74] As to which see paras 13–323 *et seq.*, above.

as mentioned in section 52(1)(b) after commencement.[75] At first sight, this appears to suggest that section 52 in its unmodified form will apply to any existing work (other than those to which section 10 of the 1956 Act applied) where relevant articles are marketed on or after August 1, 1989. However, if this were the case, an existing work which had been applied industrially before August 1, 1989 but to which section 10 had not applied[76] would become subject to section 52 merely because its marketing continued after August 1, 1989. It is submitted that this is not the effect of paragraph 20(2)[77] and that paragraph 20(2) only allows section 52 to operate in those cases where an existing work is *first* marketed within the meaning of section 52 after the commencement of the 1988 Act and, possibly, in those cases where the marketing of articles had commenced before that date but the requisite 50 articles required for section 10 of the 1956 Act to apply[78] had not yet been made when the 1988 came into force. Where articles are so marketed, then section 52 will apply to the existing work just as it does to new works.[79]

17. COPYRIGHT WORKS OF INDUSTRIAL APPLICATION CREATED BEFORE JUNE 1, 1957

A. INTRODUCTION

All works created before August 1, 1989 are referred to by the 1988 Act as existing works.[80] This Part of this Chapter is concerned only with works of industrial application created before the Copyright Act 1956 Act came into force, *i.e.* before June 1, 1957.

13–341

B. SUBSISTENCE OF COPYRIGHT

(i) An additional provision as to subsistence

Schedule 1, paragraph 6(1) of the transitional provisions. In addition to the general provisions as to subsistence of copyright in existing works, the 1988 Act contains an additional provision which excludes copyright from certain works of industrial design created before June 1, 1957.[81] Thus, paragraph 6(1) of Schedule 1 to the 1988 Act provides that:

13–342

> "Copyright shall not subsist by virtue of this Act in an artistic work made before 1st June 1957 which at the time when the work was made constituted a design capable of registration under the Registered Designs Act 1949 or

---

[75] CDPA 1988, Sch.1, para.20(2), see para. 13–321, above.
[76] Because, for example, its corresponding design had not been registrable.
[77] In *Entec (Pollution Control) Ltd v Abacus Mouldings* [1992] F.S.R. 332, an existing work had been industrially applied prior to August 1, 1989 but Copyright Act 1956, s.10 (and, therefore, CDPA 1988, Sch.1, para.20(1)) had not applied because its corresponding design was unregistrable. It was not suggested that CDPA 1988, Sch.1, para.20(2) might apply if there was any further marketing of goods after that date. In any event, as 10 years have passed since the commencement of the CDPA 1988, s.51 would operate effectively to remove copyright protection from many works of industrial design, see para. 13–317, above.
[78] See para. 13–334, above.
[79] See paras 13–306 *et seq.*, above.
[80] CDPA 1988, Sch.1, para.1(3).
[81] CDPA 1988, Sch.1, para.6(1).

under the enactments repealed by that Act, and was used, or intended to be used, as a model or pattern to be multiplied by an industrial process".[82]

In summary, therefore, no copyright will subsist in a work created before June 1, 1957 if: (1) the work in question was an artistic work; and (2) the work, at the time that it was created, constituted a design capable of registration; and (3) at the time that the work was created, the design was used or was intended to be used, as a model or pattern to be multiplied by an industrial process. These criteria are considered below. As the relevant provisions of paragraphs 6(1) and 6(2) are in substantially the same terms as their equivalents in the 1911 and 1956 Acts,[83] they will, presumably, be construed in the same way.[84]

(ii) Background to the additional provision

13–343   The need for this additional provision arose from similar provisions whereby the Copyright Acts of 1911 and 1956 had excluded copyright from such works created before June 1, 1957. Thus, section 22 of the Copyright Act 1911[85] had expressly excluded copyright from designs capable of being registered under the Patents and Designs Act 1907, except those which, though capable of being so registered, are not used or intended to be used as models or patterns to be multiplied by any industrial process.[86] When the 1911 Act was repealed by the Copyright Act 1956, the 1956 Act[87] provided that "[c]opyright shall not subsist by virtue of this Act in any artistic work made before the commencement of section 10[88] which, at the time when the work was made, constituted a design capable of registration under the Registered Designs Act, 1949, or under the enactments repealed by the Act, and was used, or intended to be used, as a model or pattern to be multiplied by any industrial process".[89] This provision thereby ensured that works from which the 1911 Act had excluded copyright did not acquire copyright under the 1956 Act,[90] although the draftsman took the opportunity to bring the wording of the exclusion up to date by replacing the reference to the Patents and Designs Act 1907 with a reference to the 1949 Act or enactments repealed by that Act. It also removed the awkward double negative and the uncertainty as to the time at which the court should determine whether copyright was excluded, which had been features of section 22 of the 1911 Act.[91]

---

[82] Sch.1, para.6(2) of the 1988 Act provides for when a design is to be deemed to have been used as a model or pattern to be multiplied by any industrial process.

[83] See paras 13–343 et seq., below.

[84] CDPA 1988, s.172.

[85] See para. 13–14, above.

[86] Under s.22(2) of the 1911 Act, r.89 of the rules made under the Patents and Designs Act 1907 applied for the purpose of determining when a design was deemed to be used or intended to have been used for these purposes. Rule 89 was in substantially the same form as CDPA 1988, Sch.1, para.6(2), see para. 13–349, below.

[87] Copyright Act 1956, Sch.7, para.8(2).

[88] Copyright Act 1956, s.10 was one of the means by which the 1956 Act sought to limit copyright protection for industrial designs. However it did not apply to works created before the 1956 Act came into force, see Sch.7, para.8(1) of that Act.

[89] Copyright Act 1956, Sch.7, para.8(3) again provided for rules by which a design was deemed to be used as a model or pattern to be multiplied by any industrial process.

[90] Such an express exclusion was required, as the 1956 Act permitted copyright to subsist in all original literary, dramatic, musical and artistic works including those created before June 1, 1957 (see ss.2(1), 3(2) and Sch.7, para.1 and Interlego A.G. v Tyco International Inc [1988] R.P.C. 343 at 361).

[91] In this respect, Copyright Act 1956, Sch.7, para.8(2) effectively followed Copyright Act 1911, s.22 as construed in King Features Syndicate v O. & M. Kleeman Ltd [1941] A.C. 417 at 427, see Interlego A.G. v Tyco International Industries Inc [1988] R.P.C. 343 at 361. As regards King Features, see para. 13–16, above.

(iii) Design capable of registration

For the additional provision to exclude copyright from a work, the relevant artistic   **13–344**
work[92] must constitute a design which, at the time that it was created, was capable
of being registered under the Registered Designs Act 1949 or the Acts repealed
by that Act. For these purposes, works fall into the following categories: (1)
those created between 1950 and June 1, 1957; (2) those created between 1919
and before 1950; (3) those created between 1907 and before 1919 and, finally, (4)
those created before 1907.

Work created between 1950 and 1957. In the case of a work created on or after   **13–345**
January 1, 1950[93] and before June 1, 1957, the question is whether that work constituted a design capable of registration under the Registered Designs Act 1949.
The test for whether a design should be treated for these purposes as being *capable
of registration* under the 1949 Act has already been considered in detail.[94]

Work created between 1919 and 1950. In the case of works created between   **13–346**
1919 and before 1950, the relevant definition of a design capable of registration
is that contained in section 93 of the Patents and Designs Act 1907 as amended
by section 19 of the Patents and Designs Act 1919.[95] This amended definition
provided that:

> "Design means only the features of shape, configuration, pattern, or orna-
> ment applied to any article by any industrial process or means, whether
> manual, mechanical or chemical, separate or combined, which in the finished
> article appeal to and are judged solely by the eye; but which does not include
> any mode or principle of construction or anything which is in substance a
> mere mechanical device".

As the wording of the 1949 Act was derived from judicial pronouncements as
to the meaning of section 19 of the 1919 Act, the test whether a design was a
design capable of registration under the 1919 Act is the same as under the 1949
Act (before its amendment by the 1988 Act).[96]

Work created between 1907 and 1919. In the case of a work created between   **13–347**
1907 and 1919, the question whether the design in question was registrable at the
time that it was created is governed by the definition of a design contained in section 93 of the Patents and Designs Act 1907 as it was prior to its amendment by
the Patents and Designs Act 1919.[97] Section 93 of the 1907 Act (in its unamended
form) provided that:

> "Design means any design ... applicable to any article, whether the design is
> applicable for the pattern, or for the shape or configuration, or for the orna-
> ment thereof, or for any two or more of such purposes, and by whatever
> means it is applicable, whether by printing, painting, embroidering, weav-

---

[92] "artistic work" would clearly bear its usual copyright meaning.
[93] The date on which the 1949 Act came into force—see s.49(2) of the 1949 Act.
[94] See paras 13–328 *et seq.*, above.
[95] It would appear that the amendment was effective from the date of the Act—December 23, 1919.
[96] See *Amp Inc v Utilux Pty Ltd* [1972] R.P.C. 103 at 113–114 referring to *Kestos Ltd v Kempat Ltd*
(1936) 53 R.P.C. 139 and *Tecalemot Ltd v Ewarts Ltd (No.2)* (1927) 44 R.P.C. 503. For the
meaning of a design under the 1949 Act before its amendment, see paras 13–328 *et seq.*, above
[97] It has been suggested (see para.209 and para.20–08, respectively, of the 12th and 13th editions of
this book) that *Pytram Ltd v Models (Leicester) Ltd* [1930] 1 Ch. 639 is authority for the proposition that the amended version of Patents and Designs Act 1907, s.93 applied to pre-amendment
(*i.e.* pre-1919 works). It is submitted that this is not correct. In *Pytram*, Clauson J. had regard to
the amended version of s.93 because he was concerned with a work created after 1919. There is
nothing in his judgment (and in particular at p.646 of his judgment) to suggest that the unamended
version of s.93 would not apply in the case of a work created between 1911 and 1919. The question was left open by Whitford J. in *Weir Pumps Ltd v CML Pumps Ltd* [1984] F.S.R. 33 at 37.

ing, sewing, modelling, casting, embossing, engraving, staining, or any
other means whatever, manual or mechanical, or chemical, separate or
combined."

This definition[98] does not expressly refer to any requirement of eye appeal nor
does it expressly exclude functional designs. It has been stated[99] that the wording
of each of the 1919 and 1949 Acts was based on judicial decisions as to its
predecessors. If so, the meaning of a design capable of registration under the
1907 Act would be substantially the same as that under the 1949 and 1919 Acts
which have already been considered.[1] However, it is by no means clear that this
was the case.[2] There were certainly cases decided prior to the 1907 Act in which
no objection was taken to the registrability of the relevant design on the grounds
of their very obvious functionality,[3] and there was nothing in the 1907 Act to
suggest that that Act changed this.

13–348   **Work created before 1907.** It seems that the definition of a design contained in
the 1907 Act will also govern whether a work created before the 1907 Act came
into force should be treated as capable of registration for these purposes.
Paragraph 6(1) of Schedule 1 to the 1988 Act refers to those Acts repealed by the
1949 Act, *i.e.* only the 1907 and the 1919 Acts and not the earlier registered
design acts which those Acts had replaced. In any event, the 1907 Act was
intended to be a consolidating Act and it would seem, therefore, that the meaning
of registrability before it was passed should have been largely the same as that
under the 1907 Act itself.[4]

(iv) Used or intended to be used as a model or pattern

13–349   Finally, for the additional provision to exclude the subsistence of copyright, it
would have to be shown that, at the time that the work in question was made, the
relevant design was either used or intended to be used as a model or pattern to be
multiplied by an industrial process. Paragraph 6(2) of Schedule 1 to the 1988 Act
provides that:

"… a design shall be deemed to be used or intended to be used as a model or
pattern to be multiplied by any industrial process—

(a) when the design is reproduced or is intended to be reproduced on
more than 50 single articles, unless all the articles in which the design
is reproduced or is intended to be reproduced together form only a
single set of articles as defined in section 44(1) of the Registered
Designs Act 1949, or

---

[98] Described as "somewhat unhelpful" by Lord Oliver in *Interlego A.G. v Tyco International Inc*
[1988] R.P.C. 343 at 353.

[99] See *Fellner on Industrial Design Law* at para.1.012.

[1] See paras 13–345 and 13–346 respectively, above.

[2] This claim was raised in argument in *British Leyland Motor Corporation v Armstrong Patents
Co Ltd* [1986] A.C. 577 but was expressly left open by Lord Bridge. The confusion appears to
derive from the use of the words "eye appeal" in some of the earlier cases. However, such use appears to have been in the context that it was the eye that was appealed to in order to determine
whether the allegedly infringing article was the same as or was an obvious imitation of the
registered design—see *Amp Inc v Utilux Pty Ltd* [1972] R.P.C. 103 at 119–121.

[3] See *Leatheries Ltd v Lycett Saddle and Motor Accessories Co Ltd* (1909) 26 R.P.C. 166, where
the design was of the base springs of a bicycle saddle; *Gillard v Worrall* (1905) 22 R.P.C. 76,
where the design of a gas jet for a baker's oven and *Werner Motors Ltd v A.W. Gamage Ltd*
(1904) 21 R.P.C. 621, where the design was of a motorcycle frame. In none of these cases was
any point taken as to the obvious functionality of the design. Instead, the main line of defence
was a lack of novelty in the design or the denial of any act of infringement. In fact ,in *Gillard*,
Hall V.C. expressly ignored the utility of the design—see at 79.

[4] See, the comments of Lord Oliver in relation to the substantially identical Sch.7, para.8(2) of the
1956 Act in *Interlego A.G. v Tyco International Inc* [1988] R.P.C. 343 at 359–363.

    (b) when the design is to be applied to—

        (i) printed paper hangings,

        (ii) carpets, floor cloths or oil cloths, manufactured or sold in lengths or pieces,

       (iii) textile piece goods, or textile goods manufactured or sold in lengths or pieces, or

       (iv) lace, not made by hand".

As is clear from the wording of paragraph 6(1), the design must be used or there must be an intention to make use of the design in the relevant way at the time that the relevant artistic work was created. In this respect, the 1988 Act (like the 1956 Act[5]) has adopted the construction of section 22 of the 1911 Act applied by the House of Lords in *King Features Syndicate Inc v O & M Kleeman Ltd*[6]

C. PERMITTED ACTS

Section 51. Section 51 of the 1988 Act operates in the same way for any work created before August 1, 1989. Its application in relation to works created before June 1, 1957 will, therefore, be no different to its application to works created while the 1956 Act was in force which have already been considered above.[7]   **13–350**

Section 52. As has been seen,[8] the application of section 52 to existing works is subject to the transitional provisions contained in paragraph 20 of Schedule 1 to the 1988 Act. However, the modified version of section 52 which may apply to 1956 Act works[9] cannot apply to any work created before June 1, 1957.[10] Thus, section 52 will only be of relevance to a work created before that date if paragraph 20(2) applies to that work, *i.e.* if there has been relevant marketing of articles after the commencement of the 1988 Act. What constitutes marketing for these purposes has already been considered in relation to 1956 Act works.[11] If section 52 applies in such a case, it applies in its unmodified form.[12]   **13–351**

Section 53. Section 53 applies to permit certain acts occurring on or after August 1, 1989 to a work created whilst the 1911 Act was in force without any qualification.   **13–352**

---

[5] See para. 13–343, above.

[6] [1941] A.C. 417. See para.13–16, above.

[7] *i.e.* those works created between June 1, 1957 and August 1, 1989—see paras 13–317 *et seq.*, above.

[8] See para. 13–321, above.

[9] Under CDPA 1988, para.20(1), s.52 applied with a modified (shorter) 15-year period in those cases where s.10 of the 1956 Act had applied to the work in question at any time prior to commencement of the 1988 Act—see paras 13–321 *et seq.*, above.

[10] Copyright Act 1956, s.10 did not apply to any work created before that Act came into force—see para.8(1) of Sch.7—thus, CDPA 1988, Sch.1, para.20(1) and its modified version of s.52 cannot apply to such a work.

[11] See para. 13–340, above.

[12] *i.e.* with its usual 25-year period rather than the modified 15-year period which applies where paragraph 20(1) operates.

PART V

MISCELLANEOUS RIGHTS

SEMICONDUCTOR TOPOGRAPHIES

1. INTRODUCTION

Background. Modern goods, such as computers, televisions, aero engines, medical equipment and machine tools often contain electronic integrated circuits, usually called "chips". Such chips are physically tiny yet may contain many hundreds of thousands of electronic components (*e.g.* transistors) and connections. Their appearance, when viewed from above under a microscope, may be likened to a complex city-street plan. Most chips contain broadly similar components and operate in broadly similar ways. However, the designer of a chip must plan the layout (or topography) of its various components and connections in a way which not only allows it to perform its particular intended function efficiently but which also minimises its size and allows for ease of manufacture; a process which may involve considerable skill and investment. This Chapter is concerned with the protection of such designs.   **14–01**

Making a semiconductor chip. A chip consists of a sandwich of materials including semiconducting material (usually called a "wafer"),[1] insulating material[2] and conductive material.[3] The chip is formed by coating the wafer of semiconductor material with an insulator. The desired layout of the components for the chip is then imparted by a process of etching through the insulator into the semiconductor material and by depositing other materials into the holes thus created so as to form the relevant components.[4] The pattern for this process of etching and depositing is determined by using a mask or a series of masks which record the desired design layout of the components.[5] The connections between these components are provided by the addition of conductive material and the layout of these connections is determined by another mask or series of masks.   **14–02**

---

[1] For example, silicon, germanium or gallium arsenide. A semiconducting material, as its name suggests, is a material whose ability to conduct electricity falls somewhere between that of a conductor such as metal on the one hand and that of an insulator on the other.

[2] *e.g.* silicon dioxide.

[3] *e.g.* aluminium.

[4] These other materials (often called "dopants") change the electrical conductivity of the part of the semiconductor wafer to which they are applied and thereby create the desired components (*e.g.* the transistors).

[5] The design of the overall layout is three-dimensional but has to be broken down into its individual separate layers. A separate mask (*i.e.* a template) is made (usually photographically) record-

14–03   **Summary of protection.** The Copyright Act 1956 made no special provision for the protection of chips. Instead, protection depended upon whether the design was recorded in something characterised as an artistic work, *i.e.* a design drawing or mask[6] recording the layout. However, in 1987, the Council of the European Communities issued a Directive[7] requiring all Member States to provide protection for the designs for semiconductor products in accordance with the terms of the Directive.[8] The United Kingdom initially sought to implement this Directive through the Semiconductor Products (Protection of Topography) Regulations 1987[9] which came into force on November 7, 1987[10] and which introduced something called a "topography right". However, the 1987 Regulations were revoked by the Design Right (Semiconductor Topographies) Regulations 1989[11] which came into force on August 1, 1989.[12] The 1989 Regulations provide that the design right provisions in Part III of the 1988 Act have effect, with certain important modifications, in relation to a design which is a semiconductor topography.[13] The modifications were required because the provisions of Part III are in some respects different to the terms of the Council Directive[14] and of later Council Decisions.[15]

2. PROTECTION OF SEMICONDUCTOR TOPOGRAPHIES

14–04   If a design is a semiconductor topography then, under the Design Right (Semiconductor Topographies) Regulations 1989,[16] the design right provisions contained in Part III of the 1988 Act apply subject to the modifications made by regulations 4 to 9 of the Regulations. The provisions of Part III have already been considered in the design right chapter of this work. This present chapter is concerned only with issues which specifically concern semiconductor topographies and, in particular, with the modifications made to Part III by the 1989 Regulations.

A. A DESIGN WHICH IS A SEMICONDUCTOR TOPOGRAPHY

14–05   **A design.** For the 1989 Regulations to apply, there must be a design which is a semiconductor topography. This means[17]:

"… a design within the meaning of section 213(2) of the Act which is a design of either of the following:

---

ing each layer of the design. The more complicated the chip, the greater the number of layers and, therefore, of masks is likely to be.

[6] Which is usually a photograph.

[7] Council Directive 87/54/EEC [1987] O.J. L24/36. See Vol.2 at H1.

[8] The need to provide for such protection arose from the fact that the United States' Semiconductor Chip Protection Act 1984, s.902 contains reciprocity provisions whereby works of semiconductor topography from other countries were only given protection in the United States if those other countries provided equivalent protection for US works.

[9] SI 1987/1497.

[10] SI 1987/1497, reg.1.

[11] SI 1989/1100, see Vol.2 at B9.i. As the 1989 Regulations and the 1987 Regulations (SI 1987/1497) were both intended to implement the Semiconductor Directive, the nature of their protection is, broadly speaking, the same. There are, however, slight differences in relation to, for example, the qualification provisions contained in reg.3 of the 1987 Regulations and reg.4 of the 1989 Regulations.

[12] SI 1989/1100, reg.1. For the position in relation to topographies created before this date, see paras 14–23 and 14–24, below.

[13] SI 1989/1100, reg.3.

[14] SI 1989/1100.

[15] Council Decisions 87/532/EEC [1987] O.J. 313/22 and 88/311/EEC [1988] O.J. 140/13.

[16] SI 1989/100, reg.3.

[17] SI 1989/1100, reg.2(1).

(a) the pattern fixed, or intended to be fixed, in or upon—

    (i) a layer of semiconductor product, or

    (ii) a layer of material in the course of and for the purpose of the manufacture of a semiconductor product, or

(b) the arrangement of the patterns fixed, or intended to be fixed, in or upon the layers of a semiconductor product in relation to one another".

For these purposes, a semiconductor product is an article the purpose, or one of the purposes of which, is the performance of an electronic function and which consists of two or more layers, at least one of which is composed of a semiconducting material and in or upon one or more of which is fixed a pattern appertaining to that or another function.[18]

Whether a design is a design within section 213(2) is considered in the design right chapter of this work.[19] A design which is a semiconductor topography is clearly a design of the shape or configuration of an article (*i.e.* of a semiconductor product). Under Part III, the design relied upon may be of any aspect of the whole or part of that product.

Excluded designs. Although section 213(3) of the 1988 Act applies to a design which is a semiconductor topography as to any other design, the so-called "must match" and surface decoration exclusions are unlikely to be of any significance in relation to a design for a semiconductor topography.[20]   **14–06**

B. SUBSISTENCE OF DESIGN RIGHT

Originality. To qualify for design right, a design which is a semiconductor topography must, like any other design, be original and not be commonplace in the design field in question at the time of its creation.[21] The meaning of these requirements has already been considered in relation to design right generally.[22] In this context, the relevant design field is that of the semiconductor industry generally.[23]   **14–07**

Qualification for design right. As has been seen,[24] design right only subsists if the relevant design qualifies for protection. Qualification may be by reference to the designer or the person by whom he was commissioned or employed. It may also be by reference to the person by whom and the country in which articles made to the design were first marketed. Finally, a design may qualify in accordance with any Order made under section 221 of the 1988 Act. These provisions as to qualification are considered in the design right chapter of this work. However, in the case of semiconductor topographies, they are subject to various modifications.   **14–08**

---

[18] reg.2(1).

[19] See paras 13–44 *et seq.*, above.

[20] For a full discussion of the exclusions contained in CDPA 1988, s.213(3), see paras 13–53 *et seq.*, above.

[21] CDPA 1988, ss.213(1) and 213(4).

[22] See paras 13–70 *et seq.*, above.

[23] Council Directive 87/54/EEC, Art. 2(2) expressly stated that the design must not be commonplace in the semiconductor industry. The 1987 Regulations (SI 1987/1497), reg.3(3) stated that a design was not original if it was commonplace among creators of topographies or manufacturers of semiconductor products.

[24] See paras 13–82 *et seq.*, above.

14–09   **Qualifying person.** The first modification is in the definition of a "qualifying person". Under section 217(1) as modified by the 1989 Regulations[25] the following are qualifying persons in relation to semiconductor topographies:

    (a) A qualifying individual, meaning a citizen or subject of or an individual habitually resident in a qualifying country. Although this wording is unaltered, the 1989 Regulations modify the definition of "a qualifying country" so that, for the purposes of semiconductor topography, it includes only the United Kingdom[26] or another Member State of the European Economic Community.[27]

    (b) A body corporate or other body having legal personality which has in any qualifying country or in Gibraltar a place of business at which substantial business activity is carried on.[28] This appears similar to section 217(1)(b) in its unmodified form.[29] However, the reference to Gibraltar is an addition and, as noted in (a) above, the definition of a "qualifying country" is somewhat narrower.

    (c) A person who falls within one of the additional classes set out in Part I of the Schedule to the 1989 Regulations.[30] These classes include (1) British Dependent Territory Citizens; (2) citizens and subjects of any country specified in Part II of the Regulations[31]; (3) habitual residents of any country specified in Part II of the Regulations[32] or the Isle of Man, the Channel Islands or any colony; and (4) firms and bodies corporate formed under the law of, or any part of, the United Kingdom, Gibraltar, another Member State of the European Economic Community of any country specified in Part II of the Regulations[33] with a place of business within any country so specified at which substantial business activity is carried on.[34]

14–10   **Semiconductor topographies created under a commission or during employment.** The second modification to the qualification provisions is where a semiconductor topography is created in pursuance of a commission or in the course of employment. In such a case, section 215 is modified[35] to allow for an agreement in writing to override the normal rule whereby the commissioner or the employer is automatically the first owner of design right. If, as a result of such an agreement, it is the designer who is the first owner of design right in a semiconductor topography, then section 217(3) as modified[36] provides that the relevant topography cannot qualify by reference to the commissioner or employer

---

[25] SI 1989/1100, reg.4(2).

[26] The reference to a person being a citizen of the United Kingdom is to be construed as a reference to that person being a British citizen, see CDPA 1988, s.217(4) as modified by SI 1989/1100, reg.4(2).

[27] CDPA 1988, s.217(3), as modified by SI 1989/1100, reg.4(2). Thus, for the purposes of semiconductor topography, a country will not be a qualifying country merely because it has been the subject of an Order under CDPA 1988, s.255 or 256.

[28] In determining whether substantial business activity is carried on at a place of business in any country, no account is taken of dealings in goods which are at all material times outside that country, CDPA 1988, s.217(5), as modified by SI 1989/1100, reg.4(2).

[29] See para. 13–98, above.

[30] As amended by the Design Right (Semiconductor Topographies) (Amendment) Regulations 1993 (SI 1993/ 2497). For earlier amendments, see SI 1989/2147, SI 1990/1003, SI 1991/2237 and SI 1992/400.

[31] *i.e.* Australia, Austria, Finland, French overseas territories, Iceland, Japan, Liechtenstein, Norway, Sweden, Switzerland, and the United States of America.

[32] See the countries listed above.

[33] See the countries listed above.

[34] See para. 14–09(b), above.

[35] SI 1989/1100, reg.5. See also para. 14–13, below.

[36] SI 1989/1100, reg.4(3).

and, that the provisions governing qualification by reference to its designer[37] will apply as if the topography had not been created in pursuance of a commission or in the course of employment.

First marketing. The next modification is to section 220. As has been seen, where a design does not qualify by reference to the designer, commissioner or employer, it may nevertheless qualify by reference to the first marketing of articles made to the design.[38] In its unmodified form, section 220(1) requires: (a) that such first marketing be by a qualifying person who is exclusively authorised to put such articles on the market in the United Kingdom and (b) that such first marketing takes place in the United Kingdom, or in a country to which the 1988 Act extends by Order made under section 255, or in another Member State of the European Economic Community. In the case of semiconductor topographies, these requirements are modified so that (a) the qualifying person must be exclusively authorised to put such articles on the market in every Member State of the European Economic Community and (b) the first marketing must take place within the territory of any Member State.[39] Further, the definition of "exclusively authorised" as modified[40] refers only to "exclusivity capable of being enforced by legal proceedings" rather than to "exclusivity capable of being enforced by legal proceedings in the United Kingdom".

14–11

Meaning of marketing. The definition of marketing has already been considered.[41] However, in the case of semiconductor topographies, the Regulations also provide that, in determining whether there has been any marketing (or whether anything has been made available for sale of hire), no account shall be taken of any sale or hire, or any offer or exposure for sale or hire, which is subject to an obligation of confidence in respect of information about the topography in question. There are, however, two exceptions to this; namely, (a) where the article or topography sold or hired or offered or exposed for sale or hire has been sold or hired on a previous occasion (whether or not subject to an obligation of confidence), or (b) where the obligation is imposed at the behest of the Crown, or of the Government of any country outside the United Kingdom, for the protection of security in connection with the production of arms, munitions or war material.[42]

14–12

C. OWNERSHIP

The first owner of design right is defined by s.215 of the 1988 Act. As has already been seen, where a topography is created pursuant to a commission or in the course of employment, section 215 is modified by the 1989 Regulations[43] so as to allow for an agreement in writing to override the normal rule whereby the commissioner or the employer is automatically the first owner of design right. The agreement may provide for any other person to be the first owner.

14–13

D. DURATION

Section 216 of the 1988 Act is modified by the 1989 Regulations so that the rules concerning the duration of design right in a semiconductor topography are some-

14–14

---

[37] *i.e.* CDPA 1988, s.218(2) to (4).
[38] See paras 13–92 *et seq.*, above.
[39] See CDPA 1988, s.220(1) as modified by SI 1989/1100, reg.4(4).
[40] CDPA 1988, s.220(4) as modified by SI 1989/1100, reg.4(4).
[41] See para. 13–92, above.
[42] SI 1989/1100, reg.7. This provision is included to give effect to the requirements of the Council Directive, 87/54/EEC, Art. 1(c).
[43] SI 1989/1100, reg.5.

what different to those for other design rights.[44] Thus, the expiry of design right in a semiconductor topography is either: (a) 10 years from the end of the calendar year in which the topography or articles made to the topography were first made available for sale or hire anywhere in the world by or with the licence of the design right owner[45]; or (b) if neither the topography nor articles made to it are made available as mentioned above within a period of 15 years commencing with the earlier of the time when the topography was first recorded in a design document or the time when an article was first made to the topography, at the end of that 15-year period.

14–15   Thus, the period of protection for a semiconductor topography may be considerably longer than that for other designs. As has been seen, the normal position is that protection is subject to a maximum period of 15 years.[46] It would seem that, for semiconductor topographies, the maximum period of protection may be up to 25 years in a case where the topography or articles made to it were first marketed just before the end of the 10-year period.

E. INFRINGEMENT

14–16   One of the most important areas of difference between the provisions for semiconductor topographies and those for other designs lies in what does and does not constitute an infringement of design right.

14–17   **Primary infringement: private non-commercial acts and acts of analysis and evaluation.** To be liable for primary infringement of design right, a person must have reproduced the relevant design by (a) making articles to that design or (b) making a design document recording that design for the purpose of enabling such articles to be made. In normal design right cases, such acts will only infringe design right if done "for commercial purposes".[47] There is no such requirement for semiconductor topographies.[48] However, section 226(1A) as added by the 1989 Regulations[49] provides for two situations where such acts will not infringe design right. The first is where the reproduction of the topography was done privately for non-commercial aims.[50] The second is where the reproduction of the topography is for the purpose of analysing or evaluating the design or analysing, evaluating or teaching the concepts, processes, systems or techniques embodied in it. This ties in with the reverse engineering provisions contained in regulation 8(4) of the 1989 Regulations which are discussed below.

14–18   **Primary infringement: reverse engineering.** Probably the most significant difference between the treatment of semiconductor topographies and the treatment of other designs is that the 1989 Regulations expressly provide that it is not an infringement of design right in a semiconductor topography to (a) create another original semiconductor topography as a result of an analysis or evaluation of the

---

[44] This modification presumably being so as to comply with the requirements of Council Directive 87/54/EEC, Arts 7(3) and (4).

[45] In determining whether there has been any relevant sale or hire for these purposes, the 1989 Regulations provide that no account shall be taken of certain sales or hire which are subject to an obligation of confidence, see para. 14–11, above.

[46] See para. 13–100, above.

[47] *i.e.* with a view to the relevant article being sold or hired in the course of a business, CDPA 1988, s.263(3). See para. 13–144, above.

[48] CDPA 1988, s.226(1) as substituted by SI 1989/1100, reg.8(1).

[49] SI 1989/1100, reg.8(1). The wording of reg.8(1) follows that of Council Directive, 87/54/EEC, Art.5(2) and 5(3).

[50] *i.e.* this is more favourable to the owners of topography design right than the normal design right requirement that the reproduction be for commercial purposes (as to which see para. 13–144, above).

first topography or of the concepts, processes, systems or techniques embodied in it or (b) to reproduce that other topography.[51] Thus, a person may obtain another's semiconductor product embodying a semiconductor topography in which design right subsists. He may analyse it (in effect decompile it) to determine its design layout (and, as appears from the preceding paragraph, may even copy the topography for this purpose). He may then use the concepts, processes, systems and techniques embodied in that layout in creating his own original topography which he can then use in the manufacture of chips. The aim of this provision appears to be to ensure that the copying of ideas embodied in another's topography is permitted but that the copying of the topography itself is not[52] and regulation 8(4) expressly provides that the topography which a person creates as a result of this process of reverse engineering must itself be original.

Infringements in relation to the whole or a substantial part of a design. The test for infringement of design right is considered in detail in the design right chapter of this work. However, the Regulations also provide that anything which would be an infringement of design right in a topography if done to a topography as a whole is an infringement of the design right in the topography if done to a significant part of the topography. It would seem, therefore, that in order to prove infringement of design right in a semiconductor topography, one may either show that the allegedly infringing topography is made exactly or substantially to the topography replied upon *or* that it is made exactly or substantially to a substantial part of that topography.[53]   **14–19**

Secondary infringement: general. Acts of secondary infringements are defined by section 227 of the 1988 Act. They comprise certain dealings with articles which the infringer knows or has reason to believe are infringing articles. The general nature of secondary infringement and the meaning of an "infringing article" have already been considered in the main design right chapterof this work.[54] For present purposes, however, it should be noted that the changes in the definition of primary infringement referred to above will affect whether or not the making of a particular article was an infringement and, therefore, whether that article is an infringing article for the purposes of section 237. Further, the 1989 Regulations alter the definition of an "infringing article" for the purposes of semiconductor topographies so that it may include a design document.[55] Thus, a mask recording the design of a part of the topography would, it is submitted, be a design document and (assuming its making was an infringement) dealings with it may constitute secondary infringements.   **14–20**

Secondary infringement: previous sale or hire. The 1989 Regulations also provide that section 227 does not apply (*i.e.* there is no act of secondary infringe-   **14–21**

---

[51] SI 1989/1100, reg.8(4) following Council Directive 87/54/EEC, Art.5(4).

[52] This is consistent with Council Directive 87/54/EEC, Art.8, which states that "The protection granted to the topographies of semiconductor products ... shall not extend to any concept, process, system technique or encoded information embodied in the topography other than the topography itself".

[53] SI 1989/1100, reg.8(5). This, it seems, brings the test for infringement for semiconductor topographies closer to the test for infringement of copyright. In other design right cases, the making of an article infringes design right in a design if that article has been made exactly or substantially to the design whereas in copyright cases, the making of a thing infringes copyright in a work if the thing in question reproduces the copyright work *or a substantial part thereof.* It may be, therefore, that a claimant in semiconductor topography does not face the sort of difficulties in framing his case which face claimants in other design right cases. See, generally, paras 13–147, 13–151 and 13–153 , above.

[54] See paras 13–157 *et seq.*, above.

[55] SI 1989/1100, reg.8(3) provides that CDPA 1988, s.228(6) (which provides that, in the case of other designs, the expression "infringing articles" does not include design documents) does not apply to semiconductor topographies.

ment) if the article in question has previously been sold or hired within (a) the United Kingdom by or with the licence of the owner of the design right in the topography in question, or within (b) the territory of any other Member State of the European Economic Community or of Gibraltar by or with the consent of the person for the time being entitled to import it into or sell or hire it within that territory.[56]

F. LICENCES OF RIGHT

14–22   **Licences of right.** The 1989 Regulations provide that section 237 of the 1988 Act does not apply in the case of a semiconductor topography.[57] Thus, licences of right are not available automatically in the last five years of the term of design right in a semiconductor topography.[58] The Regulations do not, however, exclude the possibility of licences of right arising under section 238.[59]

G. TRANSITIONAL PROVISIONS

14–23   **Semiconductor topographies created before November 7, 1987.** As mentioned above, prior to November 7, 1987,[60] the protection of semiconductor topographies was a matter (if at all) for copyright law. The application of copyright to works existing at the commencement of the 1988 Act is governed by the transitional provisions of that Act and is considered in the copyright section of this work. Under those transitional provisions, the application of section 51 to existing works was postponed until August 1, 1999.[61] In the case of copyright in topographies created before November 7, 1987, the 1989 Regulations do nothing to alter this,[62] such topographies retained full copyright protection until August 1, 1999.[63] However the 1989 Regulations did modify paragraph 19(2) of those transitional provisions so that no licences of right were available under section 237 of the 1988 Act in respect of such topographies although they may have been under section 238.[64]

14–24   **Semiconductor topographies created on or after November 7, 1987 and before August 1, 1989.** Some difficulty arises in relation to semiconductor topographies created on or after November 7, 1987 but before August 1, 1989, *i.e.* whilst the 1987 Regulations were in force. Although copyright may still subsist in artistic works recording such topographies, this will provide little protection because in respect of such topographies section 51 of the 1988 Act operated with no period of postponement.[65] Further, as the 1987 Regulations were unequivocally revoked by the 1989 Regulations, it seems clear that the

---

[56] (SI 1989/1100), reg.8(2).

[57] SI 1989/1100, reg.9.

[58] In this, the 1989 Regulations follow the requirements of Council Directive, 87/54/EEC, Art.6, which provides that the exclusive rights protecting semiconductor topographies should not be subject to the grant of automatic licences for the sole reason that a certain period of time had elapsed.

[59] For a full discussion of licences of right (including those arising under CDPA 1988, s.238), see paras 13–123 *et seq.*, above.

[60] *i.e.* the commencement date of the Semiconductor (Protection of Topography) Regulations 1987 (SI 1987/1497). See para. 14–03, above.

[61] CDPA 1988, Sch.1, para.19(1).

[62] This contrasts with the position in relation to topographies created between November 7, 1987 and August 1, 1989 as to which see para. 14–23, below.

[63] Since that date it has not been an infringement of the copyright in the relevant work to make an article to the design nor to copy an article made to the design. See para. 13–317, above.

[64] SI 1989/1100, reg.10(3).

[65] See SI 1989/1100, reg.10(2), which provided that para.19(1) of the transitional provisions of the 1988 Act (Sch.1) did not apply to topographies created between November 7, 1987 and July 31,

1987 Regulations also provide no protection in respect of events occurring after their revocation. Finally, it may be argued that the 1989 Regulations themselves provide no protection. This would seem to follow from the fact that, under the 1989 Regulations, protection for topographies is merely a modified form of the design right protection available under Part III of the 1988 Act and from the fact that, under section 213(7) of Part III, there is no design right in a design created before commencement.[66] Notwithstanding this, it is submitted that the 1989 Regulations should be construed as conferring design right protection on topographies created between November 7, 1987 and July 31, 1989. The 1989 Regulations were plainly not intended to remove protection from all topographies created before commencement, otherwise they would also have removed copyright protection from those created before November 7, 1987. Further, there is no logical reason why protection should be excluded only for those topographies which were created between November 7, 1987 and July 31, 1989, particularly given that such an exclusion would place the United Kingdom in breach of its obligation to comply with the EEC Council Directive.[67] The clear intention to exclude copyright protection suggests that protection was intended to be available under either the 1987 or the 1989 Regulations. As the 1987 Regulations are expressly revoked without any savings, it is submitted that the 1989 Regulations must have been intended to apply.

1989. Thus, since August 1, 1989, it has not been an infringement of the copyright in the relevant work to make an article to the design or to copy an article made to the design. This contrasts with the position in relation to works recording topographies created before November 7, 1987, see para. 14–23, above.

[66] CDPA 1988, s.213(7).

[67] 87/54/EEC. See Vol.2 at H1.

CIRCUMVENTION OF PROTECTION MEASURES AND RIGHTS MANAGEMENT INFORMATION

Contents

1. INTRODUCTION

Protection measures. The first part of this chapter is concerned with remedies against the circumvention of "protection measures", a term which derives from the 1988 Act as amended to give effect to the Information Society Directive. In very general terms, a protection measure is a device or technological measure which is applied to a copyright work and which prevents or restricts acts which are not authorised by the owner of the copyright. In the 1988 Act, the term is also applied to the subject-matter of rights in performances, publication right and database right. At the time of writing, the technology is in a state of almost constant development. However, it may be said that in very general terms, such devices tend to fall into one of two categories. The first is "access control", where access to the work is controlled, usually by encrypting it. The second is "copy control", where the extent or nature of copying of the work is controlled, for example by a "copy management system" like that embodied in Adobe's eBook reader.[1] Protection measures have been applied in many fields, but mainly where copies are issued to the public in digital form, such as computer games, electronic books, recorded music and DVD films. Such measures are frequently circumvented, often by the application of computer programs which are distributed on the internet. Accordingly, it has been considered necessary to provide specific legislative protection for them. The first four parts of this chapter deal with that protection. The law relating to unauthorised decoders is dealt with elsewhere.[2]

15–01

Rights-management information. The fifth part of this chapter deals with the related topic of rights management information. Works that appear in digital form are at particular risk of being altered, mutilated, misappropriated, copied or otherwise distributed without the consent of the rights holder. To combat such activities, rights holders have developed "rights management information". Such information, which is often contained in an electronic "watermark" embedded in

15–02

---

[1] See para. 15–20, below.
[2] See paras 16–09 *et seq.*, below.

the protected material, may identify the content of the work and the author and owner of the rights and may also set out the terms and conditions of use associated with the use of the work (for example details of any licence which has already been granted or the conditions under which licences may be obtained). The availability of such information obviously benefits rights holders. It also enables users to have confidence in the authenticity of the material and to be clear as to the terms and conditions under which it may be used. As is the case with any technological measure, rights management information is vulnerable to manipulation or removal (*e.g.* by so-called "watermark washing") by infringers who may go on to distribute copies of the protected material which no longer have any or any accurate rights-management information attached to them.

2. PROTECTION MEASURES: HISTORY OF PROTECTION

15–03   **Background to the 1988 Act.** At the time when the Bill which became the 1988 Act was being debated, there were growing concerns about the potential for piracy of audio and video recordings created by the introduction of the new digital technology. Particular anxiety was expressed about the fact that the reproduction of a digital recording, in contrast to that of an analogue recording, does not result in any deterioration in quality. Possible solutions to the problem of private copying or "home taping" of analogue and digital sound recordings and audiovisual material, including the introduction of a levy payable on the sale of blank recording tape and the use of spoiler or copy-protection systems, were also under discussion. Although the film and recording industries, as well as software manufacturers, had by that time succeeded in developing devices which could be built into their recordings to prevent or limit copying or at least to spoil the quality of copies made,[3] it was feared (correctly as it turned out) that pirates would be equally ingenious in creating other devices to circumvent them. At the same time, considerable concern was expressed by the computer industry about the growth of software packages which had the effect of by-passing copy-protection embodied in computer programmes.[4] In response to these concerns, limited rights and remedies in relation to such "circumvention devices" were introduced in section 296 of the 1988 Act. Those remedies extended to various acts of making and dealing with such devices, but did not apply to their possession. They were limited to cases where copies of the work in question were issued to the public in electronic form. Furthermore, no rights or remedies were introduced in respect of the act of circumvention itself.

15–04   **The Software Directive and the 1992 amendment.** On May 14, 1991 the Council of the European Communities adopted a Directive on the legal protection of computer programs ("the Software Directive").[5] This Directive requires Member States to provide appropriate remedies against any act of putting into circulation, or possessing for commercial purposes "any means the sole intended purpose of which is to facilitate the unauthorised removal or circumvention of any technical device which may have been applied to protect a computer

---

[3] Examples cited in Standing Committee E included the provision on digital tapes of a second inaudible signal which was of such high frequency that special equipment was needed to copy it; and the provision of encoding on video recordings: *Hansard*, HC, cols.733–4 (June 21, 1988) (S.C.E.).
[4] *Hansard*, HC, cols. 733–4 (June 21, 1988) (S.C.E.).
[5] [1991] O.J. L122/42. See Vol.2 at H2.

program".[6] In order to give effect to the Software Directive, section 296 was extended to cover the possession in the course of a business of a device which was designed or adapted to circumvent copy protection which had been applied to copies of a computer program.[7] The revised version of section 296 is considered in the 14th edition of this work.[8]

The WIPO Copyright Treaty and the WIPO Performances and Phonograms Treaty. In the meantime, digital technology had provided the impetus for an explosion in the use of copy-protection devices. The need to provide protection for such devices was recognised at an international level with the inclusion of provisions to that effect in the WIPO Copyright Treaty (WCT) and the WIPO Performances and Phonograms Treaty (WPPT), both adopted in December 1996.[9] Thus, Article 11 WCT and Article 18 WPPT oblige Contracting Parties to provide adequate legal protection and effective legal remedies against the circumvention of effective technological measures used by rights owners in connection with the exercise of their rights and that restrict acts, in respect of their works, performances or phonograms, respectively, which are not authorised by the respective right owner or permitted by law. These provisions are expressed in broad terms and leave considerable scope to individual states in deciding how they are to be implemented.   **15–05**

The Information Society Directive. On January 21, 1998, the European Commission submitted a proposal for a Directive on the harmonisation of certain aspects of copyright and related rights.[10] The proposal contained detailed provision for the protection of "effective technological measures". "Technological measures" were defined as "any device, product or component incorporated into a process, device or product designed to prevent or inhibit the infringement of any" copyright, related rights or database right.[11] Such measures were only deemed to be effective where "the work or other subject matter is rendered accessible to the user only through application of an access code or process, including by decryption, descrambling or other transformation of the work or other subject matter, with the authority of the rightholders".[12] On May 22, 2001, this Directive was adopted ("the Information Society Directive").[13] Detailed provisions in relation to "technological measures" remain, but their form is significantly altered from that of the draft. "Technological measures" are now defined as "any technology, device or component that, in the normal course of its operation, is designed to prevent or restrict acts, in respect of works or other subject matter, which are not authorised by the rightholder ...". Such measures are deemed "effective"   **15–06**

---

[6] Software Directive 91/250, Art.7(1).

[7] CDPA 1988, s.296(2A), inserted by the Copyright (Computer Programs) Regulations 1992 (SI 1992/3233), para.10, with effect from January 1, 1993. In *Kabushiki Kaisha Sony Computer Entertainment Inc. v Ball* [2004] EWHC 1738, Ch D at para.21, Laddie J. rejected arguments as to the construction of *ibid.*, s.296 based on the construction of the Software Directive because the 1988 Act was passed before this came into force and does not purport to give effect to it. However, this appears to overlook the fact that the object of amending s.296 was "in order to properly align its provisions with those of the Software Directive": see the Explanatory Note to the Regulations. Increasingly, however, this point will become academic as the version of s.296 as amended by the Regulations ceases to apply.

[8] At paras 15–02 to 15–05. In *Kabushiki Kaisha Sony Computer Entertainment Inc. v Ball* [2004] EWHC 1738, Ch D at para.21, Laddie J. rejected an argument that under this version of s.296 it was sufficient to prove that the defendant knew or had reason to believe that the device would be used to overcome copy protection and thus that it was not necessary to show that the defendant knew or had reason to believe that it would be used to making infringing copies.

[9] See Vol.2 at F13 and F14.

[10] [1998] O.J. C108/6.

[11] Information Society Directive 2001/29, Art.6(2).

[12] Art.6(2)

[13] [2001] O.J. L167/10.

where the use of the work or other subject-matter "is controlled by the rightholders through application of an access control or protection process, such as encryption, scrambling or other transformation of the work or other subject-matter or a copy control mechanism, which achieves the protection objective".[14] In contrast to the draft, the Directive as adopted contains detailed provision about the interrelationship between effective technological measures and permitted acts.[15] Article 1(2)(a) of the Directive expressly provides that it leaves intact and shall in no way affect the Software Directive, which is discussed above.[16] During the negotiations on the Information Society Directive, the United Kingdom Government expressed concern about the difficulties which might arise from the existence of separate regimes for computer programs and other works, not only because it is not always clear whether a work is a computer program, but also because computer programs may be used as technological protection measures for other works.[17] However, neither the Commission, nor the majority of other Member States, felt it appropriate to seek a unified approach to protection measures, although the Commission is committed to an early review of the issue.[18] Thus, although there are amendments to section 296, their main object is simply to ensure that the section conforms in style with the new sections which follow it, so as to lend coherence to this Part of the Act overall.[19]

15–07   **Implementation of the Information Society Directive.** The Information Society Directive has been implemented in the United Kingdom by the Copyright and Related Rights Regulations 2003.[20] These Regulations substitute a new section 296 of the 1988 Act and add six new sections (296ZA to 296ZF), all under the new heading "Circumvention of protection measures". In accordance with Article 1(2)(a) of the Information Society Directive,[21] there are now two separate schemes, the first relating to protection measures for computer programs only and the second relating to protection measures for all other works. In relation to computer programs only, the new section 296 provides for civil remedies in respect of the circumvention of "technical devices", which are defined as devices "intended to prevent or restrict acts that are not authorised by the copyright owner of that computer program and are restricted by copyright".[22] These remedies apply not only against those who make or deal with the means to circumvent such devices but also against those who publish information which is intended to enable or assist the removal or circumvention of such devices.[23] There are no criminal remedies. In relation to works other than computer programs, there are now both civil and criminal remedies. The new section 296ZA provides civil remedies in respect of acts of circumvention of "technological measures", which are defined as "any technology, device or component which is designed, in the normal course of its operation, to protect a copyright work".[24] At the same time, the new section 296ZD provides civil remedies in respect of devices and services designed

---

[14] Art.6(3). It has apparently been argued that this definition does not include "access control" technology because such technology does not necessarily prevent acts restricted by copyright. However, this argument seems to be precluded by the express reference to "an access control … process". See *Braun* [2003] 11 E.I.P.R. 496.

[15] Art.6(4).

[16] See para. 15–04.

[17] Consultation on UK Implementation of Directive 2001/29: Analysis of Responses and Government Conclusions, para.6.3.

[18] Analysis of Responses and Government Conclusions, para.6.3.

[19] See the Patent Office's Transposition Note in relation to the Regulations.

[20] SI 2003/2498. The Regulations came into force on October 31, 2003.

[21] See para. 15–06, above.

[22] CDPA 1988, s.296(6). See para. 15–08, below.

[23] s.296(1)(b). See para. 15–14, below.

[24] s.296ZF(1). See para. 15–18, below.

to circumvent technological measures.[25] These civil remedies also apply to technological measures designed to protect the subject-matter of rights in performances, publication right and database right.[26] The new section 296ZB creates new criminal offences in respect of devices and services designed to circumvent technological measures,[27] while the new section 296ZC contains provisions in relation to search warrants and forfeiture.[28] These criminal remedies are limited to measures to protect copyright. Finally, the new section 296ZE makes specific provision for the position where effective technological measures prevent permitted acts[29] or analogous acts in relation to the subject matter of rights in performances, database right and publication right.[30] The previous section 296 continues to apply to acts done before October 31, 2003, while the new provisions apply to acts done on or after that date.[31]

3. PROTECTION MEASURES: COMPUTER PROGRAMS

"Technical device". The new section 296 applies where a "technical device" has been "applied" to a computer program. A "technical device" is defined as "any device intended to prevent or restrict acts that are not authorised by the copyright owner of that computer program and are restricted by copyright".[32] This definition is arguably rather narrower than that contained in the Software Directive: "any technical device which may have been applied to protect a computer program".[33] However, it may be that there is little practical distinction. The definition is arguably also narrower than that of "copy protection" in the previous version of section 296: "any device or means intended to prevent or restrict copying of a work or impair the quality of copies made". *Sony v Owen* and *Sony v Ball*,[34] the only reported cases on the previous version of section 296, concerned codes embedded into CD or DVD versions of computer games for playing on Sony's Playstation consoles. On the facts of those cases, if such a CD or DVD was copied by an ordinary member of the public (for example using a CD burner), the code would not be read by the copying machine and the resulting copy would not run on the console because the console's computer program would fail to find the code. If, on the other hand, the console's process of finding the code could be bypassed (in those cases by chips known as "the Messiah" and "the Messiah 2"), the game could be run on the console. When the game was loaded onto the console, a copy was made. In *Sony v Owen* it was held under the previous version of the section that Sony's arrangements[35] were a device or means intended to prevent the making of such further copies and therefore amounted to "copy protection". In *Sony v Ball* it was held that the same applied both under the new version of the section and under the previous version. In the latter case, it was

15–08

---

[25] See para. 15–24, below.

[26] ss.296ZA(6), 296ZD(8).

[27] See para. 15–27, below.

[28] See para. 15–32, below.

[29] See para. 15–33, below.

[30] s.296ZE(11).

[31] Copyright and Related Rights Regulations 2003 (SI 2003/2498), regs 1 and 40. Further, no act done after October 1, 2003 in pursuance of an agreement made before December 22, 2002, shall be regarded as an infringement of any new or extended right arising by virtue of the Regulations, reg.32(2).

[32] CDPA 1988, s.296(6).

[33] Software Directive 91/250, Art.7(1)(c).

[34] *Sony Computer Entertainment v Owen* [2002] EWHC 45, Ch D and *Kabushiki Kaisha Sony Computer Entertainment Inc. v Ball* [2004] EWHC 1738, Ch D (the latter also involved the new version of s.296 as well as s.296ZD).

[35] The Judge stated that "the codes" amounted to copy protection. Presumably what was actually meant was Sony's arrangements including the codes.

argued that Sony's copy protection system did not amount to a technical device because it was applied primarily to the hardware (the console) rather than to the copies of the copyright works (the versions of the games). This argument was rejected for four reasons.[36] First, the court held that under the pre-amendment version of section 296 this did not matter because there was no reference to the protection being applied to a copyright work. Secondly, there was nothing in the new version of section 296 or in section 296ZD to require the protection to be "on" the software rather than in the hardware: a protection device may be "applied" to a program either by being put on the program or on the software which reads it, or both. Thirdly, there was no reason why the legislature should have been concerned as to where the copy protection system resides. Finally, in any event, as with most copy protection systems which operate on a lock-and-key basis with the hardware decrypting or unscrambling encrypted or scrambled software, the copy protection was located partly in the software and partly in the hardware. The following points should also be noted. First, it is not necessary to prove that the device is actually effective: all that need be proved is that it is intended to prevent or restrict infringements. Secondly, the definition does not make clear whose intention is in issue, but this is presumably the intention of the manufacturer or (if the manufacture is commissioned) of the person who commissions the manufacture. Thirdly, although it is necessary to show that the device was intended to prevent acts which are restricted by copyright, this is unlikely to be difficult in the case of a computer program, since any access to the work will involve copying.

15–09   **Persons with rights.** The new section 296 grants rights to three categories of person.[37] First, the person issuing the copies of the computer program to the public or communicating the program to the public.[38] Issuing to the public of copies of a work means the act of putting into circulation in the EEA copies not previously put into circulation in the EEA by or with the consent of the copyright owner, or the act of putting into circulation outside the EEA, copies not previously put into circulation in the EEA or elsewhere.[39] Communication to the public means communication to the public by electronic transmission, including making the work available in such a way that members of the public may access it from a place and at a time individually chosen by them ("on demand").[40] It is worth emphasising that exceptionally these provisions potentially give rights to non-exclusive licensees as well as copyright owners and exclusive licensees. The language of this part of section 296 could be read as confining the existence of the rights to the period during which the person seeking to exercise them is actually issuing the copies or communicating the program to the public[41]; however, it seems unlikely that this is what was intended. In practice it is likely that a person who has ceased to issue the copies to the public would remain interested in preventing their further reproduction. The second category of person with rights is the copyright owner or his exclusive licensee (if this person does not fall within

---

[36] *Kabushiki Kaisha Sony Computer Entertainment Inc. v Ball* [2004] EWHC 1738, Ch D, para.40.
[37] Contrast the previous CDPA 1988, s.296, under which the only person with a remedy was the person issuing copies to the public: s.296(2).
[38] s.296(2)(a).
[39] s.18(2), applied by s.296(8). For a full discussion of the meaning of the term "issue to the public", see paras 7–79 *et seq.*, above.
[40] s.20, applied by s.296(8). For a full discussion of the meaning of the term "communication to the public", see paras 7–98 *et seq.*, above.
[41] s.296(2) states that the person who has the rights is the person *issuing* the copies or *communicating* the work (rather than the person who *has issued them* or *has communicated* it).

the first category).[42] It is not clear from the wording of this paragraph whether the rights of the copyright owner and his exclusive licensee are intended to be concurrent or alternative. On the one hand, subsection 296(2)(b) refers to "the copyright owner or his exclusive licensee". On the other, subsection 296(3) states that the rights conferred by the section are concurrent and this provision arguably applies as much to the rights conferred on the copyright owner and his exclusive licensee as to the other rights conferred by the section. Presumably, although this is not stated, it is necessary that the claimant should be the copyright owner or exclusive licensee at the time of the act complained of rather than (for example) at the time when the program was issued to the public. The third category is the owner or exclusive licensee of any intellectual property right in the technical device itself.[43] This would no doubt extend to the owners of patents and design rights as well as of copyright. Again, although on the face of it these rights are stated to be alternative, the effect of subsection 296(3) may be that they are concurrent. Once more, it seems likely that it is necessary for the claimant to have such rights at the time of the act complained of, although again this is not made clear.

Making or dealing with means. The primary targets of section 296 are those who manufacture and deal with the means to circumvent such technical devices. Accordingly, the section creates rights which are exercisable against persons who, with a specified state of mind, manufacture for sale or hire, import, distribute, sell, let for hire, offer or expose for sale or hire, advertise for sale or hire or possess for commercial purposes[44] any means the sole intended purpose of which is to facilitate the unauthorised removal or circumvention of the technical device.[45] The state of mind in question is knowledge or reason to believe that the means in question will be used to make infringing copies.[46]

15–10

"Means". The expression "means the sole intended purpose of which is to facilitate the unauthorised removal of any technical device" derives directly from the Software Directive,[47] where it is not further defined. The use of the extremely broad term "means" is no doubt intended to protect these provisions from technological obsolescence. It is not clear whether the use of the phrase "sole intended purpose" involves a subjective or objective test. If the test is subjective, difficult questions may arise as to whose intention is meant. Where the manufacturer is sued, no doubt the relevant intention will be that of the manufacturer. Where, however, the person being sued is further down the chain of supply, the requirement that the intended purpose is "the sole intended purpose" will arguably mean that it is necessary to prove that this purpose was intended both by the manufacturer and the person sued. It seems more likely, therefore, that the test is in fact objective. The previous version of section 296 used the words "any device or means specifically designed or adapted to circumvent the form of copy-protection employed". In *Sony v Owen*,[48] which was decided under that previous version, it was argued that the Messiah had potential uses other than the making

15–11

---

[42] This fills an obvious *lacuna* in the previous law.

[43] Again, persons in this category had no remedy under the previous law. However, it remains to be seen to what extent such persons will be interested in enforcing their rights.

[44] Art.7(1)(c) of the Software Directive 91/250 envisaged that possession for commercial purposes would attract liability. A new subs.(2A) was added to the old CDPA 1988, s.296 in order to give effect to this: see para. 15–04, above.

[45] CDPA 1988, s.296(1)(b)(i).

[46] For a discussion of the meaning of these terms in the copyright context, see paras 8–08 *et seq.*, above. In *Kabushiki Kaisha Sony Computer Entertainment Inc. v Ball* [2004] EWHC 1738, Ch D at para.27, Laddie J. rejected an argument that it was sufficient to prove that the defendant knew or had reason to believe that the device would be used to overcome copy-protection.

[47] Software Directive, Art.7(1)(c).

[48] *Sony Computer Entertainment v Owen* [2002] EWHC 45, Ch D.

of infringing copies, for example to run software which had not been designed by Sony. This argument was rejected: the codes amounted to copy protection and the Messiah was specifically designed to circumvent them. In *Sony v Ball*[49] a similar argument on the new version of section 296 failed because all the intended purposes relied on by the defendant were unauthorised.

15–12　**"Unauthorised".** The term "unauthorised" is not defined in section 296. Section 296(8) provides that expressions which are defined for the purposes of the copyright part of the 1988 Act have the same meaning in section 296. The word "unauthorised" is defined in the copyright part of the 1988 Act.[50] However, the definition only applies where the word is used "as regards anything done in relation to a work" and would therefore appear to be inapplicable to the removal or circumvention of a technical device. The word "unauthorised" did not appear in the original version of section 296, nor was it added when the section was amended to give effect to the Software Directive.[51] The question therefore arises as to whether its introduction into the section makes any substantive difference. In principle it would seem to be clearly arguable that an act can only be unauthorised if there is someone who is capable of granting the authority to do it. Section 296 does not itself create a right to authorise the removal or circumvention of technical devices. It would follow that the question of authorisation would have to be considered apart from the section itself. If so, an act of removal or circumvention would only be unauthorised if done in breach of United Kingdom law, for example in breach of an effective contractual prohibition, by infringing an intellectual or other property right, by the misuse of confidential information or by otherwise acting in breach of a prohibition which exists independently of section 296. However, it is far from clear that the insertion of the word "unauthorised" was intended to effect a change in the law.[52] Furthermore, this interpretation would deprive section 296 of much of its effect.[53] Moreover, it seems doubtful that those who framed the Software Directive intended that the question whether an act of removal or cirumvention was unauthorised should depend on the vagaries of national law.[54] Finally, in *Sony v Ball*,[55] Laddie J. stated that the purpose of the revised version of section 296 was to prohibit trade in devices

---

[49] *Kabushiki Kaisha Sony Computer Entertainment Inc. v Ball* [2004] EWHC 1738, Ch D. There does not appear to have been argument about whether "purpose" was objective or subjective in this case.

[50] CDPA 1988, s.178 provides that it means "done otherwise than" (a) by or with the licence of the copyright owner; or (b) where copyright does not subsist in the work, by or with the licence of the author or (where *ibid.*, s.11(2) would have applied) his employer or persons lawfully claiming under them; or (c) pursuant to s.48.

[51] As to which, see para. 15–04, above.

[52] The Government's exact words in para.6.4 of its Analysis of Responses and Government Conclusions are as follows: "The consultation paper proposed to retain s.296, as amended on implementation of Directive 91/250, but in relation to computer programs only … This remains the intention, but in the light of comments made by parties with particular interests in computer programs, the Government has concluded that it is desirable to make some further adjustments to s.296 in order to bring its wording into closer alignment with that of Article 7(1)(c) of Directive 91/250, which it is now the sole function of s.296 to implement. These changes do not, however, alter the basic approach in s.296, and the Government has concluded that it would not be appropriate to make more substantial changes, such as the introduction of criminal sanctions …". See also the Patent Office's Transposition Note: " Section 296 has been amended principally so that it conforms in style with the new sections directly resulting from transposing Article 6 which follow it, so as to lend coherence to this Part of the Act overall. Also, this section has been expanded so that the right to bring a civil action is vested in more people than previously. Again, this conforms with the new sections. This aspect of the amendment has been made by means of further implementing Directive 91/250/EEC (Article 7)".

[53] In *BBC Enterprises Ltd v Hi-Tech Xtravision Ltd* [1991] 2 A.C. 327, a similar argument in relation to the term "not entitled" in s.298(2) of the 1988 Act succeeded at first instance but not in the Court of Appeal or the House of Lords. See para. 16–23, below.

[54] It seems improbable that the term might mean "unauthorised under EU law".

[55] [2004] EWHC 1738, Ch D, para.21.

which overcome copy protection without regard to whether that assisted copyright infringement.[56] It would seem to follow that the better view is that the term "unauthorised" means without the authority of a person with rights under the section.

Inter-relationship with permitted acts. Under sections 50A to 50C of the 1988 Act, a lawful user of a computer program is entitled to carry out certain acts in relation to a computer program which would otherwise infringe copyright. Those acts include, for example the making of back up copies.[57] In some cases, under section 296A of the 1988 Act, contractual terms which purport to prohibit or restrict such acts are void.[58] The question arises as to what happens where the existence of a technical device prevents the operation of one of these permitted acts, for example where a copy-protection device prevents the making of back-ups.[59] Unlike in the case of protection measures in respect of other rights,[60] the Government did not introduce a statutory procedure aimed at resolving the tension between technical devices on the one hand and the permitted acts on the other. In theory, of course, there is no such tension. The act of circumvention is not an infringement of the section and a supplier of means or information is only liable if he can be shown to have known or had reason to believe that it will be used to make infringing copies. In practice, however, it is impossible for a supplier to know exactly what will be done with the means or information he supplies. This may well deter suppliers from supplying those who genuinely wish only to carry out permitted acts. It is doubtful whether this is consistent with the requirement of Article 7(1) of the Software Directive that the rights in respect of technical devices should be "without prejudice to" the permitted acts. **15–13**

Publication of information. The rights under section 296 are also available against those who, again with the specified state of mind, publish information intended to enable or assist persons to remove or circumvent the technical device.[61] This category of persons is not specifically mentioned in the Software Directive, but derives from the previous version of section 296. The state of mind in question is knowledge or reason to believe that the information in question will be used to make infringing copies.[62] In this case, there is no requirement that the removal or circumvention in question should be unauthorised. **15–14**

The rights and remedies. The person with rights under section 296 has the same "rights" against the persons defined in the previous paragraph as a copyright owner has in respect of an infringement of copyright. The absence of any reference to "remedies" in the section has given rise to some uncertainty as to the **15–15**

---

[56] In that case, the defendant argued that the intended purposes of the device included acts which would be authorised by the claimant (presumably it was contended that it was implicit that if those acts were indeed authorised, the removal or circumvention would also be authorised, but this is not clear from the judgment). The judge noted that this argument could only succeed if the acts in question were authorised by Sony but held that they were not because they would infringe its copyright: see paras 28 to 33. Since this part of the argument failed, it was not necessary for the judge to consider whether the actual removal or circumvention for the purposes of these acts was authorised. Accordingly, the decision appears to leave open the question of the meaning of "unauthorised".

[57] See, generally, paras 9–132 et seq., above.

[58] See, generally, para. 9–132, above.

[59] It is obvious, for example, that a technical device cannot simply be declared "void" like a term in an agreement.

[60] See below at paras 15–33 to 15–37.

[61] CDPA 1988, s.296(1)(b)(ii).

[62] s.296(1)(b). This was the position under the previous version of s.296. For a detailed discussion of the terms "knowledge" and "reason to believe", see paras 8–08 et seq., above.

meaning of this provision, since rights are of little use without remedies.[63] However, if the point were raised, it seems inevitable that a court would conclude that the intention was that the person with rights should be entitled to the normal remedies for copyright infringement, that is an injunction, together with damages or an account of profits.[64] In addition, it seems that the person with rights will not be entitled to damages if the defendant can show that he did not know and had no reason to believe that copyright subsisted in the work to which the action relates[65]; while on the other hand he will be entitled to additional damages in the same circumstances in which such damages are available for copyright infringement.[66] Section 296(4) expressly provides that a person with rights may obtain an order for delivery up or seize without a court order means the sole intended purpose of which is to facilitate the unauthorised removal or circumvention of a technical device. These rights are the same rights as a copyright owner has in relation to infringing copies under sections 99 and 100 of the 1988 Act.[67] The rights exist where a person has the means in question in his possession, custody or control with the intention that they should be used to facilitate the unauthorised removal or circumvention of any technical device which has been applied to a computer program.[68] Where goods have been delivered up or seized under these provisions, the normal copyright provisions apply in relation to the making of disposal orders with the necessary modifications.[69]

15–16   **Concurrent nature of the rights and remedies.** The rights under section 296 are expressed to be concurrent and it is provided that certain other provisions of the copyright Part of the 1988 Act apply to proceedings under section 296 in relation to persons with concurrent rights as they apply in proceedings under those provisions in relation to a copyright owner and exclusive licensee with concurrent rights.[70] The first provision is section 101(3), which provides that in an action brought by an exclusive licensee a defendant may avail himself of any defence which would have been available to him if the action had been brought by the copyright owner.[71] Thus, for example, a defendant to an action brought by an exclusive licensee may rely on a licence granted by the copyright owner. The purpose of applying section 101(3) would appear to be to provide that if a defendant has a defence against one of the persons with rights, for example because he has a licence, he may rely on that defence in proceedings brought by another of the persons with rights against whom he would not otherwise have a defence. Presumably this also means that where a defendant would be able to raise a defence of estoppel against one person with rights, he would also be able to set up that estoppel against any other person with rights who sought to rely on the section. The other provisions of the copyright Part of the 1988 Act which are applied to section 296 are subsections 102(1) to (5), which contain provisions as to proceedings brought by a copyright owner or exclusive licensee alone.[72] The effect of the application of subsections 102(1) to (3) is that if an action is brought

---

[63] CDPA 1988, s.298, which is structured in a similar way to s.296, refers to "rights and remedies".

[64] Under s.96(2). See Ch.22. This interpretation is supported by the statement of the minister (Mr Butcher) in Standing Committee E (*Hansard*, HC, col.737 (June 21, 1988) (S.C.E.): "The remedies are to be the same as those available to a copyright owner in respect of infringement. That is analogous to the provisions of clause 277 relating to fraudulent reception of broadcasts."

[65] s.97(1). See paras 22–64 *et seq.*, below.

[66] s.97(2). See paras 22–168 *et seq.*, below.

[67] See para. 22–182 (delivery up) and paras 22–46 *et seq.* (seizure without a court order).

[68] s.296(4).

[69] s.296(7). As to these, see s.114 and paras 22–179 *et seq.*, below.

[70] CDPA 1988, s.296(3), (5).

[71] See para. 22–20, below.

[72] For the operation of these provisions, see para. 22–20, below.

by a person with rights in relation to an infringement in respect of which other persons with rights have concurrent rights of action, the action may not be proceeded with (except for the purposes of obtaining interim relief) without joining the others or obtaining the leave of the court. A person joined in accordance with this provision will not be liable for any costs in the action unless he takes part in the proceedings. Given the number and variety of persons who may have concurrent rights this provision may well cause considerable practical difficulties for a claimant who wishes to proceed to trial. Of course, such a claimant will be able to obtain the court's permission to proceed without joining others. However, the purpose of subsection 102(1) is to protect defendants from being sued by more than one claimant in separate actions. It seems likely, therefore, that a court will expect claimants to take considerable steps to identify other persons with rights before it will grant permission to proceed without their being joined. Such steps may be time-consuming and expensive. The effect of the application of subsection 102(4) is as follows.[73] First, when assessing damages the court is obliged to take into account the terms of any[74] licence between two or more persons with rights and any pecuniary remedy already awarded to or available to other persons with rights. Secondly, no account of profits shall be directed in favour of one person with rights if an award of damages has already been made or an account of profits has already been directed in favour of another person with rights. Thirdly, if an account of profits is directed, the court is obliged to apportion the profits between the persons with rights as it considers just, subject to any agreement between them. The effect of the application of subsection 102(5)[75] is that before one person with rights applies for an order for delivery up or exercises the right of seizure without a court order, he must notify any other person having rights. That person may then apply for such order for delivery up or (as the case may be) prohibiting or permitting the exercise of the right of seizure without a court order as the court thinks fit, having regard to the terms of any licence between the parties.

Other provisions about proceedings. The presumptions contained in sections 104 to 106 of the 1988 Act[76] and the withdrawal of the privilege against self-incrimination effected by section 72 of the Supreme Court Act 1981[77] apply in relation to proceedings under section 296 as they apply in relation to proceedings under the copyright Part of the 1988 Act.[78] **15–17**

4. PROTECTION MEASURES: WORKS OTHER THAN COMPUTER PROGRAMS

A. CIVIL REMEDIES

"Technological measures". As has already been explained,[79] the separate Community schemes for protection measures in respect of computer programs on the one hand and protection measures in respect of all other rights on the other have **15–18**

---

[73] See para 22–190, below, for an account of the operation of s.102(4) in the copyright context.

[74] There seems no reason to limit the application of s.102(4) to any licence between a copyright owner with rights and an exclusive licensee with rights, although this is normally the only licence which is likely to be relevant under s.296.

[75] See para. 22–190, below.

[76] As to which, see paras 22–210 et seq., below.

[77] Together with its Scottish and Northern Irish equivalents, s.15 of the Law Reform (Miscellaneous Provisions) (Scotland) Act 1985 and s.94A of the Judicature (Northern Ireland) Act 1978. See para. 22–147, below.

[78] CDPA 1988, s.296(7).

[79] See para. 15–07, above.

been implemented by creating two separate schemes in the 1988 Act. Accordingly, the new sections 296ZA and 296ZC apply where effective technological measures have been applied to a copyright work other than a computer program.[80] They also apply (with any necessary adaptations) where such measures have been applied to the subject-matter of rights in performances, publication right or database right.[81] In what follows, for ease of exposition, the new provisions of the 1988 Act will be considered as they apply to copyright. "Technological measures" are any technology, device or component which is designed, in the normal course of its operation, to protect a copyright work other than a computer program.[82] This definition is reproduced verbatim from the Information Society Directive.[83] The use of the broad term "technology" is presumably designed to deal with future developments in the field of copy protection. The term "protection" means the prevention or restriction of acts that are not authorised by the copyright owner of that work and are restricted by copyright.[84] Two points may be made. First, it is not necessary to prove that the protection of the work is the main or primary object of the measure: all that is necessary is that the measure should have been designed to achieve this in the normal course of its operation. Secondly, however, it will not be sufficient to show that the device is designed to prevent acts which are not restricted by copyright (for example, permitted acts): the main purpose of the copy protection system must be to protect a copyright work so as to prevent infringements of copyright.[85] In *Sony v Ball*[86] (discussed above)[87] the court rejected an argument that Sony's copy-protection system did not amount to a technological measure because it was directed at the hardware rather than the copyright material.[88]

15–19 **"Effective".** Technological measures are only effective if the "use" of the work is controlled by the copyright owner through one of two alternative methods which achieves "the intended protection".[89] This definition derives from the Information Society Directive,[90] although the wording has been slightly altered. For these purposes, the "use" of the work is limited to use of the work which is within the scope of the acts restricted by copyright.[91] The alternative methods of control are, first, an access control or protection process such as encryption, scrambling or other transformation of the work; and, secondly, a copy control mechanism.[92] The "intended protection" is presumably the prevention or restriction of acts that are not authorised by the copyright owner and are restricted by copyright.[93] By contrast with the position under the previous and current versions of section 296, it is not sufficient for the claimant to show that the measures are intended to achieve their object; rather, they must actually achieve it. On the other hand, it cannot be necessary to prove that the measures are completely effective in the

---

[80] CDPA 1988, ss.296ZA(1)(a) and 296ZD(1)(a).
[81] ss.296ZA(6) and 296ZD(8).
[82] s.296ZF(1).
[83] Directive 2001/29 on the harmonisation of certain aspects of copyright and related rights in the information society, [2001] O.J. L167/10, Art.6(3).
[84] s.296ZF(3)(a).
[85] *Kabushiki Kaisha Sony Computer Entertainment Inc. v Ball* [2004] EWHC 1738, Ch D, para.39.
[86] *Kabushiki Kaisha Sony Computer Entertainment Inc. v Ball* [2004] EWHC 1738, Ch D, para.43.
[87] See paras 15–08, 15–11 and 15–12.
[88] *Kabushiki Kaisha Sony Computer Entertainment Inc. v Ball* [2004] EWHC 1738, Ch D, para.43. For a more detailed account, see para. 15–08, above.
[89] CDPA 1988, s.296ZF(2).
[90] Information Society Directive, Art.6(3).
[91] s.296ZF(3)(b).
[92] s.296ZF(2).
[93] See s.296ZF(3)(a) and see para. 15–18, above.

sense of being wholly incapable of being circumvented: if that were the case there would be no need for the section in the first place.[94]

Examples of technological measures.[95] The *Sony v Owen*[96] and *Sony v Ball*[97] cases are the only reported cases in which technological measures have been the subject of litigation in the United Kingdom. *Sony v Owen* concerned computer programs and is discussed above.[98] *Sony v Ball* concerned the same technology and reliance was placed on section 296, but also on section 296ZA. Sony's arrangements were held to amount to "technological measures".[99] A number of other types of technological measure have been the subject of reported litigation in the United States. The United States legislation in this field[1] is significantly different to that contained in the 1988 Act. Accordingly, while the reported decisions provide useful illustrations of the technology, they are of little or no use in interpreting the European and United Kingdom legislation. Considerable litigation has resulted from the application of the Content Scramble System or "CSS" to DVD films. CSS employs an algorithm configured by a set of "keys" to encrypt a DVD's contents. Decryption requires a set of "player keys" as well as an understanding of the CSS encryption algorithm. Without the player keys and the algorithm, a DVD player cannot access the contents of the DVD. With the player keys and the algorithm, the player can display the film on a screen, but the viewer cannot copy the film using the copy function. The film studios distributed the CSS technology to the manufacturers of DVD players under a licensing scheme pursuant to which the manufacturers were obliged to keep the player keys confidential and prevent the transmission of CSS data from a DVD drive. Not long after DVDs began to be distributed on a wide scale, decryption programs were developed and soon became widely available on the Internet. In one case, film studios obtained injunctions against a defendant who had posted a copy of a decryption program called "DeCSS" on a website.[2] In another, film studios obtained an injunction against a company which marketed decryption programs for the purposes of making backup copies of DVDs.[3] Another form of technical measure which has been the subject of litigation in the United States is Adobe's Acrobat eBook format. Where an electronic book in this format is downloaded

15–20

---

[94] See also *Braun* [2003] 11 E.I.P.R. 496. A similar analysis has been applied to the terms "effectively controls access" and "effectively protects a right of a copyright owner", which appear in the United States Digital Millennium Copyright Act ("DMCA"): see *Universal City Studios, Inc. v Reimerdes*, 111 F.Supp.2d 346 (S.D.N.Y. 2000) and *321 Studios v Metro Goldwyn Mayer Studios Inc.*, No.C 02-1955 (N.D.Cal.), in which an argument that CSS (as to which see the next paragraph) was not effective because the access keys were widely available on the internet was characterised as "equivalent to a claim that, since it is easy to find skeleton keys on the black market, a deadbolt is not an effective lock to a door". Note, however, that in view of the considerable substantive and terminological differences between CDPA 1988, s.296ZF and the DMCA, these United States authorities are of no real assistance on the detailed construction of CDPA 1988, s.296ZF.

[95] For a general survey of the position in relation to digital works, see *Current Developments in Digital Rights Management*, a report prepared for the 10th session of WIPO's Standing Committee on Copyright and Related Rights by Jeffrey Cunard, Keith Hill and Chris Barlas. See also *Morrison & Gillies* [2002] 2 E.I.P.R. 74 (webcast content) and *Marks & Turnbull* [2000] 5 E.I.P.R. 198.

[96] *Sony Computer Entertainment v Owen* [2002] EWHC 45, Ch D.

[97] *Kabushiki Kaisha Sony Computer Entertainment Inc. v Ball* [2004] EWHC 1738, Ch D.

[98] See paras 15–08 and 15–11, above. For a United States case in relation to similar devices, see *Sony Computer Entertainment America Inc. v Gamemasters* 87 F. Supp. 2d 976 (N.D. Cal. 1999).

[99] *Kabushiki Kaisha Sony Computer Entertainment Inc. v Ball* [2004] EWHC 1738, Ch D, para.39. See also paras 15–08, 15–11 and 15–12, above.

[1] That is, the Digital Millennium Copyright Act, 17 U.S.C. § 1201 *et seq*.

[2] *Universal City Studios, Inc. v Reimerdes*, 111 F.Supp.2d 346 (S.D.N.Y. 2000); affirmed on appeal in *Universal City Studios, Inc. v Corley* 273 F.3d 429 (2d Cir. 2001). See case comment on the decision at first instance by *Goldberg and Bernstein* [2001] 3 E.I.P.R. 160.

[3] *321 Studios v Metro Goldwyn Mayer Studios Inc.* No.C 02-1955 (N.D.Cal.).

from a publisher's website, it is accompanied by an electronic "voucher" which is recognised and read by the copy of Adobe's eBook Reader program which is on the purchaser's computer. The book can then only be read on the computer onto which it has been downloaded. Furthermore, the publisher is able to restrict the purchaser's use of the book, for example to prevent its being copied, printed or distributed electronically. In one reported case the defendant sold a software program which converted eBook Reader formatted books into "naked PDF" format, thus making them easy to copy, print and distribute in electronic form.[4] A third form of technical measure which has been litigated in the United States is the encoding and security measures developed by RealNetworks to enable audio and video content to be "streamed" to consumers without permitting them to download it. This has been achieved by the operation of two security devices: the "Secret Handshake", an authentication sequence which ensures that all files encoded in RealNetworks' RealMedia format will only be sent to a RealPlayer software program; and the "Copy Switch", a piece of data in all RealMedia files which contains the content owner's preference regarding whether the stream may be copied by the consumer. The RealPlayer program reads the Copy Switch and obeys the content owner's wishes. In one reported case the defendant distributed and marketed a software product which circumvented the Secret Handshake by mimicing a RealPlayer and bypassed the Copy Switch, thus enabling streamed content to be downloaded. The court granted an interim injunction.[5] Meanwhile, in Hong Kong, Playstation discs and consoles[6] and Nintendo cartridges and Game Boy consoles[7] have been held to amount to copy protection under provisions similar to the previous version of section 296.[8] In Australia, the same result has been reached in relation to Playstation discs and consoles under legislation which defines the term "technological protection measure" in very similar terms to those of section 296ZF.[9] It seems likely that all the devices and measures referred to in this paragraph would be held to constitute "technological measures" within the meaning of subsection 296ZF(1).

15–21   **Acts of circumvention which attract liability.** Where effective technological measures have been applied to a copyright work other than a computer program, section 296ZA creates rights and remedies against a person who does anything which circumvents those measures. However, that person is only liable if he knew or had reasonable grounds to know that he was "pursuing that objective", that is, presumably, the circumvention of the measures in question.[10]

15–22   **Cryptography exception.** There is a limited exception in the case of research into cryptography. Where a person, for the purposes of research into cryptography, does anything which circumvents effective technological measures, he is only liable if in so doing or in issuing information derived from that research, he

---

[4] *United States of America v Elcom Ltd* 203 F. Supp. 2d 1111, a criminal case. This report concerns the denial of the defendant's motion to dismiss the indictment on constitutional grounds.

[5] *RealNetworks Inc. v Streambox, Inc.* 2000 U.S. Dist. Lexis 1889. This case settled in September 2000: see *Current Developments in Digital Rights Management*, a report prepared for the 10th session of WIPO's Standing Committee on Copyright and Related Rights by Jeffrey Cunard, Keith Hill and Chris Barlas.

[6] *Sony Computer Entertainment Inc v Lik Sang International Ltd* (2003) 55 I.P.R. 176.

[7] *Nintendo Co. Ltd v Lik Sang International Ltd* (2003) 55 I.P.R. 187.

[8] Hong Kong Copyright Ordinance (CAP 528), s.273.

[9] *Kabushiki Kaisha Sony Computer Entertainment v Stevens* (2003) 55 I.P.R. 161. This case contains an exhaustive history of the relevant Australian legislation (s.116A of the Copyright Act 1968 as amended).

[10] CDPA 1988, s.296ZA(1)(b). This limitation derives from Art.6(1) of the Information Society Directive 2001/29.

affects prejudicially the rights of the copyright owner.[11] In itself, the act of decrypting a technological measure for the purposes of genuine cryptographical research is unlikely to prejudice the copyright owner. The difficulty arises where the results of that research are published. In such circumstances, the rights of the copyright owner are likely have been prejudiced so that the researcher will not be able to rely on the exception.[12]

Acts of circumvention: persons with rights and the exercise of those rights.   15–23
In the case of acts of circumvention, section 296ZA gives rights to a person issuing to the public copies of the work to which the measures have been applied or communicating that work to the public and to the copyright owner or his exclusive licensee if he is not the person issuing copies of the work or communicating the work.[13] What this means is discussed above.[14] As is the case under section 296, these rights are the same as the rights of a copyright owner in respect of an infringement of copyright and are concurrent.[15] The effect of this is considered above.[16] In contrast with the position under section 296, no rights are granted to the owner or exclusive licensee of any intellectual property right in the technological measures. The presumptions contained in sections 104 to 106 of the 1988 Act,[17] the presumptions contained in Regulation 22 of the Copyright and Rights in Databases Regulations[18] and the withdrawal of the privilege against self-incrimination effected by section 72 of the Supreme Court Act 1981[19] apply in relation to proceedings under section 296ZA as they apply in relation to proceedings under the copyright Part of the 1988 Act.[20]

Devices and services: acts attracting liability. Where effective technological   15–24
measures have been applied to a copyright work other than a computer program, section 296ZD creates rights and remedies against persons who make or deal with certain devices, products or components or provide certain services.[21] The acts which attract liability are expressed in terms which are substantially identical to those contained in the Information Society Directive.[22] In relation to devices, products or components, the relevant acts are: manufacturing, importing, distributing, selling or letting for hire, advertising for sale or hire or possessing for commercial purposes. It is clear that even some non-commercial activities, such as importation for personal use and distributions which are not made in the course of a business, will attract liability under this head. In respect of services, liability occurs when the service is provided. There is no liability for offering or

---

[11] CDPA 1988, s.296ZA(2) (this derives from recital 48 to the Information Society Directive 2001/29, which states that the protection accorded to technical devices by the Directive should not hinder research into cryptography: see Analysis of Responses and Government Conclusions para.6.6). Even if the liability arises because of the prejudicial effect of the publication, it remains liability for the act of circumvention itself rather than for the act of publication.

[12] Note, further, that the publication may attract criminal liability under s.296ZB(2) or civil liability under s.296ZD(1)(b) if it can be said to amount to the provision of a service and the other conditions for liability under those provisions are satisfied. There is no cryptography defence in s.296ZB(2) or s.296ZD(1)(b).

[13] CDPA 1988, s.296ZA(3).

[14] See para. 15–09.

[15] s.296ZA(3), (4).

[16] See para. 15–16.

[17] See paras 22–210, below.

[18] SI 1997/3032.

[19] Together with its Scottish and Northern Irish equivalents, s.15 of the Law Reform (Miscellaneous Provisions) (Scotland) Act 1985 and s.94A of the Judicature (Northern Ireland) Act 1978. See para. 22–147, below.

[20] s.296ZA(5) and (6).

[21] CDPA 1988, s.296ZD(1).

[22] Directive 2001/29 on the harmonisation of certain aspects of copyright and related rights in the information society [2001] O.J. L167/10, Art.6(1).

advertising the service. There is no "knowledge" or "reason to believe" defence; accordingly, section 296ZD creates "a tort of strict liability".[23]

15–25   **Devices and services: conditions for liability.** In either case, liability only arises if one of three alternative conditions is satisfied. The first is that the goods or services are promoted, advertised or marketed for the purpose of the circumvention of the measures in question.[24] It is presumably not necessary to prove that the person making or dealing with the goods or providing the services has himself engaged in any such promotion, advertising or marketing. The second alternative condition is that the goods or services have only a limited commercially significant purpose or use other than to circumvent the measures in question.[25] Recital 48 to the Information Society Directive states that the Directive is not intended to prevent the normal operation of electronic equipment and its technological development, nor is it intended to imply an obligation to design devices, products or services to correspond to technological measures (for example, to design computers to respond to "copy control flags"). Accordingly, the object of this second condition is to "respect proportionality" and to avoid prohibiting "those devices or activities which have a commercially significant purpose or use other than to circumvent the technical protection."[26] On the face of it, the use of the term "purpose" might appear to involve an investigation of the intention of the designer of the goods or services. However, this appears to be governed by the third condition (see below). It would seem to follow that the word "purpose" is intended to mean "useful function" rather than, for example, "intended object". Thus, the court is directed to the question of the actual or potential functions or uses of the goods. It is thought that the phrase "limited commercially significant purpose or use" is intended to involve an objective test. Accordingly, the court will have to look at all the ways in which the device or service is or might be used and then decide whether uses other than the circumvention of the measures in question are or may be of more than limited commercial significance. The question of whether commercial significance is or is not "limited" will be one of fact or degree. The practical effect of this second condition will no doubt be to prevent defendants from relying on the fact that even though the goods or services can be used to circumvent the measures in question, they have another, "innocent" use, unless that use can be shown to be "commercially significant". The third alternative condition is that the goods or services are primarily designed, produced, adapted or performed for the purpose of enabling or facilitating the circumvention of the measures in question.[27] This refers to circumvention within the United Kingdom.[28] In the case of goods, this condition clearly focuses on the intention of the designer or manufacturer. In the case of services, however, the focus is also on the intention of the person who is performing them. This will raise questions of fact and degree.[29]

15–26   **Devices and services: persons with rights and the exercise of those rights.** In this case, the categories of persons with rights are identical to those under section 296.[30] These categories are discussed above.[31] Again, the rights are the same as the rights of a copyright owner in respect of an infringement of copyright and are

---

[23] *Kabushiki Kaisha Sony Computer Entertainment Inc. v Ball* [2004] EWHC 1738, Ch D, para.39.
[24] CDPA 1988, s.296ZD(1)(b)(i).
[25] s.296ZD(1)(b)(ii).
[26] See Recital 48 to the Information Society Directive 2001/29.
[27] s.296ZD(1)(b)(iii).
[28] *Kabushiki Kaisha Sony Computer Entertainment Inc. v Ball* [2004] EWHC 1738, Ch D, para.40.
[29] See, *e.g. Kabushiki Kaisha Sony Computer Entertainment Inc. v Ball* [2004] EWHC 1738, Ch D, para.40.
[30] CDPA 1988, s.296ZD(2).

concurrent.[32] The effect of this is considered above.[33] It is expressly provided that a person with rights under section 296ZD may obtain an order for delivery up or seize without a court order any device, product or component which offends the section.[34] These rights are the same rights as a copyright owner has in relation to infringing copies under sections 99 and 100 of the 1988 Act.[35] The rights exist where a person has the device, product or component in his possession, custody or control with the intention that it should be used to circumvent effective technological measures. Where goods have been delivered up or seized under these provisions, the normal copyright provisions apply in relation to the making of disposal orders, with the necessary modifications.[36] These rights as to delivery up and seizure without a court order are also concurrent.[37] Again, the effect of this is considered above.[38] Again, the presumptions contained in sections 104 to 106 of the 1988 Act,[39] the presumptions in Regulation 22 of the Copyright and Rights in Databases Regulations[40] and the withdrawal of the privilege against self-incrimination effected by section 72 of the Supreme Court Act 1981[41] apply in relation to proceedings under section 296ZD as they apply in relation to proceedings under the copyright Part of the 1988 Act.[42] Finally, it is expressly provided that section 97(1) of the 1988 Act, which provides a limited defence to a claim for damages in proceedings for infringement of copyright,[43] applies to proceedings under section 296ZD so that a defendant has a defence to a claim for damages under that section (but without prejudice to any other remedy) if he did not know or have reason to believe that his acts enabled or facilitated an infringement of copyright.[44]

B. CRIMINAL REMEDIES

Introduction. There were no criminal offences under the previous version of section 296, presumably because the Software Directive provides for "remedies" but not "sanctions" in respect of circumvention devices.[45] The Information Society Directive requires Member States to provide "adequate legal protection" both against the act of circumvention itself, and against devices and services designed to assist such circumvention.[46] It also requires Member States to provide appropriate sanctions and remedies and that sanctions shall be "effective, proportionate and dissuasive".[47] Against that background, criminal offences have been introduced in this field. However, their scope is limited.[48] First, consistently with the terms of the Software Directive and the previous position, there are no criminal offences in relation to the circumvention of technical devices applied to com-

15–27

---

[31] See para. 15–09.
[32] s.296ZD(3).
[33] See paras 15–15 and 15–16.
[34] s.296ZD(4).
[35] See para. 22–182 (delivery up) and paras 22–46 et seq. (seizure without a court order).
[36] s.296ZD(6).
[37] s.296ZD(5).
[38] See para. 15–16.
[39] See paras 22–210 et seq., below.
[40] SI 1997/3032.
[41] Together with its Scottish and Northern Irish equivalents, s.15 of the Law Reform (Miscellaneous Provisions) (Scotland) Act 1985 and s.94A of the Judicature (Northern Ireland) Act 1978. See para. 22–147, below.
[42] CDPA 1988, s.296ZD(6), (9).
[43] See paras 22–64 et seq., below.
[44] s.296ZD(7).
[45] Software Directive 91/250, Art.7(1).
[46] Information Society Directive 2001/29, Arts 6(1) and (2).
[47] Information Society Directive 2001/29, Art.8(1).
[48] This is because the Government took the view that the language of the Information Society

puter programs. Secondly, the act of circumvention itself is not a criminal offence. The criminal sanctions are limited to activities in relation to devices and services which are designed to circumvent technological measures. Thirdly, as in the case of the copyright offences, almost all the offences consist of some form of commercial activity. The only exception is activity which has a prejudicial effect on the copyright owner. Fourthly, the criminal provisions cover a more limited range of devices, products or components than are the subject of civil liability. Fifthly, there is a defence that the defendant did not know and had no reasonable grounds for believing that the device or service enabled or facilitated circumvention. Sixthly, the criminal provisions are limited to technological measures designed to protect copyright works (other than computer programs) and do not, as in the case of the civil provisions, extend to measures designed to protect the subject matter of rights in performances, database right or publication right. Finally, the penalties are relatively low. Any acts which took place prior to October 31, 2003 cannot be the subject of a prosecution under section 296ZB.[49]

15–28   **Offences in relation to devices, products or components.** Section 296ZB(1) criminalises certain acts if committed in relation to any device, product or component which is primarily designed, produced or adapted for the purpose of enabling or facilitating the circumvention of effective technological measures. The meaning of these expressions is considered elsewhere.[50] It should be emphasised that acts of making or dealing with devices which are promoted, advertised or marketed for the purpose of circumvention or which have only a limited commercially significant purpose or use other than to circumvent may attract civil liability but will not attract criminal liability. The acts which are made criminal are as follows: manufacturing for sale or hire; importing otherwise than for private and domestic use; selling or letting for hire in the course of a business; offering, exposing or advertising for sale or hire in the course of a business; possessing in the course of a business; distributing in the course of a business; and distributing otherwise than in the course of a business to such an extent as to affect prejudicially the copyright owner.[51] The wording of subsection 296ZB(1) is similar to that of subsection 107(1), which provides for offences in relation to the making of and dealing with infringing copies of copyright works. The provisions of subsection 107(1) are discussed elsewhere.[52] There appear to be only two significant differences in the range of acts which are caught. First, advertising for sale or hire is an offence under section 296ZB but not under section 107. This is no doubt because advertising for sale or hire is specifically referred to in the Information Society Directive.[53] Second, possession in the course of a business is only an offence under section 107 if the article is possessed with a view to committing an act infringing copyright.[54] Again, this difference is probably dicated by the terms of the Directive, which simply refers to possession for commercial purposes.[55]

15–29   **Offences in relation to services.** Again, the language of the criminal provisions is derived from the civil provisions. It is an offence to provide, promote, advertise or market in the course of a business or otherwise than in the course of a business

---

Directive, Art.6(2) was not sufficiently clear to be used to formulate criminal offences: Analysis of Responses and Government Conclusions, para.6.8.

[49] See Copyright and Related Rights Regulations 2003 (SI 2003/2498), regs 1 and 40.
[50] Para. 15–25.
[51] CDPA 1988, s.296ZB(1).
[52] See paras 23–10 and 23–11, below.
[53] Information Society Directive 2001/29, Art.6(2).
[54] CDPA 1988, s.107(1)(c).
[55] Information Society Directive, Art.6(2).

to such an extent as to affect prejudicially the copyright owner a service the purpose of which is to enable or facilitate the circumvention of effective technological measures.[56] This provision differs from subsection 296ZD(1) because there is no civil liability for promoting, advertising or marketing such services although there is civil liability for providing services which are promoted, advertised or marketed for the purpose of circumvention. It seems unlikely that this distinction will be of any practical importance.

Defences to criminal liability. There are two statutory defences, which apply both to the offences in relation to devices and to those in relation to services. First, it is provided that section 296ZB does not make unlawful anything done by, or on behalf of, law enforcement agencies or any of the intelligence services[57] in the interests of national security or for the purposes of the prevention or detection of crime, the investigation of an offence or the conduct of a prosecution.[58] It is thought that on general principles the burden or proving that the defendant falls within the scope of this exception will lie on the defendant (the standard being to the balance of probabilities).[59] It is also a defence for the defendant to prove that he did not know and had no reasonable ground for believing that the device, product or component or (as the case may be) the service enabled or facilitated the circumvention of effective technological measures.[60] In this case, the burden of proof clearly lies on the defendant. Again, applying general principles, the standard will be to the balance of probabilities. **15–30**

Penalties. A person guilty of any offence under section 296ZB is liable on summary conviction to imprisonment for a term not exceeding three months or a fine not exceeding the statutory maximum[61] or both; or on conviction on indictment to an unlimited fine or to imprisonment for a term not exceeding two years, or both.[62] These penalties are the maximum permitted in respect of new offences created (as these offences were) by subordinate legislation made under the European Communities Act 1972.[63] As a result, they are considerably lower than those for most other offences under the 1988 Act. **15–31**

Search warrants and forfeiture. Section 296ZC provides that certain provisions of the 1988 Act which concern search warrants and forfeiture apply to offences under section 296ZB with specified modifications. The sections are section 297B, which makes provision for the issue of search warrants where offences in relation to unauthorised decoders are suspected; and sections 297C and 297D, which make provision for the forfeiture of unauthorised decoders. The effect is as follows. First, where a justice of the peace is satisfied that there are reasonable grounds to believe that an offence under section 296ZB has been or is about to be committed in any premises or that evidence that such an offence has been or is about to be committed is in those premises, he may issue a warrant authorising a constable to enter and search the premises, using such reasonable force as is **15–32**

---

[56] CDPA 1988, s.296ZB(2).

[57] As defined in s.81 of the Regulation of Investigatory Powers Act 2000.

[58] CDPA 1988, s.296ZB(3). This defence is expressly sanctioned by Recital 51 to the Information Society Directive.

[59] For a discussion of the application of these general principles to s.107, see paras 23–58 et seq., below.

[60] s.296ZB(5). For a discussion of the terms "knowledge" and "reason to believe", see paras 8–08 et seq., above.

[61] Currently £5,000: Interpretation Act 1978, Sch.1, applying Magistrates Courts Act 1980, s.32(9) as amended by Criminal Justice Act 1991, s.17(2)(c).

[62] CDPA 1988, s.296ZB(4).

[63] See s.2(2) and Sch.2 para.1(1)(d). The offences were created by the Copyright and Related Rights Regulations 2003 (SI 2003/2498).

necessary.[64] The limitations on and manner of execution of such a warrant contained in section 297B will apply. These are considered elsewhere.[65] Secondly, where devices, products or components for the purpose of circumventing effective technological measures have come into the possession of any person in connection with the investigation or prosecution of an offence under subsection 297ZB(1) of the 1988 Act, that person may apply under section 297C for an order for forfetirue of such devices, products or components.[66] The procedure on such an application will be governed by section 297C, which is considered elsewhere.[67] There are equivalent provisions for Scotland.[68]

C. REMEDY WHERE MEASURES PREVENT PERMITTED ACTS

15–33   **Introduction.** With a view to resolving the obvious tension between the protection it grants to technological measures on the one hand and the existence of a wide range of permitted acts on the other, the Information Society Directive requires Member States to take appropriate measures to ensure that right holders allow the exercise of the permitted acts derived from Articles 5(2)(a), (2)(b), (2)(c), (2)(d), (2)(e), (3)(a), (3)(b) or (3)(e) to take place.[69] Such measures need only be taken if there are no voluntary measures taken by rightholders, including agreements between rightholders and other parties concerned.[70] The background to these provisions is considered elsewhere.[71] Section 296ZE of the 1988 Act contains a scheme for dealing with such cases. Under the scheme a complainant may make a complaint to the Secretary of State who will investigate certain matters. Depending on the outcome of that investigation the Secretary of State may give a direction requiring the owner of the rights in the work to which the measure has been applied to ensure that the complainant can benefit from the permitted act. Failure to comply with a direction will amount to a breach of statutory duty, which will be actionable by the complainant or a representative of a body of complainants.[72]

15–34   **Scope of the scheme.** Section 296ZE has a number of limitations. First, it has no application in the case of computer programs.[73] This is because the Information Society Directive expressly leaves the law as to computer programs, as contained in the Software Directive, unchanged.[74] Secondly, it does not apply to copyright works made available to the public on agreed contractual terms in such a way that members of the public may access them from a place and at a time individu-

---

[64] CDPA 1988, s.297B(1), as modified by s.296ZC(2).

[65] See para. 16–20, below, and the paras referred to there.

[66] s.297C(1), (2), as modified by s.296ZC(3), (4).

[67] See para. 16–20, below, and the paras referred to there.

[68] For search warrants, see s.297B, as modified by s.296ZC(1), (2); for forfeiture, see s.297D, as modified by s.296ZC(3), (4).

[69] Information Society Directive 2001/29, Art.6(4). For an account of how this provision has been implemented in a variety of European countries, see *Braun* [2003] 11 E.I.P.R. 496. The author discerns a trend towards the use of mediation and arbitration provisions.

[70] Art.6(4).

[71] See paras 9–09 and 9–10, above.

[72] This summary derives from the Patent Office's *Transposition Note*. During the consultation process, rightholders argued that some time should elapse before these provisions took effect in order to enable voluntary measures to be put in place. This argument gains some support from the terms of Recital 51 ("in the absence of such voluntary measures or agreements within a reasonable period of time, Member States should take appropriate measures") but less so from Art.6(4), which contains no reference to a reasonable period having elapsed before measures are taken. See Analysis of Responses and Government Conclusions, para.6.13.

[73] This follows from the definition of technological measures in CDPA 1988, s.296ZF(1).

[74] See para. 15–07, above.

ally chosen by them.[75] This exclusion would apply, for example to pay-per-use and video-on-demand services but not to non-interactive forms of online use.[76] Thirdly, in accordance with the Directive, section 296ZE only applies to the permitted acts listed in Part 1 of Schedule 5A to the 1988 Act. Fourthly, the section only applies where the complainant, or the class of persons represented by the complainant, has lawful access to the protected copyright work.[77] On the other hand, the section applies (with any necessary adaptations) to rights in performances, database right and publication right.[78]

Notice of complaint. The operation of the scheme is triggered by the issue of a notice of complaint to the Secretary of State.[79] A notice of complaint may be issued by a person on his own account or as a representative of a class of persons. In each case the basis of the complaint is that the application of an effective technological measure[80] to a copyright work[81] prevents the person or class of persons from carrying out a permitted act in relation to that work.[82] The Secretary of State may give directions as to the form and manner in which a notice of complaint may be delivered to him.[83]   **15–35**

Action on receipt of notice: is there a voluntary measure or agreement? The Secretary of State may give directions generally as to the procedure to be followed in relation to a complaint made under this section.[84] The section provides for the following procedure, which is designed to ensure, in accordance with the Directive, that measures are only taken by the Secretary of State if there are no existing voluntary or contractual arrangements.[85] Following receipt of the notice, the Secretary of State may give the owner of the copyright work or an exclusive licensee such directions[86] as appear to him to be requisite or expedient for the purpose of establishing whether there is any relevant subsisting voluntary measure or agreement.[87] For these purposes, a voluntary measure is a measure taken voluntarily by the copyright owner, his exclusive licensee or a person issuing copies of or communicating the work to the public the effect of which is to enable a person to carry out a permitted act.[88] An agreement is an agreement between the copyright owner, his exclusive licensee or a person issuing copies of or communicating the work to the public and another party which has the same effect.[89] The Secretary of State may give directions as to the form and manner in which   **15–36**

---

[75] s.296ZE(10), applying Art.7(4) of the Information Society Directive. Presumably it is thought that where matters are already regulated by contract, there are adequate other remedies.

[76] See Recital 53 to the Information Society Directive 2001/29.

[77] s.296ZE(10).

[78] s.296ZE(11). The relevant exceptions to rights in performances and database right are listed in Sch.5A, Pts 2 and 3.

[79] This is a reference to the Secretary of State for Trade and Industry.

[80] For the meaning of this term, see para. 15–18, above.

[81] The scheme does not apply to computer programs: see CDPA 1988, s.296ZE(2). On the other hand, it does apply with any necessary adaptations to the subject-matter of rights in performances, database right and publication right: s.296ZE(11).

[82] s.296ZE(2).

[83] s.296ZE(4)(a). Such directions must be published in such manner as in the Secretary of State's opinion will secure adequate publicity for them: s.296ZE(4). No such directions had been published at the time of writing.

[84] CDPA 1988, s.296ZE(3)(a). Such directions must be published in such manner as in the Secretary of State's opinion will secure adequate publicity for them: s.296ZE(4). No such directions had been published at the time of writing.

[85] See para. 15–33, above.

[86] Which must be in writing and which may be varied or revoked by a subsequent direction under s.296ZE: see s.296ZE(7), (8).

[87] s.296ZE(3)(a).

[88] s.296ZE(1)(a).

[89] s.296ZE(1)(b).

evidence of any voluntary measure or agreement may be delivered to him.[90] It is the duty of a person to whom a direction has been given under this provision to give effect to that direction.[91] By contrast with the duty to comply with a direction of the type referred to in the next paragraph, this duty is not expressed to be owed to the complainant or those whom he represents. It appears, therefore, that it is owed to the Secretary of State, who can presumably enforce it by injunctive relief (although this not stated expressly in the section). There is no express provision for an appeal against the making or refusal to make such a direction. Presumably, however, the decision to make or not to make a direction will be amenable to judicial review. It may also be possible for a person to whom a direction is addressed to challenge its validity by way of a defence to enforcement proceedings, but this is not clear.

15–37   **Action in the absence of a voluntary measure or agreement.** Where it is established that there is no subsisting voluntary measure or agreement, the Secretary of State may give such directions[92] as appear to him to be requisite or expedient for the purpose of ensuring that the copyright owner or his exclusive licensee makes available to the complainant the means of carrying out the permitted act "to the extent necessary to so benefit from the permitted act".[93] The Government's view is that a refusal by the Secretary of State to exercise his discretion to take action in a proper case would be subject to judicial review.[94] The need for the phrase "to the extent necessary to so benefit from the permitted act", which derives from the Information Society Directive, is unclear. Presumably it is intended to emphasise that any direction will be limited to the provision of the means necessary to carry out the permitted act and no further. However, this appears to be evident from the other words of the subsection. More importantly, perhaps, it is far from clear how this will work in practice. A software patch which allows a user access in order to carry out one of the permitted acts is likely to enable access for all purposes. The effect of such a direction is that the copyright owner (or exclusive licensee as the case may be) owes a statutory duty to the complainant or, in the case of a representative complaint, to the representative and each person in the class represented. A breach of that duty is actionable as a breach of statutory duty, subject to the defences and other incidents applying to actions for breach of statutory duty.[95] Typically, such a duty is likely to be enforced by a claim for injunctive relief. There seems no reason in principle why a representative action could not be brought where the duty is owed to a class. Again, there is no express provision for an appeal against the making or refusal to make such a direction. Presumably, again, the decision to make or not to make a direction will be amenable to judicial review. It seems unlikely that a copyright owner or exclusive licensee to whom a direction is addressed will be able to challenge its validity by way of a defence to enforcement proceedings, but the existing of pending judicial review proceedings might be grounds for an adjournment of such proceedings until the outcome of the judicial review.

---

[90] s.296ZE(4)(b). Such directions must be published in such manner as in the Secretary of State's opinion will secure adequate publicity for them: s.296ZE(4). No such directions had been published at the time of writing.

[91] s.296ZE(5).

[92] Which must be in writing and which may be varied or revoked by a subsequent direction under CDPA 1988, s.296ZE: see s.296ZE(7), (8).

[93] s.296ZE(3)(b).

[94] Analysis of Responses and Government Conclusions, para.6.15.

[95] s.296ZE(6).

5. RIGHTS MANAGEMENT INFORMATION

The WIPO Copyright Treaty. Article 12 of the the WIPO Copyright Treaty   **15–38**
("WCT") requires contracting parties to provide adequate and effective legal
remedies against any person who knowingly removes or alters electronic rights
management information[96] without authority. The same Article requires contracting parties to provide adequate and effective legal remedies against any person
who knowingly distributes, imports for distribution, broadcasts or communicates
to the public without authority works or copies of works knowing that electronic
rights management information has been removed without authority. In both
cases the remedies only need be provided against persons who know or (with respect of civil remedies) have reasonable grounds to believe that the act in question will induce, enable, facilitate or conceal an infringement of any right covered
by the Treaty or the Berne Convention.[97] For these purposes, "rights management
information" is defined as "information which identifies the work, the author of
the work, the owner of any right in the work, or information about the terms and
conditions of use of the work, and any numbers or codes that represent such information, when any of these items of information is attached to a copy of a work
or appears in connection with the communication of a work to the public".[98] The
Agreed Statement provides that contracting parties will not rely on Article 12 to
devise or implement rights management systems that would have the effect of
imposing formalities which are not permitted under the Berne Convention or the
WCT itself, prohibiting the free movement of goods or impeding the enjoyment
of rights under the WCT.[99]

The WIPO Performances and Phonograms Treaty. Article 19 of the WIPO   **15–39**
Performances and Phonograms Treaty ("WPPT") requires contracting parties to
provide substantially the same remedies in the field of performances and
phonograms. For the purposes of Article 19, the relevant state of mind is knowing or (with respect to civil remedies) having reasonable grounds to believe that
the act in question will induce, enable, facilitate or conceal an infringement of
any right covered by the WPPT[1]; the offending acts other than removal or
alteration of the information must be directed at copies of fixed performances or
phonograms[2]; while rights management information is defined as "information
which identifies the performer, the performance of the performer, the producer of
the phonogram, the phonogram, the owner of any right in the performance or
phonogram, or information about the terms and conditions of use of the performance or phonogram, and any numbers or codes that represent such information,
when any of these items of information is attached to a copy of a fixed performance or a phonogram or appears in connection with the communication or making available of a fixed performance or a phonogram to the public".[3] As in the
case of Article 12 of the WCT, the Agreed Statement provides that contracting
parties will not rely on Article 19 to devise or implement rights management

---

[96] See Vol.2 at F13. For background information as to the nature of rights management information,
see para. 15–02, above.
[97] WCT, Art.12(1). For the rights covered, see paras 24–04 *et seq.* (Berne) and 24–66 *et seq.* (WCT).
The Agreed Statement makes clear that the reference to "any right covered by this Treaty or by
the Berne Convention" includes both exclusive rights and rights of remuneration. See Vol.2 at
F13.
[98] WCT, Art.12(2).
[99] See Vol.2 at F13.
[1] WPPT, Art.19(1). See Vol.2 at F14. For the rights covered, see paras 24–19 *et seq.* The Agreed
Statement makes clear that the reference to "any right covered by this Treaty" includes both
exclusive rights and rights of remuneration. See Vol.2 at F14.
[2] Art.19(1)(ii).
[3] Art.19(2).

systems that would have the effect of imposing formalities which are not permitted under the Berne Convention or the WCT itself, prohibiting the free movement of goods or impeding the enjoyment of rights under the WCT.[4]

15–40   **Provisions of the Information Society Directive.**[5] Article 7 of the Directive contains provisions which are intended to implement the WIPO and WPPT Treaties. Thus, Article 7(1) sets out a list of offending acts in terms which are substantially the same as those of the Treaties, while Article 7(2) adopts the definitions of rights management information contained in the Treaties.

15–41   **Provisions of the 1988 Act.** The Directive has been implemented by adding a new section 296ZG to the 1988 Act.[6] In general, the terms of the new section follow closely those of the Directive and thus of the WCT and WPPT. Thus, the new section creates civil (but not criminal) remedies against those who tamper with electronic rights management information or deal with copies of works from which such information has been removed or in respect of which it has been altered. The terms of the section apply with the necessary adaptations to rights in performances, publication right and database right,[7] but for ease of exposition they are considered below as they apply to copyright. No act done before October 31, 2003 and no act done after October 31, 2003 in pursuance of an agreement made before December 22, 2002 is to be regarded as an infringement of the new provisions.[8]

15–42   **"Rights management information".**[9] There are three elements to the definition. First, the information must have been "provided" by the copyright owner or the holder of "any right under copyright". The latter expression is intended to transpose the Directive's term "rightholders" into English law.[10] This is a broad term, the exact scope of which is debatable. It obviously includes the copyright owner. It presumably also includes an exclusive licensee. Arguably it might be said to include non-exclusive licensees as well, but this is not clear. Secondly, the information must fall within one of two categories. Either it must identify the work, the author, the copyright owner or the holder of any intellectual property rights (whether in the work or not is not stated); or it must be information about the terms and conditions of use of the work. Thirdly, "rights management information" includes any numbers or codes which represent such information.

15–43   **Persons with rights.** Two categories of persons have rights. First, a person issuing copies of the work to the public or communicating the work to the public. Secondly, the copyright owner or his exclusive licensee if he is not the person issuing copies of the work to the public or communicating the work to the public.[11]

15–44   **Persons against whom rights are exercisable: D and E.** The rights are exercisable against two categories of person, named in the section as "D" and "E". D is a person who knowingly and without authority removes or alters electronic rights management information which is associated with a copy of a copyright work or

---

[4] See Vol.2 at F14.

[5] Directive 2001/29, [2001] O.J. L167/10.See Vol.2 at H11.

[6] This is effected by the Copyright and Related Rights Regulations 2003 (SI 2003/2498), reg.25, with effect from October 31, 2003 (SI 2003/2498, reg.1).

[7] CDPA 1988, s.296ZG(8).

[8] Copyright and Related Rights Regulations 2003 (SI 2003/2498), regs 31(2) and 32(2).

[9] CDPA 1988, s.296ZG(7)(b).

[10] The Government originally intended to limit the remedies to information provided by copyright owners, but eventually conceded that the terms of the Information Society Directive 2001/29 required a broader term: Analysis of Responses and Government Conclusions, para.7.2.

[11] CDPA 1988, s.296ZG(3), (4).

appears in connection with the communication to the public of a copyright work. D is only liable if at the time he commits the act in question, he knows or has reason to believe that by doing so he is inducing, enabling, facilitating or concealing an infringement of copyright.[12] E is a person who knowingly and without authority distributes, imports for distribution or communicates to the public copies of a copyright work from which electronic rights management information associated with the copies or appearing in connection with the communication to the public of copies of the work has been altered or removed without authority. As in D's case, E is only liable if at the time he commits the act in question he knows or has reason to believe that by so doing he is inducing, enabling, facilitating or concealing an infringement of copyright.[13] The phrase "without authority" derives from the WCT and WPPT treaties via the Information Society Directive and is not further defined in any of these documents. It is not wholly clear whose authority is relevant. On the one hand, it might be argued that since the section does not expressly create a right to prevent the removal or tampering of electronic rights management information, the relevant authority must be sought elsewhere than in the section, for example in contract. On the other hand, it is quite possible that what is intended is that any person with rights under the section may give the relevant authority.

The rights. In the case of a person issuing copies of the work to the public or communicating the work to the public, the rights are the same rights as the owner of copyright has in respect of an infringement of copyright. In the case of an exclusive licensee of the copyright, the rights are the same as he has in respect of an infringement of copyright.[14] The effect of similar provisions in respect of the circumvention of technical devices is discussed above.[15] The rights are expressed to be concurrent and sections 101(3) and 102(1) to (4) of the 1988 Act apply in proceedings under section 296ZG in relation to persons with concurrent rights as they apply, in proceedings mentioned in those provisions, in relation to a copyright owner and exclusive licensee with concurrent rights.[16] The effect of an analogous provision in relation to the circumvention of technical devices is discussed above.[17] The presumptions contained in sections 104 to 106 of the 1988 Act,[18] the presumptions in Regulation 22 of the Copyright and Rights in Databases Regulations[19] and the withdrawal of the privilege against self-incrimination effected by section 72 of the Supreme Court Act 1981[20] apply in relation to proceedings under section 296ZD as they apply in relation to proceedings under the copyright Part of the 1988 Act.[21]

15–45

---

[12] CDPA 1988, s.296ZG(1).
[13] s.296ZG(2).
[14] CDPA 1988, s.296ZG(3).
[15] Para. 15–15.
[16] s.296ZG(5).
[17] Para. 15–16.
[18] See paras 22–210 *et seq.*, below.
[19] SI 1997/3032.
[20] Together with its Scottish and Northern Irish equivalents, s.15 of the Law Reform (Miscellaneous Provisions) (Scotland) Act 1985 and s.94A of the Judicature (Northern Ireland) Act 1978. See para. 22–147., below.
[21] CDPA 1988, s.296ZG(6) and (9).

CHAPTER SIXTEEN

FRAUDULENT RECEPTION OF TRANSMISSIONS

Contents   *Para.*

1. HISTORICAL INTRODUCTION

Position before 1984. The increase in cable and satellite broadcasting inevitably **16–01** brought with it attempts to gain access to transmissions without paying the fees demanded by those who broadcast them. Satellite broadcasters attempted to limit reception to those who had paid for it by transmitting their signals in encrypted form and charging the viewer for the use of a decoding device. Pirates responded by making and distributing unauthorised decoding devices which enabled viewers to watch the programmes without paying for them. Pirates also discovered methods of "re-enabling" legitimate decoding devices which had been "disabled" because the viewer had failed to keep up the requisite subscription. In 1996 it was estimated that between five and 20 per cent of the decoding devices in circulation in the European Community were unauthorised.[1] The widespread use of such devices clearly has adverse effects both for the broadcaster, which loses subscription revenue, and for the owners of the rights in the programmes, whose income may be reduced. Before the passing of the Cable and Broadcasting Act 1984,[2] the law was thought to provide very limited protection to broadcasters in relation to such activities,[3] and the Government was concerned that those who were taking a large commercial risk in relation to the provision of cable and satellite programmes should have the reassurance that a solid legal framework was in place to prevent people enjoying the benefits of those services without paying for them.[4]

---

[1] See the European Commission's *Green Paper on the legal protection for encrypted services in the internal market*, COM (96) 76 final, March 6, 1996, p.5.

[2] (c.46).

[3] It seems that there was no legal basis on which non-subscribers could be prevented from receiving satellite broadcasts: *BBC Enterprises v Hi-Tech Xtravision Ltd* [1990] 1 Ch. 609 at 614 (Staughton L.J.). The position of cable broadcasters was stronger because the recipient of a cable programme needs to make a physical connection with the cable and an unauthorised connection would be a trespass: *BBC Enterprises v Hi-Tech Xtravision Ltd* [1990] F.S.R. 217 at 229 (Scott J.). That this was the view of the Government seems clear from the parliamentary debates on the bill: *Hansard*, HC Vol.59, col.748.

[4] *Hansard*, HC Vol.59, col.748.

16–02   **Cable and Broadcasting Act 1984.** The Cable and Broadcasting Act 1984[5] created both a new summary offence[6] and a new set of proprietary rights.[7] The provisions of the Act applied to broadcasting services in three categories: first, cable programme services; secondly, television or sound broadcasting services provided by the BBC or the IBA; and thirdly services which consisted in the sending, by means of a telecommunications system, of sounds or visual images which were provided for a person providing a service within one of the two former categories.[8] In broad terms, the new summary offence was committed by dishonestly receiving a programme included in such a service with the intention of avoiding payment of any charge applicable to its reception.[9] The new proprietary rights were infringed (again in broad terms) by the manufacture or dealing with any apparatus or device designed or adapted to enable or assist persons to receive programmes without payment; and by the publication of any information calculated to enable or assist persons to receive programmes without payment.[10]

16–03   **The 1988 Act and the Broadcasting Acts 1990 and 1996.** These provisions of the 1984 Act were repealed by the 1988 Act,[11] and replaced by similar, but not identical, provisions.[12] However, by 1989 the judgment of Scott J. in *BBC Enterprises Ltd v Hi-Tech Xtravision Ltd*[13] had cast serious doubts on the effectiveness of the new rights. Moreover, the BBC and others were concerned about the absence of a criminal remedy for the creation and use of unauthorised decoders.[14] Accordingly, a new summary offence of possessing and dealing with unauthorised decoders was inserted into the 1988 Act by the Broadcasting Act 1990.[15] The Broadcasting Act 1996 increased the scope of this offence, made it triable either way,[16] and increased the maximum penalties for it.[17]

16–04   **The Conditional Access Directive.** On November 20, 1998, the European Parliament and Council adopted a Directive on the legal protection of services based on, or consisting of, conditional access.[18] The Directive requires Member States both to take measures to prohibit, and to provide sanctions and remedies against a long list of commercial activities in relation to "illicit devices".[19] In the Directive, the term "illicit device" means any equipment or software designed or adapted to give access to a "protected service" in an intelligible form without the authorisation of the service provider.[20] For these purposes, "protected services" are: television broadcasting, radio broadcasting and information society services; provided in each case that they are provided against remuneration and on the basis of

---

[5] (c.46).
[6] s.53.
[7] s.54.
[8] s.53(2).
[9] s.53.
[10] s.54(2).
[11] CDPA 1988, s.303(2) and Sch.8.
[12] ss.297–299.
[13] [1990] F.S.R. 217. The decision was in fact overturned by the Court of Appeal [1990] 1 Ch. 609 and the Court of Appeal's decision was upheld by the House of Lords [1991] 2 A.C. 327.
[14] *Hansard*, HL Vol.521, cols 1696 *et seq.* The example was given of a person who made an unauthorised decoder available on a housing estate, thus giving rise to a large number of relatively small infringements of a type which would not warrant civil proceedings, but might be deterred by a criminal conviction: *Hansard*, HL Vol.521, col.1697.
[15] CDPA 1988, s.297A, inserted by the Broadcasting Act 1990, s.179.
[16] *i.e.* either in the Magistrates' Court or in the Crown Court.
[17] Broadcasting Act 1996, s.140(1), amending CDPA 1988, s.297A(1).
[18] [1998] O.J. L320/54. See Vol.2 at H9.
[19] Arts 3 to 5.
[20] Art.2(e).

"conditional access".[21] The term "conditional access" means any technical measure or arrangement whereby access to the protected service in an intelligible form is made conditional upon prior individual authorisation.[22] In order to comply with the Conditional Access Directive, substantial changes were made to the 1988 Act with effect from May 28, 2000.[23] Both the criminal provisions as to unauthorised decoders contained in section 297A and the scope of the right conferred by section 298 were substantially reworded. Section 297A was extended to cover information society services as well as broadcasts so as to make express reference to the circumvention of conditional access technology. Section 298 now expressly grants rights to providers of conditional access services (whether from the United Kingdom or another Member State). It also now grants rights to those who broadcast and send encrypted transmissions from Member States other than the United Kingdom. Finally, the range of infringing activities covered by the two sections has been substantially increased.

The Copyright etc. Act 2002. This Act dramatically increased the maximum penalties for the unauthorised decoder offences,[24] while at the same time making provision as to search warrants and forfeiture.[25]   **16–05**

2. POSITION UNDER THE 1988 ACT

A. THE SCHEME OF THE ACT

The scheme of the 1988 Act. The 1988 Act in its present form contains a combination of civil and criminal remedies. First, the dishonest receiver of programmes may be proceeded against in the Magistrates' Court.[26] Secondly, the person who makes, imports, distributes or carries out any of a range of commercial activities in relation to an unauthorised decoder may be proceeded against either in the Magistrates' Court or by way of trial on indictment.[27] Thirdly, there are provisions as to search warrants in relation to the unauthorised decoder offences and as to foreiture of unauthorised decoders.[28] Finally, broadcasters and others have civil remedies both against those who make, import, distribute or carry out any of a range of commercial activities in relation to unauthorised decoders or similar devices and against those who publish information which assists access to their programmes or transmissions without permission.[29] There are no civil remedies against the dishonest receiver of programmes, presumably because such remedies would be unlikely to be exercised. There are a number of minor differences between the activities which constitute offences in relation to unauthorised decoders on the one hand, and the matters which may be the subject of civil proceedings on the other. It remains to be seen whether these differences will prove to be significant in practice.   **16–06**

---

[21] Art.2(a). The term "information society services" is considered in more detail below: see paras 16–11to 16–14.

[22] Art.2(b).

[23] This was effected by substituting new CDPA 1988, ss.297A and 298: see the Conditional Access (Unauthorised Decoders) Regulations 2000 (SI 2000/1175), reg.1.

[24] s.1(4)(a).

[25] ss.2(4) and 5.

[26] s.297.

[27] s.297A.

[28] ss.297B to 297D.

[29] s.298.

B. Offence of Fraudulently Receiving Programmes

16–07   **Offence under section 297.** This section of the 1988 Act is aimed at those who knowingly receive broadcasts which they are not entitled to receive. The section makes it an offence dishonestly[30] to receive a programme included in a broadcasting service provided from a place in the United Kingdom with intent to avoid payment of any charge applicable to the reception of the programme. For this purpose, "programme", "broadcasting" and related expressions have the same meanings as in the copyright Part of the 1988 Act.[31] The 1988 Act provides that, where section 297 applies in relation to a broadcasting service, it also applies to any service run for the person providing that service, or a person providing programmes for that service, which consists wholly or mainly in the sending by means of a telecommunications system of sound or visual images, or both.[32] The offence under section 297 of the 1988 Act is entirely different to that committed by a person who installs or uses a television without a licence.[33]

16–08   **Penalty and liability of corporate officers.** A person who commits such an offence is liable on summary conviction to a fine not exceeding level 5 on the standard scale.[34] If such an offence is committed by a body corporate and is proved to have been committed with the consent or connivance[35] of a director, manager, secretary or other similar officer of the body, or a person purporting to act in any such capacity, he, as well as the body corporate, will be guilty of the offence and liable to be proceeded against and punished accordingly.[36] In relation to a body corporate whose affairs are managed by its members, "director" means a member of the body corporate.[37]

C. Offences Relating to Unauthorised Decoders

16–09   **Development of section 297A.** This section of the 1988 Act is aimed at those who carry out any of a wide array of activities in relation to unauthorised decoders. It was inserted in the 1988 Act by the Broadcasting Act 1990.[38] In its original form it created offences of making, importing, selling or letting for hire any unauthorised decoder. Section 140(1) of the Broadcasting Act 1996 extended the ambit of the section to the activities of offering or exposing for sale or hire and of advertising for sale or hire any unauthorised decoder.[39] The section was amended again with effect from May 28, 2000 to further extend the range of

---

[30] Whether an accused acted dishonestly is a question of fact. The tribunal of fact must first decide whether, according to the ordinary standards of reasonable and honest people, what was done was dishonest and, if so, whether the defendant must have realised that what he was doing was dishonest by those standards: *R. v Ghosh* [1982] Q.B. 1053. It is difficult to see what the requirement of dishonesty adds to the offence given that it is only committed if the accused intended to avoid payment of the charge.

[31] CDPA 1988, s.299(5). See *ibid.*, ss.6 and 7.

[32] s.299(4).

[33] This is a summary offence under the Communications Act 2003 (c.21), s.363(1).

[34] CDPA 1988, s.297(1). Level 5 on the standard scale is currently £5,000: Criminal Justice Act 1982, s.37(2) as substituted by Criminal Justice Act 1991, s.17(1).

[35] For the meaning of the term "connivance", see para. 23–20, below.

[36] CDPA 1988, s.297(2).

[37] s.297(2)

[38] Section 179(1) with effect from January 1, 1991: see the Broadcasting Act 1990 (Commencement No.1 and Transitional Provisions) Order 1990 (SI 1990/2347).

[39] With effect from October 1, 1996: Broadcasting Act 1996 (Commencement No.1 and Transitional Provisions) Order 1996 (SI 1996/2120).

activities covered and to extend protection to information society services as well as broadcasts.[40]

"Transmission". The section applies to apparatus designed or adapted to enable encrypted transmissions to be decoded. The term "transmission" now covers two types of transmission: first, any programme included in a broadcasting service which is provided from a place in the United Kingdom or any other Member State.[41] For these purposes, "programme", "broadcasting" and related expressions, have the same meanings as in the copyright Part of the 1988 Act.[42] The second type of transmission which is within the definition is an "information society service" which is provided from a place in the United Kingdom or any other Member State.[43] The meaning of the term "information society service" is considered in the following paragraphs. **16–10**

"Information society service": the basic definition. Section 297A incorporates by reference the definition of information society service contained in Directive 98/34/EC[44] (as amended by Directive 98/48/EC).[45] Article 1(2) of Directive 98/34/EC contains a complex and lengthy definition of the term "information society service" which in general terms is intended to include services provided over the internet while excluding traditional broadcasting activities. Obvious examples of "information society services" are (provided in each case a fee is charged) the provision of music and video files for downloading; the supply of information to subscribers via the internet; and the provision of internet access and e-mail services. The basic definition is as follows: "any service normally provided for remuneration, at a distance, by electronic means and at the individual request of a recipient of services". There are then three sub-definitions of this basic definition and Annex V to Directive 98/34 EC contains an indicative list of services not covered by the definition. Since the list in Annex V is divided into categories which correspond to the three sub-definitions, the Annex V items are listed here immediately after the sub-definitions. **16–11**

"At a distance". This means that the service is provided without the parties being simultaneously present. According to Annex V, the following services are not information society services: medical examinations or treatment at a doctor's surgery using electronic equipment where the patient is physically present; consultation of an electronic catalogue in a shop with a customer on site; plane ticket reservations at a travel agency in the physical presence of the customer by means of a network of computers; and electronic games made available in a video-arcade where the customer is physically present. **16–12**

"By electronic means". This means that the service is sent initially and received at its destination by means of electronic equipment for the processing (including digital compression) and storage of data and entirely transmitted, conveyed and received by wire, by radio, by optical means or by other electromagnetic means. Annex V states that services having material content even though provided via electronic devices are not provided "by electronic means". Examples are: automatic cash or ticket machines; and the provision of access to road networks or car parks which charge for use even where there are electronic devices at the **16–13**

---

[40] This was effected by reg.1 of the Conditional Access (Unauthorised Decoders) Regulations 2000 (SI 2000/1175), which substitutes a new CDPA 1988, s.297A.
[41] CDPA 1988, s.297A(4).
[42] s.299(5).
[43] s.297A(4).
[44] [1998] O.J. L204/37.
[45] [1998] O.J. L217/18.

entrance or exit to control access or ensure that payment is made. Other examples of services not provided "by electronic means" are the off-line provision of CD-Roms or software on disk; and services which are not provided via electronic processing or inventory systems, such as voice telephony services, fax or telex services, services provided via voice telephony or fax, telephone or fax consultation of doctors or lawyers, and telephone or fax direct marketing.

16–14   **"At the individual request of a recipient of services".** This means that the service is provided through the transmission of data on individual request. Annex V states that the following are not within this definition: services provided by transmitting data without individual demand for simultaneous reception by an unlimited number of individual receivers ("point to multipoint transmission"); television broadcasting services including near-video on demand services covered by point (a) of Article 1 of Directive 89/552/EEC;[46] radio broadcasting services; and teletext where it is televised.

16–15   **"Unauthorised decoder".** All the offences under section 297A concern activities in relation to unauthorised decoders. Relevant definitions appear in section 297A(4). The term "decoder" means any apparatus which is designed or adapted to enable (whether on its own or with any other apparatus) an encrypted transmission to be decoded. "Apparatus" includes any device, component or electronic data, including software. "Encrypted" includes subjected to scrambling or the operation of cryptographic envelopes, electronic locks, passwords or any other analogous applications. A decoder is "unauthorised" if it is designed or adapted to enable an encrypted transmission, or any service of which it forms part, to be accessed in an intelligible form without payment of the fee (however imposed) which the person making the transmission, or on whose behalf it is made, charges for accessing the transmission or service (whether by the circumvention of any conditional access technology related to the transmission or service or by any other means).[47] "Conditional access technology" means any technical measure or arrangement whereby access to encrypted transmissions in an intelligible form is made conditional on prior individual authorisation.[48]

16–16   **Offending acts.** The section embraces almost all the commercial activities which might conceivably be carried out in relation to an unauthorised decoder. Thus, an offence is committed by making, importing, distributing, selling, letting for hire, offering or exposing for sale or hire any unauthorised decoder.[49] An offence is committed by possessing such a decoder for commercial purposes.[50] A further offence is committed by installing, maintaining or replacing such a decoder for commercial purposes.[51] Yet further offences are committed by advertising such a decoder for sale or hire and otherwise promoting such a decoder by means of

---

[46] This provides as follows: "television broadcasting means the initial transmission by wire or over the air, including that by satellite, in unencoded or encoded form, of television programmes intended for reception by the public. It includes the communication of programmes between undertakings with a view to their being relayed to the public. It does not include communication services providing items of information or other messages on individual demand such as tele-copying, electronic data banks and other similar services".

[47] In *R. v Mainwaring* [2002] F.S.R. 20, it was held that a decoder which had been advertised and sold in the United Kingdom but was designed for decoding programmes broadcast from the Netherlands was "unauthorised" even though the broadcaster had no rights to charge a fee in the United Kingdom and did not seek to do so: the decoder enabled the transmission to be accessed without payment of a fee.

[48] s.297A(4).

[49] s.297(1)(a).

[50] s.297(1)(b).

[51] s.297(1)(c).

commercial communications.[52] It will be noted that some non-commercial activities are in fact caught by the section. Thus, the offences of making and importing are not qualified by the requirement that the act in question be for commercial purposes. In practice, however, it seems unlikely that such non-commercial activity would ever be the subject of a prosecution.

Enforcement regime. Contraventions of section 297A which are carried out in the course of a business and which harm the collective interests of consumers in the United Kingdom are subject to the enforcement regime laid down by Part 8 of the Enterprise Act 2002.[53] This is discussed elsewhere.[54] Furthermore, the procedural requirements contained in section 230 of the Enterprise Act 2002 must be complied with before a weights and measures authority commences a prosecution under section 297A.[55] Again, these requirements are discussed elsewhere.[56]   **16–17**

Defence. It is a defence to any prosecution for an offence under the section for the defendant to prove that he did not know, and had no reasonable ground for believing, that the decoder was an unauthorised decoder.[57]   **16–18**

Penalties and sentencing. A person who commits an offence under the section is liable on summary conviction to imprisonment for up to six months or to a fine not exceeding the statutory maximum and on conviction on indictment to imprisonment for a term not exceeding ten years or to an unlimited fine or both.[58]   **16–19**

Search warrants and forfeiture. Section 297B contains provisions as to search warrants in respect of offences under section 297A. Sections 297C and 297D contain provisions as to the forfeiture of unauthorised decoders. These sections mirror their equivalents in the copyright field, which are discussed elsewhere.[59]   **16–20**

D. APPARATUS, ETC., FOR UNAUTHORISED RECEPTION OF TRANSMISSIONS

Section 298: general. Section 298 of the 1988 Act creates what has been described as a "transmission right".[60] Its purpose has been stated to be to enable providers of broadcasting and other services to obtain recompense by giving   **16–21**

---

[52] s.297(1)(d).

[53] Enterprise Act 2002 (Pt 8 Domestic Infringements) Order 2003 (SI 2003/1593), which came into force on June 20, 2003.

[54] See para. 23–42, below.

[55] Enterprise Act 2002, s.230(2), applied by the Enterprise Act 2002 (Pt 8 Notice to OFT of Intended Prosecution Specified Enactments, Revocation and Transitional Provision) Order 2003 (SI 2003/1376) with effect from June 20, 2003.

[56] See para. 23–41, below.

[57] CDPA 1988, s.297A(3). In accordance with general principles, the standard of proof will be the balance of probabilities.

[58] CDPA 1988, s.297A(2). These penalties were increased by the Broadcasting Act 1996, s.140(1) with effect from October 1, 1996: Broadcasting Act 1996 (Commencement No.1 and Transitional Provisions) Order 1996 (SI 1996/2120) and again by the Copyright, etc. and Trade Marks (Offences and Enforcement) Act 2002, s.1(4)(a) in relation to offences committed after November 20, 2002. The statutory maximum is currently £5,000: Interpretation Act 1978, Sch.1, applying Magistrates' Courts Act 1980, s.32(9) as amended by Criminal Justice Act 1991, s.17(2)(c). In R. v Bakker [2001] EWCA Crim 2354, which predates the significant increase in penalties with effect from November 20, 2002, the appellants were a police officer and a computer engineer. They had illegally sold and distributed between 20 and 30 cable television decoder boxes, with a putative loss to cable companies of £55 per box per month. For this they were indicted for conspiracy to defraud. They had also made and sold counterfeit software causing a loss to software companies of up to £15,000. On appeal their sentences were reduced to eight and six months respectively.

[59] See paras 23–46, (search warrants) and 23–53 to 23–57 (forfeiture).

[60] British Sky Broadcasting Group Ltd v Lyons [1995] F.S.R. 357 at 362. It has been held in a criminal context that CDPA 1988, s.298 creates a right not to have others making apparatus and de-

them the right to supply apparatus designed or adapted to receive their transmissions.[61] The section gives rights and remedies in civil proceedings to broadcasters, senders of encrypted transmissions and providers of conditional access services against those who make or deal with unauthorised decoders and similar apparatus and against those who publish information to enable others to receive programmes which they are not entitled to receive.[62]

16–22   **Section 298: persons entitled to rights and remedies.** The persons entitled to relief under the section fall into three categories. The first consists of persons who make charges for the reception of programmes included in broadcasting services provided from a place in the United Kingdom or any other Member State.[63] The second consists of persons who send encrypted transmissions[64] of any other description from a place in the United Kingdom or any other Member State.[65] The third consists of persons who provide conditional access services from a place in the United Kingdom or any other Member State.[66] Under the pre-2000 wording of section 298, it was held that those within the first category are those who provide programmes included in a broadcasting service for members of the public or part of it and who make charges for the reception of such programmes; while those within the second category are those who send other kinds of transmission in an encrypted form to one or more other persons (but not the public or any part of it) and do not necessarily make charges for such sending.[67] Section 299(4) of the 1988 Act provides that, where section 298 applies in relation to a broadcasting service, it also applies to any service run for the person providing that service, or a person providing programmes for that service, which consists wholly or mainly in the sending by means of a telecommunications system of sounds or visual images, or both.

16–23   **Section 298: persons against whom relief is available.** The section gives rights and remedies against two separate categories of person. The first consists of any person who makes, imports, distributes, sells or lets for hire, offers or exposes for sale or hire, advertises for sale or hire, has in his possession for commercial purposes or installs, maintains or replaces for commercial purposes any apparatus[68] designed or adapted to enable or assist persons to access the programmes or other transmissions or circumvent conditional access technology related to them when they are not entitled to do so.[69] At the time when section 298 was confined to transmissions made from the United Kingdom, it was held that the persons referred to as being enabled or assisted to receive the transmissions included all persons who were capable of receiving such transmissions, whether in the United

---

vices designed to be of use to persons who are not authorised to receive programmes and accordingly that a conspiracy to injure that right amounts to a conspiracy to defraud: *R. v Bridgeman and Butt* [1996] F.S.R. 538 (Crown Ct).

[61] *British Sky Broadcasting Group Ltd v Lyons* [1995] F.S.R. 357 at 361.

[62] For a case on the equivalent Hong Kong provisions, see *Satellite Television Asian Region Ltd v Alpha Communications Ltd* [2003] H.K.L.R.D. 282.

[63] CDPA 1988, s.298(1)(a). The terms "programme", "broadcasting" and related expressions have the same meaning as in Pt I of the 1988 Act: s.299(5).

[64] The term "encrypted" has the same meaning as in s.297A while the term "transmission" includes transmissions as defined in that section: see s.298(7). For the definitions of "encryption" and "transmission" in s. 297A, see above at paras 16–15 and 16–10 respectively.

[65] s.298(1)(b).

[66] s.298(1)(c). The term "conditional access services" means services comprising the provision of conditional access technology: s.298(7). The term "conditional access technology" has the same meaning as in s.297A: See para. 16–15, above.

[67] *BBC Enterprises Ltd v Hi-Tech Xtravision Ltd* [1991] 2 A.C. 327 at 336C–D.

[68] The term "apparatus" has the same meaning as in CDPA 1988, s.297A: s.298(7). See para. 16–15, above.

[69] s.298(2)(a).

Kingdom or outside it. Accordingly, a British broadcaster was entitled to relief against persons who made decoders in the United Kingdom even though they were only intended to be sold outside the United Kingdom.[70] Presumably, the same would now apply to decoders which were intended to be sold outside the European Union, provided of course that they were intended to be directed at transmissions originating within it. Persons are "not entitled" to receive programmes or transmissions if they are not authorised by the provider of the programmes or the sender of the transmissions to do so.[71] It is not necessary for the claimant to prove that the apparatus or device complained of has been specifically designed to enable unauthorised use to take place or is in any way different from the claimant's own decoding devices. It is sufficient for the claimant to prove that the defendant has sold devices to persons who will then use them to receive the claimant's services without paying anything to the claimant.[72] The second category of person against whom relief is available consists of any person who publishes or otherwise promotes by means of commercial communications any information which is calculated to enable or assist persons to access the programmes or other transmissions or circumvent conditional access technology related to the programmes or other transmissions when they are not entitled to do so.[73]

Rights and remedies under section 298. The rights and remedies conferred by the section are the same rights and remedies as a copyright owner has in respect of an infringement of copyright.[74] It is expressly provided that the person entitled to rights under the section is entitled to the same rights to an order for delivery up or to seize items which would offend under the terms of the section as a copyright owner has in relation to an infringing copy.[75] In addition, the withdrawal of the privilege against self-incrimination effected by section 72 of the Supreme Court Act 1981 applies to proceedings under section 298 as to proceedings for infringement of copyright.[76] Finally, it is provided that section 97(1) of the 1988 Act, which prevents an award of damages being made in the case of an innocent infringement of copyright, applies to proceedings under section 298 with the modification that the reference in section 97(1) to the defendant not knowing or having reason to believe that copyright subsisted in the work is to be construed as a reference to his not knowing or having reason to believe that his acts infringed the rights conferred by section 298.[77]

16–24

E. EXTENT AND APPLICATION OF SECTIONS 297 TO 299

Extent. Sections 297 to 299 of the 1988 Act extend to England, Wales, Scotland and Northern Ireland.[78] They may be extended to the Isle of Man or to any of the Channel Islands by Order in Council with such exceptions and modifications as

16–25

---

[70] *BBC Enterprises Ltd v Hi-Tech Xtravision Ltd* [1991] 2 A.C. 327 at 337F.

[71] *BBC Enterprises Ltd v Hi-Tech Xtravision Ltd* [1991] 2 A.C. 327 at 338C.

[72] *British Sky Broadcasting Group Ltd v Lyons* [1995] F.S.R. 357 at 361.

[73] s.298(2)(b).

[74] CDPA 1988, s.298(2). As to these rights and remedies, see ss.96 and 97 and Ch.22 below.

[75] s.298(3). For the remedies of a copyright owner, see para. 22–182 (delivery up) and paras 22–46 *et seq.* (seizure). CDPA 1988, s.114, which deals with the disposal of infringing items which have been delivered up or seized, applies with the necessary modifications to items delivered up or seized under this section: s.298(6). For a discussion of s.114, see paras 22–179 *et seq.*, below.

[76] s.298(4). The same applies to the Scottish and Northern Irish equivalents of the Supreme Court Act 1981, s.72.

[77] s.298(5).

[78] CDPA 1988, s.304(2).

may be specified in the Order.[79] An Order in Council has been made in respect of Guernsey under section 304(5) of the 1988 Act.[80] It extends the sections to Guernsey in modified form.[81] No other such orders have been made.

16–26   **Application**. Under section 299(1) of the 1988 Act, section 297 may be applied by Order in Council in relation to programmes included in services provided from a country or territory outside the United Kingdom.[82] Section 299(1) of the 1988 Act also provides that section 298 of the Act[83] may be applied by Order in Council in relation to such programmes and to encrypted[84] transmissions sent from such a country or territory. A statutory instrument containing such an Order in Council is subject to annulment in pursuance of a resolution of either House of Parliament.[85] An Order in Council has been made in respect of Guernsey under section 299(1) of the 1988 Act relating to sections 297 and 298 of the 1988 Act.[86]

---

[79] ss.304(4)(d) (Isle of Man) and 304(5) (Channel Islands).

[80] The Copyright, Designs and Patents Act 1988 (Guernsey) Order 1989 (SI 1989/1997). See Vol.2 at A4.x. Although referring to CDPA 1988, ss.297 to 299, this Order was made on November 1, 1989, before ss.297A to 297D were inserted in the 1988 Act.

[81] Copyright, Designs and Patents Act 1988 (Guernsey) Order 1989, Sch.

[82] CDPA 1988, s.299(5) provides that the words "programme", "broadcasting" and related expressions in s.299 are to have the same meaning as in the copyright Part of the 1988 Act.

[83] As to which see paras 16–21 et seq., above.

[84] For the meaning of "encrypted", see para. 16–15, above.

[85] s.299(3).

[86] The Fraudulent Reception of Transmissions (Guernsey) Order 1989 (SI 1989/2003): see Vol.2 at A4.xi.

PUBLICATION RIGHT

1. INTRODUCTION

The Copyright and Related Rights Regulations 1996 introduced (from December **17–01** 1, 1996) a new property right equivalent to copyright, called a "publication right".[1] The right is granted without formality to any person who, after the expiry of copyright protection, publishes for the first time a previously unpublished literary, dramatic, musical or artistic work or a film. The new right therefore supplements existing rights given to publishers in their typographical arrangement of published editions.[2] However, the new publication right differs considerably from the existing right of publishers in their typographical arrangements: first, the publication right is only available in respect of previously unpublished works whereas the typographical right applies to published editions of previously published works; and, second, the rights granted by the publication right are much more extensive than the mere right to prevent facsimile copying of a typographical arrangement.[3] This new right lasts for 25 years from the end of the year in which the work was first published.

---

[1] SI 1996/2967, regs 16 and 17. Hereafter, "the Regulations". The Electronic Commerce (EC Directive) Regulations 2002 (SI 2002/2013) apply to these Regulations. See the Electronic Commerce (EC Directive) (Extension) (No.2) Regulations 2003 (SI 2003/2500), reg.2, Sch., Pt 1.

[2] CDPA 1988, ss.1(1)(c), 8.

[3] Something of an analogue to the publication right may have existed by virtue of s.3 of the Literary Property Act 1842 (c.45): "the copyright in every book which shall be published after the death of its author shall endure for the term of forty-two years from the first publication thereof, and shall be the property of the proprietor of the author's manuscript from which such book shall be first published, and his assigns." For an illustration of the operation of that provision, see *MacMillan v Dent* [1907] 1 Ch. 107, 114 (in which copyright was held to exist on publication of letters written by Charles Lamb (who had died in 1834)).

2. BACKGROUND

17–02   The Regulations implement Article 4 of the Term Directive.[4] Harmonisation in this area was considered necessary because some countries had a publication right (most notably the so-called *editio princeps* in Germany on which the Directive is mainly based[5]) and others did not. These differences presented a potential barrier to completion of the internal market. However, no proposal for harmonisation of a publication right was included in the first version of the Term Directive. This was said to be because the Commission did not feel compelled to harmonise rights which "up until now have hardly affected the internal market or that only exist in one or two Member States."[6] However, the Commission had a change of heart prior to its publication of the amended proposal.[7]

3. WHEN THE PUBLICATION RIGHT IS AVAILABLE

17–03   **Overview.** The publication right arises when a person publishes for the first time a previously unpublished work in which copyright has expired. In order to have the right, a publisher must (a) publish (b) a relevant work (c) which has not previously been published (d) in which copyright has expired and (e) which qualifies for the right.

A. PUBLISH

17–04   The right arises on publication of a previously unpublished work. The concept of publication therefore has a dual role: previous publication will defeat the right, whereas first publication after expiry of the copyright term gives rise to the right. Publication has the same meaning in both contexts,[8] subject to one important qualification. While it is clear that publication must take place in the EEA for the publication right to arise, the regulations and Directive leave it unclear whether publication outside the EEA will defeat the right (see para.17–10, below).

Publication in this context includes any making available to the public and, in particular, includes the issue of copies to the public; making the work available by means of an electronic retrieval system; the rental or lending of copies of the work to the public; the performance, exhibition or showing of the work in public; or communicating the work to the public by electric transmission.[9] A number of questions relating to this definition are considered below (see paras 17–07 *et seq.*, below).

---

[4] Council Directive 93/98 harmonising the term of protection of copyright and certain related rights. Art.4 states that "[a]ny person who, after the expiry of copyright protection, for the first time lawfully publishes or lawfully communicates to the public a previously unpublished work, shall benefit from a protection equivalent to the economic rights of the author. The term of protection of such rights shall be 25 years from the time when the work was first lawfully published or lawfully communicated to the public."

[5] Law on Copyright and Neighbouring Rights (Copyright Law) 1965, Art.71.

[6] Von Lewinski, "EC Proposal for a Council Directive Harmonizing the Term of Protection of Copyright and Certain Related Rights" (1992) 23 I.I.C. 785 at 805.

[7] It seems strange that the Commission chose to harmonise the publication right but left typographical arrangement provisions unharmonised, given that typographical arrangements were protected in the United Kingdom: CDPA 1988, ss.1(1)(c), 8; Ireland: Copyright Act 1963 (c.10), s.20; and Greece; Copyright Related Rights and Cultural Matters Law (No.2121/1993), Art.51.

[8] *cf.* Council Directive 93/98 harmonising the term of protection of copyright and certain related rights, Art.4, which provides that the right arises either where a person "lawfully publishes" or "lawfully communicates to the public" a "previously *unpublished* work", potentially suggesting that a "communication to the public" , not amounting to publication, during the copyright term will not prevent the publication right from arising on some later act.

[9] Copyright and and Related Rights Regulations 1996, reg.16(2), as amended by the Copyright and and Related Rights Regulations 2003 (SI 2003/2498). The amendments were made as part of the implementation of the Information Society Directive (2001/29/EC), and replaced the previous reference to the acts of broadcasting a work or including a work in a cable programme service

B. RELEVANT WORKS

General. The publication right arises when a person publishes for the first time a previously unpublished work. Regulation 16(7) states that in this context a "work" means a literary, dramatic, musical or artistic work or a film. **17–05**

Exclusions. No publication right arises from the publication of a work in which Crown copyright or Parliamentary copyright subsisted.[10] This limitation seems to have little basis in the Directive. However, it may be that since Article 4 refers to works, a term which is assumed to have the same meaning as in the Berne Convention, the limitation can be supported indirectly. This is because under Article 2(4) of the Berne Convention: "It shall be a matter for legislation in the countries of the Union to determine the protection to be granted to official texts of a legislative, administrative and legal nature". Under existing United Kingdom law, such works are treated differently from other literary and artistic works as regards ownership and duration, and it may be assumed that insofar as these provisions do not require modification in order to comply with Article 1 of the Term Directive, it is also legitimate to exempt such works when implementing Article 4.[11] The policy behind such an exemption is less obvious: it could be argued that Crown copyright works should be administered for the benefit of the public as a whole, and it would therefore be inappropriate to allow a private individual to obtain a property right over such a work.[12] **17–06**

C. THE REQUIREMENT THAT THE WORK BE PREVIOUSLY UNPUBLISHED

Introduction. The right is acquired only where the work is previously unpublished. As has been seen, publication in this context includes any making available to the public and, in particular, includes the issue of copies to the public; making the work available by means of an electronic retrieval system; the rental or lending of copies of the work to the public; the performance, exhibition or showing of the work in public; or communicating the work to the public by electronic transmission.[13] This definition of publication is broader than that under existing United Kingdom copyright law, most obviously in its inclusion of performance, exhibition, showing and communicating to the public by electronic transmission.[14] This presents the possibility that a work could be unpublished for copyright purposes, but published for publication right purposes. **17–07**

Sale or lending of the original. It is notable that a work is published by the issue, rental or lending of copies of a work, but not, it seems, by the sale or lending **17–08**

---

with the single act of "communicating the work to the public" and introduced a new generic description of "any making available to the public" in place of "any communication to the public."Communicating a work to the public, however, has an extended meaning, covering any communication to the public by electronic transmission, and includes wireless or cable broadcasts and any electronic transmission by way of an "on-demand" service. See further, CDPA 1988, s.20 and para. 7–98, above.

[10] Copyright and and Related Rights Regulations 1996, reg.16(5).

[11] See further, as to Crown and Parliamentary copyright, Ch.10, above.

[12] Alternatively, the justification for the exclusion may be that after a number of years such works will almost invariably have been made available to the public, for example by being placed in the Public Record Office, and this, it may be assumed, was sufficient to publish the work so that no publication right could later arise. However, the placing of a single copy of a work in a public library is probably insufficient to prevent the publication right from coming into existence: see para. 17–09, below.

[13] Copyright and and Related Rights Regulations 1996, reg.16(2).

[14] Compare CDPA 1988, s.175(4) and Berne Convention for the Protection of Literary and Artistic Works, Art.3(3).

of the original.[15] This follows from the wording of regulations 16(2)(a) and (c), which refer to the issue and rental or lending of "copies".[16] If doubt existed about this interpretation because of the non-exhaustive nature of the definition of publication, it is removed by the fact that the act of sale or lending of the original to a person would not itself amount to a communication to *the public*. Although the term "public" has been given a wide meaning in the context of "public performance" and "publication", so that in one case the exposure of six copies was held to be a publication,[17] even this wide meaning would probably not encompass the simple sale or loan of the original even if the purchaser or borrower was a "member of the public".[18]

17–09   **Single copies in public libraries**. One difficult question which the Regulations do not address is whether the placing of an original manuscript or a single copy of a work with a public library is sufficient to amount to "making available" to the public. While the words "any making available to the public" might appear broad enough to cover this situation, the better view, given the specific examples of "making available" in reg.16(2), is that such an act does not of itself constitute publication.

17–10   **Place of first publication**. The right will presumably not arise if the work has been made available to the public at any time during the term of copyright. As mentioned, it is left unclear whether there is any geographical limitation on publication which operates to prevent the publication right arising, and, in particular, whether previous publication outside the EEA prevents the publication right arising when the work is later first published in the EEA.

The failure to specify any such geographical limitation might be taken to imply that none is to operate, so that prior publication anywhere in the world prevents the right from arising.[19] Such a view would be reinforced by the fact that regulation 16(4)(a) expressly states that "a work qualifies for publication right only if first publication is in the European Economic Area".[20]

Nevertheless, it might be possible to argue that only prior publication in the EEA will operate to prevent the right arising.[21] At a general level, it might be argued that because the Directive is concerned only with the EEA, no significance is to be attached to any publication outside the EEA. Since it is only publication in the EEA that gives rise to the right, it is only prior publication in the EEA that prevents the right from arising. Such a view has the advantage that dif-

---

[15] There is no parallel to s.175(5) of the 1988 Act, which excludes from the definition of publication "publication which is merely colourable and not intended to satisfy the reasonable requirements of the public".

[16] In *Microsoft Corporation v Electro-wide Ltd* [1997] F.S.R. 580 it was argued that s.18 of the 1988 Act excluded the act of issuing a single copy, and Laddie J. proceeded on the basis that this submission was correct. The view that the term "copies" in the Regulations does not include the original is reinforced by the fact that it has been thought necessary, in order to implement the Rental Right Directive 92/100, to state explicitly in s.18(4) of the Act that issuing of copies includes issuing of the original.

[17] *Francis Day and Hunter v Feldman* [1914] 1 Ch. 728.

[18] See below as to the position where a single copy of a work is placed in a public library.

[19] In the context of contracts in restraint of trade, courts have treated a failure to specify the geographical limits of a restriction as indicating that the restriction is to operate on a worldwide basis: see, for example, *Mont v Mills* [1993] F.S.R. 577.

[20] The right therefore would not operate to provide an incentive to introduce works published outside the EEA into the EEA (as for example used to be the case with patents of importation), but only to induce first publication in the EEA.

[21] In the context of the Registered Designs Act 1949, the failure of the statute to specify where a divesting act must take place was interpreted as requiring the act to have occurred in the United Kingdom. See *Bissell AG's Design* [1964] R.P.C. 125: applicant could not rely on s.6(4) where artwork had been "applied industrially" to an article and one such article had been "sold"; held by Registrar to require sale of the article in the United Kingdom.

ficult questions will be avoided concerning virtually simultaneous publication inside and outside the EEA. In this respect, the fact that there is no explicit provision on virtually simultaneous publication outside the EEA (in contrast with the normal 30-day rule) might be taken to indicate that such publication is of no significance.[22] However, no matter how desirable this conclusion may be, the symmetry upon which this argument depends can only be sustained if regulation 16(4) is read as if it said "a work qualifies for publication right only on (a) first publication in the European Economic Area, and (b) if the publisher of the work is at the time of first publication a national of an EEA state." In other words, the reference to first publication in regulation 16(4) must be explained as indicating that no publication right arises as regards further publication in the EEA,[23] rather than that no publication right arises if the work has been previously published outside the EEA. Not only does this seem to be a highly artificial construction, it would render the word "first" in regulation 16(4) superfluous, since it is already clear from the wording of regulation 16(1) that no publication right arises as regards further publication in the EEA.

Publication of part. If part of a work has previously been published, there does not seem to be any reason why the publication right should not arise in relation to the remainder. There is authority to suggest that publication of a small part of a work will not amount to publication of a work as a whole. Thus, for example, the printing of the voice parts of a musical score contained in an arrangement for the voice and the piano would not amount to a publication of the musical composition as a whole.[24] Presumably, however, only the unpublished parts of such a work would attract the protection of the new right, so that it would not be possible to rely on publication right in the unpublished part to prevent further publication of the previously published (presumably now public domain) aspects.   **17–11**

Publication in a different medium. A related question arises as to whether publication of a work in one medium prevents the right arising in relation to publication in a different medium. For example, is an unpublished musical score to be treated as previously published as a result of publication of a phonogram which embodies a performance of the score? Since publication occurs where "copies" of the work have been issued to the public, the answer appears to depend on whether what has been already published amounts to a copy. Regulation 17(4) states that provisions contained in Chapter 1 of Part I of the 1988 Act defining expressions used generally in Part I, "apply, with any necessary adaptations, for the purpose of supplementing the substantive provisions of that Part as applied by this regulation." Hence, it might be appropriate to employ the meaning of copy from Part I. For the purposes of Part I of the 1988 Act, a copy of a musical work means a reproduction of it in any material form.[25]   **17–12**

This approach is also consistent with authorities which suggest that publication by sale of an article embodying a design is effective to publish the drawings on which the design was based.[26] Thus, it was held that a claimant was likely to be able to establish copyright in drawings as a result of first publication in the

---

[22] Copyright and and Related Rights Regulations 1996, reg.16(4). *cf.* Berne Convention for the Protection of Literary and Artistic Works, Art.3(4).

[23] This is how the word "first" is used in Council Directive 93/98 harmonising the term of protection of copyright and certain related rights, in the phrase "for the first time lawfully publishes".

[24] *Fairlie v Boosey* (1879) 4 A.C. 711 at 730.

[25] CDPA 1988, ss.17(1), (2).

[26] *Merchant Adventurers Ltd v M. Grew & Co Ltd* [1973] R.P.C. 1 at 10 (Graham J.); *British Northrop v Texteam Blackburn Ltd* [1974] R.P.C. 57, 64 (Megarry J.). It should be noted, however, that these authorities were decided in the context of qualification for copyright so that the decision that the work was published operated in favour of the plaintiff copyright owner and

United Kingdom of three-dimensional light fittings.[27] If these authorities are sound, and they are applied in the context of publication right, it would seem that no publication right will be available for publication of an artist's preliminary drawings for a sculpture, if the sculpture which faithfully reproduces the preliminary drawings, has itself been published.

A preferable interpretation of the Directive would have been that such acts do not amount to publication, and that "publication" in the context of publication right means publication of a work or a reproduction of it in the (notational and dimensional) form in which the work was brought into existence. The differences which exist between a drawing and a sculpture, or a sound recording and a score, are potentially of value to the public, and there is therefore a justification for the law providing an incentive to disclose these unpublished embodiments. In order to achieve such a construction of the publication right under the existing implementing Regulations, it would be necessary to define the term "copies" in a different way from that in the 1988 Act. This, in turn, would require a restrictive construction of regulation 17(4) as not relating to issues of acquisition of publication right but only to the limited purpose of "supplementing the substantive provisions" of Part I, that is, when defining the scope and attributes of the publication right.

17–13   **Unauthorised publication**. When determining whether the work was previously unpublished, no account is to be taken of any unauthorised act.[28] Thus, unauthorised publications are neither sufficient to give rise to publication right, nor to prevent the right arising in the case of a later authorised publication. However, a number of problems exist in defining and applying the notion of "unauthorised".

17–14   **Unauthorised publication where copyright subsists**. Where copyright subsists in a work, the term "unauthorised" is left undefined by the Regulations. However, as has been seen, regulation 17(4) states that provisions contained in Chapter 1 of Part I of the 1988 Act defining expressions used generally in Part I, "apply, with any necessary adaptations, for the purpose of supplementing the substantive provisions of that Part as applied by this regulation." The term "unauthorised" is, in turn, defined in the Act, as done without the licence of the copyright owner.[29] A work, therefore, is not to be treated as having been previously published where that publication was unlicensed. For example, if the owner of copyright in unpublished letters or diaries allowed a biographer access to the letters solely for research purposes, but the biographer published the letters, it would remain open for a person, once copyright had expired, to publish the letters and gain the publication right. Whether this would be so if the biographer's act of publishing was deemed a fair dealing or in the public interest is less clear. In those circumstances the publication would be "unauthorised" in the sense of "otherwise than with the licence of the copyright owner", even though such a licence would be unnecessary for the act to be legal. Similarly, the question arises whether publication occurs where a painting is placed on public display without the licence of the copyright owner, since such an act is "unauthorised" even though the copyright owner does not have the exclusive right to control such exhibition.

---

against a defendant who was making "technical points" (*per* Graham J., *Merchant Adventurers Ltd v M. Grew & Co. Ltd*, at 8).

[27] *Merchant Adventurers Ltd v M. Grew & Co. Ltd* [1973] R.P.C. 1.

[28] Copyright and Related Rights Regulations 1996, reg.16(3). See also CDPA 1988, s.175(6).

[29] CDPA 1988, s.178. The term is relevant when determining whether protection arises in relation to a typographical arrangement, whether the exceptions contained in ss.33, 46, 59, 60 operate, and s.105 presumptions. As to the application of this provision in relation to the publication right, see reg.17(4) of the Copyright and Related Rights Regulations 1996 and see below. Sch.1, para.46 defines "unauthorised" in a slightly different way for things done before June 1, 1957 as acts done otherwise than with the "consent or acquiescence" of the copyright owner.

An alternative interpretation is that the notion of an "unauthorised act" might suggest that no account should be taken of any act which *required* authorisation.[30] While such an interpretation seems difficult to reconcile with the terms of section 178, it would be more consistent with the Directive which employs the word "lawful".[31] Moreover, regulation 17(4) may be read as not requiring application of the defining expressions used in the 1988 Act, when (as here) considering whether publication right arises, because the regulation requires their application only when construing "the substantive provisions of that Part as applied by this regulation"—matters such as infringement or assignment of the publication right.

Unauthorised publication when copyright does not subsist. If publication takes place either before copyright subsists, or after its expiry, the statutory definition of "unauthorised" in the 1988 Act is (and could be) of no assistance, because there is no copyright owner. The Regulation therefore explains that in relation to a time when there is no copyright in the work, an unauthorised act "means an act done without the consent of the owner of the physical medium in which the work is embodied or on which it is recorded".[32] So, for example, a thief who publishes a manuscript will not obtain the new publication right.

17–15

Anonymous works. An added difficulty may arise in relation to anonymous works. Elsewhere it is explained that exceptions exist to an action for infringement of copyright where it is reasonable to assume that copyright in such a work has expired.[33] What would happen if, at this stage, a person publishes a previously unpublished work? It seems that the publisher would not benefit from the publication right if it was later shown that copyright had in fact subsisted because of the requirement of "expiry of copyright" (see paras 17–18 *et seq.*, below). However, once the copyright had expired, would the earlier publication prevent the acquisition of the publication right? Since there was no authorisation of the earlier publication, it seems it can be ignored even though it was not unlawful, because it was otherwise than with the licence of the copyright owner (see para.17–14, above).

17–16

First publication in another EEA State. Consideration also needs to be given to the question of whether the absence of authorisation must be assessed according to the law of the United Kingdom or the country of first publication. In the absence of any express provision dealing with this issue, the most convenient interpretation of the Regulations would seem to be to apply the same notion of "unauthorised", irrespective of the place of first publication, whenever publication right is claimed in the United Kingdom. As will be seen, it appears likely that publishers will be able to obtain publication right in one Member State over a work that is still protected by copyright in another Member State. Logically, therefore, it would seem to make most sense to define "unauthorised" according to the law of the country where publication right is being claimed. This would mean, for example, that a publisher in France of a previously unpublished work, in which copyright has expired, with the consent of the owner of the physical medium, would acquire the new publication right in the United Kingdom, even if the publication was in breach of the French law of *droit de divulgation*. This conclusion may, however, be in conflict with the Directive, since the Directive

17–17

---

[30] This might even mean that prior publication of a work by another should also be ignored if it constituted a breach of confidence or contract.

[31] Council Directive 93/98 harmonising the term of protection of copyright and certain related rights, Art.4.

[32] reg.16(3).

[33] CDPA 1988, ss.57, 66A and see above at para. 9–152 and para. 9–179, respectively.

requires that the work be "lawfully published".[34] Whilst it could be replied that the publication would have been lawful in the United Kingdom, the fact remains that so long as the work is only published in France there has not been a "lawful" publication.

D. THE REQUIREMENT OF EXPIRY OF COPYRIGHT

17–18 The right is only available "after the expiry of copyright protection".[35] Expiry in this context presumably means expiry in the United Kingdom as, despite harmonisation, copyright and related rights remain essentially national rights. The purpose of limiting the publication right may be presumed to have been to avoid duplication of rights in the same work, but would seem to have a number of additional consequences. These are considered below. However, the question of when copyright will expire is largely beyond the scope of this chapter.[36]

17–19 **Works in which copyright has never subsisted.** One consequence of limiting the availability of the right to cases where copyright "has expired" may be to exclude from the operation of the right works in which copyright has never subsisted,[37] as it would seem highly artificial to say that copyright in such a work has "expired". Copyright may not have "subsisted" in an unpublished work for two reasons: first, the work might have been created at a time when no statutory copyright existed; secondly, the work might have failed to attract copyright because of the author's nationality. In order fully to understand both scenarios, the history of the protection of unpublished work needs to be considered. Comments will be confined initially to a consideration of works produced by British authors.

17–20 **Lack of statutory copyright at the time of creation: common law copyright.** The requirement that copyright "subsisted" might, at first, appear to exclude all works created at a time before copyright protection existed for that category of work. Statutory copyrights were recognised in books from 1710,[38] in engravings from 1735,[39] in sculptures from 1798,[40] and in paintings, drawings and photographs from 1862.[41] Thus, for example, Shakespeare's plays were written long before the passage of the Statute of Anne, and Van Dyck's paintings were created before the passage of the Fine Arts Copyright Act. However, with the exception of the latter Act, the copyright statutes only protected *published* works, with unpublished works falling to be protected by what was called "common law copyright", a form of protection that was potentially perpetual. With the Copyright Act 1911, statutory copyright protection arose on creation rather than publication in relation to all classes of work and common law copyright was abolished.[42]

A publisher claiming "publication right" could argue that the reference to

---

[34] Council Directive 93/98 harmonising the term of protection of copyright and certain related rights, Art.4.

[35] Copyright and Related Rights Regulations 1996, reg.16(1).

[36] See Ch.6.

[37] The limitation is consistent with the terms of the Council Directive 93/98 harmonising the term of protection of copyright and certain related rights, but other countries, most notably Germany, have taken different approaches. This is considered in more detail at para. 17–27, below.

[38] Statute of Anne 1709, (8 Anne c.19).

[39] Engraving Copyright Act 1734, (8 Geo. 2 c.13).

[40] Copyright Act 1798, (38 Geo. 3 c.71).

[41] Fine Arts Copyright Act 1862, (25 & 26 Vict. c.68).

[42] This change in approach followed from the United Kingdom's ratification of the Berne Convention, which required Member States to provide protection for "Authors who are subjects or citizens of any of the countries of the Union ... whether unpublished or first published in the country of the Union." Although common law copyright probably in any event extended to

"copyright" having "expired" includes a reference to common law copyright which existed in unpublished works prior to July 1, 1912. However, it is doubtful whether such a construction is likely to be accepted. One reason for this lies in the fact that when, in the past, the legislature has intended to include the common law right within the definition of "copyright" it has said so expressly, but no such express reference is to be found in the Regulations.[43] Although the common law right was sometimes referred to as "common law copyright", it was also referred to as "the right to restrain publication at common law";[44] "quasi-copyright"; a "right analogous to copyright;"[45] and an "inchoate copyright",[46] again suggesting that "copyright" should only be taken to include the common law right where the legislation concerned says so expressly.

Moreover, whilst the common law right clearly existed with respect to unpublished literary manuscripts,[47] the exact nature, coverage and content of the common law right was never clearly established. In particular, a degree of doubt remains as to whether the common law right subsisted in unpublished artistic works, where most of the problems we are concerned with arise.[48]

On the assumption that the term "copyright" in the Regulations refers to statutory copyright only, it is necessary to see which unpublished works have been granted statutory protection. As has already been noted, prior to the Copyright Act 1911, statutory copyright applied in relation only to published works, with the exception of works covered by the Fine Art Copyright Act 1862. An important initial distinction must therefore be drawn between those unpublished works in which statutory rights were first granted in 1911, and paintings, drawings and photographs. **17–21**

Retrospective vesting of statutory copyright in most unpublished works under the Copyright Act 1911. The Copyright Act 1911 abolished common law copyright, and conferred statutory protection automatically from creation. The transitional provisions contained in the first schedule of the 1911 Act were such that this applied to pre-existing works as well as to works created after July 1, 1912.[49] As a result, all literary, dramatic and musical works and engravings which remain unpublished will have enjoyed statutory copyright protection. **17–22**

Sculptures. A different rule applied to unpublished sculptures created prior to July 1, 1912. These works were protected as if the Act had been in force at the date of their creation. Thus, unpublished sculptures were given a term of the life **17–23**

---

protect foreign authors, simply by equating protection for published and unpublished works the Berne Convention seemed to require a change in the United Kingdom's approach.

[43] *cf.* Copyright Act 1911, Sch.1.

[44] Copyright Act 1911, Sch.1.

[45] See Robertson, *The Law of Copyright* (Clarendon, Oxford, 1912), pp.v. 42.

[46] See Macgillivray, *The Copyright Act 1911* (Stevens and Sons, London, 1912), p.122. The notion of an "inchoate" copyright may be particularly significant since it seems difficult to argue that an inchoate right can, in the normal sense, have expired.

[47] See *Donaldson v Beckett* (1774) 2 Bro. P.C. 129; 4 Burr. 2408.

[48] The leading case which is said to establish the existence of common law copyright in unpublished artistic works is *Prince Albert v Strange* (1849) 18 L.J. Eq. 120, but it should be noted that this case was also decided on the grounds of breach of confidence. Furthermore, if common law copyright did subsist in unpublished artistic works this creates a difficult question as to when this copyright expired, bearing in mind that the Fine Arts Copyright Act 1862 also applied to unpublished works. The dominant view seems to have been that the common law right did subsist, but that it expired at the same time as statutory copyright (for example, see Scrutton, *The Law of Copyright* (John Murray, London, 1883), p.230), but little support for this view can be gained from the 1862 Act. Indeed, the preamble to the 1862 Act states "whereas by law, as now established, the authors of paintings, drawings and photographs have no copyrights in such their works."

[49] *i.e.* the date the 1911 Act came into force.

of the author and 50 years thereafter, with the result that sculptures would only come into copyright under the 1911 Act if the author died after July 1, 1862 (*i.e.* 50 years before the 1911 Act came into force). Sculptures not retrospectively protected by the 1911 Act, *i.e.* sculptures created by an author who died more than 50 years before, could only have enjoyed copyright on publication.

17–24 **New subject matter.** The Copyright Act 1911 also extended statutory protection to a variety of subject matter for the first time. Of such subject matter, only works of artistic craftsmanship constitute works that might now be the subject of publication right.[50] The transitional provisions of the 1911 Act did not operate so as to give unpublished works of artistic craftsmanship retrospective protection, so there was no statutory copyright protection for such works prior to July 1, 1912.[51]

17–25 **The problem of unpublished drawings, paintings and photographs.** The Fine Arts Copyright Act 1862[52] granted statutory copyright in a painting, drawing or photograph from the moment of its creation rather than publication.[53] Consequently, unpublished paintings, drawings and photographs created after the coming into force of the 1862 Act will be works in which copyright has "subsisted" for the purposes of the publication right.[54] However, the transitional provisions of the 1862 Act as regards previously created unpublished works were not as generous as those of the 1911 Act for other works. An unpublished painting, drawing or photograph, created before the coming into force of the 1862 Act received protection if it had not been "sold or disposed of before the commencement of the Act"[55] and if the term of protection under the 1862 Act had already not expired. Since the term was seven years *post-mortem auctoris*, this meant that no statutory copyright existed for any such work created by an artist or photographer who had died prior to 1855.[56]

From the above, it will be seen that the following works by British authors will have enjoyed statutory copyright protection and will thus (at some point) be eligible for publication right protection:

(a) All unpublished literary, dramatic and musical works and engravings irrespective of the date of their creation.

(b) Unpublished paintings, drawings and photographs created after the coming into force of the 1862 Act.

(c) Unpublished sculptures on which copyright was conferred by the 1911

---

[50] See para. 17–05, above.

[51] Copyright Act 1911, Sch.1.

[52] (25 & 26 Vict. c.68).

[53] *Tuck v Priester* (1887) 19 Q.B.D. 629; *Bowden Bros. v Amalgamated Pictorials* [1911] 1 Ch. 386. Also see *Copinger*, (4th ed.), p.369.

[54] Registration under that Act was only a pre-condition to bringing an action for infringement, it did not affect the question of whether copyright subsisted in the work, but it should be noted that it would be possible to argue that some forms of registration under the 1862 Act were in any event sufficient to communicate the work to the public. In particular, it should be noted that the 1862 Act provided that in addition to a written description, the registration could include "if the Person registering shall so desire a Sketch, Outline, or Photograph of the said works" (s.4). Whilst a sketch of a painting could probably not be said to communicate the final work to the public, it is less clear whether providing a photograph of a work would be sufficient. In part this question is connected with the issue of whether depositing a single copy of a work with a library is sufficient to communicate a work to the public (see para. 17–09, above). The argument that at least some forms of registration would be sufficient to communicate a work to the public would seem stronger in this case, however, because the registration of a work seems to carry with it some notion of public accessibility.

[55] Fine Arts Copyright Act 1862, s.1.

[56] It might be possible to argue that the effect of the 1862 Act was retrospectively to vest copyright in all unpublished works covered by the Act, even though on such a retrospective vesting copyright had already lapsed in many cases. However, such an argument would be highly artificial and sits uneasily with the wording of that Act: Fine Arts Copyright Act 1862, s.1. Similarly, it could be argued that the 1911 Act retrospectively vested copyright in all unpublished sculptures.

Act, *i.e.* sculptures created by an author who died within the 50 years immediately prior to the coming into force of the 1911 Act.

(d) In addition, all "British" films will have enjoyed copyright protection at some point in time. Films created before June 1, 1957 will have been protected as a series of photographs under the 1862 or 1911 Acts.[57] Films created after that date will have received express statutory protection.

Works by British authors which may never have enjoyed copyright and which may not, therefore, be eligible for publication right protection are as follows:

(a) Unpublished paintings, drawings or photographs created by an author who died before 1855.

(b) Unpublished paintings, drawings or photographs created before 1862 which had been "sold or disposed of before the commencement of the Act".[58]

(c) Unpublished sculptures that were created by an author who died more than 50 years prior to the coming into force of the 1911 Act, *i.e.* before July 1, 1862.

(d) Unpublished works of artistic craftsmanship created before July 1, 1912.

Foreign works which may never have enjoyed copyright. So far consideration   **17–26** has been restricted to works created by British authors, but consideration also needs to be given to the position of foreign works, again in order to try and determine whether there are any unpublished works which have never enjoyed copyright in the United Kingdom, with the result that they may not be eligible for publication right. In order to determine whether an unpublished foreign work has ever enjoyed copyright in the United Kingdom attention should be paid to the following principles:

(a) If the work is of a type which would not have enjoyed copyright protection if made by a British author (see above), then it is safe to assume that the work has never been in copyright in the United Kingdom.

(b) If the work was made *after* the 1911 Act came into force then the following additional principles can be applied:

   (i) If the work was created by a resident citizen of a country which has never had copyright relations with the United Kingdom then copyright will not have subsisted in the work. In this case it seems that the publication right may not be available.

   (ii) If the work was created by a citizen or resident of a Berne or Universal Copyright Convention country, or a country which has entered into a bilateral treaty with the United Kingdom after reciprocal protection was extended to that country by Order in Council, then the work will have enjoyed copyright protection in the United Kingdom.

   (iii) Even if the work was created by a citizen or resident of a Berne or Universal Copyright Convention country before reciprocal protection was extended to that country, then the work may still have been in copyright. This is because both Conventions require retrospective protection for unpublished works.[59] Thus such a work will have enjoyed copyright protection in the United Kingdom, unless the

---

[57] See *Barker v Hulton* (1912) 28 T.L.R. 496 and *Nordisk Films Co. Ltd v Onda* [1917–23] Macg. C.C. 337, respectively.

[58] Fine Arts Copyright Act 1862, s.1.

[59] Berne Convention for the Protection of Literary and Artistic Works, Art.18(1); Universal Copyright Convention, Art.VII. It would, of course, be possible for the United Kingdom to enter into a bilateral treaty which did not extend retrospective protection to unpublished works.

term of copyright had already expired.[60] In the latter case no copyright will ever have subsisted in the work and it seems that the publication right may not be available.

(c) If the work was created *before* the 1911 Act came into force then attention should be paid to the following:

    (i) If the work was a literary work created by a foreign author then it seems that the work enjoyed copyright under the 1911 Act, irrespective of whether the country of origin enjoyed copyright relations with the United Kingdom. This conclusion follows from the effect of section 24 and Schedule 1 of the 1911 Act. The effect of these provisions was to give statutory copyright to any work which enjoyed "common law copyright" protection and which could have obtained statutory copyright on publication. As common law copyright probably subsisted in foreign works, and foreign authors could probably obtain copyright protection under the 1842 Act by first publishing the work in the United Kingdom (even if resident outside the United Kingdom),[61] it seems that the effect of the 1911 Act was to grant statutory copyright protection to such works.[62]

    (ii) The above rule probably also applies to dramatic and musical works and engravings created before July 1, 1912, and to sculptures created between July 1, 1862 and July 1, 1912.

    (iii) The rule in (i), above, has no application to paintings, drawings and photographs. These works will therefore not have been able to enjoy copyright protection in the United Kingdom, except by virtue of an international agreement.

---

[60] This is most likely to have occurred in relation to artistic works. In addition, however, it should be noted that the Berne and Universal Copyright Conventions allow Member States to restrict the term of protection to that granted in the work's country of origin: Berne Convention for the protection of literary and artistic works, Art.7(8); Universal Copyright Convention (UCC), Art.IV(4). The Berne provision was implemented in the United Kingdom by the Copyright Act 1911, s.29(1)(ii) and by the Order in Council made on June 24, 1912 (S.R. & O. 1912/913) and by the subsequent Order dated March 16, 1933 (S.R. & O. 1933/253). It was maintained under the 1956 Act by the Copyright (International Conventions) Order 1957 (SI 1957/1523), but was cancelled by the Copyright (International Conventions) (Amendment) Order 1958 (SI 1958/1254) so that the normal copyright term applied thereafter to all works. However, the 1958 Order did not revive copyrights. At first this might seem to have important implications for foreign works created prior to the country of origin entering into copyright relations with the United Kingdom, where that country entered into such relations prior to the 1958 Order's coming into force as, for example, foreign unpublished literary, dramatic and musical works and engravings may not have enjoyed perpetual protection. However, it seems that all pre-existing foreign literary, dramatic and musical works and engravings were brought into copyright by the 1911 Act. Thus the above Orders could only have excluded from copyright works made between the coming into force of the 1911 Act and the coming into force of the 1958 Order. As the period between these two pieces of legislation is less than 50 years, these Orders will only act in such a way as to prevent copyright from having subsisted in a work in the United Kingdom where the country of origin provided a term of protection less than that required by the Berne Convention. This is most likely to have occurred in relation to those Universal Copyright Convention Countries which entered into copyright relations with the United Kingdom on September 27, 1957 (for example, Cuba), as a signatory to the UCC. These can provide protection for as short a period as 25 years from registration: UCC, Art.4. Therefore, to take a hypothetical example, if a Cuban author registered (but never published) a literary work in 1920 and at that time Cuba provided a period of protection for 25 years from first registration, it is probable that this work will never have been in copyright in the United Kingdom. However, even this conclusion is open to doubt since both the 1957 and 1958 Orders were repealed in 1964 (Copyright (International Conventions) Order 1964 (SI 1964/690)), and it can be argued that this Order, unlike the 1958 Order, did revive copyrights. Also see *Copinger* (10th ed.), paras 1167–1171, pp.428–430.

[61] See, in particular, the speeches of Lord Westbury and Lord Cairns in *Routledge v Low* (1868) L.R. 3 H.L. 100. It should also be noted that Lord Salisbury gave the President of the United States an assurance in a despatch of June 16, 1891 that a citizen of the United Sates did not have to be resident in the United Kingdom in order to obtain statutory copyright. Also see *Copinger* (4th ed.), pp.91–97. *cf. Jeffreys v Boosey* (1864) H.L.C. 815.

[62] *cf.* Copyright Act 1911, s.1.

(iv) Where the work in question is a painting, drawing or photograph created by a foreign author the following questions should be asked: first, would the work have been eligible for protection had it been created by a British author? (see point (a), above); secondly did the country of origin enjoy copyright relations with the United Kingdom on July 1, 1912? If the answers to these questions are yes, then prima facie the work will have enjoyed copyright protection. However, even if these conditions are satisfied, it is still possible that the work will never have been in copyright, either because the term of copyright in the country of origin had expired, or because there was no copyright protection in the country of origin because of a failure to comply with formalities required by the law in that country.[63]

An alternative way to have implemented the Directive. The preceding paragraphs demonstrate that the requirement of "expiry" of copyright often makes determining whether a work qualifies for the publication right a complex task. It would have been simpler, and might have accorded with the presumed purpose of the new right (that is, to provide an incentive for the publication of works to which the public has not had access) to have made the publication right available irrespective of whether the work has ever enjoyed copyright protection. This might have been achieved simply by saying that unpublished works could benefit from the publication right if the author of the work had died 70 or more years previously.[64] 17–27

Expiry of copyright in unpublished works. Although copyright has subsisted in most unpublished works, the publication right is only available on "expiry" thereof. One effect of the requirement of the expiry of copyright is that the publication right is unlikely to be of great significance in the United Kingdom for some time to come.[65] This is because of the dual effect of the changes made as regards unpublished works in the 1988 Act and the other changes to the copyright term introduced to give effect to the Term Directive. Again, a distinction must be drawn between three classes or works: literary, dramatic, musical works and engravings; paintings, drawings and photographs; and sculptures. 17–28

Expiry of copyright in unpublished literary, dramatic, musical works and engravings. Section 17 of the Copyright Act 1911 conferred protection on unpublished literary, dramatic and musical works and engravings for 50 years from the date of any eventual publication. This term for unpublished literary, dramatic and musical works and engravings was retained in 1956 and extended to photographs made on or after June 1, 1957.[66] This meant that there was potential perpetual copyright in these works until publication.[67] The 1988 Act ended this situation by providing that copyright in such unpublished works (unpublished as 17–29

---

[63] See International Copyright Act 1886 (49 & 50 Vict. c.33), s.2(3).

[64] The German Law on Copyright and Neighbouring Rights (Copyright Law) 1965 expressly provides that the publication right applies "to works which have not previously been published and which were never protected within the jurisdiction of this Act, but whose authors have been dead for longer than 70 years": Copyright Act 1965, Art.71(1). The question of whether a work ever enjoyed copyright protection in Germany is therefore irrelevant. Also see *Te Deum* Urteil des Bundesgerichtshofs vom 21 März 1975 Aktz.: I ZR 109/73 (Kammergericht) noted at (1975) GRUR Heft 8 at 447 and see Burrell & Haslam, "The Publication Right: Europe's First Decision" [1998] E.I.P.R. 210.

[65] Also see Williams, "Publication Right" (1997) 15 *International Media Law* 15 at 15–16.

[66] Copyright Act 1956, ss.2(3), 3(4). Under the 1911 Act copyright subsisted in photographs for a term of 50 years from the making of the original negative: Copyright Act 1911, s.21. This term was retained in 1956 for photographs made before June 1, 1957, irrespective of whether the photographs had been published by that date: Copyright Act 1956, Sch.7(2).

[67] See further, para. 6–36, above.

of August 1, 1989) was to be limited to a fixed period of 50 years from January 1, 1990, *i.e.* until December 31, 2039.[68] For some works unpublished on August 1, 1989 the relevant copyright will have been extended by the increase in the term of copyright to life and 70 years.[69] For example, if an author died in 1985 leaving unpublished copyright manuscripts (which remained unpublished on August 1, 1989), the effect of the changes made by the 1988 Act was that copyright was to last until the end of 2039. However, as a result of the increase in the duration of copyright to life plus 70 years, copyright will be extended to 2055. However, if an author died in 1940 and his works were unpublished on August 1, 1989, the extension would have no effect and the relevant date remains December 31, 2039.[70] The effect of these transitional provisions is, therefore, such that the operation of the publication right is currently restricted to unpublished artistic works (other than engravings).

17–30 Expiry of copyright in unpublished paintings, drawings and photographs. As indicated, paintings, drawings and photographs, in contrast, may well be the subject of the publication right immediately. If such a work was protected under the 1862 Act, it would have received no additional protection under the 1911 Act if copyright under the 1862 Act had expired (that is, if the author died before July 1, 1905).[71] If copyright under the 1862 Act had not expired then such works were protected as if the 1911 Act had been in force at the date of their creation.[72] In relation to unpublished artistic works (including sculptures) created after the coming into force of the 1911 Act, the term of copyright was to be the same as for published works, *i.e.* the life of the author and 50 years thereafter.

17–31 Expiry of copyright in unpublished sculptures and works of artistic craftsmanship. Unpublished sculptures and works of artistic craftsmanship were protected under the Copyright Act 1911 for an author's life plus 50 years. These periods were extended under the Duration of Copyright and Rights in Performances Regulations 1995. It will therefore be possible to establish publication right where a sculpture is first published after December 1, 1996 and that sculpture was created by a sculptor who died after July 1, 1862 but more than 70 years prior to publication. Similarly, publication right will exist where an unpublished work of artistic craftsmanship created after July 1, 1912 is first published after December 1, 1996 and that work was created by a craftsman who died more than 70 years prior to publication.

17–32 Examples of application of the publication right. The above points are perhaps best illustrated by examples:

First, an unpublished literary, dramatic or musical work created by a British author after the 1911 Act came into force. In these cases it is clear that the publication right can arise as soon as copyright expires. Thus if someone were to discover an unpublished literary work created in 1915 by T.E. Lawrence (who died in 1935), he could communicate this to the public and gain the benefit of the publication right as soon as copyright expires. However, because of the

---

[68] CDPA 1988, Sch.1, para.12(4).

[69] See further, para. 6–42, above.

[70] This appears to be the effect of reg.16(c) of the Duration of Copyright and Rights in Performances Regulations 1995, although Sch.1, para.12 of the 1988 Act has not been amended.

[71] The term of protection under the Fine Arts Copyright Act 1862 was the life of the author and seven years thereafter. Thus copyright would have expired under the 1862 Act if the author died before July 1, 1905. It should also be noted that copyright could lapse under the 1862 Act prior to the expiry of the full copyright term. In particular, copyright would lapse on transfer of the property in the physical embodiment of the work, unless copyright was expressly reserved to one of the parties: *ibid.*, s.1. A different rule applied in relation to commissioned works.

[72] Copyright Act 1911, s.24, Sch.1.

transitional provisions relating to the term of copyright in unpublished works, copyright in such a work will not expire until December 31, 2039.

Secondly, an unpublished literary, dramatic or musical work created by a British author before July 1, 1912. Such a work may or may not have been eligible for statutory copyright protection at the time of its creation. This might, therefore, seem to require the complex examination of the history of any particular work to be undertaken. However, as has been seen, the effect of section 24 of the Copyright Act 1911 would seem to be such that copyright was vested in all unpublished literary, dramatic and musical works, irrespective of the date of their creation.[73] Thus if someone were to discover an unpublished play by Shakespeare (who died in 1616), it seems that they could potentially gain the benefit of the publication right, but again because of the effect of the transitional provisions of the 1988 Act, not until December 31, 2039.

Thirdly, an unpublished artistic work (other than an engraving) produced in 1913 by Welsh painter Gwen John (who died in 1939). As the copyright in this work will have expired at the end of 1989, but then will have been revived for a further 20 years, the publication right will be available at the end of 2009. **17–33**

Fourthly, an unpublished drawing made in 1875 by Dante Gabriel Rosetti (who died in 1882). Such a work attracted copyright under the 1862 Act, and copyright expired in 1889. Therefore, publication right would arise were the drawing to be published after December 1, 1996.[74]

Fifthly, an unpublished painting created by J.M.W. Turner in 1840. Since Turner died in 1851, such a painting never attracted copyright under the Fine Arts Copyright Act 1862. It therefore seems that no publication right will arise on publication of this work.[75]

Sixthly, unpublished scores created by Austrian composer, Wolfgang Amadeus Mozart (who died in 1791). These attracted common law copyright, and, as a result of section 17 of the 1911 Act, this was converted into a copyright for 50 years from publication. In turn, the 1988 Act imposed a fixed period of 50 years from January 1, 1990. Publication right will therefore be available if the scores are first published after December 31, 2039.[76] **17–34**

Seventhly, a painting by Edward Degas (a Frenchman) who died in 1917. The work will have been protected by copyright as a result of France being a signatory to the Berne Convention.[77] Copyright will have lapsed in 1967, and publication after December 1, 1996 would give rise to the publication right.[78]

Eighthly, an unpublished painting by Spanish artist Francisco Jose de Goya y Lucientes (who died in 1828). Since such a work would not have received copyright protection in the United Kingdom,[79] it seems that publication would not give rise to the publication right.

Ninthly, an unpublished painting by American artist John Singer Sargent (who

---

[73] Copyright Act 1911, s.24, Sch.1.

[74] However, had the unpublished drawing been registered under the Fine Arts Copyright Act 1862, the question of whether registration amounted to publication would arise, see para. 17–25, n.54, above.

[75] But see para. 17–20, above.

[76] See para. 17–29, above.

[77] But also, prior to that, under bilateral arrangements made under the International Copyright Act 1844 (7 & 8 Vict. c.12).

[78] Just such a scenario appeared to have occurred when it was revealed that Degas' *Danseuses* had been located. However, that work had been previously exhibited in 1924 so that the work was not "previously unpublished". See *Guardian*, August 23, 1997.

[79] See para. 17–26, above, and see the example referring to J.M.W. Turner in para. 17–33, above.

died in 1925). Since the United States had a specific arrangement with the United Kingdom, this attracted copyright which expired in 1975.[80]

17–35 **Additional consequences.** The requirement of expiry of copyright, considered above, may also act as a disincentive to publish works in the last 25 years of the copyright term. This is because a publisher will be able to obtain a longer period of protection by waiting until copyright has lapsed and relying on the publication right.[81] This effect seems to undermine the assumed purpose of the publication right, which is to encourage and reward the bringing into the public sphere works not as yet available.[82]

Moreover, the transitional provisions may have important implications for the European single market. It seems that far from helping to create a single market for copyright works, in the short term the publication right may actually serve to create barriers to trade within Europe. This is because different countries have different transitional provisions relating to the term of copyright. As a result, it might be possible for a publisher to acquire United Kingdom publication right protection for a work which is still protected by copyright in another Member State. Bearing in mind the underlying rationale of the Term Directive, this seems to be a highly undesirable result.[83]

E. QUALIFICATION

17–36 A work qualifies for publication right protection only if first publication is in the European Economic Area and the publisher of the work is at the time of first publication a national of an EEA State.[84] The meaning of publication has already been considered.[85] Where two or more persons jointly publish the work, it is sufficient if any of them is a national of an EEA State.[86] In contrast with Articles 1 and 3 of the Term Directive, details as to qualification are not explicitly provided in relation to the publication right.[87] It is therefore possible that some Member States might make the right available in broader circumstances. That would clearly be undesirable. Interestingly, no provision is made to allow for the possible extension of the terms of regulation 16(4) allowing recognition of the rights of foreign publishers, where the country of publication provides reciprocal rights to publishers in the EEA.[88]

---

[80] See further, paras 3–225 et seq., above.

[81] It is a strange consequence of the Directive that provisions in German law designed to avoid such an undesirable situation have had to be repealed in order to implement the Directive. See, as originally enacted, German Law on Copyright and Neighbouring Rights (Copyright Law) 1965, Art.64(2). This provision was repealed by the Amendment of June 23, 1995, BGBl. I of June 29, 1995, p.842. See further, Nimmer and Geller (eds), *International Copyright Law and Practice* (Matthew Bender & Co, New York, 1996), pp.GER36, GER128-GER129.

[82] Indirectly, the right might also encourage and reward researchers who locate valuable works in archives.

[83] See Council Directive 93/98 harmonising the term of protection of copyright and certain related rights, recital 2.

[84] Copyright and Related Rights Regulations 1996, reg.16(4).

[85] See para. 17–04, above.

[86] reg.16(4). Compare CDPA 1988, s.154(3).

[87] Contrast Council Directive 93/98 harmonising the term of protection of copyright and certain related rights, Art.7.

[88] Contrast CDPA 1988, s.159. Council Directive on the legal protection of databases, Art.11(3).

4. OWNERSHIP

As noted above, the first publisher of a previously unpublished work will be the first owner of the publication right.[89] In line with the extended definition given to "publication" in this context, the first publisher of the work will be the person who first makes the work available to the public and, in particular, will include the person who first issues copies to the public; makes the work available by means of an electronic retrieval system; rents or lends copies to the public; performs, exhibits or shows the work in public; or communicates the work to the public.

The effect of these provisions would seem to be that the owner of unpublished material in which copyright has expired must think carefully before allowing others to make use of the work. For example, if the owner of an unpublished painting were to lend the work to a museum or gallery in order that it might be exhibited, then prima facie it will be the museum or gallery which will be the first owner of the publication right.[90]

5. THE NATURE OF THE RIGHT

Introduction. The publication right is a property right equivalent to copyright.[91] The publisher, however, does not get the benefit of any moral rights.[92] Otherwise, the substantive provisions of Part I of the 1988 Act relating to copyright (that is, rights of the copyright owner, acts permitted in relation to copyright works, dealings with rights in copyright works, remedies for infringement, and licensing) apply in relation to the publication right as in relation to copyright.[93] Moreover, except where the context otherwise requires, any other enactment relating to copyright, whether made before or after the Regulations, applies in relation to publication right as in relation to copyright.[94]

However, there are a number of exceptions and modifications.

Permitted acts. As regards permitted acts, while Chapter III of Part I of the 1988 Act applies in general, regulation 17(2) declares that four sections have no application to the publication right. The first is section 57 which concerns acts permitted in relation to anonymous works. This exclusion may affect the publication right in two ways. First, in assessing whether copyright has expired for the purposes of acquisition of the publication right, a publisher is unable to rely on the assumption that copyright has expired. Secondly, and more significantly, a person cannot rely on the assumption that copyright has lapsed in an underlying work to justify infringement of the publisher's right. To permit the use of such a defence in relation to the publisher's right would clearly undermine the whole effect of the publication right. The exception provided by section 66A (acts permitted on assumption as to expiry of copyright in films) is excluded for the same reason.

The other permitted acts excluded by regulation 17 appear to be of no great significance and are excluded as a housekeeping exercise. Thus section 64 (which allows an artist to repeat aspects of his or her earlier work) is excluded, as this section could have no application since the artist will in all cases have been dead

17–37

17–38

17–39

---

[89] Copyright and Related Rights Regulations 1996, reg.16(1).
[90] Also see Williams, "Publication Right" (1997) 15 *International Media Law* 15 at 15-16.
[91] Copyright and Related Rights Regulations 1996, reg.16(1).
[92] reg.17(1).
[93] reg.17(1).
[94] reg.17(5). In this context "enactment" is defined as including an enactment contained in subordinate legislation within the meaning of the Interpretation Act 1978.

for a considerable number of years. Similarly, section 67 (which permits the playing of sound recordings at clubs) is excluded because the publication right does not arise in relation to sound recordings.

17–40 **Civil remedies**. The provisions of Chapter VI of the 1988 Act apply, so that the standard remedies for copyright infringement are available for infringement of publication right,[95] including the provisions relating to additional damages.[96] However, sections 104 to 106 of the 1988 Act, which establish various presumptions, are excluded.[97]

17–41 **Criminal liability**. Sections 107(4) and (5) of the 1988 Act, which concern criminal penalties, are modified in certain circumstances, so that the severity of the punishments is reduced. More specifically, a person convicted of an offence in relation to the publication right faces a maximum punishment on summary conviction of imprisonment for a term not exceeding three months, or a fine not exceeding level 5 on the standard scale, or both.[98] This can be contrasted with the usual criminal penalties, which on summary conviction, are imprisonment for a term not exceeding six months and a variable fine (depending on the precise nature of the offence).[99] The maximum penalty on indictment is imprisonment for a term not exceeding ten years, or a fine, or both.[1]

17–42 **Licensing and the Copyright Tribunal**. In general the provisions of Chapters VII and VIII concerning the licensing and the Copyright Tribunal apply. Consequently, the exploitation of publication right is subject to the same controls as the exploitation of copyright, and thus the actions of licensing bodies are open to possible review. However a number of minor modifications have been made to these provisions. Thus section 116(4) is expressly removed. That provision, which is considered in detail elsewhere,[2] excludes certain situations from the general provisions applying to licensing schemes, so that collective works and works made by employees of a single company do not fall within references to licences or licensing schemes covering works of more than one author. Further modifications are made to sections 116(2), 117 and 124, which relate to review by the copyright tribunal of licensing schemes, so that in relation to the publication right, the words "works of more than one author" are substituted by "works of more than one publisher".

17–43 **Miscellaneous modifications**. Regulation 17(4) further provides that other relevant provisions of Part I apply, with any necessary adaptations, for the purposes of "supplementing the substantive provisions of that part as applied by the Regulations." The provisions are those:

(a) in Chapter I, defining expressions used in Part I,

(b) in Chapter IX, sections 161 (territorial waters and the continental shelf) and 162 (British ships aircraft and hovercraft), and

(c) in Chapter X, sections 171(1) and (3) (savings for other rules of law, etc.), and sections 172 to 179 (general interpretation provisions).

---

[95] In particular, note CDPA 1988, s.96(2), "In an action for infringement of copyright all such relief by way of damages, injunctions, accounts or otherwise is available to the plaintiff as in respect of any other property right." More generally, see ss.96–102 and see paras 22–113 *et seq.*, below.

[96] See s.97(2).

[97] Copyright and Related Rights Regulations 1996, reg.17(2)(b).

[98] reg.17(3)(a).

[99] See further, para. 23–17, below. The reason for the difference is that the offence was created by a provision made under the European Communities Act 1972, Sch.2, para.1(1)(d) of which provides that this is the maximum penalty on summary trial for offences created this way.

[1] CDPA 1988, s.107, as amended by the Copyright, etc. Act 2002.

[2] See para. 29–107, below.

Duration. Publication right expires at the end of the period of 25 years from the   **17–44**
end of the calendar year in which the work was first published.[3]

6. TRANSITIONAL PROVISION AND PRE-EXISTING COPIES

Pre-existing copies. Neither the Regulations nor the Directive deals with the   **17–45**
question of pre-existing copies, that is to say,they do not deal with the issue of
whether the publication right extends to control the use of copies made prior to
the publication right coming into existence. Once the publication right arises, is
the issue of pre-existing copies to the public an infringement? There are, in fact,
two related issues here: first, what is the position where a copy of a work has
been made prior to December 1, 1996 (*i.e.* before the Regulations came into
force) and second, what is the position where a person makes a copy of an unpublished work which is subsequently communicated to the public by someone else.
The first issue is essentially a matter for transitional arrangements, the second is a
matter of policy.

Transitional provisions. Regulation 25 defines "new right" as a "right arising by   **17–46**
virtue of these Regulations, in relation to a copyright work … to authorise or prohibit an act", and probably therefore includes the publication right. Regulation
27(2) explains that no act done in pursuance of an agreement made before
November 19, 1992 shall be regarded as an infringement of any new right.
Regulation 34 states that "any new right in relation to a copyright work does not
apply to a copy of the work acquired by a person before commencement for the
purpose of renting or lending it to the public". Apart from these two provisions,
there is no saving for pre-existing copies analogous to the provisions protecting
vested interests where copyright is revived by virtue of the Duration Regulations[4]
or when copyright "springs" into existence when a country becomes a party to
the Berne Union.[5] This may be an oversight on the part of the Government, but
not one that a court is likely to rectify. Consequently, it seems that any copies
made prior to December 1, 1996 may not be issued to the public without the
consent of the owner of the publication right.

Pre-existing copies made after December 1, 1996 but prior to publication of   **17–47**
the work. In Germany it has been held that copies that have been produced prior
to the publication of the work may still be used in the course of a public performance without infringing the publication right.[6] The court's reasoning was that
as a purely economic right, the publication right did not extend to control the use
of copies produced in good faith prior to the right coming into existence. Whilst
the goal of harmonisation might suggest that this approach be adopted in the
United Kingdom, the Regulations do not appear to allow for such a solution.

---

[3] Copyright and Related Rights Regulations 1996, reg.16(6). Contrast Council Directive 93/98
harmonising the term of protection of copyright and certain related rights, Arts 4 and 8.
[4] Duration of Copyright and Rights in Performances Regulations (SI 1995/3297), reg.23.
[5] See the Copyright (International Conventions) Order 1979, (SI 1979/1715), Art.6; and Copyright
(Application to Other Countries) Order 1993, (SI 1993/942), Art.7.
[6] *TE DEUM* Urteil des Bundesgerichtshofs vom 21 März 1975 Aktz.: I ZR 109/73 (Kammergericht) noted at (1975) GRUR Heft 8 at 447 and see Burrell & Haslam, "The Publication
Right: Europe's First Decision" [1998] E.I.P.R. 210.

CHAPTER EIGHTEEN

DATABASE RIGHT

Contents   *Para.*
1.   Introduction   18–01
2.   Databases as literary copyright works   18–03
3.   The *sui generis* database right   18–04

1. INTRODUCTION

Overview. The Copyright and Rights in Databases Regs 1997[1] ("the Regula-   **18–01**
tions") implemented in the United Kingdom the provisions of the EC Directive
on the legal protection of databases[2] ("the Directive"). The Regulations created a
sui generis database right which arises where there has been a "substantial investment in obtaining, verifying or presenting of the contents of the database".[3] At
the same time, a new class of literary work, namely a database, was created, but
having a different and almost certainly higher test of originality than for other
works. Thus a database will only be eligible for copyright protection if it is "original" in the sense that "by reason of the selection or arrangement of the contents
of a database" it constitutes the "author's own intellectual creation".[4] Previously
a database would have been eligible for copyright protection as a table or
compilation, provided that the relatively low test of originality applied to literary
works in general, the skill and labour criterion, was satisfied.[5] Now, however,
databases are excluded from the category of literary works consisting of tables or
compilations, and are treated as a separate category of literary works.[6]

Background. In general a database is an organised collection of information or   **18–02**
data, often stored electronically on computer disk, and is arguably comprised of
two parts: the structure and the contents.[7] It is important to note that this
fundamental distinction between structure and contents can be somewhat

---

[1] SI 1997/3032, entered into force January 1, 1998. SI 2003/ 2501. The Copyright and Rights in
Databases (Amendment) Regulations 2003, among other things extends the territorial protection
for databases to include the Isle of Man.

[2] Directive 96/9/EC of March 11, 1996.

[3] Copyright and Rights in Databases Regulations 1997, reg.13(1), implementing part of Art.7(1) of
the Directive. See further para. 18–04, below.

[4] CDPA 1988, s.3A(2) (*cf.* Reg.6 and Art.3(1) of the Directive, which continues "No other criteria
shall be applied to determine their eligibility for that protection."). See para. 3–146. As regards
the Regulations generally, see J. Adams, "'Small Earthquake in Venezuela': The Database
Regulations 1997" [1998] E.I.P.R. 129; and S. Chalton, "The Copyright and Rights in Databases
Regulations 1997: Some Outstanding Issues on Implementation of the Database Directive"
[1998] E.I.P.R. 178; Mark Davison, *The Legal Protection of Databases* (Cambridge University
Press, 2003), ch. 4.

[5] As to which, see paras 3–145 *et seq.*, above.

[6] CDPA 1988, s.3(1) as amended by reg.5(a) of the Copyright and Rights in Databases Regulations
1997, . See para. 3–21 *et seq.*

[7] The vast majority of computer databases are "relational" following the set of 12 rules for database
design originally proposed by Edgar Codd of IBM in the late 1960s. Such databases usually
consist of a series of interrelated tables of data. For example a database containing information
about a company's current customers may contain one table of data consisting of unique customer
numbers and the name of each customer and a separate table consisting of the unique customer
numbers and each customer's telephone number. By combining information from the two tables
by using the common customer numbers it is thus possible to relate each telephone number to

artificial—given a large amount of properly indexed but otherwise unstructured data, it is possible to achieve very similar functionality to a database in which the data stored is more systematically structured; it is nevertheless a distinction which underpins the Directive.[8]

In June 1988, the European Commission produced a Green Paper on copyright and the challenge of technology.[9] One of the issues identified by the Commission as requiring immediate action was the legal protection afforded to databases, defined in that paper as collections of information stored and accessed by electronic means. The Commission solicited views as to whether the selection and arrangement of the compilation within a database composed of works should itself be protected by copyright and whether a database containing material not then protected by copyright should be protected by copyright or a new *sui generis* right. However, it was not until four years later that the Commission published its proposal for a Directive on the legal protection of databases throughout the European Union, with the aim of conferring full copyright protection on databases meeting an originality test and a short term *sui generis* "right to prevent unfair extraction" for databases, whether or not they also qualified for copyright protection.[10]

The recitals to the final form of the Directive explain that the Commission considered databases not to be "sufficiently protected in all Member States by existing legislation" and stated that "such protection, where it exists, has different attributes".[11] The Commission was concerned about the effects of the differing attributes in the legislation of Member States and the negative effect this would have on the "functioning of the internal market".[12] It is notable that the final form of the Directive represents a significant widening of the rights originally proposed in the Green Paper. The Directive, which has been largely incorporated into the Regulations, seeks to remedy the problems outlined by the Commission in the Green Paper through the creation of a two-tier protection for databases.

A database is defined for the purposes of the Directive, the 1988 Act and the Regulation as a "collection of independent works, data or other materials arranged in a systematic or methodical way and individually accessible by electronic or other means".[13] At the outset it is important to note that this definition, unlike that in the initial Green Paper, is not limited to electronic databases and purportedly applies to any such collection whatever its form.[14] On January 1, 1998, the Copyright and Rights in Databases Regulations 1997[15] came into force, altering the copyright protection given to databases by the 1988 Act by incorporating into United Kingdom law the criterion of originality defined in the

---

each customer name. It is also possible, by running "queries" usually written in "Structured Query Language", to obtain selections and arrangements of the raw data that correspond to a particular request. A major benefit of relational databases is their separation between logical design and physical implementation (i.e. the computer servers upon which the database is run and the disks on which the data are stored) and consequently it is usually possible to change the physical implementation without significant software re-coding.

[8] In this context, note Recital 23 of Directive 96/9 which denies protection to the computer programs "used in the making or operation of a database", such programs being otherwise protectable as literary works.

[9] COM(88) 172 final, June 7, 1988.

[10] Original proposal: [1992] O.J. C156/4. The original proposal was for a right with a duration of 10 years.

[11] Directive 96/9, Recital 1.

[12] Directive 96/9, Recital 2, similar points are made in Recitals 3 and 4. See also the discussion in the decision of the Court of Appeal on the rationale for the Directive in *British Horseracing Board Ltd v William Hill Organisation Ltd* [2002] E.C.D.R. 4.

[13] CDPA 1988, s.3A(1), as amended by reg.6 of SI 1997/3032, implementing Art.1(2) of Directive 96/9.

[14] Directive 96/9, Art.1(1).

[15] SI 1997/3032, note that the Regulations have been amended by the Copyright and Rights in

Directive for databases protected as literary copyright works, and creating a new *sui generis* right called "database" right.

2. DATABASES AS LITERARY COPYRIGHT WORKS

Original copyright databases. Copyright databases are treated in detail elsewhere in this work.[16] Generally, however, the criterion of originality for copyright databases set out in the 1988 Act means that a literary work consisting of a database is original, if, and only if, by reason of the selection or arrangement of the contents of the database, it constitutes the author's own intellectual creation.[17] This definition should be read alongside the Directive, which provides that no criterion other than originality in the sense of the author's intellectual creation shall be applied to determine the eligibility of a database for copyright protection, and in particular, no aesthetic or qualitative criteria shall be applied.[18] This is almost certainly a higher standard of originality than that adopted for other other literary works under the 1988 Act and is consistent with other EU harmonisation measures on the criterion of originality.[19] This conclusion is supported by the facts that the Commission felt it necessary to introduce the *sui generis* right in the first place, and that the Commission considered that it had increased the threshold for copyright protection in the Directive.[20] The author of such an original database is the person who creates it, and a natural person.[21] However, many databases are probably computer-generated works, in which case under the 1988 Act the author would be the person by whom the arrangements necessary for the creation of the work are undertaken.[22] The question arises as to whether this is consistent with the requirement that the database constitutes the author's own intellectual creation.[23] The protection of original databases considered to be literary works is governed by the copyright law as laid down in the 1988 Act.

18–03

3. THE *SUI GENERIS* DATABASE RIGHT

Database right. The Regulations create a *sui generis* property right called "database right". The right can subsist whether or not the database or its contents

18–04

Databases (Amendment) Regulations 2003 (SI 2003/2501),which, among other things, extend the territorial protection for databases to include the Isle of Man.

[16] See Ch.3.

[17] CDPA 1988, s.3A(2); see also Recital 39 of Directive 96/9.

[18] Directive 96/9, Recital 15.

[19] No doubt the origin of this approach is Art.2(5) of the Berne Convention, which provides that "collections of literary or artistic works such as encyclopaedias and anthologies which, by reason of the selection and arrangement of their contents, constitute intellectual creations shall be protected as such, without prejudice to the copyright in each of the works forming part of such collections". The same approach was adopted in Directive 91/250/EEC on the legal protection of computer programs, Art.1(3) of which provides that "A computer program shall be protected if it is original in the sense that it is the author's own intellectual creation. No other criteria shall be applied to determine its eligibility for protection".

[20] Recital 60 of Directive 96/9 states that "some Member States currently protect under copyright arrangements databases which do not meet the criteria for eligibility for copyright protection laid down in this Directive ... [the] harmonisation of the criteria for determining whether a database is to be protected by copyright may not have the effect of reducing the term of protection currently enjoyed by the rightholders concerned".

[21] CDPA 1988, s.9(1).

[22] C.D.P.A. 1988, s.9(3).

[23] On this point it should be noted that, given the exclusively economic focus behind the harmonisation of the rights in Directive 96/9, it is strongly arguable that the provisions in the 1988 Act which automatically vest ownership in the hands of the person making the arrangements are compatible. See also Case C-444/02, *Fixtures Marketing Limited v Organismos Prognostikon agonon Podosfairou AE (OPAP)*, decision of the ECJ November 9, 2004, unreported, para.26 which notes that there is no requirement that a database be its maker's own intellectual creation.

is a copyright work,[24] and was apparently created to fill the gap created by raising the threshold for copyright protection with the higher criterion of originality for databases. Since the Directive was implemented into national law, there has been some litigation in the EU in which the precise scope of the *sui generis* rights has been considered.[25] In particular, four of these cases have resulted in decisions being made by the European Court of Justice under Art.234 EC.[26]

Database right will subsist in a database "if there has been a substantial investment in obtaining, veryifying or presenting the contents of the database"[27]

"Substantial" in relation to any investment, means substantial in terms of quantity or quality, or a combination of both.[28]

The investment required for a database to be eligible fir database right is defined as "any investment, whether of financial, human or technical resources"[29]; this definition in the Regulations is in line with Recital 7 of the Directive which states also that the makingof the database requires "investment of considerable human, technical and financial resources".

The ECJ has considered the meaning of the term "substantial investment" in the context of the British Horseracing Board case.[30] The ECJ noted that the purpose of the Directive was to promote and protect investment in data storage and processing systems and it therefore follows that the investment protected refers to that "in the creation of that database as such." Expanding on what that investment relates to, the ECJ concluded that it refers to the resources used to seek out pre-existing independent materials and collate them into the database, but crucially not the resources used for the primary creation of the independent materials themselves[31]. According to Mme Stix-Hackl, the Advocate General in the case, relevant factors in assessing substantiality include the scale, nature and

---

[24] Copyright and Rights in Databases Regulations 1997, reg.13(2).

[25] Some caution is required in distilling principles from this caselaw because it pre-dates the authoritative rulings of the ECJ on the scope of the Directive. Notable cases include *British Horseracing Board Ltd v William Hill Organisation Ltd* [2001] R.P.C. 31 in which Laddie J. dealt at some length with the nature of the right. On appeal the Court of Appeal ([2002] E.C.D.R. 4), without determining the appeal itself or dealing substantively with the points raised, referred the case to European Court of Justice under Art.234 EC. Other notable cases include *Royal Mail Group Plc (formerly Consignia Plc) v i-CD Publishing (UK) Ltd* [2004] EWHC 286, unreported, which concerned the licensing of mailing list databases; *France Telecom MA v MA Editions Sarl* [2001] E.C.C. 4, and *Re Unauthorised Reproduction of Telephone Directories on CD ROM* [2002] E.C.D.R. 3, in both of which it was held that unauthorised extraction from electronic telephone directory databases was prohibited; *Sietech Hearing Ltd v Borland* [2003] E.C.D.R. 26; *Danske Dagblades Forening (DDF) v Newsbooster* [2003] E.C.D.R. 5, and *Algemeen Dagblad BV v Eureka Internetdiensten* [2002] E.C.D.R. 1, both of which concerned alleged database rights in connection with internet news headlines; *Noir d'Irvoire SPRL v Home Boutiques Private Ltd Co SPRL* [2003] E.C.D.R. 29, in which palettes of colours were held not to constitute databases ; *Hit Bit Software GmbH v AOL Bertelsmann Online GmbH* [2001] E.C.D.R. 18, in which MIDI music files on AOL's website were held not to constitute databases; *Sociéteé Tigrest Sarl v Société Reed Expositions France* [2002] E.C.C. 29, [2003] E.C.D.R. 20, in which a catalogue of trade exhibitors was held to constitute a database; and *Nederlandse Omroep Stichting v Holdingmaatschappij de Telegraaf NV* [2002] E.C.D.R. 8, in which a compilation of television programme schedules in a newspaper was held not to entail any substantial investment and was thus held not to constitute a protectable database.

[26] Each of these referred cases relates to databases protecting sporting information: Case C-203/02, *The British Horseracing Board Ltd v William Hill Organisation Ltd*, unreported; Case C-46/02, *Fixtures Marketing Ltd v Oy Veikkaus AB*, unreported; Case C-444/02, *Fixtures Marketing Ltd v Organismos prognostikon agonon podosfairou (OPAP)*, unreported; Case C-338/02, *Fixtures Marketing Ltd v Svenska Spel AB*, unreported.

[27] Reg.13(1), implementing Art.7 of the Directive.

[28] Reg.12(1).

[29] Reg.12(1).

[30] Case C-203/02, *The British Horseracing Board Limited v William Hill Organisation Limited*, decision of the ECJ November 9, 2004, unreported.

[31] Case C-203/02, *The British Horseracing Board Limited v William Hill Organisation Limited*, decision of the ECJ, November 9, 2004, unreported, paras. 30-1.

contents of the database and the commercial sector to which it relates.[32] The ECJ noted that "investment in the creation of a database may consist in the deployment of human, financial or technical resources... the quantitative assessment refers to quantifiable resources and the qualitative assessment to efforts which cannot be quantified, such as intellectual effort or energy"[33]

As noted above, the *sui generis* right subsists where there has been investment in "obtaining", "verifying" or "presenting" a database. "Verification" must be understood, according to the ECJ, as referring to the resources used with a view to ensuring the accuracy of the information contained in a database by monitoring the accuracy of the materials collected when the database was created and during its operation.[34]. Given that the investment relating to the creation of the materials themselves is not protectable under the *sui generis* right, "verification" activities relating to the "stage of creation of data or other materials which are subsequently collected in a database" may not therefore be taken into account.[35] "Obtaining", on the other hand, relates to the resources used to seek out existing independent materials and collecting them into the database. It does not cover the resources used for the creation of the materials making up the contents of a database.[36] The investment in "presenting" the contents of a database relates to the resources used for the purpose of giving the database its function of processing information, as the ECJ put it "those used for the systematic or methodological arrangement of the materials contained in that database and the organisation of their individual accessibility."[37]

It is submitted that this theoretical distinction between "pre-existant" data and acts relating to the creation of a database may be difficult to discern in practice.[38] Indeed the ECJ itself notes that, where the creation of a database is linked to the creation of the materials in the database, there is nothing to preclude the sui generis right where it can be shown that there was substantial investment in the creation of the database which "was independent of the resources used to create those materials".[39] Further it is noted in a rather Delphic conclusion that, although the creator of the data in a database may not require particular resources to verify data because they were created by him, "the fact remains that the collection of those data, their systematic or methodological arrangement in the database, the organisation of their individual accessibility and the verification of

---

[32] Also relevant is Recital 40 to the Directive ("such investment may consist of the implementation of financial resources and/or the expending of time, effort and energy"). See Case C-338/02, *Fixtures Marketing Limited v Svenska Spel AB,* , AG Opinion unreported, paras 34–46.

[33] Case C-444/02, *Fixtures Marketing Limited v Organismos prognostikon agonon podosfairou AE(OPAP)*, decision of the ECJ, November 9, 2004, unreported, para 44. Identical text can be found in Case C-46/02, *Fixtures Marketing Limited v Oy Veikkaus Ab*, decision of the ECJ, November 9, 2004, unreported, para.38.

[34] Case C-203/02, *The British Horseracing Board Limited v William Hill Organisation Limited*, decision of the ECJ, November 9, 2004, unreported, paras. 34, 42.

[35] Case C-203/02, *The British Horseracing Board Limited v William Hill Organisation Limited*, decision of the ECJ,November 9, 2004, unreported, paras. 34, 42.

[36] Case C-203/02, *The British Horseracing Board Limited v William Hill Organisation Limited*, decision of the ECJ, November 9, 2004, unreported, para.42.

[37] Case C-338/02, *Fixtures Marketing Limited v Svenska Spel AB*, decision of the ECJ, 9 November 2004, unreported, para.27.

[38] Indeed it is likely that the distinction adopted by the ECJ will lead to wide variations in the scope of protection afforded to databases in different member states as national courts grapple with the problem of determining principles guiding the assessment of which data is pre-existent.

[39] Case C-203/02, *The British Horseracing Board Limited v William Hill Organisation Limited*, decision of the ECJ, November 9, 2004, unreported, para.35.

their accuracy throughout the operation of the database may require substantial investment"[40].

Thankfully the ECJ go-on to consider the facts of the case (a questionable extension of their jurisdiction under Article 234 EC)[41] and concluded that certain aspects of the British Horseracing Board's investment were not protectable under the *sui generis* right. In particular investment relating to the selection of the horses admitted to run in a race was held to concern the creation of the data which makes up the lists in the database and thus could not be taken into account.[42] Similarly checking the credentials of a potential entrant in a race (including checks on the identity of the person making the entry, the characteristics of the horse, its owner and the jockey) were also considered investment in the creation of the data and not the verification of the contents of the database.[43] These factual conclusions are important, even though they are only provisional, because the application of the theoretical distinction relied upon by the ECJ appears to be applied robustly with the result that the ambit of the sui generis right is significantly narrower than was previously assumed in litigation before the national courts of the EU member states.

A similar result was reached in the Fixtures Marketing cases which concerned the exploitation of English and Scottish football fixtures lists. Here it was concluded that the resources deployed for arranging the dates and times and identities of home and away teams were an investment in the creation of the fixtures list itself and, as it was related to the original data, could not be taken into account in assessing the scope of protection under the *sui generis* right.[44] Furthermore it was noted by the ECJ that collecting data making up a football fixtures list does not require any particular effort on the part of the professional leagues, and thus no independent investment was provided which led to a protectable database right[45] Nor was any particular effort expended in verifying the accuracy of data on league matches when the list is drawn up since the leagues are directly involved in the creation of the relevant data. Finally no substantial investment occurred in the presentation of a football fixtures list as it was too closely linked to the creation of the data as such.[46]

In the light of these robust judgments it might appear that sporting fixtures are unprotectable by means of *sui generis* database right on the basis that no sufficient investment will be made in the database *per se*. It would be wrong,

---

[40] Case C-203/02, *The British Horseracing Board Limited v William Hill Organisation Limited*, decision of the ECJ, November 9, 2004, unreported, para.36.

[41] See, for example, the decision of Laddie J. in *Arsenal Football Club v Matthew Reed (No.2)* [2003] E.T.M.R. 36). It is notable that the ECJ's findings of fact in these cases are often expressed to be provisional and determined from the facts supplied by the national court in the order for a reference under Article 234 EC. This acknowledgement arguably addresses some of the criticisms levied by Laddie J. in the Arsenal case. It should be noted, however, that findings of fact are a matter for the national courts and a resolution of this matter will not be forthcoming until the Court of Appeal gives judgment in British Horseracing Board case. Indeed it is likely that the British Horseracing Board will argue that their activities did properly constitute investments in obtaining and verification of data notwithstanding the ECJ's preliminary views.

[42] Case C-203/02, *The British Horseracing Board Limited v William Hill Organisation Limited*, decision of the ECJ, November 9, 2004, unreported, para.38.

[43] Case C-203/02, *The British Horseracing Board Limited v William Hill Organisation Limited*, decision of the ECJ, November 9, 2004, unreported, paras. 39-40.

[44] Case C-338/02, *Fixtures Marketing Limited v Svenska Spel AB*, decision of the ECJ, November 9, 2004, unreported, para.31.

[45] Case C-338/02, *Fixtures Marketing Limited v Svenska Spel AB*, decision of the ECJ, November 9, 2004, unreported, para.33.

[46] Case C-338/02, *Fixtures Marketing Limited v Svenska Spel AB*, decision of the ECJ, November 9, 2004, unreported, para.34-35. Case C-444/02, *Fixtures Marketing Limited v Organismos prognostikon agonon podosfairou AE(OPAP)*, decision of the ECJ, November 9, 2004, unreported, para.47f. Case C-46/02, *Fixtures Marketing Limited v Oy Veikkaus Ab*, decision of the ECJ, November 9, 2004, unreported, para.44f.

however, to conclude that sporting fixtures (or, for example, television listings) can no longer be protected in principle. The consequence of the ECJ's decision in those cases is that some unusual element of investment must be provided when the pre-existing data is assembled into a database in order for it to be protectable. It may well be possible, therefore, for enhanced investment in more sophisticated presentation of the data in the database by means of the compilation of enhanced indexing, for example, to satisfy the requirements for protection.

It was an objective of the Directive to give copyright protection to the structure of the database and database right protection both to the contents and the structure of the database.[47] The Commission has tried to meet this objective through separating the rights that can subsist in a database and applying two types of protection to the two parts of a database.[48] However, it is not clear whether the Regulations actually achieve those objectives.

The Regulations enable a database to gain protection either through copyright or a database right, or both, although they fail to state that any copyright subsisting in the structure will not extend to the contents and is without prejudice to any other rights subsisting in the contents. The definition of "a database" was adopted from the Directive verbatim in the Regulations.[49] This definition in the Regulations may lead to problems because a situation could arise where the contents will not be protected by copyright, not being "original", but the structure will be, by being "original". The Regulations do not appear to provide for this but such a distinction between the contents of a database and the selection or arrangement of the contents of a database is made in the Directive.[50] This distinction was discussed in the Consultative Paper on United Kingdom Implementation[51] but was not carried over into the Regulations, although the Regulations state that they "make provision for the purpose of implementing" the Directive.[52]

Definition of database. The Regulations define a database as a collection of independent works, data or other materials which are arranged in a systematic or methodical way, and are individually accessible by electronic or other means.[53] As already noted, this definition should be considered alongside the Directive and its recitals, which provide[54] that a database should be understood to include literary, artistic, musical or other collections of works, or collections of other material such as texts, sound, images, numbers, facts, and data and cover also collections of independent works, data or other materials which are systematically or methodically arranged and can be individually accessed. The Directive and Recitals also make it clear that certain types of works were specifically excluded from protection as a database; for example, computer programs used in the making or operation of databases accessible by electronic means, and recordings or audiovisual, cinematographic, literary or musical works as such, do not fall within the scope of the Directive.[55] It is also stated that "as a rule, the compilation of several recordings of musical performances on a CD[56] does not come within the scope of this Directive, both because, as a compilation, it does not meet the conditions for copyright protection and because it does not represent a substantial

18–05

---

[47] Directive 96/9, Recitals 15 and 58 and Arts 3(2) and 7(1).

[48] Whilst not being inconsistent with the other objectives of the Directive as well.

[49] CDPA 1988, s.3A(1) and Directive 96/9, Art.1.

[50] Directive 96/9, Art.3(2).

[51] "Consultative Paper on United Kingdom Implementation" dated August 1997, para.4.2.

[52] Copyright and Rights in Databases Regulations 1997, reg.2.

[53] Copyright and Rights in Databases Regulations 1997, reg.6. This definition is taken directly from Art.1 of Directive 96/9.

[54] Recital 17.

[55] Directive 96/9, Art.1(3) and Recitals 17 and 23.

[56] Despite compilations of musical performances on CD being excluded from protection, electronic

enough investment to be eligible under the *sui generis* right".[57] . The ECJ in the *Fixtures Marketing v Organismos prognostikon agonon podosfairou*case[58] explicitly noted that the fact that the information in the database related to sporting fixtures does not preclude that database from *sui generis* protection.[59] Furthermore, "it is irrelevant whether the collection is made up of materials from a source or sources other than the person who constitutes that collection, materials created by that person himself or materials falling within both those categories."[60] The materials in question must be "independent" materials which are "separable from one another" and consequently it is not possible for an audiovisual, cinematographic, literary or musical work to constitute a database[61] However, there is nothing in the Directive which requires a database to be its maker's own intellectual creation as such and the criterion of originality is only relevant to the question of whether copyright protection applies.[62] Classification of a collection as a protectable database requires systematic or methodological arrangement and individual accessibility. The ECJ noted that "While it is not necessary for the systematic or methodological arrangement to be physically apparent... that condition implies that the collection should be maintained in a fixed base, of some sort, and include technical means such as electronic, electromagnetic or electro-optical processes..., or other means, such as an index, a table of contents, or a particular plan or method of classification, to allow the retrieval of any independent material contained within it."[63] In short, what makes a protectable database different from a mere collection of materials is a means of retrieving each of its constituent materials individually from the collection. The arrangement of those data in the form of a fixtures list of the dates, times and names of teams in various football matches meets the conditions as to systematic or methodological arrangement and individual accessibility. The fact that lots are drawn to decide the pairing of teams was held not diminish that conclusion.[64] In the Fixtures Marketing cases, the date, time of, and identity of the two teams playing in football matches were held by the ECJ to constitute independent materials "in that they have autonomous informative value".[65] Indeed the ECJ noted that "although it is true that the interest of a football league lies in the overall result of the various matches in that league, the fact remains that the data concerning the date, the time and the identity of the teams in a particular match have an independent value in that they provide interested third parties with relevant information."[66] Consequently the compilation of dates, times and names of teams relating to various fixtures in a football league is a collection of indepen-

---

databases may include devices such as CD-ROM, CD-I and presumably DVD, pursuant to Recital 22 of Directive 96/9.

[57] Recital 19.

[58] Case C-444/02, decision of the ECJ November 9, 2004.

[59] Case C-444/02, *Fixtures Marketing Limited v Organismos prognostikon agonon podosfairou AE(OPAP)*, decision of the ECJ, November 9, 2004, unreported, para.23.

[60] Case C-444/02, *Fixtures Marketing Limited v Organismos prognostikon agonon podosfairou AE(OPAP)*, decision of the ECJ, November 9, 2004, unreported, para.25.

[61] Directive, 17th Recital. See also Case C-444/02, *Fixtures Marketing Limited v Organismos prognostikon agonon podosfairou AE(OPAP)*, decision of the ECJ, November 9, 2004, unreported, para.29.

[62] Case C-444/02, *Fixtures Marketing Limited v Organismos prognostikon agonon podosfairou AE(OPAP)*, decision of the ECJ, November 9, 2004, unreported, para.26.

[63] Case C-444/02, *Fixtures Marketing Limited v Organismos prognostikon agonon podosfairou AE(OPAP)*, decision of the ECJ, November 9, 2004, unreported, para.30.

[64] Case C-444/02, *Fixtures Marketing Limited v Organismos prognostikon agonon podosfairou AE(OPAP)*, decision of the ECJ, November 9, 2004, unreported, para.35.

[65] Case C-444/02, *Fixtures Marketing Limited v Organismos prognostikon agonon podosfairou AE(OPAP)*, decision of the ECJ, November 9, 2004, unreported, para.33.

[66] Case C-444/02, *Fixtures Marketing Limited v Organismos prognostikon agonon podosfairou AE(OPAP)*, decision of the ECJ, November 9, 2004, unreported, para.34.

dent materials.[67]. It would thus appear that the ECJ has adopted a very wide approach to what may constitute a database and that, aside from compilations in which the individual elements are related such as a film, establishing the required individual accessibility is a relatively low hurdle for the owner of the database to establish. One question that arises from the definition in the Regulations is whether databases other than electronic databases are covered, despite the clear guidance in the Directive that they should be. This issue turns on the meaning of "or other means". If the meaning is confined to "or other analogous means", then the Regulations cover electronic databases only and other databases such as paper databases will only be eligible for protection under copyright as a table or compilation.[68] If "or other means" is not so confined, then other databases such as paper databases will be eligible for database right. The Regulations themselves make no mention of the scope of databases that are intended to be covered and no definition is given for the meaning of "other means". Recital 14 of the Directive states that "the Directive should be extended to cover non-electronic databases" and thus it seems clear that it was the express intention of the Directive that databases other than electronic ones should be eligible for database right. It is submitted that the Regulations, therefore, cover non-electronic databases. However, if this interpretation is correct, then the requirement that the works or data be individually accessible becomes difficult to interpret.

This difficulty can be illustrated as follows: an indexed newspaper will arguably satisfy the requirements for a non-electronic database by being a collection of independent works arranged in a systematic way. Each independent work will be individually accessible by the reader as he is able to discern and discriminate with his eye one work over any other work. If this sort of individual accessibility is sufficient to yield a database right, then the threshold of this part of the criteria will be easily crossed.

It can be seen from the above illustration that problems could arise if newspapers were paper databases and therefore only eligible for copyright protection if they met the higher test for originality. It is submitted that, if the Regulations do include non-electronic databases, the new test for originality will have a much wider application than could have been intended.

Qualification for the right. Following reg. 18(1), database right does not subsist **18–06** in a database unless, at the material time, its maker, or if jointly, one or more of its makers, was:

(a) an individual who was a national of an EEA state or habitually resident within the EEA state;

(b) a body incorporated under the law of an EEA state and which, at that time, satisfied one of the conditions in subsection (2);

(c) a partnership or other unincorporated body which was formed under the law of an EEA state and which, at that time, satisfied the condition in subsection 2(a); or

(d) the analogous persons (an individual, body, partnership or unincorporated body) within the Isle of Man.[69]

The conditions in subsection (2) that are required to be satisfied for subsection 1(b) and (c) above are:

(a) that the body has its central administration or principal place of business within the EEA; or

[67] Case C-444/02, *Fixtures Marketing Limited v Organismos prognostikon agonon podosfairou AE(OPAP)*, decision of the ECJ, November 9, 2004, unreported, para.35.
[68] See para. 3–144, above.
[69] Copyright and Rights in Databases Regulations 1997, reg.18(1)(d)–(f) introduced by the Copyright and Rights in Databases (Amendment) Regulations 2003, SI 2003/2501, reg.5.

(b) that the body has its registered office within the EEA and the body's operations are linked on an ongoing basis with the economy of an EEA state.[70]

As to "foreign" databases, recital 56 of the Directive states in effect that the
maker of a database will not qualify for a database right in situations other than
those provided for under reg. 18 unless the country of which the maker of the
database is a national or where the maker is habitually resident "offers comparable protection to nationals of a Member State or those who have their habitual
residence in the territory of the Community", *i.e.* the Directive is based in this
regard on the principle of material reciprocity and protection will only be given
to non-EEA nationals on a reciprocal basis. It follows that in relation to a foreign
database, it may qualify for copyright protection but not for database right
protection. This may prove to be an important distinction in relation, for example,
to United States databases.[71]

18–07   **First ownership.** The maker of a database is the first owner of the database right
in it.[72] Pursuant to reg.14(1), the "person who takes the initiative in obtaining,
verifying or presenting the contents of a database and assumes the risks of investing in that obtaining, verification or presentation shall be regarded as the maker
of, and as having made, the database". Under reg.14(2) where "the database is
made by an employee in the course of his employment, his employer shall be
regarded as the maker of, and has having made, the database, subject to any
agreement to the contrary". The provision for databases created in the course of
employment is similar in effect, if not in form, to the provisions for copyright
works as provided for in the 1988 Act[73] and so presumably the case law that applies to the corresponding provision in the 1988 Act regarding this criteria will
apply to databases.[74] Whether an individual is an employee as opposed to an independent contractor and, if the individual is an employee, whether the database
was made in the course of his employment, will be determined in much the same
way as with copyright works.[75] While the Regulations make no provision for
joint ownership, they do provide for joint makers of a database. Regulation 14(5)
states that "a database is made jointly if two or more persons acting together in
collaboration take the initiative in obtaining, verifying or presenting the contents
of the database and assume the risk of investing in that obtaining, verification or
presentation". Clearly, therefore, there may be joint first owners of database
right.

Where a database is made by Her Majesty or by an officer or servant of the
Crown in the course of his duties, Her Majesty is to be regarded as the maker of
the database.[76] Where the database is made by, or under the direction or control
of the House of Commons or the House of Lords, the House by whom, or under
whose direction or control, the database is made is to be regarded as the maker of
the database.[77] If made by or under the direction or control of both Houses, then
the two Houses are to be regarded as joint makers of the database.[78] Where a
database is made by or under the direction or control of the Scottish Parliament,

---

[70] reg.18, reg.18(2A) applies similar requirements to qualification for the Isle of Man, although notably the link is made to the economy of the Isle of Man exclusively rather than the EEA as a
whole.
[71] In the long run, this problem is likely to be solved by an international instrument on the protection of databases by means of a system of *sui generis* protection.
[72] Copyright and Rights in Databases Regulations 1997, reg.15.
[73] CDPA 1988, s.11(2).
[74] See paras 5–12 *et seq.*, above.
[75] See paras 5–08 *et seq.*, above.
[76] Reg.14(3).
[77] Reg.14(4).
[78] Reg.14(4)(6)

the Scottish Parliamentary Corporate Body is to be regarded as the maker of the database.[79]

Transmission. The provisions in the 1988 Act governing transmission of copy-right are incorporated into the Regulations.[80]   **18–08**

Duration of right. *Prima facie*, database right subsists until the end of the period   **18–09**
of 15 years from the end of the calendar year in which the making of the database
was completed.[81] If, however, the database is made available to the public within
that 15-year period, the term of database right will expire 15 years from the date
when it was first so made available.[82] It follows that making a database available
to the public within the original 15-year term will result in the clock being re-set
and a 15 year term starting again.

If any substantial change is made to the contents of a database, including a
substantial change resulting from the accumulation of successive additions, deletions or alterations, which results in the database being considered to be a
substantial new investment, this will lead to the database resulting from that
investment having its own, new term of protection. Regulation 12 defines "investment" as including any investment, whether of financial, human or technical
resources. Article 10(3) of the Directive indicates that "substantial change"
should be evaluated "qualitatively and quantitatively". Some further guidance is
provided in the recitals to the Directive. Recital 54 states that the "burden of
proof that the criteria exist for concluding that a substantial modification of the
contents of a database is to be regarded as a substantial new investment lies with
the maker of the database resulting from such investment". Furthermore, Recital
55 states that a substantial new investment "may include a substantial verification
of the contents of the database".

In the *British Horseracing Board* case, the question issue arose as to whether
every "substantial change" made to a database resulted in a new protectable
database being created each time. This issue was not considered by the ECJ in its
judgment, however, A.G. Stix-Hackl noted that databases which are constantly
updated are "dynamic" in the sense that there is only ever one database and that
previous versions "disappear" as new data is added to it. She identified the basic
principle to be applied in determining whether the term of protection is extended
is to consider the objective of the changes, that is, to ask whether they are done to
bring the database up to date with the aim that the whole database is the object of
the new investment concerned. The consequence of this is, as A.G. Stix-Hackl
terms it, that dynamic databases enjoy a "rolling sui generis right" in which the
whole database, and not just the changes as such, enjoy a new term of protection.
Moreover, given that changes may be made to a database which, although
insubstantial when taken individually, may be sufficient to amount to a substantial
change when taken together, it will not be difficult to secure effectively unlimited
protection on a rolling right.[83] This approach is broadly consistent with that
adopted by Laddie J. at first instance.[84]

Given that the approach adopted by the ECJ was to distinguish investment in

---

[79] Reg.4A, introduced into the Regulations by SI 1999/1042.
[80] Copyright and Rights in Databases Regulations 1997, reg.23 states that ss.90–93 of the CDPA
1988 apply; see also paras 5–63 *et seq.*, above.
[81] Copyright and Rights in Databases Regulations 1997, reg.17(1). *Cf.* Directive 96/9, Art.10.
[82] Reg.17(2).
[83] Case C-203/02, *The British Horseracing Board Ltd v William Hill Organisation Ltd*, Opinion of
A.G. Stix-Hackl, paras 149–155.
[84] See *The British Horseracing Board Ltd v William Hill Organisation Ltd* [2001] R.P.C. 31, this
approach it is submitted, fails to give proper effect to Art.10(3) of Directive 96/9 which refers to
any "substantial" change, including any which would result in the database being considered to

the constituent data of the database from that of creating the database *per se*,[85]it is arguable that substantial reorganisations of the presentation of a database will be sufficient to afford an extended term of protection. To obtain a "rolling right" the investment must relate to the database *per se* rather than merely acquiring more data.

18–10   Infringement. A person will be held to infringe database right in a database if, without the consent of the owner of the right, he extracts or re-utilises all or a substantial part of its contents.[86] One interesting argument that has been advanced in connection with the scope of the *sui generis* right concerns the so-called "spin-off theory". The argument essentially runs as follows: the purpose of harmonising the law of databases through the Directive was to provide European incentives for investment by protecting that investment made in connection with preparing commercial databases; the purpose of protecting those investments is to ensure that the profits may be repaid from the principal activity for which the money was invested. Thus it is arguable that the Directive should not protect "spin-off" uses of a database which were not related to the investment creating it. This argument was made in several of the *Fixtures Marketing* cases at the European Court of Justice on the basis that the investment in the databases in issue in the proceedings was necessary for the organisation of sporting bets and not for the protection of the database *per se*—the investment would have been made in any event and the database was merely a by-product on another market. This argument was largely, and it is submitted correctly, rejected by A.G. Stix-Hackl on the grounds that there is no suggestion from the Directive that the protection for a database depends on its purpose.[87]Although no addressed explicitly by the ECJ in its judgments, the approach adopted to narrowing the scope of the investment that can be taken into consideration would appear to support a rejection of the spin-off theory.[88]

An additional form of infringement occurs where the repeated and systematic extraction or re-utilisation of insubstantial parts of the contents of a database amounts to the extraction or re-utilisation of a substantial part of those contents. An example of a situation where permission should be sought from the rightholder is given in Recital 44 of the Directive. It states: "when on-screen display of the contents of a database necessitates the permanent or temporary transfer of all or a substantial part of such contents to another medium, that act should be subject to authorisation by the rightholder."

18–11   Extraction and re-utilisation. The restricted acts are "extraction and re-utilisation". In relation to the contents of a database, "extraction" means the permanent or temporary transfer of those contents to another medium by any means

be a "substantial new investment". In British Horseracing Board itself, the database was considered as a single database by all the witnesses, and it would have been impossible and unreal to split it into a number of discrete units. Laddie J. dealt with this problem by concluding that "This does not render Art 10(3) meaningless. First it emphasises that the term keeps being renewed as the database is renewed. Secondly it makes clear that if someone takes an existing database and adds significantly to it, he obtains protection for the database incorporating his additions. This would be so even if the new author is not the same as the author of the original database." Nevertheless, this does not deal with the core point. It is suggested that the right approach, which is essentially the one which Laddie J. took, is to give the repeated extraction provisions of Art.7(5) of the Directive a purposive construction and treat them as applying to a dynamic database as much as a static one.

[85] See para. 18–04, above.
[86] The acts that infringe a database right are provided for in reg.16 of the Copyright and Rights in Databases Regulations 1997.
[87] Case C-338/02, *Fixtures Marketing Ltd v Svenska Spel AB*, Opinion of A.G.Stix-Hakl unreported, paras 42–46. See also E.Derclaye, "Databases *Sui Generis* Right: should we adopt the spin-off theory" [2004] E.I.P.R.402.
[88] See para. 18–04, above.

or in any form, and "re-utilisation" means making those contents available to the public by any means.[89] This definition should be read in the context of Article 7 of the Directive which provides that "re-utilisation" means any form of making available to the public "all or a substantial part of the contents of the database by the distribution of copies, by renting, by on-line or other forms of transmission". In relation to the various infringing acts, A.G. Stix-Hackl legitimately notes that there is potentially an error in the drafting of the Directive—the definition of "extraction" in Article 7(2)(a) requires "all or or a substantial part" and yet Article 7(5) refers to the "repeated and systematic extraction and/or re-utilization of insubstantial parts...".

One of the issues which arose in the British Horseracing Board case was whether William Hill's activities constituted acts of extraction or re-utilisation under Art. 7 of the Directive. The ECJ emphasised that the rights to prevent extraction and re-utilisation must be construed in the context of the wider objectives of the sui generis right, namely the protection of the investment of the maker of the database.[90]. Consequently it concluded that it is not relevant whether or not the act of extraction or re-utilisation is for the purpose of creating another database (whether in competition with the original database or not, of a different size, or part of wider activities)[91]. Moreover, given that the term "for commercial purposes" which had been included in the original proposal for the Directive had been dropped, the ECJ concluded that it was irrelevant whether the act in question was done for a commercial or non-commercial purpose[92]. In connection with the question of whether it was possible to infringe by means of using derived works, the ECJ concluded that there is no requirement for extraction and re-utilisation to be taken directly from the original database. Doing so would leave the maker of the database with no reasonable protection from unauthorised copying.[93] Moreover, given that unauthorised extraction and re-utilisation by a third party from a source other than the database are capable of prejudicing the maker's protected investment, there is no general requirement that extraction and re-utilisation must result from direct access to the protected database.[94] Although this would appear to significantly widen the scope of protection to include downstream derived works, mere "consultation" of a database would appear from the ECJ's judgment to have a subtly different status. Unfortunately the ECJ do not proffer an explanation of the circumstances where "consultation" drifts into "extraction". It would appear that "consultation" is intimately related to controlling access of a database - the ECJ concludes that the maker of a database can reserve access to himself or specific people. However, if the owner makes the database or part of it accessible to the public the sui generis right does not prevent third parties from "consulting" that database.[95] The same limitation applies where the owner of a database authorises a third party to re-utilise the contents of the

[89] Reg.12 of the Copyright and Rights in Databases Regulations 1997.
[90] Case C-203/02, *The British Horseracing Board Limited v William Hill Organisation Limited*, decision of the ECJ, November 9, 2004, unreported, para.45.
[91] Case C-203/02, *The British Horseracing Board Limited v William Hill Organisation Limited*, decision of the ECJ, November 9, 2004, unreported, para.47.
[92] Case C-203/02, *The British Horseracing Board Limited v William Hill Organisation Limited*, decision of the ECJ, November 9, 2004, unreported, para.48.
[93] Case C-203/02, *The British Horseracing Board Limited v William Hill Organisation Limited*, decision of the ECJ, November 9, 2004, unreported, para.52.
[94] Case C-203/02, *The British Horseracing Board Limited v William Hill Organisation Limited*, decision of the ECJ, November 9, 2004, unreported, para.53.
[95] Case C-203/02, *The British Horseracing Board Limited v William Hill Organisation Limited*, decision of the ECJ, November 9, 2004, unreported, paras. 54-5.

database "in other words, to distribute it to the public."[96] The ECJ reiterated that, according to the definition of re-utilisation in Art. 7(2)(b) of the Directive, when read in conjunction with the 41st recital, the authorisation of the maker for the re-utilisation of the database or a substantial part thereof implies that he consents to his database being made accessible to the public by the third party to whom he gave that authorisation.[97] However, the fact that a database can be consulted by third parties through someone who has authorisation for a re-utilisation from the maker of the database does not prevent that maker from recovering the costs of his investment. The ECJ concluded that "it is legitimate for the maker to charge a fee for the re-utilisation of the whole or a part of his database which reflects, inter alia, the prospect of subsequent consultation and thus guarantees him a sufficient return".[98]. Of course, the *sui generis* right does not, however, prevent a lawful user from extracting and re-utilising insubstantial parts of the contents of a database. In summary, any acts of extraction ("the transfer of the contents of the database to another medium") and acts of re-utilisation ("the making available to the public of the contents of a database") which affect the whole or a substantial part of the protected database require the authorisation of the maker, even where the database has been made accessible to public either directly or through a third party intermediary.[99] In the British Horseracing Board case the information displayed by William Hill was derived first from newspapers published before the races and subsequently from the "raw data feed" supplied by a third party. Both of these sources had their ultimate origin in the British Horseracing Board's database and the ECJ concluded in another potentially questionable finding of fact that William Hill carries out acts of extraction and re-utilisation which potentially constitute infringements subject to the requirement of substantiality.[1] Data which originated in the British Horseracing Board database was extracted by being transferred from one medium to another, and secondly William Hill re-utilised data by making it available to the public on its internet site to enable its clients to bet on horses. In summary there is no requirement for extraction and re-utilisation to be directly from the protected database and the fact that a database has been made available to the public does not mean that the maker can no longer enforce his *sui generis* right.[2]

As far as the prohibition on repeated acts of "extraction" or "re-utilisation" in Article 7(5) of the Directive is concerned, A.G. Stix-Hackl considered the provisions of Article 9 of the Berne Convention and Article 13 of the TRIPs agreement and concluded that they could not be applied as a guide to understanding the scope of Article 7(5).[3] In relation to "repeated and systematic extraction", A.G. Stix-Hackl noted that it is not entirely clear whether the two requirements are alternative or cumulative, as some language versions of the Directive link the requirements with "and" and others with "or". The majority of the language versions link the requirement with "and", which led her to conclude that they are to

---

[96] Case C-203/02, *The British Horseracing Board Limited v William Hill Organisation Limited*, decision of the ECJ, November 9, 2004, unreported, para.56.

[97] Case C-203/02, *The British Horseracing Board Limited v William Hill Organisation Limited*, decision of the ECJ, November 9, 2004, unreported, para.56.

[98] Case C-203/02, *The British Horseracing Board Limited v William Hill Organisation Limited*, decision of the ECJ, November 9, 2004, unreported, para.56.

[99] Case C-203/02, *The British Horseracing Board Limited v William Hill Organisation Limited*, decision of the ECJ, November 9, 2004, unreported, para.61.

[1] See para. 18–12below.

[2] Case C-203/02, *The British Horseracing Board Limited v William Hill Organisation Limited*, decision of the ECJ, November 9, 2004, unreported, paras. 65-67.

[3] Case C-338/02, *Fixtures Marketing Ltd v Svenska Spel AB*, Advocate General's Opinion, unreported, paras 111–116.

be understood cumulatively, as in the English text.[4] The conclusion she reached was that there was a repeated and systematic act when it is carried out at regular intervals, for example, weekly or monthly.

The ECJ reiterated that the general rule set out in Article 8(1) and the 42nd Recital to the Directive is that the maker of a database cannot prevent a lawful user of that database from extracting or re-utilising insubstantial parts of the database. Art. 7(5) should therefore be properly construed as an exception to that general rule.[5] "The provision therefore prohibits acts of extraction made by users of the database which, because of their repeated and systematic character, would lead to the reconstitution of the database as a whole or, at the very least, of a substantial part of it..."[6] Similarly "acts which conflict with the normal exploitation of [a] database or which unreasonably prejudice the legitimate interests of the maker of the database" refer to unauthorised actions "for the purpose of reconstituting, through the cumulative effect of acts of extraction, the whole or a substantial part of the contents of a database...".[7] The ECJ held that William Hill's acts took place on the occasion of each race held and were therefore repeated and systematic but only concerned insubstantial parts of the protected database. However, because William Hill's acts were not intended to circumvent to prohibition laid down in Art. 7(1), there is no possibility that William Hill might reconstitute the whole or a substantial part of the protected database and thus no infringement.[8]

Substantiality. If a database right subsists in an electronic database, then   **18–12**
downloading a substantial part of that database without authorisation from the owner of database right will amount to an infringement. Furthermore, even if a single item or value is not in itself of sufficient qualitative importance, such that its isolated downloading will not amount to infringement, its repeated and systematic downloading may be an infringement. "Substantial", in relation to any extraction or re-utilisation, means substantial in terms of quantity or quality or a combination of both.[9]

In connection with the meanings of the terms "substantial part" and "insubstantial part", the ECJ in the British Horseracing Board case confirmed that a quantitative assessment is made by comparing the volume of data extracted from the database and/or re-utilised with the volume of the contents of the whole of the database.[10]. The qualitative assessment refers to the scale of the investment in the obtaining, verification or presentation of the contents forming the subject of the extraction and/or reutilisation regardless of whether those contents are quantitatively significant relative to the whole.[11] The ECJ noted that "a quantitatively negligible part of the contents of a database may in fact represent, in terms of obtaining, verification or presentation, significant human, technical or financial

---

[4] Case C-203/02, *The British Horseracing Board Ltd v William Hill Organisation Ltd*, Advocate General's Opinion, unreported, para.39.

[5] Case C-203/02, *The British Horseracing Board Limited v William Hill Organisation Limited*, decision of the ECJ, November 9, 2004, unreported, para.84.

[6] Case C-203/02, *The British Horseracing Board Limited v William Hill Organisation Limited*, decision of the ECJ, November 9, 2004, unreported, para.87.

[7] Case C-203/02, *The British Horseracing Board Limited v William Hill Organisation Limited*, decision of the ECJ, November 9, 2004, unreported, para.89.

[8] Case C-203/02, *The British Horseracing Board Limited v William Hill Organisation Limited*, decision of the ECJ, November 9, 2004, unreported, paras. 91-92.

[9] Reg.12(1) of the Copyright and Rights in Databases Regulations 1997.

[10] Case C-203/02, *The British Horseracing Board Limited v William Hill Organisation Limited*, decision of the ECJ, November 9, 2004, unreported, para.70.

[11] Case C-203/02, *The British Horseracing Board Limited v William Hill Organisation Limited*, decision of the ECJ, November 9, 2004, unreported, para.82.

investment."[12] However, since the *sui generis* right does not affect the works, data or materials in the database, the intrinsic value of the data concerned is not a relevant criterion for making the qualitative assessment.[13].

Again, in a provisional finding of fact, the ECJ on examination of the facts of the British Horseracing Board case noted that the acts related to only a very small proportion of the whole of the database and consequently did not constitute a substantial part when evaluated quantitatively.[14]. William Hill had only used the names of the horses in the relevant race, the date, time and name of the race and the name of the racecourse. The correct test for assessing whether this was a substantial part evaluated qualitatively was to examine whether the human, technical and financial efforts put in by the maker of the database in obtaining, verifying and presenting those data constituted a substantial investment. Despite the argument that without the lists of horses running in races those races could not take place and the data are thus vital to the organisation of horse races, the ECJ reiterated that the intrinsic value of the data affected is not a relevant criterion in the assessment.[15]. Moreover, given that the resources used for the creation of the data as such are also irrelevant to the assessment,[16] the materials extracted and re-utilised by William Hill were held not to require an independent investment to that required for their creation and consequently did not constitute a substantial part in qualitative terms.[17]

18–13 **Restrictions on contractual terms affecting lawful users.** Any contractual term that purports to narrow or exclude the rights of extraction and re-utilisation of a lawful user of a database or a part of a database will be void.[18] "Lawful user", in relation to a database, means any person who (whether under a licence to do any of the acts restricted by any database right in the database or otherwise) has a right to use the database.[19]

18–14 **Permitted acts.** The Regulations permit a number of acts which would otherwise be an infringement of database right.[20] Regulation 20(1) contains a fair dealing defence,[21] which provides that database right in a database which has been made available to the public in any manner is not infringed by fair dealing with a substantial part of its contents if:

(a) that part is extracted from the database by a person who is, apart from this provision, a "lawful user of the database";

(b) it is extracted for the purpose of illustration for teaching or research and not for any commercial purpose; and

(c) the source is indicated.

This exception relates to the restricted act of "extraction" only. "Re-utilisation" for these purposes is not permitted, presumably because the permitted act does not encompass making the database available to the public.

---

[12] Case C-203/02, *The British Horseracing Board Limited v William Hill Organisation Limited*, decision of the ECJ, November 9, 2004, unreported, para.71.

[13] Case C-203/02, *The British Horseracing Board Limited v William Hill Organisation Limited*, decision of the ECJ, November 9, 2004, unreported, para.72/

[14] Case C-203/02, *The British Horseracing Board Limited v William Hill Organisation Limited*, decision of the ECJ, November 9, 2004, unreported, para.74.

[15] Case C-203/02, *The British Horseracing Board Limited v William Hill Organisation Limited*, decision of the ECJ, November 9, 2004, unreported, para.77-78.

[16] Case C-203/02, *The British Horseracing Board Limited v William Hill Organisation Limited*, decision of the ECJ, November 9, 2004, unreported, paras. 31-33, 79.

[17] Case C-203/02, *The British Horseracing Board Limited v William Hill Organisation Limited*, decision of the ECJ, November 9, 2004, unreported, para.80.

[18] Reg.19(2) of the Copyright and Rights in Databases Regulations 1997.

[19] Reg.12(1).

[20] These are permitted by Art. 6 of Directive 96/9.

[21] For the permitted acts of fair dealing in relation to copyright works, see para.9–00 *et seq.*

Schedule 1 to the Regulations provides for further exceptions to database right,[22] these exceptions relating generally to public administration. Regulation 20A(1) also provides that database right is not infringed by the copying of a work from the internet by a deposit library[23] or a person acting on its behalf where its publication on the internet, or a person publishing it there, is connected with the United Kingdom.[24] There are no exceptions to infringement relating to criticism, review and news reporting,[25] and no other exceptions for libraries and archives.[26] Generally, the Directive, and thus regulation 20, provide for far fewer exceptions to infringement of database right than the equivalent provisions of the 1988 Act relating to copyright works, and the exceptions which are created are narrower.

Permitted acts on assumption of expiry of the right. Database right is not   **18–15** infringed by the extraction or re-utilisation of a substantial part of the contents of a database at a time when, or in pursuance of arrangements made at a time when:

   (a) it is not possible by reasonable inquiry to ascertain the identity of the maker; and

   (b) it is reasonable to assume that database right has expired.[27]

Statutory presumptions. The Regulations contain two presumptions which are   **18–16** relevant in proceedings to determine who is the maker of a database. First, where the name purporting to be that of the maker appears on copies of the database as published, or on the database when it was made, the person whose name appears is to be presumed, until the contrary is proved:[28]

   (a) to be the maker of the database; and

   (b) to have made it in circumstances not falling within Regulations 14(2) to (4).

Regulations 14(2) and 14(4) refer to situations where the database was made by an employee, or by Her Majesty or by an officer or servant of the Crown, or under the direction or control of the House of Commons or the House of Lords. Consequently, if this presumption applies, the named person shall be presumed to be the maker of it and thus the first owner.

Secondly, where copies of the database as published bear a label or a mark stating:

   (a) that a named person was the maker of the database; or

   (b) that the database was first published in a specified year,

the label or mark shall be admissible as evidence of the the facts stated and shall be presumed to be correct until the contrary is proved.[29] The above presumptions apply in relation to each person alleged to be one of the makers.[30]

Remedies. The remedies available to a database owner for infringement of   **18–17** database right are the same as the civil remedies as provided under the 1988 Act

---

[22] See reg.20(2) of the Copyright and Rights in Databases Regulations 1997.

[23] "Deposit libraries" have the same meaning as in s.7 of the Legal Deposit Libraries Act 2003, see reg.20(4)(b). For permitted acts in relation to copyright and Deposit Libraries, see para.9–00 *et seq.* For Deposit Libraries generally, see para. 27–80 *et seq.*

[24] Reg.20A(1)(b) inserted by the Legal Deposit Libraries Act 2003, s.8(2) in force from February, 2004. Further provisions, including reg.20A(2), provide that no database infringement occurs in relation to any of the permitted activities under s.7 of the 2003 Act.

[25] Cf. CDPA 1988, s.30.

[26] Cf. ss.37–44.

[27] Reg.21 of the Copyright and Rights in Databases Regulations 1997.

[28] Reg.22(2) of the Copyright and Rights in Databases Regulations 1997.

[29] Reg.22(3).

[30] Reg.22(4).

for infringement of copyright,[31] except that there is no entitlement to delivery up for seizure of infringing copies.[32]It should be noted that flagrancy damages are available for infringement of database right, and that right and remedies equivalent to those available to exclusive licensees under copyright are available to exclusive licensees of database right.[33]There are no criminal offences created under the Regulations.

18–18   **Licensing schemes.** Regulations 24 and 25 refer to Schedule 2 to the Regulations and provide for licensing schemes operated by licensing bodies with respect to the licensing of database right to be referred to the Copyright Tribunal.[34]

18–19   **Transitional provisions and the retrospective effect of database right.** It should be noted that nothing in the Regulations affects any agreement made before the commencement of the Regulations on January 1, 1998.[35] No act done before commencement, or, after commencement in pursuance of an agreement made before commencement, shall be regarded as an infringement of database right in a database.[36] The Regulations also deal with databases in existence prior to commencement of the Regulations. Regulation 29(1) provides that, where a database was created on or before March 27, 1996, and was a copyright work immediately before commencement, copyright shall continue to subsist in the database for the remainder of its copyright term under the 1988 Act.[37] Databases up to 15 years old also qualify for database right: regulation 30 states that, where the making of a database was completed on or after January 1, 1983, and on commencement of the Regulations database right began to subsist in the database, then database right shall subsist in the database for the period of 15 years beginning on January 1, 1998.

---

[31] See Chapter 22, below.

[32] This is because reg.23 of the Copyright and Rights in Databases Regulations 1997 states that CPDA 1988 ss.96–98, regarding rights and remedies, apply to database right but that CPDA 1988 ss.99 and 100, regarding delivery up and seizure, are excluded.

[33] See reg.23 applying CPDA 1988, ss.121 and 102. CDPA 1988 s.97(2) which applies by virtue of reg.23.

[34] See paras 3–8 of Sch.2. Note that new provisions have been provided in para.15 of Sch.2 relating to the powers of the Competition Commission and the Enterprise Act 2002—see SI 2003/1398.

[35] Reg.28(1) of the Copyright and Rights in Databases Regulations 1997, Reg.28 was amended by the Copyright and Rights in Databases (Amendment) Regulations 2003, SI 2003/2501, reg.8.

[36] Reg.28(3), reg.28(4) provides similar savings in respect of those acts relating to Isle of Man databases protected from November 1, 2003.

[37] Note also the provisions of Recital 60 to Directive 96/9 which relate to the higher standard of originality for the copyright protection of databases and provide that "[the] harmonisation of the criteria for determining whether a database is to be protected by copyright may not have the effect of reducing the term of protection currently enjoyed by the rightholders concerned".

CHAPTER NINETEEN

PUBLIC LENDING RIGHT

Contents   *Para.*

1. PUBLIC LENDING RIGHT ACT 1979

Public lending right. After a long and chequered career a public lending right   **19–01**
Bill became law in 1979. The Public Lending Right Act 1979[1] was, however,
something of a misnomer. That is to say, although the object of the Act is to
provide payments to authors out of a central fund, the "right" is not part of the
author's copyright and is only conferred on authors if their books are lent to the
public by local library authorities in the United Kingdom.[2] Books which are not
lent do not qualify under the public lending right scheme; this will, no doubt, be
the case for many books of reference, whilst certain categories of books, *e.g.*
books of music, do not fall within the Scheme at all.

The right to control lending. The underlying position changed as a result of the   **19–02**
implementation of the Rental Rights Directive.[3] article 1 of the Directive requires
Member States to provide a right to authorise or prohibit the rental and lending of
copies of copyright works, whilst provision is made in article 5 for derogation
from that exclusive right in respect of public lending, provided that authors
receive remuneration for such lending. These provisions were implemented by
sections 18A and 40A of the 1988 Act respectively.[4] Section 18A sets out the
general principle applicable to most categories of copyright works, namely that
lending copies of a work is an act restricted by the copyright in that work.[5] The
exception to that general rule permitted by article 5 of the Directive is provided
by section 40A.[6] Thus, subsection 40A(1) provides that copyright in a work of
any description is not infringed by the lending of a book by a public library if the
book is within the public lending right scheme. Subsection 40A(1)(a) confirms
that the reference to "the public lending right scheme" means the scheme in force
under the Public Lending Right Act 1979. Subsection 40A(1)(b) seeks to define
those books which are within the public lending right scheme for the purpose of
section 40A(1), as "a book within the meaning of the provisions of the scheme
relating to eligibility, whether or not it is in fact eligible". The most natural meaning of this elliptical phrase is that the book must be a book of the type described
in article 6 or 6A of the Scheme, but need not be a book whose author is or whose

---

[1] See Vol.2 at B3.i. The Act extends to Northern Ireland and came into force on March 1, 1980 (SI
1980/83); and see the Transfer of Functions (Acts, Libraries and National Heritage) Order 1986
(SI 1986/600).

[2] Public Lending Right Act 1979, s.1(1).

[3] Council Directive 92/100 on rental and lending right and on certain rights related to copyright in
the field of intellectual property ([1992] O.J. L346/61); and see Ch.7, above, and Vol.2 at H3.

[4] Added by The Copyright and Related Rights Regulations 1996 (SI 1996/2967), regs 10(2) and
11(2), respectively.

[5] See para. 7–81, above, for a detailed discussion of CDPA 1988, s.18A.

[6] See, similarly, the provisions of CDPA 1988, s.66 relating to the compulsory licensing of lending
of literary, dramatic, musical, or artistic works, sound recordings or films and see Ch.29, below.

authors are eligible authors within the meaning of article 5 or 5A of the Scheme.[7] Alternatively, the definition may be intended to refer to books which would be eligible for registration, in terms of both the nature of the book and the eligibility of the author, but which have not been registered.[8] The difficulty is that if the former construction of the subsection is correct, then books written or illustrated by non-eligible authors lose the protection of section 18A without the potential compensation of receiving income under the public lending right scheme. If this is right, section 40A(1) does not comply in full with the provisions of article 5.1 of the Rental Rights Directive.[9]

19–03   **The Scheme**. To become eligible for a payment under the public lending right scheme, the book must be registered.[10] It is only when the Registrar of Public Lending Right has determined, in accordance with the Scheme, the sum (if any) due by way of public lending right in the case of any registered book, that the author obtains any effective right since only then is he able to recover such sums from the Registrar as a debt due.[11] The basic fund is a fixed sum for each financial year, which has from time to time been increased, and from which administration expenses and so on are to be paid,[12] so that the annual sum received by any one author is always likely to be small, as has proved to be the case in the past. Further, as such sums are dependent upon the number of times a book is lent,[13] popular authors benefit more than the less popular. Another factor which could reduce the sum per author is the fact that the Act applies to all authors, not just United Kingdom authors, so that foreign authors are also entitled to benefit under the Act unless excluded by the Scheme.[14] The right under the Scheme is to last from the date of the book's first publication (or, if later, the beginning of the year in which application is made for it to be registered) until 70 years have elapsed since the end of the year in which the author died.[15]

19–04   **Administration of public lending right**. Most of the important matters relating to the administration of the public lending right are not contained in the 1979 Act but are provided for by a scheme[16] which may be varied from time to time.[17]

Matters to be covered by the Scheme are:

(a) Classes, descriptions and categories of books in respect of which public lending right subsists.[18]

(b) Scales of payments to be made from the central fund in respect of public lending right.[19]

(c) The establishment and maintenance of a register of books in respect of which public lending right subsists and the persons entitled to the right in

---

[7] See paras 19–10, et seq., below.

[8] See paras 19–14 et seq., below.

[9] Public Lending Right Act 1979, s.40A(2) deals with lending otherwise than by a public library. See para. 7–16, above.

[10] Public Lending Right Act 1979, s.1(7) and s.4.

[11] s.1(5).

[12] s.2. The current fixed sum is £8m: see the Public Lending Right (Increase of Limit) Order 2003 (SI 2003/839). The sum for the financial year beginning April 1, 2003 was £14.252m.

[13] s.3(3).

[14] Such rights are currently limited: see para. 19–10, below.

[15] s.1(6): and see para. 19–15, below. The right initially granted by the Scheme (as specified in s.1(6)) lasted only 50 years from the author's death. The term was extended to 70 years by SI 1997/1576 with effect from July 15, 1997 to bring the term of protection into line with the extended term of copyright brought about by the Duration of Copyright and Rights in Performances Regulations 1995. See Ch.6, above.

[16] Public Lending Right Act 1979, s.3(1). See Vol. 2 at B3.ii for the present Scheme.

[17] s.3(7).

[18] s.1(2).

[19] s.1(2).

respect of any registered book, the register to be conclusive as to subsistence of and entitlement to public lending right.[20]

(d) The making and amendment of entries in the register.[21]

(e) Public lending right is:

    (i) to be established by registration,

    (ii) to be transmissible by assignment or assignation, by testamentary disposition or by operation of law, as personal or movable property,

    (iii) to be claimed by or on behalf of the person for the time being entitled, and

    (iv) to be renounced (either in whole or in part, and either temporarily or for all time) on notice being given to the Registrar of Public Lending Right to that effect.[22]

(f) Public lending right is to be dependent on, and its extent is ascertainable by reference to, the number of occasions on which books are lent out from particular libraries, to be specified by the Scheme or identified in accordance with provision made by it.[23]

(g) Local library authorities are to be required:

    (i) to give information as to loans made by them to the public of books in respect of which public lending right subsists, or of other books, and

    (ii) to arrange for books to be numbered, or otherwise marked or coded, with a view to facilitating the maintenance of the register and the ascertainment and administration of public lending right.[24]

(h) Local authorities will be reimbursed their expenses in giving effect to the Scheme. The amount of such expenditure is to be ascertained in accordance with such calculations as the Scheme may prescribe.[25]

The register. Only books which fall within a class, description or category of books prescribed by the Scheme as one in respect of which public lending right subsists can be registered.[26] An entry on the register is conclusive both as to subsistence of and entitlement to public lending right.[27] Entries on the register are to be made or amended on application made in the manner prescribed by the Scheme and supported by particulars so as to indicate, in the case of any book, who (if anyone) is for the time being entitled to public lending right in respect of it.[28] The Registrar of Public Lending Right may direct the removal from the register of every entry relating to a book in whose case no sum has become due by way of public lending right for a period of at least 10 years, but without prejudice to a subsequent application for the entries to be restored to the register.[29] The Registrar may require the payment of fees, according to scales and rates prescribed by the Scheme, for supplying copies of entries in the register; and a copy of an entry, certified under the hand of the Registrar or one of his officers with authority in

19–05

---

[20] s.1(4) and s.4(3).
[21] s.4(4).
[22] s.1(7).
[23] s.3(3).
[24] s.3(5).
[25] s.3(6).
[26] Public Lending Right Act 1979, s.4(2).
[27] s.4(3).
[28] s.4(4).
[29] s.4(5).

that behalf (which authority it is not necessary to prove) is to be admissible in evidence in all legal proceedings as of equal validity with the original.[30]

19–06   Registrar of public lending right. Public lending right is to be administered by the Registrar of Public Lending Right and his staff,[31] the Registrar being under a duty to establish and maintain the register in accordance with the Scheme and to determine the sums due by way of public lending right.[32] The central fund out of which sums will be paid in respect of public lending right will be under the control of the Registrar.[33]

19–07   Offences. The 1979 Act makes it an offence for any person, in connection with the entry of any matter whatsoever in the register, to make any statement which he knows to be false in a material particular or recklessly to make any statement which is false in a material particular. A person who commits such an offence is liable on summary conviction to a fine of not more than level 5 on the standard scale.[34] Where such an offence has been committed by a body corporate and is proved to have been committed with the consent or connivance of, or to be attributable to any neglect on the part of, a director, manager, secretary or other similar officer of the body corporate, or any person who was purporting to act in such capacity, he (as well as the body corporate) will be guilty of that offence and be liable to be proceeded against accordingly. Where the affairs of a body corporate are managed by its members, this provision applies in relation to the acts and defaults of a member in connection with his functions of management as if he were a director of the body corporate.[35]

2. THE SCHEME

19–08   History of the Scheme. The present Scheme is now found in The Public Lending Right Scheme 1982 (Commencement) Order 1982, as amended from time to time.[36]

19–09   Registration required: eligible books and posthumously eligible books. To be eligible for public lending right, a book must first be a printed and bound publication (this includes a paperback edition) and an application must be made for registration.[37] But not all books are registrable.[38] Thus, for instance, books bearing the name of a body corporate or an unincorporated association as author do not qualify, nor do serial publications such as newspapers, magazines, journals and periodicals, or books which are or are mainly musical scores.[39] No book will now qualify unless it has an ISBN number.[40]

A posthumously eligible book is a book qualifying under article 6 whose author, or one of whose authors, is a posthumously eligible person, and the book is either published within one year before his death or within 10 years after his death, and that person had successfully applied to register for Public Lending

---

[30] s.4(6).

[31] Public Lending Right Act 1979, s.1(3). The Public Lending Right Office is in Stockton-on-Tees.

[32] s.1(4), (5).

[33] s.2.

[34] Public Lending Right Act 1979, s.4(7).

[35] s.4(8).

[36] The Scheme, as amended, is set out in Vol.2 at B3.ii.

[37] Public Lending Right Scheme 1982, arts 9, 10, 14, 14A, 17, 17B and Sch.1.

[38] Arts 6 and 6A.

[39] Art.6(2).

[40] Art.6(2)(g). See the variation made to the Scheme by the Public Lending Right Scheme 1982 (Commencement of Variations) Order 1999 (SI 1999/420).

right during his lifetime, or the book consists of or incorporates a previously registered work.[41]

Eligible persons and posthumously eligible persons. To qualify for registration, the author, or at least one of the authors, must be an eligible person, or a posthumously eligible person. An eligible person must be an author of the book who at the date of the application has his only or principal home in any member State of the European Economic Area, or, if he has no home, has been present in a member State for not less than 12 months out of the preceding 24 months.[42] Under article 5A of the Scheme, in relation to an application relating to a posthumously eligible book, an author who is dead is a posthumously eligible person if, had he been an applicant for first registration of public lending right in relation to that book at the date of his death, he would have been an eligible person in accordance with article 5 of the Scheme.   **19–10**

Authors. Authors are also defined by the Scheme and include writers and translators, as well as editors and compilers who have made a sufficient contribution to the book, and illustrators.[43] Applications after an author's death are possible.[44] Books published up to 10 years after the author's death are also included.[45]   **19–11**

The register. The register has to contain particulars of the title of the book, the name or names of the persons appearing on the title page as the authors thereof, the true identity of an author if different from such name, the number given to the book by the Registrar, the name and address of each person entitled to the right in respect of the book and, if more than one, the share of each such person in such right.[46] Where a book has two or more authors, including any who are not eligible persons, the share of any non-eligible person will not be registered until he becomes and remains an eligible person and makes an application for registration.[47] Only registered owners are entitled to payment.[48] So, where only one of two authors is eligible, he will be paid 50 per cent of the share, with the balance being paid back into the Fund.   **19–12**

Inspection of the register. The right depends on registration,[49] and the register is conclusive as to whether public lending right subsists in a particular book and also as to the persons (if any) who are for the time being entitled to the right.[50] However, the Scheme gives no automatic right for the public to inspect the register.[51] On the contrary, it is provided[52] that the Registrar shall not supply a copy of any entry in the register otherwise than to a registered owner, as regards any entry which relates to his registered interest, or to such other person as the registered owner may direct, but if the entry also relates to other registered own-   **19–13**

---

[41] Art.6A.

[42] Public Lending Right Scheme 1982, Arts 5 and 5A: see Art.5 (which defines "principal home") and Sch.5, as amended by the Public Lending Right Scheme 1982 (Commencement of Variations) Order 2000 (SI 2000/933) and Public Lending Right Scheme 1982 (Commencement of Variations) Order 2004 (SI 2004/1258).

[43] Public Lending Right Scheme 1982, Art.4(1), but subject to art.4(2).

[44] Arts 5A, 6A, 14A and 17B.

[45] Arts 6 and 6A.

[46] Public Lending Right Scheme 1982, Arts 7 and 8 and see Art.9A. The register may be amended: Arts 12 and 13.

[47] Arts 2(1) "eligible author", 9(2), (3), 9A, 14 and 17. As to posthumously eligible persons see Arts 9(4), 9A, 14A and 17B.

[48] Art.47.

[49] Public Lending Right Scheme 1982, Art.10: see Art.2(1) as to "registered interest".

[50] Art.11.

[51] See Public Lending Right Act 1979, s.4(3), (6).

[52] Public Lending Right Scheme 1982, Art.35.

ers, only with the consent of all such owners. There is provision for a fee to be made payable for a copy entry, but in practice none is charged by the Registrar to registered owners. The provisions of the Scheme as to production of copy entries are intended to protect the privacy of owners, as the register includes a number of personal details, such as, for instance, the real names of those who write under a *nom de plume,* as well as details of the amounts of payments made under the Scheme, which some owners prefer to keep confidential. However, the Registrar is happy to pass on to owners requests for information from members of the public or press.

19–14   **Procedure for registration.** The Scheme sets out the procedures to be followed for registration of public lending right, or of an eligible author's share of the right, or of a posthumously eligible person's share of the right, for the transfer of a registered interest and for the renunciation of a registered interest.[53] The Registrar may require evidence to be submitted to satisfy him that a book is an eligible book, that a person applying as author for the first registration of public lending right, or the registration of a share of the right, is in fact the author of that book and is an eligible person, that any co-author who is not a party to an application for first registration of public lending right is dead or cannot be traced despite all reasonable steps having been taken to do so, and (where an application under article 17(1)(c)(iv) has been made) that there is such an agreement or arrangement as is mentioned therein and that the share of public lending right of the person making the application is as specified in that agreement or arrangement. For these purposes the Registrar may require a statutory declaration to be made.[54] The Registrar has power to treat applications as abandoned when information requested has not been given.[55] Also, under section 4(5) of the 1979 Act, the Registrar has power to remove entries from the register where no sum has become due by way of public lending right for a period of at least 10 years, although application for restoration to the register can subsequently be made.[56]

19–15   **Transmission and duration of public lending right.** The Scheme provides that a registered interest is transmissible by assignment or assignation, by testamentary disposition or by operation of law, as personal or movable property, so long, as regards a particular book, as the right in respect of that book is capable of subsisting.[57] Under the Scheme the duration of public lending right in respect of a book and the period during which there may be dealings therein is from the date of the book's first publication (or, if later, the beginning of the sampling year in which application is made for it to be registered) until 70 years have elapsed since the end of the sampling year in which the author died, or, if the book is registered as the work of more than one author, as regards dealings in the share of the right attributable to that author, the end of the year in which that author died.[58] "Sampling year" means the period of 12 months ending on June 30.[59]

The procedure for transfer is dealt with in the Scheme,[60] including provision for the transfer to an author on attaining full age, since only adults can be

---

[53] Public Lending Right Scheme 1982, Arts 3, 14, 14A, 15, 16, 17, 17A and 17B and Sch.1.
[54] Art.18.
[55] Art.33.
[56] Art.34.
[57] Public Lending Right Scheme 1982, Art.19.
[58] Art.20 as amended with effect from July 15, 1997; previously the right lasted for 50 years from the end of the relevant year.
[59] Art.36.
[60] Arts 14, 21, 22, 23 and 24 and Sch.1.

registered.[61] Procedure following death is also dealt with by the Scheme.[62] The Scheme also deals with transfer on bankruptcy, liquidation or sequestration.[63] Finally, the Scheme provides a procedure to be followed for renunciation of a registered interest.[64]

Calculation of public lending right. Public lending right is calculated by means **19–16** of two complex formulae set out in the Scheme.[65] The first formula determines the number of notional loans of a book in each sampling year. The second formula is used to calculate the sum due by way of public lending right using the number of notional loans. The basic element of the first formula in respect of any book is the number of loans of that book recorded during the sampling year at the operative sampling points in the various groups of service points. Service points which are to be operative sampling points or which are to be included in operative sampling points are designated yearly for the prescribed period by the Registrar from lists of service points (libraries and mobile libraries) supplied to the Registrar by local library authorities, with power for the Registrar to discontinue designation and designate a new sampling point. No operative sampling point is to remain an operative sampling point for more than four years. Loans are defined as loans whereby books are lent out from a service point to individual borrowers, and includes loans of books not normally held at that service point.[66] It would seem, therefore, that a book available in some libraries, but which might not be held at any of the current operative sampling points, would not qualify for public lending right. Further, even if a book was available in an operative sampling point and was used, but was not lent (the case for most reference books), it would not qualify for public lending right.

Payment in respect of public lending right. Any sum due in respect of public **19–17** lending right is to be paid without interest to the relevant registered owner as at June 30 in any financial year, and will be paid on the last day of that year unless paid earlier.[67] However, payment will not be made unless the right has been claimed by or on behalf of the person for the time being entitled, as to which the Registrar may require evidence.[68] At the end of each financial year the Registrar is to give notice to every registered owner, to whom a sum is payable by way of public lending right in respect of that year, of the notional number of lendings for that year of each book in respect of which he is a registered owner and the amount of such sum. Where no sum is payable, notice will not be given of the number of notional loans unless requested by the registered owner not later than six months after the end of the relevant financial year.[69]

[61] Arts 14, 17(3) and 25 and Sch.1.
[62] Arts 26 and 27.
[63] Arts 28, 29, 30 and 31.
[64] Arts 14 and 32 and Sch.1.
[65] Public Lending Right Scheme 1982, Arts 36– 44 and 46 and Sch.2.
[66] Art.36, and see Art.42(3)(c) entitling the Registrar to disregard any loan where an International Standard Book Number is not specified in respect of that book in the report of a local library authority.
[67] Public Lending Right Scheme 1982, Arts 47, 49 and 51 and Sch.4.
[68] Arts 48 and 50.
[69] Arts 49(3), (5).

CHAPTER TWENTY

RIGHTS OF CONFIDENCE

1. INTRODUCTION

A duty of confidence arises when confidential information comes to the knowledge of a person in circumstances where he has notice, or is held to have agreed, that the information is confidential, with the effect that it would be just in all the circumstances that he should be precluded from disclosing or using the information.[1] If a defendant is proved to have used such confidential information without the claimant's consent, express or implied, he will be liable for an infringement of the claimant's rights.[2] Equity intervenes because it is unconscionable for a person who has received information on the basis that it is confidential

20–01

---

[1] *Att-Gen v Guardian Newspapers (No.2)*, CA [1990] 1 A.C. 109 at 281B ("the broad general principle") and see 214F.

[2] *Saltman Engineering Co Ltd v Campbell Engineering Co Ltd* (1948) 65 R.P.C. 203 at 213, CA.

to reveal or otherwise misuse that information.[3] The jurisdiction is based not so much on property or on contract as on the duty of good faith.[4] Further, as a general rule, it is in the public interest that confidences should be respected.[5] This may be so even where the confider can point to no specific financial detriment to himself in disclosure.[6] As society, technology and business practice develop, so will the boundaries of the law of confidence.

A. Elements of action for breach of confidence

20–02   To succeed in an action for breach of confidence, a claimant must establish three elements:[7] first, that the information which he is seeking to protect is of a confidential nature ("confidential information");[8] second, that the information in question was communicated in circumstances importing an obligation of confidence ("confidential obligation");[9] and, third, that the defendant is about to make, or has made, an unauthorised or wrongful use or disclosure of that information ("wrongful use").[10]

B. Remedies

20–03   For past breaches of confidence a claimant can, in the discretion of the court and at the option of the claimant, obtain damages[11] or an account of profits.[12] An injunction can be obtained to restrain future breaches.[13] In addition to these remedies, the court can also make an order for delivery up of material containing confidential information.[14]

2. RELATIONSHIP BETWEEN COPYRIGHT AND CONFIDENCE

20–04   The 1988 Act, repeating in substance section 46(4) of the 1956 Act, provides that nothing in Part 1 of the 1988 Act affects the operation of any rule of equity relating to breaches of trust or confidence.[15] There are marked differences between and several similarities of copyright and the law of confidence:

---

[3] *Stephens v Avery* [1988] Ch. 449 at 456; *Att-Gen v Guardian Newspapers (No.2)*, HL (E) [1990] 1 A.C. 109 (in which the House of Lords reviewed the principles of the law of confidence); *Saltman Engineering Co Ltd v Campbell Engineering Co Ltd* (1948) 65 R.P.C. 203, CA; see also and generally Finn, *Fiduciary Obligations* (1977); Law Commission Report, *Breach of Confidence* (1981) Cmnd.8388; Gurry, *Breach of Confidence* (1984); Clarke, *Confidentiality and the Law* (1990); Coleman, *The Legal Protection of Trade Secrets* (1992); Meagher, Gummow and Lehane, *Equity: Doctrines and Remedies* (4th ed., 2002); Goff and Jones, *Law of Restitution* (6th ed., 2003); Virgo, *The Principles of the Law of Restitution* (1999); Tugendhat and Christie, *The Law of Privacy and the Media* (2002).

[4] *Fraser v Evans* [1969] 1 Q.B.D. 349 at 361, *per* Lord Denning M.R.

[5] *Att-Gen v Guardian Newspapers (No.2)*, HL (E) [1990] A.C. 109 at 256, 281.

[6] *Att-Gen v Guardian Newspapers (No.2)*, HL (E) [1990] A.C. 109 at 256.

[7] Megarry J. in *Coco v A.N. Clark (Engineers) Ltd* [1969] R.P.C. 41 at 47, relying in part on Lord Greene M.R. in *Saltman Engineering Co Ltd v Campbell Engineering Co Ltd* (1948) 65 R.P.C. 203, and widely approved; see *Att-Gen v Guardian Newspapers (No.2)*, HL (E) [1990] 1 A.C. 109 at 268; *R. v Department of Health, ex p. Source Informatics Ltd* [2001] F.S.R. 74 at 79; *Campbell v MGN Ltd* [2004] UKHL 22 at para.13; [2004] 2 W.L.R. 1232.

[8] See paras 20–05 to 20–14, below.

[9] See paras 20–15 to 20–20, below.

[10] See paras 20–21 to 20–25, below.

[11] See paras 20–30 to 20–32, below.

[12] See para. 20–33, below

[13] See paras 20–27 to 20–29, below.

[14] See para. 20–35, below

[15] CDPA 1988, s.171(1)(e).

(1) The law of confidence protects the substance of ideas and information,[16] whether communicated orally or in writing. Examples are the elaborated idea for a play before it has been performed[17] or the idea for a dramatic work which has been confided orally.[18] In contrast, there is no copyright in ideas and information, but only in the form in which they are expressed. It is no infringement of copyright to adopt or appropriate the ideas of another or to publish information received from another, provided there is no substantial copying of the form in which those ideas have, or that information has been previously embodied.[19]

(2) Copyright is good against the world generally, whereas confidentiality operates only against those who receive or acquire information or ideas in confidence, or are subsequently advised of their confidential nature.[20]

(3) Copyright subsists for a fixed period of time prescribed by statute. In practice the obligation of confidence usually ceases when the information becomes public knowledge.[21]

(4) The activities which constitute an infringement of copyright (such as reproduction, performance, rental, etc.) are prescribed by statute. The disclosure or misuse of information in breach of confidence which is the subject of case law is necessarily less specific.

(5) The statutory defences to copyright infringement claims have no parallel in the law of confidence.[22]

(6) The concept of a defence of "public interest" exists in relation to both copyright and confidence.[23] The courts will not enforce any claim to copyright by publishers of a work containing government secrets, the disclosure of which was contrary to the public interest and in breach of confidence.[24] Grossly immoral information will not be protected by the law of confidence or copyright.[25]

(7) A statutory limitation period applies to actions for infringement of copyright,[26] but not to an action for breach of confidence founded in equity. Any claim for injunctive relief is subject to the defence of delay.

(8) Different entities may own the copyright in a work and be entitled to restrain breach of confidence in respect of it.[27]

(9) Confidential information and copyright can be held in co-ownership. However, it appears that in the absence of any contractual, fiduciary or other special relationship, each of the co-owners of confidential information is entitled, as against the other co-owners, to use the information for

---

[16] See para. 20–06, below.

[17] *Gilbert v Star Newspaper Co Ltd* (1894) 11 T.L.R. 4 (where the court granted an interim injunction restraining the defendant from publishing the plot of W.S. Gilbert's comic opera *His Excellency* which was shortly due to open).

[18] *Fraser v Thames Television Ltd* [1984] Q.B.D. 44.

[19] See Chs 3 and 7, above.

[20] However, see *Venables v News Group Newspapers Ltd* [2001] Fam Div 430, in which an injunction was granted against the whole world in exceptional circumstances to restrain the publication of personal information where it was necessary to protect the human right of privacy.

[21] *Fraser v Thames Television* [1984] Q.B.D. 44 at 60; see also para. 20–08, below.

[22] This appears to be one reason why the Crown did not base its claim in the *Spycatcher* litigation on Crown copyright: see *Att-Gen v Guardian Newspapers (No.2)* HL (E) [1990] 1 A.C. 109 at 194–195; see also *Hubbard v Vosper* [1972] 2 Q.B.D. 84.

[23] See below at paras 22–82 and 20–23 respectively.

[24] *Att-Gen v Guardian Newspapers (No.2)*, HL (E) [1990] 1 A.C. 109 at 262.

[25] *Stephens v Avery* [1988] F.S.R. 510.

[26] See para. 22–228, below.

[27] *Northern Office Microcomputer (Pty) Ltd v Rosenstein* [1982] F.S.R. 124 (Sup Ct of SA) (in which it was no answer to a claim for breach of confidence in certain computer programs that the party in breach of the duty of confidence owned the copyright in the programs).

his own benefit.[28] A co-owner of copyright is not entitled to act in this way without the consent of his co-owners.[29]

(10) The distinction between copyright and confidence may be important where unpublished manuscripts have been submitted, and not accepted, for publication or use. Depending on the circumstances an obligation not to use or disclose the manuscript may be implied and enforceable under the law of confidence. This would extend to a plot or developed ideas not protected under the laws of copyright.[30]

3. CONFIDENTIAL INFORMATION

A. DEFINITION OF INFORMATION

20–05   It is not necessary for information to fall into any special category of subject-matter in order to enjoy protection under the law of confidence. However, it has been noted that there are four main classes of confidential information which have been protected by the courts[31]: trade secrets;[32] personal confidences;[33] artistic and literary confidences;[34] and Government information.[35]

Grossly immoral information will not be protected.[36] Nor will "trivial tittle-tattle (however confidential)",[37] "pernicious nonsense"[38] and "useless information".[39] However, the information need not be of any apparent commercial value.[40] Actions have succeeded in the context of personal or non-commercial confidences where no financial or other specific detriment to the claimant was obvious.[41] The absence of commercial value may affect the quantum of damages awarded or the exercise of the court's discretion in granting injunctive relief. Although the court in the *Coco* case referred to an unauthorised use of information which was to the detriment of the party communicating it,[42] the question whether detriment was an essential element of an action for breach of confidence was expressly kept open.[43] The mere simplicity of information is not a bar to its protection. The simpler an idea, the more likely it is to need protection.[44]

---

[28] *Murray v Yorkshire Fund Managers Ltd* [1998] 1 W.L.R. 951, CA.

[29] See para. 5–169, above.

[30] *Fraser v Thames Television* [1984] Q.B.D. 44 at 60. See also para. 20–13, below.

[31] *R. v Department of Health, ex p. Source Informatics Ltd* [2001] F.S.R. 74 at 82.

[32] See para. 20–10, below.

[33] See paras 20–11 to 20–12, below.

[34] See para. 20–13, below.

[35] See para. 20–14, below.

[36] *Stephens v Avery* [1988] Ch. 449 at 454.

[37] *Coco v A.N. Clark (Engineers) Ltd* [1969] R.P.C. 41 at 47. Of course what may be utterly trivial in one context might be of significance in another: *Att-Gen v Guardian Newspapers (No.2)*, CA [1990] 1 A.C. 109 at 215.

[38] *Saltman Engineering Co Ltd v Campbell Engineering Co Ltd* (1948) 65 R.P.C. 203 at 215.

[39] *Att-Gen v Guardian Newspapers (No.2)*, HL (E) [1990] 1 A.C. 109 at 282.

[40] *Nichrotherm Electrical Co Ltd v Percy* [1956] R.P.C. 272; affirmed [1957] R.P.C. 207, CA.

[41] *Prince Albert v Strange* (1849) 1 Mac & G 25; affirmed (1849) 2 DeG. Sm 652, *Pollard v Photographic Co* (1888) 40 Ch.D. 345; see also *SmithKline & French Laboratories (Australia) Ltd v Secretary to the Department of Community Services and Health* [1990] F.S.R. 617 (Federal Ct of Australia).

[42] *Coco v A.N. Clark (Engineers) Ltd* [1969] R.P.C. 41 at 47.

[43] *Coco v A.N. Clark (Engineers) Ltd* [1969] R.P.C. 41 at 48; similarly (keeping the question open), see *Att-Gen v Guardian Newspapers (No.2)*, HL (E) [1990] 1 A.C. 109 at 281H.

[44] *Coco v A.N. Clark (Engineers) Ltd* [1969] R.P.C. 41 at 47; *Cranleigh Precision Engineering Ltd v Bryant* [1965] 1 W.L.R. 1293 at 1310; *Under Water Welders & Repairers Ltd v Street and Longthorne* [1968] R.P.C. 498 at 506; *De Maudsley v Palumbo* [1996] F.S.R. 447.

If the information is in fact false, it cannot be the subject of a breach of confidence claim.[45]

B. FORM OF INFORMATION

The information need not be in any special form. Unlike copyright, it is not necessary for the information to be embodied in any document.[46] Confidential information may be conveyed orally[47] or in writing. Etchings,[48] photographs,[49] films,[50] political diaries,[51] diagrams,[52] formulae,[53] observations,[54] a judgment in arbitration proceedings[55] and even budwood twigs (containing trade secrets in propagation)[56] have been the subject of confidential information claims.

20–06

In certain circumstances the form of the information may be highly relevant to the success of proceedings or the type of relief obtained. On an application for an interim injunction the courts have restrained the publication of photographs of a claimant's activities, whilst refusing to restrain publication of a narrative account of the same events on the basis that the photographs were particularly intrusive, taken without consent and would not be expected by the claimant.[57] Arguably, some kinds of document, namely personal diaries[58] or personal correspondence,[59] may deserve protection as confidential information by reason of their form alone.

Confidential information must be reasonably specific and identifiable and this is particularly so where the information is a concept or idea.[60] This ensures that breach of confidence claims are not used as an unfair restraint of trade in the

---

[45] *Mainmet Holdings plc v Austin* [1991] F.S.R. 538, following *Berkeley Administration Inc v Mc-Clelland* [1990] F.S.R. 505.

[46] *Terrapin Ltd v Builders' Supply Co (Hayes) Ltd* [1967] R.P.C. 375; *De Maudsley v Palumbo* [1996] F.S.R. 447.

[47] In *Fraser v Thames Television Ltd* [1984] Q.B.D. 44, the idea for a television series was communicated orally. In *A v B plc* [2001] 1 W.L.R. 2341, a confession of an affair was made orally: see *A v B plc* [2003] QBD 195.

[48] *Prince Albert v Strange* (1849) 1 Mac & G 25; affirmed (1849) 2 DeG. Sm 652 (the House of Lords' source of the modern law of confidence).

[49] *Campbell v MGN Limited* [2004] UKHL 22 at paras 122–124; [2004] 2 W.L.R. 1232, *Douglas v Hello! Ltd* [2001] F.S.R. 732 at 756–757 (Brooke L.J.) and at 781 (Keene L.J.), [2001] QBD 967; *Creation Records Ltd v News Group Newspapers Ltd* [1997] E.M.L.R. 444; *Shelley Films v Rex Features Ltd* [1994] E.M.L.R. 134; *Pollard v Photographic Co* (1889) 40 Ch.D. 345.

[50] *Nicholls v BBC* [1999] E.M.L.R. 791.

[51] *Ashdown v Telegraph Group Newspapers Ltd* [2001] Ch. 685.

[52] *Nichrotherm Electrical Co Ltd v Percy* [1957] R.P.C. 207.

[53] *Johnson & Bloy (Holdings) Ltd v Wolstenholme Rink plc* [1989] F.S.R. 135, CA.

[54] *Woodward v Hutchins* [1977] 2 All E.R. 751.

[55] *Department of Economics Policy & Development of the City of Moscow v Bankers Trust Co* [2004] EWCA Civ 314; [2004] 3 W.L.R. 533.

[56] *Franklin v Giddings* [1978] Qd. R. 72.

[57] *Theakston v MGN Ltd* [2002] E.M.L.R. 398, but *cf. Service Corporation International Plc v Channel Four Television Corporation Ltd* [1999] E.M.L.R. 83 at 90, in which Lightman J. held there to be no distinction between a photograph and a written account of the same subject matter.

[58] *Ashdown v Telegraph Group Ltd* [2001] Ch. 685, CA in which a claimant's record of events at a Downing Street meeting forming part of his memoirs was confidential; *Att-Gen v Guardian Newspapers (No2)* [1990] 1 AC 109 at 281.

[59] *Thompson v Stanhope* (1774) Amb. 737; 27 E.R. 476 (private letters passed between the Earl of Chesterfield and his son); *Argyll (Duchess) v Argyll (Duke)* [1967] Ch. 302 (secrets relating to the claimant's private life communicated during her marriage to the defendant); *Beloff v Pressdram Ltd* [1973] R.P.C. 765 (memorandum written by a journalist to her editor); *Lion Laboratories Ltd v Evans* [1985] 1 Q.B. 526, CA (internal memorandum of a company); *Re Aitken* [2001] Ch. 110 at 118, in which Rattee J. observed *obiter* that the sale by a trustee in bankruptcy of a former MP's correspondence would appear to infringe Mr Aitken's Art.8 rights to "respect for … correspondence".

[60] *Fraser v Thames Television Ltd* [1984] QBD 44; *De Maudsley v Palumbo* [1996] F.S.R. 447 and see "Ideas" at para. 20–13, below.

commercial field,[61] and, more generally, injunctive relief can only be granted where the terms of the injunction can be clearly framed so that a defendant knows what he can and cannot do.[62] To this end, a litigant must carefully define in its statement of case the confidential information claimed.

Information will not be protected which has become so completely merged in the mind of the person informed that it is impossible to say from what precise source he acquired his knowledge.[63] This point is illustrated in the cases in which employers have sought to restrain former employees from disclosing or using confidential information about their employers' business acquired in the course of employment.[64]

C. Requirement of confidentiality

20–07   To be confidential, the information must not be public knowledge.[65] Once information has entered the public domain and is so generally accessible that, in all the circumstances, it cannot be regarded as confidential, then as a general rule, the principle of confidentiality can have no application to it.[66] The question whether information is in the public domain is a question of degree in each case.[67] Attempts to define what degree of publication puts a matter into the public domain have been fraught with difficulty.[68] Information has been considered confidential when already disclosed to printers,[69] when disclosed to the cast of a play which is about to open,[70] and when not disclosed to "a substantial number of people".[71] Confidentiality was lost when a foreign patent was too widely known in this country,[72] and when government secrets had been published abroad but were easily available or known in the UK.[73] Publication to the limited group to whom the information is relevant, although not to the general public, may be sufficient to deprive the information of its confidentiality.[74] There may, for example, be cases in which, even in the light of widespread publication of the information abroad, a person whom that information concerned could restrain publication by a third

---

[61] *Faccenda Chicken Ltd v Fowler* [1987] Ch. 117 at 136, *per* Neill L.J.

[62] *Printers & Finishers Ltd v Holloway* [1965] 1 W.L.R. 1; *Amway Corporation v Eurway International Ltd* [1974] R.P.C. 82; *Woodward v Hutchins* [1977] 1 W.L.R. 760; *Times Newspapers Ltd v Mirror Group Newspapers Ltd* [1993] E.M.L.R. 443 at 448.

[63] *Terrapin Ltd v Builders Supply Co (Hayes) Ltd (1959)* [1967] R.P.C. 375 at 391.

[64] *Printers & Finishers Ltd v Holloway* [1965] 1 W.L.R. 1; *Coral Index Ltd v Regent Index Ltd* [1970] R.P.C. 147; *Stevenson, Jordan & Harrison Ltd v MacDonald & Evans* [1952] 1 T.L.R. 101; *Potters-Ballotini Ltd v Weston-Baker & Ors* [1977] 1 W.L.R. 1472; *Lancashire Fires Ltd v S.A. Lyons & Company Ltd* [1996] F.S.R. 629, CA; *Ocular Sciences Ltd v Aspect Vision Care Ltd (No.2)* [1997] R.P.C. 289; and see paras 20–17 to 20–18, below.

[65] *Att-Gen v Guardian Newspapers (No.2)*, CA [1990] 1 A.C. 109 at 215 ("the basic attribute of inaccessibility"); *Saltman Engineering Co Ltd v Campbell Engineering Co Ltd* (1948) 65 R.P.C. 203 at 215; *Seager v Copydex Ltd* [1967] 1 W.L.R. 923 at 931G; *Woodward v Hutchins* [1977] 1 W.L.R. 760 at 764D.

[66] *Att-Gen v Guardian Newspapers (No.2)*, HL (E) [1990] 1 A.C. 109 at 282; *Bunn v British Broadcasting Corporation* [1999] F.S.R. 70 at 76; *Att-Gen v Times Newspapers Ltd* [2001] 1 W.L.R. 885.

[67] *Franchi v Franchi* [1967] R.P.C. 149 at 152–153, *per* Cross J. as cited in *Att-Gen v Guardian Newspapers (No.2)*, CA [1990] 1 A.C. 109 at 177D. If the gist of the information is referred to in open court, the obligation of confidence will be at an end: *Bunn v British Broadcasting Corporation* [1999] F.S.R. 70.

[68] *Att-Gen v Times Newspapers Ltd* [2001] 1 W.L.R. 885 at paras 18–23, which rehearses the arguments for defining what degree of publication amounts to putting information into the public domain. During the appeal, attempts to define this were abandoned.

[69] *Prince Albert v Strange* (1849) 1 Mac. & G. 25.

[70] *Gilbert v The Star Newspaper Co Ltd* (1894) 11 T.L.R. 4.

[71] *Michael Barrymore v News Group Newspapers Ltd* [1997] F.S.R. 600.

[72] *Franchi v Franchi* [1967] R.P.C. 149 at 153.

[73] *Att-Gen v Guardian Newspapers (No.2)*, HL (E) [1990] 1 A.C. 109.

[74] *Thomas Marshall (Exports) Ltd v Guinle* [1979] Ch. 227.

party in this country.[75] Authorities show that a breach of confidence claim in respect of personal information can survive extensive publication.[76] Information which is obtained by observation, experiment or analysis of an article cannot be the subject of a breach of confidence claim even if it remained confidential in another form (*e.g.* the written details of the manufacturer's secret process kept confidential by him).[77]

If only part of the information in question has been made public, the balance remains capable of protection.[78] If material was once public but its significance was not generally appreciated, or it was ignored, or forgotten, it may become confidential.[79] It has been held in an interim decision that because information was about to be published by the persons claiming rights of confidence it did not possess the necessary quality of confidence to restrain a "spoiling" publication.[80]

A claimant who has courted public attention in the past may have less ground to object to a later intrusion.[81] This is the corollary of the defence of waiver.

If the person to whom the duty of confidence is owed makes the information **20–08** publicly available so that it ceases to be confidential, the duty ceases to bind the confidant.[82] If, however, publication is by or with the consent of the person who owed the duty[83] or by a stranger[84] the duty of confidence may not necessarily be discharged. It may be that a confidant who, in breach of confidence, destroys the confidential nature of the information entrusted to him, remains under some limited obligation analogous to the "springboard" doctrine.[85] If a third party has put the confidential information in the public domain, the confidant may be released from his obligation without liability.[86] It is well-established that a confidant may be restrained from obtaining an unfair "head start" in circumstances where confidential information in his possession becomes public.[87]

If the stipulation of confidentiality was unreasonable at the time of making it, or if it becomes unreasonable that it should be enforced by reason of subsequent events, then the court will decline to enforce it.[88] There may thus be a limit in

---

[75] *Att-Gen v Guardian Newspapers (No.2)*, HL (E) [1990] 1 A.C. 109 at 260F.

[76] *Blair v Associated Newspapers Ltd* [2000] WL 33116509 (restraining further publication in the *Mail on Sunday* notwithstanding widespread publication in the newspaper's first edition); *Venables v News Group Newspapers Ltd* [2001] Fam Div 430 (restriction on revealing claimants' addresses would not be affected by their subsequent publication abroad or on the internet).

[77] *Mars UK v Tecknowledge* [2000] F.S.R.138 in which the defendant had obtained information by disassembly or reverse engineering of the claimant's computer chips.

[78] *Mustad & Son v Dosen (1928)* [1964] 1 W.L.R. 109, HL; but see *Bunn v British Broadcasting Corporation* [1999] F.S.R. 70.

[79] *Coco v A.N. Clark (Engineers) Ltd* [1969] R.P.C. 41 at 47.

[80] *Times Newspapers Ltd v MGN Ltd* [1993] E.M.L.R. 443; *Douglas v Hello! Ltd* [2001] Q.B.D. 967, CA at para.169, *per* Keene L.J. and para.95, *per* Brooke L.J.; but see the discussion in R.G. Toulson and C.M. Phipps, *Confidentiality* (1996), at 3–06.

[81] *A v B plc* [2003] Q.B.D. 195 at para.11(xii); *Theakston v MGN Ltd* [2002] E.M.L.R. 398 at para.68; *Campbell v MGN Ltd* [2004] UKHL 22; [2004] 2 W.L.R. 1232.

[82] *Mustad & Son v Dosen* [1964] 1 W.L.R. 109, HL (the claimant's publication of a patent specification put the information into the public domain), explained in *Att-Gen v Guardian Newspapers (No.2)*, HL (E) [1990] 1 A.C. 109 at 285; see also *Prout v British Gas plc* [1992] F.S.R. 478.

[83] *Speed Seal Products Ltd v Paddington* [1985] 1 W.L.R. 1327 at 1331 as accepted in *Att-Gen v Guardian Newspapers (No.2)*, HL (E) [1990] 1 A.C. 109 at 201B and 268D; but see the criticism of this reasoning at 285G and see 265H.

[84] *Cranleigh Precision Engineering Ltd v Bryant* [1965] 1 W.L.R. 1293 as accepted in *Att-Gen v Guardian Newspapers (No.2)*, HL (E) [1990] 1 A.C. 109 at 268D; but see the criticism of this reasoning at 285G.

[85] *Att-Gen v Guardian Newspapers (No.2)*, HL (E) [1990] 1 A.C. 109 at 288H.

[86] *Woodward v Hutchins* [1977] 1 W.L.R. 760 at 764D; and see para. 20–07, above.

[87] See "The springboard principle" at para. 20–09, below.

[88] *Dunford & Elliott Ltd v Johnston & Firth Brown Ltd* [1978] F.S.R. 143 at 148.

time after which the confidential character of the information and the duty of the court to restrain publication will lapse.[89]

D. MIXED INFORMATION—THE SPRINGBOARD PRINCIPLE

20–09   The "springboard" principle places a recipient of confidential information, which information could have been obtained from a publicly available source, under a limited obligation not to use that information. Use of it is a breach of confidence as it would give him a head start (or "springboard") over those who had lawfully gone to the public source.[90] Once a claimant has shown the initial source of information to be confidential, the burden of proof shifts to the defendant who must show that the information was obtained independently of that confidential source.[91] The springboard principle prevents the recipient of confidential information from using it as a springboard for activities detrimental to the person who made the confidential communication.[92]

The obligation on the recipient under the springboard principle remains even when all the features of the information have been published or can be ascertained by actual inspection by any member of the public.[93] While the recipient could, like anyone else, buy and analyse the article, he remains under an obligation not to shorten his labours by use of the confidential know-how he had learned.[94] Nevertheless the springboard obligation continues to bind only whilst the relevant confidential information retains its confidentiality. It is a question of degree whether and when the information has become public knowledge so the recipient has no further advantage over the public and can no longer be restrained from use of that information. The confidential obligation may thus be of limited duration.[95] It may be that some limited obligation, analogous to the springboard doctrine, may continue to rest upon a defendant who, in breach of confidence, destroys the confidential nature of the information.[96]

Where confidential information has been used by a defendant to get an illegitimate head start, that head start is still illegitimate even if, at a subsequent date, the information becomes public. Such publication affects what relief may be appropriate.[97]

E. TRADE SECRETS

20–10   Four elements may be discerned in the identification of confidential information in a commercial setting: first, the information must be information, the release of which the owner believes would be injurious to him or of advantage to his rivals or others; second, the owner must believe that the information is confidential or

---

[89] *Att-Gen v Jonathan Cape Ltd* [1976] Q.B.D. 752 at 771; *Roger Bullivant Ltd v Ellis* [1987] F.S.R. 172.

[90] *Seager v Copydex* [1967] 1 W.L.R. 923, CA.

[91] *Spencer (Earl and Countess) v UK* [1998] 25 E.H.R.R. CD 105.

[92] *Terrapin Ltd v Builders' Supply Co (Hayes) Ltd* [1967] R.P.C. 375 at 351 (the principle's original formulation). Approved in *Seager v Copydex*, above; and see *Ackroyds (London) Ltd v Islington Plastics Ltd* [1962] R.P.C. 97; *Cranleigh Precision Engineering Ltd v Bryant* [1965] 1 W.L.R. 1293; *Peter Pan Manufacturing Corpn v Corsets Silhouette Ltd* [1964] 1 W.L.R. 96; *Potter-Ballotini Ltd v Weston-Baker* [1977] R.P.C. 202 at 206, CA; *Att-Gen v Guardian Newspapers (No.2)*, HL (E) [1990] 1 A.C. 109 at 285, 288.

[93] *Terrapin Ltd v Builders' Supply Co (Hayes) Ltd* [1967] R.P.C. 375.

[94] *Saltman Engineering Co Ltd v Campbell Engineering Co Ltd* (1948) 65 R.P.C. 203 at 215, CA.

[95] *Potters-Ballotini*, above at 206–7; *Harrison v Project & Design Co (Redcar) Ltd* [1978] F.S.R. 81 at 87–8; *Peter Pan Manufacturing Corpn v Corsets Silhouette Ltd* [1964] 1 W.L.R. 96; *Prout v British Gas plc* [1992] F.S.R. 478.

[96] *Att-Gen v Guardian Newspapers (No.2)*, HL (E) [1990] 1 A.C. 109 at 288H.

[97] *Ocular Sciences Ltd v Aspect Vision Care Ltd* [1997] R.P.C. 289 at 396, explaining *Terrapin Ltd v Builders' Supply Co (Hayes) Ltd* [1967] R.P.C. 375.

secret; third, the owner's beliefs on the first two points must be reasonable; and fourth, the information must be judged in the light of the usage and practices of the particular industry or trade concerned.[98] Information satisfying these four requirements is entitled to protection.

Whether or not information is protectable will depend on the circumstances.[99] Even a collection of data collated from public sources can be classed as confidential information in its own right[1] provided that there has been some application of skill and human labour to create something novel.[2] Novelty depends on the thing itself, and not upon the quality of its component parts.[3] Further, novelty and originality have evidential value in going to show that the information is not public knowledge. The fact that the information in question is available in the sense that it could be obtained by chemical analysis of a product or by some other process of "reverse engineering", does not mean that it is public knowledge.[4] All the separate features of a product may have been published or be capable of ascertainment by inspection, but if the whole result could not be achieved, except by someone going through the same kind of process as the owner, the information remains subject to protection.[5] Such ascertainment of the features of a product does not constitute publication so as to put the whole plan or device into the public domain beyond protection.[6]

F. PERSONAL CONFIDENCES

Unlike in the United States of America, there is no over-arching and all-embracing cause of action for invasion of privacy in English law.[7] The Human Rights Act 1998 (which incorporates into domestic law the European Convention on Human Rights) has not created any new right of privacy as between private persons. However, where there is a relevant cause of action applicable, such as breach of confidence, the court as a public authority must act compatibly with the parties' Convention rights.[8] The courts must therefore give effect to the right to respect for private and family life prescribed by Article 8 and other countervailing rights, particularly, in this context, the right to freedom of expression prescribed by Article 10. A new breadth and strength has been given to the action for breach of confidence by these Articles.[9]

An action for breach of confidence will therefore normally provide protection

20–11

---

[98] *Thomas Marshall (Exports) Ltd v Guinle* [1979] Ch. 227, see also *Ansell Rubber Co Pty Ltd v Allied Rubber Industries Pty Ltd* [1972] R.P.C. 811.

[99] *Faccenda Chicken Ltd v Fowler* [1987] Ch. 117, at 136–137

[1] *Coco v A N Clark (Engineers) Ltd* [1969] RPC 41 at 47.

[2] *Ocular Sciences Ltd v Aspect Vision Care Ltd* [1997] RPC 289 at 374.

[3] *Coco v A.N. Clark (Engineers) Ltd* [1969] R.P.C. 41 at 47. But a combination of features not individually novel does not automatically become novel by being added together; see *De Maudsley v Palumbo* [1996] F.S.R. 447 at 459.

[4] But see *Cray Valley Ltd v Deltech Europe Ltd and others* [2003] EWHC 728 (Ch) in which a breach of confidence claim failed as the information was so easy to reverse engineer that a reasonable person of conscience would not regard the information as a trade secret that was not to be used.

[5] *Ansell Rubber Co Pty Ltd v Allied Rubber Industries Pty Ltd* [1972] R.P.C. 811 (Sup Ct of Victoria); *Alfa Laval Cheese Systems Ltd v Wincanton Engineering Ltd* [1990] F.S.R. 583 at 590.

[6] *Harvey Tiling Co (Pty) Ltd v Rodomac (Pty) Ltd* [1977] R.P.C. 399; *House of Spring Gardens Ltd v Point Blank Ltd* [1983] F.S.R. 213 at 250.

[7] *Wainwright v Home Office* [2003] UKHL 53; [2003] 3 W.L.R. 1137.

[8] *Campbell v MGN Limited* [2004] UKHL 22; [2004] 2 W.L.R. 1232.

[9] *A v B plc* [2003] Q.B. 195, 202, para.4; *Campbell v MGN Limited* [2004] UKHL 22; [2004] 2 W.L.R. 1232.

for an individual's privacy where such protection is justified.[10] Examples of personal information protected by the courts include the nature and frequency of a model's visits to Narcotics Anonymous meetings,[11] photographs taken covertly at a private wedding reception,[12] photographs of an individual's visit to a brothel,[13] private diaries,[14] private correspondence,[15] a patient's psychiatric report,[16] etchings of portraits made by Queen Victoria and Prince Albert,[17] secrets relating to the Duchess of Argyll's private life communicated to the Duke of Argyll during their marriage,[18] and information about the identities and whereabouts of child murderers.[19]

Note however, that where proceedings relate to journalistic, literary or artistic material, or to conduct connected with such material, section 12(4) of the Human Rights Act 1998 further requires the court to have particular regard to the importance of freedom of expression and any relevant privacy code. Rule 3(i) of the 1997 Code of Practice for members of the press, ratified by the Press Complaints Commission,[20] provides that everyone is entitled to respect for his private and family life, home, health and correspondence including digital communications, and that a publication will be expected to justify intrusions into an individual's private life. A newspaper which flouts this code is likely to have a claim to freedom of expression "trumped" by considerations of privacy.[21] However, section 12(4) of the Human Rights Act 1998 does not give either Article 8 or 10 pre-eminence over the other.[22] In the field of long-lens photography and the articles published alongside such photographs, the decisive factor in balancing the protection of private life against freedom of expression lies in the contribution, if any, that the published photographs and articles make to a debate

---

[10] *Campbell v MGN Ltd* [2004] UKHL 22; [2004] 2 W.L.R. 1232; *A v B plc* [2003] QBD 195; *Douglas v Hello! Ltd* [2001] QBD 967.

[11] *Campbell v MGN Ltd* [2004] UKHL 22; [2004] 2 W.L.R. 1232.

[12] *Douglas v Hello! Ltd* [2001] Q.B.D. 967

[13] *Theakston v MGN Ltd* [2002] E.M.L.R. 398

[14] *Ashdown v Telegraph Group Ltd* [2001] Ch. 685, CA; *Lady Archer v Williams* [2003] E.M.L.R. 38 (Q.B.D.).

[15] *Philip v Pennell* [1907] 2 Ch. 577; *Thompson v Stanhope* (1774) Amb. 737; 27 E.R. 476 (private letters passed between the Earl of Chesterfield and his son); *Hopkinson v Lord Burghley* (1866) 2 L.R. Ch. App. 447; *Cooksley v Johnson & Sons* (1906) 25 N.Z.L.R. 834; *McNicol v Sportsman's Book Stores* [1928–35] Mac.C.C. 116; *Tett Bros Ltd v Drake & Gorham Ltd* [1928–35] Mac.C.C. 492 (business letters not marked "confidential" held not to be confidential); *Beloff v Pressdram Ltd* [973] R.P.C. 765 (memorandum written by a journalist to her editor); *Lion Laboratories Ltd v Evans* [1985] 1 Q.B.D. 526, CA (internal memorandum of a company); *Re Aitken* [2001] Ch. 110 at 118, in which Rattee J. observed *obiter* that the sale by a trustee in bankruptcy of a former MP's correspondence would appear to infringe Mr Aitken's Art.8 rights to "respect for … correspondence".

[16] *Cornelius v de Taranto* [2002] E.M.L.R. 112, CA.

[17] *Prince Albert v Strange* (1849) 1 Mac. & G. 25; affirmed (1849) 2 De G. Sm 652 (widely recognised as being the origin of the English law of confidence).

[18] *Argyll (Duchess) v Argyll (Duke)* [1967] Ch. 302.

[19] *Venables v News Group Newspapers Ltd* [2001] Fam Div 430.

[20] The Code of Practice was ratified by the Press Complaints Commission on April 28, 2004 and took effect from June 1, 2004.

[21] *Douglas v Hello! Ltd* [2001] Q.B.D. 967 *per* Brooke L.J.

[22] *Re S (A Child) (Identifications: Restrictions on Publication)* [2004] Fam Div 43, para.52, *per* Hale L.J., and *Douglas v Hello! Ltd* [2001] Q.B.D. 967 at 1005, para.137, *per* Sedley L.J. Approved by *Campbell v MGN Limited* [2004] UKHL 22 at para.111; [2004] 2 W.L.R. 1232.

of general interest.[23] It will be a breach of Article 8 if no general public interest is served by the publication.[24]

A breach of confidence may involve an invasion of personal privacy without financial detriment to the claimant. For example, the publication of information which might lead to the identification of two notorious child killers (and therefore the risk of physical injury or death at the hands of those seeking retribution) may be prohibited.[25] The anonymity of a donor to a worthy cause may be protected.[26] Unauthorised publicity through the display[27] or the taking[28] of a photograph may be the subject of a claim.

20–12

In relation to sexual and other private matters, the duty of confidence is not limited to married partners[29] although its special status is recognised by the courts.[30] The more established a relationship is, the greater the protection it will be given.[31] If, however, both parties to a marriage have published details about their marriage secrets, the facts are in the public domain and no action for breach of confidence can be maintained.[32] If parties actively seek publicity for their private lives, disclosure of such matters may not be actionable.[33] Information relating to the sexual conduct of an individual may be the subject matter of a duty of confidence,[34] unless it is of "a grossly immoral tendency".[35] Cases of this kind raise fundamental conflicts between, on the one hand, the privacy which every individual is entitled to expect[36] and, on the other hand, freedom of information.

G. ARTISTIC AND LITERARY CONFIDENCES

The law of confidence protects the substance of ideas and information and so mitigates the well-established principle that there is no copyright in ideas and

20–13

---

[23] *Von Hannover v Germany* [2004] ECHR Application No.59320/00 at paras 76–77; [2004] E.M.L.R. 21 in which innocuous photographs of Princess Caroline of Monaco shopping, horse riding and skiing (amongst other things) were held to make no contribution to any debate of genuine public interest as she exercised no official function and the photographs detailed purely private activities in public places.

[24] *Von Hannover v Germany* [2004] ECHR Application No.59320/00; [2004] E.M.L.R. 21; this appears to be consistent with *Campbell v MGN Ltd* [2004] UKHL 22; [2004] 2 W.L.R. 1232 in which the House of Lords made a distinction between the lawful publication of the fact of Campbell's drug addiction and treatment (being in the public interest to correct Campbell's lies), and the unlawful publication of a photograph of Campbell attending a Narcotics Anonymous meeting and the details of the nature and frequency of those meetings, publication of which was not in the public interest.

[25] *Venables v News Group Newspapers Ltd* [2001] Fam Div 430.

[26] *Att-Gen v Guardian Newspapers (No.2)*, HL (E) [1990] 1 A.C. 109 at 256B, above.

[27] *Pollard v Photographic Co* (1888) 40 Ch.D. 345.

[28] *Creation Records v News Group Newspapers Ltd* [1997] E.M.L.R. 444.

[29] *Stephens v Avery* [1988] Ch. 449 at 455; *Michael Barrymore v News Group Newspapers Ltd* [1997] F.S.R. 600 (parties to a homosexual relationship should treat the details of the relationship as confidential irrespective of agreement).

[30] *A v B plc* [2003] QBD 195 at para.43(ii); *Theakston v MGN Ltd* [2002] E.M.L.R. 398 at para.60.

[31] *Theakston v MGN Ltd* [2002] E.M.L.R. 398 at para.11(xi).

[32] *Lennon v News Group Newspapers Ltd & Trust* [1978] F.S.R. 573.

[33] *Woodward v Hutchins* [1977] 1 W.L.R. 760, CA (press relations employee publishing details of employers' personal lives); *A v B plc* [2003] QBD 195 at para.11(xii); *Theakston v MGN Ltd* [2002] E.M.L.R. 398 at para.68; *Campbell v MGN Ltd* [2004] UKHL 22; [2004] " W.L.R. 1232 in which the facts of drug addiction and treatment were open to public comment in view of the claimant's public denials, whereas the frequency and nature of her visits to Narcotics Anonymous meetings were protectable.

[34] *Stephens v Avery* [1988] Ch. 449 at 455; *Michael Barrymore v News Group Newspapers Ltd* [1997] F.S.R. 600.

[35] *Glyn v Weston Feature Film Co* [1916] 1 Ch. 261; *Stephens v Avery* [1988] Ch. 449 at 453.

[36] See the Calcutt Committee Report on Privacy and Related Matters Cm.1102 (June 1990).

information.[37] Injunctions have been granted to prevent publication of the plot of a play before it has been performed in public,[38] or the idea for a dramatic work,[39] or the text of a play after it was taken down in writing during a performance.[40] Further, injunctions have been obtained to restrain the printing of conveyancing precedents stolen from a claimant's chambers[41]; the printing of notes lent by the claimant[42]; the selling or exhibiting of copies of a photograph without the sitter's consent[43]; and the publishing of the text of private lectures by persons attending them.[44]

An idea in the entertainment industry field will amount to confidential information if it was communicated in confidence, was clearly identifiable, sufficiently original, of potential commercial attractiveness, and sufficiently well developed to be capable of actual realisation.[45] Substantial damages may be awarded where a defendant rejects a detailed scenario for a play submitted by the claimant, but then makes use of the dramatic ideas, characters and plot contained in the scenario.[46] A developed format for a proposed television programme, even though not a full synopsis or script, can be protected by an action for breach of confidence.[47] However, the claim will fail if the claimant's ideas lack novelty and are too vague to be protected.[48]

It has been doubted whether artistic or literary information can be the subject of a duty of confidence when it is intended to be published, but publishers have a commercial interest to maintain its secrecy until publication.[49] However, the physical appearance of a "closed" film set which formed part of a scene in a film intended for public release can be the subject of an action for breach of confidence.[50] Similarly, the photographic record of a scene posed for a group's album cover where unauthorised photography was prohibited could arguably be the subject of a breach of confidence. This is so, even though the public have been allowed to observe the scene and could have disclosed or sketched the scene.[51]

H. GOVERNMENT INFORMATION

20–14 The position of the Government in its attempts to prevent disclosure of government secrets is special and was reviewed thoroughly in *Att-Gen v Guardian*

---

[37] And see "Relationship Between Copyright and Confidence" at para. 20–04, above.

[38] *Gilbert v Star Newspaper Company Ltd* (1894) 11 T.L.R. 4.

[39] *Fraser v Thames Television Ltd* [1984] 1 Q.B.D. 44.

[40] *Macklin v Richardson* (1770) 2 Amb. 694.

[41] *Webb v Rose* (1732) cited (1766) 4 Burr. 2303 at 2330; though a pupil might take copies for his own use, as long as he did not publish them; *Lamb v Evans* [1893] 1 Ch. 218.

[42] *Forrester v Waller* (1741) cited (1766) 4 Burr. 2303 at 2331; see also *Turner v Robinson* (1860) 10 Ir. Ch. 121 at 510; *Southey v Sherwood* (1817) 2 Mer. 435; *Gee (A.P.) v Pritchard (W.)* (1818) 2 Sw. 402.

[43] *Pollard v Photographic Co* (1889) 40 Ch.D. 345; *cf. Ellis v Marshall (H.) & Son* (1895) 64 L.J.Q.B.D. 757; and see para. 4–33, above. See also the statutory moral right to photographic privacy, paras 11–58 *et seq.*, above.

[44] *Caird v Sime* (1887) L.R. 12 App.Cas. 326.

[45] *Fraser v Thames Television* [1984] Q.B.D. 44 at 65; *De Maudsley v Palumbo* [1996] F.S.R. 447 at 456; *Talbot v General Television Corporation Pty Ltd* [1981] R.P.C. 1 (Sup Ct of Victoria); *Green v Broadcasting Corpn of New Zealand* [1989] 2 All E.R. 1056; *Promotivate International Inc v Toronto Star Newspapers* [1986] 23 D.L.R. (4th) 196 (Ontario High Ct).

[46] *Moore v Edwards* [1901–4] Mac. C.C. 44; *Fraser v Edwards* [1905–10] Mac.C.C. 10.

[47] *Fraser v Thames Television* [1984] Q.B.D. 44.

[48] *De Maudsley v Palumbo* [1996] F.S.R. 447 at 456 in which it was held that confidential information must be sufficiently developed and not merely aspiration such as that captured in the phrase "Wouldn't it be great if".

[49] *Times Newspapers Ltd v MGN Ltd* [1993] E.M.L.R. 443.

[50] *Shelley Films Ltd v Rex Features Ltd* [1994] E.M.L.R. 134.

[51] *Creation Records Ltd v News Group Newspapers Ltd* [1997] E.M.L.R. 444.

Newspapers (No.2),[52] the *Spycatcher* litigation, involving the publication of the memoirs of a former member of the Security Service. It is necessary to show not only that the information is confidential, but also that it is in the public interest that it should not be published.[53] Competing public interests of national security, freedom of speech and public scrutiny of government activities are weighed in the balance and play a more important part in such cases than in cases of information imparted in a private, industrial or commercial setting.[54] The reason for this additional public interest requirement appears to be that, although in the case of private citizens there is a public interest that confidential information should as such be protected, in the case of government secrets the mere fact of confidentiality is insufficient. In a free society the workings of government should be open to scrutiny and criticism.[55] The revelation of defence, intelligence or other secrets may harm the public interest by impeding the efficient achievement of proper Government ends. The Crown, however, as representing the continuing government of the country has no private life or personal feelings capable of being hurt by disclosure of confidential information.[56]

A member of the Security Service is under a lifelong duty of confidence to the Crown enforceable at the instance of the Attorney-General. The purpose of the duty is to preserve the secrets of the service which it would be against the public interest to disclose,[57] and it extends to all secret or confidential information which he acquired during his service, without discrimination between secrets of greater or lesser importance[58] and without being limited merely to information imparted under an obligation of confidence.[59] Members of the Security Service and third parties, such as the media, who receive information from them in respect of the service which they know or ought to know is confidential may be restrained from disclosing the information unless prior publication renders such an injunction pointless.[60] Such parties intending to publish information already in the public domain, if not restrained, may nevertheless be liable for damages or to an account of profits.[61] It has been said that it is very difficult to envisage a case where the defence of iniquity[62] will mean that it is in the public interest to publish al-

---

[52] *Att-Gen v Guardian Newspapers (No.2)*, HL (E) [1990] 1 A.C. 109.
[53] *Att-Gen v Jonathan Cape Ltd* [1976] 1 Q.B.D. 752 at 770 (diaries of a former minister revealing cabinet discussions); *Att-Gen v Guardian Newspapers (No.2)* HL (E) [1990] 1 A.C. 109 at 202, 218, 256, 283 (memoirs of a former officer of the Security Service); *Commonwealth of Australia v John Fairfax & Sons Ltd* (1980) 147 C.L.R. 39 at 51–53 (leaked government documents tending to prejudice foreign relations).
[54] *Att-Gen v Guardian Newspapers (No.1)* [1987] 1 W.L.R. 1248; *Att-Gen v Guardian Newspapers (No.2)*, HL (E) [1990] 1 A.C. 109; *Att-Gen v Brandon Book Publishers Ltd* [1989] F.S.R. 37 (High Ct of Ireland); *cf. Att-Gen v Turnaround Distribution Ltd* [1989] F.S.R. 169; *Lord Advocate v The Scotsman Publications Ltd* [1990] A.C. 812; see also "Justifiable Use and Public Interest", para. 20–23, below.
[55] *Att-Gen v Guardian Newspapers (No.2)*, HL (E) [1990] 1 A.C. 109, at 283.
[56] *Att-Gen v Guardian Newspapers (No.2)*, HL (E) [1990] 1 A.C. 109, at 256.
[57] *Att-Gen v Guardian Newspapers (No.2)*, HL (E) [1990] 1 A.C. 109, at 259, 265, 269, and 284; *Commonwealth of Australia v John Fairfax & Sons Ltd* (1980) 147 C.L.R. 39; *SmithKline & French Laboratories (Australia) Ltd v Secretary to the Department of Community Services and Health* [1990] F.S.R. 617 (Fed Ct of Australia: NSW Division).
[58] *Att-Gen v Guardian Newspapers (No.2)*, HL (E) [1990] 1 A.C. 109, at 269G, 284C.
[59] *Att-Gen v Guardian Newspapers (No.2)*, HL (E) [1990] 1 A.C. 109, at 144G (more a duty of secrecy than confidence).
[60] *Att-Gen v Guardian Newspapers (No.2)*, HL (E) [1990] 1 A.C. 109, at 267D.
[61] *Att-Gen v Guardian Newspapers (No.2)*, HL (E) [1990] 1 A.C. 109, at 260, 267 and 288–289; see also para. 20–15, below, on the loss of confidentiality.
[62] See para. 20–23, below.

legations in the media of iniquity in the Secret Service as opposed to pursuing the available avenues for proper complaint.[63]

There is no inconsistency between English law on this subject and Article 10 of the European Convention on Human Rights.[64] Section 6 of the Human Rights Act 1998, which provides that it is unlawful for a public authority to act in any way which is incompatible with a Convention right, requires any claim to secrecy brought by a public body to be tested against Article 10 of the Convention. If such a restriction on free speech cannot be justified under Article 10(2) (which provides exceptions), it will be unlawful.[65] However, Article 10 does not require the press to seek confirmation from the Attorney General or the court that facts it intends to publish are already in the public domain so as to remove from them the cloak of confidentiality.[66]

Opinions expressed by individual members at cabinet meetings remain confidential until such time that their disclosure would not undermine the doctrine of collective cabinet responsibility.[67] The obligation of confidence does not extend, however, to advice given by civil servants to ministers or to observations made by ministers on civil servants.[68]

4. CONFIDENTIAL OBLIGATION

A. INTRODUCTION

20–15 However secret and confidential the information may be, there can be no binding obligation of confidence unless the information is communicated or acquired in circumstances importing an obligation of confidence.[69] The law no longer requires there to be a confidential relationship between the parties for the obligation to arise,[70] but the obligation most clearly arises where there is such a relationship. These cases are considered first, below.

Confidential relationships: general. The law has long recognised that an obligation of confidence can arise out of particular relationships, such as doctor and patient,[71] solicitor and client,[72] banker and customer,[73] employer and employee,[74] and husband and wife.[75] An obligation of confidence will arise whenever the party subject to the duty is in a situation where he knows or ought as a reasonable person to know that the other person wishes to keep that information confiden-

---

[63] *Att-Gen v Guardian Newspapers (No.2)*, HL (E) [1990] 1 A.C. 109, at 187B–188H, 269B and 282–283.

[64] *Att-Gen v Guardian Newspapers (No.2)*, HL (E) [1990] 1 A.C. 109, at 283F.

[65] *London Regional Transport Ltd v The Mayor of London* [2003] E.M.L.R. 4, *per* Sedley L.J. at paras 59–61.

[66] *Att-Gen v Times Newspapers Ltd* [2001] 1 W.L.R. 885.

[67] *Att-Gen v Jonathan Cape Ltd* [1976] Q.B.D. 752 (the publishers of the diaries of former minister Richard Crossman were not enjoined after 10 years had elapsed since the cabinet discussions which were recorded).

[68] *Att-Gen v Jonathan Cape Ltd* [1976] Q.B.D. 752.

[69] *Coco v A.N. Clark (Engineers) Ltd* [1969] R.P.C. 41 at 47.

[70] See para. 20–19, below.

[71] *W. v Egdell* [1990] Ch. 359; *Hunter v Mann* [1974] Q.B.D. 767.

[72] *Parry Jones v The Law Society* [1968] Ch. 195, CA; *Re a Firm of Solicitors* [1997] Ch. 1.

[73] *Tournier v National Provincial and Union Bank* [1924] 1 K.B. 461; *Att-Gen v Guardian Newspapers (No.2)*, HL (E) [1990] 1 A.C. 109 at 255; *F.O.C.C. Ltd v Chase Manhattan Bank* [1990] H.K.L.R. 277.

[74] *Faccenda Chicken v Fowler* [1987] Ch. 117

[75] *Argyll (Duchess) v Argyll (Duke)* [1967] Ch. 302.

tial,[76] and so the existence or otherwise of such a confidential relationship should not give rise to problems as to the law.[77] For example, it will be relatively easy for a claimant to establish an obligation of confidence where information of commercial or industrial value is communicated during business negotiations with a view to a joint venture or to the joint commercial exploitation of the information.[78] In contrast, where information is communicated in a social rather than a business setting and where the purported confider refrains from referring to confidentiality, a confidential relationship is unlikely to arise.[79] The communication of information for a limited purpose may make it clear that the communication is confidential.[80] Objective standards may exist to inform a person that information is being communicated under an obligation of confidence. These include usages and practices of the particular industry or trade concerned,[81] such as relevant theatre[82] or television[83] industry custom or practice.

The obligation of confidence can terminate for a variety of reasons. The information may enter the public domain.[84] A change of circumstances may release a party from a duty of confidence as a matter of public interest.[85] A duty of confidence owed by a public authority in respect of information held by it in due performance of its public function can be overridden where, due to a change of circumstances, the interests of justice require disclosure for the purposes of legal proceedings.[86] The party confiding the confidential information can expressly or impliedly release the confidence in whole or in part.

B. CONFIDENCE IN CONTRACTS

The obligation to keep information confidential can arise from an express or an implied contract term under which the information was originally communicated.[87] The basis of the jurisdiction in these cases is contract rather than confidence.[88] "Know-how", "non-disclosure" and "confidentiality" agreements are common examples. In the case of an express covenant, questions of construction may arise.[89] Covenants of confidentiality are routinely upheld on

20–16

---

[76] *Att-Gen v Guardian Newspapers Ltd (No.2)* [1990] 1 A.C. 109 at 281. This approach has been confirmed in *Douglas v Hello! Ltd* [2001] Q.B.D. 967, CA; *Venables v News Group Newspapers Ltd* [2001] Fam Div 430; and *A v B plc* [2003] Q.B.D. 195.

[77] *A v B plc* [2003] Q.B.D. 195, 207, paras 11(ix) and (x) *per* Lord Woolf C.J., approved in *Campbell v MGN Ltd* [2004] UKHL 22 at para.85; [2004] 2 W.L.R. 1232, where Lord Hope noted that the difficulty arises in applying the relevant facts to the law.

[78] *House of Spring Gardens Ltd v Point Blank Ltd* [1983] F.S.R. 213 at 252; *Lac Minerals Ltd v International Corona Resources Ltd* [1990] F.S.R. 441 (Sup Ct of Canada); *Indata Equipment Supplies Limited v A.C. L. Ltd* [1998] F.S.R. 248, CA; *Murray v Yorkshire Fund Managers Ltd* [1998] 1 W.L.R. 951, CA.

[79] *De Maudsley v Palumbo* [1996] F.S.R. 447 at 458.

[80] *Pollard v Photographic Co* (1888) 40 Ch.D. 345 (posing for the purpose of acquiring a portrait photograph).

[81] *Thomas Marshall (Exports) Ltd v Guinle* [1979] Ch. 227 at 248.

[82] *Gilbert v Star Newspaper C Ltd* (1894) 11 T.L.R. 4.

[83] *Fraser v Thames Television Ltd* [1984] Q.B.D. 44 at 66.

[84] See para. 20–08, above, on the consequences of confidential information becoming publicly available. But the fact that information may be known to a limited number of people does not of itself prevent it retaining its confidentiality: see *Mills v News Group Newspapers Ltd* [2001] E.M.L.R. 957 at 105; *Att-Gen v Guardian Newspapers (No 2)* [1990] 1 A.C. 109 at 281.

[85] See para. 20–23, below, on justifiable use and public interest.

[86] *Soden v Burns* [1996] 1 W.L.R. 1512; *Wallace Smith Trust v Deloitte Haskins & Sells* [1997] 1 W.L.R. 257.

[87] *Yates Circuit Foil Co v Electrofoils Ltd* [1976] F.S.R. 345, *Thomas Marshall (Exports) Ltd v Guinle* [1979] Ch. 227, *Simtech Advanced Training and Simulation Systems Ltd v Jasmin Simtec Ltd* [1995] F.S.R. 475 for examples of express covenants.

[88] *Att-Gen v Barker* [1990] 3 All E.R. 257, CA at 259, 261–262.

[89] *Lansing Linde Ltd v Kerr* [1991] 1 W.L.R. 251 in which the expression "trade secrets" was held

interim injunction applications.[90] Article 10 and all of the principles applicable to the duty of confidence in equity apply with equal force to duties of confidence arising under contract.[91] Accordingly, for a contractual restriction on the freedom of expression to be upheld, it must fall within Article 10(2).[92]

C. CONTRACTS OF SERVICE

20-17 The area of the law relating to the obligation of confidence an employee or ex-employee may owe to his employer is extensive. Only an outline will be set out here. The rights and obligations of employees in regard to the disclosure and use of confidential information were re-stated by the Court of Appeal in *Faccenda Chicken Ltd v Fowler*.[93]

While an employee remains in employment, he owes a duty of good faith and confidence to his employer. If this duty is not expressly provided for in a contract of employment, the duty will readily be implied by the court.[94] The extent of the duty will vary according to the nature of the contract of employment.[95] Under such duty, an employee must not disclose information which he is expressly told is confidential or which is obviously confidential given its character.[96] This includes information which becomes part of his own skill and knowledge applied in the course of his employer's business.[97]

That duty of good faith will be broken if the employee makes or copies a list of customers of his employer for use after his employment ends or if he deliberately memorises such a list.[98] The duty includes an obligation to protect his employer's trade and commercial secrets from disclosure.[99] An employee is not entitled to steal documents or to use for his own purposes (*e.g.* for soliciting orders) information which could sensibly be regarded as confidential information contained in the stolen documents regarding the claimant's customers, customer contacts, requirements or prices charged. Neither is an employee entitled to copy such information on to scrap paper and take it away with him and use it for his own purposes.[1]

20-18 After termination of employment, the implied obligation of confidence is more restricted than a duty of good faith and only covers information which is of a suf-

---

to include not only secret formulae for manufactured products, but also the names of customers and of the goods which they would buy.

[90] *Campbell v Frisbee* [2002] E.M.L.R. 31 (personal assistant to a super model); *Adams v Attridge* [1999] CLY 2005 (ex-chauffeur to the pop group Spice Girls); *Att-Gen v Barker* [1990] 3 All E.R. 257 (employee to the Royal Household); *Barrymore v News Group Newspapers Ltd* [1997] F.S.R. 600 (sexual partner of television personality).

[91] *London Regional Transport Ltd v The Mayor of London* [2003] E.M.L.R. 4, para.46 *per* Robert Walker L.J.

[92] *London Regional Transport Ltd v The Mayor of London* [2003] E.M.L.R. 4.

[93] [1987] Ch. 117; *Lancashire Fires Ltd v S.A. Lyons & Company Ltd* [1996] F.S.R. 629; *Roger Bullivant Ltd v Ellis* [1987] F.S.R. 172; *Manor Electronics Ltd v Dickson* [1988] R.P.C. 618; *Balston Ltd v Headline Filters Ltd* [1987] F.S.R. 330, [1990] F.S.R. 385; *Johnson & Bloy (Holdings) Ltd v Wolstenholme Rink plc* [1989] F.S.R. 135; *Berkeley Administration Inc v McClelland* [1990] F.S.R. 505; *Ocular Sciences Ltd v Aspect Vision Care* [1997] R.P.C. 289; *A.T. Poeton (Gloucester Plating) Ltd v Horten* [2001] F.S.R. 169, CA; *Fibrenetix Storage Ltd v Davies (Tom)* [2004] EWHC 1359 (QBD).

[94] *Tipping v Clarke* (1843) 2 Hare 383 at 393; this principle has been applied in numerous subsequent cases: *Robb v Green* [1895] 2 Q.B.D. 315; *Reid & Sigrist Ltd v Moss* (1932) 49 R.P.C. 461 and *Faccenda Chicken Ltd v Fowler* [1987] Ch. 117.

[95] see for example *Fibrenetix Storage Ltd v Davis* [2004] EWHC 1359 (QBD), unreported.

[96] For an example of the application of these rules, see *Cray Valley Ltd v Deltech Europe Ltd* [2003] EWHC 728 (Ch), unreported.

[97] *Faccenda Chicken Ltd v Fowler* [1987] Ch. 117.

[98] *Baker v Gibbons* [1972] 1 W.L.R. 693; *Lansing Linde Ltd v Kerr* [1991] 1 All E.R. 418.

[99] *Printers & Finishers v Holloway (No.2)* [1965] 1 W.L.R. 1.

[1] *Universal Thermosensors Ltd v Hibben* [1992] 1 W.L.R. 840.

ficiently high degree of confidentiality to amount to a "trade secret", *e.g.* secret processes of manufacture, such as chemical formulae, designs or special methods of construction.[2] Regard must be had to all the circumstances of the case; in particular, to the nature of the employment (*e.g.* if the employee habitually handles sensitive material), the nature of the information (*i.e.* whether it is a trade secret or of such a highly confidential nature as to amount to the equivalent of a trade secret), whether restrictions have been imposed on the circulation of the information, whether the employer has impressed on the employee the confidentiality of the information, and whether the information in question can be easily isolated from other information which the employee is free to use or disclose.[3] To be capable of protection, information must be defined with some degree of precision; an employer will have great difficulty in obtaining protection for his business methods and practices.[4]

The overriding general principle is that, subject to the duty of confidence, every person has the right to use and exploit for the purpose of earning a living all the skill, experience and knowledge which he has at his disposal, including that which he has acquired in the course of previous periods of employment.[5] Where there is no restraint of trade clause, no injunction will be granted to restrain the use of customers' names for which the defendant relies on his memory.[6] For public policy reasons, an employee is entitled to use and put at the disposal of new employers all his acquired skill and knowledge. That is so, no matter where he acquired that skill and knowledge.[7]

The distinction between information which can be treated as the employee's acquired skill and knowledge, and that which falls within the implied term of a contract of employment so as to prevent its use or disclosure after his employment has ceased may often on the facts be very hard to draw. Much will depend on the circumstances of a particular case.[8] It is a matter of degree.[9] For example, it would be unrealistic to expect a small and informal organisation to adopt the same business disciplines as a larger and more bureaucratic concern. The court must ultimately judge whether an ex-employee has illegitimately used the confidential information which forms part of the stock-in-trade of his former employer either for his own benefit or to the detriment of the former employer, or whether he has simply used his own professional expertise, gained in whole or in part during his former employment.[10] If the information in question can fairly be regarded as a separate part of the employee's stock of knowledge which a man of honesty and intelligence would recognise to be the property of his old employer, and not his own to do with as he likes, it will be capable of protection as confidential.[11] Thus an ex-employee may be restrained from using or disclosing trade secrets which he has committed to memory.

---

[2] *Faccenda Chicken v Fowler* [1987] Ch. 117; *P.S.M. International Ltd v Whitehouse* [1992] F.S.R. 489; *United Indigo Chemical Co Ltd v Robinson* (1932) 49 R.P.C. 178; *Poly Lina Ltd v Finch* [1995] F.S.R. 751 (both technical formulae and financial or commercial information were trade secrets); *Lancashire Fires Ltd v S.A. Lyons & Company Ltd* [1996] F.S.R. 629.

[3] *Faccenda Chicken v Fowler* [1987] Ch. 117 at 137 as approved in *Lancashire Fires Ltd v S.A. Lyons & Company Ltd* [1996] F.S.R. 629 at 668.

[4] *Lancashire Fires Ltd v S.A. Lyons & Company Ltd* [1996] F.S.R. 629 at 668.

[5] *Balston Ltd v Headline Filters Ltd* [1987] F.S.R. 330 at 351.

[6] *Roberts v Northwest Fixing* [1993] F.S.R. 281, CA.

[7] *Ocular Sciences Ltd v Aspect Vision Care Ltd (No.2)* [1997] R.P.C. 289.

[8] *Lancashire Fires Ltd v S.A. Lyons & Company Ltd* [1996] F.S.R. 629 at 668–669; and see *Ocular Sciences Ltd v Aspect Vision Care Ltd (No.2)* [1997] R.P.C. 289 at 371.

[9] *P.S.M. International Ltd v Whitehouse* [1992] F.S.R. 489.

[10] *Lancashire Fires Ltd v S.A. Lyons & Company Ltd* [1996] F.S.R. 629 at 669.

[11] *Printers & Finishers v Holloway (No.2)* [1965] 1 W.L.R. 1; applied in *Lancashire Fires Ltd v S.A. Lyons & Company Ltd* [1996] F.S.R. 629 at 667 and in *Ocular Sciences Ltd v Aspect Vision Care Ltd (No.2)* [1997] R.P.C. 289 at 371.

An express covenant in a contract of employment restricting the employee's post-termination activities in order to protect the employer's trade secrets or customer connections will only be enforced if reasonably necessary and not for the purpose of merely restricting bona fide competition by such employee.[12]

D. OTHER EXAMPLES OF CONFIDENTIAL RELATIONSHIPS

20–19 If a person lends his manuscript to another, there will generally be implied an obligation that the latter shall not publish it,[13] and where an idea for a television series was communicated orally to a television company a duty of confidence arose.[14] Where information is imparted with an express confidentiality notice, a duty of confidence may be created in equity.[15] Such a non-contractual stipulation of confidentiality must be clear and manifest to the recipient of the information. If the recipient does not expressly reject the duty of confidence, the subsequent use of such information from an alternative source may give rise to complaint.[16] Where a person sits for his portrait by a photographer, there may be implied an obligation on the photographer not to sell or exhibit copies without the sitter's consent,[17] and an obligation may be implied on the part of persons attending private lectures not to take them down and publish them.[18]

An obligation of confidence may even arise where there is no "relationship" in the literal sense, as where a person has obtained the confidential information from another person without his consent such as by theft,[19] or by finding and keeping an obviously confidential document which has been lost or mislaid, or by unauthorised telephone tapping,[20] or by stealth or by a trick,[21] or even by accident.[22] Where counsel's papers were mistakenly sent to the defendant's solicitors, an injunction was granted to restrain the use of confidential information derived from the papers.[23] The court has held not only that no relationship is required to give rise to an obligation of confidence, but also that in exceptional cases an injunction may be granted against the whole world to restrain the publi-

---

[12] *Faccenda Chicken v Fowler* [1987] Ch. 117; *Herbert Morris Ltd v Saxelby* [1916] 1 A.C. 688; *Printers & Finishers v Holloway (No.2)* [1965] 1 W.L.R. 1; *Lansing Linde Ltd v Kerr* [1991] 1 W.L.R. 251; *Poly Lina Ltd v Finch* [1995] F.S.R. 751; and see *Lancashire Fires Ltd v S.A. Lyons & Company Ltd* [1996] F.S.R. 629 at 667.

[13] *Queensberry (Duke) v Shebbeare* (1761) 2 Eden 32; and see, as to letters, para. 20–11, above.

[14] *Fraser v Thames Television Ltd* [1984] Q.B.D. 44.

[15] *Stephens v Avery* [1988] Ch. 449.

[16] *Johnson v Heat and Air Systems Ltd* (1941) 58 R.P.C. 229; see also *Coco v A.N. Clark (Engineers) Ltd* [1969] R.P.C. 41.

[17] *Pollard v Photographic Co* (1889) 40 Ch.D. 345; see paras 11–58, *et seq.*, above, as to statutory moral right to privacy.

[18] *Nicols v Pitman* (1884) 26 Ch.D. 374; *Caird v Sime* (1887) 12 App.Cas. 320.

[19] *Ashburton v Pape* [1913] 2 Ch. 469; *Franklin v Giddings* [1978] 1 Q.D.R. 72 (Sup Ct of Queensland) (theft of twigs containing propagation secrets); *Church of Scientology of California v D.H.S.S.* [1979] 1 W.L.R. 723; *Union Carbide Corp v Naturin Ltd* [1987] F.S.R. 538 at 547; *Universal Thermosensors Ltd v Hibben* [1992] 1 W.L.R. 840 (ex-employee not entitled to use confidential information obtained from stolen documents or copied on to scrap paper); *Shelley Films v Rex Features Ltd* [1994] E.M.L.R. 134 (photographer who gained access to a "closed" film set without consent became subject to a duty of confidence); see also "Legislating the Criminal Code: Misuse of Trade Secrets", The Law Commission Consultation Paper No.150 (November, 1997).

[20] *Francome v Mirror Group Newspapers Ltd* [1984] 1 W.L.R. 892; *cf. Malone v Metropolitan Police Commissioner* [1979] Ch. 344.

[21] *ITC Film Distributors Ltd v Video Exchange Ltd* [1982] Ch. 431 (documents obtained by a trick excluded from evidence).

[22] *Att-Gen v Guardian Newspapers (No.2)*, HL (E) [1990] 1 A.C. 109 at 281F.

[23] *English & American Insurance Co Ltd v Herbert Smith* [1988] F.S.R. 232; see also *Re Griffin (Paul)*, The Times, November 6, 1996, CA (journalist taking counsel's papers left in court because of genuine, if mistaken belief he was authorised to do so).

cation of personal information if it is necessary to protect a countervailing convention.[24]

Under the Civil Procedure Rules, a party may only use documents disclosed through standard or specific disclosure for the purposes of the proceedings in which they are disclosed and not for any collateral or ulterior purpose.[25] This rule is the statutory enactment of the old common law implied undertaking.[26] It specifies clear exceptions where a document can be used for purposes ancillary to the proceedings; namely where the document has been read in open court,[27] where the court gives permission[28] and where the party who disclosed the document and person to whom the document belongs agree.[29] This protection is available apart from a party's private right of confidentiality as part of and in the interests of the proper administration of justice.[30] Even where a document has been read or referred to in open court, a court may make an order restricting or prohibiting it use.[31]

Benefit of confidence. The person entitled to the benefit of confidential information and to whom the duty of confidence is owed is the person who is entitled to sue as claimant for breach of confidence. If the original creator of the confidential information acted merely as agent or employee, the principal or employer will be the party able to sue.[32] Medical information about patients is subject to a duty of confidentiality owed both to the individual patients and to the carers.[33]

20–20

Where the confidential information concerns information disclosed and views expressed at cabinet meetings, the Attorney-General is entitled to enforce the obligation of confidence on behalf of the Crown.[34] Similarly, the Attorney-General is entitled to enforce the duty of confidence owed to the Crown by civil servants and former Crown servants.[35]

A claimant's right to sue has traditionally depended upon that claimant communicating confidential information to a confidant. However, as the law develops to include other situations, particularly in the privacy field, the person entitled to

---

[24] *Venables v News Group Newspapers Ltd* [2001] Fam Div 430 at para.81; applied in *Mills v News Group Newspapers Ltd* [2001] E.M.L.R. 957 at para.26 in which Lawrence Collins J. noted that it is no longer a necessary element of the law of confidence that the information arises from a confidential relationship.

[25] See CPR, r.31.22(1).

[26] *Hassneh Insurance Co of Israel v Stewart J. Mew* [1993] 2 Lloyd's Rep. 243 as an example of an implied undertaking under common law in the context of arbitration proceedings prior to the implementation of the Civil Procedure Rules.

[27] See CPR r.31.22(1)(a).

[28] See CPR, r.31.22(1)(b).

[29] See CPR, r.31.22(1) (c).

[30] *Distillers Co (Biochemicals) Ltd v Times Newspapers Ltd* [1975] Q.B.D. 613; *Riddick v Thames Board Mills Ltd* [1977] Q.B.D. 881 (document disclosed on disclosure cannot be used as basis for subsequent defamation action); *Home Office v Harman* [1983] 1 A.C. 280.

[31] See CPR r.31.22(2); and *Smithkline Beecham Plc v Apotex Europe Ltd* [2004] EWHC 2052 (in which it was held that "how to do it" documents or technical process descriptions could expect such protection without the need for a detailed explanation of why damages would be caused by their disclosure.

[32] *Fraser v Evans* [1969] 1 Q.B.D. 349 at 362 in which a consultant who had prepared a confidential report for the Greek Government was refused an injunction, as the duty of confidence was owed to the Greek Government and not to him; and see *Gartside v Outram* (1858) 26 L.J. Ch. 113 at 114; *Weld Blundell v Stephens* [1919] 1 K.B. 520; *Butler v Board of Trade* [1971] Ch. 680; *Apps v Weldtite Products Ltd* [2001] F.S.R. 703.

[33] *Ashworth Hospital Authority v Mirror Group Newspapers Ltd* [2001] 1 W.L.R. 515, CA; *Imutran v Uncaged Campaigns Ltd* [2002] F.S.R. 2; and see *Mersey Care National Health Service Trust v Ackroyd* [2003] F.S.R. 820.

[34] *Att-Gen v Jonathan Cape Ltd* [1976] Q.B.D. 752.

[35] *Att-Gen v Guardian Newspapers Ltd (No.2)*, HL (E) [1990] A.C. 109.

sue may more properly be regarded as the person to whom the confidential information relates.[36]

It appears that the benefit of confidence can, in certain circumstances, be assigned.[37] It is suggested that this is the correct position in the commercial field but is not the correct position in respect of personal information where the cause of action is intrinsically personal.[38]

5. WRONGFUL USE

20–21 Once a person has acquired confidential information under a duty of confidence, he must not misuse or threaten to misuse that information. What amounts to a wrongful use may turn on what is unconscionable for the recipient of confidential information to do with that information where his conscience is bound by that confidence.[39] Partial disclosure which is significant and substantial can amount to a breach.[40] Imperilling confidentiality may be sufficient for an injunction.[41] A particular form of disclosure may be restrained.[42] The confidant is liable even if he uses the information "subconsciously".[43] He is also liable where he has no intention of taking advantage of the information,[44] or making a financial gain, or acting out of malice.[45]

Where a defendant misuses the information maliciously to harm the claimant or for his own gain[46], the duty of confidence is more accurately expressed in a qualified form as a duty not to use the information without paying a reasonable sum for it.[47] There are often difficulties involved in granting an injunction when a defendant has added information of his own to the information he has acquired in confidence and the two have become commercially inextricable.[48] In such cases, damages may be a more appropriate remedy as compensation for the detriment suffered.

In the absence of a contractual, fiduciary or other special relationship between the co-owners of confidential information, a co-owner who is excluded from the group of co-owners ceases to have an interest in the information, so that use of

---

[36] *Venables v News Group Newspapers Ltd* [2001] Fam Div 430, in which James Bulger's murderers were entitled to an injunction prohibiting publication of facts likely to lead to their identification.

[37] *Mustad & Son v Dosen (1928)* [1964] 1 W.L.R. 109.

[38] *Ord v Upton* [2000] Ch. 352.

[39] *Douglas v Hello! Ltd* [2001] Q.B.D. 967, CA at para.65; affirmed in *R. v Dept of Health, ex p. Source Information Ltd* [2001] Q.B.D. 424, CA at para.41. See also *London Regional Transport Ltd v The Mayor of London* [2003] E.M.L.R. 4 at paras 57-59 where Sedley L.J. considers that conscience is not the determining factor in every case.

[40] *Amber Size and Chemical Co Ltd v Menzel* [1913] 2 Ch. 239.

[41] *Hivac Ltd v Park Royal Scientific Instruments Ltd* [1946] Ch. 169 (breach of confidence likely from practical point of view if workers took new employment).

[42] *Creation Records Ltd v News Group Ltd* [1997] E.M.L.R. 444 (photographic record of a scene was the subject of an interlocutory injunction even though the defendant could have sketched the scene without complaint). See also *Theakston v MGN Ltd* [2002] E.M.L.R. 398 in which photographs of the claimant visiting a brothel were injuncted, but not a narrative description of the claimant's activities in the brothel.

[43] *Seager v Copydex* [1967] 1 W.L.R. 923 (the defendants subconsciously reproduced information which the claimant had implanted in their minds).

[44] *Seager v Copydex* [1967] 1 W.L.R. 923; *Interfirm Comparisons (Australia) Pty Ltd v Law Society of New South Wales* [1977] R.P.C. 137.

[45] *British Steel Corporation v Granada Television Ltd*, [1981] A.C. 1096; innocence, malice, and intentional pursuit of financial gain are relevant to the exercise of discretionary injunctive relief; see *Coco v A.N. Clark (Engineers) Ltd* [1969] R.P.C. 41 at 50.

[46] *Mainmet Holdings plc v Austin* [1991] F.S.R. 538.

[47] *Coco v A.N. Clark (Engineers) Ltd* [1969] R.P.C. 41; *Bostitch Inc v McGarry & Cole Ltd* [1964] R.P.C. 173.

[48] *Ocular Sciences Ltd v Aspect Vision Care Ltd* [1997] R.P.C. 289 at 401 and 404.

the information by the others (or authorisation of a third party to use the information) without his consent is not a wrongful use.[49]

Detriment. There is no definitive authority on whether wrongful use may consti-   **20–22**
tute an actionable breach of confidence where no specific detriment is caused to
the claimant.[50] Persuasive *obiter* judgments suggest that no detriment is
required.[51] It is suggested that in the case of personal and non-commercial
confidences it ought to be enough for a claimant to have a legitimate interest in
protecting the information. Where there is no legitimate interest, an action should
fail. Different considerations arguably apply in the commercial field.

Justifiable use and public interest. The public interest in the preservation of   **20–23**
confidences may be outweighed by a countervailing public interest in favour of
disclosure. There are circumstances in which a party who has received confidential information has a just cause or excuse for disclosure and, indeed, it may be
his duty to reveal what he knows.[52] This has become recognised as the general
public interest defence, or defence of just cause and excuse.[53]

The courts have always refused to uphold the right to confidence when to do so
would be to cover up wrongdoing.[54] It was said that there could be no confidence
in iniquity.[55] This approach was developed by the courts to include cases in which
it is in the public interest that the confidential information should be disclosed.[56]
For example, the public interest might justify disclosure of matters, carried out or
contemplated, in breach of the country's security, or in breach of law or otherwise
destructive of the country or its people, including matters medically dangerous to
the public[57] and other misdeeds of similar gravity.[58] In such cases, the courts do
not restrain its disclosure.[59]

The inclusion into English law of Article 10 (freedom of expression) as one of
the Convention rights combined with section 12 of the Human Rights Act 1998
which requires the court to have particular regard to the importance of that right
has had an impact on the potential scope of the public interest defence. The public interest defence hinges on the principle that a genuine public interest favours
disclosure and encourages the freedom of expression. The extent to which the
Human Rights Act 1998 now requires a reappraisal of the public interest defence
remains to be fully determined. It is a developing area of the law. So far, the

---

[49] *Murray v Yorkshire Fund Managers Ltd* [1998] 1 W.L.R. 951, CA.

[50] *Coco v A.N. Clark (Engineers) Ltd* [1969] R.P.C. 41 at 48; similarly (keeping the question open),
see *Att-Gen v Guardian Newspapers (No.2)*, HL (E) [1990] 1 A.C. 109 at 281H.

[51] *Att-Gen v Guardian Newspapers (No.2)* [1990] 1 A.C. 109, at 256 *per* Lord Keith where he states
obiter that a donor to a charity ought to be able to remain anonymous; *SmithKline and French
Laboratories (Australia) Ltd v Secretary to the Dept of Community Services and Health* [1990]
F.S.R. 617 at 664, *per* Gummow J.

[52] *Schering Chemicals Ltd v Falkman Ltd* [1982] Q.B.D. 1 at 27; *Lion Laboratories Ltd v Evans*
[1985] Q.B.D. 527.

[53] *Fraser v Evans* [1969] 1 Q.B.D. 349, 362.

[54] There must be at least a *prima facie* case that the allegations of wrongdoing have substance: see
Att-Gen v Guardian Newspapers (No.2), HL (E) [1990] A.C. 109 at 222–223, 262A.

[55] *Gartside v Outram* (1857) 26 L.J. Ch. 113 as reviewed in *Att-Gen v Guardian Newspapers
(No.2)*, HL (E) [1990] 1 A.C. 109 at 268H, 282G.

[56] See *Initial Services Ltd v Putterill* [1968] 1 Q.B.D. 396, *Beloff v Pressdram Ltd* [1973] R.P.C.
765 and *Lion Laboratories Ltd v Evans* [1958] Q.B.D. 526 as reviewed in *Att-Gen v Guardian
Newspapers (No.2)*, HL (E) [1990] 1 A.C. 109 at 268H, 282G.

[57] *X v Y* [1988] R.P.C. 379 (doctor believed to have AIDS); *W. v Egdell* [1990] Ch. 359, CA,
(psychiatrist's report).

[58] *Beloff v Pressdram Ltd* [1973] R.P.C. 765 at 784 as cited in *Att-Gen v Guardian Newspapers
(No.2)*, HL (E) [1990] A.C. 109 at 222D; *Schering Chemicals Ltd v Falkman Ltd* [1982] Q.B.D.
1 at 27; *Francome v Mirror Group Newspapers Ltd* [1984] 1 W.L.R. 892.

[59] see for example *Fraser v Evans* [1969] 1 Q.B.D. 349 at 361; *Church of Scientology of California
and others v Kaufman* [1973] R.P.C. 635 (express confidentiality provision was invalid); *cf. British Steel Corporation v Granada Television Ltd* [1981] A.C. 1096.

courts have set guidelines for the granting of interim injunctions when a balance of Articles 8 and 10 is required.[60] Those guidelines emphasise the need for the courts to focus on the degree of intrusiveness required to satisfy the strict requirement of Article 10(2) if interference with the freedom of expression is to be permitted. The European Court of Human Rights has held that the decisive factor in balancing the protection of private life against freedom of expression should lie in the contribution that disclosure would make to a debate of general public interest.[61]

20–24   **Liability of third parties.** As a general rule, a third party who is in possession of information which he knows is subject to an obligation of confidence[62] or which he knows has been disclosed to him by his informant in breach of that obligation,[63] is also under an equitable duty of confidence not to use it or pass it on to anyone else.[64] The third party to whom the information has been wrongfully revealed comes under a duty of confidence to the original confider, though the extent to which that obligation is enforced will vary widely according to the circumstances of each case. The third party may be restrained from further use or disclosure[65] or be liable to an account of profits.[66]

It is uncertain whether a third party who is a bona fide purchaser for value without notice of the confidentiality of the information has a defence to a breach of confidence action. As the liability arises from the breach of an equitable obligation and not from the infringement of a proprietary right such as copyright, where ignorance is generally no defence,[67] a purchaser for value without notice ought not to be liable to restraint. In several cases it has been held that, even if a person comes by the information innocently, if he nevertheless gets to know that it was originally given in confidence, he can be restrained from breaking that confidence.[68] These cases indicate that the doctrine of bona fide purchaser for value without notice is not a defence once a purchaser becomes aware of the confidential nature of the information.[69]

In order to be fixed with an obligation of confidence, the third party must know that the information was confidential; knowledge of a mere assertion that a breach of confidence has been committed in respect of information received by him is

---

[60] *A v B plc* [2003] Q.B.D. 195; *London Regional Transport Ltd v The Mayor of London* [2003] E.M.L.R. 4 (in which disclosure was justified on public interest grounds of a report on proposed funding arrangements for the London Underground).

[61] *Von Hannover v Germany* [2004] ECHR Application No.59320/00; [2004] E.M.L.R. 21.

[62] *Att-Gen v Guardian Newspapers Ltd (No.2)*, HL (E) [1990] A.C. 109 at 268F (and see 201F and 281E) citing *Prince Albert v Strange* (1849) 1 Mac. & G. 25, affirmed (1849) 2 DeG. Sm 652;

[63] *Att-Gen v Guardian Newspapers Ltd (No.2)*, HL (E) [1990] A.C. 109 at 201F and 281E.

[64] See also *Argyll (Duchess) v Argyll (Duke)* [1967] Ch. 302; *Mustad & Son v Dosen* [1963] R.P.C. 41; *Andersen Consulting v C.H.P. Consulting Ltd*, noted at [1991] I.P.D. 15024.

[65] *Prince Albert v Strange* (1849) 1 Mac & G 25, affirmed (1849) 2 DeG. Sm 652; *Lancashire Fires Ltd v S.A. Lyons & Co Ltd* [1996] F.S.R. 629 at 675–8.

[66] *Att-Gen v Guardian Newspapers Ltd (No.2)*, HL (E) [1990] A.C. 109.

[67] *Mansell v Valley Printing Co* [1908] 2 Ch. 441; see CDPA 1988, s.97(1).

[68] *Fraser v Evans* [1969] 1 Q.B.D. 349; *Argyll (Duchess) v Argyll (Duke)* [1967] Ch. 302; *Printers & Finishers Ltd v Holloway* [1965] 1 W.L.R. 1 at 7; *Distillers Co (Biochemicals) Ltd v Times Newspapers Ltd* [1975] Q.B.D. 613; *Butler v Board of Trade* [1971] Ch. 680 at 690; *British Steel Corporation v Granada Television Ltd* [1981] A.C. 1069; see *PSM International v Whitehouse* [1992] F.S.R. 489, CA.

[69] In support of such a defence for a third party, see dicta in *Morrison v Moat* (1851) 9 Hare 241 at 263 as analysed in *Stevenson, Jordan and Harrison Ltd v Macdonald and Evans Ltd* [1951] 68 R.P.C. 190; *Tenatronics v Hauf* (1972) 23 D.L.R. (3d) 60; see also *Att-Gen v Guardian Newspapers Ltd (No.2)*, HL (E) [1990] A.C. 109 at 177F; *contra*, see *Wheatley v Bell* [1982] 2 N.S.W.L.R. 545, and *Att-Gen v Observer Ltd* [1989] 2 F.S.R. 3, *per* Nourse L.J.

insufficient.[70] It is, however, sufficient if the third party was aware of the circumstances in which the person imparting information to him acquired that information.[71] Knowledge of the circumstances includes the case where the recipient of the information has deliberately closed his eyes to the obvious.[72]

A third party is not released from his obligation because he knows that his primary confidant is about to breach his own obligation of confidence.[73]   **20–25**

The third party who deliberately procures confidential information from a confidant will be restrained.[74] Such conduct may give rise to liability outside the law of confidence, such as liability in conspiracy and for unlawful interference with contractual relations.

6. REMEDIES

Where the obligation of confidence is breached, a claimant can obtain damages   **20–26**
or an account of profits. An injunction is available to prevent future breaches. In addition, the court can also make an order for delivery up of material containing confidential information.

A. INJUNCTION

Interim[75] and final[76] injunctions may be granted. An injunction is an equitable   **20–27**
remedy and is therefore discretionary. That discretion is broad.[77] If the ingredients of the cause of action are established, and in the absence of an iniquity defence,[78] a restraint on disclosure will ordinarily be imposed unless the confider can be properly compensated by damages which the other party can pay.[79] Damages are not an adequate remedy in circumstances where there is difficulty in quantifying the loss caused by unauthorised publicity.[80] Therefore, in cases of personal information, an injunction will usually be appropriate.[81]

Interim Injunction: The effect of an interim injunction will be to postpone until trial the publication of the information, whereas publication before trial may irretrievably prejudice the position of the claimant by destroying the subject-matter of the action.[82] The court will not grant an interim injunction to restrain a breach of confidence where there is also a claim for libel, to which the defendant pleads

---

[70] *Fraser v Thames Television* [1984] Q.B.D. 44 at 58; *Union Carbide Corp v Naturin Ltd* [1987] F.S.R. 538.
[71] *Schering Chemicals Ltd v Falkman Ltd* [1982] Q.B.D. 1; *Union Carbide Corp v Naturin Ltd* [1987] F.S.R. 538 at 547.
[72] *Att-Gen v Guardian Newspapers (No.2)*, HL (E) [1990] A.C. 109 at 281C; *PCR Ltd v Dow Jones Telerate Ltd* [1998] F.S.R. 170 at 180 ("knowledge, even if Nelsonian, that the information was subject to confidentiality restrictions").
[73] *Att-Gen v Guardian Newspapers (No.2)*, HL (E) [1990] A.C. 109 at 261E.
[74] *Prince Albert v Strange* (1849) 1 Mac. & G. 25; affirmed (1849) 2 DeG. Sm 652; *Schering Chemicals Ltd v Falkman Ltd* [1982] Q.B.D. 1 as analysed in *Att-Gen v Guardian Newspapers Ltd (No.2)*, HL (E) [1990] A.C. 109 at 216G.
[75] *American Cyanamid v Ethicon* [1975] A.C. 396; *Series 5 Software Ltd v Clarke* [1996] F.S.R. 273.
[76] *Lancashire Fires Ltd v S.A. Lyons & Company Ltd* [1996] F.S.R. 629.
[77] *A v B plc* [2003] Q.B.D. 195 at para.11(i); *Venables v News Group Newspapers Ltd* [2001] Fam Div 430 at para.83 (where an injunction was granted to protect information requiring a special quality of protection).
[78] See para. 20–23, above.
[79] *Att-Gen v Guardian Newspapers (No.2)*, CA [1990] A.C. 109 at 217–8.
[80] *Schering Chemicals Ltd v Falkman Ltd* [1982] Q.B.D. 1 at 37 and 39; *cf. Graham v Deldafield* [1992] F.S.R. 313 (commercial information).
[81] *Coco v A.N. Clark (Engineers) Ltd* [1969] R.P.C. 41 at 50; *Francome v Mirror Group Newspapers Ltd* [1984] 1 W.L.R. 892 at 900, CA.
[82] *Francome v Mirror Group Newspapers Ltd* [1984] 1 W.L.R. 892; *Att-Gen v Guardian*

justification, and where it is impossible to extricate the claim for breach of confidence from the claim for defamation.[83] When determining interim injunction applications in the field of personal confidences, the courts must have regard to section 12(3) of the Human Rights Act 1998, which provides that no relief affecting the exercise of the right to freedom of expression is to be granted restraining publication before trial unless the court is satisfied that an injunction is likely to be granted at trial. The test imposed by this provision is whether a claimant's prospects of success at trial are "sufficiently favorable" to justify such an order being made in the particular circumstances of the case.[84]

Final Injunction: If a claimant is successful at trial, he will usually be granted a final injunction to prevent any future disclosure of the information being the subject matter of proceedings.

20–28   Principles: Where the likelihood of the future misuse of confidential information is established, the following principles apply[85]:

(1) A claimant is entitled to an interim or final injunction to protect him only from *further* misuse of the information. Misuse which has already taken place is a matter for damages. For example, if the defendant has already misused information by making contact with a customer and has received an order from him, an injunction to restrain him from fulfilling that order or any future order will not be granted as that would not be a case of *further* use.

(2) An interim or final injunction may be justified as fair and just if it has the effect of restoring the parties to the competitive position which they each ought to occupy and would have occupied but for the defendant's misuse of the information. This will prevent a defendant from benefiting from the springboard effect of his misuse.[86] An injunction will not, however, be appropriate if its effect would be to put a claimant into a better position for the future than he would have been in if there had been no misuse, such as where a defendant would eventually have been able to create the information for himself.

(3) An interim or final injunction is too wide if it restrains a defendant simply from soliciting, or entering into, or fulfilling a contract with a person whose name is on the claimant's confidential list of customers with whom the defendant had contact while he was in possession of the list.

(4) If it is impossible to undo what has already occurred, it may be appropriate to make an award of damages to the claimant for the use of the information, even though the claimant cannot prove that he has suffered any pecuniary loss as a result of the breach.

There is jurisdiction to grant an interim injunction which interferes with the

---

Newspapers Ltd [1987] 1 W.L.R. 1248; *Att-Gen v Newspaper Publishing Plc* [1988] Ch. 333, at 358, *per* Sir John Donaldson M.R.

[83] *Woodward v Hutchins* [1977] 1 W.L.R. 760. See also *Tillery Valley Foods v Channel Four Television Corp.* [2004] EWHC 1075 (Ch), unreported, in which Mann J. refused to grant an interim injunction as the ingredients of the cause of action in confidence did not exist and the action was a defamation action in disguise.

[84] *Cream Holdings Ltd v Banerjee* [2004] 3 W.L.R. 918 at para.22 in which it was held that the general approach should be that courts will be exceedingly slow to grant injunctions where the claimant cannot show that he will probably ("more likely than not") succeed at trial. This general approach should permit the court to dispense with this higher standard where particular circumstances, such as where the potential adverse consequences of disclosure are grave or where a short-lived injunction is needed to allow the court to give full consideration to the injunction application. And see para. 22–128, below.

[85] *Universal Thermosensors Ltd v Hibben* [1992] 1 W.L.R. 840.

[86] See para. 20–09, above, and in particular, *Ocular Sciences Ltd v Aspect Vision Care Ltd* [1997] R.P.C. 289 as to injunctive and other relief (in respect of derivative works making use of confidential information).

contractual rights of innocent third parties by, for example, restraining an ex-
employee from fulfilling a contract which he has made with the third party by the
misuse of confidential information. The jurisdiction may be exercised pending
trial if, for example:

(1) The contract was made by the defendant with the third party when he was
    employed by the claimant and he has acted in breach of his duty of fidelity
    to the claimant.

(2) It is arguable that the third party had notice of the breach of duty on the
    part of the defendant.[87]

The argument has been rejected that no injunction should be granted because
all the damage had been done and the contract had already been placed. It is not
necessary for the claimant to prove that he would suffer damages occurring after
the date of the hearing.[88]

An injunction order must identify with certainty the particular items of information covered by it, since otherwise the person restrained will not know what he
is and is not allowed to do.[89] This is particularly so in the context of trade secrets.[90]
Injunctions are normally aimed at the prevention of some specific wrong, not at
the prevention of wrongdoing in general. The court will not therefore normally
grant a wide form of injunction restraining the disclosure or misuse of any information obtained by a person in confidence.[91] Further, the injunction granted may
be of limited duration,[92] confined to the period during which the information
retains its confidential character. The term of an injunction ought not to extend
beyond the period (of the "springboard") for which the defendant's unfair
advantage through misuse of the confidential information may reasonably be
expected to continue.[93] It is possible that an injunction might be limited
geographically, to restraining publication in the United Kingdom.[94]

Once the information is made public by the confider, he is not entitled to an   **20–29**
injunction[95] or to damages for misuse occurring after publication of the
information.[96] If some of the information remains confidential, this may be
protected.[97]

It is doubtful whether a claimant must prove detriment for injunctive relief.

---

[87] *P.S.M. International Ltd v Whitehouse* [1992] F.S.R. 489.

[88] *P.S.M. International Ltd v Whitehouse* [1992] F.S.R. 489

[89] *Amway Corp v Eurway International Ltd* [1974] R.P.C. 82; *Potters-Ballotini Ltd v Weston-Baker
and others* [1977] R.P.C. 202; *Woodward v Hutchins* [1977] 1 W.L.R. 760 at 764; *John Zink Co
Ltd v Lloyds Bank Ltd* [1975] R.P.C. 385; *Ixora Trading Inc v Jones* [1990] F.S.R. 251; *Mainmet
Holdings plc v Austin* [1991] F.S.R. 538; *CMI-Centres for Medical Innovation GmbH v Phytop-
harm plc* [1999] F.S.R. 235; *Times Newspapers Ltd v Mirror Group Newspapers Ltd* [1993]
E.M.L.R. 442 at 448 where no injunction was granted to prevent premature publication of Lady
Thatcher's memoirs, as parts of the book would have to be excepted from the scope of the injunc-
tion and such exception could not be satisfactorily achieved.

[90] *P.S.M. International Ltd v Whitehouse* [1992] F.S.R. 489, applying *Lawrence David Ltd v Ashton*
[1989] F.S.R. 87 and *Lock International plc v Beswick* [1989] 1 W.L.R. 1268; and see *Raks
Holdings AS v TTPCOM Ltd* [2004] EWHC 2137 (Ch)..

[91] *Att-Gen v Guardian Newspapers (No.2)*, HL (E) [1990] A.C. 109 at 264E.

[92] *Att-Gen v Jonathan Cape Ltd* [1976] Q.B.D. 752 at 771.

[93] *Roger Bullivant Ltd v Ellis* [1987] F.S.R. 172 at 183; see "The springboard principle", para. 20–
09, above.

[94] *Att-Gen v Guardian Newspapers (No.2)*, HL (E) [1990] A.C. 109 at 260F.

[95] *Mustad & Son v Dosen* [1963] R.P.C. 41; or if the information has otherwise been made public:
Bunn v British Broadcasting Corporation [1999] F.S.R. 70.

[96] *Franchi v Franchi* [1967] R.P.C. 149.

[97] *Att-Gen v Guardian Newspapers (No.2)*, HL (E) [1990] A.C. 109; *Mustad & Son v Dosen* [1964]
1 W.L.R. 109, HL.

Private and personal information has been protected by injunction without proof of financial or other specific detriment.[98]

A party seeking equitable relief must show that he deserves the intervention of the court. An injunction will not be granted where reckless claims to confidentiality have been put forward to maximise costs, the proceedings have been conducted in an oppressive manner, and the application for injunctive relief was part of a plan to destroy the defendant's business.[99]

B. DAMAGES

20–30 Damages are available as a remedy for a past breach of confidence.[1] . Where the breach of confidence also constitutes a breach of contract or a tort, the usual principles for the award of damages apply to such cases. The purpose of an award of damages for a breach of confidence is to put the claimant in the position which he would have been in if the defendant had not wrongfully obtained and used the confidential information in question.[2] The burden is on the claimant to prove that he has suffered loss. If the act complained of also involves infringement of copyright, the damages are alternative, and not cumulative, under these two heads.[3]

Damages can compensate pecuniary loss,[4] mental distress and injury to feelings,[5] but not, it seems, damage to reputation.[6] Aggravated damages taking into account the conduct or state of mind of the defendant are recoverable.[7] It is doubtful whether exemplary damages can be awarded for breach of confidence, being a breach of an equitable obligation and not a tort.[8]

There is no one method of assessing damages applicable to all cases of breach of confidence. Damages are compensatory. Therefore, the court will seek to compensate the claimant and not to punish the defendant, and in achieving this aim will select the most appropriate method of assessment for the particular case.

20–31 The proper basis for assessing damages in a case where the person imparting the information would have licensed its use at a price, is to determine the market value of the confidential information on a sale between a willing seller and a willing buyer.[9] That value depends on the court's determination of whether the information involved a true inventive step, or was such as could have been provided

[98] See para. 20–12, above.

[99] *Ocular Sciences Ltd v Aspect Vision Care Ltd* [1997] R.P.C. 289.

[1] *Campbell v MGN Ltd* [2004] UKHL 22; [2004] 2 W.L.R. 1232; *Cornelius v de Taranto* [2002] E.M.L.R. 112 This is now settled law. Historically the position was unclear, as the jurisdiction to award damages for breach of an equitable right of confidence was conferred by Lord Cairn's Act of 1858 which gave the court power to award damages "in lieu or in addition to an injunction" and so defendants to actions had successfully argued that damages were not available where there were no grounds for an injunction.

[2] *Dowson & Mason Ltd v Potter* [1986] 1 W.L.R. 1419 (distinguishing *Seager v Copydex Ltd (No.2)*, [1969] 1 W.L.R. 809); *Cadbury Schweppes Inc v FBI Food Ltd* [2000] F.S.R. 491.

[3] *Nichrotherm Electrical Co Ltd v Percy* [1957] R.P.C. 207; *Interfirm Comparison (Australia) Pty Ltd v Law Society of New South Wales* [1977] R.P.C. 137 (Sup Ct of NSW).

[4] *Seager v Copydex (No.2)* [1969] 1 W.L.R. 809.

[5] *Cornelius v de Taranto* [2002] E.M.L.R. 112; *Lady Archer v Williams* [2003] E.M.L.R. 38 (QBD).

[6] *Lonrho v Fayed (No.5)* [1993] 1 W.L.R. 1489, 1502 in which Stuart-Smith L.J. set out the principle that no one has a right to a reputation which is unmerited and so one can only suffer an injury to reputation if what is said is false; damages for injury to reputation are available in defamation actions: see *Mahmud v Bank of Credit and Commerce International SA (In Liquidation)* [1998] A.C. 20.

[7] *Campbell v MGN Ltd* [2004] UKHL 22; [2004] 2 W.L.R. 1232 in which the House of Lords restored Morland J.'s award of £1,000 aggravated damages by reason of the newspaper's post-publication conduct (see [2002] E.M.L.R. 30, QBD).

[8] But see (1972) 12 J.S.P.T.L. (P. M. North); *Aquaculture v New Zealand Green Mussel Co Ltd (No.2)* [1987] 10 I.P.R. 319.

[9] *Seager v Copydex Ltd (No.2)* [1969] 1 W.L.R. 809; and see *Att-Gen v Guardian Newspapers*

by any competent consultant. In the former case, compensation would be the capitalised value of the royalty payable on a sale of the invention,; while in the latter case, its value would be the reasonable fee payable to such a consultant.[10] Once the compensation, as assessed, has been paid, the right to exploit the information belongs to the defendant as on an outright purchase under an agreement for sale.[11]

The measure of damages is different, however, in the case of wrongful disclosure of information by an employee to his employer's competitors who would not have been licensed by the employer to use the information. In such a case, the employer is exposed to damaging competition as a result of his employee's wrongdoing and he is entitled to damages for loss of manufacturing profits suffered as a result of the breach of confidence.[12] Similarly, where a claimant intended to use confidential information for his own purposes, damages were assessed by reference to his loss of profits.[13]

Thus in a case where a defendant's disclosure of confidential information causes a claimant to lose the prospective profit on a finance transaction for his client, the correct measure of damages is that assessed on a tortious basis, so as to put the claimant into the position he would have occupied but for the breach of confidence.[14] An award of damages may include a sum in compensation for the expense incurred by a claimant in his efforts to retrieve copies of the confidential report which has been wrongfully disclosed.[15]

While there is little guidance on setting the quantum of damages for non-pecuniary loss, the factors taken into account by the courts include the nature and detail of the confidential material disclosed, the character of the recipients of the disclosure and the extent of the disclosure.[16]

20–32

Even where it is established that the defendant has stolen documents containing confidential information and has used that information in soliciting orders, there is no irrebuttable presumption that the business resulted from the orders derived from wrongful use of the information, so as to make the defendant liable. The court looks further than the fact that the document was stolen to see whether the information was used. The claimant is entitled to fair compensation for the wrong done to him by the defendant's misuse of confidential information. Whether any particular piece of business was obtained by a defendant as a result of misuse of the claimant's confidential information is a question of fact in each case. In answering that question, the court may look with scepticism at the defendant's evidence about the actual use he has made of the information. Any doubts about his evidence are likely to be resolved in favour of the claimant.[17] A defendant cannot complain if he finds that it has become impossible to distinguish between potential customers whom he could have contacted lawfully and those whom he could not.

(No.2), HL (E) [1990] 1 A.C. 109 at 286E; *Ludlow Music v Williams (No.2)* [2002] F.S.R. 57; *SPE International Ltd v Professional Preparation Contractors (UK) Ltd* [2002] EWHC 881, unreported.

[10] *Seager v Copydex (No.2)* [1969] 1 W.L.R. 809.

[11] *Seager v Copydex (No.2)* [1969] 1 W.L.R. 809

[12] *Dowson & Mason Ltd v Potter* [1986] 1 W.L.R. 1419 (distinguishing *Seager v Copydex (No.2)* [1969] 1 W.L.R. 809).

[13] *Dowson & Mason Ltd v Potter* [1986] 1 W.L.R. 1419

[14] *Indata Equipment Supplies Ltd v A.C.L. Ltd* [1998] F.S.R. 248, CA in which the claimant was awarded a measure of damages which represented its loss of a chance of finding a financier for its client and thereby making a profit; see also *Talbot v General Television Corporation Pty. Ltd* [1981] R.P.C. 1 at 30, 31 (Sup Ct of Victoria).

[15] *Cornelius v de Taranto* [2002] E.M.L.R. 112.

[16] *Cornelius v de Taranto* [2002] E.M.L.R. 112, at para.81.

[17] *Roger Bullivant Ltd v Ellis* [1987] F.S.R. 172.

taminated by breaches of confidence, it would not be right to impose a constructive trust.[30]

E. DELIVERY UP

In its discretion, the court may make an order for delivery up of material containing confidential information.[31] This form of relief is in substance a species of injunction to be determined on the same equitable principles.[32] Delivery up may be ordered as an alternative to destruction of such material on oath and is useful where a defendant has shown, by his past conduct, that his oath is not to be relied upon.[33] A court may also award damages in lieu of an order for destruction in order to prevent unnecessary waste.[34] If a defendant has added material of his own to the information which he has obtained from a claimant in breach of confidence, he can still be ordered to deliver up the material.[35]

20–35

In principle all confidential information should be returned to a claimant, but an order for delivery up will not be made which is oppressive and would work a hardship on the defendant whilst no real benefit would be derived by the claimant.[36] A person to whom confidential documents and information have been disclosed in breach of confidence may be ordered to disclose the identity of his informant to the person entitled to the benefit of the information,[37] and, subject to the provisions of section 10 of the Contempt of Court Act 1981, to deliver up documents to enable the informant responsible for a breach of confidence to be identified.[38]

F. PROCEDURE

For the protection of a claimant who claims to be entitled to confidential information the court may require the defendant to give an undertaking that he will make no use of information disclosed in statements of case or in documents disclosed, save such use as is necessary for the purpose of the proceedings.[39] In order to reach a conclusion whether disclosure is necessary notwithstanding confidentiality, the Court should inspect the documents and consider whether justice can be done by special measures such as "covering up" or substituting anonymous references for specific names.[40] In some cases, depending on the surrounding circumstances and the state of knowledge generally in the art, the claimant may have to disclose the essential features of his process in witness statements in support of

20–36

---

[30] *Ocular Sciences Ltd v Aspect Vision Care Ltd* [1997] R.P.C. 289 at 416, *L A.C. Minerals Ltd v International Corona Resources Ltd* [1990] F.S.R. 441 (Sup Ct of Canada).

[31] *Peter Pan Manufacturing Corp v Corsets Silhouette* [1963] R.P.C. 45; *Franklin v Giddins* [1978] 1 Qd.R. 72 (Sup Ct of Queensland); *Prince Albert v Strange* (1849) 2 De Gex & Sm 652, 716.

[32] *Ocular Sciences Ltd v Aspect Vision Care Ltd* [1997] R.P.C. 289 at 410.

[33] *Ansell Rubber Industries Pty Ltd v Allied Rubber Industries Pty Ltd* [1972] R.P.C. 811.

[34] *Saltman Engineering Co Ltd v Campbell Engineering Co Ltd* (1948) 65 R.P.C. 203 at 219, CA.

[35] *Industrial Furnaces Ltd v Reaves* [1970] R.P.C. 605 at 627, 628.

[36] *Ocular Sciences Ltd v Aspect Vision Care Ltd* [1997] R.P.C. 289 at 410.

[37] *British Steel Corporation v Granada Television Ltd* [1981] A.C. 1096, applying *Norwich Pharmacal Co v Customs and Excise Commrs.* [1974] A.C. 133.

[38] *Secretary of State for Defence v Guardian Newspapers* [1985] A.C. 339.

[39] *Zink (John) & Co Ltd v Wilkinson* [1973] R.P.C. 717; *Centri-Spray Corp v Cera International Ltd* [1979] F.S.R. 175.

[40] *Science Research Council v Nassé* [1980] A.C. 1028.

his application for an interim injunction,[41] though the court can protect the confidentiality of the information by a hearing in private.[42]

Where there is a real risk that a party, exercising his right to inspect the other party's documents in legal proceedings, would use matters so disclosed for a collateral purpose, the court will exercise its inherent jurisdiction to restrict inspection, impose safeguards and prevent an abuse of the process of the court.[43] A fair balance has to be struck between the natural wish of a claimant to have his trade secrets adequately protected and the natural wish of a defendant to see any document which may support the case against him.[44] The court may order inspection, for example, of a computerised database alleged to have been made by a defendant in breach of copyright and confidence, prior to the service of a Particulars of Claim in order to enable a claimant to plead a full and proper case.[45]

[41] *Diamond Stylus Co Ltd v Baudon Precision Diamonds Ltd* [1973] R.P.C. 675.
[42] See *Yates Circuit Foil Co v Electrofoils Ltd* [1976] F.S.R. 345; *General Motors-Holden's Ltd v D. Syme & Co Ltd* [1985] F.S.R. 413 (Sup Ct of NSW).
[43] *Church of Scientology v D.H.S.S.* [1979] 1 W.L.R. 723; *Centri-Spray Corp v Cera International Ltd* [1979] F.S.R. 175; *Coflexip SA v Stolt Offshore MS Ltd (Disclosure of Documents) (No. 2)* [2004] EWHC 212, unreported.
[44] *Format Communications Mfg Ltd v ITT (U.K.) Ltd* [1983] F.S.R. 473 at 481 and 485; *Rousel Uclaf v I.C.I.* [1989] R.P.C. 59 at 62, 66; *Zink (John) & Co Ltd v Wilkinson* [1973] R.P.C. 717; *Ixora Trading Inc v Jones* [1990] F.S.R. 251.
[45] *Dun & Bradstreet Ltd v Typesetting Facilities Ltd* [1992] F.S.R. 320.

THE PROTECTION OF GOODWILL

1. INTRODUCTION

There are often cases where the interests of an author or owner of a copyright work are damaged by activities that fall outside the limits of claims for infringement of copyright. Most commonly, this is because although reference is made to a copyright work, no substantial reproduction of the work has taken place. Alternatively, the reference may only be to a name associated with the claimant or his work and there is no property in the nature of copyright in a name or word, whether invented or otherwise.[1] English law does not recognise any general tort of unfair competition[2] and it has been said that "such an action would be inconsistent with the established limits of the traditional and statutory causes of action which are available to a trader in respect of damage caused or threatened by a competitor".[3] Neither is there any tort of copying, of taking another's market or customers, or of making use of another's goodwill as such.[4]

21–01

An author or copyright owner may nevertheless have a claim in passing off if the activity has damaged, or is likely to damage, goodwill which is part of a busi-

---

[1] *Tavener Rutledge Ltd v Trexapalm Ltd* [1977] R.P.C. 275 at 278; *Star Industrial Co Ltd v Yap Kwee Kor* [1976] F.S.R. 256. See also *McCulloch v May Ltd* [1947] 2 All E.R. 845 at 849; *Exxon Corp v Exxon Insurance Consultants International Ltd* [1982] R.P.C. 69; *McCain International Ltd v Country Fair Foods Ltd* [1981] R.P.C. 69 at 77; *Kean v McGivan* [1982] F.S.R. 119 at 120; *Century Electronics Ltd v CVS Enterprises Ltd* [1983] F.S.R. 1; *My Kinda Bones Ltd v Dr Pepper's Stove Co Ltd* [1984] F.S.R. 289 at 296; *ELVIS PRESLEY Trade Marks* [1997] R.P.C. 543 at 547.

[2] *Cadbury-Schweppes Pty Ltd v The Pub Squash Co Ltd* [1981] 1 W.L.R. 193 at 201; *Harrods Ltd v Schwartz-Sackin & Co Ltd* [1986] F.S.R. 490 at 494; *Associated Newspapers Group plc v Insert Media Ltd* [1988] 1 W.L.R. 509.

[3] *Moorgate Tobacco Co Ltd v Phillip Morris Ltd* [1985] R.P.C. 219, *per* Deane J. at 240 (High Ct of Aus).

[4] *Hodgkinson & Corby Ltd v Wards Mobility Ltd* [1994] 1 W.L.R. 1564, *per* Jacob J. at 1569.

ness of his; indeed, it has been pointed out that the very purpose of a passing-off action is to vindicate the claimant's exclusive right to goodwill and to protect it against damage.[5] Passing off is one of a number of remedies which exist in this field which are complementary to actions for infringement of copyright and authors' moral rights.[6] The action is often concerned with representations relating to a title, name, or get-up but is not limited to these. It applies equally to other *indicia* or material which has given a business a distinctive character.[7] Furthermore, the tort of passing off can play an important role in the protection of characters, particularly in cases which fall outside the scope of copyright protection. While not attempting a comprehensive review of the law of passing off,[8] this chapter examines the principles and their application in the copyright related field. Despite a large volume of case law on the topic, passing-off cases generally turn on questions of fact only,[9] and indeed often the only live issue can be reduced to a single question, namely, has a misrepresentation been made?[10]

2. THE ELEMENTS OF PASSING OFF

21–02   **Introduction.** Five characteristics must be present in order to create a valid cause of action for passing off: (1) a misrepresentation, (2) made by a trader in the course of trade, (3) to prospective customers of his or ultimate consumers of goods or services supplied by him, (4) which is calculated to injure the business or goodwill of another trader (in the sense that this is a reasonably foreseeable consequence), and (5) which causes actual damage to a business or goodwill of another trader by whom the action is brought or, in a *quia timet* action, will probably do so.[11] This formulation of principles, however, does not give the same degree of assistance in analysis and decision making as the "classical trinity" of requirements namely: (1) a reputation, or goodwill, acquired by the claimant for his goods, name or mark; (2) a misrepresentation by the defendant leading to confusion (or deception), causing (3) damage to the claimant.[12] This approach highlights the essential flexibility of the tort.[13] In analysing the particular facts of a passing-off action, it is usually advantageous to take these three elements of passing off one by one, even though they are often interactive.[14]

21–03   **Goodwill.** The proprietary right which the law of passing off protects is the incorporeal property in the claimant's business reputation or goodwill. Typically, the name, mark, or get-up is the badge or vehicle that ties the goodwill to the

---

[5] *Irvine v Talksport Ltd* [2002] E.W.H.C. 367; [2002] 1 W.L.R. 2355; [2002] F.S.R. 60, para.34
[6] Others being breach of confidence (as to which see Ch.20) and malicious falsehood.
[7] See, *e.g.* the discussion relating to advertising slogans, in para. 21–34, below.
[8] See, *e.g.* Wadlow, *The Law of Passing Off: Unfair competition by misrepresentation* (3rd ed., Sweet & Maxwell).
[9] *Reckitt & Colman Products Ltd v Borden Inc* [1990] 1 W.L.R. 491, HL, at 499D, where Lord Oliver observed that most reported cases are only really of assistance by way of analogy.
[10] Of course, the other ingredients of the tort must also be established.
[11] *Erven Warnink Besloten Vennootschap v J. Townend & Sons (Hull) Ltd* [1979] A.C. 731 at 742. Care needs to be taken with some of the older authorities, decided when the principles of a passing-off action had not been fully worked out, in particular when actual fraud was considered an essential requirement of the cause of action. In addition, many of the modern reported cases are interlocutory decisions only and, where the principles of *American Cyanamid Co v Ethicon Ltd* [1975] A.C. 396 have been faithfully applied, they often do not provide a valuable guide to the strength of a plaintiff's case.
[12] *Consorzio Del Prosciutto di Parma v Marks & Spencer plc* [1991] R.P.C. 351 at 368, following the remarks of Lord Oliver in *Reckitt & Colman Products Inc v Borden Inc* [1990] 1 W.L.R. 491 at 499, and confirming a "welcome return" to the classical approach.
[13] *Irvine v Talksport Ltd* [2002] E.W.H.C. 367; [2002] 1 W.L.R. 2355; [2002] F.S.R. 60, para.13
[14] *County Sound plc v Ocean Sound Ltd* [1991] F.S.R. 367.

claimant,[15] but it is not so restricted, as it can even attach to an individual's physiognomy.[16] Goodwill has been defined as "the benefit and advantage of the good name, reputation and connection of a business. It is the attractive force which brings in custom."[17] Whilst it has no independent existence apart from the business to which it is attached,[18] it remains a commodity that may be bought and sold. In general, no goodwill attaches to the activity of a non-trader so that, for example, the courts are reluctant to interfere to prevent a person from adopting the name of a non-trader, even if annoyance and inconvenience result.[19] However, the word "trade" is widely interpreted and includes persons engaged in a professional, artistic or literary occupation,[20] political parties,[21] and those who derive income simply from their own celebrity.[22]

The claimant must prove that he has been in the market long enough for his goods or business to acquire a public reputation.[23] A reputation or goodwill can be built up by substantial sales over a short period of time,[24] or by an intensive advertising campaign.[25] In any case, there must be some sort of entry into the market.[26] Goodwill is also subject to geographical limitations, in that the reputation must exist in the same locality of the conduct complained of, and the question of to whom goodwill in a particular product will accrue is sometimes a complicated question of fact.[27] The relevant date for determining whether a claimant has established the necessary goodwill or reputation is the date of the commencement of the conduct complained of and not the date of the commencement of the proceedings,[28] and this is so even though the claimant's trade would be *prima facie* unlawful because the defendant has in the meantime registered a trade mark.[29]

Descriptive name. Where the *indicium* of the claimant's business or goods is alleged to be a name, the claimant must show that the name is distinctive of his business or goods in the eyes of the public[30] such that it is exclusively associated with his business or goods. While a fancy name can usually only indicate that the   **21–04**

---

[15] *HP Bulmer Ltd & Showerings Ltd v Bollinger SA* [1978] R.P.C. 79; *Unicorn Products Ltd v Roban Jig & Tool Co (UK) Ltd* [1976] F.S.R. 169; *Anheuser-Busch Inc v Budejovicky Budvar NP* [1984] F.S.R. 413 at 476.

[16] See paras 21–40 *et seq.*, below.

[17] *Inland Revenue Commissioners v Muller & Co Margarine Ltd* [1901] A.C. 217 at 223, 224.

[18] *Star Industrial Co Ltd v Yap Kwee Kor* [1976] F.S.R. 256, PC.

[19] *Day v Brownrigg* (1878) 10 Ch.D. 294.

[20] *Kean v McGivan* [1982] F.S.R. 119.

[21] *Burge v Haycock* [2002] R.P.C. 28.

[22] See paras 21–40 *et seq.*, below.

[23] *Licensed Victuallers' Newspaper Co v Bingham* (1888) 38 Ch.D. 139; *Oertli AG v Bowman (London) Ltd* [1957] R.P.C. 388; the plaintiff's intentions may be relevant; see *Dunlop Pneumatic Tyre Co Ltd v Dunlop Lubricant Co* (1899) 16 R.P.C. 12; *Hulton Press Ltd v White Eagle Youth Holiday Camp Ltd* [1951] R.P.C. 126; *L.R.C. International Ltd v Lilla Edets Sales Co Ltd* [1973] R.P.C. 560; *Brestian v Try* [1958] R.P.C. 161; *DC Thomson Ltd v Kent Messenger Ltd* [1975] R.P.C. 191; *BBC v Talbot Motor Co Ltd* [1981] F.S.R. 228.

[24] *Stannard v Reay* [1967] R.P.C. 589; but see as to pre-publication advertising: *Maxwell v Hogg* (1866) L.R. 2 Ch.App. 307; *Marcus Publishing plc v Hutton-Wild Communications Ltd* [1990] R.P.C. 576. See also *Mirage Studios v Counter-Feat Clothing Co Ltd* [1991] F.S.R. 145, in which it was held that a sufficient reputation had been established over a period of four months by television and radio broadcasts to a large audience, by press coverage and sales of goods.

[25] *Elida Gibbs Ltd v Colgate-Palmolive Ltd* [1983] F.S.R. 95.

[26] *My Kinda Bones Ltd v Dr Pepper's Stove Co Ltd* [1984] F.S.R. 289 at 296; *Marcus Publishing plc v Hutton-Wild Communications Ltd* [1990] R.P.C. 576.

[27] *Medgen Inc v Passion for Life Products Ltd* [2001] F.S.R. 30.

[28] *Cadbury Schweppes Pty Ltd v The Pub Squash Co Ltd* [1981] 1 W.L.R. 193 at 204; *cf. My Kinda Bones Ltd v Dr Pepper's Stove Co Ltd* [1984] F.S.R. 289; *Nationwide Building Society v Nationwide Estate Agents Ltd* [1987] F.S.R. 579 at 585, 592.

[29] *Inter Lotto (UK) Ltd v Camelot Group plc* [2003] 3 All E.R. 191; [2004] R.P.C. 171; upheld [2004] 1 W.L.R. 955; [2004] R.P.C. 186, CA.

[30] *Spalding (AG) & Bros v Gamage (AW Ltd* (1915) 32 R.P.C. 273 at 284, *Oertli (T) v Bowman*

business or goods bearing that name are derived from a particular supplier or are licensed by that supplier, a descriptive name does not usually indicate source but merely indicates the nature of the goods or business.[31] If the word or name is *prima facie* descriptive or in general use, the difficulty of establishing distinctiveness and thus the probability of deception is therefore greatly increased.[32] Inevitably, where a trader adopts words in common use for his trade name there will be some risk of confusion but that risk must be run unless the first user is allowed unfairly to monopolise the words. The law is reluctant to allow ordinary descriptive words in the English language to be fenced off so as to become the private preserve of one particular tradesman.[33] Indeed, a greater degree of discrimination may fairly be expected from the public where a trade name consists wholly or in part of words which are descriptive of the articles to be sold or the services to be rendered.[34] The court will therefore accept small differences between descriptive names of traders or their trading styles as sufficient to distinguish them.[35] A name which is *prima facie* descriptive may nevertheless become distinctive of the claimant's business or goods, and so acquire a "secondary" meaning, by the exclusive use of that name over a substantial period of time so that it in fact comes to connote a connection with the claimant and none other.[36] A secondary meaning is not established merely by showing that, before the appearance of the defendant's work, anyone who asked for the particular title would be referring to the claimant's work.[37]

21–05   **Get-up.** The get-up of a trader's goods may be an important part of his goodwill. Because of its particular connection with copyright and design right, this topic is considered separately, below.

21–06   **Misrepresentation.** It has been said that it is neither possible nor desirable to define all the different forms that actionable misrepresentations may take,[38] but in general, the defendant's conduct must be such as to mislead members of the public to believe that the goods or services offered by him are the goods or services of the claimant, or are connected with or associated with the claimant's goods or services in a way that is likely to damage the claimant's goodwill.[39] The misrepresentation must relate to the claimant's product or business. A false statement which hangs in the air is not sufficient.[40] The misrepresentation may be express or implied by conduct or get-up, conscious or unconscious. At the heart of passing off lies deception or its likelihood, in particular, deception of the ultimate

---

(EJ) (London) Ltd [1957] R.P.C. 388 at 397; *HP Bulmer Ltd & Showerings Ltd v J Bollinger SA* [1978] R.P.C. 79 at 94.

[31] *McCain International Ltd v County Fair Foods Ltd* [1981] R.P.C. 69 ("Oven Chips"), *My Kinda Town Ltd v Soll* [1983] R.P.C. 407 ("Chicago Pizza").

[32] *Burberrys v JC Cording & Co Ltd* (1909) 26 R.P.C. 693 at 701.

[33] *Marcus Publishing plc v Hutton-Wild Communications Ltd* [1990] R.P.C. 576 at 579 , per Dillon L.J.; *Pet Library (London) Ltd v Walter Ellson & Son Ltd* [1968] F.S.R. 359 at 362.

[34] e.g. *Associated Newspapers Ltd v Express Newspapers Ltd* [2003] EWHC 1322, Ch.D, para.38.

[35] *Office Cleaning Services Ltd v Westminster Window and General Cleaners Ltd* (1946) 63 R.P.C. 39.

[36] *Reddaway v Banham* [1896] A.C. 199.

[37] *Mathieson v Sir I Pitman & Son Ltd* (1930) 47 R.P.C. 541.

[38] *HP Bulmer Ltd & Showerings Ltd v Bollinger SA* [1978] R.P.C. 79 at 99.

[39] *HP Bulmer & Showerings Ltd v J Bollinger SA* [1978] R.P.C. 79 at 99; *Morning Star Co-operative Society Ltd v Express Newspapers Ltd* [1979] F.S.R. 113 at 114; *Newsweek Inc v BBC* [1979] R.P.C. 441 at 447; *Mirage Studios v Counter-Feat Clothing Co Ltd* [1991] F.S.R. 145 at 155.

[40] *Schulke & Mayr UK Ltd v Alkapharm UK Ltd* [1999] F.S.R. 161; *British Broadcasting Corporation v Talksport Ltd* [2001] F.S.R. 53.

consumer.[41] The misrepresentation must be made to members of the public in such a way that it is likely to cause confusion amongst them between the claimant's and the defendant's goods or business.[42] The judge has to decide whether the public at large or a particular relevant section of the public is likely to be deceived and what would be the effect of the misrepresentation made by the defendant upon reasonable prospective purchasers or clients.[43] The test is whether ordinary sensible members of the public would be confused and it is not sufficient that the confusion would be confined to a small, unobservant section of society,[44] remembering that people often have an imperfect recollection of names and marks. When considering the likelihood of confusion, it may be relevant to consider the education and intelligence of the particular sector of the public concerned.[45] No protection is available against mere confusion, only confusion caused by misrepresentation, which is quite a different thing.[46] Confusion may result from the collision of two independent rights and, where this is the case, neither party can complain; it must put up with the results of the confusion as one of the misfortunes which occur in life.[47]

Common fields of activity. There is no requirement that there be any similarity between the fields of business activities of the claimant and the defendant,[48] though it may be of important evidential value in assessing confusion and deception,[49] in which context it goes to two of the three elements of a passing-off action, namely whether any misrepresentation has been made[50] and whether any damage is likely to result.[51] Thus, if the claimant has acquired his reputation in one field and the defendant is operating in another, it may be that the public will not assume that there is any connection between the two. Alternatively, if the claimant is not active in the field complained of, then, in the absence of a defamatory statement, it may be that he will not suffer any loss even if a connection is assumed. The issue of separate fields of activity becomes particularly relevant where the claimant wishes to expand from one field into a different field, and it is common for creators of artistic or literary works to exploit their works through the granting of merchandising licences for use on a very wide range of goods and

21–07

---

[41] *Hodgkinson & Corby Ltd v Wards Mobility Ltd* [1994] 1 W.L.R. 1564 at 1570.

[42] *HP Bulmer & Showerings Ltd v J Bollinger SA* [1978] R.P.C. 79. The court may, given appropriate evidence, infer that the intention of the buyer was to acquire a genuine article: see *Mirage Studios v Counter-Feat Clothing Co Ltd* [1991] F.S.R. 145 at 159.

[43] *Colgate Palmolive Ltd v Pattron* [1978] R.P.C. 635; *Berkeley Hotel Co Ltd v Berkeley International (Mayfair) Ltd* [1972] R.P.C. 237; *John Hayter Motor Underwriting Agencies Ltd v RBHS Agencies Ltd* [1977] F.S.R. 285 at 293.

[44] *Newsweek Inc v BBC* [1979] R.P.C. 441 at 447; *DC Thomson & Co Ltd v Kent Messenger Ltd* [1975] R.P.C. 191 at 199. This corner of the field of passing off is rich in descriptions of people whose possible confusion can be discounted. See, *e.g. Norman Kark Publications Ltd v Odhams Press Ltd* [1962] 1 W.L.R. 380, at 393, *per* Wilberforce J., leaving out of account "careless and indifferent persons"; *Cowen v Hulton* (1882) 46 L.T. 897, *per* Jessel M.R.: "I am unable to see how anyone, who does not deserve the name of an idiot, could be induced to buy the defendant's paper for the plaintiff's"; *Morning Star Co-operative Society Ltd v Express Newspapers Ltd* [1979] F.S.R. 113 at 117, *per* Foster J.: "Only a moron in a hurry would be confused".

[45] *C Arthur Pearson Ltd v TP O'Connor* [1905–10] Mac.C.C. 43 (no readers of periodical entitled "M.A.P." (short for "Mainly about People") likely to think that a similar periodical entitled "P.T.O." (short for "People talked of") was connected.

[46] *County Sound plc v Ocean Sound Ltd* [1991] F.S.R. 367, CA, applying *Marengo v Daily Sketch and Sunday Graphic Ltd* (1946) [1992] F.S.R. 1, CA.

[47] *Marengo v Daily Sketch and Sunday Graphic Ltd* (1946) [1992] F.S.R. 1, CA, *per* Lord Greene M.R. at 2.

[48] *Irvine v Talksport Ltd* [2002] E.W.H.C. 367; [2002] 1 W.L.R. 2355; [2002] F.S.R. 60, paras 24 to 29; *Mirage Studios v Counter-Feat Clothing Co Ltd* [1991] F.S.R. 145.

[49] *Annabel's (Berkeley Square) Ltd v Schock* [1972] R.P.C 838; *Lego System Aktieselskab v Lego M Lemelstrich Ltd* [1983] F.S.R. 155 at 187; *Mirage Studios v Counter-Feat Clothing Co Ltd* [1991] F.S.R. 145 at 157.

[50] *Nice and Safe Attitude Ltd v Piers Flook* [1997] F.S.R. 14 at 20.

[51] *Mecklermedia Corp v DC Congress Gessellschaft mbH* [1997] F.S.R. 627, *per* Jacob J. at 633.

services. The areas of activity are not confined to those in which the claimant is actually engaged on the date at which he brings his proceedings, but extend to potential trade in other allied areas to which his business might reasonably extend, or, at least, be thought by the public to have extended. In such cases, it will be easier to establish confusion and thus damage if it can be shown that those fields are closely related, and so much part of the normal and natural expansion of the claimant's business that confusion is likely to be occasioned among members of the public, particularly with modern commercial practices of licensing and franchising of business operations.[52] In cases of celebrity endorsement, of course, this element is of little significance.[53]

21–08   **Damage.** Damage is the gist of the action. The damage suffered may take a number of forms, though it is not always possible to draw strict distinctions between different heads of damage.[54] Moreover, some heads of damage are more uncertain than others and may be harder to establish. The most common is that the claimant loses sales of his goods or services which he might otherwise have made.[55] In addition, the general reputation which the claimant's goods and business enjoy for quality and other characteristics may be depreciated by confusion so that the strength of his mark is eroded and his competitive position in the market is weakened.[56] Alternatively the claimant may claim to have suffered damage through a loss of control over his own reputation.[57] Any erosion or dilution of the distinctiveness or exclusiveness of a name or mark may also be a form of damage to the goodwill of a business.[58] The claimant may also claim that the defendant's activities have restricted the claimant's potential for expanding his business into another field,[59] possibly through granting merchandising licences,[60] although such claims are often regarded with suspicion as being too speculative. The situation is different where the claimant is already in the business of granting licences, relating to, for example, characters or literary works. The loss of a licence fee will be a relevant head of damage, either because of the actual loss of a fee or because potential licensees will go elsewhere and the claimant will no longer be able to ensure that the licences actually granted will be exclusive licences.[61] It is not necessary to prove an adverse effect on the goodwill resulting from, for

---

[52] *L.R.C. International Ltd v Lilla Edets Sales Co Ltd* [1973] R.P.C. 560; *Ames Crosta Ltd v Pionex International* [1977] F.S.R. 46; *John Walker & Sons Ltd v Rothmans International Ltd* [1978] F.S.R. 357; *DC Thomson & Co Ltd v Kent Messenger Ltd* [1975] R.P.C. 191 at 199; *Sterwin A.G. v Brocades (Great Britain) Ltd* [1979] R.P.C. 481 at 490; *Television Broadcasts Ltd v Home Guide Publication Co* [1982] F.S.R. 505 (Sup Ct of HK).

[53] See paras 21–40 *et seq.*, below.

[54] For a review, see Carty, "Heads of Damage in Passing Off" [1996] E.I.P.R. 490.

[55] *Spalding (AG) & Bros v AW Gamage Ltd* (1915) 32 R.P.C. 273.

[56] *HP Bulmer Ltd & Showerings Ltd v J Bollinger SA* [1978] R.P.C. 79 at 94. See also *Alfred Dunhill Ltd v Sunoptic SA & C Dunhill* [1979] F.S.R. 337 at 362, 365; *Lowenbrau Munchen v Grunhalle Lager International Ltd* [1974] R.P.C. 492 at 501; *Annabel's (Berkeley Square) Ltd v Schock* [1972] R.P.C. 838 at 845; *Totalizator Agency Board v Turf News Pty Ltd* [1972] R.P.C. 579 (Sup Ct of Victoria); *News Group Newspapers Ltd v The Rocket Co Ltd* [1981] F.S.R. 89.

[57] *British Legion v British Legion Club (Street) Ltd* (1931) 48 R.P.C. 555 at 564; *Lego System Aktieselskab v Lego M Lemelstrich Ltd* [1983] F.S.R. 155 at 190 and 195; *Mirage Studios v Counter-Feat Clothing Co Ltd* [1991] F.S.R. 145 at 152; *Totalizator Agency Board v Turf News Pty Ltd* [1972] R.P.C. 579 at 582–3 (Sup Ct of Victoria); *The Financial Times Ltd v Evening Standard Co Ltd* [1991] F.S.R. 7 at 12, where the principle was accepted. See also *Associated Newspapers plc v Insert Media* [1991] 1 W.L.R. 571 at 580.

[58] *Taittinger SA v Allbev Ltd* [1993] F.S.R. 641 at 670, 674 and 678; *Irvine v Talksport Ltd* [2002] E.W.H.C. 367; [2002] 1 W.L.R. 2355; [2002] F.S.R. 60.

[59] *Newsweek Inc v BBC* [1979] R.P.C. 441 at 448; *cf. Hulton Press Ltd v White Eagle Youth Holiday Camp Ltd* (1951) 68 R.P.C. 126.

[60] *Stringfellow v McCain Foods (GB) Ltd* [1984] R.P.C. 501 at 545. See also *Lyngstad v Anabas Products Ltd* [1977] F.S.R. 62 at 66.

[61] *Mirage Studios v Counter-Feat Clothing Co Ltd* [1991] F.S.R. 145 at 152. However, there is a danger of circularity where the loss of a licence fee is the only damage: the defendant would not

example, poor quality goods.[62] However, where there are no underlying rights which might form the subject matter of a licence, for example in the case of a mere name, in which no copyright subsists, different considerations may apply.[63]

3. CLAIMS BY AUTHORS AND COPYRIGHT OWNERS GENERALLY

Work not the claimant's. An action in passing off will lie to prevent an author's name being used on a work that is not his own.[64] The mere fact that an author may not have approved of a publication of his work is not enough if there is no misrepresentation as to the contents or authorship.[65] The action is available not only to the author but to anyone whose business involves exploitation of the author's work, for example subsequent owners of the copyright[66] or the publisher of the work. After his death, a passing-off action will be maintainable by the author's personal representative,[67] or whoever succeeds to the goodwill. A nice question arises as to the position after the copyright in the author's works has expired, since then anyone may exploit the author's actual works. It is suggested that in such a situation anyone whose business included the exploitation of his works would have a cause of action against a defendant who misrepresented a work to be by the author, assuming damage was caused thereby.

21–09

False attribution: the moral right. The cause of action in passing off now exists alongside the statutory moral right which provides a remedy for false attribution of authorship.[68] There is not, however, a complete overlap between the two rights. For example, the moral right is conferred on every person, whether an established author or not,[69] and there is thus no need to prove an established reputation. Moreover, the statutory cause of action is actionable *per se*, without the need to prove damage.[70] On the other hand, it is only the person who has been wrongly attributed as the author who has any claim for infringement of the moral right. Others, such as publishers or the copyright owner, who may have been damaged by the wrong attribution and thus have a claim in passing off, have no claim under the moral right. The moral right is also limited in time to the life of a person and a period of 20 years after his death, whereas there is in principle no such limitation in a passing-off action, so long as goodwill continues to subsist.

21–10

---

need a licence unless his conduct would otherwise be passing off, but if the claimant suffers no other damage, passing off is not established. See *Tot Toys Ltd v Mitchell* [1993] 1 N.Z.L.R. 325, *per* Fisher J. at 362 (High Ct of NZ).

[62] The plaintiff does not have to prove damage to the goodwill caused, for example, by inferior goods (see *Children's Television Workshop Inc v Woolworths (N.S.W.) Ltd* [1981] R.P.C. 187 at 195) and the court will often assume it: *Paramount Pictures Corp v Howley* (1991) 39 C.P.R. (3d) 419 (High Ct of Ontario).

[63] *Mirage Studios v Counter-Feat Clothing Co Ltd* [1991] F.S.R. 145, at 158, *per* Browne-Wilkinson V.C. See also *Stringfellow v McCain Foods (GB) Ltd* [1984] R.P.C. 501 at 544.

[64] *Lord Byron v Johnston* (1816) 2 Mer. 29; *Ridge v The English Illustrated Magazine* [1911–16] Mac.C.C. 91; *Alan Clark v Associated Newspapers Ltd* [1998] R.P.C. 261.

[65] *Kipling v Putnam's Sons* (1903) 120 Fed. Rep. 631; [1901–04] Mac.C.C. 37 (US Circuit Ct of Appeal), where a publisher bound up non-infringing copies of an author's work together with copies of his non-copyright works and sold the edition in competition with the plaintiff's. Today the issue of such copies to the public would be an infringement of copyright. See para. 7–03, above.

[66] *Wood v Butterworth* [1901–04] Mac.C.C. 16 (action by copyright owner, the executor and trustee of authoress).

[67] *Wood v Butterworth* [1901–04] Mac.C.C. 16 (action by copyright owner, the executor and trustee of authoress); *Conan Doyle v London Mystery Magazine Ltd* (1949) 66 R.P.C. 312; *Sweeney v Macmillan Publishers Ltd* [2002] R.P.C. 35.

[68] CDPA 1988, s.84. See para. 11–52, above.

[69] See CDPA 1988, s.84 for the full extent of the beneficiaries of the right.

[70] *Alan Clark v Associated Newspapers Ltd* [1998] R.P.C. 261 at 269.

21–11   **Claimant's work represented to be another's.** It can also be passing off to represent a work which *is* the claimant's as being the work of someone else (so-called "reverse passing off").[71] This remedy has parallels with the moral right of a person to be identified as the author of a work.[72]

21–12   **Professional name or *nom de plume*.** It is common for performers and other artistes to use professional names in which there may subsist a valuable goodwill[73] and an author or artist who has acquired a reputation under a *nom de plume* is entitled to protect it by a passing-off action.[74] In several cases, the point has arisen whether someone who, while employed or engaged by another, has acquired a reputation under a *nom de plume* or in a fictional character under whose name he has written or performed, was entitled to the exclusive use of it after the relationship has ended. In the absence of some clear term to the contrary, the name is the property of the individual who has acquired the reputation, and he alone is entitled to use it after the severance of his relationship.[75]

21–13   **Alterations and revisions not the author's.** The exploitation of a work as the author's but which has been altered or revised without the author's consent may amount to passing off.[76] So, a claim by an author succeeded where he had written two editions of a textbook under his own name and then sold the copyright to the defendant, who then published a third edition with many mistakes as if it had been edited by the plaintiff.[77] In *Sweeney v Macmillan Publishers Ltd*,[78] the claim failed, but only because the claimants could not identify with sufficient clarity the class of goods identified in the mind of the public by the name of the work and author.[79] This remedy is in addition to any remedies which the author may have for infringement of his moral right of integrity,[80] defamation,[81] or, where he has retained the copyright and merely licensed use of the work, a claim for infringement of copyright on the basis that such use is beyond the terms of the licence[82] and perhaps also a breach of contract.

---

[71] *John Robert Powers School Inc v DB Tessensohn* [1995] F.S.R. 947 (High Ct of Singapore) (plaintiff's study notes used in defendant's school represented to be the defendant's), following *Bristol Conservatories Ltd v Conservatories Custom Built Ltd* [1989] R.P.C. 455; *Pasterfield v Denham* [1999] F.S.R. 168 (where the claim failed because of no likelihood of confusion or damage).

[72] CDPA 1988, s.77. See generally as to moral rights, Ch.11, above.

[73] As in *Fleetwood Mac Promotions Ltd v Clifford Davis Management Ltd* [1975] F.S.R. 150 (name of pop group).

[74] *Marengo v Daily Sketch Ltd* [1948] 1 All E.R. 406; *Maitland-Davidson v The Sphere and Tatler Ltd* [1917–23] Mac.C.C. 128.

[75] *Landa v Greenberg* (1908) 24 T.L.R. 441; *Hines v Winnick* [1947] Ch. 708; *Modern Fiction Ltd v Fawcett* (1949) 66 R.P.C. 230; *Forbes v Kelmsley Newspapers Ltd* [1951] 2 T.L.R. 656.

[76] See further at para. 21–09, above, as to this problem.

[77] *Archbold v Sweet* (1832) 1 M.Rob. 162. Some of the cases in this area decided before the law of passing off was fully developed need to be regarded with caution. For example, in *Lee v Gibbings* (1892) 67 L.T. 263, where an edited and mutilated version of an author's work had been published as his (the defendant had obtained the uncut sheets of the full version of the plaintiff's work and cut them down) it was held that his only remedy was in libel, there being no remedy for injury to his reputation as such. In *Humphreys v Thomson & Co Ltd* [1905–10] Mac.C.C. 148, where substantial alterations had been made to the plaintiff's work for the purposes of serial publication, the jury was directed that what had been done probably did not amount to passing off. It is suggested that this was eminently a question for the jury, who in fact returned a verdict for the plaintiff on the ground that what had happened was injurious to her reputation.

[78] [2002] R.P.C. 35.

[79] The problem lay in the fact that other versions of the work (James Joyce's *Ulysses*) had been published after the author's death. It was unacceptable to define the class by reference to those works which had been approved by the author or his estate, or by some body of academic opinion.

[80] See para. 11–36, above.

[81] See *e.g. Moseley v Stanley Paul & Co* [1917–23] Mac.C.C. 341 (vulgar and offensive dust jacket a libel on author).

[82] See para. 5–202, above.

Old work as new. It is not uncommon for a publisher, whether in the literary or   **21–14**
musical fields, to attempt to capitalise on the new-found popularity of an author
or artiste by publishing older material which the publisher still has the right to
exploit. There can be no objection to this unless there is some misrepresentation
that the material is in fact new and this suggestion is damaging, for example
because of the immature character of the work. In *Harris & Co v Warren and
Phillips*[83] the action failed on the ground that there could be no clear demarcation
in quality or merits between songs written at different times in the composer's
career. Given a clear and damaging representation that an old work was in fact a
new work, it is thought that a different decision would be reached today.[84]

Sequels and spin-offs. It is a common phenomenon for a successful novel, featur-   **21–15**
ing settings and a character or characters which are the creation of the author, to
spawn a series of such works. The same applies to television programmes, films
and the like. So also, the popularity of a work published in one medium, such as a
book, may give rise to a public appetite for derivative works in other media. A
common theme of such works may be a similar title, a topic considered in more
detail below, but usually use will also be made of the same fictional characters or
settings. The creator of such works will thus often develop a highly marketable
property in the name or features of the fictional characters and settings which he
has created.[85] There is no right in a character or settings as such, only in the
goodwill which has become attached to the author's business,[86] but a fictional
character and settings created by an author are clearly capable of being an "attractive force" to bring in custom, and thus part of the goodwill of the business.
Even in the case of films or broadcast plays, where the actor portraying the
character may change, the continued portrayal of that character may nevertheless
induce the public to continue to watch or listen to the presentation, and thus there
is goodwill which attaches to the business and which can loosely be said to constitute property in the character.[87] Another who produces a work which makes
use of those features will be in danger of causing the public to think that his work
is another in the same series and therefore from the same stable. Much will
depend on how the work is presented.

Generally, however, the goodwill which belongs to an author is the goodwill
in the actual stories[88] and to pass off, the defendant must impinge on that goodwill.
Thus, merely to publish a magazine featuring stories expressed to be in the tradition of a well-known fictitious character, but not featuring him, is not actionable
because there is no misrepresentation.[89] If the stories were actually to feature the
character, however, the position would be different if there was also an implied
representation that they were by the same author, and no doubt where a defendant
attempts to cash in on the popularity of a character developed by another author,

---

[83] (1918) 35 R.P.C. 217.
[84] See, generally, *Spalding (AG) & Bros v Gamage (AW) Ltd* (1915) 32 R.P.C. 273 and, for example,
Westinghouse Brake & Saxby Signal Co Ltd v The Varsity Eliminator Co Ltd (1935) 52 R.P.C.
295 (altered goods sold as plaintiff's goods); *Morris Motors Ltd v Lilley* [1959] 1 W.L.R. 1184
(car which was not new sold as new); *Doan v American Book Co* (1901) 105 Fed. Rep. 772,
[1901–04] Mac.C.C. 1 (US Circuit Ct of Appeal) (second-hand books rebound and passed off as
new). In *Coogan v Odhams Press Ltd* [1928–35] Mac.C.C. 1, undertakings were given not to
print old material about the plaintiff as if it were new.
[85] The related topic of character merchandising is considered separately, at para. 21–44, below.
[86] *Shaw Bros (Hong Kong) Ltd v Golden Harvest (HK) Ltd* [1972] R.P.C. 559 at 563 (claim by film
producer to fictitious character "the One-Armed Swordsman" popularised in a series of films).
[87] *Shaw Bros (Hong Kong) Ltd v Golden Harvest (HK) Ltd* [1972] R.P.C. 559 at 564.
[88] *Conan Doyle v London Mystery Magazine Ltd* (1949) 66 R.P.C. 312.
[89] *Conan Doyle v London Mystery Magazine Ltd* (1949) 66 R.P.C. 312 (magazine of stories in the
tradition of Sherlock Holmes, but which did not feature the character, although purportedly
published from his fictitious address of 221B Baker Street).

by publishing a work featuring the character, the court will readily conclude that some members of the public will be misled into thinking that it is indeed by the original author.

21–16   **"Authorised" works.** Just as it may amount to passing off to sell goods as having been approved by the owner of the relevant goodwill, so the publication of a biography or other work as having been authorised or approved by its subject may amount to passing off.[90] Where the claim is brought by a claimant who is already engaged in exploiting the goodwill associated with his name by activities such as merchandising or endorsement, the claim may be easily established. Where the plaintiff is simply well known, it may be more difficult to establish any relevant business to which any goodwill is attached. Thus a well known actor failed in passing off to stop the publication of an interview with him which suggested he had consented to it, since he was not a trader in relation to stories about him[91] Nevertheless, it may be easier today to persuade a court that a celebrity has a relevant business.[92]

21–17   **Inserts.** It is common today for newspapers to have various advertising materials inserted into them. This will often imply that the material has been inserted with the proprietor's consent in which case the unauthorised insertion of material will amount to passing off.[93]

21–18   **Artist's style imitated.** An artist cannot complain if another artist chooses to adopt a similar style or characteristics, except perhaps where a particular style or characteristic has become associated with an artist and another has so nearly copied it as to lead to confusion.[94] Thus, in *Gordon Fraser Gallery Ltd v Tatt*,[95] the court refused to grant an injunction to the plaintiff, who published a distinctive style of greetings card, restraining the defendants from offering for sale cards bearing a distinct resemblance to the plaintiff's. The defendant's cards were not copies of, but were obviously derived from, the plaintiff's cards. The court held there was no likelihood of confusion. Similarity of artistic style and content, not amounting to breach of copyright, were not sufficiently defined features on which to base an allegation that somebody would be persuaded to buy the defendant's goods in the belief that they were the plaintiff's goods.

21–19   **Literary parody.** Where an author's literary style is parodied, it will often be difficult to draw the line between what is a permissible degree of imitation and what is actionable in passing off or under the statutory tort of false attribution of authorship. A successful parody must be sufficiently close to the claimant's work to evoke elements of his literary style, for comical or satirical effect, without going so far as to deceive members of the public that the work in question is in fact the claimant's. Where a parody represents that the claimant is the author of the work in question, while simultaneously attempting to represent that the claimant is not the author of the work, it is necessary to look at the work as a whole to

---

[90] *Lord Brabourne v Hough* [1981] F.S.R. 79 (interlocutory only).

[91] *Kaye v Robertson* [1991] F.S.R. 62 (although an injunction was granted on the basis of a claim in malicious falsehood). In *Coogan v Odhams Press Ltd* [1928–35] Mac.C.C., the damage alleged was injury to the plaintiff's reputation by the publication of untrue stories and the inability to sell his story to another newspaper. (In the event, undertakings were given not to print old material about the plaintiff as if it were new.).

[92] *Irvine v Talksport Ltd* [2002] E.W.H.C. 367, [2002] 1 W.L.R. 2355, [2002] F.S.R. 60; and see further paras 21–41 *et seq.*, below.

[93] *Associated Newspapers plc v Insert Media Ltd* [1991] 1 W.L.R. 571; *Illustrated Newspapers Ltd v Publicity Services (London) Ltd* (1938) 55 R.P.C. 172.

[94] See *Marengo v Daily Sketch and Daily Graphic Ltd* [1992] F.S.R. 1, CA; (1948) 65 R.P.C. 242, HL.

[95] [1966] R.P.C. 505.

determine whether the latter representation is sufficient to ensure that members of the public are not deceived. Thus, "[a] parody which occasions only a momentary and inconsequential deception is both successful and permissible; but a parody which contains an enduring deception is neither".[96]

4. PROTECTION OF TITLES

No copyright in titles. The titles of books, newspapers, periodicals and other copyright works are not generally in themselves the subject of copyright.[97] The reason is that there is usually no original literary work in the formation of several ordinary words into a title. The words or phrases chosen may be original in their application to the subject-matter of the work, and may require much skill and judgment to produce. However, that skill and judgment is generally employed in choosing and selecting from common words and phrases, and not in putting together words in an original form, or in affording to others information, instruction, or pleasure.[98] Where, as will usually be the case, the title forms part of a larger work or compilation, the copying of the title will rarely, if ever, amount to the taking of a substantial part.[99]

21–20

Goodwill in titles. Although there will almost certainly be no copyright in a title, there will often be a valuable proprietary right in the goodwill which the title has helped to generate and which has come to be associated with it. There is little discussion in the cases as to who is entitled to the goodwill in the title of a book or magazine. It is suggested that the goodwill associated with a successful title may be an asset of both the author's and the publisher's business and so both may be entitled to bring a passing-off action, depending on the precise nature of the misrepresentation.

21–21

A. NEWSPAPERS AND PERIODICALS

Until recently, it was often difficult for a newspaper proprietor to restrain the use of similar titles by others, on the grounds that the names of most newspapers, such as "Star",[1] "Advertiser",[2] "Herald",[3] "Times",[4] "Chronicle",[5] "Express",[6]

21–22

---

[96] *Alan Clark v Associated Newspapers Ltd* [1998] R.P.C. 261, *per* Lightman J. at 272.

[97] See para. 3–16, above.

[98] *Exxon Corp v Exxon Insurance Consultants International Ltd* [1982] Ch. 119. Some early authorities appear to support the proposition that the title of, for example, a literary work is protected by copyright (*Weldon v Dicks* (1878) 10 Ch.D. 247; *Mack v Petter* (1872) L.R. 14 Eq. 431). Those cases have subsequently been overruled so far as short titles of unoriginal character are concerned: *Dicks v Yates* (1881) 18 Ch.D. 76; *Licensed Victuallers' Newspaper Co v Bingham* (1888) 38 Ch.D. 139, *per* Lindley L.J.; *Miss World (Jersey) Ltd v James Street Productions Ltd* [1981] F.S.R. 300; *Exxon Corp v Exxon Insurance Consultants International Ltd* [1982] Ch. 119. Copyright, however, may well subsist in a whole page of title or something of that kind requiring original labour (*Dicks v Yates* (1881) 18 Ch.D. 76; *Francis Day and Hunter Ltd v Twentieth Century Fox Corp Ltd* [1940] A.C. 112 at 123; *Ladbroke (Football) Ltd v William Hill (Football) Ltd* [1964] 1 W.L.R. 273 at 286) or be infringed by the taking of headings forming part of a larger work (*Lamb v Evans* [1893] 1 Ch. 218—elaborate headings given in each case in English, French, German and Spanish).

[99] *Francis Day and Hunter Ltd v Twentieth Century Fox Corp Ltd* [1940] A.C. 112; *Ladbroke (Football) Ltd v William Hill (Football) Ltd* [1964] 1 W.L.R. 273.

[1] *Morning Star Co-operative Society Ltd v Express Newspapers Ltd* [1979] F.S.R. 113.

[2] *Baylis & Co (The Maidenhead Advertisers) Ltd v Darlenko Ltd* [1974] F.S.R. 284.

[3] *Tamworth Herald Co Ltd v Thomson Free Newspapers Ltd* [1991] F.S.R. 337.

[4] *George Outram and Co Ltd v The London Evening Newspapers Co Ltd* (1911) 27 T.L.R. 231.

[5] *Cowen v Hulton* (1882) 46 L.T. 897.

[6] *Dillon v Pearson* [1901–04] Mac.C.C. 17.

and "Post"[7] were taken to be descriptive. Doubt was cast on this suggestion, however, in *Associated Newspapers Ltd v Express Newspapers*,[8] in which it was held, without reference to any of the authorities mentioned above, but after extensive evidence of the public's understanding of such titles, that "Mail" was not descriptive of a newspaper because newspapers are not called 'mails'.[9] The court went on to hold that there was a likelihood that the public would confuse the "*Evening Mail*" with the "*Daily Mail*".[10] That, together with a finding that damage might be caused to the reputation of the *Daily Mail* if the new newspaper ran a controversial campaign,[11] is directly contrary to earlier authority.[12] Nonetheless, it is suggested that the decision, on its facts, was correct and consistent with the modern application of the tort of passing off.[13] Where a title is purely,[14] or partly,[15] descriptive, however, small variations in the defendant's title,[16] or dif-

---

[7] *DC Thomson & Co Ltd v Kent Messenger Ltd* [1975] R.P.C. 191.

[8] [2003] EWHC 1322, Ch.D; [2003] F.S.R. 51.

[9] [2003] EWHC 1322 at para.26.

[10] [2003] EWHC 1322 at para.43.

[11] [2003] EWHC 1322 at para.47.

[12] *Borthwick v Evening Post* (1888) 37 Ch.D. 449.

[13] e.g. *Taittinger SA v Allbev Ltd* [1993] F.S.R. 641, and see especially para. 21–39, below.

[14] *Kelly v Byles* (1880) 13 Ch.D 682 (where the plaintiff published a series of "Post Office" directories, including the Post Office Directory of West Riding of Yorkshire, and the defendant proposed to publish "The Post Office Bradford Directory"; held: the name "Post Office" when used in relation to directories was not synonymous with the plaintiff); *Dale Reynolds & Co v Trade Press Publishing Co* [1901–04] Mac.C.C. 32 (*The Plumber and Decorator* and *The Decorators' and Painters' Magazine* descriptive, but an injunction was granted to restrain the defendant from selling their newspaper without clearly distinguishing it from the plaintiffs'); *Pearl Cooper Ltd v Richmond Hill Press Ltd* [1957] R.P.C. 363 (where the plaintiff's magazine was called *Sports Car and Lotus Owner*, which had become known as *Sports Car*; no injunction to restrain publication of *Sports Cars Illustrated*, the title being highly descriptive and not likely *per se* to cause confusion); *cf. Emap National Publications Ltd v Security Publications Ltd* [1997] F.S.R. 891 (*Practical Classics* and *Classics* names not in themselves distinctive, but similarity in a combination of features in the magazine formats amounted to passing off); *Norman Kark Publications Ltd v Odham Press Ltd* [1962] 1 W.L.R. 380 (no sufficient distinctiveness remaining in the title *Today*' after its amalgamation and publication as *"Courier" incorporating "Today"*).

[15] *Ridgeway Co (The) v The Amalgamated Press Ltd* (1911) 28 T.L.R. 149 (*Everybody's Magazine*, and *Everybody's Weekly*, "everybody" in this context meaning that the magazine was suitable for everyone and would commend itself to everyone, the magazines being otherwise distinguishable and not in competition); *The Cricketer Ltd v Newspapers Pty Ltd* [1974] V.R. 477 (Sup Ct of Victoria) (no one familiar with the plaintiff's *The Cricketer* magazine, published mainly in England and about English cricket, would confuse it with the *Cricketer*, published in Australia with a different get-up and mostly about cricket in Australia); *DC Thomson & Co Ltd v Kent Messenger Ltd* [1975] R.P.C. 191 (differences in appearance, content and area of circulation (parts of south-east Kent) of the defendant's *The South East Sunday Post*, where it already published *The Evening Post*, meant no confusion likely with the plaintiff's *The Sunday Post*, published mainly in Scotland); *World Athletics & Sporting Publications Ltd v ACM Webb (Publishing) Ltd* [1981] F.S.R. 27 (no confusion between *Athletics Weekly* and *Athletics Monthly* because the content and look of each different and aimed at different readership); *Tamworth Herald Co Ltd v Thomson Free Newspapers Ltd* [1991] F.S.R. 337 (no relevant confusion likely between *Tamworth Herald* and *Tamworth Herald and Post*; any confusion which did arise was likely to be because both papers used the word "Tamworth").

[16] *Bradbury v Beeton* (1869) 18 W.R. 33; (1869) 21 L.T. 323 (reputation of *Punch*, so strong that no one would assume any connection with *Punch and Judy*); *The Ridgeway Co v Hutchinson* (1923) 40 R.P.C. 335 (*Hutchinson's Adventure Story Magazine* clearly distinguishable from the plaintiff's *Adventure*; "… one of the boldest actions that I have ever had to deal with …", *per* Sargant J.); *Brittain Publishing Co (London) Ltd v Trade & Commercial Press Ltd* [1957] R.P.C. 134 and 271 (*National Weekly* for an advertising paper sufficiently distinguishable from both *London Weekly Advertiser* and *National Advertiser*; an undertaking had been obtained that the defendant would not publish without taking sufficient steps to distinguish its publication from the plaintiff's and the issue was whether the defendant had done so); *Baylis & Co (The Maidenhead Advertiser) Ltd v Darlenko Ltd* [1974] F.S.R. 284 (the word "new" in the defendant's free newspaper *The New Advertiser* sufficient to distinguish it from the plaintiff's long established, paid-for local newspaper entitled *The Maidenhead Advertiser*, often shortened to *The Advertiser*); *Advance Magazine Publishing Inc v Redwood Publishing Ltd* [1993] F.S.R. 449 (*BBC Gourmet Good Food* distinguishable from *Gourmet*).

ferences between the publications' price, get-up,[17] and mode of distribution,[18] may suffice to prevent confusion arising. Alternatively, if there is confusion, this may not be attributable to the defendant's misrepresentation, but to the descriptiveness of the title. No question of descriptiveness arises where the title is a "fancy" one.[19] The question in each case must be whether the defendant, by reason of the name of its newspaper, is representing that it is associated with the claimant's.[20] Where there has been a deliberate attempt to mislead the public, the court will be reluctant to assume that the defendant's efforts will have been unsuccessful.[21] Sometimes cases are decided on the basis that although there may be confusion, there is no damage.[22]

B. Books

A distinction can be drawn between, first, titles which are arbitrary and capable **21–23** of being distinctive, second, titles which on the one hand are descriptive, but are capable of acquiring a secondary meaning, and third, titles that are purely descriptive and inherently incapable of being distinctive.[23] If the title is an invented fancy title, as the title of a work of fiction will often be, it will be relatively easy to establish distinctiveness. The difficult cases are those where the titles, though

---

[17] *Local Sunday Newspapers Ltd v Johnston Press plc*, unreported, June 19, 2001; *Spottiswoode v Clarke* (1846) 2 Phil. 154 (the differences in the size, colour and engravings of the defendant's *Old Moore's Family Pictorial Almanack* such that no one could mistake it for the *The Pictorial Almanack*); *Cowen v Hulton* (1882) 46 L.T. 897 (*The Sporting Chronicle* clearly distinguishable from the *The Newcastle Daily Chronicle*, occasionally shortened to *The Chronicle*); *Dillon v Pearson* [1901–04] Mac.C.C. 17 (the plaintiff published *The Evening Express* as an evening paper in Liverpool, and the proprietors of the *Daily Express*, published in London, proposed to publish a morning paper in Liverpool under the title *The North Express*; there was some confusion as a result of people referring to the single word "Express" but this was momentary and no one was confused having opened the paper); *Cox v Sports Publishing Co.* [1901–04] Mac.C.C. 27 (*The Field*, *The Field and Kennel*); *George Outram and Co Ltd v The London Evening Newspapers Co Ltd* (1911) 27 T.L.R. 231 (confusion unlikely between the plaintiff's *Evening Times*, published in Glasgow, and the *Evening Times* published in London, where there were virtually no sales of the plaintiff's paper); *Morning Star Co-operative Society Ltd v Express Newspapers Ltd* [1979] F.S.R. 113 (the differences in name, style and content of the defendant's proposed tabloid, *The Daily Star*, sufficient to avoid confusion with the plaintiff's broadsheet, *The Morning Star*, often shortened *The Star*).
[18] *Associated Newspapers Ltd v Express Newspapers* [2003] EWHC 1322, Ch.D; [2003] F.S.R. 51.
[19] *Clement v Maddick* (1859) 1 Giff. 98 (publishers of the newspaper *Bell's Life* entitled to an injunction to stop publication of *Penny Bell's Life*); *Chancellor, Masters and Scholars of Oxford University v Pergamon Press Ltd* (1977) 121 S.J. 758: *Oxford Dictionary* and *Oxford Dictionary of Perfect Spelling*.
[20] *Tamworth Herald Co Ltd v Thomson Free Newspapers Ltd* [1991] F.S.R. 337.
[21] *Hogg v Kirby* (1803) 8 Ves. 215 (*The Wonderful Magazine, New Series Improved* clearly held out to be a continuation of a periodical entitled *The Wonderful Magazine*); *Prowett v Mortimer* (1856) 4 W.R. 519 (*The True Britannia* deliberately misrepresented to be continuation of *The Britannia*, which had recently merged with another title to become *The John Bull and Britannia*).
[22] *Borthwick v The Evening Post* (1888) 37 Ch.D. 449 (the defendant proposed to publish an evening paper under the title *Evening Post* and although a connection might be made with the plaintiff's paper *Morning Post*, no damage would be suffered in terms of lost sales); *Rubber & Technical Press Ltd v Maclaren & Sons Ltd* [1961] R.P.C. 264 (*Rubber and Plastics Age, Rubber and Plastics Weekly*: the confusion was "postal" only and not regarded as likely to lead to any loss of custom or other damage to the goodwill); *Norman Kark Publications Ltd v Odhams Press Ltd* [1962] 1 W.L.R. 380 ("*Courier*" incorporating "*Today*" and *Today, The New John Bull*; although there might be some embarrassment and inconvenience, this was not enough if there was no resulting loss of trade).
[23] *Mathieson v Sir I Pitman & Sons Ltd* (1930) 47 R.P.C. 541 at 550. As to the acquisition of a secondary meaning in the present context, the principle is that: "The name of a person or words forming part of the common stock of language, such as the description of the contents of a book, may become so far associated with the book of a particular author that it is capable of proof that the use of it by itself, without explanation or perhaps qualification, by another publisher, would deceive a purchaser into the belief that he was getting a book written by A, when he was in fact getting an entirely different book written by B.": *ibid*.

descriptive, have "an element of fancy".[24] It may of course happen that the publisher of a book will find that it is alleged that its title will cause confusion in some other field, for example the claimant's retail business, although any misrepresentation or damage may be hard to establish in such circumstances.[25]

21–24 Examples of descriptive titles of books. Clearly descriptive and thus not distinctive were two titles of the claimant's, respectively, *How to appeal against your rates in the Metropolis* and *How to appeal against your rates outside the Metropolis*. Some confusion with the defendant's books entitled *How to appeal against your rates within the Metropolis* and *How to appeal against your rates without the Metropolis* was inevitable but unavoidable.[26] Again, a book of housing statistics entitled *Cottage Homes of England* was distinguishable from a book with the same title but of entirely different character, being a study work for artists.[27] And where the plaintiff sold a style of photographic album decorated with pictures of castles, which was called the *Castle Album*, along with other similar albums in the range, the use was not sufficient for the title to have acquired a secondary meaning, *i.e.* it had not come to mean albums of the plaintiff's and none other.[28] On the other hand, the publishers of a work entitled *My Life and Loves by Frank Harris* were held to have acquired a distinctive reputation in the title although it was descriptive. The defendants' publication of an expurgated version under the same title was therefore calculated to deceive the public into buying copies of the defendants' book in the belief that they were copies of the plaintiff's book.[29]

21–25 Series of books and sequels. In the case of a series of books published under a common title, the allegation will usually be that the defendant's book is a further publication in the series. Here, it may be easier to establish goodwill, since use of such a common title is more likely to be use in a trade-mark sense, *i.e.* as indicating a trade source. Thus, it was held that the use of the words *Dark Future* as the common title of a series of books was significantly different from its use as the title of a single book and, in this respect, might be considered comparable to the title of a periodical or magazine.[30] When, however, the title chosen consists of common words, as will often be the case, it will be more difficult for the claimant to succeed. Thus plaintiffs who marketed a series of books called *The Pet Library* failed to restrain the defendants from displaying their books on a stand bearing the legend *Ellson's Pet Library* because, in the case of common descriptive

[24] *Mathieson v Sir I Pitman & Sons Ltd* (1930) 47 R.P.C. 541. See *International Press Ltd v Tunnell* [1938] 1 D.L.R. 393 (Ont. C.A.).

[25] As in *Mothercare UK Ltd v Penguin Books Ltd* [1988] R.P.C. 113, where likelihood of confusion was alleged between the plaintiff's "Mothercare" business and the book *Mother Care/Other Care*. Held: although descriptive, there was an established goodwill in the plaintiff's name but the title of the defendant's book implied no association with the plaintiff's business and the suggested damage was far-fetched.

[26] *Mathieson v Sir I Pitman & Sons Ltd* (1930) 47 R.P.C. 541. Note that the plaintiff's titles were held to have an element of fancy in the sense that it was possible to think of other descriptive titles for them, albeit that books with "How to ..." as part of their titles were common.

[27] *Crotch v Arnold* [1905–10] Mac.C.C. 227.

[28] *Schove v Schmincké* (1886) 33 Ch.D 546.

[29] *W.H. Allen & Co v Brown Watson Ltd* [1965] R.P.C. 191. The expurgated version of the work had previously been published under the title *Frank Harris: My Life and Adventures* and the plaintiff had obtained much pre-publication publicity for the unexpurgated work under the new title. The defendants had acquired the right to publish the expurgated version. There could of course have been no objection to the defendants publishing the book under the old title.

[30] *Games Workshop Ltd v Transworld Publishers Ltd* [1993] F.S.R. 705. An interlocutory injunction was granted on the basis of infringement of a registered trade mark, but the principle is equally applicable to passing-off actions.

words, comparatively small differences are accepted as sufficient to avert confusion.[31]

Work published in several editions. A reference work which is published through several editions will usually acquire a distinctive reputation even though its title will be largely descriptive. Here, the aggrieved party may be the previous editor, who claims that the work of a new edition is represented to be his,[32] or the publishers, who claim that a new work is likely to be confused with the established one. Whatever the precise nature of the claim, it is always necessary to show that the representation complained of is untrue. So where an author had published four editions of a work during his lifetime, the publisher of the posthumous fifth edition was refused an injunction against the defendant who proposed to publish a reprint of the fourth edition,[33] there being no misrepresentation as to the nature of its contents.[34] But where the plaintiffs were the publishers of a well-known work published in several editions entitled "Hemy's Royal Modern Tutor for the Pianoforte", of which Hemy was the author and which was commonly known as *Hemy's Pianoforte Tutor*, the defendants were stopped from publishing a work entitled *Hemy's New and Revised Edition of Jousse's Royal Standard Pianoforte Tutor*, based on an old and out of date work which they had employed Hemy to update, the word "Hemy" being displayed on the cover in disproportionately conspicuous type and dishonestly calculated to deceive.[35]

21–26

No misrepresentation. It is always important to ask what precisely is the representation said to have been made by the defendant. For example, a plaintiff produced a selection of 13 of Hazlitt's essays, together with a specially written introduction and notes, which was published as: "Hazlitt. Selected Essays, edited by George Sampson". The edition was selected as an examination text by London University. The defendant subsequently published a selection of 20 of Hazlitt's essays, including those selected in the plaintiff's work, with its own introduction and notes, which it published as "Hazlitt's Selected Essays, Edition Hollingworth". The 13 essays which had been selected for examination were also indicated. The evidence was that when asked for the edition prescribed for the University examination, the defendant had supplied its own edition. It was alleged that the defendant had published its work in a manner calculated to deceive purchasers into thinking it was the prescribed edition and thus that it was the plaintiff's work. The claim failed.[36] Although it was accepted that the defendant was selling its book as that prescribed for examination, this misrepresentation went only to the quality of the book and did not imply any suggestion that it was the book published by or connected with the plaintiff.[37]

21–27

Spin-offs. The misrepresentation alleged may be that a work in another medium, such as a play or film, is based on the claimant's work. So an injunction was

21–28

---

[31] *The Pet Library (London) Ltd v Walter Ellson & Son Ltd* [1968] F.S.R. 359 at 362.

[32] *Archbold v Sweet* (1832) 1 Moo. & R. 162 where an author had written two editions of a textbook under his own name and then sold the copyright to the defendant, who then published a third edition with many mistakes and as if it were edited by the plaintiff. See also para. 21–13, above, dealing with alterations and revisions to a work.

[33] It by then being out of copyright.

[34] *Seeley v Fisher* (1841) 11 Sim. 581.

[35] *Metzler v Wood* (1878) 8 Ch.D 606.

[36] *Cambridge University Press v University Tutorial Press* (1928) 45 R.P.C. 335. A claim for infringement of copyright based on the plaintiff's selection of the essays failed (at 344). The purchasers of the book had a valid complaint, however, in that the defendant's book was not the prescribed edition (at 345) and so could presumably have set aside the contract of sale.

[37] It is suggested that today the result might be different, bearing in mind the scope of the tort as now explained in *Erven Warnink Besloten Vennootschap v J Townend & Sons (Hull) Ltd* [1979] A.C. 731.

granted to prevent the showing of a film entitled *This Man is Dangerous* on the grounds that the film's title would suggest that it was based on the plaintiff's novel of the same title.[38] There must, however, be a likelihood of a connection being made between the two works, so that a claim failed where it was inconceivable that anyone going to see the film entitled *The Man Who Broke the Bank at Monte Carlo* would do so believing they were going to hear a performance of a well-known song of the same name.[39]

C. PLAYS AND FILMS

21–29 The title of a play or film will often be a fancy name and therefore capable of being distinctive of the claimant's work. Disputes over unrelated plays or films with identical or similar titles are not common, but the problem may arise in the case of remakes of films or with films based on the same public domain work. In the case of a remake of a film where the film or the underlying rights are still in copyright, the new film will usually infringe that copyright. Where the film does not infringe it may nevertheless amount to passing off where the effective representation is that it is in fact a remake, i.e. a film based on material which the owners of the rights in the original film have the exclusive right to exploit.[40] In the case of two films based on a public domain work it will clearly be very difficult to establish any misrepresentation in the absence of something close to fraud, such as, for example, a deliberate attempt to associate the later film with the earlier film's publicity.

21–30 **Spin-offs.** More commonly, the claim will be that the defendant's work is misrepresented to be a spin-off or new version of the claimant's work in another medium. Thus, a defendant was restrained from publishing a musical work whose title and cover falsely conveyed the impression that the work was taken from the music of a play[41] and, where a professional playwright had achieved great musical-hall success with a dramatic sketch entitled "*The New Car*", a defendant was injuncted where it falsely represented in advertisements that its film entitled *His First Car* was a version of the plaintiff's sketch.[42] Again, where a film-maker had released two films, entitled *Alvin Purple* and its sequel *Alvin Rides Again*, featuring a fictional character called Alvin Purple, it was held that a television series entitled *Alvin*, based on the same character and using the same principal actor would amount to a deception.[43] Where a film is part of a series, possibly with a common title, then it may bear closer analogy to a newspaper or periodical than a single publication such as a book and, consequently, it may be easier for the claimant to establish goodwill and that the use of the name amounts to use in a trade-mark sense.

---

[38] *Cheyney v Rialto Productions Ltd* [1936–45] Mac.C.C. 386. This was despite the fact that there was no evidence of any confusion even though over 12 million people had seen the film. The decision was interlocutory only.

[39] *Francis Day & Hunter Ltd v Twentieth Century Fox Corp Ltd* [1940] A.C. 112, PC, Lord Wright observing (at 126): "A frying pan cannot be passed off as a kettle".

[40] See the reasoning in *Samuelson v Producer's Distributing Co Ltd* (1932) 48 R.P.C. 580 (film based on revue sketch).

[41] *Elkin & Co v Francis Day & Hunter* [1905–10] Mac.C.C. 294. The action was brought by the composer and publisher of the music. It seems that the connection of the defendant's work with the plaintiff's would not have been denied but for a general practice in the trade being alleged whereby use of the name in such circumstances did not imply any such connection.

[42] *Samuelson v Producer's Distributing Co Ltd* (1932) 48 R.P.C. 580. The film was not in fact based on the sketch so the plaintiff's copyright was not infringed. The plaintiff had no plans for the making of a film version but the relevant misrepresentation was that the defendant's production was one which the plaintiff alone had the right to authorise.

[43] *Hexagon Pty Ltd v Australian Broadcasting Commission* [1976] R.P.C. 628. The plaintiff's claim in fact failed on the grounds of estoppel.

In all such cases the essence of the action remains a sufficient misrepresentation. So where a defendant intended to release a film entitled *Irish and Proud of it*, the author of a play of the same name which had last been produced some 12 years previously and which was otherwise unrelated was refused an injunction on the grounds that no ordinary member of the public would think that the film was a version of the play.[44] Again, the owners of the copyright in a successful play entitled *The Younger Generation* failed to stop the exhibition of a film of the same name some 16 years after the play's last professional run, it being held that the general public would not make any connection.[45] And it was held that no one going to see a film entitled *Alternative Miss World*, which was a satire or skit on the well-known "Miss World" beauty contest, would think there was any connection.[46]

D. Musical Works

It is unusual for a musical work to be passed off as the claimant's by use of a similar title. Where the same title is used, the position is likely to be either that the defendant's work is the same as the claimant's, in which case there will be no misrepresentation although issues of copyright may arise, or else it will be plain that they are different works. One such case arose where the plaintiff was the publisher of a song entitled "Minnie", which was a song with new words based on an old, non-copyright tune entitled "Lillie Dale", and which had become popular as sung by a particular artiste. The defendants were stopped from publishing songs respectively entitled "Minnie Dale" and "Minnie, dear Minnie", each having different words from the plaintiff's song but with the same tune, and each falsely represented to be sung by the singer of the plaintiff's work and thus implicitly to be the plaintiff's song.[47] On a related point, there may also be passing off by the misleading use of the name of a musician or group.[48]

21–31

E. Television and Radio

Again, there will be no copyright in the mere title of a television or radio programme[49] but where a claimant can establish that a title of a radio or television programme is sufficiently distinctive he may be able to prevent the use of a similar title by a competitor. Thus, the producer of a children's television quiz show, *It's Academic*, was entitled to an injunction to restrain the defendant from adopting the title *John Bailey's It's Academic* in relation to a similar quiz show.[50] Often, however, the title will be wholly or partly descriptive, in which case it may not serve to distinguish the claimant's programme at all[51] or the public may easily be able to distinguish the two, as where viewers of a locally produced tal-

21–32

---

[44] *O'Gorman v Paramount Film Service Ltd* [1937] 2 All E.R. 113. *Samuelson v Producer's Distributing Co Ltd* (1931) 48 R.P.C. 580, was distinguished on the grounds that the author had no immediate prospect of a film version of his work being made. But this was also the position in *Samuelson* and it is suggested that the sound basis for the decision is that stated in the text.

[45] *Houghton v Film Booking Offices Ltd* (1931) 48 R.P.C. 329. The action was brought by the trustees of the will of the author.

[46] *Miss World (Jersey) Ltd v James Street Productions Ltd* [1981] F.S.R. 309.

[47] *Chappell v Sheard* (1855) 2 K. & J. 117; *Chappell v Davidson* (1855) 2 K. & J. 123.

[48] *Byford v Oliver* [2003] F.S.R. 704 ("Saxon"); *Sutherland v V2 Music Ltd* [2002] EWHC 14, Ch.D; [2002] E.M.L.R. 28 ("Liberty").

[49] *Green v Broadcasting Corp of New Zealand* [1989] R.P.C. 469 (High Ct of N.Z. at first instance, at 472): "Opportunity Knocks".

[50] *Willard King Organisation Pty Ltd v United Telecasters (Sydney) Ltd* [1981] 2 N.S.W.L.R. 547 (Sup Ct of NSW), the difference in names not being sufficient to distinguish.

[51] As in *County Sound plc v Ocean Sound Ltd* [1991] F.S.R. 367, where the plaintiff's radio programme *Gold AM* was held to be descriptive, meaning "Golden Oldies on AM radio". No sec-

ent programme entitled *Opportunity Knocks* would not have been confused with the foreign version from which it was derived.[52]

21–33   **Spin-offs.** Where the programme is successful, there will often be profitable spin-offs available into other markets, such as books and merchandise.[53] Whether attempts by others to take commercial advantage of the popularity of the programme amounts to passing off depends on whether any misrepresentation is made, in particular, that the book or other merchandise is made or authorised by the makers of the programme. Mere use of the title of the programme, in a book about the programme and its characters, will not usually amount to any such misrepresentation.[54]

5. ADVERTISING SLOGANS

21–34   Although the task of devising advertising slogans often requires a high level of skill and judgment, as with titles, they will usually not qualify for copyright protection as original literary works.[55] However, the value of an advertising slogan lies in its role in generating additional goodwill for a product or service and in acting as a badge or vehicle for that goodwill, and, in appropriate circumstances, a slogan may be protected as part of that goodwill. Thus, passing off is not limited to names but is wide enough to encompass other descriptive material, such as slogans or visual images, which radio, television or newspaper advertising campaigns can lead the market to associate with a claimant's product, provided always that such descriptive material has become part of the goodwill of the product.[56] The test is whether the product has derived from the advertising a distinctive character which the market recognises.[57] In most cases, claimants have failed to establish that their slogan is distinctive.[58] It may be, of course, that the defendant's advertisement as a whole is deceptive.[59]

---

ondary meaning had been acquired and so no injunction was granted to stop the defendant's programme of the same name.

[52] *Green v Broadcasting Corp of New Zealand* [1989] R.P.C. 469 (High Ct of NZ). The plaintiff had the added difficulty that the original programme was hardly known in New Zealand, *i.e.* there was no local goodwill. Assuming there had been, it is suggested that no one would have taken the New Zealand programme to be the actual UK programme since one of the features of the UK programme was the personality of its presenter, the plaintiff. It is suggested that the relevant question would therefore have been whether the public would take the New Zealand programme to have been licensed by the proprietors of the UK programme. See also, *Baywatch Production Co Inc v The Home Video Channel* [1997] F.S.R. 22 (no evidence of confusion between the plaintiff's *Baywatch* programme and the defendant's *Babewatch* programme). As to format rights generally, see para. 3–42, above.

[53] As to character merchandising generally, see paras 21–44 *et seq.*, below.

[54] *Grundy Television Ltd v Startrain Ltd* [1988] F.S.R. 581 (book about the characters in the television "soap" *Neighbours*).

[55] *Sinanide v La Maison Kosmeo* (1928) 139 L.T. 365 ("Beauty is a social necessity, not a luxury"); *Kirk v J & R Fleming Ltd* (1928–35) Mac.C.C. 44 (28 words arranged in four short, ordinary and commonplace sentences). See para. 3–15, above.

[56] *Cadbury Schweppes Pty Ltd v Pub Squash Co Ltd* [1981] 1 W.L.R. 193.

[57] *Cadbury Schweppes Pty Ltd v Pub Squash Co Ltd* [1981] 1 W.L.R. 193.

[58] *Midgley (ST) and Sons Ltd v Morris and Cowdery* (1904) 21 R.P.C. 314, where the slogan "Fair Wear or a Free Pair" was held not to be distinctive of the plaintiff's product due to prior user; *cf. RHM Foods Ltd v Bovril Ltd* [1983] R.P.C. 275, where it was held that the plaintiffs had an arguable though not a strong case relating to similar packaging and advertising including the slogan "It browns, it seasons and thickens".

[59] *R & C Products Pty Ltd v SC Johnson & Sons Pty Ltd* (1993) 26 I.P.R. 98, where the plaintiff's advertisements had featured a well-known actor and a slogan "When you are on a good thing stick to it". The defendant's advertisements for a competing product featured the same actor and the slogan "When you find a better thing, switch to it". Held: that the defendant's advertisement was the type which the manufacturer of the plaintiff's product might use had it developed a new product which it wished to put onto the market and therefore evoked a connection with the plaintiff's product which was likely to mislead or deceive.

6. GET-UP AND APPEARANCE OF GOODS

The means by which consumers may be deceived include not only such *indicia*   **21–35**
as the name of the product but also the labels, logos, wrappings and containers
with which, or in which, the product is sold and even, exceptionally, the shape or
appearance of the article itself. These features may be the subject of copyright[60]
or design right but where they are not, a claimant's only remedy may be in passing off. As to this, the get-up[61] may proclaim an article's origin just as much as a
particular name attached to it.[62] There is, however, no property in get-up as such[63]
and to copy is not to pass off.[64] The distinction between passing off and other proprietary causes of action is that the right protected is the goodwill and not the
get-up itself.[65] Mere copying does not imply any representation that such activity
is licensed.[66]

Packaging and containers. Where it is the design of the printed material or   **21–36**
packaging which is alleged to deceive, a claimant must in the ordinary way establish that such get-up is associated exclusively with him.[67] Deception in such cases
may take the form of imitation of the lettering used,[68] the shape or appearance of
the container in which the goods are sold,[69] or combinations of these, perhaps in
conjunction with a similar name.[70] As to distinctiveness of the shape or appearance of the container, this may be relatively easy to establish where the shape of
the container has elements which are not just utilitarian but have an element of
fancy,[71] although this is not essential. Thus, a claim succeeded where the shape in
question was a plastic container for preserved lemon juice in the shape, colour
and size of a natural lemon.[72] The evidence established that the public made a
100 per cent association of the shape of the packaging with the claimant's product and the crucial point of reference for shoppers was the shape and not any

---

[60] Thus copyright may be claimed for the artistic part of a trade-mark (*Karo Step Trade Mark*
[1977] F.S.R. 260), designs for labels (*Charles Walker & Co Ltd v The British Picker Co Ltd*
[1961] R.P.C. 57; *Tavener Rutledge Ltd v Specters Ltd* [1959] R.P.C. 83 and 355, CA; *R & A
Bailey & Co Ltd v Boccaccio Pty Ltd* (1988) 77 A.L.R. 177), logos (*AUVI Pte Ltd v Seah Siew
Tee* (1991) 24 I.P.R. 41 (High Ct. of Singapore); *Roland Corp v Lorenzo & Sons (Pty) Ltd* (1991)
22 I.P.R. 245 (Fed Ct of Aus)) or wrappings (*Frank & Hirsch (Pty) Ltd v A. Roopanand Brothers
(Pty) Ltd* [1993] E.I.P.R. D–241 (CA of S.A.)). As to copyright in labels and logos generally, see
para. 3–16, above, and for a review of the protection afforded to trade marks by the law of copyright, see Lyons "Copyright in Trade Marks" [1990] 1 E.I.P.R. 21.
[61] "Get-up" is a loose expression but a working definition is "those non-verbal features of a product
and its presentation which are relied upon by traders to distinguish their products from those of
their competitors". See *Tot Toys Ltd v Mitchell* (1991) 5 I.P.R. 337 at 347 (High Ct of NZ).
[62] *F Hoffmann-La Roche & Co AG v DDSA Pharmaceuticals Ltd* [1972] R.P.C. 1 at 20.
[63] *Reckitt & Colman Products Ltd v Borden Inc* [1990] 1 W.L.R. 491, *per* Oliver L.J. at 505.
[64] *Benchairs Ltd v Chair Centre Ltd* [1974] R.P.C. 429 at 435.
[65] *Reckitt & Colman Products Ltd v Borden Inc* [1990] 1 W.L.R. 491 at 511, *per* Lord Jauncey.
[66] *Merchandising Corp of America v Harpbond Ltd* [1983] F.S.R. 32.
[67] As, for example, in *Taverner Rutledge Ltd v Specters Ltd* [1959] R.P.C. 83 and 355, CA.
[68] As in *Weingarten Bros v Charles Bayer & Co* (1905) 22 R.P.C. 341.
[69] As to a parallel proprietary claim in such cases, it is today likely, if anything, to be founded in
design right. See Ch.13 as to the phasing out of claims for infringement of copyright where the
copyright work consists of the design of any aspect of the shape or configuration of an article but
also note the limitation of design right claims, for example, where the design is commonplace or
is dictated by "must-fit" considerations.
[70] *United Biscuits (UK) Ltd v Asda Stores Ltd* [1997] R.P.C. 513 ("Penguin" and "Puffin" biscuits).
[71] For example *Coca-Cola Co v Barr (AG) & Co Ltd* [1961] R.P.C. 387 (shape of bottle having
twist and thin waist distinctive); *John Haig & Co Ltd v Forth Blending Co Ltd* (1953) 70 R.P.C.
259 (dimple bottle distinctive of plaintiff's whisky). But such features must be capable of
distinguishing. See for example *Williams & Co v Bronnley & Co Ltd* (1909) 26 R.P.C. 765
(shape and colour of containers for shaving soap common to the trade); *Sodastream Ltd v Thorn
Cascade Ltd* [1982] R.P.C. 459 (grey colour of plaintiff's gas cylinders not inherently apt to
distinguish, although a matter for trial).
[72] *Reckitt & Colman Products Ltd v Borden Inc* [1990] 1 W.L.R. 491 at 504. Lord Oliver approached
the case on the basis that it was a true "get-up" case, *i.e.* one concerned with the shape of the

labelling.[73] Even where the container has novel elements, however, it is not enough to show that the feature is recognised by the public. It must also be shown that those elements have become distinctive such that use of them by the defendant is deceptive.[74] Where confusion is possible a defendant must take sufficient steps to prevent any deception which might otherwise arise although often differences in additional elements in the get-up of the two rival containers, such as the colouring, labelling, and use of the trader's own name will be sufficient to distinguish them.[75] Exceptionally, however, the association of the shape with the claimant may be so strong that steps such as the display of the defendant's name or brand may not be adequate.[76]

21–37   **Shape of article itself.** It is notoriously difficult to succeed where the only instrument of deception is the shape or appearance of the article itself, particularly if the shape is a utilitarian one[77] The reason is that members of the public usually do not buy such an article because they associate the shape with a particular manufacturer but because they want an article of that shape, either for what it does or because the shape is attractive.[78] A successful action requires proof that the get-up has come to mean that the product has just one source[79] and the position usually is that the public are not moved to buy such articles "by reference to source".[80] Although the strict statement of principle is that "anyone is entitled, subject to some monopoly or statutory right preventing him, to copy and sell any article on the market, and a false representation and passing off only arise if he does something *further* which suggests that the article which he is selling is that of the claimant",[81] this requires some modification, since there is in fact no rule of law that a passing-off claim cannot succeed where the claimant proves that it is the shape and the shape alone which has become exclusively associated with his business.[82] Nor, despite earlier statements to the contrary,[83] is there in fact any rule of law which prevents such a claim succeeding where the shape is utilitarian

---

container in which the product was sold, not of the product itself. Lord Jauncey dealt with it on both footings (at 518). The other Law Lords agreed with both of them.

[73] The claim therefore succeeded even though a careful purchaser would not be confused once the label was read.

[74] *Adcock-Ingram Products Ltd v Beecham SA (Pty) Ltd* [1978] R.P.C. 232 (Sup Ct of SA) (aerosol container with domed closing device not distinctive despite its reputation).

[75] There are numerous examples in the cases. See, *e.g. Tetrosyl Ltd v Silver Paint & Lacquer Co Ltd* [1980] F.S.R. 68; *Malaysia Dairy Industries Pte Ltd v Yakult (Singapore) Ltd* [1980] F.S.R. 43; *Rizla Ltd v Bryant & May Ltd* [1986] R.P.C. 389; *Dalgety Spillers Foods Ltd v Food Brokers Ltd* [1994] F.S.R. 504.

[76] *Reckitt & Colman Products Ltd v Borden Inc* [1990] 1 W.L.R. 491.

[77] It is suggested in law there is no distinction to be made between cases concerning the shape of the article itself, and the shape of packaging or the container for it. See, *e.g. Tot Toys Ltd v Mitchell* (1991) 25 I.P.R. 337 at 350 (although drawing a distinction there between features of shape which are capricious, even though serving a purpose, and those which are not). The difference in the factual situation merely affects the difficulty of proof. Although the distinction may sometimes help with an analysis of the facts, it can lead to unhelpful arguments such as whether the lemon juice container in *Reckitt & Colman Products Ltd v Borden Inc.* [1990] 1 W.L.R. 491, was concerned with the shape of an article or get-up.

[78] *British American Glass Co Ltd v Winston Products (Blackpool) Ltd* [1962] R.P.C. 230; *George Hensher Ltd v Restawile Upholstery (Lancs) Ltd* [1972] F.S.R. 557.

[79] *Jarman & Platt Ltd v Barget (I) Ltd* [1977] F.S.R. 260.

[80] *Hodgkinson & Corby Ltd v Wards Mobility Services Ltd* [1995] F.S.R. 169 at 178. Such motivation is essential: *Tot Toys Ltd v Mitchell* (1991) 25 I.P.R. 337 at 366 (High Ct of NZ).

[81] *Benchairs Ltd v Chair Centre Ltd* [1974] R.P.C. 429 at 435 (emphasis added).

[82] *Reckitt & Colman Products Ltd v Borden Inc* [1990] 1 W.L.R. 491 at 519; *Hodgkinson & Corby Ltd v Wards Mobility Services Ltd* [1995] F.S.R. 169 at 176.

[83] Most notably in *Williams v H Bronnley & Co Ltd* (1909) 26 R.P.C. 765, *per* Fletcher Moulton J. at 773 "... I strongly object to look at anything, that has value in use, as part of the get-up of an article".

rather than fancy.[84] It is simply that in the former case the burden of proving distinctiveness will be that much harder to discharge since functional features,[85] or features characteristic of the product itself or copied from pre-existing artistic styles are not inherently distinctive, and the law leans against conferring a monopoly on such features.[86] The fact that the claimant has a large share or even a monopoly of the market does not prove that the public are attracted to the product because of their knowledge or belief that it comes from a particular trade source.[87] Reputation may be more easily established, however, where the article is shaped or coloured in an unusual way, not for practical purposes, but to give it a distinctive appearance.[88]

Cases where a claimant has discharged the burden are understandably rare, the most notable being the *Dolly Blue* case,[89] where the plaintiff established distinctiveness for its "dye-sticks", consisting of a bag of dye attached to a stick.[90] So also where sales of the plaintiff's coloured capsules over a period of time were held to have come to mean a drug manufactured by the plaintiff and no one else[91] and again where it was held arguable that the combination of utilitarian features of an electric fan was capable of being distinctive.[92] Cases in which such claims have failed are much more common, as where distinctiveness was claimed for the shape of ornamental dogs,[93] toy building bricks,[94] a child's "buzzy bee" toy,[95] three-piece suite,[96] stacking chairs,[97] reproduction furniture,[98] prefabricated buildings,[99] ordinary domestic houses with flint facias,[1] chocolate bars,[2] and utilitarian cushions to relieve pressure sores.[3]

Get-up of publication. Mere similarity in the style of a publication will rarely, if ever, be sufficient to found a passing-off action in this field, although it may **21–38**

---

[84] *Hodgkinson & Corby Ltd v Wards Mobility Services Ltd* [1995] F.S.R. 169 at 177, citing the utilitarian features of the article on which the plaintiff succeeded in *Edge (William) & Sons Ltd v Niccolls* (1911) 28 R.P.C. 582 (the *Dolly Blue* case). But *cf. Reckitt & Colman Products Ltd v Borden Inc* [1990] 1 W.L.R. 491 at 511, *per* Lord Jauncey: "Any monopoly which a plaintiff may enjoy in get-up will only extend to those parts which are capricious and will not embrace ordinary matters which are in common use".

[85] *Komesaroff v Mickle* [1988] R.P.C. 204 (Sup Ct of Victoria).

[86] *Jarman & Platt Ltd v Barget (I) Ltd* [1977] F.S.R. 260.

[87] *Jarman & Platt Ltd v Barget (I) Ltd* [1977] F.S.R. 260.

[88] *F Hoffmann-La Roche & Co AG v DDSA Pharmaceuticals Ltd* [1972] R.P.C. 1 at 20; *Benchairs Ltd v Chair Centre Ltd* [1974] R.P.C. 429.

[89] *William Edge & Sons Ltd v William Niccolls & Sons Ltd* (1911) 28 R.P.C. 582.

[90] See the report at 558 for illustrations of the products. The plaintiff's product carried no manufacturer's name so that although the defendant put its name on its product this did not serve to distinguish it (at 596). In *Reckitt & Colman Products Inc v Borden Inc* [1990] 1 W.L.R. 491 at 504, Lord Oliver regarded this case as one where the distinctiveness was to be found in something other than the principal object sold (*i.e.* in the stick rather than the dye bag).

[91] *F Hoffmann-La Roche & Co AG v DDSA Pharmaceuticals Ltd* [1972] R.P.C. 1 at 20, although arguably this was a "get-up" or "container" case rather than one concerned with the appearance of an article itself. It was distinguished on the facts in subsequent "pill" cases, where the features in question were held not sufficient to distinguish, either because they were common in the field (*Roche Products Ltd v Berk Pharmaceuticals* [1973] R.P.C. 473; *John Wyeth & Brothers Ltd v M & A Pharmachem Ltd* [1988] F.S.R. 26) or because the plaintiff's previous monopoly had lead to a quite different result, namely, to signify what the product was, rather than its trade origin (*John Wyeth & Brothers Ltd v M & A Pharmachem Ltd* [1988] F.S.R. 26).

[92] *Kemtron Properties Ltd v Jimmy's Co Ltd* [1979] F.S.R. 86 (Sup Ct of HK).

[93] *British American Glass Co Ltd v Winston Products (Blackpool) Ltd* [1962] R.P.C. 230.

[94] *Interlego AG v Tyco Industries* [1987] F.S.R. 409 (CA of HK).

[95] *Tot Toys Ltd v Mitchell* (1991) 25 I.P.R. 337.

[96] *George Hensher Ltd v Restawile Upholstery (Lancs) Ltd* [1972] F.S.R. 557.

[97] *Benchairs Ltd v Chair Centre Ltd* [1974] R.P.C. 429.

[98] *Jarman & Platt Ltd v Barget (I) Ltd* [1977] F.S.R. 260.

[99] *Terrapin Ltd v Arriston Buildings Ltd* [1964] F.S.R. 218.

[1] *Charles Church Developments plc v Cronin* [1990] F.S.R. 1.

[2] *Cadbury Ltd v Ulmer GmbH* [1988] F.S.R. 385.

[3] *Hodgkinson & Corby Ltd v Wards Mobility Services Ltd* [1995] F.S.R. 169.

increase the likelihood of deception when, for example, combined with a confusingly similar title.[4] Thus, where the plaintiff's well-known financial newspaper was published on pink paper, the risk of deception by the defendant's use of the same shade of paper for the business section of its newspaper was too remote to justify the granting of an interlocutory injunction.[5] However, although use of individual features of a publication may not amount to passing off, use of a particular combination of features, such as the size and choice of colourings, and the positioning of such features as logos, straplines, and bylines may, given appropriate evidence, lead to confusion between the claimant's and the defendant's publications.[6]

7. PRODUCT ENDORSEMENT AND CHARACTER MERCHANDISING

21–39 Endorsement and merchandising are two distinguishable concepts; though they often overlap, they may be differentiated by asking what the relevant representation to the public is. Endorsement occurs when someone, typically a celebrity, "tells the relevant public that he approves of the product or service or is happy to be associated with it. In effect he adds his name as an encouragement to members of the relevant public to buy or use the service or product".[7] This may be done by using the person's name, voice or likeness. It is a form of advertising for an otherwise unconnected product. Merchandising, by contrast, "involves exploiting images, themes or articles which have become famous"[8] by creating products bearing an associated name or image, for instance garments bearing an image from a popular film. Some merchandising involves endorsement, as in a pop group's "official" calendar, but it is by no means a necessary inference.

Where there is no remedy in copyright infringement against such use, supplementary protection may be available through a passing-off action. English law has historically been slow to provide such protection but cases of passing off in this particular field are no different in principle from any other passing-off case and should be assessed in the light of the modern formulation of the law in the *Jif Lemon* decision[9] and the classical trinity of the constituent elements of the tort, namely, goodwill, misrepresentation and damage.

A. NAME, LIKENESS OR VOICE OF REAL PERSON

21–40 It now seems established that falsely to represent that one's product is endorsed by a celebrity is passing off.[10] Older cases found defamation on similar facts,[11] but as public taste generally no longer considers it to be disreputable to appear in commercials and the like, these decisions may no longer be good law. This development now complements defamation, along with the torts of malicious

---

[4] Often, the case is put the other way, *i.e.* differences in get-up are said to be sufficient to distinguish publications with similar and partly descriptive titles. See para. 21–22, above, and the footnotes thereto.

[5] *The Financial Times Ltd v Evening Standard Co Ltd* [1991] F.S.R. 7. See also *Associated Newspapers plc v Insert Media* [1991] 1 W.L.R. 571 at 580.

[6] *Emap National Publications Ltd v Security Publications Ltd* [1997] F.S.R. 891.

[7] *Irvine v Talksport Ltd* [2002] E.W.H.C. 367; [2002] 1 W.L.R. 2355; [2002] F.S.R. 60; para.9, upheld [2003] EWCA Civ. 423; [2003] 2 All E.R. 881; [2003] F.S.R. 35.

[8] *Irvine v Talksport Ltd* [2002] E.W.H.C. 367; [2002] 1 W.L.R. 2355; [2002] F.S.R. 60; para.9, upheld [2003] EWCA Civ. 423; [2003] 2 All E.R. 881; [2003] F.S.R. 35.

[9] *Reckitt & Colman Products Ltd v Borden Inc* [1990] 1 W.L.R. 491; see para. 21–02, above.

[10] . *Reckitt & Colman Products Ltd v Borden Inc* [1990] 1 W.L.R. 491, para.9.

[11] *e.g. Tolley v JS Fry and Sons Ltd* [1931] A.C. 333 (defamation); *cf. Corelli v Wall* (1906) 22 T.L.R. 532 (defamation); *Kaye v Robertson* [1991] F.S.R. 62 (malicious falsehood).

falsehood and breach of confidence,[12] and means that the courts should no longer feel the need to stretch the boundaries of those torts to correct perceived injustices. It may also avoid the need for the courts to create a distinct right to personality,[13] privacy or, conversely, publicity.[14] There is no property in a person's name as such[15] and the mere unauthorised use of a person's name or likeness in an advertisement does not amount to passing off.[16] Again, doubts as to the commercial morality of the unauthorised commercial exploitation should not bear upon the question whether the core elements of goodwill, misrepresentation and damage can be established.

(i) Goodwill

It was held important in *Irvine v Talksport* that the claimant, a Formula 1 racing driver, was well known by name and appearance to the public.[17] Indeed, almost anyone engaged in a profession or business which brings him before the public will have a name, likeness or voice[18] which is associated exclusively with him. It matters not in what field the celebrity's primary business is, provided that he is sufficiently well known to have an actual subsidiary business in offering endorsement. Despite suggestions to the contrary,[19] this will now almost certainly be the case even when the celebrity does not in fact do so, because such activities are today such a common feature of the business of well-known personalities who are exposed to the public in the course of earning their livelihood that even the potential for such activity will, it is suggested, be regarded as an adjunct of the core business (though this may be relevant to the quantum of damage). It is arguable, in principle, that the estate of a deceased person might be able to establish that it has goodwill in a business involving the licensing of the image of the decedent, although this involves a circularity in establishing misrepresentation.[20]

21–41

---

[12] See *e.g.* para. 20–11, above.

[13] *cf.* the position in Canada, where a *sui generis* common law tort of appropriation of personality has developed: *Krouse v Chrysler Canada Ltd* (1971) 25 D.L.R. (3d) 49 (High Ct of Ontario); *Athans v Canadian Adventure Camps Ltd* (1977) 80 D.L.R. (3d) 583 (High Ct of Ontario); *Heath v Weist-Barron School of Television Canada Ltd* (1981) 62 C.P.R. (2d) 236 (High Ct of Ontario); *Dowell v Mengen Institute* (1983) 72 C.P.R. (2d) 238 (High Ct of Ontario); *Joseph v Daniels* (1986) 11 C.P.R. (3d) 544 (Sup Ct of British Columbia); *Baron Phillipe De Rothschild S.A. v Casa De Habana Inc.* (1987) 19 C.P.R. (3d) 114 (High Ct of Ontario); *Gould Estate v Stoddart Publishing Co* (1997) 30 O.R. (3d) 520 (Ontario Ct, General Division); *Shaw v Berman et al.* (1997) 72 C.P.R. (3d) 9 (Ontario Ct, General Division).

[14] *Sony Music Australia Ltd v Tansing* (1994) 27 I.P.R. 649 at 653–6 (Fed Ct of Aus), denying the existence of a right of publicity in Australia, although acknowledging the possibility for future development of such a cause of action). For the position in the United States, see *Zacchini v Scripps Howard Broadcasting Co* 433 U.S. 562 (1977) (US Sup Ct) and see generally, McCarthy, *The Rights of Publicity and Privacy* (Clark Boardman Callaghan, New York).

[15] *Dockrell v Dougall* (1899) 15 T.L.R. 333 at 334; *DuBoulay v DuBoulay* (1869) L.R. 2 P.C. 430 at 440.

[16] *10th Cantanae Pty Ltd v Shoshana Pty Ltd* (1988) 79 A.L.R. 299 (Fed Ct of Aus) at 306.

[17] [2002] E.W.H.C. 367; [2002] 1 W.L.R. 2355; [2002] F.S.R. 60, para.56.

[18] In *Sim v HJ Heinz & Co Ltd* [1959] 1 W.L.R. 313 it was held arguable that an actor's voice was part of his stock-in-trade and protectable as part of his business. It is suggested that this is clearly so.

[19] Thus, in *Kaye v Robertson* [1991] F.S.R. 62, the claim by an actor that an interview was misrepresented to have been given with his consent failed *inter alia* because he had no existing business in the giving of interviews to which any goodwill attached, a very restrictive view of the notion of the relevant business; *Lyngstad v Anabas Products Ltd* [1977] F.S.R. 62 at 68 where the court placed great emphasis on the absence of evidence that the plaintiff pop singers carried on a relevant business in the United Kingdom.

[20] See para. 21–42, below.

(ii) Misrepresentation

21–42 The misrepresentation in cases of false endorsement is said to be that the celebrity recommends, or associates himself with, the product.[21] This can be criticised on the grounds that in the majority of cases the celebrity is paid to use or speak of his approval, and that the public are probably fully aware that this is so. However, this is a fiction the law is prepared to entertain, as its effectiveness in practice cannot be questioned. It is suggested that the more sophisticated way of framing the representation—that the celebrity has licensed the product's manufacturer to use his name in relation to it—should be avoided where possible, as it gives rise to circularity.[22] Where the name or image of a deceased person is used, that circularity becomes unavoidable, as it is unlikely that a misrepresentation as to an endorsement by, or connection with, the person in question will be made out.[23] However, it may still be possible for the estate of a deceased person to establish that the public believe that the goods in question are licensed by the estate.[24] With the increasing use of licensing and endorsement as a method of advertising, the public may increasingly come to make such assumptions, although, as in the case of fictitious characters, the question whether such a misrepresentation has been made will largely be a question of fact.[25]

Formerly, claimants in English courts have had difficulty in establishing such a misrepresentation. Thus where photographs of well-known pop stars were used on merchandise it was held that there was no real possibility that a reasonable person might be misled into believing that there was some sort of connection between the plaintiff's business as entertainers and the defendant's merchandising business, in the form of a licensing or endorsement agreement.[26] The Australian courts, by contrast, have been open to the arguments deployed in *Irvine* for some time, and where defendants misrepresented that well-known professional ballroom dancers endorsed or recommended the defendants' record, by using a photograph of them on the record sleeve, it was held that the defendants had wrongfully appropriated the plaintiff's professional reputation.[27] On the other hand, a well-known television presenter who complained of the use of her name in an advertisement, in conjunction with an actress who resembled her, failed in her claim because the evidence did not establish the necessary misrepresentation.[28] Moreover, there are clearly circumstances in which use of a person's image will not imply any representation as to the product, for example

---

[21] Accepted as possible in *Taverner Rutledge Ltd v Trexapalm Ltd* [1975] R.P.C. 179.

[22] That is, that logically it is a necessary part of the representation that the claimant requires a licence for his conduct to be lawful. In *Mirage Studios v Counter-Feat Clothing Co Ltd* [1991] F.S.R. 145, a case concerned with fictitious characters, it was said that a misrepresentation relating to the existence of a licensing arrangement was actionable, although the court distinguished the clearer case of the licensing of rights in copyright material from a case involving the licensing of a mere name, in which no copyright subsists. It was stated that different considerations may apply in the latter case, which, given the change in trading habits, may require reconsideration in the future. (*ibid.*, at 158).

[23] *Irvine v Talksport Ltd* [2002] E.W.H.C. 367; [2002] 1 W.L.R. 2355; [2002] F.S.R. 60, para.44.

[24] See *ELVIS PRESLEY Trade Marks* [1997] R.P.C. 543.

[25] *Mirage Studios v Counter-Feat Clothing Co Ltd* [1991] F.S.R. 145. *cf. ELVIS PRESLEY Trade Marks* [1997] R.P.C. 543 at 553–4.

[26] *Lyngstad v Anabas Products Ltd* [1977] F.S.R. 62. The photographs used were licensed by a third party (*ibid.*, at 65).

[27] *Henderson v Radio Corporation Pty Ltd* [1969] R.P.C. 218 (High Ct of NSW): "In our view once it is proved that A is falsely representing his goods as the goods of B or his business to be the same as, or connected with the business of B, the wrong of passing off has been established and B is entitled to relief", *per* Evatt C.J. at 234. See also, *Hutchence v South Seas Bubble Co Pty Ltd* (1986) 64 A.L.R. 330 (Fed Ct of Aus); *Pacific Dunlop Ltd v Hogan* (1989) 87 A.L.R. 14 (Fed Ct of Aus).

[28] *i.e.* that it was she who was endorsing or was otherwise associated with the product: *10th Cantanae Pty Ltd v Shoshana Pty Ltd* (1988) 79 A.L.R. (Fed Ct of Aus). The use of the plaintiff's

where a photograph of someone taking part in a public event is used, although much will depend in such a case on precisely how the image is used.

(iii) Damage

To succeed in an action for passing off by endorsement, the claimant must show damage to his business in licensing his name or image. Whilst a claimant might argue that he has suffered damage by way of an injurious association between his business or profession and the business of the defendant,[29] or that he has suffered damage through the loss of control of his own reputation,[30] the simpler route is to argue that he has suffered damage through the loss of a licensing opportunity, since it is normally only possible to endorse one brand of a particular product at any one time. The loss of a licence fee which the claimant could have charged, but for the defendant's misrepresentation, is the most relevant form of damage in such a case.[31] Where the fields of activity of the celebrity and the product are far apart, however, the court might regard such an alleged head of damage as being too speculative.[32] The apparent circularity in claiming such a head of damage on its own, noted above,[33] is, it is suggested, illusory in this context; the loss of a licence fee is a mode of quantifying the damage, not the damage itself.

21–43

B. FICTIONAL CHARACTERS

In a case where what has been used is an image which recalls the character, effective protection will often be provided by the law of copyright.[34] However, a claim will fail if the claimant cannot show that the defendant has taken a substantial part of the copyright work.[35] Alternatively, an action for copyright infringement will not be available if the intended claimant does not own the copyright. Where alternative or parallel protection is sought, a passing-off action may provide a remedy. Clearly, a fictional character cannot "endorse" a product in any sense, although its maker, through his creations, can, and the public awareness of that character is capable of forming part of the goodwill of its maker's business. The unauthorised use of that character in the same media or in "spin-offs" into other media may therefore amount to passing off.[36] Whether the use of the character in merchandising activities constitutes passing off will usually turn on what representation is made by use of the character. As has been pointed out,[37] the deliberate reference by a trader to a fictional character created by another does not necessarily imply a trade connection. The intention may be merely to take advantage of the beneficial associations of the character.

21–44

---

name, "Sue Smith", by the defendant was, perhaps surprisingly, accepted to have been coincidental and not deliberate. See also *Honey v Australian Airlines Ltd* (1990) 18 I.P.R. 185 (Fed Ct of Aus) where a misrepresentation as to endorsement was not sufficiently established on the facts.

[29] *Harrods Ltd v R Harrod Ltd* (1924) 41 R.P.C. 74; *Annabel's (Berkeley Square) Ltd v Schock* [1972] R.P.C. 838.

[30] *British Legion v British Legion Club (Street) Ltd* (1931) 48 R.P.C. 555 at 564; *Lego System Aktieselskab v Lego M Lemelstrich Ltd* [1983] F.S.R. 155 at 190, 195.

[31] As in *Irvine v Talksport Ltd* [2002] EWHC 367, [2002] 1 W.L.R. 2355, [2002] F.S.R. 60. The appropriate way of calculating such a fee was set out by the Court of Appeal at [2003] EWCA Civ. 423, [2003] 2 All E.R. 881, [2003] F.S.R. 35. See also *Henderson v Radio Corporation Pty Ltd* [1969] R.P.C. 218 (High Ct of NSW).

[32] *Stringfellow v McCain Foods (GB) Ltd* [1984] R.P.C. 501 at 544.

[33] See para. 21–42, n.20, above.

[34] As in *King Features Syndicate v Kleeman (O & M) Ltd* [1941] A.C. 417 (dolls, toys and brooches based on "Popeye" drawings).

[35] *cf. Mirage Studios v Counter-Feat Clothing Co Ltd* [1991] F.S.R. 145 at 154.

[36] As to such possibilities, see paras 21–28, 21–30 and 21–33, above.

[37] *Tot Toys Ltd v Mitchell* (1991) 25 I.P.R. 337 at 376 *et seq.* (High Ct of NZ); *The New Zealand Olympic and Commonwealth Games Association Inc v Telecom New Zealand Ltd* [1996] F.S.R. 757 at 763.

(i) Goodwill

21–45   The originator of a cartoon character or other literary or artistic work may have a valuable goodwill not only in the business of the creation of cartoons, videos and films of his characters but also of granting licences for others to exploit the creations as a marketable commodity.[38] In this respect, it is important to establish that the claimant's business is dual in nature, namely that it consists both of the creation and exploitation of the character, or cartoon, or film in question, and also the licensing of the right to use such creations on goods sold by other people. It does not matter that the claimant is not himself a manufacturer of the goods of the type which the defendant is marketing. It is sufficient if he is in the business of licensing such use, provided that the public assumes the character would not normally appear without the licence of some person, such as the claimant.[39] If established, this link between the goods being sold and the claimant is sufficient to found a case.

It now seems probable that mere use of the name of a fictional character would support a passing-off action. Although there is no copyright in a mere name, and there can be no business capable of being carried on by licensing the use of the name alone,[40] a court ought to recognise that the public could perceive there to be an endorsement by the character's creators. The issue of whether a claimant has goodwill which may be damaged by the defendant's misrepresentation will need to be approached according to the facts of each case and the prevailing trading habits[41] and if the claimant can clearly establish the existence of goodwill, the question whether copyright material is being licensed may be immaterial.

(ii) Misrepresentation

21–46   Given appropriate evidence, it may be possible to show that a substantial number of the purchasing public expect and know that where a famous fictional character is reproduced on goods, the reproduction is normally governed by a licence granted by the owner of the copyright or other rights in the character.[42] In such a case there may therefore be two misrepresentations rolled into one: (a) the goods are "genuine", that is, they are the claimant's or derived from the claimant, and (b) they are licensed. Nevertheless, at this stage, the greatest care needs to taken in examining the evidence. The public may make the association between the image used by the defendant and the claimant's character, in the sense that people recognise that a reference is being made, perhaps intentionally. But it does not

---

[38] *Mirage Studios v Counter-Feat Clothing Co Ltd* [1991] F.S.R. 145.

[39] See also *Children's Television Workshop Inc v Woolworths (NSW) Ltd* [1981] R.P.C. 187 at 193 and *Fido Dido Inc v Venture Stores (Retailers) Pty Ltd* 16 I.P.R. (Fed Ct of Aus), both regarded as sound law in *Mirage Studios v Counter-Feat Clothing Co Ltd* [1991] F.S.R. 145. It seems that this proviso was not satisfied in *Lorimar Productions Inc v Sterling Clothing Manufacturers (Pty) Ltd* [1982] R.P.C. 395 at 415 (Sup Ct of SA).

[40] See *Mirage Studios v Counter-Feat Clothing Co Ltd* [1991] F.S.R. 145 at 157, where the previous English decisions on the subject (*Wombles Ltd v Womble Skips Ltd* [1977] R.P.C. 99; *Tavener Rutledge Ltd v Trexapalm Ltd* [1975] F.S.R. 179; *Lyngstad v Anabas Products Ltd* [1975] F.S.R. 488) were distinguished on this basis. In *Lyngstad*, however, both the name "Abba" and photographs of the band were used on the defendants' merchandise. Nevertheless, it is suggested that the names, and indeed the photographs, were not being used to identify the trade source of the goods and no misrepresentation of a licensing connection between the plaintiffs and the defendants was established on the facts. See further the discussion of this case in para. 21–42, above.

[41] *Mirage Studios v Counter-Feat Clothing Co Ltd* [1991] F.S.R. 145 at 158.

[42] As in *Children's Television Workshop Inc v Woolworths (NSW) Ltd* [1981] R.P.C. 187, at 190 (Sup Ct of NS), approved in *Mirage Studios v Counter-Feat Clothing Co Ltd* [1991] F.S.R. 145 (toy representations being sold of plaintiffs' three well-known puppet characters, the "Muppets": evidence that public assume that representations of well-known fictional characters sold under licence).

follow from this that the public believes that the image is the same as the claimant's character and has been used under licence.[43] Although, in principle, it may be possible to show that consumers are motivated by the desire to obtain "genuine", or licensed products, there is no universal rule that a defendant will always be making a misrepresentation by offering competing goods which are "non-genuine", or unlicensed and that consumers will always rely on such a misrepresentation.[44] Much will depend on the evidence in each case.

(iii) Damage

The misrepresentation that the goods are genuine, or licensed, is calculated to injure the business or goodwill of the owner of the rights in a character, provided his business includes that of licensing the use of such characters for profit. The damage may take the form of a direct loss of royalties or, alternatively, the value of the licence right may be diminished by the application of the characters to inferior goods.[45]   **21–47**

8 WEBSITES AND THE INTERNET

A fertile source of passing off in recent years has been the internet. "Cyber-squatting"—registering a domain name with the name of another company, individual or work—has frequently been held to be passing off.[46] This is the same principle as that which deems the incorporation of similarly named company to be "an instrument of fraud".[47] However, where the domain name will not inevitably lead to confusion, and has been registered without any intention to take advantage of the claimant's goodwill or reputation, the domain name is not an instrument of fraud.[48] So too it is possible to pass off not only by means of the domain name itself, but also by means of the content of a web page if it falsely represents there to be a connection with the claimant's business. However, there is no passing off merely by means of "metatags", because they are only read by computers and not consumers, even if they cause the defendant's website to be retrieved by search engines when a search under the claimant's name is made,   **21–48**

---

[43] See *e.g. Lorimar Productions Inc v Sterling Clothing Manufacturers (Pty) Ltd* [1982] R.P.C. 395 (Sup Ct of SA), where there was no evidence that the public would assume those behind the well-known TV series *Dallas* would have any business connection with defendants who were using names such as "Dallas", "Southfork" and "Ritchie" in their businesses and on merchandise.

[44] *ELVIS PRESLEY Trade Marks* [1997] R.P.C. 543 at 553–4.

[45] In some cases, the courts may be willing to presume that the plaintiff has suffered some damage to the goodwill of his licensing business, even though no actual damage can be shown. See, *e.g. Paramount Pictures Corp v Howley* (1991) 39 C.P.R. (3d) 419 (High Ct of Ontario).

[46] *British Telecommunications plc v One-in-a-Million* [1999] 1 W.L.R. 903; [1999] F.S.R. 1, followed in *Easygroup IP Licensing v Sermbezis* [2003] EWHC 2645, Ch.D; *Musical Fidelity Ltd v Vickers* [2003] F.S.R. 898, CA; *Bonnier Media Ltd v Smith*, (OH), *The Times*, July 10, 2002; *Tropical Resorts Management Ltd v Morgan*, *Independent*, October 8, 2001; *Easyjet Airline Co Ltd v Dainty* [2002] FSR 6; *MBNA American Bank NA v Freeman*, unreported, July 17, 2000; *Lawyers Online Ltd v Lawyer online Ltd*, unreported, July 7, 2000, *Britannia Building Society v Prangley*, unreported, June 6, 2000.

[47] See for instance *Glaxo plc v Glaxowellcome Ltd* [1996] F.S.R. 388; *Direct Line Group Ltd v Direct Line Estate Agency Ltd* [1997] F.S.R. 374; *Halifax plc v Halifax Repossessions Ltd* [2002] E.W.H.C. 2518; [2002] S.T.C. 402, appealed as to remedy only [2004] EWCA Civ 331; [2004] B.C.C. 281; *cf. Ben & Jerry's Home Made Inc v Ben & Jerry's Ice Cream Ltd* (no interim injunction where defendant not trading, now disapproved); *Petroliam Nasional Bhd v Kho Nee Kiong* [2003] 4 *Malaysian Law Journal* 216.

[48] *Radio Taxicabs (London) Ltd v Owner Drivers Radio Taxi Services Ltd* [2004] R.P.C. 19, though it is suggested that the result in this case turned on its own facts.

provided that it is clear to the consumer when he clicks on the link retrieved that he is not being directed to the claimant's website.[49]

PART VI

REMEDIES

Chapter Twenty Two

CIVIL REMEDIES

Contents

Contents *Para.*

1. OVERVIEW

22–01 **Scope of this Chapter.** This Chapter covers the non-criminal remedies and procedure in respect of infringements of all the rights covered in this work with the following exceptions and qualifications. First, remedies for breach of confidence fall into a separate category and are dealt with elsewhere.[1] This Chapter does, however, deal with some of the procedural questions which arise in confidential information cases. Second, this work only deals in outline with registered designs and Community registered designs. Accordingly, remedies and procedure for infringement of those rights do not feature in this Chapter. Finally, it should be emphasised that this Chapter is not intended to be anything like a comprehensive treatise on the subject of civil procedure. Rather it is intended to highlight and discuss those aspects of civil procedure which are specifically relevant to the enforcement of the rights covered in this work.

22–02 **Other remedies.** Where the infringement also constitutes a criminal offence, a potential claimant should always consider whether or not the expense of civil litigation might be avoided by reporting the infringement to the appropriate authority or even by commencing a private prosecution.[2] For criminal remedies, reference should be made to Chapters 15 and 16, above and Chapter 23, below. Consideration should also be given, where relevant, to reporting the matter to the Commissioners of Customs and Excise.

---

[1] See paras 20–26 *et seq.*, above.
[2] For a discussion of the advantages and disadvantages of criminal proceedings, see paras 23–44 and 23–45, below.

The Enforcement Directive. On April 29, 2004, the European Parliament and   **22–03**
the Council adopted a Directive on the enforcement of intellectual property
rights.[3] Member States are obliged to implement the Directive by April 28, 2006.[4]
The declared object of the Directive is to reduce or eliminate the prejudice caused
to the functioning of the single market and the weakening of the substantive
intellectual property law which is believed to be caused by the disparities between national procedural regimes.[5] This is to be achieved by the approximation
of national enforcement systems so as to ensure a "high, equivalent and
homogeneous level of protection in the Internal Market".[6] The Directive applies
to all intellectual property rights.[7] Although the Directive contains numerous provisions, it is not thought that many of them will involve a change in English law.
The main changes which are likely to result appear to be as follows. First, an
extension of the categories of persons entitled to sue for infringement to non-
exclusive licensees, collective rights management bodies and professional
defence bodies.[8] Secondly, provision for the publication of judicial decisions at
the infringer's expense.[9] Thirdly, the requirement that Member States encourage
the development by trade or professional associations of codes of conduct at
Community level aimed at the enforcement of intellectual property rights.[10] At
the time of writing, the Government was preparing a consultation in relation to
the implementation of the Directive.

Scope of this section. The remainder of this section of this Chapter gives a gen-   **22–04**
eral outline of the statutory provisions as to civil remedies in relation to each individual right covered in this work. There are no statutory provisions relevant to
passing off, which is actionable as a tort.

Copyright and publication right. An infringement of copyright is actionable by   **22–05**
the copyright owner.[11] An infringement occuring after the grant of an exclusive
licence is also actionable by the exclusive licensee.[12] Certain infringements are
also actionable by a non-exclusive licensee.[13] In an action for infringement all
such relief, by way of damages, injunctions, accounts or otherwise, is available to
the claimant as is available in respect of the infringement of any other property
right.[14] However, that general rule is subject to a number of statutory
qualifications. Two relate to damages. First, there is a defence to a damages claim
in the very limited number of cases where the defendant did not know and had no
reason to believe that copyright subsisted in the work in question.[15] Secondly, the
court may award a species of damages called "additional damages" which is peculiar to this field.[16] Two further qualifications concern injunctions. First, there is
a defence to claims for an injunction and for an order for delivery up where the
defendant undertakes to take a licence of right which is available under section

---

[3] [2004] O.J. L 157/45. For background, see the Green Paper on combating counterfeiting and
piracy in the single market, COM (98) 569 final; the follow-up to the Green Paper, COM (2000)
789 final; and the proposal for the Directive, COM(2003) 46 final.

[4] Art.20(1).

[5] Recitals 7–9. For criticism, see Cornish *et al.* [2003] EIPR 447.

[6] Recital 10.

[7] Art.1.

[8] Art.4(1).Note that some non-exclusive licensees may already sue: see paras 22–23 *et seq.*, below.

[9] Art.15.

[10] Art.17.

[11] CDPA 1988, s.96(1).

[12] s.101.

[13] s.101A.

[14] s.96(2).

[15] s.97(1).

[16] s.97(2).

144 of the 1988 Act.[17] Secondly, as well as granting an injunction against the infringer, the court may also grant an injunction against a service provider who has actual knowledge that another person is using its service to infringe copyright.[18] The court's equitable power to order delivery up of infringing articles is amplified by an express statutory power, which extends to articles specifically designed or adapted for making copies of a particular copyright work.[19] Finally, in certain limited circumstances, a copyright owner can seize infringing copies without the need to obtain a court order.[20] Publication right is a property right equivalent to copyright and the same provisions as to remedies apply as apply to copyright.[21] In the remainder of this Chapter, statements about copyright apply to publication right unless otherwise stated.

22–06   **Moral rights**. Unlike copyright, moral rights are not property rights. Infringements of moral rights are actionable as a breach of statutory duty owed to the person entitled to the right.[22] In proceedings for infringement of the right to object to derogatory treatment the court may grant an injunction prohibiting the doing of an act unless a disclaimer is made, dissociating the author or director from the treatment of the work.[23]

22–07   **Performers' property rights**. Like copyright, performers' property rights (as their name suggests) are property rights.[24] An infringement is actionable by the rights owner.[25] An infringement occuring after the grant of an exclusive licence is also actionable by the exclusive licensee.[26] There is no provision for an action by a non-exclusive licensee. As in the case of copyright, in an action for infringement all such relief, by way of damages, injunctions, accounts or otherwise, is available to the claimant as is available in respect of the infringement of any other property right.[27] By analogy with the copyright position, there is a defence to a damages claim where the defendant did not know and had no reason to believe that the rights subsisted in the recording to which the action relates;[28] the court has the power to award additional damages;[29] there is a defence to claims for an injunction and delivery up where the defendant undertakes to take a licence of right which is available under paragraph 17 of Schedule 2A of the 1988 Act;[30] and the court may grant an injunction against a service provider who has actual knowledge that another person is using its service to infringe a performer's property right.[31] Again, by analogy with the position in relation to copyright, there is a statutory right to an order for delivery up of illicit recordings (although not of articles specifically designed or adapted for making copies of a particular

---

[17] s.98. For a discussion of s.144, see para. 29–131, below. If this provision operates there is also a limit on the financial remedies available: s.98(1)(c).
[18] s.97A.
[19] s.99.
[20] s.100.
[21] Copyright and Related Rights Regulations 1996 (SI 1996/2967), regs.16(1) and 17(1).
[22] CDPA 1988, s.103(1).
[23] s.103(2).
[24] CDPA 1988, s.191A.
[25] s.191I(1).
[26] s.191L.
[27] s.191I(2).
[28] s.191J(1).
[29] s.191J(2).
[30] s.191K.
[31] s.191JA.

recording).[32] There is also a right in limited circumstances to seize illicit recordings without a court order.[33]

Performers' non-property rights and recording rights. In contrast to performers' property rights, these rights are not property rights and, like moral rights, are actionable by the person entitled to the right as a breach of statutory duty.[34] A person having performers' non-property rights or recording rights can, however, apply for an order for delivery up of illicit recordings[35] or (in limited circumstances) seize such recordings without a court order.[36]

22–08

Unregistered design right and semi-conducter topographies. Unregistered design right is a property right.[37] An infringement is actionable by the design right owner.[38] An infringement occuring after the grant of an exclusive licence is also actionable by the exclusive licensee.[39] There is no provision for an action by a non-exclusive licensee. As in the case of copyright, in an action for infringement all such relief, by way of damages, injunctions, accounts or otherwise, is available to the claimant as is available in respect of the infringement of any other property right.[40] By analogy with the copyright position, there is a defence to a damages claim where the defendant did not know and had no reason to believe that design right subsisted in the design to which the action relates.[41] Uniquely to design right, where in an action for secondary infringement, the defendant shows that the infringing article was innocently acquired by him or a predecessor in title, the only remedy is a reasonable royalty.[42] In other respects, the provisions of the 1988 Act are similar to those for copyright. Thus, the court has the power to award additional damages;[43] there is a defence to claims for an injunction and delivery up where the defendant undertakes to take a licence of right under section 237 or 238 of the 1988 Act;[44] and there is a statutory right to an order for delivery up.[45] On the other hand, there is no right to seize infringing articles without a court order. Certain uses of unregistered designs by the Crown are not infringements but give rise to a right to compensation which, in the absence of agreement, may be determined on a reference to the court.[46] Rights in respect of semiconductor topographies are governed by the design right provisions of the 1988 Act with the modifications set out in Chapter 14, above.[47] In the remainder of this Chapter, statements about design right apply to rights in respect of semiconductor topographies unless otherwise stated.

22–09

Community designs. To some extent, rights under Community designs raise different issues to the other rights covered in this work and reference should be

22–10

---

[32] s.195.
[33] s.196.
[34] CDPA 1988, s.194.
[35] s.195.
[36] s.196.
[37] CDPA 1988, s.213(1).
[38] s.229(1).
[39] s.234.
[40] s.229(2).
[41] s.233(1).
[42] s.233(2).
[43] s.229(3).
[44] s.239.
[45] s.230.
[46] ss.240–252.
[47] See the Design Right (Semiconductor Topographies) Regulations 1989 (SI1989/1100) reg.3.

made to Chapter 13, above.[48] In general, however, the same remedies are available for infringement of Community designs as are available in respect of infringement of copyright. In particular, the Community Designs Regulation provides that where a Community design court[49] finds that a defendant has infringed or threatened to infringe a Community design, it is obliged, in the absence of special reasons, to grant an injunction; to order the seizure of the infringing products and materials and implements predominantly used to manufacture the infringing goods;[50] and to make an order imposing "other sanctions appropriate under the circumstances which are provided by the law of the Member State in which the acts of infringement or threatened infringement are committed".[51] The court is also obliged to take such measures in accordance with its national law as are aimed at ensuring that such orders are complied with.[52]

22–11 **Rights in respect of protection measures, rights management information and unauthorised decoders.** In each of these cases, the person with rights has the same rights and remedies in respect of an infringement as a copyright owner has in respect of an infringement of copyright.[53] Thus, in an action for infringement all such relief, by way of damages, injunctions, accounts or otherwise, is available to the claimant as is available in respect of the infringement of any other property right.[54] In addition, a person with rights in respect of protection measures (whether in relation to computer programs or otherwise) has the same right to apply for an order for delivery up of circumvention devices or to seize them without a court order as a copyright owner has in relation to infringing copies.[55] Finally, in the case of protection measures other than those relating to computer programs, there is a defence to a damages claim where the defendant did not know and had no reason to believe that his acts enabled or facilitated an infringement of the right in question.[56]

22–12 **Database right.** Database right is a property right.[57] The remedies available to the owner and an exclusive licensee of database right are the same as those for infringement of copyright save that there is no right to a statutory order for delivery up or to seize infringing articles.[58]

22–13 **Equitable remuneration.** The appropriate remedy for an author or performer wishing to fix the amount of the equitable remuneration or dissatisfied with the amount payable is an application to the Copyright Tribunal. This is discussed elsewhere.[59]

---

[48] See paras 13–242 *et seq.*, above

[49] That is, the Chancery Division of the High Court, a Patents County Court or a County Court where there is a Chancery District Registry: see CPR 63.13(3) and PD63, para.18.1.

[50] Provided their owner knew the effect for which such use was intended or if such effect would have been obvious in the circumstances.

[51] See Art.89(1) of Council Regulation No.6/2002 on Community designs: [2002] O.J. L3/1.

[52] See Art.89(2) of Council Regulation No.6/2002 on Community designs [2002] O.J. L3/1.

[53] CDPA 1988 ss.296(2) (circumvention of technical devices applied to computer programs); 296ZA(3) (circumvention of technological measures applied to works other than computer programs); 296ZD(3) (devices and services designed to circumvent technological measures applied to works other than computer programs); 296ZG(3) (rights management information); and 298(2) (apparatus, etc. for unauthorised reception of transmissions).

[54] s.96(2).

[55] s.296(4) (computer programs) and s.296ZD(4) (other works).

[56] s.296ZD(7). See para. 22–74, below.

[57] Copyright and Rights in Databases Regulations 1997 (SI 1997/3032), reg.13.

[58] Copyright and Rights in Databases Regulations 1997 (SI 1997/3032), reg.23.

[59] See paras 29–133 and 29–152 *et seq.*, below.

Terminology in this Chapter. In the remainder of this Chapter, the term "non-property rights" means: moral rights, performers' non-property rights, recording rights, and rights in respect of protection measures, rights management information and unauthorised decoders.

22–14

2. WHO MAY SUE

A. LEGAL OWNER OR PERSON WITH RIGHTS

Copyright, performers' property rights, unregistered design right and database right. These rights are property rights and accordingly the remedies are given to the owner, that is to say, the original owner, or a person deriving title under him by a valid assignment or otherwise. Where different persons are (whether in consequence of a partial assignment or otherwise) entitled to different aspects of the right, the owner for this purpose is the person who is entitled to the relevant aspect of the right.[60]

22–15

Non-property rights. In the case of the non-property rights, the remedies are given to the person entitled to the right, whose identity is specified in the relevant legislation, or a person to whom that right has been lawfully transmitted.

22–16

B. EQUITABLE OWNER

Copyright. As to equitable ownership generally, see paragraphs 5–170 et seq., above. A person entitled to the copyright in equity may start an action and seek interim relief relying on his equitable title. He will not, however, be entitled to final relief unless he has either joined the legal owner as a party (co-claimant or defendant) or obtained an assignment of the legal title.[61] The purpose of the rule is to protect the defendant from the possibility of being sued again by the legal owner, in particular a bona fide assignee of the copyright for value without notice of the equitable owner's rights. It follows that there may be cases where the Court can be satisfied that there is no real possibility of a claim by the legal owner or for some other reason the rule, which is a rule of practice, not law, can be relaxed.[62] It is thought that such cases will rarely arise. If the equitable owner chooses to get in the legal title, as opposed to joining the legal owner, a mere assignment of copyright is insufficient. The assignment must include accrued rights

22–17

---

[60] CDPA 1988, s.173(1) for copyright, s.191A(3) for performer's property rights and s.258(1) for design right.

[61] *Merchant Adventurers Ltd v Grew & Co Ltd* [1972] Ch. 242 at 252; *Performing Right Society Ltd v London Theatre of Varieties Ltd* [1924] A.C. 1 at 14, 15 and 35; *EM Bowden's Patents Syndicate Ltd v Herbert Smith & Co* [1904] 2 Ch. 86 at 91; *Ward Lock & Co Ltd v Long* [1906] 2 Ch. 550; *University of London Press Ltd v University Tutorial* [1916] 2 Ch. 601; *Hexagon Pty Ltd v Australian Broadcasting Commission* [1976] R.P.C. 628; *Roban Jig & Tool Co Ltd v Taylor* [1979] F.S.R. 130 at 135; *Wah Sang Industrial Co v Takmay Industrial Co Ltd* [1980] F.S.R. 303; *John Richardson Computers Limited v Flanders* [1993] F.S.R. 497; *Bookmakers' Afternoon Greyhound Services Ltd v Wilf Gilbert (Staffordshire) Ltd* [1994] F.S.R. 723; *Batjac Productions Inc v Simitar Entertainment (UK) Limited & Another* [1996] F.S.R. 139; *Orwin v Attorney-General* [1998] F.S.R. 415 at 423, CA; *Comprop Ltd v Moran*, Royal Court of Jersey, March 20, 2002, unreported; *cf. Roland Corporation v Lorenzo & Sons Pty Ltd* (1991) 22 I.P.R. 245 (Fed Ct of Australia) where it was said that a plaintiff could obtain declaratory and injunctive relief, even though he had no title, legal or equitable, at the date of issue of the writ.

[62] See *Performing Right Society Ltd v London Theatre of Varieties Ltd* [1924] A.C. 1, at 18; *William Brandt's Sons & Co v Dunlop Rubber Co Ltd* [1905] A.C. 454 at 462; *Weddell v Pearce & Major* [1988] Ch. 26 at 43; *Batjac Productions Inc v Simitar Entertainment (UK) Limited & Another* [1996] F.S.R. 139; *Musical Fidelity Ltd v Vickers* [2002] EWHC 1000, Ch D; Lawtel 28/8/02: final relief granted to equitable owner after legal owners, a firm of solicitors, undertook to assign the copyright to the claimant (not challenged on appeal: [2002] EWCA Civ 1989).

of action in order to perfect the equitable owner's title to sue,[63] although in a *quia timet* action where the only remedy sought is a permanent injunction, a mere assignment of copyright without accrued causes of action should be sufficient. It appears that, if the defendant wishes to take the point, he can apply for the action to be stayed until the claimant perfects his title or joins the legal owner.[64] It also appears that an equitable owner is entitled to the remedies available under the 1988 Act as against the bare legal owner.[65] In *Orwin v Attorney-General*,[66] the claimant in copyright infringement proceedings claimed to be the legal, alternatively the equitable owner of various copyrights. In support of his claim to equitable ownership, he relied on an agreement between him and a company of which he had been a director. The company had been struck off the Register. He brought separate proceedings against the Attorney-General (representing the Crown) for an order pursuant to section 51 of the Trustee Act 1925, vesting the copyrights in him, claiming that the Crown held the copyrights on trust for him. The order was refused on the basis that (a) it was not at all clear from the evidence that the legal estate was vested in the Crown on trust for the claimant (in which case there would be no jurisdiction to make the order) and (b) the order should not be made in the absence of the defendant in the copyright proceedings, who was entitled to adduce evidence, cross-examine and make representations. The Court of Appeal made an order consolidating the Trustee Act proceedings with the copyright proceedings.

22–18 **Performers' property rights, design right and database right**. It seems that an equitable owner of a performer's property right, design right, or database right will have the same rights to sue as an equitable owner of copyright. The classic situation in which an equitable title arises is where a person commissions another to create a work and there is an express or implied term of the contract of commission that the intellectual property rights in the work will belong to the commissioner. In the case of design right, of course, such a situation will not normally arise because the 1988 Act provides that where a design right is created in pursuance of a commission, the person commissioning the design is the first owner of any design right.[67] A similar provision applies to database right.[68]

22–19 **Non-property rights.** There can be no "equitable owner" of these rights. They are not assignable, but only capable of transmission, if at all, on death.[69] Upon death, performers' non-property rights and moral rights pass to the person entitled, but recording rights do not pass even on death.[70]

---

[63] *Batjac Productions Inc v Simitar Entertainment (UK) Limited & Another* [1996] F.S.R. 139.
[64] *Weddell v Pearce & Major* [1988] Ch. 24 at 41. However, in *E.M. Bowden's Patents Syndicate Ltd v Herbert Smith & Co* [1904] 2 Ch. 86 and 122, the authority relied upon by Scott J. in the *Weddell* case, the action was not stayed in terms; the trial, which had commenced before the point was taken, was adjourned to enable the legal owner as at the date of the Writ to be joined.
[65] *Cableship Ltd v Williams* noted at [1991] I.P.D. 14205; *John Richardson Computers Ltd v Flanders* [1993] F.S.R. 497. It is not clear whether the remedies were available as a matter of equity. In *Ibcos Computers Ltd v Barclays Mercantile Highland Finance Ltd* [1994] F.S.R. 275, no point was taken.
[66] [1998] F.S.R. 415.
[67] CDPA 1988, s.215(2) and see para. 13–108, above.
[68] Copyright and Rights in Databases Regulations 1997 (SI 1997/3032), reg.14(1).
[69] CDPA 1988, ss.94 (moral rights not assignable), 95 (when moral rights pass on death), 192A (performers' non-property rights only pass on death) and 192B (rights of persons having recording rights are not assignable or transmissible at all).
[70] See the previous footnote and above at paras 12–41 (performers' non-property rights), 11–66 (moral rights) and 12–42 (recording rights).

C. EXCLUSIVE LICENSEE

Copyright. For the definition of "exclusive licensee" (which includes an **22–20**
exclusive importer or distributor[71]) see paragraphs 5–203 *et seq*, above. Section
101 of the 1988 Act provides that an exclusive licensee has the same rights and
remedies, except against the copyright owner, in respect of matters occurring after the grant of the licence as if the licence had been an assignment.[72] This right is
purely procedural—the exclusive licensee has no property right. Presumably the
words "except against the copyright owner" are there to ensure that the exclusive
licensee cannot sue the copyright owner for infringement of copyright, but is
restricted to his contractual remedies under the exclusive licence. Without these
words, the copyright owner would be treated as an assignor of the copyright and
any act of infringement by him would be "without the licence of the copyright
owner", in the words of section 16(2). The rights and remedies of an exclusive licensee are concurrent with those of the copyright owner and references in Part I
of the 1988 Act to the copyright owner are to be construed accordingly.[73] In an
action brought by an exclusive licensee, a defendant may avail himself of any
defence which would have been available to him if the action had been brought
by the copyright owner.[74] Where a copyright owner and an exclusive licensee
have concurrent rights of action, the one may not proceed with the action without
the leave of the court,[75] unless the other is joined as a claimant or added as a
defendant.[76] A copyright owner or exclusive licensee may apply for an interim
injunction without joining the other or obtaining the leave of the court.[77] For a
fuller discussion of the position of statutory exclusive licensees, see paragraphs
5–203 *et seq.*, above.

Performers' property rights, design right and database right. There are cor- **22–21**
responding provisions giving the same remedies to exclusive licensees of
performers' property rights,[78] design right[79] and database right.[80]

Non-property rights. There are no provisions in respect of statutory exclusive **22–22**
licences for these rights. A non-statutory exclusive licensee will have no right to
bring proceedings.

D. NON-EXCLUSIVE LICENSEES AND AGENTS

Section 101A of the 1988 Act: background. The essence of a licence is a **22–23**
contractual or personal relationship whereby the licensee is permitted to do an act
or acts which would, but for the licence, be an infringement. A non-exclusive licensee is not the owner of the copyright or any interest in it. For these reasons,
prior to October 31, 2003, non-exclusive licensees had no right to bring proceedings for infringement.[81] Since October 31, 2003, however, some non-exclusive
licensees have had the right to bring proceedings under section 101A of the 1988

[71] *Biotrading & Financing Oy v Biohit Ltd* [1998] F.S.R. 109.
[72] CDPA 1988, s.101(1).
[73] s.101(2).
[74] s.101(3).
[75] For an example of where leave was given by consent, see *Bodley Head Ltd v Flegon* [1972] R.P.C. 587. See para. 5–203, above.
[76] s.102(1). A copyright owner or exclusive licensee who is joined as a defendant in pursuance of this provision is not liable for any costs of the action unless he takes part in the proceedings: s.102(2). For special provisions which apply where a copyright owner and exclusive licensee have concurrent rights of action, see para. 22–190, below.
[77] s.102(3).
[78] CDPA 1988, ss.191L and 191M.
[79] ss.234 and 235.
[80] Copyright and Rights in Databases Regulations 1997 (SI 1997/3032), reg.23.
[81] *Nicol v Barranger* [1917–23] Mac.C.C. 219.

Act.[82] This results from representations made by broadcasters during the consultation in relation to the implementation of the Information Society Directive. Prior to the implementation of the Directive, broadcasts and cable programmes (including programmes transmitted in "on-demand" services) were protected under sections 6 and 7 of the 1988 Act respectively. The Government's draft implementing regulations proposed the complete removal of the term "cable programme service" from the 1988 Act and the alteration of the definition of "broadcast" to as to include internet transmisions of a broadcast character. In their representations on the draft regulations,[83] many broadcasters expressed concern that this would reduce the amount of protection for on-demand services. They argued that where (as, for example in the case of acquired programming such as films), the broadcaster was not the owner or exclusive licensee of the rights in the underlying works, it would be unable to take action against infringers. Licensors might become reluctant to grant licences or they might charge higher fees. Licensors might be reluctant to take action themselves or not have the funds to do so. Where the on-demand service consisted of a large number of clips, it might not be feasible for the numerous owners in the rights to take action but it would be vital for them to be able to do so. The Government did not accept that the existing law protected the service as such rather than the programmes provided in it, which were protected in other ways.[84] Nevertheless, it considered that it would be reasonable for service providers to be able to act against infringements connected to their activities in circumstances where they were neither the owner or exclusive licensee but the owner of the copyright in the content wished them to act.[85] Accordingly, the Government considered it appropriate to introduce such provision, but applying to non-exclusive licensees in general.[86] The Patent Office's Transposition Note states that the purpose of the new section is to ensure that all right holders are able to protect their rights, in line with article 8(2) of the Information Society Directive.[87]

22–24   **Non-exclusive licensees with a right of action.** For these purposes, the expression "non-exclusive licensee" means the holder of a licence authorising the licensee to exercise a right which remains exercisable by the copyright owner.[88] However, not every such licensee has a right of action. First, it is necessary for the non-exclusive licence to be in writing and signed by or on behalf of the copyright owner.[89] Secondly, it is necessary that the licence expressly grants the licensee a right of action under section 101A of the 1988 Act.[90]

---

[82] CDPA 1988, s.101A, inserted by reg.28 of the Copyright and Related Rights Regulations 2003 (SI 2003/2498). Regulation 31(2) provides that no act done before commencement (October 31, 2003) shall be regarded as an infringement of any new or extended right arising by virtue of the Regulations. It is thought that this does not prevent a licensee suing in respect of an act which occurred prior to October 31, 2003, because the act in respect of which the licensee will be suing will not be an infringement of a new or extended right but an infringement of copyright. The question may well be academic given that the licensee only has the right to sue in respect of infringing acts which are directly connected to a prior licensed act of the licensee and only if the licence expressly grants the licensee a right of action under s.101A. It is unlikely in practice that any licence granted prior to October 31, 2003 will make express reference to s.101A.

[83] See in particular the BBC's representations, which were supported by the Producers' Rights Agency, ITC, Channel 4 and Channel 5 (all submissions to the consultation can be viewed at the Patent Office).

[84] Consultation: Analysis of Responses and Government Conclusions, para.8.5.

[85] Consultation: Analysis of Responses and Government Conclusions, para.8.6.

[86] *ibid.*

[87] This provides that Member States shall provide "appropriate" sanctions and remedies in respect of infringements of the rights and obligations set out in the Directive. See Vol.2 at H11.

[88] CDPA 1988, s.101A(6).

[89] s.101A(1)(b)(i).

[90] s.101A(1)(b)(ii).

Infringing acts in respect of which there is a right of action. Even if these two   **22–25**
requirements are met, the licensee only has a right of action if the infringing act
was "directly connected to a prior licensed act of the licensee".[91] This formulation clearly gives broadcasters the rights they sought in the course of the
consultation.[92] However, as the Government intended, the right is not restricted
to broadcasters. Accordingly, for example, it would seem that a record company
which pressed a CD under a non-exclusive licence from MCPS would be able to
sue a person who made further copies from that CD but not otherwise.

Rights concurrent. As in the case of an exclusive licensee, the rights of a non-   **22–26**
exclusive licensee and the copyright owner are concurrent. The consequences are
the same as where the rights of an exclusive licensee and the copyright owner are
concurrent.[93]

Agents. A mere agent acting on behalf of the copyright owner has not such an   **22–27**
interest in the work as to entitle him to claim relief.[94] For example, the Mechanical Copyright Protection Society Ltd (MCPS), unlike the Performing Right Society Ltd (PRS) and Phonographic Performance Ltd (PPL), does not take assignments of copyright from its members and cannot, therefore, bring proceedings in
its own name for infringement of its members' rights.[95] It merely acts as agent for
its members when granting so-called mechanical licences. However, where a
body exists to represent copyright owners who are its members, representative
proceedings for copyright infringement may be brought by a limited selection of
those members.[96]

Other rights. Non-exclusive licensees in respect of other rights have no rights to   **22–28**
sue for infringement. Again, presumably, a mere agent acting on behalf of an
owner of such a right cannot bring an action in his own name.

E. JOINT OWNERS

Copyright, performers' property rights, design right and database right.   **22–29**
Where copyright (or any aspect of copyright) is owned by more than one person
jointly, references to the copyright owner are to all the owners.[97] There are similar provisions for performers' property rights and design right.[98] The effect of
these provisions is that one joint owner can sue to prevent a third party[99] or even
another joint owner[1] from carrying out a restricted act without his licence. Where
a third party is sued, there is no requirement to join the other joint owner.[2] It
seems that one joint owner can only obtain damages for the injury done to his
share.[3] Although there is provision for joint ownership of database right,[4] the
Database Regulations do not contain any equivalant provisions to those for copyright, performers' property rights and design right. Nevertheless, it is thought that

---

[91] CDPA 1988, s.101A(1)(a).
[92] See para. 22–23, above.
[93] CDPA 1988, s.101A(2) to (5). For the position in relation to exclusive licensees, see para. 22–20, above.
[94] *Nicol v Stockdale* (1818) 3 Swans.687; *Petty v Taylor* [1897] 1 Ch. 465.
[95] For MCPS, the PRS and PPL, see below at paras 28–56, 28–59 and 28–60respectively.
[96] See *e.g. Independiente Ltd and others v Music Trading On-Line (HK) Ltd* [2003] EWHC 470, Ch D, which concerned members of the British Phonographic Industry Ltd.
[97] CDPA 1988, s.173(2).
[98] ss.191A(4) and 258(2).
[99] See para. 5–169, above.
[1] See para. 5–169, above.
[2] See para. 5–169, above.
[3] See para. 5–169, above.
[4] Copyright and Rights in Databases Regulations 1997 (SI 1997/3032), regs.14(6) and 15.

the position is the same as for copyright, performers' property rights and design right.

22–30   **Non-property rights.** There is no provision for joint ownership of these rights.

3. RELEVANT DATE OF TITLE

22–31   It is essential that, at the date of the issue of the claim form, the claimant has a legal or equitable title to the relevant right, for title is an essential ingredient of the cause of action for infringement and, without any title, the claimant has no cause of action.[5] A cause of action must exist at the date of the issue of the claim form.[6] The claimant may commence proceedings relying on his equitable title to the copyright and get in the legal title afterwards or join the legal owner; but a claimant with no title at all cannot sue, acquire a title by written assignment subsequently and then obtain the permission of the court to amend so as to validate the claim form *ex post facto*.[7] A claim form which is issued before the claimant has acquired any title and before, therefore, the claimant has any cause of action, is incurably bad.[8] The claimant's proper course in such a case is to issue a new claim form founded on his new cause of action.[9] This does not affect the principle that the court has jurisdiction to grant the claimant permission to amend his claim form and particulars of claim so as to plead a cause of action arising after the issue of the claim form.[10]

4. WHO MAY BE SUED?

A. COPYRIGHT AND DESIGN RIGHT: PRIMARY INFRINGERS

22–32   For copyright and design right purposes, the persons who are primarily liable to be sued are individuals and companies who, without the licence of the owner of the right in question, do, or authorise others to do, any one or more of the separate and distinct acts which are restricted by the right in question.[11] Thus, for example, in relation to a published book which is alleged to infringe copyright, the author, printer and publisher are all liable to be sued for infringement of copyright, regardless of whether they knew or had reason to believe that the book infringed copyright. A person who has personally committed primary infringements of copyright (and presumably design right) cannot escape personal liability simply because he has committed them in the course of carrying out his

---

[5] *Beloff v Pressdram Ltd* [1973] 1 All E.R. 241; [1973] R.P.C. 765.

[6] *Arrowin Ltd v Trimguard (UK) Ltd* [1984] R.P.C. 581.

[7] *Roban Jig & Tool Co Ltd & Elkadart Ltd v Taylor & Others* [1979] F.S.R. 130; *Acorn Computers v MCS Micro Computer Systems* (1984–85) 57 A.L.R. 389; see also *Nicol v Barranger* [1912–23] Mac.C.C. 219.

[8] *Belegging-en Exploitatiemaatschappij Lavender BV v Witten Industrial Diamonds Ltd* [1979] F.S.R. 59.

[9] *Form Tubes Ltd v Guinness Brothers Plc* [1989] F.S.R. 41.

[10] *Vax Appliances Limited v Hoover Plc* [1990] R.P.C. 656; *Banks v CBS Songs Ltd* [1992] F.S.R. 278; *Chiron Corp. v Organon Teknika Ltd (No.4)* [1994] F.S.R. 252; *Beecham Group Plc v Norton Healthcare Ltd* [1997] F.S.R. 81. See CPR Part 17.

[11] CDPA 1988, ss.16(1) and (2) and 226(1) and (3); doing and authorising the doing are separate acts of infringement: *Ash v Hutchinson* [1936] Ch. 489; *MCA Records Ltd v Charly Records Ltd* [2000] E.M.L.R. 743 at 807. It has been said that a claimant must plead specific authorisation of an actual breach of copyright affecting him: *A & M Records Inc & Others v Audio Magnets Incorporated (UK) Ltd* [1979] F.S.R. 1. See, however, para. 7–134, above.

duties as an employee or agent or as the director of a company.[12] It is not essential to be able to identify the infringer by name.[13]

B. COPYRIGHT AND DESIGN RIGHT: SECONDARY INFRINGERS

Persons may also be liable for secondary acts of infringement such as importation and sale of infringing copies.[14] Liability depends on proof of the requisite knowledge or reason to believe. Thus, for example, in order to establish that a retailer of books or records is liable for infringement of copyright by selling or offering for sale books or records, it must be proved that the retailer knew at the relevant time or had reason to believe that the book or record was an infringing copy of the work.[15] The most common way of fixing the retailer with the requisite knowledge is by giving him express notice by letter of the claimant's allegation of infringement.[16] A reasonable time should be allowed for the prospective defendant to investigate the claim.[17] It is thought that as in the case of primary infringements, a person who has personally committed a secondary infringement cannot escape personal liability simply because he has committed it in the course of carrying out his duties as an employee or agent or as the director of a company. Although it is not possible to "authorise" a secondary infringement, a person authorising such an act may be liable as a joint tortfeasor.[18]

22–33

C. OTHER RIGHTS: DIRECT INFRINGERS

For other rights, there is no distinction between primary and secondary infringements and whether it is necessary to prove that the defendant had a particular state of mind depends on the right in question. Some infringements of moral rights depend on a particular state of mind while others do not.[19] For performers' property and non-property rights and the rights of persons having recording rights, the Act sets out various acts which, if committed without the licence of the person entitled to enforce the right, are infringements irrespective of the question of whether the person committing the act knew or had reason to believe that he was infringing.[20] Some infringements of rights in respect of protection measures, rights management information and unauthorised decoders depend on a particular state or mind and others do not.[21] Again, it is thought that a person who has personally committed an infringement cannot escape personal liability simply because he has committed it in the course of carrying out his duties as an employee or agent or as the director of a company.

22–34

---

[12] *C Evans & Sons Ltd v Spritebrand Ltd* [1985] F.S.R. 267 at 271.

[13] In *Bloomsbury Publishing Group Ltd v News Group Newspapers Ltd* [2003] EWHC 1205, Ch D, the claimant knew that copies of a book which it proposed to publish had been offered to the press but had been unable to identify the person concerned. The Court granted an interim injunction against 'the person or persons who have offered the publishers of the *Sun*, the *Daily Mail*, and the *Daily Mirror* newspapers a copy of the book " *Harry Potter and the Order of the Phoenix*" by JK Rowling or any part thereof and the person or persons who has or have physical possession of a copy of the said book or any part thereof without the consent of the claimants". See also *Hampshire Waste Services Ltd v Persons Unknown*, [2003] EWHC 1738, Ch D (injunction restraining unnamed persons from entering or remaining without the claimant's consent on named incinerator sites).

[14] See Ch.8, above.

[15] CDPA 1988, s.23.

[16] See para. 8–10, above.

[17] See para. 8–10, above..

[18] See paras 22–35 *et seq.*, below.

[19] See Ch.11, above.

[20] See Ch.12, above.

[21] See Chs 15 and 16, above.

D. JOINT TORTFEASORS

22–35 **General.** In certain circumstances a person may be liable for infringement of copyright by reason of having been a joint tortfeasor. It is sometimes said that this will be the case in two situations. The first is where an infringing act has been committed pursuant to a common design between the actual infringer (who is primarily liable) and some other person, who is therefore liable as a joint infringer. The second is where the infringing act has been procured by another person, who is likewise liable as a joint infringer. It is an open question whether these are distinct torts, or whether they are simply different examples of the kind of factual circumstances which will give rise to joint liability.[22]

22–36 **Common design.**[23] If there is a concerted design by two persons to sell goods which they know or have reason to believe infringe copyright, then the parties, who have such a design and execute it, are joint tortfeasors and are both liable for infringement.[24] It is suggested that where the infringement alleged is secondary, so that the claimant has to establish "guilty knowledge", a person without such knowledge cannot be a joint tortfeasor, whether he is the person committing the secondary act (in which case there is, of course, no tort) or the other party to the common design. Both must have the requisite degree of knowledge.[25] In relation to patents, the law was reviewed in *Unilever plc v Chefaro Proprietaries Ltd.*[26] There must be shown some act in furtherance of the design, not a mere agreement. It is not necessary to show a design to infringe deliberately. It is sufficient to show that the design related to acts which constitute infringement. The mere capacity of a parent company to control a subsidiary does not make the two companies joint tortfeasors. What matters is the extent of control actually exercised by one over the other.[27] The same principles presumably apply to primary infringements of copyright. Provided that an act of infringement is in fact committed in the United Kingdom and it is proved that the defendants had a common design to commit that act, it does not matter whether the agreement which is the basis of such design was made within or outside the jurisdiction, nor does it matter that the defendant himself has not done any act within the jurisdiction which, taken by itself, could be said to amount to a several infringement.[28] It is a case of one tort committed by one of them on behalf of and in concert with the other. If, however, the claimant is suing in respect of the infringement of his foreign copyrights (as he now can[29]), the court will apply the relevant foreign law of joint tortfeasorship.[30]

[22] *MCA Records Inc v Charly Records Ltd* [2001] EWCA Civ 1441 para.36.
[23] In *Unilever plc v Gillette (UK) Ltd* [1989] R.P.C. 583, where the development of the law is analysed, Mustill L.J. said that the phrases "concerted action" or "agreed on common action" would serve just as well.
[24] *Morton-Norwich Products Inc v Intercen Ltd* [1978] R.P.C. 501; *Ash v Hutchinson* [1936] Ch. 489; *PRS Ltd v Mitchell, etc. Ltd* [1924] 1 K.B. 762; *Ravenscroft v Herbert & Another* [1980] R.P.C. 193; *Cadbury Ltd v Ulmer GmbH.* [1988] F.S.R. 385; *Crystal Glass Industries Ltd v Alwince Products Ltd* [1986] R.P.C. 259 (CA of New Zealand); *CBS Songs Ltd v Amstrad Consumer Electronics plc* [1988] A.C. 1013; *Grower v BBC* [1990] F.S.R. 595 at 607–612; *MCA Records Inc v Charly Records Ltd* [2001] EWCA Civ 1441.
[25] *Mattel Inc v Tonka Corp.* [1992] F.S.R. 28.
[26] [1994] F.S.R. 135, applying *Mölnycke AB v Proctor-Gamble Ltd (No.6)* [1992] R.P.C. 21; [1992] 1 W.L.R. 1112, CA and *Unilever plc v Gillette (UK) Ltd* [1989] R.P.C. 583, CA.
[27] *Intel Corporation v General Instrument Corporation & Others (No.2)* [1991] R.P.C. 235.
[28] See *Morton-Norwich Products Inc v Intercen Ltd* [1978] R.P.C. 501.
[29] See para. 22–116, below.
[30] *Coin Controls Ltd v Suzo International (UK) Ltd* [1997] F.S.R. 660.

Procurement. A person who procures a particular infringement by inducement, incitement or persuasion[31] of an identifiable individual, is jointly and severally liable with the infringer for the damage suffered by the person entitled to sue. On the other hand, there is no liability for facilitating an infringement by another,[32] in the sense of conferring on another person a power to copy as distinct from granting him the right to copy. There is no general duty on a person under the 1988 Act, or at common law, actionable by the copyright owner, to prevent or discourage or warn others against infringement, giving rise to an action in negligence for failing to do so.[33]   **22–37**

Supply of equipment which may be used to infringe. A person who sells and advertises to the public a product, such as a tape recorder, which might be used for either lawful or unlawful purposes, does not procure a breach of copyright by the purchaser or user who makes the decision as to use.[34] He may persuade the person to purchase the product, but does not procure him to use it to infringe copyright. Each must act with the other in the commission of the tort as where two or more persons are closely involved in the design, production and manufacture of the infringing article. There is no common design and, therefore, no joint liability between a manufacturer and purchaser of recording equipment capable of being used to make infringing tapes. The manufacturer has no control over or interest in the equipment after sale.[35] Exceptionally, however, where copyright is infringed by a public performance of the work or by the playing or showing of the work in public by means of apparatus for playing sound recordings, showing films or receiving visual images by electronic means, those who supplied the apparatus may, if they can be shown to have the appropriate state of mind, be liable as secondary infringers.[36]   **22–38**

Liability in respect of file sharing networks. As discussed below (at paragraph 27–186) the growth of high speed internet access, the widespread availability of hardware for the making and storing of digital copies of sound recordings and the development of so-called "file sharing" or "peer to peer" networks have made it possible for millions of individuals to exchange copies of sound recordings and other works in digital form. Following the effective shutting down of the unlicensed service provided by Napster as a result of action in the United States (see paragraph 27–170, below), a second generation of such networks has been developed. The Napster system involved a centralised indexing software architecture in which an index of files was maintained on servers which were owned and operated by Napster. By contrast, the second generation networks involve decentralised indexing systems.[37] In some instances, each user maintains his or her own index (as in the case of StreamCast's Morpheus system). In others, a number of select computers on the network are designated as indexing servers (as in the case of Grokster's FastTrack system). In either case, the distributor of the software on which the file sharing takes place does not host any files or   **22–38A**

---

[31] See *CBS Songs Ltd v Amstrad Comsumer Electronics Plc* [1988] A.C. 1013, *per* Lord Templeman at 1058.

[32] *Belegging-En Exploitatiemaatschappij Lavender BV v Witten Industrial Diamonds Ltd* [1979] F.S.R. 59; *CBS Songs Ltd v Amstrad Comsumer Electronics Plc* [1988] A.C. 1013; *PLG Research Ltd v Ardon International Ltd* [1993] F.S.R. 197. See, also, *Credit Lyonnais Bank Nederland NV v Export Credit Guarantee Dept.* [1998] 1 Lloyd's Rep.19.

[33] *CBS Songs Ltd v Amstrad Comsumer Electronics Plc* [1988] A.C. 1013; *Paterson Zochonis Ltd v Merfarken Packaging* [1983] F.S.R. 273.

[34] *CBS Songs Ltd v Amstrad Consumer Electronics Plc* [1988] A.C. 1013.

[35] *ibid.*

[36] CDPA 1988, s.26(2). An occupier of the premises and the supplier of the sound recording or film may also be liable: ss.26(3) and (4). See above, paras 8–16, above.

[37] The account which follows is derived from the decision in *Metro-Goldwyn-Mayer Studios Inc v Grokster Ltd*, United States Court of Appeals 9th Circuit, Thomas C.J., August 19, 2004.]

indexes of infringing files and does not regulate or provide access. These file sharing networks are used both for infringing purposes, such as the unlicensed downloading of copyright sound recordings and for non-infringing purposes, such as the sharing of music files which are licensed for distribution in this way[38] and of literary works and films which are in the public domain.[39] Actions against those who distribute the software for such systems have failed in the United States courts on the grounds that the distributors are not liable either for contributory copyright infringement or for vicarious copyright infringement.[40] Depending on the precise facts, it seems likely that a similar result would be reached here. Like the tape recorder in the *Amstrad* case (see the previous paragraph), the file sharing software may be used for lawful and unlawful purposes; its distributor has no control over its use after it has been passed to the user; the user decides whether or not to infringe; and accordingly the distributor cannot be said to procure the infringement and there cannot be said to be a common design to infringe.

22–39　**Choice of defendant.** The claimant can choose which tortfeasor to sue. He does not have to sue all of them. The defendant cannot dictate whom a claimant shall sue or make the choice for him. The claimant can also choose which joint tortfeasor to enforce his judgment against. It is permissible to join an alleged joint tortfeasor for the purpose of obtaining disclosure against him.[41]

E. Conspiracy

22–40　Parties to a conspiracy to infringe copyright or the other rights covered by this Chapter are also liable to be sued.[42] There are two torts or two species of the same tort, depending on the means used.[43] A conspiracy to injure by lawful means is actionable where the claimant proves that he has suffered loss or damage as a result of action taken pursuant to a combination or agreement between the defendant and another person or persons to injure him, where the predominant purpose of the defendant is to injure the claimant. A conspiracy to injure by unlawful means is actionable where the claimant proves that he has suffered loss or damage as a result of unlawful action taken pursuant to a combination or agreement between the defendant and another person or persons to injure him by unlawful means, whether or not it is the predominant purpose of the defendant to do so. Damages for injury to reputation or feelings are not recoverable in an action for conspiracy.[44]

---

[38] An example given in the *Grokster* litigation was the music of the band Wilco, whose record company refused to release one of its albums on commercial grounds. The band repurchased the work and made it available for free downloading. This sparked widespread interest and Wilco obtained another record contract.

[39] Examples given in the *Grokster* litigation included literary works made available through Project Gutenberg and films released by the Prelinger Archive.

[40] *Metro-Goldwyn-Mayer Studios Inc v Grokster Ltd* 259 F. Supp. 2d 1029 (C.D. Cal. 2003), upheld on appeal United States Court of Appeals 9th Circuit, Thomas C.J., August 19, 2004. Note, however, that the decision was limited to the software in use at the time of the District Court decision, *i.e.* April 2003, and did not cover previous versions which (according to the Court of Appeals) contain differences which may be significant.

[41] *Mölnlycke AB v Procter & Gamble Ltd* [1992] 1 W.L.R. 1112; [1992] R.P.C. 21, CA.

[42] See generally *Clerk & Lindsell on Torts*. What follows is only the barest outline.

[43] *Kuwait Oil Tanker Co SAK v Al Bader*, [2000]EWCA Civ 160, summarising *Lonrho Ltd v Shell Petroleum Co Ltd* [1982] A.C. 173; *Lonrho Plc v Fayed* [1992] 1 A.C. 448 and *Rookes v Barnard* [1964] A.C. 1129 at 1209; see *Valor International Ltd v Application des Gaz & Another* [1979] R.P.C. 281, for pleading conspiracy.

[44] *Lonhro Plc v Fayed (No.5)* [1993] 1 W.L.R. 1489.

F. DIRECTORS AND CONTROLLING SHAREHOLDERS OF COMPANIES

Basis for liability. If a company has committed an act of infringement, the direc- **22–41**
tors and controlling shareholders may in certain circumstances be personally
liable. Of course, if the director or shareholder himself has actually committed an
infringing act (albeit on behalf of the company) he is liable. For example, a director of a music publishing company would be liable if he were to photocopy sheet
music without the licence of the copyright owner and it would be no defence to
say that he did it on behalf of the company. Also, a director may be liable for
having authorised an act of infringement.[45] However, directors of a company are
not liable simply because they are directors.[46] Furthermore, in general, a director
will not be liable if he does no more than carry out his constitutional role in the
governance of the company, that is to say by voting at board meetings.[47] By the
same token, a shareholder who does no more than exercise his power of control
through the constitutional organs of the company by, for example, voting at general meetings or exercising his power to appoint directors, will not be liable
either.[48] The position is different if the director or shareholder is exercising control
otherwise than through the company's constitutional organs. If that is the case, he
will be liable as joint tortfeasor if the circumstances are such that he would be so
liable if he were not a director or controlling shareholder.[49] It will not be a defence
for him to contend that he could have procured the same acts through the exercise
of constitutional control.[50] Thus, for example, if a director exercising control
otherwise than through the company's constitutional organs personally orders or
procures the commission of an infringing act, he is liable.[51] So too if in some
other way he and the company join together in a concerted action to secure that
the infringing act is done.[52] It is not essential to establish a knowing, deliberate,
wilful participation in the alleged tort. Each case depends on its own particular
facts.[53] However, if the company's infringing act is a secondary act of infringement so that so-called "guilty knowledge" is an essential ingredient of the tort, it
is likely that the director will only be liable for having ordered or procured that
act if he himself had the same "guilty knowledge".[54] Finally, if a company is
formed for the express purpose of committing infringing acts, the individuals
promoting the company will be personally responsible for the consequences.[55]

---

[45] See paras 7–130 *et seq.*, above, for the meaning of "authorise".
[46] *Cropper, etc. Ltd v Cropper* (1906) 23 R.P.C. 388; *Rainham Chemical Works v Belvedere Fish Guano Co Ltd* [1921] 2 A.C. 465 at 488; *Prichard & Constance (Wholesale) Co Ltd v Amata Ltd* (1924) 42 R.P.C. 63; *Evans & Sons Ltd v Spritebrand Ltd* [1985] F.S.R. 267.
[47] *MCA Records Inc v Charly Records Ltd* [2001] EWCA Civ 1441, para.49. There may be exceptions to this rule, but they will be "rare indeed": *ibid.*
[48] *MCA Records Inc v Charly Records Ltd* [2001] EWCA Civ 1441, para.49. Again, exceptions will be "rare indeed": *ibid.*
[49] *MCA Records Inc v Charly Records Ltd* [2001] EWCA Civ 1441, para.50. See also *Australasian Performing Right Association Ltd v Valamo Pty Ltd* (1990) 18 I.P.R. 216 (Fed. Ct. of Australia).
[50] *MCA Records Inc v Charly Records Ltd* [2001] EWCA Civ 1441, para.50.
[51] *MCA Records Inc v Charly Records Ltd* [2001] EWCA Civ 1441, para.50; *British Thomson-Houston Co Ltd v Sterling Accessories Ltd* [1924] 2 Ch. 33; *Betts v De Vitre* 3 Ch. App.441; *Mentmore Manufacturing Co Ltd v National Merchandising Manufacturing Co Inc* (1978) 89 D.L.R. (3d) 195 (Can.).
[52] *MCA Records Inc v Charly Records Ltd* [2001] EWCA Civ 1441 paras 52 and 53.
[53] *Evans & Sons Ltd v Spritebrand Ltd* [1985] F.S.R. 267; *White Horse Distillers Ltd v Gregson Associates Ltd* [1984] R.P.C. 61 at 90, 91; *A.P.Besson Ltd v Fulleon Ltd* [1986] F.S.R. 319; *Canon Kabushiki Kaisha v Green Cartridge Co Ltd* [1996] F.S.R. 874.
[54] *Evans & Sons Ltd v Spritebrand Ltd* [1985] F.S.R. 267; *MCA Records Inc v Charly Records Ltd* [2001] EWCA Civ 1441 para.51; and see, by analogy, *Mattel Inc v Tonka Corp.* [1992] F.S.R. 28.
[55] *Rainham Chemical Works v Belvedere Fish Guano Co* [1921] 2 A.C. 465 at 475; *P.S.Johnson & Associates Ltd v Bucko Enterprises Ltd* [1975] 1 N.Z.L.R. 311; *Prichard, etc. Ltd v Amata Ltd* (1925) 42 R.P.C. 63.

Similarly, where exceptionally the company is a mere tool or "cat's paw" of the director or other officer.[56]

22–42 Procedural issues. The fact that an application to join a director is made because it is feared that damages and costs may be irrecoverable against a corporate defendant is not, by itself, considered a mere tactical ruse, putting unfair pressure on the defendant to settle.[57]

G. VICARIOUS LIABILITY

22–43 Where an employee of a person, firm or company personally commits an act of infringement in the course of his employment, the employer will usually be vicariously liable.[58]

H. PERSONS IN POSSESSION OF INFRINGING COPIES, INFRINGING ARTICLES OR ILLICIT RECORDINGS

22–44 The court has power in certain circumstances,[59] on application by any of the following, namely, a copyright owner, a person having performers' rights (whether property or non-property), a person having recording rights, a design right owner, or an exclusive licensee within the meaning of the Act, to make an order for the delivery up to the applicant or to such other person as the court may direct of infringing copies, illicit recordings or infringing articles (as the case may be). As will be seen,[60] the power is only exercisable against a person who has infringing copies or illicit recordings in his possession, custody or control in the course of a business or infringing articles in his possession, custody or control for commercial purposes. Of course, if such a person knows or has reason to believe that an article in his possession in the course of a business (or, for design right, in his possession for commercial purposes) is an infringing copy, illicit recording or infringing article (as the case may be) he is liable to be sued as a secondary infringer in any event. Even if such a person did not have "guilty knowledge" at the time he acquired the article, it is usually easy to notify him of the relevant facts so that, after a reasonable time to make inquiries, continued possession will amount to a secondary act of infringement. However, it is *not* a necessary ingredient of the right to apply for an order for delivery up of infringing copies, illicit recordings or infringing articles that the person in possession of the item in question has the "guilty knowledge" necessary to make him a secondary infringer.[61] There is analogous provision in relation to articles specifically designed or adapted for making copies of a particular copyright work, or articles to a particular design (but not copies of a particular illicit recording). In these cases, however, it is necessary to show 'guilty knowledge' and, accordingly, that the defendant has infringed the copyright or design right as the case may be. There are analogous provisions in relation to unauthorised decoders and circumvention devices (although in the latter case it must be shown that the defendant intended that the device should be used for the purposes of circumvention).[62] There is no provision of this kind in relation to database right or moral rights.

---

[56] *Townsend v Haworth*, reported as a note to *Sykes v Haworth* at (1875) 48 L.J. Ch. (NS) 770, at 772
[57] *PLG Research Ltd v Ardon International Ltd* [1992] F.S.R. 59.
[58] See *Clerk & Lindsell on Torts* (18th ed.), Chapter 5.
[59] For the detail of these provisions see para. 22–182, below.
[60] See para. 22–182, below.
[61] *Lagenes Ltd v It's At (UK) Ltd* [1991] F.S.R. 492.
[62] See above at paras 16–24 (decoders) and 15–15 and 15–26 (circumvention devices).

I. Service Providers

Specific provision is made for the grant of injunctions against service providers. This is dealt with below.[63]

22–45

5. RIGHT OF SEIZURE WITHOUT COURT ORDER

Introduction. The 1988 Act confers on the following persons, namely, copyright owners (including exclusive licensees), persons having performers' rights (including exclusive licensees in the case of performers' property rights) and persons having recording rights, the right to seize infringing copies[64] and illicit recordings[65] without the need for a court order,[66] such as a search order.[67] As to the exercise of this remedy where an exclusive licensee has concurrent rights, see paragraph 22–190, below. This remedy was introduced at the instigation of popular music groups and record companies to deal with, for example, persons selling infringing T-shirts on the street outside a pop concert venue. In such cases, a search order is of no use because the trader may well have disappeared by the time the order has been obtained. Because of the restricted circumstances in which and the stringent conditions under which this right may be exercised, the search order will continue to be an important judicial remedy. There is no right of seizure without a court order in relation to design right, database right or moral rights. However, the copyright provisions are applied to unauthorised decoders and circumvention devices (although in the latter case it must be shown that the defendant intended that the device should be used for the purposes of circumvention).[68] In what follows, the infringing copy, illicit recording, decoder or device as the case may be is referred to as an "offending article".

22–46

Circumstances in which the right may be exercised. A person having such a right, or a person authorised by him, may seize an offending article in specified circumstances. First, the offending article must be found exposed or otherwise immediately available for sale or hire.[69] Second, the offending article must be one in respect of which the person entitled to the right would be entitled to apply for an order for delivery up under section 99 or section 195.[70] Broadly speaking, this means that the person from whom the article is to be seized must have it in his possession, custody or control in the course of a business and it must have been made less than six years prior to the seizure. In the case of copyright, performers' rights, design right and unauthorised decoders, such a person need not be an infringer himself, as where he does not possess the necessary 'guilty knowledge'. In the case of circumvention devices, 'guilty knowledge' must be shown. For a full discussion of the entitlement to an order under section 99 or section 195, see paragraph 22–182, below.

22–47

Conditions for exercise of the right. The right to seize and detain is exercisable subject to certain conditions:

22–48

---

[63] See paras 22–108 et seq., below.
[64] For the definition of infringing copy, see para. 8–03, above.
[65] For the definition of illicit recording, see para. 12–69,above.
[66] CDPA 1988, ss.100 and 196.
[67] See para. 22–141, below.
[68] CDPA 1988 ss.298(3) (decoders); 296(4) (circumvention devices in respect of computer programs); 296ZD(4) (other circumvention devices).
[69] CDPA 1988, ss.100(1) and 196(1).
[70] ss.100(1) and 196(1)

(1) Before anything is seized, notice of the time and place of the proposed seizure must be given to a local police station.[71]

(2) Although a person may, for the purpose of exercising the right, enter premises to which the public have access, he may not seize anything in the possession, custody or control of a person at a permanent or regular place of business of his.[72] "Premises" includes land, buildings, moveable structures, vehicles, vessels, aircraft and hovercraft.[73] This is an important condition which precludes "self help" seizure of goods from shops, offices, warehouses and other similar business premises.

(3) A person exercising the right may not use any force.[74] Like the requirement of prior notification to a local police station, this requirement has been imposed in the interests of maintaining public order.

(4) At the time when anything is seized there must be left at the place where it was seized a notice in the prescribed form containing the prescribed particulars as to the person by whom or on whose authority the seizure is made and the grounds on which it is made.[75] The forms and particulars are prescribed by order of the Secretary of State made by statutory instrument subject to annulment in pursuance of a resolution of either House of Parliament.[76]

(5) The exercise of the right to seize and detain is subject to any decision of the court in the exercise of its jurisdiction to make an order as to the disposal of an offending article.[77] Under that jurisdiction, the court may make an order that offending articles seized or detained shall be forfeited to the copyright owner or destroyed or otherwise dealt with as the court may think fit.[78]

22–49   Practical considerations. It can be seen at once that it might be difficult for a person wanting to exercise this right to know whether or not the conditions are satisfied. For example, whilst in some cases it might be obvious that the articles he intends to seize were made less than six years ago,[79] in others it may well not be obvious. What is meant by the expression "a permanent or regular place of business"? It is suggested that a market trader who runs a market stall every week in the same location has a regular (albeit not permanent) place of business. What if he has no right to a particular location for his stall within the market, but sets up his stall each week according to whatever space is available? Does "place of business" refer to the market generally or to a particular site within the market? It is suggested that the former is more likely to be correct, because the right is designed to catch the fly-by-night trader who disappears off the scene and cannot easily be traced. A market-stall holder can be served with a seizure order if he regularly uses the same market, albeit that the precise location of his stall may change from week to week. Furthermore, what is the position in respect of record fairs, which are held annually at each of three or four different locations around the country? It is suggested that a person who regularly attends each such venue year on year has many "regular places of business" and that the right cannot be exercised at any of those places. Presumably a trader just starting out in business

---

[71] CDPA 1988, ss.100(2) and 196(2).

[72] ss.100(3) and 196(3).

[73] ss.100(5) and 196(5).

[74] ss.100(3) and 196(3).

[75] ss.100(5), (6) and 196(5), (6). See SI 1989/1006, Vol.2 at A4.i.

[76] *ibid.*

[77] ss.100(1) and 196(1).

[78] Under s.114 or 204 as the case may be; see paras 22–179 *et seq.*, below.

[79] For example, an illicit recording of a performance only given within the previous six years.

and operating his stall at any such record fair for the first time has no "permanent or regular place of business". In many cases it must be difficult for a person wishing to exercise the right of seizure to know whether or not the trader is trading from his regular place of business. Because of these difficulties and, no doubt, other difficulties which could arise on the particular facts of each individual case, this right is, in practice, used sparingly and only in the most obvious of cases. The risk of an action for unlawful interference with goods and the possibility of aggravated or exemplary damages in such an action is a deterrent to those contemplating the self-help powers in sections 100 and 196.

6. DEFENCES

It is, of course, always an answer to a claim of infringement that the claimant has failed to establish an essential ingredient of his cause of action. Defendants frequently put in issue (by non-admission) and sometimes deny subsistence and ownership of the relevant right. Copying is often denied or, if the defendant admits to having copied, he sometimes pleads that the part taken was not substantial. General equitable defences such as waiver, estoppel, acquiescence and "clean hands" are often raised. There are, however, several specific points worth noting relevant to defences.   **22–50**

A. Licences and Permitted Acts

Copyright. Copyright is not infringed if the person who does, or authorises another to do, acts restricted by the copyright has the licence of the copyright owner to do the act in question.[80] A licence from the copyright owner is also a defence to acts which would otherwise be secondary acts of infringement.[81] If the copyright is owned by more than one person jointly, there will be an infringement unless the licence has been obtained from all the joint owners.[82]   **22–51**

Moral rights. Similarly, moral rights are not infringed if the person entitled to the right has consented to the act in question[83] or if the right has been waived.[84]   **22–52**

Performers' rights. Again, consent is a defence to a claim for infringement of performers' property and non-property rights and of the rights of persons having recording rights.[85] If a performer's property right is owned by more than one person jointly, there will be an infringement unless the consent has been obtained from all the joint owners.[86]   **22–53**

Design right. Design right is not infringed if the person who does, or authorises another to do, any act which would otherwise be a primary infringement has the licence of the owner to do the act in question[87] or if the owner has licensed an act which would otherwise be a secondary infringement.[88]   **22–54**

Circumvention of protection measures. Licence or consent is not a specific defence to liability in respect of the circumvention of protection measures.   **22–55**

---

[80] CDPA 1988, s.16(2) and see paras 5–194 et seq., above.
[81] ss.22–24 and see para. 8–02, above.
[82] s.173(2).
[83] CDPA 1988, s.87(1) and see para. 11–75, above..
[84] s.87(2) and see para. 11–76, above.
[85] See para. 12–50, above.
[86] CDPA 1988, s.191A(4).
[87] CDPA 1988, s.226(3) and see para. 13–119, above.
[88] s.227(1) and see para. 13–119, above.

However, it is a defence to an allegation of making or dealing with the means of circumventing a technical device applied to a computer program or publishing information intended to enable or assist such circumvention that the defendant did not know or have reasonable grounds to believe that it was to be used to make infringing copies.[89] It would seem to follow that it will also be a defence to show that the copies which were intended to be made would not in fact have been infringing, for example because there was a licence to make them. It is also a defence to an allegation of making or dealing with such means to show that any intended removal or circumvention of the technical device was authorised.[90] It is a defence to an allegation of circumvention of technical measures applied to a work other than a computer program to show that the device prevents or restricts acts which are in fact not an infringement of copyright, for example because they are licensed.[91] The same applies to the acts of making or dealing with devices aimed at circumventing such measures.[92]

22–56 **Rights management information**. The existence of authority is a defence to liability for removing or altering rights management information.[93]

22–57 **Unauthorised decoders.** As with liability for the circumvention of protection measures, there is no specific defence of licence or consent to liability in respect of unauthorised decoders. However, it is a defence to an allegation of making or dealing with an unauthorised decoder that the access which it is designed to achieve will in fact be access to which the person in question is entitled.[94]

22–58 **Database right**. The consent of the owner of the right is a defence.[95]

22–59 **Permitted acts.** There are also many acts which may be done without the licence of the rights owner and without infringing his rights. For copyright, they are dealt with in Chapter III of Part I of the 1988 Act and are described as "Acts Permitted in relation to Copyright Works". For moral rights they are set out in the main body of the section of the Act dealing with those rights. For rights in performances they are dealt with in Schedule 2 to the 1988 Act. For design right, they are set out Chapter III of Part III of the 1988 Act. These are not strictly speaking defences, since the Act provides that these acts can be done without infringing the right in question. There are no specific "permitted acts" in respect of the circumvention of protection measures, rights management information or unauthorised decoders apart from a limited exception for liability in respect of the circumvention of protection measures for acts done for the purposes of research into cryptography.[96] A small number of acts may be done without infringing database right. These are set out in the Regulations.[97]

---

[89] CDPA 1988, s.296(1)(b). See paras 15–10 and 15–14, above.
[90] s.296(1)(b)(i). See para. 15–12, above.
[91] This follows from the definition of "effective technical measure" in s.296ZF.
[92] *ibid.*
[93] CDPA 1988, s.296ZG(1). See para. 15–44, above.
[94] CDPA 1988, s.298(2). See para. 16–23, above.
[95] Copyright and Rights in Databases Regulations 1997 (SI 1997/3032), reg.16(1). See para. 18–10, above.
[96] CDPA 1988, s.296ZA(2).See para. 15–22, above.
[97] Copyright and Rights in Databases Regulations 1997 (SI 1997/3032).

B. Ignorance not Necessarily a Defence

Copyright and design right. Ignorance is no excuse for primary infringement of **22–60** copyright,[98] and the same is no doubt true of design right. If the defendant has in fact derived his work, either directly or indirectly, from the work in which the claimant has rights, the fact that the defendant was unaware that the work he has copied existed (for instance, where he made copies of a play which, unknown to him, had been copied from a novel of which he had no knowledge), or was the claimant's, or was the subject of copyright, affords no defence to the action for primary infringement, although it may affect the remedy.[99] Similarly, it is no defence to liability for primary infringement of copyright or design right that the defendant has relied upon a licence or assignment, which he believed had been granted by the owner of the right, if this is not the case; though, again, it may affect the remedy. Liability for secondary infringement, such as by importation or sale, is, of course, dependent on proof that the defendant knew or had reason to believe that he was dealing in infringing or illicit copies or infringing articles. Plainly "ignorance" is a defence for secondary infringement.

Acts permitted on assumption of expiry of rights. In certain cases, acts which **22–61** would otherwise infringe the copyright in anonymous or pseudonymous works, films and database right are permitted if where it is reasonable to assume that the right has expired. These permitted acts are considered elsewhere.[1]

Other rights. For the other rights covered in this Chapter, there is no distinction **22–62** between primary and secondary infringements. Whether ignorance will amount to a defence will depend on the provisions establishing the right in question and the facts of the individual case.

C. Defences to Damages Claims

Introduction. There are a number of different types of defence to claims for **22–63** damages in respect of the rights covered in this Chapter. In the case of copyright, performers' property rights, design right and database right, a defendant will have such a defence if he can show that he did not know or have reasonable grounds to believe that the relevant right subsisted ("the subsistence defence"). This defence is dealt with in paragraphs 22–65 to 22–71, below. There are then certain specific defences to damages in respect of certain infringements of performers' non-property rights and recording rights (paragraph 22–72, below), design right (paragraph 22–73, below), and rights in respect of protection measures, rights management information and unauthorised decoders (paragraphs 22–73 to 22–74, below). In most cases, these defences are of limited application, both because of their expressed scope and because they are without prejudice to other remedies.

Scope of the subsistence defence. A claimant is not entitled to damages in re- **22–64** spect of an infringement of copyright if it is shown that, at the time of the infringement, the defendant did not know, and had no reason to believe, that copyright subsisted in the work to which the action relates.[2] There are similar

---

[98] *Mansell v Valley Printing Co* [1908] 2 Ch. 441; *Lee v Simpson* (1847) 3 C.B. 871; *Wittman v Oppenheim* (1884) 27 Ch.D. 260; *Byrne v Statist Co* [1914] 1 K.B. 622; *Sony Music Entertainment (UK) Ltd v Easyinternetcafe Ltd* [2003] EWHC 62, Ch D.

[99] For example, an injunction might well not be granted against an innocent infringer who makes it clear, once he knows the true position, that he does not intend to continue infringing; also, there will be no grounds for an award of additional damages against an innocent infringer and the court may refuse to order an account of profits.

[1] See above at paras 9–152 (literary, dramatic, musical and artistic works), 9–179 (films) and 18–15 (databases).

[2] CDPA 1988, s.97(1).

provisions for performers' property rights,[3] design right[4] and database right.[5] In each case, the onus is on the defendant to establish these matters by evidence.[6] This defence to damages is, however, without prejudice to any other remedy, such as delivery up or an account of profits.[7] There has been a defence to damages for copyright claims similar to this provision since the 1911 Act[8] and the authorities are all under the old law.

22–65   **The subsistence defence: application to secondary infringers of copyright and design right.** It is difficult to see how this defence could apply to a secondary infringer. Anyone who knows or has reason to believe that he is dealing in infringing copies must know or have reason to believe that copyright subsists, because that is an essential part of the meaning of "infringing copies". He cannot, therefore, be said to have no reason to believe that copyright subsists in the work.

22–66   **The subsistence defence: direct infringers.** When can a direct infringer have no reason to believe that the relevant rights subsisted? It is suggested that a defendant can only have no reason to believe that the relevant rights subsist if he has grounds for thinking that (a) the term of protection has run out; or (b) the work, recording, design or database is of such a character that it ought not to be a subject of protection; or (c) possibly, because the work, recording, design or database is a foreign work.

22–67   **The subsistence defence: belief that term has run out.** In a copyright case, if an infringer were to ascertain that the author of the original work was born 160 years ago but, after due inquiry, he could not discover the date of the author's death, he might have reason to believe that the copyright had run out. Or, again, if a copyright work bearing no author's or publisher's name, is pronounced by experts to be the work of A, who died 80 years ago, whereas it is, in fact, the work of B, who died only 60 years ago, this, perhaps, is another case in which this section might be successfully pleaded.[9] Different considerations apply in the case of performers' property rights, design right and database right because the term of these rights does not depend on when the author died but on the date when the protected material came into being or was publicly released. Where such a date appears on what reasonably appears to be an official version, a defendant will presumably be able to rely on that date as a basis for a reasonable belief that the rights have run out. Where, however, no such date appears, a defendant will be expected to have made all reasonable enquiries as to the date the protected material came into being or was released. Whether he has done so will be a question of fact. It is suggested that no person has a right to assume, without inquiry, that a copyright work published anonymously is not the subject of rights.

22–68   **The subsistence defence: belief that material not entitled to protection.** If the defendant contends that he did not think the material in question was of a character which ought to be entitled to protection, upon the court holding the contrary, the defendant may have some difficulty in convincing the court that he had no reason for anticipating the court's decision.[10] Of course, it might be different if the defendant's belief was based upon a decision of the court which was subsequently overruled.

---

[3] s.191J(1).
[4] s.233(1).
[5] The Copyright and Rights in Databases Regulations 1997 (SI 1997/3032), reg.23.
[6] *James Arnold & Co Ltd v Miafern Ltd* [1980] R.P.C. 397 at 410.
[7] s.97(1).
[8] 1911 Act, s.8 and 1956 Act, s.17(2).
[9] See *J Whitaker & Sons Ltd v Publishers' Circular Ltd* [1946–47] Mac.C.C. 10.
[10] See *Pytram Ltd v Models, etc. Ltd* [1930] 1 Ch. 639, where a mistaken view of the construction

The subsistence defence: foreign works, performances, designs and databases. In respect of copyright, if the work was a foreign work, it is likely that it would be entitled to protection in this country, either because the 1988 Act had been extended or applied to the works of such countries by Order in Council, or because the work was simultaneously published in this country. It is thought that, while a defendant would not be able to rely on ignorance of an Order in Council, he might, depending on the precise facts, be able to say that he was unaware of simultaneous publication. Similarly, it is likely that a foreign performance would be entitled to protection in this country, either because it took place in another member State or another country to which Part II of the 1988 Act has been extended by Order in Council or because the performer was a citizen or subject of or resident in another member State or another such country. A defendant is more likely to be able to rely on the defence in respect of foreign designs and databases, in respect of which there is less reciprocal protection.

22–69

The subsistence defence: mistake as to identity of owner of right or existence of the protected material. The defence does not apply if the defendant publishes a copyright work under a wrong impression as to who is the copyright owner.[11] In one case a publisher published the work of X which, unknown to the publisher, contained large extracts from the work of Y, whose identity was well known to the publisher. The publisher was unable to contend successfully that he did not know and had no reason to believe copyright did not subsist in Y's work. All he could urge was that he did not believe that X had copied from Y's work, and that was held not to bring him within the section.[12] Nor, it is suggested, is ignorance of the existence of the copyright work (in a case of indirect copying),[13] a good basis for alleging ignorance that copyright subsisted in the work.

22–70

The subsistence defence: other considerations. In deciding whether a defendant did not know and had no reason to believe that copyright subsisted in a work, the court will take into account all the relevant circumstances, for example: the nature of the claimant's work, the fact that the claimant's name was or was not printed on it, the fact that the work bore or did not bear a claim to copyright in it,[14] any legal advice which the defendant received[15] and the fact that there may have been a long-standing practice of copying works of the character of the claimant's work without complaint. A general practice of copying would not, however, provide a defence to liability,[16] as distinct from a defence to damages.

22–71

Defence to damages for infringement of performers' non-property rights and recording rights. There is a totally separate defence to damages available to a person charged with contravening section 182(1) (recording or broadcasting a

22–72

---

of s.22 of the 1911 Act was stated by Clauson J. not to afford a defence under s.8 of that Act; he later held that, in fact, the view was not mistaken so that it was unnecessary to rely upon s.8 of that Act. See also *Field v Lemaire* (1939) 4 D.L.R. 561.

[11] *Byrne v Statist Co* [1914] 1 K.B. 622. See also *Gribble v Manitoba Free Press Ltd* [1932] 1 D.L.R. 169.

[12] *John Lane The Bodley Head Ltd v Associated Newspapers Ltd* [1936] 1 K.B. 715.

[13] See para. 7–15, above.

[14] *Swinstead v R. Underwood & Sons* [1923–28] Mac.C.C. 39 (copyright in a tombstone; defendant not liable for infringement damages).

[15] A defence based on erroneous advice allegedly given by a patent agent failed in *AP Besson v Fulleon Ltd* [1986] F.S.R. 319 because the defendant's evidence as to the question which was asked and the advice given was insufficiently specific.

[16] *Walter v Steinkopff* [1892] 3 Ch. 489; *Banier v News Group Newspapers Limited* [1997] F.S.R. 812 (this case is irrelevant for the purposes of a s.97(1) defence, but mentioned here as it establishes the proposition that the apparent wide-spread practice amongst newspapers of publishing photographs without a licence and then seeking to obtain a licence retrospectively, provides no defence to liability).

live performance without the consent of the performer) or section 186(1) (making a recording of a performance without the consent of the performer or person having recording rights) of the 1988 Act.[17] No damages shall be awarded against a defendant who shows that at the time of the infringement he believed on reasonable grounds that consent had been given.

22–73 **Defence to damages for infringement of design right**. Where a person obtains a licence of right in circumstances where the identity of the design right owner is unknown and it is subsequently established that a licence was not available as of right, the licensee is not liable in damages for, or for an account of profits in respect of, anything done before he was aware of any claim by the design right owner that a licence was not available.[18]

22–74 **Defence to damages: protection measures and rights management information.** In general, the persons with these rights have the same rights against those who breach their rights as a copyright owner has in respect of infringement of copyright.[19] It follows that section 97(1) of the 1988 Act should apply so that a defendant would have a defence to a claim for damages where he could show that he did not know and had no reason to believe that the relevant right (copyright, publication right, rights in performances or database right as the case might be) subsisted in the work, performance or database which was protected by the protection measure or with which the rights management information was associated (as the case might be).[20] This appears to be the case in relation to claims to enforce rights in respect of protection measures for computer programs, claims in respect of the acts of circumventing protection measures for works or protected material other than computer programs and all claims in respect of rights management information. However, where proceedings are brought in respect of devices and services designed to circumvent protection measures other than those applied to computer programs, the defence is made out if the defendant shows that he did not know or have reason to believe that his acts enabled or facilitated an infringement of the copyright or other protected material in question.[21] This is likely to be a much easier test to satisfy than that applicable to the other claims mentioned in this paragraph.

22–75 **Defence to damages: unauthorised decoders.** In proceedings in respect of unauthorised decoders, it is a defence to a claim for damages that the defendant did not know or have reason to believe that his acts infringed the rights conferred by section 298 of the 1988 Act.[22]

D. WHEN ABSENCE OF DAMAGE IS A DEFENCE

22–76 In a copyright case, the fact that the infringement has not caused the claimant copyright owner any damage is irrelevant to liability for infringement. Copyright is a right of property and a copyright owner is entitled to take legal proceedings for the protection of that property, even though he has not suffered or cannot

---

[17] CDPA 1988, ss.182(3) and 186(2).
[18] CDPA 1988, s.248(4).
[19] CDPA 1988, ss.296(2), 296ZA(3), 296ZD(2) and 296ZG(3).
[20] If this were not the intention, s.296ZD(7) would not refer to " section 97(1) … as it applies to proceedings for infringement of the rights conferred by this section".
[21] s.296ZD(7).
[22] CDPA 1988, s.298(5).

prove actual loss or damage.[23] The same is presumably true of performers' property rights, design right and database right. Furthermore, damage does not appear to be essential to the causes of action under the provisions as to protection measures, rights management information and unauthorised decoders. Nevertheless, a claimant who commences proceedings without having suffered damage does so at his own risk as to costs. By contrast, infringements of moral rights, performers' non-property rights and the rights of persons having recording rights are treated as breaches of statutory duty,[24] where damage is usually an essential ingredient of the tort.[25]

E. Undertaking to Take Licence of Right

Introduction. The 1988 Act imposes restrictions on the availability of certain remedies in cases where an undertaking is given by a defendant to infringement proceedings to take a licence of right in respect of copyright, performers' property rights, design right and database right.[26]
22–77

When the restrictions apply. The restrictions apply where[27] :
22–78
(1) There are in existence proceedings for infringement of copyright, performers' property rights, design right or database right, as the case may be;
(2) In respect of that copyright, performer's property right, design right or database right a licence is available as of right under section 144 or paragraph 19 of Schedule 1 to the 1988 Act (copyright),[28] paragraph 17 of Schedule 2A to the 1988 Act (performers' property rights),[29] sections 237 or 238 of the 1988 Act (design right),[30] or paragraph 15(1) of Schedule 2 to the Copyright and Rights in Databases Regulations 1996;[31] and
(3) The defendant to the proceedings undertakes to take a licence on such terms as may be agreed or, in default of agreement, settled by the Copyright Tribunal (in the case of copyright, performers' property rights or database right) or comptroller (in the case of design right).

Procedure. The defendant may give the undertaking at any time before final order in the proceedings and he may give it without any admission of liability.[32] The defendant is therefore entitled to continue to contest the action both on grounds of liability for infringement and *quantum*. The effect of the defendant giving the undertaking is as follows: First, the statutory provisions provide that no injunction shall be granted against him.[33] However, it has been held that where there are doubts as to the financial ability of the party giving the undertaking to comply with its terms, it is necessary for that party to show that the undertaking is one which he can reasonably be expected to honour.[34] Second, no order for delivery up shall be made under sections 99, 195 or 230 of the 1988 Act (as the
22–79

---

[23] *Weatherby & Sons v International Horse Agency and Exchange Ltd* [1910] 2 Ch. 297; *Hawkes & Son (London) Ltd v Paramount Film Service Ltd* [1934] Ch. 593, at 603, 608.
[24] CDPA 1988, ss.103(1) and 194.
[25] See generally, *Clerk & Lindsell on Torts.*
[26] CDPA 1988, ss.98, 191K and 239. Copyright and Rights in Databases Regulations 1997 (SI 1997/3032), reg.23, applying s.98 to database right.
[27] CDPA 1988, ss.98(1), 191K(1) and 239(1).
[28] See para. 29–131, below.
[29] See para. 29–131, below.
[30] See paras 13–124 and 13–125 *et seq.*, above.
[31] SI 1997/3032. See para. 29–131, below.
[32] CDPA 1988, ss.98(2), 191K(2) and 239(2).
[33] ss.98(1)(a), 191K(1)(a) and 239(1)(a).
[34] *Dyrlund Smith A/S v Turverville Smith Ltd* [1998] F.S.R. 774, CA. It is not clear how this approach can be reconciled with the clear terms of the sections.

case may be)[35] . Third, the amount recoverable against the defendant by way of damages or on an account of profits shall not exceed double the amount which would have been payable by him as licensee if such a licence on those terms had been granted before the earliest infringement.[36] The giving of the undertaking thus operates to provide a ceiling to the amount of payment which the defendant is liable to make to the claimant for infringement.

22–80   **Prior infringements.** These provisions do not affect the remedies available in respect of an infringement committed before the relevant licence of right was available.[37]

F. INNOCENTLY ACQUIRED ILLICIT RECORDINGS AND INFRINGING ARTICLES

22–81   There is a "remedy" defence to the secondary acts of infringement contained in section 184(1) (infringement of performers' rights by importing, possessing or dealing with illicit recordings) and section 188(1) (infringement of recording rights by importing, possessing or dealing with illicit recordings). In subsection (2) of those sections it is provided that, where the defendant shows that the illicit recording was innocently acquired by him or by a predecessor in title of his, the only remedy available against him in respect of the infringement is damages not exceeding a reasonable payment in respect of the act complained of. "Innocently acquired" means that the person acquiring the recording did not know and had no reason to believe that it was an illicit recording.[38] There is a similar provision in the case of secondary infringement of design right.[39]

G. PUBLIC INTEREST

22–82   **Introduction**. There has long been recognised a defence to a claim for copyright infringement based on the fact that the immorality or similar impropriety of the claimant's work itself is such as to prevent its enforcement. That defence is dealt with elsewhere.[40] Further, since 1972, the courts have also recognised a more general defence of public interest to claims for copyright infringement.[41] Although this defence was not expressly referred to in the 1956 Act, subsection 171(3) of the 1988 Act provides that nothing in Part I of the Act (which concerns copyright) affects any rule of law preventing or restricting the enforcement of copyright on grounds of public interest or otherwise. Even before the Human Rights Act 1998 came into force, this more general defence was held to extend not only to cases where the defendant had infringed the claimant's copyright in

---

[35] ss.98(1)(b), 191K(1)(b) and 239(1)(b). There is no provision for statutory delivery up in respect of database right.

[36] ss.98(1)(c), 191K(1)(c) and 239(1)(c).

[37] CDPA 1988, ss.98(3), 191K(3) and 239(3).

[38] CDPA 1988, ss.184(3) and 188(3).

[39] s.233(2)—the expression used in this sub-section is "not exceeding a reasonable *royalty* in respect of the act complained of".

[40] See paras 3–260 *et seq.*, above.

[41] See *Beloff v Pressdram Ltd* [1973] 1 All E.R. 241; *Lion Laboratories Ltd v Evans* [1985] Q.B. 526; *Church of Scientology of California v Miller The Times*, October 23, 1987; *Attorney-General v Guardian Newspapers (No.2)* [1990] 1 A.C. 109; *Beggars Banquet Records Ltd v Carlton Television Ltd* [1993] E.M.L.R. 349; *ZYX Music Gmbh v King* [1995] E.M.L.R. 281; [1995] F.S.R. 566; *PCR Ltd v Dow Jones Telerate Ltd* [1998] F.S.R. 170; *Service Corp. International Plc v Channel Four Television Corp. The Independent*, May 14, 1998. The defence has been recognised in Australia: *Acohs v RA Bashford* (1997) 37 I.P.R. 542. See also *Aztech Systems Pte Ltd v Creative Technology Ltd* [1996] F.S.R. 54 (High Ct of Singapore), where the public interest was a factor taken into account in considering a fair dealing defence. The leading case is now *Ashdown v Telegraph Group Ltd* [2001] EWCA Civ 1142.

order to reveal some form of impropriety on the part of the claimant, but also to cases where disclosure was otherwise in the public interest.[42] The passing of the Human Rights Act 1998 has given the defence new definition and accordingly, the authorities decided before it came into force must be approached with caution.[43] The public interest defence to claims for breach of confidence is considered elsewhere.[44] There is no equivalent to subsection 171(3) for the other rights considered in this Chapter. Nevertheless, the existence of a public interest in disclosure may well give rise to a defence to injunctive relief in respect of such claims.[45]

Tension between copyright and freedom of expression. The Court of Appeal's decision in *Ashdown v Telegraph Group Ltd*[46] is now the leading case. Where the infringement at issue involves a disclosure of information which was previously not in the public domain, there is a fundamental tension between the claimant copyright owner's right to peaceful enjoyment of his property on the one hand and the defendant's right to free expression on the other. Both these rights are enshrined in the European Convention on Human Rights.[47] In *Ashdown*, the Court of Appeal held that the right to free expression will only "trump" the copyright owner's right to peaceful enjoyment of his property where the infringement in question is actually necessary in the public interest.[48] As the Court of Appeal pointed out, this will not usually be the case.[49] For example, the information conveyed by a literary work may well be capable of being disclosed without there being any need to reproduce the actual words in which that information was expressed. On the other hand, in some cases some verbatim reproduction will be necessary, for example in order to demonstrate the authenticity of the document in question.[50] Accordingly, the court must look closely at the facts of each case.[51] **22–83**

First solution: refusal of injunction. It will usually be sufficient in order to give effect to the right of freedom of expression for the court to refuse as a matter of discretion to grant the claimant copyright owner injunctive relief, leaving the copyright owner to his remedies by way of damages or an account of profits.[52] This is not an application of the public interest defence, but rather an application of the 1988 Act in a way which accommodates the right of freedom of expression.[53] As the Court of Appeal put it: "freedom of expression should not normally carry with it the right to make free use of another's work".[54] **22–84**

Second solution: public interest defence. The Court of Appeal went on to hold that in the rare case where it is in the public interest that the copyright work should be reproduced without any sanction, this is permissible under the public **22–85**

---

[42] See *Lion Laboratories Ltd v Evans* [1985] Q.B. 526, as explained in *Ashdown v Telegraph Group Ltd* [2001] EWCA Civ 1142 para.58, not following dicta of the majority in *Hyde Park Residence Ltd v Yelland* [2001] Ch. 143; *PCR Ltd v Dow Jones Telerate Ltd* [1998] F.S.R. 170 at 187 (Lloyd J.).

[43] For a discussion, see *Copinger*, 14th ed., para. 22–48.

[44] See para. 22–109, below.

[45] See para. 22–154, below.

[46] [2001] EWCA Civ 1142; [2002] Ch. 149.

[47] See Art.1 of the First Protocol and Art.10 respectively.

[48] paras 43, 59, 81.

[49] paras 39 and 59.

[50] On the facts, the Court of Appeal held that the extensive reproduction of an eight-page minute was unjustified because the publication of "one or two extracts" would have sufficed to demonstrate the authenticity of the minute in question: see para.59.

[51] para.45.

[52] para.46. For these remedies, see below at paras 22–162 *et seq.* and 22–175 *et seq.*, respectively.

[53] paras 45–47.

[54] para.46.

interest defence provided by subsection 171(3).[55] This follows from the fact that this defence is not limited to cases where the defendant has infringed the claimant's copyright in order to reveal some form of impropriety and in fact "the circumstances in which public interest may override copyright are not capable of precise categorisation or definition".[56] The Court of Appeal stated that a refusal to grant an injunction would "usually" be sufficient, because where a newspaper considered it necessary to copy the exact words of another there was no reason in principle why it should not indemnify the author for any financial loss suffered or account to him for any profit made.[57] However, where the defendant is not a newspaper, it is not at all clear from the *Ashdown* decision in what circumstances the court is likely to consider it sufficient for the claimant to be refused injunctive relief as opposed to being deprived of his other remedies by the application of the public interest defence. Presumably much will depend on the nature of the work in question and the defendant's financial circumstances. For example, where a notional royalty is likely to be very high and the defendant is a person of limited means, it may be appropriate to apply the full public interest defence and deprive the claimant of his right to financial compensation. The opposite result may occur where a notional royalty would be low but the defendant, however impoverished, stands to make a considerable profit from the disclosure.

22–86 **Related defences.** Where public interest issues arise, defendants frequently seek to rely on one of the permitted acts. In particular, in a freedom of expression case, a defendant may, depending on the facts, be able to rely on the defence of fair dealing for the purposes of reporting current events or (although this is less likely) for the purposes of criticism or review.[58] Even if these defences are not available, a defendant may be able to resist injunctive relief on the grounds that the claimant does not come to the court with clean hands.

22–87 **Interim relief.** The principles governing the grant of interim injunctions where the right to freedom of expression is engaged are discussed below (paragraph 22–128).

H. USE IN ELECTRONIC NETWORKS: MERE CONDUIT, CACHING AND HOSTING.

(i) Introduction

22–88 **Introduction.**[59] The Electronic Commerce, or E-Commerce, Directive[60] provides, amongst other things, for "horizontal" exclusions of the liabilities of service providers which may arise out of the transmission and storage of information in their electronic networks. The exclusions are horizontal in the sense that they apply to liabilities of all kinds and thus not just in respect of infringements of copyright or other intellectual property rights. The underlying rationale is that exposure to such claims would have a chilling effect on the functioning of networks. The effect of the Directive is that, subject to various safeguards, any "liability" of a service provider in respect of the activities of "mere conduit",

---

[55] para.47.
[56] para.58, not following dicta of the majority in *Hyde Park Residence Ltd v Yelland* [2001] Ch. 143.
[57] para.58.
[58] See above at paras 9–44 *et seq.* and 9–45 *et seq.*, respectively.
[59] See, generally, Strachan: "The Internet of Tomorrow: The New-Old Communications Tool of Control" [2004] E.I.P.R. 123.
[60] Directive 2000/31/EC [2000] O.J. L178/1.See Vol.2 at H10.

"caching" and "hosting" of information is to be exempted, while retaining the possibility of their being subject to injunctive relief. All these acts may involve the transient or permanent reproduction of material in computer memory. Where copies made in this way are temporary, they may come within the exception provided for by section 28A of the 1988 Act, provided they are "transient or incidental", and their making is "an integral and essential part of a technological process" and for the sole purpose of enabling "a transmission of a work in a network between third parties by an intermediary". This provision is discussed elsewhere.[61] Otherwise, however, service providers will have to rely on the E-Commerce Directive, which has been implemented in the United Kingdom with effect from August 21, 2002, by the Electronic Commerce (EC Directive) Regulations 2002.[62]

The aim of the E-Commerce Directive. The overall aim of the E-Commerce Directive in this area can be gathered from Recital 42, which provides that: "The exemptions from liability ... cover only cases where the activity of the service provider is limited to the technical process of operating and giving access to a communication network over which information made available by third parties is transmitted or temporarily stored, for the sole purpose of making the transmission more efficient; this activity is of a mere technical, automatic and passive nature, which implies that the information society service provider has neither knowledge of nor control over the information which is transmitted or stored". **22–89**

Review. The Directive required the Commission to review the application of the Directive by July 17, 2003.[63] That review has taken place.[64] The Commission has concluded that in general this part of the Directive has been satisfactorily implemented. It proposes to continue to monitor and analyse new developments and to examine any future need to adapt the present framework, including whether there is a need for further exemptions of liability, for example in relaton to hyperlinks and search engines.[65] **22–90**

The Regulations: general. The Regulations closely follow the provisions of the Directive. Their effect is to provide a defence to claims for damages or any other kind of pecuniary remedy in defined situations. Technically the acts in question remain infringements and so any copies made in the process which, the regulations apart, would be infringing copies, remain so. The consequences so far as criminal proceedings are concerned are dealt with elsewhere.[66] Nothing in the regulations is to prevent a person agreeing contractual terms which differ from the terms of the regulations.[67] Neither the Directive nor the Regulations specifically deal with the position of providers of such services as hyperlinks, location tools or content aggregation. **22–91**

Key definitions. The Regulations and Directive contain certain key definitions, namely a "service provider", "information society services" and a "recipient of the service." A "service provider" means any person providing an information **22–92**

---

[61] See para. 9–16, above.
[62] SI 2002/2013. See Vol.2 at B10.i. reg.16, which concerns "Stop Now Orders" came into force on October 23, 2002.
[63] E-Commerce Directive 2000/31, Art.21(1).
[64] COM 2003(702) final.
[65] COM 2003(702), para.4.6.
[66] See para. 23–22, below.
[67] SI 2002/2013, reg.20(1).

society service[68] The term "information society service" is defined in the same way as in section 297A of the 1988 Act (which concerns unauthorised decoders) and is considered elsewhere.[69] "Recipient of the service" is defined to mean any person who, for professional ends or otherwise, uses an information society service, in particular for the purposes of seeking information or making it accessible.[70] This effectively repeats the wording of the Directive,[71] which also makes it clear that a "person" includes any natural or legal person. This definition emphasises that "recipient" means a recipient of the service provider's service, not just of the information supplied, and it thus includes the third parties who provide the information.

(ii) The defence of mere conduit

22–93   **The defence of mere conduit.** Regulation 17(1) provides that where an information society service is provided which consists of the transmission in a communication network of information provided by a recipient of the service or the provision of access to a communication network, the service provider shall not be liable for damages or for any other pecuniary remedy or for any criminal sanction as a result of that transmission where the service provider (a) did not initiate the transmission; (b) did not select the receiver of the transmission; and (c) did not select or modify the information contained in the transmission. This follows the wording of Article 12(1). These acts of transmission and of provision of access are to include the automatic, intermediate and transient storage of the information transmitted where: (a) this takes place for the sole purpose of carrying out the transmission in the communication network, and (b) the information is not stored for any period longer than is reasonably necessary for the transmission (see regulation 17(2)). Again, this follows the wording of Article 12(2).

22–94   **The Directive.** Regulation 17 and Article 12 must be read in conjunction with the Recitals to the Directive. Recital 43 states that a service provider can benefit from the exemptions for "mere conduit" (and for "caching") when it is "in no way involved" with the information transmitted. The Recital adds that this is conditional, among other things, on the service provider not modifying the information that it transmits, although this does not include manipulations of a technical nature which take place in the course of the transmission, since they do not alter the "integrity" of the information contained in the transmission. Recital 44 adds that a service provider who deliberately collaborates with one of the recipients of its service in order to undertake illegal acts goes beyond the activities of "mere conduit" (or "caching") and as a result cannot benefit from the liability exemptions. This provision is not repeated in the Regulations but no doubt they must be interpreted consistently with this Recital.

22–95   **The operation of the defence.** The intention is therefore to provide a defence to any pecuniary claim (or to any criminal charge) in the case of such passive and intermediate acts of a service provider. The defence extends to all acts of the service provider which would otherwise be infringing, and thus not only to the transient reproduction of works in the service provider's servers but also to possession of infringing copies of the information on its servers and acts of transmission of works by it (for example by acts which would infringe the communication and making available to the public rights). As already noted, a service

---

[68] reg.2(1), repeating Art.2(b) of the Directive.
[69] See paras 16–11 *et seq.*, above.
[70] SI 2002/2013, reg.2(1).
[71] E-Commerce Directive 2000/31, Art.2(d).

provider may be liable as a joint tortfeasor where it has deliberately collaborated with a third party to commit infringing acts but otherwise, provided the conditions in the regulation are satisfied, any pecuniary liability of the service provider which might otherwise arise in respect of the infringing acts of a third party is excluded. It appears that a service provider is not liable if it suspects or even knows that its networks are being used as a conduit for infringing material, unless perhaps the making available of its networks in such circumstances could be construed as deliberate collaboration. As to the possibility of injunctive relief, however, see paragraphs 22–108 *et seq.*, below.

The requirement that the information should not be stored for any period longer than is reasonably necessary for the transmission makes it clear that storage, even transient storage, for some longer period will take the activity outside the defence. To the extent that storage takes place for caching purposes, this is dealt with by regulation 18 andArticle 13. The element of passivity required of the service provider is also underlined by the references to the "automatic", "intermediate" and "transient" storage of information, and the requirement that such storage is only to be for the sole purpose of carrying out the transmission. "Automatic" is intended to refer to the requirement that the act of storage occurs through the ordinary operation of the technology, "intermediate" to the fact that the storage takes place in the course of transmission and "transient" to the fact that it is for a limited time. The element of intermediacy is further underlined by the fact that the regulation applies only in relation to information provided by a recipient of the service. This means that to the extent that any infringing material is provided by the service provider itself there will be no defence. Further emphasis as to both these matters is given by the three conditions in regulation 17(1). As to these:

(a) No initiation of the transmission by the service provider. The reference to initiation shows that although the service provider may be the transmitter of the information, or the first in line in an integrated network transmission, provided it does not take the decision to start off the process its actions will fall within the defence. This will include an automatic transmission in response to a request.

(b) No selection of the receiver of the transmission. A service provider may well carry out the process of directing the information to the recipient, but if this is done as an automated response to a request from the provider of the information it will not have "selected" the recipient.

(c) No selection or modification of the information contained in the transmission. This speaks for itself although, as seen, manipulations of a technical nature which take place in the course of the transmission can take place without losing the benefit of the defence (Recital 43).

(iii) The defence of caching

The defence of caching. "Caching" is the local storing of information in a   **22–96**
network that is in frequent demand by users, such that users may access the information more quickly so as to avoid the network being slowed up by repeated access to the source of the information.[72] Caching may take place in the user's own system or locally in the network. In practice, it is a technical and automatic process. Regulation 18 provides that where an information society service is provided which consists of the transmission in a communication network of in-

---

[72] See generally, Hugenholtz, "Caching and Copyright: The Right of Temporary Copying" [2000] E.I.P.R. 482 and Julia-Barceló, "On-line intermediary liability issues: comparing EU and US frameworks" [2000] E.I.P.R. 106.

formation provided by a recipient of the service, the service provider shall not be liable for damages or for any other pecuniary remedy or for any criminal sanction as a result of that transmission where: (a) the information is the subject of automatic, intermediate and temporary storage where that storage is for the sole purpose of making more efficient onward transmission of the information to other recipients of the service upon their request; and where (b) the service provider: (i) does not modify the information; (ii) complies with conditions on access to the information; (iii) complies with any rules regarding the updating of the information, specified in a manner widely recognised and used by industry; (iv) does not interfere with the lawful use of technology, widely recognised and used by industry, to obtain data on the use of the information; and (v) acts expeditiously to remove or to disable access to the information he has stored upon obtaining actual knowledge of the fact that the information at the initial source of the transmission has been removed from the network, or access to it has been disabled, or that a court or an administrative authority has ordered such removal or disablement.[73] The wording closely follows that of the Directive.[74]

22–97   **Additional guidance and condition (i).** Recital 43 to the Directive states that a service provider can benefit from the exemptions for "caching" when it is "in no way involved" with the information transmitted. The Recital adds that this is conditional, among other things, on the service provider not modifying the information that it transmits. The Recital goes on to say that the condition that the information is not modified does not include manipulations of a technical nature which take place in the course of the transmission, since they do not alter the "integrity" of the information contained in the transmission. Recital 44 adds that a service provider who deliberately collaborates with one of the recipients of its service in order to undertake illegal acts goes beyond the activities of "caching" and as a result cannot benefit from the liability exemptions. These provisions (apart from the condition that the information is not modified) are not repeated in the Regulations but no doubt the latter must be interpreted consistently with this Recital. As to the possibility of an injunction, see paragraph 22–108 *et seq.*, below.

22–98   **Condition (ii): compliance with conditions on access to the information.** This is not further defined, either in the Directive or the Regulations. It is thought that it means conditions imposed by the provider of the information, for example a requirement to pay a fee before the information may be accessed. If service providers were to permit users to access information supplied as part of a conditional access service from a cache without paying the fee, this would obviously undermine the business of the provider of the information.

22–99   **Condition (iii):compliance with industry rules regarding updating of information.** The object of this condition is evidently to ensure that the caching does not result in the provision of "stale" information. However, the references to industry rules and practice may clearly lead to uncertainty as to whether or not a provider has complied with them and has therefore infringed. The Directive expressly encourages the drawing up of relevant codes of conduct.[75]

22–100   **Condition (iv): non-interference with technology to obtain data on use of the information.** The reason for this condition is that web-pages which are delivered directly from caches do not register "hits". As a result, where advertising income

---

[73] SI 2002/2013, reg.18.
[74] E-Commerce Directive 2000/31, Art.13.
[75] E-Commerce Directive 2000/31, Art.16.

or royalties are paid on a "per-hit" basis, the provider of the information will lose out unless it is able to obtain data on the use of the information in the cache.

Condition (v): acting to remove or disable access. The requirement to act expeditiously to remove or disable access to the information arises where the service provider has knowledge of any one of three alternative matters. It must be emphasised that what is relevant for this purpose is not knowledge or reasonable grounds to believe that the cached material is infringing or otherwise unlawful, or even that it is so, with the result that any such knowledge would be immaterial (compare the test in relation to hosting, below). Indeed, as will be seen, the Directive makes it clear that a general obligation is not to be imposed on providers, when providing caching services, to monitor the information which they transmit, nor a general obligation actively to seek facts or circumstances indicating illegal activity.[76] As to whether a service provider has the knowledge relevant for the purposes of the caching defence, it might have been thought better to leave matters as they stood in the regulation, which merely repeats the wording of the Directive,[77] and seems reasonably clear.

22–101

Caching: knowledge:Regulation 22: background. In its response to the consultation process, however, the Government said:

22–102

"The limitations on liability for caches and hosts apply if an intermediary does not have actual knowledge of illegal activity or information. In line with the Directive, the draft Regulations did not propose specifying how actual knowledge is obtained. A number of comments sought further detail on what constitutes actual knowledge and what type of notice would give rise to it. Others recognised the inherent difficulties of providing a definition of actual knowledge but requested that some attention instead be given to what would *not* constitute actual knowledge. The Government remains of the view that providing a positive definition would risk creating loopholes that could be exploited to avoid liability inappropriately. Being too prescriptive about what does not constitute actual knowledge raises similar concerns. However, it recognises that intermediaries face difficulties in assessing whether they are likely to be deemed to have actual knowledge. Given that the courts will ultimately decide individual cases, the Government believes it appropriate for them to have regard at least to whether a notice has been sent to the intermediary in question and, if so, whether it contains key information about the sender, where the relevant information is stored and why it is considered unlawful ...". There appears to be some confusion in this response between the different types of knowledge required for the caching and hosting defences, and to what extent each requires "actual" or "deemed" knowledge. As already pointed out, the knowledge, whether actual or deemed, of unlawful activity is irrelevant for the purposes of the caching defence. Actual knowledge of one of the three specified matters is all that is relevant.

Caching: terms of regulation 22. Despite this, therefore, the Government added regulation 22, which provides that in determining whether a service provider has actual knowledge for the purposes of regulation 18(b)(v) (and also of regulation 19(a)(i)—the hosting defence), a court shall take into account all matters which appear to it in the particular circumstances to be relevant and, among other things, shall have regard to whether a service provider has received a notice through a means of contact made available in accordance with regulation 6(1)(c). This regulation provides that a person providing an information society service shall make available to the recipient of the service and any relevant enforcement

22–103

---

[76] See E-Commerce Directive 2000/31, Art.15(1).
[77] Art.13(1)(e).

authority, in a form and manner which is easily, directly and permanently accessible, the details of the service provider, including his electronic mail address, which make it possible to contact him rapidly and communicate with him in a direct and effective manner. Further, under regulation 22, a court is to have regard to the extent to which any such notice includes: (i) the full name and address of the sender of the notice; (ii) details of the location of the information in question; and (iii) details of the unlawful nature of the activity or information in question. As will be seen, this provision, particularly (iii), seems relevant only to the hosting defence. Information about the location of the information might be relevant to whether or not the service provider had acted expeditiously to remove the information from cache memory, but this is not to what the regulation is directed. It is suggested that regulation 22 adds nothing to the caching defence and should not construed as doing so since otherwise it would go beyond the terms of the Directive.

(iv) Hosting

22–104 **The defence of hosting.** "Hosting" is the provision of space to users for content, such as web sites, news groups or bulletin boards. Regulation 19 provides that where an information society service is provided which consists of the storage of information provided by a recipient of the service, the service provider shall not be liable for damages or for any other pecuniary remedy or for any criminal sanction as a result of that storage where: (a) the service provider: (i) does not have actual knowledge of unlawful activity or information and, where a claim for damages is made, is not aware of facts or circumstances from which it would have been apparent to the service provider that the activity or information was unlawful; or (ii) upon obtaining such knowledge or awareness, acts expeditiously to remove or to disable access to the information, and (b) the recipient of the service was not acting under the authority or the control of the service provider.The wording closely follows that of the Directive.[78]

22–105 **"Unlawful information".** Presumably, this term in the present context means information whose storage would involve the infringement of an intellectual property right.[79]

22–106 **Knowledge.** The regulation, like the Directive, makes a distinction between different kinds of knowledge in relation to different kinds of liability. In relation to civil claims for damages (which presumably should be read as including claims for other civil pecuniary remedies), the fact that there are grounds on which the unlawfulness might be apparent to the service provider will be enough to remove the defence, irrespective of the service provider's actual knowledge. In relation to criminal liability, however, actual knowledge is required before the defence is removed. The same provision is made for the purposes of determining whether a service provider has actual knowledge for these purposes as for the caching defence.[80] This provision only relates to the issue of actual knowledge in the first limb of regulation 19(a)(i), and not the "reasonable grounds" issue in the second limb. Again, it is suggested that it adds nothing to the defence. Presumably the issue of actual knowledge and knowledge on the "reasonable grounds" basis will be approached in the same way as the issue of knowledge for the purposes of sec-

---

[78] E-Commerce Directive 2000/31, Art.14(1).
[79] E-Commerce Directive 2000/31, Art.14(1)(a) speaks of "illegal" information.
[80] See para. 22–103, above.

ondary infringement of copyright.[81] The Directive enables Member States to establish procedures governing the removal or disabling of access to information, i.e. notice-and-take-down procedures.[82] Following consultation, the Government has decided that in the first place this should be a matter for industry codes of conduct rather than statutory regulation, something which in turn is encouraged by the Directive.[83] It is difficult to see, however, how such codes could affect the question of knowledge or whether the service provider had acted expeditiously to remove or disable access to cached material, both being primarily issues of fact.

(v) Injunctions and other provisions

Mere conduit, caching and hosting: termination of infringement. In the case   **22–107** of all acts of conduit, caching and hosting, the Directive provides that it is not to affect the possibility for a court or administrative authority, in accordance with Member States' legal systems, requiring the service provider to terminate or prevent an infringement.[84] This is supplemented by Recital 45 which states that the Directive does not affect the possibility of injunctions of different kinds, in particular ones requiring the termination or prevention of any infringement, including the removal of illegal information or the disabling of access to it. The regulations provide that nothing in regulations 17, 18 and 19 shall affect the rights of any party to apply to a court for relief to prevent or stop infringement of any rights.[85] The Regulations also provide that any power of an administrative authority to prevent or stop infringement of any rights shall continue to apply notwithstanding regulations 17, 18 and 19.[86]

No doubt these provisions were included as a matter of caution but it is not clear what they add to the general law. As already noted, the general effect of the Regulations is not to make the acts of service providers permitted acts of the kind referred to in Chapter III of the 1988 Act. They remain infringements but there is now a defence in relation to pecuniary claims and criminal proceedings. If an infringement is being committed because the service provider is acting outside the scope of any defence granted by the Regulations, then an injunction can be granted on normal principles. If a service provider is acting within the Regulations in relation to its hosting activities but it is subsequently given sufficient notice of a likely infringement, then unless it acts to remove or to disable access to the information the defences will not apply and the service provider will be liable to the normal remedies, including the grant of an injunction, in respect of any infringement which is continuing or which is likely to be committed in the future. As has been seen, in relation to the caching defence the relevant kind of notice required is rather different, and perhaps an injunction might be justified where the service provider unreasonably refused to co-operate in disabling the activities of a known and persistent infringer. Again as already noted, it appears that in the case of mere conduit a service provider is not liable in respect of any pecuniary remedy even if it knows or suspects that a third party is using its networks to transmit infringing material, provided no deliberate collaboration has occurred, and it is a prerequisite of the defence that any storage ends once it is no longer reasonably necessary for the transmission. In such a case, it may be that an injunction might be appropriate against an uncooperative service provider so as to

---

[81] See paras 8–08 *et seq.*, above.
[82] E-Commerce Directive 2000/31, Art.14(3).
[83] Art.16(1).
[84] E-Commerce Directive 2000/31, Arts 12(3), 13(2) and 14(3).
[85] SI 2002/2013, reg.20(1)(a).
[86] reg.20(2).

prevent access to its network by a third party where it was likely that infringing material was to be transmitted.

22–108   **Injunctions against service providers who are not infringing: background.** Article 8(3) of the Information Society Directive[87] requires Member States to ensure that rightholders are in a position to apply for an injunction against intermediaries whose services are used by a third party to infringe a copyright or related right. The reason for this provision appears from Recital 59, which notes that in a digital environment the services of intermediaries may increasingly be used by third parties and that in many cases such intermediaries are best placed to bring such infringing activities to an end. Accordingly, the Recital continues, rightholders should have the possiblity of applying for an injunction against an intermediary who carries a third party's infringement in a network, even when the intermediary's acts are exempted under Article 5 (that is, because they constitute a permitted act). The Government's initial view was that there was no need for specific legislative implementation of Article 8(3) because injunctions would be available at common law. However, during the consultation on the implementation of the Directive, right owner organisations generally expressed concern that unless specific provision was made to implement Article 8(3), there would be uncertainty as to their rights to apply for injunctions, particularly where intermediaries themselves were not infringing because of the Article 5(1) exemption, which permits temporary acts of copying.[88] Accordingly, in order to avoid uncertainty, the Government decided to implement Article 8(3) specifically.

22–109   **Injunctions against service providers who are not infringing: the provisions.** Sections 97A and 191JA were therefore introduced into the 1988 Act by the Copyright and Related Rights Regulations 2003.[89] These sections give the High Court[90] power to grant an injunction against a service provider[91] where that service provider has actual knowledge of another person using its service to infringe copyright or (as the case may be) a performer's property right. It seems clear that this provision is not intended to cut down the power to grant injunctions at common law, but rather to create a new power which will be exercisable when there is no power to grant an injunction at common law.

22–110   **Injunctions against service providers who are not infringing: actual knowledge.** In determining whether a service provider has actual knowledge for these purposes, the court is obliged to take into account: first, all matters which appear to it in the particular circumstances to be relevant; secondly, whether a service provider has received a notice through a means of contact made available in accordance with regulation 6(1)(c) of the E-Commerce Regulations; and thirdly, the extent to which any such notice includes (i) the full name and address of the sender and (ii) details of the infringement in question.[92] It is thought that the question of whether a service provider has actual knowledge for these purposes will be determined in the same way as for secondary infringement of copyright.[93]

---

[87] 2001/29, [2001] O.J. L 167/6.See Vol.2 at H11.

[88] See the Analysis of Responses and Government Conclusions, para.8.3

[89] SI 2003/2498, Vol.2 at A3.iv, with effect from October 31, 2003.

[90] In Scotland, the Court of Session.

[91] For these purposes, service provider has the same meaning as in the Electronic Commerce Regulations (SI 2002/2013), as to which see para. 22–92, above.

[92] CDPA 1988, ss.97A(2) and 191JA(2).

[93] See paras 8–08, *et seq.*, above.

Monitoring of information. Although the caching and hosting exemptions in   22–111
particular may be affected by the service provider's knowledge of any infringement, the Directive makes it clear that a general obligation is not to be imposed
on providers, when providing conduit, caching and hosting services, to monitor
the information which they transmit or store, nor a general obligation actively to
seek facts or circumstances indicating illegal activity.[94] This is not repeated in the
Regulations since it there is no such obligation under United Kingdom law in the
first place. Nevertheless, it should be noted that Recital 44 provides that the
Directive does not affect the possibility of Member States requiring service
providers who host information provided by recipients of their service to apply
such duties of care as can reasonably be expected from them and which are specified by national law, in order to detect and prevent certain types of illegal
activities.

Disclosure of information about infringers. The Directive enables Member   22–112
States to "establish" obligations whereby service providers must provide information about infringing activities of users of their services.[95] Presumably *Norwich Pharmacal*[96] orders fall within the scope of this, so that nothing in the
Regulations affords a defence in relation to the exercise of this jurisdiction.

7. REMEDIES AND PROCEDURE

A. Jurisdiction

Extent of the 1988 Act. Parts I (copyright and moral rights), II (rights in perfor-   22–113
mances), III (design right) and VII (which includes the provisions as to protection measures, rights management information and decoders) all extend (so far as
relevant) to England and Wales, Scotland and Northern Ireland.[97] The Database
Regulations extend to the United Kingdom.[98] For the purposes of Parts I to III,
the territorial waters of the United Kingdom are treated as part of the United
Kingdom.[99] These Parts apply to things done in the United Kingdom sector of the
continental shelf on a structure or vessel which is present there for purposes
directly connected with the exploration of the sea bed or subsoil or the exploitation of their natural resources as they apply to things done in the United Kingdom.[1]
The United Kingdom sector of the continental shelf means the areas designated
by order under section 1(7) of the Continental Shelf Act 1964.[2] Part I and Part II
of the 1988 Act apply to things done on a British ship, aircraft or hovercraft as
they apply to things done in the United Kingdom.[3] Curiously, there is no equivalent provision for design right. However, the courts have jurisdiction over torts
committed on British ships[4] and statutes normally extend thereto.[5]

---

[94] E-Commerce Directive 2000/31, Art.15(1).
[95] E-Commerce Directive 2000/31, Art.15(2).
[96] See para. 22–142 *et seq.*, below.
[97] See, respectively, CDPA 1988, ss.157, 207, 255 and 304.
[98] SI 1997/3032, reg.1(3).
[99] CDPA 1988, ss.161(1), 209(1) and 257(1).
[1] ss.161(2), 209(2) and 257(2).
[2] ss.161(3), 209(3) and 257(3).
[3] ss.162(1) and 210(1). For definitions of British ship, aircraft and hovercraft see subss.(2) of those
sections.
[4] *Lloyd v Guibert* (1865) L.R. 1 Q.B. 115; *Davidson v Hill* [1901] 2 K.B. 606.
[5] *Schwartz v The India Rubber, etc. Co Ltd* [1912] 2 K.B. 299.

22–114   **Extent of the 1988 Act may be increased.** Parts I and III of the Act may be extended to any of the Channel Islands, the Isle of Man or any colony.[6] Similarly, the provisions in respect of fraudulent reception of transmissions may be extended to the Isle of Man and any of the Channel Islands.[7] These provisions have scarcely been used.[8] Otherwise, there is no provision for extending the provisions in respect of the other rights covered in this Chapter.

22–115   **Acts committed outside the United Kingdom.** In addition to the provisions mentioned in paragraph 22–113, above, various provisions of the 1988 Act make it clear that acts committed outside the United Kingdom cannot be infringements of copyright under the 1988 Act. For example, copyright is defined in territorial terms, as the exclusive right to do the restricted acts "in the United Kingdom".[9] The distribution right, which is expressed (in section 18(2) of the 1988 Act) in terms of the act of putting copies into circulation in the EEA, might appear to constitute an exception to this rule. However, it is thought that this does not give any rights in respect of activities outside the United Kingdom as defined in the 1988 Act.[10] By contrast, a person who, when outside the United Kingdom, authorises the commission of a restricted act in the United Kingdom will infringe.[11] It is thought that similar principles apply to the other rights covered in this work.

22–116   **Jurisdiction over foreign rights and infringements thereof: general.** A claim that acts done outside the United Kingdom constitute an infringement of the copyright law of a foreign country was not, until relatively recently, considered to be justiciable in the English courts.[12] However, the position is now changed with regard to actions claiming infringement of intellectual property rights to which either the Judgments Regulation, the Brussels Convention or the Lugano Convention applies.[13] Moreover, doubt has been cast on the main authority which states that such issues are not justiciable in proceedings which are not subject to the Regulation or the Conventions.[14]

22–117   **Position under the Judgments Regulation and the Brussels and Lugano Conventions.** If the action is properly constituted in the English courts under the terms of the Regulation or the relevant Convention[15] and the court has jurisdiction over the defendant (usually because of his domicile), the court must entertain the action on its merits, thereby giving full effect to the intellectual property laws

---

[6] CDPA 1988, ss.157(2), and 255(2).

[7] s.304(4) and (5).

[8] An order has been made extending the provisions of the 1988 Act with modifications to Bermuda: the Copyright (Bermuda) Order 2003 (SI 2003/1517).

[9] CDPA 1988, s.16(1). *Def Lepp Music v Stuart-Brown* [1986] R.P.C. 273; *Jonathan Cape Ltd v Consolidated Press Ltd* [1954] 1 W.L.R. 1313; *Pearce v Ove Arup Ltd* [2000] Ch. 403 at 438 (*obiter*).

[10] See above, para. 7–80, above. The same applies to the distribution right in respect of performers' rights: see s.182B(2).

[11] *ABKCO Music & Records Inc v Music Collection International Ltd* [1995] R.P.C. 657.

[12] *Tyburn Productions Ltd v Conan Doyle* [1991] Ch. 75.

[13] Council Regulation (EC) No.44/2001 on jurisdiction and the recognition and enforcement of judgments in civil and commercial matters [2000] O.J. L 12/1 (which, so far as relevant, governs actions against defendants domiciled in EU Member States other than Denmark), the Brussels Convention on Jurisdiction and Enforcement of Judgments in Civil and Commercial Matters (which, so far as relevant, governs actions against defendants domiciled in Denmark) and the Lugano Convention on Jurisdiction and the Enforcement of Judgments in Civil Matters (which, so far as relevant, governs actions against defendants domiciled in EFTA states). The position as between different parts of the United Kingdom is governed by the Civil Jurisdiction and Judgments Act 1982 (c.27), Sch.4.

[14] See para. 22–118, below.

[15] For example, there is no *lis pendens* (Judgments Regulation, Art.27; Brussels Convention, Art.21; Lugano Convention, Art.22).

of other states.[16] Where the Judgments Regulation applies, this principle will apply to rights equivalent to those covered in this work unless Article 22(4) of the Regulation applies. Article 22(4) provides that in proceedings concerned with the registration or validity of patents, trade marks, designs, or other similar rights required to be deposited or registered, the courts of the contracting state in which the deposit or registration has been applied for, has taken place or is under the terms of a Community instrument or international convention deemed to have taken place have exclusive jurisdiction, regardless of domicile. Similar provision is made by Article 16(4) of the Brussels Convention and Article 16(4) of the Lugano Convention.

Position in other cases. In actions which are not subject to the Judgments Regulation or the Conventions, the position is less clear. There is no doubt that (subject to questions of personal jurisdiction[17] and *forum non conveniens*[18] and the provision of evidence as to foreign law[19]) the English courts will grant relief in respect of acts in those counties which would amount to passing off if committed in England.[20] As to copyright, in *Tyburn Productions Ltd v Conan Doyle*[21] Vinelott J held that the question whether a defendant had any copyright in the United States so as to be able to prevent the distribution of the claimant's film was not justiciable in England. His decision was based in part on a finding that the *Moçambique* rule applies to copyright.[22] This rule provides that the English court has no jurisdiction to entertain proceedings for the determination of title to or the right to the possession of immovable property situated outside England.[23] However, this part of the reasoning in the *Tyburn* case has been doubted.[24] Nevertheless, the *Tyburn* decision has been approved by the Court of Appeal on the basis that the Judge was right to regard the relief sought as "an exercise in futility" because there was no evidence that the English court's decision would be treated as binding in the United States.[25] At least in the Court of Appeal, therefore, there is certainly scope for argument that an English court may rule on questions of title to foreign rights equivalent to copyright, provided it can be shown that such an order would have some practical effect. Furthermore, the *Tyburn* deci-

22-118

---

[16] *Gareth Pearce v Ove Arup Partnership Limited* [2000] Ch. 403; *Coin Controls Ltd v Suzo International (UK) Ltd* [1997] 3 All E.R. 45; [1997] F.S.R. 660; *Fort Dodge Animal Health Ltd & Others v Akzo Nobel NV & Another* [1998] F.S.R. 222, CA.

[17] Which are governed by the common law rule that a defendant who is liable to be served with a claim form is subject to the jurisdiction of the court: Dicey & Morris, *The Conflict of Laws* (13th ed.) Rule 24. As to service out of the jurisdiction, see CPR Part 6 and the relevant Practice Direction.

[18] That is, the court's power to stay English proceedings on the ground that there is another forum in another jurisdiction which is clearly more appropriate: Dicey & Morris, *The Conflict of Laws* (13th ed.) Rule 31.

[19] Where necessary under the Private International Law (Miscellaneous Provisions) Act 1995 (c.42), s.11.

[20] See *e.g. Alfred Dunhill Ltd v Sunoptic SA* [1979] F.S.R. 337. Note that the so-called "double actionability" rule has been abolished by the Private International Law (Miscellaneous Provisions) Act 1995 (c.42), s.10; accordingly, there is no longer any requirement that acts complained of should be actionable in the United Kingdom. See *Clerk & Lindsell on Torts* (18th ed.), para.6-09.

[21] [1991] Ch. 75.

[22] In doing so, he followed the Australian case of *Potter v Broken Hill Pty Co Ltd* (1906) 3 C.L.R. 479 in which it had been held that the *Moçambique* rule applied to a case where the validity of a foreign patent was put in issue. It was conceded that if the rule applied to patents, it also applied to copyright: see *Tyburn Productions Ltd v Conan Doyle* [1991] Ch. 75 at p.84D.

[23] Dicey & Morris, *The Conflict of Laws* (13th ed.) Rule 114(3). For some exceptions to this, see the next paragraph.

[24] See *Pearce v Ove Arup Ltd* [2000] Ch. 403 at pp.439–40 and *R. Griggs Group Ltd v Evans* [2004] EWHC 1088, Ch D (Peter Prescott Q.C.) at paras 135–139.

[25] *Pearce v Ove Arup Ltd* [2000] Ch. 403 at pp.439–40 . See also *R. Griggs Group Ltd v Evans* [2004] EWHC 1088, Ch D (Peter Prescott Q.C.) at para.139.

sion was probably limited to cases where subsistence or title are in issue.[26] Accordingly, the question whether an infringement claim of this type would be justiciable where subsistence or validity are not in issue seems to be an open one. In that context, it should be noted that the *Moçambique* rule does not apply to proceedings for trespass to or any other tort affecting immovable property unless the proceedings are principally concerned with a question of title to, or the right to possession of that property.[27] If applied by analogy to infringements of rights equivalent to copyright, this exception would mean that an action for infringement which was not principally concerned with subsistence or title would be justiciable in England.

22–119   **The court's *in personam* jurisdiction.** If, in accordance with the *Tyburn* decision, the *Moçambique* rule applies to copyright, the court nevertheless has jurisdiction by way of exception to the *Moçambique* rule to make orders *in personam* which would result in the transfer from one party to another of foreign intellectual property.[28] Such orders may be made where the claim is based on a contract or equity between the parties.[29] The precise extent of this jurisdiction is unclear.[30] However, it has been held that where a defendant legal owner of copyright has assigned the United Kingdom copyright together with all foreign copyrights to a third party with notice of the equitable owner's title, the court has jurisdiction to order the assignee to assign to the equitable owner not only the United Kingdom copyrights but also the foreign copyrights even though the assignee has not assumed any express personal obligation to do so.[31]

B. Interim Relief

(i) Injunction

22–120   **General.** In many cases, the most important remedy for infringement of the rights covered in this Chapter is an injunction. An injunction may be either interim, that is one granted prior to the trial and only until after judgment or further order, or it may be final and permanent. Most injunctions sought are of a negative or prohibitory nature. However, an interim mandatory injunction may also be granted, to require a person to do something. The criteria for the grant of such injunctions are considered below.[32] Applications for interim injunctions are frequently made in actions for infringement of copyright and similar rights, since damages are often not an adequate remedy for the injury suffered by the claimant.[33] In order to justify applying for a *quia timet* injunction, a claimant does not necessarily have

---

[26] *Pearce v Ove Arup Ltd* [2000] Ch. 403 at p.440B.

[27] Civil Jurisdiction and Judgments Act 1982 (c.27), s.30(1).

[28] Dicey & Morris, *The Conflict of Laws* (13th ed.) Rule 114(3)(a).

[29] *ibid.*

[30] See Dicey & Morris, *The Conflict of Laws* (13th ed.), paras 23–040 to 23–048.

[31] *R. Griggs Group Ltd v Evans* [2004] EWHC 1088, Ch D. It should be noted that because of the way the issue developed in this case, the court assumed (unless and to the extent that it would be unreasonable to do so) in favour of the equitable owner both that all relevant local laws as to the equitable owner's entitlement to an order transferring the copyright to him were the same as English law and that no relevant local courts would consider it a breach of comity to make the order sought: see paras 25, 114 and 141.

[32] See para. 22–138, below.

[33] *Coral Index Ltd v Regent Index Ltd* [1970] R.P.C. 147; *Annabel's (Berkeley Square) Ltd v G Schock* [1972] R.P.C. 838 at 845; *Slick Brands (Clothing) Ltd v Jollybird Ltd* [1975] F.S.R. 470; *Foseco International Ltd v Fordath Ltd* [1975] F.S.R. 507; *Combe International Ltd v Scholl (UK) Ltd* [1980] R.P.C. 1; *Monet of London Ltd v Sybil Richards Ltd* [1978] F.S.R. 368 at 375; *cf. Aljose Fashions Ltd v Alfred Young & Co Ltd* [1978] F.S.R. 364; *Foster v Mountford and Rigby Ltd* [1978] F.S.R. 582 (breach of confidence—Supreme Court of Northern Territory, Australia).

to show a real threat of future infringement. Prevarication by the defendant may be enough.[34]

Without notice applications. An application for an injunction may be made without notifying the party against whom relief is sought. The grant of such an injunction involves making an order against a defendant before he has had an opportunity to put his case. Accordingly, such applications should only be made where there is grave urgency, possible risk of irreparable damage or some other particular circumstances which would justify the grant of relief at this early stage, *e.g.* that the purpose of the injunction would be frustrated if the defendant was warned.[35] Except where secrecy is essential, an applicant must put the respondent on informal notice.[36]

22–121

Interim injunctions: general considerations.[37] The object of an interim injunction is to give to the claimant temporary protection against injury by the continuing violation of his rights for which he cannot be adequately compensated in damages in the action. This need to protect the claimant must be weighed against the corresponding need of the defendant to be protected against injury resulting from his being prevented from exercising his legal rights and for which injury he could not be adequately compensated under the claimant's cross-undertaking in damages. An interim injunction is thus a temporary, discretionary remedy. In general, it is not part of the court's function at this early stage in the litigation to try to resolve conflicts of evidence or difficult questions of law which call for detailed argument and mature consideration. In brief, at the interim stage the court usually has to make a decision when the existence of the right or the violation of it or both is uncertain and will remain uncertain until final judgment is given in the action. The court seeks to achieve a balance of justice, rather than of convenience. While the court disregards fanciful claims, it must contemplate that either party may succeed and do its best to ensure that nothing occurs pending trial which will prejudice their rights. This is difficult because both parties are often asserting wholly inconsistent claims.[38] Nevertheless the court should attempt to hold the ring until a just decision on the validity of the claim can be made.[39]

22–122

American Cyanamid v Ethicon. In this, the leading case, the House of Lords set out certain general princples to be applied on applications for interim injunctions. Those principles may be summarised as follows. The first question is whether the claimant has shown that there is a serious question to be tried. If not, the application will be refused. If so, the next question is whether, if the claimant were to obtain a permanent injunction at trial, he would be adequately compensated by an award of damages for the loss he had sustained before the trial as a result of the continuing acts of the defendant. If damages would be an adequate remedy, the court will normally refuse to grant an interim injunction, however strong the claimant's claim appears to be.[40] If damages would not be an adequate remedy for the claimant, the court goes on to consider whether the defendant, if he were

22–123

---

[34] *Linpac Mouldings Ltd v Eagleton Direct Export Ltd* [1994] F.S.R. 545, CA.

[35] *Hoffmann-La Roche & Co AG v Secretary of State for Trade and Industry* [1975] A.C. 295; *American Cyanamid Co v Ethicon Ltd* [1975] A.C. 396; *Morning Star Co-operative Society Ltd v Express Newspapers Ltd* [1979] F.S.R. 113; *Whitbread v Calder Valley Inns,* unreported, cited in *Square Moves Limited v Moorcroft* [1992] I.P.D. 15122; *TRP v Thorley,* CA (1993) noted in the *Supreme Court Practice 1999,* para.29/1A/21 and [1993] 8 SCP News.

[36] *Practice Direction—Interim Injunctions,* para.4.3(3); *Chancery Guide,* para.5.4.

[37] See, generally, *American Cyanamid Co v Ethicon Ltd* [1975] A.C. 396.

[38] *Francome v Mirror Group Newspapers Ltd* [1984] 1 W.L.R. 892.

[39] *Att.-Gen. v Guardian Newspapers Ltd* [1987] 1 W.L.R. 1248.

[40] *American Cyanamid Co v Ethicon Ltd* [1975] A.C. 396; *British Association of Aesthetic Plastic*

to succeed at the trial, would be adequately compensated under the claimant's cross-undertaking in damages for the loss which he had sustained before the trial by being prevented from doing the acts sought to be restrained. If damages in the measure recoverable under the undertaking would be an adequate remedy and the claimant would be in a financial position to pay them, there would be no reason upon that ground for refusing an interim injunction. If the court is in doubt as to the adequacy of the respective remedies in damages available to either the claimant or the defendant or both, the question of the balance of convenience arises. The expression "balance of justice" may be better.[41] At this stage, the court considers the potential injustice to the claimant if the injunction is withheld and the potential injustice to the defendant if the injunction is granted. The course to be taken is that which would involve the least risk of ultimate injustice, having regard to the actual and potential rights and liabilities of the parties on both sides.[42] Many factors may be relevant, including the extent to which the disadvantages to each party would be incapable of being compensated in damages in the event of his succeeding at trial. If the extent of such uncompensatable damage would not differ widely, it is relevant to consider the strength of the parties' respective cases, at least if it is apparent on undisputed evidence that the strength of one party's case is disproportionate. In the last resort, where other factors appear to be evenly balanced, it is the prudent course to take such measures as are calculated to preserve the *status quo*.[43]

22–124 *Series 5 Software v Ltd v Clarke*.[44] In this case, Laddie J. sought to reformulate the principles applicable to the grant of interim injunctions, as follows: (1) The grant of an interim injunction is a matter of discretion and depends on all the facts of the case. (2) There are no fixed rules as to when an injunction should or should not be granted. The relief must be kept flexible. (3) Because of the practice adopted on the hearing of applications for interim relief, the court should rarely attempt to resolve complex issues of disputed fact or law. (4) Major factors to bear in mind are (a) the extent to which damages are likely to be an adequate remedy for each party and the ability of the other party to pay, (b) the balance of convenience, (c) the maintenance of the *status quo*, and (d) any clear view the court may reach as to the relative strength of the parties' cases.[45] This decision is frequently cited,[46] but the Court of Appeal has left open the question whether or not it is correct.[47]

Surgeons v Cambright Ltd [1987] R.P.C. 549; *Baltimore Aircoil Co Inc & Others v Evapco & Another* (1994) I.P.D. 17081. There is nothing to stop a claimant who is confident about the merits of his case seeking summary judgment and an interim injunction in the alternative.

[41] *Francome v Mirror Group Newspapers Ltd* [1984] 1 W.L.R. 892 at 899.

[42] *Fleming Fabrications Ltd v Albion Cylinders Ltd* [1989] R.P.C. 47; *Mail Newspapers Plc v Express Newspapers Plc* [1987] F.S.R. 90; *Shelley Films Ltd v Rex Features Ltd* [1994] E.M.L.R. 134.

[43] *American Cyanamid Co v Ethicon Ltd* [1975] A.C. 396.

[44] [1996] F.S.R. 273.

[45] [1996] F.S.R. 273, at 286.

[46] See, *e.g.*, *Antec International Ltd v South Western Chicks (Warren) Ltd* [1997] F.S.R. 278 (passing off, Laddie J: *Series 5* contains the reasons why the merits may be taken into account); *Barnsley Brewery Company Ltd v RBNB* [1997] FSR 462 (passing off, Walker J.: *Series 5* a valuable reminder of the background and context of *American Cyanamid Co v Ethicon Ltd* [1975] A.C. 396 and its basic message—avoidance of mini-trials and doing least injustice); *Intelsec Systems Ltd v Grech-Cini* [2001] 1 W.L.R. 1190 (Nicholas Warren Q.C. as a result of *Series 5* it may be that the court can consider the strength of the parties' cases "more widely" in relation to the balance of convenience); *Wyeth Holdings Corporation v Alpharma* [2003] EWHC 3196 (Pat) (patents; Laddie J stated that he did not resile from anything he said in *Series 5*, but was unable to form a clear view on the merits).

[47] *Guardian Media Group plc v Associated Newspapers Ltd*, unreported, January 20, 2000, para.18.

Application of the *American Cyanamid* principles: general. The paragraphs **22–125**
immediately following deal with certain cases where the *American Cyanamid*
principles do not apply to the grant of interim injunctions or apply in modified
form. Thereafter, an attempt is made to discuss the application of the *American
Cyanamid* principles so far as they are relevant to the rights covered in this work.

Where decision will determine the case. Where the case will in effect be decided **22–126**
on the application for interim relief, the principles in *American Cyanamid* do not
apply.[48] This is frequently the case when the court is considering a contractual
provision which restrains certain activity (*e.g.* the use of confidential information) for a short period. Depending on the facts, the same may apply in a copyright case. The precise significance of the fact that the grant or refusal of an
injunction will determine the case appears to depend on the facts. In *NWL Ltd v
Woods*,[49] Lord Diplock stated that in such a case the degree of likelihood that the
claimant will succeed is a factor to be brought into the balance when weighing
the risks that injustice will result from deciding the application one way or the
other. In some cases this has been held to mean that the court should attempt to
reach a view on the merits.[50] In others, however, where the court has not been
able to reach such a view, the fact that the grant of an injunction would be
determinative of the case has led it to refuse one altogether.[51]

Passing-off cases. In some passing-off cases it has been argued that the outcome **22–127**
of the application for an interim injunction will determine the case because the
grant of an injunction is likely to lead to a permanent change of name by the defendant (or the permanent adoption of a different name from that intended).
However, there is no rule of law that in a passing-off case the claimant must establish a stronger case than a serious issue to be tried.[52] Nevertheless, in a
passing-off case the Court of Appeal has held that the *American Cyanamid* rules
have a "degree of flexibility" and do not prevent the court from giving proper
weight to any clear view of the merits, where this can be reached without the
need for a mini-trial.[53] Such a clear view may not be difficult to reach where all
that is required is a comparison of the parties' respective packaging. In the same
case, the Court of Appeal held that it is particularly important to give "proper
weight" to the merits when the grant or refusal of an injunction will affect the
commercial outcome of the case.[54] In general, moreover, the strength of the parties' respective cases may be taken into account because it affects the likelihood
that they will suffer damage between the grant or refusal of the interim injunction
and the trial and is therefore relevant to the balance of convenience.[55]

Cases involving freedom of expression. Section 12 of the Human Rights Act **22–128**
1998[56] applies where a court is considering whether to grant any relief which, if

---

[48] *NWL Ltd v Woods* [1979] 1 W.L.R. 1294; *Cayne v Global Natural Resources plc* [1984] 1 All
E.R. 225; *Lawrence David Ltd v Ashton* [1989] F.S.R. 87; *Lansing Linde v Kerr* [1991] 1 W.L.R.
251; *Entec Pollution Control Ltd v Abacus Mouldings* [1992] F.S.R. 332; *Instance v Denny Bros
Printing Ltd* [2000] F.S.R. 869.

[49] [1979] 1 W.L.R. 1294.

[50] See, *e.g. Lansing Linde v Kerr* [1991] 1 W.L.R. 251; *Sun Valley Foods Ltd v Vincent* [2000]
F.S.R. 825; *Instance v Denny Bros Printing Ltd* [2000] F.S.R. 869; *BBC v Talksport Ltd* [2001]
F.S.R. 6.

[51] *Cayne v Global Natural Resources plc* [1984] 1 All E.R. 225; *Entec Pollution Control Ltd v
Abacus Mouldings* [1992] F.S.R. 332.

[52] *Elan Digital Systems Ltd v Elan Computers Ltd* [1984] F.S.R. 373; *CPC (United Kingdom) Ltd v
Keenan* [1986] F.S.R. 527.

[53] *Guardian Media Group plc v Associated Newspapers Ltd*, unreported, January 20, 2000, para.18.

[54] *ibid.*

[55] See below, para. 22–133, below.

[56] c.42.

granted, might affect the exercise of the right to freedom of expression.[57] Where this is the case, no such relief is to be granted so as to restrain publication before trial unless the court is satisfied that the applicant is likely to establish that publication should not be allowed.[58] The effect of this is that the *American Cyanamid* test does not apply. After considerable uncertainty as to the correct test,[59] the House of Lords has now held that "likely" has an extended meaning which sets the normal standard higher than the Cyanamid standard but which permits the court to dispense with that higher standard where particular circumstances make this necessary.[60] In general, therefore, the standard is one of "probably" or more likely than not. However, there will be cases where a lesser degree of likelihood will suffice. Examples include cases where the potential adverse consequences of disclosure would be particularly graveSuch as a case where the claimant's claim depended on a question of fact on which he had an arguable but distinctly poor case, but where the disclosure of the information would lead to a grave risk of personal injury: *Cream Holdings Ltd v. Banerjee* [2004] UKHL 44; [2004] 3 W.L.R. 918, at para.19. and where a short-lived injunction is necessary in order to enable the court to hear and give proper consideration to an application for interim relief. *Cream Holdings Ltd v. Banerjee* [2004] UKHL 44; [2004] 3 W.L.R. 918, para.22. Section 12(3) goes on to provide that the court must have particular regard to the importance of the Convention right of freedom of expression.[61] It then provides that where the proceedings relate to material which the respondent claims, or which appears to the court, to be journalistic, literary or artistic material (or to conduct connected with such material), the court must have particular regard to the following three matters: the extent to which the material has, or is about to become available to the public; the extent to which it is or would be in the public interest for the material to be published; and any relevant privacy code.[62] Section 12 does not apply to defamation cases where rights of privacy or confidence are not involved.[63]

22–129 **Section 12 of the Human Rights Act and privacy cases: *A v B*.[64]** In this case, which concerned a confidential information claim, the Court of Appeal, with a view to reducing the number of authorities necessary on interim applications

---

[57] That is, the right to free expression laid down by Art.10 of the European Convention on Human Rights: see Human Rights Act 1998, s.12(1).

[58] Human Rights Act 1998, s.12(3). s.12(2) provides that where the respondent is neither present nor represented, no such relief is to be granted unless the court is satisfied that the applicant has taken all practical steps to notify the respondent or there are compelling reasons why the respondent should not be notified.

[59] In *Imutran Ltd v Uncaged Campaigns Ltd* [2002] F.S.R. 2, Morritt V.-C. noted that the word "likely" suggested a higher standard than the ordinary Cyanamid standard but doubted whether the difference would be significant in most cases. In *Cream Holdings Ltd v. Banerjee* [2003] EWCA Civ 103, paras. 61 and 121, the Court of Appeal held that the phrase "is likely to establish" meant "has a real prospect of establishing" rather than "is more likely than not to establish".

[60] *Cream Holdings Ltd v. Banerjee* [2004] UKHL 44; [2004] 3 W.L.R. 918, para.20.

[61] For an example of an application of this subsection, see *Psychology Press Ltd v Flanagan* [2002] EWHC 1205, QBD.

[62] Human Rights Act 1998, s.12(4)(a), (b).

[63] *Greene v Associated Newspapers Ltd* [20004] EWCA Civ 1462: *Bonnard v Perryman* [1891] 2 Ch. 269 still applies in such cases. Accordingly, in a defamation case where the defendant contends that the words complained of are true and swears he will plead and prove the defence of justification, the court will not grant an interim injunction unless (exceptionally) it is satisfied that the defence cannot succeed.

[64] [2002] EWCA Civ 337; [2003] Q.B. 195. The House of Lords refused leave to appeal on May 30, 2002.

involving privacy and section 12, set out guidelines for the determination of such applications.[65] They are as follows:

(1) General. Whether any injunction is granted is a matter for the discretion of the judge, to be exercised in accordance with well-established principles, including the need to establish that after trial it is likely that an injunction will be granted, while recognising that the interim decision may well determine the outcome of the proceedings.

(2) Balance. If an injunction is refused, the claimant may be deprived of his or her only remedy of any value. However, this must be weighed against the defendant's rights of freedom of expression as embodied in section 12.

(3) "... likely to be established that publication should not be allowed". As to the word "likely", useful guidance was provided in *Imutran v Uncaged Campaigns Ltd*.[66]

(4) Press freedom. The fact that if an injunction is granted it will interfere with the freedom of the press is a matter of particular importance.[67]

(5) Relevance of public interest. The fact that under section 12(4) the court must have particular regard to whether it would be in the public interest for the material to be published does not mean that the court can interfere with the freedom of the press where there is no identifiable public interest. Regardless of the quality of the material, *prima facie* the court should not interfere with publication.

(6) Legal basis. In all or the great majority of situations, an action for breach of confidence will provide the necessary protection. Accordingly, at first instance it can be readily accepted that it is unnecessary to tackle the "vexed question" of whether there is a separate cause of action based on a new tort of infringement of privacy.

(7) Protectable interest. In most cases the question whether there is an interest capable of being the subject of a claim for privacy should not be allowed to be the subject of detailed argument. Usually the answer will be obvious. Where it is not, to answer the question will often be unnecessary because the weaker the claim for privacy the more likely that it will be outweighed by the claim based on freedom of expression.

(8) Public interest. The same is true where the public interest is relied on to oppose the grant of an injunction. In the majority of cases it will be obvious whether a public interest is involved. If it is not, the public interest is unlikely to be decisive. In any event, the citation of authority on this issue is unlikely to be helpful.

(9) Existence of duty. The question whether there is a confidential relationship should not give rise to problems of law: a duty of confidence will arise whenever a party knows or ought to know that the other person can reasonably expect his privacy to be protected.[68] The difficulty will be as to the relevant facts. Whether a duty exists will depend on all the circumstances of the relationship between the parties at the time of the threatened or actual breach.

---

[65] Although these guidelines were not expressly approved by the House of Lords in *Campbell v MGN Ltd* [2004] UKHL 22, they received generally favourable comment in that decision.

[66] Note, however, that since *A v B* was decided, the *Imutran* decision (*Imutran Ltd v Uncaged Campaigns Ltd* [2002] F.S.R. 2) has been overtaken by that in *Cream Holdings Ltd v Banerjee* [2003] EWCA Civ 103. See the previous paragraph.

[67] Applying the dictum of Hoffmann L.J. in *R. v Central Independent Television PLC* [1994] Fam. 192 at 201–204.

[68] Applying the dictum of Lord Goff in *Att-Gen v Guardian Newspapers (No.2)* [1990] 1 A.C. 109, HL at 281.

(10) Mode of obtaining the information. If there is an intrusion in a situation where a person can reasonably expect his privacy to be respected then that intrusion will be capable of giving rise to liability in an action for breach of confidence unless it can be justified.[69] Obvious examples of such intrusion are the bugging of someone's home or the use of other surveillance techniques. However, the fact that information is obtained as a result of unlawful activities does not mean that its publication should necessarily be restrained.[70] Depending on the nature of the activity there may be other remedies. On the other hand, the fact that unlawful means have been used to obtain the information could well be a compelling factor when it comes to exercising discretion.

(11) Sexual relationships. More difficult is the situation where the alleged intrusion is as a result of the reporting of information to a third party by a party to the relationship which creates the privacy. This is a material factor where two people have shared a sexual relationship outside marriage. If one wishes to exercise his or her Article 10 rights this must impact on the other's rights to maintain confidentiality. Where the parties are married, special considerations may arise. Where they are not, the fact that the confidence is a shared confidence which only one of the parties wishes to preserve does not extinguish the other's right to have the confidence respected, but it does undermine that right. The more stable the relationship, the greater will be the significance attached to it.

(12) Public figures. A public figure is entitled to a private life but must recognise that his actions will be more closely scrutinised by the media. Even trivial facts about a public figure can be of great interest to the public. Conduct which in the case of a private individual would not be the appropriate subject of comment can be the proper subject of comment in the case of a public figure. The public figure may hold a position where higher standards of conduct are expected by the public, may be a role model or may set the fashion. The higher the public figure's profile the more likely that this will be the position. Whether or not he has courted publicity, he may be a legitimate subject of public attention. However, if he has courted publicity, he may have less ground to object to the intrusion which follows. In many of these situations it would be overstating the position to say that there is a public interest, but if the public have an understandable and so a legitimate interest in being told the information, then this may properly be taken into account. The courts must not ignore the fact that if newspapers do not publish information which the public are interested in, there will be fewer newspapers.[71]

(13) Issues of taste. In drawing up a balance sheet between the parties' respective interests, courts should not act as censors or arbiters of taste. If there is no case for restraining publication, the fact that a more lurid approach will be adopted by the publisher or broadcaster than the court would regard as unacceptable is irrelevant.

(14) Codes of practice. Section 12(4) requires the court to take account of any relevant privacy code, but that is only one of a number of factors to be taken into account. Courts may well find the Press Complaints Commis-

---

[69] Applying *Venables v News Group Newspapers Ltd* [2001] 2 W.L.R. 1038 at para.81.

[70] Following *Australian Broadcasting Corporation v Lenah Game Meats Pty Ltd* [2001] H.C.A. 63.

[71] Referring to Council of Europe Resolution 1165 of 1998, paras 6–12. For the application of these principles to the facts of individual cases, see *A v B* itself, *Campbell v MGN Ltd* [2004] UKHL 22 and *Archer v Williams* [2003] EWHC 1670, QB. For a detailed summary at first instance of the recent authorities in this area, see *Douglas v Hello! Ltd* [2003] EWHC 786, Ch D, at paras 186–193.

sion Code of Practice, and in particular its provisions as to privacy, harassment and public interest to be of assistance. Relevant extracts are as follows:

> "3. *Privacy* (i) Everyone is entitled to respect for his or her private and family life, home, health and correspondence. A publication will be expected to justify intrusions into any individual's private life without consent. (ii) The use of long-lens photography to take pictures of people in private places without their consent is unacceptable. Note—Private places are public or private property where there is a reasonable expectation of privacy.

> "4. *Harassment* ... (ii) [Journalists and photographers] must not photograph individuals in private places (as defined by the note to clause 3) without their consent; must not persist in telephoning, questioning, pursuing or photographing individuals after having been asked to desist; must not remain on their property after having been asked to leave and must not follow them.

> "*Public interest* 1. The public interest includes: (i) Detecting or exposing crime or a serious misdemeanour. (ii) Protecting public health and safety. (iii) Preventing the public from being misled by some statement or action of an individual or organisation ...".

A newspaper which flouts the privacy provisions of the Code is likely to have its claim to freedom of expression trumped by Article 10(2) considerations of privacy.[72] However, the court should discourage advocates from relying on individual decisions of the Press Complaints Commission which are at best no more than illustrative of how it performs its functions.

The Court went on to state that frequently what is required is not a technical approach to the law but a balancing of the facts. The weight to be attached to each relevant consideration will vary depending on the precise circumstances. If the balance does not point clearly in either direction, interim relief should be refused.

Public interest cases. Where a defendant wishes to raise a public interest defence, special rules apply. They are considered above.[73] **22–130**

American Cyanamid: **Adequacy of damages.** In actions in respect of the rights covered in this work, damages are often not an adequate remedy since there are difficulties both in ascertaining and in quantifying such damage as injury to the claimant's property, business, commercial opportunity, reputation and goodwill.[74] The court will take into account the fact that the defendant might not be in a **22–131**

---

[72] Applying *Douglas v Hello! Ltd* [2001] Q.B. 967.

[73] See paras 22–82 *et seq.*, above.

[74] Examples include: *Elanco Products Ltd v Mandops (Agrochemical Specialists) Ltd* [1979] F.S.R. 46 (copyright); *Mothercare Ltd v Robson Books Ltd* [1979] F.S.R. 446 (passing off); *Rolls Royce Motors Ltd & Another v Zanelli & Others* [1979] R.P.C. 148 (copyright and trade mark); *News Group Newspapers Ltd v The Rocket Record Co Ltd* [1981] F.S.R. 89 at 106 (trade mark and passing off); *Elan Digital Systems Ltd v Elan Computers Ltd* [1984] F.S.R. 373 (passing off); *Games Workshop Ltd v Transworld Publishers Ltd* [1993] F.S.R. 705 (trade mark); *Ciba-Geigy Plc v Parke Davis & Co Ltd* [1994] F.S.R. 8 at 22 (passing off and injurious falsehood); *Jian Tools for Sales Inc v Roderick Manhattan Group Ltd & Another* [1995] F.S.R. 924 (passing off); *Antec International Ltd v South Western Chicks (Warren) Ltd* [1997] F.S.R. 278 (passing off); *P.G. Mavros (Private) Ltd v Ponter*, unreported, Laurence Collins Q.C., July 7, 1999 (copyright); *Quad International Inc v Goldstar Publications Ltd* [2003] EWHC 2081 (passing off). See, however, *IVS Technologies (PVT) Ltd v APM Technologies SA*, Michael Briggs Q.C., April 7, 2003, *Audi Performance Racing v Revo Technick Ltd* [2003] EWHC 1668, Ch D and *Vollers Corsets Company Ltd v Cook* [2003] EWHC 2693, Ch D, all copyright cases in which it was held that damages would be an adequate remedy for the claimant but not the defendant.

financial position to meet a claim for substantial damages against him.[75] Conversely, the court will take into account the ability or otherwise of the claimant to compensate the defendant on the cross-undertaking in damages.[76] The mere fact that a party is of slender means is not, however, conclusive.[77]

22–132 *American Cyanamid*: **Balance of convenience**. There are many factors varying from case to case which will influence the court's decision on the balance of convenience. For example, in some cases the court has held it against a defendant, in granting an injunction, that the defendant has walked into an existing situation with his eyes open and taken a calculated risk.[78] The court will discount obligations incurred by the claimant with a view to bolstering up his case on the balance of convenience.[79] On the other hand, it has been held against a claimant that the effect of the injunction would be disastrous to the defendant and disrupt his business,[80] even though it appears that the defendant has acted in a surreptitious way in the manner that he has gone about establishing his business.[81]

22–133 **The relevance of the merits to the balance of convenience**. In *American Cyanamid*, it was held that if the extent of the uncompensatable damage would not differ widely as between the two respective parties, it is relevant to consider the strength of their respective cases, provided that it is apparent on undisputed evidence that the strength of one party's case is disproportionate. In practice, the strength of the parties' respective cases is often taken into account on the balance of convenience because it affects the likelihood that they will suffer damage between the grant or refusal of the interim injunction and the trial.[82]

---

[75] *Missing Link Software v Magee* [1989] F.S.R. 361 at 368; *Mirage Studios v Counter-Feat Clothing Company Ltd* [1991] F.S.R. 145 at 152; *Dyrlund-Smith A/S v Turberville Smith Ltd* [1998] F.S.R. 774.

[76] *Morning Star Co-operative Society Ltd v Express Newspapers Ltd* [1979] F.S.R. 113. In some cases, the court may require the provision of a bond (*Anton Piller KG v Manufacturing Processes Ltd* [1976] R.P.C. 719; *JC Penney Co Inc v Penneys Ltd* [1975] R.P.C. 367; *Harman Pictures NV v Osborne* [1967] 1 W.L.R. 723; *Globelgance BV v Sarkissian* [1974] R.P.C. 603) or a payment into court (*Vernon & Co (Pulp Products) Ltd v Universal Pulp Containers Ltd* [1980] F.S.R. 179 at 191; *CPC (United Kingdom) Inc v Keenan* [1986] F.S.R. 527 at 536; *Brupat Ltd v Sandford Marine Products Ltd* [1983] R.P.C. 61 at 67).

[77] *Apple Corps Ltd v Lingasong Ltd* [1977] F.S.R. 345; *Allen v Jambo Holdings Ltd* [1980] 1 W.L.R. 1252; [1980] 2 All E.R. 502, CA.

[78] *Hymac v Priestman Bros.Ltd* [1978] R.P.C. 495; *Netlon v Bridport* [1979] F.S.R. 530; *News Group Newspapers Ltd v The Rocket Record Co Ltd* [1981] F.S.R. 89 at 107; *BBC v Talbot Motor Co Ltd* [1981] F.S.R. 228; *Elida Gibbs Ltd v Colgate-Palmolive Ltd* [1983] F.S.R. 95; *Elan Digital Systems Ltd v Elan Computers Ltd* [1984] F.S.R. 373; *Reckitt & Colman Products Inc v Borden Inc* [1987] F.S.R. 228 at 240; *Consorzio del Prosciutio di Parma v Marks & Spencer Plc* [1990] F.S.R. 530 at 541.

[79] *Raindrop Data Systems Ltd v Systemics Ltd* [1988] F.S.R. 354.

[80] *Fison Ltd v E J Godwin (Peat) Industries Ltd* [1976] R.P.C. 653; *Baskin Robbins Ice Cream Co v Gutman* [1976] F.S.R. 545; *IVS Technologies (PVT) Ltd v APM Technologies S.A.*, Michael Briggs Q.C., April 7, 2003; *Audi Performance Racing v Revo Technick Ltd* [2003] EWHC 1668 (Ch) and *Vollers Corsets Company Ltd v. Cook* [2003] EWHC 2693 (Ch).

[81] *Potters-Ballotini v Weston Baker* [1977] R.P.C. 202.

[82] See the following first instance decisions: *Series 5 Software Ltd v Clarke* [1996] F.S.R. 273 (restrictive covenants and confidential information); *Antec International Ltd v South Western Chicks (Warren) Ltd* [1997] F.S.R. 278 (passing off); *Barnsley Brewery Company Ltd v RBNB* [1997] FSR 462 (passing off); *CMI Centres for Medical Innovation GmbH v Phytopharm plc* [1999] F.S.R. 235 (confidence); *Wyeth Holdings Corporation v Alpharma* [2003] EWHC 3196, Pat Ct (patents and passing off,); *Quad International Inc v Goldstar Publications Ltd* [2003] EWHC 2081 (passing off). In *Red Bull GmbH v Mean Fiddler Music Group Plc*, Lewison J, April 28, 2004 (passing off), the Judge held that the grant of an injunction would effectively determine the action but that the correct test was whether there was a serious issue to be tried, albeit that he should scrutinise the evidence with particular care. However, it seems the defendant did not argue that the court should give a judgment on the merits, but rather that the correct test was whether there was a "*prima facie* case". It is not clear what authorities were cited to the Judge.

American Cyanamid: Status quo. Where other factors appear to be evenly bal-   **22–134**
anced, the court will often take such measures as are calculated to preserve the
status quo. If, on the one hand, the defendant is enjoined temporarily from doing
something which he has not done before, the only effect of the interim injunction
in the event of his succeeding at the trial may be to postpone the date at which he
is able to embark on a course of action which he has not previously found it necessary to undertake. If, on the other hand, the defendant is interrupted in the
conduct of an established enterprise, the injunction would cause much greater inconvenience to him since he would have to start again to establish it in the event
of his succeeding at the trial.[83] The preservation of the *status quo* particularly
favours the grant of an injunction in those cases where the defendant has only
just begun to do the act complained of and where he has no established business
or his sales and capital investment have been small, while the claimant has an
established business.[84] In such cases it is often easier to calculate the damage
which the defendant will suffer by reason of the injunction than it is to calculate
the damage which will be done to the claimant if the defendant is not restrained.
For example, it may be easier to calculate the expenditure thrown away by a defendant in printing and promoting a book, the publication of which is restrained
by injunction, than it is to calculate the injury which will be done to the sales and
goodwill of the claimant's existing book if publication by the defendant is not
restrained.[85] The courts will generally, as a temporary measure, protect a long-
established business against the activities of an interloper.[86]

There are, however, some cases in which the courts will take the view that the
damage to the claimant can be readily calculated by reference to the sales made
by the defendant and that the damage which would be done to the defendant by
preventing him from getting a foot in the market as soon as possible is not easily
quantifiable.[87] The defendant may undertake to keep an account of his sales.[88]
Where there is only a risk of unquantifiable damage to the claimant and a certainty
of unquantifiable damage to the defendant the court will often refuse to maintain
the *status quo* and dismiss a claim for an injunction.[89] One course taken by the
court in such cases is to grant or refuse an injunction and order a speedy trial of
the action.[90]

---

[83] *American Cyanamid Co v Ethicon Ltd* [1975] A.C. 396.
[84] *Elanco Products Ltd v Mandops (Agrochemical Specialists) Ltd* [1979] F.S.R. 46; *Polydor Ltd v
Harlequin Record Shop Ltd* [1980] 1 C.M.L.R. 669 at 676; *Sodastream Ltd v Thorn Cascade Co
Ltd* [1982] R.P.C. 459; *Biba Group Ltd v Biba Boutique* [1980] R.P.C. 413; *Esanda Ltd v Esanda
Finance Ltd* [1984] F.S.R. 96 (High Ct. of New Zealand); *Mail Newspapers Plc v Insert Media
Ltd* [1987] R.P.C. 521; *Fleming Fabrications Ltd v Albion Cylinders Ltd* [1989] R.P.C. 47; *Miss-
ing Link Software v Magee* [1989] F.S.R. 361 at 368; *Alfa Laval Cheese Systems Ltd v Wincanton
Engineering Ltd* [1990] F.S.R. 583 at 594; *Wyeth Holdings Corporation v Alpharma* [2003]
EWHC 3196.
[85] *Mothercare Ltd v Robson Books Ltd* [1979] F.S.R. 466.
[86] *Chill Foods (Scotland) Ltd v Cool Foods Ltd* [1977] R.P.C. 522.
[87] *Catnic Components Ltd v Stressline Ltd* [1976] F.S.R. 157; *Kwik Lok Corporation v WBW
Engineers Ltd* [1975] F.S.R. 237; *Belfast Ropework Co Ltd v Pixdane Ltd* [1976] F.S.R. 337;
Temple Instruments Ltd v Hollis Heels Ltd [1973] R.P.C. 15; *Polaroid Corp. v Eastman Kodak
Co* [1976] F.S.R. 530; [1977] F.S.R. 25, CA; *Netlon v Bridport-Gundry* [1979] F.S.R. 530;
Hunter v Fitzroy Robinson & Partners [1978] F.S.R 167; *Potters-Ballotini Ltd v Weston Baker*
[1977] R.P.C. 202; *Corruplast Ltd v George Harrison (Agencies) Ltd* [1978] R.P.C. 761; *Taverner Rutledge Ltd v Trexapalm Ltd* [1977] R.P.C. 275; *The Boots Co Ltd v Approved Prescrip-
tion Services Ltd* [1988] F.S.R. 45; *John Wyeth & Bro. Ltd v M & A Pharmachem* [1988] F.S.R.
26.
[88] *Catnic Compenents Ltd v Stressline Ltd* [1976] F.S.R. 157 at 160, 163; *Concrete Systems v Devon Symonds Holdings* [1978] S.A.S.R. 79.
[89] *John Walker & Sons Ltd v Rothmans International Ltd* [1978] F.S.R. 357; *Unider Ltd v Marks &
Spencer Plc* [1988] R.P.C. 275.
[90] *Lawrence David Ltd v Ashton* [1989] F.S.R. 87; *Johnson & Bloy (Holdings) Ltd v Wolstenholme
Rink Plc* [1989] F.S.R. 135. (both cases where an injunction was granted to enforce a restrictive

22–135   **The time factor.** One problem which has arisen in determining the *status quo* is the fixing of the relevant time. It has been suggested[91] that the relevant date for determining the *status quo* may variously be the date on which the defendant first did the offending act, or the date on which the claimant first learned of that act, or the date on which the claimant first ought to have been aware of the defendant's act, or the date when the claimant first complained to the defendant, or the date when the claimant sent his letter before action or the date when the claimant issued his claim form. There is much to be said in favour of the view that the *status quo* to be preserved by an injunction is that state of affairs which existed before the defendant first began to do the act which the claimant seeks to restrain by injunction.[92] However, in *Garden House Foods Limited v Milk Marketing Board*,[93] Lord Diplock said (*obiter*[94]):

> "In my opinion, the relevant *status quo* to which reference was made in *American Cyanamid* is the state of affairs existing during the period immediately preceding the issue of the Writ claiming the permanent injunction, or if there be unreasonable delay between the issue of the Writ and the motion for an interlocutory injunction, the period immediately preceding motion. The duration of that period since the state of affairs last changed must be more than minimal, having regard to the total length of the relationship between the parties in respect of which the injunction is granted; otherwise the state of affairs before the last change would be the relevant *status quo*".

It may be very difficult to identify the *status quo* in a rapidly changing commercial situation; for example, at the outset of a character merchandising operation.[95] Where there is no letter before action and there is delay after the issue of the claim form before service, the date of service of the claim form may be the relevant date for deciding what represents the *status quo*.[96] Although a defendant who chooses to continue with a course of action after a dispute arises cannot gain any benefit thereby, if the defendant was substantially committed to a course of action when the dispute arose and continued along that course, the status quo is represented by the defendant being committed to that course of action. The position is not analogous to the building cases where the defendant builder presses ahead as quickly as possible with construction after complaint is made so as to present a court with a *fait accompli*. That type of situation represents a change of course.[97]

22–136   **Other relevant considerations.** As well as the interests of freedom of speech (as to which, see above), the interests of the public in general may also be taken into account in the exercise of the court's discretion.[98] Unexplained delay in applying

---

covenant or obligation of confidence by ex-employees, pending a speedy trial); *Alfa Laval Cheese Systems Ltd v Wincanton Engineering Ltd* [1990] F.S.R. 583 at 594.

[91] *Alfred Dunhill Ltd v Sunoptic SA* [1979] F.S.R. 337; see *Alfa Laval Cheese Systems Ltd v Wincanton Engineering Ltd* [1990] F.S.R. 583 at 594.

[92] *Metric Resources Corp. v Leasemetric Ltd* [1979] F.S.R. 571; *John Walker & Sons Ltd v Rothmans International Ltd* [1978] F.S.R. 357; *Consorzio del Prosciutto di Parma v Marks & Spencer Plc* [1990] F.S.R. 530 at 541; *The British Diabetic Association v The Diabetic Society* noted at [1992] I.P.D. 15103.

[93] [1984] 1 A.C. 130 at 140; see also *Jian Tools for Sales Inc v Roderick Manhattan Group Ltd* [1995] F.S.R. 924.

[94] See *The British Diabetic Association v The Diabetic Society* noted at [1992] I.P.D. 15103.

[95] *Mirage Studios v Counter-Feat Clothing Company Ltd* [1991] F.S.R. 145 at 153.

[96] *Graham v Delderfield* [1992] F.S.R. 313.

[97] *Management Publications Ltd v Blenheim Exhibitions Group Plc* [1991] F.S.R. 550.

[98] *R. v Secretary of State for Transport, ex p. Factortame Ltd (No.2)* [1991] A.C. 603; *Cambridge Nutrition Ltd v BBC* [1990] 3 All E.R. 523; *Beggars Banquet Records Ltd v Carlton Television Ltd* [1993] E.M.L.R. 349.

for interim relief will weigh heavily against the claimant and is often fatal.[99] However, the court will take into account whether or not the defendant has been led into expense, or lulled into security, or misled by the inaction of the claimant.[1] The question is whether the delay is culpable or unreasonable so as to make it unjust to grant the injunction sought. Delay is not prejudicial, for example, if it is explicable by attempts to settle the dispute.[2] A claimant is not precluded from asserting his rights, even by way of interim injunction, merely because he has tolerated some acts which have infringed his rights.[3] Section 239 of the 1988 Act provides that where, in a design right case, a defendant undertakes to take a licence of right, no injunction shall be granted against him. However, this does not mean that no injunction may be granted in any case where the defendant offers immediately to take a licence of right. Where a question can reasonably be raised as to the financial ability of the defendant to comply with the financial obligations that would be imposed by the licence, it is incumbent on him to show that the undertaking is one which he can reasonably be expected to honour.[4] Furthermore, if the offer is to enter into a licence of right at the end of the trial if the defendant loses, the application for an injunction should be decided on *American Cyanamid* principles.[5]

Cross-undertaking in damages. The court will normally refuse to grant an interim injunction unless the claimant is willing to furnish an undertaking by himself or by some other willing and responsible person to pay any which the defendant (or any other person served with or notified of the order) sustain which the court considers the claimant should pay.[6] A claimant should specifically give evidence as to his ability to meet his liability on the cross-undertaking.[7] The court retains a discretion as to whether and when to enforce the undertaking[8] and may not do so if it considers that the conduct of the defendant makes it inequitable to do so. If the undertaking is enforced, damages are assessed on the same basis as if the undertaking had been a contract between the claimant and the defendant that the claimant would not prevent the defendant from doing that which he was

22-137

[99] *Southey v Sherwood* (1817) 2 Mer. 435; *Mawman v Tegg* (1826) 2 Russ. 385, 393; *Lewis v Chapman* (1840) 3 Beav. 133; *Kenitex Chemicals Inc v Kenitex Textured Coating Ltd* [1965] 2 F.S.R. 109 (three months' delay—no injunction); *Bravington Ltd v Barrington Tennant* [1957] R.P.C. 183 (three months' unexplained delay); *Park Court Hotel Ltd v Trans-World Hotels Ltd* [1970] F.S.R. 89; *Celanese Corporation v Akzo Chemie UK Ltd* [1976] F.S.R. 273 (no injunction—six months' delay between launching of motion and hearing of motion); *Radley Gowns Ltd v Costas Spyrou* [1975] F.S.R. 445; *Russel-Uclaf v G. P. Searle & Co Ltd* [1977] F.S.R. 125; *Foseco International Ltd v Fordath Ltd* [1975] F.S.R. 507; *Nichols Advanced Vehicle Systems Inc & Others v Rees, Oliver & Others* [1979] R.P.C. 127; *My Kinda Town v Soll* [1983] R.P.C. 407 at 418; *Century Electronics Ltd v CVS Enterprises Ltd* [1983] F.S.R. 1 (four months' delay after becoming aware of defendant's activities); *The Quaker Oats Company v Alltrades Distributors Ltd* [1981] F.S.R. 9 (two months' delay after learning of imports of infringing goods); *Hoover Plc v George Hulme Ltd* [1982] F.S.R. 565 at 587, 588; *Dalgety Spillers Foods Ltd v Food Brokers Ltd* [1994] F.S.R. 504; *Baltimore Aircoil Co Inc & Others v Evapco & Another* (1994) I.P.D. 17081; *BASF Plc v CEP (UK) Plc* (1996) I.P.D. 19030.
[1] See previous note and *Byford v Rainbow Communications Ltd* (1995) I.P.D. 18132; *Express Newspapers Plc v Liverpool Daily Post & Echo Plc* [1985] 3 All E.R. 680.
[2] *CPC (United Kingdom) Ltd v Keenan* [1986] F.S.R. 527.
[3] *News Group Newspapers Ltd v The Mirror Group Newspapers (1986) Ltd* [1989] F.S.R. 126; *Raychem Corp. v Thermon (UK) Ltd* [1989] R.P.C. 423.
[4] *Dyrlund Smith A/S v Turberville Smith Ltd* [1998] F.S.R. 774.
[5] *ibid.*
[6] *Hoffmann-La Roche & Co AG v Secretary of State for Trade and Industry* [1975] A.C. 295. Practice Direction—Interim Injunctions, para.5.1.
[7] *Brigid Foley Ltd v Elliott* [1982] R.P.C. 433.
[8] *Cheltenham & Gloucester Building Society v Ricketts* [1993] 1 W.L.R. 1545; *Balkanbank v Taher & Others* [1995] 1 W.L.R. 1056.

restrained from doing by the terms of the injunction.[9] If the interim order restrains the defendant in wider terms than prove at trial to have been justifiable, then the court will normally order an inquiry on the claimant's cross-undertaking even though he has been successful in proving infringement.[10] Even if the claimant chooses not to pursue his action at trial, the defendant is not entitled to an inquiry on the cross-undertaking as of right and no such inquiry will be ordered if the court is satisfied that the defendant did in fact infringe copyright.[11] The cross-undertaking is automatically implied, both in cases of the grant of an injunction and also on the giving of an undertaking to the court by the defendant,[12] whether by consent or otherwise.

22–138   **Interim mandatory injunctions.** Different principles govern the court's discretion to grant interim mandatory injunctions which are usually more drastic in their effects. According to Phillips L.J. in *Zockoll Group Ltd v Mercury Communications Ltd*,[13] the following passage from the judgment of Chadwick J. in *Nottingham Building Society v Eurodynamics Systems*[14] is all the citation that should be necessary on the question of mandatory injunctions:

> "In my view the principles to be applied are these. First, this being an interlocutory matter, the overriding consideration is which course is likely to involve the least risk of injustice if it turns out to be 'wrong' in the sense described by Hoffman J.[15]
>
> Secondly, in considering whether to grant a mandatory injunction, the court must keep in mind that an order which requires a party to take some positive step at an interlocutory stage, may well carry a greater risk of injustice if it turns out to have been wrongly made than an order which merely prohibits action, thereby preserving the *status quo*.
>
> Thirdly, it is legitimate, where a mandatory injunction is sought, to consider whether the court does feel a high degree of assurance that the claimant will be able to establish this right at a trial. That is because the greater the degree of assurance the claimant will ultimately establish his right, the less will be the risk of injustice if the injunction is granted.
>
> But, finally, even where the court is unable to feel any high degree of assurance that the claimant will establish his right, there may still be circumstances in which it is appropriate to grant a mandatory injunction at an interlocutory stage. Those circumstances will exist where the risk of injustice if this injunction is refused sufficiently outweigh the risk of injustice if it is granted".[16]

An interim mandatory injunction may be granted to require a defendant to take all practical steps to recover allegedly infringing items which have

---

[9] *Hoffmann-La Roche & Co AG v Secretary of State for Trade and Industry* [1975] A.C. 295; *Novello v James* (1854) 24 L.J. Ch. 111; *Air Express Ltd v Ansett Transport Industries (Operations) Pty* (1979) 146 C.L.R. 249 at 267 (High Ct of Australia); *Finansiera Avenida SA v Shiblaq*, *The Times*, January 14, 1991. See, also, *Helitune Ltd v Stewart Hughes Ltd* [1994] F.S.R. 422.

[10] *John Richardson Computers Limited v Flanders (No.2)* [1994] F.S.R. 144.

[11] *Waterlow Publishers Ltd v Rose & Another* [1995] F.S.R. 207.

[12] *Catnic Components Ltd v Bainbridge Bros (Engineers) Ltd* [1976] F.S.R. 112.

[13] [1998] F.S.R. 360 at 366.

[14] [1993] F.S.R. 468 at 474.

[15] A reference to *Films Rover Ltd v Cannon Film Sales Ltd* [1987] 1 W.L.R. 670.

[16] These principles were applied in *Psychometric Services Ltd v Merant International Ltd* [2002] F.S.R. 8 (If source code was not delivered up claimant likely to go into liquidation; delivery up ordered).

been distributed. Where title has passed, the court may order the defendant to ask for them back.[17]

Procedure. The application is made under CPR Part 23.[18] The following points may be made in relation to the rights covered in this work. First, on any application, whether with or without notice, a party is not entitled to rely on confidential evidence which has not been or will not be revealed to the other side.[19] Thus a defendant against whom a without notice injunction has been granted is entitled to see all the evidence on which the injunction was granted, so that he can comment on it and adduce contrary evidence. Secondly, the evidence should deal with questions as to what damage the claimant would suffer if the injunction is refused and what damage the defendant will suffer if the injunction is granted[20] and it is now common for evidence to be filed as to the respective financial means of the claimant and the defendant.[21] Thirdly, except where secrecy is essential an applicant for an interim injunction should take steps to notify the respondent informally of the application.[22] Fourthly, on a without notice application, the applicant is under a duty to make full and frank disclosure of all relevant facts. Breach of this duty may lead to the discharge of the order.[23] The applicant's advocate should also draw to the court's attention any defence (whether of fact or law or mixed fact and law) which could be advanced on behalf of the respondent in opposition to the application. Fifthly, it is desirable that an interim injunction is expressed in words which the person restrained can readily understand, particularly if he is not in court when it is granted, and that the terms of the injunction should be clear.[24] It is also desirable that an injunction is not expressed in terms such as the "claimant's copyright", since it has been held that this means that in order to succeed on an application to commit the defendant for contempt, the claimant is obliged to prove the very things which are in issue in the action.[25]

22–139

Costs of applications. Where the application is determined on the balance of convenience, the normal order is that costs are reserved to the trial judge.[26] However, the court may depart from that principle, for example where the outcome of the hearing of the application was so plain that the court should conclude that a party had wasted time and money in fighting the issue[27] or where the court forms a realistic view that the case is not likely to go to trial and the substantive merits are very plain.[28]

22–140

---

[17] *British Broadcasting Corporation v Precord Ltd* noted at [1991] I.P.D. 15023.
[18] For draft entries for the application notice, see Vol.2 at J2.vi. See, generally, CPR Part 25: *Practice Direction—Interim Injunctions*; and Ch.5 of the *Chancery Guide*.
[19] *VNU Business Publications BV v Ziff Davies (UK) Ltd* [1992] R.P.C. 269, following *Re K* [1963] Ch. 381, CA, and *WEA Records v Visions Channel 4* [1983] 1 W.L.R. 721, CA.
[20] *Antec International Ltd v South Western Chicks (Warren) Ltd* [1997] F.S.R. 278.
[21] *Standex International Ltd v CB Blades* [1976] F.S.R. 114.
[22] *Practice Direction—Interim Injunctions*, para.4.3(3); *Chancery Guide*, para.5.4.
[23] *R. v Kensington Income Tax Commissioners, ex parte Princess Edmond de Polignac* [1917] 1 Q.B. 486 at 509; *Brink's Mat Ltd v Elcombe* [1988] 1 W.L.R. 1350.
[24] *Staver Co Inc v Digitext Display Ltd* [1985] F.S.R. 512; *Video Arts Limited v Paget Industries Ltd* [1988] F.S.R. 501; *Khorasandrijan v Bush* [1993] Q.B. 727; *Hunter Kane Ltd v Watkins*, Ch D, February 12, 2003 (Bernard Livesey Q.C.).
[25] *The Staver Company Inc v Digitext Display Ltd* [1985] F.S.R. 512; *Video Arts Limited v Paget Industries Ltd* [1988] F.S.R. 501; see, however, *Spectravest Inc v Aperknit Ltd* [1988] F.S.R. 161, in which the first of these authorities was not followed, although the point was academic (see at p.170). For standard forms of injunction, see Vol.2 at J2.vii and viii.
[26] *Desquenne et Giral UK Ltd v Richardson* [2001] F.S.R. 1.
[27] As in the pre- CPR case of *Bushbury Land Rover v Bushbury Ltd* [1997] F.S.R. 709, referred to in *Picnic at Ascot v Derigs* [2001] F.S.R. 2.
[28] As in the pre- CPR case of *Direct Line Group Ltd v Direct Line Estate Agency Ltd* [1997] F.S.R. 374, also referred to in *Picnic at Ascot v Derigs* [2001] F.S.R. 8.

(ii) Search (formerly Anton Piller) orders

22–141   **Search orders.** The High Court has jurisdiction, on an application made to the court by a claimant without notice and in private, to make a mandatory order requiring a defendant to permit or allow the claimant and his representatives to enter the defendant's premises, as specified in the order, so as to inspect articles and documents relevant to the proceedings and to remove them or take copies of them[29] and even to take the proceeds of infringing articles.[30] A draft form of order is annexed to *Practice Direction—Interim Injunctions*.[31] There are many decided cases on seizure orders and reference should be made to the relevant specialist works. However, the following points can be made. First, this form of order has, in many copyright, confidence and passing-off cases, proved to be one of great efficacy, because the defendant is taken completely by surprise before he is able to deal further with the documents and articles relating to the offending acts. The defendant knows nothing of the proceedings until he is required by the order to admit the claimant and his representatives to the premises. Secondly, three conditions must be satisfied before the court will make an order: first, the claimant must show that he has an extremely strong *prima facie* case; secondly, the claimant must show that he has suffered, or is likely to suffer, very serious and irreparable damage if an order is not made; and, thirdly, there must be clear evidence that the defendant has in his possession incriminating documents or things and that there is a real possibility that he may destroy such material before any application can be made on notice.[32] Thirdly, the order must be served and carried out in the presence of a supervising solicitor, who is experienced in the workings of search orders and who is wholly independent of the claimant and his solicitors.[33] The introduction of this requirement has considerably increased the cost and complexity of such applications. Fourthly, if the defendant wishes to apply to the court to discharge the order as having been improperly obtained, he is allowed to do so.[34] Fifthly, the order will only normally be made in respect of precisely defined premises.[35] Sixthly, as a matter of the law of evidence, information derived or obtained as a result of a search order which ought never have to have been obtained is admissible.[36] The court, however, has a jurisdiction *in personam* to restrain the use made of such information where it would be inequitable for the claimant to do so.[37] Seventhly, the applicant is under a duty to make full disclosure to the court and to act in the utmost good faith.[38] The court may discharge a search order on the grounds of non-disclosure and order costs to be

---

[29] Civil Procedure Act 1997, s.7; CPR 25.1(1)(h); *Anton Piller KG v Manufacturing Processes Ltd & Others* [1976] Ch. 55; *EMI Ltd v Pandit* [1976] R.P.C. 333; *Pall Europe Ltd v Microfiltrex Ltd* [1976] R.P.C. 326; *Rank Film Distributors Ltd & Others v Video Information Centre & Others*, [1982] A.C. 380; *International Electronics Ltd v Weigh Data Ltd, The Times*, March 13, 1980; *Gates v Swift* [1981] F.S.R. 57; *Booker McConnell Plc v Plascow* [1985] R.P.C. 425; *Columbia Picture Industries Inc v Robinson* [1987] Ch. 38; [1986] F.S.R. 367; *Manor Electronics Ltd v Dickson* [1988] R.P.C. 618; *Swedac Ltd v Magnet & Southern Plc* [1989] F.S.R. 243; *Universal Thermosensors Ltd v Hibben* [1992] 1 W.L.R. 840.

[30] *CBS United Kingdom Ltd v Lambert* [1983] Ch. 37.

[31] Certain specified paragraphs of the standard form should be deleted in intellectual property cases as a result of the withdrawal in such cases of the privilege against self-incrimination (see para. 22–147, below).

[32] *Anton Piller K.G. v Manufacturing Processes Ltd* [1976] Ch. 55.

[33] *Practice Direction—Interim Injunctions*, para.7.2.

[34] Standard form order, paras 10 and 27.

[35] *Protector Alarms Ltd v Maxim Alarms Ltd* [1978] F.S.R. 442; *Cook Industries Inc v Galliher* [1979] Ch. 439; *Universal City Studios Inc v Mukhtar & Sons Ltd* [1976] 2 All E.R. 330.

[36] *Helliwell v Piggot-Sims* [1980] F.S.R. 356.

[37] *Lord Ashburton v Pape* [1913] 2 Ch. 469. *Guess? Inc v Lee Seck Mon* [1987] F.S.R. 125 (CA of Hong Kong); *English & American Insurance Co Ltd v Herbert Smith* [1988] F.S.R. 232; *Naf Naf SA v Dickens (London) Ltd* [1993] F.S.R. 424.

[38] *Booker McConnell Plc v Plascow* [1985] R.P.C. 425; see also *Dormeuil Frères SA v Nicolian*

awarded on an indemnity basis, with immediate assessment. For the operation of the privilege against self-incrimination in these applications, see below.[39]

(iii) Identity of infringers

General. In an action for infringement of copyright or related rights, the court now frequently exercises its jurisdiction, on an interim application, to make an order requiring a defendant to make an affidavit setting out the names and addresses of the suppliers and purchasers of infringing material and articles known to him.[40] He is also required to state in the affidavit the dates and quantities supplied, and to exhibit documents relating to supplies and purchases.[41] This is a valuable form of order because it enables the claimant in a copyright action, for example, to obtain from retailers of infringing goods details as to the wholesale or manufacturing sources of supply. The basis of the jurisdiction is that a person, whether he is himself an infringer, or has become innocently involved without personal liability in the wrongdoing[42] of others, is under a duty to assist those injured by those acts to give full information by way of disclosure of documents and of the identity of the wrongdoers.[43] It matters not if they are out of the jurisdiction.[44] The application should be made promptly.[45]

22–142

Conditions. The jurisdiction to order disclosure exists if three conditions are satisfied: First, the third party has become mixed up in the transactions of which disclosure is required.[46] It is sufficient if it can be shown that there is "a good indication" of wrongdoing but not every piece of a pleaded case is in position.[47] Secondly, the order for disclosure must be for a legitimate purpose. It is not necessary for the applicant to show that he intends to sue the person so identified. It is sufficient that (for example) he intends to dismiss a wrongdoer who is an

22–143

International (Textiles) Ltd [1989] F.S.R. 255. This duty includes a duty to point out to the judge any differences between the order sought and the standard order annexed to *Practice Direction—Interim Injunctions* (see *The Gadget Shop Ltd v The Bug.com Ltd* [2001] F.S.R. 26) and to inform a judge of the Queen's Bench Division in a copyright and breach of confidence case that the natural forum is the Chancery Division (see *Elvee Ltd v Taylor* [2001] EWCA Civ 1943). See generally *Civil Procedure 2004*, para.25.3.5.

[39] See para. 22–147, below.

[40] Such orders are not included in the list of interim remedies in CPR 25.1(1). However, the list is not intended to be exhaustive: CPR 25.1(3).

[41] *Radio Corporation of America v Reddington's Rare Records* [1974] 1 W.L.R. 1445; *Harry Freedman v Hillingdon Shirts Co Ltd* [1975] F.S.R. 449; *EMI Ltd & Another v Sarwar* [1977] F.S.R. 146; *Loose v Williamson* [1978] 1 W.L.R. 639; *EMI Ltd & Others v Pandit* [1976] R.P.C. 333.

[42] In *Ashworth Hospital Authority v MGN Ltd* [2001] 1 W.L.R. 515, the Court of Appeal held that the jurisdiction applied in breach of confidence cases. In the House of Lords (*Ashworth Hospital Authority v MGN Ltd* [2002] UKHL 29), it was held (*obiter*) that it did not matter whether the wrongdoing was tortious, in breach of contract, a civil wrong or a crime (paras 34, 53). In *Financial Times Ltd v Interbrew SA* [2002] EWCA Civ 274, the Court of Appeal held that the jurisdiction applies in relation to equitable as well as common law wrongs, in particular in breach of confidence cases.

[43] *Norwich Pharmacal Co v Customs and Excise Commissioners* [1974] A.C. 133; *British Steel Corp. v Granada Television Ltd* [1981] A.C. 1096; *X Ltd v Morgan-Grampian Plc* [1990] 2 W.L.R. 1000.

[44] *Smith Kline & French Laboratories Ltd v Global Pharmaceutics Ltd* [1986] R.P.C. 394 and *Jade Engineering Ltd v Antiference Window Systems* [1996] F.S.R. 461.

[45] *Wilmot Breeden Ltd v Woodcock Ltd* [1981] F.S.R. 15.

[46] In *The Coca-Cola Company v British Telecommunications Plc* [1999] F.S.R. 518, the claimant wished to sue a third party who had been involved in the delivery of infringing goods. The court was satisfied that it was very probable that a mobile telephone had been used by the third party in connection with the delivery. The respondent service provider was ordered to disclose the address of the third party. See also *Totalise plc v The Motley Fool Ltd* [2001] 4 E.M.L.R. 750 (order made against operators of website on whose discussion boards defamatory material had been posted anonymously).

[47] *Carlton Film Distributors Ltd v. VCI PLC* [2003] F.S.R. 47.

employee. However, it is necessary for the applicant to identify the purpose for which the information is sought and the use of the material will then be restricted to that purpose unless the court orders otherwise.[48] Thirdly, the procedure must not offend against the "mere witness" rule which prevents a person from obtaining disclosure from someone who would be compellable to give the information as a witness, either orally or on a summons to produce document under CPR 34.3(2). Finding out the identity of the tortfeasor falls outside that rule.

22–144   **Scope of order.** The jurisdiction is not confined to cases of identifying wrongdoers.[49] It has been used to discover the names and addresses of persons to whom the defendant had sent a letter which the claimant alleged contained false statements.[50] It may be exercised to discover what has happened to property and in aid of a freezing order, where it is just and convenient to make the order.[51] The jurisdiction to order disclosure against a person who has become mixed up in the torts of others applies *a fortiori* against the wrongdoer himself.[52] Disclosure may therefore be ordered against a defendant if there is a reasonable cause of action pleaded against him.[53]

In *Roberts v Jump Knitwear*[54] it was held that no disclosure order would be made to reveal the names of innocent third parties who had been supplied with allegedly infringing articles. It is doubtful whether that decision was correct.[55] Under section 99(1) of the 1988 Act there is a right to apply for an order for delivery up and under that jurisdiction an order for delivery up may be made regardless of the existence of any knowledge of the defendant that the copy is an infringing copy. In those circumstances the court has jurisdiction to make an order against the person who has allegedly put infringing copies into circulation requiring him to disclose the identity of the persons to whom such copies have been supplied. The fact that it has not yet been established that the copies are infringing copies is not a bar to this jurisdiction. The issue will not be decided between the claimant and the third party until proceedings under section 99 have been brought and determined.[56]

In appropriate cases, the disclosure of names of the defendant's customers may be refused or limited to the claimant's advisers so as to protect the defendant from approaches to his customers by the claimant which might damage his goodwill or might amount to a misuse of confidential information.[57]

The obligation to give information extends to all information necessary to enable the claimant to decide whether it is worth suing the wrongdoer or not.[58] In principle, a defendant may be ordered to state whether the order for goods has

---

[48] *Ashworth Hospital Authority v MGN Ltd* [2002] UKHL 29, at paras 45 to 53, overruling *Financial Times Ltd v Interbrew SA* [2002] EWCA Civ 274.
[49] *Jade Engineering Ltd v Antiference Window Systems* [1996] F.S.R. 461; *cf. Arab Monetary Fund v Hashim* [1992] 2 All E.R. 911, suggesting that the jurisdiction in *Norwich Pharmacal Co v Customs and Excise Commissioners* [1974] A.C. 133 extends only to identifying the wrongdoers and no further.
[50] *CHC Software Care Ltd v Hopkins & Wood* [1993] F.S.R. 241.
[51] *Mercantile Credit (Europe) AG v Aiyela* [1994] Q.B. 366 and [1993] F.S.R. 745 (Hobhouse J.); *cf. Arab Monetary Fund v Hashim* [1992] 2 All E.R. 911, suggesting that the *Norwich Pharmacal* jurisdiction extends only to identifying the wrongdoers and no further.
[52] *Norwich Pharmacal Co v Customs and Excise Commissioners* [1974] A.C. 133 at p.175C–D.
[53] *CFC Software Care Ltd v Hopkins & Wood* [1993] F.S.R. 241.
[54] [1981] F.S.R. 527.
[55] *Lagenes Ltd v It's At (UK) Ltd* [1991] F.S.R. 492; it was not followed in *Jade Engineering Ltd v Antiference Window Systems* [1996] F.S.R. 461.
[56] *Lagenes Ltd v It's At (UK) Ltd* [1991] F.S.R. 492.
[57] *Kentron Properties Pty Ltd v Jimmy's Co Ltd* [1979] F.S.R. 86 at 96; *Sega Enterprises Ltd v Alca Electronics & Others* [1982] F.S.R. 516; *Moore & Craven* [1871] 7 L.R. Ch. App.94; *Jade Engineering Ltd v Antiference Window Systems* [1996] F.S.R. 461.
[58] *Société Romanaise de la Chaussure SA v British Shoe Corporation Ltd* [1991] F.S.R. 1.

been solicited by the manufacturer or whether the defendant has initiated the order, and to give disclosure of all relevant documents. In *Société Romanaise de la Chaussure SA v British Shoe Corporation Ltd*,[59] the defendant was ordered to state the grounds of its belief that it was the only customer for the goods and that the manufacturer held no other stocks. The defendant was also ordered to give disclosure of all documents relevant to the grounds of belief. It was pointed out that the information was disclosable in due course in any case. It was not harmful to the defendant to order the information to be produced now, but it was harmful to the claimant if left to speculate in the absence of the information.

Costs. Normally, where the respondent is in no way implicated with the unlawful act in question, the applicant will be ordered to pay the respondent's costs, including the costs of complying with the order. There may be exceptions to this rule, but not where the respondent had a genuine doubt as to whether the applicant was entitled to the order; the respondent was under a legal obligation not to reveal the information (or the legal position was not clear and the respondent had a reasonable doubt as to his obligations); the respondent might be subject to proceedings if disclosure was given voluntarily; the respondent would or might suffer damage by giving the disclosure; or the disclosure would or might infringe a legitimate interest of another.[60]   **22–145**

Section 10 of the Contempt of Court Act 1981.[61] Section 10 provides that no Court may require a person to disclose, nor is any person guilty of contempt of court for refusing to disclose, the source of information contained in a publication for which he is responsible, unless it be established to the satisfaction of the court that disclosure is necessary in the interests of justice or national security or for the prevention of disorder or crime. The leading case on section 10 is now *Ashworth Hospital Authority v MGN Ltd.*[62] In this case, the House of Lords held that section 10 must now be applied in accordance with the jurisprudence of Article 10 of the European Convention on Human Rights.[63] Accordingly, the court must start from the proposition that freedom of expression constitutes one of the essential foundations of a democratic society and that the safeguards to be afforded to the press are of particular importance. Protection of journalistic sources is one of the basic conditions for press freedom since without such protection sources may be deterred from assisting the press in informing the public on matters of public interest. As a result, the vital watchdog role of the press may be undermined and the ability of the press to provide accurate and reliable information may be adversely affected. Accordingly, an order for source disclosure cannot be compatible with Article 10 unless it is justified by an overriding requirement in the public interest.[64] It is "in the interests of justice", in the sense in which the phrase is used in section 10, that persons should be enabled to exercise important legal rights and to protect themselves from serious legal wrongs whether or not resort to legal proceedings in a court of law will be necessary to attain those objectives.[65] The courts will normally protect journalists' sources from identification. Disclosure will only be ordered when it is necessary and proportionate. The necessity for any restriction of freedom of expression must be convincingly established. Limitations on the confidentiality of journalistic   **22–146**

---

[59] [1991] F.S.R. 1..
[60] *Totalise plc v The Motley Fool Ltd* [2001] 4 E.M.L.R. 750.
[61] c.49.
[62] [2002] UKHL 29.
[63] As set out in *Goodwin v United Kingdom* (1996) 22 E.H.R.R. 123.
[64] [2002] UKHL 29 at para.38.
[65] [2002] UKHL 29, para.39.

sources call for the most careful scrutiny by the court.[66] Any restriction on freedom of expression must meet a pressing social need and the restriction must be proportionate to a legitimate aim which is being pursued.[67] In *Ackroyd v Mersey Care NHS Trust*[68] , the Court of Appeal held that in most cases where a source disclosure order was sought against a journalist, it would not be appropriate to make the order on a summary judgment application.[69]

22–147   **Self-incrimination.** The frequent use of search orders in proceedings for infringement of copyright coupled with orders to give disclosure of names and addresses of suppliers and related documents used to give rise to problems with the privilege against self-incrimination. The circumstances in which infringement takes place frequently involves the commission of criminal offences or subjects the defendant to penalties. The infringement may even involve a criminal conspiracy to defraud. In such cases, the defendant used to be able to claim the privilege against self-incrimination to set aside an order for disclosure or production of documents or information.[70]

In order to meet that situation the position as to the privilege against self-incrimination was altered by the provisions of section 72 of the Supreme Court Act 1981 (as amended by Schedule 7 to the 1988 Act).[71] The privilege has been withdrawn from a party and his or her spouse in the proceedings and circumstances specified in section 72. A person is not excused from answering questions put to him or from complying with an order by reason that to do so would tend to expose him or his or her spouse to proceedings for a related offence or the recovery of a related penalty. The withdrawal of the privilege applies to civil proceedings in the High Court for infringement of rights pertaining to any "intellectual property"—*i.e.* "patent, trademark, copyright, design right, registered design, technical or commercial information or other intellectual property"—or for passing off. It also applies to proceedings to obtain disclosure of information relating to the infringement of such a right.

The defendant is, however, given the safeguard that no statement or admission by a person in answering a question or complying with an order is, in proceedings for a related offence, admissible against the person or his spouse.[72] It is admissible in proceedings for perjury or contempt of court. A "related offence" is one which is committed by or in the course of the infringement or passing off to

---

[66] [2002] UKHL 29, para.61.

[67] [2002] UKHL 29, para.62. The case concerned the publication by a newspaper of verbatim extracts from the medical records of Ian Brady, one of the Moors murderers, who was a patient at Ashworth Security Hospital. The extracts appeared to have come from the hospital's confidential computer database and to have been provided to the newspaper by an employee at the hospital in exchange for a cash payment. The hospital wished to identify the employee for the purposes of dismissing him. It was agreed that the integrity of the database was vital for the care and safety of individual patients. On the facts, the House of Lords upheld the disclosure order.

[68] [2003] EWCA Civ 663 at para.68.

[69] This case arose out of the disclosure made in *Ashworth Hospital Authority v MGN Ltd* [2002] UKHL 29. It had been anticipated that compliance with the order would result in the disclosure of the identity not only of the intermediary from whom the newspaper had received the information but also of the person, almost certainly an employee at Ashworth, who obtained the information from the database and passed it on to the newspaper. In the event, the newspaper, complying with the order, disclosed that the intermediary was a freelance journalist. That disclosure did not, however, reveal the identity of the original source. Accordingly, the hospital sought an order compelling the freelance journalist to disclose his source, who (it was accepted) was a person within the hospital who obtained the information about Brady from the database. The journalist resisted disclosure on the grounds that his position was distinguishable from that of the newspaper. It was argued that the journalist could not have a defence in the light of the decision in the *Ashworth Hospital* case. However, the Court of Appeal permitted the case to go to trial because the focus in the journalist's case was substantially different.

[70] *Rank Film Distributors Ltd v Video Information Centre* [1982] A.C. 380.

[71] *Crest Homes Plc v Marks* [1987] A.C. 829.

[72] The court may, however, permit the claimant, upon application, to inform the police of any al-

which the proceedings relate or "any offence" revealed by the facts on which the claimant relies in the proceedings. The effect of the definition of "related offence" is that it is only where there is a risk of further damage to the claimant that the defendant is denied the right to claim the privilege in respect of self-incrimination for offences not committed by or in connection with the alleged infringement. The "related offence" is defined in different and much wider terms in the case of proceedings to prevent future torts than in the case of proceedings for past or present infringements.[73]

In cases where section 72 does not apply, the privilege against self-incrimination still applies. It was held *in Tate Access Floors Inc v Boswell*[74] that the privilege applies in fraud actions where there is a real risk that the defendant may be prosecuted for perjury. It is not necessary for the defendant to claim the privilege: an order whereby the defendant may be incriminated should never be made. However, such an order can usually be made against a foreign corporation because there is no risk of prosecution. The defendant is not entitled to claim the privilege if he is adequately protected against prejudice.[75] Thus, an order may properly be made whose execution is conditional (a) upon the defendant being advised of his right to claim privilege and (b) upon his expressly declining the right.[76] The privilege should be claimed by the defendant himself on oath.[77] A defendant served with a search order is entitled to supply all documents which he claims may be incriminating to the supervising solicitor. If the latter decides that they are incriminating they will be excluded from the search.[78]

(iv) Freezing (formerly Mareva) injunctions

The court also has a wide discretionary jurisdiction to make restraint and disclosure orders in respect of a defendant's assets both in and outside England and Wales and both before and after judgment, in order to prevent a defendant from taking action, such as disposal of assets, designed to frustrate subsequent orders of the court in favour of a claimant. Many cases continue to be reported on the grant and discharge of freezing injunctions and reference should be made to more specialised works for a full account of this jurisdiction. As in the case of search orders, there are now standard forms of freezing injunctions.[79]

22–148

C. FINAL RELIEF

(i) Declaratory judgment

The court will not make a declaratory order to the effect that copyright will subsist in documents not yet in existence, but which it is anticipated will be brought into existence. There must be before the court specific documents, the character of which can be established.[80] The court will not make declarations of right amount-

22–149

---

leged theft of his property or of any admissions made by the defendant—see *Process Development Ltd v Hogg* [1996] F.S.R. 45.

[73] *Universal City Studios Inc v Hubbard* [1984] Ch. 225.
[74] [1991] Ch. 512.
[75] *AT & T Istel v Tully* [1993] A.C. 45, HL.
[76] *IBM United Kingdom Ltd v Prima Data International Ltd* [1994] 1 W.L.R. 719.
[77] *Downie & Others v Coe & Others*, The Times, November 28, 1997.
[78] See the standard order annexed to *Practice Direction—Interim Injunctions*, para.11.
[79] See *Practice Direction—Interim Injunctions*. Note that paragraph 9(2) of the standard form may require modification to take account of the withdrawal of the privilege against self-incrimination (as to which, see para. 22–147, above).
[80] *Odhams Press Ltd v London and Provincial Sporting News Agency, etc. Ltd* [1936] Ch. 357.

ing to conclusions of fact from hypothetical or assumed states of fact.[81] Nor will the court grant declaratory relief against a person who has not asserted any right.[82] There must be put before the court evidence of an actual or intended infringement of copyright and the court will not attempt an exhaustive enunciation of the factual circumstances in which infringement has or has not occurred.[83] The court will not normally grant on application for summary judgment a declaration that the defendant's work does not infringe the claimant's work. A declaration as to non-infringement is, like other forms of declaration, discretionary.[84] On the other hand, a declaration may be granted where a judgment is obtained without a trial (*e.g.* a default judgment), when full justice cannot otherwise be done. For example, a declaration may be granted that a publishing agreement is at an end, so facilitating an author in his efforts to sell his work elsewhere. It is important that the declaration in question should not effect the rights of anyone other than the defendants or the persons claiming through them.[85]

(ii) Permanent injunction

22–150   **General.** If the claimant succeeds at the trial in establishing infringement of copyright, he will normally be entitled to a permanent injunction to restrain future infringements.[86] There is no need for the claimant to prove actual damage.[87] The question whether an injunction ought to be granted permanently is one which is determined by reference to the circumstances and state of the law existing at the date when the question falls to be determined and the court's consideration is not confined to those circumstances existing at the date of the claim form. An injunction is a discretionary remedy, and general equitable principles will apply, for example, the "clean hands" principle.[88] The claimant must show positively that the defendant is likely to continue his infringement in cases where the prima facie position is that the infringement has occurred once and for all and is finished and done with.[89] If, in addition, the defendant had given a bona fide undertaking not to repeat the infringement, that is an important factor which would influence the court in refusing an injunction. In the majority of such cases, it would be very difficult for a claimant, whose rights had been infringed, to prove positively a definite likelihood of a repetition of the infringement. On the other hand, if the letter containing the undertaking contains a false justification of the infringement and the defendant persists in putting the claimant's rights in issue and maintain-

---

[81] *Wyke Group plc v Cooper Roller Bearings Co Ltd* [1996] F.S.R. 126.

[82] *ibid.*

[83] *Moorehouse & Angus Robertson (Publishers) Pty Ltd v University of New South Wales* [1976] R.P.C. 51.

[84] *Della Reed Ltd v Delkim Developments* [1988] F.S.R. 329.

[85] *Patten v Burke Publishing Co Ltd* [1991] F.S.R. 483; [1991] 1 W.L.R. 541, followed in *Aitbelaid v Nima, The Times,* July 19, 1991.

[86] *Weatherby & Sons v International Horse Agency and Exchange Ltd* [1910] 2 Ch. 297; *Performing Right Society Ltd v Ciryl Theatrical Syndicate Ltd* [1923] 2 K.B. 146; *Samuelson v Producers Distributing Co Ltd* (1931) 48 R.P.C. 580 at 593; *Performing Right Society Ltd v Mitchell and Booker (Palais de Danse) Ltd* [1924] 1 K.B. 762, 774; *Pride of Derby and Derbyshire Angling Association Ltd v British Celanese Ltd* [1953] Ch. 149, 181, 194; *Morris v Redland Bricks Ltd* [1970] A.C. 652 at 664D, 665F; *Colgate Palmolive Ltd v Markwell Finance Ltd* [1990] R.P.C. 197 at 200 and *Performing Right Society Ltd v Berman* [1975] F.S.R. 400 at 403; *Phonographic Performance Ltd v Maitra* [1998] 1 W.L.R. 870, CA; *Ludlow Music Inc v Williams* [2002] EWHC 638, Ch D. For an exceptional case where the court refused an injunction, see *Banks v EMI Songs Ltd (No.2)* [1996] E.M.L.R. 452 discussed in the next paragraph.

[87] *Smith v Johnson* (1863) 33 L.J.Ch. 137; *Campbell v Scott* (1842) 11 Sim. 31; *Weatherby & Sons v International Horse Agency and Exchange Ltd* [1910] 2 Ch. 297 at 305; *Hawkes & Son (London) Ltd v Paramount Film Service Ltd* [1934] Ch. 593 at 608.

[88] *Ocular Sciences Ltd v Aspect Vision Care Ltd* [1997] R.P.C. 289.

[89] *Performing Right Society Ltd v Berman* [1975] F.S.R. 400 (High Ct of Rhodesia); *P.R.S. v Butcher* [1975] F.S.R. 405 (High Ct of Rhodesia).

ing "a quite hopeless justification of its reprehensible conduct", justice requires that the claimant be protected by an injunction.[90] In *Performing Right Society Ltd v Berman*[91] infringement was alleged by the playing by a band of music at a club operated by the defendants. No undertaking had been given not to repeat the infringement. An injunction was granted notwithstanding that the club had subsequently closed down.

Damages in lieu. In the nineteenth century case of *Shelfer v City of London Electric Lighting Co*,[92] it was stated to be a "good working rule" that if the injury to the claimant's rights is small and capable of being estimated in money and can be adequately compensated by a small money payment and the case is one in which it would be oppressive to grant an injunction, the court may award damages in substitution for an injunction. In *Jaggard v Sawyer*, the Court of Appeal emphasised that the test is one of oppression and not merely the balance of convenience.[93] In *Banks v CBS Songs Ltd (No.2)*,[94] a record company argued that a songwriter's claim to an injunction should be refused on the basis of the *Shelfer* decision. The court rejected this submission on the grounds that since the copyright might last another century it was impossible to say that the claimant could be adequately compensated by a small money payment.[95] The court nevertheless refused an injunction because although the case was outside the working rule set out in *Shelfer*, it was "wholly exceptional": the defendants had been exploiting the lyrics for some 11 years; it was accepted that most of the commercial use had probably already occurred; and the claimant had made plain that what she really wanted was money—the claim for an injunction was made not because she wanted to stop the commercial exploitation but in order to negotatiate a price.

22–151

Statutory limits on grant of injunction. In proceedings for infringement of the right to object to derogatory treatment of a work,[96] the Court may, if it thinks it is an adequate remedy in the circumstances, grant an injunction on terms prohibiting the doing of any act unless a disclaimer is made, dissociating the author or director from the treatment of the work.[97] Occasionally, the 1988 Act provides that an injunction should not be granted.[98]

22–152

Delay in taking proceedings. The tendency of the court is not to refuse an injunction at the hearing of the action merely on account of delay in instituting proceedings,[99] subject to the provisions of the Limitation Act 1980. Of course, such delay may be a factor in establishing general equitable defences such as laches, acquiescence, waiver and estoppel. Under certain circumstances delay might be held to amount to a tacit permission to reproduce the work.[1]

22–153

---

[90] *Banier v News Group Newspapers Ltd* [1997] F.S.R. 812 at 816.
[91] [1975] F.S.R. 400 (High Ct of Rhodesia).
[92] [1895] 1 Ch. 287.
[93] [1995] 1 W.L.R. 269.
[94] [1996] E.M.L.R. 452.
[95] See, to the same effect, *Ludlow Music Inc v Williams* [2002] F.S.R. 57, where an attempt to invoke the *Shelfer* principle failed.
[96] CDPA 1988, s.80.
[97] s.103(2).
[98] See "undertaking to take licence of right", paras 22–77 *et seq.*, above and "innocently acquired illicit recordings and infringing articles", para. 22–81, above.
[99] *Hogg v Scott* (1874) L.R. Eq. 444; *Morris v Ashbee* (1868) L.R. 7 Eq. 34; *Fullwood v Fullwood* (1878) 9 Ch.D. 176; *Reliance Rubber Co Ltd v Reliance Tyre Co Ltd* (1925) 42 R.P.C. 91; *Aktiebologet Manus v R.J. Fullwood & Bland Ltd* (1948) 65 R.P.C. 329.
[1] *Rundell v Murray* (1821) Jac. 311; *Saunders v Smith* (1838) 3 My. & Cr. 711. See also *Ludlow Music Inc v Williams* [2001] F.S.R. 271 (summary judgment): arguable acquiescence defence and *Ludlow Music Inc v Williams* [2002] EWHC 638, Ch D (trial): if injunction had been sought

22–154   **Public policy, public interest and privacy cases.** An injunction may be refused on the grounds of public policy or public interest.[2] The principles set out in *A v B*[3] in relation to the grant of interim injunctions in cases involving privacy apply equally to the grant of final injunctions.[4]

22–155   **Scope of injunction: future and other works.** It has been held that an injunction will not be granted to restrain infringements of future numbers of a periodical, although the defendants have systematically copied from numbers already published[5] and that no injunction will be granted against copying a future football fixture list.[6] These cases probably do not represent the current state of the law and it is suggested that there is no reason in principle why an injunction should not be granted to protect future copyrights or other rights.[7]

22–156   **Scope of injunction: injunction post expiry of right.** In *Dyson Appliances Ltd v Hoover Ltd (No.2)*[8] , the defendant had infringed the claimant's patent by various forms of development activity, thus obtaining a "springboard" in the market which the court assessed at 12 months. Because of this, the claimant would have been entitled to "springboard" damages in respect of the period of 12 months after the expiry of the patent.[9] Because those damages would be very difficulty to quantify, the claimant was granted an injunction to restrain acts which would otherwise have infringed the patent for a period of 12 months after its expiry. It is not yet clear whether this decision will be applied to the rights covered in this work.[10]

22–157   **Scope of injunction: acts in respect of existing rights.** In general, where the claimant has established an infringement of his rights, and subject to the points made above, he is entitled to an injunction to restrain any future infringement of those rights.[11] Exceptionally, the court may grant relief in a narrower form. Thus, for example, in one passing-off and trade mark case, the Court of Appeal upheld

---

in respect of existing pressings of infringing CDs it would have been refused on grounds of acquiescence.

[2] See paras 22–82 *et seq.*, above.

[3] See para. 22–129, above.

[4] See e.g. at first instance *Douglas v Hello! Ltd* [2003] EWHC Civ 1373, Ch D, and *Archer v Williams* [2003] EWHC Civ 1670, QBD.

[5] *Cate v Devon, etc. Newspaper Co* (1889) 40 Ch.D. 500 at 507; *Sweet v GW Bromley & Co* [1905–10] Mac.C.C. 203; but see *Bradbury v Sharp* [1891] W.N. 123 and *TM Hall & Co v Whittington & Co* [1892] 18 V.L.R. 525.

[6] *Football League Ltd v Littlewoods Pools Ltd* [1959] Ch. 637.

[7] *Phonographic Performance Ltd v Amusement Caterers (Peckham) Ltd* [1963] 3 All E.R. 493 (in that case the court extended an existing injunction, so that it was not confined to works in the claimant's repertoire when the writ was issued; it is not clear from the report whether the injunction was granted against infringing future copyrights, or merely those copyrights owned by the claimant at the date of the injunction, as opposed to the date of the claim form); *Independent Television Publications Ltd v Time Out Ltd* [1984] F.S.R. 64; *Microsoft Corporation v Electro-Wide Ltd* [1997] F.S.R. 580 (injunction in respect of any of the claimant's copyrights in operating system software); *cf. Columbia Picture Industries v Robinson* [1987] Ch. 38; [1986] F.S.R. 367, where the court refused to grant an injunction extending to copyright in future films because it was often difficult to identify the owner or exclusive licensee of film copyright and it would therefore be impossible for the defendant to know what films were covered.

[8] [2001] R.P.C. 27.

[9] See *Gerber Garment Technology v Lectra Systems Ltd* [1997] R.P.C. 443.

[10] Note, however, that the injunction was granted under s.61(1) of the Patents Act 1977 (c.37), which is in rather different terms ss.96, 1911 and 229 of the 1988 Act. Furthermore, the *Dyson* decision (*Dyson Appliances Ltd v Hoover Ltd (No.2)* [2001] R.P.C. 27) was based in part on European patents jurisprudence.

[11] *Microsoft Corporation v Plato Technology Ltd*, CA, unreported, July 15, 1999. In *Coflexip SA v Stolt Comex Seaways MS Ltd* [1999] F.S.R. 483, a patent case, Laddie J. had held that where the defendant was an honest trader, the injunction should generally be limited to the acts found to infringe rather than to any acts of infringement of the whole patent. This decision was distinguished in *Aktiebolget Volvo v Heritage (Leicester) Ltd* [2000] F.S.R. 253 (trade marks; defendant had not acted in accordance with honest commercial practies) but followed in *Beautimatic International Ltd v Mitchell International Pharmaceuticals Ltd* [2000] F.S.R. 267 (trade

an injunction limited to dealing with software which the defendant knew or had reason to believe to be counterfeit.[12] It should, however, be noted that the court emphasised that this decision was confined to its facts. In another case involving passing off and trade marks, the court rejected undertakings which were qualified so that the defendant would not be in breach of them if it had at all times maintained in force a regulatory procedure to the satisfaction of the court and if it dealt expeditiously with any complaints from the claimant.[13]

Where portion only of the defendant's work is copied. Where only part of a work has been copied, and the part which has been copied from the claimant's work can be separated from that which has not been copied, an injunction will be granted only against the objectionable part or parts.[14] But even where a very large proportion of a work of a piratical nature is unquestionably non-infringing, if the parts which have been copied cannot be separated from those which are non-infringing without destroying the use and value of the original matter, he who has made an improper use of that which did not belong to him must suffer the consequences of so doing, and an injunction will be granted against the whole.[15] He has only himself to blame for the consequences of mixing another person's work with his own in such a way that they cannot be separated. Where the claim is for a permanent injunction, as distinct from an interim injunction, it will not usually be appropriate to weigh the damage which the defendant will suffer by reason of the injunction (for example, through the loss of non-infringing material), against the damage which the claimant will suffer if the injunction is refused.[16]

22–158

Form of injunction. The modern form of interim injunction contains provisions that:

22–159

"1. A defendant who is an individual who is ordered not to do something must not do it himself or in any other way; he must not do it through others acting on his behalf or on his instructions or with his encouragement.

2. A defendant which is a corporation and which is ordered not to do something must not do it itself or by its directors officers employees or agents or in any other way".[17]

Final injunctions are usually expressed in similar terms.[18]

The terms of the injunction must be clear, otherwise the court will not grant it. The defendant is entitled to know precisely what acts he is prohibited from committing.[19]

Enforcement of injunctions. Injunctions may be enforced against a defendant who is an individual by committal and sequestration; and against a defendant which is a body corporate, by sequestration; and also by committal and sequestra-

22–160

---

marks). However, Laddie J's decision was overruled by the Court of Appeal: *Coflexip S.A. v Stolt Comex Seaways MS Ltd* [2001] 1 All E.R. 952. Accordingly, the authority of the *Beautimatic* decision is doubtful.

[12] *Microsoft Corporation v Plato Technology Ltd*, CA, unreported, July 15, 1999.

[13] *British Telecommunications plc v Nextcall Telecom plc* [2000] F.S.R. 679: the proposed undertakings would have involved the court descending into the commercial arena in order to decide whether there had been a breach.

[14] *Jarrold v Houlston* (1857) 3 K. & J. 708; *Lamb v Evans* [1892] 3 Ch. 462.

[15] *Advanced Vehicle Systems Inc & Others v Rees, Oliver & Others* [1979] R.P.C. 127 at 141.

[16] *Macmillan Publishers Ltd v Thomas Reed Publications Ltd* [1993] F.S.R. 455 at 366, 467.

[17] See draft order in Vol.2 at J2.viii.

[18] See *e.g.* Vol.2 at J2.xii.

[19] *Staver Co Inc v Digitext Display Ltd* [1985] F.S.R. 512; *Columbia Picture Industries v Robinson* [1987] Ch. 38; [1986] F.S.R. 367; *Video Arts Limited v Paget Industries Ltd* [1988] F.S.R. 501; *Khorasandjian v Bush* [1993] Q.B. 727.

tion against its directors and other officers.[20] In less serious cases the court may, instead of these penalties, impose a fine and payment of costs,[21] or merely the payment of costs.[22] Breach of an undertaking to the court is punishable in the same way as breach of an injunction.[23] To establish contempt of court it is sufficient to prove that the defendant's conduct was intentional and that he knew all the facts which made it a breach of the order. It is not necessary to prove that the defendant knew it was a breach.[24] The court has to decide what the defendant has done, even if that involves deciding issues in the action.[25] If there is a dispute as to whether the defendant's conduct is a breach of an order or undertaking the defendant can apply to the court for guidance.[26] The court has a discretion to decline to hear a litigant's appeal where he has wilfully and contumaciously failed to comply with an order of the court.[27] Where, on an application to commit for contempt of court, the court is satisfied that the breach of the undertaking to the court is also a breach of contract by the contemnor, in respect of which there is no defence to a claim for damages, the court may make a summary award of damages in addition to an order for costs on an indemnity basis.[28]

(iii) Election between damages and account of profits

22–161 A successful claimant is usually entitled to an inquiry as to damages[29] or, at his election, an account of profits.[30] He is not entitled to both, since the principle which lies behind the equitable remedy of an account of profits is that the claimant condones the infringement and takes the profits made by the infringer for the use of his property.[31] The remedies are, therefore, mutually inconsistent and the claimant must elect between the two. Furthermore, a claimant who has chosen to sue more than one member of a chain of distribution may not elect for damages against one defendant and profits against another.[32] Once a clear, unequivocal election has been made, for example the entering of judgment for one or the

---

[20] RSC, Ord.45, r.5, Ord.46, r.5 and Ord.52, preserved by the CPR. *Att-Gen for Tuvalu v Philatelic Distribution Corporation Ltd* [1990] 1 W.L.R. 926.

[21] RSC, Ord.52, r.9; *Phonographic Performance Ltd v Amusement Caterers (Peckham) Ltd* [1964] Ch. 195; *Steiner Products Ltd v Willy Steiner Ltd* [1966] 1 W.L.R. 986; *Ronson Products Ltd v Ronson Furniture Ltd* [1966] R.P.C. 497; *Re Mileage Conference Group, etc. Ltd's Agreement* [1966] 1 W.L.R. 1137; *Re W. (B.) (An Infant)* [1969] 2 Ch. 50; *GCT (Management) Ltd v The Laurie Marsh Group Ltd* [1973] R.P.C. 432; in *Re Grantham Wholesale, etc. Ltd* [1972] 1 W.L.R. 559; *Jennison v Baker* [1972] 2 Q.B. 52.

[22] *Ronson Products Ltd v Ronson Furniture Ltd* [1966] R.P.C. 497. In contempt proceedings costs are usually awarded on an indemnity basis.

[23] *Re Mileage Conference Group, etc. Ltd's Agreement* [1966] 1 W.L.R. 1137; *Biba Ltd v Stratford Investments Ltd* [1973] R.P.C. 799.

[24] *British Telecommunications plc v Nextcall Telecom plc* [2000] F.S.R. 679.

[25] *Spectravest Inc v Aperknit Ltd* [1988] F.S.R. 161. Note, however, that it is desirable to avoid this by phrasing interim injunctions in terms which refer to specific acts rather than, for example, to "the claimant's copyright". See para. 22–139, above.

[26] *Spectravest Inc v Aperknit Ltd* [1988] F.S.R. 161.

[27] *X Ltd v Morgan Grampian Ltd* [1991] 1 A.C. 1, HL. However, this is a jurisdiction which should be exercised only exceptionally: *Atlantic Capital Corporation v Johnson* Independent, July 15, 1994.

[28] *Midland Marts Ltd v Hobday* [1989] 1 W.L.R. 1143.

[29] See paras 22–162 *et seq.*, below.

[30] See paras 22–175 *et seq.*, below.

[31] *Caxton Publishing Co Ltd v Sutherland Publishing Co Ltd* [1939] A.C. 178 at 198; *De Vitre (JD) v Betts (W)* (1873) L.R. 6, HL 319; *Island Records Ltd v Tring International Plc* [1995] F.S.R. 560. But see Laddie J.'s rejection of this justification in *Cala Homes (South) Ltd v Alfred McAlpine Homes East Ltd* [1996] F.S.R. 36; according to Laddie J. there is no need for the legal fiction of condoning the infringement—the claimant has to elect for the simple reason that the two remedies are inconsistent.

[32] *Spring Form Inc v Toy Brokers Ltd* [2002] F.S.R. 276. This is because once the claimant has elected to be compensated in damages for the appearance in commerce of the infringing article,

other,[33] the claimant cannot change his mind and opt for the other remedy. A claim form claiming only damages does not amount to such an election and the claimant will usually be permitted to amend at any time before judgment to include a claim for an account.[34] The election should be made at the latest when infringement is established,[35] but the claimant cannot be forced to make an election before then.[36] Prior to making his election, the claimant is entitled to disclosure and inspection of those documents and an order for the provision of that information which are necessary to enable him to make an informed choice.[37] This should not be an over-lengthy or unnecessarily sophisticated exercise. The claimant is not entitled to know exactly the amount of any damage or profits, but only to such information as the court considers to be a fair basis in the circumstances of the particular case for an election.[38]

(iv) Damages

General. Subject to any special defence as to damages,[39] a successful claimant is entitled to recover damages for the infringement of his right. Actions for infringement of moral rights, performers' non-property rights and the rights of persons having recording rights are treated as breaches of statutory duty[40] and, presumably, damages are assessed using the same principles as those applicable to the commission of any other breach of statutory duty.[41] For actions for infringement of copyright, design right and performers' property rights, the 1988 Act provides that all such relief by way of, *inter alia*, damages is available to the claimant as is available in respect of the infringement of any other property right.[42] It is often said that the measure of damage for copyright infringement is the depreciation caused by the infringement to the value of the copyright as a chose in action.[43] It has now been held that the principles set out in the patent case of *General Tire and Rubber Company v Firestone Tyre and Rubber Company Ltd* are applicable in copyright cases.[44] Accordingly, the general rule, as in the case of any other "economic" tort, is that the measure of damages is to be, so far as possible, that sum of money which will put the injured party in the same position

22–162

---

the compensation which he receives reflects all the commercial stages through which the article goes: see *Gerber Garment Technology v Lectra Systems Ltd* [1997] R.P.C. 443.

[33] *Island Records Ltd v Tring International Plc* [1995] F.S.R. 560, 563 (Lightman J.); *Led Builders Pty Ltd v Eagle Homes Pty Ltd (No.3)* (1996) 36 I.P.R. 293.

[34] *Thornton Hall Manufacturing Ltd v Shanton Apparel Ltd* (1988) 12 I.P.R. 48 (High Ct of NZ).

[35] *Redrow Homes Ltd v Betts Bros Plc* [1997] F.S.R. 828 at 831 (Court of Session (Inner House)); *Led Builders Pty Ltd v Eagle Homes Pty Ltd (No.3)* (1996) 36 I.P.R. 293.

[36] *Dr Martens Australia Pty Ltd v Bata Shoes Co of Australia Pty Ltd* (1997) I.P.R. 163; but see *Zupanovich Pty Ltd v Beale Nominees Pty Ltd* (1995) 32 I.P.R. 339 at 355 (Carr J.); however, it seems that Carr J. was contemplating cases where liability was not in issue. See also *Gentry Homes Pty Ltd v Diamond Homes Pty Ltd* (1993) A.I.P.C. 91–008.

[37] *Minnesota Mining & Manufacturing Co v C Jeffries Pty Ltd* [1993] F.S.R. 189 (Fed. Ct of NSW); *Island Records Ltd v Tring International Plc* [1995] F.S.R. 560; *Led Builders Pty Ltd v Eagle Homes Pty Ltd (No.3)* (1996) 36 I.P.R. 293.

[38] *Island Records v Tring International Plc* (above); *Brugge v Medicaid* [1996] F.S.R. 362.

[39] See paras 22–63 *et seq.*, above.

[40] CDPA 1988, ss.103(1) and 194.

[41] Reference should be made to the standard textbooks on torts such as *Clerk & Lindsell*.

[42] CDPA 1988, ss.96(2), 229(2) and 191I(2).

[43] *Sutherland Publishing Co Ltd v Caxton Publishing Co Ltd* [1936] Ch. 323 *per* Lord Wright M.R., at 336; *Prior v Landsdowne Press Pty Ltd* [1977] R.P.C. 511 (Sup.Ct. of Victoria); *Interfirm Comparison (Australia) Pty Ltd v Law Society of New South Wales* [1977] R.P.C. 137; *Infabrics Ltd v Jaytex Shirt Co Ltd* [1984] R.P.C. 405 at 457; *Paterson Zochonis Ltd v Merfarken Packaging Ltd* [1983] F.S.R. 273 at 281, 287, 294; *International Writing School Inc v Rimila Pty Ltd* (1994) 30 I.P.R. 250 (Fed Ct of Aus); *Claydon Architectural Metalwork v D.J. Higgins & Sons* [1997] F.S.R. 475.

[44] [1976] R.P.C. 197, applied in *Blayney v Clogau St David's Gold Mines Ltd* [2003] F.S.R. 19.

as he would have been in if he had not sustained the wrong.[45] It seems, therefore, that damages for all the rights covered in this work are now to be assessed on the same footing.[46]

22–163   **General Tire.** There are two essential principles in valuing the claim: first, that the claimant has the burden of showing his loss; and secondly, that the defendant being a wrongdoer, damages should be liberally assessed but that the object is to compensate the claimant and not punish the defendant.[47] There are three main groups of reported cases which exemplify the court's approach to typical situations. The first is where the claimant is a manufacturer, who exploits his right to make articles or products which he sells at a profit. The benefit of the right is realised through the sale of the article or product. In such a case, the infringement diverts sales from the right owner to the infringer. The measure of damages is then normally the profit which would have been realised by the owner of the right if the sales had been made by him.[48] The second group of cases is where the right is exploited by the grant of licences for royalty payments. If the infringer uses the right without a licence, the measure of damages is the amount he would have had to pay by way of royalty instead of acting illegally.[49] The amount of such a royalty is a matter of evidence. However, before a "going rate" can be taken as the basis on which the infringer ought to pay damages, it must be shown that the circumstances in which the going rate was paid are the same as or comparable with those in which the rightholder and infringer are assumed to strike their bargain. In the third group of cases, there is no normal rate of profit and no normal royalty. In such a case it is for the claimant to adduce evidence to guide the court. The evidence may consist of the practice in the trade or other trades, expert opinion, evidence as to the profitability of the right and any other factor on which the judge can decide the measure of loss. The ultimate process is one of judicial estimation of the available indications. In this third group of cases, the court is seeking to assess the price which could reasonably have been charged for a licence.[50] The hypothesis is that the actual licensor and the actual infringer are willing to negotiate with each other as they are, with their strengths and weaknesses, in the market as it exists.[51] In a case within this group, the court may have to call into play "inference, conjecture and the like", and apply "a sound imagina-

---

[45] Applying *Livingstone v Rawyards Coal Co* (1880) 5 A.C. 25 at p.39.

[46] See as to passing off, *Irvine v Talksport Ltd* [2003] F.S.R. 35. Note, however, that this was an endorsement case where the "user" principle applied without difficulty. In *Reed Executive plc v Reed Business Information Ltd* [2004] EWCA Civ 159 at para.165, Jacob L.J. doubted whether the "user" principle automatically applied in passing-off cases, especially when the mark concerned is not the sort of mark available for hire: "The ordinary case is just one that protects goodwill. For damages to be awarded on the user principle is close to saying there is no damage so some will be invented. It is not the same sort of thing as having to pay for use of an invention (the basis of the user principle in patents)".

[47] Applying *Pneumatic Tyre Co Ltd v Puncture Proof Pneumatic Tyre Co Ltd* (1899) 16 R.P.C. 209 at p.215.

[48] Examples in copyright cases being *Birn Bros Ltd v Keene & Co Ltd* [1918] 2 Ch. 281 and *Columbia Pictures Industries v Robinson* [1988] F.S.R. 531. Note, however, that these are both cases under the 1956 Act pursuant to which conversion damages were also available.

[49] Examples in copyright cases being *Performing Right Society Ltd v Bradford Corporation* [1917–23] Mac.C.C. 309; *Chabot v Davies* [1936] 2 All E.R. 221; *Stovin-Bradford v Volpoint Ltd* [1971] Ch. 1007 at 1016, 1020; *Lewis Trusts v Bambers Stores Ltd* [1983] F.S.R. 453 at 469; *Devefi Pty Ltd v Mateffy Perl Nagy Pty Ltd* [1993] R.P.C. 193 (Fed. Ct. of Australia); and *Nottinghamshire Healthcare National Health Service Trust v News Group Newspapers Ltd* [2002] EWHC 409; [2002] E.M.L.R. 33. See also *Irvine v Talksport Ltd* [2003] F.S.R. 35, para.106.

[50] See *Meters Ltd v Metropolitan Gas Meters Ltd* (1911) 28 R.P.C. 157 at p.164–5.

[51] *General Tire and Rubber Company v Firestone Tyre and Rubber Company Ltd* [1976] R.P.C. 197 at p.221. However, any impecuniosity on the part of the licensee is disregarded: *Irvine v Talksport Ltd* [2002] F.S.R. 60, para.74.

tion and the practice of the broad axe".[52] In some cases it may be appropriate to award as damages the cost of producing or commissioning the material in a form which did not infringe copyright.[53]

General Tire groups not exhaustive. The three groups of case referred to in **22–164** *General Tire* were not intended to be exhaustive.[54] Accordingly, for example, where the claimant is in competition with the defendant, there is no reason why he cannot recover lost profits on sales made by the defendant which he can show he would have made but for the infringement (*General Tire* group 1) and a notional licence fee (calculated in accordance with *General Tire* group 2 or 3 as appropriate) in respect of all other sales made by the defendant.[55] Moreover, the fact that the pirated work may have injured the reputation of and vulgarised the original may be taken into consideration in assessing the amount of damages.[56] In *Mansell (V.) & Co Ltd v Wesley (H.) Ltd*,[57] it was held that the claimant was justified in withdrawing his stock, the design of which had been vulgarised, and adding to his claim for damages the loss so suffered. The fact that the defendant could have achieved the same result without using the claimant's work is not relevant when assessing the claimant's loss.[58] In a patent case, a claimant has recovered damages to represent lost profits on sales of associated non-patented goods, spare parts and servicing and profits lost in the period after the expiry of the patent as a result of the competitive "bridgehead" built up by the defendant's infringements during the subsistence of the patent.[59] It is possible to recover as damages the costs of employing inquiry agents.[60] In a passing off case where the claimant cannot show lost sales or loss of business, his damages need not necessarily be assessed on a "user" or "notional licence fee" basis.[61] Furthermore, there is nothing to stop the court awarding an additional sum in respect of aggravated damages to take account of injury to the claimant's proper feelings of pride and dignity, humiliation, distress, insult or pain caused by the circumstances of the defendant's conduct.[62] Finally, following the overruling of *AB v South West Water Services*[63] it appears that the court now has power to award exemplary damages in cases involving copyright and the other rights covered in

---

[52] *Watson, Laidlaw & Co Ltd v Pott, Cassells and Williamson* (1914) 31 R.P.C. 104 at 118 per Lord Shaw (a patent case). For the application of this approach in copyright cases, see *SPE International Ltd v Professional Preparation Contractors (UK) Ltd* [2002] EWHC 881, Ch D; *Ludlow Music Inc v Williams* [2002] F.S.R. 868 and *Blayney v Clogau St David's Gold Mines Ltd* [2003] F.S.R. 19.

[53] *Peninsular Business Services Ltd v Citation plc* [2004] F.S.R. 17 (His Honour Judge Maddocks). See also *Pollock v Williamson* [1923] V.L.R. 225 (court awarded the cost of obtaining a non-infringing translation by a person of the highest competence).

[54] *General Tire and Rubber Company v Firestone Tyre and Rubber Company Ltd* [1976] R.P.C. 197, at p.212; see *Blayney v Clogau St David's Gold Mines Ltd* [2003] F.S.R. 19 at para.12.

[55] *Blayney v Clogau St David's Gold Mines Ltd* [2003] F.S.R. 19, at para.20.

[56] *Hanfstaengl v W. H. Smith & Sons* [1905] 1 Ch. 519; *Lewis Trusts v Bambers Stores Ltd* [1983] F.S.R. 453 at 469; *Allibert S.A. v O'Connor* [1982] F.S.R. 317 (High Ct of Ireland) and see *Milpurrurru v Indofurn Pty Ltd* (1994) 30 I.P.R. 209 (Fed. Ct of Aus.).

[57] [1936–45] Mac.C.C. 288.

[58] See, *e.g. Work Model Enterprises Ltd v Ecosystem Ltd* [1996] F.S.R.356.

[59] *Gerber Garment Technology Inc v Lectra Systems Ltd* [1995] R.P.C. 383; [1997] R.P.C. 443, CA.

[60] *British Motor Trade Association v Salvadori* [1949] Ch. 556; *South African Music Rights Organisation Ltd v Trust Butchers (Pty) Ltd* (1978) 1 S.A.L.R. 1052. See also *Morton-Norwich Products Inc v Intercen Ltd (No.2)* [1981] F.S.R. 337 (claimant entitled to recover costs of *Norwich Pharmacal* application). For the difficulties which a claimant may face in recovering its internal costs of investigation by way of damages, see *Admiral Management Services Ltd v Para Protect Europe Ltd* [2002] EWHC 233, Ch D.

[61] *Reed Executive plc v Reed Business Information Ltd* [2004] EWCA Civ 159, para.165.

[62] *Nottinghamshire Healthcare National Health Service Trust v News Group Newspapers Ltd* [2002] EWHC 409; [2002] E.M.L.R. 33, para.51. As to aggravated damages generally, see the current edition of *Clerk & Lindsell on Torts*.

[63] [1993] Q.B. 507.In this case it was held that exemplary damages were not available in respect of

this work, provided the case falls into one of the three categories identified by Lord Devlin in *Rookes v Barnard*.[64]

22–165   **Limits on amount of damages.** The damages will not, however, include loss suffered because of the commission by a third party of another tort, such as passing off,[65] which has been facilitated by the defendant's infringement of copyright. The ordinary rules as to causation, foreseeability and remoteness will be applied.[66] If it was reasonably foreseeable that the defendant's acts of infringement would cause a particular head of damage to the claimant, damages under that head ought to be recoverable. But the infringement must be an effective cause of the damage. Where a defendant copied the claimant's technical brochure and used the infringing copy for the purpose of selling a competing product, it was held that the claimant's loss of sales was due to lawful competition and was not caused by the infringement.[67] The burden is on the claimant to prove damage, but not to a degree of certainty. Once it is shown that pirate marketing has taken place, some loss of sales will be assumed.[68]

22–166   **Practice.** Damages are usually assessed on an inquiry before the Master after liability for infringement has been established at the trial of the action, with costs of the inquiry reserved. It does not follow automatically that, because a claimant has succeeded on liability, he should be entitled to an inquiry as to damages. If the court is satisfied that an inquiry would be fruitless, it may refuse an order one. However, an inquiry will be ordered even if the claimant can only show a *prima facie* or arguable case that he will recover damages.[69] If the court thinks the damages are likely to be negligible or small, it can use its case management powers to stop the case getting out of hand.[70] Furthermore, because the remedy of an inquiry is discretionary,[71] the court may decide to assess the damages in a very

---

torts in respect of which such damages had not been awarded before 1964. It was thought that there was no such award in a copyright case. However, *AB v South West Water Services* was overruled by the House of Lords in *Kuddus v Chief Constable of Leicestershire* [2001] UKHL 29; [2002] 2 A.C. 122. Accordingly, there seems to be no reason why exemplary damages cannot be awarded in a copyright case.

[64] [1964] A.C. 1129. The two relevant categories are: first, oppressive, arbitrary or unconstitutional action by government servants; and second, where the defendant's conduct has been calculated by him to make a profit which may well exceed the compensation payable to the claimant. See, generally, *Clerk & Lindsell on Torts*.

[65] *Paterson Zochonis Ltd v Merfarken Packaging Ltd* [1983] F.S.R. 273.

[66] *Gerber Garment Technology Inc v Lectra Systems Ltd* [1995] R.P.C. 383; [1997] R.P.C. 443, CA (a patent case); *Claydon Architectural Metalwork v DJ Higgins & Sons* [1997] F.S.R. 475.

[67] *Work Model Enterprises Ltd v Ecosystem Ltd & Clix Interiors Ltd* [1996] F.S.R. 356; see also *Peninsular Business Services Ltd v Citation plc* [2004] F.S.R. 17 (manuals not used in sales process) and *A-One Accessory Imports Pty Ltd v Off Road Imports Pty Ltd* (1996) 34 I.P.R. 332: infringing brochure was the key to sales; defendant would have taken six months to make non-infinging version; claimant entitled to lost profits for six months.

[68] *Columbia Pictures Industries v Robinson* [1988] F.S.R. 531.

[69] *McDonald's Hamburgers Ltd v Burger King (UK) Ltd* [1987] F.S.R. 112 (inquiry ordered even though *quantum* "speculative"); *Brain v Ingledew Brown Bennison & Garret (a firm)* [1997] F.S.R. 511 (inquiry ordered although prospects of recovery "weak" on current evidence); *Prince Plc v Prince Sports Group Inc* [1998] F.S.R. 21 (application adjourned to enable claimant to adduce evidence); *Reed Executive plc v Reed Business Information Ltd* [2004] EWCA Civ 159 para.164 (criteria unchanged by introduction of the CPR).

[70] *Reed Executive plc v Reed Business Information Ltd* [2004] EWCA Civ 159, para.164. For example, the court can require the claimant to put in a statement of case and supporting evidence without requiring the defendant to do anything with a view to encouraging a claimant who has little to gain to think twice; it can order the trial to be on paper unless a case for cross-examination is made out; disclosure can be restricted or done away with; a time-limit for the hearing can be imposed: *ibid.*

[71] *Allied Maples Group Ltd v Simmons & Simmons* [1995] 1 W.L.R. 1602 at 1622; *Brain v Ingledew Brown Bennison & Garret (a firm)* [1997] F.S.R. 511.

simple case at trial in order to save the costs of a separate inquiry.[72] For that reason, and notwithstanding the fact that it is the court's practice to try intellectual property cases on liability alone, leaving damages to be assessed on an inquiry if the claimant is successful, it is prudent for a claimant to apply at the Case Management Conference for an order for a split trial so that there is no possibility of his being caught by surprise at trial should the judge subsequently decide to refuse to order an inquiry.[73] An application to dismiss an inquiry as to damages for want of prosecution is not governed by the same considerations as on an application to strike out proceedings before an order has been made.[74] Other than in simple cases, it is usually prudent to have formal statements of case in the inquiry.[75]

Special cases. For special provisions in the case where the copyright owner has granted an exclusive licence which encompasses the defendant's infringing acts, see section (x), below. For the right to information from the defendant before electing between an inquiry as to damages and an account of profits, see paragraph 22–161, above. Where performers' rights or the rights of persons having recording rights are infringed by the making of a broadcast of a performance or recording, then, if the broadcast is made from a place in the United Kingdom and is received and immediately retransmitted by cable, the fact of such retransmission is to be taken into account in assessing damages for the infringement.[76] Any damages recovered by a personal representative in respect of infringement of performers' rights in respect of an infringement after a person's death devolve as part of his estate as if the right (or right of action) had subsisted and been vested in him immediately before his death.[77] **22–167**

(v) Additional damages

General. In actions for infringement of copyright, design right and performers' property rights, the court has power, having regard to all the circumstances, and in particular to the flagrancy of the infringement and any benefit accruing to the defendant by reason of the infringement, to award such additional damages as the **22–168**

---

[72] See, *e.g.*, *Michael O'Mara Books Ltd v Express Newspapers Plc* [1998] E.M.L.R. 383 (an application for summary judgment).

[73] This also has the advantage of ensuring that disclosure is limited to the issues relating to liability, as opposed to quantum—see para. 22–161, below.

[74] *Nichols Advanced Vehicle Systems Inc v Rees, Oliver & Others (No.2)* [1985] R.P.C. 445.

[75] *Gerber Garment Technology Inc v Lectra Systems Ltd & Another* [1994] F.S.R. 471 (a patent case).

[76] CDPA 1988, Sched. 2, para.19(2).

[77] s.192A(5); Duration of Copyright & Rights in Performances Regulations, (SI 1995/3297) Reg.31(3); Copyrights & Related Rights Regulations (SI 1996/2967) reg.30(2).

justice of the case may require.[78] The remedy is discretionary.[79] Additional damages cannot be awarded to a claimant who has elected for an account of profits.[80]

22–169   **Flagrancy.** Flagrancy implies scandalous conduct or deceit, including deliberate and calculated infringement where a defendant reaps a pecuniary advantage in excess of the damages he would otherwise have to pay.[81] Where the infringement has been carried out in breach of a court order, it is fairly to be described as flagrant.[82] Flagrancy is not a necessary ingredient of additional damages. It is merely a factor to take into account if it is present.[83]

22–170   **Benefit to the defendant.** It has been held that the presence of this factor permits the court to include an element of restitution in its award, having regard to the benefit gained by the defendant, for example where the normal compensation awarded to the claimant leaves the defendant still enjoying the fruit of his infringement.[84] Such an award overlaps to a certain extent with the remedy of an account of profits,[85] but is not co-extensive with it because it permits the court to take account of benefit which is not profit, for example where a defendant has established himself in the market and generated a goodwill by a flagrant infringement.[86] It has been suggested (obiter) that the inclusion of a restitutionary element in an award of additional damages might be appropriate in two specific circumstances. The first was where a defendant who had declined the claimant's offer of a licence went on and deliberately infringed. In such a case, an award of additional damages might be made to bring the total of damages up to the fee originally sought by the claimant or even to enable the claimant to participate in the profits made by the defendant while also recovering damages for the invasion of his right. The second was where the copyright owner is not in the business of granting licences. In those circumstances, an award of strictly compensatory damages might be accompanied by an award of additional damages reflecting the benefit derived by the defendant. Thus, if the correct approach to infringement damages was to calculate a royalty on a "profits available" basis, then in a case of

---

[78] CDPA 1988, ss.97(2), 229(3) and 191J(2). The provisions of the 1988 Act are wider than s.17(3) of the 1956 Act. For a summary of the principles for awarding damages under s.17(3), see *Noah v Shuba* [1991] F.S.R. 14 at 29–31. The 1988 Act has removed that part of s.17(3) which required the court to be satisfied that "effective relief was not otherwise available to the plaintiff" before an award of additional damages could be made. Under s.17(3), if, for example, effective relief was available to the plaintiff in respect of another cause of action, such as libel or breach of confidence, or because conversion damages, as well as infringement damages, were available, relief might not be given by an award of additional damages for infringement of copyright—see *Beloff v Pressdram Ltd* [1973] R.P.C. 765; *Prior v Landsdowne Press (Pty) Ltd* [1977] R.P.C. 511; *Ravenscroft v Herbert & Another* [1980] R.P.C. 193. See also para.704 of the report of the Whitford Committee (Cmnd.6732) as explained in *Nottinghamshire Healthcare National Health Service Trust v News Group Newspapers Ltd* [2002] EWHC 409; [2002] E.M.L.R. 33, para.41.

[79] *Raben Footwear Pty Ltd v Polygram Records Inc* [1997] I.P.R. 417; *Pro Sieben Media AG v Carlton UK Television Ltd* [1998] F.S.R. 43; [1997] E.M.L.R. 509. For a summary of the law in Australia, see *Sullivan v FNH Investments Pty Ltd* [2003] F.C.A. 323; (2003) 57 I.P.R. 6, but note that the statutory power to award additional damages (s.115(4) of the Copyright Act 1968) is in very different terms from s.97(2).

[80] *Redrow Homes Ltd v Betts Brothers plc* [1998] F.S.R. 345.

[81] *Ravenscroft v Herbert & Another* [1980] R.P.C. 193, at 206; *ZYX Muisc Ltd v King* [1995] F.S.R. 566.

[82] *Sony Computer Entertainment Inc v Owen* [2002] EWHC 45 [2002] E.M.L.R. 34 at para.28.

[83] *Cala Homes (South) Limited v Alfred McAlpine Homes East Ltd* [1995] F.S.R. 818 at 838; *ZYX Music Ltd v King* [1995] F.S.R. 566.

[84] *Nottinghamshire Healthcare National Health Service Trust v News Group Newspapers Ltd* [2002] EWHC 409; [2002] E.M.L.R. 33, para.51 (Pumfrey, J.).

[85] *cf. ZYX Music Ltd v King* [1995] F.S.R. 566, in which the Judge ordered that the award of additional damages should include a sum representing the extent to which ordinary damages would not adequately reflect *inter alia* the defendant's profit.

[86] *cf. ZYX Music Ltd v King* [1995] F.S.R. 566; see also the observations of Lord Clyde in *Redrow Homes Ltd v Betts Brothers plc* [1998] F.S.R. 345 at p.353 and *cf.* the 1956 Act case of *Nichols Advanced Vehicle Systems Inc & Others v Rees Oliver & Others* [1979] R.P.C. 127.

flagrant infringement it might be right to take a larger share of the available profits for the claimant's account than might otherwise be taken.[87] Again, the benefit to the defendant is not a necessary ingredient of a claim for flagrancy damages. It is merely a factor to take into account.[88]

Can the award include a punitive element? After much uncertainty, it has been **22–171** held at first instance that an award of additional damages may not contain a purely punitive element.[89] The reasons for this include the existence of a relevant statutory offence (under section 107 of the 1988 Act[90]) and the risk that an infringer might in a case of concurrent copyrights be exposed to successive actions by the owners of the different copyrights, each seeking punishment in respect of his own interest.[91] It should be noted, however, that exemplary damages, which may include a punitive element, are probably now available for infringement of copyright and the other rights covered in this work.[92]

Other relevant considerations. Section 97(2) is drafted in the widest terms. The **22–172** court is clearly permitted to take account of the factors admitted as aggravation at common law, that is damages intended to take account of injury to the claimant's proper feelings of pride and dignity, humiliation, distress, insult or pain caused by the circumstances of the defendant's conduct.[93] However, the section permits an aggravation of the award on a basis far wider than that.[94] Thus, for example, the courts have taken into account, sometimes under the heading of flagrancy and sometimes not: the fact that the material reproduced was obviously stolen from the claimant;[95] the destruction of evidence by the defendant;[96] the fact that the infringement continued in the face of a warning;[97] attempts to conceal the infringement by disingenuous correspondence;[98] the absence of an apology;[99] and upset caused to the claimant's employees.[1] On the other hand, it appears that the court may take account any "mitigating circumstances";[2] the defendant's means;[3] rea-

---

[87] See *Ludlow Music Inc v Williams* [2002] EWHC 638, Ch, Pumfrey, J.
[88] *Cala Homes (South) Limited v Alfred McAlpine Homes East Ltd* [1995] F.S.R. 818 at 838; *ZYX Music Ltd v King* [1995] F.S.R. 566.
[89] *Nottinghamshire Healthcare National Health Service Trust v News Group Newspapers Ltd* [2002] EWHC 409; [2002] E.M.L.R. 33, para.51.
[90] See Ch.23, below.
[91] *Nottinghamshire Healthcare National Health Service Trust v News Group Newspapers Ltd* [2002] EWHC 409; [2002] E.M.L.R. 33, para.51.
[92] See para. 22–164, above.
[93] *Nottinghamshire Healthcare National Service Trust v News Group Newspapers Ltd* [2002] EWHC 409; [2002] E.M.L.R. 33, para.51; *cf.* the 1956 Act cases of *Nichols Advanced Vehicle Systems Inc & Others v Rees Oliver & Others* [1979] R.P.C. 127 and *Beloff v Pressdram Ltd* [1973] R.P.C. 765.
[94] See the previous note.
[95] *Nottinghamshire Healthcare National Health Service Trust v News Group Newspapers Ltd* [2002] EWHC 409; [2002] E.M.L.R. 33, para.60. The way the defendant obtained the copied material was also held to be relevant (under the heading of flagrancy) in the 1956 Act case of *Beloff v Pressdram Ltd* [1973] R.P.C. 765.
[96] *Nottinghamshire Healthcare National Health Service Trust v News Group Newspapers Ltd* [2002] EWHC 409; [2002] E.M.L.R. 33.
[97] *Peninsular Business Services Ltd v Citation plc* [2004] F.S.R. 17 (His Honour Judge Maddocks).
[98] *ibid.*
[99] *Nottinghamshire Healthcare National Health Service Trust v News Group Newspapers Ltd* [2002] EWHC 409; [2002] E.M.L.R. 33, para.51; *cf.* the 1956 Act case of *Beloff v Pressdram Ltd* [1973] R.P.C. 765—lack of regret.
[1] *Nottinghamshire Healthcare National Health Service Trust v News Group Newspapers Ltd* [2002] EWHC 409; [2002] E.M.L.R. 33, para.51.
[2] *Michael O'Mara Books Ltd v Express Newspapers Plc* [1998] E.M.L.R. 383; *Sony Computer Entertainment Inc v Owen* [2002] EWHC 45, [2002] E.M.L.R. 34 at para.28.
[3] *Michael O'Mara Books Ltd v Express Newspapers Plc* [1998] E.M.L.R. 383.

sonable doubts about the claimant's title;[4] provocation by the claimant;[5] and whether the defendant reasonably believed that the claimant would grant him a licence.[6]

22–173 **Quantum.** Each case obviously depends on its own facts. However, the reader may be assisted by some examples of actual awards. Additional damages have been awarded in a number of reported cases under the 1988 Act.[7] In one case, which concerned the manufacture and sale of infringing CDs, and the infringement had not been particularly beneficial to the defendants, the court had in mind a sum of £1 per infringing CD produced and not sold and £5 per infringing CD sold.[8] In another, when a newspaper had published a stolen photograph of an inmate of a mental hospital, ordinary damages were assessed at £450 and additional damages were assessed at £9,550.[9] In a third, a consultant in employment law and other fields had deliberately infringed the manuals of a competitor. Ordinary and additional damages were assessed at £9,000 each. The amount of the additional damages was described as a "premium" or "mark-up".[10] Two awards are reported in cases under the 1956 Act[11]: a sum of £2,000 where the conduct of the defendant had been deceitful and treacherous, thereby obtaining benefits for himself and inflicting on the claimant humiliation for which it was difficult to compensate;[12] and an award of £1,000 against a photographer, who sold to the Press photographs taken by him for a client in circumstances in which the copyright vested in the client.[13]

22–174 **Procedure.** Where a claim is made for additional damages under section 97(2) or section 229(3) of the 1988 Act, the particulars of claim must include a statement to that effect and the grounds for claiming them.[14] There is no set rule as to whether the question of flagrancy should be dealt with at trial or on an inquiry as to damages; accordingly it is for the court to lay down a sensible procedure in each case.[15] The assessment of additional damages will usually be made by the Master in the course of the conduct of the inquiry as to damages for infringement

---

[4] *MCA Records Inc v Charly Records Ltd* [2000] E.M.L.R. 743 at 814: "It may be that the difficulties about MCA's title are at least part of the circumstances to which I am required to have regard; but in my view they rank low on the list".

[5] *Beloff v Pressdram Ltd* [1973] R.P.C. 765 (a 1956 Act case).

[6] *Ludlow Music Inc v Williams* [2002] EWHC 683 (Ch).

[7] Note, however, that the *quantum* of additional damages is often left to the Master and that such decisions are not usually reported.

[8] *Springsteen v Flute International Ltd* [1999] E.M.L.R. 180.

[9] *Nottinghamshire Healthcare National Health Service Trust v News Group Newspapers Ltd* [2002] EWHC 409; [2002] E.M.L.R. 33, para.60. The court observed that if this exceeded the sum which was appropriate under s.97(2) having regard to the benefit to the defendant, no further infringements of that kind would take place; but that if further such infringements took place it would show that the advantage to the newspaper still exceeded the award of damages.

[10] *Peninsular Business Services Ltd v Citation plc* [2004] F.S.R. 17 (His Honour Judge Maddocks). The judge used as a yardstick s.1 of the Landlord and Tenant Act 1730, pursuant to which a landlord may recover "double value" against a tenant who wilfully holds over after the termination of a lease. However, this section is a penal provision (see the terms of the section and *e.g. Lloyd v Rosbee* (1810) 2 Camp.453) and accordingly it is not clear how far the *Peninsular* decision is consistent on this point with the *Nottinghamshire Healthcare* case (*Nottinghamshire Healthcare National Health Service Trust v News Group Newspapers Ltd* [2002] EWHC 409), which is not referred to in the judgment. See also *Microsoft Corp. v Able System Development Ltd* [2002] 3 H.K.L.R.D. 515 (High Court of Hong Kong): additional damages representing 10 per cent of ordinary damages.

[11] Note, however, that the criteria were different: see the notes to para. 22–168, above.

[12] *Nichols Advanced Vehicle Systems Inc v Rees (No.3)* [1988] R.P.C. 71.

[13] *Williams v Settle* [1960] 1 W.L.R. 1072

[14] CPR PD63, para.25.1. Curiously, there is no reference to section 191J(2) which permits an award of additional damages in respect of performers' property rights. No doubt the same principle applies.

[15] *Condé Nast Publications Ltd v MGN Ltd* [1998] F.S.R. 427.

of copyright.[16] However, where the trial judge has made a finding as to flagrancy, he should direct the court taking the inquiry to have particular regard to the findings as to the flagrancy of the infringement made in the judgment.[17] In general, the trial judge may indicate in his judgment that additional damages should be awarded and the considerations which are relevant to the assessment of the additional damages.[18]

(vi) Account of profits

General. An alternative remedy to damages is an account of profits, which was originally an equitable remedy incidental to the right to an injunction.[19] The account is of net profit[20] ; for example, the sale price of the infringing article, less manufacturing and delivery costs.[21] As an account is an equitable remedy, it is liable to be defeated by the usual equitable defences such as acquiescence, unclean hands and laches. It is desirable that the court should consider the practical consequences of ordering the remedy of profits in the particular case.[22] The court will readily grant an account where there has been deliberate, knowing infringement, but it appears that it may refuse an account if the infringement has been entirely innocent.[23] The court will not refuse to grant an account merely because damages might be an adequate remedy (such that the claimant may benefit from a "windfall").[24]

The principles upon which such an account is granted were thus stated by Wigram V.C. in *Colburn v Simms*.[25]

"It is true," he said, "that the court does not, by an account, accurately measure the damage sustained by the proprietor of an expensive work from the invasion of his copyright by the publication of a cheaper book. It is impossible to know how many copies of the dearer book are excluded from sale by the interposition of the cheaper one. The court, by the account, as the nearest approximation which it can make to justice, takes from the wrongdoer all the profits he has made by his

22–175

---

[16] *The Lady Anne Tennant v Associated Newspapers Group Ltd* [1979] F.S.R. 298; *Microsoft Corporation v Electro-Wide Ltd & Another* [1997] F.S.R. 580.

[17] *MCA Records Inc v Charly Records Ltd* [2001] EWCA Civ 1441.

[18] *ZYX Music GmbH v Chris King & Others* [1995] F.S.R. 566.

[19] CDPA 1988, s.96(2); *Hogg v Kirby* (1803) 8 Ves.215; *Grimson v Eyre* (1804) 9 Ves.341 at 346; *Baily v Taylor* (1830) 1 R. & M. 73; *Sheriff v Coates* (1830) 1 R. & M. 159; *Kelly v Hooper* (1840) 4 Jur. 21. For a review of the principles involved in taking an account of profits see *Kirby* in [1991] 10 E.I.P.R. 367 and *Bently* in [1991] 1 E.I.P.R. 5. See also *Bently* in [1990] 3 E.I.P.R. 106 on *Potton Ltd v Yorkclose Ltd* [1990] F.S.R. 11.

[20] *Delfe v Delamotte* (1857) 3 K. & J. 581; *cf. Pike v Nicholas* (1869) L.R. 5 Ch. 251. If the claimant has paid tax on the profits, the profits will be net of tax, subject to an obligation to account for any tax reclaim or tax credit which may subsequently arise: *Celanese International Corp. v BP Chemicals Ltd* [1999] R.P.C. 203, para.137.

[21] *My Kinda Town v Soll* [1983] R.P.C. 15 at 49. *House of Spring Gardens Ltd v Point Blank Ltd* [1985] F.S.R. 327 (Supreme Ct. of Ireland); *Potton Ltd v Yorkclose Ltd* [1990] F.S.R. 11; *Van Camp Chocolates Ltd v Milsbrooks Ltd* [1984] 1 N.Z.L.R. 354. Where the claimant sues two or more defendants in a chain of distribution, a defendant who is obliged to indemnify another defendant who is further down the chain may deduct the amount of the indemnity from his profits: *Spring Form Inc v Toy Brokers Ltd* (2001) I.P.D. 24073 (for procedural issues arising from this, see para. 22–178, below).

[22] *Allied Signal Inc v Du Pont Canada Inc* (1995) 33 I.P.R. 511 at 531–532.

[23] *Sir Terence Orby Conran v Mean Fiddler Holdings Ltd* [1997] F.S.R. 856 at 861 (Robert Walker J.); an account was refused in that case (which concerned infringement of trade marks), the infringement having been initially innocent and ceased upon commencement of proceedings, and where discussions between the parties might have made proceedings unnecessary. It was held that whether to grant an account lay within the discretion of the court. However, the fact that the defendant's infringement was done innocently will not necessarily preclude the granting of an account: see *Wienerworld Ltd v Vision Video Ltd* [1998] F.S.R. 832, a copyright case.

[24] *Wienerworld Ltd v Vision Video Ltd* [1998] F.S.R. 832.

[25] (1843) 2 Ha. 543, 560; see *Pike v Nicholas* (1870) L.R. 5 Ch. 251 and *International Credit Control Ltd v Axelion* [1974] 1 N.Z.L.R. 695.

piracy, and gives them to the party who has been wronged. In doing this the court may often give the injured party more, in fact, than he is entitled to, for *non constat* that a single additional copy of the more expensive book would have been sold, if the injury by the sale of the cheaper book had not been committed. The court of equity, however, does not give anything beyond the account". The basis on which an account is ordered is that there should not be any unjust enrichment on the part of the defendant, and that the defendant should be deprived of any profit (even including an unrealised profit) attributable to wrongful acts committed in breach of the claimant's rights.[26] Accordingly, an account of profits will not extend to matters not quantifiable as "profits", such as the acquisition of an enhanced position in the market.[27] For these purposes, the accounting defendant is treated as if he had carried on his business on behalf of the claimant.[28] It is not the purpose of the account to identify what saving the defendant has made by adopting the infringing activity instead of a non-infringing activity.[29] By the same token, a claimant cannot increase his claim by arguing that the defendant could or should have generated higher profits.[30] It is no answer to a claim for an account that the defendant could have made the same profits by following an alternative, non-infringing course.[31]

22–176 **Where defendant has mixed infringing and non-infringing material**. While an account of profits may be a useful remedy in a simple case, it is very difficult to take where part only of the defendant's material infringes the claimant's copyright. In such a case an attempt must be made to apportion profits according to the relative value of the infringing and non-infringing material. For example, in a case of infringement of copyright in architectural drawings by the construction of houses, there would be excluded from the account profits attributable to the purchase, landscaping and sale of the land on which the houses were built, any increase in the value of the houses during the interval between the completion of the houses and sale, and profits attributable to the advertising, marketing and selling of the houses.[32] In the absence of some special reason to the contrary, the profits of a single project should be apportioned to different parts or aspects of the project in the same proportions as the costs and expenses are attributed to them.[33] However, the court may depart from this rule if, for example, the costs and expenses of a particular part are not an accurate reflection of the contribution made by that part to the whole.[34]

---

[26] See *e.g. Celanese International Corp. v BP Chemicals Ltd* [1999] R.P.C. 203 (a patent case) at para.37: the court is trying to determine what profits have been caused, in the legal sense, by the defendant's wrongful acts.

[27] *Redrow Homes Ltd v Betts Brothers Plc* [1999] 1 A.C. 197 at p.209D–E; [1988] F.S.R. 345 at 353 (Lord Clyde).

[28] *Celanese International Corp. v BP Chemicals Ltd* [1999] R.P.C. 203, para.36.

[29] *Celanese International Corp. v BP Chemicals Ltd* [1999] R.P.C. 203, paras 39–40 and 63–72, following *Peter Pan Manufacturing Corporation v Corsets Silhouette* [1963] R.P.C. 45, *Baker Energy Resources Corp. v Reading & Bates Construction* (1998) 58 C.P.R. (3d) 359 and *Potton Ltd v Yorkclose Ltd* [1990] F.S.R. 11.

[30] *Celanese International Corp. v BP Chemicals Ltd* [1999] R.P.C. 203, para.42, following *Dart Industries Inc v Decor Corporation Pty Ltd* (1993) 26 I.P.R. 193.

[31] *Celanese International Corp. v BP Chemicals Ltd* [1999] R.P.C. 203, para.39.

[32] *Potton Ltd v Yorkclose Ltd* [1990] F.S.R. 11. See also *Dart Industries Inc v Decor Corporation Pty Ltd* (1993) 26 I.P.R. 193 (High Ct of Aus) (a patent action), where the defendant was held liable to account for the profits made from the manufacture and sale of plastic canisters where only the lids infringed. The sales were attributable to the lid, without which the canisters would never have been made.

[33] *Potton Ltd v Yorkclose Ltd* [1990] F.S.R. 11 at p.19.

[34] *Celanese International Corp. v BP Chemicals Ltd* [1999] R.P.C. 203, para.55. A particular part or process may be very cheap but add a lot of value (*ibid.*), as in *The Wellcome Foundation Ltd v Apotex Inc*, Fed Court of Canada, August 26, 1998 (MacKay, J.) where the court (at para.57)

Infringment part of a larger enterprise. Where the infringement was only part **22–177** of a larger enterprise which generated profits, it is for the defendant to show that it is inequitable to order an account of the whole profits, by demonstrating that only a proportion of the profits were made by means of the infringement.[35] If the defendant cannot establish that not all of the profits made were attributable to the infringement, the result will be that it must account for the whole of the profit made by the enterprise.[36] However, once the need for an apportionment has been established, there is no onus on either party in relation to the question of what apportionment should take place.[37]

In *Dart Industries Inc v Decor Corporation Pty Ltd*[38] it was held on the facts of that case that the proportion of overhead costs which were attributable to the obtaining of the relevant profit might be deducted in arriving at a profit figure. It was pointed out that where the manufacture of a product constituted a side line of the defendant's business and made use of spare capacity, it would not be right to deduct a proportion of overhead costs since these would have been incurred in any event. Where, however, the product was an integral part of the defendant's range, such that if the product in question had not been manufactured, some alternative product would have been, it would be wrong in principle to deny the defendant a deduction of a proportion of his overheads. Otherwise the defendant would be in a worse position than if he had never manufactured the infringing article. Again, if it is shown that overheads were increased by the production of the infringing article, or would have been reduced had it not been produced, it may be appropriate to attribute the difference to the infringing product.

In the patent case of *Celanese International Corp. v BP Chemicals Ltd*,[39] the defendant divided its business into units. The infringing process was used in two plants which were both included in one of the units, the BPC Acetyls Business Unit. Each plant used a different mix of starting materials to produce different final product mixes in differently designed hardware with different overall capital and running costs and different overall profitabilities. Some of the overheads of the BPC Acetyls Business Unit were attributable to the two plants; others were not. Three major issues arose. First, whether the plants should be treated separately or whether a loss made on one could be set off against a profit made on another. The court held that the plants should be treated as separate businesses which happened to be run on the same site and shared some common upstream and downstream plant and services.[40] Secondly, how overheads should be apportioned. The claimant contended that the defendant should not be allowed to deduct any overheads which would have been incurred if the infringement had not taken place. However, the judge accepted the defendant's submission that the proportion of overheads which were attributable to the plants should be

---

rejected an apportionment based on the relative costs of infringing and non-infringing ingredients of a combination drug because the infringing ingredient was "the major potentiating ingredient". Another situation where the court may wish to depart from the general rule is where there is a standard process involving a number of steps and where one step is replaced by an infringing process which results in an increase in profits: *Celanese International Corp. v BP Chemicals Ltd* [1999] R.P.C. 203, para.58. If the court is able to depart from the general rule, it is released from mathematical constraints and has a wide discretion to pick whatever figure it thinks is fair (*ibid.*, para.57).

[35] *Zupanovich Pty Ltd v Beale Nominees Pty Ltd* (1995) 32 I.P.R. 339; *Warman International Ltd v Dwyer* (1995) 128 A.L.R. 201 at 211–212; *Celanese International Corp. v BP Chemicals Ltd* [1999] R.P.C. 203, para.73.

[36] *Zupanovich Pty Ltd v Beale Nominees Pty Ltd* (1995) 32 I.P.R. 339 at pp.358–359 (Carr J.).

[37] *My Kinda Town v Soll* [1983] R.P.C. 15 at p.57; *Celanese International Corp. v BP Chemicals Ltd* [1999] R.P.C. 203, para.73.

[38] (1993) 26 I.P.R. 193 (High Ct of Aus.) (a patent action). See also *LED Builders Pty Ltd v Eagle Homes Pty Ltd* (1999) 44 I.P.R. 24 (F.C.A., Lindgren J) where a building company was permitted an allowance for general overheads.

[39] [1999] R.P.C. 203.

[40] paras 78 and 87.

deducted.[41] Thirdly, the defendant's overheads included research and development costs. The claimant contended that the defendant was only entitled to deduct such costs if they were useful and were used during the period of infringement. This argument was rejected.[42]

22–178 **Procedure**. A claimant is obliged to elect between the alternative remedies of damages and an account and is entitled to disclosure before doing so.[43] A account will be refused if it is clear that there are no profits.[44] Where a claimant is awarded an account of profits, he cannot also be awarded additional damages.[45] The account is normally taken by the Master. Where an account is sought against two or more defendants in a chain of distribution who may be obliged to indemnify each other, the accounts must be taken together and no order must be made for payment in respect of any infringing article until the claimant undertakes not to make a claim in respect of that article against any other defendant.[46] A claimant is entitled to disclosure for the purposes of the account. In general, the defendant will be obliged to give full particulars, upon oath, of the number of copies printed and sold, and the cost of publication and distribution, verified by the production of all proper vouchers and receipts.[47] For special provisions in the case where the copyright owner has granted an exclusive licence which encompasses the defendant's infringing acts, see section (x) below.

(vii) Forfeiture

22–179 **The power**. The court has power[48] to make orders as to the disposal of infringing copies and other articles, illicit recordings, and infringing articles and other things which have been delivered up in pursuance of an order,[49] or which have been seized or detained by the owner of the relevant right or a person authorised by him.[50] The application may be brought in the High Court or a county court.[51] Where there is no pending action, the application is by Part 8 claim form.[52] Where there is a pending action, it is thought that the application should be made by notice under Part 23.[53]

The application may be for an order that the material in question shall be:

---

[41] paras 88–94.
[42] paras 96–101.
[43] See above, para. 22–161, above.
[44] *Lee v Alston* (1789) 1 Ves.78; *Colburn v Simms* (1843) 2 Ha. 543; *Powell v Aiken* (1857) 4 K. & J. 343.
[45] *Redrow Homes Ltd v Betts Brothers Plc* [1998] 2 W.L.R. 198; [1998] F.S.R. 345; see para. 22–168, above.
[46] *Spring Form Inc v Toy Brokers Ltd* (2001) I.P.D. 24073.
[47] *Stevens v Brett* (1863) 12 W.R. 572.
[48] ss.114, 204 and 231 of the 1988 Act. s.114 applies with the necessary modifications to means for facilitating the unauthorised removal or circumvention of technical devices applied to computer programs (see CDPA 1988, s.296(7)) and to devices designed to circumvent technical measures in relation to other works (CDPA 1988, s.296ZD(6)).
[49] *i.e.* an Order under ss.99 or 118, 195 or 199 or 230 of the 1988 Act, as the case may be.
[50] *i.e.* seized or detained under ss.100 or 196 of the 1988 Act, as the case may be. Note the lack of a seizure provision in respect of design right.
[51] ss.115(1), 205(1) and 232(1) of the 1988 Act. There is no financial limit: High Court and County Courts Jurisdiction Order 1991 (SI 1991/724), art.2(1)(n). It is provided that the provisions giving jurisdiction to county courts are not to affect the High Court's jurisdiction: CDPA 1988, ss.115(3), 205(3) and 232(3).
[52] This is because before April 26, 1999 (the date when the CPR came into force), such an application in the High Court would have been brought by originating summons (under RSC, Ord.93, r.24(2)) and no Act, rule or practice direction makes any additional or contrary provision: see PD8, para.A.1(3) and A.2(1).
[53] Following the repeal of RSC, Ord.93 r.24 and CCR, Ord.49 r.4A, there does not seem to be any specific provision about such claims. However, prior to the introduction of the CPR, applications in pending actions were made by summons or motion in the action: RSC, Ord.93 r.24(2). More-

(1) forfeited to the owner of the relevant right; or

(2) destroyed; or

(3) otherwise dealt with as the court may think fit.[54]

   An application may also be made (for example, by a defendant) for a decision that no such order should be made.[55] If the court decides that no order should be made, the person in whose possession, custody or control the material was before being delivered up or seized is entitled to its return.[56]

Procedure and decision. In considering what order (if any) should be made, the court is to consider whether other remedies available in an action for infringement of copyright, infringement of the rights conferred by Part II of the 1988 Act or infringement of design right would be adequate to compensate the owner of the relevant right and to protect his interests.[57] Provision is made for the protection of the interests of third parties. The procedure for making an order includes service of notice on persons having an interest in the material.[58] Any such person is entitled to appear in proceedings for such an order, whether or not he was served with notice, and to appeal against any order made, whether or not he appeared.[59] An order is not to take effect until the end of the period within which notice of an appeal may be given or, if before the end of that period, notice of appeal is duly given, until the final determination or abandonment of the proceedings on the appeal.[60] For special provisions in the case where the copyright owner has granted an exclusive licence which encompasses the defendant's infringing acts, see section (x) below.

22–180

Where more than one person interested. Where there is more than one person interested in the material, the court is to make such order as it thinks just and may, in particular, direct that the material be sold, or otherwise dealt with, and the proceeds divided.[61] A person has an interest for the purposes of these provisions if an order could be made in his favour in respect of it under certain other provisions.[62] Apart from that express provision, the 1988 Act does not define what is meant by "an interest" or a "person interested". The expressions would obviously embrace a person who has a legal or equitable title to or interest in the material, or to rights in it or an exclusive licence but are not necessarily so confined and may extend to persons who have "commercial interests" which would be damaged or prejudiced by orders for forfeiture, destruction or disposal.

22–181

---

over, PD63, para.26.1 (discussed below,) makes provision for service of "the claim form, *or application notice,* where appropriate" (emphasis added).

[54] CDPA 1988, ss.114(1), 204(1) and 231(1).

[55] *ibid.*

[56] ss.114(5), 204(5) and 231(5).

[57] CDPA 1988, ss.114(2), 204(2) and 231(2).

[58] PD63, para.26.1. This is expressed in terms of all identifiable persons who have an interest in the goods, material or articles within the meaning of ss.114 or 204 of the 1988 Act, thus omitting any reference to those with an interest in infringing articles or things within the meaning of s.231. This appears to be accidental. RSC, Ord.93 r.24(1) was not so limited. Moreover, para.26.1 is expressed to apply when an application is made under s.231 as well as ss.114 and 204. Furthermore, all three sections permit rules of court to be made which provide for service of notice of the proceedings on persons having an interest in the relevant material: CDPA 1988, ss.114(3), 204(3) and 231(3). In any event, service would appear to be the prudent course in all cases.

[59] CDPA 1988, ss.114(3), 204(3) and 231(3).

[60] *ibid.*

[61] CDPA 1988, ss.114(4), 204(4) and 231(4).

[62] In the case of each of the three types of right being described here, (*i.e.* (1) copyright, (2) performer's rights and recording rights and (3) design right), the other provisions being referred to are the equivalent provisions for the other two types of right together with s.19 of the Trade Marks Act 1994 (c.26).

(viii) Delivery up

22–182   The court has a statutory power to make an order for delivery up. A copyright owner (or exclusive licensee[63]) may apply for an order for delivery up to him or to such other person as the Court may direct of (a) infringing copies[64] in a person's possession, custody or control in the course of a business and (b) articles in a person's possession, custody or control specifically designed or adapted for making copies of a copyright work which that person knows or has to reason to believe have been used or are to be used to make infringing copies.[65] Note that there is no "guilty knowledge" provision under (a).[66] An example of (b) would be a mould or template. A person having performers' rights (including an exclusive licensee of a performer's property right[67]) or having recording rights in relation to a performance may apply to the Court for an order that an illicit recording[68] in another person's possession, custody or control in the course of a business be delivered up to him or to such other person as the court may direct.[69] A design right owner (or exclusive licensee[70]) may apply for an order for delivery up to him or to such other person as the court may direct of (a) infringing articles[71] in a person's possession, custody or control for commercial purposes[72] and (b) anything in a person's possession, custody or control specifically designed or adapted for making articles to a particular design which that person knows or has to reason to believe has been used or is to be used to make infringing articles.[73] The court has jurisdiction to make a mandatory order for delivery up on an interim application, if there is a high degree of assurance that the claimant will establish his entitlement at trial and the risk of injustice, if the injunction were refused, sufficiently outweighs the risk of injustice if it were granted.[74]

This power does not affect any other power of the court[75]; for example, its equitable jurisdiction. The power is not available where a defendant in infringement proceedings undertakes to take a licence of right where such a licence is available,[76] nor when the defendant shows that an illicit recording was "innocently acquired" by him.[77]

A person to whom an infringing copy or other article, illicit recording or infringing article or other thing is delivered in pursuance of an order must retain

---

[63] CDPA 1988, s.101(1) and (2).

[64] As to which see CDPA 1988, s.27 and para. 8–03, above.

[65] CDPA 1988, s.99(1). In relation to means for facilitating the unauthorised removal or circumvention of technical devices applied to computer programs which a person has in his possession, custody or control with the intention that it should be used to facilitiate the unauthorised removal of any technical device which has been applied to a computer program, a person with rights under CDPA 1988, s.296(2) has the same rights as a copyright owner has under s.99(1) in respect of infringing copies: see CDPA 1988, s.296(4). For s.296 generally, see paras 15–08 *et seq.*, above. In relation to a device, product or component which a person has in his possession, custody or control with the intention that it should be used to circumvent effective technological measures, a person with rights under CDPA 1988, s.296ZD(2) has the same rights as a copyright owner has under s.99(1) in respect of infringing copies: see CDPA 1988, s.296ZD(4).

[66] *Lagenes Ltd v It's At (UK) Ltd* [1991] F.S.R. 492.

[67] CDPA 1988, s.191L(1) & (2).

[68] As to which see CDPA 1988, s.197 and para. 12–69, above.

[69] CDPA 1988, s.195(1).

[70] CDPA 1988, s.234(1) and (2).

[71] As to which see CDPA 1988, s.228 and para. 13–158, above.

[72] For the definition of "commercial purposes" see para. 13–144, above.

[73] CDPA 1988, s.230(1).

[74] *Nottingham Building Society v Eurodynamics Systems Plc* [1993] F.S.R. 468 at 474, and see para. 22–138, above.

[75] CDPA 1988, ss.99(4), 195(4) and 230(7).

[76] CDPA 1988, ss.98, 191K and 239.

[77] See para. 22–81, above.

it pending the making of an order, or the decision not to make an order, as to its disposal under sections 114, 204 or 231 of the 1988 Act, as the case may be.[78]

An order for delivery up must not be made unless the court also makes, or it appears to the court that there are grounds for making, an order for the disposal of the infringing copy or other article under sections 114, 204 or 231 of the 1988 Act, as the case may be.[79] Delivery up is a discretionary remedy and will not be ordered in cases where its effect is disproportionate and would cause greater harm than is necessary in order to safeguard the legitimate interests of the claimant.[80]

In general,[81] an application for an order for delivery up may not be made after the end of the period of six years from the date on which the infringing copy or article, illicit recording or infringing article or thing in question was made.[82]

The court still has an equitable[83] jurisdiction to order delivery up of articles which have been created in violation of a claimant's right, but only for the purposes of destruction.[84] This principle could be used, for example, to support an order for delivery up of a derogatory treatment of a work where there was reason to believe that the defendant might not obey the terms of an injunction or, perhaps, where the defendant intended to make use of the derogatory treatment without infringing the moral right. In fact, it is frequently used in copyright cases generally. The jurisdiction extends to articles which are not in themselves infringing copies, if they were brought into being as the result of the use of infringing copies.[85]

The basis of the equitable jurisdiction is not that the infringing copies belong to the claimant, but the protection of the claimant's rights by preventing their use by the defendant.[86] The relief should therefore be limited to what is necessary for the protection of the claimant's rights, not the punishment of the defendant.[87] Thus the relief will not be granted if the articles can be rendered non-infringing,[88] nor if the articles have been taken out of the jurisdiction and there is no evidence of an intention to reimport them.[89]

Where a defendant has mixed the claimant's work with work of his own, then, if it is physically possible to sever one from the other, the order for delivery up

---

[78] CDPA 1988, ss.99(3), 195(3) and 230(6).

[79] CDPA 1988, ss.99(2), 195(2) and 230(2).

[80] *Ocular Sciences Ltd v Aspect Vision Care Ltd (No.2)* [1997] R.P.C. 289; see also, *Valeo Vision SA v Flexible Lamps Ltd* [1995] R.P.C. 205, where delivery up was refused on the grounds that it was a commercial nonsense and not in the interests of justice—a licence of right was available to the defendant very soon and any advantage to the defendant in being able to retain infringing copies could be reflected in the inquiry.

[81] For exceptions, which are (broadly) similar to ss.28 and 32 of the Limitation Act 1980, see CDPA 1988, ss.113(2), (3), 203(2), (3) and 230(4), (5).

[82] CDPA 1988, ss.99(2) and 113, 195(2) and 203 and 230(2) *et seq.*

[83] And therefore discretionary: *Ocular Sciences Ltd v Aspect Vision Care Ltd (No.2)* [1997] R.P.C. 289 at pp. 410 and 420.

[84] *Hole v Bradbury* (1879) L.R. 12 Ch. D. 886; *cf. Delfe v Delamotte* (1857) 3 K. & J. 581; *Stannard v Harrison* (1871) 11 W.R. 811. The statutory provisions as to delivery up are stated not to affect any other power of the court: CDPA 1988, ss.99(4), 195(4) and 230(7).

[85] *Chappell & Co Ltd v Columbia Graphophone Co* [1914] 2 Ch. 124.

[86] It is in substance a species of injunction: *Ocular Sciences Ltd v Aspect Vision Care Ltd* [1997] R.P.C. 289 at pp.410 and 420.

[87] *Vavasseur v Krupp* (1879) 9 Ch.D. 351 at 360; *Mergenthaler Limotype Co Ltd v Intertype Co Ltd* (1926) 43 R.P.C. 381 (both patent cases).

[88] *Electrical & Musical Industries Ltd v Lissen Ltd* (1936) 54 R.P.C. 5 at 35; *British United Shoe Machinery Co Ltd v Gimson Shoes Machinery Co Ltd* (1928) 45 R.P.C. 85 at 105; *Geodesic Constructions Pty Ltd v Gatson* (1976) S.A.S.R. 453 at 471.

[89] *Roussel Uclaf v Pan Laboratories Pty Ltd* (1994) 29 I.P.R. 556 (Fed. Ct. of Aus.).

will apply only to the infringing material,[90] but where the parts are physically in-separable the order for delivery up may extend to the whole of the article.[91]

The exercise of the jurisdiction to make an order for delivery up, particularly at the interim stage, may be affected by the provisions of the Contempt of Court Act 1981 relating to disclosure of sources of information.[92]

For special provisions in the case where the copyright owner has granted an exclusive licence which encompasses the defendant's infringing acts, see section (x) below.

(ix) Points as to costs

22–183   **Scope.** There are no specific rules as to costs in actions concerning the rights covered in this work, and the reader is referred to the relevant Civil Procedure Rules and specialist works. The following paragraphs cover certain specific ap-plications of those rules to actions concerning the rights covered in this work.

22–184   **Pre-action behaviour.** Pre-action behaviour may be crucial to the final costs order.[93] Pre-action behaviour in relation to the enforcement of the rights covered in this work is discussed below.[94]

22–185   **Defendants' pre-action offers.** In the previous edition of this work, it was stated that as a general rule a claimant in a copyright case was not obliged to rest satis-fied with the defendant's promise not to infringe and was entitled to go to court to vindicate his right.[95] The introduction of the Civil Procedure Rules has swept away the old rules as to costs and it seems unlikely that this proposition remains correct as a general rule. Much will depend on the nature of the infringement and the infringer. If a respectable and financially strong defendant, who has been guilty of innocent infringement, offers suitable contractual undertakings together with such other relief as the claimant may reasonably expect to recover at trial (such as delivery up, *Tring*-type disclosure and a money offer), a claimant who nevertheless commences proceedings may well do so at his own risk as to costs. By contrast, where the defendant's offer can be shown to be worthless, for example because the infringement was deliberate and flagrant, a claimant may well be considered to be justified in commencing proceedings (after complying with such requirements as to pre-action behaviour as may be applicable).

22–186   **Part 36 offers.** In actions concerning the rights covered in this work, the issues of liability and quantum will normally be tried separately. If the claimant suc-ceeds at trial, he can expect to obtain an injunction, together (at his election) with an order for an inquiry as to damages or an account of profits.[96] The question arises as to how a defendant who wishes to make a Part 36 offer should frame his offer. It is not clear whether a claim for an inquiry or an account is a "money claim" within the meaning of Part 36. It is probably unsafe to assume that it is not. Accordingly, a defendant who wishes to obtain the protection of Part 36

---

[90] *Warne & Co v Seebohm* (1888) 39 Ch.D. 73; *Nichols Advanced Vehicle Systems Inc v Rees* [1979] R.P.C. 127.
[91] *Stevens v Wildy* (1850) 11 L.J. Ch. 190; *Secretary of State for Defence v Guardian Newspapers* [1985] A.C. 339.
[92] Contempt of Court Act 1981 (c.49), s.10; see above, para. 22–146, above.
[93] CPR 44.3(5)(a).
[94] See paras 22–192 *et seq.*, below.
[95] *Copinger*, 14th ed. para.22–101.
[96] See above, para. 22–161, above.

should make a Part 36 payment in respect of the claim for damages or profits and a Part 36 offer in respect of the rest of the claim.[97]

Costs of split trials. Where there is an order for a split trial and the only relief the claimant obtains is an enquiry as to damages or an account of profits, but it is uncertain whether the claimant will recover more than nominal damages, the trial judge may well be justified in deferring any order as to costs until the final outcome is known.[98]   **22–187**

Costs of internal experts. In the patent case of *Re Nossen's Patent*[99], the court permitted the claimant to recover, by way of costs, a sum in respect of experiments conducted by its employees for the purposes of the proceedings. It has been held that this principle applies generally in intellectual property proceedings.[1] Thus, a corporate claimant may in principle recover a reasonable sum in respect of expert services performed by its own staff in investigating, formulating and presenting its claim. Whether these costs are recoverable will depend on whether the employees concerned are truly experts.   **22–188**

Joinder pursuant to section 102(1) of the 1988 Act. A copyright owner or exclusive licensee added as a defendant pursuant to section 102(1) of the 1988 Act is not liable for any costs unless he takes part in the proceedings.[2] There are similar provisions in respect of performers' property rights and design right.[3]   **22–189**

(x) The position of exclusive licensees

In cases where an exclusive licensee has concurrent rights with a copyright owner, owner of a performer's property right or design right, special considerations apply to the remedies of delivery up, seizure without a court order, damages and account of profits.   **22–190**

First, the owner of the right must notify the exclusive licensee before applying for an order for delivery up under sections 99, 195 or 230 and (in the case of copyright and performer's property rights) before exercising the right of seizure under sections 100 or 196, as the case may be.[4] The exclusive licensee can then apply to the court and the court may make such order for delivery up under sections 99, 195 or 230 as it thinks fit having regard to the terms of the licence. In the case of copyright and performer's property rights, the court may also make such order as it thinks fit, having regard to the terms of the licence, prohibiting or permitting the exercise by the rights owner of the right of seizure under sections 100 or 196, as the case may be.[5]

Secondly, in an action for infringement of copyright, performer's property rights or design right which relates wholly or partly to an infringement in respect of which the owner of the right and an exclusive licensee have or had concurrent rights of action:

   (a) the court is directed to take into account, when assessing damages, the terms of the licence and any pecuniary remedy already awarded or available to either of them in respect of the infringement;

---

[97] CPR 36.4(2).

[98] *Weill v Mean Fiddler Holdings Ltd* [2003] EWCA Civ 1058 at para.34.

[99] [1969] 1 W.L.R. 638.

[1] *Admiral Management Services Ltd v Para Protect Europe Ltd* [2002] EWHC 233 (Ch).

[2] CDPA 1988, s.102(2).

[3] ss.191M(2) and 235(2).

[4] CDPA 1988, ss.102(5), 191M(5) and 235(5).

[5] *ibid.*

(b) the court may not direct an account of profits if an award of damages has been made, or an account of profits has been directed in favour of the other of them in respect of the infringement;

(c) if an account of profits is directed the court must apportion the profits between them as the court considers just, subject to any agreement between them.

These provisions apply whether or not the owner of the right and the exclusive licensee are both parties to the action.[6]

8. PROCEDURAL AND RELATED MATTERS

A. INFRINGEMENT OF EACH RIGHT A SEPARATE TORT

22–191 The various rights conferred upon a copyright owner, including the right to authorise any of the restricted acts are separate and distinct rights, and the infringement of each is a distinct and separate tort. The same is true of moral rights, rights in performances and design right. Consequently, for example, judgment against the author of an infringing work for having authorised its printing is no bar to an action against the printer.

B. PRE-ACTION CONDUCT

22–192 **General.** There are no pre-action protocols in respect of claims involving the rights covered in this Chapter. The position is therefore governed by paragraphs 4.1 to 4.10 of *Practice Direction—Protocols*, which provides amongst other things that parties to a potential dispute should use a reasonable procedure, suitable to their particular circumstances, which is intended to avoid litigation.

22–193 **The pre-action Code of Practice.** An Intellectual Property Pre-Action Protocol Committee was established by the Law Society some time ago to develop pre-action protocols for intellectual property cases. However, before the final drafts were published, the Committee was informed that no such protocols were now required.[7] Nevertheless, the Committee has published its drafts in the form of a Code of Practice.[8] The Code does not have the force of law,[9] but it seems likely that its contents will be taken into account in considering whether parties have complied with *Practice Direction—Protocols*. The Code applies to all intellectual property disputes.[10] The aim of the Code is to ensure that the parties inform each other about their cases before proceedings commence with a view to avoiding litigation and (if litigation is unavoidable) keeping costs to a proportionate level.[11] Accordingly, the Code sets out certain prescribed information which a prospective claimant must include in a letter of claim and which a prospective defendant must include in a letter of response. This information is described in the following paragraphs. The Code first sets out general requirements which all such letters should conform to. It then sets out specific requirements for certain types of claim. The Code also requires the parties to show that they have

---

[6] CDPA 1988, ss.102(4), 191M(4) and 235(4).

[7] See the Introduction to the Code of Practice referred to in the next note.

[8] *Code of Practice for pre-action conduct in intellectual property disputes*, January 2004. The text is available at *www.richardsbutler.com*.

[9] Although it was published with the support of Sir Hugh Laddie who was a member of the Committee

[10] para.2.1. In the case of a mixed claim (e.g. infringement of copyright and breach of contract) it provides that the parties should follow the requirements of any applicable pre-action protocols and codes of practice as far as possible.

[11] para.1.2.

considered alternative methods of resolving their dispute.[12] In the Code, a person making a claim is referred to as a claimant and a person responding to a claim as a defendant.

When the Code may be departed from. There are a number of such circumstances.[13] The examples given in the Code are: where it is reasonable for the claimant to apply for interim relief in a manner and timescale which is inconsistent with the Code; where there is a reasonable and urgent need to issue proceedings in order to found jurisdiction; where the limitation period is about to expire; where a claim for threats might arise; and where it would not be reasonable to expect compliance with the Code having regard to the parties' previous dealings. Since a threats claim might arise in many cases of alleged design right infringement, it seems likely that the Code will seldom be used in this field. 22–194

Letters of claim and response under the Code: general.[14] A letter of claim under the Code should state that it follows the Code and the defendant should also do so; should enclose a copy of the Code where the defendant is unrepresented; should identify the claimant; should list the remedies the claimant seeks; and should give details of any funding arrangements entered into.[15] The letter of response should be sent within 14 days or any shorter time specified by the claimant.[16] If this cannot be done, the defendant should contact the claimant and supply an alternative date.[17] The letter of response should state whether and to what extent the claim is accepted or rejected.[18] If the claim or any part of it is accepted, the defendant should state what remedies the defendant is prepared to offer, including whether he is prepared to stop the acts complained of and offer undertakings.[19] If the defendant is prepared to offer a financial remedy, the letter should provide the claimant with the relevant information to enable the claimant to know the basis on which the sum offered has been calculated.[20] If the defendant requires more information the letter should identify the information required and state why it is needed.[21] If the claim is rejected, the letter should explain why, giving a sufficient indication of any facts on which the defendant currently relies in support of any substantive defence.[22] Where the defendant is considering making a counterclaim, it should give the same details of the counterclaim as would be required if it were a claimant.[23] Finally, the letter should give details of any funding arrangements entered into.[24] 22–195

---

[12] The examples given in the Code (para.6) are: without prejudice discussion, determination by an independent expert, mediation and arbitration.

[13] Para.2.2. Para.2.1 also provides that in more complex cases it may be reasonable to extend the time limits provided for in the Code.

[14] These documents are not intended to have the same status as a statement of case. They should be sufficiently detailed to enable each party to understand the other's case, but their preparation should not place an unreasonable or disproportionate cost burden on either party: para.2.3.

[15] para.3.2.

[16] para.4.2.

[17] para.4.2. In almost all cases the defendant will be expected to have responded within 28 days of receipt of the letter of claim: *ibid.*

[18] para.4.2(a).

[19] para.4.2(b).

[20] para.4.2(c). In some cases, it will be reasonable for the the respondent to require the claimant and its advisers to keep this material confidential: *ibid.*

[21] para.4.2(d).

[22] para.4.2(e).

[23] para.4.2(f).

[24] para.4.2(g).

22–196   **Letters of claim and response: additional provisions for copyright, moral rights, database right and unregistered design right.** As well as the matters referred to in the previous paragraph, a letter of claim in relation to claims for infringement of these rights should also contain the following where appropriate.[25] First, sufficient information to identify the work or design in question,[26] including where possible a copy. Secondly, the date of creation (in the case of copyright) or the year of first marketing (in the case of UK unregistered design right). Thirdly, an explanation of how and by whom the claimant's work was created; in the case of a moral right, the letter should identify the author or director as appropriate and how any paternity right relied on was asserted. Fourthly, details of the claimant's title. Fifthly, details of any other person with an interest in the work and of the interest itself. Sixthly, details of the infringing actions or threatened infringing actions and why that activity has infringed or will infringe. Seventhly, in cases of alleged infringement by copying, sufficient details to enable the defendant to identify the infringing work. Eighthly, the relevant parts of the infringing work which are or will be copied. Ninthly, the relevant parts of the claimant's work which have been or will be copied. Tenthly, how the defendant obtained access to the claimant's work. Finally, whether there is to be a claim for additional damages and if so what acts are relied on. A letter of response in relation to these claims should, where appropriate, explain why the defendant disputes that the right in issue subsists, that the work is original, is owned by the claimant or has been copied and why the work which is claimed to be an infringement is not an infringement; should state whether the defendant is prepared to enter into a licence agreement; and should inform the claimant, in accordance with the Code, whether the defendant intends to make a claim for unjustified threats.[27]

22–197   **Letters of claim and response: additional provisions for breach of confidence.** In breach of confidence cases, the letter of claim should where appropriate do the following.[28] First, it should identify the nature of the confidential information, including why it is confidential. If it is difficult for the claimant to disclose details in the absence of a formal confidentiality regime, the letter should seek to establish such a regime. Secondly, it should state how the confidential information came into existence. Thirdly, it should provide details of the claimant's title. Fourthly, it should provide details of the how the defendant came into possession of the information. Fifthly, it should provide details of why the information was communicated to the defendant in circumstances imposing a duty of confidence, including details of any contractual provisions on which the claimant wishes to rely. Finally, it should provide details of how the defendant has breached or will breach the duty of confidence including, if known, to whom it is believed the defendant has disclosed or will disclose the information, and in what form. Where appropriate, a letter of response in a breach of confidence case should explain why the defendant was or is entitled to use or disclose the information, including where appropriate an explanation as to why the defendant disputes that the information is confidential, is owned by the claimant or has been or will be disclosed to or by the defendant.[29]

22–198   **Letters of claim and response: additional provisions for passing off.** In passing-off cases, the letter of claim should do the following, where appropri-

---

[25] App.B.
[26] In a copyright case the letter should identify the type of work in accordance with the descriptions set out in sections 1(1) and 3 to 8 of the 1988 Act.
[27] App. B.
[28] App.A.
[29] App. A.

ate:[30] First, it should provide sufficient details to identify the mark or get-up of the claimant and enclose a copy where practicable. Secondly, it should provide sufficient details to identify the goods or services associated with the mark or get-up relied on and how it has been used in respect of goods and services. Thirdly, it should provide details of the date on which the claimant started to use the mark or get-up relied on. Fourthly, in relation to the goods or services relied on it should provide sufficient details to identify the size and geographical extent of the reputation or goodwill associated with the mark or get-up relied on and how long that reputation or goodwill has been in existence. Fifthly, it should identify the mark or get up complained of, including the goods or services to which it is or will be applied. Sixthly, it should identify the activities of the defendant complained of. Seventhly, it should identify the confusion those activities have caused or are likely to cause. Eighthly, it should set out any examples of instances of confusion currently relied on. A letter of response to such a letter should where appropriate:[31] first, where the defendant does not agree with the claimant's description of its goodwill or get-up or goods or services relied on, state the defendant's reasons for so disagreeing; secondly, where the defendant does not agree with the claimant's description of the defendant's mark or get-up or goods or services complained of, give sufficient details to identify the defendant's mark or get-up or goods or services; thirdly, identify the date when the defendant started use of its mark or get-up on its goods or services and give sufficient details to identify the size and geographical extent of any reputation or goodwill associated with the defendant's mark or get-up or goods or services and how long that reputation or goodwill has been in existence. Finally, it should state whether the defendant is prepared to enter into a licence agreement.

Letters of claim and response: additional provisions for threats claims. In these cases, the letter of claim should additionally where appropriate identify the correspondence or other activities of the defendant complained of, where possible enclosing copies and identify the relevant statutory provision relied on.[32] Where the defendant does not agree with the claimant's characterisation of the meaning of any words complained of, the letter of response should state the defendant's reasons for so disagreeing.[33] **22–199**

C. COMMENCEMENT OF PROCEEDINGS

The Code of Practice. This provides that a claimant should not issue proceedings until either he has received a letter of response from the defendant or 14 days have elapsed since the letter of claim was sent and the defendant has not responded, nor given a reasonable explanation for his failure to respond.[34] **22–200**

Jurisdiction of County Courts. The County courts have jurisdiction under their general jurisdiction in tort to hear and determine cases of infringement of copyright.[35] It is suggested that the same can be said of cases of infringement of the other rights covered in this Chapter. Special jurisdiction is given to the county courts to make orders for the delivery up and final disposal of infringing copies, **22–201**

---

[30] App.C.
[31] App.C.
[32] App.F.
[33] App. F.
[34] para.5.
[35] See *PSM International Plc v Specialised Fastener Products (Southern) Ltd* [1993] F.S.R. 113 and *McDonald & Another v Graham* [1994] R.P.C. 407 at 435; *Gerber Garment Technology Inc v Lectro Systems Ltd* [1997] R.P.C. 443 (infringement of a patent a statutory tort).

illicit recordings and infringing articles.[36] This jurisdiction also extends to means of circumventing protection measures for computer programs, devices for circumventing protection measures for other works and unauthorised decoders.[37] With the exception of the Patents County Court, County Courts do not have jurisdiction to grant seizure orders,[38] while except in the case of a nominated Judge of the Mercantile List of the Central London County Court, their jurisdiction to grant freezing orders is limited (relevantly) to circumstances where the property to be frozen forms or may form the subject-matter of proceedings or where the order is sought in aid of execution.[39]

22–202 **High Court or County Court: the rules and practice directions.** The rules about where proceedings may be commenced are not entirely clear. A claim where the claimant expects to recover more than £15,000 may be started in the High Court.[40] However, in many cases involving the rights covered in this work, it cannot be said that the claimant expects to recover more than £15,000. Examples include: where only *quia timet* relief is sought; where the alleged infringement has only just begun; and where the claimant is unclear as to the extent of the damage. Prior to the introduction of the Civil Procedure Rules, claims of this nature were usually commenced in the High Court because of the availability there of specialist judges and facilities for swift interlocutory relief. The present position is uncertain. On the one hand, paragraph 2.1 of PD7 states: "Proceedings (whether for damages or for a specified sum) may not be started in the High Court unless the value of the claim is more than £15,000", while CPR 16.3(5) (so far as it relates to matters other than personal injuries) states that where a claim form is to be issued in the High Court it must state either that the claimant expects to recover more than £15,000; or that some other enactment provides that the claim may only be commenced in the High Court; or that the claim is to be in one or more of the specialist High Court lists. There are no relevant enactments which require ordinary actions concerning the rights dealt with in this work to be commenced in the High Court, nor is there a relevant specialist list. Accordingly, the effect of PD7 paragraph 2.1 and CPR 16.3(5) would appear to be that cases where the claimant does not expect to recover over £15,000 must be commenced in a County Court. On the other hand, paragraph 2.5 of PD7 provides that a claim relating to Chancery business may, subject to any enactment, rule or practice direction, be dealt with in the High Court or a County Court. Both copyright and design right are Chancery business for these purposes.[41] Although PD7 paragraph 2.5 is expressed to be subject to any enactment, rule or practice direction, it is certainly arguable as a matter of construction that is not intended to be read subject to PD7 paragraph 2.1 (the terms of which are set out above). Unlike paragraph 2.4, paragraph 2.5 is not expressly stated to be subject to paragraph 2.1. If this analysis is correct, copyright and design right claims will be correctly brought in the High Court whatever the value of the action. Claims for the other rights covered in this Chapter are not stated to be Chancery business in Schedule 1 to the Supreme Court Act 1981. However, the list in Schedule 1 is not

---

[36] CDPA 1988, ss.115, 205 and 232. This jurisdiction has no financial limit: High Court and County Courts Jurisdiction Order 1991 (SI 1991/724), art.2.

[37] This is because CDPA 1988 ss.99 and 114 are applied to such articles by ss.296(4) and (7) (means of circumventing protection measures for computer programs), 296ZD(4) and (6) (devices for circumventing protection measures for other works) and 298(3) and (6) (decoders). s.115 simply gives County Courts jurisdiction to make orders under ss.99 and 114.

[38] County Court Remedies Regulations 1991 (SI 1991/1222), reg.3(1), (2).

[39] County Court Remedies Regulations 1991 (SI 1991/1222), reg.3(3).

[40] CPR PD7, para.2.1.

[41] See para.1 of Sch.1 to the Supreme Court Act 1981 (c.54).

exhaustive. As the Chancery Guide makes clear,[42] proceedings for passing off "are heard" in the Chancery Division. It is certainly arguable that proceedings for breach of confidence are "Chancery business" although it should be recognised that such claims are often brought in the Queen's Bench Division. One potential difficulty with this argument is that none of the matters set out in CPR 16.3(5) (above) is the fact that the claim concerns Chancery business.

High Court or County Court: argument based on the value of the claim. A **22–203** further argument which can be used by claimants is that the value of the claim is not the amount of damages or profits sought but the value to the claimant of an injunction. The value to the claimant of an injunction can be said to be the amount of loss which its existence can be expected to prevent. This will often exceed £15,000. PD7 paragraph 2.1 speaks of the "value" of the claim. However, this argument is also inconsistent with CPR 16.3(5), which requires a High Court claim form to state that the claimant expects to "recover" more than £15,000.

High Court or County Court: conclusion. It seems therefore that there is a risk **22–204** that a technical objection may be made where the claimant is unable to say that he expects to recover more than £15,000. However, there is no reported case in which this has occurred. CPR 3.10 provides that errors of procedure such as a failure to comply with a rule or practice direction do not invalidate any step taken in the proceedings unless the court so orders and that the court may make an order to remedy the error. If a point as to jurisdiction were successfully taken against a claimant after a claim form had been issued it is likely that the court would simply transfer the case to a County Court with appropriate directions in the meantime.

Allocation: CPR 63 and PD63. CPR 63.13 when read in conjunction with **22–205** para.18.1 of PD 63 provides that claims in respect of the rights covered in this Chapter other than confidential information claims which do not involve technical trade secrets[43] must be brought either in the Chancery Division or in a Patents County Court or in a county court where there is also a Chancery District Registry. There are Chancery district registries at Birmingham, Bristol, Cardiff, Leeds, Liverpool, Manchester and Newcastle upon Tyne.[44] It is thought that this provision does not resolve the uncertainty mentioned above, but simply has the effect that if a claim is brought in a county court it must be brought either in a Patents County Court or in a county court where there is also a Chancery District Registry.

The claim form. Claims will almost always be brought as Part 7 claims. The **22–206** claim form must contain a concise statement of the nature of the claim, specify the remedy which the claimant seeks and, where money is claimed, contain a statement of value.[45] A claim which is expressed in such general terms as "infringement of unregistered design right" would be unlikely to comply with this rule, and claimants will have to be more precise. What is required is a brief statement of the right in question and of the remedies sought. Except in the case of a claim in respect of confidential information brought in the Queen's Bench Divi-

---

[42] See Sch.1, para.23.9.
[43] See PD63, para.18.1(12). Historically, breach of confidence claims have frequently been brought in the Queen's Bench Division.
[44] See PD63, para.18.2.
[45] CPR 16.2(1). The statement of value must be in accordance with CPR 16.2(3).

sion, a claim form must be marked "Chancery Division, Intellectual Property" in the top right-hand corner below the title of the court in which it has been issued.[46]

22–207   **The particulars of claim.** A claimant who seeks additional damages under section 97(2) or section 229(3) of the 1988 Act must so state in the particulars of claim form and state the grounds for claiming them.[47] Otherwise, there are no specific provisions relating to the rights covered in this Chapter. However, it is worth noting that paragraph 8.3(1) of PD16 provides that where a claim is based on a written agreement, a copy of the contract or document constituting the agreement should be attached to or served with the particulars of claim. It is thought that this provision does not require a claimant to attach copies of his or her documents of title to the particulars of claim. The reference to "claims based upon a written agreement" is almost certainly a reference to claims brought to enforce a contract or to recover damages for its breach. Appendix 1 to the Chancery Guide contains guidelines on statements of case. In the previous edition of this work it was stated that a claimant in a copyright action was expected to indicate in particulars to a statement of claim, by reference to parallel passages or otherwise, the parts he mainly relied upon as constituting an infringement, but that he might well reserve the right, at the trial, to rely upon general similarities as further evidence of piracy.[48] Following the introduction of the Civil Procedure Rules, it seems unlikely that such an approach would be considered acceptable. In a nineteenth century case, it was held that if a claimant brings an action to protect a work, being only entitled to copyright in a small part of such work, he ought to tell the defendant, in his claim, what that part is, otherwise costs unnecessarily incurred must be borne by the claimant.[49] It seems inevitable that the same principle would be applied today.

D. FORM OF DEFENCE

22–208   In his defence a defendant must state which of the allegations he denies, which he is unable to admit and which he denies. Where he denies an allegation he must state his reasons for so doing and if he intends to put forward a different version of events from that given by the claimant, he must state his own version.[50] Where a defendant fails to deal with an allegation in his defence, he shall be taken to admit it unless either he has set out in his defence the nature of his case in relation to the issue to which that allegation is relevant or the allegation relates to the amount of money claimed.[51] Accordingly, the defendant to an action for infringement of the rights covered in this chapter should, if he desires to dispute the subsistence of the right or the claimant's title to the right or both, specifically raise the point in his defence. He may do this by non-admission, leaving the claimant to prove his case at trial, or by denial. Any positive case to be advanced by the defendant (for example, an assertion that the right belongs to a third party and not

---

[46] PD63, para.19.1. Taken literally, this would mean that the words "Chancery Division" will appear in claims brought in a County Court. However, PD7 para.2.5 provides that a claim relating to "Chancery business" which is brought in a County Court should be marked "Chancery Business". Although by no means all the claims covered by PD63 are strictly "Chancery business", it seems likely that what is intended that this should apply to all claims brought in a County Court pursuant to PD63, para.18.1.

[47] PD63, para.25.1.
[48] *Copinger on Copyright* (14th Ed.), para.22–120.
[49] *Page v Wisden* (1869) 17 W.R. 483.
[50] CPR 16.5(1) and (2).
[51] CPR 16.5(3) to (6).

to the claimant) should be specifically pleaded. Also any other specific defence should be pleaded with supporting facts.[52]

E. SUMMARY JUDGMENT

The general principles which are applicable in summary judgment applications are set out in CPR Part 24 and the numerous authorities under that Part.[53] The following specific points can be made as to summary judgment applications in respect of claims involving the rights covered in this Chapter. First, if the relief sought on the application for summary judgment includes an injunction (as it usually will in intellectual property cases) the application should be made made directly to the Judge instead of the Master.[54] Secondly, where the issue is whether a substantial part of the claimant's work has been taken, that should normally go to trial since it is a matter of fact and degree.[55] However, this will not be the case where the court is satisfied on the application for summary judgment that no further evidence is likely to emerge and, therefore, that there is no point in the matter going to trial.[56] Thirdly, where a claimant alleges infringement of copyright in a number of works, he is entitled to apply for summary judgment in respect of some of them, leaving the others to a trial.[57] Fourthly, where on an application under CPR Part 24, a claimant succeeds in establishing that there is no triable issue that part of the defendant's work infringes, it will not normally be correct to deny the claimant a permanent injunction against that part because the defendant argues that such an injunction may not be granted after a full trial.[58] Fifthly, if a claimant in his supporting affidavit claims to be the owner of the copyright without giving full details of each and every fact underlying the claim to subsistence and ownership, and if there is no reason to believe, from the defendant's evidence or otherwise, that the claimant's claim is not true, the court will not give the defendant permission to defend on the basis that something may turn up during the course of disclosure or Part 18 Answers.[59] The judgment will usually contain a permanent injunction and an order for an inquiry as to damages, including, if appropriate, additional damages. The inquiry will normally be conducted before a Master.

22–209

F. PRESUMPTIONS

Introduction. The 1988 Act contains a series of presumptions designed to assist a claimant in a copyright action whether on an application for interim relief, or at the trial.[60] These presumptions apply in proceedings under sections 296 (circumvention of technical devices applied to computer programs), 296ZA and 296ZD (circumvention of technological measures applied to other works and de-

22–210

---

[52] As to pleading of "Euro defences" see *Ransburg-Gema AG v Electrostatic Plant Systems Ltd* [1990] F.S.R. 287.

[53] See the current edition of *Civil Procedure*. For a recent example in the field, see *Celador Productions Ltd v Melville* [2004] EWHC 2362 (Ch).

[54] *Chancery Guide*, para.6.26.

[55] *Total Information Processing Systems Ltd v Daman Ltd* [1992] F.S.R. 171, applying *Leco Instruments UK Ltd v Land Pyrometers Ltd* [1982] R.P.C. 133.

[56] *Ludlow Music Inc v Williams* [2001] F.S.R. 271.

[57] *Macmillan Publishers Ltd v Thomas Reed Publications Ltd* [1993] F.S.R. 455. This case predates the CPR but the principle should still hold good.

[58] *Macmillan Publishers Ltd v Thomas Reed Publications Ltd* [1993] F.S.R. 455, applying *Mawman v Tegg* (1826) 2 Russ.385. Again, this case predates the CPR but the principle should still hold good.

[59] *Microsoft Corporation v Electro-Wide Ltd & Another* [1997] F.S.R. 580.

[60] CDPA 1988, ss.104–106. See also s.27(4) for a presumption as to infringing copies and see ss.93A and 191F for presumptions as regards the transfer of rental right in the case of a film production agreement.

vices and services designed to circumvent such measures) and 296ZG (rights management information).[61] The presumptions do not apply to publication right.[62] There are similar presumptions in relation to database right,[63] but none in respect of the other rights dealt with in this Chapter.

22–211   **Literary, dramatic, musical and artistic works: name purporting to be that of the author.** Where a name purporting to be that of the author appeared on copies of a literary, dramatic, musical or artistic work as published or appeared on the work when it was made, the person whose name so appeared is to be presumed, until the contrary is proved, to be the author of the work.[64] If, however, the name purports to be that of an "arranger", the only presumption is that the "name" in question did some work of arrangement.[65] It is further to be presumed, until the contrary is proved, that the work was made in circumstances not falling within the provisions relating to works produced in the course of employment, or the provisions relating to Crown copyright, parliamentary copyright or copyright of certain international organisations.[66] The effect of this provision is that, where an author's name appears in the circumstances indicated, it will not be necessary for the claimant to prove that the person so named as author actually wrote, composed or created the work. It will be sufficient for the claimant to establish a documentary title commencing from such author. Where the work is alleged to be a work of joint authorship, a similar presumption is made in relation to each person alleged to be one of the authors of the work.[67] In the equivalent provision in the 1956 Act, it was expressly provided that the "name" must be either the true name of the person whose name so appeared, or a name by which he was commonly known.[68] It is suggested that the absence of these words in the 1988 Act is a change of expression and not a change of substance[69] and that if a name by which a person is commonly known appears on copies of the work as author, then the presumption will still apply. The whole purpose of the presumption is to identify "a person" who is to be presumed to be the author. Such a person could not be identified except by reference to his actual name or a name by which he was commonly known. The situation of a person who is commonly known by some name other than his real name falls, it is suggested, within the natural meaning of the presumption, even without the words which appeared in the equivalent provision of the 1956 Act. To take a fictitious example, it is suggested that the court would not refuse to apply the presumption in the case of a book entitled *My Early Life by ABCD*, merely because *ABCD* is not the author's real name. Clearly there is a name purporting to be that of the author on the book, so the first part of the presumption is satisfied. All that is left to do is to identify the actual person to whom that name refers. That must be the author known as *ABCD*, because it couldn't be anyone else.

22–212   **Literary dramatic, musical and artistic works: name purporting to be that of the publisher.** Where the provision discussed in the previous paragraph does not apply, that is to say, where an author's name does not appear on the work, but the work qualifies for copyright protection by virtue of first publication in the

---

[61] See, respectively, CDPA 1988 ss.296(7)(a), 296ZA(5)(a), 296ZD(6)(a) and 296ZG(6)(a).

[62] Copyright and Related Rights Regulations 1996 (SI 1996/2967), reg.17(2)(b).

[63] Copyright and Rights in Databases Regulations 1997 (SI 1997/3032), reg.22. See para. 22–219, below.

[64] CDPA 1988, s.104(2)(a).

[65] *per* Cross J. in *Roberton v Lewis* [1976] R.P.C. 169.

[66] CDPA 1988, s.104(2)(b).

[67] s.104(3).

[68] s.20(2) of the 1956 Act.

[69] See s.172(2).

United Kingdom, or in another country to which the relevant provision of the 1988 Act extends, and a name purporting to be that of the publisher appeared on copies of the work as first published, the person whose name so appeared is presumed to have been the owner of the copyright at the time of publication.[70] Again, this presumption applies until the contrary is proved.[71] If the publisher is to be presumed to have been the owner of the copyright at the time of publication, it follows that it is to be presumed that the author did not own the copyright at that time. The onus is on the person challenging the publisher's presumed ownership of the copyright to prove affirmatively that the person named as publisher did not own the copyright when the work was published.[72]

Deceased or anonymous authors. In the case of a literary, dramatic, musical or artistic work, if the author of the work is dead, or the identity of the author cannot be ascertained by reasonable inquiry, the work is to be presumed to be an original work in the absence of evidence to the contrary.[73] Furthermore, in such cases, it is to be presumed, in the absence of evidence to the contrary, that the claimant's allegations as to what was the first publication of the work and as to the country of first publication are correct.[74]   22–213

Works for films. Where the work is a screenplay or dialogue for a film, or music specifically created for and used in a film, some of the presumptions regarding films may apply.[75]   22–214

Sound recordings. There are further presumptions which can be relied upon in any action brought with respect to the copyright in a sound recording.[76] Where copies of the recording as issued to the public bear a label or other mark stating (a) that a named person was the owner of copyright in the recording at the date of issue of the copies; or (b) that the recording was first published in a specified year or in a specified country, the label or mark shall be admissible as evidence of the facts so stated and shall be presumed to be correct until the contrary is proved. This presumption applies equally in proceedings relating to an infringement alleged to have occurred before the date on which the copies were issued to the public.[77]   22–215

Films: presumption arising from issue of copies to the public. In proceedings brought with respect to a film, where copies of the film as issued to the public bear a statement containing specified facts, that statement is admissible as evidence of the facts stated and is presumed to be correct until the contrary is proved.[78] The facts in question are, first, that a named person was the director or producer of the film[79]; secondly, that a named person was the principal director, the author of the screenplay, the author of the dialogue or the composer of music specifically created for and used in the film[80]; thirdly, that a named person was the owner of the copyright in the film at the date of issue of the copies[81];or fourthly, that the film was first published in a specified year or in a specified   22–216

---

[70] See CDPA 1988, s.104(4).
[71] ibid.
[72] Warwick Film Productions Ltd v Eisinger [1969] 1 Ch. 508.
[73] CDPA 1988, s.104(5)(a).
[74] s.104(5)(b).
[75] See paras 22–217 and 22–218, below.
[76] CDPA 1988, s.105(1).
[77] s.105(4).
[78] CDPA 1988, s.105(2).
[79] s.105(2)(a).
[80] s.105(2)(aa).
[81] s.105(2)(b).

country.[82] As in the case of the presumption in relation to sound recordings, this presumption applies equally in proceedings relating to an infringement alleged to have occurred before the date on which the copies were issued to the public.[83] For the purpose of this presumption, a statement that a person was the director of a film shall be taken, unless a contrary indication appears, as meaning that he was the principal director of the film.[84]

22–217 **Films: presumption arising from showing in public or communication to the public.** A presumption also applies to proceedings with respect to a film where the film as shown in public or communicated to the public bears a statement that a named person was the director or producer of the film, that a named person was the principal director, the author of the screenplay, the author of the dialogue or the composer of music specifically created for and used in the film or that a named person was the owner of the copyright in the film immediately after it was made.[85] This presumption equally applies in proceedings relating to an infringement alleged to have occurred before the date on which the film was shown in public, or communicated to the public.[86] Again, a statement that a person was the director of a film shall be taken, unless a contrary indication appears, as meaning that he was the principal director of the film.[87]

22–218 **Computer programs.** A similar provision applies in the case of a computer program where copies of the program are issued to the public in electronic form bearing a statement that a named person was the owner of the copyright in the program at the date of issue of the copies or that the program was first published in a specified country or that copies of it were first issued to the public in electronic form in a specified year.[88]

22–219 **Database right.** Where proceedings are brought in respect of database right, similar presumptions apply. First, where a name purporting to be that of the maker appeared on copies of the database as published, or on the database when it was made, the person whose name appeared shall be presumed, until the contrary is proved, to be the maker of the database and to have made it in circumstances not falling within regulations 14(2) to (4), and not to have made it in the course of employment, in the course of duties as an officer or servant of the Crown or under the direction or control of the House of Commons or House of Lords.[89] Secondly, where copies of a database as published bear a label or mark stating that a named person was the maker of the database or that the database was first published in a specified year, that label or mark shall be admissible as evidence of the facts stated unless the contrary is proved.[90] In the case of a database alleged to have been made jointly, these provisions apply in relation to each person alleged to be one of the makers.[91]

22–220 **Crown copyright.** Special provision is made for presumptions relating to works subject to Crown copyright. In proceedings brought with respect to a literary, dramatic or musical work in which Crown copyright subsists, where there ap-

[82] s.105(2)(c).
[83] s.105(4).
[84] s.105(6).
[85] CDPA 1988, s.105(5).
[86] s.105(4) and 105(5).
[87] s.105(6).
[88] CDPA 1988, s.105(3).
[89] Copyright and Rights in Databases Regulations (SI 1997/3032), reg.22(2).
[90] Copyright and Rights in Databases Regulations (SI 1997/3032), reg.22(3).
[91] Copyright and Rights in Databases Regulations (SI 1997/3032), reg.22(4).

pears on printed copies of the work a statement of the year in which the work was first published commercially, that statement shall be admissible in evidence of the fact stated and shall be presumed to be correct in the absence of evidence to the contrary.[92]

G. PROOF OF COPYING

Whether copying has occurred or not is a matter of fact.[93]Direct evidence of copying is rarely available and reliance frequently has to be placed on inference drawn from circumstantial evidence.[94] The basis of secondary proof of copying normally lies in the establishment of similarities between the claimant's work and the defendant's work, combined with proof of the possibility of access by the author of the defendant's work to the claimant's work. Inferences may properly be drawn from the surrounding circumstances and from the nature of the similarities themselves.[95] It is good practice for the claimant to particularise at an early stage in an action the alleged points of similarity between his work and the defendant's work.[96] The existence of a striking general similarity coupled with evidence of the opportunity to copy will establish a *prima facie* case of copying which the defendant then has to answer.[97] The evidential burden shifts to the defendant who then may seek to adduce evidence of some alternative explanation of the similarities between the two works, for example, evidence of independent creation or common source.[98] The Court has declined to order interrogatories seeking evidence of the detailed history of the defendant's development of their copyright work on the grounds that they were "fishing" for information which would be the subject of evidence at the trial.[99] The task of the judge is then to consider the evidence as a whole and decide whether there has been copying or not.[1] An appellate court will not normally interfere with the judge's findings of fact.[2]

22–221

Similar fact evidence. The general rule in civil cases is that the court will admit evidence of similar facts if it is logically probative, that is, if it is logically relevant in determining the matter which is in issue, provided that it is not oppressive or unfair to the other side, and provided that the other side has fair notice of it and is able to deal with it.[3] Thus, where the issue in a copyright case is whether the similarity between the claimant's work and the defendant's work is due to copy-

22–222

---

[92] CDPA 1988, s.106.
[93] For the admissibility of expert evidence on this issue, see para. 22–223, below.
[94] *Sifam Electrical Instrument Co Ltd v Sangamo Western Ltd* [1973] RPC 899.
[95] *John Richardson Computers Ltd v Flanders* [1993] F.S.R. 497 at 543.
[96] *N&P Windows Ltd v Cego Ltd* [1989] F.S.R. 56.
[97] In *Francis Day & Hunter Ltd v Bron* [1963] 1 Ch. 587 at 614, Willmer LJ (with whom Upjohn LJ agreed) stated that where there is a substantial degree of objective similarity between C's and D's work, that *of itself* will afford *prima facie* evidence of a causal connection between C's and Ds' work, or at least is a circumstance from which such an inference can be drawn. See also *Cadieux v Beauchimin* [1901–4] Mac.C.C.4 (Sup of Canada) and *Mathieson v Universal Stock Exchange* [1901–4] Mac.C.C. 4 (Buckley J).
[98] For a fuller discussion, see para. 7–17, above. For the position in relation to artistic works, see para. 7–56, above.
[99] *Rockwell International Corp. v Serck Industries Ltd* [1988] F.S.R. 187.
[1] *L. B. (Plastics) Ltd v Swish Products Ltd* [1979] R.P.C. 551, HL; *Antocks Lairn Ltd v I. Bloohn Ltd* [1971] F.S.R. 490 at 493; *Catnic Components Ltd & Another v Hill and Smith Ltd* [1979] F.S.R. 619 at 626; *The Duriron Co Inc v Hugh Jennings & Co Ltd* [1984] F.S.R. 1; *Wham-O Manufacturing Co v Lincoln Industries Ltd* [1985] R.P.C. 127 (Court of Appeal of New Zealand); and see *Francis Day & Hunter Ltd v Bron* [1963] Ch. 587 (proof of copying from memory).
[2] *L.B. (Plastics) Ltd v Swish Products Ltd* [1979] R.P.C. 551, HL.
[3] *Mood Music Publishing Co Ltd v De Wolfe Ltd* [1976] Ch. 119, *R. v Scarrott* [1978] Q.B. 1016; *Omega v Africio Textile* [1982] 1 S.A.L.R. 951; *Berger v Raymond Sun Ltd* [1984] 1 W.L.R. 625; *Perrin v Drennan* [1991] F.S.R. 81; *Designers Guild Ltd v Russell Williams (Textiles) Limited*

ing or is a coincidence, it is relevant to know that the defendant has produced works which bear a close resemblance to works other than the work in question which are the subject of copyright. Whereas similarity between two works might be mere coincidence in one case, it is unlikely that there could be coincidental similarity in, say, four cases. The probative force of several resemblances together is much better than one alone. It does not matter in such cases that the claimant has not alleged that infringement of copyright has occurred in the other cases. It is sufficient to allege that copying has occurred. Depending on the circumstances, such evidence may be just as probative, especially if it is likely that copyright subsists in the other works and the defendant would have known of or was reckless as to this.[4] It seems that the similar facts do not need to be pleaded in the claimant's reply, provided that the defendant is not taken by surprise at the trial.[5] Although similar fact evidence is admissible to establish the possibility or probability of infringement, the court will not, in the absence of an allegation that the defendant has made a practice of copying others' work, order disclosure of documents which are directed solely towards the credit of the defendant.[6]

H. EXPERT EVIDENCE

22–223   **Copying.** Expert evidence may be called (with the permission of the court[7]) to point out coincidences, similarities or identical omissions with a view to establishing copying,[8] but it is not proper, unless the expert is suitably qualified,[9] for an expert witness to state, as a matter of opinion, that the work was copied from another.[10] That is a question for the judge.[11]

22–224   **Artistic craftsmanship.** Expert witnesses may also be called with permission to give evidence on the question whether a particular work is a work of artistic craftsmanship. The experts should be persons with special capabilities and

---

[1998] F.S.R. 275, where the learned judge held that it was *prima facie* oppressive to seek, at least to a limited extent, to turn a case about infringement of copyright in one design to a case concerning copying (even if not copyright infringement) of two other designs. If by that the learned judge meant no more than that the *prima facie* oppressiveness consisted of an extension of the length (and therefore the costs) of the trial, which would have to be balanced against the probative value of the evidence, then that is in line with the previous cases. If, however, he meant more, it is difficult to see what he had in mind. All attempts to introduce similar fact evidence involve an allegation of copying other works. The particular instances of similar fact which the learned judge disallowed on this ground could have been (and indeed were) disallowed on other grounds (the claimants disclaimed any infringement of copyright and never satisfactorily put their case in a clear and comprehensible way). See also *Stoddard International Plc v William Lomas Carpets Ltd* [2001] F.S.R. 44: similar fact evidence must be clear in order to be probative; and *Mattel Inc v Woolbro (Distributors) Ltd* [2003] EWHC 2412, Ch D: showing that various products of the defendant are very similar to earlier products of the claimant may only show that the defendant gets inspiration from the claimant or that both get inspiration from current fashion trends. To prove a habit of copying may involve a very detailed analysis of the precise degree of similarity and surrounding fashion trends which may justify its exclusion on grounds of proportionality.
[4] *Perrin v Drennan* [1991] F.S.R. 81, where leave was given to amend pleadings to allege similar facts.
[5] *Designers Guild Ltd v Russell Williams (Textiles) Limited* [1998] F.S.R. 275.
[6] *EG Music & Another v SF (Films) Distributors Ltd & Another* [1978] F.S.R. 121.
[7] See, generally, CPR Part 35 and PD35. The question of expert evidence should be raised at the Case Management Conference.
[8] *LB (Plastics) Ltd v Swish Products Ltd* [1979] R.P.C. 551, HL at 619; *Billhofer Maschinen Fabrik GmbH v Dixon & Co Ltd* [1990] F.S.R. 105.
[9] Civil Evidence Act 1972, s.3; *Mölnlycke AB v Proctor & Gamble (No.5)* [1994] R.P.C. 49 at 113; *Glaverbel SA v British Coal Corp. & Another* [1995] R.P.C. 254 at 271.
[10] *Deeks v Wells* [1928–35] Mac.C.C. 353 (PC); *Bauman v Fussell* [1978] R.P.C. 485.
[11] *Monsoon Ltd v India Imports of Rhode Island Ltd* [1993] F.S.R. 486. See also para. 7–18, above.

qualifications for forming an opinion on the matter in question, although it will still be a question for the decision of the judge at the end of the day.[12]

Passing off cases. Opinion evidence from members of the trade as to the likelihood of confusion is inadmissible. However, it is legitimate to call evidence from persons skilled in a particular market to explain any special features of that market of which the judge may otherwise be ignorant and which may be relevant to the likelihood of confusion.[13]

22–225

I. DISCLOSURE AND INSPECTION

The general principles which are applicable to disclosure are set out in CPR Part 31 and the numerous authorities under that Part.[14] The following specific points can be made as to disclosure in cases involving the rights covered in this Chapter. First, if, as is common, there is a split trial as to liability and quantum of damages, the court will not normally require disclosure of documents relating only to quantum before liability has been established. Thus, where there is to be a split trial, disclosure will not be ordered before liability is established merely to enable a party to form an estimate of the amount in issue or to enable information to be given to the Legal Services Commission.[15] Special circumstances must be shown,[16] such as, possibly, a genuine wish by the defendant to make a bona fide offer to settle.[17] Secondly, if confidential documents are relevant the court may, in its discretion, require the defendant to give an undertaking not to make use of the information disclosed thereby and limit the right to take away documents or make copies of them.[18] Inspection of documents relating to trade secrets may be ordered subject to safeguards as to where and by whom the documents may be inspected. A fair balance has to be struck between the natural wish of a party to have his confidential documents adequately protected and the natural wish of the other party to see any documents which may support his case.[19] Thirdly, in intellectual property cases, the defendant is not entitled to privilege from giving disclosure on the ground that he would tend to incriminate himself. This privilege was withdrawn by section 72 of the Supreme Court Act 1981, as amended.[20] Finally, it has been held that a claimant may confine his claim in copyright to part of an unpublished work and, in that case, he will not be required, on disclosure, to disclose the remainder.[21] For disclosure for the purpose of making an informed election between an inquiry as to damages and an account of profits, see paragraph 22–161, above.

22–226

---

[12] *George Hensher Ltd v Restawile Upholstery (Lancs.) Ltd* [1976] A.C. 64 at 82.
[13] *The European Ltd v The Economist Newspaper Ltd* [1998] F.S.R. 283.
[14] See, generally, the current edition of *Civil Procedure*.
[15] *Baldock v Addison* [1995] 1 W.L.R. 158; [1994] F.S.R. 665 and *Kapur v JW Francis & Co & Another, The Times*, March 4, 1998, not following *Hazeltine Corp. v British Broadcasting Corporation* [1979] F.S.R. 523. See also *De La Rue v Dickinson* 3 K. & J. 388; *Fennessy v Clark* [1887] 37 Ch.D. 184; *Lea v Saxby* 32 L.T.R. 731 and *William Gaynor & Son Ltd v HP Bulmer Ltd, The Times*, January 19, 1984.
[16] See previous note.
[17] *Kapur v JW Francis & Co, The Times*, March 4, 1998, CA.
[18] *Centri-Spray v Cera International Ltd & Others* [1979] F.S.R. 175; see also on confidentiality *R. v NSPCC* [1978] A.C. 171; *Science Research Council v Nasse* [1980] A.C. 1028.
[19] *Format Communications Mfg Ltd v ITT (UK) Ltd* [1983] F.S.R. 473; *Zink (John) and Co Ltd v Wilkinson* [1973] R.P.C. 717; *Roussel Uclaf v ICI* [1989] R.P.C. 59; *Atari v Philips Electronics and Associated Industries Ltd* [1988] 5 F.S.R. 416; *Roussel Uclaf v ICI (No.2)* [1990] R.P.C. 45; *Ixora Trading v Jones* [1990] F.S.R. 251.
[20] See paras 22–147 *et seq.*, above.
[21] *Sitwell v Sun Engraving Co Ltd* (1938) 107 L.J. Ch. 68.

J. PRODUCTION OF ORIGINAL WORK

22–227　In an action for infringement of copyright in a work it is not necessary to produce the original from which the alleged copy has been derived[22] if it can be proved by other satisfactory evidence.[23] Indeed, in many cases, the original work has disappeared or been destroyed before the action is commenced or comes to trial.[24]

K. PERIOD OF LIMITATION

22–228　The 1988 Act provides no special limitation period (except in respect of applications for delivery up[25]), so that the six-year period provided in the Limitation Act 1980[26] for actions for tort operates in respect of actions for infringement of all the rights covered in this Chapter. It is important to note that each act of infringement is a separate tort. The fact that the claimant's remedy for one act of infringement is barred does not extinguish the claimant's copyright: he may sue for subsequent or continuing infringements committed within the limitation period.

---

[22] *Lucas v Williams & Sons* [1892] 2 Q.B. 113.
[23] *Wham-O Manufacturing Co v Lincoln Industries Ltd* [1985] R.P.C. 127.
[24] *George Hensher Ltd v Restawile Upholstery (Lancs) Ltd* [1976] A.C. 64 at 79H; *James Arnold & Co Ltd v Miafern Ltd* [1980] R.P.C. 397 at 402; *Allibert SA v O'Connor* [1981] F.S.R. 613 at 621; *Wham-O Manufacturing Co v Lincoln Industries Ltd* [1985] R.P.C. 127 at 142; *Plix Products Ltd v Frank M. Winstone (Merchants) Ltd* [1986] F.S.R. 608.
[25] See para. 22–182, above.
[26] (c.58), s.2.

CRIMINAL REMEDIES AND CUSTOMS SEIZURE

1. CRIMINAL REMEDIES

A. HISTORICAL INTRODUCTION

Early history. From the Copyright Act of 1709[1] to the end of the nineteenth
century, infringers were not liable to be imprisoned. However, under many of the
Copyright Acts in force during this period,[2] infringers were liable in summary
proceedings brought by the copyright owner to financial penalties and infringing
copies were liable to be forfeited. These remedies were in addition to any liability
for damages. The extent to which these provisions created criminal offences
varied. For example, section 6 of the Fine Art Copyright Act 1862[3] was held to
create a criminal offence[4] while the Dramatic Copyright Act 1833[5] was held not
to do so.[6] Criminal remedies similar to those of the present day were first
introduced in the Musical (Summary Proceedings) Copyright Act 1902 as
amended by the Musical Copyright Act 1906.[7]

23–01

The Musical Copyright Act 1906. The origins of the Musical Copyright Act
1906[8] are to be found in the Musical (Summary Proceedings) Copyright Act
1902,[9] which was directed at pirated copies of musical works, and in particular at
preventing what was perceived to be a growing practice of selling pirated sheet
music in the streets at very low prices.[10] The main point of concern was that the
pirated copies did not carry the name of their printer and accordingly copyright

23–02

---

[1] 8 Anne c.19.

[2] As to which see paras 2–18 *et seq.*, above.

[3] 25 & 26 Vict. c.68. See Vol.2 at E5.ix.

[4] *Ex p. Graves* (1868) L.R. 3 Ch. App.642. See however *Re Johnson* 15 W.R. 160 where a Commissioner in Bankruptcy held that a penalty recoverable under this Act was analogous to damages for assault.

[5] Vol.2 at E5.v.

[6] *Adams v Batley* (1887) 18 Q.B.D. 625.

[7] 2 Edw. 7, c.15. See *Copinger* (5th ed.), p.212. See also *R. v Willets* (1906) 70 J.P. 127 in which the Common Sergeant observed, apparently on the basis of a concession by the prosecution, that the Copyright Act 1842 (5 & 6 Vict. c.45) did not create criminal offences.

[8] 6 Edw. 7, c.36.

[9] 2 Edw. 7, c.15.

[10] For the background to this provision, see *Copinger* (5th ed.), pp.214–216. It seems that at that time copyright sheet music sold at 2s. per sheet but infringing copies were being sold at 2d. per

owners experienced difficulties in finding a substantial person to proceed against.[11] The 1902 Act provided for the seizure of such copies by constables and for their destruction, forfeiture or delivery up by order of a court of summary jurisdiction. However, it did not create criminal offences. For a variety of reasons,[12] the Act was a failure. Under the 1906 Act, making or dealing with pirated copies of sheet music became punishable on summary conviction by a fine.[13] Second offenders were liable to imprisonment for up to two months.[14] The burden of proving lack of guilty knowledge was on the defendant.[15] Constables were given powers to arrest street hawkers.[16] Provision was made for courts of summary jurisdiction to issue search warrants and to order the forfeiture or destruction of pirated copies so seized.[17]

23-03   **The 1911 and 1956 Acts.** The framers of the 1911 Act originally intended that all the provisions of the 1902 and 1906 Acts should be extended, in consolidated form, to all categories of copyright work.[18] However, this provoked considerable opposition in Parliament and substantial modification proved necessary.[19] As a result, new criminal provisions were introduced in respect of infringements of the copyright in all categories of work.[20] Making or dealing with an infringing copy, making or possessing a plate for the purposes of making infringing copies, and causing works to be performed in public without a licence were all made offences punishable in the case of a first offender by a fine and in the case of a second offender by imprisonment for up to two months.[21] The burden of proving guilty knowledge on the prosecutor and the powers of arrest, search and seizure contained in the 1902 and 1906 Acts were not applied more generally. Meanwhile, the 1902 and 1906 Acts were left in place.[22] The provisions of the 1911 Act were substantially reproduced in the 1956 Act,[23] but the 1902 and 1906 Acts were repealed by it.[24]

23-04   **The Whitford Committee and amendments to the 1956 Act.** In 1977 the Whitford Committee heard evidence that because of the difficulties of proving guilty knowledge and the small size of the penalties, the criminal provisions of the 1956 Act were seldom used.[25] The Committee recommended that there be a new of-

---

sheet: see the speech of Lord Monkswell introducing what was to become the 1902 Act: *Hansard*, Vol.106, col.456.

[11] See *Copinger* (4th ed.), p.331. It seems that copyright owners ultimately decided to take the law into their own hands by seizing copies of pirated sheet music from the street hawkers. It was only when this led to fights in the streets that the 1902 Act was passed, in the face of considerable opposition: Scrutton, *The Law of Copyright* (4th ed.), pp.v and 107.

[12] Which are summarised in *Copinger* (5th ed.) pp.215–216. For detailed analysis of the causes of the Act's failure, see the debate on the abortive Copyright Bill of 1904, in particular at *Hansard*, Vol.130, cols 1158–59, 1167–68 and 1191–93. In the course of the debate it was claimed that the sale of pirated copies of sheet music had actually increased since the 1902 Act had been passed.

[13] 1906 Act, c.36, s.1(1).

[14] *ibid.*

[15] *ibid.*

[16] s.1(2).

[17] s.2.

[18] See *Copinger* (5th ed.) p.212.

[19] See *Copinger* (5th ed.) p.212. See also MacGillivray, *The Copyright Act 1911, Annotated* (1912), p.94.

[20] Copyright Act 1911, s.11, Vol.2 at E3.

[21] Copyright Act 1911, s.11(1) and (2).

[22] Copyright Act 1911, s.11(4).

[23] Copyright Act 1956, s.21.

[24] Copyright Act 1956, s.50 and Sch.9.

[25] Cmnd. 6732, paras 708 *et seq.*

fence of possessing an infringing copy in the course of trade;[26] that the burden of proof on the issue of knowledge should be placed on the defendant;[27] and that fines for copyright infringement should "at least be kept in line with penalties under the Performers' Protection Acts and offences against property generally".[28] The Committee also recommended that the public performance of sound recordings and films should be made an offence.[29] By 1981, none of these recommendations had been implemented and concerns about sound recording and video piracy were mounting. In 1982 and 1983, two statutes were passed with a view to deterring these activities. The Copyright Act 1956 (Amendment) Act 1982[30] made possession by way of trade of an infringing copy of a sound recording or a film an offence. The Copyright (Amendment) Act 1983[31] made the offences of making for sale or hire, importing and distributing infringing copies of films or sound recordings triable either way[32] with a maximum penalty of two years' imprisonment.[33] Both the 1982 and the 1983 Acts were presented[34] as interim measures pending the full revision of the law of copyright which was ultimately to be effected by the 1988 Act.[35] During the debates that led to the 1983 Act, it was acknowledged by the Government[36] that video piracy was spreading rapidly,[37] that it was under the control of substantial criminals,[38] and that London had become the world centre of pirate video production.[39] In 1985, the increased penalties for sound recordings and films contained in the 1983 Act were extended to offences in relation to computer programs.[40]

The Performers' Protection Acts. The criminal offences of making recordings   **23–05**
of a performance without the performer's consent and dealing with such recordings were created by the Dramatic and Musical Performers' Protection Act 1925.[41] This Act was introduced to deter what was perceived to be a growing practice of making recordings of radio broadcasts of performances for further reproduction and sale. Parliament's main concern was that this was deterring good performers from appearing on radio; but anxiety was also expressed about the effect on the artistes' reputations of the poor quality of such recordings.[42] There was some opposition to the introduction of criminal sanctions in this area.[43] However, the Bill's supporters pointed out that there were criminal sanctions in the Copyright Act 1911 and that there was a defence where the copying was not for the purpose

---

[26] Cmnd. 6732, para.711.

[27] The Committee appears to have intended that it should be for the accused to prove both that he did not know and that he had no reasonable grounds to suspect that the copy in question was infringing: Cmnd. 6732, para.711.

[28] Cmnd. 6732, para.711.

[29] Cmnd. 6732, para.713.

[30] (c.35).

[31] (c.42).

[32] *i.e.* either in the Magistrates' Court or the Crown Court.

[33] This was effected by the introduction of new subss. 21(7A) and (7B) into the 1956 Act.

[34] In both cases, the Bills were sponsored by private members.

[35] See, as to the 1982 Act, *Hansard*, HC Vol.27, col.590 and, as to the 1983 Act, *Hansard*, HC Vol.35, col.605.

[36] Which ultimately supported both Bills, albeit in limited form.

[37] *Hansard*, HC Vol.35, col.619.

[38] *Hansard*, HC Vol.41, col.1137.

[39] *Hansard*, HC Vol.41, cols 1114–1115.

[40] By the Copyright (Computer Software) Amendment Act 1985 (c.41) (see Vol.2 at E7. Like the 1982 and 1983 Acts, this statute originated as a private member's bill but was supported by the Government as an interim measure pending the introduction of what was to become the 1988 Act. See *Hansard*, HC Vol.73, col.1371.

[41] 15 & 16 Geo. 5, c.46.

[42] See *Hansard*, HC Vol.185, cols 1970–71 and HL Vol.62, cols 18–19.

[43] See *e.g., Hansard*, HC Vol.185, col.1971.

of trade, and the opposition was overcome.[44] The 1925 Act was later modified and then replaced by the Performers' Protection Acts 1958–1972.[45] By 1972, a conviction on indictment for making a recording of a performance without the performer's consent or for dealing with such a recording carried a maximum penalty of two years' imprisonment.[46] On their face, these Acts created criminal sanctions only, but the civil courts were able to hold that their breach was actionable as a breach of statutory duty.[47]

23–06   **Background to the 1988 Act.** In its 1986 White Paper[48] the Government asserted that the deterrent effect of the increased penalties for offences in relation to sound recordings, films and computer programs had been very successful, particularly in relation to video piracy, and that it therefore proposed to extend the increased penalties to all categories of copyright material.[49] The Government also proposed, in accordance with the Whitford Committee report, to make unauthorised public performance of sound recordings and films an offence,[50] and to make possession in the course of trade of infringing copies of any type of work an offence.[51] In addition, the Government observed that establishing guilty knowledge could be a major and costly obstacle for the prosecution, as for a civil plaintiff, and that this could discourage the initiation of proceedings. It accordingly proposed a "relaxation" of the requirements of guilty knowledge in criminal proceedings in identical terms to that proposed in respect of civil proceedings for secondary infringements.[52] Finally, it proposed that offences in relation to rights in performances should be brought into line with those in relation to copyright both in terms of the types of activities which would be offences and in relation to penalties.[53] As will be seen, all these proposals were implemented in the 1988 Act.

23–07   **The policy of the 1988 Act.** The parliamentary debates on the criminal provisions of the 1988 Act demonstrate that when drafting the new section 107 the Government was concerned both to increase protection for the rights of the copyright owner and to protect consumers from poor quality counterfeit goods. Thus, Government spokesmen in both Houses of Parliament made it clear that they regarded copyright infringement as equivalent to theft.[54] However, the point was also made that pirate or counterfeit goods are seldom of the same quality as the originals and in the case of counterfeit goods such as electrical appliances or brake shoes "there is a very real safety problem".[55] The consumer protection aspects of section 107 were emphasised by the proposed new sections 107A and 198A of the 1988 Act[56] which were intended to impose a duty on local weights and measures authorities to enforce the criminal provisions in their area and ap-

---

[44] See, *e.g., Hansard*, HC Vol.185, cols 1971, 1974 to 1975.

[45] See Vol.2 at E6.

[46] Dramatic and Musical Performers' Protection Act 1958 (6 & 7 Eliz. 2, c.44), s.1, as amended by the Performers' Protection Act 1972 (c.32). See Vol.2 at E6.

[47] See the discussion at para. 12–07, above.

[48] *Intellectual Property and Innovation*, Cmnd. 9712.

[49] para.12.8.

[50] para.12.10.

[51] para.12.11.

[52] For what is a secondary infringement, see Ch.8, above.

[53] *Intellectual Property and Innovation*, Cmnd. 9712, para.14.3.

[54] See *e.g. Hansard*, HL Vol.491, col.420, *per* Lord Beaverbrook.

[55] *Hansard*, HL Vol.491, col.420. Note, however, that the creation of criminal offences for design right infringement was not being considered.

[56] Prospectively added by Criminal Justice and Public Order Act 1994 (c.33), s.165, but not yet in force.

ply certain sections of the Trade Descriptions Act 1968[57] to such enforcement.[58] This aspect of Government policy is also emphasised by the fact that the penalties under section 107, while in most cases greater than before, were originally commensurate with those found in consumer protection statutes such as the Trade Descriptions Act 1968[59] and the Food Safety Act 1990[60] rather than with those for offences against property generally.[61] The first of the Government's concerns ("infringement is equivalent to theft") has been echoed by the Court of Criminal Appeal in a statement that the making and distribution of counterfeit video films is a serious offence amounting in effect to theft of the copyright owner's intellectual property.[62] Furthermore, it has been held that section 107 of the 1988 Act is not confined to cases of "piracy"[63] and that the section may therefore be used by a collecting society against a person who is alleged to have distributed infringing copies of copyright works belonging to one of the society's members even though there has been a pre-existing commercial relationship between the society and the alleged infringer.[64]

The Copyright, etc. and Trade Marks (Offences and Enforcement) Act **23–08**
2002.[65] This Act came into force on November 20, 2002.[66] The bill which later became the Act was introduced as a private member's bill but at all times had Government support. It emerged in the context of a perception that the existing penalties for the offences under the 1988 Act were insufficient, as a result of which organised criminals had entered the field. There were also concerns about inconsistencies between the copyright and trade mark regimes. Accordingly, the penalties for the either-way offences under the 1988 Act were brought into line with those under the Trade Marks Act 1994; search warrants were made available in respect of all the main 1988 Act offences rather than only a selection; and the forfeiture provisions in force in respect of trade marks were applied to the offences under the 1988 Act. It should be noted that the intended harmonisation between the copyright and trade marks regimes was only partially achieved. All offences under the Trade Marks Act 1994, including those of selling goods bearing a sign identical to a registered trade mark, are triable either way (that is, in the Magistrates' Court or in the Crown Court) and carry a maximum penalty of ten years' imprisonment. By contrast, many offences under the 1988 Act, including the offence of selling an infringing copy of a copyright work, remain triable only summarily (that is, in the Magistrates' Court) and carry a maximum penalty of two years' imprisonment.[67] Perhaps the most significant effect of the 2002 Act is that because of the increase in penalties, the more serious offences under the 1988 Act are now "arrestable offences" as defined in the Police and Criminal Evidence

---

[57] (c.29).
[58] See para. 23–41, below. As a result of conflicts between the Department of the Environment and the Department of Trade and Industry as to resourcing and cost allocation, these sections were never brought into force. It is not clear whether they will ever be brought into force.
[59] (c.29).
[60] (c.16).
[61] This is no longer the case. See below, para. 23–08.
[62] *R. v Carter* [1993] F.S.R. 303.
[63] *i.e.* for these purposes cases where the alleged infringement is carried out by persons who have and have had no previous commercial relationship with the copyright owner.
[64] *Thames and Hudson Ltd v Design and Artists Copyright Society Ltd* [1995] F.S.R. 153.
[65] c.25.
[66] See the Copyright, etc. and Trade Marks (Offences and Enforcement) Act 2002 (Commencement) Order 2002, SI 2002/2749.
[67] See below, para. 23–17.

Act 1984.[68] As a result, in respect of those who commit such offences, ordinary citizens and police officers have extensive powers of arrest without warrant.[69]

23–09 **The Copyright and Related Rights Regulations 2003.**[70] These Regulations came into force on October 31, 2003. As well as introducing new offences in relation to the circumvention of protection measures, which are dealt with elsewhere,[71] they also introduced new offences of infringing copyright by communicating a work to the public and of infringing a performer's making available right.[72] Since there was no previous offence which covered these activities, a loophole has been closed. However, at present the penalties for these offences are low. In accordance with general principles, these provisions do not apply to pre-commencement acts.[73]

B. CRIMINAL OFFENCES AND PENALTIES

(i) Copyright offences

23–10 **Section 107(1): offences involving making, possessing or dealing with infringing copies.** A person commits an offence who, without the licence of the copyright owner,[74] does any of a number of acts in relation to an article which is, and which he knows or has reason to believe is, an infringing copy[75] of a copyright work. The acts in question are making for sale or hire;[76] importing into the United Kingdom otherwise than for his private and domestic use;[77] possessing in the course of a business with a view to committing any act infringing the copyright;[78] in the course of a business selling or letting for hire, offering or exposing for sale or hire, exhibiting in public or distributing;[79] and distributing otherwise than in the course of a business to such an extent as to affect prejudicially the owner of the copyright.[80] The wording of section 107(1) of the 1988 Act is similar to that of the sections of the Act which create civil liability and the reader is referred to the relevant chapters for a detailed discussion of those provisions. The following points may be made. First, with one exception,[81] the only types of infringement which are made criminal offences are infringements with obvious commercial purposes. Thus, for example, in contrast to the position in civil proceedings, no liability attaches to the making of an infringing copy unless the copy has been made for sale or hire.[82] Secondly, no offence is committed by doing any act unless the accused has the requisite state of mind. This applies as much to "primary" as to "secondary" infringements.[83] Thirdly, the state of mind required to be proved by the prosecution is expressed in identical terms to that required to be proved by a claimant in a civil action for secondary infringement, namely knowl-

---

[68] c.60, s.24(1)(b).
[69] Police and Criminal Evidence Act 1984, s.24(4) to 24(7).
[70] SI 2003/2498.
[71] See para. 15–27 et seq.
[72] New CDPA 1988, ss.107(2A) and 198(1A), introduced by reg.26.
[73] reg.40(3).
[74] As to which, see CDPA 1988, ss.173 and 101(2), and paras 5–194 et seq., above.
[75] See CDPA 1988, s.27 and paras 8–03 et seq., above for the meaning of infringing copy.
[76] CDPA 1988, s.107(1)(a).
[77] CDPA 1988, s.107(1)(b).
[78] CDPA 1988, s.107(1)(c).
[79] CDPA 1988, s.107(1)(d).
[80] CDPA 1988, s.107(1)(e).
[81] The offence of distributing infringing copies to such an extent as to affect prejudicially the owner of the copyright.
[82] CDPA 1988, s.107(1)(a).
[83] As to the distinction, see para. 7–02, above.

edge or reason to believe that the copy is an infringing one.[84] The test for "reason to believe" is an entirely objective one.[85]

"With a view". The offence of possession in the course of a business is limited to possession "with a view to committing any act infringing the copyright". It is not clear whether "with a view" means "with the intention of" or something less. In *R. v Zaman*,[86] which concerned criminal offences under the Trade Marks Act 1994,[87] it was held that the words "with a view" in the expression "with a view to gain" were not to be equated with the words "with intent to". The Court of Appeal therefore upheld the trial judge's direction that the prosecution had to satisfy the jury that gain "was [the defendant's] idea, ... was in his mind as a real possibility, something that might realistically happen". The Court's reasoning derives from a close reading of the Trade Marks Act 1994. Nevertheless, some of that reasoning may yet apply by analogy to section 107. In particular, it is clearly arguable that the choice of the phrase "with a view to committing" rather than "with intent to commit" was deliberate and that therefore something less than intention was envisaged.   **23–11**

Section 107(2): offences in relation to articles designed for making copies of copyright works. Other offences are committed by a person who makes an article specifically designed or adapted for making copies of a particular copyright work,[88] or has such an article in his possession,[89] if in either case he knows or has reason to believe that the article is to be used to make infringing copies for sale or hire in the course of a business. Section 107(2) is similar to section 24 of the 1988 Act,[90] but contains several differences. First, *dealing* with articles designed for making copies of copyright works is not a criminal offence. It is doubtful whether this difference is of any practical importance since anyone dealing with an article is likely to have had it in his possession. Secondly, section 24 requires possession to have been in the course of a business while section 107(2) merely requires the possessor to know or have reason to believe that the article is to be used to make infringing copies for sale, hire or use in the course of a business. The criminal provision will therefore apply to a person who is merely looking after the article for the real infringer if the former has the requisite state of mind. Thirdly, section 107(2) requires the possessor to know or have reason to believe that the infringing copies to be made with the article are to have a commercial purpose whereas section 24 simply requires the possessor to know or have reason to believe that infringing copies are to be made. Finally, the terms of section 107(2) make clear beyond doubt that the only articles to which the subsection applies are articles designed or adapted for making copies of a particular copyright work. It follows that articles such as photocopiers, video recorders and cassette   **23–12**

---

[84] Compare CDPA 1988, ss.22 and 23. Note also that despite the recommendations of the Whitford Committee (referred to in para. 23–04, above), there was no reversal of the burden of proof on this issue and accordingly it lies on the prosecution.

[85] See the civil case of *LA Gear Inc v Hi-Tec Sports plc* [1992] F.S.R. 121; the view expressed in the text was upheld by Mr Recorder Harman in *R. v Mudd* (unreported, Crown Court at Middlesex Guildhall, September 20, 1995), who ruled that the prosecution had to prove that a reasonable man with the defendant's background and experience of the field in which he was operating would have had reason to believe that the article was infringing.

[86] Unreported, July 1, 2002.

[87] See s.92(1) of the Trade Marks Act 1994 (c.26).

[88] CDPA 1988, s.107(2)(a).

[89] CDPA 1988, s.107(2)(b).

[90] See paras 8–02 *et seq.*, above.

recorders are excluded from its ambit. On the other hand, a computer onto which a file or program has been loaded so as to copy it may fall within the section.[91]

23–13   **Section 107(2A): communicating to the public.** Article 3 of the Information Society Directive[92] makes provision in respect of the communication of copyright works to the public ("communication right"). Article 8(1) provides that Member States shall provide appropriate sanctions and remedies in respect of infringements of the rights and obligations set out in the Directive and that sanctions thus provided for must be effective, proportionate and dissuasive. The Government decided that in order properly to implement the Directive it was necessary to create a new criminal offence. Accordingly, the Copyright and Related Rights Regulations[93] introduced a new subsection 107(2A) which makes it an offence to infringe the copyright in a work by communicating that work to the public either in the course of a business or to such an extent as to affect prejudicially the copyright owner. The offence is only committed if the accused knew or had reason to believe that copyright in the work would thereby be infringed. The term "communication to the public" is defined in section 20 of the 1988 Act as "communication to the public by electronic transmission" and is stated to include broadcasting and "the making available to the public of the work by electronic communication in such a way that members of the public may access it from a place and at a time individually chosen by them", that is "on-demand" services. These terms are the same in civil and criminal proceedings and reference should be made to the discussion of them in the civil context.[94] Section 107(2A) does not apply to acts committed before October 31, 2003.[95]

23–14   **Section 107(3): offences in relation to public performances.** Criminal offences may also be committed in relation to the public performance of works. Where copyright is infringed (otherwise than by reception of a communication to the public[96]) by the public performance of a literary, dramatic or musical work or by the playing or showing in public of a sound recording or film, any person who caused the work to be so performed, played or shown is guilty of an offence if he knew or had reason to believe that copyright would be infringed.[97] Section 107(3) differs from section 19 of the 1988 Act[98] in that liability falls on a person who has "caused" the work to be performed, played or shown.[99] Questions as to the meaning of "causing" arose in a number of reported cases under the Dramatic Copyright Act 1833[1] as extended by the Copyright Act 1842.[2] These statutes imposed liability on a person who caused a musical or dramatic work to be represented without the licence of the copyright owner, and accordingly these authorities are relevant to the interpretation of section 107(3). In general, as might be expected, a person was not liable for causing a work to be represented unless he was actually responsible for bringing the representation about. Thus, a company which made and supplied film versions of a dramatic work to music halls and theatres which were then shown to the public did not cause the dramatic work to be

---

[91] *cf.* the wording of CDPA 1988, s.24(1), although the effect is almost certainly the same. See para. 8–15, above.

[92] Directive 2001/29/EC, [2001] O.J. L167/10.

[93] SI 2003/2498.

[94] See para. 7–98 *et seq.*, above.

[95] See reg.40(3) of the Copyright and Related Rights Regulations (SI 2003/2498).

[96] For the meaning of this term, see the previous paragraph.

[97] CDPA 1988, s.107(3)(a), (b).

[98] As to which see paras 7–91 *et seq.*, above.

[99] A person who caused a performance would no doubt be liable in civil proceedings as a joint tortfeasor. See paras 22–35 *et seq.*, above.

[1] 3 Wm. 4, c.15. See Vol.2 at E5.v.

[2] 5 & 6 Vict. c.45. See Vol.2 atE5.vii0.

represented, even though the supplier knew (and presumably intended) that the films would be so shown.[3] This decision (if correct) would no doubt be of equal application to those who supply sound recordings to discotheques and night clubs.[4] Similarly, where the landlord of a tavern hired a room to S who put on a series of infringing performances of a musical work, the landlord was held not to have caused the performances to be represented even though he had supplied S with equipment, had advertised and sold tickets in the bar, and had been put on notice of the copyright owner's rights after the performances began.[5] Again, where the owner of a theatre let it out to D who put on an infringing production of a play, the owner was held not to have caused the performance to be represented even though he had supplied equipment and scene shifters, had paid for printing and advertising, and was paid by a share of the gross receipts.[6] A different result was reached where the performer was an agent of the owner of the premises. Thus, where the owner of a theatre who also employed its company, including his son, who was the stage manager, let out the theatre and the company to his son, who put on an infringing production of a play, the owner was held to have caused the play to be represented because he retained control and because what was done by his son was done with his permission.[7] Similarly, where the owner of a music hall engaged a singer to sing whatever songs the singer wished and the singer performed a song without a licence to do so, the owner was held liable on the grounds that the singer sang as his agent.[8] In *French v Day, Gregory and others*[9] it was held that the general manager of a theatre who had no power to engage or dismiss its artistes, who acted at all times in accordance with the proprietors' instructions, and who obtained no financial benefit from the production did not cause a work to be represented even though he had authority to stop it: he was merely the "mouthpiece" of the proprietor. If this decision is correct, it would seem to follow that a cinema projectionist or disc jockey who was an employee would not be liable if, following his employer's instructions, he projected a film or played a sound recording without the licence of the copyright owner, even though he actually caused the film to be shown or the sound recording to be played. It seems unlikely that this result was intended by Parliament. The brief report in *French's* case does not make clear to what extent the defendant was actually involved in or knew about the infringing performance.[10] Moreover, in the earlier case of *Parsons v Chapman*,[11] which was not cited in *French's* case, it was held that the acting manager of a theatre, who paid the actors' salaries and dismissed them, caused a play to be performed, and that it made no difference that he did so as agent of the proprietor. For these reasons, it seems unlikely that *French's* case would be followed today.

Sound recordings. If a sound recording qualifies for copyright protection only because either its author was a national of one of a number of specified countries (including the United States of America) or because it was first published in one of those countries or for both reasons, then no offence is committed by playing it

23–15

---

[3] *Karno v Pathé Frères* (1908) 99 L.T. 114. The decision is *obiter* on this point: *ibid.* at 119.

[4] This is treated as a special case for the purposes of civil liability: CDPA 1988, s.26.

[5] *Russell v Briant* (1849) 8 C.B. 836.

[6] *Lyon v Knowles* (1863) B. & S. 556; affirmed (1863) B. & S. 566.

[7] *Marsh v Conquest* (1864) 17 C.B.N.S. 418.

[8] *Monaghan v Taylor* (1886) 2 T.L.R. 685.

[9] (1893) 9 T.L.R. 548.

[10] Reference is made to the "introduction" of the piece in question, but it is not clear what this means.

[11] (1831) 5 C. & P. 33, a case under 10 Geo. 2, c.28.

in public.[12] The specified countries are those which are not either parties to the Rome Convention for the Protection of Performers, Producers of Phonograms and Broadcasting Organisations, members of the European Community or otherwise considered to give adequate protection for sound recordings.[13]

23–16   **Trap purchases.** An offence is only committed if the relevant act is done without the licence of the copyright owner. Many prosecutions are likely to be commenced as a result of a trap purchase by the copyright owner or some person acting on his behalf or with his licence. The question arises whether a defendant to an allegation of selling an infringing copy would be able to rely on these facts to argue that no offence had been committed. It is well established that entrapment is not a defence to a criminal charge.[14] It also seems unlikely in normal circumstances that evidence of a trap purchase would be excluded under section 78 of the Police and Criminal Evidence Act 1984.[15] However, it might be argued that the sale took place with the licence of the copyright owner and therefore did not constitute an offence.[16] It seems that by analogy with authorities on consent under the Patents Acts this is likely to be treated as a question of fact turning in particular on the authority given to the actual purchaser and what he does. In one case, the plaintiff was the proprietor of a patent in a telescopic ladder which consisted of two ladders combined with each other, the inner being raised or lowered by means of an endless cord. In order to obtain evidence of infringement, the plaintiff sent his agent to order such a ladder from the defendant. The defendant initially made a telescopic ladder without a cord but the plaintiff's agent refused to accept it without the cord and the defendant ultimately added a cord. It was held that the plaintiff by his agent had consented to the infringement.[17] On the other hand, where the proprietor of a patent in a particular type of tyre sent his agent to the defendant to repair a worn-out version of the tyre and the defendant repaired it in infringement of the patent, it was held that no consent had been given. On the facts, the plaintiff's agent's authority was limited to seeing whether the defendant was infringing the patent[18] and did not extend to ordering an infringing repair.[19] It

---

[12] Copyright (Application to Other Countries) Order 1999 (SI 1999/1751) Art.3. See Vol.2 at C1.iv.

[13] SI 1999/1751, Sch.2, heading.

[14] *R. v Sang* [1980] A.C. 402.

[15] 1984, (c.60). *cf. Director of Public Prosecutions v Marshall* [1988] 3 All E.R. 683 in which a refusal to exclude evidence that plain clothes police officers had purchased liquor from the premises was upheld on a charge of selling liquor without a licence; and *LB Ealing v Woolworths Plc* [1995] Crim. L.R. 58 in which a refusal to exclude evidence of the purchase of an 18 certificate video film by an 11-year-old boy was upheld even though the boy had been sent into the shop by a trading standards officer to buy the film. In *Nottingham City Council v Amin* [2000] 1 W.L.R. 1071, a taxi driver had been hailed by two plain clothes police officers while driving in an area not covered by his licence and had picked them up. He was charged with plying for hire without a licence. A Stipendiary Magistrate excluded the evidence of the officers under s.78 having regard to Art.6 of the European Convention on Human Rights and on the ground that they were agents provocateurs. The Divisional Court quashed this decision because there was no evidence that the officers had prevailed on, incited or pressured the defendant to commit the offence, and the admission of the evidence would not render the proceedings unfair. For a detailed review of the inter-relationship between entrapment, s.78, and the Human Rights Act 1998, see *Attorney-General's Reference No.3 of 2000: R. v Loosely* [2001] UKHL 53 in which *Amin's Case* was approved. See also the discussion in *Blackstone's Criminal Practice* 2004 at para.F2.17.

[16] This issue will not usually arise in civil proceedings because evidence of a trap purchase is likely to be sufficient to persuade a court to grant an injunction and an enquiry or an account. The prosecution can prevent the issue arising in criminal proceedings by charging the defendant with offences other than sale in relation to the goods sold in the trap purchase, *e.g.* possession in the course of a business, or offering or exposing for sale.

[17] *Kelly v Batchelar* (1893) 10 R.P.C. 289.

[18] " ... it was employment of an agent for the purpose of seeing what the defendant would do under given circumstances", *per* North J. at 250.

[19] *Dunlop Pneumatic Tyre Company Ltd v Neal* (1899) 16 R.P.C. 247.

is worth noting[20] that in this case there was no evidence that the plaintiff's agent had specified any particular method of repair.

Mode of trial and penalties. The more serious offences of making for sale or hire, importation and distribution (whether or not in the course of a business) are triable both summarily (*i.e.* in the Magistrates' Court) and on indictment (*i.e.* in the Crown Court). They carry a maximum penalty on summary conviction of imprisonment for a period not exceeding six months or a fine not exceeding the statutory maximum[21] or both; but on conviction on indictment carry a maximum penalty of imprisonment for ten years or an unlimited fine or both.[22] The communication to the public offence[23] is triable either way with a maximum penalty on summary conviction of three months' imprisonment or a fine not exceeding the statutory maximum or both and on indictment of an unlimited fine or imprisonment for a term not exceeding two years or both.[24] All the other offences under section 107 of the 1988 Act are triable only summarily and carry a maximum penalty of six months' imprisonment or a fine not exceeding level 5 on the standard scale[25] or both.[26]

23–17

Sentencing for offences committed before November 20, 2002. As has already been made clear, in respect of most either-way copyright and performers' rights offences committed before November 20, 2002, the maximum penalty on conviction following trial on indictment was imprisonment for two years or an unlimited fine or both. From time to time during this period, the courts imposed prison sentences for video piracy on a substantial scale. A suspended sentence of nine months' imprisonment for a medium-scale video piracy operation involving the use of three video recorders to make infringing video tapes was upheld on appeal in 1992;[27] an immediate sentence of seven months' imprisonment was upheld in respect of a larger operation involving the use of 17 video recorders in 1994;[28] and an immediate sentence of 18 months was reduced to 12 months on appeal in respect of a larger still operation involving the use of 50 video recorders in 1996.[29] Although video piracy has given way to DVD piracy, it is thought that there is little material difference between the two. Sentences of similar severity were imposed for offences relating to computer programs and CD-ROMS. Thus, in 1996, the operator of a computer bulletin board which had been used for exchanging infringing copies of computer games on a relatively large scale[30] received a sentence of 27 months' immediate imprisonment which was reduced by the Court

23–18

---

[20] Although this was not part of North J.'s decision.

[21] Currently £5,000: Interpretation Act 1978 (c.30), Sch.1 applying Magistrates Courts Act 1980 (c.43), s.32(9) as amended by Criminal Justice Act 1991 (c.53), s.17(2)(c).

[22] CDPA 1988, s.107(4). These penalties apply in respect of offences committed on or after November 20, 2002: see the Copyright, etc. and Trade Marks (Offences and Enforcement) Act 2002, s.1(2) and (5). For commencement, see the Copyright, etc. and Trade Marks (Offences and Enforcement) Act 2002 (Commencement) Order 2002, SI 2002/2749. For offences committed before November 20, 2002, the maximum penalties on summary trial are the same but on trial on indictment the maximum term of imprisonment is two years.

[23] CDPA 1988, s.107(2A). See para. 23–13, above.

[24] This is because this offence was created by statutory instrument under the European Communities Act 1972 and these are the maximum penalties available when offences are created in this way: European Communities Act 1972 (c.68), Sch.2, para.1(1)(d).

[25] Also currently £5,000: Criminal Justice Act 1982 (c.48) , s.37(2) as substituted by Criminal Justice Act 1991 (c.53), s.17(1).

[26] CDPA 1988, s.107(5).

[27] *R. v Carter* [1993] F.S.R. 303. The defendant had no relevant previous convictions.

[28] *R. v Gibbons* (1995) 16 Cr. App.R. (S.) 398.

[29] *R.v Gross* [1996] 2 Cr.App.R. (S.) 189. Seven hundred and fifty three infringing copies were found.

[30] During a period of about three months, over 900 games were downloaded and over 500 uploaded. Ninety five per cent of these were infringing copies of games which retailed at £40 each. The

of Appeal to 12 months.[31] In another case in 1996, a sentence of 12 months' immediate imprisonment was reduced by the Court of Appeal to six months for a man of good character who had been found guilty of making copies on compact disc of computer programs.[32] In 1997, a sentence of 27 months' immediate imprisonment was upheld by the Court of Appeal for offences of distributing pirate CD-ROM discs.[33] The Court of Appeal has made clear its view that counterfeiting is equivalent to theft[34] and that such offences should "normally attract at least a short sentence of imprisonment".[35]

23–19   **Sentencing for offences committed after November 20, 2002.** As has already been stated, in respect of most either-way copyright and performers' rights offences committed on or after November 20, 2002, the maximum penalty on conviction following trial on indictment is imprisonment for ten years or an unlimited fine or both. At the time of writing, there are no reported cases in which defendants have been sentenced for such offences under this regime. However, since the maximum penalties for trade mark offences are the same and since many trade mark offences could (subject to evidential considerations) equally have been prosecuted as copyright offences, sentencing decisions in relation to such cases may well have relevance in the copyright field. Two reported cases are of particular significance. In one, the defendant, a man of good character, had operated a rather unsophisticated but profitable business from home producing infringing copies of games, DVDs, VCDs and videos over a period of two years. His turnover was about £27,000 per year. A total sentence of 21 months' imprisonment was upheld by the Court of Appeal.[36] In the other, the defendant had a business producing high quality CD counterfeits. He admitted to having produced between 3,000 and 4,000 and stated that he was intending to produce 2,000 per week. He had no relevant previous convictions. He claimed that initially he thought he was exploiting a loophole in the law, but admitted that he had come to realise that this was not so. A sentence of 30 months' imprisonment was upheld.[37] Each sentencing decision (unless it is a guideline decision) depends on its own facts. Nevertheless, it seems clear that the increase of sentence effected in 2002 is unlikely to result in sentences which are vastly greater than those passed under the previous regime.

23–20   **Criminal liability of company officers and others.** Where an offence under section 107 of the 1988 Act committed by a body corporate is proved to have been

---

defendant's premises were raided and he was found to have a library of some 990 games (it is not clear from the report whether these were infringing). The defendant was of previous good character.

[31] *R. v Lewis* [1997] 1 Cr.App.R. (S.) 208.

[32] *R. v Lloyd* [1997] 2 Cr.App.R. (S.) 151.

[33] *R. v DuKett* [1998] 2 Cr.App.R. (S.) 59.

[34] *R. v Carter* [1993] F.S.R. 303. See also *R. v DuKett* [1998] 2 Cr.App.R. (S.) 59: "Infringement of copyright is widespread. It does, in an ethical sense, involve stealing other men's property, and in its cumulative effect is able to cause serious damage to legitimate commercial and proprietary interests …. A serious view is to be taken of the distribution by way of business and the recording for such distribution of pirated material which, if bought legitimately, would cost substantial sums of money" (Jowitt J.).

[35] *R. v Kemp* (1995) 16 Cr. App.R. (S.) 941. Note, however, that this case also involved trade mark offences in respect of which the maximum sentence is 10 years' imprisonment and the Court of Criminal Appeal may well have had this in mind when making this observation (see however the first paragraph of Hooper J.'s judgment in which he appears to suggest that all the offences were under CDPA 1988, s.107 and carried a maximum of two years).

[36] *R. v Passley* [2003] EWCA Crim 2727; [2004] 1 Cr.App.R. (S.) 70. The Court considered the cases of *R. v Carter* [1993] F.S.R. 303, *R. v Gibbons* (1995) 16 Cr.App.R.(S.) 398 and *R. v Kemp* (1995) 16 Cr.App.R.(S.) 941. See para. 23–18, above.

[37] *R. v Gleeson* [2001] EWCA Crim 2023; [2002] 1 Cr.App.R. (S.) 112.

committed with the consent or connivance of a director, manager,[38] secretary or other similar officer of the body, or a person purporting to act in such a capacity, that person is guilty of the offence and liable to be proceeded against and punished accordingly.[39] The effect of this provision is that the consenting or conniving officer is deemed to be guilty of the same offence as the company and is subject to the same penalties. A director consents to the commission of an offence where "he is well aware of what is going on and agrees to it", while he connives in the commission of an offence where "he is equally well aware of what is going on but his agreement is tacit, not actively encouraging what happens but letting it continue and saying nothing about it".[40]

Publication right. Section 107 applies equally to publication right[41] with the single modification that on summary conviction the maximum penalty is three months' imprisonment or a fine not exceeding level 5[42] on the standard scale or both.[43]

23–21

The "mere conduit", "caching" and "hosting" defences. These defences, which were introduced in order to implement the E-Commerce Directive, apply to criminal proceedings as much as to civil proceedings.[44] Their substantive provisions are considered elsewhere.[45] The Regulations which implement the Directive provide that where a service provider relies on one of these defences, it bears an evidential burden of proof in relation to the defence. Accordingly, where evidence is adduced which is sufficient to raise an issue with respect to the defence, the court or jury is to assume that the defence is satisfied unless the prosecution proves beyond reasonable doubt that it is not.[46] It is thought that this "reverse burden" does not offend the presumption of innocence enshrined in Article 6(2) of the European Convention on Human Rights and is accordingly valid.[47]

23–22

(ii) Offences in relation to rights in performances under the 1988 Act

Offences of making, dealing with and using illicit recordings under section 198 of the 1988 Act. These offences fall into three broad categories. First, a person commits an offence if, without sufficient consent,[48] he does one of a number of acts in relation to a recording which is, and which he knows or has

23–23

---

[38] It seems that Parliament intended that this expression would continue to be interpreted by the courts to mean a senior manager who did not have a seat on the board of directors: *Hansard*, HL Vol.493, col.1370. The earlier case law is summarised in *R. v Boal* [1992] 1 Q.B. 591 where it was held in relation to a provision similar to CDPA 1988, s.110 that the word "manager" referred only to a person who was in a position of real authority in the company with both the power and the responsibility to decide corporate policy and strategy.

[39] CDPA 1988, s.110(1).

[40] *Huckerby v Elliott* [1970] 1 All E.R. 189 at 194 (*obiter*).

[41] See the Copyright and Related Rights Regulations 1996 (SI 1996/2967) reg.17(1), Vol.2 at A3.iii.

[42] Currently £5,000: Crimnal Justice Act 1982 (c.48), s.37(2) as substituted by Criminal Justice Act 1991 (c.53), s.17(1).

[43] Copyright and Related Rights Regulations 1996 (SI 1996/2967) reg.17(3). This offence was created by statutory instrument under the European Communities Act 1972 and these are the maximum penalties available when offences are created in this way: European Communities Act 1972 (c.68), Sch.2, para.1(1)(d). No attempt was made to increase these penalties in the Copyright, etc. and Trade Marks (Offences and Enforcement) Act 2002 (c.25) so they remain anomalous.

[44] See the Electronic Commerce (EC Directive) Regulations 2002 (SI 2002/2013), regs 17 to 19.

[45] See para. 22–88 *et seq.*, above.

[46] Electronic Commerce (EC Directive) Regulations 2002 (SI 2002/2013), reg.21(2).

[47] Note, however, that the law is in a state of development: see para. 23–59, below.

[48] As to which see para. 23–26, below.

reason to believe is, an illicit recording.[49] Those acts are as follows: making for sale or hire;[50] importing into the United Kingdom otherwise than for his private and domestic use;[51] possessing in the course of a business with a view to infringing any of the rights conferred by Part II of the 1988 Act;[52] and in the course of a business selling or letting for hire, offering or exposing for sale or hire, or distributing.[53] Secondly, a person who infringes a performer's making available right after October 31, 2003 in the course of a business or otherwise, so as to affect prejudicially the owner of the making available right, commits an offence if he knows or has reason to believe that by doing so he is infringing the making available right in the recording.[54] Thirdly, a person also commits an offence who causes a recording of a performance made without sufficient consent to be shown or played in public or communicated to the public, thereby infringing any of the rights under Part II of the 1988 Act if he knows or has reason to know that those rights are thereby infringed.[55]

23–24   **Comparison with civil provisions**. Subsections 198(1)–(3) of the 1988 Act have the effect of making most civil infringements of rights in performances criminal offences, albeit using different terminology to that used in the civil provisions.[56] The main differences are as follows.[57] First, all the criminal offences require "guilty knowledge". Many civil infringements do not.[58] Secondly, the civil infringement of broadcasting live a qualifying performance without consent[59] is not made a criminal offence. Thirdly, rights at civil law are infringed by the possession of an illicit recording in the course of a business;[60] a criminal offence is only committed by a person who possesses an illicit recording in the course of a business if that possession is with a view to infringing any rights in performances.[61] Fourthly, there are no criminal provisions in relation to performers' property rights.[62] Finally, the offences in the first broad category referred to inthe previous paragraph are committed by making and dealing with "illicit recordings" without "sufficient consent". The offence in the third broad category referred to above is committed in relation to recordings made without "sufficient consent". The term "illicit recording" is defined differently for the purposes of criminal and civil proceedings.[63] The term "sufficient consent" is not relevant to civil proceedings. The two terms are dealt with in the next two paragraphs.[64]

---

49 As to which, see para. 23–25, below.
50 CDPA 1988, s.198(1)(a).
51 CDPA 1988, s.198(1)(b).
52 CDPA 1988, s.198(1)(c). Pt II of CDPA 1988 is the part headed "Rights in Performances". For a discussion of the term "with a view", see para. 23–11, above.
53 CDPA 1988, s.198(1)(d)(i) to (iii).
54 CDPA 1988, s.198(1A), inserted by the Copyright and Related Rights Regulations 2003 (SI 2003/2498) reg.26 (for commencement, see *ibid.*, reg.40(3)). The "making available right" is the right to authorise or prohibit the making available of a recording by electronic transmission in such a way that members of the public may access it from a place and at a time individually chosen by them (*i.e.* "on demand"): see CDPA 1988. s.182CA and para. 12–66, above.
55 CDPA 1988, s.198(2)(a), (b).
56 For discussion of the civil provisions, see Ch.12, above.
57 There are others, but they are unlikely to be of any practical effect.
58 See, *e.g.* CDPA 1988, ss.182(1)(a) and 186(1).
59 CDPA 1988, s.182(1)(b).
60 CDPA 1988, ss.184(1)(b) and 188(1)(b).
61 CDPA 1988, s.198(1)(c).
62 *i.e.* under ss.182A to 182C.
63 Compare CDPA 1988, s.197(4) with CDPA 1988, s.197(2) and (3).
64 See below at paras 23–25 and 23–26 respectively.

"Illicit recording". A recording is only illicit if it is a recording of the whole or a **23–25**
substantial part of a performance[65] and has been made otherwise than for private
purposes.[66] If those pre-conditions are satisfied, then so far as concerns criminal
proceedings, the recording is illicit whether it is illicit "for the purposes of" a
performer's rights or "for the purposes of" a person having recording rights in the
performance.[67] A performer will only have rights in a qualifying performance,[68]
i.e. a performance which is given by a qualifying individual or takes place in a
qualifying country.[69] "For the purposes of" the performer's rights, the recording
is illicit if made without the performer's consent.[70] A person will have recording
rights in a performance (whether or not it is a qualifying one) if he is a qualifying
person and is a party to and has the benefit of an exclusive recording contract in
relation to the performance or he is an assignee of such a person.[71] If the recording is subject to an exclusive recording contract but the person with the benefit of
the contract or his assignee is not a qualifying person, then a licensee of that
person or an assignee of such a licence will have the recording rights provided
the licensee or assignee is a qualifying person.[72] "For the purposes of" the rights
of the person having recording rights, the recording is illicit if it was made without
the consent of the person having recording rights or of the performer.[73] It seems
that the consent of one will suffice. The extended definition of "illicit recording"
contained in section 197(5) of the 1988 Act applies to criminal proceedings.[74] It
is provided[75] that for the purposes of determining whether a recording is an illicit
one it is immaterial where it was made. This cannot have been intended to make
it a criminal offence to make for sale or hire an illicit recording outside the United
Kingdom: there is a rule of construction that in the absence of express words to
the contrary the conduct prohibited by a criminal statute shall be an offence under
English law only if it took place within the jurisdiction.[76] Rather, the intention
appears to be that it should be an offence both to import into the United Kingdom
an illicit recording which has been made abroad and to deal with such a recording
within the United Kingdom.

"Sufficient consent". In the case of a qualifying performance (*i.e.* a performance **23–26**
which is given by a qualifying individual or takes place in a qualifying country),[77]
sufficient consent means the consent of the performer.[78] In the case of a non-
qualifying performance subject to an exclusive recording contract,[79] the meaning
of sufficient consent depends on the offence charged. In the case of an offence of
making an illicit recording, sufficient consent means the consent of the performer
or of the person having recording rights at the time the consent is given.[80] If there
is more than one person with recording rights the consent must be the consent of

---

[65] The term "performance" is defined in CDPA 1988, s.180(2). See para. 12–23, above.
[66] CDPA 1988, s.197(2) and (3), applied by s.197(4).
[67] CDPA 1988, s.197(4).
[68] CDPA 1988, ss.182–184.
[69] CDPA 1988, s.18. Qualifying individual and country are defined in s.206. See para. 12–24,
above.
[70] CDPA 1988, s.197(2).
[71] CDPA 1988, s.185(2).
[72] CDPA 1988, s.185(3).
[73] CDPA 1988, s.197(3).
[74] See para. 12–69, above, for a full discussion.
[75] By CDPA 1988, s.197(6).
[76] *Blackstone's Criminal Practice* 2004, para.A8.2.
[77] CDPA 1988, s.181. Qualifying individual and country are defined in s.206. See para. 12–24,
above.
[78] CDPA 1988, s.198(3)(a).
[79] Defined in CDPA 1988, s.185. See para. 12–28, below.
[80] CDPA 1988, s.198(3)(b)(i). The consent of one of them will suffice.

both or all of them.[81] In the case of all the other offences under section 198(1) (possessing or dealing with a recording) and the offences under section 198(2) (showing, playing or communicating the recording), sufficient consent means the consent of the person having recording rights or, if there is more than one such person, of both or all of them.[82]

23–27   **Penalties for offences under section 198.** The offences of making for sale or hire, importing and distributing are triable either way (*i.e.* both summarily and on indictment). They carry a maximum penalty on summary conviction of imprisonment for a term not exceeding six months or a fine not exceeding the statutory maximum[83] or both; but on conviction on indictment they carry a maximum penalty of imprisonment for ten years or an unlimited fine or both.[84] The "making available" offence is also triable either way. The maximum penalty on summary conviction is imprisonment for a term not exceeding three months or a fine not exceeding the statutory maximum[85] or both; but on conviction on indictment, the maximum penalty is imprisonment for two years or an unlimited fine or both.[86] The other offences under section 198 are triable only summarily and carry a maximum penalty on summary conviction of six months' imprisonment or a fine not exceeding level 5 on the standard scale[87] or both.[88]

23–28   **Liability of officers.** Where an offence under section 198 of the 1988 Act committed by a body corporate is proved to have been committed with the consent or connivance of a director, manager, secretary or other similar officer of the body, or a person purporting to act in such a capacity, that person is guilty of the offence and liable to be proceeded against and punished accordingly.[89] The effect of this provision is that the consenting or conniving officer is deemed to be guilty of the same offence as the company and is subject to the same penalties. Section 198 is identical in effect to section 110 of the 1988 Act.[90]

23–29   **False representations of authorisation.** It is an offence for a person (such as an artiste's agent) to represent falsely that he is authorised by any person to give consent for the purposes of Part II of the 1988 Act in relation to a performance, unless he believes on reasonable grounds that he is so authorised.[91] The maximum

---

[81] CDPA 1988, s.198(3)(b).

[82] CDPA 1988, s.198(3)(b)(ii).

[83] Currently £5,000: Interpretation Act 1978 (c.30), Sch.1, applying Magistrates' Courts Act 1980 (c.43), s.32(9) as amended by Criminal Justice Act 1991 (c.53), s.17(2)(c).

[84] CDPA 1988, s.198(5), as amended by the Copyright, etc. and Trade Marks (Offences and Enforcement) Act 2002, s.1(3), in respect of offences committed on or after November 20, 2002: see the Copyright, etc. and Trade Marks (Offences and Enforcement) Act 2002 (Commencement) Order 2002, SI 2002/2749. For offences committed before November 20, 2002, the maximum term of imprisonment on trial on indictment is two years.

[85] Currently £5,000: Interpretation Act 1978 (c.30), Sch.1, applying Magistrates' Courts Act 1980 (c.43), s.32(9) as amended by Criminal Justice Act 1991 (c.53), s.17(2)(c).

[86] CDPA 1988, s.198(5A). This offence was created by statutory instrument under the European Communities Act 1972 (the new Copyright and Related Rights Regulations 2002, SI 2003/2498) and these are the maximum penalties available when offences are created in this way: European Communities Act 1972 (c.68), Sch.2, para.1(1)(d).

[87] Also currently £5,000: Criminal Justice Act 1982 (c.48), s.37(2) as substituted by Criminal Justice Act 1991 (c.53), s.17(1).

[88] CDPA 1988, s.198(6).

[89] CDPA 1988, s.202(1).

[90] As to which see para. 23–20, above.

[91] CDPA 1988, s.201(1).

penalty on summary conviction is six months' imprisonment or a fine not exceeding level 5 on the standard scale[92] or both.[93]

Defences. No offence is committed by the doing of an act which by virtue of any provision in Schedule 2 to the 1988 Act (which sets out various "permitted acts") may be done without infringing any of the rights under Part II of the Act.[94] Furthermore, the "mere conduit", "caching" and "hosting" defences provided for by the E-Commerce Directive apply to these offences.[95] Their substantive provisions are considered elsewhere.[96] The burden of proof in relation to these defences is considered above.[97] **23–30**

(iii) Some other relevant offences

Aiding, abetting, counselling and procuring. The terms of the 1988 Act do not expressly exclude criminal liability as an accessory for the offences contained in the statute. It follows that a person may be criminally liable for an offence under the 1988 Act on the basis that he has aided, abetted, counselled or procured its commission.[98] Aiding, abetting, counselling or procuring a summary offence is triable summarily, while aiding, abetting, counselling or procuring an offence triable either way[99] is itself triable either way.[1] **23–31**

Incitement. The common law offence of incitement is committed by a person who knowingly solicits, encourages, pressurises, threatens or endeavours to persuade another to do what would be an offence if carried out by the person incited, with intent that the offence should be carried out.[2] Mode of trial for incitement is the same as for the offence alleged to have been incited.[3] The penalty following conviction on indictment is in the discretion of the court, while the maximum penalty following summary conviction is the same as that for the offence incited.[4] **23–32**

Attempts. It is an offence to do an act which is more than preparatory to the commission of a relevant substantive offence with intent to commit that offence.[5] However, there can be no attempt to commit an offence which is triable only summarily,[6] as are many of the offences under the 1988 Act.[7] In general, the maximum penalties on conviction of attempting to commit an offence are the same as those on conviction of the offence attempted.[8] **23–33**

---

[92] £5,000: see Criminal Justice Act 1982 (c.48), s.37(2) as substituted by Criminal Justice Act 1991 (c.53), s.17(1).
[93] CDPA 1988, s.201(2).
[94] CDPA 1988, s.198(4). See paras 12–74 *et seq.*, above, for permitted acts.
[95] See the Electronic Commerce (EC Directive) Regulations 2002 (SI 2002/2013), regs 17–19.
[96] See para. 22–88 *et seq.*, above.
[97] See para. 23–22, above.
[98] *R. v Jefferson* [1994] 1 All E.R. 270; Accessories and Abettors Act 1861 (24 & 25 Vict. c.94), s.8; Magistrates' Courts Act 1980 (c.43), s.44(1).
[99] *i.e.* triable either summarily (in the Magistrates' Court) or on indictment (in the Crown Court).
[1] Magistrates' Courts Act 1980 (c.43), s.44(2). Whether an offence under CDPA 1988 is triable only summarily or is triable either way is stated in the relevant paragraph above.
[2] See *Blackstone's Criminal Practice* 2004, paras A6.1 *et seq.*
[3] *ibid.*
[4] *ibid.*
[5] Criminal Attempts Act 1981 (c.47), s.1.
[6] s.1(4) and Interpretation Act 1978 (c.30), Sch.1.
[7] Whether an offence is triable only summarily or is triable either way is stated iᵣ paragraph above.
[8] Criminal Attempts Act 1981, s.4(1)(c).

23–34   **Statutory conspiracy.** With the exceptions of conspiracy to defraud,[9] conspiracy to outrage public decency and conspiracy to corrupt public morals, the offence of conspiracy at common law was abolished by the Criminal Law Act 1977[10] and replaced by the offence of statutory conspiracy. If a person agrees with another that a course of conduct shall be pursued which, if the agreement is carried out in accordance with their intentions, will necessarily involve the commission of an offence (or would do so but for a factual impossibility), he is guilty of the offence of statutory conspiracy.[11] The offence is triable only on indictment.[12] The consent of the Director of Public Prosecutions is required before proceedings can be brought in respect of a conspiracy to commit a summary offence.[13] The maximum penalty on conviction of conspiracy to commit an offence under the 1988 Act is the same as that for the offence itself.[14]

23–35   **Conspiracy to defraud.** The offence is constituted by an agreement, by two or more, by dishonesty to deprive a person of something which is his, or to which he is or would be or might be entitled; or an agreement by two or more by dishonesty to injure some proprietary right of that person.[15] Such rights include copyright,[16] and no doubt also design right and the rights in a performance. It is permissible to charge a person with conspiracy to defraud even though the conspiracy alleged was also a conspiracy to commit a substantive offence.[17] The offence of conspiracy to defraud is triable on indictment only.[18] The maximum sentence is 10 years' imprisonment or a fine or both.[19]

23–36   **Theft and deception.** Theft is defined as the dishonest appropriation of property belonging to another with the intention of permanently depriving that other of it.[20] An assumption by a person of any of the rights of an owner amounts to an appropriation.[21] It is also an offence dishonestly to obtain property by deception.[22] For these purposes, "property" includes "money and all other property, real or personal, including things in action and other intangible property".[23] By section 1(1) of the 1988 Act, copyright is defined as a "property right" and by section 90(1) it is transmissible as personal or moveable property. At first sight it would seem that a person who dishonestly dealt with the copyright in a work as if it were his own would commit the offence of theft because he had assumed one of

---

[9] As to which see para. 23–35, below.

[10] (c.45), s.5.

[11] Criminal Law Act 1977, s.1(1).

[12] Criminal Law Act 1977, s.3(1).

[13] Criminal Law Act 1977, s.4.

[14] Criminal Law Act 1977, s.3(1).

[15] *Scott v Metropolitan Police Commissioner* [1975] A.C. 819.

[16] In *Rank Film Distributors v Video Information Centre* [1982] A.C. 380, a majority of the House of Lords held that "the risk of those who deal in or manufacture illicit films being prosecuted for [conspiracy to defraud]" was "by no means remote or fanciful". There have been a number of reported prosecutions of conspiracy to defraud copyright owners. See, in particular, *R. v Willets* (1906) 70 J.P. 127; *R. v Whiteley* (1907) 148 C.C.C. Sessions Papers 267; *R. v Bokenham* [1905–10] Mac.C.C. 290 and *Scott v Metropolitan Police Commissioner* [1974] 1 Q.B. 733. In *R. v Bridgeman and Butt* [1996] F.S.R. 538 (H.H. Judge Halbert, Chester County Court), it was held that a conspiracy to re-enable disabled smartcards for the reception of satellite transmissions amounted to a conspiracy to defraud the transmitting company because it would prejudice its rights under CDPA 1988, s.298(2). See paras 16–21 *et seq.*, above.

[17] Criminal Justice Act 1987 (c.38), s.12(1).

[18] Criminal Justice Act 1987 (c.38), s.12(3).

[19] Criminal Justice Act 1987 (c.38), s.12(3).

[20] Theft Act 1968 (c.60), s.1(1).

[21] Theft Act 1968 (c.60), s.3(1) as interpreted by the House of Lords in *DPP v Gomez* [1993] A.C. 442.

[22] Theft Act 1968 (c.60), s.15(1).

[23] Theft Act 1968 (c.60), s.4(1).

the rights of the copyright owner;[24] and that where a person obtained an assignment of copyright by a fraudulent misrepresentation, that would amount to an offence of obtaining property by deception. However, the House of Lords has held that the definition of property in the Theft Act 1968[25] does not appear to include copyright[26] and it might be difficult to persuade a court to depart from this finding, even though it does not appear to have been based on full argument.[27] Theft and obtaining by deception carry maximum sentences of imprisonment following trial on indictment of seven and 10 years' imprisonment respectively.[28]

Design right. The 1988 Act creates no offences in relation to design right. However, design right, like copyright, is a property right[29] and it might therefore be open to a prosecutor to charge a defendant with theft of design right or with obtaining design right by deception.[30] It would also seem likely that the offence of conspiracy to defraud[31] would be committed by the parties to a conspiracy to deprive a person of his design right.   23–37

Other offences under the 1988 Act. The 1988 Act also creates criminal liability in respect of devices and services designed to circumvent technological measures and in respect of unauthorised decoders. These offences are dealt with elsewhere.[32]   23–38

The "mere conduit", "caching" and "hosting" defences. These defences, which are considered above,[33] apply in all criminal proceedings.   23–39

C. SOME PROCEDURAL MATTERS

(i) Introduction

This section of this work is only intended to deal with procedural matters which are specifically relevant to the offences under the 1988 Act. For a comprehensive account of criminal procedure and evidence, the reader is referred to the standard texts.[34]   23–40

---

[24] In *The Theft Acts* (7th ed., 1995) Edward Griew states (at para.2–18): "There is no doubt that, for example, intangibles such as shares and copyright are property ....". See also Smith, *The Law of Theft* (8th ed., 1997) at para.2–105.

[25] (c.60).

[26] *Rank Film Distributors v Video Information Centre* [1982] A.C. 380 at 445.

[27] A further potential difficulty arises from the fact that a theft is only committed if the accused has the intention *permanently* to deprive the true owner of the property. A person who purports to assign a copyright belonging to another may well know that such assignment will be of no legal effect and thus not intend any permanent deprivation of the copyright (he will of course intend permanently to deprive the purported assignee of his money). In those circumstances, the prosecution would need to rely on Theft Act 1968, s.6(1) which provides so far as relevant: "A person appropriating property belonging to another without meaning the other permanently to lose the thing itself is nevertheless to be regarded as having the intention of permanently depriving the other of it if his intention is to treat the thing as his own to dispose of regardless of the other's rights; ... ". See *Blackstone's Criminal Practice* 2004, paras B4.39 *et seq.* for the relevant case law.

[28] Theft Act 1968 (c.60), ss.1(7) and 15(1).

[29] CDPA 1988, s.213(1).

[30] But note the points made in the previous paragraph.

[31] As to which see para. 22–35, above.

[32] See paras 15–27 *et seq.* and 16–09 *et seq.*, respectively..

[33] See para. 23–22, above.

[34] See, *e.g. Blackstone's Criminal Practice, Archbold Criminal Pleading, Evidence and Practice, Stones' Justices Manual*, Andrews and Hirst, *Criminal Evidence*.

(ii) Enforcement methods

23–41   **The proposed new sections 107A and 198A.** In 1994, it was intended that it should become the duty of every local weights and measures authority to enforce the provisions of sections 107 and 198 of the 1988 Act within its area.[35] To assist authorities in fulfilling these new duties, Parliament provided that various sections of the Trade Descriptions Act 1968[36] were to apply in relation to the enforcement of sections 107 and 198 as they apply in relation to the enforcement of that Act.[37] Those sections give officers the power to make test purchases,[38] inspect goods, enter premises, require the production of documents, seize and detain goods and break open containers.[39] Various types of obstruction of officers are made an offence.[40] There is provision for an owner of goods who has suffered loss by reason of their seizure or detention to obtain compensation[41] if he is not convicted of an offence committed in relation to the goods.[42] If proceedings are to be brought by a local authority under these sections, it is obliged to give the OFT notice of its intention to commence them and to inform it of their outcome.[43] However, as a result of conflicts between the Department of the Environment and the Department of Trade and Industry as to resourcing and cost allocation, sections 107A and 198A have never been brought into force. At the time of writing, there is no indication that they will ever be brought into force. Accordingly, local weights and measures authorities have no duty to enforce the criminal provisions of the 1988 Act.[44]

23–42   **Civil enforcement under the Enterprise Act 2002.** Contraventions of sections 107 and 198 of the 1988 Act which are carried out in the course of a business and which harm the collective interests of consumers in the United Kingdom are now subject to the enforcement regime laid down by Part 8 of the Enterprise Act 2002.[45] Part 8 permits certain bodies ("enforcers") to apply to the court for "enforcement orders", which are similar to injunctions.[46] As well as prohibiting further contraventions, such orders may also require the person against whom

---

[35] CDPA 1988, ss.107A and 198A, introduced by Criminal Justice and Public Order Act 1994 (c.33), s.165.

[36] (c.29).

[37] CDPA 1988, ss.107A(2) and 198A(2).

[38] Trade Descriptions Act 1968 (c.29), s.27.

[39] Trade Descriptions Act 1968 (c.29), s.28(1).

[40] Trade Descriptions Act 1968 (c.29), s.29.

[41] The right to and amount of which is to be determined by arbitration: Trade Descriptions Act 1968 (c.29), s.33(2).

[42] Trade Descriptions Act 1968 (c.29), s.33.

[43] Enterprise Act 2002, s.230(2), applied by the Enterprise Act 2002 (Part 8 Notice to OFT of Intended Prosecution Specified Enactments, Revocation and Transitional Provision) Order 2003 (SI 2003/1376). These provisions reflect the existing requirements about notices of intended prosecution contained in s.130 of the Fair Trading Act 1973, which concerns offences under the Trades Description Act 1968 and other consumer protection statutes. Their purpose is to reinforce the OFT's co-ordination role in respect of the legislation to which Pt 8 of the Enterprise Act 2002 applies. For example, the OFT would be able to inform one authority that another was already prosecuting or that an enforcement order had been granted. This might lead the first authority to decide that it was not necessary to prosecute: see Explanatory Notes to the Enterprise Act 2002, para.576.

[44] When local authorities do prosecute, they must have regard to their own public protection enforcement policies. Failure to comply with such a policy may lead to a stay on the grounds of abuse of process: *R v Adaway*, CA (Crim Div) November 4, 2004. For the Government's strategy on IP crime, see its IP Crime Group's document *IP Crime Strategy* (August 10, 2004), which is available on the Patent Office website (www.patent.gov.uk).

[45] Enterprise Act 2002 (Pt 8 Domestic Infringements) Order 2003 (SI 2003/1593), Art.2 and Schedule, applying to infringements committed on or after June 20, 2003.

[46] Enterprise Act 2002, s.217.

they are made to publish their terms and a corrective statement.[47] An undertaking may be accepted instead.[48] A "consultation" machinery, which is designed to prevent further infringement without the need for an application to the court, must be gone through before an application is made.[49] The OFT[50] and all local weights and measures authorities are "general enforcers" for the purposes of Part 8.[51] Other bodies may be designated as enforcers by the Secretary of State.[52] At the time of writing, certain statutory regulators had been so designated.[53] In future, private organisations may also be so designated if they satisfy certain criteria.[54]

Private prosecution. There are no restrictions on who may prosecute an offender   **23–43** for an offence under the 1988 Act[55] and there have been many private prosecutions under the Act since it was introduced. Most private prosecutions are brought by local authorities, but some have been brought by private individuals. The right to bring a private prosecution is of considerable antiquity and is perceived by the courts as a valuable safeguard against inertia or partiality on the part of the authorities.[56] However, there are certain constraints on the exercise of the right. First, the Magistrates' Court before which it is sought to commence the proceedings by the issue of a summons may refuse to do so on the grounds that the proceedings are frivolous, vexatious or an abuse of the process of the court.[57] Secondly, the Director of Public Prosecutions is given statutory powers to take over the conduct of private prosecutions[58] and this power may be used to effect the discontinuance of a prosecution which is considered to be contrary to the public interest.[59] Thirdly, the court has the power to stay the proceedings on the ground that they amount to an abuse of its process. This power is generally exercised on one of two grounds: either because the defendant has been or will be prejudiced in the preparation or conduct of his defence by delay on the part of the prosecution, or because the prosecution has manipulated or misused the process

---

[47] Enterprise Act 2002, s.217(8).
[48] Enterprise Act 2002, s.217(9).
[49] Enterprise Act 2002, s.214.
[50] See para. 29–255, below.
[51] Enterprise Act 2002, s.213(1)(b).
[52] s.213.
[53] By the Enterprise Act 2002 (Part 8 Designated Enforcers: Criteria for Designation, Designation of Public Bodies as Designated Enforcers and Transitional Provisions) Order 2003 (SI 2003/1399).
[54] i.e. the criteria set out in the Order cited in the previous note.
[55] In its Consultation Paper No.149: *Consents to Prosecution* (The Stationery Office, 1997), the Law Commission invited discussion as to whether the consent of the DPP ought to be required before a private prosecution for copyright infringement could be commenced (see in particular paras 6.47–6.51). In its final report (*Consents to Prosecution*, Law Commission 255), the Commission concluded that it would not be appropriate to impose a consent requirement in copyright cases: see at para.5–51.
[56] *Gouriet v Union of Post Office Workers* [1978] A.C. 435 at 477 and 497.
[57] In practice, this power is rarely used. See, generally, *Blackstone's Criminal Practice 2004*, para.D2.34.
[58] Prosecution of Offences Act 1985 (c.23), s.6(2).
[59] In *R. v Tower Bridge Magistrates' Court* [1994] Q.B. 340 it was observed that this power could be used if there was insufficient evidence, or the prosecution would be contrary to the public interest, or to avoid duplication, or for "any other good reason". The power was used by the DPP under earlier legislation (which was in similar terms) to bring an end to a private prosecution of a defendant who had been given an undertaking by the DPP that he would not be prosecuted in exchange for giving evidence for the Crown (*Turner v DPP* (1979) 68 Cr. App.R. 70); and also where the defendant to pending criminal proceedings brought a private prosecution against one of the Crown's witnesses and the DPP was satisfied that the proceedings were a vexatious attempt to discredit that witness (*R. v DPP, Ex p. Raymond* (1980) 70 Cr. App.R. 233; *Raymond v Attorney-General* [1982] Q.B. 839). The DPP's current policy is only to intervene on evidential grounds if there is clearly no case to answer: see *R. v DPP, Ex p. Duckenfield* [2000] 1 W.L.R. 55, where the Divisional Court refused to interfere with this policy.

of the court so as to deprive the defendant of a protection provided by the law or to take advantage of a technicality.[60]

(iii) Choice of remedy

23–44   **Advantages of criminal proceedings.** Criminal proceedings have two obvious advantages to a copyright owner faced with an infringement.[61] For some defendants, a criminal conviction may be more of a deterrent to future infringement than an injunction limited to a particular work or works. It is recognised that penalties for second and further offences are generally greater than those for first offences.[62] In addition, the rules as to costs in respect of indictable offences (*i.e.* offences which are triable either way,[63] thus including the more serious copyright and rights in performances offences) are generally quite favourable to a prosecutor who is not a public authority. First, in any case the court may order the defendant to pay a successful prosecutor's costs. On the other hand, in determining the amount of any costs order, the court is obliged to take account of a number of factors (including the defendant's means) which would not be relevant in a civil case.[64] Secondly, however, in proceedings for an indictable offence, the court has the power[65] to make an award of prosecution costs out of Central (*i.e.* government[66]) Funds whether the defendant is convicted or acquitted. The practice is that such an order should be made save where there is good reason for not doing so, for example, where proceedings have been instituted or continued without good cause.[67]

23–45   **Disadvantages of criminal proceedings.** First, there is no entitlement to an injunction or to an inquiry as to damages or an account of profits.[68] Secondly, subject to what is said below about the burden of proof, the prosecution must establish guilt beyond reasonable doubt rather than merely on the balance of probabilities. Thirdly, it is necessary in criminal proceedings for copyright offences to prove knowledge or reason to believe even in respect of primary infringements.[69] Fourthly, the presumptions contained in sections 104 and 105 of the 1988 Act do not apply in criminal proceedings.[70] Fifthly, all persons charged

---

[60] See the detailed discussion in *Archbold Criminal Pleading Evidence and Practice* 2004 at paras 4–48 *et seq.* and note *R. v Leominster Magistrates' Court and Another Ex p. Aston Manor Brewery Co.*, *The Times*, January 8, 1997 as to the difficulties which may arise where there are concurrent civil and criminal proceedings. See as to local authorities' obligations to comply with their own policies, failure to do which may render a prosecution an abuse, *R. v Adaway*, CA (Crim Div), November 4, 2004.

[61] A possible further advantage, *i.e.* that the prosecution may not have to prove the absence of a licence or consent, is dealt with in detail in paras 23–58 *et seq.*, below.

[62] In this context, it is worth noting that it has now been held that the court has no jurisdiction to include a penal element in an award of additional damages under CDPA 1988, s.97(2): *Nottinghamshire Healthcare NHS Trust v News Group Newspapers Ltd* [2002] EWHC 409 (Ch).

[63] See Interpretation Act 1978 (c.30), Sch.1.

[64] For an example in this field, see *R. v Bow Street Magistrates' Court, Ex p. Mitchell* [2001] F.S.R. 267.

[65] Under Prosecution of Offences Act 1985 (c.23), s.17(1).

[66] Interpretation Act 1978 (c.30), Sch.1.

[67] *Practice Direction on Costs in Criminal Proceedings* [2004] 2 All E.R. 1070, para.III.1.1.

[68] It is true that the criminal court may make an order for compensation under the Powers of Criminal Courts (Sentencing) Act 2000 (c.6), s.130: see *Blackstone's Criminal Practice*, 2004, paras E18.1 *et seq.* However, this will be confined to the matters proved or admitted by the defendant. On a fully contested trial, it would be usual to seek to prove a small number of offences only, while on a guilty plea the number of matters admitted by the defendant may well be small. Note also the availability of forfeiture orders under Powers of Criminal Courts (Sentencing) Act 2000, s.143 and confiscation orders under the Proceeds of Crime Act 2002 (c.29).

[69] See para. 23–10, above.

[70] By CDPA 1988, s.107(6). Note however, that the presumption contained in s.27(4) does apply.

with the duty of investigating offences,[71] whether before or after proceedings have been begun, are obliged to have regard to the Code of Practice under the Criminal Procedure and Investigations Act 1996.[72] The Code contains detailed requirements as to the conduct of investigations. Among its provisions are a duty to pursue all reasonable lines of inquiry, whether they point towards or away from the suspect;[73] a duty to record and retain all information, including negative information, which has a bearing on the offence being investigated;[74] a duty to retain draft witness statements where their content differs from the final version;[75] and a duty to retain communications with experts.[76] Sixthly, the prosecution in criminal proceedings have extensive duties of disclosure. In the main these are not significantly different in scope from a claimant's obligations as to disclosure in civil proceedings.[77] However, having applied the Code of Practice, the prosecution may well have in their possession more disclosable material of a damaging nature than would a claimant in civil proceedings.[78] Seventhly, the defence duties of disclosure remain limited. Where the case is to be tried summarily, the defence is not obliged to provide a defence statement;[79] accordingly, the basis of the defence may not become apparent until late in the trial, leaving the prosecu-

---

[71] It was held on the similar wording in the Police and Criminal Evidence Act 1984 (c.60), s.67(9), that the question whether a person was "charged with the duty of investigating offences or charging offenders" was one of fact: *R. v Seelig* (1992) 94 Cr. App.R. 17 at 26. In that case, the Court of Appeal was not prepared to interfere with a finding that DTI inspectors were not within s.67(9). It has subsequently been held that store detectives (*R. v Bayliss* (1994) 98 Cr. App.R. 235) and commercial investigators employed by a betting shop (*R. v Twaites* (1991) 92 Cr. App.R. 106) may be within the subsection while the officers of the Federation Against Copyright Theft are within it (*Joy v Federation Against Copyright Theft* [1993] Crim. L.R. 588). It is clear from these cases that the "duty" may arise simply from an ordinary contract. It follows that officers of a collecting society charged with investigating cases of criminal infringement or solicitors instructed to prepare criminal proceedings in respect of an infringement may well (depending on the facts) be subject to the Code of Practice.

[72] (c.25). See s.26(1) of the Act. The Code of Practice is reproduced in App.6 to *Blackstone's Criminal Practice*, 2004. Persons charged with a duty of investigating offences are also obliged to have regard to the Codes of Practice under the Police and Criminal Evidence Act 1984 (c.60): see s.67(9) of that Act. The 1984 Act Codes concern, *inter alia*, searches, seizure of property, detention and questioning, identification and tape recording of interviews. They are reproduced as App.2 to *Blackstone's Criminal Practice*, 2004. It has been held that the provisions of the Codes concerning the interviewing of detained persons or persons attending police stations voluntarily do not apply to interviews conducted by persons other than police officers elsewhere than in police stations: see *R. v South Central Division Magistrates' Court, Ex p. Secretary of State for Social Security*, Q.B.D. Administrative Court, unreported, October 23, 2000, (interview with officers of benefits agency at their premises) and *R. v South East Wiltshire Magistrates, Ex p. Beale*, DC, unreported, December 11, 2002, (interview with trading standards officers at their office). In such circumstances the suspect has no right to free legal advice but may be entitled to advice under the Green Form scheme, which is means tested. The limit of a trading standards officer's obligations in such circumstances is to give the suspect the opportunity to consult a solicitor. It would be wholly inappropriate to advise on the availability of legal assistance: see *Ex p. Beale*.

[73] Code of Practice, para.3.4.

[74] paras 4.1–4.4.

[75] para.5.4.

[76] para.5.4.

[77] The extensive prosecution disclosure obligations which formerly existed at common law were replaced in limited form by the Criminal Procedure and Investigations Act 1996 (c.25). S.3 provides that any material which in the prosecutor's opinion might undermine the case for the prosecution against the accused must be disclosed. If the accused gives a defence statement (which is obligatory in the case of trial on indictment but voluntary in summary proceedings), the prosecution must also disclose any material which might reasonably be expected to assist the accused's defence: Criminal Procedure and Investigations Act 1996, s.7. For the definition of "criminal investigation", see Criminal Procedure and Investigations Act 1996, s.1(4). See also the Attorney-General's Guidelines on Disclosure in Criminal Proceedings, *Blackstone's Criminal Practice* 2004, App.6.

[78] This is of course only correct since the interests of justice outweigh those of the parties in criminal proceedings. In practice, the CPS and other prosecuting agencies often give wider disclosure than is required by the terms of the Criminal Procedure and Investigations Act 1996 and the Attorney-General's Guidelines.

[79] They may however supply a voluntary statement under Criminal Procedure and Investigations

tion little or no time to prepare cross-examination or evidence in rebuttal. Where the case is to be tried on indictment, the defence duties of disclosure are more extensive. A written statement must be provided, setting out in general terms the nature of the defence, indicating the matters on which the accused takes issue with the prosecutor and the reasons for so taking issue, and giving particulars of any alibi.[80] Once more, however, there is no requirement on the defence to give disclosure. Finally, the time limit for commencing summary proceedings[81] is only six months.[82] This may cause difficulties if a lengthy investigation is necessary before proceedings can be commenced.

(iv) Search warrants under the 1988 Act

23–46   **Background.** Search warrants in this field were first introduced in the Musical Copyright Act 1906, which empowered justices to issue them in respect of pirated sheet music.[83] Specific provision for the issue of search warrants in relation to other copyright offences was first made by the Copyright (Amendment) Act 1983,[84] which provided for the issue of warrants in respect of the offences of making, importing and distributing infringing copies of sound recordings and films.[85] Sections 109 and 200 of the 1988 Act extended these powers to offences of making, importing and distributing infringing copies of copyright works of all types and illicit recordings.[86] By the Copyright, etc. and Trade Marks (Offences and Enforcement) Act 2002 these powers were extended to all offences of making or dealing with infringing copies, all offences in relation to articles specifically designed for making copies of a copyright work and all offences of making or dealing with illicit recordings.[87] At the same time as the new offences of infringement of copyright by communication to the public and infringement of the performers' making available right were introduced, these powers were again extended to cover these offences.[88]

23–47   **When a warrant may be issued.** Sections 109 and 200 provide that where a justice of the peace is satisfied by information on oath given by a constable that there are reasonable grounds for believing that an offence of making, importing or distributing an infringing copy, communication to the public, making, importing or distributing an illicit recording or making available has been or is about to be committed in any premises and that evidence that such an offence has been or is about to be committed is in the premises, he may issue a search warrant.[89] The

---

Act 1996 (c.25), s.6. Such a statement is only likely to be served where the defence are seeking further disclosure from the prosecution pursuant to s.7 of the Act.

[80] Criminal Procedure and Investigations Act 1996 (c.25), s.5.

[81] As to which offences are triable only summarily, see the relevant paragraphs above.

[82] Magistrates' Court Act 1980 (c.43), s.127. There is no time limit for commencing proceedings for an either-way offence, but prosecution delay may justify a stay on grounds of abuse of process.

[83] See para. 23–02, above.

[84] (c.42).

[85] A new section 21A was added to the Copyright Act 1956.

[86] CDPA 1988, ss.109(1)(a) and 200(1)(a). In general Police and Criminal Evidence Act 1984 (c.60), s.8, which gives justices a general power to issue search warrants, does not apply to offences under the 1988 Act.

[87] Copyright, etc. and Trade Marks (Offences and Enforcement) Act 2002 (c.25), s.2. The powers do not apply to the offences under s.107(3) (public performance of works, sound recordings or films) or 198(2) (causing a recording made without consent to be show or played in public or communicated to the public).

[88] Copyright and Related Rights Regulations 2003 (SI 2003/2498), reg.26, with effect from October 31, 2003.

[89] CDPA 1988, ss.109(1) and 200(1).

word "premises" is defined as including land, buildings, fixed or moveable structures, vehicles, vessels, aircraft and hovercraft.[90]

Effect of warrants. The effect of the warrant is to authorise a constable to enter   **23–48** and search the premises, using such reasonable force as is necessary.[91] However, the warrant may not authorise the constable to search for items which are subject to legal privilege[92] or which constitute "excluded" or "special procedure" material consisting of documents or records as defined in the Police and Criminal Evidence Act 1984.[93] The definitions of "excluded" and "special procedure" material are lengthy and complex.[94] In broad terms, so far as is likely to be relevant to the field of copyright and rights in performances, the effect of this limitation is that the warrant may not authorise a search for journalistic material[95] consisting of documents or records; or for documents or records which are in the possession of a person who acquired or created them in the course of a trade, business, profession or other occupation or for the purposes of any office and who holds them subject to any express or implied undertaking to hold them in confidence[96] or subject to any statutory restriction on disclosure or obligation as to secrecy. The warrant may authorise persons (such, no doubt, as the right owner or his representative) to accompany any constable who is executing it. Warrants remain in force for 28 days from the date of their issue.[97] In executing a warrant issued on the basis that there are grounds that a copyright offence has been or is about to be committed, the constable may seize an article if he reasonably believes that it is evidence that *any* offence under section 107(1), (2) or (2A) of the 1988 Act has been or is about to be committed, *i.e.* not merely an offence on the basis of which the warrant was obtained.[98] Where the warrant has been issued on the basis of an offence in relation to rights in performances, the constable may seize an article if he reasonably believes that it is evidence that any offence under section 198(1) or (1A) has been or is about to be committed.[99]

(v) Delivery up under the 1988 Act

Delivery up under section 108 of the 1988 Act: copyright.[1] The court before   **23–49** which proceedings are brought against a person for an offence under section 107 of the 1988 Act may, if satisfied that at the time of his arrest or charge he had in his possession, custody or control in the course of a business an infringing copy

---

[90] CDPA 1988, ss.109(5) and 200(4).

[91] CDPA 1988, ss.109(1) and 200(1).

[92] As defined in Police and Criminal Evidence Act 1984 (c.60), s.10. Note that items held with the intention of furthering a criminal purpose are not within the definition of items subject to legal privilege: *ibid.* s.10(2).

[93] See CDPA 1988, ss.109(2) and 200(2).

[94] See Police and Criminal Evidence Act 1984, ss.11 to 14.

[95] Defined by Police and Criminal Evidence Act 1984, s.13 as material acquired or created for the purposes of journalism if it is in the possession of the person who acquired it or created it for the purposes of journalism.

[96] Except in the case of personal records (*i.e.* records concerning an individual and relating to his physical or mental health or to certain types of counselling or assistance which have been given to him: Police and Criminal Evidence Act 1984, s.12), an undertaking to hold documents or records in confidence is of no effect for these purposes if it arises as between employer and employee or between a company and an associated company: Police and Criminal Evidence Act 1984, s.14(3)–(6).

[97] CDPA 1988, ss.109(3) and 200(3).

[98] CDPA 1988, s.109(4). This covers all the offences under s.107 except those involving the public performance of works, sound recordings or films.

[99] CDPA 1988, s.200(3A), inserted by the Copyright, etc. and Trade Marks (Offences and Enforcement) Act 2002 (c.25), s.2. This covers all the offences under s.198 except that of causing a recording made without consent to be played or shown in public or communicated to the public.

[1] For delivery up in civil proceedings, see paras 22–182 *et seq.*, above.

of a copyright work, order the infringing copy to be delivered up to the copyright owner or to such other person as the court may direct.[2] A conviction is not a pre-condition for the making of an order for delivery up. The same provision applies to articles specifically designed or adapted for making copies of a particular copyright work, provided the person knew or had reason to believe that the article had been or was to be used to make infringing copies.[3] The presumptions contained in sections 104 to 106 of the 1988 Act apply on an application for delivery up.[4] For the purposes of these provisions a person is treated as charged with an offence when he is orally charged or is served with a summons or indictment.[5] An order may be made by the court of its own motion or on the ap-plication of the prosecutor.[6] However, no order may be made after the time limited for the making of a delivery up order in civil proceedings[7] or if it appears unlikely that a disposal order will be made.[8] An appeal against a delivery up or-der made by a Magistrates' Court lies to the Crown Court.[9] A person to whom an article is delivered up pursuant to the section is obliged to retain it pending the making of a disposal order or the decision not to make one.[10] The powers to order delivery up under section 108 of the 1988 Act are expressly without prejudice to the powers of the court under section 143 of the Powers of Criminal Courts (Sentencing) Act 2000,[11] which gives the court extensive powers to make an or-der depriving a person of his rights in property which has been or was intended to be used for the purpose of committing or facilitating[12] the commission of an of-fence and is discussed below.[13]

23–50   **Delivery up under section 199 of the 1988 Act: rights in performances.** The court's powers to order delivery up of illicit recordings in criminal proceedings are substantially the same as those relating to infringing copies of copyright works.[14]

(vi) Forfeiture in criminal proceedings

23–51   **General provisions as to forfeiture.** Statutory provisions as to forfeiture apply generally to all criminal cases. These provisions are now contained in section 143 of the Powers of Criminal Courts (Sentencing) Act 2000.[15] There are two regimes which are relevant to the offences under the 1988 Act. The first (section 143(1)) applies where a person has been convicted of an offence. In such a case the court may order forfeiture of any property which it is satisfied has been lawfully seized from that person or was in his possession or control at the time when he was ap-prehended for the offence or when a summons was issued in respect of it. Before a forfeiture order may be made under this provision, the court must be satisfied that the property in question has been used for the purpose of committing or

---

[2] CDPA 1988, s.108(1). Compare the similar provisions in civil proceedings under *ibid.* s.99.
[3] CDPA 1988, s.108(1).
[4] CDPA 1988, s.107(6). As to these presumptions, see paras 22–210 *et seq.*, above.
[5] CDPA 1988, s.108(2).
[6] CDPA 1988, s.108(3).
[7] CDPA 1988, s.108(3)(a); for the time limit see CDPA 1988, s.113 and para. 22–182, above.
[8] CDPA 1988, s.108(3)(b); for disposal orders see s.114.
[9] CDPA 1988, s.108(4).
[10] CDPA 1988, s.108(5); as to disposal orders see s.114.
[11] c.6. See CDPA 1988, s.108(6), as amended by the Powers of Criminal Courts (Sentencing) Act 2000, Sch.9, para.115.
[12] Which expression includes steps taken after the offence to dispose of property or to avoid ap-prehension or detection: Powers of Criminal Courts (Sentencing) Act 2000, s.143(8).
[13] See para. 23–51 *et seq.*, below.
[14] As to which see the previous paragraph.
[15] c.6.

facilitating the commission of an offence or was intended by the defendant to be used for that purpose. The second regime (section 143(2)) applies where a person has been convicted of an offence and that offence, or another offence which has been taken into consideration on sentence, consists of the unlawful possession of property which has been lawfully seized from the defendant or was in his possession at the time of arrest or the issue of a summons. In that case, the court may make a forfeiture order irrespective of whether the property had been or was intended to be used for the commission or to facilitate the commission of an offence. Under each regime, the forfeiture power is discretionary and the court is obliged to have regard to the value of the property and to the likely effect of a forfeiture order on the offender.[16] The former provision would theoretically permit the court to order the forfeiture of equipment (*e.g.* a computer or photocopier) which had been used to manufacture infringing copies. However, it seems unlikely that a court would make such an order if the defendant's livelihood depended on his keeping the equipment for legitimate uses.[17]

Extension of these powers in other contexts. It will be apparent that these general provisions, although extensive, have their limitations. First, it is necessary that the defendant should have been convicted of an offence. Thus, no application may be made where the investigation does not lead to a prosecution or where the defendant is acquitted. Secondly, the property must have been lawfully seized or have been in the defendant's possession at the time of his arrest or of the issue of the summons. No application may be made where the property has come into an investigator's possession by other means. Thirdly, there is no provision which expressly enables the court in a case where a large number of items have been seized to draw inferences from samples. For reasons of this type, specific forfeiture provisions were introduced in a variety of fields, including most relevantly in the field of trade marks,[18] which sought to remove each of the three limitations set out above.

23–52

Forfeiture under the 1998 Act: general. The Copyright, etc. and Trade Marks (Offences and Enforcement) Act 2002[19] introduced new provisions in respect of the forfeiture of infringing copies, articles specifically designed for making copies, illicit recordings and unauthorised decoders. These provisions, which came into force on November 20, 2002, are modelled on section 97 of the Trade Marks Act 1994 and their introduction was intended to further the aim of harmonising the criminal provisions in respect of copyright, performers' rights and decoders with those in respect of trade marks.[20]

23–53

Forfeiture proceedings: threshold conditions and venue. Section 114A of the 1988 Act[21] applies where infringing copies or articles specifically adapted or designed for making copies of a particular copyright work have come into the possession of any person in connection with the investigation or prosecution of a "relevant" offence.[22] Thus they apply not only where a police officer has seized an infringing copy in the course of an arrest but also, for example, where a private investigator has been handed an infringing copy by an informer. The application for forfeiture must be made by the person into whose possession the copies or

23–54

---

[16] Powers of Criminal Courts (Sentencing) Act 2000, s.143(4).
[17] See *e.g. Blackstone's Criminal Practice*, 2004, para.E20.2.
[18] Trade Marks Act 1994 (c.26), s.97.
[19] c.25.
[20] See *Hansard* HC Vol.375 cols 628–9 (second reading).
[21] The equivalent provision for Scotland is in s.114B.
[22] CDPA 1988, s.114A(1).

articles have come.[23] The definition of "relevant offence" extends beyond offences under section 107(1), (2) or (2A) of the 1988 Act to offences under the Trade Descriptions Act 1968 and offences involving dishonesty or deception.[24] Therefore, forfeiture may take place even if there is in fact no intellectual property content to the investigation or prosecution, for example if it is really concerned with a burglary or the handling of stolen goods. Furthermore, an application for forfeiture may be made whether or not proceedings have been brought. Thus, for example, where an authority accumulates a large number of infringing articles as a result of a raid but is unable to prosecute because the offender has absconded or given a false name, forfeiture can nevertheless be sought.[25] If proceedings have been brought for a relevant offence relating to some or all of the infringing articles, the application must be made to the court where those proceedings are taking place.[26] Otherwise, the application must be brought by way of complaint to a Magistrates' Court.[27]

23–55   **Forfeiture proceedings: the decision.** The court may only make a forfeiture order if it is satisfied (presumably to the civil rather than the criminal standard, although this is not stated) that a relevant offence has been committed in relation to the infringing copies or articles.[28] In reaching its decision, the court is expressly permitted to infer that a relevant offence has been committed in relation to any infringing copies or articles if it is satisfied that such an offence has been committed in relation to infringing copies or articles of which the infringing copies or articles in question are representative (whether by reason of being of the same design or part of the same consignment or batch or otherwise).[29] It is not clear what this subsection is intended to achieve, since even in the absence of such a provision there would be no obstacle to the court reaching its conclusions from inference. Moreover, the subsection fails to make clear exactly what type of inferences may be drawn. Take, for example, a consignment of 1,000 counterfeit music CDs which is found in a defendant's possession. Suppose that the consignment is made up of 100 batches, each of which consists of 10 identical CDs. In this case, for practical reasons, the prosecution may be forced to limit the charges to possession of one CD from each of (say) 15 of the 100 batches. On conviction, it will certainly be open to the court to order forfeiture of the whole contents of those 15 batches. However, does the mere fact that the court has found that the contents of those batches are counterfeit entitle it to infer that the contents of the other 85 batches (which may include copies of entirely different copyright works) are also counterfeit? Much will depend on the facts. In practice, defendants in this position are seldom unduly concerned to retain possession of the goods in question and can frequently be persuaded to sign a disclaimer in respect of any rights they may have in them.

23–56   **Forfeiture proceedings: form of order and appeals.** The court's powers as to the terms of the order are very wide: it may order the copies or articles to be destroyed in accordance with such directions as it may give; alternatively it may direct that the copies or articles shall be forfeited to the owner of the copyright in

---

[23] CDPA 1988, s.114A(1).
[24] CDPA 1988, s.114A(2).
[25] *Hansard* HC, Standing Committee C, January 9, 2002, col.9.
[26] CDPA 1988, s.114A(3)(a).
[27] CDPA 1988, s.114A(3)(b).
[28] CDPA 1988, s.114A(4).
[29] CDPA 1988, s.114A(4).

question or dealt with in such way as it considers appropriate.[30] Any person aggrieved by the grant or refusal of an order by a Magistrates' court will be permitted to appeal to the Crown Court.[31] In the Crown Court the position as to appeals is less clear. Where the defendant has been convicted, an appeal by him will presumably lie to the Court of Criminal Appeal under section 9(1) of the Criminal Appeal Act 1968.[32] However, where the defendant has been acquitted but a forfeiture order has nevertheless been made, or where someone other than a defendant to criminal proceedings wishes to appeal, it is less clear what jurisdiction the Court of Criminal Appeal would have to hear the appeal. The court will be permitted to delay implementation of the order pending an appeal or an appeal by case stated.[33]

Forfeiture of illicit recordings and unauthorised decoders. The copyright provisions discussed above are mirrored by provisions in respect of illicit recordings (section 204A of the 1988 Act)[34] and unauthorised decoders (section 279C of the 1988 Act).[35] In the case of unauthorised decoders, if the court does not order the destruction of the decoders, it may direct that they shall be forfeited to the person with rights and remedies under section 298 of the 1988 Act.[36] **23–57**

(vii) The burden of proof

Introduction. In criminal proceedings, the burden generally lies on the prosecution to prove every element of the offence beyond reasonable doubt. Juries are often directed that they must not convict unless they are "sure" or "satisfied so that they feel sure" of the defendant's guilt.[37] On the other hand, where the defendant relies for his defence on any "exception, exemption, proviso, excuse or qualification", the burden of proving such exception, etc. on the balance of probabilities is on him.[38] Thus, for example, in the case of driving without a licence, it has been held that the prosecution must prove that the accused was driving, but the burden is on the accused to prove that he had a driving licence.[39] This "reverse burden" is a "legal" burden rather than an "evidential" burden.: the defendant is required to prove the facts necessary to establish the defence on the balance of probabilities, rather than merely to raise an issue with respect to the defence.[40] The question arises whether any of the ingredients of the criminal offences under the 1988 Act fall into this category and if so whether this is compatible with the right to a fair trail enshrined in the Human Rights Act 1998. The following paragraphs will consider first phrases such as "without the licence of the copyright owner" in section 107 and "without sufficient consent" in section 198;[41] secondly to the term "a person who infringes" in sections 107(2A) and 198(1A);[42] thirdly to the "permitted act" defence to liability under section 198;[43] and finally to the terms "infringing copy" in section 107 and "illicit recording" in section 198.[44] The burden of proof in relation to the "mere conduit", "caching" and "hosting" defences is considered above.[45] **23–58**

General legal propositions. The law as to so-called "reverse burdens" of proof is in a state of development following the coming into force of the Human Rights **23–59**

---

[30] CDPA 1988, s.114A(8), (9).
[31] CDPA 1988, s.114A(6).
[32] c.19.
[33] CDPA 1988, s.114A(7).
[34] In Scotland, s.204B.
[35] In Scotland, s.297D.
[36] For s.298, see para. 16–21 et seq., above.
[37] For the authorities, see *Blackstone's Criminal Practice* 2004, para.F3.17.
[38] Magistrates' Courts Act 1980 (c.43), s.101 (summary proceedings); *R. v Hunt* [1987] A.C. 352 (trial on indictment).
[39] *John v Humphreys* [1955] 1 W.L.R. 325.
[40] *The Queen on the application of Grundy & Co Excavations Ltd* [2003] EWHC Admin 272 (QB).
[41] See para. 23–61, below.
[42] See para. 23–62, below.

Act 1998, which incorporates into English law the presumption of innocence provided for by Article 6(2) of the European Convention on Human Rights. It seems, however, that there are two separate questions in each case. First, irrespective of the Human Rights Act, does the provision in question, as a matter of construction, impose a burden of proof on the defendant? Secondly, if it does, what is the impact of the Human Rights Act on the provision?[46] The first question is one of construction, but if the "linguistic construction" is unclear, the court may take account of policy considerations including in particular the parties' respective abilities to discharge the burden in question.[47] As to the second question, the Convention jurisprudence has been summarised as follows[48]:

> "The overriding concern is that a trial should be fair, and the presumption of innocence is a fundamental right directed to that end. The Convention does not outlaw presumptions of fact or law but requires that these should be kept within reasonable limits and should not be arbitrary. It is open to states to define the constituent elements of a criminal offence, excluding the requirement of mens rea. But the substance and effect of any presumption adverse to a defendant must be examined, and must be reasonable. Relevant to any judgment on reasonableness or proportionality will be the opportunity given to the defendant to rebut the presumption, maintenance of the rights of the defence, flexibility in application of the presumption, retention by the court of a power to assess the evidence, the importance of what is at stake and the difficulty which a prosecutor may face in the absence of a presumption. ... The justifiability of any infringement of the presumption of innocence cannot be resolved by any rule of thumb, but on examination of all the facts and circumstances of the particular provision as applied in the particular case."

The trade mark case of *R. v Johnstone*[49] is a useful illustration of the application of these principles in a similar field. The House of Lords upheld a provision which imposed a legal burden on a defendant under section 92 of the Trade Marks Act 1994, which creates various offences in relation to the use of signs identical or similar to trade marks with a view to gain and without consent. Section 92(5) provides that it is a defence to a charge under section 92 for the defendant to prove that he believed on reasonable grounds that the use of the sign in the manner in which it was used, or was to be used, was not an infringement of the registered trade mark. The reasons given for the decision in *R. v Johnstone* were: the urgent international pressure, in the interest of consumers and traders alike, to restrain fraudulent trading in counterfeit goods; the framing of offences against section 92 as offences of "near absolute liability"; the dependence of the defence on facts within the defendant's own knowledge; the fact that those who trade in brand products are aware of the need to be on guard against counterfeit goods, to deal with reputable suppliers and keep records and of the risks they take if they do not; and the fact that it is to be expected that those who supply traders with counterfeit products, if traceable at all by outside investigators, are unlikely to be co-operative so that, in practice, if the prosecution were obliged to prove that a trader acted dishonestly, fewer investigations would be undertaken and fewer prosecutions would take place.[50]

---

[46] This was the approach adopted in *The Queen on the application of Grundy & Co Excavations Ltd* [2003] EWHC Admin 272 (QB).

[47] *R. v Hunt* [1987] A.C. 352.

[48] *Attorney General's Reference No. 4 of 2002* [2004] UKHL 43; [2004] 3 W.L.R. 976 at para.21. This is now the leading case.

[49] [2003] UKHL 28; [2003] 1 W.L.R. 1736.

[50] *R. v. Johnstone* [2003] UKHL 28; [2003] 1 W.L.R. 1736 at paras 52 and 53. See the analysis of

Authorities. In the leading case on the criminal copyright provisions of the 1956 **23-60**
Act,[51] it was conceded by the prosecution that the burden of proving that the copies were infringing copies lay on them, while there was no issue as to whether the defendant had a licence to possess them. There are no reported cases on the incidence of the burden of proof in relation to offences relating to performers' rights. Accordingly, in each case, the question remains open.

"Without the licence of the copyright owner" and "without sufficient **23-61**
consent". Applying the principles set out above, it is thought that in relation to all the offences under section 107(1) of the 1988 Act, the burden of showing that he had a licence to do the act in question lies on the defendant; and that in relation to all the offences under section 198 of the 1988 Act the burden of showing that he had sufficient consent to do what he did also lies on the defendant. In the one case the offence is constituted by doing an act "without the licence of the copyright owner", and in the other it is constituted by doing an act "without sufficient consent". In both cases, the defendant alleging a licence or consent will be raising an "exception, exemption, proviso, excuse or qualification". Thus, the provision creates an offence plus an exception. Furthermore, the accused should have no difficulty proving the existence of the licence or consent, whereas the prosecution may have considerable difficulties proving its absence. For reasons similar to those outlined in *R. v Johnstone*[52] it is thought that such a reverse is unlikely to offend the defendant's right to a fair trial.

"Person who infringes". The offences of communicating a copyright work to **23-62**
the public and of making a recording available to the public (sections 197(2A) and 198(1A)) are committed by a person who infringes copyright or a performer's making available right, as the case may be. Each of these provisions hides an exemption, exception, proviso, excuse or qualification, because it is of the essence of the copyright infringement that the act of communication to the public should have been committed without a licence, and it is of the essence of the infringement of the making available right that the act of making available should have been committed without the performer's consent. It is suggested that these provisions are analogous to those discussed in the previous paragraph, and accordingly that the legal burden in respect of them lies on the defendant.

Permitted acts defences. As has been stated above, no offence is committed **23-63**
under section 198 of the 1988 Act by the commission of a permitted act.[53] It is thought that a defendant seeking to rely on this provision is clearly raising a proviso and that the burden of showing that what he did was a permitted act will therefore lie on him. Once again, the provision in question is creating an offence plus an exception. Furthermore, the accused should have no difficulty proving that what he did was a permitted act, whereas the prosecution may have considerable difficulties proving it was not. Again, it is thought that such a reverse burden is unlikely to infringe the defendant's right to a fair trial.

"Infringing copy" and "illicit recording". More difficult issues are raised by **23-64**
the offences of dealing with "infringing copies" and "illicit recordings". An infringing copy of a copyright work is in effect a copy made without the licence of the copyright owner,[54] while an illicit recording is a recording made without

---

this decision in *Attorney General's Reference No. 4 of 2002* [2004] UKHL 43; [2004] 3 W.L.R. 976 at para.27.
[51] *Musa v Le Maitre* [1987] F.S.R. 272.
[52] [2003] UKHL 28, discussed in para. 23–59, above.
[53] CDPA 1988, s.198(4). For permitted acts, see CDPA 1988, Sch.2 and paras 12–74 *et seq.*, above.
[54] By CDPA 1988, s.27(2), an article is an infringing copy if its making constituted an infringement

the consent of the performer or a person having recording rights or both.[55] It follows that a "dealing" offence will not occur if the article dealt with has been made with a licence or with consent. It is clearly arguable therefore that the wording of both sections 107 and 198 contains a hidden "exception, exemption, proviso, excuse or qualification". The same point arises where a defendant seeks to contend that an allegedly infringing copy with which he has dealt was not in fact infringing because its making was a permitted act (*e.g.* fair dealing);[56] or that an allegedly illicit recording with which he has dealt was not in fact illicit because its making was a permitted act.[57] It is thought that these provisions are much less likely to be construed as imposing a burden on the defendant, for the following reasons. First, the effect of placing the burden on the defendant would be far-reaching. In a case where dealing with an infringing copy was alleged, the prosecution would not need to prove who owned the copyright infringed either at the time the infringing copy was made or at the time of the act of dealing complained of.[58] In a case where dealing with an illicit recording was alleged, the prosecution would not be obliged to prove who owned any of the rights in the performance either at the time the recording was made or at the time it was dealt with. It would follow that in some cases it would be easier to establish criminal than civil liability. Secondly, the question of ease of proof[59] provides some further guidance. It would not be unreasonable to expect a defendant charged with selling an infringing or illicit article to be able to prove that he had a licence or a consent so to deal with it. However, there is clearly scope for unfairness if a defendant charged with selling an infringing or illicit article is obliged to prove that the article, which he may have purchased through a long chain of suppliers, was made by licence or with consent, or indeed that its making was a permitted act. It is thought that a criminal court would be likely to wish to avoid such unfairness. Thirdly, the terms of the Act are such that the prosecution have to prove in all cases that the defendant knew or had reason to believe that the article was infringing or illicit. It is difficult to see how this could be done without also proving that the article was indeed infringing or illicit. On balance, therefore, it is thought likely that in these cases a court would certainly place the legal and evidential burden of proving that the article was infringing or illicit on the prosecution. Even if this construction were not adopted, it seems likely that a court would hold that such a reverse burden infringed the defendant's right to a fair trial.

2. SEIZURE BY CUSTOMS OF IMPORTED COPIES

A. OVERVIEW AND HISTORICAL INTRODUCTION

23–65   **Overview.** Before the passing of the 1911 Act, provision already existed for a copyright owner to notify Customs of his interest with a view to prohibiting the importation of infringing books.[60] The 1911 Act extended this to copies of all

---

of the copyright in question. By *ibid.* s.16(2), copyright in a work is infringed by a person who does a restricted act without the licence of the copyright owner. By *ibid.* s.17(1), the copying of a work is a restricted act.

[55] See the definition in CDPA 1988, s.197(4) and para. 23–25, above.

[56] For permitted acts, see Ch.8, above.

[57] Under CDPA 1988, Sch.2. This is unlikely in practice.

[58] Of course, the prosecution would still have to prove that copyright subsisted; and this might depend on identifying a qualifying author who might also have been the owner of the copyright at the time the infringing copy was made.

[59] For the relevance of this, see para. 23–59, above.

[60] Customs Consolidation Act 1876, s.42; Table of Prohibitions.

copyright works.[61] Similar provision was made by the 1956 Act,[62] but this was expressly limited to infringing copies of published literary, dramatic and musical works. Section 111 of the 1988 Act re-enacted these provisions of the 1956 Act and extended them to infringing copies of sound recordings and films. However, these provisions were seldom used.[63] Since July 1, 1995, a new regime has been in force under EC legislation, although this has been subject to frequent amendment. It covers goods which infringe most of the rights covered in this work, but does not apply to parallel imports or overruns. For reasons which will become apparent, many more rights owners have taken advantage of this scheme than that under the 1988 Act. Nevertheless, section 111 remains in force, although its scope remains limited to printed copies of published literary dramatic and musical works, and copies of sound recordings and films, and it only applies where the EC legislation does not apply. Neither regime applies to goods imported for genuine private or domestic use. It should be emphasised that this part of this chapter deals only with the seizure of imported copies. A copyright owner's rights to seize infringing copies which are exposed or immediately available for sale or hire are dealt with elsewhere.[64]

The 1986 Regulation. The first Community legislation of this type was the Council Regulation of 1986,[65] which was aimed at preventing the importation into the Community of goods which infringed a trade mark registered in a Member State.[66] This Regulation permitted a trade mark owner to notify the customs authorities of his interest; if an attempt was made to import goods which infringed the trade mark, the customs authorities could seize and destroy or otherwise dispose of them. There were perceived to be a number of defects in the system.[67] First, it applied only to trade marks and not to other intellectual property rights. Secondly, it made no provision for the customs authorities to act on their own initiative, as opposed to at the request of the rights owner. Thirdly, it did not apply to goods which were entered for export or re-export from the Community, or to goods otherwise under customs control in the Community.   **23–66**

TRIPS obligations. Section 4 of the TRIPS agreement[68] contains "special requirements related to border measures", which may be briefly summarised as follows. First, Members are obliged to enable right-holders who have valid grounds for suspecting that the importation of counterfeit trade mark or pirated copyright goods may take place, to apply for the suspension of the release into free circulation of such goods.[69] Such measures may be applied to other intellectual property rights and to exports.[70] Right-holders are to be obliged to provide *prima facie* evidence of infringement[71] and may be obliged to provide security.[72] If the applicant has not commenced proceedings within 10 working days of   **23–67**

---

[61] Copyright Act 1911, s.14. See Vol.2 at E3.

[62] Copyright Act 1956, s.22. See Vol.2 at E3.

[63] It seems that no more than 10 or 12 notifications were made each year under the 1988 Act before July 1995. This and some of the other information which follows was very kindly provided by Mr Ronald Bann of HM Customs and Excise.

[64] See CDPA 1988, s.100 and paras 22–46 *et seq.*, above.

[65] Council Regulation 3842/86 laying down measures to prohibit the release for free circulation of counterfeit goods, [1986] O.J. L375/1.

[66] Council Regulation 3842/86, Arts 1(2)(a) and 2.

[67] See, in particular, the recitals to Reg.3295/94 laying down measures to prohibit the release for free circulation, export and re-export from the Community of goods infringing certain intellectual property rights, [1994] O.J. L 341/8 and the Opinion of the Economic and Social Committee on the less extensive proposed Regulation, [1994] O.J. C52/37, para.2.6 and para.3.2.

[68] See Vol.2 at F11.

[69] Art.51.

[70] Art.51.

[71] Art.52.

receiving notice of the suspension, or any extended period of 10 days, the goods must be released.[73] Provision is to be made for affording the right-holder an opportunity to inspect the goods.[74] The mechanics to be applied where action is taken by customs authorities on their own initiative ("ex officio") are laid down.[75] Competent authorities are to have power to order the destruction or disposal of infringing goods.[76] Finally, provision may be made to exclude from the application of these provisions small quantities of goods of a non-commercial nature contained in travellers' personal luggage or sent in small consignments.[77]

23–68   **The 1994 Regulation.** The 1986 Regulation was repealed by Council Regulation 3295/94 ("the 1994 Regulation"), which was directly applicable in all Member States from July 1, 1995.[78] The 1994 Regulation was intended to address the defects referred to above and to take account of TRIPS.[79] Thus, the general structure of the Regulation was based on the TRIPS provisions referred to above, customs authorities were permitted to act on their own initiative, the number of categories of rights protected was increased and the range of circumstances in which goods might be seized was extended. In 1995, the 1994 Regulation was supplemented by Commission Regulation 1367/95 ("the 1995 Implementing Regulation").[80] The Counterfeit and Pirated Goods (Customs) Regulations 1995[81] ("the 1995 Customs Regulations") and the Counterfeit and Pirated Goods (Consequential Provisions) Regulations 1995[82] ("the 1995 Consequential Regulations") contained provisions designed to implement the Council and Commission Regulations in the United Kingdom. In 1999, the 1994 Regulation was amended in order to increase the range of circumstances in which goods might be seized.[83] In order the give effect to this, the 1995 Customs Regulations and the 1995 Consequential Regulations were revoked and replaced by the new customs and consequential provisions regulations ("the 1999 Customs Regulations" and "the 1999 Consequential Provisions Regulations").[84] The 1999 Customs Regulations were amended by further Regulations in 2003, which abolished fees for applications to the Commissioners ("the 2003 Regulations") with effect from October 1, 2003.[85]

23–69   **The Council Regulation and the Domestic Regulations.** Against a background of mounting concerns about the extent of the trade in counterfeit and pirated goods,[86] the 1994 Regulation was in turn replaced by a new Council Regulation

---

[72] Art.53. They may be required to indemnify the importer, consignee and owner for injury caused by wrongful detention of the goods: Art.56.

[73] Art.55.

[74] Art.57. The competent authorities may be allowed to inform the right-holder of the names and addresses of the consignor, importer and consignee and the quantity of the goods where a positive determination has been made as to the merits: Art.57.

[75] Art.58.

[76] Art.59.

[77] Art.60.

[78] Art.17.

[79] See the sixth recital.

[80] Commission Regulation 1367/95 laying down provisions for the implementation of Council Regulation (EC) No.3295/94 laying down measures to prohibit the release for free circulation, export, re-export or entry for a suspensive procedure of counterfeit and pirated goods, [1995] O.J. L133/2.

[81] SI 1995/1430.

[82] SI 1995/1447.

[83] By Council Regulation 241/99, [1999] O.J. L27/1.

[84] SI 1999/1601 and 1618, respectively.

[85] SI 2003/2316. These Regulations were introduced in anticipation of the 2004 Council Regulation, which is dealt with below.

[86] According to the Explanatory Memorandum to the draft regulation (COM (2003) 20 final), there

("the Council Regulation") with effect from July 1, 2004.[87] The Council Regulation retains the structure of its predecessor, but introduces certain changes. The main changes which are relevant to the rights covered by this work are as follows. First, there is to be a standard application form. Secondly, application fees have been abolished (although this had already occurred in the United Kingdom). Thirdly, there is provision for supplying additional information to the rightholder at an earlier stage. Finally, sanctions are introduced for the misuse of information so supplied. Although it is directly applicable, the Council Regulation envisaged that a further, implementing regulation would be introduced by the Commission.[88] On October 21, 2004 an implementing regulation ("the 2004 Implementing Regulation") was adopted.[89] The 2004 Implementing Regulation is directly applicable. It repeals the 1995 Implementing Regulation[90] and appears to apply retroactively from July 1, 2004.[91] The Government has introduced new regulations which implement parts of the Council Regulation in the United Kingdom ("the Domestic Regulations").[92] With effect from July 1, 2004, the Domestic Regulations revoke the 1999 Customs Regulations, the 1999 Consequential Regulations and the 2003 Regulations. Those parts of the Council Regulation which have not been implemented by the Domestic Regulations are directly applicable, and in most cases guidance as to their application has been given by the Commissioners of Customs and Excise ("the Commissioners").[93]

B. THE COUNCIL REGULATION AND THE DOMESTIC REGULATIONS

The types of goods to which the Council Regulation applies. The Council   **23–70**
Regulation applies both to "counterfeit" and to "pirated" goods. Broadly speak-

---

was a ninefold increase in the number of infringing items intercepted at the EU's external frontiers over the four years from 1998 to 2001 (from 10 million to 100 million). Counterfeiters had become more interested in quantity than quality, concentrating less on items with a high value added, and more on household objects produced on a commercial scale. There had been particular increases in seizures of foodstuffs and CDs. Organised crime was increasingly active in the field.

[87] Council Regulation 1383/2003 concerning customs action against goods suspected of infringing certain intellectual property rights and the measures to be taken against goods found to have infringed such rights, [2003] O.J. L196/7 (see Vol.2 at B7.ai). See generally Daele: "Regulation 1383/2003: A New Step in the Fight against Counterfeit and Pirated Goods at the Borders of the European Union" [2004] E.I.P.R. 214.

[88] See Arts 20, 21.

[89] Commission Regulation (EC) No. 1891/2004 of October 21, 2004 laying down provisions for the implementation of Council Regulation (EC) No. 1383/2003 concerning customs action against goods suspected of infringing certain intellectual property rights and the measures to be taken against goods found to have infringed such rights [2004] O.J. L328/16. See Vol.2 at B7.aii.

[90] Art.10.

[91] Art.11. "Applications for action" lodged before July 1, 2004 are to remain valid until their legal expiry date and shall not be renewed: Art.9. The reference to the "legal expiry date" suggests that this is a reference to decisions made on applications lodged before July 1, 2004, although this is far from clear. Such "applications" must "be accompanied" by an Art.6 declaration (as to which, see para. 23–78, below): *ibid.* This presumably means that such a declaration must now be supplied in respect of such applications. The provision of the declaration has the effect of releasing any deposit or fee: *ibid.* In the United Kingdom, the requirement for fees was abolished with effect from October 1, 2003: SI 2003/2316 (see para. 23–68, above). However, the power to require a deposit (under SI 1999/1601, reg.4) remained in existence until July 1, 2004, when SI 1999/1601 was revoked by SI 2004/1473. Art.9 also provides that where proceedings brought before the competent authority on a matter of substance before July 1, 2004 are still under way on that date, the deposit shall not be released before the close of those proceedings. Presumably this refers to a situation where legal proceedings are in force to determine whether particular goods are infringing, *e.g.* in the United Kingdom, condemnation proceedings or court proceedings. Curiously, no provision is made in respect of applications lodged between July 1 and October 21, 2004.

[92] The Goods Infringing Intellectual Property Right (Customs) Regulations 2004, SI 2004/1473. See Vol.2 at B7.bii.

[93] Customs Notice 34 Intellectual Property Rights, July 2004 ("Customs Notice 34"). See Vol.2 at B7.biii.

ing, "counterfeit goods" are defined as goods which infringe a registered trade mark.[94] "Pirated goods" are defined as goods "which are or contain copies made without the consent of the holder of a copyright or related right[95] or design right, regardless of whether it is registered in national law, or of a person duly authorised by the right-holder in the country of production, in cases where the making of those copies would constitute an infringement of that right under the Community Design Regulation[96] or the law of the Member State in which the application for action by the customs authorities is made".[97] The term "pirated goods" also includes goods which infringe patents, supplementary protection certificates, plant variety rights, designations of origin or geographical indication and geographical designations.[98] Moulds or matrices specifically designed or adapted for making pirated goods are treated as pirated goods if the use of such moulds or matrices infringes the right-holder's rights under Community law or the law of the Member State in which the application for action by the customs authorities is made.[99] The discussion which follows is confined to those categories of counterfeit goods which infringe the rights covered in this work.

23–71   **The "right-holder".** For the purposes of the Council Regulation, this term is broadly defined as meaning (relevantly): the holder of a copyright, related right or design right; any other person authorised to use the right; or "a representative of the right-holder or authorised user".[1] The 2004 Implementing Regulation provides that the latter term includes a collecting society which has as its sole or principal purpose the management or administration of copyrights or related rights.[2]

23–72   **Excepted goods.** Goods which are protected by a copyright, related right or design right and have been manufactured with the consent of the right-holder are not within the definition of "pirated goods".[3] Accordingly, the Council Regulation has no application to parallel imports. Goods "which have been manufactured or are protected by another intellectual property right [to which the Council Regulation applies] under conditions other than those agreed with the right-holder" are also excluded.[4] This appears to exclude over-runs and similar goods. Finally, as permitted under TRIPS,[5] the Council Regulation does not apply to goods of a non-commercial nature contained in travellers' personal luggage within the limits laid down in respect of relief from customs duty, provided there are no material indications to suggest the goods are part of commercial traffic.[6]

23–73   **When the Council Regulation applies to goods.** The Council Regulation applies when goods have been "entered for release for free circulation, export or re-

---

[94] The full definition is in Art.2 (1)(a). See Vol.2 at B7.ai.

[95] By reg.2(2) of the Goods Infringing Intellectual Property Rights (Customs) Regulations 2004 (SI 2004/1473) (Vol.2 at B7.bii), the term "copyright or related right" is to be construed as a reference to "copyright, rights in performances, publication rights or database rights".

[96] Council Regulation 6/2002 on Community designs [2002] O.J. 3/1.

[97] Regulation 1383/2003, Art.2 (1)(b). See Vol.2 at B7.ai.

[98] Art.2(1)(c).

[99] Art.2(3).

[1] Regulation 1383/2003, Art.2(2).

[2] Art.1(2).

[3] Art.3(1).

[4] Art.3(1).

[5] See Art.60.

[6] Art.3(2). The limit as at July 2004 was £145: HM Customs Notice 34: *Customs: Intellectual Property Rights*, July 2004 (see Vol.2 at B7.biii). This figure is subject to review. According to the Commission's website, the purpose of the proviso was to allow for checks on travellers to make sure that the use of couriers or 'mules' does not conceal a large flow of goods.

export";[7] or have been "found during checks on goods entering or leaving the Community customs territory[8] ..., placed under a suspensive procedure[9] ..., in the process of being re-exported subject to notification",[10] or placed in a free zone or free warehouse[11] ("an Article 1(1) situation"). These terms are derived from Council Regulation (EC) No.2913/92 which established the Community Customs Code.[12] Broadly speaking, goods "entered for release for free circulation" are non-Community goods which it is intended to import into the Community but which have not yet been released by Customs.[13] Goods "entered for export" are goods which are intended to be exported from the Community, but which have not yet cleared Customs.[14] Goods "entered for re-export" are non-Community goods[15] which it is intended to re-export from the Community but which have not yet cleared customs.[16] Checks may be made on goods when they enter or leave the Community Customs territory.[17] The relevant categories of "suspensive procedure" under which goods may be placed are as follows.[18] First, the "external transit" procedure, which permits the movement from one point to another within the customs territory of the Community of non-Community goods without such goods being subject to import duties or commercial policy measures; and of Community goods subject to a Community measure involving their export to third countries and in respect of which the corresponding customs formalities for export have been carried out.[19] Secondly, the "customs warehousing" procedure, which permits the storage in a customs warehouse of non-Community goods without such goods being subject to import duties or commercial policy measures; and of Community goods where Community legislation provides that their being placed in a customs warehouse shall attract the application of measures normally attaching to the export of such goods.[20] Thirdly, the "inward processing" procedure, which permits non-Community goods which are intended to be re-exported from the Community in processed form to be used without their being subject to import duties or commercial policy measures; and permits goods released for free circulation to be used with repayment or remission of the import duties chargeable on them if they are exported from the customs territory of the Community in processed form.[21] Fourthly, the procedure for "processing under customs control", which permits non-Community goods to be used in the customs territory of the Community in operations which alter their nature or state and allows the products of such operations to be released for free circulation.[22] Finally, the "temporary importation" procedure, which allows the use in the customs territory of the Community of non-Community goods intended for re-export without having undergone any change except normal depreciation with total or partial

---

[7] In accordance with Art.61 of Council Regulation (EC) No.2913/92 establishing the Community Customs Code, as amended [1992] O.J. L302/1 (" Regulation 2913/92").
[8] In accordance with Arts 37 and 183 of Reg.2913/92.
[9] Within the meaning of Art.84(1)(a) of Reg.2913/92.
[10] Under Art.182(2) of Reg.2913/92.
[11] Within the meaning of Art.166 of Reg.2913/92. See Art.1(1) of Reg.1383/2003.
[12] [1992] O.J. L302/1.
[13] Arts 37(1), 59(1) and 79.
[14] Arts 161 and 162.
[15] As defined in Art.4(8).
[16] Art.182(1).
[17] Arts 37 and 183.
[18] Art.84(1)(a).
[19] Art.91(1).
[20] Art.98(1).
[21] Art.114.
[22] Art.130.

relief from import duties and without their being subject to commercial policy measures.[23]

23–74   **Action by customs authorities on their own initiative: Article 4: general.** Article 4 contains two provisions. The first (Article 4(1)) enables customs authorities who have come across goods which they suspect to be pirated to notify right-holders who have not made an application for action under Article 5 (or who have made an application which has not yet been granted) and to hold the goods in order to enable such an application to be made.[24] The second (Article 4(2)) enables customs authorities to seek information from the right-holder in order to "confirm" their suspicions.

23–75   **Article 4(2): confirming suspicions.** It seems logical to consider Article 4(2) first. This provides that the customs authorities may, in accordance with the rules in force in the Member State concerned, without divulging any information other than the actual or supposed number of items and their nature, and before informing the right-holder of the possible infringement, ask the right-holder to provide them with any information they may need to confirm their suspicions. Two difficulties arise. First, it is not clear how this is to work in practice: giving the prescribed information to the right-holder is virtually bound to alert him to the possible infringement. Secondly, the phrase "confirm their suspicions" is ambiguous. It could refer to strengthening existing suspicions. On the other hand, it could refer to making those suspicions definitively valid. It seems likely that the object of the Article 4(2) procedure is to provide sufficient support for the authorities' suspicions to justify invoking the Article 4(1) procedure (it is not clear what other purpose there might be). Given that Article 4(2) appears to apply where there is thought to be a "possible infringement", it seems likely that the phrase refers to strengthening existing suspicions.

23–76   **Article 4(1): action.** Article 4(1) provides that where, before an application has been made by a right-holder (or, if one has been made, before it has been granted), in the course of checks carried out on goods in an Article 1(1) situation,[25] the customs authorities have "sufficient grounds for suspecting" that goods are pirated goods, they are permitted to take certain action. The Regulation does not state what grounds are "sufficient". However, Article 4(1) appears to be intended to reflect Article 58 of TRIPS, which sets out the procedure which is to be applicable if Members require competent authorities to act on their own initiative and suspend the release of goods in respect of which they have acquired *prima facie* evidence that an intellectual property right is being infringed. This would suggest a test of whether there is a *prima facie* case. Such a test would be consistent with the wording of Article 4 for two reasons. First, it would seem to follow from the interpretation of Article 4(2) suggested above that the standard is more than a mere possibility. Secondly, however, the use of the words "grounds for suspecting" suggests it is not necessary to establish a belief that it is more probable than not that the goods are pirated. If there are sufficient grounds, Article 4(1) permits the customs authorities to suspend the release of the goods or detain them for three working days "from the moment of receipt of the notification by the right-holder and by the declarant or holder of the goods, if the latter are known" in or-

---

[23] Art. 137.

[24] Art.6 of the 2004 Implementing Regulation provides that in the case of perishable goods the procedure for suspension of release or detention shall be initiated primarily in respect of products for which an application has already been lodged. This is presumably because of the practical difficulties involved in operating this procedure quickly enough to prevent damage to the goods.

[25] For the Art.1(1) of Regulation 1383/2003 situations, see para. 23–73, above.

der to enable the right-holder to make an application under Article 5(1).[26] This appears to envisage that both the right-holder on the one hand and the declarant or holder of the goods on the other will be notified by the customs authorities that the goods have been suspended or detained. Curiously, however, the Regulation does not lay down any express power to do this. The purpose of taking the action is stated to be to enable the right-holder to submit an application for action in accordance with Article 5.

Article 4: Domestic Regulations and Customs Notice. Regulation 4 of the Domestic Regulations is intended to implement Article 4. The conditions for action are expressed in the same terms as in Article 4. Accordingly, action may be taken if goods are in an Article 1(1) situation, no application has been made under Article 5, or one has been made but not granted and the Commissioners have sufficient grounds for suspecting that the goods are pirated goods. Again, the term "sufficient grounds" is left undefined but for the reasons stated in the previous paragraph, it is thought that the test is whether there is a *prima facie* case. If these conditions are satisfied, the Commissioners have four powers, which are stated to be exercisable in accordance with Article 4 of the Council Regulation.[27] First, they may notify a right-holder of the nature of the items and of the actual or supposed number of items and ask a right-holder to provide any information they may need to confirm their suspicions. This clearly derives from Article 4(2). However, unlike in the case of Article 4(2) there is no restriction on divulging other information. Moreover, it seems that the threshold for acting under this power is the same as that for acting under the other three powers in regulation 4: "sufficient grounds". This seems inconsistent with the object of Article 4(2), which is to enable the customs authorities to obtain sufficient grounds to act under Article 4(1) (see the previous paragraph). This inconsistency could, however, be resolved and the requirement to act "in accordance with Article 4" satisfied if the word "sufficient" could be construed differently depending on which power was being used. Secondly, the Commissioners may notify a right-holder and a declarant of the possible infringement of the right. As stated in the previous paragraph, this power appears to be implicit in Article 4. Thirdly, they may suspend the release of, or detain the goods. Unlike in Article 4(1), which limits this power to a period of three working days from receipt of notification by the right-holder, declarant or holder, there is no apparent limitation on the time for which the release may be suspended or the goods detained.[28] Finally, if the Commissioners do suspend or detain, they may invite the right-holder, in the absence of an existing application, to make an application within three working days of the notification of the suspension or detention. This power appears to be implicit in Article 4(1), the purpose of which is to enable the right-owner to submit an application for action under Article 5. Regulation 4 goes on to provide that if at any time during the period of suspension or detention an application is granted covering the goods, the decision granting the application shall be taken to have applied at the time the goods entered the Article 1(1) situation.[29] The effect of such a decision is that the goods are deemed to have been liable to forfeiture at

23–77

---

[26] Art.5 of the 2004 Implementing Regulation apparently seeks to clarify this provision by stating that if the customs service informs the declarant or holder of the goods that they have been detained or their release suspended pursuant to Art.4(1) of the Council Regulation, the time limit of 3 working days is to be counted only from the time the right-holder is notified. As to Art.5(1) applications, see para. 23–78, below.

[27] reg.4(1)(a) to (d).

[28] Note, however, that the Commissioners take the view that there is a time limit of three days: Notice 34, July 2004, para.3.4.

[29] reg.4(2).

that time.[30] The significance of this provision is that goods which are liable to forfeiture may be seized or detained by the Commissioners under the general law.[31]
Thus, the grant of a decision operates retroactively to legitimate the original
suspension or detention of the goods.

23–78 **Application for action: Articles 5 and 6.** The Council Regulation provides that
a right-holder may apply in writing to the competent customs department for action to be taken when goods are found in an Article 1(1) situation.[32] It also
provides that Member States are to designate the customs department competent
to receive and process applications and to encourage right-holders to lodge applications electronically where electronic data interchange systems exist.[33] It
goes on to provide that where the applicant is the right-holder of a Community
design right, the application may, as well as requesting action in the Member
State in which it is lodged, also request action by the customs authorities of one
or more other Member States.[34] It then states that the application must be made
out on a form established in accordance with the procedure set out in Article
21(2) and which contains all the information needed to enable the goods in question to be readily recognised by the customs authorities and in particular three
types of mandatory information: an accurate and detailed technical description of
the goods; any specific information the right-holder may have concerning the
type or pattern of fraud; and the name and address of the right-holder's contact
person.[35] Article 21(2) envisages that the Commision will introduce an implementing Regulation to deal with this.[36] This has been done.[37] The Council Regulation goes on to say that the application must also include the declaration required
by Article 6.[38] This is a declaration accepting: (i) liability to the persons involved
in the Article 1(1) situation if a procedure to determine whether the goods are
pirated is discontinued owing to an act or omission by the right-holder or the
goods are found not to be pirated;[39] (ii) liability for costs incurred in keeping the
goods under customs control;[40] and (iii) liability for the costs of translations

---

[30] reg.3.

[31] *i.e.* the Customs and Excise Management Act 1878 (c.2) s.139(1). The section refers to any thing
liable to forfeiture under "the customs and excise Acts". The latter term is defined as the Customs
and Excise Act 1979 and any other enactment for the time being in force relating to customs or
excise: *ibid.*, s.1. There seems little doubt that this includes the Domestic Regulations.

[32] Art.5(1). For the Article 1(1) situations, see para. 23–73, above.

[33] Arts 5(2) and (3). See also Art.8(1) of the 2004 Implementing Regulation, which provides that
Member States must inform the Commission as soon as possible of the competent customs depart-
ment, and Art.8(6) which provides for publication of a list of such departments in the Official
Journal. The remainder of Art.8 makes provision for the exchange of information between the
Commission and competent customs departments.

[34] Art.5(4). If action is sought in other Member States, the application form must indicate them and
the contact details of the right-holder in each Member State so indicated: *ibid.* Art.5(5).

[35] Art.5(5). Compare the requirements of Art.52 of TRIPS, which states that the application must
provide adequate evidence to satisfy the competent authorities that there is a *prima facie* case of
infringement and a detailed description of the goods to make them readily recognisable.

[36] Art.21(2) states that when reference is made to that paragraph, Arts 4 and 7 of Decision 1999/
468/EC shall apply. The latter (Council Decision of June 28, 1999 [1999] O.J. L184/23) lays
down the procedures for the exercise of implementing powers conferred on the Commission.

[37] Reg.1891/2004 [2004] O.J. L328/16 ("the 2004 Implementing Regulation"). The relevant forms
are at Annexes I and II. The forms contain detailed notes as to their completion and submission,
as to which see also the requirements of Art.3 of the 2004 Implementing Regulation.

[38] Art.5(5). A representative applicant must produce such a declaration signed by the right-holder or
person authorised to use the right; or a document authorising him to bear any costs arising from
customs action on their behalf in accordance with Art.6 of the Council Regulation: see Art.2(3)
of the 2004 Implementing Regulation. Presumably what is meant is a document pursuant to
which the representative undertakes to be liable for such costs.

[39] Art.6(1).

[40] Art.6(1).

where the application is for action in more than one Member State.[41] Next, the Council Regulation provides that the application must contain proof that the applicant holds the right for the goods in question.[42] Right-holders are also encouraged to forward other information, such as the value of the "original"[43] goods on the legitimate market; the location of the goods or their intended destination; particulars identifying the consignment or packages; the scheduled arrival or departure date; the means of transport; the identity of the importer, exporter or holder; the country of production and the routes used by traffickers; and the technical differences between the authentic and suspect goods.[44] The Regulation states that details may be required which are specific to the type of intellectual property right referred to in the application for action.[45]

Articles 5 and 6: Domestic Regulations and Customs Notice. These Articles are not covered in the Domestic Regulations, but are referred to in Customs Notice 34.[46] There is no formal designation of a customs department to receive and process applications, but this role clearly devolves on the Commissioners of Customs and Excise. There are two application forms, one for applications for action in the United Kingdom, and the other for action in two or more Member States.[47] The information required by the forms largely complies with what is required by Article 5 and the forms have an annex containing an undertaking to pay all costs and liabilities incurred under the 2003 Regulation.[48] Given that the 2004 Implementing Regulation contains forms and is directly applicable, it seems inevitable that these forms will be withdrawn.[49]   **23–79**

Decision on an application: Articles 5(7), 5(8) and 8. The Council Regulation provides that the application must be processed and the applicant must be notified of the decision within 30 working days of its receipt.[50] The right-holder may not be charged a fee.[51] Where the application does not contain the mandatory information which it is required to include, the competent customs department may   **23–80**

---

[41] Art.6(2). The relevant forms are at Annexes I-A and II-A to the 2004 Implementing Regulation. In each case, the undertaking to pay costs extends to the costs occasioned by the destruction of infringing goods pursuant to Art.17.

[42] As to this, the 2004 Implementing Regulation provides as follows. First, where the application is lodged by the holder of a copyright, related right or unregistered design right, the proof required is evidence of authorship or of the applicant's status as right-holder: Art.2(1)(a). Presumably what is meant is that if the applicant is the right-holder because he is the author, then he must provide proof of authorship; whereas if he is the right-holder as a result of transmission of title, then he must provide some document of title. It is not clear in either case precisely what will suffice. Secondly, where the application is lodged by any other person authorised to use the right, the proof required is that which is required of a right-holder together with the document by which the applicant is authorised to use the right in question: Art.2(1)(b). Thirdly, where the application is lodged by a representative of the right-holder or person authorised to use the right, the proof required is that required of a right-holder together with the representative's authorisation to act: Art.2(1)(c).

[43] The forms at Annexes I and II to the 2004 Implementing Regulation, refer to "authentic" goods.

[44] Reg.1383/2003, Art.5(5).

[45] Art.5(6). The 2004 Implementing Regulation provides that such details may include the place of manufacture or production, the distribution network and the names of licensees: see Art.4.

[46] July 2004 edition.

[47] Forms C1340 and C1340A respectively.

[48] These are stated in HM Customs Notice 34 para.3.7 to include (by way of example): storage charges where goods correctly detained have been found not to be infringing; storage charges where the detention or seizure results in a notice of claim and the outcome of proceedings is awaited; storage charges for correctly detained and seized goods which have had to be stored in commercial warehouse facilities due to their nature and quantity; legal costs and compensation for "any loss suffered" if the right-holder or the courts confirm that the goods are not infringing; and costs incurred in the destruction of the goods.

[49] For the forms in the 2004 Implementing Regulation, see the previous paragraph.

[50] Art.5(7). The form of the decision is prescribed by the Implementing Regulation: see Annex I Box 14 and Annex II Box 15.

[51] Reg.1383/2003, Art.5(7).

decide not to process it. If so, it must provide reasons for its refusal and include information on the appeal procedure.[52] If an application is granted, the department is obliged to specify the period during which the authorities are to take action. The period must not exceed one year from the date of adoption of the decision.[53] On expiry of that period and if all liabilities under the Regulation have been paid, the period may be extended.[54] The right-holder is obliged to notify the department if his right ceases to be validly registered or expires.[55] A decision granting the application is to be forwarded to those customs offices of the Member State or States likely to be concerned by the relevant goods.[56] If asked, the applicant is obliged to provide any additional information necessary to the implementation of the decision.[57]

23–81   **Articles 5(7), 5(8) and 8: Domestic Regulations and Customs Notice.** Again, these provisions are not dealt with in the Domestic Regulations but are covered in Customs Notice 34. The Notice provides as follows. Where possible, the application should be submitted 30 working days before the right-holder expects the infringing goods to be imported or exported or the right-holder wants the monitoring period to commence.[58] If the application is made as a result of a notification under Article 4(1) and regulation 4, it must be submitted within three working days of the notification.[59] No fee is charged.[60] The application will be determined as soon as possible and in any event within 30 days of receipt.[61] If the application is rejected, reasons will be given and the applicant will be given the opportunity to ask the Commissioners to reconsider.[62] If the application is accepted, this will be confirmed in writing by means of a formal decision.[63] If the application was made in response to an invitation, the customs officer concerned will be notified if the application has been accepted.[64] When the application concerns a Community Design, the applicant will need to forward it to the customs authorities of the other Member States concerned. It may be necessary for the applicant to arrange for a translation.[65] If a decision is granted, it will operate for 12 months but this period may be extended for further 12-month

---

[52] Art.5(8). The application may only be resubmitted when duly completed.

[53] Art.8(1), (2), (3).

[54] Art.8(1), (2). The same rules apply *mutatis mutandis* to an extension as apply to an initial application: *ibid.*, Art.7.

[55] Art.8(1). The Article 6 undertakings at Annexes I-A and II-A to the 2004 Implementing Regulation include an undertaking to notify the designated customs department of any "alteration to or loss of" the relevant rights.

[56] Art.8(2). It seems that the primary obligation to do this (and to forward any translations) lies on the applicant, but that with his consent it may be forwarded directly by the department which has taken the decision: *ibid.* The 2004 Implementing Regulation provides that on receipt of "the extract of a decision", the Member State shall complete without delay the "acknowledgement of receipt" section of the form and return a copy of the extract to the designated customs department: see Art.3.

[57] Art.8(2).

[58] para.3.4.

[59] para.3.4. This is because Art.4(1) provides that the goods may only be detained for three working days. As has been pointed out, however, no such time limit appears in reg.4 (see para 23–77, above).

[60] para.3.6.

[61] para.5.1, Step 1.

[62] Step 2.

[63] Step 3. Presumably this will now be in the form prescribed by the Implementing Regulation: see Annex I Box 14 and Annex II Box 15.

[64] Step 4.

[65] Step 5. The 2004 Implementing Regulation provides that on receipt of "the extract of a decision", the Member State shall complete without delay the "acknowledgement of receipt" section of the form and return a copy of the extract to the designated customs department: see Art.3.

periods.[66] However, the Domestic Regulations provide that a decision shall cease to have effect where either a change in the ownership or authorised use of the right specified in the application is not communicated in writing to the Commissioners or that right expires.[67]

Immediate action when goods are found following a decision: Article 9. Use of information: Article 12. Article 9 provides that where a customs office which has received the decision granting an application is satisfied, after consulting the applicant if necessary, that goods in an Article 1(1) situation are suspected of being pirated, it is obliged to suspend their release or detain them.[68] The customs office is obliged immediately to inform the department which processed the application.[69] The office or department must inform the right-holder and the declarant of its action and may inform them of the actual or estimated quantity and the actual or supposed nature of the goods.[70] With a view to establishing whether an intellectual property right has been infringed, and in accordance with national provisions on the protection of personal data, commercial and industrial secrecy and professional and administrative confidentiality, the office or department is obliged to inform the right-holder of the names and addresses of the consignor, consignee, declarant or holder of the goods and their origin and provenance.[71] Information supplied under this provision (Article 9(3)) may be used only for the purposes of Article 10 (which states that national law shall apply when deciding whether the goods are pirated), Article 11 (agreed disposal) and Article 13(1) (which refers to release of the goods if proceedings have not been commenced).[72] It is thought that the references to Article 10 and Article 13(1) mean that the information may be used by the right-holder in proceedings to decide whether the goods are pirated, but the wording is not entirely clear. Any other use of such information, unless permitted by national law, may, on the basis of national law, result in civil liability and lead to the suspension of the application for the remaining period of its validity (it is assumed that the word "application" should read "decision").[73] In the event of any further misuse, the department may refuse to renew the application (again, it is thought that "application" should read "decision"). The right-holder and the consignor, consignee, declarant or holder must be allowed to inspect the goods.[74] The office may take samples and, according to the rules of the Member State concerned, hand them over to the right-holder at his express request, strictly for the purposes of analysis and to facilitate the subsequent procedure.[75]

23–82

Articles 9 and 12: Domestic Regulations and Customs Notice. Customs Notice 34 provides that if the Commissioners detect goods suspected of infringing intellectual property rights they will detain them and notify the application and the declarant, providing details of the actual or estimated quantity and the nature

23–83

---

[66] para.3.6.
[67] reg.4. There is nothing expressly to this effect in the Council Regulation.
[68] Art.9(1).
[69] Art.9(1)
[70] Art.9(2).
[71] Art.9(3).
[72] Art.12. It has been said that the purpose of this restriction is to prevent right-holders from contacting the holder of the goods and authorising their release on payment of a fee, thus permitting counterfeit goods to come on to the market and providing a disincentive to customs officers to exercise their powers: see Daele: "Regulation 1383/2003: A New Step in the Fight against Counterfeit and Pirated Goods at the Borders of the European Union" [2004] E.I.P.R. 214.
[73] Art.12
[74] Art.9(3).
[75] Art.9(3). Where circumstances allow, samples must be returned on completion of analysis and, where applicable, before the goods are released or their detention ended. Any analysis is to be carried out under the sole responsibility of the right-holder: *ibid.*

of the goods.[76] The Notice goes on to state that if the applicant has a valid application in force (it is thought that this should be a reference to a valid decision), at the applicant's request the Commissioners will (where known) supply the name and address of the declarant, consignee, consignor, importer or exporter and manufacturer.[77] The Domestic Regulations make provision as to the misuse of information, as follows.

"Misuse of information" is defined as use of information supplied under Article 9(3) otherwise than for the purposes specified in Articles 10, 11 and 13(1) of the Council Regulation or pursuant to an enactment or order of the court.[78] Insofar as it refers to an enactment or an order of the court, this provision goes beyond the terms of Article 12. Regulation 11(1) provides that where the Commissioners have reasonable grounds for believing that there has been a misuse of information by the right-holder, they may suspend the decision in force at the time of the misuse in relation to a relevant intellectual property right for the remainder of the period of its validity. Three points may be noted. First, suspension may occur where the Commissioners have reasonable grounds to believe that misuse has taken place rather than when it has actually taken place. Arguably this goes beyond what is permitted by the Council Regulation. Secondly, the suspension is limited to a "relevant intellectual property right", that is a right in relation to which information was supplied under Article 9(3) and in relation to which the Commissioners have reasonable grounds to believe that a misuse has taken place.[79] Where a decision involves more than one intellectual property right but the misuse involves only one right, the suspension will be limited to that right. This appears to be a limitation on the scope of the remedy (which is, of course, permitted by the terms of the Council Regulation). Thirdly, the reference in the definition of misuse to orders of the court appears to be a further limitation on the scope of the remedy. The Domestic Regulations go on to provide that where the Commissioners have reasonable grounds for believing that there has been a further misuse of information within three years of a previous misuse, they may suspend the decision in force at the time of the misuse in relation to a relevant intellectual property right for the remainder of the period of its validity and refuse to renew it or accept a new application in relation to a relevant intellectual property right for a period of up to one year from its expiry.[80] No provision is made for civil liability for the misuse of information. The Domestic Regulations also provide for the making available of samples in accordance with the Council Regulation.[81]

23–84   **Destruction by consent: Article 11.** The Council Regulation permits Member States to provide that rather than undergoing the legal process of determining whether the goods are infringing,[82] it should be open to the parties to agree that the goods are simply destroyed. The process is to comply with the following conditions. First, within 10[83] working days of receipt of notification that release of the goods has been suspended or the goods have been detained, the right-holder is to inform the authorities that the goods infringe.[84] At the same time, he must supply the written agreement of the declarant, holder or owner of the goods

---

[76] para.3.8.
[77] para.3.8.
[78] reg.11(3)(a).
[79] reg.11(3)(b).
[80] reg.11(2).
[81] reg.6.
[82] As to which, see above at paras 22–85 to 22–88.
[83] Three working days if the goods are perishable.
[84] The 2004 Implementing Regulation provides that where an application for action is lodged in accordance with Art.4(1) of the Council Regulation before the expiry of the time limit of three

to abandon them for destruction. If the authorities agree, this agreement may be supplied directly. Secondly, agreement is to be presumed if the declarant, holder or owner has not specifically opposed destruction within "the prescribed period",[85] that is, presumably, the period of 10 days from receipt of notification.[86] Thirdly, destruction is to be carried out, unless national legislation provides otherwise, at the expense and under the responsibility of the right-holder. It is to be "systematically preceded" by the taking of samples for keeping by the customs authorities in such conditions that they constitute evidence admissible in legal proceedings in the Member State in which they might be needed. Article 11 is not covered in the Domestic Regulations or the Customs Notice. Accordingly, since its implementation is left to the discretion of Member States, it would appear that it does not apply in the United Kingdom.

Court determination of whether goods are pirated: Articles 10 and 13. If the goods are not destroyed by consent, it is necessary to determine whether they are pirated. Article 10 of the Council Regulation provides simply that the law in force in the Member State within the territory of which the goods are placed in the Article 1(1) situation shall apply to this determination. However, Article 13 provides that if within 10 working days of receipt of the notification of suspension of release or detention, the customs office has not been notified that proceedings have been initiated to determine whether the goods are pirated or an Article 11 agreement has not been received, release of the goods shall be granted or their detention shall be ended as appropriate.[87] The period may be extended by up to 10 working days.[88] It follows that proceedings must be implemented within this time limit in order to prevent the release of the goods. **23–85**

Articles 10 and 13: Domestic Regulations and Customs Notice—general. Under the Domestic Regulations, there are two procedural methods for the determination of whether the goods are pirated. The method used depends on the nature of the right which the decision specifies as subsisting in the goods. For these purposes, rights are divided into two categories. The first ("Category 1") consists of design rights, Community designs, registered designs, patents, supplementary protection certificates, plant variety and breeders' rights, designations of origin, geographical indications and geographical designations. The second ("Category 2") consists of all the other rights covered by the Council Regulation, that is: copyright, rights in performances, publication right, database right, and trade marks. If the decision specifies a Category 1 right as subsisting in respect of the goods, then even if a Category 2 right is also so specified, the matter has to go to the relevant court (the same is true of patents, registered designs and similar **23–86**

working days and that application has been accepted, the period of 10 (or three, as the case may be) working days runs from the day after the application is received: see Art.5.
[85] Which may be extended by a further 10 days where circumstances warrant it.
[86] Or, as the case may be, receipt of the Art.4(1) application (see Art.5 of the 2004 Implementing Regulation), together with any extension of the period (as to which, see previous note).
[87] Subject to completion of all customs formalities: Art.13. In the case of perishable goods, this period is three days: *ibid.* The 2004 Implementing Regulation provides that where an application for action is lodged in accordance with Art.4(1) of the Council Regulation before the expiry of the time limit of three working days and that application has been accepted, the period of 10 (or three, as the case may be) working days runs from the day after the application is received: see Art.5. See also Art.7(1) of the 2004 Implementing Regulation.
[88] Art.13. In the case of perishable goods, no extension is permitted: *ibid.* See also Arts. 7(1) and (2) of the 2004 Implementing Regulation, which provide respectively that if there is insufficient time to apply for such proceedings, an extension may be deemed to be appropriate and that where an extension has already been granted under Art.11 of the Council Regulation, no further extension may be granted under Art.13(1).

rights).[89] Otherwise, the matter proceeds by way of condemnation proceedings under the general Customs and Excise law.[90] The object of the distinction appears to be to ensure that in cases where specialist technical knowledge may be relevant, the matter is dealt with in the Chancery Division of the High Court or the Patents County Court rather than by way of ordinary condemnation proceedings, which may be brought in the Magistrates' Court. Where rights in both categories are alleged to be infringed, the right-holder may waive any Category 1 rights in the goods with the result that the matter will proceed by way of condemnation proceedings. The waiver must be given by notice in writing to the Commissioners within 10 working days of notification of the suspension or detention.[91] The waiver is for the purposes of the Council Regulation and the Domestic Regulations only, and its effect is that for the purposes of the Domestic Regulations the right-holder is treated as if he did not have the right concerned.[92] The fact that in condemnation proceedings the burden lies on the person alleging that the goods are not pirated[93] and the potential difficulties in relation to time limits outlined below[94] are powerful incentives to waive any Category 1 rights where Category 2 rights also exist.

23–87   **Category 1 rights: court proceedings.** Where court proceedings are appropriate, the Council Regulation provides that if the office has not been notified within 10 working days of receipt by the right-holder of notification of suspension or detention that proceedings have been initiated, the goods must be released or their detention ended.[95] The 10-working-day period may be extended for a further 10 days.[96] For these purposes, the only proceedings that will do are proceedings commenced in the relevant court by the right-holder alleging that the goods infringe an intellectual property right of his and seeking relief which that court has the power to grant after a finding of such infringement.[97] The relevant court is the High Court or the Patents County Court.[98] Regulation 9(3) of the Domestic Regulations goes on to provide that without prejudice to "any provision" of the Council Regulation, the suspension of release or detention shall cease if at any time the Commissioners are not satisfied, or cease to be satisfied that such proceedings have been commenced or are satisfied that such proceedings have been withdrawn or otherwise terminated without other such proceedings being commenced.[99] Regulation 9(3) provides that "for the purposes of this Regulation" proceedings shall be taken not to have been commenced before a claim

---

[89] reg.9.

[90] reg.7.

[91] reg.8(2). If the goods are perishable, the time limit is three days: reg.8(3).

[92] reg.8(4).

[93] See para. 23–88, below.

[94] See para. 23–87, below.

[95] Art.13(1). In the case of perishable goods, the period is three working days: Art.13(2). The 2004 Implementing Regulation provides that where an application for action is lodged in accordance with Art.4(1) of the Council Regulation before the expiry of the time limit of three working days and that application has been accepted, the period of 10 (or three, as the case may be) working days runs from the day after the application is received: see Art.5.

[96] Art.13(1). No extension is permitted in the case of perishable goods: *ibid*. See also Arts 7(1) and (2) of the 2004 Implementing Regulation, which provide respectively that if there is insufficient time to apply for such proceedings, an extension may be deemed to be appropriate and that where an extension has already been granted under Art.11 of the Council Regulation, no further extension may be granted under Art.13(1). HM Customs Notice 34 provides that if an extension is required, written reasons must be supplied: para.5.2(b).

[97] Goods Infringing Intellectual Property Rights (Customs) Regulations 2004 (SI 2004/1473), reg.9(2).

[98] reg.9(6). In Scotland, the relevant court is the Court of Session and in Northern Ireland, the High Court: *ibid*.

[99] The reference to "other such proceedings" is presumably a reference to fresh proceedings com-

form has been issued[1] and served on all other parties in accordance with the rules of court.[2] It seems clear that regulation 9(3) is irrelevant for the purposes of deciding whether proceedings have been initiated under the Council Regulation. Accordingly, the requirements of that Regulation will be satisfied if proceedings are issued within the time limit laid down by Article 13, that is in normal cases 10 working days together with any extension thereof or in the case of perishable goods, three working days. However, if proceedings are not served within those time limits (which, if the defendant is abroad or the goods are perishable is quite likely), this appears to mean that the suspension or detention "shall cease" pursuant to regulation 9(3). Does this mean that the goods must be handed back to their owner? Regulation 10(1) provides that nothing in the Domestic Regulations shall be taken to affect any power which the Commissioners have to suspend the release of or detain any goods apart from the Domestic Regulations. The Commissioners might therefore argue that they are entitled to continue to detain the goods under their general powers.[3] However, this would then presumably mean that the normal condemnation procedure applies, thus creating two parallel sets of proceedings and defeating the object of distinguishing between Category 1 and Category 2 goods.[4] It seems therefore that the right-holder might have to invoke regulation 10(2), which states that nothing in the Domestic Regulations is to be taken to affect the court's power to grant interim relief, and seek an interim order for the detention of the goods pending determination of the proceedings. Again, it seems unlikely that this was intended. The Commissioners have stated that they will need to be satisfied not only that the suspected infringement has been referred to a court, but also that the proceedings are being actively pursued. Accordingly, they may contact the right-holder from time to time. If they are not satisfied that the proceedings are being actively pursued, the goods will be released.[5]

Category 2 rights: condemnation proceedings. Customs Notice 34 states that   **23–88** in relation to goods suspected of infringing copyright or a right in a performance,[6] once the right-holder has been given a sample, the Commissioners will then ask him to give a written opinion as to whether the goods are pirated and (if so) the reasons why they infringe. This opinion must be given within 10 working days of the date on which the right-holder was notified of the detention, but the period may be extended for a further 10 days on request. If the Commissioners are then satisfied that the goods are liable to forfeiture, they will seize them.[7] The general Customs and Excise law provides that notice of the seizure must then be given to the owner of the goods.[8] Any person claiming that the goods were not liable to seizure then has one month from service of the notice of seizure to give notice of a claim to the Commissioners.[9] In the absence of such a notice, the goods will be treated as condemned.[10] If such a notice is given, the Commissioners are obliged

---

menced because, for example, the existing proceedings are against the wrong defendant. See also HM Customs Notice 34, para.5.2(b).

[1] Or in Scotland, a summons has been signeted or in Northern Ireland a writ has been issued: reg.9(5).

[2] reg.9(4), (5).

[3] *e.g.* Customs and Excise Management Act 1979, s.139.

[4] As to which, see above.

[5] Customs Notice 34, para.5.2(a). This provision does not appear to derive from either the Council Regulation or the Domestic Regulations.

[6] Presumably this is also intended to apply to goods suspected of infringing publication right and database right as well, but this is not stated.

[7] Customs Notice 34, para.5.2(a).

[8] Customs and Excise Management Act 1979 (c.2), Sch.3, para.1.

[9] Sch.3, para.3.

[10] Under Sch.3, para.5.

to take proceedings for condemnation of the goods.[11] The proceedings may be in the Magistrates' Court or the High Court.[12] The burden of showing that the goods are not or were not liable to forfeiture, that is that they are not pirated goods, lies on the person so alleging.[13] The right-holder may be asked to provide further assistance, for example by providing further witness statements and attending the hearing.[14] According to the Commissioners, the right-holder may be liable for the expenses incurred by them in connection with such proceedings.[15] It will be evident that the Government's decision to implement the 2003 Council Regulation by applying these provisions of the general Customs and Excise law leads to a result which does not accord with the exact terms of Article 13, which envisage that the right-holder will initiate proceedings and then notify the customs office that this has been done.

23–89   **Interim release of the goods: Article 14 of the Council Regulation.** This Article provides (relevantly) that the declarant, owner, importer, holder or consignee of goods suspected of infringing design rights shall be able to obtain their release or an end to their detention on provision of security. There are three preconditions: first, the customs office or department must have been notified that a procedure has been initiated within the prescribed period to determine whether the goods are pirated goods; secondly, the authority "empowered for this purpose" must not have authorised precautionary measures before expiry of that time limit; and thirdly, all customs formalities must have been completed.[16] The security must be sufficient to protect the interests of the right-holder and its payment is not to affect his other remedies.[17] Article 14 goes on to provide that where the procedure to determine whether the goods are pirated has been commenced otherwise than by the right-holder, the security shall be released if the person initiating "the said procedure" does not exercise his right to institute legal proceedings within 20 working days of the date on which he receives notification of the suspension of release or the detention. Finally, Article 14 provides that where the second subparagraph of Article 13(1) applies, that is, where the time for the right-holder to initiate proceedings has been extended from 10 to 20 working days, the 20-day period may be extended to 30 working days.[18] It is not easy to understand how the latter provisions are intended to interact with those of Article 13.

23–90   **Article 14: Customs Notice.** The Domestic Regulations do not deal with Article 14. Customs Notice 34 states that the owner, importer or consignee has the right to take delivery of the goods against a security, provided that the matter has been referred to the court within the required period, the court has not issued an injunction or imposed any other interim measure and all customs formalities have been completed. It goes on to say that the security should be sufficient to protect the right-holder's interests and that the Commissioners will look to the right-holder to provide a realistic estimate, with supporting evidence, of the appropriate

---

[11] Under Sch.3, para.8.

[12] Sch.3, para.8(1)(a). The various procedural provisions contained in Customs and Excise Management Act 1979, ss.145, 146 and 152 to 155 are applied by the Goods Infringing Intellectual Property Rights (Customs) Regulations 2004 (SI 2004/1473), reg.7(1)(b).

[13] SI 2004/1473, reg.7(2).

[14] Customs Notice 34, para.5.2(a).

[15] Customs Notice 34, para.5.3, citing the scope of the indemnity which must be given on application.

[16] Art.14(1).

[17] Art.14(2).

[18] Art.14(2).

monetary amount. The Commissioners may also seek corresponding "advice" from the owner, importer or consignee.[19]

Storage of the goods. Article 15 of the Council Regulation provides that the conditions of storage of the goods are for Member States to decide but that they shall not give rise to costs for the customs administration. The Domestic Regulations make no provision for storage or storage costs, but Customs Notice 34 makes clear that storage will be at the expense of the applicant.[20]   **23–91**

Final disposal of the goods. Article 16 of the Council Regulation provides that goods found to be pirated shall not be allowed to enter the Community customs territory, released for free circulation, removed from the Community customs territory, exported, re-exported, placed under a suspensive procedure or placed in a free zone or free warehouse. Article 17(1) provides that without prejudice to the other legal remedies open to the right-holder, Member States shall adopt the measures necessary (a) to allow the competent authorities to destroy the goods or dispose of them outside commercial channels in such a way as to preclude injury to the right-holder, without compensation and, unless otherwise specified in national legislation, at no cost to the exchequer; and (b) to take any other measures effectively depriving the persons concerned of any economic gains from the transaction. No specific provision is made in the Domestic Regulations. However, this does not appear to be necessary. If the determination that the goods are pirated is taken in court proceedings, the court can give effect to Articles 16 and 17 under its normal powers. If on the other hand, the goods are condemned in condemnation proceedings, the Commissioners have a discretion as to how to dispose of them[21] but they will normally be destroyed.[22] If the right-holder then wishes to seek an account of profits in accordance with Article 17(1)(b), then he can no doubt bring a separate action claiming such an account.   **23–92**

Article 19: liability of customs authorities and right-holder. This Article provides that except as provided by national laws, the customs authorities shall not be liable to (i) a right-holder for failing to detect pirated goods or to suspend their release or to detain them or (ii) to the persons involved in the Article 1(1) situation for the exercise of their powers.[23] Article 19 goes on to provide that the right-holder's civil liability shall be governed by the law of the Member State in which the goods in question were placed in the Article 1(1) situation.[24] Depending on the facts, such liability might arise under the English law of malicious falsehood.   **23–93**

C. SECTION 111 OF THE 1988 ACT

The scope of section 111 of the 1988 Act. Section 111, which contains similar provisions to those in the Council Regulation, originally applied to all infringing printed copies of published literary, dramatic or musical works and to all infringing copies of sound recordings or films which were imported into the United Kingdom (there was an exception for goods imported for private or domestic use). However, in 1995, at the same time as the Council Regulation came into force, the scope of the section was severely curtailed in order to give effect to the   **23–94**

---

[19] Customs Notice 34, para.5.2(b).
[20] Customs Notice 34, para.3.7.
[21] Customs and Excise Management Act 1979 (c.2), s.139(5).
[22] HM Customs Notice 34: *Customs: Intellectual Property Rights*, para.5.3.
[23] Art.19(1).
[24] Art.19(2).

Community obligation to establish the internal market .[25] The section as amended does not apply to goods placed or expected to be placed in an Article 1(1) situation in respect of which an application may be made under the Council Regulation,[26] nor does it apply to infringing copies which arrive in the United Kingdom from within the European Economic Area unless they have not been entered for free circulation.[27] The section remains restricted to infringing printed copies of published literary dramatic and musical works, and to copies of sound recordings and films.[28] The exception for goods imported for private or domestic use also remains. Unlike the Council Regulation, the section applies to all "infringing copies", including parallel imports and over-runs, and it seems likely that this is in fact the only area in which the section is now of any practical effect.

23–95   **Notice procedure under section 111 of the 1988 Act.**[29] The owner of the copyright in any published literary, dramatic or musical work may give notice[30] to the Commissioners of Customs and Excise requesting them to treat as prohibited goods printed copies of the work which are infringing copies.[31] The notice must state that the person giving it is the owner of the copyright in the work and must specify the period during which the goods are to be treated as prohibited. The period must not exceed five years, and shall not extend beyond the period for which copyright is to subsist.[32] The owner of the copyright in a sound recording or film may also give notice[33] in writing to the Commissioners with a view to preventing the importation of infringing copies. The notice must state that he is the owner of the copyright in the work, that infringing copies of the work are expected to arrive in the United Kingdom at a time and place specified in the notice,[34] and that he requests the Commissioners to treat the copies as prohibited goods.[35] In all cases, a copy of the copyright work must be supplied to the Commissioners with the notice.[36] At the same time, or at the time the goods to which the notice relates are imported, the person giving the notice must provide the Commissioners with such evidence as they may reasonably require to enable them to establish that he is the owner of the copyright in the work and that any goods detained are infringing copies.[37] The person giving the notice must give the Commissioners such security as they may require against liability and expense they may suffer as a result

---

[25] The amendments were effected by the Copyright (EC Measures Relating to Pirated Goods and Abolition of Restrictions on the Import of Goods) Regulations 1995 (SI 1995/1445).
[26] CDPA 1988, s.111(3B), added with effect from July 1, 1995 by The Copyright (EC Measures Relating to Pirated Goods and Abolition of Restrictions on the Import of Goods) Regulations 1995 (SI 1995/1445), reg.2 and amended by the Goods Infringing Intellectual Property Rights (Customs) Regulations 2004 (SI 2004/1473), reg.12. For the meaning of the term Art.1(1) situation, see para. 23–73, above.
[27] CDPA 1988, s.111(3A), added with effect from July 1, 1995 by The Copyright (EC Measures Relating to Pirated Goods and Abolition of Restrictions on the Import of Goods) Regulations 1995 (SI 1995/1445), reg.2.
[28] CDPA 1988, s.111(1) and (3).
[29] See generally HM Customs Notice 34: *Customs: Intellectual Property Rights*, July 2004 (Vol.2 at B7.biii).
[30] In the form contained in Sch.1 to the Copyright (Customs) Regulations (SI 1989/1178) (Vol.2 at B7.bi). A separate notice must be given in respect of each work: *ibid.*, reg.2(1). There is a fee of £30 + VAT per notice: *ibid.*, reg.4.
[31] CDPA 1988, s.111(1); see *ibid.* s.27 for the definition of an infringing copy.
[32] CDPA 1988, s.111(2).
[33] In the form contained in Sch.2 to the Copyright (Customs) Regulations (SI 1989/1178). A separate notice must be given in respect of each work and in respect of each expected importation: *ibid.* reg.2(2). There is a fee of £30 + VAT per notice: *ibid.* reg.4.
[34] In this respect the requirements are much more onerous than those relating to published literary, dramatic or musical works.
[35] CDPA 1988, s.111(3); see *ibid.* s.27 for the definition of an infringing copy.
[36] The Copyright (Customs) Regulations 1989 (SI 1989/1178), reg.5.
[37] SI 1989/1178, reg.5.

of the notice,[38] and must keep them indemnified against such liability and expense.[39] The person giving the notice must inform the Commissioners of any change in the ownership of the copyright and of any other change affecting the notice within 14 days of such change.[40] The notice is deemed to have been withdrawn within 14 days of any change in the ownership of the copyright or if the person giving the notice fails to comply with any requirement of the Regulations.[41] There is a right of appeal against a refusal by the Commissioners to accept a notice.[42]

Effect of a notice under section 111. When a notice under section 111 of the   **23–96**
1988 Act is in force, the importation of goods to which it applies (otherwise than for the private and domestic use of the importer) is prohibited.[43] The prohibition does not, however, render the importer liable to any penalty other than the forfeiture of the goods.[44] The normal Customs law will apply. Accordingly, the owner of the goods must be notified of the seizure.[45] Any person claiming that the goods were not liable to seizure then has one month to give notice of a claim to the Commissioners.[46] In the absence of such a notice, the goods will be treated as condemned.[47] If such a notice is given, the Commissioners are obliged to take proceedings for condemnation of the goods.[48] If the goods are condemned, or deemed to be condemned, the Commissioners have a discretion as to how to dispose of them[49] but they will normally be destroyed.[50]

---

[38] SI 1989/1178, reg.6.
[39] SI 1989/1178, reg.7.
[40] SI 1989/1178, reg.8.
[41] SI 1989/1178, reg.9.
[42] The appeal process is via the Excise and Customs appeal procedure laid down by HM Customs and Excise Notice 990.
[43] CDPA 1988, s.111(4).
[44] CDPA 1988, s.111(4).
[45] Customs and Excise Management Act 1979 (c.2), Sch.3, para.1(2). There is no obligation to notify the owner if he or his servant or agent was present at the seizure or if the seizure was in a ship or aircraft and took place in the presence of the master or commander: *ibid.*
[46] Customs and Excise Management Act 1979 (c.2), Sch.3, para.3. The month runs from the date of service of notice of seizure or (in the absence of such service) from the date of the seizure itself.
[47] Under Customs and Excise Management Act 1979 (c.2), Sch.3, para.5.
[48] Under Customs and Excise Management Act 1979 (c.2), Sch.3, para.8. The proceedings may be in the Magistrates' Court or the High Court: *ibid.* para.8(1)(a).
[49] Customs and Excise Management Act 1979 (c.2), s.139(5).
[50] HM Customs Notice 34: *Customs: Intellectual Property Rights*, July 2004 (see Vol.2 at B7.biii), p.7.

PART VII

INTERNATIONAL ASPECTS

CHAPTER TWENTY FOUR

INTERNATIONAL TREATIES

1. INTRODUCTION—SCOPE OF INTERNATIONAL COPYRIGHT

24–01 **Relationship between international conventions, treaties and agreements, and domestic law.** International copyright is concerned with treaties, conventions or agreements between nations requiring their Contracting States to respect, in their own countries, the copyright of nationals of other Contracting States. There is no general principle of international law requiring such protection[1] and, before the making of international agreements regarding the matter, a book written by a foreigner and published abroad could obtain no protection in this country.[2] Similarly, no protection was afforded abroad to the works of British nationals.

In some countries, such conventions, treaties or agreements are regarded as self-executing, becoming automatically part of the law of the land following adherence to the convention in question, and are so regarded by the courts. However, in the United Kingdom, since 1911, this is not the case, and domestic legislation is required to give effect to the treaty obligations undertaken. The courts are not concerned, therefore, except in very limited circumstances (such as where an Act is ambiguous and the Parliamentary record shows the intention was to implement the Convention),[3] to interpret such treaties, conventions or agreements, but only the Acts of Parliament and Orders in Council made for the purpose of giving effect thereto.[4]

As regards the international scope of copyright, there are a number of different

---

[1] See *Def Lepp Music v Stuart-Brown* [1986] R.P.C. 273.

[2] *Guichard v Mori* (1831) 9 L.J.Ch. 227. The question of how far under the Acts of Anne and of 1842 an alien could obtain copyright at all in England (apart from the International Copyright Acts) was discussed in *Jefferys (C) v Boosey (T)* [1855] 4 H.L.C. 815, and *Routledge v Low* [1868] L.R. 3 H.L. 100.

[3] See Ch.3 as regards the protection of works of foreign origin. As to the Treaty of Rome 1957, see also Ch.25.

[4] *The Jade* [1976] 1 W.L.R. 430. See also *Smith Kline & French Laboratories Ltd v RD Harbottle (Mercantile) Ltd* [1980] R.P.C. 363 and *E's Applications* [1983] R.P.C. 231.

aspects to be taken into consideration. In this Chapter, the general body of conventions, treaties and agreements regulating the copyright and related rights relations between different countries at the universal and regional levels are discussed. The protection afforded to copyright and related rights under the law of the European Union is dealt with in Chapter 25, below. The protection of works of United Kingdom origin in foreign countries is covered in Chapter 26, below. Finally, the protection actually afforded to foreign works by the law of the United Kingdom is explained elsewhere in Chapter 3, above.

Major copyright Conventions. The two major copyright Conventions are the Berne Convention for the Protection of Literary and Artistic Works, first adopted in 1886, and the Universal Copyright Convention of 1952. Other Conventions and Agreements to which this country is a party and which have taken on increasing importance in international copyright and related rights relations in recent years include the Rome Convention for the Protection of Performers, Producers of Phonograms and Broadcasting Organisations 1961 (the Rome Convention), the Convention for the Protection of Producers of Phonograms against the Unauthorised Duplication of their Phonograms 1971 (the Phonograms Convention), and the Agreement on Trade-Related Aspects of Intellectual Property Rights, 1994 (the TRIPs Agreement). **24–02**

In December 1996, the Berne and Rome Conventions were supplemented and updated by the adoption of two new instruments, the WIPO Copyright Treaty and the WIPO Performances and Phonograms Treaty.

All these treaties are discussed in this Chapter.[5]

Other copyright and related rights conventions. There are a number of other Conventions of lesser importance because of either their limited membership and scope, or their regional character. These are briefly discussed in Parts 9 and 10 of this Chapter and include the Convention Relating to the Distribution of Programme-Carrying Signals Transmitted by Satellite (Brussels, 1974),[6] the Vienna Typefaces Convention,[7] the Madrid Double Taxation Convention,[8] the Pan-American Conventions,[9] and a number of Council of Europe Conventions and Recommendations.[10] **24–03**

There are also a series of European Union Directives on the subject of copyright and related rights, most of which have already been implemented in the United Kingdom. Legislation is under preparation with regard to others and more European Union legislation may be expected in the future. Current European Union legislation and the programme of the Commission concerning copyright and related rights is dealt with in Chapter 25, below.

2. THE BERNE CONVENTION AND ITS REVISIONS

A. HISTORY

Early treaties. Prior to 1886, international copyright was regulated to a limited **24–04**

---

[5] The full texts of these Conventions are reproduced in Vol.2 of this work.
[6] See paras 24–158 *et seq.*, below.
[7] See paras 24–162 *et seq.*, below.
[8] See paras 24–164 *et seq.*, below.
[9] See paras 24–165 *et seq.*, below.
[10] See paras 24–168 *et seq.*, below.

extent by bilateral treaties between a number of European nations.[11] During the nineteenth century, international copyright relations developed gradually as the need was perceived to prevent international piracy of copyright works.[12] In England, the Crown was authorised, by the International Copyright Act 1844,[13] and various amending Acts,[14] by Order in Council, to direct that works first published in foreign countries should be entitled to copyright in the United Kingdom, and, between 1846 and 1886, the United Kingdom entered into a series of bilateral treaties with other European countries providing for reciprocal protection to authors of the respective countries. A large number of Orders in Council were promulgated under the 1844 Act to give effect to these treaties. The general purpose of the treaties entered into by the United Kingdom was to give the authors of works first published in one of the States party thereto the same privileges in the other States as would have been enjoyed if the work had been first published there. By the mid-nineteenth century, the United Kingdom had entered into bilateral agreements on copyright with Belgium, France, Hanover, Prussia, Sardinia-Italy and Spain.[15]

24–05 **Berne Convention.** These early treaties gave rise to a complicated situation, for the rights of a foreign author in the United Kingdom and of a British national elsewhere varied according to the particular treaty or Order in Council concerned and it was difficult for an author to establish the extent to which he was protected in a country other than his own. In 1884 and 1885, at the initiative of the Swiss Government, conferences were held in an attempt to draw up an international copyright treaty.[16] The United Kingdom was a party to these Conferences, which resulted at the Diplomatic Conference held at Berne in 1886 in the framing of a Convention, known as the Berne Convention, whereby the Contracting States were "constituted into a Union for the protection of the rights of authors over their literary and artistic works".[17] To enable the United Kingdom to give effect to this Convention by Orders in Council, the International Copyright Act 1886[18] was passed.

The Berne Convention has been revised[19] periodically to take account of new technologies, the development of which in turn gave rise to new uses of copy-

---

[11] S. Ricketson, *The Berne Convention for the protection of literary and artistic works: 1886–1896* (Queen Mary College, University of London, 1987), paras 1.29 *et seq.*

[12] S. Ricketson, *The Berne Convention for the protection of literary and artistic works: 1886–1896* (Queen Mary College, University of London, 1987), para.1.30.

[13] 7 & 8 Vict. c.12. See also I. Davis, "A Century of Copyright: the United Kingdom and the Berne Convention", [1986] *Copyright* 177.

[14] 15 & 16 Vict. c.12; 25 & 26 Vict. c.68; 38 & 39 Vict. c.12.

[15] S. Ricketson, *The Berne Convention for the protection of literary and artistic works: 1886–1896* (Queen Mary College, University of London, 1987), para.1.30.

[16] S. Ricketson, *The Berne Convention for the protection of literary and artistic works: 1886–1896* (Queen Mary College, University of London, 1987), paras 2.19 *et seq.* and paras 2.38 *et seq.*

[17] Berne Convention 1886, Art.1. The UK adhered to this Convention on November 28, 1887. The new Convention Convention entered into force on December 5, 1887, with the following membership: Belgium, France, Germany, Haiti, Italy, Spain, Switzerland, Tunisia and the UK. The UK ratified the Convention on behalf also of its colonial possessions and principal self-governing dominions. As to the history and development of the Berne Convention, see: C. Masouyé, *Guide to the Berne Convention for the Protection of Literary and Artistic Works (Paris Act, 1971)* (WIPO, Geneva, 1978); A. Bogsch, "The First Hundred Years of the Berne Convention for the Protection of Literary and Artistic Works", [1986] *Copyright* 291, and S. Ricketson, *The Berne Convention for the protection of literary and artistic works: 1886–1896* (Queen Mary College, University of London, 1987).

[18] 49 & 50 Vict. c.33.

[19] Art.17 of the 1886 Act provided for periodic revisions. The history of the various Acts of the Berne Convention is as follows:—September 9, 1886: Berne Convention (entry into force December 5, 1887);—May 4, 1896: Additional Act of Paris (entry into force on December 9, 1897);—November 13, 1908: Berlin Act (entry into force September 9, 1910);—March 20, 1914: Additional Protocol of Berne (entry into force on April 20, 1915);—June 2, 1928: Rome

right protected works, and of political, economic and social changes. Over the years, new rights for copyright owners have been recognised, raising the level of protection and increasing the uniformity of treatment of rights owners in the Contracting States. These revisions are discussed below.

Additional Act of Paris 1896. In 1896, a further Diplomatic Conference was held in Paris[20] to consider certain modifications aimed at clarifying and consolidating the original Convention and which experience had shown to be necessary or expedient. For example, it was made clear that the expression "published" meant "published for the first time" and that authors being nationals of countries not party to the Berne Convention but whose works were first published in a Berne country were protected under the Convention. Posthumous works were expressly protected. This Conference resulted in what was called the "Additional Act of Paris 1896", which was adopted by the United Kingdom on March 7, 1898. The revision took the form of a separate instrument, the Additional Act, as opposed to a revised Berne Convention, because a number of the proposed amendments were unacceptable to some Contracting States. A major and lasting consequence of this for the future of the Berne Union was the replacement of one single treaty by several different Acts of the Convention, each with restricted membership as various countries became bound by slightly different texts.[21] A further Interpretative Declaration[22] was also adopted, containing certain authentic interpretations of the Act agreed by the majority of the States present. These included that protection should depend only on compliance with formalities in the country of origin and a definition of "published", limiting the concept to the making available of copies and making it clear that "performance" of a work did not constitute publication. The United Kingdom did not accept the Declaration, its contents being at variance with its domestic law at the time.

24–06

The revised Berne Convention of Berlin 1908. In 1908, a further Diplomatic Conference was held in Berlin,[23] the object of which was "to secure, if possible, a general agreement to such a revision of the Berne Convention and the Additional Act of Paris as would enable the Contracting States to sign a single new instrument containing stipulations of a more complete and simple character, with a view, not only to affording a more effectual protection to the author, but also to removing the more salient difficulties which had been encountered in the working of the existing arrangements".[24] The result of the Conference was the Revised Berne Convention or Berlin Act 1908, which replaced the original Convention of 1887, and the Additional Act of Paris 1896, except that States who were signatories to the original Convention and the Additional Act of Paris could still elect to be bound by the provisions of these Conventions in preference to those of

24–07

Act (entry into force August 1, 1931);—June 26, 1948: Brussels Act (entry into force August 1, 1951);—June 14, 1967: Stockholm Act (revised substantive provisions never entered into force; they were themselves revised in 1971; administrative provisions entered into force in 1970);—July 24, 1971: Paris Act (entry into force October 10, 1974). The WIPO Copyright Treaty adopted by the Diplomatic Conference on December 20, 1996, is not a revised Act of the Berne Convention but a new treaty, which is a special agreement within the meaning of Art.20 of the Berne Convention.

[20] S. Ricketson, *The Berne Convention for the protection of literary and artistic works: 1886–1896* (Queen Mary College, University of London, 1987), paras 3.1 to 3.7.

[21] See paras 24–61 to 24–65, below, and "General Table of Copyright and Related Rights Conventions and National Laws", Ch.26, below.

[22] *The Berne Convention for the Protection of Literary and Artistic Works from 1886 to 1986* (WIPO, Geneva, 1986) texts, p.229.

[23] S. Ricketson, *The Berne Convention for the Protection of Literary and Artistic works: 1886–1896* (Queen Mary College, University of London, 1987), paras 3.8 to 3.20.

[24] Report of British Commissioners, Blue Book 1909, Miscellaneous (No.2) Cd.4467, p.5.

the Revised Convention.[25] Among the most important changes agreed were the inclusion of architectural, choreographic and pantomime works; the grant of a translation right for the full term of the copyright in the original work,[26] adaptations, musical arrangements and other reproductions in altered form of a literary or artistic work, as well as collections of works, as original works, without prejudice to the rights of the authors of the original works. Authors of musical works were protected with regard to mechanical reproduction by the new recording techniques and cinematographic works of sufficient originality were also accorded protection for the first time. It further embodied three basic principles which have been regarded as pillars of the Convention ever since: the principle of national treatment, which entitles authors of one Union country to the same rights in other Union countries as those accorded by the laws of those countries to their own nationals; the principle of the absence of formalities, according to which the enjoyment and exercise of rights were not to be subject to any formality, such as registration; and the principle of independence of protection, according to which the enjoyment and exercise of rights, as well as their enforcement, was to be governed exclusively by the laws of the country in which protection was claimed. For the first time, the term of protection was fixed at the life of the author plus 50 years; however, this term was not obligatory and it was open to Union countries to adopt a different term. The United Kingdom ratified the Berlin text in 1912.[27]

An additional Protocol was agreed to on March 20, 1914. The 1896 Paris Act had admitted to the benefits of the Convention authors from non-Union countries who first published their works in a Union country. However, this presented a problem because often authors from Union countries did not receive adequate reciprocal protection for their works in non-Union countries. The most notorious case was that of the United States of America, whose nationals benefited from the Berne Convention by first publishing over the border in Canada. However, nationals of Union countries were generally not afforded protection in the United States. The 1914 additional Protocol was promoted by the United Kingdom at the instigation of Canada (at the time a self-governing Dominion) and permitted the government of a Union country to restrict protection in the case of authors from non-Union countries which failed to protect the authors from the Union country in an adequate manner. Only Canada availed itself of this facility.

24–08   **Rome and Brussels Acts.** The Berne Convention was revised at Rome in 1928[28] and again at Brussels in 1948.[29] Two important modifications were adopted at Rome: the recognition for the first time of moral rights (specifically, the right to claim authorship of a work and the right to claim respect for its integrity) and the right of authors to control the use of their works in broadcasting (the exclusive right of radiodiffusion). The copyright protection available to films was extended to cover films which did not possess an original character, these enjoying protection under the new text as photographic works rather than as cinematographic works. As regards moral rights, Contracting States were left free to determine the way in which these rights should be protected and it was not mandatory for such rights to be protected through the copyright law. Thus the United Kingdom was able to continue to protect such rights by other means, such as passing off, defa-

---

[25] Berlin Act, Art.27.

[26] See Art.VI of the original Berne Convention of 1886, which provided for a translation right of 10 years following publication of the work in the original language in a country of the Union. See I. Davis, "A Century of Copyright: the United Kingdom and the Berne Convention" [1986] *Copyright* 177, p.179.

[27] [1912] *Le Droit d'Auteur*, 90. The new Act had entered into force on September 9, 1910.

[28] The Rome Act came into force on August 1, 1931.

[29] The Brussels Act came into force on August 1, 1951.

mation and slander of goods.[30] The Rome Act was considered to have achieved relatively little to advance the cause of authors. Work on a further revision started early in the 1930s but was interrupted by the Second World War.

After the war, work resumed and the Brussels Act was adopted at a conference in 1948.[31] The latter revision was limited to refining and consolidating the changes made by the Berlin and Rome Acts; among other changes, cinematographic works (without qualification) and photographic works were included in the primary list of works protected, along with works of applied art. Perhaps the most significant change related to the term of protection; the option to derogate from the standard minimum term of life plus 50 years was removed. No fundamental extensions to authors' rights were introduced but a number of other important changes were made. These included: modification of the definition of publication, so that publication within 30 days was considered as being simultaneous; assimilation of rebroadcasting, relaying and public playing of broadcasts to the basic broadcasting right introduced in the Rome Act, extension of the author's right in relation to the filming of his work to cover distribution and public performance of the film; and the guarantee of an author's right to equitable remuneration in respect of the mechanical recording of his work, in countries which did not recognise an exclusive recording right. These various amendments involved alterations to which effect could only be given in the United Kingdom by new legislation. Thus, one of the reasons for the passing of the 1956 Act was to enable the United Kingdom to ratify the Brussels Act.[32] During the Brussels Conference, motions were adopted calling for protection (without prejudice to the rights of authors) to be included in the Convention for sound recordings, broadcasts and performers.[33] These led in due course to the adoption of the Rome Convention in 1961.[34]

It should also be noted that, at the Rome Conference in 1928, a resolution had been adopted calling for world unification of authors' rights through an accommodation between the Berne Convention and the two most important inter-American Conventions, the Buenos Aires and Havana Conventions[35] and to discuss the formation of an international copyright convention of wider geographical scope, the Berne Convention membership being limited at that time to European countries and their colonies and dominions in other parts of the world. Although this idea was not taken up at the Brussels Conference, it was not abandoned, and, under the auspices of the United Nations Educational, Scientific and Cultural Organisation (UNESCO), the Universal Copyright Convention was later concluded in Paris in 1952.[36]

Stockholm Act. The Berne Convention was again revised at Stockholm in 1967.[37] **24–09** This introduced the controversial Protocol Regarding Developing Countries[38] designed to meet the wishes of certain developing countries which considered the

[30] See Ch.11, above.
[31] See S. Ricketson, *The Berne Convention for the Protection of Literary and Artistic Works: 1886–1896* (Queen Mary College, University of London, 1987), paras 3.33 *et seq.*
[32] For text see *Copinger* (10th ed.), paras 1681, *et seq* .
[33] *Actes de la Conference de Bruxelles*, 587 (votes VI, VII and VIII).
[34] See paras 24–88 *et seq.*, below.
[35] *Actes de la Conference de Rome*, 350. See also S. Ricketson, *The Berne Convention for the Protection of Literary and Artistic Works: 1886–1896* (Queen Mary College, University of London, 1987), para.3.31. The Buenos Aires and Havana Conventions are discussed at paras 24–165 *et seq.*, below.
[36] Regarding the UCC, see para. 24–79 *et seq.*
[37] Cmnd.4412. For text see *Copinger* (11th ed.), paras 1681 *et seq.* See *Records of the Intellectual Property Conference of Stockholm* (WIPO, Geneva, 1971) and S. Ricketson, *The Berne Convention for the Protection of Literary and Artistic Works: 1886–1896* (Queen Mary College, University of London, 1987), paras 3.49 to 3.65.
[38] See R.F. Whale, *The Stockholm Act of the Berne Copyright Union. Protocol Regarding the*

extent of protection provided by the Berne Convention too great in the light of the particular domestic circumstances of such countries. The Protocol therefore provided that any such country which ratified or acceded to the Convention could make reservations in respect of certain matters, particularly in relation to reproduction and translation rights, broadcasting for non-profit making purposes and compulsory licensing of protected works for educational purposes, which would have the effect of giving less protection in that country than was afforded in other countries of the Berne Union.

The adoption of the Protocol, despite opposition from the developed nations, led to a serious situation in the international copyright community. Thus, although Article 21 of the Stockholm Convention made the Protocol an integral part of the Convention, Article 28 provided that any country ratifying or acceding to the Convention could declare that its ratification or accession was not to apply to the substantive provisions of the Convention and the Protocol. As a result, by 1970, none of the major developed countries had ratified or acceded to the substantive provisions of these instruments. The United Kingdom, for instance, acceded only to the administrative provisions and final clauses, namely Articles 22 to 38, linked to the new Convention establishing the World Intellectual Property Organisation (WIPO).[39]

Article 26 of the Stockholm Act provided the possibility of amending the administrative clauses, including Article 26 itself, by the Assembly of the Union. The entry into force of any such amendment required that three-fourths of the countries members of the Assembly had notified their acceptance of it to the Director General of WIPO.

24–10   **Paris Act.** This situation was particularly unfortunate since it had been hoped that one of the results of the Stockholm revision would have been that the United States of America would eventually join the Berne Union after revising its domestic law. However, such hopes faded as a result of what transpired at Stockholm. Serious attempts were therefore made, following Stockholm, to try to resolve this situation, including proposals to revise the Universal Copyright Convention and to revise further the Berne Convention. In fact both Conventions were revised in Paris in 1971, Articles 22 and 23 of the Paris revision of Berne being amended later in October 1979, in accordance with the procedure provided for by Article 26. The main change, in 1971, as regards the Berne Convention, was the dropping of Article 21 relating to the Protocol Regarding Developing Countries and the Protocol itself and, instead, the inclusion of acceptable special provisions in favour of developing countries in Article 21 and an Appendix in the Paris revision of Berne. As a result, many countries, among them some of the major countries (including the United Kingdom) subsequently adhered to the Paris Act. So far as the United States of America is concerned, that country acceded to the Paris Act with effect from March 1, 1989.[40] Some of the changes to the Paris Act required amendments to the 1956 Act before the United Kingdom could ratify it.[41] The necessary changes to the law were made in the 1988 Act (the copyright provisions of which came into force on August 1, 1989) and this country eventually ratified the Paris Act on September 29, 1989, with effect from

---

Developing Countries, (British Copyright Council, London, 1968); and D.M. Schrader, "Analysis of the Protocol Regarding Developing Countries", [1970] 17 *Bulletin of the Copyright Society of the USA* 160.

[39] The UK ratified the Stockholm Act on February 26, 1970, and made a declaration to the effect that its ratification did not apply to Arts 1 to 21 and to the Protocol Regarding Developing Countries.

[40] [1988] *Copyright* 444.

[41] See Report of the 1977 Copyright Committee, Cmnd.6732, paras 50–60 and 85 and *Intellectual Property and Innovation* (White Paper) 1986 Cmnd.9712.

January 2, 1990.[42] The substantive provisions of the Paris Act,[43] which remain in force today, are examined below.[44]

WIPO Copyright Treaty. The substantive provisions of the Paris Act have recently been supplemented by the WIPO Copyright Treaty, adopted on December 20, 1996. The Treaty is a special agreement within the meaning of Article 20 of the Berne Convention and does not derogate in any way from the existing obligations that Contracting States of the Berne Convention have to each other under the Paris Act.[45] The new Treaty is discussed below.[46]   **24–11**

B. SUBSTANTIVE PROVISIONS OF PARIS ACT

Principles underlying the Convention. Two systems are possible for an international copyright convention. Theoretically, the most satisfactory system would be a complete copyright code to be applied in each country of the Union both for nationals and subjects of other countries of the Union.[47]   **24–12**

A less satisfactory system is one which merely requires each Member State to give to the nationals of other Member States the same protection as it gives to its own nationals, so-called national treatment, with the result that the measure of protection will vary from state to state. The system in fact adopted in the Berne Convention represented a compromise of the two systems and the revisions of the Convention referred to above have tended to extend the principle of the common code. In fact the Paris Act embodies a reasonably complete code but, as will be seen, specifically reserves to members the right to deal with certain matters according to their own legislation.

Eligibility for protection. Articles 4, 5 and 6 of the Berlin, Rome and Brussels Conventions contained the fundamental dual principle of mutual protection, by means of national treatment, and code protection. Articles 4, 5 and 6(1) of the Brussels Convention have been redrafted and rearranged to form Articles 3, 4 and 5 of the Paris Act.[48]   **24–13**

Article 3 contains the general criteria for eligibility for protection and provides as follows:

"(1) The protection of this Convention shall apply to:

(a) authors who are nationals of one of the countries of the Union, for their works, whether published or not;

(b) authors who are not nationals of one of the countries of the Union, for their works first published in one of those countries, or simultaneously in a country outside the Union and in a country of the Union.

(2) Authors who are not nationals of one of the countries of the Union but who have their habitual residence in one of them shall, for the purposes of this Convention, be assimilated to nationals of that country".

---

[42] [1989] *Copyright* 287.

[43] For text see Vol.2 at F1 *et seq.* For an examination of the equivalent provisions of the Brussels Convention, see *Copinger* (10th ed.), Ch.24, and of the Stockholm Convention see *Copinger* (11th ed.), Ch.24.

[44] See paras 24–12 *et seq.*, below.

[45] WIPO Copyright Treaty, Art.1. Art.20 Berne Convention provides:"The Governments of the countries of the Union reserve the right to enter into special agreements among themselves, in so far as such agreements grant to authors more extensive rights than those granted by the Convention, or contain other provisions not contrary to this Convention. The provisions of existing agreements which satisfy these conditions shall remain applicable".

[46] See paras 24–119 *et seq.*, below.

[47] See paras 25–14, *et seq.*, below.

[48] See C. Masouyé *Guide to the Berne Convention for the Protection of Literary and Artistic Works (Paris Act, 1971)* (WIPO, Geneva, 1978), pp.26–38.

This Article is broader in scope than the Brussels Act, since works of nationals of Union countries are to be protected, even if first publication takes place in a non-Union country. The previous position was that first publication in a non-Union country would have meant loss of protection: Article 4 of Brussels. Further, protection is to be afforded to nationals of non-Union countries habitually resident in a Union country.[49] It is to be noted that the Paris Act provides, in a similar way to the Brussels Act, that it is open to any country of the Union to restrict protection to works whose authors are nationals of a non-Union country which does not give reciprocal rights and are not habitually resident in a country of the Union: Article 6.[50]

The Paris Act (Article 4) contains special criteria of eligibility for protection in respect of cinematographic works and works of architecture (new in Stockholm). This Article provides:

"The protection of this Convention shall apply, even if the conditions of Article 3 are not fulfilled, to:

(a) authors of cinematographic works the maker of which has his headquarters or habitual residence in one of the countries of the Union;

(b) authors of works of architecture erected in a country of the Union or of other artistic works incorporated in a building or other structure located in a country of the Union".

24–14 **What is "publication"?** As has been seen, under Article 3 of the Paris Act, protection, in the case of authors who are not nationals of one of the countries of the Union, depends upon first publication of the work in a Union country, or publication simultaneously in a non-Union country and in a Union country. Article 3(3) defines the expression "published works" as follows:

"works published with the consent of their authors, whatever may be the means of manufacture of the copies, provided that the availability of such copies has been such as to satisfy the reasonable requirements of the public, having regard to the nature of the work. The performance of a dramatic, dramatico-musical, cinematographic or musical work, the public recitation of a literary work, the communication by wire or the broadcasting of literary or artistic works, the exhibition of a work of art and the construction of a work of architecture is not to constitute publication".

This definition has been changed in certain respects from that in Article 4(4) of the Brussels Act. Thus the present definition is to apply generally whereas, under Article 4(4), the definition was only to apply for the purposes of Articles 4, 5 and 6 of the Brussels Act. Again, whereas previously it had been understood that there could be no publication unless it was authorised, the new definition expressly limits publication to works published with the consent of the authors. Finally, the language used is now more suitable to cover various kinds of works, in that publication depends, to some extent, on the nature of the work.[51] The concept of publication in the Paris Act is, therefore, similar to that adopted by the 1988 Act,[52] and all that is required to constitute publication in a particular country is that copies should be made available for sale in that country, with the consent of the copyright owner, in sufficient quantity to satisfy the reasonable requirements of the public there, having regard to the nature of the work.

It will have been noted that, under the Paris Act, the construction of a work of

---

[49] See CDPA 1988, s.154.
[50] See C. Masouyé, *Guide to the Berne Convention for the Protection of Literary and Artistic Works (Paris Act, 1971)* (WIPO, Geneva, 1978), pp.39–40.
[51] See C. Masouyé, *Guide to the Berne Convention for the Protection of Literary and Artistic Works (Paris Act, 1971)* (WIPO, Geneva, 1978), pp.27–28.
[52] See CDPA 1988, s.175.

architecture does not constitute publication. However, the 1988 Act provides that the construction of a work of architecture in the form of a building is to be the equivalent of publication of the work.[53]

Simultaneous publication. The alternative to first publication in a Union   **24–15**
country, to entitle authors who are nationals of non-Union countries to the protection of the Paris Act, is simultaneous publication in a non-Union country and in a Union country: Article 3(1). Prior to the Brussels Act the only provision dealing with "simultaneous publication" was Article 4 in connection with country of origin. As there was no definition of this term, "simultaneous" *prima facie* appeared to involve publication on the same day. However, Article 4(3) of the Brussels Act added a definition which is substantially repeated in Article 3(4) of the Paris Act. According to this definition, a work is to be considered as having been published simultaneously in several countries, if it has been published in two or more countries within 30 days of its first publication.[54]

Extent of protection. The extent of protection is dealt with in Article 5 of the   **24–16**
Paris Act which lays down the principle of national treatment and provides as follows:

"(1) Authors shall enjoy, in respect of works for which they are protected under this Convention, in countries of the Union other than the country of origin, the rights which their respective laws do now or may hereafter grant to their nationals, as well as the rights specially granted by this Convention.

...

(3) Protection in the country of origin is governed by domestic law. However, when the author is not a national of the country of origin of the work for which he is protected under this Convention, he shall enjoy in that country the same rights as national authors".

A distinction is made between the extent of protection in the country of origin and in other countries of the Union, since protection in the country of origin is governed by the domestic law but, in countries other than the country of origin, the author is given not only the rights which are given under their domestic laws, but also the rights granted by the Convention. In theory, therefore, an author can be worse off in the country of origin than in other countries of the Union.[55]

Country of origin. It will be noted that, under Article 5 of the Paris Act, authors   **24–17**
are protected in countries other than the country of origin, and that a distinction is made as to the type of protection afforded in the country of origin and in other countries.[56] Country of origin is defined in Article 5(4) as follows:

"The country of origin shall be considered to be:

(a) in the case of works first published in a country of the Union, that country; in the case of works published simultaneously in several countries of the Union which grant different terms of protection, the country whose legislation grants the shortest term of protection;

(b) in the case of works published simultaneously in a country outside the Union and in a country of the Union, the latter country;

(c) in the case of unpublished works or of works first published in a country outside the Union, without simultaneous publication in a

---

[53] Compare s.175(3) and Copyright Act, 1956, s.49(2)(a). See para.3–127, above.
[54] See CDPA 1988, s.155(3).
[55] See C. Masouyé, *Guide to the Berne Convention for the Protection of Literary and Artistic Works (Paris Act, 1971)* (WIPO, Geneva, 1978), pp.32–34.
[56] See C. Masouyé, *Guide to the Berne Convention for the Protection of Literary and Artistic Works (Paris Act, 1971)* (WIPO, Geneva, 1978), pp.35 et seq.

country of the Union, the country of the Union of which the author is a national provided that:

    (i) when these are cinematographic works the maker of which has his headquarters or his habitual residence in a country of the Union, the country of origin shall be that country, and

    (ii) when these are works of architecture erected in a country of the Union or other artistic works incorporated in a building or other structure located in a country of the Union, the country of origin shall be that country".

24–18   **Rights of nationals of a Union country.** The result of the above Articles is that nationals of a Union country are to be accorded protection in every Union country for: (a) unpublished works, (b) works published in the Union country in which protection is sought, (c) works published in another Union country, and (d) works published in a non-Union country. This last is a change from the Brussels Act under which, subject to simultaneous publication, protection was lost if a work was first published in a non-Union country: Article 4(1) of Brussels. Thus, a British subject can claim in, say, France, national treatment both for his unpublished works and for his published works wherever published.

It has been mentioned above (paragraph 24–00) that nationals of non-Union countries, but who are habitually resident in one of them, are to be assimilated to nationals of that country (Article 3(2) of Paris); also that cinematographic works and works of architecture may be protected in certain circumstances irrespective of the nationality of their authors.

24–19   **Rights of nationals of a non-Union country.** Nationals of a non-Union country, other than those habitually resident in a Union country, are to be accorded protection for their works first published in a Union country, or simultaneously published in a non-Union country and in a Union country. No protection is, therefore, given to unpublished works of nationals of non-Union countries unless they are habitually resident in a Union country.[57] This means that an author, being a national of a non-Union country, habitually resident in, say, France, is protected in France under the Convention for his unpublished works, which would not be the case if he were habitually resident in his own country. However, it has been mentioned above (paragraph 24–00) that cinematographic works and works of architecture may be protected, in certain circumstances, irrespective of the nationality of their authors.

24–20   **No formalities.** It was provided by Article 2 of the original Berne Convention that enjoyment of the rights conferred by the Convention should be "subject to the accomplishment of the conditions and formalities prescribed by the law of the country of origin of the work", and, in order to make it clear that the formalities of the country in which protection was sought need not be complied with, the Interpretative Declaration of Paris provided that the copyright should depend upon these conditions and formalities "solely". It followed from these provisions that it was always necessary, where a foreigner sought protection in a country other than that in which he first published his work, to inquire as to what formalities were prescribed by the country of origin of the work. Moreover, the question was raised whether, if a work was totally unprotected in its country of origin, it could claim any protection in other Union countries. Obviously, such a question might involve inquiries into difficult points of foreign law upon which the local

---

[57] See CDPA 1988, ss.154 and 155. As to the meaning of "publication", and "simultaneous publication", see paras 24–14 and 24–15, above.

tribunal might find it hard to pronounce a correct decision.[58] The Berlin Act, however, marked a considerable advance in principle by providing, in Article 4,[59] that "the enjoyment and exercise of" copyright in the various countries "shall not be subject to the performance of any formality", and that "such enjoyment and such exercise are independent of the existence of protection in the country of origin of the work"—that is to say, there are not to be any formalities precedent to obtaining copyright, for instance, reservation of copyright, nor any formalities precedent to the bringing of an action for infringement, such as the registration which was necessary under the repealed English legislation—prior to the commencement of proceedings to enforce copyright in a literary work. "Consequently"—as the paragraph proceeded—"apart from the express stipulations of the present Convention, the extent of protection, as well as the means of redress secured to the author to safeguard his rights, shall be governed exclusively by the laws of the country where protection is claimed".

However, it is to be noted that this paragraph, now Article 5(2) of Paris, only applies to the rights conferred in Article 5(1) of Paris, that is to say, to the rights enjoyed in countries other than the country of origin of the work. The equivalent Article 4(2) of the Brussels Act only applied to the rights in Article 4(1) of that Act which was concerned with the rights of nationals of a Union country. Article 5(1) of the Paris Act, however, applies both to the rights of nationals of non-Union countries as well as to the rights of nationals of Union countries.

The term of protection. Article 7(1) of the Paris Act lays down a minimum term   **24–21**
of protection granted by the Convention and binding on all countries of the Union for the life of the author and 50 years after his death with respect to literary and artistic works. This term was introduced at the Berlin Revision (1908) but only became an obligation under the Brussels Act, 1948.[60] By Article 2, paragraph (2), of the original Convention it was provided that copyright "must not exceed, in the other countries, the duration of the protection granted in the said country of origin". At the Diplomatic Conference at Berlin in 1908, an effort was made to induce the States represented there to agree to a uniform term of protection as a condition of membership of the Union. This effort did not, however, entirely succeed, and Article 7 (subsequently revised and made obligatory in the Brussels Act) of the Berlin Convention was agreed to as a compromise.

Article 7 was again revised in the Stockholm Act, repeated in the Paris Act, and contains some new provisions. The basic term of protection is still to be the life of the author and 50 years after his death: Article 7(1). However, unlike the Brussels Act, minimum terms of protection have now been laid down for cinematographic works, photographic works and works of applied art. Thus, in the case of cinematographic works, the countries of the Union may provide that the term of protection is to expire 50 years after the work has been made available to the public with the consent of the author,[61] or, failing such an event within 50 years from the making of such a work, 50 years after the making: Article

---

[58] For instance, the point was raised in the German courts as to whether Oscar Wilde's work, *Salome*, would have been debarred from copyright in England upon the ground that the work was blasphemous. In England it was provided by s.2(3) of the International Copyright Act 1886 (now repealed), that "the International Copyright Acts and an Order made thereunder shall not confer on any person any greater right or longer term of copyright in any work than that enjoyed in the foreign country in which such work was first published". As to the difficulties that arose upon the words "any greater right", see *Hanfstaengl v Empire Palace* [1894] 3 Ch. 109; and as to compliance with the conditions of the country of origin, *Sarpy v Holland* [1908] 2 Ch. 198.

[59] Equivalent provisions are contained in the Rome, Brussels, Stockholm and Paris Acts.

[60] See C. Masouyé, *Guide to the Berne Convention for the Protection of Literary and Artistic Works (Paris Act, 1971)* (WIPO, Geneva, 1978), pp.45 *et seq.*

[61] See para. 24–23, below.

7(2).[62] In the case of photographic works and works of applied art in so far as they are protected as artistic works, it is to be a matter for legislation in the countries of the Union to determine the term of protection thereof; however, this term is to last at least until the end of a period of 25 years from the making of such a work: Article 7(4). In the case of anonymous or pseudonymous works where the identity of the author remains undisclosed, the period is 50 years after the work has been lawfully made available to the public: Article 7(3). Article 7(4) of the Brussels Act referred to 50 years from the date of publication. However, the Paris Act (like Stockholm) now provides that countries of the Union are not required to protect anonymous or pseudonymous works in respect of which it is reasonable to presume that their author has been dead for 50 years: Article 7(3).[63]

Article 7(5) of the Paris Act provides that the term of protection subsequent to the death of the author and the terms provided by paragraphs (2) (cinematographic works), (3) (anonymous and pseudonymous works), and (4) (photographic works and works of applied art) are to run from the date of death or of the event referred to in those paragraphs, but such terms are to be deemed to begin on January 1 of the year following the death or such event.

As stated above, the Brussels Act omitted the provisions of Article 7(2) of the Rome Act which entitled countries of the Union to provide a shorter period of protection than those laid down in Article 7, and this necessitated the abolition in the United Kingdom, by the 1956 Act, of the proviso to section 3 of the 1911 Act allowing works to be published under a compulsory licence at the expiration of 25 years from the death of the author. On the other hand, a provision of the Paris Act (new in Stockholm) permits those countries of the Union bound by the Rome Act of the Convention, which grant in their domestic legislation shorter terms of protection than those in Article 7, to maintain such terms when ratifying or acceding to the Paris Act: Article 7(7).

24–22   The Paris Act further provides that the countries of the Union may grant a term of protection in excess of those provided by Article 7: Article 7(6). Again, the Paris Act provides that in any case the term is to be governed by the legislation of the country where protection is claimed, but unless the legislation of that country otherwise provides, the term is not to exceed the term fixed in the country of origin of the work: Article 7(8).

It will be noted that the Paris Act does not, in respect of the basic term of protection, draw any distinction between published and unpublished works.

The Rome Act added, for the first time, provisions with regard to the minimum term of copyright in works of joint authorship, namely one expiring with the death of the author who dies last. However, the Brussels Act dropped this provision and, instead, provided that, in the case of a work of joint authorship, the term of protection was to be calculated from the date of the death of the last surviving author: Article 7 *bis*. As a result, the maximum term of 50 years from the death of the last surviving author became obligatory and this again resulted in an alteration in English law under the provisions of the 1956 Act, continued by the 1988 Act. The Paris Act contains an equivalent provision: Article 7 *bis*.

24–23   **Protected works.** What are the works which must be protected? Article 1 of the

---

[62] See CDPA 1988, s.13.
[63] See ss.9(4) and 12(2).

Paris Act[64] states that the countries to which the Convention applies are constituted into a Union for the protection of the rights of authors in their "literary and artistic works". Article 2(1) then provides that:

"The expression "literary and artistic works" shall include every production in the literary, scientific, and artistic domain, whatever may be the mode or form of its expression, such as books, pamphlets, and other writings; lectures, addresses, sermons and other works of the same nature; dramatic or dramatico-musical works, choreographic works and entertainments in dumb show, musical compositions with or without words; cinematographic works to which are assimilated works expressed by a process analogous to cinematography; works of drawing, painting, architecture, sculpture, engraving and lithography; photographic works to which are assimilated works expressed by a process analogous to photography; works of applied art, illustrations; maps, plans, sketches, and three-dimensional works relative to geography, topography, architecture or science".

This definition presents something of a trap to the English lawyer accustomed to the general words "literary, dramatic, musical and artistic works" in the English Copyright Acts who may therefore think, mistakenly, that the words "literary and artistic works" appearing in the Convention do not include dramatic or musical works. Prior to the Berlin Act, there was no obligation to protect choreographic works or works of architecture, but, in countries where such works received protection, the other Union countries were entitled to the benefit of such protection. Photographic and cinematographic works were included in the definition of "literary and artistic works" for the first time by the Brussels Act. Photographic works were previously protected under Article 3 which was not repeated in the Brussels Act. Prior to the Brussels Act, cinematographic productions were protected under Article 14, but only as literary or artistic works if the author had given the work an original character: in the absence of such an original character, they were protected as photographic works. This qualification was adopted in this country by the 1911 Act, and the change brought about by the Brussels Act of the Convention was followed here in the 1956 Act by the introduction of a special section dealing with the copyright in cinematograph films.[65] This definition differed slightly from that in the Brussels Act, in particular the deletion of the words "the acting form of which is fixed in writing or otherwise" after the reference to "entertainments in dumb show". This is because Article 2(2) of the Paris Act provides that it shall be a matter for legislation in the countries of the Union to prescribe that works in general, or any specified categories of works, shall not be protected unless they have been fixed in some material form.[66]

The Paris Act expressly provides, however, that the protection of the Convention is not to apply to news of the day, nor to miscellaneous facts having the character of mere items of press information: Article 2(8). Article 9(3) of the Brussels Act was slightly differently worded in that it provided that the protection of the Convention was not to apply to news of the day nor to miscellaneous information having the character of mere items of news. Thus, no copyright protection is afforded by the Convention to news or facts constituting press information. There are no equivalent provisions of English law, and material published in the press is afforded the same protection as other literary material, subject only to the qualification that information is not protected as such by copyright law, but only the form in which the information is expressed.

---

[64] See C. Masouyé, *Guide to the Berne Convention for the Protection of Literary and Artistic Works (Paris Act, 1971)* (WIPO, Geneva, 1978), pp.12 *et seq.*

[65] Copyright Act 1956, s.13, and see CDPA 1988, s.1(1)(b).

[66] See CDPA 1988, s.3(2) and (3).

24–24   Translations, adaptations and arrangements, collections, works of applied art. Article 2(3) of the Paris Act[67] then goes on to provide that "Translations, adaptations, arrangements of music and other alterations of a literary or artistic work shall be protected as original works without prejudice to the copyright in the original work". The countries of the Union are therefore bound to make provision for the protection of the above-mentioned works and also for collections such as encyclopedias and anthologies: Article 2(5). On the other hand, it is a matter for legislation in the countries of the Union to determine the protection to be granted to official texts of a legislative, administrative and legal nature, and to official translations of such texts: Article 2(4).

The provisions of Article 2 as to adaptations must be read in conjunction with Article 12, which declares that authors of literary or artistic works are to enjoy the exclusive right of authorising adaptations, arrangements and other alterations of their works. Article 2(7) provides that it is a matter of domestic legislation as to how far works of applied art and industrial designs and models are protected, subject to Article 7(4), which provides for a minimum term of protection of 25 years from the making of a work of applied art.[68]

24–25   Speeches. Lectures and speeches first received protection, as such, under the Rome Act; previously, unless constituting literary works, they would not have fallen within the protection of the existing Convention. As a consequence, it is provided (Article 2 *bis*)[69] that the domestic legislation of any country may limit protection in respect of political speeches and speeches delivered in the course of legal proceedings and may determine the conditions under which lectures and addresses delivered in public may be reproduced by the press, broadcast, communicated to the public by wire and made the subject of public communication as envisaged in Article 11 *bis*(1),[70] when such use is justified by the informatory purpose. Article 2 *bis* of the Brussels Act was limited to reproduction by the press. On the other hand, such Article was not restricted to public lectures and addresses, nor did it contain a reference to the use being justified by the informatory purpose.

24–26   Translation rights. It will be noted that translations are to be protected, and this is so, apparently, whether or not they are authorised translations, subject to the rights of the author of the original work: Article 2(3). Article 8[71] deals with the rights of the author of the original work, stipulating that:

> "Authors of literary and artistic works protected by this Convention shall enjoy the exclusive right of making and of authorising the translation of their works throughout the term of protection of their rights in the original works".

The question of translations is of prime importance from the international point of view, for it is only by means of translations that an author of a literary or scientific work can practically make his work known in a country speaking another language than his own. Complete rights in respect of authorising translations were only gained for the first time under the Berlin Act. The original Convention only gave the exclusive right of translation for a period of 10 years from publication of the original work, and this only to authors who were subjects

---

[67] See C. Masouyé, *Guide to the Berne Convention for the Protection of Literary and Artistic Works (Paris Act, 1971)* (WIPO, Geneva, 1978), pp.19 *et seq.*

[68] See para. 24–21, above.

[69] See C. Masouyé, *Guide to the Berne Convention for the Protection of Literary and Artistic Works (Paris Act, 1971)* (WIPO, Geneva, 1978), p.24.

[70] See paras 9–155 *et seq.*, above, and para. 24–31, below.

[71] See C. Masouyé, *Guide to the Berne Convention for the Protection of Literary and Artistic Works (Paris Act, 1971)* (WIPO, Geneva, 1978), p.53.

of a Union country. The Additional Act of Paris gave to such authors the exclusive right of translation during the whole period of copyright in the original work, subject, however, to the condition that an authorised translation, in the language for which protection was claimed, should be published in a Union country within 10 years from the first publication of the original work. Under the Berlin, Rome, Brussels, Stockholm and Paris Acts, authors—whether citizens of a Union country or not—who first published in a Union country, enjoy the exclusive right of authorising a translation during the entire period of copyright in the original work, free from any such conditions as to publication of an authorised translation. Under the Stockholm, and now Paris, Acts authors of a Union country would enjoy this right even if they had published in a non-Union country. Citizens of non-Union countries, however, have no right to protection against translations of their unpublished works. The exclusive right of translation is, however, limited in so far as compulsory licences for developing countries are foreseen in Article II of the Appendix to the Paris Act.[72]

Reproduction rights. Prior to Stockholm the Convention did not contain a provision expressly recognising a right of reproduction, notwithstanding that such a right was commonplace in the legislation of many countries of the Union.[73] To correct this anomaly the Stockholm Act provided, and that of Paris now provides, that authors of literary and artistic works protected by the Convention are to have the exclusive right of authorising the reproduction of these works in any manner or form: Article 9(1). All methods of reproduction and processes known or yet to be discovered are envisaged. Further, any sound or visual recording is to be considered as a reproduction for the purposes of the Convention: Article 9(3). Because of the introduction of Article 9(3), it has not been necessary to repeat Article 13(1) of Brussels giving authors of musical works the right to authorise the recording of such works.

    24–27

However, both the Stockholm and Paris Acts go on to provide that the countries of the Union may permit the reproduction of such works in certain special cases, provided that such reproduction does not conflict with a normal exploitation of the work and does not unreasonably prejudice the legitimate interests of the author: Article 9(2).[74] This provision has become of great importance in international copyright and the same principle, now known as "the 3-step test of the Berne Convention" has been incorporated also into the TRIPs Agreement and the World Copyright Treaty (WCT), where the scope of the principle has been extended from the reproduction right to all exclusive rights in the case of TRIPs and the exclusive rights of authors in the case of the WCT. The principle has also been included in the World Performances and Phonograms Treaty (WPPT) so far as the rights provided for in that Treaty are concerned.[75] The 3-step test is discussed below.

Exceptions. The Paris Act of the Berne Convention contains, in Articles 10 and 10 *bis*, provisions giving limited freedom to use works by means of exceptions to the rights granted by the Convention.[76] These specific exceptions and limitations sanctioned by the Paris Act concern quotations, the use of works by way of illustration for teaching, reproduction by the media for information purposes and

    24–28

---

[72] See para., 24–53 below.

[73] See C. Masouyé, *Guide to the Berne Convention for the Protection of Literary and Artistic Works (Paris Act, 1971)* (WIPO, Geneva, 1978), pp.54 *et seq.*

[74] See CDPA 1988, ss.28–76.

[75] WPPT, Art.16.

[76] See C. Masouyé, *Guide to the Berne Convention for the Protection of Literary and Artistic Works (Paris Act, 1971)* (WIPO, Geneva, 1978), pp.58 *et seq.*

reporting current events, as well as non-voluntary (compulsory) licensing systems.

(a) *Quotations*

24–29 Article 10(1) provides:

"It shall be permissible to make quotations from a work which has already been lawfully made available to the public, provided that their making is compatible with fair practice, and their extent does not exceed that justified by the purpose, including quotations from newspaper articles and periodicals in the form of press summaries".

In this provision, "quotation" means including one or more passages from someone else's work in one's own. Quotation consists of reproducing extracts from a work either to illustrate a theme or defend some proposition or to describe or criticise the work quoted from. The use of quotations is not confined to literature: it may be from a book, a newspaper, a review, a cinematograhic film, a recording or a radio or television programme.[77] This is wider than Article 10(1) of the Brussels Act, which was new and only permitted quotations from newspaper articles and periodicals, and "short" quotations at that. However, when a work is quoted, the source and name of the author, if given, must be mentioned: Article 10(3).[78]

There are three limits on these licences to quote. In the first place, the work from which the extract is taken must have been lawfully made available to the public. Secondly, the quotation must be "compatible with fair practice", implying an objective appreciation of what is normally considered acceptable. The fairness or otherwise of the quotation is ultimately a matter for the courts to decide. Thirdly, the quotation must only be to the extent justified by the purpose, which again is a matter for the courts.

(b) *Use of Works by Way of Illustration for Teaching*

24–30 The right to use a work for teaching purposes is laid down in Article 10(2), which revises Article 10(2) of the Brussels Act. This right is subject to the same conditions as exist for quotations. It provides that it is to be a matter for legislation in the countries of the Union and for special agreements existing or to be concluded between them, to permit the utilisation, to the extent justified by the purpose, of literary or artistic works by way of illustration in publications, broadcasts or sound or visual recordings for teaching, provided such utilisation is compatible with fair practice. Again this is subject to mention being made of the source and name of the author, if given: Article 10(3).[79]

It should be noted that since the Stockholm Act the word "extracts" no longer appears, so that the utilisation is not limited to extracts as before. It would seem, therefore, that entire works can be used for teaching purposes, assuming fair practice and no greater use than is justified by the purpose. The word "teaching" includes teaching at all levels, in educational institutions generally but excludes scientific research.[80]

---

[77] See *Guide to the Berne Convention for the Protection of Library and Artistic Works* (Paris Act, 1971) (WIPO, Geneva, 1978, p.58.

[78] See CDPA 1988, ss.29 and 30.

[79] CDPA 1988, ss.24–36.

[80] See C. Masouyé, *Guide to the Berne Convention for the Protection of Literary and Artistic Works (Paris Act, 1971)* (WIPO, Geneva, 1978), p.60.

(c) *Use by the Media and Reporting Current Events*

Article 10 *bis*(1) and (2)[81] provide for certain exceptions for the benefit of the **24–31** media. Under Article 10 *bis*(1) it is to be a matter for legislation in the countries of the Union to permit the reproduction by the press, the broadcasting or the communication to the public by wire of articles published in newspapers or periodicals on current economic, political or religious topics, and of broadcast works of the same character, in cases in which the reproduction, broadcasting or such communication thereof is not expressly reserved, providing the source is indicated. The legal consequences of a breach of this obligation are to be determined by the legislation of the country where protection is claimed. Article 9(2) of the Brussels Act contained a similar provision except that it was confined to reproduction by the press.

Article 10 *bis*(2) provides further that it is also to be a matter for such legislation to determine the conditions under which, for the purpose of reporting current events by means of photography, cinematography, broadcasting or communication to the public by wire, literary or artistic works seen or heard in the course of the event may, to the extent justified by the informatory purpose, be reproduced and made available to the public. This provision is wider than Article 10 *bis* of the Brussels Act, which was new and which it replaces, and, in particular, is no longer limited to "short extracts" from literary and artistic works. However, the use is limited to the extent justified by the informatory purpose and the works must have been seen or heard in the course of the event.[82] Under this provision the conditions prescribed may dispense with the need to seek prior permission and, in some cases, the payment of a fair remuneration.[83]

(d) *Compulsory licences to record*

Article 13(1)[84] of the Brussels Act, which provided that the authors of musical **24–32** works were to have the exclusive rights of recording such works and the public performance by means of mechanical instruments of the work thus recorded, was not repeated in the Stockholm Act as the first right was covered by Article 9 of the Stockholm Act, repeated in Paris, and the second right by Article 11 of the Stockholm Act, repeated in Paris. However, the Stockholm Act, like that of Brussels, contained provisions, repeated in Paris, permitting the countries of the Union to impose reservations and conditions on the rights of authors of musical works to record their works, so as to permit compulsory licences to record such music: Article 13(1). However, such Article makes clear that compulsory licences may also extend to words accompanying the music, whereas, under Article 13 of the Brussels Act, this was not clear. But such reservations and conditions are not to be prejudicial to the rights of the authors of the music and words to obtain equitable remuneration. The 1911 Act gave the right to record on royalty terms in respect of any work which had previously been recorded, and this right was repeated in the 1956 Act, but abolished by the 1988 Act.[85]

The 3-step test of the Berne Convention. As mentioned above in paragraph 24– **24–33** 27, Article 9(2) of the Berne Convention permits other exceptions to the principle

---

[81] See C. Masouyé, *Guide to the Berne Convention for the Protection of Literary and Artistic Works (Paris Act, 1971)* (WIPO, Geneva, 1978), p.61.

[82] See CDPA 1988, s.30: and see paras 9–35 and 9–44, *et seq.*, above.

[83] See C. Masouyé, *Guide to the Berne Convention for the Protection of Literary and Artistic Works (Paris Act, 1971)* (WIPO, Geneva, 1978), pp.62 *et seq.*

[84] See C. Masouyé, *Guide to the Berne Convention for the Protection of Literary and Artistic Works (Paris Act, 1971)* (WIPO, Geneva, 1978), p.79.

[85] See CDPA 1988, Sch.1, para.21.

of the exclusive right of reproduction in certain special cases, provided that the permitted reproduction does not conflict with a normal exploitation of the work and does not unreasonably prejudice the legitimate interests of the author. It is the assessment whether any given exception satisfies the criteria laid down in Article 9(2) that has come to be known as the "3-step test": first, the reproduction must be for a specific purpose and is allowed only in certain special cases; secondly, the reproduction should not conflict with a normal exploitation of the work; and thirdly, the use must not unreasonably prejudice the legitimate interests of the author. These three conditions are cumulative, all three having to be satisfied before reproduction is allowed and each condition raises problems of interpretation.

As regards the first condition, the words "in certain special cases" indicate that the circumstances justifying the making of an exception must, in themselves, be special or exceptional. The use must be for a specific, designated purpose: a broadly framed exemption, for example, for private or personal use, generally, would not be justified here. Secondly, there must be something "special" about this purpose; "special" here meaning that the use is justified by some clear reason of public policy or other exceptional circumstance.[86]

However, even where a special case is established, if the contemplated reproduction would be such as to conflict with a normal exploitation of the work, it is not permitted at all under Article 9(2). No guidance is given in the Convention as to the meaning of the expression "normal exploitation" of a work, but in the records of the Stockholm Diplomatic Conference leading to the adoption of Article 9(2) an example is given of a use which would conflict with such normal exploitation, namely the photocopying of a "very large number of copies" for a particular purpose.[87] Masouyé gives another example: "Novels, schoolbooks, etc. are normally exploited by being printed and sold to the public. This Article does not permit member countries to allow this, *e.g.* under compulsory licences, even if payment is made to the copyright owner".[88].

24–34 If there is no such conflict, then the next step is to consider whether there is unreasonable prejudice to the legitimate interests of the author. "In cases where there would be serious loss of profit for the copyright owner, the law should provide him with some compensation", such as, for example, a system of compulsory licensing with equitable remuneration.[89]

The 3-step test provides the legislator with certain guidelines to follow when shaping exceptions to the copyright law. However, it provides a rather flimsy basis for legislation in the light of all the new digital, high-speed and global reproduction techniques available to the public in the world of the internet.[90]

24–35 **Performing rights and recitation rights.** The performing rights of authors of dramatic, dramatico-musical and musical works are required to be protected by Article 11 of the Paris Act.[91] Under the original Convention these rights had to be specially reserved by notice on the title page, if the work was published, but the

---

[86] See S. Ricketson, *The Berne Convention for the protection of literary and artistic works: 1886–1896* (Queen Mary College, University of London, 1987), pp.482 *et seq.*

[87] *Records of the Intellectual Property Conference of Stockholm (1967)*, WIPO Geneva, 1971, Main Committee I-Report, at 1145 *et seq.*

[88] See C. Masouyé, *Guide to the Berne Convention for the Protection of Literary and Artistic Works (Paris Act, 1971)* (WIPO, Geneva, 1978), p.55.

[89] See C. Masouyé, *Guide to the Berne Convention for the Protection of Literary and Artistic Works (Paris Act, 1971)* (WIPO, Geneva, 1978), p.56.

[90] See also paras 24–72, 24–132and 24–142, below.

[91] See C. Masouyé, *Guide to the Berne Convention for the Protection of Literary and Artistic Works (Paris Act, 1971)* (WIPO, Geneva, 1978), pp.64 *et seq.*

Berlin, Rome and Brussels Acts provided that authors, to enjoy protection, should not be bound to forbid the public presentation or performance thereof. This provision was deleted in the Stockholm Act as being superfluous and is not repeated in the Paris Act. The Stockholm Act, and now the Paris Act, makes clear that the public performance of a work by sound recordings is included so that the part of Article 13(1) of the Brussels Act relating thereto was not repeated in Stockholm, nor is it repeated in the Paris Act. Apart from public performance, the Article also covers any communication to the public of the performance of such works. By the same Article, authors of dramatic or dramatico-musical works are required to be protected, during the existence of their rights in the original works, against the unauthorised public performance or communication of translations of their works: Article 11(2).

Rights relating to the recitation of literary works were given to the authors thereof by Article 11 *ter* of the Stockholm Act, repeated in Paris, which expanded Article 11 *ter* of the Brussels Act to equate recitation rights to performing rights under Article 11. Thus Article 11 *ter* covers the public recitation of literary works and also any communication to the public of the recitation of such works. Also, by the same Article, authors of literary works are required to be protected, during the existence of their rights in the original works, against the unauthorised public recitation or communication of translations of their works.

Copyright Tribunal. In connection with Article 11 of the Brussels Act, the   **24–36**
United Kingdom delegation at Brussels declared that they accepted the provisions of Article 11 on the understanding that HM Government remained free to enact such legislation as they might consider necessary, in the public interest, to prevent or deal with any abuse of the monopoly rights conferred upon owners of copyright by the law of the United Kingdom.[92] It was in reliance upon this declaration that the 1956 Act introduced a Performing Right Tribunal with powers to modify and enforce licences granted by licensing bodies for the public performance of works controlled by such bodies.[93] This declaration was not repeated at Stockholm (or Paris), but it was agreed that countries were free to enact measures to restrict possible abuses of monopoly.[94] The Performing Right Tribunal has now been renamed as the Copyright Tribunal with a much wider jurisdiction.[95]

Broadcasting rights. The Rome Act first introduced provisions with regard to   **24–37**
radio communication, but these were substantially amplified by the Brussels Act and repeated in the Stockholm and Paris Acts. Article 11 *bis* of the Paris Act provides that authors of literary and artistic works are to have the exclusive right of authorising the broadcasting of their works and communication of their works to the public by wireless, the communication of their works to the public by wire or by rebroadcasting of the broadcast of the work when the communication is made by an organisation other than the original one, and the communication of their works to the public by loudspeaker or other instrument transmitting the

---

[92] *Actes de la Conference de Bruxelles* (1951), p.82.
[93] Copyright Act 1956, ss.23–30.
[94] Records of the Intellectual Property Conference of Stockholm (1967), Geneva, 1971, Vol.II, Report of Main Committee I, para.263. See also Summary Minutes (Main Committee I), paras 1407 to 1427 and see C. Masouyé, *Guide to the Berne Convention for the Protection of Literary and Artistic Works (Paris Act, 1971)* (WIPO, Geneva, 1978), p.99.
[95] CDPA 1988, ss.116–152: and see paras 29–93 *et seq.*, below. This jurisdiction now covers the compulsory licence to include sound recordings (but not the music on the sound recordings) in broadcasts and cable programme services created by an amendment of the CDPA 1988 introduced by s.175 of the Broadcasting Act 1990 (c.42), and the compulsory licence to provide information about broadcast programmes introduced by s.176 of and Sch.17 to the 1990 Act. As to the coming into force of these provisions, see the Broadcasting Act 1990 (Commencement No.1 and Transitional Provisions) Order 1990 (SI 1990/2347), vol.2 at A2.ii.

broadcast of the work. The conditions for the exercise of these rights are left to the legislation of individual countries, provided that such legislation does not affect the right of the author to obtain equitable remuneration. Thus, Member States may substitute for the authors' exclusive rights a system of compulsory licences.[96]

The Paris Act, therefore, confers upon authors three distinct rights in respect of broadcast performances of their works: namely, first, the right to restrict the original broadcast, secondly, the right to restrict any diffusion of the broadcast by an independent receiving authority, and thirdly, the right to restrict the public performance of the broadcast at the receiving end. The first two rights were clearly conferred by the 1956 Act,[97] but, after much discussion during the passing of that Act, the right to restrict the operation of a diffusion service was considerably qualified by section 40(3) of that Act.[98]

24–38 **Recordings of broadcasts.** It is further provided, by Article 11 *bis*(3) of the Paris Act, that a permission to broadcast is not to imply permission to record the broadcast. But there then follows a somewhat ambiguous paragraph as follows:

"It shall, however, be a matter for legislation in the countries of the Union to determine the regulations for ephemeral recordings made by a broadcasting organisation by means of its own facilities and used for its own broadcasts. The preservation of these recordings in official archives may, on the ground of their exceptional documentary character, be authorised by such legislation".

Section 6(7) of the 1956 Act was designed to give effect to the provisions of the Article as to ephemeral recordings, but there was no provision for the preservation of recordings in official archives.[99]

24–39 **Cinematographic rights.** As has already been pointed out,[1] cinematographic works are now treated as of the class of literary and artistic works receiving general protection under Article 2 of the Paris Act. But the rights of authors of literary or artistic works, whose material may be included in a cinematograph film, are dealt with in Article 14 of the Paris Act,[2] and it is expressly stated, by Article 14 *bis*(1) thereof, previously Article 14(2) of the Brussels Act, that the protection of a cinematographic work as an original work is without prejudice to the rights of the author of the work adapted or reproduced. The author is required to be given the exclusive right of authorising, first, the cinematographic adaptation and reproduction of his works, and the distribution of the works thus adapted or reproduced and, secondly, the right of public performance and communication to the public by wire of the works thus adapted or reproduced. The latter right was new in the Stockholm Act. Article 14 further provides that the adaptation into any other artistic form of a cinematographic production derived from literary or artistic works is, without prejudice to the authorisation of the author of the cinematographic production, to remain subject to the authorisation of the authors of the original works. Section 13(7) of the 1956 Act provided that, where the copyright in a cinematograph film had expired, a person who caused the film to be seen, or to be seen and heard, in public did not thereby infringe any copyright

---

[96] See C. Masouyé, *Guide to the Berne Convention for the Protection of Literary and Artistic Works (Paris Act, 1971)* (WIPO, Geneva, 1978), p.70.

[97] Copyright Act 1956, ss.2(5)(d) and (e) and 3(5)(c) and (d).

[98] ss.2, 3 and 40, Copyright Act 1956, were amended by the Cable and Broadcasting Act 1984 (c.46). See now CDPA 1988, ss.16(1), 72 and 73.

[99] See now CDPA 1988, ss.68 and 75, which latter section provides for recording for archival purposes. See para. 9–213 above.

[1] See para. 24–23, above.

[2] See C. Masouyé, *Guide to the Berne Convention for the Protection of Literary and Artistic Works (Paris Act, 1971)* (WIPO, Geneva, 1978), pp.82 *et seq.*

subsisting in any literary, dramatic, musical or artistic work. Since the film copyright may well have expired before that in the works included in them, it is difficult to see how this provision accorded with Article 14 of the Paris Act. The 1988 Act contains no such provision.

Soundtracks of films. Article 14(3) of the Paris Act provides that the provisions   **24–40**
of Article 13(1) are not to apply with respect to films, so no compulsory licences for musical works and associated words to be incorporated in films are permitted. Article 14(3), therefore, was designed to prevent countries restricting in any manner the rights of authors of musical works to have these works included in the soundtracks of cinematograph films. While there was some doubt whether, under section 19(2) of the 1911 Act, the compulsory licence provisions thereby enacted could be utilised for the purpose of cinematograph films, it is clear that the similar provisions of section 8 of the 1956 Act did not apply, since they applied only where a manufacturer intended to sell a record by retail. Section 8 of the 1956 Act has been repealed by the 1988 Act, which contains no equivalent provision.

Cinematograph films. It has been mentioned above[3] that cinematographic works   **24–41**
are included in the class of works protected under Article 2, and that Article 14 *bis*(1) provides that such protection is without prejudice to the copyright in any work adapted or reproduced.[4] Article 14 *bis*(1) goes on to make clear what was previously understood to be the position, namely that the owner of the copyright in a cinematographic work is to have the same rights as the author of an original work, including the rights under Article 14.[5]

Article 14 *bis*(2)(a), which was new to Stockholm, leaves the question of ownership of the copyright in a cinematographic work to the legislation of the country where protection is claimed. However, the rest of Article 14 *bis*(2) and Article 14 *bis*(3), which also were new to Stockholm, contain provisions dealing with the rights of authors of contributions to a cinematographic work in countries where they are included among the owners of the copyright in such a work. Section 13(4) and (10) of the 1956 Act, however, provided that the maker of a cinematograph film, that is the person by whom the arrangements necessary for the making of the film are undertaken, was the initial owner of the copyright in the film. Section 9(2) and (11) of the 1988 Act contained the same definition until amended by the Copyright and Related Rights Regulations 1996[6]; the law now provides that such owner is the author, which in the case of a film shall be taken to be the producer and the principal director.

"Moral rights". The Rome Act, for the first time, introduced provisions intended   **24–42**
to extend an author's rights beyond those generally understood in common law countries to be included in the term "copyright". These provisions cover what is known in Continental law countries as the author's *"droit moral"* or moral right. These provisions were extended by the Brussels Act,[7] Article 6 *bis*, and provided, first, that, even after the assignment of his copyright, the author should have the right during his lifetime to claim authorship of the work, and to object to any "distortion, mutilation or other alteration thereof or any other action in relation to the said work which would be prejudicial to his honour or reputation". Secondly,

---

[3] See paras 24–23 and 24–39, above.
[4] See C. Masouyé, *Guide to the Berne Convention for the Protection of Literary and Artistic Works (Paris Act, 1971)* (WIPO, Geneva, 1978), p.85.
[5] See para. 24–39 , above.
[6] SI 1996/2967.
[7] See C. Masouyé, *Guide to the Berne Convention for the Protection of Literary and Artistic Works (Paris Act, 1971)* (WIPO, Geneva, 1978), pp.41 *et seq.*

it was provided that the rights granted to the author as aforesaid should, after his death, be maintained at least until the expiry of the copyright. Thirdly, the means of redress for safeguarding the rights granted by this article was left to the national law. These provisions were, with amendments, repeated in the Stockholm and Paris Acts.

Thus, the Stockholm Act, in Article 6 *bis*, whilst preserving the author's right to claim authorship of the work (the right of paternity), has made slight changes in the wording, repeated in the Paris Act, of the right to object to mutilation (the right of integrity) which now covers the right of the author to object to any "distortion, mutilation or other modification of, or other derogatory action in relation to, the said work, which would be prejudicial to his honour or reputation". A further amendment, introduced by Article 6 *bis* of the Stockholm Act and repeated in the Paris Act, is to make the grant of such rights compulsory at least until the expiration of the copyright, rather than during the author's lifetime and optional thereafter until the expiration of copyright as under Article 6 *bis* of the Brussels Act.

24–43 **Obligation to safeguard moral rights by legislation.** It will be observed, first, that the Brussels, Stockholm and Paris Acts make the grant of such rights compulsory for the period prescribed and, secondly, that the Convention requires the rights to be safeguarded by the legislation of the country where protection is claimed. It would seem to follow from this that, not only are countries of the Union bound to grant such rights, but that they must be granted by statute law. So far as this country is concerned, prior to the 1988 Act the only statute law at all concerned with either of these rights was section 43 of the 1956 Act. But even this section, whilst going some way to grant a right of integrity, only did so in respect of artistic works. Further, not only did such section not grant a right of paternity to authors but, instead, made it an offence to ascribe paternity to a non-author. Other than this, and actions for passing off, defamation and slander of goods, English law did not, before the 1988 Act, afford protection for the rights provided for in Article 6 *bis*.[8]

It has been argued, therefore, that, prior to the 1988 Act, this country had not complied with the obligations of Article 6 *bis*; it is interesting to note, in this regard, that the 1952 Copyright Committee stated that, in the 20 years since the Rome Act had been accepted, no other Union country had complained that this country had failed to discharge its obligations under Article 6 *bis*.[9] However, the 1977 Copyright Committee, after having considered the matter in detail, in particular the question whether this country had failed to discharge such obligations,[10] recommended that the Copyright Act should be amended to make proper provision for moral rights under copyright law.[11] It is to be noted that Article 36 of the Paris Act provides that it is understood that, at the time a country becomes bound by that Act, it will be in a position under its domestic law, to give effect to the provisions thereof, and the 1988 Act now, for the first time in this country, provides statutory protection for moral rights, by granting a paternity right, an integrity right and a right to privacy of certain photographs and films, as well as providing for false attribution of authorship.[12] This was done as from August 1, 1989, just before the United Kingdom deposited its instrument of ratification of the Paris Act on September 29, 1989, with effect from January 2, 1990.

24–44 **"*Droit de suite*" (Artists' Resale Right).** A further new right, which was

---

[8] See Ch.11.
[9] Cmnd.8662, para.220.
[10] Cmnd.6732, paras 50–57.
[11] Cmnd.6732, para.85(vi).
[12] CDPA 1988, ss.2(2), 77–89, 94, 95, 103, and Sch.1, paras 22, 23 and 24; and see Ch.11.

introduced for the first time in the Brussels Act, deals with what is known in Continental-law countries, as the "*droit de suite*", the so-called "artists' resale right". Article 14 *ter* of the Stockholm Act, replacing Article 14 *bis* of the Brussels Act, provided, and now Article 14 *ter* of the Paris Act provides,[13] that the author or, after his death, the persons or institutions authorised by national legislation are, with respect to original works of art and original manuscripts, to enjoy the inalienable right to an interest in any sale of the work subsequent to the first transfer thereof by the author. This matter, however, is left to the legislation of individual members[14] and enjoyment of the right depends on reciprocity. It cannot be claimed in any country introducing such legislation by an author belonging to a country which does not have such legislation. The 1977 Copyright Committee recommended that "*droit de suite*" should not be introduced in the United Kingdom,[15] and the 1988 Act made no provision for such a right. However, the situation is about to change since a Directive of the European Parliament and of the Council on the resale right for the benefit of the author of an original work of art was adopted by the European Parliament and Council of the European Communities after many years of negotiation on September 27, 2001. According to the Directive, in principle, Member States must bring their domestic laws into conformity with the Directive before January 1, 2006.[16]

Protection of rights. The remedy of a person whose work has been pirated is to be governed by the local law. Article 4(2) of Brussels, replaced by Article 5(2) of Stockholm, and now by Article 5(2) of Paris provides that, "apart from the provisions of this Convention, the extent of protection, as well as the means of redress afforded to the author to protect his rights, shall be governed exclusively by the laws of the country where protection is claimed".[17]   **24–45**

However, seizure of the pirated copies is a remedy which ought to be secured to authors by the legislation of every Union country, for Article 16[18] provides as follows:

"(1) Infringing copies of a work shall be liable to seizure in any country of the Union where the work enjoys legal protection.

(2) The provisions of the preceding paragraph shall also apply to reproductions coming from a country where the work is not protected, or has ceased to be protected.

(3) The seizure shall take place in accordance with the legislation of each country".

---

[13] See C. Masouyé, *Guide to the Berne Convention for the Protection of Literary and Artistic Works (Paris Act, 1971)* (WIPO, Geneva, 1978), p.90.

[14] See as to " *droit de suite*" in the European Union, C. Doutrelepont, " *Le Droit et l'objet d'art: le droit de suite des artistes plasticiens dans l'Union européenne*" (Bruylant, Brussels, 1996); in France and certain other countries, R. Plaisant, "The ' *droit de suite*'" [1969] *Copyright* 157; in Germany, A. Dietz, "Letter from the Federal Republic of Germany" [1980] *Copyright* 85. See also W. Duchemin, "The Community Directive on the Resale Right" [2002] 191 *RIDA* 3.

[15] Cmnd.6732, para.805.

[16] The Commission of the European Communities first presented a proposal for a European Parliament and Council Directive on the resale right for the benefit of an original work of art (document COM(96) 97 final) on March 13, 1996. Finally adopted on September 27, 2001, the Directive entered into force on October 13, 2001 ([2001] O.J. L272/32, October 13, 2001). For more information and the text of this Directive and on its likely impact on UK law, see Ch.25, paras 25–91 *et seq.*, below and Vol.2, Appendix , H–12 below.

[17] An important and instructive case came before the Paris Court of Appeal which, affirming the decision of the Seine Civil Tribunal, held that the manager of the Paris branch and representative in Paris of an Argentine newspaper was liable in damages for putting on sale in France copies of the newspaper printed in Buenos Aires, and containing pirated portions of a novel written by a French author. This liability, the court stated, would exist "even if the legislation of the country of publication accorded no protection to copyright": *Foley v Cazaux*, [1913] Le Droit d'Auteur 100.

[18] See also Brussels Act, Art.13(3) as to seizure of recordings: and see CDPA 1988, ss.100 and 114.

Notwithstanding the provisions of the Convention, each Union country is to be at liberty "to permit, to control, or to prohibit, by legislation or regulation, the circulation, presentation, or exhibition of any work or production in regard to which the competent authority may find it necessary to exercise that right"; Article 17 of the Paris Act.

24–46 **Presumptions.** Article 15 of the Paris Act,[19] as did Article 15 of the Brussels Act and Article 15 of the Stockholm Act, provides for certain presumptions as to authorship.[20] Thus, Article 15(1) provides that, in order that the author of a literary or artistic work protected by the Convention shall, in the absence of proof to the contrary, be regarded as such and consequently entitled to institute infringement proceedings in the countries of the Union, it is to be sufficient for his name to appear on the work in the usual manner.

Article 15(1) is to be applicable even if the name is a pseudonym, where the pseudonym adopted by the author leaves no doubt as to his identity. Article 15(3), however, provides that, in the case of anonymous and pseudonymous works, other than those referred to in Article 15(1), the publisher whose name appears on the work, in the absence of proof to the contrary, is to be deemed to represent the author, and in that capacity he is to be entitled to protect and enforce the author's rights. These provisions are to cease to apply when the author reveals his identity and establishes his claim to authorship of the work.

Article 15 of the Stockholm Act, now Article 15 of the Paris Act, also contained certain new provisions. Thus, Article 15(2) provides that the person or body corporate whose name appears on a cinematographic work "in the usual manner" shall, in the absence of proof to the contrary, be presumed to be the maker of such work.[21]

Again, Article 15(4) provides that, in the case of unpublished works where the identity of the author is unknown, but where there is every ground to presume that he is a national of a country of the Union, it is to be a matter for legislation in that country to designate the competent authority who shall represent the author and shall be entitled to protect and enforce his rights in the countries of the Union.[22]

24–47 **Retrospective effect.** An alteration was made as regards retrospective effect in the Berlin Act, and is repeated in the Rome, Brussels, Stockholm and Paris Acts. Under the original Convention it was provided that its provisions should apply to all works which, at the time of its coming into force, had "not yet fallen into the public domain in their country of origin". The Berlin, Rome, Brussels, Stockholm and Paris Acts (Article 18(1)) only except works which have, at the moment of their coming into force, fallen into the public domain in their country of origin "through the expiry of the term of protection". Works, therefore, which have, in the country of their origin, lost their protection owing to failure to comply with formalities, such as registration and so forth, are intended to be protected under the Convention, as also, apparently, are works which were previously entitled to no protection whatsoever, for instance (in some countries), works of architecture and photographs.[23] On the other hand, Article 18(2) provides that if, through the expiry of the term of protection which was previously granted, a

---

[19] See C. Masouyé, *Guide to the Berne Convention for the Protection of Literary and Artistic Works (Paris Act, 1971)* (WIPO, Geneva, 1978), p.93.

[20] See CDPA 1988, ss.104–106.

[21] See s.105.

[22] See s.169.

[23] The 1911 Act did not comply with the provisions as to retrospective effect and, in adhering to the Berlin Act, the UK made a reservation upon the point. This reservation was not maintained when

work has fallen into the public domain of the country where protection is claimed, that work is not to be protected anew. These provisions are to apply also in the case of new accessions to the Union, and to cases in which protection is extended by the application of Article 7 or by the abandonment of reservations: Article 18(4).

Article 18(3), however, provides that the application of the principle laid down in Article 18(1) and (2) is to take effect subject to any provisions contained in special conventions to that effect existing or to be concluded between countries of the Union, and that, in the absence of such provisions, the respective countries are to determine, so far as they are respectively concerned, the conditions of application of such principle.

Convention not to limit wider protection. Article 19 of the Paris Act[24] expressly   **24–48**
states that the Convention is not to preclude authors from the benefit of any greater protection granted by the local law, and Article 20 thereof preserves the right of Member States to make special agreements with other Member States giving greater protection to their respective nationals than is required under the Convention.[25] The various Directives adopted by the European Union on the subject of copyright and the new WIPO Copyright Treaty[26] are examples of such special agreements.

C. ADMINISTRATIVE PROVISIONS AND FINAL CLAUSES OF PARIS ACT

Administrative provisions and final clauses. Articles 22 to 26 of the Stockholm   **24–49**
Act, now Articles 22 to 26 of the Paris Act,[27] contain the administrative provisions, and Articles 27 to 38,[28] the final clauses of the Convention, contain certain general provisions. Articles 22 and 23 of the Paris Act providing for the Assembly of the Union and its Executive Committee were amended in October 1979.[29] Article 24 of the Paris Act provides that the administrative tasks with respect to the Union are to be performed by the International Bureau, being the International Bureau of Intellectual Property referred to in the Convention establishing the World Intellectual Property Organisation[30]: Article 22(2)(ii).

This latter Convention was framed at Stockholm in 1967 and was signed by the United Kingdom on July 14, 1967. The objects of the Organisation established by the Convention are stated to be to promote the protection of intellectual property throughout the world through co-operation among States and, where appropriate, in collaboration with any other international organisation, and to ensure administrative co-operation among the various Unions, including the Berne

---

the UK ratified the Rome Act, presumably on the ground that it was not necessary to do so in view of the fact that the Convention did not make necessary any alteration of English law previously in force. The Acts of 1956 and 1988 appear, in substance, to comply with this Article.

[24] See C. Masouyé, *Guide to the Berne Convention for the Protection of Literary and Artistic Works (Paris Act, 1971)* (WIPO, Geneva, 1978), p.103.

[25] See C. Masouyé, *Guide to the Berne Convention for the Protection of Literary and Artistic Works (Paris Act, 1971)* (WIPO, Geneva, 1978), p.104.

[26] See Ch.25 and paras 24–66 *et seq.*

[27] See C. Masouyé, *Guide to the Berne Convention for the Protection of Literary and Artistic Works (Paris Act, 1971)* (WIPO, Geneva, 1978), pp.106–120.

[28] See C. Masouyé, *Guide to the Berne Convention for the Protection of Literary and Artistic Works (Paris Act, 1971)* (WIPO, Geneva, 1978), pp.121–145.

[29] Amendments to Arts 22 and 23 were adopted in 1979 by the Assembly of the Berne Union, when it decided to adopt biennial, instead of triennial, budgets and to hold its ordinary sessions every two years. These amendments entered into force on November 19, 1984. See A. Bogsch, "The First Hundred Years of the Berne Convention for the Protection of Literary and Artistic Works", [1986] *Copyright* 291 at 314, and S. Ricketson, *The Berne Convention for the protection of literary and artistic works: 1886–1896* (Queen Mary College, University of London, 1987), paras 13.12 and 13.47.

[30] For text see Vol.2 below, at F7.

Union: Article 3. Article 12(1) of this Convention provides that the Organisation is to enjoy on the territory of each Member State, in conformity with the laws of that State, such legal capacity as may be necessary for the fulfilment of the Organisation's objectives and for the exercise of its functions. Accordingly the United Kingdom has provided by statutory instrument,[31] which came into operation on the date on which the Convention entered into force with respect to this country, that the Organisation is to have the legal capacities of a body corporate. The Convention was ratified by the United Kingdom on February 26, 1969, and entered into force on April 26, 1970.

D. STOCKHOLM PROTOCOL REGARDING DEVELOPING COUNTRIES

24–50 **Protocol.** As has been mentioned,[32] the Stockholm revision of the Berne Convention introduced the controversial Protocol Regarding Developing Countries[33] which provided that any developing country which ratified or acceded to the Stockholm Act could make reservations in respect of certain matters, which would have the effect of giving less protection in that country than was afforded in other countries of the Union. Because of this controversy, however, although Article 21 of Stockholm made the Protocol an integral part of the Convention, this was subject to the provisions of Article 28 of Stockholm which enabled any country ratifying or acceding to the Act to declare that its ratification or accession was not to apply to the substantive provisions of the Act and the Protocol. Since today no country of the Union remains bound by the substantive provisions of the Stockholm Act and its Protocol, the Protocol has become of historical interest only and for that reason its substantive provisions are not considered further here. For a detailed account of these provisions of the Protocol, the reader is referred to paragraphs 24–53 to 24–58 of the 14th edition of the present work.

E. APPENDIX TO PARIS ACT

24–51 **Appendix.** As has been mentioned,[34] the Paris Act has dropped Article 21 relating to the Protocol Regarding Developing Countries and the Protocol itself, and substituted another Article 21 and an Appendix containing provisions dealing with developing countries, such Article providing that the Appendix forms an integral part of the Paris Act. However, this is subject to Article 28 under which any country may declare that its ratification or accession shall not apply to the substantive provisions of the Paris Act and the Appendix.

24–52 **Mode of operation of Appendix.** Article I of the Appendix provides that any country regarded as a developing country in conformity with the established practice of the General Assembly of the United Nations which ratifies or accedes to the Paris Act and which, having regard to its economic situation and its social or cultural needs, does not consider itself immediately in a position to make provision for the protection of all the rights as provided for in the Paris Act, may declare that it avails itself of one or both faculties in Articles II and III; or instead of availing itself of the faculty in Article II may make a declaration according to Article V(1)(a) relating to Article 30 of the Paris Act. Any such declaration notified before the expiration of the first 10 years from the entry into force of the

---

[31] The World Intellectual Property Organisation (Immunities and Privileges) Order 1968 (SI 1968/890).
[32] See para., 24–09 above.
[33] S. Ricketson, *The Berne Convention for the Protection of Literary and Artistic Works: 1886–1896* (Queen Mary College, University of London, 1987), pp.609 *et seq.*
[34] See para. 24–10, above.

substantive provisions of the Paris Act and the Appendix lasts until the expiration of such period. Any notification after the expiration of that period lasts for 10 years. Any such declarations may be renewed in whole or in part for further periods of 10 years.

Any country which has ceased to be regarded as a developing country cannot renew its declaration and, whether or not it withdraws its declaration, it is precluded from availing itself of such faculties after the expiration of the 10-year period then running, or from the expiration of a period of three years after it has ceased to be regarded as a developing country, whichever period expires later. Notwithstanding a declaration ceases to be effective, copies in stock made under a licence granted by virtue of the Appendix may be disposed of. Further, where a country avails itself of any of such faculties, no country may give less protection to works originating in the former country than it is obliged to give under the substantive provisions of the Paris Act.

The faculty under Article II; translation rights.[35] This enables a developing **24–53** country, in relation to works published in printed or analogous form of reproduction, to substitute for the exclusive right of translation provided for in Article 8 of the Paris Act, a system of non-exclusive and non-transferable licences, granted by the competent authority, subject to certain conditions and the provisions of Article IV. As the latter largely apply also to Article III licences, they are dealt with below after the faculty under Article III.

The first condition is one of time. Thus, if after the expiration of a period of three years, or any longer period determined by the national legislation of such country, commencing on the date of first publication of the work, a translation of the work has not been published in a language in general use in that country by the owner of the translation rights, or with his authorisation, any national of such country may obtain a licence to make a translation of the work in the said language and publish the translation in printed or analogous forms of reproduction. Alternatively a licence may be granted if all the editions of the translation published in the language concerned are out of print. A further alternative arises in the case of translations into a language which is not in general use in one or more developed countries who are Union members; in which case one year is to be substituted for the period of three years above mentioned. But any developing country availing itself of this faculty may, with the unanimous agreement of the developed countries which are Union members and in which the same language is in general use, substitute, in the case of translations into that language for the said period of three years an agreed shorter period of not less than one year; this provision will not apply where the language in question is English, French or Spanish. However, these time limits only bring the faculty into operation. That is to say, no licence obtainable after a three-year period is to be granted until a further period of six months has elapsed or nine months in the case of a one-year period, in each case from the date the applicant complies with the requirements of Article IV(1), or, where the identity or address of the owner of the translation rights is unknown, from the date on which the applicant sends copies of his application submitted to the competent authority as provided by Article IV(2).

Apart from the condition as to time, Article II imposes other conditions. Thus, if during such six- or nine-month period a translation in the language in respect of which the application was made is published by the owner of the translation rights or with his authorisation, no licence can be granted. Any licence in fact granted can only be for the purpose of teaching, scholarship or research. If a

---

[35] See para. 24–26, above.

licence is granted, but a translation of the work is published by the owner of the translation rights or with his authorisation at a price reasonably related to that normally charged in the country for comparable works, the licence will terminate if such translation is in the same language and with substantially the same content as the translation published under the licence. However, existing stocks may be disposed of. No licence may be granted when the author has withdrawn all copies of the work from circulation.

Article II also contains provisions dealing with licences in respect of works with illustrations as well as text, and translations for the purposes of use in broadcasts.

24–54 **The faculty under Article III; reproduction rights.**[36] This enables a developing country to substitute for the exclusive right of reproduction provided for in Article 9 of the Paris Act a system of non-exclusive and non-transferable licences, granted by the competent authority, subject to certain conditions and the provisions of Article IV dealt with below. The works to which this faculty applies are works published in printed or analogous forms of reproduction and to the reproduction in audiovisual form of certain lawfully made audiovisual fixations and to the translation of any incorporated text.

As with Article 2, the first condition is one of time. Thus, a licence may be obtained by a national of such country to reproduce and publish a particular edition of a work at a price reasonably related to that normally charged in the country for comparable works or a lower price for use in connection with systematic instructional activities if, after the expiration of the prescribed period, copies of such edition have not been distributed in that country to the general public or in connection with systematic instructional activities, by the owner of the reproduction rights or with his authorisation, at such first-mentioned price. A licence may also be obtained to reproduce and publish an edition of the work which has been so distributed if, after the expiration of the applicable period, no authorised copies of the edition have been on sale for a period of six months in such country to the general public or in connection with systematic instructional activities at a price reasonably related to that normally charged in that country for comparable works.

The commencing date for the various prescribed periods is the date of first publication of the edition in question and the periods are, subject to any longer periods determined by the legislation of the country in question: for works of the natural and physical sciences, including mathematics, and of technology, three years; for works of fiction, poetry, drama and music, and for art books, seven years; for all other works, five years. Again, these periods only bring the faculty into operation. Thus no licence obtainable after a three-year period is to be granted until six months from the date the applicant complies with the requirements of Article IV(1) or, where the identity or the address of the owner of the reproduction rights is unknown, from the date on which the applicant sends, as provided by Article IV(2), copies of his application submitted to the competent authority. In respect of other periods there appears to be no extra time-factor unless the owner of the rights cannot be found and Article IV(2) applies. In which case no licence is to be granted until three months from the date of the dispatch of the copies of the application.

Article III imposes other conditions apart from time. Thus, if during the extra periods of six or three months above mentioned a distribution of copies of the edition in question has taken place in the country of the kind mentioned above, no licence is to be granted. Further, no licence is to be granted if the author has

---

[36] See para. 24–27 , above.

withdrawn from circulation all copies of the edition in question. Again, a licence to reproduce and publish a translation of a work is not to be granted if, either the translation was not published by the owner of the translation rights or with his authorisation, or the translation is not in a language in general use in the country concerned. Also if a distribution of copies of the edition in question has taken place in the country of the kind mentioned above, any licence granted is to terminate if such edition is in the same language and with substantially the same content as the edition which was published under the licence. However, existing stocks may be disposed of.

The provisions of Article IV. The provisions of Articles II and III are subject to Article IV which contains certain provisions relating to procedural matters and licence terms.   24–55

As to procedure, Article IV provides that a licence under Articles II or III may only be granted if the applicant, in accordance with the procedure of the country concerned, establishes, either that he has requested, and been denied, the necessary authorisation by the owner of the relevant rights, or that, after due diligence, he was unable to find such owner. He must also, when making his request, inform any designated national or international information centre. If the owner cannot be found, then Article IV requires the applicant to send copies of his application to the competent authority for a licence to various persons.

As to licence terms, Article IV contains certain provisions which, it would seem, would have to be contained in a licence or, at least, taken into account when the licence is granted. Thus, it is provided that the name of the author is to be indicated in all copies of the translation or reproduction published under the licence. The title of the work and, in the case of a translation, the original title of the work is to appear on all such copies. Further, licences to export are not permitted and all such copies are to bear a notice in the appropriate language stating that the copies are available for distribution only in the country or territory to which the licence applies. Also, the licence must provide for just compensation of the owner of the relevant rights and for payment and transmittal of such compensation. Finally, national legislation must ensure a correct translation of the work, or an accurate reproduction of the particular edition, as the case may be.

F. ENTRY INTO FORCE OF STOCKHOLM ACT

Ratification or accession. Because of the controversy over the introduction into the Stockholm revision of the Berne Convention of the Protocol Regarding Developing Countries,[37] which was made an integral part of the Stockholm Act (Article 21), the Act permitted any country of the Union ratifying or acceding thereto to declare that its ratification or accession was not to apply to the substantive provisions of the Convention (Articles 1 to 21) and the Protocol: Article 21(1)(b)(i). Alternatively, such a country might declare that its ratification or accession was not to apply to the administrative provisions of the Act (Articles 22 to 26): Article 28(1)(b)(ii). Ratification or accession in either way carried with it the final clauses of the Stockholm Act (Articles 27 to 38): Article 28(3). There were, therefore, two distinct ways in which a country of the Union might have become a party to the Stockholm Act but, as a result, none of the major developed countries ratified or acceded to the substantive provisions of the Stockholm Act.   24–56

The substantive provisions of the Stockholm Act and its Protocol. Articles 1   24–57

---

[37] See para. 24–50, above.

to 21 and the Protocol were to come into force with respect to the first five countries which had ratified or acceded to it without declaring that their ratification or accession should not apply to such Articles and Protocol, and without making the declaration permitted by paragraph (1)(b)(i) of the Protocol, three months after the deposit of the fifth instrument of ratification or accession: Article 28(2)(a). As Articles 1 to 21 and the Appendix to the Paris Act came into force on October 10, 1974, no country may now ratify or accede to Stockholm; Article 34(1) Paris. However, the previous Acts remain in force in relations with countries of the Union which do not ratify or accede to the Paris Act; Article 32(1) Paris.

24–58 **The Protocol.** However, the Protocol could be applied before the entry into force of the Stockholm Act (Article 28(2)(d)) and, therefore, Article 28(2)(a) was made subject to the provisions of Article 5 of the Protocol. Article 5 provided that any country of the Union might declare, at any time before becoming bound by Articles 1 to 21 and the Protocol, either: (a) in the case of a developing country, that it intended to apply the provisions of the Protocol to works whose country of origin is a country of the Union which admits the application of the reservations under the Protocol; or (b) that it admitted the application of the provisions of the Protocol to works of which it is the country of origin by countries which, on becoming bound by Articles 1 to 21 and by the Protocol, or on making a declaration of application of the Protocol by virtue of the provision of (a), have made reservations permitted by the Protocol. If a country had already separately accepted the Protocol in accordance with Article 5 thereof, its declaration under Article 28(1)(b)(i) might only relate to Articles 1 to 20; Article 28(1)(c).

24–59 **The administrative provisions.** The administrative provisions of the Stockholm Act, Articles 22 to 26, were to come into force with respect to the first seven countries that had ratified or acceded without declaring that their ratification or accession did not apply to such Articles, three months after the deposit of the seventh instrument of ratification or accession: Article 28(2)(b).

24–60 **Declarations and notifications.** The Stockholm Act provided for various declarations or notifications. For instance, Article 7(7) provided that any country of the Union bound by the Rome Act, which grants shorter terms of protection than those provided for in Article 7 of the Stockholm Act, might maintain such terms when ratifying or acceding to the Stockholm Act. Again, Article 33, which provided, in paragraph (1), for the settling of disputes about the interpretation or application of the Stockholm Act, provided, in paragraph (2), that a country, when ratifying or acceding to the Stockholm Act, might declare that it did not consider itself bound by paragraph (1). Further, Article 38(2) provided that countries of the Union not bound by Articles 22 to 26 (the administrative provisions of the Stockholm Act) might, until five years after the entry into force of the Convention establishing the World Intellectual Property Organisation[38] exercise, if they so desired, the rights provided under such Articles as if they were bound by such Articles, by giving written notification thereof as prescribed by Article 38(2).

24–61 **State of ratifications or accessions.** The only countries which adhered to the substantive provisions of the Stockholm Act and the Protocol in due time, *i.e.* prior to October 10, 1974, were Chad, the former East Germany, Mauritania, Pakistan, Romania and Senegal. Notwithstanding that this was more than five

---

[38] See para. 24–49, above.

countries, the substantive provisions never entered into force in view of the declarations made by Pakistan and Mauritania.[39]

On the other hand, the administrative provisions of the Stockholm Act did come into force, the following countries having adhered thereto: Australia, Austria, Belgium, Canada, Chad, Denmark, Fiji, Finland, Germany,[40] Ireland, Israel, Liechtenstein, Morocco, Pakistan, Romania, Senegal, Spain, Sweden, Switzerland and the United Kingdom.

Romania's ratification was accompanied by declarations under Articles 7(7) and 33(2). Pakistan and Senegal made declarations under Article 5(1)(a) of the Protocol. Bulgaria and Sweden made declarations under Article 5(1)(b) of the Protocol. Pakistan's accession was accompanied by a declaration that Pakistan availed itself of the reservations in Article 1 of the Protocol other than that in Article 1(a): Mauritania's accession was accompanied by a declaration that Mauritania availed itself of the reservations in Article 1 of the Protocol. Finally, the following countries availed themselves of the provisions of Article 38(2): Argentina, Belgium, Brazil, Bulgaria, Cameroon, Chile, the then Czechoslovakia, Dahomey, France, Gabon, Greece, the Holy See, Hungary, Italy, the then Ivory Coast, Japan, Luxembourg, Malta, Monaco, the Netherlands, Niger, Norway, Portugal, South Africa, Tunisia, Turkey and Yugoslavia.

G. ENTRY INTO FORCE OF PARIS ACT

Ratification or accession. The method of entry into force of the Paris Act was complicated. Thus, under Article 28(2)(a), Articles 1 to 21 (the substantive provisions) and the Appendix were to come into force three months after both the following conditions had been fulfilled. First, at least five countries of the Union must have ratified or acceded to the Paris Act without making a declaration under paragraph (1)(b) of Article 28. Secondly, France, Spain, the United Kingdom and the United States of America must have become bound by the Paris revision of the Universal Copyright Convention. Such entry into force applied to those countries of the Union which, at least three months before the coming into force, had deposited instruments of ratification or accession not containing a declaration under paragraph (1)(b) of Article 28. With regard to any other Union country which ratifies or accedes to the Paris Act without making such a declaration, Articles 1 to 21 and the Appendix are to come into force three months after the date on which the Director General of the World Intellectual Property Organisation (WIPO) has notified the deposit of the relevant instrument of ratification or accession, unless a subsequent date has been indicated in the instrument deposited, in which case entry into force takes place on the date indicated.

The declaration under Article 28(1)(b) is to the effect that the ratification or accession of the country concerned is not to apply to Articles 1 to 21 and the Appendix. However, if such country has previously made a declaration under Article 6(1) of the Appendix, then it may declare only that its ratification or accession is not to apply to Articles 1 to 20. Any country which has made such a declaration may at a later time declare that it extends the effects of its ratification or accession to those provisions.

So far as Articles 22 to 38 (the administrative and final provisions) are concerned, Article 28(3) provides that, as regards any country which ratifies or accedes to the Paris Act with or without a declaration under Article 28(1)(d), Articles 22 to 38 are to come into force three months after the date on which the

24–62

---

[39] See para. 24–58, above.

[40] Both Germany (Democratic Republic) and Germany (Federal Republic) adhered to the administrative provisions of the Stockholm Act.

Director General has notified the deposit of the relevant instrument of ratification or accession, unless a subsequent date has been indicated in the instrument deposited, in which case entry into force takes place on the date indicated.

Articles 29 and 30(2)(b) contain provisions for accession by non-Union countries.

Article 29 *bis* provides that the ratification or accession to the Paris Act by any country not bound by Articles 22 to 38 of the Stockholm Act is, for the sole purposes of Article 14(2) of the Convention establishing the World Intellectual Property Organisation, to amount to ratification of or accession to the Stockholm Act with the limitation set forth in Article 28(1)(b)(i) thereof.

Article 30(2)(a) enables any country ratifying or acceding to the Paris Act, subject to Article 5(2) of the Appendix, to retain the benefit of the reservations it has previously formulated.

24–63 Finally, Article 6(1) of the Appendix (relating to developing countries) provides that any Union country may declare, as from the date of the Paris Act, and at any time before becoming bound by Articles 1 to 21 and the Appendix, as follows: (i) if it is a country which, were it bound by Articles 1 to 21 and the Appendix, would be entitled to avail itself of the faculties referred to in Article 1(1) of the Appendix, that it will apply the provisions of Article 2 or of Article 3 of the Appendix or of both to works whose country of origin is a country which, pursuant to (ii), admits the application of those Articles to such works, or which is bound by Articles 1 to 21 and this Appendix; such declaration may, instead of referring to Article 2, refer to Article 5 of the Appendix; (ii) that it admits the application of the Appendix to works of which it is the country of origin by countries which have made a declaration under (i) or a notification under Article 1 of the Appendix.

Articles 1 to 21 and the Appendix entered into force on October 10, 1974, by which time the requirements of Article 28(2)(a) had been complied with. Articles 22 to 38 are also now in force. The United Kingdom ratified the Paris Act with effect from January 2, 1990.

24–64 As of August 20, 2004, the following countries have ratified or acceded to the whole of the Paris Act including the Appendix: Albania, Algeria, Andorra, Antigua and Barbuda, Argentina, Armenia, Australia, Austria, Azerbaijan, Bahrain, Bangladesh, Barbados, Belarus, Belgium, Belize, Benin, Bolivia, Bosnia and Herzegovina, Botswana, Brazil, Bulgaria, Burkina Faso, Cameroon, Canada, Cape Verde, Central African Republic, Chile, China,[41] Colombia, Congo, Costa Rica, Côte d'Ivoire, Croatia, Cuba, Cyprus, Czech Republic, Democratic People's Republic of Korea, Democratic Republic of the Congo, Denmark, Djibouti, Dominica, Dominican Republic, Ecuador, Egypt, El Salvador, Equatorial Guinea, Estonia, Finland, France, Gabon, Gambia, Georgia, Germany, Ghana, Greece, Grenada, Guatemala, Guinea, Guinea-Bissau, Guyana, Haiti, the Holy See, Honduras, Hungary, Iceland, India, Indonesia, Israel, Italy, Jamaica, Japan, Jordan, Kazakhstan, Kenya, Kyrgyzstan, Latvia, Lesotho, Liberia, Libyan Arab Jamahiriya, Liechtenstein, Lithuania, Luxembourg, Macedonia (the former Yugoslav Republic of), Malawi, Malaysia, Mali, Mauritania, Mauritius, Mexico, Micronesia (Federated States of), Monaco, Mongolia, Morocco, Namibia, the Netherlands (for the Kingdom in Europe only), Nicaragua, Niger, Nigeria, Norway, Oman, Panama, Paraguay, Peru, Philippines, Poland, Portugal, Qatar, Republic of Korea, Republic of Moldova, Romania, Russian Federation, Rwanda,

---

[41] The Paris Act applies also to the Hong Kong and Macau Special Administrative Regions of China.

Saint Kitts and Nevis, Saint Lucia, Saint Vincent and the Grenadines, Saudi Arabia, Senegal, Serbia and Montenegro, Singapore, Slovakia, Slovenia, Spain, Sudan, Suriname, Swaziland, Sweden, Switzerland, Syrian Arab Republic, Tajikistan, Thailand, Togo, Tonga, Trinidad and Tobago, Tunisia, Turkey, Ukraine, United Arab Emirates, United Kingdom (with the Isle of Man), United Republic of Tanzania, United States of America, Uruguay, Venezuela, Viet Nam and Zambia.

The following countries have now ratified or acceded to the Paris Act, other than Articles 1 to 21 and the Appendix, by reason of having made a declaration under Article 28(1)(b): Bahamas, Malta, South Africa, Sri Lanka and Zimbabwe. Articles 22 to 38 of the Paris Act apply also to the Netherlands Antilles and Aruba.

Algeria, Bahamas, Cuba, Democratic People's Republic of Korea, Egypt, Guatemala, India, Indonesia, Israel, Jordan, Lesotho, Liberia, Libyan Arab Jamahiriva, Lithuania, Malta, Mauritius, Mongolia, Oman, Saint Lucia, South Africa, Thailand, Tunisia, United Republic of Tanzania, Venezuela and Viet Nam have made declarations that they do not consider themselves bound by Article 33(1) concerning the settlement of disputes by the International Court of Justice. Bosnia and Herzogovina, Cyprus, Serbia and Montenegro and Slovenia have made reservations concerning the right of translation. Portugal has declared that its ratification shall not apply to Article 14 *bis*(2)(c) to the effect that the undertaking by authors to bring contributions to the making of a cinematographic work must be in a written agreement. India has made a declaration under Article 14 *bis*(2)(b) (presumption of legitimation for some authors who have brought contributions to the making of the cinematographic work). Algeria, Bahrain, Bangladesh, Cuba, Democratic People's Republic of Korea, Jordan, Mongolia, Philippines and Singapore have availed themselves of the faculties provided for in Articles II and III of the Appendix. The relevant declarations are effective until October 10, 2004. Jordan, Oman, Philippines, Sudan, Thailand and Viet Nam have availed themselves of the same faculties with effect until October 10, 2014. The United Kingdom, Germany and Norway have declared that they admit the application of the Appendix of the Paris Act to works of which they are the state of origin by states that have made a declaration under Article VI(1)(i) of the Appendix or a notification under Article 1 of the Appendix.

H. PRESENT MEMBERS OF THE COPYRIGHT UNION

Countries forming the Copyright Union. As of August 20, 2004,[42] the following 156 countries form the Copyright Union: Albania, Algeria, Andorra, Antigua and Barbuda, Argentina, Armenia, Australia, Austria, Azerbaijan, Bahamas, Bahrain, Bangladesh, Barbados, Belarus, Belgium, Belize, Benin, Bolivia, Bosnia and Herzegovina, Botswana, Brazil, Bulgaria, Burkina Faso, Cameroon, Canada, Cape Verde, Central African Republic, Chad, Chile, China, Colombia, Congo, Costa Rica, Côte d'Ivoire, Croatia, Cuba, Cyprus, Czech Republic, Democratic People's Republic of Korea, Democratic Republic of the Congo, Denmark, Djibouti, Dominica, Dominican Republic, Ecuador, Egypt, El Salvador, Equatorial Guinea, Estonia, Fiji, Finland, France (including overseas territories and the territorial entity of Mayotte), Gabon, Gambia, Georgia, Germany,[43] Ghana, Greece, Grenada, Guatemala, Guinea, Guinea-Bissau, Guyana, Haiti, the Holy See,

24–65

---

[42] The situation is constantly changing and the current position can be obtained by consulting the World Intellectual Property Organisation website: *http://www.wipo.int.*

[43] The Treaty of Union of August 31, 1990 (BGBL, 1990, Pt II, 885 *et seq.*) between the former Federal Republic of Germany and the former German Democratic Republic, which effected the reunification of Germany, provided that, in the case of copyright, the law of the former Federal

Honduras, Hungary, Iceland, India, Indonesia, Ireland, Israel, Italy, Jamaica, Japan, Jordan, Kazakhstan, Kenya, Kyrgyzstan, Latvia, Lebanon, Lesotho, Liberia, Libyan Arab Jamahiriva, Liechtenstein, Lithuania, Luxembourg, Macedonia (the former Yugoslav Republic of), Madagascar, Malawi, Malaysia, Mali, Malta, Mauritania, Mauritius, Mexico, Micronesia (Federated States of), Monaco, Mongolia, Morocco, Namibia, the Netherlands, New Zealand, Nicaragua, Niger, Nigeria, Norway, Oman, Pakistan, Panama, Paraguay, Peru, Philippines, Poland, Portugal, Qatar, Republic of Korea, Republic of Moldova, Romania, Russian Federation, Rwanda, Saint Kitts and Nevis, Saint Lucia, Saint Vincent and the Grenadines, Saudi Arabia, Senegal, Serbia and Montenegro, Singapore, Slovakia, Slovenia, South Africa, Spain, Sri Lanka, Sudan, Suriname, Swaziland, Sweden, Switzerland, Syrian Arab Republic, Tajikistan, Thailand, Togo, Tonga, Trinidad and Tobago, Tunisia, Turkey, Ukraine, United Arab Emirates, United Kingdom,[44] United Republic of Tanzania, United States of America (including the territories of American Samoa, Guam, the Northern Mariana Islands, Puerto Rico and the US Virgin Islands), Uruguay, Venezuela, Viet Nam, Zambia and Zimbabwe.

3. THE WIPO COPYRIGHT TREATY 1996

A. History

24–66 **Need for new international regulations.** In the course of the 1980s, a consensus developed that there was a need for new international regulations concerning the application of the Berne Convention. There were two main reasons for this. The first was the need to update the level of protection afforded by the Convention to deal with the technical developments which had emerged since the adoption of the Paris Act 1971. Secondly, the shortcomings of the Convention with respect to standards of protection and the lack of any mechanism therein for enforcing the obligations of Member States or for the settlement of disputes between them were brought into focus in the context of the GATT Multilateral Trade Negotiations (the Uruguay Round). The deliberations of the GATT Working Group on Trade-Related Aspects of Intellectual Property (TRIPs) resulted, in December 1993, in agreement on the text of a new international instrument which, following the successful outcome of the Uruguay Round, was formally adopted at Marrakesh in April 1994. The TRIPs Agreement contains enforceable copyright treaty obligations, which include the requirements of the Paris Act of the Berne Convention and impose additional standards of protection exceeding those of the Berne Convention.[45]

A new substantive revision of the Berne Convention was ruled out, however. A formal revision would require unanimity among the Member States. At the time, such unanimity was perceived to be politically impossible in view of the widely differing standards and objects of protection in the then more than 100 Member States (on January 1, 1997, the Berne Union comprised 121 States). Thus, work proceeded on the basis that any new instrument would be an independent multilateral treaty, possibly in the form of a Protocol to the Convention, and that such an instrument would be likely to take the form of a special agreement under Article 20 of the Convention.

Republic of Germany (*i.e.* the Copyright Law of September 9, 1965, as amended), was to apply in the territory of the former German Democratic Republic with effect from October 3, 1990.

[44] The UK extended the application of the Paris Act of the Berne Convention to the Isle of Man with effect from March 18, 1996.

[45] See paras 24–135 *et seq.*, below.

Work on a possible Protocol to the Convention began in 1991. According to the relevant WIPO programme items for the years 1990–91 and 1992–93,[46] the purpose of the Protocol would be to clarify the existing or establish new international standards where, under the Paris Act of the Berne Convention, doubts may exist as to the extent to which the Convention applies. It was considered that such clarification was required because governments interpret their obligations under the Convention differently. Discrepancies had arisen in respect of certain subject-matters of protection (*e.g.* computer programs, sound recordings, computer-generated works); certain rights (*e.g.* rental right, public lending right, right of distribution of copies of any kind of works, right of display); the applicability of the conventional minima (no formalities, term of protection, etc.); and the obligation of granting national treatment (without reciprocity) to foreigners. The desirability of covering the rights of producers of sound recordings in the protocol was also to be examined.

Terms of reference of possible Protocol. Following two sessions of the Committee of Experts responsible for the preparation of the possible Protocol, held in 1991 and 1992 respectively,[47] its terms of reference were modified,[48] due mainly to the fact that agreement could not be reached on the inclusion of the protection of producers of sound recordings in the possible Protocol, as had been proposed by WIPO.[49] According to the modified terms of reference, the issues agreed to be discussed in connection with the possible Protocol were the following: (1) computer programs, (2) databases, (3) rental right, (4) non-voluntary licences for the sound recording of musical works, (5) non-voluntary licences for primary broadcasting and satellite communication, (6) distribution right, including importation right, (7) duration of the protection of photographic works, (8) communication to the public by satellite broadcasting, (9) enforcement of rights, and (10) national treatment. A separate Committee of Experts on a Possible Instrument for the Protection of the Rights of Performers and Producers of Phonograms (sound recordings) was established to discuss all questions concerning the effective international protection of the rights of performers and producers of sound recordings. A third session of the Committee of Experts on the possible Protocol to the Berne Convention[50] and a first session of the Committee of Experts on the possible Instrument[51] were held in 1993. The nature of the relationship, if any, between the possible Protocol and the possible Instrument, when and if adopted, and between the latter and the Rome Convention for the Protection of Performers, Producers of Phonograms and Broadcasting Organisations 1961, and the Convention for the Protection of Producers of Phonograms Against Unauthorised Duplication of Their Phonograms 1971, were also the subject of discussion. **24–67**

The digital agenda. Further sessions of the Committees of Experts were convened in 1994 and 1995[52] in the course of which the need to address also issues connected with the exploitation of works in the digital environment of the **24–68**

---

[46] Programmes adopted by the Assembly and Conference of Representatives of the Berne Union, October 1989 and October 1991 (see WIPO documents AB/XX/2, item PRG. 02(2) and AB/XX/20, paras 152 and 199, for the 1990/1991 biennium, and document AB/XXII/22, para.197, for the 1992/1993 biennium).

[47] For the reports of these sessions, see Copyright 1992: First Session at 30 and Second Session at 66 and 93.

[48] The terms of reference of the Committee of Experts were modified by the Assembly and the Conference of Representatives of the Berne Union in September 1992 (see WIPO document B/A/XIII/2, para.22).

[49] WIPO Programme 1992/3 (document AB/XXII/2, item 03(2)).

[50] See Report of the third session, (Geneva, June 1993), Copyright 1993, 179.

[51] See Report of the first session (Geneva, June/July, 1993), Copyright 1993, 196.

[52] See Copyright 1994, 44, and Industrial Property and Copyright 1995, 107, 110 and 427.

so-called Global Information Infrastructure was recognised (the Digital Agenda). Following the publication in September 1996 by WIPO of "basic proposals" for the substantive provisions of three treaties dealing respectively with authors' rights, the rights of phonogram producers and performers and *sui generis* intellectual property protection of databases (*i.e.* non-copyright protection), a Diplomatic Conference on Certain Copyright and Neighbouring Rights Questions was held in Geneva from December 2 to 20, 1996; the "basic proposals" formed the basis for negotiation. On December 20, 1996, two new international instruments were adopted and opened for signature: the WIPO Copyright Treaty and the WIPO Performances and Phonograms Treaty.[53] The issue of *sui generis* protection for databases was postponed. The Conference also adopted a number of agreed statements concerning the WIPO Copyright Treaty[54] and the WIPO Performances and Phonograms Treaty,[55] a Resolution concerning audiovisual performances[56] and a Recommendation concerning databases calling for further discussion of the issue.[57]

There follows in this chapter a summary of the WIPO Copyright Treaty and its related statements in view of the close relationship of the new Treaty with the Paris Act of the Berne Convention. The WIPO Performances and Phonograms Treaty and its related statements are discussed below, in section 7 of this Chapter, following the discussion of the Rome and Phonograms Conventions in sections 5 and 6.[58] The status of the related statements in relation to interpreting the Treaties may be evaluated in the light of the Vienna Convention on the Law of Treaties and, in particular, section 3 thereof concerning interpretation of treaties.[59]

B. SUBSTANTIVE PROVISIONS OF THE WIPO COPYRIGHT TREATY

24–69   **The Treaty and its explanatory statements.** The Diplomatic Conference adopted the Treaty and a series of explanatory statements, representing the agreed interpretation to be given to certain provisions of the Treaty. With one exception, the explanatory statements were adopted by consensus. The exception was that

---

[53] The Final Act of the Diplomatic Conference (CRNR/DC/98) was signed by the following 57 states on December 20, 1996: Angola, Argentina, Australia, Austria, Azerbaijan, Belgium, Bolivia, Brazil, Burkina Faso, Canada, Chile, China, Colombia, Croatia, Cuba, Denmark, Ecuador, El Salvador, Finland, Germany, Honduras, Hungary, Indonesia, Ireland, Italy, Jamaica, Japan, Kazakhstan, Kenya, Mexico, Mongolia, Namibia, the Netherlands, New Zealand, Nicaragua, Norway, Peru, Philippines, Republic of Korea, Republic of Moldova, Romania, Russian Federation, Singapore, Slovakia, Slovenia, Spain, Sudan, Sweden, Switzerland, Togo, Trinidad and Tobago, UK, USA, Uzbekistan, Venezuela, Zimbabwe. The European Communities also signed the Final Act. The following also signed the WIPO Copyright Treaty and the WIPO Performances and Phonograms Treaty: Bolivia, Burkina Faso, Chile, Germany, Indonesia, Italy, Kenya, Mongolia, Namibia, Spain, Togo, Venezuela, European Communities.
[54] Document CRNR/DC/96 of December 20, 1996.
[55] Document CRNR/DC/97 of December 20, 1996.
[56] Document CRNR/DC/99 of December 20, 1996.
[57] CRNR/DC/100 of December 20, 1996, and see para. 24–78, below.
[58] See also the following accounts of the results of the Diplomatic Conference: "WIPO Diplomatic Conference on Certain Copyright and Neighbouring Rights Questions", [1997] *Copyright* 97; J. Reinbothe, M. Martin-Prat and S. von Lewinski, "The New WIPO Treaties: A First Résumé" [1997] 4 E.I.P.R. 171; T.C. Vinje, "The New WIPO Copyright Treaty: A Happy Result in Geneva" [1997] 5 E.I.P.R. 230; M. Fabiani, "The Geneva Diplomatic Conference on Copyright and the Rights of Performers and Phonogram Producers" [1997] 3 Ent. L.R. 98. See also J. Reinbothe and S. von Lewinski, "The WIPO Treaties 1996: Ready to Come into Force" [2002] E.I.P.R. 199.
[59] See Arts 31 to 33. Art.31 (2) and (4) are of particular relevance: "2. The context for the purpose of the interpretation of a treaty shall comprise, in addition to the text, including its preamble and annexes: (a) any agreement relating to the treaty which was made between all the parties in connection with the conclusion of the treaty; (b) any instrument which was made by one or more parties in connection with the conclusion of the treaty and accepted by the other parties as an instrument related to the treaty. 4. A special meaning shall be given to a term if it is established that the parties so intended".

relating to the reproduction right. In the following discussion, these statements are taken into account. As already stated, the Treaty is a special agreement within the meaning of Article 20 of the Berne Convention[60] and does not derogate from existing obligations that Contracting Parties have to each other under that Convention (Article 1). Parties shall comply with Articles 1 to 21 and the Appendix of the Paris Act of the Convention (Article 1(4)). The statement concerning Article 1(4) makes it clear that the reproduction right as provided for in Article 9 of the Berne Convention, and the exceptions permitted thereunder, fully apply in the digital environment, in particular to the use of works in digital form. Moreover, the storage of a protected work in digital form in an electronic medium constitutes a reproduction within the meaning of Article 9 of the Berne Convention.

Article 2 defines the scope of copyright protection as extending to expressions and not to ideas, procedures, methods of operation or mathematical concepts as such.

Article 3 provides that Contracting Parties shall apply *mutatis mutandis* the provisions of Articles 2 to 6 of the Berne Convention, concerning protected works, conditions of protection, including criteria of eligibility, national treatment and the possibility of restricting protection in the case of works made by nationals of certain non-Union countries, respectively, in respect of the protection provided for in the Treaty. According to the related statement, the expressions "country of the Union" and "country outside the Union" in the Berne Convention are to be read as references to countries that are respectively members or non-members of the Treaty.

New protected works. Computer programs are protected as literary works within the meaning of Article 2 of the Berne Convention (Article 4); this provision is of a declaratory nature since it confirms the existing understanding that such programs were already protected under Berne. Compilations of data or other material, in any form, which by reason of the selection or arrangement of their contents constitute intellectual creations are protected as such. This protection does not extend to the data or material itself and is without prejudice to any copyright subsisting in the data or material contained in the compilation (Article 5). The accompanying statements to these two articles assert that the scope of protection provided is consistent with Article 2 of the Berne Convention and on a par with the relevant provisions of the TRIPs Agreement.[61]   **24–70**

Newly recognised rights. An express right of distribution is recognised giving authors the exclusive right to authorise or prohibit the making available to the public of the original and copies of their works through sale or other transfer of ownership (Article 6). According to the accompanying statement, the expressions "original" and "copies" refer exclusively to fixed copies that can be put into circulation as tangible objects. The right may be made subject to exhaustion after the first sale or other transfer of ownership (Article 6(2)). This right is new to the Berne Convention and is also not recognised in the TRIPs Agreement, although it is provided for in a number of national laws and considered in some jurisdictions as a component of the reproduction right.   **24–71**

Subject to certain limitations, a right to authorise commercial rental is recognised in favour of authors of computer programs, cinematographic works and works embodied in phonograms (sound recordings (Article 7)). The accompanying statement explains that Contracting Parties are not required under this Article

---

[60] In the Treaty, reference to the Berne Convention means the Paris Act thereof (Art.1(3)).
[61] Art.10 (1) and (2) of the TRIPs Agreement.

to provide an exclusive right of commercial rental to authors who, under the domestic law of that country, are not granted such rights with respect of sound recordings and that the obligation is consistent with Article 14(4) of the TRIPs Agreement. As regards computer programs, the right is excluded where the program itself is not the essential object of the rental. As for films, the right only applies where commercial rental has led to widespread copying which has materially impaired the exclusive right of reproduction. However, Contracting Parties which on April 15, 1994, had and continue to have a system of equitable remuneration of authors for rental may maintain that system unless the reproduction right is being materially impaired (Article 7(3)).[62]

Finally, to deal with new means of communication over services such as the internet, Article 8 provides authors with the exclusive right to authorise any communication to the public of their works, by wire or wireless means, including the making available to the public of their works in such a way that members of the public may access these works from a place and at a time individually chosen by them, *i.e.* online transmissions over interactive services. Thus authors have obtained a valuable right to authorise on-demand transmissions. However, to allay the fears of mere electronic communication systems service providers, who feared that they would be made responsible for clearing copyright in programs sent over their networks, the accompanying statement explains that it is understood that the mere provision of physical facilities for enabling or making a communication does not in itself amount to communication within the meaning of the Treaty or the Berne Convention. It is also pointed out that Contracting Parties may apply Article 11 *bis*(2) of the Berne Convention and provide for compulsory licensing.

In respect of photographic works, the possibility provided by Article 7(4) of the Berne Convention to limit the term of protection to 25 years shall no longer apply (Article 9), the general term of protection of 50 years *post mortem auctoris* being applicable instead.

24–72   **Limitations and exceptions: Extension of the Three-Step Test of the Berne Convention.** As regards limitations and exceptions to authors' rights, the limitation of Article 9(2) of the Berne Convention to the effect that limitations and exceptions to the reproduction right must not conflict with a normal exploitation of the work nor unreasonably prejudice the legitimate interests of the author (the so-called 3-step test of the Berne Convention) is extended to apply not merely to the reproduction right but also to all authors' rights (Article 10).[63] According to the accompanying statement, this provision neither reduces nor extends the scope of Article 9(2) of the Berne Convention, but permits Contracting Parties to carry forward and appropriately extend into the digital environment limitations and exceptions in their national laws, which have been considered acceptable under the Berne Convention. Similarly, it is to be understood as permitting them to devise new exceptions and limitations appropriate in the digital network environment.[64]

24–73   **Technical protection.** The importance of the use of technical anti-copying devices in the fight against piracy of works of all kinds is recognised in Article 11, which provides for the Contracting Parties to provide adequate legal protection and effective legal remedies against the circumvention of effective technological measures used by authors to prevent unauthorised use of their works. Certain

---

[62] *cf.* Art.11 of the TRIPs Agreement, which has a parallel provision.

[63] *cf.* Art.13 of the TRIPs Agreement and see para. 24–33, above.

[64] This statement was adopted not by consensus but by majority vote. It is therefore of more limited value than the other statements to which all present agreed.

obligations concerning electronic rights management information are included with the same aim; thus Contracting Parties must provide adequate and effective legal remedies against acts which may induce, enable, facilitate or conceal an infringement of any right protected under the Treaty or the Berne Convention, both exclusive rights and rights of remuneration,[65] and including acts such as the removal or alteration of electronic rights management information without authority; the distribution, importation for distribution, broadcast or communication to the public, without authority, of works or copies of works knowing that electronic rights management information has been removed or altered without authority. "Rights management information" is defined as information that "identifies the work, the author of the work, the owner of any right in the work, or information about the terms and conditions of use of the work, and any numbers or codes that represent such information, when any of these items of information is attached to a copy of a work or appears in connection with the communication of a work to the public" (Article 12). Contracting Parties may not rely on this Article to devise or implement rights management systems that would have the effect of imposing formalities, which are not permitted under the Berne Convention or the Treaty, prohibiting the free movement of goods or impeding the enjoyment of rights under the Treaty (accompanying statement concerning Article 12).

Retroactive effect and enforcement. Article 13 of the Treaty provides that the rules of Article 18 of the Berne Convention concerning retroactive effect, or the way in which the Convention applies to works already in existence when their country of origin first joins the Convention, shall apply to the protection provided for under the Treaty. Thus the Treaty applies to all works which, at the moment of its coming into force, have not yet fallen into the public domain in the country of origin through the expiry of the term of protection.   **24–74**

Article 14 deals with enforcement of rights, obliging the Contracting Parties to ensure that enforcement procedures are available to permit effective action against infringement, including remedies to prevent infringements and remedies which constitute a deterrent to further infringements. This provision is of a very general nature and does not include any reference to the more effective enforcement provisions contained in Articles 41 to 61 of the TRIPs Agreement. The Diplomatic Conference specifically rejected a "basic proposal" to either include the TRIPs enforcement provisions in an annex or by reference (which would have simply required Contracting Parties to apply the relevant provisions of the TRIPs Agreement).

C. SIGNATORIES AND ENTRY INTO FORCE

Parties to the Treaty. Any Member State of the World Intellectual Property Organisation (WIPO) may become party to the Treaty, as well as any intergovernmental organisation competent in respect of, and having legislation binding on its Member States on, matters dealt with by the Treaty. The European Union has signed the Treaty on this basis (Article 17). The Treaty entered into force three months after the deposit of 30 instruments of ratification or accession by states with the Director General of WIPO (Article 20). Thereafter, new parties are bound by the Treaty three months from the date on which they deposit their instruments (Article 21). No reservations to the Treaty are permitted (Article 22), although it may be denounced on giving one year's notice (Article 23). The Treaty   **24–75**

---

[65] Accompanying statement concerning Art.12 of the Treaty.

is administered by the International Bureau of WIPO[66] (Article 16) and supervised by an Assembly, which deals with matters concerning the maintenance and development of the Treaty and its application and operation.[67]

The Treaty was open for signature until December 31, 1997, at which date 51 States had signed the Treaty as well as the European Community.[68]

As of August 20, 2004, the following 48 countries had ratified or acceded to the Treaty: Argentina, Belarus, Bulgaria, Burkina Faso, Chile, Colombia, Costa Rica, Croatia, Cyprus, Czech Republic, Ecuador, El Salvador, Gabon, Georgia, Guatemala, Guinea, Honduras, Hungary, Indonesia, Jamaica, Japan, Jordan, Kazakhstan, Kyrgyzstan, Latvia, Lithuania, Macedonia (the former Yugoslav Republic of), Mali, Mexico, Mongolia, Nicaragua, Panama, Paraguay, Peru, Philippines, Poland, Republic of Korea, Republic of Moldova, Romania, Saint Lucia, Senegal, Serbia and Montenegro, Slovakia, Slovenia, Togo, Ukraine, United Arab Emirates, United States of America.[69]

The Council of the European Community approved the Treaty with regard to matters within its competence by decision dated March 16, 2000.[70]

D. PENDING ISSUES NOT ADDRESSED BY THE TREATY

24–76   **Problems left unresolved.** It will be noted that of the list of matters considered by the Committees of Experts on a possible Protocol to the Berne Convention, some did not find solutions in the Treaty. For example, the proposal to include an additional specific right to authorise or prohibit importation in the context of the new distribution right was rejected. Likewise, agreement could not be reached on a rule concerning the international exhaustion of the distribution right, leaving the question of national or international exhaustion to national law. The proposals to abolish the non-voluntary licences for broadcasting of literary and artistic works and for the sound recording of musical works, permitted respectively by Article 11 *bis*(2) and Article 13 of the Berne Convention, were also abandoned.

24–77   **The digital agenda.** As regards the digital agenda, two important issues for which solutions were proposed in the "basic proposals" were not resolved. First, agreement could not be reached on the proposal to make it clear that acts such as temporary storage in electronic communications media constitute acts of reproduction.[71] Similarly, the proposal to clarify the concept of "publication", by specifically providing that making a work available to the public through on demand interactive systems should be treated as publication, was not followed.[72]

24–78   **Databases.** In particular, the Conference was unable to reach a sufficient consensus on the subject of the *sui generis* protection of databases, which require

---

[66] The Director General of WIPO is the depository of the Treaty (Art.25).

[67] WCT, Art.15(2)(a).

[68] Argentina, Austria, Belarus, Belgium, Bolivia, Burkina Faso, Canada, Chile, Colombia, Costa Rica, Croatia, Denmark, Ecuador, Estonia, Finland, France, Germany, Ghana, Greece, Hungary, Indonesia, Ireland, Israel, Italy, Kazakhstan, Kenya, Kyrgyzstan, Luxembourg, Mexico, Moldova (Republic of), Monaco, Mongolia, Namibia, the Netherlands, Nigeria, Panama, Portugal, Romania, Senegal, Slovakia, Slovenia, South Africa, Spain, Sweden, Switzerland, Togo, United Kingdom, United States of America, Uruguay, Venezuela, European Community.

[69] The situation is constantly changing and the current position can be obtained by consulting the WIPO website: *http://www.wipo.int.*

[70] Council Decision of March 16, 2000, on the approval, on behalf of the European Community, of the WIPO Copyright Treaty and the WIPO Performances and Phonograms Treaty([2001] O.J. L89/6). See Vol.2, Appendix H11. The decision authorised the President of the Council to deposit the instrument of ratification as from the date by which Member States are obliged to implement the Directive.

[71] See Basic Proposal 7.

[72] See Basic Proposal 3.

significant investment but do not necessarily qualify for protection as a literary work (non-original databases), to be able to adopt an international instrument on the subject. Instead, a recommendation was adopted by the Conference in which the participants expressed interest in examining further the possible implications and benefits of a *sui generis* system of protection of databases at the international level and recommended that the competent authorities of WIPO should, in the first quarter of 1997, decide on a schedule for further preparatory work on a Treaty on Intellectual Property in Respect of Databases.[73] In doing so, the recommendation recognised that databases are a vital element in the development of a global information infrastructure and the need to strike a balance in relation thereto between the interests of the producers of databases in protection from unfair copying and the interests of users in having appropriate access to the benefits of a global information infrastructure. Meanwhile, discussions have continued on the issue under the auspices of WIPO, but to date no consensus on the need for a new international instrument on the subject has emerged.[74]

4. THE UNIVERSAL COPYRIGHT CONVENTION AND ITS REVISION

A. HISTORY

Object of Convention. Largely with the object of creating a bridge between the Berne Convention countries on the one hand and the Pan-American Convention countries on the other hand,[75] and particularly in the hope that the United States of America might be persuaded to enter into copyright relations with the Berne Union countries, a draft International Convention was prepared under the auspices of the United Nations Organisation for Education, Science and Culture (UNESCO), which resulted in the Universal Copyright Convention (UCC), signed at Geneva on September 6, 1952.[76] The Convention entered into force on September 16, 1955.

24–79

At the time, the Convention represented a turning point in intergovernmental copyright relations and was hailed by many scholars and experts in the copyright field as one of the most significant milestones in the entire history of copyright.[77] For the United States of America it "marked the culmination of a seven years' effort ... to improve its copyright relations with the rest of the world".[78]

The great advantage of the Convention was that it established a set of minimum standards for copyright throughout the world, which could be accepted by countries with very different copyright systems: those which conformed to the

---

[73] WIPO Document CRNR/DC/100 of December 20, 1996.

[74] In March 1997, the Governing Bodies of WIPO decided to convene an Information Meeting concerning intellectual property in databases. This took place in September 1997 and called upon WIPO to undertake further studies of the issue and for consultations to take place with WIPO Member States and the European Community ([1997] Industrial Property and Copyright, 187 and 349). Five studies have been completed and were discussed at the 7th session of WIPO's Standing Committee on Copyright and Related Rights between May 13 and 17, 2002: see its report dated May 30, 2002. The Standing Committee decided that the issue would be carried forward to the agenda of its 8th session (November 4–8, 2002). At its June 2003 meeting the Standing Committee decided that the matter would next be considered in mid-2004, at which time it decided to postpone the matter again until 2005 (WIPO Press Release 386/2004, June 10, 2004).

[75] See paras 24–163 *et seq.*, below.

[76] As a result the Convention is variously referred to as the Universal, Geneva or UNESCO Convention. As regards the 1952 text of the UCC, see *Records of the Intergovernmental Conference*, Geneva, 1952, UNESCO, Paris, 1954; see also T.R. Kupferman and M. Foner (eds.), *Universal Copyright Convention Analysed* (Federal Legal Publications, Inc., New York, 1955).

[77] *cf.* C.B. Seton in Kupferman and Foner, xi.

[78] *per* the Hon. Arthur Fisher, US Register of Copyrights, in Kupferman and Foner, Universal Copyright Convention Analysed (Federal Legal Publications, Inc. New York, 1955).

principle of the Berne Convention requiring the granting of copyright protection without formalities and those countries with copyright laws which made protection dependent on compliance with formalities such as notice, deposit, registration or other formal requirements.

24–80   The Convention was a success and has attracted many members, for many years outstripping the membership of the Berne Convention, its lower level of protection being of particular interest to developing countries. Administered by UNESCO, the progress of the Convention is monitored by the Intergovernmental Committee established thereunder.[79] The latter co-operates closely with the Executive Committee of the Berne Union in copyright matters.

In due course, in parallel with moves to revise the Berne Convention, recommendations were made for the holding of a revision Conference in mid-1971 for the purpose of revising this Convention in an attempt to resolve the unfortunate situation which had arisen over the Protocol Regarding Developing Countries to the Stockholm revision of the Berne Convention. The Universal Copyright Convention, like the Berne Convention, was revised in Paris in 1971.[80]

Following the accession of the United States of America to the Paris Act of the Berne Convention with effect from March 1, 1989, as well as those of large numbers of developing countries over the past 25 years, including many in Latin America, the Universal Copyright Convention has lost part of its *raison d'être* and importance. The accession of the Russian Federation in 1995 to the Paris Act of the Berne Convention has further reduced its importance in providing copyright links between major countries. It is of interest to note that, in 1971, at the time of the adoption of the Paris Acts of the Berne Convention and the Universal Copyright Convention, both Conventions had 59 Member States. As of August 20, 2004, by contrast, the Berne Union comprises 156 Member States as compared with the 99 Member States of the UCC.

B. SUBSTANTIVE PROVISIONS

24–81   **Main provisions.** Basically, the effect of the revised Universal Copyright Convention[81] is that each Contracting State undertakes to give to the unpublished works of the nationals of all other Contracting States the same protection as it gives to the unpublished works of its own nationals as well as the protection specially granted by the Convention, and further undertakes to give to the published works of nationals of the other Contracting States wherever first published, and to published works of the nationals of any country if first published in one of the other Contracting States, the same rights as it gives to works first published in its own territory as well as the protection specially granted by the Convention. Furthermore, such published works, if first published outside the territory of the Contracting State in question and not being the work of a national author, are to enjoy such protection without formality, such as registration or the deposit of copies, provided only that from the time of first publication all copies published bear the symbol © accompanied by the name of the copyright proprietor and the year of first publication, placed in such manner and location as to

---

[79] UCC, Art.XI.

[80] *Records of the Conference for Revision of the Universal Copyright Convention*, Paris, July 5–24, 1971, UNESCO, Paris 1973. See also A. Bogsch, *The Law of Copyright Under the Universal Copyright Convention* (3rd rev. ed., Sijthoff, Leyden and Bowker, New York, 1972).

[81] For the text of the 1971 Convention see Vol.2 at F2.

give reasonable notice of claim of copyright.[82] The Convention is not to apply to works which, at the effective date of the Convention in a Contracting State where protection is claimed, are permanently in the public domain in that State.

Term of copyright. The Convention provides for a minimum term of protection, namely, the life of the author and 25 years after his death. It is, however, provided that any Contracting State which, upon the effective date of the Convention in that State, does not compute the term of protection upon the basis of the life of the author, shall be entitled to compute the term of protection from the date of first publication of the work or from its registration prior to publication, provided that the term of protection is not to be less than 25 years from the date of first publication or registration. "Publication" is defined in the Convention as meaning the reproduction in tangible form and the general distribution to the public of copies of a work from which it can be read or otherwise visually perceived.

24–82

Minimum protection required. As to the nature of the protection to be afforded, the Convention provides that each Contracting State shall give adequate and effective protection to the rights of authors and other copyright proprietors in literary, scientific and artistic works, including writings, musical, dramatic and cinematographic works, and paintings, engravings and sculpture. It is further provided that these rights are to include the basic rights ensuring the author's economic interests, including the exclusive right to authorise reproduction by any means, public performance and broadcasting, and are to extend to the work either in its original form or in any form recognisably derived from the original. Any Contracting State may make exceptions to such rights, provided these do not conflict with the spirit and provisions of the Convention, but shall nevertheless accord a reasonable degree of effective protection to each of the rights to which exception has been made. It is also provided that such rights include the exclusive right to make, publish and authorise the making and publication of translations of works, but the Contracting State may make provision for compulsory licences to translate if, after the expiration of a period of seven years from the date of first publication, a translation has not been published in a language in general use in that state.

24–83

While promising protection on the general lines above indicated, this Convention does not describe the details of protection which are to be afforded by the Contracting States and substantially leaves the mode and extent of protection to the separate legislation of each state. It only extended further than the Berne Convention in requiring protection to be given to published works, not only if first published in a Contracting State, but if first published anywhere, if the author is a national of a Contracting State.[83] To meet this requirement of the Convention, and in order to enable the United Kingdom to ratify the Convention, the 1956 Act altered the law of the United Kingdom so as to protect the published works of nationals of Contracting States although first published outside the United Kingdom and the Convention area.[84] The most important amendment in the Paris revision of this Convention was to provide for various forms of compulsory licence in favour of developing countries similar to those in the Appendix to the Paris revision of the Berne Convention.[85] This did not call for any revision of this country's law and the United Kingdom has, in fact, ratified the Paris revision of this Convention.

---

[82] The positioning of such notice on various types of works is considered in the UNESCO Copyright Bulletin, 1957, vol.X, No.2, pp.225 and 247.

[83] But see now Art.3(1) of the Paris Act of Berne, para. 24–13, above.

[84] Copyright Act 1956, ss.2(2) and 3(3) and see CDPA 1988, ss.154 and 155.

[85] See paras 24–51 *et seq.*, above.

C. RELATIONSHIP WITH THE BERNE CONVENTION

24–84   **Safeguards for the Berne Convention.** The relationship between the Universal Copyright Convention and the Berne Convention is expressed in the text of the UCC itself, which provides:

> "This Convention shall not in any way affect the provisions of the Berne Convention for the Protection of Literary and Artistic Works or membership in the Union created by that Convention".[86]

To that Article in both the 1952 and 1971 texts is annexed a Declaration, which is an integral part of the Convention for the States bound by the Berne Convention. According to the 1952 text, works which, according to the Berne Convention, have as their country of origin a country which has withdrawn from the Berne Union, shall not be protected by the Universal Copyright Convention in the countries of the Berne Union. Moreover, as between members of the Berne Union, only the Berne Convention will apply. In the 1971 text, these rules are relaxed in favour of countries which at the time of withdrawal from the Berne Union are recognised as developing countries availing themselves of the provisions of Article 5 *bis* of the 1971 text concerning compulsory licences to translate.

These provisions, the aim of which was to deter withdrawal from the Berne Union and to exclude the application of the Universal Copyright Convention between Berne Member States, responded to the fear of certain members of the Berne Union that the existence of the UCC might encourage defections by Berne Union Member States seeking to downgrade the level of protection of their international copyright obligations.[87]

D. ENTRY INTO FORCE OF THE 1952 AND 1971 CONVENTIONS

24–85   **Ratification or accession.** Countries, may ratify, accept or accede to this Convention which originally came into force three months after the deposit of 12 instruments of ratification, acceptance or accession, including such deposit by four non-Berne Union members, on September 16, 1955.[88] Subsequently, the Convention came into force in respect of any state three months after that state deposited its instrument of ratification, acceptance or accession.

Accession to the 1971 Convention by a state not party to the 1952 Convention also constitutes accession to that Convention; but, if its instrument of accession was deposited before the 1971 Convention came into force, such state could make its accession to the 1952 Convention conditional upon the coming into force of the 1971 Convention. After the coming into force of the 1971 Convention, no state may accede solely to the 1952 Convention. Relations between states party to the 1971 Convention and states that are party only to the 1952 Convention, are to be governed by the 1952 Convention. However, any state party only to the 1952 Convention may, by a notification deposited with the Director General, declare that it will admit the application of the 1971 Convention to works of its nationals or works first published in its territory by all states party to the 1971 Convention.

The 1971 Convention in fact came into force on July 10, 1974, three months after the deposit of 12 instruments of ratification, acceptance or accession.

---

[86] UCC, 1952 and 1971 texts, Art.XVII and see also Declaration annexed to that Article.

[87] *cf.* A. Bogsch, "Co-existence of the Universal Copyright Convention with the Berne Conventions", in Kupferman and Foner, *Universal Copyright Convention Analysed* (Federal Legal Publications, Inc., New York, 1995), p.141 and S. Ricketson, *The Berne Convention for the Protection of Literary and Artistic Works: 1886–1896* (Queen Mary College, University of London, 1987), paras 15.27 *et seq.*

[88] UCC 1952 text, Art.IX.

The following 64 countries have now ratified or acceded to the 1971 Convention **24–86** as of August 20, 2004: Albania, Algeria, Australia, Austria, Bahamas, Bangladesh, Barbados, Bolivia, Bosnia and Herzegovina, Brazil, Bulgaria, Cameroon, China, Colombia, Costa Rica, Croatia, Cyprus, Czech Republic, Denmark, Dominican Republic, Ecuador, El Salvador, Finland, France, Germany, Guinea, the Holy See, Hungary, India, Italy, Japan, Kenya, Liechtenstein, Macedonia (the former Yugoslav Republic of), Mexico, Monaco, Morocco, the Netherlands, Niger, Norway, Panama, Peru, Poland, Portugal, Republic of Korea, Russian Federation, Rwanda, Saint Vincent and the Grenadines, Saudi Arabia, Senegal, Serbia and Montenegro, Slovakia, Slovenia, Spain, Sri Lanka, Sweden, Switzerland, Togo, Trinidad and Tobago, Tunisia, United Kingdom, United States of America, Uruguay and Venezuela.

The following countries have availed themselves of the exceptions in favour of developing countries: Algeria, Bangladesh, China, Mexico, Republic of Korea and Tunisia.

E. PARTIES TO THE UNIVERSAL COPYRIGHT CONVENTION

Convention countries.[89] As of August 20, 2004, the following 99 countries are **24–87** parties to the Universal Copyright Convention 1952: Albania, Algeria, Andorra, Argentina, Australia, Austria, Azerbaijan, Bahamas, Bangladesh, Barbados, Belarus, Belgium, Belize, Bolivia, Bosnia and Herzegovina, Brazil, Bulgaria, Cambodia, Cameroon, Canada, Chile, China, Colombia, Costa Rica, Croatia, Cuba, Cyprus, Czech Republic, Denmark, Dominican Republic, Ecuador, El Salvador, Fiji, Finland, France, Germany,[90] Ghana, Greece, Guatemala, Guinea, Haiti, the Holy See, Hungary, Iceland, India, Ireland, Israel, Italy, Japan, Kazakhstan, Kenya, Lao People's Democratic Republic, Lebanon, Liberia, Liechtenstein, Luxembourg, Macedonia (the former Yugoslav Republic of), Malawi, Malta, Mauritius, Mexico, Monaco, Morocco, Netherlands, New Zealand, Nicaragua, Niger, Nigeria, Norway, Pakistan, Panama, Paraguay, Peru, Poland, Portugal, Republic of Korea, Republic of Moldova, Russian Federation, Rwanda, Saint Vincent and the Grenadines, Saudi Arabia, Senegal, Serbia and Montenegro, Slovakia, Slovenia, Spain, Sri Lanka, Sweden, Switzerland, Tajikistan, Togo, Trinidad and Tobago, Tunisia, Ukraine, United Kingdom[91] (extended to British Virgin Islands, Gibraltar, Isle of Man and Saint Helena), United States of America (extended to American Samoa, Guam, the Northern Mariana Islands, Puerto Rico, the US Virgin Islands), Uruguay, Venezuela, Yugoslavia and Zambia.

5. THE ROME CONVENTION

A. HISTORY

The Convention for the Protection of Performers, Producers of Phonograms **24–88** **and Broadcasting Organisations** (the Rome Convention) was adopted in Rome on October 26, 1961,[92] at a Diplomatic Conference convened by the International Labour Organisation (ILO), the United Nations Organisation for Education, Sci-

---

[89] The situation is constantly changing and the current position can be obtained by consulting the UNESCO website: http:// firewall.UNESCO.org.

[90] See n.142, above.

[91] The effective date for the UK was September 27, 1957, and, as regards the 1971 Convention, it was July 10, 1974.

[92] The Final Act of the Conference and the Convention were signed by the following States: Argentina, Austria, Belgium, Brazil, Cambodia, Chile, Denmark, France, Federal Republic of Germany, the Holy See, Iceland, India, Italy, Mexico, Spain, Sweden, UK and Yugoslavia. See

ence and Culture (UNESCO) and the United International Bureaux for the Protection of Intellectual Property (BIRPI), the predecessor organisation of WIPO. These three organisations constitute the Secretariat of the Intergovernmental Committee set up under the Convention to monitor its application and operation.[93]

24–89 **Neighbouring rights.** The rights of the beneficiaries of the Rome Convention are widely referred to as "neighbouring rights", although the term appears nowhere in the Convention. This expression is often used for ease of reference and is the term favoured by the World Intellectual Property Organisation (WIPO) to describe the rights. The term appears to have been coined during the many years work leading to the adoption of the Convention, and derives from the French expression "*droits voisins du droit d'auteur*". In 1956, already, a study group of the Berne Union considered the question and concluded:

> "Although most participants felt that "neighbouring rights" was probably not an entirely correct term, no agreement was possible on any other term. It was therefore decided that the term "neighbouring rights" which, because of its long use has the advantage of having become a generally known expression may, at least for the time being, be retained in the form of "so-called neighbouring rights".[94]

The expression is inappropriate as regards the rights granted in the United Kingdom and other common law countries. Such rights are generally a property right, which may vest in individuals or in a legal entity, and are described as copyright. For example, in such countries the rights of producers of phonograms and broadcasters are invariably described as copyrights. However, in civil law countries it serves the purpose of defining rights, such as those of the beneficiaries of the Rome Convention, which have a close connection with authors' rights, but relate to works, productions and other subject-matter which are considered not to qualify for authors' rights because such rights are linked to the personality of the creator, and thus may only be granted to a natural person.

24–90 **Related rights.** In recent years, there has been a growing consensus that the term "related rights" is to be preferred. This is the term used by the Commission of the European Union to describe the rights of the beneficiaries of the Rome Convention and it is the term used throughout this book.

24–91 **Preparation of the Convention.** The Rome Convention was the result of many years of discussion and preparation, the work of several inter-governmental committees and the involvement of the three inter-governmental organisations mentioned above, the ILO, UNESCO and BIRPI.[95] The ILO had first become involved with the problems faced by performers as a result of technological change in the 1920s. Traditionally, a performance had been ephemeral, perishing

---

Records of the Diplomatic Conference on the International Protection of Performers, Producers of Phonograms and Broadcasting Organisations, ILO, UNESCO, BIRPI, 1968.

[93] Rome Convention, Art.32(1) and (5).

[94] Report of the Study Group on so-called "neighbouring rights" (intermediate intellectual rights), Paris, May 1956, para.I.

[95] For a detailed review of the history of the Convention, see C. Masouyé, *Guide to the Rome Convention and to the Phonograms Convention* (WIPO, Geneva, 1981), pp.7 *et seq.* (hereafter " WIPO RC and PC Guide"); see also C. Masouyé, "Performers' Rights in the Rome Convention", XXXXVI RIDA (1965) 162; Stewart, *International Copyright and Neighbouring Rights* (Butterworths, London, 1983) Ch.8, and S. Ricketson, *The Berne Convention for the protection of literary and artistic works: 1886–1896* (Queen Mary College, University of London, 1987), paras 15.45 *et seq.*, and H.H. von Rauscher auf Weeg, "The Rome Convention Rights: a Comparative Review of Legislation and International Developments over Twelve Years" [1974] *Bulletin of the Copyright Society of the USA* 237.

"in the very instant of its production".[96] With the development of recording techniques, cinema, radio and television, performances could be recorded in permanent form and the performances repeated and distributed by broadcast and gramophone records to a wider audience. The performers claimed that these developments deprived them of employment opportunities as their physical presence and live performances could be and were being replaced by the exploitation of their recorded performances. The subject of performers' rights was considered at the Berne Convention Revision Conference, which took place at Rome in 1928. That Conference considered that an international convention on the subject was premature, but called on governments to consider measures to protect performers. The subject of protecting sound recordings under the Berne Convention was first advocated by the United Kingdom at the Berlin Revision Conference of 1908, and at each such Conference thereafter, in 1928 at Rome and 1948 at Brussels. For their part, representatives of producers and broadcasters, both of whom sought protection for their productions against unauthorised use, continued to press for international action. A meeting of experts was convened in Samadan, Switzerland in 1939 by the Secretariat of the Berne Union and the International Institute for the Unification of Private Law. Two draft treaties were produced, one on performers and producers of phonograms and the other on broadcasting organisations. After the Second World War, the issues were raised again at the Berne Convention Revision Conference held in Brussels in 1948, which adopted a series of separate *voeux* calling on governments to consider means for providing protection for performers, producers of phonograms and broadcasting organisations, in each case without prejudice to the rights of authors.[97] At that stage, the issues were still seen as separate problems:

"The Convention was based from the outset on social objectives. The origins of the Convention in the 1920s and 1930s were based on a need recognised, not only by performers but also by certain governments, to protect performers' rights in the light of the increased use of recording devices. The decision to protect all three beneficiaries in a single Convention was taken many years later".[98]

Following a series of conferences during the 1950s, which produced various drafts of a convention,[99] in 1960, a committee of experts convened jointly by the ILO, UNESCO and BIRPI, met at the Hague and drew up a draft convention (the Hague draft), which brought together provisions for the protection of the three future beneficiaries of the Rome Convention in one instrument and served as a basis for the work of the Diplomatic Conference in Rome the following year.

A pioneer Convention. The Rome Convention has often been referred to as a pioneer Convention in that, at the time of its adoption, it was not a Convention that merely reflected existing national legislation but it broke new ground and

24–92

[96] *per* Adam Smith, *The Wealth of Nations*, quoted by E. Thompson in: "Twenty Years of the Rome Convention: Some Personal Reflections" [1981] *Copyright* 270 at 274.
[97] *Voeux VI (Protection des fabricants des phonogrammes), VII (Protection des radioémissions) and VIII (Droits voisins du droit d'auteur et notamment protection des artistes exécutants): Documents de la Conférence réunie à Bruxelles du 5 au 26 juin 1948, Bureau de l'Union Internationale pour la protection des oeuvres littéraires et artistiques* (Berne, 1951), p.428. For Resolutions concerning the protection of performers, phonograms and broadcasts between 1927 and 1935, see pp.455 *et seq.* and 477 *et seq.*; for Resolutions on the subject adopted between 1936 and 1948, see pp.493, 505 and 509.
[98] Recommendations Concerning the Protection of Performers, Producers of Phonograms and Broadcasting Organisations, adopted in February 1979 by a Sub-committee of the Intergovernmental Committee of the Rome Convention, [1979] *Copyright* 105.
[99] Draft Conventions adopted by Committees of Experts of the ILO in 1951, [1951] *Le Droit d'Auteur*, 137 and 1956, [1956] *Le Droit d'Auteur* 93; draft prepared by a Committee of Governmental experts convened by UNESCO and the Secretariat of the Berne Union, [1957] *Le Droit d'Auteur* 72 and Supplement April 1957.

there were very few countries whose legislation was compatible with it. In this sense, it was ahead of its time and set minimum standards of protection for the three beneficiaries which governments were obliged to incorporate in their national legislation before they could adhere to it.[1] Its pioneer character, however, had the necessary corollary that, to obtain a consensus, the level of protection provided for was low.

24–93   Reasons for slow growth of membership. The Rome Convention, after its difficult birth, remained controversial. It was, and still is to some extent, opposed by organisations representing the authors and broadcasting organisations. The former opposed the granting of exclusive rights to other categories of right owners both for reasons of principle and on practical grounds. The authors have argued that the beneficiaries are not truly creative and that they should not therefore benefit from the same kind of protection as authors do. It has also been suggested that performance rights in sound recordings compete with and diminish the value of authors' performance rights.[2] The broadcasters have taken the view that the rights they enjoy under the Rome Convention are of no great benefit and have been opposed to certain of the rights of the other beneficiaries provided for in the Convention, in particular, those of performers and the concept of the payment of equitable remuneration to performers and producers for the broadcasting of sound recordings.[3]

As a result, the membership of the Convention grew slowly. 15 years after its adoption, in 1976, it had only 17 Member States. However, in the 1970s the Intergovernmental Committee of the Rome Convention acted as a catalyst for the promotion of the Convention by undertaking a series of initiatives with a view to promoting adherence to the Convention. In 1974, a model law for the implementation of the Rome Convention in national legislation was agreed by the Intergovernmental Committee[4] and endorsed by the representative organisations of the three beneficiaries of the Convention, who pledged themselves to support any legislation which might be introduced in the future based on the provisions of the model law. The European Broadcasting Union formally withdrew its opposition to the Convention, in general terms, but maintained its opposition to the provisions thereof relating to performance rights in sound recordings. Subsequently, in 1979, following an enquiry into the practical implementation of the Convention undertaken by its Intergovernmental Committee between 1975 and 1978, a series of conclusions and recommendations were adopted with the aim of promoting wider acceptance of the Convention and of providing guidance to States as to how the Convention may be applied in practice.[5]

The work undertaken to promote the Convention in the 1970s bore fruit. By its

---

[1] The Rome Convention, Art.26.

[2] This assertion has been rejected by the Intergovernmental Committee of the Rome Convention following a study of the matter: "It is therefore clear that there is no evidence to support the proposition that authors' revenue has decreased as a result of neighbouring rights ... In addition, the Sub-committee believes that a possible adverse effect on authors' royalties would not in any event constitute a sufficient reason for opposing the rights provided for in the Rome Convention since justice demands that performers and producers of phonograms should enjoy secondary rights in phonograms". Recommendations Concerning the Protection of Performers, Producers of Phonograms and Broadcasting Organisations, para.28.

[3] cf. J.F. da Costa, "Some Reflexions on the Rome Convention", [1976] Copyright 80; G. Davies, "The Rome Convention 1961—A Brief Summary of its Development and Prospects", [1979] E.I.P.R. 154; Thompson, "Twenty years of the Rome Convention: Some Personal Reflections" [1981] Copyright 270 n.195, above.

[4] Model Law Concerning the Protection of Performers, Producers of Phonograms and Broadcasting Organisations, published by ILO, UNESCO and WIPO in 1974; for text see [1974] Copyright 163.

[5] Recommendations, Concerning the Protection of Performers, Producers of Phonograms and Broadcasting Organisations, above.

20th anniversary in October 1981, its membership had grown to 32 and, as of August 20, 2004, the Convention had 77 Member States.

Present relevance of the Convention. Although the possibility of revision of the Convention is foreseen,[6] no revision has taken place in spite of the fact that technical developments have greatly reduced the value of its protection to the three beneficiaries. The main reason for a reluctance to revise the Convention is the fear that the compromise it represented between conflicting interests would be reopened and that the balance achieved therein between those interests risked being upset in any revision. However this may be, the Rome Convention is outdated in many respects. The extent of the protection provided for in the Convention and the balance of interests among the three beneficiaries reflected in the Convention were determined in the light of the technology existing and foreseen in 1961. "… Technological development in the past two decades in the areas of concern to the beneficiaries has occurred at an unprecedented pace and has introduced new techniques (especially satellites, cable television, videograms) none of which could have been foreseen at the time of the drafting of the Convention".[7] Nearly two further decades have passed since the Intergovernmental Committee of the Rome Convention made that statement and the proliferation of new technologies affecting the rights of the three beneficiaries of the Rome Convention have grown exponentially. These problems have recently been considered in the context of the new WIPO Performances and Phonograms Treaty 1996, discussed below in section 7 of this Chapter.

24–94

Under the auspices of WIPO, since 1997 consideration has been given to the adoption of a new instrument aimed at strengthening the protection of the rights of broadcasting organisations. It is recognised that new technological developments have changed both the ways in which broadcast signals are transmitted and the potential means by which such signals can be retransmitted by third parties and that the rights of broadcasters need to be reassessed. There is a growing signal piracy problem in many parts of the world, including piracy of digitised pre-broadcast signals, which has made this need more acute.To date there is no draft instrument. However, in June 2004, WIPO's Standing Committee on Copyright and Related Rights (SCCR) adopted a Recommendation calling on WIPO's governing body to convene a diplomatic conference at an appropriate time. Meanwhile, the SCCR will discuss a new draft instrument at a meeting scheduled to take place in November 2004 and is expected to recommend dates for the proposed diplomatic conference.[8]

B. SUBSTANTIVE PROVISIONS

Definition of the beneficiaries of the Rome Convention. As already mentioned, the Convention deals with the rights of three beneficiaries: performers, producers of phonograms and broadcasting organisations.

24–95

Performers are defined as: "actors, singers, musicians, dancers, and other persons who act, sing, deliver, declaim, play in, or otherwise perform literary or

---

[6] Rome Convention, Art.32(1)(b).

[7] *cf.*, Recommendations Concerning the Protection of Performers, Producers of Phonograms a d Broadcasting Organisations, above.

[8] WIPO Press Release 386/2004 of June 10, 2004. See also on the current state of negotiations, R. Owens, "Protection of the Rights of Broadcasting Organisations", paper presented at the Fordham University School of Law, Twelfth Annual Conference on International Intellectual Property Law and Policy, April 2004. A consolidated text of treaty proposals is available on the WIPO website (*www.wipo.int/news/en/conferences.html*).

artistic works".[9] The limitation to artists who perform literary and artistic works results in the exclusion of variety and circus artists but the Convention provides that a state may extend protection to such artists.[10]

The term *producer of phonograms* requires explanation. A phonogram, in plain terms, is an original sound recording which is reproduced and made available to the public in the form of records (LPs, CDs, minidiscs) cassettes or other media such as DVDs. The Convention defines it as follows: "'phonogram' means any exclusively aural fixation of sounds of a performance or of other sounds".[11] This means mainly recordings of performances of music or the spoken word but also covers recordings of other sounds such as bird song, wildlife sounds and sound effects. The "producer of phonograms" means "the person who, or the legal entity which, first fixes the sounds of a performance or other sounds".[12] In practice, this is usually a record company although there are also many independent producers who produce original recordings and then sell or license them to record companies.

Broadcasting organisations needs no explanation but the definition of broadcasting has given rise to some difficulty. It is defined in the Convention as meaning "the transmission by wireless means for public reception of sound or of images and sounds".[13] Technical developments since 1961 have rendered the definition restrictive in that, for example, cable distribution of broadcasts is excluded. It has also been argued that transmission of broadcast programmes by satellite is not covered,[14] although a majority of the members of the Intergovernmental Committee of the Rome Convention take the view that the definition of the Convention does include satellite transmissions.[15]

24–96   **National treatment.** The protection given by the Convention is based on the principle of national treatment, which means the treatment accorded by the domestic law of the Contracting State in which protection is claimed. Thus, each Contracting State extends the same protection to beneficiaries from other Contracting States as it does to its own nationals.[16] National treatment is that accorded by the Contracting State (i) to performers who are its nationals, as regards performances taking place, broadcast, or first fixed on its territory; to producers of phonograms who are its nationals, as regards phonograms first fixed or first published on its territory; to broadcasting organisations which have their headquarters on its territory, as regards broadcasts transmitted from transmitters situated on its territory. Contracting States shall grant national treatment to performers if any of the following conditions are met: the performance takes place in another Contracting State; the performance is incorporated in a phonogram which

---

[9] Rome Convention, Art.3(a).

[10] Art.9.

[11] Art.3(b).

[12] Art.3(c).

[13] Art.3(f).

[14] According to the European Broadcasting Union: " Article 13 does not protect broadcasters against distribution by cable, and this is so serious a deficiency that, in Europe, at least, the broadcasting organisations have had to seek a remedy from the Council of Europe under the aegis of which an intergovernmental agreement [European Agreement on the Protection of Television Broadcasts, see para. 24–167, below] has come into existence whose main object is to protect television broadcasts against cable distribution. Nor is the Rome Convention applicable to the transport of programmes by satellite, and a separate convention concluded in 1974 was needed to shore up this gap in protection" [Convention Relating to the Distribution of Programme-Carrying Signals Transmitted by Satellite, see paras 24–155 et seq., below]. (See EBU observations on the Implementation of the Rome Convention, Annex II of doc. ILO/UNESCO/WIPO/ICR/SC.1/IMP/2, 1979.)

[15] See Report of the Fourth Ordinary Session of the Intergovernmental Committee of the Rome Convention, [1974] *Copyright* 41, paras 19 et seq.

[16] Rome Convention, Art.2.

is protected under the Convention; the performance, not being fixed on a phonogram, is carried by a broadcast protected by the Convention.[17] The points of attachment for the protection of producers of phonograms are the following: the producer is a national of another Contracting State (criterion of nationality); the first fixation of the sound was made in another Contracting State (criterion of fixation)[18]; the phonogram was first published in another Contracting State (criterion of publication).[19] The criterion of publication includes simultaneous publication in a Contracting State within 30 days of first publication.[20] The points of attachment for national treatment for broadcasters are either that the headquarters of the broadcasting organisation is situated in another Contracting State or that the broadcast was transmitted from a transmitter situated in another Contracting State.[21]

The general rule of national treatment may be modified, however, by principles of reciprocity with regard to the performance rights in phonograms provided for under Article 12, since States are permitted to make various reservations concerning these rights and the rights of broadcasters with respect to the performance in public of their television broadcasts, which include limiting protection by insisting on material reciprocity. This also applies to the duration of Article 12 rights.[22]

Performers' rights. The principal protection provided for performers in the Convention is contained in Article 7, which gives performers the possibility of preventing certain acts done without their consent: for example, the broadcasting and communication to the public of their live performance; the fixation of their unfixed performance; the reproduction of a fixation of their performance, subject to certain conditions. However, once a performer has consented to the incorporation of his performance in a visual or audiovisual fixation, Article 7 has no further application.[23] These rights are not exclusive rights to authorise or prohibit the acts in question. The protection is defined as giving performers "the possibility of preventing" the acts in question; this means that Member States are free to protect performers not only by means of specific rights, but also by the application of the laws of unfair competition or the imposition of criminal sanctions. Indeed, prior to the 1988 Act, the United Kingdom protected performers by means of criminal sanctions.[24]   **24–97**

Rights of producers of phonograms. The exclusive rights of producers of phonograms are dealt with in Article 10, which gives them the right to authorise or prohibit the direct or indirect reproduction of their phonograms. This is the right that enables producers to combat piracy, counterfeiting and the like.   **24–98**

Performance rights in phonograms. Article 12 provides for performance rights in phonograms and concerns both performers and producers of phonograms. Article 12 provides a right to equitable remuneration in favour of producers of phonograms, or performers, or both, for the use of phonograms both for public performances (such as at cafés, hotels, theatres, in juke boxes and other public   **24–99**

---

[17] Art.4.

[18] Art.17 provides that any state that, on the date of the adoption of the Convention on October 26, 1961, granted protection to producers of phonograms solely on the basis of the criterion of fixation may declare that it will apply the criterion of fixation alone.

[19] Art.5.

[20] Art.5(2).

[21] Art.6. However, a Contracting State may declare that it will protect broadcasters only if the headquarters of the broadcasting organisation is situated in another Contracting State and the broadcast was transmitted from a transmitter situated in the same Contracting State.

[22] Art.16(1)(a)(iv) and (b).

[23] Rome Convention, Art.19.

[24] See Ch.12, above.

places) and in broadcasting, by sound or television services. States are, however, free to reserve Article 12 altogether or to give the right to producers alone, to performers alone, or to give the right to one with the obligation to share with the other or to both with the obligation to share equally. States, therefore, have a great deal of freedom as to how they apply Article 12. It should also be noted that unlike the performance rights of authors under the copyright conventions, Article 12 does not give performers and producers of phonograms the right to authorise or prohibit the communication to the public or the broadcasting of their phonograms, but gives a mere right to receive equitable remuneration. This differs from the position in the United Kingdom where, since 1934, the producers' right to authorise or prohibit such use has been recognised.[25]

24-100   **Exclusive rights of broadcasting organisations.** Article 13 deals with the rights of broadcasting organisations which are granted the right to authorise or prohibit: the rebroadcasting of their broadcasts; the fixation of their broadcasts; the reproduction of fixations of their broadcasts made without their consent; and the communication to the public of their television broadcasts, if such communication is made in places accessible to the public against payment of an entrance fee.

24-101   **Duration.** The minimum term of protection provided for by the Convention is 20 years computed from the end of the year in which:

    (a) the fixation was made, for phonograms and performances incorporated therein;

    (b) the performance took place, for performances not incorporated in phonograms;

    (c) the broadcast took place, for broadcasts.

24-102   **Common provisions.** Certain exceptions to the protection granted by the Convention are permitted as regards private use; use of short excerpts in connection with the reporting of current events; ephemeral fixations made by broadcasting organisations, by means of their own facilities and for their own broadcasts; use solely for the purposes of teaching or scientific research. Moreover, a Contracting State may provide for the same kinds of limitations with regard to the beneficiaries of the Convention as are permitted in connection with copyright in literary or artistic works.[26]

24-103   **Formalities.** Where Contracting States require compliance with formalities as a condition of protection in relation to phonograms, these shall be considered as fulfilled if all authorised duplicates of the phonogram or their containers bear a notice consisting of the symbol vP, accompanied by the year date of the first publication. The container or notice must also identify the producer, his successor in title or his exclusive licensee.[27]

24-104   **No retroactivity.** The Convention has no retroactive effect; rights acquired before the date it comes into force for any state are not prejudiced and no state is obliged to apply its provisions before that date.[28]

C. RELATIONSHIP WITH THE BERNE CONVENTION

24-105   **Safeguard for authors' rights.** The relationship of the Rome Convention with that of Berne is dealt with in Article 1 of the Convention which contains a safeguard for copyright proper, providing that the:

---

[25] See Ch.3, above.
[26] Rome Convention, Art.15.
[27] Rome Convention, Art.11.
[28] Rome Convention, Art.20.

"Protection granted under this Convention shall leave intact and shall in no way affect the protection of copyright in literary and artistic works. Consequently, no provision of this Convention may be interpreted as prejudicing such protection".

This is a key provision of the Rome Convention. Throughout the long negotiations leading to the adoption of the Convention, the authors' societies had:

"looked with some fear and suspicion on the proposals to protect the neighbouring rights. They claimed that a convention on this subject was useless or at least superfluous; most problems could be dealt with by contract; and in any case it was premature since the function of international treaties was to follow, and not to precede, national legislation, and, on this subject, few countries had passed laws. This being so, these bodies were determined to maintain the integrity of copyright, fearing the impact the creation of these new rights would have on the rights authors already enjoyed".[29]

Two examples of the kind of situation which the authors had in mind and in which conflict may arise will illustrate the problem. The first is where, as a result of the beneficiaries of the Rome Convention having rights, more than one authorisation becomes necessary for the use of a work, for example, where both the author of a work and the producer of a phonogram incorporating the work have the right to authorise a use such as broadcasting or rental. It has been argued that, if the author wishes to authorise the use but the producer refuses, this "affects" the rights of the author because the exercise of the right is prevented. Secondly, users may require two licences in respect of performance rights, one from the authors'society and one from the society representing producers and/or performers; here the authors feared that their income from this source would therefore be diminished.

Thus, Article 1 was introduced as a preliminary provision to make it clear that the legal situation of the copyright owner is unaffected by the rights of the beneficiaries of the Rome Convention. However, the possible effects of the Convention on the economic interests of authors is another matter.[30] Article 1 does not mean that the rights of the beneficiaries of the Rome Convention must be subordinated to the exercise of the rights of authors. As Masouyé stated:

"It does not proclaim [copyright's] superiority by laying down that neighbouring rights may never be stronger in content or scope than those enjoyed by authors ... Whenever, by virtue of the copyright law, the authorization of the author is necessary for the reproduction or other use of his work, the need for this authorisation is not affected by the Convention. Conversely, when, by virtue of this Convention, the consent of the performer, recorder or broadcaster is necessary, the need for his consent does not disappear because authorisation by the author is also necessary".[31]

It is clear that this does not altogether solve the authors' problem, since the *existence* of other rights may have an impact on the *exercise* of their rights. It would hardly be equitable, however, if they had won the argument on this point and succeeded in preventing the present beneficiaries of the Rome Convention from obtaining any protection.

Closed Convention. A further safeguard for authors is built into the Rome Convention. Only states which are members of either the Berne Convention or of the Universal Copyright Convention may adhere to it; it is thus a so-called closed convention, the aim of the relevant provisions being to ensure that no state will

24–106

---

[29] WIPO RC and PC Guide, para.1.4.
[30] Records of the Rome Conference, p.38; WIPO RC and PC Guide, para.1.5.
[31] WIPO RC and PC Guide, paras 1.10 and 1.12. See also Records of the Rome Conference, p.38.

protect the beneficiaries of the Rome Convention without already having in place legislation for the protection of authors.[32] Thus so-called neighbouring rights may not be given precedence over copyright.

D. PARTIES TO THE ROME CONVENTION

24–107   **States which may adhere to the Convention.** The Convention is open to adherence by any state member of the United Nations, which is also a member of the Berne Convention or the Universal Copyright Convention. It entered into force three months after the date of deposit of the sixth instrument of ratification, acceptance or accession on May 18, 1964.

24–108   **Present membership.** As of August 20, 2004, the following 77 states were party to the Convention: Albania, Argentina, Armenia, Australia, Austria, Barbados, Belarus, Belgium, Bolivia, Brazil, Bulgaria, Burkina Faso, Canada, Cape Verde, Chile, Colombia, Congo, Costa Rica, Croatia, Czech Republic, Denmark, Dominica, Dominican Republic, Ecuador, El Salvador, Estonia, Fiji, Finland, France, Germany, Greece, Guatemala, Honduras, Hungary, Iceland, Ireland, Israel, Italy, Jamaica, Japan, Kyrgyzstan (from August 13, 2003), Latvia, Lebanon, Lesotho, Liechtenstein, Lithuania, Luxembourg, Macedonia (the former Yugoslav Republic of), Mexico, Monaco, the Netherlands (for the Kingdom in Europe), Nicaragua, Niger, Nigeria, Norway, Panama, Paraguay, Peru, Philippines, Poland, Portugal, Republic of Moldova, Romania, Russian Federation, Saint Lucia, Serbia and Montenegro, Slovakia, Slovenia, Spain, Sweden, Switzerland, Togo, Turkey, Ukraine, United Kingdom, Uruguay and Venezuela.[33] .

6. THE PHONOGRAMS CONVENTION

A. HISTORY

24–109   **The Convention for the Protection of Producers of Phonograms Against Unauthorised Duplication of their Phonograms** (the Phonograms Convention) was adopted on October 29, 1971, in Geneva, at a Diplomatic Conference convened jointly by the United Nations Organisation for Education, Science and Culture (UNESCO) and the World Intellectual Property Organisation (WIPO).[34] The purpose of the Convention was limited and specific: to provide international protection against what had become during the late 1960s the widespread and increasing problem of piracy of phonograms.[35] Piracy may be defined as the manufacture of duplicates of legitimately produced phonograms without the authorisation of the original producer of the phonogram and the importation, distri-

---

[32] Rome Convention, Art.23 (on signature and deposit) and Art.24 (on ratification and accession).

[33] Under the Rome Convention, Member States may make certain reservations. A complete list of these reservations appears at *www.wipo.org/treaties/documents/english/word/k-rome.doc.*

[34] *Records of the International Conference of States on the Protection of Phonograms*, Geneva, October 18 to 29, 1971, UNESCO, WIPO, 1975. See also A.L. Kaminstein, "Convention for the Protection of Producers of Phonograms Against Unauthorised Duplication of their Phonograms" 19 *Bulletin of the Copyright Society of the USA* [1972] 175; E. Ulmer, "The Convention for the Protection of Producers of Phonograms Against Unauthorised Duplication of their Phonograms" [1972] 3 I.I.C. 317; S. Ricketson, *The Berne Convention for the protection of literary and artistic works: 1886–1896* (Queen Mary College, University of London, 1987), para.15.55, *et seq.;* Stewart, *International Copyright and Neighbouring Rights,* (Butterworths, London, 1983), Ch.9.

[35] Film and video piracy was excluded from the outset. Cinematographic works are protected under the Berne and Universal Copyright Conventions and governments took the view that authors of such works, including film producers as copyright owners or successors in title to the authors of such works, were adequately protected against piracy under national legislation and the copyright conventions.

bution, or sale to the public of such unlawful duplicates for commercial gain.[36] It was generally recognised that piracy damages the interests not only of the producers of phonograms but also those of the authors and performers whose works and performances are incorporated in phonograms, since the pirate who copies phonograms pays nothing to the authors and composers whose music and lyrics are copied, nothing to the recording artists and musicians and, nothing, of course, to the producer of the legitimate recording. Better protection against piracy would, therefore, be in the long-term interests of all these categories of right owners.

The need for the Convention. International action to combat piracy was first **24–110** called for at a meeting of experts, which had gathered in 1970 to prepare for the revision of the Berne and Universal Copyright Conventions, due to take place the following year. In view of the urgency of the piracy problem, a committee of governmental experts convened by UNESCO and WIPO met in March 1971 and prepared a draft convention, which served as the basis for the Diplomatic Conference held later that same year. The speed with which agreement was reached on this international instrument was unprecedented, reflecting the serious nature of the problem. While authors and composers had legal protection against piracy of their works incorporated in phonograms under national laws and the Berne and Universal Copyright Conventions, Governments recognised that the existing international conventions did not provide those most affected, the producers of phonograms themselves, with adequate legal tools to deal with the widespread piracy which was destroying their markets. The Rome Convention provided producers of phonograms with the right to authorise or prohibit the direct or indirect reproduction of their phonograms, but did not provide any protection in respect of importation or distribution of unauthorised copies, unless these acts were linked with the act of reproduction itself. Moreover, the Rome Convention was open only to Member States of the Berne and Universal Copyright Conventions and had a very limited membership at the time, only 11 Member States in 1971, whereas piracy was and remains an international problem requiring the co-operation of as many countries as possible worldwide.

Furthermore, national legislation protecting phonograms varied greatly. Some countries protected them by means of specific rights: copyright or related rights; others protected them under the law of unfair competition or by means of penal sanctions. International protection was afforded in common law countries under the Berne and Universal Copyright Conventions on the basis of national treatment under these conventions, while elsewhere the only international protection available to producers was afforded by the Rome Convention. The proponents of the Phonograms Convention, therefore, sought an urgent solution by means of a new, simple international instrument, which as many countries as possible would be able to join. Such an instrument with a broad membership would create "a kind of *cordon sanitaire...* by providing that in case of an unauthorised duplica-

---

[36] Two different kinds of piracy of phonograms should be distinguished: "Piracy"— *stricto sensu*—is the unauthorised duplication of an original phonogram distributed to the public with labels, artwork, trade marks and packaging different from, although often similar to, those of the original legitimate phonogram; the legitimate producer's trade mark is not used. "Counterfeiting" is the unauthorised duplication and distribution of an original phonogram and its packaging as a whole. The legitimate producer's original label, artwork, trade marks and packaging are copied as well as the sounds contained in the original legitimate recording. A third illegal activity is also described as piracy, namely "bootlegging", which means the unauthorised recording of an artist's performance. Bootlegging is not covered by the Phonograms Convention. *cf.* G. Davies, "Piracy of Phonograms" (2nd ed., ESC Publishing Ltd., Oxford, 1986) pp.4 *et seq.*, and generally.

tion the importation and distribution in the Contracting States can also be prohibited".[37]

B. SUBSTANTIVE PROVISIONS

24–111 **Obligations of Member States.** The heart of the Convention is Article 2 which establishes the obligations of Member States as to whom they must protect and against what:

"Each Contracting State shall protect producers of phonograms who are nationals of other Contracting States against the making of duplicates without the consent of the producer and against the importation of such duplicates, provided that any such making or importation is for the purpose of distribution to the public, and against the distribution of such duplicates to the public".

The terms "producers of phonograms" and "phonograms" are defined in the same way as in the Rome Convention,[38] and the only criterion for protection is the producers' nationality. Unlike the Rome Convention, the Phonograms Convention is not based on national treatment. Contracting States are obliged to provide the required protection to nationals of other Contracting States regardless of their domestic law. This obligation may have the result that foreign repertoire from another Contracting State of the Phonograms Convention enjoys a higher standard of protection than national repertoire. The means by which the Phonograms Convention is to be implemented is left by its Article 3 to the domestic law of each Contracting State and shall include one or more of the following: protection by means of the grant of a copyright or other specific right, which secure an exclusive right to the producer; protection by means of the law relating to unfair competition; protection by penal sanctions. The term "other specific right" refers to rights in the nature of copyright or authors' rights but known as "neighbouring" or "related" rights. Unfair competition is defined in the Paris Convention for the Protection of Industrial Property as meaning "any act of competition contrary to honest practices in industrial or commercial matters".[39] As far as penal sanctions are concerned, any state choosing this method of protection must make it a criminal offence to do any of the acts referred to in Article 2 punishable by fines and imprisonment.

24–112 **Duration of the protection.** Like in the Rome Convention, the minimum term of protection under the Convention is 20 years. This may be computed either from the end of the year of first fixation, as in the Rome Convention, or of the year in which the phonogram was first published.[40] However, the 20-year minimum only applies if the national law prescribes a specific term. Thus, the Convention recognised the fact that under the law of unfair competition, for example, protection may not be limited in time. The Convention does not provide for material reciprocity with regard to term.

24–113 **Formalities and exceptions.** Where Contracting States require compliance with formalities as a condition of protection in relation to phonograms, as in the Rome Convention, these shall be considered as fulfilled if all authorised duplicates of the phonogram or their containers bear a notice consisting of the symbol (P), accompanied by the year date of first publication. The container or notice must also

---

[37] Ulmer, "The Convention for the Protection of Producers of Phonograms Against Unauthorised Duplication of their Phonograms" [1972] 3.I.I.C., 317, para.4.

[38] Phonograms Convention, Art.1, Rome Convention, Art.3.

[39] Paris Convention, Art.10 *bis*.

[40] Phonograms Convention, Art.4.

identify the producer, his successor in title or his exclusive licensee.[41] The Convention also provides that Contracting States may make the same kinds of limitations as are permitted with respect to the protection of authors of literary and artistic works. However, no compulsory licences are allowed, except in the following circumstances: the duplication is for use solely for the purpose of teaching or scientific research; the licence is valid only within the territory of the Contracting State whose competent authority has granted the licence and shall not extend to the export of duplicates; and finally any such licence must give rise to equitable remuneration.[42]

No retroactivity. Like the Rome Convention, there is no obligation to afford the protection of the Convention retroactively to phonograms fixed before the Convention entered into force with respect to them, although Contracting States are free to do so, if they so wish.[43]   **24–114**

C. RELATIONSHIP WITH THE COPYRIGHT CONVENTIONS AND THE ROME CONVENTION

Safeguard for copyright and related rights. The Convention contains a clause for the safeguard of copyright and related rights, providing that the Convention shall in no way be interpreted to limit or prejudice the protection otherwise secured to authors, to performers, to producers of phonograms or to broadcasting organisations under any domestic law or international agreement.[44] The relevant international agreements are the Berne Convention, the Universal Copyright Convention, the Rome Convention and the Paris Convention. A further link with these agreements is provided by the fact that WIPO provides the administration for all services relating to the Convention and its Secretariat.[45]   **24–115**

Relationship to the Rome Convention. The reasons why it was considered necessary to adopt a special Convention to deal with piracy have been noted in para.24–110, above. The Convention is not a special agreement concluded under Article 22 of the Rome Convention; such a special agreement would have been limited to the existing Member States of the Rome Convention and, as seen above, the Phonograms Convention was intended to be open to adherence by as many states as possible. The Convention may be seen, therefore, as complementary to that of Rome. It contains no provision which is contrary thereto. So far as states which are party to both Conventions are concerned, the relations between them will be governed by both Conventions. Article 21 of Rome provides that the protection provided by that Convention shall not prejudice any protection otherwise secured to performers, producers of phonograms and broadcasting organisations. This being so, countries party to both conventions must each accord the other the benefits of both cumulatively, applying whichever gives the greater protection.[46] There is also a safeguard clause for performers, confirming that Contracting States are free to legislate as they see fit for the protection of performers whose performances are recorded on phonograms.[47]   **24–116**

---

[41] Phonograms Convention, Art.5.
[42] Phonograms Convention,, Art.6.
[43] Phonograms Convention, Art.7(3).
[44] Phonograms Convention, Art.7 (1).
[45] Phonograms Convention, Art.8.
[46] *cf. WIPO RC and PC Guide*, para.7.5.
[47] Phonograms Convention, Art.7(2).

D. PARTIES TO THE PHONOGRAMS CONVENTION

24–117 **States which may adhere to the Convention.** Unlike the Rome Convention whose membership is limited to states members of one or other of the two copyright conventions, and in order to secure the greatest possible number of Contracting States so as to put an end to international piracy, the Convention is open to adherence by any state member of the United Nations, or of any of its Specialised Agencies, or of the International Atomic Energy Agency, or any state party to the Statute of the International Court of Justice. Any state joining the Convention must be in a position to give effect to its obligations under the Convention in accordance with its domestic law.[48]

24–118 **Entry into force and membership.** The Convention came into force following the deposit of the fifth instrument of ratification or accession on April 18, 1973. Membership of the Convention grew relatively quickly and, as ofAugust 20, 2004, the following 73 states were party to the Convention: Albania, Argentina, Armenia, Australia, Austria, Azerbaijan, Barbados, Belarus, Brazil, Bulgaria, Burkina Faso, Chile, China,[49] Colombia, Costa Rica, Croatia, Cyprus, Czech Republic, Democratic Republic of the Congo, Denmark, Ecuador, Egypt, El Salvador, Estonia, Fiji, Finland,[50] France, Germany, Greece, Guatemala, the Holy See, Honduras, Hungary, India, Israel, Italy,[51] Jamaica, Japan, Kazakhstan, Kenya, Kyrgyzstan, Latvia, Liechtenstein, Lithuania, Luxembourg, Macedonia (the former Yugoslav Republic of), Mexico, Monaco, the Netherlands (for the Kingdom in Europe), New Zealand, Nicaragua, Norway, Panama, Paraguay, Peru, Republic of Korea, Republic of Moldova, Romania, Russian Federation, Saint Lucia, Serbia and Montenegro, Slovakia, Slovenia, Spain, Sweden, Switzerland, Togo,Trinidad and Tobago, United Kingdom, United States of America, Ukraine, Uruguay and Venezuela.

7. WIPO PERFORMANCES AND PHONOGRAMS TREATY 1996

A. HISTORY

24–119 **Background.** The advances in technology of recent years have revolutionised the media and the means of exploitation of works protected by copyright and the subject-matter of related rights. The events leading to the adoption of the new WIPO Treaties on Copyright and Performances and Phonograms have been described in section 3 of this Chapter. As there mentioned, in 1992, a separate Committee of Experts on a Possible Instrument for the Protection of the Rights of Performers and Producers of Phonograms was established to discuss all questions concerning the effective international protection of the rights of performers and producers of phonograms.[52] The first session of the Committee of Experts on

---

[48] Phonograms Convention, Art.9(4).

[49] The Phonograms Convention applies also to the Hong Kong Special Administrative Region of China with effect from July 1, 1997.

[50] Finland has declared, in accordance with Art.7(4) of the Convention, that it will apply the criterion according to which it affords protection to producers of phonograms solely on the basis of the place of first fixation instead of the criterion of the nationality of the producer.

[51] Like Finland, Italy has declared in accordance with Art.7(4) of the Convention that it will apply the criterion according to which it affords protection to producers of phonograms solely on the basis of the place of first fixation instead of the criterion of the nationality of the producer.

[52] Terms of Reference of the Committee of Experts on a Possible Instrument on the Protection of the Rights of Performers and Producers of Phonograms, see "Questions Concerning a Possible

the Possible Instrument was held in 1993[53] and altogether six sessions were held.[54] The WIPO Performances and Phonograms Treaty was adopted by the Diplomatic Conference on Certain Copyright and Neighbouring Rights Questions, held in Geneva in December 1996, which also adopted the WIPO Copyright Treaty.

The question of the protection of producers of phonograms was removed from the terms of reference of the Committee of Experts on a Possible Protocol to the Berne Convention because agreement could not be reached on including such rights in the Protocol. Civil law countries which protect producers of phonograms by means of related rights objected, in principle, to producers' rights being dealt with in the context of the Berne Convention. At the same time, there was agreement that it would not be appropriate to discuss questions related to the protection of producers of phonograms without also discussing the protection of performers, whose performances are embodied in phonograms.[55] Thus, the decision not to consider the rights of producers of phonograms and performers in the context of the Protocol to the Berne Convention was influenced by the international classification of the rights of producers and performers as related rights protected by the Rome Convention, rather than authors' rights or copyrights, protected by the Berne Convention.

The most important issues to be discussed in relation to the new instrument were the following: of specific interest to performers, moral rights, the economic rights of performers in their unfixed (live) performances; of interest to both categories of right owners were, rights of reproduction, modification, rights of distribution and importation, rights to make available phonograms and performances to the public for interactive and on-demand access systems, rental rights, rights to remuneration for broadcasting or communication to the public, term of protection and enforcement of rights. There was broad agreement that the level of protection provided for producers and performers under the Rome and Phonograms Conventions was in need of improvement to bring the protection into line with the realities of contemporary technology, which had created new means for creating, storing, performing and disseminating phonograms and performances. However, the question whether the rights of performers in respect of audiovisual fixations, *i.e.* in film, television broadcasts and video, should be covered by the new instrument was and remained controversial until the closing stages of the Diplomatic Conference in 1996; in the event, as a result of the sustained opposition of the film and broadcasting industries, the decision was made to confine the Treaty to performances fixed in phonograms.

Relation to the WIPO Copyright Treaty. The Performances and Phonograms   **24–120** Treaty parallels many of the provisions of the WIPO Copyright Treaty. The Preamble of the new Treaty reflects the concern to update and strengthen the protection of producers and performers by recognising the need to introduce new international rules to provide adequate solutions to the questions raised by economic, social, cultural and technological developments, and the profound impact of the development and convergence of information and communication technologies on the production and use of performances and phonograms.

As in the case of the WIPO Copyright Treaty, a series of agreed statements

---

Instrument for the Protection of the Rights of Performers and Producers of Phonograms", para.5 (WIPO Memorandum, [1993] *Copyright* 142).

[53] Report of the First Session, Geneva, June 28 to July 2, 1993, [1993] *Copyright* 196.

[54] November 1993, [1994] *Copyright* 44; December 1994, [1995] *Industrial Property and Copyright* 110; September 1995, [1995] *Industrial Property and Copyright* 425; February 1996, [1996] *Industrial Property and Copyright* 118; and May 1996, [1996] *Industrial Property and Copyright* 236.

[55] WIPO memorandum, [1993] *Copyright* 142.

were adopted at the same time as the WIPO Performances and Phonograms Treaty concerning the interpretation of the various articles of the Treaty. The following analysis of the Treaty takes account of these statements.[56]

B. SUBSTANTIVE PROVISIONS

24–121   **Beneficiaries of the Convention**. The beneficiaries of protection under the Treaty are performers and producers of phonograms, as defined in the Treaty. These definitions differ from those of the Rome Convention. That of performers is expanded to include those who perform expressions of folklore in addition to literary or artistic works. The new definition of "producer of phonograms" does not appear to involve any substantive change. The definition reads: "'Producer of a phonogram' means the person, or the legal entity, who or which takes the initiative and has the responsibility for the first fixation of the sounds of a performance or other sounds, or the representations of sounds". The words "or the representations of sounds" are new. The definition of phonogram is also new. In the Rome and Phonograms Conventions, "'phonogram' means any exclusively aural fixation of sounds of a performance or of other sounds"; the words "exclusively aural" have been deleted and the following words added at the end of the definition instead: "other than in the form of a fixation incorporated in a cinematographic or other audiovisual work". This is clarified by an agreed statement according to which this definition "does not suggest that rights in the phonogram are in any way affected through their incorporation into a cinematographic or other audiovisual work".

The performers and producers protected are nationals of the Contracting Parties, who would meet the criteria for eligibility for protection provided for by the Rome Convention (see para.24-00, above). In relation to these criteria, which include the criteria of nationality, fixation and publication, definitions are provided of fixation[57] and publication. Fixation is not defined in either the Rome or Phonograms Conventions. Here it is defined as "the embodiment of sounds, or of the representations thereof, from which they can be perceived, reproduced or communicated through a device"[58] and an agreed statement provides a further explanation of the term: "it is understood that fixation means the finalisation of the master tape ('bande-mère')".[59] Publication of a fixed performance or a phonogram means the offering of copies of the fixed performance or the phonogram to the public, *with the consent of the right holder*, and provided that copies are offered to the public in reasonable quantity.[60] The words in italics are new as compared to the definition of the Rome and Phonograms Conventions.

24–122   **National treatment.** Protection under the Treaty is based on the principle of national treatment, defined as meaning Contracting Parties shall accord to nationals of other Contracting Parties the treatment it accords to its own nationals with

---

[56] See also the following accounts of the results of the Diplomatic Conference: "WIPO Diplomatic Conference on Certain Copyright and Neighbouring Rights Questions" [1997] *Copyright* 97; J. Reinbothe, M. Martin-Prat and S. von Lewinski, "The New WIPO Treaties: A First Résumé" [1997] 4 *E.I.P.R.* 171; T.C. Vinje, "The New WIPO Copyright Treaty: A Happy Result in Geneva, [1997] 5 *E.I.P.R.* 230, M. Fabiani, "The Geneva Diplomatic Conference on Copyright and the Rights of Performers and Phonogram Producers" [1997] 3 Ent. L.R. 98; V. A. Espinel, "Harmony on the Internet: The WIPO Performances and Phonograms Treaty and United Kingdom Copyright Law" [1998] Ent. L.R. 21. See also J. Reinbothe and S. von Lewinski, "The WIPO Treaties 1996: Ready to Come into Force" [2002] E.I.P.R. 199.

[57] The possibility of applying only the criterion of fixation in accordance with Art.17 of the Rome Convention is maintained (Treaty, Art.3(3)).

[58] Treaty, Art.2(c).

[59] Statement concerning Art.3(2).

[60] Treaty, Art.3(e).

regard to the exclusive rights specifically granted in the Treaty, subject to certain permitted reservations concerning performance rights in phonograms.[61]

Performers' rights. Moral rights are recognised in favour of performers for the   **24–123**
first time at international level, as regards a performer's live aural performances fixed in phonograms.[62] A performer has the right to be identified as the performer of his performances, except where omission is dictated by the manner of the use of the performance, and to object to any distortion, mutilation or other modification of his performances that would be prejudicial to his reputation. If the legislation of the Contracting Party permits, such rights may also be maintained after the performer's death.

Performers are also guaranteed certain exclusive rights for the first time by international treaty. These are the exclusive right of authorising:

(i) the broadcasting and communication to the public of their unfixed performances (except where the performance is already a broadcast performance) and the fixation of their unfixed performances[63];

(ii) the direct or indirect reproduction of their performances fixed in phonograms in any manner or form[64];

(iii) subject to national rules relating to exhaustion of rights, the making available to the public of the original and copies of their performances fixed in phonograms through sale or other transfer of ownership[65];

(iv) the commercial rental to the public of the original and copies of their performances fixed in phonograms, except that a Contracting Party that has a system of equitable remuneration of performers for the rental of copies of their performances may maintain such a system, provided that the commercial rental of phonograms is not giving rise to the material impairment of the exclusive right of reproduction of performers[66];

(v) the making available to the public of their performances fixed in phonograms, by wire or wireless means, in such a way that members of the public may access them from a place and at a time individually chosen by them.[67]

Rights of producers of phonograms. Producers of phonograms are guaranteed   **24–124**
the following exclusive rights to authorise:

(i) the direct or indirect reproduction of their phonograms, in any manner or form[68];

(ii) subject to national rules of exhaustion of rights, the making available to the public of the original and copies of their phonograms through sale or other transfer of ownership (right of distribution)[69];

(iii) subject to the same proviso mentioned above in relation to performers, the commercial rental to the public of the original and copies of their phonograms[70];

(iv) the making available to the public of their phonograms, by wire or wire-

---

[61] Treaty, Art.4.
[62] Treaty, Art.5.
[63] Treaty, Art.6.
[64] Treaty, Art.7.
[65] Treaty, Art.8.
[66] Treaty, Art.9.
[67] Treaty, Art.10.
[68] Treaty, Art.11.
[69] Treaty, Art.12.
[70] Treaty, Art.13.

less means, in such a way that members of the public may access them from a place and at a time individually chosen by them.[71]

For the first time, performers are granted an exclusive right to reproduction of their performances by international convention. Under the Rome Convention,[72] the rights afforded to performers were not exclusive rights but the possibility of preventing the doing of certain acts without their consent. The reason for this was to leave complete freedom of choice as to the means used to implement the Convention to the Member States.

The words "in any manner or form" in the reproduction rights of both performers and producers are new as compared with the Rome and Phonograms Conventions.[73] This expression is already found in Article 9(1) of the Berne Convention concerning the right of reproduction enjoyed by authors. It has been included to make it clear that there is no difference between the rights of the beneficiaries and those of authors in this respect.[74] An agreed statement clarifies the extent of the reproduction rights granted to the beneficiaries, as follows: "The reproduction right, as set out in Articles 7 and 11, and the exceptions permitted thereunder through Article 16, fully apply in the digital environment, in particular to the use of performances and phonograms in digital form. It is understood that the storage of a protected performance or phonogram in digital form in an electronic medium constitutes a reproduction within the meaning of these articles".

As regards the new exclusive right to "make available" performances and phonograms to the public, this right is not the equivalent of the right of communication to the public established in Article 8 of the WIPO Copyright Treaty for authors of literary and artistic works.[75] There is no agreed statement concerning this new right but the preparatory documents for the Diplomatic Conference make it clear that the intention behind the provision is to provide performers and producers with exclusive rights to authorise the use of their performances and phonograms in situations where, in the electronic marketplace, retail sales of phonograms are replaced by a database open to the public for the direct delivery of music via communication networks to home computers, and members of the public are able to access such phonograms from a place and at a time individually chosen by them, in the context of online, on-demand interactive services.[76] The right is intended to cover both directly interactive ways of making available and subscription services with similar effects.[77]

24–125   **Common provisions.** Both performers and producers of phonograms shall enjoy the right to a single equitable remuneration for the direct or indirect use of phonograms published for commercial purposes for broadcasting or for any com-

---

[71] Treaty, Art.14.

[72] Rome Convention, Art.7.

[73] Art.7 of the Rome Convention gives performers the possibility of preventing "the fixation, without their consent, of their unfixed performances"; Art.10 thereof gives producers "the right to authorise or prohibit the direct or indirect reproduction of their phonograms". Under the Phonograms Convention, producers are protected "against the making of duplicates without the consent of the producer" (Art.2).

[74] Basic Proposal for the Substantive Provisions of the Treaty for the Protection of the Rights of Performers and Producers of Phonograms to be considered by the Diplomatic Conference (hereinafter "Basic Proposal"), WIPO document CRNR/DC/5, Notes on Art.14, para.14.06.

[75] See para. 24–71, above.

[76] Basic Proposal for the Substantive Provisions of the Treaty for the Protection of the Rights of Performers and Producers of Phonograms to be considered by the Diplomatic Conference (hereinafter "Basic Proposal"), WIPO document CRNR/DC/5, notes on Art.18, paras 18.01–18.12.

[77] Basic Proposal, paras 18.06 and 18.08.

munication to the public.[78] Such remuneration may be claimed from the user by the performer or the producer or by both. In the absence of agreement between the parties, national legislation may set the terms according to which such remuneration shall be shared. However, reservations may be made with regard to these provisions, in respect of certain uses or other limitations, and the provisions may be excluded altogether, as in the Rome Convention. It had been proposed that the various rights of reservation given by Article 16(1)(a) of the Rome Convention should not apply in the case of broadcasting or communication to the public by wire or wireless means when the broadcasts or communication can only be received on subscription and payment.[79] This proposal was rejected and the situation under the Rome Convention has been perpetuated. An agreed statement gives some recognition to the problem, providing that it is understood that nothing precludes a Contracting Party from providing exclusive rights to a performer or producer of phonograms beyond those required to be provided under this Treaty.[80]

The term "published for commercial purposes" includes phonograms made available to the public by wire or wireless means in such a way that members of the public may access them from a place and at a time individually chosen by them.[81]

"Broadcasting" is defined with a wider meaning than in the Rome Convention, as follows:

> "'broadcasting' means the transmission by wireless means for public reception of sounds or of images and sounds *or of the representations thereof; such transmission by satellite is also 'broadcasting'; transmission of encrypted signals is 'broadcasting' where the means for decrypting are provided to the public by the broadcasting organisation or with its consent"*.[82]

(The words in italics are new). The Treaty also includes the following definition of communication to the public of a performance or a phonogram:

> "the transmission to the public by any medium, otherwise than by broadcasting, of sounds of a performance or the sounds or the representations of sounds fixed in a phonogram ... communication to the public includes making the sounds or representations of sounds fixed in a phonogram audible to the public".[83]

An agreed statement regarding these rights to equitable remuneration reads as follows:

> "It is understood that Article 15 does not represent a complete resolution of the level of rights of broadcasting and communication to the public that should be enjoyed by performers and phonogram producers in the digital age. Delegations were unable to achieve consensus on differing proposals for aspects of exclusivity to be provided in certain circumstances or for rights to be provided without the possibility of reservations, and have therefore left the issue to future resolution".[84]

A further agreed statement states that rights to equitable remuneration may

---

[78] Treaty, Art.15.
[79] Basic Proposal, paras 12.04 and 19.04.
[80] Agreed Statement Concerning Art.1.
[81] Treaty, Art.15(4).
[82] Art.2(f).
[83] Art.2(g).
[84] Agreed Statement Concerning Art.15.

also be granted to performers of folklore and producers of phonograms recording folklore where such phonograms have not been published for commercial gain.[85]

24–126 **Limitations and exceptions: Application of the 3-step test of the Berne Convention.** The same kinds of limitations may be made by Contracting Parties with respect to the rights of performers and producers of phonograms as are provided for in their national legislation in connection with the protection of literary and artistic works.[86] Such limitations shall be subject to the principle of the 3-step test of the Berne Convention and are, therefore, confined to certain special cases which do not conflict with a normal exploitation of the performance or phonogram and do not unreasonably prejudice the legitimate interests of the performer or of the producer of the phonogram.[87] According to an agreed statement,[88] this means that, as with respect to the WIPO Copyright Treaty, Contracting Parties may carry forward and appropriately extend into the digital environment limitations and exceptions in their national laws which have been considered acceptable under the Berne Convention and that they may devise new exceptions and limitations that are appropriate in the digital network environment.

24–127 **Term of protection.** The duration of the protection shall last, in the case of performers, for 50 years computed from the end of the year in which the performance was fixed in a phonogram. With respect to producers, who are also afforded a 50-year term of protection, the term is computed from the end of the year in which the phonogram was published, or, failing such publication within 50 years from fixation of the phonogram, 50 years from the end of the year in which the fixation was made.[89] This provision represents progress in comparison with the Rome and Phonograms Conventions, both of which provide for a minimum period of protection of only 20 years.[90]

24–128 **Obligations concerning technological measures and rights management information.** As in the Copyright Treaty,[91] Contracting Parties undertake certain obligations to provide adequate legal protection and effective legal remedies against:

(a) the circumvention of effective technological measures that are used by performers or producers of phonograms in connection with the exercise of their rights under the Treaty and that restrict acts, in respect of their performances or phonograms, which are not authorised by the performers or the producers of phonograms concerned or permitted by law[92];

(b) any person knowingly performing any of the following acts knowing, or with respect to civil remedies having reasonable grounds to know, that it will induce, enable, facilitate or conceal an infringement of any right covered by the Treaty:

(i) to remove or alter any electronic rights management information[93] without authority;

---

[85] Agreed Statement Concerning Art.15.

[86] cf. Berne Convention, Arts 10 and 11.

[87] Berne Convention, Art.9(2); cf. para. 24–33, above.

[88] Agreed Statement concerning Art.16: "The agreed statement concerning Art.10 (on Limitations and Exceptions) of the WIPO Copyright Treaty is applicable *mutatis mutandis* also to Art.16 (on Limitations and Exceptions) of the WIPO Performances and Phonograms Treaty".

[89] Treaty, Art.17.

[90] Rome Convention, Art.14; Phonograms Convention, Art.4.

[91] See discussion of the equivalent provisions concerning the WIPO Copyright Treaty, para. 24–73, above.

[92] Treaty, Art.18.

[93] Rights management information is defined as meaning: "information which identifies the performer, the performance of the performer, the producer of the phonogram, the phonogram, the

(ii) to distribute, import for distribution, broadcast, communicate or make available to the public, without authority, performances, copies of fixed performances or phonograms knowing that electronic rights management information has been removed or altered without authority.[94]

Formalities and reservations. The enjoyment and exercise of the rights provided for by the Treaty may not be made subject to any formality.[95] No reservations may be made under the Treaty except in relation to performance rights in phonograms.[96]   **24–129**

Retroactive effect and enforcement. The Treaty provides that the provisions of Article 18 of the Berne Convention concerning retroactive effect, shall apply *mutatis mutandis* to the protection provided for under the Treaty.[97] Thus, the Treaty applies to all performances and phonograms which, at the moment of its coming into force, have not yet fallen into the public domain in the country of origin through the expiry of the term of protection.   **24–130**

The Treaty also contains identical provisions concerning enforcement to those of the WIPO Copyright Treaty.[98] Thus, Contracting Parties are obliged to ensure that enforcement procedures are available to permit effective action against infringement, including remedies to prevent infringements and remedies which constitute a deterrent to further infringements. This provision is of a very general nature and does not include any reference to the more effective enforcement provisions contained in Article 41 to 61 of the TRIPs Agreement. The Diplomatic Conference specifically rejected a "basic proposal" to either include the TRIPs enforcement provisions in an annex or by reference (which would have simply required Contracting Parties to apply the relevant provisions of the TRIPs Agreement).[99]

C. RELATIONSHIP TO COPYRIGHT CONVENTIONS AND THE ROME AND PHONOGRAMS CONVENTIONS

No derogation from existing obligations. The relation of the Treaty to the copyright and related rights conventions is laid down in Article 1. This provides that nothing in the Treaty shall derogate from existing obligations that Contracting Parties have to each other under the Rome Convention[1] or prejudice any rights and obligations under any other treaties.[2] The protection granted shall also leave intact and in no way affect the protection of copyright in literary and artistic works; nor may any provision of the Treaty be interpreted as prejudicing such protection.[3]   **24–131**

An agreed statement concerning Article 1 seeks to clarify the provisions on the relationship between rights in phonograms under the Treaty and copyright in works embodied in the phonograms. In cases where authorisation is needed from

---

owner of any right in the performance or phonogram, any numbers or codes that represent such information, when any of these items of information is attached to a copy of a fixed performance or a phonogram or appears in connection with the communication or making available of a fixed performance or a phonogram to the public" (Art.19).

[94] Art.19.
[95] Art.20.
[96] Art.21.
[97] Treaty, Art.22.
[98] Treaty, Art.23.
[99] Basic Proposal, Notes on Art.27, paras 27.01 to 27.03.
[1] Treaty, Art.1(1).
[2] Art.1(3).
[3] Art.1(2).

both the author of a work embodied in the phonogram and a performer or producer owning rights in the phonogram, the need for the authorisation of the author does not cease to exist because the authorisation of the performer or producer is also required, and vice versa.

As already mentioned,[4] the statement also makes it clear that nothing in the copyright safeguard provisions precludes a Contracting State from providing exclusive rights to a performer or producer of phonograms beyond those required to be provided under the Treaty.

D. SIGNATORIES AND ENTRY INTO FORCE

24–132   **Parties to the Treaty.** Any Member State of the World Intellectual Property Organisation (WIPO) may become party to the Treaty, as well as any intergovernmental organisation competent in respect of, and having legislation binding on its Member States on, matters dealt with by the Treaty.[5] The European Union has signed the Treaty on this basis. The Treaty entered into force three months after the deposit of 30 instruments of ratification or accession by States with the Director General of WIPO.[6] Thereafter, new parties are bound by the Treaty three months from the date on which they deposit their instruments.[7] The Treaty may be denounced on giving one year's notice.[8]

The Treaty is administered by the International Bureau of WIPO[9] and supervised by an Assembly, which deals with matters concerning the maintenance and development of the Treaty and its application and operation.[10]

The Treaty was open for signature until December 31, 1997, at which date 50 states had signed it as well as the European Community.[11]

24–133   By February 20, 2002, instruments of ratification of or accession to the Treaty had been deposited by 30 states. Accordingly, the Treaty entered into force on May 20, 2002.

As at August 20, 2004, the following 44 states were parties to the Treaty: Albania, Argentina, Belarus, Bulgaria, Burkina Faso, Chile, Colombia, Costa Rica, Croatia, Czech Republic, Ecuador, El Salvador, Gabon, Georgia, Guatemala, Guinea, Honduras, Hungary, Jamaica, Japan, Jordan, Kazakhstan, Kyrgyzstan, Latvia, Lithuania, Mali, Mexico, Mongolia, Nicaragua, Panama, Paraguay, Peru, Philippines, Poland, Republic of Moldova, Romania, Saint Lucia, Senegal, Serbia and Montenegro, Slovakia, Slovenia, Togo, Ukraine, United States of America. The Council of the European Community approved the Treaty with regard to matters within its competence by decision dated March 16, 2000.[12]

---

[4] See para., 24–125 above.
[5] Treaty, Art.26.
[6] Art.29.
[7] Art.30.
[8] Art.31.
[9] Art.25.
[10] Art.24.
[11] Argentina, Austria, Belarus, Belgium, Bolivia, Burkina Faso, Canada, Chile, Colombia, Costa Rica, Croatia, Denmark, Ecuador, European Communities, Estonia, Finland, France, Germany, Ghana, Greece, Hungary, Indonesia, Ireland, Israel, Italy, Kazakhstan, Kenya, Luxembourg, Mexico, Monaco, Mongolia, Namibia, the Netherlands, Nigeria, Panama, Portugal, Republic of Moldova, Romania, Senegal, Slovakia, Slovenia, South Africa, Spain, Sweden, Switzerland, Togo, United Kingdom, United States of America, Uruguay, Venezuela.
[12] See para. 24–75, above. The Council decision authorised its President to deposit the instrument of ratification as from the date by which Member States are obliged to implement the Directive ([2001] O.J. L89, p.6); see Vol.2, App.HI1.

E. PENDING ISSUES NOT ADDRESSED BY THE TREATY

Problems left unresolved. A major drawback of the Treaty is the failure to cover   **24–134**
the rights of performers in the audiovisual fixations of their performances. This
was recognised in the resolution adopted by the Diplomatic Conference, which
noted "that the development of technologies will allow for a rapid growth of audiovisual services and that this will increase the opportunities for performing artists to exploit their audiovisual performances that will be transmitted by these
services" and drew attention to the need to ensure an adequate level of protection
for audiovisual performances, in particular in the new digital environment. To
that end, the resolution called for work to be started on a protocol to the Treaty
concerning audiovisual performances, with a view to the adoption of such a
protocol not later than in 1998.[13] The issue proved too controversial for the 1998
deadline for a new instrument to be met. It was not until December 2000[14] that a
Diplomatic Conference on the Protection of Audiovisual Performances convened
by WIPO took place but the Conference ended in failure.[15] Provisional agreement
was reached on a number of issues including national treatment, economic rights
of performers in their unfixed performances, the exclusive rights of reproduction,
distribution and rental, the right of making available of fixed performances, the
right of broadcasting and communication to the public and protection against the
circumvention of technological protection measures. It was also agreed that audiovisual performers would be granted moral rights protection, including the
right to be identified as the performer of their performances and to object to any
distortion, mutilation or other modification of their performances which would be
prejudicial to their reputations, taking due account of the nature of audiovisual
fixations. The issue which led to the breakdown of the negotiations was the law
applicable to a transfer of economic rights from the performer to the film producer or others. The USA insisted on the US concept of "work made for hire" being explicitly recognised in the new instrument by the inclusion of a mandatory
although rebuttable presumption of transfer of all exclusive economic rights to
the producer, once the performer had consented to the audiovisual fixation of his
performance. In the interests of the powerful US film industry, the USA also
argued that the statutory transfer provisions of the law of the country where a film
is produced should have extraterritorial application in the country of exploitation.
This was opposed by many countries with a civil law approach, including the
European Community and its Member States; the latter defended the position
that contractual transfer provisions should be given only limited recognition in
the country of exploitation and that in any case the law in the country of exploitation should be respected.

The Diplomatic Conference concluded by recommending to the Assemblies of
Member States of WIPO, in their September 2001 session, that they reconvene
the Diplomatic Conference for the purpose of reaching agreement on outstanding

---

[13] Resolution Concerning Audiovisual Performances, adopted by the Diplomatic Conference on
December 20, 1996. In March 1997, the Governing Bodies of WIPO established a Committee of
Experts on the protocol concerning audiovisual performances.

[14] The Committee of Experts on a Protocol concerning Audiovisual Performances met twice in
September 1997 and June 1998. Subsequently, the matter was considered by the WIPO Standing
Committee on Copyright and Related Rights, which met in November 1998, May 1999,
November 1999 and April 2000 (see WIPO docs. SCCR/1/9, SCCR/2/11, SCCR/3/11 and SCCR/
4/6.

[15] The Diplomatic Conference on the Protection of Audiovisual Performances met in Geneva from
December 7 to 20, 2000. See also S. von Lewinski, "The WIPO Diplomatic Conference on Audiovisual Performances: A First Resume" [2001] *E.I.P.R.* 333 and "International protection for
audiovisual performers: a never-ending story? A résumé of the WIPO Diplomatic Conference
200" [2001] 189 *RIDA* 3.

issues.[16] At that meeting, the Assemblies of Member States of WIPO noted the Chairman's observations that a great deal of work needed to be done before agreement could be reached on this question. The Assemblies decided that the matter would remain on the agenda for their future meetings in September 2002, at which the Chairman would report on progress.[17] At the Assemblies' 2002 meeting it was decided to convene an ad hoc informal meeting relating to this issue in 2003 to assess possible ways of resolving the outstanding issues. The informal meeting took place in November 2003, but no results thereof were published. The subject is on the agenda of the Assemblies of the Member States of WIPO to be held in September 2004.

Other questions of importance which were not dealt with in the Treaty contrary to expectations were: the proposal to include an additional specific right to authorise or prohibit importation in the context of the new distribution right; exhaustion of the distribution right (a question left to national law); the proposed exclusive right to authorise modification of performances and phonograms (this right was proposed in order to cover any possible situation in which digital or other technological manipulation might be used to circumvent traditional notions of reproduction)[18]; proposals to afford exclusive rights of broadcasting and public performance of phonograms, at least in the digital environment.

As regards the digital agenda, as in the WIPO Copyright Treaty, two important issues for which solutions were proposed in the "basic proposals" were not resolved. First, agreement could not be reached on the proposal to clarify that acts such as temporary storage in electronic communications media constitute acts of reproduction.[19] Similarly, the proposal to clarify the concept of "publication", by specifically providing that making a work available to the public through on demand interactive systems should be treated as publication, was not followed.[20]

8. THE TRIPS AGREEMENT

A. HISTORY

24–135   **The Uruguay Round of the GATT** (General Agreement on Tariffs and Trade (the GATT Agreement) was concluded on December 15, 1993, after seven years of negotiations, and the final act was signed in Marrakesh, Morocco, on April 15, 1994. Thus, the Round, had a successful outcome, adopting the Agreement establishing the World Trade Organisation (WTO) to replace the GATT Agreement administration, and Annex 1C thereto, the Agreement on Trade-Related Aspects of Intellectual Property Rights, (the TRIPs Agreement): see below, Volume 2 at F11.

24–136   **Scope of the Agreement.** The TRIPs Agreement is concerned, *inter alia*, with copyright and related rights. It sets standards for the Member States of the WTO ("Members") concerning the availability, scope and use of intellectual property rights generally, covering not only copyright and related rights but also trade marks, geographical indications, industrial designs, patents, layout designs (topographies) of integrated circuits, the protection of know-how (undisclosed information) and control of anti-competitive practices in contractual licences. It

---

[16] Summary Minutes (Plenary) of the Diplomatic Conference on the Protection of Audiovisual Performances, Geneva, December 7–20, 2000.
[17] WIPO doc. A/36/15, para.186.
[18] Basic Proposal, Notes on Art.8, para.8.04.
[19] Notes on Art.7, para.7.07.
[20] Notes on Art.2, para.2.20.

includes also provisions for the enforcement of intellectual property rights and dispute prevention and settlement measures.[21]

According to the Agreement, WTO Members are obliged to legislate to provide the standards of protection laid down therein for the various categories of intellectual property right owners covered by the Agreement. Members are free to determine the appropriate method of implementing the provisions of the Agreement within their own legal system and practice.[22] They are obliged to accord the treatment provided for in the Agreement to the nationals of other Members[23] and to accord most categories of intellectual property rights owners treatment no less favourable than it accords to its own nationals with regard to the protection of intellectual property (national treatment).[24] As regards performers, producers of phonograms (sound recordings), and broadcasting organisations, however, the latter obligation (national treatment) only applies in respect of the rights provided under the Agreement. The Agreement also provides for most-favoured-nation treatment, according to which, subject to certain defined exceptions, any advantage, favour, privilege or immunity granted by a Member to the nationals of any other country shall be accorded immediately and unconditionally to the nationals of all other Members.[25] This is a principle not recognised by the copyright and related rights conventions.

B. SUBSTANTIVE PROVISIONS

The standards of protection to be afforded in relation to copyright and related rights may be summarised as follows: Members shall comply with Articles 1–21 of, and also the Appendix to, the Paris Act 1971 of the Berne Convention,[26] with the one exception of the provisions of the Convention concerning moral rights, which were expressly excluded from the scope of the Agreement.[27] Copyright protection under the Agreement extends to expressions and not to ideas, procedures, methods of operation or mathematical concepts as such.[28]

Computer programs shall be protected as literary works under the Berne

24–137

---

[21] On the TRIPs Agreement generally, see D. Gervais, *The TRIPS Agreement—Drafting History and Analysis*, 2nd Ed. (Sweet and Maxwell, London, 2003); M. Blakeney, *Trade Related Aspects of Intellectual Property Rights: A Concise Guide to the TRIPs Agreement* (Sweet and Maxwell, London, 1996); as regards the relationship between the TRIPs Agreement and the copyright and related rights conventions, see "Implications of the TRIPs Agreement on Treaties Administered by WIPO", memorandum prepared by the International Bureau of WIPO, [1996] *Copyright*, 164. For further reading, see: F.K. Beier and G. Schricker, *From GATT to TRIPs—The Agreement on Trade-Related Aspects of Intellectual Property Rights* (1996); J.H.J. Bourgois, "The EC in the WTO and Advisory Opinion 1/94: An Echternach Procession."; C.M. Correa, "TRIPs Agreement: Copyright and Related Rights", [1992] 25 *I.I.C.* 543; P.E. Geller, "Intellectual Property in the Global Marketplace: Impact of TRIPs Dispute Settlements?" (1995) 29 *The International Lawyer*" 99; N. Khlestov, "WTO-WIPO Co-operation: Does it have a Future" [1997] 10 *E.I.P.R.* 560; P.Samuelson, "Challenges for the WIPO and the Trade-related Aspects of IP Rights Council in Regulating IP Rights in the Information Age" [1999] *E.I.P.R.* 578; S.K. Verma "TRIPs--Development and Transfer of Technology", IIC, vol.27, N. 31, 1996, 331; A. Otten, "The Fundamental Importance of the TRIPs Agreement for a Better Enforcement of Copyright", records of the ALAI Berlin Congress, June 16–19, 1999, 41.

[22] The TRIPs Agreement, Art.1(1).

[23] TRIPs Agreement, Art.1(3). In respect of the relevant intellectual property right, the nationals of other Members shall be understood as those natural or legal persons that would meet the criteria for eligibility for protection provided for in the Paris Convention (1967), the Berne Convention (1971), the Rome Convention and the Treaty on Intellectual Property in Respect of Integrated Circuits, if all Members of the WTO were members of those conventions.

[24] TRIPs agreement, Art.3. (This provision is subject to the exceptions provided for in the international, intellectual property conventions, including the Berne Convention and the Rome Convention.)

[25] Art.4.

[26] See paras 24–10, *et seq.*, above.

[27] The TRIPs Agreement, Art.9.

[28] Art.9(2).

Convention and compilations of data or other material (databases), which by reason of the selection or arrangement of their contents constitute intellectual creations, shall be protected as such,[29] without prejudice to any copyright subsisting in the data or material itself.

24–138 **Rental rights.** In principle, the right to authorise or prohibit the commercial rental to the public of originals or copies of their works are to be provided for authors and their successors in title in respect of at least computer programs and cinematographic works. However, as regards cinematographic works, Members are excepted from this obligation unless such rental has led to widespread copying of such works which is materially impairing the exclusive right of reproduction conferred in that Member's territory on authors and their successors in title. In respect of computer programs, this obligation does not apply to rentals where the program itself is not the essential object of the rental.[30]

24–139 **Terms of protection** calculated on a basis other than the life of a natural person, shall be no less than 50 years from authorised publication, or in the absence of such publication, from making.[31] Limitations shall not conflict with a normal exploitation of the work or unreasonably prejudice the legitimate interests of the right holder.[32]

24–140 **Performers, producers of phonograms (sound recordings) and broadcasting organisations** are specifically protected. Performers shall have the following rights: the possibility of preventing the unauthorised fixation of their unfixed performance and the reproduction of such fixation as well as the unauthorised broadcasting and communication of their live performances. Producers of phonograms shall enjoy the right to authorise or prohibit the direct or indirect reproduction, and the rental of, their phonograms. Other right holders in phonograms may also enjoy a rental right therein under national law.[33] The term of protection of performers and producers shall be not less than 50 years computed from the end of the year in which the fixation was made or the performance took place. The TRIPs Agreement contains no provisions relating to the broadcasting and public performance rights of producers and performers.[34]

Broadcasting organisations shall have the right to prohibit the fixation, the reproduction of fixations, and the rebroadcasting by wireless means of broadcasts, as well as the communication to the public of television broadcasts of the same. The term of protection shall be 20 years from the end of the calendar year in which the broadcast took place.[35]

24–141 **Limitations and exceptions.** The Agreement provides that, with respect to literary and artistic works, Members shall confine limitations or exceptions to exclusive rights to certain special cases which do not conflict with a normal exploitation of the work and do not unreasonably prejudice the legitimate

---

[29] Art.10.
[30] TRIPs Agreement, Art.11.
[31] TRIPs Agreement, Art.12. (This does not apply to photographic works or works of applied art).
[32] Art.13. (*cf.* the Berne Convention, Art.9(2)).
[33] If on April 15, 1994, a Member had in force a system of equitable remuneration of right holders in respect of the rental of phonograms, it may maintain such system provided that the commercial rental of phonograms is not giving rise to the material impairment of the exclusive rights of reproduction of right holders (TRIPs Agreement, Art.14(4)).
[34] *cf.* The Rome Convention, Art.12.
[35] The TRIPs Agreement, Art.14.

interests of the right holder. This provision is in line with Article 9(2) of the Berne Convention ("the 3-step test"), which is expressed in similar terms.[36]

In relation to the rights of performers, producers of phonograms and broadcasting organisations guaranteed by the TRIPs Agreement, any member may provide for conditions, limitations, exceptions and reservations to the extent permitted by the Rome Convention.[37] However, this is qualified by the application of the Three-Step Test of the Berne Convention also to limitations on related rights.[38] The rule of retroactivity of Article 18 of the Berne Convention shall also apply, *mutatis mutandis*, to the rights of performers and producers of phonograms in phonograms, so that all phonograms not in the public domain at the date of entry into force of the Agreement with respect to any Member will be protected.[39] This provision goes further than the Rome Convention which does not require retroactive application of its provisions.

The Application of the 3-step test by a WTO Panel. Of particular interest in connection with limitations under the TRIPs Agreement, is the application of the "3-step test" of the Berne Convention by a World Trade Organisation Panel in its report on a complaint brought against the United States of America by the European Union[40] under the TRIPs dispute prevention and settlement procedure.[41] This report would appear to be the first judicial interpretation of the 3-step test. The panel found that the term "special cases" in the first condition requires that a limitation or exception in national legislation should be clearly defined and should be narrow in its scope and reach. However, a limitation or exception may be compatible with the first condition even if it pursues a special purpose whose underlying legitimacy in a normative sense cannot be discerned. Thus, the first condition does not imply passing a judgment on the legitimacy of the exceptions in dispute (as had been argued by the European Union).[42] As regards the second condition, that an exception should not conflict with the normal exploitation of a work, the panel considered that a conflict arises when the exception or limitation enters into economic competition with the ways that right holders normally extract economic value from that right to the work (*i.e.* the copyright) and thereby deprives them of significant or tangible commercial gain.[43] The panel finally gave its opinion on the third condition of the 3-step test, that the exception or limitation must not unreasonably prejudice the legitimate interests of the right holder, finding that there is unreasonable prejudice where an exception or limitation causes or has the potential to cause an unreasonable loss of income to the copyright holder.[44]

24–142

---

[36] TRIPs Agreement, Art.13.
[37] *cf.* the Rome Convention, Art.15, which permits exceptions for: private use; use of short excerpts in connection with the reporting of current events; ephemeral recordings by broadcasting organisations; use solely for purposes of teaching or scientific research. Moreover, the same kinds of limitations are permitted as are provided for in respect of literary and artistic works. Compulsory licenses are only permitted to the extent they are compatible with the Convention.
[38] TRIPs Agreement, Art.14(6); *cf.* para. 24–33, above.
[39] Art.14(6).
[40] Panel Report WT/DS160/R of June 15, 2000: United States— s.110(5) of the Copyright Act.
[41] See para. 24–147, below.
[42] Panel Report., para.6.112.
[43] *ibid.*, para 6.183.
[44] Concerning the Panel Report, see J.C.Ginsburg, "Toward Supranational Copyright Law? The WTO Panal Decision and the "Three–Step Test" for Copyright Exceptions", (2001) 187 RIDA 3; D.J. Brennan, "The Three–Step Test Frenzy—Why the TRIPs Panel Decision might be considered Per Incuriam",[2002] IPQ 2, 212; Y.Gaubic, "Les exceptions au droit d'auteur: un nouvel avenir, in [2001] Communicaion Commerce électronique, no.6, 12; B.C.Goldmann, "Victory for Songwriters in WTO Music Royalties Dispute between U.S. and E.U.—Background of the Conflict Over the Extension of Homestyle Exemption", (2001) 32 *IIC*412; M.Ficsor, "How

24–143   **Anti-competitive practices.** The Agreement also permits Members to provide in their national legislation for control of anti-competitive practices in contractual licences.[45] This is of particular relevance in the copyright and related rights field to the practices of collecting societies.

24–144   **General obligations concerning enforcement measures.** As regards enforcement, Members are obliged to ensure that enforcement procedures are available under their national laws to permit effective action against any act of infringement of the intellectual property rights covered by the agreement, including remedies to prevent infringements, which are expeditious and constitute a deterrent to further infringements but without creating barriers to legitimate trade or allowing abuse.[46] Such procedures shall be fair and equitable, simple, cheap and timely.[47] Parties to a proceeding shall have an opportunity for review by a judicial authority of final administrative decisions and, subject to national jurisdictional rules, of at least the legal aspects of initial judicial decisions on the merits of a case. However, there is no obligation to provide for review of acquittals in criminal cases.[48]

24–145   **Standards of procedure and remedies.** The Agreement also lays down standards with regard to civil and administrative procedures and remedies,[49] in order to guarantee fair and equitable procedures for the enforcement of intellectual property rights. Included are *inter alia* rules concerning evidence, injunctions, damages, disposal of infringing goods and right of information concerning the identity of those engaged in infringing practices.[50] The adoption of provisional measures by Members is foreseen to prevent infringements, and in particular to prevent the entry into the channels of commerce in their jurisdiction of goods, including imported goods immediately after customs clearance.[51] There are also special requirements related to border controls to enable a right holder, who has valid grounds for suspecting that the importation of counterfeit trademark or pirated copyright goods may take place, subject to various conditions, to lodge an application in writing with the competent authorities, administrative or judicial, for the suspension by the customs authorities of the release into free circulation of such goods.[52]

24–146   **Criminal procedures.** Members are obliged also to provide for criminal procedures and penalties to be applied at least in cases of wilful trademark counterfeiting or copyright piracy on a commercial scale. Remedies available shall include imprisonment and/or monetary fines sufficient to provide a deterrent, consistently with the level of penalties applied for crimes of a corresponding gravity. Where appropriate, remedies shall also include the seizure, forfeiture and

---

much of What? The "Three–Step Test" and its application in two recent WTO dispute settlement cases", (2002) 192 RIDA 110; and J. Bornkamm, "Copyright and teh Public Interest–The Three–Step Test in International Copyright", paper delivered at the Fordham University School of Law 10th Annual Conference on International Intellectual Property Law and Policy, New York, April 4– 5, 2002.

[45] *ibid.* TRIPs Agreement, Art.40.
[46] *ibid.* TRIPs Agreement, Art.41(1).
[47] Art.41(2).
[48] Art.41(4).
[49] TRIPs Agreement, ss.2–5, Arts 42–61.
[50] Arts 42 to 49.
[51] Art.50.
[52] Arts 51–60.

destruction of the infringing goods and of any materials and implements the predominant use of which has been in the commission of the offence.[53]

Dispute prevention and settlement. The Agreement provides for a dispute settlement procedure under the WTO,[54] according to which, should a dispute arise regarding the obligations of a Member, there is the possibility of taking action under the GATT Understanding on Rules and Procedures Governing the Settlement of Disputes. This aspect of the agreement is of particular importance in view of the sanctions which may be imposed under that procedure on a Member which fails to comply with its obligations under the TRIPs Agreement. The fact that under the Berne Convention there are no sanctions whatsoever should a Member State thereof be in breach of its obligations thereunder was an important reason for the GATT TRIPs negotiations.[55] This difference is one of the strengths of the TRIPs Agreement. Under the Berne Convention, disputes between countries of the Union may be brought by one of the countries in question before the International Court of Justice.[56] The provision is not obligatory and there are no sanctions. "An adverse decision of the International Court carries no condemnation; the Court merely makes a finding as to the law and it is then a matter for the countries in question to solve by diplomatic or legislative means, as they wish".[57]

24–147

The TRIPs dispute settlement mechanism may be invoked both in the areas of minimum standards of protection and of enforcement. To date, it has been invoked in a number of cases concerning copyright and related rights (*inter alia* the complaints by the United States of America and European Communities filed against Japan in 1996 concerning the protection of sound recordings under TRIPs[58]; the complaints filed by the United States of America in 1998 against the European Communities and Greece in respect of the lack of effective remedies against copyright infringement in Greece[59]; a complaint by the European Communities filed in 1999 against the United States of America concerning exemptions in the US Copyright Act permitting communication to the public of broadcast works by certain commercial establishments without the authorisation of right-holders or payment of royalties.[60] The USA also filed complaints against Denmark and Sweden concerning the lack of provisional measures in the context

---

[53] TRIPs Agreement, Art.61.

[54] TRIPs Agreement, Art.64. The settlement of disputes under the Agreement will be subject to the provisions of Articles XXII and XXIII of the General Agreement on Tariffs and Trade 1994 as elaborated and applied by the understanding on Rules and Procedures Governing the Settlement of Disputes.

[55] It should be noted, however, that, under the auspices of WIPO, a Committee of Experts on the Settlement of Intellectual Property Disputes Between States held eight sessions to discuss a draft Treaty on the subject in the mid-1990s. The aim of the Treaty, to be administered by WIPO, was to establish procedures for the amicable settlement of disputes. However, disagreement about the need for such a Treaty led to a Diplomatic Conference scheduled to take place in the biennium 1994/1995 being shelved. For a report of the 8th Committee of Experts see [1996] *Industrial Property and Copyright* 319. For the draft Treaty and proposed Regulations, see [1995] *Copyright* 168 and 205. Meanwhile, the WIPO Arbitration and Mediation Center was established in 1994 to offer arbitration and mediation services for the resolution of international commercial disputes between private parties in the field of intellectual property. The Center has focused on establishing an operational and legal framework for the administration of disputes relating to the Internet and electronic commerce (for further information see *http:// arbiter.wipo.int/center*).

[56] Berne Convention, Art.33.

[57] See C.Masouyé, *Guide to the Berne Convention for the Protection of Literary and Artistic Works (Paris Act, 1971)* (WIPO, Geneva, 1978), para.33.5.

[58] WT/DS28 and WT/DS42.

[59] WT/DS/124/1 and WT/DS/125/1.

[60] WT/DS/160/1.

of civil proceedings in TRIPs matters[61] and against Ireland for failure to comply with TRIPs provisions on copyright and related rights.[62] Some of these cases have been the subject of consultations; on some, mutually agreed solutions have been found, and others have led to WTO dispute settlement panel or Appellate Body reports upholding the complaints and determining that the copyright legislation of the country in question should be amended.[63]

24–148   **Exhaustion.** It should be noted that, for the purposes of dispute settlement under the TRIPs Agreement, nothing in the Agreement "shall be used to address the issue of the exhaustion of intellectual property rights".[64] Thus, like the copyright and related rights conventions, the TRIPs Agreement leaves the question of exhaustion of rights to national law.

24–149   **Transitional arrangements** are provided for to give Members time to bring their legislation into line with the Agreement. In particular, the least-developed-country Members are not obliged to apply the provisions of the Agreement with regard, *inter alia*, to copyright and related rights for a period of 10 years, which may be extended on motivated request.[65]

24–150   **The TRIPs Council.** Finally, the Agreement establishes a Council for Trade-Related Aspects of Intellectual Property Rights to monitor the operation of the Agreement and, in particular, Members' compliance with their obligations thereunder. In carrying out its functions, the Council is required to establish, within one year of its first meeting, appropriate arrangements for co-operation with the World Intellectual Property Organisation (WIPO).[66] To that end, an Agreement between WIPO and WTO was reached in December 1995.[67]

It should also be noted that the TRIPs Agreement is due to be reviewed in the context of the Doha Trade Negotiations launched under the auspices of the World Trade Organisation in 2001. The issues for review at present concern industrial property.

C. DIRECT EFFECT OF TRIPs IN TRIPs MEMBER STATES

24–151   Reference is made in Chapter 25 to decisions of the European Court of Justice in which the question whether the TRIPs Agreement can have direct effect in the European Union is discussed.[68] The question has also arisen at the national level where, within the European Union, there are diverging views on the direct applicability of TRIPs, depending on the legal order of the individual Member States. Direct effect is only possible in states whose constitutions accord domestic legal effect to international agreements. The different approaches may be illustrated by the following examples. Germany: The German Government takes the view that TRIPs may have direct effect in Germany. In the memorandum introducing the German Draft Act for the Ratification of the WTO Agreement, it said the following: "Domestic law by and large is in conformity with the results of the negotiations; in addition some of the provisions, at least those of the Agree-

[61] WT/DS/83 and WT/DS/86.
[62] WT/DS/82.
[63] An overview of the state of play of WTO disputes is available on the WTO website *www.wto.org*. As at August 20, 2004, 21 TRIPs-related disputes had been settled or were still pending, of which six concerned copyright or related rights issues.
[64] TRIPs Agreement, Art.6.
[65] TRIPs Agreement, Arts 65 and 66.
[66] TRIPs Agreement, Art.68.
[67] For text, see [1996] *Industrial Property and Copyright, Bilateral Treaties, Text 03*, 001.
[68] *cf.* Ch. 25, para. 25–104.

ment on Trade-Related Aspects of Intellectual Property Rights, are directly applicable".[69] Ireland: The Irish High Court has given direct effect to TRIPs in a patent case. It based its judgement not on Community law but on the domestic law according to which any treaty supersedes domestic law in relation to certain patents.[70] United Kingdom: The High Court has held that TRIPs could not have direct effect in the United Kingdom for several reasons: the language of Article 1(1) of TRIPs was not that of a treaty intended by the signatories to have direct effect; the fundamental character of the WTO and TRIPs was merely an agreement among nations and thus was not self-executing by way of conferring private rights on citizens. WTO and TRIPs were not capable of having direct effect and, even if some provisions of TRIPs were capable of having such effect, Article 32 at issue was not sufficiently clear and precise to do so; the Court found these points so self-evident as to fall within the *acte claire* doctrine.[71]

D. PARTIES TO THE TRIPs AGREEMENT

All Member Countries of the Agreement establishing the World Trade Organization (WTO) are automatically Members of the TRIPs Agreement, which as mentioned above is Annex C1 to that Agreement. As of August 20, 2004, there were 147 Members of WTO and 31 Observer governments, which must start accession negotiations within five years of becoming observers.   **24–152**

E. WIPO/WTO AGREEMENT

This agreement, signed on December 22, 1995, entered into force on January 1, 1996. It provides *inter alia* for WTO Members and their nationals to have access to copies of laws and regulations in the WIPO collection, and copies of translations thereof, on the same terms as apply to Member States of WIPO and nationals of those states. Access is also guaranteed on the same terms to any computerised database of the International Bureau of WIPO containing laws and regulations. The WTO Secretariat is also given access free of charge to any such database.[72] Provision is further made for the WTO Secretariat and the Council for TRIPs to have access to the laws and regulations of WTO members in the WIPO collection. The International Bureau shall not put any restrictions on the use that the WTO Secretariat may make of the copies of laws, regulations and translations transmitted accordingly.[73] Reciprocal arrangements are made for WTO to transmit laws and regulations received by them to WIPO, under the same conditions.[74] WIPO will give WTO Members which are developing countries but not Member States of WIPO the same assistance for translation of laws and regulations as it provides to its own Members which are developing countries.[75]   **24–153**

Similar arrangements are provided for developing countries which are Members of WTO but not of WIPO as regards legal-technical assistance relating to the TRIPs Agreement.[76] Finally, the WTO Secretariat and the International Bureau of WIPO are to enhance co-operation in their legal-technical assistance and technical co-operation activities relating to the TRIPs Agreement for

---

[69] *Entwurf eines Gesetzes zu dem Übereinkommen vom 15. April 1994 zur Errichtung der Welthandelsorganisation, Denkschrift,* para.6, Bundestagdrucksache 12/7655(neu).
[70] *Allen & Hanbury's Ltd v Controller of Patents, Designs, and Trademarks,* [1997] 1N.Ir. 416 (High Ct 1996).
[71] In *Lenzing AG's European Patent (UK)* ([1997] R.P.C. 245).
[72] WIPO-WTO Agreement, Art.2 (1) and (2).
[73] Art.2(3).
[74] Art.2(4).
[75] Art.2(5).
[76] Art.4(1).

developing countries, keep in regular contact and exchange non-confidential information.[77]

9. OTHER CONVENTIONS OF RELEVANCE TO THE COPYRIGHT AND RELATED RIGHTS CONVENTIONS

A. INTRODUCTION

24–154   There are a number of other Conventions of relevance to the copyright and related rights conventions, to which the United Kingdom has not adhered. For the sake of completeness, these are briefly discussed below.

B. THE SATELLITE CONVENTION

24–155   **The Convention relating to the distribution of programme-carrying signals transmitted by satellite**, known as the Satellite Convention, was adopted on May 21, 1974, in Brussels.[78] The Convention differs from the copyright and related rights conventions in that it is an international *public* law Convention as opposed to an international *private* law convention and thus grants no private rights, imposing instead certain obligations on States. The reason for this approach was that many governments took the view that "if affirmative rights were to be accorded to originating broadcasting organisations as a matter of private law under a new international convention, these should be counterbalanced by granting correlative rights to contributors to programmes, particularly authors and other copyright owners". Moreover, there was concern that any new convention should not prejudice the Rome Convention.[79] Granting further private rights to broadcasters would have upset the balance between the three beneficiaries of the Rome Convention.[80]

The aim of the Convention was to regulate potential legal problems raised by intercontinental transmissions of television programmes by satellite. It provides measures to prevent ground stations belonging to broadcasters and cable distribution companies within the satellite footprint from poaching and distributing programme-carrying signals transmitted by satellite which were not intended for them.[81] The problem arose during the late 1960s when the European Broadcasting Union sought protection of its members' programmes transmitted by point-to-point and distribution satellites to ground stations. In the main, the programmes transmitted were not copyright material but live sporting events, news items, etc., transmitted between broadcasting organisations and not designed for reception by the public. Such transmissions were vulnerable to poaching, or piracy, and the question arose whether the rights of broadcasters under the Rome Convention gave the broadcasters protection with respect to satellite distribution. The Rome

---

[77] Art.4 (2) and (3).

[78] For text, see [1974] *Copyright* 151. See also *Records of the International Conference of States on the Distribution of Programme-Carrying Signals Transmitted by Satellite*, UNESCO/WIPO, 1977; S.M. Stewart, "International Copyright and Neighbouring Rights" (Butterworths, London, 1983), Ch.10; S. Ricketson, *The Berne Convention for the protection of Literary and Artistic Works: 1886–1896* (Queen Mary College, University of London, 1987), para.15.57, *et seq.*; E. Ulmer, "Protection of authors in relation to the transmission via satellite of broadcast programmes" LXXXXII *RIDA* 4 (1977).

[79] See Report of the General Rapporteur, Barbara Ringer, in the *Records of the Diplomatic Conference*, para.10.

[80] *Records of the Diplomatic Conference*, para.11.

[81] Preamble to the Convention, para.4: "Convinced that an international system should be established under which measures would be provided to prevent distributors from distributing programme-carrying signals transmitted by satellite which were not intended for those distributors".

Convention defines broadcasting as the transmission by wireless means *for public reception* of sounds or of images and sounds[82] and the transmitted broadcasts concerned were not necessarily for direct reception by the public. There was general agreement that broadcasts transmitted to the public by means of direct broadcasting satellites were covered by the Convention and many took the view that, since point-to-point and distribution satellite broadcasts were ultimately destined for reception by the public, these were also protected.[83] However, sufficient doubt remained for the broadcasters to seek specific protection against piracy of their programmes transmitted by point-to-point and distribution satellites. Following a series of meetings starting in 1968,[84] the Convention was adopted in 1974.[85]

Substantive provisions. The scope of the Convention is limited; it provides that   **24–156**
each Contracting State undertakes to take adequate measures to prevent the distribution on or from its territory of any programme-carrying signal by any distributor for whom the signal emitted to or passing through the satellite is not intended. The obligation applies where the originating organisation is a national of another Contracting State and where the signal distributed is a derived signal (*i.e.* a signal obtained by modifying the technical characteristics of the emitted signal).[86] The term "take adequate measures" leaves Contracting States free to decide on the kind of protection to be provided; it may be by a specific right, but may also be by means of administrative measures, penal sanctions or telecommunications laws or regulation[87]; the duration of the protection is also left to domestic legislation.[88] Exceptions are provided for news reporting, quotations and educational use.[89]

The Convention specifically does not apply where the signals emitted by or on behalf of the originating organisation are intended for direct reception from the satellite by the general public.[90] The Convention does not have retrospective effect.[91]

Relationship to the Berne and Rome Conventions. The Satellite Convention   **24–157**
itself stipulates that its provisions are in no way to be interpreted to limit or prejudice the protection secured to authors, performers, producers of phonograms, or broadcasting organisations, under any domestic or international agreement.[92] Furthermore, the Preamble to the Convention refers to the need not to impair or prejudice in any way wider acceptance of the Rome Convention.[93] In practice, problems in this connection do not appear to have arisen, the number of Member States of the Rome Convention having increased from 14 at the time of the adop-

---

[82] Rome Convention, Art.3(f).
[83] Ringer, *Records of the Diplomatic Conference*, para.37.
[84] Working Group on Copyright Problems of Satellite Communications (Geneva, October 14–16, 1968), [1968] *Copyright* 230; UNESCO/BIRPI Committee of Governmental Experts on Problems in the Field of Copyright and of the Protection of Performers, Producers of Phonograms and Broadcasting Organisations Raised by Transmission via Space Satellites, which met on the following occasions: Lausanne/Ouchy, April 21–30, 1971 [1971] *Copyright* 102; Paris, May 9–11, 1972 [1972] *Copyright* 142; and Nairobi, July 2–11, 1973 [1973] *Copyright* 147.
[85] The Convention was signed on May 21, 1974, the date of its adoption, by the following States: Belgium, Brazil, Cyprus, Germany (Federal Republic), Israel, Italy, the then Ivory Coast, Kenya, Lebanon, Mexico, Morocco, Senegal, Spain, Switzerland, USA.
[86] The Satellite Convention, Art.2(1).
[87] Ringer, *Records of the Diplomatic Conference*, para.79.
[88] The Satellite Convention, Art.2(2).
[89] Art.4.
[90] Art.3.
[91] Art.5.
[92] Satellite Convention, Art.7.
[93] Preamble, para.5.

tion of the Satellites Convention in May 1974[94] to 77 states on August 20, 2004.[95] The progress of the Satellites Convention is monitored by the Assembly and Executive Committee of the Berne Union, in the absence of any intergovernmental committee of its own.

24–158 **Entry into force and parties to the Satellite Convention.** The Convention entered into force on August 25, 1979, following the deposit of the fifth instrument of ratification or accession. As of August 20, 2004, the following 24 states were party thereto: Armenia, Australia, Austria, Bosnia and Herzogovina, Costa Rica, Croatia, Germany, Greece, Italy, Jamaica, Kenya, Macedonia (the former Yugoslav Republic of), Mexico, Morocco, Nicaragua, Panama, Peru, Portugal, Russian Federation, Slovenia, Switzerland, Trinidad and Tobago, United States of America and Yugoslavia. The United Kingdom did not sign the Convention at the time of its adoption[96] and has not subsequently acceded to it.[97]

C. THE VIENNA TYPEFACES AGREEMENT

24–159 **The Vienna Agreement for the Protection of Typefaces and their International Deposit** (the Vienna Agreement), was adopted on June 12, 1973, in Vienna. A Protocol to the Agreement was also adopted on that day concerning the term of protection to be accorded to typefaces. The Agreement constituted a Union for the protection of typefaces,[98] which are defined as sets of designs, intended to provide means for composing texts by any graphic technique, of the following: letters and alphabets as such with their accessories such as accents and punctuation marks; numerals and other figurative signs such as conventional signs, symbols and scientific signs; ornaments such as borders, fleurons and vignettes. The term "typefaces" does not include typefaces of a form dictated by purely technical requirements.[99]

According to the Agreement, the Contracting States undertake to ensure the protection of typefaces, by establishing a special national deposit, or by adapting the deposit provided for in their national industrial design laws, or by their national copyright provisions. These kinds of protection may be cumulative.[1] The Agreement is based on the principle of national treatment.[2] To qualify for protection, typefaces must be novel, or original, or both.[3] The protection afforded by the Agreement confers on the owner, who may be a natural person or legal entity,[4] the right to prohibit the making without consent of any reproduction of the typeface as well as the commercial distribution and importation of such

---

[94] [1975] *Copyright* 32.

[95] Status of the Convention, WIPO, August 20, 2004.

[96] [1975] *Copyright* 106.

[97] The UK made it clear at the Diplomatic Conference that it considered the Convention unnecessary, would not sign it and was unlikely to accede to it thereafter. As the Head of the UK delegation said: "The United Kingdom ... adheres firmly to the view that satellite broadcasts come within the scope of the Rome Convention and, therefore, this is the proper instrument to which countries should look for their protection ... The United Kingdom comes to this Conference with no powers to sign ... But our own attitude is that until we see actions, we are not ourselves willing to accede to it". The actions referred to were evidence that the broadcasters would abandon their campaign of opposition to the Rome Convention (*cf. verbatim* Records of the Conference, in Records of the Diplomatic Conference, para. 24–155, above, paras 37–3 and 37–8 to 37–12).

[98] Vienna Agreement, Art.1. Report of the Diplomatic Conference and text, see [1973] *Copyright* 122 and 132. See also S. Ricketson, *The Berne Convention for the protection of literary and artistic works: 1886–1896* (Queen Mary College, University of London, 1987), para.15.62.

[99] Vienna Agreement, Art.2.

[1] Art.3.

[2] Art.5.

[3] Art.7.

[4] Art.4.

reproductions.[5] The term of protection provided for in the Agreement is a minimum of 15 years.[6] However, according to the Protocol to the Agreement, States party to the Protocol shall provide a minimum of 25 years instead.[7] The Agreement also provides for a system of international deposit and recording thereof in an international register to be administered by the International Bureau of the World Intellectual Property Organisation (WIPO).[8]

Detailed Regulations concerning the international deposit of typefaces are annexed to the Agreement.[9]

Entry into force and parties to the Convention. The Agreement has never entered into force. For it to do so would require that five states had deposited their instruments of ratification or accession. To date, only France and Germany have done so.[10] It is a closed Convention; only states party to either the Paris Union for the Protection of Industrial Property, the Berne Convention or the Universal Copyright Convention may become party to the Agreement. Although the United Kingdom signed the Agreement on the date of its adoption, it has not ratified it.   **24–160**

D. THE MADRID DOUBLE TAXATION CONVENTION

The Convention for the Avoidance of Double Taxation of Copyright Royalties (the Madrid Convention) was adopted in Madrid on December 13, 1979, under the auspices of the United Nations Organisation for Education, Science and Culture (UNESCO) and the World Intellectual Property Organisation (WIPO).[11] The subject-matter of the Convention is of importance to authors who earn royalties from the exploitation of their works and are liable to pay tax thereon in more than one country. However, the Convention has no impact on the creation and subsistence of authors' rights.   **24–161**

Under the Convention, each Contracting State undertakes to make every possible effort, in accordance with its Constitution and certain guiding principles laid down in the Convention: "to avoid double taxation of copyright royalties, where possible, and, should it subsist, to eliminate it or to reduce its effect … by means of bilateral agreements or by way of domestic measures".[12] The guiding principles relate to matters such as fiscal sovereignty and equality of rights of states to tax copyright royalties and fiscal non-discrimination.[13]

A model of a bilateral agreement, comprising several alternative provisions, is attached to the Convention but does not form an integral part thereof.

The administration of the Convention is entrusted to UNESCO and WIPO jointly.

An additional Protocol was adopted at the same time as the Convention, providing for its provisions to apply also to the taxation of royalties paid to performers,   **24–162**

---

[5] Art.8.

[6] Art.9.

[7] Protocol, Art.1.

[8] Ch.II, Arts 12–25.

[9] Art.29 and Regulations Under the Vienna Agreement for the Protection of Typefaces and their International Deposit.

[10] As of August 20, 2004; information received from WIPO.

[11] For the report of the Diplomatic Conference and text of the Convention and its Protocol, see [1980] *Copyright* 12. See also S. Ricketson, *The Berne Convention for the Protection of Literary and Artistic Works: 1886–1896* (Queen Mary College, University of London, 1987), para.15.60.

[12] The Madrid Convention, Art.8.

[13] Arts 5–7.

producers of phonograms and broadcasting organisations in respect of rights related to copyright or "neighbouring rights".

In order to enter into force, the Convention requires the adherence of 10 states.[14] To date, only seven have done so and the Convention remains a dead letter.[15] The United Kingdom did not sign the Convention, its delegate declaring that, while endorsing the aims of the Convention, it objected to the method employed—a multilateral Convention—which was unrealistic and risked being ineffective.[16] For these reasons, the United Kingdom could not accept the texts, at that time,[17] and has not since changed its attitude.

10. REGIONAL CONVENTIONS

A. PAN-AMERICAN CONVENTIONS

24–163   As seen above at paragraphs 24–79*et seq.*, the principal purpose of the Universal Copyright Convention (UCC) was to provide a conventional link to govern copyright relations between the countries of the Berne Union, on the one hand, and the Member States of the various multilateral copyright conventions which had been adopted between 1889 and 1928 by certain of the States on the American continent, including in some cases the United States of America, on the other.[18] These include the Montevideo Convention and the so-called Pan-American Conventions.[19] The Universal Copyright Convention provides specifically that the Convention shall not abrogate any copyright relations in effect exclusively between two or more American Republics and that in the event of any difference between the provisions of the UCC and any Pan-American Convention the most recently formulated shall prevail.[20]

The Pan-American Conventions were all influenced by the Berne Convention and reflected the aim of their signatories to obtain a copyright treaty which would

---

[14] Madrid Convention, Art.13.

[15] The Convention was signed by: Cameroon, the then Czechoslovakia, the Holy See and Israel. As of August 2004, the following states have adhered to the Convention: Czech Republic (1993); Ecuador (1994); Egypt (1982); India (1983); Iraq (1981); Peru (1988); Slovakia (1993). The Protocol was signed by Cameroon, the Holy See and Israel. As of August 2004 the following states have adhered to it: Czech Republic and Slovakia. Information received from WIPO.

[16] General Report of the Diplomatic Conference on the Double Taxation of Copyright Royalties, Madrid, November 26 to December 13, 1979, [1980] *Copyright* 12 *et seq.*, at para.175.

[17] General Report of the Diplomatic Conference on the Double Taxation of Copyright Royalties, Madrid, November 26 to December 13, 1979, [1980] Copyright 12, *et seq.*, at para.179.

[18] "The Conference [for the adoption of the UCC] was the logical development of the desire expressed by many nations for many years and on many different occasions for some international agreement on the rights of authors which would be acceptable to the Member States of the Berne Union for the Protection of Literary and Artistic Works, and to the members of the Organisation of American States, and, if possible, also to other States which were not members of either." Report of the Rapporteur-General (Sir John Blake) of the Intergovernmental Conference of States for the adoption of the Universal Copyright Convention, Geneva, August 18 to September 6, 1952, in T.R. Kupferman and M. Foner (eds.), *Universal Copyright Convention Analysed* (Federal Legal Publications Inc., New York, 1955), p.214.

[19] The full text of these Conventions, and information concerning the states to which they apply, will be found in "Copyright Laws and Treaties of the World", published by UNESCO. They are also reproduced in T.R. Kupferman and M. Foner, *Universal Copyright Convention Analysed* (Federal Legal Publications Inc., New Yorker 1995), 614 *et seq.* See also H.G. Henn, "Interrelation Between the UCC and the Pan-American Copyright Conventions" in T.R. Kupferman and M. Foner, 125; S. Ricketson, *The Berne Convention for the protection of literary and artistic works: 1886–1896* (Queen Mary College, University of London, 1987), paras 15.3 *et seq.* and S.P.Ladas, "Patents, Trademarks, and Related Rights; National and International Protection" (Harvard University Press, Cambridge, 1975). See also "Les Conventions pan-américaines concernant la protection de la propriété intellectuelle: Mexico (1902), Rio de Janeiro 1906, Buenos Aires 1910" [1911] *Le Droit d'Auteur*, 58.

[20] Art.XVIII of the 1952 and 1971 texts.

attract all the States of the Americas.[21] However, all the Conventions differed fundamentally from the Berne Convention in that they provided that copyright protection, at least for published works, be subject to compliance with formalities.[22] With the passage of time, and the adherence of many of the Latin-American States as well as the United States of America to the Berne Convention and the UCC, these conventions are no longer of more than historical interest. The United Kingdom was never party to any of them.

The Montevideo Convention[23] (January 11, 1889) was influenced by and largely   **24–164** modelled on the Berne Convention. However, it rejected the principle of national treatment and adopted a wholly different principle to that of the Berne Convention, conferring upon an author belonging to one country of the Union in the other countries of the Union the rights which he enjoys in the country where he first publishes, not the rights which authors enjoy in the country where the infringement takes place. Thus, under this Convention, the law of the country of origin follows the work into the other countries of the Union. Membership was limited to signatory states which ratified the Convention; as far as non-signatory states were concerned, these could accede to the Convention but only benefited from conventional relations with signatory states which accepted their accession. This limited the value of the Convention, since of the five signatory states that ratified it (Argentina, Bolivia, Paraguay, Peru and Uruguay), Peru and Uruguay refused to recognise accessions by non-Latin American states.[24]

The Pan-American Conventions are those of Mexico City[25] (1902), Rio de Ja-   **24–165** neiro[26] (1906), Buenos Aires[27] (1910), Caracas[28] (1911), Havana[29] (1928) and Washington[30] (1946). These all had the aim of attracting the adherence of all American States, an aim in which none of them succeeded. The later of these Conventions are all modifications of the original Convention of 1902, and all adopt the Berne principle of according national protection to works published in any of the countries of the Union (principle of national treatment). But under the Convention of 1902, in order to obtain copyright in another country, it was an "indispensable" condition that the author or his representatives should address a petition to the official department of each government, claiming the recognition of the right. This was modified by the later Conventions, and, under the Convention of 1910, it simply provided that "the acknowledgment of a copyright obtained in one state, in conformity with its laws, shall produce its effects of full right, in all the other states, without the necessity of complying with any other formality, provided always there shall appear in the work a statement that indicates the reservation of the property right".[31] The Convention of 1902 was ratified by Costa Rica, the Dominican Republic, El Salvador, Guatemala,

---

[21] With the exception of the Montevideo Convention, the Pan-American Conventions were open to adherence only by countries of the Western Hemisphere, *i.e.* American States.

[22] See H.G. Henn, "Interrelation Between the UCC and the Pan-American Copyright Conventions" in T.R. Kupferman and M. Foner, p.137.

[23] Convention of Montevideo on Literary and Artistic Property, January 11, 1889.

[24] [1889] *Le Droit d'Auteur*, 52.

[25] Convention for the Protection of Literary and Artistic Property, January 27, 1902.

[26] Convention for the Protection of Patents of Invention, Drawings and Industrial Models, Trade-Marks and Literary and Artistic Property, August 23, 1906.

[27] Convention Concerning Literary and Artistic Copyright, August 11, 1910.

[28] Agreement on Literary and Artistic Property, July 17, 1911.

[29] Revision of the Conference of Buenos Aires Regarding Literary and Artistic Copyright, February 18, 1928.

[30] Inter-American Convention on the Rights of the Author in Literary, Scientific and Artistic Works, 1946.

[31] Buenos Aires Convention, Art.3.

Honduras, Nicaragua and the United States of America. The Convention of 1906 was ratified by Brazil, Chile, Costa Rica, Ecuador, El Salvador, Guatemala, Honduras, Nicaragua and Panama. The Convention of 1910 was ratified by 14 states, making it the most successful of these conventions; namely, Argentina, Bolivia, Brazil, Chile Colombia, Costa Rica, the Dominican Republic, Ecuador, Haiti, Guatemala, Honduras, Mexico, Nicaragua, Panama, Peru, Paraguay, Uruguay and the United States of America. The 1911 Convention, which was modelled on the Montevideo Convention, was signed by Bolivia, Colombia, Ecuador, Peru and Venezuela but ratified only by the last three of these.[32] Finally, the Convention of 1928, which was a revision of the Buenos Aires Convention, was ratified by only Costa Rica, Ecuador, Guatemala, Nicaragua and Panama.

Many years later, a further Convention was concluded at Washington in 1946 under the auspices of the Pan-American Union, according to which rights of copyright set out in some detail are to be conferred as between the signatory countries without formality or restriction. This Convention replaced, in relations between the Contracting States, the Conventions of Buenos Aires (1910), Havana (1928) and all earlier inter-American Conventions on copyright but did not affect rights acquired under those Conventions.[33] The Washington Convention was ratified by Argentina, Bolivia, Brazil, Chile, Colombia, Costa Rica, Cuba, Dominica, Ecuador, Guatemala, Haiti, Honduras, Mexico, Nicaragua and Paraguay.

B. COUNCIL OF EUROPE CONVENTIONS AND RECOMMENDATIONS

24–166   **Interest of the Council of Europe in Copyright and Related Rights.** Since the 1950s, the Council of Europe has adopted a series of European Agreements on broadcasting, aimed at promoting a "European audiovisual area" and at safeguarding intellectual property rights on a European basis (see the Table of Council of Europe Copyright and Related Rights Conventions, in para.24–167, below).[34] More recently, it has also undertaken studies of a number of copyright and related rights law questions, which have resulted in the adoption by the Council of Ministers of a series of recommendations and declarations.[35] The United Kingdom is a member of the Council of Europe and party or signatory to these instruments.

The Council of Europe's policy in these matters has been expressed as follows: "copyright and neighbouring rights are at the basis of the creation, production and circulation of audiovisual works in Europe and…it is necessary to provide for a minimum harmonisation of national rules in the area of copyright and neighbouring rights so as to guarantee adequate protection of rights holders, while facilitating the public's access to audiovisual creations through the new opportunities offered by technical developments".[36] The value to the international community of the Council of Europe's involvement in these matters lies in its efforts to promote copyright and related rights throughout its 47 Member States in

---

[32] "L'Union bolivienne et la protection de la propriété intellectuelle", [1912] *Le Droit d'Auteur* 58.

[33] Washington Convention, Art.XVII.

[34] Council of Europe activities concerning the protection of copyright and neighbouring rights in the media sector (doc. DH-MM(96) 4), para.8. A table showing these parties to there conventions is contained in para. 24–167, below.

[35] Doc. DH–MM (96) 4, for an account of Council of Europe activities to 1996. The Agreements, Resolutions and Declarations mentioned are all available from the Publications Section, Council of Europe, F-67075 Strasbourg Cedex, France.

[36] Resolution No.1 on media economics and political and cultural pluralism, 3rd. European Ministerial Conference on Mass Media Policy (October 1991).

Western and Eastern Europe.[37] The agreements are also open to signature and ratification by non-Member States.

European agreements on broadcasting. The European Agreement concerning Programme Exchanges by means of Television Films, 1958, aims to facilitate the exchange of television films, *inter alia*, in the framework of the European Broadcasting Union.[38]   **24–167**

The European Agreement on the Protection of Television Broadcasts, 1960, with its Protocol, 1965, and three additional Protocols (1974, 1983 and 1989),[39] was adopted as a temporary, regional arrangement with limited objectives. It was foreseen that it would remain in force only until such time as an international convention on related rights, including the protection of television broadcasts, was established.[40] Broadcasting organisations have the right to authorise the following acts in relation to their television broadcasts: re-broadcasting, cable distribution, communication to the public and audiovisual recording in another country. The parties can make protected utilisations subject to given reservations, and, in particular, can withhold completely the protection of cable distribution. The adoption of the Rome Convention in 1961 led to the adoption of the 1965 Protocol to the Agreement, which urged Contracting Parties to accede to the Rome Convention; the slow pace of adherence to the Rome Convention subsequently resulted in the adoption of the three Additional Protocols of 1974, 1983 and 1989, which had the same aim. They all provided that, after a prescribed date, no state could remain or become a party to the Agreement unless it had become a party to the Rome Convention. The date prescribed by the second Protocol was January 1, 1990 and, since the third Protocol (aimed at postponing the deadline once more) had not entered into force on that date, four states then ceased to be members.

The European Agreement for the Prevention of Broadcasts transmitted from Stations outside National Territories 1965, reinforces, within Europe, compliance with the International Telecommunication Union (ITU) Radio Regulations. The Agreement aims to prevent the establishment of broadcasting stations on board ships, aircraft or other objects, such as platforms and artificial islands outside national territories (pirate stations) , which transmit broadcasts intended for reception within the territory of one of the parties and requires all broadcasting to be licensed.[41]

The European Convention relating to Questions on Copyright Law and Neighbouring Rights in the Framework of Transfrontier Broadcasting by Satellite was

---

[37] The Council of Europe has the following 47 Member States: Albania, Andorra, Armenia, Austria, Azerbaijan, Belgium, Bosnia and Herzegovina, Bulgaria, Croatia, Cyprus, Czech Republic, Denmark, Estonia, Finland, France, Georgia, Germany, Greece, Hungary, Iceland, Ireland, Italy, Latvia, Liechtenstein, Lithuania, Luxembourg, Macedonia (the former Yugoslav Republic of), Malta, Moldova, the Netherlands, Norway, Poland, Portugal, Romania, Russian Federation, San Marino, Serbia and Montenegro, Slovakia, Slovenia, Spain, Sweden, Switzerland, Turkey, Ukraine, UK.

[38] Adopted in Paris on December 15, 1958, this Agreement entered into force on July 1, 1961. As of August 20, 2004, the following 15 Member States of the Council of Europe were party thereto: Belgium, Cyprus, Denmark, France, Greece, Ireland, Luxembourg, the Netherlands, Norway, Spain, Sweden, Turkey and the United Kingdom. The Agreement is open to non-Member States and Israel and Tunisia have adhered thereto.

[39] Adopted in Strasbourg on June 22, 1960, this Agreement entered into force on July 1, 1961. As of August 20, 2004, it is in force in six Member States: Denmark, France, Germany, Norway, Sweden and the United Kingdom.

[40] Agreement, Art.13.

[41] Adopted in Strasbourg on January 22, 1965, this Agreement entered into force on October 19, 1967. The following Member States of the Council of Europe were party thereto as of August 20, 2004: Belgium, Cyprus, Denmark, France, Germany, Greece, Ireland, Italy, Liechtenstein, the Netherlands, (including the Netherlands, Antilles and Aruba), Norway, Poland, Portugal, Spain, Sweden, Switzerland, Turkey and the United Kingdom.

adopted on February 17, 1994 but has not yet entered into force.[42] The Convention indicates the criteria for identifying the applicable national law governing relations between broadcasters and rights holders in respect of the transmission of works and other contributions by direct broadcasting satellite (DBS) or by fixed satellite services (FSS) under conditions which are comparable to direct broadcasting by satellite. The Convention also deals with ways and means of acquiring rights in works which are used for broadcasting by satellite. Furthermore, it establishes a minimum harmonisation of the level of protection of the various categories of rights holders (authors, composers, audiovisual producers, performers, phonogram producers, broadcasting organisations).[43]

24–168 **Convention on Cybercrime.**[44] This is the first international treaty to address criminal law and procedural aspects of various types of behaviour directed against computer systems, networks and data. It contains provisions concerning offences related to infringements of copyright and neighbouring rights (Article 10). It was opened for signature on November 23, 2001, and has been signed by 32 Member States of the Council of Europe as well as by Canada, Japan, South Africa and the United States of America. It entered into force on July 1, 2004, following ratification by five countries, including at least three Member States of the Council of Europe. As at August 20, 2004, it had been ratified by six States: Albania, Croatia, Estonia, Hungary, Lithuania and Romania.

An additional Protocol to the Convention on Cybercrime, concerning the criminalisation of acts of a racist and xenophobic nature committed through computer systems,[45] was adopted on January 28, 2003. It will enter into force following five ratifications.[46]

24–169 **Recommendations and Declarations.** These identify key issues for priority action and lay down principles designed to guide Member States in improving the level of protection provided by their national laws and relate to copyright law questions in the following fields: copyright law principles to be respected in the field of television broadcasting by satellite and cable,[47] the protection of related rights,[48] the legal protection of encrypted television services,[49] sound and audiovisual private copying,[50] measures to combat piracy in the field of copyright and neighbouring rights,[51] measures against sound and audiovisual piracy,[52] principles relating to copyright law questions in the field of reprography,[53] the promotion of education and awareness in the area of copyright and neighbouring rights

---

[42] As of August 20, 2004, the Convention has been signed, by nine Member States of the Council of Europe: Belgium, Cyprus, Germany, Luxembourg, Norway, San Marino, Spain, Switzerland and the United Kingdom. It has also been signed on behalf of the European Union. It will enter into force after its ratification by seven States, including at least five Member States. To date, it has been ratified only by Cyprus, with effect from December 21, 1998 and Norway, with effect from June 19, 1998.

[43] Council of Europe activities concerning the protection of copyright and neighbouring rights in the media sector (doc.DH–MM(94)(4), paras 18 et seq.

[44] Convention on Cybercrime (CETS No.185).

[45] CETS No.189.

[46] As of August 20, 2004, the Protocol had been signed by 23 Member States of the Council of Europe.

[47] Recommendation No.R (86) 2 of February 14, 1986.

[48] Declaration on the protection of neighbouring rights (adopted by the Committee of Ministers of the Council of Europe on February 17, 1994).

[49] Recommendation No.R(91) 14 of September 27, 1991.

[50] Recommendation No.R (88) 1 of January 18, 1988.

[51] Recommendation No.R (88) 2 of January 18, 1988.

[52] Recommendation No.R (95) 1 of January 11, 1995.

[53] Recommendation No.R(90) 11 of April 25, 1990.

concerning creativity,[54] copyright and cultural policy[55] and on measures to protect copyright and neighbouring rights and combat piracy, especially in the digital environment.[56]

European agreements on related topics, including the information society. A number of European Conventions on topics having an impact on copyright and related rights have been adopted in the years since the 14th edition of this work was published. These do not deal directly with copyright and related rights but concern aspects of the information society and broadcasting.   **24–170**

The European Convention on Transfrontier Television ,[57] adopted on May 5, 1989, and which entered into force on May 1, 1993, creates a legal framework for the free circulation of trans-frontier television programmes in Europe, through minimum common rules, in fields such as programming, advertising, sponsorship and the protection of certain individual rights, such as the right to exercise the right to reply to TV programmes. The Convention has been amended by a Protocol,[58] which entered into force on March 1, 2002.

The Convention on Information and Legal Cooperation concerning "Information Society Services"[59] was adopted on October 4, 2001. The aim of the Convention, which was prepared in close co-operation between the Council of Europe and the European Commission, is to set up a legal information and co-operation system in the area of new communication services, following the example of Directive 98/34/EC[60] and extending it beyond the borders of the European Union. According to the Council of Europe, it will enable it to act as a clearing house for draft legislation in the field of "Information Society Services", in order to provide a harmonised approach to the regulation of online services at the pan-European level. The Convention will enter into force after the expression of their consent to be bound by five signatories of which at least one is not a Member State of the European Economic Area. As of August 20, 2004, the Convention had not entered into force.

The European Convention for the Protection of the Audiovisual Heritage and its Protocol on the Protection of Television Productions[61] were adopted on November 8, 2001. They will enter into force following ratification by five countries, including at least four Member States of the Council of Europe. The Convention concerns the principle of compulsory legal deposit and conservation in film archives of all moving-image material produced or co-produced and made available to the public in each signatory state. The material has to be available for consultation for academic or research purposes, subject to the international or national rules on copyright. As of August 20, 2004, the Convention had not entered into force.   **24–171**

The European Convention on the Legal Protection of Services Based on, or

---

[54] Recommendation No.R (94) 3 of April 5, 1994.

[55] Recommendation No.R (86) 9 of May 1986.

[56] Recommendation No.R (2001) 7.

[57] CETS No.132.

[58] CETS No.171.

[59] CETS No.180.

[60] Directive 98/34/EC of the European Parliament and of the Council of June 22, 1998, laying down a procedure for the provision of information in the field of technical standards and regulations and of rules on Information Society services ([1998] O.J. L204, July 21, 1998, p.37). Directive as amended by Directive 98/48/EC of the European Parliament and of the Council ([1998] O.J. L217, of August 5, 1988, p.18.

[61] CETS Nos 183 and 184.

Consisting of, Conditional Access,[62] was adopted on January 24, 2001, and entered into force on July 1, 2003. The Convention seeks to protect operators and providers of paid radio, TV and online services against unlawful reception of such services. It supplements a European Community Directive[63]on the same subject by extending protection throughout Europe. Under the Convention, it is a criminal offence to manufacture, import, distribute, sell, offer for hire, possess or install decoders or smart cards enabling access to be obtained unlawfully to the above-mentioned services. The promotion, marketing or advertising of illicit devices are also prohibited. Penalties include seizure and confiscation of devices or material and of any profits or financial gain resulting from the unlawful activity. The aim of the Convention is to help European providers of audiovisual and online services to reduce financial losses sustained as a result of electronic and computer piracy, in the interest of both service operators and the public.

As of August 20, 2004, the Convention had the following Member States: Bulgaria, Cyprus, Moldova, Netherlands and Romania.

[62] CETS No.178.

[63] Directive 98/84/EC of the European Parliament and of the Council of November 20, 1998, on the legal protection of services based on, or consisting of, conditional access (cf. Ch. 25–91, below and Vol.2, App.H9).

TABLE OF COUNCIL OF EUROPE COPYRIGHT AND RELATED RIGHTS CONVENTIONS[1]

Member States of the Council of Europe	European Agreement Concerning Programme Exchanges by Means of Television Films 1958[2]	Agreement on the Protection of Television Broadcasts 1960[3]	European Agreement for the Prevention of Broadcasts Transmitted from Stations Outside National Territories 1965[4]	European Convention Relating to Questions of Copyright Law and Neighbouring Rights in the Framework of Transfrontier Broadcasting by Satellite 1994[5]	Convention on Cybercrime 2001[6]
	Date of entry into force	(E) Date of entry into force (D) Date denunciation took effect	Date of entry into force	(a) Date of signature (b) Date of ratification	(a) Date of Signature (b) Date of entry into force or ratification
Albania					(b) July 1, 2004
Andorra					
Armenia					(a) November 23, 2001
Austria					(a) November 23, 2001
Azerbaijan					
Belgium	April 8, 1962	March 8, 1968 (E) January 1, 1990	October 19, 1967	(a) August 6, 1998	(a) November 23, 2001
Bosnia and Herzogovina					

Member States of the Council of Europe	European Agreement Concerning Programme Exchanges by Means of Television Films 1958[2]	Agreement on the Protection of Television Broadcasts 1960[3]	European Agreement for the Prevention of Broadcasts Transmitted from Stations Outside National Territories 1965[4]	European Convention Relating to Questions of Copyright Law and Neighbouring Rights in the Framework of Transfrontier Broadcasting by Satellite 1994[5]	Convention on Cybercrime 2001[6]
Bulgaria					(a) November 23, 2001
Croatia					(b) July 1, 2004
Cyprus	February 20, 1970	February 22, 1970 (E) January 1, 1990 (D)	October 2, 1971	(a) February 10, 1995 (b) December 21, 1998	(a) November 23, 2001
Czech Republic					
Denmark	November 25, 1961	November 27, 1961 (E)	October 19, 1967		(a) April 22, 2003.
Estonia					(b) July 1, 2004
Finland					(a) November 23, 2001
France	July 1, 1961	July 1, 1961 (E)	April 6, 1968		(a) November 23, 2001
Georgia					

Member States of the Council of Europe	European Agreement Concerning Programme Exchanges by Means of Television Films 1958[2]	Agreement on the Protection of Television Broadcasts 1960[3]	European Agreement for the Prevention of Broadcasts Transmitted from Stations Outside National Territories 1965[4]	European Convention Relating to Questions of Copyright Law and Neighbouring Rights in the Framework of Transfrontier Broadcasting by Satellite 1994[5]	Convention on Cybercrime 2001[6]
Germany		October 9, 1967(E)	February 28, 1970	(a) April 18, 1997	(a) November 23, 2001
Greece	February 9, 1962		August 14, 1979		(a) November 23, 2001
Hungary					(b) July 1, 2004
Iceland					(a) November 30, 2001
Ireland	April 4, 1965		February 23, 1969		(a) February 28,2002
Italy			March 19, 1983		(a) November 23, 2001
Latvia					(a) May 5, 2004
Liechtenstein			February 14, 1977		
Lithuania					(b) July 1, 2004
Luxembourg	October 31, 1963			(a) May 11, 1994	(a) January 28, 2003

Member States of the Council of Europe	European Agreement Concerning Programme Exchanges by Means of Television Films 1958[2]	Agreement on the Protection of Television Broadcasts 1960[3]	European Agreement for the Prevention of Broadcasts Transmitted from Stations Outside National Territories 1965[4]	European Convention Relating to Questions of Copyright Law and Neighbouring Rights in the Framework of Transfrontier Broadcasting by Satellite 1994[5]	Convention on Cybercrime 2001[6]
Macedonia (the former Yugoslav Republic of)					(a) November 23, 2001
Malta	October 31, 1963				(a) January 17, 2002.
Moldova					(a) November 23, 2001
Netherlands	March 5, 1967		September 27, 1974		(a) November 23, 2001
Norway	March 15, 1963	August 10, 1968 (E)	October 17, 1971	(a) May 11, 1994 (b) June 19, 1998	(a) November 23, 2001
Poland			November 11, 1994		(a) November 23, 2001
Portugal			September 7, 1969		(a) November 23, 2001
Romania					(a) November 23, 2001 (b) September 1, 2004
Russia					
San Marino				(a) May 11, 1994	

Member States of the Council of Europe	European Agreement Concerning Programme Exchanges by Means of Television Films 1958[2]	Agreement on the Protection of Television Broadcasts 1960[3]	European Agreement for the Prevention of Broadcasts Transmitted from Stations Outside National Territories 1965[4]	European Convention Relating to Questions of Copyright Law and Neighbouring Rights in the Framework of Trans-frontier Broadcasting by Satellite 1994[5]	Convention on Cyber-crime 2001[6]
Serbia and Montenegro					
Slovakia					
Slovenia					(a) July 24, 2002
Spain	January 4, 1974	October 23, 1971 (E) January 1, 1990 (D)	March 11, 1988	(a) May 11, 1994	(a) November 23, 2001
Sweden	July 1, 1961	July 1, 1961 (E)	October 19, 1967		(a) November 23, 2001
Switzerland			September 19, 1976	(a) May 11, 1994	(a) November 23, 2001
Turkey	March 28, 1964	January 20, 1976 (E) January 1, 1990 (D)	February 17, 1975		
Ukraine					(a) November 23, 2001

Member States of the Council of Europe	European Agreement Concerning Programme Exchanges by Means of Television Films 1958[2]	Agreement on the Protection of Television Broadcasts 1960[3]	European Agreement for the Prevention of Broadcasts Transmitted from Stations Outside National Territories 1965[4]	European Convention Relating to Questions of Copyright Law and Neighbouring Rights in the Framework of Transfrontier Broadcasting by Satellite 1994[5]	Convention on Cybercrime 2001[6]
United Kingdom	July 1, 1961	July 1. 1961 (E)	December 3, 1967	(a) October 2, 1996	(a) November 23, 2001
EC				(a) June 26, 1996	
Non-Member States[7]					
Belarus					
Canada					(a) November 23, 2001
Holy See					
Israel	February 15, 1978				
Japan					(a) November 23, 2001
Monaco					
Morocco					
South Africa					(a) November 23, 2001
Tunisia	February 22, 1969				

Member States of the Council of Europe	European Agreement Concerning Programme Exchanges by Means of Television Films 1958[2]	Agreement on the Protection of Television Broadcasts 1960[3]	European Agreement for the Prevention of Broadcasts Transmitted from Stations Outside National Territories 1965[4]	European Convention Relating to Questions of Copyright Law and Neighbouring Rights in the Framework of Transfrontier Broadcasting by Satellite 1994[5]	Convention on Cybercrime 2001[6]
USA					(a) November 23, 2001

[1] See Ch.24(10)(B). This Table is up to date as of August 20, 2004.

[2] CETS No.027. The Agreement is open for accession by the following non-Member States: Israel, Morocco and Tunisia.

[3] CETS No.034. As regards the Protocol to this Agreement (CETS No.054, 1965) and the three additional Protocols thereto (CETS No.081, 1974; CETS No.113, 1983 and CETS No.131, 1989), see para.24–167 , above.

[4] CETS No.053. The Agreement is open for accession by Morocco.

[5] CETS No.153. This Convention has not yet entered into force. It is open for signature and ratification by the Member States, the other states party to the European Cultural Convention (Belarus, Holy See and Monaco), and on behalf of the European Community.

[6] CETS No.185. This Convention has not yet entered into force. It is open for signature and ratification by the Member States of the Council of Europe and by non-Member States which participated in its elaboration, namely, Canada, Japan, South Africa and the United States of America.

[7] Note that some of the treaties listed are open for signature and ratification by one or more states not party to the Council of Europe (*cf.* nn.2, 4, 5 and 6, above).

CHAPTER TWENTY FIVE

COMMUNITY LAW

Contents

1. INTRODUCTION

Creation and enlargement of the EC and EEA. The European Economic Community was created by the Treaty of Rome of March 25, 1957.[1] Together with the Treaties creating the European Coal and Steel Community and the European Atomic Energy Community, the Treaty set up a framework for economic and political co-operation among the original six founder Member States,[2] leading to the development of a Common Market. The United Kingdom of Great Britain and Northern Ireland, Denmark and the Republic of Ireland acceded to the European Communities on January 1, 1973. The United Kingdoms accession to the Treaty was implemented in the United Kingdom legal system by the European Communities Act 1972,[3] under which, as since amended, much of the legislation required to implement Community Directives and Regulations has been introduced.

25–01

---

[1] Which, as amended, is referred to in this work as "the Treaty".

[2] Belgium, France, Federal Republic of Germany, Italy, Luxembourg and the Netherlands.

[3] c.68; the combined effect of ss.2(1) and 3 (1) of the Act is that Community law, as a body of provisions of the Treaty and its implementing measures and judicial decisions interpreting and applying those provisions, is fully integrated into the laws of the United Kingdom and, since January 1, 1973, has formed part of the national legal order.

Subsequently, membership of the Communities has expanded to 25. First came the accession of Greece on January 1, 1981, followed by those of Spain and Portugal on January 1, 1986, and those of Austria, Sweden and Finland on January 1, 1995. More recently, on May 1, 2004, the following 10 new Member States acceded to what has meanwhile become the European Union: Czech Republic, Estonia, Cyprus, Latvia, Lithuania, Hungary, Malta, Poland, Slovenia and Slovakia. With the accession of these 10 new Member States, the overall EU population has increased from 375 million to 450 million. Negotiations are formally under way also with Bulgaria and Romania which are expected to be admitted to the EU in 2007. In addition, Turkey has been recognised as a candidate for membership. The Accession Treaty provides that the 10 new Member States must have complied with EU law by May 1, 2004 (the date of their accession), including the *acquis communautaire* (existing body of Community law) with regard to copyright and related rights.

The Treaty on European Union (TEU),[4] which came into force on November 1, 1993,[5] created a new structure, the European Union, with separate legal powers, but within which the existing communities, including the European Economic Community (EEC), now renamed the European Community (EC),[6] continue to operate. The TEU enlarged the aims of the Treaty and substantially amended its provisions, principally in the areas concerned with economic and monetary union. Meanwhile, the Treaty of Amsterdam has entered into force, following completion of the ratification process in the Member States. The Articles, titles and sections of the Treaty on European Union (TEU) and of the Treaty establishing the European Community (the Treaty), as amended by the Treaty of Amsterdam, have been renumbered in accordance with tables of equivalences annexed to the Treaty of Amsterdam and forming an integral part thereof[7]. All references in this Chapter to the Articles of the Treaty are to the Consolidated Version of the Treaty establishing the European Community, incorporating the changes made by the Treaty of Amsterdam.[8]

The Treaty of Nice has meanwhile revised the Treaties once more with the aim of adapting the way in which the European institutions operate in order to facilitate the entry into the EU of the new Member States. The Treaty of Nice, adopted on December 11, 2000 and signed on February 26, 2001, entered into force on February 1, 2003, after being ratified by the then 15 Member States of the EU according to their respective constitutional rules.[9] The institutional reforms achieved by the Treaty of Nice do not drastically change the institutional balance, but make some adjustments to the functions and composition of the institutions and further enhanced co-operation.

---

[4] Otherwise known as the Maastricht Treaty, negotiated at Maastricht in December 1991 and formally signed by the Member States at Maastricht on February 7, 1992.

[5] The changes to the European Communities Act 1972 consequent on the UK's accession to the TEU were effected by the European Communities (Amendment) Act 1993, c.32.

[6] Strictly speaking, all of the legislative measures taken by the Community have been in terms of EEC (now EC) law, rather than EU law; in this work the term Community law is used to describe both the past body of EEC and EC measures and law, as well as those resulting from the TEU. For a useful summary of the new (and old) terminology, see [1994] 1 C.M.L.R. 4.

[7] Art.12, Treaty of Amsterdam. These tables are reproduced in App.G2

[8] Signed at Amsterdam on October 2, 1997; [1997] O.J. C340/173–308, November 10, 1997). The Treaty entered into force on May 1, 1999. The legislation necessary to give domestic legal effect to the Treaty in the United Kingdom is contained in the European Communities (Amendment Act) Act 1998, c.21). The consolidated version is available on-line at europa.eu.int/eur-lex/en/treaties. Relevant Articles of the Treaty of Rome, as amended, are reproduced in App.G1.

[9] Treaty of Nice, [2001] O.J. C80/1, March 10, 2001.

The European Economic Area was created by the EEA Agreement,[10] which came into force on January 1, 1994.[11] It included Austria, Finland and Sweden, before their accession to the EU,[12] and thus now comprises all the Member States of the EU together with Iceland, Liechtenstein and Norway.[13]

The new EU Member States were obliged by the Accession Treaty to become members of the EEA with effect from May 1, 2004.

Scope of this section. It is the purpose of this chapter to consider the effect of Community law on the various rights enjoyed under the 1988 Act by the owner of copyright and related rights subsisting under that Act. It is beyond the scope of this chapter to describe in any detail the functions and workings of the Community and its institutions, or of the relationship between Community law and the national law of Member States.[14] **25–02**

The application of Community competition law to copyright and related rights, is not the subject of the present chapter but is dealt with at Chapter 29, paras 29–210 *et seq.*, below. However, it should be noted that the interface between intellectual property rights and EC competition law (Arts 81 and 82 of the Treaty dealing respectively with prohibited anti-competitive agreements and practices and abuse of dominant positions (ex Arts 85 and 86)) has become a topic of increasing importance in the last ten years and the impact of this interface needs to be borne in mind when considering the scope of the exclusive rights granted by the 1988 Act. Efforts to balance these rights have resulted in a body of case law of the European Court of Justice affecting the exercise of copyright and related rights. For many years such case law was mainly concerned with the control of the activities of collecting societies, which by their nature normally occupy a dominant position on the market (see Chapter 29, paras 29–253 *et seq*, below). More recently, the court has developed its case law to deal with conflicts arising when the exercise of an intellectual property right threatens to thwart competition on a given market. In such cases, it has put curbs on the exploitation of exclusive rights where, in the view of the court, a particular exercise of copyright by its owner conflicts with Art.82 of the Treaty, amounting to abuse of a dominant position. The court does not question the extent and terms of intellectual property rights granted by Member States but reserves the right "in exceptional circumstances" to limit the owner's freedom to exercise the right as he sees fit and to force him to grant a licence to competitors (compulsory licence).[15]

Before dealing with the impact of Community law on the exercise of copyright and related rights in the United Kingdom, it is necessary first to give a brief description of the relevant principles upon which the Community is based.

---

[10] The Agreement on the European Economic Area, signed at Oporto on May 2, 1992, as adjusted by the Protocol signed at Brussels on March 17, 1993.

[11] The legislation necessary to give domestic legal effect in the UK to the Agreement is contained in the European Economic Area Act 1993, c.51.

[12] Of the EFTA countries, only Switzerland opted not to join the EEA.

[13] With effect from January 1, 1994, therefore, most Community law (including all the copyright and related rights measures discussed in this Chapter) extends to the EFTA countries (except Switzerland, and, for the time being, Liechtenstein).

[14] The reader is referred to specialist works on these subjects, see: Lasok and Bridge, *Law and Institutions of the European Union*, (6th ed., Butterworths); Wyatt and Dashwood, *European Community Law*, (3rd ed., Sweet & Maxwell); Toth, *The Oxford Encyclopaedia of European Community Law* (OUP).

[15] *IMS Health GmbH & Co OHG v NDC Health GmbH & Co KG*, Case C-418/01 of April 29, 2004, see para. 25–70, below.

2. THE FREE MOVEMENT OF GOODS AND SERVICES WITHIN THE COMMUNITY

25–03   **Principal aims of the Community: realisation of a common market.** Article 2 (ex Article 2) of the Treaty establishing the European Community provides that the Community's task includes the promotion throughout the Community of: a harmonious development of economic activities; a high degree of convergence of economic performance; the raising of the standard of living and quality of life; and the economic and social cohesion and solidarity among Member States. This task is to be achieved by the establishment of a common market and an economic and monetary union. The establishment of a common market is therefore expressed as a means to an end, rather than an end in itself, but it is this preliminary aim which implies before all else the removal of all obstacles to the free movement of goods, persons, services and capital within the territory of the common market, and therefore across the boundaries of the Member States.

25–04   **Measures to remove obstacles to the common market.** Obstacles to the free movement of goods between Member States may be found in a variety of measures adopted by national governments, for example in customs duties, import quotas and subsidies for a particular national industry. Obstacles to the creation of a common market may also be found in practices adopted by private bodies trading within the common market, which are aimed at restricting competition and isolating national markets. It is with these obstacles in mind that Art.3 (ex Art.3) describes the activities to be undertaken by the Community as including:

     (a) the elimination, as between Member States, of customs duties and of quantitative restrictions on the import and export of goods, and of all other measures of equivalent effect;

     (c) an internal market characterised by the abolition, as between Member States, of obstacles to the free movement of goods, persons, services and capital; and

     (g) [16] the institution of a system ensuring that competition in the Common Market is not distorted.

These objectives find more detailed expression in later parts of the Treaty.

25–05   **Free movement of goods.** This objective is the subject of Arts 23 to 31 of the Treaty (ex Arts 9 to 37; (ex Arts 11 and 13 to 27 have been repealed)), forming the title Free Movement of Goods, which is the first title of Part Three of the Treaty, devoted to the policies of the Community. The position of this title reflects the fundamental importance attributed to this objective in the framework of the Treaty, although the objective of free movement of goods was not itself expressed as a principle in any Article of the Treaty in its original form.[17] The principle is now expressly referred to in Arts 4 and 14 (ex Arts 3 (a) and 7a) of the Treaty.[18] Nevertheless, well before this amendment to the Treaty, the Court of Justice, in its judgments in cases which came before it raising the issue of free movement of goods, stressed the importance of this principle, which was to be deduced from the wording, spirit and structure of this title. By such case law, the court

---

[16] This paragraph was re-lettered by the TEU; previously it was para.(f).

[17] Art.3(c), as originally worded, referred only to the removal of obstacles to the free movement of persons, service and capital.

[18] Inserted (originally as Art.8a) by the Single European Act, which came into force on July 1, 1987; later Arts 3(a) and 7a) of the Treaty.

established this principle as a rule of Community law as firmly as if it had from the beginning been expressly set out as such in an Article of theTreaty.[19]

Free movement of services. The general provisions governing the freedom to provide services are contained in Arts 49 to 55 (ex Arts 59 to 66; ex Art.62.has been repealed). Where, however, the principle of free movement of services touches on the field of transport or the liberalisation of banking and insurance services, the general provisions are subject to the particular provisions of the titles governing transport and the free movement of capital respectively. The principle of free movement of goods was not expressly contained in any Article of the original Treaty, and yet has been the area in which the Community has experienced the fastest development. In contrast, the principle of free movement of services was, from the beginning, contained in Art.3, but it is only in recent years that the Community has begun to focus its attention on the development of an effective regime for the free movement of services, in particular in relation to economic rather than professional services.   **25–06**

In essence, the framework of the provisions on services requires the abolition of restrictions imposed on nationals established in one Member State who provide services to persons established in another Member State. The basic principles are set out in Arts 49 and 50 (ex Arts 59 and 60), both of which are directly effective Treaty provisions. Article 50(2), (ex Art.60(2)) defines services as including, in particular, activities of an intellectual or commercial character, and activities of craftsmen and of the professions. The Court of Justice has further stated that the restrictions to be abolished pursuant to Arts 49 and 50 include all requirements imposed on the person providing the service by reason, in particular, of his nationality, or the fact that he does not habitually reside in the state where the service is provided, and which do not apply to persons established within the national territory, or which may prevent or otherwise obstruct the activities of the person providing the service.[20]

3. CONFLICT BETWEEN COPYRIGHT AND RELATED RIGHTS AND THE FREE MOVEMENT OF GOODS AND SERVICES

Copyright as an intellectual property right. The preferred term in early Community law for what are more usually now called intellectual property rights was intellectual and commercial property rights. This was the term used in the original Art.36 of the Treaty (now Art.30)[21] and in Reg.17.[22] The term copyright is nowhere mentioned in the Treaty. Despite the absence of any express reference to copyright, there was little doubt that copyright was to be considered as an intellectual property right for the purposes of the Treaty and its implementing measures.[23] This was confirmed by the Court of Justice in the case of *Musik-*   **25–07**

---

[19] For a full treatment of the subject of the free movement of goods, see Oliver and Jarvis, *Free Movement of Goods in the European Community*, (4th. ed., Sweet & Maxwell, London, 2002).

[20] Case 33/74 *Van Binsbergen v Bedrijfsvereniging Metaalnijverheid* [1974] E.C.R. 1299 at 1309, para.10.

[21] See further para. 25–20, below.

[22] Reg.17/62; [1962] O.J. 13/204, providing the procedure for enforcement of the competition rules (see further para. 29–208, below); see Art.4(2)(b), where the reference to intellectual and commercial property is followed by the description "in particular, patents, utility models, designs or trade marks".

[23] See the discussion in A. Dietz, *Copyright Law in the European Community*, (Alphen aan den Rijn, Sijthoff & Noordhoff, 1978), p.13, paras 27–31. See also the submissions of Advocate General Roemer in Case 78/70, *Deutsche Grammophon GmbH v Metro-SB-Grossmarkte GmbH*

Vertrieb Membran v GEMA,[24] in which the court rejected the argument that its
case law on intellectual property rights could not extend to copyright because
copyright was aimed at protecting the author's moral rights as much as his economic rights. The court, while recognising the presence of both economic and
moral rights behind the protection of copyright in national legislation, stated that
the questions before it concerned the economic aspect of copyright and that the
commercial exploitation of copyright raised the same issues as any other form of
intellectual and commercial property right in relation to the control of markets by
the author and those acting under him. Subsequently, the court has applied the
principles laid down in *Musik-Vertrieb Membran v GEMA* to related rights, and
in particular performers' rights.[25]

As between the different intellectual property rights it has been pointed out that
copyright is closer in nature to a patent than a trade mark.[26] It has been suggested
that as between patents and trade marks, the underlying justification for the
protection is stronger in the case of the former than the latter, and to the extent
that this is correct, the same may apply to copyright.[27] However, one important
difference between patents and copyright is that whereas the exercise of a patent
right will necessarily involve the creation of a material object either itself the
subject of the patent, or made by a process the subject of the patent, the exercise
of copyright will not always do so, since copyright gives not only the right to
control the production of products reproducing the copyright work, but also, for
instance, the right to control performance of the copyright work. The same applies to related rights. Unlike the right to control production, which is exhausted
once a product is produced, the right to control performance is not exhausted
upon the occasion of the first performance of the work. It is a right that will accrue in respect of each performance of the work, allowing an author to exercise a
continuing control over the performance of his work.[28]

25–08   **Territoriality.** However, it is a common characteristic of all intellectual property
rights that they confer some degree of monopoly or exclusivity, and that the
extent in content, time and territory of that monopoly or exclusivity is in the first
instance a matter for the national law of the state granting the right in question.[29]
The fact that an intellectual property right is the creature of the national laws of
the state granting the right necessarily places limits on the territory within which
such a right is effective. This has been referred to as the "territoriality principle"
of intellectual property rights,[30] but it is really no more than a necessary reflection
of the territorial limit to the sovereignty of the state concerned. In the present
context, an act which is complained of as being an infringement of an intellectual

[1971] E.C.R. 487; [1971] C.M.L.R. 63 1 at 646–647; Lord Denning M.R. in *Application des Gaz S.A. v Falks Veritas Ltd* [1974] Ch. 381; [1974] 2 C.M.L.R. 75 at 82 [23]; *Yate Security Products Ltd v Newman* [1990] F.S.R. 320.
[24] Cases 55 & 57/80, [1981] E.C.R. 147; [1981] 2 C.M.L.R. 44; see also Case 402/85, *Basset v SA-CEM* [1987] E.C.R. 1747 [11]; [1987] 3 C.M.L.R. 173 [11].
[25] Joined Cases C92-326/92, *Phil Collins v Imtrat HandelsGmbH* and *Verwaltungsgesellschaft mbH v EMI Electrola GmbH* [1993] 3 C.M.L.R. 773.
[26] Advocate General Roemer in Case 78/70, *Deutsche Grammophon GmbH v Metro-SB-Grossmarkte GmbH* [1971] E.C.R. 487; [1971] C.M.L.R. 631 at 649. See also Case 40/70, *Sirena S.R.L. v Eda S.R.L.* [1971] E.C.R. 69; [1971] C.M.L.R. 260 at 273 [7].
[27] See the views expressed by Advocate General Dutheillet de Lamothe in *Sirena S.R.L. v Eda S.R.L.* [1971] E.C.R. 69 at 87; [1971] C.M.L.R. 260 at 264–265.
[28] See further, as to the importance of this distinction, para. 25–27, below.
[29] See Case 144/81 *Keurkoop B.V. v Nancy Kean Gifts B.V.* [1982] E.C.R. 2853; [1983] 2 C.M.L.R. 47; Case 341/87 *EMI Electrola GmbH v Patricia Im- und Export Verwaltungsgesellschaft GmbH* [1989] E.C.R. 79; [1989] 2 C.M.L.R. 413; Case 53/87 *Maxicar v Renault* [1988] E.C.R. 6039; [1990] 4 C.M.L.R. 265.
[30] Advocate General Roemer in Case 78/70 *Deutsche Grammophon GmbH v Metro-SB-Grossmarkte GmbH* [1971] E.C.R. 487; C.M.L.R. 631 at 647–648.

property right, but which was committed in France, must be judged by French law.[31] Such an act is not an infringement of any rights granted under the 1988 Act.

International conventions in the field of copyright and related rights have helped to increase the protection available for the foreign owner of copyright and related rights in the states adhering to such conventions, but this is achieved by each state according copyright to the works of foreign authors under its own national laws.[32] It is not the aim (or effect) of such conventions to create a unitary right recognised throughout the combined territories of the signatories.

Monopoly or exclusivity. Whilst international conventions have achieved a   **25–09** measure of harmonisation in certain aspects of the extent of the exclusivity granted by the laws of each state to the owner of copyright and related rights, and notably, in the case of copyright, in the duration of such exclusivity, the extent, particularly of the content, of such exclusivity remains a matter for the laws of each state. It should be noted, however, that the extensive EC programme of harmonisation of the law of copyright and related rights has set standards in relation also to the extent of certain rights.[33] In the present context, the exclusive rights granted to the owner of copyright under the 1988 Act as amended to date generally include the right to copy the work the subject of copyright, issue copies thereof to the public, rent or lend it, perform, show or play the work in public, communicate it to the public and adapt it, all in the manner and forms appropriate to the type of work in question, and also the right to authorise others to exercise such rights, or any one or more of the acts which the copyright owner has the exclusive right to do, and for part or all of the life of the copyright.

Justification for monopoly or exclusivity: "exhaustion of rights". The   **25–10** justification for the monopoly or exclusivity accorded to the owner of an intellectual property right is that it gives him the protection necessary to allow him to obtain just recompense for his expenditure of time, effort and money in the creation or invention of the matter the subject of the right. Thus, where the exercise of the right can result in the production of a material object which will then be the subject of commerce, as is the case with a patent and, to a large extent with copyright, the owner of the right is able, in the territory of the state according such right, to control the production of such material objects, either by producing them himself, or by licensing another to do so, and in either case he is able to extract his recompense on the occasion of the first sale with his consent of such products in that territory. Thereafter, in principle, as a general rule, such products can be freely sold by way of trade within the territory of that state (apart from any enforceable contractual terms preventing such resale) and the owner of the right cannot assert his monopoly or exclusivity to prevent such resale.[34] This is a characteristic common to all intellectual property rights. In terminology developed in continental jurisdictions, the owner of the right has "exhausted his rights" by such authorised first sale.

Territorial monopoly or exclusivity and the prevention of imports. The right   **25–11** of first sale accorded to the owner of an intellectual property right under the national laws of state A usually carries with it the right to prevent the importation

---

[31] This is a separate issue from whether such a complaint is justiciable in the courts of a territory other than that in which the alleged infringement was committed; see, as to the position in England: para. 22–115, above.

[32] See Ch.24.

[33] See paras 25–41 *et seq*, below.

[34] It should be noted here, however, that not all rights are exhausted on first sale (see paras 25–27 *et seq*, below).

into the territory of state A of products protected in state A by the right in question, which have been manufactured in state B without the authority of the owner of the right in state A. Without this additional protection the monopoly or exclusivity could be rendered valueless as a result of such international trade, and the whole purpose of the monopoly or exclusivity would be defeated.

Whether this protection, for the owner's home market in state A can also be invoked against imports of products in respect of the manufacture of which in state B the owner could not complain, either because they were manufactured by him under an equivalent right accorded to him by the laws of state B, or by someone deriving title to such equivalent right from him, or by a licensee under such right, either of himself or of his successor in title, is a question which depends on the intellectual property right concerned and on the national laws of state A under which such right is enforced. The question may be put in continental terms as whether such a sale, or disposition of the right of sale, abroad can properly be said to exhaust the owner's rights under the laws of the home market. In the United Kingdom the question turns, apart from considerations of Community law, entirely on the precise terms in which the right to prevent imports is given by the relevant statute to the owner of the intellectual property right.

25–12   Imports into the United Kingdom. Under the Copyright Act 1956,[35] the position appeared to turn on the answer to the hypothetical question whether the product being imported was manufactured in the foreign country by a person who, had he manufactured the product in the United Kingdom, would not thereby have infringed copyright. If this question was answered affirmatively, then importation of the product could not be prevented, but if this question was answered in the negative, then importation could be prevented, even though the manufacture was in fact not an infringement of copyright under the copyright laws of the country where the product was actually manufactured.[36]

The 1988 Act maintained and tightened this rule.[37] Under the 1956 Act, the contractual nature of an exclusive licence prevented an exclusive licensee of the copyright in the United Kingdom from restraining the importation into the United Kingdom of products manufactured abroad by the copyright owner or by anyone under licence from him or his successor in title.[38] Importation of such products into the United Kingdom might have rendered the copyright owner in breach of his contract with the licensee, but it was not an infringement of the copyright, and consequently the restrictions on importation under the 1956 Act did not apply. The 1988 Act amended this prohibition on importation to include, in its definition of an infringing copy of a work, imported products the manufacture of which in the United Kingdom would have been a breach of an exclusive licence agreement in relation to that work.[39]

However, the 1988 Act also makes express provision for imports which are subject to Community law.[40] The definition of an infringing copy of a work in section 27(3) of the Act is not to be construed as applying to an article which may

---

[35] Copyright Act 1956, ss.5 (2) and 16 (2).

[36] *Polydor Ltd and R.S.O. Records Inc v Harlequin Record Shop Ltd and Simons Records Ltd* [1980] 2 C.M.L.R. 413, CA; [1980] F.S.R. 194; (for the decision of the ECJ on the effect of Community law, see [1982] E.C.R. 329; [1982] 1 C.M.L.R. 677; [1982] F.S.R. 358); *CBS United Kingdom Ltd v Charmdale Record Distributors Ltd* [1981] Ch. 91; [1980] 2 All E.R. 807; *The Who Group Ltd and Polydor Ltd v Stage One (Records) Ltd* [1980] 2 C.M.L.R. 429; [1980] F.S.R. 268.

[37] CDPA 1988, ss.22, 27(1) and 27(3).

[38] Copyright Act 1956, s.19(4).

[39] CDPA 1988, s.27 (3)(b).

[40] CDPA 1988, s.27(5). Similar provisions exist in relation to design right, see CDPA 1988, s.228(3) and (5).

be lawfully imported into the United Kingdom by virtue of any enforceable Community right.[41]

The prevention of imports: conflict with the aims of the Community. The **25–13**
exercise of copyright, and other intellectual property rights to prevent imports
into a state has so far been considered only in a national context, where the boundaries of the state define the limits for the purposes both of the enforcement of the
right in question and of the state's control of its trade with other countries. In the
context of the Community, copyright continues to be accorded by the separate
national laws of each of the Member States,[42] with the consequence that national
boundaries continue to determine the limits to the enforcement of each of these
copyrights, but, as has been explained above,[43] the national boundaries are no
longer allowed to present an obstacle to the free movement of goods and services
within the Community. However, it should readily be appreciated, from the
discussion above, that nationally-held intellectual property rights such as copyright, by the very combination of their twin characteristics of territoriality and
exclusivity, are capable of being used to prevent imports into one Member State
of copies of a work lawfully on the market in another Member State, and thus
constituting in themselves an obstacle to the free movement of goods and services within the Community.[44]

4. RESOLUTION OF THE CONFLICT BETWEEN INTELLECTUAL PROPERTY RIGHTS AND THE AIMS OF THE EC

A. CREATION OF COMMUNITY INTELLECTUAL PROPERTY RIGHTS

Creation of unitary rights. One solution to the problem of ensuring that intel- **25–14**
lectual property rights do not present an obstacle to the realisation of the Common Market is to create a unitary right covering the combined territories of the
Member States,[45] the content of which is determined by Community law, not by
the national laws of the separate Member States, and to which effect is given in
identical manner in the national courts of each Member State.

Community Patent Convention. Such was the objective in relation to patents of **25–15**
the Community Patent Convention, signed by the then nine Member States of the
Community on December 15, 1975.[46] The Convention applied, by Arts 32 and
81, the principle of exhaustion of rights to patents, in that a Community patent
could not be asserted to prevent the importation into one Member State of a product marketed in another Member State by the patentee or with his express consent.
The Convention was subject to ratification by the then nine Member States, which
did not happen.[47] Subsequent enlargement of the Community caused further difficulties in the Convention being ratified, and has, in effect, removed any chance
of the Convention entering into force. The concept of a unitary Community patent was seen in the 1970s as a means of preventing patents being used to restrict

---

[41] As defined by the European Communities Act 1972 (as amended), s.2(1); see para. 25–01, above.
[42] References in this chapter to Member States are effectively references to EEA States, see para. 25–01, above.
[43] See paras 25–03 *et seq.*, above.
[44] As was stated in relation to patents by the Court of Justice in Case 24/67 *Parke, Davis v Probel* [1968] E.C.R. 81; [1968] C.M.L.R. 47 at 58 [2]; and in relation to copyright in Cases 55 & 57/80 *Musik-Vertrieb Membran v GEMA* [1981] E.C.R. 147 [13]; [1981] 2 C.M.L.R. 44.
[45] See para. 25–12, above.
[46] [1976] O.J. L17/1.
[47] Denmark was unable to ratify the Convention.

intra-Community trade. The considerable progress which has been made since then in the harmonisation of national patent laws and the success of the 29-Member State European Patent Convention (EPC) removed any urgent need to establish a unitary Community patent.[48] However, on August 1, 2000, the European Commission put forward a proposal for a Regulation on the Community Patent.[49] Under the proposal, upon grant, Community patents would be single patents legally valid throughout the European Union and the Regulation would be the applicable framework. It is proposed that Community patents would be granted by the European Patent Office and therefore a revision of the European Patent Convention (EPC) is required. Thus, the effective establishment of the Community patent does not depend solely on the adoption of the Regulation on the Community Patent, but also requires the convening of a Diplomatic Conference to revise the EPC to accommodate it. However, negotiations have stalled on the question of languages and the jurisdiction of the proposed Community Patent Courts of first and second instance. Agreement on the Community Patent continues to elude the EU Council and in May 2004 the matter was put on hold indefinitely.[50] Meanwhile, a Diplomatic Conference to revise the EPC has been twice scheduled to be held (in June 2002 and in November 2004) but each time has had to be postponed. To date (August 20, 2004), no new date for a Diplomatic Conference has been set.

25–16   Community Trade Mark. A proposed Regulation on a Community Trade Mark was put forward in 1980 and amended in 1984.[51] A Regulation was finally adopted by the Council of Ministers on January 14, 1994.[52] Once registered, a Community trade mark is valid for the entire Community. The Regulation applies exhaustion of rights to the Community trade mark, in that a Community trade mark cannot be used to prohibit its use in relation to goods marketed in the Community under that mark by the proprietor of the mark or with his consent.[53]

25–17   Copyright. So far as copyright is concerned, to date there have been no proposals for a full codification of Community copyright law. Moreover, this intellectual property right enjoys the special position that no registration system is required in any of the laws of the Member States for the subsistence of copyright under those laws, and also that a certain degree of harmonisation as to the content of the right in the Member States had already been achieved as a result of a succession of international conventions. It was therefore argued that there was no need for a special agreement between Member States (such as the Community Patent Convention) but that the further harmonisation necessary to allow for the

---

[48] For the subsequent difficulties experienced by the Community in progressing this Convention, see Tritton, *Intellectual Property in Europe* (2nd. ed. Sweet & Maxwell, London 2002), para.2–168 *et seq.*

[49] Proposal for a Council Regulation on the Community Patent (presented by the Commission), COM(2000) 412 final, August 1, 2000. On April 10, 2002, the European Parliament voted in favour of a resolution approving the Commission's then proposal. Meanwhile, on February 20, 2002, the Commission put forward a proposal for a Directive on the Patentability of Computer-Implemented Inventions (COM (2000) 92 final). A common position concerning the latest proposal on this subject (IP/04/659) was adopted by the Council in May 2004 and is now before the Parliament.

[50] See Commission Press Release *http:/ue.eu.int/ueDocs/cms_Data/docs/pressData/en/intm/80522.pdf*

[51] [1980] O.J. C351/1; [1984] O.J. C230/1; [1981] 1 C.M.L.R. 365 (original text).

[52] Council Reg.40/94/EC; [1994] O.J. L11/1. The Regulation came into force on April 14, 1994.

[53] Council Reg.40/94/EC; [1994] O.J. L11/1, Art.13 (1). The principle of exhaustion does not apply where there are legitimate reasons for the proprietor to oppose further commercial exploitation of the goods: Council Reg.40/94/EC; [1994] O.J. L11/1, Art.13 (2).

realisation of the Common Market could be achieved by appropriate directives issued by the Council.[54]

Thus, in spite of the programme of harmonisation undertaken in recent years, the *acquis communautaire* in the field of copyright remains limited in its scope and does not cover the whole field of copyright and related rights.

B. CASE LAW OF THE COURT OF JUSTICE DEVELOPING THE PRINCIPLE OF EXHAUSTION OF RIGHTS AND THE SPECIFIC OBJECT OF THE INTELLECTUAL PROPERTY RIGHT

Role of the Court of Justice. In the absence of a unitary system of intellectual property rights, it was left to the Court of Justice to resolve the conflict between the national intellectual property rights and the aims of the Community. The court's solution had to take account of the protection afforded to national property rights, in particular to intellectual and commercial property rights, under Arts 295 and 30 (ex Arts 222 and 36) of the Treaty. **25–18**

Article 295 of the Treaty. Article 295 (ex Art.222), which is found in Part 6 of the Treaty, devoted to general and final provisions, provides that the Treaty shall in no way prejudice the rules in Member States governing the system of property ownership.[55] However, the object of this Article is to guarantee, in a general manner, the freedom of the Member States to organise their own systems of property, but not to guarantee that the Community institutions may not intervene in the subjective right of property, as was affirmed by the Court of Justice by its judgment in *Consten & Grundig v Commission*.[56] **25–19**

Article 30 of the Treaty. Article 30 (ex Art.36) allows for exceptions to the principle of free movement of goods, in that the provisions of Arts 28 and 29 (ex Arts 30 to 34) are not to preclude prohibitions on imports and exports justified on specified grounds, which include the protection of industrial and commercial property, provided that such measures do not constitute a means of arbitrary discrimination or a disguised restriction on trade between Member States.[57] The Court of Justice has stated that, in so far as Art.30 provides exceptions to the fundamental rule of free movement of goods between Member States, the exceptions are to be interpreted strictly.[58] **25–20**

Distinction between the existence or substance of intellectual property rights and their exercise. The solution adopted by the Court of Justice was to draw from the interpretation of these Arts a distinction between the existence of nationally held intellectual property rights and their exercise. This distinction was first drawn in *Consten & Grundig v Commission*,[59] in which the court was considering an appeal against a decision of the Commission which prohibited, under Art.81(1) **25–21**

---

[54] Under what are now Arts 94 and 95 (ex Arts 100 and 100A) of the Treaty. As to the considerable progress that has been made in recent years in harmonising national copyright and related rights laws of the Member States through this means, see the discussion at paras 25–41 *et seq.*, below.

[55] For the text of Art.295 (ex Art.222), see Vol.2 at G1.

[56] Cases 56 & 58/64 *Consten & Grundig v EC Commission* [1966] E.C.R. 299; [1966] C.M.L.R. 418; and see the Opinion of Advocate General Roemer at [1966] C.M.L.R. 443. See also Cases C-241 & 242/GIP *RTE and ITP v Commission* [1995] E.C.R. I-743; 4 C.M.L.R. 718.

[57] For the text of Art.36, see Vol. 2 at G1.

[58] Case 7/68 *Re Export Tax on Art Treasures* [1968] E.C.R. 423; [1969] C.M.L.R. 1; Case 35/76 *Simmenthal SpA v Amministrazione delle Finanze dello Stato* [1976] E.C.R. 1871; [1977] 2 C.M.L.R. 1; Case 113/80 *Commission v Ireland* [1981] E.C.R. 1625; [1982] 1 C.M.L.R. 706; Case 95/81 *Commission v Italy* [1982] E.C.R. 2187.

[59] For a commentary on subsequent developments, see G. Friden, "Recent Developments in EEC Intellectual Property Law: The distinction between Existence and Exercise revisited." [1989] C.M.L.Rev.193. For criticism of the distinction, see Beier, "Industrial Property and Internal Mar-

(ex Art.85(1)), an agreement relating to the exercise of trade marks. The distinction was then developed in a number of cases, in relation to trade marks,[60] copyright,[61] and similar rights of protection under German law,[62] design rights,[63] patents[64] and performers' rights.[65] The essence of the distinction is that Community law does not affect the grant, substance or existence of such rights, which remain a matter for the respective national laws of the Member States.[66] However, Community law may interfere with the exercise of such rights to the extent that such exercise is contrary to a fundamental rule of Community law.

25–22   **Development of distinction into principle of Community law.** Although the distinction was primarily developed by reference to Art.30 (ex Art.36) and the derogation in that Art for the protection of industrial and commercial property, the extension of the distinction to the free movement of services and to the application of competition policy required the court to develop the doctrine as a principle of Community law, of which Art.30 is an express example relating to the free movement of goods. This was a progression from *Consten & Grundig v Commission*,[67] where the Court of Justice pointed out that Art.30 had, by its very terms and position in the Treaty, no application to the rules on competition.[68] The foundation for this extension by the Court of Justice of the distinction between the exercise of the rights of intellectual property to fields beyond the free movement of goods was not fully explained in its reasoning,[69] and there are no parallel exceptions in the chapters of the Treaty on the freedom to provide services or the application of the competition rules. Nevertheless, in *Coditel S.A. v Cine Vog Films S.A.*[70] the Court of Justice stated that whilst Art.49 (ex Art.59) prohibits restrictions upon the freedom to provide services, it does not thereby mean restric-

---

ket" (1990) 2 I.I.C. 131 and Reindl, "The Magic of Magill: TV Program Guides as a Limit of Copyright Law?" (1993) 1 I.I.C. 60. See also T.C.Vinje, "The Final Word on Magill" [1995] 6 EIPR 297.

[60] Case 40/70 *Sirena S.R.L. v Eda S.R.L.* [1971] E.C.R. 69; [1971] C.M.L.R. 260; Case 16/74 *Centrafarm B.V. v Winthrop B.V.* [1974] E.C.R. 1183; [1974] 2 C.M.L.R. 480; Case 51/75 *EMI Records Ltd v CBS United Kingdom Ltd* [1976] E.C.R. 811; [1976] 2 C.M.L.R. 235; Case 58/80 *Dansk Supermarked A/S v A/S Imerco* [1981] E.C.R. 181; [1981] 3 C.M.L.R. 590.

[61] Case 62/79 *Coditel S.A. v Cine Vog Films S.A.* [1980] E.C.R. 881; [1981] 2 C.M.L.R. 362; Case 262/81 *Coditel S.A. v Cine Vog Films S.A. (No. 2)* [1982] E.C.R. 3381; [1983] 1 C.M.L.R. 49; Case 270/80 *Polydor Ltd and R.S.O. Records Inc v Harlequin Record Shop Ltd and Simons Records Ltd* [1982] E.C.R. 329; [1982] 1 C.M.L.R. 677; Case T-69/89 *Radio Telefís Éireann v Commission* [1991] 4 C.M.L.R. 586 at 617 para.71 and Cases C-241 & 242/91P *Radio Telefís Éireann and ITP v Commission* [1995] E.C.R. I-743; [1995] 4 C.M.L.R. 718 at 790 paras 49 to 50.

[62] Case 78/70 *Deutsche Grammophon GmbH v Metro-SB-Grossmarkte GmbH* [1971] E.C.R. 487; [1971] C.M.L.R. 631.

[63] Case 144/81 *Keurkoop B.V. v Nancy Kean Gifts B.V.* [1982] E.C.R. 2853; [1983] 2 C.M.L.R. 47.

[64] Case 24/67 *Parke, Davis v Probel* [1968] E.C.R. 55; [1968] C.M.L.R. 47; Cases 15 & 16/74 *Centrafarm B.V.v Sterling Drug Inc* [1974] E.C.R. 1147, 1183; [1974] 2 C.M.L.R. 480; Case 35/87 *Thetford Corporation v Fiamma SpA* [1988] E.C.R. 3585; [1988] 3 C.M.L.R. 549.

[65] Joined Cases C 92-326/92 *Phil Collins v Imtrat HandelsGmbH* and *Verwaltungsgesellschaft mbH v EMI Electrola GmbH* [1993] 3 C.M.L.R. 773 at 796 para.17.

[66] As stated by the ECJ in: Case 35/87 *Thetford Corporation v Fiamma SpA* [1988] E.C.R. 3585; [1988] 3 C.M.L.R. 549; Case 144/81 *Keurkoop B.V.v Nancy Kean Gifts B.V.* [1982] E.C.R. 2853; [1983] 2 C.M.L.R. 47; Case 341/87 *EMI Electrola GmbH v Patricia Im- und Export Verwaltungsgesellschaft GmbH* [1989] E.C.R. 79; [1989] 2 C.M.L.R. 413; Cases C-30/90 and 235/89 *Commission v United Kingdom and Italy* [1992] E.C.R. I-777; [1992] C.M.L.R. 709; Case C-317/91 *Deutsche Renault AG v Audi AG* [1993] E.C.R. I-6277; [1995] 1 C.M.L.R. 461 para.31; Case C-9/93 *IHT Internazionale Heiztechnik GmbH v Ideal-Standard GmbH* [1994] E.C.R. I-2789; [1994] 2 C.M.L.R. 857; Joined Cases C 92-326/92 *Phil Collins v Imtrat HandelsGmbH* and *Verwaltungsgesellschaft GmbH v EMI Electrola GmbH* [1993] 3 C.M.L.R. 773 at 796 para.22.

[67] Cases 56 & 58/64 [1966] E.C.R. 299; [1966] C.M.L.R. 418.

[68] Cases 56 & 58/64 [1966] C.M.L.R. 418 at 476.

[69] See, *e.g.* Case 40/70 *Sirena S.R.L. v Eda S.R.L.* [1971] E.C.R. 69; [1971] C.M.L.R. 260 at 273 para.5.

[70] Case 62/79 [1980] E.C.R. 881 [15]; [1981] 2 C.M.L.R. 362 at 400 para.15; see also Case 262/81 *Coditel S.A. v Cine Vog Films S.A. (No. 2)* [1982] E.C.R. 3381; [1983] 1 C.M.L.R. 49.

tions upon the exercise of certain economic activities which have their origin in the application of national legislation for the protection of intellectual property, save where such application constitutes a means of arbitrary discrimination or disguised restriction on trade between Member States. The explanation for this teleological interpretation of the Treaty may simply be the willingness of the Court of Justice to develop principles for the application of Community law to ensure uniformity in its sectors of influence. Moreover, the Court of Justice has stressed repeatedly that the goal of the Treaty is a single market. To the extent that the Court of Justice develops limits on the ability of national intellectual property laws to derogate from that goal, it would be illogical for the Court to apply different rules in respect of the market in goods to those applied in respect of the market in services.

Development of the concept of the specific object of an intellectual property   25–23
right. The case law of the Court of Justice has made it clear that the existence of intellectual property rights is not affected by the Treaty. Only the exercise of those rights requires justification as a derogation from the principle of free movement of goods or services, in that such derogation must not constitute a means of arbitrary discrimination or a disguised restriction on trade between Member States. In *Deutsche Grammophon GmbH v Metro-SB-Grossmärkte GmbH & Co K.G.*[71] the court gave detailed consideration to the terms of Art.30 and held that the Art. only permits restrictions on the freedom of trade to the extent that they are justified for the protection of the rights that form the specific object of that property.[72] The court thereby further developed the concept of the distinction between the existence or substance and the exercise of the right, by introducing the concept of the specific object of the intellectual property right. The specific object of the right is a matter of its substance, and the exercise by the owner of the right of what is no more than the specific object of the right will be protected by the derogation from the principle of free movement in Art.36. Anything further done by the owner of the right which restricts the free movement of goods or services between Member States will be struck down as incompatible with Community law.

Since its judgment in the *Deutsche Grammophon* case, the court has affirmed the concept of the specific object of the intellectual property right as governing the limits of the exceptions in Art.36 in favour of intellectual property rights, in relation to patents,[73] trade marks,[74] copyright,[75] and registered designs.[76]

The Deutsche Grammophon Case. Whilst the position was therefore quickly   25–24

---

[71] Case 78/70 [1971] E.C.R. 487; [1971] C.M.L.R. 631.

[72] Case 78/70 [1971] C.M.L.R. 631 at 657 para.11; repeated by the court in a later trade mark case: Case 119/75, *Terrapin (Overseas) Ltd v Terranova Industrie* [1976] E.C.R. 1039; [1976] 2 C.M.L.R. 482 at 505 para.5.

[73] Case 15/74 *Centrafarm B.V. v Sterling Drug Inc.* [1974] E.C.R. 1147 at 1183; [1974] 2 C.M.L.R. 480; Case 187/80 *Merck & Co Inc v Stephar B.V.* [1981] E.C.R. 2063; [1981] 3 C.M.L.R. 463; Case 19/84 *Pharmon B.V. v Hoechst AG* [1985] E.C.R. 2281; [1985] 3 C.M.L.R. 775; Case 193/83 *Windsurfing International Inc v EC Commission* [1986] E.C.R. 611, [1986] 3 C.M.L.R. 489; *Allen & Hanburys v Generics UK* [1988] E.C.R. 1245; [1988] 1 C.M.L.R. 701 at 714 paras 11 to 13; Cases C-30/90 and 235/89 *Commission v United Kingdom and Italy* [1992] E.C.R. I-777; [1992] 2 C.M.L.R. 709 at 759 para.21.

[74] Case 16/74 *Centrafarm B.V. v Winthrop B.V.* [1974] E.C.R. 1183; [1974] 2 C.M.L.R. 480; Case 3/78, *Centrafarm B.V. v American Home Products Inc* [1978] E.C.R. 1823; [1979] 1 C.M.L.R. 326; Case C-10/89, *S.A. CNL-Sucal NV v Hag GF AG.* [1990] 3 C.M.L.R. 571 at 608, para.14.

[75] Case 62/79 *Coditel S.A. v Cine Vog Films S.A.* [1980] E.C.R. 881; [1981] 2 C.M.L.R. 362; Cases 55 & 57/80 *Musik-Vertrieb Membran GmbH v GEMA* [1981] E.C.R. 146; [1981] 2 C.M.L.R. 44; Case 262/81 *Coditel S.A. v Cine Vog Films S.A. (No. 2)* [1982] E.C.R. 3381; [1983] 1 C.M.L.R. 49; Case 402/85 *Basset v SACEM* [1987] E.C.R. 1747; [1987] 3 C.M.L.R. 173; see also the Opinion of Advocate General Jacobs in Case 395/87 *Ministère Public v Tournier* [1989] E.C.R. 2521; [1991] 4 C.M.L.R. 248; and Cases 110/88 241/88 and 242/88 *Lucazeau v SACEM* [1989] E.C.R. 2811; [1991] 4 C.M.L.R. 248 at paras 22–26.

clarified in relation to patents and trade marks, the Court of Justice was not so clear, in its earlier judgment in the *Deutsche Grammophon* case, in relation to a right under German law similar to copyright. The court merely stated that it conflicted with the provisions regarding the free movement of goods in the Common Market if a producer of sound recordings so exercises the exclusive right granted to him by the legislation of a Member State to market protected Arts (in this case records) so as to prohibit the marketing in that Member State of products that have been sold by himself or with his consent in another Member State, solely because this marketing has not occurred in the territory of the first Member State.[77] The court did not take the opportunity of defining in more precise terms the specific object of copyright,[78] yet clearly accepted that in the case before it the attempt by Deutsche Grammophon to prevent the re-importation of the products into Germany went beyond the specific object of the right in question.

When the case came back before the German court, issues arose on the facts as to whether there had been a marketing of the records in France by Polydor S.A. (a wholly-owned subsidiary of Deutsche Grammophon) and as to whether Deutsche Grammophon was responsible for, and had therefore consented to, that marketing. The German court decided against Deutsche Grammophon on these issues, and applied the ruling of the Court of Justice to prevent Deutsche Grammophon from asserting its exclusive distribution rights in Germany, under the German Copyright Act, to prevent the re-importation of the records in question from France.[79]

25–25   Subsequent development by national courts. After the *Deutsche Grammophon* case,[80] it was left to the national courts to define what they considered to be the specific object of copyright under their laws, guided by the rulings of the Court of Justice in that case and the *Centrafarm/Sterling*[81] and *Centrafarm/Winthrop*[82] cases. In *Time Limit S.A. v SABAM*,[83] the Belgian Court of Appeal was called on to consider the validity of certain royalties levied by the Belgian performing right society SABAM. Following the guidance laid down by the Court of Justice in the above cases, the Belgian Court defined the specific object of copyright in a musical work as including the right of reproduction, but not the right to lay down the territorial limits within which the product embodying the reproduction may be marketed.

25–26   Further development by the Court of Justice. The first case concerning the right of reproduction and the exercise of copyright to come before the Court of Justice after the *Deutsche Grammophon* case was *Musik-Vertrieb Membran v GEMA*.[84] This case raised the question of the compatibility with Community law of the practice of the German authors' and composers' collecting society of collecting the difference between the royalty fees paid to authors in the exporting Member State and the royalty fees payable in Germany when records were

---

[76] Case 144/81 *Keurkoop B.V. v Nancy Kean Gifts B.V.* [1982] E.C.R. 2853; [1983] 2 C.M.L.R. 47; Case 238/87 *Volvo AB v Eric Veng (UK) Ltd* [1988] E.C.R. 6211; [1989] 4 C.M.L.R. 122.

[77] Case 78/70 *Deutsche Grammophon GmbH v Metro-SB-Grossmärkte GmbH* [1971] E.C.R. 487; [1971] C.M.L.R. 631.

[78] Case 78/70 *Deutsche Grammophon GmbH v Metro-SB-Grossmärkte GmbH* [1971] E.C.R. 487; [1971] C.M.L.R. 631 at 657–658 [13].

[79] See also the Opinion of Advocate General Roemer, Case 78/70 *Deutsche Grammophon GmbH v Metro-SB-Grossmärkte GmbH* [1971] C.M.L.R. 631, at 647–648.

[80] *Deutsche Grammophon GmbH v Metro-SB-Grossmärkte GmbH* [1972] C.M.L.R. 107.

[81] Case 15/74 *Centrafarm B.V. v Sterling Drug Inc.* [1974] E.C.R. 1147, 1183; [1974] 2 C.M.L.R. 480.

[82] Case 16/74 *Centrafarm B.V. v Winthrop B.V.*. [1974] E.C.R. 1183; [1974] 2 C.M.L.R. 480.

[83] [1979] 2 C.M.L.R. 578 at 582 [9].

[84] Cases 55 & 57/80 [1981] E.C.R. 147; [1981] 2 C.M.L.R. 44.

imported into Germany from another Member State. The court, after rejecting the argument that the moral rights aspect of copyright required it to be treated differently to other intellectual property rights,[85] stated that the right involved in the case was the right to exploit commercially the marketing of the protected work, particularly in the form of licences granted in return for payment of royalties. In respect of the exercise of such an economic right, the court reaffirmed, in accordance with its development of the doctrine of exhaustion of rights for other forms of intellectual property, and without therefore needing to define further the specific object of copyright, that the copyright owner could not rely on the exclusive exploitation right conferred by copyright to restrict the importation of the sound recordings which had been lawfully marketed in another Member State by the copyright owner or with his consent. In *Parfums Christian Dior*,[86] the court held that the rights of a copyright holder to restrain the reproduction of a protected work in a reseller's advertising could not be greater than those conferred on a trade mark proprietor in similar circumstances.[87]

Divisibility of copyright: reproduction right and performance right. As has already been stated,[88] copyright, unlike other forms of intellectual property, is a divisible right, in that copyright in a work gives separate rights to control the reproduction and performance of the work. The Court of Justice has acknowledged that these two separate rights form divisible elements of the specific subject-matter of copyright, and that exhaustion of the right to control reproduction will not necessarily exhaust the right to control performance.[89] The two *Coditel* cases[90] raised the question of whether the owner of a copyright work could rely on that copyright to prevent the transmission in one Member State of the work lawfully broadcast in another Member State. In the first *Coditel* case, the court was asked to consider the question in relation to former Arts 30, 36, 59 and 60 (new Arts 28, 30, 49 and 50). The court held that films differ from those literary and artistic works for which the placing of the work at the disposal of the public is inseparable from the circulation of the material object in which the work is reproduced, such as a book or a record. Rather, films belong to that category of literary and artistic works which are made available to the public by performance which can be infinitely repeated. The commercial exploitation of such works falls within the domain of movement of services. In these circumstances, the court held that it is part of the essential function of copyright that the owner of the copyright in a film and his assigns may require fees for any showing of that film.[91] Consequently, the court decided that the provisions of the Treaty relating to the freedom to provide services would not prevent the assignee of the performing right in a film from exercising his right to prohibit exhibition of the film in a Member State without his authority, if the film was picked up and transmitted af-

25–27

---

85 In Case T-69/89 *Radio Telefís Éireann v Commission* [1991] 4 C.M.L.R. 586 at 617, para.71, the court stressed that the specific object of copyright is to protect both the economic and moral rights of the copyright owner.

86 Case C-337/95 *Parfums Christian Dior S.A. v Evora B. V* [1998] 1 C.M.L.R. 737.

87 Case C-337/95 *Parfums Christian Dior S.A. v Evora B.V.* [1998] 1 C.M.L.R. 737, paras 55–59. Further consideration was given to the issue by the court in the *Magill* case; see para. 29–57, below.

88 See para. 25–07, above.

89 Case 62/79 *Coditel S.A. v Cine Vog Films S.A.* [1980] E.C.R. 881; [1981] 2 C.M.L.R. 362; Case 262/81 *Coditel S.A. v Cine Vog Films S.A. (No. 2)* [1982] E.C.R. 3381; [1983] 1 C.M.L.R. 49; Case 402/85 *Basset v SACEM* [1987] E.C.R. 1747; [1987] 3 C.M.L.R. 173; Case 158/86 *Warner Brothers Inc v Erik Christiansen* [1988] E.C.R. 2605; [1990] 3 C.M.L.R. 684; Case 395/87 *Ministère Public v Tournier* [1989] E.C.R. 2521; [1991] 4 C.M.L.R. 248.

90 Case 62/79 *Coditel S.A. v Cine Vog Films S.A.* [1980] E.C.R. 881; [1981] 2 C.M.L.R. 362; Case 262/81 *Coditel S.A. v Cine Vog Films S.A. (No. 2)* [1982] E.C.R. 3381; [1983] 1 C.M.L.R. 49.

91 Case 62/79 *Coditel S.A. v Cine Vog Films S.A.* [1980] E.C.R. 881; [1981] 2 C.M.L.R. 362 at 400.

ter being broadcast in another Member State by a third party with the consent of the original owner.[92]

25–28 Distinction applied to records and video cassettes. Since the *Coditel* cases, the Court of Justice has further considered the specific subject-matter of copyright in the context of performances of sound recordings on records and of films on video cassettes. Both records and video cassettes are media where the commercial exploitation of the performance right in the copyright work cannot be separated from the distribution of the material product, subject to the right of reproduction. For both forms of reproduction of the copyright work, the court has upheld the right of the copyright owner to continue to exploit the commercial performance of his work despite the exhaustion of the right of reproduction in the material form of the copyright work.[93] In *Ministére Public v Tournier*,[94] the Court of Justice held that national copyright legislation which prevented the public performance of sound recordings from records, without the payment of royalties in respect of such performance, even when royalties have already been paid for the reproduction of the work in the form of such records in another Member State, is not incompatible with former Articles 30 and 59 (new Arts 28 and 49).

The Court of Justice adopted a similar approach in *Warner Brothers Inc v Erik Christiansen*[95] to Danish legislation which allowed the owner of the Danish copyright to prevent the rental on the Danish market, without his consent, of video cassettes purchased in another Member State, where there was no legislation governing the exercise of copyright upon the rental of the cassettes and where they had been marketed with the consent of the owner of the copyright in that Member State. The Danish legislation was not, the court held, incompatible with former Arts 30 and 36 (new Arts 28 and 30).

Nevertheless this case provided greater difficulty in defining the border between the continuous right of exploitation in the performance of a work and the right of reproduction and first distribution of a work. In reaching its decision in the *Warner Brothers* case, the court avoided expressly classifying the protection of the rental right under Danish law as falling either under the continuing right of exploitation in the performance of the copyright work, or as being a departure from the principle that the right of reproduction and first marketing of a work is exhausted with respect to a product reproducing that work following the first placing of that product on the market by or with the consent of the copyright owner.

However, in *Metronome Musik GmbH v Music Point Hokam GmbH*,[96] the Court of Justice confirmed that the release into circulation of a sound recording on disc or cassette cannot render lawful other forms of exploitation of the protected work, such as rental, that are of a different nature from sale or any other lawful form of distribution.

Thus, while the first marketing of a copyright work in a material form by or with the consent of the copyright owner within the Community will exhaust, in relation to that product, the right of exploitation in the reproduction of the copy-

---

[92] Case 62/79 *Coditel S.A. v Cine Vog Films S.A* [1981] 2 C.M.L.R. 362 at 400.

[93] Case 402/85 *Basset v SACEM* [1987] E.C.R. 1747; [1987] 3 C.M.L.R. 173 and *per* Advocate General Lenz at 180 para.26; Case 158/86 *Warner Brothers Inc v Erik Christiansen* [1988] E.C.R. 2605; [1990] 3 C.M.L.R. 684; see also paras 24 and 25 of the Opinion of Advocate General Jacobs in *Ministère Public v Tournier* [1989] E.C.R. 2521; [1991] 4 C.M.L.R. 248 and Cases 110/88, 241/88 and 242/88 *Lucazeau v SACEM* [1989] E.C.R. 2811; [1991] 4 C.M.L.R. 248.

[94] Case 395/87 *Ministère Public v Tournier* [1989] E.C.R. 2521; [1991] 4 C.M.L.R. 248 at para.15. Contrast the court's decision in Cases 55 & 57/80 *Musik-Vertrieb Membran v GEMA* [1981] E.C.R. 147; [1981] 2 C.M.L.R. 44.

[95] Case 158/86 [1988] E.C.R. 2605; [1990] 3 C.M.L.R. 684.

[96] Case C-200/96 [1998] E.C.R. I-1953.

right work, the right of exploitation in relation to the performance or rental of the work thereby remains unaffected, even in respect of performance by means of, or rental of, that product. Meanwhile, in *Foreningen af Danske Videogramdistribu- torer v Laserdisken*,[97] , the Court of Justice has held that it is not contrary to for- mer Arts 30 and 36 of the Treaty or to the Council Directive on rental right and lending right and on certain rights related to copyright in the field of intellectual property[98] for the holder of an exclusive rental right to prohibit copies of a film from being offered for rental in a Member State, even where the offering of those copies for rental has been authorised in the territory of another Member State, Thus, the court has made it clear that the exclusive right to authorise or prohibit the rental of a film is comparable to the right of public performance and, unlike the right of distribution, is not exhausted as soon as it has been exercised.

C. LIMITATIONS ON THE PRINCIPLE OF EXHAUSTION OF RIGHTS

(i) Goods originating outside the EC.

International exhaustion: goods originating outside the EC. The question has   **25–29** arisen whether the principle of exhaustion of rights applies to prevent a right owner in a Member State from asserting his right against the importation into that Member State of goods which were marketed by him or with his consent outside the EC.[99] In *EMI Records Ltd v CBS United Kingdom Ltd*,[1] CBS, who owned the mark "Columbia" in the United States and other non-Member States, imported goods under the mark into the EC, and EMI, who owned the mark in various Member States, sought to prevent such imports. The mark had once been in com- mon ownership. The Court of Justice held that the principle of exhaustion of rights had no application to goods originating from outside the Community. The court explained this limitation to the principle on the ground that it is the free movement of goods within the Community which is the aim of the Common Market, and the exercise of intellectual property rights to prevent the importation into a Member State of goods manufactured or first marketed outside the Com- munity in no way jeopardises the unity of the Common Market which Arts 28 to 30 (ex Arts 30, 34, 36 and 37) and the principle embodied in them are intended to ensure.[2]

The court adopted a similar approach in *Silhouette International Schmied GmbH & Co KG v Harlauer Handels GmbH*,[3] in which it confirmed that Art.7 of

---

[97] Case C-61/97, judgement of September 22, 1998 [2000] E.C.D.R. 139.

[98] Council Directive 92/100/EEC of November 19, 1992 [1992] O.J. L346/61.

[99] The territory of the EC comprises the national territories of the 25 Member States of the EU The EEA Agreement contains equivalent provisions to Arts 30–36 of the Treaty, and it is thought that the principle of exhaustion will be applied throughout the EEA, that is, in addition, to the ter- ritories of the three EEA States who are not members of the E.U, *i.e.* Iceland, Norway and Liecht- enstein (although not applying to Liechtenstein for the time being); see para. 25–01, above. As to whether this assumption is correct, see, however, the discussion in Tritton, *Intellectual Property in Europe* (2nd ed., Sweet & Maxwell, London, 2002) paras 7. 555 *et seq.* Note that the EFTA Court, in an advisory opinion in Case E- 2/97, *Mag Instrument Inc v California Trading Company Norway* (judgment of December 3, 1997 [1998] E.T.M.R. 85), held that it is for the EFTA States to decide whether they wish to introduce or maintain the principle of international exhaustion of rights conferred by a trade mark with regard to goods originating outside the EEA.

[1] Case 51/75 *EMI Records Ltd v CBS United Kingdom Ltd* [1976] E.C.R. 811; [1976] 2 C.M.L.R. 235. N.B. Ex Arts 31 to 33 and 35 have been repealed.

[2] Case 51/75 *EMI Records Ltd v CBS United Kingdom Ltd* [1976] 2 C.M.L.R. 235 at 265.

[3] Case C-355/96 [1998] E.C.R. I-4799: (The opinion of Advocate General Jacobs, which was fol- lowed by the court, is reported at [1998] F.S.R. 474).

the Trade Marks Directive[4] precluded Member States from providing that trade mark rights became exhausted in a Member State by virtue of the marketing of the goods in a non-Member State with the proprietor's consent. The *Silhouette* judgment established the absolute principle of EEA-wide exhaustion, finding that Member States are precluded from extending the principle of EEA-wide exhaustion by means of national rules providing for international exhaustion.[5] Although the judgment related to the exhaustion of trade mark rights, the principle applies also to other intellectual property rights, including copyright. The *Silhouette* judgment was confirmed by the Court of Justice in *Sebago and Another v GB-Unic*, the court adding that the legal consequence of exhaustion can arise only if the consent extends to every individual item of the goods in respect of which exhaustion is pleaded.[6]

In the last few years, there has been much discussion of the issue of exhaustion of trade mark rights and, in particular, of the implications of a change from the existing Community/EEA exhaustion régime, as confirmed by *Silhouette* and *Sebago* to that of international exhaustion. Following discussions in the Internal Market Council, the Commission announced in May 2000 that it had decided not to propose a change to the current EEA-wide exhaustion approach.[7] Subsequently, on October 3, 2001, the European Parliament called on the Commission to produce by December 31, 2002, a report including a detailed study of the implications of a possible transition to the principle of international exhaustion for European manufacturers and consumers, as well as jobs.[8] The report in the form of a Commission Staff Working Paper was duly published on May 21, 2003,[9] and concluded that there were no "deficiencies in current legal provision relating to possible abuses of trade marks within the EU".

25–30 **Goods in free circulation in the EC** In the *EMI* case, above, the Court of Justice had to consider the further problem of the exercise of an intellectual property right in Member State A, against the importation into that state of goods from Member State B but which had been manufactured outside the EC. It was argued that the combined effect of Arts 23(2) (ex Art.9(2)) and Art.24(1) (ex Art.10(1)) of the Treaty was to place such goods for all purposes on an equal footing with goods manufactured in Member State B. Article 23(2) (ex Art.9(2)) provides that the provisions, *inter alia*, of Arts 28 to 31 (ex Arts 30, 34, 36 and 37) shall apply to products originating from non-Member States which are in free circulation in Member States. Article 24(1) provides that products originating from a non-Member State shall be considered in free circulation in a Member State if all import formalities and customs duties have been complied with and paid. The Court of Justice held, however, that neither the rules of the Treaty on the free movement of goods, nor those on the putting into free circulation of products

---

[4] Directive 89/100/EEC of December 21, 1988, to approximate the laws of the Member States relating to trade marks; [1989] O.J. L40/1.

[5] As regards the EEA, see paras 25–01 and 25–103, below.

[6] Case C-173/98, *Sebago and Maison Dubois* [1999] E.C.R. I-4103.

[7] See "Exhaustion of Trade Mark Rights—Working document from the Commission services on exhaustion of trade mark rights" submitted to the Council and the European Parliament on December 9, 1999, and communiqué from Commissioner Bolkestein on the issue of exhaustion of trade mark rights, June 2, 2000. See also NERA Study "The Economic Consequences of the Choice of Regime of Exhaustion in the Area of Trade Marks", published by the Commission on February 8, 1999, and House of Commons Select Committee on Trade and Industry Report on "Trade Marks, Fakes and Consumers", Eighth Report, Session 1998–99 June 29, 1999, H.C. 380. See also A. Carboni, "Cases about Spectacles and Torches: Now Can We See the Light" [1998] E.I.P.R. 470; W.R. Cornish,"Silhouette"—Through a Glass Darkly", in *Festschrift Till Gunnar Karnell*, (Gotab AB, Stockholm, 1999) 99.

[8] Document A5-0311/2001.

[9] Document SEC(2003) 575, entitled: "Possible abuses of trade mark rights within the EU in the context of Community exhaustion".

from third countries, nor the principles governing the common commercial policy,[10] prohibit the proprietor of a mark in all Member States of the Community from exercising his right in order to prevent the importation of similar products bearing the same mark and coming from a non-Member State.[11] However, in the case of trade marks, Article 7 of the Trade Marks Directive does apply to prevent the proprietor from exercising his rights where goods manufactured in a non-Member State have been marketed in a Member State with his consent (or the consent of a person with whom he has economic links, such as a member of the same corporate group).[12]

The CDPA 1988. Applying the *EMI* decision to copyright, therefore, the owner of copyright in the United Kingdom may exercise his right under the 1988 Act to prevent the unlicensed importation into the United Kingdom of products manufactured outside the EEA, for example in the United States of America, where such manufacture may have been lawful, but was not by or with the consent of such owner of the United Kingdom copyright within the meaning of the relevant provisions of the 1988 Act.[13] This remains so, even if importation is being effected via another Member State, at least where the rights in that other Member State are owned by the same person.[14]

25–31

(ii) Goods originating in the territory of States associated with the EC

Agreements between third countries and the EC. The EC has entered into agreements with a number of third countries, in some cases with a view to such third countries becoming members of the Community,[15] in other cases with a view to developing trade and other links between the Community and such third countries.[16] The form of such agreements varies depending on the closeness of the commercial, political and economic links which the agreement is intended to create between the Community and the third country in question. However, nearly all such agreements seek to improve the flow of trade between the Community and such third country, and to this end include provisions similar to those in Arts 28 to 31 (ex Arts 30, 34, 36 and 37 of the Treaty.[17]

25–32

The question therefore arises in the case of each third country which has entered into such an agreement with the Community, whether the provisions of the agreement in question are such as to give rise to a principle of free movement

---

[10] Found in Arts 131 to 135 of the Treaty (ex Arts 110, 112, 113, 115 and 116; (ex Arts 111 and 114 have been repealed)), under which agreements have been concluded between the Community and certain third countries; see further paras 25–32 *et seq.*, below.

[11] Case 51/75 *EMI Records Ltd v CBS United Kingdom Ltd* [1976] 2 C.M.L.R. 235 at 266 [21].

[12] Case C-352/95 *Phytheron International S.A. v Jean Bourdon S.A.* [1997] E.C.R. I-1729.

[13] See para. 25–12, above. See also CDPA 1988, s.18 (2), discussed at paras 7–76 *et seq.*, above.

[14] As to where this is not the case, see para. 25–38, below.

[15] As in the case of the original treaties with Greece and Turkey, of July 9, 1961 and September 12, 1963, respectively.

[16] For example, the Treaties concluded with the EFTA countries, setting up a free trade area between the Community and those countries: Austria, Iceland, Sweden, Switzerland, all of July 22, 1972; Norway, May 14, 1973; and Finland, October 5, 1973. Others include: Malta, December 5, 1970; Cyprus, December 19, 1972; Israel, May 11, 1975; Mexico, July 15, 1975; Tunisia, April 25, 1977; Algeria, April 26, 1977; Morocco, April 27, 1976; Jordan, Syria and Egypt, January 18, 1977; Lebanese Republic, May 3, 1977; and Lomé Convention, December 15, 1989. There are also a number of agreements concluded with European states, some of which are now EU Member States: Poland and Hungary, December 16, 1991; Romania, July 28, 1980; Albania, October 26, 1992; Bulgaria, March 8, 1993; Czech Republic and Slovakia, October 4, 1993; and Slovenia, April 5, 1993. Free Trade Agreements have also been entered into with Latvia, Lithuania and Estonia, July 18, 1994; and Faroe Islands, December 6, 1996.

[17] As in the case of the original treaties with Greece and Turkey, of July 9, 1961 and September 12, 1963, respectively. As to the EEA Agreement, see para. 25–29, above. N.B. Ex Arts 31–33 and 35 have been repealed.

of goods between the Community and such third country which can be invoked as being of directly applicable effect to prevent the exercise of intellectual property rights affecting that trade, in the same way as the principle has been applied to trade between Member States of the Community, as discussed above.[18]

25–33 **Association Agreement between Portugal and the EC.** This question came before the Court of Justice in *Polydor Ltd v Harlequin Record Shop Ltd*,[19] on a request by the Court of Appeal for a preliminary ruling as to the interpretation and effect of the Agreement of July 22, 1972 between Portugal (at the time not a member of the Community) and the Community. Article 4(2) of the Areement, which came into force on January 1, 1973, provided for the abolition of measures having an effect on imports equivalent to quantitative restrictions by January 1, 1975. Article 23 of the Agreement provided in terms identical to Art.30 (ex Art.36) of the Treaty that the Agreement should not preclude prohibitions or restrictions on imports or exports justified on grounds of the protection of intellectual property.

The plaintiffs, who were the owners of the exclusive right to manufacture records of certain sound recordings in the United Kingdom, sought to prevent the importation into the United Kingdom by the defendants of records embodying such sound recordings manufactured lawfully in Portugal under licence from a company associated with the plaintiffs, which was the holder of the exclusive right to manufacture records of the sound recordings in Portugal. It was argued, on an application for interlocutory relief, that Art.14(2) of the Agreement provided the defendants with a complete defence to the action. Reversing the decision at first instance, the Court of Appeal refused the grant of an interlocutory injunction and referred the issues of interpretation and effect of Arts 14(2) and 23 of the Agreement to the Court of Justice.

To reach its decision, the Court of Justice returned to first principles and examined the objectives of the Agreement of July 22, 1972, in comparison with the Treaty of Rome. The court noted that the Agreement with Portugal was a Free Trade Agreement, the aims of which were different to those of the Treaty, which were to unite the national markets into a single market reproducing the conditions of a domestic market by establishing a common market and progressively approximating the economic policies of the Member States. The court held that in the circumstances of the Agreement of July 22, 1972, restrictions on trade in goods might be justifiable on the grounds of protection of intellectual property within the Community. Consequently in the framework of the free trade arrangement, a prohibition on the importation into the Community of products from a non-Member State based on copyright could be justified. Art.14(2) of the Agreement could not therefore be relied on to prohibit the enforcement of that right as a restriction on trade.

25–34 **Direct effect of such agreements.** Although the Court of Justice did not consider the question of direct effect in this case, the court has subsequently held in rela-

---

[18] See para. 25–03, above and see paras 29–173 *et seq.*, below. See also Bellamy and Child, *European Community Law of Competition* (5th ed., Sweet & Maxwell, 2001), paras 2–158 to 2–168. See also Arts: N. March Hunnings, "Enforceability of the EEC-EFTA Free Trade Agreements" (1977) 2 E.L.Rev. 163; M. Waelbrook "A Reply", (1978) 3 E.L.Rev 27 and N. March Hunnings, "A Rejoinder" (1978) 3 E.L.Rev 278.

[19] Case 270/80 *Polydor Ltd and R.S.O. Ltd v Harlequin Record Shop Ltd and Simons Records Ltd* [1982] E.C.R. 329; [1982] 1 C.M.L.R. 677; and see *Adams v Public Prosecutor, Canton Basle* [1978] 3 C.M.L.R. 480 in which the Swiss Supreme Court decided that Art.23 of the EEC-Switzerland Treaty (in terms similar to Art.81 of the Treaty, ex Art.85) does not create any right of action for private persons in the Swiss courts; see also, in respect of the EEC-Austria Treaty, *Austro-Mechana Gesellschaft v Gramola Winter & Co* [1984] 2 C.M.L.R. 626 (decision of the Austrian Supreme Court).

tion to other treaties, for example Art.2(1) of the Yaoundé Convention of 1963, that directly effective rights may arise within the Member States from a treaty with associated states.[20] The Court of Justice has made it clear that all agreements with third countries may be capable of giving rise to directly effective provisions. Further, the court has rejected the argument that the question of direct effect is linked to the question of reciprocity. Failure by a third state to accord direct effect to the provisions of an agreement will not prevent those provisions having direct effect within the Community.[21]

(iii) Spurious goods

Right to oppose infringement part of substance of intellectual property right. **25–35**
The limits introduced to the exercise of intellectual property rights by the principle of free movement of goods, as set by the test of exhaustion of rights, have no application to the exercise of an intellectual property right by the owner of that right against merely spurious goods, and this is so whatever the country of origin of such spurious goods. The reason for this is that it is part of the substance, or specific object, of an intellectual property right to be able to prevent others making unauthorised use of the subject-matter protected by the intellectual property right, in a manner which directly usurps the primary exclusive rights granted to the owner of the intellectual property right. This was expressly confirmed by the Court of Justice in the *Centrafarm/Sterling* and *Centrafarm/Winthrop* cases,[22] in which it stated that the right to oppose infringement was part of the specific object of patents[23] and the right to prevent others taking advantage of a mark by selling goods improperly bearing the mark was part of the specific object of trade marks.[24] There has been no case before the Court of Justice expressly raising the protection of copyright works against spurious infringement. However, presumably a similar protection will be afforded to copyright works where the rights sought to be asserted against the spurious goods are part of the specific subject of copyright, whether relating to the right of reproduction or the right of performance.

Imported spurious goods. This right of protection arises both when the owner **25–36**
of an intellectual property right in Member State A seeks to assert that right in state A against goods produced in state A, and when he seeks to assert that right in state A against goods manufactured in state B being imported into state A. In the latter case it does not matter whether state B is a Member State of the Community or not. So long as the goods have not been brought into existence with the consent of the owner in state A of the intellectual property right, he has not, in connection with the creation of the goods, exercised that intellectual property right, or any equivalent intellectual property right he may enjoy in state B, so that the question of having exhausted either right cannot arise.[25] Thus, the owner of copyright under the CDPA 1988 may still assert his rights under that Act to prevent the importation into the United Kingdom of goods which reproduce his

---

[20] Case 87/75 *Conceria Daniele Bresciani v Amministrazione delle Finanze* [1976] E.C.R. 129; [1976] 2 C.M.L.R. 62; *cf.* Cases 518, 86/75, *EMI Records Ltd v CBS United Kingdom Ltd* and *EMI Records Ltd v CBS Grammofon A/s*, [1976] E.C.R. 811 at 871; [1976] 2 C.M.L.R. 235 at 265–266.

[21] Case 104/81 *Hauptzollamt Mainz v Kupferberg* [1982] E.C.R. 3641; [1983] 1 C.M.L.R. 1.

[22] Cases 15 & 16/74 [1974] E.C.R. 1147 at 1183; [1974] 2 C.M.L.R. 480.

[23] Case 15/74 [1974] 2 C.M.L.R. 503.

[24] Case 16/74 [1974] 2 C.M.L.R. 508; see also *Centrafarm v American Home Products Corporation* [1978] E.C.R. 1823; [1979] 1 C.M.L.R. 326.

[25] See para. 25–37, below.

copyright work and which have been manufactured without his consent abroad, whether in the territory of a Member State of the Community or not.[26]

D. EXHAUSTION OF RIGHTS: ASSOCIATED PROBLEMS

25–37   **The principle of exhaustion of rights, consent and associated problems.** For copyright works legitimately marketed within the Community the essential problem remains the determination of the degree of connection required between the marketing of the work in Member State B and the person who seeks to exercise an intellectual property right in Member State A to prevent the importation of that work, before the principle of the exhaustion of rights applies to preclude him from doing so. In its development of the theory of the specific object of the various intellectual property rights,[27] the court has emphasised that the owner of such a right will be considered to have exhausted his rights when they have been exercised within the Community by the owner himself or with his consent, or by a person connected with him by ties of legal or economic dependence. Nevertheless the use of the notion of consent to determine the exhaustion of the rights by their owner does not provide a clear solution to all the problems that arise in seeking to resolve the conflict between the principles of free movement and the territorial nature of national intellectual property regimes. In connection with copyright, three particular problems may be mentioned:

 (a) where copyright protection afforded by the various national laws of the Member States differs in some material respect;[28]

 (b) where the owner of exclusive rights held in each Member State has dealt with them in some states so as to lose his exclusivity in those states;[29] and

 (c) where the exclusive rights in different Member States are held by different persons, but were once held by the same person.[30]

(i) Differing protection among Member States

25–38   The absence of complete harmonisation among the Member States in the field of intellectual and commercial property rights causes some uncertainty as to the position of the owner of a right in one Member State seeking to prevent the import of the protected work from another Member State which provides for a lesser degree of protection for that right. Initially the question arose in connection with attempts to prevent the import of products from countries which either provided no equivalent intellectual property right[31] or provided for such a right but subject to a system of compulsory licensing.[32] More recently the division of the specific object of copyright into two elements, the right of reproduction and the right of performance, has generated further complexities that have had to be resolved.

The importance of the notion of consent in addressing the dilemma of differing levels of protection appeared early in the court's case law. In *Parke, Davis & Co*

---

[26] Principally under CDPA 1988, ss.22 and 27; previously under ss.5(2) and 16(2) of the 1956 Act.
[27] See para. 25–23, above.
[28] See para. 25–38, below.
[29] See para. 25–39, below.
[30] See para. 25–40, below.
[31] Such as in Case 24/67 *Parke, Davis & Co v Probel* [1968] E.C.R. 55; [1968] C.M.L.R. 47.
[32] Such as in Cases 55 & 57/80 *Musik-Vertrieb Membran GmbH v GEMA* [1981 E.C.R. 146; [1981] 2 C.M.L.R. 44; and Case 19/84 *Pharmon B.V. v Hoechst A.G.* [1985] E.C.R. 2281; [1985] 3 C.M.L.R. 775 and see also *Ramsberg-Gema A.G. v Electrostatic Plant Systems Ltd* [1990] F.S.R. 287.

v Probel,[33] the Court of Justice was asked for its preliminary ruling on a number of questions concerning the proposed exercise by the patentee in the Netherlands of his patent rights in that country to prevent the import into and sale in the Netherlands of medicine manufactured in Italy. At that time, no patent protection was available in Italy in respect of the medicine. The Dutch patentee had no connection with and had not consented to the manufacture of the medicine in Italy. The answer given by the Court of Justice was that the principle of free movement of goods had no application to such a case, and the Dutch patentee was not prohibited by such principle from exercising his patent rights in the Netherlands to prevent the import and sale of such medicine.

Later, in *Merck & Co Inc v Stephar B.V.*,[34] the Court of Justice considered the position where a Dutch patentee was seeking to prevent the import into and sale in the Netherlands by an importer of pharmaceutical products which the Dutch patentee had himself marketed in Italy. The Court of Justice, reaffirming its previous definition of the specific object of a patent right, refused to allow the principle of free movement of goods to be restricted so as to uphold the prohibition under national law of the importation of the goods. The crucial factor was that the patentee had chosen to market the product on the Italian market. Once he had made this choice, he had exhausted his patent rights in all territories of the Community in respect of those products so marketed. The court stated that it is for the proprietor of the patent to decide, in the light of all the circumstances, which include the absence of patent protection in a given Member State, under what conditions he will market his product. If he chooses to do so in a Member State which does not provide patent protection, then he must accept the consequences of his choice as regards the free movement of those goods within the Common Market.[35] The Court of Justice viewed this as the logical extension of the principle established through its developing case law that the proprietor of an intellectual property right protected by a national law cannot rely on that law to protect the importation of a product which has been lawfully marketed in another Member State by the proprietor himself or with his consent.[36] This position was confirmed in *Merck & Co Inc v Primecrown Limited*.[37]

Part of the developing case law to which the court was referring in *Merck v Stephar* is the case of *Musik-Vertrieb Membran GmbH v GEMA*.[38] GEMA, a German management collecting society, had brought separate actions in the German courts against Membran and against K-Tel International on the grounds that they had infringed the distribution rights of the authors represented by GEMA by importing into Germany sound recordings of musical works protected under German copyright. The sound recordings were already in free circulation in other Member States, *inter alia*, in the United Kingdom, but GEMA claimed damages equivalent to the difference between the licence fees already paid in another Member State and the royalty in force in Germany. On a request by the German Federal Court of Justice for a preliminary ruling, the Court of Justice ruled that Arts 28 and 30 (ex Arts 30 and 36) of the Treaty precluded the exercise of rights granted under national legislation which enabled a copyright management society, empowered to exercise the copyright of composers of musical works reproduced on sound recordings in other Member States, to invoke those rights on the distribution of the sound recordings in the national market following their

---

[33] Case 24/67 [1968] E.C.R. 55; [1968] C.M.L.R. 47.
[34] Case 187/80 [1981] E.C.R. 2063; [1981] 3 C.M.L.R. 463.
[35] Case 187/80 [1981] E.C.R. 2063, at 2081.
[36] Case 187/80 [1981] E.C.R. 2063, at 2082.
[37] Case C-267/95 [1996] E.C.R. I-6285; [1997] 1 C.M.L.R. 83.
[38] Cases 55 & 57/80 [1981] E.C.R. 146; [1981] 2 C.M.L.R. 44.

circulation in that other Member State by or with the consent of the owners of those copyrights, in order to claim the payment of a fee equal to the royalties ordinarily paid for the marketing on the national market less the lower royalties already paid in the Member State of manufacture.[39]

It is to be noted that part of the factual background in the *Musik-Vertrieb* case, above, was that the United Kingdom legislation enforced a statutory licensing scheme, taking effect after records of the work had been made with a view to sale by or with the licence of the author. This scheme included a fixed rate of royalty payment as a consequence of which contractual royalties tended to be agreed at the same level as the statutory rate. The Court of Justice refused to allow this statutory restriction on the freedom of the copyright owner to affect its decision. The court's reasoning for this was twofold. First, the existence of a disparity between national laws which is capable of distorting competition between Member States cannot justify a Member State giving legal protection to practices of a private body which are incompatible with the rules concerning the free movement of goods. Second, within the Common Market an author has the right to choose the place in which, in the light of all the circumstances, he wishes to put the work in circulation. In making that choice, the author looks to his best interests which may include not only the level of remuneration but other factors such as opportunities for distributing his work and the marketing facilities.[40]

In both the *Merck v Stephar* and *Musik-Vertrieb* cases, above, the court refused to allow the exercise of national legislation to protect the owner of a right in one Member State from the effects of differing levels of protection under the laws of another Member State because the circulation of that work in that other Member State had been by, or with the consent of, the owner of the right. The importance of the existence of such consent is reinforced by the decision of the Court of Justice in *Pharmon B.V. v Hoechst A.G.*[41] Under the United Kingdom patent legislation, the holder of the patent for the drug "frusemide" was required to grant a compulsory licence for the manufacture, importation and sale of "frusemide" within the territory of the United Kingdom to a local undertaking. The licence contained a prohibition upon the exportation of the drugs manufactured under the licence. The licensee sold the drug to a Dutch undertaking which sought to market the drug in Holland in response to which the patentee, Hoechst, instituted proceedings for an injunction. The Court of Justice, on a request for a preliminary ruling as to the compatibility of the Dutch patent legislation with Arts 28 and 30 (ex Arts 30 and 36) of the Treaty, upheld the right of the patentee on the ground that, when a patentee is required by the legislation of a Member State to grant a compulsory licence for the manufacture and marketing of the patented product, the patentee cannot be deemed to have consented to the operation of that third party, as he has been deprived of the right freely to determine the conditions under which he markets his products. Only in this way did the court feel that the patentee would be able to protect the substance of his exclusive rights under the patent. However, where the patentee was under no legal obligation to market his product in a particular Member State, but did so because he felt ethically obliged to, his rights were thereby exhausted: *Merck & Co Inc v Primecrown Limited.*[42]

The Court of Justice returned to the doctrine of consent in the case of *EMI*

---

[39] Cases 55 & 57/80 [1981] E.C.R. 146, at 166.

[40] Cases 55 & 57/80 [1981] E.C.R. 146, at 165.

[41] Case 19/84 [1985] E.C.R. 2281; [1985] 3 C.M.L.R. 775.

[42] Case C-267/95 [1996] E.C.R. I-6285; [1997] 1 C.M.L.R. 83. See also W. Alexander,"Intellectual Property and the Free Movement of Goods—1996 Case Law of the European Court of Justice", [1998] 28 IIC 16.

Electrola GmbH v Patricia Im-und Export Verwaltungsgesellschaft GmbH.[43] At issue was whether EMI Electrola, the copyright holder in Germany for a particular sound recording still protected by German copyright, could prevent the import of copies of the sound recording marketed in Denmark. Although the copies of the sound recording had been marketed in Denmark without the consent of the holder of the Danish rights of reproduction and distribution for the sound recording, the marketing was lawful as the period of copyright protection in Denmark had expired. The defendants argued that since the works were lawfully marketed in Denmark, they were entitled to export them to Germany. In this instance, the court upheld the right of EMI Electrola to rely on their exclusive rights of reproduction and distribution of the work in Germany. The expiry of the copyright protection in Denmark did not alter the absence of consent by the German right-holder to the marketing of the work in another Member State.

It would therefore seem that disparities between national legal systems for the protection of intellectual property will not affect the court's decision that the primary factor for deciding whether the principles of free movement override national protection for copyright works is the absence or presence of the consent of the right-holder to the marketing of the work in the other Member State.[44]

Nevertheless, the application of the test of consent can be complicated. As the Court of Justice observed in the *EMI Electrola v Patricia* case,[45] the state of Community law at the time was characterised by a lack of harmonisation or approximation of legislation on the protection of literary and artistic property. It was, and still is for the national legislatures to specify the conditions and rules of that protection.

Leaving the determination of conditions and rules of protection to the national legislatures raised two separate problems. First, apart from differing periods of protection, differences in the nature of that protection lead to a variance between the rights protected in the different Member States.[46] Second, it might not be straightforward to determine whether the right being invoked is part of the existence and exercise of the right of reproduction in a copyright work, or whether the right is part of the existence and exercise of the right of performance in a copyright work. If it is the latter, the right may not be exhausted by a single exercise, but would appear to be capable of repeated exploitation.[47] The degree of harmonisation of national legislation in the field of copyright and related rights achieved in recent years has in some measure solved these problems.[48]

The present state of the case law of the Court of Justice suggests not only that consent will be the dominant factor in determining whether the holder of copyright has exhausted his rights, but also that the copyright owner will remain free to decide when to exercise that consent. The proviso to this remains the second sentence of Art.30 (ex Art.36), namely: the prohibitions or restrictions allowed or imposed by the national legislation must not be such as to constitute a means of arbitrary discrimination or a disguised measure for restricting trade between Member States.

---

[43] Case 341/87 [1989] E.C.R. 79; [1989] 2 C.M.L.R. 413.

[44] See the Opinion of Advocate General Darmon, Case 341/87 [1989] E.C.R. 79, at 418 *et seq.* Such disparities have, of course, led to measures being taken at Community level to harmonise the content of national copyright and related rights laws; see paras 25–41 *et seq.*, below.

[45] Case 341/87 *EMI Electrola GmbH v Patricia Im- und Export Verwaltungsgesellschaft GmbH* [1989] E.C.R. 79; [1989] 2 C.M.L.R. 413 at 423.

[46] See, for example, the decision of the Court in Case 158/86 *Warner Brothers Inc v Erik Christiansen* [1988] E.C.R. 2605; [1990] 3 C.M.L.R. 684, which leaves unclear the nature of the right protected by the Danish copyright laws relating to the rental of video cassettes, referred to at para. 25–28, above.

[47] See para. 25–27, above.

[48] See paras 25–41, *et seq.*, below.

So far, the Court of Justice has not been asked to consider the situation where the proprietor of an intellectual property right in one Member State, either by deliberate choice or otherwise, has not obtained equivalent protection in other Member States where such rights are available. In such a case, would the principles of free movement permit the owner of the right to prevent the import of products marketed by another, when it was his failure to obtain equivalent right protection which allowed that other to market the products in another Member State? Applying the test of consent as developed in the Court of Justice's case law discussed above, this question would be answered in the negative. But, in the case of patents, if the failure to obtain such a parallel patent were due to a deliberate choice, then could it be said that the exercise of the rights under the patent laws of one Member State, where patent protection had been obtained, amounted, in the circumstances, to an arbitrary discrimination or a disguised restriction on trade between Member States?

Similarly, if the holder of copyright in, say the Netherlands, does not act to assert his rights against manufacture and sale of goods in the Netherlands known to him to be taking place in infringement of his rights, it cannot be said that he has consented in a positive sense to such manufacture and sale, but can it be said that in such circumstances that the exercise of his rights under the CDPA 1988 to prevent importation of those goods into the United Kingdom amounts to arbitrary discrimination or disguised restriction on such trade?[49]

Whether the proviso to Art.30 (ex Art.36) is satisfied, it is suggested, is in any case a matter for the consideration of the national court which is asked to enforce the intellectual property right in question.[50] There may be sound commercial reasons why, in the first example, the owner of the patent right in the Netherlands does not wish to take out patent protection in a particular country, and, in the second example, the owner of the copyright in the United Kingdom does not wish to exercise his parallel rights in the Netherlands to prevent the infringement at source. If so, then it is difficult to see how such action could be found to be arbitrary or, indeed, to be aimed at trade between Member States at all.[51]

Although no direct answer to these problems has been given by the Court of Justice, recent developments, as discussed above, would suggest that, in such a situation, the court would uphold the prohibition on the imports. The Court of Justice has repeatedly stressed, that in the absence of harmonisation, it will not interfere with the existence or structure of national intellectual property rights. Thus, in *Keurkoop B.V. v Nancy Kean Gifts B.V.*,[52] the Court of Justice was asked to pronounce on the compatibility of Dutch design rights with Arts 28 and 30 (ex Arts 30 and 36). The design rights in question could be acquired by the first person to register them, without inquiry as to whether that person was also the author of the design or a person claiming title under the author. The only right of challenge to that registration vested in the author of the design or the person commissioning the design from the author. No creative or artistic activity was therefore required as a condition for a person to register a design. The question was raised for the Court of Justice's preliminary ruling by the Dutch Regional Court of Appeal, in proceedings in the Dutch courts in which the proprietor of the

---

[49] See the arguments raised in *British Leyland Motor Corporation Ltd v Wyatt Interpart Company Ltd* [1979] F.S.R. 39; [1979] 1 C.M.L.R. 395; and [1979] F.S.R. 583; [1979] 3 C.M.L.R. 79, CA; see also Case 53/87 *Maxicar v Renault* [1988] E.C.R. 6039; [1990] 4 C.M.L.R. 265.
[50] As was confirmed by the Court of Justice in Case 3/78 *Centrafarm B.V. v American Home Products Corporation* [1978] E.C.R. 1823; [1979] 1 C.M.L.R. 326 at 343. See also *British Leyland Motor Corporation Ltd v T.I. Silencers Ltd* [1979] F.S.R. 591.
[51] See *Lerose Ltd v Hawick Jersey International Ltd* [1973] F.S.R. 15; [1973] C.M.L.R. 83; *Lowenbrau Munchen v Grunhalle Lager International Ltd* [1974] F.S.R. 1; [1974] C.M.L.R. 1 at 12.
[52] Case 144/81 [1982] E.C.R. 2853; [1983] 2 C.M.L.R. 47; see also Case 53/87 *Maxicar v Renault* [1988] E.C.R. 6039; [1990] 4 C.M.L.R. 265.

Dutch design right sought to prevent the importation into Holland of products manufactured in another Member State lawfully but, without his authority, and which were identical to the registered design. The Court of Justice held that the design legislation in issue fell within the scope of the provisions of Art.30 (ex Art.36) on the protection of industrial and commercial property, and that the proprietor of the Dutch design right could prevent the importation into Holland from another Member State of products identical in appearance to the protected design, provided that they had not been marketed by him or with his consent, and that the rights of the respective proprietors of the designs had been created independently of one another.

The problem of exhaustion of the rights conferred by a trade mark was referred once again to the Court of Justice in *Zino Davidoff SA v A&G Imports Ltd*.[53] The context again concerned so-called "grey re-imports", *i.e.* goods which have been marketed for the first time by the right-holder, or with his consent, outside the EEA and are then imported into the EEA. In its judgment, the court characterised the issue before it as the determination of the circumstances in which the proprietor of a trade mark may be regarded as having consented, directly or indirectly, to the importation and marketing within the EEA by third parties who currently own them of products bearing that mark, which have been placed on the market outside the EEA by the proprietor of the mark or with his consent. The court observed that consent, which was tantamount to the renunciation by the proprietor of his exclusive right to prevent imports into the EEA, was the decisive factor in the extinction of that right. It went on to reject a suggestion that questions of consent should be a matter for the national laws of Member States, since if that were so, protection for trade mark proprietors would vary according to the legal system concerned. Accordingly, it concluded, it was for the court to supply a uniform interpretation of the concept of consent. In view of its serious consequences, the court held that consent must be so expressed that an intention to renounce the rights of the trade mark proprietor is unequivocally demonstrated. Such an intention will normally be gathered from an express statement of consent. However, it is conceivable that consent might be inferred from facts and circumstances before, during or after the placing of the goods on the market outside the EEA which unequivocally demonstrate that the trade mark proprietor has renounced his rights. It is for the trader alleging consent to prove it and not for the trade mark proprietor to prove its absence. Accordingly, implied consent cannot be inferred from mere silence on the part of the proprietor; from the fact that the proprietor has not communicated his opposition to marketing within the EEA; from the fact that the goods do not carry a warning that placing them on the market in the EEA is prohibited; from the fact that the proprietor transferred title to them without imposing contractual restrictions on the transferee; or from the fact that, according to the law governing that contract, in the absence of such restrictions, the property right transferred includes an unlimited right of resale or at least a right to market the goods in the EEA. It is irrelevant that the importer of the goods is not aware that the proprietor does not consent to their being placed on the market in the EEA or being sold there by traders other than authorised retailers. It is also irrelevant that the authorised retailers or wholesalers in the EEA have not imposed contractual restrictions on their own purchasers setting out such opposition, even if they have been informed of it by the trade mark proprietor.

---

[53] Joined Cases C-414/99, C-415/99 and C-416/99, *Zino Davidoff SA v A & G Imports Ltd*; *Levi Strauss and Co, Levi Strauss (UK) Ltd v Tesco Stores*; *Tesco plc and Costco Wholesale UK Ltd* (references for a preliminary ruling from the High Court of Justice of England and Wales, Chancery Division (Patent Court)). Judgment of November 20, 2001: [2000] 2 W.L.R. 321

Subsequently, in *Levi Strauss & Co v Tesco Stores Ltd*, before the UK Patents Court, Pumfrey J. stated that the clear thrust of the Court of Justice's decision was that only express consent to the subsequent marketing within the EEA would suffice.[54] He went on to accept that the effect of the decision was to create a presumption of infringement; to require that presumption to be rebutted by evidence which in most cases the defendant would not be able to provide, that is, evidence of unambiguous consent; and to condemn genuine goods of the proprietor to the status of counterfeit goods. In his view, these consequences were "certainly striking but they are inevitable".[55]

The European Court of Justice has dealt in a recent judgment in the case *Van Doren v Lifestyle Sports*[56] with the question of the extent to which national courts may decide the question whether goods have been placed on the market in the EEA with the trade mark owner's consent by reference to national rules as to the allocation of the burden of proof, since the case turned on where the goods in question "had been put on the market by the trade mark owner or with his consent". As the court established in *Zino Davidoff and Levi Strauss*, it is the trader who relies on consent to prove it. In its judgment, however, the court held that a national rule of evidence according to which a defendant relying on a plea of exhaustion of the trade mark had to prove the existence of the conditions for such exhaustion was consistent with Community law. Nevertheless, such a rule of evidence might have to be qualified in the light of the Community principles on the protection of the free movement of goods. Where a party succeeded in establishing that there was a "real risk of partitioning national markets" if he bore that burden of proof, particularly where the proprietor marketed his products in the EEA under an exclusive distribution system, it was for the proprietor to establish that the products were initially placed on the market outside the EEA by him or with his consent. If such evidence was adduced, it was for the defendant to prove the proprietor's consent to subsequent marketing of the products in the EEA.

(ii) Loss of exclusivity in some Member States

25–39 It has not been unusual for the owner of copyright in a work in those countries of the world recognising his right, to divide the world into primary and secondary markets. Such has often been the case, for example, with literary works where language has a greater importance in determining markets than national boundaries. Thus, an English author, or more usually the British publisher who has acquired his rights, might exploit his copyright by licensing the exclusive right of publication in the English language in North America to a North American publisher, reserving to himself the exclusive right of publication in the English language in the United Kingdom, whilst allowing either party to sell their copies of the work in the English language in other secondary markets such as the rest of Europe. What if the North American publisher, or someone else, then imports into Holland a large quantity of copies of the work in the English language, which were lawfully produced in North America, and someone then seeks to import these into the United Kingdom? Is the British publisher entitled to assert his exclusive rights against such imports? It may be that the copies in question were first sold in North America, in which case the British publisher would have received royalties calculated on the higher rate appropriate to a pri-

---

[54] [2002] EWHC 1556 (Ch).

[55] [2002] EWHC 1556 (Ch)., paras 17 and 19.

[56] Case C-244/00 *Van Doren and Q. GmbH v Lifestyle Sports + Sportswear Handelsgesellschaft GmbH* [2003] E.C.R. 1-3051

mary, exclusive, market, but even so, on the principle in *EMI Records Ltd v CBS United Kingdom Ltd*,[57] why should a first sale in a non-Member State have any effect on exclusive rights enjoyed in a Member State? On the other hand, the copies in question may have been the subject of a first sale by the North American publisher in Holland, from which the British publisher would have received royalties calculated on the lower rate appropriate to a secondary, non-exclusive, market. In such a case, the first marketing of the works in Holland took place with the consent of the British publisher, and applying the test of consent, as currently developed, he could be considered to have exhausted his exclusive rights within the Community by such first marketing, notwithstanding that he received only the lower royalty.[58] Should this be the correct analysis of the application of the principle of the exhaustion of rights and the notion of consent to the division between primary and secondary markets, the distinction between markets, when both are within the Common Market, becomes one that is difficult, if not impossible, to protect through the use of exclusive national copyright.

The case law of the Court of Justice has shown a growing awareness of the commercial difficulties inherent in the use of the notion of consent within a market lacking harmonisation. However, the concept of exhaustion of rights, in its present state of development does not provide ready answers to the problems which may arise from the complex manner in which copyright is capable of exploitation in different countries, for what, in the past, have been considered justifiable commercial reasons.[59] The concept requires a good deal more definition before these questions can be answered with any confidence.[60]

(iii) Common origin of rights

The divisibility of copyright and related rights geographically by reference to national boundaries, or even in areas which cut across national boundaries, allows the owner of such rights in various Member States to dispose of his rights in relation to particular territories to different persons by way of outright assignments or by licences. Once this has occurred, the question arises of whether Community law prevents the assignee or licensee of the owner of the copyright under the CDPA 1988 from asserting his right to prevent imports into the United Kingdom of products made in, *e.g.* France, by the assignee or licensee from the same person of the French copyright?[61]

25–40

In relation to trade marks, the "common origin" principle was developed early in the case law of the Community.[62] No distinction was made between direct and indirect sales, nor did the application of the principle depend on a previous marketing. It was sufficient in the case of trade marks for the principle of free

[57] Case 51/75 [1976] E.C.R. 811; [1976] 2 C.M.L.R. 235.

[58] Cases 55 & 57/80 *Musik-Vertrieb Membran GmbH v GEMA* [1981] E.C.R. 146; [1981] 2 C.M.L.R. 44; Case 58/80 *Dansk Supermarked A/S v Imerco A/S* [1981] E.C.R. 181; [1981] 3 C.M.L.R. 590; Case 187/80 , *Merck & Co Inc v Stephar B.V.* [1981] E.C.R. 2063; [1981] 3 C.M.L.R. 463.

[59] See, for example, the concern expressed in relation to these problems by the 1977 Copyright Committee, Cmnd. 6732, paras 83–84.

[60] See, for example, the discussion on Distribution Right, Exhaustion and Rental Right, in Chapter 4 of the Commission's Green Paper on Copyright and the Challenge of Technology, Commission (COM (88) 172 final).

[61] *i.e.* under CDPA 1988, s.27(5).

[62] Case 40/70 *Sirena S.R.L. v Eda S.R.L.* [1971] E.C.R. 69; [1971] C.M.L.R. 260; Case 192/73 *Van Zuylen Freres v Hag* [1974] E.C.R. 731; [1974] 2 C.M.L.R. 127; Case 119/75 *Terrapin (Overseas) Ltd v Terranova Industrie* [1976] E.C.R. 1039; [1976] 2 C.M.L.R. 482 at 506. See also *Re the Persil Trade Mark* [1978] F.S.R. 348; [1978] 1 C.M.L.R. 395; Case 3/78 *Centrafarm B.V. v American Home Products Corporation* [1978] E.C.R. 1823; [1979] 1 C.M.L.R. 326. See also Bellamy and Child, *European Community Law of Competition* (5th ed., Sweet & Maxwell, 2001), paras 8–031—8–034.

movement of goods within the Community to apply in order to prevent the exercise of a trade mark in Member State A against goods bearing that mark and lawfully originating in Member State B, that the two marks should have had a common origin. This left it unclear how far this principle extended to other intellectual property rights. The Court of Justice's decision, that the principle did not apply to patents granted under compulsory licence,[63] allowed the premise that by analogy it did not apply to other intellectual property rights such as copyright and designs.[64] The Court of Justice has now clarified the position and reconsidered the "common origin" principle. The principle no longer has a role to play in the resolution of the conflict between the free movement of goods and national intellectual property rights. In its ruling in *S.A. CNL-Sucal N.v v Hag GF A.G* ("*Hag II*"),[65] the court rejected the principle of common origin, and confirmed its doctrine that exceptions to the principle of free movement of goods in the Common Market will be allowed only in so far as the exceptions are justified for safe guarding rights which are the specific subject-matter of that property.[66] This ruling does not resolve all the unanswered problems raised by the court's notion of exhaustion of rights, but it does remove the uncertainty that was caused by the parallel existence of the independent doctrine of common origin.

In *IHT Internazionale Heiztechnik GmbH v Ideal-Standard GmbH*,[67] the Court of Justice held that the effect of *Hag II* was that where the unitary control of the mark in different Member States had been lost by a voluntary assignment, the assignee in one Member State cannot be said to have consented to another economically independent undertaking having placed the products on the market in another Member State. In such a case, the assignee had no power to determine the products to which the mark might be affixed in the other Member State nor to control their quality. This reasoning appears to be equally applicable to the assignment of copyright in a work for one Member State by the person who holds the copyright in that work in other Member States.

5. HARMONISATION OF NATIONAL COPYRIGHT AND RELATED RIGHTS LAWS IN THE EUROPEAN UNION

A. Background and History of the Commission's harmonisation PROGRAMME

25–41   **Introduction.** Prior to the accession of the United Kingdom to the European Economic Community[68] on January 1, 1973,[69] the Commission of the European Communities (the Commission) had not initiated any measures for the harmoni-

---

[63] See Bellamy and Child, *European Community Law of Competition* (5th ed., Sweet & Maxwell, 2001), para.8–033; Case 19/84 *Pharmon B.V. v Hoechst A.G.* [1985] E.C.R. 2281; [1985] 3 C.M.L.R. 775.

[64] In Case 119/75 *Terrapin (Overseas) Ltd v Terranova Industrie* [1976] E.C.R. 1039; [1976] 2 C.M.L.R. 482, the Court of Justice justified the application of the common origin doctrine to trade marks on the ground that the basic function of a trade mark, that is to guarantee to consumers that the product has the same origin, is already undermined where the original right has been subdivided (at 506 [6]). Such reasoning would not appear to be applicable to the subdivision of copyrights or patents. See also the remarks of Advocate General Roemer, Case 78/70 *Deutsche Grammophon GmbH v Metro-SB-Grossmärkte GmbH & Co K.G.* [1971] E.C.R. 487; [1971] C.M.L.R. 631 at 649, to the effect that copyright is more closely related to patent rights than to the trade mark right. This was later reaffirmed by Advocate General Darmon in Case 341/87 *EMI Electrola GmbH v Patricia Im- und Export Verwaltungsgesellschaft GmbH* [1989] E.C.R. 79; [1989] 2 C.M.L.R. 413 at 417.

[65] Case C-10/89 [1990] 3 C.M.L.R. 571.

[66] Case C-10/89 [1990] 3 C.M.L.R. 571 at 607.

[67] Case C-9/93 [1993] E.C.R. I-2789, para 43ff.

[68] As to the terminology used in this work, see para. 25–01 and n.6, above.

sation of national laws in the field of copyright. However, in the 1990s, following a period of studies and consultations over the previous ten years, the Commission embarked on a programme of harmonisation of national copyright laws by means of Directives which, when fully implemented, likely to have led to far-reaching changes to the United Kingdom copyright law, similar in impact to the changes brought about in United Kingdom legislation following the United Kingdom's participation in the work leading to the adoption of the Berne Convention,[70] and subsequent membership thereof.[71] This EC harmonisation programme had little impact on the 1988 Act, but in the intervening years that Act has been amended on a number of occasions to bring the law of the United Kingdom into conformity with a series of EC Directives adopted in the field of copyright and related rights since 1991, and described below in paras 25–46, *et seq.*

Directives for the harmonisation of national laws adopted by the Council of Ministers under Arts 100 and 100a of the Treaty[72] are addressed to the Member States, which are obliged to modify their national laws so as to bring into force such laws, regulations and administrative provisions as may be necessary to comply with the particular directive by a certain date. Thus, the existing and future Community legislation on copyright has exerted considerable influence on the copyright law of the United Kingdom already, and future legislation will continue to do so. Since the United Kingdom and Ireland are the only two countries in the European Union whose copyright laws follow the Anglo-American copyright tradition, the United Kingdom has already been obliged to incorporate certain concepts of the Mainland-European author's right approach to copyright into its law on the subject, and this trend is likely to continue so that in the long-run the character of the copyright law of the United Kingdom is likely to change.

Distinction between *copyright* and *authors' rights*. For newcomers to the field   **25–42** of copyright, it should be explained that within the European Union there are two basic approaches to the protection of the categories of right owners afforded protection in the United Kingdom under the Copyright, Designs and Patents Act 1988. The Continental-European approach to author's right (*le droit d'auteur*) is based on the protection of the individual author. A work is considered to be an expression of the author's personality and it follows, therefore, that only individual, natural persons may be accorded an author's right. The Anglo-American approach of *copyright* admits protection both of individuals and of corporate bodies, and thus permits a wide variety of creative endeavour to benefit from copyright protection. Thus, in Mainland-European countries, as a general rule legal entities, as opposed to natural persons, are not accorded authors' rights under the *droit d'auteur* system so that, for example, neither producers of films and sound recordings, nor broadcasting organisations are considered to be authors. To the extent that the beneficiaries of the Rome Convention,[73] and film producers are afforded protection in *droit d'auteur* countries, they are protected

---

[69] For a discussion of the effect of the accession of the UK to the Treaty, in the light of the subsequent development of Community law, on the exercise of various rights enjoyed under the Copyright, Designs and Patents Act 1988 by the owner of copyright subsisting under that Act, see paras 25–03 *et seq.*, above.

[70] The Convention for the Protection of Literary and Artistic Works signed at Berne on September 9, 1886, as subsequently amended.

[71] See paras 24–04 *et seq.*, above. See also *Guide to the Berne Convention*, (World Intellectual Property Organisation (WIPO), Geneva, 1978) and S. Ricketson, *The Berne Convention for the Protection of Literary and Artistic Works: 1886–1986*, (Centre for Commercial Law, Queen Mary College; Kluwer, London, 1987).

[72] The Treaty, as amended by the Treaty on European Union, referred to in this work as the Treaty.

[73] The International Convention for the Protection of Performers, Producers of Phonograms and Broadcasting Organisations, signed at Rome on October 26, 1961. The Convention entered into

by means of rights related to copyright, known as related or neighbouring rights (*droits voisins du droit d'auteur*).

A further distinction between *copyright* and *droit d'auteur* systems concerns the requirement, common to both, that only original works may be protected. The requirement of originality is defined differently in the various Member States. In Mainland-European countries, originality requires a degree of creativity reflecting the individuality of the author's personality, whereas in the United Kingdom, original means only that the work originates with the author and is not copied. The interpretation of the notion of originality has traditionally been reserved to the courts in both systems.[74]

The copyright harmonisation programme of the Commission thus has to steer a difficult course between the copyright and author's right approaches. The task is facilitated, however, by the existing common ground between the Member States in the field of copyright resulting from their common membership of the Berne Union.[75]

25–43   History of EC interest in copyright and related rights. In the following, the history of Community interest in copyright is reviewed and attention is drawn to the impact that Community legislation has already had and is likely to have in the future on the law of the United Kingdom.

Detailed analyses of those Directives which have already been adopted, and either implemented or which are in the course of being implemented in United Kingdom law, are to be found in the relevant chapters of this work.[76]

The first call for action by the Commission in relation to copyright came from the European Parliament in a Resolution on the Preservation of the European Cultural Heritage in 1974. This asked the Commission "to propose measures to be adopted by the Council to approximate the national laws on the protection of the cultural heritage, royalties and other related intellectual property rights".[77] In response to this Resolution, the Commission put forward a series of policy documents on the subject of Community action in the cultural sector,[78] including some aspects of copyright law, and commissioned a number of comparative law stud-

---

force on May 18, 1964 (see paras 24–88 *et seq.*, above). The Rome Convention is not to be confused with the Rome Act revising the Berne Convention 1928. See also *Guide to the Rome Convention and the Phonograms Convention*, (World Intellectual Property Organisation (WIPO), Geneva, 1981).

[74] On the question of originality and other distinctions (formalities, ownership and assignability of rights, moral rights and related rights) between copyright and *droit d'auteur*, see G. Davies, "The Convergence of Copyright and Authors' Rights-Reality or Chimera?" (1995) 26 I.I.C. 964; see also T.K. Dreier, "Authorship and New Technologies from the Point of View of the Civil Law Traditions" (1995) 26 I.I.C. 989; D.M. Rose, "Copyright in Stage Production Elements: Requirements of Originality and Record under English Law" [1998] Ent. L.R. 30.

[75] The Berne Union consists of those States which are signatories to the various Acts of the Berne Convention, which was adopted in 1886 and revised at Berlin (1908), Rome (1928), Brussels (1948), Stockholm (1967) and Paris (1971). Each revised text of the Convention is known as an Act, *e.g.* the Paris Act, etc. "The creation of a single Union, based on the principle of the assimilation of foreigner to national, with certain minimum standards of protection, and capable, by means of revision, of meeting world changes, allows recently joined countries to have international relationships with all the Union countries including those not yet bound by the most recently revised text of the Convention." *Guide to the Rome Convention and the Phonograms Convention*, (World Intellectual Property Organisation (WIPO), Geneva, 1981), above, para.1.7, n.52, above. See also paras 24–04 *et seq.*, above.

[76] See Chs 3, 6, 7, 12, 14, 17 and 18.

[77] Resolution of May 13, 1974, para.11: [1974] O.J. C62/6 and [1974] 5 EC Bull., point 2406.

[78] *Community Action in the Cultural Sector*, Commission Communication to the Council: [1977] 6 EC Bull. Supp.; *Stronger Community Action in the Cultural Sector*, Commission Communication to the Council, 1982, COM(82) 590 final, October 16, 1982.

ies[79] to examine various aspects of the protection of authors of literary and artistic works, producers of phonograms and performers[80] within the EEC.

The need for a degree of harmonisation of the copyright laws of Member States came into focus during the late 1970s and the 1980s in the context of litigation which opposed the directly applicable provisions of the Treaty concerning the free movement of goods and freedom to provide services within the Community and the exclusive rights granted by national copyright laws, which were territorial in nature.[81] The need for such harmonisation became more urgent following the political decision to complete the internal market (defined by the Single European Act of July 1, 1987, as being "an area without frontiers in which the free movement of goods, persons, services and capital is ensured in accordance with the provisions of the Treaty") by January 1, 1993.[82]

More recently, beginning with the Commission's action plan entitled "Europe's Way to the Information Society", published in 1994,[83] the Commission has identified intellectual property protection as a key issue given the critical role creative content and innovation will play in the further development of the so-called "Information Society", and has addressed the challenges to copyright and related rights brought about by new technologies such as digitisation and multimedia.,

The action plan resulted in a proposal for further harmonisation of copyright and related rights, in the form of the draft Directive on the harmonisation of certain aspects of copyright and related rights in the information society (Information Society Directive) published in December 1997,[84] which also had the aim of bringing Community legislation into conformity with the new WIPO Treaties, the WIPO Copyright Treaty (WCT) and the WIPO Performances and Phonograms Treaty (WPPT).[85] These two Treaties, adopted in 1996, had established new international standards for the protection of authors, performers and producers of phonograms and imposed fresh obligations on Member States of the European Union. Meanwhile, the Information Society Directive came into force in May 2002([86]) and was supposed to be implemented in the national laws of EU

---

[79] See the following in the Cultural Studies Series: A. Dietz, *Copyright Law in the European Community: A comparative investigation of national copyright legislation with special reference to the provisions of the Treaty establishing the European Economic Community*, document COM. XII/125/76 (published in English by Sijthoff and Noordhoff, 1978). A. Dietz, *Le droit primaire des contrats d'auteur dans les États membres de la Communauté européenne*, document COM. SG-Culture/4/81FR (1981); also published in German: *Das primäre Urhebervertragsrecht in der Bundesrepublik Deutschland und in den anderen Mitgliedsstaaten der EG*, (Schweitzer Verlag, 1984). F. Gotzen, *Performers' Rights in the European Economic Community*, document COM. XII/52/78. F. Gotzen, *Performing Rights Contracts*, document COM. XII/47/80. G. Davies, *Piracy of Phonograms*, document COM. XII/235/80, (published for the Commission by ESC Publishing Ltd, 1981; rev 2nd ed., 1986). G. Davies, *Piracy of Phonograms*, document COM. XII/235/80, (published for the Commission by ESC Publishing Ltd, 1981; rev 2nd ed., 1986). G. Davies, *The Private Copying of Sound and Audiovisual Recordings*, document COM. SG-Culture/39/83 (published for the Commission by ESC Publishing Ltd, 1984). See also W. Duchemin, *Copyright Protection for Photographs in the European Economic Community* (1977). See also W. Duchemin, "Suggestions with a view to improving the protection of photographs within the European Economic Community" [1980] 105 RIDA 2 and 25.

[80] See also, with particular reference to the rights of producers of phonograms and performers, G. Davies, and H.H. von Rauscher auf Weeg, *Challenges to Copyright and Related Rights in the European Community* (ESC Publishing Ltd, 1983).

[81] See paras 25–07 *et seq.*, above.

[82] Art.8A: for the text see Vol. 2 at G1 *et seq.* See also the Commission's White Paper, *Completing the Internal Market*, COM(85) 310 final.

[83] COM(94) 347 final of July 19, 1994.

[84] *Proposal for a Directive on the Harmonisation of Certain Aspects of Copyright and Related Rights in the Information Society* (COM(97) 628 final) of December 10, 1997, see paras 25–79 *et seq*, below.

[85] See paras 24–72 *et seq.* and 24–115 *et seq.*, above.

[86] Directive 2001/29/EC of the European Parliament and of the Council ([2001] O.J. L167/10); see Vol.2 at H11 and paras 25–96 *et seq.*, below.

Member States before December 22, 2001.[87] The deadline was not met by the United Kingdom whose necessary implementing legislation only entered into force on October 31, 2003.[88]

The EC Council has also formally approved the WCT and WPPT and authorised the President of the Council to ratify the Treaties on behalf of the European Community, as from the deadline for implementation by the Member States.[89]

B. THE CHALLENGE OF TECHNOLOGY: THE ACQUIS COMMUNAUTAIRE 1991–1996

25–43A   The following account of the Commission's past and present programme for harmonisation of copyright and related rights is presented for convenience in three parts: first, the original harmonisation programme put in motion by the Commission's first Green Paper, published in 1988, entitled "Copyright and the Challenge of Technology: Copyright Issues Requiring Immediate Action"[90] and its follow-up, most of which has now been implemented by a first generation of Community legislation, which now represents the *acquis communautaire*; second, the new generation of Community legislation which had its origins in the Commission's Green Paper "Copyright and Related Rights in the Information Society", issued in 1995 and is still in the course of implementation;[91] and, finally, the latest proposals of the Commission for further action in the field of copyright and related rights in the future.[92]

25–44   **The 1988 Green Paper and its follow-up.** The Commission's first major step towards harmonisation was the Green Paper published in 1988, entitled "Copyright and the Challenge of Technology: Copyright Issues Requiring Immediate Action".[93] In it the Commission suggested a minimalist approach, taking the view that many issues of copyright law did not need to be the subject of action at Community level. Since all Member States were party to the Berne Convention and to the Universal Copyright Convention, a fundamental convergence of many areas of their copyright laws had already been achieved.[94] The Community's approach, therefore, should be marked by a need to address Community problems, and any temptation to engage in law reform for its own sake should be resisted.[95] The Green Paper therefore focused attention on six issues which it considered required immediate action. These were: piracy (unauthorised reproduction of works and related subject-matter for commercial gain); private copying (home taping) of sound and audiovisual recordings; the distribution right, its exhaustion and rental rights; the legal protection of computer programs; legal problems relating to the operation of databases; and the role of the Community in multilateral and bilateral external relations affecting these matters. In the Commission's view,

---

[87] Directive 2001/29/EC of the European Parliament and of the Council, Art.13.

[88] Copyright and Related Rights Regs 2003 (SI 2003/2498).

[89] Council Decision of March 16, 2000, on the approval, on behalf of the European Community, of the WIPO Copyright Treaty and the WIPO Performances and Phonograms Treaty ([2000] O.J. EC 189/6); see Vol.2 at I. Due to the Association Agreements that the European Community has concluded with third countries, ratification by the European Community and its Member States will trigger ratification by as many as 42 countries.

[90] COM(88) 172 final. [1988] 6 EC Bull, points 1.2.1 *et seq.*

[91] *Green Paper on Copyright and Related Rights in the Information Society* (hereinafter "Green Paper"), COM(95) 382 final of July 19, 1995: see also *Follow-up to the Green Paper on Copyright and Related Rights in the Information Society* (hereinafter "Follow-up to the Green Paper"), COM(96) 568 final of November 20, 1996.

[92] See para. 25–99, *et seq.*, below.

[93] See para. 25–43A, above.

[94] Green Paper, para. 25–43A, above, para.1.4.9, and see, paras 24–04 *et seq.* and 24–79 *et seq.*, above.

[95] Green Paper, para. 25–43A, above, para.1.4.10.

legislative solutions to these issues would promote, at the Community level, the protection, the increased status and the stimulation of intellectual and artistic creativity, which it considered a precious asset, the source of Europe's cultural identity and that of each individual state.[96]

Of particular interest were the general comments of the Commission, in the introduction to the Green Paper, as to the overall objectives which the then EEC should seek to achieve in its legislative programme for copyright protection. These were described as four-fold. First, to ensure the proper functioning of the Common Market, so that creators and providers of copyright goods and services should be able to treat the Community as a single internal market. Secondly, to improve the competitiveness of the EEC economy in relation to its trading partners, particularly in areas such as the media and information.Thirdly, the intellectual property of Community nationals, which represented considerable investment in terms of finance and effort, should not be misappropriated by others outside its external frontiers.[97] Fourthly, in developing Community rules on copyright, due regard should be had to ensuring that copyright was not used to create monopolies of undue scope and duration, and, therefore, to the limitations to be imposed on the rights granted in the interests of third parties and the public at large.[98] The central theme of these concerns, that of using copyright to create a favourable environment to stimulate and protect the creativity and investment of individuals for the benefit of the EEC economy, balanced against the potential danger, inherent in copyright, of creating anti-competitive monopolies, is one that mirrors the conflicts with which the European Court of Justice has been faced in developing its case law in the field of industrial property rights.[99]

The Green Paper was a consultative document, intended to provide a basis for discussion. It was not a definitive statement of the Commission's position, nor an exhaustive study of all problems requiring attention. The views of governments and interested parties (authors, performers, the film, recording and broadcasting industries, and consumers) were sought and a series of hearings held.[1] The Green Paper was generally welcomed but gave rise to criticism in some quarters for concentrating on issues, such as piracy, home taping and computer programs, said to be of more concern to industry than to authors.[2] It should be noted, however, that the legal basis for any action by the Community is restricted under the Treaty. Harmonisation of the laws of Member States may only be undertaken to the extent required for the proper functioning of the internal market (Art.3(g), former Art.3(h)). Thus, the Community may only legislate where differences in the legal protection provided by the laws and practices of Member States represent sources of barriers to trade and distortions of competition which impede the achievement and proper functioning of the internal market, and to prevent such

---

[96] Green Paper, para. 25–43A above, para.1.4.4.

[97] See, in respect of one possible method of challenging misappropriation of intellectual property by others outside the EU, "Re Unauthorised Reproduction of Sound Recordings in Indonesia" [1988] 1 C.M.L.R. 387, concerning the use of the New Commercial Policy Instrument, Reg. 2641/84: [1984] O.J. L252/1, against illicit commercial practices.

[98] Green Paper, para. 25–43A above, paras 1.3.1 to 1.3.6.

[99] See para. 25–07, above.

[1] (1.) Hearing on the Legal Protection of Computer Programs (October 1988). (2.) Hearing on Audiovisual Home Copying (December 1988). (3.) Hearing on Rental Rights and Certain Aspects of Piracy (September 1989). (4.) Hearing on the Protection of Databases (April 1990). (5.) Hearing on Moral Rights (November/December 1993). Further hearings and consultations have been held in connection with the Commission's later proposals for directives on the artist's resale right and copyright and related rights in the information society, discussed later in this Chapter.

[2] See M. Möller, "Author's Right or Copyright?" in F. Gotzen ed., Copyright and the European Community (1989); G. Schricker, "Harmonisation of Copyright in the European Economic Community" (1989) 20 I.I.C. 466. See also on the Green Paper generally, T. Dreier, and S. von Lewinski, "The European Commission's Activities in the Field of Copyright" (1991) Journal of the Copyright Society of the U.S.A., 96.

differences becoming greater. It may not, therefore, harmonise legislation for the sake of it, but only to eliminate differences with the objective of introducing the single internal market and ensuring that competition in that market is not distorted (*cf* Art.3(f) of the Treaty).

The differences in the level of protection afforded to related rights within the Community were very much greater than any differences in the protection of authors' rights and there was, therefore, at that time a correspondingly greater need for action by the Community in the field of related rights.

25–45   **Follow-up to the Green Paper.** In January 1991, the Commission issued a document, entitled *Follow-up to the Green Paper*,[3] which put forward a comprehensive working programme in the field of copyright (in the sense of author's, rights) and so-called "neighbouring" or "related" rights.[4] In it, the Commission stressed the need to harmonise copyright and related rights at a high level of protection, arguing that such rights are fundamental to intellectual creation, their protection ensuring the maintenance and development of creativity in the interest of authors, cultural industries, consumers and society as a whole. It was proposed that the following legislative action be taken by December 31, 1991:

(i) A decision that the Member States should adhere to the 1971 Paris Act of the Berne Convention and to the Rome Convention.[5]

(ii) Proposals for directives on the following subjects to be laid before the Council on:

(1) rental right, lending right and certain related rights;

(2) home copying of sound and audiovisual recordings;

(3) harmonisation of the legal protection of databases;

(4) harmonisation of the term of protection for copyright and certain related rights;

(5) harmonisation of copyright rules applicable to satellite broadcasting and cable transmission.[6]

Of these six proposals, one, private copying of sound and audiovisual recordings, remained outstanding until the adoption of the Information Society Directive. This proved a controversial issue to which solutions were hard to find. The Commission's position shifted more than once and the issue is not yet fully resolved.[7]

The Commission also announced its intention to study the need for action on the following issues before the end of 1992: moral rights, reprography, artist's resale right, as well as the collective management of copyright and related rights and collecting societies. In the meantime, the Commission has put forward a pro-

---

[3] *Follow-up to the Green Paper: Working Programme of the Commission in the Field of Copyright and Neighbouring Rights* (hereinafter "Follow-up to the Green Paper"), Commission Communication to the Council, document COM(584) 90 final, January 17, 1991.

[4] Terms applied to the rights of the beneficiaries of the Rome Convention for the Protection of Performers, Producers of Phonograms and Broadcasting Organisations 1961. Hereinafter, the term "related rights", also used by the Commission in recent directives, is used.

[5] All Member States are party to the Berne Convention. However, Ireland is not party to the Paris Act 1971 thereof. On March 19, 2002, the European Court of Justice declared that in failing to adhere to the Paris Act, Ireland had failed to fulfil its obligations under Art.300(7) of the Treaty of Rome, in conjunction with Art.5 of Protocol 28 to the Agreement on the EEA.: Case C-13/00 *Commission v Ireland*. On July 14, 2003, the Commission announced that since Ireland had still failed to adhere to the Paris Act, it had decided to send it a reasoned opinion under Art.228 of the Treaty: Press Release IP/03/1005. As of August 20, 2004, Ireland had still not adhered to the Paris Act.

[6] *Follow-up to the Green Paper*, p.39.

[7] The present position is discussed in paras 25–99 *et seq.*, below. See also J. Reinbothe,"Private Copying, Levies and DRMs against the Background of the EU Copyright Framework", speech delivered at the DRM Levies Conference, September 8, 2003.

posal for a Directive on only one of these issues, namely artist's resale right.[8] The other matters remain under consideration.[9] By that date, the Commission also proposed to consolidate the role of the Community in the field of bilateral and multilateral external relations and to establish an inventory of the intellectual property situation in certain non-Member States.[10] The Commission stated that, in its work, it would be guided by two principles: the need to strengthen the protection of copyright and related rights, and the need for a comprehensive approach, aiming at a basic level of harmonisation, common to all Member States, of those aspects of copyright and related rights which might have implications for the creation of the internal market.

Legislative measures adopted to date. Eight legislative texts have been adopted   **25–46** so far by the Council of Ministers and one proposed text rejected. Of these texts, six represent the first generation of measures adopted to harmonise the copyright laws of the Member States, originating as they do from the original 1988 Green Paper. The seventh, the Information Society Directive, is the first of the second generation of harmonisation measures, initiated by the 1995 Green Paper on copyright and related rights in the information society. The six first-generation Directives, the five earliest of which represent the "*aquis communautaire*" in the field of copyright and related rights having been implemented by all the Member States, are the following: (1) the Directive on the legal protection of computer programs of May 14, 1991;[11] (2) the Directive on rental right and lending right and on certain rights related to copyright in the field of intellectual property, of November 19, 1992;[12] (3) the Directive on the co-ordination of certain rules concerning copyright and rights related to copyright applicable to satellite broadcasting and cable re-transmission of September 27, 1993;[13] (4) the Directive harmonising the term of protection of copyright and certain related rights of October 29, 1993;[14] (5) the Directive on the legal protection of databases of March 11, 1996;.[15] and the Directive on the resale right for the benefit of the author of an original work of art adopted on June 6, 2001.[16] Two Directives of the second generation following on the Green Paper on the Information Society have been adopted meanwhile: first, the Directive on the harmonisation of certain aspects of copyright and related rights in the information society of May 22, 2001[17] and the Directive on the enforcement of intellectual property rights of April 19, 2004.[18]

The state of implementation of these Directives by the Member States as of August 1, 2004, is set out in the Table showing the implementation of EC Directives on copyright and related rights in the Member States of the EU, EEA and Switzerland.[19]

The proposal which did not obtain the support of the Council of Ministers was that concerning the adherence of Member States to the Paris Act 1971 of the Berne Convention and the Rome Convention. It should also be noted that, in a

---

[8] See para. 25–72, below.
[9] See paras 25–98 *et seq.*, below.
[10] *Follow-up to the Green Paper*, p.39.
[11] Directive 91/250; [1991] O.J. L122/4246. See Vol. 2 at H2 *et seq.*
[12] Directive 92/100; [1992] O.J. L346/61. See Vol. 2 at H3 *et seq.*
[13] Directive 93/83; [1993] O.J. L248/15. See Vol. 2 at H4 *et seq.*
[14] Directive 93/98; [1993] O.J. L290/9. See Vol. 2 at H5 *et seq.*
[15] Directive of the Parliament and Council 96/9/EC: [1996] O.J. L77/20. See Vol. 2 at H6 *et seq.*
[16] Directive 2001/84/EC ([2001] O.J. L272/32 . See Vol. 2 at H12.
[17] Directive 2001/29/E.C. ([2001] O.J. L167/10) See Vol. 2 at H11 .
[18] Directive 2004/48/EC ([2004] O.J. L195/16. See Vol. 2 at H14.
[19] See para. 25–105, below. Referred to in this section as the Directive Implementation Table.

separate, but related field, the Council of Ministers adopted a Directive on the legal protection of semi-conductor products as long ago as 1986.[20]

25–47   **Proposed Decision Concerning Adherence to the Berne and Rome Conventions**. This was the first proposal for Community legislation in this field and was put forward to the Council in December 1990. It would have required all Member States to adhere to and comply with the Paris Act 1971 of the Berne Convention and the Rome Convention before the end of 1992. The proposal was rejected for political reasons in December 1991.

The Commission made the proposal, considering that adherence of all the Member States to the Conventions would provide a harmonised basis on which rules for copyright and related rights could be built. It would also have represented a step forward in the fight against piracy of sound recordings and audiovisual works. At the time, Belgium and Ireland were not parties to the Paris Act of the Berne Convention, while Belgium, Greece, the Netherlands, Portugal and Spain had not ratified the Rome Convention.[21] Since the standard of protection, therefore, varied considerably among the Member States, the Commission's proposal aimed at eliminating the consequent distortions and at clearing the way for the internal market.

The proposal was rejected by the Council of Ministers, having been opposed by the Member States. It would have incorporated the Conventions into Community law, thus bringing them under EC (now EU) responsibility. This would have given the Commission negotiating authority on behalf of the Member States in the administrative bodies of the Conventions, at a time when there was no Community legislation on the subject-matter of the Conventions, and would have subjected the latter to surveillance by the European Court of Justice. The EC Member States were reluctant to relinquish responsibility on these issues to the Community and considered that other measures could be adopted to achieve the goal of copyright harmonisation and to ensure that all Member States adhered to the Conventions. The Council, therefore, in May 1992 adopted a Resolution instead, in which the Member States concerned undertook to adhere to the Paris Act of the Berne Convention and the Rome Convention by January 1, 1995, and to introduce national legislation to ensure effective compliance therewith.[22] Given the problem of piracy, this Resolution also invited the Commission, when negotiating agreements with third countries on behalf of the Community, to pay particular attention to encouraging such third countries to adhere to the Conventions and to comply effectively with the standards of protection provided for therein.

25–48   **Council Directive on the Legal Protection of Computer Programs (the Software Directive).**[23] The final text of the Directive was adopted on May 14, 1991, following a two-year legislative process[24] and the deadline for its

---

[20] Directive 87/54: [1986] O.J. L24/36. See Vol. 2 at H1 *et seq.* and, as to the position in the United Kingdom, Ch.14, above.

[21] Belgium, Greece and the Netherlands had no legislation at that time on related rights. Now, all three have legislated on the subject and all have meanwhile ratified the Rome Convention. However, Ireland has not yet adhered to the Paris Act of the Berne Convention. On March 19, 2002, the European Court of Justice declared that in failing to adhere to the Paris Act, Ireland had failed to fulfil its obligations under Art.300(7) of the Treaty of Rome, in conjunction with Art.5 of Protocol 28 to the Agreement on the EEA: Case C-13/00 *Commission v Ireland*. There is still no date for implementation.

[22] Council Resolution on increased protection for copyright and neighbouring rights of May 14, 1992; [1992] O.J. C138/01.

[23] Directive 91/250/EEC; [1991] O.J. L122/42.

[24] The first draft of the Directive was published in January 1989: *Proposal for a Council Directive*

implementation by the Member States was set at January 1, 1993, the date of the establishment of the internal market.[25]

Background. The Directive had been foreshadowed in the Green Paper, in which the Commission had announced its intention to submit a proposal for a Directive for the protection of computer programs within the framework of copyright and related rights.   **25–49**

Terms of the Directive. The Directive establishes that computer programs are to **25–50** be protected under copyright law as literary works within the meaning of the Berne Convention,[26] thus following an international trend.[27] The aim was to secure clear and effective copyright protection for computer programs in all Member States, to remove differences in protection which had negative effects on the functioning of the common market and to avoid any such differences arising in the future by harmonising such issues as the beneficiaries and subject-matter of protection, the exclusive rights on which protected persons should be able to rely in order to authorise or prohibit certain acts, and the duration of protection.

By specifying that computer programs were to be protected as literary works within the meaning of the Berne Convention, the Directive effectively achieved an equally important aim for the Member States: that of integrating programs into an established system of international protection, bringing with it the advantages of certain minimum standards of protection and national treatment for Community software in the Contracting States of the Berne Convention.

On the question of authorship, the Directive defines the author of a computer program as the natural person or group of natural persons having created the program or, where the legislation of the Member State permits, the legal person designated as the right-holder by that legislation. The restricted acts include reproduction, translation, adaptation, arrangement and any form of distribution to the public, including rental.[28] During the legislative process, the draft Directive gave rise to considerable controversy.[29] It opposed the interests of the major manufacturers of computer software on the one hand, and companies specialising in developing computer products compatible with those of the market leaders and software users on the other. The major manufacturers sought a high level of copyright protection, whereas the developers wanted to be able to analyse existing programs by means of reverse engineering, and software users were concerned that the protection afforded would hinder the use and maintenance of software. The final text is a compromise which permits exceptions to the restricted acts in certain limited circumstances, *inter alia*, where necessary for the use of the computer program by the lawful acquirer in accordance with its intended purpose, including error correction, and to make it possible to connect all

---

on the legal protection of computer programs, COM(88) 816 final-SYN 183: [1989] O.J. C91/4, submitted by the Commission on January 5, 1989.

[25] See the Directive Implementation Table, para. 25–105, below.

[26] Directive 91/250, Art.1(1).

[27] See para. 24–70, above.

[28] Directive 91/250, Art.4.

[29] See, *inter alia*, W.R. Cornish, "Interoperable Systems and Copyright" [1989] 11 E.I.P.R. 391 and "Computer Program Copyright and the Berne Convention" [1990] 4 E.I.P.R. 129; W.T. Lake, *et al*, "Seeking Compatibility or Avoiding Development Costs? A Reply on Software Copyright in the EC" [1989] 12 E.I.P.R. 431; M. Colombe, and C. Meyer, "Interoperability Still Threatened by EC Software Directive: A Status Report" [1990] 9 E.I.P.R. 325; C.G. Miller, "The Proposal for an EC Council Directive on the Legal Protection of Computer Programs" [1990] 10 E.I.P.R. 347; T. Dreier, "The Council Directive of 14 May 1991 on the Legal Protection of Computer Programs" [1991] 9 E.I.P.R. 319.

components of a computer system, including those of different manufacturers, so that they can work together.[30]

On April 10, 2000, the Commission submitted a report on the implementation of the Directive to the other Community institutions. According to the report, the objectives of the Directive have been achieved and the effects on the software industry are satisfactory (as demonstrated for example by industry growth and a decrease in software piracy). It concluded that no amendment of the Directive was appropriate or necessary.[31]

25–51 **Implementation in the United Kingdom.** The Directive has been implemented in the United Kingdom by the Copyright (Computer Programs) Regulations 1992, which entered into force on January 1, 1993.[32]

25–52 **Directive on Rental Right and Lending Right and on Certain Rights Related to Copyright in the Field of Intellectual Property (the Rental and Related Rights Directive).**[33] This Directive was adopted on November 19, 1992, having first been proposed by the Commission to the Council in December 1990. Member States were given until July 1, 1994, to bring their laws into line with it.[34]

25–53 **Background.** The Directive deals with two major topics which were already addressed in the Green Paper, the threat of piracy, and rental and lending of, *inter alia*, books, films and sound recordings.[35] However, it goes much further by providing for a harmonised legal framework for the protection of performers, producers of phonograms and broadcasting organisations throughout the European Union.

One of the major areas where differences existed hitherto between Member States is in the nature and level of protection afforded to performers, producers of phonograms and broadcasting organisations. In the United Kingdom and Ireland, producers of phonograms and broadcasting organisations were protected under the copyright law, while performers enjoyed related rights protection. In the other Member States, the situation varied widely; some countries afforded a high level of protection under related rights legislation to these categories of right owners while others afforded them little or no specific protection. Likewise, the term of protection for related rights varied between 20 and 50 years[36] and it was not until 2002 that the last of the then 15 EC Member States adhered to the Rome Convention of which related rights owners are the beneficiaries.[37] The aim of the Directive, therefore, was twofold: to eliminate the differences which existed between the various Member States as regards the legal protection afforded to

---

[30] Directive 91/250, Arts 5 and 6.

[31] COM(2000) 199 final, April 10, 2000

[32] SI 1992/3233. For a detailed analysis of the implementation of the Directive in UK law, see paras 3–19 *et seq.*, above. See also A. Mosawi, "Some Implications of the New Regulations Regarding Rental Rights" [1995] 8 Ent. L.R. 307; R. Fry, "Rental Rights Derailed: Performers and Authors Lose Out on Rental Income for Old Productions" [1997] 2 Ent. L.R. 31 and P. Kamina, "British Film Copyright and the Incorrect Implementation of the EC Copyright Directives" [1998] E.I.P.R. 109.

[33] Council Directive 92/100/EEC; [1992] O.J. L346/61.

[34] Directive 92/100, Art.15. In 1998, the EC Commission referred Ireland to the Court of Justice for failure to communicate national measures for transposing the Directive into national law. Meanwhile, Ireland has adopted a new law, the Copyright and Related Rights Act 2000 (No. 28 of 2000), which entered into force on January 1, 2001 and complies with the Directive. See the Directive Implementation Table, para. 25–105, below.

[35] See Chs 2 and 4 of the Green Paper.

[36] See para. 25–62 and 25–63, below. On the Directive, see also J. Reinbothe, and S. von Lewinski, *The EC Directive on Lending Rights and on Piracy* (Sweet & Maxwell, London, 1993).

[37] Portugal became party to the Rome Convention on July 17, 2002.

authors and owners of related rights with respect to rental and lending rights by providing a harmonised level of legal protection for all right owners; and to strengthen the position of right owners in the fight against piracy by establishing a minimum standard of rights of fixation, reproduction, distribution, broadcasting and communication to the public for owners of related rights.

Terms of the Directive. As regards rental and lending, exclusive rights to autho- **25–54** rise or prohibit rental and lending are granted to authors, performers, film and phonogram producers in respect of their works, performances, films and sound recordings.[38] The Court of Justice has held that the exclusive rental rights guaranteed by the Directive are not exhausted in a Member State even where the offering of those copies for rental has been authorised in the territory of another Member State.[39]

However, Member States are free to derogate from the exclusive right in respect of public lending, provided that authors at least obtain a remuneration for such lending.[40] The Directive also seeks to protect authors and performers from signing away their rights by providing that, where they have transferred or assigned their rental right in a film or sound recording, they retain an inalienable right to obtain an equitable remuneration for the rental.[41]

Chapter II of the Directive concerns related rights and affords the basic rights of the Rome Convention in relation to rights of fixation,[42] reproduction,[43] broadcasting and communication to the public.[44] Art.8 of the Directive provides for the payment of equitable remuneration to performers and producers when a sound recording published for commercial purposes or a reproduction of such a recording is used for broadcasting or other communication to the public. There is no definition of the term "equitable remuneration" in the Directive. The Court of Justice has held that the Directive requires Member States to lay down rules ensuring that users pay equitable remuneration and that Member States are not bound by any particular criteria in the way this is done, although it stressed that the concept of equitable remuneration in the Directive must be interpreted uniformly in all EU Member States.[45] In the absence of any Community definition of the term "equitable remuneration", there is no objective reason to justify the court in laying down such criteria. To do so would necessarily entail its acting in the place of Member States. Accordingly, it is for Member States alone to determine, in their own territories, the most appropriate criteria for assuring, within the limits imposed by Community law and the Directive, adherence to that Community concept. Such a conclusion is consistent with Art.12 of the Rome Convention for the Protection of Performers, Producers of Phonograms and Broadcasting Organisations, 1961 (as to which, see para.24–109, above). The court concluded that Art.8 did not preclude the application by the Dutch Courts of a model for calculating the amount of equitable remuneration which operated by reference to variable and fixed factors, such as the number of hours of phonograms broadcast, viewing and listening densities achieved, the tariffs fixed by agreement in the field, the tariffs set by public broadcasting organisations in bordering Member States and the amounts paid by commercial stations. More-

---

[38] Directive 92/100, Art.2.
[39] See para. 25–35 , above.
[40] Directive 92/100, Art.5.
[41] Art.4.
[42] Art.6.
[43] Art.7.
[44] Art.8.
[45] In *Stichting ter Exploitatie van Naburige Rechten (SENA) v Nederlandse Omroep Stichting (NOS)*, Case C-245/00,

over, whether the remuneration was equitable was to be assessed, in particular, in the light of the value of the use of a commercial phonogram in trade.

In addition, the Directive provides for an exclusive distribution right which is without prejudice to the rental and lending right and which may only be exhausted within the Community where the first sale in the Community is made by the right-holder or with his consent.[46] The Directive also introduces related rights to authorise or prohibit reproduction and distribution for film producers with respect to their films.

25–55 **Authorship of cinematographic or audiovisual works.** The Directive also tackled the issue of the authorship of cinematographic or audiovisual works in the Community by providing that the director of such a work is to be regarded as a co-author in addition to other possible co-authors, including the producer. According to Art.2(2) of the Directive: "For the purposes of this Directive, the principal director of a cinematographic or audiovisual work shall be considered as its author or one of its authors. Member States may provide for others to be considered as its co- authors". Those Member States which did not provide for author's rights for film directors were fundamentally opposed to this provision due to concern that it would cause difficulties for the exploitation of films in their territories. Accordingly, on the occasion of the adoption of the Directive, the Commission made a political commitment to produce a report on the question of authorship of cinematographic or audiovisual works in the Community. That report was published on December 6, 2002.[47]

In the meantime, the limited effect of Art.2(2) has been significantly extended. Art.2(2) is limited to "the purposes of this Directive", that is the harmonisation of the rental and lending right. However, Art.. 1(5) of Directive 93/83/EEC on the co-ordination of certain rules concerning copyright and rights related to copyright to satellite broadcasting and cable re-transmission extended the effect of Art.2(2) to the right to authorise the communication to the public by satellite. Soon after, Art.2(1) of Directive 93/98/EEC Harmonising the Term of Protection of Copyright and Certain Related Rights applied Art.2(2) to all rights in cinematographic and audiovisual works.

In its report, the Commission concludes that there is no evidence that the vesting of original authorship in the principal director has caused difficulties in the exploitation or distribution of films or in the effective tackling of piracy or other unauthorised use. In practice, relevant exploitation rights are transferred to the producer, either by operation of law or by contract. Potential difficulties resulting from disparities in national legislation are "levelled" by contractual arrangements. Nevertheless, the Commission announced its intention to keep under review not only the issue of first ownership of rights but also the contractual arrangements between producers and other right-holders together with the increasingly complex area of rights administration in this field.

25–56 **Public Lending Right.** Article 5 of the Directive requires that the authors of books, films and any other copyright works and (at Member States' discretion) other right-holders, either have the right to authorise or refuse lending of their works by institutions such as public libraries, or that they be remunerated for such public lending. Member States have discretion to determine the level of remuneration to be paid to right-holders, and also are entitled to exempt completely

---

[46] Directive 92/100, Art. 9. On February 4, 2002, the Commission announced that it intended to pursue infringement proceedings against Denmark for a partial failure to implement these provisions of the Directive: europa.eu.int/comm/internal__ market/en/intprop/news/02-191.htm. Press Release IP/02/191 of that date. These proceedings have since been closed.

[47] COM (2002) 691 final.

some types of lending establishments from both the exclusive lending right and the remuneration right. Article 5(4) of the Directive called for the Commission to draw up a Report on public lending in the Community before July 1, 1997. Because of delays in the implementation of the Directive, this was postponed and published finally in September 2002.[48] The Commission considers harmonisation of the PLR to be important for the internal market because the lending activities of public institutions can have a significant and negative effect on the commercial rental market, particularly for music and films. The report assessed the implementation of the PLR provisions under the Directive and concluded ,*inter alia*, that, although there has been an improvement compared to the situation prior to the adoption of the Directive, the public lending right (PLR) is being applied differently in the various EU Member States and in some cases is not being applied properly.[49] Moreover, there had been serious delays in the implementation of the Directive on this subject. It reiterated the Commission's commitment to ensuring that the PLR is effective in all Member States and to monitoring the way increasing use of new technologies is affecting the application of PLR.

Infringement proceedings under Art.226 of the Treaty have been opened against a number of Member States and, in 2002, the Commission referred Belgium to the European Court of Justice for failing to implement the provisions of the Directive on PLR. In 2004, the Commission opened infringement proceedings against another six Member States, France, Italy, Ireland, Luxembourg, Portugal and Spain regarding their national implementation of the public lending right and, in the case of Portugal, regarding rental rights, stating that—as guardian of the Treaties— it is determined to ensure the correct application of the PLR by all the Member States. This was followed up in July 2004 in the second stage of the infringement procedure by reasoned opinions addressed to the governments in question. If no satisfactory response is received in due time, the next step is for the Commission to take the Member States concerned to the European Court of Justice.[50]

Implementation in the United Kingdom. The United Kingdom implemented the Directive by the Copyright and Related Rights Regulatios 1996,[51] which entered into force on December 1, 1996, and implemented also the Satellite and Cable Directive as well as certain provisions of the Duration Directive, which were not covered by the Duration of Copyright and Rights in Performances Regulations 1995.[52] The latter entered into force on January 1, 1996.   **25–57**

The majority of the rights provided for in the Directive were already provided for by United Kingdom law, but a number of changes to domestic legislation were needed to comply with it. For example, the 1988 Act did not give authors exclusive rental and lending rights in respect of all literary, musical and dramatic works and artistic works or provide for similar rights for performers. Under the Directive, the principal director of a film must be treated as an author in addition to the producer thereof, who alone was considered the author under the 1988 Act. Performers were also given a statutory right to claim from producers of phonograms a share in the remuneration paid for the broadcasting or other communica-

---

[48] COM (2002) 502 final of September 9, 2002, "Report from the Commission to the Council, the European Parliament and the Economic and Social Committee on the public lending right in the European Union."

[49] COM (2002) 502 final, paras 4, 4.2, 5.1 and 5.2.

[50] Press Releases IP/04/60 and IP/04/891, dated January 16, 2004 and July 13, 2004, respectively.

[51] SI 1996/2967. The UK missed the deadline under Art.15 of the Directive, according to which implementing legislation should have been in place by July 1, 1994. For a detailed analysis of the implementation of the Directive in UK law, see Chs 3, 6, 7 and 12, above. See also A. Sutcliffe, "Equitable Remuneration for Rental: Areas of Uncertainty Analysed" [1998] Ent. L.R. 59.

[52] SI 1995/3297.

tion to the public of commercially published phonograms of their performances, whereas previously such remuneration was shared with performers on a voluntary basis; performers were also granted exclusive rights in respect of distribution of recordings of their performances.

On July 26, 2001, the European Commission decided to refer the United Kingdom to the Court of Justice for incomplete implementation of this Directive. According to the Commission, the United Kingdom was not respecting Art.8(2) thereof, which entitles performers and producers of phonograms to equitable remuneration each time their music is broadcast in a place accessible to the public. The United Kingdom has argued that it is possible to set aside these rights in the case of broadcasting free of charge to the public, as is the case, for example, with background music in shops.[53]

25–58   **Directive on the Co-ordination of Certain Rules Concerning Copyright and Rights Related to Copyright Applicable to Satellite Broadcasting and Cable Re-transmission (the Satellite and Cable Directive).**[54] This Directive was adopted on September 27, 1993, having first been proposed by the Commission to the Council in October 1991. Member States were given until January 1, 1995, to bring their laws into line with it.[55]

25–59   **Background.** The problem of harmonising Community copyright and related rights legislation in the field of cable re-transmission had first been addressed by the Commission in its Green Paper on the establishment of a common market in the field of broadcasting, published in 1984 and known as "Television Without Frontiers".[56] There, the Commission had proposed that, in order to eliminate obstacles to the free flow of radio and television programmes by cable throughout the European Union, once a programme had been broadcast in one of the Member States, the exclusive rights of authors and other rights owners to authorise or prohibit cable re-transmission should be replaced by a system of compulsory licences. Right owners would have had a right to receive equitable remuneration for such cable re-transmission but would have been obliged to exercise the right through collecting societies. A system of compulsory arbitration in the event that the parties failed to agree was also envisaged. Thus, once a right owner had consented to the broadcasting of his work in one Member State, it could have been rebroadcast throughout the Community. This proposal, the aim of which was to overturn the *Coditel* decisions of the European Court of Justice,[57] found almost no support. The court had ruled that the owner of a copyright work could rely on his right to prohibit transmission of the work without his authority in one Member State, even where the work had been lawfully broadcast in another Member State with the consent of the right owner in that State. As a result of the strong opposition to the copyright chapter manifested during the consultation process, it was dropped from the final Directive "Television Without Frontiers", as adopted in October 1989.[58] The Commission subsequently returned to the

---

[53] Pending case 458/2002, *Commission v UK*. This case is still pending before the court. However, in view of the amendments made to s.72 of the 1988 Act by the Copyright and Related Rights Regulations 2003 (SI 2003/2498) it may be that the Commission will not pursue it.

[54] Council Directive 93/83/EEC; [1993] O.J. L248.

[55] Directive 93/83, Art.14(1). See the Directive Implementation Table, para. 25–105, below.

[56] *Television Without Frontiers*, Commission Communication to the Council, COM(84) 300 final, June 14, 1984.

[57] Case 62/79 *Coditel S.A. v Ciné-Vog Films S.A.* [1980] E.C.R. 881; [1981] 2 C.M.L.R. 362; and Case 262/81 *Coditel S.A. v Ciné-Vog Films S.A. (No. 2)* [1982] E.C.R. 3381; [1983] 1 C.M.L.R. 49.

[58] Directive 89/552, on the co-ordination of certain provisions laid down by law, regulation or

subject in 1990 in its Communication on Audiovisual Policy[59] and in a discussion paper "Broadcasting and Copyright in the Internal Market".[60] The first draft of the Satellite and Cable Directive followed in October 1991.[61]

Terms of the Directive. The principal feature of the Directive is that, in the case   **25–60** of communication to the public by satellite, it requires the broadcaster to obtain, by agreement, the authorisation of all the copyright and related rights' owners concerned in the Member State where the broadcast originates, *i.e.* the law applicable to the communication to the public is that of the country of origin.[62] Thus, the broadcaster is obliged to clear the rights for the whole footprint in one negotiation, so avoiding the cumulative application of several national laws to one single act of broadcasting. In such negotiations, however, the Directive provides that, in arriving at the amount of the payment to be made for the rights acquired, the parties should take account of all aspects of the broadcast, such as the actual audience, the potential audience and the language version.[63] With regard to cable re-transmission of simultaneous, unaltered and unabridged programmes, the Directive provides for compulsory, collective administration of rights.[64] These proposals were not foreseen in the Green Paper.

The Directive provides for a common minimum standard of protection to be afforded to authors and owners of related rights in all the Member States in order to remove existing obstacles to cross-border broadcasting by satellite (whether by direct satellite or communications satellite) and cable re-transmission caused by the differences between national laws. According to its preamble, the Directive sets out to harmonise legislation so as to ensure a high level of protection for authors, performers, phonogram producers and broadcasting organisations and to prevent a broadcasting organisation taking advantage of differences in levels of protection by relocating their activities.[65] As regards protection for the beneficiaries of related rights, the Directive provides for it to be aligned with the rights accorded to them under the Directive on rental right and lending right and certain rights related to copyright in the field of intellectual property, referred to above.[66] This guarantees performers and phonogram producers remuneration for satellite broadcasting of sound recordings, but not a right to authorise or prohibit such broadcasting, rights which producers enjoy at present under the national laws of certain Member States, including the United Kingdom.[67]

The Directive guarantees authors the exclusive right to authorise satellite broadcasting and to exercise that right by agreement; owners of related rights are entitled to equitable remuneration.[68] Except in the case of cinematographic and audiovisual works, however, collective agreements may be extended in certain

---

administrative action in Member States concerning the pursuit of television broadcasting activities; [1989] O.J. L298/23.

[59] COM(90) 78 final, February 21, 1990.

[60] SEC. (90) 2194, November 8, 1990.

[61] [1991] O.J. C255/3.

[62] Directive 93/83/EEC see para. 25–58, above. Recital 14 and Arts 2(b) and (3). It should be noted that the majority of Member States grant producers of phonograms and performers only rights to equitable remuneration for the broadcasting of their phonograms and recorded performances, as opposed to exclusive rights to authorise or prohibit use thereof, in line with the minimum standards of the Rome Convention (Art.12) and the Rental Rights Directive (Art.8(2)).

[63] Directive, Recital 17.

[64] Directive, Art.8.

[65] Directive 93/83, Recital 24.

[66] Directive 93/83, Recital 25.

[67] Producers of phonograms enjoy the right to authorise or prohibit the satellite broadcasting of sound recordings in Portugal, Spain and the UK.

[68] Directive 93/83, Arts 2 and 4.

circumstances to right-holders not represented by the collecting society.[69] Existing agreements concerning satellite broadcasting were permitted to remain in force until January 1, 2000.

As regards re-transmission by cable of broadcasts, the applicable copyright and related rights are to be observed, and authorisation obtained, on the basis of individual or collective contractual agreements between authors, holders of related rights and cable operators. Existing statutory licence systems were to be phased out by December 31, 1997.[70] However, such rights are only to be exercised through a collecting society and, where a right-holder has not transferred the management of his rights to a collecting society, the collecting society which manages rights of the same category shall be deemed to be mandated to manage his rights. If there is more than one such society, the right owner shall have a choice. In the case of failure to agree, the Directive provides for either party to seek the assistance of mediators.[71]

The Court of Justice has handed down a decision in response to a referral asking whether a system for the reception of television programmes broadcast terrestrially or by satellite and their exclusive distribution to the guests occupying the rooms of a hotel constitutes an "act of communication to the public" or "reception by the public" for copyright infringement purposes. The court concluded that the issue in question was not governed by the Directive and must consequently be decided in accordance with national law.[72]

Finally, the Commission undertook to submit a report, not later than January 1, 2000, on the application of the Directive and, if necessary, to make further proposals to adapt it to developments in the audio and audiovisual sector.[73] This provision originated in an amendment of the European Parliament, which was concerned that the Directive should keep pace with developments in digital broadcasting technology. In the future, digital broadcasting by satellite and cable will be increasingly used to operate new electronic delivery systems direct to consumers, becoming in fact a new means of distribution. Phonogram producers and performers argue that such electronic delivery systems will displace sales of recordings in the form of hard copies (pre-recorded discs and cassette tapes), thus undermining revenues and leading to a reduction in investment in recorded music. To enable them adequately to control this future market and preserve their reproduction and distribution rights, they seek the right to authorise communication to the public of sound recordings by satellite and cable instead of a mere right to remuneration.

The report was published on July 26, 2002.[74] The Commission has identified two important areas of action. First, citizens have increasingly been encountering difficulties in accessing satellite channels transmitted outside the Member State in which they are resident, for example, because the programmes transmitted by the channel are encrypted so as to prevent reception beyond national borders. The Commission considers that this is contrary to the principle of the Directive, which involves moving beyond a purely national approach. It therefore intends to carry out a study with a view to resolving this problem. Second, the Commission intends to assess the existing methods of managing the rights to cable retransmission before considering whether or not to revise the Directive. In this context, the Commission identifies a number of issues which it considers may require resolu-

---

[69] Art.3.

[70] Art.8.

[71] Art.9.

[72] Case C- 293/98, *Entidad de Gestion de Derechos de los Productores Audiovisuales (Egeda) v Hosteleria Asturiana SA (Hoasa)* [2000] E.C.D.R. 231.

[73] Directive 93/83/EEC, para. 25–58, above.

[74] COM(2002) 430 final of July 26, 2002.

tion, including: difficulties in resolving disputes as to payment for rights linked to retransmission by mediation; difficulties in negotiating those rights in the first place; the possible establishment of a "one-stop shop" for cable retransmission; and the possible rationalisation of the management of rights relating to the installation of shared antennas, for example, in blocks of flats. The Commission has also considered whether it is necessary to extend the scope of the Directive to take account of ongoing technological developments (including digital television and the Internet) but has concluded that it is too early to gauge the impact and content of these changes and therefore too early to determine whether such an extension is necessary. The report has been followed by two working sessions of interested parties and the revision process is ongoing.[75]

Implementation in the United Kingdom. The Directive has been implemented in the United Kingdom by the Copyright and Related Rights Regulations 1996, which entered into force on December 1, 1996.[76] However, under the 1988 Act, the United Kingdom granted rights to holders of related rights which went beyond the minimum standards of the Directive. For example, producers of films and sound recordings are protected as authors and enjoy the right to authorise or prohibit satellite broadcasting and cable distribution. Moreover, whereas most right owners are represented by and exercise their rights through collecting societies, this is done voluntarily and they are under no obligation to do so.   **25–61**

Directive Harmonising the Term of Protection of Copyright and Related Rights (the Term Directive). The Directive was adopted on October 29, 1993, and the deadline for implementation by Member States was July 1, 1995.[77]   **25–62**

Background. The subject of term of protection was not discussed in the Green Paper. This was surprising since, at the time, the periods of protection for authors and, particularly, for holders of related rights varied widely in the Community. Minimum periods of protection are laid down in the Berne Convention (50 years after the death of the author (*post mortem auctoris*, hereinafter pma)) and the Rome Convention (20 years), but Contracting States were free to provide longer periods of protection and some Community Member States had done so. A majority granted authors 50 years pma, but France (for musical works only) and Germany granted 70 years pma and Spain 60 years pma. As regards related rights, no less than five different durations applied across the Member States ranging from 20 to 50 years from publication and/or fixation.[78]   **25–63**

These disparities clearly created obstacles to the free movement of goods and services and led to distortions of competition, since the same work could at the same time be protected in one Member State and not in another. Commission action on this subject was precipitated by the European Court of Justice, which in the *Patricia* case[79] ruled that, in the absence of harmonisation of national laws, it was for the national legislature to determine the conditions of such protection, including its duration. In so far as disparities between national laws might lead to restrictions on intra-Community trade, those restrictions were justified under Art.36 of the Treaty as long as they were due to the disparity between the rules

---

[75] See document SEC (2004) 995 of July 19, 2004 "Commission Working Paper on the review of the EC legal framework in the field of copyright and related rights, para.1.2.

[76] SI 1996/2967. For an analysis of the implementation of the Directive in UK law, see Ch.7, above.

[77] See Directive 93/98, Art.13. See the Directive Implementation Table, para. 25–105, below.

[78] At the end of 1993, the periods in force were: 50 years in Denmark (from fixation), France (from fixation), Greece (from fixation), Ireland (from publication), Netherlands (from fixation), Portugal (from publication) and the UK (from publication); 40 years in Spain (from publication); 30 years in Italy (from deposit); 25 years in Germany (from publication or fixation) and 20 years in Luxembourg (from fixation).

[79] Case 341/87 *EMI Electrola v Patricia and Others* [1989] E.C.R. 79; [1989] 2 C.M.L.R. 413.

concerning the period of protection and this was inseparably linked to the existence of the exclusive right.

In its Follow-up to the Green Paper, therefore, the Commission announced its intention of drawing up a directive on this subject,[80] and a proposal was put forward to the Council in March 1992.[81]

25–64　　Terms of the Directive. The Directive provides for a uniform period of protection for authors of 70 years pma, thus harmonising upwards to the longest period of protection in any Member State. The main justification for this prolongation was stated[82] to be that, under the Berne Convention, 50 years pma had been intended to provide protection for the author and the first two generations of his descendants. Since the average lifespan in Member States had increased, 50 years was no longer sufficient to cover two generations. Moreover, due regard to established rights was a general principle of law established by the Community legal order and, therefore, harmonisation of the terms of copyright and related rights could not have the effect of reducing the protection then enjoyed by any right-holders in the Community.[83] The Directive does not apply to moral rights, presumably because in some Member States, for example, France,[84] such rights are perpetual. As regards related rights, the Directive set the period of protection at 50 years after lawful publication or communication to the public. This was also the period advocated by the Commission for related rights in the Uruguay Round negotiations under the General Agreement on Tariffs and Trade(GATT), which resulted, *inter alia*, in the Agreement on Trade-Related Aspects of Intellectual Property Rights, Including Trade in Counterfeit Goods (the TRIPs Agreement).[85]

In order to ensure full harmonisation, the date from which each term of protection is to be calculated was fixed, in conformity with the Berne and Rome Conventions, at the first day of January of the year following the death of the author or other relevant event, such as publication.[86] The relevant event so far as related rights are concerned is the performance, fixation, transmission, lawful publication or communication to the public.

The preceding directives on copyright and related rights made provision for minimum terms of protection only, subject to further harmonisation. The Directive therefore repealed the provisions of those Directives as regards term and substituted its own rules.

The new terms applied to all works and other subject-matter of protection still protected in at least one Member State on July 1, 1995.

It is to be noted that film producers are treated, like in the Directive on rental and related rights,[87] as owners of related rights in this Directive, being granted a period of protection of 50 years calculated from first fixation or, if published, from publication or communication to the public. The Directive provides that the 70 years pma of protection for authors of cinematographic or audiovisual works will begin with the death of the last survivor of the following persons: the director, the screen writer (*i.e.* the author of the scenario), the scriptwriter (*i.e.* the

---

[80] *Follow-up to the Green Paper*, see para. 25–45, above.
[81] COM(92) 33 final-SYn.395: [1992] O.J. C92/6.
[82] Directive 93/98, Recital 5.
[83] Directive 93/98, Recital 9.
[84] Law on the Intellectual Property Code (Legislative Part), No.92597 of July 1, 1992, as last amended by Law No.921336 of December 16, 1992, Art.L.1211: "An author shall enjoy the right to respect for his name, his authorship and his work. This right shall attach to his person.It shall be perpetual, inalienable and imprescriptible. It may be transmitted *mortis causa* to the heirs of the author."
[85] See paras 24–135 *et seq.* and specifically para. 24–139, above.
[86] Directive 93/98, Art.8.
[87] See paras 25–63, above.

author of the dialogue), and the composer of the music. This does not include the producer, previously considered the sole author under the laws of the United Kingdom. Photographs are to be protected for 70 years as works, if they are original in the sense that they are the author's own intellectual creation.[88] The Directive represents a departure from the standards of the Berne Convention which provides for a minimum of 50 years pma for works (maintained in the new WIPO Copyright Treaty[89]) but only 25 years for photographs.[90]

The trend towards extending the term of protection of authors from 50 to 70 years pma has not met with unanimous approval. It has been pointed out that it is seldom the descendants of an author who benefit from copyright after his death, but rather his publisher, and that no adequate debate has taken place in recent years on the justifications for longer terms in the light of the public interest.[91]

ECJ Case Law. In the case of *Butterfly Music v Caroselli Edizione*, the Court of Justice addressed transitional provisions for the introduction of a harmonised 50-year term of protection for rights of performers and of producers of phonograms pursuant to the Directive in Italy, where the period of protection was increased from 30 to 50 years.[92] As a result, rights in a sound recording which had fallen into the public domain were revived and enforced against *Butterfly Music*. The latter contended that, even if the rights had revived, the Italian law did not comply with the obligation on Member States to "adopt the necessary provisions to protect in particular acquired rights of third parties" as laid down in the Directive. The Italian law provided, in the event of revival of rights, for a three-month period in which previously legally made copies could be distributed after the entry into force of the new period of protection. The court held that the three-month period for distribution was reasonable having regard to the objective pursued, namely to provide transitional measures which would not frustrate the application of the new term of protection. The judgment has been criticised on the ground that three months is a short period for third parties who have legally acquired rights which they have exercised in good faith.

25–65

The term of copyright protection was addressed by the court also in a further case *Land Hessen v Ricordi*.[93] . The case concerned the term of protection granted by German law to Puccini's "La Bohème". The court held that it was contrary to the prohibition of discrimination on grounds of nationality in Art.12 of the EC Treaty for the term of protection granted by the legislation of one Member State to the works of an author who was a national of another Member State to be shorter than the term granted to the works of its own nationals. Thus, the full 70 years, copyright protection of the German law applied to "La Bohème" in Germany.

---

[88] Directive 93/98, Art.6.

[89] At the time Directive 93/98 was adopted, there was a movement towards prolonging the period of protection under the Berne Convention to 70 years pma. See "Memorandum of the International Bureau of WIPO on Questions concerning a possible Protocol to the Berne Convention", (BCP/CE/I/3), October 1991. In the event, however, the WIPO Copyright Treaty did not alter the term of protection of literary and artistic works.

[90] The WIPO Copyright Treaty (see paras 24–66 *et seq.*, above) extended the minimum term of protection for photographic works to 50 years pma.

[91] See, for example, S. Ricketson, "The Copyright Term" (1992) 6 I.I.C. 755; S. von Lewinski, in (1992) 6 I.I.C. 785; G. Dworkin, "Authorship of Films and the European Commission Proposals for Harmonising the Term of Copyright" [1993] 5 E.I.P.R. 151; G. Davies, *Copyright and the Public Interest*, (2nd. ed., Sweet & Maxwell, London, 2002).

[92] Case C- 60/98, *Butterfly Music Srl v Carosello Edizioni Musicale Discografiche SRL (Federazione Industria Musicale Italiana Intervening)* [2000] E.C.D.R. 1

[93] Case C-360/00, *Land Hessen v G. Ricordi & Co*, [2002] E.C.R. I-5089

25–66 **Implementation in the United Kingdom.** The Directive has been implemented in the United Kingdom by the Duration of Copyright and Rights in Performances Regulations 1995, which entered into force on January 1, 1996,[94] and by the Copyright and Related Rights Regulations 1996, which entered into force on December 1, 1996.[95] The Directive obliged the United Kingdom to extend the period of protection of literary, dramatic, musical and artistic works in the United Kingdom to 70 years pma and to change the manner in which the duration of copyright in films is calculated to 70 years, based on the life not of the author of a film under the 1988 Act, (the producer), but of certain persons connected with the film.

The Copyright and Related Rights Regulations 1996 introduced a further provision of the Duration Directive into the law of the United Kingdom, the new 25-year protection for works in which the copyright has expired but which have never before been published (the so-called "publication right").[96]

25–67 **Directive on the Legal Protection of Databases (the Database Directive).**[97] The Directive was adopted on March 11, 1996, having originally been put forward in 1992.[98] Member States were given until January 1, 1998, to implement the Directive.[99] The Directive is to be distinguished from the Directive on Data Protection adopted on October 23, 1995, which harmonises the treatment in the Member States of the protection of personal data (defined as any data relating to an identifiable natural person) held on individuals.[1]

25–68 **Background.** The 1988 Green Paper contained a chapter on databases and in it the Commission, without reaching any firm conclusions itself on these issues, requested comments on the following questions:

(a) whether the mode of compilation within a database of works should be protected by copyright; and

(b) whether that right to protect the mode of compilation, in addition to possible contractual arrangements to that effect, should be extended to databases containing material not protected by copyright and whether this protection should be copyright or a right *sui generis*.[2]

The response indicated strong interest in the harmonisation of the protection of databases and, at a hearing held in April 1990, right owners expressed overwhelming support for protection of databases by means of copyright. There was no support for a *sui generis* or related rights approach.

In its *Follow-up to the Green Paper*, therefore, the Commission concluded that a uniform and stable legal environment for the creation of databases within the Community should be established without further delay, given the economic importance of the sector and the risk of distortions arising within the internal

---

[94] SI 1995/3297.

[95] SI 1996/2967. For a detailed analysis of the implementation of the Directive in UK law, see Chs 6 and 12, above. See also P. Kamina, "Authorship of Films and Implementation of the Term Directive: The Dramatic Tale of Two Copyrights" [1994] 8 E.I.P.R. 319; D. Bradshaw, "The EC Copyright Duration Directive: Its Main Highlights and Some of its Ramifications for Businesses in the UK Entertainment Industry", [1995] 5 Ent. L.R. 171; J.N. Adams, "The Duration of Copyright in the United Kingdom after the Regulations", [1997] 1 Ent. L.R. 23; A. Robinson, "The Life and Terms of UK Copyright in Original Works" [1997] 2 Ent. L.R. 60.

[96] See Ch.17, above.

[97] Directive 96/9/EC of the European Parliament and of the Council; [1996] O.J. L77/20.

[98] Original proposal: [1992] O.J. C156/4.

[99] Directive 96/9, Art.16. The Commission referred Luxembourg to the European Court for failure to implement the Directive in time, *cf.* The *Commission of the European Communities v Luxembourg* [2000] E.C.D.R. 246. See the Directive Implementation Table, para. 25–105, below.

[1] Directive 95/46/EC on the protection of individuals with regard to the processing of personal data and on the free movement of such data, [1995] O.J. L281/31.

[2] *Green Paper*, para. 25–44, above.

market.[3] The Commission recognised also the danger that, without such a uniform legal environment, investment in modern information storage and retrieval systems would not take place within the Community.

Terms of the Directive. The Directive defines the term "database" as "a collec-   **25–69** tion of independent works, data or other materials arranged in a systematic or methodical way and individually accessible by electronic or other means".[4] The databases protected under the Directive are collections or compilations of data, works or other materials, arranged, stored and accessed by electronic means or analogous processes. The Directive adopts a two-tier approach to the protection of such databases. Copyright protection will apply if the database is *original*, in the sense that, by reason of the selection or arrangement of its contents, it constitutes the author's own intellectual creation. No other criteria are to be applied to determine their eligibility for protection,[5] aesthetic or qualitative criteria being expressly excluded.[6] In such cases, the database will be considered a collection within the meaning of Art.2(5) of the Berne Convention. However, the Commission, recognising that many databases are unlikely to meet this requirement of originality, has sought to safeguard also the position of makers of such *non-original* databases against misappropriation by providing for a *sui generis* right to protect against unauthorised extraction or re-utilisation of the whole or of a substantial part of the contents of a database. This right depends on the maker of the database showing that there has been qualitatively and/or quantitatively a substantial investment in either the obtaining, verification or presentation of its contents.[7]

The copyright in existing works incorporated into the database is not affected by the Directive, the owners of copyright therein retaining their exclusive rights.[8] Moral rights remain outside the scope of the Directive also, this aspect of protection being left to national laws.[9] The author of a database protected by copyright is defined as being the natural person or group of natural persons who created the database, or, where national legislation permits, the legal person designated as the right-holder by that legislation. Where collective works are recognised by the legislation of a Member State, the economic rights shall be owned by the person holding the copyright.[10] Arrangements applicable to the copyright ownership of databases created by employees are left to national legislation.[11]

The duration of protection for original databases protected by copyright is covered by the Duration Directive and thus the same as that afforded to literary works, *i.e.* 70 years pma. As regards the *sui generis* right to prevent unauthorised extraction or re-utilisation, the period of protection runs from the date of completion of the non-original database and lasts for 15 years from January 1 of the year following the date of completion. Any substantial change to the contents of a

---

[3] *Follow-up to the Green Paper*, para. 25–45, above.

[4] Directive 96/9, Art.1. However, this definition is expanded by Recital 17, which states: "Whereas the term 'database' should be understood to include literary, artistic, musical or other collections of works or collections of other material such as texts, sound, images, numbers, facts, and data; whereas it should cover collections of independent works, data or other materials which are systematically or methodically arranged and can be individually accessed; whereas this means that a recording or an audiovisual, cinematographic, literary or musical work as such does not fall within the scope of this Directive".

[5] Directive 96/9, Art.3(1).

[6] Recital 16.

[7] Art.7.

[8] Art.3(2).

[9] Recital 28.

[10] Art.4.

[11] Recital 29.

database, which would result in the database being considered to be a substantial new investment, will give rise to a new period of protection.[12]

The usual exceptions to copyright protection permitted by the Berne Convention, including private use of a non-electronic database, use for teaching or scientific research and other non-profit making purposes, are foreseen, subject, in the case of databases protected by copyright, to the safeguards of Art.9(2) of the Berne Convention.[13] Moreover, a person having the right to use a database will not infringe copyright by the performance of any act necessary for the purposes of access to and normal use of the contents of the database.[14]

The beneficiaries of the *sui generis* right are the makers of non-original databases, who are nationals of, or have their habitual residence in, a Member State.[15] As regards the extension of the *sui generis* right to databases produced in third countries, the Directive provides for the conclusion by the Council of agreements on the subject. The term of protection extended to databases produced in third countries shall not exceed 15 years.[16]

While the objective of the Directive to provide a harmonised system of protection for databases has been generally welcomed, certain of its provisions have been the subject of controversy.[17] Perhaps the most difficult question in the preparatory work was the proposal that a database shall be protected by copyright if it is original, in the sense that it is a collection of works or materials which, by reason of the selection or arrangement of their contents, constitutes the author's own intellectual creation (Art.3). Although originality is a common requirement for copyright protection of works in all Member States, the standards for originality vary.[18] In the United Kingdom, originality means only that the database is not copied and that it originates or emanates from the author, whereas under the Mainland-European approach originality means something more: the work must show some creativity. Originality was formerly defined in Germany, for example, in relation to computer programs:

"The minimum requirements of copyrightability are met only at a somewhat higher level; they presuppose a significant amount of creativity with respect to selection, accumulation, arrangement and organisation, as compared to the general, average ability."[19]

The phrase *author's own intellectual creation* is the same as that used in the Directive on the protection of computer programs (Art.1(3)) which was appar-

---

[12] Art.10.

[13] Re Art.9(2) Berne Convention, see paras 24–04 *et seq.* and specifically para. 24–27, *et seq.*, above.

[14] Directive 96/9, Arts 6 & 9.

[15] Art.11(1).

[16] Art.11(3).

[17] See, *inter alia*, M. Pattison, "The European Commission's Proposal on the Protection of Computer Databases" [1992] 4 E.I.P.R. 113; J. Hughes, and E. Weightman, "EC Database Protection: Fine Tuning the Commission's Proposal" [1992] 5 E.I.P.R. 147; P. Cerina, "The Originality Requirement in the Protection of Databases in Europe and the United States" (1993) 5 I.I.C. 579. See also L. Kaye, "The Proposed EU Directive for the Legal Protection of Databases: A Cornerstone of the Information Society?" [1995] 17 E.I.P.R. 583; S. Chalton, "The Amended Database Directive Proposal: A Commentary and Synopsis" [1994] 3 E.I.P.R. 94 and "The Effect of the EC Database Directive on United Kingdom Copyright Law in Relation to Databases: A Comparison of Features" [1997] 6 E.I.P.R. 278; W.R. Cornish, "1996 European Community Directive on Database Protection" (1996) 21 *Columbia-VLA Journal of Law and the Arts* 1; S. Beutler, "The Protection of Multimedia Products through the European Community's Directive on the Legal Protection of Databases" [1996] 8 Ent. L.R. 317; S. Smith, "Legal Protection of Factual Compilations and Databases in England—How will the Database Directive Change the Law in this Area?" [1997] I.P.Q. No. 4, 450; S. Lai, "Database Protection in the United Kingdom—The New deal and its Effect on Software Protection" [1998] 1 E.I.P.R. 32.

[18] See Cerina, *The Originality Requirement in the Protection of Databases in Europe and the United States* (1993) 51.1.C. 579.

[19] This definition of the Federal Supreme Court of May 9, 1985, (Case No. 1 ZR52/83), was handed

ently adopted to indicate that the United Kingdom concept of originality was intended.[20] Recital 16 indicates this is also the case in this Directive, stating that no aesthetic or qualitative criteria should be applied to determine eligibility for protection. However, even if this is the intention, originality of content, according to the present United Kingdom concept, will not be sufficient to provide protection to a database. The author will have to show originality in the selection or arrangement of the content of the database. The selection or arrangement criteria derive from Art.2(5) of the Berne Convention relating to collections and compilations but appear to pose problems in the context of databases.

It has been pointed out that many databases are of value for the very reason that they are complete collections of the relevant materials, being comprehensive rather than selective in their contents. Likewise the arrangement requirement needs clarification, since the arrangement of material in a database is normally dictated by the computer program running the database and by the operating system being used on the computer and is not controlled by the author of the database.

Now that the criterion of originality in the selection or arrangement has been retained in the final Directive as the basis for copyright protection, many commercially valuable databases will fall outside the protection of the copyright law and will benefit only from the new *sui generis* right to prevent unauthorised extraction or re-utilisation of a database for a period of 15 years.

ECJ Case Law. Databases have been the subject of two decisions by the European Court of Justice in cases concerning the balance to be struck between intellectual property rights and EC competition law.[21] These cases are discussed more fully in Chapter 29. They establish that the exclusive right of reproduction forms part of the owner's rights, so that refusal to grant a licence, even if it is the act of an undertaking holding a dominant position, cannot in itself constitute abuse of a dominant position. This principle applies to all intellectual property rights.[22] Nevertheless, exercise of an exclusive right by the owner may, in exceptional circumstances, involve abusive conduct and justify compulsory licences being imposed by the European Commission pursuant to Art.82 of the Treaty.[23] In *Magill*, Radio Telefís Éireann and ITP (as agent for the ITV companies) refused on the basis of copyright protection to grant licences to third parties to reproduce their programme listings (recognised as protected databases). The court found that this amounted to an abuse of their dominant positions and that exceptional circumstances were present. These were that the refusal concerned a product the supply of which was indispensable for carrying on the new business (the publishing of a general weekly television guide); without the information it would be impossible to publish and sell the guide; the refusal

25–70

---

down prior to the adoption of the computer programs Directive (Directive 91/250). See English text in [1986] I.I.C. 688.

[20] See Czarnota and Hart, *Legal Protection of Computer Programs in Europe: A Guide to the EC Directive* (Butterworths, London 1991) p.44.

[21] *Volvo AB v Erik Veng (UK) Ltd*, Case 238/87 [1988] E.C.R. 6211; [1989] 4 C.M.L.R. 122; *RTÉ and ITP v Commission (Magill)*, Cases C–241 & 242/91P [1995] E.C.R. I-734; [1995] 4 C.M.L.R. 718; *IMS Health GmbH & Co OHG v NDC Health GmbH & Co KG*, Case C-418/01, [2004] E.C.D.R. 9. See also T.C. Vinje, "The Final Word on Magill", [1995] 6 E.I.P.R. 297; T. Ramsauer, "Just Another Brick?—The European Court of Justice on the Interface between European Competition Law and Intellectual Property", e.Copyright Bulletin, Paris, Unesco, April-June 2004.

[22] Case 238/87 *Volvo AB v Erik Veng (UK)* [1988] E.C.R. 6211; [1989] 4 C.M.L.R. 122, para.8 and Cases C–241 & 242/91P *RTE and ITP v Commission (Magill)* [1995] E.C.R. I–734; [1995] 4 C.M.L.R. 718, para.49.

[23] Case 238/87 *Volvo AB v Erik Veng (UK)* [1988] E.C.R. 6211; [1989] 4 C.M.L.R. 122, para.9 and Cases C-241 & 242/91P *RTE and ITP v Commission (Magill)* [1995] E.C.R. I–734; [1995] 4 C.M.L.R. 718, para.50.

prevented the emergence of a new product for which there was a potential consumer demand and was not justified by objective considerations; it was also likely to exclude all competition in the secondary market.[24] More recently, in *IMS Health v NDC Health*, the court was concerned with the refusal to license data on regional sales of pharmaceutical products in Germany contained in a particular database within the meaning of the German copyright law. In finding the refusal abusive, the court identified three cumulative conditions which are sufficient to determine the existence of exceptional circumstances: that the refusal is preventing the emergence of a new product for which there is a potential consumer demand; that it is unjustified; and that it is such as to exclude any competition on a secondary market.[25] The secondary market may be a potential market or even a hypothetical market.[26]

A recent Opinion of Advocate General Stix-Hackl relating to the interpretation of the Database Directive, is also of interest.[27] It takes the view, *inter alia*, that the term database, as the fundamental criterion for the applicability of the Directive, should be interpreted widely and, for example, covers lists of football fixtures. The right provided by the Directive allows the maker of a database to prevent the use of the data it contains under certain circumstances. It is intended to protect databases or their contents without protecting the information they contain as such. It thus indirectly protects the investment involved in the making of the database. It is for the national court to assess whether there was a substantial investment. The purpose of the database is not a criterion for the assessment of its eligibility for protection. However, only investment in the obtaining, verification and presentation of the contents of a database is capable of protection.

25–71   **Implementation in the United Kingdom.** The Directive has been implemented in the United Kingdom by means of the Copyright and Rights in Databases Regulation 1997, which entered into force on January 1, 1998.[28]

The 1988 Act made no specific provision for databases, but made provision for protection of copyright in compilations and a database may be considered to be a type of compilation. The Regulations bring the law into line with the Directive, by defining databases and providing that copyright protection should only be accorded to a database which, by virtue of the selection or arrangement of the contents, constitutes the author's own intellectual creation. Thus, the definition of literary work has been modified to include a database, as defined in the Directive; and the meaning of "original" has been defined in relation to databases in accordance with the Directive.[29] Provision is also made as required for the *sui generis* database right.[30]

---

[24] Cases C-241 & 242/91P *RTE and ITP v Commission (Magill)* [1995] E.C.R. I–734; [1995] 4 C.M.L.R. 718, paras 53–56.
[25] Cases C-418/01 *IMS Health GmbH & Co OHG v NDC Health GmbH & Co KG* [2004] E.C.R. 9, para.38.
[26] Cases C-418/01 *IMS Health GmbH & Co OHG v NDC Health GmbH & Co KG* [2004] E.C.R. 9, para.44.
[27] Opinion of Advocate General Stix-Hackl in Cases C-46/02, C-203/02, C-338/02 and C-444/02, *Fixtures Marketing Ltd v Oy Veikkaus AB The British Horseracing Board Ltd and Others v William Hill Organisation Ltd Fixtures Marketing Limited v Svenska Spel AB Fixtures Marketing Ltd v Organismos prognostikon agonon podosfairou (OPAP)*, Press Release No. 46/04/EN, June 8, 2004.
[28] SI 1997/3032; see Ch.18, above.
[29] regs 5 and 6.
[30] regs 12–25; and see Ch.18, above.

**Directive 2001/84/EC on the resale right for the benefit of the author of an   25–72
original work of art (the Artists' Resale Right or *Droit de Suite* Directive).**[31]
The Directive was adopted on September 27, 2001, and the deadline for
implementation by Member States is, in principle, January 1, 2006. However,
those Member States, including the UK, which did not provide for artists' resale
rights when the Directive came into force (on the day of its publication in the *Office Journal* of the European Communities)[32] will be able to restrict its application to living artists only, for a further four years until January 1, 2010. Thereafter, at the request of a Member State it will be possible to extend that period for a
further two years subject to certain conditions. These unprecedented rules reflect
the fact that the Directive was strongly resisted by some Member States, including the United Kingdom, and the result represents a hard-fought compromise.[33]

Background. Community action on this subject was first put forward in the Com-   25–73
mission's follow-up to the 1988 Green Paper. In that document, the Commission
announced its intention of carrying out a study on artist's resale right (often
referred to as "*droit de suite*"). Following a number of consultation exercises
based on questionnaires and public hearings,[34] and after having conducted studies[35] into the legal and economic aspects of the matter, in 1996 a first proposal for
a Parliament and Council Directive on this subject was put forward by the
Commission[36]. Due to the controversy surrounding the proposal, the draft Directive went through a number of drafts between 1996 and 2001[37].

Terms of the Directive. The Directive introduces harmonised legal arrange-   25–74
ments for the artist's resale right Community-wide. The *raison d'être* of the
artist's resale right is essentially to provide authors of original works of art with
financial support linked to the value of their works on the market. This is achieved
on the basis of price bands focusing on the resale price of works with declining
royalty scales. The right is defined as "an unassignable and inalienable right,
enjoyed by the author of an original work of graphic or plastic art, to an economic interest in successive sales of the work concerned" *i.e.* a right to receive a
royalty based on the sale price obtained for any resale of protected works of the
visual arts, subsequent to the first transfer of the work by the author.[38] The right
applies to all acts of resale involving art market professionals such as sellers,
buyers, dealers or intermediaries, and covers sales in salesrooms and art galleries
and, in general, any dealing in works of art. Transactions effected by individuals
acting in their private capacity without the participation of an art market profes-

---

[31] Directive 2001/84/EC, on the resale right for the benefit of the author of an original work of art
[2001] O.J. L272/32 of October 13, 2001; see also Vol. 2, H12.
[32] Directive 2001/84/EC, Art.13
[33] Austria, Ireland, the Netherlands and Luxembourg also opposed the introduction of artists' resale
rights.
[34] Hearings were held in July and November 1991, August 1994 and February 1995.
[35] *Le droit de suite dans l'Union européenne, Analyse juridique, Eléments économiques*, Brussels
1995, study carried out by the Commission. See also, *Das Folgerecht der bildenden Kunstler*, ifo
Institut für Wirtschaftsforschung, Munich, 1994.
[36] Original Proposal and Explanatory Memorandum: COM(96) 97 final [1996] O.J. C178/16.
[37] See Opinion of the Economic and Social Committee, [1997] O.J. C75/17, March 10, 1997;
Opinion of the European Parliament, [1997] O.J. C132/88, April 28, 1997; see also S. Hughes,
"Droit de Suite: A Critical Analysis of the Approved Directive" [1997] 12 E.I.P.R., 694; amended
Proposal of the Commission, COM(98) 78 final, March 12, 1998 ([1998] O.J. C125/8, April 23,
1998); Council Common Position of June 19, 2000 ([2000] O.J. C300/1, of October 20, 2000 and
Decision of the European Parliament of December 13, 2000 ([2000] O.J. C232/173), Decision of
the European Parliament of July 3, 2001 and Decision of the Council of July 19, 2001.
[38] Directive 2001/84/EC, Recital 1 and Art.1(1).

sional, as well as acts of resale by such individuals to museums, which are not for profit and open to the public, are excepted.[39]

The artist's resale right is recognised by the Berne Convention, pursuant to which countries of the Union are free to decide whether or not to introduce the right into their domestic law. The right is therefore not governed by the rule of national treatment, but subject to reciprocity; thus countries of the Berne Union may only claim protection for their nationals in other such countries when they themselves have national legislation providing for such a right for nationals of other Union countries.[40] However, it is pointed out in the Directive that it follows from the case law of the Court of Justice of the European Communities that reciprocity clauses in the Community context run counter to the principle of equal treatment resulting from the prohibition of any discrimination on grounds of nationality.[41] At the time of the adoption of the Directive, 11[42] of the then 15 Member States of the European Union recognised the artist's resale right in principle and nine applied it in practice.[43] In each of these Member States, the right is included as a property right in the legislation on copyright and is limited in duration.[44] There are substantial differences in these laws as regards the works covered by the right, the holders of the right, the transactions giving rise to payment of a royalty, the rates applied and the basis on which these are calculated.[45] The Commission concluded, therefore, that, in relation to the free movement of goods and distortions of competition, the substantial differences between the various laws of the Member States and the uncertainty about the application of the artist's resale right in the various provisions of the Member States have a direct negative impact on the proper functioning of the internal market in works of art[46] and that, therefore, Community legislation was required under Art.95 of the Treaty.[47]

The resale right royalty shall be payable by the seller. The right shall not apply to acts of resale where the seller has acquired the work directly from the author less than three years before the resale and where the resale price does not exceed EUR 10,000.[48]

The aim of the Directive is to ensure that artists share in the economic success of their works and, to this end, the right is to be inalienable so that it is impossible to waive it or assign it to another party. The original works of art to which the artist's resale right relates are: works of graphic or plastic art such as pictures, collages, paintings, drawings, engravings, prints, lithographics, sculptures, tapestries, ceramics, glassware and photographs, provided they are made by the artist himself or are copies considered to be original works of art.[49] Copies are to be considered original works of art if they have been made in limited numbers by the artist himself or under his authority. Such copies will normally have been

[39] Recital 18 and Art.1(2).
[40] Art.14 *ter*, Berne Convention. However, Recital 7 of the Directive proposes that the EC take action in the external sphere to make Art.14 *ter* compulsory in order to introduce obligatory resale rights at international level.
[41] Resale Right Directive, Recital 6.
[42] Belgium, Denmark, Finland, France, Germany, Greece, Italy, Luxembourg, Spain, Portugal, Sweden (*cf.*Explanatory memorandum, Table 5).
[43] Italy and Luxembourg recognise the artists' resale right but do not yet apply it in practice. Austria, Ireland, the Netherlands and the United Kingdom do not recognise the right.
[44] Explanatory memorandum, para.1(6), p.2.
[45] para.1(7), p.3.
[46] para.1(7), p.3.
[47] Resale Right Directive, Recital 10.
[48] Art.1(3).
[49] Art.2(1).

numbered, signed or otherwise duly authorised by the artist.[50] Original manuscripts of writers and composers are excluded.[51]

The minimum threshold for the payment of royalties in application of the right is to be set by the Member States, but may not exceed EUR 3,000.[52] Royalties are payable to the author of the work, and, after his death to his legal heirs,[53] on the sales price net of taxes.[54] The royalty rates to be paid by the seller[55] are set at the following rates for the various sale price bands: four per cent for the portion of the sale price up to EUR 50,000; three per cent for the portion of the sale price from EUR 50,001 to 200,000; one per cent for the portion of the sale price from EUR 200,001 to 350,000; 0.5 per cent for the portion of the sale price from EUR 350,001 to 500,000; 0.25 per cent for the portion of the sale price exceeding EUR 500.[56] However, the total amount of the royalty may not exceed EUR 12,500. Member States are also free to apply a rate of five per cent for the portion of the sale price up to EUR 50,000.[57] If the minimum sale price set is lower than EUR 3,000, the Member State shall also determine the rate applicable to the portion of the sale price up to EUR 3,000, but this may not be lower than four per cent.[58]. Member States may provide for compulsory or optional collective management of royalties paid over by virtue of the artist's resale right.[59] They are also under an obligation to make arrangements for payment to be made to nationals of third countries, provided that authors from EU Member States enjoy reciprocal treatment in the third countries concerned.[60] For three years from the date of any transaction in the work, any dealer and commercial agent, sales director or organiser of public sales is obliged to supply right owners with all necessary information in order to enable them to secure payment of royalties in respect of the sale of works.[61]

The Directive also makes provision for adjusting the minimum threshold and the rates of royalties, including the maximum rate; the Commission is obliged to present a report on the implementation of the Directive by January 1, 2009, and every four years thereafter, in order that account can be taken of its impact on the competitiveness of the European market in modern and contemporary art and adjustments made, where appropriate.[62]

The duration of the right is 70 years pma as provided for in the Term Directive.[63]

Implementation in the United Kingdom. Throughout the negotiations leading to the adoption of the Directive, the proposal was much criticised in the United Kingdom because of London's pre- eminence in the international art market. It is feared that, once the artists' resale right is introduced, the result will be that art sales will be conducted in non-EU countries, in particular, Switzerland (Geneva) and the United States of America (New York), thus putting London in an unfair competitive position in relation to Geneva and New York, damaging the United

25–75

---

[50] Art.2(2)).
[51] Recital 19.
[52] Art.3.
[53] Art.6(1).
[54] Art.5.
[55] Art.1(4).
[56] Art.4(1).
[57] Art.4(2)
[58] Art.4(3).
[59] Art.6(2).
[60] Art.7.
[61] Art.9.
[62] Art.11.
[63] Art.8; *cf.* paras 25–62, *et seq.*

Kingdom art market and leading to a loss of art works, revenue and jobs. The UK Government also argued that the administrative burden of collecting the royalty would outweigh by far any benefit to artists.[64]

To date, the United Kingdom has not taken steps to implement the Directive.

C. THE INFORMATION SOCIETY

25–76   **The 1995 Green Paper on Copyright and Related Rights in the Information Society and its Follow-up**, The Bangemann report on "Europe and the Information Society"[65] led to the adoption of an action plan[66] by the Commission, which identified intellectual property protection as a key issue, given the critical role creative content and innovation was likely to play in the development of the information society. The Green Paper on Copyright and Related Rights in the Information Society[67] was essentially a further step in a process of consultation, seeking the views of interested parties and Member States on the extent to which there was a need to adapt the legal environment for intellectual property within the Single Market in order to respond to the developing information society. The information society is nowhere defined but is described as being the result of technological progress, which by combining information technology, high-speed telecommunications and television has made it possible "to process, store, retrieve and communicate information in whatever form it may take, whether oral, written or visual, unconstrained by distance, time and volume".[68] The Green Paper saw the information society as a reality, in that, thanks to digital communications technology, the information superhighways (publicly accessible networks capable of transferring large amounts of information at high speed between users) had already begun to transmit works and other subject-matter protected by copyright and related rights in interactive services. The Green Paper was concerned, therefore, to describe how the information society was expected to develop, and with the implications of the development of these new technologies for the system of copyright and related rights. According to the Commission, while respecting the principle of subsidiarity, the Community has an obligation to take measures in respect of copyright and related rights in order to guarantee the free movement of goods, the freedom to provide services and to avoid creating distortions of competition.[69]

The Commission identified nine areas in which it considered harmonisation of the laws of Member States on copyright and related rights should be given priority in order to ensure that the information society could operate properly. These were: the applicable law when a work is exploited; the question of exhaustion of rights (Community-wide exhaustion is part of the *acquis communautaire*; the question arises whether the Community should apply international exhaustion); the reproduction right, and the exceptions to it, particularly for private copying; the definition of the right of communication to the public; the possible introduction of a new exclusive right to digital dissemination or transmission; the introduction of a new exclusive right to authorise digital broadcasting for holders

---

[64] See, *e.g. The Times*, leading article, June 8, 1998; *The Times*, "Artists gain but markets lose", Supplement, p.3, July 17, 2001.]

[65] *Europe and the Global Information Society. Recommendations to the European Council*, by the High-Level Group on the Information Society, May 26, 1994.

[66] *Europe's Way to the Information Society-An Action Plan*, COM(94) 347 final July 19, 1994.

[67] COM(95) 382 final of July 19, 1995. See also T. Hoeren, "The Green Paper on Copyright and Related Rights in the Information Society" [1995] 10 E.I.P.R. 511 and M. Pullen, "The Green Paper on Copyright and Related Rights in the Information Society (Is it all a Question of Binary Numbers)" [1996] 2 Ent. L.R. 80.

[68] Bangemann report, n.1.

[69] *Green Paper*, para.12.

of related rights (as opposed to a right to equitable remuneration); moral rights; the acquisition and management of rights so as to facilitate access to works and related matter; and technical systems of identification and protection of works and other protected matter.

Following publication of the Green Paper, many submissions were received from, and hearings held with, interested parties.[70] Thereafter, the Commission drew up its Single Market policy in the area of copyright and related rights in the information society, which was published as a follow-up to the Green Paper in November 1996.[71]

Follow-up to the 1995 Green Paper. The Commission concluded from the process of consultation referred to, that there was a need for further harmonisation of copyright and related rights, pointing out that "The use of computer technology, digitisation and the convergence of communication and telecommunication networks are already having an enormous impact on the transborder-wide exploitation of literary, musical or audio-visual works and other protected subject-matter such as phonograms or fixed performances".[72] In proposing readjustment of the existing legal framework, it asserted that the traditionally high level of copyright protection should be maintained and further developed to meet the needs and practices of copyright markets. Four issues were identified for priority action, the reproduction right (including exceptions thereto), the right of communication to the public, the legal protection of the integrity of technical identification and protection schemes and the distribution right (including the principle of exhaustion), and, indeed, these issues are dealt with in the subsequently-adopted European Parliament and Council Directive on the harmonisation of certain aspects of copyright and related rights in the Information Society, discussed below.[73]

25–77

Issues requiring further evaluation. Several other issues discussed in the 1995 Green Paper were identified as requiring further evaluation before any action could be taken. As regards the proposal to strengthen the right of certain holders of related rights (producers of phonograms and performers) to control broadcasting, notably in its new form of multichannel broadcasting, by the grant of exclusive rights to replace the present right at Community level to equitable remuneration, the Commission took the view at the time that the case for such new rights had not yet been made out.[74] It put forward two reasons why such rights might need strengthening at a future date: the fact that more Member States might wish to grant such exclusive rights in the future to particular holders of related rights; and that multichannel broadcasting might become a primary market for the exploitation of phonograms and fixed performances. However, since digital broadcasting and multichannel broadcasting were only in their infancy at the time, the Commission expressed its intention to continue to evaluate developments in the market and to take the necessary legislative action, should it prove

25–78

---

[70] Hearings were held in January 1996 and the consultation process was concluded by a conference "Copyright and Related Rights on the Threshold of the 21st Century", held in June 1996 in Florence.

[71] *Follow-up to the Green Paper on Copyright and Related Rights in the Information Society,* COM(96) 568 final of November 20, 1996.

[72] *Follow-up to the Green Paper on Copyright and Related Rights in the Information Society,* Chs 1, 3.

[73] COM(97) 628 final of December 10, 1997 (see paras 25–79 *et seq.,* below).

[74] It should be noted that the majority of Member States grant producers of phonograms and performers only rights to equitable remuneration for the broadcasting of their phonograms and recorded performances, as opposed to exclusive rights to authorise or prohibit such, in line with the minimum standards of the Rome Convention (Art.12) and the Rental Rights Directive (Art.8(2)).

necessary at a future date.[75] The Commission's decision not to legislate for these new rights was much criticised by the rights owners concerned, who argued that exclusive rights to authorise or prohibit broadcasting are essential in the digital environment.

Another issue on which no action was recommended was that of the applicable law and law enforcement in the digital environment, *i.e.* the question as to which country's law applies to transnational acts of exploitation. The consultation process had indicated that the majority of interested parties took the view that the problems which might be created by the transfrontier nature of acts of digital transmission could be taken care of through contractual freedom and the application of existing private international law; nevertheless, in view of the complex legal situation, it was indicated that guidance on existing rules rather than outright harmonisation would be welcomed. The Commission, therefore, stated that it was considering issuing a clarifying Communication on the subject, which would address the applicable-law issues as well as the enforcement of rights. The Commission also expressed its intention to study the enforcement-related issue of liability for copyright infringements to evaluate the need for an initiative at EU level.[76] In the Green Paper of 1995, the Commission had appeared to favour the applicable law being defined as the country of origin.[77] After consultation, the Commission's view changed; in the Explanatory memorandum to the Proposal for the Information Society Directive,[78] the Commission stated that potential infringements were governed by the national laws under which the right had been granted and where protection was sought. Thus, in the case of transnational acts of exploitation, several national laws might apply in parallel.[79]

A further issue on which no action was recommended at the time was management of rights. The consultation process had indicated that the majority of interested parties took the view that management of rights should in principle be left to the market, irrespective of the introduction of digitisation. The usefulness of collective management is not called into question. Some parties, however, were calling for harmonised measures to adequately control the behaviour of collecting societies, both in terms of licensing and competition rules. Others had requested a clarification of the application of Community competition rules to collecting societies and collective management, through a code of conduct or voluntary guidelines. The Commission intended, therefore, to continue to study the issue in the light of the development of the market with particular regard to the Single Market. A future Community initiative was envisaged to define, both under the Single Market and the competition rules of the EC Treaty, the rights and obligations of collecting societies, in particular with respect to the methods of collection. Issues to be tackled would include the calculation of tariffs, supervision mechanisms, and the application of the rules on competition to collecting societies and collective management.[80]

Finally, the Commission took the view that the time was not yet ripe for Community action on moral rights, although it was recognised that moral rights had an economic impact and would be affected by the exploitation of works and other protected subject-matter by digital technology. However, at that time, consultations had shown that moral rights were not posing any real problem so far as the Single Market was concerned. The situation might change with the emergence of

---

[75] *Follow-up to the Green Paper*, Chs 3, 1.
[76] *Follow-up to the Green Paper*, Chs 3, 2.
[77] *cf.* Arts 2 & 3 of the Cable and Satellite Directive 93/83, see para. 25–60, above.
[78] See para. 25–79, below.
[79] Explanatory memorandum, Ch.2, 8.
[80] Ch.3, 3 and see para. 25–100, below.

the digital environment and, therefore, the Commission proposed to further study the development of the market and see whether existing disparities in legislation constituted significant obstacles to the exploitation of protected subject-matter, which might require action at Community level.[81]

The Commission also drew attention to the international dimension of the information society and to the negotiations underway at that time under the auspices of WIPO to set minimum standards of protection at the international level in the context of the work which led to the subsequent adoption in December 1996 of the WIPO Copyright Treaty (hereafter referred to as WCT) and the WIPO Performances and Phonograms Treaty (hereafter referred to as WPPT).[82]

In relation to moral rights, it should be noted that the WPPT provides that performers should enjoy moral rights with respect to their live audio performances fixed in phonograms and this is, therefore, an issue the Commission will have to address sooner or later.[83]

Directive on the harmonisation of certain aspects of copyright and related rights in the information society (the Information Society Directive). The Directive was adopted on May 22, 2001,[84] having first been proposed by the Commission in December 1997.[85] Member States were given until December 22, 2002, to comply with the Directive.[86] Only Greece and Denmark met the deadline. Italy and Austria implemented the Directive in April and June 2003, respectively. In July 2003, the Commission sent reasoned opinions to the other 11 Member States which were in the course of implementation. In the meantime, the Directive has been transposed into domestic law by Germany, Luxembourg and the United Kingdom, but the Commission has referred Belgium, Spain, France, the Netherlands, Portugal, Finland and Sweden to the Court of Justice for failure to implement. It has also referred the United Kingdom for failure to apply the Directive to Gibraltar. Eight of the "new" Member States (*i.e.* all except Cyprus and Estonia) have notified the Commission of the national measures intended to implement the Directive.[87]

25–79

Background. In its original proposal, the Commission announced that its aim was not only to ensure a level playing field within the Community for goods and services containing material protected by copyright in the digital environment, but also to implement a significant number of the obligations set out in the two new Treaties already referred to, the WCT and WPPT.[88] The legal basis for the Directive rests on Arts 47(2), 55 and 95 of the Treaty of Rome, as amended.[89] As is the case with other Directives in the field of copyright and related rights, the Directive does not aim at a general harmonisation of laws but at harmonising those matters which are necessary for the smooth functioning of the internal market. The Directive recognises that liability for activities in the network environment concerns not only copyright and related rights but other areas of the law, such as defamation, misleading advertising, or infringement of trademarks.

25–80

---

[81] Ch.3, 4 and see para. 25–101, below.

[82] Ch.4.

[83] WPPT, Art.5

[84] Directive 2001/29/EC of the European Parliament and of the Council ([2001] O.J. L167/10); see App.H11, below.

[85] COM(97) 628 final, December 10, 1997; [1998] O.J. C108/6.

[86] Information Society Directive Art.13, see para. 25–79, above. See the Directive Implementation Table, para. 25–105, below.

[87] Press Release IP/O4/891, July 13, 2004.

[88] Both Treaties have been signed on behalf of the European Community (*cf.* Decision of the Council authorising accession of the EC to the WCT and WPPT, April 24, 1998 [1998] O.J. C165/8), Vol.2, App.I, below. For a full treatment of both Treaties, see Ch.24, above.

[89] Preamble to the Information Society Directive, para.1.

These matters are addressed in another Directive on certain legal aspects of information society services, in particular electronic commerce, which clarifies and harmonises various legal issues on this subject.[90] At the time of the adoption of the Directive, the Commission announced: "Not only is this Directive the most important measure ever to be adopted by Europe in the copyright field but it brings European copyright rules into the digital age. The Directive will stimulate creativity and innovation by ensuring that all material protected by copyright, including books, films, music are adequately protected by copyright. It provides a secure environment for cross-border trade in copyright protected goods and services, and will facilitate the development of electronic commerce in the field of new and multimedia products and services (both online and offline via, *e.g.* CDs)."[91]

25–81 **Terms of the Directive.** The Information Society Directive focuses on the four issues for which Community legislation was forecast in the Follow-up to the Green Paper, the reproduction right, the right of communication to the public of works and right of making available to the public other subject-matter, the distribution right, exceptions and limitations to these rights and the legal protection of technological measures and rights-management information.[92]

The reproduction right. The Directive defines the scope of the acts covered by the reproduction right with regard to the different beneficiaries in conformity with the *acquis communautaire*.[93] It seeks to provide all right owners with the exclusive right to authorise or prohibit direct or indirect,[94] temporary or permanent reproduction by any means and in any form, in whole or in part,[95] of their works, fixed performances, phonograms, films and broadcasts, respectively.[96] This provision aims at ensuring that all authors, performers, phonogram and film producers and broadcasting organisations benefit from the same level of protection for their works or other subject-matter as regards the acts protected by the reproduction right.[97] The definition aims at covering all relevant acts of reproduction, whether online or offline, in material or immaterial form and is in line with the WCT and the WPPT.[98]

25–83 **Right of communication to the public of works and right of making available to the public other subject-matter.** The Directive provides authors with the exclusive right to authorise or prohibit any communication to the public of their works, by wire or wireless means, including the making available to the

---

[90] Information Society Directive, Recital 16; see Directive 2000/31/EC of the European Parliament and of the Council of June 8, 2000, on certain legal aspects of information society services, in particular electronic commerce, in the internal market (Directive on electronic commerce, [2000] O.J. L178/1, July 17, 2000). See para. 25–91 , below, and App.H10 *et seq.*

[91] Commission Press Release, April 9, 2001.

[92] On the Proposed Directive, see: S. von Lewinski, "A Successful Step towards Copyright and Related Rights in the Information Age: The New EC Proposal for a Harmonisation Directive" [1998] E.I.P.R. 135; M. Hart, "The Proposed Directive for Copyright in the Information Society: Nice Rights, Shame about the Exceptions" [1998] E.I.P.R. 169; G.P. Cornish, "Libraries and the Harmonisation of Copyright" [1998] E.I.P.R. 241; T. Heide, "The Berne Three-step Test and the Proposed Copyright Directive" [1999] E.I.P.R. 103; M. Doherty and I. Griffiths, "The Harmonisation of European Union; Copyright Law for the Digital Age" [2000] E.I.P.R. 17; B. Hugenholtz, "Why the Copyright Directive is Unimportant and Possibly Invalid" [2000] E.I.P.R. 499; T.C. Vinje, "Should we Begin Digging Copyright's Grave" [2000] E.I.P.R. 551

[93] Information Society Directive, Recital 21.

[94] *cf.* Art.7, Rental and Related Rights Directive 92/100 (see para. 25–52 , above).

[95] *cf.* Art.4a, Software Directive 91/250 (see para. 25–48 , above) and Art.5a of the Database Directive 96/9 (see para. 25–67, above).

[96] Information Society Directive, Art.2.

[97] Explanatory memorandum, comments on Art.1, para.1 (now Art.2).

[98] As regards the harmonisation of exceptions to the reproduction right, see para. 25–85, below.

public thereof in such a way that members of the public may access them from a place and at a time individually chosen by them.[99] The other right owners, performers, phonogram producers, film producers and broadcasting organisations, are provided with the exclusive right to authorise or prohibit the making available to the public, by wire or wireless means, in such a way that members of the public may access them from a place and at a time individually chosen by them.[1] These rights are not to be exhausted by any act of communication to the public or making available to the public[2] as defined in the Directive. The authors' right of communication to the public is to be understood in a broad sense as covering all communication to the public not present at the place where the communication originates. It covers any transmission or retransmission of a work to the public by wire or wireless means, including broadcasting.[3] The right of the other right owners to make subject-matter available to the public should be also understood as covering all acts of making available such subject-matter to members of the public not present at the place where the act of making available originates.[4] Thus the interactive environment is addressed, implementing the relevant provisions of the WCT and WPPT at Community level,[5] all right-holders being given an exclusive right to make available to the public copyright works or any other subject-matter by way of interactive on-demand transmissions. Such interactive on-demand transmissions are characterised by the fact that members of the public may access them from a place and at a time individually chosen by them. The right applies also in circumstances where several unrelated members of the public may have individual access, from different places and at different times, to a work which is on a publicly accessible site. It is irrelevant whether any individual member of the public has actually retrieved it or not. Since the provision of services, and online services in particular, does not give rise to exhaustion of rights, every online service is an act which will always require authorisation.[6]

Distribution right: The Directive provides authors, in respect of the original of their works or of copies thereof, with the exclusive right to authorise or prohibit any form of distribution to the public by sale or otherwise, thus harmonising the distribution right for authors of all categories of works.[7] The first sale in the Community of the original of a work or copies thereof by the right-holder or with his consent exhausts the right to control resale of that object in the Community but it should not be exhausted outside the Community.[8] This reflects the established case law of the European Court of Justice and excludes the possibility of Member States applying international exhaustion. In *Silhouette International Schmied GmbH & Co KG v Hartlauer Handelsgesellschaft Gmbh*,[9] the European Court of Justice decided that there is no international exhaustion of trade mark rights as a result of products being put on the market by the proprietor or with his consent in the EEA. It should be noted in this connection that the Rental and Related Rights Directive[10] has already harmonised the distribution right for four groups of rights owners (performers, broadcasters, phonogram producers and film producers).

25–84

---

[99] Information Society Directive, Art.3(1).
[1] Art.3(2).
[2] Art.3(3).
[3] Recital 23.
[4] Recital 24.
[5] *cf.* Art.8 WCT and Arts 10 and 14 WPPT.
[6] Information Society Directive, Recital 29.
[7] *cf.* Art.6(1) WCT.
[8] Information Society Directive, Art.4.
[9] *cf Silhouette International Schmied GmbH & Co KG v Hartlauer Handelsgesellschaft Gmbh* (Case C-355/96 "Silhouette/Hartlauer", see para. 25–29.
[10] *cf.* The Rental and Related Rights Directive, Art.9, and see para. 25–52, above.

25–85   **Exceptions.** The exceptions and limitations to the reproduction right and the communication to the public right, including the right of making available to the public by interactive means have been harmonised and reassessed in the light of the new electronic environment. This was considered important to avoid divergent interpretations in Member States and the risk of obstacles to trade within the Community as well as to safeguard a fair balance of rights between right-holders themselves and between right-holders and users of protected subject-matter.[11] The Directive also seeks to promote learning and culture by protecting works and other subject-matter, while permitting exceptions or limitations in the public interest for the purpose of education and teaching.[12] The Directive contains, first, mandatory exceptions with respect to temporary, transient or incidental acts of reproduction, which are an integral and essential part of a technological process, such as transmissions between networks, where such acts have no economic importance. This exception includes acts which enable browsing as well as acts of caching, including those which enable transmission systems to function efficiently, provided that the intermediary does not modify the information and does not interfere with the lawful use of technology to obtain data on the use of the information.[13]

Second, the Directive provides for an exhaustive, closed list of permitted exceptions and limitations to the reproduction right and the right of communication to the public. These exceptions are optional and Member States will be free to keep or introduce them at national level or not to do so; however, no further exceptions will be permitted. It is understood that all these exceptions are subject to the "three-step test" laid down in Art.9(2) of the Berne Convention, *i.e.* limitations to the reproduction right are only permitted in "certain special cases", which do not "conflict with a normal exploitation of the work" and do not "unreasonably prejudice the legitimate interests of the author"[14].

As regards the reproduction right, Member States may provide for exceptions or limitations to the right: "in respect of reprography (except in the case of sheet music, the paper reproduction of which remains prohibited), provided that the right-holders receive fair compensation; in respect of reproductions on any medium made by a natural person for private use and for ends that are neither directly nor indirectly commercial, on condition that the right-holders receive fair compensation, which takes account of the application or non-application of technological measures".[15]

Member States may provide for fair compensation for right-holders also when applying the optional provisions on exceptions and limitations, which do not require such compensation.[16] As regards the reproduction right, Member States may also provide for limitations with respect to: acts of reproduction made by publicly accessible libraries, educational establishments, museums or archives, which are not for direct or indirect economic or commercial advantage; ephemeral recordings made by broadcasting organisations by means of their own facilities and for their own broadcasts; reproductions of broadcasts made by social institutions pursuing non-commercial purposes, such as hospitals or prisons, subject, in the latter case, to the payment of fair compensation to the right-holders.

The exceptions permitting reprography and private copying are not manda-

---

[11] Information Society Directive, Recital 31.
[12] Recital 14.
[13] Recital 33.
[14] On the "three-step test" see para. 24–33 *et seq.*, above.
[15] Information Society Directive, Art.5(2).
[16] Recital 35.

tory; where such exceptions are provided for, then the right-holders are to be entitled to fair compensation, which, in the case of private copying, is to take account of the application or non-application of technological protection measures. However, the Directive does not impose harmonisation of remuneration schemes. As regards reprography, the existing remuneration schemes, where they exist, are not considered to create major barriers to the internal market, and are to be permitted to continue.[17] As regards private copying, no distinction is made in the Articles of the Directive between analogue and digital technology, contrary to expectations.[18] However, private copying may not be permitted without fair compensation being paid, and Member States are to be free to introduce or continue remuneration schemes to compensate for the prejudice to right-holders. A Recital acknowledges that differences between those remuneration schemes affect the functioning of the internal market but asserts that, with regard to analogue private reproduction, those differences should not have a significant impact on the development of the information society. By contrast, digital private copying is recognised in the Recital as likely to be more widespread and to have a greater economic impact. It is suggested, therefore, that due account should be taken of the differences between digital and analogue private copying and it is stated that a distinction should be made in certain respects between them.[19] Thus, when applying the exception or limitation on private copying, Member States are called on to take due account of technological and economic developments, in particular with respect to digital private copying and remuneration schemes, when effective technological protection measures are available. At the same time, such exceptions or limitations should not inhibit the use of technological measures or their enforcement against circumvention.[20]

So far as determining the form, detailed arrangements and possible level of fair compensation, account is to be taken of the particular circumstances of each case. When evaluating these circumstances, it is suggested in a Recital that a valuable criterion would be the possible harm to the right-holders resulting from the act in question. In cases where right-holders have already received payment in some other form, for instance as part of a licence fee, no specific or separate payment may be due. The level of fair compensation should take full account of the degree of use of technological protection measures referred to in the Directive. In certain cases where the prejudice to the right-holder would be minimal, no obligation for payment may arise.[21]

Further limitations to both the right of reproduction and the right of communication to the public are provided for, all of which are commonly to be found in the present legislation of Member States and are also envisaged by the international copyright and related rights conventions. These include standard exceptions concerning, for example, use for teaching or scientific research, use

---

[17] Recital 37.

[18] In the *Green Paper*, the Commission had pointed out that a situation in which private copying is legal in some Member States and not in others would create serious difficulty and place barriers in the way of trade. It had stated that a degree of harmonisation would be required to resolve the problems, suggesting that "Where the technology does not allow copying to be prevented, a valid response may continue to be that levies should be charged on the equipment and recording medium, and private copying declared permissible. But where there is the technical means to limit or prevent private copying, there is no further justification for what amounts to a system of statutory licensing and equitable remuneration." *Green Paper*, section III, reproduction right, paras 1 and 3. Likewise, in the *Follow-up to the Green Paper*, the Commission outlined its intention to make private copying a fully restricted act, with respect to certain acts of exploitation in the digital environment, whereas in other situations, such as analogue copying, private copying might be permitted Community-wide, be it with or without remuneration. *Follow-up*, p.12.

[19] Information Society Directive, Recital 38.

[20] Recital 39.

[21] Recital 35.

by persons with disabilities and the use of quotations for the purpose of criticism or review, etc.[22] A far-reaching exception is included permitting reproduction by the press, the communication to the public or making available of published Articles on current economic, political or religious topics or of broadcast works or other subject-matter of the same character, in cases where such use is not expressly reserved, and as long as the source, including the author's name is indicated. Similarly, it is permissible to use works or other subject-matter in connection with the reporting of current events, to the extent justified by the informatory purpose and as long as the source and author's name are given, where possible. This is a far-reaching exception in that it is not restricted to the reproduction of short extracts but appears to allow reproduction of complete works.[23]

The Directive further provides a long list of other optional, permitted exceptions and limitations to the reproduction right, and rights of communication and making available to the public. This list represents, in practice, all the specific exceptions presently to be found in the copyright laws of the Member States, including some common to many Member States, such as incidental use and use for the purpose of caricature, parody or pastiche, as well as some more unusual exceptions, peculiar to particular Member States, for example, use of works, such as works of architecture or sculpture, made to be located permanently in public places[24] and use for the purpose of advertising the public exhibition or sale of artistic works.[25]

25–86   **Obligations concerning technological measures.** As forecast in the Green Paper and its follow-up, and in order to comply with the WCT and WPPT, right-holders are to be permitted to make use of technological measures designed to prevent or restrict acts not authorised by them.[26] Thus, Member States are to provide adequate legal protection against illegal activities which enable or facilitate the circumvention of any effective technological measures, which the person concerned carries out in the knowledge or with reasonable grounds to know that he or she is pursuing that objective.[27] . The obligation on States is to protect against any of the following activities: manufacture, import, distribution, sale, rental, advertisement for sale or rental, or possession for commercial purposes of devices, products or components or the provision of services which are promoted, advertised or marketed for the purpose of circumvention of, or which have only limited commercially significant purpose or use other than to circumvent,[28] or are primarily designed, produced, adapted or performed for the purpose of enabling or facilitating the circumvention of any effective technological measures.[29] The term technological measure is defined as meaning any technology, device, product or component incorporated into a process, device or component that, in the normal course of its operation, is designed to prevent or restrict acts, in respect of works or other subject-matter, which are not authorised by the right-holder.[30] Technological measures are deemed effective where the use of a protected work or other subject-matter is controlled by the right-holders through application of an access control or protection process, such as encryption, scrambling or other

---

[22] Art.5(3).
[23] Art.5(3)(c).
[24] cf. Art.59, German Copyright Act 1965 (as amended in 1998).
[25] cf. Art.L122-5(3)(d) of the French Intellectual Property Code (1992).
[26] Information Society Directive 2001/29, Recital 47.
[27] Art.6(1).
[28] Thus, circumvention equipment which is an accessory function of a multipurpose machine is not covered. This lacuna has been criticised.
[29] Art.6(2).
[30] Art.6(3).

transformation of the work or other subject-matter or a copy control mechanism, which achieves the protection objective.[31]

Notwithstanding the legal protection of technological measures apparently guaranteed by the Directive, the normal operation of electronic equipment and its technological development should not be prevented.[32] Moreover, the legal protection of such measures is to apply without prejudice to public policy, as reflected by the provisions of the Directive concerning exceptions and limitations. Thus, it is provided that, in the absence of voluntary measures taken by right-holders, including agreements between right-holders and other parties concerned, Member States shall take appropriate measures to ensure that right-holders make available to beneficiaries of certain exceptions or limitations the means of benefiting from that exception or limitation. This applies, *inter alia*, to reprography, non-commercial reproduction by libraries, the making of ephemeral recordings by broadcasting organisations and non-commercial reproductions of broadcasts in hospitals and prisons. In this respect, an obligation is imposed on Member States to take such measures.[33]

In the case of private copying, the Directive is more cautious. Voluntary measures to facilitate private copying are to be promoted by Member States but, in their absence, Member States are permitted to take measures to enable beneficiaries of a private use exception to take advantage thereof but are not obliged to do so. At the same time, it is also stipulated that right-holders are not to be prevented from using technological measures in order to control the number of reproductions made.[34]

It is also specifically provided that the technological measures applied voluntarily by right-holders, including those applied in implementation of voluntary agreements, and those applied in implementation of measures taken by Member States, shall be protected.[35]

Finally, it is recognised that the protection of technological measures should ensure a secure environment for the provision of interactive on-demand services. Thus, it is made clear that the provisions enabling Member States to take measures to give beneficiaries of exceptions access to works do not apply to works or other subject-matter made available to the public on agreed contractual terms in such a way that members of the public may access them from a place and at a time individually chosen by them.[36]

The apparent guarantee in the proposed Directive that exceptions permitting private copying should not inhibit the use of technological measures or their enforcement against circumvention is welcome.[37] However, it is open to doubt whether the legal protection of technological measures prevails over the exceptions permitted under the proposed Directive or not. Moreover, Member States are to be free to set their own rules on this issue; this will inevitably lead to the various industries involved being obliged to adapt their protection systems to comply with differing national definitions of what private copying is and how much should be allowed.

According to the statement of the Council's reasons for its amendments to the

---

[31] *loc. cit.*
[32] Information Society Directive, Recital 48
[33] Art.6(4), para.1 and Recital 51.
[34] Art.6(4), para.2 and Recital 52.
[35] Art.6(4), para.3.
[36] Art.6(4), para.5.
[37] Recital 39, last sentence: "Such exceptions or limitations should not inhibit the use of technological measures or their enforcement against circumvention."

Commission's earlier, amended proposal,[38] the European Parliament had suggested that it be stipulated in Art.5(4) (current Art.5(5)) that the legal protection of technological measures prevailed over the exceptions listed in Art.5. The Commission had disagreed and, in its amended proposal,[39] the exceptions provided for in Art.5 prevailed over the legal protection of technological measures. The Council, however, has stated that its version of Art.6(1) makes it "clear that Art.6(1) protects against circumvention of all technological measures designed to prevent or restrict acts not authorised by the right-holder, regardless of whether the person performing the circumvention is a beneficiary of one of the exceptions provided for in Art.5".[40] Thus, it seems the intention is to allow technological measures to prevail over, *inter alia*, the exception permitting private use. But this rule has been qualified by the introduction of so-called "safeguards for the protection of the legitimate interests of beneficiaries of exceptions" in Art.6(4);[41] these appear to be contradictory provisions obliging right-holders to make available to beneficiaries of exceptions and limitations, including reproduction for private use, the means of benefiting therefrom, thus precluding the use of technological measures to stop private copying altogether. As noted above, only agreed contractual terms for on-demand supply of works or other subject-matter are to prevail over these provisions.[42]

The Recitals shed some light on these provisions. As stated in Recital 47, technological development will allow right-holders to make use of technological measures designed to prevent or restrict acts not authorised by the right-holders. Harmonised legal protection against circumvention of effective technological measures and against provision of devices and products or services to this effect is therefore required. However, Recital 51 lays down the principle that the legal protection of technological measures applies without prejudice to public policy and that Member States should promote voluntary measures by right-holders to accommodate achieving the objectives of certain exceptions and limitations. In the absence of such voluntary measures within a reasonable period of time, Member States are under an obligation to take appropriate measures to ensure that right-holders provide beneficiaries of such exceptions or limitations with appropriate means of benefiting from them, *by modifying an implemented technological measure or by other means* [emphasis added][43].

With specific reference to private copying, however, Recital 52 calls for voluntary measures to make reproduction for private use possible and provides that, in the absence of such voluntary measures, Member States may impose solutions "to enable beneficiaries of the exception or limitation concerned to benefit from it" but they are not obliged to do so. Both voluntary measures and measures imposed by Member States "do not prevent right-holders from using technological measures which are consistent with the exceptions or limitations on private copying in national law in accordance with Art.5(2)(b), taking account of the condition of fair compensation under that provision and the possible differentiation between various conditions of use in accordance with Art.5(5), such as controlling the number of reproductions. In order to prevent abuse of such measures,

---

[38] Council Common Position (EC) No. 48/2000 adopted by the Council on September 28, 2000. Statement of the Council's Reasons ([2000] O.J. C344/1, December 1, 2000).

[39] COM(1999) 250 final ([1999] O.J. C180/6, June 25, 1999).

[40] Council Common Position, see above, para.43.

[41] Council Common Position, see above, para.44 and see also Information Society Directive, para. 25–79, above, Recitals 51 and 52.

[42] Council Common Position, see above, para.44 and see also Directive, Art.6(4), para.4.1.

[43] Directive, Recital 51.

any technological measures applied in their implementation should enjoy legal protection."[44]

The upshot of these confused and confusing provisions appears to be that the use of technological measures to prevent private copying altogether is allowed in principle but not in practice. Where a Member State provides for a private use exception, the public must be allowed to make copies for private use, *"on condition that the right-holders receive fair compensation which takes account of the application or non-application of technological measures"*.[45]. Presumably, the suggestion here is that the right-holders would get more compensation if no technological controls are used and less if, say, as hinted at in Recital 52, the number of reproductions is controlled. However, these proposals beg a number of questions. How can electronic distribution of works be controlled, if a right to private use overrides exclusive reproduction rights and prevents right-holders from using technological measures to stop consumers making copies from the new online digital multimedia services which dominate the Internet? If technological measures must permit private use, and must be adapted to differing national legal requirements, what will be the impact on commercial piracy? Where is the technology that can handle these situations? Furthermore, is it compatible with the three-step test of the Berne Convention embodied in the Directive: "The exceptions and limitations ... shall only be applied in certain special cases which do not conflict with a normal exploitation of the work or other subject-matter and do not unreasonably prejudice the legitimate interests of the right-holders"[46] and with the WIPO Treaties of 1996[47] to prevent the use of technological measures to stop private copying?

Obligations concerning rights management information. On this subject, the Directive follows the structure of the relevant Articles of the WCT and WPPT.[48] It recognises that important progress has been made in the international standardisation of technical systems of identification of works and protected subject-matter in digital format. It aims at encouraging the use of compatible systems of identification of works, which provide information about the terms and conditions of use of works so as to facilitate the management of rights, as well as at the protection of such systems in the networked environment.[49] It therefore imposes an obligation on Member States to provide adequate legal protection against any person knowingly performing without authority any of the following acts: the removal or alteration of any electronic rights-management information; the distribution, importation for distribution, broadcasting, communication or making available to the public of works or other protected subject-matter from which electronic rights-management information has been removed or altered without authority. The qualification "knowingly performing" an act means knowing, or having reasonable grounds to know, that by so doing the person concerned is inducing, enabling, facilitating or concealing an infringement of any copyright or related right (including the *sui generis* database right).[50] Rights-management is defined as information provided by right-holders which identifies the work or other subject-matter, the author or other right-holder, or information about the

25–87

---

[44] The Directive, Recital 52.
[45] Art.5(2)(b).
[46] Art.5(5).
[47] Art.10(2) WIPO Copyright Treaty (WCT) and Art.16(2) WIPO Performers and Phonograms Treaty (WPPT), 1996.
[48] Art.13 WCT and Art.19 WPPT.
[49] Information Society Directive, Recitals 54–57.
[50] Art.7(1).

terms and conditions of the use of the work or other subject-matter, and any numbers or codes that represent such information.[51]

25–88   **Sanctions and remedies.** The provisions of the Directive are to be backed up by Member States with effective sanctions and remedies in respect of infringements of the rights and obligations set out in the Directive. Member States are to take all measures necessary to ensure that the sanctions and remedies are applied and they are effective, proportionate and dissuasive.[52] Among the remedies to be provided must be an action for damages, the possibility to apply for an injunction and, where appropriate, the seizure of infringing material and circumvention devices.[53] Furthermore, Member States are to ensure that right-holders are in a position to apply for an injunction against intermediaries whose services are used by a third party to infringe a copyright or related right.[54] This possibility is necessary because in the digital environment the services of intermediaries may increasingly be used by third parties for infringing activities and in many cases such intermediaries are best placed to bring such infringing activities to an end.[55]

25–89   **Continued application of other legal provisions.** The protection provided under the Directive is without prejudice to national or Community legal provisions in other areas, such as industrial property, data protection, etc.[56]

25–90   **Implementation in the United Kingdom**. The Directive was implemented in the United Kingdom by the Copyright and Related Rights Regulations 2003, which came into force on October 31, 2003.[57] and amended the 1988 Act substantially. These amendments are discussed in the relevant chapters of this work, in particular, in Chs 4, 7, 9, 12, 15, 22 and 23,

25–91   **Other EU Initiatives Relevant to the Information Society.** Two further EU non-intellectual property initiatives associated with the information society are relevant in the context of copyright.

     The EC Directive on the legal protection of conditional access services (the Conditional Access Directive)[58] aims to create a uniform legal environment for the protection of television and radio broadcasting and conditional access services, that is, services offered to the public where access is subject to payment of subscriptions, such as pay-television. It provides protection against illicit devices which enable or facilitate the circumvention of technological measures designed to protect legally provided services. Specifically prohibited are the manufacture, import, distribution, sale, rental or possession for commercial purposes of illicit devices such as pirate decoders, their installation, maintenance or replacement for commercial purposes, and also the use of commercial services to promote such devices. Member States were given until May 28, 2000, to implement the Directive.[59]

     The second initiative is the **EC Directive on electronic commerce** (the

---

[51] Art.7(2).

[52] Information Society Directive Art.8 (1) and Recital 58.

[53] Art.8(2).

[54] Art.8(3).

[55] Recital 59.

[56] Information Society Directive, Art.9 and Recital 60.

[57] M. Hart and S. Holmes, "Implementation of the Copyright Directive in the UK" [2004] E.I.P.R. 254.

[58] Directive 98/84/EC of the European Parliament and of the Council on the legal protection of services based on, or consisting of, conditional access (The Conditional Access Directive [1998] O.J. L320/54 November 28, 1998). See Vol.2 at H9.

[59] Directive 98/84/EC, Art.6. For implementation in the United Kingdom, see above, para. 16–03,

E-Commerce Directive).[60] The Directive seeks to establish specific harmonised rules only where strictly necessary to ensure that businesses and citizens can supply and receive information society services throughout the EU regardless of frontiers. These areas include definition of where operators are established, transparency obligations for operators, transparency requirements for commercial communications, conclusion and validity of electronic contracts, liability of Internet intermediaries, online dispute settlement and the role of national authorities. Member States are required to provide for fast, efficient legal redress appropriate to the online environment and to ensure that sanctions for violations of the rules established under the Directive are effective, proportionate and dissuasive. Most importantly, the Directive lays down that information society services should be supervised at the source of the activity and that such services should therefore be subject to the law of the Member State in which the service provider is established, i.e. the country of origin principle applies. Member States were given until January 17, 2002, to implement the Directive.[61]

In 2002, the Commission commenced proceedings in the European Court of Justice against Spain and Greece for failure to notify implementing legislation[62] On July 10, 2003, Advocate General Geelhoed expressed the opinion that Spain had failed properly to implement the Directive. As at April 24, 2003, the Commission remained unclear as to whether the Directive had been completely implemented in a compatible form in several other Member States. A report on the implementation of the Directive contains a detailed summary of recent developments in the field and sets out the action which the Commission intends to take to strengthen the effect of the Directive.[63] First, the Commission intends to make vigorous efforts to ensure that the Directive is fully implemented. Second, it intends to consult with Member States on the practical difficulties they have encountered when enforcing the Directive. Third, it intends to encourage industry and national authorities to work together to combat piracy. Fourth, it intends to continue to co-operate with other European countries and international organisations in order to enforce the coherent application of European rules against piracy. In this context, the Commission notes that the Commission's proposal for a Council Framework Decision on attacks against information systems,[64] if implemented in accordance with the Commission's intentions, would create a new offence of illegal access to information systems. This offence would be committed by any person who unlawfully accessed a conditional access service.[65] The Commission also intends to work towards the ratification of European Convention ETS No.178 on the legal protection of services based on, or consisting of, conditional access.[66] Finally, the Commission notes that much piracy in the field derives from the fact that providers often limit access to their services to subscribers in a particular Member State, thus preventing access to residents of other states even though they are willing to pay.[67] The Commission recommends

---

above. On June 12, 2002, the Commission commenced an action in the European Court of Justice (Case C-219/02) against Greece on the grounds that it had failed fully to implement the Directive.

[60] Directive 2000/31/EC of the European Parliament and of the Council of June 8, 2000, on certain legal aspects of information society services, in particular electronic commerce, in the Internal Market (The E-Commerce Directive [2000] O.J. L178/1, July 17, 2000). See Ch.9 , above, and Vol.2 at H10.

[61] Directive 2000/31/EC, Art.22.

[62] Cases C-58/02 and C-219/02 respectively

[63] COM (2003) 198 final, para.3.2 and 7.2.

[64] COM 2002 (173) final of April 19, 2002

[65] COM 2002 (173), para.5.4.

[66] COM 2002 (173), para.6.2.

[67] COM 2002 (173), para.4.4.

that right-holders and service providers seek contractual solutions to this problem.[68]

25–92 **Directive on the enforcement of intellectual property rights (the Enforcement Directive)**

The Directive was adopted on April 29, 2004,[69] having been first proposed by the Commission in January 2003.[70] Member States have been given until April 29, 2006, to comply with the Directive.[71]

25–93 **Background.** The Commission had first signalled its intention to legislate on enforcement in the *Follow-up to the 1995 Green Paper*.[72] Thereafter, in October 1998, the Commission adopted a Green Paper on Combating Counterfeiting and Piracy in the Single Market.[73] It considered that these practices jeopardised the proper functioning of the Single Market, deflected trade and distorted competition, and were prejudicial to the development of all forms of creativity and to the growth and competitiveness of European industry. The aim of the *Green Paper* was to evaluate the economic impact of counterfeiting and piracy in the Single Market, to assess the effectiveness of legislation, in the field and to examine possible initiatives to improve the situation. Initiatives envisaged included: monitoring by the private sector, technical devices for safety and authentification, sanctions and other means of enforcing intellectual property rights, as well as improved administrative co-operation between the competent authorities. The publication of the *Green Paper* marked the start of a wide-ranging consultation of all the interested parties concerned, the Member States and the institutions of the European Union. A hearing of interested parties was held in March 1999 and a report on the responses to the *Green Paper* was published in June 1999.[74]

25–94 **Follow-up to the Green Paper**. As a result of the responses to the Green Paper, in November 2000 the Commission published a follow-up to the *Green Paper*,[75] announcing that counterfeiting and piracy were major problems in most economic and industrial sectors in the Single Market and that the European Community should take steps to strengthen and improve the fight against counterfeiting and piracy. It estimated that EU businesses which operate internationally were losing between EUR 400 million and EUR 800 million in the Single Market and EUR 2,000 million in non-member countries. It concluded also that, in addition to its economic and social consequences, the phenomenon seemed to be increasingly linked to organised crime and was continuing to spread via the Internet. The *Follow-up* contained an action plan, identifying actions that should be carried out as a matter of urgency, medium-term actions and other initiativels. In particular, it was proposed to introduce a Directive as a matter of urgency aimed at strengthening the means for enforcing intellectual property rights.

---

[68] COM 2002 (173), para.7.2.

[69] Directive 2004/48/EC of the European Parliament and of the Council of April 29, 2004, on the enforcement of intellectual property rights ([2004] O.J.L157 of April 30, 2004, as corrected in [2004] O.J.L195/16 of June 2, 2004.

[70] COM (2003) 46 final of January 30, 2003, entitled "Proposal for a Directive of the European Parliament and of the Council on measures and procedures to ensure the enforcement of intellectual property rights". See C.H. Massa and A. Strowel, "The Scope of the Proposed IP Enforcement Directive: Torn between the Desire to Harmonise Remedies and the Need to Combat Piracy" [2004] E.I.P.R. 244.

[71] Directive 2004/48, Art.20.

[72] *cf* 25–76, above.

[73] COM(98) 569 final of October 15, 1998.

[74] *Final Report on responses to the European Commission Green Paper on Counterfeiting and Piracy*, June 1999, by Amédée Turner Q.C. and Christopher Jackson.

[75] Communication from the Commission to the Council, the European Parliament and the Economic and Social Committee, *Follow-up to the Green Paper on Combating Counterfeiting and Piracy in the Single Market*, COM(2000) 789 of November 17, 2000.

Medium-term actions planned included: the setting up of administrative co-operation mechanisms, particularly between the competent national authorities, but also between these authorities and the Commission; examination of the need to submit proposals to harmonise the maximum thresholds for criminal sanctions, extending Europols powers to include combating counterfeiting and piracy, and improving access to information by establishing a structure permitting access—via an Internet site, for example—to judgments of national courts.

Other proposed long-term initiatives aimed at making better use of existing information systems, strengthening co-operation and exchange of information between the private sector and public authorities and promoting European judicial co-operation. In regard to the latter, the Commission proposed to address the problem of counterfeiting and piracy enforcement in connection with work in progress on civil and criminal judicial co-operation.[76] Consideration would also be given to establishing a specialised intellectual property rights tribunal with jurisdiction over cases concerning the validity and infringement of such rights.[77]

Objectives of the Directive. As emphasised in its Preamble, the Directive seeks to create a level playing field for the enforcement of intellectual property rights in the EU Member States by eliminating existing disparities in national legislations and by ensuring a high, equivalent and homogeneous level of protection in the internal market.[78] It covers infringement of all intellectual property rights, including both copyright and industrial property rights, which have been the subject of harmonisation within the EU. It aims to build on Member States' international obligations,[79] and notably on the TRIPs Agreement,[80] and concentrates on infringements carried out for commercial purposes or which cause significant harm to right-holders. In addition to helping to combat illegal practices, the Directive is designed to foster legitimate trade and the development of the information society. In proposing the Directive, the Commission suggested that ever-increasing harm was being done to business (lower investments, closure of SMEs), society (job losses, consumer safety, threat to creativity) and governments (loss of tax revenue) because of increasing counterfeiting and piracy. The Directive does not aim to establish harmonised rules for judicial co-operation, jurisdiction, the recognition and enforcement of decisions in civil and commercial matters, or deal with applicable law.[81] **25–95**

Terms of the Directive. The Directive is without prejudice to the specific provisions on the enforcement of rights and on exceptions contained in existing Community legislation.[82] It is based on best practice in the legislation of the Member States and requires all Member States to provide for the measures, procedures and remedies necessary to ensure the enforcement of intellectual property rights; such measures shall be effective, proportionate and dissuasive.[83] The Directive provides, *inter alia:* for provisional and precautionary measures, including interlocutory injunctions intended to prevent any imminent infringement of rights;[84] for measures for preserving evidence giving powers to judicial authorities to or- **25–96**

---

[76] *Follow-up to the Green Paper*, para.25; *cf.* COM(2000) 495, July 26, 2000.
[77] *Follow-up to the Green Paper. cf.* also doc. COM(2000) 109 final, March 1, 2000.
[78] Enforcement Directive, Recitals 7 and 10.
[79] Recital 6.
[80] Recitals 4 and 5.
[81] Recital 11.
[82] Enforcement Directive 2004/48, Art.2 .
[83] Art.3.
[84] Art.9.

der discovery of documents[85] as well as provisional measures to preserve evidence, and to order the seizure and delivery up of infringing goods and, in appropriate cases, the materials and implements used in the production and/or distribution of the goods and documents relating thereto; these measures may be taken, if necessary, without the other party having been heard;[86] and for powers to force offenders to pay damages appropriate to the actual prejudice suffered by the right-holders to compensate for lost income.[87]

The Directive follows a "TRIPs plus" approach (cf. paras 24–140 et seq., above). The TRIPs Agreement provides for minimum common standards on enforcement of rights to be applicable at international level and implemented in all the EU Member States. The Directive supplements TRIPs by the following: it establishes the right for collective rights-management bodies and professional defence bodies, such as trade associations, as well as right-holders and their licensees directly, to initiate legal proceedings;[88] it provides for presumptions of authorship or ownership of rights for the benefiaries of copyright and related rights;[89] it gives judicial authorities the power to force those selling pirated or counterfeit goods to disclose information on where the goods come from, on quantities ordered, produced and delivered and on prices, as well as to identify people involved in production and distribution networks;[90] the publication of judgments for deterrent purposes; and corrective measures including the withdrawal at the offender's expense of goods found to be infringing from channels of commerce.[91]

The implementation of the Directive is to be kept under review. Member States are to report to the Commission on its implementation three years from its entry into force (May 20, 2006) on the basis of which the Commission is to assess the effectiveness of the measures taken and evaluate the need for amendments to the Directive.[92]

25–97   Implementation of the Directive in the United Kingdom. To date, the implementation process has not begun.

D. FORECAST FOR FUTURE COMMUNITY INITIATIVES

25–98   Outstanding issues. The Community legislative framework in the field of copyright and related rights remains under review by the Commission, which is continuing to evaluate the need for further legislation on a number of subjects. As mentioned above,[93] a number of other future Community initiatives in the field of copyright were forecast in the 1988 Green Paper and the Follow-up thereto published in 1990 as well as in the 1995 Green Paper on Copyright in the Information Society and its Follow-up. In the Follow-up to the 1988 Green Paper, the Commission announced that legislative action was to be taken on six issues by the end of 1991.[94] Although the Commission's timetable slipped somewhat, as seen in paras 25–74, et seq., above, action has been taken in the meantime on all of these issues.

The last outstanding issue, private copying, was tackled rather half-heartedly

---

[85] Art.6.
[86] Art.7.
[87] Art.11.
[88] Art.4.
[89] Art.5.
[90] Art.8.
[91] Art.10.
[92] Art.18.
[93] See paras 25–44, 25–45 and 20–76, above.
[94] See para. 25–45, above.

in the Information Society Directive.(see paras 25–85 and 25–86, above) but no attempt has been made to date to harmonise existing national legislation providing for remuneration schemes for private copying . Since Art.12 of the Information Society Directive calls for regular review of the application of the Directive in general and, in particular, of its provisions concerning exceptions in the light of the development of the digital market, further legislation on this subject cannot be excluded. For this reason, the history of Community activities on this matter remains relevant and is summarised in para.25–99, below.[95]

As already noted,[96] the Commission, in the *Follow-up to the 1995 Green Paper*, discussed the desirability of harmonisation in some other areas and announced its intention of continuing to evaluate the need for Community legislation on the following issues: the introduction of exclusive rights for the benefit of holders of related rights (performers and producers) to control broadcasting; applicable law and law enforcement; the collective management of copyright and related rights and collecting societies; and moral rights.[97] On two of these issues, exclusive broadcasting rights and applicable law, no proposal for action has been published by the Commission to date. The exclusive broadcasting right was discussed at the International Conference on Intellectual Property Rights, "Creativity and Intellectual Property Rights: Evolving Scenarios and Perspectives", Vienna, July 12–14, 1998, where divergent views were expressed as to the need to update the current legal framework for the protection of works and other subject matter.[98] However, the Commission has been active in the other areas. The issue of law enforcement has been dealt with by the Enforcement Directive[99] as described in para.25–104 et seq., above , and recent developments on the subject of the collective management of rights and moral rights are discussed below in paras 25–106 and 25–106.1—25–106.3, respectively.

Most recently, on July 19, 2004, the Commission has published a staff working paper on the review of the EC legal framework in the field of copyright and related rights.[1] The objective of the review is twofold: to improve the operation of the *acquis communautaire* in the field of copyright and its coherence; and to safeguard the good functioning of the Internal Market. It is foreseen that the review will lead to further legislation in due course. This document is discussed in para.25–106.2—25–106.3, below.

Private copying of sound and audiovisual recordings. The issue of private   **25–99** copying[2] has proved one of the most difficult to resolve, and the Commission's position on the subject has shifted more than once. Because of the importance of the topic, for both legal and economic reasons, the Commission's changing response to the issue is briefly discussed here.

In the 1988 Green Paper, the Commission pointed out that the topic of audiovi-

---

[95] See also Ch.13, above, for European Community Protection for Designs.

[96] See para. 25–76, above.

[97] See *Follow-up to the Green Paper*, Chs 8.3, 8.4 and 8.5 and p.39.

[98] See records of the Conference published by the European Commission, DG Internal Market, conclusions of the first panel. On the subject of applicable law, see S. Plenter, "Choice of Law Rules for Copyright Infringements in the Global Information Infrastructure: A Never-ending Story?" [2001] E.I.P.R. 313.

[99] Enforcement Directive, see para. 25–92, *et seq.*, above.

[1] SEC(2004) 995 of July 19, 2004, Commission staff working paper on the review of the EC legal framework in the field of copyright and related rights.

[2] Private copying (sometimes called home taping) is the non-commercial copying of sound and audiovisual recordings for personal domestic use; in other words, it is the act of recording, in the home, the music from a pre-recorded record or tape, the film from a pre-recorded video cassette tape or video disc, or a radio or television programme as broadcast. For an international comparative study of this practice, see G. Davies, and M. Hung, *Music and Video Private Copying: An International Survey of the Problem and the Law* (Sweet & Maxwell, London, 1993).

sual private copying was ripe for discussion at the Community level for three principal reasons:[3]

(1) The industries most concerned claimed that private copying was causing them economic harm and had negative effects on right owners generally and sought greater protection.[4] These interests were opposed by interests favouring freedom for the public to engage in home copying, including manufacturers of blank tape and recording equipment and consumer organisations.[5]

(2) Measures had been introduced at the national level by some, but not all, Member States,[6] and by a number of trading partners among non-Member States[7] to compensate right owners, thus creating new divergencies in intellectual property law among Member States. That situation gave rise to concern that "the divergencies may have significant, negative effects on the functioning of the internal market".[8]

(3) "New technical developments are increasing the ease and attractiveness of home copying of audiovisual material: high-speed copying, improvements in the quality of home made copies, and now the arrival of digital audio tape (DAT) with its capacity for making perfect copies both rapidly and cheaply, have raised new questions as to how copyright laws should deal with the matter." The question also arose how to secure the investment in time, effort and money needed for the creation of audiovisual works if technical developments make it possible to produce perfect, rapid and cheap copies on machines accessible to almost anyone.[9]

In its conclusions, the Commission recognised that the practice of home copying might cause losses to right-holders to the extent that it could be a substitute for sales of pre-recorded material.[10] It concluded, however, that while royalty or "levy" schemes in existence should be retained where they already existed, if Member States considered such schemes the best way to remunerate right owners,[11] there was no need for action by the Commission at that time to make such schemes mandatory by harmonising existing schemes with respect to audio analogue products, taking the view that analogue products were becoming obsolete.[12] As regards video home taping, the Commission also considered that any initiative to generalise levy schemes would not be justified. It undertook to keep national legislation and technical developments under review to ensure that "appropriate action is taken if it becomes necessary".[13]

The Commission, however, did conclude that, with regard to digital audio tape, DAT, "Community measures to require a degree of technical protection

---

[3] COM(88) 172 final, paras 3.1.3 to 3.1.6.

[4] The main argument put forward by right owners today is that the practice of private copying is a new and widespread method of exploitation of works with respect to which they should enjoy protection. Moreover, private copying combined with the perfect-quality reproduction made possible by digital technology, has given the problem a completely new dimension so that it is no longer equitable for the practice to be permitted as an exception to the reproduction right.

[5] These interests deny that any prejudice is caused to right owners by private copying. See, for example, publication of the Home Taping Rights Campaign Office, London, 1987; D.G. Jerrard, "The Case for Digital Audio Tape: an Opportunity, not a Problem" [1987] 10 E.I.P.R. 279.

[6] The following Member States have introduced private copying legislation providing for remuneration to be paid to right owners: Austria, Belgium, Denmark, Finland, France, Germany, Greece, Italy, the Netherlands, Portugal and Spain.

[7] See Davies and Hung, *Music and Video Private Copying: An International Survey of the Problem and the Law* (Sweet & Maxwell, 1993), Ch.7.

[8] *Green Paper*, para.3.1.5.

[9] para.3.1.6.

[10] para.3.12.1.

[11] para.3.12.3.

[12] para.3.10.22.

[13] para.3.12.4.

would be desirable provided that they are technically feasible and properly balanced in respect of all the interests concerned".[14] Accordingly, the Commission invited comments on the desirability of technical solutions in general and, in particular, as regards digital audio recordings.[15]

The Commission also asked for the views of interested parties "as to whether it is accepted that levies should remain in those Member States which have introduced them, and could be introduced if Member States so wish in those countries which have not yet introduced them".[16]

Subsequently, the Commission continued to study the matter and to consult with interested parties. A hearing was held in December 1988,[17] and a further meeting with interested parties took place in November 1989. During those consultations, the Commission's conclusion that there was no need to harmonise legislation on remuneration for private copying was much criticised. In its 1990 document, *Follow-up to the Green Paper*, the Commission announced that, given the need to complete the internal market, it intended to lay a proposal for a Directive before the Council on private copying in 1991. It stated also that it was favourably disposed to the general use of a technical system, known as SCMS (the serial copying management system),[18] which limits the copying capabilities of consumer DAT recording equipment, saying:

> "New technology is to be encouraged, but not where it would damage the interests of right-holders and consumers. The SCMS satisfies these requirements by allowing copies to be made while at the same time limiting the practice; the user thus has the full benefit of technical progress. It also allows right-holders to keep at least partial control of the exploitation of their works by preventing the making of the unlimited series of copies permitted by DAT technology."[19]

Thereafter, the Commission has continued to waver, continuing to consider the issue and to consult thereon. It submitted a working document to the Council in 1992, on which no consensus was reached, and a consultation paper was issued to interested parties in 1993.[20] Meanwhile, the Commission again addressed the issue in its 1995 Green Paper on the Information Society and the Follow-up thereto. There it indicated that it would legislate on private copying in the context of harmonising the exceptions permitted in Member States to the reproduction right and that it would be necessary to distinguish between "digital" and "analogue" private copying. Proposed action was that, with respect to certain acts of exploitation of copyright (in the digital environment), private copying would

---

[14] para.3.10.5.

[15] para.3.13.1.

[16] para.3.13.2.

[17] Record of the hearing on Audio-Visual Home Copying, Brussels, December 12, 1988 (Document 11/D/5069/89).

[18] SCMS operates by codes embedded into the digital information received by a DAT recorder and circuitry controlling the functions of the recorder. Based on the nature of the codes, the DAT recorder either permits unrestricted copying, or permits copying while labelling the copy with codes to restrict further copying, or prevents copying altogether. The technical standards for DAT systems, the Digital Audio Interface Standard (IEC958) and the DAT Standard (IEC60A124), were modified in 1991 to incorporate the system. In May 1990, the Japanese Government introduced administrative measures to implement SCMS with regard to DAT recorders. In October 1992, America adopted the Audio Home Recording Act which makes the incorporation of a technical control mechanism to prevent unauthorised serial copying of protected works in digital recording equipment and interface devices obligatory. The legislation applies not only to SCMS but to any other future system with the same functional characteristics certified by the Secretary of Commerce. See also Davies and Hung, *Music and Video Private Copying: An International Survey of the Problem and the Law* (Sweet & Maxwell, 1993), ss.5.1.4.3. and 5.2.3.

[19] *Follow-up to the Green Paper*, para.3.4.

[20] *Consultation Paper on Private Copying*, Directorate General XV of the European Commission 1993, para.2.2.

become a fully restricted act, in other situations (analogue) it would be permitted Community-wide, be it with or without remuneration.[21] However, as described above,[22] in the Information Society Directive, the Commission came down against legislating on the subject, leaving Member States free to maintain or introduce exceptions for private copying, with or without remuneration schemes.

The Commission's position on this matter has been criticised. In view of the fact that no less than 11 of the Member States have already introduced private copying legislation and the new dangers to right owners caused by the perfect quality of digital copies, it would be surprising if the Commission does not eventually take action to harmonise national legislation on this subject. If such harmonisation does take place, the United Kingdom would be obliged to reconsider its position and follow suit. To date, the United Kingdom has resisted the trend towards private copying legislation within the European Union, although, like the Commission, the United Kingdom Government has wavered on the issue. Following the recommendation of the Whitford Committee in 1977[23] that a "levy" on recording equipment, similar to that operated in the Federal Republic of Germany at the time, should be implemented, the United Kingdom Government in its Green Paper published in 1981,[24] invited public debate on the issue, but said that it was not convinced of the need for it.

Following this consultation, the government published a White Paper in 1986[25] in which it stated that it had decided to introduce a "levy" on blank audio tapes. This decision, which was announced in the Queen's speech[26] setting out the government's programme in June 1987, was subsequently overturned and the subject was dropped from the Copyright Bill introduced later that year and from the 1988 Act.

25–100 **Collective Management of Copyright and Related Rights**. As foreseen in the *Follow-up to the 1995 Green Paper on Copyright and Related Rights in the Information Society*, the issue of the management of rights has continued to be addressed in the ongoing consultation process initiated by the *Green Paper*. A study on certain aspects of collective management carried out by a private consultant at the Commission's request and completed in early 2000.[27] The subject was also on the agenda of two Conferences organised by the Commission in 1998[28] and 2000[29] respectively. Subsequently, a public hearing on collective management of rights was held in November 2000.[30] These discussions showed broad support for the dominant position of collecting societies and general agree-

---

[21] *Follow-up to the Green Paper*, pp.11 and 12.

[22] See para. 25–85, above.

[23] *Copyright and Designs Law, Report of the Committee to consider the Law on Copyright and Designs*; Chairman, the Hon. Mr Justice Whitford, Cmnd. 6732 (1977).

[24] *Reform of the Law Relating to Copyright, Designs and Performer's Protection: A Consultative Document*, Cmnd 8302 (1981) Chapter 3, para.23.

[25] *Intellectual Property and Innovation, presented to Parliament by the Secretary of State for Trade and Industry by Command of Her Majesty*, Cmnd. 9712 (1986).

[26] Queen's Speech: June 25, 1987. The Copyright Bill, without provisions for royalties for private copying, was introduced in October 1987.

[27] *"Étude sur la gestion collective des droits d'auteur dans l'Union Européenne"*,(Study on collective management of copyright in the European Union), Deloitte and Touche, ITEC Group 2000.

[28] Vienna Conference on Creativity and Intellectual Property Rights: Evolving Scenarios and Perspectives, July 12–14, 1998 (Conclusions, Panel 5).

[29] Strasbourg Conference on Management and Legitimate Use of Intellectual Property, July 9–11, 2000 (Conclusions, Panel 3).

[30] Hearing on Collective Management, Brussels, November 13–14, 2000. Issues discussed in the context of the internal market included: rules relating to the establishment of collecting societies and freedom to provide services; appropriate exercise of collective management; supervision and settlement of disputes; new forms of collective licensing models and the need for a level playing field for collective management.

ment on the essential place of collective management in the administration of rights but were inconclusive on the need for Community legislation.

However, in April 2004, the Commission brought the consultation process to an end with the publication of a communication entitled "The Management of Copyright and Related Rights in the Internal Market"[31] in which it argues in favour of the need for Community legislation in the field of collective management of rights. The Commission's communication explains that following the harmonisation brought about by the various Directives in the field of intellectual property, it is now crucial to ensure a level playing field at Community level of rules and conditions for effective rights management in the internal market. The Commission's communication thus addresses issues such as Community-wide licensing, the need for the large-scale introduction of Digital Rights Management systems acceptable to all stakeholders, and the establishment and status of collecting societies. In relation to individual rights management, the Commission has found that there is sufficient common ground in the Member States so that differences in national laws have not given rise to concern with respect to the functioning of the internal market and that immediate action at Community level is not called for. On the subject of the collective management of rights, by contrast, the Commission has concluded that the efficiency, transparency and accountability of collecting societies are crucial for the functioning of the Internal Market ; thus, as regards the cross-border marketing of goods and provision of services based on copyright and related rights, legislative action is required to harmonise those aspects of collective management which affect cross-border trade and have been identified as impeding the full potential of the Internal Market. The Commission therefore intends to propose a legislative instrument on certain aspects of collective management and good governance of collecting societies. Public consultation on the proposal is planned. No timetable for the proposed legislation has been set.[32]

Moral rights. Moral rights is another subject which the Commission has been keeping under review and holding consultations on in order to determine whether or not there is a need for Community action on the subject. The subject was discussed at the Vienna and Strasbourg Conferences held in 1998 and 2000, respectively, and referred to in the previous paragraph. In 1998, divergent views were expressed as regards further harmonisation at Community level and it was agreed to continue to study the matter. Meanwhile, a comparative study on the subject was supported by the Commission and published in April 2000.[33] The study concluded that Community-wide harmonisation of moral rights is not necessary or desirable at present for a number of reasons. First, most interested parties are very cautious about any initiative to harmonise moral rights; this results from fears that any agreed text would be such a compromise that the level of protection of moral rights would be lower than is the case at present and could lead, for example, to waivable moral rights Community-wide. Secondly, there is a general perception among the interested parties that the present differences in national legislations on the subject of moral rights have no impact on the functioning of the internal market. Thirdly, governments do not appear to consider it necessary to harmonise moral rights. Instead, it was proposed that the European

25–101

---

[31] Document COM (2004) 261 final of April 16, 2004, "Communication from the Commission to the Council, the European Parliament and the European Economic and Social Committee".

[32] For a more detailed discussion of the Commission's proposals and conclusions on this subject, see Ch.28, paras 28–20 et seq., below.

[33] A. Strowel and M. Salokannel, with the assistance of E. Derclaye, "Moral rights in the context of the exploitation of works through digital technology", Final Report, April 2000 (Study contract No. ETD/99/B5-3000/E 28).

Community should promote collective agreements dealing with "good practices" in the field of moral rights, either at national or Community level.[34]

The Commission has recently confirmed that at present there is no apparent need to harmonise moral rights protection in the Community. In its opinion, in practice, the international legal framework seems to provide an adequate level playing field for the markets to operate, taking into account the protection for moral rights both in the analogue and digital environments.[35]

25–102   Current Review of the EC Legal Framework in the Field of Copyright and Related Rights. On July 19, 2004, the Commission published a staff working paper on the review of the EC legal framework in the field of copyright and related rights.[36] The objective of the review is twofold: first, to improve the operation of the *acquis communautaire* in the field of copyright and its coherence; and second to safeguard the good functioning of the internal market.

As regards the first objective, the paper assesses whether any inconsistencies on the definitions or on rules on exceptions and limitations between the different Directives hamper the operation of the *acquis communautaire* or have a harmful impact on the fair balance of rights and other interests, including those of users and consumers. The various Directives are therefore reviewed and compared with the standard set by the Information Society Directive with a view to approximation but only minor adjustments are envisaged at present. The Commission is committed to updating and simplifying the *acquis communautaire* as anounced in its Annual Policy Strategy for 2004 and in the Better Regulation Action Plan.[37] It considers that initiatives to simplify the copyright and related rights *acquis* will ease the enforcement thereof for the 10 new Member States. In this connection, 10 Commission announces in the paper that it is also working towards the objective of codifying the *acquis communautaire*. At present, it is working on the codification of the Software Directive, the Rental Right Directive and the Term Directive.[38] The Database Directive will be the subject of a separate report, due to be submitted pursuant to its Art.16(3) in the summer of 2005.[39]

The second objective is addressed by an analysis of whether the Community legislative framework in this area still contains shortcomings having a negative impact on the functioning of the internal market. It concludes that for the time being there is only a need to harmonise the criteria used to determine the beneficiaries of protection in the field of related rights (the so-called "points of attachment"). These have an impact on the internal market and are also relevant to the adherance of the Community and its Member States to the WIPO Performances and Phonograms Treaty (WPPT).[40]

The Commission proposes to consult on these issues and to put forward legislative proposals for the amendment of existing Directives and to harmonise the points of attachment in the course of 2005.

---

[34] A. Strowel and M. Salokannel, with the assistance of E. Derclaye, "Moral rights in the context of the exploitation of works through digital technology", VI Conclusion, pp.226 *et seq.*

[35] Document SEC(2004) 995 of July 17, 2004, Commission Staff Working Paper on the review of the EC legal framework in the field of copyright and related rights, para.3.5.

[36] Document SEC(2004) 995 of July 17, 2004, Commission Staff Working Paper on the review of the EC legal framework in the field of copyright and related rights, para.3.5.

[37] COM (2002) 278 final, of June 5, 2002.

[38] Document SEC (2004) 995, para.1.3.

[39] Document SEC (2004) 995, para.2.2.4.

[40] Document SEC (2004) 995, para.3.4.

E. EXTERNAL RELATIONS OF THE EUROPEAN UNION

The 1995 Follow-up document also drew attention to the international dimension **25–103** of the information society and the corresponding need for a truly international level playing field as regards the protection of copyright and related rights. For some years now, the Community, represented by the Commission, has played an active role in multilateral external relations in this field, for example, in the nego- tiations leading to the adoption of the TRIPS Agreement in the context of the Uruguay Round of GATT, and now in the Doha Round of negotiations under the auspices of the WTO. The European Union also claims competence to represent the views of the Member States, through the Commission, so far as it, concerns matters upon which the European Union has legislated, in inter-governmental meetings on the subject of copyright and related rights convened by the World Intellectual Property Organisation (WIPO), which administers the Berne and Rome Conventions.[41] Thus, the Commission played an active role in the negotia- tions which led to the adoption of the WCT and WPPT under the auspices of WIPO in December 1997.[42]

In the meantime, a Council Decision was adopted in March 2000 on the ap- proval, on behalf of the European Community, of the WIPO Copyright Treaty and the WIPO Performances and Phonograms Treaty.[43] The decision gives the President of the Council the authority to deposit the instruments of conclusion with the Director General of WIPO as from the date by which the Member States have to bring into force the Information Society Directive, referred to above.[44]

In so far as intellectual property matters upon which the European Union has legislated are concerned, the Commission claims competence to represent the Member States at the inter-governmental level.[45] Thus, the Commission has continued to represent the Member States in inter-governmental meetings on the subject of copyright and related rights and has actively participated, *inter alia*, in the negotiations concerning the draft WIPO Treaty on the Protection of the Rights of Broadcasting Organisations and the draft WIPO Treaty on the Protection of Audiovisual Performances.[46]

Furthermore, as a result of the establishment of the European Economic Area, which entered into force on January 1, 1994, embracing the European Com- munity and its then Member States on the one hand; and Austria, Finland, Iceland, Norway and Sweden and, under the conditions laid down in Art.1(2) of the Protocol Adjusting the Agreement on the European Economic Area, Liechten- stein[47] on the other, the EEA States undertook to accept the relevant *acquis com- munautaire*, that is, the general principles of the European Union Treaties and

---

[41] The administration of the Rome Convention is tripartite and shared between WIPO, the International Labour Organisation (ILO) and the United Nations Educational, Scientific and Cultural Organisation, (UNESCO).

[42] See paras 24–66 *et seq.* and 24–119 *et seq.*, above.

[43] Council Decision 2000/278/EC of April 11, 2000 ([2000] O.J. L89/6)

[44] Council Decision 2000/278, Art.2, and see para. 25–79, above.

[45] K.H. Pilny and B.R. Eagle, "The Significance of Intellectual Property at the Community Level *vis-à-vis* Non-EU Trading Nations" [1998] E.I.P.R. 4.

[46] See paras 24–94 and 24–134, above, respectively.

[47] In relation to the EEA Agreement, these countries are referred to as the "EFTA States". At pres- ent, following the accession of Austria, Finland and Sweden to the EU, the following EFTA States are parties to the Agreement: Iceland, Liechtenstein and Norway. Switzerland, which is a Member State of the European Free Trade Association (EFTA), is not a Contracting State to the EEA Agreement and is not in a position to become a party to it, following the negative outcome of a referendum on the subject, which took place on December 6, 1992. For details of the various EC Directives adopted and implemented by the EFTA States, see the Directive Implementation Table, para. 25–105, below.

other legislation, including the existing and future directives on copyright and related rights, as interpreted by the Court of Justice of the European Union.[48]

25–104 **Community competence with respect to the TRIPs Agreement.** The Court of Justice has had occasion to consider the question of the competence of the Community and the jurisdiction of the court in respect of TRIPs, as well as the question whether TRIPs has direct effect in the Member States. In 1994, the court delivered an Opinion, holding that the Community and the Member States shared competence to conclude the TRIPs Agreement, except with respect to its provisions on the release into free circulation of counterfeit goods.[49]. In *Hermès International v FHT Marketing Choice BV*,[50] the jurisdiction of the court to interpret TRIPs was questioned by a group of Member States on the ground that, as the Community had still not adopted any harmonising measures in the area in question (Art.50, TRIPs, which deals with provisional measures against intellectual property infringement), that provision of the TRIPs Agreement did not fall within the scope of application of Community law. The court held that it did have jurisdiction on two grounds: first, the Community had concluded and the Member States had ratified the WTO without distinction as to competence *vis-à-vis* other contracting parties. Second, since the Community is a party to the TRIPs Agreement and since that agreement applies to the Community trade mark (and national trade marks), the courts when called upon to apply national rules with a view to ordering provisional measures for the protection of rights arising under a trade mark, are required to do so, as far as possible, in the light of the wording and purpose of Art.50 of the TRIPs Agreement. Jurisdiction was based, therefore, to some extent, on the internal harmonisation of trade mark law.

In joined cases *Parfums Christian Dior SA and Assco Geruste GmbH*,[51] the court held that its jurisdiction to interpret Art.50 of TRIPs is not restricted solely to situations covered by trade mark law but extends to intellectual property rights falling within the scope of the TRIPs Agreement; the judicial bodies of the Member States and the Community are obliged for practical and legal reasons to give the TRIPs Agreement a uniform interpretation.

On the question of the direct effect of TRIPs, the court held that the provisions of TRIPs, an annex to the WTO Agreement, are not such as to create rights upon which individuals may rely directly before the courts of the Member States by virtue of Community law. The court then drew a distinction between fields to which TRIPs applies in respect of which there is Community legislation and areas where there is none. In the first case, the judicial authorities of both the Member States and the Community must apply national rules as far as possible in conformity with the relevant provisions of TRIPs. Where the Community has not legislated, competence for the protection of intellectual property remains with the Member States and does not fall within the scope of Community law. In this latter case, Community law neither requires nor forbids that the legal order of a Member State should accord to individuals the right to rely directly on a rule laid down by TRIPs or that it should oblige the courts to apply that rule of its own motion.[52]

In its bilateral relations, the Community (now the EU) has also been active in

---

[48] See *Follow-up to the Green Paper*, Chapter 7.5.

[49] Opinion 1/94 of November 15, 1994 [1994] E.C.R. I-5267

[50] Case C-53/96, *Hermès International v FHT Marketing Choice BV* [1998] E.C.R. I-3603

[51] Joined Cases C-300/98 and C-392/98, *Parfums Christian Dior SA v TUK Consultancy BV* and *Assco Gerüste GmbH and Rob van Dijk v Wilhelm Layher GmbH & Co KG and Layher BV* [2001] ECD.R. 159.

[52] Joined Cases C-300/98 and C-392/98, *Parfums Christian Dior SA v TUK Consultancy BV* and *Assco Gerüste GmbH and Rob van Dijk v Wilhelm Layher GmbH & Co KG and Layher BV* [2001] ECD.R. 159, para.49.

the field of copyright and related rights. For example, in the trade and co-operation agreements concluded in 1989 and 1990 between the Community and most of the countries of central and eastern Europe, the question of intellectual, industrial and commercial property was given particular attention, especially because of its implications for direct investment in those countries by Community businesses and for the transfer of technology:[53] In its accession negotiations with candidate countries, including the 10 new Member States, the EU has treated the internal market as an important area for the accession process and insisted on full implementation of the *acquis communautaire* Directives over the whole field of intellectual property by the candidate countries.

---

[53] Follow up to the Green Paper, Ch.7.6.

25–105

TABLE SHOWING THE IMPLEMENTATION OF EC DIRECTIVES ON COPYRIGHT AND RELATED RIGHTS IN THE MEMBER STATES OF THE EU, EEA AND SWITZERLAND

Member States	Computer Programmes Dir. 91/250/EEC	Rental and Lending Right Dir. 92/100/EEC	Satellite Broadcasting & Cable Re-transmission Dir. 93/83/EEC	Duration of Copyright Protection Dir. 93/98/EEC	Protection of Databases Dir. 96/9/EC	Information Society Directive Dir. 2001/29/EC	Artists' Resale Right Dir. 2001/84/EC	Enforcement of Intellectual Property Rights Dir. 2004/48/EC
EU Countries[1]								None to date
Austria	01.11.1993	11.02.1993	02.05.1996	29.03.1996	09.01.1998	06.06.2003	-	-
Belgium	27.07.1994	27.07.1994 14.05.2004	27.07.1994	27.07.1994	14.11.1998	-	-	-
Cyprus*	19.07.2002	19.07.2002 18.10.2002	19.07.2002	19.07.2002	19.07.2002	30.04.2004	-	-
Czech Republic*	12.05.2000	12.05.2000	12.05.2000	12.05.2000	08.12.1961 05.03.1964 18.05.1990 18.12.1991 12.05.2000	08.12.1961 18.05.1990 12.05.2000	-	-
Denmark	19.12.1992	13.06.1995 14.06.1995 17.12.2002	13.06.1995 12.03.2003	14.06.1995	26.06.1998	17.12.2002	-	-
Estonia*	18.11.2002	18.11.2002 10.04.2004	18.11.2002	18.11.2002	18.11.2002	-	-	-

Member States	Computer Programmes Dir. 91/250/EEC	Rental and Lending Right Dir. 92/100/EEC	Satellite Broadcasting & Cable Re-transmission Dir. 93/83/EEC	Duration of Copyright Protection Dir. 93/98/EEC	Protection of Databases Dir. 96/9/EC	Information Society Directive Dir. 2001/29/EC	Artists' Resale Right Dir. 2001/84/EC	Enforcement of Intellectual Property Rights Dir. 2004/48/EC
Finland	07.05.1993 22.12.1993	24.03.1995	24.03.1995	22.12.1995	03.04.1998 22.10.2003	-	-	-
France	11.05.1994	01.07.1992 18.06.2003	28.03.1997	28.03.1997	01.07.1998	-	-	-
Germany	23.06.1993	29.06.1995	20.05.1998	23.06.1995	28.07.1997	10.09.2003	-	-
Greece	04.03.1993	04.03.1993	04.03.1993 24.12.1997	04.03.1993 24.12.1997	15.03.2000	10.10.2002	-	-
Hungary*	06.07.1999 27.11.2003	06.07.1999 27.11.2003	06.07.1999 27.11.2003	06.07.1999 27.11.2003	17.11.2001 27.11.2003	06.07.1999 27.11.2003	-	-
Ireland	02.02.1993	01.03.2001	01.03.2001	01.07.1995	01.03.2001	19.01.2004	-	-
Italy	31.12.1992	16.12.1994	18.11.1996	27.02.1996 13.06.1997	30.04.1999 06.05.1999	14.04.2003	-	-
Latvia*	27.04.2000 01.05.2004	27.04.2000 01.05.2004	27.04.2000 01.05.2004	27.04.2000 01.05.2004	27.04.2000 01.05.2004	27.04.2000 01.05.2004	27.04.2000 01.05.2004	-
Lithuania*	21.03.2003	21.03.2003	21.03.2003	21.03.2003	21.03.2003	21.03.2003	21.03.2003	-
Luxembourg	28.04.1995	16.09.1997	16.09.1997 30.04.2001	16.09.1997	30.04.2001	29.04.2004	-	-
Malta*	01.01.2001	01.01.2001	-	01.01.2001	01.01.2001 10.01.2003	23.12.2003	-	-

Member States	Computer Pro-grammes Dir. 91/250/EEC	Rental and Lending Right Dir. 92/100/EEC	Satellite Broadcast-ing & Cable Re-transmis-sion Dir. 93/83/EEC	Duration of Copyright Protection Dir. 93/98/EEC	Protection of Databases Dir. 96/9/EC	Informa-tion Society Directive Dir. 2001/29/EC	Artists' Resale Right Dir. 2001/84/EC	Enforce-ment of Intellectual Property Rights Dir. 2004/48/EC
Netherlands	07.07.1994	28.12.1995	18.07.1996	28.12.1995	21.07.1999	-	-	-
Poland*	23.05.1994 07.07.2000	23.05.1994 27.11.2002	23.05.1994 07.07.2000 27.11.2002	23.05.1994 07.07.2000 27.11.2002	23.05.1994 09.11.2001	30.04.2004	-	-
Portugal	17.06.1994 20.10.1994	03.09.1997 27.11.1997	03.09.1997 27.11.1997	03.09.1997 27.11.1997	04.07.2000	-	-	-
Slovakia*	31.12.2003	31.12.2003	31.12.2003	31.12.2003	31.12.2003	31.12.2003	31.12.2003	-
Slovenia*	14.04.1995	14.04.1995	14.04.1995	14.04.1995 09.02.2001	14.04.1995 09.02.2001	14.04.1995 09.02.2001	14.04.1995	-
Spain	24.12.1993	31.12.1994	13.10.1995 22.04.1996 07.03.1998	13.10.1995	07.03.1998	-	-	-
Sweden	01.01.1993	01.06.1995	07.12.1995	07.12.1995	01.01.1998	-	-	-
United Kingdom	01.01.1993	01.12.1996	01.12.1996	19.12.1995	01.01.1998	31.10.2003 (Gibraltar is missing)	-	-
EFTA Countries[2]								

Member States	Computer Pro-grammes	Rental and Lending Right	Satellite Broadcast-ing & Cable Re-transmis-sion	Duration of Copyright Protection	Protection of Databases	Informa-tion Society Directive	Artists' Resale Right	Enforce-ment of Intellectual Property Rights
	Dir. 91/250/ EEC	Dir. 92/100/ EEC	Dir. 93/83/ EEC	Dir. 93/98/ EEC	Dir. 96/ 9/EC	Dir. 2001/ 29/EC	Dir. 2001/ 84/EC	Dir. 2004/ 48/EC
Iceland	fully implemented	fully implemented	fully implemented	fully implemented	fully implemented	?	?	
Liechtenstein	fully implemented	fully implemented	fully implemented	fully implemented	fully implemented	?	?	
Norway	fully implemented	fully implemented	fully implemented	fully implemented	fully implemented	?	?	
Switzerland[3]	compatible law	partially implemented[4]	compatible law	compatible law	not yet implemented	?	?	

[1] The date refers to the date of publication in a State's official journal or, failing that, to the date of adoption or the date of entry into force (where the law so provides)—Concerning the new Member States (*), the implementing measures notified to the Commission have not yet been accepted as complete or in conformity with the respective Directive.

[2] See EFTA website: *www.efta.int*. As regards the EEA Agreement, see para.25–01 and n.8, above.

[3] The revision of the Swiss national copyright law in 1994 contained provision to make the law compatible with EC copyright directives in force at that time. On September 15, 2004, the Swiss Government published a draft revised Copyright Law 1992 as a basis for consultation with a view to updating the law in the light of the Information Society Directive and to enable Switzerland to ratify the WCT and WPPT. (See *www.ige.ch*.)

[4] The rental right applies to date only to computer programs.

CHAPTER TWENTY SIX

THE PROTECTION OF COPYRIGHT WORKS
ABROAD

General Table of Copyright and Related Rights Conventions and National 26–01
Laws. The following Table shows the extent to which copyright works protected
under the 1988 Act are protected in other countries in accordance with the
principal international treaties to which the United Kingdom is party, and which
have entered into force on August 20, 2004. The substantive provisions of each
of these treaties are discussed in detail in Chapter 24, above. The aim of this table
is to present in a readily accessible form the basic information the reader requires
to establish whether a work is protected in the 188 countries listed. The information provided by the Table is explained below.

Berne Convention for the Protection of Literary and Artistic Works, 1886. 26–02
The Table shows the membership, if any, of the Berne Union and the latest Act(s)
of the Berne Convention to which the country in question is party; the Table also
shows which countries have made declarations with regard to certain provisions
of the Convention affecting the protection they afford to nationals of other
Member States; these declarations are explained in the footnotes to the Table.
This column of the Table is up to date to August 20, 2004.

Universal Copyright Convention, 1952. The Table shows the membership, if 26–03
any, of the Universal Copyright Convention and whether the country in question
is party to the 1952 Geneva Act of the Convention or to the 1971 Paris Act.
Countries which have availed themselves of the exceptions to protection in favour of developing countries are also indicated. This column of the Table is up to
date to August 20, 2004.

Other treaties. The Table also gives the dates of the adherences of each country 26–04
(where appropriate) to the following additional treaties:

The Agreement on Trade Related Aspects of Intellectual Property
(TRIPs), 1994. This column of the Table is up to date to August 20, 2004.

The Rome Convention for the Protection of Performers, Producers of
Phonograms and Broadcasting Organisations (the Rome Convention),
1961. This column of the Table is up to date to August 20, 2004.

The Convention for the Protection of Producers of Phonograms against
the Unauthorised Duplication of their Phonograms (the Phonograms
Convention), 1971. This column of the Table is up to date to August 20,
2004

The Convention Relating to the Distribution of Programme-Carrying
Signals Transmitted by Satellite (the Satellite Convention), 1974. This
column of the Table is up to date to August 20, 2004.

The WIPO Copyright Treaty, 1996. This column of the Table is up to date
to August 20, 2004.

The WIPO Performances and Phonograms Treaty, 1996. This column of
the Table is up to date to August 20, 2004.

National laws. The international treaties included in the Table oblige the Member 26–05
States to provide nationals of other Member States with the minimum standards
of protection guaranteed by the treaties and, in the case of the Berne Convention,

the UCC, the TRIPs Agreement, the Rome Convention, the WIPO Copyright Treaty and the WIPO Performances and Phonograms Treaty, with so-called national treatment.[1] This means that a Member State gives to nationals of other Member States not only the minimum standards of protection provided for by the international treaty in question but also the same protection as it gives to its own nationals under its domestic law.[2] To establish whether any given work is protected in a particular country, it is necessary, therefore, to know not only which international treaties the country in question is party to but also to be able to identify the copyright law in force in that country.

The Table gives the date of the principal copyright laws in force in the countries listed, with the date of the most recent amendments to the laws in brackets. Since the Supplement to the 14th Edition of the present work was published in 2002, it is of interest to note that no less than 38 entirely new laws on copyright and related rights have been adopted and 44 more national laws have been amended.

The period of protection for literary and artistic works (as defined in the Berne Convention (Article 2(1)) is shown also in the Table.[3] Here it may be noted that the number of countries which now grant literary and artistic works a period of protection of 70 years pma or more have increased from 29 in 1999, when the 14th Edition of this work was published, to 53 as shown in the Table.

Where a given country has adhered to one or other of the treaties listed, it is included in the Table, even if it has no domestic copyright law or no information is available about such law. In these cases, under the heading "Date of the principal law", the remark "No legislation" or "Unknown" is made, as the case may be, and the period of protection shown corresponds to the minimum period required by the treaty to which the country is party. In principle, rights owners are guaranteed all the rights which the treaty in question expressly gives them and, where the treaty to which the country is party provides for a specific, minimum period of protection for nationals of other Member States, that period will apply in accordance with the provisions of the treaty in question.

26–06   **Sources.** The information given on the membership of the various conventions and treaties listed above is based on their current status as published on August 20, 2004, on the websites of WIPO (World Intellectual Property Organisation), Unesco (United Nations Organisation for Science, Education and Culture) and the WTO (World Trade Organisation), as well as, in some cases, on additional more up-to-date information from the organisations themselves. The date of the latest law applicable in the countries in question and the term of protection is based mainly on the most recently available information in the following collections of laws: WIPO's "Collection of Laws for Electronic Access" (CLEA); WIPO's Cumulative Index of Copyright and Related Rights Laws and Treaties; and Unesco's "Collection of National Copyright Laws".

---

[1] See Ch.24, above, regarding the national treatment provisions of the various Conventions.
[2] The United Kingdom implements its obligations under these international agreements by extending protection to the works of nationals of other countries by means of statutory instruments issued pursuant to the CDPA 1988, ss.159 and 208; see Apps, Part C, below.
[3] See Table, n.7.

GENERAL TABLE OF COPYRIGHT AND RELATED RIGHTS CONVENTIONS[1]

Signatories	Berne Convention[2] September 9, 1886 and Subsequent Acts	UCC[3] September 6, 1952 revised in Paris, July 24, 1971	TRIPS April 15, 1994	Rome Convention October 26, 1961	Geneva Phonograms Convention October 29, 1971	Satellite Convention May 21, 1974	WIPO Copyright Treaty[4]	WIPO Performances and Phonograms Treaty[5]	Date of Principal Law (most recent amendment)[6]	Period of Protection[7]
Albania	Paris A	Paris	September 8, 2000	September 1, 2000	June 26, 2001			May 20, 2002	1992	70 years pma
Algeria	Paris A, C, H	Paris*	observer[8]						2003	50 years from January 1 pma
Andorra	Paris A	Geneva	observer[8]						1999	70 years pma
Angola			November 23, 1996						1990	50 years pma (from end of year)
Antigua and Barbuda	Paris A		January 1, 1995						2002	50 years pma
Argentina	Paris A	Geneva	January 1, 1995	March 2, 1992	June 30, 1973		March 6, 2002	May 20, 2002	1933 (1998)	70 years pma
Armenia	Paris A		February 5, 2003	January 31, 2003	January 31, 2003	December 13, 1993			2000	50 years from January 1 pma

Signatories	Berne Convention[2] September 9, 1886 and Subsequent Acts	UCC[3] September 6, 1952 revised in Paris, July 24, 1971	TRIPS April 15, 1994	Rome Convention October 26, 1961	Geneva Phonograms Convention October 29, 1971	Satellite Convention May 21, 1974	WIPO Copyright Treaty[4]	WIPO Performances and Phonograms Treaty[5]	Date of Principal Law (most recent amendment)[6]	Period of Protection[7]
Australia	Paris A	Paris	January 1, 1995	September 30, 1992	June 22, 1974	October 26, 1990			1968 (2003)	50 years pma (from end of year)
Austria	Paris A	Paris	January 1, 1995	June 9, 1973	August 21, 1982	August 6, 1982			1936 (2003)	70 years pma
Azerbaijan	Paris A	Geneva	observer[8]		September 1, 2001				1996	50 years pma
Bahamas	Paris B,H Brussels	Paris	observer[8]						1956	50 years pma (from end of year)
Bahrain	Paris A, C		January 1, 1995						1993	50 years pma
Bangladesh	Paris A, C, D	Paris*	January 1, 1995						1962 (1978)	50 years from January 1, pma
Barbados	Paris A	Paris	January 1, 1995	September 18, 1983	July 29, 1983				1998	50 years pma
Belarus	Paris A	Geneva	observer[8]	May 27, 2003	April 17, 2003		March 6, 2002	May 20, 2002	1998	50 years pma

Signatories	Berne Convention[2] September 9, 1886 and Subsequent Acts	UCC[3] September 6, 1952 revised in Paris, July 24, 1971	TRIPS April 15, 1994	Rome Convention October 26, 1961	Geneva Phonograms Convention October 29, 1971	Satellite Convention May 21, 1974	WIPO Copyright Treaty[4]	WIPO Performances and Phonograms Treaty[5]	Date of Principal Law (most recent amendment)[6]	Period of Protection[7]
Belgium	Paris A	Geneva	January 1, 1995	October 2, 1999					1994 (1998)	70 years from January 1 pma
Belize	Paris A	Geneva	January 1, 1995						2000	50 years pma (from end of year)
Benin	Paris A		February 22, 1996						1984	50 years pma (from end of year)
Bhutan			observer[8]							
Bolivia	Paris A	Paris*	September 12, 1995	November 24, 1993					1992	50 years pma (from end of year)
Bosnia and Herzegovina	Paris A, E	Paris	observer[8]			March 6, 1992			2002	70 years from January 1 pma
Botswana	Paris A		May 31, 1995						1965	50 years pma

Signatories	Berne Convention[2] September 9, 1886 and Subsequent Acts	UCC[3] September 6, 1952 revised in Paris, July 24, 1971	TRIPS April 15, 1994	Rome Convention October 26, 1961	Geneva Phonograms Convention October 29, 1971	Satellite Convention May 21, 1974	WIPO Copyright Treaty[4]	WIPO Performances and Phonograms Treaty[5]	Date of Principal Law (most recent amendment)[6]	Period of Protection[7]
Brazil	Paris A	Paris	January 1, 1995	September 29, 1965	November 28, 1975				1998	70 years from January 1, pma
Brunei Darussalam			January 1, 1995						1999	50 years pma (from end of year)
Bulgaria	Paris A	Paris	December 1, 1996	August 31, 1995	September 6, 1995		March 6, 2002	May 20, 2002	1993 (2002)	70 years pma
Burkina Faso	Paris A		June 3, 1995	January 14, 1988	January 30, 1988		March 6, 2002	May 20, 2002	1983 (1984)	50 years pma (from end of year)
Burundi			June 23, 1995						1978	50 years pma (from end of year)
Cambodia		Geneva	observer[8]						2003	50 years pma
Cameroon	Paris A	Paris	December 13, 1995						2000	50 years pma (from end of year)

Signatories	Berne Convention[2] September 9, 1886 and Subsequent Acts	UCC[3] September 6, 1952 revised in Paris, July 24, 1971	TRIPS April 15, 1994	Rome Convention October 26, 1961	Geneva Phonograms Convention October 29, 1971	Satellite Convention May 21, 1974	WIPO Copyright Treaty[4]	WIPO Performances and Phonograms Treaty[5]	Date of Principal Law (most recent amendment)[6]	Period of Protection[7]
Canada	Paris A	Geneva	January 1, 1995	June 4, 1998					1985 (2004)	50 years pma (from end of year)
Cape Verde	Paris A		observer[8]	July 3, 1997						
Central African Republic	Paris A		May 31, 1995						1985	50 years pma (from end of year)
Chad	Stockholm B Brussels		October 19, 1995						Unknown	50 years pma minimum of BC
Chile	Paris A	Geneva	January 1, 1995	September 5, 1974	March 24, 1977		March 6, 2002	May 20, 2002[9]	1970 (1992)	50 years pma
China	Paris A[10]	Paris*	December 11, 2001		April 30, 1993[10]				1990 (2001)	50 years pma
Colombia	Paris A	Paris	April 30, 1995	September 17, 1976	May 16, 1994		March 6, 2002	May 20, 2002	1982 (1993)	80 years pma
Congo	Paris A		March 27, 1997	May 18, 1964					1982	50 years pma (from end of year)

Signatories	Berne Convention[2] September 9, 1886 and Subsequent Acts	UCC[3] September 6, 1952 revised in Paris, July 24, 1971	TRIPS April 15, 1994	Rome Convention October 26, 1961	Geneva Phonograms Convention October 29, 1971	Satellite Convention May 21, 1974	WIPO Copyright Treaty[4]	WIPO Performances and Phonograms Treaty[5]	Date of Principal Law (most recent amendment)[6]	Period of Protection[7]
Costa Rica	Paris A	Paris	January 1, 1995	September 9, 1971	June 17, 1982	June 25, 1999	March 6, 2002	May 20, 2002	2000	70 years pma
Côte d'Ivoire	Paris A		January 1, 1995						1996	99 years pma (from end of year)
Croatia	Paris A	Paris	November 30, 2000	April 20, 2000	April 20, 2000	October 8, 1991	March 6, 2002	May 20, 2002	2003	50 years from January 1, pma
Cuba	Paris A, C, D, H	Geneva	April 20, 1995						1977 (1994)	50 years from January 1, pma
Cyprus	Paris A, E	Paris	July 30, 1995		September 30, 1993		November 4, 2003		1976 (2002)	50 years pma (from end of year)
Democratic People's Republic of Korea	Paris A, C								Unknown	50 years pma minimum of BC

Signatories	Berne Convention[2] September 9, 1886 and Subsequent Acts	UCC[3] September 6, 1952 revised in Paris, July 24, 1971	TRIPS April 15, 1994	Rome Convention October 26, 1961	Geneva Phonograms Convention October 29, 1971	Satellite Convention May 21, 1974	WIPO Copyright Treaty[4]	WIPO Performances and Phonograms Treaty[5]	Date of Principal Law (most recent amendment)[6]	Period of Protection[7]
Czech Republic	Paris A	Paris	January 1, 1995	January 1, 1993	January 1, 1993		March 6, 2002	May 20, 2002	2000	70 years pma (from January 1 pma)
Democratic Republic of the Congo	Paris A		January 1, 1997		November 29, 1977				1986	50 years pma (from end of year)
Denmark	Paris A	Paris	January 1, 1995	September 23, 1965	March 24, 1977				1995	70 years pma
Djibouti	Paris A		May 31, 1995						1996	25 years pma
Dominica	Paris A		January 1, 1995	November 9, 1999					2003	70 years pma
Dominican Republic	Paris A	Paris	March 9, 1995	January 27, 1987					2000	50 years from January 1 pma
Ecuador	Paris A	Paris	January 21, 1996	May 18, 1964	September 14, 1974		March 6, 2002	May 20, 2002	1998	70 years pma
Egypt	Paris A, H		June 30, 1995		April 23, 1978				1954 (1994)	50 years pma

Signatories	Berne Convention[2] September 9, 1886 and Subsequent Acts	UCC[3] September 6, 1952 revised in Paris, July 24, 1971	TRIPS April 15, 1994	Rome Convention October 26, 1961	Geneva Phonograms Convention October 29, 1971	Satellite Convention May 21, 1974	WIPO Copyright Treaty[4]	WIPO Performances and Phonograms Treaty[5]	Date of Principal Law (most recent amendment)[6]	Period of Protection[7]
El Salvador	Paris A	Paris	May 7, 1995	June 29, 1979	February 9, 1979		March 6, 2002	May 20, 2002	1993	50 years pma
Equatorial Guinea	Paris A		observer[8]						Unknown	50 years pma minimum of BC
Estonia	Paris A		November 13, 1999	April 28, 2000	May 28, 2000				1992 (2002)	70 years pma
Ethiopia			observer[8]						1960	50 years pma (from end of year)
European Community			January 1, 1995						Directives cf. Ch. 25, above	70 years pma Dir. 93/98/EEC
Fiji	Stockholm B Brussels	Geneva	January 14, 1995	April 11, 1972	April 18, 1973				1956	70 years pma
Finland	Paris A	Paris	January 1, 1995	October 21, 1983	April 18, 1973				1961 (1998)	50 years pma (from end of year)

Signatories	Berne Convention[2] September 9, 1886 and Subsequent Acts	UCC[3] September 6, 1952 revised in Paris, July 24, 1971	TRIPS April 15, 1994	Rome Convention October 26, 1961	Geneva Phonograms Convention October 29, 1971	Satellite Convention May 21, 1974	WIPO Copyright Treaty[4]	WIPO Performances and Phonograms Treaty[5]	Date of Principal Law (most recent amendment)[6]	Period of Protection[7]
France	Paris A	Paris	January 1, 1995	July 3, 1987	April 18, 1973				1992 (2003)	70 years pma (from end of year)
Gabon	Paris A		January 1, 1995				March 6, 2002	May 20, 2002	1987	
Gambia	Paris A		October 23, 1996						Unknown	50 years pma minimum of BC
Georgia	Paris A		June 14, 2000				March 6, 2002	May 20, 2002	1999	70 years pma
Germany	Paris A, I	Paris	January 1, 1995	October 21, 1966	May 18, 1974	August 25, 1979			1965 (1998)	70 years pma (from end of year)
Ghana	Paris A	Geneva	January 1, 1995						1985	50 years pma
Greece	Paris A	Geneva	January 1, 1995	January 6, 1993	February 9, 1994	October 22, 1991			1993 (2002)	70 years pma (from end of year)
Grenada	Paris A		February 22, 1996						1956	50 years pma

Signatories	Berne Convention[2] September 9, 1886 and Subsequent Acts	UCC[3] September 6, 1952 revised in Paris, July 24, 1971	TRIPS April 15, 1994	Rome Convention October 26, 1961	Geneva Phonograms Convention October 29, 1971	Satellite Convention May 21, 1974	WIPO Copyright Treaty[4]	WIPO Performances and Phonograms Treaty[5]	Date of Principal Law (most recent amendment)[6]	Period of Protection[7]
Guatemala	Paris A, H	Geneva	July 21, 1995	January 14, 1977	February 1, 1977		February 4, 2003	January 8, 2003	1998 (2000)	75 years pma
Guinea	Paris A	Paris	October 25, 1995				May 25, 2002	May 25, 2002	1980	80 years pma (from end of year), thereafter paying public domain
Guinea-Bissau	Paris A		May 31, 1995						Unknown	50 years pma minimum of BC
Guyana	Paris A		January 1, 1995						1956 (1966)	50 years pma
Haiti	Paris A	Geneva	January 30, 1996						1968	25 years pma (50 years under Convention)

Signatories	Berne Convention[2] September 9, 1886 and Subsequent Acts	UCC[3] September 6, 1952 revised in Paris, July 24, 1971	TRIPS April 15, 1994	Rome Convention October 26, 1961	Geneva Phonograms Convention October 29, 1971	Satellite Convention May 21, 1974	WIPO Copyright Treaty[4]	WIPO Performances and Phonograms Treaty[5]	Date of Principal Law (most recent amendment)[6]	Period of Protection[7]
Holy See	Paris A	Paris	observer[8]		July 18, 1977				1960 (1996)	70 years pma (from end of year)
Honduras	Paris A		January 1, 1995	February 16, 1990	March 6, 1990		May 20, 2002	May 20, 2002	1999	75 years pma
Hong Kong (SAR of China)[10]	Paris A		January 1, 1995		July 1, 1997				1997 (1999)	50 years pma
Hungary	Paris A	Paris	January 1, 1995	February 10, 1995	May 28, 1975		March 6, 2002	May 20, 2002	1999	70 years from January 1, pma
Iceland	Paris A	Geneva	January 1, 1995	June 15, 1994					1972 (2000)	70 years pma (from end of year)
India	Paris A, F, H	Paris	January 1, 1995		February 12, 1975				1957 (1999)	60 years from January 1, pma
Indonesia	Paris A, H		January 1, 1995				March 6, 2002		2000	50 years pma

Signatories	Berne Convention[2] September 9, 1886 and Subsequent Acts	UCC[3] September 6, 1952 revised in Paris, July 24, 1971	TRIPS April 15, 1994	Rome Convention October 26, 1961	Geneva Phonograms Convention October 29, 1971	Satellite Convention May 21, 1974	WIPO Copyright Treaty[4]	WIPO Performances and Phonograms Treaty[5]	Date of Principal Law (most recent amendment)[6]	Period of Protection[7]
Iran									1970	30 years pma
Iraq			observer[8]						1971	25 years pma or 50 years from publication, whichever is longer
Ireland	Stockholm B Brussels	Geneva	January 1, 1995	September 19, 1979					2000	70 years pma
Israel	Paris A, H	Geneva	April 21, 1995	December 20, 2002	May 1, 1978				1911 (1999)	50 years pma (from end of year)
Italy	Paris A, H	Paris	January 1, 1995	April 8, 1975	March 24, 1977	July 7, 1981			1941 (2001)	70 years pma
Jamaica	Paris A		March 9, 1995	January 27, 1994	January 11, 1994	January 12, 2000	June 12, 2002	June 12, 2002	1993 (1999)	50 years pma
Japan	Paris A	Paris	January 1, 1995	October 26, 1989	October 14, 1978		March 6, 2002	October 9, 2002[11]	1970 (2002)	50 years pma
Jordan	Paris A, C, D, H		April 11, 2000				April 27, 2004	May 24, 2004	1992	30 years pma

Signatories	Berne Convention[2] September 9, 1886 and Subsequent Acts	UCC[3] September 6, 1952 revised in Paris, July 24, 1971	TRIPS April 15, 1994	Rome Convention October 26, 1961	Geneva Phonograms Convention October 29, 1971	Satellite Convention May 21, 1974	WIPO Copyright Treaty[4]	WIPO Performances and Phonograms Treaty[5]	Date of Principal Law (most recent amendment)[6]	Period of Protection[7]
Kazakhstan	Paris A	Geneva	observer[8]		August 3, 2001		November 12, 2004*	November 12, 2004*	1996	50 years pma
Kenya	Paris A	Paris	January 1, 1995		April 21, 1976	August 25, 1979			2001	50 years pma (from end of year)
Kuwait			January 1, 1995						1999	50 years pma
Kyrgyzstan	Paris A		December 20, 1998	August 13, 2003	October 12, 2002		March 6, 2002	August 15, 2002	1998 (2001)	50 years from January 1 pma
Lao People's Democratic Republic		Geneva	observer[8]						No legislation	25 years pma minimum of UCC
Latvia	Paris A		February 10, 1999	August 20, 1999	August 23, 1997		March 6, 2002	May 20, 2002	2000	70 years pma
Lebanon	Rome	Geneva	observer[8]	August 12, 1997					1999	50 years pma (from end of year)

Signatories	Berne Convention[2] September 9, 1886 and Subsequent Acts	UCC[3] September 6, 1952 revised in Paris, July 24, 1971	TRIPS April 15, 1994	Rome Convention October 26, 1961	Geneva Phonograms Convention October 29, 1971	Satellite Convention May 21, 1974	WIPO Copyright Treaty[4]	WIPO Performances and Phonograms Treaty[5]	Date of Principal Law (most recent amendment)[6]	Period of Protection[7]
Lesotho	Paris A, H		May 31, 1995	January 26, 1990					1989	50 years pma (from end of year)
Liberia	Paris A, H	Geneva							1972	25 years pma (50 years under Convention)
Libyan Arab Jamahiriya	Paris A,H		observer[8]						1968	25 years pma or 50 years from first publication, which-ever is the longer
Liechtenstein	Paris A	Paris	September 1, 1995	October 12, 1999	October 12, 1999				1928 (1996)	50 years pma
Lithuania	Paris A,H		May 31, 2001	July 22, 1999	January 27, 2000		March 6, 2002	May 20, 2002	1999 (2000)	70 years pma

Signatories	Berne Convention[2] September 9, 1886 and Subsequent Acts	UCC[3] September 6, 1952 revised in Paris, July 24, 1971	TRIPS April 15, 1994	Rome Convention October 26, 1961	Geneva Phonograms Convention October 29, 1971	Satellite Convention May 21, 1974	WIPO Copyright Treaty[4]	WIPO Performances and Phonograms Treaty[5]	Date of Principal Law (most recent amendment)[6]	Period of Protection[7]
Luxembourg	Paris A	Geneva	January 1, 1995	February 25, 1976	March 8, 1976				1972 (1997)	70 years from January 1, pma
Macau (SAR of China)[10]	Paris A		January 1, 1995		December 20, 1999				1999 (2000)	50 years pma
Madagascar	Brussels		November 17, 1995						1995	70 years pma (from end of year)
Malawi	Paris A	Geneva	May 31, 1995						1989	50 years after year of author's death
Malaysia	Paris A		January 1, 1995						1987 (2000)	50 years pma
Maldives			May 31, 1995						No legislation	50 years pma minimum of TRIPs
Mali	Paris A		May 31, 1995				April 24, 2002	May 20, 2002	1984	50 years pma

Signatories	Berne Convention[2] September 9, 1886 and Subsequent Acts	UCC[3] September 6, 1952 revised in Paris, July 24, 1971	TRIPS April 15, 1994	Rome Convention October 26, 1961	Geneva Phonograms Convention October 29, 1971	Satellite Convention May 21, 1974	WIPO Copyright Treaty[4]	WIPO Performances and Phonograms Treaty[5]	Date of Principal Law (most recent amendment)[6]	Period of Protection[7]
Malta	Paris B, H Rome	Geneva	January 1, 1995						2000	50 years pma (from end of year)
Mauritania	Paris A		May 31, 1995						Unknown	50 years pma minimum of BC
Mauritius	Paris A, H	Geneva	January 1, 1995						1997	50 years pma
Mexico	Paris A	Paris*	January 1, 1995	May 18, 1964	December 21, 1973	August 25, 1979	March 6, 2002	May 20, 2002	1997 (1999)	75 years pma
Micronesia (Federated States of)	Paris A								Unknown	50 years pma minimum of BC
Monaco	Paris A	Paris		December 6, 1985	December 2, 1974				1948	50 years pma
Mongolia	Paris A, C, D, H		January 29, 1997				October 25, 2002	October 25, 2002	1993 (1999)	50 years pma
Morocco	Paris A	Paris	January 1, 1995			June 30, 1983			2000	50 years pma (from end of year)

Signatories	Berne Convention[2] September 9, 1886 and Subsequent Acts	UCC[3] September 6, 1952 revised in Paris, July 24, 1971	TRIPS April 15, 1994	Rome Convention October 26, 1961	Geneva Phonograms Convention October 29, 1971	Satellite Convention May 21, 1974	WIPO Copyright Treaty[4]	WIPO Performances and Phonograms Treaty[5]	Date of Principal Law (most recent amendment)[6]	Period of Protection[7]
Mozambique			August 26, 1995						2001	70 years pma
Myanmar			January 1, 1995						2001	50 years pma
Namibia	Paris A		January 1, 1995						2002	50 years pma (from end of year)
Nauru									1956 (1971)	50 years pma
Nepal			April 23, 2004						1965 (1997)	50 years pma
Netherlands	Paris A[12]	Paris	January 1, 1995[12]	October 7, 1993[12]	October 12, 1993[12]				1912 (1995)	70 years pma (from end of year)
New Zealand	Rome	Geneva	January 1, 1995		August 13, 1976				1994 (1999)	50 years pma
Nicaragua	Paris A	Geneva	September 3, 1995	August 10, 2000	August 10, 2000	August 25, 1979	March 6, 2003	March 6, 2003	1999	70 years from January 1 pma

Signatories	Berne Convention[2] September 9, 1886 and Subsequent Acts	UCC[3] September 6, 1952 revised in Paris, July 24, 1971	TRIPS April 15, 1994	Rome Convention October 26, 1961	Geneva Phonograms Convention October 29, 1971	Satellite Convention May 21, 1974	WIPO Copyright Treaty[4]	WIPO Performances and Phonograms Treaty[5]	Date of Principal Law (most recent amendment)[6]	Period of Protection[7]
Niger	Paris A	Paris	December 13, 1996	May 18, 1964					1993	50 years pma (from end of year)
Nigeria	Paris A	Geneva	January 1, 1995	October 29, 1993					1988 (1999)	70 years pma (from the end of the year)
Norway	Paris A, I	Paris	January 1, 1995	July 10, 1978	August 1, 1978				1961 (1995)	70 years pma (from end of year); 50 years for certain works
Oman	Paris A, D		November 9, 2000						2000	50 years from January 1 pma
Pakistan	Stockholm B Rome	Geneva	January 1, 1995						1962 (1992)	50 years from January 1, pma

Signatories	Berne Convention[2] September 9, 1886 and Subsequent Acts	UCC[3] September 6, 1952 revised in Paris, July 24, 1971	TRIPS April 15, 1994	Rome Convention October 26, 1961	Geneva Phonograms Convention October 29, 1971	Satellite Convention May 21, 1974	WIPO Copyright Treaty[4]	WIPO Performances and Phonograms Treaty[5]	Date of Principal Law (most recent amendment)[6]	Period of Protection[7]
Panama	Paris A	Paris	September 6, 1997	September 2, 1983	June 29, 1974	September 25, 1985	March 6, 2002	May 20, 2002	1994 (1997)	50 years pma
Papua New Guinea			June 9, 1996						2000	50 years pma
Paraguay	Paris A	Geneva	January 1, 1995	February 26, 1970	February 13, 1979		March 6, 2002	May 20, 2002	1998 (1999)	70 years pma
Peru	Paris A	Paris	January 1, 1995	August 7, 1985	August 24, 1985	August 7, 1985	March 6, 2002	July 18, 2002	1996	70 years pma
Philippines	Paris A, D	Geneva	January 1, 1995	September 25, 1984			October 4, 2002	October 4, 2002	1998	50 years pma
Poland	Paris A	Paris	July 1, 1995	June 13, 1997			March 23, 2004	October 21, 2003	1994	50 years pma
Portugal	Paris A, G	Paris	January 1, 1995	July 17, 2002		March 11, 1996			1985 (2000)	70 years pma
Qatar	Paris A		January 13, 1996						2002	50 years pma
Republic of Korea	Paris A	Paris*	January 1, 1995		October 10, 1987		June 24, 2004		1986 (1995)	50 years from January 1, pma

Signatories	Berne Convention[2] September 9, 1886 and Subsequent Acts	UCC[3] September 6, 1952 revised in Paris, July 24, 1971	TRIPS April 15, 1994	Rome Convention October 26, 1961	Geneva Phonograms Convention October 29, 1971	Satellite Convention May 21, 1974	WIPO Copyright Treaty[4]	WIPO Performances and Phonograms Treaty[5]	Date of Principal Law (most recent amendment)[6]	Period of Protection[7]
Republic of Moldova	Paris A	Geneva	July 26, 2001	December 5, 1995	July 17, 2000		March 6, 2002	May 20, 2002	1994	50 years from January 1, pma
Romania	Paris A		January 1, 1995	October 22, 1998	October 1, 1998		March 6, 2002	May 20, 2002	1996	70 years pma
Russian Federation	Paris A	Paris	observer[8]	May 26, 2003	March 13, 1995	January 20, 1989			1993 (1995)	50 years from January 1, pma
Rwanda	Paris A	Paris	May 22, 1996						1983	50 years pma
Saint Kitts and Nevis	Paris A		February 21, 1996						Unknown	50 years pma minimum of BC
Saint Lucia	Paris A, H		January 1, 1995	August 17, 1996	April 2, 2001		March 6, 2002	May 20, 2002	1956	50 years pma
Saint Vincent and the Grenadines	Paris A	Paris	January 1, 1995						1989	50 year pma (from end of year)
Samoa			observer[8]						1998	75 years pma

Signatories	Berne Convention[2] September 9, 1886 and Subsequent Acts	UCC[3] September 6, 1952 revised in Paris, July 24, 1971	TRIPS April 15, 1994	Rome Convention October 26, 1961	Geneva Phonograms Convention October 29, 1971	Satellite Convention May 21, 1974	WIPO Copyright Treaty[4]	WIPO Performances and Phonograms Treaty[5]	Date of Principal Law (most recent amendment)[6]	Period of Protection[7]
San Marino									1991	50 years pma (from end of year)
Sao Tome and Principe			observer[8]							
Saudi Arabia	Paris A	Paris	observer[8]						1989	50 years pma
Senegal	Paris A	Paris	January 1, 1995				May 18, 2002	May 20, 2002	1973 (1986)	50 years pma (from end of year)
Separate Customs Territory of Taiwan, Penghu, Kinmen and Matsu			January 1, 2002						Unknown	50 years pma minimum of TRIPs

Signatories	Berne Convention[2] September 9, 1886 and Subsequent Acts	UCC[3] September 6, 1952 revised in Paris, July 24, 1971	TRIPS April 15, 1994	Rome Convention October 26, 1961	Geneva Phonograms Convention October 29, 1971	Satellite Convention May 21, 1974	WIPO Copyright Treaty[4]	WIPO Performances and Phonograms Treaty[5]	Date of Principal Law (most recent amendment)[6]	Period of Protection[7]
Serbia and Montenegro	Paris A, E	Paris	observer[8]	June 10, 2003	June 10, 2003	April 27, 1992	June 13, 2003	June 13, 2003	Unknown	50 years pma minimum of BC
Seychelles			observer[8]						1984 (1991)	25 years pma (from end of year)
Sierra Leone			July 23, 1995						1965	50 years pma (from end of the year)
Singapore	Paris A, C		January 1, 1995						1987 (1999)	50 years pma (from end of year)
Slovakia	Paris A	Paris	January 1, 1995	January 1, 1993	January 1, 1993		March 6, 2002	May 20, 2002	1997	70 years pma
Slovenia	Paris A, E	Paris	July 30, 1995	October 9, 1996	October 15, 1996	June 25, 1991	March 6, 2002	May 20, 2002	1995	70 years pma
Solomon Islands			July 26, 1996						1987	50 years pma

Signatories	Berne Convention[2] September 9, 1886 and Subsequent Acts	UCC[3] September 6, 1952 revised in Paris, July 24, 1971	TRIPS April 15, 1994	Rome Convention October 26, 1961	Geneva Phonograms Convention October 29, 1971	Satellite Convention May 21, 1974	WIPO Copyright Treaty[4]	WIPO Performances and Phonograms Treaty[5]	Date of Principal Law (most recent amendment)[6]	Period of Protection[7]
South Africa	Paris B, H Brussels		January 1, 1995						1978 (2002)	50 years pma (from end of year)
Spain	Paris A	Paris	January 1, 1995	November 14, 1991	August 24, 1974				1996 (1998)	70 years pma
Sri Lanka	Paris B Rome	Paris	January 1, 1995						1979	50 years pma (from end of year)
Sudan	Paris A, D		observer[8]						1996	50 years pma; 25 years pma for certain works
Suriname	Paris A		January 1, 1995						Unknown	50 years pma minimum of BC
Swaziland	Paris A		January 1, 1995						No legislation	50 years pma minimum of BC

Signatories	Berne Convention[2] September 9, 1886 and Subsequent Acts	UCC[3] September 6, 1952 revised in Paris, July 24, 1971	TRIPS April 15, 1994	Rome Convention October 26, 1961	Geneva Phonograms Convention October 29, 1971	Satellite Convention May 21, 1974	WIPO Copyright Treaty[4]	WIPO Performances and Phonograms Treaty[5]	Date of Principal Law (most recent amendment)[6]	Period of Protection[7]
Sweden	Paris A	Paris	January 1, 1995	May 18, 1964	April 18, 1973				1960 (2000)	70 years pma
Switzerland	Paris A	Paris	July 1, 1995	September 24, 1993	September 30, 1993	September 24, 1993			1992 (1995)	70 years pma, 50 years for certain works (both from end of year)
Syrian Arab Republic	Paris A								2001	50 years pma
Taipei (China)			January 1, 2002						Unknown	50 years pma minimum of TRIPs
Taiwan									1992 (1993)	50 years pma
Tajikistan	Paris A	Geneva	observer[8]						Unknown	50 years pma minimum of BC
Thailand	Paris A, D, H,		January 1, 1995						1994	50 years pma

Signatories	Berne Convention[2] September 9, 1886 and Subsequent Acts	UCC[3] September 6, 1952 revised in Paris, July 24, 1971	TRIPS April 15, 1994	Rome Convention October 26, 1961	Geneva Phonograms Convention October 29, 1971	Satellite Convention May 21, 1974	WIPO Copyright Treaty[4]	WIPO Performances and Phonograms Treaty[5]	Date of Principal Law (most recent amendment)[6]	Period of Protection[7]
The former Yugoslav Republic of Macedonia	Paris A	Paris	April 4, 2003	March 2, 1998	March 2, 1998	November 17, 1991	February 4, 2004		1996 (1998)	70 years pma
Togo	Paris A	Paris	May 31, 1995	June 10, 2003	June 10, 2003		May 21, 2003	May 21, 2003	1991	50 years pma (from end of year)
Tonga	Paris A		observer[8]						1985	50 years pma (from end of year)
Trinidad and Tobago	Paris A	Paris	March 1, 1995		October 1, 1988	November 1, 1996			1997 (2000)	50 years pma; 75 years from publication for certain works
Tunisia	Paris A, H	Paris*	March 29, 1995						1994	50 years from January 1, pma

Signatories	Berne Convention[2] September 9, 1886 and Subsequent Acts	UCC[3] September 6, 1952 revised in Paris, July 24, 1971	TRIPS April 15, 1994	Rome Convention October 26, 1961	Geneva Phonograms Convention October 29, 1971	Satellite Convention May 21, 1974	WIPO Copyright Treaty[4]	WIPO Performances and Phonograms Treaty[5]	Date of Principal Law (most recent amendment)[6]	Period of Protection[7]
Turkey	Paris A, H		March 26, 1995	April 8, 2004					1951 (1995)	70 years pma
Uganda			January 1, 1995						1964	50 years pma or from publication, whichever latest
Ukraine	Paris A	Geneva	observer[8]	June 12, 2002	February 18, 2000		March 6, 2002	May 20, 2002	2001	70 years pma
United Arab Emirates	Paris A, D		April 10, 1996				July 14, 2004		1992	25 years pma
United Kingdom	Paris A, I (extended to Isle of Man from March 18, 1996)	Paris	January 1, 1995	May 18, 1964 (extended to Isle of Man from July 28, 1999)	April 18, 1973				1988 (2003)	70 years pma
United Republic of Tanzania	Paris A, H	Geneva	January 1, 1995						1999	50 years pma (from end of year)

Signatories	Berne Convention[2] September 9, 1886 and Subsequent Acts	UCC[3] September 6, 1952 revised in Paris, July 24, 1971	TRIPS April 15, 1994	Rome Convention October 26, 1961	Geneva Phonograms Convention October 29, 1971	Satellite Convention May 21, 1974	WIPO Copyright Treaty[4]	WIPO Performances and Phonograms Treaty[5]	Date of Principal Law (most recent amendment)[6]	Period of Protection[7]
United States of America	Paris A	Paris	January 1, 1995		March 10, 1974	March 7, 1985	March 6, 2002	May 20, 2002[13]	1976 (2003)	50 years pma; for works for hire 75 years from first publication or 100 years from creation, whichever expires first
Uruguay	Paris A	Paris	January 1, 1995	July 4, 1977	January 18, 1983				1937 (1994)	40 years pma or 50 years under BC
Uzbekistan			observer[8]						1996	50 years from January 1, pma
Vanuatu			observer[8]							

Signatories	Berne Convention[2] September 9, 1886 and Subsequent Acts	UCC[3] September 6, 1952 revised in Paris, July 24, 1971	TRIPS April 15, 1994	Rome Convention October 26, 1961	Geneva Phonograms Convention October 29, 1971	Satellite Convention May 21, 1974	WIPO Copyright Treaty[4]	WIPO Performances and Phonograms Treaty[5]	Date of Principal Law (most recent amendment)[6]	Period of Protection[7]
Venezuela	Paris A, H	Paris	January 1, 1995	January 30, 1996	November 18, 1982				1993 (1995)	60 years from January 1, pma
Viet Nam	Paris A, D, H		observer[8]						1995 (1996)	50 years pma (from end of year)
Yemen			observer[8]						1994	30 years from January 1, pma or 25 years from January 1, of year of production for certain works
Zambia	Paris A	Geneva	January 1, 1995						1994	50 years pma (from end of year)

1371

Signatories	Berne Convention[2] September 9, 1886 and Subsequent Acts	UCC[3] September 6, 1952 revised in Paris, July 24, 1971	TRIPS April 15, 1994	Rome Convention October 26, 1961	Geneva Phonograms Convention October 29, 1971	Satellite Convention May 21, 1974	WIPO Copyright Treaty[4]	WIPO Performances and Phonograms Treaty[5]	Date of Principal Law (most recent amendment)[6]	Period of Protection[7]
Zimbabwe	Paris B Rome	Paris 64 Geneva 99	March 5, 1995						1967 (1982)	50 years pma
Total number of Member States	156		147	77	73	24	48	44	188	

1. This table reflects the status of ratifications and accessions to the Conventions as of August 20, 2004. An asterisk * indicates a future date on which the ratification or accession will enter into force.

2. Berne Convention: "Paris" means the Berne Convention as revised at Paris on July 24, 1971 (Paris Act); "Stockholm" means the said Convention as revised at Stockholm on July 14, 1967 (Stockholm Act); "Brussels" means the said Convention as revised at Brussels on June 26, 1948 (Brussels Act); "Rome" means the said Convention as revised at Rome on June 2, 1928 (Rome Act). Paris Revision Countries which have ratified or acceded to the entire Paris Act of the Berne Convention, including the Appendix, are indicated as "Paris A". Countries which have declared that their ratification or accession does not apply to Arts 1–21 and the Appendix are indicated as "Paris B". Countries which have availed themselves of one or both of the faculties in Arts II and III of the Appendix until October 10, 2004, are indicated as "Paris C". Countries which have availed themselves of one or both of the faculties in Arts II and III of the Appendix until October 10, 2014, are indicated as "Paris D". Countries which have made a declaration concerning the right of translation under Art.V of the Appendix are indicated as "Paris E". Countries which have made a declaration under Art.14*bis*(2)(b) are indicated as "Paris F" (presumption of legitimation for some authors who have brought contributions to the making of the cinematographic work). Countries which have made a declaration under Art.14*bis*(2)(c) are indicated as "Paris G" (undertaking by authors to bring contributions to the making of a cinematographic work must be in writing). Countries which have made a declaration under Art.33(2) relating to the International Court of Justice are indicated as "Paris H". Countries which have made a declaration that they admit the application of the Appendix of the Paris Act to works of which it is the State of origin are indicated as "Paris I".

Stockholm Revision: The substantive provisions of the Stockholm revision did not, and now cannot, come into force. However, previous Acts remain in force in relations with those countries of the Union which have not ratified or acceded to the Paris Act. For countries which have ratified or acceded to the whole of the Paris Act and the Appendix, no reference is made to either Stockholm or earlier revisions. Those countries which declared that their ratification or accession does not apply to Arts 1–21 of the Stockholm Act and the Protocol Regarding Developing Countries are indicated as "Stockholm B". This also indicates countries which ratified or acceded to the entire Stockholm Act, the substantive provisions of which have not come into force.

3. UCC: Countries that have ratified or acceded to the 1971 Paris revised Convention are indicated as "Paris" (most of these are party also to the Geneva Convention); others are shown as "Geneva". Countries which have availed themselves of the exceptions in favour of developing countries are indicated as "Paris*".

4. The WIPO Copyright Treaty came into force on March 6, 2002. See para.24–75, above.

5. The WIPO Performances and Phonograms Treaty came into force on May 20, 2002. See para.24–133, above.

6. The date of the principal law is given, with the date of the most recent amendment in brackets.

7. The period of protection is for literary and artistic works (as defined in Art.2(1) of the Berne Convention), and is indicated as either *post mortem auctoris* (pma), pma from the end of the calendar year, or pma from January 1 of the following year. Many countries have different periods of protection for different works, *e.g.* for photographs, computer programs, collective works, works where the author is a legal entity and for the subject-matter of related rights. For some works the period of protection runs from the date of publication. In some countries the period of protection is less than that required by international convention. In such cases the indicated period does not apply to foreign works. This Table is up to date as of August 1, 2004. It is intended as a general guide only, and more detailed information can be obtained at *http://wipo.org/clea/en/index.html* and *http://portal.unesco.org/culture* (Collection of National Copyright Laws).

8. An "observer" state must start accession negotiations within five years (except Holy See).

9. Pursuant to Art.15, para.3 of the Treaty, the Republic of Chile will apply the provisions of Art.15, para.1 of the Treaty only in respect of direct uses of phonograms published for commercial purposes for broadcasting or for any communication to the public. Pursuant to Art.15, para.3 of the Treaty, as regards phonograms the producer or performer of which is a national of another Contracting Party which has made a declaration under Art.15, para.3 of the Treaty, the Republic of Chile will apply, notwithstanding the provisions of the preceding declaration, the provisions of Art.15, para.1 of the Treaty to the extent that Party grants the protection provided for by the provisions of Art.15, para.1 of the Treaty.

10. The Paris Act of the Berne Convention and the Geneva Phonograms Convention apply to Hong Kong from July 1, 1997 and to Macao from December 20, 1999.

11. Pursuant to Art.3(3), Japan will not apply the criterion of publication concerning the protection of producers of phonograms. Pursuant to Art.15(3), Japan will not apply the provisions of Art.15(1) to the extent that Party grants the protection provided for by Art.15(1); and Japan will apply the provisions of Art.15(1) in respect of direct uses for broadcasting or for wire diffusion, but Japan will not apply the provisions of Art.15(1) to the phonograms made available to the public, by wire or wireless means, in such a way that members of the public may access them from a place and at a time individually chosen by them.

12. Accession for the Kingdom in Europe. Arts 22–38 of the Paris Act of the Berne Convention apply also to the Netherlands Antilles and Aruba.

13. Pursuant to Art.15(3) of the WIPO Performances and Phonograms Treaty, the United States will apply the provisions of Art.15(1) of the WIPO Performances and Phonograms Treaty only in respect of certain acts of broadcasting and communication to the public by digital means for which a direct or indirect fee is charged for reception, and for other retransmissions and digital phonorecord deliveries, as provided under the United States law.

PART VIII

EXPLOITATION AND CONTROL OF RIGHTS

EXPLOITATION OF RIGHTS IN PARTICULAR INDUSTRIES

1. THE PUBLISHING INDUSTRY

A. THE GENERAL NATURE OF THE PUBLISHING INDUSTRY

The publishing industry in the United Kingdom is a vibrant and diverse industry, **27–01** producing a wide variety of material both in conventional printed form and in various electronic forms, such as CD-ROMs, online journals and material published over the internet. The principal sectors of the publishing industry, are: book publishing, magazine publishing, journal publishing, electronic publishing and newspaper publishing. Electronic publishing is an aspect of all the other areas of publishing, and can involve offline (*e.g.* CD-ROM) or online publishing (including internet) and will be dealt with briefly in the context of book publishing, magazine publishing and journal publishing. Newspaper publishing is considered in depth in a separate section.[1]

Book publishing. Book publishing is big business. In 2002, the sales of books by **27–02** the United Kingdom publishing industry amounted to approximately £3,240 million.[2] Books are published in hardback and paperback form in a wide variety of shapes and sizes. Some (particularly works of fiction) consist only of text; others are illustrated. Of those that are illustrated, the illustrations range from simple line drawings or tables through to complex hand-drawn full colour artwork, colour and black-and-white photographs, and "pop-up" illustrations. The book publishing industry has for a long time generally been considered to consist of two principal sectors, namely "trade publishers" (*i.e.* those who publish books for the general public, and whose books are primarily made available through retail bookshops) and those who publish for the professions (*e.g.* legal, accountancy, medical, engineering, etc.), academic works (*e.g.* for schools, colleges and universities) and encyclopaedias. Of course, within each of these two broad divisions, various publishers specialise in particular subject areas. Whilst it is still fair to describe the industry as consisting of these two principal sectors, electronic publishers are increasingly becoming a significant sector in their own right, as well as forming part of the above two sectors. The Publishers' Association has established the Electronic Publishers' Forum to provide a means through which electronic publishers can meet and discuss matters of particular interest to their sector. The distinction between "trade publishers" and other publishers is important, since it affects the rights which are generally acquired by these different groups of publishers.

Over the last 15 years or so there has been a marked tendency towards so-called "vertical publishing", whereby the hardback and paperback editions of a particular book are published by the same publisher. Hardback books generally command a higher selling price (and usually also a higher profit margin) than paperback books, and many books are often published originally in hardback, with a paperback edition being published a year or so later, once the demand for the hardback edition has fallen off. In the past, publishers tended to specialise either in publishing in hardback or in paperback. It is now far more common for publishers to have the facility to publish both hardback and paperback editions, perhaps under different imprints but within the same corporate group.

A further tendency within the last 15 years or so has been towards the concentration of book publishing within the hands of a few multinational corporations, often having interests not only in book publishing but also in other media

---

[1] See paras 27–93 *et seq.*, below.
[2] For up-to-date statistics of the UK book publishing industry, see the website of The Publishers' Association at *www.publishers.org.uk*.

such as television, music and film production and distribution. Notwithstanding the dominance of the multinational publishers, there is still a wide range of small to medium-sized independent publishers, often concentrating on specialised sectors of the book market. In addition, there are a number of "book packagers", who create books for publication under publishers' imprints, and oversee the whole process from concept through to delivery of the finished books to the publisher or to the publisher's distributor. Very often the books in question will have been conceived by the packager and the idea "sold" to publishers both in English-language markets and in foreign-language markets, and the development and production of the books is financed by stage payments from the publishers. This process is particularly suited to highly illustrated works, where the surrounding text can be produced in a number of different languages.

With developments in computer and printing technology, it is now feasible for books to be created using desktop publishing software, and small print runs can be economically viable. This makes it possible for even an individual to carry out every aspect of the publishing process, from writing the book to designing the page layout and printing and publishing.

There are also so-called "vanity publishers", who will publish a work provided that the author pays all or a substantial part of the cost of producing and publishing the book. In general, this does not represent a good deal for the author, and authors will usually only resort to this if they cannot get a conventional publisher to publish the book at the publisher's own risk and expense.

27–03   **Book distribution.** Books may reach the ultimate purchaser by a number of different routes, the most common of which are as follows:

(a) *Retailers*

Many bookshops purchase direct from the publishers, often ordering through an electronic ordering system, which enables bookshops to order precisely the number of books which they expect to be able to sell or for which they have actual requests from customers. In general, bookshops purchase on a "sale-or-return" basis, but where large quantities of any particular title are involved, some publishers are prepared to offer booksellers a higher discount off the "published price" or "recommended retail price" in return for the transaction being on a "firm sale" basis. Booksellers in the United Kingdom are now free to sell books to the ultimate purchaser at whatever price they choose, since the abolition of the Net Book Agreement. In practice, relatively few titles are sold at a discount from the publisher's recommended retail price, and those that are sold at a discount from the recommended price tend to be best-sellers or special promotions at the largest chain booksellers.

(b) *Wholesalers*

Many bookshops are supplied largely by wholesalers. If wholesalers purchase books from publishers in bulk and supply bookshops they need to obtain a substantial discount from the publishers in order to enable them to supply bookshops at a price which enables the bookshop in turn to make a profit on those books.

(c) *Distributors*

Distributors provide warehousing and distribution services for publishers, including invoicing and collection of payment from bookshops, in return for commission.

(d) *Book clubs*

There are a number of general and special interest book clubs which operate throughout the United Kingdom, whereby members of the public can obtain books by mail order, many of them being at prices lower than are available through bookshops. Book clubs attract new members by means of an introductory special offer, with a number of books at very cheap prices, in return for which the purchaser generally makes a commitment to buy a minimum number of books over a given period of time. The books sold by book clubs may, if quantities are small, be the publisher's original editions or, in the case of larger quantities, they will be the book clubs' own editions with their own imprint. The book clubs' own editions may either be produced for them by the publisher at the same time as it arranges the printing of its own edition (in which case the longer print run thereby made possible will reduce unit costs) or they may be manufactured by the book club itself. This will affect the terms on which the book club deals with the publisher and will also affect the amount which the author receives from the sale of copies through the book club.

(e) *Direct sales*

There are a number of organisations that sell books direct to individual members of the public, particularly at people's offices. The books sold in this way may be the publishers' regular editions or they may be editions specifically produced for and with the imprint of the direct seller. This method of sale has become increasingly popular and now constitutes a significant part of the market for some books. However, there is considerable concern amongst authors and their representatives that publishers are selling books to direct sellers (including book clubs) too soon after first publication and at very reduced prices, which damages bookshop sales and therefore reduces the royalties authors can expect to receive.

(f) *Internet sales*

Increasingly, books are being sold through online booksellers such as *Amazon.co.uk*, *WHSmith.co.uk* and *bol.com*. Although online booksellers currently represent only a small proportion of the total retail market for books,[3] they are increasing their share, and they also supply other products, such as computer games, software and music.

Magazine publishing. There are varying estimates of the number of magazine titles published in the United Kingdom, but BRAD (British Rate and Data) lists nearly 8,500 separate titles which take advertising, of which 5,108 were "business and professional" titles and 3,229 were "consumer" titles. In the last 10 years, the total number of magazine titles has increased by 25 per cent. Total expenditure (consumer and advertiser) on consumer magazines in the United Kingdom was over £2.6 billion in 2002. As well as the distinction between "business and professional" titles on the one hand and "consumer" titles on the other, in recent years there has emerged the so-called "customer magazines" sector, comprising publications produced under contract for companies and distributed either free of charge or offered for sale to customers. This sector has enjoyed rapid growth and the total value of the customer magazine sector was put at more than £366 million by the Advertising Association in 2003.[4]

27–04

The United Kingdom magazine publishing industry is dominated by a small number of major companies who publish a large and often diverse range of titles. Some titles are produced in different versions for different markets, either in the same language (*e.g.* separate English-language editions for the American and United Kingdom markets) or in different languages for various different countries,

[3] It was thought that *Amazon.co.uk* had a share of about 5 per cent or 6 per cent of the UK market around the beginning of 2004.
[4] For up-to-date statistics of the UK magazine publishing industry, see the website of The Periodical Publishers' Association at *www.ppa.co.uk*.

while retaining the same overall identity and brand, notwithstanding differences in content. The United Kingdom magazine publishing industry also has a large number of small independent publishers, often producing magazines for special interests, and there are a large number of new titles published on a regular basis.

27–05   **Magazine distribution.** The vast majority (about 89 per cent) of magazines are sold in the United Kingdom through retail outlets. In general, magazines tend to be distributed through a number of large or independent distributors. The distributors make arrangements with the printers of the magazines for the magazines to be shipped to wholesalers who in turn distribute to individual newsagents. At present, relatively small numbers of consumer magazines are sold in the United Kingdom on subscription by mail order, either by the publisher directly or through subscription agents, but often at a substantial discount from the cover price charged in newsagents. However, the proportion of magazines sold in this way is likely to increase. Some magazines are *only* available on subscription. About 24 per cent of business and professional magazines are sold through subscriptions, and as much as 90 per cent of so-called "business-to-business" magazines are sold by subscription. In addition, a number of magazine publishers are making all or parts of their magazines available, in some cases at a charge, over the internet. Sometimes this is to enable them to present information in a way which cannot be done on the printed page; sometimes this is to enable additional background information to be published; often it also enables the publishers to present up-to-the-minute news, which cannot be done in a printed monthly magazine. The more comprehensive the material available on the internet, the more likely the publisher will charge to access it. Even if there is a charge to access all of the material, some of it will usually be available free of charge as a "taster".

27–06   **Journal publishing.** This sector mainly comprises the publication of professional (including scientific) and academic journals. It is difficult to obtain clear and up-to-date statistics of the scale of the journal publishing sector.[5] The total turnover of all journals for the years 1999 and 2000 was £554.29 million: Of this, £286.3 million represented UK-only publishers and £267.99 million represented the turnover of international publishers. As with book and magazine publishing, there are a number of major players in this market sector, as well as independent publishers. Journals tend to be sold on subscription, either by direct arrangement between the publisher and the subscriber or through subscription agents acting on behalf of the publisher. Something under 50 per cent of revenue is earned from subscriptions in this way.[6] Traditionally, journals have been made available only in printed form, but there is now a move towards making journals available online.[7] A number of major journal publishers are involved in arrangements with academic institutions to provide their journals online pursuant to a "site licence",

---

[5] Some statistics for UK Journal publishing for 1999 and 2000 are contained in a survey conducted in 2001 and published in August 2002 by TFPL Ltd on behalf, and amongst the membership, of the Publishers' Association ("PA") and the Association of Learned and Professional Society Publishers ("ALPSP"). The TFPL survey is available on the ALPSP website at *www.alpsp.org/resources/pubstats.pdf*, and many other useful resources are also available on the ALPSP web site.

[6] See the TFPL survey.

[7] In the TFPL surveys for 1999 and 2000, 91 of the 169 respondents published some, or all, of their journals electronically, and those electronic journals represented 70 per cent of the total number of titles covered in the survey. Some of the respondents published all of their journals electronically; some publish some, but not all, of their journals electronically; and some publish only in print.

permitting unlimited access to the journals in question for all students and staff of the licensed academic institutions.[8]

B. SOURCES OF COPYRIGHT WORKS

(a) All sections of the publishing industry involve the creation of literary works. These are created by "authors"[9] and notably a particular type of author, namely journalists. While authors of books are generally unlikely to be employees of the publisher (although there are some exceptions to this), it is common for journalists to be employees of magazine and newspaper publishers, although there are substantial numbers of freelance journalists. Where an author (including a journalist) is an employee, then the copyright in works created in the course of his or her employment are owned by the employer, subject to any agreement to the contrary.[10] Many authors are represented by literary agents, who will negotiate contracts with book, newspaper and magazine publishers on behalf of their client authors. Authors' agents do not usually have authority to sign contracts on behalf of their authors.

27–07

(b) In the case of illustrated works, specialist illustrators, artists and photographers are the primary sources of the illustrations. Depending on the publishers in question, some illustrators may be in-house employees, in which case the employer will own the copyright in their work, but in general illustrators, artists and photographers are more likely to be freelance. Many specialist illustrators and photographers are represented by agents, who provide the link between the illustrator or photographer on the one hand and the publisher on the other hand and who can provide the right person for the particular task in hand. The agent will also negotiate on behalf of the illustrator/photographer the terms upon which the work will be created specifically for the publisher or otherwise made available to the publisher. In the case of photographs, many photographers place their existing work with photographic libraries, some of which specialise in particular subject areas, and publishers use picture researchers to find the required images from these libraries, who are authorised to grant copyright licences as agent for the photographers.

27–08

(c) All sections of the publishing industry use editors to a greater or lesser extent, and an editor may contribute to the overall copyright in a literary work, depending on the nature of the work and the extent of the editor's contribution. Where the work consists of contributions from a number of different authors, under the general editorship of one person, the editor's contribution is likely to be substantial and result in the creation of a new copyright work, of which the editor will be the author.[11] Where, on the other hand, the editor's function is more of a copy-editing role, then the editor's work may not be sufficient to make him an "author".[12] Editing and copy-editing is frequently carried out by in-house employees, so that the copyright in any work created by them will be owned by the publisher, but copy-editing is often out-sourced to freelancers, and so publishers should be made aware that they need to acquire an assignment of copyright in such cases. Even where the amount of copy-editing is sufficient to result in the creation of a new copyright work, the publisher is unlikely to assert copyright in it (quite apart from the effect of any assignment by the "true" author).

27–09

---

[8] See para. 27–76, below.

[9] In the technical sense as used in CDPA 1988, s.9 and in the colloquial sense.

[10] See CDPA 1988, s.11(2), and paras 5–08 *et seq.*, above.

[11] See para. 4–24, above.

[12] See *Fylde Microsystems Ltd v Key Radio Systems Ltd*, [1998] F.S.R. 449, by analogy.

27–10 (d) Designers and typesetters are responsible for creating the overall "look" of a publication. Design work is normally done in-house, particularly with the desktop publishing software which is now widely used, and much of the work previously done by typesetters is also carried out in-house, so that the work created on computer by the publisher is sent to the repro-house (if applicable) and printer to produce the finished product. To the extent that any copyrights are created in this process, they should be owned by the publisher, although publishers should check the standard terms and conditions of business of the repro-houses and printers with whom they deal. The publisher is the "author" of the typographical arrangement of the published edition of a work and hence the first owner of the copyright in it.[13]

C. WORKS CREATED AND MAIN RIGHTS REQUIRED FOR EXPLOITATION

(i) Books

27–11 The end product in the book publishing process is a book written by one or more authors and edited either in-house or by an independent editor or panel of editors. The rights required by the publisher will depend on the nature of the book in question, and may differ according to whether the book is a "trade" publication or a professional, academic or encyclopaedia publication:

(a) "Trade" publications

27–12 The publisher will require the following rights to be granted by each author and any other individual who has contributed copyright material to the work (*e.g.* by way of editing) by way of exclusive licence and usually for the full period of copyright. The publisher may also seek a complete or partial waiver of moral rights, particularly for the purpose of exercising electronic-form publication rights and licensing serial rights and subsidiary rights. Authors may well resist such a request, if professionally advised.

27–13 **(1) Volume form publication rights.** *i.e.* the right to publish the work as a printed book. For the purposes of calculating the royalties payable to the author, this right is often sub-divided into very specific types of volume form, *e.g.* trade hardback, trade paperback, mass market paperback, book club, etc. and different royalty rates will apply to the different types of volume form publication and according to whether particular copies are sold in the "home" territory or in "export" markets.

27–14 **(2) Electronic form publication rights.** *i.e.* the right to publish the work in any electronic form (whether online or offline) whether in conjunction with any other works or not, and by means of any technology now known or subsequently developed.

27–15 **(3) Serialisation rights.** These are commonly divided into first serial rights and second serial rights, meaning the right to publish a serialisation commencing before and after publication of the book respectively.

27–16 **(4) Translation rights.** *i.e.* the right to translate the work into foreign languages and to publish the foreign language editions.

27–17 **(5) Various "subsidiary rights"**. These are rights which the publisher will usually license to third parties, including:

---

[13] CDPA 1988, ss.9(2)(d), 11(1). See paras 4–77 and 5–61, above.

— electronic publishing rights (insofar as not directly exercised by the publisher);

— the mechanical reproduction of the work (*i.e.* audio tapes of undramatised readings of the work);

— quotation and extract rights (*i.e.* the right to authorise others to publish quotations or extracts from the work in other works);

— reprographic reproduction rights (these are often granted by the publishers to the Copyright Licensing Agency (CLA)[14] to authorise photocopying and other forms of reprographic reproduction under various blanket licensing schemes and individual licences);

— condensation rights (*i.e.* the right to produce and publish a condensed version of the work—this right might be expressly subject to the author's prior written consent, as a condensation might, unless expressly authorised, infringe an author's integrity right)[15];

— film, television and live stage dramatisation rights (*i.e.* the right to dramatise the work and present that dramatisation by means of film, television or live stage although these rights are more commonly reserved by authors and negotiated on the author's behalf through specialist agents);

— database right where the work in question constitutes a database for the purposes of the Copyright and Rights in Databases Regulations 1997[16];

— Braille rights[17] have for many years been granted to UK publishers. In anticipation of the Copyright (Visually Impaired Persons) Act 2002, which is dealt with elsewhere,[18] the Publishers' Association and other representatives of rights holders produced a set of guidelines on access to books, magazines and journals for visually-impaired persons.[19] In addition, the CLA has introduced a Visually Impaired Persons Licence designed specifically for not-for-profit organisations wishing to make and to circulate copies of copyright works in a format accessible to visually impaired persons. The CLA has also made alternative provision for educational establishments wishing to make similar copies available for their own staff and students.[20]

(b) *Professional, academic and encyclopaedia works*

The publisher will require an assignment of the entire copyright in the work for the full period of copyright together with a waiver of all moral rights. This is particularly so in relation to works which have several authors or editors and works which are expected to go into a number of editions in the future, so that the material can freely be used in future editions, whatever the form those editions may take. In addition, in relation to professional or academic works, the publisher will require the express right (but probably without a corresponding obligation) to continue using the author's name on and in relation to any number of future editions. This is because this type of work often comes to be known by the author's name

27–18

---

[14] As to the CLA, see para. 28–52, below.

[15] *i.e.* under CDPA 1988, s.80. See paras 11–34 *et seq.*, above.

[16] See Ch.18, above.

[17] *i.e.* the right to convert the work in question into Braille or to record the work for the sole use of the blind and print-handicapped, on a free-of-charge basis, where the author receives no payment.

[18] See para. 9–63 *et seq.*, above.

[19] These guidelines are available on the Publishers' Association website at *www.publishers.org.uk/ paweb/paweb.nsf/pubframe!Open*.

[20] Details are available on the CLA web site, *http://www.cla.co.uk/have_licence/he/ helicenceamendmentsnotice.doc*.

With this type of work, the publisher will also require an obligation on the part of the author to revise the work when the publisher considers it necessary, in order to keep the work up to date. This is particularly important where a work has already been associated with a particular author, but if the original author is unable or fails to revise the work, the publisher invariably retains the right to engage someone else to do so. This illustrates why the publisher requires to have the complete copyright in the work and a waiver of all of the author's moral rights: a new author brought in to revise the work must have the freedom to reuse and amend all or any of the work as thought fit, without the new author or the publisher being exposed to a claim by the original author for infringement of copyright or of moral rights or passing off.

(ii) Magazines

27–19　Employed writers and editors and regular contributors to magazines will normally be expected to assign the full copyright in their work to the publisher. With regard to occasional articles, the publisher will probably require no more than first British publication rights (although the period of exclusivity should be spelt out) unless the magazine circulates elsewhere or the publisher requires to syndicate the article to other magazines (*e.g.* foreign editions of the same magazine, possibly involving translation into foreign languages), in which case wider rights will be required. Furthermore, if the magazine is available electronically, *e.g.* over the internet, then the publisher might insist on a full assignment of copyright in relation to all material which it publishes (perhaps on the basis that it would license the author to reuse the material elsewhere after a certain period).

(iii) Journals

27–20　Journals vary in the rights that they require. Academic and scientific journals tend to require a full assignment of copyright from all contributors, albeit that they authorise contributors to reuse their material, *e.g.* in books written or co-written by or with contributions from the authors, subject to giving credit to the journal where the work is first published. This gives the publisher the ability to publish the material in all media without further consultation with the authors of the articles. Journals aimed at other professions, however, tend to require no more than the simple non-exclusive right to publish—this assumes that there is limited opportunity for the reuse of material in competing journals. Assuming that the journals in question are currently published in printed form only, then, unless wider rights were explicitly acquired by the publisher, a licence to publish in printed form is all that is likely to be implied. Accordingly, if, for example, the publisher then wanted to publish back issues over the internet, it would need further consents from all the authors.

(iv) Electronic publishers

27–21　Because of the rapid developments in technology, which make new forms of electronic delivery available, electronic publishers require maximum flexibility to exploit works in whatever way they can. Works which are published electronically will often be updated very regularly (ranging from daily to quarterly), and this again requires maximum flexibility. For this reason, and because works published electronically frequently have many authors, electronic publishers usually require a complete assignment of copyright in all material which they publish. It is particularly important for them to obtain a world-wide assignment of copyright, consisting of the equivalent rights throughout the world. With the advent of satellite broadcasting and further exploration of outer space, one can imagine rights being required even beyond the world.

Where a full assignment of copyright is, for any reason, not obtainable, an electronic publisher will require an exclusive licence of "electronic publication rights". The rights should be defined widely, giving as many examples as possible, stipulating that these are by way of example only and not by way of limitation and are to include all media and means of exploitation now known or subsequently developed. If the licence is governed by English law, this should be effective.[21]

D. TRADE UNIONS AND TRADE ASSOCIATIONS WHICH REPRESENT SOURCES OF WORKS AND ORGANISATIONS THAT EXPLOIT THEM

Authors. There are two main bodies representing authors: the Society of Authors ("SoA")[22] and the Writers Guild of Great Britain ("WGGB").[23] The SoA tends to represent authors of books, whereas the WGGB tends to represent authors of material intended primarily for film and television exploitation. The SoA has entered into so-called "Minimum Terms Agreements" with a number of book publishers, specifying the minimum terms that the publisher will offer to members of the SoA. The WGGB has entered into agreements with broadcasters and unions representing film producers, specifying minimum terms that would be offered to WGGB members.   **27–22**

Author's agents. Quite apart from being entitled to join the SoA or the WGGB, many authors are represented by an agent, who will negotiate terms with publishers and others who exploit the author's material. The author's agents themselves have a body called the Authors' Agents Association,[24] through which they discuss matters of interest to authors' agents generally and develop policies to recommend to their members.   **27–23**

Illustrators. Illustrators are represented by the Association of Illustrators.[25]   **27–24**

Publishers. The following organisations represent various types of publishers[26]:   **27–25**
  — the Publishers Association represents book publishers (the vast majority of book publishers are members);
  — the Independent Publishers Guild represents a number of small, independent book publishers;
  — the Scottish Publishers Association represents independent Scottish book publishers;
  — the Periodical Publishers Association represents magazine publishers; and
  — the Association of Learned and Professional Society Publishers represents the publishers of professional and academic journals.

---

[21] As to the construction of agreements in relation to new technologies, see para. 5–225, above.
[22] www.societyofauthors.org.
[23] www.writersguild.org.uk.
[24] For more information about the Association of Authors' Agents, including a copy of their Code of Practice, see its website at www.agentsassoc.co.uk.
[25] For more information about the Association of Illustrators, see its website at www.aoi.co.uk.
[26] For more information about the organisations representing publishers, and for useful links, see their respective websites: The Publishers' Association: www.publishers.org.uk; The Independent Publishers' Guild: www.ipg.uk.com; The Scottish Publishers' Association: www.scottishbooks.org; The Periodical Publishers Association: www.ppa.co.uk; The Association of Learned and Professional Society Publishers: www.alpsp.org.

27–26 **Printers.** Printers are represented by the British Printing Industries Federation.[27]

27–27 **Booksellers.** Booksellers are represented by the Booksellers Association.[28]

27–28 **Actors.** Actors (*e.g.* in relation to sound recordings of works on tape) are represented by British Actors Equity (commonly known as "Equity").[29] Although Equity has agreements with most organisations that use its members' talent, specifying minimum terms, it does not have any such arrangements with publishers of sound recordings.

E. COLLECTING SOCIETIES AND LICENSING AGENCIES RESPONSIBLE FOR ADMINISTERING RIGHTS

27–29 **Authors' societies.** The Authors Licensing and Collecting Society ("ALCS")[30] administers a number of rights on behalf of authors, primarily the reprographic reproduction right (which it grants to the Copyright Licensing Agency ("CLA"),[31] and it distributes income received from the CLA amongst its author members. ALCS also administers the foreign lending right, cable retransmission right, private recording right, off-air recording right and public reception of broadcasts on behalf of its members.[32]

27–30 **Artists' and illustrators' societies.** Design and Artists' Copyright Society ("DACS")[33] administers the right to make copies of artistic works on behalf of its members (which include the estates of deceased artists).[34]

27–31 **Publishers' societies.** The members of Publishers Licensing Society ("PLS")[35] are the Publishers Association, the Periodical Publishers Association and the Association of Learned and Professional Society Publishers. PLS administers the reprographic reproduction right on behalf of publishers, and grants it to the CLA, so that the CLA is able to administer such rights on behalf of both publishers and authors. The CLA has established various blanket licensing schemes, *e.g.* for educational establishments and for business, and also licenses larger scale photocopying (with the prior consent of the rights owners) through its CLARCS (rapid clearing system) system. The CLA has reciprocal arrangements with similar organisations outside the United Kingdom.[36] PLS distributes income received from CLA amongst its publisher members.

27–32 **Educational users.** There are two licensing schemes for the purposes of section 35 of the 1988 Act which have been certified pursuant to section 143 of the Act, both of which were most recently amended as of April 1, 2003. The scheme operated by Educational Recording Agency Limited allows the recording of certain broadcasts and cable programmes by educational establishments for the educational purposes of such establishments in return for specified payments.

---

[27] For more information about the British Printing Industries Federation, see its website at *www.bpif.org.uk.*

[28] For more information about the Booksellers Association, see its website at *www.booksellers.org.uk.*

[29] For more information about British Actors Equity, see its website at *www.equity.org.uk.*

[30] For more information about the Authors' Licensing and Collecting Society, and for useful links, see its website at *www.alcs.co.uk.*

[31] For more information about the Copyright Licensing Agency, see its website at *www.cla.co.uk*

[32] See, further, as to the CLA, para. 28–52, below.

[33] For more information about Design and Artists' Copyright Society, see its website at *www.dacs.co.uk.*

[34] See, further as to DACS, para. 28–53, below.

[35] For more information about Publishers Licensing Society, see its website at *www.pls.org.uk*

[36] See, further, as to CLA, para. 28–52, below.

The scheme operated by Open University Educational Enterprises Limited allows the recording off air of Open University television programmes by schools and further and higher education establishments in return for specified fees.[37]

F. PUBLISHING AGREEMENTS

(i) Formalities of publishing arrangements

No formalities required. In the United Kingdom, contracts between authors and publishers are not, as in some countries, regulated by any special law, but their validity, construction and enforcement depend upon the ordinary rules of law governing contracts relating to dealings with personal property. Such contracts do not even have to be in writing, unless they are to effect an assignment of copyright or are to constitute an exclusive licence.[38] In practice, publishing arrangements vary from the most informal, for example an oral or an implied licence to publish a single article, to a formal, full-length publishing agreement. It is with the informal agreement, where many (or perhaps all) of the essential terms are left to implication, that it is often most difficult to determine the respective rights of the parties.[39] Some guidance may be found in the Publishers' Association Code of Practice (the great majority of book publishers in the United Kingdom are members of the Association) which seeks to establish general principles for its members to follow, rather than uniformity of contract.[40]

27–33

(ii) Formal agreements: common forms of publishing arrangements

Questions which may arise on the construction of assignments and licences are dealt with elsewhere.[41] This section is concerned with problems peculiar to the publishing industry. Agreements between authors and publishers fall commonly into two principal classes:

27–34

(a) outright disposals of copyright, whether for a fixed sum or on royalty terms; and

(b) licences for a period on royalty terms.

More rarely, such agreements may take the form of profit-sharing agreements.

Agreement for outright disposal of copyright. The consequences for the author of making an outright disposal of his copyright in consideration of receiving royalties are discussed elsewhere.[42] Where copyright is sold for a single payment, the matter is relatively simple, because the rights of the parties are concluded at once. If the copyright in the work is to belong to the publisher (whether upon payment of a fixed sum or royalties), an assignment in writing of the copyright by the author to the publisher should be made even though the work has been written to the order of the publisher, since the copyright will vest, in the first instance, in the author unless the author is an employee of the publisher.[43] If no assignment

27–35

---

[37] As to licensing schemes, see paras 29–78 *et seq.*, below. For the schemes themselves, see Vol.2 at B2.

[38] See CDPA 1988, ss.90(3) and 92(1) and paras 5–82 and 5–204, above, respectively.

[39] See, *e.g. Ray v Classic FM* [1998] F.S.R. 622.

[40] See para. 27–39, below.

[41] See para. 5–221, above.

[42] See para. 5–73 *et seq.*, above.

[43] CDPA 1988, s.11(1) and (2). As to what would amount to an assignment, see paras 5–82 and 5–107, above.

has been executed, however, the publisher may none the less have acquired certain equitable rights in the commissioned work.[44]

Under the 1988 Act, an assignment in writing of the copyright in a work not yet created will operate to vest the copyright in the work in the assignee as soon as the work comes into existence and without further assurance.[45] Consequently, if an author has made an agreement with one publisher to assign the copyright in his next book to that publisher, and subsequently, when about to write that book, he agrees to assign the copyright in it to a second publisher, the copyright will, upon the book being written, vest in the first publisher and not in the second publisher. Both agreements will operate as agreements only until the work is in fact created, so that their priority will depend merely upon the dates of the respective agreements and be unaffected by any question of notice.[46]

After an author has parted with the copyright in a book he is not at liberty to reproduce substantially the same matter in another work. In the absence of any special agreement, the second publication would be an infringement of the copyright in the first.[47]

27–36   **Agreements conferring licences.** In the case of a royalty agreement, the advisability (from the author's point of view) of securing that a licence only is granted to the publisher is discussed elsewhere.[48] If the royalty payable to the author is a certain proportion of the published or recommended retail price of the work, the agreement may specify a minimum price at which the book is to be published, but with the abolition of the Net Book Agreement, a publisher can no longer guarantee that the book will be sold in retail shops at no less than that price.[49] Whilst the Net Book Agreement was in force, it was common for author's royalties on copies sold in the "home" market to be calculated upon the retail price at which books were sold in shops. However, since the abolition of the Net Book Agreement, some publishers calculate royalties on the recommended retail price, while others calculate all royalties on the publisher's net receipts.

27–37   **Profit-sharing agreement.** Nowadays, profit-sharing is not a very common arrangement between author and publisher, although it has been suggested that it might be a suitable way of providing appropriate compensation to a very successful author. In such an agreement, generally the publisher takes the whole risk of the costs of publication,[50] and the net profits are divided between the parties. This may create a partnership, and the right to publish the work will be a partnership asset; whether an assignment or licence of the copyright will be granted will depend upon the express or implied terms of the agreement. A profit-sharing agreement between an author and a publisher may establish a fiduciary relation-

---

[44] See para. 5–174, above.

[45] CDPA 1988, s.91. As to assignment of future copyright, see para. 5–107, above.

[46] See, as to the position under an option to publish an author's next work, *Macdonald (E) Ltd v Eyles* [1921] 1 Ch. 631.

[47] *Colburn v Simms* (1843) 2 Hare 543; see, as to artistic works, CDPA 1988, s.64.

[48] See paras 5–75 and 5–77, above.

[49] The publishing industry has for some years been debating whether or not recommended retail prices ("RRPs") should continue to be shown on book covers. Whether the practice of stipulating RRPs could infringe competition law, given that in the vast majority of cases books will be sold in retail shops at the recommended retail prices specified by publishers, especially if printed on the book covers, is yet to be decided. However, there is considerable opposition amongst authors to the abolition of RRPs, mainly because it is feared that calculation of royalties would then have to move entirely to the "net receipts" basis and that authors would lose out. The removal of RRPs could also result in an increase in costs to independent booksellers, putting them at a further disadvantage compared with the large chains and supermarkets.

[50] *Reade v Bentley* (1858) 4 K. & J. 656 where an argument that the publisher was merely an agent was rejected because he had taken those risks.

ship between the parties, and the author will then be entitled to an account from the publisher.[51]

Whether a joint venture is terminable by notice. The author's right to determine the profit-sharing agreement will depend upon the express or implied terms of the agreement. If the agreement grants no more than a licence, then the author may be able to determine it on giving reasonable notice.[52]

27–38

G. MATTERS TO BE CONSIDERED IN DRAFTING PUBLISHING AGREEMENTS

(i) The Publishers' Association Code of Practice.

In 1982 the Publishers' Association first issued its Code of Practice to its members, who constitute the vast majority of book publishers in the United Kingdom. The Code, revised and reissued subsequently, is intended as a guide to good publishing practice which the Publishers' Association recommends to its members in their dealings with authors. Since it cannot deal with every possible situation that can arise in the course of dealings between publishers and authors (and as so much depends on the type of work involved, the market it is aimed at, the standing of the author, and so on), the Publishers' Association stress the importance of following the general principles of the Code. They add that it is impractical to expect "total uniformity of contract or practice". The purpose of the Code is to assist in developing and preserving a constructive and co-operative relationship between authors (and the agents and the representatives acting for them) and their publishers, this being vital to successful publishing.

27–39

The Code sets out 20 principles (which apply only to agreements whereby an author assigns or licenses an interest in the copyright of a work to a publisher) with explanatory comment by way of example (which is not intended to be an exhaustive explanation). These principles serve as guidance only, and do not have any contractual effect, except to the extent that publishers embody them in their contracts with authors. The principles are as follows (the commentary here is not taken verbatim from the Code):

(a) *The publishing contract must be clear, unambiguous and comprehensive, and must be honoured in both the letter and the spirit*

The contract should in particular define: the work by some means sufficient to identify it or, where it is not yet completed, by specifying the nature, agreed length and scope of the work; the rights granted; the time scale for delivery and publication; payments to the author; provisions for sub-licensing; responsibility for index, etc. and for clearing and paying for third-party copyright permissions; and termination and reversion of rights.

27–40

(b) *The author should retain ownership of the copyright, unless there are good reasons otherwise*

An exclusive licence is normally sufficient for a publisher, but with some works

---

[51] *Barry v Stevens* (1862) 31 Beav. 258. As to the creation and consequences of such a fiduciary relationship generally.

[52] See *Reade v Bentley*, (1858) 4 K. & J. 656, where notice was validly given at a time when the publisher had not incurred expenses on a new edition; approved in *Abrahams v Herbert Reiach Ltd* [1922] 1 K.B. 477 at 480. Contrast *Holland v Methuen & Co Ltd* [1928–35] Mac.C.C. 247: no right to determine on notice (otherwise than for breach of contract) where the agreement was to pay royalties rather than for profit-sharing.

(*e.g.* encyclopedias and reference works, certain types of academic works, publishers' compilations edited from many outside contributions, some translations and works particularly vulnerable to copyright infringement because of their extensive international sale) there may be good reason for the publisher to acquire the copyright.

(c) *The publisher should ensure that an author who is not professionally represented has a proper opportunity for explanation of the terms of the contract and the reasons for each provision*

All too often, contracts are submitted by publishers to authors without any explanation at all, and publishers do not tend to advise authors that it would be in their interests to seek expert advice. Many publishing agreements are therefore not subjected to any negotiation at all.

(d) *The contract must set out reasonable and precise terms for the reversion of rights*

This is intended to be the safeguard to the author who grants a licence to the publishers for the full period of copyright. Rights should revert to the author on a serious breach of contract by the publisher (which, if remediable, is not promptly remedied) or if the book is out of print for a substantial time. Particular rights might also revert if they have not been successfully exploited during a given period (*e.g.* certain translation rights) provided this does not affect other retained rights and provided the publisher has recouped any advance made to the author.

(e) *The publisher must give the author a proper opportunity to share in the success of the work*

For example, royalty rates might escalate after sales reach certain specified levels.

(f) *The publisher must handle manuscripts promptly, and keep the author informed of progress*

27–41   Manuscripts and synopses should be acknowledged as soon as received by the publisher, and authors should get at least a progress report within six weeks. It is important, however, for the publisher to know if the manuscript or synopsis is being simultaneously submitted to any other publisher.

(g) *The publisher must not cancel a contract without good and proper reason*

This includes the situation where the author fails to deliver on time or fails to deliver a work suitable for publication. In the latter case, the publisher must give the author sufficiently detailed reasons for rejection. If there is a change in the publisher's circumstances or policies such that they no longer wish to publish the work (however good it may be), the publisher must compensate the author.

(h) *The contract must set out the anticipated timetable for publication*

The contract should make clear the time scale within which the author undertakes to deliver the completed manuscript and within which the publisher undertakes to publish it.

(i) *The publisher should be willing to share precautions against legal risks not arising from carelessness by the author*

This refers primarily to libel risks, which can be minimised by having the book read for libel by a specialised lawyer or by libel insurance. In practice, a number of major publishers carry libel insurance that covers their authors as well as themselves, and also have books read for libel.

(j) *The publisher should consider assisting the author by funding additional costs involved in preparing the work for publication*

This would cover, *e.g.* cost of indexing and costs of third-party copyright permissions, which could be recouped out of royalties payable subsequently to the author.

(k) *The publisher must ensure that the author receives a regular and clear account of sales made and money due*

Accounts should be rendered at least annually, and more commonly twice yearly. **27–42** The contract should specify the accounting periods, and stipulate when royalty statements should be delivered and royalties paid. The publisher should pay the author on request the appropriate share of any substantial advances received from major sub-licensing agreements by the end of the month following the month of receipt (provided advances have been recouped and proper allowance made for returned stock).

(l) *The publisher must ensure that the author can clearly ascertain how any payments due from sub-licensing agreements will be calculated*

(m) *The publisher should keep the author informed of all important design, promotion, marketing and sub-licensing decisions*

There should be full consultation with the author on these matters, including, e.g. the jacket design, jacket text, promotional and review activities and sale of major subsidiary rights.

(n) *The integrity of the author's work should always be protected*

This is clearly important, given an author's moral rights. No significant alterations to the work should be made without the author's consent, particularly where the author has retained the copyright. The author who has retained ownership of the copyright is entitled also to be credited with the authorship of the work, and to retain the ownership of the manuscript.

(o) *The publisher should inform the author clearly about opportunities for amendment of the work in the course of production*

It is much more expensive to alter a work that has been typeset than one which has not yet been typeset. The contract should make clear whether proofs will be provided, whose responsibility it is to check them, and what scale of author's revisions to proofs will be acceptable.

(p) *It is essential that both the publisher and the author have a clear common understanding of the significance attaching to the option clause in a publishing contract*

27–43   The option for the publisher to acquire rights over the author's next work or works is important. It should be carefully negotiated and fully understood by both parties. It is not usually desirable for an option to cover more than one work.

(q) *The publisher should recognise that the remaindering of stock may effectively end the author's expectations of earnings*

Before remaindering a work, the publisher should inform the author and give him the opportunity to purchase all or part of the stock at the remainder price. Whether the author should receive a royalty on such copies is to be determined by the contract.

(r) *The publisher should endeavour to keep the author informed of changes in the ownership of the publishing rights and of any changes in the imprint under which a work appears*

(s) *The publisher should be willing to help the author and the author's estate in the administration of literary affairs*

By way of example, the publisher should agree to act as an expert witness on questions of the valuation of a literary estate.

(t) *Above all, the publisher must recognise the importance of co-operation with the author in an enterprise in which both are essential*

This relationship can only be fulfilled in an atmosphere of confidence, in which authors get the fullest possible credit for their work and achievements.

(ii) Minimum Terms Agreements

27–44   The Society of Authors and The Writers' Guild of Great Britain have negotiated Minimum Terms Agreements ("MTAs") with a number of book publishers, whereby the publishers agree that the terms and conditions which they offer to authors who are members of the Society or Guild will be no less favourable to the author than those specified in the MTA to which they are a party. In practice, all the MTAs vary a little, but they do have most of their provisions in common. The following is a summary of the main terms covered by recent MTAs.

27–45   **Term granted and review.** Traditionally, publishers expected to be granted a licence for the full period of copyright, subject to reversion of rights to the author in certain circumstances. This is reflected in some of the MTAs. However, one form of MTA provides that the duration of the licence granted to the publisher is a matter for negotiation (although in practice the licence is likely to be for the full period of copyright). Another MTA, however, provides for an initial term not exceeding 30 years from first publication of the book, with a right to initiate negotiations for (but not an absolute right to acquire) a further period.

    MTAs generally also provide for a review of the terms of the agreement on every tenth anniversary of the publication date. This review may be limited in some cases to terms relating to royalties or subsidiary rights. When the review has been initiated, the terms involved are to be considered in the light of comparable terms prevailing in the trade and altered to the extent that may be just and equitable. In the absence of agreement on what is just and equitable, the matter is to be referred to arbitration.

Consultation. MTAs may provide for the author to have a contractual right to all or any of the following: **27–46**
  (a) consultation on and approval of copy editing and the final number and type of illustrations (such approval not to be unreasonably withheld);
  (b) consultation on publication date;
  (c) sight of roughs or proofs of the jacket and of the jacket blurb;
  (d) no change in the title or text to be made by the publisher without the author's consent (except, in some cases, in order to conform with house style);
  (e) information, on request, as to the number of copies printed in the first and subsequent print-runs;
  (f) an opportunity to see and approve the edited typescript before it is sent to the printers;
  (g) two compete sets of the proofs of the work (one to be corrected and returned to the publisher within a specified period);
  (h) to make corrections to the proofs up to 15 per cent of the cost of composition.

Royalties. MTAs vary, and the following is a guide, but is regarded as reason- **27–47**
ably typical. Different considerations may apply according to the nature of the book (for example, the royalty rates will be lower for heavily illustrated works and for children's books).

(a) *The advance*

This is usually not less than 65 per cent of the author's estimated receipts from **27–48**
the sale of the projected first printing if the work is to be published by the publisher only in hardback or only in paperback, or 55 per cent if it is to be published by the publisher both in hardback and in paperback.

If the work is commissioned by the publisher, then the advance is usually payable as to one third on signature of contract; one third on delivery of final and revised typescript; and one third within one year of delivery or on publication, whichever is the sooner.

If the work is not commissioned, the advance is usually paid half on signature of contract and the other half within one year of signature of contract or on publication, whichever is the sooner.

(b) *Hardback royalties*

The basic scale of royalties may be as follows, but there may be situations where **27–49**
other rates of royalty will apply:
  Home market.
      On the first 2,500 copies: 10 per cent of published price
      On the next 2,500 copies: 12.5 per cent of published price
      On all further copies sold: 15 per cent of published price
  Export market.
      On the first 2,500 copies: 10 per cent of price received
      On the next 2.500 copies: 12.5 per cent of price received
      On all further copies sold: 15 per cent of price received

(c) *Paperback royalties*

27–50   A typical royalty scale is as follows:
> **Home market.**
> > On the first 40,000 copies: 7.5 per cent of published price
> > On all further copies sold: 10 per cent of published price
>
> **Export market.**
> > On the first 50,000 copies: 6 per cent of published price
> > On all further copies sold: 8 per cent of published price

(d) *United States rights*

27–51   If the publisher arranges publication of an American edition on a royalty basis, the publisher retains a maximum of 15 per cent of the proceeds, inclusive of any sub-agent's commission.

(e) *Translation rights*

27–52   The publisher retains not more than 20 per cent of the proceeds from any foreign language edition, inclusive of any sub-agent's commission.

(f) *Subsidiary rights*

27–53   Receipts from sale or licensing of some of the major subsidiary rights are often divided as follows:

	Author	Publisher
First Serial	90 per cent	10 per cent
Second Serial	75 per cent	25 per cent
Merchandising	80 per cent	20 per cent
TV and radio readings	75 per cent	25 per cent

27–54   **General matters.** MTAs also deal with issues such as payment of copyright fees for agreed illustrations, sharing the cost of an index, the number of free copies of each edition that the author should receive from the publisher, requirements as to rendering statements of account, and the situations in which rights will revert to the author (such as failure by the publisher to comply with the terms of the contract, liquidation or receivership of the publisher, the work being out of print, and in some cases, where annual sales of the work fall below specified levels).

H. TERMS FOUND IN PUBLISHING AGREEMENTS

(i) Effect of submission of manuscript

27–55   The simplest form of contract is where a manuscript is sent to a publisher without anything being said about terms. A non-exclusive licence may be made orally or implied by conduct from the circumstances of the case. For example, if a person writes a letter to the editor of a newspaper, there is an implied licence to publish the letter in the absence of any express indication to the contrary (*e.g.* where the letter is marked "Not for Publication"). Similarly, if an author submits an article to the editor of a journal or periodical, the submission of the manuscript may by custom, or necessary implication, be treated as an offer of a licence to publish in consideration of payment on the usual terms for that publication. Such an offer can at once be accepted by the editor or publisher of that journal or periodical without further communication with the author.[53]

On the other hand, if an author submits the typescript of a book to a publisher without anything more, then it will probably amount to no more than an offer to enter into negotiations for a publishing contract, and would not constitute an offer capable of immediate acceptance so as to form a binding contract. Accordingly, in that situation, the publisher would not be entitled simply to accept the book and publish it without reaching agreement with the author on terms. What, short of actual publication, amounts to an acceptance of an author's manuscript will depend upon the circumstances of the case. In *Malcolm v Chancellor, Masters and Scholars of the University of Oxford*,[54] it was held that an oral agreement had been reached on the telephone between the author and the publisher for the publication of the book at a fair royalty. The Court of Appeal held that the fact that the parties had not agreed on matters such as the print run, the price of the book or the format for publication did not mean that no contract existed. The Court considered, after receiving expert evidence on the plaintiff's behalf that was not contradicted, that these matters would either be agreed later between the parties or would be decided by the publishers.[55] If, however, before publication, there are detailed discussions about the form of publication and these never come to fruition, no licence to publish will be implied.[56] In *Myers v Macmillan Press Ltd*[57] the plaintiff author sued for failure to publish. There was no written contract between the parties for the work in question, but the defendant, having considered a specimen part of the work, had instructed the plaintiff to "go ahead" with the work. By the date of the trial the defendant had conceded that there was a contract: the parties had previously entered into two written contracts for other books and it was accepted by both parties at trial that the same terms would govern the work in question.

(ii) Obligations as to manuscript

In the absence of agreement to the contrary, where a manuscript submitted to a publisher is lost or destroyed through his negligence, or that of his employees, the author may recover its value.[58] Once there is an agreement to publish, whether ownership of the manuscript itself passes to the publisher depends on the terms of any contract between the publisher and the author, but the grant of a licence to publish alone does not confer ownership of the manuscript upon the publisher. Whether an author who is willing to leave his manuscript in the hands of the publisher for a substantial period after its initial publication will, where the publishing agreement is silent as to its ownership, be treated as abandoning it, is an open question.[59] In practice, a book publishing agreement will often stipulate whether or not the manuscript is to be returned to the author when no longer required for production purposes. In addition, the agreement will usually provide

27–56

---

[53] As to such a trade custom, see *Hall-Brown v Iliffe & Sons* [1928–35] Mac.C.C. 88 (where the custom was found not to apply, as the parties were negotiating terms).

[54] [1994] E.M.L.R. 17.

[55] The decision relies on the assumption underlying *Abrahams v Herbert Reiach Ltd*, [1922] 1. K.B. 477, that an agreement between a publisher and an author for the publication of a book for a stated consideration and no more is a complete and enforceable contract. For commentary on *Malcolm* see *Nyman* in [1991] 3 Ent.L.R.84.

[56] *Hall-Brown v Iliffe & Sons Ltd* [1928-35] Mac. C.C. 88.

[57] Unreported, March 3, 1998.

[58] *Stone v Long* [1901–04] Mac.C.C. 66. But contrast *Howard v Harris* (1884) Cababé & Ellis 253 in which the defendant was held to owe no duty of any sort to the plaintiff to preserve the manuscript.

[59] In *Moorhouse v Angus & Robertson (No.1) Pty* [1981] 1 N.S.W.L.R. 700, the Court of Appeal of New Zealand reversed a finding of abandonment at first instance ([1980] F.S.R. 231), leaving the

expressly that the publisher is not liable to the author for any loss of or damage to the manuscript (and any accompanying materials) while in the possession of the publishers, and authors should keep copies of everything that they submit to a publisher.

27–57 **Whether obligation to publish.** Where the copyright in a work is sold outright, the publisher is under no obligation to publish, unless there is an express or implied term to that effect in the agreement.[60] However, if the author is tied to the publisher for a period of time or a number of works, the absence of an obligation to publish may be an indication that the agreement is in restraint of trade or may indicate such inequality of bargaining power as to render the agreement unenforceable.[61] But where there is an agreement to publish, without stating any date of publication, an undertaking to publish within a reasonable time will be implied.[62] If publication is delayed beyond that period, the author is entitled to damages resulting from that delay and possibly also to damages for loss of publicity or opportunity to enhance his reputation.[63] In *Moorhead v Paul Brennan*[64] the author granted the publisher an exclusive world-wide publishing contract for her book for the legal term of copyright. The publisher had an obligation to publish the work within a stated time but had no resources to publish abroad. It was held that although no term was to be implied into the contract that the publisher should himself publish abroad, a term was to be implied that the publisher would not impede or obstruct opportunities to receive royalties from persons willing to publish under licence abroad. The publisher was in breach by refusing to grant a licence to the only likely sub-publisher abroad except on unreasonable terms.

(iii) Meaning of "edition"

27–58 In current publishing practice, the word "edition" is used to denote all the copies of a work that are published in exactly the same form, both as to the content and the medium of publication. Copies of a work are frequently issued in batches according to demand, and copies are frequently supplied in small quantities to meet specific orders from members of the general public. Where a work is reprinted, with no alterations, the reprint is sometimes referred to as a new "impression". Where, however, any substantive change is made, *e.g.* in updating a work or adding a new preface, this is now regarded as a new "edition".[65]

27–59 **The number of copies.** Where the agreement is for the exclusive publication of a specified number of copies, that number only can be printed and sold, and, until

---

question of law open. See also *Copyright*, No.5, May 1966, p.144; as to letters, see para. 5–220, above.

[60] The absence of such an express or implied term means that the publisher need not publish and the author may have no remedy. However, the court would clearly wish to imply such a term, to avoid an unreasonable result: contrast *Nichols v The Amalgamated Press* [1905–10] Mac.C.C. 166 with *Hole v Bradbury* (1897) 12 Ch. D. 886 at 895.

[61] *AS Schroeder Music Publishing Co Ltd v Macaulay* [1974] W.L.R. 1308; [1974] 3 All E.R. 616; *Clifford Davis Management Ltd v WEA Records Ltd* [1975] 1 All E.R. 237. For a full discussion of the restraint of trade doctrine see para. 29–304 *et seq.*, below.

[62] *Crane v C Arthur Pearson Ltd* [1936–45] Mac.C.C. 125; *Barrow v Chappell & Co Ltd* [1976] R.P.C. 355.

[63] *Crane v C Arthur Pearson Ltd* [1936–45] Mac.C.C. 125; *Barrow v Chappell & Co Ltd* [1976] R.P.C. 355; and *Abrahams v Herbert Reiach Ltd* [1922] 1 K.B. 477.

[64] [1991] 20 I.P.R. 161 (Sup Ct of NSW).

[65] It is unlikely that *Reade v Bentley* (1858) 4 K. & J. 656, where the meaning of "edition" was extensively discussed, has any application today. In another old case, *Blackwood v Brewster* [1860] 23 Sess.Cas. (2nd Ser.) 142, it was held that an editor, who was to be paid for preparation of every new edition of a work, was not entitled to superintend, or to claim payment for, reprinting the work to replace copies destroyed by fire. The copies reprinted did not form a new edition, but replaced the part of the edition destroyed.

their sale, the author cannot revoke the authority given to the publishers, or himself publish the work.[66] A term that the publisher shall publish a second edition, if demanded by the public, and print as many copies as he can sell, gives the publisher the right, when such demand arises, to publish and sell as many copies as can properly be considered to belong to that edition, and to prevent the author, or any other person, from publishing until such copies have been sold. If the agreement is silent as to the number of copies to be published, the publisher must publish as many as is reasonable in all the circumstances.[67]

Number of editions. When the number of editions or copies to be published is not specified, the publisher is not bound to publish more than one edition. The further rights of the parties depend upon the provisions, express or implied, of the contract. In principle, where no term of the contract is specified, the parties may determine the agreement upon giving reasonable notice.[68]   **27–60**

(iv) The meaning of "volume form"

A publishing agreement will traditionally grant to the publisher the right to publish the work in "volume form". The expression "volume form" is generally understood in the book publishing industry to connote publication in the form of a printed book. It would not include publication in any electronic format. The expression "volume form" also distinguishes between publication of a work as a whole and publication by instalments in "serial form", so that the exclusive right to publish in volume form would be infringed by publication of substantially the whole of the work in a single issue of a magazine.[69] A grant of the exclusive right to produce, print, publish and sell a work in "volume" form has been held to give the grantee sufficient title to sue for infringement where the defendant merely had in his possession an infringing copy of a proof of the book, and had offered it for sale to a newspaper: the copies were copies of the work in volume form.[70]   **27–61**

(v) "Electronic" form

Many publishers have for a number of years been careful to acquire (where the authors or their agents would agree) electronic rights alongside traditional print publication rights, even if they did not have any immediate intention of publishing in an electronic form. Where the contract contains no express clause dealing with publication in this form, it will be a question of construction whether the rights granted extend this far.[71] Clearly, and as cases in the United States have shown,[72] old-style contracts which merely grant rights limited, for example, to publication "in book form" may well not extend to publication in electronic form.   **27–62**

---

[66] He may be entitled to publish a second edition: see *Warne v Routledge* (1874) L.R. 1 8 Eq. 497.

[67] *Abrahams v Herbert Reiach Ltd*, n.64; and see *Malcolm v Chancellor, Masters & Scholars of the University of Oxford* [1994] E.M.L.R., 17, above, where failure to specify the number of copies to be printed did not prevent there being a binding contract to publish the work.

[68] See, *e.g. Reade v Bentley*, n.66; contrast with *Holland v Methuen & Co Ltd*, [1928-35] Mac.C.C. 247, where there was no right to determine until the publisher was in breach of contract.

[69] *Jonathan Cape Ltd v Consolidated Press Ltd* [1954] 1 W.L.R. 1313; [1954] 3 All E.R. 253.

[70] *Michael O'Mara Books Ltd v Express Newspapers plc* [1999] F.S.R. 49.

[71] See para.5–00 as to construction of licences in the face of new technologies.

[72] See, e.g. *Random House Inc v Rosetta Books* (July 11, 2001,unreported), where "the right to print, publish and sell the work[s] in book form" was held not to include the right to publish the books in electronic form; *Tasini v New York Times* (June 25, 2001, unreported) where work of freelancers which was originally produced for printed publications was infringed by being included in various electronic databases. For a review of the United States cases affecting this issue, see Radcliffe, "New Media Convergence: Acquiring Rights to Existing Works for the Internet under U.S. Law" [2001] E.I.P.R. 172.

(vi) Price and style of publication

27–63   The contract may provide for the manner and style of the publication and the price at which it is to be issued to the public, but if the price at which the work is to be sold is not fixed by agreement, or otherwise arranged by the author and publisher, the publisher is the proper person to fix it.[73] At the same time, he would not be permitted to fix upon a style, or sell at a price, which would be clearly injurious either to the literary reputation or the pecuniary interests of the author without his consent.

27–64   **Right to alter.** Whether a publisher has the right to alter an author's work will depend upon whether the agreement amounts to an assignment or a licence, the terms of that assignment or licence, and on the extent to which the author's moral right of integrity is affected, or has been waived. These are points discussed elsewhere.[74] Subject to the terms of the contract, the writer of a signed article is entitled to complain of alterations in the text made without his consent.[75] On the other hand, if an author is employed to write a work of a particular description, and does so, the employer may have no right to complain if the result is unsatisfactory where he has agreed to accept the product of the skill and taste of the author.[76]

(vii) Whether benefit assignable.

27–65   A publishing contract is usually regarded as a personal contract, and thus unassignable. The point is discussed elsewhere.[77]

(viii) Stock in hand

27–66   It is a common situation that, after the end of the term of a publishing agreement, a publisher has a remaining stock of the work lawfully made during the term. The position under the older cases was that since copies printed during the term of the agreement would not have been infringing copies, they could be sold without infringing copyright, although the author might have had a remedy in breach of contract if excessive printing had taken place towards the end of the term of the agreement with a view to stockpiling. Today, the sale of such copies will almost certainly amount to an issue of copies to the public within the meaning of section 18 of the 1988 Act,[78] and thus will be an infringement, unless licensed. Whether such an act is licensed will depend upon the terms, express or implied, of the contract.

(ix) Non-compete clause

27–67   Publishing contracts frequently contain a clause stipulating that the author should not write or have published a work that, in the publisher's opinion, would compete with or affect prejudicially the sales of the work that is the subject of the

---

[73] *Benning v Dove* (1831) 5 C. & P. 427; and see *Abrahams v Herbert Reiach Ltd*, [1922] 1 K.B. 477, and also *Malcolm v Chancellor, Masters and Scholars of the University of Oxford* [1994] E.M.L.R.17, where it was held that the failure to agree upon the format of publication (*i.e.* hardback or paperback, or both) and/or the price at which the book would be published did not, of itself, prevent the existence of a binding contract to publish the work.
[74] See paras 5–202 and 5–224, above, but see also *Barrow v Chappell & Co Ltd*, [1976] R.P.C. 355.
[75] *Joseph v National Magazine Co Ltd* [1959] Ch.14.
[76] *Ellis v British Filmcraft Productions Ltd* [1928–35] Mac.C.C. 51.
[77] See para. 5–223, above.
[78] See para. 7–76, above.

contract. Assuming that no question of restraint of trade arises,[79] such clauses will usually be enforced by way of injunction.[80] Although they are arguably not appropriate in a contract for a novel, they are today a standard clause, inserted by the publisher in its standard form of publishing contract, and intended solely for the benefit of the publisher. These clauses are seldom questioned by the author (unless the author is represented by a literary agent or lawyer) and are therefore almost invariably not specifically negotiated. What is at issue, of course, is whether the author is entitled to write a new but competing work, not whether the author is entitled to write a work which reproduces a substantial part of the work which is subject to the publishing contract, this being a breach of the exclusive rights granted to the publisher.

I. CONSEQUENCES OF BREACH OF A PUBLISHING AGREEMENT

(i) Failure to supply the work

Specific performance. The court will not order specific performance of an agreement to create a work. Such an agreement is a contract to provide personal services and there would be no means of enforcing such an order.[81] However, the court can order specific performance of an agreement to assign copyright, or can order an author to deliver a completed manuscript to the publisher.[82]

27–68

If the author undertakes to write a work and dies before completing it, his executors or administrators will usually be discharged from the contract, for the undertaking was merely personal in its nature, and has become impossible to perform[83] but it may be that if the author has assigned the copyright in the work, the copyright in any completed part may pass to the publisher, depending on the wording of the contract.

Damages. Problems arise where the agreement does not make express provision for failure to deliver the manuscript. In practice, publishing agreements will nowadays provide that if the author fails to supply the work by the agreed date, or by any mutually agreed subsequent date, the publisher will have the right to terminate the contract and obtain repayment of any advance previously paid to the author. It is sometimes also a condition that the author will not arrange for the publication of the work in question by any other publisher, without first offering it to the original publisher upon the terms set out in the original publishing contract. If, however, the author delivers part, but not all, of the work, the agreement will usually give the publisher the express right to engage someone else to complete the work, and to pay the cost of doing so out of monies otherwise payable to the author under the agreement.

27–69

---

[79] See para. 29–304, below.

[80] See, *e.g. Psychology Press Ltd v Flanagan* (June 19, 2002, unreported). The public policy exemplified in the law of contract whereby the court regularly enforces provisions for the restriction of unfair competition (provided always that they are reasonable and proportionate) outweighed any freedom of expression considerations under Art.10 of the European Convention on Human Rights. It is not clear whether it was argued on behalf of the defendants that the "competing works" clause of the contract was an unjustifiable restraint of trade, on the basis that it might unfairly restrict the extent to which the author could earn a living from writing books on her specialist subject.

[81] *Clarke v Price* (1819) Wils. 157; see *Page One Records Ltd v Britton* [1968] 1 W.L.R. 157 where an injunction was refused when it would have amounted to a decree of specific performance.

[82] *Thombleson v Black* (1837) 1 Jur. 198; and see *Macdonald (E) Ltd v Eyles* [1921] 1 Ch. 631 at 638, where Peterson J. construed the agreement as a contract to sell the products of the author's labour or industry, and granted an injunction requiring the author to deliver the completed manuscript to the publisher and restraining her from disposing of the work in breach of the agreement; see also *Transatlantic Records Ltd v Bulltown Ltd* [1980] CA transcript 164.

[83] *Marshall v Broadhurst* (1831) 1 Tyrwh. 348 at 350.

If the author fails or refuses to supply the manuscript, in breach of contract, the publisher will have a remedy in damages.[84] Where the author fails to supply the manuscript, the publisher can recover as damages any outlay made in reliance on the contract and the estimated loss of profit, or any other consequential loss.[85]

(ii) Failure to publish a work

27–70 **Specific performance.** While a publishing agreement remains completely unperformed, it may be impracticable for the court to order specific performance by the publisher of his agreement to publish, although where the order could be enforced without practical difficulty, such an order may be made. This may depend upon how far the exact terms of publication have been agreed. The court cannot order specific performance of an agreement to publish where it would require supervision of the editing process.[86] In *Malcolm v Chancellor, Masters and Scholars of the University of Oxford*,[87] where the judge at first instance would not have ordered specific performance of the contract (had he found one to exist, which he did not), the Court of Appeal (which, by a majority, held that a contract did exist) approved the judge's decision on this point, and ordered an inquiry as to damages. Whether it would ever be in an author's interest to obtain an order for specific performance of a contract to publish his work, is a moot point. If the parties have fallen out to the extent that the author has had to litigate in order to establish that the publisher is in breach of a contract to publish, it may not be sensible for the author to have that publisher publish his work (in particular, presumably, under the terms of an exclusive licence).

27–71 **Damages.** Damages may be awarded against publishers in respect of delay in publication, amounting to a breach of contract, a failure to publish by an agreed date or within a reasonable time thereafter[88] or a refusal to publish amounting to a repudiatory breach of contract. Damages for failure to publish by an agreed date or a refusal to publish at all may be based upon an estimate of what the plaintiff would have got if the defendant had carried out its bargain.[89] In *Joseph v National Magazine Co Ltd*,[90] damages were assessed on the loss to the plaintiff as an expert in jade of the enhancement of his reputation which would have resulted from the publication. In *Malcolm v Chancellor, Masters and Scholars of the University of Oxford*, an inquiry as to damages was ordered both to recompense the author for loss of the opportunity for him to enhance his reputation by securing the imprimatur of the Oxford University Press on his work[91] and to compensate the author for loss of royalties. An author may also claim remuneration on a *quantum*

---

[84] *Gale v Leckie* (1817) 2 Stark. N.P. 107.

[85] See general principles formulated in *Anglia TV v Reed* [1972] 1 Q.B. 60. For an example of such a claim, see *Times Newspapers Ltd v George Weidenfeld & Nicholson Ltd* (March 28, 2001, unreported).

[86] *See Joseph v National Magazine Co Ltd* [1959] Ch.14, above, in which specific performance was refused, as editing of the article was necessary, distinguishing *Barrow v Chappell & Co Ltd*, [1976] R.P.C. 355 (decided in 1951) where the score of the musical work was ready for publication and the judge found that the publisher was not entitled to edit it without the composer's consent, and the publisher had offered an undertaking to publish if found to be bound by the agreement.

[87] [1994] E.M.L.R. 17.

[88] See *White v Constable & Co* [1901–04] Mac.C.C. 2.

[89] See *Abrahams v Herbert Reiach Ltd*, [1922] 1 K.B. 477.

[90] See [1959] Ch.14. See also *Tedesco v Bosa* (1993) 10 O.R. (3d) 799, noted at [1993] 3 Ent.L.R. 58 (Ontario Ct Gen Div).

[91] On the inquiry as to damages ordered by the Court of Appeal, a substantial sum was awarded under this head. The findings are reported at *www.akme.btinternet.co.uk*. The entire history of the litigation is the subject of Andrew Malcolm's book *The Remedy* (AKME Publications).

meruit basis for work done on a publication which is abandoned,[92] as an alternative to damages for loss of royalties.

Where the time of publication, number of copies and price and form of the book are left to the discretion of the publisher, the damages for failure to publish are based on a reasonable estimate of the amount that the author would have earned if the publisher had complied with his contract to publish. This will require consideration of everything likely to affect the amount of the profit, such as the nature and popularity of the subject matter, the reputation of the author, the cost of producing a book on that subject, the price of such a book, the business capacity of the publishers and the chances of earning profits by sales of the book.[93] It will involve examining the publishing history of books deemed to be comparable to the one in suit and estimating how many copies would have been sold in each format, in each applicable language, at what prices and at what times. The courts are able to consider the conflicting evidence adduced by each party and form their own view, which they did in *Malcolm*[94] and in *Myers v Macmillan Press Ltd.*[95] In *Myers*, it was accepted by both parties that if the plaintiff succeeded on liability, he could elect between two alternative bases for assessing damages. The first is the loss of profits which, on the court's assessment, he would have made had the defendant performed its obligations under the publishing agreement. The second basis is a *quantum meruit*. The judge said that the second basis is less satisfactory, as it involves carrying out an exercise which does not reflect what happens in practice, *i.e.* assessing what would have been a reasonable number of hours for the plaintiff to have spent in writing the work and what would have been a reasonable hourly rate to pay for that work. In the event, the first basis of assessment would clearly have resulted in a higher award, and so damages for loss of profits were awarded. If the author has incurred specific expenses in connection with the agreement, such as preparing illustrations for the text, these can be claimed as special damages.[96] Where a publishing agreement requires the defendant to publish the first edition of the claimant's book, and the agreement also contemplates that further editions will be published, the failure by the defendant to publish the first edition of the book will entitle the claimant to damages both for failure to publish the first edition and also for the loss of the chance to establish the title, by the success of the first edition, which would lead to repeat editions in the future, and hence generate royalties on those further editions.[97] Where the breach by the publisher is otherwise than a failure to publish, the measure of damages will be the loss sustained by the author by reason of the publisher's breach.

Account of profits. In limited circumstances an account of profits can be awarded as a remedy for breach of contract.[98] **27–72**

Damages for breach of obligation to "use all reasonable endeavours" to obtain right of first negotiation. An obligation to use all reasonable endeavours to obtain a right of first negotiation from any assignee of the purchaser for the author to do specified work, in good faith, may be legally binding[99]. Such an obligation, if clear and certain, does not become any less clear or certain because of the wide range of routes by which the obligation can be discharged. **27–73**

---

[92] *Planché v Colburn* (1831) 8 Bing. 14.
[93] *Abrahams v Herbert Reiach Ltd,* [1922] 1 K.B. 477 .
[94] *Malcolm v Chancellor, Masters and Scholars of the University of Oxford*, [1994] E.M.L.R. 17.
[95] Unreported, March 3, 1988.
[96] As in *Joseph v National Magazine Co Ltd*, [1959] Ch.14.
[97] *Thornton v Tulett* [2000] EWCA unreported.
[98] *Attorney-General v Blake* [2001] 1 A.C. 268.
[99] *Lambert v HTV Cymru (Wales) Ltd* [1998] FSR 874.

J. PARTICULAR PROBLEMS OR POINTS WHICH CONFRONT THE PUBLISHING INDUSTRY

27–74   **Territorial rights.** The question of territorial rights is one that particularly concerns United Kingdom book publishers, because English language books are read in many countries around the world, and exclusivity of publishing rights is an essential factor in the economics of publishing any particular work. In relation to works which are suitable for sale in the English language both in the United Kingdom and in the United States of America, rights are generally shared between United Kingdom and American publishers as follows: the United Kingdom publisher will have the exclusive rights to publish in the United Kingdom and the Republic of Ireland, Australia, New Zealand, South Africa, the Middle East and Commonwealth countries (other than Canada); the American publisher will have the exclusive right to publish in the United States, its territories and dependencies, Canada and the Philippines; the rest of the world is treated as an "open market", where both the United Kingdom publisher and the American publisher have the non-exclusive right to publish. It is particularly important to note that, in general, the countries of the EEA, other than the United Kingdom and the Republic of Ireland, form part of the "open market", and so copies of a work placed on sale in any of those countries by or with the consent of the copyright owner can be imported into the United Kingdom, against the wishes of the United Kingdom publisher who has exclusive rights for the United Kingdom territory. American editions of books tend to be significantly cheaper than the corresponding United Kingdom editions[1] and can therefore undercut the corresponding United Kingdom editions if they can find their way into the United Kingdom market. United Kingdom publishers could avoid this potential problem if they were able to secure exclusive publishing rights throughout the EEA but this does not seem to happen in practice.

A fairly recent development is the emergence of bookshops operating via the Internet. This offers the opportunity to anyone in the world to order books (generally American editions) via the Internet at discounted prices, which are substantially lower than those applying, for example, in the United Kingdom. However, if an internet-based bookshop were to sell copies of an American edition to someone in the United Kingdom, in circumstances where a United Kingdom publisher has exclusive rights to publish that work in the United Kingdom, then this may amount to infringement of copyright,[2] depending on where the sale takes place and who is the importer. A comprehensive Rights Database is currently being developed by Book Data Limited, which aims to identify clearly which United Kingdom editions have an exclusive right to be sold in the United Kingdom, so that distributors and online booksellers can readily distinguish between these and potentially infringing American editions. This is supported by the Publishers' Association representing the United Kingdom book publishers.

27–75   **Territory: are worldwide rights enough?** With satellite broadcasting now commonplace and with the establishment of a base on the moon becoming a real possibility, the question arises whether it is still sufficient for publishers and other users of copyright material to acquire rights on no more than a worldwide basis. For many years the American film and television industries have routinely acquired

---

[1] This may in part be explained by the fact that the larger American territory enables American publishers to print larger quantities and hence have lower unit costs, although this advantage of the American publishers can be affected by the exchange rate between the US dollar, sterling and the euro.

[2] See CDPA 1988, ss.18(1), (2), 22, 23.

rights "throughout the universe". Precisely what the legal effect of this is, bearing in mind that rights of copyright do not at present extend beyond the earth, may be open to debate, but such a grant should at least be binding as a matter of contract as between the grantor and the grantee, if not as against third parties. Perhaps it is now also time for United Kingdom publishers (particularly electronic publishers) to acquire rights in copyright works on a universe-wide basis.

Site licensing of journals. The publishing of journals electronically and making them available to educational establishments throughout the United Kingdom on the basis of a site licence represents a major step forward in educational publishing. Previously, site licensing had been adopted on an individual basis between higher education institutions ("HEIs") and publishers, but never before on a national basis. Trials of site licensing on a national basis are currently being carried out by a few publishers, with government assistance. The initial scheme (known as the Higher Education Funding Councils United Kingdom Pilot Site Licence Initiative ("PSLI")), ran from 1995 to 1997, aiming to offer greater access to research and teaching materials through a combination of reduced prices and the lifting of restrictions on the use of materials (such as photocopying for course packs). The scheme also sought to assess different site licence models (as each of the publishers involved used a slightly different arrangement) and whether this is a way forward for the future, and also to evaluate the use of different media (*e.g.* paper and electronic). The PSLI was followed by the United Kingdom National Electronic Site Licence Initiative ("NESLI"), for a period of three years from January 1, 1999. In contrast with the PSLI, the NESLI was run by a managing agent, which carried out negotiations with publishers, managed delivery of the electronic material and oversaw the day-to-day operation of the programme. NESLI has now been followed by NESLi2, for the period 2003–2006, building on the experience of the earlier initiatives.[3]

27–76

The electronic distribution of journals via a site licence arrangement raises a number of important copyright issues. First, it involves the digitisation of the works in question. The publisher therefore has to ensure that it owns the necessary right to do this, or to authorise others to do so, in relation to all of the material in question before it proceeds, since digitisation without consent of the copyright owner could amount to infringement. The publisher will also want to ensure that the site licence specifies very particularly the limitations of the rights granted to the educational establishments that are being licensed and the users who are entitled to use the material pursuant to the site licence. The site licence should also specify what rights are to be granted to print any of the material that is made available electronically. The site licence should also contain provisions for the protection of the intellectual property in the material, particularly given that the digitisation and electronic communication of the material renders it vulnerable to piracy. The site licence may authorise some people to access the material off-site, *e.g.* at home, and this has particular implications for the security of the intellectual property. This raises a question for academic institutions to consider whether the abuse of electronically available copyright material should, in the case of a student, lead to expulsion from the course, and in the case of a member of staff, to dismissal.

Electronic publishing generally. The issues currently being tackled in relation to the site licensing of electronically published journals are also being dealt with in relation to the digitisation of other works required by libraries in academic

27–77

---

[3] For up-to-date information on various licensing initiatives, see the website of the Association of Learned and Professional Society Publishers: *www.alpsp.org*

institutions. Publishers are increasingly being met with requests for the right to digitise all or parts of various works. This involves the publishers in checking that they either have the rights or can clear the necessary rights. It also involves consideration of how the digitisation takes place and by whom it is carried out. For example, an increasing number of "photocopiers" are now, in fact, digital copiers, although this may not be widely realised by rights owners. It is assumed that these "digital copiers" are generally being used to prepare materials for the production of printed materials, although they could be used as a delivery mechanism for on-screen display. The way in which these copiers work does not, however, constitute true "digitisation", and would not allow the flexibility of usage that true digitisation can afford.

The making available of materials in digital form raises issues as to how the material should be paid for. This in turn depends on a number of elements, including the degree of risk to the publisher or other rights owner in terms of protection of intellectual property and possible loss of direct sales which might otherwise have been made.

27–78   In March 1998 it was announced that agreement had been reached between the Joint Information Systems Committee of the United Kingdom Higher Education Funding Councils and the Publishers Association, making it possible for HEIs to have ready access to digital versions of academic publications. This involves the creation of a model licence to enable HEIs to disseminate digital versions of publications within agreed sites; agreement on the charging formula to be applied by publishers when HEIs digitise existing printed material; and publishing guidelines on what is meant by the concept of "fair dealing" in a digital environment. The Copyright Licensing Agency ("CLA") offers a licence to HEIs to digitise extracts from books, journals and periodicals and to make them available to students and staff over a network. Charges are set by the rightsholders, either on a per-student basis (particularly suitable for textbooks) or on a flat-fee basis of a fee per page multiplied by the number of pages. A further and complementary development is the HERON scheme. HERON offers a national service to the UK academic community for copyright clearance, digitisation and delivery of book extracts and journal articles. In addition, HERON has also developed a resource bank of digitised materials for rapid reuse (subject to copyright permissions). HERON's status as a designated Trusted Repository means that it is entitled to hold copies of CLA-cleared digitised texts. These texts form the basis of HERON's resource bank of archived pre-digitised material. The remaining content comprises copies of material requested through HERON, where the rightsholder has given permission for a master copy to be stored. The HERON charging structure has a number of elements:

> *Institutional Subscription*: Each institution pays an annual subscription fee to HERON in order to use the service.
>
> *Copyright clearance*: This payment is dictated by the rightsholder. The majority of requests are calculated on a 'per-student-per-page' basis for use by students on a specific course. Only those students on the specified course can be directed to the material (although other students may use the material should they come across it during their own private study or research. 5p is the most common rate but charges can still vary quite a lot. Some requests (especially for journal articles) are charged on a flat-fee basis which allows any student registered at the institution to be directed to the material.
>
> *Supply fee*: This fee will vary depending on whether or not the document is a resupply from HERON's existing archive or a new document, requiring digitisation.

Completion fee: HERON adds a completion charge on extracts for carrying out this work and to cover the development of the HERON service.

Privacy and Confidentiality Publishers, particularly of magazines and newspapers, face difficult decisions over whether to publish certain material in the light of developments in the law of confidentiality, which are discussed in more detail elsewhere.[4]

27–79

Scientific publications: free for all. In July 2004 the House of Commons Select Committee on Science and Technology published its report "Scientific Publications: free for all?". The Committee's aim was to: examine the provision of scientific journals to the academic community and wider public; to establish whether the market for scientific publications was working well; how trends in journal pricing affected libraries and other users; the impact that new publishing trends would have on the scientific process; and what provisions were in place to support a secure national archive. This investigation took place in the context of intense scrutiny of the scientific, technical and medical ("STM") publishing industry. Whilst the volume of research output and the price of scientific journals has been steadily increasing, library budgets have seen funding decreases. As a consequence, the ability of libraries to purchase journals has come under severe pressure.

27–79A

Technology has made possible a fundamental change to the way scientific articles are published. By removing some of the non-editorial overheads associated with print publications, digitisation makes it relatively cheap to set up and run new journals. The internet makes it feasible, in theory, for readers to access the articles they need online, without charge. Several publishing models based around the central concept of free online access have emerged: collectively their proponents form the "Open Access" movement.

Traditionally, STM publishing works on the "subscriber-pays" publishing model, as follows: Authors submit articles to journals, usually free of charge. The publishers send the articles out for peer review. Those articles that are deemed to be of a sufficiently high standard are edited and published. The journal is then sold to readers, usually by means of a subscription. Commercial, learned and professional society and academic publishers all currently use this model, although some of them are also experimenting with the "author-pays" model. The "author-pays" model works in this way: Authors, or more usually their research funders, pay to publish their article in a journal. The publishers send the articles out for peer review. Those articles that are deemed to be of a sufficiently high standard are edited and published. The journal is disseminated free of charge, primarily via the internet, although sometimes in paper form too. In some cases the author, or funder, pays a submission fee in advance of the publication fee in order to cover the administrative costs of processing their article, whether or not it is accepted for publication.

The Select Committee Report recommended:

27–79B

(a) All UK higher education institutions establish institutional repositories on which their published output can be stored and from which it can be read, free of charge, online.

(b) Research Councils and other Government funders mandate their funded researchers to deposit a copy of all of their articles in this way.

(c) The Government to appoint a central body to oversee the implementation of the repositories; to help with networking; and to ensure compli-

---

[4] See para. 20–11, above.

ance with the technical standards needed to provide maximum functionality.

(d) Whilst institutional repositories will help to improve access to journals, a more radical solution may be required in the long term, and early indications suggest that the author-pays publishing model could be viable—but further experimentation is necessary.

(e) In order to encourage such experimentation, Research Councils each to establish a fund to which their funded researchers can apply should they wish to pay to publish.

(f) The British Library to receive sufficient funding to enable it to carry out the preservation of digital material.

(g) Work on new regulations for the legal deposit of non-print publications to begin immediately.

The government response was a distillation of responses from all the government departments and other government organisations that have an interest in the Report. Whilst the government said that it endorses much of the Report "in principle", in practice it undertook to implement none of the main recommendations. The Select Committee declared itself disappointed with the "unsatisfactory" government response. The Committee said that the government argued against the wholesale adoption of the "author-pays" publishing model as if that is what the Committee had recommended, whereas the Committee points out that it had not in fact made such a recommendation. The Committee instead recommended further investigation and has asked the government to reconsider its position.[5] A similar debate is taking place within the American STM publishing industry.

K. DEPOSIT OF PRINTED AND NON-PRINTED PUBLICATIONS

(i) Deposit of books

27–80   **History of the privilege.** The 1911 Act, in obedience to Article 4 of the Revised Convention of Berne, which provided that the enjoyment and exercise of the rights conferred by the Convention should not be subject to the performance of any formality, abolished all necessity for registration of copyright, but substantially re-enacted sections 6 to 9 of the Copyright Act 1842[6] relating to the deposit of published books at the British Museum and other libraries.[7] The old law was slightly extended by the 1911 Act inasmuch as the National Library of Wales was added to the list of libraries which can, under certain circumstances, demand delivery of a copy of a published book.

Representations were made to the 1952 Copyright Committee that the delivery of copies of books to the libraries free of charge was unfair to publishers, but the Committee recommended that the privilege of the libraries of deposit to receive copies of published works should be continued.[8] The 1956 Act in fact left unrepealed section 15 of the 1911 Act under which this privilege was conferred.[9]

Although the 1977 Copyright Committee received evidence on a number of topics relating to libraries of deposit, it considered that, since the link between

---

[5] The Select Committee Report and the government response can be accessed on the UK Parliament website at: *www.publications.parliament.uk/pa/cm/cmsctech.htm.*

[6] 5 & 6 Vict. c. 45.

[7] Copyright Act 1911, s.15.

[8] Cmnd.8662. para.58.

[9] Copyright Act 1956, s.50(2) and Sch.9, both repealed by the Statute Law (Repeals) Act 1974 (c. 22).

the legal recognition of property rights in published literary matter and its deposit in one or more designated libraries ceased to exist at a date now remote, there was no reason why the law of copyright should any longer concern itself with the subject of legal deposit. The Committee therefore made no formal recommendations on the subject although the Report set out the Committee's views on certain matters,[10] for instance that all deposit libraries should be on the same footing. The 1988 Act also left unrepealed section 15 of the 1911 Act.[11]

Background to the Legal Deposit Libraries Act 2003: the future of Legal Deposit. Advances in publication technology and the rising popularity of non-print media prompted the Government to review the then current legal deposit requirements. A consultation paper was published in February 1997, inviting comments on whether legislation should be extended to cover electronic publications, sound recordings, film and video recordings, and microfilm. Following the extensive responses to the paper, a working party was set up in December 1997 which reported in July 1998 to the Secretary of State for Culture, Media and Sport. It concluded that in the longer term only statutory deposit could secure a comprehensive national published archive. It recommended that the archive should be a distributed one, including (but not necessarily restricted to) the six current legal deposit libraries. The Secretary of State, in a parliamentary answer in December 1998, accepted that the report "makes a convincing case for moving towards legislation for the legal deposit of non-print publications on the basis of minimum burden on publishers and minimum loss of sales". He asked the chairman of the Working Party to do further work on definitions and the impact on business through the medium of the technical group of library and publishing experts, with a view to then moving towards legislation. He asked that in the meantime a code of practice for the voluntary deposit of non-print publications should be drawn up and agreed between publishers and the deposit libraries and that a Regulatory Impact Assessment of the costs and benefits of the statutory deposit of non-print publications should be prepared before the proposed legislation was drafted. Following the Secretary of State's request, a code of practice was drawn up and agreed by representatives of the legal deposit libraries and publishing trade bodies.[12]

27–81

The code of practice applies to new publications published after January 4, 2000, but publishers are also encouraged to deposit publications which were published before this date. The scheme is voluntary and publishers are under no legal obligation to comply with it, but publishers are requested to do so in order to help plug the gap in the national published archive before new legislation eventually comes into force. In addition, the scheme operates as a pilot phase during which various issues can be agreed and monitored, so that when the new legislation is is brought into force, it should be workable and effective.

The code of practice applies to UK non-print publications in microform and offline electronic media, which are primarily text-based or which are intended as information rather than entertainment products. Publications originally published abroad, but distributed in the UK, are liable for deposit as well as those first published in the UK. Online publications do not formally come within the code of practice, but it does contain recommendations for arrangements relating to online publications which are substantially fixed at the time of first publication, and the online elements of hybrid offline/online publications. Continuously updated

---

[10] Cmnd.6732, paras 833 and 834.
[11] CDPA 1988, s.303 and Sch.8.
[12] A copy of the code of practice, and other resources relating to legal and voluntary deposit of works, can be found on the web site of the Association of Learned and Professional Society Publishers at *www.alpsp.org*.

publications, such as 'dynamic' databases, are not addressed in the code of practice.

27–82   The code of practice does not cover film, sound or Ordnance Survey digital mapping products, which are subject to separate voluntary schemes. Publishers are not requested to deposit any publication which substantially duplicates the content of a print publication from the same publisher which has already been deposited, nor a publication published only for private internal use within an organisation, nor certain categories of publications specified by the legal deposit libraries as not being required for deposit, such as computer software and computer games. Publishers are asked to deposit a minimum of one copy of all new microform or offline electronic publications, normally to the British Library, who will in turn issue a list of items received to the other deposit libraries. These other deposit libraries may then each request the deposit to them of an additional copy, and publishers are asked, at their discretion, to deposit such copies if so requested.

The code of practice makes proposals for access arrangements for the deposited publications and for printing out up to the limits for photocopying from printed publications. However, the code of practice does not allow for electronic downloading and saving from deposited publications by users. The code of practice assumes, in the absence of an express prohibition by the publisher, that the holding deposit libraries may copy a publication onto other media for preservation purposes only, subject to the preservation of the individual publication's identity and integrity, and so that the copied version may not be used to provide user access. This is to help ensure the long-term accessibility and usability of offline media, such as CD-ROMs, which cannot otherwise at present be assured because of the frequent advances in technology, which render older technologies obsolete and leads to the hardware necessary to access the software becoming unavailable.

27–83   **The Legal Deposit Libraries Act 2003.** The Legal Deposit Libraries Act 2003 ("the 2003 Act") repeals section 15 of the 1911 Act but effectively re-enacts it so far as printed publications are concerned and extends it to cover works published in non-print form. The 2003 Act has necessitated amendments to the 1988 Act to ensure that the various acts required or enabled by the 2003 Act do not infringe copyright. These are dealt with elsewhere.[13]

27–84   **The libraries entitled to the privilege.** Section 1(1) of the 2003 Act requires a person who publishes in the United Kingdom a work to which the 2003 Act applies to deliver, at his own expense, a copy of the work to an address (being an address in the UK or an electronic address) specified (generally or in a particular case) by any deposit library entitled to delivery under the section. If a deposit library has not specified an address, the copy is to be delivered to the library.[14] Generally the copy to be delivered should be in the same medium as that in which the work was published.[15] The deposit libraries are the British Library Board, the National Library of Scotland, the National Library of Wales, the Bodleian Library, Oxford, the University Library, Cambridge and the Library of Trinity College, Dublin.[16] In the case of works published in print, the 2003 Act applies (subject to any prescribed exception) to—

(a) a book (including a pamphlet, magazine or newspaper);

---

[13] See paras 9–114, *et seq.*, above.
[14] Legal Deposit Libraries Act 2003, s.1(2).
[15] Legal Deposit Libraries Act 2003, s.1 (6), the exception being works published online, where Regulations under s.6(h) may specify the medium in which the copy is to be delivered.
[16] Legal Deposit Libraries Act 2003, s.14.

(b) a sheet of letterpress or music;

(c) a map, plan, chart or table; and

(d) a part of any such work.[17]

In relation to a work published otherwise than in printed form, the 2003 Act applies to a work of a prescribed description,[18] but that must not include works that consist only of a sound recording or film or such material and other material which is merely incidental to it.[19]

The 2003 Act does not apply to a work which is substantially the same as one already published in the same medium in the UK.[20] Where substantially the same work is published in the UK in more than one medium, the obligation to deliver a copy to the deposit libraries applies only to publication in one of those media, and the question of which medium is to be determined in accordance with regulations to be made by the Secretary of State, and the regulations may also provide for how to determine whether or not particular works are or are not to be regarded as substantially the same.[21]

The British Library Board is entitled to delivery of a copy of every work published in print[22] and the copy must be delivered within one month of the date of publication.[23] The Board must give a written receipt (which may be sent by electronic or other means). The Bodleian Library, Oxford, the University Library, Cambridge, the National Library of Scotland, the Library of Trinity College, Dublin and the National Library of Wales, are entitled to delivery of a copy of any work published in print which it requests (by electronic or other means) in writing. Such copy is to be delivered at any time within a month after such request, which must be made within 12 months after publication or within one month after publication if the request is made before publication.[24] In the case of an encyclopaedia, newspaper, magazine or other work, the written request may include all numbers or parts of the work which may be subsequently published.[25]   **27–85**

What copies are to be delivered. The copy to be delivered to the British Library Board must be one of the best copies produced for publication in the UK,[26] but the copy for each of the other libraries is to be one of the copies of which the largest number have been produced for publication in the UK.[27]   **27–86**

Effect of failure to deliver copies. The 2003 Act does not make delivery of the copies a condition of copyright. If the publisher, upon whom the duty is imposed of delivering the requisite copies of the work, fails to deliver a copy to a particular library, that library may apply to the county court (or to the sheriff in Scotland) for an order requiring the publisher to comply.[28] If on an application to the court (or sheriff) it appears that the publisher is unable to comply or for any other reason it is not appropriate to make an order requiring the publisher to comply, then the court or the sheriff can order the publisher instead to pay to the library an   **27–87**

---

[17] Legal Deposit Libraries Act 2003, s.1(3).
[18] Legal Deposit Libraries Act 2003, s.1(4).
[19] Legal Deposit Libraries Act 2003, s.1(5).
[20] Legal Deposit Libraries Act 2003, s.2(1).
[21] Legal Deposit Libraries Act 2003, s.2(2) and (3).
[22] Legal Deposit Libraries Act 2003, s.(1).
[23] Legal Deposit Libraries Act 2003, s.4(2).
[24] Legal Deposit Libraries Act 2003, s.5(5).
[25] Legal Deposit Libraries Act 2003, s.5(3)(b).
[26] Legal Deposit Libraries Act 2003, s.4(3).
[27] Legal Deposit Libraries Act 2003, s.5(6).
[28] Legal Deposit Libraries Act 2003, s.3(2).

amount up to the cost of making good the failure to comply.[29] There is no criminal penalty, unlike under the previous legislation.

27–88   Foreign works published in England. The 2003 Act applies to works published in the United Kingdom, making no requirement that they must be entitled to copyright protection in the United Kingdom, nor that they be "first published" in the United Kingdom. It is understood that in the past, while the libraries of deposit did not claim that every book, copies of which are issued to the public in the United Kingdom, falls within the obligation to deliver copies, they have made this claim where the imprint of a London publisher appears on the work, whether alone or jointly with a foreign publisher, and whether or not the work has been first published in another country.[30]

In the wake of the enactment of the 2003 Act, the Joint Committee on Legal Deposit ("JCLD") has been established to (amongst other things)—

  (a) further the mutual understanding between publishers and the legal deposit libraries of their respective positions and interests regarding the legal and voluntary deposit of printed, offline and online material, and to promote collaboration in the implementation of the 2003 Act;

  (b) resolve issues that might arise between publishers and the libraries;

  (c) maintain and monitor the voluntary code of practice[31];

  (d) develop and administer pilot schemes for online material considered to be a priority for libraries; and

  (e) advise government on the way forward regarding the establishment of a Legal Deposit Advisory Panel and to inform the Panel and government of the interests and requirements of publishers and libraries with respect to legal deposit.

The JCLD is made up of interested parties, including representatives from the British Library and the other deposit libraries, the Publishers Association, the ALPSP and the Digital Content Forum. One of the JCLD's priorities will be to provide input on proposed regulations under the 2003 Act.

27–89   Further developments in preserving electronic works. In September 1999 Book Industry Communication ("BIC") published a study entitled "Digital Preservation: an introduction to the standards issues surrounding the deposit of non-print publications". It is available on the BIC website,[32] which contains information about technical standards in relation to the publishing industry and also useful links. It is also available on the website of The Association of Learned and Professional Society Publishers.[33]

There are many digital initiatives currently in progress grappling with the complex issues involved in promoting the wide dissemination of works in digital formats and the preservation of electronically published works. One project is the UK Web Archiving Consortium[34], comprising six leading UK institutions (the British Library, The National Archives, the National Library of Wales, the National Library of Scotland, the Joint Information Systems Committee ("JISC") and the Wellcome Trust), working collaboratively to develop a test-bed for selective archiving of UK websites. Using software developed by the National Library of Australia, consortium members will archive sites (once appropriate permis-

---

[29] Legal Deposit Libraries Act 2003, s.3(3).
[30] See discussion in the Report of 1952 Copyright Committee, Cmnd. 8662, paras 60–65.
[31] See paras 27–81 *et seq.*, above.
[32] *www.bic.org.uk.*
[33] *www.alpsp.org.*
[34] *www.webarchive.org.uk.*

sions have been obtained from website owners) relevant to their interests. For example, the Wellcome Library will focus on collecting medical sites, whilst the National Library of Wales will collect sites that reflect life in contemporary Wales. The British Library will focus on sites of cultural, historical and political importance. Once sites have been archived, catalogued and checked for completeness, they will be made accessible through the consortium website. Users will be able to browse the archive—using broad subject headings—or search for specific sites and topics.

Another initiative is the Digital Preservation Coalition[35]. It was established in 2001 "to foster joint action to address the urgent challenges of securing the preservation of digital resources in the UK and to work with others internationally to secure our global digital memory and knowledge base" and members include the British Library, The National Archives, Consortium of University Research Libraries, JISC and the Council for Museums, Archives and Libraries.

Information about and links to these and other initiatives are available from various industry websites, including those listed in this section.

(ii) Deposit of scripts

Deposit of scripts of new plays. Quite apart from the above provisions relating to deposit, the Theatres Act 1968[36] requires delivery of copies of scripts of plays to the Trustees of the British Museum. In practice, delivery was made to the British Museum's Department of Manuscripts. Since the British Library Act 1972[37] makes no reference to the 1968 Act, strictly speaking, delivery should still be made to the Trustees and not to the Board. Thus, the 1968 Act provides that,[38] with certain limited exceptions,[39] where there is given in Great Britain a public performance of a new play, being a performance based on a script, a copy of the actual script on which that performance was based must be delivered to the Trustees of the British Museum free of charge within the period of one month beginning with the date of the performance; the Trustees are required to give a written receipt for every script so delivered. However, delivery continues to be made to the Department of Manuscripts (the collections of which were transferred under the 1972 Act from the Trustees to the Board).

27–90

Definitions. The 1968 Act contains definitions of "script", "play", "public performance" and "public performance of a new play". Thus, "script" is defined as the text of the play (whether expressed in words or in musical or other notation) together with any stage or other directions for its performance, whether contained in a single document or not.[40] "Play" is defined as (a) any dramatic piece, whether involving improvisation or not, which is given wholly or in part by one or more persons actually present and performing and in which the whole or a major proportion of what is done by the person or persons performing, whether by way of speech, singing or action, involves the playing of a role, and (b) any ballet given wholly or in part by one or more persons actually present and performing, whether or not it falls within paragraph (a) of this definition.[41] "Public performance" is defined as including any performance in a public place within the

27–91

---

[35] www.dpconline.org.
[36] c.54.
[37] c.54.
[38] Theatres Act 1968, s.11(1).
[39] Theatres Act 1968, s.11(4).
[40] Theatres Act 1968, s.9(2).
[41] Theatre Act 1968 s.18(1).

meaning of the Public Order Act 1936,[42] and any performance which the public or any section thereof are permitted to attend, whether on payment or otherwise.[43] Section 18 of the London Local Authorities Act 1990[44] extends the definition of "public performance" in the 1968 Act. The extended definition is confined to performances in London boroughs and takes effect in a particular borough on a date appointed by resolution of the relevant borough council.[45] In a borough where the extension is in force, the expression "public performance" includes "any performance which is not open to the public but which is promoted for private gain".[46] The phrase "promoted for private gain" is defined in a new section 18A of the 1968 Act which is inserted by section 18(3) of the 1990 Act. Finally, "public performance of a new play" is defined as a public performance of a play of which no previous public performance has ever been given in Great Britain, but does not include a public performance of a play which either is based on a script substantially the same as that on which a previous public performance of a play given there was based, or is based substantially on a text of the play which has been published in the United Kingdom.[47]

27–92   **Effect of failure to deliver copies.** If the above-mentioned requirements as to delivery are not complied with, then any person who presented the relevant performance is liable, on summary conviction, to a fine not exceeding level 1 on the standard scale.[48] However, it is provided that a person is not to be treated as presenting a performance of a play by reason only of his taking part therein as a performer.[49]

2. THE NEWSPAPER INDUSTRY

A. General Nature of the Industry

27–93   The United Kingdom has a lively and diverse printed press industry, incorporating not only a range of national broadsheets and tabloids, but also some 1,300 regional and local newspapers. There has been a phenomenal degree of change in the development of the industry over the last 20 years or so; trends have included a rapid growth in free weekly newspapers, beginning during the 1980s, which has impacted on the industry's structure; a trend towards consolidation of ownership and cross-media ownership (accelerated by the Broadcasting Act 1996); structural changes in employment patterns as a result of technological changes and shifts in trade union power; and a recent rapid expansion into "electronic media" including audio text services, joint ventures with cable, fax-on-demand, and online publications.

    The industry is also facing unprecedented competition for advertising revenue from other media sectors. Classified advertising, in particular, is beginning to migrate to electronic publications, multi-channel television and cable and satellite networks. The industry is responding to these challenges not only by expanding into online publications, but also by increasing promotional and marketing

---

[42] 1 Edw. 8 and 1 Geo. 6, s.9; see now Criminal Justice Act 1972 (c. 71), s.33 and Roads (Scotland) Act 1984 (c. 54), Sch.9.
[43] Theatres Act 1968, s.18(1).
[44] c.13.
[45] London Local Authorities Act 1990, ss.3 and 18(1).
[46] London Local Authorites Act 1990, s.18(2).
[47] Theatres Act 1968, s.11(3).
[48] Theatres Act 1968, s.11(2); as amended by Criminal Justice Act 1982 (c.48), ss.37 and 38. In relation to offences committed on or after October 1, 1992 the figure for level 1 on the standard scale is £200: see Criminal Justice Act 1991 (c.53), ss.17(1) and 101(1) and Sch.12, para.6.
[49] Theatres Act 1968, s.18(2).

activity in respect of their print-on-paper publications, and diversifying into broadcast media.

National and regional press sectors. The newspaper market in 2001 was estimated to be worth some £7.55 billion, with the national press generating 55.2 per cent of total revenue, and the regional press generating 44.8 per cent.[50] Well over half of newspaper revenue comes from advertising, the exact proportion being significantly affected by the strength of advertising demand. Total national newspaper advertising revenue in 2003 was just over £1.95 billion.[51] The national sector comprises 11 daily newspapers and nine Sunday newspapers. Total circulation is 12,162,589 copies for daily newspapers and 12,752,933 for Sunday newspapers.[52] The local and regional press sector alone comprises approximately 1,300 titles in the United Kingdom, takes close to £3 billion in advertising revenue.[53] Each week, 37 million regional paid-for newspapers are sold and 29 million free newspapers are delivered.[54] Just over 85 per cent of the population read a regional or local newspaper, compared with just over 70 per cent who read a national newspaper.[55] Together the national and regional press sector employ approximately 67,800 people.[56]

27–94

General regulatory regime. There is no single definition of a newspaper, statutory or otherwise. Rather, newspapers are defined differently for different purposes, including libel,[57] for tax purposes,[58] for media ownership,[59] and other purposes.[60] Neither is there a specific regulatory regime governing the industry in the form of licensing or other permissions to publish a newspaper. In contrast with the broadcasting industries that are subject to a statutory licensing regime,[61] the newspaper sector regards its freedom from government control licensing systems as an essential historical prerequisite to maintain the tradition of a free press.[62] General legal and commercial constraints exist in the context of choosing a title (trade-mark law, passing-off law), acquiring a newspaper company or group of companies,[63] distribution networks (such as competition law considerations in respect of acceptance or refusal to supply particular outlets) and the need to ensure an imprint appears on the first or last page of each newspaper edition.[64] There is a requirement that any person who prints "any paper for hire, reward, gain or profit" preserves at least one copy for a period of six months and to mark on it in "fair and legible" letters the name and address of the person who

27–95

---

[50] Source: Key Note at *http://www.keynote.co.uk/*.

[51] See *http://www.newspapersoc.org.uk/facts-figures/AdvExp-03.pdf*.

[52] Source: Audit Bureau of Circulations for May 31, 2004 to June 27, 2004 (figures include *The Evening Standard*).

[53] Advertising Association and The Newspaper Society Intelligence Unit, 2004.

[54] ABC circulation figures, Newspaper Society Intelligence Unit; Advertising Statistics Yearbook 2004.

[55] BMRB/TGI 2004.

[56] Labour Force Survey, seasonally adjusted, Spring 2001.

[57] Newspaper Libel and Registration Act 1881, to the extent not repealed by the Defamation Act 1996.

[58] See for example, Value Added Tax Act 1994, Sch.8, Pt II.

[59] Enterprise Act 2002; Communication Act 2003, repealing Fair Trading Act 1973, s.57.

[60] Statutory definitions may also be found in, for example, the Betting, Gaming and Lotteries Act 1963, Lotteries and Amusements Act 1976, and the Accommodation Agencies Act 1953.

[61] Communication Act 2003. See generally, as to broadcasting industry, paras 27–235 *et seq.*, below.

[62] As to relevant self-regulatory controls, see paras 27–118 *et seq.*, below. As to protection of titles by a passing off action, see paras 21–22 *et seq.*, above.

[63] Communications Act 2003, amending the Enterprise Act 2002 specifying new public interest considerations to be applied to mergers involving newspaper enterprises.

[64] Newspapers, Printers and Reading Rooms Repeal Act 1869, Sch.2 of which re-enacted s.2, Printers and Publishers Act 1839, as amended by Criminal Law Act 1977, s.31(6).

employed him to print it.[65] Failure to do so may incur a fine of up to £500 per copy (level 2).[66] One copy must be given to the British Library. The Libraries of Oxford, Cambridge, Scotland, Wales and Trinity College, Dublin are entitled to copies on demand. A myriad of statutory, case law and self-regulatory restrictions on content of published material exists.[67]

27–96 **Increasing relevance of copyright.** For the past 150 years or so, the newspaper industry's task of bringing editorial and advertising content to both domestic and business customers has been limited to the distribution of text and images by means of the printed page. During the last 15 years, however, the industry has witnessed a rapid expansion in both the formats in which information may be presented and the media by which it can be delivered. This developing structure of delivery systems has accentuated the commercial importance of copyright to the industry as a result of the shift in focus away from the traditional printed-on-paper product and toward the intellectual property rights in content which can be exploited through a number of different media products.[68] Thus, newspaper publishers are increasingly viewing themselves and their market more broadly by emphasising their function as providing an information service as opposed to sale of printed product. "New media services" such as online publications, CD-ROM and CD-i ventures are providing an increasing proportion of the revenue mix for newspaper companies relative to traditional print products. However, as a consequence, rights-clearance issues are becoming more complex and time-consuming than previously. Publishers are finding it necessary to make increasing use of collecting societies where, for example, multi-media ventures use music and moving images, and are dealing with new and increasing layers of copyright in clearance matters, for example, for the first time to deal with performers' rights and recording rights.[69] This wider commercial focus has prompted many newspaper companies to reassess their copyright position in relation to traditional contributors and in some cases to redraft agreements with newsagencies, freelancers, employees and advertisers to ensure that appropriate rights are in place for future ventures in new media formats.

27–97 Certain unique characteristics of the newspaper industry have impacted upon the way in which it has urged copyright legislation to be developed in the United Kingdom and Europe. The industry has played a major role in government consultations relating to the formation and amendment of key aspects of copyright legislation since the 1956 Act. Its inherent characteristics of multi-contributorship (the product of the labours of researchers, journalists, copy editors, sub-editors, advertisement designers and photographers), rapid rate of dissemination of information, space constraints, the need to ensure clear presentation of newspaper layout and readability, and volume and diversity of information processed (editorial and advertising) have been cited as important factors to take into account during past reviews of the legislation as a whole or aspects of it. The industry is also an active participant in the current debate on the domestic, european and international level in respect of the ongoing adjustment of the copyright framework which has been spurred by the need for a legal regime

---

[65] Newspapers, Printers and Reading Rooms Repeal Act 1869, re-enacting the Unlawful Societies Act 1799, s.29.
[66] Criminal Law Act 1977, s.31; Criminal Justice Act 1982, s.46.
[67] The most important of which include contempt of court, defamation, and advertising regulation, both statutory and self-regulatory, in respect of advertisement content, and see paras 27–314, and 27–318, below.
[68] This shift has been referred to as the "paradigm shift".
[69] As to these rights, see Ch.12, above. As to the role of collecting Societies, see Ch.28, below.

capable of accommodating the new media.[70] The industry's participation in this debate is rooted in its increasing commercial interest in digital as well as analogue production, and in the notion that newspaper publishers will be key players in the new media environment, both as providers of content and as investors in new media products and infrastructure. The ongoing evaluation of the applicability of current copyright law to new technology is prompting many companies to reassess their copyright position in the context of possible "new media" projects they expect to undertake, to develop new and improved procedures for recording and monitoring licence terms and conditions and, in some cases, to redraft their current agreements with newsagencies, freelancers, employees and advertisers.

Much of the industry's representation takes place through its trade association links. The United Kingdom's national press is represented by the Newspaper Publishers' Association.[71] The Newspaper Society, representing regional and local publishers in the United Kingdom,[72] is a member of the European Newspaper Publishers' Association (ENPA), based in Brussels,[73] as well as the World Association of Newspapers (WAN) based in Paris.[74] ENPA and WAN operate a joint copyright committee which plays an active part in oral and written consultations by the European Commission, the European Parliament and WIPO (World Intellectual Property Organisation). The Newspaper Society was also instrumental in an all-industry challenge in 1993 before the Copyright Tribunal[75] to the royalty levels set by the BBC, ITV companies and Channel Four in respect of their television listings following the ending of the duopoly in seven-day television listings.[76]

B. SOURCES OF COPYRIGHT

General. The fundamental tenet that there is no copyright in ideas, only in the form in which they are expressed, manifests itself in the newspaper context by the principle that there is no copyright in "news". There is nevertheless copyright in the form in which it is expressed in particular articles and reports.[77] Copyright will also subsist in the whole newspaper by way of the compilation of these items[78] and, in addition, in the typographical arrangement of the published newspaper.[79] This latter right protects a publisher's skill and effort in creating the layout of each edition, and may form the basis of an infringement action in circumstances in which a substantial portion of a printed page (perhaps comprising third-party copyright in editorial or advertising material), has been copied for use in another publication. The photocopying of individual articles, none of which sufficiently reproduces the layout of any page to amount to a substantial part of

27–98

---

[70] Most recently in response to the Council Directive on Copyright and Related Rights in the Information Society (2001/29/EC) now implemented in the form of the Copyright and Related Rights Regulations 2003 (SI 2003/2498).

[71] Newspaper Publishers Association, 34 Southwark Bridge Road, London, SE1 9EU, Tel: 020 7207 2200. Fax: 020 7928 2067.

[72] Newspaper Society, Bloomsbury House, 74–77 Great Russell Street, London, WC1B 3DA, Tel: 020 7636 7014. Fax: 020 7631 5119. *www.newspapersoc.org.uk.*

[73] ENPA, Rue des Pierres 29, bte 8, 1000 Brussels, Belgium, Tel: 003225 510190. Fax: 00 322 5510199. *www.enpa.be.*

[74] WAN, 25 Rue d'Astorg, 75008, Paris, France. Tel: 00 331 47428500. Fax: 00 331 47424948. *www.wan-press.org.*

[75] *News Group Newspapers Ltd v Independent Television Productions* [1993] E.M.L.R. 1.

[76] See paras 27–265 *et seq.*, below.

[77] See Ch.7, above, as to the protection generally afforded to literary and artistic works.

[78] As to copyright in compilations, see paras 3–21 *et seq.*, above.

[79] As to such copyright, see paras 3–102 *et seq.*, above.

its typographical arrangement, has been held not to infringe the copyright in the layout.[80]

27-99 **Multiplicity of sources.** The content incorporated into a published edition of a newspaper originates from a wide variety of sources: salaried employees (including journalists, photographers and illustrators); freelance journalists; news agencies and photo libraries; occasional contributors (the most common examples being readers' letters to the editor and classified advertising); advertising agencies; and third-party contributors of databases of information such as weather and sport information, arts and entertainment and the like. Where newspapers have introduced ancillary electronic services such as recorded audiotext material, there may be other third-party right-holders in recorded music or sports, weather messages, or other recorded information.

27-100 **Employee's works.** The rule whereby an employer is normally the first owner of works created by employees during the course of their employment[81] is now regarded by newspaper proprietors as axiomatic.[82] It gives a newspaper publisher wide scope to deal with employed journalists' works, both in-house and commercially, without the financial and administrative burden of entering into a substantial number of licence agreements or negotiating royalty fees over and above paid salaries. Its practical effect is to permit, in the absence of an agreement to the contrary,[83] use of employed journalists' material in electronic media, magazines, spin-off publications, and to enable newspaper proprietors to publish in book form, to sell articles or photographs to radio or television companies or pass to other media owned by the same group and to store and retrieve such works in databases for internal or external use, all without the need to obtain licences from employees.

27-101 **Employee or independent contractor?** Given that the ownership of copyright in the works of journalists depends upon the employment status of the journalist, the question of whether a journalist is working under a contract for service or contract for services is of crucial importance in the industry. Although as a general rule the status is clear, the gradual extension over recent years of "employee-style" benefits to freelancers, new ways of working and varying methods of payment has in some cases blurred the original, relatively distinct freelance status, and may create a risk that freelancers might be deemed to be employees. There is much general case law on the subject of the criteria and consequences of the differing status of employees and independent contractors.[84]

27-102 **Commissioned and unsolicited works.** The exception to the general rule in the 1988 Act that the author of a work is the first owner of the copyright applies only to employees' works. Copyright ownership of material submitted by anyone other than an employee of the newspaper (whether journalist, graphic artist, illustrator and whether commissioned or unsolicited material) is therefore dependent upon such contractual arrangements as may exist between the parties.[85] Copy from advertising agencies and private advertisers (whether domestic or business) will generally be subject to a newspaper's standard terms and condi-

---

[80] *Newspaper Licensing Agency Ltd v Marks & Spencer Plc* [2001] UKHL 38, HL.

[81] CDPA 1988, s.11(2). See paras 5–08 *et seq.*, above.

[82] Compare with the position under the 1911 and 1956 Acts where, in some circumstances, the copyright was split between the journalist and his publisher-employer: see para.5–000. The point is still important in the case of works made under the 1956 and 1911 Acts.

[83] Agreements to the contrary are very rare in the newspaper industry.

[84] See paras 5–11 *et seq.*, above.

[85] As may ownership of materials produced by an employee otherwise than during the course of his employment.

tions of acceptance of advertising, subject to contractual principles relating to incorporation of such terms. Copyright in unsolicited published materials such as letters to the editor will normally remain with the author[86] although some national newspapers have sought to obtain assignments of the copyright in such letters and to accept them only on the basis that they have not been submitted for publication elsewhere. Agreements with news agencies and external photolibraries will govern permitted use of material received by virtue of a subscription service. Such agreements generally reserve to the agency copyright and all other intellectual property rights in material supplied by them, granting subscribers to their services non-exclusive, non-transferable licences for a set time period, normally between three to five years. Newspapers are generally able under the terms of the licence to extract from the stream of material received via the service as much or as little as is relevant to them, to edit the material, and publish it for the duration of the licence. Downloading of agency material onto a newspaper's database is normally prohibited.

Journalists' interviews. Spoken words qualify for copyright protection once recorded in any manner, in writing or otherwise, provided they constitute a "literary" work and are "original".[87] Thus, copyright may well subsist in the words of an interviewee, once recorded by a reporter.[88] Because the "author" of and thus owner of the copyright in the interviewee's words is the interviewee himself and not the person recording the spoken words,[89] an infringement action might lie[90] by the speaker following publication of the words were it not for the exception in section 58 of the 1988 Act.[91] The effect of this section is that, provided no relevant prohibitions were imposed by the interviewee before the reporter made the recording, no express agreement need be obtained for subsequent use of the recording for the purpose of reporting current events or communicating the words to the public. It appears that any prohibition must be expressly made[92] and it is suggested that the stipulation by an interviewee that his comments were "off the record" would usually constitute a valid prohibition, given the well accepted understanding that such words are meant to prohibit use in the form of news reports or otherwise.

27–103

It is a further condition that the person who is lawfully in possession of the record must consent to the use of it.[93] This would appear to indicate that publication of the interview requires the consent of the reporter in order to ensure that the proprietor or other officer of the newspaper company does not infringe the interviewee's copyright. It is likely, however, that the reporter's consent would be inferred from the fact that the particular story had been submitted by him for publication. Presumably, also, where this tape is in "possession" of an employed reporter his "possession" is that of his employer.

There is a quite separate copyright which may subsist in the journalists' work,

---

[86] The submission of a letter or article for publication will however usually imply a licence to publish. See paras 5–220 *et seq.*, above.

[87] CDPA 1988, s.3(2). As to "originality", see paras 3–127 *et seq.*, above.

[88] "Record" is not defined but would include a record in any form including writing or a sound recording. "Writing" includes any form of notation or code: CDPA 1988, s.178.

[89] See para. 4–20, above. As to the separate copyright belonging to the interviewer, see further in the text and para. 4–21, above.

[90] Often, of course, publication of the interview will have been impliedly licensed by the interviewee.

[91] For a detailed discussion of this section, see paras 9–000 *et seq.* and see CDPA 1988, s.58(2)(b), (c).

[92] Where an interviewee is unaware that a recording is being made, the law of confidence may apply. See Ch.20, above.

[93] CDPA 1988, s.58(2)(d).

consisting of his record of the interview.[94] The standard of independent skill and labour required of a reporter in the taking down of notes to a speech or interview for the separate work to qualify for copyright protection is low. The mere taking of a *verbatim* shorthand note of an oral speech not previously written down has been held sufficient for the written record to qualify for copyright protection.[95]

27–104   **News stories obtained from other sources.** It is a relatively commonplace practice for media to take note of other media sources for news stories to be then either followed up independently or rewritten by their own staff for publication. The rewriting of news stories may be permissible, provided that this does not involve the substantial reproduction of an article from another newspaper or radio, television or cable broadcast, which would infringe the copyright in that item. Even where the taking has been of a substantial part, however, this can sometimes be justified on the basis of fair dealing for the purposes of reporting current events, provided a sufficient acknowledgment is included.[96] Where the defence does not apply, and what has been taken are extracts consisting of an interviewee's own words, it is sometimes argued that a custom exists in the industry whereby it is accepted that this will happen.[97]

27–105   **Advertisements and other marketing ventures.** Insofar as newspaper employees expend sufficient skill and labour in the creation of text, design and illustration for an advertisement, whether classified or display, the newspaper proprietor will *prima facie* own the copyright subsisting in the work. Where advertisements are created in part by newspaper staff and in part by a private advertiser or agency, copyright in the advertisement will be split accordingly. The same is true for newspaper promotions or other marketing tools in the form of games or competitions, many of which may contain sufficient skill and labour to qualify for copyright protection as a compilation.[98] Newspaper-compiled business directories and other lists of, say, restaurants, entertainments, educational courses or facilities may also qualify for protection provided newspaper staff expend sufficient skill and effort in creating or compiling the list from previous published advertisers or original research and endeavour.[99] Alternatively, they may qualify for protection under database right.[1]

C. RIGHTS REQUIRED FOR EXPLOITATION

27–106   Whilst the employer-ownership provisions in the 1988 Act, together with generally clear contractual agreements with external contributors, have meant that rights-clearance issues have been relatively straightforward for the traditional print-on-paper newspaper, rights-clearance issues are becoming increasingly complicated as publishers begin to invest in digitised products. Uncertainty as to the scope of existing terms and conditions, and as to future technological develop-

---

[94] See paras 3–127 *et seq.*, above, as to the requirement of sufficient skill and labour, or originality.
[95] *Walter v Lane* [1900] A.C. 539; *Express Newspapers Plc v News (UK) Ltd* [1990] 1 W.L.R. 1320.
[96] CDPA 1988, s.30(2).
[97] See, e.g. *Express Newspapers Plc v News (UK) Ltd* [1990] 1 W.L.R. 1320. This is because it would be contrary to pubic interest if further dissemination of news items was prohibited absolutely as a copyright infringement. But the argument has never succeeded, for good reason it is suggested. See *Walter v Steinkopff* [1892] 3 Ch. 489; *Banier v News Group Newspapers Ltd* [1997] F.S.R. 812.
[98] CDPA 1988, s.1(1)(c) and see, for example, *Express Newspapers v Liverpool Daily Post and Echo* [1985] 1 W.L.R. 1089 where copyright was held to subsist in a game consisting of reader cards comprising a five-letter sequence and daily varying grid-letter sequences.
[99] See, for example, *Waterlow Directories Ltd v Reed Information Services Ltd* [1992] F.S.R. 409.
[1] See Ch.18, above.

ment, has led many publishers in recent years to review their procedures for commissioning work and securing rights from contributors. Despite attempts at establishing industry-wide standard terms,[2] each publisher or publishing group tends to have developed the procedures and documents most suited to its own business.

Employees. Notwithstanding the employee provisions of section 11(2) of the 1988 Act, it is common practice to include an express assignment of copyright in any work created by an employee at any time while in the newspaper's employment. There are a number of reasons for this. First, an express assignment avoids arguments about whether a particular piece of work was produced "in the course of employment".[3] Express and clear provision in an employment contract can render less likely subsequent disputes about whether a verbal agreement was made as to copyright ownership, or whether a course of conduct was such that in respect of a particular article, photograph or illustration, there was a contrary agreement as to ownership. Lastly, an express assignment is useful in cases where other jurisdictions are involved, particularly in the event that the newspaper wishes to secure foreign rights in the material.

27–107

Freelances. Although industry practice is becoming more attuned to the need for written agreements in a rights-clearance context, it remains the position that frequently there is no written agreement between the newspaper and a freelance. Rather, articles and photographs are submitted by freelances at short notice for insertion in the next publication. In return, contributors receive a fee, the level of which is often agreed after the event. In these circumstances a publisher will have an implied permission "to use the work in the manner and for the purpose in which and for which it was contemplated between the parties that it would be used at the time of the engagement".[4] This implied permission will generally be regarded by custom and practice as including a non-exclusive licence to publish the work in printed form. In addition, it is possible that the non-exclusive right to permit photocopying of the article, post it up as part of the online version of the newspaper and store it on archival databases may also be implied into the arrangement, since these are now likely to be understood as the normal consequences of publication in a newspaper. However, there is always a risk that the terms of the implied contract with the contributor may remain unclear, including the scope, permitted media of publication, territorial limitations, syndication rights and duration of the licence. An implied licence may also not extend to syndication of the newspaper's commercial databases to third parties, including news agencies or other media companies. With time, assuming a custom develops, the courts may be willing to imply a wider licence to permit reproduction in other formats.

27–108

In the meantime, the general practice, as a minimum action, is to notify contributors in advance of intentions to reproduce. Clearly, a written agreement with an express assignment or licence is preferable. An assignment or exclusive licence of copyright will not be effective unless in writing and signed.[5] Some publishers are beginning to commission work using electronic terms which may

---

[2] For example, following the agreement reached by Guardian Newspapers Ltd and the National Union of Journalists in 1999.

[3] For example, if an employee created a particular piece of work outside official working hours or if an employee argued that his work was outside his ordinary duties.

[4] *Robin Ray v Classic FM plc* [1998] FSR 622, at 643.

[5] CDPA 1988, ss.90(3) and 92(1).

satisfy the requirement as to writing,[6] although it is less clear that the requirement for a signature would be met. Often, where the negotiating position of a particular freelance journalist is strong, licences rather than assignments are the norm, but this may simply reflect the publisher's chosen approach. Depending upon the relative negotiating power between the parties there may initially be an exclusive licence for a set duration followed by a non-exclusive licence. Increasingly, syndication rights to publish in foreign territories (particularly in the context of online transmissions which do not respect geographical boundaries) and foreign languages are sought. Particular media platforms over and above printed publications are often specified including, most recently, mobile communications platforms.[7]

For a newspaper proprietor to have *locus standi* to institute infringement proceedings relating to the work, a written, signed agreement would be required from the freelancer either making the proprietor an exclusive licensee or amounting to an assignment of copyright.[8]

27–109   **Rights to exploit advertising material.** For the avoidance of doubt, newspapers may insert in their standard terms and conditions of acceptance of advertising a provision that the copyright for all purposes in all artwork, copy, and other material which the newspaper company or its employees have originated, contributed to or reworked belongs to the company. Such terms and conditions also authorise the company to record, reproduce, publish, distribute and broadcast (or permit such acts) in respect of all advertisements accepted for publication (including, but not limited to text, artwork and photographs) and to include and make them available in any information service, electronic or otherwise. A warranty to the effect that advertising copy submitted does not infringe any third party intellectual property rights is another common provision, as is an indemnity from advertisers and advertising agencies in respect of all costs, damages and other charges falling upon the newspaper company in respect of legal actions or threatened legal actions arising from the publication of advertisements accepted for publication.[9]

27–110   **Photographs.** In-house photographic libraries, the content of which comprise photographs taken solely by staff photographers after August 1, 1989, will generally be free from ownership restrictions on use. However, rights-clearance issues become more complicated where libraries comprise photographs taken by freelances (where use will be governed by contractual terms or implied licences) or in respect of older photographs where the law in force at the time the photograph was taken will apply. External photo libraries are becoming increasingly concerned that once their photographs have been digitised, there is almost unlimited scope for them to be copied, digitised and altered. Photographers and agencies have therefore become more reluctant to grant licences for online newspaper publications without strict limitations on the right to adapt or alter the works. Where ancillary services are offered by newspaper companies, such as audiotext facilities linking newspaper text to telephone facilities, such commercial

---

[6] Electronic Communications Act 2000, s.8.

[7] Newspapers may also be affected by the rental right introduced into United Kingdom Law by the Copyright and Related Rights Regulations 1996 (SI 1996/2967) to the extent that they produce audio-visual works. The unwaivable right to equitable remuneration applies to authors of literary, artistic, dramatic or musical works. Any contractual term purporting to exclude or restrict this right would be deemed to be of no effect.

[8] CDPA 1988, ss.101(1) and 96(1), respectively. The new s.101A (see Ch.22, above) is unlikely to be of much application to the newspaper industry because, while non-exclusive licences are not unusual in freelance commissioning terms, they are often not signed by the contributors.

[9] No case law exists on this point as yet.

projects are increasingly becoming integrated in newspaper operations, there may be a need for clearing rights via collecting societies such as the Performing Rights Society (PRS) or the Mechanical Copyright Protection Society (MCPS).[10]

The defence of "fair dealing" for the purposes of reporting current events does not apply to photographs.[11] Nor is it acceptable, in circumstances in which publication is time-critical, to reproduce photographs and pay licence fees for publication after the event.[12] In such circumstances the court may reach a finding of flagrancy and award additional damages.

The moral right restricting publication of photographs commissioned for private and domestic purposes[13] means that in certain circumstances waiver of this right will be required if such a photograph is to be included in a newspaper. Section 85 created a very limited exception to the general common law position that there is no right to prevent a photographer from taking a photograph of a person and subsequently using the photograph commercially for publication and distribution. The section is narrow in scope and was intended to cover, for example, commissioned wedding photographs and family portraits in a non-commercial context.[14] Nevertheless, developments in the law of privacy and data protection may in due course require that greater care will need to be taken in the use of photographs of a private nature, even if section 85 does not apply.[15]

Exceptions to paternity and integrity right. In specific circumstances the 1988 Act gives the author of a literary, dramatic, musical or artistic work the right to be identified as author of that work[16] (the "paternity right") and to object to the work being subjected to "derogatory treatment", (the "integrity right").[17] A number of exceptions to the paternity and integrity rights that are relevant to publication of a copyright work in a newspaper apply, namely:

    27–111

   (i) Where a work is made for the purpose of reporting current events.[18]

   (ii) In relation to the publication in a newspaper, magazine or similar periodical of any literary, dramatic musical or artistic work (including photographs, illustration, editorials, news stories) made for the purposes of such publication, or made available with the consent of the author for the purposes of such publication.[19]

   (iii) Where the employer of the author is the first owner of the copyright pursuant to section 11(2) and where what is done has the authority of the copyright owner.[20]

---

[10] As to such societies see paras 28–59 and 28–56, below.

[11] CDPA 1988, s. 30(2).

[12] *Banier v News Group Newspapers Ltd* [1997] F.S.R. 812.

[13] CDPA 1988, s.85.

[14] In May 1993, the Photographs and Films (Unauthorised Use) Bill sought to extend the moral rights provision in s.85 to create what was in effect a right of privacy. The Bill, ultimately withdrawn, would have extended the moral right to cover non-commissioned photographs, effectively covering all photographs intended for commercial exploitation. The Bill would have created severe restrictions on use of journalistic material in the ordinary course of newspaper production.

[15] *Caroline von Hannover v Germany* [2004] ECHR (Application No. 59320/00).

[16] CDPA 1988, ss.77, 78.

[17] CDPA 1988, s.80(1) and 80(2)(b). The treatment would have to be held to amount to a "distortion or mutilation" of the work or be otherwise prejudicial to the honour or reputation of the journalist or photographer.

[18] CDPA 1988, ss.81(3) and 79(5).

[19] CDPA 1988, s.81(4)(a) and 79(6)(a).

[20] CDPA 1988, ss.79(3), 82. In the case of derogatory treatment, a disclaimer may have to be published if the author has been named. See s.82(2). Note, that where a newspaper publishes only with a licence of the copyright owner, the licence may not extend to publication in altered form. See para. 5–224, above.

27–112   Implications of exceptions of paternity right. One practical effect of the Act's exceptions to the paternity right is that no action will lie where a freelance or employed journalist is not identified in a published article by way of a by-line. In the case of freelancers, the exception applies whether the published work was specifically commissioned by the newspaper or whether it was an unsolicited work submitted to the newspaper. The rationale behind the exception lies partly in the practical difficulties which can ensue in ascertaining which of the persons who contributed to a final published version of an article (researchers, journalists, contributions, sub-editors) should be accorded a by-line. It has also been argued that the clarity of representation of newspapers and the flexibility of editors and publishers to determine an attractive format and appearance may be hindered if a paternity right imposed an obligation to provide by-lines to journalists. In some cases publishers and editors identify authors voluntarily or in satisfaction of a contractual obligation. Because it is arguable that the exception to the paternity right would not extend to electronic publications, express waivers are frequently included in contractual agreements.

27–113   Implications of exceptions to integrity right. The Act's exceptions to the integrity right mean that staff journalists, freelancers and readers who have submitted letters for publication and agencies who have submitted illustrations or text in advertising copy (subject to contractual agreements) cannot object to the editing of their contributions.[21] The exception also applies to subsequent exploitation of the work elsewhere, for example online, without modification to the published version.[22] Photographers cannot sue in respect of alterations to the size, colour or proportions of their published photographs. The electronic or manual alteration of a photograph, including cropping, has been justified in terms of the requirement to conform to space constraints or to align with the content of a particular news story. Some journalists' employment contracts may contain waivers of the integrity right (conditional or unconditional, and sometimes expressed to be subject to revocation). These are unlikely to be necessary, given that the moral right of integrity does not apply to a work prepared for publication in a newspaper, magazine or similar periodical.

27–114   False attribution. Contracts with freelancers and employees (whether in respect of text, photographs, graphic illustrations or design) frequently contain a waiver of the moral right not to have work falsely attributed to the author.[23] In a newspaper context, such a right could be infringed by normal distribution to the public of a newspaper containing an article, photograph or advertising material where a false attribution has been made. The attribution may be express or implied. In contrast with the paternity and integrity rights, there is no exception applicable in a news-reporting context.[24]

27–115   Literary reviews. Although not an authoritative legal source, it is common practice for newspapers to pay regard to the guidance issued by the Society of Authors as to what constitutes "fair dealing" in respect of newspaper reviews of

---

[21] CDPA 1988, s.82(2) and s.79(3)(a). Note that where an author, journalist or photographer is or has been previously identified at the time of the relevant act (*i.e.* publication), without a sufficient disclaimer, then the integrity right may apply. To constitute a sufficient disclaimer, there would have to be a prominent indication at the time of publication that, if the author has been identified, the work has been subjected to treatment to which the author has not consented. CDPA 1988, s.84. See generally as to these rights, Ch.11, above.

[22] CDPA 1988, s.81(4).

[23] CDPA 1988, s.85.

[24] See, for example *Clark v Associated Newspapers Ltd* [1998] 1 All E.R. 959.

books and other literary works.[25] The position taken by the Society of Authors and the Publishers Association[26] is that they will normally regard as "fair dealing" the use of a single extract of up to 400 words or a series of extracts (of which none exceed 300 words) to a total of 800 words from a prose work, or of extracts to a total of 40 lines from a poem, provided that this does not exceed a quarter of the poem. The words must be quoted in the context of "criticism or review".[27]

D. REPRESENTATIVE COLLECTING SOCIETIES AND LICENSING AGENCIES RESPONSIBLE FOR ADMINISTERING THE RIGHTS

In marked contrast with the industrial relations position in a number of member states, there is little involvement in the print industry in the United Kingdom with systems of pooled copyright management, house agreements, collective agreements and the like. Rights are generally agreed and exploited on the basis of bilateral agreements between creators of commissioned works and publishers. That is, individual management is the norm.   **27–116**

The Newspaper Licensing Agency. In January 1996, a number of national newspapers launched the Newspaper Licensing Agency (NLA).[28] The NLA was designed to complement the service offered by the Copyright Licensing Agency (CLA) which licenses the copying of magazines, books and periodicals. The NLA is a limited company which sells licences to companies and organisations which photocopy press cuttings for internal purposes. The NLA has estimated that 160–320 million copies of newspaper articles published by its members are made each year for internal management information, representing up to £6 million per annum potential revenue. The scheme is designed to cover organisations whose use is unlikely to fall within the fair dealing exceptions of the 1988 Act. The NLA offers a selection of licences dependent upon the type of organisation and its requirements.[29]   **27–117**

The NLA now represents all the national newspapers and more than 700 regional and foreign newspapers. By 2003 it was estimated that cumulative distributions to newspapers since 1996 would exceed £51 million.[30] Following the litigation in the case of *The Newspaper Society Ltd v Marks & Spencer Plc*[31] the NLA amended the terms of its mandate and licences to cover the grant of licences of the copyright in individual articles, where that copyright had not been assigned to the applicable publisher. Its Distribution Scheme aims to identify contributors who have not assigned copying rights to the publisher ("Special Contributors"), who are entitled to a share of the sums paid by the NLA to newspaper publishers.[32]

The European Commission have published a communication[33] which foreshadows a legislative proposal in the area of collective rights management and in particular on the governance of copyright collecting societies. In an associated letter

---

[25] The Society of Authors, 84 Drayton Gardens, London SW10 9SB. Tel. 020 7373 6642. Fax 020 7373 5768. *www.societyofauthors.net.*

[26] Publishers Association, 29B Montague Street, London WC1B 5BW. Tel. 020 7691 9191. Fax 020 7691 9199. *www.publishers.org.uk.*

[27] The Society of Authors "Permissions Quick Guide" available online.

[28] The Newspaper Licensing Agency Ltd, Wellington Gate, Church Road, Tunbridge Wells, TN1 1NL. Tel. 01892 525273. Fax 01892 525275. *www.nla.co.uk.*

[29] See 'How to Apply—Type of Licence Required' on the NLA website.

[30] "Publishers Flyer", on the NLA's website.

[31] See [2001] UKHL 38, [2003] 1 A.C. 551.

[32] "Distribution of Revenues to Publishers and Special Contributors", published by the NLA on its website.

[33] Communication on management of copyright and related rights in the Internal Market (COM(2004)261) published on April 19, 2004.

and press notice, the Commission asked for comments on the course of action proposed in the Communication. The communication illustrates the continuing interest of the European Commission in technical systems for the management of rights, notably digital rights management ("DRM"). The NLA responded to the communication, arguing that legislation was unnecessary. In its response, ENPA[34] emphasised the crucial importance of rights management to the newspaper industry, and insisted that newspapers should retain the freedom to opt for individual or collective management, rather than being obliged to follow a particular model by legislation.

E. OTHER INDUSTRY CONTROLS

27–118   **Self-regulatory controls.** In both the editorial and advertising spheres, there are well-established self-regulatory controls in respect of content. Editorial content is overseen by the Press Complaints Commission (PCC), funded by means of a levy on all British newspapers, magazines and periodicals. The PCC enforces a Code of Practice with provisions relating to accuracy, payment for articles, harassment, opportunity to reply, interviewing or photographing children, intrusion into grief or shock and other matters.[35] The PCC was created in 1991 to replace the old Press Council in response to recommendations to the Home Office by The Committee on Privacy and Related Matters.[36] Self-regulation in the advertising and marketing area is administered by the Advertising Standards Authority (ASA)[37] on the basis of an industry formulated British Code of Advertising, Sales Promotion and Direct Marketing.[38] This topic is dealt with in more detail elsewhere.[39]

F. CURRENT INDUSTRY ISSUES

27–119   The major current issues of concern to the newspaper sector generally relate either to the application of existing law to new industry technology or to the introduction of new copyright law emanating from the European Commission or WIPO. So far as possible in both cases, the industry has sought to resolve concerns by united (trade association and industry) activity, in the latter case in the form of representational work and in the former case by way of liaison with the relevant industry sectors or representative organisations including FAST and other specially formed industry groups.[40]

27–120   **"Videograbbing".** A current concern of publishers (and news agencies) is the practice of using video technology to capture images from broadcast material (either live or film footage) for subsequent use in print publications. This should be understood in the context of the increasing use of video technology by newspaper journalists as a routine means of gathering information. The capture and publication of such images without authorisation is *prima facie* an infringement of

---

[34] As to the ENPA, see para. 27–97, above.

[35] The most recent version took effect on June 1, 2004 and is obtainable online from the PCC's website at *www.pcc.org.uk*.

[36] Chaired by Sir David Calcutt (Cmnd.1102) July 1990.

[37] Advertising Standards Authority, Brook House, 2 Torrington Place, London WC1E 7HW. Tel. 020 7580 5555. Fax: 020 7631 3051. *www.asa.org.uk*.

[38] The eleventh edition of the British Code of Advertising, Sales Promotion and Direct Marketing came into force on March 4, 2003.

[39] See the section on the Advertising Industry, paras 27–301 *et seq.*, below.

[40] For example DATIC (Digital Advertisement Transfer Industry Committee) formed in the early 1990s and comprising representatives from the NPA (Newspaper Publishers' Association), BPIF (British Printing Industries Federation) IPA (Institute of Practitioners in Advertising), ISBA (Incorporated Society of British Advertisers), The Newspaper Society, the PPA (Periodical Publishers' Association), PIRA and the Pre-Press Association.

copyright.[41] In the absence of licence agreements, therefore, publishers are limited to reliance on the defence of fair dealing for the purpose of reporting current events, relying on the fact that a frame from a broadcast film is not a photograph.[42] Clearly, such reliance brings with it numerous limitations on the commercial use of such images by newspapers. Given that the defence applies only to the reporting of current events, care must be taken as to the nature of newspaper articles accompanied by a videograbbed image. General features or documentary material on historical events, for example, unless relevant to a current topical issue fall outside the fair dealing provisions.[43] The specific exclusion in section 30(2) of photographs means that publication of videograbbed images which reproduce broadcast photographs would not be subject to the fair dealing defence, although it may be possible in certain circumstances to rely on the defence of incidental inclusion of the image.[44] In an effort to remove the uncertainty and limitation on use of such material occasioned by reliance solely on the fair dealing defence, some newspaper publishers have given serious consideration to entering into licences for publication of such images and other material, such licences being increasingly offered by broadcasters as part of a general subscription service.

Electronic databases copyright litigation. The question of which rights should now be secured from freelance journalists in order to meet the demands of modern newspaper publishing was thrown into relief by a class action brought against a group of US database publishers in 2000.[45] Although the litigation was solely concerned with infringement of US copyright in the literary works of freelance journalists, many United Kingdom newspaper and magazine publishers have been drawn into a consideration of the issues because material originally commissioned by them from freelances had been supplied or syndicated to US database publishers and had been offered or displayed in electronic form by the US database publishers. The parties to the class action were ordered to enter into mediation, the result of which is a settlement in which UK newspaper publishers or their parent companies are potentially capable of participating. It is likely, however, that the implications of the class action and its settlement will prove relatively impermanent, since most, if not all, newspaper publishers have amended their commissioning terms to include the right to store and display commissioned material on electronic databases, and to authorise others to do the same. Nevertheless, the issue is an example of a recurrent theme, namely the need to secure rights in respect of new forms of exploitation of commissioned works. Another current example arises from the recent launch of 'e-papers'. These are electronic facsimiles of the offline editions of newspapers, together with advertisements, in which the layout and content of the print edition will be preserved. Again, commissioning terms need to be reviewed and, if necessary, adjusted, to ensure that the right to publish in this format is secured from freelances.

27–121

---

[41] CDPA 1988, s.17(4).

[42] CDPA 1988, s.4(2).

[43] In any event, a sufficient acknowledgement would be required on the reproduced image to fall within the defence.

[44] CDPA 1988, s.31, and see para. 9–56, above.

[45] *In re Freelance Works in Literary Databases Copyright Litigation* MDL No.1379 (S.D.N.Y). This class action was launched in 2001 following the Supreme Court decision in *New York Times Co v Tasini*, 121 S. Ct. 2381 (2001), in which the Court held that, absent express consent, the republication of print periodicals in electronic formats infringed the copyrights in freelances' contributions.

27–122   **Electronic commissioning of material.** Publishers are increasingly looking to streamline the commissioning process, both to ensure that the commissioning terms are binding on freelance journalists, and to make the process easier to administer for commissioning editors. Commissioning freelances by electronic means is the inevitable result of combining these objectives with new technology. The question arises of whether electronic commissioning terms are capable of meeting the statutory requirements for a valid assignment of copyright or grant of an exclusive licence.[46] Section 8 of the Electronic Communications Act 2000 allows ministers to amend the statute book, statutory instrument, to authorise or to facilitate the use of electronic communications or storage. As yet, no statutory instrument has been laid down to resolve the ambiguity in the law at present relating to whether signatures in an electronic form will suffice as a signature for the purposes of section 90 (3) . However, it could be argued that an effect of EU legislation[47] and international model laws[48] is that the status of a "signature" must not be prejudiced solely by virtue of its electronic form. In the absence of definitive guidance a publisher commissioning material using electronic terms can argue that any agreement to assign or grant an exclusive licence is contractually enforceable by the publisher against the contributor.

27–123   **Public interest defence.** The availability of a public interest defence to a claim for infringement of copyright has been the subject of recent consideration on at least two occasions[49] and is of particular interest to newspaper publishers and editors. It is now clear that the question must be considered in the context of an analysis of the defences available and whether these conflict with the right to freedom of expression, and that in these rare cases it is necessary to have close regard to the facts of the individual case. The court is required to apply the 1988 Act in a way that accommodates the right to freedom of expression. However, the right to freedom of expression does not normally include a right to make free use of another person's work. Where a newspaper considers it necessary to use exact extracts, it is appropriate for it to indemnify the author of such extracts or provide him with any profits that stems from the use of them. But it has been observed that since there is a clear public interest in giving effect to the right of freedom of expression, where such right overrides the rights conferred under the 1988 Act, s.171(3) does permit the defence of public interest to be raised.[50]

3. THE MUSIC INDUSTRY

A. Overview

27–124   In 2000 the value of the music sector to the United Kingdom economy was estimated to be £3.6 billion (up from £2.5 billion in 1995), including overseas earnings.[51] Copyright and related rights provide the legal framework and foundation on which the industry is built. This section will concentrate on rights in

---

[46] CDPA, s.90(3) and s.92(1).

[47] Directive 2000/31/EC ('the Electronic Commerce Directive') and Directive 1999/93/EC ('the Electronic Signatures Directive').

[48] UNCITRAL Model Law on Electronic Signatures 2001, Art.6.

[49] *Hyde Park Residence Ltd v Yelland* [2001] Ch. 143 and *Ashdown v Telegraph Group Ltd* [2002] Ch. 149. See para. 22–82, above.

[50] *Ashdown v Telegraph Group Ltd* [2002] Ch. 149.

[51] "Counting the Notes', National Music Council 2002, 60–62 Clapham Road London SW9 0JJE. This revenue is generated from several sectors of activity including (a) concerts and other live performances; (b) the production and sale of carriers of sound recordings; (c) the administration of rights in musical and literary works, sound recordings and performances; (d) the manufacture and distribution of musical instruments; (e) the provision of music education and training.

musical and literary works (the music publishing business), rights in audio recordings of performances of those musical and literary works (the recording business)
and the related rights and business practices that are built around them.

The music industry has historically profited from the introduction of new forms
of exploitation and advances in technology. For example, the introduction of
digital (as opposed to analogue) sound recordings in the form of compact discs
was responsible for an increase in the industry's revenues. Perversely, the
ubiquity of compact disc digital recordings combined with the widespread use of
personal computers and the connectivity provided by communication networks
(primarily the internet) has resulted in a dramatic threat and challenge to the
music industry and the legal framework within which it operates.

The industry has been dominated by a limited number of multinational
companies that control so called "major" record companies (which own and/or
exploit sound recordings) and "major" publishing companies (which own and/or
exploit musical and literary works).[52] Independent record companies and independent publishers compete with the majors and have often been (a) more
responsive to new forms of music and (b) able to offer artists and writers more
flexible terms. The dominance of the majors has generally been preserved by
virtue of their access to funds and resources as well as their ownership of a large
proportion of the most valuable catalogues of copyright works and sound
recordings. These companies generally operate on such a scale as to afford them
advantages in terms of distribution (both domestically and internationally) and
the ability to lobby for changes to industry practice and applicable legislation.

At the time of writing, the traditional music industry faces significant change.
It has witnessed a global decline in sales of physical copies of sound recordings[53]
which has been accompanied by an increase in alternative forms of personal
entertainment and an increase in the ease with which high quality pirate copies of
music are made on a micro and macro level, be it through counterfeit compact
discs or file sharing. Digital means of distribution threaten to make a key record
company's "raison d'être"—the access to the means to manufacture and distribute physical copies—redundant. Despite these difficulties, legitimate means for
the exploitation of music in various new media are showing promise. Industry
practice and the applicable laws are adapting to recognise new forms of exploitation and develop the licensing regimes necessary to allow them to flourish. It is
likely that there will be a further change to established industry structures with
the increase in new means for the delivery and exploitation of music.

B. THE MUSIC PUBLISHING BUSINESS

The copyrights in musical and literary works were the earliest of the rights that   **27–125**
underpin the music industry to have been recognised and are the underlying
rights on which much of the remainder of the industry is built. With the exception
of works that are in the public domain, practically any commercial exploitation
of sound recordings or performances requires a licence of the copyright in the
original musical and literary works which are embodied in those recordings or
performed by the performers. The fact that these rights endure for the life of the
author plus 70 years (the longest period of protection afforded to any of the rights
examined in this section) means that the vast majority of works that are the
subject of significant commercial exploitation (with the notable exception of a
substantial proportion of classical compositions) remain in copyright.

---

[52] At present there are five major international companies operating in the United Kingdom—EMI,
BMG, Sony, Universal and Warner. At the time of writing Sony and BMG are in the process of
combining their record company divisions into one joint venture operation although the publishing arms of both companies will remain independent.
[53] Global music sales declined by 7.6 per cent in 2003: IFPI April 7, 2004.

With the exception of the printing of sheet music, all of the mainstream sources of income for the publishing industry are reliant on performances being made of the relevant copyright works, which performances are either live or, more typically, recorded for further exploitation. The principle forms of exploitation are:

(i) the printing of sheet music;

(ii) the public performance of the works[54];

(iii) the manufacture for distribution and sale to the public of physical copies of audio or audio visual recordings of the works[55];

(iv) the communication and making available to the public of the works[56];

(v) the inclusion or combination of the works in or with other copyright works or goods or services.[57]

First Owner of Copyright

27–126   The copyright in a musical or literary work will ordinarily vest on creation in the composer or lyricist (usually referred to in the popular music business as a songwriter or simply a writer).[58] Typically, key rights in the relevant copyrights will be regulated by one or more agreements with collecting societies if the works have been the subject of any commercial exploitation or the writer has had previous success.[59] A writer may also enter into a publishing agreement with a music publisher which will regulate the writer's copyrights and may also regulate certain of the writer's services.[60] The writer and, to the extent applicable, the collecting societies and/or publisher will own and/or control and/or administer the rights in the copyright work.

Collecting Societies

27–127   Writers and, if applicable, publishers will typically rely on collecting societies to license the exploitation of certain of their rights. The key rights in this context are the right to publicly perform a musical or literary work,[61] the right to communicate to the public that work[62] and the right to reproduce and issue to the public copies of that work, including in the form of copies audio or audio visual recordings such as compact discs.[63] The licensing of these rights collectively enables exploitation which could not in practice take place on a commercial basis if clearances from writers and/or publishers required negotiation on each occasion.

The majority of United Kingdom writers will seek to become members of the

---

[54] Whether in the form of live performances or the playing in public of sound recordings embodying the relevant works.

[55] Being predominantly traditional audio products (such as compact discs) released by record companies and consisting of commercial sound recordings, but also in other formats including DVDs, CD-ROMs and promotional sound carriers distributed with other goods or services.

[56] This includes traditional radio and television broadcasting as well as the more recent forms of communication and making available to the public, ranging from streaming music (akin to broadcasts) to the making available of downloadable copies by means of telecommunication devices and networks.

[57] This includes the synchronisation of the works with moving images such as films, advertisements and computer games.

[58] For exceptions to first ownership of copyright see para. 5–08, et seq., above.

[59] As to collecting societies, see para 27–127, below.

[60] As to music publishers, see para 27–129, below.

[61] CDPA 1988, s,16(1)(c).

[62] CDPA 1988, s.16(1)(d).

[63] s.16(1)(a) and (b).

Performing Rights Society ('PRS')[64] and by virtue of their membership will exclusively assign to the PRS their so-called "performing rights", being the right to authorise the public performance and communication to the public of their copyright works. The PRS operates a number of licensing schemes, the most important of which are the licences offered to broadcasters (including radio and television), venues where live or other public performances take place (including live venues, clubs, bars and retailers) and, in conjunction with the Mechanical Copyright Protection Society ('MCPS'), licences to operators of music services in new media.[65] Tariffs are set by negotiation between a licensee and PRS but are subject to referral to the Copyright Tribunal[66] and are intended to reflect the level or type of usage and the licensee's revenues. The PRS makes quarterly distributions of the monies it receives from licensees after deducting an administration charge. Distributions are apportioned between writers based on information included in accounts or returns PRS receives from its licensees.[67]

A writer or publishing company may also appoint a collecting society to issue so called "mechanical" licences on its behalf. In the United Kingdom the relevant collecting society is the MCPS.[68] The MCPS is an organisation representing music publishers and songwriters which licenses the reproduction right of its members and administers some limited synchronisation licences. The MCPS acts as an agent in respect of the "mechanical" rights unlike the PRS which benefits from a full assignment of its members' "performing" rights. MCPS operates a range of licensing schemes the most important of which is the licensing of the rights to manufacture and distribute physical audio or audiovisual products in many formats including CD, video and DVD. Different schemes apply to different forms of distribution, so that, for example, retail sales are treated differently to product given away with other goods or services such as compact discs distributed with newspapers or magazines. MCPS also licenses a range of new media activities often under a joint licence granted with PRS. The terms upon which the MCPS grants licences vary between different licensing schemes. The schemes are approved by the MCPS board but may be referred to the Copyright Tribunal. The current scheme for licensing the manufacture of commercial audio product has been approved by the Copyright Tribunal.[69] The scheme provides for payment of a fixed percentage of the dealer price of the record in question.[70] The MCPS charges commission for its services on a variety of different scales.[71] A writer or publisher does not have to appoint a collecting society as its agent. It could issue or refuse to issue licences itself for some or all of the works in its catalogue. However, once it has appointed a collecting society as its agent, whilst it may reserve some rights to itself, the primary task of issuing mechanical licences will then fall to the collecting society.

---

[64] MCPS—PRS Alliance, Copyright House, 29–33 Berner's Street, London, W1T 3AB. See also para. 28–59, below.

[65] Including internet or mobile telephone streaming and/or download services.

[66] As to the Copyright Tribunal see para. 29–93, below.

[67] PRS bases its distributions on returns it receives from its licensees detailing the specific copyright works that have been exploited. The level of detail in returns will depend on the licensee. Major licensees including broadcasters such as the BBC and large live venues are typically required to submit a complete list of all copyright works broadcast or publicly performed. Medium-sized licensees are only required to provide samples and very small licensees may be exempt from submitting returns. The combination of the data is used to determine the distribution of revenue to PRS' members.

[68] MCPS—PRS Alliance, Copyright House, 29–33 Berner's Street, London, W1T 3AB. See also para. 28–56, below.

[69] As to the Copyright Tribunal see para. 29–93, below.

[70] As to the dealer price see para. 27–147, below. For details of the three types of schemes, AP1, AP2 and AP2A, reference should be made to the MCPS.

[71] As to the commission rates payable, refer to MCPS.

27–128   Similar collecting societies to the PRS and the MCPS operate in most territories of the world. In many cases there is one single society that licenses both the performing right and the reproduction right, for example GEMA (Germany).[72] These societies offer licensing schemes of a similar type. The collecting societies have detailed reciprocal agreements that permit each society to license the repertoire of the other affiliated societies in its local territory, ensuring relevant licences include not only local repertoire but a vast body of copyrights from around the world.

Whilst public performance and national broadcast rights are generally licensed from the society in the territory in which the public performance or broadcast takes place, collecting societies (particularly within the EU) compete with each other to offer favourable terms to the major international record companies for reproduction rights. These competitive terms have encouraged major record companies to deal direct with one European society for all of its European manufacturing licenses.[73]

Publishers

27–129   Commercially successful composers and lyricists will usually enter into an agreement with a music publisher to regulate their rights in original music and lyrics as well as their services as writers.[74]

The music publisher may be a "major" international company with branches or affiliated group companies in all countries where the songs are likely to be exploited. Such a company is more likely to be in a position to administer copyrights on an international basis through its networks of overseas companies in an economic and efficient manner. Through intra-group arrangements these companies specify how much of the locally generated income a local affiliate may retain and enable more speedy accounting through of income to the United Kingdom.[75] The network of international affiliates also means that to the extent that profits are made at a local level, such profits benefit the group as a whole. The size of these companies and their inter-company arrangements usually enable a major international music publisher to offer higher advances and calculate royalties due to the songwriter on an "at-source" basis.[76] This means that compared with an independent publisher they can generally offer a more competitive deal to the songwriter.

Smaller companies may only have a presence in a limited number of countries or indeed only in the United Kingdom. In order, therefore, to be able to exploit songs and collect revenue in other countries these music publishers have to enter into sub-publishing arrangements. These agreements are generally on armslength, commercial terms and not only will the independent publisher not benefit in any way from any profits retained by its sub-publishers, it may suffer a greater reduction in its receipts from foreign territories than that retained by a local affil-

---

[72] Gesellschaft für Musikalische Aufführungs und Mechanische Vervielfältigungsrechte.

[73] At the time of writing, the Universal group of record companies has terminated its so-called central European licensing arrangements with MCPS in favour of a new licence with SABAM (Spain).

[74] See para. 27–130 to 27–137, below.

[75] Foreign accounting arrangements have a definite impact on the speed in which a writer is paid. For example, a sub-publisher in Germany may account to the UK music publisher every six months, accounting for example for income received in the period January 1 to June 30 within 90 days, i.e. by September 30. Assuming the UK music publisher also accounts to the writer at the same six-monthly intervals, the income received in the UK on September 30 is finally paid through to the writer on March 30 of the following year, i.e. 90 days after December 31. Thus it can take a year or more for the income to reach the songwriter. If the UK publisher received accounting quarterly within 60 days the writer would be accounted to 6 months earlier.

[76] As to "at source", see para. 27–137, below.

iate of a major United Kingdom publisher. In these circumstances it is more common for the music publisher to offer a "receipts" basis for calculating royalties[77] or, if it offers an "at-source" deal it is less likely to be on competitive terms, particularly outside its home territory. Whilst it is not necessarily the case, smaller publishers are often perceived as being more "writer friendly" and, since they generally control smaller catalogues, as being more determined to secure exploitation of and full accounting for their copyrights.

Publishing Agreements

Agreements licensing or assigning copyrights in musical and literary works vary significantly. This section will be limited to an examination of agreements whereby substantially all of the rights of the owner of copyright are assigned or exclusively licensed to a publisher.[78] A licence may be for the world or a specified territory, and for the life of copyright[79] or for a shorter period. These agreements fall broadly into one of three types: the exclusive songwriter agreement, the single song assignment and the administration agreement,[80] in addition to which there are commissioning agreements. The publisher or owner of the relevant rights may then enter into agreements with third parties for specified forms of exploitation, for example, the printing of sheet music.   **27–130**

Types of Agreement

(i) Exclusive Songwriter Agreement. An exclusive songwriter agreement regulates a common form of relationship between a writer and a publisher. In addition to effecting the assignment of existing and/or future copyrights to the publisher this type of agreement grants the publisher exclusive rights over the writer's services and the products thereof during the term of the agreement.   **27–131**

The term of an exclusive songwriter agreement may be for a fixed contract period but it is commonly for a period that extends by reference to a specified event.[81] This event is typically the fulfilment of a minimum requirement known as the "minimum commitment". A writer's minimum commitment will vary depending on the circumstances and the relative bargaining power of the writer and publisher. It is common for the agreement to include options to extend the term by further contract periods each of equal or similar length to the initial period. The publisher will not usually have more than three such options (four contract periods in total). The options are generally only exercisable by the publishing company.

For a writer who is not also a performer able to record his songs for a record company which is able to procure a commercial release, a fixed contract period with no minimum commitment may be more appropriate. If there is a minimum commitment it is likely to be that the writer wholly writes a specified number of songs. There may be no requirement that the songs be commercially exploited or there may be a requirement that a minimum number of them be exploited.[82]

---

[77] As to the "receipts", see para. 27–137, below.

[78] As to licence versus assignment, see paras 5–201, above.

[79] As to duration of copyright, see Ch.6, above.

[80] For a detailed discussion of publishing agreements, see Bagehot on Music Business Agreements (Sweet & Maxwell, 1998).

[81] The period will often be for a minimum of one year and the extension will normally be capped so that each period does not exceed 3 to 5 years.

[82] Typically by being recorded by a third party as a "cover".

For a so-called "singer songwriter",[83] the minimum commitment is typically a requirement not only that the writer write and deliver a number of new and original songs but also that they be commercially released as audio recordings. In order to fulfil the minimum commitment the publisher will in addition usually require that these songs be included in an album[84] and that they be sufficient in number to enable the publisher to collect a minimum percentage of the total mechanical royalties payable in respect of that album. This percentage will vary, with a typical range being between 100 per cent to 50 per cent, but it may be less, particularly if the writer is one of several in a band and can therefore only hope to control a low percentage of the works embodied in an album.

Where the writer is a member of a group of performing artists the publisher may choose to enter into one exclusive agreement with all members of the group and the writers' obligations (including minimum commitment) are typically joint and several. A well-drafted agreement will determine the rights of parties if one or more members leave the group. A balance has to be struck between the wish of the publishing company to protect its investment by retaining exclusive rights over all the writers and the interests of the writers who will wish to ensure that the agreement applies in a manner that reflects the changes to the group.[85]

27–132   **(ii) Single Song.** This type of agreement does not include any rights over a songwriter's services, nor does it include a minimum commitment. The single-song assignment or licence provides for an assignment or licence of the copyright in one or more specified songs (or a part thereof) to the music publisher. This is typically done in return for an entitlement to receive a royalty and, in some cases, in return for an advance against those royalties.

27–133   **(iii) Administration.** This type of agreement is intended to grant the rights to administer the copyright in certain songs. The rights may be granted by a songwriter, publisher (typically a small publisher) or other owner of or licensee of the relevant copyrights to an administrator, principally so that the administrator may effect the registration of the songs with all relevant collecting societies and collect any income generated by exploitation of the works. The rights granted may take the form of an assignment or licence of copyright and in some cases consist solely of an appointment of the administrator as an agent on behalf of the copyright owner.

It is unusual for the administrator actively to seek additional exploitation for the songs or to be obliged to do so. The percentage of income retained by the administrator is typically less than that retained by a publisher under any other publishing agreement[86] which is reflected in the fact that there is rarely an advance paid.

The administration agreement must be distinguished from a sub-publishing agreement. A sub-publishing agreement usually grants the sub-publisher materially all of the rights that the publisher has in certain songs albeit that it may be for a limited territory or duration. An advance may often be payable against royalties

---

[83] For these purposes this would mean a writer who is also a vocalist or a musician or a member of a band.

[84] The album or long play record is currently a more profitable format than the single, which as a format has in recent years seen a substantial drop in volume sales as well as price. It remains to be seen whether new forms of exploitation will reduce the relative importance of albums.

[85] This will include changes to the minimum commitment to reflect what may be reasonably expected from the new group and, if appropriate, the departing members as well as changes to the treatment of songs (and the related income) to the extent that they are written prior to and after the change(s) in the group.

[86] 10–15 per cent of "at source" income as opposed to the 20–30 per cent that a publisher would expect to retain under an exclusive publishing agreement.

and there is usually an obligation on the sub-publisher to do more than merely administer the songs. The sub-publisher will usually retain a larger percentage of income than an administrator.[87]

(iv) Commissioning Agreement. This type of agreement is similar in many ways to a songwriter agreement but is specific to a particular project such as a film or theatrical production. The commissioning agreement will not normally include a requirement of exclusivity but will include very specific requirements for the writing and delivery by the writer of the material required for the relevant project. The term will be linked to the delivery of the commissioned works. The delivery requirements will typically include the making and delivery or the overseeing of the making of recordings of the relevant copyright works.

Rights

The publishing agreement will regulate the extent of the rights of the publisher and the publisher will usually seek to maximise the scope of its rights. The duration of the publisher's rights will vary. A rights period equal to the life of copyright is often sought by independent publishing companies[88] or under a commissioning agreement. The duration of rights granted to a major publisher under an exclusive songwriter agreement is likely to be between 10 and 25 years following the expiry of the term of the agreement. Under an administration agreement, it is common for the rights to be granted for periods as short as one to three years. The publisher's rights may be limited to specified territories, although this is usually resisted by publishers and is rarely accepted by major international publishers.

The principle rights a publisher will seek to control are:

  (i) The exclusive right to license mechanical reproduction and the issue of copies to the public. These rights are most commonly administered on behalf of the publisher by collecting societies such as the MCPS.[89] Licences are typically granted by such collecting societies at standard rates[90] and without a requirement for the consent of the publisher or the writer. It is common for a writer who is also a performer to seek to restrict the granting of a first mechanical licence by the publisher or a collecting society so that no third party may successfully apply for and obtain a mechanical licence to record a "cover" of the writer's song before the writer has had the opportunity to do so.

  (ii) The exclusive right to collect income from public performance and com-

27–134

27–135

27–136

---

[87] Usually about 15–25 per cent of income "at source".

[88] Often mindful of building a catalogue of rights, which forms a valuable asset of the business.

[89] As to collecting societies, see paras 27–126 and Ch.28, below.

[90] The rates applied in the UK have been determined by the Copyright Tribunal and are currently 8.5 per cent of the "dealer price" (as to the dealer price see para.[]) of the records in question. In other territories there are similar standard rates established by law or by agreement between industry bodies. Rates are commonly calculated either by reference to the price of the records themselves or the number or duration of the copyright works that are embodied in them. In the USA and Canada, the rate is set by statute and paid by reference to the number and duration of the copyright works on a record with a minimum set amount, regardless of duration. It is possible to contract out of the statutory rate in the USA and Canada. It is therefore common for a North American record company to seek to limit its exposure to a maximum amount per record. This is typically equal to 75 per cent of the minimum statutory of each of the compositions with an artificial cap on the maximum number of compositions (typically between 10 and 12 for an album). A music publishing agreement will usually prohibit the songwriter from entering into a recording agreement which seeks to reduce the mechanical royalty payable without the music publisher's consent. The publishing company uses this provision to enable it to negotiate the best terms possible with the record company. If the exclusive publishing agreement is entered into after the recording agreement, then the publisher will either have to accept any reduced mechanical royalty provisions in North America or seek to renegotiate, but from a weaker position.

munication to the public (but not the "grand rights"[91]). These rights are, however, almost always devolved to the performing right societies such as PRS. If the writer is a member of PRS, the publisher takes subject to PRS's rights and the publisher's right is limited to an entitlement to receive a proportion of the revenues distributed by PRS[92] . The PRS or similar societies in turn regulate the collecting of income and the granting of licences by centrally negotiated "blanket" licence schemes with licensees, including broadcasters, live venues and, more recently, forms of new media exploitation.[93] Under blanket licences all of a collecting society's repertoire is licensed and neither the publisher nor the writer exercises any rights of approval over licensees or licence terms.

(iii) The exclusive right to grant licences to synchronise the works with visual images. Some synchronisation licences are granted under licence schemes administered by collecting societies[94] however the most commercially significant of these licenses[95] are granted by the publisher on terms negotiated by the publisher and are often subject to a writer's approval;

(iv) The exclusive right to reproduce the song graphically and to license that reproduction. This includes the right to publish or license the publication of sheet music. This right is particularly important in the context of classical music where the publisher licenses and is paid for the various sheet music "parts" printed for orchestras. A writer will rarely be entitled to exercise a right of approval over the exercise by the publisher of this right.

(v) The exclusive right to authorise alterations, adaptations, translations and the use of extracts from a song.[96] A writer will commonly seek to be entitled to exercise rights of approval over material alterations to a work or the granting of "sample" clearances.

(vi) The exclusive right to authorise the public performance outside of the scope of collecting society licensing. This consists of "grand rights" exploitation, being the right to publicly perform the work as part of a theatrical production where the work is being performed in a dramatico-musical context. A writer will typically seek to approve grand rights exploitation.

Remuneration

27–137   It is common for a publisher to pay a writer advances in the context of an exclusive songwriter agreement.[97] The amount of such advance will depend on a combination of three factors, being the anticipated income from the relevant songs (which may not yet be written), the songwriter's bargaining power (this will often depend on the number of publishers competing to sign the writer) and

---

[91] As to grand rights see para. 27–135, above at (vi)..

[92] A writer's membership of PRS assigns to PRS exclusively the public performance and communication to the public rights of the writer. The PRS's membership rules prevent a writer from assigning to a publisher these rights and restrict the amount of income the publisher may claim directly from PRS to 50 per cent of the relevant income. This 50 per cent of PRS income is commonly referred to as the "publisher's share" and the other 50 per cent is referred to as the "writer's share".

[93] As to the PRS see para. 27–127, above.

[94] Major UK broadcasters such as the BBC will benefit under their blanket licences from a synchronisation licence for their own productions for limited uses such as recordings of live performances and background use.

[95] Including licences for the inclusion of songs in motion pictures, advertisements and computer games.

[96] This could include authorisation of the inclusion of a sample of the work in another work or of the use of the title of the song or an extract from it.

[97] Advances may equally be payable under any other publishing agreement.

the publisher's budget. Different amounts may be payable by way of advance during the term of a publishing agreement. These will often be linked to certain events most commonly one or more of (i) signature of the agreement; (ii) the exercise by the publisher of options to extend the term; and (iii) the satisfaction of the minimum commitment for a particular contract period. The amounts of such advances may either be specified in the publishing agreement or, for option periods, may be determined by means of a formula, most often as a percentage of the revenue generated from previous songs subject to minimum and maximum amounts.[98] Advances paid under publishing agreements are typically recoupable from the writer's share of any income under the publishing agreement but are generally not repayable by the writer. The publisher bears the risk that insufficient income may be generated from exploitation of the songs to recoup the advances and any other recoupable payments they may have made under the agreement.

Subject to recoupment of any advances (if applicable), a publishing agreement will regulate the royalties and other remuneration payable to the songwriter. There are two fundamentally different bases on which royalties are usually calculated: on an "at source" basis and on a "receipts" basis. In an "at source" agreement, the royalties are calculated on the basis of the gross amounts generated by the exploitation of the songs net only of certain very limited deductions. These deductions are typically limited to sales taxes, fees paid to collecting societies for actually collecting in the income[99] and fees paid to arrangers and translators on industry standard terms. In a "receipts" agreement, the publisher pays the royalty on the basis of an amount which is equal to the "at source" amount but after deduction of other costs or amounts retained by third parties including amounts retained by sub-publishers or licensees. The royalty rate itself will vary from one agreement to another and from one form of exploitation to another.[1]

The publishing agreement should also set out how the income is to be accounted, in what form and how regularly. Typically, accounting will be every 6 months.

Representative Bodies

The main organisation in the United Kingdom that represents the interests of songwriters is BASCA.[2] BASCA was founded in 1947 as the Songwriters Guild. It represents the interests of contemporary songwriters and is represented on the boards of the industry bodies such as PRS and MCPS. BASCA runs regular legal and creative workshops. It also operates an online enquiry service using a direct link with the MCPS' computerised database. BASCA sponsors annual awards and competitions and makes available a standard songwriter agreement to members at a nominal fee.

27–138

The Music Publisher's Association (MPA) represents 90 per cent of all United

---

[98] Referred to as a "mini-max" formula.

[99] As to collecting societies, see Ch.28, below.

[1] A songwriter could expect to receive, from a United KingdomUnited Kingdom music publisher, a royalty for most forms of exploitation of between 60 per cent and 80 per cent. In a commissioning agreement this rate is likely to be in the region of 50 per cent, and in an administration agreement the rights owner will typically receive between 85 per cent and 95 per cent. Different considerations apply to publishing agreements outside the UK, where percentages as low as 50 per cent are not uncommon. Lower percentages also tend to apply to publishing agreements in the classical music field.

[2] British Academy of Songwriters, Composers and Authors: British Music House, 25–27 Berners Street, London, W1T 3LR. Tel: 0207 636 2929.

Kingdom music publishers.[3] The MPA represents the interests of music publishers and on their behalf lobbies the government, the remainder of the music industry, the media and the public. They also administer International Standard Music Numbers to identify songs.

C. THE RECORDING BUSINESS

27–139   For present purposes, a sound recording is a fixation of a performance of a musical and/or literary work. This recording creates a separate property right from the right in the underlying work or the rights in the performances that are embodied in it.[4] It is fundamental to the exploitation of rights in a sound recording that the underlying publishing and performance rights are cleared or are capable of being cleared.

This right to control the exploitation of a sound recording is at the heart of a record company's business. The principle forms of exploitation of sound recordings are:

  (i) the public performance of the sound recordings[5];
 (ii) the manufacture for distribution and sale to the public of physical copies of the recordings[6];
(iii) the communication and making available to the public of the sound recordings[7];
 (iv) the inclusion or combination of the recordings in or with other recordings or products.[8]

In 2003 the global music market was worth $US32 billion (28.5 billion euros) with total unit sales (including music video) of 2.7 billion.[9]

First Owner of Rights in A Sound Recording

27–140   The first owner of copyright in the sound recording is the producer.[10] The producer is the person by whom the arrangements necessary for the making of the sound recording are undertaken[11] and is in most circumstances the person or entity that has paid for or made available the facilities for the creation of the sound recording. Depending on the circumstances, this person may be the performer, record company, publisher, manager, record producer or studio owner.

Collecting Societies

27–141   In the same way as writers and publishers rely on collecting societies to license

---

[3] MPA, 3rd Floor Strandgate, 20 York Buildings, London WC2N 6JU, Fax: 020 7839 7776, Tel: 020 7839 7779.

[4] See Ch.12, above.

[5] Unlike publishing, this does not include live performances which, by definition, do not rely on recordings. It does include the playing in public of recordings.

[6] For present purposes this is predominantly in the form of traditional audio products (such as compact discs) released by record companies and consisting of commercial sound recordings.

[7] This includes traditional radio and television broadcasting as well as the more recent forms of communication and making available to the public in various forms, from streaming (which is akin to broadcasts) to the making available of downloadable files by means of telecommunication devices and networks.

[8] This includes the synchronisation of the recordings with moving images such as films, advertisements and computer games.

[9] IFPI April 7, 2004.

[10] CDPA 1988 s.9(2)(aa).

[11] CDPA 1988, s.178. The term "producer" as used in the context of the ownership of sound recordings should not be confused with the technical "producer", who is engaged to oversee the creation of the sound recording in the recording studio. As to record producers, see para. 27–161, below.

the exploitation of certain of their rights, the owners of rights in a sound recording, albeit to a lesser extent, typically rely on collecting societies to license collectively the rights in sound recordings for certain purposes. The key rights in this context are the right to publicly perform and broadcast a sound recording.[12] In contrast with writers and publishers, the owners of rights in sound recordings generally seek either to exploit or to license any reproduction of their works directly and will generally only do so if the circumstances and commercial terms of such exploitation meet with their approval.

The owners of commercial sound recordings will in the UK typically mandate Public Performance Limited (PPL)[13] to administer and license on their behalf similar rights in the sound recording as those licensed by PRS on behalf of writers and publishers. PPL operates a number of licensing schemes[14] the most important of which are the licences offered to broadcasters (including radio and television), venues where public performances take place (including clubs, bars and retailers). Tariffs are set by negotiation between a licensee and PPL and, after deducting an administration charge, PPL distributes 50 per cent of its revenues to the owners of the copyright in the sound recordings on whose behalf it administers and the other 50 per cent as equitable remuneration[15] to performers and/or collecting societies mandated by performers to collect such income. Distributions are based on information included in accounts or returns which PPL receives from its licensees, from which PPL determines to what extent specific sound recordings have been exploited.

Similar collecting societies to PPL operate in many territories of the world, administering the rights of owners of sound recordings and/or performers in the context of public performance and broadcast. Unlike the collecting societies representing writers and publishers, these societies have not at the time of writing established full and detailed reciprocal agreements and rights owners seeking accurate and regular payments will generally seek to register their interests with each local society. It is of note that in the United States of America owners of sound recordings and performers are not entitled to receive payment for the broadcast of recordings on radio or television.

Record Companies

A record company is typically engaged in the creation or acquisition of rights in sound recordings, their promotion and their exploitation, primarily through distribution for sale of physical copies of recordings to the public. Each of these aspects of a record company's business has to date generally required substantial investment due to the costs associated with the creation, promotion and distribution of those sound recordings. The record industry has therefore tended to involve substantially greater financial risk than the publishing industry, where a publisher's financial exposure tends to be limited to advance payments (if applicable) and overhead and administration costs.

With the advent of affordable computer-based recording facilities it is now possible for performers to produce first-class sound recordings at home or in a

27–142

---

[12] CDPA 1988, ss.19 and 20.

[13] 1 Upper James Street, London, W1F 9DE. Tel: 020 7534 1000. Fax: 020 7534 1111. As to the MCPA, see para. 28–56, below.

[14] These include radio and television (analogue and digital), cable, satellite and internet simulcasts, suppliers of jukeboxes, background music systems or music services to business sites or users and licensing premises, such as night-clubs, pubs or even an individual using music such as a dance teacher or aerobics instructor.

[15] Payable by the copyright owners to performers pursuant to CDPA 1988, s.182D as to performer's equitable remuneration. See para. 27–160, below.

non-commercial studio at relatively low cost. With this first potential barrier to entry lowered, performers may decide to act as a record company themselves. They may take on the obligation to promote their own records and may employ others to act as press, promotion and sales agents. They may also seek a distributor[16] to manufacture and distribute copies of the sound recordings or distribute copies via the internet.

In order to exploit sound recordings a record company must:

> acquire rights in sound recordings. This is achieved either by virtue of the record company being the first owner of rights in those sound recordings or by acquiring the relevant rights pursuant to an assignment or licence of the relevant rights in the sound recordings;

> clear the underlying rights in the songs that are embodied in the sound recordings it controls for the forms of exploitation it intends to undertake. The most important of these rights, the right to mechanically reproduce and distribute copies to the public, is typically available at standard rates through the MCPS or an equivalent collecting society;

> secure the consents it requires from the performers whose performances are embodied in the sound recording. This is done either pursuant to a recording agreement with the featured performers by reference to whom the recordings will be marketed or, in the case of non-featured performers, agreements with those performers securing their consents.[17]

Acquiring Rights in Recordings—Exclusive Recording Agreements

27–143   Due to the level of investment that is often required in order to create, promote and distribute sound recordings, a record company will generally seek to enter into exclusive arrangements with the performer or group of performers whose performances it intends to record and/or commercially release and by reference to whom those recordings will be marketed and promoted.[18] These agreements tend to regulate exclusively such performer's entire recording output during the term of the agreement. The record company will usually seek to ensure that the recording agreement confirms that the rights in the resulting recordings will vest in the record company as first owner of copyright and to the extent that any such rights vest in the performer that such rights are assigned to the record company.

Exclusivity, Term and Minimum Commitment

27–144   A recording contract will generally seek to control exclusively the performers' rights in recordings made for a period of time. Generally the record company will seek to control all such recordings but where a performer operates in different and distinct genres of music or under distinct and different professional names, the record company will occasionally limit the scope of the recording agreement to one genre or one title, leaving the performer free to enter into separate agreements in relation to the excluded category of performances. This is generally resisted by record companies who prefer to control exclusively all of a performer's output in all genres.

---

[16] As to distributors, see para. 27–166, below.

[17] As to agreements with performers see para. 27–143 and 27–159, below.

[18] This is to be distinguished from circumstances where record labels acquire the rights in specified recordings by assignment or licence of those recordings. For a description of such agreements see paras 27–149 and 27–152, below.

The term of an agreement will typically be for an initial period which is linked in duration to the required minimum commitment. There will usually be options exercisable by the record company to extend the term by further contract periods of equal length.[19]

The performer will in most cases be required to deliver to the record company a minimum number of recordings of performances in each contract period. The minimum commitment for each contract period is typically the recording and delivery of a new studio recorded album[20] although the commitment for the initial period may consist of one or more singles. Each contract period is usually extendible by the record company until a fixed period of time after the delivery[21] or release of the minimum commitment for that period. The record company will prefer the period to end by reference to release[22] in order to evaluate the performance of the relevant album before deciding whether to exercise its option for the next album. It is usual for a performer to seek (i) to limit the periods of extension so that each contract period is not capable of being extended indefinitely and (ii) a commitment from the record company to make the recordings commercially available for sale to the public within a fixed period of time from delivery.[23]

A number of high-profile cases culminating in the George Michael case[24] brought significant changes to the way in which the music industry operated. After the decisions in the Gilbert O'Sullivan[25] and Holly Johnson[26] cases, record contracts which tied a performer to one company exclusively for up to seven or eight albums became open to criticism as being unreasonably restrictive. Record companies have too much invested to risk having an unenforceable contract and, as a result, recording agreements in the United Kingdom now tend to be for a maximum of five or six albums in the popular music industry, with some record companies, particularly those in the independent sector, often agreeing to have options for three albums or fewer. In the classical music field, long-term deals are uncommon. A conductor or soloist will occasionally sign a "tie-in" deal for a two or three album series of a particular type of music. "Popular" classical performers, who are perceived as having the commercial potential to cross over from the classical music market into the mainstream marketplace, often have recording contracts similar to pop performers.

In the case of a group of performers, the recording contract should also make provision for the possibility that the group may decide to cease performing together either because one or more leave the group or the entire group disbands. As with similar provisions under a publishing agreement,[27] the record company will seek to protect its investment by securing options to continued exclusivity over not only those performers remaining together as the group but also the individuals who may have left. The continued use of the professional name of the

---

[19] For a detailed discussion of recording contract terms, see *Bagehot on Music Business Agreements* (Sweet & Maxwell, 1998).

[20] Other recordings, including live recordings will typically be agreed to belong to the record company but will not satisfy the minimum commitment. If recordings in excess of the minimum commitment are made during the term these will also typically be subject to the recording agreement and belong to the record company.

[21] Delivery is determined by reference to the standard of the recordings. This will usually require that the recordings are technically satisfactory for manufacture of recordings for commercial sale and of a reasonable artistic standard, sometimes fixed by reference to the standard of previous recordings by that performer.

[22] Between three and six months after release is common.

[23] A period of between three and six months is common. This is referred to as the "release commitment".

[24] *Panayiotou v Sony Music Entertainment (UK) Ltd* [1994] E.M.L.R 220.

[25] *O'Sullivan v Management Agency and Music Ltd* [1985] Q.B. 428.

[26] *Zang Tumb Tum Records Ltd v Holly Johnson* [1993] E.M.L.R. 61.

[27] See para. 27–131, above.

group is a matter of fundamental importance not only to the group but also to the record company since it is often central to the promotion of the group and their recordings. The contract should therefore detail not only the record company's rights to the performers' services and how the group name is dealt with but also the manner of division of income from recordings made before and after the change to the group has occurred.

Rights

27–145   An exclusive recording agreement will typically result in the ownership by the record company of all the rights in recordings of musical performances made by the performer during the term of the agreement and confirm the grant by the performer of performer's rights and consents. The agreement will also typically restrict the performer from rerecording the songs recorded and delivered for the record company within a certain period of the end of the term of the agreement.[28] Whilst the record company will wish for unfettered rights of exploitation, it is common for the agreement to provide for restrictions on certain aspects of the exploitation of the sound recordings together with obligations on the record company. Restrictions or consents will relate to matters including:

(i) artistic matters—these may include choice of artwork, choice of singles, choice of producer or remixer, the choice of songs for an album and their order, the concept and directors of promotional videos;

(ii) financial matters—these will typically include matters which affect the amount of advances or royalties payable to the performer, for example, as to amounts which may be recoupable from or reduce payments to a performer, including recording costs, remix costs and video budgets;

(iii) exploitation outside the context of singles or albums—performers will seek to have approval over exploitation which is not part of the mainstream exploitation of sound recordings by the record company. These may include synchronisation with advertisements and feature films, and over premiums where recordings are given away with or to promote another product or service.

The featured performer will also typically seek certain agreements and undertakings from the record company. The most important of these will be an obligation to pay (as applicable) advances, recording costs and royalties, and an obligation to commercially release the minimum commitment recordings. This release commitment is often limited to particular territories and in some cases to the "home" territory of the record company only.[29]

In addition to the rights over the performer's recording services and the sound recordings, the exclusive recording agreement may also seek to govern the performers' rights in relation to audio-visual recordings of musical performances and will generally grant the record company rights to require that the performer is available to make so-called promotional videos to promote the sale of the sound recordings. The agreement will usually contain obligations on the

---

[28] This is intended to protect the record company against new recordings by the performer of the songs performed for the record label made by the performer after the expiry of the recording agreement being made available in direct competition with the record company's recordings. This restriction is typically limited to recordings which are commercially released by the record company during or within a certain period (often one year) after the end of the term and generally applies for a fixed period from the end of the term only (often five years).

[29] A performers' remedies for a record company's failure to release may vary but generally they will include a right to terminate the term of the agreement (and therefore any further options) and/or a right to either require an assignment of the rights in the sound recordings to the performer or a right to require the record company to license the sound recordings to a third party willing to release them.

performer to make themselves available to promote the product of their services. The contract will also usually place an obligation on the performer to procure that the record company will be entitled to acquire a mechanical licence from the owner of the copyright in the works to be recorded and that this licence will be available on the terms accepted as standard in the industry.[30] This will be the case whether or not the performer is the writer of the works to be recorded since the record company will need such licences to release the recordings. The MCPS and similar societies outside the United Kingdom have established licensing schemes for the terms on which licences will be granted and administered.[31]

Remuneration

A performer or group of performers will in most cases receive advances under an exclusive recording agreement. As with the advances payable to a writer under a publishing agreement, such advances (i) are recoupable but typically non-returnable; (ii) will vary in amount considerably; (iii) may be payable at various points during the term[32] either in amounts fixed under the agreement or determined by a formula specified in the agreement.[33] The advances paid to a performer are either inclusive or exclusive of recording costs for the minimum commitment recordings. Whether they are inclusive or exclusive will generally depend on the circumstances and in particular whether the performer already has access to recording facilities or wishes to control the recording process. Unless the performer has access to recording facilities of sufficient quality to deliver the minimum commitment recordings to the record company's satisfaction, the performer in an inclusive deal is taking a risk that the advances will either be insufficient to meet the recording costs or that there may not be a significant sum available to the performer personally after the payment of recording costs. An advance that is exclusive of recording costs is generally referred to as the "personal advance".   **27–146**

The performer's personal advance is typically fully recoupable from the performer's royalties. Whether other amounts are also recoupable from the performer's royalties depends on the type of royalty arrangement provided for by the agreement. There are two principle methods of paying royalties to a performer from the exploitation of the recordings:

(i) Royalties based on the price of records. This is the method typically adopted by major record companies and larger independent record companies. Royalties from the most significant form of exploitation, being the sale of "records",[34] are calculated according to a formula by reference to the number of records sold and the price of those records. The price used is almost always either the "dealer price" or the "retail price" of those records.[35] In respect of exploitation other than in the form of "records"—for example use in an advertisement or motion   **27–147**

---

[30] As to mechanical licences and controlled composition clauses, see para. 27–135 , above (see footnotes).

[31] As to the MCPS and other collecting societies, see Ch.28, below, and para. 27–127, above.

[32] Most commonly the advances will be paid on some or all of the following (i) signature of the agreement, (ii) commencement and/or completion of recording of the minimum commitment; (iii) the exercise of an option; (iv) success milestones, including achieving certain chart positions or numbers of sales.

[33] Often under what is commonly known as a mini-max formula, which typically sets advances for option periods by reference to the royalties accrued to the artist in respect of the recordings made in the preceding contract period subject to a minimum and a maximum amount.

[34] Meaning various formats of sound recordings—the compact disc album format is at the time of writing the most popular format.

[35] The dealer price is usually defined as the price which distributors of records charge to retailers and the retail price is defined as the price at which the records are sold to the public. The royalty

picture—the record company will typically account to the performer for a percentage of its actual or its net receipts from such exploitation. Under this method of calculation of royalties the record company will typically seek to recoup from the performer's royalties not only the performer's advances but also recording costs.[36] Other costs which are incurred by the record company do not however affect the performer's royalty. These may be substantial and include the costs of marketing, promotion, manufacture (including mechanical royalties) and distribution of recordings.

27–148   **(ii) Royalties based on net receipts.** This basis is more typically applied by independent record companies and under so called "production agreements". A production agreement commonly refers to an exclusive recording agreement entered in to by a performer with a party that intends to fund the making and/or promotion of recordings but hopes to secure a licence agreement with a record company to distribute those recordings[37] . In a so called "net receipts" agreement the performer's royalty is based on a percentage[38] of the total income derived from the relevant recordings after deduction of the total costs incurred in making and exploiting the recordings. Under this model the only amounts typically recoupable from the performer's share of income are the performer's personal advances with all other costs, including recording costs (recoupable against the artist in the alternative, above), marketing, promotion, manufacture and distribution costs (not recoupable in the alternative, above) being deductible from gross income.

Acquiring Rights in Recordings—Other Examples

27–149   Whilst record companies will seek to enter into exclusive recording agreements with performers in whose careers they intend to make a substantial investment, record companies and third parties may acquire rights in sound recordings under a variety of agreements:

Exclusive Licences and Assignments

27–150   These will be relevant where the party seeking to exploit the rights wishes to control them exclusively but is not the first owner of those rights. Examples include:
- A performer who makes the relevant recordings and thereby is the first owner of the rights in such recordings. The performer may seek to license the recordings in order to provide for a reversionary interest on the expiry of the licence or to restrict the rights licensed to certain territories or certain forms of exploitation.

---

rate payable will typically be in the range of 15 per cent to 21 per cent for popular music if it is calculated on the dealer price, and approximately 30 per cent lower if calculated on a retail-price basis. The rate itself is slightly misleading in that it is usually subject to detailed calculation provisions that seek either to reduce the base price of the records—typically for example the dealer price is reduced by a 25 per cent packaging deduction in the case of a CD format—or to reduce the rate itself for certain types of sale.

[36] These will typically include recording costs of any nature, including studio costs, payments to producers, engineers and session musicians, mastering costs, remix costs and video costs, although video costs are typically only partly recoupable from audio-only forms of exploitation, the remainder being recoupable from audiovisual exploitation.

[37] The royalty paid by a record company for such recordings will often be higher than the royalty it would otherwise pay since the creative and financial risk involved in the making of the recordings has already been taken. Royalties in these circumstances are often more than 20 per cent of the dealer price.

[38] The percentage is typically 50 per cent or more in favour of the performer with increases up to 70 per cent or more relatively common, particularly in later contract periods.

- An agreement for the acquisition of a catalogue of recordings by one record company from another.
- A commissioning agreement whereby recordings are made for a specific purpose and are assigned or licensed to the party commissioning them. This could include a film producer commissioning original music for a motion picture.

Non-exclusive licences

These will be relevant where the party exploiting the recordings only requires certain non-exclusive rights. Examples include licences of recordings for the purpose of inclusion in a compilation, an advertisement or a computer game.   **27–151**

Non-exclusive recording agreements

With the exception of "popular" classical performers whose recordings are a "crossover" success, recording agreements for the creation of classical recordings rarely include ongoing exclusive rights over a performer's services. It is also common that only certain performers such as the conductor or a soloist receive royalties from the exploitation of the recordings, with other musicians being paid session fees according to rates fixed with the Musician's Union.[39] The royalties that are payable to the "featured" performers are also generally lower than those payable to pop performers. This reflects the fact that the financial return to the record industry from classical recordings is generally below that of pop records, due to the size of the market.   **27–152**

Representative Bodies

The representative bodies for United Kingdom record companies are the British Phonographic Industry ('BPI')[40] and the Association of Independent Music ('AIM').[41] The BPI membership consists of the major labels and some of the larger independents. The BPI is affiliated with similar organisations in other territories through a global umbrella organisation, the International Federation of the Phonographic Industry ('IFPI').[42] AIM represents independent record companies. Both organisations generally lobby on behalf of their members, take action against piracy and in some cases negotiate arrangements on behalf of their members (see for example the BPI/MU agreement at paragraph 27–159, below).   **27–153**

D. PERFORMERS

The rights of performers were the last of the three rights examined in this section to have been recognised. In this context, a "performer" includes vocalists, musicians and conductors. Performers may either perform publicly or "live" (for example on stage) or perform for the purpose of their performances being recorded for further exploitation. Performers will broadly fall into two categories, described here as contracted (or featured) performers, and session performers. A typical example of a contracted performer is one who is a party to an exclusive recording agreement. A session performer is a performer who will typically be   **27–154**

---

[39] As to the Musicians' Union, see para. 27–159, below.
[40] BPI, Riverside Building, County Hall, Westminster Bridge Road, London, SE1 7JA. Tel: 020 7803 1300, Fax: 020 7803 1310.
[41] AIM, Lamb House, Church Street, London, W4 2PD. Tel: 020 8994 5599. Fax: 020 8994 5222.
[42] IFPI (UK), 54 Regent Street, London, W1B 5RE. Tel: 020 7878 7900. Fax: 020 7878 7950.

engaged for a specific performance or series of performances, more often on than not on the basis of his ability rather than public renoun.

Consent

27–155   Quite apart from a performer's right and ability to impose by contract any condition to rendering a performance, all performers have the right to grant or withhold their consent to certain forms of exploitation of their performance including, but not limited to:

  (i)   the making of a recording of a live performance[43];
  (ii) the copying of a recording of a performance (the reproduction right)[44];
  (iii) the issue of a copy of a recording of a performance to the public[45];
  (iv) the making available of a recording of a performance to the public.[46]

Equitable remuneration

27–156   In addition to the right to grant or withhold consent as described above a performer has a right to receive equitable remuneration from the relevant copyright owner in respect of the public performance and communication to the public of a commercially published recording of their performance, except where that communication to the public constitutes the act of a "making available".[47] Communication to the public for these purposes therefore includes all traditional forms of broadcast and any form of transmission of a recording that is akin to a broadcast—in other words where the recipient is not able to determine when and where they receive the transmission. This right to receive equitable remuneration may not be assigned by the performer except to a collecting society.[48]

Moral Rights

27–157   There are provisions contained in the 1996 WIPO Performances and Phonograms Treaty extending moral rights to performers.[49] At the time of writing 43 states had ratified the treaty, but the United Kingdom and the countries of the EC have not.

Recording rights under Exclusive Recording Agreements

27–158   It shoule be noted that a record company with the benefit of an exclusive recording agreement with a performer will have certain rights akin to the performers' rights by virtue of that agreement.[50]

The clearance of performer's rights

The performer's consent.

27–159   Consents are typically secured through the medium of a contract with the

---

[43] s.182.
[44] s.182A.
[45] s.182B.
[46] CDPA 1988, s.182CA.
[47] s.182D.
[48] s.182D(2).
[49] WIPO CRMR/DC/95— WIPO Performances and Phonograms Treaty Ch.II, Art.5. See Vol.2 at F14.
[50] See CDPA 1988, ss.185–188. See Ch.12, above. As to more detailed provisions usually found in exclusive recording contracts, see paras 27–143 and 27–148, above.

performer although certain consents may be implied by conduct, for example, where a performer willingly performs in a recording studio, knowing that that his performance will be recorded with the intention that the recording be commercially exploited. In the case of featured performers subject to an exclusive recording agreement, their agreement will typically provide for the broadest possible consents in favour of the record company. Outside the context of a recording agreement or in the case of a session performer, the performer will usually be contracted for a specific performance or recording session. The contract should provide as a minimum for his consent to the exploitation of the product of his services that is anticipated but will often confirm the grant of all possible consents to any form of exploitation.

The agreement with the performer will regulate the remuneration payable for the performance and the forms of exploitation for which the consents are granted. In the case of a session musician the remuneration is usually a one-off fee. Many session performers will be members of the Musicians' Union ("MU").[51] The MU sets minimum rates for the remuneration of its members in respect of certain forms of exploitation of their performances. Industry bodies will often formally adopt and agree these rates by negotiation with the MU. If, for example, a recording is made by or for a record company which is a member of BPI or by or for a film or TV programme producer which is a member of Producers Alliance for Cinema and Television (PACT), the minimum rates be will be set down in collective agreements negotiated between the MU and the BPI or PACT.

The MU was set up to represent the interests of performers. Its objects are "to secure the complete organisation of all persons eligible for membership for their mutual protection and advancement, to regulate their relations with their employers and with each other, to improve the state and remuneration of its members and their dependants, to advance the knowledge and skills of members in order to improve and maintain their standard of musical competence and conduct". Another body which represents the interests of musicians is the Incorporated Society of Musicians ("ISM").[52] ISM has as its overall aim the promotion of the art of music, of higher standards in the musical profession and the provision of advice and service to its members.

The right to receive equitable remuneration

Prior to the introduction of the right to equitable remuneration under the Copyright and Related Rights Regulations 1996,[53] performers had no statutory right to equitable remuneration from the broadcast and public performance of their performances. Record companies at that time collected public performance and broadcast income in the United Kingdom through collecting societies such as PPL.[54] A proportion of the record company income was paid *ex gratia* to performers.[55] The right to equitable remuneration when introduced did not entitle performers to license the broadcast and public performance of their performances, since the claim to equitable remuneration could only be made against the record companies.[56] The previous system of *ex gratia* payments from PPL was extended so that PPL income was split as to 50 per cent to the record companies and 50 per

27–160

---

[51] Musicians' Union, 60/62 Clapham Road, London SW9 0JJ. Tel: 0207 582 5566. Fax: 0207 582 9805.

[52] ISM: 10 Stratford Place, London W1C 1AA. Tel: 0207 629 4413. Fax: 0207 408 1538.

[53] SI 1996/2967.

[54] As to PPL see para. 27–141, above.

[55] 20 per cent to featured performers and 12.5 per cent to the Musicians' Union on behalf of non-featured performers.

[56] CDPA 1988, s.182D.

cent to the performers. The regulations do not specify such a split or what constitutes equitable remuneration. In the event of a disagreement between performers and the record companies the Copyright Tribunal has jurisdiction.[57]

Two performers' collecting societies have been established in the United Kingdom, seeking not only to collect income on behalf of performers but also to use their collective bargaining power to lobby for performers and to secure a fair distribution of the income between featured and session performers. The two societies are PAMRA[58] and AURA.[59] Performers are equally able to register with and collect their income directly from PPL. This is an area which is currently in flux, not only in the United Kingdom but also in terms of the collecting of performers' similar entitlements from other territories where such income is available. Outside of the European Community, Japan is probably the most significant source of such income. There is no entitlement to such income in North America.

E. RECORD PRODUCERS, MIXERS AND REMIXERS

27–161   Traditionally viewed as being responsible for the technical aspects of the making of recordings, record producers, mixers and remixers are now often recognised as much for their creative role as for their technical expertise, often more so.

The traditional role of the record producer is to be primarily responsible for overseeing the recording process to ensure that the sound recordings produced are of a standard suitable for release to the public. The producer is often also responsible for ensuring that the sound recording is completed on time and within budget and that all consents have been obtained from session performers and other contributors to the recordings.[60] Whilst this traditional role is filled by many record producers, certain producers[61] have become well known for the artistic as well as the technical quality of their recordings. These producers will often determine key creative matters and be involved in the writing of the underlying musical works embodied in the recordings. In some cases these producers may not be technically proficient or be actively involved in the organisation of recording sessions, leaving such tasks to studio engineers or A&R[62] co-ordinators respectively.

The role of the record producer is usually governed by a contract with the person commissioning the making of the recordings. This will usually be the record company seeking to exploit the sound recording. The producer contract will usually stipulate the services required of the producer and require that the producer complete an agreed number of recordings for delivery to the record label. The agreement will typically require the producer to acknowledge that the record company is the "producer" (as the term is used in the 1988 Act) of the sound recording and therefore the first owner of the sound recording copyright, and will also require the producer to assign all rights in the sound recordings. This will include a grant of consent and assignment of all rights in any performances of the producer.

27–162   The remuneration payable to the producer will be one or more of (i) a (non-

---

[57] CDPA 1988, s.182D(4).

[58] Performing Artists' Media Rights Association—161 Borough High Street, London, SE1 1HR. Tel: 020 7940 0410. Fax: 020 7407 2008.

[59] Association of United Recording Artists—1 York Street, London, W1U 6PA. Tel: 0870 8505200. Fax: 0870 8505201.

[60] As to consents, see para. 27–155, above.

[61] Particularly in the area of pop and R&B, where producers have become as famous as and, in some cases more important than, the featured artist.

[62] Artist and Repertoire.

recoupable) fee, (ii) a recoupable advance and (iii) a royalty[63] . These amounts may or may not include some or all of the recording costs. The royalty will usually be calculated and paid in the same way and at the same time as the featured performers royalties are paid.

The producer of a sound recording may or may not also be the "mixer". The mixer will usually become involved once the performances that constitute the recording have been recorded and will be engaged to ensure that the sound quality of the whole recording, each individual performance and the level of volume of each of the performances relative to the others is optimised. As with producers, some mixers have developed a reputation for achieving a particular quality of sound and are highly sought after and very well remunerated. The agreement with a mixer will typically provide for the assignment of rights to the person commissioning the mix (generally the record company) with remuneration most likely to consist of a fixed fee but occasionally to include an advance and/or a royalty.[64]

A remixer is usually a producer or mixer engaged to rework or alter a sound recording to produce a different sound. Traditionally a remix would take the elements of the original recording and change the quality of their sound or the arrangement to produce a recording that either changed the emphasis of the relevant performances, altered the order of the performances or extended or shortened certain sections. More recently, remixers have been engaged to produce a recording which in many cases shares little in common with the original recording, often using nothing more than a vocal performance or only a part of it. Depending on the degree of change, a new musical or literary copyright work may be created.[65] As a matter of practice, however, it is extremely unusual, regardless of the contribution of the remixer, for the remixer to be acknowledged as a writer or to be recognised as the owner of any new musical or literary works embodied in the remix, ownership of which is usually attributed to the writers of the works embodied in the original recording.

The contract with the remixer will usually specify that any rights in a new sound recording are assigned to the person commissioning the remix. The remixer will typically only receive a one-off fee and will waive any applicable moral rights. The remixer will usually be entitled to receive a credit on the packaging of the sound recordings.

F. MANAGERS

A manager in this context is a representative of a performer, songwriter, producer, mixer or remixer (referred to here as the "artist"). Managers of classical performers are often referred to as agents. The precise nature of the role will vary from artist to artist and may include advising and assisting an artist to raise their profile, seeking opportunities from record companies and publishers, making arrangements for live performances and promotional appearances[66] and negotiating agreements on behalf of the artist either alone or in conjunction with a lawyer specialising in the entertainment industry. Whilst it is not essential that a manager is appointed by an artist, most successful artists will retain a manager with experience who is able to advance the artist's career, resolve differences between the

27–163

---

[63] A UK producer's royalty will vary but will typically be between 2 and 5 per cent of the dealer price, depending on the standing of the producer.

[64] The royalty payable to a mixer, if any, will be in the region of 1 per cent of the dealer price and will rarely exceed 2 per cent of the dealer price.

[65] As to the requirement of originality, see para. 3–127, above. The new sound recording will inevitably be a new copyright work.

[66] A live agent and/or tour manager may also be engaged to assist with live work.

artist and third parties such as record labels and publishers, and seek to enforce the terms of the agreements to which the artist is party.

It is common for a manager to have a formal written contract with the artist.[67] A management contract will usually deal with two key aspects:

(a) The scope of the agreement

27–164   The appointment is usually exclusive and will apply to certain of the artist's activities. The activities may be very broad and extend to anything relating to "the entertainment industry" or be limited to "the music industry" or even to a specific activity such as songwriting. The term of the agreement will vary from a rolling period terminable by either side on notice, to a fixed term[68] or a period determined by milestones in the artist's career.[69] The manager may be appointed throughout the world or for a specified territory. If it is a worldwide arrangement, an artist appointing a United Kingdom based manager may seek to secure an option to require the appointment of a manager in North America.

(b) The remuneration payable to the manager.

27–165   The manager will receive a fee, commonly described as commission which is a percentage of the artist's earnings from the activities in respect of which the manager has been appointed. The percentage for a United Kingdom manager is typically 20 per cent[70] and is generally calculated on the artist's gross income, net only of a limited number of costs. The manager will seek to receive commission in respect of activities carried out during the term but will also seek to ensure that commission is payable even if the income from those activities arises after the term. The artist will seek to limit the manager's entitlement to receive this post term commission.[71] The artist may account to the manager directly. Alternatively, the manager may seek to receive the artist's income directly or may require the appointment of an accountant to receive the income and to account to the manager for his commission. In addition to commission, the manager will usually also be entitled to reimbursement of certain out-of-pocket expenses which arise in the course of his services.

The United Kingdom representative body for managers is the Music Managers Forum (MMF).[72]

G. DISTRIBUTORS

27–166   In the present context, "distributors" means distributors of physical copies of sound recordings—predominantly in compact disc format—to retail outlets. The sale of sound recordings is still dominated by physical products. Efficient distribution systems to ensure that retail customers receive supplies of records are vitally important to the music industry. A record company's agreement with a distributor may be limited to the distribution of product manufactured by the rec-

---

[67] Some managers, including very successful ones, dispense with formal contracts altogether and rely simply on a relationship of trust with the artist.

[68] This is often between three and five years.

[69] These are often "album cycles", referring to the time from commencement of recording of an album to the end of the main promotional activity in relation to that album after its commercial release.

[70] Rates of between 15 per cent and 25 per cent are possible and rates in the USA are typically 15 per cent.

[71] A typical compromise will see the manager receiving commission at the full rate for a period of five years following the end of the term and at half rate for a period of five years thereafter.

[72] MMF: 1 York Street, London, W1U 6PA. Tel: 0870 850 7800. Fax: 0870 850 7801.

ord company or it may also appoint the distributor to be responsible for manufacture. The latter is referred to as a "production and distribution" agreement or a P&D deal.

The major international record companies will either own their own manufacturing and distribution companies[73] or will benefit from advantageous terms negotiated for the manufacture and distribution of their products with large manufacturers and distributors. The large distributors will in turn have advantageous relationships with retailers and in particular retail chains that are responsible for the sale of large volumes of the most "commercial" product. Smaller independent record companies tend to have less advantageous distribution terms and may not have access to a large distributor. In some cases these record companies will enter into agreements with small distributors that aggregate products from several independent record companies in order to create sufficient volume to be distributed by a larger distributor.

A distribution agreement will normally provide for the distributor to be appointed exclusively by a record company in respect of its entire catalogue of recordings for a specified territory for a specified duration. It is common for a distributor to seek international rights even if the distributor is based in one territory. The distributor will in those circumstances seek to distribute the product outside their territory either through connected distributors in other territories or by the sale of product to exporters based in its home territory. The agreement will provide for the distributor to be granted the right to issue copies of recordings to the public and, in a P&D deal, the right to make copies of the recordings. A United Kingdom based distributor will typically receive a percentage of the dealer price[74] in respect of records sold and will, in addition, charge the record company for other costs or services. These may include, charges for manufacturing (in a P&D deal), charges for promotional activities, charges for storage and charges in respect of records distributed and then returned.

H. New Threats or New Opportunities

New technologies have always had an impact on the music industry. In some cases the impact has been profound. The invention of the means for making recordings of performances of musical works resulted in the eventual creation of a new category of rights on which the entire recording business is built. Whilst some technologies such as the introduction of the compact disc format have been embraced by the industry, other developments have been less welcome. The hostile reactions to the introduction of the first "tape-to-tape" recording devices are echoed in the various disputes that have surrounded the software and hardware that now facilitate the making and dissemination of high quality copies of sound recordings.[75] One of the key differences with the most recent developments has been the speed at which the technology is advancing and the relative ease with which consumers have access to many of the latest possible applications.

27–167

Most previous technological developments were reliant on specialised hardware, much of which was initially expensive. The time required for any technology to reach a significant market penetration often allowed the music industry and, if applicable, the law, the opportunity to develop a model for dealing with the technology. Much of the current technology relies on software which

---

[73] With recent changes in the industry, for example the sale of Sony and Warner's distribution joint venture TEN, it is no longer true to say that the majors tend to own manufacturing and distribution facilities.

[74] This will normally be between 5 per cent and 25 per cent although higher and lower percentages are possible. For "dealer price", see para. 27–147, above.

[75] See para. 27–169 to 27–171, below.

is freely available and can operate on hardware that already has substantial market penetration in the western world, such as personal computers and mobile telephones. Whilst new technologies still represent potential opportunities for the music industry, the rapid rate of growth and the speed at which this technology becomes readily available to consumers is one of the fundamental challenges that it faces today.

Piracy—the digital age and Peer-to-Peer networks

27–168   Piracy has always represented a challenge to the music industry. Copyright developed precisely to allow rights owners the ability to prohibit the unauthorised copying and distribution of their work. The traditional threat for the music industry has principally been from the organised wholesale manufacture and distribution of pirated physical copies. The compact disc format has meant that it is possible for pirate copies to be all but indistinguishable in quality from authorised copies. Whilst this remains a very real threat, the possibilities (in many cases the reality) offered by new technology are of an entirely different order. Unauthorised copying by individuals has always been a concern, but it has recently been seen as a threat to the very existence of the industry.

The internet and in particular the introduction of high speed or broadband access for domestic consumers[76] together with the widespread availability of hardware for the making or storage of digital copies of sound recordings[77] have made it possible for individual consumers not only to make unauthorised copies with ease but to distribute them in previously unimaginable quantities at negligible cost. So-called "file-sharing" or "peer-to-peer" networks[78] have made it possible for millions of individuals to exchange copies of sound recordings, videos, computer games and even complete feature films.

The industry has adopted several approaches to combat the perceived threat from new technology with varying degrees of success and failure:

The hardware:

27–169   Initial efforts were targeted at outlawing devices that allowed the copying and storage of digital sound recordings. The Recording Industry Association of America (RIAA)[79] attempted and failed to ban one of the then most widely adopted devices,[80] the RIO MP3 player.[81] It is clear from this and other cases both in the United States and the United Kingdom that attempts to ban hardware that has legitimate as well as illegitimate applications are almost certainly doomed to failure where the distributor of the hardware has no effective means of policing the end user.[82]

The P2P networks:

27–170   Perceived by most in the music industry and other entertainment industries to be

---

[76] This permits the fast and cheap downloading of large audio and audiovisual files.

[77] This includes "burning" CD copies or storing such copies on a personal computer's hard-disk storage or on portable playback devices.

[78] These networks allow their users or "peers" to search the hard-drive storage of the personal computers of each user on the network and take copies of files from those hard drives.

[79] The BPI equivalent record company representative body in the United States of America.

[80] *Recording Industry Association of America Inc Diamond Multimedia Systems Inc* 180F 3d 1072 (1999) (9th Circ (US)).

[81] MP3 refers to a common format used to encode sound recordings into digital files.

[82] See *CBS Songs Ltd v Amstrad Consumer Electronics* [1988] A.C. 1013, HL, where attempts to outlaw tape to tape recorders failed and *Sony Corp of America v Universal City Studios Inc* 104 SCt 774 (1984) (Sup Ct (US)) where attempts to ban Betamax video recorders failed.

a much greater threat than devices capable of making or storing digital copies of sound recordings or other materials, the peer-to-peer file-sharing networks were targeted next. Although it is now the name of a licensed service, Napster was the first of the peer-to-peer services that came to prominence and provided simple and effective means for its users to exchange files of copyrighted sound recordings. Napster was estimated to have had 70 million users at its peak. The original Napster was effectively shut down following a series of legal challenges.[83] Amongst the arguments unsuccessfully advanced by Napster was a defence based on the "Amstrad" or "Betamax" defence which had been successfully used in the *Diamond Multimedia* RIO case. However, whilst the service was capable of legitimate applications the overwhelming evidence was that it was used to trade unlicensed recordings. Crucially, however, the service itself operated through servers under Napster's control and therefore Napster had access to information about its users and was in a position both to monitor the exchange of files and to terminate user accounts, thereby preventing infringement.

The following generation of P2P networks with names like Kazaa,[84] Aimster, Blubster, Morpheus and Grokster were more resilient to legal challenge. These new variants eschewed centrally based directories of users in favour of decentralised networks over which there was effectively no control. Without control over the users these new services argued that they should benefit from a "Betamax" type defence on the basis that they supplied software to users which could have legitimate application but unlike Napster they did not then have control over users or the ability to prevent infringement. This approach has so far been relatively successful. Despite the fact that Aimster was found guilty of contributory infringement due to its operation of ancillary services that supported infringing users, both Kazaa and Grokster have had some successes defending themselves.[85]

The individual users:

Frustrated by the relative ineffectiveness of its attempts against hardware manufacturers and the continued availability of file-sharing services, the music industry's attention has turned to individual users in the hope that bringing high-profile claims against individuals using file-sharing networks would act as a deterrent. The RIAA has led the charge against individual users issuing proceedings against many users accused of being serial copyright infringers. In many cases users' identities were discovered following controversial procedures under the DMCA.[86] Punitive damages have been sought in many cases and the RIAA has been accused of adopting bullying tactics in the conduct of many of the claims. The BPI has at the time of writing indicated that it too is taking action against individual users in the United Kingdom. Despite the concerns that have been raised about the approach itself and some of the negative publicity that it has provoked, there are indications that the use of file-sharing networks is on the

27–171

---

[83] These culminated in two successful applications by the recording industry in *A&M Records Inc v Napster Inc* 114F. Supp. 2d 896 (N.D. Cal 2000) and *A&M Records Inc v Napster Inc* 239 F3d 1004 (9th Cir 2001).

[84] By the end of 2002 Kazaa estimated it had 140 million users.

[85] See *Recording Industry Association of America v Verizon Internet Services Inc* 351 F3d 1229 (2003) (DC Circ (US)) where Verizon successfully challenged subpoenas issued under the 1998 Digital Millennium Copyright Act requiring Verizon reveal the identity of a Kazaa user and *Metro-Goldwyn-Mayer Studios Inc v Grokster Ltd* 380F 3d (9th Circuit 2004) *confirming* 259 F Supp 2d 1029 (2003) (CD Cal (US)) where Grokster was granted a summary judgment motion largely based on the fact that despite notices of infringement Grokster had no control over the network and could do nothing to prevent the infringement.

[86] The Digital Millennium Copyright Act 1998.

decline. This decline has coincided with an increased availability of legitimate music services, so it is difficult to determine to what extent the decline is attributable to this or to the industry's recent targeting of individuals.

Developing and licensing legitimate services:

27–172   Much of the criticism initially levelled at the music industry focussed on the fact that there was little alternative to pirated music in the new media environment. Understandably sceptical about the possibility of operating a commercially viable service in a market flooded with free pirated copies and fearful that once legitimate digital copies were made available online those copies would themselves be pirated, the industry has only relatively recently become fully engaged in and committed to the new forms of distribution of music. Whilst not abandoning the enforcement route, rights owners are now licensing multiple services in the online and mobile telecommunications environment and these services are already showing promise. With a shift in emphasis from prohibition to control, rights owners are focussed on the development of copyright protection mechanisms that can offer comfort that, once disseminated, digitised "content" will be secure. Security has been generally sought under two headings—encryption and digital rights management ('DRM'), the former relating to encrypting the files so that only authorised users may access them and latter focussing on establishing certain permitted uses for the files.[87] There are three main challenges facing secure delivery.

(i) The continued susceptibility of any security measures to being "cracked" by determined "hackers", with software designed to circumvent protection often being freely available on the internet.

(ii) The lack of universally accepted and adopted fixed standards that apply to devices and to methods of encoding files. At the time of writing there are several formats used for the encoding of files for delivery, storage and playback and new or updated formats are constantly offered to consumers as they are developed.

(iii) The concern that digital rights management impairs the consumer experience by limiting the way in which legitimate music may be used by the consumer. In many cases the most restrictive forms of DRM compare very unfavourably with the unrestricted use offered by pirate copies.

Legitimate New Forms of Exploitation—New Opportunities

The Online Boom

27–173   Apple's iTunes online music download service in the United States reached a landmark 100 million downloads in July 2004 since its launch in April 2003.[88] Apple also distributed 800,000 downloads within 1 week of the launch of its European service, of which 450,000 were sold to consumers in the United Kingdom.[89] Such are the positive indicators at the time of writing of the potential of online distribution of music that the world's second-largest music group, EMI, predicted that digital distribution could account for 25 per cent of sales within three to five years. In this climate, a multiplicity of legitimate services has

---

[87] DRM will commonly seek to restrict the number and type of storage or playback devices to which files may be copied and/or the number of times a file may be copied onto a physical format such as recordable compact disc.

[88] BBC News *BBC.co.uk* report dated July 12, 2003.

[89] BBC News *BBC.co.uk* report dated June 23, 2004.

developed and continue to be announced on a regular basis. The types of services fall broadly into the following categories:

(i) Download services. These permit users to receive and retain copies of sound recordings for future playback subject to certain DRM restrictions. Unlike the purchase of a physical copy (the most analogous form of traditional exploitation), download services can vary widely. Most current download services will offer a combination of usage rights which may include the right to make a copy on one (or more) personal computer, one (or more) storage device or portable player, and one (or more) copy onto a recordable compact disk. Some downloads are purchased outright on the basis that they will be available to the buyer for an unlimited period of time. Some downloads are intended to function on a more restricted basis. The restriction may be by reference to a specified period of time or some other condition such as the user maintaining a subscription with the applicable service.[90]

27–174

(ii) Streaming services. These permit users to listen to a sound recording which is transmitted to their personal computer or similar device but without a copy being made for later playback. As with download services there are wide range of streaming services. They include services that are akin to traditional radio broadcasts[91] insofar as they consist of continuous non-interactive transmissions which are communicated to all users at one time determined by the service. At the other end of the spectrum are complete "on-demand" services where specific sound recordings selected by the consumers are received by them at a time and place of their choosing. In between these two models lie a range of possible services that include archives of broadcast programmes that are available to members of the public on demand and online radio services that offer multiple channels aimed at different types of listener that in some cases even adapt to the listener's feedback and requirements.

27–175

Mobile Music

Exploitation which is akin to internet download and streaming services is at the time of writing becoming established for use with mobile telephones. Similar models to those detailed above are developing for mobile applications. The delivery of downloads or the streaming of music via mobile telecommunication networks is a natural extension of delivery via the (typically) wired internet and is a symptom of the convergence of technologies and hardware. The latest mobile phones have a similar functionality to a personal computer or portable digital music storage device and player. The medium offers new forms of exploitation, which have already generated significant revenues for companies offering content for mobile users and the music industry. There are currently two key types of exploitation of music which are mobile phone-specific:

27–176

(i) Ringtones. The global ringtones market for the year 2003 was estimated to have a value of US$ 3 billion with revenues in excess of US$ 4.7 billion forecast

27–177

---

[90] Napster, for example, are at the time of writing offering an "à la carte" full download service with payments made per copy of recording purchased and an alternative subscription-based service with access to downloaded music, limited to the time during which the consumer is a subscriber. The downloads offered under the Napster subscription service are "tethered"—the files are encrypted so as to remain capable of playback, the file requires regular authentication to confirm that the user is a subscriber.

[91] Many traditional terrestrial broadcasters now offer "simulcasts"—simultaneous transmissions of their terrestrial broadcast online.

for 2008.[92] A ringtone refers to the sound made by a telephone to alert the user to an incoming call. Early examples were referred to as monophonic ringtones which consisted of a basic series of single tones reproducing a melody. More advanced telephones permitted the use of so-called polyphonic ringtones. These also consisted of a series of tones but were more complex and rich in texture than a monophonic tone. As handsets developed, it became possible for them to reproduce a faithful copy of a studio recording,[93] as opposed to a series of electronic tones.

27–178   **(ii) Ring-back.** A more recent development which at the time of writing was becoming established in the United Kingdom are the so called "ring-back" services. These allow a consumer to substitute the tone heard by a caller which signified that the phone of a recipient of the calls was ringing with music individually selected by the recipient.

Changes in the Industry

27–179   As has been seen, the traditional music industry is both highly organised and relatively regimented in terms of the arrangements between the various rights owners. New forms of exploitation have brought with them challenges to the way in which the industry is organised, how rights are licensed and how the remuneration from those licences is split between the various participators. The new technologies have also challenged the established business models and relationships between publishers, record companies, performers, collecting societies, distributors and retailers.

(i) *The publishing business*

27–180   The publishers have generally been proactive as regards new media exploitation and have sought, principally through collecting societies, to make licences available for most mainstream forms of new media exploitation. Writers and publishers have in fact benefitted from new forms of exploitation in circumstances where others have not. Ringtones in particular have previously consisted predominantly of monophonic and polyphonic ringtones that exploit neither the commercial sound recordings owned by record companies nor the performances embodied in them. The capability of mobile phones has now enabled the reproduction of studio recordings, and the record companies are licensing Truetones or Mastertones. There has also, however, been a proliferation of so-called "sound-alike" ringtones.[94] Sound-alikes do not generate revenue for the record labels or their performers, payments instead being due to the publishers and writers, with fees payable to the session musicians (often on a buy-out rather than ongoing royalty basis) performing the sound-alike recordings. There are however tensions in relation to the publishing business. Record labels and the operators of online and mobile phone services are seeking to establish a favourable business model, and there is a pressure on publishers and collecting societies to reduce their share of revenues from new exploitation.[95]

One of the features of these new forms of exploitation (the internet in particu-

---

[92] Mobile Music (2nd Ed.), June 2004, Informa Media Group.
[93] Commonly referred to as Truetones or Mastertones.
[94] Which consist of studio recordings made by session musicians that are intended to be faithful cover versions of the commercially available sound recordings.
[95] Typical combined MCPS/PRS licences for online or mobile phone downloads or streaming for a UK-based service is charged at 12 per cent (currently at a reduced introductory rate of 8 per cent) of the price paid by consumer less VAT; combined ringtones licences are at 15 per cent of the

lar) is that they do not readily recognise geographical boundaries. The MCPS and PRS have entered into multilateral agreements (for example the "Santiago Agreement" in October 2000) with mechanical and performing rights societies in other countries with the principle aim of making it possible for collecting societies to license each others' repertoire to services based in their territory, even if those services disseminate music to users based outside the territory. This is not an easy goal to achieve, and the detail of the arrangements remains imperfect. These arrangements are at the time of writing being scrutinised by the European Commission on the basis that preventing licensees from having a freedom of choice over which society to apply to for a licence may be in breach of competition rules.

(ii) *The record companies*

Whereas the traditional role of record companies has been seen as crucial to a successful career as a recording artist, due principally to their ability to fund the recording and promotion of records and their access to means for the distribution of those records, this is now in question. Whilst it remains the case that launching a successful career as a performer of popular music still typically requires a substantial investment in promotion, it is now possible to make high-quality sound recordings without the need for substantial funds or access to expensive recording studios. New media also offer artists the means to promote and distribute their recordings at relatively low cost. Whilst the distribution of albums in compact disc form and traditional forms of marketing remain at the time of writing key to most artists, new forms of distribution may well change this emphasis on physical products and the importance of the album format.

27–181

In addition to the threat from new forms of distribution, where the record companies' royalty basis is more difficult to justify,[96] global sales of physical formats have seen a decline in recent years.[97] Considering the substantial investment that is often necessary to launch a successful international artist, record companies have in some cases suggested that they should share in other forms of artist income[98] which they claim are only possible due to the artist's increased profile arising out of their investments in marketing and promotion. Such a drastic change in the way in which a record company operates has yet to become a reality, although it is not uncommon for a record company to seek to secure rights over an artist's website or domain name.

(iii) *The performers*

Performers who are party to recording agreements with record labels are concerned at the manner in which they may in future be remunerated from new forms of exploitation. It is common for the royalty payable to an artist for the sale of recordings under a traditional recording agreement to be a percentage of the "dealer price".[99] The concern for the performers is that the licence fee or price charged by record companies in the context of online or mobile distribution of downloads will be treated as a *de facto* "dealer price" for that form of distribution. The traditional dealer price of a CD on which an artist's royalty is calculated is gross of elements of cost that are absorbed by the record company such as

27–182

---

price paid by the consumer. This is much lower than the current rates sought by major record labels for the licensing of Mastertones or Truetones.

[96] See para. 27–182, below.
[97] Down by 7.6 per cent in 2003: IFPI April 2004.
[98] Such as income from live performances and merchandising.
[99] As to dealer price, see para. 27–147, above.

mechanical licence fees, manufacturing costs and distribution fees. These costs are commonly absorbed by the online or mobile distributor (although some record companies are seeking to pay for publishing clearances themselves). The net result may well be that record companies retain as profit a far greater percentage of the "dealer price" from non-physical sales whilst the performer sees the same or worse[1] percentage.

Other performers are as a matter of practice relatively unaffected by new technology. Whilst they are entitled to grant or withhold their consent to the making available of recordings of their performances,[2] these consents will typically be secured when recordings are made. The recent expansion of the right to equitable remuneration to cover communication to the public specifically excludes circumstances where recordings of performances are made available and therefore excludes download services and any streaming service that is "on demand".

(iv) *The distributors and retailers*

27–183   The challenge to the existence and profitability of traditional distributors and retailers is obvious. The new forms of exploitation have effectively created new distributors and retailers. There is often no advantage gained for these new media from traditional "bricks-and-mortar" strengths of geographic location and an investment in an infrastructure designed to deliver physical products from record company to distributor to retailer to consumer. As new forms of distribution become accepted, there is a significant risk for traditional distributors and retailers of a reduction in sales of physical product. These distributors and retailers are already operating in an environment where margins are under threat from the reduction of the retail price of compact discs and the substantial decline in the sale of singles.

The music industry is currently facing some potentially dramatic changes in the way it operates. New media may forever change the way in which music is made, delivered and "consumed". It remains to be seen whether these changes will lead to a stronger or weaker industry although historically dramatic changes attributable to technology have led to increased strength and prosperity for the industry.

4. THE FILM INDUSTRY

A. THE GENERAL NATURE OF THE INDUSTRY

27–184   In excess of 170 films intended for theatrical exhibition (feature-length, otherwise known as "feature" films) with budgets in excess of £500,000 were produced in 2003 by United Kingdom producers either acting alone or in co-production with those from other countries. This total includes indigenous United Kingdom film production, films originating overseas but filmed mainly in the United Kingdom and co-productions filmed both in the United Kingdom and abroad using British crew and expertise. The total cost of production of these films was about £1.17 billion, representing an increase in excess of 100 per cent over the figure for 2002,[3] although the proportion of films made with co-producers from the United States of America (about 25 per cent of the total) was responsible for just over 70

---

[1] Many recording agreements provide for the reduction of royalty rates from new formats or for a high "packaging deduction" to be applied to reduce the dealer price from new formats.

[2] CDPAs.182A .

[3] Source: UK Film Council.

per cent of such cost. These bald statistics do not include those films made overseas, particularly in Hollywood, where writers, directors or actors from the United Kingdom make a creative contribution to any film.

There are three stages involved in turning an initial idea into a film which is exhibited in theatres, on television screens and exploited in various DVD, video cassette[4] and other formats around the world: development, production and distribution. Each stage raises different copyright issues. Film creation is a collaborative process in which artistic and technical contributions are made by many people. As a general rule, the director is responsible for refining the screenplay,[5] taking charge of filming the scenes and editing the footage shot into the completed work. The producer is responsible for raising the funding, engaging the director, camera crew and actors and arranging distribution of the completed work. The following outline is intended to simplify what can be an extremely intricate and complicated process.

(i) Development

The development of a film includes all the activity on the part of the producer   **27–185** which is necessary to prepare a film project for the production stage. It consists of:

(a) acquisition of the necessary rights in any literary or dramatic work on which the film is to be based; this may be a novel or play (usually referred to as an "underlying work"), a story outline or "treatment" upon which a screenplay might be based, or simply a screenplay itself;

(b) engaging personnel required at the development stage, for example the writer of the screenplay, then the casting director who will conduct auditions for the actors;

(c) creation of works necessary to make the film, *e.g.* screenplay, production or costume designs;

(d) scouting possible filming locations and negotiating for use of studio facilities;

(e) preparation of a production budget and shooting schedule, financing plan and cash-flow schedule.

Development finance for the above may be provided by a film distributor, a broadcaster or the United Kingdom Film Council (the "Film Council"). In return for this, the financier will usually expect to take an assignment by way of security or a charge over the producer's rights in any underlying work and the copyright in works and other materials created for the film project.[6] Unless the development financier is also financing the production of the film,[7] these rights will be reassigned to the producer once all sums lent by the development financier have been repaid.[8]

---

[4] "DVD" or digital versatile disc has replaced video cassette as the home-viewing format of choice. In 2003 the global DVD market was estimated to be worth US$50 billion.

[5] "Screenplay" is the script for the film including dialogue and scene directions.

[6] For mortgages and charges of copyright, see paras 5–190 *et seq.*, above.

[7] See Production, paras 27–186 *et seq.*, below.

[8] Some development financiers have been known to require credit and an ongoing financial participation.

(ii) Production

27–186   Production itself can be divided into three phases. First, there is *pre-production*, which involves activities such as storyboarding,[9] casting, engaging the production crew, set building, hire or manufacture of costumes and props and securing locations or studios. Next is the *production* phase, commonly referred to as "principal photography". During this phase, in addition to the filming or "shooting", prints are taken from each section of negative that has been shot to create the "rushes".[10] Additional scenes may be filmed by a second unit, often away from the principal location. The soundtrack is recorded, usually towards the end. Lastly, during the *post-production* phase at a studio, the editing, dubbing and recording of any voice-overs are undertaken, music and sound effects are added, and a scene may be reshot if appropriate. The first version of the film assembled during post-production is commonly called the "rough cut". The second is called the "director's cut", which is the version delivered by the director to the producer. Thereafter the producer will make such changes as he may wish, or be permitted, to make before delivering the final version (or "final cut") to one or more distributors.

The decision whether or not to proceed with production will usually depend upon whether someone can be found to finance the budget for that production. Frequently the development financier will also finance all or part of production, so retaining his investment and any rights previously acquired in the project. The producer will charge a producing fee to the budget and will receive a share (typically 50 per cent) of any eventual profits derived following the recoupment from receipts of the cost of marketing and production of the film.

The producer may, before commencement of principal photography, agree to sell rights in the film by way of pre-sale to a theatrical or DVD/video distributor or broadcaster. The distributor will acquire certain rights of exploitation in the film once it has taken delivery of materials from the producer. In return the distributor will pay an advance on account of receipts from the exploitation of the film which advance will be paid on or by reference to delivery.

In order to fund the costs of production of the film, the producer may seek bank finance which can be raised against the security of completed distribution agreements which provide for the payment of an advance on a date certain. In return for a fee and an interest margin, the bank will usually agree to advance funds on the strength of bankable distribution agreements coupled with additional security over the copyright and other rights in the film.

27–187   An investor or the financier of a film will usually require a security interest, often by a mortgage of the copyright in the film and in the underlying rights, together with the benefit of the agreements entered into by the production company. This arrangement will result in ownership of the copyright in the film being assigned to the financier by way of security only and therefore subject to reassignment to the producer on repayment of the loan. The documentation may afford certain rights of approval but a bank will typically not wish to become involved in creative aspects of the project. It will not want to exercise any of those rights except in extreme circumstances.

In addition to the sources of repayment, the bank considering the financing of a film will need to consider the security which is available and is being offered to it

---

[9] A "storyboard" is a plot outline.

[10] "Rushes" are the prints of all material which has been filmed, which are viewed on a daily basis by the director in order to ensure the quality of what has been filmed and that no retakes are required. Digital technology is facilitating greater use of shooting on high definition (HD) videotape, although celluloid remains the technology of choice at present.

by the producer. While the bank may require a fixed and floating charge over the assets of the production company, in many cases the independent production company may have no other assets than the film being produced. The bank will need to look for repayment of its loan to the distribution agreements concluded by the producer and the advances payable under those agreements, together with its security over the copyright in the film and other rights and the benefit of insurance (such as a completion bond).[11]

The production agreement between the producer and the financier will not merely involve provision of production finance, the grant of rights and the taking of security. It will also be concerned with such issues as the financier's approval rights, liability for cost overruns, ownership or sale of any artwork or props, allocation of any budgetary underspend, insurances (with particular reference to the financier's interest in payment of any claim), administration of the production account, entitlements to credits and the producer's delivery obligations.

(iii) Distribution

After completion, the producer will then want to exploit the finished film and, unless he or his financier is a distributor or has been granted distribution rights, he will be looking to secure a distribution agreement. Often he will do this through a sales agent (formerly called a producer's "rep" or representative), who will charge expenses and a commission of typically between 10 per cent and 25 per cent of the income realised from the distribution agreements which he procures on the producer's behalf. The distributor will generally receive an exclusive licence from the producer of those rights in the film that are necessary for its exploitation, including the right to cut (usually for reasons of length or because of censorship requirements) and to dub or sub-title the sound track of the film into other languages and the right to promote the film, *e.g.* by creating "trailers". The distributor will also want the right to license to sub-distributors, as he may not have the necessary infrastructure in all the territories in which the film is to be distributed, and to authorise such sub-distributors themselves to cut, dub or sub-title and promote the film.

27–188

The master negative of the film will normally be retained at the processing laboratory. The distributor can only expect to own the original negative outright if he has distribution rights in all media worldwide. The producer will arrange for the laboratory to provide copies of the negative and other materials to distributors in particular territories, as appropriate. The distributor will often own the materials delivered to it on the agreed date by the producer and will supply copies of the film to exhibitors. If further materials have to be ordered from the laboratory, the distributor will be permitted to do so direct if he holds a "laboratory access letter" from the producer authorising this.

The distributor's income (known as "gross income") will principally consist of receipts from the cinema box office, fees paid by licensed broadcasters and revenue from the sale of copies of the film by DVD and video cassette retailers. Once the cinema exhibitors and retailers have deducted their cut (for which there is currently no typical percentage or fixed fee), the distributor will deduct from the gross income ("distributor's gross") all distribution expenses as well as his commission (typically 25 to 30 per cent of distributor's gross) before passing on the balance ("distributor's net income") to the financier.

---

[11] As to completion bonds, see para. 27–221, below.

B. THE SOURCES AND RIGHTS

27–189   The producer must acquire from the rights owners sufficient rights to produce and exploit the film. These may be obtained from the creators of the works or their successors in title. The rights may be in pre-existing or "underlying" works, or in specially created works, such as an original screenplay. The main sources upon which the film will be based are as follows:

(i) Underlying works

27–190   If underlying works (such as a novel, play or biography) are to be reproduced in or adapted for the screenplay and the film, the film producer must acquire the necessary rights in them so as not to infringe the rights of the copyright owner.[12] The rights needed are those to:

(i) adapt the work in the form of a screenplay[13] ;

(ii) reproduce the work in the form of a film[14] ;

(iii) perform the work in public by exhibition of such film[15] ;

(iv) broadcast the work or include it in a cable programme service[16] ;

(v) issue copies of the work (in the form of the film) to the public, *i.e.* usually in DVD or video cassette form[17] ;

(vi) rent or lend copies of the work (in the form of the film) to the public, *i.e.* usually in DVD or video cassette form.[18]

There are other (often referred to as "ancillary" or "subsidiary") rights which may need to be acquired, namely the rights to:

(a) adapt the work in the form of scripts for a television series or serial or "movie-of-the-week" (often referred to as "TV spin offs");

(b) adapt the work in the form of a dramatic work for radio broadcast or performance on stage;

(c) adapt the work in the form of a synopsis (for promotional purposes);

(d) adapt the screenplay for publication in the form of a "novelisation";

(e) publish the screenplay in the form of a "book of the film"[19] ;

(f) copy the work in the form of a remake[20] of the film;

(g) copy the work in the form of a prequel[21] or sequel to the film.

---

[12] In theory it would be possible for the producer to acquire the entire copyright in any underlying work. In practice, the entire copyright is rarely acquired and the copyright owner reserves to himself rights not required for film purposes (*e.g.* book and other publication rights).

[13] CDPA 1988, s.21.

[14] s.17.

[15] s.19.

[16] s.20.

[17] s.18 as amended by reg.10(2) of the Copyright and Related Rights Regulations 1996 (SI 1996/2967).

[18] CDPA 1988, s.18A as amended by reg.10(2) of the Copyright and Related Rights Regulations 1996 (SI 1996/2967).

[19] "Book of the film" is generally understood to be a publication in which the screenplay is juxtaposed with other writing (such as director's notes) and with still photographs taken on the production set.

[20] A film is remade when the screenplay of the earlier film is filmed a second time, invariably by a different director; one of the best examples is "Ben Hur".

[21] A "prequel" to a film is another film using one or more of the characters, the characterisations, the designs and the genre (perhaps even some of the plot lines or settings) of the script of the original, but portraying the characters at an earlier moment in time. The more customary "sequel" to a film portrays the characters at a later moment in time than the original. The extent to which either a prequel or a sequel infringes the copyright in the original work is a moot point since it is invariably the custom to seek a grant of such rights where contemplated.

To the extent that the rights owner has the capacity to grant them, the producer **27–191** will also be concerned to acquire the right to produce and distribute a soundtrack music album, to use the writer's name and likeness, and the "merchandising rights".[22] Merchandising rights are often pieced together from disparate sources, for example the name and features of characters described in the underlying work, the set or costume designer's drawings, specially designed artwork and logos, and registered trade marks.

It would be usual for the producer to require the author either to hold back from granting film (or television) rights in any sequel or prequel to the underlying work written by him, or at least to afford to the producer the right to match the terms of any third-party offer to acquire such rights. Provided that the grant of rights from the author to the producer is drafted sufficiently widely, this restriction will not arise in respect of sequels or prequels to the film based on the characters and settings of the original film because the copyright in them (to the extent that the same subsists) will vest in the producer.

At the start of the development stage it is common for a producer to acquire an option to purchase the film rights in the underlying work for a consideration which is typically 10 per cent of the agreed purchase price. This sum will be on account of and deductible from the purchase price due on exercise of the option. An initial option period of one year is customary, which might be extended by further periods for an additional consideration which may or may not be deductible from the purchase price. The producer thus ensures that his initial financial exposure is not massive and he has a window of opportunity to develop the project, but the rights are available to enable him to make the film and he can grant security over such option to any funding source.

(ii) Original screenplay

Where a writer is commissioned to write an original screenplay, as opposed to a **27–192** film based on a pre-existing work, it is usual for the producer to take a full assignment of any rights the writer may have in his screenplay. No such assignment would technically be required where the writer is employed by the producer under a contract of service.[23] However, even in such circumstances, the prudent producer will use a full assignment incorporating provisions dealing with entitlements to credits and moral rights. A producer with insufficient funds to pre-purchase all rights, or who only envisages certain types of exploitation, may choose simply to acquire those rights which are required for immediately foreseeable uses.

Unless he is deemed to be employed by the producer under a contract of service, the writer has the moral right to be identified as the author of the work (his paternity right).[24] This obligation will normally be satisfied by giving the writer a screen credit, *e.g.* in accordance with the provisions of the current WGGB/PACT Screenwriting Credits Agreement. The producer must also have regard to the writer's integrity right, protecting him from "derogatory treatment" of his work (which might result from editing, dubbing, etc. of the film).[25] Since moral rights are unassignable, producers should ensure that they are waived by their owners if

---

[22] The producer will require the right to register the copyright in the film in those jurisdictions in which it is necessary to do so, *e.g.* the United States of America.

[23] CDPA 1988, s.11(2). This remains a rarity outside the United States of America where such works are frequently written by screenplay writers contracted under so-called "work-for-hire" agreements.

[24] CDPA 1988, s.77. See Ch.11, above.

[25] CDPA 1988, s.80. Again, see Ch.11, above.

there is any possibility of their being infringed.[26] The application of moral rights is examined in more detail at paragraph 27–202, below.

(iii) Musical works

27–193   Although music will frequently not be added to the sound track until the film has been edited in the post production stage, it may be featured or performed as part of the live action. Whether the producer uses a pre-existing musical work or a work specially commissioned for use within the soundtrack of the film, it will be necessary to obtain a "synchronisation" licence to record (or "dub") the music (and naturally any lyrics to be performed alongside the music) onto the soundtrack. In the case of pre-existing music, this will be under the control of the owner of the copyright in the work or, in the case of music specially composed for the film, the composer.[27] If the composer has an exclusive publishing contract, the publisher will also have to be party to the licence. The producer will also require a grant of the "mechanical" right, that is the right to copy or transpose the work onto other media, *e.g.* DVDs, and for all media of distribution (including those technologies not yet invented). Both such rights—synchronisation and mechanical—are often administered by the Mechanical-Copyright Protection Society ("MCPS") on its behalf.[28]

A recurrent problem is that music for the soundtrack is invariably left to a later stage in the production process (sometimes because the composer wishes to view the "rough cut" first); requests for synchronisation licences are given a low priority by publishers and record companies (resulting in delays) and the budget available to "clear" music is usually small. All these factors can often combine to reduce the strength of the producer's negotiating position with the copyright owner. A similar timing problem can also occur where the score is commissioned from a composer. Whether or not the producer pays for the recording of the score (and especially if he does not), it is imperative to agree in advance issues such as the composer's duties; the grant (or waiver) of rights; the engagement of, and obtaining grants and consents from, musicians.

(iv) Sound recordings

27–194   Where an existing sound recording is to be used as part of the sound track, a synchronisation (or "recording synchronisation" or "master use") licence will be required in respect of such sound recording from the owner of the copyright in that recording, usually a record company. A grant of the right to copy the recording onto other carriers will also be required from the record company.

(v) Artistic works

27–195   Copyright in the set and costume designs and any storyboard should be expressly assigned in the producer's agreements with the relevant "behind the camera" personnel. Copyright in such artistic works as appear in the background of a film (architectural works, paintings, etc.) will usually not be infringed in a film which displays those works since the Act allows for the *incidental* inclusion of artistic

---

[26] As permitted by CDPA 1988, s.87.
[27] As to which see para. 27–200, below.
[28] As to the MCPS, see para. 28–56, below.

works[29] in a film and the making of a film of works of architecture and sculpture on public display.[30] The producer will, however, still need a grant of rights or "clearance" from the copyright owner in order to feature an artistic work prominently in his film.

(a) *Assignments from actors/director*

Contracts for the services of all performers and the director should contain an express assignment of the copyright in any material which may be created during the course of filming. In this way copyright in "on-the-floor" dialogue changes suggested by such individuals and incorporated into the film will vest in the production company.

27–196

(b) *Public domain works*

A producer may wish to use material in which the copyright has expired. Although it will not be necessary for the producer to acquire rights in such public domain material, it will be necessary to establish the position in all countries in which the film is to be distributed.

27–197

(c) *Duration of grant of rights*

A producer would certainly be advised to take an outright assignment of copyright or film rights for the full period of copyright to enable the film to be exploited without reference to the owners of the underlying rights. In addition the assignment should be expressed to include all renewals, reversions and extensions or revivals of the period of copyright because, although the Berne and Universal Copyright Conventions provide minimum periods of copyright, it may be that national laws provide varying degrees of protection.

27–198

C. THE WORKS WHICH ARE CREATED AND THE MAIN RIGHTS WHICH ARE REQUIRED FOR EXPLOITATION

The film

A producer, as part of the development process of his film project, will need to acquire all of the rights in the film which are necessary to enable him to exploit it in all media of exploitation. The principal media are theatrical exhibition, free or pay television broadcasts (including the relay of such signal over cable television networks) and the sale ("sell-through") or rental of DVDs and video cassettes.[31] The best position is for the producer to acquire the copyright or the exclusive film, television and video rights in the work throughout the world together with the sole right to exploit the film based on the work in any and all media for the full period of copyright plus any renewals, extensions or revivals.[32]

27–199

---

[29] CDPA 1988, s.31. See paras 9–56 *et seq.*, above, for a discussion of the "incidental inclusion" exception.

[30] CDPA 1988, s.62.

[31] These rights are those contained in CDPA 1988 (as amended), ss.18, 19 and 20.

[32] If the film is never made, there may be a "turnaround" provision requiring these rights to be returned to the previous owner after a fixed period. Such return must be by way of reassignment, although the prudent owner will include a power of attorney in his favour to enable him to execute the reassignment, in the event that the producer fails to reassign when the provision becomes operative.

The soundtrack

27–200   Notwithstanding that the soundtrack of a film is to be treated as part of the film,[33] film soundtracks are entitled to copyright separately as sound recordings under the Act. The film producer should therefore ensure that he takes either an assignment of copyright from the soundtrack owner of or a licence entitling him to reproduce the work in any material form. In many cases, he alone arranges for the soundtrack to be made.[34]

The right to perform any music or lyrics in public (the "performance right"), as opposed to the sound recording of that work, will invariably have been assigned by the composer (assuming he is British) to the Performing Right Society (the "PRS"). This assignment will also include the right to synchronise specially commissioned music with the film soundtrack. In an ideal world, the composer will be required in his agreement with the producer to procure the grant of such synchronisation right by the PRS to the producer. Since no royalty is collected for public performance in the United States of America, the PRS in practice refuses to grant a film synchronisation licence unless the producer agrees to provide for payment of fees to the composer via the PRS in respect of the theatrical exhibition of the film in the United States.

As the assignee of the right to perform any composition in public (assuming the composer is British—there are similar affiliated societies in other countries), the PRS controls the performance right of works of its members. However, since the public performance of such works will be undertaken by others, e.g. theatrical exhibitors, it is not the producer who obtains performing right licences from the PRS.

If the producer intends to issue a recording of the soundtrack or "soundtrack album", this may prove lucrative if the requisite rights are obtained in a timely manner and on favourable terms. If the producer has to return to negotiate this right with the composer, if he does not own the copyright in the sound recording of the score, if the fullest consents have not been obtained from the performers, or if he intends to use various recordings owned by different recording companies, he may find that to release such a soundtrack album presents grave difficulties.

Ancillary rights

27–201   As explained at paragraph 27–191, above, the producer would be well advised to acquire as far as possible all ancillary or subsidiary rights, including the right to exploit recordings of the soundtrack, the merchandising elements of the underlying works, the right to publish synopses of the works and the right to make adaptations from them. Although the "merchandising rights"[35] (i.e. the right to sell products bearing attributes of a film, such as a toy or T-shirt) are potentially lucrative, there is no generic merchandising right. Nevertheless, a book of a film may infringe copyright or another intellectual property right in the screenplay, or a toy based on an animated film character may infringe copyright in the drawings or designs used in the film. There is no copyright in film titles, although the film owner can benefit from the sale of goods bearing the film title by registration of trade marks of particular classes of goods. The tort of passing off may offer further protection to film owners.[36] Sequel rights to the film made by the producer should be acquired in order to prevent the situation where such rights are granted

[33] CDPA 1988, s.5B(2).
[34] For first owner of copyright in soundtrack, see paras 5–06 et seq., above.
[35] As to merchandising rights in relation to the film industry, see para. 27–191, above.
[36] As to protection of the goodwill in titles by a passing-off action, see Ch.22, above.

to a third party who may go on to produce a film the commercial success of which is derived almost entirely from the success of the earlier film.

Moral rights

A waiver of the moral rights of authors, without which it may not be possible to make desired changes or "cuts" to the film and thus ensure its successful exploitation, should be included in any agreement to acquire film rights.[37] It should be noted that in certain circumstances the right to object to derogatory treatment may still apply even if the work is created under a contract of service.[38]

27–202

Performers' property rights

Following the creation of the performers' property rights by the Duration of Copyright and Rights in Performances Regulations 1995,[39] it is imperative that the producer obtains the written consent of all performers in the film. This is usually obtained by a clause to this effect in the contract of engagement. These rights extend to all performers whether they are seen in the film or whether their performance is only included in the soundtrack. Where a performing artiste with an exclusive recording contract appears, the consent of the person having the benefit of such contract, *i.e.* the record company, must also be obtained.[40]

27–203

Rental and lending right

Following the creation of the rental and lending right by the Copyright and Related Rights Regulations 1996[41] it is anticipated that, in due course, one or more test cases, and possibly collective bargaining agreements, will ensue. The potential problem areas for the film industry are:

27–204

  (a) the lack of a presumption of transfer of rental right in a film production agreement with the film director;

  (b) the uncertainty created by the jurisdiction of the Copyright Tribunal generally and, in particular, the outlawing of provisions purporting to prevent a person from questioning the amount of equitable remuneration[42];

  (c) the fact that the rental right is partly retrospective in scope,[43] resulting in difficulty in tracing the successors in title of rights owners years after the event and difficulty in assessing the impact of the right on the operations and valuations of film libraries and catalogues.

Copyright notice

To secure protection in those countries which are not party to the Berne Convention, but are members of the Universal Copyright Convention,[44] it is essential to ensure that the © symbol, the name of the copyright owner and the year of first publication appear on all film prints and negatives.

27–205

---

[37] As to moral rights generally, see Ch.11, above.

[38] See CDPA 1988, s.82.

[39] As to performers' property rights generally, see Ch.12, above.

[40] As to such right of a record company, see para. 27–143, above.

[41] As to rental and lending right generally, see para. 7–81, above.

[42] As to which see s.93C(5) of the CDPA 1988 (as amended by reg.14 of the Copyright and Related Rights Regulations 1996) (SI 1996/2967).

[43] Reg.26 of the Copyright and Related Rights Regulations 1996 (SI 1996/2967).

[44] As to which, see Ch.24, above. Note also that the United States of America is now a member of Berne.

D. THE ORGANISATIONS BY MEANS OF WHICH FILMS ARE EXPLOITED

27–206   Distributors (including so-called "majors", or Hollywood film studios). These are the companies which market the film and incur significant expenditures on the cost of prints of the film and on advertising in the press, on posters and billboards, on television and through other publicity. Unless they control their own means of distribution they license the film through some or all of the other media, as follows:

(a) Theatre owners. Films are booked into cinemas through which the film can achieve a "theatrical"' release. Some cinemas are part of a chain, others are independently owned/operated.

(b) Non-theatrical distribution. This is the term given to describe all means of distribution, other than those specifically identified in (a) and (c)–(g). The most obvious are exhibition on airlines, ships and oil rigs, or by relay to bedrooms in a hotel. Other methods include exhibition in institutions such as hostels, schools, colleges or prisons.

(c) Dial-up online distributors ("video on demand" or "pay per view"). This is a growing market by which a customer can order the viewing of a film by connection to an interactive network.

(d) DVD and video cassette rental outlets. These outlets have grown up since the early 1980s, some operating under the brand name of a chain, others independently owned.

(e) "Sell through" retailers. Many DVDs or video cassettes are offered for sale by retailers also offering copies to rent. Increasing numbers of units are sold by large high-street retail stores.

(f) Pay TV broadcasters and pay cable TV. These are the broadcasting channels and cablecasting networks which will offer films to their subscribers.

(g) Free TV broadcasters and basic cable TV. Exhibitions of the film on "free-to-air" television and by basic (*i.e.* free) cable can deliver the largest audiences, but yield no return to the producer/distributor other than the basic licence fee.[45]

E. THE TRADE UNIONS OR TRADE ASSOCIATIONS WHICH REPRESENT VARIOUS INTERESTS

27–207   Bodies representing producers or their representatives:

(a) AFMA, formerly known as the American Film Marketing Association, represents more than 170 independent film producers and their representatives;

(b) Motion Picture Association of America represents seven major producers and distributors of films in the United States of America;

(c) Producers Alliance for Cinema and Television ("PACT") represents independent feature film companies operating in the United Kingdom;

(d) New Producers Alliance represents young film producers.

27–208   Bodies representing creators:

(a) Music Publishers Association represents music publishers;

(b) British Academy of Composers and Songwriters represents composers of music and lyrics;

(c) Directors Guild of Great Britain represents film, television and theatre directors;

---

[45] Distribution online is anticipated, but not yet a reality.

(d) Society of Authors represents principally novelists and dramatists;

(e) Writers' Guild of Great Britain ("WGGB") represents all freelance writers in the United Kingdom but principally writers for film and television;

(f) British Film Designers Guild represents film designers.

Bodies representing performers: **27–209**

(a) Equity represents actors and other performers including singers and dancers. As well as negotiating in traditional TV and film works, Equity negotiates individual agreements for the use of its members' services in developing media such as interactive CD-ROM games;

(b) Film Artistes Association, now operating as a sub-division of BECTU, represents film "extras";

(c) Musicians' Union represents performing musicians.

Bodies representing film technicians: **27–210**

(a) Broadcasting, Entertainment, Cinematograph and Theatre Union ("BECTU"), formed by a merger between ACTT and NATKE, represents the technical staff used in film productions (*e.g.* set designers, cameramen, editors, etc.) throughout the United Kingdom;

(b) Production Managers Association represents film production managers;

(c) Guild of Location Managers represents those who scout for film locations;

(d) British Society of Cinematographers represents cinematographers or assistant directors;

(e) Guild of British Camera Technicians represents camera operator technicians;

(f) Production Guild of Great Britain, formed by a merger between the Guild of Film Production Accountants and Financial Administrators and the Guild of Film Production Executives, represents film production accountants

Bodies representing distributors or those involved in the distribution process: **27–211**

(a) British Phonographic Industry represents the producers and distributors of sound recordings in the United Kingdom and internationally through the International Federation of the Phonographic Industry;

(b) Cable Communications Association represents the major companies holding licences to operate cable programme services in the United Kingdom;

(c) Cinema Exhibitors Association represents operators of cinemas in the United Kingdom;

(d) Independent Television Association represents those companies holding regional and national licences to broadcast on Channel 3;

(e) Film Distributors' Association represents theatrical film distributors (currently 13) in the United Kingdom;

(f) Videogram Producers Association represents the producers and distributors of video cassettes.

Guild agreements

The various individuals involved in film production are represented by different   **27–212**
professional bodies which agree minimum terms and conditions of service. PACT
has collective bargaining agreements with Equity, Film Artistes Association,
Musicians' Union, BECTU and WGGB governing the employment of their respective members. There is at present no standard agreement between film directors and PACT, since the director's authorship of a film was not recognised by
statute in the United Kingdom until the coming into force of the Copyright and

Related Rights Regulations 1996.[46] These standard film industry agreements are worth a brief examination insofar as they differ regarding the treatment of copyright and other similar rights.

27–213 **PACT—Equity agreement for cinema.**[47] Actors have performers' property rights but no copyright in their work. These rights allow performers to control the reproduction, distribution, and the rental and lending of recordings of their performances. The text of the PACT—Equity agreement grants all consents necessary under the Act for exploitation of such recordings although, since the agreement pre-dated the coming into force of the Copyright and Related Rights Regulations 1996, it is advisable to ensure that the producer's agreement with the individual actor confirms this.

27–214 **PACT—WGGB agreement.**[48] According to this agreement, full copyright in the work for which the writer is engaged vests in the producer. However, the writer is given the right to buy back an original script for 50 per cent of sums paid if principal photography has not begun within two years of delivery of the last material for which the writer had been commissioned.

27–215 **PACT—BECTU agreement.**[49] Again, this agreement grants to the producer all the necessary grants and consents under the Act as he may reasonably require. This might be in respect of copyright in a set or costume design.

27–215A The American principal professional organisations involved in film production are:

    (a) Writers Guild of America ("WGA")—the counterpart of WGGB;

    (b) Directors Guild of America ("DGA")—the counterpart of the Directors Guild of Great Britain;

    (c) Screen Actors Guild ("SAG")—the counterpart of Equity.

Generally, each of the above three bodies negotiates a standard agreement with the Alliance of Motion Picture and Television Producers ("AMPTP"), which is the multi-employer bargaining unit representing the "major" film studios and the leading independents. Production companies are obviously only bound by such agreements if they are signatories to them. This has resulted in the practice of requiring in addition co-producers, distributors or other parties contracting with AMPTP members to execute so-called "affiliation" agreements. The intended effect of such an "affiliation" agreement is to extend the provisions of the agreement between the guild and AMPTP so as to bind the non-member for the purposes of the specific film.

F. COLLECTING SOCIETIES/LICENSING AGENCIES WHICH ARE RESPONSIBLE FOR ADMINISTERING THE RIGHTS

27–216 [50] Authors Licensing and Collecting Society administers photocopying, lending and certain recording and retransmission rights on behalf of authors in the United Kingdom;

Compact administers the rights to cable retransmission and private copying of works for film and television producers;

Design and Artists Copyright Society administers the rights of painters, sculptors, photographers and other visual artists;

---

[46] (SI 1996/2967), Reg.18.
[47] Dated July 1, 1993.
[48] Dated February 3, 1992.
[49] Dated December 1, 1995.
[50] As to Collecting Societies generally, see Ch.28, below.

Directors' and Producers' Rights Society administers authorial rights payments received from United Kingdom broadcasters and via agreements with collecting societies overseas on behalf of film and television directors;

Educational Recording Agency administers the recording of works for educational use in educational establishments;

MCPS administers the rights to broadcasting and public use of music recordings and issues licences to film companies allowing them to include their members' works in films and commercials;

PRS administers the rights to perform a work in public, broadcast it or include it in a cable programme service and any film synchronisation rights if a work has been commissioned for a film soundtrack;

Phonographic Performance Limited administers the rights to broadcasting and the public use of sound recordings and issues licences to radio and television broadcasters and performance venues, such as dance halls and discotheques;

Videogram Performance Limited, administers the rights to sound recordings contained in music videos.

G. RELEVANT INDUSTRY CONTROLS

Licensing of films

For a film to be shown in cinemas it must be licensed. The British Board of Film Classification ("BBFC") was established in 1912 to bring a degree of uniformity to the censorship standards imposed by Local Authorities in the exercise of their licensing function . The BBFC has for many years regulated the content of films distributed in the United Kingdom. Local Authorities retain the right to ban a film which may have been passed by the BBFC, to alter the category for a film to be exhibited under their jurisdiction or to impose or waive cuts to be made to a film. However, in general, Local Authorities accept the decisions of the BBFC. Since 1985 the BBFC has also classified and controlled the content of video recordings offered for sale or hire commercially in the United Kingdom, which definition was later expanded to include computer games.[51] It does this in conjunction with the Video Standards Council, which was established in 1989 and administers a voluntary scheme making age-suitability recommendations for computer and video games that do not require legal classification.

27–217

The BBFC is responsible for the certification of films to be exhibited in cinemas. There are a number of tests laid down within its memorandum which must be applied before the granting of a certificate. There are six categories of certificate: U-Universal; PG-Parental Guidance; 12A, 15, 18 and R18 for restricted distribution only. If a film or video is obscene within the meaning of the Obscene Publications Acts or offends against other provisions of the law in such a manner that in the view of the BBFC no amount of cutting can make it acceptable, the work will be refused a certificate altogether[52] . Film companies are free to submit their product to any Local Authority if it is felt that a different view might be taken.[53] For videos, there is the Video Appeals Committee.

---

[51] Video Recordings Act 1984. See also Sch.9, para.22(a) of the Criminal Justice and Public Order Act 1994 which extends the definition of video recordings to include computer-generated games and works.

[52] The age definition in the Protection of Children Act 1978 of a "child" as portrayed in a film was raised to age 18 by the Sexual Offences Act 2003. This makes it an offence to portray onscreen the sexual exploitation of an under-18, irrespective of the actual age of the actor.

[53] An example of a Local Authority taking a different view was in the case of David Cronenberg's film "Crash".

Quotas

27–218   The "Television Without Frontiers" Directive[54] was intended to serve as a means to promote European productions and the distribution of audio-visual products. Article 4 of the Directive obliges all television channels licensed in Europe to devote to European works a majority of certain parts of the transmission schedule (this rule does not apply to those parts of the schedule devoted to news, sports events, games, advertising and teletext services). "European works" are, broadly speaking, works made, or at least supervised and controlled, by producers established in EU Member States.[55] However, the obligation to make transmissions involving 51 per cent European works is qualified insofar as it only applies "where practicable".[56]

Films Act 1985

27–219   Schedule 1 of the Films Act 1985 sets out the circumstances in which a film will be regarded as a British film under the Act and therefore can be certified as a qualifying film for the purpose of certain tax and other legislation.[57] For a film to qualify as a British film, each of the following three requirements must be satisfied:

  (a) The maker of the film must, throughout the time the film was made, be either: (i) a person ordinarily resident in an EU Member State; or (ii) a company registered in an EU Member State, being a company whose central management and control is exercised in an EU Member State. The maker is defined as the person (*i.e.* the legal entity) by whom the arrangements necessary for the making of the film are undertaken.

  (b) At least 70 per cent of the expenditure on production of the film must have been incurred on activity carried out in the United Kingdom.

  (c) Not less than the requisite amount of labour costs must have been paid to: (i) Commonwealth citizens or citizens of any EU Member State; or (ii) persons ordinarily resident in a Commonwealth country or an EU Member State.[58]

H. PROBLEMS WHICH CONFRONT THE INDUSTRY IN PRACTICE

(i) Colourisation

27–220   The case of *Turner Entertainment v Huston*[59] highlights a potential problem which can arise in relation to colourisation of monochrome films. Turner Entertainment had acquired the rights to the 1950 film "Asphalt Jungle" and had "colourised" the film, which had originally been created in black and white. Turner Entertainment applied to register copyright in the new version and consented to the broadcast of the colourised version on French television. The heirs to the estate of the film's director, John Huston, tried to prevent its broadcast

---

[54] The Co-ordination of Certain Provisions Laid Down by Law, Regulation or Administrative Action in Member States Concerning the Pursuit of Television Broadcasting Activities: 89/552/EC and 97/36/EC.

[55] Art.6 of Directive 89/552.

[56] Art.4 of Directive 89/552.

[57] For tax treatment of "British" films, see paras 30–11 *et seq.*, below.

[58] Sch.1, para.4 (2)(c) to Films Act 1985. Sch.1, para.7 to Films Act 1985 sets out in detail how the requisite amount of labour costs is to be calculated.

[59] *Turner Entertainment v Heirs to the Estate of John Huston*, Court of Appeal of Versailles, *Revue Internationale des droits d'auteur* No.164 April 1995 at p.389.

on the basis that the colourisation was an infringement of the author's moral right not to have his work subjected to derogatory treatment. The issue turned on whether the disputed modification was compatible with the original artistic concept of the film. The Court of Appeal of Versailles felt there was evidence to suggest that John Huston would have opposed the broadcast of a colourised version of one of his works and so held that his moral right of integrity had been infringed. The case represents persuasive authority that colourisation may constitute derogatory treatment of a film under the Act. It added colourisation to a list of technical alterations held by the French courts to constitute an infringement of a film-maker's right of integrity. Previous illustrations had involved the addition of credits, the addition of a sound track, excessive editing and the superimposing of a logo on the broadcast of a film.

(ii) Completion bonds

A financier will frequently obtain a performance guarantee or "completion bond" from an independent guarantor that the film will be completed and delivered to the distributors, or in the alternative the financier's investment will be repaid. In return for providing such bond, the completion guarantor might expect a fee of approximately 3 per cent of the "negative cost" (*i.e.* all the cost up to the completion of the master negative and delivery of the film). This negative cost figure is commonly known as the "strike price". The guarantor will also seek an agreement with the producer to protect his position, which agreement will grant to the guarantor the ultimate right to take over production of the film if the producer should run into insoluble difficulties. Problems have occurred[60] in circumstances where the distributor refuses to accept delivery and to pay the distribution advance, the guarantee of repayment is called under the completion bond and the guarantor has to pursue the remedies under his agreement with the producer.

27–221

(iii) Co-productions

Because film is such an international commodity, and funding difficult to come by, it is hardly surprising that producers should want to shoot or edit their films in different territories or to co-produce with producers from other countries. This process can create difficulties in various different ways, for example availability of work permits for cast and crew, attribution of nationality for subsidy or awards purposes, and so on. These difficulties have been reduced by the creation of a series of bilateral co-production treaties. The United Kingdom has seven treaties with, respectively, Australia (June 1990), Canada (July 1991), France (June 1995), Germany (November 1975), Italy (June 1967), New Zealand (April 1993) and Norway (May 1983). These treaties facilitate co-productions between co-producers resident in the respective countries, which qualify according to the treaty regulations to be treated as a production of each such country (at least to the extent of the expenditure in such country). Although each treaty is bilateral, it is possible to construct three-way co-productions using the provisions of each of any two treaties. Since 1992, the European Convention on Cinematographic Co-productions has been promoted by the Council of Europe and 31 countries have now adhered to it. The Convention can operate as a framework either for a three-way co-production between producers located in signatory states, or for a bilateral co-production between two such producers.

27–222

Although these treaties (and the Convention) have facilitated the production of

---

[60] An example was a film entitled "Mesmer".

international films, actual and potential problems remain, many resulting from the conflicts between the applicable legal regimes. For instance, could a completion guarantor enforce its contractual right to replace the director of a co-production film in both jurisdictions, including one where the moral rights of authors carry great weight?

(iv) Copyright in characters and titles

27–223   Where characters from a film are copied borrowing the name and other identifying features but without details of plot or dialogue, a claim for infringement of copyright is unlikely to be successful. A claim for passing off a different film as a sequel to, or spin-off from, the original film by reason of the unauthorised use of the character will be the most likely cause of action available to the owner.[61] It is very difficult to protect titles of films by an action for infringement of copyright due to the requirements of originality and that a substantial part of a work be copied.[62] If a well-known title of a film is used without authority, the owner's remedy is likely to lie in passing off.[63] Protection by registration as a trade mark may be available provided the title is sufficiently distinctive.

The MPAA, the global representative of the "major" film studios, has a voluntary subscription registration scheme for titles of theatrical motion pictures. Over 125,000 titles have been registered since 1925. The primary purpose of the MPAA Title Registration Bureau is not to assist copyright owners but to avoid confusion in the US theatrical marketplace. The register, which can be used for a fee by non-MPAA members, helps prevent the release of two or more films with similar or identical titles. Subscribers agree to resolve disputes through arbitration, and any arbitration decision can be enforced by a court.

(v) Incidental inclusion

27–224   A substantial part of a copyright work, such as a painting or a film clip, but not music or lyrics, may be included in the film even though the owner may not have consented to its use. In such a case the defence of "incidental inclusion" may be available, but it will be a matter of degree.[64] In practice, permission for inclusion (or "clearance") is usually sought.

(vi) ISAN system

27–225   The ISAN system is a voluntary standard numbering system for the unique and international identification of audiovisual works. Any such work to which the system applies is allocated a 16-digit ISAN (International Standard Audio-visual Number). Plans for the introduction of the system are advanced but not yet set in concrete. If and when introduced the system could be used to assist allocation of royalties among rightholders, to track use of audio-visual works and for anti-piracy purposes such as verifying title registrations.

(vii) Plagiarism

27–226   The issue of plagiarism, particularly allegations of plagiarism, is ever-present in

---

[61] As to such a remedy, see Ch.21, above.
[62] As to copyright in titles, see para. 3–16, above.
[63] As to passing off generally, see Ch.21, above.
[64] As to incidental inclusion and CDPA 1988, s.31, see paras 9–56 *et seq.*, above.

the film industry.[65] Screenplays are often submitted on an unsolicited basis. Nevertheless it is the desire of some production companies to read or review all such screenplays. In response to the former trend, some companies have adopted a policy either to return all such unsolicited screenplays marked "unread" or to invite the writer to sign a waiver of all appropriate rights as a condition precedent to the reading of any such unsolicited screenplay.

(viii) Portrayal of living persons

There is no copyright infringement if a living person is portrayed in a film. However, a film-maker undertaking such a project should beware of a possible claim for infringement of privacy or for defamation by such a person who may feel the film has lowered his reputation in the eyes of others. This is why the credits of a film (other than a biographical study) usually purport to state that any resemblance of any character to a living person is entirely coincidental. One sure way to avoid the possibility of a defamation action where the film portrays a living person is to collaborate with such person when making the film. Such collaboration should involve the agreement of those depicted in the film not to work with any other film-maker who is considering making a competing film. It is also advisable to acquire the exclusive rights to use any published biography on which the portrayal is to be based, not only to avoid any copyright infringement, but also to avoid such material being available for use in any competitive project.

27–227

(ix) Public domain films

A film producer will always be advised to take an assignment or an irrevocable licence for the full term of copyright in the underlying rights he seeks to acquire, especially where the underlying works were not originally created for the purposes of the film. This is because the periods of copyright of the underlying works may, in theory, extend beyond the expiry of copyright in the film and its exploitation could thereafter be subject to the licence of the owners of the copyright in the underlying works. Given the recent extension of the term of copyright in films,[66] this issue may in the future pose less of a problem in practice.[67]

27–228

(x) Publishers' quitclaims

It is standard in many publishing agreements for a book publisher to take some interest (either a licence or an agency) in the film, television and radio rights to the published work. A "quitclaim" is often sought from the publisher(s) in all major territories in order to confirm that no such interest is asserted by such publisher(s).

27–229

(xi) Screen credits

The author of a literary, dramatic, artistic or musical work has the right under

27–230

---

[65] The authors of a 1987 stage play entitled "Ladies Night" commenced proceedings in California against the makers of "The Full Monty", claiming that the award-winning film plagiarised the setting, premise and some character development of the earlier work. "Errors and omissions" insurance was devised with this type of claim in mind.

[66] Duration of Copyright and Rights in Performances Regulations 1995 (SI 1995/3297), reg.6(1).

[67] It is intended to extend the period of copyright in the United States of America, thus also reducing the scale of the problem there.

certain circumstances to be identified as the author of that work.[68] This right extends to an author from whose work an adaptation has been made, which would include for example where a screenplay has been adapted from a novel. The director of a film has the right to be identified as the director in similar circumstances.[69]

Credits are the lifeblood of the film industry. Although they (and their order, size, whether sole or shared, etc.) are sometimes negotiated at great length, no standard industry credits have evolved. Only select directors will command a "possessory" credit.[70] However, the provisions of the WGGB/PACT Screenwriting Credits Agreement will sometimes be incorporated into an agreement with a writer, even where the parties are not contracting in accordance with the terms of the PACT/WGGB Agreement, and the DGA has very strict requirements to be adhered to for distribution in the United States of America. Thus, certain conventions have become established-for example that the director will have a credit on the final card, *i.e.* the final frame on which credits appear, whether at the beginning or end of the film. The issue remains a contractual art, not a science.

(xii) Storylines

27–231   Since there is no monopoly of source material and no copyright in an idea, there is frequently a multiplicity of projects concerning a topical or popular subject in development at any time. There are several independent registration services for writers. These accept registrations of screenplays and scripts submitted for a limited period of time so that the author can verify his authorship with effect from an independently certifiable date. Registration with one of these services does not however confer any proprietary rights.[71] It is rare, however, for more than two similar big-budget projects to reach the screen at the same or similar time.[72] The MPAA title register,[73] although technically available only to MPAA members, can alert a film producer to the existence of a storyline which may resemble one he is thinking of using in his next project.

(xiii) United States Library of Congress

27–232   The United States of America is the most important source of making films and frequently the most lucrative market—at least for American films. It is also one of the few jurisdictions to maintain a register of copyrights.[74] Although registration is no longer a prerequisite for subsistence of copyright, the register is extensively used and offers several benefits to producers of United Kingdom films:

(a) a search against the title of an underlying work may reveal interests other than those of the copyright owner, for example that of a mortgagee or owner of a prior contractual option;

(b) registration of the producer's interest in an underlying work or a

---

[68] CDPA 1988, s.77(1).

[69] CDPA 1988, s.77(2)(a) and (b).

[70] For example "John Carpenter's 'The Thing'", "A film by John Carpenter" or "A John Carpenter film".

[71] Examples of such registration services include the Raindance Script Registration Service and the Script Factory Script Registration Service.

[72] The Robin Hood films were a notable exception to this generalisation.

[73] See para. 27–223, above.

[74] The register is kept at the United States Library of Congress in Washington, DC.

screenplay would operate as notice of it to third parties who conduct similar searches[75];

(c) a search against the title will reveal the existence of any work with the same or a similar title.

(xiv) Video and DVD piracy

This problem remains a major cause of concern for all those in the film industry, approaching 30 years since it first manifested itself. There are a number of laws dealing with counterfeiting in the United Kingdom and an agency, Federation Against Copyright Theft (FACT), which acts to combat piracy and other forms of copyright theft. The manufacture of pirate DVD and video cassette copies is prevalent in the Asia Pacific and Eastern Europe regions, where it is frequently controlled by organised crime.

27–233

(xv) WIPO Register

The World Intellectual Property Organisation ("WIPO") has sponsored a Treaty on the International Registration of Audiovisual Works, which entered into force on February 27, 1991.[76] The Treaty has established a self-supporting International Film Register ("IFR") to record statements concerning rights in audiovisual works. These statements show who owns the work or which other rights in the work exist, the territory for which the rights are valid and other details concerning the work.

27–234

Two problems have dogged the scheme. The MPAA and AFMA have expressed concern about the possibility of false filings being used so as to undermine the rights of the legitimate owner. Also, the eligibility of persons to file registration applications is limited to natural persons or legal entities which have their domicile or seat in a country which is a member of the Treaty establishing the Register. As at November 15, 1996, only 12 countries had become signatories to the Treaty, which inhibits the usefulness and effectiveness of the Register. The United Kingdom is not a signatory and apparently has no immediate plan to become one. The United States of America is not a signatory and as a result the Register is not used by the "major" film studios.

5. THE BROADCASTING INDUSTRY

A. OVERVIEW

The broadcasting industry, both in the United Kingdom and worldwide, is a user on a massive scale of copyright works and of performances of actors and musicians. Its expenditure on acquiring the rights to broadcast such works and performances forms a significant proportion of the annual revenues that flow from copyright users to rights owners. For example, UK radio and television broadcasters paid the Performing Right Society ("PRS")[77] some £89.6 million in 2003 for the right to broadcast musical works, representing 53 per cent of the

27–235

---

[75] To facilitate such registration and to preserve confidentiality, the practice has grown up of executing a supplemental or "short-form" document which reflects the principal grant of rights but not the commercial terms contained in the long-form documents.

[76] "International Property Laws and Treaties, Multilateral Treaties 1–01"; *Copyright*, June 1989 published by WIPO.

[77] As to the PRS, see para. 28–59, below.

PRS's revenues in that year from its UK licensing activity[78] . The BBC's payments to copyright collecting societies amounted to £54.4 million in 2003/4[79] . UK television broadcasters spent over £1.2 million in 2002 on acquiring rights from Hollywood studios and other overseas producers to broadcast feature films and other acquired programmes.[80]

Broadcasters are not merely users of existing copyright works and of live or recorded performances by actors and musicians. They also commission and finance the creation of new works for use in their services: new television and radio programmes, and the music, screenplays, scripts and other works and performances they may include. Broadcasters own the copyright or hold extensive rights in such specially created works and they turn that ownership to account not only by broadcasting them but also by licensing their secondary use by others in a variety of media. The turnover in 2003/4 of BBC Worldwide Limited derived from programme distribution and channel licensing was £254 million.[81] The UK's television programme export industry earned revenues of $921 million in 2003, giving an increase of more than 80 per cent over the past five years.[82]

Broadcasters create programme services designed to appeal to mass, minority or special-interest audiences. The broadcasters own the copyright in their broadcasts and need adequate legislation to enable them to protect the economic value of their rights. With the development of encryption, which allows broadcasters to limit reception of their services to those prepared to pay to receive them, there has proved to be a need to supplement broadcasters' basic protection under copyright law with additional "associated rights" to enable them to take effective action against those who manufacture or market devices designed to circumvent encryption controls. These were introduced, along with related criminal law sanctions, in the 1988 Act, and were then supplemented by the Broadcasting Acts of 1990 and 1996, and again by the Copyright and Related Rights Regulations 2003.[83]

B. THE STRUCTURE OF THE BROADCASTING INDUSTRY IN THE UNITED KINGDOM

Regulation

27–236   Broadcasting is, in most countries, a highly regulated industry. In part this is because, until recent years, the limited range of frequencies available for broadcasting restricted the number of broadcasters able to operate without unacceptable levels of signal interference. Further, it was, and still is, considered that the right to use these limited public assets, the frequencies, should be allocated according to the public interest. A third principal reason for the high degree of regulation results from the pervasive and invasive nature of broadcasting. Radio and television signals enter every home; if individuals in the home turn on a radio or television set they hear or see whatever is being broadcast at that moment on the channel to which their set is tuned. Regulation of the content of broadcasting services is aimed, at the minimum, to ensure that what they hear or see is within acceptable political and cultural limits. At the maximum, regulation is intended

---

[78] PRS press release, June 9, 2004.
[79] BBC Annual Report and Accounts 2003/2004.
[80] Office for National Statistics: International Service Transactions of the Film and Television Industries, 2002.
[81] BBC Annual Report and Accounts 2003/2004.
[82] British Television Distributors Association press release, May 2004.
[83] See Ch.15, above.

to enhance the quality of life. For instance, the BBC's primary objects include, in the language of its Charter, the provision as public services of "sound and television programmes of information, education and entertainment". Likewise, the chief European regulatory instrument, the EC Directive "Television without Frontiers" of October 1989,[84] seeks to regulate broadcasting across frontiers because such broadcasting is, according to the Directive's preamble, one of the ways of pursuing such Community objectives as establishing a closer union between the peoples of Europe, contributing to social and economic progress by eliminating the barriers which divide Europe, and ensuring the preservation and strengthening of peace and liberty.

Commercial broadcasters

The regulation of commercial broadcasting in this country is undertaken by the Office of Communications—Ofcom—under powers vested in it by the Communications Act 2003. It is an offence for anyone other than the BBC to operate a broadcasting service in the UK without a licence from Ofcom. Licensed broadcasters are required by the terms of their licences to observe Ofcom's codes as to programme content, as to advertising standards and the duration and placement of advertising,[85] and as to impartiality and other matters. Some of these obligations reflect the terms of the "Television without Frontiers" Directive and the parallel European Convention on Transfrontier Television.   **27–237**

The BBC

The provision of publicly funded broadcasting in this country is undertaken by the BBC. Established by Royal Charter, with its Governors appointed by the Queen in Council, the BBC is essentially self-regulating. The Communications Act 2003 has, however, subjected the BBC to regulation by Ofcom in respect of programme content standards and certain quantifiable elements of its public service obligations, such as the requirement that 25 per cent of its television programmes be commissioned from independent producers.[86]   **27–238**

Range of services

As of mid-2003, the broadcasting services being provided in the United Kingdom were as follows:—   **27–239**

Television
- Five channels are broadcast on the available analogue terrestrial broadcasting frequencies and, in consequence of being allocated those frequencies, have public service broadcasting obligations. These channels are now also broadcast from digital terrestrial and digital satellite transmitters. Government policy is that analogue broadcasting should cease around 2010–2012. The five channels are—
  - BBC1 and BBC2;
  - ITV comprising:
    — the national breakfast-time service broadcast by GMTV;
    — the 15 regional ITV services—the majority of which are now

[84] Directive 89/552/EEC.
[85] As to the advertising codes, see para. 27–318, below.
[86] ss.198 and 338 Communications Act 2003.

owned by Granada—which together finance and provide a national network with a substantial amount of regional variation;

- Channel 4 and, in Wales, the Welsh-language S4C;
- Five.

- Numerous services are broadcast via satellite; over 240 are made available by BSkyB in its basic package offering to subscribers to its platform. Services broadcast by satellite include—
  - services intended for reception in the UK, such as the public service channels mentioned above, or in the UK and Ireland, for example, the UKTV channels and the Sky channels;
  - services intended for reception in the UK and the rest of Europe: for example, CNN International, MTVEurope, Discovery;
  - services not intended for reception in the UK but only elsewhere in Europe—for example, BBC Prime and BBC World, TV3 (aimed at Scandinavia);

  Some of these services are general entertainment and information channels, others are thematic channels (e.g. predominantly feature films, or news, sport, children's or music programming).

  - A limited number of the channels carried by BSkyB on its satellite platform are also broadcast via digital terrestrial transmitters and on cable networks for reception only in the UK. These transmission systems have significantly less channel capacity than BSkyB's satellite platform.

Radio

- The BBC provides—

  10 national radio services, 5 of which are broadcast in analogue as well as digital form;

  3 national regional services, for Scotland, Wales and Northern Ireland, together with services in Welsh and Gaelic;

  over 40 local and community radio services;

  The World Service.

- There are 3 national commercial radio services broadcasting on analogue frequencies—

  Virgin 1215;

  Classic FM;

  Talksport.

- National digital commercial stations have also commenced broadcasting.

- There are over 250 local commercial radio stations. Most of these provide music-based services.

Other broadcasting services

These include—

- teletext services of general interest, such as the BBC's CEEFAX;
- data broadcasting services, most conveying information services for commercial customers.[87]

---

[87] These broadcast the "other information" referred to in the definition of broadcasting in s.6 of the 1988 Act. See para. 3–93, above.

Programme production

Until the arrival of Channel Four in the early 1980's the UK television industry was vertically integrated. That is, the broadcasters also had substantial programme-making capacity to provide their programming requirements. Channel Four adopted the so-called publisher-broadcaster model, commissioning almost all its programming from independent production companies. The Broadcasting Act 1990 further encouraged the growth of an independent production sector by imposing on the BBC and the ITV companies a requirement that a minimum of 25 per cent of the time they allocate to the broadcasting of certain defined categories of programmes should be reserved for the broadcasting of a range and diversity of independent productions. The Communications Act 2003 has given further support to production companies by limiting the scope of the rights which broadcasters can insist on acquiring when commissioning independent productions.

27–240

Radio remains by and large a vertically-integrated sector, although independent production has secured a foothold.

Cable

By March 2004, over 3.3 million homes in the United Kingdom received television broadcasts by way of cable rather than through off-air reception from terrestrial or satellite transmitters.[88] All but a few of the channels transmitted are of UK origin and are also broadcast over-the-air from terrestrial and satellite transmitters. Also offered on cable networks are a small number of cable-exclusive television programme services, including some video-on-demand services. A number of radio services are also transmitted.

27–241

Internet broadcasting

A very large number of sound broadcasting services are transmitted via the internet. Many are "simulcasts" of services also being broadcast over the air, while others are transmitted only in this medium. Internet relays from concerts and sports events—also now treated as acts of broadcasting under the 1988 Act—have also become common. The provision of television services over the Internet is in its infancy, but the rapid pace of technical development means that this form of broadcasting is likely to be widespread before the next edition of this book appears. Of course, internet technology is ideally suited to the provision of programming on demand, and many individual television and radio programmes are now made available in this way.

27–242

C. THE USE OF COPYRIGHT WORKS AND PROTECTED PERFORMANCES IN BROADCASTING

Rights usage

A given hour of broadcasting may use almost no copyright works or protected performances at all, while another may involve the use of a multiplicity of works and performances, many simultaneously. For instance, a live broadcast of an hour of cricket from Lord's or tennis from Wimbledon will as a rule not involve the use of protected works of third parties, other than to a trivial extent. An hour

27–243

[88] Ofcom—Digital Television Update, Quarter 1, 2004.

of football coverage may include some singing by the crowd of well-known tunes,[89] but little else in the way of copyright material. Advertisers' logos and other copyright works may appear in shot, but the broadcaster's contract with the event organiser will generally place the onus on the organiser to effect any necessary clearances of them; their inclusion will usually, of course, be intended by the advertiser. Synchronised swimming may cross the borderline between sport and performance of a dramatic work, provided, of course, that it is choreographed.[90] At the other extreme, an hour of a television drama-documentary programme, for example a dramatisation of the life of a public figure, could well involve all of the following—

- The use of a biography or other source material as the basis for the programme;
- The commissioning of a researcher to analyse other sources or to carry out fresh research into the subject, and to provide a written report for the screenplay writer to use;
- The commissioning of a writer to provide a dramatic screenplay;
- The clearance of rights in extracts from letters, speeches, diaries or other literary works to be quoted in the programme;
- The engaging of a director to direct the filming[91];
- The use of existing photographs and the commissioning of a photographer to take fresh ones for use in the production;
- The use of historic film or television footage of the events, period or characters being portrayed;
- The commissioning of a composer to write opening, closing and incidental music;
- The use of existing music, to be played by musicians in or out of vision, or to be dubbed into the programme from commercial records or CDs;
- The use of such commercial sound recordings, which are themselves copyright works in their own right;
- The engaging of actors and musicians to perform in the production, who will have rights in respect of the fixations made of their performances.[92]

Rights clearances

27–244   Just as the extent to which various types of programmes use copyright works and performances may differ markedly, so too may the rights clearances which broadcasters and their programme suppliers obtain. A commercial radio broadcaster may need to acquire nothing more than the right to give one live broadcast of a work, because the broadcast will have little or no prospect of further exploitation in any way. Conversely, a television production company will typically acquire very extensive rights in order to be able to realise the full commercial value of the programme over a period of many years.

To take the example of a television drama-documentary again, the following rights clearances will typically be required—

- The right to adapt the source material as required for the purposes of the programme. In this connection a waiver of the author's moral right of integrity will usually be sought;

---

[89] Accompanied sometimes by rather less-well-known words.
[90] Note, however, the rejection of the argument that there is a copyright in a sports game such as American football, in which individual movements are intended to follow a pre-set plan, in *FWS Joint Sports Claimants v Copyright Board* (1991) 22 I.P.R. 429 (Fed Ct App Canada).
[91] Following the implementation of the EC Term and Rental Directives (93/98 and 92/100), the principal director will be a co-author of the programme. See para. 4–58, above.
[92] See Ch.12, above.

- The right to copy all the works and performances to be used. This is needed to permit them to be recorded or filmed in the course of production of the programme. Apart from being reproduced in the final master recording, there will be a number of intermediate reproductions which the clearance must permit;
- The right to broadcast each work and performance included in the programme, and the programme itself, by all methods of broadcast transmission;
- Secondary exploitation rights including—
- The right to make and distribute copies of the programme in the form of videograms, both by way of sale and by way of rental and lending;
- The right to make and distribute copies of the soundtrack of the programme in the form of CDs;
- The right to permit the programme to be transmitted via cable, either by way of licensing of the programme for inclusion in a third party's cable channel or by way of cable retransmission (by reception and immediate retransmission) of broadcasts;
- The right to permit the programme to be included in internet services, including on-demand services;
- The right to adapt and distribute the programme in nonlinear media (e.g. CD-ROM or CDi);
- The right to permit the programme to be shown in public, certainly to non-paying audiences and, in some instances, to paying audiences too;
- The right to publish the screenplay or an adaptation of it in a book related to the programme and likewise the right to publish in such book other elements such as photographs and extracts from the source material;
- The right to publish the screenplay in the form of a novelisation of it;
- The right to use any of the works or performances in connection with the promotion and advertising of the programme;
- The right to make further recordings of any of the works or performances, as recorded for the purposes of the programme, for archival purposes[93];
- The right to produce and market merchandise related to the programme.

Acquisition of rights

The acquisition of such rights can be extremely straightforward. Some may be **27–245** acquired by the simple method of acquiring the complete copyright in the work throughout the world, in perpetuity, in return for payment of a single fee at the outset. More often, the clearance process will involve the painstaking negotiation of the acquisition of specified rights, for limited territories and for limited periods, not infrequently from several rightsowners for a single work, and against payment of an initial fee payable in instalments at different stages of the production process, with further fees or royalties becoming due upon further exploitation of the programme. The parties' freedom to negotiate may, moreover, be constrained by the terms of agreements between, on the one hand, trade unions or collecting societies representing rightsowners, and on the other hand the broadcaster or a trade association representing producers. Some of these are minimum terms agreements, setting the minimum rates that must be paid and the working prac-

---

[93] CDPA 1988 s.75, which enables designated broadcasts to be recorded for archival purposes can at present only be taken advantage of by The British Film Institute, The British Library, The Music Performance Research Centre, The National Library of Wales and The Scottish Film Council. See para. 4–213, above and Vol.2 at A4.xvi.

tices that must be observed when writers are commissioned or performers engaged for productions. Others set out standard terms for certain uses of certain types of works. Others again are "blanket agreements" allowing specified uses to be made of a body of works in a collecting society's repertoire, against payment of annual lump sums or fixed rates per unit of usage.

The following is a representation in schematic form of the collecting society and trade union agreements that govern the process of rights clearances for broadcasting in the UK.

TYPE OF WORK OR PERFORMANCE	ARE CLEARANCES PRIMARILY MADE INDIVIDUALLY RATHER THAN UNDER A COLLECTIVE AGREEMENT?	ARE ANY CLEARANCES (OR PAYMENTS) MADE UNDER COLLECTIVE AGREEMENTS?	WHICH TRADE UNION OR COLLECTING SOCIETY IS INVOLVED?
Source Material	Yes	Only for certain cable retransmissions of terrestrial broadcasts, some BBC satellite television programme services and for the radio channel BBC7[94]	Authors Licensing and Collecting Society ('ALCS')[95]
Screenplays and radio drama scripts	Yes	Only for certain cable retransmissions of terrestrial broadcasts, some BBC satellite television broadcasts and for radio channel BBC7	ALCS. In addition, the Writers Guild of Great Britain[96] has minimum terms agreements with the Producers Alliance for Cinema and Television ('PACT'), ITV, and the BBC for the writing of drama scripts

[94] The retransmissions concerned are of UK terrestrial broadcasts in Ireland, but would also include any foreign terrestrial broadcasts retransmitted in the UK.
[95] As to the ALCS, see para. 28–49, below.
[96] www.writersguild.org.uk.

TYPE OF WORK OR PERFORMANCE	ARE CLEARANCES PRIMARILY MADE INDIVIDUALLY RATHER THAN UNDER A COLLECTIVE AGREEMENT?	ARE ANY CLEARANCES (OR PAYMENTS) MADE UNDER COLLECTIVE AGREEMENTS?	WHICH TRADE UNION OR COLLECTING SOCIETY IS INVOLVED?
Directors	Yes	No. However, the Directors and Producers Rights Society ('DPRS')[97] collects remuneration for British directors in respect of cable retransmissions in Europe of British television programmes	The Broadcasting, Entertainment, Cinema and Theatre Union ('BECTU'),[98] the Directors Guild[99] and DPRS have agreements with PACT, the BBC, ITV, Channel Four, S4C, Five and BSkyB relating to the engagement of directors
Commissioned Composers	Yes, other than for broadcasting, cable and public performance rights pre-assigned by the composer to the Performing Right Society ('PRS')	For broadcasting and public performance rights	PRS[1]

[97] As to the DPRS, see para. 28–54, below.
[98] www.bectu.org.uk.
[99] www.dggb.co.uk.
[1] As to the PRS see para. 28–59, below.

TYPE OF WORK OR PERFORMANCE	ARE CLEARANCES PRIMARILY MADE INDIVIDUALLY RATHER THAN UNDER A COLLECTIVE AGREEMENT?	ARE ANY CLEARANCES (OR PAYMENTS) MADE UNDER COLLECTIVE AGREEMENTS?	WHICH TRADE UNION OR COLLECTING SOCIETY IS INVOLVED?
Existing music	Only if "grand rights"[2] usage is involved, or for secondary exploitation rights falling outside the scope of the mandate given by composers and publishers to the Mechanical Copyright Protection Society ("MCPS")[3] or outside the scope of the blanket agreements referred to in column 4	Yes, for (a) broadcasting and public performance rights, and (b) synchronisation and recording rights	(a) The Music Publishers Association[4] has negotiated agreements on synchronisation and broadcasting fees for grand rights use (b) PRS has negotiated blanket agreements with broadcasters for broadcasting and public performance rights (c) MCPS has negotiated blanket agreements for synchronisation and recording rights with broadcasters and some independent producers

[2] As to the meaning of this expression, see para. 27–288, below.
[3] As to the MCPS, see para. 28–56, below.
[4] www.mpaonline.org.uk

TYPE OF WORK OR PERFORMANCE	ARE CLEARANCES PRIMARILY MADE INDIVIDUALLY RATHER THAN UNDER A COLLEC- TIVE AGREEMENT?	ARE ANY CLEAR- ANCES (OR PAY- MENTS) MADE UNDER COLLEC- TIVE AGREEMENTS?	WHICH TRADE UNION OR COLLECTING SOCIETY IS INVOLVED?
Commercial sound recordings	The consent of individual record companies may be required for certain fur- ther exploitation of tele- vision programmes containing dubbed com- mercial records, even if a blanket agreement has been entered into be- tween the commissioning broadcaster and Phonographic Perfor- mance Limited ('PPL')[5]	For dubbing and broadcasting rights	PPL has blanket agreements with both radio and television broadcasters

[5] As to PPL, see para. 28–60, below.

TYPE OF WORK OR PERFORMANCE	ARE CLEARANCES PRIMARILY MADE INDIVIDUALLY RATHER THAN UNDER A COLLECTIVE AGREEMENT?	ARE ANY CLEARANCES (OR PAYMENTS) MADE UNDER COLLECTIVE AGREEMENTS?	WHICH TRADE UNION OR COLLECTING SOCIETY IS INVOLVED?
Music videos	Yes, except to the extent that usage may be covered by a blanket agreement between a broadcaster and Video Performance Limited ('VPL')[6]	For broadcasting rights	VPL has negotiated blanket agreements or standard rates with some broadcasters and producers
Artistic works	Yes	Only for certain cable retransmissions, through the Design and Artists Copyright Society ('DACS')[7]	DACS has negotiated a model form of clearance agreement with the BBC. Likewise, the British Association of Picture Libraries and Agencies ('BAPLA')[8] has negotiated a model form of agreement with the BBC for the use of its members' photographs
Film and television programme footage	Yes	For cable retransmission of foreign broadcasts	The Association de Gestion Internationale Collective des Oeuvres Audiovisuelles ('AGICOA') is mandated to license cable retransmission

[6] As to VPL, see para. 28–61, below.
[7] As to DACS, see para. 28–53 , below.
[8] www.bapla.org.uk.

TYPE OF WORK OR PERFORMANCE	ARE CLEARANCES PRIMARILY MADE INDIVIDUALLY RATHER THAN UNDER A COLLECTIVE AGREEMENT?	ARE ANY CLEARANCES (OR PAYMENTS) MADE UNDER COLLECTIVE AGREEMENTS?	WHICH TRADE UNION OR COLLECTING SOCIETY IS INVOLVED?
Actors	Yes	No	British Actors Equity Association ('Equity')[9] has negotiated minimum terms agreements with PACT, the BBC and the ITV companies for the engagement of actors
Musicians	Yes	No	The Musicians' Union[10] has negotiated minimum terms agreements with PACT, the BBC and the ITV companies for the engagement of musicians

9 www.equity.org.uk.
10 www.musiciansunion.org.uk.

Copies of the agreements entered into by the Writers' Guild, the Musicians' Union and Equity can be obtained from those unions. The Producers Rights Agency[11] should be contacted for information on the agreements entered into by PACT and the ITV companies. For information about the blanket and other agreements entered into by the various collecting societies, application should be made to the societies themselves.

D. REGULATORY CONTROLS RELEVANT TO RIGHTS-CLEARANCES

Copyright Tribunal

A critically important role is played by the Copyright Tribunal[12] in relation to the terms on which collecting societies license the use of works in their repertoires by broadcasters.

27–246

Noteworthy references to the Tribunal in the broadcasting field have been—

PARTIES	REFERENCE NUMBER	OUTCOME
1. The British Broadcasting Corporation 2. The Performing Right Society Limited	24/71	Established a formula whereby the BBC would pay 2 per cent of its licence fee income (and of its Foreign Office grant in aid for the World Service) for the broadcasting of music in its radio and television services
1. The Association of Independent Radio Contractors Limited. 2. Phonographic Performance Limited	35/78	For the right to broadcast commercial records, the Tribunal decided that commercial radio stations should pay PPL 4 per cent of the first £650,000 of net advertising revenue and 7 per cent of the remainder
1. The Independent Television Companies Association Limited 2. Independent Television News Limited 3. The Performing Right Society Limited	38/81	The Tribunal rejected PRS's claim for a percentage of ITV's net advertising revenue

---

[11] www.pact.co.uk/pra.

[12] As to the Copyright Tribunal and its predecessor, the Performing Right Tribunal, generally, see para. 29–88, below.

PARTIES	REFERENCE NUMBER	OUTCOME
1. The Association of Independent Radio Companies & Others 2. Phonographic Performance Limited	9/91	The Tribunal altered the formula under which the commercial radio broadcasters pay percentages of their net advertising revenue so that they would pay as follows—Music stations: 5 per cent of relevant revenue; Speech stations: 1 per cent of relevant revenue
1. BSkyB and Sky TV 2. The Performing Right Society Limited	38/96	In this reference, BSkyB sought a continuation of the terms on which its predecessors were licensed to broadcast music. The PRS sought a percentage (1 per cent initially, rising to 3 per cent after two years) of BSkyB's net advertising revenues and (discounted) revenues from cable operators. The Tribunal rejected a revenue-based approach and awarded a flat fee, adjustable for the future as to one part by percentage changes in viewer hours and RPI and as to another part by an incremental payment for each new channel

Licensing of performers' rights

27–247   The Copyright Tribunal was given another important jurisdiction by the 1988 Act, one for which broadcasters had lobbied in order to overcome difficulties they had experienced in exploiting their programme archives. The difficulties arose from the need to obtain additional consents from performers for the making of copies of programmes for supply to new categories of users, such as satellite broadcasters. The 1988 Act empowered the Tribunal to grant consent on behalf of a performer to the making of a copy of a recording which includes the performer's performance, if the performer could not be identified or traced after reasonable enquiry.[13] This provision was invoked to enable a 1954 BBC radio production of Dylan Thomas's "Under Milk Wood" to be used as the sound-track of an animated television production of this work.[14]

For the same reason, the Tribunal was also given power under the 1988 Act to give consent to the making of further recordings in the case of a performer who was unreasonably withholding consent.[15] It was considered unacceptable that a "tenth spear carrier" (*i.e.* a minor member of the cast) should be able to prevent exploitation of a production by withholding his consent unreasonably when all other cast members might have consented to the making of the necessary copies. This power was abolished on implementation of the EC Directive on Rental and Lending Rights[16]. The overall enhancement of performers' rights required by the Directive was considered to be incompatible with this compulsory licence mechanism.

E. RIGHTS-CLEARANCE ISSUES IN THE BROADCASTING FIELD

Overview of developments

The 1988 Act introduced, as broadcasters had requested, a number of provisions designed to facilitate their use of copyright works and protected performances. The process continued in the Broadcasting Act 1990, which made a number of amendments to the 1988 Act. Although the thrust of subsequent EC legislation has been to enhance the rights of authors and performers, the Satellite Broadcasting and Cable Retransmission Directive[17] recognised that the rights-clearance burden on satellite broadcasters needed to be lightened in the interests of encouraging the development of transfrontier television services. Likewise the transitional provisions of the Regulations implementing that Directive, the Rental and Lending Rights Directive[18] and the Term Directive[19] bear the imprint of representations made by producers and broadcasters concerned to ensure that the making of productions for which they had already entered into commitments, and the exploitation of productions already completed, should not be impeded. Although producers and broadcasters regretted the loss of section 190(1)(b) of the 1988 Act because of its incompatibility with the terms of the Rental and Lending Rights Directive, their representations in respect of the drafting of the transitional provisions succeeded to a degree in ensuring that their programme archives should not be locked up by rights-clearance difficulties, just at the point at which the new media were promising to offer fresh opportunities for their exploitation. No sooner had broadcasters achieved these concessions, however, than they found themselves having to make representations to the European Parliament and Commission over the treatment, in the proposed Directive on Copyright and Related Rights in the Information Society, of the key exceptions to copyright protection. Once that Directive[20] had been adopted, their attention focussed on ensuring that the UK's regulations implementing it dealt appropriately with the new forms of broadcasting then coming onstream. The salient features of these developments are outlined below.

27–248

---

[13] CDPA 1988, s.190 (1)(a).

[14] *Ex p. Sianel Pedwar Cymru* [1993] E.M.L.R. 251.

[15] CDPA 1988, s.190 (1)(b).

[16] Reg.23, The Copyright and Related Rights Regulations 1996 (SI 1996/2967).

[17] 93/83/EEC.

[18] 92/100/EEC.

[19] 93/98/EEC.

[20] 2001/29/EC.

The 1988 Act

27–249   The most important of the facilitating provisions introduced by the 1988 Act were as follows:

Recording of the spoken word

27–250   The 1988 Act put it beyond doubt that a speaker's words, recorded on tape as he spoke, could constitute a literary work.[21] The making of such recordings is an everyday activity for broadcasters, who were therefore concerned that the implied licences on which they would often have to rely would not protect them in all circumstances. For instance, would a speaker who regretted what he had said be entitled to revoke such a licence? What would be the position as regards recordings made surreptitiously, for which no implied licence could be invoked? The validity of such concerns was recognised and dealt with by section 58 of the 1988 Act, which provides that where a recording of spoken words is made for the purposes of broadcasting, it is not an infringement of copyright in the words as a literary work to use the recording (or to copy it and use the copy) for broadcasting, provided certain conditions are met. These conditions have not detracted from the protection which s.58 gives to broadcasting journalism.[22]

Fair dealing

27–251   Under the Copyright Act 1956 the fair dealing exceptions did not apply to sound recordings or films. Further, the civil rights of performers which had been recognised by the court in *Rickless v United Artists Corp*[23] were not subject to a statutory fair dealing exception. These defects were remedied by the 1988 Act.[24] The BBC, having pressed for these changes to be introduced, mounted the first challenge to their scope, but failed to convince the court that the broadcasting by British Satellite Broadcasting of highlights from the BBC's coverage of the 1990 Football World Cup was not fair dealing for the purpose of reporting a current event.[25]

The availability of this fair dealing exception was underpinned by the inclusion in the Broadcasting Act 1996 of a provision making void any clause in an agreement which seeks to prohibit the taking of visual images from a broadcast in circumstances where the exception would apply.[26]

The application to films of the exception allowing criticism or review has also been tested by a broadcaster, Channel Four, which succeeded in persuading the Court of Appeal that the use of excerpts from Stanley Kubrick's film "A Clockwork Orange" in a programme evaluating the film and arguing that Kubrick's ban on its showing in the UK should be lifted, fell within the scope of the exception.[27]

These fair dealing exceptions have been the subject of further amendments introduced by the Copyright and Related Rights Regulations 2003, most notably

---

[21] See CDPA 1988, s.3(1) and para. 3–14, above.

[22] As to these conditions and s.58 generally, see para. 9–155 *et seq.*, above.

[23] [1988] Q.B. 40.

[24] By CDPA 1988, s.30 for films, sound recordings and broadcasts and by s.189 and Sch.2 para.2 for performances.

[25] *BBC v British Satellite Broadcasting Ltd* [1992] Ch. 141. As to the fair dealing provisions, see para. 9–44 *et seq.*, above.

[26] s. 137, Broadcasting Act 1996.

[27] *Time Warner Entertainment Co v Channel Four Television Corp* [1994] E.M.L.R. 1, CA. See paras 9–35. *et seq.*, above.

in the new requirement that fair dealing with a work for the purposes of reporting a current event by way of a broadcast must be accompanied by a sufficient acknowledgement, except where this would be impossible for reasons of practicality or otherwise. There are not likely to be many instances where it can safely be said that it would be impossible to give an acknowledgement.[28]

Incidental inclusion

Broadcasters gave a warm welcome to the introduction of a defence of incidental inclusion in the Bill that became the 1988 Act. Had the Act included only the wording of section 31(1) from the Bill (*i.e.* "Copyright in a work is not infringed by its incidental inclusion in an artistic work, sound recording, film, broadcast or cable programme") the defence would have produced a very satisfactory degree of protection for broadcasters against claims from copyright owners for payments for the use of their works in such *de minimis* circumstances. However, lobbying by music copyright owners resulted in the inclusion in the Act of section 31(3), which provides that a musical work, words spoken or sung with music, or so much of a sound recording, broadcast or cable programme as includes a musical work or such words, shall not be regarded as incidentally included in another work if it is deliberately included. This has complicated the analysis that needs to be made when a producer or broadcaster is considering whether this exception is applicable.[29] Broadcasters were dismayed to find that the exception did not appear at all in the exhaustive list of exceptions permitted by the Information Society Directive in its draft form, but their concerted lobbying succeeded in having it included in the final version.

27–252

Artistic works on public display

Broadcasters filming in public places or in premises open to the public are at risk of including artistic works that happen to be "in shot". Section 62 of the 1988 Act is a useful safeguard to them in circumstances where they might not readily be able to argue that they are covered by the exception for "incidental inclusion". It provides that the copyright in (a) buildings and (b) sculptures, models for buildings and works of artistic craftsmanship, if permanently situated in a public place or in premises open to the public, will not be infringed by making a film of them or broadcasting or including in a cable programme service a visual image of them.[30] This exception too survived unscathed the Information Society Directive.

27–253

The Broadcasting Act 1990: use of sound recordings

The Broadcasting Act 1990 introduced into the 1988 Act an important change to the basis on which broadcasters may acquire the right to use sound recordings.[31] This followed an enquiry by the Monopolies and Mergers Commission[32] into practices in the collective licensing of public performance and broadcasting rights in sound recordings, which recommended that Phonographic Performance Limited ("PPL")[33] should be obliged to permit the use of its repertoire in return for equitable remuneration, and that users should be entitled to a statutory licence.

27–254

---

[28] See para. 9–29, above.
[29] As to CDPA 1988, s.31 generally, see para. 9–56, above.
[30] As to CDPA 1988, s.62 generally, see para. 9–169, above.
[31] CDPA 1988, ss.135 A–G. See, generally paras 29–25. *et seq.*, below.
[32] CM 530. December 1988.
[33] As to PPL, see para. 28–60, below.

The statutory licence is available when the licensing body refuses to grant a licence whose terms as to payment would be acceptable to the broadcaster, or a licence allowing unlimited "needletime" or such needletime as the broadcaster has demanded (needletime being the amount of time in any period in which the sound recordings may be broadcast). The reference to the Tribunal made in 1991 by the Association of Independent Radio Companies[34] was made under the terms of this new provision, not surprisingly since it had been the Association which had made the representations which led to the reference of PPL's practices to the Monopolies and Mergers Commission. The Copyright and Related Rights Regulations, 2003 have restricted the scope of this statutory licence so that it will not apply to on-demand services, nor to internet broadcasts other than simulcasts.

EC copyright harmonisation Directives

27–255   The key provisions of the EC copyright harmonisation Directives facilitating broadcasters' rights clearances are as follows—

Place of broadcast

27–256   The Satellite Broadcasting and Cable Retransmission Directive[35] adopts the "emission theory" of broadcasting, that is, that a broadcast receivable in more than one country should be deemed to take place only in the country where the broadcast originates, rather than in each country where the broadcast is receivable. This means that a broadcaster only has to clear rights in one territory, not wherever the signal may be received. This was already the position as far as the United Kingdom was concerned under the 1988 Act, although further, refining amendments were introduced by the Copyright and Related Rights Regulations 1996.[36] This principle now applies throughout the EC and EEA. In practice, of course, the commercial terms on which rights are licensed to the satellite broadcaster will reflect the fact that audiences in other countries within the satellite footprint will be reached. It is noteworthy that in relation to the forms of Internet transmission defined as broadcasting by the Copyright and Related Rights Regulations 2003, there is no similar adoption of the emission theory.[37]

Exemption from collective licensing

27–257   The Satellite Broadcasting and Cable Retransmission Directive includes a provision[38] that broadcasters are not obliged to exercise their rights as against cable operators through collecting societies, in respect of the rights which have been transferred to them in copyright works of whatever type. Without this provision, transfrontier satellite broadcasters would be unable to achieve Europe-wide cable retransmission of their broadcasts on the basis of a single clearance made with a copyright owner able to grant a licence for the entire geographic area covered by the broadcast. Instead, they would be faced with the daunting prospect of having to obtain clearance country by country from the collecting societies in each country mandated to grant cable retransmission rights in works of the type in question. Broadcasters rather than cable operators have this clearance burden because under present market conditions in many countries cable operators are

---

[34] para. 27–246, above.
[35] 93/83/EEC, Art.1.2(b).
[36] See para. 7–111, above.
[37] But see para. 7–116, above.
[38] 93/83, Art.10.

able to require the broadcasters to deliver their programme services free and clear of charges for copyright and related rights. However, while trans-frontier satellite broadcasters have to date been able to obtain single clearances for the whole of Europe to cover the cable retransmission of most types of work included in their services, they have not as yet been able to do so in respect of copyright music. The national performing right societies have not been prepared to allow one another to grant to broadcasters such Europe-wide licences for cable retransmissions.

Transitional provisions

The three copyright Directives adopted in the 1990s contained a number of other **27–258** transitional provisions intended to give protection to persons with "legitimate expectations", that is, persons who had entered into contractual arrangements on the basis of existing law and who would be adversely affected by a change in the law applicable to those arrangements which resulted from implementation of the Directives.[39] In giving effect to the transitional provisions, the UK Government responded in a number of respects to concerns expressed by producers and broadcasters wishing to ensure that rights clearances for production and exploitation of programmes should not be complicated. Key provisions which reflect these concerns include the following—

- The revival of copyright in a work included in or adapted by a film or television or radio programme at a time before July 1, 1995 when that work was out of copyright will not affect the continued exploitation of the film or programme;
- The revived copyright in a work will not be infringed by acts done after 1 January 1996 in pursuance of arrangements to exploit the work entered into before January 1, 1995 when it was in the public domain;
- The revived copyright in a work will not be infringed by a restricted act done at a time when, or done in pursuance of arrangements made at a time when, the name and address of a person entitled to authorise the act cannot be ascertained by reasonable enquiry;
- A copyright licence subsisting on December 31, 1995 which was valid for the entire period of the copyright under the 1988 Act is extended so as to have effect throughout the duration of any extended copyright (subject to any agreement to the contrary);
- The presumption of transfer of rental rights is applied to agreements concluded before December 1, 1996, with no exclusion in relation to screenplay, dialogue or music specifically created for the film.

F. PROTECTION OF BROADCASTERS' RIGHTS

The 1988 Act introduced a number of specific protections of broadcasters' rights **27–259** additional to the protection of the broadcast themselves. Two in particular are worth special attention.

Protection of encrypted broadcasts

The 1988 Act included, at the request of broadcasters, specific protection in re- **27–260** spect of fraudulent reception of broadcast programmes, which was made a crimi-

---

[39] For a discussion of the transitional arrangements, see paras 5–136 *et seq.*, above.

nal offence,[40] and in respect of dealings in equipment or publishing of information to enable or assist unauthorised reception, which was made the subject of civil rights and remedies.[41] Broadcasters of pay television services had foreseen that such a package of criminal and civil law deterrents would be needed to deal with circumvention of payment for reception of their encrypted services. These provisions were strengthened by amendments introduced by the Broadcasting Act 1990, which made it a criminal offence to make, import, sell or let for hire an unauthorised decoder, and by further amendments in the Broadcasting Act 1996 adding offences of offering, exposing or advertising such decoders for sale or hire, and increasing the penalties for the offences.[42] These provisions, and such counterparts as had been enacted in other EU Member States, were reinforced by the EU Directive on the legal protection of services based on, or consisting of, conditional access.[43] The Directive requires Member States to prohibit the manufacture, import, sale or possession for commercial purposes of illicit devices; their installation, maintenance or replacement for commercial purposes; and the use of commercial communications to promote them. An illicit device is defined as any equipment or software designed or adapted to enable unauthorised access to a radio, television or online service where these are provided on the basis of conditional access. Broadcasters were concerned that conditional access was defined in the Directive in such a way that it would only be protected when it is aimed at ensuring remuneration for provision of a service. Broadcasters want conditional access to be protected when it is used to restrict access for other reasons, such as territorial rights limitations.

Cable retransmission

27–261   The 1988 Act also narrowed the scope, just in time for the new era of satellite broadcasting and the proliferation of television channels it ushered in, of the provision which had made its first appearance as section 40(3) of the Copyright Act 1956. This had provided that a cable operator would not infringe the copyright in a work included in a UK television or radio broadcast by retransmitting the broadcast to its subscribers. The justification for this exception was that cable operators were under obligation to retransmit BBC and ITV television broadcasts; the so-called "must-carry" rule. They were therefore seen as vulnerable to claims from copyright owners for excessive fees.

Section 73 of the 1988 Act continued the exception and further extended it to the copyright in the broadcasts themselves. However, the Act restricted the exception to the retransmission only of unencrypted broadcasts from terrestrial transmitters and to retransmissions of broadcasts intended for reception in the area where the cable operator's network is located or to broadcasts which a (diminishing) number of cable operators are obliged to carry as a condition of their operating licences granted under the Cable and Broadcasting Act 1984. The Broadcasting Act 1996 substituted a new section 73, applying the exception only to "must-carry" broadcasts (it was envisaged that some digital terrestrial broadcasts would be in this category) and to a defined list of public service channels , namely those of the BBC, ITV, Channel 4, Channel 5, S4C and the teletext services associated with them. Other commercial television broadcasters are

---

[40] See CDPA 1988, s.297 and para. 16–07, above.
[41] See s.298 and para. 16–21, above.
[42] See s.297A and para. 16–09, above.
[43] 98/84/EC.

therefore at liberty to negotiate terms for the carriage of their services with cable operators.[44]

G. Other Specific Provisions Dealing with Broadcasting

The 1988 Act dealt with three particular issues concerning broadcasting that had been the subject of controversy in the years prior to its adoption— **27–262**

Off-air recording

Off-air recording of television and radio broadcasts for private purposes had become a commonplace activity by 1988. Almost all of it constituted an infringement of copyright; only a recording made of a "live" broadcast containing no copyright works would not infringe, and only a very small proportion of broadcasts fell into this category. Rejecting calls for introduction of levies on blank tapes and recording equipment, the Government legalised home taping for "time-shifting" purposes, enabling the broadcast to be viewed or listened to at a more convenient time.[45] **27–263**

Off-air recording for educational purposes

Educational establishments wishing to make use for educational purposes of the wealth of material broadcast on radio and television had been frustrated by the inability of broadcasters to license them to do so. The broadcasters understandably did not see it as their function to spend their resources on acquiring rights from their programme contributors for the benefit of the educational sector. The 1988 Act found an innovative solution to the impasse, in the form of section 35. This provides, in effect, that unless copyright owners create officially approved licensing schemes for off-air recording by educational establishments, such recording will be treated as not infringing copyright. Presented with this challenge, the UK copyright collecting societies, performers' unions and broadcasters formed the Educational Recording Agency[46] and negotiated licence schemes with the educational sector that have produced significant revenues where none previously flowed.[47] **27–264**

Programme listings

For many years prior to 1988, newspaper and magazine publishers lobbied for compulsory licences to be imposed on the BBC, ITV and Channel 4 to allow publication of their weekly programme listings. Weekly listings were published for BBC programmes only in the BBC's own magazine "*Radio Times*", and for ITV and Channel 4 only in the "*TV Times*". Newspapers and other magazines were only allowed to print listings for the day of publication, with the right to print listings for additional days at weekends and public holidays. A Monopolies and Mergers Commission enquiry in 1985 decided, on the casting vote of the Chairman, that the refusals to license, although anti-competitive, were not against the public interest. The BBC and ITP Publications (who held the publication rights in the ITV and Channel Four listings) argued that they were merely exercis- **27–265**

---

[44] s.138 and Sch.9, Broadcasting Act 1996. See para. 9–205, above.

[45] CDPA 1988, s.70, and see para. 9–192, above.

[46] *www.era.org.uk*.

[47] As to CDPA 1988, s.35 generally, and the licensing schemes, see paras 9–97, above, and 28–55, below, respectively.

ing their rights as copyright owners of the listings and that, since these were literary works, compulsory licences could not be imposed in any event. They took
proceedings in the European Court of First Instance in an ultimately unsuccessful
attempt to overturn a European Commission Statement of Objections ordering
them to permit publication.[48]

The 1988 Act paved the way for a licence of right to be imposed by ministerial
Order by providing in section 144 that this could be done following a Competition Commission finding that a refusal to grant licences on reasonable terms may
be expected to operate or had operated against the public interest. In recognition
of the point made by the broadcasters that compulsory licences could not be
imposed on owners of copyright in literary works, section 144(3) provided that a
minister shall only exercise the power to provide for a licence as of right if satisfied that to do so would not contravene any Convention relating to copyright to
which the United Kingdom is a party. The Broadcasting Act 1990 finally settled
the controversy by requiring broadcasters to make their weekly listings available
to publishers who wished to publish them, and by allowing publication to commence on payment of such fees as the publisher proposed.[49] If the fee was not
agreed by the copyright owner, the publisher would have to apply to the Copyright Tribunal for the fee to be determined. Such a reference was duly made to
the Tribunal which, after an appeal had been settled by agreement, ultimately
ordered a rate per publication of 0.004 pence for each day in respect of which the
listings were published, multiplied by the average circulation figure for each issue of the publication.[50]

Programme formats

27–266   In 1989 the Privy Council decided that the unifying features of the television talent show "Opportunity Knocks" did not constitute a work protected by copyright
law.[51] This sparked a debate which is still continuing on whether new legislation
is needed to afford protection to so-called programme formats and, if so, what
form the protection should take.

In 1994 the Patent Office published a Consultative Document identifying what
appeared to be the main underlying factors and difficulties, and appending a
private Member's Bill which had been drafted by proponents of the introduction
of express copyright protection for formats. The responses received ranged from
those desiring greater protection, or a different type of protection, than was being
proposed by the proponents of the Bill, to those who wished to see no legislative
change. In 1996 a Further Consultative Document[52] was published by the Patent
Office inviting comments on a different approach, one that would not involve
introducing express copyright protection for formats as such, either as a category
of literary work or as a new category of work. Instead, the proposal was that
where one or more of the existing categories of copyright work embodies a
format, then the copyright in the work would be infringed by making a programme in accordance with that format. A format would be defined as a sufficiently elaborated scheme or plan for a series of programmes setting out those
factors which are to be present in each programme in the series. For an infringement to occur, the work or series of works recording the scheme or plan would

---

[48] *British Broadcasting Corp v EC Commission* [1991] 4 C.M.L.R. 669, CFI; *Independent Television Publications Ltd v EC Commission*: T-76/89 [1991] 4 C.M.L.R. 745, CFI.

[49] Broadcasting Act 1990, s.176, and see para. 29–09, below.

[50] *News Group Newspapers Ltd v Independent Television Publications Ltd* [1993] R.P.C. 173.

[51] *Green v New Zealand Broadcasting Corp* [1989] R.P.C. 700. As to this decision, and the protection of formats generally, see para. 3–42, above.

[52] See [1996] 5 Ent. L.R at p.216.

have to have been wholly set out in material form which pre-dated the first programme made to that scheme or plan.

This new approach received a somewhat warmer welcome from the television industry, but in the intervening years there has been no indication from the Patent Office that legislation will be forthcoming.

H. INTERNATIONAL PROTECTION OF BROADCASTERS' RIGHTS

Many broadcasters consider that, at the international level, insufficient recognition is given to their status as copyright owners of the broadcasts they create, and in particular to their need for enhanced protection in the face of the challenges posed by the new technologies. Whereas many of those challenges were addressed for other rights owners and for performers in the WIPO Treaties adopted in December 1996,[53] broadcasters' rights were not on the agenda.

27–267

In April 1997, WIPO held a World Symposium on Broadcasting, New Communication Technologies and Intellectual Property, at which a catalogue of rights was identified as a core for up to date neighbouring rights protection of broadcasters. Subsequent meetings of the WIPO Standing Committee on Copyright and Related Rights have taken matters forward to the point where, as at June 2004, it appears that a Diplomatic Conference may be convened as the final step in developing a new international treaty. Differences remain on whether only traditional broadcasters should be protected or whether protection should also be extended to webcasters and cablecasters. Likewise, there is still argument over whether the rights of broadcasters should be limited to those necessary to fight "signal piracy", and what the term of protection should be. Nonetheless, the Committee considered that the differences could be narrowed in a reasonable time frame.

The rights that would be accorded to broadcasters under the Treaty text in respect of their broadcasts are the right to authorise or prohibit—

> rebroadcasting
> retransmission by any means
> communication to the public, in places accessible to the public against payment of an entrance fee
> fixation
> reproduction of fixations
> distribution of the original or copies of the fixations and of reproductions
> transmission of fixations
> making available (on demand)

In addition, broadcasters would have to be given protection against any of these acts in relation to their signals prior to broadcasting.

Broadcasters' rights would be subject to the same kind of limitations and exceptions as are applicable to literary and artistic works. The term of protection would be 50 years computed from the end of the year in which the broadcasting took place. Adequate legal protection and remedies must be provided against circumvention of effective technological measures, and against removal or alteration of rights management information and against certain uses made with knowledge that such information had been removed without authority.

Many of these rights and protections are embodied in the 1988 Act, particularly following implementation of the EU Information Society Directive. While the impact of any new treaty will therefore be limited in terms of any changes likely to be required to United Kingdom copyright legislation, at the international level

---

[53] As to the WIPO Treaties, see para. 24–66, above.

the new protections will provide some assurance to broadcasters that they can engage in and expand their international broadcasting activities with greater confidence that they will be able to protect their services from unauthorised use.

6. THE THEATRE, THE OPERA AND THE BALLET

A. THE AUTHORS OF COPYRIGHT MATERIAL

27–268   The law of copyright in its application to the practical and contractual aspects of the theatre, opera and ballet as giving rise to dramatic works within the meaning of ,section 1 of the 1988 Act[54] can best be illustrated by reference to a live stage musical, which usually contains all the elements of drama, speech, music, song and dance (or choreographed movement) and production design, one or more of which may be missing from other forms, namely a non-musical play, an opera or a ballet. The principal parties or *dramatis personae* involved in the creation or acquisition of copyright and other rights in relation to the production of a stage musical are as follows:

    (i) Writers and composers
    (ii) Creative team:
        (a) Stage director
        (b) Choreographer or musical stager
        (c) Designers of:
            (i) Sets and properties
            (ii) Costumes and wigs
            (iii) Lighting
            (iv) Sound
        (d) Orchestrator and musical "arrangers"
    (iii) Logo and artwork designers
    (iv) Performers
    (v) Translators
    (vi) Producer.

(i) Writers and composers

27–269   Clearly the fundamental elements of these works are the basic words and music which are to be performed. Rarely will there be just one playwright or dramatist who has written the entire work and also composed the music. More often the music, text and lyrics will be composed or written by different persons, and even one such element alone may involve a number of collaborators.[55] In addition, there may be separate individuals who have created the conceptual treatment, some or all of the plot or the characterisation.[56] Sometimes adaptors or new writers will be engaged to adapt or make changes in a pre-existing novel, film or play on which a new work is to be based. The different bases for the acquisition of

---

[54] For meaning of "dramatic work" see s.2 of CDPA 1988 and *Norowzian v Arks Ltd (No.2)* [2000] F.S.R. 363, [2002] E.M.L.R. 67 and para. 3–35, above. The CA held that the meaning of dramatic work is at large, whose natural and ordinary meaning is "a work of action, with or without words or music, which is capable of being performed before an audience", and could thus include a film.

[55] As to whether such collaborators will be "joint" authors, see paras 4–47 *et seq.*, above, *Brighton v Jones* [2004] EWHC 1157. See also *Beckingham v Hodges* [2002] E.M.L.R. 45 and *Bambgoye v Reed* [2004] E.M.L.R. 5.

[56] As to the protection given by the law of copyright to such elements, see para. 3–41, above.

writers' and composers' rights by the producer are considered below.[57] Note also that where the writer or composer is a member of the Performing Right Society Ltd ("PRS"),[58] the PRS will have acquired certain rights in his work, including in particular, in this context, the so-called "small" performing right.[59] Authors also have important moral rights in respect of their work.[60]

Often the contractual terms between authors and producers will be governed by the minimum terms of a collective bargaining agreement between bodies representing the two sides respectively.[61] However, it will be noted that there is no such standard collective bargaining agreement for commercial West End of London theatre productions, where the usual practice is for terms to be negotiated between the parties to suit individual circumstances.[62] Typically such agreements will provide for an advance and royalties, comprising a percentage of net weekly box office receipts,[63] payable to the author or other copyright owner[64] Royalties may be expressed to escalate after recoupment of pre-production capital expenditure, or to be "capped" or "pooled" prior to such recoupment, or in some cases may be calculated on "weekly running surplus" rather than box office receipts. The advance will usually be expressed as non-returnable but recoupable in whole or in part from royalties. The producer will be granted an option to present the production within a specific period, possibly extendible by payment of further advances. If the production is presented within the option period and continued for a specified number of consecutive performances (usually 21), the producer may acquire specified subsidiary rights to produce in other territories or to exploit the work in other media. The producer's rights may be limited to a specified period of time, or they may be open-ended and subject to lapse only if, after the closure of the initial run or another specified period, less than a specified number of performances per annum (usually 50) are presented by the producer, or if no payment is made to the author in lieu of any shortfall in order to preserve the rights for a further period.

The grantor of the rights will, usually, be expected to "hold back" on releasing other stage rights or subsidiary rights so long as the producer's rights subsist or for a specified period or territory, and even when such other rights are released from hold-back, it is frequently agreed that the producer will share in revenue from their exploitation on the ground that such revenue is generated in part by his contribution to the reputation of the work, at least in the case of new work as distinct from "revivals".[65]

Other typical provisions commonly found in such agreements relate to warranties as to title and as to non-obscene and non-defamatory content, billing credits, house-seats allocation (seats held back for management disposal or priority

---

[57] para. 27–283 to 27–286, below.

[58] As to the role of the PRS, see Ch.28, below, and in particular para. 27–288, below.

[59] See paras 27–288 and 27–293, below. As to the full extent of the rights administered by the PRS, see the Society's Handbook.

[60] As to these, see Ch.11, above.

[61] For details of relevant collective bargaining agreements see para. 27–298, below.

[62] The expression "West End" of London in a theatrical context is normally taken to mean those theatres which are represented in the Society of London Theatre, as distinct from the geographical location of London's West End. Such theatres may not necessarily have a West End postal address.

[63] Usually defined as subject to certain standard deductions, such as VAT, credit card and ticket agents' commissions and block-booking discounts.

[64] In theatrical contracts, as the copyright ownership often becomes fragmented and the subject of sub-licensing arrangements, the obligation to pay royalties to a variety of royalty participants is frequently passed on to licensees and sub-licensees, but the possibly unwelcome effect in this context of the Contracts (Rights of Third Parties) Act 1999 should be noted, and the appropriate steps taken to negate its impact, if desired.

[65] For contractual restrictions on authors generally see para. 29–304, below.

reservation), approval or consultation rights, attendance at auditions and rehearsals, expenses, payment and accounting procedures.

(ii) The creative team

27–270   The creative team, together with and in consultation with the producer, is
responsible for converting the basic written work (that is to say the music, text
and lyrics) into the audio-visual representation of that basic work which is presented on stage. Inevitably this often involves a considerable degree of creativity.
It may also involve the creation of new copyright works, such as the set or
costume designs, in so far as these contain a sufficient degree of originality. The
creative team will usually be engaged as self-employed independent contractors
under contracts for services and will therefore start off as owners of the copyright
in their works,[66] although occasionally they may be employees under a contract
of service, for example if part of a resident stage company, when the copyright
will vest in the employer unless otherwise agreed.[67] It is also not uncommon for
individual members of the creative team to contract their services through their
own so-called "lend-out" companies which have the exclusive right to dispose of
such services,[68] in which case a personal guarantee of his company's contractual
obligations by the individual concerned, in what is often called an "inducement
letter", will usually be required.

The creative team will usually be remunerated by a fixed fee, possibly payable
by instalments at fixed intervals. Usually such fees are expressed as being non-
returnable but recoverable, in whole or in part, from the whole or part of future
royalties. The use of their copyright material or the product of their services on a
repetitive basis will usually be remunerated by reference to royalties expressed as
a fixed percentage of box office receipts (after standard deductions such as VAT
and credit card and ticket agency commissions and block-booking discounts),
possibly in some cases escalating after a specified number of performances or after so-called "recoupment" of the pre- production capital costs incurred prior to
opening.[69]

(a) *Directors*

27–271   There seems no reason in principle why a director's stage directions, whether relating to vocal or facial expressions, gestures or movements, should not attract
copyright as part of the whole dramatic work,[70] provided that they add significantly to the dramatic content, are original and are recorded in some permanent
form.[71] No doubt where a director adds stage directions which are commonplace
or largely dictated by the script, no question of copyright will arise, there being

---

[66] As to the rights acquired by the producer, see paras 27–281 and 27–283 to 27–286, below.

[67] CDPA 1988, s.11(2). As to works of employees generally, see paras 5–11 *et seq.*, above, and
para. 27–300, below, and note in particular *Intercase UK Ltd v Time Computers Ltd* (2003) [BLD
1712034628] and *Ultraframe (UK) Ltd v Fielding* [2003] EWCA 1805.

[68] Such companies generally employ their "owners" under a contract of service and so will in the
first instance own the copyright in any work made by the employee.

[69] See para. 27–269, above, as to basis of royalty calculation.

[70] As to what constitutes a dramatic work, see para. 3–35, above, and s.2 of CDPA 1988 and *Norowzian v Arks Ltd (No.2)* [2000] F.S.R. 363, [2002] E.M.L.R. 67 and para. 3–35, above. The CA
held that the meaning of dramatic work is at large, whose natural and ordinary meaning is "a
work of action, with or without words or music, which is capable of being performed before an
audience", and could thus include a film.

[71] The view has been expressed (see L. E. Cotterell, *Performance* (3rd ed.), p.371) that despite a
stage director giving life and vitality to the printed text of a dramatic work, his creative contribution has no protection in law. This view needs to treated with caution as a statement of principle.
As indicated in the text, it depends on the circumstances. As a matter of practice, the collective

no sufficient contribution to the dramatic work as a whole or no originality. In each case it will be a matter of degree. In many cases it will be fortuitous whether the further requirement, namely that the directions be recorded in some permanent form, is satisfied, depending on whether the stage directions were noted down at any stage or whether, for example, the production was filmed.[72] In practice, the point may not be important since the stage director's contract will usually provide for him to be remunerated whenever and wherever "the product of his services"[73] is used by the other contracting party. It is only where his work is described for the purpose of remuneration as being confined to that which is protected by copyright, or where he has placed some limitation on the right to use his copyright material, that a problem may arise.

(b) *Choreographers and musical stagers*

The work of choreographers will be protected if the usual conditions for subsistence of copyright apply.[74] The function of a choreographer is, of course, similar to that of a stage director, but relates specifically to dance and movement. Consequently, similar considerations apply as in the case of a director, save that, in contrast to the stage director, the choreographer's position is expressly recognised by section 3(1) of the 1988 Act.   **27–272**

Stage fights. Stage fights, although not works of "dance", are clearly capable of constituting one of the elements of a dramatic work. Fight direction has developed into a separate specialist art form of its own to such an extent that a standard form of Agreement for Fight Directors was set up in 1991 and updated in January 1995 between the Theatres National Committee (TNC)[75] and British Actors Equity Association ("Equity"), applicable to theatrical productions throughout the United Kingdom. It requires TNC members presenting a production which involves a fight to engage a suitably qualified fight director, and any member of the Equity Fight Director's Register is regarded as qualified. A "fight" for this purpose is defined by such agreement as "a specialised performance involving two or more people using fists, implements or weapons, which requires choreography[76] and supervision for safety".   **27–273**

(c) *Designers*

Costumes and stage sets. Clearly the room for originality is limited in, for example, the exact re-creation of military uniforms and period costumes, the   **27–274**

---

bargaining agreements for directors between the Society of London Theatre (SOLT) and Equity, and between the Theatrical Management Association (TMA) and Equity proceed on the basis that copyright subsists in the product of a stage director's services, which may or may not be justified (*cf.* the position of a film director as a joint copyright owner under ss.9(2)(ab) and 10(1A) of CDPA 1988). The absence of any similar provision in relation to the work of a live stage director appears to leave it an open question. However, *cf. Brighton v Jones* [2004] EWHC 1157, where a stage director's textual and non textual changes to the play, incorporated at rehearsals into the final version, were held to be not of sufficient substance to justify copyright protection, although the principle of stage directions being in the right circumstances capable of copyright protection seems to have been accepted by the court.

[72] As to the requirement that a copyright work be recorded, in writing or otherwise, see CDPA 1988, s.3(2) and paras 3–105 *et seq.*, above. As to the operation of this requirement in relation to dramatic works, see para. 3–115, above, and note that a film director is accorded the status of a joint copyright owner by ss.9(2)(ab) and 10(1A) of the 1988 Act.

[73] The expression "product of his services" is one which appears frequently in this field.

[74] As to subsistence of copyright in works of dance, see para. 3–35, above, and CDPA 1988, s.3.

[75] For the composition of the TNC see para. 27–296, below.

[76] Although strictly (according to the O.E.D), choreography refers to the act of dancing. However, fight movement may be regarded as "mime" and therefore a dramatic work within the meaning of s.3(1) of CDPA 1988.

design and colours of which are dictated by historical fact and are to be found in most public libraries. Similarly, a playwright's description of a scene in a play may in some instances leave the set-designer little room for manoeuvre to demonstrate much originality of design, particularly where commonplace "props" or a spartan set are required. However, there are many cases where considerable scope for originality[77] exists in relation to the design of costumes and stage sets. Costume and sets designs will normally qualify for design right rather than copyright,[78] but copyright protection may be available for such works as works of artistic craftsmanship.[79]

The question was considered in some depth in *Shelley Films Ltd v Rex Features Ltd*[80] which related to an alleged infringement of copyright by the taking of photographs of a scene of actors in costume on a film set. The plaintiff claimed copyright in the set and costumes and prostheses as works of artistic craftsmanship. It was held that there was a serious question to be tried as to the subsistence of copyright in those works as works of artistic craftsmanship. For example, the evidence was that the script's perception of a particular character had led the designer of his costume to base it upon a Prussian military uniform which he then adapted, using his researches into contemporary artwork and the sort of fabrics, buttons and braiding appropriate for the period and partly his own imaginative conceptions of what the character should look like. There then followed a process of fabric and colour selection, distressing and breaking down in order to produce a garment which would have been worn by the character concerned. In this way, he had created some 120 costumes so that, besides being technically correct, they blended in and constituted part of the overall artistic texture of the film.[81] It was also held that it was plainly arguable that copyright could subsist in a film set as a work of artistic craftsmanship.[82] Here, the evidence was that the set and every detail of it were the result of hundreds of little drawings, loosely based on the designer's researches, yet imaginatively conceived as original creations bearing in mind the artistic concepts of the film. Although that case related to a film, there can be no difference in principle for present purposes between a film set and a stage set.

As in the case of directors and choreographers, there are collective bargaining agreements,[83] which proceed on the basis of the existence of copyright in designs of stage sets and costumes. Indeed, most commercial contracts between designer and producer will ignore the difficulties in establishing copyright by assuming its existence and providing for payment by the producer whenever the product of the designer's services is used. Problems are likely to arise in such cases, however, when, for example, a designer alleges that his designs have been used without his consent, in response to which it is said that only commonplace, public domain elements of the designs, if any, have been used to which no copyright protection attaches. The outcome of each such case will turn on its own facts. Clearly designers should beware of warranting that *all* parts of their designs are wholly original, when this may be open to challenge. Warranties as to originality are commonly requested in creative team contracts, but ought to be confined to the totality of the

---

[77] As to the meaning of originality in this context, see Ch.3, above.

[78] See Ch.13, above.

[79] See *Guild v Eskander* [2001] F.S.R. 645.

[80] [1994] E.M.L.R. 34.

[81] The scrupulous re-creation of an authentic, albeit well used uniform cannot, however, be an original work. See para. 3–131, above.

[82] Depending on the circumstances it might also be capable of being a work of architecture, being a fixed structure or part of a fixed structure: see CDPA 1988, s.4(1)(b) and para. 3–61, above. Very often of course, there will be preliminary drawings for the set.

[83] See para. 3–298, above.

work (as distinct from its component parts) and to the absence of breach of any third party's copyright.

Lighting design. Lighting design has long been recognised as a means of contributing to the appearance of the stage, sets and costumes, which in turn contribute to the dramatic impact of the visual presentation to the audience. Lighting designs will usually be recorded in the form of a specification of the equipment required, a "plot" or plan of the positioning of that equipment and lighting cues. It is obviously desirable in particular that there be some record of the form and sequence of lighting effects., Whether they are capable of forming an element of the dramatic work as a whole, and thus in principle capable of copyright protection, is an open question which remains to be tested.[84]

27–275

Sound design. Sound design is of comparatively recent origin, and is a manifestation of the huge advances in sound technology during the last 50 years or so, which has made the role of the sound designer in the production of a stage musical one of primary and increasing importance. The West End of London has recently seen the advent of recorded music to replace or partially replace live orchestral accompaniment of a stage musical, despite initial strenuous opposition from the Musicians' Union. This and the continuing development of new sound technology, such as digital audio systems, is expected to enhance even further the important role of sound designers in musical theatre.

27–276

There are three basic elements of sound design, namely the specification of equipment, the positioning of that equipment in the theatre, and the movement of certain parts of the equipment (such as microphones) during the performance. The "sound desk" with its console of myriad moveable keys is a very important piece of sound equipment in a first class production of a stage musical, usually displacing a block of seats in the back of the auditorium, and being operated during the performance by a sound engineer in accordance with instructions given to him by the sound designer. Some elements of sound design are peculiar to the structure and configuration of the theatre. Others are peculiar to the production itself, irrespective of venue, and other elements to the voice characteristics of individual performers. There may also be special sound effects, such as those created by a motor car or aeroplane, to be reproduced at the appropriate time in the course of a performance. All these various elements will be plotted, specified and cued by the sound designer. The extent to which they are capable of copyright protection as part of a dramatic or musical work may be arguable, but his diagrams, written specifications and "plots" clearly will be protected under section 4 of the 1988 Act, which provides that diagrams, maps, charts and plans are regarded as artistic works for copyright purposes, irrespective of artistic quality.[85]

(d) *Orchestrators*

The function of an orchestrator is usually to create musical, instrumental and vo-

27–277

---

[84] If a written record of the lighting designs is protected by copyright as a literary or dramatic work, which itself is arguable and remains to be determined, then it may be argued that the use of such designs in a dramatic performance on stage will likewise be protected under s.16(1)(c) of CDPA 1988. The same can be said also of stage directions and sound designs. Clearly, when standing alone lighting and sound designs, of themselves can hardly be dramatic works, and it is questionable whether by introducing the implementation of such designs into the performance of a dramatic work, the designs themselves somehow acquire copyright protection as being an integral part of a dramatic work. Lighting design, unlike sound design, creates a visual image, and this may possibly in certain circumstances be regarded as a work of artistic craftsmanship, intended to convey instructions from which, either the designer himself or another person (*e.g.* a lighting engineer) can create an artistic work—see *Vermaat v Boncrest Ltd* [2001] FSR 43, and as to works of artistic craftsmanship generally see para. 3–65, above.

[85] See previous note.

cal arrangements from a piano-vocal score to full orchestral and vocal rendering. Invariably this process involves the creation of new musical sounds and therefore a new copyright work by the orchestrator.[86] An orchestrator will usually be engaged to carry out his work by someone, possibly the original composer, but more probably a producer who has acquired the right to create or commission the creation of orchestrations,[87] since the contents of orchestrations for a stage production are to some extent dictated by the venue of the performance. Orchestrations are an important element in the presentation of a stage musical, and orchestrators for that reason are customarily treated in much the same way as other members of the creative team. They are usually remunerated by substantial fees for their initial work and by performance fees or box -office royalties in relation to future use of their orchestrations in the production. In return for a substantial fee they may well be expected to assign the copyright in their orchestrations to whoever commissioned them, since they will be working as adaptors of pre-existing copyright material, namely the music of the composer Sometimes vocal, instrumental and dance "arrangements" of the musical score will (possibly by inadvertence) be created separately and attract separate copyright protection from the orchestrations by individuals separately engaged for that purpose.[88]

(iii) Logo and artwork designers

27–278   The importance of a distinctive logo and artwork to the marketing and promotion of modern stage musical production has grown greatly, and has given rise to exploitation in other important areas such as merchandising and commercial usage. A kind of livery or uniform is frequently created for the musical, which is intensively used as a means of enhancing the reputation of the work in all its possible means of exploitation. Thus, the producer of a stage musical will, at a comparatively early planning stage, devote a great deal of time and thought to the graphic designer's work, which he will usually commission on the basis that the copyright will vest in or be assigned to the producer. The use of such artwork will often lead to its being identified by the public exclusively with the particular production, so establishing a valuable goodwill, protectable in a passing-off action.[89]

(iv) Performers

27–279   Although performers have extensive rights in relation to their performances, these are not of immediate concern to live stage producers since they relate to their fixation or broadcast only,[90] and do not therefore attract copyright protection as such. Performers' rights will, however, assume great significance to a stage producer if it is desired to make a film or sound recording of the stage production, or to make a live broadcast.

Performers are usually engaged on standard printed collective contracts in one

---

[86] See paras 3–137 et seq., above, and, e.g. Redwood Music Ltd v Chappell & Co Ltd [1982] R.P.C. 109; Godfrey v Lees [1995] E.M.L.R. 307; Sawkins v Hyperion Records Ltd [2004] EWHC 1530.
[87] See CDPA 1988, ss.21 (3)(b) and 16(1)(e).
[88] See, for example, Beckingham v Hodges [2002] E.M.L.R. 45, where a session musician, performing a violin part, was held on the facts to be a joint author of a musical arrangement and entitled to a royalty by virtue of having made a "significant and original" contribution to the arrangement. See also Bambgoye v Reed [2004] E.M.L.R. 5 to similar effect in relation to a copyright contribution by a tape operator and sound engineer, and Sawkins v Hyperion Records Ltd [2004] EWHC 1530, Ch, as to copyright in a new edition of an out-of-copyright work.
[89] As to such goodwill, see Ch.21, above. See also Griggs v Evans [2003] EWHC 2914 and para. 5–174, above, as to ownership of copyright in commissioned logos.
[90] For a full discussion of performer rights, see Ch.12, above

or other of the forms agreed by their trade union, Equity, with various bodies representing producers and theatre managers, such as Society of London Theatre (SOLT), Theatre Managers Association (TMA), Independent Theatre Council (ITC), and Variety and Allied Entertainments Council (VAEC). There are separate forms for play actors, variety artists and musicians, the latter being agreed by the Musicians Union rather than Equity.

(v) Translators

The lyrics and text of a finished work written in one particular language may be required to be translated into another language or languages for the purposes of foreign productions. The right to make or authorise such a translation will in the first instance belong to the original author.[91] Where, for example, the right is assigned or licensed to a stage producer, it is usual for the author or copyright owner to reserve a right of approval over such translation as well as over the translator, although the producer will usually seek to provide that any right of approval by the author will not be unreasonably withheld. Although constituting an adaptation of a pre-existing copyright work, the translation will itself be a new copyright work,[92] and where it has been commissioned[93] it is usual for the party engaging the translator to stipulate that the copyright in the translation will vest in or be assigned to that party or as he may direct.[94]

27–280

(vi) The producer

The role of the producer in relation to a live stage production is manifold and varied. It embraces all arrangements necessary or desirable for presenting a play, a musical, an opera, a ballet or other work to the paying public on the live stage. The principal aspects in which the producer will be involved may be summarised as follows, although the list is not intended by any means to be exhaustive:

27–281

(1) *Acquiring the rights, i.e.* acquiring the legal right to present the work from the authors and all other copyright owners such as the creative team, including the negotiation of remuneration, the extent and duration of the producer's copyright licence or assignment and all other contractual terms between the parties.

(2) *Preparing the budget.*

(3) *Raising the money.*

(4) *Selecting the creative team and cast.*

(5) *Organising auditions and rehearsals.*

(6) *Selecting and hiring the theatre.*

(7) *Arranging logo and artwork design and printing.*

(8) *Promotion, publicity and advertising.*

(9) *Ticket retailing arrangements.*

(10) *Arrangements for sets and properties.*

(11) *Managing the administration and accounts of the production.*

---

[91] See CDPA 1988, s.21(3)(a)(l) and paras 7–121 *et seq.*, above. It must also be borne in mind that the person who has the right to authorise performances of a work in a foreign jurisdiction will be determined by the law of that jurisdiction.

[92] As to copyright in translations, see para. 3–135, above.

[93] As to ownership of copyright in commissioned works, see para. 5–174, above.

[94] And see para. 27–286, below, as to "commissioned works", and *Griggs v Evans* [2003] EWHC 2914 and para 5–174, above, as to ownership of copyright in commissioned logos. A comparison may be made with orchestrations and arrangements of pre-existing music, where the same position applies.

27–282 As to raising the money for the production, non-profit-making production companies (usually having charitable status) are likely to be heavily subsidised by grants from public bodies such as the Arts Council of England, the National Lottery and local authorities or by public donation. Commercial production companies which are unable to self-finance their own productions will usually seek financial investment from backers who are colloquially known as "angels". In such cases the producer will estimate the cost of preparing the production up to the first paid public performance. This estimate is referred to as the "capitalisation" to which investors are invited to contribute by purchasing units, each of which units is entitled to a pro rata share of (usually) 60 per cent of production profits, the remainder being reserved to the producer, who will also usually reserve for himself a producer's royalty (expressed as a percentage of box office receipts) and a weekly office management fee.

A producer will usually be more involved with the acquisition or licensing of copyright works than with their creation. It is more than likely, however, that in the course of preparing to mount a production, and particularly during the consultation process with his creative team and during rehearsals, the producer will contribute ideas and suggestions which may lead to changes in the creative material or its manner of presentation. The producer will, however, rarely claim copyright for himself in the product of his ideas and suggestions.[95] If they are adopted, they are in practice likely to be recorded as the original contributions of the authors and creative team.

A commercial producer of a stage musical is usually remunerated in a variety of ways. He will usually charge the production with a producer's royalty, up to about 2 per cent of net weekly box-office receipts[96] after prior deduction from such receipts of VAT, block-blocking discounts, credit card and agency commissions, and he will usually share any "profits" (as contractually defined) with his investors on the basis of 40 per cent for himself and 60 per cent for his investors, unless of course he finances the production himself or with the aid of loan capital without any profit-sharing arrangements. He will also usually charge to the production a weekly office management fee, usually from two weeks prior to first rehearsal until two weeks after closure. If he has obtained the right to subsidiary exploitation, such as merchandising, cast album sound recording, and motion picture, he will control, and therefore expect to retain a substantial share of the net revenue generated by any such exploitation. On the other hand, any losses in excess of the amount contributed by his "investors" will have to be borne by him.

B. LICENCE OR ASSIGNMENT?

27–283 A grant of the right to present a single specific production of a live stage play, stage musical, opera or ballet at a specified venue, for a fixed term or even an open-ended run, with no wish to promote the work any further, would normally be expected to be granted by way of an exclusive licence for a specified period. An alternative would be an exclusive licence for an indefinite period, subject to lapse by reference to predetermined criteria, such as failure to present a minimum number of performances over a specified period or make payment in lieu. Usually such a licence would be expressed to be exclusive within a defined territory

---

[95] In any event, suggestions or "inspiration" from another work, etc. will rarely be of sufficient substance to qualify for copyright protection. See para. 4–40, above; *Ultra Marketing and Scott v Universal Components* [2004] EWHC 468; *Stoddard International plc v William Lomas Carpets Ltd* [2001] FSR 14.

[96] As to basis of calculation of royalties see para. 27–555, above.

for the obvious reason that the producer would not wish to find himself in competition with other producers of the same work.[97]

The authors and composers. In the case, however, of a production of a major, big-budget stage musical which is expected, if successful, to have a relatively long life under the stewardship of the producer to whom the rights are originally being granted, the producer may ask for an assignment of the right to present performances of the work, either worldwide or within a specified territory or territories,[98] as distinct from a mere licence, exclusive or otherwise. The point may be the subject of much contention, but the distinction between an assignment and an exclusive licence (particularly if the licence is described as "perpetual", *i.e.* for the full period of copyright) may be largely negated if, as is sometimes the case, an exclusive licence stipulates that the licensor's remedies for breach shall be confined to an action for damages and shall not give rise to any right of termination.[99] Alternatively, an outright assignment may contain provision for reverter or reassignment in specified circumstances such as, for example, failure either to present a minimum number of performances per annum or to pay compensation instead. Any exclusive licence or assignment must be in writing.[1] It is important to make clear what the intended legal effect is.

27–284

The creative team. The same point frequently arises in relation to the copyright material of the creative team. They will obviously be willing to grant licences for the use of their material in the particular production concerned, and may even be prepared to grant a general exclusive licence (limited to use in connection with the musical or play or other work concerned) for a long or indefinite period. On the other hand, they may be resistant to assigning their rights in creative material, even with reverter or reassignment provisions, and most of their collective bargaining agreements reserve copyright to them, although some provide for the parties to elect between outright assignment of copyright to the producer or manager (either in perpetuity or for a restricted period) on the one hand and a mere copyright licence on the other, which suggests that either course may be regarded as reasonable, depending on the circumstances and the relative bargaining strengths of the parties.[2]

27–285

Commissioned work. The question of whether to seek a licence or an assignment also frequently arises where one party engages or commissions another to create copyright material for a particular purpose, for example the logo and artwork for a stage musical or the music to go with the lyrics of a partly written work.[3] In these circumstances the party doing the commissioning will often insist, as a condition of the engagement, that the other agrees in advance to the copy-

27–286

---

[97] As to the distinction between licencing or assignment, see para. 5–200, above.

[98] He may fear that with only a licence, which may be terminable on breach, the production may be forced to close after a minor or disputed violation.

[99] In *Harbinger v GE Information* [2000] 1 P.L.C. 56 the High Court held that the use of the words "in perpetuity" as the term of the licence negated any possibility of termination on reasonable notice and meant that the licence continued until the licensee no longer required it. This was despite termination procedures in the licence itself, thus, in effect, making even more ephemeral the distinction between an assignment and an exclusive licence in perpetuity. The negation of any right to terminate a licence for breach was given judicial sanction in *NIC v PW Allen* [2004] BL 0/026/04. For judicial consideration and rejection of a submission that a termination-for-breach clause constituted an unenforceable contract penalty see *Python (Monty) Pictures Ltd v Paragon Entertainment Corporation* [1998] E.M.L.R. 640 at 686.

[1] See ss.90(3) and 92(1) of CDPA 1998.

[2] See, for example, the SOLT/Equity Agreement for West End Theatre Designers (1989) and the TMA/Equity/BECTU Agreement for Theatre Designers outside West End (1999) and the SOLT/Equity Agreement for West End Theatre Choreographers (2003).

[3] As to the ownership of copyright in a commissioned work, see para. 5–174, above, and as to copyright in a logo see para. 27–277, above, and *Griggs v Evans* [2003] EWHC 2914.

right in the product of his services vesting in or being assigned to the commissioning party, a concession which is often made where there are others who would be willing to do the work.

C. Classification of Rights

27–287   The rights in the various works may be classified in a number of different ways, the importance of which is two-fold. First, copyright is divisible,[4] and one particular classification of rights may be licensed, assigned or otherwise disposed of differently from another. Secondly, the exploitation of one class of rights may be differently remunerated than another. Again, it is proposed to take the classification of rights in a stage musical as the example with the widest scope.

27–288   **"Grand rights" and "small rights".** This classification is solely concerned with performing rights. As a matter of convention the expression "grand rights" is usually understood to mean the right to present performances of dramatico-musical works and ballets.[5] In contrast, the "small performing right", or "small right", usually means the right to perform non-dramatic performances of individual songs or short excerpts from a dramatico-musical work. The Performing Right Society, ("PRS")[6] limits its jurisdiction in respect of these "small rights" to circumstances where:

(i) the performance is not dramatic[7] ; and

(ii) it does not exceed 25 minutes or 25 per cent of the total length of the work; and

(iii) it is not a performance of a complete act of the work; and

(iv) it is not a so-called "potted" or condensed version of the whole work.[8]

Thus, for example, a non-vocal performance of the music alone, or the singing of one or two songs from a dramatico-musical work by a singer in street dress on a plain stage in cabaret or on television or in a variety bill will not be within the domain of the grand rights owner.

The distinction between the two rights is important because the grand rights are usually not within the rights which are assigned to the PRS by its members, so that even in the case where the author, composer or publisher is a member of the PRS, these rights will be controlled by the author, etc. and not the PRS, unless the author as a matter of convenience to himself, with PRS approval, unusually chooses to vest the grand rights also in the PRS. In contrast, the small rights are assigned to the PRS by its members and so are controlled by the PRS. The distinction between the two types of rights has been brought into sharp relief by a proliferation in recent years of so-called "compilation shows", featuring short excerpts from a number of well known stage musicals. Often such shows are presented with dramatic staging and costume, and thus dramatically, without the consent of the grand rights owner and so potentially in infringement of copyright.

In addition to the small rights, the PRS also administers the performing rights

---

[4] As to divisibility of copyright, see paras 5–93 *et seq.*, above.

[5] The PRS Rules define a dramatico-musical work as "an opera, operetta, musical play, review or pantomime, in so far as it consists of words and music written expressly therefore", and a ballet as "a choreographic work having a story, plot or abstract idea, devised or used for the purpose of interpretation by dancing and/or miming, but does not include country or folk dancing, nor tap dancing, nor precision dancing sequences".

[6] As to the Performing Right Society Ltd and its affiliated societies overseas, see para. 28–59, below.

[7] Whether or not it is dramatic depends on all the circumstances, including the use of costume, stage scenery, dramatic movement or mime and any other means to convey the dramatic impact of the piece to the audience, such as narration of the plot or storyline, either as part of the performance itself or in a theatre programme. For further details see the PRS Rules.

[8] See the PRS Rules.

in dramatico-musical works and ballets of its members when such works are performed by means of films made primarily for the purpose of exhibition in cinemas, and the television broadcasting of such films.[9] It also controls performances of such works when given in public by means of radio or television sets (for example in a hotel lounge or public house).[10]

It should be noted, however, that not every author, composer and music publisher is necessarily a member of the PRS and that the separation of grand rights and small rights into different ownerships (if any) is essentially a contractual matter for the original copyright owner.

Professional rights and amateur rights. These classifications mostly speak for themselves. Professional rights are performing rights which are exercised with the use of only paid professional performers. Amateur rights relate to performances using amateur performers. It is rare for amateur rights in a new work to be released before at least the initial first-class professional production has run its course. Amateur rights, at least in relation to well known, established works, will often be administered through a specialist agency, offering a "catalogue" of such works available to amateur production companies. Sometimes a performance may be classified as a "pro-am", meaning that both professional and amateur performers are used. In such a case a licence will be required from whoever controls each of the professional and amateur rights.

27–289

First-class and second-class rights. There is no standard uniform definition of the expression "first-class" in relation to a theatrical production, but it is widely recognised that the size, location and importance of the theatre are essential elements, as also are the use of exclusively professional performers and an experienced, professional creative team. A theatre with fewer than 400 seats would not normally be regarded as a first-class venue. The size of the budgeted capitalisation of pre-production costs and the length of the production run, whether open-ended or for a fixed season or touring, will also be relevant factors. Amateur, concert-version, cabaret-version, condensed, tabloid, and dinner-theatre performances will all usually be regarded as second-class, and the same frequently applies to repertory performances. The expression "repertory" is usually applied to performances either by a "resident" stage company under the same management, or as part of a repertoire of a number of works pre-programmed for a fixed season at a fixed venue or venues or both. In the final analysis, contracts which deal separately with first-class and second-class rights should provide their own definitions of the meaning of such expressions.

27–290

Subsidiary rights. A production contract for a major stage production will often be expected to include the grant to the producer, conditional upon his presenting a first-class live stage production for a specified minimum number of performances, within a specified period at a specified venue or in a specified place or territory, of one or more so called "subsidiary" or "ancillary" or "residual" or "secondary" rights, in addition to the specified live performance rights. These subsidiary rights may include any one or more of the following, namely the right to exploit the work by:

27–291

  (i) merchandising and commercial usage;
  (ii) motion picture (film, television, home-video (whether "as staged" or as an adaptation of the live stage version));
  (iii) second-class stage performances;

---

[9] See the PRS Rules.
[10] See the PRS Rules. As to what constitutes a performance "in public" in such circumstances, see para. 7–95, above.

(iv) cast album sound recording, featuring members of the cast of the specified production or productions; and

(v) electronic transmission (CD-ROM, internet and other multi-media).

Merchandising and commercial usage exploitation will in practice usually relate to the title, logo and artwork of a show, rather than the text or lyrics or music, although the latter may sometimes be used as, for example, in respect of a book about the history and origins of a work. Copyright in the logo and artwork will probably be acquired by the producer from the graphic designer in any event,[11] and will rarely have originated from the author or composer and other copyright owner. As to the title of the show, there will rarely be any copyright in it,[12] and so the consent of the author or composer to merchandising exploitation will rarely be needed. Nevertheless, it is usual for the author, composer or copyright owner of the written work to require and be given a share of merchandising revenue on the ground that the reputation of the written work contributes materially to the generation of the revenue concerned. Multimedia rights are, of course, a modern phenomenon, akin to motion picture rights and in certain respects indistinguishable from them. As a matter of practicality it may be convenient simply to include them in the same contractual definition as motion picture rights, since attempts at separation can cause problems of both technological and remunerative differentiation.

27–292   **New productions, reproductions, revivals and transfers.** "New production" is an expression which may be used either to describe a production of a work which may be long established and may already have been presented on the live stage before, but is now to be presented in a different way with a different creative team and with different production designs and other elements than before, or it may be used to describe a new work which is now to be presented for the first time.

"Reproductions" used to be a comparatively rare phenomenon, but are becoming increasingly common. Since about 1985 the global reproduction market has opened up, such that it is now common for "reproductions", namely recreations of the original stage production, which perhaps is still being presented to the public at its original location, to be presented at the same time in a number of different countries and languages around the world, either directly by the original producer or under licence from him on a kind of franchise basis. For this purpose, of course he has to acquire the necessary rights from the creative team as well as the authors, bearing in mind the various territories in which rights may need to be exploited.

It follows that the copyright elements of the work of the creative team in relation to stage musicals have assumed far greater importance. As a result, copyright terms are usually much more complex and difficult to negotiate in respect of a contract geared to the worldwide reproduction market in stage musicals than a simple licence for a single production run at a single specified theatre. Licensed reproductions, where the original producer licenses another to recreate the same production elements of stage directions, choreography and designs at another venue, are akin to franchise operations, and usually involve conditions of close artistic quality control. The creative team will usually require to be given options for their engagement in reproducing their work at other venues, and also to be involved in the appointment of "deputies" engaged to re-create their work if they do not take up their option due to non-availability or otherwise.

A "revival", as the word implies, refers to a production of an established work

---

[11] As to this, see paras 27–278 and 27–281, above.
[12] As to copyright in titles, see para. 3–16, above, and as to their protection by a passing-off action, see para. 21–20, above.

which has been presented before, perhaps many times, but has been out of production for a long time and is now being "revived".

A "transfer" refers to an entire production with its physical assets, and possibly including the whole of the original stage company, being transferred from one venue to another, possibly even from one country to another, as from the West End of London to Broadway or vice versa, or from an out-of-town venue to a major West End or Broadway theatre.

Reserved rights and music publishing rights. Most contracts between author **27–293** and producer can be expected to stipulate that all other rights apart from the specific rights expressly granted are reserved to the grantors. Even where a full range of subsidiary rights is granted to the producer, however, the authors or copyright owners will expect to reserve to themselves the so-called "music publishing rights" which are usually expressed to include sound recording rights, motion-picture-with-music synchronisation rights, the publication of sheet music and the "small" non-dramatic performance rights in the individual musical compositions, such as are customarily administered by music publishers or local collection societies. It is, however, up to the contracting parties to establish what they mean by such expressions in each individual case.

D. MORAL RIGHTS

Authors have important moral rights in this field, including in particular, the right **27–294** not to have their work subjected to derogatory treatment and the right to be identified as the author of their work.[13] Although the moral rights of authors cannot be assigned,[14] they may be waived or be the subject of consent, but only by the original author during his lifetime.[15] Frequently a stage play or musical is adapted from a film, novel or other original work, a process that involves a risk of the author claiming that his work has been subjected to derogatory treatment within the meaning of the Act.[16] Consequently, an adaptor will be at risk unless either a waiver of the moral right or consent in some form to make the adaptation is obtained. Where an author is persuaded to waive his moral rights in a particular work, it is not uncommon for him to stipulate that, in the event of his considering that his work is being subjected to derogatory treatment, he should be entitled to require cancellation of his accreditation as the author of a work of which he no longer approves. Indeed, certain collective bargaining agreements provide specifically for a designer to have such a right of cancellation of his accreditation.[17]

The translation of a lyric set to music needs to be in harmony with the corresponding musical composition, requiring a certain amount of poetic licence and freedom of expression on the part of the translator, whose task is to maintain the right balance between being faithful to the sense and object of the original words, whilst finding the best way of expressing the meaning in harmony and synchronisation with the music, even if this means departing from a more literal translation.

---

[13] As to moral rights generally, see Ch.11, above.

[14] See paras 11–66 et seq., above.

[15] CDPA 1988, s.94. As to waiver of moral rights, see s.87 and paras 11–76, et seq., above. As to the position following the author's death, see s.95 and paras 11–66, et seq., above. The position varies in other jurisdictions.

[16] But see the next sub-paragraph.

[17] See, for example, the TMA/Equity/BECTU Agreement for Theatre Designers (1999).

However, a translation of a literary or dramatic work is in any event excluded from the scope of derogatory treatment.[18]

E. Theatre Premises and Deposit of Scripts

27–295   The Theatres Act, 1968, provides, among other things, for the prohibition of obscene performances in public, and requires delivery of scripts of new plays to the Trustees of the British Museum free of charge (for archiving purposes) within one month of the first public performance.

F. Unions, Trade Associations and other Organisations

27–296   The principal "trade union"[19] or trade association for performers is Equity (formerly called British Actors Equity Association), and for theatre staff and technicians is the Broadcasting, Entertainment, Cinematograph and Theatre Union (BECTU). The principal trade associations for theatre managers are the Society of London Theatre (SOLT) formerly called the Society of West End Theatre (SWET), the Theatrical Management Association (TMA) which is to provincial theatre managers and subsidised repertory theatre managers what SOLT is to managers of theatres in the West End of London and pre-West End touring managers, and the Independent Theatre Council (ITC) which covers small scale independent theatres. The Theatres National Committee (TNC) comprises representatives of each of SOLT, TMA and ITC.

There are, however, a great many other representative bodies in the theatre industry such as, for example, the Theatre Writers Union (TWU), the British Academy of Songwriters, Composers and Authors (BASCA), the British Ballet Association and the Musicians' Union. A full list of theatre-related societies and organisations is to be found in the British Theatre Directory,[20] which is updated annually. Among these organisations are listed separate associations for, by way of example, lighting designers, choreographers, theatre designers and stage managers. The same directory also contains details of Arts Councils and Regional Arts Boards which are dedicated to providing financial support to the subsidised sector of the theatre. Other organisations include:

> The London Theatre Council and its sister organisation in the provinces, which are run by representatives of Equity and SOLT/TMA, their purpose being to regulate relations between managers and artists in the West End and provincial theatre respectively and, most importantly, to provide a structure for conciliation and arbitration.

> The Theatres Trust, established by Act of Parliament in 1976 to promote the better protection of theatre for the benefit of the nation. It administers a charitable fund and maintains contact with other organisations with related concerns.

> The Theatres Advisory Council, a federation of a large number of national bodies, which represents various interests in the theatre industry, and provides a discussion forum and an advisory and representative function on behalf of the industry as a whole.

> The Performing Artists' Media Rights Association (PAMRA), an organisation dedicated to the protection of performers' rights in all media on behalf of its members.

---

[18] CDPA 1988, s.80(2)(a)(i).

[19] The expression "trade union" may be regarded as a misnomer when applied to those performers, who are self-employed and enter into contracts for services rather than contracts of service.

[20] Published by Richmond House Publishing Company Ltd of Douglas House, 3 Richmond Buildings, London W1V 5AE.

G. COLLECTING SOCIETIES AND LICENSING AGENCIES

The role of the Performing Right Society Ltd (PRS) in relation to live stage per-   **27–297**
formances of dramatico-musical works has already been considered above.[21] A
licence from both the PRS and Phonographic Performance Ltd (PPL) will also be
required for the playing of recorded music incidental to the action of a live stage
non-musical play, assuming the content of the recording is not out of copyright
and that the author/composer is a member of those societies. In the absence of
such membership a licence would be needed from the author/composer or his
assignees. The same applies to incidental recorded music prior to curtain-up or in
the interval or between scene changes. There are collective bargaining agreements between SOLT/TMA and the Musicians' Union which contain detailed
provisions for reporting to, and in some cases obtaining prior approval of the
Union for the use in a stage production of recorded music (including archive
recordings) and as to use in such production of electronic instruments. However,
there are important and substantial differences between the SOLT and TMA
agreements with the Union in this respect, which require careful study and the
reasons for which are not obvious, the current SOLT Agreement having been
made in December 2003 and seeming more favourable to the producer than that
of the TMA made in June 2002.

There are a number of privately owned and operated agencies, which specialise in the licensing of plays (including stage musicals) to repertory companies,
schools, colleges, amateur dramatic societies and the like, that is to say in the
licensing of so-called "second-class rights"[22] . This is regarded as a convenient
method of marketing and exploiting such second-class rights with a view to maximising the revenue from such exploitation in a way which the rights owners
would find difficult to do themselves. Agencies of this kind will frequently reach
out to the market by issuing "catalogues" of the available works in their licensing
"repertoire", and will set standard tariffs, sometimes by reference to a percentage
of box office receipts and sometimes fixed performance fees or a mixture of both.
They operate off commission which will be deducted when accounting to their
principals, the rights owners. Often they are appointed on fixed, long-term
contracts at specified commission rates.

H. COLLECTIVE BARGAINING AGREEMENTS

There are a great many collective bargaining agreements relating to live stage   **27–298**
performances. All of them regulate the minimum remuneration and other minimum terms and conditions of engagement of the members of the contracting organisations concerned. Some relate only to performers, stage managers and theatre staff, and are accordingly outside the scope of this work as having no
particular copyright significance. The principal agreements relating to creators of
copyright material are as follows:

Date	
1987	SOLT/TMA/Equity Agreement for Pro- ducers and Directors of Opera in the United Kingdom.

---

[21] In 1996 the PRS formed an alliance with the MCPS (The Mechanical Copyright Protection Society, which administers and collects royalties on music recordings on behalf of its members)
called "The MCPS-PRS Alliance" or simply "The Music Alliance," but each remains a separate
society in terms of income, constitution, membership and guardianship of rights.

[22] As to the use of the expression "second-class rights" see para. 27–290, above.

Date	
1989	SOLT/EQUITY Agreement for West End of London Theatre Designers.
1993	TNC/Writers Guild of GB/Theatre Writers Union Agreement for authors of plays to be staged by Royal National Theatre, Royal Shakespeare Theatre and the English Stage Companies.
1993	TMA/Writers Guild of GB/Theatre Writers Union/Scottish Society of Playwrights Agreement for Writers of works to be produced by a member in the provinces.
1995	TNC/Equity Agreement for Fight Directors.
1999	TMA/Equity/BECTU Agreement for Designers outside West End of London.
2000	TMA/EQUITY Agreement for Choreographers in subsidised repertory and provincial commercial contracts.
2001	SOLT/EQUITY Agreement for engagement of Freelance Directors and Assistant Directors for theatrical productions at a West End of London theatre (including any pre-West End tour).
2002	TMA/EQUITY Agreement for Directors and Assistant Directors of subsidised repertory and provincial theatres.
2002	SOLT/EQUITY Agreement for West End Theatre chCoreographers.
2003	ITC/Writers Guild of GB/Theatre Writers Union Agreement for Writers of plays first professioanlly presented in the provinces by ITC approved managers.

I. OPERA AND BALLET

27–299   In theory there is no reason why both opera and ballet should not follow the same course as stage musicals, and indeed precisely the same copyright considerations apply in all three cases. Many productions, however, tend to be of classical works which are out of copyright, and are most often presented by national or regional, heavily subsidised opera or ballet companies, with "resident" or "semi-resident" performers, management and production personnel. Nevertheless contemporary dance and opera works by new writers do play a significant part in the continuing development of these performing arts. Sometimes classical ballet may be rechoreographed almost as a wholly new work. The choreography will usually be recorded by notation or other appropriate means, in which case, it will ordinarily be protected as a dramatic work.[23]

---

[23] CDPA 1988, s.3(1) which defines a "dramatic work" as including a work of dance or mime. See para. 3–35, above.

The creative team. In the case of opera and ballet productions the creative team **27–300** of director, choreographer[24] and designers are more likely to be employed as part of a resident company than in the case of stage musicals or regular theatre. If so, the copyright in their work, created in the course of such employment, will usually vest in the employer, *i.e.* the production company.[25] If independent and self-employed, they will be expected to assign any copyright in their work to the company engaging them.[26]

Just as the role of the choreographer in ballet assumes a heightened importance, so in the case of opera does the role of the musical director. Making a written record of choreography for copyright and reproduction purposes in the form of special choreographer's "notation" is a highly skilled task, the result of which is likely to unintelligible to the uninitiated. An opera, however, as with a stage musical, is usually recorded in permanent form by written music and words, and thus unlikely to present any problems of establishing an adequate permanent record for copyright purposes.

Opera producers are usually regarded by national and major opera companies in much the same way as members of the creative team of a stage musical. They are engaged to perform the function of producer either for a single production or series of productions for which they will usually be remunerated by fees or a salary, plus expenses but no royalties. They will not have to raise finance for the production but will be expected to put together all the artistic elements required. They will usually be engaged under the standard form of agreement established by SOLT/TMA/EQUITY in 1987 which also includes opera directors. This agreement refers to the copyright in the producer's services being assigned to the production company which presupposes that there is some creative element of the producer's services which is capable of copyright protection.[27] This supposition is open to question, although sometimes an opera "producer" will also fulfil the director's role.[28] The agreement gives the producer a right to additional remuneration from any transfer or revival of his production and from any exploitation in another medium.

Apart from the above, there is no standard agreement for commercial productions of contemporary opera and ballet, the producers of which will either adopt or adapt one or other of the SOLT/ TMA/Equity forms of agreement for opera or regular theatre productions, or negotiate special terms for such copyright licences as they require.

7. THE ADVERTISING INDUSTRY

A. COMPONENTS OF ADVERTISING

(i) Television, radio and cinema commercials

A television or cinema commercial is typically the product of the creative and **27–301**

---

[24] In ballet the roles of director and choreographer are often combined under the title of "artistic director".

[25] CDPA 1988, s.11(2). As to works of employees, see paras 5–00 *et seq* and note in particular *Intercase UK Ltd v Time Computers Ltd* (2003) [BLD 1712034628] and *Ultraframe (UK) Ltd v Fielding* [2003] EWCA 1805.

[26] The 1987 SOLT/TMA/Equity Agreement referred to above requires copyright in the product of a freelance producer's and director's services to be assigned to the opera company concerned on specified terms. This assumes the existence of copyright in such services but such assumption may not be justified, as to which see paras and 27–271 and 27–282, above (and the footnotes thereto).

[27] See para. 27–270, 27–271, 27–272and 27–275, above.

[28] See para. 27–271, above.

administrative work of many separate individuals. The intellectual property rights involved are often complex. Many of the rights will vest in the advertiser or its advertising agency, but advertisers are often surprised to learn what rights remain with other contributors.

27–302   **Production companies**. Most television and cinema commercials are produced for an advertising agency by one of a relatively small number of specialist production companies. Advertising agency creative staff are the initial source of a joint creative enterprise which is then managed by the agency in conjunction with the production company. The first work involved in this process and the most important work underlying the end product is the script, which may be either a literary or dramatic work. Its author will typically be a copywriter employed by the advertising agency and the copyright in the script will in such cases usually vest initially in the advertising agency.[29] In some cases, storyboards will be produced by agency staff or by artists commissioned for this purpose.[30] These graphic representations of scenes from the intended film may be significant in infringement actions as artistic works underlying the end product.

The division of labour between advertising agency and production company varies. The production company will assemble a team of film technicians and a director approved by the advertising agency. The advertising agency may be responsible for selecting and hiring actors and for commissioning or licensing any music required. It may be difficult to determine whether the producer of the resulting film is the production company, the advertising agency or both.[31] The author of the film will be the producer and the principal director.[32] The first owner of the copyright in the film will be the producer and the principal director, or their employers.[33] The sound track of the commercial is treated as part of the film.[34]

A television commercial can be not only a film but also a dramatic work if, as is often the case, it is a work of action which is capable of being performed before an audience.[35] The author of the commercial, *qua* dramatic work, will be the person who creates it. This may include different persons, for example the writer of the script, from the authors of the commercial *qua* film (the producer and principal director).

In most cases the identity of the producer will be of little significance since production companies and advertising agencies normally contract on standard terms approved by their respective trade associations.[36] These provide for an assignment to the advertising agency of "all copyright and similar rights throughout the world for all purposes and for their full duration in the Commercial(s) and in all other footage shot by the production company in the production of the Commercial(s) whether or not included in the completed Commercial(s)".[37] As to the director, he is normally an employee or sub-contractor of the production company and it is the production company's duty to ensure that it procures from the direc-

---

[29] CDPA 1988, s.11(2), see para. 5–08, *et seq.*, above.

[30] As to the ownership of copyright in commissioned works, see para. 5–174, above.

[31] As to who is the "producer" of a film and a sound recording, see paras 4–49 and 4–59, above.

[32] CDPA 1988, s.9(2) and see para. 4–58, above.

[33] CDPA 1988, ss.11(2) and 10(1A). See para. 5–48, above.

[34] CDPA 1988, s.5B(2), but see s.5B(5). See also para. 3–76, above.

[35] *Norowzian v Arks Ltd (No. 2)* [2000] F.S.R. 363.

[36] The Advertising Producers Association, 26 Noel Street, London W1F 8GT and the Institute of Practitioners in Advertising, 44 Belgrave Square, London SW1X 8QS.

[37] But note that animation "exclusively designed and created by the production company" remains the property of the production company unless a copyright assignment is separately agreed; see Agreement for the Production of Commercials (2003), Clause 12(b).

tor and passes on to the advertising agency an assignment of the director's interest, if any, in the copyright.[38]

Many of the individuals employed or hired by the production company, such as cameramen, lighting and sound technicians, will have no copyright interest. Others, such as set designers and model makers, may be the authors of copyright artistic works. The standard contract provides that the copyright in underlying works such as these must, if created by the production company, be assigned by it to the advertising agency. Except in the case of animated cartoon characters and models created by third parties for the commercial, if they are created by third parties the production company undertakes to obtain from the third party either an assignment of copyright or, if an assignment cannot be negotiated on reasonable terms, a licence on terms to be approved by the advertising agency.[39]

It is also the production company's responsibility to procure the irrevocable and unconditional waiver of all moral rights, wherever in the world enforceable, vesting in the director and all other persons engaged in the creation or production of the commercial.[40] It is provided, however, that the use of the commercial in connection with the production of any other commercial for a different advertiser is subject to the production company's prior written consent.[41]

Music. Many commercials include music in their soundtrack. That music may be original or it may be copied from an existing sound recording. Alternatively, an existing musical work may be adapted and rerecorded so as to fit the timing and other requirements of the commercial. Where a music production company is commissioned by the advertising agency to produce a sound recording incorporating either original music or a version of an existing work, the music production company will normally be the producer of the resulting sound recording and therefore its author and the first owner of the copyright in it.[42] If the sound recording embodies an original musical work the author of that work will be the composer hired or employed by the music production company. **27–303**

Copyright in a sound recording created by a music production company and in any musical work created for the commercial is dealt with quite differently from the copyright in the film itself and its associated sound recording. Under the terms of the standard agreement approved by the trade associations of the music production companies[43] and advertising agencies[44] the copyrights in both the sound recording and the musical work are retained by the music production company.[45] An exclusive licence is granted to the advertising agency to exploit the works in specified media and territories and for a specified period of time. With one limited qualification relating to credits,[46] however, the music production company warrants that all moral rights of all persons engaged in the production of the work have been waived.

Where an existing copyright musical work, or a version reproducing any

---

[38] Agreement for the Production of Commercials (2003), Clause 12(c).

[39] Agreement for the Production of Commercials (2003), clause 12(c).

[40] Agreement for the Production of Commercials (2003), clause 12(e). International advertisers should note that, notwithstanding the terms of the production company's warranty, a waiver of moral rights may be unenforceable under the laws of certain other jurisdictions including France and Germany.

[41] Clause 12(f).

[42] CDPA 1988, s.9(2)(aa). See para. 5–41, above.

[43] Producers and Composers of Applied Music (PCAM).

[44] Agreement for the Production and Licensing of Original Musical Composition (February 2003).

[45] As between the production company and the composer, the production company will usually have taken the copyright either as the composer's employer or under the terms of his engagement.

[46] The composer and his publisher/agent are entitled to a printed credit wherever the advertising agency, advertiser and film director receive such a credit.

substantial part of an existing musical work, is to be included in an advertisement the advertising agency must obtain a licence from the copyright owner, normally a music publishing company. The standard terms of such licences vary from publisher to publisher. If an extract from an existing sound recording is to be used rather than a new version, the advertising agency must also obtain a licence from the owner of the copyright in that sound recording, normally a record company. Phonographic Performance Limited ("PPL")[47] takes an assignment of the performing right and dubbing right under its standard form agreement with member record companies. In practice, however, PPL does not grant dubbing licences for advertisements or where the sound recording is to be associated with brands or trade marks, but leaves this to the individual record companies.

27–304   **Actors.** An entirely separate set of rights is created when an actor's audio or visual performance is recorded for inclusion in a commercial.[48] An actor engaged by an advertising agency will necessarily give consent, either expressly or impliedly, for the recording of his live performance. Subsequent exploitation of the commercial is subject to contractual restrictions agreed by the advertising agency, normally under the terms of a standard contract agreed with Equity.[49] The actor's ability to enforce those restrictions is in practice reinforced by his reproduction right to authorise or prohibit the making of direct or indirect copies of the original master recording made by the production company.[50] The reproduction right is a property right[51] but is retained by the actor under the terms of the standard Equity agreement.[52] Under this agreement the actor grants consent for the exploitation of the commercial "limited to television transmission in the United Kingdom for the purpose of advertising the product(s) or service(s) specified". Any extension to other media such as cinema, radio or press advertising, or inclusion in a film or television documentary or other programme, or use outside the United Kingdom, requires the actor's further consent.

The Equity agreement requires the advertising agency to obtain the actor's specific consent for use of still photographs in "paid-for advertising space, packaging, or point-of-sale material". Exploitation of stills from a commercial in this manner without such consent would not, however, infringe an actor's reproduction right.[53]

(ii) Printed advertisements

27–305   Copyright will often subsist in press and poster advertisements, either as artistic or literary works (including compilations) or both. They are frequently the work of a number of individuals, some of whom may have copyright interests. As with broadcast and cinema advertising, the creative process typically starts within an advertising agency. Copy for the advertisement will be written within the agency and employees of the agency may also produce a "concept" or "visual" to il-

---

[47] 1 Upper James Street, London, W1F 9DE.

[48] As to rights in performances generally, see Ch.12, above.

[49] Agreements for the Employment of Artists in Television Commercials (November 1, 1991). These Agreements are not officially approved but are used in practice, as supplemented by further standard terms approved by the Advertising Producers Association, the Institute of Practitioners in Advertising and the Incorporated Society of British Advertisers.

[50] CDPA 1988, s.182A. See para. 12–62, above.

[51] CDPA 1988, s.191A(1).

[52] Agreement for the Employment of Featured Artists in Television Commercials.(November 1, 1991). This Agreement is not officially approved but is used in practice, as supplemented by further standard terms approved by the Advertising Producers Association, the Institute of Practitioners in Advertising and the Incorporated Society of British Advertisers.

[53] Stills would not amount to a recording of part of an actor's "performance". cf. the position in relation to infringement of copyright in a film, para. 7–70, above.

lustrate how the advertisement is intended to look. If the advertisement is to include photographic or other graphic material, external creative suppliers will be commissioned by the agency.

Advertising copy. Copyright does not subsist in advertising slogans.[54] More substantial copy, however, may be protected as a literary work. As in the case of scripts for television commercials, the copyright in advertising copy written by copywriters employed by an advertising agency will normally vest initially in the advertising agency,[55] unless assigned by the advertising agency to the advertiser.

27–306

Photographs and illustrations. The author of a photograph is the person who creates it and this will normally be the photographer. The role of the photographer in the creation of some advertising photographs may, however, be largely technical, the main creative input coming from the advertising agency's art director who may specify the precise content of the photograph. In these circumstances authorship may be joint, particularly if each has collaborated in the creation of the work and each has contributed a significant part of the skill and labour protected by the copyright.[56]

27–307

Photographs and illustrations are usually commissioned by an advertising agency from outside photographers and artists. The copyright in such circumstances is frequently retained by the photographer or illustrator. The Association of Photographers[57] has agreed a negotiating framework with representatives of advertising agencies under which the copyright in commissioned photographs is retained by photographers whose works are licensed for use for specified media, territories and time periods. Most advertisers will require exclusive use of commissioned photographs and other artistic works, at least in the field of advertising and for the duration of the campaign in question. It is likely that exclusivity is, at least to this extent, implied in most commissions.

B. ISSUES BETWEEN RIGHTS OWNERS

(i) Rights of action against third parties

Since advertisements are often made up of a number of distinct copyright works and ownership of the copyright in some of these works will not always vest in the advertiser or its agency, complex questions may arise when an advertisement is copied without permission by some third party. Who, for example, has rights of action when a commissioned artistic work included in an advertisement is reproduced without permission in a television drama and copyright has been retained by the artist?

27–308

Unauthorised use for non-advertising purposes of an image associated with a particular advertising campaign may be damaging to the campaign itself. In extreme cases the image may need to be replaced and a new work commissioned for the campaign. This will involve substantial additional costs for the advertiser. If the artist has retained copyright in the work, the advertiser will be unlikely to have any right of action against the infringer, even if an exclusive licence has been granted by the artist. This is because the licence will have given the

---

[54] *Sinanide v La Maison Kosmeo* (1928) 139 L.T. 365; *Kirk v Fleming* (1928–35) MacG. Cop. Cas. 44. It is, however, common for advertising slogans to be registered as trade marks.
[55] CDPA 1988, s.11(2).
[56] See para. 4–33, above, where the question of authorship of photographs is discussed.
[57] 81 Leonard Street, London, EC2A 4QS.

advertiser exclusive rights only in the field of advertising[58] : the advertiser has no cause of action where the infringement is outside the scope of the exclusive licence (unless the infringing act was directly connected to a prior licensed act and the artist has expressly granted a right of action in respect of non-exclusive rights).[59] The artist will be able to sustain an infringement action, but will only be able to recover damages referable to the damage to his own interest in the copyright. Such damage may be limited, for example, to the loss of opportunity to negotiate a reuse fee in the event that the advertiser decided to renew the licence at the end of its term. The artist will not be able to recover damages by reference to the far greater costs incurred by the advertiser in replacing the advertisement with one based on a different, uncompromised image.

(ii) Rights in physical works

27–309   Title to photographic transparencies, original illustrations and models incorporated in photographs is a matter for agreement, just as with the copyright in such works.[60] There is no fixed trade practice. Disputes as to ownership of transparencies are unusual owing to the widespread use in the production process of digital technology. If an advertising agency has a digital scan of a photograph it is unlikely to have any further requirement for the transparency. Original physical materials are generally regarded by photographers as belonging to themselves. The value of an original illustration, unlike a photographic transparency or negative, lies primarily in its status as an *objet d'art*. An illustration commissioned for an advertisement may be a desirable object for the advertiser to display in its boardroom. It is normal trade practice, however, for illustrators to grant advertisers and their agencies reproduction rights only. The original artwork is owned by the illustrator and an additional price must usually be paid for its purchase. Some models created for advertising photographs may have equivalent status to illustrations as physical objects. Trade practice in relation to models is less clear. A model of artistic value is more likely to be regarded as belonging to the model maker.

(iii) Rights of advertisers vis-à-vis agencies

27–310   The suggested contract provisions published in 2002 by the Incorporated Society of British Advertisers,[61] the Chartered Institute of Purchasing and Supply[62] and the Institute of Practitioners in Advertising have gone some way towards standardising the terms of contracts between advertisers and agencies. They make it clear that there are many different ways in which intellectual property rights can be handled. Different scenarios are therefore provided for: (a) rights to be assigned to the advertiser on request at any time, (b) rights to be assigned to the advertiser immediately and (c) rights to be assigned on request on termination of the contract provided the advertiser has performed its obligation. The third of these scenarios is said to reflect "the underlying legal position whereby, in the absence of any assignment, copyright will be owned by the Agency insofar as its employees create material or outside suppliers of material assign copyright to the Agency in writing."

Where no written contract is entered into, the copyright in materials created by

---

[58] As to the rights of an exclusive licensee, see para. 5–205, above.

[59] CDPA 1988, s.101A.

[60] As to the distinction between ownership of physical materials and the copyright in the works embodied in them, see paras 5–02 and 5–65, above.

[61] Langham House, 1b Portland Place, London, W1B 1PN.

[62] Easton House, Easton on the Hill, Stamford, Lincolnshire, PE9 3NZ.

an advertising agency's employees (and by sub-contractors such as television commercial production companies who have assigned copyright to the agency) will normally belong to the advertising agency. In particular circumstances, for example, where the design of a logo is commissioned,[63] the advertising agency may be held to have assigned copyright to the advertiser in equity.[64] In many cases it may be possible to imply a licence for advertising created by the advertising agency to continue to be used by the advertiser after the termination of the contract, but this will depend upon a number of factors including the manner in which the advertising agency has been remunerated. Advertising agencies will not be in a position to assign to the advertiser copyright in materials created by third parties who have retained copyright, for example licensors of existing or commissioned musical works.

Where an advertising agency presents creative proposals to an advertiser as part of a "pitch", copyright will remain with the advertising agency if the pitch is unsuccessful. Where a pitch is successful and an advertising agency agrees to assign to the advertiser "copyright in work created by [it] for [the advertiser's] advertising", this will only extend to material created after the appointment of the advertising agency.[65] Copyright will not protect ideas imparted by advertising agencies to advertisers during a pitch, although an action for breach of confidence would in many circumstances lie against an advertiser who made use of ideas disclosed to it by an advertising agency in the course of an unsuccessful pitch.[66]

Advertising agencies are under an implied obligation to their clients to carry out their work with reasonable skill and care. This would include a duty to use reasonable care not to include material knowingly copied from a third party. Alternatively, the copying of material from a third party without a licence may breach an implied obligation to deliver work to the advertiser which is fit for the purpose for which it was commissioned.[67]

C. COPYING OF OTHER ADVERTISEMENTS

(i) Copyright and passing off

Copyright. It is unusual for one advertiser simply to reproduce material included in another advertiser's advertisement. When this occurs, the other advertiser may be concerned to prevent any damage to the integrity of its campaign or the advertising agency whose work has been plagiarised may wish to warn off a competing agency from taking further liberties in future. In either case, issues as to title may arise and appropriate assignments may need to be executed in order to give appropriate rights of action to the party who wishes to take proceedings.

27–311

Imitations or parodies. More commonly, one advertiser will merely imitate or parody another's campaign, whether to score points against a competitor in a comparative campaign or simply to entertain its audience by a witty cultural reference. The main issue raised by a parody of an advertisement is the same as

27–312

---

[63] *R Griggs Group Ltd v Evans* [2003] EWHC 2914, CH.
[64] *Drabble (Harold) Ltd v Hycolite Manufacturing Co* (1928) 44 T.L.R. 264. But see also *Robin Ray v Classic FM plc* [1998] F.S.R. 622; see para. 5–174, above.
[65] *Hutchison Personal Communications Ltd v Hook Advertising Ltd* [1996] F.S.R. 549.
[66] See Ch.20, above.
[67] *Antiquesportfolio.com v Rodney Fitch Y Co Ltd* [2001] F.S.R. 345.

in any other infringement claim. Neither the fact of parody nor the advertising context affects the issue of substantiality.[68]

27–313   **Passing off.** Similarities between the campaigns of competing advertisers may give rise to a passing-off claim. The tort of passing off is wide enough to encompass slogans or visual material associated with an advertiser's product by means of an advertising campaign.[69] The product must have derived from the advertising a distinctive character recognised by the market.[70] An advertisement which makes use of a competitor's brand name in such a manner as to give rise to confusion as to the source or origin from which that product may be obtained may also amount to a passing off.[71]

(ii) Advertising codes

27–314   Broadcast and non-broadcast advertisements are governed by codes of practice for which the Advertising Standards Authority[72] and Ofcom[73] are responsible. These codes contain provisions concerning the imitation of others' advertisements.

D. REFERENCES TO INDIVIDUALS

(i) Defamation and passing off

27–315   In many other countries unauthorised references in advertising to living (and in some cases deceased) individuals are restricted by clearly defined privacy laws. The United Kingdom has a developing law of privacy but the extent to which this will govern advertising is uncertain. The use of photographs of individuals in advertisements may arguably be controlled under the Data Protection Act 1998 in certain circumstances. References to deceased individuals will rarely infringe any legal rights of their heirs. Unauthorised references to living individuals do, however, give rise to clear defamation or passing off claims in certain circumstances.

27–316   **Defamation.** An advertisement may defame an individual either directly or indirectly. Both types of defamation were held to have been present when a photograph of a policeman on duty bore the caption: "Phew! I am going to get my feet into a Jeyes' Fluid foot-bath." Not only did this suggest that the policeman's feet smelt, but also that he was engaged in publicity for which the public would assume that he had received payment, this being inconsistent with his position as a public servant.[74] The following have also been held to be defamatory: to portray an amateur golfer in such a manner as to suggest a paid endorsement, thereby imperilling his amateur status[75] ; the superimposition of a professional model's head and shoulders upon some other woman's legs, thereby implying that the model had consented to being photographed in an indecent

---

[68] *AGL Sydney Ltd v Shortland County Council* (1990) A.I.P.C. 90–661. As to parodies generally, see para. 7–34, above. See below as to Codes of Practice.
[69] See para. 21–34, above.
[70] *Cadbury Schweppes Pty Ltd v Pub Squash Co Pty Ltd* [1981] All E.R. 213.
[71] *McDonald's Hamburgers Ltd v Burgerking (UK) Ltd* [1986] F.S.R. 45.
[72] 2 Torrington Place, London, WC1E 7HW.
[73] Riverside House, 2A Southwark Bridge Road, London, SE1 9HA.
[74] *Plumb v Jeyes Sanitary Compounds Co Ltd, The Times*, April 15, 1937.
[75] *Tolley v Fry* [1931] A.C. 333.

manner, in an advertisement for silk stockings[76] ; the use of a person's features on the body of a very tall man dressed in an exaggeratedly foppish manner[77] ; a circular stating that a professional footballer would give advice on football pool entries, footballers being forbidden by the Football Association from gambling in this manner.[78]

The principle of strict liability for unintentional defamation, in relation to "lookalikes" of persons whose photographs are included in advertisements, has been held to be incompatible with a publisher's right to freedom of speech under Article 10 of the European Convention on Human Rights.[79] Although this decision is open to criticism it would appear to apply also to the more usual problem of unintentional references in advertising to individuals and companies when real names are used in fictional contexts, giving rise to "namesake" claims.

Passing off. A passing-off claim may arise when a celebrity is portrayed or referred to in an advertisement without permission in such a manner as to suggest to the public that permission has been given for reference to be made to that person.[80] The claimant must show not only that the advertisement contains an express or implied misrepresentation to this effect but also that a business goodwill of his has been damaged. This is unlikely to be the case in the case of a private individual or of a person such as a senior politician who, although prominent, is not in the business of accepting fees for commercial endorsements.   27–317

A passing-off claim may also lie when a copyright work is used in an advertisement without permission if it will be wrongly assumed that permission has in fact been granted.

(ii) Advertising codes

Broadcast and non-broadcast advertisements are governed by codes of practice for which the Advertising Standards Authority and Ofcom are responsible. These codes contain important provisions concerning the circumstances in which permission should be obtained for portrayals of or references to individual living persons.   27–318

8. THE COMPUTER SOFTWARE INDUSTRY

A. THE INDUSTRY

Once confined to bulky machines operated by technicians in air-conditioned rooms, software is now embedded in a wide range of consumer products, as well as providing the means of managing ever-more complex processes in the financial and business worlds and in scientific research. Software producers create products for an enormously diverse range of uses and budgets. Consciously or unconsciously, virtually everyone in the developed world today uses computer software on a regular basis.   27–319

Large organisations continue to make use of powerful mainframe computers and supercomputers for large scale applications. Meanwhile, middle-sized machines, personal computers, and networked communications have opened up everyday computing for large sectors of the population in the work and home

---

[76] *Griffiths v Bondor*, *The Times*, December 11, 1935.
[77] *Dunlop Rubber Co v Dunlop* [1921] 1 A.C. 367.
[78] *Rutherford v Turf Publishers Ltd*, *The Times*, October 30, 1925.
[79] *O'Shea v MGN Ltd* [2001] E.M.L.R. 943.
[80] *Irvine v TalkSport Ltd* [2002] EWHC 367, Ch; [2003] EWCA Civ 423.

environment. The 1980s were the decade of the widespread adoption of stand alone personal computers, while the 1990s saw the penetration of networked communications, and the popularisation of online computing and the internet. In the 2000s, wireless computing and the widespread adoption of mobile telephones and other mobile communications devices are further extending the reach of software into people's daily lives.

The software industry shaped copyright law relating to exploitation of products in digital form. It was the application of copyright law to computer programs, that first established the concept that reproduction which was incidental to use and/or transient implicated the reproduction right, meaning that use of copyright software required a licence. This concept became clear as regards programs in Europe from adoption of Directive 91/250 on the legal protection of computer programs ("the Software Directive"). It has since been extended to databases and to all forms of work by Directive 96/9/EC on the legal protection of databases ("the Database Directive") and Directive 2001/29/EC on the 1996 harmonisation of certain aspects of copyright and related rights in the information society ("the Information Society Directive"—implementing similar principles from the WIPO Copyright and Performances and Phonograms Treaties of 1996). Software was also the testbed for copyright law reinforcement of the use of copy-protection technologies by making it unlawful to take steps to circumvent copy protection applied to programs, or to deal in programs from which copy protection had been removed. This type of protection was first introduced in Europe by the Software Directive, and has since been elaborated and extended to works of all types, through the WIPO Copyright and Performances and Phonograms Treaties and the Information Society Directive.

27–320   Key issues in the protection of programs by copyright today tend to result from the nature of software and its creation, and from methods of distribution and use. The methods of creation of software vary and there have been enormous developments in the way software is written and used. In a world of rapidly changing terminology and technology, there has been understandable reluctance to engage in precise legal definition of terms—the term "computer program" is not defined at all in the 1988 Act, for example, and only partially defined the Software Directive.

Some software is bespoke (or "custom")—*i.e.* purpose written. Other software is "off-the-shelf", *i.e.* a standard package intended for supply to multiple users on a non-exclusive basis. Other software may be a mix of "off-the-shelf" and bespoke elements. Many "off-the-shelf" packages are intended for widespread commercial distribution. Traditionally, this has mainly occurred by means of the supply of copies in electronic form on physical media such as floppy discs or CD-ROMs, often through intermediary wholesalers and retailers. The mixed physical and intangible nature of the product generated enormous debate about the legal nature of the transaction and how a software publisher could effectively establish direct contractual relations with the user in order to establish limitations on liability and scope of licence. In mass-market sectors, the practice grew up of "shrink-wrap licensing" *i.e.* the supply of contractual terms as between software publisher and user in conjunction with product "sold" though intermediaries in the distribution channel.

More recently, there is a clear trend in the distribution of software towards direct electronic distribution, bypassing the need to provide a physical copy, or to have intermediary suppliers. Software distribution is ideally suited to all-electronic commerce, subject to there being adequate legal and technological infrastructure to prevent unlicensed copying. "Click-wrap" agreements in electronic distribution (which require the acquirer positively to assent to terms and conditions before goods are supplied) may provide a more secure contractual basis for software licensing than their shrink-wrap precedessors.

Another trend in licensing has been the growth of so-called "open-source" software. Open-source licensing began as a reaction to closed licensing models based on ownership of copyright and trade secrets in program code. In open-source licensing, software suppliers make their source code available and permit its modification and inclusion in derivative products, provided that the recipient agrees that if it decides to redistribute derivative code it will similarly make available its source code and will pass on the terms of licence and any notices applicable to the original code. By doing this, software developers potentially allow their software to evolve, grow and be disseminated much more rapidly and simply. Open-source software licensing has particularly taken off in the areas of operating systems, core internet applications, and programming tools. Methods of open-source licensing are subject to a commonly understood set of principles as to the rules of open-source licensing, which can be found in documents published on the internet (see *e.g. www.opensource.org*), but terms of licence vary between products.

B. WRITING SOFTWARE

(i) Authorship/ownership

One feature of the industry is that, while most software is the product of teamwork, the programming labour force is relatively mobile, with people often moving employment and working on a freelance, consultancy basis. It is common to find that there are problems in proving legal title to software, and it is no coincidence that in both *Richardson (John) Computers Ltd v Flanders*[81] and *Ibcos Computers Ltd v Barclays Mercantile Highland Finance Ltd*,[82] the first two reported English software copyright trials, the plaintiffs had problems in establishing full legal title and had to rely on title in equity to parts of their software.   **27–321**

The mobility of programmers means that questions frequently arise about possible copying of software in which a previous employer owns rights. This may be a clear infringement resulting from programmers innocently or deliberately bringing copied software with them and reusing it extensively in their new employment. On the other hand, there may be much more subtle arguments about whether similarities between two separate pieces of software represent infringing copying, or are merely the natural result of the same person doing something similar in a similar way. In *Cantor Fitzgerald v Tradition (UK) Ltd*[83] programmers who wrote the defendants' program modules had also previously written the claimants'. They were held to have infringed copyright and misused confidential information by loading the claimants' source code on to the defendants' computers and to have infringed by some, but not all, of the alleged acts of copying of the claimants' code, including uses involving consulting the claimants' code during development and using the claimants' code during testing and debugging.

Methods of writing software have evolved extensively over the years. Things which were once hand-coded can now be generated automatically through the use of programming tools. Increasingly "intelligence" is being built into computer programs and data. These trends tend to exacerbate the already inherent difficulties in determining the boundary between "idea" and "expression" in computer programs, and may also challenge concepts of originality. Inbuilt

---

[81] [1993] F.S.R. 497.
[82] [1994] F.S.R. 275.
[83] [2000] RPC 95.

intelligence has also raised questions about the concept of authorship. In a simple case it is easy to draw an analogy between a computer program used to achieve a result and a pen or other tool, which does not challenge human authorship of the result.[84] But, as the 1988 Act has already recognised,[85] there may be a need for a rule to determine the deemed human author in cases where the machine appears to be the author, rather than any human being.

(ii) Bug fixing and maintenance

27–322 Computer programs tend to evolve, both during initial development, and subsequently, to enhance their functionality or to correct programming errors or "bugs". Testing and bug fixing are important in all but the most trivial software development programme. Even after extensive testing, few software publishers would ever warrant that their software is "bug-free". Among other things, most programs are designed to work with other programs in an overall computer environment, in response to input, such that their operation is affected by factors outside the control of the developer.

Because software is not generally warranted bug-free, maintenance and error correction are important issues for users of software. The Software Directive recognised these concerns by specifically requiring member states to provide that "in the absence of specific contactual provisions" it is not an infringement of copyright to carry out acts restricted by copyright in a computer program where this is necessary for the use of the computer program by the lawful acquirer in accordance with its intended purpose, including for error correction.[86]

Because programs can fail, and may require to be reloaded into computer memory, many users also require the right to make "back-up copies" of programs supplied to them. This practice was also recognised by the Software Directive, which required that national laws provide that the making of a back-up copy of a program by a person who has the right to use it may not be prevented by contract in so far as it is necessary for that use.[87]

In its April 2000 communication on the implementation and effect of the Software Directive, the Commission clarified its position as regards the scope of the back-up copy exception. The Commission is of the opinion that the wording and objective of Article 5(2) means that only "a" (*i.e.* one) copy is permitted and that the purpose may not be other than as a "back-up" to ensure that normal use of the program can continue in the event of loss or defect of the original. The making of unauthorised copies for private use is not permitted, and consitutes an act of software piracy.

C. RELEVANT WORKS

27–323 The 1988 Act[88] makes computer programs a subset of "literary works", as does the Software Directive. The international status of computer programs as literary works appears to have been confirmed by adoption in December 1996 of the

[84] This was the approach taken in *Express Newspapers plc v Liverpool Daily Post and Echo plc* [1985] F.S.R. 306.
[85] See CDPA 1988, s.9(3) and the definition of "computer-generated work" in s.178.
[86] Directive 91/250, Art.5.1. See CDPA 1988, s.50C, added by the Copyright (Computer Programs) Regulations 1992 (SI 1992/3233).
[87] Directive 91/250, Art.5.2. See CDPA 1988, ss.50A and 296A, added by The Copyright (Computer Programs) Regulations 1992 (SI 1992/3253) and para.9–00. In practice, where software is acquired on a physical medium for loading into computer memory, it is common for the original copy to be kept as the back-up copy.
[88] See CDPA 1998, s.3.

WIPO Copyright Treaty.[89] However, as mentioned above, there is considerable scope for debate over what is, and is not, a computer program for these purposes. The 1988 Act does not define the term at all, while the Directive only does so partially, by including "preparatory design material" for computer programs[90] but excluding from protection "ideas and principles which underlie any element of a computer program, including those which underlie its interfaces".[91]

Methods of program development vary depending upon the programming environment, and have evolved over time as programs have become more powerful and more complex in response to repeated and drastic falls in cost of memory and processing power. Programs can be expressed at multiple levels, from levels which involve methods of expression which are more intelligible to the human mind, such as code written in popular programming languages of their day, to the lowest levels of machine-intelligible code. Subject to any questions of substantiality and originality which may arise, any level of code should be protectable as a computer program for copyright purposes. The 1988 Act confirms that making a version of a program in which it is converted into or out of a computer language or code into a different computer language or code may be an act of infringing adaptation.[92]

There are levels, however, at which it is not so clear what is within the scope of a computer program for these purposes. One of these is the reference to "preparatory design materials" in the Software Directive. Does this embrace, for example, manuscript notes or flow diagrams which a programmer might have generated in sketching out initial design thoughts, and, if so, how much is protection for high-level design precluded by virtue of this being "idea" and not "expression"? A second area of uncertainty is the boundary between programs and data on which they operate. For example, in an electronic database, where is the boundary between what is protected as "program" and what is protected as a protected database or under the *sui generis* right created as a result of the Database Directive.[93] This is not just a theoretical problem under the 1988 Act. Among other things, the scope of protection and the acts permitted in relation to copyright works vary depending on the work involved. For example, the "back-up right" contained in section 50A is limited to computer programs, suggesting that it may not be permissible to back up data. Similarly, sections 79 and 81 of the 1988 Act exclude computer programs from the moral rights to be identified as author and to object to derogatory treatment of the work, but these rights may still apply to non-program elements. Following implementation of the Information Society Directive, the statutory provisons applicable to circumvention of copy-protection technology in relation to programs are also differently worded from those applicable to other types of work.[94]

At the user interface level it is also very unclear what is protected as a computer program. At its broadest, this could include input commands, screen layouts, text or images on screen generated by the program, or other forms of

27–324

---

[89] Directive 91/250, Art.4 provides that computer programs are protected as literary works within the meaning of Art.2 of the Berne Convention.

[90] Directive 91/250, Art.1.1.

[91] Directive 91/250, Art.1.2.

[92] See CDPA 1988, s.21.

[93] Dir. 91/250 is silent on this issue. Dir. 96/9 specifically excludes protection under that Directive for "computer programs used in the making or operation of databases accessible by electronic means" (Art.1.3).

[94] As was highlighted in *Sony v Ball* [2004] EWHC 1738, Ch D. S.296 of the 1988 Act has been retained in relation to computer prgrams only; new ss.296ZA–F apply to other types of work. The retention of different treatment for programs was thought to be required by the terms of the Information Society Directive 2001/29.

data output to devices to which the computer is connected. There is also enormous scope for overlapping protection for different aspects of digital products. Screen outputs are clear examples of items which can easily be characterised as other forms of work, such as (non-program) literary works,[95] or artistic works. The 1988 Act defines a "film" as "a recording on any medium from which a moving image may by any means be reproduced",[96] a definition which obviously embraces many multimedia products, which also are or include computer programs. The provisions of the 1988 Act dealing with films differ significantly from those dealing with literary works generally, and, particularly, computer programs. This affects many aspects of the right, including authorship and ownership,[97] the restricted acts,[98] and the permitted acts.[99] So, in a case involving partial copying, for example, complex and difficult questions could arise about the limits of protection for computer programs and the interrelationship of that protection with the protection available for other forms of works.

D. RELEVANT TRADE ASSOCIATIONS, COLLECTING SOCIETIES/LICENSING AGENCIES

27–325   The software industry has not established significant collective licensing. It is a very dynamic and varied market in terms both of products and of means of distribution and exploitation. These conditions have militated against the establishment of collective licensing. On the other hand, because there is interdependency between software products which are designed to work together, and between software products and hardware products, it is common in the industry for products of different vendors to be combined prior to sale to end users. For example, manufactures of hardware may act as resellers of third-party software (and vice versa). Reference has already been made to the practice of open-source licensing.

There has been collective activity in connection with enforcement in the United Kingdom and elsewhere. For example, FAST, the Federation Against Software Theft[1] was established in the mid-1980s, when the United Kingdom first enacted legislation confirming subsistence of copyright in computer programs, to act as an anti-piracy body acting on behalf of the industry. The video games industry has since established ELSPA, the European Leisure Software Publishers Association,[2] which manages anti-piracy investigations and enforcement on behalf of its members. The Business Software Alliance (BSA)[3] has also carried out anti-piracy work in the United Kingdom on behalf of its members. All of these bodies, and other computer industry bodies such as Intellect (formerly the CSSA, (Computing Services and Software Association) and BCS (British Computer Society), take an active role in representing their members on issues which affect them.

---

[95] For example, in the form of text on screen generated by the program, or "compilations".

[96] CDPA 1988, s.5B, introduced by The Duration of Copyright and Rights in Performances Regulations 1995 (SI 1995/3297).

[97] See CDPA 1988, ss.9 and 10, as amended by The Copyright and Related Rights Regulations 1996 (SI 1996/2987).

[98] See, for example, subs.17(2), which applies only to literary, dramatic, musical or artistic works, or subs.17(4), which applies only to films.

[99] There are many examples in Ch.III of permitted acts which apply only to limited categories of work, such that films are treated differently from literary works. Implementation of Dir.91/250 has also led to the introduction of various permitted acts which apply only to computer programs.

[1] Clivemont House, 54 Clivemont Road, Maidenhead, Berkshire, SL 6 7 BZ, www. fast.org.uk.

[2] Suite 1, Haddonsacre, Station Road, Nr. Evesham, Worcs, WR11 5LW, www. elspa.com.

[3] BSA Europe, 79 Knightsbridge, London, SW1X 7RB, www.bsa.org.

E. CONTROLS ON THE INDUSTRY

There are no specific controls on the exercise of copyright in computer software **27–326** outside the normal principles of competition law. It is clear, however, that there are certain areas of particular sensitivity so far as the application of competition law is concerned, and in particular in the areas of interoperability, the making available of interface specifications and bundling of products. Software maintenance is also an area in which competition issues may arise, in particular because third parties carrying out maintenance may need to perform restricted acts of copying by running some or all of the software on their customer's machine in the process of performing their service.[4]

F. PROBLEMS AND ISSUES

(i) Problems of subsistence and infringement inherent in the nature of software

Most lawyers and judges have read books, listened to music, seen plays, watched **27–327** films, and visited museums and art galleries. Traditional forms of work are relatively familiar to them. This assists in forming judgments about questions such as whether a work or an aspect of a work is sufficiently original to be protected by copyright, or about whether a substantial part has been copied. Most lawyers and judges are much less familiar with computer programs and computer programming. As a result, in those software copyright disputes which involve comparison of non-identical products, it is common for there to be detailed and extensive expert evidence going to matters of originality and substantiality. The functional nature of software, and trends in types of software for different uses, also tend to raise difficult questions about whether similarities result from copying protected expression or underlying idea.

There has been very limited United Kingdom case law on these issues. Courts in the United States, on the other hand, have decided a number of cases exploring these issues under United States law. Given that country's important role in the development of the software industry, these cases have tended to have the effect of determining the development of the industry's understanding of what aspects of a program may be protected by copyright. As a very broad generalisation, early United States cases tended to confirm protection of software under copyright law, whereas later cases have tended to qualify its scope. A consequence of the tendency for United States cases to develop industry thinking on these issues was that in the first reported English software copyright infringement trial, *John Richardson Computers Ltd v Flanders*,[5] Ferris J. based his approach to analysing originality and infringement on the "abstraction and filtration" analysis from the United States case of *Computer Associates In v Altai In*[6] This analysis seeks to exclude systematically from consideration elements dictated by efficiency, elements dictated by external factors, and elements taken from the public domain. In *Ibcos Computers Ltd v Barclays Mercantile Highland Finance Ltd*[7] Jacob J. rejected this route as unhelpful, pointing out that United States copyright law is different in certain material respects from the copyright law of the United Kingdom. He went back to basic principles of United Kingdom copyright law to

---

[4] See *Digital Equipment Corp v LCE Computer Maintenance Ltd* (Mervyn Davies J., May 22, 1992 (transcript available on LEXIS)).

[5] [1993] F.S.R. 497.

[6] 982 F. 2d. 693, 23 U.S.P.Q. 2d. 1241 (1992).

[7] [1994] F.S.R. 275.

determine considerations of the distinction between idea and expression in the context of deciding whether a substantial part had been copied. He reconfirmed that only "mere general ideas" and "general principles" are excluded from protection, but that "detailed ideas" may be protected. He found that the test of substantiality was a question of degree, "where a good guide is the notion of overborrowing of the skill, labour and judgment which went into the copyright work". He analysed the various programs which were common between the parties' software and determined infringement or non-infringement of each on its specific facts.

(ii) Protection of user interfaces

27–328   Another aspect of the difficulties of determining what is and is not a computer program is the protection of user interfaces such as screen displays. In considering whether the reproduction of elements which are output on screen infringe copyright, it is normally necessary to consider the screen output both as an independent work or works (such as a literary work or artistic work) and as part of the program as such. In the case of programs with video elements, it may also be necessary to consider the screen output as a "film" as defined in the 1988 Act, section 5B. This may raise questions of different authorship and ownership of these aspects of the software, as well as questions of different scope of protection.

There are additional questions about whether prescribed forms of user inputs for a program, such as the use of a particular keyboard function key or keystroke to achieve a particular result, form part of the protected work, or whether these should be excluded from consideration of whether a substantial part has been copied. Arguments for exclusion could be that these are not of their nature protectable under United Kingdom copyright law, or because they are not sufficiently original. It is also sometimes argued that such features of computer systems should be deprived of protection because they have become "industry standard".

(iii) Compatibility; protection of interfaces; reverse engineering

27–329   The fact that programs do not work in isolation has various implications. Programmers have to make their programs work with the hardware and software with which they are designed to run, and have to enable them to operate on the types of inputs they may receive. So, they have to understand the environments in which their programs will be used. Producers of hardware and software commonly recognise that it is in their own interests to make available information about at least some of the "interfaces" to their products to enable third parties to develop "compatible" or "interoperable" products. This reflects the industry symbiosis between hardware and software manufacturers, and developers of "operating" and "applications" software—nobody would buy computers unless good applications and peripheral devices were available for them. This applies right across the range, from suppliers of the most powerful hardware and most sophisticated software applications, to the manufacturers of simple commercial applications, networking tools, or video games devices.

The Software Directive reflected these issues, both in describing the limits on the scope of copyright in a computer program,[8] and in establishing a limited exception to the restricted acts where reproduction of copyright code "is "indis-

---

[8] Directive 91/250, Art.1.2 provides "Protection in accordance with this Directive shall apply to the expression in any form of a computer program. Ideas and principles which underlie any element of a computer program, including those which underlie its interfaces, are not protected by copyright under this Directive". CDPA 1988 does not specifically include this language.

pensable to obtain the information necessary to achieve the interoperability of an independently created computer program with other programs" subject to numerous limiting conditions.[9] In *Mars UK Ltd v Teknowledge Ltd*[10] the defendants had used reverse engineering techniques to establish the communications protocol used to communicate with program-controlled coin receiving and changing mechanisms. Parts of the communications process involved encryption to protect data contained in the mechanisms from unauthorised modification. The defendents' purpose in doing this was to enable them to offer after-sales services in relation to the mechanisms, including updating and changing coinset data contained in the mechanisms to enable the mechanisms to accept or change different coins from those originally programmed into them.

The defendants' main argument in defence was based on an implied licence to repair (*British Leyland*) argument. Jacob. J. held that the Software Directive and Database Directive did not provide for such a defence, and that—had it otherwise been applicable on the facts—the defence was not available in relation to programs and databases (see, also, paragraph 5–00, above). Accordingly, various acts carried out by the defendants both during the reverse engineering process and subsequently in developing their own reprogramming software and in reprogramming mechanisms infringed the claimant's copyrights and database rights. There was no detailed consideration of which acts specifically infringed and the judge did not consider the claimant's allegation of infringement by circumvention of copy-protection. In the United States case of *Sony v Connectix*,[11] it was held that intermediate copies of software made and used by the defendant during the defendant's reverse engineering of the plaintiff's software were "protected fair use", necessary to permit the the defendant to make its non-infringing product. Article 6 of the Software Directive requires that acts of reproduction during decompilation be limited to those parts of the program necessary to achieve interoperability, something which may be difficult to do until one has established what the different parts of the program do. This preliminary analysis may, however, be permitted under Article 5(3) of the Software Directive (which permits lawful users to observe, study or test the functioning of a program in order to determine the ideas and principles which underlie any element of it, so long as this is done in the course of performing acts which the user is permitted to do). Article 5 (3) is now expressly implemented in the 1988 Act, by the introduction of section 50BA. The wording in Article 6 which limits permitted decompilation to those parts of the program necessary to achieve inter-operability is not implemented verbatim in section 50B. Instead, that section provides[12] that the defence does not apply where the lawful user of the program "does not confine the decompiling to such acts as are necessary to achieve the permitted objective".

(iv) Protection for hardware implementations/circuit designs

At their most basic level, computer programs consist of very simple instructions   **27–330**
to hardware to carry out very simple functions. These instructions may be stored as program instructions, or by hardware implementation, for example, in a semiconductor chip. As noted above, there is no comprehensive definition of "computer program". Arguably, a hardware implementation of a set of instructions which could also be implemented in program code should benefit from the

---

[9] Directive 91/250, Art.6. See CDPA 1988, s.50B, introduced by The Copyright (Computer Programs) Regulations 1992 (SI 1992/3233).
[10] [2000] F.S.R. 138.
[11] 203 F. 3d 596 (9th Cir. 2000).
[12] CDPA 1988, s.50B(3)(b).

same form of protection. This appears to be confirmed by recital 7 of the Software Directive, although not expressly imported into the Act.

In the mid-1980s, the United States enacted[13] *sui generis* protection for semiconductor chip-masks works, being a series of related images, however fixed or encoded, representing the patterns on the layers of a semiconductor chip. Protection for foreign mask works was based on reciprocity. In response to this, Council Directive 87/54/EEC on the legal protection of topographies of semiconductor products was adopted in December 1986. Directive 87/54/EEC required Member States to provide protection for the topographies of semiconductor chips. The Directive includes, *inter alia*, specific limitations relevant to reverse engineering of semiconductor topographies. It is currently implemented in the United Kingdom via a modified form of the design right.[14]

At the same time, industry has continued to seek patent protection for inventions involving circuits for computers, including in the semiconductor area. In addition, there is potential for reliance on circuit layout diagrams and lists of electronic components included in the circuitry as artistic or literary (non-program) works.[15]

(v) Enforceability of shrink-wrap licences

27–331   In mass-market software distribution, many aspects of the transaction are approached as a contractual licence directly between rightholder and end user, but there is typically a "channel" of wholesalers and retailers through whose hands passes the physical item on which the software is recorded, *i.e.* floppy discs or CD-ROM, plus associated documentation. As between retailer and purchaser, the transaction is one of sale and purchase. It is not normal for the customer to be asked to read and sign the licence terms before buying the product. In many cases, the terms are not even visible until the user has made the purchase and opened the box. Although licensor terms and conditions typically cover similar issues, such as scope of licence and limitations and exclusions of the software publisher's liability, the details of the terms and conditions vary and certainly could not be said to be "industry standard".

In that copyright law makes it clear that incidental and transitory copying is *prima facie* restricted unless licensed, copyright owners are in a strong position to argue that the sale of a copy of a program does not imply an unlimited licence to do any act restricted by the copyright and that it is clearly within the contemplation of users that their use will be subject to the scope of licence restrictions.[16] However, traditional contract analysis requires offer and acceptance between vendor and purchaser, or licensor and licensee, for terms to be agreed. The fact these terms are not agreed to at time of purchase therefore raises questions about enforceability of shrink-wrap licence terms.

Nonetheless, the practice of shrink-wrap licensing has been widely used. In 1996, an important test case was fought in the United States, *Pro CD v Zeidenberg*.[17] The outcome appears to have brought some measure of certainty to enforceability of shrink-wrap licence terms in the United States, although there is ongoing discussion about reform of the Uniform Commercial Code in this area.

---

[13] Semiconductor Chip Protection Act 1984.

[14] See, The Design Right (Semiconductor Topographies) Regulations 1989 (SI 1989/1100), as amended. For a detailed discussion of the right, see Ch.14, above.

[15] See *Anacon Corp Ltd v Environmental Research Technology Ltd* [1994] F.S.R. 659.

[16] See *Creative Technology v Aztech Systems Pte Ltd* 1997–1 S.L.R. 621; 1996 S.L.R. LEXIS 486.

[17] United States Court of Appeals (7th Cir.) 86 F. 3d. 1447.

The Scots Court of Session decision of *Beta Computers v Adobe Systems*,[18] also recognised the industry practice.

Electronic distribution reduces or removes the need for a distribution channel, enabling software publishers to deal directly with their customers without establishing traditional distribution infrastructure. Electronic distribution has grown rapidly, and is expected to grow further, with consequential reduction of shrink-wrap distribution. None the less, electronic commerce will not sweep away physical distribution for some time. Furthermore, in the online environment related questions will continue to arise, as to whether, for example, notices as to licence limitations necessarily have contractual effect. In this respect, the use of "click-wrap" agreements (requiring licensees positively to indicate acceptance of licence terms) may increase.

(vi) Scope of licensed use

There are many different types of software, and many different types of use of software. So, it is not surprising that there is no single type of licence. On the other hand, many licences cover similar issues. Typical software licences cover: **27–332**

1. type of machine on which the software may be used (*e.g.* model of mainframe, or whether stand-alone or networked, in the case of personal computer software);
2. restrictions on types of use (*e.g.* internal data processing or bureau use or permitted number of users on a network);
3. maintenance, right to make back ups and, in some cases, escrow of source code (*i.e.* a copy to be deposited with a third party on terms that it will be made available to the customer on specified triggering events, such as insolvency of the licensor).

These, and other, scope of licence issues are frequently covered with a fairly high level of specificity in supplier standard-form licences.

As is discussed elsewhere, the ability of a software copyright owner to restrict scope of use is to some extent circumscribed by statute, in particular as a result of the implementation of the Software Directive. For example, the "decompilation right" cannot be excluded by contract, any more than the right to make back-ups where this is necessary for the licensed use. However, the circumstances in which the exceptions to the restricted acts arise have been carefully defined, such that it may be possible to limit their application by the manner in which the licence is drafted or by establishing business practices which obviate their application, such as the routine publication of interface specification information.[19]

---

[18] [1996] F.S.R. 367.

[19] Art.6 of Dir.91/250/EEC only applies, *inter alia*, to the extent the information necessary to achieve interoperability has not previously been readily available.

CHAPTER TWENTY EIGHT

COLLECTING SOCIETIES

Contents

Contents   *Para.*

1. INTRODUCTION

A. RATIONALE FOR COLLECTING SOCIETIES

28–01 **Individual exercise of rights.** Copyright confers exclusive rights which are vested in the copyright owner and give him the right to forbid others to exploit the work without authorisation. Ideally these rights are exercised on an individual basis by agreement between the copyright owner and the individual user of the work and there are many cases in which rights continue to be exercised individually. Such individual exercise of rights is the norm, for example, so far as agreements between authors of literary works and publishers are concerned with respect to the conditions for publication of the author's work. Similarly, the author of a dramatic work will likely have no difficulty in making an individual contract with a theatre company. Producers of cinematographic works also generally control the use of their works directly. Likewise, owners of rights in computer programs manage their products themselves.

28–02 **Need for collective administration of certain rights.** There are, however, certain rights which are difficult if not impossible to exercise individually and in respect of which rights owners have for many years banded together to exercise rights on a collective basis. The need for such collective administration of rights was felt first in the second half of the nineteenth century[1] by composers and music publishers as regards the performance in places of public entertainment of non-dramatic musical works. Since then, new technologies have given rise to new, high-volume markets for works in respect of which individual exercise and control of rights is at worst impossible, or at best impractical. Public performance and broadcasting of works were the first uses to give rise to collective licensing, and in that area collective administration has been traditional. In recent years, the emergence of secondary mass usage by new means of exploitation of works such as reprographic reproduction of literary and graphic works, commercial rental, satellite broadcasting, cable distribution of television programmes and films, and the use of powerful computer technology to digitise and store protected works of all kinds and to transmit them in non-material digital form throughout the world, by means of a combination of computer, telephone and satellite and cable technologies on the new global information infrastructure that has produced the internet,[2] has made the need for collective administration of rights even more acute. Increasingly, therefore, since 1990, when the first commercial provider of

---

[1] See para. 28–08.

[2] "The Internet is a global network of computers linked mainly via the telephone system and the academic, research and commercial computing networks. The Internet is a fledgling superhighway network which is limited by the rate at which the network components can transmit and handle data. The Internet is not a genuine superhighway because it does not offer the basic capability of two-way real-time video transmission and interactivity. It is, however, widely available and highly functional as an information exchange and electronic mail service. The Internet also provides a useful prototype from which a full information superhighway might evolve. Part of that evolution has been the development of a user-friendly interface in the form of the World Wide Web (www). The www allows access to a global network of computers by millions of people with no formal training in computer technology". The House of Lords Select Committee on Science and Technology, in its report entitled *Information Society: Agenda for Action in the United Kingdom*, HL Paper 77, See ss.1995–96, 5th. Report, July 1996, paras 1.8 and 1.9. For a

Internet dial-up access came on line, and the invention of the world+ wide web a year later,[3] collective administration has become the most realistic way for copyright owners to exercise many of their rights.

Collecting societies. The term "collecting societies" is generally used internationally to describe the organisations set up by the various categories of rights owners to administer their rights collectively. A collecting society has been defined by the EU to mean "any organisation which manages or administers copyright or rights related to copyright as its sole purpose or as one of its main purposes".[4]

As regards the United Kingdom, the 1988 Act uses the term licensing body, with the following similar, but more precise definition:

> "A 'licensing body' means a society or other organisation which has as its main object, or one of its main objects, the negotiation or granting, either as owner or prospective owner of copyright or as agent for him, of copyright licences, and whose objects include the granting of licences covering works of more than one author."[5]

Copyright licences are defined as meaning 'licences to do, or authorise the doing of, any of the acts restricted by copyright.'[6]

In the United Kingdom and other EU Member States, collecting societies or licensing bodies are private sector organisations established and controlled by the rights owners' themselves. However, in most countries, for the protection of the public, there is some kind of government supervision or control over the practices of collecting societies. In the United Kingdom, the 1988 Act provides a regulatory framework for the operation of licensing schemes and licensing bodies in certain areas and also provides for the Copyright Tribunal to oversee the proper functioning of such licensing schemes and the activities of the licensing bodies generally.[7]

Purposes of collective administration. Collective administration of copyrights serves two principal purposes:

(a) to do for members of collecting societies what they cannot practically and economically do for themselves by providing a service to enable rights owners to enforce and administer certain of their copyrights effectively and cheaply, and

(b) to provide a service to users by facilitating access to copyright works and making it possible for users to comply with their obligations under the law to obtain licences for the use of copyright works.

As the Monopolies and Mergers Commission stated in 1988:

> 'The principal functions of collective licensing bodies are to license the use of the copyrights they manage; to monitor that use in order to enforce the conditions upon which the licence has been granted; and to collect and distribute the royalties payable as the result of licensed use. The licensing function includes the negotiation of appropriate rates of royalty with the prospective user, and is inevitably contentious because it is concerned with how much the user should pay for the copyright material. Collective licensing should provide a mechanism so that payment of the required royalty:

28–03

28–04

---

brief history of the Internet, see Cunard, Hill and Barlas, "Current Developments in the Field of Digital Rights Management", WIPO doc. SCCR/10/2, August 1, 2003, p.5, *et seq.*.

[3] Cunard, Hill and Barlas, "Current Development in the Field of Digital Rights Management", WIPO doc. SCCR/10/2, August 1, 2003, *p.6.*

[4] Satellite and Cable Directive 93/83, Art.1(4).

[5] CDPA 1988, Chapter VII, Copyright Licensing, s.116(2); see paras 29–30 and 29–107, below.

[6] CDPA 1988, s.116(3).

[7] CDPA 1998, Ch.VII. See also paras 28–15and 28–19and Ch.29, paras 29–88 *et seq.*

    (a) guarantees users immediate access to the licensor's repertoire;

    (b) keeps to a minimum the administrative costs incurred by users and owners;

    (c) provides for the use of copyright of recordings that have yet to be made (and hence are of unknown value); and

    (d) meets the needs of owners and users whatever the scale of their business."[8]

The Commission concluded that collective licensing bodies are the best available mechanism for licensing copyright works provided they can be restrained from using their monopoly unfairly.[9]

In a system of collective administration, rights owners authorise one or more collecting societies to administer their rights on their behalf. The societies then generally organise and make available to prospective users, or associations of users, blanket licences, which authorise the users to make use of the entire repertoire, national and foreign, represented by the society in question, for certain purposes and for a prescribed period. Blanket licences are granted on a take-it-or-leave-it basis with respect to the society's entire repertoire; societies do not license the use of a part only of their repertoire. Such blanket licences generally cover "commercially marketable repertoires, in which the value of the whole is greater than the sum of the values of the parts: the difference reflects the benefit of the aggregation" to the user.[10] In some circumstances, collecting societies issue individual licences, although on standard terms.

Licences are granted in return for royalties or fees and the collecting societies collect and distribute the resulting remuneration among the copyright owners. Such organisations either acquire copyrights from their members by assignment or act as agents or licensees on behalf of their members to enforce copyright. Collecting societies are also empowered to monitor the uses made of the works to ensure that unauthorised uses of the works controlled by them do not take place. Where necessary, they enforce the rights of their members by legal action for infringement. For example, in the field of music, no individual composer, producer of a sound recording or other copyright owner has the resources, in practice, to secure adequate protection for his work or deal with the very large number of broadcasters and the many thousands of different public performance users in thousands of different places wishing to exploit such works.

Various collecting societies undertake additional activities on behalf of their members, other than collective administration of rights. Such activities include the provision of social and legal services to rights owners, educational and public relations activities aimed at ensuring a better understanding and respect on the part of the public and users for the rights they administer and representation of their members' interests in relation to government departments and intergovernmental organisations.

28–05   **Advantages of collecting societies.** Collecting societies are practically, economically and legally both viable and essential: practically, because copyright owners cannot be in an indefinite number of places at the same time exercising individual

---

[8] Monopolies and Mergers Commission, *Collective Licensing, A report on certain practices in the Collective Licensing of Public Performance and Broadcasting Rights in Sound Recordings*, Cm. 530 HMSO December 1988, para.7.12. The report referred specifically to the activities of PPL in relation to the licensing of sound recordings but its conclusions on the merits of collective licensing are equally applicable in respect of other works protected by copyright. The reference in point (c) of the passage quoted refers to the fact that licences cover the use of both existing sound recordings and those yet to be produced.

[9] Cm. 530 HMSO December 1988, para.7.14.

[10] Cm. 530 HMSO December 1988, para.7.15.

rights, and foreign rights owners would be unable to exercise their rights outside their country of origin without extreme expense and difficulty; economically, because it is cheaper to share the financial expenses of negotiation, supervision and collection among the greatest possible number of rights owners; and, legally, because it is impossible for users of works to obtain permission from every individual copyright owner, both national and foreign. From the point of view of the user, there is a clear advantage in being able to obtain a licence from a national collecting society, giving him the right to use virtually any work from its worldwide repertoire. Given that national collecting societies control the rights administered by their sister societies in other countries by means of the reciprocal representation agreements already referred to, the user with a Performing Right Society (PRS) or Phonographic Performance Ltd (PPL) licence (see para.28–09, below) is generally safe from actions for infringement, whatever music or sound recordings he uses.

There is an additional advantage to the individual right owner whose personal standing or size would put them in a weak bargaining position in relation to powerful users, if they were to try to exercise their rights on an individual basis. Collective licensing increases their marketing power, putting them on the same footing as their better known or more influential colleagues.

In certain cases, there is a need for rights owners to mandate more than one collecting society. This lies in the fact that some of these societies administer only one particular right for one category of right owner. For example, the Mechanical Copyright Protection Society (MCPS) administers composers' reproduction rights, whereas the Performing Right Society (PRS) administers their public performance, broadcasting and cable distribution rights.[11] These rights are collectively referred to as performing rights.

The public interest. There is a general consensus that such collective administration bodies provide the best available mechanism for licensing and administering copyrights and is to be encouraged wherever individual licensing is not practicable. They represent the best means of protecting the rights owners' interests, enabling copyright owners to license and monitor the use of their works, to collect and distribute royalties, and to bring actions for infringement. At the same time, they facilitate access to copyright protected works for the consumer and minimise the number of persons with whom users must negotiate licensing contracts.

    28–06

The convenience offered by such bodies both to the owner and user of copyright cannot be matched by any other means and, in their absence, in a totally free market, individual users and copyright owners would be at a serious disadvantage in negotiating and subsequently enforcing contractual arrangements for the exploitation of rights. Thus, collecting societies make the copyright system more effective and efficient, promote the dissemination of works and tend to enlarge the choice of works made available to the public. They benefit rights owners and users alike and in principle operate for the benefit of the public.

Collective administration of rights through such societies operates worldwide. While the precise nature, representation and practices of collecting societies vary from country to country, collective administration of copyright by licensing bodies is standard practice.

---

[11] For details of the activities of these societies, see para. 28–09 and Section 4 of this Chapter below. Since 1997, these two bodies have been brought under joint management. Meanwhile, the PRS and MCPS have formed an alliance, although retaining their separate identities in terms of membership and the rights they license. The MCPS-PRS Alliance services both societies and is jointly owned by them. For further information about the PRS and MCPS, see paras 28–59 and 28–56,

Technical progress is such that in the modern world there exist innumerable possibilities for the exploitation of protected works. Such technology, whilst facilitating access to works by the consumer, has increased the difficulties of enforcing exclusive rights. Collective administration provides the only practical means for rights owners to safeguard their rights and, in particular, those new rights introduced to enable rights owners to control new methods of exploitation of their works. Indeed, the law now provides that certain rights may only be exercised through collecting societies both in the United Kingdom and elsewhere. For example, under the amendments introduced by the Copyright and Related Rights Regulations 1996,[12] which implement, *inter alia*, the EU Directive on rental right and that on satellite broadcasting and cable distribution,[13] the cable-redistribution rights of copyright owners may be exercised against a cable operator only through a licensing body.[14] Other examples of rights in respect of which legislation makes their exercise conditional on collective administration are the reprographic reproduction right, the right to remuneration in respect of private copying of works (a right which has been introduced in a majority of Member States of the EU and elsewhere but which has yet to be introduced in the law of the United Kingdom), and the artists' resale right (*droit de suite*), which is also not yet part of the law of the United Kingdom.

Following the adoption of the new EC Directives on the harmonisation of certain aspects of copyright and related rights in the information society and on the resale right for the benefit of the author of an original work of art, the situation may change in the United Kingdom. As regards remuneration for private copying, the United Kingdom is in a position to maintain its opposition to the payment of such remuneration, as it is not obligatory under the Directive for Member States to introduce such a right. However, so far as the artists' resale right is concerned, Member States will be obliged to introduce the right in due course.[15]

28–07 **Benefits of collective administration for foreign nationals.** Collective administration of rights also greatly facilitates the exercise of the rights of foreign rights owners, entitled to national treatment under the international copyright and related rights conventions and pursuant to EC law (see Part VII, Chapters 24 and 25, above). Most established collecting societies belong to international networks, consisting of federations of societies representing the same categories of rights owners and which enter into reciprocal representation agreements for the exercise of rights in their respective members' repertoire.[16] Thus, one collecting society in any given country is able to represent both foreign and national rights owners within its territory and to license practically the entire world repertoire of the rights owners it represents; at the same time a rights owner will be able to exercise his rights and receive royalties when his work is used abroad. The system is thus of benefit both to United Kingdom and non-United Kingdom nationals.

---

[12] SI 1996/2967.

[13] Directive on rental right and lending right and on certain rights related to copyright in the field of intellectual property of November 19, 1992 (Directive 92/100[1992] O.J. L346/61); Directive on the co-ordination of certain rules concerning copyright and rights related to copyright applicable to satellite broadcasting and cable retransmission of September 27, 1993 (Directive, 93/83, [1993] O.J. L248/15).

[14] CDPA 1988, s.144A. See paras 29–74 *et seq.*, below.

[15] For details of these developments, see respectively paras 25–79 *et seq.* and 25–72 *et seq.*, above.

[16] See also paras 28–23 *et seq.* below.

B. ORIGINS OF COLLECTING SOCIETIES

The first collecting societies. The establishment of the first collective licensing **28–08**
body predates the adoption of the Berne Convention for the Protection of Literary and Artistic Works in 1886 (the Berne Convention).[17] SACEM (Society of
Authors, Composers and Music Publishers), the French society representing
authors and composers, was established in France in 1852 to administer public
performance rights in musical works. Following the adoption of the Berne
Convention, which recognised the public performance right as a principal feature
of the protection to be afforded to all authors from the Berne Union countries, it
became apparent to authors in many other countries that, in practice, it was impossible to safeguard such a right on an individual basis. The need for collective
licensing bodies was soon felt, therefore, in every country in Europe and led to
the establishment of more such bodies representing, in the first place, authors and
composers. Subsequently, by the turn of the century, technical developments led
to the advent of new categories of works protected by copyright, such as
photographs, films and sound recordings. Following the recognition of public
performance rights in sound recordings, collective licensing bodies representing
producers and performers were set up in the countries which recognised these
rights. The emergence of radio and television broadcasting as a major user of
copyright works in the first half of the twentieth century,[18] as well as the other
new technologies which have developed in the meantime and given rise to new
uses of works, such as reprography, satellite transmission and cable distribution,
commercial rental, computer storage of protected works in databases and nowadays digital storage and distribution of works online over the internet and so on,
has led to the extension of collective licensing schemes to new areas. Likewise,
new categories of works have emerged and been afforded copyright protection,
such as computer programs, broadcasts, cable programmes and databases. As a
result of all these developments, new collecting societies have been set up to
safeguard, enforce and obtain payment for the exploitation of new rights recognised by legislation in favour of authors and other copyright owners.

The establishment of collecting societies in the United Kingdom. In the United **28–09**
Kingdom, the first collecting societies to be set up were the Mechanical Copyright Licences Company Ltd (Mecolico), now the Mechanical Copyright Protection Society (MCPS), and the Performing Right Society Ltd (PRS). Mecolico
was established by music publishers at the time of the 1911 Act to collect and
distribute royalties from producers of sound recordings for the recording rights in
music and lyrics (these rights are sometimes referred to as "mechanical rights").
The PRS was set up in 1914 to administer the public performance rights of
authors, composers and music publishers in musical works, which at the time
were published mainly in the form of sheet music. At that time, music publishers
derived most of their income from theatrical performances of their works and
from the sale of sheet music; the recording industry was still in its infancy. The
PRS now administers all non-dramatic performing rights in musical works,
including broadcasting, cable distribution and non-theatrical use of excerpts from
dramatico-musical works (these rights are known as "small" rights as opposed to
"grand" rights). Grand rights are the rights of authors and composers in dramatic

---

[17] As to the Berne Convention, generally, see s.2, Ch.24.
[18] Marconi developed wireless communication (radio) in the closing years of the last century. The
first radio programme broadcast in the USA took place in 1906. The BBC was established by
charter in 1927 with a monopoly over sound broadcasting. Television was invented by Baird in
1926 and the first television programmes to be broadcast in the UK took place in July 1936.

and dramatico-musical works,[19] which it is feasible to exercise individually since the use of such works is limited to a comparatively small number of users and locations. The PRS also plays a limited role in the licensing of its members' film synchronisation rights. Phonographic Performance Ltd (PPL) came into being in 1934 to administer performing rights in sound recordings on behalf of record producers, following the decision in the *Cawardine*[20] case, which decided that the rights conferred on record producers by the 1911 Act included public performance and broadcasting rights. Organisations equivalent to those in the United Kingdom are established in most other European countries and, outside Europe, particularly in the English-speaking world, including, for example, in Australia, Canada and the United States of America.

28–10   **Collecting societies operating in the United Kingdom in 2004.** Today, the following additional collective licensing bodies are operating in the United Kingdom; their activities, as well as those of the MCPS, PRS and PPL, are described in more detail in Section 4 of the Chapter, below:

    (a) Authors' Licensing and Collecting Society Ltd (ALCS) administers a wide variety of rights in literary and dramatic works on behalf of authors, including *inter alia* the reprographic right, the cable distribution right and the private recording right.

    (b) Association of United Recording Artists (AURA) collects equitable renumeration arising from the exploitation of phonograms on behalf of performers.

    (c) British Equity Collecting Society Ltd (BECS) administers performers' remuneration;

    (d) Compact Collections Ltd collects secondary television royalties for film and television content owners;

    (e) Copyright Licensing Agency Ltd (CLA) licenses the reprographic rights of authors and publishers in published literary and artistic works;

    (f) Design and Artists Copyright Society Ltd (DACS) administers rights in artistic works;

    (g) Directors and Producers Rights Society (1992) Ltd (DPRS) administers certain rights on behalf of film and television directors and producers;

    (h) Educational Recording Agency Ltd (ERA) licenses the recording by educational establishments of broadcasts and cable programmes;

    (i) Newspaper Licensing Agency Ltd (NLA) licenses the reprographic rights of newspaper publishers in news articles;

    (j) Performing Artists' Media Rights Association Ltd (PAMRA) collects recorded performance remuneration on behalf of performers;

    (k) Video Performance Ltd (VPL) administers the rights of producers of music videos.

A number of other trade associations, including the Music Publishers' Association (MPA), the British Phonographic Industry (BPI) and the International Federation of the Phonographic Industry (IFPI) also administer certain rights on behalf of their members. The Open University Educational Enterprises Ltd licenses the off-air recording of Open University programmes.

---

[19] Opera, operetta and ballet.
[20] *Gramophone Co Ltd v Stephen Cawardine and Co* [1934] Ch. 450.

C. CHARACTERISTICS OF EFFECTIVE COLLECTING SOCIETIES

Structure and functions of collecting societies. There have been a number of   **28-11**
studies carried out at the international level under the auspices of the World Intellectual Property Organisation (WIPO, Geneva) into the structure and functions of
appropriate and effective collecting societies. These gave rise to the adoption in
1979 of guidelines for the establishment and operation of collecting societies for
the rights of producers of phonograms and performers under the Rome Convention for the Protection of Performers, Producers of Phonograms and Broadcasting
Organisations 1961 (the Rome Convention).[21] In 1983, WIPO published model
statutes for organisations administering authors' rights.[22] Subsequently, both
WIPO and Unesco published studies on the establishment and operation of collective administration organisations to serve as a basis for advice to
governments.[23]

In the United Kingdom, the activities of the PRS and PPL in particular have
been under scrutiny in recent years as a result of investigations by and subsequent
recommendations of the Monopolies and Mergers Commission.[24]

From the foregoing, some characteristics of effective collecting societies may
be identified.

Benefits of a single organisation representing a single category of rights   **28-12**
owner. As a rule, there should be only one organisation for any one category of
rights owners open for membership to all rights owners of that category on reasonable terms. A long-established exception to this principle is the alliance between authors and publishers in performing right societies such as the PRS. By
means of reciprocal representation agreements with foreign societies or federations of societies, a collecting society should represent in its territory both
national and foreign rights owners.

The existence of two or more organisations in the same field may diminish the
advantages of collective administration for both rights owners and users. For the
rights owners, competing societies lead to duplication of functions and reduction
in economies of scale in operation and thus are unlikely to bring benefits to their
members.[25] For the user, a multiplicity of societies representing a single category
of rights owner would also cause uncertainty, duplication of effort and extra

---

[21] Recommendations concerning the protection of performers, producers of phonograms and
broadcasting organisations, adopted by the Intergovernmental Committee of the Rome Convention in 1979 [1979] *Copyright* 105. As to the Rome Convention, generally, see s.5, Ch.24.

[22] Model Statutes for Public Institutions Administering Authors' Rights and for Private Societies
Administering Authors' Rights, October 1983, [1983] *Copyright* 351 and 353.

[23] WIPO, *Collective administration of copyright and neighbouring rights*, Geneva 1990 (WIPO
publication No.688(E)); P. Schepens, *Guide to the collective administration of authors' rights
(The Administration Society at the Service of Authors and Users)*, Unesco, 2002 (doc. CLT-2000/
WS/4).

[24] Monopolies and Merger Commission, *Performing rights—A report on the supply in the United
Kingdom of the services of administering performing rights and film synchronisation rights*,
(Cm. 3147 HMSO, London 1996). Monopolies and Mergers Commission, *Collective Licensing—A report on certain practices in the Collective Licensing of Public Performance and
Broadcasting Rights in Sound Recordings*, (Cm. 530 HMSO, London 1988). The Monopolies
and Mergers Commission has meantime been replaced by The Competition Commission,
established by The Competition Act 1998, see para. 29–255below.

[25] As noted in para.9–1 of the MMC PRS report (see previous note), there are only two major
jurisdictions, Brazil and the USA, where there are competing societies. In Brazil, in 2002 there
were 12: ABRAC (*Associação Brasileira de Autores, Compositores, Intérpretes e Mùsicos*),
ABRAMUS (*Associação Brasileira de Mùsicos*); AMAR (*Associação de Mùsicos, Arranjadores
e Regentes*); ANACIM (*Associação Nacional de Autores, Compositores e Intérpretes de Mùsica*);
ASSIM (*Associação de Intérpretes e Mùsicos*); ATIDA (*Associação de Titulares de Direitos Au-
torais*), SADEMBRA (*Sociedade Administradora de Direitos de Execução Musical do Brasil*);
SBACEM (*Sociedade Brasileira de Autores, Compositores e Escritores de Mùsica*); SBAT (*Sociedade de Autores Brasileira Teatrais*) which administers "grand rights"; SICAM (*Sociedade*

expense. The user would have to check, for each work he wished to use, which society controlled it and whether he had the appropriate licence. For both parties, administration costs would be greater, reducing the revenue available for distribution to rights owners and increasing the overall cost of obtaining licences for the user.

28–13 **Adequate mandates.** Collecting societies should have valid mandates to act as agent or licensee of their members, or take assignments of their individual rights, and have the legal personality required:

> (a) to enter into binding contracts, both at the national and international level;
> (b) to exercise the mandates or assignments received from their members;
> (c) to enforce their members' rights by means of legal action, where necessary.

Societies should provide an efficient, transparent and equitable service to their members. Monitoring of uses and the collection of royalties should be as comprehensive as possible, subject to reasonable costs. Members should receive regular and sufficiently detailed information about the manner in which their rights are being exercised. Such information should also be available to foreign collecting societies with which the society has entered into reciprocal representation contracts. Societies should provide for a suitable internal appeal procedure to deal with matters of dispute between them and their members.

28–14 **Collection and distribution of revenue.** Decisions about the methods and rules of collection and distribution of remuneration, on the basis of statistically valid sampling procedures, should be taken by the rights owners concerned. There should be no discrimination between rights owners, members or non-members, nationals or foreigners. Indeed, foreign rights owners should receive the same treatment in all respects as national rights owners. Remuneration collected should be distributed among individual rights owners as much in proportion to the actual use of their works as possible, subject only to deduction of the actual costs of administration and of any other deductions (*e.g.* for cultural or social purposes) which have been expressly agreed by the members. Such costs should be subject to the effective scrutiny of the membership.

Government supervision of, and interference in, the establishment and operation of tariffs and other licensing conditions applied by collective administration organisations, which are in a *de facto* monopoly position vis-à-vis users, is justified to the extent that such supervision is required to prevent abuse of such a monopoly position.[26]

D. PRINCIPLES GOVERNING THE REGULATION OF COLLECTING SOCIETIES

28–15 **Public interest and need for public control.** Any collecting society by its nature and as a matter of fact, will be in a dominant position because it will represent the rights of a majority of a particular category of rights owners, both national and

---

Independente de Compositores e Autores Musicais); SOCINPRO (*Sociedade Brasileira de Administração e Protecão de Direitos Intelectuais*) and UBC (*União Brasileira de Compositores*). In the USA, there are three: ASCAP (American Society of Composers, Authors and Publishers), BMI (Broadcast Music Inc.) and SESAC (Society of European Stage Authors and Composers). In Brazil, so far as rights in musical works and phonograms are concerned, the situation is different from that in the USA. Collection is effected by one organisation, ECAD, a private monopoly organisation imposed by law, which collects remuneration on behalf of six of the above music societies (AMAR, ABRAMUS, SPACEM, SICAM, SOCINPRO and UBC) and distributes it to rights owners through the specific society to which the rights owner is affiliated (Law No.9.610/98). As to the position in the USA, see paras 28–17.

[26] Monopolies and Mergers Commission Cm. 3147 HMSO 1996. Cm. 3147; Conclusions, para.306 (m); see also paras 29–73 *et seq.*, below.

foreign in any given territory. Thus, collective administration may not be in the public interest if there is no mechanism for ensuring that monopolistic collecting agencies do not abuse this position. As mentioned above, the existence of collecting societies is considered to be of advantage to the public as being the most effective means of, on the one hand, administering and protecting rights owners' interests whilst, on the other, facilitating the ease of access of copyright protected works to the consumer. The potential conflict between the public interest in collective administration and the *de facto* monopolistic nature of collecting societies has on occasion been illustrated by users challenging their role on the grounds that they are monopolies and abuse their monopoly position. In the United Kingdom, there have been complaints of abuse of monopoly rights against, in particular, the PRS and PPL, since virtually all popular music is now controlled by these organisations and their counterparts in other countries. It has therefore come to be felt, in a number of countries and at the international level, that to ensure against abuse of monopoly some measure of public control over the activities of such organisations is necessary in the public interest;[27] and that:

"... it is better to accept the usefulness, in the public interest, of the fact of monopoly but to control it in other ways".[28]

Supervision of establishment and operation of collecting societies. In many countries, therefore, collecting societies are subject to some form of supervision which may be exercised in a variety of ways. Some countries make the establishment of a collecting society conditional upon the approval of a competent authority (*e.g.* the Ministry of Culture, the Ministry of Justice or the Patent Office); this is the case, for example, in France, Germany and Spain.[29] In France, the Ministry of Culture is responsible; but if for any reason it opposes the incorporation of a society, the courts have jurisdiction to decide the matter after assessing the professional qualifications of the founders of such society, the human and material means that they intend to use to collect royalties and to exploit their repertoire. By law, such societies are obliged to make available blanket licences covering the complete repertoire of the French and foreign rights owners they represent.[30] In Germany, the supervising authority for collecting societies is the Patent Office.[31] In Spain, as in France, authorisation to operate as a collecting society must be obtained from the Ministry of Culture. Due account is taken, in particular, of the degree to which the proposed society is representative of the category of right owner it purports to represent, the volume of potential users, the suitability of its statutes and the means whereby it proposes to achieve its aims, the potential efficiency of its administration abroad, and the views of existing collecting societies operating in Spain.[32] Where such systems for supervision by a competent authority of the establishment and operation of collecting societies exist, provision is made for continued monitoring of the societies' activities. In the United Kingdom, the means of control are the Copyright Tribunal the Office of

28–16

---

[27] See, as to the position of such organisations under Arts 81 and 82 (ex Arts 85 and 86) of the Treaty of Rome, para. 28–20 and para. 29–253, below.

[28] See Wallace, W., "Control over the Monopoly Exercise of Copyright" [1973] I.I.C. 382.

[29] See Dietz, "Legal Regulation of Collective Management of Copyright (Collecting Societies Law) in Western and Eastern Europe) *Journal of the Cop. Soc. of the USA*, No.4 [2002] 49, 897.

[30] Law on the Intellectual Property Code (No.92–597 of July 1, 1992, as amended up to January 3, 1995), Title II concerning royalty collection and distribution societies, Arts L.321–3 and L.321–7.

[31] Law of September 9, 1965, on the Administration of Copyright and Related Rights, as amended to May 23, 1985, Art.18(1).

[32] Revised Law on Intellectual Property, regularising, clarifying and harmonising the applicable statutory provisions (approved by Royal Legislative Decree 1/1996 of April 12, 1996, Arts 142 *et seq.*).

Fair Trading and the Competition Commission, whose respective powers are considered in detail below.[33]

28–17 **The monopoly position of collecting societies.** Various jurisdictions have dealt differently with the reality that collecting societies, having a *de facto* monopoly position, may abuse that position. Some provide for settlement of disputes by the civil courts. Elsewhere, governments have opted to establish, as in the United Kingdom and Australia,[34] some form of compulsory arbitration or specialist tribunal having jurisdiction to review the activities of collecting societies and power to determine or vary the rates charged and to order the grant of licences. Others provide for review of licensing conditions by an administrative authority.

In Germany, collecting societies are specifically exempted from the antitrust law, in recognition of the fact that the very nature of a collective licensing body is by necessity a monopoly. In order to avoid any abuse of this monopoly, a special arbitration board (*Schiedstelle*) was established to control the activities of collective licensing bodies and to settle any conflicts which might arise between them and users.[35] As a rule, claims may not be asserted in court proceedings unless they have been preceded by proceedings before the arbitration board.[36] The Canadian Government has also recognised the need to exempt collecting societies from certain provisions of its Competition Act and has set up a system of voluntary submission to regulatory review; the Competition Act does not apply in respect of any royalties or related terms and conditions arising under an agreement submitted for review.[37]

In 1985, the Australian Trade Practices Commission had to decide whether to allow the Phonographic Performance Company of Australia Ltd (PPCA) to become the collective licensing body representing copyright owners in sound recordings throughout Australia. The Commission concluded that there was public benefit in terms of efficiencies and cost savings and that such benefit outweighed any detriment to competition. Since this collective arrangement was justified on "public benefit" grounds, it was found to be eligible for exemption from the Trade Practices Act of 1974. This finding is equally applicable to collecting societies representing other rights owners.[38]

In the United States of America, litigation concerning the operations of collecting societies has given rise to an exhaustive examination of the question whether the operations of these societies are contrary to the public interest by reason of incompatibility with US antitrust law. The benefits to rights owner and user alike of collective licensing is recognised and the societies' activities are not *per se* considered to be unlawful.[39] There is, however, competition for the collective administration of performing rights in music in the United States of America, where three competing organisations, ASCAP, BMI and SESAC, exist. ASCAP is a composers' society, representing and controlled by its members. BMI is a corporate body with full trading powers owned and managed by broadcasters, *i.e.* music users, with the writers and publishers it represents playing no part in its

[33] See paras 29–93and 29–255 *et seq.*
[34] Copyright Act 1968, Part IV. For a comparative law study of the role of copyright tribunals, see M. Freegard, " *Quis Custodiet?* The Role of Copyright Tribunals" [1994] 7 E.I.P.R. 286.
[35] The Law of September 9, 1965, on the Administration of Copyright and Related Rights, Arts 14, 14a–14c, and 15.
[36] The Law of September 9, 1965 on the Administration of Copyright and Related Rights, Art.16.
[37] Copyright Act 1988, s.50.5(3).
[38] Determination of the Trade Practices Commission of Australia on applications for authorisation under s.88(1) of the Trade Practices Act 1974 by EMI Records (Australia) Ltd on their own behalf and that of Phonographic Performance Company of Australia Ltd dated August 28, 1985.
[39] For an authoritative finding on this issue, see *Broadcast Music Inc v Columbia Broadcasting Sys., Inc*, 441 US 1, 201 U.S.P.Q. 497 (1979), 5.9.

operations. SESAC is a privately owned corporation representing writers and publishers. These organisations carry out identical functions, competition between them lying in competing for members. Users have to obtain licences from all three.

Collective administration and the copyright conventions. The international **28–18** conventions on copyright and related rights do not explicitly address the question of collective administration of rights.[40] Their basic philosophy is the protection of individual rights owners and individual exercise of rights. Article 2(6) of the Berne Convention provides that "protection shall operate for the benefit of the author and his successors in title". According to this principle, collective administration should not operate in such a way as to reduce the protection established by the Convention. However, the Berne Convention provides that members of the Union may determine by legislation the conditions under which certain rights may be exercised, in particular, the broadcasting and cable distribution rights as well as the right of recording musical works (both of which may be subject to compulsory licensing in certain circumstances).[41] These provisions provide a basis in convention law for non-voluntary licences or for obligatory collective administration. Collective administration is also considered appropriate in other cases where the right is established as a mere right to remuneration[42] or where it represents a compromise between an exclusive right and a fair use exception to it, permitted under the conventions, as in the case of remuneration schemes established to compensate for home taping and reprography.

The compatibility of tribunals, supervisory authorities, etc. with the Berne **28–19** **Convention.** It is relevant here to mention Article 17 of the Berne Convention, which deals with the right of governments to take measures to control the circulation, performance and exhibition of works for the preservation of public order. According to the WIPO Guide to the Berne Convention, "Authors may exercise their rights only if that exercise does not conflict with public order. The former must give way to the latter".[43] The Article is mainly but not solely concerned with censorship; according to the report on the discussions relating to Article 17 at the Stockholm Conference in 1967, "questions of public policy should always be a matter for domestic legislation" and "the countries of the Union would therefore be able to take all necessary measures to restrict possible abuse of monopolies".[44] It is, therefore, understood that under the Berne Convention, tribunals and other supervisory bodies may only interfere with the setting of tariffs and other licensing conditions in cases where there is an actual abuse of monopoly position and should only serve the purpose of taking measures against possible abuses of monopolies.[45] Thus, such tribunals may not be used arbitrarily as a means to impose a régime of statutory control over the exercise of the exclusive rights guaranteed to authors under the Berne Convention.

---

[40] The WIPO Copyright Treaty (WCT) and the WIPO Performances and Phonograms Treaty (WPPT), both adopted on December 20, 1996, contain respectively Arts 12 and 19, which impose certain obligations on Contracting Parties concerning the protection of rights management information; for further details, see paras 24–73 *et seq.* and paras 24–128 *et seq.*, above.

[41] Art.11 *bis* (2) and Art.13(1) of the Berne Convention.

[42] For example, Art.12 of the Rome Convention, which provides for equitable remuneration to be paid to producers of phonograms and performers for the broadcasting and public performance of sound recordings in certain circumstances.

[43] *WIPO Guide to the Berne Convention*, [1978] Geneva 99.

[44] Records of the Stockholm Conference, 1967, Report of Main Committee I, para.263.

[45] See WIPO, *Collective Administration of Copyright and Neighbouring Rights*, [1990] Geneva, para.281.

E. COLLECTIVE ADMINISTRATION AND EC LAW

28–20 **Community action on collecting societies.** The Commission of the European Community (the Commission) first announced its intention to study the need for action within the EC on the subject of the collective management of copyright and related rights and collecting societies in its document *Follow-up to the Green Paper* issued in January 1991.[46] To date, no firm proposals for legislation relating to collective administration have been published by the Commission, but a legislative proposal is foreshadowed in a recent communication dated April 2004 entitled "The Management of Copyright and Related Rights in the Internal Market.[47] The communication is the result of a wide-ranging process of consultation with interested parties begun in 1995/96 and continued through 2002 on the basis of its Green Paper entitled: "Copyright and Related Rights in the Information Society", published in July 1995.[48] The Green Paper included a chapter concerning questions on the exploitation of rights, in which it raised issues for discussion with regard to the acquisition and management of rights and technical systems of identification and protection, having regard particularly to new multimedia works and the exploitation of works on digital networks.[49] That paper did not comment on the structure of collecting societies. Following consultation with interested parties, in November 1996, the Commission issued a Communication, *Follow-up to the Green Paper on Copyright and Related Rights in the Information Society* (1996 Follow-up Communication),[50] which set out the Commission's Single Market policy at the time in the area of copyright and related rights in the Information Society.[51] The document identified management of rights as an issue requiring further evaluation, rather than as a priority item for legislative action.[52] This further evaluation included a study on certain aspects of collective management carried out at the Commission's request and completed in early 2000.[53] Discussions continued at a series of conferences organised by the European Union in the year 2000, culminating in a hearing on collective management, held in Brussels in November 2000, with a view to assisting the Commission to determine appropriate action in the field.[54]

In its latest communication published in April 2004,[55] the Commission announced that it has now concluded that Community legislation on the collec-

---

[46] *Follow-up to the Green Paper: Working Programme of the Commission in the Field of Copyright and Neighbouring Rights*, Commission Communication to the Council, document COM(90) 584 final, January 17, 1991.

[47] Communication from the Commission to the Council, the European Parliament and the European Economic and Social Committee, document COM (2004) 261 final of April 16, 2004.

[48] *Green Paper: Copyright and Related Rights in the Information Society*, presented by the Commission, Brussels, July 19, 1995, (COM(95) 382 final).

[49] ibid. Ch.2, Part Three, ss.VIII and IX, at pp.69 *et seq.*

[50] Communication from the Commission, *Follow-up to the Green Paper on Copyright and Related Rights in the Information Society*, Brussels, November 20, 1996 (COM(96) 568 final).

[51] See also the answer given by Mr M. Monti in the European Parliament on behalf of the Commission on November 12, 1996, to a written question (E 2255/96) by Mr K.-L. Lehne to the Commission on the subject of "Competition between copyright management societies (music collecting societies" [1997] O.J. C105/5.

[52] 1996 Follow-up to the Green Paper (Com (96) 568 final), at 3.

[53] *"Etude sur la gestion collective des droits d'auteur dans l'Union européenne"*, Deloitte & Touche, ITEC Group 2000.

[54] Conference organised by the Portuguese Presidency at Evora, March 2000; International Conference organised by the Commission entitled "The Management and Legitimate Use of Intellectual Property", Strasbourg, July 2000; Public Hearing on Collective Management, Brussels, November 2000; the conclusions of the Hearing are available on the Commission website: *http://europa.eu.int*.

[55] Com (2004) 261 final of April 16, 2004. Note also that the European Parliament adopted a resolution on January 15, 2004, on a Community framework for collective management societies in the field of copyright and neighbouring rights. The resolution noted, *inter alia*, "that collecting societies require a degree of regulation, bringing greater harmonisation, democratisation and

tive management of rights, and particularly on the governance of collecting societies, would be highly desirable, stating that the marketing of intellectual property rights needs to be facilitated in order to create a true single market in this area. Following the publication of the document, the Commission launched a further consultation exercise on what such legislation might consist of.

It should be recalled that the issue of collective management has been addressed in several Community instruments. There is a definition of collecting societies in the Satellite and Cable Directive (Art.1(4)); it is stated to be for the purposes of that particular Directive but is clearly of general application. Directives in the field of copyright and related rights explicitly tolerate or recommend the mandatory assignment of certain rights, such as the rights of authors and performers to equitable remuneration for rental, to collecting societies.[56] Community law also stipulates mandatory rights administration by collecting societies in the case of cable distribution: "Member States shall ensure that the right of copyright owners and holders of related rights to grant or refuse authorisation to a cable operator for a cable retransmission may be exercised only through a collecting society".[57] Likewise Community law provides for the extension of a collective agreement with a collecting society to unrepresented right-holders.[58] In several cases, the Directives refer to collecting societies as an accepted way of rights management. However, Recital 17 of the Directive on the harmonisation of certain aspects of copyright and related rights in the information society[59] states: "It is necessary, especially in the light of the requirements arising out of the digital environment, to ensure that collecting societies achieve a higher level of rationalisation and transparency with regard to compliance with competition rules." This is followed by a qualifying statement to the effect that the Directive is without prejudice to the arrangements in the Member States concerning the management of rights such as extended collective licences.[60]

Recognition of advantages of collective administration. The Commission and **28–21** the Court of Justice have long acknowledged the factual dependence of rightholders on collective licensing in relation to certain rights, accepting that in practice an individual rights owner does not have the resources or power to exercise his rights himself and cannot avoid joining a collecting society. Moreover, rights owners depend on such societies to counterbalance the users' market strength.[61] However, as stated in the 1996 Follow-up document:

"copyright licensing and collecting societies as such are subject to the EU

---

transparency in relation to the management of copyright and neighbouring rights, and … a Community approach in the area of the exercise and management of copyright and neighbouring rights must be pursued while respecting and complying with the principles of copyright and competition law and in accordance with the principles of subsidiarity and proportionality". Bull. EU 1/2–2004 para.1.3.61. See also Report on a Community Framework for collecting societies for authors' rights adopted by the Committee on Legal Affairs and the Internal Market, December 11, 2003 (doc. A5–0578/2003 final).

[56] Art.4(3) and (4) of the Rental Right Directive 92/100.

[57] Art.9 of the Cable and Satellite Directive 92/183.

[58] Art.3(2) of the Cable and Satellite Directive to the benefit of collecting societies. *cf.* Lewinski, "Mandatory Collective Administration of Exclusive Rights— A Case Study on its Compatibility with International and EC Copyright Law", E.Copyright Bulletin, No.1, January-March 2004.

[59] Directive 2001/29/EC of May 22, 2001 [2001] O.J. L167/10; see para. 25–79 above.

[60] Directive 2001/29/EC Recital 18.

[61] See, *e.g.*: Case 127/73 *BRT v SABAM & FONIOR* [1974] E.C.R. 51 and 313; [1974] 2 C.M.L.R. 238; *Re GEMA (No.I)* [1971] O.J 1971 L134/15; [1971] C.M.L.R. D 35; *Re GEMA (No.2)* [1972] O.J 1972 L182/24; [1971] C.M.L.R. D 115; *GEMA Statutes* [1982] O.J. 1982 L94/12; [1982] 2 C.M.L.R. 482. In 1994, the Commission, however, issued a statement of objections (no decision has been issued) against the collective licensing activities of VPL and IFPI, with respect to their members' broadcasting rights in music videos. Following a complaint from MTV, which had previously negotiated a collective licence covering the whole repertoire of VPL and IFPI for its pan-European satellite broadcasting service but which, at the conclusion of a five-year contract,

competition rules. Collecting societies are 'undertakings' for the purposes of applying Article 85 (restrictive agreements) and 86 (abuse of dominant position) of the Treaty. They cannot be regarded as "undertakings entrusted with the operation of services of general economic interest" benefiting from the special regime laid down in Article 90(2) of the Treaty".[62]

Thus, collecting societies, drawing up their rules, must take account of all relevant interests in such a way that a balance is ensured between the requirement of maximum freedom for authors, composers and publishers to dispose of their works and that of the effective management of their rights. They should not, therefore, impose obligations on its members which are not absolutely necessary for the attainment of the object of collective licensing and which encroach unfairly on a member's freedom to exercise his copyright.[63] A number of practices of collective licensing bodies have been found to be an abuse under Article 82 (ex Article 86) of the Treaty, including the following:

(a) imposing an obligation on members to assign all their rights, present and future, to the licensing body[64] ;

(b) unreasonable refusal to supply services to persons in need of the licensing body who do not come within a certain category of persons defined by that body on the basis of nationality or residence[65] ;

(c) conducting their activities so that their effect is to partition the common market and thereby restrict the freedom to supply services which constitute one of the objectives of the Treaty[66] ;

(d) discriminating between persons seeking services or customers on the ground of nationality alone.[67]

For a full discussion of these issues, see paras 29–173 *et seq*. and para.29–253 , below.

28–22 **Future EC legislative action.**.The legislative proposal foreshadowed in the Commission's communication on the management of copyright and related rights in the internal market already referred has come to four main conclusions:[68]

— An internal market for collective rights management will be more firmly established if a legislative framework on the governance of collecting societies is implemented at Community level. Such a framework would address the issues surrounding the establishment and use of collecting societies, the relationship they have with right-holders and commercial users, and lastly, their external supervision. This would make it possible to

---

alleging that the collective licensing of their members' repertoire by VPL and IFPI represented an abuse of monopoly, it wished to replace by separate licences from major, individual record companies, the Commission stated that the refusal of the major companies to negotiate individually had the result "that competition between the members of VPL, and between the majors in particular, is restricted since by giving an exclusive mandate to VPL ... they refrained from conducting price negotiations on an individual basis". The position of the small independent record companies was completely overlooked in the Commission's statement. The Commission's attitude in this case is at variance with its past decisions on the subject of collective licensing and with the case law of the Court. See H. Porter, "European Union Competition Policy: Should the Role of Collecting Societies Be Legitimised? *MTV v. VPL*", [1996] 12 E.I.P.R. 672. C. Jackson, "European Union Competition Policy: Collecting Societies", [1997] 3 E.I.P.R. 161.

[62] *Follow-up to the Green Paper* (COM(96) 568 final), at p.25. Note that the Articles referred to are now Articles 81 and 82, respectively.

[63] *BRT v SABAM & FONIOR* [1974] E.C.R. 51 and 313; [1974] 2 C.M.L.R. 238.

[64] *Re GEMA (No.1)* [1971] O.J. L134; [1971] C.M.L.R. D 35.See also *Bangalter v SACEM*, COMP/C2/37.219;cf para. 29–254, below.

[65] Case 7/82, *GVL v Commission* [1983] E.C.R. 483.

[66] Case 22/79 *Greenwich Film Production v SACEM* [1979] E.C.R. 3275.

[67] *Re GEMA (No.1)*, [1071] O.J. L134; [1971] C.M.L.R D 35; GVL [1983] E.C.R 483; Case 402/85 *Basset v SACEM* [1983] E.C.R. 483.

[68] Commission Press release IP/04/492.

ensure that collecting societies are transparent, and that established Community law in the field of intellectual property is properly applied. It would foster the emergence of Community-wide licensing for the exploitation of rights via one-stop shops.

— The development of Digital Rights Management (DRM) systems should, in principle, be based on their acceptance by all stakeholders, including consumers, as well as on copyright policy of the legislature. A prerequisite to ensure Community-wide accessibility to DRM systems and services by right-holders as well as users and, in particular, consumers, is that DRM systems and services are inter-operable.

— For the time being, there is no need for action at Community level with regard to individual rights management, as differences in national law have not given rise to concern with respect to the functioning of the internal market; national developments will, however, be kept under review.[69] An internal market in the collective management of rights can be best achieved if the monitoring of collecting societies under competition rules is complemented by the establishment of a legislative framework on good governance. Common ground on the following features of collective rights management would be required: the establishment and status of collecting societies (persons who may establish a society, the status thereof, the necessary evidence of efficiency, operability, accounting obligations, and a sufficient number of represented right-holders); the relation of collecting societies to users (users must be in a position to contest tariffs, through the courts, specially created mediation tribunals or with the assistance of public authorities); however, use without payment should not be permitted. These principles would promote and safeguard access to protected works on appropriate terms.[70]

F. RELATIONS WITH FOREIGN COLLECTING SOCIETIES

Application of principle of national treatment. The principle of national treatment under the copyright conventions[71] requires that authors of literary and artistic works protected under the Berne Convention or the Universal Copyright Convention shall enjoy the same rights of protection of their works in all the other States of the Berne Union or UCC as do nationals of those States.[72] Article 5, paragraph (1) of the Berne Convention defines the principle of national treatment as follows:

28–23

"Authors shall enjoy, in respect of works for which they are protected under this Convention, in countries of the Union other than the country of origin, the rights which their respective laws do now or may hereafter grant to their nationals, as well as the rights specially granted by this Convention."

Article II of the Universal Copyright Convention similarly lays down:

"Published works of nationals of any Contracting State and works first published in that State shall enjoy in each other Contracting State the same protection as that other State accords to works of its nationals first published in its own territory, as well as the protection especially granted by this Convention."

The principle of national treatment in relation to copyright works and perform-

---

[69] (Com (96) 568 final), para.2.3.

[70] Com (96) 568 final, para.3.5.

[71] See Ch.24.

[72] Art.3 of the WIPO Copyright Treaty (WCT) of December 20, 1996, and Art.4 of the WIPO Performances and Phonograms Treaty (WPPT) of the same date, also provide for the application of the national treatment principle.

ers' rights is recognised also by the Agreement Establishing the World Trade Organisation (including the Agreement on Trade-related Aspects of Intellectual Property Rights), 1994.[73] , and by the Rome Convention.[74] The United Kingdom implements its obligations under these international agreements by extending protection to the works of nationals of other countries by means of statutory instruments issued pursuant to sections 159 and 208 of the 1988 Act.[75]

28–24   **Need for international co-operation to implement national treatment.** The principle of national treatment was incorporated in the original text of the Berne Convention adopted in 1886. In order for this principle to be fully applied, the need was felt from the early days of the Convention for international co-operation between organisations representing rights owners in different countries in order to enforce the rights of their members not only in their countries of origin but elsewhere. International co-operation with regard to the performing rights of authors and composers of musical works was the first to develop. In the last years of the nineteenth century and in the first quarter of the twentieth century, performing rights societies were established in nearly all European countries as well as overseas. Co-operation developed rapidly between these organisations and in 1926 an international confederation of such societies was established, the International Confederation of Societies of Authors and Composers (CISAC), which groups some 210 societies in 109 countries,[76] representing rights owners of musical, dramatic, literary and audio-visual works and of works of graphic and visual art.[77] Subsequently, as new collecting societies were formed at the national level to administer rights in new categories of works and in respect also of new uses of works in response to new technical developments, these new collecting societies also established international non-governmental organisations to co-ordinate their activities.

28–25   **International federations of collecting societies.** Thus, most of the collecting societies operating in the United Kingdom belong to such international federations of societies representing the same category of rights owners in other countries. The United Kingdom societies have reciprocal representation agreements with the other member societies of such federations for the exercise of rights in their respective members' repertoire. Agreements in the field of performing rights in works, where the network of collecting societies is the most developed, are based on the CISAC "Model Contract of Reciprocal Representation between Public Performance Rights Societies" (the CISAC Model Contract). Under Article 3(1) of that contract:

> "each of the contracting parties undertakes to enforce, within the territory in which it operates, the rights of the members of the other party in the same way and to the same extent as it does for its own members, and to do this within the limits of the legal protection afforded to a foreign work in the country where protection is claimed, unless, in virtue of the present contract,

---

[73] TRIPs Agreement, Art.1(3): "Members shall accord the treatment provided for in this Agreement to the nationals of other Members."

[74] Art.2, Rome Convention. However, national treatment is subject to the protection specifically guaranteed, and the limitations specifically provided for, in the Convention (Art.2(2)). So far as performing rights in phonograms are concerned, which are protected under Art.12, reservations are permitted under Art.16 excluding such protection in whole or in part and there is no obligation to give national treatment.

[75] The Copyright (Application to Other Countries)(Amendment) Order 2003 (SI 2003/774) and the Performances (Reciprocal Protection) (Convention Countries and Isle of Man) Order 2003 (SI 2003/773) respectively, both of which entered into force on April 22, 2003. See Vol II, Part C1.

[76] As at September 15, 2001.

[77] The address of CISAC is 20–26 Boulevard du Parc, 92200 Neuilly-sur-Seine, France. www.cisac.org. It has two regional offices in Buenos Aires and Singapore.

such protection not being specifically provided in law, it is possible to ensure an equivalent protection ...

In particular, each society shall apply to works in the repertoire of the other society the same tariffs, methods and means of collection and distribution of royalties as those which it applies to works in its own repertoire."[78]

A second powerful international organisation, which groups some 44 national societies in 42 countries concerned with the collective administration of authors' rights to authorise the reproduction of works in the form of recordings (sound recordings or audiovisual fixations), sometimes referred to as mechanical rights, is the International Bureau of Societies Administering the Rights of Mechanical Recording and Reproduction (BIEM—*Bureau international des Sociétés gérant les droits d'enregistrement et de reproduction mécanique*), founded in 1929.[79] BIEM's principal function is to act as a centralised negotiating body fixing the conditions for the use of the repertoire of its member societies. Its main negotiating partner is the International Federation of the Phonographic Industry (IFPI), established in 1933.[80] The objects of IFPI are to create and promote the rights of producers of phonograms (sound recordings) and videograms (music videos) nationally through statutes, case law or contract, and internationally through conventions and agreements and, where such rights already exist, to defend, preserve and develop them.[81] A standard contract exists between IFPI and BIEM governing the conditions under which IFPI members (all recording companies) are authorised to use the BIEM repertoire of musical works.[82] The contract is renegotiated from time to time and is implemented by means of individual contracts between national BIEM societies and individual producers and is subject to some nationally negotiated variations.

Other international organisations representing collecting societies operating in non-musical fields include AGICOA[83] and IFFRO.[84] The Association for the International Collective Management of Audiovisual Works (AGICOA), established in 1981, groups national associations and societies of producers of audiovisual works. Its purpose is the representation and defence, within collective management, of its members' interests.[85] AGICOA has two principal functions, namely negotiations in co-operation with its national member organisations in respect of the simultaneous, cable retransmission of unchanged broadcasts including the audiovisual works in AGICOA's repertoire, and the collection and distribution of remuneration resulting from such negotiations. The International Federation of Reproduction Rights Organisations (IFRRO) was established in 1988. Its statutory purpose is to facilitate, on an international basis, the collective and/or centralised management of reproduction and other relevant rights in copyright-able works through the co-operation of national Reproduction

---

[78] CISAC document "CISAC/40.700, July 1974", updated to July 1, 1974. According to the CISAC Secretariat, this remains the applicable text.

[79] Membership as of August 20, 2004 . The address of BIEM is 20–26 Boulevard du Parc, 92200 Neuilly-sur- Seine, France. *www.BIEM.org*.

[80] IFPI has more than 1450 members in 75 countries. The IFPI Secretariat is located at 54 Regent Street, London W1R 5PJ, UK. It has regional offices also in Beijing, Brussels, Hong Kong, Miami (for Latin America) and Moscow. The RIAA (Recording Industry Association of America) is affiliated to IFPI. (See *www.ifpi.org* and *www.riaa.org*.)

[81] IFPI statutes, Ch.1.3.

[82] BIEM/IFPI Standard Contract for the Phonographic Industry (Discs, Tapes and Cassettes). The current contract dated June 30, 1998, was negotiated for the period July 1, 1997, to June 30, 2000, but remains in force.

[83] AGICOA has 42 member associations in 23 countries. Its address is 26, rue de Saint-Jean, 1203 Geneva, Switzerland. *www.Agicoa.org*.

[84] IFFRO groups 41 member organisations and 68 associate members in more than 50 countries. Its address is rue du Prince Royal 87, B-1050 Brussels, Belgium. *www.iffro.org*.

[85] By-Laws of IOA, Art.3.

Rights Organisations (RROs).[86] Its main objectives are: (1) to foster the creation of RROs worldwide; (2) to facilitate formal and informal agreements and relationships between and on behalf of its members; and (3) to increase public and institutional awareness of copyright and the role of RROs in conveying rights and royalties between right-holders and users.

In the field of the performing rights of producers of sound recordings and performers, foreign producers and performers are entitled to receive their share of remuneration derived from performing rights in sound recordings in keeping with the principle of national treatment in certain cases or, where applicable, on the basis of material reciprocity in accordance with national laws and the Rome Convention.[87] International co-operation between national collecting societies is promoted and supervised by means of the joint activities of three international non-governmental organisations, the International Federation of Musicians (FIM)[88] (representing mainly session musicians and members of orchestras), the International Federation of Actors (FIA)[89] (representing soloists, conductors and singers) and the International Federation of the Phonographic Industry (IFPI), which represents producers of sound recordings and music videos.

2. THE CONTROL OF COLLECTING SOCIETIES IN THE UNITED KINGDOM

28–26 **Variety of controls over collecting societies.** Control over the operations of collecting societies is exercised in a variety of ways. First, there is the democratic control exercised by the members of such societies through their governing bodies by means of guarantees for their protection written into the memoranda and articles of association of the various societies. Secondly, the collecting societies' activities are subject to compliance with the copyright licensing provisions of the 1988 Act[90] and to the international obligations of the United Kingdom under the Copyright Conventions.[91] Thirdly, the terms of licences and licensing schemes operated by collecting societies may be referred to the Copyright Tribunal for review, confirmation or variation by actual or potential licensees.[92]Fourthly, collecting societies are subject to powers exercisable under UK domestic legislation to control anti-competitive or monopolistic practices.[93]Finally, as seen above,[94] collecting societies are subject to the EU competition rules. Each of these means of control is discussed briefly below.

---

[86] Statutes of the International Federation of Reproduction Rights Organisations, Art.1.

[87] Countries enjoying full protection for sound recordings, including performing rights, are listed in Sch.2 of the Copyright (Application to Other Countries) (Amendment) Order 2003 (SI 2003/774).

[88] FIM , founded in 1948, has more than 200.000 members who are members of 72 musicians' organisations in 60 countries. Its objects are to protect and further the economic, social and artistic interests of musicians organised in its member unions. Its address is 21bis, rue Victor Massé, 75009 Paris, France. *www.Fim-musicians.com*.

[89] FIA, established in 1952, has 100 member organisations in 70 countries. Its objects are the protection and promotion of the artistic, economic, social and legal interests of the actors, singers, dancers, variety and circus artists, choreographers, directors, professional broadcasters, etc. organised in its affiliated or associated unions. Its address is Guild House, Upper St. Martin's Lane, London, WC2H 9EG, UK. *www.fia-actors.com*.

[90] CDPA 1988, Ch.VII, ss.116–144.

[91] See Ch.24 and paras 29–06 *et seq*. below.

[92] CDPA 1988, Ch. VII, ss. 145-152.

[93] CDPA 1988, Ch. VII, s. 144; and see paras 28–28 , 29–54and 29–254, *et seq*., below.

[94] See paras 28–20 *et seq*., above and 29–178 *et seq*., and in particular, para. 29–253,below.

A. INTERNAL CONTROLS EXERCISED BY THE MEMBERS OF COLLECTING SOCIETIES

Effect of *de facto* monopoly position of collecting societies on their members. **28–27**
The *de facto* monopoly position of collecting societies prevails generally in respect both of the rights owners, who are the members of the organisations, and of the users. Rights owners, as a rule, do not have any choice other than to entrust the administration of their rights to the particular collecting society representing their respective category of rights owner. For this reason, as seen above,[95] in some countries there is government supervision of the establishment and operation of collecting societies in order to guarantee their effective and proper operation for the benefit of their members. In the United Kingdom, there are no legislative provisions making the establishment or recognition of collecting societies conditional on the approval of a government department. Collecting societies are private companies, established and controlled by their members and subject to the requirements of United Kingdom company law, including the obligations imposed thereby on the directors of companies.

The rights owners who make up the membership of collecting societies have the ability to influence the way in which their rights are administered and to control the operating methods of such societies, provided that certain guarantees to that effect are written into the constitutions of the collecting societies in question. There should be guarantees therefore for the rights owners who are members of any given society to participate democratically in the policy-making process of the society's operations. In conformity with EU law, members should retain the option of managing certain rights themselves, where appropriate, or of mandating the society to administer them on their behalf.[96] Decisions concerning terms of membership, and the methods and rules of monitoring uses of works, collecting and distributing remuneration and enforcing rights should be taken by all the individual rights owners represented by the society, or by bodies representing them. Members should also have access to regular, full and detailed information enabling them to judge whether the rules are being correctly applied, whether the costs of administration are reasonable and whether the distribution of remuneration is actually taking place as prescribed. There is also a need for appeal procedures enabling members to challenge distributions on the ground that the distribution policies of the society have been incorrectly implemented. Members should also expressly authorise any decisions to use fees collected by their society to undertake additional activities for the defence and promotion of their members' interests, such as, for example, anti-piracy campaigns or the promotion of cultural or social activities.

Monopolies and Mergers Commission recommendations concerning rights **28–28**
of members. Guidance to collecting societies with regard to maintaining correct relations with their members emerged following a 1995 report of the Monopolies and Mergers Commission into the practices of the PRS. In 1994, complaints that the PRS was operating against the interests of certain of its members were referred to the Monopolies and Mergers Commission. Complaints had been received from writers of "less popular" forms of music to the effect that: they were receiving inadequate royalty payments; under the Society's rules, they lacked sufficient representation to be able to pursue their interests effectively; and the revenue policies adopted by the Society unduly favoured the writers and publishers of "more popular" forms of music. Criticisms were also made by some

---

[95] See para. 28–16.
[96] *GEMA (No.1)* [1971] J.O. L134; [1971] C.M.L.R. D35.

of the highest-earning members of the Society about the exclusive nature of their assignment of performing rights to the Society and the restrictions applied to members who wished to leave. Concerns were also raised about the amounts spent on administration and whether the Society was managed efficiently.[97] In November 1995, the Commission issued a report into the PRS' activities, in which it came to a number of conclusions concerning the Society's management practices and decided that the PRS had failed to provide adequate information to its members and to operate with sufficient transparency. It had failed to make clear to its members: its responsibilities to them, its policies and procedures and the limitations of its services; how it allocated costs; and their right to self-administer certain performance rights in accordance with the *GEMA* decision.[98] The Society had also failed to consult the membership adequately in order to allow them to contribute to policy-making and to choose whether they wished cross-subsidies from one group of members to another to occur or not. It had also failed to ensure that its members had a right of appeal in matters of dispute to deal with their grievances and had refused to allow members to administer their own rights in respect of live performances. To remedy these deficiencies, the Commission made a series of recommendations[99] to strengthen the position and influence of members within the Society, including: the establishment of an Appeals Board to resolve disputes which members may have from time to time with the Society about their personal rights; the introduction of a formal consultative process to take members' views on proposed changes in policy or strategy; the amendment of voting rules to allow writer members to send representatives to speak and vote for them at meetings; amendment of the Articles of Association to allow self-administration of the live performance right and to make it clear that members have the right to self-administer the categories of performing rights specified in the *GEMA* decision.[1]

The PRS Memorandum and Articles of Association have been revised to take account of the Commission's recommendations. These recommendations may also be expected to serve as guidelines for the operational practices of other United Kingdom collecting societies in the future.

B. PUBLIC CONTROL OF COLLECTING SOCIETIES IN THE UNITED KINGDOM

28–29 **Public control of collecting societies in the public interest.** As seen above,[2] some measure of public control over the activities of collecting societies is now considered to be necessary in the public interest. Some mechanism is required to guard against the possibility that monopoly rights are abused in the conditions demanded for licensing their use, and to prevent the customer suffering from

---

[97] *Performing Rights: A report on the supply in the United Kingdom of the services of administering performing rights and film synchronisation rights*, (Cm. 3147) London, HMSO, paras 2.2 and 2.3. Note that the IMMC has in the meantime been replaced by the Competition Commission, established by the Competition Act 1998, see para. 29–255, below.

[98] These rights are listed in the MMC report, (Cm. 3147) HMSO, p.52, as follows: the general performing right; the broadcasting right; the public performing right of broadcast works; the televising right; the public performing right of televised works; the right of cinematographic exhibition; the right of mechanical reproduction and diffusion; the public performing right of mechanically reproduced works; the cinematographic production right; the right to produce, reproduce and diffuse on video tape; the public performing right of works reproduced on video tape; and the exploitation rights resulting from technical development or future change in the law. See *Re GEMA (No.1)* O.J 1971 L134/15; [1971] C.M.L.R. D35; *Re GEMA (No.2)* [1972] O.J L182/24; [1972] C.M.L.R. D115.

[99] MMC report, (Cm. 3147) HMSO, summary of recommendations, pp.34–36.

[1] *cf.* n.88.

[2] See para. 28–15.

unjustifiably high prices, since collecting societies may in some cases control worldwide repertoires over which they exercise a *de facto* monopoly in any given country.

The position prior to the 1956 Act. Prior to the 1956 Act, there were no controls over the activities of collecting societies of which there were only four operating at the time (the PRS, MCPS, PPL and the Sound Film Music Bureau). The PRS and PPL were then, as now, concerned respectively with the control of performing rights in musical works and sound recordings. The other two were solely concerned with the exercise of the right to record the music under their control.

28–30

Brussels Act of the Berne Convention. The exclusive right of the author to authorise the public performance and transmission of dramatic, dramatico-musical or musical works was formally established in the Berne Convention in a new text of Article 11 at the Brussels Conference in 1948.[3] At the time, the United Kingdom delegation made the following Declaration:

28–31

> "The United Kingdom Delegation accepts the provisions of Article 11 of the Convention on the understanding that His Majesty's Government remains free to enact such legislation as it may consider necessary in the public interest to prevent or deal with any abuse of the monopoly rights conferred upon owners of copyright by the law of the United Kingdom."[4]

This declaration by the United Kingdom would appear to have been prompted by representations made to it by a number of organisations as regards the licensing practices of PRS and PPL.[5] Complaints were also made to the 1952 Copyright Committee,[6] to the effect that these two societies had exercised their rights to fix and to alter their tariffs of charges in an arbitrary way, and that one of them had unjustifiably withheld its licences or only issued them subject to unduly restrictive conditions.[7] In view of the Government Declaration made at Brussels, it was open to the Gregory Committee, notwithstanding that it was recommending adherence to the Brussels Act of the Berne Convention, to make proposals for the compulsory adjustment of tariffs charged by the copyright organisations. One method suggested was that of compulsory arbitration, but this did not seem wholly satisfactory, in that it was necessary to envisage not only disputes between a collecting society and organisations representing performers, but also cases where individual persons were aggrieved, and moreover, what was really required was some method of arriving at tariffs which would be binding not only between the parties, but also in respect of any other persons wishing to exercise similar rights. The Committee therefore proposed that a standing tribunal should be established to decide disputes between collecting societies and would-be users of controlled works.[8] This proposal was accepted by the legislature and was embodied in sections 23 to 30 of the 1956 Act.

Performing Right Tribunal. Section 23 of the 1956 Act established the Performing Right Tribunal (PRT) with the jurisdiction conferred by the provisions of the

28–32

---

[3] These rights were made subject, however, to minor reservations allowing Member States to preserve their law on exceptions covering performances at religious ceremonies and performances by military bands at public fêtes.

[4] See Records of the Brussels Conference June 5–26, 1948, *Documents de la Conférence*, Bureau de l'Union internationale pour la protection des oeuvres littéraires et artistiques, Berne, 1951, pp.82 and 264. See also Ricketson, *The Berne Convention for the Protection of Literary and Artistic Works 1886-1986*, 3.43.

[5] Report of the Gregory Committee, HMSO 1952 (Cmd. 8662), Pt VIII, para.205.

[6] Report of the Gregory Committee, HMSO 1952 (Cmd. 8662), Pt VII, paras 137 *et seq.* and see Pt VIII, paras 204 *et seq.*

[7] Report of the Gregory Committee, HMSO 1952 (Cmd. 8662), paras 204 and 205.

[8] Report of the Gregory Committee, HMSO 1952 (Cmd. 8662), paras 210 *et seq.*

1956 Act.[9] The PRT had two principal functions.[10] The first was to confirm or vary licence schemes put into operation by organisations under which licences were to be granted to the public in certain classes of cases.[11] The second was to deal with applications by individuals who were aggrieved, either because an organisation operating a licence scheme refused or failed to grant the individual a licence in accordance with the scheme, or to procure the grant to him of such a licence, or because the individual claimed that he required a licence in a case where there was no applicable licence scheme and the organisation refused or failed to grant him a licence, or the terms and conditions proposed were unreasonable.[12] The PRT was concerned with licences dealing with only three types of right. First, the right to perform in public, broadcast or diffuse, a literary, dramatic or musical work or an adaptation thereof.[13] Secondly, the right to cause a sound recording to be heard in public or to be broadcast.[14] Thirdly, the right to cause a television broadcast to be seen or heard in public.[15] The rights, therefore, covered in effect the whole of the performing and broadcasting rights conferred by the 1956 Act, other than the right to include an artistic work in a television broadcast, the right to cause a film to be seen or heard in public or to be broadcast, and the right to re-broadcast a sound or television broadcast.

28–33   **Proposals for reform.** The functions of the PRT were considered by the Whitford Committee,[16] which recommended that it should be given jurisdiction over a wider range of matters, including reprographic licences, video recording, licences to use music on film sound-tracks, and copyright clearances where the copyright owner cannot be traced.[17] The Committee also proposed that the tribunal's name should be changed to the Copyright Tribunal, in view of the recommended increase in its jurisdiction. The 1986 White Paper, in its belated response to the Committee's report, generally followed these recommendations in relation to the change of name of the tribunal and the extension of its functions,[18] and also made recommendations as to the introduction of more specific criteria for the tribunal to base its decisions on, and for improvements in the procedure before the tribunal. These recommendations were enacted in the 1988 Act, Chapter VIII of which established the Copyright Tribunal as the successor to the PRT.

C. THE COPYRIGHT TRIBUNAL

28–34   **The Copyright Tribunal.** The constitution of the Copyright Tribunal established under the 1988 Act is described elsewhere,[19] as also is its procedure under the Copyright Tribunal Rules 1989.[20] The Copyright Tribunal has been given an extended jurisdiction, covering not only the functions previously carried out by the PRT, but also a number of new specific functions introduced by the 1988 Act, as amended by the Broadcasting Act 1990. Since the 1988 Act came into force, the functions of the Copyright Tribunal have more than doubled as a result of

---

[9] 1956 Act, ss.24–27A.
[10] s.24(1).
[11] ss.25 and 26.
[12] ss.27(1) and (2) and 27A.
[13] s.24(2)(a); a right (as to musical works and associated works) usually controlled by PRS.
[14] s.24(2)(b) a right usually controlled by PPL.
[15] s.24(2)(c) a right controlled by broadcasting organisations, such as the BBC.
[16] Report of the Committee to consider the Law on Copyright and Designs, HMSO, March 1977 (Cmnd. 6732).
[17] Cmnd. 6732, paras 788–790.
[18] Cmnd. 9712 (1986) Ch.18, broadly following proposals set out in the 1981 *Green Paper*, Cmnd. 8302.
[19] See para. 29–93, below.
[20] See paras 29–96 and 29–159, *et seq.*, below.

new legislation, including *inter alia* the *Broadcasting Act 1996* and the Copyright and Related Rights Regulations 1996. The functions and procedures concerning the control of exercise of rights by the Copyright Tribunal are described in detail in Chapter 29[21]. It should be noted that the Tribunal's jurisdiction does not extend to all copyright licences. It would be contrary to the Berne Convention to subject the exercise of all the exclusive rights of authors of literary, dramatic, musical and artistic works and films to public control by the Tribunal. Licences offered by individual authors do not fall within the Tribunal's jurisdiction. Thus, as regards the works protected by the Berne Convention, jurisdiction relates to licences and schemes of a licensing body, such as a collecting society, having as its main object the negotiating or granting of licences, including licences covering works of more than one author in relation to copying the work, rental or lending of copies of the work to the public, performing, showing or playing the work in public, or communicating the work to the public. In summary, the proceedings heard by the Tribunal and which concern collecting societies are *inter alia* proceedings brought by, or on behalf of, actual or potential licensees, relating to the following: applications to determine remuneration payable with respect to cable re transmission and rental; proposed or existing licensing schemes;[22] entitlement to a licence under licensing scheme;[23] licensing by a licensing body;[24] coverage of a licensing scheme or licence in respect of reprographic copying by an educational establishment;[25] terms of a copyright licence available as of right consequent on the exercise of their powers by the Secretary of State, the Office of Fair Trading and the Competition Commission[26] and applications to settle the terms of payment as to the reasonableness of any condition in relation to the use as of right of sound recordings in broadcasts or cable programme services.[27] The Tribunal's jurisdiction also extends to applications concerning the exercise and licensing of the rights of performers and the determination of royalties and equitable remuneration payable in relation thereto.[28]

D. UNITED KINGDOM COMPETITION LAW

The Office of Fair Trading and the Competition Commission. The role of these bodies under the United Kingdom legislation aimed at anti-competitive practices is discussed in Chapter 29.[29] Such legislation has particular application to collecting societies as regards both their dealings with their members and with their licensees.[30]

28–35

E. EC LAW

Application of EC Competition Law. The application of EC competition law to the exercise of intellectual property rights is discussed elsewhere.[31] Again, such

28–36

---

[21] See paras 29–93, *et seq.*, below.

[22] CDPA 1988, ss.73(4), 73A, 118, 119 and 120; and see further paras 29–108, *et seq.*, below.

[23] ss.121 and 122; and see further paras 29–116, *et seq.*, below.

[24] ss.125, 126 and 127; and see further paras 29–119, *et seq.*, below.

[25] s.139; and see further para. 29–129, below.

[26] s.144(4); and see further para. 29–297, below.

[27] ss.135D, 135E and 135F, introduced into the CDPA 1988 and into s.149 of the CDPA 1988 by amendment of the Broadcasting Act 1990, s.175(1) and (2); see further paras 29–25, *et seq.*, below.

[28] See para. 29–95, below.

[29] See para. 29–255, below, *et seq.*

[30] See para. 29–272, *et seq.*

[31] See paras 29–173, *et seq.*, below.

law has particular application to collecting societies, as regards their dealings both with their members and with their licensees.[32]

3. THE FUTURE OF COLLECTING SOCIETIES

A. THE IMPACT OF TECHNICAL DEVELOPMENT AND THE INFORMATION SOCIETY ON COLLECTING SOCIETIES AND THE MARKET

28–37 **The Information Society.**
"The world is undergoing a technological revolution and entering the age of the Information Society. The combination of information technology and high-speed communications is breaking down the traditional barriers to the movement of information (distance, location, time and volume) at an unprecedented rate. Information technology is becoming widely accessible and as a result a vast new range of applications and opportunities is arising".[33]

As the 1996 Select Committee of the House of Lords pointed out, these developments have exacerbated the well-established tensions between copyright owners and those who wish to use works subject to copyright. The internet has increased these problems exponentially. A networked, digital environment making use of digital recording and transmission techniques gives users access to large quantities of material for inspection, down-loading, storing, printing and dissemination.[34] Copyright law has changed over the years in response to technical development and the copyright owners and their collecting societies are in the process of responding to these latest changes, which present not so much new problems as problems of scale and technical control to the copyright owner.

28–38 **Expansion of fields of collective administration.** As already discussed,[35] collective administration is justified when use of protected works takes place on such a scale and in such circumstances that it is impractical for the rights owners and the users to negotiate on an individual basis. In recent years, the fields in which individual exercise of rights have become impractical or impossible have been constantly expanding as a result of technical developments which have led to new uses and methods of exploitation of works. Collective administration by performing rights societies no longer applies only in the field of music but has expanded to embrace rental rights, broadcasting rights, satellite transmission and cable distribution of broadcasts and audiovisual works. Under the increasing pressure of technical developments, other categories of rights owners have established collective licensing systems to control repeated, high volume uses; one example is the blanket licensing of the reprographic copying of literary works; another is the administration of remuneration schemes for private copying where these are in place. Film producers have also established mechanisms for negotiating collectively as regards cable television use.

28–39 **The impact of digital technology on the market.** In the 1990s, new methods of exploitation of protected works developed rapidly and the digital and communica-

---

[32] See paras 29–193and 29–253, et seq., below.
[33] House of Lords, Select Committee on Science and Technology, report entitled *Information Society: Agenda for Action in the United Kingdom*, HL Paper 77, See ss.1995–96, 5th Report, July 1996, para.1.6.
[34] House of Lords, Select Committee on Science and Technology, report entitled *Information Society: Agenda for Action in the United Kingdom*, HL Paper 77, See ss.1995–96, 5th Report, July 1996, paras 2.18 and 2.19.
[35] See para. 28–02, above.

tions revolution continues to transform the ways in which works are made available to the public. Digital storage media has been essential to the growth of eCommerce in digital goods but it is also used to store large quantities of copyright infringing material. In the United Kingdom, the BBC and commercial broadcasters are entering the digital broadcasting market and the consumer already has access via his computer and telephone to the internet,[36] from which he is able to obtain access to copyright works of all kinds to use, store, transmit and copy at will. As the 2003 WIPO report has put it, "The situation becomes even more problematic when the personal computer is linked to the internet, because the owner's compilations can then be made available to anyone else on a file-sharing network. ... All content is now vulnerable to illegal copying and distribution over the internet, irrespective of media type".[37] Meanwhile, digital technology also makes possible widespread, interactive legitimate services making all kinds of works available on a commercial basis to consumers. Such digital services are beginning to get established on the internet. which these days is operating worldwide and reaches over 600 million people.[38] Thus, the packaged product, the CD or video cassette, for example, is fast being displaced by delivery to the consumer by electronic means in interactive services such as video-on-demand, pay-per-view and musical juke boxes online. In the new electronic networks, households have direct access to multimedia works and services and interactive technology enables the consumer to play an active role; they are no longer passive recipients of programmes but are able to communicate directly with the distribution network, to select their favourite films and music from a wide range of databases to copy and even edit them.

The challenge to collecting societies. The exact way in which the information society will develop over the next decades cannot be predicted with any certainty. Collecting societies are facing the challenge of monitoring and securing reward for the use of their members' works in all these new services. It is clear, however, that an important element for the successful development of the information society will be the ability of right owners to control access to protected works by means of technological copy protection measures and to monitor and obtain payment for use of such works through digital rights management (DRM) techniques. The role, organisation and operation of collecting societies in the management of rights must evolve to adapt to this new environment ."The challenge is both to secure reward for use and also to ensure that securing that reward is for the users as fast, simple and painless as possible."[39] Moreover, it is plain that international co-operation between collecting societies will play a vital role in meeting this challenge. "No one country can protect the intellectual property of its citizens satisfactorily: global agreement and enforcement will be ever more necessary in

28–40

---

[36] Over two million people accessed the internet in the year to August 1995, para.3.39. By 2002, it was estimated that about 10 per cent of the world's population was online, representing more than 605 million users. It was also predicted that by 2005 the world online population could reach one billion (cf. *Intellectual Property on the internet: A Survey of Issues*, WIPO, December 2002, para.7.

[37] Cunard, Hill & Barlas, "Current Developments in the Field of Digital Rights Management", WIPO doc. SCCR/10/2, August 1, 2003, paras 1.2.3 and 1.2.6.

[38] The number of countries connected to the internet has increased significantly in the past ten years. Whereas at the beginning of the 1990s, a little over ten countries were connected to the internet, this figure stood at 214 at the end of 2001. See International Telecommunication Union (ITI), "World Telecommunication Development Report", (March 2002).

[39] C. Clark, *The Copyright Environment for the Publisher in the Digital World, (International Publishers' Association)* , March 1996. See also T.C. Vinje, "A Brave New World of Technical Protection Systems: Will there Still Be Room for Copyright?" [1996] 8 E.I.P.R. 431. See also *The Future of Copyright in a Digital Environment*, B. Hugenholtz, ed. (Kluwer, The Hague, 1996) and Copyright in the New Digitals, London, Environment, I.A.Stamatoudi and P.L.C. Torremans, eds (Sweet and Maxwell, 2000).

the digital age,"[40] and this applies not only to the legislative framework for copyright but also to collective administration.

28–41 **Supranational central licensing schemes.** Hitherto, collective licensing has been effected mainly at national level by national societies separately representing the traditional sectors of music, text and picture, with foreign repertoire being protected by means of reciprocal representation agreements with sister collecting societies in other countries. However, the harmonisation of copyright and related rights in the European Union has paved the way, for example, for a real single market in satellite broadcasting and cable distribution and national boundaries are irrelevant in the context of the internet and the information society. The territorial basis for the operations of collecting societies is becoming outdated and inappropriate and the desirability of supranational or pan-European central licensing schemes being established to clear rights is increasingly recognised. "In the long term it is difficult to see the need for separate national societies in each Community Member State. A single community society could achieve the same results more efficiently than the present over-complex structure, and might not be significantly less competitive."[41] The suggestion has even been made that a single, worldwide, international collecting society for rights in works in digital form should be founded to license all repertoires on a central basis to avoid compatibility problems. "One central institution will then install the international numbering system, provide necessary information on the product and licensing terms, collect and distribute royalties and deliver digital copies of the work".[42]

28–42 **Multimedia works.** Multimedia works pose a particular problem for collective administration due to the large number of licences required to produce them. They bring together in one product, text, music and images, all these components having different rights owners from whom licences have to be obtained by the maker of the multimedia work. The multimedia work, moreover, is itself a work in its own right and has an author or producer of its own, the natural or legal person who created it, and the user must obtain a licence from him.[43] The rights in the various components have traditionally been represented by different collecting societies divided according to the traditional distinctions between music, text and image. To cope with the changing situation, it has been suggested that "one-stop-shops" be established by rights owners to represent them all and facilitate access to works. As the Commission has suggested:

> "With the development of the Information Society, currently adequate means of administering rights must be reassessed. In particular, the question must be addressed of whether and how copyright administration needs to be rationalised in view of the possibilities created by digital technology for creating complex works or other protected matter, such as multimedia products or services. In fact, the creation and exploitation of multimedia

---

[40] House of Lords Select Committee Report, Information Society: Agenda for Action in the United Kingdom, HL Paper 77, para.5.45.

[41] Temple Lang J., "Media, Multimedia and European Community Antitrust Law", paper delivered at 24th Annual Conference of the Fordham Corporate Law Institute on International Antitrust Law and Policy, October 16–17, 1997.

[42] Hoeren, T., "An assessment of long-term solutions in the context of copyright and electronic delivery systems and multimedia products", European Commission DG XIII E-1, document EUR 16069 EN, p.35 et seq., and 50.

[43] Art.5 of the new WIPO Copyright Treaty of December 20, 1996, contains the following provision relating to compilations of data, which is applicable to multimedia works: "Compilations of data or other material, in any form, which by reason of the selection or arrangement of their contents constitute intellectual creations, are protected as such. This protection does not extend to the data or the material itself and is without prejudice to any copyright subsisting in the data or material contained in the compilation."

products and services may imply that the individual exercise of rights will become even less practicable than it is today due to the great number of new or pre-existing works, productions and uses involved. This may call for new forms of centralised administration which facilitate rights management or, in some cases, for more collective management."[44]

The concept of a one-stop-shop. In this context it is worth noting that within the European Union a number of national one-stop-shops have been set up by coalitions of national collecting societies which have pooled their resources and repertoires in new joint representative organisations, the purpose of which is to manage the rights of their members in multimedia works or, in the case of the music industry, for example, to licence joint repertoires for cross-border use.[45] The Commission has suggested that such alliances "would give authors, performers and also editor/producers, a tool which would allow them to identify the origin of very diverse works, by bringing together the repertoires which might be valuable to the new technologies. Users could obtain information which interested them, such as the level of the fees and the rights given. Such provision of information could be possible if different societies operated together and combined their databases and systems if identification were progressively introduced".[46] Such one-stop-shops are envisaged as being the means to centralise the identification of individual rights; they would not replace the collecting societies but would make the current system more efficient and easier to deal with for the user. The European Commission takes the view that the creation and development of one stop shops for "Multimedia Rights Clearance Systems" should be left to the market but this has not prevented it from supporting studies and pilot projects financially and a number of these projects are ongoing.[47]

28–43

B. EU APPROACH TO THE ROLE OF COLLECTING SOCIETIES IN THE INFORMATION SOCIETY

The approach of the EU. As seen above, the EU has already addressed the issue of collective management in several Community instruments, endorsing their role in rights management and in some situations providing for mandatory rights administration by collecting societies, as in the Satellite and Cable Directive.[48] It is likely that the Commission will continue to favour collective management of rights in order to ensure that potential users should not encounter unreasonable difficulty in identifying the source which can grant or refuse them a licence. Moreover, in its *Follow-up to the Green Paper on Copyright and Related Rights in the Information Society*, the Commission referred to the fact that, while in some Member States a particular work may be managed individually, it may be

28–44

---

[44] *Follow-up to the Green Paper on Copyright and Related Rights in the Information Society*, Communication from the Commission, Brussels, November 20, 1996 (COM(96) 568 final), p.24.

[45] These new coalitions include: SESAM (France); *Clearingstelle Multimedia* (CMMV GmbH) (Germany); *Centrum voor Dienstveerlening Auteurs-en aanverwante rechten* (CEDAR) (Netherlands); *Oficina Multimedia* (OM) (Spain); *Copyswede* (Sweden) and *KOPIOSTO* (Finland). For further information on these developments, see Clark, C. and Koskinen-Olsson, T., "New Alternatives for Centralised Management One-Stop-Shops—A Review", paper delivered at the WIPO International Forum on the Exercise and Management of Copyright and Neighbouring Rights in the Face of the Challenges of Digital Technology, Seville, May 1997. For an account of the Commission's recent decision in relation to a new one-stop licensing scheme for simulcasts, see paras 29–210.

[46] *Green Paper: Copyright and Related Rights in the Information Society*, presented by the Commission, Brussels, July 19, 1995 (COM(95) 382 final), p.76.

[47] See M. Schippan, "Purchase and Licensing of Digital Rights: The VERDI Project and the Clearing of Multimedia Rights in Europe" [2000] E.I.P.R. 24; Multimedia Rights Clearance Systems, published by the European Commission, DG XIII/E.

[48] See paras 28–20 and 28–36 , above. See also Chapters 25 and 29.

subject to collective management in another.[49] Furthermore, substantial differences exist with respect to licensing conditions as such. It suggested that the consequences of the existence of a wide variety of different regimes in the Member States would have to be kept under review to avoid barriers to trade arising which could impede the effective exploitation of rights across Member States. On this issue, it concluded: "It seems essential that the Single Market provides both rightholders and users with similar and transparent conditions (level playing field) for the exploitation/management of rights, both with respect to individual and collective licensing conditions."[50]

There is certainly a need for a clarification of the application of Community competition rules to collecting societies and collective management, if centralised, voluntary licensing schemes to facilitate rights clearance on a pan-European basis are to be encouraged in the form of one-stop-shops. The need for such clarification was brought into focus as a result of the intervention of the Commission competition authorities in the activities of Video Performance Ltd (VPL), which administers the rights in its members' videos, and the International Federation of the Phonographic Industry, representing international music video repertoire. In 1987, VPL and IFPI entered into pan-European licensing agreements with satellite broadcasters, including MTV for a period of five years, in which they licensed the use of their members' music videos for the entire satellite footprint. At that time, MTV had welcomed the opportunity given by VPL and IFPI to obtain such a licence, which enabled them to clear the entire worldwide music video repertoire by one licence in what represented a real "one-stop-shop". Without the licence, MTV would not have been able to enter the market so quickly and effectively. As has been pointed out, in this case, a collecting society not only facilitated competition within the European Community, but also acted as a springboard to promote the emergence of a new pan-European broadcaster.[51] In 1992, however, MTV approached the major record companies seeking to make individual direct deals with them and to avoid taking the VPL/IFPI licence. The majors demurred, preferring to continue to licence their repertoire collectively. MTV then lodged a complaint with the Commission competition authorities alleging that VPL and IFPI were acting in breach of Article 81(1) (former Article 85(1)) of the Treaty of Rome. In 1994, the Commission issued a statement of objections in response to the complaint in which they said that the refusal of the five major companies to negotiate individually and the fact that they had instead given a mandate to VPL and IFPI to conduct collective negotiations on their behalf and to conclude blanket, rather than individual licences, restricted competition between members of VPL and between the majors in particular and was contrary to the Community's competition rules. No decision of the Commission has been issued in this case but the statement of objections leaves the law on collective licensing in some doubt and it would appear that the policy of the competition directorate is inconsistent with the views that the Commission has expressed in other contexts about the usefulness of collective management. For example, in its *Green Paper on Copyright and Related Rights in the Information Society*, the Commission said:

> "It is reasonable to suppose that certain alliances would be a major step forward for collecting societies, which are currently organised by category of work or class of right holder (*e.g.* authors, performers, etc.). To allow

---

[49] *Follow-up to the Green Paper on Copyright and Related Rights in the Information Society (Com (96) 568 final*, p.26.
[50] *Follow-up to the Green Paper*, p.26.
[51] For a full account of these proceedings, see H. Porter, "European Union Competition Policy: Should the Role of Collecting Societies be Legitimised?" [1996] 12 E.I.P.R. 672 at 674.

centralised management or administration of the rights over all works, performances and other protected matter incorporated into multimedia works, the collecting societies and other rights managers ought to be encouraged to set up joint bodies allowing a simplification of right management. ...[52] The competition rules are fundamental, but there is no reason why they should be in contradiction with the idea of centralised schemes, at least so far as the creation of 'one-stop-shops' are concerned. ...[53] Centralised schemes for the administration of rights, which would be voluntary in character, would be an appropriate response to the information society."[54]

In a more recent decision, the Commission held that

"The absence of territorial boundaries in the on-line environment induced by the internet and digital format of the products enables users to choose any collecting society in the EEA which is a member of the one-stop-shop mechanism for the delivering of the licence. ... This way, commercial users will be able to recognise the most efficient societies in the EEA and seek their licences from the collecting societies that provide them at lower cost".[55]

C. THE POTENTIAL CONTRIBUTION OF DIGITAL TECHNOLOGY TO COLLECTIVE ADMINISTRATION

Technical systems of identification and protection. In the new world of the information society, technical systems of identification and protection will have the potential to facilitate the administration of rights in the digital environment to and allow more individual management of certain rights. Digital technology offers scope for identifying, controlling access to, tracing, monitoring and rewarding all uses of works. It provides rights owners for the first time with tools to control uses such as private copying, which could not be monitored or controlled before. As the Commission has stated "at least with respect to some new forms of copyright applications, new digital means of identification of protected material and of automatic licensing of their uses may allow more individualised management".[56] The need for compulsory statutory licensing of certain rights, often in the past introduced because of the perceived difficulty of clearing rights on an individual basis, and for private copying levies on the sale of blank tapes and equipment to provide remuneration of previously uncontrollable private use, could be replaced by payments for use paid directly by the user to the rights owner. In relation to multimedia products, where thousands of rights-holders may be involved, Hoeren has suggested that electronic clearing of rights is essential. In his view, "technical devices have no disadvantages *per se*; they are instead mandatory for solving multimedia licensing problems".[57]

The organisations and collecting societies representing the various copyright owners are fully aware of these possibilities and the development of digital rights management systems (DRM systems) has become a key issue. DRM systems can be used to identify works and right owners, "to clear rights, to secure payment, to

28–45

---

[52] *Green Paper on Copyright and Related Rights in the Information Society (Com (95) 382 final,,* p.76.

[53] *Green Paper, ,* p.77.

[54] *Green Paper*, p.77.

[55] Case COMP/C2/38.014 IFPI Simulcasting, Decision of October 8, 2002, OJ L 107 of April 30, 2003, p.58.

[56] Green Paper, (Com (95) 382 final, p.75.

[57] Hoeren "An assessment of long-term solutions in the context of copyright and electronic delivery systems and multimedia products", European Commission DG–XIII E-1, document EUR 16069EN, p.43.

trace behaviour and to enforce rights .... [They] are, therefore, crucial for the development of new high volume, low transactional value business models".[58]

In the past few years much work has been done by right owners to establish product identification codes which take advantage of digital technology to provide for digital identification of works. Such digital identification is the first step in building DRM systems, which will enable the use of copyright materials to be tracked, the users to be identified, recorded and charged in order for appropriate payment to be made for the use made.[59]

In 1995, the US NII Report pointed out that digital identification of works would be critical to the efficient operation and success of the information superhighway:

"Copyright management information will serve as a kind of license plate for a work on the information superhighway, from which a user may obtain important information about the work. The accuracy of such information will be crucial to the ability of consumers to find and make authorised uses of works on the NII. Reliable information will also facilitate efficient licensing and reduce transaction costs for licensable uses of copyright works (both fee-based and royalty-free)."[60]

For copyright identification systems to be useful, all works and protected subject-matter need to carry identification of the work and its respective rights owner. Moreover, international standards for such codes are necessary if they are to be recognised and to be effective globally. The European Commission has provided funds for research projects and efforts towards establishing open standards and envisages an EC recommendation to reinforce the requirement for interoperability of DRM systems and services.[61] To date, identification codes, most of which are recognised by the International Standards Organisation (ISO), are in use for books (ISBN),[62] journals (ISSN),[63] recorded music tracks (ISRC),[64] CDs (SID),[65] sheet music (ISMN), musical works (ISWC—,)[66] electronic music releases (GRid—Global Release Identifier), interested party number (IPN) which is a new identifier for composers, authors and publishers ("compositeurs, auteurs, éditeurs", previously identifed as CAE) and performers (IPDN—International Performers' Database Number). BIEM and CISAC have also developed a Common Information System (CIS), which is a standardised identification system for the works administered by their member societies and in use via the CIS network

---

[58] EC Communication, p.10.

[59] See generally D.J. Gervais, "Electronic Rights Management Systems (ERMS): The Next Logical Step in the Evolution of Rights Management", paper delivered at the WIPO International Forum on the Exercise and Management of Copyright and Neighbouring Rights in the Face of the Challenges of Digital Technology, Seville, May 1997.

[60] Report of the Working group on Intellectual Property Rights (NII Report), B.A. Lehman, Assistant Secretary of Commerce and Commissioner of Patents and Trademarks, Chair, Washington, September 1995, p.235.

[61] EC Communication, p.11.

[62] The International Standard Book Number (ISBN) consists of 10 digits identifying the group, publisher and title.

[63] The International Standard Serial Number (ISSN) is used to identify periodicals.

[64] The International Standard Recording Code (ISRC) consists of twelve digits including information on the original producer, the year of recording and the country of origin.

[65] The Source Identification (SID) uses nine digits representing the manufacturer, the country and city of manufacture and the manufacturing equipment identifier. This is a code used to control unauthorised reproduction. For details of such systems, see papers of a meeting held by the International Bureau of WIPO in 1994 on "Questions concerning the Establishment of a Voluntary International Numbering System for Certain Categories of Literary and Artistic Works and for Phonograms". The idea of an international digital numbering system has been part of the program of WIPO since 1994.

[66] The International Standard Music Number and the International Standard Work Code.

around the world.[67] Such universal product identification codes are a pre-requisite for electronic copyright clearance systems. Some of these codes are insufficient because they identify, for example like the ISBN, the packaging (the book) not the work or works contained therein. In such cases, the codes need to be adapted to the new requirements. Suitable codes, of global application, would in principle make it possible to establish signalling methods, incorporated in the subcodes of digital works, which would provide encoded business information capable of being automatically read electronically. The rights owners would be identified and paid by means of schemes of individual invoicing to consumers in respect of the actual use made by them of protected works. For such schemes to work, the systems sold to consumers would have to incorporate systems for the reading of the codes.

Electronic licensing and clearance systems are the future; at present, they are not in widespread use. However, the situation is evolving rapidly in this area. There is a great deal of research and experimentation on the subject being undertaken by interested parties in Europe, Japan and the United States of America.[68] Under the auspices of the Commission, a system known as CITED (Copyright in Transmitted Electronic Data) is being developed. This is a generic harmonised reference model applicable to all kinds of possible distribution of digital information. It is not yet implemented. In another initiative on a global scale, the international trade bodies BIEM, CISAC, IFPI and the RIAA, representing music publishers, authors, composers and the recording industry, are working jointly to develop a global infrastructure to support the efficient management of the electronic delivery of music in an online environment. The project is known as the Music Integrated Identification Project (MI3P).[69] The system will be fully integrated with existing industry identifiers already in common use, such as the CIS, ISRC and ISWC.

Anti-copying devices. Another positive result of digital technology is its application to anti-piracy measures. New types of anti-copying devices, such as encryption and scrambling systems, designed to prevent unauthorised copying of copyright works distributed over the internet have been developed and are constantly being perfected. Likewise, devices permitting the limitation of reproductions made for private purposes such as the serial copy management system (SCMS), an ISO standard for digital sound recording machines which permits such machines to copy from a CD or digital tape but prevents copies being made from those first copies, are being developed. In this area also, uniform standards which are inter-operable and recognised throughout the world are a prerequisite for success.

28–46

Much work is being done in developing systems to deliver digital files of copy-

---

[67] See "CIS, The Common Information System", plan proposed by the BIEM/CISAC Information Systems Steering Committee in December 1994 and approved by the Executive Bureau at Cannes, February 1995. Updated in July 1995, available from CISAC, 11, rue Keppler, 75116 Paris. See K. Hill, "CIS-A Collective Solution for Copyright Management in the Digital Age" [1997] 76 *Copyright World*, 18–25.

[68] See generally with regard to Europe, Japan and the USA: R. Oman, "Technological Means of Protection and Rights Management Information", paper delivered at the WIPO International Forum on the Exercise and Management of Copyright and Neighbouring Rights in the Face of the Challenges of Digital Technology, Seville, May 1997. As regards Europe, see "Handbook listing the various initiatives and existing techniques for the identification of rights holders and works in the context of management and clearance of rights in the digital area", Council of Europe, doc. MM-S-PR 4 Rev., February 13, 1998 and *inter alia*, D. S. Marks and B. H. Turnbull, "Technical Protection Measures: The Intersection of Technology, Law and Commercial Licences" [2000] E.I.P.R. 198; N. Hanbridge, "DRM: Can it Deliver? [2001] Ent. L.R. 138; J. Selby, "The Legal and economic implications of the digital distribution of music" [2000] E.I.P.R. 4 and 25.

[69] See *www.mi3p-standard.org*.

right subject-matter over the internet, to receive payment for that delivery and to protect the file from unauthorised distribution and reproduction. All the research and development activity under way will no doubt lead to the adoption of effective technical protection measures in due course, which will benefit in the European Union from the legal protection afforded by the Information Society Directive, already referred to.[70]

D. LEGISLATIVE BACK-UP FOR TECHNICAL SYSTEMS OF IDENTIFICATION AND PROTECTION

28–47 Internationally, there is a consensus that legislative back-up is needed to provide effective legal remedies against the circumvention of copyright protection systems and the removal or alteration of electronic copyright management information without authority. The two new WIPO instruments adopted on December 20, 1996, the WIPO Copyright Treaty and the WIPO Performances and Phonograms Treaty include provisions to this effect.[71]

In the USA, legislative back-up for such systems was introduced in 1998 in the "Digital Millenium Copyright Act" (DMCA). The Act provides that the following should give rise to criminal offences and penalties: the circumvention of copyright protection systems, the providing of false copyright management information, and the removal or alteration of copyright management information.[72]

Within the EU, the adoption of the Information Society Directive provides for legal protection of electronic information attached to works and related subject-matter for the purpose of copyright management and protection systems and to prevent any circumvention, removal or alteration of such electronic information without authority.[73]

Community law first legislated in this area in the context of the Computer Programs Directive. Article 7(1)(c) thereof stipulates that Member States are to provide appropriate remedies against persons putting into circulation, or possessing for commercial purposes, "any means the sole intended purpose of which is to facilitate the unauthorised removal or circumvention of any technical device which may have been applied to protect a computer program".

Finally, this is one area of the law where the United Kingdom was in advance of its Community partners. The 1988 Act already provided rights owners with protection equivalent to the rights obtaining in respect of infringement against devices designed to circumvent electronic copy-protection systems.[74]

---

[70] See also Marks and Turnbull, "Technical Protection Measures: The Intersection of Technology, Law and Commercial Licences" [2000] E.I.P.R 198, G. Davies, "Technical Devices as a Solution to Private Copying" in P. Torremans and I. Stamatoudi, *Copyright in the New Digital Environment, The Need to Redesign Copyright* (Sweet and Maxwell, London, 2000); G. Davies, "Copyright in the Information Society-Technical Devices to Control Private Copying", in *Festschrift für Adolf Dietz* (Verlag C.H. Beck, Munich, 2001); L. Jones, Artist's Entry into Cyberspace: Intellectual Property on the internet" [2000] E.I.P.R. 79.
[71] Arts 11 and 12 of the WIPO Copyright Treaty (WCT); Arts 18 and 19 of the WIPO Performances and Phonograms Treaty (WPPT). Both Treaties were adopted at Geneva on December 20, 1996 (see Vol.2 at F13 and F14, below).
[72] Pub.L. No.105–304, 112 Stat. 2860 (1998), adding new paras 512 and 1201–1203 to the Copyright Act 1976.
[73] The relevant provisions of the Directive are Arts 6 and 7. See also paras 25–99 *et seq.*, above.
[74] CDPA 1988, s.296 (see Ch.15).

4. INDIVIDUAL COLLECTING SOCIETIES OPERATING IN THE UNITED KINGDOM

A. ASSOCIATION OF UNITED RECORDINGS ARTISTS ("AURA")

AURA is a company limited by guarantee. It was founded in 1995. Its members, **28–48** most of whom are featured performers, appoint AURA as their exclusive agent to collect equitable remuneration arising in accordance with the terms of the Copyright and Related Rights Regulations 1996[75] and equivalent legislation applicable in other territories from the exploitation of sound recordings embodying their performances and their right to remuneration in respect of blank tape levy, rental, public performance, broadcast and cable transmission in such territories as they specify.[76] As at August 2004, AURA had some 500 members, and collected royalties from seven foreign countries through the "single pipeline" operated by PPL.[77] Membership is free, but AURA charges a commission of five per cent. AURA's website is at *www.aurauk.com*.[78]

B. AUTHORS' LICENSING & COLLECTING SOCIETY LTD ("ALCS")

The ALCS administers a wide variety of rights in literary and dramatic works on **28–49** behalf of authors, their heirs and personal representatives and of its corporate members (the Society of Authors and the Writers' Guild of Great Britain).[79] The main rights administered as at August 2004 were as follows. First, the reprographic right, defined as the right exercisable anywhere in the world to reproduce or authorise the reproduction of a work by means of any appliance or process capable of producing multiple copies of the work in such a form that the work may be perceived visually.[80] This right is administered by ALCS through the CLA (as to which see paragraph 28–52, below), which acts as agent for ALCS. Second, the cable retransmission right, defined by the ALCS as the simultaneous showing via cable network of one country's television programmes in another country.[81] Third, the educational off-air recording right. This right is administered by the ALCS as a member of the ERA (as to which see paragraph 28–55, below).[82]

---

[75] SI 1996/2967 (Vol.2 at A3.iii) implementing the Rental and Related Rights Directive [1992] O.J. L346/61 (Vol.2 at H3). The 1996 Regulations introduced two relevant rights. First, a performer's right to equitable remuneration in respect of the playing in public or inclusion in a broadcast or cable programme of a commercially published sound recording: CDPA 1988, s.182D. Section 182D has now been amended (by the Copyright and Related Rights Regulations 2003 (SI 2003/2498), reg.7) to refer to playing in public or communicating to the public otherwise than by way of being made available by an electronic on-demand service. See para. 12–46, above. This right is also administered by PAMRA, as to which see para. 28–58, below. The second right is a performer's right to equitable remuneration in respect of the rental of copies of a sound recording (CDPA 1988, s.191G). See para. 12–48, above. Section 182D(2) and s.191G(2) provide that these rights to equitable remuneration may not be assigned except to a collecting society for the purpose of enabling it to enforce them on the performer's behalf. This right falls within PAMRA's remit as well. See para. 28–58, below.

[76] See membership application form.

[77] The seven countries were: Germany, Japan, Switzerland, the United States (for digital only), Holland and Ireland. AURA expected that Brazil, Canada, Denmark, Finland and Norway would soon be added to this list. Discussions were ongoing with French societies and AURA hoped to receive French royalties some time in 2005.

[78] The editors are grateful to Jake Beaumont-Nesbitt of AURA for his assistance with the contents of this paragraph.

[79] Articles of Association, Arts 3 and 4.

[80] Art.1(xvii).

[81] Art.7(c)(iv).

[82] Art.7(c)(v).

Fourth, the German and Dutch public lending right.[83] Fifth, the private recording right, which gives ALCS the right to recover monies from blank tape levies where they exist.[84] A number of other rights were also administered.[85] As at August 2004, the ALCS had over 16,500 full members and over 33,000 associate members[86] and had arrangements with similar societies in 38 other countries.[87] The ALCS is a company limited by guarantee incorporated under the Companies Act 1985. Full members assign to the ALCS the rights specified in the Articles of Association.[88] The current membership fee for United Kingdom residents is £10 plus VAT per year. The ALCS levies a commission of 11 per cent which is charged on fees at the point of distribution.[89] In the year 2003/4, the ALCS distributed royalties of about £12.5 million gross. Most of the royalties distributed were attributable to photocopying, cable retransmission, off-air recording, over-

---

[83] *i.e.* the entitlement of authors to a fee in respect of loans of copies of their works by a public library. This right is administered through the German collecting society VG Wort and the Dutch society Stichting Leenrecht. See Articles of Association, Arts 7(c)(i) and 7(d)(i).

[84] Articles of Association, Arts 7(c)(iii) and 7(d)(i). As at August 2004, monies from blank tape levies were collected from France, Germany, Switzerland, Austria and Belgium.

[85] The ALCS also collected remuneration for its members from the following sources: payments for the public reception of broadcasts; remuneration for the use of audio tapes for the blind in Norway; payment for the use of extracts of published editions on radio in Denmark, France, Germany, Hungary, Poland and Switzerland; the German rental right; income from "small literary rights", that is income from miscellaneous sources such as readings of excerpts of literary works on television and radio in certain countries; and the right to read poems at poetry festivals (administered under an agreement with the British Federation of Music and Drama Festivals). ALCS also licenses BBC Worldwide Ltd for the use of BBC programmes containing literary and dramatic material. These licences cover the direct reception and cable retransmission of the BBC's entertainment satellite channel, BBC PRIME, in Europe and Africa, the information satellite channel, BBC WORLD worldwide, and the satellite transmission of BBC digital channels from the Republic of Ireland. Fees received from BBC Worldwide Ltd are distributed to writers for every transmission of programmes falling within the ALCS repertoire.

[86] Whose rights it administers as their agent, charging a commission of 14 per cent at the point of distribution.

[87] The list is as follows: Australia, Austria, Belgium, Bulgaria, Canada, Chile, the Czech Republic, Denmark, France, Finland, Georgia, Germany, Greece, Hong Kong, Hungary, Ireland, Italy, Jamaica, Japan, Kenya, Latvia, Lithuania, Mexico, the Netherlands, New Zealand, Nigeria, Poland, Portugal, Romania, Russia, Singapore, Slovakia, Spain, South Africa, Sweden, Switzerland, the USA and Zimbabwe .

[88] Articles of Association, Art.7(a). The rights assigned to the ALCS are broader in scope than those actually administered. The full list is as follows: "(i) the lending right; (ii) the reprographic right in each published work; (iii) the private recording right; (iv) the right to communicate the work to the public by means of cable diffusion which expression includes diffusion over any path provided by a material substance or by re-transmission or rebroadcasting of the work to the public by the technical means known as MMDS or any similar technical means of omnidirectional microwave or ultra high frequency transmission using terrestrial transmitters or other terrestrial equipment; (v) the off-air recording right; (vi) the right to perform the work in public by means of apparatus for receiving visual images or sounds conveyed by electronic means; (vii) the right to communicate the work to the public by means of the satellite broadcasts of the programme services of BBC World Service Television including the terrestrial retransmission thereof; (viii) the rights of exploitation by all or any electronic means or in electronic form, capable of or amenable to collective administration; (ix) the rental right; (x) the performing right; (xi) the right for educational establishments to reproduce the work for use in enlarged text format and onto acetate for use with overhead projectors only, in each case solely for the purposes determined by the Secretary of State for Education and Employment (or otherwise the Minister of the Crown responsible for Education in either Scotland or Wales) in connection with the teaching of the United Kingdom National Curriculum and/or any other national literacy initiatives instituted by such Secretary of State; (xii) the right (1) to reproduce the work in text form in the Braille and/or the Moon systems; (2) to store such text electronically (including the right to reproduce the same electronically but only for purposes ancillary to the reproduction of text in such systems); and (3) to issue such reproductions exclusively and solely to visually impaired persons for non-commercial purposes; and (xiii) the right to (1) mechanically reproduce the work (but excluding the right to mechanically reproduce any work which has been sung, spoken or performed with music); and (2) to issue such mechanical reproductions exclusively and solely to visually impaired persons for non-commercial purposes in formats available exclusively for registered blind persons." (Art.7(c)). There is scope to extend the list (Arts 7(d) and (e)). The extent to which these rights are administered abroad is in the discretion of the Board of ALCS: Art.7(d).

[89] A legal fund deduction of 0.5 per cent is also levied on certain sources of income.

seas public lending and private copying .The ALCS website is at www.alcs.co.uk.[90]

C. BRITISH EQUITY COLLECTING SOCIETY LTD ("BECS")

BECS was incorporated in April 1998 with the principal object of collecting, distributing and administering "performers' remuneration".[91] "Performers' remuneration" is defined by BECS as any income or remuneration arising or payable to performers in any of the following ways: first, in respect of the rental of a sound recording or film either by way of the exercise of the rental right under section 182C of the 1988 Act or of the right to equitable remuneration where the rental right has been transferred under section 191G of the 1988 Act or of any equivalent rights in other countries; secondly, from any blank tape levy or other levies on copying media or devices; and thirdly, in respect of the cable retransmission of programmes incorporating their performances.[92] There is power to add to the definition any income or remuneration which is of a similar collective character and which the Board of Management resolves should be collected by BECS.[93] Members sign a mandate appointing BECS as their exclusive agent to collect this remuneration on their behalf. There is no membership charge, but BECS charges commission, the amount of which depends on the source of revenue, but may be as much as 15.6 per cent. As at April 5, 2004, BECS had some 17,000 members. As at January 1, 2004, BECS had reciprocal arrangements with nine foreign collecting societies in Belgium, Denmark, France, Greece, Italy, the Netherlands, Norway, Spain and Switzerland. BECS is a company limited by guarantee incorporated under the Companies Act 1985. Its website is at www.equitycollecting.org.uk.[94]

28–50

D. COMPACT COLLECTIONS LTD

Compact Collections Ltd was incorporated in 1995 for the purposes of collecting secondary television royalties for film and television content owners. It is a limited company incorporated under the Companies Act 1985. As at January 2004 it administered rights on behalf of some 150 members worldwide, many of which were production or distribution companies. The rights administered were as follows: the cable retransmission right;[95] the private copying right;[96] the educational off-air recording right;[97] the German rental right; and the right to show films by televised broadcast in public places. It also collected the theatrical box office levy from Spain. Compact Collections Ltd does not collect royalties in respect of the exercise of any United Kingdom rights. Members appoint Compact Collections Ltd to be their exclusive representative for the purposes of adminis-

28–51

---

[90] The editors are grateful to Richard Combes, Legal Assistant of ALCS, for his assistance in updating this paragraph.

[91] Memorandum of Association, Art.4(1).

[92] Art.3(1)–(4).

[93] Art.3(5).

[94] The editors are grateful to Laurence Oxenbury, Chief Executive of British Equity Collecting Society for his assistance in updating this paragraph.

[95] This right is administered in respect of royalties arising in Austria, Belgium, Canada, Denmark, the Republic of Ireland, Finland, France, Germany, Liechtenstein, Luxembourg, the Netherlands, Norway, Spain, Sweden, Switzerland and the USA.

[96] This right is administered in respect of Austria, Belgium, Denmark, France, Germany, the Netherlands, Spain, Sweden and Switzerland.

[97] This right is administered in respect of Australia, New Zealand and Switzerland.

tering these rights. The website of Compact Collections Ltd is at *www.compactcollections.com*.[98]

E. COPYRIGHT LICENSING AGENCY LTD ("CLA")

28–52   CLA represents the copyright interests of authors and publishers in the United Kingdom. Its Articles of Association permit it to license the copying of published literary, dramatic, musical and artistic works[99] using photocopiers and other methods of multiple copying such as scanning.[1] Artistic works are licensed under an agency agreement with DACS.[2] As at June 2004, CLA represented over 1,500 United Kingdom publishers,[3] including all the major publishers in the United Kingdom, and had bilateral agreements with similar societies in 20 other countries.[4] It also represented some 120,000 authors.[5] CLA is a company limited by guarantee registered under the Companies Act 1985. Its members are the Authors' Licensing and Collecting Society[6] ("the ALCS") and Publishers Licensing Society Ltd. It is empowered by its Articles of Association to negotiate the terms of and to grant licences, to collect royalties and to institute and prosecute such proceedings as may be necessary for the enforcement of the rights entrusted to it.[7] Its licences typically authorise the licensee and those authorised by the licensee to make reprographic copies for the licensee's own purposes at specified premises over a particular period in return for a specified sum. Most of CLA's licences are granted to schools, colleges and universities.[8] Where a group of schools or universities is represented by a negotiating body,[9] CLA will grant a collective licence to that body. CLA also issues increasing numbers of licences to Government Departments, local authorities, other public bodies and private businesses.[10] Finally, CLA operates a special licensing scheme ("the CLA VIP Licensing Scheme") in respect of the making by bodies not conducted for profit of multiple copies for visually impaired persons for circulation outside their organisations.[11] In order to enable CLA to distribute royalties in proportion to actual use, many licences require the licensee to take part in a survey of the copy-

---

[98] The editors are grateful to J. O'Sullivan, Director and General Manager of Compact Collections Ltd for his assistance in updating this paragraph.

[99] Articles of Association, Art.9(a).

[1] See Articles of Association, Art.1(a)(v) which defines "reprographic right" as "the right to reproduce or authorise the reproduction of the work by means of any appliance or process capable of producing multiple copies of the work in such a form that the work may be perceived visually", and *cf.* the definition of reprographic copying in CDPA 1988, s.178.

[2] For DACS, see para. 28–53, below.

[3] As agent for Publishers Licensing Society Ltd, which takes a non-exclusive licence from its members to authorise the making of reprographic copies: see PLS Form A.

[4] They were as follows: Australia, Canada (including Quebec), Denmark, Finland, France, Germany, Greece, Iceland, the Republic of Ireland, Jamaica, the Netherlands, New Zealand, Norway, Singapore, South Africa, Spain, Sweden, Switzerland and the USA.

[5] As agent for the ALCS, as to which see para. 28–49, above.

[6] As to which see para. 28–49, above.

[7] Articles of Association, Art.10.

[8] This scheme is the subject of a decision of the Copyright Tribunal: *Universities UK v Copyright Licensing Agency Ltd and Design and Artists Copyright Society Ltd*, CT71/00, 72/00, 73/00, 74/00, 75/01, [2002] I.P.D. 25021. The availability of licences from the CLA for educational establishments means that s.36 of the CDPA 1988 is of very limited practical effect: see s.36(3).

[9] Such as the Association of Metropolitan Authorities or Universities UK.

[10] CLA attempts where possible to agree a model licence with each trade or representative body. As at June 2004, rates for businesses ranged from £9.56 to £28.68 per year per professional, managerial or technical employee or partner, depending in part on the type of industry or profession concerned and in particular on the amount of research involved in that industry or profession.

[11] This scheme covers books, journals and periodicals published in the United Kingdom, together with some foreign works. It also includes databases where these are included in books, journals and periodicals. There is a list of excluded works. The scheme is intended to comply with CDPA 1988, s.31D, with the effect that s.31B (which provides for the making of multiple copies for visually impaired persons) is disapplied by s.31D(1). For s.31B, see para. 9–78 *et seq.*, above.

right works copied on its premises over a specified period.[12] All licences contain conditions as to the proportion of a work which may be copied.[13] Some categories of works[14] and a number of specific works are excluded altogether.[15] Licensees are provided with an indemnity by CLA in respect of infringement claims which is expressed to be in addition to the indemnity implied by section 136 of the 1988 Act.[16] Royalties in respect of the copying of books are divided equally between Publishers Licensing Society Ltd and ALCS.[17] In the year to March 2003, the CLA received royalties totalling £36 million and distributed over £38 million. During the year, the CLA's administration costs were £4.5 million. CLA's website is at *www.cla.co.uk.*[18]

F. DESIGN AND ARTISTS COPYRIGHT SOCIETY LTD ("DACS")

DACS exists to protect and promote the copyright and similar rights in artistic works of artists and other visual creators[19] and their successors in title.[20] DACS is a company limited by guarantee registered under the Companies Act 1985 and operates as a not for profit organisation. Licensing is divided into "primary" and "collective" licensing. Primary licensing means the exercise on behalf of members of those rights which are exercisable individually such as the right to make copies of the work, the right to issue copies of the work to the public and moral rights. Collective licensing concerns those rights which it is impractical or impossible for a member to exercise individually. Rights administered by DACS by way of collective licensing as at August 2004 included certain reprographic rights,[21] the educational off-air recording right[22] and the satellite and cable retransmission right.[23] DACS intends to administer the artist's resale right when that comes into existence in 2006. As at June 2004, DACS represented some 36,000 artists, other visual creators and their successors in title for the purposes of primary licensing. Licence fees received in respect of collective licensing are distributed via the relevant organisations of visual creators. Members are divided

28–53

Where educational establishments make copies for visually impaired persons for internal use only, this will be covered by an extension of the existing CLA licence: see para.8 of the scheme.

[12] This may be up to six weeks.

[13] In particular, with minor exceptions, no more than five per cent or one complete chapter of a book may be copied at a time; *cf.* CDPA 1988, s.36(2).

[14] They are as follows: works published outside the UK or one of the countries in relation to which a reciprocal arrangement exists; printed music (including the words); public examination papers; newspapers (as to which see para. 28–57, below); privately-owned documents issued for tuition purposes and limited to clientèle who pay fees (other than those published by the Open University or the National Extension College); maps, charts, and books of tables; workbooks, workcards and assignment sheets; separate photographs, illustrations and diagrams; industrial house journals; Bibles, liturgical works and orders of service.

[15] *i.e.* works specifically excluded by a special notice, mentioning the CLA, on the work itself and works included in the list contained in the CLA's publication, *Excluded Works*, February 1998.

[16] Note the limited application of s.136.

[17] As to which see para. 28–49, above.

[18] The editors are grateful to Siobhan Sherry, Public Relations Manager of the CLA, for her assistance in updating this paragraph.

[19] Including sculptors, photographers and other visual creators of artistic works as defined by CDPA 1988, s.4.

[20] Memorandum of Association, para.3.

[21] Administered through the CLA, as to which see para. 28–52, above.

[22] Which DACS administers as a member of the ERA, as to which see para. 28–55, below.

[23] In respect of retransmissions in the Republic of Ireland, revenue is collected through the Irish Music Rights Organisation, a group of broadcasters and collecting societies. In respect of retransmissions in Belgium, France and Holland, revenue is collected through the relevant local collecting society. The full list of rights which DACS may administer collectively is as follows (see Articles of Association, Art.1.18): cable retransmission right, digital and electronic imaging rights, lending right, off-air recording right, private audio-visual recording right, public display right, rental right, reprographic right, resale right (*droit de suite*), terrestrial and satellite broadcast rights, and such other rights as may hereafter come into existence.

into ordinary members (the authors of the works and their nominees) and successor members (defined as surviving spouses and relatives, beneficiaries under a will or personal representatives of the authors).[24] As at June 2004, membership cost a one-off fee of £25 including VAT.[25] An ordinary member grants to DACS an exclusive licence to exercise and to authorise others to exercise all the primary and secondary rights in all that member's artistic works throughout the world for primary and collective advertising purposes.[26] Members retain the right to exercise any of the primary or secondary rights on notice to DACS.[27] In addition, a member may if he or she wishes retain control over the grant of licences in respect of any type of use which he or she specifies in the membership agreement. DACS automatically refers requests for licences for the use of works in advertising or merchandising to the member concerned.[28] DACS agrees to use its reasonable endeavours to preserve the member's rights[29] and to collect royalties,[30] but is not obliged to institute legal proceedings.[31] However, if proceedings are commenced in the name of the member, DACS is granted the right to have the conduct of those proceedings and to compromise them as it sees fit.[32] Licences are granted both on an individual basis by reference to a standard published tariff (which varies in accordance with the type of reproduction) and on a collective basis where appropriate. In general, royalties are distributed every six months. DACS operates a special blanket licensing scheme[33] for the reproduction of artistic works on to slides, acetates and transparencies by educational establishments. DACS retains a commission of 25 per cent from all royalties. Royalties in respect of works which have been licensed individually are distributed on the basis of actual use. DACS' turnover in 2003 was over £3m. The DACS website is at *www.dacs.org.uk*.[34]

G. Directors and Producers Rights Society (1992) Ltd ("DPRS")

28–54   DPRS represents individual film and television directors and producers and their estates. As at July 2004, it administered on their behalf the cable retransmission right, the private copying right and the video rental right through collecting societies in the European Community and Switzerland.[35] DPRS also represents freelance television directors in respect of the exploitation of their works in the United Kingdom. As a matter of industry practice, such directors are required to assign all their rights in programmes of which they are the authors to the producer. The fee paid on such assignment is deemed to cover the first transmission. However, in July 2001, DPRS reached an agreement with the United Kingdom broadcasters and producers[36] ("the Rights Agreement") in relation to remuneration for any further transmissions within the United Kingdom ("secondary use"). Under an initial

---

[24] Articles of Association, Arts 4.1 and 4.2.

[25] "A Guide to Membership of the Design and Artists Copyright Society Ltd" (DACS) ("Membership Guide").

[26] Membership Agreement (Ordinary Member), Arts 1 and 2m.

[27] Membership Agreement (Ordinary Member), Arts 3 and 5.

[28] Membership Guide, para.11.

[29] Membership Agreement (Ordinary Member), Art.9.

[30] Membership Agreement (Ordinary Member), Art.10.

[31] Membership Agreement (Ordinary Member), Art.9.

[32] Membership Agreement (Ordinary Member), Art.9.

[33] The Slide Collection Licensing Scheme.

[34] The editors are grateful to Steve Vaid, Director of Operations of DACS and John Robinson, Director of Services of DACS for their assistance in updating this paragraph.

[35] As at July 2004 it had agreements with collecting societies in Austria, Belgium, the Czech Republic, Denmark, Finland, France, Germany, Hungary, Italy, the Netherlands, Poland, Portugal, Slovakia, Spain and Switzerland.

[36] The BBC, ITV Network, Channel 4, Channel 5, BSkyB, PACT, S4C and TAC.

five-year arrangement, DPRS receives a fixed annual sum in respect of such secondary use. Payments are distributed to individual directors in accordance with a scheme devised and administered by DPRS.[37] DPRS is a company limited by guarantee. As at July 2004, it had over 2,500 members. The DPRS website is at *www.dprs.org.*[38]

H. EDUCATIONAL RECORDING AGENCY LTD ("ERA")

Section 35(1) of the 1988 Act, as amended by the Copyright and Related Rights Regulations, permits educational establishments[39] and persons acting on their behalf to make recordings of cable or broadcast programmes and to copy such recordings for educational purposes without infringing copyright. Section 35(1A) provides that where a recording is made in this way without infringing copyright, copyright is not infringed if it is communicated to the public within the premises of an educational establishment provided that the communication cannot be received by any person situated outside the premises of that establishment. However, these provisions do not apply if or to the extent that there is a certified licensing scheme in force.[40] On May 30, 1990, a certified licensing scheme operated by ERA came into force.[41] The scheme is limited to the works and performances in respect of which the licensor members of ERA (who include the BBC, the ITV Network, Channel Four and Channel Five)[42] own or control the copyright.[43] It does not apply to Open University programmes[44] (the Open University has its own licensing scheme[45]). ERA offers individual or blanket licences to record or make copies of recordings for educational purposes only. At the time of writing, proposals were being prepared to extend the scheme to cover the communication to students within educational establishments under section 35(1A) of the 1988 Act. Licence fees are calculated on a per capita basis, to which tariffs (based on the level of education provided by the establishment) are applied.[46] ERA has negotiated discounted licence fees with umbrella organisations representing large numbers of educational establishments.[47] Under the terms of ERA's licence, all recordings or copies must be marked with a statement that the recording is to be used only for educational purposes.[48] ERA reserves the right to require licensees to carry out a survey of the material they copy and rec-

28–55

---

[37] The terms of the scheme are available on DPRS's website, *www.dprs.org.*

[38] The editors are grateful to Suzan Dormer of DPRS for her assistance in updating this paragraph.

[39] Which expression includes schools and any other educational establishment specified by order of the Secretary of State: CDPA 1988, s.174(1). The Secretary of State has specified universities and institutions providing further or higher education under this section: see the Copyright (Educational Establishments) (No.2) Order 1989 No.1068. ERA has published a statement on the meaning of the term "educational establishment".

[40] CDPA 1988, s.35(2).

[41] Under the Copyright (Certification of Licensing Scheme for Educational Recording of Broadcasts and Cable Programmes) (Educational Recording Agency Ltd) Order 1990, (SI 1990/879). See Vol.2 at B2.i. This has been amended by the following statutory instruments: SI 1992/211, SI 1993/193, SI 1994/247, SI 1996/191, SI 1998/203, SI 1999/3452 and SI 2003/188.

[42] The full list is: the ALCS (see para. 28–49, above), BBC Worldwide Ltd, Channel Four Television Corporation, DACS (see para. 28–53, above), the BPI, Independent Television Network Ltd, MCPS (see para. 28–56, below) and Sianel Pedwar Cymru: see para.4 of the ERA Scheme, which is the Schedule to SI 1990/879, as amended

[43] See para.3 of the ERA Scheme, which is the Schedule to SI 1990/879.

[44] ERA Scheme, para.4.

[45] Certified under the Copyright (Certification of Licensing Scheme for Educational Recording of Broadcasts)(Open University) Order 2003 (SI 2003/187). See Vol.2 at B2.ii.

[46] For licences taking effect on or after April 1, 2003, primary schools pay 23p per capita; secondary schools pay 47p per capita; further education establishments pay 88p per capita; while universities pay £1.40 per capita: see SI 2003/188.

[47] *Off-Air Recording for Educational Establishments*, ERA, 1999.

[48] See para.6 of the ERA licensing scheme, which is the Schedule to SI 1990/879.

ord[49] and to inspect all recordings and copies made by licensees under the terms of the licence.[50] ERA is a limited company registered under the Companies Act 1985. Its turnover in the year ending March 31, 2004 was £5.3m. It charges a commission of about 4.5 per cent. Its website is at *www.era.org.uk*.[51]

I. MECHANICAL-COPYRIGHT PROTECTION SOCIETY LTD ("MCPS")

28–56   MCPS exists to protect the "mechanical" copyright in musical works. This is defined in its current membership agreement as the right to make sound-bearing copies of musical works, to issue such copies to the public, to import such copies and to authorise any of these things.[52] As at July 2004, it had about 12,700 composer members and about 4,800 publisher members. In 2004, it had reciprocal arrangements with similar societies in 47 other countries[53] and agency arrangements with similar societies in five other countries.[54] MCPS is a limited company registered under the Companies Act 1985. It is a wholly-owned subsidiary of Music Publishers' Association Ltd, a company limited by guarantee. The normal membership agreement,[55] involves the appointment of MCPS as the member's agent to manage and administer its mechanical copyright in the United Kingdom and (in certain circumstances) throughout the world.[56] The agreement empowers MCPS to grant licences and collect royalties on the member's behalf[57] and obliges MCPS to use its best endeavours to prevent infringement.[58] It entitles (but does not oblige) MCPS to take proceedings for infringement in the member's name.[59] MCPS's licensing arrangements in relation to phonorecords[60] were the subject of a Copyright Tribunal decision in 1992,[61] which fixed royalty rates at 8.5 per cent of that part of the published price for dealers attributable to music the copyright in which is administered by MCPS. Pursuant to the Copyright Tribunal decision, MCPS offers three types of licence agreement to record companies.[62] The AP.1 agreement[63] permits the record company to record any work within MCPS's repertoire provided MCPS is notified at least seven working days before release. Royalties are paid quarterly in arrears. However, consent for a first recording must still be obtained in advance.[64] The AP.2A agreement is intended for companies which have a trading history with MCPS but do not fulfil the financial and accounting criteria for the AP.1 agreement. The record company must obtain a licence before manufacture, but is given a 60-day credit period up to an agreed sum for the payment of royalties. The AP.2 agreement is similar to the AP.2A

---

[49] ERA licensing scheme, para.7. As at July 2004, about two per cent of educational licensees were subject to this requirement.

[50] See para.8 of the ERA licensing scheme.

[51] The editors are grateful to Helen Nicholson, Chief Executive of ERA, for her assistance in updating this paragraph.

[52] cl.16.21 of MA2. Note, however, that authorising the importation of infringing copies is not an infringement of copyright.

[53] Including Australia, Austria, Belgium, Canada, France, Germany, Greece, Hong Kong, Hungary, Israel, Italy, Japan, the Netherlands, New Zealand, Poland, Portugal, South Africa, Spain and Switzerland.

[54] Bulgaria, Canada, Croatia, the USA and Zimbabwe.

[55] Agreement MA2 dated August 1994.

[56] cl.1.1.

[57] cl.1.2.

[58] cl.9.1.

[59] cl.11.

[60] *i.e.* CDs, cassettes, and vinyl records made for the purpose of retail sale to the public.

[61] *BPI v MCPS* [1993] E.M.L.R. 86, 139.

[62] Terms and Conditions of Business, Product Licensing (MCPS).

[63] Which, as at August 2004, was held by about 134 record companies and their associated labels.

[64] In addition, there are specific restrictions as to the making of adaptations of works. The licence does not cover reproduction where the licence of the owner of the sound recording copyright or the consent of the performer has not been obtained.

agreement but there is no credit period. There are other standard agreements for other specialist areas, such as videos, music-DVD videos and newspaper/magazine covermounts.[65] There are blanket licensing arrangements with substantially all United Kingdom television and radio stations,[66] schools[67] and many other specialist music providers, such as in-flight radio programme providers, online music service providers, karaoke disc producers, mobile phone ringtone suppliers and video jukebox software suppliers.[68] MCPS levies commission on royalties before they are distributed to members. During 2003, commission rates were fixed at between 3.15 per cent and 20 per cent depending on the product and the nature of the licensing agreement. The average commission rate in 2003 was 6.1 per cent. In that year, royalties of over £230 million were collected, royalties of over £226 millon were distributed and commission of over £13.8 million was levied. MCPS administers the off-air educational recording right on behalf of its members through the ERA.[69] Some time ago, MCPS established an operational alliance with the PRS under which both societies are managed by a limited company which is jointly owned by them. This company employs the staff and owns assets such as buildings. However, the rights continue to be vested in or administered by the societies separately and there is no intention to merge the two organisations. The MCPS website is at *www.mcps.co.uk.*[70]

J. NEWSPAPER LICENSING AGENCY LTD ("NLA")

The NLA was launched in January 1996 in order to license certain types of copying of newspaper articles. Its repertoire comprises works appearing in all the national newspapers and over 1,000 regional newspapers in the United Kingdom, together with a number of foreign newspapers.[71] It is a limited company registered under the Companies Act 1985. Since January 1, 1998, its remit has extended to most types of copying of the typographical arrangement of the published editions of any works appearing in the newspapers in its repertoire and of the literary and artistic works appearing in those newspapers. As a result of the decision of the House of Lords in *Newspaper Licensing Agency Ltd v Marks & Spencer plc*[72] the NLA now concentrates on enforcing its literary and artistic copyrights rather than those in the typographical arrangements of the newspapers of its members. Newspaper publishers assign to the NLA that part of the copyright in the typographical arrangement of the published editions of any works appearing in their newspapers and that part of the copyright in the literary and artistic works so appearing which consists of the right to license their copying and to pursue infringement claims in respect of unlicensed copying.[73] There is a basic licence fee which covers ad hoc copying of national newspapers and is based on the size of

28–57

[65] Terms and Conditions of Business, Product Licensing (MCPS).
[66] Terms and Conditions of Business, Broadcast Blanket Licensing (MCPS).
[67] Through the ERA. See para. 28–55, above.
[68] Terms and Conditions of Business, Other Licensing (MCPS).
[69] See para. 28–55, above.
[70] The editors are grateful to Nick Kounoupias and Michael Lynch of MCPS/PRS for their assistance in updating this paragraph.
[71] Including the major newspapers in France, the Republic of Ireland and the United States.
[72] [2001] UKHL 38. This case is discussed at length at para. 3–104, above. It is understood that Marks & Spencer plc has now taken a standard NLA licence to copy newspaper cuttings for its internal management and information purposes.
[73] Publisher Mandate, cl.1(a). For these purposes, "works" are defined as including advertisements, photographs, cartoon and strip illustrations, graphic designs, drawings, illustrations, charts, diagrams, paintings and other works of fine art: Publisher Mandate, cl.1(c). The full list of reproduction rights assigned is: photocopying; faxing; digital scanning and transmission; and any copying, reproduction or other act which takes place as a necessary incident to one of these acts throughout the world: Publisher Mandate, cl.1(a). The right to pursue claims of copyright infringement in respect of unlicensed copying extends to all these forms of reproduction together

the licensee.[74] Additional fees are payable for the copying of other newspapers, for systematic copying, for digital copying, and for public relations consultancies and trade or professional organisations who make copies for their clients. The licences expressly do not permit the reproduction of photographs, illustrations or advertisements.[75] There is a limit of 250 copies of any particular article.[76] Special licences are available for professional partnerships[77] and educational establishments.[78] Non-educational charities are entitled to apply for a discount.[79] Except in the case of public relations consultancies, trade or professional organisations, professional partnerships and educational establishments, licensees are not generally permitted to use copies of press cuttings otherwise than for distribution to personnel for their internal use.[80] By March 2004, the NLA had issued licences to over 30,000 companies and other organisations. In the last financial year the NLA collected royalties of over £12 million. Royalties are distributed to publishers on the basis of licensees' audits. There is a standard commission of 20 per cent, but different rates may apply in respect of foreign newspapers.The NLA's website is at *www.nla.co.uk*.[81]

K. PERFORMING ARTISTS' MEDIA RIGHTS ASSOCIATION LTD ("PAMRA")

28–58   PAMRA was incorporated in December 1995 for the purposes of collecting, distributing and administering on behalf of performers all and any remuneration arising from the implementation in the United Kingdom of the Rental and Related Rights Directive,[82] PAMRA is a company limited by guarantee. Its members appoint it as their agent for the purposes of collecting "recorded performance remuneration".[83] The latter term is defined as including the performer's share of the statutory equitable remuneration paid on the broadcast or communication to the public of a phonogram published for commercial purposes (or a reproduction of such a phonogram). It also includes such other types of remuneration for performances[84] as PAMRA may resolve to collect.[85] In addition, PAMRA is appointed its members' agent to enter into agreements with performers' or producers' organisations within or outside the United Kingdom with a view to obtaining recorded performance remuneration and to negotiate and settle with producers' organisations that such monies may be shared between performers' and produc-

---

with any other unlicensed act of copying or reproduction. By cl.1(c) the assignment extends to all works previously published in the newspaper.

[74] Thus, for example, in the year commencing May 10, 2004, a company with 51 to 100 employees with a turnover of less than £10m paid an annual fee of £540.

[75] Standard licence, cl.2.2.

[76] Standard licence, cl.3.4.

[77] The licence contains specific provisions as to the supply of copies to clients.

[78] Schools where the normal admission age is under 16 can obtain a licence free of charge: cl.6.7 of the Newspaper Copying Licence for Educational Establishments.

[79] See cl.8 of the standard licence.

[80] Standard licence, cl.1.

[81] The editors are grateful to Guy MacNaughton, Managing Director of the NLA, for his assistance in updating this paragraph.

[82] The same rights are also administered by AURA, whose members are mainly featured artists. For AURA, and a more detailed account of the rights in question, see para. 28–48 and notes thereto, above.

[83] Membership Scheme, para.1.1(a).

[84] Whether arising as a result of rights in respect of the rental and/or lending of fixed performances or as a result of levies on copying devices or media or as a result of other measures intended to recompense, *inter alia*, performers: Membership Sheme, para.14.

[85] Membership Scheme, para.1.1(a), 14.

ers' bodies.[86] PAMRA is also entitled to enter into agreements with foreign collecting societies to collect income arising abroad in respect of the broadcast and public performance of their recorded performances.[87] Between 1996 and 2003, PAMRA entered into reciprocal arrangements with collecting societies in Austria, Belgium, Canada, Croatia, Denmark, Estonia, Germany, Greece, the Republic of Ireland, Italy, Malaysia, Mexico, the Netherlands, Poland, Romania, Russia and Spain; and exclusive agreements with societies in Japan and Switzerland. In addition, under the terms of its membership scheme, PAMRA has powers to represent its members in the Copyright Tribunal, to enter into blanket licensing arrangements, and to seek to recover remuneration by action in the Courts.[88] There is no membership fee, but PAMRA charges a 9.5 per cent administration fee on United Kingdom equitable remuneration. By 2004, PAMRA had a membership of over 17,000 performers. In 2003, PAMRA distributed a total of over £12m to its members. PAMRA's website is at *www.pamra.org.uk.*[89]

L. PERFORMING RIGHT SOCIETY LTD ("PRS")

The PRS exists to administer the performing rights in musical works (which expression includes any words associated with musical works,[90]) *i.e.* the rights to perform such works in public, to communicate them to the public and to authorise others to do the same.[91] It also administers the film synchronisation right in musical works, which is defined as the exclusive right in any part of the world to record them on the soundtrack of a film.[92] As at the end of 2003, the PRS had a United Kingdom membership of over 40,000, of whom over 35,000 were living composers and about 3,000 were music publishers.[93] At the same time it represented foreign music copyright owners[94] through affiliated organisations in over 75 other countries throughout the world.[95] The PRS has claimed that its licence is necessary for practically every public performance[96] of copyright music[97] in the United Kingdom.[98] The PRS is a company limited by guarantee registered under the Companies Act 1985. The Articles of Association require

28–59

---

[86] Membership Scheme, para.1.1(b). Note that by CDPA 1988, s.182D(1), equitable remuneration is payable by the copyright owner (*i.e.* in most cases by the record company); by s.182D(3) the amount payable by way of equitable remuneration is as agreed by or on behalf of the persons by whom and to whom it is payable; and by s.182D(4) in default of agreement, the amount may be determined by the Copyright Tribunal.

[87] Membership Scheme, para.1.1(c).

[88] Membership Scheme, para.1.1(g), (h) and (j).

[89] The editors are grateful to Jo Laverty, Communications Manager at PAMRA for her assistance in updating this paragraph.

[90] Art.1(a)(xvii) of the PRS Articles of Association defines "musical work" as including "(a) any part of a musical work, (b) any vocal or instrumental music recorded on the soundtrack of any film, (c) any musical accompaniment to non-musical plays, (d) any words or music of monologues having a musical introduction or accompaniment, [and] (e) any other words (or part of words) which are associated with a musical work even if the musical work itself is not in copyright, or even if the performing rights in the musical work are not administered by [the PRS]".

[91] Articles of Association, Art.1(xix). See CDPA 1988, ss.19 and 16(2).

[92] Articles of Association, Art.1(a)(xii). In *Music Gallery Ltd v Direct Line Insurance PLC* [1998] E.M.L.R. 551, it was held that the film synchronisation right granted to the PRS by its members in works written primarily for the purpose of being included in the soundtrack of a particular film or films in contemplation when the work was commissioned, applies only to that film or those films and not to any film.

[93] For eligibility, see Articles of Association, Art.4.

[94] In 2003, over £58 million was allocated to affiliated societies abroad.

[95] Royalties of over £48m were allocated to copyright owners in France, Germany and the USA during 2003, while royalties of over £76m were received from the following countries during the same period: Austria, Belgium, Canada, Denmark, France, Germany, Ireland, Italy, Japan, the Netherlands, Spain, Switzerland and the USA.

[96] As to what constitutes a performance "in public" see paras 7–91 *et seq.*, above.

[97] As defined in the PRS Articles of Association, Art.1(a)(xvii).

[98] *PRS Member Information Pack "What is PRS? A guide to the Performing Right Society".*

members on election (or at any time thereafter if so requested) to assign or cause to be assigned to the PRS the following rights in "all or any works or parts of works,[99] present or future, of which the member is the writer, publisher or proprietor", namely: the performing right; (in the case of writer members only) the film synchronisation right in every work composed or written primarily for the soundtrack of a film; and such other rights as the Board of the PRS may direct.[1] Provision is made for members to reserve to themselves on admission one or more "categories of rights" or "forms of utilisation" of their rights in all of their works,[2] and for existing members to require the PRS on notice to reassign any such rights to them.[3] It is further provided that any assignment of the film synchronisation right must expressly require the PRS at the request of the composer or author of a work to assign or license the film synchronisation right in the work to the film producer or any other person who commissioned the composition or writing of the work on terms as to the payment to the PRS by the film producer of royalties in respect of cinema showings of the film in the United States of America.[4] It is also provided that any member may require the PRS to reassign the right to perform the work live in public.[5] Finally, it is provided that the PRS may "decline to exercise" the performing right in a specified work or works.[6] The PRS is obliged by the Rules to enforce the rights assigned to it.[7] As well as individual licences, there are a number of different licensing schemes, the tariff for each of which depends on the category of user.[8] Because blanket licences are granted, the system of royalty distribution is complex and sophisticated. Some licensees (including the BBC, ITV and many concert venues) are required to submit a full census of all performances. Otherwise, licence fees are distributed on the basis of sample returns from users together with analogous data such as radio usage. Royalties in respect of a particular work are divided between publishers and authors in a set proportion, subject to any prior agreement there may be between them.[9] In 2003, the PRS collected royalties of over £280 million and had over £240 million available for distribution to its members.[10] On February 1, 1996, the

---

[99] Presumably this is intended to be a reference to musical works as defined in Art.1(a)(xvii).

[1] Articles of Association, Arts 7(a) and 7(c). The terms of Art.7(c)(iii) are intended to permit the Board of the PRS to specify particular parts of the performing and film synchronisation right which are not to be administered by it. If they are not to be administered by the PRS then they are not within the ambit of any assignment to it: Art.7(a). The Board has directed that the PRS shall not in fact administer the so-called "grand rights", *i.e.* the performing right in "dramatico-musical works" (defined in the Rules of the PRS as "an opera, operetta, musical play, revue or pantomime, in so far as it consists of words and music written expressly therefor": see Rule 1(e)) or ballets. For a more detailed account of the rights which the PRS does not administer, see its *Member Information Pack "Dramatic presentations of music"*.

[2] Arts 7(cc) and (cd). The terminology derives from *Re Gema* [1971] C.M.L.R. (R.P. Supplement) D35 at D49 and *Re Gema (No.2)* [1972] C.M.L.R. (R.P. Supplement) D115 at D116. The "categories of rights" are expressed as follows "(i) the general performing right; (ii) the broadcasting right, including the public performing right of broadcast works (transmission right); (iii) the right of cinematographic exhibition; (iv) the right of mechanical reproduction and diffusion, including the public performing right of mechanically reproduced works (transmission right); (v) the cinematographic production right; (vi) the exploitation rights resulting from technical developments or future change in the law." The "forms of utilisation of rights" are the same as the categories of rights but also include the "televising right", the "public performing right of televised works" and the "public performing right of works reproduced on video tape".

[3] Articles of Association, Arts 7(cc) and (cd). For the notice periods, which may be up to three years, see Art.9(f).

[4] Art.7(b).

[5] Art.7(g).

[6] Art.7(f). See also *Member Information Pack "Dramatic presentations of music"*. This right is in practice exercised at the member's request.

[7] Rules and Regulations, Rule 2(a).

[8] See in respect of Tariff D (dance halls) *PRS v BEDA* [1993] E.M.L.R. 325.

[9] For details see *Member Information Pack "Registering works and agreements"*.

[10] Directors' Report and Accounts 2003.

Monopolies and Mergers Commission ("MMC") published a report on the PRS.[11] It found that a monopoly situation existed in favour of PRS and made 44 recommendations, all of which have now been implemented.[12] Some years ago, the PRS established an alliance with MCPS, although the two organisations have not been merged at the level of rights or membership.[13] The PRS website is at *www.prs.co.uk*.[14]

M. Phonographic Performance Ltd ("PPL")

PPL was established in 1934 to administer certain rights in sound recordings on behalf of its record company members. PPL is a company limited by guarantee registered under the Companies Act 1985. As at August 2004, PPL had over 3,000 record company members. Members assign to PPL (or, where they are not the owner of the relevant rights, appoint PPL as their exclusive agent in respect of) all their current and future broadcast and public performance rights together with the related "dubbing" rights, that is the rights to make copies for the purposes of subsequent broadcasts or public performances. By its Articles of Association, PPL is granted sole power and authority in the name of its members to collect licence fees, to recover damages for infringement of the broadcasting, public performance or dubbing right and to take, defend and compromise proceedings in relation to such rights.[15] Like the PRS, PPL operates a variety of licensing schemes which depend on the category into which the user of the sound recordings falls. For example, the BBC pays a lump sum, while a night club's blanket licence fee is assessed on a sliding scale depending on the amount of record usage and the numbers attending on each evening. The way in which revenue is distributed depends on the user. The BBC submits full returns of all its sound recording use and revenue received from the BBC is therefore distributed in proportion to actual use. Commercial radio revenue is distributed in proportion to the amount of use evidenced by sample returns. The samples in fact consist of full returns from radio stations which represent 60 per cent of the total licensed sound recording use on independent radio and are therefore thought to be representative. Revenue from the use of records as "specially featured entertainment" (*i.e.* mainly discos and clubs) is distributed on the basis of a combination of selected BBC and commercial radio returns on the one hand and the information provided by specially commissioned play charts and dance record sales charts on the other. Revenue from juke box operators is distributed according to a combination of BBC and commercial radio returns on the one hand and returns from the relevant dubbing operators on the other. Revenue from background music operators is distributed on the basis of returns from those operators. For many years, PPL made an ex gratia payment to performers of 32.5 per cent of the total money distributed after deducting running costs. Following the implementation of the Rental and Related Rights Directive on December 1, 1996, PPL has paid equitable remuneration to some 30,000 performers. The split between the record company as owner of the copyright in the sound recording and the performer has

28–60

---

[11] Cm. No.3147.

[12] Examples are the member's entitlement to require a reassignment of the right to perform the work in public.

[13] The editors are grateful to Nick Kounoupias and Michael Lynch of MCPS/PRS for their assistance in updating this paragraph.

[14] The PRS has been a party to the following decisions of the Copyright Tribunal: *The Working Mens Club and Institute Union Ltd v The PRS* [1992] R.P.C. 227; *National Association of Holiday Centres Ltd v The PRS*, unreported CT 3/89; *British Hotels Restaurants and Caterers Association v The PRS*, unreported CT 6/90; *PRS v BEDA* [1993] E.M.L.R. 325; *British Sky Broadcasting and Another v The PRS* [1998] E.M.L.R. 193; *British Airways Plc v The PRS* [1998] E.M.L.R. 556.

[15] Articles of Association, Art.7(i).

been agreed at 50:50. There are agreed rules as to how to distribute the performer's share. In the year ending December 31, 2003, PPL's gross revenue amounted to about £80 million while its administration costs were about £30 million.[16] PPL's website is at *www.ppluk.com*.[17]

N. VIDEO PERFORMANCE LTD ("VPL")

28–61   VPL exists to exercise and enforce certain rights in music videos. Its members are the owners or exclusive licensees of the rights to broadcast and perform music videos in public together with the "dubbing right" which permits the copying of videos for the purpose of subsequent broadcast or public performance. As at August 2004, VPL had over 900 members (including the major record companies in the United Kingdom) and controlled the copyright in over 50,000 music videos. VPL is a company limited by guarantee registered under the Companies Act 1985. VPL's gross revenue in the seven-month accounting period to December 31, 2003 was over £4.5 million, of which about 15 per cent was spent on administrative and other expenses. The website of VPL is at *www.vpluk.com*.[18]

---

[16] For Copyright Tribunal cases to which PPL has been a party, see the notes to para. 29–99, below.
[17] The editors are grateful to Peter Leathem, Director of Legal and Business Affairs at PPL, for his assistance in updating this paragraph.
[18] The editors are grateful to Peter Leathem, Director of Legal and Business Affairs at VPL, for his assistance in updating this paragraph.

CHAPTER TWENTY NINE

CONTROL OF THE EXERCISE OF COPYRIGHTS AND RELATED RIGHTS

29–01   **Scope of chapter.** The exercise of copyright and related rights by their owner is subject to a variety of legal restraints. It is the purpose of this Chapter to examine the different legal restraints which may operate to fetter the free exercise of exclusive rights accorded under the 1988 Act and the Database Regulations. The first section deals with nine situations where the owner's right may be, or become, subject to a compulsory licence. The second section deals with certain anomalous circumstances where there is some interference with the free exercise of such rights, but which stop short of a compulsory or statutory licence. The third section sets out the jurisdiction of the Copyright Tribunal, and its control over the exercise of rights in a wide variety of different circumstances. The procedure before the Tribunal is also described in this section. The fourth and fifth sections describe the effect of rules of European and domestic competition law and the doctrine of restraint of trade on the exercise of such rights.

1. COMPULSORY LICENCES

A. INTRODUCTION

Although copyright is a property right, in certain limited circumstances the law permits uses of works without the consent of the copyright owner if the user complies with specified conditions, including the payment of a fee.[1] In such circumstances, the copyright owner is compelled to license the particular use of the work and the licence is referred to as a "compulsory licence" or "licence of right".[2] Although the conceptual distinction is sometimes blurred,[3] such licences differ from permitted acts in that payment is required. The effect of a compulsory licence is not dissimilar to the refusal by a court of injunctive relief or to a statutory right of "equitable remuneration" in that the right owner is left with the possibility of financial compensation for uses of the work rather than control over such uses. A further useful distinction can be drawn between statutory licences and compulsory licences properly so called. In the case of a statutory licence the rate is fixed by law, in the case of a compulsory licence the rate is left to be negotiated, but in neither case can use be refused or prevented.[4] Collectively these licences can be referred to as non-voluntary licences.

29–02

Under existing domestic law compulsory licences are available in eight distinct circumstances: where the copyright work comprises broadcast schedules and a person wishes to reproduce those schedules[5]; where the work is a sound recording, and it is proposed to broadcast it or include it in a cable programme[6]; where copyright had lapsed but has been revived by the Duration Regulations[7]; where the work is a document embodying a design which was in existence on January 1, 1989 and therefore subject to transitional provisions[8]; where the Secretary of State has made an order regarding the lending of works[9]; where a copyright work is included in a wireless broadcast which is retransmitted by cable under a statutory requirement but beyond the original broadcast area[10]; where the work is of

29–03

---

[1] Thus, in jurisprudential terms, the grant of a compulsory licence converts a property rule into a liability rule. See further, Ayres and Talley, "Solomonic Bargaining: Dividing a Legal Entitlement to facilitate Coasean Trade," (1995) 104 Yale L.J. 1027; Kaplow and Sharell, "Property Rules Versus Liability Rules: An Economic Analysis," (1996) 109 Harv. L.Rev. 713. For consideration in the context of intellectual property, see Merges, "Contracting into Liability Rules: Intellectual Property Rights and Collective Rights Organizations" (1996) 84 Cal. L.Rev. 1293.

[2] Compare Patents Act 1977 (c.37), ss.46–54.

[3] In particular, note that a number of the permitted acts only take effect in the absence of a licensing arrangement, thereby encouraging the grant of licences: CDPA 1988, ss.31B, 35, 36, 60, 74.

[4] Historically, the United Kingdom has adopted a mixture of statutory and compulsory licences, although since 1989 the preference has clearly been for compulsory licences.

[5] Broadcasting Act 1990 (c.42), s.175–6, Sch.17, paras 29–09 *et seq.*, below.

[6] CDPA 1988, ss.135A–H, paras 29–25 *et seq.*, below.

[7] Duration of Copyright and Rights in Performances Regulations (SI 1995/3297), reg.24(1), paras 29–41 *et seq.*, below.

[8] CDPA 1988, Sch.1, para. 29–44, below.

[9] s.66, paras 29–45 *et seq.*, below.

[10] s.73(4), paras 29–48 *et seq.*, below.

"enemy origin"[11]; and where the Secretary of State, the Office of Fair Trading or the Competition Commission so provide under their statutory powers in relation to competition.[12] Compulsory licences may also be made available if a copyright owner is found to have violated Article 82 of the Treaty of Rome.[13] Further compulsory licences exist in relation to unregistered design right, in particular, to allow for the reproduction of a design during the last five years of its protection, but these provisions are dealt with elsewhere.[14]

B. OVERVIEW

(i) History of compulsory and statutory licences in the United Kingdom

29–04   Apart from the existing provisions, the United Kingdom has historically recognised four other situations where non-voluntary licences were made available. The first compulsory licence was introduced into the United Kingdom by the Literary Copyright Act 1842.[15] This provision was aimed at preventing the newly increased term of protection from being used in such a way as to be detrimental to the public interest. It gave the Judicial Committee of the Privy Council a power to grant compulsory licences any time after the death of the author where the owner of the copyright was preventing a work that had previously been published from being republished. This provision was re-enacted in the 1911 Act and the powers of the Judicial Committee of the Privy Council were extended to cover cases where the owner was refusing to grant a licence to allow a work to be performed in public.[16] These provisions were not repeated in the 1956 Act.[17] A second non-voluntary licence was available after 1847 to permit the importation of reprints of works into the colonies, on payment of a customs duty which was to be redistributed to authors.[18] This scheme was abandoned in 1911.[19] A third such licence was introduced by the proviso to section 3 of the 1911 Act and gave a statutory licence to reproduce for sale any work after the expiration of 25 (or, in the case of pre-1911 works, 30) years from the date of death of the author, with the rate being calculated at 10 per cent on the price at which the work was published. Concern existed as to whether such a provision conflicted with the

---

[11] The Patents, Designs, Copyright and Trade Marks (Emergency) Act 1939 (c.107), s.2, paras 29–52 et seq., below.

[12] CDPA 1988, s.144, paras 29–54 et seq., below.

[13] "Where the Commission ... finds that there is infringement of Article 85 or Article 86 of the Treaty, it may by decision require the undertakings or associations of undertakings concerned to bring such infringement to an end": Radio Telefis Eireann v EC Commission [1995] F.S.R. 530, ECJ; [1995] 4 C.M.L.R 718 and see Van der Wal, "Article 86 EC: The Limits of Compulsory Licensing". (1994) E.C.L.R. 230; Goraere, The Use and Abuse of Intellectual Property Rights (Sweet & Maxwell, London, 1996) pp.135–150; and paras 29–56 et seq., below.

[14] See paras 13–123 et seq., above.

[15] Literary Copyright Act 1842 (5 & 6 Vict. c.45), s.5. It might be noted, however, that the Statute of Anne 1709, (8 Anne c.19) contained a provision which allowed for a maximum price to be set on the sale of particular books, a provision which has been described as "analogous" to a compulsory licence. See Latman, Gorman & Ginsburg, Copyright for the Nineties (3rd ed., Matthew Bender, New York, 1989) p.4.

[16] Copyright Act 1911, s.4.

[17] The powers under the 1911 Act were never in fact used and repeal occurred in the light of the recommendations of the Gregory Committee: Report of the Copyright Committee, 1952 (Cmnd. 8662). This enabled the United Kingdom to comply with the Brussels Act (1971) revising the Berne Convention. As to the international concern these provisions had caused, see Ricketson, The Berne Convention for the Protection of Literary and Artistic Works: 1886–1986 (Kluwer, London, 1987), para.7.11.

[18] Colonial Copyright Act 1847, (10 & 11 Vict. c.95). This was introduced primarily at the behest of the Canadians, who subsequently charged a duty of 12.5 per cent. However, very little was collected: Report of the Commission on Copyright, 1878 (C-2036) paras 182–197.

[19] Copyright Act 1911, s.37; Sch.2

requirements of the Berne Convention, and the provision was not re-enacted in the 1956 Act.[20]

The fourth licence—the statutory recording licence—was introduced in 1911 and was maintained in the 1956 Act.[21] Under this licence manufacturers were entitled to make records of musical works which had previously been recorded with the consent of the copyright owner, provided the manufacturer gave the copyright owner notice of his intention to do so and paid a royalty. Further provision was made so that words previously associated with such a recording might also be reproduced.[22] The 1956 Act fixed the royalty payable at an amount equal to 6.25 per cent of the ordinary retail selling price of the record,[23] although this was subject to alteration following a public inquiry.[24] Regulations were prescribed setting out the particulars to be given by the manufacturer, including the estimated number of records intended to be sold or supplied.[25] This licence was originally introduced to encourage the growth of the then infant recording industry.[26] Despite the Whitford Committee's recommendation that the licence should remain (subject to alterations of detail),[27] the 1981 Green Paper suggested[28] and the 1986 White Paper recommended[29] its abolition. Consequently, the provisions of the 1956 Act were repealed by the 1988 Act and no equivalent scheme was substituted.[30] The decision to abolish the statutory recording licence was taken in recognition of the fact that the conditions of the market had long since changed and that there had been a breakdown of the consensus in its

---

[20] Again, repeal occurred in the light of the recommendations of the Gregory Committee: Report of the Copyright Committee, 1952 (Cmnd.8662), para.23. However, it should be noted that although the 1956 Act repealed s.3 of the 1911 Act it maintained the effect of the proviso as a defence after 1956 in relation to reproductions of pre-1957 works in respect of which the requisite notice had been given. As there was no limit set on the time before which the requisite notice could be given, it is conceivable that a notice could have been given before June 1, 1957 in respect of a work the copyright in which had then more than 25 years still to run. In such a case a licence could still be available today, despite the repeal of Sch.7 to the 1956 Act, since the general words of para.25(1) of Sch.1 to the 1988 Act would appear sufficient to preserve such a "defence". In practice, however, it is considered extremely unlikely that the proviso to s.3 of the 1911 Act continues to have any application. A suggestion that the statutory licence should be revived was rejected by the Whitford Committee: Report of the Committee to consider the Law on Copyright and Designs, 1977 (Cmnd 6732) paras 875–7.

[21] Copyright Act 1956, s.8; Copyright Act 1911, s.19. For a detailed discussion of the provisions, see *Copinger*, (12th ed.) para.827 et seq. See also *Discount Inter-Shopping Co Ltd v Micrometre Ltd* [1984] Ch. 369.

[22] Copyright Act 1956, s.8(5).

[23] s.8(2).

[24] s.8(3). An inquiry was held in 1977, but no change in the rate resulted.

[25] Copyright Royalty System (Records) Regulations, 1957 (SI 1957/866): *Copinger*, (12th ed.) paras 1737 et seq.

[26] Intellectual Property and Innovation, 1986 (Cmnd.9712) para.11.2. In the United States of America the introduction of a statutory mechanical recording licence was a response to the acts of the Aeolian Company, a piano-roll manufacturer, in purchasing the exclusive recording rights from over 80 music publishers. It was feared that this would give the Company an unbreakable hold on the market. The recording licence was thus introduced to ensure that, subject to the payment of a reasonable royalty, potential competitors would be free to release their own versions of popular recordings. See further, Rosenlund, "Compulsory Licensing of Musical Compositions for Phonorecords Under the Copyright Act of 1976," (1979) 30 Hastings L.J. 683 at 686–7.

[27] Whitford Committee: Report of the Committee to consider the Law on Copyright and Designs, 1977 (Cmnd.6732), paras 341–368.

[28] Reform of the Law relating to Copyright, Designs and Performers Protection, 1981 (Cmnd.8302), pp.18–21.

[29] Intellectual Property and Innovation 1986 (Cmnd.9712), para.11.5.

[30] The 1988 Act contained transitional provisions such that the provisions of the 1956 Act continued to apply where the prescribed notice was given by the manufacturer before August 1, 1989, but only in respect of the making of records within one year of that date and up to the number of records stated in the notice as intended to be sold. As regards licences thereafter, the matter is one of negotiation between the owners of copyright and the recording company. In general, this is effected in the UK by the Mechanical Copyright Protection Society (as to which, see para. 28–56. above). In 1991, on a reference from British Phonographic Industry Ltd the Copyright Tribunal set the rate at 8.5 per cent. This remains the rate.

favour.[31] Nor was the Government convinced that the statutory recording licence was necessary in order to maintain diversity within the recording industry.[32]

29–05   **Proposed licences.** A number of proposals for the introduction of other non-voluntary licences have been made, but not adopted: these have included proposals to replace the copyright system with a system of royalties,[33] as well as more specific proposals for compulsory licences to publish foreign works,[34] to televise any event,[35] to use musical works in television programmes,[36] for the inclusion of sound recordings in cinematographic works,[37] for the making of ephemeral recordings,[38] for use of works where it is difficult to trace the copyright owners,[39] and for the public performance and broadcasting of musical and literary works.[40] More recently interest has focused on the need for compulsory licences to be made available to allow for the creation of multimedia works. This proposal is considered in detail, below.[41]

(ii) International standards and policy considerations

29–06   **International standards: Berne Convention..**[42] One reason why so few non-voluntary licences exist in the United Kingdom is that international standards to which the United Kingdom has committed itself are generally antipathetic to such provisions. However, two provisions of the Berne Convention explicitly permit the national legislature to grant such licences.[43] Article 13 empowers each country to restrict the right of the authors of musical works and accompanying lyrics to authorise the sound recording of their works to a right to equitable remuneration.[44] Similarly, Article 11 *bis*(2) allows the author's exclusive right to authorise the communication to the public of the work, by broadcasting or related means, to be restricted to a right of equitable remuneration.[45] Although the WIPO

---

[31] Intellectual Property and Innovation 1986 (Cmnd.9712), para.11.4.

[32] Intellectual Property and Innovation 1986 (Cmnd.9712), para.11.4.

[33] Such a proposal was considered, but rejected, in the Report of the Royal Commission on Copyright, 1878 (C-2036), paras 16–22. Recently, however, there has been renewed interest in this proposal, with some commentators arguing that this might be the best way of ensuring remuneration for authors over electronic networks. For example, see Rheingold, *The Virtual Community* (Minerva, London, 1995), p.103.

[34] Scrutton, *The Law of Copyright* (John Murray, London, 1883), pp.276–77. But compare the United Kingdom's obligations under the Berne Convention. These are considered below.

[35] Gregory Committee: Report of the Copyright Committee, 1952 (Cmnd.8662), para.159

[36] Whitford Committee: Report of the Committee to consider the Law on Copyright and Designs, 1977 (Cmnd.6732), para.357.

[37] Whitford Committee: para.357.

[38] Whitford Committee: paras 359–60.

[39] Whitford Committee: paras 774–5.

[40] Monopolies and Merger Commission: A Report on the supply in the UK of the services of administering performing rights and film synchronisation rights, 1996 (Cm.3147) paras 2.96, 2.131, 10.5, 10.21, 10.31, 10.38, 10.41, 10.48, 14.134.

[41] See paras 29–69 *et seq.*, below.

[42] As to the Berne Convention generally, see paras 26–04 *et seq*, above.

[43] For a useful analysis of Berne in the context of the US jukebox licence, see Martin, "The Berne Convention and the US Compulsory License for Jukeboxes: Why the Song Could not remain the Same" (1990) J Copyright Socy USA 262 at 296–307.

[44] "Each country of the Union may impose for itself reservations and conditions on the exclusive right granted to the author of a musical work and to the author of any words, the recording of which together with the musical work has already been authorised by the latter, to authorise the sound recording of that musical work, together with such words, if any." Art.14 makes it explicit that this does not apply to cinematographic reproductions. For the full text of the Berne Convention (Paris Act, 1971), see Vol.2 at F1.

[45] "It shall be a matter for legislation in the countries of the Union to determine the conditions under which the rights mentioned in the preceding paragraph may be exercised, but those conditions ... shall not in any circumstances be prejudicial to the moral rights of the author, nor to his right to

Treaty adopted at Geneva in December 1996[46] had proposed to remove these provisions, in the end the *status quo* was maintained.[47] It may be possible to justify certain other licences under Article 9(2) as regards reproduction of works "provided that such reproduction does not conflict with a normal exploitation of the work and does not unreasonably prejudice the legitimate interests of the author"; and under Article 10(2) as regards use by way of illustration in publications for teaching provided such utilisation is compatible with fair practice.[48] It has also been suggested[49] that there might be a power to grant compulsory licences under Article 17 of the Convention, which provides that "the provisions of this Convention cannot in any way affect the right of the Government of each country of the Union to *permit*, to control, or to prohibit, by legislation or regulation, the circulation, presentation, or exhibition of any work or production".[50] The better view, however, seems to be that Article 17 is not intended to permit any general system of compulsory licences but to cover such things as the maintenance of public order and morality.[51] Over and above these provisions the United Kingdom delegation made a declaration (as opposed to a reservation) in relation to Article 11 of the Brussels Act to the effect that the Government remained free to enact such legislation as it might consider necessary in the public interest to prevent or deal with any abuse of the monopoly rights conferred upon owners of copyright.[52] It seems, therefore, that compulsory licences can be imposed to control an abuse of monopoly.[53]

Rome and Phonograms Conventions.[54] The Rome Convention states that   **29–07**
Contracting States are permitted to provide for the same kinds of limitations in respect of the works covered by the Convention "as it provides for, in its domestic laws and regulations, in connection with the protection of copyright in literary and artistic works", but that "compulsory licences may be provided for only to the extent to which they are compatible with this Convention".[55] Consequently, compulsory licences may not be imposed as regards reproduction of phonograms

---

obtain equitable remuneration." Note that Arts 13 and 11 *bis* state that the right to equitable remuneration shall " *in the absence of agreement* be fixed by competent authority" (emphasis added). A literal reading of these provisions would suggest that countries of the Union are only entitled to grant compulsory licences, they are not free to introduce a statutory licence (see para. 29–02, above). This is not, however, how the effect of this provision has historically been understood. For the full text of the Berne Convention (Paris Act, 1971), see Vol.2 at F1.

[46] See paras 24–66 *et seq*, above.

[47] Art.11 of the draft Treaty proposed the abolition of Certain Non-Voluntary Licenses within three years. It stated, "(1) Within three years of ratifying or acceding to this Treaty, Contracting Parties shall no longer provide for non-voluntary licenses under Art.11 *bis*(2) of the Berne Convention in respect of the broadcasting of a work. (2) Within three years of ratifying or acceding to this Treaty, Contracting Parties shall no longer apply the provisions of Art.13 of the Berne Convention". At the meeting in Geneva, several delegations proposed a longer phase-out period and others favoured eliminating para.(2), many expressing concerns over possible anti-competitive conduct by recording companies. Ultimately, it was agreed that the Article be deleted in its entirety and the existing provisions of the Berne Convention were maintained.

[48] See further, Ricketson, *The Berne Convention for the Protection of Literary and Artistic Works: 1886–1986* (Kluwer, London, 1987), para.16.28.

[49] See Ricketson, *The Berne Convention for the Protection of Literary and Artistic Works: 1886–1986* (Kluwer, London, 1987), para.9.72.

[50] Berne Convention (Paris Act, 1971), Art.17 (emphasis added); Vol.2 at F1. See also para. 28–19, above.

[51] See further, Ricketson, *The Berne Convention for the Protection of Literary and Artistic Works: 1886–1986* (Kluwer, London, 1987), para.9.72. It should also be noted that attempts by the UK and Australian Governments to amend Art.17 in this respect were rejected at the Stockholm revision conference in 1967, at least partly on the grounds that the amendment was superfluous: *ibid.*, para.9.73.

[52] Ricketson, *The Berne Convention for the Protection of Literary and Artistic Works: 1886–1986* (Kluwer, London, 1987), para 9.73.

[53] See para. 29–54, below.

[54] As to these, see paras 24–88 *et seq*. and 24–109 *et seq.*, above, respectively.

[55] Rome Convention for the Protection of Performers, Producers of Phonograms and Broadcasting

since that would be inconsistent with Article 10, nor in relation to the rebroadcasting, fixation or reproduction of broadcasts (which would be inconsistent with Article 13) but may be imposed as regards secondary uses of phonograms under Article 12, since this Article only requires that Contracting States ensure that a remuneration is paid for the broadcasting or communication to the public of phonograms.[56]

Article 6 of the Convention for the Protection of Producers of Phonograms Against Unauthorised Duplication of their Phonograms (1971)[57] states that compulsory licences to make or import duplicates of phonograms may not be permitted unless (a) duplication is for use solely for the purpose of teaching or scientific research; (b) the licence does not permit export of the duplicates; and (c) an equitable remuneration, linked to the number of duplicates to be made, is paid.

29–08   Policy considerations. A second reason why the law has rarely allowed for non-voluntary licences is that they are seen as a "suspect device in copyright law generally".[58] They are "administratively cumbersome, unlikely to arrive at a correct rate,[59] and contrary to copyright's overall free market philosophy".[60] Nevertheless, such licences provide a compromise of the unrestricted exercise of intellectual property rights that the legislature occasionally finds attractive. It is not possible to characterise by way of a single principle the circumstances in which the legislature has in the past made copyright subject to such licences. Rather they have been employed to deal with a number of difficult situations. Some of the factors which seem to influence the choice of non-voluntary licences are as follows:

   (i)   where a change in the law (such as extension of the term of copyright, or the addition of new rights) alters the assumptions upon which owners may have acquired copyright and potential users planned their activities[61] ;

   (ii) where in the light of technological change (such as the emergence of sound recordings), the refusal to license the use of copyright works might impede the emergence of certain industries or activities, or a negotiated price might give the copyright owner an unjustified windfall[62] ;

 (iii) where the copyright owner has failed to supply the needs of the public and other producers and distributors are available[63] ;

 (iv) where copyright owners have refused to license use of their works or have

---

Organisations, 1961, Art.15(2). For the text of the Convention, see Vol.2 at F5. It might also be possible to justify a limited number of compulsory licences under Art.15(1), which allows for exceptions to the protection guaranteed as regards private use, reporting of current events, ephemeral recordings and teaching and scientific research.

[56] See para. 29–25, below.

[57] The text of the Convention is set out in Vol.2 at F8.

[58] Ginsburg, "Creation and Commercial Value: Copyright Protection of Works of Information" (1990) 90 Col. L.Rev. 1865 at 1872.

[59] See further, Scrutton, *The Law of Copyright* (John Murray, London, 1883), at 14.

[60] Ginsburg, "Creation and Commercial Value: Copyright Protection of Works of Information" (1990) 90 Col. L.Rev. 1865 at 1924.

[61] See, for example, the provisions relating to revived copyright (see paras 29–41 *et seq.*, below).

[62] See, for example, the provisions relating to the statutory recording licence (see para. 29–04, above) and the proposals for a multimedia licence (see para. 29–69, below).

[63] Scrutton, *The Law of Copyright* (John Murray, London, 1883), suggests that compulsory licences should be available in the following exceptional circumstances (i) as regards works first published abroad where the author's interests do not immediately lead them to supply the work; (ii) where the social organisation of a country is in its infancy; and (iii) where a publisher fails to supply works within a reasonable time at a reasonable price. Also note the special regime for developing countries contained in the Berne Convention, as to which, see Ricketson, *The Berne Convention for the Protection of Literary and Artistic Works: 1886–1986* (Kluwer, London, 1987), Ch.11. See also, Ch.24.

imposed conditions which do not reflect the purposes for which copyright is granted;

  (v) where there is evidence of abuse of monopoly[64] ;

 (vi) where there exist otherwise insuperable transaction costs or delays[65] ;

(vii) where a negotiated price would be too high and it is deemed desirable to subsidise users, for example those which are public institutions.[66]

C. EXISTING COMPULSORY LICENCES

(i) Information about programmes

Introduction. The Broadcasting Act 1990 introduced provisions into the 1988 Act entitling publishers, once certain conditions are satisfied, to reproduce information about programmes which are to be broadcast. The scheme of the Broadcasting Act is that these provisions are to take effect as if they were included in Chapter III of Part I of the 1988 Act (acts permitted in relation to copyright works).[67] Some minor amendments to these provisions were made by the Broadcasting Act 1996 and the Communications Act 2003.[68] More important are the likely implications of the Copyright and Rights in Databases Regulations[69] for these provisions. It seems that the Database Regulations may affect these provisions in two key respects: first, they may affect the question of whether copyright can subsist in listings of programmes and second, it seems that the compulsory licence is not available in relation to the database right. However, since the precise effect of the Database Regulations is unclear and since an understanding of the background to introduction of the compulsory licence remains important, the compulsory licence as it affects copyright in programme listings will first be considered. But when reading this section it should be remembered that it may be that copyright no longer subsists in such listings.

29–09

Background. The proprietors of the *Radio Times* and *TV Times* had a long-standing policy of asserting copyright in the listings of their programmes. By refusing to grant licences to publish such listings more than two or three days prior to broadcast they were each able to use this copyright to create a monopoly over weekly listings of their respective programmes. As a result, no comprehensive weekly guide to programme schedules was available. This remained the position until the owners of *Time Out* magazine decided to produce a comprehensive weekly listing by publishing in advance details of dates, titles and times of trans-

29–10

---

[64] See paras 29–54 *et seq.* below and para. 29–06, above.

[65] See further, Cassler, "Copyright Compulsory Licences—are they Coming or Going?" (1990) 37 Jo. Copyright Socy USA 231 at 249–250. Professor Merges, has criticised the use of compulsory licences in these circumstances, arguing that copyright owners will often form collecting societies in order to overcome transaction cost problems and that such societies tend to be more efficient than compulsory licence schemes, in particular, because of their ability to tailor schemes to the needs of different classes of user. It should be noted, however, that Professor Merges' criticisms are primarily aimed at statutory licensing schemes, that is where the rate is fixed by statute. Although Professor Merges argues that collective licensing will still tend to be more efficient than "judicially administered" schemes he only refers in passing to the possibility of setting up a "a special rate court" (such as the Copyright Tribunal). See Merges, "Contracting into Liability Rules: Intellectual Property Rights and Collective Rights Organizations" (1996) 84 Cal. L.Rev. 1293, in particular, at 1316–1317.

[66] See, *e.g.* the Australian Copyright Act 1968 (Cth). See further, Lahore, *Copyright and Designs* (Butterworths, Sydney, 1996) paras 28,005; 28,170–28,205; 28,230–28,370.

[67] Broadcasting Act 1990, Sch.17, para.7(1): "This Schedule and the Copyright, Designs and Patents Act 1988 shall have effect as if the Schedule were included in Ch.III of Pt I of that Act, and that Act shall have effect as if proceedings under this Schedule were listed in s.149 of that Act (jurisdiction of the Copyright Tribunal)." The provisions of the 1990 Act are set out at in Vol.2 at A2.i.

[68] 1996 (c.55) and 2003 (c.21) respectively.

[69] SI 1997/3032.

mission of selected television programmes for the following week, those details having been taken from the proprietors' listings. In the resulting litigation[70] *Time Out* argued that the listings were not protected by copyright on the basis that there is no copyright in information. This argument was rejected, however, and the injunctions sought by the proprietors were granted.[71] This case caused some disquiet,[72] and in 1984 the Office of Fair Trading produced a report in which it concluded that broadcasters were involved in a course of conduct which constituted an anti-competitive practice which affected the public interest and therefore referred the situation to the Monopolies and Mergers Commission (MMC) under section 5 of the Competition Act 1980.[73] In 1985, the MMC reported. While it found that refusal to grant licences amounted to an anti-competitive practice within section 2 of the Competition Act, it was divided equally as to whether it was contrary to the public interest.[74]

Despite the MMC's inconclusive report, the Government decided to take action to bring the two monopolies to an end following the findings of the Select Committee on Home Affairs in June 1988, and a ruling of the European Commission in relation to an analogous situation in the Republic of Ireland in December 1988.[75] The Home Secretary thus announced in September 1989 the Government's intention of introducing a compulsory licensing scheme. Accordingly, the Broadcasting Act 1990 introduced provisions into the 1988 Act entitling publishers, provided certain conditions are satisfied, to reproduce information about programmes which are to be broadcast. These provisions are to be found in section 176 of and Schedule 17 to the Broadcasting Act 1990.[76]

29–11   **The duty.** By section 176(1) a person providing a programme service to which the section applies has a duty to make available information relating to the programmes to be included in the service to any person wishing to publish in the United Kingdom any such information. The term "making available" is distin-

---

[70] *ITP v Time Out and Elliott* and *BBC v Time Out and Elliott* [1984] F.S.R. 64.

[71] The position in the United Kingdom is this respect was quite different from that which operated in most other countries, except the Republic of Ireland (as which see *Radio Telefis Eireann and others v Magill TV Guide Ltd* [1990] F.S.R. 561). See *Copinger* (14th ed.) para.29–10, n.72.

[72] Earlier criticism of the publishing arrangements appeared in the Third Report of the House of Commons Estimates Committee (Session 1968–9) P.P. Vol.13 xxvii, para.71 (suggesting a single combined weekly listings journal) and Report of the Committee on the Future of Broadcasting, 1977 (Cmnd.6753) paras 29.33–29.42 (the majority taking the view that the monopoly did not operate in the public interest and that the broadcasters should be obliged to waive their copyright in programme information, if necessary on payment of an agreed fee).

[73] *BBC and ITP Ltd : The Publication of Programme Information*, Office of Fair Trading, December 13, 1984.

[74] *The British Broadcasting Corporation and Independent Television Publications Limited: A report on the policies and practices on the BBC and ITP of limiting the publication by others of advance programme information*, 1985 (Cmnd. 9614). It should be noted that the European Court of First Instance and the European Court of Justice later declared that a refusal to license the use of such listings was an abuse of dominant position and contrary to Art.86 of the Treaty of Rome. See paras 29–57 *et seq.* below.

[75] Commission Decision 89/205/EEC of December 21, 1988 [1989] OJ L78/43; [1989] 4 C.M.L.R. 757. In July 1991, the Court of First Instance of the European Communities (Second Chamber) decided *Radio Telefis Eireann v EC Commission* [1991] 4 C.M.L.R. 586, rejecting the broadcasting organisations' appeal against the finding of the Commission that it had infringed Art.86. In June 1994, Advocate-General Gulmann delivered his opinion in support of the broadcasters, but in April 1995 the ECJ upheld the decision of the Commission and the Court of First Instance. See paras 29–57 *et seq.* below.

[76] Set out in Vol.2 at A2.i. The original Bill (Broadcasting Bill No. 9 (1989–90) December 12, 1989) did not include such provisions, which were added in Standing Committee. See further, the Report of the Debates of House of Commons Standing Committee F in 1990, cols 1346–1384; cols 1465–1501.

guishable from that of supplying, since making available suggests notions of accessibility rather than delivery.[77]

The providers. Persons providing a programme service to which the section applies are[78] : the BBC for television and national radio services provided for reception in the United Kingdom; licensees of television programme services subject to regulation by OFCOM[79] ; the Welsh Authority for public television services provided by it[80]; and licensees of any national service subject to regulation by Ofcom,[81] any simulcast radio service,[82] and any national digital sound programme service subject to regulation by Ofcom.[83]   **29–12**

The information. The information which is to be provided consists of the titles of the programmes and the time of their proposed inclusion in a programme service,[84] but need not include information about any advertisement.[85] This matches the information with respect to which copyright was claimed in the *Time Out* case.[86] There is no requirement that the person make available "billing" material, that is the copyright material which adds flesh to this skeleton,[87] though this may be available from a variety of sources.[88] However, it may be more significant that the Act fails to provide any duty to provide information as to bar codings which set automatic video recording machines.[89]   **29–13**

Timing. The duty is to make the information available as soon after it has been prepared as is reasonably practicable. Moreover, this general requirement is limited by a principle of equity between publishers to the effect that information must be made available to any publisher not later than when it is made available to any other publisher. Failure to provide listings to all publishers at the same   **29–14**

---

[77] *News Group Newspapers v ITP Ltd* [1993] R.P.C. 173 at 190. Thus a broadcaster could meet the obligation by allowing staff or agents to copy the master copy, although in practice copies are made and sent to broadcasters: *ibid*. However, where the broadcaster has assigned future copyright it may be that the making and supplying of copies will infringe that copyright, as there is no obligation to make such copies and thus no defence of statutory authority will apply. (As to the defence of statutory authority see CDPA 1988, s.50: para. 9–131).

[78] Broadcasting Act 1990, s.176(7).

[79] OFCOM (the Office of Communications) was established under s.1 of the Office of the Communications Act 2002 (c.11). The ITC's functions under Pt I of the Broadcasting Act 1990 (as to which see *Copinger* (14th ed.) n.80 to para.29–13) were transferred to OFCOM by s.2 of the Communications Act 2003 (c.21) with effect from December 29, 2003: see the Office of Communications Act 2002 (Commencement No.3) and Communications Act 2003 (Commencement No.2) Order 2003, SI 2003/3142, reg.3(1) and Sch.1. The television services regulated by OFCOM are now listed in s.211 of the Communications Act 2003. They include independent terrestrial services (Channels 3, 4 and 5), cable services, and domestic and non-domestic satellite broadcasting services. Satellite and digital services provided by persons under the jurisdiction of the United Kingdom for the purposes of the Television Without Frontiers Directive (Directive 89/552/EEC) are also included: see s.211(2)(a) and (b).

[80] Within the meaning of Pt 2 of Sch.12 to the Communications Act 2003.

[81] See Broadcasting Act 1990, s.126(1) and Communications Act 2003, s.245(4)(a).

[82] Added by the Broadcasting Act 1996, s.148(1), Sch.10, para.10. "Simulcast radio service" means a service provided by a person for broadcasting in digital form and corresponding to a service which is a national radio service within the meaning of Pt 3 of [the Broadcasting Act 1990] and is provided by that person: Broadcasting Act 1996, s.41(2), as substituted by s.256(1) of the Communications Act 2003.

[83] Added by the Broadcasting Act 1996, s 148(1), Sch.10, para.10.

[84] Broadcasting Act 1990, s.176(2).

[85] s.176(8).

[86] *ITP v Time Out and Elliott* and *BBC v Time Out and Elliott* [1984] F.S.R. 64. Also see *Hansard*, HL Vol.521, col.1700. The *Magill* decision was also limited to consideration of this information.

[87] *News Group Newspapers v ITP Ltd* [1993] R.P.C. 173.

[88] Consequently, it is probably not information with respect to which the broadcasting companies have a dominant position.

[89] Report of the Debates of the House of Commons Standing Committee F in 1990, col.1375 (Mr Gale).

time would thus be a breach of statutory duty.[90] As regards weekly listings, the statute also lays down a minimum period. It says that in the case of information in respect of all the programmes to be included in the service in any period of seven days, the duty is to make the information available not later than the beginning of the preceding period of 14 days, or such other number of days as may be prescribed by the Secretary of State by order.[91] Early versions of the Bill referred simply to a duty to make available at the publisher's request such information as he might reasonably require.[92] However, the issue of timing was sensitive, since the aim was to provide a realistic opportunity of allowing others to publish a rival weekly publication, without giving unwarranted information to rival broadcasters who could then alter their schedules.[93] The period of 14 days reflected previous practice according to which the final listings went to the *TV Times* 10–17 days before transmission.[94] A publisher may ask for skeleton schedules before that point and the general duty applies. There does not appear to be an entitlement to updating information.[95]

29–15   **Conditions.** The obligation to provide information is not satisfied if the information is provided on terms, other than terms as to copyright, prohibiting or restricting publication in the United Kingdom by the publisher.[96]

29–16   **The recipient/licensee.** The information is to be made available to a publisher, not in respect of each publication, so when calculating the terms of payment one flat fee is paid per publisher, with rates thereafter calculated according to circulation and usage—not per title.[97]

29–17   **The compulsory licence.** The Broadcasting Act 1990 makes further provision to enable information provided under the duty outlined above to be reproduced and published, by providing for a compulsory licence scheme, the provisions of which are set out in Schedule 17 to that Act.[98]

29–18   **The licensor.** For the purposes of the compulsory licence, the Broadcasting Act proceeds on the basis that the provider of the programme service has the right to grant licences. Thus the person to be approached for the licence is the programme service provider, even though the copyright in works containing information as to scheduling may have been assigned to another person. Schedule 17 to the Broadcasting Act 1990 therefore provides that the person providing the programme service, rather than the assignee, is to be treated as the owner of the copyright for the purposes of licensing any act restricted by the copyright,[99] but

[90] *Hansard*, HL Vol.521, col.1701.
[91] Broadcasting Act 1990, s.176(3)(b).
[92] House of Commons Bill No. 100, Parliamentary Papers Vol.3 (1989–90), Clause 164(1).
[93] Report of the Debates of the House Standing Committee F in 1990, cols 1351–2; 1376; *Hansard*, HL Vol.521, col.1701.
[94] Report of the Debates of the House of Commons Standing Committee F in 1990, col.1371. This was a House of Lords' Amendment: Lords Amendments to the Broadcasting Bill, House of Commons Bill No. 202, 26 October 1990 Parliamentary Papers (1989–90) Vol.5.
[95] *News Group Newspapers v ITP Ltd* [1993] R.P.C. 173 at 190.
[96] Broadcasting Act 1990, s.176(5). Note that this provision does not appear broad enough to prevent a broadcaster from relying on database right. See further para. 29–24, below.
[97] *News Group Newspapers v ITP Ltd* [1993] R.P.C. 173 at 184–5.
[98] For transitional provisions, see *Copinger* (14th ed.) para.29–19.
[99] Broadcasting Act 1990, Sch.17, para.1(2). Prior to the Broadcasting Act such assignments had been made by BBC to BBC Enterprises, and by ITV and Channel 4 to ITP, which in turn had been acquired by Reed International.

the broadcaster must then account to the assignee for payments received for the rights to publish.[1]

Obtaining the compulsory licence. The compulsory licence is available where the programme service provider[2] refuses to grant the publisher a licence on terms as to duration and payment which are acceptable to the publisher.[3] The publisher must first give notice of his intention to exercise the right to the programme service provider, asking him to propose terms of payment.[4] After receipt of any such proposal (assuming that it is unacceptable) or after the expiry of a reasonable time, the publisher must then give the programme service provider reasonable notice of the date on which he proposes to begin exercising the right and the terms of payment which he proposes. It seems that one month's notice would in most situations be reasonable.[5] The publisher must also give reasonable notice to the Copyright Tribunal of his intention to exercise the right and of the date on which he proposes to do so, and also apply to the Tribunal to settle terms of payment.[6] **29–19**

The licence. Once a publisher has done all these things, and whether or not the Tribunal has yet settled terms of payment, the publisher, after the date specified in his notice to the programme service provider, and if he makes the required payments, shall be in the same position as if he held a licence.[7] Thus, where the publisher "does any act in circumstances in which the paragraph applies", he shall be in the same position as regards infringement of copyright as if he had at all material times been the holder of a licence granted by the programme service provider to do such acts. This licence also covers anything done on his behalf,[8] and applies to any act restricted by the copyright in works containing the information. Thus where, for example, the information is contained in a literary work, it apparently follows that the licence will extend to any act restricted by the copyright in such work. The publisher may therefore reproduce and publish the information in a newspaper or magazine (though this involves the restricted acts of reproduction, adaptation and issuing)[9] and presumably may broadcast the information, including, for example, on teletext. **29–20**

Payment. The required payments, which are to be made at not less than quarterly intervals in arrears,[10] are those determined by the Copyright Tribunal. If no such determination has yet been made, the required payments are those proposed by the programme service provider in response to the request from the publisher or, **29–21**

---

[1] See the Report of the Debates of the House of Commons Standing Committee F in 1990, cols 1358, 1377.

[2] Or the assignee in the case of an assignment made before September 29, 1989: Broadcasting Act 1990, Sch.17, para.1(3)(b).

[3] Broadcasting Act 1990, Sch.17, para.2(1)(b). Note that the reference to refusing to grant a licence includes failing to do so within a reasonable time of being asked: Broadcasting Act 1990, Sch.17, para.2(2).

[4] Broadcasting Act 1990, Sch.17, para.3(1).

[5] An amendment proposed in the Committee stage of the House of Lords suggested requiring a prospective publisher to give both the broadcaster and the Copyright Tribunal three months' notice. This was rejected as unduly slanting the scheme against the publisher: *Hansard*, HL Vol.521, col.1702–3. The Government suggested that one month's notice would be reasonable as regards notice to the broadcaster and the Tribunal: *Hansard*, HL Vol.522, col.852. In *News Group Newspapers v ITP Ltd* [1993] R.P.C. 173, MGN applied on February 28, 1991 to publish commencing on March 1, 1991. No objection was made, but this hardly appears to be reasonable notice. In contrast, ITP had applied on January 30, 1991, to commence on March 1, 1991.

[6] Broadcasting Act 1990, Sch.17, para.3(2).

[7] Broadcasting Act 1990, Sch.17, para.4(1).

[8] Broadcasting Act 1990, Sch.17, para.7(2).

[9] *News Group Newspapers v ITP Ltd* [1993] R.P.C. 173 at 180.

[10] Broadcasting Act 1990, Sch.17, para.4(2).

if no such proposal has been made or is considered by the publisher to be unreasonably high, those proposed by the publisher in his notice to the programme service provider.[11] If the publisher were to offer a derisory sum, the Tribunal might well award costs against him.[12]

29–22 **The Copyright Tribunal.** Where an application is made to the Copyright Tribunal to settle terms of payment, the Tribunal may make such order as it may determine to be reasonable in the circumstances.[13] During the passage of the Broadcasting Act calls were made for the Copyright Tribunal to be provided with guidance to help it with its "Solomonic task" of determining rates of payment.[14] More specifically, it was suggested that the statute should make clear whether the purpose of the payment was to reimburse costs incurred by the broadcaster or to compensate for loss of copyright.[15] The Government declined to include any such directions, arguing that it was for the parties to a dispute to bring any relevant considerations to the Tribunal's attention. In particular, it rejected an amendment requiring the Tribunal to distinguish between the copyright and information elements of the value of a work and to ignore the latter when assessing the licence fee. The jurisdiction is thus "wide and unfettered"[16] and previous decisions over licensing schemes do not provide a compelling analogy.[17]

In *News Group Newspapers v ITP Ltd*[18] a number of publishers sought to have the terms of payment set for use of information concerning BBC and ITV schedules.[19] The publishers argued that the terms should not exceed the cost of supply of the information, whereas the broadcasters asserted that the rates should reflect the value of the copyright in the statutory information. This represented "a great gulf both in terms of principle and of money".[20] The Copyright Tribunal, in exercising its discretion, was concerned about evidence that after the enactment of the 1990 Act a large number of local papers had stopped publishing listings. Indeed the Copyright Tribunal called this "a serious matter, contrary to the public interest and not in accordance with the policy and objects of the 1990 Act". The Tribunal saw its task as being to promote dissemination of the information, rather than to protect the financial interests of the broadcaster as copyright owner.[21] This was because "[t]he objects of the 1990 Act include making a wide range of programmes and types of broadcasting available and that is only worth doing if individuals can easily find out what is on so that they can choose for themselves what they want to see and hear". It rejected the relevance of any exercise to

---

[11] Sch.17, para.4(3). The publisher's fee was preferred to the copyright owner's "because the principal reason for the legislation is to open up the market:" Report of the Debates of the House of Commons Standing Committee F in 1990, col.1381.

[12] See previous note.

[13] Broadcasting Act 1990, Sch.17, para.5(1). As to the Copyright Tribunal generally, see paras 29–93 *et seq.* below, and as to its procedure see paras 29–159 *et seq.*, below.

[14] See *Hansard*, HL Vol.521, col.1704. Also see the Report of the Debates of the House of Commons Standing Committee F in 1990, col.1353.

[15] Report of the Debates of the House of Commons Standing Committee F in 1990, col.1383; *Hansard*, HL Vol.521, col.1700.

[16] *News Group Newspapers v ITP Ltd* [1993] R.P.C. 173 at 180.

[17] *News Group Newspapers v ITP Ltd* [1993] R.P.C. 173 at 187.

[18] See previous note.

[19] The Tribunal held there was no reason to treat the BBC and ITV differently: *News Group Newspapers v ITP Ltd* [1993] R.P.C. 173 at 185.

[20] *News Group Newspapers v ITP Ltd* [1993] R.P.C. 173 at 186.

[21] *News Group Newspapers v ITP Ltd* [1993] R.P.C. 173 at 186. Thus, although the interests of the broadcasters were taken into account, these were considered to be of only secondary importance: see at 188.

second guess what "free negotiations" would have produced as "entirely theoretical and unreliable".[22]

The Tribunal indicated that little assistance was provided by analogies with other licensing schemes or patent licences.[23] Moreover, it took the view that the inclusion of the statutory information could not been shown to be responsible for any "significant and calculable incremental profit" to publishers. However, while the Tribunal said that the problem of proving a causative link between the use of the information and the profits made by newspapers was insuperable, it held that the rate to be paid should relate to the extent of usage by the publisher. This was best calculated by reference to circulation and to the number of days for which the information was published, with a minimum set to ensure that the marginal costs of supply were met. The Tribunal assessed the basic costs of the broadcasters at £125,000 each and the administrative costs at £200 per publisher. Consequently, it imposed a rate of 0.003p for each day multiplied by the circulation with a £200 minimum per publisher. It calculated that this would give a return to the broadcasters of £500,000 above costs, but stated that even were this as high as £1,600,000 that would not be unreasonable. The BBC and ITP appealed, but a hearing was avoided by a compromise of 0.004p.[24]

The Order. The order has effect from the date the publisher begins to exercise **29–23** the right, so that any necessary adjustments in the amounts which have fallen due must be made.[25] An application may subsequently be made to review the order.[26] However, an application for review shall not be made, except with the special leave of the Tribunal, within 12 months from the date of the order or of the decision on a previous application. Similarly, for orders intended to be in force for 15 months or less, no review is to take place until the last three months before expiry.[27] The provisions relating to such applications are analogous to those relating to the Tribunal's jurisdiction over licensing schemes, which are dealt with elsewhere.[28] On such an application, the Tribunal shall consider the matter and confirm or vary the original order as it may determine to be reasonable in the circumstances.[29] The order made on such an application is to have effect from the date on which it is made or such later date as may be specified by the Tribunal.[30]

The Database Regulations. As has been noted, the Database Regulations may **29–24** affect the provisions considered above in two key respects:

(1) The Regulations may affect the question of whether copyright can subsist in listings of programmes. Here two subsidiary questions need to be asked: (a) do programme listings fall within the definition of a "database"? and, if so, (b) are programme listings likely to satisfy the new originality test?

As to (a), it should be noted that a database is defined as "a collection of independent works, data or other materials which are arranged in a systematic or methodical way, and are individually accessible by electronic or other means".[31] As a collection of information about television programmes that are to be shown, arranged according to time and date, television listings would seem to fall squarely within this definition.

---

[22] *News Group Newspapers v ITP Ltd* [1993] R.P.C. 173 at 187.
[23] *News Group Newspapers v ITP Ltd* [1993] R.P.C. 173 at 187.
[24] [1993] E.M.L.R. 133.
[25] Broadcasting Act 1990, Sch.17, para.5(2).
[26] Sch.17, para.6(1).
[27] Sch.17, para.6(2).
[28] See para. 29–108, below.
[29] Sch.17, para.6(3).
[30] Sch.17, para.6(4).
[31] CDPA 1988, s.3A(1), as inserted by the Copyright and Rights in Databases Regulations 1997 (SI

As to (b), as is explained in detail elsewhere,[32] henceforth copyright will only subsist in a database if the database satisfies a new originality test, that is, where "by reason of the selection or arrangement of the contents of the database the database constitutes the author's own intellectual creation".[33] This test of originality was introduced in order to bring the position in the United Kingdom in line with the Database Directive.[34] Since the Directive seeks to harmonise the test of originality for databases throughout Europe and since, as has been seen, programme listings would not qualify for copyright protection in most European countries, it is suggested that programme listings may well not now normally qualify for copyright protection.[35]

(2) If the above analysis is correct then it seems that copyright no longer subsists in programme listings, thus rendering redundant the compulsory licence in so far as it affects *copyright* in the database.[36] However, it is also important to consider the likely impact of the database right. Again two subsidiary questions need to be asked: (a) does the database right subsist in programme listings? and, if so, (b) does the compulsory licence apply to the database right?

As to (a), as is explained in detail elsewhere,[37] the database right subsists in a database if there has been a "substantial investment in obtaining, verifying or presenting the contents of the database".[38] It is suggested that (depending on the facts) television listings probably do not fall within this definition, because the investment concerned relates directly to the *production* of the information, rather than to obtaining, verifying or presenting it.[39]

As to (b), it seems clear that the compulsory licence available under the Broadcasting Act will not extend to the database right, given that the Act refers to the copyright owner and does not mention the database right, and

---

1997/3032); the text of the Regulations, in so far as not inserted into the 1988 Act, is set out in Vol.2 at A3.iv; and see, generally, Ch.18.

[32] See para. 3–146, above.

[33] CDPA 1988, s.3A(2) and see para. 3–146, above. Copyright continues to subsist in existing databases (*i.e.* databases created on or before March 27, 1996). However, because of the short commercial life of television listings this is not important for present purposes.

[34] Council Directive No. 96/9 of March 11, 1996 on the legal protection of databases, Art.3 [1996] O.J. L77; for the full text of the Directive, see Vol.2 at H6.

[35] However, it is impossible to be certain about this conclusion, in particular, because courts in the United Kingdom have historically been prepared to look at the originality that lies "behind" the work. See, in particular, *Ladbroke v William Hill* [1964] 1 All E.R. 465.

[36] Even if this analysis is incorrect, and it is held that copyright continues to subsist in programme listings, it will still be important to determine whether the compulsory licence applies to the database right, since copyright and database right apply independently of each other: Database Regulations (SI 1997/3032), reg.13(2).

[37] See Ch.18.

[38] Database Regulations (SI 1997/3032), reg.13(1).

[39] See in particular the *Fixtures Marketing* cases (Case 46/02 *Fixtures Marketing Ltd v Oy Veikkaus AB*; Case C-338-02 *Fixtures Marketing Ltd v Svenska Spel AB*; and Case C-444/02 *Fixtures Marketing Ltd v Organismos prognostikon agonon podosfairou AE (OPAP)*) and Case C-203/02 *The British Horseracing Board Ltd v William Hill Organization Ltd*. In the *Fixtures Marketing* cases, the question was whether database right subsisted in Premier League fixture lists. On the facts, considerable investment was involved in determining the dates, times and team pairings for particular matches. However, the ECJ held that this investment was irrelevant because it did not relate to the obtaining, verification and presentation of the data but rather to the creation of the data which formed the subject matter of the database. At the same time, the obtaining, verification and presentation of the data did not require any significant independent investment. Accordingly, no database right subsisted in such lists. See also Ch.18. Depending on the facts, it seems likely that a similar result would be reached in respect of television listings.

there is no general provision in the Database Regulations which extends such a licence to incorporate the database right.[40]

If, contrary to what is suggested above, database right does subsist in programme lists, at first this might seem to present the possibility that broadcasters would seek to use the database right to re-establish their previous monopoly. However, this would be unlikely, since to do so would be a breach of competition law and the Competition Commission (and in some cases the Secretary of State) has a separate power to order that licences in respect of the database right shall be available as of right following an adverse market investigation report.[41] Moreover, the market for weekly television listings has changed beyond all recognition since the compulsory licence was introduced and it is by no means certain that broadcasters would wish to return to the previous position, even if they could legally do so. Nevertheless, it might well be possible for broadcasters to argue for a higher licence fee for use of their programme listings. In particular, it could be said that the rate set by the Tribunal under the compulsory licence applicable to the copyright in the database is not appropriate for a licence of database right, since, as has been seen, in arriving at a rate the Tribunal saw its task as being to promote dissemination of the information, rather than to protect the financial interests of the broadcaster, a conclusion which was based on the objects of the Broadcasting Act 1990, which (it could be argued) have no relevance to the database right.

(ii) Use as of right of sound recordings in broadcasts and cable programme services

General. The Broadcasting Act 1990 introduced a new compulsory licence allowing persons to include sound recordings in broadcasts or cable programme services.[42] The statutory right is available against a licensing body which either restricts the amount of needletime, that is imposes restrictions on the total or proportionate time in which such recordings can be played, or imposes unacceptable terms as to payment. After complying with certain procedural formalities, the broadcaster may broadcast the recording and "shall be in the same position as regards infringement of copyright as if he had at all material times been the holder of a licence granted by the owner of the copyright in question".[43] Some minor amendments to these provisions were made by the Broadcasting Act 1996 and the Copyright and Related Rights Regulations 2003.[44] These limitations on the copyright in sound recordings are permissible under the Rome Convention, which merely requires Contracting States to guarantee to the producers of phonograms

29–25

---

[40] Note that the Database Regulations (SI 1997/3032) do provide a general defence of statutory authority (Sch.1, para.6). However, this would not assist a publisher since the compulsory licence only refers to infringement of copyright. As has been seen, the compulsory licence provisions apply as if they were included in Ch.III of Pt 1 of the 1988 Act and s.28(1) of that Act provides that "the provisions of this Chapter ... relate only to the question of infringement of copyright and do not affect any other right or obligation".

[41] Database Regulations (SI 1997/3032), Sch.2, para.15(1), as amended by the Enterprise Act 2002 (Consequential and Supplemental Provisions) Order 2003 (SI 2003/1398) Art.2 and Sch., para.31, with effect from June 20, 2003. This provision closely follows the wording of s.144, as to which see paras 29–54 *et seq.* and paras 29–297 *et seq.*, below.

[42] These provisions are additional to the general jurisdiction of the Copyright Tribunal to control licensing bodies and licensing schemes, as to which see paras 29–105 *et seq.*, below.

[43] CDPA 1988, s.135C(1).

[44] SI 2003/2498.

an equitable remuneration from (as opposed to exclusive right to control) the broadcasting or communication to the public of published phonograms.[45]

29–26   **Background.** Under the 1911 Act sound recordings were equated with musical works, but the scope of this copyright was initially unclear. In the *Cawardine* case decided in 1934[46] it was held that the right conferred on the manufacturers of sound recordings by the 1911 Act included a public performance right. Thereafter, these performance rights were administered on behalf of most record companies by Phonographic Performance Limited (PPL).[47] It remained unclear whether the broadcasting of a work amounted to a public performance, but to the extent that the right to control broadcasts existed, these rights fell to be administered on behalf of record companies by PPL, as part of its collective exercise of public performance rights more generally.[48] Hence, when the Copyright Act 1956 expressly granted the owner of copyright in a sound recording the exclusive right to broadcast the work, these rights also came to be administered by PPL. It remains the case that broadcasting rights, together now with cablecasting rights, in respect of sound recordings are usually exercised collectively in the United Kingdom by PPL. The licensing terms are therefore subject to review by the Copyright Tribunal (formerly the Performing Right Tribunal).

Prior to 1988 the licences granted by PPL to radio broadcasters were typically limited as regards the length of the periods in which the broadcaster could perform PPL's repertoire.[49] In 1988 the Monopolies and Mergers Commission (MMC) was requested to report on practices relating to the collective licensing of sound recordings for broadcasting and public performance. Pending the completion of the Report moves to introduce provisions to force an end to needletime restrictions were stifled.[50] The MMC Report[51] concluded that the needletime restriction was an anti-competitive practice which adversely affected radio licensees and that it should be abandoned.[52] The MMC therefore recommended the imposition of an obligation on PPL to permit the use of its repertoire in return for equitable remuneration, initially on the basis of what the licensee thought "appropriate", pending determination by the Copyright Tribunal as to equitable remuneration.[53]

29–27   **The 1988 Act amended.** The 1990 Broadcasting Act gave effect to the recommendations of the MMC.[54] With effect from February 1, 1991, a compulsory licence of the kind proposed, with unlimited needletime, was incorporated into the 1988 Act by introducing into it seven new sections, sections 135A to 135G, which provided for a statutory right to include sound recordings in broadcasts and cable programme services. The scheme of the new provisions followed that

---

[45] Rome Convention for the Protection of Performers, Producers of Phonograms and Broadcasting Organisations, Art.12 (and see para. 24–99, above).

[46] *Gramophone Co. Ltd v Stephen Cawardine & Co.* [1934] Ch.450.

[47] As to PPL, see para. 28–60, above.

[48] See *Copinger* (13th ed.) para.8–102, n.8 and further discussion in earlier editions.

[49] These "needletime" restrictions were first imposed in 1946 in response to pressure from the Musicians' Union. Independent radio companies were generally limited to a total of nine hours per day: MMC Report, Collective Licensing: A Report on Certain Practices in the Collective Licensing of Public Performances and Broadcasting Rights in Sound Recordings, 1988 (Cm. 530) paras 7.44–7.48.

[50] See, *Hansard*, HL Vol.491, cols 509–511.

[51] Collective Licensing: A report on certain practices in the collective licensing of public performances and broadcasting rights in sound recordings, 1988 (Cm.530).

[52] Collective Licensing: Report, 1988 (Cm.530), paras 7.44, 7.48, 7.49.

[53] Collective Licensing: Report, 1988 (Cm.530), para.7.49.

[54] The original Bill did not include such provisions, which were added in Standing Committee. See the Report of the Debates of the House of Commons, Standing Committee F in 1990, cols 1454–1464.

of the provisions dealing with the right to use information about programmes. This has already been considered.[55] Sections 135A to 135G were further amended by the Copyright and Related Rights Regulations 2003.[56] The sections now apply only to non-internet "broadcasts" within the meaning of section 6 of the 1988 Act and to "simulcasts", that is transmissions taking place simultaneously on the internet and by other means (section 6(1A)(a)).[57] The result is a significant narrowing of the ambit of the sections. Before the amendment, the sections applied to cable programmes as well as broadcasts. As a result, they almost certainly applied to the other two forms of internet transmission which are within the new definition of "broadcast" (that is, concurrent transmissions of live events (section 6(1A)(b)) and transmissions of recorded moving images or sounds forming part of a programme service offered by the person responsible for making the transmission, being a service in which programmes are transmitted at scheduled times determined by that person (section 6(1A)(c)). They also applied to "on-request" or "on-demand" services. This is no longer the case.[58]

Given that prior to 1991 the terms of licences granted by PPL for the broadcast of its sound recordings were reviewable by the Copyright Tribunal,[59] the critical change effected by the introduction of sections 135A to 135G concerned "needletime". Under the provisions in effect prior to 1991, conditions concerning needletime were subject only to a reasonableness requirement. Therefore, as long as PPL could demonstrate a legitimate reason to restrict needletime, the Tribunal could not object to it. Under the new law, the term "needletime" means the time in any period (whether determined as a number of hours in the period or a proportion of the period, or otherwise) in which recordings may be included in a broadcast.[60]

Scope. The provisions are confined to uses of "sound recordings". Consequently, **29–28** they do not confer any right to include in the broadcast the musical works or associated lyrics embodied in the recording, which must therefore be the subject of a separate agreement with the owner of these rights.[61] Nor do the provisions allow for the broadcasting of "music videos" since these are cinematographic works.[62] Moreover, section 135A(5) states that the term "sound recording" does not include a film sound track when accompanying a film. However, the Secretary of State may now extend the scope of these provisions by Order so as to include works of any description.[63] For example, as a result of recent controversies, the Secretary of State might wish to extend the system to music videos[64] and

---

[55] See paras 29–09 et seq. above.

[56] SI 2003/2498.

[57] CDPA 1988, s.135A(5).

[58] See Consultation on UK Implementation of Directive 2001/29/EC on Copyright and Related Rights in the Information Society : Analysis of Responses and Government Conclusions, para.3.15.

[59] See generally, paras 29–105 et seq., below.

[60] CDPA 1988, s.135A(5).

[61] These will be administered in the main by the Performing Right Society, as to which, see para. 28–59, above.

[62] The Association of Independent Radio Companies Ltd (AIRC) v Phonographic Performance Ltd [1994] R.P.C. 143 at 173.

[63] CDPA 1988, s.135H(1)(a), added by the Broadcasting Act 1996, s.139(1); no order has yet been made under this provision.

[64] MTV Europe objected to the collective licensing practices of Video Performance Limited (VPL) since it wished to obtain Europe-wide licences directly from the record companies. Consequently, MTV complained to the European Commission which in turn issued a statement of objections to VPL's practices in 1994. The dispute is referred to at p.173 of the AIRC case (Association of Independent Radio Companies Ltd v Phonographic Performance Ltd [1994] R.P.C. 143). It seems that since the Commission's statement, VPL allows bilateral negotiations, so the objection raised

it has been suggested that a parallel licence should apply as regards the performance or broadcast of musical and literary works.[65]

29–29   **Licensed acts.** The licence is only available where the licensee intends to "broadcast" the sound recording. This terms bears the same meaning as in section 6 of the 1988 Act save that the only form of internet transmission to which the sections apply is a "simulcast".[66] The licence thus covers both radio and television broadcasts, whether national or local, as well as satellite broadcasts and digital broadcasts. From November 1, 1996, the Secretary of State may by order amend these provisions so as to limit the types of broadcast to which the licence applies.[67] This provision was enacted so that digital broadcasts and broadcasts designed to provide background music in shops (sometimes referred to as "narrowcasts") can be excluded from the scope of the licence should that prove necessary.[68]

29–30   **The licensor.** The licence is only available where the rights are administered by a licensing body, as defined in section 116(2) of the 1988 Act.[69] The section is drafted to cover the situation both where the licensing body has been given the right to grant licences, but also where it has the ability to procure the grant of such a licence.[70] The requirement that the rights be administered by a licensing body may prove significant if changes in commercial practice lead individual record companies to license the broadcasting of records themselves (for example on a Europe-wide basis). In such a situation the question will arise as to whether a record company with a catalogue of recordings itself constitutes a licensing body. This may raise difficult questions about whether a record company has such licensing activities as one of its "main objects", and whether the record company grants licences only relating to works of which it is the "author".[71]

The licensing body may not refuse the licence, it seems, even if the prospective licensee is of dubious financial standing or if it has engaged in activities damaging to the record companies (*e.g.* encouraging home taping).[72]

29–31   **Necessary conditions.** A person who wishes to include sound recordings in a broadcast must then show that one of two sets of conditions is satisfied. These two sets of conditions differentiate between the situations where a broadcaster

---

by MTV no longer exists. See *Music and Copyright* Vol.68/1 21.6.1995. Also see Porter, "European Union Competition Policy: should the role of collecting societies be legitimised?" [1996] 12 E.I.P.R. 673.

[65] Such an extension was considered by the MMC: A Report on the supply in the UK of the services of administering performing rights and film synchronisation rights, 1996 (Cm.3147) paras 10.5, 10.21, 10.31, 10.38, 10.48, 14.134. The MMC concluded, however, that such an extension was not necessary: *ibid.* paras 2.96, 2.131. Such an extension to literary, dramatic, musical or artistic works or films would not contravene the Berne Convention, as Art.11 *bis*(2) allows for limitations to be placed on an author's right to authorise the broadcasting or communication to the public of the work (whether by wireless or by wire or by public communication of a broadcast): "It shall be a matter for legislation in the countries of the Union to determine the conditions under which the rights mentioned in the preceding paragraph [Broadcasting and Related Rights] may be exercised, but these conditions ... shall not in any circumstances be prejudicial to the moral rights of the author, nor to his right to obtain equitable remuneration".

[66] CDPA 1988, s.135A(5). For the background to this, see para. 29–27 above.

[67] s.135H(1)(b), added by the Broadcasting Act 1996, s.139(1); no order has yet been made under this provision.

[68] See *Hansard*, HL Vol.568, cols 547–8; Vol.569, cols 761–3. See also *AEI Rediffusion Music Ltd v Phonographic Performance Ltd* [1998] R.P.C. 335.

[69] As to which, see para. 29–107, below.

[70] CDPA 1988, s.135A(1)(a).

[71] As to the definition of "author" in relation to a sound recording see CDPA 1988, s.9(2) (aa) and see para. 5–41, above.

[72] *cf.* MMC Report, Collective Licensing: A Report on Certain Practices in the Collective Licensing of Public Performances and Broadcasting Rights in Sound Recordings, 1988 (Cm.530). paras 7.16.–7.17, suggesting an injunction should be available in such circumstances.

has obtained a licence but is unhappy with the terms thereof and where a licence does not exist (for example, because it was never granted or has lapsed without being renewed). Where the broadcaster already has a licence, the statutory right only applies if the licence limits the needletime available to the broadcaster. In those circumstances, if the broadcaster is refused greater (including unlimited) needletime, or is only offered extended needletime on terms as to payment which are unacceptable or is not offered different terms within a reasonable time, then the statutory licence will potentially be available.[73] Where a broadcaster does not hold a licence the statutory licence will be available if the licensing body refuses within a reasonable time to grant a licence either on terms as to payment which would be acceptable to the broadcaster (or on terms laid down in an order of the Copyright Tribunal under section 135D) or if the licensing body restricts the needletime that the broadcaster has demanded.[74]

Proposal of terms. Before a broadcaster can avail itself of the statutory licence, various steps must be taken.[75] These involve at least three stages, and they are mandatory not directory.[76] First, the broadcaster must give notice to the licensing body of its intention to use the right and ask the body to propose terms of payment.[77] This gives the licensing body the opportunity to set the rate which the broadcaster will have to pay pending the determination by the Copyright Tribunal. Secondly, once the proposed terms have been received from the licensing body (or a reasonable period has passed), the broadcaster must give reasonable notice of the date on which it proposes to commence broadcasting of sound recordings under the right, and the terms of payment that the broadcaster intends to employ.[78] At this time, the broadcaster must also give reasonable notice to the Copyright Tribunal of its intention to exercise the right, and of the date on which it proposes to begin to do so, and apply to the Tribunal under section 135D to settle the terms of payment.[79]   **29–32**

The licence. Once all these conditions are satisfied, then, after the date that was specified in the notice, if a person includes in a broadcast any sound recordings, he is to be in the same position as regards infringement of copyright as if he had at all material times been the holder of a licence granted by the owner of the copyright, provided three further conditions are satisfied[80] : (a) he complies with any reasonable condition, notice of which has been given to him by the licensing body, as to the inclusion of those recordings[81] ; (b) he provides the licensing body with such information about their inclusion in the broadcast as it may reasonably require; and (c) the broadcaster makes payments as required at not less than   **29–33**

---

[73] CDPA 1988, ss.135A(3), (4).

[74] s.135A(2) and (4).

[75] CDPA 1988, s.135B

[76] However, where a broadcaster fails to comply with these requirements it is questionable whether the broadcaster's liability for damages for infringement of copyright in the sound recording will exceed what is awarded by the Copyright Tribunal, together with any interest the Court may award. In certain circumstances, this could have substantial implications as to costs. See further, *Phonographic Performance Ltd v Retail Broadcast Services Ltd* [1995] F.S.R. 813 at 817, *per* Jacob J.

[77] CDPA 1988, ss.135B(1)(a). In *Phonographic Performance Ltd v Retail Broadcast Services Ltd* [1995] F.S.R. 813, the defendant and PPL had been in voluntary negotiations during which PPL proposed terms for payment. Jacob J. held that the requirement that the licensing body be asked to propose terms of payment had not been satisfied: " Section 135B(1) sets up a particular machinery. The person intending to avail themselves of the right must send the notice called for by subsection (1)(a). Some other notice or negotiation will not do". [1995] F.S.R. 813 at 816.

[78] s.135B(1)(b).

[79] s.135B(3).

[80] CDPA 1988, s.135C(1).

[81] See further, paras 29–35, *et seq.*, below.

quarterly intervals in arrears. The terms of payment are to be either those specified by the Copyright Tribunal or, if there are none, those proposed by the licensing body or if those are "unreasonably high", those specified in the broadcaster's notice to the licensing body. Once a person is treated as being the holder of a licence in accordance with these provisions, any existing licence is replaced.[82]

29–34 **The Copyright Tribunal.** As has been seen, before being entitled to the licence the broadcaster must have applied to the Copyright Tribunal to settle the terms of payment. The provisions relating to the application to the Copyright Tribunal to settle the terms of payment, and the right to apply for review of any order, follow the same form as those which relate to the right to use information about programmes.[83] Section 135D requires the Copyright Tribunal to consider such applications and provides it with a discretion to make such order as it may determine to be reasonable in the circumstances. In addition, a person exercising the right may also request that the Copyright Tribunal consider the reasonableness of any conditions or requirements as to information imposed by the licensing body and again the Tribunal is given the power to make such order as it may determine to be reasonable in the circumstances.[84] The Tribunal does not have jurisdiction to limit the forms of broadcast by which the sound recording may be transmitted, for example, by excluding digital audio broadcasting (but see para.29–29, above).

29–35 **References about conditions, etc.** The test as to whether a condition may be attached to the exercise of the statutory right is that of reasonableness. This presumably means reasonable from both parties' point of view, judged by reference to the objective which the statutory right was intended to achieve. A condition as to providing security for the licence fees would probably not be deemed reasonable, given that the provisions are intended to assist the establishment of niche radio stations which may well lack the resources to provide such security.[85] However, the Tribunal has held that a requirement that a licensee identify which programmes are supplied by third parties and the identity of the supplier is reasonable.[86] During the passage of these provisions through Parliament, it was suggested that conditions could be imposed so as to prohibit certain disreputable practices which might be damaging to record companies. Thus, for example, it would, no doubt, be reasonable to impose conditions so as to prevent the playing of a particular record whenever a particular product is advertised in such a way as to imply an endorsement of that product by the artist involved.[87] Moreover, the MMC took the view that conditions designed to restrict home taping were reasonable.

The power to review the conditions of the licence does not enable the Tribunal to require the licensing body to grant related ancillary rights, such as the right to dub[88] recordings and keep copies indefinitely,[89] or to provide to other stations copies of programmes compiled by the licensee. Pending a finding by the Tribunal

---

[82] CDPA 1988, s.135C(4).

[83] See paras 29–22 et seq., above and as to the procedure of the Tribunal, see paras 29–159 et seq., below.

[84] CDPA 1988, s.135E.

[85] During the passage of the Broadcasting Bill there were attempts to introduce an amendment which would have required a broadcaster to provide security for the differences between the amount asked for by the licensing body and the amount the broadcaster declared it was willing to pay. This amendment was rejected by the Government because of the adverse affect this might have on small broadcasters. See *Hansard*, HL Vol.521, cols 1678–80.

[86] *The Association of Independent Radio Companies Ltd (AIRC) v Phonographic Performance Ltd* [1994] R.P.C. 143 at 188–189.

[87] See *Hansard,* HL Vol.521, col.1671; Vol.522, col.840.

[88] That is to make a further copy of recorded music.

that a condition is unreasonable, the licensee should comply with it. If it declined to do so, the licensing body might seek injunctive relief requiring compliance with the condition. However, were the condition unreasonable, it is unlikely that such relief would be forthcoming.[90]

Payment: general approach. It has been said that it is "notoriously difficult to arrive at a decision as to an appropriate royalty in the absence of equivalent consensual licences".[91] Ultimately, the decision will be "a 'judgment call' taking into account a large number of factors".[92]   **29–36**

In *AIRC v PPL*[93] the Copyright Tribunal considered the effect of the removal of needletime restrictions on the terms of licences between PPL and the AIRC. PPL sought a substantial increase in the rates that had been determined when airplay was restricted to nine hours per day. PPL argued that such an increase was justified by the huge increase in the applicant's use of its records since the rates were last set by the Tribunal. AIRC argued that PPL's proposals were unreasonable as they represented a 54 per cent increase on the expiring licence and that the promotional benefit to the respondent's members should be taken into account, as should lower royalty rates in other European countries. In reaching its decision the Tribunal held that the position in other European countries was not helpful as the structure and function of the radio industries there was so different.[94] It also thought existing agreements on video licensing by VPL to MTV Europe and patent licences were of no assistance. It held that the most useful comparator was the PRS agreement with the AIRC, particularly as regards the overall yield which the Tribunal considered "should be in the same general range".[95] In rejecting the respondent's argument for a substantial increase the Tribunal held that, whilst the amount of needletime was a relevant consideration in assessing payment, on the facts, the abolition of needletime had worked not only to the benefit of the broadcasters but also to the benefit of PPL.[96] Nor could such an increase be justified by reference to the loss of revenue caused by home taping.[97]

AEI Rediffusion v PPL[98] involved a dispute between PPL and the operators of a subscription narrowcast service delivered by satellite. The Tribunal had to consider the appropriate royalty rate and the revenue on which it should be based. The Tribunal emphasised that it had a duty to arrive at a figure "which is both fair to the licensor in terms of the value to the licensee of having access to the copy-

---

[89] In *Phonographic Performance Ltd v AEI Rediffusion Music Ltd* [1998] Ch. 187 it was held that there was no right to make copies under s.135C of the Act. Broadcasters must therefore rely on s.68 of the Act which requires copies to be destroyed within 28 days (see para. 9–186) or they must negotiate a separate dubbing licence. During the passage of the Broadcasting Bill some concern was expressed that the dubbing right might be used to reimpose needletime restrictions: *Hansard,* HL Vol.521, col.1658. However, a review of dubbing licence arrangements might fall within the general powers of the Tribunal. See further, *AEI Rediffusion Music Ltd v Phonographic Performance Ltd* [1998] R.P.C. 335, in particular, at 358 and see para. 29–119, below.

[90] See *Hansard*, HL Vol.542, col.841.

[91] *AEI Rediffusion Music Ltd v Phonographic Performance Ltd* [1998] R.P.C. 335 at 343.

[92] *AEI Rediffusion Music Ltd v Phonographic Performance Ltd* [1998] R.P.C. 335 at 343 and see the cases cited at para. 29–99, below.

[93] *The Association of Independent Radio Companies Ltd (AIRC) v Phonographic Performance Ltd* [1994] R.P.C. 143. Also see Arnold, (1993) Ent. L.Rev. 145.

[94] But note that the MMC has emphasised the potential importance of international comparisons: MMC, *A Report on the supply in the UK of the services of administering performing rights and film synchronisation rights*, 1996 (Cm.3147) para.2.91.

[95] *The Association of Independent Radio Companies Ltd (AIRC) v Phonographic Performance Ltd* [1994] R.P.C. 143 at 185.

[96] *Association of Independent Radio Companies Ltd v Phonographic Performances Ltd* [1994] R.P.C. 143 at 183–4.

[97] *Association of Independent Radio Companies Ltd v Phonographic Performances Ltd* [1994] R.P.C. 143 at 184.

[98] *AEI Rediffusion Music Ltd v Phonographic Performance Ltd* [1998] R.P.C. 335.

right sound recordings, and also fair to the licensee in giving him a proper reward for the effort put into the exploitation of the licensor's intellectual property rights. This includes in particular making full allowance for the added value provided by the licensee".[99] The Tribunal also said that where the licensee makes part of its profit from equipment sales or rental then it will be appropriate to take this into account in cases where "without the provision of the music the opportunity to sell or lease equipment would not arise".[1] Moreover, it seems that in cases where a licensor's rights are to be exploited overseas under a licence granted in the United Kingdom, the right to broadcast in the United Kingdom will be made subject to conditions that a proper royalty rate should be paid in respect of all sites taking the service. In this case this meant that the rate payable for use of the copyrights overseas should be the same as that charged domestically.[2] When deciding on a useful comparator the driving consideration should be commercial reality. Thus the decision in the *AIRC* case that patent licences were of no assistance could not be taken to have decided as a matter of principle that licences of different legal rights could be of no assistance.[3] However, the best comparator in this case was the existing commercial dubbing licences, even though the markets for delivery on tape or CD or delivery by satellite were "not exactly co-terminous".[4]

Virgin v PPL[5] concerned Virgin Megastores Radio, a radio station located in Virgin's Oxford Street store, which played music introduced by disc jockeys for satellite broadcast to all Virgin's stores. The Tribunal rejected comparisons with the *AEI* decision because, in its view, the activities of Virgin's radio station (which involved "live"[6] music, DJs, news bulletins and advertisements) did not constitute narrowcasting.[7] By contrast, it accepted that there were enough similarities between Virgin's radio station and an independent local radio station for the royalty rates ordered in the *AIRC* case to provide useful guidance.[8] Never-theless, because Virgin's radio station did not have to make a profit and its advertising revenue might be lower than a comparable local radio station, the royalty rate was set at a higher level than for a local radio station with compara-ble advertising revenue.[9] The Tribunal rejected an argument that there should be a discount because Virgins's radio station was itself involved in marketing the re-cords of PPL's members.[10] It also held that it should ignore the possibility that if too high a royalty was charged, this might force Virgin to discontinue its radio station.[11] Finally, to guard against the possibility that Virgin might cease to pursue a policy of maximising advertising revenue, thus reducing the royalty, the

---

[99] *AEI Rediffusion Music Ltd v Phonographic Performance Ltd* [1998] R.P.C. 335 at 343.

[1] *AEI Rediffusion Music Ltd v Phonographic Performance Ltd* [1998] R.P.C. 335 at 343.

[2] *AEI Rediffusion Music Ltd v Phonographic Performance Ltd* [1998] R.P.C. 335 at 343.

[3] *AEI Rediffusion Music Ltd v Phonographic Performance Ltd* [1998] R.P.C. 335 at 348.

[4] *AEI Rediffusion Music Ltd v Phonographic Performance Ltd* [1998] R.P.C. 335 at 353.

[5] *Virgin Retail Ltd v Phonographic Performance Ltd* [2000] E.M.L.R. 323.

[6] In the sense that it was played "live" by a DJ.

[7] *Virgin Retail Ltd v Phonographic Performance Ltd* [2000] E.M.L.R. 323 at para.50. The Tribunal defined "narrowcasting" by reference to the *AEI* decision. It noted that AEI had originally been a "commercial dubber", that is it had delivered background music to its subscribers in the form of a hard copy, typically a tape, which was then played by the subscriber on commercially available equipment. It went on to point out that the service which was the subject of the *AEI* decision, *AEI Rediffusion Music Ltd v Phonographic Performance Ltd* [1998] R.P.C. 335, was exactly the same as this except that material was broadcast rather than supplied in hard copy. Accordingly, the Tribunal defined narrowcasting as "the business analogous to a commercial dubber of a company which uses the broadcasting medium to supply pre-recorded material to its clients rather than supplying them with hard copies of the pre-recorded material" (para.43).

[8] *Virgin Retail Ltd v Phonographic Performance Ltd* [2000] E.M.L.R. 323, para.64.

[9] *Virgin Retail Ltd v Phonographic Performance Ltd* [2000] E.M.L.R. 323, para.68.

[10] *Virgin Retail Ltd v Phonographic Performance Ltd* [2000] E.M.L.R. 323, para.71.

[11] *Virgin Retail Ltd v Phonographic Performance Ltd* [2000] E.M.L.R. 323, para.73; but the Tribunal stated that it was "singularly unimpressed" by Virgin's evidence as to this: para.72.

Tribunal imposed a minimum royalty on Virgin, based on square footage of Virgin's sites.[12] On appeal, the Judge accepted that the Tribunal was entitled to reject the comparison with the *AEI* decision, but held that there was no evidence to support its finding that the *AIRC* decision provided useful guidance: the whole commercial *raison d'être*, commercial financing and business of an independent local radio station was completely different from that of Virgin's radio station.[13] Accordingly, he remitted the matter to the Tribunal. The dispute was then settled and the application withdrawn.

Factors to be taken into account. In considering what is reasonable on any application to review the conditions of the licence or to settle or review the terms of payment, the Tribunal is expressly required to consider certain factors:[14] **29–37**

(i) **Non-discrimination.** The Copyright Tribunal is required to have regard to the terms of any orders which it has made in the case of persons in similar circumstances exercising the right conferred by section 135C, and to exercise its powers so as to ensure that there is no unreasonable discrimination between persons exercising that right against the same licensing body.[15] In the *AIRC* case, the Copyright Tribunal declined to discriminate on the basis of usage, except in determining whether a station was a music station or talk station. It held that talk stations should be able to make reasonable use of recorded music without incurring the full rigours of normal rates. It also held that low revenue stations should benefit from a lower rate, so that the tariff encouraged "small and specialist incremental stations which add to the diversity in broadcasting".[16] Apart from those two concessions, it imposed a single standard revenue-based roya¹·· applicable to the generality of stations. In *Virgin v PPL*, the *AIRC* decision was taken into account by the Tribunal, but this decision was overruled on appeal.[17]

(ii) **Other orders.** Secondly, the Tribunal is directed, when settling the terms of payment, not to be guided by any order it has made under any enactment other than section 135D.[18] This might appear to exclude from consideration comparisons with voluntary licensing schemes, the compulsory licence for broadcast information, as well as decisions made by the Performing Rights Tribunal and the Copyright Tribunal prior to 1991. However, the requirement that the Tribunal is not to be "guided by" previous orders[19] does not require it to ignore previous decisions; it merely indicates that the Tribunal should not regard such orders as the basis or starting-point for determination of a decision under the section.[20] The Tribunal should not simply extrapolate, but should consider matters

---

[12] *Virgin Retail Ltd v Phonographic Performance Ltd* [2000] E.M.L.R. 323, para.77.

[13] *Phonographic Performance Ltd v Virgin Retail Ltd* [2001] E.M.L.R. 139 at para.38.

[14] These factors do not expressly include those set out in s.129 of CDPA 1988. Nevertheless, the wide language of s.135D ("reasonable in the circumstances") requires those factors to be taken into account: *Phonographic Performance Ltd v Virgin Retail Ltd* [2001] E.M.L.R. 139, para.11.

[15] CDPA 1988, s.135G(1).

[16] *Association of Independent Radio Companies Ltd (AIRC) v Phonographic Performance Ltd* [1994] R.P.C. 143 at 179. This reflects Government policy as represented in the Green Paper, *Radio: Choices and Opportunities*, 1987 (Cm.92) and the White Paper, *Broadcasting in the '90s: Competition, Choice and Quality*, 1988 (Cm.517). The MMC Report, *Collective Licensing: A Report on Certain Practices in the Collective Licensing of Public Performances and Broadcasting Rights in Sound Recordings*, 1988 (Cm.530) also suggested that new stations should be given preferential rates: para.7.42.

[17] For a fuller account, see the previous paragraph.

[18] CDPA 1988, s.135G(2).

[19] For criticism of the width of this phrase see *Hansard*, HL Vol.522, col.842 (Lord Jenkins).

[20] *The Association of Independent Radio Companies Ltd (AIRC) v Phonographic Performance Ltd* [1994] R.P.C. 143 at 175.

afresh. In the *AIRC* case, the terms of the agreement between the parties had been reviewed in 1980 by the PRT and again in 1986.[21] The Copyright Tribunal considered that it could refer to these previous orders as "an essential part of the history of the matter", but that in this case the previous orders were of little help because of changes in the independent radio and record industries and because of difficulty in following the reasoning of the PRT.[22]

   (iii) **Re-transmissions.** The Act makes further provision to deal with the situation where a broadcast is further broadcast by reception and immediate retransmission.[23] Where the retransmission is confined to the original broadcast area, the Act provides that the Copyright Tribunal, in considering what charges (if any) should be paid for licences for either transmission, should have regard to the extent to which the owner of copyright in the sound recording has already received, or is entitled to receive, payment for the other transmission in that area.[24] Where a retransmission extends beyond the original broadcast area, the Tribunal is further directed to leave out of consideration of the terms of the licence for the first transmission any further transmission to an area outside that to which the first transmission was made.[25] The aim of these provisions is thus to ensure that the copyright owner is not remunerated twice over, and to protect the original broadcaster from having to pay royalties for transmission beyond its service area.[26]

29–38   **Effect of the Order.** The effect of the order is retrospective, relating back to the date when the applicant began to use the statutory licence. If the Tribunal increases the financial remuneration due to the licensing body from that which the applicant has been paying pending determination, the broadcaster is liable for the amounts that have fallen due. If the broadcaster has been paying the licensing body too much, the difference must be repaid.[27] In *AIRC v PPL* the Tribunal held that since there was no express provision in the 1990 scheme permitting the Tribunal to order that interest be paid, such power was not available.[28] Following criticism of this by the Monopolies and Mergers Commission,[29] the Broadcasting Act 1996 introduced a new section 151A into the 1988 Act empowering the Tribunal to award simple interest at such rate and for such period after the first payment became due as the Tribunal thinks reasonable in the circumstances.[30] The power is only available where the reference or application to the Tribunal is

---

[21] *AIRC v PPL*, Decision of July 15, 1980; *AIRC v PPL*, Decision of October 23, 1986.

[22] *The Association of Independent Radio Companies Limited (AIRC) v Phonographic Performance Ltd* [1994] R.P.C. 143 at 175.

[23] CDPA 1988, ss.135G(3) and 134.

[24] s.134(2).

[25] s.134(3).

[26] These provisions should thus be compared to the provisions relating to the re-transmission of broadcasts in a cable programme service, as to which see paras 29–48 *et seq.*, below.

[27] CDPA 1988, s.135D(2).

[28] *The Association of Independent Radio Companies Ltd (AIRC) v Phonographic Performance Ltd* [1994] R.P.C. 143 following *Swift v Board of Trade* [1925] A.C. 520 and distinguishing *Knibb v NCB* [1987] 1 Q.B. 906.

[29] MMC, A Report on the supply in the UK of the services of administering performing rights and film synchronisation rights 1996 (Cm.3147) para.2.93, 2.130. But note the BBC evidence that the absence of such a power provides an incentive for matters to be dealt with expeditiously: para.10.5. See also, The Reports of the Debates of the House of Commons Standing Committee D in 1996, col.760.

[30] CDPA 1988, s.151A, added by the Broadcasting Act 1996, s.139(2). More generally see para. 29–114 and notes, below.

made after the commencement of the section.[31] Having set out the basis on which the order is to be made, the Tribunal usually refers the matter back to the parties to produce an agreed form of licence which in due course is incorporated in the Tribunal's final order. If the parties fail to do so, the Tribunal will determine the form of wording of the order.

Costs. The Tribunal has considerable discretion over the award of costs.[32] The MMC suggested that, where the licensee adopted an unreasonably low figure the Copyright Tribunal should order it to bear the costs of both parties[33] ; the same would apply if the licensing body made an unreasonably high demand.[34]   **29–39**

Review. The Order is open to review at the behest of either party. On such an application the Tribunal must consider the matter and make such order confirming or varying the original order as it may determine to be reasonable in the circumstances.[35] Such an application cannot be made without special leave within 12 months following an existing order or decision.[36] Similarly, if the order was made so as to be in force for 15 months or less, or as a result of a decision on a previous application is due to expire within 15 months of that decision, no application for review is permitted (without special leave) until the last three months before the expiry date.[37]   **29–40**

(iii) Duration: transitional provisions

General. As is noted elsewhere, the effect of the implementation of the Term Directive has been that certain copyrights which had lapsed are revived.[38] In the United Kingdom the revived right is, however, limited, if certain conditions are satisfied, to a right to remuneration. The regulations thus provide that in the case of a work in which revived copyright subsists any acts restricted by the copyright shall be treated as licensed by the copyright owner, subject only to the payment of such reasonable royalty or other remuneration as may be agreed or determined in default of agreement by the Copyright Tribunal.[39] A person intending to avail himself of this right, must give reasonable notice of his intention to the copyright owner, stating when he intends to begin to do the acts.[40] If he fails to give such notice his acts shall not be treated as licensed.[41] If he does give such notice, the acts are to be treated as if they were licensed and a reasonable royalty or other remuneration shall be payable in respect of them despite the fact that the amount of such royalty or other remuneration is not yet agreed or determined.[42] Thus, for example, when the United Kingdom copyright lapsed in Joyce's *Ulysses* in 1991 and was revived on January 1, 1996, a person wishing to publish a copy of that work was obliged to give notice of his intention to the owner of the copyright and   **29–41**

---

[31] CDPA 1988, s.151A(3), *i.e.* where the reference is made on or after November 1, 1996.

[32] CDPA 1988, s.151; Copyright Tribunal Rules 1989 (SI 1989/1129), regs 48, 26B(3) and see para. 29–170, below.

[33] MMC Report, Collective Licensing: A Report on Certain Practices in the Collective Licensing of Public Performances and Broadcasting Rights in Sound Recordings, 1988 (Cm.530) para.7.19(e).

[34] *Hansard,*HL Vol.521, col.1664; Vol.522, col.840.

[35] CDPA 1988, s.135F(3).

[36] s.135F(2)(a).

[37] s.135F(2)(b).

[38] para. 6–11, above. As to what is revived copyright, see para. 6–75, above.

[39] Duration of Copyright and Rights in Performances Regulations 1995 (SI 1995/3297), reg.24(1).

[40] reg.24(2).

[41] reg.24(3).

[42] reg.24(4).

agree a royalty or apply to the Copyright Tribunal to settle a reasonable royalty.[43] This compulsory licence does not, however, apply if or to the extent that a licence to do the acts could be granted by a licensing body,[44] whether under a licensing scheme or otherwise.[45] Moral rights, which are also revived, continue to be subject to any waiver which subsisted immediately before the expiry of the old term and are otherwise exercisable as with any other copyright work.[46] For equivalent provisions for rights in performances, see notes to para.29–155, below.

29–42   **The notice**. The Regulations require the notice to state the date on which the person giving it intends to do the acts in question.[47] However, a notice which fails to state that date may be sufficient where it can be shown that when the notice was served the copyright owner knew that date by other means, for example as a result of publicity material or having been informed of it orally.[48] Since the copyright owner cannot stop the publication, the purpose of the requirement to give notice appears to be to ensure that the acts in question are open and not clandestine and that a person who hoped to get away with an infringement in secret cannot justify his act retrospectively by reference to the Regulations. Accordingly, it is arguable that only a short period of notice need be given.[49] The notice does not need to include a copy of the intended publication.[50] There is no reason why a notice should not be expressed in contingent terms, for example, that it is without prejudice to an argument that the acts in question would not infringe, for example because Regulation 23 applies.[51]

29–43   **The Copyright Tribunal.** An application to settle the royalty or other remuneration payable in respect of the right outlined above may be made to the Tribunal by either the owner or the licensee.[52] The Tribunal is required to consider such applications and may make such an order as it may determine to be reasonable in the circumstances.[53] Either party may subsequently apply to the Tribunal to vary the order, and the Tribunal shall consider the matter and make such order confirming or varying the original order as it may determine to be reasonable in the circumstances.[54] Restrictions exist, similar to those already considered, so that an application for review may not normally be made within 12 months from the date of the original order.[55]

(iv) Copyright in design documents

29–44   As is explained in detail elsewhere, where copyright subsists in a document or model embodying a design for anything other than an artistic work or a typeface, section 51 of the 1988 Act provides a "defence" to an action for infringement to any person who makes an article to the design or copies such an article.[56] This is effective as regards design documents created after January 1, 1989. However, to

[43] *Sweeney v Macmillan Publishers Ltd* [2002] R.P.C. 35.
[44] For the definition of a licensing body see CDPA 1988, s.116(2) and para. 29–107, below.
[45] Duration of Copyright and Rights in Performances Regulations 1995 (SI 1995/3297), reg.24(5).
[46] reg.22. See further, Ch.11, above.
[47] Duration of Copyright and Rights in Performances Regulations 1995 (SI 1995/3297), reg.24(2).
[48] *Sweeney v Macmillan Publishers Ltd* [2002] R.P.C. 35, para.62.
[49] *Sweeney v Macmillan Publishers Ltd* [2002] R.P.C. 35, para.63. On the facts, notice in March in respect of publication in June was held to be reasonable "on any basis".
[50] *Sweeney v Macmillan Publishers Ltd* [2002] R.P.C. 35, para.63.
[51] *Sweeney v Macmillan Publishers Ltd* [2002] R.P.C. 35, paras 64 to 65.
[52] Duration of Copyright and Rights on Performances Regulations 1995 (SI 19953297), reg.25(1).
[53] See further, para. 29–98, below.
[54] reg.25(3).
[55] reg.25(4).
[56] See further, para. 9–142 and paras 13–278 *et seq.*, above.

avoid the drastic effects that the introduction of such a defence would have on established rights in works already in existence, paragraph 19 of Schedule 1 to the 1988 Act provided that section 51 should not apply to designs recorded in design documents or models prior to August 1, 1989 for 10 years thereafter. The effect of this provision wass that full copyright protection was maintained during this period. However, paragraph 19(2) provided that licences of right were available in relation to such design documents on the same conditions as such licences are available in relation to unregistered designs under sections 237 to 239 of the 1988 Act.[57] Paragraph 19(3) explained that section 237 was to be read as applying to the last five years of the 10 year period. The net effect of this was that from August 1, 1989 until July 31, 1994 full copyright applied (subject to the non-derogation from grant doctrine) but that from then until July 31, 1999, licences of right were available in relation to such design documents. The scope of the licence was confined to acts which would have been permitted under section 51 had it applied.[58] Since July 31, 1999, section 51 has applied fully to design documents created before August 1, 1989.

(v) Lending to public of copies of certain works

Overview. Under section 66 of the 1988 Act, power is provided to the Secretary of State to subject the lending of certain works to compulsory licensing. The new section 66 was introduced by the Copyright and Related Rights Regulations 1996[59] and came into force on December 1, 1996. It replaced the power given to the Secretary of State under the 1988 Act to subject the rental of sound recordings, films or computer programs to such licences. The new power has not been exercised.[60]

29–45

Background. The implementation of the Rental and Related Rights Directive[61] required extension of the rental right to include lending, and the works to which the right applies to include literary, dramatic, musical and some artistic works as well as sound recordings and films.[62] The amended section 66 extends the Secretary of State's power to order compulsory licences to all such works, but confines the power to deal only with cases of lending. Such a limitation is consistent with the provisions of the Directive[63] and existing international conventions.[64] Rental remains an exclusive right outside the scope of any potential order, as is required under the Directive.

29–46

The amended section also repeals, but does not replace, former section 66(5).

---

[57] For examples of such applications, see the cases referred to in paras 13–126 *et seq.*, above, and *In the matter of an application by Stafford Engineering Services Ltd* [2000] R.P.C. 797. These provisions were challenged on the grounds that they contravened GATT-TRIPS, which requires Member States to protect industrial designs for at least 10 years. This argument was rejected on the grounds that the Registered Designs Act 1949 fulfilled the United Kingdom's obligations in this respect. The unregistered design right grants additional protection over and above that required by TRIPS. See *Re Azrak-Hamway International Inc. Licence of Right (Design Right and Copyright) Application* [1997] R.P.C. 134 at 150–1.

[58] CDPA 1988, Sch.1, para.19(7).

[59] SI 1996/2967, reg.11(3)

[60] Neither has the original power.

[61] Council Directive 92/100 on rental and lending right and on certain rights related to copyright in the field of intellectual property ([1992] O.J. L346/61); see also paras 7–81 *et seq.*, above.

[62] Art.1, Art.2.

[63] Art.5; the text of the Directive is set out at Vol.2, H3. For background see Reinbothe and von Lewinski, *The EC Directive on Rental and Lending Rights and on Piracy* (Sweet & Maxwell, London, 1993) pp.34–35, 77–83.

[64] There is no lending right under either the Berne or Rome Conventions. *cf.* the exclusive rental right under the WIPO Copyright Treaty, 1996, Art.7; and under the WIPO Performances and Phonograms Treaty, 1996, Art.13.

This stated that copyright in a computer program would not be infringed by the rental of copies to the public after the end of a period of 50 years from the end of the calendar year in which copies of it were first issued to the public in electronic form. The effect of this repeal is that the rental right in such works is retained for the full copyright term.

29–47   **The Order.** The Secretary of State may by order specify that in certain situations the lending to the public of copies of literary, dramatic, musical or artistic works, sound recordings or films shall be treated as licensed by the copyright owner subject only to the payment of such reasonable royalty or other payment as may be agreed or determined in default of agreement by the Copyright Tribunal.[65] No such order shall apply if, or to the extent that, there is a licensing scheme certified for the purposes of this section under section 143 providing for the grant of licences.[66] The order shall be made by statutory instrument; and laid before and approved by a resolution of each House of Parliament.[67] The terms of the order may make different provision for different cases and may specify cases by reference to any factor relating to the work, the copies lent, the lender or the circumstances of the lending.[68] Such an order would not operate to exempt from liability a person lending or renting infringing copies.[69]

(vi) Cable retransmission

29–48   **Overview.** A further compulsory licence is available permitting the retransmission by cable of copyright works and performances included in certain wireless broadcasts, where the cable area falls outside the original broadcast area. The licence represents a compromise between copyright owners, cable service providers and broadcasters where the cable provider is obliged to carry certain broadcasting services. These provisions were introduced by the Broadcasting Act 1996. They supplement the exceptions available under section 73(2) and 73(3) of the 1988 Act.[70] Section 73(2) deals with copyright in the broadcasts themselves, and provides a defence where the retransmission is in pursuance of a "must-carry" requirement or is in the same service area. Section 73(3) and (4) concern copyright in the works included in the broadcast. Thus, section 73(3) provides a defence to an action for infringement of copyright in works contained in the broadcast as regards retransmissions within the broadcast area.[71] Section 73(4) provides for a compulsory licence where inclusion is pursuant to a relevant requirement, but diffusion extends beyond the broadcast area. The compulsory licence under section 73(4) is therefore of no application where the retransmission is within the broadcast area and the section 73(3) defence applies, nor does it have any relevance to copyright in the broadcast itself. These provisions have been amended by the Copyright and Related Rights Regulations 2003[72] in order to give effect to the new definition of "broadcast" introduced by those Regulations. The provisions as amended continue to be confined to wireless broadcasts. Accordingly, the amendments appear to be purely ones of terminology.

These provisions must also be viewed alongside section 144A of the 1988 Act. This section applies to the right of the owner of copyright in a literary, dramatic,

---

[65] CDPA 1988, s.66(1).
[66] s.66(2). No such scheme has yet been certified.
[67] s.66(4).
[68] s.66(3).
[69] s.66(5).
[70] See *Hansard*, HL Vol.570, cols 194–5; HC July 1, 1996, col.593. See paras 9–205 *et seq.*, above.
[71] See further, para. 9–209, above.
[72] SI 2003/2498.

musical or artistic work, sound recording or film to control the cable retransmission of a wireless broadcast from another EEA State.[73] This right can only be exercised against a cable operator through a licensing body.[74]

It should also be noted that equivalent provisions exist as regards the retransmission of performances.[75]

The licence. The licence applies to works included in a broadcast which has been retransmitted beyond the original broadcast area in fulfilment of a "must-carry" obligation. In these circumstances, the Act provides that the retransmission by cable shall be treated as licensed by the owner of the copyright in the work, subject only to the payment to him by the person making the broadcast of such reasonable royalty or other payment as may be agreed or determined in default of agreement by the Copyright Tribunal. The idea appears to be that the original broadcaster must pay a royalty to the copyright owner of a work included in the broadcast because the original licence negotiated between the broadcaster and the owner of copyright may not have accounted for the additional audience reached by the retransmission.[76] At first sight it may perhaps seem surprising that it is the broadcaster who has to pay the royalty to the copyright owner and not the person operating the retransmission service, in particular because the broadcaster's potential liability is dependent upon the actions of a third party over whom the broadcaster has no control. The justification for this arrangement is that the "must-carry" provisions are designed to protect traditional broadcasters by ensuring that their broadcasts remain widely available, whereas the person operating the retransmission service might well prefer not to have to include the broadcasts concerned. Moreover, in the case of broadcasters whose income depends upon advertising revenue, such retransmission may allow the broadcaster to charge more for advertising time, as the advertisements will reach a larger audience. Further justification for placing the obligation on the broadcaster can be obtained by reference to the relative transaction costs: identifying and locating all the relevant copyright holders might involve considerable extra expense for the cable retransmitter, whereas the broadcaster will in any event have to negotiate with the copyright owners to get permission to include their works in the broadcast.

29–49

Qualification. In order to qualify for the licence a number of conditions must be satisfied:

29–50

First, the retransmission must be of a wireless broadcast made from a place in the United Kingdom and it must be received and immediately retransmitted by cable.[77] However, this restriction should be viewed alongside section 144A, considered above, which mandates the collective administration of cable retransmission rights in respect of wireless broadcasts made in another EEA State.[78]

Secondly, the inclusion of the broadcast in the cable retransmission must be in pursuance of a relevant requirement. This is defined as a requirement imposed under either section 78A of the Broadcasting Act 1990, or paragraph 4 of Part III of Schedule 12 to that Act. Section 78A deals with the inclusion of certain services in local delivery services provided by digital means. Paragraph 4 deals with

---

[73] As to which countries are EEA States, see para. 25–01, above.
[74] CDPA 1988, s.144A(3). This section was introduced in order to comply with Art.9 of the Directive on the co-ordination of certain rules concerning copyright and rights related to copyright applicable to satellite broadcasting and cable retransmission 93/83/EEC [1993] O.J. L248/15 (see paras 25–58 *et seq.*, above); see generally as to s.144A, para. 29–75, below.
[75] CDPA 1988, Sch.2, para.19 inserted by the Broadcasting Act 1996, Sch.9, para.5.
[76] The compulsory licence does not operate where the retransmission of the work by cable is licensed by the owner of copyright in the work: CDPA 1988, s.73(5), and see below.
[77] CDPA 1988, s.73(1).
[78] See further, para. 29–75, below.

inclusion of certain services in diffusion services originally licensed under the Cable and Broadcasting Act 1984.[79]

Thirdly, the section only operates where the area in which the cable retransmission takes place ("the cable area") falls outside the area for reception in which the broadcast is made ("the broadcast area"). To the extent that it falls within the broadcast area, an absolute defence exists under section 73(3).[80]

Finally, the licence does not apply if, or to the extent that, the retransmission of the work by cable is licensed by the owner of the copyright in the work.[81]

29–51   **The Copyright Tribunal.** An application to settle the royalty or other sum payable in respect of the compulsory licence may be made to the Copyright Tribunal by the copyright owner or the person making the broadcast.[82] The Tribunal is required to consider such applications and may make such order as it determines to be reasonable in the circumstances.[83] Either party may subsequently apply to the Tribunal to vary the order, and the Tribunal shall consider the matter and make such order confirming or varying the original order as it may determine to be reasonable in the circumstances.[84] Restrictions exist, similar to those already considered, so that an application for review may not normally be made within 12 months from the date of the original order.[85]

(vii) Works of enemy origin

29–52   **Background: The First World War.** Where works were made or published before or during the First World War the copyright in this country, if the property of an enemy, became vested in the Public Trustee as the Custodian of Enemy Property under the Trading with the Enemy Acts 1914 to 1918.[86] After the termination of the war such copyrights were revested, but this was subject to a complex system of disabilities and restrictions.[87] In the light of these complexities, the emergency legislation adopted on the outbreak of war in 1939,[88] created a simpler system so that the war did not affect the continuance or creation of British copyrights in works originating in enemy countries. The 1939 provisions remain in force[89] and have been amended by successive Acts of Parliament dealing with intellectual property matters.

29–53   **The Patents, Designs, Copyright and Trade Marks (Emergency) Act 1939.** Under the 1939 Act, enemy owned copyrights are preserved[90] but made subject to the possibility of compulsory licensing. Power is vested in the Comptroller to grant licences in respect of copyrights owned by an enemy or enemy subject on

---

[79] CDPA 1988, s.73(7).

[80] See further, para. 9–209, above.

[81] CDPA 1988, s.73(5).

[82] CDPA 1988, s.73A(1).

[83] s.73A(2). Such an order has effect from the date on which it is made or such later date as may be specified by the Tribunal: s.73A(5). For the procedure before the Tribunal see paras 29–159 *et seq.*, below. It should also be noted that s.134 of the 1988 Act (duty of the Copyright Tribunal to leave retransmission out of account in considering what charges should be paid for licences for the original transmission) does not apply in relation to such applications: s.134(3A) (added by the Broadcasting Act 1996, Sch.9, para.2(3)).

[84] CDPA 1988, s.73A(3).

[85] s.73A(4).

[86] 4 & 5 Geo. 5, c.87; 5 Geo. 5, c.12; 5 & 6 Geo. 5, c.79; 5 & 6 Geo. 5, c.98; 5 & 6 Geo. 5, c.105; 8 & 9 Geo. 5, c.31.

[87] See *Copinger* (10th ed.) para.1186.

[88] The Patents, Designs, Copyright and Trade Marks (Emergency) Act 1939, c.107.

[89] For a discussion of this see *Novello & Co Ltd v Hinrichsen Edition Ltd* [1951] Ch. 1026 at 1032.

[90] The Patents, Designs, Copyright and Trade Marks (Emergency) Act 1939, s.5.

any terms that the comptroller may think expedient.[91] This power also applies where an enemy or enemy subject is a joint owner of copyright.[92] Owners of copyright to which the Act applies remain free to exercise their rights unless and until some order affecting them is made by the Comptroller. Where an order has been made by the Comptroller this will override any exercise of the owner's rights which is inconsistent with the terms of that licence. But, provided the Comptroller has granted a non-exclusive licence, there is nothing to stop the owner, if not disqualified by trading with the enemy legislation, from granting additional non-exclusive licences.[93]

Before making an order the Comptroller is under a duty to give any interested party an opportunity to be heard, except in cases where this would be impossible or inexpedient.[94] Where the Comptroller orders royalties to be paid he shall also give directions as to the person to whom or the manner in which the licensee is to pay or deal with such royalties.[95] For these purposes the "Comptroller" means the Comptroller-General of Patents, Designs and Trade Marks and "enemy" and "enemy subject" have the meanings assigned to them by the Trading with the Enemy Act 1939.[96]

(viii) Control of monopoly: powers exercisable under domestic law

Licences as of right. The 1988 Act and the Rights in Databases Regulations supplement, with reference to copyright, design right, performers' property rights and database right, the general controls under United Kingdom legislation over anti-competitive or monopolistic practices.[97] Thus, section 144 of the 1988 Act provides that where whatever needs to be remedied, mitigated or prevented by the Secretary of State, the Office of Fair Trading or (as the case may be) the Competition Commission under various specified statutory provisions consists of or includes (a) conditions in copyright licences restricting the use of the work by the licensee or the right of the copyright owner to grant other licences, or (b) a refusal on the part of the copyright owner to grant licences on reasonable terms, then the Secretary of State, Office of Fair Trading or Competition Commission as the case may be is given the power to cancel or modify the licensing conditions, and (instead or in addition) the power to provide that licences shall be available as of right.[98] However, these powers may only be exercised if the person or body exercising them is satisfied that to do so does not contravene any Convention relating to copyright to which the United Kingdom is a party.[99] Equivalent provi-

29–54

---

[91] s.2. Note that the Comptroller also has the power to vary existing licences by virtue of this provision.

[92] s.2(1).

[93] See *Novello & Co Ltd v Hinrichsen Edition Ltd* [1951] Ch. 1026, in particular, at 1038.

[94] The Patents, Designs, Copyright and Trade Marks (Emergency) Act 1939, s.8.

[95] s.2(6). Note that under s.2(5) of the Act a licensee also has exceptional powers to "institute proceedings in his own name as though he were the owner of copyright". See, as to the effect of this provision, *Novello & Co. Ltd v Eulenberg* [1950] 1 All E.R. 44.

[96] s.10.

[97] See, generally, as to such legislation, para. 29–254, below.

[98] CDPA 1988, s.144 (1A), as amended by the Enterprise Act 2002 (c.40) Sch.25 para.18(2) with effect from June 20, 2003: see the Enterprise Act (Commencement No. 3, Transitional and Transitory and Savings) Order 2003 (SI 2003/1397), Art.2 (except for the purposes of references under s.32 of the Water Industry Act 1991: see Art.3(1)). This provision is discussed at paras 29–297 *et seq.*, below.

[99] CDPA 1988, s.144(3); see further para. 29–301, below.

sion is made in respect of design right,[1] performers' property rights[2] and database right.[3]

29–55   The Copyright Tribunal. If the terms of a licence available under any of these provisions except section 238 cannot be agreed, then the person requiring the licence may apply to the Copyright Tribunal to settle the terms.[4] The licence, as so settled, must authorise the licensee to do everything in respect of which a licence under the relevant provision is available.[5] When the terms of the licence have been settled by the Tribunal, the licence takes effect from the date of application to the Tribunal.[6] The terms of a licence under section 238 are to be settled by the comptroller in default of agreement.[7]

(ix) Control of monopoly: European Law

29–56   Overview. In addition to the domestic provisions, considered above, it is important to note that compulsory licences may also be made available under European law, where a copyright owner is found to have violated Article 82 (formerly 86) of the Treaty of Rome. The prohibition contained in the Article against abuse of a dominant position is considered elsewhere.[8] This section only considers the extent to which compulsory licences may be made available as a remedy for a breach of this Article.

29–57   The *Magill* decision.[9] In May 1986 the Irish publisher, Magill TV Guide Limited, began to publish a comprehensive weekly TV listings guide in the Irish Republic and in Northern Ireland. This led to an injunction being granted by the Irish High Court on the grounds that Magill was infringing copyright in the broadcasters' programme schedules.[10] By this time Magill had lodged a complaint with the European Commission which commenced an investigation under Council

---

[1] CDPA 1988, s.238, as amended by the Enterprise Act 2002 (c.40) Sch.25 para.18(3) with effect from June 20, 2003: see the Enterprise Act (Commencement No. 3, Transitional and Transitory and Savings) Order 2003 (SI 2003/1397), Art.2 (except for the purposes of references under s.32 of the Water Industry Act 1991: see Art.3(1)). Since design right is not covered by any relevant international convention, there is no requirement that the powers in respect of it should only be exercised if the person or body exercising them is satisfied that to do so does not contravene such a convention.

[2] CDPA 1988, Sch.2A para.17, as amended by the Enterprise Act 2002 (c.40) Sch.25 para.18(5) with effect from June 20, 2003: see the Enterprise Act (Commencement No. 3, Transitional and Transitory and Savings) Order 2003 (SI 2003/1397), Art.2 (except for the purposes of references under s.32 of the Water Industry Act 1991: see Art.3(1)).

[3] The Copyright and Rights in Databases Regulations 1997 (SI 1997/3032), Sch.2, para.15, as amended by the Enterprise Act 2002 (Consequential and Supplemental Provisions) Order 2003 (SI 2003/1398), art.2 and Sch., para.31 with effect from June 20, 2003 (except for the purposes of references under s.32 of the Water Industry Act 1991: *ibid.*, art.3(1)). Since database right is not covered by any relevant international convention, there is no requirement that the powers in respect of it should only be exercised if the person or body exercising them is satisfied that to do so does not contravene such a convention.

[4] CDPA 1988, s.144(4), CDPA 1988, Sch.2A para.17(4) and Sch.2, para.15 (3) of the Regulations, respectively; as to the Copyright Tribunal generally, see paras 29–93 *et seq.*, below, and as to such applications and the procedure before the Tribunal see paras 29–159 *et seq.*, below.

[5] CDPA 1988, s.144 (4), CDPA 1988, Sch.2A para.17(4) and Sch.2, para.15 (3) of the Regulations, respectively.

[6] CDPA 1988, s.144(5) CDPA 1988, Sch.2A para.17(5) and Sch.2, para.15 (4) of the Regulations, respectively.

[7] s.238(3).

[8] See paras 29–183 *et seq.*, below.

[9] Joined Cases C-241 & 242/91P, *Radio Telefis Eireann and Independent Television Publications Ltd v E.C. Commission* [1995] E.C.R. I-743; [1995] 4 C.M.L.R. 718, paras 3–10 (opinion of Advocate-General Gulman) and paras 7–15 (Judgment). See Aitman & Jones: "Competition Law and Copyright: Has the Copyright Owner Lost the Ability to Control his Copyright?" [2004] E.I.P.R. 137.

[10] Also see paras 29–10 *et seq.*, above.

Regulation 17 implementing Articles 85 (now 81) and 86 (now 82) of the Treaty. In its decision[11] the Commission held that the policies of the BBC, ITP and RTE in refusing to grant licences to publish weekly listings of their television programmes amounted to an infringement of Article 86 (now 82). The Commission therefore ordered that the broadcasters bring this infringement to an end by granting such licences on request. The broadcasters appealed, but the Commission's decision was upheld by the European Court of First Instance.[12] The reasoning of the Court of First Instance caused some controversy and ITP and RTE, but not the BBC, appealed to the European Court of Justice.[13] Advocate-General Gulman then delivered an opinion which supported the broadcasters' case and recommended that the appeal be allowed.[14]

In upholding the decision of the Commission[15] and the Court of First Instance the Court of Justice considered both the circumstances in which a refusal to grant licences could amount to a breach of Article 86 (now 82) and the extent to which compulsory licences could be made available as a remedy for such a breach. The Commission accepted that a refusal to grant licences could not, in itself, constitute an abuse of a dominant position. Thus the question was whether "there may exist such special circumstances in connection with a refusal to license that it can no longer be regarded as a refusal to license in itself".[16] The Court of Justice held that such special circumstances may occasionally exist and thus "the exercise of an exclusive right by the proprietor may, in exceptional circumstances, involve abusive conduct".[17] The Court of First Instance had said that the existence of such special circumstances must be judged against the "essential function" of copyright. This "essential function" was said to be providing protection for the moral rights in the work and ensuring a reward for creative efforts.[18] The Court of First Instance had further said that "where the copyright is no longer exercised in a manner which corresponds to its essential function the primacy of Community law prevails over any use of rules of national intellectual property law contrary to the principles of the free movement of goods and freedom of competition".[19] Although the Court of Justice declined to expand on this aspect of the Court of First Instance's decision, it did not expressly disapprove of it. In this case it was enough that the "applicants were using their copyright in the programme listings produced as part of the activity of broadcasting in order to secure a monopoly in the derivative market of weekly television listings".[20] The broadcasters were thus abusing a dominant position.

Having found that the broadcasters had abused a dominant position the Court of Justice then had to consider whether the Commission had the power to order

---

[11] December 21, 1988; *Magill TV Guide/ITP, BBC and RTE* [1989] O.J. L78/43; [1989] 4 C.M.L.R. 749.

[12] Case T-69/89, *Radio Telefis Eireann v Commission* [1991] 4 C.M.L.R. 586; Case T-70/89, *BBC v Commission* [1991] 4 C.M.L.R. 669; and Case T-76/89, *Independent Television Publications Ltd v Commission* [1991] 4 C.M.L.R. 745.

[13] See further, Tritton, *Intellectual Property in Europe* (Sweet & Maxwell, London, 1996), p.646; Myrick, "Will Intellectual Property on Technology still be viable in a unitary market?" [1992] 9 E.I.P.R. 298.

[14] [1995] 4 C.M.L.R. 718 at 725–781.

[15] Joined Cases C-241 & 242/91P *Radio Telefis Eireann and Independent Television Publications Ltd v EC Commission* [1995] E.C.R. I-743; [1995] 4 C.M.L.R. 718.

[16] Joined Cases C-241 & 242/91P *Radio Telefis Eireann and Independent Television Publications Ltd v EC Commission* [1995] E.C.R. I-743; [1995] 4 C.M.L.R. 718, para.40 (opinion of Advocate-General Gulman).

[17] Joined Cases C-241 & 242/91P *Radio Telefis Eireann and Independent Television Publications Ltd v EC Commission* [1995] E.C.R. I-743; [1995] 4 C.M.L.R. 718, para.50.

[18] Case T-69/89 *Radio Telefis Eireann v Commission* [1991] 4 C.M.L.R. 586, para.71.

[19] Case T-69/89 *Radio Telefis Eireann v Commission* [1991] 4 C.M.L.R. 586, para.71.

[20] Joined cases C-241 & 242/91P *Radio Telefis Eireann and Independent Television Publications Ltd v EC Commission* [1995] 4 C.M.L.R. 718, para.56.

that licences be made available in order to bring this abuse to an end. The Court had little difficulty in finding that such a direction from the Commission fell within its powers under Article 3 of Regulation 17,[21] pointing out that it had previously been held that the Commission's powers under this Article included the power to issue an order requiring the person in violation of Article 86 (now 82) to do certain acts. Furthermore, the Court of Justice stressed that in this case there was no other way in which the abuse could be brought to an end.[22] The *Magill* decision has been considered by the courts in Europe in three important subsequent cases:

29–58   ***Tiercé Ladbroke.***[23] This case concerned a refusal by the owners of the exclusive television rights in respect of French racing to provide a Belgian betting company (Ladbroke) with the sound and pictures of French races for its betting outlets in Belgium. The Court of First Instance held that *Magill* was not in point. In *Magill*, the refusal to licence prevented the applicant from entering the market. By contrast, Ladbroke had the largest share of the betting market in Belgium. Furthermore, the refusal to supply would not fall within the prohibition of Article 86 (now 82) unless it concerned a product or service which was either essential for the exercise of the activity in question (in that there was no real or potential substitute) or was a new product the introduction of which might be prevented despite specific, constant and regular demand. In this case, the availability of televised broadcasts was not indispensable for the taking of bets. Accordingly there was no abuse of dominant position.

29–59   ***Bronner.***[24] This case concerned the question whether a refusal by a newspaper proprietor in a dominant position to include another's product in its home-delivery scheme could amount to an abuse of that position. The Court of Justice emphasised that it would only be in exceptional circumstances that the refusal by a dominant owner to license another would amount to an abuse. It stated that in *Magill* those exceptional circumstances were that the refusal concerned a product (information on the schedules) the supply of which was indispensable for carrying on the business in question (publication of a television guide); prevented the appearance of a new product for which there was potential demand; was not justified by objective considerations; and was likely to exclude all competition in the secondary market of television guides. The Court went on to state that the effect of *Magill* was that three cumulative requirements needed to be satisfied before an abuse existed: elimination of competition, absence of objective justification and the fact that the service being refused is indispensable to the proposed business inasmuch as there is no actual or potential substitute. On the facts, at least the third of these requirements was not satisfied and accordingly there could be no abuse.

29–60   ***IMS Health.***[25] In this case, both parties were engaged in the business of tracking sales of pharmaceutical and healthcare products and marketing the resulting

---

[21] Council Regulation 17/62 [1959–62] O.J. 87. As from May 1, 2004, this has been repealed and replaced by Council Regulation (EC) No. 1/2003 on the Implementation of the Rules of Competition Laid Down in Articles 81 and 82 of the Treaty: [2003] O.J. L1/1 ("the Modernisation Regulation"). Art.7(1) of the Modernisation Regulation is in similar terms to Art.3 of Reg.17. See para. 29–205 below.

[22] Joined cases C-241 & 242/91P *Radio Telefis Eireann and Independent Television Publications Ltd v EC Commission* [1995] 4 C.M.L.R. 718, paras 90–91.

[23] *Tiercé Ladbroke SA v Commission*, Case T-504/93, [1997] E.C.R. II-923; [1997] 5 C.M.L.R. 309.

[24] Case C-7/97 *Oscar Bronner GmbH & Co KG v Mediaprint Zeitungs- und Zeitschriftenverlag GmbH & Co KG* [1998] E.C.R. I-7791, [1999] 4 C.M.L.R. 112.

[25] Case C-418/01 *IMS Health GmbH & Co. OHG v NDC Health GmbH & Co KG* [2004] 4 C.M.L.R.

regional sales data to pharmaceutical companies. At issue was the assumed copyright in a "brick structure" which had been developed by the claimant ("IMS") in conjunction with a working group which included many of its clients and which had become the *de facto* industry standard for the presentation of such data. The defendant ("NDC") had attempted to market data based on a different brick structure, but clients were reluctant to use it. It therefore contended that IMS's refusal to grant it a licence to use the brick structure infringed Article 82.

Indispensability: questions and arguments. Two of the questions referred by   **29–61**
the German court concerned the criteria for determining whether the refusal of
access concerned a product or service which was indispensable for carrying on a
particular business (the first exceptional circumstance identified in *Bronner* as
having applied in *Magill*). The first of these questions was as to the relevance of
the degree of participation by users in the development of IMS's brick structure.[26]
The second was as to the relevance of the outlay, particularly in terms of cost,
which potential users would have to provide in order to be able to purchase sales
data based on a different brick structure.[27] IMS contended that the participation
referred to in the first question was evidence of competition, representing the
manufacturer's efforts to meet its clients' needs. The cost to clients of changing
to a competing product would be offset by the advantage of the competing
product. NDC and the Commission, on the other hand, contended that the
considerable role played by users in the design of the IMS's brick structure had
contributed to a relationship of dependency by them on the structure. Relying on
Bronner, they contended that the criterion for determining whether the structure
was indispensable is whether a competitor could create a viable alternative. In
this case, they contended, legal and economic constraints made this impossible.[28]

Indispensability: the decision. The Court held, applying *Bronner*, that it is nec-   **29–62**
essary to determine whether there are products or services which provide alternative solutions even if they are less advantageous, and whether there are technical,
legal or economic obstacles capable of making it impossible or at least unreasonably difficult for any undertaking to create such alternatives. Economic obstacles
are only relevant to the extent that the creation of such alternatives is not
economically viable for production on a scale comparable to that of the copyright
owner. Accordingly, in considering the question of indispensability, any
dependency on the part of clients (if proven) would be relevant. If there were
such dependency, it would be likely that such clients would have to make
exceptional organisational and financial efforts in order to acquire the sales data
presented on the basis of a different brick structure. The supplier of such a
structure might therefore be obliged to offer terms which were such as to rule out
any economic viability of doing business on a scale comparable to the copyright
owner.[29]

Abuse: the three conditions. The other question referred by the German court   **29–63**
was whether there was an abuse where potential clients rejected any competing
product not based on IMS's brick structure because their set-up relied on products

---

28. See Stothers, " *IMS Health* and its implications for compulsory licensing in Europe" [2004]
10 E.I.P.R. 467.

[26] Case C-418/01 *IMS Health GmbH & Co OHG v NDC Health GmbH & Co KG* [2004] 4 C.M.L.R.
28, para.17.

[27] Case C-418/01 *IMS Health GmbH & Co OHG v NDC Health GmbH & Co KG* [2004] 4 C.M.L.R.
28.

[28] The arguments are recited at Case C-418/01 *IMS Health GmbH & Co OHG v NDC Health GmbH
& Co KG* [2004] 4 C.M.L.R. 28, paras 26 and 27.

[29] Case C-418/01 *IMS Health GmbH & Co OHG v NDC Health GmbH & Co KG* [2004] 4 C.M.L.R.
28, paras 28 and 29.

manufactured on the basis that structure.[30] In answering this question, the Court began by stating that it was clear from the case law that in order for a refusal by a copyright owner to give access to a product or service which was indispensable for carrying on a particular business to be abusive, it was sufficient for three cumulative conditions to be satisfied. Those conditions were as follows: First, that the refusal was preventing the emergence of a new product for which there was a potential consumer demand. Secondly, that the refusal was unjustified. Thirdly, that the refusal was such as to exclude any competition on a secondary market.[31] It will be noted that the Court stated that the conditions were "sufficient", not "necessary". In the English case of *Intel v Via Technologies*, which was decided before final judgment was given in *IMS Health*, the Court of Appeal held that the decisions in *Bronner* and at an interim stage in *IMS Health*[32] indicated the circumstances in which the European Court of Justice and the President of the Court of First Instance respectively regarded as exceptional in the cases before them.[33] The Court of Appeal went on to state that it did not follow that other circumstances in other cases might not be regarded as exceptional.[34] It is suggested that nothing in the final decision in *IMS Health* detracts from the force of this observation.

29–64   **The first condition: new product or service**. The parties disputed whether NDC was intending to produce a new product or service. The Court emphasised that free competition would only prevail (in the form of a compulsory licence) where the refusal to grant a licence prevented the development of a secondary market to the detriment of consumers. It was not sufficient that the competitor merely intended to duplicate the copyright owner's goods and services. The competitor must intend to produce new goods and services not offered by the copyright owner and for which there is a potential consumer demand.[35] It was for the national court to resolve this issue.

29–65   **The second condition: unjustified**. The Court reiterated that it was for the national court to decide on the facts whether the refusal was justified by objective considerations.[36] However, it did not provide further guidance on this point, as to which no specific observations were made by the parties.

29–66   **The third condition: exclusion of competition on a secondary market**. IMS contended that this condition was not met because NDC was attempting to supply its product on the same market. By contrast, NDC argued that it was not essential that there were two different markets and that it was sufficient that the copyright owner should have a monopoly on an infrastructure which was indispensable in order to compete with it on the market in which it carried on business. The Commission, in turn, argued that it was not necessary for the infrastructure to be on a separate market: it was sufficient that it was at a stage of upstream production.[37] The Court noted that in *Bronner*, the national court had been invited to determine whether home-delivery schemes constituted a separate market on

---

[30] Case C-418/01 *IMS Health GmbH & Co OHG v NDC Health GmbH & Co KG* [2004] 4 C.M.L.R. 28, para.17.

[31] Case C-418/01 *IMS Health GmbH & Co OHG v NDC Health GmbH & Co KG* [2004] 4 C.M.L.R. 28, para.38.

[32] *IMS Health Inc v European Commission* [2002] 4 C.M.L.R. 58.

[33] *Intel Corporation v Via Technologies Inc.* [2002] EWCA Civ 1905, para.48.

[34] *Intel Corporation v Via Technologies Inc.* [2002] EWCA Civ 1905, para.48.

[35] paras 48 and 49.

[36] Case C-418/01 *IMS Health GmbH & Co OHG v NDC Health GmbH & Co KG* [2004] 4 C.M.L.R. 28, para.51.

[37] For the arguments, see Case C-418/01 *IMS Health GmbH & Co OHG v NDC Health GmbH & Co KG* [2004] 4 C.M.L.R. 28, paras 32 and 33.

which the owner of the scheme held a dominant position. Accordingly, it had been relevant to distinguish an upstream market for a product or service (in *Bronner*, the market for home delivery) and a (secondary) downstream market on which the upstream product or service was used for the production of another product or supply of another service (in *Bronner*, the market for daily newspapers). The Court noted that in *Bronner* the fact that the home-delivery service was not marketed separately did not preclude the possibility of identifying it as a separate market. It followed, according to the Court, that it was sufficient that a potential, even hypothetical, market could be identified. If two different stages of production could be identified, even if they were interconnected, the condition would be fulfilled provided the upstream product was indispensable for the supply of the downstream product. On the facts of the case, therefore, the question for the national court was whether IMS's brick structure constituted, upstream, an indispensable factor in the downstream supply of regional sales data. If so, the question was whether IMS's refusal to grant a licence was capable of excluding all competition on the market for sales data.[38] In the English case of *Intel v Via Technologies*, which was decided before final judgment was given in *IMS Health*, the Court of Appeal held that the decisions in *Bronner* and at an interim stage in *IMS Health* did not mean that all competition had to be excluded on the secondary market: it was sufficient that competition from the person requesting the licence was excluded.[39] It is suggested that this view is no longer sustainable given the clear statements in *IMS Health* that "all" or "any" competition must be excluded.[40]

Application in the United Kingdom. Article 82 is drectly enforceable in the English courts and is regularly raised by way of a defence in proceedings for infringement of intellectual property rights. Reference has already been made to the patent case of *Intel v Via Technologies*.[41] In that case, the Court of Appeal made some general observations as to the way in which arguments based on the *Magill* line of cases should be dealt with in the United Kingdom. First, so-called "Euro-defences" demand careful scrutiny so as to avoid defences without merit going to what is likely to be a long and expensive trial; on the other hand, cases involving Article 81 or 82 often involve questions of mixed law and fact which are not suitable for summary determination.[42] Second, where the jurisprudence of the European Court of Justice is in the course of development, it is dangerous to assume that it is beyond argument with real prospect of success that the existing case law will not be extended or modified so as to encompass the defence being advanced.[43] Finally a Euro-defence which is likely at some stage to be the subject of a reference to the European Court of Justice is likely to be one which for that reason should only be disposed of at a trial.[44]   **29–67**

Enforcement by the Commission. One of the Commission's most important functions is to ensure that European law is properly implemented, and thus it is   **29–68**

---

[38] Case C-418/01 *IMS Health GmbH & Co OHG v NDC Health GmbH & Co KG* [2004] 4 C.M.L.R. 28, paras 40 to 47.

[39] *Intel Corporation v Via Technologies Inc.* [2002] EWCA Civ 1905 para.49.

[40] See *Intel Corporation v Via Technologies Inc.* [2002] EWCA Civ 1905 at paras 37, 39, 40 (heading), 47, 52.

[41] *Intel Corporation v Via Technologies Inc.* [2002] EWCA Civ 1905. See paras 29–63 and 29–66 above.

[42] *Intel Corporation v Via Technologies Inc.* [2002] EWCA Civ 1905, para.32.

[43] *Intel Corporation v Via Technologies Inc.* [2002] EWCA Civ 1905, para.32.

[44] *Intel Corporation v Via Technologies Inc.* [2002] EWCA Civ 1905, para.35.

the responsibility of the Commission to ensure that Article 82 is enforced.[45] It must be expected, therefore, that compulsory licences will be made available under European law following a ruling by the Commission, whenever the Commission considers that the circumstances justify this.[46]

D. REFORM: PROPOSALS FOR MULTIMEDIA COMPULSORY LICENCES

29–69   **Background.** As has been seen, a wide range of compulsory licences has been proposed, although very few of these proposals have ever been implemented.[47] Most recently attention has focused on the need for compulsory licences as a response to the advent of the "information society". Aside from some of the more radical proposals, a number of commentators have argued for compulsory licences to be made available in respect of multimedia products.[48] It is these more limited proposals which are beginning to be given serious consideration.

Although the term "multimedia" is incapable of precise definition, in general it is used to refer to products consisting of a mixture of digitally stored text, graphics and music, irrespective of whether these works are made available on CD-ROM, DVD or over electronic networks. In copyright terms a multimedia work is likely to include a mixture of literary, musical and artistic works, films and sound recordings, hence they are sometimes referred to as "hybrid" works.[49] In order to create a multimedia product it is normal to incorporate the whole or part of a number of pre-existing works, as only using original material would usually be prohibitively expensive. Moreover, the most successful multimedia works have so far proved to be derivative products comprising abridgements or abstracts, which it will often not be possible to produce without obtaining a series of copyright licences.

This section will examine the arguments that surround the introduction of compulsory licences for multimedia products and some of the more recent responses to this debate.

29–70   **Why might compulsory licences for multimedia products be necessary?** The principal argument for the introduction of compulsory licences for multimedia products concerns the transaction costs of having to negotiate licences for all the different works that might be included in a multimedia product.[50] Compulsory licences, it is argued, could significantly reduce these transaction costs with the result that many more products would become available.[51] Moreover, concern has been expressed that, even when it has proved possible to get all the relevant licences, multimedia producers have been overcharged. In particular, it has been said that copyright owners have been able to charge substantial sums for relatively small sections of their works. Risk-averse publishers will tend to pay what is

---

[45] See further para. 29–205, below.

[46] See, *e.g. Microsoft,* C (2004) 900 final. It should be noted that although the Commission will often act following a complaint (as in *Magill*) it also has the power to initiate an investigation.

[47] See further, para. 29–05, above.

[48] For example, see Tang, "Multimedia information products and services" in Loader (ed.), *The Governance of Cyberspace* (Routledge, London, 1997); Reichmann, "Legal Hybrids Between the Patent and Copyright Paradigms" (1995) 94 Colum. L. Rev. 2432. Also see Merges, "Contracting into Liability Rules: Intellectual Property Rights and Collective Rights Organizations" (1996) 84 Cal. L.Rev. 1293 at 1376. *cf.*Dixon and Hansen, "The Berne Convention Enters the Digital Age" [1991] 11 E.I.P.R. 605.

[49] For example, see the *Multimedia Industry Advisory Report,* Department of Trade and Industry, December 1995, p.13.

[50] See further, Merges, "Contracting into Liability Rules: Intellectual Property Rights and Collective Rights Organizations" (1996) 84 Cal. L.Rev. 1293 at 1376–1377; Hoeren, *Copyright in Electronic Delivery Services and Multimedia Products* (Luxembourg, European Commission, 1995).

[51] See para. 29–69, above.

demanded by the copyright owner, with the result that the cost of the final products is increased, even if the taking would arguably fall within one of the exceptions (for example, fair dealing for the purpose of criticism or review) or if the material taken arguably does not form a substantial part of the owner's work.[52] The "bewildering differences in national copyright Acts in the area of exemptions and limitations"[53] make it still more likely that the producers of multimedia works will be unwilling to rely on the exceptions: they will have to be confident that their use of any underlying works is permitted in every country in which they intend to market their product. Further difficulties are created by the absence of a *bona fides* defence. One of the dangers in having to obtain a very large number of licences is that it is easy to overlook the need to obtain a particular licence. In the absence of a such a defence (or a compulsory licence) there is a danger that the producer of the multimedia work will be held to ransom by the copyright owner whose prior consent was not obtained.[54]

A second argument put forward by those in favour of the introduction of compulsory licences concerns perceived difficulties with collecting societies. In particular, it is said that collecting societies are national in nature and they only tend to deal with a limited range of rights, which makes them inappropriate to deal with rights clearance for multimedia works.[55]

Finally, concern is sometimes expressed that right owners are reluctant to license their works for use in multimedia products, particularly where these are to be made available over electronic networks, because of a fear that they will lose control over their work.[56] By replacing copyright with a right to equitable remuneration, these difficulties would disappear.

In addition to the arguments outlined above, those in favour of compulsory licences tend to point out that multimedia products pose a number of other difficulties for copyright law. For example, it has been said that the role of moral rights may have to be re-examined in relation to multimedia works.[57] Whilst these problems do not provide direct evidence of the need for compulsory licences, they might suggest a need to think again about how multimedia works are dealt with.

Reasons to wait and see. On behalf of those opposed to the introduction of compulsory licences for multimedia works it can be said that there are at least four reasons why it would be prudent to wait before attempting to reform the copyright system in this respect.   **29–71**

First, it is said that the "unique nature" of the problems posed by multimedia works has been exaggerated. Certainly, it is possible to point to other types of product, particularly films, which incorporate a range of copyright works. Moreover, there already seems to be some evidence of the voluntary formation of ap-

---

[52] See further, Goldberg, "Now that the future has arrived maybe the law should take a look: multimedia technology and its interaction with the fair use doctrine" (1995) 44 Am. U.L. Rev.

[53] Hoeren, *Copyright in Electronic Delivery Services and Multimedia Products* (Luxembourg, European Commission, 1995), pp.5–7.

[54] Hoeren, *Copyright in Electronic Delivery Services and Multimedia Products* (Luxembourg, European Commission, 1995), pp.5–7.

[55] See Henry, *Publishing and Multimedia Law* (Butterworths, London, 1994).

[56] See Hoeren, *Copyright in Electronic Delivery Services and Multimedia Products* (Luxembourg, European Commission, 1995), p.10.

[57] For example, see Gaster, "Copyright and Neighbouring Rights in the European Information Society" in *Copyright in Multimedia: Papers from the Aslib Conference held on July 18 & 19, 1995* (Aslib, London, 1995).

propriate collecting societies. For example, the German societies GVL and GEMA have merged for purposes of supplying a "one-stop multimedia service".[58]

Secondly, the introduction of a compulsory licence for multimedia works would be incompatible with existing international copyright agreements and the predominant international mood is clearly not in favour of the extension of compulsory licences.[59]

Thirdly, it is important to wait and see how the market for multimedia works is affected by changes in technology. Digitisation may give rise to more effective ways of administering rights.[60] One of the advantages of the developments in information processing may therefore be that the transaction costs of obtaining licences will be reduced.

Finally, it should be noted that some commentators have challenged the assumption that the most effective way of reducing transaction costs is to introduce compulsory licences. In particular, it has been argued that the collective administration of rights is often more efficient than compulsory licensing schemes, as collecting societies are able to tailor licensing schemes to meet the needs of different classes of user.[61]

29–72   **Current proposals.** Although none of the major industrialised nations has attempted to introduce compulsory multimedia licences, the need to try to find ways of reducing transaction costs has been given widespread consideration.

In the United Kingdom this issue was touched upon in the Report of the Multimedia Industry Advisory Group.[62] However, although the Group noted the problems that the producers of multimedia works face in respect of transaction costs, it did not make any definite proposals as to how to overcome these difficulties, other than to suggest that a format right for multimedia works be introduced which would "vindicate producers' efforts".[63]

In Europe the matter has most recently been considered by the Commission in its White Paper on copyright and related rights in the information society.[64] In this document the Commission concluded that the management of rights in an information society was an issue that required further evaluation.[65] Nevertheless, the Commission accepted that "The creation and exploitation of multimedia products and services may imply that the individual exercise of rights will become even less practicable than it is today due to the great number of new or pre-existing works, productions and uses involved. This may call for new forms of centralised administration which facilitate rights management or, in some cases, for more collective management".[66] Whilst stressing that for the time being licensing should be left to the market, the Commission went on to point out that

---

[58] *Music and Copyright,* Vol.110/15 (March 26, 1997). Also see Merges, "Contracting into Liability Rules: Intellectual Property Rights and Collective Rights Organizations" (1996) 84 Cal. L.Rev. 1293 at 1378–1380. For other such developments, see Schippan, *Purchase and Licensing of Digital Rights: the Verdi Project and the Clearing of Multimedia Rights in Europe* [2000] E.I.P.R. 24.

[59] See further, para. 29–06, above.

[60] For example, see Merges, "Contracting into Liability Rules: Intellectual Property Rights and Collective Rights Organizations" (1996) 84 Cal. L.Rev. 1293 at 1380–1383.

[61] Merges, "Contracting into Liability Rules: Intellectual Property Rights and Collective Rights Organizations" (1996) 84 Cal. L.Rev. 1293 at 1380–1383.

[62] Department of Trade and Industry, December 1995.

[63] Report of the Multimedia Industry Advisory Group (DTI, December 1995), p.22.

[64] *Follow-Up to the Green Paper on Copyright and Related Rights in the Information Society,* COM(96)final (Brussels, November 20, 1996). See further paras 25–77 *et seq.,* above.

[65] *Follow-Up to the Green Paper on Copyright and Related Rights in the Information Society,* Ch.3, Pt 3.

[66] *Follow-Up to the Green Paper on Copyright and Related Rights in the Information Society,* Ch.3, Pt 3.

"In some situations Community law stipulates mandatory rights administration by collecting societies or the extension of a collective agreement with a collecting society to unrepresented right holders".[67] The forced collective administration of rights bears a close resemblance to making compulsory licences available.[68] The main European development in this field since the White Paper is the MMRCS Strategic Analysis Study within the framework of the INFO 2000 programme. This study, which was funded by the Commission, involved ten different pilot projects aimed at enhancing multimedia rights clearance processes.[69] However, the study has not resulted in any specific legislative proposals or other new initiatives.

There has also been interest in Japan in the need to reform the administration of rights, with plans for the creation of a centralised body to administer multimedia rights. Fears have been expressed by US officials that this might include an element of compulsory licensing.[70]

Thus, although no concrete proposals for the introduction of compulsory licences have yet been put forward, interest is beginning to be shown in finding ways of reducing transaction costs for the producers of multimedia works. While the issue of transaction costs remains unresolved, it is likely that proposals for compulsory licences for multimedia works will continue to be floated.

2. MISCELLANEOUS CONTROLS ON THE EXERCISE OF RIGHTS

Introduction. There are two areas where the legislature has interfered with the exercise of exclusive rights accorded under the 1988 Act, but stopping short of imposing a compulsory or statutory licence. In these two cases, the Act has left the right to be exercised consensually, but has provided how it is to be exercised. In the first case, that of the exercise of the cable retransmission right, the Act provides that the right may only be exercised by a collecting society. In the second case, that of the exercise of the reproduction right by reprographic copying of published literary, dramatic, musical and artistic works and typographical arrangements of published editions, the Act provides that existing consensual arrangements for the exercise of such right in respect of certain such works may be compulsorily extended to include other such works. In a third area, the Act provides a procedure for the certification or (in one case) notification of licensing schemes for certain works for the purpose of displacing the permitted acts which would otherwise apply to those works. In a fourth area, the Act provides a procedure for compulsory notification of proposed licences or licensing schemes to the Secretary of State, who may decide to refer them to the Copyright Tribunal. The effect in all these cases is to subject the exercise of such rights to the control of the Copyright Tribunal.

29–73

---

[67] *Follow-Up to the Green Paper on Copyright and Related Rights in the Information Society*, Ch.3 Pt 3. See further, Council Directive 93/83 on the co-ordination of certain rules concerning copyright and rights related to copyright applicable to satellite broadcasting and cable retransmission [1993] O.J. L248/15, Art.9, Art.3(2); and see further para. 29–74, below.

[68] Also see para. 29–48, above.

[69] See the account in Schippan, *Purchase and Licensing of Digital Rights: the Verdi Project and the Clearing of Multimedia Rights in Europe* [2000] E.I.P.R. 24 and the Final Evaluation of the Info 2000 Programme at *http://europa.eu.int/information_society/programmes/evaluation/pdf/report1info2000_en.pdf*.

[70] See Merges, "Contracting into Liability Rules: Intellectual Property Rights and Collective Rights Organizations" (1996) 84 Cal. L.Rev. 1293 at 1378.

A. COMPULSORY COLLECTIVE ADMINISTRATION OF RIGHTS: THE CABLE RETRANSMISSION RIGHT

29–74   **Cable retransmission right.** The Satellite and Cable Directive[71] was adopted as part of the programme of harmonisation of the national laws of Member States of the European Union undertaken at the instigation of the Commission,[72] aimed, in the case of this Directive, at the creation of a single audio visual area.[73] One of the aims of the Directive was to facilitate the cable retransmission across national boundaries of broadcast and cable transmissions. For these purposes the Directive defined cable retransmission as "the simultaneous, unaltered and unabridged retransmission by a cable or microwave system for reception by the public of an initial transmission from another Member State, by wire or over the air".[74] The Directive required Member States to ensure that when programmes from other Member States are retransmitted by cable in their territory the applicable copyright and related rights are observed, and that such retransmission takes place on the basis of individual or collective contractual agreements between right owners and cable operators.[75] However, the Directive also required that the cable retransmission right should only be capable of being exercised as regards a cable operator through a collecting society.[76] Where a right owner had not transferred the management of the cable retransmission right in his work to a collecting society, he was to be treated as having mandated the collecting society which manages rights of the same category to manage his right. Where there was more than one such collecting society, the right owner was to have the right to choose which he wished to be mandated to manage his right.[77] A right owner who had not mandated his right to a collecting society was to have the same rights and obligations arising from an agreement between a collecting society and a cable operator as one who had.[78]

29–75   **Section 144A of the 1988 Act.** These provisions of the Satellite and Cable Directive were implemented in the United Kingdom by the Copyright and Related Rights Regulations 1996,[79] which introduced into the 1988 Act, with effect from December 1, 1996, section 144A. Although the wording of the section often closely follows the provisions of the Directive, it remains questionable whether the section properly implements the Directive in all respects. Section 144A has in turn been amended to give effect to the Information Society Directive.[80]

The section first identifies as a specific right in a work, being part of the bundle of rights comprising the copyright in that work under the 1988 Act, the right to grant or refuse authorisation for cable retransmission of a wireless broadcast

---

[71] September 27, 1993, [1993] O.J. L248/15; for the text of the Directive, see Vol.2 at H4.
[72] See generally paras 25–41 *et seq.*, above and for a discussion of the Directive, see paras 25–58 *et seq.*, above.
[73] See Council Directive 89/552, [1989] O.J. L298/23, on the co-ordination of certain provisions laid down by law, regulation or administrative action in Member States concerning the pursuit of television broadcasting activities.
[74] Directive 89/552, Art.1(3).
[75] Art.8(1).
[76] Art.9(1). This was considered necessary in order to ensure the smooth operation of contractual arrangements for retransmission in other Member States of the broadcast and cable transmissions; see Recital (28).
[77] Art.9(2).
[78] Art.9(2).
[79] SI 1996/2967; those provisions of the Regulations not incorporated into the 1988 Act are set out in Vol.2 at A3.iii.
[80] The amendments are effected by the Copyright and Related Rights Regulations 2003, SI 2003/2498, with effect from October 31, 2003.

from another EEA State in which the work is included.[81] A "cable retransmission" is defined as the reception and immediate retransmission by cable, including the transmission by microwave energy between terrestrial fixed points, of a wireless broadcast.[82] This right is defined as the cable retransmission right and the works in respect of which it exists are all literary, dramatic, musical and artistic works, sound recordings and films.[83] The policy behind the Directive was that collective administration of the cable retransmission right was only required in relation to the numerous underlying works reproduced in the broadcast, but was not necessary in respect of the broadcast itself, as the broadcaster should remain free to decide for itself whether to grant or refuse authorisation for the cable retransmission of its broadcast in another EEA State. Thus this list does not include the broadcast itself, and it is expressly provided that the section does not affect any rights exercisable by the maker of the broadcast, either in respect of the broadcast, or any underlying works included in it.[84] The omission of cable programmes from this list is explained on the same basis. What is less easy to understand is why the cable retransmission right is expressed to be limited to the retransmission of a wireless broadcast, thus excluding cable retransmission where the initial transmission is by cable, since such a retransmission would also appear to be within the terms of the Directive.[85]

The section then provides that the cable re-transmission right may only be exercised against a cable operator through a licensing body.[86] For these purposes a cable operator means a person responsible for cable retransmission of a wireless broadcast[87] ; this is the person who will be committing the act restricted by the copyright in the work when re-transmitting the initial broadcast by means of cable.[88] The meaning of the expression "exercised against" is unclear. The definition of the cable retransmission right speaks of the right to grant or refuse authorisation, and therefore the exercise of that right would naturally include granting authorisation to a cable operator, and the grant of the right to a cable operator should therefore be included in the expression, notwithstanding the awkwardness caused by the word "against". On the other hand, the expression may be interpreted to mean that the copyright owner no longer may institute proceedings for infringement of the right against a cable operator, this being now the exclusive remit of whichever collecting society is deemed to be mandated to manage the right. If the cable operator does, in fact, have the appropriate licence from a collecting society, then it will have a defence to an action for infringement, but if it has no such licence, then its retransmission is an infringement. In that case why should the owner of the right (who has not transferred it to a collecting society) be entitled to institute proceedings?

A copyright owner who has not transferred the management of the cable retransmission right in his work to a licensing body is deemed to have mandated the licensing body which manages rights of the same category to manage his right.[89] Where there are two or more such licensing bodies, the copyright owner

---

[81] CDPA 1988, s.144A (1); as to which countries are EEA States, see para. 25–01, above.

[82] CDPA 1988, s.144A (7); the term does not appear elsewhere in the 1988 Act and the definition is therefore expressed to be for the purposes of s.144A.

[83] s.144A(1).

[84] s.144A(6).

[85] See the definition in Art.1(3) of Directive 93/83, cited in para. 29–74 above, which governs the extent of Art.9(1).

[86] CDPA 1988, s.144A(2); as to the definition of a licensing body, see para. 29–107, below.

[87] s.144(7); again, the term cable operator is not one which appears elsewhere in the 1988 Act, and the definition is expressed to be for the purposes of this section.

[88] See ss.16(1)(d) and 20.

[89] s.144A(3).

may specify which of them is to manage the right in his work.[90] Such a copyright owner who has not transferred the management of the cable retransmission right to a licensing body nevertheless has the same rights and obligations resulting from any relevant agreement between the cable operator and the licensing body as those who have transferred their right to that body,[91] but he must claim those rights within the period of three years from the date of the cable retransmission of his work.[92]

B. COMPULSORY EXTENSION AND CREATION OF LICENSING SCHEMES AND LICENCES FOR REPROGRAPHIC COPYRIGHT OF CERTAIN WORKS

29–76   **Reprographic copying by educational establishments.** The 1988 Act provides a special regime in sections 137 to 141 in respect of reprographic copying[93] of published literary, dramatic, musical or artistic works or of typographical arrangements of published editions by educational establishments.[94] Where a licensing scheme, to which sections 118 to 123 of the 1988 Act apply,[95] or a licence, to which sections 125 to 128 of that Act apply,[96] exists and provides for the licensing of reprographic copying of such works by educational establishments, then the Secretary of State has power to extend the coverage of such scheme or licence to works which he considers to be of a description similar to those covered but unreasonably excluded from it.[97] The Secretary of State may not exercise this power in relation to a work unless he considers that to do so would not conflict with the normal exploitation of the works or unreasonably prejudice the legitimate interests of the copyright owners.[98]

Where the Secretary of State proposes to make such an order, he must give notice to the copyright owners, the licensing body in question and appropriate persons or organisations representative of educational establishments.[99] Such notice must inform the persons of their right to make written or oral representations to the Secretary of State within six months of the notice, and if any person wishes to make oral representations, the Secretary of State will appoint a person to hear them.[1] The Secretary of State, in making his decision, must take into account representations made to him and all other matters as appear to him to be relevant.[2] There is provision for the variation or discharge by the Secretary of State of any order previously made by him under section 137 of the 1988 Act on the applica-

---

[90] s.144A(3).

[91] s.144A(4).

[92] s.144A(5); the Directive gave Member States the freedom to stipulate the length of this period, subject to a minimum of three years. In implementing this provision the Government simply applied this minimum.

[93] Reprographic copying means copying by a process for making facsimile copies or involving the use of an appliance for making multiple copies, or, in the case of a work held in electronic form, copying by electronic means: CDPA 1988, s.178.

[94] Educational establishment means any school (as further defined) and other description of educational establishment specified for such purpose by an order of the Secretary of State: CDPA 1988, s.174.

[95] See para. 29–108, below.

[96] See para. 29–119, below.

[97] CDPA 1988, s.137(2)(a).

[98] s.137(2)(b); this provision is necessary for the derogation of the owner's rights in such works not to be in breach of the Berne Convention, and follows the wording of the permitted exception to the owner's exclusive rights in such works: see Berne Convention (Paris Act, 1971) Art.9(2), the text of which is set out in Vol.2 at F1.

[99] s.137(3).

[1] s.137(4).

[2] s.137(5).

tion of the copyright owner.[3] Such variation cannot be made within two years of the original order or of a previous application seeking to vary it, unless the Secretary of State is satisfied that the circumstances are exceptional.[4] The Secretary of State may proceed to confirm the previous order on considering the grounds for the application without further representations,[5] but if he does not, the procedure to be followed is the same as that described above for the making of a decision under section 137 of the 1988 Act.[6] The Secretary of State's decision under each of these sections is subject to a right of appeal to the Copyright Tribunal.[7]

Inquiry whether scheme or licence required. The Secretary of State may appoint a person to inquire into whether new provision is required, by way of a licensing scheme or general licence, to authorise the making by or on behalf of educational establishments of reprographic copies of published literary, dramatic, musical or artistic works or of the typographical arrangements of published editions.[8] The procedure to be followed on such an inquiry is to be laid down by regulation by statutory instrument.[9] The person holding the inquiry is not to recommend the making of new provision unless he is satisfied that it would be to the advantage of educational establishments and that to do so would neither conflict with the normal exploitation of the works nor unreasonably prejudice the legitimate interests of the copyright owners.[10] A recommendation for new provision shall also specify any terms, other than terms as to charges payable, on which authorisation under the new provision should be available.[11] Where provision has not been made in accordance with such a recommendation within one year,[12] the Secretary of State has power to order that the making of reprographic copies of the works to which the recommendation relates by educational establishments for the purposes of instruction shall be treated as if licensed by the owners of the copyrights in the works.[13] The order is to be made by statutory instrument, and shall not come into force until at least six months after it is made.[14] The order may provide that any existing more restrictive licence shall cease to have effect, and shall provide for the terms of the licence, which shall be royalty-free.[15] The order may also provide that copies made pursuant to the order (and, therefore, when made not infringing copies[16]) are to be treated as infringing copies if sold, let for hire, offered or exposed for sale or hire or exhibited in public.[17]

29–77

C. Certification or Notification of Licensing Schemes for Purposes of Excluding Permitted Acts

Certification of licensing schemes. The Secretary of State is given power to certify a licensing scheme on the application of the person operating or proposing

29–78

---

[3] s.138(1).
[4] s.138(2).
[5] s.138(3).
[6] s.138(4).
[7] s.139; see, as to the procedure, paras 29–159 et seq., below.
[8] CDPA 1988, s.140; as to the meaning of reprographic copying and educational establishments, see para. 29–76, above.
[9] s.140(2), (3) and (6).
[10] s.140(4).
[11] s.140(5).
[12] i.e. no licensing scheme or licence complying with the recommendation has been established or granted: s.141(2).
[13] CDPA 1988, s.141(1).
[14] s.141(7) and (8).
[15] s.141(3) and (4).
[16] s.27.
[17] s.141(5).

to operate it for the purposes of displacing other provisions of the 1988 Act which permit certain acts in relation to the works the subject of the scheme.[18] The sections affected are: section 35 (educational recording of broadcasts),[19] section 60 (copying or issuing to the public copies of abstracts of scientific or technical articles),[20] section 66 (lending to the public of copies of certain works),[21] section 74 (sub-titled copies of broadcasts for people who are deaf or hard of hearing)[22] and section 141 (reprographic copying of published works by educational establishments).[23] The scheme may be certified if the Secretary of State is satisfied that it enables the works to which it relates to be identified with sufficient certainty by persons likely to require licences and sets out clearly the charges, if any, payable and other terms on which licences will be granted.[24] The order is made by statutory instrument and the scheme is to be scheduled to the order; the order is not to take effect before eight weeks after it is made.[25] A certified scheme may not be effectively varied unless a corresponding amendment is made to the order; the Secretary of State must make such an amendment where the scheme has been varied by the Copyright Tribunal.[26] The Secretary of State may revoke an order if it appears to him that the scheme has ceased to be operated, or is no longer being operated according to its terms.[27]

29–79   **Notification of licensing schemes.** Rather different provision is made in respect of licensing schemes which may displace the permitted acts provided for in section 31B of the 1988 Act, which permits in certain circumstances the making or supplying of multiple accessible copies of works to visually impaired persons. It is provided that section 31B does not apply if a licensing scheme is in force, is not unduly restrictive and the scheme and any modification to it have been notified to the Secretary of State.[28] Section 31D(2) provides that a scheme is "unreasonably restrictive" if it includes a term or condition which purports to prevent or limit the steps which may be taken under section 31B or 31C or has that effect.[29] However, section 31D(2) does not apply if the work in question is no longer published by or with the authority of the copyright owner and there are reasonable grounds for preventing or restricting the making of accessible copies of the work.[30] It appears, therefore, that where, for example, a book is out of print, the scheme will not be unreasonably restrictive if it prevents or restricts the making of copies provided there are reasonable grounds for doing so. It is not clear what grounds might be considered to be reasonable. Where sections 31B and 31C are displaced by a licensing scheme, section 31D(4) applies the normal

---

[18] CDPA 1988, s.143(1).

[19] s.35(2); Two schemes have so far been certified under this provision. The relevant statutory instruments to which they are scheduled are, (1) the Copyright (Certification of Licensing Scheme for Educational Recording of Broadcasts and Cable Programmes) (Educational Recording Agency Limited) Order 1990 (SI 1990/879) (which has been amended by SI 1992/211, SI 1993/193, SI 1994/247, SI 1996/191, SI 1998/203, SI 1999/3452 and SI 2003/188) and (2) the Copyright (Certification of Licensing Scheme for Educational Recording of Broadcasts) (Open University) Order 2003 (SI 2003/187). For the Educational Recording Agency Limited, see para. 28–55, above.

[20] S.60(2); and see para. 9–163, above.

[21] s.66(2); and see para. 9–178, above.

[22] s.74(4); and see para. 9–211, above.

[23] See para. 9–98, above and para. 29–76, above.

[24] CDPA 1988, s.143(2).

[25] s.143(3).

[26] s.143(4).

[27] s.143(5).

[28] CDPA 1988, s.31D(1). See para. 9–86, above.

[29] s.31D(2). S.31C permits the holding of intermediate copies of the master copy used to make copies under s.31B.

[30] s.31D(3).

provisions of the 1988 Act concerning references of the scheme to the Copyright Tribunal and applications to the Copyright Tribunal for individual licences under the scheme.[31]

D. COMPULSORY NOTIFICATION OF SOUND RECORDING LICENSING SCHEMES TO THE SECRETARY OF STATE

Background. Before the coming into force of the Copyright and Related Rights Regulations 2003,[32] the showing or playing in public of a broadcast or cable programme to an audience who had not paid for admission to the place where this occurred (*e.g.* a shop or public house) did not infringe any copyright in any sound recording included in the broadcast.[33] This has now changed. Such showing or playing does infringe the sound recording copyright if the recording is an "excepted" recording, that is a recording of music whose author is not the author of the broadcast (there are exceptions where the playing is by a non-profit-making organisation or is necessary for demonstrating or repairing equipment).[34] As will be apparent, most recordings which are likely to be played in these circumstances are in fact "excepted" recordings and accordingly a licence will be necessary. In practice, such a licence will need to be obtained from PPL, which owns the United Kingdom rights to play substantially all commercially released sound recordings in public.[35]

29–80

New section 128A of the 1988 Act: general. Given the large number of persons who will require a licence to play excepted recordings in public, it was inevitable that PPL would introduce a licensing scheme. Any such scheme would ordinarily have been subject to review by the Copyright Tribunal under the general provisions as to licensing schemes.[36] However, the 2003 Regulations do not simply leave the position subject to the general law. Rather, they make provision (in a new section 128A of the 1988 Act) for any proposed licence or licensing scheme to be referred to the Secretary of State before it comes into operation. The Secretary of State then has a choice as to whether to notify the proposed licence or scheme to the Copyright Tribunal or to allow it to be implemented. The purpose of adopting this machinery is not wholly clear. However, it may be that the Government considered that the users of broadcasts might not have sufficient resources to make a reference to the Tribunal under the ordinary law. At the time of writing it is understood that PPL and the Secretary of State are in the course of discussions about a proposed scheme.

29–81

Notification of licence or scheme to the Secretary of State. The provisions of section 128A apply to a proposed licence or licensing scheme that will authorise the playing in public of excepted sound recordings included in broadcasts where that would otherwise infringe the copyright in them.[37] For these purposes, the term "licence" means a licence granted by a licensing body otherwise than in pursuance of a licensing scheme and which covers works of more than one

29–82

---

[31] This is effected by providing that ss.119 to 122 of CDPA 1988 apply to the scheme as if it were one to which they applied under s.117. As to ss.119 to 122, see paras 29–111 *et seq.*, below.

[32] SI 2003/2498, which came into force on October 31, 2003.

[33] CDPA 1988, s.72(1)(b).

[34] s.72(1)(b), (1A).

[35] As to which, see para. 28–60, above. For a more detailed discussion of these provisions, see paras 9–198 *et seq.*, above.

[36] See paras 29–108 *et seq.*

[37] CDPA 1988, s.128A(1). For the term "excepted recording", see para. 29–80, above.

author.[38] The meaning of the terms "licensing scheme" and "licensing body" are discussed below.[39] A licensing body that wishes to operate such a licence or scheme must notify its details to the Secretary of State before it comes into operation and may not operate such a licence or licensing scheme until 28 days have elapsed since the notification.[40] The Secretary of State may then refer the licence or scheme to the Copyright Tribunal for a determination of whether it is reasonable in the circumstances. Alternatively, he may notify the licensing body that he does not intend to refer it to the Tribunal.[41] The only sanction for failure to notify the licence or scheme to the Secretary of State before it comes into operation or for operating the licence or scheme before the 28-day period has elapsed is that if the Secretary of State becomes aware of this, he may refer the licence or scheme to the Tribunal for a determination as above.[42] It is clear that once the 28-day period has elapsed, the licence or scheme may come into operation even though the Secretary of State has referred it to the Copyright Tribunal.[43] These provisions apply to a proposed modification of an existing licence or scheme as they apply to proposed licences or schemes.[44]

29–83   **Factors the Secretary of State must take into account.** The Secretary of State is obliged to take into account five factors, as follows. First, whether the terms and conditions of the proposed licence or scheme have taken into account four additional factors. These are considered in the next paragraph. Secondly, any written representations received by the Secretary of State. No doubt this will include any representations from the licensing body and potential licensees. However, there is no obligation on the Secretary of State to engage in a public consultation.[45] Thirdly, previous determinations of the Tribunal. This is not limited in any way. However, presumably the Secretary of State is only obliged to take account of determinations about licences or schemes which are genuinely similar or comparable to the licence or scheme in question. Fourthly, the availability of other schemes, or the granting of other licences, to persons in similar circumstances, and the terms of those schemes or licences. Clearly, this is directed at comparables. It does not appear to be limited to comparables in the United Kingdom, although in practice there may be few genuine comparables abroad. Fifthly, the extent to which the licensing body has consulted any persons who would be affected by the proposed licence or scheme, or organisations representing such persons, and the steps, if any, it has taken as a result. It is not entirely clear what "steps" are meant here. Presumably, however, this is a reference to changes made to the terms of the licence or scheme as a result of representations made by record companies and potential licensees.

29–84   **The four additional factors.** As has been stated in the previous paragraph, the Secretary of State is obliged to take account of whether the terms and conditions of the proposed licence or scheme themselves have taken into account four additional factors.[46] These are as follows. First, the extent to which the broadcasts to be shown or played by a potential licensee are likely to include excepted sound

---

[38] s.128A(13).

[39] See paras 29–106 and 29–107.

[40] CDPA 1988, s.128A(2), (3).

[41] s.128A(4).

[42] s.128A(5).

[43] See, *e.g.*, s.128B(4) which gives the Tribunal a power to backdate its order and provides for the repayment of excessive licence fees which have been paid prior to the date of the order.

[44] s.128A(12).

[45] Note, however, that the existence of the fifth factor (discussed below) will have the effect that the licensing body will be obliged to consult.

[46] CDPA 1988, s.128A(7).

recordings. The presence of this factor is presumably aimed at avoiding a scheme under which charges are based solely on the number of hours of broadcasting. However, it is not easy to see how it will be applied in practice. Secondly, the size and nature of the audience that the licence or scheme would permit to hear the excepted sound recordings. This is already a factor in PPL's licensing scheme in respect of the playing of sound recordings in night clubs and public houses. Thirdly, what commercial benefit a potential licensee is likely to obtain from playing the excepted sound recordings. No doubt this factor is aimed at distinguishing between situations where the playing of the sound recording can be shown to encourage the public to enter the premises (for example, the playing of an appropriate radio station in a specialist music shop) and situations where the fact that the broadcast is being played is unlikely to have any bearing on the number of customers who attend (for example, a radio which is played in the kitchen of a café but is audible at the counter).[47] Fourthly, the extent to which the owners of the copyright in the sound recordings will receive equitable remuneration from sources other than the proposed licence or scheme for the inclusion of their recordings in the broadcasts.

Interaction with the Copyright Tribunal's general jurisdiction. As has already been made clear, in the absence of this machinery, the Tribunal would have jurisdiction over the licence or scheme under its general jurisdiction, which is discussed below.[48] Accordingly, it was necessary for provision to be made as to the interaction of the two regimes. That provision is as follows. First, the terms of a licence or scheme which must be notified to the Secretary of State under section 128A may be referred to the Tribunal under its general jurisdiction over *proposed* licences or schemes (under sections 118 and 125 of the 1988 Act), but only if this is done before the notification to the Secretary of State takes place.[49] If this occurs, two special provisions apply. First, the reference is not to be considered premature[50] merely because the licence or scheme has not been notified to the Secretary of State. Secondly, if the Tribunal decides to entertain the reference, the section 128A machinery ceases to have effect; thus, there is no obligation to refer the proposed licence or scheme to the Secretary of State and the Secretary of State has no power to refer it to the Tribunal.[51] The second express provision in relation to the interaction of the two regimes is that if a proposed licensing scheme has been notified to the Secretary of State, but has then come into operation, the entitlement to refer it to the Copyright Tribunal under section 119 of the 1988 Act (that is, as an *existing* scheme) is postponed until the Secretary of State has notified the licensing body that he does not intend to refer it to the Tribunal.[52] Finally, it is provided that nothing in section 128A is to prejudice any right to make a reference or application to the Tribunal under certain specified sections of the 1988 Act. These sections, which are all considered below,[53] provide for the following (in brief): the right to refer a scheme back to the Tribunal after it has already ruled on it under sections 118, 119 or 128A (section 120); the right to apply for a licence under an existing scheme (section 121) and to apply for a review

29–85

---

[47] In its Analysis of Responses and Government Conclusions on this point, the Government emphasised that "the circumstances in which broadcasts are heard in commercial situations will vary considerably, and will not always be the same as with [sic] a conscious or deliberate decision to play sound recordings in public by way of CDs, tapes or the like": see at para.5.20.

[48] paras 29–108 *et seq.*, below.

[49] CDPA 1988, s.128A(8).

[50] s.128(10)(a). This is a reference to the Tribunal's power under ss.118(2) and 125(2) to refuse to entertain a reference on the ground that it is premature.

[51] s.128(10)(b).

[52] s.128A(9).

[53] See paras 29–115 *et seq.*, below.

of a decision made on such an application (section 122); the right to refer an expiring licence to the Tribunal (section 126); and the right to apply for a review of an order of the Tribunal made under sections 125, 126 or 126B of the 1988 Act, in the latter case where the order did not relate to a licensing scheme (section 127).[54]

29–86   **Decision to the Copyright Tribunal.** If a proposed licence or scheme is referred to the Copyright Tribunal, it is empowered to make "appropriate enquiries" to establish whether the licence or scheme is reasonable in the circumstances.[55] This appears to envisage it undertaking an inquisitorial role, but precisely how this is intended to operate is not clear. The Tribunal is obliged to take account of whether the terms and conditions of the scheme have taken into account the four additional factors referred to above. It is also obliged to take into account any other factors it considers relevant.[56] In the case of a licensing scheme, it is then obliged to make an order either confirming or varying the scheme, either generally or so far as it relates to cases of any description. In the case of a licence, it is obliged either to confirm or vary the licence.[57] The Tribunal may direct that the order, so far as it reduces the amount of the charges payable, has effect from a date before the date on which it is made. If it so directs, any necessary payments shall be repaid and the Tribunal may award simple interest on the repayments.[58]

29–87   **Review of Copyright Tribunal's order.** The normal provisions apply as to the review of the order. Thus, while the order remains in force, the operator of the scheme, a person claiming that he requires a licence in a case to which the order applies or an organisation claiming to be representative of such persons may refer the scheme again to the Tribunal so far as it relates to cases of that description.[59] Special leave is required if the reference is sought to be made within 12 months of the order or, if the order was made for 15 months or less, before the start of the last three months before its expiry.[60] The scheme remains in operation until proceedings on the reference are concluded.[61] The Tribunal may make such order either confirming, varying or further varying the scheme so far as it relates to cases of the description to which the reference relates as the Tribunal may consider to be reasonable in the circumstances.[62] The order may be made so as to be in force indefinitely or for such period as the Tribunal may determine.[63] Analogous provision is made in respect of licences.[64]

3. CONTROL OF THE EXERCISE OF COPYRIGHT AND RELATED RIGHTS BY THE COPYRIGHT TRIBUNAL

A. INTRODUCTION

29–88   **Organisations controlling the exercise of copyright.** In most countries a development in the field of copyright has been the creation of organisations to control the exercise of specific rights restricted by the copyright in particular

---

[54] S.125 provides for the reference to the Tribunal of the terms of a proposed licence.
[55] CDPA 1988, s.128B(1).
[56] s.128B(2).
[57] s.128B(3).
[58] s.128B(4), (5).
[59] CDPA 1988, s.120(1).
[60] s.120(2).
[61] s.120(3).
[62] s.120(4).
[63] s.120(5).
[64] s.127.

types of works, collectively, on behalf of the various authors and owners of the copyright in such works. In particular the rights so controlled have been the performing,[65] broadcasting and recording rights in musical works and sound recordings. Such organisations either acquire the relevant rights from their members, or act as agents on behalf of their members to enforce such rights. They issue licences in respect of the works of all their members and, in the last resort, enforce the rights of their members by legal action. Because their principal activity is to exercise the rights under their control by granting licences and collecting royalties due under such licences, such organisations are often referred to as Collecting Societies.[66] From the point of view of composers of music and owners of musical copyright the system has great advantages, in that no individual composer or copyright owner can, in practice, secure adequate protection for his work, or deal with the very large number of persons and bodies wishing to exploit such works. The system also has considerable advantages, from the point of view of those wishing to exploit such works, in that licences relating to all of a great number of works ("blanket licences") can be obtained from a single organisation, whereas, without such a system, it would be necessary to obtain individual licences from a large number of owners of copyright, and the delay and inconvenience, and the risk of exploiting such works without having obtained a licence from the person entitled to give one, would greatly add to the difficulty and expense of exploiting such works.[67] A number of such organisations have been established in the United Kingdom. The longest established and largest of these are Performing Right Society Limited (PRS),[68] controlling the right to perform musical works in public, Mechanical-Copyright Protection Society Limited (MCPS),[69] controlling the right to make recordings of musical works, and Phonographic Performance Limited (PPL),[70] controlling the right to play sound recordings in public, and broadcast them and, in limited circumstances, to rerecord them. There are also equivalent organisations established in most other European countries and in the United States, Canada and Australia.

Public interest and need for public control. The existence of such organisations is therefore to the advantage of the public in facilitating wider access by the public to such works, but it has also given rise to complaints of the abuse of what have become monopoly rights, since (for example) virtually all popular music is now controlled by such organisations. It therefore came to be felt, in a number of

29–89

---

[65] The performing right under the law of the United Kingdom is, with regard to literary dramatic or musical works: the right to perform them in public by any mode of visual or acoustic presentation, including presentation by means of a sound recording, film or broadcast of the work; with regard to sound recordings: the right to play them in public; and with regard to films or broadcasts: the right to show them in public; see CDPA 1988, ss.16(1)(c) and 19 which correspond to the provisions of the previous law contained in the Copyright Act 1956, ss.2(5)(c), 12 to 14A and 48(1).

[66] For a detailed consideration of the role and workings of the different Collecting Societies, see Ch.28.

[67] See the 1977 Copyright Committee, Cmnd. 6732, para.390 in relation to musical works. The respective advantages of collective licensing of specific rights in copyright works to authors and copyright owners on the one hand and users of copyright works on the other are however the same whenever works of various authors are likely to be regularly used by a number of different users. Accordingly Collecting Societies, for example, exist to control the exercise of the right to photocopy literary and artistic works, to photocopy material from newspapers and to make recordings of broadcast or cable programmes for educational purposes: see Ch.28.

[68] See para. 28–59, above.

[69] See para. 28–56, above.

[70] See para. 28–60, above.

countries, that some measure of public control over the activities of such organisations was necessary in the public interest.[71]

29–90   **Copyright Committee 1952.** At the Brussels Copyright Conference, the United Kingdom, in accepting the provisions of Article 11 of the Brussels Act (1948), declared that it remained free to enact such legislation as it might consider necessary in the public interest to prevent or deal with any abuse of the monopoly rights conferred upon owners of copyright by the law of the United Kingdom.[72] It was therefore open to the 1952 Copyright Committee, notwithstanding that it was recommending adherence to the Brussels Act, to make proposals for the compulsory adjustment of tariffs charged by such copyright organisations. One method suggested was that of compulsory arbitration, but the Committee did not consider this wholly satisfactory, in that it was necessary to envisage not only disputes between a collecting organisation and an organisation of potential users of copyright works, but also cases where individual persons were aggrieved, and moreover, what was really required was some method of arriving at tariffs which would be binding not only between the parties to the reference, but also in respect of any other persons wishing to exercise similar rights. The Committee therefore proposed that a standing tribunal should be established to decide disputes between collecting organisations and would-be users of controlled works.[73] This proposal was accepted by the legislature and was embodied in sections 23 to 30 of the 1956 Act.

29–91   **Performing Right Tribunal.** Section 23 of the 1956 Act established the Performing Right Tribunal (PRT) with the jurisdiction conferred by the provisions of the 1956 Act. The PRT had three principal functions.[74] The first was to confirm or vary licence schemes put into operation by organisations under which licences to do certain acts restricted by the copyright in particular works were to be granted to the public in certain classes of cases.[75] The second was to deal with applications by persons who were aggrieved because an organisation operating a licence scheme refused to grant them a licence in accordance with the scheme,[76] and the third was to deal with applications by persons who were aggrieved because they claimed that there was no licence scheme applicable to them and that the organisation concerned with granting licences of the type required unreasonably refused to grant them a licence or proposed terms that were unreasonable.[77] The PRT was concerned with licences dealing with only three types of right. First, the right to perform in public, broadcast or diffuse, a literary, dramatic or musical work or an adaptation thereof.[78] Secondly, the right to cause a sound recording to be heard in public or to be broadcast.[79] Thirdly, the right to cause a television broadcast to be seen or heard in public.[80] The rights, therefore, covered in effect, the whole of the performing and broadcasting rights conferred by the 1956 Act, other than the right to include an artistic work in a television broadcast, the right to cause a film

---

[71] See, as to the position of such organisations under Art.82 of the Treaty of Rome, para. 29–253, below.

[72] This declaration was not repeated in relation to the Stockholm Act (1967), since it was accepted at the Stockholm Conference that questions of ordre public are always a matter of domestic law and that Convention countries remain free to enact measures to restrict possible abuses of monopoly.

[73] Cmnd.8662, para.210.

[74] Copyright Act 1956, ss.24 to 27A.

[75] s.24(1).

[76] ss.27(1) and (2) and 27A.

[77] s.27(3).

[78] s.24(2)(a); a right (as to musical works and associated words) usually controlled by PRS.

[79] s.24(2)(b); a right usually controlled by PPL.

[80] s.24(2)(c); a right then controlled by the BBC or the IBA.

to be seen or heard in public or to be broadcast, and the right to rebroadcast a sound or television broadcast.

Proposals for reform. The functions of the PRT were considered by the 1977   **29–92** Copyright Committee, which recommended that it should be given jurisdiction over a wider range of matters, including reprographic licences, video recording, licences to use music on film sound-tracks, and copyright clearances where the copyright owner cannot be traced.[81] The Committee also proposed that the tribunal's name should be changed to the Copyright Tribunal, in view of the recommended increase in its jurisdiction. The White Paper generally followed these recommendations in relation to the change in name of the tribunal and the extension of its functions,[82] and also made recommendations as to the introduction of more specific criteria for the tribunal to base its decision on, and for improvements in the procedure before the tribunal. These recommendations were enacted in the 1988 Act, Chapter VIII of which established the Copyright Tribunal as the successor to the PRT.

B. THE COPYRIGHT TRIBUNAL

The Copyright Tribunal. By section 145 of the 1988 Act the Tribunal   **29–93** established under section 23 of the 1956 Act was renamed the Copyright Tribunal.[83] The Tribunal's membership was enlarged in view of its increased jurisdiction, and now consists of a chairman and two deputy chairmen appointed by the Lord Chancellor. Each must have a seven-year general qualification within the meaning of section 71 of the Courts and Legal Services Act 1990[84] ; or be an advocate or solicitor in Scotland of at least seven years' standing; or a barrister or solicitor in Northern Ireland of at least seven years' standing; or a person who has held judicial office. In addition, the Tribunal must consist of not less than two and not more than eight ordinary members appointed by the Secretary of State.[85]

Constitution of the Copyright Tribunal. For the purposes of any proceedings   **29–94** the Copyright Tribunal shall consist of a chairman (who shall be either the chairman or a deputy chairman of the Tribunal) and two or more ordinary members.[86] In the absence of unanimity, decisions are arrived at by majority, with the chair-

---

[81] Cmnd. 6732, paras 788–90; the Committee also recommended that the Tribunal should have jurisdiction in respect of royalties payable under s.8 of the 1956 Act (assuming the statutory licence was to be retained) and over the amount of levy on blank tape (assuming that such levy was to be introduced).

[82] Cmnd.9712 (1986) Ch.18, broadly following proposals set out in the 1981 Green Paper, Cmnd.8302.

[83] Proceedings pending before the PRT before August 1, 1989 therefore fell to be heard by the Copyright Tribunal and were subject to the Copyright Tribunal Rules 1989; see r.55 made pursuant to CDPA 1988, Sch.1, para.34, and see *The Performing Right Society Ltd v British Entertainment and Dancing Association* [1991] I.P.D. 14178 (hearing before PRT but decision given on August 1, 1989 by the Copyright Tribunal).

[84] 1990 (c.41). By the Courts and Legal Services Act 1990, s.71(3)(c) a person has a general legal qualification if he has a right of audience in relation to any class of proceedings in any part of the Supreme Court, or all proceedings in county courts or magistrates' courts.

[85] CDPA 1988, ss.145(2), (3) as amended by the Courts and Legal Services Act 1990, s.71(2), Sch.10, para.73.

[86] CDPA 1988, s.148(1), derived from Copyright Act 1956, Sch.4, para.3. Para.3 of the Tribunal's *Practice Direction* (Vol.2 at B1.ii) provides that substantive hearings will be taken by a Tribunal consisting of the Chairman or a Deputy Chairman and at least two and ordinarily not more than four other members while procedural hearings will be taken by the Chairman or one of the Deputy Chairmen sitting alone. It is not clear how the latter provision can be reconciled with CDPA 1988, s.148(1), which provides that "for the purposes of *any* proceedings" (emphasis added) the Tribunal shall consist of a chairman and two or more ordinary members.

man exercising a casting vote.[87] There are provisions ensuring that the Tribunal remains duly constituted where a member is unable to continue after proceedings are part heard,[88] and for the appointment of one of the ordinary members to act as chairman together with a suitably qualified person to advise on law, where it is the chairman who is unable to continue.[89]

29–95   **Jurisdiction of the Copyright Tribunal.** Following the proposals for reform discussed above,[90] the Copyright Tribunal was given an extended jurisdiction, covering not only the three functions previously carried out by the PRT in relation to licence schemes and licences by licensing bodies (but in relation to a wider variety of copyright licences), but also five further specific functions introduced by the 1988 Act and two further specific functions subsequently introduced into the 1988 Act by the Broadcasting Act 1990.[91] Subsequently, the jurisdiction of the Copyright Tribunal was again extended and extended very considerably. As to the functions inherited from the PRT in relation to licensing schemes and licensing bodies dealing with copyright licences, the variety of copyright licences in relation to which the functions are exercisable has been further extended. Furthermore, principally as a result of (1) the introduction of performers' property rights[92] and the right to equitable remuneration for the playing in public or broadcasting of sound recordings of performances,[93] (2) the introduction of rights for authors to receive equitable remuneration for the rental of sound recordings and films,[94] (3) the increase in the duration of copyright and of rights in performances (and consequent provisions for use as of right, subject to a reasonable royalty, of works in which revived copyright subsists and performances in which revived performance rights subsist),[95] (4) the introduction of the database right[96] , and (5) the introduction of the publication right for those who publish previously unpublished works in which copyright has expired,[97] the number of specific functions of the Copyright Tribunal has more than doubled since the 1988 Act came into force. Accordingly in addition to the 10 specific functions which the Tribunal had in 1990 it now has no fewer than 17 further functions. Specifically it now has jurisdiction to hear and determine:

    (1) Jurisdiction under Part I of the 1988 Act

        (a) applications to determine the royalty or other remuneration to be paid to a copyright owner with respect to the cable re-transmission in certain circumstances of a wireless broadcast including a work owned by him[98] ;

        (b) applications to determine the amount of equitable remuneration payable to authors of literary, dramatic, musical and artistic works and principal directors of films where their rental right concerning a

---

[87] CDPA 1988, s.148(2), derived from Copyright Act 1956, Sch.4, para.3.

[88] s.148(3).

[89] s.148(4) and (5).

[90] See para. 29–92, above.

[91] For a list of the specific functions of the Tribunal as at the beginning of 1991, see *Copinger* (13th ed.) para.15–57.

[92] See para. 12–20, above and para. 29–134, below.

[93] Under CDPA 1988, s.182D, see para. 12–45, above and para. 29–152, below.

[94] Under CDPA 1988, s.93B, see para. 7–89, above and para. 29–133, below.

[95] See paras 6–15, 12–37 and 29–41, above and para. 29–155, below.

[96] See Ch.18, above and para. 29–157, below.

[97] See Ch.17, above and para. 29–158, below.

[98] CDPA 1988, ss.73(4) and 73A, introduced into the 1988 Act and into s.149 of the 1988 Act by the Broadcasting Act 1996, s.138 and Sch.9; see further paras 29–48 *et seq.*, above.

sound recording or film has been transferred to the producer of the sound recording or film[99];

(c) references of proposed or existing licensing schemes dealing with copyright licences[1];

(d) applications with respect to entitlement to a copyright licence under a licensing scheme[2];

(e) references or applications with respect to licensing by a licensing body dealing with copyright licences[3];

(f) references by the Secretary of State of licences or licensing schemes in relation to the playing of sound recordings under section 128A of the 1988 Act[4];

(g) applications to settle the terms of payment or as to the reasonableness of any condition in relation to the use as of right of sound recordings in broadcasts[5];

(h) appeals against an order by the Secretary of State as to the coverage of a licensing scheme or licence in respect of reprographic copying by an educational establishment[6];

(i) applications to settle a royalty or other sum payable for lending of certain works to the public[7];

(j) applications to settle the terms of a copyright licence available as of right consequent on the exercise of their powers by the Secretary of State, the Office of Fair Trading and the Competition Commission[8];

(k) applications to settle the terms of payment under a compulsory licence in respect of information about a programme service[9];

(2) Jurisdiction under Part II of the 1988 Act

(l) applications to determine the amount of equitable remuneration payable to performers where commercially published sound recordings of their performances are played in public or communicated to the public[10];

---

[99] CDPA 1988, s.93C, introduced into Ch. V of Part I and s.149 of the 1988 Act by the Copyright and Related Rights Regulations 1996 (SI 1996/2967), para.14; and see para. 7–89 above and para. 29–133, below.

[1] CDPA 1988 ss.118, 119, 120 and 128A; and see further paras 29–108 *et seq.*, below. s.128A was introduced into the 1988 Act by the Copyright and Related Rights Regulations 2003 (SI 2003/2498), reg.21.

[2] ss.121 and 122; and see further paras 29–116 *et seq.*, below.

[3] ss.125, 126, 127 and 128A; and see further paras 29–119 *et seq.*, below. s.128A was introduced into the 1988 Act by the Copyright and Related Rights Regulations 2003 (SI 2003/2498), reg.21.

[4] See above, paras 29–81 *et seq.*, above.

[5] CDPA 1988, ss.135D and 135E, introduced into Ch.III of Pt I, and s.149 of the 1988 Act by the Broadcasting Act 1990, Sch.17, para.7(1) and amended by the Copyright and Related Rights Regulations 2003 (SI 2003/2498), Sch.2, para.1; see further paras 29–25 *et seq.*, above.

[6] CDPA 1988, s.139; and see further para. 29–129, below.

[7] s.142, as inserted by the Copyright and Related Rights Regulations 1996 (SI 1996/2967), reg.13(2); and see further para. 29–130, below.

[8] s.144(4) as amended by the Enterprise Act 2002 (c.40), Sch.25 para.18; and see further paras 29–131 and 29–297 *et seq.*, below.

[9] Broadcasting Act 1990, Sch.17 paras 5 and 6 introduced into Ch.III of Pt I and s.149 of the 1988 Act by the Broadcasting Act 1990, Sch.17, para.7(1); see further paras 29–09, *et seq.*, above.

[10] CDPA 1988, 182D, introduced into the 1988 Act by the Copyright and Related Rights Regulations 1996 (SI 1996/2967), reg.20, as amended by the Copyright and Related Rights Regulations 2003 (SI 2003/2498), reg.7(2); and see further para. 29–152, below.

(m) applications to give consent to the making of a recording of a performance on behalf of a performer who cannot be traced[11];

(n) applications to determine the amount of equitable remuneration payable to performers where their rental right concerning a sound recording or film has been transferred to the producer of the sound recording or film[12] ;

(o) applications to determine the royalty or other remuneration to be paid to the owners of the rights conferred by Part II of the 1988 Act in relation to a performance or recording of a performance with respect to the re-transmission by cable of a wireless broadcast including the performance or recording[13] ;

(p) references of proposed or existing licensing schemes relating to performers' property right licences, namely for copying a recording of a performance or renting or lending of copies of such a recording to the public[14];

(q) applications with respect to entitlement to a licence under a licensing scheme relating to performers' property right licences[15];

(r) references and applications with respect to licensing by a licensing body dealing with performers' property right licences[16];

(s) applications to settle the royalty or other sum payable for the lending of certain recordings treated as licensed by performers by virtue of an order of the Secretary of State[17] ;

(t) applications to settle the terms of licences in respect of performers' property rights available as of right consequent on the exercise of their powers by the Secretary of State, the Office of Fair Trading and the Competition Commission[18];

(3) Other jurisdiction

(u) applications to settle the royalty or other remuneration payable in respect of the use as of right of works in which revived copyright subsists[19];

(v) applications to settle the remuneration payable in respect of the doing as of right with regard to performances in which revived performance right subsists of any acts which require the consent of the owner of such rights[20];

(w) references and applications with respect to licensing schemes, licences and licensing bodies relating to licences in respect of the

---

[11] s.190, as amended by the Copyright and Related Rights Regulations 1996 (SI 1996/2967), reg.23; and see further para. 29–154, below.

[12] s.191G and 191H, introduced into the 1988 Act by the Copyright and Related Rights Regulations 1996 (SI 1996/2967), reg.21; and see further para. 29–153, below.

[13] Sch.2, paras 19 and 19A, introduced into the 1988 Act by the Broadcasting Act 1996, s.138 and Sch.9, as amended by the Copyright and Related Rights Regulations 2003 (SI 2003/2498), reg.22; and see further para. 29–155, below.

[14] Sch.2A, paras 3, 4 and 5 introduced into the 1988 Act by the Copyright and Related Rights Regulations 1996 (SI 1996/2967), reg.22; and see further paras 29–137 *et seq.*, below.

[15] Sch.2A, paras 6 and 7; and see further para. 29–144, below.

[16] Sch.2A, paras 10, 11 and 12; and see further paras 29–148 *et seq.*, below.

[17] Sch.2A, para 15; and see para. 29–155, below.

[18] Sch.2A, para.17, as amended by the Enterprise Act 2002 (c.40), Sch.25 para.18; and see paras 29–297 *et seq.*, below.

[19] Under the Duration of Copyright and Rights in Performances Regulations 1995 (SI 1995/3297), reg.25; and see further paras 29–41 *et seq.*, above.

[20] Under the Duration of Copyright and Rights in Performances Regulations 1995 (SI 1995/3297), reg.35; and see further para. 29–155, below.

database right conferred in respect of the contents of databases ("database right licences")[21]; and in particular:

(i) references of proposed or existing licensing schemes relating to database right licences[22];

(ii) applications with respect to entitlement to licences under a licensing scheme relating to database right licences[23];

(iii) references or applications with respect to licensing by a licensing body dealing with database right licences[24];

(iv) applications to settle the terms of a database right licence available as of right consequent on the exercise of their powers by the Secretary of State, the Office of Fair Trading and the Competition Commission[25];

(x) equivalent references and applications with respect to licensing schemes, licences and licensing bodies relating to licences in respect of the publication right conferred on publishers of previously unpublished works in which copyright has expired[26];

(y) applications to determine the royalty or other remuneration payable to the trustees for the Hospital for Sick Children in respect of the use of the play "Peter Pan" by Sir James Matthew Barrie.[27]

Procedure before the Copyright Tribunal. The Lord Chancellor, in the exercise of powers conferred under the 1988 Act,[28] has made certain rules regulating the procedure to be followed in respect of proceedings before the Copyright Tribunal.[29] The Chairman has also issued a Practice Direction, giving guidance on a number of procedural matters.[30] The principal aspects of the procedure before the Copyright Tribunal are discussed further below.[31] The Copyright Tribunal has statutory power to order any party to proceedings before it to pay the costs of any other party.[32]   **29–96**

Appeal to the Court on point of law. Under the 1956 Act[33] any question of law arising in the course of proceedings before the PRT could be referred by the PRT, at the request of any party, to the High Court[34] for decision, whether before or after the PRT gave its decision in the proceedings. The procedure was by way of   **29–97**

---

[21] Under the Copyright and Rights in Databases Regulations 1997 (SI 1997/3032), reg.25 and Sch.2; and see further para. 29–157, below.

[22] Copyright and Rights in Databases Regulations 1997 (SI 1997/3032), Sch.2, paras 3, 4 and 5.

[23] Sch.2, paras 6 and 7.

[24] Sch.2, paras 10, 11 and 12.

[25] Sch.2, para.15(3), as amended by the Enterprise Act 2002 (Consequential and Supplemental Provisions) Order 2003 (SI 2003/1398) with effect from June 20, 2003.

[26] Under the Copyright and Related Rights Regulations 1996 (SI 1996/2967), reg.17; and see further para. 29–158 below and Ch.17.

[27] CDPA 1988, Sch.6, para.5, as amended by the Copyright and Related Rights Regulations 1996 (SI 1996/2967); and see further para. 29–132, below.

[28] CDPA 1988, s.150 (as amended by the Arbitration Act 1996).

[29] The Copyright Tribunal Rules 1989 (SI 1989/1129), see Vol.2 at B1.i (based, to a large extent, on the Performing Right Tribunal Rules (as amended), made under the Copyright Act 1956) as amended by The Copyright Tribunal (Amendment) Rules 1991 (SI 1991/201) and The Copyright Tribunal (Amendment) Rules 1992 (SI 1992/467). These rules are under review: see the Copyright Tribunal Practice Direction as amended (April 7, 2004 version), para.1.

[30] See Vol.2 at B1.ii.

[31] See paras 29–159 et seq., below.

[32] CDPA 1988, s.151; and see r.48, and see further para. 29–170, below.

[33] Copyright Act 1956, s.30.

[34] In Scotland, the Court of Session.

case stated.[35] The legislature did not adopt this approach in the 1988 Act,[36] which makes provision for an appeal to the High Court on any point of law arising from a decision of the Copyright Tribunal.[37] Such an appeal can therefore be made only after the Copyright Tribunal has made a decision, and the Court has no power to refuse to entertain the appeal.[38] Provision is made for such appeal under the Copyright Tribunal Rules, and for suspension of the Copyright Tribunal's order pending the outcome of the appeal.[39] In so far as an appeal is in respect of the amount of royalty determined by the Copyright Tribunal, establishing an error of law is likely to be difficult. If the Tribunal has expressly directed itself in accordance with the requirement to make such order as is reasonable[40] then it will only have erred in law if it did something which no Tribunal, if it thought about the matter, could have regarded as reasonable. Such irrationality could be shown either if the royalty fixed by the Tribunal was so large or so small that no rational Tribunal could have arrived at such a figure, or if the reasons given by the Tribunal disclosed some *non sequitur* which invalidated the reasoning,[41] or if there was no evidential basis for an essential factual finding.[42]

29–98   **Factors the Copyright Tribunal is required to take into account in all proceedings.** Under the 1956 Act the PRT was required to make such orders as were reasonable in all the circumstances,[43] but the 1956 Act set out no guidance as to what was reasonable. The general requirement under the 1988 Act remains that the Copyright Tribunal should make such orders as are reasonable in all the circumstances.[44] However, the 1988 Act, whilst providing that the Copyright Tribunal has a general obligation in any case to have regard to all relevant considerations,[45] gives further general guidance by providing that the Copyright Tribunal shall, in determining what is reasonable, have regard to the availability and the terms of other schemes or licences to other persons in similar circum-

---

[35] Copyright Act 1956, s.30(5); and see rr.19 to 21 of the Performing Right Tribunal Rules 1965 (as amended), *Copinger* (12th ed.), paras 1776–1778.

[36] In the light of representations made by the Council on Tribunals.

[37] CDPA 1988, s.152. There is no restriction on further appeals from the decision of the Court. A decision for these purposes includes, it would seem, an interim decision. Appeals under s.152 on a point of law have been made to the High Court in *The Performing Right Society Limited v British Entertainment and Dancing Association* [1993] E.M.L.R. 325; *AEI Rediffusion Music Limited v Phonographic Performance Ltd* [1999] E.M.L.R. 129, a successful appeal in relation to costs ordered to be paid by the Tribunal in accordance with an erroneous principle applied by it (appeal to the Court of Appeal dismissed: [1999] 1 W.L.R. 1507); *Phonographic Performance Ltd v Virgin Retail Ltd* [2001] E.M.L.R. 139, see para. 29–36 above; and *Phonographic Performance Ltd v Candy Rock Recording Ltd* [1999] E.M.L.R. 806.

[38] Under the 1956 Act, a case could be stated on a point of law at any time in the proceedings, and the Court could refuse to entertain the reference where the PRT refused to state a case (but see *AIRC Ltd v Phonographic Performance Ltd* [1983] F.S.R. 637).

[39] Copyright Tribunal Rules 1989, rr.42–45, Vol.2 at B1.ii.

[40] See para. 29–98, below.

[41] *The Performing Right Society v British Entertainment and Dancing Association* [1993] E.M.L.R. 325 at 330, *per* Hoffmann J. See also *The British Phonographic Industry v Mechanical-Copyright Protection Society* [1993] E.M.L.R. 86 at 97 where the Tribunal itself acknowledged that it was bound not to take into account irrelevant circumstances.

[42] As was found in *Phonographic Performance Ltd v Virgin Retail Ltd* [2001] E.M.L.R. 139 at para.38.

[43] Copyright Act 1956, ss.25(5), 26(4), 27(5) and 27A(4).

[44] CDPA 1988, ss.73A(2), 93C(3), 118(3), 119(3), 120(4), 121(4), 122(3), 125(3), 126(4), 127(3), 135D(1), 135E(2), 142(2), 182D(6), 191H(3), Sch.2, para.19A(2), Sch.2A, paras 3(3), 4(3), 5(4), 6(4), 7(3), 10(3), 11(4), 12(3), 15(3) and Sch.6, para.5(1). The requirement that the Tribunal should make such orders as are reasonable in the circumstances is also contained in paras 25(2) and 35(3) of the Duration of Copyright and Rights in Performances Regulations 1995 (SI 1995/3297) (jurisdiction to settle the royalty or other remuneration payable in respect of the use as of right of works and performances in which revived copyright and performance rights subsist) and the Copyright and Rights in Databases Regulations 1997 (SI 1997/3032) (jurisdiction with respect to licensing schemes, licences and licensing bodies dealing with the database right).

[45] CDPA 1988, s.135.

stances, and shall exercise its powers so as to secure that there is no unreasonable discrimination between the actual or prospective licensees making the application and licensees under alternative schemes or licences being operated or granted by the same person.[46] Beyond this, the 1988 Act gives no further general guidance but the Copyright Tribunal has itself expressly acknowledged that the *Wednesbury* principle applies to it as much as to any inferior tribunal and that as a matter of principle the Tribunal could not take into account irrelevant circumstances.[47]

Factors the Copyright Tribunal has taken into consideration. Since 1989 the Copyright Tribunal has adjudicated substantively on twelve references or applications relating to licensing schemes and licensing bodies.[48] These individual decisions (all but two of which related to the playing in public or broadcasting of musical works or sound recordings by various categories of music users) show

29–99

---

[46] s.129, (and see Sch.2A, para.14 with regard to applications concerning licensing of performers' rights and see the Copyright and Rights in Databases Regulations 1997 (SI 1997/3032), Sch.2, para.14 with regard to applications relating to database right licensing). *Candy Rock Recording Ltd v Phonographic Performance Ltd* [1999] E.M.L.R. 155 (on appeal [1999] E.M.L.R. 806 and on further appeal [2000] E.M.L.R. 618) concerned the terms of a proposed licence to "dub", that is rerecord, sound recordings onto cassettes and CDs for hire to public houses, restaurants and chain stores for use as background music. The Tribunal held that it was entitled to take account of the *AEI* decision (above, para. 29–36) because narrowcasters and dubbers were in competition. However, it took into account the fact that the customer of a dubber has to pay PPL a further fee in order to play its recordings in public whereas a narrowcaster (in reliance on s.72 CDPA 1988) does not. Accordingly, it set a fee at a level which it stated would permit Candy Rock to compete with narrowcasters. On appeal, the Court of Appeal [2000] E.M.L.R. 618 held that the Tribunal was obliged to ensure that there was no unreasonable discrimination but not to secure fair competition. Nevertheless, although the use of the word "compete" was unfortunate, the Tribunal had not erred. The product to be licensed was the same but the way PPL obtained recompense for its use was different. The effect of s.72 was a relevant factor for the Tribunal in seeking to avoid unreasonable discrimination between licensees. Read in context, the Tribunal was attempting to avoid unreasonable discrimination between dubbers and narrowcasters and this was the correct approach. The Court of Appeal also stated that s.129 was not limited to a comparison between licences granted by the same person.

[47] *The British Phonographic Industry v Mechanical-Copyright Protection Society Limited* [1993] E.M.L.R. 86 at 97. See also *Phonographic Performance Ltd v Candy Rock Recording Ltd* [2000] E.M.L.R. 618 (CA) at para.29: "Nothing is excluded provided it is relevant to determining the terms of the licence".

[48] *The Performing Right Society Ltd v British Entertainment and Dancing Association* noted at [1991] I.P.D. 14178 (licensing scheme relating to the performance of musical works in discotheques); *British Amusement Catering Trades Association v Phonographic Performance Ltd* [1992] R.P.C. 149 (licensing scheme relating to the performance of sound recordings on jukeboxes); *Working Men's Club and Institute Union Ltd v The Performing Right Society Ltd* [1992] R.P.C. 227 (licensing scheme relating to the performance of musical works in working men's clubs); *The British Phonographic Industry Ltd v Mechanical-Copyright Protection Society Ltd* [1993] E.M.L.R. 86 and 139 (licensing scheme relating to the reproduction of musical works on records); *The Association of Independent Radio Companies Ltd v Phonographic Performance Ltd* [1994] R.P.C. 143 (application to settle the terms relating to the right to include sound recordings in broadcasts under ss.135D and 135E of the 1988 Act, see para. 29–36, above); *AEI Rediffusion Music Ltd v Phonographic Performance Ltd*, [1998] R.P.C. 335 (another application under ss.135D and 135E; discussed at length at para. 29–36, above); *British Sky Broadcasting Ltd and Sky Television Ltd v The Performing Right Society Ltd* [1998] R.P.C. 467 (licence to broadcast musical works on satellite television); *British Airways Plc v The Performing Right Society*, [1998] R.P.C. 581 (licensing scheme relating to the performance of musical works on aircraft); *Romeike & Curtice Ltd v The Newspaper Licensing Agency Ltd*, [1999] E.M.L.R. 142, (licence relating to the photocopying of newspaper articles); *Virgin Retail Ltd v Phonographic Performance Ltd* [2000] E.M.L.R. 323; on appeal [2001] E.M.L.R. 139 (terms of payment for broadcasting sound recordings on radio station in record shops — discussed at para. 29–36 above); *Candy Rock Recording Ltd v Phonographic Performance Ltd* [1999] E.M.L.R. 155; on appeal [1999] E.M.L.R. 806 and on further appeal [2000] E.M.L.R. 618 (terms of a proposed licence to "dub", that is rerecord, sound recordings onto cassettes and CDs for hire to public houses, restaurants and chain stores for use as background music); and *Universities UK v Copyright Licensing Agency Ltd and Design and Artists Copyright Society Ltd*, CT71/00, 72/00, 73/00, 74/00, 75/01 [2002] I.P.D. 25021 (reprographic copying in Universities). See also *News Group Newspapers Ltd v Independent Television Publications Ltd* [1993] R.P.C. 173 (application to settle the terms of payment for the use as of right of information relating to a programme service under the jurisdiction conferred by the Broadcasting Act 1990, Sch.17, see para. 29–22, above).

that in assessing what payment should be made for a particular form of exploitation of copyright works and how it should be calculated the Tribunal has had regard to a diverse range of factors. The nature and extent of the use of the works in question has been considered in each case. Specifically, however, in cases where the licensing body seeks to base payment for a licence on the revenue or profits of the licensee the Tribunal has considered whether there is a sufficient causal link between the use by the licensee of the copyright work in question and the revenue or profits of that licensee.[49] Moreover even where the basis of the payment is not in issue the available profits of the licensee may be taken into account in order to ensure that the impact on the licensee's business is not disproportionate.[50] As to comparables the Tribunal is specifically directed to have regard to and has had regard to other schemes and licences.[51] In this regard the Tribunal has therefore considered royalties payable by other licensees in respect of the same right in the same works both in the United Kingdom and elsewhere[52]

---

[49] See *British Sky Broadcasting Ltd and Sky Television Ltd v The Performing Right Society Ltd* [1998] R.P.C. 467, where PRS' contention that the licence fee for the broadcasting of musical works in its repertoire on Sky should be a percentage of Sky's relevant revenues was rejected on the ground that there was no sufficient correlation between the use of the works and Sky's revenues (which were derived mainly from subscribers who paid to watch programmes the main feature of which was sport or which otherwise contained many different elements). It was further held relevant that Sky's revenues were a product of substantial capital investment made at high risk which risk PRS had not shared. The Sky case is to be contrasted with *AEI Rediffusion Music Ltd v Phonographic Performance Ltd* [1998] R.P.C. 335, where the question was the amount to be paid by AEI for the compulsory licence to include sound recordings in "narrowcast" broadcasts to particular outlets. There the Tribunal set a minimum royalty to take into account not only revenue of the licensee generated directly by the narrowcasts (which consisted preponderantly of recordings) but also income generated by sales of equipment to receive the narrowcasts which the licensee was only able to make by reason of supplying the narrowcasts. In some cases whether the royalty is to be a percentage of income is not of concern to the licensee, the real issue being not the basis of the calculation but the result, see *British Airways Plc v The Performing Right Society Ltd* [1998] R.P.C. 581. See also J. Rayner James and A. Norris, "A Common Thread in Collective Licensing?" [1998] Ent. L.R. 205.

[50] See *British Phonographic Industry Ltd v Mechanical-Copyright Protection Society Ltd* [1993] E.M.L.R. 86 at 124, referring to dicta in *Smith Kline & French Ltd's (Cimetidine) Patents* [1990] R.P.C. 203. This does mean that rich licensees should pay more or that licensees who make a loss should pay nothing but is a cross check to ensure that the royalty is not too high. In *AEI Rediffusion Music Ltd v Phonographic Performance Ltd* [1998] R.P.C. 335, in a passage which it approved in *Candy Rock Recording Ltd v Phonographic Performance Ltd* [1999] E.M.L.R. 155 at 168, the Tribunal stated that ultimately what it had to determine was how much of the licensee's total profit should be paid by way of licence fee. In so doing, the Tribunal had to arrive at a figure from the total receipts which was both fair to the licensor in terms of the value of the licensee having access to the copyright works and fair to the licensee in giving him a proper reward for the effort put into the exploitation of the licensor's intellectual property rights. In *Virgin Retail Ltd v Phonographic Performance Ltd* [2000] E.M.L.R. 323 (on appeal [2001] E.M.L.R. 139), the Tribunal refused to take any account of the possibility (which it found was not made out on the facts) that a high royalty might force Virgin to discontinue its radio service. In that case, however, the radio station was a marketing tool rather than a profit-making exercise in its own right (see at para.68). By contrast, in *Candy Rock Recording Ltd v Phonographic Performance Ltd* [1999] E.M.L.R. 155 (upheld on appeal [1999] E.M.L.R. 806 and not pursued on the further appeal [2000] E.M.L.R. 618) the Tribunal took account of the state of health of the dubbing business.

[51] CDPA 1988, s.129. However as regards other schemes and licences in the UK the Tribunal has pointed out that its task is not made easier by the well-established and wholly understandable practice of licensing bodies of negotiating tariffs sequentially, relying upon gains achieved in each negotiation to support later increases in other tariffs. The Tribunal has therefore said that this approach makes it necessary for the Tribunal to consider carefully the circumstances surrounding any particular negotiated tariff as there may be special considerations depriving a particular negotiated rate of its cogency in support of the tariff under review. See *Working Men's Club and Institute Union Ltd v The Performing Right Society Ltd* [1992] R.P.C 227 at 238. Nevertheless, in *AEI Rediffusion Music Ltd v Phonographic Performance Ltd* [1998] R.P.C. 335 at 347, in a passage which was approved by the Tribunal itself in *Candy Rock Recording Ltd v Phonographic Performance Ltd* [1999] E.M.L.R. 155 at 168, the Tribunal stated that it was well established that if it is satisfied that there exist other licences which are sufficiently comparable to the licence it is being asked to settle, the Tribunal should adopt a similar rate absent any special circumstances.

[52] CDPA 1988, s.129. During the passage of the Bill through Parliament an amendment requiring

as well as royalties paid by licensees for other rights.[53] Other factors which the Tribunal has taken into account include the audience for musical works and sound recordings,[54] the incidental benefit derived by the licensor from the public exploitation of its copyright works,[55] profits which the licensee has been able to make out of the sale of ancillary equipment and out of the jurisdiction,[56] the strength of the market in which the licensee operates[57] and guidelines laid down for similar tribunals in other jurisdictions and decisions from other jurisdictions.[58] Ultimately, however, because the Tribunal is seeking to fix a price for a commodity where there is no market in the conventional sense, it has also paid particular regard to previously negotiated agreements between the parties.[59]

Particular factors the Copyright Tribunal is required to take into account in certain proceedings. The 1988 Act also sets out a number of other particular factors, in addition to the general requirements discussed above,[60] which the Copyright Tribunal is required to take into account in proceedings dealing with specific matters.[61] In all cases concerned with the control of licensing schemes and licensing bodies the aim of the 1988 Act is to seek to maintain a fair balance between the interests of those seeking licences under licence schemes and from licensing bodies, and those whose rights in the copyright works or other subject-matter involved are affected. The relevant provisions of the 1988 Act with regard to control of licensing schemes and licensing bodies dealing with copyright licences, which are contained in sections 130 to 134, fall into three types of case: the first two are each individual situations which are singled out for special consideration, and the third comprises a number of situations each involving a subsequent copyright work that includes in it other copyright works where (1) the licence in respect of the subsequent copyright work has been obtained (or is not

29–100

---

the Tribunal to look specifically at data from other Member States of the EEC was resisted on the grounds that there was nothing in what became section 129 to preclude it from considering comparisons from anywhere in the world if they were relevant (*Hansard*, Reports of Standing Committee E, 1988, col.432). In *British Phonographic Industry Ltd v Mechanical-Copyright Protection Society Ltd* [1993] E.M.L.R. 86, the royalty payable in Europe for making recordings was held not to be a meaningful comparator as the British record industry was of a different order of magnitude and the commercial risks were commensurately greater.

[53] In *AEI Rediffusion Music Ltd v Phonographic Performance Ltd* [1998] R.P.C. 335, the Tribunal expressly stated that it was entitled to find a licence of a different right to the one in dispute as being a comparator if in all the circumstances that was appropriate (licences to "dub" sound recordings for playing in public held to be a relevant comparator to narrowcast licence to broadcast recordings for playing in public). See also for comparison of rates under PRS licences in respect of musical works and PPL licences in respect of sound recordings, *The Manx Radio Case* PRT 18/64, where it was held that as regards the PRS rights in musical works and those of PPL in sound recordings neither was superior to the other.

[54] See *British Sky Broadcasting Ltd and Sky Television Ltd v The Performing Right Society Ltd* [1998] R.P.C. 467.

[55] See *Association of Independent Radio Contractors Ltd v Phonographic Performance Ltd* [1994] R.P.C. 143. However, in *Virgin Retail Ltd v Phonographic Performance Ltd* [2000] E.M.L.R. 323 (on appeal [2001] E.M.L.R. 139), an application under s.135D CDPA 1988, the Tribunal refused to award a discount to reflect the fact that Virgin's business was to a significant extent involved in selling the records of PPL's record company members, which were marketed on Virgin's radio station.

[56] See *AEI Rediffusion Music Ltd v Phonographic Performance Ltd* [1998] R.P.C. 335.

[57] *Candy Rock Recording Ltd v Phonographic Performance Ltd* [1999] E.M.L.R. 155; upheld on appeal [1999] E.M.L.R. 806; point not pursued on further appeal [2000] E.M.L.R. 618.

[58] See *British Phonographic Industry Ltd v Mechanical-Copyright Protection Society Ltd* [1993] E.M.L.R. 86, and *British Sky Broadcasting Ltd and Sky Television Ltd v The Performing Right Society Ltd* [1998] R.P.C. 467.

[59] See *British Phonographic Industry Ltd v Mechanical-Copyright Protection Society Ltd* [1993] E.M.L.R. 86, and *British Sky Broadcasting Ltd and Sky Television Ltd v The Performing Right Society Ltd* [1998] R.P.C. 467.

[60] See para. 29–98, above.

[61] The particular factors required to be taken into account by CDPA 1988, s.135G, in relation to applications in respect of the use as of right of sound recordings in broadcasts and cable programme services are discussed at para. 29–37, above.

required) but the licence in respect of the underlying works is itself the subject of the proceedings or (2) the terms of the licence in respect of the underlying works are specifically declared to be relevant to the terms of the licence in respect of the subsequent copyright work. Similarly, in cases concerning the determination of the amount payable by way of equitable remuneration to authors of literary, dramatic, musical or artistic works, to directors of films and to performers in respect of the rental of sound recordings or films including their work or concerning the amount of such remuneration payable to performers where sound recordings including their performances have been played in public or included in a broadcast or cable programme, the aim of the 1988 Act is again to maintain a fair balance between the persons entitled to the remuneration and those obliged to pay it and the Tribunal is directed to take into account particular factors to achieve this.

29–101   **Particular factors: (i) licences for reprographic copying.** Proceedings relating to the licensing for reprographic copying of published literary, dramatic, musical or artistic works or of the typographical arrangement of published editions may come before the Copyright Tribunal either under the general provisions relating to licensing schemes or under the provisions relating to licences granted by licensing bodies,[62] or, where the party seeking the licence is an educational establishment, under the specific provisions relating to such copying by educational establishments.[63] In all such proceedings the Copyright Tribunal shall have regard to the extent of the availability of other published editions of the work, the proportion of the work to be copied and the nature of the use to which the copies are likely to be put.[64] These factors are clearly of importance not only to whether it is reasonable that a licence is not available (*e.g.* because too large a part of the work is to be photocopied and published editions are available, or because the use to which the photocopies are to be put is damaging to the copyright owner's own commercial exploitation of his copyright), but also to what is a reasonable fee for the licence sought. This provision provides the means for the Copyright Tribunal to ensure that excessive photocopying does not become a substitute for the normal access to such works through the purchase of published editions.

29–102   **Particular factors: (ii) licences in respect of recordings, films, broadcasts or cable programmes including an entertainment or event.** In proceedings relating to licences for sound recordings, films or broadcasts which include any entertainment or other event,[65] the Copyright Tribunal shall have regard to any conditions imposed by the promoter of the entertainment or other event (other than conditions which seek to regulate the charges to be imposed in respect of licences or which relate to payment for the grant of facilities to make the recording, etc.),[66] and shall not regard the refusal or failure to grant a licence as unreasonable if it could not have been granted consistently with those conditions.[67] The situation envisaged here is analogous to those discussed under (iii) below, except that there may be no underlying work by means of the copyright in which the promoter can control the subsequent exploitation of his entertainment or event, and his only opportunity to do so is through the contract with the maker of the recording. The aim of the 1988 Act is, therefore, to ensure that the reasonable

---

[62] CDPA 1988, ss.116–128; see paras 29–105 *et seq.*, below.

[63] s.139; see para 29–129, below.

[64] s.130.

[65] *i.e.* proceedings brought under the general provisions applying to licensing schemes and licences granted by licensing bodies, see paras 29–105 *et seq.*, below.

[66] CDPA 1988, s.132(3).

[67] s.132(2); this provision is based on s.29(4) of the 1956 Act which applied to television broadcasts, and is now extended to cover sound recordings, films, cable programmes and sound broadcasts.

rights of the promoter of the entertainment or event to control the making of a recording of his entertainment or event and its further use, by means of contractual terms imposed on the maker of the recording, are not circumvented by the possibility of others being entitled to obtain licences from the maker to exploit the recording under the general provisions of the 1988 Act in relation to licensing schemes and licences granted by licensing bodies. Unless promoters of such entertainments and events can be assured that such conditions will be respected, they might well be unwilling to permit the recording to be made and exploited at all.

Particular factors: (iii) Payments in respect of underlying copyright works **29–103** **and other rights.** In these cases the aim of the 1988 Act is to ensure that any consideration already received or stipulated for by the owner of the copyright in the underlying work or other right at the time he authorises the making and showing of the subsequent copyright work, or which he may otherwise be entitled to obtain in respect of any further use by others of that subsequent copyright work, is taken into account, so as to ensure, in effect, that his overall remuneration from the licensing of his work, both directly by himself and indirectly by the owner of the subsequent copyright work, is neither unreasonably high (because he is paid in respect of some uses twice), nor unreasonably low (because he is not paid at all in respect of some uses).

This principle applies to proceedings relating to licences for educational establishments for the recording by them or on their behalf of broadcasts which include copyright works, or for the making of copies of such recordings, for educational purposes[68] ; proceedings relating to licences in respect of the rental or lending of copies of a work[69] ; proceedings relating to licences in respect of the copyright in sound recordings, films or broadcasts[70] ; and proceedings relating to licences in respect of works to be included in immediate retransmissions of broadcasts.[71]

In the last mentioned case, there are further special provisions which apply, depending on whether the retransmission is to be in the same area as that of the original transmission, or partly or wholly in an area outside that of the original transmission. Where the retransmission is to be in the same area as the original transmission, the Copyright Tribunal, in considering what charges, if any, should be made in respect of either transmission, must take into account any charges the copyright owner is entitled to receive in respect of the other transmission, thus preventing the copyright owner obtaining remuneration twice over in respect of the same area.[72] Where the retransmission is to an area wholly or partly outside the area of the original transmission, then, to the extent that it is, the Copyright Tribunal must leave the further transmission out of account in considering what charges, if any, should be paid in respect of the first transmission, thus leaving

---

[68] CDPA 1988, s.131(1) and (2); such proceedings would be brought under the general provisions applying to licensing schemes and licences granted by licensing bodies, see paras 29–105 *et seq*, below.

[69] CDPA 1988, s.133(1) as amended by the Copyright and Related Rights Regulations 1996 (SI 1996/2967); and see further para. 29–130, below.

[70] CDPA 1988, s.133(2); such proceedings would be brought under the general provisions applying to licensing schemes and licences granted by licensing bodies, see paras 29–105 *et seq.*, below. Foreign broadcasts and cable transmissions may therefore be relevant where charges under UK licences or foreign licences have been negotiated to take account of foreign retransmission (see as to the former position under s.28 of the 1956 Act: *Copinger* (12th ed.) para.1271).

[71] CDPA 1988, s.134; such proceedings would be brought under the general provisions applying to licensing schemes and licences granted by licensing bodies, see paras 29–130 *et seq.*, below. Reception and retransmission may be a permitted act, see CDPA 1988, s.73 and para. 9–205, above; and see further below.

[72] CDPA 1988, s.134(2).

the copyright owner to make his own terms with the party making the retransmission.[73] (These special provisions do not, however, apply in relation to any applications to the Tribunal to determine the reasonable royalty or other sum payable to a copyright owner by a broadcaster in respect of works included in a wireless broadcast which is retransmitted by cable where or to the extent that the retransmission falls outside the area of the original transmission and occurs as a result of the statutory obligations imposed under the Broadcasting Act 1990.[74] In the case of such retransmissions the inclusion in the retransmission (to the extent that it falls outside the area of the original transmission) of any work included in the broadcast is treated as licensed by the copyright owner subject to the payment to him by the person making the broadcast of a reasonable royalty and the Copyright Tribunal has a separate specific jurisdiction to determine the amount of such royalty).[75]

Finally, with regard to payments in respect of underlying copyright works, such payments made by the owners of subsequent works (such as sound recordings, films and broadcasts) in which the underlying works are included are an expense incurred by the owners of such subsequent works in creating those works and, as such, relevant to the licence fees that they should receive for their exploitation.

29–104   **Particular factors: (iv) factors relevant to determining equitable remuneration.** On applications to determine the amount payable by way of equitable remuneration to the author of a literary, dramatic, musical or artistic work or the principal director of a film for the rental of a sound recording or film (where such author or director has transferred his rental right concerning the recording or film) the Copyright Tribunal, in being directed to make such order as to the method of calculating and paying such remuneration as it may determine to be reasonable in all the circumstances, is specifically directed to take into account the importance of the contribution of the author or director to the recording or film.[76] Similarly, on applications to determine the amount of equitable remuneration payable to performers for rental of sound recordings or films where they have transferred their rental rights concerning such recordings or films the Tribunal is directed to take into account the importance of the contribution of the

---

[73] CDPA 1988, s.134(3). The purposes of s.134(2) and (3) were explained in Parliament as being, "intended, first, to ensure that if copyright owners license inclusion of their material in a foreign broadcast or cable programme service on terms which cover retransmission of that broadcast or service in the United Kingdom, any tribunal award that they may obtain in the UK in respect of royalties due from UK cable operators or broadcasters for retransmitting the foreign broadcast are (sic) abated to the extent that this retransmission was allowed for in the terms of the initial licence. The intention is to avert double payments to rights owners in respect of what is essentially a single transmission (or chain of transmissions) reaching the same audience. This policy is unchanged from the 1956 Act, where it is implemented by Section 28. The second objective is to ensure that, when broadcasts or cable programme services are retransmitted within the intended reception area of the broadcast or service (and this applies particularly to 'in area' retransmissions abroad of UK satellite broadcasts), and rights owners obtain payment from the cable operator for the retransmission under local law, tribunal decisions on licences in respect of the original broadcast shall take this into account. The third objective is to ensure that when broadcasts or cable programme services are retransmitted beyond or outside the intended reception area of the broadcast or service, the broadcaster or provider of the cable programme service which is retransmitted cannot be made to pay royalties in respect of the retransmission. It is up to the rights owners concerned to use any rights available in the country or area of the retransmission to reach an agreement with those responsible for it. If such rights do not exist it should not fall to the broadcaster to reimburse copyright owners for that fact" (*Hansard*, HL Vol.491, cols 524, 525).

[74] Section 78A and Sch.12, Part III, para.4; see CDPA 1988, s.134(3A) as inserted into the 1988 Act by s.138 and Sch.9 of the Broadcasting Act 1996.

[75] Under CDPA 1988, ss.73(4) and 73A, inserted into the 1988 Act by s.138 and Sch.9 of the Broadcasting Act 1996. See para. 29–51, above.

[76] CDPA 1988, s.93C(3), inserted into the 1988 Act by the Copyright and Related Rights Regulations 1996 (SI 1996/2967).

performers to the recording or film,[77] and the Tribunal is given a similar direction when determining the equitable remuneration payable to performers where sound recordings containing their performances are played in public or included in a broadcast or cable programme.[78]

C. CONTROL BY THE COPYRIGHT TRIBUNAL OF LICENSING SCHEMES AND LICENSING BODIES DEALING WITH COPYRIGHT LICENCES

Introduction. The aim of the provisions establishing control by the Copyright Tribunal over licensing schemes and licences by licensing bodies is to prevent copyright owners abusing what has come to be recognised as a monopoly or near monopoly power in their dealings with those wishing to be licensed to exploit their copyright works. However, this control is only exercisable (apart from certain other situations discussed below[79]) in a situation involving either a licensing scheme or a licensing body, as these terms are defined.[80] A copyright owner is not obliged to operate or join a licensing scheme,[81] or to agree to a licensing body exercising or administering his copyright,[82] and, in general, if he does neither and refuses to grant a licence, then such refusal is not subject to the overriding jurisdiction of the Copyright Tribunal. It is only, therefore, when a copyright owner himself chooses to operate a tariff for licences of his works, or agrees to his works being owned or administered by a collecting society acting on his behalf, that the grant and the terms of a licence affecting his works may be referred to the Copyright Tribunal.

29–105

(i) Definitions

Licensing scheme. "Licensing scheme" is defined[83] as a scheme setting out the classes of cases in which the operator of the scheme, or the person on whose behalf he acts, is willing to grant copyright licences and the terms on which licences would be granted in those classes of cases. The term "scheme" is to include anything in the nature of a scheme, whether described as such, or as a tariff, or by any other name.[84] The question of whether a licensing scheme exists depends on the circumstances of each case, and thus where a particular type of licence was not available on demand from a licensing body and each inquiry for such a licence was considered individually there was no scheme even though each inquiry was dealt with in the same methodical manner.[85] Where a scheme which has been properly referred to the Tribunal contains a restriction on certain

29–106

---

[77] s.191H(3) inserted into the 1988 Act by the Copyright and Related Rights Regulations 1996 (SI 1996/2967).

[78] s.182D(6) inserted into the 1988 Act by the Copyright and Related Rights Regulations 1996 (SI 1996/2967).

[79] See para. 29–128, below.

[80] See paras 29–106 and 29–107, below.

[81] But, in relation to the making in some cases of copies for the visually impaired, the educational recording of broadcasts, the copying of abstracts of scientific or technical articles, the lending of certain works and adding sub-titles to broadcasts for the hard of hearing, certain acts are deemed not to be infringements if there is no licensing scheme in existence under which royalties are payable: CDPA 1988, ss.31B, 35, 60, 66 (as amended by the Copyright and Related Rights Regulations 1996 (SI 1996/2967) and 74; see paras 9–86, 9–97, 9–163, 9–211 and 29–45, above.

[82] But in relation to the cable re-transmission right, this may only be exercised against a cable operator by a collecting society: see paras 29–48 *et seq.*, above.

[83] CDPA 1988, s.116(1): derived from Copyright Act 1956, s.24(4) where the term defined was "licence scheme".

[84] CDPA 1988, s.116(1).

[85] *Candy Rock Recording Ltd v Phonographic Performance Ltd*, CT 34/96; and see *The Performing Right Society Ltd v Working Men's Club and Institute Ltd* [1988] F.S.R. 586. See also *Universities UK v Copyright Licensing Agency Ltd and Design and Artists Copyright Society Ltd*, CT71/

types of copying which would otherwise fall within the scheme, the Tribunal has jurisdiction to consider whether that restriction is reasonable,[86] even if the operator has no mandate to license those types of copying.[87] A "copyright licence" is a licence to do, or to authorise the doing of,[88] any of the acts restricted by copyright.[89]

29–107 **Licensing body.** "Licensing body" is defined[90] as meaning a society or other organisation which has as its main object, or one of its main objects, the negotiation or granting of copyright licences,[91] either as owner or prospective owner of copyright, or as agent for the owner or prospective owner of copyright, and whose main objects include the granting of licences covering works of more than one author. Collective works[92] are not "works of more than one author" for these purposes, nor are works made by employees of one person, firm, company or group of companies.[93] The definition is therefore intended to cover collective licensing societies and agencies rather than individual publishers or authors, whose activities fall within the jurisdiction of the Copyright Tribunal only if they operate a licensing scheme.

00, 72/00, 73/00, 74/00, 75/01 [2002] I.P.D. 25021 at para.58. The reference concerned reprographic copying at educational establishments. The CLA operated a scheme which covered all such copying except when it involved the creation of "course packs" (defined compilations of photocopied material provided to support a course of study). Although it was possible to obtain a licence from the CLA to create a course pack (under the "CLARCS" scheme), the CLA did not hold itself out as willing to grant licences in respect of course packs because it did not have a mandate from all its members to license them; furthermore, the terms of the licences for course packs varied depending on the transaction. Accordingly, the Tribunal held that CLARCS was not a licensing scheme (para.58). Nevertheless, it went on to hold that it had jurisdiction over the CLARCS system: see next footnote.

[86] *Universities UK v Copyright Licensing Agency Ltd and Design and Artists Copyright Society Ltd*, CT71/00, 72/00, 73/00, 74/00, 75/01 [2002] I.P.D. 25021, para.59. The basis for this finding was that one of the terms of the CLA's licensing scheme was a specific restriction on copying course packs. The scheme having been properly referred to it, the Tribunal held that it had jurisdiction to consider the reasonableness of that restriction and if it considered it unreasonable, to require its removal (para.59). The Tribunal considered an argument based on the terms of CDPA 1988, ss.119(1) and (3). s.119(1) allows a reference on behalf of a person who claims he requires a licence in a case of "a description to which the scheme applies". S.119(3) allows the Tribunal to vary the scheme but only so far as it relates to cases of the description to which the reference relates. The scheme which had been referred related only to copying which did not involve the creation of course packs. Accordingly, the Tribunal thought it arguable that its powers were limited to copying which did not involve the creation of course packs. However, the Tribunal rejected this argument on the grounds that it involved too narrow a view of the phrase "a case of a description to which the Scheme applies". The copying involved in the creation of Course Packs involved copying of the same material, by the same people as were involved when copying took place under the licensing scheme.

[87] *Universities UK v Copyright Licensing Agency Ltd and Design and Artists Copyright Society Ltd*, CT71/00, 72/00, 73/00, 74/00, 75/01 [2002] I.P.D. 25021, para.60.

[88] The express inclusion of these words reverses the decision of Whitford J. on the different wording of s.24(2) of the 1956 Act to the effect that the PRT's jurisdiction was limited to the right itself and not the right to authorise as well: *Reditune Limited v PRS* [1981] F.S.R. 165.

[89] CDPA 1988, s.116(3); compare the much narrower definition under the 1956 Act in s.24(2), and see para. 29–91, above; but see the further definitions in ss.117 and 124 (as inserted by the Copyright and Related Rights Regulations 1996 (SI 1996/2967) which limit the schemes and licences which fall within the jurisdiction of the Copyright Tribunal, paras 29–109 and 29–119, below.

[90] CDPA 1988, s.116(2); derived from Copyright Act 1956, s.24(3), but without drawing the distinctions previously made as between the different forms of licences set out in s.24(2) of that Act. See also para. 29–91, above.

[91] That is a licence to do, or to authorise the doing of any of the acts restricted by copyright: CDPA 1988, s.116(3); compare the much narrower definition under the 1956 Act in s.24(2), and see paras 29–91 and 29–106, above.

[92] That is a single work of more than one author, or a number of such works where the authors are the same.

[93] CDPA 1988, s.116(4).

(ii) References and applications with respect to licensing schemes

References and applications involving licensing schemes. The distinction, **29–108**
introduced in the 1956 Act, between references and applications relating to general tariffs and those relating to individual complaints, is maintained in the 1988
Act. Under sections 118, 119 and 120 of the 1988 Act the subject of the reference
is the scheme itself whereas under sections 121 and 122 of that Act the subject of
the application is the availability of an individual licence to a person claiming to
be covered by the scheme or claiming to have been unreasonably excluded from
it.

Jurisdiction over licensing schemes. The jurisdiction of the Copyright Tribunal **29–109**
over licensing schemes depends both on the licensing scheme being operated by
a licensing body and on the nature of the right the subject of the licensing scheme.
Thus the Tribunal has jurisdiction over licensing schemes operated by licensing
bodies, covering works of more than one author, in so far as they relate to licences
for copying the works, rental or lending of the works to the public or performing,
showing or playing the works in public or communicating them to the public.[94]

Reference of a proposed scheme. Under the 1956 Act, a licence scheme could **29–110**
be referred to the PRT at any time whilst in operation.[95] The 1988 Act, whilst
retaining this jurisdiction,[96] has, in section 118, introduced the possibility of
referring a proposed licensing scheme to the Copyright Tribunal before it has
begun to be operated.[97] A proposed scheme may be referred to the Copyright
Tribunal by an organisation claiming to be representative of persons claiming
that they require licences in cases of a description to which the scheme would
apply.[98] The validity of such an organisation's claim to be representative of such
class of persons is a matter which the Copyright Tribunal will decide.[99] The
Copyright Tribunal must first consider whether the reference is premature, in
which case it will refuse to entertain it.[1]

Reference of an existing scheme. In the case of an existing scheme, where a **29–111**
dispute arises with respect to the scheme between the licensing body operating it
and any person claiming that he requires a licence in cases of a description to
which the scheme applies, or an organisation claiming to be representative of
persons requiring such licences, the scheme may be referred to the Copyright
Tribunal either by such person or by such organisation.[2] An existing scheme
which has been referred to the Copyright Tribunal remains in operation until the
reference has been determined.[3]

Order confirming or varying the scheme. Where an existing or proposed licens- **29–112**

---

[94] CDPA 1988, s.117, as amended by the Copyright and Related Rights Regulations 1996 (SI 1996/
2967) and the Copyright and Related Rights Regulations 2003 (SI 2003/2498).
[95] Copyright Act 1956, s.25(1); and see *The Performing Right Society Ltd v Working Men's Club
and Institute Union Ltd* [1988] F.S.R. 586.
[96] CDPA 1988, s.119; see para. 29–111, below.
[97] Proposed schemes were referred to the Tribunal in *British Amusement Catering Trades Association v Phonographic Performance Ltd* [1992] R.P.C. 149 and *The British Phonographic Industry
Ltd v Mechanical-Copyright Protection Society Ltd* [1993] E.M.L.R. 139.
[98] s.118(1); Copyright Tribunal Rules 1989, r.3(1), Form 1, Vol.2 at B1.i.
[99] See as to "credentials", Copyright Tribunal Rules 1989, rr.2(1) and 6, Vol.2 at B1.i.
[1] CDPA 1988, s.118(2) and r.3(3), see Vol.2 at B1.i. The Tribunal will normally consider the matter on the basis of written submissions only (*Practice Direction*, para.4, Vol.2 at B1.ii). For a decision as to whether a reference in respect of a proposed licence was premature, see the *Candy
Rock* decision, CT 35/96, noted at para. 29–120, below.
[2] CDPA 1988, s.119(1); The Copyright Tribunal Rules 1989, r.3(1), Form 1, see Vol.2 at B1.i.
[3] CDPA 1988, s.119(2).

ing scheme is referred under section 118 or 119 of the 1988 Act, the Copyright Tribunal is empowered to make such order, either confirming or varying the scheme, in so far as it relates to cases of the description to which the reference relates, or, in the case of a proposed scheme, generally, as the Tribunal may determine to be reasonable in the circumstances.[4] There is no presumption that a referred scheme should either be confirmed or varied.[5] The Copyright Tribunal's order may be either for an indefinite period, or for such period as the Tribunal may determine.[6]

29–113   **Effect of order.** A licensing scheme confirmed or varied by the Copyright Tribunal remains in operation (or in the case of a proposed scheme comes into and remains in force) for so long as the Tribunal's order remains in force.[7] The effect of an order of the Copyright Tribunal with respect to a licensing scheme is that if, during the continuance of the order, a person has complied with the terms and conditions which, in accordance with the licensing scheme as confirmed or varied by the order, would be applicable to a licence granted in accordance with the scheme, and has paid any charges payable in respect of such licence (or, if the amount payable could not be ascertained, has given an undertaking to pay such charges) then he is to be in the same position as if he had at all material times been the holder of a licence granted by the owner of the copyright in question in accordance with the scheme.[8] The exact effect of these provisions will therefore depend on the precise form of any scheme as varied or confirmed by the Tribunal. It would seem, however, that once a licensing scheme has been confirmed or varied by the Tribunal, as covering a particular description of cases, it will not be necessary for an actual licence to be issued to a person wishing to carry out activities falling within the scheme with regard to a case covered by that description, since it will be sufficient if he complies with the terms and conditions of the licensing scheme and pays fees as required under it. If, however, a licence is actually issued, the parties are bound by the terms of the licence and the protection of the order is irrelevant.

29–114   **Date from which order takes effect. Interest.** Under the 1956 Act the PRT had no power to backdate its order, which took effect on the scheme from the date the order was made.[9] The 1988 Act introduced a limited ability for the Copyright Tribunal to backdate the effect of its order on the scheme referred to it. Thus, where the order of the Tribunal varies the amount of charges payable under a licensing scheme, the Tribunal may direct that the order has such effect from a date earlier than that on which the order is made, but not earlier than the date on which the reference was made or, if later, on which the scheme came into

---

[4] CDPA 1988, s.118(3) and 119(3); as to reasonableness, see s.129 and para. 29–98, above and as to other factors to be considered, see paras 29–100 to 29–104, above.

[5] *The British Phonographic Industry Ltd v Mechanical-Copyright Protection Society Limited* [1993] E.M.L.R. 56 at 99.

[6] CDPA 1988, ss.118(4), 119(4). Once the Tribunal has made a final order either confirming or varying the scheme under ss.118(4) or 119(4), then while such order remains in force it can only be reviewed on a further reference under s.120, see para. 29–115, below. See *The Working Men's Club and Institute Union Ltd v The Performing Right Society Ltd* [1992] R.P.C. 227 in which a matter of months after the Tribunal's order varying the tariff in question until further notice, an attempt was made to substitute, by agreement, a revised version of the tariff. There was no attempt to invoke s.120 or to vary the substance of the order but merely to make presentational and stylistic changes to the licensing scheme set out in it. The Tribunal accordingly held that in such circumstances it had no jurisdiction to vary the order it had made.

[7] CDPA 1988, s.123(1).

[8] s.123(2); presumably protecting such person both from proceedings for infringement of copyright and from prosecution for offences under s.107.

[9] See *The Performing Right Society Ltd v Working Men's Club and Institute Union Ltd* [1988] F.S.R. 586; *The British Broadcasting Corporation v The Performing Right Society Ltd* (1967) PRT 22/67.

operation.[10] Any necessary repayments, or further payments, in respect of charges already paid must then be made.[11] Where the Tribunal directs that the order varying the amount of charges payable under a licensing scheme relating to licences for communicating works to the public has effect from a date earlier than that on which it is made the Tribunal has power to award simple interest.[12] Interest may be awarded for such period, beginning not earlier than the date on which the reference was made and ending not later than the date of the order, as the Tribunal thinks is reasonable in the circumstances.[13] The power of the Tribunal to award interest when directing that the order varying the charges payable under a licensing scheme is backdated, is limited to schemes relating to licences for communicating works to the public.[14] There is also a power to award interest where the Tribunal settles the terms of payment for the use as of right of sound recordings in broadcasts or confirms or varies such an order.[15]

Further reference. Where the Copyright Tribunal has made an order with respect to a licensing scheme,[16] the scheme may be referred again to the Tribunal in relation to cases of the description to which the order applies.[17] On the second and any subsequent reference, application may be made not only by such an organisation or person as may initiate a first reference, but also by the licensing body operating the scheme.[18] In order, however, to avoid constant references with regard to the same description of cases, a licensing scheme may not, without the special leave of the Copyright Tribunal, be referred back to the Tribunal within 12 months from the date of the order on the previous reference, or, if the previous order was made so as to be in force for 15 months or less, until the last three months before expiry of the order.[19] An application for special leave must be made to the Copyright Tribunal on the appropriate form together with a statement of the grounds for the application.[20] A licensing scheme which is made the subject of a further reference remains in operation until the reference is

29–115

---

[10] CDPA 1988, s.123(3); as a matter of construction of s.123 it would appear that this provision does not apply to an application under s.121.

[11] CDPA 1988, s.123(3).

[12] s.151A(1)(a) and (b) inserted into the 1988 Act by s.139(2) of the Broadcasting Act 1996, as amended by the Copyright and Related Rights Regulations 2003.

[13] CDPA 1988, s.151A(1).

[14] On the passage of the Broadcasting Bill through Parliament the Government spokesman stated that because of the scope of the Bill the new s.151A (giving the Tribunal power to award interest) had been limited to cases involving broadcasting and cable programmes, but that when a suitable legislative opportunity arose the Government intended to apply the change to all disputes that can be heard by the Tribunal. To date no such change has been introduced. That the Tribunal has no general power to award interest was made clear in *The Association of Independent Radio Companies Ltd v Phonographic Performance Ltd* [1994] R.P.C. 143.

[15] Under s.135D or 135F. See s.151A(1)(c) and (d) inserted into the 1988 Act by s.139(2) of the Broadcasting Act 1996. It had been held in the *AIRC* case (*The Association of Independent Radio Companies Ltd v Phonographic Performance Ltd* [1994] R.P.C. 143), which was a reference under s.135D but was decided before the introduction of s.151A, that the provisions of s.135D (which are similar to those of s.123(3) in that they provide for backdating and the making of any necessary payments by way of adjustment but are themselves silent as to interest) impliedly excluded a power to award interest.

[16] *i.e.* under any of ss.118, 119 or 120 of the 1988 Act.

[17] CDPA 1988, s.120(1); Copyright Tribunal Rules 1989, r.3(1), Form 1, see Vol.2 at B1.i. This statutory provision deals with subsequent referral of a scheme in relation to the same description of classes previously the subject of the order; the same scheme may be referred any number of times to the Tribunal under s.119, quite apart from this provision, if the reference is in relation each time to a description of classes within the scheme but not the subject of a previous order (*cf.* s.26(7) of the 1956 Act, not specifically re-enacted).

[18] CDPA 1988, s.120(1); this allows the operator of the scheme to seek to have the terms as to payment, or other terms, varied.

[19] s.120(2).

[20] The Copyright Tribunal Rules 1989, r.3(1), Form 3, see Vol.2 at B1.ii; such grounds might consist of a material change of circumstances, or new arguments raised by another applicant but are not limited to such cases, see *Hansard*, HL Vol.493, col.137, as noted in para. 29–118.

determined.[21] On a further reference, the Copyright Tribunal has the same powers with regard to the order it can make as in the case of an initial reference.[22]

29–116　Application for individual licence where scheme exists. Under the 1956 Act, an application for an individual licence in relation to a scheme could only be made where the scheme applied, but the licensing body operating the scheme would not grant a licence to the applicant in accordance with the scheme.[23] Thus, no application could be made in relation to the scheme where it contained terms or conditions, other than those relating to the amount of a charge for a licence, which excluded from the scheme the class of case in respect of which the applicant sought a licence.[24] Under the 1988 Act, however, an applicant may make an application to the Copyright Tribunal for an individual licence where a licensing scheme exists in two situations, depending, again, whether the licence sought is or is not covered by the scheme. The first, which re-enacts the position under the 1956 Act, is where the applicant claims, in a case covered by the scheme, that the operator has refused or failed within a reasonable time to grant to him, or to procure the grant to him of, a licence in accordance with the scheme.[25] The second, which was new, is where the applicant seeks a licence in respect of a case which is excluded from the scheme and claims that the operator of the scheme either has refused to grant a licence, and that in the circumstances it is unreasonable that a licence should not be granted, or has proposed terms for a licence which are unreasonable.[26] A case is treated as excluded from a licensing scheme for this purpose if either the case falls within exceptions provided for in the scheme or is so similar to a case in which a licence is granted under the scheme that it is unreasonable that it should not be dealt with in the same way.[27] On an application under section 121 of the 1988 Act, the Copyright Tribunal, if satisfied that the claim is well founded, must make an order declaring that, in respect of the matters specified in the order, the applicant is entitled to a licence on such terms and conditions as the Tribunal may determine to be applicable in accordance with the scheme, or, as the case may be, reasonable in the circumstances.[28] The order may be made either for an indefinite period, or for such period as the Tribunal may determine.[29]

29–117　Effect of order. Where the Copyright Tribunal has made an order under section 121, and, during the continuance of the order, the person in whose favour the or-

---

[21] CDPA 1988, s.120(3).
[22] s.120(4) and (5); see para. 29–112, above.
[23] Copyright Act 1956, s.27(2).
[24] This being the effect of ss.24(5) and 27(1) of the 1956 Copyright Act.
[25] CDPA 1988, s.121(1); The Copyright Tribunal Rules 1989, r.3(1), Form 2, see Vol.2 at B1.i.
[26] s.121(2); The Copyright Tribunal Rules 1989, r.3(1), Form 2. No application may be made under this subsection by an organisation claiming to be representative of persons requiring a licence: *Universities UK v Copyright Licensing Agency Ltd and Design and Artists Copyright Society Ltd*, CT71/00, 72/00, 73/00, 74/00, 75/01 [2002] I.P.D. 25021, para.29.
[27] s.121(3). On the passage of the legislation through Parliament and in speaking to an amendment to substitute the word "excluded" for the word "excepted" in what is now subs.121(3) the Minister stated: "The point to bear in mind is that the word "cases" does not refer to "works" which may be outside a licensing scheme but types of licensing situations which may not be covered by it. For example, where a scheme covers the use of the licensing body's repertoire in village halls but not in church halls. Substituting the word "excluded" for the word "excepted" should help to bring out the fact that we are dealing with cases where a particular class of potential licensee has been prevented from having access to the works in question under the terms of the scheme. This exclusion is unreasonable. Thus it might be held that the circumstances in which church halls required a licence to use music or records were sufficiently similar to those in which village halls might do so for it to be unreasonable not to treat them in the same way." (*Hansard*, HL Vol.493, col.1375.).
[28] CDPA 1988, s.121(4); as to reasonableness, see s.129 and para. 29–98, above and as to other factors to be considered, see paras 29–100 to 29–104, above.
[29] s.121(5).

der is made pays any charges payable in accordance with the order (or, if the amount payable cannot be ascertained, gives an undertaking to pay such charges) and complies with the other terms of the order, then such person is to be in the same position as if he had at all material times been the holder of a licence granted by the owner of the copyright in question.[30]

Further reference. Where the Copyright Tribunal has made an order under section 121 of the 1988 Act that a person is entitled to a licence under a licensing scheme, the operator of the scheme or the original applicant may apply to the Tribunal for a review of its order.[31] As with other provisions in the 1988 Act dealing with subsequent references,[32] such an application may not be made, without the special leave of the Copyright Tribunal, within 12 months from the date of the order on the previous reference, or, if the previous order was made so as to be in force for 15 months or less, until the last three months before expiry of the order.[33] An application for special leave must be made to the Copyright Tribunal on the appropriate form together with a statement of the grounds for the application.[34] On an application for review the Copyright Tribunal is empowered to confirm or vary its previous order as the Tribunal may determine to be reasonable having regard to the terms applicable in accordance with the licensing scheme, or, as the case may be, reasonable in all the circumstances.[35] **29–118**

(iii) References and applications with respect to licensing bodies

Jurisdiction over licences by licensing bodies. Where no licensing scheme exists or is proposed, the Copyright Tribunal has jurisdiction in relation to the granting and terms of licences only when the party from whom the licence is sought is a licensing body.[36] The jurisdiction of the Tribunal then depends, as in the case of licensing schemes,[37] on the nature of the right the subject of the licence. Thus, the Copyright Tribunal has jurisdiction over licences to copy works, rent or lend works to the public, to perform, play or show works in public or communicate works to the public.[38] **29–119**

Reference of a proposed licence. A person seeking a licence[39] from a licensing body may refer the terms of the proposed licence to the Copyright Tribunal under **29–120**

---

[30] CDPA 1988, s.123(5), presumably protecting such person both from proceedings for infringement of copyright and from prosecution for offences under s.107; and see s.123(2), para. 29–113, above. As a matter of construction of s.123 it would appear that subs.(3) does not apply to an application under s.121, so that there is no ability to backdate the effect of the order as to the amount payable.

[31] CDPA 1988, s.122(1); The Copyright Tribunal Rules 1989 r.3(1), Form 2, see Vol.2 at B1.i. This allows the operator of the scheme to seek to have the terms as to payment, or other terms, varied.

[32] See paras 29–115, above, and 29–125, below.

[33] CDPA 1988, s.122(2). The Tribunal's jurisdiction is not, however, limited to cases where there has been a material change of circumstances. An amendment to the Bill which would have had this effect was resisted, it being said on behalf of the Government that there might be other cases in which an early return to the Tribunal might be appropriate, such as where it turned out that it had been misled, inadvertently or deliberately, about the facts or an existing error of fact was subsequently discovered. (*Hansard*, HL Vol.491, col.496).

[34] The Copyright Tribunal Rules 1989, r.3(1), Form 3, see Vol.2 at B1.i; such grounds might consist of a material change of circumstances, or new arguments raised by another applicant but are not limited to such cases, see the previous note.

[35] CDPA 1988, s.122(3).

[36] CDPA 1988, s.124. as amended by the Copyright and Related Rights Regulations 1996 (SI 1996/2967). As to the definition of a licensing body, see para. 29–107, above.

[37] See para. 29–109, above.

[38] CDPA 1988, s.124, as amended by the Copyright and Related Rights Regulations 1996 (SI 1996/2967) and the Copyright and Related Rights Regulations 2003 (SI 2003/2498).

[39] *i.e.* one falling within the jurisdiction of the Tribunal; see para. 29–119, above.

section 125(1) of the 1988 Act.[40] As with a reference of a proposed licensing scheme,[41] the Tribunal must first decide whether the reference is premature, in which case it will refuse to entertain it.[42] If the Tribunal does entertain the reference, it may make such order, either confirming or varying the terms of the proposed licence, as the Tribunal may determine to be reasonable in the circumstances.[43] The Copyright Tribunal's order may be either for an indefinite period or for such period as the Tribunal may determine.[44]

29–121 **Reference of an expiring licence.** A licensee under a licence[45] which is due to expire, whether by effluxion of time or as a result of notice given by the licensing body, may apply under section 126(1) of the 1988 Act to the Copyright Tribunal within the last three months before the licence is due to expire,[46] on the ground that it is unreasonable in the circumstances that the licence should cease to be in force.[47] The effect of such an application is to continue the licence in force until the application has been determined.[48] On such an application the Copyright Tribunal may make such order, either confirming or varying the terms of the proposed licence, as the Tribunal may determine to be reasonable in the circumstances.[49] The Copyright Tribunal's order may be either for an indefinite period or for such period as the Tribunal may determine.[50]

29–122 **Effect of order.** Where the Copyright Tribunal has made an order under section 125 or section 126 of the 1988 Act, and, during the continuance of the order, the person entitled to the benefit of the order pays any charges payable in accordance with the order (or, if the amount payable cannot be ascertained, gives an undertaking to pay such charges) and complies with the other terms of the order, then such person is to be in the same position as if he had at all material times been the holder of a licence granted by the owner of the copyright in question.[51]

29–123 **Date from which order takes effect.** As in the case of orders relating to licensing schemes,[52] the 1988 Act introduced a limited ability for the Copyright Tribunal to backdate the effect of its order under section 125 or section 126 of the

---

[40] The Copyright Tribunal Rules 1989, r.20(1), Form 7, see Vol.2 at B1.i.

[41] See para. 29–110, above.

[42] CDPA 1988, s.125(2) and The Copyright Tribunal Rules 1989, r.20(3), see Vol.2 at B1.i. In *Candy Rock Recording Ltd v Phonographic Performance Ltd* CT 35/96, November 6, 1996, the Tribunal held on a preliminary issue that a letter which stated that a licensing body was prepared in principle to grant a licence provided that the intended licensee gave certain undertakings contained terms on which a licensing body proposed to grant a licence and thus that the Tribunal had jurisdiction to hear the reference. The Tribunal will normally consider the matter on the basis of written submissions only (*Practice Direction*, para.4, Vol.2 at B1.ii). In the *Candy Rock* decision, the Tribunal stated that its discretion whether to entertain the reference was an unusual discretion which was to be exercised sparingly and judicially on a practical view of the disputes between the parties.

[43] CDPA 1988, s.125(3); as to reasonableness, see s.129 and para. 29–98, above, and as to other factors to be considered, see paras 29–100 to 29–104, above.

[44] s.125(4).

[45] *i.e.* one falling within the jurisdiction of the Tribunal; see para. 29–119, above.

[46] CDPA 1988, s.126(2).

[47] The Copyright Tribunal Rules 1989, r.20(1), Form 7, see Vol.2 at B1.i.

[48] CDPA 1988, s.126(3).

[49] s.126(4); as to reasonableness, see s.129 and para. 29–98, above, and as to other factors to be considered, see paras 29–100 to 29–104, above. For a reference of an expiring licence, see *British Sky Broadcasting Ltd and Sky Television Ltd v The Performing Right Society Ltd* [1988] R.P.C. 467.

[50] CDPA 1988, s.126(5).

[51] CDPA 1988, s.128(1); presumably protecting such person both from proceedings for infringement of copyright and from prosecution for offences under s.107; and see s.123(2), and para. 29–113, above.

[52] See para. 29–114, above.

1988 Act with regard to the charges payable.[53] Thus, the Tribunal may direct that the order has effect with regard to the charges payable from a date earlier than that on which the order is made, but not earlier than the date on which the reference was made or, if later, on which the licence was granted or, as the case may be, was due to expire.[54] Any necessary repayments, or further payments, in respect of charges already paid must then be made.[55] Where the direction relates to a licence for communicating works to the public the Tribunal has power to award simple interest.[56]

Transfer of benefit of order. The benefit of an order made by the Copyright Tribunal under section 125 or section 126 of the 1988 Act may be assigned, provided such assignment was not prohibited under the terms of the order, or the original licence, as the case may be.[57]   **29–124**

Further reference. Where the Copyright Tribunal has made an order with respect to a licence,[58] the licence may be referred back to the Tribunal for review.[59] On the second and any subsequent reference, application may be made not only by the licensee who initiated the initial reference (or by a person subsequently becoming entitled to the benefit of the order),[60] but also by the licensing body.[61] In order, however, to avoid constant references, a licence may not, without the special leave of the Copyright Tribunal, be referred back to the Tribunal within 12 months from the date of the order on the previous reference, or, if the previous order was made so as to be in force for 15 months or less, until the last three months before expiry of the order.[62] An application for special leave must be made to the Copyright Tribunal on the appropriate form together with a statement of the grounds for the application.[63] On an application for review the Tribunal is directed to confirm or vary its previous order as it may determine to be reasonable in the circumstances.[64]   **29–125**

(iv) Implied indemnity in certain licensing schemes and licences

Implied indemnity. In the case both of licensing schemes and licences granted by licensing bodies which license the reprographic copying[65] of published literary, dramatic, musical or artistic works, or the typographical arrangement of published editions, there is implied into the scheme or the licence an undertaking by the operator of the scheme, or the licensing body granting the licence, as the case may be, to indemnify the licensee against any liability, including as to costs,[66]   **29–126**

---

[53] CDPA 1988, s.128(3).
[54] s.128(3).
[55] s.128(3).
[56] s.151A.
[57] CDPA 1988, s.128(2).
[58] *i.e.* under CDPA 1988, ss.125, 126 or 127.
[59] s.127; The Copyright Tribunal Rules 1989, r.20(1), Form 8, see Vol.2 at B1.i.
[60] See para. 29–124, above.
[61] CDPA 1988, s.127(1); this allows the licensing body to seek to have the terms as to payment, or other terms, varied.
[62] s.127(2).
[63] The Copyright Tribunal Rules 1989, r.21, Form 3, Vol.2 at B1.i; such grounds might consist of a material change of circumstances, or new arguments raised by another applicant but are not limited to such cases, see para. 29–118, above.
[64] CDPA 1988, s.127(3).
[65] As defined in CDPA 1988, s.178.
[66] Which include those reasonably incurred in relation to actual or contemplated proceedings: CDPA 1988, s.136(4).

which he may incur by infringing copyright by making or authorising the making of reprographic copies of a work within the apparent scope of his licence.[67]

29–127   **Conditions for availability of indemnity.** A licensee is taken to act within the scope of his licence in respect of a work which is not in fact within the licence where it is not apparent, from an inspection both of the licence and of the work, that the work does not fall within the description of works to which the licence applies.[68] It is to be noted that, whilst it is not a condition of availability of the indemnity that the licensee should in fact have checked the terms both of the licence and the work, he would in all cases be wise to do so. The scheme or licence may also contain provisions, provided they are reasonable,[69] regulating the manner in which and the time within which the licensee may make a claim under the indemnity,[70] and for the operator of the scheme or the licensing body to take over the conduct of the licensee's defence in any proceedings affecting the amount of the liability under the indemnity.[71]

D. CONTROL BY THE COPYRIGHT TRIBUNAL OF OTHER COPYRIGHT LICENSING AND OF THE RIGHT TO EQUITABLE REMUNERATION FOR RENTAL

29–128   **Other controls exercised by the Copyright Tribunal.** In addition to its general jurisdiction in respect of licensing schemes and licences granted by licensing bodies, discussed above,[72] the Copyright Tribunal exercises control over licensing of copyright works in a number of other areas. It is given such control by reason of various provisions in the 1988 Act, dealing with schemes for reprographic copying by educational establishments,[73] the lending right in respect of literary, dramatic, musical or artistic works, sound recordings or films,[74] licences of right available consequent on the exercise of their powers by the Secretary of State, the Office of Fair Trading or the Competition Commission,[75] and the determination of a royalty payable to the trustees of the Hospital for Sick Children in respect of the play "Peter Pan",[76] compulsory licences in respect of works included in wireless broadcasts which are re-transmitted by cable,[77] compulsory licences in respect of information about a programme service[78] and compulsory licences in respect of use as of right of sound recordings in broadcasts.[79] Additionally, control over copyright licensing is conferred on the Copyright Tribunal by provisions dealing with compulsory licences in respect of works in which copyright had

---

[67] s.136(1) and (2). This provision, which was new in the 1988 Act, gives statutory force to the scheme previously operated voluntarily by the Copyright Licensing Agency (an association of publishers and authors; see para. 28–52, above); see the White Paper, Cmnd.9712, para.8.7.

[68] CDPA 1988, s.136(3)(a). Given the terms of this sub-paragraph, it is not clear what sub-para.(b) adds.

[69] s.136(5); presumably a court would refuse to give effect to any conditions which it considered unreasonable.

[70] s.136(5)(a).

[71] s.136(5)(b).

[72] See paras 29–105 et seq., above.

[73] CDPA 1988, s.139; see para. 29–129, below.

[74] s.142, as amended by the Copyright and Related Rights Regulations 1996 (SI 1996/2967); see para. 29–130, below.

[75] s.144(4); see para. 29–131, below.

[76] Sch.6, para.5; see para. 29–132, below.

[77] s.73A inserted into the 1988 Act by the Broadcasting Act 1996, s.138 and Sch.9; see further paras 29–48 et seq., above.

[78] Broadcasting Act 1990, Sch.17, paras 5 and 6, introduced into Ch.III of Part I, and s.149, of the 1988 Act by the Broadcasting Act 1990, Sch.17, para.7(1); see further paras 29–09 et seq., above.

[79] CDPA 1988, ss.135D, 135E and 135F, introduced into the 1988 Act and into s.149 of the 1988 act by amendment by the Broadcasting Act 1990, s.175(1) and (2); see further paras 25–25 et seq., above.

lapsed but has been revived.[80] Lastly, the Tribunal is given control over the rights of authors of certain works and directors of films to equitable remuneration for rental of films and sound recordings, where such persons have transferred their rental rights concerning such films or recordings by the specific provisions of the 1988 Act introducing the right to such remuneration in such circumstances.[81]

Power to extend coverage of scheme or licence for reprographic copying.   **29–129**
The 1988 Act establishes a system of control by the Secretary of State over licensing schemes and licences granted by a licensing body which license educational establishments to make reprographic copies of published literary, dramatic, musical or artistic works or of the typographical arrangements of published editions.[82] The Copyright Tribunal is given jurisdiction to hear appeals from orders made by the Secretary of State in the exercise of this control.[83] Thus, where the Secretary of State has made an order extending the coverage of a scheme or licence[84] or an order confirming, varying or discharging any previous such order,[85] the owner of the copyright in a work which is the subject of the order and, in the case of a subsequent order, any organisation representative of educational establishments which was given notice of the initial application for the order and made representations in respect of it, may appeal to the Tribunal.[86] The appeal must be brought within six weeks of the making of the order (which does not take effect for such period).[87] Although the Tribunal has power to entertain an appeal brought after such period, its decision will not then affect the validity of anything done in reliance on the order before the decision of the Tribunal takes effect.[88] In deciding the appeal the Tribunal is required to have regard, in addition to all other relevant circumstances,[89] to the extent to which published editions of the works in question are otherwise available, to the proportion of the work to be copied and to the nature of the use to which the copies are likely to be put.[90]

Settling royalty in respect of lending right. Section 66 of the 1988 Act empow-   **29–130**
ers the Secretary of State to subject the lending of certain types of work to compulsory licensing by order.[91] In such cases, where no scheme exists, the acts may be carried out subject only to the reasonable royalties.[92] In default of agreement between the copyright owner and the person claiming to be treated as being licensed by him under section 66(1) of the 1988 Act, either of them may apply to the Copyright Tribunal to determine the royalty or other sum to be paid to the copyright owner.[93] Upon such an application, the Tribunal shall make such order

---

[80] The Duration of Copyright and Rights in Performances Regulations 1995 (SI 1995/3297), regs 24 and 25; see further paras 29–41 et seq., above.
[81] CDPA 1988, ss.93B and 93C, inserted into the 1988 Act by the Copyright and Related Rights Regulations 1996 (SI 1996/2967); see paras 7–89 above and 29–133, below.
[82] CDPA 1988, ss.137–141; see paras 29–76 and 29–77, above.
[83] CDPA 1988, s.139(1) and (2).
[84] Under CDPA 1988, s.137.
[85] Under CDPA 1988, s.138.
[86] s.139(1) and (2); The Copyright Tribunal Rules 1989, r.24, Form 9 or 10, see Vol.2 at B1.i.
[87] s.139(3) and (4).
[88] s.139(5).
[89] s.135; see para. 29–98, above.
[90] s.130; see para. 29–101, above and, as to considering other relevant circumstances, see ibid. s.135 and para. 29–98, above.
[91] See para. 29–45, above.
[92] CDPA 1988, s.66(1), as amended by the Copyright and Related Rights Regulations 1996 (SI 1996/2967); see paras 29–45 et seq., above.
[93] s.142(1) as amended by the Copyright and Related Rights Regulations 1996 (SI 1996/2967); The Copyright Tribunal Rules 1989, r.27, Form 11, see Vol.2 at B1.i.

as it may determine to be reasonable in all the circumstances,[94] and such order takes effect from the date on which it was made, or such later date as the Tribunal shall specify.[95] Either party may subsequently apply to the Tribunal to vary its order,[96] but not, without the special leave of the Tribunal, within 12 months of the original order or previous application. An application for special leave must be made to the Tribunal on the appropriate form together with a statement of the grounds for the application.[97] On a further application the Copyright Tribunal has the same powers with regard to the order it can make as in the case of an initial application.[98]

29–131   **Settling terms of licence of right consequent on the exercise of their powers by the Secretary of State, the Office of Fair Trading or the Competition Commission.** Section 144 of the 1988 Act supplements, with reference to copyright, the general controls under United Kingdom legislation over anti-competitive or monopolistic practices.[99] Under this section,[1] where whatever needs to be remedied, mitigated or prevented by the Secretary of State, the Office of Fair Trading or (as the case may be) the Competition Commission under various specified statutory provisions consists of or includes conditions in licences granted by a copyright owner restricting the use by the licensee of the copyright work or preventing the copyright owner granting other licences, or a refusal of a copyright owner to grant licences on reasonable terms, then the powers conferred on the Secretary of State, the Office of Fair Trading or (as the case may be) the Competition Commission by Schedule 8 to the Enterprise Act 2002 include the power to cancel or modify those conditions as well as the power to provide (in addition or instead) that licences in respect of the copyright shall be available as of right.[2] The Secretary of State, the Office of Fair Trading or (as the case may be) the Competition Commission may only exercise such powers if he or it is satisfied that to do so will not contravene any Convention relating to copyright to which the United Kingdom is a party.[3] If the terms of a licence available under this section cannot be agreed, then the person requiring the licence may apply to the Copyright Tribunal to settle the terms,[4] and the licence, as so settled, takes effect from the date of application to the Tribunal.[5] There are analogous provisions in respect of performers' property rights and database right.[6]

---

[94] s.142(2), as amended by the Copyright and Related Rights Regulations 1996 (SI 1996/2967); as to reasonableness, see s.135 and para. 29–98, above, and as to the other factors to be considered, see s.133(1) and para. 29–103, above.

[95] s.142(5) as inserted by the Copyright and Related Rights Regulations 1996 (SI 1996/2967).

[96] s.142(3) and (4); as amended by the Copyright and Related Rights Regulations 1996 (SI 1996/2967); The Copyright Tribunal Rules 1989, r.27, Form 12, see Vol.2 at B1.i.

[97] The Copyright Tribunal Rules 1989, r.28, Form 3, see Vol.2 at B1.i; such grounds might consist of a material change of circumstances, or new arguments raised by another applicant, but are not limited to these, see para. 29–118, above.

[98] CDPA 1988, s.142(3), as amended by the Copyright and Related Rights Regulations 1996 (SI 1996/2967).

[99] This legislation is discussed, together with the background to the enactment of s.144, at paras 29–297 et seq., below. As to the possible application of EC law see paras 29–172 et seq., below.

[1] A provision which is closely modelled on Patents Act 1977 (c.37), s.53. The section has been significantly amended by para.18 of Sch.25 to the Enterprise Act 2002 (c.40).

[2] CDPA 1988, s.144(1A).

[3] s.144(3); the exercise of such powers in respect of the exercise of copyright may be inconsistent with the Berne Convention; see Greaves [1987] 1 E.I.P.R. 3, 5; and see further para. 29–06, above.

[4] s.144(4); The Copyright Tribunal Rules 1989, r.31, Form 13, see Vol.2 at B1.i. As to the factors to be considered by the tribunal, see paras 29–98 to 29–103, above.

[5] s.144(5).

[6] CDPA 1988, Sch.2A, para.17 and the Copyright (Rights in Databases) Regs 1997 (SI 1997/3032), Vol.2 at A3.iv, Sch.2, para.15.

Settling the royalty or other remuneration payable to the trustees for the Hospital for Sick Children in respect of the use of the play "Peter Pan". The Copyright Tribunal has a similar jurisdiction to that discussed above in relation to the lending right, to settle the royalty or other remuneration payable to the trustees of The Hospital for Sick Children, Great Ormond Street, London in respect of the public performance, commercial publication, or communication to the public of the play "Peter Pan" written by Sir James Barrie, under the right conferred by the 1988 Act on the trustees.[7] In default of agreement as to the amount to be paid to the trustees, an application may be made to the Copyright Tribunal to determine the royalty or other remuneration to be paid,[8] and the Tribunal shall make such order as it considers reasonable in all the circumstances.[9] Application may be made to the Tribunal subsequently to vary its order,[10] but not, without the special leave of the Tribunal, within 12 months from the original order or application. An application for special leave must be made to the Tribunal on the appropriate form together with a statement of the grounds for the application.[11] On a further application the Copyright Tribunal has the same powers with regard to the order it can make as in the case of an initial application,[12] and any variation made by the Tribunal has effect from the date when made or such later date specified by the Tribunal.[13]

29–132

Control exercised by the Copyright Tribunal over rights of authors and principal directors of films to equitable remuneration for rental. Section 93B of the 1988 Act[14] provides that authors of literary, dramatic, musical or artistic works copies of whose works have been included in a sound recording or film and who have transferred their rental right concerning the sound recording or film[15] to the producer of such recording or film (or are deemed to have done so[16]) retain a right to equitable remuneration for the rental.[17] Equally, if principal directors of films[18] have transferred their rental rights concerning the films, they too retain the right to equitable remuneration for the rental.[19] In default of agreement as to the amount payable by way of equitable remuneration, the person by

29–133

---

[7] CDPA 1988, s.301 and Sch.6, para.2(1); see para. 6–50, above.

[8] Sch.6, para.5(1); The Copyright Tribunal Rules 1989, r.38, Form 15, see Vol.2 at B1.i.

[9] Sch.6, para.5(1); as to reasonableness, see s.135 and para. 29–98, above.

[10] The Copyright Tribunal Rules 1989, r.38, Form 16, see Vol.2 at B1.i.

[11] The Copyright Tribunal Rules 1989, r.39, Form 3, see Vol.2 at B1.i; such grounds might consist of a material change of circumstances, or new arguments raised by another applicant but are not limited to such cases, see para. 29–118, above.

[12] CDPA 1988, Sch.6, para.5(2).

[13] Sch.6, para.5(4).

[14] As inserted into the 1988 Act by the Copyright and Related Rights Regulations 1996 (SI 1996/2967).

[15] *i.e.* the exclusive right arising under CDPA 1988, s.18A (inserted into the 1988 Act by the Copyright and Related Rights Regulations 1996 (SI 1996/2967)) to rent copies of their works (which in this case would be constituted by the film or recording in which the works were included) to the public.

[16] Where an agreement concerning film production is concluded between the author or prospective author of a literary, dramatic, musical, or artistic work and a film producer, the author is to be presumed, unless the agreement provides to the contrary, to have transferred to the film producer any rental right in relation to the film arising by virtue of the inclusion of a copy of the author's work in the film: CDPA 1988, s.93A(1) and (2) (inserted into the 1988 Act by the Copyright and Related Rights Regulations 1996 (SI 1996/2967) and see para. 5–103, above. This does not apply to any rental right arising by virtue of the inclusion in the film of the screenplay, dialogue or music specifically created for and used in the film: s.93A(3)).

[17] CDPA 1988, s.93B(1)(a), inserted into the 1988 Act by the Copyright and Related Rights Regulations, above; and see para. 7–89, above.

[18] Who would be co-authors of the films under CDPA 1988, s.9(2)(ab), inserted into the 1988 Act by the Copyright and Related Rights Regulations 1996 (SI 1996/2967).

[19] CDPA 1988, s.93B(1)(b) and see para. 7–89, above.

or to whom it is payable[20] may apply to the Copyright Tribunal to determine the amount payable[21] and such persons may also apply to the Tribunal to vary a previous agreement or previous determination of the Tribunal as to the amount of such remuneration[22] but such application may not, except with the special leave of the Tribunal be made within 12 months from the date of a previous determination.[23] On an application to it regarding equitable remuneration, the Tribunal is directed to make such order as to the method of calculating and paying such remuneration as it may determine to be reasonable in the circumstances, specifically taking into account the importance of the author, or, in the case of a film, the director, to the recording or film.[24] Moreover it is specifically also provided that remuneration is not to be considered inequitable merely because it is paid by way of a single payment or at the time of the transfer of the rental right.[25]

E. CONTROL BY THE COPYRIGHT TRIBUNAL OF PERFORMERS' RIGHTS AND OVER EQUITABLE REMUNERATION PAYABLE TO PERFORMERS

29–134   **Introduction.** The creation of performers' property rights giving performers rights, analogous to copyright, to prevent the copying, issue to the public or rental or lending to the public of copies of recordings of their performances[26] gave performers, collectively, the same monopoly or near monopoly power with regard to those wishing to be licensed to exploit their performances as that collectively enjoyed by copyright owners with regard to those wishing to be licensed to exploit their copyright works.[27] Accordingly, at the same time as such rights were conferred upon performers, the Copyright Tribunal was given control over licensing schemes and licensing bodies dealing with performers' property right licences, equivalent to that which it has over such schemes and bodies dealing with copyright licences.[28] In addition to performers' property rights, amendments to the 1988 Act also conferred upon performers the right to equitable remuneration, where sound recordings of their performances are played in public or included in a broadcast or cable programme,[29] and the right to such remuneration

---

[20] Equitable remuneration is payable by the person for the time being entitled to the rental right, that is the person to whom the right was transferred or any successor in title of his: CDPA 1988, s.93B(3) (*i.e.* in the first instance the producer of the recording or film). As regards the person to whom it is payable, this is the person on whom the right is conferred and it is provided that the right may not be assigned by the author or film director except to a collecting society for the purpose of enabling it to enforce the right on his behalf: *ibid.* s.93A(2). (It is understood that the Authors Licensing and Collecting Society ("ALCS", see para. 28–49, above) has the power to administer the right to such remuneration on behalf of authors of literary works and that the Directors and Producers Rights Society (1992) Limited ("DPRS", see para. 28–54, above) has been established to administer such rights on behalf of film directors. The right is, however transmissible by testamentary disposition or by operation of law as personal or moveable property and may be assigned or further transmitted by any person into whose hands it passes: *ibid.*

[21] CDPA 1988, s.93C(1).

[22] s.93C(2).

[23] s.93C(2).

[24] s.93C(3).

[25] s.93C(4).

[26] *i.e.* under CDPA 1988, ss.182A, 182B and 182C, inserted into the 1988 Act by the Copyright and Related Rights Regulations 1996 (SI 1996/2967), para. 12–19, above.

[27] See para. 29–89, above.

[28] The Tribunal was given control over licensing schemes and licensing bodies concerned with performers' property right licences by CDPA 1988, Sch.2A, inserted into the 1988 Act by the Copyright and Related Rights Regulations 1996 (SI 1996/2967); and see paras 29–135 *et seq.*, below.

[29] CDPA 1988, s.182D, inserted into the 1988 Act by the Copyright and Related Rights Regulations 1996 (SI 1996/2697).

for rental of sound recordings or films,[30] and control over the amount of such remuneration was given to the Copyright Tribunal. Finally, the Copyright Tribunal is given control over licensing of performers' rights in a number of other specific situations, most of which mirror situations in which the Tribunal exercises control over copyright licensing.[31]

(i) Control by the Copyright Tribunal of licensing schemes and licensing bodies dealing with performers' property right licences

Licensing scheme. A "licensing scheme" is defined as a scheme setting out: (a) the classes of case in which the operator of the scheme, or the person on whose behalf he acts, is willing to grant performers' property right licences, and (b) the terms on which licences would be granted in those classes of case.[32] The term "scheme" is to include anything in the nature of a scheme, whether described as a scheme or a tariff or by any other name.[33] A "performers' property right licence" is a licence to do or authorise the doing of any of the acts for which consent is required under sections 182A, 182B, 182C or 192CA of the 1988 Act.[34]

29–135

Licensing body. A "licensing body" is defined as a society or other organisation which has as its main object, or one of its main objects, the negotiating or granting, whether as owner or prospective owner of a performer's property rights or as agent for him, of performers' property right licences, and whose objects include the granting of licences covering the performances of more than one performer.[35] Licences or licensing schemes covering the performances of more than one performer do not include licences or schemes covering only performances recorded in a single recording, or performances recorded in more than one recording where the performers giving the performances are the same or the recordings are made by, or by employees of or commissioned by, a single individual, firm, company or group of companies.[36]

29–136

(a) *References and applications with respect to licensing schemes*

References and applications involving licensing schemes. Licensing schemes operated by licensing bodies may be referred to the Copyright Tribunal. Applications for licences in connection with such schemes may be made to the Tribunal, so far as they relate to licences for copying a recording of the whole or any substantial part of a qualifying performance, making such a recording available

29–137

---

[30] CDPA 1988, s.191H, inserted into the 1988 Act by the Copyright and Related Rights Regulations 1996 (SI 1996/2697); see further para. 29–153, below. This right corresponds to the right conferred upon authors of copyright works under CDPA, ss.93B and 93C, see paras 29–133, above.

[31] See para. 29–155, below.

[32] CDPA 1988, Sch.2A, para.1(1). Sch.2A was inserted into the 1988 Act by the Copyright and Related Rights Regulations 1996 (SI 1996/2957). See the parallel definition of "licensing scheme" in relation to copyright rights in CDPA 1988, s.116(1) and para. 29–106, above.

[33] CDPA 1988, Sch.2A, para.1(1). Whether a licence scheme exists depends on the circumstances of each case, see para. 29–106, above.

[34] *i.e.* making, issuing to the public, renting, lending or making available to the public copies of recordings of performers' performances; see further Ch.12. The reference to the "making available" right was added by the Copyright and Related Rights Regulations 2003 (SI 2003/2498), reg.7(4)(a).

[35] CDPA 1988, Sch.2A, para.1(2). See the parallel definition of "licensing body" in relation to copyright rights in CDPA 1988, s.116(2) and para. 29–107, above.

[36] Sch.2A, para.1(4).

to the public in the way mentioned in section 182CA(1) of the 1988 Act, or renting or lending copies of a recording to the public.[37]

29–138   **Reference of a proposed licensing scheme.** The terms of a proposed licensing scheme may be referred to the Copyright Tribunal by an organisation claiming to be representative of persons claiming that they require licences in cases of a description to which the scheme would apply.[38] The Tribunal may decline to entertain the reference on the ground that the reference is premature.[39] The Tribunal must decline to entertain the reference unless it is satisfied that the organisation is reasonably representative of the class of persons it claims to represent.[40]

29–139   **Reference of an existing scheme.** If a licensing scheme is already in operation, a reference to the Copyright Tribunal may be made by a person claiming that he requires a licence in a case of a description to which the scheme applies, or by an organisation claiming to be representative of such persons.[41] The scheme remains in operation until all proceedings on the reference are concluded.[42] Where the reference is made by an organisation, the Tribunal must decline to entertain the reference unless it is satisfied that the organisation is reasonably representative of the class of persons it claims to represent.[43]

29–140   **Order confirming or varying the scheme.** Where an existing or proposed scheme is referred to the Copyright Tribunal, the Tribunal is empowered to make such order either confirming or varying the scheme, in so far as it relates to cases of the description to which the reference relates, and additionally in the case of a proposed scheme, generally, as the Tribunal may determine to be reasonable in the circumstances.[44] The Tribunal's order may be either for an indefinite period, or for such period as the Tribunal may determine.[45]

29–141   **Effect of order.** A licensing scheme confirmed or varied by the Copyright Tribunal remains in operation (or in the case of a proposed scheme comes into and remains in force) for so long as the Tribunal's order remains in force.[46] Where the Tribunal has made an order confirming or varying a licensing scheme following a reference or application, a person who, in a case of a class to which the order applies, pays the scheme's operator any charges payable under the scheme in respect of a licence covering the case in question (or, if the charges cannot be ascertained, gives an undertaking to pay them when ascertained) and complies

---

[37] CDPA 1988, Sch.2A, para.2, as amended by the Copyright and Related Rights Regulations 2003 (SI 2003/2498), reg.7(4)(b).
[38] CDPA 1988, Sch.2A, para.3(1). See the parallel jurisdiction of the Tribunal with regard to proposed licensing schemes dealing with copyright licences, CDPA 1988, s.118 and para. 29–110, above.
[39] CDPA 1988, Sch.2A, para.3(2).
[40] CDPA 1988, s.205B(3) provides for the making of provision to this effect by rules. The relevant rule is r.6 of the Copyright Tribunal Rules 1989 (SI 1989/1129).
[41] CDPA 1988, Sch.2A, para.4(1).
[42] CDPA 1988, Sch.2A, para.4(2).
[43] CDPA 1988, s.205B(3) and r.6 of the Copyright Tribunal Rules 1989 (SI 1989/1129).
[44] CDPA 1988, Sch.2A, paras 4(3) and 3(3). As to reasonableness, see para. 29–151, below and paras 29–98 and 29–100, above dealing with the requirement that the Tribunal should make such orders as are reasonable in all the circumstances in relation to licensing schemes dealing with copyright licences.
[45] Sch.2A, paras 4(4) and 3(4).
[46] CDPA 1988, Sch.2A, para.8(1).

with any other applicable terms, is deemed to be licensed as regards performers' property rights.[47]

Date from which order takes effect. Where the order of the Tribunal varies the amount of the charges payable under a licensing scheme, the Tribunal may direct that the order has such effect from a date earlier than that on which the reference was made, or, if later, on which the scheme came into operation.[48] Any necessary repayments, or further payments, in respect of charges already made must then be made.[49] The Tribunal does not have power to award interest when backdating its order.[50] **29–142**

Further reference. Where the Tribunal has made a previous order in respect of a licensing scheme under paragraphs 3, 4 or 5 of Schedule 2A, any of the following may make a further reference to the Tribunal: the operator of the scheme: a person claiming that he requires a licence in a case of the description to which the order applies, or an organisation claiming to be representative of such persons.[51] However, without the special leave of the Tribunal, such further reference may not be made within 12 months from the date of the previous order, or (if the order was made to be in force for 15 months or less) within three months of the expiry of the previous order.[52] Again, where the reference is made by an organisation, the Tribunal must decline to entertain the reference unless it is satisfied that the organisation is reasonably representative of the class of persons it claims to represent.[53] A licensing scheme which is made the subject of a further reference remains in operation until the reference is determined.[54] On a further reference the Tribunal has the same powers with respect to the order it can make as in the case of an initial reference.[55] **29–143**

Applications for individual licences in connection with licensing scheme. A person may make an application to the Copyright Tribunal for an individual licence where a licensing scheme exists in two situations, depending on whether the licence sought is or is not covered by the scheme. A person who claims, in a case covered by a licensing scheme, that the operator of the scheme has refused to grant him, or procure the grant to him of, a licence in accordance with the scheme, or has failed to do so within a reasonable time after being asked, may apply to the Tribunal for a declaration that he is entitled to a licence.[56] Alternatively if the case is excluded from the scheme, either because it falls within an exception to the scheme or because it falls outside the scheme altogether, an application for a declaration may still be made. If the case falls outside the scheme altogether, the case must be so similar to those in which licences are granted that it is unreasonable that it should not be dealt with in the same way.[57] In such cases (*i.e.* where the case falls within an exception or outside the scheme), application **29–144**

---

[47] Sch.2A, paras 8(2) and (5), mirroring CDPA 1988, s.123(2), see para. 29–113, above.

[48] CDPA 1988, Sch.2A, para.8(3).

[49] Sch.2A, para.8(3)(a).

[50] The power to order further payments or repayments impliedly excludes the power to award interest; see notes to para. 29–114, above, discussing directly equivalent provisions relating to licensing schemes relating to copyright licences. However in the case of copyright licensing schemes the 1988 Act gives the Tribunal express power to award interest in limited circumstances, see Sch.2A, para.8(3)(a).

[51] CDPA 1988, Sch.2A, para.5(1).

[52] Sch.2A, para.5(2).

[53] CDPA 1988, s.205B(3) and r.6 of the Copyright Tribunal Rules 1989 (SI 1989/1129).

[54] Sch.2A, para.5(3).

[55] Sch.2A, para.5(4).

[56] CDPA 1988, Sch.2A, para.6(1), mirroring CDPA 1988, s.121(1), see para. 29–116, above.

[57] Sch.2A, paras 6(2) and (3), mirroring CDPA 1988, s.121(2), see para. 29–116, above.

for a declaration may be made not only where the operator has refused or failed to grant a licence, but also where the operator proposes terms for a licence which are claimed to be unreasonable.[58] The Tribunal may make an order declaring that the applicant is entitled to a licence, either on the terms applicable under the scheme, or on such terms as it considers reasonable.[59] Again the order may be indefinite or for a fixed period.[60]

29–145 **Further reference.** Where the Tribunal has made a previous order in respect of the entitlement of a person to a licence in connection with a licensing scheme, either the operator of the scheme or the original applicant may make a further reference to the Tribunal.[61] However, without the special leave of the Tribunal, such further reference may not be made within 12 months from the date of the previous order, or (if the order was made to be in force for 15 months or less) within three months of the expiry of the previous order.[62]

(b) *References and applications with respect to licensing by licensing bodies*

29–146 **Jurisdiction over licensing by licensing bodies.** The Copyright Tribunal also has jurisdiction over references and applications in respect of licences relating to a performer's property rights which cover the performance of more than one performer granted by a licensing body otherwise than in connection with a licensing scheme, in so far as the licences authorise the copying of a recording, the electronic "on-demand" transmission of a recording or the rental and lending of copies of a recording to the public.[63]

29–147 **Reference to Tribunal of proposed licence.** The terms on which a licensing body proposes to grant a licence may be referred to the Copyright Tribunal by the prospective licensee.[64] The Tribunal may decline to entertain the reference on the ground that the reference is premature.[65] If the Tribunal decides to entertain the reference it may make such order as it thinks reasonable in the circumstances, either confirming or varying the terms of the licence.[66] The order may be indefinite or for a fixed period determined by the Tribunal.[67]

29–148 **Reference to Tribunal of expiring licence.** Where a licence is due to expire, either by effluxion of time or as a result of notice given by the licensing body, the licensee may apply to the Copyright Tribunal on the ground that it is unreasonable in the circumstances that the licence should cease to be in force.[68] The application may not be made until the last three months before the licence is due to expire.[69] The licence remains in operation until the proceedings on the reference

---

[58] Sch.2A, para.6(2).

[59] Sch.2A, para.6(4).

[60] Sch.2A, para.6(5).

[61] CDPA 1988, Sch.2A, para.7(1).

[62] Sch.2A, para.7(2); and see para. 29–118, above, as to the parallel provisions relating to copyright licensing.

[63] CDPA 1988, Sch.2A, para.9, as amended by the Copyright and Related Rights Regulations 2003 (SI 2003/2498), reg.7(4)(b). S.182CA(1) refers to "on-demand" transmissions. For the definition of "licensing body" see para. 29–136, above.

[64] CDPA 1988, Sch.2A, para.10(1).

[65] Sch.2A, para.10(2).

[66] Sch.2A, para.10(3).

[67] Sch.2A, para.10(4).

[68] CDPA 1988, Sch.2A, para.11(1). This mirrors the provisions of CDPA 1988, s.126(1), see para. 29–121, above.

[69] Sch.2A, para.11(2).

are concluded.[70] The Tribunal may make an order declaring that the licensee continues to be entitled to the benefit of the licence on such terms as the Tribunal determines to be reasonable in the circumstances.[71] The order may be indefinite or for a fixed period.[72]

Effect of order of Tribunal as to licence. Where the Tribunal has made an order on a reference or application relating to a licence not under a licensing scheme, the person entitled to the benefit of the order is deemed to be licensed as regards performers' property rights if he pays the licensing body any charges payable in accordance with the order (or, if the charges cannot be ascertained, gives an undertaking to pay them when ascertained) and complies with any other applicable terms.[73] In so far as it varies the charges payable, the order may be backdated to the date when the reference or application was made, or, if later, the date on which the licence was granted or was due to expire.[74]   **29–149**

Further reference. Where the Tribunal has made a previous order in respect of a licence under paragraphs 10 or 11 of Schedule 2A, either the licensing body or the person entitled to the benefit of the order may apply to the Tribunal to review its order.[75] However, without the special leave of the Tribunal, such further application may not be made within 12 months from the date of the previous order, or (if the order was made to be in force for 15 months or less) within three months of the expiry of the previous order.[76]   **29–150**

General considerations: unreasonable discrimination. When considering a reference or application, whether relating to a licensing scheme or licence, in determining what is reasonable the Tribunal must have regard to the same factors. These are: the availability of other schemes, or the granting of other licences, to other persons in similar circumstances; and the terms of those schemes or licences. The Tribunal must exercise its powers so as to secure that there is no unreasonable discrimination between licensees, or prospective licensees, under the scheme or licence to which the reference or application relates and licensees under other schemes operated by, or other licences granted by, the same person.[77] The Tribunal also has a general obligation to have regard to all relevant circumstances.[78]   **29–151**

(ii) Control by the Copyright Tribunal of performers' rights to equitable remuneration and other performers' rights

Section 182D of the 1988 Act: playing in public and communication to the public. Under this section, the Tribunal is given control over the amount of equitable remuneration payable to performers by owners of the copyright in commercially published sound recordings including the performers' performances, where such sound recordings are played in public or communicated to the public   **29–152**

---

[70] Sch.2A, para.11(3).
[71] Sch.2A, para.11(4). As to reasonableness, see para. 29–151, below.
[72] Sch.2A, para.11(5).
[73] CDPA 1988, Sch.2A, para.13(1).
[74] Sch.2A, para.13(3).
[75] CDPA 1988, Sch.2A, para.12(1).
[76] Sch.2A, para.12(2).
[77] CDPA 1988, Sch.2A, para.14 (1).
[78] Sch.2A, para.14(2). See also para. 29–98, above dealing with the requirement that the Tribunal should make such orders as are reasonable in all the circumstances in relation to copyright licensing schemes and licences.

otherwise than by way of electronic "on-demand" transmission.[79] In default of agreement as to the amount payable by way of equitable remuneration, the person by or to whom equitable remuneration is payable may apply to the Tribunal to determine the amount.[80] Such persons may also apply to the Tribunal either to vary any agreement as to the amount payable or any previous determination by the Tribunal, but no such application may be made within 12 months of a previous determination except with the special leave of the Tribunal.[81] There is no power to back-date an order varying any agreement or previous determination by the Tribunal as to the amount of remuneration. On an application, the Tribunal is directed to make such order as to the method of calculating and paying equitable remuneration as the Tribunal may determine to be reasonable in the circumstances, specifically taking into account the importance of the contribution of the performer to the sound recording.[82] In *Stichting ter Exploitatie van Naburige Rechten v Nederlandse Omroep Stichting*,[83] the European Court of Justice had to consider the method used in the Netherlands to calculate the amount of equitable remuneration. It held as follows. Although the concept of equitable remuneration must be interpreted in the same way in all Member States, there is no universally applicable method for determining the amount of such remuneration for all Member States. It is for each Member State to determine the relevant criteria consistent with the objectives of the Directive, which are to enable a proper balance to be achieved between, on the one hand, the interests of performing artists and producers in obtaining remuneration for the broadcast of a particular sound recording and, on the other, the interests of third parties in being able to broadcast the sound recording on terms that are reasonable. Whether the remuneration is equitable is to be assessed, in particular, in the light of the value of the use of the sound recording in trade. The European Court of Justice therefore has no role in laying down the criteria for determining equitable remuneration, only to provide the national courts with direction in order for them to assess whether the criteria actually used are such that they ensure that performers and record producers receive equitable remuneration in a manner that is consistent the Directive. The Dutch model for calculating equitable remuneration by reference to variable and fixed factors, such as the number of hours of broadcasts of recordings, the viewing and listening numbers, agreed tariffs in the relevant field, tariffs set in bordering states and the amounts paid by commercial broadcasters, having as its object the achievement of a proper balance of the respective interests, did not therefore contravene Community Law.

29–153   **Section 191H of the 1988 Act: rental.** Under this section,[84] the Tribunal is given control over the amount payable by way of equitable remuneration to performers

---

[79] CDPA 1988, s.182D(4), as amended by the Copyright and Related Rights Regulations 2003 (SI 2003/2498), reg.7(2), with effect from October 31, 2003; and see further Ch.12. The right to such remuneration is collectively controlled on behalf of performers by PAMRA (The Performing Artists Media Rights Association, see para. 28–58, above) and AURA (the Association of United Recoring Artists, see para. 28–48, above), which, it is understood, have reached an agreement as to the amount of remuneration currently payable with Phonographic Performance Limited (which controls the public performance rights in sound recordings on behalf of the owners of the copyright in such recordings (see para. 28–60, above)).

[80] CDPA 1988, s.182D(4). The person to whom such remuneration is in the first instance payable is the performer, and he may not assign his right to such remuneration except to a collecting society: s.182D(1) and (2). The right is however transmissible by testamentary disposition or operation of law as personal or moveable property and may be assigned or further transmitted by any person into whose hands it passes: s.182D(2).

[81] CDPA 1988, s.182D(5).

[82] s.182D(6).

[83] Case C- 245/00, [2003] E.C.R. I-1251.

[84] Inserted into the 1988 Act by the Copyright and Related Rights Regulations 1996 (SI 1996/2967).

for the rental of sound recordings or films including recordings of their performances, where they have transferred (or are presumed to have transferred) their rental right concerning such recordings or films.[85] Again, an application to determine the amount of such remuneration may be made by the person by or to whom it is payable,[86] and such persons may also apply to the Tribunal to vary a previous agreement or previous determination of the Tribunal as to the amount of such remuneration.[87] Again, without the special leave of the Tribunal, no application may be made within 12 months from the date of a previous determination.[88] As with remuneration for public exploitation of commercial sound recordings, the Tribunal on an application with respect to equitable remuneration for rental is directed to make such order as it determines to be reasonable in the circumstances, taking into particular account the importance of the contribution of the performer to the film or sound recording.[89] It is however specifically provided that remuneration is not to be considered inequitable merely because it is paid by way of a single payment or at the time of the transfer of the rental right.[90]

Granting consent on behalf of a performer to the making of a copy of a recording of a performance. The Copyright Tribunal has power to grant consent on behalf of a performer to the making of a copy of a recording of a performance, where the identity or whereabouts of the person entitled to the reproduction right in the performance cannot be ascertained by reasonable inquiry.[91] The consent has effect as consent of the person entitled to the reproduction right for the purposes of the provisions of Part II of the 1988 Act relating to performers' rights and as consent of the performer for the purposes of the criminal provisions of the 1988 Act in relation to rights in performances.[92] The Tribunal shall not give consent except after the service or publication of such notices as are required by The Copyright Tribunal Rules or by direction of the Tribunal.[93] In deciding whether to grant consent on behalf of the performer, the Tribunal is bound to take into account two factors, namely whether the original recording was made with his consent and is lawfully in the possession or control of the person wishing to make the further recording, and whether the making of the further recording is consistent with the obligations of the parties to the arrangements under which the original recording was made.[94] Where the Tribunal gives consent on behalf of a performer, it may attach such conditions as it considers appropriate,[95] and, in default of agreement between the applicant and the person entitled to the reproduction right, the Tribunal shall also determine what payment is to be made

29–154

---

[85] CDPA 1988, s.191H(1); and see further para. 12–48, above.

[86] s.191H(1). The remuneration is payable in the first instance to the performer, and he may not assign it except to a collecting society (though it is transmissible by testamentary disposition or by operation of law): s.191G(2). The British Equity Collecting Society Limited ("BECS") has been formed to collect such remuneration, see para. 28–50, above. The collection of such remuneration also falls within the remit of PAMRA (see para. 28–58, above) and AURA (see para. 28–48, above). It is payable by the person for the time being entitled to the rental right, namely, the person to whom the rental right was transferred or any successor in title: s.191G(3).

[87] CDPA 1988, s.191H(2).

[88] s.191H(2)

[89] s.191H(3).

[90] s.191H(4).

[91] CDPA 1988, s.190, as amended by the Copyright and Related Rights Regulations 1996 (SI 1996/2967); see para. 12–52, above. The application is made by Form 14: The Copyright Tribunal Rules 1989, r.34, Form 14, see Vol.2 at B1.i.

[92] Thus enabling the applicant to copy the recording (s.182A), issue those copies to the public (s.182B), or rent or lend those copies to the public (s.182C).

[93] CDPA 1988, s.190(3); and see r.35, The Copyright Tribunal Rules 1989, Vol.2 at B1.i.

[94] s.190(5).

[95] s.190(2).

to such person.[96] To date there is only one reported case in relation to the Tribunal's power to grant consent on behalf of performers.[97]

29–155 **Other controls exercised by the Copyright Tribunal over performers' rights.** In addition to the jurisdiction of the Tribunal, discussed above, with regard to licensing schemes and licensing bodies dealing with performers' property rights and its jurisdiction with regard to equitable remuneration and the granting of consent on behalf of performers who cannot be identified or traced, the Tribunal exercises control over the licensing of performers' rights in a number of other specific situations. These largely mirror the other controls exercised by the Tribunal over licensing of copyright works[98] and the Tribunal is given such control by various provisions inserted into the 1988 Act dealing with the lending right in respect of sound recordings or films treated as licensed by performers by virtue of an order of the Secretary of State,[99] licences of right of performers' property rights available as a result of the exercise of powers consequent on a competition report[1] and compulsory licences in respect of performances or recordings of performances included in wireless broadcasts which are retransmitted by cable pursuant to statutory requirement but beyond the original broadcast area.[2] In one further case control over the licensing of performers' rights is conferred upon the Copyright Tribunal by regulations providing for compulsory licences in respect of performances in which performance rights had lapsed but have been revived.[3]

---

[96] s.190(6). If the Tribunal is satisfied that the identity or whereabouts of a performer cannot be ascertained by reasonable enquiry and that all particulars required (including particulars of the terms upon which the previous recording was made) have been supplied, the Tribunal may make an Order simply giving consent, with a provision for liberty to apply for an Order as to payment or other terms as the Tribunal may think fit: see Copyright Tribunal Practice Direction (April 7, 2004) para.18. An example is *Chris Sawyer*, CT 63/98.

[97] *Ex p. Sianel Cymru* [1993] E.M.L.R. 251, where the applicant (the Welsh Fourth Television Channel Authority) wished to make an animated version of *Under Milk Wood* and rerecord the original 1954 BBC radio production onto the soundtrack. (The copyright owner of that recording had no objection to the proposed rerecording.) The cast of the radio production had included members of a school. The applicant had managed to ascertain the identity of some of the school children but not all. It applied to the Tribunal under s.190(1) for consent on behalf of those performers whose identity or whereabouts could not be ascertained and also for consent on behalf of the personal representatives of one deceased performer whose identity could not be ascertained. The order of the Tribunal giving consent included an express liberty for the performers and the personal representatives to apply to the Tribunal for payment. See also the unreported case of *Chris Sawyer*, CT 63/98, where a similar order was made and see Vol.2 at B1.iii.

[98] See para. 29–95, above.

[99] CDPA 1988, Sch.2A, para.15. The provisions of para.15 mirror the provisions in s.142 of the 1988 Act relating to the settling of a royalty in respect of the lending of copies of certain copyright works treated as licensed by the copyright owner by order of the Secretary of State (see para. 29–130, above) but the subject matter of para.15 is a royalty in respect of the lending of recordings or films containing performers' performances treated as licensed by the Secretary of State's order (under CDPA 1988 Sch.2, para.14A) in the absence of a licensing scheme.

[1] CDPA 1988, Sch.2A, para.17, as amended by the Enterprise Act 2002 (c.40) Sch.25, para.18. The provisions of para.17 giving the Tribunal power to settle the terms of licences of right of performers' property rights directed consequent on a competition report mirror the provisions in s.144 of the 1988 Act giving the Tribunal power to settle the terms of a licence of right in respect of copyright; see para. 29–131, above.

[2] CDPA 1988, Sch.2, paras 19 and 19A as amended by the Copyright and Related Rights Regulations 2003 (SI 2003/2498), reg.22. Again, these provisions mirror provisions of the 1988 Act dealing with copyright works (*i.e.* s.73A giving the Tribunal power to settle the royalty payable to copyright owners under the compulsory licence of their works where such works are included in a wireless broadcast which is by statutory requirement retransmitted by cable outside the broadcast area) discussed at para. 29–51, above.

[3] The Duration of Copyright and Rights in Performances Regulations 1995 (SI 1995/3297), regs 34 and 35. In the case of a performance in which revived performance rights subsist any acts which require the consent of any person under Pt II of the 1988 Act are treated as having that consent subject only to the payment of such reasonable remuneration as may be agreed or in default of agreement determined by the Copyright Tribunal (reg.34(1)). In order for a person to

F. CONTROL BY THE COPYRIGHT TRIBUNAL OF THE LICENSING OF DATABASE RIGHT AND PUBLICATION RIGHT

Introduction. The creation of new intellectual property rights, analogous to copyright (1) in respect of the contents of databases ("the database right")[4] and (2) conferred on those who, after the expiry of copyright protection, for the first time publish previously unpublished works ("the publication right"),[5] also gives the owners of such rights as a group the same kind of monopoly power with regard to those wishing to exploit their works as that enjoyed by copyright owners. Thus, as with the new performers' rights, the provisions introducing the database and publication rights at the same time also provided for control of their licensing by the Copyright Tribunal.[6]

29–156

Database right licensing. With regard to database right there exist provisions, equivalent to those under the 1988 Act regulating copyright licensing schemes and licensing bodies,[7] giving the Copyright Tribunal control over licensing schemes and licensing bodies dealing with database right licences,[8] and in respect of database right licences available as of right consequent on a report of the Monopolies and Mergers Commission.[9] Again, following the provisions of the 1988 Act with regard to copyright licensing, the Tribunal in exercising its jurisdiction in relation to references and applications relating to licensing schemes and licensing bodies concerned with database right licences is directed to make such order as it may determine to be reasonable in the circumstances.[10] Further, again imitating the provisions of the 1988 Act regulating copyright licensing, the Tribunal in determining what is reasonable on a reference or application relating to a licensing scheme or licence dealing with the database right is to have regard to the availability of other schemes or the granting of other licences in similar circumstances and the terms of those licences. The Tribunal must then exercise its powers so as to secure that there is no unreasonable discrimination between licensees or prospective licensees under the scheme or licence to which the reference or application relates and licensees under other schemes operated by, or other licences granted by, the same person.[11]

29–157

Publication right licensing. With regard to control over licensing of publication

29–158

---

take advantage of such compulsory licence he must give reasonable notice to the rights owner stating when he intends to begin to do the acts (reg.34(2)). If he does so his acts are treated as having consent and reasonable remuneration shall be payable in respect of them despite the fact that its amount is not agreed or determined until later (reg.34(4)). An application to settle the remuneration payable may be made to the Tribunal by the rights owner or the person claiming to be treated as having his consent and on an application the Tribunal may make such order as it may determine to be reasonable in the circumstances (reg.35(1) and (2)). For the equivalent copyright provisions see paras 29–41 *et seq.*, above.

[4] See Ch.18.

[5] See Ch.17.

[6] Copyright and Rights in Databases Regulations 1997 (SI 1997/3032), regs 24 and 25 and Sch.2; and the Copyright and Related Rights Regulations 1996 (SI 1996/2967), reg.17.

[7] See paras 29–105 *et seq.*, above.

[8] Copyright and Rights in Databases Regulations 1997 (SI 1997/3032), Sch.2, regs 1 to 14. As to the database right, see Ch.18. The form and wording of these provisions dealing with licensing schemes and licensing bodies concerned with database right licences follows the form and wording of the provisions of the 1988 Act dealing with such schemes and bodies concerned with copyright licences; see paras 29–105 to 29–125, above. Thus there is provision for reference of proposed or existing licensing schemes (Sch.2, paras 3 to 5), for applications for the grant of individual licences in connection with a licensing scheme (Sch.2, paras 6 to 8), for references and applications with respect to the grant of licences by licensing bodies not in connection with a licensing scheme (Sch.2, paras 9 to 13).

[9] Copyright and Rights in Databases Regulations 1997 (SI 1997/3032), Sch.2, para.15; and see equivalent provisions relating to copyright licences paras 29–131, above and 29–297, below.

[10] Sch.2, paras 3(3), 4(3), 5(3), 6(3), 7(3), 10(3) and 11(3).

[11] Sch.2, para.14. See also paras 29–98 and 29–100, above, dealing with the requirement that the

right, the substantive provisions of Chapter VII of the 1988 Act (*i.e.* those dealing with copyright licensing) are, with minor amendments, simply applied in relation to publication right as in relation to copyright.[12] Moreover the provisions of Chapter VIII, dealing with the constitution and procedure of and appeals from the Copyright Tribunal are also applied for the purpose of supplementing such substantive provisions as so applied.[13] The modifications of the substantive provisions are twofold. First, section 116(4)[14] (which excludes from licences and licensing schemes over which the Tribunal has jurisdiction, licences or schemes covering only a single collective work or collective works of which the authors are the same or the works of employees of a single individual firm or company or group of companies) does not apply.[15] Licensing schemes dealing with licences of the publication right relating to such works are accordingly within the jurisdiction of the Tribunal. Secondly, in sections 116(2), 117 and 124 (which define the schemes and licences subject to the Tribunal's jurisdiction) the words "works of more than one author" are replaced by the words "works of more than one publisher."[16] This is necessary since the right is given to the publisher, and in the same way that copyright licensing schemes have to cover the works of more than one author to come within the jurisdiction of the Tribunal, publication right licensing schemes have to cover freshly published works of more than one publisher.

G. PROCEDURE BEFORE THE COPYRIGHT TRIBUNAL

29–159 **Provisions governing procedure.** The procedure before the Tribunal is governed by The Copyright Tribunal Rules,[17] made by the Lord Chancellor in the exercise of powers conferred under the 1988 Act.[18] Subject to the provisions of the Act and of the Rules, the Tribunal has power to regulate its own procedure,[19] and in exercise of this power the Chairman has issued a Practice Direction giving further guidance as to the procedure which will be followed by the Tribunal.[20] The Rules have not been amended since 1992 and accordingly only regulate applications and references under the jurisdictions then exercised by the Tribunal and do not deal with the additional jurisdictions discussed in this chapter.[21] So far as the Rules themselves are concerned, these first set out the full procedure on refer-

---

Tribunal should take such factors into account in relation to copyright licensing schemes and licences.

[12] The Copyright and Related Rights Regulations 1996 (SI 1996/2967), reg.17.

[13] reg.17(4).

[14] See para. 29–107, above.

[15] The Copyright and Related Rights Regulations 1996 (SI 1996/2967), reg.17(2)(c).

[16] reg.17(3)(b).

[17] SI 1989/1129; see Vol.2 at B1.i. The Copyright Tribunal Rules were amended by The Copyright Tribunal (Amendment) Rules 1991 (SI 1991/201), which were introduced to deal with applications (under ss.135D and 135E of the 1988 Act) relating to the use as of right of sound recordings in broadcasts and cable programme services and applications (under Broadcasting Act 1990, Sch.17) relating to compulsory licences in respect of information about programme services and were themselves amended in one minor respect by The Copyright Tribunal (Amendment) Rules 1992 (SI 1992/467); see Vol.2 at B1.i. These rules are under review: see the Copyright Tribunal Practice Direction as amended (April 7, 2004 version) para.1, Vol.2 at B1.i.

[18] CDPA 1988, s.150.

[19] Copyright Tribunal Rules (SI 1989/1129), r.54.

[20] The procedure set out in the Practice Direction is stated (para.1) to be compulsory, subject to a direction of the Tribunal to the contrary. See Vol.2 at B1.ii.

[21] Thus, for example, no specific procedural framework currently exists to regulate the Tribunal's jurisdiction with regard to compulsory licences in respect of works in which copyright has lapsed but been revived, with regard to equitable remuneration for rental, with regard to performers' rights, or with regard to database right or publication right licensing. The Rules have been under review for many years. A consequence of the Rules not having been updated is not only that procedure under the new jurisdictions conferred on the Tribunal is not specifically dealt with (which deficiency might be overcome by the Tribunal's power to regulate its own procedure) but also

ences and applications with respect to copyright licensing schemes[22] ; this follows largely, but with some modifications, the procedure set out in the former Performing Right Tribunal Rules made under the 1956 Act. It is this procedure which is, in general, described below. The Rules then deal separately with certain of the other jurisdictions exercised by the Tribunal,[23] setting out the procedure for commencing such proceedings and providing for any specific matters relevant to that jurisdiction,[24] and then applying such of the Rules relating to references and applications with respect to licensing schemes as are appropriate to the particular jurisdiction. The final provisions of the Rules contain provisions of general application as to appeal, costs, and other procedural matters. The constitution of the Tribunal is dealt with above.[25]

Secretary and service of documents. The Tribunal has an office,[26] and its business is administered by the Secretary. Under the Rules a variety of documents are required to be served, sometimes directly by a party on another party or person. Where direct service is required, the document may be sent by prepaid post to the person (or to his solicitor or agent[27]) at his address for service, or, where no such address has been given, at his registered office, principal place of business or last known address.[28] In other cases service must be effected on the Secretary, by prepaid post at his office,[29] and the Secretary then has to serve copies on others. In the latter case, the Secretary will stipulate the number of copies required.[30]

29–160

Commencement and withdrawal of proceedings. All types of proceedings dealt with by the Rules are to be commenced by notice in one of the prescribed

29–161

---

that there is now uncertainty as to the applicability of provisions of the Arbitration Act 1996 to proceedings before the Tribunal. The Rules, by r.46, specifically provide that certain provisions of Pt I of the Arbitration Act 1950 (dealing with the examination of parties and witnesses on oath, the power (under that Act) of the High Court to issue subpoenas and make orders, inter alia, as to security for costs, discovery and interrogatories and the power of the arbitrator to make interim awards and correct slips in any award) apply to proceedings before the Tribunal. The provisions are then specifically set out in Sch.2 to the Rules. Pt I of the Arbitration Act has, however, been repealed by the Arbitration Act 1996 which contains similar (but not identical) provisions to those referred to in the Rules and while it is possible that the references in the Rules to the 1950 Act may be construed as references to the corresponding provisions of the 1996 Act (see Interpretation Act 1978, ss.17 and 23) it is not certain that they would be. If not, the Tribunal could itself only deal with such of the above matters as were appropriate to be dealt with under its power (under r.54) to regulate its own procedure. The Arbitration Act 1996 does, however, amend s.150 of the 1988 Act so that for the future any new rules may expressly apply any of the provisions of Pt I of the Arbitration Act 1996 in relation to proceedings before the Tribunal.

[22] Rules 3 to 19. Based on the former Performing Right Tribunal Rules (1965) under the 1956 Act, for which see *Copinger* (12th ed.) paras 1758 *et seq.*

[23] For the different jurisdictions of the Tribunal, see para. 29–95, above. For the jurisdictions which the Tribunal exercised at the time of the last amendment of the rules (*i.e.* 1992) and which are therefore, the only jurisdictions specifically regulated by the rules, see *Copinger* (13th ed.) para.15–57.

[24] For example, in the case of proceedings under s.190(1) (application for Tribunal's consent on behalf of a performer whose identity and whereabouts are unknown), the inquiries which the Tribunal makes to establish that the identity and whereabouts cannot be ascertained.

[25] See para. 29–94.

[26] The address is: Room 1/8, Harmsworth House, 13–15 Bouverie Street, London EC4Y 8DP. Telephone: 020 7596 6510 Fax: 020 7596 6526, email: copyright. tribunal@patent.gov.uk. Furthermore information about the Tribunal is given on the Patent Office's website: *www.patent.gov.uk.* The office is open from 10.00 to 16.00 each weekday except Good Friday, Christmas Day and Bank Holidays (r.52, Vol.2 at B1.i).

[27] Copyright Tribunal Rules 1989 (SI 1989/1129), r.50(5), Vol.2 at B1.i; *i.e.* a solicitor or agent appointed to act in the proceedings by notice in writing to the Secretary in accordance with r.15.

[28] Copyright Tribunal Rules 1989 (SI 1989/1129), r.50(1), Vol.2 at B1.i.

[29] r.50(1), Vol.2 at B1.i.

[30] *Practice Direction*, para.2, Vol.2 at B1.ii.

forms served on the Secretary.[31] In each case the applicant has to serve with the form a statement of his case.[32] The Secretary then, as soon as is practicable, serves copies on the appropriate persons, being, in the case of a reference or application with respect to a licensing scheme, the operator of the licensing scheme named in the application, or, where the application is for review of a previous order, every person who was a party to the proceedings when the previous order was made.[33] Where the application relates to a proposed scheme,[34] the Tribunal will first consider whether the reference is premature.[35] For this purpose the respondent will be invited to comment in writing and the Tribunal will normally reach a decision without hearing oral submissions.[36] A reference or application may be withdrawn by the applicant at any time before it has been finally disposed of, by notice in writing served on the Secretary and on every other party to the proceedings.[37] Such withdrawal does not prevent the Tribunal making an order as to the payment of costs incurred up to the time such notice is served,[38] or from proceeding to determine the reference or application if it decides to do so on the application of any other party to the proceedings.[39]

29–162   **Advertisement of proceedings.** Except where the Tribunal has declined to entertain a reference on the grounds that it is premature,[40] or the Chairman in any other case otherwise directs, the application or reference is then advertised.[41] The advertisement gives details of the application or reference, and the names and addresses of the applicant and any other organisation or person served with notice of the proceedings.[42] The advertisement states the time within which any objection to the applicant's credentials must be received,[43] and within which any other organisation or person may apply to intervene in the proceedings.[44]

29–163   **Intervention in the proceedings.** Any organisation or person may apply to be made a party to the proceedings by serving a notice on the Secretary in the prescribed form within the time stated in the advertisement.[45] On being served with such notice the Secretary must, as soon as practicable, serve copies of the

---

[31] Copyright Tribunal Rules 1989 (SI 1989/1129), rr.3, 20, 24, 26A 27, 31, 34, 38 and 41A. In each case a fee is payable in accordance with r.49 and Sch.1.

[32] Para.5(a) of the *Practice Direction* (Vol.2 at B1.ii) provides that the Applicant's Statement of Case required by r.3 should specify exactly what variation of an existing scheme or proposed scheme, or existing licence or proposed licence is sought. It suggests that this may conveniently be done (particularly in a complicated case) by setting out the existing scheme or proposed scheme on the right hand side of the page and indicating the portions sought to be deleted by italicising or striking out or otherwise. Proposed additions can be set out on the left-hand side of the page. Under the former Rules governing the procedure of the PRT (r.3(2), The Performing Right Tribunal Rules 1965, *Copinger* (12th ed.) para.1760), the applicant also had to serve with his application a list of relevant documents in his possession. This burdensome requirement has been dropped, and indeed there is no automatic disclosure at any stage under the new Rules or in the standard form of directions, although a party can seek such a direction where appropriate.

[33] Copyright Tribunal Rules 1989 (SI 1989/1129), r.3(2).

[34] Under CDPA 1988, s.118; the same applies in the case of an application with respect to a licence proposed to be granted by a licensing body, under CDPA 1988, s.125. See paras 29–110 and 29–120, above.

[35] Pursuant to CDPA 1988, s.118(2) and r.4 (or s.125(2) and r.20(3)).

[36] *Practice Direction*, para.4, Vol.2 at B1.ii.

[37] Copyright Tribunal Rules 1989 (SI 1989/1129), r.16(1), Vol.2 at B1.i.

[38] r.16(1). As to costs, see para. 29–170, below.

[39] Rule 16(2).

[40] See para. 29–161, above.

[41] Copyright Tribunal Rules 1989 (SI 1989/1129), r.5(1); advertisement is only required for an application or reference relating to a licensing scheme, but may be directed under r.35 in respect of an application under s.190 of the 1988 Act for the Tribunal's consent on behalf of a performer.

[42] r.5(2).

[43] See para. 29–164, below.

[44] See para. 29–163, below.

[45] Copyright Tribunal Rules 1989 (SI 1989/1129), r.7(1) and Form 5; such notice may be served af-

notice on every other party to the proceedings and must serve on the intervener a copy of the applicant's reference or application and statement of case and any other notice of intervention.[46] These provisions are substantially repeated (taking account of the difference that there is no advertisement, and therefore no time within which the intervention must be made) in relation to references and applications with respect to licensing bodies,[47] and in that form they are applied to intervention in each of the other types of proceedings before the Tribunal by any organisation or person claiming to have a substantial interest in those proceedings.[48]

Objections to applicant's credentials. A licensing scheme may be referred to the Tribunal by an organisation claiming to be representative of persons claiming that they require licences in cases of a description to which a licensing scheme applies or, in the case of a proposed scheme, would apply.[49] The organisation's credentials, that is the validity of its claim to be representative of a class of persons,[50] may be challenged by any other organisation or person, within the time stipulated in the advertisement of the proceedings,[51] by serving on the Secretary a notice, or by the Tribunal of its own motion.[52] The Secretary must then serve notice of the objections on every party to the proceedings and the proceedings are automatically stayed from that moment until further order.[53] The Chairman then gives directions for the parties to make written representations on the issue of the validity of the credentials.[54] The Tribunal may decide the issue on the basis of the written submissions, or may give any objector and any other party the opportunity of making oral representations at a hearing.[55] If, after considering the objections, the Tribunal is not satisfied as to the credentials, it will direct that no further proceedings are to be taken on the reference or application, except in relation to any order for costs which the Tribunal may make.[56] If, on the other hand, the Tribunal is satisfied as to the credentials, it will direct that the reference or application shall proceed, and the Tribunal may give such consequential directions as are appropriate.[57]

29–164

Objections to intervener's credentials. Objections may also be made to an intervener's credentials, that is, the possession by the intervener of a sufficient interest in the matter in dispute.[58] In relation to proceedings with respect to licensing schemes, the party intending to object to an intervener's credentials must serve notice in the prescribed form on the Secretary, who will then serve copies on every other party.[59] The Tribunal may of its own motion object to an intervener's credentials, in which case the Secretary must serve notice of such

29–165

---

ter the expiry of such time with the leave of the Chairman or the Tribunal. See also, as to intervening in other proceedings, rr.23, 26, 26D, 30, 33, 37, 41, 41D and 44.

[46] Rule 7(2).

[47] Rule 23.

[48] Rules 26, 26D, 30, 33, 37, 41, 41D and, in respect of an application under r.43 (for suspension of Tribunal's order pending appeal), r.44. As to what is a substantial interest, see para. 29–165, below.

[49] CDPA 1988, ss.118(1), 119(1), and 120(1); only such an organisation may refer a proposed scheme.

[50] Copyright Tribunal Rules 1989 (SI 1989/1129), r.2(1).

[51] See para. 29–162, above; such time may be extended by the Tribunal or Chairman: r.6(1).

[52] In Form 4: r.6(1).

[53] Rule 6(2).

[54] Rule 6(3).

[55] Rule 6(3).

[56] Rules 6(4) and 48.

[57] Rule 6(5).

[58] Copyright Tribunal Rules 1989 (SI 1989/1129), r.2(1).

[59] In Form 6: rr.8(1) and (2).

objection, together with a statement of the reasons for it, on every other party.[60] Unless the Chairman makes such a direction on the hearing for directions,[61] an objection to an intervener's credentials does not operate as a stay of the proceedings, and is considered by the Tribunal at the same time as the reference or application in question.[62] These provisions also apply to objecting to the credentials of an organisation or person seeking to intervene in each of the other types of proceedings before the Tribunal.[63]

29–166   **Completion of written cases.** In the case of proceedings with respect to a licensing scheme, the operator of the scheme must, within 28 days of being served with the applicant's statement of case, serve on the Secretary a written answer to the applicant's case.[64] An intervener has 21 days from the time limited in the advertisement[65] within which to serve on the Secretary a statement of the case he intends to make.[66] The Secretary must then serve copies of such answer and case on every other party.[67] This completes the written statements of case in the proceedings, save that a party may, without leave, amend his statement of case or answer at any time prior to the date fixed by the Chairman on the hearing for directions, after which leave is required.[68] The amendment is made by serving a copy on the Secretary, who must, as soon as practicable, serve a copy on every other party.[69] In the case of other types of proceedings before the Tribunal, the respondent has 21 days after service on him of the applicant's statement of case within which to serve his written answer on the Secretary,[70] who must then serve a copy of the same on every other party.

29–167   **Directions.** Upon the expiry of the time limited by the Rules for the service of a statement of case by an intervener or of the answer by the respondent, the Chairman is to appoint a date and place for the attendance of the parties for the purpose of his giving directions as to the further conduct of the proceedings.[71] The Secre-

---

[60] Rule 8(3).

[61] See para. 29–167, below.

[62] Rule 8(4); *cf.* the position in relation to an applicant's credentials, para. 29–164, above.

[63] See rr.23, 26, 26D 30, 33, 37, 41, 41D and 44. In relation to other proceedings rule 23 governs an intervener's application and provides that in order successfully to intervene the intervener must have a substantial interest in respect of the reference or application in question. In a recent case the Tribunal considered such provision and held that, "a substantial interest in the proceedings" required an intervener to have a direct interest in the specific subject matter of the dispute. The Tribunal further held that a substantial interest of such a direct and specific nature was not established, in the case of an application in relation to an individual licence, merely because the proceedings in question might have some persuasive or precedent effect on a possible future case involving the intervener and one of the parties. The situation was contrasted with possible intervention in proceedings concerning a scheme which would affect many potential licensees: *British Sky Broadcasting Ltd and Sky Television Plc v The Performing Right Society Limited*, CT 38/96 (interim decision on application by Turner Entertainment Networks International to intervene). In this case the Tribunal also held that notwithstanding that an intervener established a sufficient interest, the Tribunal still had a discretion to grant or refuse the application to intervene. See also the interim decision of the Tribunal in *Candy Rock Recording Ltd v Phonographic Performance Ltd*, CT 34/96 in which the application of AEI Rediffusion Ltd to intervene was refused on similar grounds.

[64] Copyright Tribunal Rules 1989 (SI 1989/1129), r.9(1). Para.5(b) of the *Practice Direction* (Vol.2 at B1.ii) provides that the Respondent's Answer should "specify exactly what the Respondent wants". Time may be extended by consent or by the Tribunal or the Chairman: r.51.

[65] See para. 29–162, above.

[66] Rule 9(2).

[67] Rule 9(3).

[68] Rule 10(1) and (3); as to the hearing for directions, see para. 29–167, below.

[69] Rule 10(2).

[70] See rr.22(1), 25(1), 29(1), 32(1), 36(1) and 40(1). Time may be extended by consent or by the Tribunal or the Chairman: r.51.

[71] Copyright Tribunal Rules 1989 (SI 1989/1129), r.11(1). These provisions are applied to all types of proceedings before the Tribunal: rr.22(2), 25(2), 26C(2), 29(2), 32(2), 36(2), 40(2) and 41C(2).

tary is to give every party and every intervener 21 days' notice of such hearing.[72] In a two-party case, the applicant must, not less than 14 days before the hearing, send to the respondent and to the Secretary his written proposals for directions, and the respondent must send the applicant not less than 7 days before the hearing a written statement stating whether he agrees the directions, and if not what directions he counter-proposes.[73] A draft of the directions normally to be made in a two-party case is scheduled to the Practice Direction.[74] Where there are more than two parties, each party should send its written proposals to the other parties and to the Secretary not less than 10 days before the hearing.[75] The parties may agree the directions to be made, in which case the Chairman may make an order accordingly.[76] Where the directions are not agreed in advance, and the hearing for directions proceeds, the Chairman shall give every party attending an opportunity to be heard and shall consider the oral and written representations, and shall make such directions as will lead to the just, expeditious and economical disposal of the proceedings.[77] The Chairman may give directions as to the date and place of the substantive hearing, if one is requested by any party[78]; the procedure to be followed in regard to the submission and exchange of written arguments[79]; the date after which no amended statement of case or answer is to be served without leave[80]; the preparation and delivery by the applicant of an agreed schedule setting out the issues to be determined and the contentions of each party in relation thereto[81]; the admission of facts and documents and the discovery and inspection of documents[82]; the giving of evidence on affidavit[83]; and the consideration by the Tribunal of any objection made to an intervener's credentials.[84] Although not mentioned specifically in rule 11, the normal directions provide for the exchange between the parties and service on the Tribunal of written evidence prior to the hearing, in the form of witness statements.[85] It was envisaged that this would shorten the length of the hearing, and go some way to meeting the criticism made in the past that hearings before the PRT were too long

---

[72] r.11(1).

[73] *Practice Direction*, para.6(c), Vol.2 at B1.ii.

[74] *Practice Direction*, para.6(a). The normal directions provide that evidence shall be by written witness statement (para.1); lay down a timetable for service of such statements (paras 3 to 5); provide that although there will be a hearing, the parties may rely on written submissions (para.6); provide that notice must be given if a party wishes to cross-examine a witness (para.8); and state that it shall not be necessary to cross-examine a witness in order to challenge his evidence (para.9).

[75] *Practice Direction*, para.6(d).

[76] *Practice Direction*, para.6(g).

[77] Rule 11(2).

[78] Rule 11(2)(i). Any party requesting a date to be set should make inquiries of the other parties and the Secretary as to suitable dates, and the parties should provide an estimate or estimates of the likely length of the hearing: *Practice Direction*, para.6(e). The Chairman will normally set a date but if no party wishes for a date to be set at this time, normally the Chairman will not do so: *ibid.*

[79] Rule 11(2)(ii). Para.10 of the *Practice Direction* (Vol.2 at B1.ii) provides that not less than 7 days before the date appointed for the hearing each party should send to the other and to the Secretary a skeleton argument setting out briefly that party's arguments, including references to all portions of evidence particularly relied upon and any legal authorities relied upon. The skeleton argument should also have annexed to it a concise summary of the written evidence of each of that party's witnesses: *ibid.* Para.11 provides that a skeleton argument will not be taken as binding.

[80] Rule 11(2)(iii).

[81] Rule 11(2)(iv).

[82] Rule 11(2)(v). Disclosure is referred to specifically in *Practice Direction* para.6(b), although not in the draft order. For the agreement of facts, see *Practice Direction*, para.9.

[83] Rule 11(2)(vi).

[84] Rule 11(2)(vii).

[85] Para.7 of the *Practice Direction* contains detailed provisions as to the form and content of witness statements.

and costly.[86] Further directions may be given at a later date.[87] Failure to comply with a direction may result in the party concerned being debarred from taking any further part in the proceedings without the leave of the Tribunal.[88] Core bundles and bundles of copies of authorities should also be lodged with the Secretary at least seven days before the hearing date.[89] Any jurisdictional points should be raised no later than the hearing for directions.[90] The Tribunal may order a pre-trial review once the evidence is complete.[91]

29–168   **The substantive hearing.** The hearing is to be in public, unless the Tribunal or the Chairman otherwise orders.[92] Every party (which includes an intervener whose application is pending) to a reference or application which is considered at an oral hearing before the Tribunal is entitled to attend the hearing and to address the Tribunal and to give evidence and call witnesses.[93] Any party may authorise some other person (who may be a solicitor) to act for him in the proceedings[94] and may be represented at the hearing by solicitor or counsel or any other person allowed by the Tribunal or the Chairman to appear on his behalf, or, except in the case of a corporation or unincorporated body, may appear in person.[95] According to the Copyright Tribunal Rules, evidence is to be given orally or, if agreed, or the Tribunal or the Chairman so orders, by affidavit, but the Tribunal may at any stage of the proceedings require the attendance of any deponent for examination and cross-examination.[96] However, the normal directions order annexed to the *Practice Direction* makes clear that evidence will now be given by witness statement unless notice to cross-examine has been given.[97] On the basis that the Tribunal will have read in advance the statements of case, written evidence and the skeleton arguments,[98] substantial opening speeches are not required, and each party will normally be allowed no more than one hour for its opening speech.[99] Lengthy closing speeches are discouraged, and each party is encouraged to provide at the beginning of its closing speech a written summary of the main points to be made.[1] Lengthy cross-examination is also discouraged, and an order may be obtained to the effect that a witness need not be cross-examined merely

---

[86] See the 1986 White Paper, Cmnd. 9712, para.18.19. It is doubtful whether this objective has been achieved. In *Universities UK v Copyright Licensing Agency Ltd and Design and Artists Copyright Society Ltd*, CT71/00, 72/00, 73/00, 74/00, 75/01 [2002] I.P.D. 25021, the Copyright Tribunal reported the parties' perception that proceedings in the Tribunal were "necessarily extremely costly, intolerably lengthy and highly complex" and accordingly that a reference to the Copyright Tribunal was regarded as "a last resort: a failure of a most serious kind" (para.16). The Tribunal suggested that time and cost could be saved by restricting the scope of the second round of written evidence (para.13) and by ensuring that evidence was limited to the issues raised by the statements of case (para.14).

[87] Copyright Tribunal Rules 1989 (SI 1989/1129), r.11(3).

[88] Rule 11(4) and 53.

[89] *Practice Direction*, para.12.

[90] *Practice Direction*, para.6(b).

[91] *Practice Direction*, para.8(a). The *Practice Direction* goes on to provide (under the heading "Pre-Trial Review") that the parties may be required by the Tribunal before or during a hearing to calculate the aggregate royalty product of the parties' proposals and the product on such alternative bases as the Tribunal may specify and in computer readable form as prescribed (para.8(b)); and that the Tribunal may direct that issues are separated into separate topics — for example the rates separated from the licence terms — and heard separately (para.8(c)).

[92] Copyright Tribunal Rules 1989 (SI 1989/1129), r.14(2).

[93] Rule 14(1).

[94] Rule 15(1); such agent must be appointed by notice in writing to the Secretary: r.15(2).

[95] Rule 15(5).

[96] Rule 14(3).

[97] See paras 1 and 8.

[98] See para. 29–167, above.

[99] *Practice Direction*, para.13, Vol.2 at B1.ii.

[1] *Practice Direction*, para.15.

for the purpose of challenging his evidence.[2] The normal order for directions contains an order that a party wishing to cross-examine another party's witness must give prior notice to that effect.[3]

The decision. The Copyright Tribunal is to give its decision in writing, including **29–169** a statement of its reasons, and, where on a reference the Tribunal has varied the scheme, a copy of the scheme so varied is to be annexed to the decision.[4] Unless the operation of the decision is suspended,[5] the Secretary is to send a copy of the decision to every party[6] and is to make a copy available for inspection at the office.[7] Short particulars of the decision may be advertised if the Chairman so directs.[8] Except where the operation of the order is suspended,[9] the Tribunal's order takes effect from such date and shall remain in force for such period as shall be specified in the order.[10]

Costs. The costs of and incidental to any proceedings are in the discretion of the **29–170** Copyright Tribunal which may make any order for the payment of costs by one party to another in respect of the whole or part of the proceedings.[11] Such an order may be for payment of a lump sum by way of costs or such proportion of the costs as may be just, and, in the latter case, the Tribunal may direct that the amount be assessed by the Chairman or be taxed by a taxing officer.[12] Orders for the payment of costs by one party to another were rarely made by the PRT. In its first Practice Direction, made in early 1990, the Copyright Tribunal gave warning that it would consider exercising this power against any party which it considered responsible for undue prolixity in its evidence at the hearing, and that, whilst it was not the Tribunal's practice that in all cases costs would follow the event, the fact that a party's case might have been unreasonably maintained would be an important factor in considering the exercise of its discretion as to costs. This warning was repeated in the current Practice Direction made in 1995 and amended in 2004.[13] Subject to this point, however, the Tribunal's jurisdiction as to costs differs from that of the courts in two important respects. First, there is no general rule that the unsuccessful party shall pay the successful party's costs. Second, the breadth of the Tribunal's discretion means that the outcome is often one in which there is no clear winner or loser. Accordingly, there is far more room for flexibility in relation to costs in the Tribunal than in the ordinary courts.[14] The Tribunal further specifically stated in its initial Practice Direction and has repeated in its current Practice Direction that offers "without prejudice as to costs"[15] would be considered in relation to any application for costs.[16] In accor-

---

[2] *Practice Direction*, para.14 and see para.9 of the normal order for directions in the Schedule to the *Practice Direction*.

[3] Para. 8.

[4] Copyright Tribunal Rules 1989 (SI 1989/1129), r.17.

[5] Under rr.42 or 43; see para. 29–171, below.

[6] Rule 17.

[7] Rule 18; as to the office, see para. 29–160, above. Members of the public may obtain copies of decisions on request from the Secretary on payment of photocopying costs.

[8] Rule 18.

[9] See para. 29–171, below.

[10] Rule 19; subject to the statutory provisions which govern the earliest date from which the order may take effect (see para. 29–114, above).

[11] Copyright Tribunal Rules 1989 (SI 1989/1129), r.48(1).

[12] Rule 48(2).

[13] *Practice Direction*, para.16.

[14] *AEI Rediffusion Music Ltd v Phonographic Performance Ltd* [1999] 1 W.L.R. 1507.

[15] So-called *"Calderbank"* letters, following the procedure commended by the Court of Appeal in *Calderbank v Calderbank* [1976] Fam. 93.

[16] *Practice Direction*, para.17.

dance with such indications the Tribunal has since 1989 made orders for costs in six cases.[17]

29–171 **Appeal.** The substantive provisions which now provide for an appeal on a point of law from the Copyright Tribunal to the High Court, rather than the procedure formerly applicable of referring proceedings before the PRT to the High Court by way of case stated, have been discussed above.[18] Such appeal is to be brought within 28 days of the date of the decision of the Tribunal.[19] There are two separate procedures to be observed in order to bring such an appeal. The appeal itself is instituted by the filing and service of an appellant's notice,[20] under CPR 52.4.[21] The procedure of the appeal is then governed by the CPR Part 52 as modified by paragraph 17 of PD52.[22] In addition, a notice of appeal in the prescribed form[23] must be served on the Secretary and on every other party.[24] On receipt of the notice of appeal the Tribunal may, of its own motion, suspend the operation of its order,[25] and any party to the proceedings may apply to the Tribunal for it to do so.[26] A copy of such application must be served on every other party by the Secretary, and objections to a suspension may be lodged by any other party within 14 days of his being served with such notice.[27] The procedure for determining such an application is then the same as set out above, including the possibility for intervention by a person or organisation not previously a party to the proceedings.[28] If the Tribunal refuses the application, it must give reasons for its decision.[29] If the Tribunal does suspend its order, then sections 123 and 128 of the 1988 Act do not have effect for the duration of the suspension.[30]

---

[17] Orders requiring one party to pay a proportion of the costs of the other have been made in *The Performing Right Society Ltd v British Entertainment and Dancing Association* noted at [1991] I.P.D. 14178 (PRS ordered to pay 60 per cent of BEDA's costs down to the date of a *"Calderbank"* letter and 100 per cent thereafter): *British Amusement Catering Trades Association v Phonographic Performance Ltd* [1992] R.P.C. 149; *The British Phonographic Industry Ltd v Mechanical-Copyright Protection Society Ltd* [1993] E.M.L.R. 139 (where regard was again had to a *"Calderbank"* letter); *AEI Rediffusion Music Limited v Phonographic Performance Ltd* [1999] E.M.L.R. 129 (appeal to the Court of Appeal dismissed: [1999] 1 W.L.R. 1507); *British Airways Plc v The Performing Right Society Ltd* [1998] R.P.C. 581; and *Universities UK v Copyright Licensing Agency Ltd and Design and Artists Copyright Society Ltd*, CT71/00, 72/00, 73/00, 74/00, 75/01; [2002] I.P.D. 25021.

[18] See para. 29–97, above.

[19] Copyright Tribunal Rules 1989 (SI 1989/1129), r.42(1); the court (but not the Tribunal: r.51) has power to extend time.

[20] PD52, para.17.3.

[21] All causes and matters relating to copyright are assigned to the Chancery Division (Supreme Court Act 1981, Sch.1, para.1 (i)) and therefore appeals in relation to copyright must be brought in the Chancery Division. "Claims" in respect of rights in performances must be brought in the Chancery Division (PD63 para.18.1). Even if this provision does not literally apply to appeals from the Copyright Tribunal in respect of rights in performances, it seems inevitable that such appeals will be made to the Chancery Division.

[22] There are two relevant modifications. First, the time for filing the appellant's notice is 28 days after the date of the decision (para.17.3) or, where a statement of reasons is given later than the notice of the decision, 28 days after that statement is received by the appellant (para.17.4). Second, as well as serving the appellant's notice on the respondent, the appellant must serve it on the Chairman of the Tribunal (para.17.5). This requirement seems unnecessary in view of Rule 42(2) of the Copyright Tribunal Rules (see below).

[23] In Form 17.

[24] Copyright Tribunal Rules 1989 (SI 1989/1129), r.42(2).

[25] Rule 42(4).

[26] By Form 18; r.43(1).

[27] Rule 43(2).

[28] Rules 43(3) and 44.

[29] Rule 43(4).

[30] See paras 29–113, 29–117 and 29–122, above.

4. COMPETITION LAW AND THE EXERCISE OF COPYRIGHT AND OTHER RIGHTS COVERED IN THIS WORK

Introduction. This section considers the restraints which are imposed on the free exercise of copyright and other rights covered in this work by competition law and related legislative and common law rules, dealing first with European Community competition law, then United Kingdom competition law and, lastly, the common law doctrine of restraint of trade. The restraint imposed on the free exercise of copyright and related rights by the Community law principle of free movement of goods and services is dealt with elsewhere.[31]   **29–172**

A. EUROPEAN COMMUNITY COMPETITION LAW

Introduction. As has been discussed elsewhere,[32] the principal aims of the European Union require the establishment within the Union of a common market, and this in turn requires the removal of all obstacles to the free movement of goods, persons, services and capital within the territory of the European Union, and therefore across the boundaries of the Member States. Such obstacles may be caused by the trading activities of undertakings which seek to restrict competition and isolate national markets. The institution of a system which ensures that competition within the common market is not distorted in this way is one of the primary activities which the Community is charged by the Treaty to undertake. Articles 81 to 89 of the Treaty, comprising Chapter 1 (the Rules on Competition) of Title VI of the Treaty, are the specific provisions directed at achieving this.[33] Of this Chapter of the Treaty, Articles 81 and 82 in Section 1 (the rules applying to undertakings), are the most important Articles for present purposes. This section of the work discusses these Articles and their application to the exercise of copyright and the other rights covered in this work.   **29–173**

(i) Article 81: general

General. Article 81 comprises three paragraphs: Article 81 (1) prohibits certain restrictive agreements; Article 81 (2) declares prohibited agreements to be void; and Article 81 (3) provides for exemption in certain cases of individual agreements or types of agreements from the prohibition in Article 81(1). Article 81 is effectively reproduced in Article 53 of the EEA Agreement[34] with respect to restrictive agreements that may affect trade between the EEA States.[35]   **29–174**

Agreements, decisions and concerted practices. Article 81(1) applies to agreements, decisions and concerted practices. There is little need to draw any hard-and-fast line between these concepts, which often overlap.[36] An agreement may be oral.[37] It need not be legally binding, but can consist of an informal understand-   **29–175**

---

[31] See Ch.25.

[32] See Ch.25.

[33] In what follows, all references to provisions of the Treaty are to those provisions as renumbered by the Treaty of Amsterdam.

[34] The Agreement on the European Economic Area, signed at Oporto on May 2, 1992, as adjusted by the Protocol signed at Brussels on March 17, 1993.

[35] That is to say, the 25 Member States of the EU and Iceland, Liechtenstein and Norway (that is to say all the EFTA States other than Switzerland, which decided not to take part in the EEA).

[36] See, *e.g.*, the remarks of Advocate General Reischl in Case 209/78 *Van Landewyck v Commission* [1980] E.C.R. 3125 at 3310; [1981] 3 C.M.L.R. 134.

[37] *e.g.* Case 28/77 *Tepea v Commission* [1978] E.C.R. 1391; [1978] 3 C.M.L.R. 392.

ing between the parties.[38] It may also exist, for the purposes of Article 81(1), in the terms of a compromise of legal proceedings brought by the owner of an industrial property right for the enforcement of such right.[39] A concerted practice will exist where there is no agreement between undertakings, but where undertakings by one means or another have reached the stage where they are knowingly co-ordinating their behaviour so as to substitute practical co-operation between them for the risks of competition.[40]

29–176   **Apparently unilateral behaviour.** What at first sight appears to be unilateral conduct may, particularly in the context of distribution arrangements, turn out on analysis to infringe Article 81(1). Thus, if an undertaking chooses to operate a selective distribution system (for example, where dealers are appointed only if (a) they satisfy certain criteria and (b) they agree not to supply to dealers outside the authorised network), the undertaking's decisions as to whom it is prepared to admit to its dealer network may be considered as part of the agreement between the undertaking and its dealers, and, therefore, as potentially falling under Article 81(1).[41] In another case, a supplier who stamped "Not for export" on invoices to his dealers was held to infringe Article 81(1), as the dealers tended to comply with that indication.[42] However, where a supplier refused to supply dealers with as much product as they wanted on the ground that some of what they wanted would be exported but the dealers, while reducing their orders, continued to do their best to export what they could, there was no agreement within Article 81(1) because there was no relevant "concurrence of wills", nor was there any tacit acquiescence by the dealers in anti-competitive practices on the part of the suppliers.[43]

29–177   **Undertakings.** There is no definition of the term "undertaking" in the treaty. However, it has been held that every entity engaged in economic activity is an undertaking, regardless of its legal status or how it is funded.[44] Sole traders may be undertakings.[45] However, an employee of an undertaking, being incorporated into and forming an economic unit with it, cannot himself be an undertaking.[46] Non-profit-making organisations may be undertakings.[47] State corporations may be undertakings, although not in so far as they are exercising what are essentially the sovereign functions of the state.[48]

29–178   **Single economic entity.** Two or more legal persons may be treated as a single

---

[38] e.g. Case 41/69 *ACF Chemiefarma v Commission* [1970] E.C.R. 661, grounds 110–114.

[39] Case 258/78 *Nungesser v Commission* [1982] E.C.R. 2015, grounds 82–89; [1983] 1 C.M.L.R. 278.

[40] Case 48/69 *ICI v Commission* [1972] E.C.R. 619, para.64; [1972] C.M.L.R. 557 ("Dyestuffs").

[41] Case 107/82 *AEG v Commission* [1983] E.C.R. 3151; [1984] 3 C.M.L.R. 325.

[42] Case C-277/87 *Sandoz v Commission* [1990] E.C.R. I-45.

[43] *Bayer v Commission* [2000] E.C.R. II-3383, [2001] 4 C.M.L.R. 126 (C.F.I.); upheld on appeal: Joined Cases C-2/01P and C-3/01P *Bundesverband der Arzneimittel-Importeure eV v Commission*, January 6, 2004.

[44] See, e.g. Case C-41/90, *Höfner v Macroton GmbH* [1991] E.C.R. I-1979; [1994] C.M.L.R. 306 at para.21. The term undertaking includes individuals such as authors, artists, artistes, inventors and plant breeders: *Re Unitel*, [1978] O.J. L157/39; [1978] 3 C.M.L.R. 306; *A.O.I.P. v Beyrard* [1976] O.J. L6/8; [1976] 1 C.M.L.R. D14; *H. Vaessen B.V. v Alex Morris* [1979] O.J. L19/32; [1979] 1 C.M.L.R. 511; Case 258/78 *Nungesser v Commission* [1982] E.C.R. 2015; [1983] 1 C.M.L.R. 278. A performer's service company is, of course, an undertaking for these purposes: *Panayiotou v Sony Music Entertainment (UK) Ltd* [1994] E.M.L.R. 229, para.B1.

[45] e.g. *COAPI* [1995] O.J. L122/37 (Spanish intellectual property agents).

[46] e.g. Case C-22/98 *Becu* [1999] E.C.R. I-5665, [2001] 4 C.M.L.R. 968.

[47] e.g. Case C-244/94 *Fédération Française des Sociétés d'Assurance* [1995] E.C.R. I-4013 (organisation entrusted with managing a voluntary State supplementary old-age insurance scheme).

[48] e.g. Case C-364/92 *Eurocontrol* [1994] E.C.R. I-43 (body co-ordinating air-traffic control across the EU was not an undertaking); note that the activities of State entities are to some extent protected against the application of the competition rules by Art.86(2) of the Treaty, which lies outside the scope of this work.

undertaking if they form part of the same economic unit. If the only parties to an agreement that engage in economic activity are all part of a single undertaking, Article 81(1) will not apply, as the conduct is essentially unilateral. The test for determining whether one company is part of the same economic unit as another is whether that company enjoys real autonomy in determining its course of action in the market, or whether it carries out the instructions of its parent company.[49]

Object or effect of preventing, distorting, or restricting competition within the common market: general. Examples of the types of restrictions that fall within Article 81(1) are given in sub-paragraphs (a) to (e) of Article 81(1). These restrictions, which are often known as the "hardcore" restrictions, can be broadly summarised as terms fixing selling prices or conditions, limiting or controlling production, sharing markets, applying dissimilar conditions to equivalent transactions and tying the other party to extraneous obligations. However, this list is expressly not exhaustive. The issue of what restrictions will be regarded as having the object or effect of preventing, distorting, or restricting competition under Article 81(1) is the most complex question in Community competition law, and it is beyond the scope of this work to examine it in detail. However, in the context of intellectual property rights generally, and the rights covered in this work in particular, a number of points can be made.

29–179

Distinction between horizontal and vertical agreements. Although the distinction defies precise legal definition, horizontal agreements are agreements between undertakings at the same level of trade, whereas vertical agreements are between undertakings at different levels of trade. In the present context, the best example of a vertical agreement would be a copyright licensing agreement between an author and a publisher. On the other hand, an agreement between publishers in different countries to grant each other licences in certain works in their respective countries would be regarded as a horizontal agreement, or as a mixed horizontal/vertical agreement. It has been clear since 1966 that Article 81(1) applies to vertical as well as horizontal agreements,[50] but the distinction is still of importance in analysing the applicability of Article 81(1).[51]

29–180

The "object"/"effect"distinction. Article 81 applies where the agreement either has as its object the prevention, restriction of distortion of competition or where that is its effect. These criteria are alternative.[52] Accordingly, the Court of Justice has held on numerous occasions that where an agreement can be shown to have an anti-competitive object, it is not necessary to prove in addition that it might have an anti-competitive effect.[53] By contrast, where such an object cannot be proved, it is necessary to show, usually by market analysis, that the agreement would have such an effect.[54] However, the distinction is not quite as straightforward as it seems because in any case there is only an infringement of Article 81 if, in addition to meeting one of the criteria referred to above, the agreement appreciably affects competition *and* has an appreciable effect on trade between

29–181

---

[49] Case 15/74 *Centrafarm v Sterling Drug* [1974] E.C.R. 1147; [1974] 2 C.M.L.R. 480; Case C-73/95P *Viho Europe v Commission* [1997] 4 C.M.L.R. 419 at 450.

[50] Cases 56 & 58/64 *Consten and Grundig v Commission* [1966] E.C.R. 299; [1966] C.M.L.R. 418.

[51] See, for example, the Commission's notice on agreements of minor importance [2001] O.J. C368/07, paras 7 to 9, where differing guidance is given as to the application of Art.81(1) depending on whether the agreement is horizontal or vertical.

[52] Case 56/65, *Société Technique Minière v Machinenbau Ulm* [1966] E.C.R. 235 at 249; [1966] C.M.L.R. 357 at 375.

[53] *e.g.* Case 56/65, *Société Technique Minière v Machinenbau Ulm* [1966] E.C.R. 235 at 249; [1966] C.M.L.R. 357 at 375.

[54] Cases T-374/94 etc., *European Night Services v Commission* [1998] E.C.R. II-3141; [1998] 5 C.M.L.R. 718, para.136.

Member States.[55] Some analysis of the market may therefore be necessary even in a case where the agreement has been shown to have an anti-competitive object.[56] Finally, it should be said that even if all these criteria are satisfied, Article 81 will not be infringed if it is declared inapplicable under Article 81(3).[57]

29–182   **Provisions which are intrinsically likely to have the object or effect of preventing, distorting, or restricting competition.** Horizontal agreements to fix prices or to share out markets have consistently been held to have the object of preventing, distorting, or restricting competition. Similarly, vertical agreements that contain absolute restrictions on dealers supplying outside their allocated territories,[58] or which fix resale prices, have consistently been found to have such an object. Even where an agreement is between undertakings with such a low aggregate market share that the Commission would not usually hold an agreement between them to be capable of falling within Article 81(1), an agreement containing such "hardcore" provisions may be held to have the object of preventing, distorting, or restricting competition.[59] Such restrictions are sometimes referred to as " *per se*" restrictions on competition. This term (which is derived from American anti-trust law) is acceptable shorthand provided that it is remembered: (a) that there is no restriction on competition that cannot be exempted under Article 81(3)[60] ; and (b) that if the effect of the restriction on competition or on trade between Member States is insignificant, there will be no contravention of Article 81(1).[61]

29–183   **Proof of anti-competitive effect.** In the previous edition of this work it was stated that the cases revealed essentially two approaches to this issue. First, there were cases where the European Courts had emphasised the importance of a full market analysis before a significant adverse effect on competition could be established. Secondly, there were cases where there might be such an adverse effect, but that effect was counter-balanced by the pro-competitive aspects of the agreement.[62] The Court of First Instance has now held that it is inappropriate to weigh the anti-competitive effects of the agreement against the pro-competitive effects at this stage of the analysis.[63] Rather, it held, this exercise should be car-

---

[55] See Whish, *Competition Law*, 5th ed., pp.110–111, where the jurisprudence is described as "somewhat confused and confusing on this issue". For these requirements, see paras 29–185 and 29–188 respectively, below.

[56] See Whish, *Competition Law*, 5th ed., pp.110–111.

[57] See below para. 29–190.

[58] In Case C-306/96 *Javico AG v Yves Saint Laurent Parfums SA* [1999] Q.B. 477, the Court of Justice discussed the applicability of Art.81(1) to a restriction imposed on a dealer based in the EEA requiring him to supply only in a territory outside the EEA. In essence, the Court held that, in contrast to the case where the territory was a part of the EEA, such a restriction was not intrinsically likely to contravene Art.81(1), although it might do so if competition in the relevant market was limited in the EEA, there was a marked difference in prices between the EEA and outside it, and the volume of products covered by such a clause was not very small in comparison to the market for the products in the EEA.

[59] Notice on Agreements of Minor Importance [2001] O.J. C368/07, para.11. See paras 29–185 *et seq.* below.

[60] Case T-17/93 *Matra Hachette v Commission* [1994] E.C.R. II-595, para.85.

[61] *e.g.* Case 5/69 *Volk v Vervaecke* [1969] E.C.R. 295; [1969] C.M.L.R. 273, in which, since the supplier's market share was between 0.2 and 0.5 per cent, a provision conferring absolute territorial protection on a distributor did not contravene Art.81(1). Note, though, that an agreement with an anti-competitive object, but which failed to achieve that object because it was not implemented properly, will be regarded as falling under Art.81(1): Case T-13/89 *ICI v Commission* [1992] E.C.R. II-1021, para.293.

[62] *Copinger*, 14th ed., para.29–164.

[63] Case T-112/99, *Métropole Télévision v Commission* [2001] E.C.R. II-2459, [2001] 5 C.M.L.R. 1236, para.72.

ried out later, when considering the applicability of Article 81(3).[64] It would seem to follow that cases in this second category are more properly analysed as cases where, although the agreement contained restrictions, it did not result in a restriction of competition.[65]

Market analysis. The Court of First Instance has said that a full analysis of the relevant market is necessary before any finding can be made of anti-competitive behaviour under Article 81 or Article 82.[66] This proposition, however, has to be approached with caution in the context of Article 81(1). If the parties to an agreement are clearly of a substantial size, or if the restriction in question is a so-called *per se* restriction, then it may not be necessary to conduct any detailed market analysis.[67] However, as has been said above, even so-called *per se* restrictions may be regarded as having no appreciable effect on competition if an analysis of the parties' positions on the relevant markets shows that they have insignificant market power[68] . Where the restrictions are not *per se* restrictions, an analysis of the parties' positions on the relevant market may reveal that they have an aggregate share of the market which is low enough to benefit from the presumptions in the Commission's notice on agreements of minor importance[69] (as to which, see below[70]). Moreover, market analysis has been held to be essential where it is alleged that the agreement in question has to be considered in the light of other similar agreements. The leading case on this point is *Delimitis v Henniger Bräu*.[71] In that case, the owner of a bar agreed to purchase his supplies of beer exclusively from one supplier. In analysing that restriction, the Court of Justice stated that it was first necessary to define the relevant market (being, in that case, "on-licence" beer), and then it was necessary to examine how far access to that market was foreclosed to potential new suppliers of beer for "on-licence" sale, taking account of the agreement in question and the other similar agreements between breweries and outlets. Finally, the Court stated that the agreement in question would only contravene Article 81(1) if it significantly contributed to that foreclosure.

29–184

The Commission's notice on agreements of minor importance: general.[72] The Court of Justice has consistently held that Article 81(1) is not applicable unless there is an appreciable effect on competition. The purpose of this notice is to quantify, with the help of market share thresholds, what is not an appreciable restriction on competition. The notice is not concerned with the requirement that the agreement be shown to have an appreciable effect on trade between Member States. However, in the notice the Commission acknowledges that agreements between small and medium-sized undertakings (that is, undertakings with fewer than 250 employees and either an annual turnover not exceeding EUR 40 million or an annual balance-sheet total not exceeding EUR 27 million) are rarely capable of appreciably affecting trade between Member States.[73] In cases covered by the notice, the Commission will not institute proceedings either on application or on

29–185

---

[64] Case T-112/99, *Métropole Télévision v Commission* [2001] E.C.R. II-2459, [2001] 5 C.M.L.R. 1236, para.74.
[65] Whish, *Competition Law*, 5th ed., pp.117–119.
[66] Cases T-68/89, T-77/89 and T-78/89 *Società Italiana Vetro v Commission* [1992] E.C.R. II-1403, para.159.
[67] Cases 100–103/80 *Musique Diffusion Française v Commission* [1983] E.C.R. 1825, para.87; [1983] 3 C.M.L.R. 221.
[68] Case 5/69 *Volk v Vervaecke* [1969] E.C.R. 295; [1969] C.M.L.R. 273.
[69] [2001] O.J. C368/13.
[70] Paras 29–185 *et seq.*, below.
[71] Case C-234/89, [1991] E.C.R. I-935; [1992] 5 C.M.L.R. 210. This case was followed in the English case of *Crehan v Inntrepreneur Pub Company CPC* [2004] EWCA Civ 637.
[72] [2001] O.J. C368/13.
[73] Notice, para.3.

its own initiative.[74] Where undertakings assume in good faith that an agreement is covered by the notice, the Commission will not impose fines.[75] Although not binding on them, the notice is intended to give guidance to the national courts and authorities.[76]

29–186   **The Commission's notice on agreements of minor importance: specific provisions.** The notice applies to agreements between undertakings which affect trade between Member States.[77] Where such an agreement is between actual or potential competitors[78] on the relevant markets affected by the agreement, the Commission's view is that it will not appreciably restrict competition if the aggregate market share held by the parties does not exceed 10 per cent on any relevant market.[79] Where such an agreement is between non-competitors, it will not appreciably restrict competition if the market share held by each of the parties does not exceed 15 per cent on any relevant market.[80] Where it is difficult to classify the parties as competitors or non-competitors, the 10 per cent threshold applies.[81] Where, in a relevant market, competition is restricted by the cumulative effect of agreements for the sale of goods or services entered into by different suppliers or distributors,[82] the thresholds are both reduced to 5 per cent.[83] Agreements are also not restrictive of competition if they do not exceed the relevant threshold by two per cent during 2 successive years.[84] However, these provisions do not apply to agreements containing any of a list of "hardcore" restrictions. If the agreement is between competing undertakings, the hardcore restrictions may be summarised as follows: price fixing, the limitation of output or sales and the allocation of customers.[85] Between non-competing undertakings, they are (in summary): the restriction of the buyer's ability to determine its sale price (but genuine maximum and recommended prices are permitted), territorial restrictions (with significant exceptions), certain restrictions in relation to selective distribution systems and restrictions on a supplier's ability to sell components as spare parts.[86]

29–187   **Agreement contains restrictions but has no anti-competitive effects.** The Court of Justice has in some cases been prepared to regard *prima facie* restric-

---

[74] para.4.

[75] para.4.

[76] para.4. The Notice is without prejudice to any interpretation of Art.81 which may be given by the Court of Justice or the Court of First Instance: para.6.

[77] Ntoice [2001] O.J. C368/13, para.7.

[78] An undertaking is an actual competitor if it is either active on the same relevant market or in the absence of the agreement it is able to switch production to the relevant products and market them in the short term without incurring significant additional costs or risks in response to a small and permanent increase in relative prices ("immediate supply-side substitutability"). An undertaking is a potential competitor if there is evidence that, absent the agreement, the firm could and would be likely to undertake the necessary additional investments or other necessary switching costs so that it could enter the relevant market in response to a small and permanent increase in relative prices: *ibid.*, n.4, citing the Commission's guidelines on the applicability of Art.81 to horizontal cooperation agreements [2001] O.J. C 3/2, nn.8 and 9.

[79] Notice on agreements of minor importance, para.7(a).

[80] para.7(b).

[81] para.7.

[82] This is called a "cumulative foreclosure effect of parallel networks of agreements having similar effects on the market". Individual suppliers or distributors with a market share not exceeding 5 per cent are not generally considered to contribute significantly to a such an effect. Furthermore, such an effect is unlikely to exist if less than 30 per cent of the relevant market is covered by parallel networks of agreements having similar effects: Notice on agreements of minor importance, para.8.

[83] Notice on agreements of minor importance, para.8.

[84] para.9.

[85] para.11(1).

[86] para.11(2).

tions on competition as not having an appreciable anti-competitive effect under Article 81(1) because they are necessary to facilitate a commercial activity such as the penetration of a new market or the successful operation of a purchasing cooperative. In the present context, the best example of this approach is *Nungesser v Commission*.[87] The Court of Justice there held that an agreement by which the holder of certain plant breeder's rights granted Nungesser the exclusive right to produce and sell the relevant seeds in West Germany did not contravene Article 81(1). The Court accepted that without such an agreement it would be commercially impossible to introduce the new seeds onto the West German market, and hence that the agreement promoted competition between the new seeds and existing products. However, the Court drew a clear distinction between that case, and a case where the agreement, or the parties' behaviour, sought to prevent any competition between the exclusive licensee and parallel exporters into the licensee's territory. A similar approach can be seen in the more recent case of *Gøttrup-Klim v Dansk Landbrugs Grovvareselskab AmbA*,[88] where a rule of a Danish agricultural purchasing co-operative that prevented members from joining other purchasing co-operatives was held not to contravene Article 81(1) if it went no further than was necessary to maintain the position of the co-operative in relation to producers. An analogous approach was adopted in *Wouters v Algemene Raad van de Dederlandsche Orde van Advocaten*[89] in which the Court of Justice held that Article 81(1) might not be infringed by a professional rule which restricted lawyers' freedom of action if it could reasonably be considered necessary in order to ensure the proper practice of the profession.

Effect on trade between Member States.[90] Articles 81(1) and 82 apply only where the agreement[91] or conduct has an actual or potential effect on trade between Member States. This test serves to define the boundary between agreements and conduct which are subject to the Community competition rules and agreements which are left to be dealt with exclusively by national competition law.[92] The Court of Justice has consistently held that the test is satisfied if "it is possible to foresee, with a sufficient degree of probability on the basis of a set of objective factors of law or of fact, that the agreement [or conduct] in question may have an influence, direct or indirect, actual or potential, on the pattern of trade between Member States".[93] It is enough that the pattern of trade between two Member States is affected, *e.g.* the pattern of trade between the United Kingdom and Ireland[94] (a point of some practical importance when the relevant products are English-language publications). It is irrelevant that the effect of the agreement or conduct is to increase, rather than reduce, trade between Member

29–188

---

[87] Case 258/78 *Nungesser v Commission* [1982] E.C.R. 2015; [1983] 1 C.M.L.R. 278.

[88] Case C-250/92 [1996] E.C.R. I-5641.

[89] Case C-309/99 [2002] C.M.L.R. 913; [2002] E.C.R. I-1577.

[90] See generally the Commission's guidelines on the effect on trade concept contained in Arts 81 and 82 of the Treaty, O.J. [2004] C101/81.

[91] Note that a provision of an agreement that does not affect trade between Member States when viewed in isolation may nonetheless be subject to Art.81(1) if the agreement as a whole has such an effect: Case 193/83 *Windsurfing International v Commission* [1986] E.C.R. 611; [1986] 3 C.M.L.R. 489.

[92] Case 22/78 *Hugin v Commission* [1979] E.C.R. 1869, para.17; [1979] 3 C.M.L.R. 345.

[93] This phrase, which appears in Case 56/65, *Société Technique Minière v Machinenbau Ulm* [1966] E.C.R. 235 at 249; [1966] C.M.L.R. 357 at 375, is to be found in a number of judgments of the Court; see, for example, Case 99/79 *Lancôme v Etos* [1980] E.C.R. 2511, para.23; [1981] 2 C.M.L.R. 164. The phrase "such as might prejudice the aim of a single market in all the Member States" is sometimes appended to the test (see *e.g.* Case 30/87 *Bodson v Pompes Funèbres* [1988] E.C.R. 2479, para.25; [1989] 4 C.M.L.R. 984) but it is not clear what, if anything, this adds.

[94] See, for example, *Irish Sugar* [1997] O.J. L258/1, para.159 ("border rebate" affected pattern of imports from Northern Ireland to Ireland), and Case T-66/89 *Publishers' Association v Commission* [1992] E.C.R. II-1995, para.56; [1992] 5 C.M.L.R. 120 (annulled on appeal on other grounds, Case C-360/92P [1995] E.C.R. I-23).

States.[95] An agreement or conduct which has the effect of partitioning national markets will be particularly likely to have an effect on trade between Member States.[96] One way in which an agreement or conduct may be found to have an effect on trade between Member States is if it affects the structure of competition within the common market.[97] However, the fact that an agreement or conduct prevents transactions which could in theory have been attempted, or which in fact have been attempted, is not of itself enough to show an effect on trade between Member States for these purposes, if the transactions affected would be or are entirely abnormal transactions (*e.g.* transactions attempted in order to demonstrate an effect on trade between Member States).[98] In the United Kingdom, the practical importance of this aspect of Articles 81(1) and 82 is much diminished following the enactment of the Competition Act, as the Chapter I and II prohibitions substantially replicate Articles 81(1) and 82 respectively, but without the reference to an effect on trade between Member States.[99]

29–189   **Article 81(2): effects of prohibition.** An agreement which contravenes Article 81(1) is automatically void under Article 81(2). Article 81(2) does not, however, affect provisions of an agreement that are severable from those provisions that fall under Article 81(1)[1] ; whether provisions are severable is a matter of national law.[2] The only agreements falling under Article 81(1) that are not affected by Article 81(2) are those which have been declared inapplicable under Article 81(3), or which fall into a category of agreements which, pursuant to Article 81(3), has been prescribed as exempt from the prohibition of Article 81(1) pursuant to a block exemption.

29–190   **Article 81(3).**[3] From what has been said above, it will be appreciated that a large number of agreements fall under Article 81(1). It may, of course, be that the anti-competitive aspects of many such agreements are more than offset by their beneficial aspects. Article 81(3) provides the legal framework for conducting such a balancing exercise. Under Article 81(3), Article 81(1) can be "declared inapplicable" to an agreement or category of agreements if it satisfies each of four conditions, namely that:

> (i) it may contribute to an improvement in the production or distribution of goods or services,[4] or to technical or economic progress[5] ;

---

[95] *e.g. Napier Brown* [1988] O.J. L284/41; [1990] 4 C.M.L.R. 196.

[96] *e.g.* Case 19/77 *Miller v Commission* [1978] E.C.R. 131; [1978] 2 C.M.L.R. 334.

[97] *e.g.* Cases 6 & 7/73 *Commercial Solvents v Commission* [1974] E.C.R. 223; [1974] 1 C.M.L.R. 309.

[98] Case 22/78 *Hugin v Commission* [1979] E.C.R. 1869; [1979] 3 C.M.L.R. 345.

[99] See below, paras 29–261 *et seq.* For the English decisions on Art.81 prior to the introduction of the Competition Act, see *Copinger*, (14th ed.), para. 29–167.

[1] Case 56/65 *Société Technique Minière v Machinenbau Ulm* [1966] E.C.R. 235 at 249; [1966] C.M.L.R. 357.

[2] Case 319/82 *Société de Vente de Ciments et Bétons v Kerpen & Kerpen* [1983] E.C.R. 4173; [1985] 1 C.M.L.R. 511.

[3] See generally the Commission's guidelines on the application of Article 81(3) of the Treaty [2004] O.J. C101/8.

[4] Although Art.81(3) refers to "goods", there is no doubt that improvements relating to services are also covered; see *e.g. BT/MCI* [1994] O.J. L223/36 (improvements relating to telecommunications) and the Commmission's Guidelines on the application of Art.81(3), [2004] O.J. C101/97, para.48 (which states that this provision applies by analogy to services).

[5] The Commission has interpreted this phrase widely, to include such matters as: cost savings (*LH/SAS* [1996] O.J. L54/36; see also the Commmission's guidelines on the application of Art.81(3), [2004] O.J. C101/97, paras 64 to 68); the protection of a large investment (*Eurotunnel III* [1994] O.J. L354/66); the restructuring of an industry under acceptable social conditions (*Stichting Baksteen* [1994] O.J. L131/15); and qualitative efficiencies (see the Commmission's guidelines on the application of Art.81(3), [2004] O.J. C101/97, paras 69 to 72).

(ii) a fair share of the resulting benefit is passed on to consumers;[6]

(iii) the restrictions are indispensable to the achievement of the aims of agreement;[7] and

(iv) the agreement does not eliminate competition in a particular sector.[8]

These conditions are cumulative in that all must be satisfied before the benefit of Article 81(3) may be claimed.[9] They are also exhaustive, in that the objectives of other Treaty provisions may only be taken into account to the extent that they are subsumed under the four conditions.[10]

Article 81(3): procedure before May 1, 2004. Before May 1, 2004, Article 81(3)[11] operated by the grant of individual exemptions, which could only be granted by the Commission.[12] In particular, a national court could not apply Article 81(3); if it believed that an agreement before it could benefit from the application of the provision, it could only stay proceedings pending a decision by the Commission.[13] An agreement (except an agreement falling within Article 4(2) of Regulation 17)[14] could not receive an individual exemption for a period before its notification to the Commission.[15] The Commission granted very few individual exemptions; in the vast majority of cases where it believed that Article 81(3) was satisfied, it would issue no more than a "comfort letter" indicating that belief. The Commission's view was that national courts should "take account of these letters as factual elements".[16] However, an agreement that fell within a block exemption made under Article 81(3) was automatically exempt without the need to notify it.

29–191

Article 81(3): current procedure. Since May 1, 2004, a new procedure has been in operation. Article 81(3) is now "directly effective". Thus, agreements which are caught by Article 81(1) but which satisfy the conditions of Article 81(3) are not prohibited, and no prior decision to that effect is required.[17] Furthermore, Article 81(3) can now be applied by national competition authorities and courts as well as the Commission. As before, however, an agreement that falls within a

29–192

---

[6] Commission's guidelines on the application of Art.81(3), [2004] O.J. C101/97, paras 83 to 104.

[7] Commission's guidelines, paras 73 to 82.

[8] paras 105 to 116.

[9] para.42.

[10] para.42.

[11] Exemptions under Art.53(3) of the EEA Agreement were (and at the time of writing still are) granted by the EFTA Surveillance Authority where (a) the only trade affected is between participating EFTA Member States or (b) where (i) there is no effect on trade between EU Member States and (ii) the turnover of the undertakings concerned equals 33 per cent or more of their EEA turnover: Art.56 of the EEA Agreement. These provisions are currently under review.

[12] Reg.17, First Regulation implementing Arts 85 and 86 of the Treaty [1962] O.J. Sp. Ed. No. 204/87, Art.9(1).

[13] Notice on co-operation between national courts and the Commission, [1993] O.J. C39/5, paras 28–31.

[14] For the purposes of the present work, the most relevant provision of Art.4(2) was Art.4(2)(b), which covered agreements to which not more than two undertakings were party and which only imposed restrictions on the exercise of the rights of the assignee or user of industrial property rights. In *Re Advocaat* [1974] O.J. L237/12; [1974] 2 C.M.L.R. D79, the Commission held that a licence to use a trade mark was outside the exemption because restrictions were accepted by the licensor; this will always be so, for example, where the licence is exclusive. Further, in *H Vaessen BV v Alex Morris* [1979] O.J. L19/32; [1979] 1 C.M.L.R. 511, a patent licensing agreement contained a no-challenge clause and a clause imposing an exclusive purchasing obligation relating to products not covered by the patent. The Commission held that these restrictions went beyond those referred to in Art.4(2)(b), and that the agreement was not exempt from notification. The parties to an agreement which was exempt from notification might, nevertheless, notify it to the Commission: Arts 4(2) and 5(2).

[15] Reg.7, Art.6(1).

[16] Notice on co-operation between national courts and the Commission, [1993] O.J. C30/5, para.25.

[17] Council Regulation (EC) No 1/2003 on the implementation of the rules of competition laid down in Arts 81 and 82 of the Treaty ("the Modernisation Regulation"), [2003] O.J. L1/1, Art.1(2).

block exemption is automatically exempt from the operation of Article 81(3).[18] It is thought that existing individual exemptions remain in force while existing comfort letters, although not capable of remaining in force since they have no legal effect, will continue to have much the same effect as they had before May 1, 2004.[19] As before, the burden of proving that the conditions of Article 81(3) apply lies on the undertaking claiming the benefit of Article 81(3).[20]

(ii) Article 82: general

29–193   **Article 82.** Whereas Article 81 in essence deals with agreements between undertakings, Article 82 regulates unilateral behaviour by single undertakings.[21] Article 82 prohibits the abuse by an undertaking of a dominant position within the common market or a substantial part of it, where that abuse may affect trade between Member States. It should be noted at the outset that Article 82 does *not* prohibit dominance; it addresses abuses of that dominance. In the words of the Court of Justice:

> "A finding that an undertaking has a dominant position is not in itself a recrimination but simply means that, irrespective of the reasons for which it has such a dominant position, the undertaking concerned has a special responsibility not to allow its conduct to impair genuine undiluted competition on the common market".[22]

Article 82 is effectively reproduced in Article 54 of the EEA Agreement.[23]

29–194   **Dominant position.** The classic definition of a dominant position is that it is:

> A position of economic strength enjoyed by an undertaking which enables it to prevent effective competition being maintained on the relevant market by giving it the power to behave to an appreciable extent independently of its competitors, customers and, ultimately, of its consumers.[24]

In practice, there are two key elements in assessing whether an undertaking enjoys such a position of economic strength.

29–195   **Relevant market.** The first element is the assessment of the correct relevant market; this element is so important a constituent of the analysis of conduct under Article 82 that an error will vitiate any finding of breach.[25] There are two aspects to the definition of the relevant market: the product market and the geographical market. The relevant market comprises those goods (or services) to which the conduct relates and those goods (or services), defined by their nature and their geographical location, which are interchangeable or substitutable for them. This can be looked at from the point of view of the customer[26] (what other goods or services could he buy instead, and from where?) and of the supplier (what suppli-

---

[18] All existing block exemption regulations remain in force: Commission Guidelines on the application of Art.81(3), [2004] O.J. C101/97, para.2.

[19] Whish, *Competition Law* (5th ed.), pp.165 (exemptions) and 167 (comfort letters).

[20] Modernisation Regulation 1/2003, Art.2.

[21] See, however, "collective dominance" below, para. 29–197. For the meaning of the term "undertaking", see para. 29–177, above.

[22] Case 322/81 *Michelin v Commission* [1983] E.C.R. 3461, para.57; [1985] 1 C.M.L.R. 282.

[23] The Agreement on the European Economic Area, signed at Oporto on May 2, 1992, as adjusted by the Protocol signed at Brussels on March 17, 1993.

[24] Case 27/76 *United Brands Company v Commission* [1978] E.C.R. 207; [1978] 1 C.M.L.R. 429, para.65.

[25] *e.g.* Case 6/72 *Continental Can v Commission* [1973] E.C.R. 215, para.32.

[26] It may be that some customers can use alternatives but others cannot; if relatively few can use an alternative to the product in question, the product in question is more likely to be a relevant market. In Case 322/81 *Michelin v Commission* [1983] E.C.R. 3461; [1985] 1 C.M.L.R. 282, the fact that some customers could easily use retread tyres did not prevent new tyres from being the

ers could easily switch from production of other goods or services to those goods or services, and where could they do this?).[27] It is beyond the scope of this work to enter further into these questions, but a valuable guide to the Commission's thinking on can be found in its Notice on the definition of the relevant market.[28]

Dominance. The obvious case where an undertaking is dominant in a relevant market is where it is unlawful to compete with that undertaking on that market.[29] This point is important in the context of copyright, since the essence of that right is that others are unable to supply copies of a work in which such a right is held, without permission of the right holder. In most cases, of course, the work to which the right relates is not a relevant market, since a number of alternative works exist, each of which is an acceptable substitute from the point of view of the customer.[30] But this may not be the case with some works, *e.g.* TV listings information.[31] In cases where there is no legal restriction on competition, the starting point is to consider the undertaking's share of the relevant market. As the Court of Justice has observed,[32] a high market share makes an undertaking an unavoidable trading partner for most customers (unless smaller competitors can rapidly expand production). However, there is no hard-and-fast market share above which an undertaking can be said to be dominant.[33] Other things being equal, an undertaking is more likely to be dominant if: its market share has been stable over time[34] ; it faces no competitors of any size,[35] or only one or two large competitors[36] ; its size, financial strength and reputation confer advantages on the relevant market[37] ; or there are no large purchasers of the product in a position to exercise countervailing market power.[38]

29–196

Collective dominance. Since Article 82 refers to an abuse "by one or more undertakings", it is clear that two or more undertakings can hold a collective dominant position. Such a position may exist if the entities present themselves or act together on a particular market as a collective entity.[39] The existence of such a position may flow from the existence of an agreement or from other links between the undertakings in question. However, the existence of an agreement or such links is not essential: a finding of collective dominance may be based on

29–197

---

relevant market. Similarly, spare parts or software packages designed for particular equipment are not in the same relevant market as equivalent parts or packages designed for other equipment if customers are unable to change the equipment that they have; see *e.g.* Case 22/78 *Hugin v Commission* [1979] E.C.R. 1869; [1979] 3 C.M.L.R. 345.

[27] In Case 6/72 *Continental Can v Commission* [1973] E.C.R. 215, above, the Court of Justice accepted that the market for light metal containers for meat and fish was not a relevant market unless manufacturers of other metal containers were unable easily to switch production into making such containers.

[28] [1997] O.J. C372/3; [1998] 4 C.M.L.R. 177.

[29] *e.g.* Case 311/84 *CBEM v CLT and IPB* [1985] E.C.R. 3261 ("Telemarketing").

[30] Case 24/67 *Parke, Davis v Probel* [1968] E.C.R. 81; [1968] C.M.L.R. 47.

[31] Cases C-241 & 242/91P *RTE and ITP v Commission* [1995] E.C.R. I-743; [1995] 4 C.M.L.R. 718 ("Magill TV Guide"); discussed more fully at paras 29–57 *et seq.* above.

[32] Case 85/76 *Hoffmann-La Roche v Commission* [1979] E.C.R. 461, para.41; [1979] 3 C.M.L.R. 211.

[33] Hence, in the Commission decision in *Tetra Pak II* [1992] O.J. L72/1; [1992] 4 C.M.L.R. 551, the Commission found that a market share of 48–52 per cent did not confer dominance; but in Case 27/76 *United Brands v Commission* [1978] E.C.R. 207; [1978] 1 C.M.L.R. 429, a market share of 40–45 per cent was found to do so.

[34] Case 85/76 *Hoffmann-La Roche v Commission* [1979] E.C.R. 461, para.58.

[35] Case 27/76 *United Brands v Commission* [1978] E.C.R. 207; [1979] 1 C.M.L.R. 429, para.111.

[36] Case 85/76 *Hoffmann-La Roche v Commission* [1979] E.C.R. 461, para.51.

[37] Case 85/76 *Hoffmann-La Roche v Commission* [1979] E.C.R. 461, paras 45–47; Case 322/81 *Michelin v Commission* [1983] E.C.R. 3461, para.55; [1985] 1 C.M.L.R. 282.

[38] *Alcatel/Teletra* [1991] O.J. L122/48; [1991] 4 C.M.L.R. 778.

[39] Joined Cases C-395/96 P and C-396/96 P *Compagnie Maritime Belge Transports SA v Dafra-Lines A/S* [2000] E.C.R. I-1365, [2000] 4 C.M.L.R. 1076, para.36.

other connecting factors; it is necessary to make an economic assessment and, in particular, an assessment of the market in question.[40] An example of a case where such a position of collective dominance has been established is the relationship between members of a liner shipping conference.[41]

29–198   **Relationship between the dominance and the abuse.** Four situations can be distinguished; in each of them, an undertaking may be found to be abusing its dominant position.

(i) The abuse affects the market in which the undertaking is dominant ("the dominated market"). In this case there is no need to show any causal link between the dominance and the abuse.[42]

(ii) The undertaking uses its position in the dominated market to produce effects in another market (*e.g.* by refusing in the dominated market to supply competitors in the other market), a practice often known as "leveraging".[43]

(iii) The undertaking behaves in the other market in a way designed to protect its position in the dominated market.[44]

(iv) The undertaking behaves on another market in a way that produces effects on that other market. This is at first sight a surprising case, as the conduct does not appear to relate to the dominant position at all. However, there is a breach of Article 82 in such cases if the other market is "associated" with the dominated market, and if there are "special circumstances".[45]

29–199   **Abuse.** Article 82 itself contains a non-exhaustive list of practices that may be considered to be abuses. The following are examples of practices that have been considered to be abuses; the list concentrates on those abuses which are likely to be of most relevance in the context of this work.

29–200   **Excessive prices.** Although this might be thought to be the most obvious way in which a monopolist might seek to abuse his market power, there are relatively few cases[46] where excessive pricing has been found to be an abuse, even though the setting of unfairly high prices is listed as an abuse in Article 82(a). The principal difficulty is that in the absence of appropriate comparators[47] in order to determine whether a price is excessive, a comparison has to be made with the costs of production[48]; but these costs can be very difficult to determine objectively.

29–201   **Price discrimination.** There are a number of cases where it will almost certainly

---

[40] Joined Cases C-395/96 P and C-396/96 P *Compagnie Maritime Belge Transports SA v Dafra-Lines A/S* [2000] E.C.R. I-1365, [2000] 4 C.M.L.R. 1076, paras 41 to 45.

[41] Joined Cases C-395/96 P and C-396/96 P *Compagnie Maritime Belge Transports SA v Dafra-Lines A/S* [2000] E.C.R. I-1365, [2000] 4 C.M.L.R. 1076.

[42] Case 6/72 *Continental Can v Commission* [1973] E.C.R. 215; the ability to acquire a competitor did not depend on the undertaking's dominance.

[43] *e.g.* Case 311/84 *CBEM v CLT and IPB* [1985] E.C.R. 3261 ("Telemarketing"). Another example in this category is Case T-219/99 *British Airways plc v Commission*, ECJ December 17, 2003.

[44] *e.g.* Case C-310/93P *BPB v Commission* [1995] E.C.R. I-865, para.11; see also Cases C-241 & 242/91P, *RTE and ITP v Commission* [1995] E.C.R. I-743; [1995] 4 C.M.L.R. 718.

[45] Case C-333/94P *Tetra Pak v Commission* [1996] E.C.R. I-5951. In that case, the markets were associated because both T and its competitors were present on both markets; T was the leading supplier in both; the customers in one were at least potential customers in the other; and T's position in the dominated market allowed it to concentrate on protecting its position in the other market.

[46] One being Case 27/76 *United Brands v Commission* [1978] E.C.R. 207; [1978] 1 C.M.L.R. 429. Note, however, that in this case the Commission's decision was quashed by the ECJ.

[47] As to which, see, *e.g.* Case 30/87 *Bodson v Pompes Funèbres* [1988] E.C.R. 2479; [1989] 4 C.M.L.R. 984.

[48] Case 27/76 *United Brands v Commission* [1978] E.C.R. 207; [1978] 1 C.M.L.R. 429, para.251.

be regarded as an abuse for a dominant undertaking to charge different prices[49] to different purchasers for his product. One is where the favoured purchasers are those that have purchased, or are particularly liable to purchase, from the dominant undertaking's competitors.[50] Another is where discounts are given to dealers who buy all or a high proportion of their supplies from the dominant undertaking,[51] or who achieve a large turnover in the dominant undertaking's products.[52] Price discrimination based on the nationality of the purchaser with a view to maintaining national boundaries between markets is very likely to be considered to be an abuse.[53] Differing royalty fees charged by a dominant copyright owner may well constitute price discrimination in the absence of objective justification.

Refusal to supply. It will be an abuse for a dominant undertaking to refuse to supply raw material to a purchaser because that purchaser will use it to compete with the dominant undertaking on another, ancillary market.[54] So, for example, it was an abuse for a company dominant in the supply of TV listings information to refuse to supply a company that wished to compete with it on the market for weekly TV guides[55] ; and it was an abuse for a broadcasting company to refuse to accept advertisements showing telephone numbers of a telemarketer that competed with the broadcaster's own telemarketing arm.[56]

29–202

Essential facilities. In a line of cases which can be seen as a development of the cases discussed in the previous two paragraphs, an abuse has been found where the owner of an "essential facility"—and thereby dominant in the supply of that facility—refused to grant access to that facility to a potential competitor, or discriminated in price against that competitor. Thus, in *Port of Rødby*,[57] the Commission found that it was an abuse of a ferry company's dominant position in the market for port facilities at Rødby (where it owned the port) for it to refuse to allow a potential competitor to use the port on reasonable terms. There have been similar decisions concerning other ports and airports.[58] A similar line of reasoning was employed in the *Magill* case,[59] where TV listings information was regarded as "essential" to the publication of weekly TV guides. It will be seen in the context of this work that this line of case-law could affect the conduct of copyright and related right owners if the right that they possess can be described as an "essential facility".[60]

29–203

---

[49] Or to treat more favourably in other ways, such as shorter delivery times; *e.g.* Case C-310/93P *BPB Industries v Commission* [1995] E.C.R. I-865 (priority given to those who purchased plasterboard from the dominant undertaking).

[50] *e.g.* Case C-62/86 *AKZO v Commission* [1991] E.C.R. I-3359 (discounts to purchasers who have bought from a competitor); *Irish Sugar* [1997] O.J. L258/1 (discounts to customers who were particularly accessible to competing cross-border suppliers).

[51] *e.g.* Case 40/73 *Suiker-Unie v Commission* [1975] E.C.R. 1663 at 2003; [1976] 1 C.M.L.R. 295; Case 85/76 *Hoffmann-La Roche v Commission* [1979] E.C.R. 461; [1979] 3 C.M.L.R. 211.

[52] *e.g.* Case 322/81 *Michelin v Commission* [1983] E.C.R. 3461, para.57; [1985] 1 C.M.L.R. 282.

[53] *e.g.* Case 27/76 *United Brands v Commission* [1978] E.C.R. 207; [1978] 1 C.M.L.R. 429; Case 226/84 *British Leyland v Commission* [1986] E.C.R. 3263; [1987] 1 C.M.L.R. 184.

[54] *e.g.* Case 6/73 *Commercial Solvents v Commission* [1974] E.C.R. 223.

[55] Cases C-241 & 242/91P *RTE and ITP v Commission* [1995] E.C.R. I-743; [1995] 4 C.M.L.R. 718.

[56] Case 311/84 *CBEM v CLT and IPB* [1985] E.C.R. 3261 ("Telemarketing").

[57] [1994] O.J. L55/52.

[58] *e.g. Brussels Airport* [1995] O.J. L216/8; *Sea Containers/Stena Sealink* [1994] O.J. L15/8.

[59] Cases C-241 & 242/91P *RTE and ITP v Commission* [1995] E.C.R. 1-743; [1995] 4 C.M.L.R. 718.

[60] See paras 29–57 *et seq.* above, for a discussion of the *Magill* decision and subsequent ECJ cases; see also para. 29–251, below.

29–204   Miscellaneous abuses. Other abuses include: making the supply of products conditional on the purchase of some other product[61] ("tying"); and pricing below the average variable cost[62] of producing a product, or pricing at below average total cost with the intent of eliminating a competitor ("predatory pricing").[63]

(iii) Enforcement and direct effect of Articles 81(1) and 82

29–205   Enforcement. The Modernisation Regulation provides that Articles 81 and 82 are to be enforced not only by the Commission, but also by the competition authories and courts of the Member States.[64] The Commission's powers are as follows. First, where, acting on a complaint[65] or on its own initiative, it finds that there is an infringement, it may by decision impose any behavioural or structural remedies which are proportionate to the infringement and necessary to end it.[66] In the case of intentional or negligent infringements of Articles 81 and 82, it may also impose a fine of up to 10 per cent of the preceding year's turnover of the relevant undertaking.[67] In cases of urgency, it may order interim measures.[68] It may accept binding "commitments" in lieu of imposing remedies.[69] Where the Community public interest so requires, it may, acting on its own initiative, by decision find that Article 81 is not applicable to a particular agreement or that Article 82 does not apply.[70] In addition, the Commission is empowered to investigate a particular sector of the economy or a particular type of agreement across various sectors.[71] For these purposes, the Commission may compel undertakings and associations to supply information,[72] and may take statements[73] and conduct all necessary inspections.[74] The Modernisation Regulation grants similar enforcement powers to the competition authorities of Member States.[75] In addition, it provides that national courts shall have the power to apply Articles 81 and 82.[76]

29–206   Relationship between the work of the Commission and the national competition authorities: general.[77] The Modernisation Regulation requires Member States to designate the authority or authorities responsible for the application of Articles 81 and 82 in such a way that its provisions are effectively complied

---

[61] *e.g.* Case T-30/89 *Hilti v Commission* [1991] E.C.R. II-1439; [1992] 4 C.M.L.R. 16 (upheld on appeal Case C-53/92P [1994] E.C.R. I-667) (supply of nail guns made conditional on purchase of nails).

[62] That is to say, costs such as energy and raw materials that are not fixed in the short term however much is produced; contrast management overheads and depreciation, which do not vary with the amount produced.

[63] Case C-62/86 *AKZO v Commission* [1991] E.C.R. I-3359.

[64] Arts 4, 5 and 6 of the Modernisation Regulation 1/2003.

[65] Which may be made by any person with a legitimate interest or a Member State: Modernisation Regulation, Art7(2).

[66] Art.7(1).

[67] Art.23(2)(a).

[68] Art.8(1). The Commission may impose fines for intentional or negligent breaches of such measures: Art.23(2)(b).

[69] Art.9(1). For the first example of the procedure in operation, see Commission Notice 2004/C 229/04 [2004] O.J. C229/13 concerning the joint selling of media rights to the German Bundesliga. Again, the Commission may impose fines for intentional or negligent breaches of such commitments where they have been made binding by a decision: Art.23(2)(c).

[70] Art.10.

[71] Art.17.

[72] Art.18. There are financial penalties for supplying incorrect or misleading information: Art.23.

[73] Art.19. Only those who consent may be interviewed.

[74] Arts 20 and 21. This provision includes sweeping powers of search and seizure.

[75] Art.5.

[76] Art.6 .

[77] See, generally, the Commission Notice on co-operation within the Network of Competition Authorities [2004] O.J. C101/43.

with.[78] It also provides that the Commission and the national authorities shall apply the Community competition rules in close cooperation.[79] To that end, it contains detailed provision for the exchange of information, including confidential information,[80] and requires the Commisson to consult with an Advisory Committee on Restrictive Practices and Dominant Positions consisting of representatives of the national authorities before taking enforcement or investigatory action.[81] It also contains provisions to avoid duplication in enforcement procedures.[82] Finally, it expressly provides that when national authorities make rulings on agreements, decisions or practices which are already the subject of a Commission decision, they cannot take decisions which would run counter to the Commission's decision.[83]

Enforcement of Articles 81 and 82 by national competition authorities in the United Kingdom. In accordance with the requirements of the Modernisation Regulation, the Office of Fair Trading ("OFT") and certain regulators have been designated as national competition authorities for the United Kingdom.[84] Since May 1, 2004, the OFT has been empowered to conduct an investigation where there are reasonable grounds to suspect an infringement of either Article 81 or Article 82.[85] For the purposes of such an investigation, the OFT is given extensive powers to require the production of documents and information[86]; to enter premises[87]; to accept commitments in lieu of enforcement[88]; to make decisions that Article 81 or Article 82 have been infringed; and to give directions for the purposes of ending the infringements and enforcing those directions.[89] Appeals from the OFT lie to the Competition Commission.[90] The OFT is also given extensive powers in relation to the enforcement of inspections under Articles 20(4), 21 and 22(2) of the Modernisation Regulation.[91]

29–207

[78] Modernisation Regulation 1/2003, Art.35. For the United Kingdom authorities, see the next paragraph.
[79] Art.11(1).
[80] Arts 11(2) and 12. See also the Commission Notice on cooperation within the Network of Competition Authorities [2004] O.J. C101/43, paras 26 to 30.
[81] Modernisation Regulation 1/2003 Art.14. See also the Commission Notice on co-operation within the Network of Competition Authorities [2004] O.J. C101/43, paras 58 to 68.
[82] Arts 11 and 13. See also the Commission Notice on cooperation within the Network of Competition Authorities [2004] O.J. C101/43, paras 6 to 25, 31 to 57.
[83] Art.16(2).
[84] The Competition Act 1998 and Other Enactments (Amendment) Regulations 2004 (SI 2004/1261), reg.3(1). The regulators are those referred to in s.54(1) of the Competition Act 1998 (c.41), i.e. (at the time of writing) the Office of Communications; the Gas and Electricity Markets Authority; the Director General of Electricity Supply for Northern Ireland; the Director General of Water Services; the Office of Rail Regulation; the Director General of Gas for Northern Ireland; and the Civil Aviation Authority.
[85] Competition Act 1998, s.25(3) and 25(5), inserted by the Competition Act 1998 and Other Enactments (Amendment) Regulations 2004 (SI 2004/1261), Sch.1, para.10.
[86] Competition Act 1998, s.26. Failure to comply may be an offence under ibid., s.42.
[87] ss.27 to 29. Again, failure to comply may be an offence under s.42.
[88] ss.31A to 31E, inserted by the Competition Act 1998 and Other Enactments (Amendment) Regulations 2004 (SI 2004/1261), Sch.1, para.18.
[89] ss.32 to 34. There is power to take interim measures in s.35 and power to impose penalties in ss.36 to 38.
[90] s.46.
[91] These powers are set out in Pts 2 and 2A of the Competition Act, as amended by the Competition Act 1998 and Other Enactments (Amendment) Regulations 2004 (SI 2004/1261), Sch.1. Arts 20(4) and 21 concern inspections by the Commission. Art.22 concerns investigations by competition authorities of other Member States.

29–208   **Relationship between the work of the Commission and litigation in national courts.**[92] Before the introduction of the Modernisation Regulation, neither negative clearance nor infringement decisions as a matter of law precluded a national court from making contrary findings as to the application of Article 85(1) or 86. However, the Commission had stated its view that even where its decisions on competition matters were not formally binding on national courts, they provided national courts with significant information for reaching a judgment.[93] Further, it had been held to be an abuse of process to seek to reargue in English courts matters fully argued before and determined by the Commission and which had been raised on appeal to the Community courts.[94] The present position is that when national courts rule on agreements, decisions or practices which are already the subject of a Commission decision, they are expressly prohibited by the terms of the Modernisation Regulation from taking decisions running counter to the decision adopted by the Commission.[95] They must also avoid giving decisions which would conflict with a decision contemplated by the Commission in proceedings it has initiated and in order to do so may consider whether to stay the proceedings.[96] At the same time, the Modernisation Regulation provides for three forms of co-operation between the Commission and national courts. First, national courts may ask the Commission to transmit to them information which is in its possession,[97] Secondly, they may ask the Commission for its opinion on questions concerning the applicability of the Community competition rules.[98] Thirdly, the Commission may make written or (if they request) oral observations to the national courts.[99] The application of Articles 81 and 82 in the English Courts is governed by a Practice Direction.[1]

29–209   **Direct effect.** The Modernisation Regulation makes clear that, as before, Articles 81(1) and 82 have direct effect in the national courts of the Member States.[2] Prior to 2001, the English courts (including the House of Lords) had held that a right to damages would arise from breach of Article 82 on the basis of breach of statutory duty.[3] In 2001, the European Court of Justice held in *Courage v Crehan* that the

---

[92] See, generally, the Commission Notice on the co-operation between the Commisison and the courts of the EU Member States in the application of Arts 81 and 82 EC , [2004] O.J. C101/54.

[93] Commission Notice on co-operation between national courts and the Commission in applying Arts 85 and 86 of the EEC Treaty [1993] O.J. C39/6, para.20.

[94] *Iberian UK v BPB Industries* [1996] 2 C.M.L.R. 601 (English High Court).

[95] Modernisation Regulation 1/2003, Art.16(1).

[96] Modernisation Regulation 1/2003, Art.16(1). This is stated to be without prejudice to the rights and obligations under Art.234 of the Treaty (which gives the ECJ jurisdiction to make preliminary rulings as to the Treaty etc.).

[97] Art.15(1). See also Commission Notice on the co-operation between the Commission and the courts of the EU Member States in the application of Articles 81 and 82 EC [2004] O.J. C101/54, paras 21 to 26.

[98] Art.15(1). See also Commission Notice on the co-operation between the Commisison and the courts of the EU Member States in the application of Articles 81 and 82 EC [2004] O.J. C101/54, paras 27 to 30.

[99] Modernisation Regulation, Art.15(3). See also Commission Notice on the co-operation between the Commisison and the courts of the EU Member States in the application of Arts 81 and 82 EC [2004] O.J. C101/54, paras 31 to 35.

[1] Practice Direction — Competition Law — Claims relating to the application of Arts 81 and 82 of the EC Treaty. See *Civil Procedure 2004* para.B12–001.

[2] Modernisation Regulation 1/2003, Art.6. For the previous case law, see, *e.g.* Case 127/73 *BRT v SABAM* [1974] E.C.R. 51, para.16; [1974] 2 C.M.L.R. 238. There are certain exceptions to the applicability of Arts 81 and 82, but these apply in the transport sector and are unlikely to be material to the rights covered in this work. For agreements notified to the Commission prior to March 13, 1962 (or the relevant date of accession) see *Copinger* (14th ed.), para.29–183, note 45.

[3] *Garden Cottage Foods v Milk Marketing Board* [1984] A.C. 130; [1983] 3 C.M.L.R. 43; *Bourgoin v Ministry of Agriculture* [1986] Q.B. 716; [1986] 1 C.M.L.R. 267; see also *Cutsforth v Mansfield Inns* [1986] 1 W.L.R. 588.

same applies in respect of a breach of Article 81.[4] The main issue in *Courage v Crehan* was whether a claimant was precluded from claiming damages under Article 81 if he was a party to the agreement and thus arguably *in pari delicto* with the defendant. The Court of Justice stated the general principle that in the absence of Community rules governing the matter, it is for the domestic legal system of each Member State to lay down the detailed procedural rules governing actions for safeguarding rights which individuals derive directly from Community law, provided that such rules are not less favourable than those governing similar domestic actions (the principle of equivalence) and that they do not render practically impossible or excessively difficult the exercise of rights conferred by Community law (the principle of effectiveness).[5] Having regard to these principles, the Court confirmed that a remedy in damages for breach of Article 81 was necessary in order to give the provision its full effectiveness.[6] The Court went on to hold that Article 81 precludes a rule of national law which disqualifies a claimant from claiming damages merely because he was a party to the agreement in question.[7] However, it held, Community law does not preclude a rule of national law which disqualifies a claimant from relying on his own unlawful acts to obtain damages where it is established that he bore significant responsibility for the distortion of competition.[8] In deciding whether the claimant bore such responsibility, it is relevant to consider such matters as the parties' respective bargaining positions, their conduct and whether the agreement in question was part of a network of agreements which had a cumulative effect on competition and to which the claimant was not a party.[9] It has now been held by the Court of Appeal that although the claim under Article 81 is a claim for breach of statutory duty, it is not necessary for the claimant to establish that the duty imposed by Article 81 exists in respect of the kind of loss he has suffered.[10] Otherwise, it appears that damages are assessed in accordance with the normal tort principles.[11] Again applying general principles, there seems no reason why the court should not grant an injunction to prevent a breach or threatened breach of Articles 81 or 82.

---

[4] Case C-453/99 *Courage Ltd v Crehan* [2001] E.C.R. I-6297, [2001] 5 C.M.L.R. 1058.

[5] Case C-453/99 *Courage Ltd v Crehan* [2001] E.C.R. I-6297, [2001] 5 C.M.L.R. 1058, para.29.

[6] Case C-453/99 *Courage Ltd v Crehan* [2001] E.C.R. I-6297, [2001] 5 C.M.L.R. 1058, para.26.

[7] Case C-453/99 *Courage Ltd v Crehan* [2001] E.C.R. I-6297, [2001] 5 C.M.L.R. 1058, para.36.

[8] Case C-453/99 *Courage Ltd v Crehan* [2001] E.C.R. I-6297, [2001] 5 C.M.L.R. 1058, para.36.

[9] Case C-453/99 *Courage Ltd v Crehan* [2001] E.C.R. I-6297, [2001] 5 C.M.L.R. 1058, paras 32–34, 36. The case concerned two beer-tie agreements to which Crehan (as publican) was a party. The judge held that he was not significantly responsible for the distortion of competition and this was upheld by the Court of Appeal [2004] EWCA Civ 637 at para.153: "He was not of course compelled to enter into any agreement with Inntrepreneur. To that extent he had bargaining power. But he was dealing with the single largest tied-house landlord in the United Kingdom who made it clear that the offending tying terms in their agreement were not negotiable. There was no equality of bargaining power in any real sense. Mr. Crehan was in a markedly weaker position than Inntrepreneur: if he wanted to lease the pubs he had to agree to the tie. In practice Inntrepreneur imposed the tie on him".

[10] *Crehan v Inntrepreneur Pub Company CPC* [2004] EWCA Civ 637 at paras 162 and 167. Thus, on the facts of that case, the tie agreements offended against Art.81 because they had adverse effects on the market for the distribution of beer. The claimant was not a beer distributor and had not suffered loss as a result of those adverse effects. His claim was that as a result of having entered into the tie agreements he was obliged to pay more for beer than independent competitors. Applying the normal principles in respect of damages for breach of statutory duty (as stated in *South Australia Asset Management Corporation v York Montague Ltd* [1997] A.C. 191 at 211), his loss would have been irrecoverable. The Court of Appeal held that as a matter of construction of the ECJ's decision and in accordance with the principle of effectiveness, this loss was nevertheless recoverable.

[11] In *Crehan v Inntrepreneur Pub Company CPC*, [2004] EWCA Civ 637, the Court of Appeal, in ruling on questions of causation and *quantum*, did not suggest otherwise: see at paras 169–183.

(iv) Application of Community competition law to copyright and related rights

29–210   **Introduction.** There are three main areas where Community competition law can affect the exercise of the rights covered in this work. The first is that Article 81(1) of the Treaty can affect the agreements by which a right holder assigns his rights or licenses others to make copies of the work in which he has those rights. The second is that Article 82 of the Treaty can restrict the ability of rightholders to decline to license others to copy the work, and can restrict the terms on which they can license, and their ability to discriminate between licensees, if they do grant a licence. Finally, both Articles 81 and 82 can affect the activities of copyright collecting societies.

29–211   **The effect of the competition rules on copyright.** The first holder of an industrial property right enjoys the right as a result of a legal status granted by a state to his invention, product or work, and such ownership itself has nothing to do with the elements of agreement, decision or concerted practice mentioned in Article 81(1).[12] However, the Court of Justice has made it clear that Article 81(1) will apply when there is an agreement for the exercise of that ownership or even its creation, and that, although the industrial property right, as a legal entity, will not fall within the class of agreements, decisions or concerted practices prohibited by Article 81(1), the exercise of that right may be subject to the prohibitions in the Treaty when it is the purpose, the means or the result of an agreement, decision or concerted practice.[13]

The Court of Justice in *Sirena SRL v Eda SRL*[14] held that the exercise of trade mark rights may come within the prohibition of Article 81(1) if it is "the object, means or consequence of an agreement", and that the agreement for these purposes could comprise an assignment. The Court held that the simultaneous assignment to several concessionaires of national trade mark rights for the same product may prejudice trade between Member States and distort competition in the Common Market, if this has the effect of re-establishing rigid frontiers between Member States. However, the Court of Justice went on to state that it was sufficient for Article 81(1) to apply, in that case to an agreement concluded before the date the Treaty took effect, if the effects of the agreement continued after that date. The judgment in *Sirena* left it unclear when an agreement such as an assignment could be considered as continuing to have its effects. What if the assignment were a bare assignment containing no other terms as to the future exercise of the right by the assignee, or if any such terms as it may have contained had become spent by the passing of time? In *EMI Records Ltd v CBS United Kingdom Ltd*[15] the Court of Justice repeated the principle that the exercise of a trade mark may fall within the prohibition of Article 82(1) if it were to manifest itself as the subject, means or consequence of a restrictive agreement. The Court then stated that an agreement could continue to produce its effects after it had formally ceased to be in force, but should only be regarded as doing so if, from the behaviour of the persons concerned, there might be inferred the existence of elements of concerted practice peculiar to the agreement and producing the same result as that envisaged by the agreement. The Court added that such an inference should not be drawn when the effects do not exceed those flowing from the mere exercise of the national trade-mark rights.

---

[12] Case 24/67 *Parke, Davis v Probel* [1968] E.C.R. 55; [1968] C.M.L.R. 47; Case 51/75 *EMI Records Ltd v CBS United Kingdom Ltd* [1968] E.C.R. 811.

[13] Case 144/81 *Keurkoop BV v Nancy Kean Gifts BV* [1982] E.C.R. 2853 at 2873; [1983] 2 C.M.L.R. 47.

[14] Case 40/70, [1971] E.C.R. 69; [1971] C.M.L.R. 260.

[15] Case 51/75, [1976] E.C.R. 811; [1976] 2 C.M.L.R. 235.

(a) *Application of Article 81 to assignments or licences of copyright and related rights: general issues.*

General issues. It might be thought that restrictions on the assignee[16] or licensee   **29–212**
as to their use or reproduction of the work in question under a copyright assignment or licence should raise few competition issues, given that in the absence of the agreement the assignee or licensee would not have been able to reproduce or use the work at all.[17] However, it is unlikely that such an approach can be relied upon. Thus, in *Windsurfing*,[18] the Court of Justice upheld the Commission's view (in a patents case) that a restriction on the licensee to the effect that he could mount the patented rig only on a particular type of surfboard was contrary to Article 81(1). It might also be thought that if a licensor or licensee would not have entered into an agreement at all in the absence of a particular clause (thus preventing the dissemination of the work at all), then that should be an argument against its being regarded as anti-competitive. That argument does carry some weight under Article 81(1), as the case of *Nungesser v Commission*[19] shows; it may also affect the analysis under Article 81(3).

(b) *Application of Article 81 to assignments of licences of copyright and related rights: relevant block exemptions*

The technology transfer block exemption ("TTBER"): background.[20] As has   **29–213**
been seen, Article 81(3) of the Treaty provides that Article 81(1) may be declared inapplicable in the case of any category of agreements between undertakings. Article 1(1)(b) of Regulation 19/65/EEC[21] provides that the Commission may by regulation declare that Article 81(1) shall not apply to categories of agreements to which only two undertakings are party and which include restrictions imposed in relation to the acquisition or use of industrial property rights, in particular of patents, utility models, designs or trade marks, or to the rights arising out of contracts for assignment of, or the right to use, a method of manufacture or knowledge relating to the use or application of industrial processes. In 1984, pursuant to this provision, the Commission made a Regulation in respect of patent licensing agreements.[22] In 1988, it made a further Regulation in respect of know-how licensing agreements.[23] In 1996, these provisions were repealed and replaced by a new Regulation covering technology transfer agreements.[24] This Regulation in turn has now been repealed and replaced with effect from May 1, 2004 but subject to transitional provisions.[25] The aim of the new Regulation is to simplify the regulatory framework and its application. The Commission considered it ap-

---

[16] In *Panayiotou v Sony Music Entertainment (UK) Ltd* [1994] E.M.L.R. 229 at 425–426, Jonathan Parker J. drew a distinction between a full assignment (which he did not regard as being concerned with the exercise of rights but with their transfer) and a licence or a partial assignment. He therefore concluded that Art.295 of the EC Treaty protected the full assignment at issue in that case from Art.81(1), *sed quaere*.

[17] Compare, under the UK Restrictive Trade Practices Act 1976, *Ravenseft Properties v DGFT* [1978] Q.B. 352, where it was held that a restriction of this type upon the licensee or assignee was not a relevant restriction for the purposes of that Act. The Commission's 1964 Patent Notice reflected this approach until it was withdrawn in 1984.

[18] Case 193/83, [1986] E.C.R. 611; [1986] 3 C.M.L.R. 489.

[19] Case 258/76, [1982] E.C.R. 2015; [1983] 1 C.M.L.R. 278.

[20] Commission Regulation 772/2004/EC [2004] O.J. L123/11. For the previous law, which remains in force at the time in writing so far as concerns the EEA, see *Copinger* (14th ed.), para.29–189.

[21] [1965] O.J. 036/533 as amended by Council Regulation 1215/99/EC [1999] O.J. L 148/1.

[22] Reg.2349/84/EEC.

[23] Reg.556/89/EEC.

[24] Reg.240/96 EC [1996] O.J. L31/2. See *Copinger* (14th ed.), para.29–189.

[25] Commission Regulation No. 772/2004/EC on the application of Art.81(3) to categories of technology transfer agreements [2004] O.J. L123/1, "the TTBER". Art.9 repeals Reg.240/96 EC.

propriate to move away from the previous approach which involved listing exempted clauses and to place greater emphasis on defining the categories of agreements which are exempted up to a certain level of market power and on specifying the restrictions or clauses which are not to be contained in such agreements. The Commission considered that this was consistent with an "economics-based" approach which assesses the impact of agreements on the relevant market.[26] The block exemption of categories of agreement is based on a presumption that to the extent that they are caught by Article 81(1) they fulfil the four conditions laid down by Article 81(3).[27] Block exempted agreements are legally valid and enforceable. They can only be prohibited for the future and only on withdrawal of the block exemption by the Commission or a national competition authority. They cannot be prohibited under Article 81 by national courts in the context of private litigation.[28]

29–214   **The TTBER: direct application to the rights covered in this Work.** The 1996 block exemption did not apply to licences of intellectual property rights other than patents unless they were ancillary to patent or know-how licences.[29] This caused a lack of certainty in the computer software field, which the Commission considered particularly regrettable in view of the economic importance of software products.[30] Accordingly, for the first time, the technology transfer block exemption applies to copyright licences, albeit only to licences relating to computer software. Since the Regulation applies to patent licensing agreements and for these purposes, the term "patent" includes designs and semiconductor topographies,[31] the Regulation also applies to licensing agreements in respect of these rights as well.

29–215   **The TTBER: application by analogy to the rights covered in this work.** Moreover, although the block exemption does not apply to copyright other than software copyright, the Commission has made clear that as a general rule it will apply the principles set out in the Regulation to copyright licences which are granted for the purpose of the reproduction and distribution of copies of a copyright work, that is, the production of copies for resale.[32] On the other hand, the Commission does not intend to apply the TTBER by way of analogy to rights in performances or "other rights related to copyright" (this appears to be a reference

---

Art.10 provides that where an agreement was in force on April 30, 2004 and was exempt from Art.81 under Reg.240/96 EC on that date, but does not satisfy the conditions of the TTBER, Art.81(1) shall nevertheless not apply to it until March 31, 2006.

[26] TTBER, Recital 4. See also the Commission's Evaluation Report on Reg.240/96 EC, COM(2001) 786 final.

[27] Guidelines on the application of Art.81 of the EC Treaty to technology transfer agreements [2004] O.J. C101/2 ("TTBER Guidelines"), para.35.

[28] TTBER, para.34. As to withdrawal, see para. 29–229, below.

[29] Reg.240/96, Art.1(1).

[30] The Commission's Evaluation Report COM(2001) 786 final, refers to two forms of uncertainty (para.114). First, a single licence often includes a complex package of intellectual property rights and it may be difficult to determine what is the preponderant element of the licence. Secondly, while the Commission was generally inclined to treat copyright licences in the same way as patent licences (as in *Sicasov* [1999] O.J. L4/27, [1999] C.M.L.R. 192), it had never clearly stated that all the principles applicable to patents were also applicable to copyright. The Report goes on to say that this is of particular importance to the software industry, because many software licensing agreements do not fall within the block exemption for vertical agreements (Reg.2790/99), for example if they involve distribution licences where the distributor duplicates the software and provides the physical medium on which the program is stored; or so-called "value-added" licences, whereby the software producer allows the licensee to modify the software for particular purposes, such as the creation of a local language version (*ibid.*, para.115).

[31] TTBER, Art.1(h).

[32] TTBER Guidelines, para.51.

to copyright in sound recordings and broadcasts).[33] Such rights are considered to raise different considerations. The Commission's reasoning is not always easy to follow. According to the Commission, in the case of "the various rights related to performances", value is created not by the reproduction and sale of copies of a product but by each individual performance of the protected work. Such exploitation can take various forms including the performance, showing or renting of protected material such as films, music or sporting events.[34] The Commission goes on to emphasise the importance of taking account of "the specificities of the work and the way in which it is exploited".[35] In that context, the Commission believes that resale restrictions may give rise to fewer competition concerns,[36] while particular concerns may arise where licensors impose on their licensees to extend to each of the licensors more favourable conditions obtained by one of them.[37]

The TTBER: general. Recital 5 to the Regulation states that technology transfer agreements usually improve economic efficiency and are usually pro-competitive because they can reduce duplication of research and development, strengthen the incentive for initial research and development, spur incremenal innovation, facilitate diffusion and generate product market competition. Accordingly, Article 2 of the Regulation declares that Article 81(1) of the Treaty does not apply to technology transfer agreements entered into between two undertakings[38] permitting the production of contract products (that is, products produced with the licensed technology).[39] The term "technology transfer agreement" means a patent licensing agreement, a know-how[40] licensing agreement, a software copyright licensing agreement or a mixed patent, know-how and software copyright licensing agreement. For these purposes, the term "patent" includes designs and semiconducter topographies.[41] Such agreements are included even if they contain provisions which relate to the sale and purchase of products or the licensing of other intellectual property rights provided that those provisions do not constitute the primary object of the agreement and are directly related to the production of the contract products.[42] The definition also includes assignments of patents, know-how, software copyright or a combination thereof where part of the risk associ-

29–216

---

[33] TTBER Guidelines, para.52. When used by the Commission, the term "related rights" usually refers to the rights granted by the 1961 Rome Convention for the Protection of Performers, Producers of Phonograms and Broadcasting Organisations: see below, paras 24–88 *et seq.*, above.

[34] Presumably a protected sporting event is an event in respect of which exclusive broadcasting rights have been granted.

[35] Citing Case 262/81 *Coditel SA v Ciné Vog Films SA* [1982] E.C.R. 3381; [1983] 1 C.M.L.R. 49, discussed at para. 29–240, below.

[36] The reason for this is not stated.

[37] Again, the Commission does not elaborate.

[38] In the TTBER Guidelines, the Commission notes that the block exemption does not apply to agreements between more than two undertakings but states that the principles in the Regulation will be applied to agreements between more than two undertakings which are of the same nature as those covered by the block exemption (paras 39 and 40).

[39] TTBER, Art.1(f). The term "product" means a good or service, including both intermediary and final goods or services. In the TTBER Guidelines, the Commission notes that in order to be covered by the block exemption the licence must permit the licensee to exploit the licensed technology (para.41). It goes on to say that the exemption does not cover "technology pools" (agreements whereby the parties agree to pool their respective technologies and license them as a package or authorise a third party to license them on (*ibid.*)). Guidance as to technology pools is given in the TTBER Guidelines at paras 210 to 235.

[40] "Know-how" is defined a a package of non-patented practical information resulting from experience and testing, which is secret, substantial and identified: TTBER, Art.1(i).

[41] See above, para. 29–214.

[42] TTBER, Art.1(b). Thus, according to the Commission, an agreement containing provision for the sale and purchase of products would be included in the exemption where, for example, the tied products take the form of equipment or process input which is specifically tailored to exploit the licensed technology efficiently: TTBER Guidelines, para.49. Similarly, where an agreement

ated with the exploitation of the technology remains with the assignor.[43] The exemption applies to the extent that the agreement contains restrictions on competition falling within Article 81(1) and as long as to the intellectual right in question has not expired, lapsed or been declared invalid or (in the case of know-how) ceased to be secret.[44]

29–217   **The TTBER: "competing undertakings".** This term, which appears regularly in the TTBER, is defined in Article 1(j) to mean undertakings which compete on the relevant technology market and/or the relevant product market. There are lengthy sub-definitions as follows. Competing undertakings on the relevant technology market are undertakings which license out competing technologies without infringing each others' intellectual property rights. The relevant technology market includes technologies which are regarded by the licensees as interchangeable with or substitutable for the licensed technology, by reason of the technologies' characteristics, royalties and intended use.[45] Potential competition on the technology market is not taken into account for these purposes.[46] Competing undertakings on the relevant product market are undertakings which, in the absence of the technology transfer agreement, are both active on the relevant product and geographic market(s) on which the contract products are sold without infringing each others' intellectual property rights; or would on realistic grounds undertake the necessary additional investments or other necessary switching costs so that they could timely enter, without infringing each others' intellectual property rights, the relevant product and geographic markets in response to a small and permanent increase in relative prices (thus, to this extent, potential competition is relevant).[47] The relevant product market comprises products which are regarded by the buyers as interchangeable with or substitutable for the contract products, by reason of the products' characteristics, prices and intended use.[48]

29–218   **The TTBER: "reciprocal agreements".** This term also appears frequently in the TTBER. An agreement is reciprocal where the parties grant each other in the same or separate contracts a patent, know-how or software copyright licence or a mixed patent, know-how or software copyright licence and where these licences concern competing technologies or can be used for the production of competing products.[49] An agreement is not reciprocal merely because it contains a grant back obligation or because the licensee licenses back its own improvements to the licensed technology.[50] An agreement is non-reciprocal where one party grants the other a patent, know-how or software copyright licence or a mixed patent, know-how or software copyright licence or where the parties grant each other

---

contains a provision for a licence in respect of copyright other than software copyright, it will only be block exempted to the extent that the copyright licence serves to enable the licensee better to exploit the licensed technology: *ibid.*, para.50.

[43] TTBER, Art.1(b). A particular example of this is stated to be where the consideration is dependent on the turnover obtained by the assignee in respect of products produced with the assigned technology, the quantity of such products produced or the number of operations carried out using the technology: *ibid.*

[44] TTBER, Art.2. Where the know-how becomes publicly known as a result of action by the licensee, the exemption applies for the duration of the agreement: *ibid.*

[45] TTBER, Art.1(j)(i).

[46] TTBER Guidelines, para.66.

[47] TTBER, Art.1(j)(ii). TTBER Guidelines, para.67.

[48] TTBER, Art.1(j)(ii).

[49] , TTBER Art.1(c). The TTBER Guidelines use the term "cross-licensing agreement": para.78.

[50] TTBER Guidelines, para.78.

such a licence but those licences do not concern competing technologies and cannot be used for the production of competing products.[51]

The TTBER: market share thresholds. The block exemption of restrictive **29–219**
agreements is subject to market share thresholds. Outside the "safe harbour" created by these thresholds, individual assessment is required. However, the fact
that market shares exceed the thresholds does not give rise to any presumption
that the agreement is caught by Article 81(1) or does not fulfil the conditions of
Article 81(3).[52] The threshold depends on whether the parties to the agreement
are competing. Where they are competing, the exemption only applies if their
combined market share is less than 20 per cent on the affected relevant technology and product market.[53] Where the parties are not competing, the exemption
applies if the market share of each of the parties does not exceed 30 per cent on
the affected relevant technology and product market.[54] The Regulation contains
specific rules as to the calculation of market share.[55]

The TTBER: hardcore restrictions: general. The TTBER contains a list of so- **29–220**
called "hardcore" restrictions, which the Commission considers to be restrictive
of competition by their very object.[56] Where a technology transfer agreement
contains a hardcore restriction, the agreement as a whole falls outside the block
exemption; for the purposes of the Regulation, such restrictions cannot be
severed.[57] The list of hardcore restrictions depends on whether the parties are or
are not competing undertakings.[58] Where the parties to the agreement are not
competing at the time it is concluded but become competitors afterwards, they
are to be treated as if they are competing undertakings for the full length of the
agreement unless it is materially amended.[59] Where the parties are competing
undertakings, the exemption does not apply to agreements which directly or
indirectly, in isolation or in combination with other factors under the parties'
control, have any of the following objects[60]: restrictions on the prices at which
the product is to be sold[61]; the limitation of output[62]; the allocation of markets or
customers (but there are numerous exceptions to this)[63]; and the restriction of the
licensee's ability to exploit its own technology or of the ability of any party to
carry out research and development unless the latter is indispensable to prevent
the disclosure of the licensed know-how to third parties.[64] Where the parties are
not competing undertakings,[65] the exemption does not apply to agreements which
directly or indirectly, in isolation or in combination with other factors under the
control of the parties have any of the following objects: first, the restriction of a

---

[51] TTBER, Art.1(d).
[52] TTBER Guidelines, para.65.
[53] TTBER, Art.3(1). For these purposes, the market share of a party on the relevant technology market(s) is defined in terms of the presence of the licensed technology on the relevant product market(s). A licensor's market share is the combined market share on the relevant product market of the contract products produced by the licensor and its licensees: TTBER, Art.3(3).
[54] TTBER, Art.3(2). For the definition of market share, see the previous footnote.
[55] TTBER, Art.8.
[56] TTBER Guidelines, para.14.
[57] TTBER Guidelines, para.75.
[58] For when undertakings are competing, see above, para. 29–217.
[59] TTBER, Art.4(3).
[60] TTBER, Art.4(1). These are analogous to the so-called "blacklisted" restrictions which appeared in Art.3 of Reg. 240/96/EC (see *Copinger*, (14th ed.), para.29–189). See generally the TTBER Guidelines, paras 77 to 95.
[61] TTBER, Art.4(1)(a). See para. 29–221, below.
[62] TTBER, Art.4(1)(b). See para. 29–222, below.
[63] TTBER, Art.4(1)(c). See para. 29–223, below.
[64] TTBER, Art.4(1)(d). See para. 29–224, below.
[65] For the meaning of the term "competing undertakings", see para. 29–217, above.

party's ability to determine its prices when selling products to third parties (but this is without prejudice to the possibility of imposing a maximum sale price or recommending a sale price, provided it does not amount to a fixed or minimum sale price as a result of pressure from, or incentives offered by, any of the parties)[66]; secondly, the restriction of the territory into which, or the customers to whom, the licensee may passively sell the contract products (but there are numerous exceptions to this)[67]; and thirdly, the restriction of active or passive sales to end-users by a licensee which is a member of a selective distribution system and which operates at the retail level (but this is without prejudice to the possibility of prohibiting a member of the system from operating out of an unauthorised place of establishment).[68]

29–221   **Competing undertakings: price fixing**. The exemption does not apply where the agreement has as its object the restriction of a party's ability to determine its prices when selling products to third parties,[69] including products incorporating the licensed technology.[70] According to the Commission,[71] it is immaterial whether the agreement concerns fixed, minimum or maximum prices. Direct restrictions which will offend include direct agreement on the price to be charged and direct agreement on a price list with certain allowed maximum rebates. Price-fixing may also be implemented indirectly by applying disincentives to deviate from an agreed price level, for example by providing that the royalty rate will increase if product prices are reduced below a certain level. However, an obligation to pay a certain minimum royalty does not in itself amount to price-fixing.[72] Where royalties are calculated on the basis of individual product sales, the amount of the royalty has a direct impact on product prices. Accordingly, competitors can use cross-licensing with reciprocal running royalties as a means of co-ordinating prices on downstream product markets. The Commission will only treat such cross licences as price-fixing where the agreement is devoid of competitive purpose.[73] The restriction on price fixing also applies to agreements whereby royalties are calculated on the basis of all products sold irrespective of whether the licensed technology is being used.[74] Such agreements restrict competition because they raise the cost of using the licensee's own technology and reduce competition which would otherwise have existed.[75] Exceptionally, however, Article 81(3) may apply to such an agreement, for example where, in the absence of the restriction, it would be impossible for the licensor to calculate and monitor royalties because the licensor's technology leaves no visible trace in the final product and there are no practicable alternative monitoring methods.[76]

29–222   **Competing undertakings: limitation of output**. The exemption does not apply where the agreement has as its object the limitation of output,[77] that is a restric-

---

[66] TTBER, Art.4(2)(a). See below, para. 29–225.

[67] TTBER, Art.4(2)(b). See below, paras 29–226 to 29–227.

[68] TTBER, Art.4(2)(c). See below, para. 29–227.

[69] TTBER, Art.4(1)(a).

[70] TTBER Guidelines, para.79.

[71] TTBER Guidelines, para.79.

[72] TTBER Guidelines, para.79.

[73] TTBER Guidelines, para.80.

[74] TTBER Guidelines, para.81. Such agreements are also caught by Art.4(1)(d): see para. 29–224, below.

[75] See the *Windsurfing* case, Case 193/83 *Windsurfing International v Commission* [1986] E.C.R. 611; [1986] 3 C.M.L.R. 278.

[76] TTBER Guidelines, para.81.

[77] TTBER, Art.4(1)(b).

tion on how much a party may produce or sell.[78] However, limitations on the output of contract products imposed on the licensee in a non-reciprocal agreement or imposed on only one of the licensees in a reciprocal agreement are permissible.[79] The effect is that the TTBER identifies as hardcore restrictions reciprocal output restrictions on both parties and output restrictions on the licensor in respect of his own technology.[80] According to the Commission, when competitors agree to impose reciprocal output limitations, the object and likely effect of the agreement is to reduce output in the market. The same is true of agreements which reduce the parties' incentive to expand output, for example by obliging each other to make payments if a certain level of output is exceeded.[81] However, a "one-way" restriction on the licensee does not necessarily lead to a lower output. Rather, it is likely that the agreement leads to a real integration of complementary technologies or an efficiency enhancing integration of the licensor's superior technology with the licensee's productive assets.[82] Where an output restriction is imposed on only one of the licensees in a non-reciprocal agreement, the Commission considers that this is likely to reflect the higher value of the technology licensed by one of the parties and may serve to promote pro-competitive licensing.[83]

Competing undertakings: allocation of markets or customers. The exemption does not apply where the agreement has as its object the allocation of markets and customers.[84] This applies whether or not the licensee remains free to use its own technology.[85] However, there are numerous exceptions: first, an obligation on the licensee or licensees to produce with the licensed technology only within one or more technical fields of use or one or more product markets[86]; secondly, an obligation on either party to a non-reciprocal agreement not to produce with the licensed technology within one or more technical fields of use or one or more product markets or one or more exclusive territories reserved for the other[87]; thirdly, an obligation on the licensor not to license the technology to another licensee in a particular territory[88]; fourthly, the restriction in a non-reciprocal agreement of active or passive sales by either party into the exclusive territory or to the exclusive customer group reserved for the other party[89]; fifthly, the restriction in a non-reciprocal agreement of active sales by the licensee into the

29–223

---

[78] TTBER Guidelines, para.82.

[79] TTBER, Art.4(1)(b). For what is a reciprocal agreement, see above, para. 29–218. In general, the hardcore list is stricter for reciprocal agreements than for non-reciprocal agreements: TTBER Guidelines, para.78.

[80] TTBER Guidelines, para.82.

[81] TTBER Guidelines, para.82.

[82] TTBER Guidelines, para.83.

[83] TTBER Guidelines, para.83.

[84] TTBER, Art.4(1)(c).

[85] TTBER Guidelines, para.85. This is because once the licensee has tooled up to use the licensor's technology it may be costly to maintain a separate production line using another technology in order to serve customers covered by the restrictions. Furthermore, given the anti-competitive potential of the restraint, the licensee may have little incentive to produce under its own technology: *ibid.*

[86] It is, however, a condition of the exemption that the field of use restrictions do not go beyond the scope of the licensed technologies: TTBER Guidelines, para.90. It is also a condition that licensees are not limited to use of their own technology: TTBER, Art.4(1)(d): see para. 29–224, below.

[87] For what is a reciprocal agreement, see para. 29–218 above. The reason for this exception is that the purpose of the agreement may be to give the licensee an incentive to invest in and develop the licensed technology rather than to share markets: TTBER Guidelines, para.86.

[88] This exception permits the licensor to appoint a sole licensee in a particular territory. The exemption applies whether or not the agreement is reciprocal because it does not affect the parties' abilities fully to exploit their own technology in the respective territories: TTBER Guidelines, para.88.

[89] Again, the reason for this exception is that the purpose of the agreement may be to give the licensee an incentive to invest in and develop the licensed technology rather than to share markets:

exclusive territory or to the exclusive customer group allocated by the licensor to another licensee provided the latter was not a competing undertaking of the licensor at the time of the grant of its own licence[90]; sixthly, a "captive use restriction", that is an obligation on the licensee to produce the contract products only for its own use, provided the licensee is not restricted in selling the contract products actively and passively as spare parts for its own products[91]; and seventhly, an obligation on the licensee in a non-reciprocal agreement to produce the contract products only for a particular customer where the licence was granted in order to create an alternative source of supply for that customer.[92]

29–224   **Competing undertakings: restrictions on licensee's ability to exploit its own technology and on research and development.** The exemption does not apply where the agreement has as its object the restriction of the licensee's ability to exploit its own technology.[93] When restrictions are imposed on the licensee's use of its own technology the competitiveness of that technology is reduced.[94] Accordingly, when the licensee is using its own technology, it is not to be subject to limitations as to where it produces or sells, how much it produces or sells or at what price it sells; it must not be obliged to pay royalties on products produced with its technology; and must not be restricted in licensing its technology to third parties.[95] The exemption is also inapplicable where the agreement has as its object the restriction of either party's ability to carry out research and development, unless that restriction is indispensable to prevent the disclosure of the licensed know-how to third parties.[96] This applies whether or not the restriction concerns the licensed technology.[97] The Commission considers that each party must be free to carry out independent research and development.[98] However, it considers that the mere fact that the parties agree to provide each other with future improvements of their respective technologies does not amount to a restriction on independent research and development.[99] Restrictions imposed to protect know-how must be necessary and proportionate. For example, where the agreement designates particular employees to be trained in and responsible for the use of the

---

TTBER Guidelines, para.87. Active selling to an exclusive territory or group involves making active approaches to customers in that territory or group or establishing a warehouse or distribution outlet in that territory; passive selling to an exclusive territory or group involves making supplies to that territory or group in response to unsolicited requests together with general advertising which reaches that territory, provided it is a reasonable way to reach the seller's own public or the public in non-exclusive territories: see para.50 of the Commission's Guidelines on Vertical Restraints [2000] O.J. C291/1.

[90] The Commission believes that such restrictions are likely to induce the licensee to exploit the licensed technology more efficiently: TTBER Guidelines, para.89. However, if the licensees agree between themselves not to sell into certain territories or to certain customer groups, that agreement amounts to a cartel: *ibid.*

[91] Captive use restrictions are permitted because they may be necessary to encourage the dissemination of technology, particularly between competitors: TTBER Guidelines, para.92. Thus, where the contract product is a component, the licensee can be obliged to produce that component only for incorporation in its own products: *ibid.* However, the licensee must not be prohibited from supplying third parties that perform after-sale services on the contract products: *ibid.*

[92] The Commission considers that the potential of such agreements to share markets is limited and that it cannot be assumed that the agreement will cause the licensee to cease exloiting his own technology: TTBER Guidelines, para.93. The Commission points out that it is not a condition for the operation for this exception that only one such licence is granted and that this exception includes situations where more than one person is licensed to supply the same specified customer: *ibid.*

[93] TTBER, Art.4(1)(d).

[94] TTBER Guidelines, para.95.

[95] TTBER Guidelines, para.95.

[96] TTBER, Art.4(1)(d).

[97] TTBER Guidelines, para.94.

[98] TTBER Guidelines, para.94.

[99] TTBER Guidelines, para.94.

licensed know-how, it may be sufficient to oblige the licensee to prohibit those employees from being involved in research and development with third parties.[1]

Non-competing undertakings: price-fixing. The exemption does not cover agreements between non-competitors which have as their object the restriction of a party's ability to determine its prices when selling products to third parties.[2] However, this is stated to be without prejudice to the possibility of imposing a maximum sale price or recommending a sale price, provided it does not amount to a fixed or minimum sale price as a result of pressure from, or incentives offered by any of the parties.[3] This category of hardcore restriction includes agreements that directly establish the selling price. It also includes indirect price-fixing, for example by fixing the margin, fixing the maximum level of discounts, linking the sales price to that of a competitor, threats, intimidation, warnings, penalties or contract terminations in relation to observance of a given price level.[4] The Commission notes that direct or indirect means of price-fixing can be made more effective when combined with measures to identify price-cutting, such as the implementation of a price-monitoring system or imposing an obligation on licensees to report price deviations.[5] It also notes that price-fixing may be made more effective when combined with measures that reduce the licensee's incentive to reduce its selling price, for example where the licensor obliges the licensee to apply a most-favoured-customer clause.[6] The Commission goes on to state that the same means can be used to make maximum or recommended prices work as fixed or minimum selling prices, but that the provision of a list of recommended prices or the imposition of a maximum price is not considered in itself as leading to fixed or minimum prices.[7]

29–225

Non-competing undertakings: the general rule as to territorial restrictions. The exemption does not cover agreements between non-competitors which have as their object the restriction of the territory into which, or the customers to whom, the licensee may passively sell the contract products.[8] Passive sales restrictions may be the result of direct obligations (including an obligation to refer orders from particular customers or customers in particular territories to other licensees) or of indirect obligations aimed at inducing the licensee to refrain from making such sales, such as financial incentives or the implementation of a monitoring system aimed at verifying the effective destination of the licensed products.[9] The Commission notes that quantity sales may be an indirect means to restrict passive sales. However, it will not assume that this is the case unless the limitations are used to implement an underlying market partitioning agreement. Indications of such an agreement include: the adjustment of quantities over time to cover only local demand; the combination of quantity limitations and an obligation to sell minimum quantities in the territory; minimum royalty obligations linked to sales in the territory; differentiated royalty rates depending on the destination of the products; and the monitoring of the destination of products sold

29–226

---

[1] TTBER Guidelines, para.94.
[2] TTBER Art.4(2)(a).
[3] TTBER Art.4(2)(a).
[4] TTBER Guidelines, para.97.
[5] TTBER Guidelines, para.97.
[6] TTBER Guidelines, para.97.
[7] TTBER Guidelines, para.97.
[8] TTBER, Art.4(2)(b). For the meaning of the term "passive sales", see notes to para. 29–223, above.
[9] TTBER Guidelines, para.98.

by individual licensees.[10] It will be seen that sales restrictions on the licensor are not treated as hardcore restrictions. The same applies in general to restrictions on active sales by the licensee (other than by a licensee in a selective distribution system).[11] The block exemption of restrictions on active selling is based on the assumption that such restrictions promote investments, non-price competition and improvements in the quality of services provided by licensees by solving "free-rider" problems and "hold-up" problems.[12]

29–227   **Non-competing undertakings: exceptions to the general rule as to territorial restrictions.** There are the following exceptions to the general rule. First, the restriction of passive sales into an exclusive territory or to an exclusive customer group reserved for the licensor.[13] Secondly, the restriction of such sales into an exclusive territory or customer group allocated by the licensor to another licensee during the first two years that that other licensee is selling the contract products in that territory or to that contract group.[14] Thirdly, an obligation on the licensee to produce the contract products only for its own use (provided that the licensee is not restricted in selling the contract products actively and passively as spare parts of its own products).[15] Fourthly, the obligation to produce the contract products only for a particular customer, where the licence was granted in order to create an alternative source of supply for that customer.[16] Fifthly, the restriction of sales to end-users by a licensee operating at the wholesale level.[17] Finally, the restriction of sales to unauthorised distributors by the members of a selective distribution system.[18]

29–228   **The TTBER: excluded restrictions.**[19] The Regulation also lists four types of restriction which are not block exempted and require individual assessment.[20] Unlike the hardcore restrictions, these restrictions may be severed.[21] The rationale behind the exclusion of the first three of the four restrictions is to avoid block

---

[10] TTBER Guidelines, para.98.

[11] TTBER Guidelines, para.99.

[12] TTBER Guidelines, para.99. A "free-rider" problem arises if a licensee takes a free ride on the investment of another in building up the brand and creating a demand for it. A "hold-up" problem arises where a licensee will not commit the investment necessary to sell the contract products without the protection of an exclusive distribution agreement, usually because of fears that its business will be dominated or expropriated by the licensor.

[13] TTBER, Art.4(2)(b)(i). It is presumed that such restraints promote pro-competitive dissemination of technology and the integration of such technology into the production assets of the licensee: TTBER Guidelines, para.100.

[14] TTBER, Art.4(2)(b)(ii). Given the amount of investment often required in order for a licensee to start up in a particular territory, the Commission believes that it is often the case that a licensee would not enter into the licence agreement without protection for a certain period of time against sales into its territory from other licensees: TTBER Guidelines, para.101.

[15] TTBER, Art.4(2)(b)(iii). The effect of this is that where the product is a component, the licensee can be obliged to use it only for incorporation into its own products and not to sell it to other producers. However, the licensee must be able to sell the products as spare parts for its own products and therefore to be able to supply third parties that perform after sales services on those products: TTBER Guidelines, para.102.

[16] TTBER, Art.4(2)(b)(iv).

[17] TTBER, Art.4(2)(b)(v).

[18] TTBER, Art.4(2)(b)(vi). This permits the licensor to impose on licensees an obligation to form part of a selective distribution system. However, in that case licensees must be allowed to sell to end users (unless restricted to a wholesale function under Art.4(2)(b)(v)): *ibid.*, Art.4(2)(c); TTBER Guidelines, para.105. The Commission notes that the agreements between the licensee and its buyers must comply with the Vertical agreements block exemption Regulation (EC 2790/1999): *ibid.* See below, paras 29–234 *et seq.*

[19] See generally TTBER Guidelines, paras 107 to 116.

[20] TTBER, Art.5.

[21] TTBER Guidelines, para.107.

exemption of agreements which may reduce licensees' incentives to innovate.[22] They are as follows. First, any direct or indirect obligation on the licensee to grant an exclusive licence to the licensor or to a third party designated by the licensor in respect of its own severable improvements to or its own new applications of the licensed technology.[23] Secondly, any direct or indirect obligation on the licensee to assign, in whole or in part, to the licensor or a third party designated by the licensor, rights to its own severable improvements to or its own new applications of the licensed technology.[24] Thirdly, any direct or indirect obligation on the licensee not to challenge the validity of intellectual property rights which the licensor holds in the common market (without prejudice to the possibility of providing for termination of the technology transfer agreement in the event that the licensee challenges the validity of one or more of the licensed intellectual property rights).[25] The fourth exclusion applies where the parties are not competing and concerns any direct or indirect obligation limiting the licensee's ability to exploit its own technology or limiting the ability of any of the parties to the agreement to carry out research and development, unless the latter restriction is indispensable to prevent the disclosure of the licensed know-how to third parties.[26]

Withdrawal and disapplication of the TTBER. In certain circumstances, the benefit of the Regulation may be withdrawn by the Commission if it finds in any particular case that an agreement to which it applies nevertheless has effects which are incompatible with Article 81(3).[27] Particular examples given in the Regulation are as follows: first, where the access of third parties' technologies to the market is restricted, for example by the cumulative effect of parallel networks of similar restrictive agreements restricting licensees from using third parties' technologies; secondly, where potential licensees' access to the market is restricted, for example by the cumulative effect of parallel networks of similar restrictive agreements prohibiting licensors from licensing to other licensees; and third where without any objectively valid reason, the parties do not exploit the licensed technology.[28] National competition authorities are given an analogous power of withdrawal where a particular agreement has effects which are incompatible with Article 81(3) in the territory of a Member State or a part thereof, which has all the chracteristics of a distinct geographic market.[29] The Commission is also given power by Regulation to declare that where parallel networks of similar technology transfer agreements cover more than 50 per cent

29–229

---

[22] TTBER Guidelines, para.108.

[23] TTBER, Art.5(1)(a). Non-exclusive grant-backs are considered to promote innovation: TTBER Guidelines, para.109.

[24] TTBER, Art.5(1)(b).

[25] TTBER, Art.5(1)(c). Intellectual property rights are defined as including "industrial property rights, know-how, copyright and neighbouring rights": *ibid.*, Art.1(g). Note that in *Neilson Hordell / Reichmark* Commission XIIth Report on Competition Policy, points 88–89, the Commission had objected to a no-challenge clause. The Commission's reasoning is that invalid intellectual property stifles innovation and the licensee is likely to be in the best position to say whether a particular right is or is not valid: TTBER Guidelines, para.112. However, the Commission takes a favourable view of no-challenge clauses relating to know-how where once disclosed it is likely to be impossible or very difficult to recover the licensed know-how. In such a case, a no-challenge clause promotes innovation, in particular by allowing weaker licensors to license stronger licensees without fear of a challenge once the know-how has been absorbed by the licensee: *ibid.*

[26] TTBER, Art.5(2); *cf.* para. 29–224, above. See also TTBER Guidelines paras 114–116.

[27] TTBER, Art.6, applying Art.29(1) of the Modernisation Regulation 1/2003. TTBER Guidelines paras 117 to 122.

[28] TTBER, Art.6(1)(a) to (c).

[29] TTBER, Art.6(2).

of a relevant market, the block exemption Regulation does not apply to technology transfer agreements containing specific restraints relating to that market.[30]

29–230   **Non-block exempted agreements: the TTBER Guidelines.** Where a technology transfer agreement is not block exempted, then unless it contains hardcore restrictions, there is no presumption that it infringes Article 81, and individual assessment is necessary.[31] The Commission has issued guidelines as to how it will approach such agreements. As is the case with the TTBER, the Commission will apply the guidelines by analogy to copyright licensing, but not to the licensing of rights in performances or other related rights.[32] The guidelines are lengthy and detailed and accordingly no more than a brief sketch will be presented here.

29–231   **A further safe harbour.** The guidelines make clear that outside the area of hardcore restrictions, Article 81 is unlikely to be infringed where there are four or more independently controlled technologies in addition to the technologies controlled by the parties to the agreement, provided that these independent technologies may be substitutable for the licensed technology at a comparable cost to the user.[33] Where this condition is met, there is a further "safe harbour". Otherwise, individual assessment is required.

29–232   **Individual assessment: general.** The guidelines begin by emphasising the need to take due account of the way in which competition operates on the market in question. The Commission considers the following factors to be particularly relevant in this respect: the nature of the agreement; the market position of the parties; the market position of competitors; the market position of buyers of the licensed products; entry barriers; and the maturity of the market. This list is not, however, exhaustive.[34] The guidelines go on to note the potential negative effects on competition which may arise from restrictive technology transfer agreements. They are stated to be as follows (again the list is not exhaustive): the reduction of inter-technology competition on a technology market or on a market for the products in question; the foreclosure of competitors by raising their costs, restricting their access to essential inputs or otherwise raising barriers to entry; and the reduction of intra-technology competition between undertakings that produce products on the basis of the same technology.[35] The guidelines then note that even restrictive licence agreements mostly also produce pro-competitive effects in the form of efficiencies which may outweigh their anti-competitive effects.[36] There follows a detailed discussion of when such efficiencies will be sufficient to satisfy Article 81(3).[37]

29–233   **Types of clause covered by the guidelines.** The guidelines go on to discuss specific types of clause. First, there is a non-exhaustive list of obligations which the Commission believes are generally not restrictive of competition within the meaning of Article 81. The list, which is similar to but shorter than the so-called "white list" contained in the previous block exemption regulation,[38] is as follows: confidentiality obligations; obligations not to use the licensed technology after the expiry of the agreement, provided that the technology remains valid and in

[30] TTBER, Art.7(1). TTBER Guidelines paras 123 to 129.
[31] TTBER Guidelines, para.37.
[32] TTBER Guidelines, para.52.
[33] TTBER Guidelines, para.131.
[34] TTBER Guidelines, para.132.
[35] para.141.
[36] para.146.
[37] paras 146 to 152.
[38] See *Copinger*, (14th ed.), para.29–189.

force; obligations to assist the licensor in enforcing the licensed intellectual property rights; obligations to pay minimum royalties or to produce a minimum quantity of products incorporating the licensed technology; and obligations to use the licensor's trade mark or indicate the name of the licensor on the product.[39] There is then guidance on the application of Article 81 to a variety of different types of clause.[40] The types of clause are as follows: royalty obligations; exclusive and sole licences which restrict production within a given territory; restrictions on sales into a given territory or to a given customer group; output restrictions; "field of use restrictions", that is restrictions under which the licensee is limited to one or more technical fields of application or one or more product markets; "captive use restrictions", that is obligations on the licensee to limit its production of the licensed product to the quantities required for the production of its own products and the maintenance and repair of its own products; "tying", that is making the licensing of one technology conditional on the licensee taking a licence for another technology or purchasing a particular product; "bundling", which occurs where two technologies or a technology and a product are only sold together as a bundle; and "non-compete obligations", that is obligations on the licensee not to use third-party technologies which compete with the licensed technology. The guidance on these particular clauses is detailed and defies summary. The reader is accordingly referred to the Commission's text itself.[41] Finally, the guidelines deal with licensing in settlement and non-assertion agreements (which are treated like other licence agreements)[42] and technology pools.[43]

The vertical agreements block exemption. The Commission's view is that in relation to most vertical restraints, competition concerns can only arise if there is insufficient inter-brand competition, that is if there is some degree of market power at the level of the supplier, the buyer or both.[44] In that context, Council Regulation (EC) No. 2790/99 ("the VABER")[45] provides block exemption to vertical agreements, subject to certain qualifications and exceptions. For these purposes, a vertical agreement is an agreement entered into between two or more undertakings each of which operates for the purposes of the agreement at a different level of the production or distribution chain and relating to the conditions under which the parties may purchase, sell or resell certain goods or services.[46] The block exemption applies to such agreements provided that the market share of the supplier does not exceed 30 per cent of the relevant market or (if the agreement contains exclusive supply obligations) the market share of the buyer does not exceed 30 per cent of the relevant market.[47] However, the exemption does not apply to an agreement which has as its object one of a list of "hardcore" restrictions, including price-fixing, territorial restrictions and certain restrictions relating to exclusive distribution systems.[48] The exemption also does not apply to certain specified obligations contained in vertical agreements, such as certain

29–234

---

[39] TTBER Guidelines, para.162.

[40] TTBER Guidelines, paras 156 to 203.

[41] [2004] O.J. C 101/2.

[42] TTBER Guidelines, paras 204 to 209.

[43] TTBER Guidelines, paras 210 to 235.

[44] Commission Notice Guidelines on Vertical Restraints [2000] O.J. C291/1, para.6.

[45] Commission Regulation (EC) No. 2790/99 on the application of Art.81(3) of the Treaty to categories of vertical agreements and concerted practices [1999] O.J. L336/21. See also Commission Notice: Guidelines on Vertical Restraints [2000] O.J. C291/1, paras 21 to 99.

[46] VABER, Art.2(1).

[47] VABER Art.3. For the calculation of market share, see *ibid.*, Art.9.

[48] VABER Art.4. If a "hardcore" restriction is present, the whole agreement is void: see Commission Notice Guidelines on Vertical Restraints [2000] O.J. C291/1, para.46.

non-compete obligations.[49] The benefit of the exemption may be withdrawn by the Commission or by a national authority.[50]

29–235   **Provisions of the VABER relating to intellectual property rights.** The exemption applies to vertical agreements containing provisions which relate to the assignment to the buyer or use by the buyer of intellectual property rights, but only if those provisions do not constitute the primary object of such agreements and are directly related to the use, sale or resale of goods or services by the buyer or its customers.[51] For these purposes, the term "intellectual property rights" includes industrial property rights, copyright and neighbouring rights,[52] and thus the vast majority of the rights covered in this work including copyright. It is clear, however, that the exemption does not apply to a copyright assignment between an author and a publisher because the assignment would be the primary object of the agreement.

29–236   **Application of the vertical agreements block exemption to intellectual property rights: general guidance.** The Commission has issued a Notice[53] giving guidance as to the application of the block exemption. It notes that five conditions must be fulfilled before an agreement containing provisions in relation to intellectual property rights will fall within the exemption and then gives examples of the types of agreement which, in the Commission's opinion, are and are not exempt.[54] First, in order to be exempt, the intellectual property provisions must be part of a vertical agreement, that is an agreement with conditions under which the parties purchase, sell or resell goods or services. Accordingly, neither an agreement concerning the assignment or licensing of intellectual property rights for the manufacture of goods nor a pure licensing agreement is exempt. Examples of agreements which are not exempt for this reason are as follows: where one party provides another with a recipe and licenses that other to produce a drink with it; where one party provides the other with a mould or master and licenses the other to produce or distribute copies; the "pure" licence of a trade mark or sign for the purposes of merchandising; sponsorship contracts concerning the right to advertise oneself as the official sponsor of an event; and copyright licensing such as broadcasting contracts concerning the right to record or broadcast an event. Secondly, the intellectual property rights must be assigned to or for use by the buyer. Accordingly, the exemption does not apply when the rights are supplied by the buyer to the supplier, even if the rights concern the manner of manufacture or distribution. Thus, for example, sub-contracting involving the transfer of know-how to the sub-contractor is not exempt. However, vertical agreements under which the buyer provides the supplier with no more than specifications which describe the goods or services to be supplied are exempt. Thirdly, the assignment or licensing of the intellectual property rights must not constitute the primary object of the agreement. The primary object must be the purchase or distribution of goods or services and the intellectual property provision must serve the implementation of the vertical agreement. Fourthly, the intellectual property provisions must be directly related to the use, sale or resale of goods or services by the buyer or his customers. They will normally concern the marketing of goods and services. Examples include: a franchise agreement where the fran-

---

[49] VABER, Art.5. Provided that an obligation in this category is severable, its presence does not mean that the whole agreement is void, merely that the obligation itself is not exempt: Commission Notice Guidelines on Vertical Restraints [2000] O.J. C291/1, para.57.

[50] VABER, Arts 6 and 7.

[51] VABER Art.2(3).

[52] VABER Art.1(e).

[53] Commission Notice: Guidelines on Vertical Restraints [2000] O.J. C291/1.

[54] Guidelines on Vertical Restraints, paras 30 to 37.

chisor sells the franchisee goods for resale and licenses to the franchisee the use
of his trade mark and know-how to market the goods; and a contract under which
the supplier of a concentrated extract licenses the buyer to dilute and bottle the
extract before selling it as a drink. Finally, the intellectual property provisions
must not contain restrictions on competition having the same object or effect as
vertical restraints which are not exempted under the Regulation.

Application of the vertical agreements block exemption to copyright: specific **29–237**
provisions which are exempt. The Notice goes on to give specific examples of
provisions in agreements concerning copyright which the Commission considers
will be exempt to the extent that they fall within Article 81(1) at all.[55] First, an
obligation imposed by a copyright owner on a reseller of goods covered by copyright (for example, books or software) under which the reseller may only resell
on condition that the buyer (whether another reseller or the end user) shall not
infringe the copyright. Second, agreements under which hard copies of software
are supplied for resale and under which the reseller does not acquire a licence to
any rights over the software (such rights being granted to the end-user, for
example under a "shrink-wrap" licence). These are agreements for the supply of
goods for resale for the purposes of the Regulation and are exempt. Thirdly,
obligations imposed by a software copyright owner on the buyers of hardware
incorporating that software not to make copies of the software for resale or for
use in combination with other hardware.

Block-exempted horizontal agreements.[56] There are two relevant horizontal **29–238**
block exemptions. The first concerns categories of specialisation agreement.[57]
The term "specialisation agreement" includes a joint production agreement by
virtue of which two or more parties agree to produce certain products jointly.[58]
Again, the exemption may apply to provisions concerning the assignment or use
of intellectual property rights, but only if they do not constitute the primary
object of the agreement and are directly related to and necessary for their
implementation.[59] The second exemption concerns categories of research and
development agreement.[60] The kinds of agreement which may be exempt are
agreements which relate to the conditions under which the parties pursue either
joint research and development of products or processes and joint exploitation of
the results of that research and development or joint exploitation of the results of
research and development carried out by them pursuant to a prior agreement between them.[61] It is clear that the exemption may include provisions as to the
licensing of intellectual property rights between the parties to a research and
development agreement as defined. Any licences granted by way of the exploitation of the research and development will be governed by the TTBER so far as
they concern rights to which it applies.[62]

---

[55] Guidelines on Vertical Restraints, paras 39 to 41.
[56] See, generally, Commission Notice: Guidelines on the applicability of Art.81 of the EC Treaty to horizontal co-operation agreements [2001] O.J. C3/2.
[57] Commission Regulation (EC) No. 2658/2000 on the application of Art.81(3) of the Treaty to categories of specialisation agreements.
[58] Commission Regulation (EC) No. 2658/2000, Art.1(1)(c).
[59] Commission Regulation (EC) No. 2658/2000, Art.1(2). The term "intellectual property" is not defined.
[60] Commission Regulation (EC) No. 2659/2000 on the application of Art.81(3) of the Treaty to categories of research and development agreements.
[61] Commission Regulation (EC) No. 2659/2000, Art.1(1).
[62] See TTBER Guidelines, para.60. For the rights to which the TTBER applies, see above, para. 29–216.

(c) *Application of Article 81 to assignments or licences of copyright and related rights: relevant case law and Commission decisions*

29–239 **The *Nungesser* principle: "open" exclusive licences.** An important distinction was drawn in the *Nungesser* case[63] between so-called "open" exclusive licences (which prevent the licensor from competing with the licensee in the licensee's territory or from granting further licences in respect of that territory, but do not preclude other licensees selling into the territory) and "closed" exclusive licences (where the agreement is designed to protect the licensee from any competition with respect to the licensed goods). "Open" exclusive licences may well not fall under Article 81(1) at all, provided that (as in *Nungesser*) they do not last for an undue period of time,[64] are necessary to provide the licensee with the degree of protection that he needs in order to develop a market for the product,[65] and relate to a new product with which purchasers may not be familiar.[66] The Court of Justice accepted the argument that this was a case where the licensee would not have been prepared to take the risk of developing and marketing the licensed product without protection of this kind; as a result, competition was not affected by the restriction and Article 81(1) did not apply to it. In any event, an open exclusive licence which is not unlimited in time is likely to benefit from an exemption under Article 81(3) even if the conditions in *Nungesser* do not apply.[67] The Commission may be more inclined to take an adverse view of such a clause if the effect of the exclusivity is that a product is not supplied at all in a part of the common market.[68]

29–240 **Right to perform a copyright work.** In *Coditel II*,[69] the Court of Justice stated that an exclusive licence to exhibit a film would not, as such, be subject to Article 81. The Court of Justice took the view that the right of the owner of the copyright in a film to require fees for the showing of that film was part of the essential function of copyright; unless the grant of a sole and exclusive licence to show a film could be shown to be the purpose, the means or the result of an agreement prohibited by the Treaty, the restriction was unaffected by Article 81. However, the Court of Justice also held[70] that if artificial and unjustifiable barriers were created, or if there was a possibility of charging excessive royalties, or if the period of exclusivity was disproportionate, then the agreement would fall under Article

---

[63] Case 258/78 *Nungesser v Commission* [1982] E.C.R. 2015; [1983] 1 C.M.L.R. 278.

[64] See *RAI/Unitel* [1978] O.J. L157/39; [1978] 3 C.M.L.R. 306, Commission XIIth Report on Competition Policy, point 90; the Commission held that Unitel's exclusive contract for opera singers for one operatic work and one means of exploitation was not caught by Art.81(1); it is not clear what period may be imposed.

[65] In *Velcro/Aplix* [1985] O.J. L233/22; [1989] 4 C.M.L.R. 157, the Commission held that *Nungesser* did not apply to take an exclusive licence outside Art.81(1) once the technology in question had ceased to be novel. See also Commission Decision 88/501, *Tetra Pak I (BTG Licence)* [1990] 4 C.M.L.R. 47, upheld on appeal: Case T-51/89 *Tetra Pak Rausing SA v Commission* [1990] E.C.R. II-309; [1991] 4 C.M.L.R. 334, where it was held that an open exclusive patent licence would have infringed Art.81 even though it fell within the block exemption provided for by Reg.2349/84 because the licensee was dominant in the field of activity which was the object of the licence and barriers to entry were particularly high.

[66] Compare Art.4 of the TTBER, which does not include open exclusive licences in the list of hardcore restrictions. Note also *Knolle-Hill Form*, Commission XIIIth annual report on competition policy, point 142, where the Commission records its view that neither the newness of the product nor the necessary investment justified an "open" exclusive licence with a duration of eight years. Given the market position of the companies involved, the Commission would not have been prepared to grant an exemption under Art.81(3).

[67] Compare Art.4 of the TTBER, and para. 29–223, above.

[68] See *The Old Man and the Sea* [1977] 1 C.M.L.R. D121.

[69] Case 262/81 *Coditel v Cine Vog Films* [1982] E.C.R. 3381; [1983] 1 C.M.L.R. 49.

[70] Case 262/81 *Coditel v Cine Vog Films* [1982] E.C.R. 3381; [1983] 1 C.M.L.R. 49, para.19.

81. This dictum was applied in *Film Purchases for German Television Stations*,[71] where the Commission held that the purchase of the exclusive right to show a large number of films in Germany and Luxembourg for a long period was contrary to Article 81(1), and required modification of the agreement to allow third parties to show films at times that did not clash with those chosen by the licensees.

Other objectionable provisions in the case-law and Commission decisions. A   **29–241** restriction on the licensee selling copyright works outside the allocated territory is at first sight contrary to Article 81(1).[72] However, such a restriction may well not be a "hardcore" restriction within the meaning of Article 4 of the TTBER. Where the agreement is between competitors, a provision which allocates markets is generally a hardcore restriction. However, where the agreement is a non-reciprocal agreement, a restriction of active sales by the licensee into the exclusive territory allocated to another licensee is not a hardcore restriction, provided the latter was not a competing undertaking of the licensor at the time of the conclusion of its own licence.[73] Where the agreement is between non-competitors, restrictions of the territory into which the licensee may actively sell the contract products are not deemed to be hardcore restrictions. Restrictions on the territory into which passive sales may be made are generally deemed to be hardcore. However, a restriction of passive sales into the exclusive territory allocated by the licensor to another licensee during the first two years that the other licensee is selling the contract products in that territory is not a hardcore restriction.[74]

The Commission has also held the following clauses to be objectionable: a royalties clause extending to goods which are not the subject of the licensed rights[75]; a "no-challenge" clause preventing the licensee from challenging the licensor's rights[76]; clauses in licensing agreements for the development of games compatible with Sega and Nintendo's consoles which required the licensee to obtain the licensor's approval of any game before it was marketed, restricted the range of sub-contractors the licensee could use and limited the number of games licensees could release per year[77]; and terms of agreements between Microsoft and Internet service providers for the licensing and distribution of Microsoft's Internet Explorer products which provided for termination if minimum distribution volumes or percentages of the Internet Explorer were not achieved and which restricted ISPs from promoting and advertising competing browser software.[78] The Commission has also recently objected to so-called "most favoured nation"

---

[71] [1989] O.J. L284/36; [1990] 4 C.M.L.R. 841.

[72] See para. 29–179, above.

[73] TTBER Art.4(1)(c)(v).

[74] TTBER Art.4(2)(b)(ii).

[75] *NeilsonHordell/Reichmark* Commission XIIth Report on Competition Policy, points 88–89.

[76] *NeilsonHordell/Reichmark* Commission XIIth Report on Competition Policy, points 88–89.

[77] *Sega and Nintendo* Commission XXVIIth Report on Competition Policy (1997), pp.125–6. These cases were resolved by comfort letter following deletion of the offending clauses. The following year, the Commission dealt with the following restrictions in Sony's game development licensing agreements: a requirement that the licensee obtain Sony's approval before starting development and before launching the game; a requirement that all developing and publishing sub-contractors be approved by Sony; and a requirement that the licensee have its games manufactured by Sony: *Sony*, Commission XXVIIIth Report on Competition Policy (1998), pp.159–160. Proceedings were terminated on the basis that these restrictions were removed and replaced with "non-restrictive" pre-release approval rights. All game software would be tested either by an independent testing service or by Sony's testing service, but only for compliance with clear, non-objectionable specifications and well-defined criteria.

[78] *Microsoft* Commission XXIXth Report on Competition Policy (1999), point 56 and p.162. This case was resolved by comfort letter on deletion of the offending clauses.

clauses in agreements between Hollywood film studios and pay-TV companies in Europe.[79]

29–242   **Sports broadcasting and Article 81.** There have been a number of recent Commission cases involving the broadcasting of sporting events:[80]

Eurovision[81] concerned the European Broadcasting Union ("EBU"), an association of radio and television organisations which coordinates and supports television programme exchanges among its members through the Eurovision system. The notified arrangements were the rules governing the joint acquisition of sport television rights; the sharing of the jointly acquired sport television rights; the exchange of the signal for sporting events; the access scheme for non EBU members to Eurovision sports rights; and the sub-licensing rules relating to exploitation of Eurovision rights on pay-TV channels. The Commission held that the rules fell within the scope of Article 81(1) but, having regard to their provision for the grant of sublicences to non EBU members, adopted a decision conditionally exempting them under Article 81(3).[82]

Telefónica/Sogecable/Audiovisual Sport[83] followed the notification to the Commission by a Spanish pay-TV company ("Sogecable") and a Spanish telecommunications operator ("Telefónica") of an agreement concerning a joint venture company ("AVS") which had been set up by them to exploit the broadcasting rights to the Spanish "Liga" and "Copa" football matches. In broad terms, under the agreement, Sogecable, which held exclusive pay-per-view broadcasting rights in respect of the Liga, granted Telefónica and its cable subsidiaries a licence to broadcast Liga matches. In return, Telefónica, which held pay-per-view rights to Champions League matches, granted a licence to Sogecable to broadcast such matches jointly with Telefónica. It was agreed that the parties would cooperate in the exploitation of these rights through AVS, which determined the prices and conditions for their exploitation. The Commission's preliminary view was that the agreement might have as its object and effect both price-fixing and the sharing of markets.[84] Following notification of this, the parties agreed to grant access to the relevant rights to new cable and digital terrestrial television entrants, to modify their agreements and to introduce contractual guarantees that the competitors were free to set the prices of pay-per-view matches to viewers. The investigation was suspended when it was announced that Via Digital would merge with Sogecable. Following the merger, Sogecable agreed to buy Telefónica's stake in AVS, thus terminating the agreement notified to the Commission.[85]

GTR/FIA[86] concerned amongst other things the broadcasting rights in respect of the FIA Formula One Championship. Following a notification by the Commission, the organisers and promoters of the championship made various alterations

---

[79] These clauses give the studios the right the enjoy the most favourable terms agreed between a pay-TV company and any one of them; the cumulative effect is an alignment of prices: Commission Press Release IP/04/1314.

[80] See, generally, Aitman & Jones: "Competition Law and Copyright: Has the Copyright Owner Lost the Ability to Control his Copyright?" [2004] E.I.P.R. 137. The Commission has launched a sector inquiry into the sale of sports right to Internet and 3G mobile phone operators. It will consider both Arts 81 and 82 and in particular: refusals to supply; the bundling of TV rights with new media/UMTS rights; the existence of embargos favouring TV coverage over new types of coverage; and the purchase of new media/UMTS rights on an exclusive basis: Press Release IP/04/144, January 30, 2004.

[81] Case COMP/C2/32.150.

[82] [2000] O.J. L151/18.

[83] Case COMP/C2/37.652.

[84] Press Release IP/00/372, April 12, 2000.

[85] Press Release IP/03/655, May 8, 2003.

[86] Case COMP/C2/36.776.

to their broadcasting arrangements. These included the removal of provisions which would have entitled the organisers to appropriate all media rights in a given championship together with a reduction in the length of periods of exclusivity granted to individual broadcasters. Accordingly, the Commission indicated that it intended to take a favourable view of the arrangements.[87] It later closed its investigation.[88]

UEFA's broadcasting regulations[89] concerned UEFA regulations which enable national football associations to "block" a limited number of hours during which football may not be broadcast on television. Their purpose is to provide national football associations with a limited opportunity to schedule domestic football fixtures at times when attendance and amateur participation are not liable to be disrupted by contemporaneous broadcasting. The Commission decided that UEFA's regulations did not have any anti-competitive object: the object was to promote the development of football and the variety of the competition rather than restricting broadcasters' possibilities of acquiring rights to football events or of competing for advertising revenues or subscribers. Nor was there an appreciable restriction of competition. Accordingly, the Commission decided that it had no grounds for action under Article 81(1).[90]

UEFA: Champions League[91] concerned the sale of media rights in respect of that league. UEFA applied for negative clearance or exemption in respect of its proposed arrangements for the sale of these rights. Under the proposed arrangements, UEFA was granted the exclusive right to sell these rights, thus excluding the football clubs from taking independent commercial actions relating to their exploitation. UEFA's commercial policy was to sell the television rights in a single package on an exclusive basis to a single broadcaster per Member State. The Commission issued a statement of objections finding that the notified arrangement restricted competition. Subsequently, UEFA notified a new commercial policy which would give the football clubs much greater control over the sale of these rights. The Commission's preliminary view was that its concerns would be met by the new policy.[92] The Commission later made a final decision exempting the policy.[93]

In *Joint Selling of the media rights of the FA Premier League*,[94] the Commission concluded (following its own initiative investigation and thereafter an application for negative clearance or exemption) that certain aspects of the agreement between the Premier League clubs and Football Association Premier League Limited ("FAPL", a company owned by the clubs) restricted competition. The clubs granted FAPL the exclusive right to sell the media rights to the Premier League. Any sale of the rights required approval of two thirds of the clubs in general meeting. Thus, individual clubs were prevented from taking independent commercial actions regarding the exploitation of the rights. The Commission found that this restricted competition in the upstream market for the acquisition of media rights and that this also affected the downstream markets on which those rights are used to provide services to consumers, in particular the television markets where free-TV broadcasters compete for advertisers and pay-TV broadcasters compete for subscribers. In response to the Commission's objections, FAPL offered commitments which would involve the television rights be-

---

[87] [2001] O.J. C169/5.
[88] Press Release IP/01/1523, October 30, 2001.
[89] Case COMP/C2/37.576.
[90] [2001] O.J. L171/12.
[91] Case COMP/C.2/37.398.
[92] [2002] O.J. C196/03.
[93] Press Release IP/03/1105.
[94] Cases COMP/C2/38.173 and 38.453.

ing offered in several packages and would give the individual clubs greater rights to exploit the broadcasting rights themselves. The Commission has invited observations on these commitments.[95]

29–243   *IFPI "Simulcasting".*[96] This case arose from the notification by the IFPI[97] of a model agreement between record companies' collecting societies in relation to the simultaneous broadcast via the internet in multiple territories of sound recordings incorporated in radio and television programmes. The purpose of the agreement was to enable broadcasters to obtain a single multi-territorial licence from a single collecting society rather than having to obtain a separate licence in respect of each territory in which the broadcasts would be received. In its original form, the agreement required broadcasters to obtain a licence from the collecting society for the territory in which the signal in question originated. Following discussions with the Commission, the agreement was amended so that broadcasters whose signals originate anywhere in the EEA will be able to approach any participating EEA collecting society for a licence, thus encouraging competition between the various collecting societies (there are participating societies in all EEA countries except France and Spain; other participants include societies in the Far East, Latin America and New Zealand). In 2001, the Commission indicated that it took a favourable view of the amended agreement[98] and in 2002 it issued a decision exempting the agreement until its expiry.[99] The Commission's reasoning can be summarised as follows. There were two relevant product markets: "multi-territorial simulcasting rights administration services between record producers' collecting societies" and "multi-territorial and multi-repertoire licensing of the record producers' simulcasting right".[1] In respect of each product market, the geographical market was the whole of the EEA apart from France and Spain.[2] The proposed agreement was an agreement between undertakings.[3] Article 5(2) of the agreement, which provided that the tariff applicable to the clearance of rights was that of the country of destination, appreciably restricted competition.[4] The proposed agreement was clearly capable of affecting trade between Member States.[5] Although the agreement would create a new product, improve the distribution of music and benefit the consumer,[6] the Commission identified two major concerns in respect of Article 5(2). The first was that neither the national tariffs nor the global licence fee distinguished between the copyright royalty and the administration fee. The parties resolved this concern by undertaking to separate these two elements and to identify them separately when charging users. This could not be done immediately and the parties undertook to achieve it by December 31, 2004. The Commission accepted that this time period was in-

---

[95] Notice [2004] O.J. C115/3. Similar issues have arisen is respect of the German Bundesliga: see Commission Notice 2004/C 229/04 [2004] O.J. C229/13.

[96] Case COMP/C2/38.014. See Capobianco: "Licensing of Music Rights: Media Convergence, Technological Developments and EC Competition Law" [2004] E.I.P.R. 113 and Aitman & Jones: "Competition Law and Copyright: Has the Copyright Owner Lost the Ability to Control his Copyright?" [2004] E.I.P.R. 137.

[97] For the IFPI, see para. 28–25, above.

[98] [2001] O.J. C231/18.

[99] [2003] O.J. L107/58.

[1] Case COMP/C2/38.014 *IFPI*, para.32. The term "multi-repertoire licence" was defined by the Commission as "a multi-territory licence to a user including, beside its own, the repertoire of a represented sister-society": *ibid.*, para.16.

[2] paras 39 and 44.

[3] para.60.

[4] para.76.

[5] para.83.

[6] paras 87, 92 and 95 respectively.

dispensable within the meaning of Article 81(3)[7] . The Commission's second concern was that the global licence fee to be charged in respect of multi-territory/multi-repertoire licences would include a royalty element which resulted from the aggregation of all the copyright royalties determined at national level. As a result, the royalty element would remain predetermined and unchangeable by the society granting the licence. Ultimately, however, the Commission accepted that such a provision was indispensable within the meaning of Article 81(3).[8] The Commission further concluded that the agreement did not eliminate competition in respect of a substantial part of the relevant products within the meaning of Article 81(3).[9]

The Santiago Agreement. In April 2001, BUMA, GEMA, PRS and SACEM (which were later joined by all similar societies in the EEA apart from SPA in Portugal) notified to the Commission a proposed amendment to their existing bilateral reciprocal representation agreements[10] to cover the licensing of the public performance of music on the Internet ("the Santiago agreement").[11] The amendment authorises each society to grant non-exclusive licences for the online public performance (including webcasting, streaming, music on demand and music included in online video transmission) of musical works in the repertoire of all the other societies on a worldwide basis. The licence is granted by the society operating in the country where the content provider has its economic residence. In its Notice of Objections, the Commission stated that it supports the "one-stop-shop" principle embodied in the agreement, but that the agreement fails to provide for competition between collecting societies and thus hampers the achievement of a genuine single market in the field of copyright management services. The Commission believes that this may result in unjustified inefficiencies as regards the offer of online music services to the ultimate detriment of consumers. It also considers that the territorial exclusivity embodied in the agreement is not justified by technical reasons and is irreconcilable with the worldwide reach of the internet.[12]

29–244

(d) *Application of Article 82 to the exercise of copyright and related rights*

Article 82 and industrial property rights. The question of industrial property rights and Article 82 first arose in the *Parke, Davis* case,[13] where the Court of Justice held that the ownership and exercise of a patent right does not in itself give its holder a dominant position for the purpose of Article 82. This was repeated in the *Deutsche Grammophon* case[14] in relation to the right analogous to copyright there in issue. However, if the subject matter of the right is itself a relevant market (*i.e.* in essence, where there is no substitute for the work in ques-

29–245

---

[7] para.107.

[8] para.115.

[9] para.123.

[10] As to which, see the Case C-395/87 *Tournier v Ministere Public* and Cases C-110, 241 and 242/88 *Lucazeau v SACEM; SACEM v Deiselle; SACEM v Sougmagnac* [1989] E.C.R. 2521; [1991] C.M.L.R. 248, para. 29–253, below.

[11] Case COMP/C2/38.126, [2001] O.J. C145/2. For the rights administered by PRS, see para. 28–59, above. See also Capobianco: "Licensing of Music Rights: Media Convergence, Technological Developments and EC Competition Law" [2004] E.I.P.R. 113.

[12] Press release IP/04/586. The Commission contrasts the Santiago agreement unfavourably with the IFPI Simulcasting agreement (see para. 29–243, above) and the standard agreement produced in 2003 by the record companies' collecting societies, pursuant to which commercial users will also have freedom of choice as regards the licensor society in Europe.

[13] Case 24/67 *Parke, Davis v Probel* [1968] E.C.R. 55; [1968] C.M.L.R. 47.

[14] Case 78/70 *Deutsche Grammophon GmbH v Metro-SB-Grossmärkte GmbH & Co.* [1971] E.C.R. 487; [1971] C.M.L.R. 631.

tion) then the owner of a copyright is likely to have a dominant position and Article 82 will potentially apply. Moreover, if an undertaking enjoys a dominant position for reasons unconnected with the right, it may find that its behaviour with respect to copyright is restrained by Article 82. In *Tetra Pak I*[15] the Commission held that it was an abuse of Tetra-Pak's dominant position in aseptic packaging for it to purchase the company that held the exclusive licence to use a competing technology.

29–246   **Types of abusive conduct: excessive pricing.** In *Basset v SACEM*[16] the Court of Justice upheld the right of a copyright management society to charge a supplementary mechanical reproduction royalty in addition to the performance royalty for the public performance of sound recordings, as this was a power granted to it by national legislation, even though that right was not provided for by the Member State where the recordings were lawfully placed on the market. But the Court added that it was possible for the level of royalties to be such that Article 82 might be invoked. Since the national court had found that SACEM had a dominant position, it followed that its conduct would be contrary to Article 82 if anything it did amounted to an abuse, particularly by imposing unreasonable conditions.[17]

29–247   **Terms of licences.** It may be an abuse of an undertaking's dominant position for it to enter into licence agreements which have the effect of preventing or restricting the other party from dealing with a competitor. Thus, in the *Microsoft* case,[18] the Commission intervened to prevent the following conduct by Microsoft: entering into "per-processor" licences under which equipment manufacturers had to pay a licence fee to Microsoft based on the number of computers sold, whether or not they were loaded with Microsoft software; entering into long licences going beyond the lifetime of most operating systems; and entering into confidentiality agreements with software firms that had the effect of preventing their dealing with competitors. Microsoft agreed to desist from such conduct in future.

29–248   **Infringement actions.** Another example of an abusive exercise of industrial property is where a number of undertakings owning similar industrial property rights, and together enjoying a dominant position, commence several infringement actions against a competitor, which are then stayed on condition that the competitor enter into an agreement with such undertakings.[19]

29–249   **Refusal to licence or supply.** Further, it can amount to an abuse within Article 82 for an undertaking which occupies a dominant position in spare parts for its products to refuse to supply such spare parts.[20] Spare parts for industrial machines are often the subject of drawings in which intellectual property rights subsist, and such rights may be exercised in such a way as to seek to maintain a dominant position enjoyed in respect of the spare parts; such exercise may, in certain circumstances, amount to an abuse of the dominant position, and be prohibited by Article 82.

---

[15] [1988] O.J. L272/27; [1990] 4 C.M.L.R. 47.

[16] Case 402/85, [1987] E.C.R. 1747; [1987] 3 C.M.L.R. 173.

[17] See also Case 238/87 *Volvo v Veng* [1988] E.C.R. 6211; [1989] 4 C.M.L.R. 122 and Case T-30/89 *Hilti v Commission* [1991] E.C.R. II-1439; [1992] 4 C.M.L.R. 16 (upheld on appeal Case C-53/92P [1994] E.C.R. I-667).

[18] Commission press release IP/94/653.

[19] *Zip Fasteners* [1977] 3 C.M.L.R. 44.

[20] Case 22/78 *Hugin v Commission* [1979] E.C.R. 1869; [1979] 3 C.M.L.R. 345, upholding the Commission decision ([1978] O.J. L122/23) on finding of abuse, but quashing the decision on the basis that there was no effect on trade between Member States.

Volvo v Veng. In *Volvo AB v Erik Veng (UK) Ltd*[21] the Court of Justice had to **29–250** consider the question of a refusal to license the manufacture of spare body panels for cars in connection with registered design rights. Volvo, the registered proprietor in the United Kingdom for the design of the body panels, sought to prevent Veng importing into the United Kingdom Volvo body panels manufactured without authority from Volvo. The Court of Justice in a brief judgment, answering only one of the three questions referred to it, stated that in the absence of harmonised laws within the Community, the individual is entitled to the protection of the subject-matter of his rights to the extent determined by the national legislature. In this case the right of a proprietor of a registered design included, as part of the subject-matter of his exclusive right, the right to prevent third parties manufacturing and selling, or importing, products identical to the design. Thus, forcing a proprietor to grant a licence, even in return for a reasonable royalty, would deprive the proprietor of the substance of his rights. However, the Court added that the exercise of an exclusive right by the proprietor of a registered design in respect of car body panels may be prohibited by Article 82 if it involves, on the part of an undertaking holding a dominant position, certain abusive conduct, such as the arbitrary refusal to supply spare parts to independent repairers, the fixing of prices for spare parts at an unfair level or a decision no longer to produce spare parts for a particular model, even though many cars of that model are still in circulation, provided such conduct is liable to affect trade between Member States.

The *Magill* line of cases. However, in *Magill*,[22] the Court of Justice, upholding **29–251** the Court of First Instance,[23] held that the refusal by Radio Telefis Eireann and ITP (as agent for the ITV companies) to grant licences to third parties to reproduce their schedules amounted to an abuse of their dominant positions in the supply of that information.[24] The Court accepted that refusal to grant a licence could not "in itself" amount to an abuse.[25] However, there were exceptional circumstances in the *Magill* case: the refusal prevented the emergence of a product for which there was potential consumer demand (a comprehensive TV guide); there was no justification for the refusal; and by refusing, the undertakings reserved the TV guide market to themselves.[26] Although the Court did not itself allude to this point, it may well be that the Court had in mind the nature of the "work" in question; it was difficult to argue that the copyright at issue protected any substantial investment or provided a reward for creativity. The Court went on to hold that the Commission was entitled, under Article 3 of Council Regulation 17/62, to require RTE and ITP to put an end to the infringement of Article 86 by ordering them to supply the scheduling information at issue.[27] Subsequent decisions have demonstrated that the principle in *Magill* remains a valid one, but that its application is extremely limited.[28]

---

[21] Case 238/87, [1988] E.C.R. 6211; [1989] 4 C.M.L.R. 47.

[22] Cases C-241& 242/91P *RTE and ITP v Commission* [1995] E.C.R. I-743; [1995] 4 C.M.L.R. 718; and see, for a fuller discussion of the background to this case, paras 29–57 *et seq.*, above.

[23] Case T-69/89 [1991] E.C.R. II-485.

[24] The Court found that these undertakings enjoyed a " *de facto* monopoly over [that] information"; (para.47) there were, in effect, no substitutes for that information, which could not be obtained in any other way but from the undertakings.

[25] Cases C-241& 242/91P *RTE and ITP v Commission* [1995] E.C.R. I-743; [1995] 4 C.M.L.R. 718, para.49.

[26] Cases C-241& 242/91P *RTE and ITP v Commission* [1995] E.C.R. I-743; [1995] 4 C.M.L.R. 718, paras 53–56.

[27] Cases C-241& 242/91P *RTE and ITP v Commission* [1995] E.C.R. I-743; [1995] 4 C.M.L.R. 718, paras 88–94.

[28] See above, paras 29–57 *et seq.* See also *Microsoft* C(2004) 900 final: refusal to supply interface

29–252   **The Berne Convention.** In *Magill*, the Court of Justice rejected a submission to the effect that the decision appealed from was contrary to the Berne Convention. The Court observed that the Community was not a party to that convention, and noted that provisions of an international agreement entered into before the Treaty could not be relied on if the rights of non-Member States were not involved.

29–253   **Collecting societies.** Collecting societies have come under particular scrutiny under Article 82.[29] In *Re GEMA*[30] the Commission held that the German performing right society had a dominant position within the meaning of Article 82, and had abused that position by the following practices: discriminating against authors from other Member States; binding its members to unjustified obligations, such as the assignment by the author of all his rights to GEMA; preventing foreign publishers from becoming ordinary members of GEMA; extending copyright through contractual means to non-copyright works; and discriminating against (i) independent importers of gramophone records as compared with manufacturers of records and (ii) importers of tape and optical sound recorders as compared with German manufacturers of such recorders.

In *BRT v SABAM*[31] the Court of Justice had to consider questions referred to it raising the validity under Article 82 of practices carried out by the Belgian association of authors, composers and publishers, SABAM. The Court held that in determining whether a national copyright society is imposing unfair conditions on its members or on third parties, account is to be taken of all relevant interests so as to ensure a balance between the needs of the members for freedom from restraint, and for effective management of their rights.[32] The Court went on to hold that for the society to require a compulsory assignment by an author to it of all his copyrights, present and future, may amount to an unfair condition, especially if the assignment is to remain effective for a considerable time after the author has left the society.[33]

In *GVL v Commission*[34] the Court was asked to overturn the Commission's decision[35] that the German collecting society GVL had abused a dominant position by refusing to conclude management contracts or otherwise manage the performer's rights for artistes of other Member States not resident in Germany. Upholding the Commission's decision and finding that GVL had a monopoly on the relevant market for the secondary exploitation of copyright, the Court held that a refusal by a *de facto* monopoly to provide its services to all who might be in need of them, but who are not in a category defined by that undertaking by nationality or residence, is an abuse of a dominant position. Thus GVL could not refuse its services to foreign artistes not resident in Germany; they might also wish to assert rights of secondary exploitation. GVL knew it was preventing those artistes from being paid the royalties they were entitled to.

---

information necessary to develop Microsoft-compatible products resulted in an order for disclosure. The order is subject to an action for annulment: Case T-201/04, [2004] O.J. C179/18. This case also involved the "tying" of Windows Media Player with the Windows operating system. Microsoft was asked to cease doing this. This order is also subject to Case T-201/04.

[29] For the Commission's current thinking in this area, see its Communication The Management of Copyright and Related Rights in the Internal Market COM (2004) 261 final, April 16, 2004. See further as to the application of the rules of competition to performing right societies, Ernst-Joachim Mestmacker, *Journal of World Trade Law* 1976 Special Supplement No.3, Ch.IV.

[30] [1971] O.J. L134/15; [1971] C.M.L.R. D35; see also *Re Gema (No.2)* [1972] O.J. L166/22; [1972] C.M.L.R. D115.

[31] Case 127/73 [1974] E.C.R. 313; [1974] 2 C.M.L.R. 238.

[32] Case 127/73 *BRT v SABAM* [1974] 2 C.M.L.R. 238 at 283[8].

[33] Case 127/73 *BRT v SABAM* [1974] 2 C.M.L.R. 238 at 283[12]; see also *Greenwich Films SA v SACEM* [1979] 2 C.M.L.R. 535 and Case 22/79 [1979] E.C.R. 3275; [1980] 1 C.M.L.R. 629.

[34] Case 7/82 [1983] E.C.R. 483; [1983] 3 C.M.L.R. 645.

[35] [1981] O.J. L370/49; [1982] 1 C.M.L.R. 221.

In *Basset v SACEM*,[36] the Court held that the French copyright management society SACEM would not be infringing Article 82 by exercising the powers granted to it by national legislation. However, it was possible that the level of royalty or combined royalties charged by the society might be such as to bring Article 82 into operation. The French court had already found that the royalties charged by SACEM were not unreasonable, so the Court of Justice made no further comment in this particular case.

The practices of SACEM received further attention from the Court of Justice in a series of cases[37] challenging the restrictions it imposed on discotheques using the repertoire of authors registered with SACEM and collecting societies in other Member States having reciprocal agreements with SACEM. The challenge under Article 82 was to the level of royalties charged by SACEM to discotheques for the performance of the protected works in comparison with copyright societies in other Member States. In the judgment of the Court, if those rates were significantly higher than those charged by the other copyright societies, when compared on an equal basis, the difference would be an indication of abuse. It would then be for the society in question to justify the difference objectively.[38] An attempt by SACEM to justify the difference on the basis of its greater administrative zeal was rejected by the Court as also being capable of explanation by the lack of competition on the market, allowing SACEM to develop an unnecessarily burdensome administration. In *Ministère Public v Tournier*[39] the Court went slightly further than in the other cases by adding that the imposition of any inequitable contractual term by a dominant undertaking is an abuse of Article 82.

In *Banghalter v SACEM*,[40] the Commission held that a mandatory requirement in the statute of a collecting society that all rights of an author, including those of online exploitation, be assigned, amounted to an abuse since it corresponded to the imposition of an unfair trading condition.

B. UNITED KINGDOM COMPETITION LAW

(i) Introduction

Current United Kingdom legislation. United Kingdom competition law is now   **29–254**
governed by the Competition Act 1998 and the Enterprise Act 2002, which repealed and replaced the patchwork of provisions contained in the Restrictive Trade Practices Act 1976,[41] the Resale Prices Act 1976,[42] Parts IV and V of the Fair Trading Act 1973[43] and sections 2 to 10 of the Competition Act 1980.[44] The relevant provisions of these repealed statutes are discussed in the previous edi-

---

[36] Case C-402/85 [1987] E.C.R. 1717; [1987] 3 C.M.L.R. 173.

[37] Case 395/87 *Ministère Public v Tournier* [1989] E.C.R. 2521; Cases 110/88, 241/88 & 242/88 *Lucazeau v SACEM; SACEM v Debelle; SACEM v Sougmagnac* [1989] E.C.Rl. 2811; [1991] 4 C.M.L.R. 248.

[38] Case 395/87 *Ministère Public v Tournier* [1989] E.C.R. 2521; Cases 110/88, 241/88 & 242/88 *Lucazeau v SACEM; SACEM v Debelle; SACEM v Sougmagnac* [1989] E.C.Rl. 2811; [1991] 4 C.M.L.R. 248, paras 38 and 25 of the respective judgments.

[39] [1989] E.C.R. 251, para.34 of the judgment.

[40] Case COMP/C2/37.219, as reported in the Commission's Communication The Management of Copyright and Related Rights in the Internal Market, COM (2004) 261 final, April 16, 2004, pp.16 to 17.

[41] Repealed by Competition Act 1998, s.74(3) and Sch.14, with effect from March 1, 2000: see the Competition Act 1998 (Commencement No.5) Order 2000 (SI 2000/344), Art.2 and Sch.

[42] Repealed by the provisions referred to in the previous note.

[43] These provisions (with the exception of ss.57–62, which covered newspaper merger references and were repealed by the Communications Act 2003) were repealed by Enterprise Act 2002, s.278(2) and Sch.26 with effect from June 26, 2003: Enterprise Act 2002 (Commencement No.3, Transitional and Transitory Provisions and Savings) Order 2003 (SI 2003/1397), Art.2 and Sch.

tion of this work.[45] In broad terms, the Competition Act now covers anti-competitive agreements and conduct,[46] while the Enterprise Act now covers issues of market structure, in particular, mergers[47] and market investigations.[48] A residual part of the Competition Act 1980 remains in force and covers the regulation of the conduct of certain public bodies.[49]

29–255   **The Office of Fair Trading and the Competition Commission.** The two major institutions of relevance to the rights covered in this work are the Office of Fair Trading ("OFT") and the Competition Commission. The OFT is a body corporate established under the Enterprise Act 2002.[50] It took over the functions of the Director General of Fair Trading ("DGFT"), an office which was established by the Fair Trading Act 1973. The OFT is not the same as the former "OFT", which was not a statutory body, but simply the administrative staff which grew up around the office of the DGFT.[51] Its role so far as relevant to this work includes the enforcement of the Chapter I and II prohibitions in the Competition Act 1998 and the conduct of preliminary investigations into mergers and markets and decisions as to whether to make references to the Competition Commission. The Competition Commmission is body corporate established by the Competition Act 1998.[52] It replaced the Monopolies and Mergers Commission ("MMC"). The Commission conducts inquiries into mergers, markets and the regulation of the major regulated industries in response to references by the OFT, the Secretary of State, or specific regulators. The Commission has no power to conduct inquiries on its own initiative.[53] Its rules of procedure are available on its website.[54]

(ii) The Competition Act 1998

(a) *Transitional provisions and general principles*

29–256   **The Competition Act: transitional provisions: general.** As explained above,[55] the Restrictive Trade Practices Act 1976 has been repealed by the Competition Act 1998. As explained below,[56] the Competition Act replaces the 1976 Act by prohibitions closely modelled on Articles 81 and 82 of the Treaty ("the Chapter I prohibition" and the "Chapter II prohibition" respectively.) Schedule 13 to the Act sets out the transitional provisions in respect of the Chapter I prohibition (the Act contains no transitional provisions in respect of the Chapter II prohibition).[57]

---

[44] Repealed by Competition Act 1998, s.17 and Sch.14 with effect from March 1, 2000: see the Competition Act 1998 (Commencement No. 5) Order 2000 (SI 2000/344), Art.2 and Sch.
[45] See *Copinger*, 14th ed., paras 29–202 to 29–214 and 29–230 to 29–236 and 29–242.
[46] See below, paras 29–256 *et seq.*
[47] See below, paras 29–279 *et seq.*
[48] See below, paras 29–290 *et seq.*
[49] See below, paras 29–296 *et seq.*
[50] Enterprise Act 2002, s.1(1).
[51] See Explanatory Notes to the Enterprise Act 2002, paras.18 to 20. The OFT's website is at *www.oft.gov.uk.*
[52] Competition Act 1998, s.45.
[53] See the article "What is the Competition Commission?" on its website *www.competition-commission.org.uk.*
[54] Publication CC1 at *www.competition-commission.org.uk.*
[55] See para. 29–254, above.
[56] See paras 29–259 *et seq.* below.
[57] The OFT published a guideline (OFT 406) explaining its interpretation of the transitional provisions and setting out the DGFT's approach to his powers in relation to agreements affected by them. This guidance has now been updated in draft form by the OFT's draft guideline on the major provisions (OFT 400a, April 2004), paras 12.8 to 12.29. See the OFT's website (*www.oft.gov.uk*).

Transitional periods. The Chapter I prohibition came into force on March 1,   **29–257**
2000.[58] Most agreements made before that date which complied with the then
current legislation benefited from transitional periods during which the prohibition did not apply. Most of these transitional periods were only for a period of
one year and are considered in the previous edition of this work.[59] However, in
some cases, the transitional period lasts for five years from March 1, 2000. Those
cases are as follows: agreements to the extent to which they contain provisions
which, immediately before March 1, 2000, have been found by the Restrictive
Practices Court not to be contrary to the public interest[60]; agreements relating to
goods which, immediately before March 1, 2000, were exempt under section 14
of the Resale Prices Act 1976, to the extent that the agreement consists of exempt
provisions[61]; certain agreements which have been subject to scrutiny under the
Financial Services Act 1986 or the Broadcasting Act 1990[62]; and certain agreements relating to regulated utilities.[63] The OFT's draft guideline notes that agreements which benefit from these transitional periods are not immune from the application of Articles 81 and 82.[64] The OFT is able to extend the transitional
periods for a period of up to six months.[65] Its draft guideline states that an extension will only be granted if the agreement may infringe the Chapter I prohibition
but not seriously and there are good reasons why the extension is required, for
example the agreement is being renegotiated or is due to expire shortly after the
end of the transitional period.[66] The OFT also has the power to terminate these
transitional periods.[67] Its draft guideline suggests that it is likely to exercise this
power when it is concerned that an agreement may be having an appreciable effect on competition such that it is appropriate to review it under Chapter I rather
than waiting for the transitional period to run its course.[68]

Agreements benefiting from a section 21(2) direction. Agreements which, im-   **29–258**
mediately before March 1, 2000, benefited from a direction under section 21(2)
of the Restrictive Trade Practices Act were excluded from the Chapter 1 prohibition for their duration.[69] However, this exclusion has been repealed with effect
from May 1, 2007.[70] In the meantime, the OFT has the power to "claw back" the
exclusion.[71] It should also be noted that the exclusion will be lost if there is a material variation after March 1, 2000.[72]

General principles of interpretation. Section 2 of the Act provides for a prohi-   **29–259**
bition ("the Chapter I prohibition") of anti-competitive agreements closely

---

[58] See the Competition Act 1998 (Commencement No. 5) Order 2000, SI 2000/344, Art.2 and Sch.
[59] See *Copinger* (14th ed.) para. 29–215.
[60] Competition Act 1998, Sch.13, para.23(1). Presumably what is meant is that the agreement
contained such terms immediately before March 1, 2000. Note that the effect of the words "to the
extent that" is that the transitional period may only apply to certain provisions of the agreement
rather than to the whole agreement: OFT 400a, para.12.15. Where an agreement is only partly
covered by a transitional period, the OFT can have regard to the whole agreement in considering
whether the Ch.I prohibition has been breached: Competition Act 1998, Sch.13, para.1(5).
[61] Competition Act 1998, Sch.13, para.24(1). For the effect of the use of the words "to the extent
that", see previous Note.
[62] Sch.13, para.26.
[63] Sch.13, paras 27 to 34.
[64] OFT 400a, para.12.13.
[65] Competition Act 1998, Sch.13, para.36.
[66] OFT 400a, para.12.25.
[67] Competition Act 1998, Sch.13, para.37.
[68] OFT 400a, para.12.28.
[69] Competition Act 1998, Sch.3 para.2.
[70] By the Competition Act 1998 and Other Enactments (Amendment) Regulations 2004 (SI 2004/
1261), reg.4 and Sch.1, para.50(a).
[71] Competition Act 1998, Sch.3, para.2(3).
[72] Sch.3, para.2(2).

modelled on Article 81(1) of the Treaty,[73] although without the reference to an effect on trade between Member States. Likewise, section 18 provides for a prohibition ("the Chapter II prohibition") on abuse of a dominant position closely modelled on Article 82 of the Treaty.[74] In interpreting these provisions, the starting point is section 60 of the Act. That section is as follows:

"(1) The purpose of this section is to ensure that so far as is possible (having regard to any relevant differences between the provisions concerned), questions arising under this Part in relation to competition within the United Kingdom are dealt with in a manner which is consistent with the treatment of corresponding questions arising in Community law in relation to competition within the Community.

(2) At any time when the court determines a question arising under this Part, it must act (so far as is compatible with the provisions of this Part and whether or not it would otherwise be required to do so) with a view to securing that there is no inconsistency between:

(a) the principles applied, and decision reached, by the court in determining that question; and

(b) the principles laid down by the [EC] Treaty and the European Court,[75] and any relevant decision of that Court, as applicable at that time in determining any corresponding question arising in Community law.

(3) The court must, in addition, have regard to any relevant decision or statement of the [European] Commission.

(4) Subsections (2) and (3) also apply to—

(a) the [OFT][76]; and

(b) any person acting on behalf of the OFT, in connection with any matter arising under this Part.

(5) In subsections (2) and (3), 'court' means any court or tribunal.

(6) In subsections (2)(b) and (3), 'decision' includes a decision as to

(a) the interpretation of any provision of Community law;

(b) the civil liability of an undertaking for harm caused by its infringement of Community law".

The effect of this provision is that in applying the Act both the courts and the OFT will, in essence, be required to interpret the Act in the same way as equivalent provisions of Community law are interpreted by the European Community Courts and the European Commission. Thus, concepts such as "agreement", "undertaking", "prevention, distortion or restriction of competition", "abuse", and "dominant position" are left undefined in the Act. In order to extract their meaning, reference must be made to the case law of the European Community Courts, and (on the basis that its views have, by virtue of section 60(3), persuasive authority) to decisions and statements of the European Commission.[77] It is therefore suggested that the reader should refer, before reading the following

---

[73] As to which, see paras 29–174 et seq., above.

[74] As to which, see paras 29–193 et seq., above.

[75] That is to say, the Court of Justice and the Court of First Instance: Competition Act 1998, s.59(1).

[76] The Act originally gave powers to the Director General of Fair Trading. However, with effect from April 1, 2003, this post was abolished by s.2(2) of the Enterprise Act 2002 (c.40) and its functions were transferred to the Office of Fair Trading by s.2(1) of the same Act. For commencement, see the Enterprise Act 2002 (Commencement No. 2, Transitional and Transitory Provisions) Order 2003, SI 2003/766, Art.2 and Sch. S.60 was amended to give effect to this: Enterprise Act 2002, Sch.25, para.38, also with effect from April 1, 2003: ibid. The powers of the OFT under the Act are shared with a number of specialist utility regulators in their respective fields. This complication is unlikely to affect the rights that are the subject of this work, and is ignored in what follows.

[77] The OFT has stated that in its view this is limited to decisions or statements which have the authority of the European Commission as a whole, such as, for example, decisions on individual

discussion of the Act, to the discussion above of European Community competition law.[78] The following discussion will concentrate mainly on matters where there is or may be a difference in approach between the Act and equivalent provisions of Community competition law, or where there is no equivalent provision of Community law. In addition, however, reference will be made to the OFT's guidelines where that assists in illuminating the understanding that body has of the Community law.

Market integration. One area where the approach of the OFT and of the courts under the Act may well differ from the approach of the Community authorities under Articles 81 and 82 is that of agreements and conduct that have the effect of segmenting the market. The Community authorities have consistently condemned vertical agreements that confer absolute territorial protection on distributors or licensees, and have condemned as abusive conduct by a dominant undertaking that is intended to partition the market for its products on a geographical basis.[79] However, it is doubtful that this strict approach to such agreements or conduct will be appropriate in the context of the Act; there is no evidence that United Kingdom legislators or policy-makers have shared in relation to the United Kingdom the concern to promote market integration that is evident in the Treaty. It remains to be seen how this distinction is developed.

29–260

(b) *The Chapter I prohibition*

The Chapter I prohibition. Subsections 2(1) and (2) of the Act set out the Chapter I prohibition[80] in terms that substantially replicate Article 81(1) of the Treaty.[81] Agreements[82] between undertakings[83] that (a) may affect trade within the United Kingdom[84] and (b) have as their object or effect the prevention, restriction or distortion of competition within the United Kingdom are prohibited

29–261

---

cases under Arts 81 and 82 together with clear statements about its policy approach which the European Commission has published in the Annual Report on Competition Policy: see the OFT's Guideline on The Major Provisions, OFT 400, para.6.2. The draft revised version of this Guideline (OFT 400a) is to the same effect save that it refers additionally to Commission Notices as "clear statements of [the Commission's] policy approach": see para.4.13.

[78] See paras 29–173 *et seq.*, above.

[79] See *e.g.* paras 29–182 and 29–234, above.

[80] The OFT has published a guideline as to its interpretation of the Ch.1 prohibition (OFT 401). In April 2004 it published a draft revised guideline (OFT 401a) Both the original and the draft revised guideline are available on its website (*www.oft.gov.uk*).

[81] See paras 29–174 *et seq.*, above.

[82] The section refers (as does Art.81(1)) to agreements between undertakings, decisions by associations of undertakings and concerted practices; in what follows, references to agreements include references to decisions and concerted practices. According to the OFT, the term "agreement" "has a wide meaning and covers agreements whether legally enforceable or not, written or oral; it includes so-called gentlemen's agreements. There does not have to be a physical meeting of the parties for an agreement to be reached: an exchange of letters or telephone calls may suffice if a consensus is arrived at as to the action each party will, or will not, take": see the OFT's Guideline 401, para.2.7. The draft revised version of this Guideline (OFT 401a, April 2004) is to the same effect. The OFT has published a Guideline on the application of the Ch.I and II prohibitions to the activities of trade associations, professional bodies and self-regulatory organisations: OFT 408 and OFT 408a (draft revised guideline, April 2004).

[83] According to the OFT, the term "undertaking" "includes any natural or legal person capable of carrying on commercial or economic activities relating to goods or services, whatever its legal status. It includes companies, firms, businesses, partnerships, individuals operating as sole traders, agricultural co-operatives, trade associations and non-profit-making organizations": see the OFT's Guideline 401, para.2.5. The draft revised Guideline (OFT 401a, April 2004) is to substantially the same effect but includes in the list of undertakings "(in some circumstances) public entities that offer goods or services on a given market" (para.2.6). As under Community law, the prohibition is not applied to agreements between undertakings which form a single economic unit: Guideline OFT 401, para.2.6 (draft Guideline OFT 401a para.2.7 is to the same effect).

[84] The effect of this provision is rather obscure. Art.81(1) refers (as does Art.82) to an effect on

unless exempt. However, there is no reference to an effect on trade between Member States; the Act therefore applies to agreements that have a purely domestic effect. Subsection 2(4) renders void any agreement or decision prohibited by subsection 2(1); it is analogous to Article 81(2).

29–262 **Territorial effect.** In addition to the requirements of subsection 2(1) (to the effect that an agreement must affect trade and competition within the United Kingdom to be caught by the prohibition), subsection 2(3) provides that an agreement will not be prohibited unless it is, or is intended to be, implemented in the United Kingdom. This provision is intended to replicate the test at Community level set out by the Court of Justice in *Wood Pulp*.[85]

29–263 **Appreciability.** Although the Act makes no mention of it, the requirement that the effect on competition should be appreciable is implicit in the application of established Community case law to the Chapter I prohibition by section 60 of the Act. At the time of writing, the OFT's guidance provides as follows. In general, an agreement will not have an appreciable effect on competition if the parties' combined share of the relevant market is less than 25 per cent.[86] Where that combined share is below 25 per cent, an agreement will nevertheless be capable of having an appreciable effect if it directly or indirectly fixes prices or shares markets; imposes minimum resale prices; or is one of a network of similar agreements which have a cumulative effect on the market in question.[87] Of course, even where the parties' combined market share exceeds 20 per cent, the agreement may not have an appreciable effect, for example because of its content and the structure of the affected market or markets (for example entry conditions or the characteristics of buyers and the structure of the buyers' side of the market).[88] For these purposes, the relevant market share is the combined market share not only of the parties to the agreement but also of other undertakings belonging to the same group of undertakings as the parties to the agreement.[89] However, this guidance is likely to be superseded shortly by new guidance, which applies the much lower thresholds contained in the European Commission's Notice on agreements of minor importance.[90] Once this guidance has been adopted, if the thresholds in the Commission's Notice have not been reached, and provided the agreement does not contain any of the hardcore restrictions referred to in the Commission's Notice, the OFT is likely to take the view that the agreement does not fall within the Chapter I prohibition.[91] Where the OFT considers that undertakings have in good faith relied on the terms of the Notice, it will not

---

trade between Member States; it is clear that this imposes an additional requirement to the requirement that there be an effect on competition within the common market, because it is clearly possible to have both effect on competition in the common market and yet no effect on trade between Member States (where the effect is confined to one Member State forming part of the common market). But it is not clear how an agreement or conduct could affect competition within the UK but not affect trade within the UK. In para.2.16 of Guideline OFT 401, the OFT acknowledges that in practice it is very unlikely that an agreement which restricts competition in the United Kingdom does not also affect trade in the United Kingdom and states that in applying the Ch.I prohibition the focus will be on the effect on competition (para.2.21 of OFT 401a is to the same effect).

[85] Case C-89/95 *Åhlström v Commission* [1993] E.C.R. I-1307.
[86] Guideline OFT 401, para.2.19.
[87] Guideline OFT 401, para.2.20.
[88] Guideline OFT 401, para.2.21. See the Guideline OFT 415 on Assessment of Market Power (see also the draft revised version of this: Guideline OFT 415a).
[89] Guideline OFT 401, para.2.22.
[90] See draft Guideline OFT 401a, paras 2.26 and 2.27. For the Commission's Notice, see paras 29–185 *et seq.*, above.
[91] Draft Guideline OFT 401a, para.2.27.

impose penalties for breach of the Chapter I prohibition.[92] As before, the OFT will approach the matter on the basis that even where the relevant threshold is exceeded, the agreement may not have an appreciable effect.[93]

Exemptions. Section 4 of the Act originally gave the OFT power to exempt individual agreements notified to it from the Chapter I prohibition on the grounds set out in section 9. Following the abolition of the system of individual notifications at European level,[94] the Government decided to abolish the corresponding domestic system.[95] Accordingly, since May 1, 2004 it has no longer been possible to notify an agreement under section 4.[96] Section 6 of the Act gives the Secretary of State power, on the recommendation of the OFT, to exempt a class of agreements which are likely in the view of the OFT to be ones to which section 9 applies. The effect of these provisions is to reproduce the substance of Article 81(3) of the Treaty, although set out in a different way. To date, no block exemptions have been made which are of any relevance to the rights covered in this work.

29–264

Parallel exemptions. Subsection 10(1) provides that an agreement that is exempt from Article 81(1) by virtue of a Commission or Council Regulation (such as a block exemption regulation)[97] or because of a decision by the Commission under Article 10 of the Modernisation Regulation[98] is exempt from the Chapter I prohibition. Such Regulations and decisions only apply where Article 81(1) is otherwise satisfied, and in particular where the agreement in question affects trade between Member States. In order to exempt agreements which only fall outside such Regulations and decisions because they have no actual or potential effect on trade between Member States, subsection 10(2) provides that an agreement is exempt from the Chapter I prohibition if it does not affect trade between Member States but otherwise falls within a category of agreement which is exempt from the Community prohibition by virtue of a Commission or Council Regulation. The 1998 Act gives the OFT power to cancel such a "parallel exemption".[99] The power is exercisable where the OFT finds that the agreement nevertheless has effects in the United Kingdom, or a part of it, which are incompatible with the conditions laid down in section 9 of the 1998 Act.[1]

29–265

Exclusions. A number of agreements (and various types of conduct) are excluded

29–266

---

[92] Draft Guideline OFT 401a, para.2.27.

[93] Draft Guideline OFT 401a, para.2.28.

[94] See para. 29–205, above.

[95] The Government's reasoning was as follows (see the DTI's Consultation document of April 1, 2003 on proposals to amend the Competition Act 1998 to give effect to the Modernisation Regulation, paras 1.9, 1.10 and 3.18 to 3.21). First, the alignment of European and domestic law would create greater transparency and certainty for business. Secondly, there was a risk that undertakings from across the EU would seek to use the domestic notification system in order to obtain a degree of comfort in relation to the application of Articles 81 and 82. Finally, as was the case in the EU, the system of individual notification was little used. In the three years since the Competition Act came into force, the OFT only received 19 notifications (by contrast, in the same period it gave informal advice in over 190 cases).

[96] The effect of Reg.4 and para.2 of Sch.1 to the Competition Act and Other Enactments (Amendment) Regulations 2004 (SI 2004/1261) was that on May 1, 2004, s.4 ceased to have effect. Individual exemptions granted before May 1, 2004 and still in force on that day remain effective, but this does not permit the OFT to extend the period of the exemption under s.4(6) of the Competition Act 1998 after May 1, 2004: *ibid.*, Reg.6(2).

[97] *e.g.* Commission Regulation 2790/99 which creates a block exemption for certain vertical agreements (see above, paras 29–234 *et seq.*).

[98] Council Regulation (EC) No. 1/2003, [2003] O.J. L1/1. Art.10 gives the Commission the power, acting on its own initiative and where the Community public interest requires, to make findings that Art.81 or 82 is inapplicable.

[99] Competition Act 1998, s.10(5).

[1] See r.12 in the Schedule to the Competition Act (Office of Fair Trading's Rules) Order 2004 (SI 2004/2751).

from the Chapter I prohibition (and the Chapter II prohibition). These relate to mergers and concentrations (Schedule 1); agreements and conduct scrutinised for competition implications under other enactments, such as the Financial Services Act 1986[2] (Schedule 2); planning obligations and other general exclusions (Schedule 3)[3]; and professional rules (Schedule 4). The exclusion that has been most likely to be important in practice to readers of this work does not, however, appear on the face of the Act. This is the exclusion relating to vertical agreements, where the Act proceeds by granting the Secretary of State the power to prescribe exclusions and exemptions in relation to both the Chapter I and Chapter II provisions by subordinate legislation; see section 50. Such exclusions may, however, be made subject to withdrawal by the OFT.[4] The meaning of "vertical agreement" is itself left to be prescribed by the Secretary of State.[5]

29–267   **Vertical agreements: scope of the exclusion.** The power to exclude vertical agreements was exercised by the making of an Order ("the Exclusion Order").[6] The definition of the term "vertical agreement" in the Exclusion Order is based on the terminology of Commission Regulation 2790/99,[7] which provides for a block exemption for certain vertical agreements ("the VABER"). Accordingly, for these purposes, a vertical agreement is an agreement between undertakings, each of which operates, for the purposes of the agreement, at a different level of the production or distribution chain, and relating to the conditions under which the parties may purchase, sell or resell certain goods or services.[8] The term also includes provisions contained in such agreements which relate to the assignment to the buyer or use by the buyer of intellectual property rights, provided that those provisions do not constitute the primary object of the agreement and are directly related to the use, sale or resale of goods or services by the buyer or its customers.[9] The effect of this provision in the VABER is discussed above.[10] The Exclusion Order provides that the Chapter I prohibition does not apply to a vertical agreement unless it directly or indirectly, in isolation or in combination with other factors under the control of the parties, has the object or effect of restricting the buyer's ability to determine its sale price, without prejudice to the possibility of the supplier imposing a maximum sale price or recommending a sale price, provided that these do not amount to a fixed or minimum sale price as a result of pressure from, or incentives offered by, any of the parties.[11] Again, this term is based on the terminology of the VABER.[12] However, unlike the VABER, which contains numerous "hardcore restrictions" which will take the agreement out of the scope of the block exemption (including, for example, territorial restrictions), the Exclusion Order only contains this single hardcore restriction. Furthermore, there are no excluded obligations in the Exclusion Order. By analogy with the

---

[2] (c.60).

[3] Exclusions in this Schedule that may be worth noting are: the exclusion for agreements which have benefited from a direction by the Secretary of State under RTPA 1976, s.21(2)—see *Copinger* (14th ed.), para.29–207 and para. 29–258, above; and the exclusion for an agreement entered into or conduct engaged in so as to comply with a legal requirement having legal effect in the UK.

[4] Competition Act 1998, s.50(3). See also r.14 of the Office of Fair Trading's Rules (Sch. to SI 2004/2751).

[5] Competition Act 1998, s.50(5).

[6] The Competition Act 1998 (Land and Vertical Agreements Exclusion) Order 2000 (SI 2000/310).

[7] [1999] O.J. L336/21. See above, paras 29–234 *et seq.*

[8] Exclusion Order (SI 2000/310), Art.2.

[9] Exclusion Order (SI 2000/310), Art.2

[10] See para. 29–235, above.

[11] Exclusion Order (SI 2000/310), Arts 3 and 4.

[12] VABER Art.4(a). See above, para. 29–234.

Commission's powers under the VABER, the OFT has power to withdraw the benefit of (or "claw back") the exclusion in respect of a particular agreement;[13] if this is done, an agreement between the same parties which is to the like object and effect cannot benefit from the exclusion.[14] The following other points should be noted.[15] First, unlike the VABER, the United Kingdom exclusion is not subject to a market share threshold.[16] Secondly, the Exclusion Order provides that the Chapter I prohibition is disapplied "to the extent that" the agreement is a vertical one.[17] Accordingly, some provisions may benefit while others may not. Thirdly, the Exclusion Order does not preclude the consideration of an agreement as part of the conduct of an undertaking under the Chapter II prohibition.[18] Finally, the Exclusion Order does not preclude the application of Article 81 when there may be an effect on trade between Member States.

The revocation of the vertical agreements exclusion. The Exclusion Order is revoked with effect from May 1, 2005.[19] As a result, vertical agreements will only be exempt if they satisfy the requirements of the VABER, which will apply by way of parallel exemption.[20] Accordingly, a vertical agreement which may affect trade between Member States but satisfies the requirements of the VABER will continue to be exempt. Furthermore, a vertical agreement which has no actual or potential effect on trade between Member States but otherwise satisfies the requirements of the VABER will also be exempt. The application of the VABER to the rights covered in this work is considered above.[21]   **29–268**

Guidance from the OFT. Prior to May 1, 2004, a party to an agreement who thought it might infringe the Chapter I prohibition was able to notify it to the DGFT for guidance[22] or for a decision.[23] This system has now been swept away.[24] The following transitional provisions apply. First, if an agreement was notified for guidance or for a decision before May 1, 2004, and the notification had not been determined by that date, the notification is treated as a request for informal advice.[25] Secondly, no penalty may be imposed in respect of any infringement   **29–269**

---

[13] Exclusion Order (SI 2000/310), Art.7.

[14] Exclusion Order (SI 2000/310), Art.8.

[15] See the OFT's Draft competition law guideline on Vertical Agreements, OFT 419, April 2004.

[16] However, the DTI has stated that agreements between parties with some degree of market power are precisely those which could face "claw-back" under the Exclusion Order as well as potentially falling within the Ch.II prohibition: Consultation document on Modernisation, June 2003, para.4.13.

[17] Exclusion Order (SI 2000/310), Art.3.

[18] See below, paras 29–272 et seq.

[19] By the Competition Act (Land Agreements Exclusion and Revocation) Order 2004 (SI 2004/1260), Art.2.

[20] For the VABER, see paras 29–234 et seq., above. For parallel exemptions, see para. 29–2650, above. For the Government's reasoning, see the DTI's consultation on Modernisation, published on June 17, 2003 and its updated Response to the consultation, both of which are available on the DTI's website. The Government believes first, that the revocation will reduce the risk of confusion; second, that in its emphasis on market power and hardcore restrictions, the VABER more precisely reflects agreed economic analysis across the EU of the effects of vertical agreements; third, that only a limited number of agreements will be affected by the revocation; and finally that the revocation achieves "maximum visible correspondence" with EU law and avoids an undesirable system of dual regulation. The transitional period until May 1, 2005 is intended to give businesses time to consider relevant provisions in their agreements.

[21] See paras 29–234 et seq., above.

[22] Competiton Act 1998, s.13.

[23] Competition Act 1998, s.14.

[24] By reg.4 of and para.9 of Sch.1 to the Competition Act and Other Enactments (Amendment) Regulations 2004 (SI 2004/1261).

[25] See the OFT's draft guideline to the major provisions, OFT 400a, para.12.3.

under Part I of the Act between the date of notification and May 1, 2004.[26] Thirdly, individual exemptions granted before May 1, 2004 continue in force until they expire; however, the OFT retains the power to cancel them.[27] Fourthly, by the same token, an individual exemption made by the European Commission prior to May 1, 2004 is binding on the OFT in its application of Articles 81 and 82 until the expiry date of the exemption. The operation of the Competition Act parallel exemption provisions will continue to apply.[28] The OFT has issued a considerable amount of guidance as to how it operates the provisions of the Competition Act. Furthermore, it has stated that it will continue to offer informal advice.[29] Finally, where a case raises novel or unresolved questions about the application of the Chapter I or Chapter II prohibitions, and where the OFT considers there is an interest in issuing clarification for the benefit of a wider audience, it may publish written guidance in the form of an opinion.[30] Such an opinion cannot prejudice the assessment of the same question by the Competition Appeal Tribunal and does not bind any court having the power to apply the prohibitions in the Competition Act[31]; nor can it bind the subsequent assessment of the same or similar issues, although the OFT will have regard to its opinion when carrying out the assessment.[32]

29–270   **The OFT's draft guideline on intellectual property rights: general.** The OFT has issued a draft guideline in respect of the application of the Competition Act to intellectual property rights.[33] According to this guideline, the OFT recognises the importance of intellectual property rights, since they tend to encourage innovation and thus benefit consumers.[34] The OFT acknowleges that much of the European case law concerning intellectual property rights has been driven by the single market objective. It considers that it is not obliged by section 60 to follow that case law. In practice, however, it intends to follow the principles developed in the European case law in relation to intellectual property rights where they are relevant in a domestic context.[35] The guideline contains a statement of the general approach which the OFT expects to take when assessing the most common forms of restrictions in intellectual property licensing agreements. It emphasises that in practice, each agreement will be assessed on a case by case basis by examining it in its market and economic context.[36] The OFT's main concerns in respect of such agreements are price-fixing, market sharing and provisions which foreclose the market.[37]

29–271   **The OFT's draft guideline on intellectual property rights: specific provisions in licences.** Specific guidance is given as to the application of the Chapter I prohibition to intellectual property licences as follows. First, any provisions in a licence which directly or indirectly impose minimum resale prices for the

---

[26] Competition Act and Other Enactments (Amendment) Regulations 2004 (SI 2004/1260), reg.9(2).

[27] Competition Act and Other Enactments (Amendment) Regulations 2004 (SI 2004/1260), reg.6.

[28] Competition Act and Other Enactments (Amendment) Regulations 2004 (SI 2004/1260), reg.7. For parallel exemption, see para. 29–265, above.

[29] See the OFT's draft competition law guideline on Modernisation (OFT 442, April 2004), para.3.4, 3.17.

[30] OFT 442, April 2004, para.3.15. See also the OFT's draft competition law guideline on The Major Provisions (OFT 400a, April 2004), paras 6.6 to 6.21

[31] OFT 442, April 2004, para.3.16.

[32] OFT 442, April 2004, para.3.16.

[33] OFT 418. Although this guideline was issued in draft in November 2001 and consultation closed on February 28, 2002, no final version of the guideline has ever been published.

[34] OFT 418, para.1.3.

[35] para.1.8.

[36] para 2.17.

[37] para.2.18.

products or services covered by the licensed intellectual property right are likely to infringe the prohibition. The OFT considers that the licensee must remain free to determine its own pricing policy. The setting of royalty rates in a way intended to fix the prices at which the goods or products are sold is likely to infringe.[38] Secondly, any provisions which share markets are likely to infringe. However, the grant of an exclusive right to manufacture and sell the goods in a particular territory and/or the grant of a particular field of exploitation are unlikely to infringe unless, having regard to the conditions of competition in the relevant market, they have the effect of foreclosing competition in that market and therefore have an appreciable effect on competition.[39] Thirdly, a provision preventing sub-licensing or assignment will generally not infringe.[40] Fourthly, a provision which requires a licensee to grant back to the licensor the exclusive right to improvements may infringe.[41] Fifthly, any provision preventing the exploitation of the right after the expiry of the licence will infringe if it exceeds the lifetime of the right. Other provisions in a licence which continue to apply even after the right has expired, such as a royalty obligation, may also infringe.[42] Sixthly, an obligation to meet certain specifications as to minimum quality of the licensed product (including provisions as to marketing and labelling) is unlikely to infringe.[43] Seventhly, provisions which require the licensee to purchase certain products from the licensor may infringe where they have the effect of foreclosing the market, but not if they are necessary for quality control.[44] Finally, a requirement that the licensee produce a minimum quantity of products made using the right may infringe if it prevents the licensee from using other intellectual property rights to compete with products made using the right and if it forecloses the market and therefore has an appreciable effect on competition.[45]

(c) The Chapter II prohibition

The Chapter II prohibition. Section 18[46] prohibits any "conduct" which amounts to the abuse of a dominant position "in a market ... if it may affect trade within the United Kingdom [or any part of it]".[47] Although the word "conduct" does not appear in Article 82, it is not thought that its inclusion should lead to any difference between the interpretation of section 18 and that of Article 82. The dominant position must be within the United Kingdom or any part of it.[48] As in relation to the Chapter I prohibition, there is no reference to an effect on trade between Member States; the Act therefore potentially applies to conduct that has a purely domestic effect. An illustrative list of abuses—identical to the equivalent list in Article 82—is set out in section 18(2).

29–272

---

[38] OFT 418, para.2.19.
[39] para.2.21.
[40] para.2.22.
[41] para.2.23.
[42] para.2.24.
[43] para.2.25.
[44] para.2.26.
[45] para.2.27.
[46] The OFT has published a guideline as to its interpretation of the Ch.II prohibition (OFT 402). In April 2004, the OFT produced a draft revised guideline (OFT 402a). Both guidelines are available on the Office's website (www.oft.gov.uk).
[47] See Competiton Act 1998, s.18(3).
[48] Competiton Act 1998, s.18(3).

29–273   **Exclusions.** Schedules 1 and 3 to the Competiton Act set out a number of exclusions from the Chapter II prohibition. These exclusions also apply in relation to the Chapter I prohibition and are set out above.[49]

29–274   **Notifications.** As in the case of the Chapter I prohibition, the Competition Act originally provided for the possibility of notifying conduct for guidance or a decision as to whether it contravened the Chapter II prohibition. Again, however, this system has been abolished with effect from May 1, 2004[50] and replaced by the same system of published guidance, informal advice and Opinions as applies in respect of the Chapter I prohibition.[51]

29–275   **Enforcement.** The Competition Act gives the OFT wide powers to require the production of documents and information where it suspects that there has been a breach of one of the prohibitions.[52] It also has wide powers to enter premises (with or without a warrant) in order to seek documents.[53] Once the OFT has established the existence of an infringement, it may impose a penalty of up to 10 per cent of an undertaking's annual turnover.[54] It will also issue directions requiring the undertaking concerned to bring the infringement to an end[55] ; such directions may also be made on an interim basis pending a final determination of whether there has been an infringement.[56] An appeal on the merits and on the law lies to the Competition Commission established by section 45 and Schedule 7[57]; a further appeal on a point of law or on penalty lies to the Court of Appeal, with the permission of that court.[58]

29–276   **Civil liability.** The effect of section 60(6)(b)[59] appears to be that the existence of, and conditions attaching to, civil liability by undertakings in breach of the prohibitions to third parties depend on the existence of, and conditions attaching to, an equivalent liability in Community law under Articles 81(1) and 82.[60]

29–277   **The OFT's draft guideline on intellectual property rights: general points about the Chapter II prohibition.** This draft guideline is introduced elsewhere.[61] In applying the Chapter II prohibition, the OFT accepts the general Community law position that ownership of an intellectual property right does not necessarily create a dominant position. However, the OFT believes that whether dominance results from the ownership of an intellectual property right depends on the extent to which there are substitutes for the product, work or process to which it relates.[62] In assessing dominance, the OFT will follow the approach set out in its guidelines

---

[49] See para. 29–266, above.

[50] By Reg.4 of and para.9 of Sch.1 to the Competition Act and Other Enactments (Amendment) Regulations 2004 (SI 2004/1261).

[51] See para. 29–269.

[52] Competition Act 1998, s.27.

[53] ss.28–29.

[54] s.36. See the OFT's draft guideline (OFT 423a, April 2004). The OFT may not, however, impose a penalty where the agreement is a "small agreement" or abusive conduct is "of minor significance": ss.39 and 40 respectively. These terms are defined in the Competition Act 1998 (Small Agreements and Conduct of Minor Significance) Regulations 2000 (SI 2000/262).

[55] ss.33 and 34. These provisions are analogous to Art.3(1) of Council Reg.17/62 (now Art.7(1) of the Modernisation Regulation 1/2003), which was held in the circumstances of the *Magill TV Guides* case to permit the Commission to require the compulsory licensing of copyright material; see paras 29–57 *et seq.*, above.

[56] Competition Act 1998, s.35.

[57] s.46.

[58] s.49.

[59] Set out at para. 29–259, above.

[60] As to which see para. 29–209, above.

[61] See above, para. 29–270.

[62] Draft Guideline OFT 418, Intellectual property rights, para.3.3.

on market definition and the Chapter II prohibition and will take account of factors such as the market shares of the undertaking in question as well as barriers to entry in the relevant market. It will also consider whether there are other constraints on the behaviour of the undertaking in question, such as strong buyer power or government regulation.[63] The draft guideline goes on to state that although the existence of an intellectual property right may impede entry into a market in the short term, any other undertaking may in the long term be able to enter the market with its own innovation. A persistently high market share may indicate no more than persistently successful innovation. Accordingly, dominance will be assessed on a case-by-case basis.[64]

The OFT's draft guideline: specific types of conduct. The draft guideline goes on to identify certain types of conduct which may or may not infringe the Chapter II prohibition. They are as follows. First, refusal to licence. The OFT states that this will not generally infringe, but may do so if there is no objective justification for the refusal and the intellectual property right relates to a product or service which is (a) essential for the exercise of the activity in question because there is no real or potential substitute or (b) relates to a new product or service whose introduction might be prevented, despite specific, constant and regular potential demand on the part of consumers.[65] This part of the draft guideline should be treated with caution since it predates the Court of Justice's decision in *IMS Health*.[66] In particular, to the extent that conditions (a) and (b) are stated to be alternative rather than cumulative, it appears that this statement of the law is not correct. Moreover, there is no reference to the new product or service having to be on a separate market. Secondly, tying and bundling.[67] The draft guideline states that tying and bundling may be an abuse if imposed by a dominant undertaking, but that such provisions are unlikely to infringe where they are necessary for a satisfactory exploitation of the licensed right or for ensuring that the licensee conforms with quality standards.[68] Thirdly, other contractual provisions of the type listed in the guideline as potentially infringing the Chapter I prohibition may also infringe the Chapter II provision.[69] Fourthly, pricing. The OFT's view is that intellectual property rights provide an incentive to innovate by preventing for a period of time the commercial appropriation of ideas that have resulted from that innovation. Successful innovation will naturally lead to an undertaking earning post-innovation profits which are significantly higher than those of its competitors. Accordingly, there will not necessarily be an infringement if the owner of the right holds a dominant position and charges a higher selling price or royalty rate for a product, process or work protected by its right as compared with that of an unprotected product, process or work.[70]

29–278

(iii) Mergers: Part 3 of the Enterprise Act 2002

The Fair Trading Act 1973 and its repeal. Before the introduction of the Enterprise Act, mergers were covered by Part V of the Fair Trading Act 1973. In

29–279

---

[63] Draft Guideline OFT 481. The guideline on market definition is OFT 403. The guideline on the Ch.II prohibition is OFT 402. Draft revised versions of both were published in April 2004 (OFT 403a and 402a). All these documents are available on the OFT's website.
[64] Draft Guideline OFT 418, Intellectual property rights, para.3.4.
[65] Draft Guideline OFT 418, Intellectual property rights, para.3.7.
[66] Discussed above, paras 29–60 *et seq*.
[67] For definitions of these terms, see para. 29–233, above.
[68] Draft Guideline OFT 418, Intellectual property rights, para.3.8.
[69] Draft Guideline OFT 418, Intellectual property rights, para.3.9. For these, see above, para. 29–271.
[70] Draft Guideline OFT 418, Intellectual property rights, para.3.11.

summary, the position was as follows. There were two regimes, a general regime and a special regime relating to newspaper mergers. The general regime was triggered by a reference by the Secretary of State to the Monopolies and Mergers Commission, which was obliged to report on whether a "merger situation" had been created and if so whether the creation of that situation operated or might be expected to operate against the public interest. The report was then laid before Parliament and the Secretary of State was empowered to prohibit the merger or impose conditions in relation to it. Special rules applied to newspaper mergers. In summary, transfers to newspaper proprietors of newspapers whose circulation exceeded a prescribed figure were void unless made with the written consent (which might be given subject to conditions) of the Secretary of State. Except in some cases where he was satisfied that the newspaper was not economic as a going concern and as a separate newspaper or where he was satisfied that its circulation was less than a prescribed figure, the Secretary of State was obliged to refer the matter to the Monopolies and Mergers Commission ("MMC") for a report prior to acting. The provisions relating to the general regime have been repealed with effect from June 26, 2003,[71] while those relating to newspaper mergers have been repealed with effect from December 29, 2003.[72]

29–280   **When the OFT may make a reference.**[73] A reference may be made by the OFT[74] if a "relevant merger situation" exists or is anticipated. Such a situation exists if two or more enterprises have ceased to be distinct enterprises and either (a) the value of the turnover in the United Kingdom of the enterprise being taken over exceeds £70 million ("the turnover test") or (b) at least one quarter or all the goods or services of a particular description which are supplied in the United Kingdom or a substantial part of the United Kingdom are supplied by or to one and the same person or are supplied by or to the persons by whom the enterprises concerned are carried on ("the share of supply test").[75] If the OFT believes that a relevant merger situation has been or will be created and a substantial lessening of competition within any United Kingdom market or markets for goods or services has resulted or may result, it is obliged to make a reference to the Competition Commission.[76] However, the OFT may decide not to make a reference if the market is or the markets concerned are not of sufficient importance to justify it,

---

[71] By the Enterprise Act 2002, s.278(2) and Sch.26. For commencement, see Enterprise Act 2002 (Commencement No. 3, Transitional and Transitory Provisions and Savings) Order 2003 (SI 2003/1397), Art.2 and Sch. For transitional provisions, see Enterprise Act 2000, Sch.24, paras 13 and 15 to 18.

[72] By the Communications Act 2003 (c.21) s.373 and Sch.19(1). For commencement, see the Office of Communications Act 2002 (Commencement No.3) and Communications Act 2003 (Commencement No.2) Order 2003 (SI 2003/3142), Art.3 and Sch.1. For transitional provisions, see Communications Act 2003, Sch.18. paras 59 to 61.

[73] See, generally, OFT Guidance, 516: Mergers — Substantive Assessment Guidance, May 2003 (as amended by OFT Guidance Note 516a, October 2004) and OFT 526: Mergers — Procedural Guidance, May 2003.

[74] This is a significant change. Under the old law, the Secretary of State made the decision as to whether to refer: Fair Trading Act 1973, s.64(1).

[75] Enterprise Act 2002, s.23.

[76] Enterprise Act 2002, s.22(1) and 33(1). The "substantial lessening of competition" test did not appear in the Fair Trading Act 1973. In *OFT v IBA Health Ltd* [2004] EWCA Civ 142, the CAT had held that in reaching a decision as to whether to make a reference under 33(1) (anticipated mergers) the OFT was obliged to decide first, whether as far as it was concerned there was a significant prospect of a substantial lessening of competition ("SLC") and secondly (if not) whether there was a significant prospect of an alternative view being taken in the context of a fuller investigation by the Commission. The CA rejected this: the relevant belief is that the merger may be expected to result in SLC, not that the Commission may in due course decide that it may be expected to result in SLC. Further, the body which is to hold that belief is the OFT, not the Commission (see para.38). The test is one of belief, not mere suspicion (para.44). The belief must be reasonable and objectively justified by relevant facts (para.45). The likelihood of a substantial lessening of competition must be more than merely fanciful but need not be as high as "a significant prospect" (para.48). More than an arguable issue of SLC is required (para.84). By contrast,

any relevant consumer benefits outweigh the substantial lessening of competition (or any effects thereof) or (in the case of an anticipated merger) the arrangements are not sufficiently far advanced or likely to proceed to justify the reference.[77] For these purposes relevant customer benefits are: lower prices, higher quality or greater choice of goods or services and greater innovation in relation to goods or services.[78] The OFT may also make a reference if the European Commission has by decision referred the whole or part of a case to it under Article 4(4) or 9 of the EC Merger Regulation, or is deemed to have taken such a decision, unless an intervention notice is in force in relation to that case.[79]

When the OFT may not make a reference. The OFT is prohibited from making   **29–281**
a reference under the following circumstances. First, while it is considering whether to accept undertakings in lieu of a reference.[80] Secondly, once it has accepted undertakings in lieu of making a reference, provided all material facts were notified to it or made public before the undertakings were accepted.[81] Thirdly, the Act contains a "merger notice procedure" pursuant to which notice may be given to the OFT of proposed arrangements which might result in the creation of a relevant merger situation.[82] In general, no reference may be made in respect of such arrangements if the period for considering the merger notice has expired without a reference being made.[83] Fourthly, if the Secretary of State has accepted undertakings in lieu of making a reference under sections 45 or 63 of the Enterprise Act, provided all material facts were notified to the Secretary of State or the OFT or made public before the undertakings were accepted.[84] Fifthly, if there is in force an intervention notice under section 42 of the Enterprise Act, or the matter to which such a notice relates has been finally determined under Chapter 2 otherwise than in circumstancs where a notice is given to the OFT under section 56(1).[85] Sixthly, where the matter is being considered or has been dealt with by the European Commission.[86]

Undertakings in lieu of reference. The power to accept undertakings in lieu of a   **29–282**
reference may be exercised if the OFT considers that it is under a duty to make a reference.[87] The power must be exercised for the purpose of remedying, mitigating or preventing the substantial lessening of competition concerned or any

---

where the Competition Commission has to decide under ss.35(1) or 36(1) whether the merger may be expected to result in SLC, the test is the balance of probabilities (paras 46 and 81).

[77] Enterprise Act 2002, ss.22(2) and 33(2).

[78] s.30.

[79] s.34A(1). The Merger Regulation is Council Regulation (EC) No. 139/2004 of 20 January 2004 on the control of concentrations between undertakings [2004] O.J. L24/1. For intervention notices, see below, para. 29–281.

[80] Enterprise Act 2002, ss.22(3)(b) and 33(3)(b). The power to accept undertakings is considered in the next paragraph.

[81] ss.22(3)(a), 33(3)(a), 74(1) and 74(2).

[82] ss.96 to 102. See also the Enterprise Act 2002 (Merger Prenotification) Regulations 2003 (SI 2003/1369).

[83] Enterprise Act 2002, ss.22(3)(a), 33(3)(a) and 96(3). Note, however, that there are numerous exceptions to this: see s.100.

[84] ss.22(3)(a), 33(3)(a) and Sch.7, para.4. For ss.45 and 63, see para. 29–288 below, respectively. The Secretary of State's power to accept undertakings derives from Sch.7, para.3.

[85] Enterprise Act 2002, s.22(3)(d).

[86] Pursuant to a request by the United Kingdom under Art.22(1) of the EC Merger Regulation 139/2004: Enterprise Act 2002, s.22(3)(e); or where a reasoned submission requesting referral to the European Commission has been submitted to the European Commission under Art.4(5) of the EC Merger Regulation 139/2004 and no Member State competent to examine the concentration under its national competition law has, within the time permitted by Art.4(5) of the EC Merger Regulation, expressed its disagreement as regards the request to refer the case to the European Commission: *ibid.*, s.22(3)(f).

[87] Enterprise Act 2002, s.73(1).

adverse effect thereof.[88] In exercising its power, the OFT is obliged to have particular regard to the need for as comprehensive a solution as is reasonable and practicable and may have particular regard to the effect of any action on any relevant customer benefits in relation to the creation of the relevant merger situation.[89] Neither the OFT nor the Secretary of State may make a reference in relation to the creation of a relevant merger situation if it is the situation by reference to which the undertakings were accepted.[90] Where the OFT considers that an undertaking has not been or will not be fulfilled or that false or misleading information has been given to it in relation to an undertaking, it may make an order instead.[91]

29–283 **Determination by the Competition Commission.**[92] On a reference the Commission is obliged to decide whether a relevant merger situation has been created or will be created and if so whether that has resulted or may be expected to result in a substantial lessening of competition within any market or markets in the United Kingdom ("an anti-competitive outcome").[93] If the Commission decides that there is an anti-competitive outcome, it must decide whether to take action itself, or recommend action to be taken by others, for the purpose of remedying, mitigating or preventing the substantial lessening of competition or any adverse effect thereof.[94] If it decides that action should be taken, it must also decide what action should be taken and what is to be remedied, mitigated or prevented.[95] Like the OFT when considering whether to accept undertakings in lieu, the Commission is obliged to have particular regard to the need for as comprehensive a solution as is reasonable and practicable and may have particular regard to the effect of any action on any relevant customer benefits in relation to the creation of the relevant merger situation.[96] The Commission's decisions must be published in a report on the reference.[97]

29–284 **Action on the report.** Following publication of the report, the Commission is under a duty to take such action as it considers to be reasonable or practicable in order to remedy, mitigate or prevent the substantial lessening of competition and any adverse effects thereof.[98] Again it must have particular regard to the need for as comprehensive a solution as is reasonable and practicable and may have particular regard to the effect of any action on any relevant customer benefits in relation to the creation of the relevant merger situation.[99] To that end, it may accept undertakings or make an order, which may contain anything permitted by Schedule 8 of the Act, together with such supplementary, consequential or incidental provision as the Commission considers appropriate.[1] Where the Commission considers that an undertaking has not been or will not be fulfilled or that false or

---

[88] s.73(2).

[89] s.73(3), (4).

[90] Enterprise Act 2002, s.74(1). However, this prohibition does not apply if material facts were not notified to the OFT or made public before the undertaking was accepted: s.74(2).

[91] s.75(2).

[92] See, generally, Merger References: the Competition Commission's Guidelines, CC 2, June 2003.

[93] Competition Act 1998, ss.35(1) and 36(1). This is a significant departure from the "public interest" test in s.84 of the Fair Trading Act 1973. In *OFT v IBA Health Ltd* [2004] EWCA Civ 142, the CA held that where the Competition Commission has to decide under ss.35(1) or 36(1) whether the merger may be expected to result in a significant lessening of competition, the test is the balance of probabilities (paras 46 and 81).

[94] Competition Act 1998, ss.35(3) and 36(2).

[95] ss.35(3)(c), 36(2)(c).

[96] ss.35(4), (5) and 36(3), (4).

[97] s.38.

[98] Competition Act 1998, s.41.

[99] Competition Act 1998, s.41(4), (5).

[1] Enterprise Act 2002, ss.82 to 84.

misleading information has been given to it in relation to an undertaking, it may make an order instead.[2]

Schedule 8: general restrictions and obligations. Schedule 8 also applies where authorities other than the Competition Commission are taking action. Accordingly, some of its provisions are expressed in terms of what "the authority", rather than "the Competition Commission", may do. The range of permitted provisions is extensive. Under the heading "General restrictions on conduct", it includes provisions prohibiting: the making or performance of an agreement[3]; the withholding from any person of any goods or services or any orders for goods or services[4]; the requiring as a condition of the supply of goods or services the buying of any goods, the making of any payment in respect of services other than the goods or services supplied or the doing of or refraining from the doing of any other such matter[5]; discrimination (or anything which the authoriy considers to be discrimination) between persons in the prices charged for goods or services[6]; giving or agreeing to give any preference (or anything which the authoriy considers to be a preference) in respect of the supply of goods or services or of orders for goods or services[7]; or charging prices for goods or services which differ from those in any published list or notification or doing anything which the authority considers to be charging such prices.[8] An order may regulate the prices charged for goods or services, provided the relevant report identifies the prices as requiring remedial action.[9] An order may prohibit the exercise of a right to vote exercisable by virtue of the holding of any shares, stocks or securities.[10] Under the heading "General obligations to be performed", an order may require a person to supply goods or services or to do anything which the relevant authority considers appropriate to facilitate the supply of goods or services.[11] An order may require a person to supply goods or services to a particular standard or in a particular manner or to do anything which the relevant authority considers appropriate to facilitate the provision of goods or services to that standard or in that manner.[12]

29–285

Schedule 8: acquisitions and divisions. Under this head an order may: prohibit or restrict the acquisition by any person of the whole or part of an undertaking or assets of another person's business or the doing of anything which will or may result in two or more bodies corporate becoming interconnected bodies corporate[13]; require that if such an acquisition occurs or the bodies corporate become interconnected, the persons concerned shall observe any prohibitions or restric-

29–286

---

[2] Enterprise Act 2002, s.83(2).

[3] Or ordering a party to terminate an agreement Sch.8, para.2(1). However, such an order may not affect an agreement (or proposed agreement) so far as it relates to the terms and conditions of employment of any workers or to the physical conditions in which any workers are required to work: *ibid.*, Sch.8, para.2(2).

[4] Sch.8, para.3(1). References to withholding include references to agreeing or threatening to withhold and procuring others to withhold or to do such acts: *ibid.*, Sch.8, para.3(2).

[5] Sch.8, para.4.

[6] Sch.8, para.5. The order may also prohibit the procuring of such acts: *ibid.*

[7] Sch.8, para.6. Again, the order may also prohibit the procuring of such acts: *ibid.*

[8] Sch.8, para.7.

[9] Sch.8, para.8.

[10] Sch.8, para.9.

[11] Sch.8, para.10(1).

[12] Sch.8, para.10(2).

[13] Sch.8, para.12(1). Bodies corporate are "interconnected" if one is a subsidiary of the other or if both are subsidiaries of the same parent: Enterprise Act 2000, s.129(2).

tions[14]; or provide for the division of any business or group of interconnnected bodies corporate.[15]

29–287 **Schedule 8: supply and publication of information.** Under this head, an order may: require a supplier of goods or services to publish or otherwise notify prices and other information[16]; prohibit the notification of recommended or suggested prices[17]; require a supplier of goods or services to publish accounting information about the goods or services as well as information as to the quantities supplied and the geographical areas in which they are supplied[18]; and require information to be supplied to the relevant authority.[19]

29–288 **Public interest, special public interest cases and European merger cases.** In exceptional circumstances, the Secretary of State may give the OFT an "intervention notice" where he considers that one or more public interest considerations is or may be relevant to a consideration of a merger situation.[20] A "public interest consideration" is one which is specified in section 58 of the Act or is not so specified but in the opinion of the Secretary of State ought to be so specified.[21] The only specified public interest consideration (except in the case of media mergers, which are considered below)[22] specified in section 58 of the Act is the interests of national security. The effect of an intervention notice is that the OFT is obliged to report to the Secretary of State on both the competition and the public interest considerations.[23] On receipt of the report, the Secretary of State may make a reference to the Commission,[24] which is then obliged to report to the Secretary of State on competition and public interest considerations and remedies.[25] The Secretary of State may then take such action under paragraph 9 or 11 of Schedule 7 to the Act as he considers to be reasonable or practicable to remedy, mitigate or prevent any of the effects adverse to the public interest which have resulted from or may be expected to result from the creation of the relevant merger situation.[26] A similar procedure applies to "special public interest cases" concerning merger situations which involve government contractors holding confidential information relating to defence matters.[27] The Secretary of State's powers to take action are set out in section 66(6). A similar procedure also applies where there is a relevant merger situation which is also a concentration with a Community dimen-

---

[14] Sch.8, para.12(2).

[15] Sch.8 para.13(1). Such an order may contain such provision as the relevant authority considers appropriate to effect or take account of the division, *e.g.* provision as to transfer of property, rights, liabilities or obligations: *ibid.* Sch.8, para.13(3).

[16] Sch.8, para.15. The order can also prohibit the publication or notification of information: *ibid.*

[17] Sch.8, para.16.

[18] Sch.8, para.17.

[19] Sch.8, para.19.

[20] Enterprise Act 2002, s.42.

[21] s.42(3).

[22] See below, para. 29–289.

[23] Enterprise Act 2002, s.44.

[24] Enterprise Act 2002, s.45. The Secretary of State may accept an undertaking in lieu of making a reference: Sch.7, para.3. If he considers that the undertaking has not been or will not be fulfilled or that false or misleading information has been given in relation to it, he may make an order instead: para.5(2).

[25] Enterprise Act 2002, s.50.

[26] s.55. Para.9 gives the Secretary of State power to accept final undertakings. Para.10(2) gives the Secretary of State power make an order in the event of the non-fulfilment of the final undertakings or if false or misleading information has been supplied in relation to them. Para.11 gives the Secretary of State power to make orders containing anything permitted under Sch.8 (see paras 29–285 to 29–287 above) together with such supplementary, consequential or incidental provision as the Secretary of State considers appropriate.

[27] ss.59 to 66. The Secretary of State's powers to accept undertakings and make orders are the same as in relation to public interest mergers.

sion and the Secretary of State wishes to take appropriate measures to protect legitimate interests as permitted by Article 21(4) of the EC Merger Regulation.[28]

Media mergers.[29] Media mergers are now assimilated to the general mergers regime, but special rules apply to them.[30] First, additional public interest considerations are specified for the purposes of section 58 of the Act, such as the need for accurate presentation of news and free expression of opinion in newspapers.[31] This will bring many media mergers into the category of public interest mergers. When that occurs, OFCOM is obliged to report to the Secretary of State.[32] Secondly, certain media mergers are now subject to the "special public interest cases" regime.[33] Again, OFCOM is to report to the Secretary of State.[34] Finally, in relation to newspaper mergers, the Schedule 8 powers are supplemented by the addition of new powers, including the power to alter the constitution of a body corporate, and attach conditions to the operation of a newspaper.[35]

29–289

(iv) Market investigations: Part 4 of the Enterprise Act 2002

Background. Part IV of the Fair Trading Act provided for the reference to the Monopolies and Mergers Commission ("the MMC") of "monopoly situations". References might be made (save in a very few cases)[36] by the DGFT,[37] and the vast majority of references under Part IV were made by him; however, they might also be made by the Secretary of State for Trade and Industry, or the Secretary of State acting jointly with appropriate Ministers.[38] The MMC reported on a reference to the Secretary of State. If it found certain matters referred to it to be contrary to the public interest, the Secretary of State might make an appropriate order under Schedule 8 to the Act or section 144 of the 1988 Act.[39] These provisions, which are discussed in the previous edition of this work,[40] have been repealed by the Enterprise Act 2002 with effect from June 26, 2003.[41] There are two main changes. First, references are now made by the OFT (or, if he is not satisfied with the decision of the OFT not to make a reference, the appropriate Minister) to the Competition Commission. Secondly, there need not be a "monopoly situation" as defined in the Fair Trading Act 1973; rather, it is sufficient that there be prevention, restriction or distortion of competition.

29–290

---

[28] Council Regulation (EC) No.139/2004 of January 20, 2004 on the control of concentrations between undertakings, [2004] O.J. L24/1, which came into effect on May 1, 2004. For the Secretary of State's powers in this regard, see Enterprise Act 2002, ss.67 to 68 and the Enterprise Act 2002 (Protection of Legitimate Interests) Order 2003 (SI 2003/1592).

[29] See, generally, the DTI's Guidance Document: Enterprise Act 2002: Public Interest Intervention in Media Mergers, May 2004, which is available on the DTI's website, *www.dti.gov.uk*.

[30] By the insertion in the Enterprise Act 2002 of a number of additional sections by the Communications Act 2003, with effect from December 29, 2003: see the Office of Communications Act 2002 (Commencement No. 3) and Communications Act 2003 (Commencement No. 2) Order 2003 (SI 2003/3142), Art.3 and Sch.1.

[31] Enterprise Act 2002, s.58(2A) to (2C).

[32] s.44A.

[33] s.59(3) to (3D).

[34] s.61A.

[35] Sch.8 para.20A.

[36] Set out in RTPA 1976, Schs 5 and 7.

[37] FTA 1973, s.50.

[38] FTA 1973, s.51.

[39] See paras 29–297 *et seq.*, below.

[40] *Copinger*, (14th ed.), paras 29–232 *et seq.*

[41] Enterprise Act 2002, s.278(2) and Sch.26. For commencement, see Enterprise Act 2002 (Commencement No.3, Transitional and Transitory Provisions and Savings) Order 2003 (SI 2003/1397), Art.2 and Sch. For transitional provisions, see Enterprise Act 2002, Sch.24, paras 14 to 18.

29–291   **Power of OFT and Minister to make references.**[42] The OFT may make a reference to the Commission if it has reasonable grounds for suspecting that any feature, or combination of features, of a market in the United Kingdom for goods or services prevents, restricts or distorts competition in connection with the supply or acquisition of any goods or services in the United Kingdom or a part of the United Kingdom.[43] For these purposes, the following are features of the market: the structure of the market or any aspect of that structure; any conduct (whether or not in the market concerned) of one or more than one person who supplies or acquires goods or services in the market; and any conduct in relation to the market concerned of customers of any person who supplies or acquires goods or services.[44] A reference may not be made by the OFT where a reference by the appropriate Minister is pending.[45] The appropriate Minister has the power to make a reference (a) in the same circumstances as the OFT,[46] (b) where he is not satisfied with a decision of the OFT not to make a reference[47] or (c) when he has brought to the OFT's attention information which he considers relevant to the question of whether it should made a reference, but is not satisfied that it will decide within such period as he considers reasonable whether to make such a reference.[48] The effect of an earlier acceptance of undertakings in lieu of a reference on these powers to refer is dealt with in the next paragraph.

29–292   **Undertakings in lieu of reference.** The power to accept undertakings in lieu of a reference may be exercised if the OFT considers that it has the power to make a reference and otherwise intends to make one.[49] The power must be exercised for the purpose of remedying, mitigating or preventing any adverse effect on competition concerned or any detrimental effect on customers so far as it has resulted from or may be expected to result from the adverse effect on competition.[50] In exercising its power, the OFT is obliged to have particular regard to the need to achieve as comprehensive a solution as is reasonable and practicable and may have particular regard to the effect of any action on any relevant customer benefits of the feature or features of the market concerned.[51] Neither the OFT nor the relevant Minister may make a reference in relation to any feature of a market for goods or services where the OFT has accepted undertakings in lieu of a reference within the previous 12 months in relation to the same description of goods or services to which the feature relates[52]

29–293   **Questions to be decided on reference.**[53] On receipt of a reference, the Competition Commission is obliged to decide whether any feature or combination of features of each relevant market prevents, restricts or distorts competition in con-

---

[42] See, generally, OFT 511: Market Investigation References, March 2003. The OFT mya decide to make such a reference as a result of a market study prusuant to s.5 of the Enterprise Act. For market studies, see generally, "Market Studies: Guidance on the OFT approach" (OFT, November 2004).

[43] Enterprise Act 2002, s.131(1).

[44] Enterprise Act 2002, s.131(2). "Conduct" includes any failure to act, whether intentional or not, and any other unintentional conduct: *ibid.*, s.131(3).

[45] s.131(4)(b).

[46] s.132(3).

[47] s.132(1).

[48] s.132(2).

[49] Enterprise Act 2002, s.154(1).

[50] s.154(2).

[51] ss.154(3) and (4).

[52] Enterprise Act 2002, s.156(1), unless the OFT considers that any undertaking concerned has been breached or the person responsible for giving the undertaking concerned gave the OFT false or misleading information in connection with the matter: *ibid.*, s.156(2).

[53] See, generally, Market Investigation References: Competition Commission Guidelines, CC3, June 2003.

nection with the supply or acquisition of any goods or services in the United Kingdom or a part of the United Kingdom.[54] If the Commission decides that there is such an adverse effect on competition, it must also decide whether action should be taken by itself for the purposes of remedying, mitigating or preventing the adverse effect on competition or any resultant detrimental effect on customers.[55] For these purposes, the term "detrimental effect on customers" means higher prices, lower quality of goods or services or less innovation.[56] If the Commission decides that action should be taken, it should decide what action is to be taken and what is to be remedied, mitigated or prevented.[57] Like the OFT when considering whether to accept undertakings, the Commission is obliged to have particular regard to the need to achieve as comprehensive a solution as is reasonable and practicable and may have particular regard to the effect of any action on any relevant customer benefits of the feature or features of the market concerned.[58] The Commission is obliged to prepare and publish a report on its decisions.[59]

Action on report. Following publication of the report, the Commission is under a duty to take such action as it considers to be reasonable or practicable in order to remedy, mitigate or prevent the adverse effect on competition and any detrimental effects on customers.[60] Again it must have particular regard to the need for as comprehensive a solution as is reasonable and practicable and may have particular regard to the effect of any action on any relevant customer benefits of the feature or features of the market concerned.[61] To that end, it may accept undertakings or make an order, which may contain anything permitted by Schedule 8 of the Act, together with such supplementary, consequential or incidental provision as the Commission considers appropriate.[62] The provisions permitted by Schedule 8 are considered above.[63] Where the Commission considers that an undertaking has not been or will not be fulfilled or that false or misleading information has been given in relation to an undertaking, it may make an order instead.[64]

29–294

Public interest cases. Where the OFT is considering whether to accept undertakings in lieu of a reference or the Commission is considering a reference, the Secretary of State may serve an "intervention notice" if he considers that it is or may be the case that a public interest consideration is relevant to the case.[65] For these purposes, a public interest consideration is a consideration specified as such in the Act or which is not so specified but which the Secretary of State considers ought to be so specified.[66] At the time of writing, the only consideration which is specified is the interests of national security.[67] If an intervention notice is served at a time when the OFT is considering whether to accept undertakings in lieu, the Secretary of State obtains a power of veto over the undertakings which the OFT

29–295

---

[54] Enterprise Act 2002, s.134(1).
[55] s.134(4)(a), (b).
[56] s.134(5).
[57] s.134(4)(c).
[58] s.134(6), (7).
[59] s.136(2).
[60] Enterprise Act 2002, s.138(2). For the meaning of the expression "detrimental effects on customers", see the previous paragraph.
[61] s.138(4), (5).
[62] ss.159 to 161.
[63] See paras 29–285 to 29–287.
[64] Enterprise Act 2002, s.160(2).
[65] Enterprise Act 2002, s.139.
[66] s.139(5).
[67] s.153(1).

may accept.[68] Where an intervention notice is served at a time when the Commission is considering a reference, the Commission is obliged determine the same questions as in a normal case, but to decide whether the Secretary of State should take action.[69] If the Commission's report contains a decision that there is an adverse effect on competition and that action should be taken, the Secretary of State must then decide whether a public interest consideration is relevant to any action recommended by the Commission.[70] If so, he may take remedial action,[71] by way of accepting undertakings or making an order in accordance with Schedule 8.[72] Where the Secretary of State considers that an undertaking has not been or will not be fulfilled or that false or misleading information has been given to him in relation to an undertaking, he may make an order instead.[73] If the Secretary of State does not act, the matter reverts to the Commission to be dealt with in the normal way.[74]

(v) The Competition Act 1980.

29–296   **Competition Act 1980, section 11.** Sections 2 to 10 of this Act conferred powers of investigation and control on the DGFT in relation to "anti-competitive practices".[75] These provisions were repealed by the Competition Act 1998 with effect from March 1, 2000.[76] However, section 11 remains in modified form.[77] This section empowers the Secretary of State to refer to the Competition Commission any question relating to the efficiency and costs of or the service provided by certain public bodies.[78] Following a reference, the Commission must report on the questions referred and any recommended action.[79] On receipt of the report, the Secretary of State has the power to make an order for the purpose of remedying or preventing what he considers are the adverse effects of any course of conduct specified in the report as operating against the public interest.[80] An order made under this power may contain anything permitted by Schedule 8 of the Enterprise Act 2002 with some specified omissions.[81]

---

[68] s.150.
[69] s.141.
[70] s.146.
[71] s.147.
[72] s.147.
[73] s.160(2).
[74] s.148.
[75] See *Copinger*, (14th ed.), para.29–242.
[76] Competition Act 1998, s.17 and Sch.14. For commencement, see the Competition Act 1998 (Commencement No. 5) Order 2000 (SI 2000/344), Art.2 and Sch. For transitional provisions, see Competition Act 1998, Sch.13, para.43.
[77] As amended by Enterprise Act 2002, Sch.25 para.10, with effect from June 20, 2003: see the Enterprise Act 2002 (Commencement No. 3, Transitional and Transitory Provisions and Savings) Order 2003 (SI 2003/1397), Art.2 and Sch. For savings, see Art.8.
[78] Competition Act 1980, s.11(1). The public bodies are as follows: any body corporate that supplies goods or services by way of business, whose affairs are managed by its members and whose members hold office by virtue of a statutory appointment by a Minister (*ibid.*, s.1(3)(a)); certain public transport companies and service providers (s.1(3)(aa) to (bb)); the Environment Agency (s.1(3)(c)); a board administering a scheme under the Agricultural Marketing Act (s.1(3)(d)); any body corporate with a duty to promote and assist the supply of goods and services by any of these bodies (s.1(3)(e)); and any subsidiary of such a body (s.1(3)(f)).
[79] Competition Act 1980, s.11(8), (10).
[80] Competition Act 1980, s.12(5).
[81] Competition Act 1980, s.12(5A). The omitted paras are 8 (regulation of prices charged for goods or services), 13 (division of business or group) and 14 (division by sale of part of an undertaking).

(vi) Section 144 of the 1988 Act

Introduction. This section introduced special powers exercisable in cases where   **29–297**
the matters identified by the Monopolies and Mergers Commission as operating
against the public interest included conditions in licences granted by the owner of
copyright in a work restricting the use of the work by the licensee or the right of
the copyright owner to grant other licences; or a refusal of a copyright owner to
grant licences on reasonable terms. Section 144 has now been amended to take
account of the changes introduced by the Enterprise Act 2002.[82] Its provisions
now apply where whatever neeeds to be remedied, mitigated or prevented by the
Secretary of State, the OFT or (as the case may be) the Competition Commission
under a list of specified provisions consists of or includes conditions in licences
granted by the owner of copyright in a work restricting the use of the work by the
licensee or the right of the copyright owner to grant other licences; or a refusal of
a copyright owner to grant licences on reasonable terms.[83] In such a case, the
powers conferred by Schedule 8 of the Enterprise Act 2002 include power to
cancel or modify those conditions and, instead or in addition, to provide that
licences in respect of the copyright be available as of right.[84]

Circumstances where section 144 may apply. As has been explained, section   **29–298**
144 applies where something needs to be remedied by the Secretary of State, the
OFT or the Competition Commission under a list of specified provisions. They
are as follows: section 12(5) of the Competition Act 1980, which empowers the
Secretary of State to make an order to remedy or prevent the adverse effects of a
course of conduct by certain public authorities[85]; section 41(2) of the Enterprise
Act 2002, which obliges the Competition Commission in some circumstances to
take action in relation to mergers[86]; sections 55(2) and 66(6) of the Enterprise
Act, which empower the Secretary of State to take action in relation to mergers in
public interest cases[87] and special public interest cases[88]; section 75(2) of the
Enterprise Act, which empowers the OFT to make orders in relation to mergers
when undertakings in lieu of a reference are not or will not be fulfilled or false or
misleading information has been given[89]; section 83(2) of the Enterprise Act,
which gives the same powers to the Commission in relation to final undertakings[90]; section 138(2) of the Enterprise Act, which obliges the Competition Commission in some circumstances to take action following a market investigation[91];
section 147(2) of the Enterprise Act, which empowers the Secretary of State to
take action following a market investigation to which a public interest consideration applies[92]; section 160(2) of the Enterprise Act, which permits the Competition Commission or the Secretary of State to make orders following a market

---

[82] By the Enterprise Act 2002, Sch.25, para.18(2) and (3) with effect from June 20, 2003: see the
Enterprise Act 2002 (Commencement No.3, Transitional and Transitory Provisions and Savings)
Order 2003 (SI 2003/1397), Art.2 and Sch. Note, however, that the amendments have not come
into effect for purposes relating to the making by the Secretary of State of references under s.32
of the Water Industry Act 1991 (duty to refer merger of water or sewerage undertakings), or any
references so made: Art.3(1) and Sch.

[83] CDPA 1988, s.144(1).

[84] CDPA 1988, s.144(1A). For Sch.8, see paras 29–285 to 29–287 above.

[85] See para. 29–296, above.

[86] See para. 29–284, above.

[87] See para. 29–288, above.

[88] See para. 29–288, above.

[89] See para. 29–282, above. The reference to s.66(6) has effect as if it includes a reference to
Art.12(7) of the Enterprise Act 2002 (Protection of Legitimate Interests) Order 2003 (SI 2003/
192): see Sch.4, para.7. For this Order, see note to para. 29–189, above.

[90] See para. 29–284 above.

[91] See para. 29–294, above.

[92] See para. 29–295, above.

investigation where undertakings are nor or will not be fulfilled or false or misleading information has been given[93]; and paragraphs 5(2) and 10(2) of Schedule 7 to the Enterprise Act, which empower the Secretary of State to make orders in relation to public interest and special public interest mergers when undertakings in lieu of a reference or final undertakings are not or will not be fulfilled or false or misleading information has been given.[94]

29–299   **Exercise of powers under section 144.** The powers available under section 144 may only be exercised if the Secretary of State, the OFT or (as the case may be) the Competition Commission is satisfied that to do so does not contravene any Convention relating to copyright to which the United Kingdom is a party.[95] The terms of any licence available by virtue of these provisions fall to be settled, in default of agreement, by the Copyright Tribunal on an application by the person requiring the licence.[96] The terms so settled shall authorise the licensee to do everything in respect of which a licence is so available.[97] Where the terms of a licence are so settled by the Tribunal, the licence has effect from the date on which the application to the Tribunal was made.[98]

29–300   **Application to design right, rights in performances and database right.** Section 238 of the 1988 Act[99] contains parallel powers in relation to design right. The section is in substantially the same terms as section 144 but there are the following differences. First, there is no reference to compliance with international Conventions, no doubt because the United Kingdom is not a party to any relevant Convention in respect of design right. Secondly, in default of agreement the terms of the licence are to be settled by the comptroller rather than the Copyright Tribunal.[1] Paragraph 17 of Schedule 2A to the 1988 Act[2] contains parallel powers in relation to performers' property rights. These are in substantially identical terms to those of section 144. Finally, paragraph 15 of Schedule 2 to the Database Regulations[3] contains parallel powers in relation to database right. This paragraph is in substantially the same terms but again, since there is no relevant convention in respect of database right, there is no reference to compliance with international conventions.

29–301   **Background.** The above provisions were introduced following two reports from the MMC. The first of these reports concerned the licensing of copyright in re-

---

[93] See paras 29–294 and 29–295, above.

[94] See para. 29–288, above. The references to paras 5(2) or 10(2) have effect as if they included a reference to paras 5(2) or 10(2) to the Enterprise Act 2002 (Protection of Legitimate Interests) Order 2003 (SI 2003/192): see *ibid.*, Sch.4, para.7. For this Order, see above, para. 29–189.

[95] CDPA 1988, s.144(3).

[96] CDPA 1988, s.144(4); as to the Copyright Tribunal generally, see paras 29–88 *et seq.*, and as to an application under this provision see para. 29–131, above.

[97] CDPA 1988, s.144(4)

[98] CDPA 1988, s.144(5).

[99] As amended by the Enterprise Act 2002 (c.40) Sch.25 para.18(3) with effect from June 20, 2003: see the Enterprise Act (Commencement No.3, Transitional and Transitory and Savings) Order 2003 (SI 2003/1397), Art.2 (except for the purposes of references under s.32 of the Water Industry Act 1991: see Art.3(1)).

[1] CDPA 1988, s.238(3).

[2] As amended by the Enterprise Act 2002 (c.40) Sch.25 para.18(5) with effect from June 20, 2003: see the Enterprise Act (Commencement No.3, Transitional and Transitory and Savings) Order 2003 (SI 2003/1397), Art.2 (except for the purposes of references under s.32 of the Water Industry Act 1991: see Art.3(1)).

[3] As amended by the Enterprise Act 2002 (Consequential and Supplemental Provisions) Order 2003 (SI 2003/1398), art.2 and Sch., para.31 with effect from June 20, 2003 (except for the purposes of references under s.32 of the Water Industry Act 1991: *ibid.*, Art.3(1)).

spect of spare body panels for cars by the Ford Motor Company Limited.[4] The MMC concluded that Ford's refusal to grant licences to would-be manufacturers of replacement parts was anti-competitive and contrary to the public interest.[5] However, the MMC went on to say that there was no remedy against such practices under existing legislation because "the ability to make an order for the grant of a licence is not among the limited powers exercisable by the Secretary of State following a report of the Commission".[6] The MMC also pointed out that whilst an order prohibiting Ford from engaging in this practice might appear to oblige Ford indirectly to grant licences, there would be nothing to stop Ford from only offering licences at a prohibitively high rate.[7]

The second report concerned the refusal of the owners of the *Radio Times* and *TV Times* to license newspapers and magazines to publish comprehensive weekly listings of television programmes.[8] Although the MMC concluded that the BBC and ITP were engaged in an anti-competitive practice, in this case the MMC was equally divided on the question of whether this practice operated against the public interest.[9] Nevertheless, the MMC also made it clear that even if it had concluded that the practice did operate in the public interest it would not have been able to recommend an effective course of action.[10] Section 144 was thus introduced to ensure that in future a remedy would be available in these circumstances.

Prior to the introduction of this provision there was some concern that such a power would contravene the United Kingdom's international obligations under the Berne Convention.[11] It might be thought that such a power would fall within Article 17 of the Convention, which provides that "The provisions of this Convention cannot in any way affect the right of the Government of each country of the Union to permit, to control, or to prohibit, by legislation or regulation, the circulation, presentation, or exhibition of any work or production". The better view, however, seems to be that Article 17 should be confined to matters of public order and morality.[12] Nevertheless, the regulation of monopolistic activity may still be justified under the general principle, agreed at the Rome, Brussels and Stockholm revision conferences, that Member States remain free to regulate certain matters in the public interest, and that this includes restricting potential

---

[4] Ford Motor Company Ltd: A report on the policy of the Ford Motor Company of not granting licences to manufacture or sell in the United Kingdom certain replacement body parts for Ford Vehicles, 1985 (Cmnd 9437). This Report followed an investigation under Competition Act 1980 s.3 (as to which see *Copinger*, (14th ed.), para.29–242) by the DGFT, who concluded that Ford was engaged in an anti-competitive practice and who referred the matter to the MMC. See further, *Ford Motor Company Ltd, Licensing for the Manufacture or Sale of Replacement Body Parts*, published on March 21, 1984 by the Office of Fair Trading: paras 9.1–9.4.

[5] Cmnd.9437, paras 6.51; 6.29–6.50.

[6] MMC Report, Cmnd.9437, para.6.57.

[7] MMC Report, Cmnd.9437, paras 6.58–6.59.

[8] The British Broadcasting Corporation and Independent Television Publications Limited: A report on the policies and practices on the BBC and ITP of limiting the publication by others of advance program information, 1985 (Cmnd 9614). Again, this Report followed an investigation under Competition Act 1980, s.3 (as to which see *Copinger*, 14th ed., para.29–242) by the Director General of Fair Trading who referred the matter to the MMC. See further, British Broadcasting Corporation and Independent Television Publications: The Publication of Programme Information, published on December 13, 1984 by the Office of Fair Trading. See further, paras 29–10 *et seq.*, above.

[9] Cmnd.9614, paras 6.11; 6.26–6.36; 6.37–6.40.

[10] MMC Report, Cmnd.9614, para.6.42.

[11] See para. 29–06, above and see further, Greaves, "Copyright: Public interest and statutory powers under the CA 1980", [1987] 1 E.I.P.R. 3 at 5.

[12] See further, Ricketson, *The Berne Convention for the Protection of Literary and Artistic Works: 1886–1986* (Kluwer, London, 1987), para.9.72. It should also be noted that attempts by the UK and Australian Governments to amend Art.17 so as to include expressly a reference to the control of monopolies were rejected at the Stockholm revision conference (1967), at least partly on the grounds that any such amendment would be superfluous.

abuses of monopoly. Moreover, the Act expressly provides that the powers under section 144 and paragraph 17 of Schedule 2A shall only be exercised if the person exercising them is satisfied that to do so does not contravene any Convention relating to copyright to which the United Kingdom is a party.[13]

(vii) References to the MMC under the old law

29–302   **The *Video Games* reference.** An example of the use by the DGFT and the MMC of their powers under the Fair Trading Act 1973,[14] after the coming into force of section 144 of the Copyright, Designs and Patents Act 1988, which is of relevance to the subject-matter of this work is the reference of video games to the MMC.[15] The investigation concerned the practices of Sega and of Nintendo, which provided, and licensed others to provide, software for use on consoles supplied by them. The MMC was concerned at the conditions on which the companies licensed others to produce games; those conditions enabled the companies to control the pricing and time of release of the games and enabled the segmentation of markets. The MMC held that this was not an appropriate way of seeking a reward for research and development of the consoles; such a reward could be obtained from manufacturers of the consoles. The MMC recommended that if necessary[16] section 144 of the 1988 Act should be used to ensure that software companies could obtain licences on terms to be settled by the Copyright Tribunal if not agreed; the MMC also recommended that licences should no longer contain conditions as to the number of games to be produced, or as to prior approval of their contents or packaging.

29–303   **The report into collective licensing.**[17] This report resulted from "general" references under section 78 of the Fair Trading Act 1973. The MMC were requested to report on practices relating to the collective licensing of sound recordings for broadcasting and public performance, and in particular, the practice of owners of copyright assigning their rights to collecting bodies, and those bodies stipulating royalties, common tariffs and restrictions on competition. At the time of the report there were a number of bodies concerned directly or indirectly with the licensing of sound recordings for broadcasting and public performance,[18] but only Phonographic Performance Limited (PPL) actually fell within the terms of reference. The MMC concluded that collective licensing bodies are the best available mechanism for licensing sound recordings, provided they can be restrained from using their monopoly power unfairly. The MMC identified a number of respects in which the activities of collecting societies, and in particular PPL, might have effects adverse to the public interest and included a number of recommendations in its report. Amongst the main recommendations made by the MMC were that PPL should be obliged to permit the use of its repertoire in return for equitable remuneration; users should be entitled to a statutory licence; PPL's injunctive rights should be curtailed; the Copyright Tribunal should be strengthened; and PPL should abandon its needletime restraints.

---

[13] CDPA 1988, s.144(3), Sch.2A, para.17(3).

[14] The 1973 Act has now been repealed and replaced: see para. 29–254 above.

[15] *Video Games* (1995) Cm.2781.

[16] Although in fact both Sega and Nintendo gave appropriate undertakings to the Secretary of State.

[17] Collective Licensing: A Report on certain practices in the collective licensing of public performances and broadcasting rights in sound recordings, 1988, (Cm.530).

[18] Phonographic Performance Limited (PPL); the International Federation of Phonogram and Videogram Producers (IFPI); the Mechanical Rights Society Limited and the Mechanical Copyright Protection Society Limited (MCPS) which were due to merge at the time; and British Phonograph Industry Limited (BPI); as to PPL and MCPS, see paras 28–60 and 28–56, respectively.

5. RESTRAINT OF TRADE

General principles. The common law doctrine of restraint of trade is an example   **29–304**
of the application of public policy to contracts. Under the doctrine, covenants
which are in restraint of trade are prima facie unenforceable at common law and
are enforceable only if they are reasonable as between the parties and so far as
the public interest is concerned.[19] Covenants in restraint of trade are void in the
sense that the courts will not enforce them, but the parties are not acting illegally
if they choose to do so.[20] The doctrine is one to be "applied to factual situations
with a broad and flexible rule of reason".[21]

The case of *Macaulay v Schroeder Music Publishing Co Ltd*[22] dispelled whatever doubts may previously have existed as to the applicability of the principles
established in cases on agreements in restraint of trade to agreements for the
exclusive provision of services for a definite period. It is therefore now clear that
the doctrine is capable of applying to agreements relating to publishing and
recording.[23]

In *Macaulay v Schroeder*, above, the House of Lords, affirming the Court of
Appeal and Plowman J., held that an agreement between a songwriter and music
publishers, whereby the publishers engaged the songwriter's exclusive services
for the term of the agreement was, having regard to all its terms, unduly restrictive and in unreasonable restraint of trade and was therefore contrary to public
policy and unenforceable, and that this was so, notwithstanding that the agreement was in the publishers' standard form, which was a form in common use between music publishers and songwriters.

Whilst the agreement in *Macaulay v Schroeder*, above, was in the form of an
agreement for exclusive services, which contained an express restriction on the
songwriter's ability to work for any other music publishers, with an assignment
of the product of the writer's talent created during the period of the agreement,[24]
it was the restriction inherent in this assignment of future works which was
throughout seen as the restriction which brought the agreement within the
principles applicable to agreements in restraint of trade. It follows, therefore, that
these principles are equally applicable to an agreement which in its form is simply
an assignment of present and future works, or even of future works only, to be
composed during the period of the agreement, and which contains no express
restrictions on the songwriter's ability to pursue his profession, but only terms
directly connected with the assignment, such as for the payment by the publishers
of royalties on works published under the agreement. All such agreements and
assignments have therefore to be considered in the light of the decision in *Macaulay v Schroeder*, above. What is required is a consideration of the agreement
as a whole, and an assessment of the cumulative effect of the restrictions in it,
whether such restrictions are expressed, or merely follow, by necessary implication, from the very fact of an assignment of future works. An artist's contract is
in restraint of trade if the artist can effectively be prevented by the contract from

---

[19] See in particular *Esso Petroleum Ltd v Harper's Garage (Stourport) Ltd* [1968] A.C. 269. For a
general discussion of the principles of the doctrine see *Chitty on Contracts* (29th ed., Sweet &
Maxwell) at paras 16–075 *et seq.*
[20] *Boddington v Lawton* [1994] I.C.R. 478.
[21] *Per* Lord Reid in *Esso Petroleum Ltd v Harper's Garage (Stourport) Ltd* [1986] A.C. 269 at 331.
[22] [1974] 1 W.L.R. 1308, HL. See also *Clifford Davis Management Ltd v WEA Records Ltd* [1975]
1 W.L.R. 61, CA.
[23] See also *Zang Tumb Tuum Records Ltd v Johnson* [1993] E.M.L.R. 61.
[24] The material terms of the agreement are set out in the speech of Lord Reid: *Macaulay v Schroeder* [1974] 1 W.L.R. 1308 at 1310.

reaching the public over a prolonged period. It makes no difference that meanwhile the artist has a living wage.[25]

In *Sunshine Records (Pty) Ltd v Frohling*,[26] the court held that an exclusive recording contract for an initial term of three years renewable for a further three years was in undue restraint of trade, because of the nature, extent and duration of the obligations and restrictions imposed on the artists, together with the absence of any real reciprocal obligation on the recording company.

29–305   More recently, the doctrine of restraint of trade was considered in *Panayiotou v Sony Music Entertainment (UK) Ltd*.[27] In that case the pop star, George Michael, alleged that his exclusive recording agreement dated January 4, 1988, with the defendant, Sony, (the 1988 Agreement) was void or unenforceable (in so far as it remained unperformed) as being in unreasonable restraint of trade. The allegation that the agreement was void was not pursued at first instance. The plaintiff further alleged that the agreement was prohibited by Article 85(1) of the Treaty of Rome.[28] Although the only agreement in issue was the 1988 Agreement, the background to that agreement was important. The plaintiff and one Ridgeley, who at the time were both young, unknown and inexperienced, had entered into an exclusive recording agreement dated March 25, 1982, with Melodyshire Ltd, trading as Inner Vision (the 1982 Agreement). The 1982 Agreement was for their exclusive performances for up to four singles and 10 albums. Inner Vision had a licence agreement with Sony, and the 1982 Agreement incorporated Sony's then standard artists' conditions. In late 1983 the plaintiff and Ridgeley were in dispute with Inner Vision, claiming that the 1982 Agreement was unenforceable as being in restraint of trade. Inner Vision commenced proceedings, which in due course were compromised by the plaintiff and Ridgeley entering into a recording agreement with Sony (the 1984 Agreement) on Sony's then standard form of recording contract, including an option to acquire the exclusive recording services of each artist if they ceased to perform together as a group. The plaintiff and Ridgeley subsequently ceased to perform together as a group, and in 1986 Sony exercised its option against the plaintiff, thereby acquiring the exclusive right to his performances as a solo artist. Sony took delivery of the plaintiff's first solo album, *Faith*, which was very successful.

The plaintiff then renegotiated the terms of his recording agreement with Sony, and entered into the 1988 Agreement, whereupon the 1984 Agreement ceased to have effect. The plaintiff was obliged to deliver three albums in the initial period of the 1988 Agreement. *Faith* was treated as the first, and the plaintiff delivered *Listen Without Prejudice* as the second in July 1990. Further variations were negotiated and agreed to in the 1988 Agreement. Before delivery of the third album, the present dispute arose and the plaintiff commenced proceedings in October 1992.[29]

The terms of the 1988 Agreement were held to contain restraints of trade, as

---

[25] See *Silvertone Records Ltd v Mountfield* [1993] E.M.L.R. 152 and *Provident Financial Group plc v Hayward* [1989] 3 All E.R. 298.

[26] [1990] (4) S.A.782. See also *Watson v Prager* [1991] 1 W.L.R. 726, in which Scott J. applied the principles laid down in *Macaulay v Schroeder* [1974] 1 W.L.R. 1308, holding that an exclusive three-year contract between a boxer and his manager was, on its terms, unreasonable and unenforceable.

[27] [1994] E.M.L.R. 229, Parker J.

[28] Now Art.81(1). See paras 29–174 *et seq.*, above.

[29] The material terms of the 1988 Agreement were: it covered the plaintiff's worldwide performing services for the production of records; it was for an initial contract period and five further contract periods at Sony's option; each contract period continued until after delivery of a minimum commitment for that period; the agreement was for an overall maximum term of 15 years; the total minimum commitment, assuming that all options were exercised, was sufficient for eight albums; Sony could reject product on the ground that it was not of the artistic or commercial quality of

understood for the purposes of the common law doctrine, which were not dispensed from the necessity of justification, so that, apart from arguments based on public policy, the restraint of trade doctrine was applicable to the 1988 Agreement and its provisions required to be justified by reference to the test in *Nordenfelt v Maxim Nordenfelt Guns and Ammunition Company Ltd.*[30]

However, the judge then went on to hold that the 1988 Agreement had to be considered as a renegotiation of the 1984 Agreement, which was itself a compromise of proceedings which raised the issue of the enforceability of the 1982 Agreement. The plaintiff had expressly not sought to assert the unenforceability of the 1984 Agreement in the current proceedings. The court concluded that the 1984 Agreement had to be treated for the purposes of the current proceedings as an enforceable agreement. In these circumstances the court accepted Sony's argument that reasons of public policy relating to the compromise of disputes precluded the plaintiff from alleging that the 1988 Agreement was in restraint of trade. For that reason, the plaintiff's claim failed.[31]

The judge then proceeded to consider whether, on the basis that the restraint of trade doctrine did apply to the 1988 Agreement, its terms were justified. His conclusion, after considering each of the relevant terms and the evidence before him, was that the restrictions contained were reasonably necessary for the protection of the legitimate interests of Sony and were commensurate with the benefits secured to the plaintiff under the agreement.[32]

It is clear that, for the purposes of deciding whether an agreement is in unreasonable restraint of trade or unduly restrictive, the agreement must be considered as at the date it is entered into.[33] The court is not therefore entitled to have regard to how the agreement has in practice been operated, nor to the motives of the party under the restraint who now wishes to be free of his bargain.

In *Macaulay v Schroeder*, above, certain terms were singled out as pointing to a conclusion that the agreement in that case was unduly restrictive; they are set out in the speech of Lord Reid, and are a helpful guide for those seeking to avoid entering into a publishing agreement which may subsequently be found to be unduly restrictive.[34] Of particular importance is the duration of the term of the agreement,[35] and this will include any possible extension, whether automatic in certain events, or at the option of the publishers. Then the exclusivity of the ser-

29–306

---

prior recorded performances; Sony was entitled to copyright in the master recordings throughout the world for the full period of copyright; the plaintiff was not entitled to perform for recording purposes any composition contained in a master recording before the later of three years after expiry of the agreement or five years from release of the master recording of the composition; Sony's obligation to exploit the product of the plaintiff's services was limited to the release of no less than three and no more than four single play records; Sony was free to assign its copyrights and, indirectly, its contractual rights under the agreement.

[30] [1894] A.C. 535.

[31] *Panayiotou v Sony Music Entertainment (UK) Ltd.* [1994] E.M.L.R. 229 at 345–347.

[32] *Panayiotou v Sony Music Entertainment (UK) Ltd.* [1994] E.M.L.R. 229 at 380.

[33] *Macaulay v Schroeder Music Publishing Co Ltd* [1974] 1 W.L.R. 1308, *per* Lord Reid at 1309H.

[34] In *Silvertone Records Ltd v Mountfield* [1993] E.M.L.R. 152 the following terms of an exclusive recording agreement were held to be unfair: the term of the agreement which made it possible to sterilise the artist's output for seven years; a rerecording restraint of 10 years; the record company's unrestricted right to authorise the use of the artist's records to endorse products; the right to withhold advances in the event of a breach of any kind; the unequal power to terminate the agreement; the record company's right to decide on all aspects of the recording process and the denial of any artistic control to the artists; the record company's unlimited right of assignment, given the degree of co-operation required.

[35] *Macaulay v Schroeder Music Publishing Co. Ltd* [1974] 1 W.L.R. 1308, *per* Lord Reid at 1312G. The term under consideration was for five years, extendable for a further five years on royalties payable in the first five years exceeding a stated amount. Such agreements often contain a string of option clauses enabling the publisher or record company to prolong the agreement. If the total possible length of the agreement is such as to make it unfair, the publisher or record company will not be able to save the agreement by arguing that some of the option clauses can be severed:

vices and the extent of the works covered by the agreement must be considered. Are all outlets for the writer's creative talents covered, or only those in certain fields, leaving him free to exploit his talents in other fields? Are all the writer's past and future works created during the term of the agreement covered? Clearly the narrower the scope of the restriction in these two respects, the less likely that it would be found unreasonable. The right to assign the benefit of the agreement may be a relevant consideration; an unqualified right in this respect on the part of the publishers, coupled with a qualified right or an express prohibition against such assignment on the part of the writer may well be unreasonable. Are the publishers under any meaningful obligation to publish and exploit any of the writer's works?[36] If it is not practicable to provide for such an obligation, it may be advisable to give the writer a right to terminate the agreement, and to call for reassignment of the copyright in unpublished works, if the publishers do not publish his works.[37]

Looked at as a whole, can it be said that the agreement could, whether by deliberate manipulation or not, result in the sterilisation of the earning output of the writer for a considerable time?[38] If so, it will be for the party imposing the restrictions to show that they are both reasonably necessary for the protection of that party's legitimate interests, and commensurate with the benefits secured to the party restricted. This brings the test applicable to such agreements closer to the approach of Lord Diplock in *Macaulay v Schroeder*, above, who agreed with Lord Reid's analysis of the restrictive effect of the terms of the agreement, and stated that the question to be asked was the same as in all cases where the court was faced with a bargain that on its face appeared unconscionable, by reason of the unequal bargaining power of the parties, that is, "was the bargain fair?".[39]

29–307 Whichever formulation was adopted, the publishers in *Macaulay v Schroeder*, above, were held not to have discharged the onus on them in the light of the restrictive nature of the agreement, to justify its restrictions, or to show that the agreement as a whole was fair. Lord Reid summarised the position as follows:

"Any contract by which a person engages to give his exclusive services to

---

see *Silvertone Records Ltd v Mountfield* [1993] E.M.L.R. 152. A publisher is entitled to a reasonable period to obtain a proper reward for taking on a new writer, with all the incidental costs involved: *John v James* [1991] F.S.R. 397 at 451. In that case, six years was considered too long, even in respect of unknown artists. In the case of the recording agreement, a five-year tie was held to be reasonable in respect of unknown artists, given the expense involved in breaking a new artist and the low success rate: *ibid.* at 452.

[36] As to which see Lord Reid, *Macaulay v Schroeder Music Publishing Co. Ltd* [1974] 1 W.L.R. 1308 at 1313H; as to the meaning of an undertaking to use "best endeavours", see *IBM United Kingdom Ltd v Rockware Glass Ltd* [1980] F.S.R. 335 and *Imasa Ltd v Technic Incorporated* [1981] F.S.R. 554.

[37] Such a provision would considerably mitigate the otherwise restrictive effect of the agreement: per Lord Reid, *Macaulay v Schroeder Music Publishing Co. Ltd* [1974] 1 W.L.R. 1308 at 1314A/B; see for a case where the reassignment provisions failed to save the agreement *Zang Tumb Tuum Records Ltd v Johnson* [1993] E.M.L.R. 61; see also *Silvertone Records Ltd v Mountfield* [1993] E.M.L.R. 152.

[38] For examples of cases where that was held to be so see *Zang Tumb Tuum Records Ltd v Johnson* [1993] E.M.L.R. 61, above, and *Silvertone Records* [1993] E.M.L.R. 152.

[39] *Macaulay v Schroeder Music Publishing Co. Ltd* [1974] 1 W.L.R. 1308 at 1315H–1316A. And see further as to the court's jurisdiction to refuse to enforce such bargains, *Lloyd's Bank v Bundy* [1975] Q.B. 326, CA and *Clifford Davis Management Ltd v WEA Records Ltd* [1975] 1 W.L.R. 61; but see *National Westminster Bank plc v Morgan* [1985] A.C. 686 disapproving Lord Denning M.R. in *Bundy, ibid.* at 339, to the effect that English courts will grant relief where there has been "inequality of bargaining power". But see also *John v James* [1991] F.S.R. 397, where it was held that an experienced and successful publisher assumed a dominating influence over young inexperienced writers. Even after a short acquaintance they were apprehensive of the publisher and anxious to have him as their publisher, trusting and relying on him that the terms of the contract proposed were reasonable. The publisher took charge of the arrangement and failed to explain the terms of the agreement. The agreement was liable to be set aside even though the publisher had acted in good faith and had made no conscious attempt to obtain an unfair bargain (see *ibid.* at 451; similar considerations applied to the recording agreement: *ibid.* at 453).

another for a period necessarily involves extensive restriction during that period of the common law right to exercise any lawful activity he chooses in such manner as he thinks best. Normally the doctrine of restraint of trade has no application to such restrictions: they require no justification. But if contractual restrictions appear to be unnecessary or to be reasonably capable of enforcement in an oppressive manner, then they must be justified before they can be enforced. In the present case the respondent assigned to the appellants 'the full copyright for the whole world' in every musical composition 'composed, created or conceived' by him alone or in collaboration with any other person during a period of five or it might be 10 years. He received no payment (apart from an initial £50) unless his work was published and the appellants need not publish unless they chose to do so. And if they did not publish he had no right to terminate the agreement or to have copyrights reassigned to him. I need not consider whether in any circumstances it would be possible to justify such a one-sided agreement. It is sufficient to say that such evidence as there is falls far short of justification. It must therefore follow that the agreement, so far as unperformed, is unenforceable".[40]

The declaration granted in *Macaulay v Schroeder*, above, was that the agreement was contrary to public policy and void. However, agreements found to be in restraint of trade are usually voidable, not void and it may be that such an agreement is better described as unenforceable.[41] Clearly the writer is not bound by the agreement from the moment it is held to be in restraint of trade, and it would follow that any assignment in the agreement of the copyright in future works would not be effective to vest in the publishers the copyright in works brought into existence after the agreement is held to be in restraint of trade. What the position is regarding copyrights in works already brought into existence at that date is far from clear.[42] If such an agreement were truly void, it would follow that no assignment of such copyright would have taken place but if, as it is thought, such an agreement is merely voidable as to the future, then the position may be that the legal title to such works in existence before the agreement is avoided is effectively assigned to the assignee at law by such agreement, and notwithstanding the subsequent avoidance of the agreement remains vested in the assignee, subject to the Court ordering, in the exercise of its equitable jurisdiction, reassignment of the copyright in such works. This question will be particularly important in the case of any such works which the publishers have already at that date exploited, either themselves, or by granting rights to others. A further unanswered problem arises in connection with any separate assignment of copyright in particular works in which a songwriter engaged under such an agreement is asked by the publishers to execute. Such assignments are often taken, for no further consideration than the publishers' promise to pay royalties on the work being published, usually in the same terms as in the principal agreement. In themselves such individ-

29–308

---

[40] *Macaulay v Schroeder Music Publishing Co. Ltd* [1974] 1 W.L.R. 1308 at 1314H.

[41] See Lord Reid, *Macaulay v Schroeder Music Publishing Co. Ltd* [1974] 1 W.L.R. 1308 at 1315A/B; see also *Clifford Davis Management Ltd v WEA Records Ltd* [1975] 1 W.L.R. 61 and *Zang Tumb Tuum Records Ltd v Johnson* [1993] E.M.L.R. 61. Severance of objectionable clauses is not permissible where it is the whole agreement which is objectionable, and the court will not strike out clauses so as to change the nature of the contract: *Silvertone Records Ltd v Mountfield* [1993] E.M.L.R. 152.

[42] The judgment of the Court of Appeal in *Macaulay v Schroeder Music Publishing Co. Ltd*, delivered by Russell L.J., [1974] 1 All E.R. 171 at 181f, confirmed that the assignment was ineffective as to the copyright in works not in existence at the time the agreement was avoided, but the statement that the assignment of copyright in works already brought into existence at that time remained effective, *per* Russell L.J. [1974] 1 All E.R. 171 at 181e/f, was based on a concession made to such effect by counsel for the plaintiffs. Compare the position where the agreement is set aside in equity for undue influence and breach of fiduciary duty: *O'Sullivan v Management Agency and Music Ltd* [1985] Q.B. 428 at 459 C/D.

ual assignments are clearly not within the principles applied in *Macaulay v Schroeder*, above, but, in that the only reason for their execution is the pre-existing obligation under the principal agreement, if this latter agreement is subsequently found to be unenforceable, should not the same apply to any such individual assignments?[43]

---

[43] This was the court's approach in *O'Sullivan v Management Agency and Music Ltd* [1985] Q.B. 428, at 459C/D.

CHAPTER THIRTY

TAXATION

Contents   *Para.*

Contents | Para.

1. INCOME TAX

A. INTRODUCTION

30–01 This chapter is principally concerned with the tax treatment of copyright and other related forms of intellectual property covered by this work, whose exploitation may give rise to taxable receipts. Save where specific rights are dealt with, these rights are referred to collectively as intellectual property.

Exactly how such receipts are taxed depends upon the manner in which a number of factors are combined. At the outset it may be helpful to summarise the most important of these:

(a) whether the recipient is or has been carrying on a trade, profession or vocation which involves the creation or exploitation of intellectual property, etc. for example, authors, composers, designers, publishers, film producers, record companies, etc.;

(b) whether the receipt is a royalty or a lump sum;

(c) whether the recipient is resident or domiciled in the United Kingdom;

(d) whether the receipt has a United Kingdom source.

It is convenient to treat (a) above as the primary classification and to categorise taxpayers as either traders or non-traders. The other factors are considered as each of the two categories are dealt with.

B. TRADES, PROFESSIONS AND VOCATIONS

30–02 Technically trades in the strict sense are taxed under Case I of Schedule D while "professions or vocations" are taxed under Case II.[1] However, as there is no material difference between the rules applicable to Cases I and II of Schedule D, it is convenient to classify as "traders" not only persons who carry on a trade which involves the creation or exploitation of intellectual property, for example, persons involved in publishing, film and record production or distribution, etc. but also individuals who carry on a profession or vocation which involves the creation or exploitation of intellectual property for example, authors, composers and designers. Although companies resident in the United Kingdom[2] pay corporation tax on their profits and not income tax, profits for corporation tax are computed according to income tax principles.[3] Accordingly, the rules discussed below are relevant to companies as well as to individuals, save that they generally have no application to employees who produce intellectual property in the course of their

---

[1] Income and Corporation Taxes Act 1988 ("ICTA 1988"), s.18.

[2] And non-resident companies trading in the United Kingdom through a permanent establishment: ICTA 1988, s.11 (as amended by FA 2003, s.149(1)).

[3] ICTA 1988, s.9.

employment. This is because the rights usually vest in the employer[4] and so it is the employer who is usually taxable on any receipts generated by the exploitation of the rights. The employee is taxable under Schedule E on his emoluments from the employment. The distinction between works made by employees in the course of their employment under a contract of service and other works is discussed elsewhere.[5]

It is outside the scope of this work to discuss in any detail what constitutes a trade, profession or vocation and reference should be made to specialist works on income tax for a full treatment of the topic.[6] In most cases it will be relatively clear whether the creator or owner of intellectual property is carrying on a trade, profession or vocation. Examples, noted above, include professional authors, composers, recording artists, designers and others who systematically exploit their creative activities on a commercial basis. The more difficult cases concern people whose creative activities are casual or sporadic, for example, individuals who create a copyright work by an isolated piece of writing.

In *Billam v Griffith*,[7] an individual who had written three or four plays in his   **30–03**
spare time, only one of which was successful, was held to be carrying on the profession of a dramatist. By contrast, in *Nethersole v Withers*,[8] an actress who dramatised a single novel was held not to have been carrying on the profession or vocation of a dramatist when she subsequently disposed of the film rights. In *Beare v Carter*,[9] there was no suggestion that a taxpayer who merely edited five versions of one book over a 36-year period was carrying on the profession or vocation of authorship.

The fact that a person creates a copyright work by an isolated piece of writing, rather than in the course of a profession, does not mean, in itself, that any profit escapes tax.[10] Where, for example, an independent individual collaborates with a journalist to produce a series of articles, the individual is taxable upon sums received from the transaction unless the individual is being paid mainly for publication rights, any services that he renders being incidental.[11]

C. TRADING RECEIPTS

A person who is resident in the United Kingdom and carrying on a trade, profes-   **30–04**
sion or vocation here which involves exploiting intellectual property is taxable upon *any* sums which he receives from such exploitation whether or not they are received in the United Kingdom.[12] This includes royalties and licence fees. It also includes lump sums for the grant of a licence to exploit the right or for the total or partial assignment of the right[13] or as compensation or damages for infringements.[14]

---

[4] For example see CDPA 1988, s.11(2). This rule is subject to any agreement to the contrary. Also see generally, paras 5–08 *et seq.*, above.

[5] See paras 5–12 *et seq.*, above.

[6] See, *e.g. Whiteman on Income Tax* (3rd ed., Sweet & Maxwell, 1988), Ch.4.

[7] (1941) 23 T.C. 757.

[8] (1948) 28 T.C. 501.

[9] [1940] 2 K.B. 187; 23 T.C. 353.

[10] But the appropriate Case of Sch.D would be VI, rather than II: ICTA 1988, s.18(3).

[11] Compare *Hobbs v Hussey* [1942] 1 K.B. 491 with *Housden v Marshall* 38 T.C. 233. See also *Alloway v Phillips* [1980] 1 W.L.R. 888.

[12] See paras 30–22 to 30–24, below, for the position of a non-resident.

[13] *Glasson v Rougier* [1944] 1 All E.R. 535; 26 T.C. 86; *Housden v. Monsell* [1950] 2 All E.R. 1239; 31 T.C. 529. The principle is that a professional receipt is incapable of being capital for tax purposes. See also *Billam v Griffith* 23 T.C. 752 and *Mackenzie v Arnold* 33 T.C. 363.

[14] Because any sum which a trader derives from carrying on of his trade is income. See *Raja's*

D. PRIZES AND AWARDS

30–05 The Revenue accept that literary, etc. prizes which are both unsolicited and awarded as "a mark of honour, distinction or public esteem in recognition of outstanding achievement in a particular field" are not taxable receipts.[15] Any other prizes, awards, grants or bursaries received by a professional author, musician, etc. will be taxable on the basis that entering competitions or seeking awards is a normal part of the profession of authors and other creative persons.[16]

The Revenue also accepts that the following awards made by the Arts Council are not taxable:

(i) Training bursaries to trainee directors, associate directors, actors and actresses, technicians and stage managers, students attending the City University Arts Administration Courses, people attending full-time courses in arts administration (the practical training course) and in-service bursaries for the theatre designers scheme.

(ii) "Buying Time Awards" to dramatists, authors, composers and artists to maintain the recipient to enable him to take time off to develop and explore his personal talents. These at present include the awards and bursaries known as the:

Theatre Writing Bursaries;

Awards and Bursaries to Composers;

Awards and Bursaries to Painters, Sculptors and Printmakers;

Literature Awards and Bursaries.[17]

It is understood that the Arts Council will normally indicate whether a particular award is taxable.

E. THE BASIS OF TAXATION

30–06 Historically, trading profits have been assessed to income tax on the preceding year basis, *i.e.* by reference to the income of the accounting period which ends in the preceding year of assessment, except where the special commencement or discontinuance rules applied. With effect from the 1996/97[18] year of assessment, the preceding year basis has been replaced by the so-called "current year" basis under which tax is assessed by reference to the income of the accounting period which ends in the year of assessment concerned. Where the trade or profession was commenced on or before April 5, 1994, special transitional rules apply in relation to the 1996/97 year of assessment. In the case of trades or professions commenced on or after April 6, 1994, the current year basis applies from commencement.

The change from preceding year basis to current year basis was made to facilitate "self-assessment". Under the system of self-assessment, which is effective from the 1996/97 year of assessment, individuals are required to file annual tax returns which include a self-assessment of that individual's income tax and capital gains tax liabilities. The tax self-assessed in the return is due for payment automatically. No further action is required on the part of the Revenue.

Commercial College v Gian Singh & Co Ltd [1977] A.C. 312; [1976] S.T.C. 282; *Rolfe v Nagel* [1982] S.T.C. 53 and *Deeny v Gooda Walker Ltd* [1996] S.T.C. 299. For a case concerning a theatrical production company, see *Vaughan v Archie Parnell and Alfred Zeitlin Ltd* 23 T.C. 505.

[15] *IR Manuals Business Income Manual*, para.BIM50710.

[16] *IR Manuals Business Income Manual*, para.BIM50710.

[17] *IR Manuals Business Income Manual*, para.BIM50715.

[18] The commencement of the current year basis coincides with the introduction of a system of self-assessment, to replace the previous system of assessment by the Revenue.

F. Cash or earnings basis

There are two basic ways of ascertaining the taxable income of a person carrying **30–07** on a trade or profession. The first, known as the "cash" basis, requires income to be arrived at by reference to sums actually received during the relevant accounting period. The second, known as the "earnings" basis, requires the trader to bring in debits, credits and stock (or work in progress) at the beginning and end of the accounting period. It was common for authors and others carrying on similar professions to adopt the "cash" basis because they were remunerated by royalties which could not accurately be calculated in advance. However, section 42 of the Finance Act 1998 requires that from April 6, 1999 the "earnings basis" will be the appropriate accounting basis applicable.

Section 44 of the Finance Act 1998 sets out transitional rules governing the move from the "cash basis" to the "earnings basis".

G. Gifts

Where a trader disposes of an item of trading stock otherwise than in the course **30–08** of his trade (for example by giving an item away otherwise than to forward the interests of the trade), he is treated for tax purposes as if he had earned, as a trading receipt, an amount equal to the market value of the item at the time of the disposal.[19] It has been held that this rule does not apply to persons carrying on a profession who are taxed on a cash basis.[20] Given that from April 6, 1999, the cash basis only applies to barristers and advocates in the early years of practice, this exception is of limited impact.

H. Deductible expenses

Traders are not taxed on their gross receipts, but on their profits. Such profits are **30–09** computed in accordance with ordinary principles of commercial accounting and adjusted to reflect the statutory disallowances contained in section 74 of the Taxes Act.[21] Section 74 contains a list of deductions which are prohibited. In so far as such deductions are made in drawing up the taxpayer's accounts, they must be added back to establish the taxpayer's taxable profits. The prohibitions most relevant to persons carrying on a trade, profession or vocation which involves exploiting intellectual property are the prohibitions on deducting:

(1) Disbursements or expenditure not wholly and exclusively laid out or expended for the purposes of the trade, profession or vocation;[22]

(2) Capital expenditure[23];

(3) Annuities or other annual payments (other than interest) payable out of profits.[24]

The deductibility of royalties and lump sums is discussed further at paragraph 30–00 below.

Capital expenditure incurred by a trader may qualify for capital allowances, for example, capital expenditure on plant or machinery.

---

[19] *Sharkey v Wernher* [1956] A.C. 58; 36 T.C. 275.

[20] *Mason v Innes* [1967] Ch. 1079.

[21] See *Odeon Associated Theatres Ltd v Jones* 48 T.C. 257, CA and *Gallagher v Jones* [1993] S.T.C. 537, CA.

[22] ICTA 1988, s.74(1)(a).

[23] s.74(1)(f).

[24] s.74(1)(m). This does not prohibit a trader who pays a royalty which is an annual payment in the hands of the recipient from claiming a deduction for that payment, provided it is a trading expense: *Paterson Engineering Company Ltd v Duff* 25 T.C. 43.

I. EXPENDITURE ON FILMS, TAPES AND DISCS

30–10   Expenditure which is incurred on the production or acquisition of a master version of a film[25] which is not held as trading stock is regarded as revenue expenditure, notwithstanding that it would be capital under general revenue law.[26] Such expenditure is not necessarily deductible in the accounting period in which it is incurred. It is allocated to such of the taxpayer's accounting periods as is "just and reasonable".[27] The allocation may result in part of the expenditure incurred in a particular year not being allocated to that year. The taxpayer is entitled to elect that unallocated expenditure be allocated to an accounting period ending not more than two years before the date on which the election was made.[28] There is a limit to the amount of unallocated expenditure which can be relieved in this way: it cannot exceed the difference between (a) the value realised from the film, etc. in the year to which the carry back claim relates and (b) the amount of expenditure originally allocated to that period.[29] The effect is to ensure that no profit from a film, etc. need be brought into account until all the production costs have been recouped out of income relating to that production.[30]

Where the above rules apply to treat expenditure on the production or acquisition of a film, tape or disc as revenue expenditure, any receipts from the subsequent disposal of the film, tape or disc are subject to tax as revenue receipts.[31]

Special treatment for "British" films

30–11   There are two provisions which give preferential treatment in relation to expenditure on a film which is certified[32] as a British film. They provide two alternative ways in which expenditure on such films can be relieved, provided the resultant film is not held as trading stock.

(i) *Election to treat as capital expenditure*

30–12   A person who carries on a trade or business which consists of or includes the exploitation of the master version of a film[33] may elect for the treatment discussed above not to apply to expenditure[34] on the production or acquisition of the master version of a film which has been certified[35] as a British film. Such an election may

---

[25] *i.e.* expenditure on the production or acquisition of the master version of a film: Finance (No.2) Act 1992, s.40A(1); Finance Act 2000, s.113(1), (6); Capital Allowance Act 2001, Sch.2, para.82. According to the Revenue this includes expenditure on the costs of adapting a story for film purposes, normal production expenses such as wages and salaries, costumes, studio hire and the costs of filming, processing and editing but not expenditure on the provision of assets such as film cameras, lights and sound equipment as the latter items are not "used up in the process of production": see *IR Manuals*, para.BIM56335. Expenditure on the latter items should qualify for capital allowances, as expenditure on plant and machinery.

[26] Finance (No.2) Act 1992, s.40A(1).

[27] s.40B; *IR Manuals*, paras BIM56210, 56215.

[28] s.40B.

[29] s.40B

[30] See *IR Manuals*, paras BIM56000 *et seq.*

[31] Finance (No.2) Act 1992, s.40A(2)

[32] By the Secretary of State under Sch.1 to the Films Act 1985.

[33] The Revenue accepts that the activities of a finance lessor of master versions may amount to the carrying on of a trade, depending on the degree of organisation with which the activities are carried on; see *Barclays Mercantile Industrial Finance Ltd v Melluish* [1990] S.T.C. 314.

[34] See for eligible expenditure, *IR Manuals*, para.BIM56335.

[35] By the Secretary of State under Sch.1 to the Films Act 1985.

only be made if the value of the master version of the film is expected to be realisable over a period of at least two years.[36]

The election must be made by written notice to the Board of Inland Revenue and must relate to all of the expenditure incurred on the production or acquisition of the master version of the film in question.[37] Where the liability is to corporation tax or income tax on the preceding year basis, the election must be made within two years after the completion of the film, tape or disc. Where the liability to income tax is under the current year basis, the claim must be made on or before the first anniversary of January 31 next following the year of assessment in which ends the relevant period in which the master version of the film is completed. "Relevant period" has the meaning given in section 40B, Finance (No.2) Act 1992.[38] The effect of the election is to enable the expenditure to qualify for capital allowances as expenditure on plant.[39]

(ii) *Alternative method of set off*

A person who carries on a trade or business which consists of or includes the exploitation of films is entitled, on making a claim,[40] to deduct the costs of certain pre-production expenditure in the year in which it is incurred or an earlier period.[41] Only expenditure which can reasonably be said to have been incurred with a view to enabling a decision to be taken as to whether or not to make the film qualifies for such treatment.[42] It must be payable before the first day of principal photography and it must not be repayable in the event of the film not being made.[43] Not more than 20 per cent of the budgeted total expenditure on the film can be deducted in this way.[44]

30–13

A person who carries on a trade or business which consists of or includes the exploitation of films is also entitled to claim[45] a deduction in the year in which the film is completed[46] (or an earlier year) of up to one-third of the total expenditure incurred by the claimant on the production of the film or the acquisition of the master negative, tape or disc (less any expenditure deducted by virtue of section 41 of the Finance (No.2) Act 1992).[47]

The deduction is increased to the whole of the production expenditure for a British film completed on or after July 2, 1997 where the expenditure on production or acquisition was incurred on or after July 2, 1997 and before July 2, 2000 and the total production expenditure on the film is £15 million or less.[48]

The Finance Bill 2004, clauses 114 to 118 inclusive set out an anti-avoidance measure. This applies to individuals who have carried on a trade, either alone or in partnership, where the profits and losses of such trade have been calculated in accordance with the film tax relief set out at sections 40A to 40C and sections 41

30–14

---

[36] Finance (No.2) Act 1992, s.40D(3)(4).
[37] s.40D
[38] s.40D(5) and see s.40D(6) as to when a master version of a film is "completed".
[39] See *IR Business Income Manual*, para.BIM56015.
[40] The claim must be made within two years of the end of the period in which the expenditure in question becomes payable: Finance (No.2) Act 1992, s.41(6).
[41] s.41(1).
[42] s.41(2)(a).
[43] s.41(2)(b), (c).
[44] s.41(5).
[45] The claim must be made within two years after the end of the period to which the claim relates: s.42(6).
[46] *i.e.* the year in which it is first in a form in which it can reasonably be regarded as ready for copies of it to be made and distributed for presentation to the general public: s.43(3)(a).
[47] Finance (No.2) Act 1992, s.42(1)–(5).
[48] Finance (No.2) Act 1997, s.48.

to 43 of the Finance (No.2) Act 1992 and section 48 of the Finance (No.2) Act 1997. This measure is aimed at tackling schemes which are used by individuals to convert a tax deferral into a permanent tax gain. The new rules apply with effect from December 10, 2003. Clause 114 details the necessary conditions for the measure to take effect. It also raises a charge to income tax where those conditions are met.

The measures will apply to any individual who has claimed loss relief under sections 380 or 381of the ICTA 1988 or section 72 of the Finance Act 1991 in relation to losses arising from such a trade. A charge to income tax arises where there is a disposal, after December 10, 2003, of rights of an individual to profits in the trade where the individual either receives non-taxable consideration, or the amount of his losses claimed are more than his net contribution to the trade. Clause 115 describes what is meant by the term "disposal of a right of the individual to profits arising from the trade". Clause 116 defines the terms "the losses claimed" and "the individual's capital contribution to the trade". The "losses claimed" are "film-related losses". An indiviudal's capital contribution to the trade includes all amounts contributed by the individual less any amounts which that individual receives from the business or which is reimbursed to him or which he receives from somebody else. Clause 117 deals with the computation of the chargeable amount for the purposes of clause 114. The aim is to prevent double counting of any amounts which have already been brought into charge under clause 114. Clause 118 defines "film-related losses" as losses that result from computations made in accordance with any of sections 40A to 40C of Finance (No.2) Act 1992, sections 41 to 43 of Finance (No.2) Act 1992 and section 48 of Finance (No.2) Act 1997. Clause 118 also defines what is meant by "non-taxable" consideration. This means consideration that is not chargeable to income tax apart from section 114.

J. TOP-SLICING RELIEF

30–15 It has already been noted that lump sums received by a taxpayer in the course of his profession, for the disposal or assignment of intellectual property rights are subject to income tax. This can distort the taxpayer's taxable profits for the year of receipt, giving rise to a disproportionate charge to tax. The rules set out below for the spreading of lump sums and royalties for copyright were superseded, for payments actually receivable after April 5, 2001, by the Finance Act 2001 (see para.30–00 below). Sections 534 to 538 relieve the consequences of this, by permitting certain receipts to be spread over a period of years for tax purposes. This relief applies in four situations:

(i) Lump sums for the sale of copyrights and public lending rights 10 years or more after their creation

30–16 The first situation is where the author[49] of a literary, dramatic, musical or artistic work assigns the copyright in the work (wholly or partially) or grants any interest in the copyright at least 10 years after the first publication of the work.[50] Provided such an assignment or grant is for a period of at least two years and the consideration for it consists wholly or partially of a lump sum payment,[51] the taxpayer can make a claim requiring that the lump sum be taxed as if it were receivable in a number of equal yearly instalments.

---

[49] Or joint author: ICTA 1988, s.535(11). As to joint authorship, see paras 4–37 *et seq.*
[50] ICTA 1988, s.535(1). The first publication of the work is the first occasion on which the work or a reproduction of it is published, performed or exhibited: *ibid.*, s.535(11).
[51] Including an advance on account of royalties which is not returnable: s.535(11).

The number of yearly instalments depends upon the period of the assignment or grant. If the assignment or grant is for between two and six years, the payment will be treated as if it were receivable in a number of instalments equal to the number of years of whole years in the grant.[52] Thus a payment for a grant or assignment for three and a half years would be taxed as if it were receivable in three annual instalments, each being one-third of the total payment. If the assignment or grant is for six years or more, the payment will be treated as if it were receivable in six equal instalments, the first of which being receivable on the date the lump sum became receivable.[53]

If the author dies or discontinues his profession or vocation after the payment is made, any instalments which would be treated as becoming receivable after the death or discontinuance are treated as becoming receivable on the date when the last instalment before the death or discontinuance is treated as becoming receivable.[54]

This relief applies equally to the public lending right, but not to design right.[55] It must be claimed within a year after January 31, following the year of assessment in which the lump sum is actually receivable,[56] and a claim cannot be made if a prior claim has been made in relation to the lump sum under s.534,[57] (see the following paragraph).

(ii) Payments for the sale of copyrights and public lending rights which take more than 12 months to create.

The second situation is where the author[58] of a literary, dramatic, musical or artistic work assigns (wholly or partially) or grants any interest in the copyright of the work for a consideration which consists of a payment which would otherwise be included in his profits for a single year of assessment.[59] Provided the author was engaged on the making of that work for a period of at least 12 months, he may make a claim requiring that only half of the consideration be treated as if it were receivable when that consideration actually became receivable.[60] The remaining half will be treated as if it were receivable 12 months *before* the date on which the consideration actually became receivable.[61] If the author was engaged on the making of the work for a period in excess of 24 months, he may make a claim requiring that one-third of the consideration be treated as if it were receivable when that consideration actually became receivable.[62] One third of the payment is treated as if it were receivable 12 months *before* the date on which the consideration actually became receivable and the balance is treated as if it were receivable 24 months *before* the date on which the consideration actually became receivable.[63]

This relief applies to lump sum payments, including advances on account of

30–17

---

[52] s.535(3). The first instalment being treated as receivable on the date when the lump sum is actually paid: *ibid.*, s.535(3).
[53] s.535(2).
[54] s.535(4) and (6).
[55] s.537.
[56] ICTA 1988, s.535(8A), as respects claims made in relation to 1996/97 and later years of assessment: Finance Act 1996, s.128(8) and (11).
[57] ICTA 1988, s.535(9).
[58] Or joint author: ICTA 1988, s.534(7)(a).
[59] s.534(1).
[60] s.534(2).
[61] s.534(2)
[62] s.534(3).
[63] s.534(3)

royalties which are not returnable.[64] In relation to such payments, the relief must be claimed within a year after January 31, following the year of assessment in which the payment in question is actually receivable.[65]

The relief also applies to payments of royalties, payments on account of royalties and sums payable periodically,[66] but only if they are receivable within two years after first publication of the work.[67] A claim in respect of any such payment extends to all such payments receivable by the claimant in respect of the copyright in the same work.[68] Where these payments are receivable over two or more tax years, the claimant is treated as having made separate claims for the payments receivable in each tax year.[69] Such claims must be made within a year after January 31, following the latest year of assessment in which such payments are receivable.[70]

This relief applies equally to the public lending right, but not to design right.[71] No relief will be given if a prior claim has been made under section 535 in relation to any of the payments.[72]

(iii) Payments for the sale of registered designs and design rights which take more than 12 months to create

30–18 The third situation concerns designers[73] of designs in which design right subsists and authors of registered designs who assign such rights (wholly or partly) or grant an interest in such rights by licence for a consideration which consists of a payment which would otherwise be included in computing the amount of their profits for a single year of assessment.[74] Provided the designer or author was engaged in the creation of the design for a period of more than 12 months, he may make a claim requiring that only half of the amount of the payment be treated as if it were receivable when it actually became receivable.[75] The remaining half will be treated as if it were receivable 12 months *before* the date on which the payment actually became receivable.[76] If the designer was engaged in the creation of the design for a period of more than 24 months, he may make a claim requiring that one-third of the payment be treated as if it were receivable when the payment actually became receivable.[77] One third of the payment will be treated as it were receivable 12 months *before* the date on which the payment actually became receivable and the balance is treated as if it were receivable 24 months *before* the date on which the payment actually became receivable.[78]

This relief applies to lump sum payments, including advances on account of royalties which are not returnable.[79] In relation to such payments, the relief must

---

[64] s.534(4)(a).
[65] s.534(5A)(b).
[66] s.534(4)(b).
[67] s.534(4). The first publication of a work is the first occasion on which it, or a reproduction of it is published, performed or exhibited; see s.534(7)(b).
[68] s.534(5)(a).
[69] s.534(5)(b).
[70] s.534(5A)(a), as respects claims made in relation to 1996/97 and later years of assessment: Finance Act 1996, ss.128(5) and (11).
[71] ICTA 1988, s.537.
[72] s.534(6). For the position of partnerships see s.534(6A).
[73] Including joint designers: ICTA 1988, s.537A(6)(a).
[74] s.537A(1).
[75] s.537A(2).
[76] s.537A(2)
[77] s.537A(3).
[78] s.537A(3)
[79] s.537A(4)(a).

be claimed within a year after January 31, following the year of assessment in which the payment in question is actually receivable.[80]

The relief also applies to payments of royalties, payments on account of royalties and other sums payable periodically, but only in so far as they are receivable within two years after articles made to the design (or to which the design is applied) are first made available for sale or hire.[81] A claim in respect of any such payment extends to all such payments receivable by the claimant in respect of rights in the design in question.[82] Where these payments are receivable over two or more tax years, the taxpayer is treated as having made separate claims for the payments receivable in each year.[83] Such claims must be made within a year after January 31, following the latest year of assessment in which such payments are receivable.[84]

(iv) Artists' receipts for works of art which take more than 12 months to create

The final situation concerns artists who obtain a sum for the sale of a painting, sculpture or other work of art or by way of commission or fee for the creation of the work of art.[85] If the artist was engaged on the making of that work of art for at least 12 months, he may make a claim requiring that only half of the payment be treated as if it were receivable when that payment actually became receivable.[86] The remaining half will be treated as if it were receivable 12 months *before* the date on which the payment actually became receivable.[87] If the artist was engaged on the making of the work for more than 24 months, he may make a claim requiring that one third of the payment be treated as if it were receivable on the date on which the payment actually became receivable.[88] One third of the payment is then treated as if it became receivable 12 months *before* the date on which the payment actually became receivable, and the balance is treated as if it became receivable 24 months *before* the date on which the payment actually became receivable.[89]

30–19

This relief is also available where an artist spent less than 12 months engaged on the making of the work of art in question, provided the work was one of a number of works which he was engaged for a period of at least 12 months in making for an exhibition.[90] Claims for this relief must be made within a year after January 31, following the year of assessment in which the payment is actually receivable.[91]

Finance Act 2001, section 71 and Schedule 24 enacted new rules to deal with the fluctuation of profits over consecutive years in respect of profit from copyright, designs, public lending rights and other creative artisitic works. The new rules are set out at ICTA 1988, section 95A and Schedule 4A. These rules apply from 2000–2001. Under the new provisions, an individual can, in appropriate circum-

30–20

---

[80] s.537A(5A)(b).
[81] s.537A(4)(b). Articles are made available for sale or hire as soon as they are made available by or with the licence of the design right owner or proprietor of the registered design: s.537A(6)(b).
[82] s.537A(5)(a).
[83] s.537A(5)(b).
[84] s.537A(5A)(a).
[85] ICTA 1988, s.538(1).
[86] s.538(1)(a), (2).
[87] s.538(1)(a), (2).
[88] s.538(3).
[89] s.538(3).
[90] s.538(1)(b).
[91] s.538(4).

stances, make a claim to average his profit if those profits are from a qualifying trade, profession or vocation ("relevant profits") and a "tax year" is a year of assessment.[92] For these purposes, a "qualifying trade, profession or vocation" is defined as an activity the profits from which are taxable under Schedule D Case I and are derived wholly or mainly from qualifying creative works.[93] Qualifying creative works are literary, dramatic, musical or artistic works or designs created by taxpayers personally, or where the trade, profession, vocation is carried on by a partnership, by one or more of the partners personally.[94]

An averaging claim may be made if the taxpayer has been carrying on the qualifying trade, profession or vocation in two consecutive tax years and either his relevant profits for one of the tax years are less than 75 per cent of his relevant profits for the other tax year or his relevant profits for one (but not both) of the tax years are nil.[95] No claim can be made for a tax year if an averaging claim in respect of the same qualifying trade, profession or vocation has already been made in relation to a later tax year.[96] But a tax claim can be made in relation to a tax year that was the later tax year on a prior averaging claim.[97] No claim can be made in relation to a tax year in which the taxpayer starts or ceases to carry on the trade, profession or vocation or that in which the trade, profession or vocation ceases to be a qualifying trade, profession or vocation.[98]

The averaging claim must be made within 12 months after January 31, next following the end of the later of the two years to which it relates.[99] If the taxpayer's profits for one year amount to 70 per cent or less of the relevant profits for the other year or if the relevant profits for one (but not both) of the years are nil, the amount of the adjusted profits for each of the years is the average of the relevant profits.[1] Schedule 4A, paragraph 6(3) sets out the formula that applies to determine the adjusted profits where the relevant profits for one of the two years amounts to more than 70 per cent but less than 75 per cent of the relevant profits for the other year.[2]

K. POST-CESSATION RECEIPTS

30–21 As a matter of general Revenue law, a person carrying on a trade, profession or vocation is not taxable on:

(a) Lump sums received pursuant to contracts entered into *after* the discontinuance of his or her trade, profession or vocation;[3] or

(b) Lump sums, royalties, etc. received after the discontinuance of his or her trade, profession or vocation which are paid pursuant to contracts made *before* that discontinuance.[4]

Sums falling within (b) are, however, taxable under the "post-cessation

---

[92] ICTA 1988, Sch.4A, para.14.
[93] Sch.4A, para.2(1).
[94] Sch.4A, para.2(2).
[95] Sch.4A, para.3(1).
[96] Sch.4A, para.4(1).
[97] Sch.4A, para.4(3).
[98] Sch.4A, para.4(2).
[99] Sch.4A, para.5.
[1] Sch.4A, para.6(2).
[2] Sch.4A, para.6(3).
[3] Such sums will only be taxable as capital receipts: see paras 30–36 and 30–43, below. Note, however, that where a trader who has permanently discontinued his trade transfers, the right to receive sums to which the post-cessation receipts provisions apply, he is taxable on the amount or value of the consideration received for the transfer or (if the transfer is not at arm's length) on the value of the right transferred: ICTA 1988, s.106.
[4] *Purchase v Stainers Executors* [1952] A.C. 280; 32 T.C. 367; *Carson v Peter Cheyney's Executors* [1959] A.C. 412; 38 T.C. 240.

receipts" rules[5] which apply to "... sums arising from the carrying on of the trade, profession or vocation during any period before the discontinuance (not being sums otherwise chargeable to tax)".[6] Although it is widely believed that sums falling within (a) above are also caught, it is far from clear that this is correct. It is suggested that such sums "arise" from the sale of intellectual property rights after discontinuance, not from the carrying on of the profession before the discontinuance, and thus fall outside the "post-cessation receipts" rules. However, so long as significant sales continue to take place, it may be difficult for a person carrying on a trade, profession or vocation which involves creating and exploiting such rights to establish that a discontinuance has occurred.[7]

As will be inferred from their exclusion from (b) above, royalties paid under a royalty contract entered into *after* the discontinuance of a trade, profession or vocation are taxable on general principles.[8]

L. NON-RESIDENTS: TRADING IN THE UNITED KINGDOM

Income from a trade, profession or vocation carried on in the United Kingdom by a non-United Kingdom resident is *prima facie* liable to United Kingdom taxation, and will generally be liable to tax in the country of residence as well. Where there is a double tax treaty between the United Kingdom and the country of residence, there will normally be exemption from United Kingdom tax unless the trade or profession is carried on through a permanent establishment in this country.

30–22

The test for determining where a trade profession or vocation is carried on is: where do the operations take place from which the profits in substance arise?[9] The test was applied in *Commissioners of Inland Revenue v HK-TVB International Ltd*,[10] where a company incorporated and carrying on business in Hong Kong was granted the sole and exclusive right to exploit the copyright in Chinese dialect video films outside Hong Kong which it exercised by granting sub-licences to customers abroad. The company argued that this did not amount to carrying on a trade or business in Hong Kong: the company was either providing services to its customers in the overseas territories concerned, or it was exploiting property assets outside Hong Kong by sub-licensing rights which were only capable of use in the overseas territories concerned. The Court rejected the company's argument, saying "the relevant business of the taxpayer company was the exploitation of film rights exercisable overseas and it was a business carried on in Hong Kong. The fact that the rights which they exploited were only exercisable outside Hong Kong was irrelevant in the absence of any financial interest in the subsequent exercise of the rights by the sub-licensee". It was held to be a factor of great importance that the company's principal place of business was in Hong Kong.

The "post-cessation receipts" rules apply to non-residents whose trade or

---

[5] ICTA 1988, ss.103 and 104, which treat such receipts as income assessable under the rules applicable to Case VI of Schedule D (see *ibid.*, s.18(3)).

[6] ICTA 1988, s.103(2) and *cf.* s.104(2).

[7] Because it is just as much part of such a person's trade, profession or vocation to turn such rights to account as it is to create such rights: see *Carson v Peter Cheyney's Executors* [1959] A.C. 412; 38 T.C. 240.

[8] See paras 30–36 *et seq.*, below.

[9] *FL Smith v Greenwood* [1921] 3 K.B. 583. The place where contracts are concluded is not decisive: *Firestone Tyre and Rubber Co. v Llewellin* [1957] 1 W.L.R. 464; 37 T.C. 111. See also *IRC v Padmore* [1987] S T.C. 36.

[10] [1992] S.T.C. 723, PC.

profession was being carried on in the United Kingdom at the time when it was discontinued, for example, authors who emigrate on retirement.[11]

M. RESIDENCE

30–23 Historically, it has been a feature of United Kingdom tax law that there is no statutory test of residence, and that "resident" must be given its ordinary meaning.[12] Accordingly, the question of whether an individual is resident or not is generally determined by reference to such factors as the regularity, purpose and duration of his visits to the United Kingdom. Whilst a comprehensive survey of the meaning of residence is beyond this work, attention is drawn to the following points:

(a) A person who is present in the United Kingdom for six months or more in any financial year is resident in that year;[13]

(b) A person who lives and works abroad with a full-time contract of employment for a period including a full financial year will not be resident or ordinarily resident in the United Kingdom in that year;[14]

(c) It is the Revenue's view that a person who visits the United Kingdom for periods averaging at least three months per year becomes resident after four years of such visits, unless his arrangements indicated from the start that regular visits of such duration were to be made, in which case he would be resident from the first year;[15]

(d) If a British subject who has hitherto been resident leaves the United Kingdom for some temporary purpose only, he does not cease to be resident here.[16]

Different rules apply to companies. A company incorporated in the United Kingdom is automatically deemed to be resident here.[17] Foreign incorporated companies are resident where their central management and control is located.[18]

N. FOREIGN TRADES, PROFESSIONS, ETC.

30–24 A trade or profession carried on wholly outside the United Kingdom by a non-resident is outside the scope of United Kingdom taxation.[19] This is so even if the trade is one that had previously been carried on in the United Kingdom: the post-cessation receipts rules will not apply because there will have been no discontinuance.

The taxation of an individual who is resident in the United Kingdom, but carries on a trade, profession or vocation wholly abroad, depends upon whether or

---

[11] Save that the rules do not catch receipts which represent income arising outside the United Kingdom: ICTA 1988, ss.103(3) and 104(3).

[12] In July 1988, the Revenue produced a consultative document entitled "Residence in the United Kingdom: The Scope of UK Taxation for Individuals" which proposed the introduction of a statutory test of residence based on days of presence in the UK The proposals were subsequently shelved.

[13] ICTA 1988, s.336(1).

[14] See *Reed v Clark* [1986] Ch.1; [1985] S.T.C. 323.

[15] See the Inland Revenue booklet on "Residents and non-residents" (IR 20, 1996).

[16] In *Reed v Clark* [1986] Ch.1; [1985] S.T.C. 323, a British subject who lived and worked abroad for a period of one year was held not to have left the United Kingdom for a temporary purpose only.

[17] Finance Act 1988, s.66. See also Finance Act 1994, s.249 which treats certain dual resident companies as non-resident.

[18] *Unit Construction Ltd v Bullock* [1960] A.C. 351 and see Revenue Statement of Practice SP1/90.

[19] See *Colquhoun v Brooks* 2 T.C. 490, where the so-called "principle of territoriality" was established.

not he is domiciled in the United Kingdom. If he is domiciled here, he will be subject to United Kingdom income tax on the whole of his profit; but because the income is taxed under Case V of Schedule D (rather than Cases I or II), the post-cessation receipts rules[20] cannot apply. Accordingly, sums arising after discontinuance of the trade, profession or vocation escape the charge to tax.

If the individual is resident but not domiciled in the United Kingdom,[21] he is liable to tax only to the extent that income from the trade or profession is remitted to the United Kingdom.[22] Sums are remitted to the United Kingdom if they are received here in cash or, having been converted abroad into non-cash form, are brought into the United Kingdom and converted into cash here. There is also a deemed remittance where money borrowed in the United Kingdom, or borrowed abroad and remitted to the United Kingdom, is repaid abroad out of unremitted income.[23] Remittances in a year of assessment after the trade or profession has been discontinued escape the charge to tax, because there is no longer any taxable source. Because the remittance basis only applies to individuals, United Kingdom resident companies are fully taxable on the profits of a foreign trade (subject to any available double taxation relief).

O. Royalties received otherwise than in the course of a trade, profession or vocation

As a matter of general revenue law, a third party or a personal representative is only taxable[24] upon royalties derived from a royalty contract if the contract from which the royalties derive was entered into otherwise than in the course of a trade, profession or vocation, i.e. by a third party or personal representative or by a trader after he has permanently discontinued his trade. Royalties paid under a contract which was originally entered into in the course of a trade, profession or vocation and later assigned to a third party, or which later vest in personal representatives, escape the charge to income tax,[25] unless they are caught by the anti-avoidance provisions discussed at paragraphs 30–00 to 30–00 below.   **30–25**

Finance Bill 2004 includes clauses 93 to 101, which together seek to implement the EU Interest and Royalties Directive (Council Directive 2003/49/EC of June 3, 2003. The terms of the Directive have effect from January 1, 2004. The aim of the Directive and indeed clauses 92 to 101 is to remove source-state taxation on interest and royalty payments between associated companies in different Member States of the EU.

P. Lump sums received otherwise than in the course of a trade, profession or vocation

A lump sum received by a person otherwise in the course of trade, profession or   **30–26**

---

[20] ICTA 1988, ss.103 and 104 (discussed at para. 30–21, above), which only apply to the receipts of a trade, profession or vocation which was assessable under Cases I or II.

[21] Or, being a Commonwealth citizen or a citizen of the Republic of Ireland, is not ordinarily resident in the United Kingdom.

[22] ICTA 1988, s.65(5): the "remittance" basis of taxation.

[23] s.65(6) to (9).

[24] Generally under Case III of Schedule D (see *Asher v London Film Productions Ltd* [1944] K.B. 133 and *Hume v Asquith* [1969] 2 Ch. 58; 45 T.C. 251), unless the royalties are not pure income profit in the hands of the recipient, in which case they will be subject to tax under Case VI; see *Curtis Brown Ltd v Jarvis* 14 T.C. 744, *Lawrence v IRC* 23 T.C. 333 and the dictum of Pennycuick J. in *Noddy Subsidiary Rights Co Ltd v IRC* [1966] 3 All E.R. 459; 43 T.C. 458. In *Mitchell v. Rosay* 35 T.C. 496, a share in the gross receipts of a film were held to be taxable as income under Case III.

[25] *Hume v Asquith* [1969] 2 Ch. 58; 45 T.C. 251.

vocation[26] for the assignment or partial assignment of an intellectual property right is a capital receipt.[27] Accordingly, it will generally be subject to capital gains tax, rather than income tax. By contrast, a lump sum received otherwise in the course of a trade, profession or vocation for the grant of a licence may be either capital or income, depending upon the true character of the transaction.[28] Thus, a lump sum has been held to be capital where the grant of the licence substantially diminished the value of a copyright work.[29] But a lump sum, which is quantified by reference to some anticipated quantum of user,[30] which is received for or on account of royalties[31] or represents a share of gross receipts[32] will normally be income.

Damages for infringement of an intellectual property right may also be taxable as income if they represent compensation for the unauthorised use of the right rather than the diminution of its capital value.[33] Where damages are not subject to tax, tax may in some circumstances be taken into account in determining the quantum of the damages payable (see paragraph 30–00 below).

Q. ANTI-AVOIDANCE PROVISIONS

30–27 It will be apparent from the foregoing discussion that one way for a trader to minimise the income tax consequences of exploiting his intellectual property would be to arrange for the receipts of such exploitation to accrue to a person not carrying on a trade, profession or vocation (for example, the author's spouse). However, there are a number of provisions in the Taxes Act which prevent such avoidance. All of them operate by taxing the receipts as income of someone (typically the author) other than the person to whom they actually accrue.

(i) Section 775: Sale of income derived from personal activities

30–28 A person such as an author, musician or composer who is carrying on a profession or vocation will be chargeable to income tax[34] on any capital amounts received by another person which come into the recipient's hands as a result of arrangements which:

(a) Are designed to exploit the earning capacity of the person carrying on the profession or vocation; and

(b) Have as one of their main objectives the avoidance or reduction of liability to income tax.[35]

Thus, an author, musician or composer can be assessed to income tax on capital sums paid for the grant of a licence to exploit his copyright in a work, even though

---

[26] *cf. Shiner v Lindblom* 39 T.C. 367 at 373, in which it was held that the taxpayer did not receive a lump sum in the course of his profession as an actor. Nor was he trading in copyrights. Accordingly, the sum in question was not taxable.

[27] *Nethersole v Withers* [1948] 1 All E.R. 400; 28 T.C. 501, which involved a partial assignment of a copyright.

[28] *Nethersole v Withers* [1948] 1 All E.R. 400; 28 T.C. 501. The principle is the same as applies to patent licences: compare *Rustproof Metal Window Co. Ltd v IRC* [1947] 2 All E.R. 454; 29 T.C. 243 with *Murray v ICI Ltd* [1967] Ch. 1038; 44 T.C. 175.

[29] *Haig's Trustees v IRC* [1939] S.C. 676; 22 T.C. 725.

[30] *Nethersole v Withers* [1948] 1 All E.R. 400; 28 T.C. 501.

[31] Compare *IRC v Longmans Green & Co. Ltd* 17 T.C. 272 with *Beare v Carter* [1940] 2 K.B. 187; 23 T.C. 353.

[32] *Mitchell v Rosay* (1954) 35 T.C. 496.

[33] *Raja's Commercial College v Gian Singh & Co Ltd* [1977] A.C. 312; [1976] S.T.C. 282. What matters is the character of the payment and not the authority under which it is paid.

[34] Under ICTA 1988, Sch.D, Case VI.

[35] ICTA 1988, s.775. The taxpayer has a statutory right to recover the tax payable under s.775 from the person who actually receives the capital sum: *ibid.*, s.777(8)(a).

those capital sums may be payable to a service company or to members of his family.

(ii) Part XV of the Taxes Act: The settlement provisions

Any income arising under a settlement during the lifetime of the settlor is treated **30–29** for the purposes of the Taxes Acts as the settlor's income unless it derives from property in which he has no interest.[36] The same applies to income arising under a settlement which is paid to or for the benefit of an unmarried minor child of the settlor during his lifetime.[37] Settlement is widely defined in section 660G of ICTA 1988 to include "any disposition, trust, covenant, agreement, arrangement or transfer of assets", although the width of the definition is limited by the rule that there must be an element of bounty before there can be a "settlement".[38] The term "settlor" is also widely defined to include any person who has contributed funds directly or indirectly for the purposes of the settlement.[39] Accordingly, if an author, musician or composer settles intellectual property rights, he will be subject to income tax on any income arising during his lifetime which *could* be applied for the benefit of himself or his spouse (*e.g.* by virtue of the exercise of a power). He will also be subject to income tax on any income which is *actually* used during his life to benefit an unmarried minor child of his.[40]

(iii) Sections 739 and 740: Transfers of assets abroad

Sections 739 and 740 prevent avoidance of United Kingdom tax by a transfer of **30–30** assets to non-residents. Where an individual who is ordinarily resident in United Kingdom seeks to avoid tax[41] by transferring (or procuring the transfer of) assets to a non-resident, section 739 deems the income of the non-resident to be income of the transferor if either (a) the transferor or his spouse has power to enjoy the income concerned, or (b) the transferor or his spouse receives a capital sum which is in any way connected with the transfer. The section also applies where the transferor is not ordinarily resident at the time of the transfer if he or his spouse subsequently becomes ordinarily resident.[42] Section 740 applies where income-producing assets are transferred to a non-resident and an individual ordinarily resident in the United Kingdom who is not within section 739 receives any benefit out of assets available for the purpose. The recipient is taxed on the value of the benefit. Neither section applies where there is no tax avoidance motive.[43]

The anti-avoidance provisions are not confined to transfers of income producing assets. In *Brackett v IRC*,[44] there was held to be a transfer of assets for the purpose of section 739 where the taxpayer entered into a service contract with a Jersey company whose shares were owned by a settlement created by the taxpayer. As a result the trading income of the Jersey company derived from the taxpayer's activities was deemed to be the taxpayer's income. The case consider-

---

[36] ICTA 1988, s.660A(1). A person has an interest in settled property if it may become payable to or applicable for the benefit of him or his spouse: s.660A(2) and note the exceptions in s.660A(4)(5). Capital sums paid to the settlor out of undistributed income which is not otherwise taxable in his hands are also charged to income tax: *ibid.*, ss.677–682.

[37] s.660B(1). Payments out of accumulated income are also caught: s.660B(2).

[38] See *Bulmer v IRC* [1967] Ch. 145; *IRC v Plummer* [1979] S.T.C. 793.

[39] ICTA 1988, s.660G(1), (2); *IRC v Mills* [1974] S.T.C. 130, HL.

[40] *Crossland v Hawkins* [1961] Ch. 539.

[41] The intention need not be to avoid income tax; the avoidance of any form of United Kingdom taxation is sufficient; see ICTA 1988, ss.739(1A)(b) and 741.

[42] s.739(1A)(a).

[43] s.741. See now *IRC v Willoughby* [1995] S.T.C. 143; [1997] S.T.C. 995, HL.

[44] [1986] S.T.C. 521.

ably restricts the scope for high-earning United Kingdom residents, for example, entertainers, sportsmen, etc. to avoid United Kingdom income tax by entering into a service contract with an offshore company.

(iv) Post-cessation receipts

30–31 The "post-cessation receipts" rules discussed at paragraph 30–00 above, apply to lump sums and royalties received by third parties, as well as by the person who previously carried on the trade, profession or vocation concerned. Accordingly, a lump sum or royalties received by a third party or personal representatives[45] will be subject to income tax under these provisions if payable under a contract entered into by a person carrying on a trade, profession or vocation prior to discontinuance. As the "post-cessation receipts" rules only apply to sums received after the discontinuance, only royalties and lump sums received after the original author, musician or composer has ceased carrying on his trade, profession or vocation will be caught. Accordingly, sums received by a third party under a contract assigned to him by an author, composer or musician are not subject to tax under the post-cessation receipts rules *so long as the original author, etc. continues to practise*. Further, where a trader who has permanently discontinued his trade, profession or vocation transfers the right to receive sums to which the post-cessation receipts provisions apply, for example the benefit of an existing royalty contract, the trader is taxable on the amount or value of the consideration received for the transfer or (if the transfer is not at arm's length) on the value of the right transferred.[46] No further liability falls on the transferee.

It is considered that lump sums received by persons who are not carrying on a trade, profession or vocation on the sale by them of intellectual property rights fall outside the "post-cessation receipts" rules altogether.[47] In the case of lump sums paid to the personal representatives of the author of a literary, dramatic, musical or artistic work or as consideration for the assignment by them, wholly or partially, of the copyright in the work, it is expressly provided that the "post-cessation receipts" rules do not apply.[48] In the authors' view, this is a declaratory provision, intended for the avoidance of doubt,[49] and does not imply that such sums would be caught if received by a person who used to carry on a trade, profession or vocation or by a third party other than the personal representatives of a person who used to carry on a trade, profession or vocation.[50]

R. Anti-avoidance: limited partnerships

30–32 Sections 117 and 118 of the Income and Corporation Taxes Act 1988 restrict the amount of tax relief[51] available to a partner in a limited partnership where tax relief is claimed on amounts in excess of the limited partner's contribution to the partnership. The excess cannot be set against the partner's other income but

---

[45] This includes the personal representatives of a person who previously carried on a trade, profession or vocation, as the deceased's trade, profession or vocation will have been discontinued on his death.

[46] ICTA 1988, s.106.

[47] Post-discontinuance sales by a person who used to carry on a trade, profession or vocation are discussed at para. 30–21, above. The position of third parties is *a fortiori*.

[48] ICTA 1988, ss.103(3)(b) and 104(3). This exclusion also has effect in relation to assignments of public lending right (*ibid.*, s.103(3)) and there is a corresponding provision relating to design rights; *ibid.*, s.103(3)(bb) inserted by CDPA 1988, Sch.7, para.36(6).

[49] *cf.* the dictum of Lord Herschell in *West Derby Union v Metropolitan Life Assurance Society* [1897] A.C. at 656.

[50] For example, a legatee of a copyright, design right or public lending right.

[51] In respect of trading losses, interest relief and capital allowances.

remains available for carry forward against income from the partnership. The provisions were introduced to deal with the sort of arrangements that were common currency in the world of film finance during the 1980s and were held to be effective for tax purposes in *Reed (Inspector of Taxes) v Young*.[52] In that case, the taxpayer was one of a number of limited partners in a film production partnership. She contributed £10,000 to the capital of the partnership, which in commercial terms was her maximum exposure to loss, but her share of partnership trading losses for tax purposes, which she could set against her other income, was well in excess of that figure.[53] However, in *Ensign Tankers (Leasing) Ltd v Stokes*,[54] arrangements for financing a film through a limited partnership, designed to exploit the rules relating to first-year allowances, were held to be partially ineffective for tax purposes on the ground that the arrangements involved an artificial tax avoidance scheme which fell foul of the new approach to tax avoidance laid down in *W T Ramsay Ltd v IRC*[55] and *Furniss (Inspector of Taxes) v Dawson*.[56]

S. POSITION OF THE PAYER

30–33

A royalty paid by a trader will be deductible in computing the profits of his trade provided it is a trading expense, that is to say expenditure which is neither capital[57] nor disallowed by section 74 of the Taxes Act 1988.[58] The same principle applies to a lump sum paid by a trader for the grant of a licence to exercise intellectual property rights. Such a sum may be either a revenue expense or a capital expense, depending on the circumstances of the case, in particular the nature and duration of the rights granted by the licence and the purpose for which they have been acquired.[59] Damages paid by a trader for infringement of an intellectual property right will normally be deductible in computing the profits of his trade if the infringement was incidental to the carrying on of the trade.[60]

Copyright royalties paid by a person who is not carrying on a trade, and royalties paid by traders which are not trading expenses are not allowable for income tax purposes, even if they are annual payments in the hands of the recipient.[61] Such royalties must be paid gross unless the recipient is normally resident abroad,[62] in which case the payer is obliged to deduct tax at the basic rate from

---

[52] [1986] S.T.C. 285, HL.

[53] Because the partnership's expenditure was largely financed by non-recourse loans.

[54] [1992] S.T.C. 226, HL.

[55] [1984] A.C. 474; [1984] S.T.C. 153.

[56] [1979] 1 W.L.R. 974; [1979] S.T.C. 582.

[57] Deduction of royalties will not generally be disallowed as a capital expenditure, even if the intellectual property right is a capital asset of the trader concerned and the royalties are consideration for its acquisition: see *Wharf Properties v CIR* [1997] S.T.C. 351, where the Privy Council held that interest payments on a loan used to acquire an income-producing capital asset were deductible as a revenue expense (but only after the asset had been acquired and was producing income).

[58] A royalty which is an annual payment in the hands of the recipient will not be disallowed under ICTA 1988, s.74(1)(m) if it is a trading expense: *Paterson Engineering Co. Ltd v Duff* 25 T.C. 43.

[59] See *Vodafone Cellular Ltd v Shaw* [1997] S.T.C. 734, CA. For a full treatment of the distinction between capital and revenue expenses, see *Whiteman on Income Tax* (3rd ed., Sweet & Maxwell, 1988) paras 7–02 to 7–11.

[60] See *Herald and Weekly Times Ltd v Federal Commissioner of Taxation* [1932] 48 C.L.R. 113 (concerning the deductibility of libel damages by a newspaper).

[61] ICTA 1988, s.125 (ousting the general rule that annual payments are deductible in computing the total income of an individual, or are a charge on income in the case of a company).

[62] ICTA 1988, s.536, which also applies to public lending right: *ibid.*, s.537. The section does not apply to non-resident professional authors: see *Hansard*, HC Written Answer, Vol.791, col.31 (November 10, 1969). Nor does it apply to payments in respect of copyright in a cinematographic film or video recording, or the soundtrack of such a film or recording so far as it is not separately exploited: *ibid.*, s.536(2) as substituted by CDPA 1988, Sch.7, para.36(5).

the payment and account to the Revenue for the taxes.[63] It is then up to the non-resident, if entitled to do so, to claim from the Revenue the tax deducted. Any agreement for making such a payment without deduction of income tax is rendered void.[64] Where any royalty payment is made through the hands of an agent resident in the United Kingdom who is entitled to deduct commission from the payment, the agent need only deduct basic rate tax from the residue of the royalty payment remaining *after deduction of his commission*.[65] If the amount of the commission is not ascertained at the time of the payment, tax is deductible from the gross amount of the payment.[66]

Corresponding provision is made for payments of royalties to non-resident owners of design rights and non-resident owners of the right in a registered design.[67]

Every person carrying on a trade or business may be required by notice to make a return of periodical or lump sum payments made in respect of any copyright, public lending right, design right or the right in a registered design.[68] The same applies to any person carrying on an activity which does not constitute a trade or a business.[69]

T. Double Taxation Relief

30–34 The United Kingdom is party to a comprehensive range of Double Tax Treaties, the majority of which deal expressly with royalties arising in one contracting state which are paid to a resident of the other contracting state.[70] The majority of treaties, though by no means all, give exclusive taxing rights to the contracting state where the recipient is resident; the other contracting state may not then impose a withholding tax.[71] Most treaties contain two exceptions to the general rule. First, relief is not available if the recipient carries on business in the contracting state where the royalties arise through a permanent establishment or fixed base of business and the right or property in respect of which the royalties are paid is effectively connected with the permanent establishment or fixed base. Secondly, where there is a special relationship between the payer and the recipient, and the royalties exceed the amount that would have been agreed upon in the absence of any special relationship, there is no treaty relief for the excess. Where treaty relief is not available, the country of residence usually gives unilateral relief for the foreign tax.

---

[63] ICTA 1988, s.536(1), which does not apply to royalties paid in respect of works which have been exported from the United Kingdom for distribution outside the United Kingdom: *ibid.*, s.536(2). Nor does it apply if the Revenue agrees that tax need not be deducted. It has been held that a lump sum may be a royalty payment for the purposes of this provision; see *IRC v Longmans Green & Co Ltd* 17 T.C. 272.

[64] ICTA 1988, s.536(6).

[65] s.536(3). In *Rye & Eyre v CIR* [1935] A.C. 274, a firm of solicitors who paid an advance of royalties to a non-resident on behalf of a client were held to be persons "by or through whom" the payment was made.

[66] s.536(4).

[67] s.537B, inserted by CDPA 1988, Sch.7, para.13.

[68] Taxes Management Act 1970, s.16(1) (as amended by CDPA 1988, Sch.7, para.13).

[69] Taxes Management Act 1970, s.16(2) (as amended by CDPA 1988, Sch.7, para.13).

[70] See Art.12 of the OECD Draft Model Convention which includes payments of any kind received as consideration for the use of, or the right to use, any copyright of literary, artistic or scientific work, including cinematographic films, any patent, trademark design or model. Rents for the use of tapes and films in cinemas or on radio are often included in the definition of royalties.

[71] Where royalties are paid by a United Kingdom resident to a person who is entitled to the benefit of treaty relief, application may be made to the Financial Intermediaries and Claims Office (now the Center for Non-residents) to pay the royalty gross.

U. THE TAX ELEMENT IN DAMAGES

It was established in *British Transport Commission v Gourley*[72] that where a **30–35** plaintiff receives compensation for loss of income which would have been taxable and the compensation is not itself subject to tax, the defendant is entitled to have the damages reduced by an amount equivalent to the tax which the plaintiff would have had to pay. The reason behind the *Gourley* principle is to prevent the plaintiff from being over-compensated. However, the principle only applies where the court is satisfied that the compensation is not subject to either income tax or capital gains tax[73] and will not in practice be applied where calculation of the appropriate deduction will be unduly complex.[74]

2. CAPITAL GAINS TAX

A. INTRODUCTION: THE SCOPE OF CAPITAL GAINS TAX

Capital gains tax is payable on gains realised from the disposal of assets. All **30–36** forms of property are assets for this purpose including incorporeal property such as copyrights and other forms of intellectual property.[75] Indeed the Taxation of Chargeable Gains Act 1992 makes express reference to copyright, design rights or licences to use any copyright work or design in which design right subsists.[76]

A person who is resident or ordinarily resident[77] in the United Kingdom is chargeable to capital gains tax on the disposal[78] of assets wherever situated, save that an individual who is not domiciled in the United Kingdom is taxable only on a remittance basis[79] in respect of gains arising on the disposal of intellectual property situated abroad.[80] Non-residents are outside the scope of capital gains tax, save that a non-resident carrying on a trade profession or vocation in the United Kingdom through a branch or agency here is subject to capital gains tax on assets used for the purpose of the trade or held for the purposes of the branch or agency.[81]

Although a person who disposes of intellectual property is *prima facie* liable to capital gains tax, there are special rules designed to prevent double taxation

---

[72] [1956] A.C. 185, HL.

[73] *Pennine Raceway Ltd v Kirklees Metropolitan Council (No.2)* [1989] S.T.C. 122.

[74] See *John v James* [1986] S.T.C. 352, where damages received by Elton John against a music publisher who failed to account for sums due under various publishing and recording agreements were not reduced under the *Gourley* principle.

[75] See the Taxation of Chargeable Gains Act 1992 ("TCGA 1992"), s.20. Where a third party disposes of the benefit of a royalty contract he will generally be subject to capital gains tax; *cf.* TCGA 1992, s.237(c) and *Rank Xerox v Lane* [1981] A.C. 629; S.T.C. 740; [1980] R.P.C. 385. But an author who commutes royalties for a lump sum is liable to income tax; *Glasson v Rougier* [1944] 1 All E.R. 535; 26 T.C. 86.

[76] TCGA 1992, s.275(j); see also the reference to registered designs in *ibid.*, s.275(h).

[77] "Resident" and "ordinarily resident" have the same meanings as for income tax; see TCGA 1992, s.9 and the discussion at para. 30–23 above. Although it is arguable that a person cannot be ordinarily resident in the United Kingdom unless he is resident here, it is known that the Revenue does not share this view.

[78] Or part disposal; see *ibid.*, s.21(2)(a). There is a part disposal of an asset where an interest or right in or over an asset is created and where any property derived from the asset remains undisposed of: see TCGA 1992, s.21(2)(b). The copyright in a work is regarded as a single asset (para.78204 of the Revenue's *Capital Gains Tax Manual*), so that any partial assignment is a part disposal. On a part disposal, only part of the acquisition cost of the asset is deductible; see para. 30–62 below.

[79] TCGA 1992, s.12(1) and see s.12(2) for the definition of remittance for these purposes.

[80] Copyright, design right and franchises, and rights or licences to use any copyright work or design in which design right subsists, are situated in the United Kingdom if they or any right derived from them, are exercisable in the United Kingdom: TCGA 1992, s.275(j). And see *Redwood Music Ltd v B. Feldman & Co. Ltd* [1979] R.P.C. 1.

[81] TCGA 1992, s.10.

which ensure that sums taken into account for income tax purposes are left out of account for capital gains tax.[82] So a professional author, musician, etc. who disposes of copyright will not be subject to capital gains tax if the consideration is taken into account for income tax as a professional receipt.[83] The same principle applies to a dealer in copyright.

B. SALES

30–37   Unless the consideration is chargeable to income tax, an arm's length disposal of intellectual property to a person who is not connected[84] to the vendor will give rise to a capital gains tax charge on the difference between (a) the consideration for that disposal and (b) any allowable expenditure[85] attributable to the right plus the appropriate indexation allowance for disposals before April 1998. Taper Relief will apply to later disposals.[86]

The requirement that any sums chargeable to income tax must be excluded from the consideration received for the disposal does *not* require the Revenue to exclude the capitalised value of any right to receive royalties.[87] If the right is such that it cannot be valued, the vendor's liability to capital gains tax is computed on the basis that he received the market value of the right.[88] Market value is also substituted for the actual consideration where there is a sale of copyright otherwise than by way of a bargain at arm's length or to a connected person.[89]

C. GIFTS

30–38   A gift of intellectual property is a disposal otherwise than by way of bargain at arm's length and is therefore treated as a disposal at market value. The donor will be subject to capital gains tax on the difference between (a) the market value of the right at the date of the gift[90] and (b) the acquisition cost[91] of that asset plus the appropriate indexation allowance for other gifts made before April 1998. For later periods, the gains will be subject to Taper Relief.[92]

The donor may be able to postpone part or all of the capital gains tax arising on a gift, or any other disposal at an undervalue, by claiming hold-over relief.[93] Hold-over relief is available in two situations. The first is where the gift amounts to a chargeable transfer for inheritance tax purposes (for example, where the right

---

[82] s.37(1).

[83] *cf.* para. 30–07 above.

[84] Broadly, a person is connected with his relatives, his spouse's relatives, the trustees of any settlement of which he (or anyone connected to him) is settlor, his partners (and their spouses) and any companies of which he has control; see TCGA 1992 s.286.

[85] See paras 30–41— 30–43, below.

[86] See TCGA 1992, s.2A and Sch.A1.

[87] TCGA 1992, s.37(3). Thus, where intellectual property is assigned in return for royalties, the assignor (whether author or third party) is exposed to the risk of double taxation, namely capital gains tax on the capitalised value of the royalties and income tax on the royalties as they come in. No case is known in practice where the Revenue have invoked this subsection in the context of copyright royalties, and it may be that the Revenue view the rather odd words "are not precluded" as being permissive. However, then the provisions in declaratory and confers no such discretion on the Revenue.

[88] TCGA 1992, s.17(1)(b).

[89] S.18(2). Broadly, a person is connected to his relatives, his spouse's relatives, the trustees of any settlement of which he (or anyone connected to him) is settlor, his partners (and their spouses) and any companies of which he has control; see s.286.

[90] TCGA 1992, s.17(1)(a).

[91] See paras 30–41— 30–43, below.

[92] See TCGA 1992, s.2A and Sch.1A.

[93] Hold-over relief operates by reducing both the chargeable gain accruing to the donor and the donee's acquisition cost; TCGA 1992, ss.165(4) and 260(3). Accordingly, the gain becomes chargeable when the donee disposes of the right (or emigrates; see *ibid.*, s.168).

is given to a company or to discretionary trustees).[94] The second is where the right is used for the purposes of a trade, profession or vocation carried on by (a) the donor, (b) his personal company[95] or (c) a member of a trading group of which the holding company is the donor's personal company.[96]

Where a person makes a gift of a right to receive intellectual property as and when it comes into existence, it is considered that the gift of the right is not a disposal. The reason lies in the fact that in order for property to be disposed of, it must exist at the time of the purported gift, and the person making the gift must have a beneficial or proprietary right in that property.[97]

D. Deemed Disposals: Capital Sums Derived From Assets

A person is deemed to have disposed of intellectual property whenever he or she derives a capital sum from that asset.[98] Thus, unless it is taxable as income, any sum received on the grant of (or under the terms of) a licence to exploit such a right or as damages for infringement[99] will be subject to capital gains tax.   **30–39**

Moral and performers' rights

It is suggested that because moral rights are personal and not proprietary rights,[1]   **30–40** they are not a form of property and hence do not count as "assets" for capital gains tax.[2] Sums received in return for a waiver of, or by way of compensation for infringement of, moral rights would not on this view be derived from "assets" and would therefore escape the charge to capital gains tax. The point may be of limited practical significance because in infringement cases the exemption for compensation or damages "for any wrong or injury suffered by an individual in his person" is likely to apply given the wide meaning attributed by the Revenue to the phrase "in his person".[3] Further, in the case of professional authors, etc. sums received by way of compensation for infringement of moral rights are liable to be taxed, if at all, as income.

In the authors' view, performers' rights and recording rights are commercial in nature and would be held to be an asset for capital gains tax purposes.

E. Allowable Expenditure

For capital gains tax purposes, the gain on a disposal is arrived at by deducting   **30–41** from the actual or notional consideration the amount of any allowable expenditure. Allowable expenditure for capital gains tax purposes consists of

---

[94] TCGA 1992, s.260(2) and see para. 30–46 as to what is a "chargeable transfer".

[95] *i.e.* a company in which the donor exercises at least five per cent of the voting rights: TCGA 1992, s.165(8)(a).

[96] TCGA 1992, s.15(2)(a).

[97] See *Kirby v Thorn EMI* [1986] S.T.C. 200 and *Whiteman on Capital Gains Tax* (4th ed., Sweet & Maxwell, 1988), paras 5–105 *et seq.*

[98] TCGA 1992, s.22. Particular examples of situations where capital sums are derived from assets are set out in *ibid.*, s.22(1)(a)–(d). Where this occurs there is a part disposal of the asset.

[99] The concessionary treatment by which the Revenue does not tax certain damages awards does not apply to damages for infringement of an intellectual property right because there is an "underlying asset"; see Extra-Statutory Concession D33.

[1] See paras 11–05 and 11–65, above.

[2] Some support for this view is found in para.12 of Extra-Statutory Concession D33. *cf.* the view expressed in the previous edition of this work that, although moral rights are not assignable (CDPA 1988, s.94), they are nonetheless "assets" for the purposes of capital gains tax because they can be waived (*ibid.*, s.87) and thus turned to account.

[3] See Extra-Statutory Concession D33 para.12 where it is stated that the words "in his person" embrace more than physical injury so that distress, embarrassment, loss of reputation or dignity are covered; damages for libel or slander are given as an example.

acquisition cost plus enhancement expenditure and incidental costs of acquisition. For periods before April 1998, the allowable expenditure would be increased by the available indexation allowance. For later periods, Taper Relief will apply.

Where a person disposes of intellectual property which he has owned since March 31, 1982, the acquisition cost of that asset is its market value on March 31, 1982.[4] In any other case, the acquisition cost of the right *acquired* depends on the circumstances in which the acquisition took place. If the acquisition was from a connected person[5] or otherwise than by way of a bargain at arm's length, the acquisition cost will be the market value of the asset at the time of acquisition.[6] Otherwise it will be the amount of the consideration actually given for the right or in the case of the creator of the right, the expenditure incurred in its creation. Allowable enhancement expenditure is any expenditure wholly and exclusively incurred on the right for the purpose of enhancing the value of the asset, being expenditure reflected in the state or nature of the asset at the time of disposal, and any expenditure wholly and exclusively incurred in establishing, preserving or defending title to, or a right over the intellectual property.[7]

Any expenditure which is allowable for income tax purposes, such as expenditure incurred in the creation of copyright by a professional author, is not allowable expenditure for capital gains tax.[8]

Personal representatives are treated as having acquired assets from the deceased at their market value at the date of death.[9] Accordingly, the acquisition cost of any intellectual property deemed to be so disposed and re-acquired by the personal representatives will be the market value of the intellectual property at the date of the deceased's death.

F. ACQUISITION COST: WASTING ASSETS AND PART DISPOSALS

30–42 Intellectual property rights with less than 50 years to run are "wasting assets."[10] The acquisition cost of such assets is written off (on a straight line basis) from the date of acquisition to the date on which it expires.[11]

Where an intellectual property right is only disposed of in part (*e.g.* by the grant of a right to exploit the right for a limited period or in a limited location), only part of the acquisition cost is deductible in computing the chargeable gain. Each element of the acquisition cost is deductible in computing the chargeable gain. Each element of the acquisition cost is reduced according to an A/A+B formula, where A is the consideration for the disposal and B is the market value of the right remaining undisposed of.[12]

G. INDEXATION ALLOWANCE

30–43 Indexation allowance is designed to prevent gains due to inflation from being subject to capital gains tax. The allowance is given by means of a deduction in

---

[4] TCGA 1992, s.35.
[5] Broadly, a person is connected with his relatives, his spouse's relatives, the trustees of any settlement of which he (or anyone connected to him) is settlor, his partners (and their spouses) and any companies of which he has control; see TCGA 1992, s.286.
[6] TCGA 1992, ss.17(1)(a) and 18(1)(2).
[7] s.38(1).
[8] s.37(1).
[9] s.62(1)(a). Where the value of any assets has been ascertained for the purposes of inheritance tax (see para. 30–44 below) that value is taken to be their market value at the date of death for the purposes of capital gains tax: TCGA 1992, s.274.
[10] TCGA 1992, s.44.
[11] s.46.
[12] s.42.

computing the chargeable gain accruing on a disposal.[13] The amount deductible is a fraction of each component of the asset's allowable expenditure, that fraction being given by dividing (a) the increase in the RPI between the date on which the expenditure was incurred and the date on which the asset is disposed of by (b) the RPI on the date when the expenditure was incurred.[14] The indexation allowance is only available to reduce or extinguish a gain, and not to create a loss.[15]

However, as a result of Finance Act 1998 changes, indexation allowance has been frozen with effect from April 1998 for non-corporate taxpayers. Specifically, indexation allowance does not apply to any expenditure incurred after April 1, 1998 by any non-corporate taxpayer. Further, a non-corporate taxpayer only gets the benefit of indexation allowance on allowable expenditure up to April 1998 on asset disposals occurring after April 6, 1998.

The impact of the loss of indexation allowance for periods after April 1998 is alleviated by Taper Relief introduced by the Finance Act 1998. The taper will reduce the amount of chargeable gains arising on a disposal in line with the length of period of ownership of the asset after April 5, 1998. The taper relief varies according to whether the asset is a business or non-business asset. Gains on the disposal of non-business assets are taxed at a higher level. Non-business assets held before March 17, 1998 are given a bonus holding period of one year. This bonus period is added to the period post-April 1998 during which the asset is held in order to determine the full period of ownership of the asset.

3. INHERITANCE TAX

A. DEATH

When a person dies, inheritance tax will be payable on the value of any intellectual property which immediately before his death was vested in him or comprised in a settlement in which he had an interest in possession.[16] Further, inheritance tax will be payable on the value of any intellectual property which the deceased gave away during his lifetime, if he reserved a benefit in the gifted property.[17] The value of property given away by a person to another individual or to particular settlements within seven years of his death will also form part of that person's estate on his death.[18]

30–44

The value of the property for inheritance tax purposes is the price which it might reasonably be expected to fetch if sold in the open market immediately before the deceased's death.[19] A valuation by the publisher or literary agent is evidence[20] of open market value, although the Capital Taxes Office is not bound to accept it.

B. LIFETIME GIFTS AND SETTLEMENTS BY THE HOLDER

It is not uncommon for people to make *inter vivos* gifts or settlements of intellectual property. Such gifts and settlements will not divest the donor's estate of the property (for the purposes of inheritance tax) if he reserves a benefit in the

30–45

---

[13] TCGA 1992, s.53(1).

[14] s.54(1).

[15] Finance Act 1994, s.93, amending TCGA 1992, s.53.

[16] Inheritance Tax Act 1984 ("IHTA 1984"), ss.4(1), 5 and 49(1).

[17] Finance Act 1986, s.102(2).

[18] IHTA 1984, s.3A(4).

[19] IHTA 1984, s.160. If the death of the holder affects the value of the property, the change in value is taken into account as though it had occurred immediately before the death: *ibid.*, s.171.

[20] It is admissible as expert evidence.

gifted property[21] or settles such property on trusts in which he retains an interest in possession.[22]

As inheritance tax is payable on certain *inter vivos* gifts, a gift or settlement of intellectual property may give rise to an inheritance tax charge. If the gift is to an individual, or to a settlement in which an individual has an interest in possession or an accumulation or maintenance trust, the gift or settlement will be a "potentially exempt transfer".[23] A potentially exempt transfer only gives rise to an inheritance tax charge if the donor dies within seven years of making the gift or settlement.[24] Although the tax charge is calculated by reference to the value of the property at the time of the gift (less the value of any consideration received by the donor), it will be charged at the rate in force when the donor dies[25] and, if tax is chargeable, tapering relief will be available if the donor survives for at least three years after making the gift or settlement.[26]

30–46 Any other gift or settlement will be a "chargeable transfer"[27] at the time it is made, and inheritance tax will be payable at the lifetime rates[28] on the value of the rights comprised in the gift or settlement. If the donor dies within seven years, the tax payable on the chargeable transfer is recomputed at the full death rates in force at the time of death and, if this results in a higher amount of tax, the balance becomes payable.[29]

Where there is an effective assignment of future copyright or design right, it is apprehended that the Revenue may invoke the so-called "associated operations" provisions[30] if (as will usually be the case) it can be said that the assignment and the creation of the right were effected with reference to one another. If so, the assignment will be treated as having taken place at the time when the right comes into existence.

In order for a transfer of a right to attract inheritance tax there must be an intention to confer gratuitous benefit. Consequently, a sale of intellectual property at arm's length will not attract inheritance tax even if the sale is at an undervalue.[31]

C. Exemptions

30–47 There is no charge to inheritance tax where intellectual property passes to the owner's spouse or a charity.[32] This is so, whether the copyright passes by way of *inter vivos* gift, settlement or on the holder's death.

---

[21] Finance Act 1986, s.102.
[22] IHTA 1984, s.49(1).
[23] IHTA 1984, s.3A.
[24] s.3A.
[25] IHTA 1984, Sch.2, para.1A.
[26] IHTA 1984, s.7(4).
[27] *i.e.* a chargeable transfer is a transfer of value made by an individual other than an exempt transfer (IHTA 1984, s.2). A transfer of value is any disposition which reduces the value of the transferor's estate. Apart from the exemptions mentioned in para. 30–47 below, there is also an exemption for transfers not exceeding £3,000 in any one year: *ibid.*, s.19.
[28] Lifetime transfers are charged at half of the death rates: IHTA 1984, s.7(2).
[29] Because of tapering relief, tax at the death rates may be lower; but there is no refund in that event: IHTA 1984, s.7(5).
[30] IHTA 1984, s.268.
[31] IHTA 1984, s.10.
[32] IHTA 1984, ss.18 and 23.

D. BUSINESS PROPERTY RELIEF

30-48

In the absence of any authority on the point, it is unclear whether intellectual property comprised in the estate of a person whose trade, profession or vocation involves exploiting such rights (*e.g.* an author, musician, composer, etc.) qualifies for business property relief.[33] However, it is understood that in practice the Revenue do afford business property relief on the death of such a person provided he was carrying on his trade, profession or vocation at (or shortly before) his death. Although the Revenue regard this treatment as concessionary, it is suggested that there are persuasive arguments in favour of the view that, on the death of a professional author, musician, composer, artist, etc., the rights comprised in his estate qualify for business property relief as a matter of law.[34] On the other hand, where an author, musician, etc. makes an *inter vivos* gift or settlement of copyright, etc. it is difficult to see how business property relief can be available because there is no transfer of a business, merely a transfer of individual business assets.[35]

E. PERSONS DOMICILED OUTSIDE THE UNITED KINGDOM

30-49

There are two special rules in relation to intellectual property rights held by non-United Kingdom domiciled persons. First, inheritance tax is only payable in respect of intellectual property rights held by persons who are domiciled outside the United Kingdom where such rights are situated in the United Kingdom.[36] Second, where the intellectual property is comprised in a settlement and is situated outside the United Kingdom, no inheritance tax is payable on a transfer of such property if the settlor of that settlement was not United Kingdom domiciled at the time the settlement was created.

In respect of any particular work, separate copyrights or equivalent rights subsist in different territories throughout the world. Copyright is only situated here in so far as it is protected here by the Copyright, Designs and Patents Act 1988. The rights in works which are protected in other countries by other laws are situate in those countries and not in the United Kingdom.[37] Such rights, if held by a non-United Kingdom domiciled person or within a settlement created by a non-domiciled person, will be outside the scope of inheritance tax.

4. STAMP DUTY

30-50

The Finance Act 2000, section 129 and Schedule 34 abolished stamp duty in respect of instruments for the sale, transfer or other disposition of intellectual property. This abolition applies to instruments executed on or after March 28, 2000. The Finance Act 2002, section 116 abolished stamp duty in respect of an instrument for the sale transfer or other disposition of goodwill. The abolition applies to instruments executed on or after April 23, 2002.

---

33 IHTA 1984, s.103 *et seq.*

34 See *Dymonds Capital Taxes* at paras 24.710 to 711.

35 *cf.* the capital gains tax cases of *McGregor v Adcock* [1977] 3 All E.R. 65, [1977] S.T.C. 206, 51 T.C. 692; *Mannion v Johnston* [1988] S.T.C. 758; *Pepper v Daffurn* [1993] S.T.C. 466 and *Wase v Bourke* [1996] S.T.C. 18.

36 A person is domiciled in the United Kingdom if (a) he is domiciled here as a matter of general law (see *Dicey and Morris on the Conflict of Laws* (12th ed., Sweet & Maxwell, 1993) at pp.124–158), (b) he was domiciled here within the previous three years (IHTA 1984, s.267(1)(a) or (c) he was resident in the United Kingdom in 17 of the previous 20 years of assessment (*ibid.*, s.267(1)(b)).

37 IHTA 1984, s.6(1).

38 For inheritance tax purposes, there is no "situs" code comparable to TCGA 1992, s.275 (discussed at para. 30–36, above.)

5. VALUE ADDED TAX

A. THE SOURCES OF VAT LAW

30–51   One of the treaty obligations assumed by the United Kingdom on joining the European Economic Community in 1972 was an obligation to introduce the common system of VAT.[39] VAT is an indirect tax levied on consumption which is administered in the United Kingdom by the Commissioners of Customs and Excise. It is collected at each stage in the commercial chain from the supplier, who must account for tax on the supply he makes ("output tax") but can recover tax on supplies made to him ("input tax"). The result is that the burden of VAT falls on the person who is unable to recover the tax charged on supplies made to him. This is generally the ultimate consumer, but in the case of an exempt supply[40] is the person making the exempt supply.

The principal current source of United Kingdom VAT legislation is the consolidating Value Added Tax Act ("VATA 1994"), together with regulations made under statutory instrument. The domestic legislation is designed to give effect to the common system of VAT, in particular the Sixth Directive of May 17, 1977 which is required to be implemented in all Member States' VAT legislation. The domestic legislation is construed where possible so as to give effect to the Sixth Directive. In case of conflict between domestic and directly applicable Community legislation, taxpayers (but not the Commissioners of Customs and Excise) may rely on the latter.

B. THE CHARGE TO VAT

30–52   VAT is charged on any supply of goods or services made in the United Kingdom where it is a taxable supply made by a taxable person in the course or furtherance of any business carried on by him.[41] VAT is currently charged at 17.5 per cent on the value of the supply and is a liability of the person making the supply.[42]

The grant or assignment of copyright or any other intellectual property right is a supply of services if done for a consideration.[43] An author, musician, composer, etc., who assigns or licenses copyright will thus be subject to VAT if the other conditions for chargeability are met.

30–53   First, the supply must be a taxable supply. To constitute a taxable supply, the supply must be made in the United Kingdom and can be any supply of goods or services other than an exempt supply.[44]

30–54   Secondly, the person granting or assigning the right must be a taxable person.[45] A taxable person is a person who is either registered for VAT or is required to be so registered.[46] A person is required to be registered if, at the end of any month, he

---

[39] The European Communities Act 1972 provides for the implementation of Community legislation in United Kingdom law and for it to take precedence over domestic law.
[40] *i.e.* supplies of goods and services within Sch.9 to the Value Added Tax Act 1994 ("VATA 1994").
[41] VATA 1994, s.4.
[42] VATA 1994, s.2.
[43] VATA 1994, s.5(2). A gift of a right will not be a supply because "supply" does not include anything done otherwise than for consideration: *ibid.*, s.5(2).
[44] VATA 1994, s.4. The place of supply rules are discussed at para. 30–57, below.
[45] VATA 1994, s.4(1).
[46] VATA 1994, s.3(1).

has made taxable supplies exceeding the VAT threshold[47] in the preceding year or there are reasonable grounds for believing that the value of his taxable supplies in the next 30 days will exceed the VAT threshold.[48] So, for example, an author who is about to receive an advance of £60,000 would become a taxable person even if he was previously below the threshold for registration.

Thirdly, the supply must be made by the taxable person in the course or further-ance of a business carried on by him.[49] The term "business" extends beyond trades, professions or vocations,[50] to include any occupation or function actively pursued with a reasonable and recognisable continuity and which involves the making of taxable supplies,[51] even if it is not done with the object of making profit.[52] However there are limits. Merely exercising rights of ownership does not amount to the carrying on of a business, for example, the buying and selling of securities in the course of managing an investment portfolio.[53] Difficult questions may therefore arise where a copyright or the benefit of a royalty agreement is inherited or acquired by gift. It is thought that the mere receipt of royalties does not amount to the carrying on of a business. However, the Commissioners of Customs and Excise have stated that the heir or testamentary beneficiary of a deceased member of the Performing Rights Society must be registered for VAT if his receipts from the Society exceed the registration limits.[54] The Society has accepted this view with some reservations.

30–55

Finally, the supply must be made for a consideration, which may be in monetary or non-monetary form and includes everything received in return for the supply. VAT is charged on the "value" of the supply, namely the amount which, with the addition of VAT thereon, equals the consideration.[55] Where the consideration for the grant of a right takes the form of royalties, there is a separate supply of services on each occasion when payment is received or, if earlier, when an invoice is issued.[56]

30–56

C. PLACE OF SUPPLY

The general rule is that a supply of services is made in the United Kingdom if the supplier belongs here.[57] There are, however, important exceptions to the general rule which are of relevance in the present context. First, some supplies of services are treated as made where the supplies are physically carried out. These include cultural, artistic, sporting, scientific, educational or entertainment services.[58] Secondly, some supplies of services are treated as made where the recipient of the supply belongs if the recipient belongs outside the EC or belongs in the EC and receives the supply for the purpose of a business carried on by him. The supplies concerned are listed in Schedule 5 to the Value Added Tax Act 1994 and include transfers and assignments of copyrights, patents, licences,

30–57

[47] £58,000 from April 1, 2004.
[48] Sch.1, para.1(1).
[49] VATA 1994, s.4(1).
[50] s.94(1).
[51] See *C&E Commissioners v Morrison's Academy* [1978] S.T.C. 1.
[52] *C&E Commissioners v Morrison's Academy* [1978] S.T.C. 1. at 5c–d.
[53] *Wellcome Trust v C&E Commissioners* [1996] S.T.C. 945.
[54] See the *Commissioners' Internal Manual on VAT*, Pt 3, App.A, para.2a.
[55] VATA 1994, s.19.
[56] VAT Regulations 1995 (SI 1995/2518), regs 90 and 91.
[57] VATA 1994, s.7(10).
[58] VAT (Place of Supply of Services) Order 1992 (SI 1992/3121), art.15.

trademarks and similar rights, as well as the acceptance of any obligation to refrain from pursuing or exercising any such rights.[59]

The Value Added Tax Act 1994 contains detailed rules to determine where a person belongs. The supplier will belong in the United Kingdom if he has his only business establishment or fixed establishment in the United Kingdom.[60] If the supplier has business establishments or fixed establishments in more than one country, the supplier is treated as belonging in that country which is most directly concerned with the supply in question.[61] If the supplier has no business establishment or fixed place of business anywhere, he is treated as belonging in the country where he has his usual place of residence.[62] Similar rules apply to determine where the recipient of the supply belongs save that, where a supply of services is made to an individual and is received by him otherwise than for the purposes of any business carried on by him, he is treated as belonging where he has his usual place of residence.[63]

D. THE REVERSE CHARGE (ON SUPPLIES FROM ABROAD)

30–58 As mentioned in the previous paragraph some supplies of services, including transfers and assignments of copyright, patents, licences, trademarks and similar supplies, are supplied where received.[64] These supplies are subject to the so-called "reverse charge". For example, the reverse charge will apply where supplies are made by a person who belongs in a country other than the United Kingdom and are received by a person who belongs in the United Kingdom for the purpose of any business carried on by him.[65] The "reverse charge" rules treat the recipient as if he had himself supplied the services in the United Kingdom in the course or furtherance of his business and the supply were a taxable supply. If the recipient is a taxable person, he is both liable to account for output tax and eligible for input tax credit (to the extent that the services which are the subject matter of the reverse supply are attributable to taxable supplies). So, for example, a publishing company which acquires copyright from an author who belongs abroad will have to pay VAT on the consideration for the copyright but (assuming the company is entitled to full credit for its input tax) will be able to recover the VAT as input tax in exactly the same way as if the VAT had been charged by a third-party supplier.

Other supplies which are subject to the reverse charge include advertising services, the services of consultants, lawyers, accountants and other similar services, data processing and the provision of information, banking, financial and insurance services as well as any services supplied to a recipient who is registered for VAT.[66]

---

[59] VAT (Place of Supply of Services) Order 1992 (SI 1992/3121), arts 1 and 4.
[60] VATA 1994, s.9(2)(a). A person carrying on business through a branch or agency in any country is treated as having a business establishment there: *ibid.*, s.9(5)(a). As to fixed establishment, see *C&E Commissioners v DFDS A S* [1997] S.T.C. 384.
[61] VATA 1994, s.9(2).
[62] s.9(2)(b). In the case of a body corporate, this means the place where it is legally constituted.
[63] s.9.
[64] Supplies are not taxable supplies for reverse charge purposes, if the recipient belongs outside the EC or belongs in the EC and receives the supply otherwise than for the purpose of a business carried on by him.
[65] VATA 1994, s.8.
[66] Sch. 5.

E. BOOKS, ETC.

Books, booklets, brochures, pamphlets, leaflets, newspapers, journals, periodicals, **30–59**
children's picture books and painting books, music (printed, duplicated or manuscript), maps, charts and topographical plans (excluding plans or drawings for
industrial, architectural, engineering, commercial or similar purposes) are all
zero-rated.[67] This means that the supplier does not need to account for VAT but is
entitled to credit for input tax attributable to the supply.[68]

F. THE MUSIC INDUSTRY

The Commissioners of Customs &Excise have published their views of how **30–60**
VAT affects the various societies involved in the administration of copyright in
the music industry.[69]

The Performing Rights Society ("PRS").[70] There are two supplies involved:
the assignment of the performing right to PRS by the member on joining, the
consideration being the payments receivable from PRS; and the grant of licences
by PRS, the consideration being the fees received by PRS (which form the basis
of PRS's distribution to its members). The Commissioners of Customs & Excise's
view is that successor members, *i.e.* the heir or testamentary beneficiary of the
original writer, make supplies in their own right and have to be registered if their
receipts from PRS exceed the registration limits.[71]

Phonographic Performances Ltd ("PPL").[72] There are three supplies involved:
the assignment of public performing and broadcasting rights from the record
companies to PPL; the granting of licences by PPL; and the supply of taxable services by the International Federation of the Phonographic Industry to the record
producers. The consideration for the supply by the record producers to PPL is the
total amount receivable by PPL less PPL's administration charge only. The
consideration for the supply by PPL is the fee received for the granting of
licences. The consideration for the supply by the International Federation of the
Phonographic Industry is the amount paid to them by PPL on behalf of the record
producers. *Ex gratia* payments by PPL to music publishers, the Musicians Union
and artistes are outside the scope of VAT.

Mechanical Rights Society Ltd. The annual subscription charged to members
is the consideration for a taxable supply of the services provided to members.

Mechanical Copyright Protection Society Ltd ("MCPS").[73] The commission
charged to holders of music copyright is the consideration for a continuous supply of services under regulation 90 of the VAT Regulations.

---

[67] VATA 1994, s.30 and Sch.8.
[68] Zero-rated supplies are those supplies described in VATA 1994, Sch.8. Unlike exempt supplies,
are "taxable supplies". So input tax attributable to zero-rated supplies is recoverable: input tax attributable to exempt supplies is irrecoverable. Zero-rating is also referred to as "exemption with
credit".
[69] See the *Commissioners' Internal Manual on VAT*, Pt 3, App.A, para.2.
[70] As to the PRS, see para.28–60.
[71] See the *Commissioners' Internal Manual on VAT*, Pt 3, App.A, para.2.
[72] As to PPL, see para. 28–61, above.
[73] As to the MCPS, see para. 28–57, above.

G. CREDIT FOR INPUT TAX

30–61 It is a fundamental principle of the VAT system that a taxable person is entitled to recover VAT on supplies made to him to the extent that the supplies are attributable to taxable supplies he makes.[74]

---

[74] VATA 1994, ss.24–26. There are detailed rules for attributing input tax between taxable supplies and supplies which are either outside the scope of VAT or are exempt: See Pt XIV of the VAT Regulations 1995 (SI 1995/2518).

Index

References are to paragraph numbers

Cable re-transmission
compulsory licences. *see Compulsory licences*
Cable re-transmission right
compulsory collective administration 29–74, 29–75
Cable, reception and re-transmission of wireless broadcast by
performances, rights in, and 12–100, 12–101
Cable transmissions, 3–86, 3–87. *see also Broadcasts*
Caching 22–96—22–103
acting to remove or disable access 22–101
additional guidance 22–97
compliance with conditions on access to information 22–98
compliance with industry rules regarding updating of information 22–99
defence of 22–96
knowledge 22–102
non-interference with technology to obtain data on use of information 22–100
terms of regulation 22, 22–103
Capital gains tax 30–36—30–43
acquisition cost
part disposals 30–42
wasting assets 30–42
allowable expenditure 30–41
acquisition cost 30–41
personal representatives 30–41
assets
moral rights 30–40
performers' rights 30–40
capital sums derived from assets 30–39
deemed disposals 30–39
gifts 30–38
indexation allowance 30–43
sales 30–37
scope 30–36
Car exhaust
design right 13–60
Car wheels
design right 13–60
Caricature
fair dealing, and 9–41
Case summaries
originality 3–139
Catalogues
infringement 7–45
Channel Islands
protection of copyright 3–256
Character merchandising
passing off. *see Passing off*
Charges 5–190—5–193
equitable 5–193
Charitable organisation
meaning 9–183
Chips. *see Semiconductor topographies*
Church of England
Measures of Synod
Crown copyright 10–19, 10–20

Circumvention devices
protection measures, and 15–03
Civil law systems
authorship, and 4–03—4–05
Civil remedies 22–01—22–228
agents 22–23—22–28
Community designs 22–10
conspiracy 22–40
controlling shareholders 22–41, 22–42
copyright and design right: primary infringers 22–32
copyright and design right: secondary infringers 22–33
criminal offences, and 22–02
database right 22–12
date of title 22–31
defences, 22–50—22–112. *see also Defences*
direct infringers 22–34
directors 22–41, 22–42
Enforcement Directive 22–03
equitable owner 22–17—22–19
copyright 22–17
database right 22–18
design right 22–18
non-property rights 22–19
performers' property rights 22–18
equitable remuneration 22–13
exclusive licensee 22–20—22–22
copyright 22–20
database right 22–21
design right 22–21
non-property rights 22–22
performers' property rights 22–21
infringement of copyright 22–05
joint owners 22–29, 22–30
joint tortfeasors, 22–35—22–39. *see also Joint tortfeasors*
legal owner 22–15, 22–16
moral rights 22–06
non-exclusive licensees 22–23—22–28
infringing acts 22–25
right of action 22–24
rights concurrent 22–26
section 101A, Act of 1988, 22–23
performers' non-property rights 22–08
performers' property rights 22–07
performers' recording rights 22–08
person with rights 22–15, 22–16
persons in possession of infringing copies, infringing articles or illicit recordings 22–44
publication right 22–05
rights in respect of protection measures 22–11
rights management information 22–11
seizure without court order 22–46—22–49
semi-conductor topographies 22–09
service providers 22–45
terminology 22–14
unauthorised decoders 22–11
unregistered design right 22–09
vicarious liability 22–43
who may be sued 22–32—22–45
who may sue 22–15—22–30